Webster's Contemporary Spanish-English Dictionary

Webster's Contemporary Spanish-English Dictionary

Created in Cooperation with the
Editors of Merriam-Webster

FEDERAL STREET PRESS

A Division of Merriam-Webster, Incorporated
Springfield, Massachusetts

Federal Street Press is a trademark of Federal Street Press, a division of Merriam-Webster, Incorporated.

This 2009 edition published by
Federal Street Press
A Division of Merriam-Webster, Incorporated
P.O. Box 281
Springfield, MA 01102

Federal Street Press books are available for bulk purchase for sales promotion and premium use. For details write the manager of special sales, Federal Street Press, P.O. Box 281, Springfield, MA 01102

ISBN 13 978-1-59695-055-9

Printed in the United States of America

09 10 11 12 13 5 4 3 2 1

Contents

Preface

The book you are holding is a new edition of a dictionary designed to meet the needs of English and Spanish speakers in a time of ever-expanding communication among the countries of the Western Hemisphere. It is intended for language learners, teachers, office workers, tourists, business travelers—anyone who needs to communicate effectively in the Spanish and English languages as they are spoken and written in the Americas. This new dictionary provides accurate and up-to-date coverage of current vocabulary in both languages, as well as abundant examples of words used in context to illustrate idiomatic usage. The selection of Spanish words and idioms was based on evidence drawn from a wide variety of modern Latin-American sources and interpreted by trained Merriam-Webster bilingual lexicographers. The English entries were chosen by Merriam-Webster editors from the most recent Merriam-Webster dictionaries, and they represent the current basic vocabulary of American English.

All of this material is presented in a format which is based firmly upon and, in many important ways, is similar to the traditional styling found in the Merriam-Webster monolingual dictionaries. The reader who is familiar with Merriam-Webster dictionaries will immediately recognize this style, with its emphasis on convenience and case of use, clarity and conciseness of the information presented, precise discrimination of senses, and frequent inclusion of example phrases showing words in actual use. Other features include pronunciations (in the International Phonetic Alphabet) for all English words, full coverage of irregular verbs in both languages, a section on basic Spanish grammar, tables of the most common Spanish and English abbreviations, and a detailed Explanatory Notes section which answers any questions the reader might have concerning the use of this book.

This dictionary represents the combined efforts of many members of the Merriam-Webster Editorial Department, along with advice and assistance from consultants outside the company. The primary defining work was done by Charlene M. Chateauneuf, Seán O'Mannion-Espejo, Karen L. Wilkinson, and Jocelyn Woods; early contributions to the text were also submitted by Cèsar Alegre, Hilton Alers, Marién Díaz, Anne Gatschet, and María D. Guijarro, with Victoria E. Neufeldt, Ph.D. and James L. Rader providing helpful suggestions regarding style. Proofreading was done by Susan L. Brady, Daniel B. Brandon, Charlene M. Chateauneuf, Deanna Chiasson, Seán O'Mannion-Espejo, James L. Rader, Donna L. Rickerby, Adrienne M. Scholz, Amy West, Karen L. Wilkinson, and Linda Picard Wood. Brian M. Sietsema, Ph.D. provided the pronunciations. Cross-reference services were provided by Donna L. Rickerby, Karen L. Levister assisted in inputting revisions. Carol Fugiel contributed many hours of clerical assistance and other valuable support. The editorial work relating to typesetting and production was begun by Jennifer S. Goss and continued by Susan L. Brady, who also offered helpful suggestions regarding format. Madeline L. Novak provided guidance on typographic matters. John M. Morse was responsible for the conception of this book was well as for numerous ideas and continued support along the way.

Eileen M. Haraty
Editor

Explanatory Notes

Entries

1. Main Entries

A boldface letter, word, or phrase appearing flush with the left-hand margin of each column of type is a main entry or entry word. The main entry may consist of letters set solid, of letters joined by a hyphen, or of letters separated by a space:

cafetalero[1], **-ra** *adj* . . .

eye–opener . . . *n* . . .

walk out *vi* . . .

The main entry, together with the material that follows it on the same line and succeeding indented lines, constitutes a dictionary entry.

2. Order of Main Entries

Alphabetical order throughout the book follows the order of the English alphabet, with one exception: words beginning with the Spanish letter *ñ* follow all entries for the letter *n*. The main entries follow one another alphabetically letter by letter without regard to intervening spaces or hyphens; for example, *shake-up* follows *shaker.*

Homographs (words with the same spelling) having different parts of speech are usually given separate dictionary entries. These entries are distinguished by superscript numerals following the entry word:

hail[1] . . . *vt* . . .

hail[2] *n* . . .

hail[3] *interj* . . .

madrileño[1], **-ña** *adj* . . .

madrileño[2], **-ña** *n* . . .

Numbered homograph entries are listed in the following order: verb, adverb, adjective, noun, conjunction, preposition, pronoun, interjection, article.

Homographs having the same part of speech are normally included at the same dictionary entry, without regard to their different semantic origins. On the English-to-Spanish side, however, separate entries are made if the homographs have distinct inflected forms or if they have distinct pronunciations.

3. Guide Words

A pair of guide words is printed at the top of each page, indicating the first and last main entries that appear on that page:

factura • faringe

4. Variants

When a main entry is followed by the word *or* and another spelling, the two spellings are variants. Both are standard, and either one may be used according to personal inclination:

jailer *or* **jailor** . . . *n* . . .

quizá *or* **quizás** *adv* . . .

Occasionally, a variant spelling is used only for a particular sense of a word. In these cases, the variant spelling is listed after the sense number of the sense to which it pertains:

electric . . . *adj* **1** *or* **electrical** . . .

Sometimes the entry word is used interchangeably with a longer phrase containing the entry word. For the purposes of this dictionary, such phrases are considered variants of the headword:

bunk[2] *n* **1** *or* **bunk bed** . . .

angina *nf* **1** *or* **angina de pecho** : angina . . .

Variant wordings of boldface phrases may also be shown:

madera *nf*. . . **3 madera dura** *or* **madera noble** . . .

atención[1] *nf* . . . **2 poner atención** *or* **prestar atención** . . .

5. Run-On Entries

A main entry may be followed by one or more derivatives or by a homograph with a different functional label. These are run-on entries. Each is introduced by a boldface dash and each has a functional label. They are not defined, however, since their equivalents can be readily derived by adding the corresponding foreign-language suffix to the terms used to define the entry word or, in the case of homographs, simply substituting the appropriate part of speech:

illegal . . . *adj* : ilegal — **illegally** *adv* (the Spanish adverb is *ilegalmente*)

transferir . . . *vt* trasladar : to transfer — **transferible** *adj* (the English adjective is **transferable**)

Bosnian *n* : bosnio *m,* -nia *f* — **Bosnian** *adj* (the Spanish adjective is *bosnio, -nia*)

On the Spanish side of the book, reflexive verbs are sometimes run on undefined:

enrollar *vt* : to roll up, to coil — **enrollarse** *vr*

The absence of a definition means that *enrollarse* has the simple reflexive meaning "to become rolled up or coiled," "to roll itself up."

6. Bold Notes

A main entry may be followed by one or more phrases containing the entry word or an inflected form of the entry word. These are bold notes. Each bold note is defined at its own numbered sense:

álamo *nm* **1 :** poplar **2 álamo temblón :** aspen

hold[1] . . . *vi* **. . . 4 to hold to : . . . 5 to hold with : . . .**

If the bold note consists only of the entry word and a single preposition, the entry word is represented by a boldface swung dash **~**.

pegar . . . *vi* **. . . 3 ~ con :** to match, to go with . . .

The same bold note phrase may appear at two or more senses if it has more than one distinct meaning:

wear[1] . . . *vt* **. . . 3 to wear out :** gastar ⟨he wore out his shoes . . . ⟩ **4 to wear out** EXHAUST : agotar, fatigar ⟨to wear oneself out . . . ⟩ . . .

estar . . . *vi* **. . . 15 ~ por :** to be in favor of **16 ~ por :** to be about to ⟨está por cerrar . . . ⟩ . . .

If the use of the entry word is commonly restricted to one particular phrase, then a bold note may be given as the entry word's only sense:

ward[1] . . . *vt* **to ward off : . . .**

Pronunciation

1. Pronunciation of English Entry Words

The matter between a pair of brackets [ ] following the entry word of an English-to-Spanish entry indicates the pronunciation. The symbols used are explained in the International Phonetic Alphabet chart on page 58a.

The presence of variant pronunciations indicates that not all educated speakers pronounce words the same way. A second-place variant is not to be regarded as less acceptable than the pronunciation that is given first. It may, in fact, be used by as many educated speakers as the first variant, but the requirements of the printed page are such that one must precede the other:

tomato [tə'meɪt̬o, -'mɑ-] . . .

When a compound word has less than a full pronunciation, the missing part is to be supplied from the pronunciation at the entry for the unpronounced element of the compound:

gamma ray ['gæmə] . . .

ray ['reɪ] . . .

smoke[1] ['smo:k] . . .

smoke detector [dɪ'tɛktər] . . .

In general, no pronunciation is given for open compounds consisting of two or more English words that are main entries at their own alphabetical place:

water lily *n* : nenúfar *m*

Only the first entry in a series of numbered homographs is given a pronunciation if their pronunciations are the same:

dab[1] ['dæb] *vt* . . .

dab[2] *n* . . .

No pronunciation is shown for principal parts of verbs that are formed by regular suffixation, nor for other derivative words formed by common suffixes.

2. Pronunciation of Spanish Entry Words

Spanish pronunciation is highly regular, so no pronunciations are given for most Spanish-to-English entries. Exceptions have been made for certain words (such as foreign borrowings) whose Spanish pronunciations are not evident from their spellings:

pizza ['pitsa, 'pisa] . . .

footing ['fu,tɪŋ] . . .

Functional Labels

An italic label indicating a part of speech or some other functional classification follows the pronunciation or, if no pronunciation is given, the main entry. The eight traditional parts of speech, adjective, adverb, conjunction, interjection, noun, preposition, pronoun, and verb, are indicated as follows:

daily[2] *adj* . . .

vagamente *adv* . . .

and . . . *conj* . . .

huy *interj* . . .

jackal . . . *n* . . .

para *prep* . . .

neither[3] *pron* . . .

leer . . . *v* . . .

Verbs that are intransitive are labeled *vi,* and verbs that are transitive are labeled *vt.* Entries for verbs that are both transitive and intransitive are labeled *v;* if such an entry includes irregular verb inflections, it is labeled *v* immediately after the main entry, with the labels *vi* and *vt* serving to introduce transitive and intransitive subdivisions when both are present:

deliberar *vi* **:** to deliberate

necessitate . . . *vt* **-tated; -tating :** necesitar, requerir

satisfy . . . *v* **-fied; -fying** *vt* . . . — *vi* . . .

Two other labels are used to indicate functional classifications of verbs: *v aux* (auxiliary verb) and *v impers* (impersonal verb).

may . . . *v aux, past* **might** . . .

haber[1] . . . *v aux* **1 :** have . . . — *v impers* **1 hay :** there is, there are . . .

Gender Labels

In Spanish-to-English noun entries, the gender of the entry word is indicated by an italic *m* (masculine), *f* (feminine), or *mf* (masculine or feminine), immediately following the functional label:

magnesio *nm* . . .

galaxia *nf* . . .

turista *nmf* . . .

If both the masculine and feminine forms are shown for a noun referring to a person, the label is simply *n:*

director, -tora *n* . . .

Spanish noun equivalents of English entry words are also labeled for gender:

amnesia . . . *n* : amnesia *f*

earache . . . *n* : dolor *m* de oído

gamekeeper . . . *n* : guardabosque *mf*

Inflected Forms

1. Nouns

The plurals of nouns are shown in this dictionary when they are irregular, when plural suffixation brings about a change in accentuation or in the spelling of the root word, when an English noun ends in a consonant plus *-o* or in *-ey,* when an English noun ends in *-oo,* when an English noun is a compound that pluralizes any element but the last, when a noun has variant plurals, or whenever the dictionary user might have reasonable doubts regarding the spelling of a plural:

tooth . . . *n, pl* **teeth** . . .

garrafón *nm, pl* **-fones** . . .

potato . . . *n, pl* **-toes** . . .

abbey . . . *n, pl* **-beys** . . .

cuckoo[2] *n, pl* **-oos** . . .

brother–in–law . . . *n, pl* **brothers–in–law** . . .

quail[2] *n, pl* **quail** *or* **quails** . . .

hábitat *nm, pl* **-tats** . . .

tahúr *nm, pl* **tahúres** . . .

Cutback inflected forms are used for most nouns on the English-to-Spanish side, regardless of the number of syllables. On the Spanish-to-English side, cutback inflections are given for nouns that have three or more syllables; plurals for shorter words are written out in full:

shampoo[2] *n, pl* **-poos** . . .

calamity . . . *n, pl* **-ties** . . .

mouse . . . *n, pl* **mice** . . .

sartén *nmf, pl* **sartenes** . . .

hámster *nm, pl* **hámsters** . . .

federación *nf, pl* **-ciones** . . .

If only one gender form has a plural which is irregular, that plural form will be given with the appropriate label:

campeón, -ona *n, mpl* **-ones** : champion

The plurals of nouns are usually not shown when the base word is unchanged by the addition of the regular plural suffix or when the noun is unlikely to occur in the plural:

apple . . . *n* : manzana *f*

inglés[3] *nm* : English (language)

Nouns that are plural in form and that regularly occur in plural constructions are labeled as *npl* (for English nouns), *nmpl* (for Spanish masculine nouns), or *nfpl* (for Spanish feminine nouns):

knickers . . . *npl* . . .

enseres *nmpl* . . .

mancuernas *nfpl* . . .

Entry words that are unchanged in the plural are labeled *ns & pl* (for English nouns), *nms & pl* (for Spanish masculine nouns), *nfs & pl* (for Spanish feminine nouns), and *nmfs & pl* (for Spanish gender-variable nouns):

deer . . . *ns & pl* . . .

lavaplatos *nms & pl* . . .

tesis *nfs & pl* . . .

rompehuelgas *nmfs & pl* . . .

2. Verbs

ENGLISH VERBS

The principal parts of verbs are shown in English-to-Spanish entries when they are irregular, when suffixation brings about a change in spelling of the root word, when the verb ends in *-ey*, when there are variant inflected forms, or whenever it is believed that the dictionary user might have reasonable doubts about the spelling of an inflected form:

break[1] . . . *v* **broke** . . . ; **broken** . . . ; **breaking** . . .

drag[1] . . . *v* **dragged; dragging** . . .

monkey[1] . . . *vi* **-keyed; -keying** . . .

label[1] . . . *vt* **-beled** *or* **-belled; -beling** *or* **-belling** . . .

imagine . . . *vt* **-ined; -ining** . . .

Cutback inflected forms are usually used when the verb has two or more syllables:

multiply . . . *v* **-plied; -plying** . . .

bevel[1] . . . *v* **-eled** *or* **-elled; -eling** *or* **-elling** . . .

forgo *or* **forego** . . . *vt* **-went; -gone; -going** . . .

commit . . . *vt* **-mitted; -mitting** . . .

The principal parts of an English verb are not shown when the base word is unchanged by suffixation:

delay[1] . . . *vt*

pitch[1] . . . *vt*

SPANISH VERBS

Entries for irregular Spanish verbs are cross-referenced by number to the model conjugations appearing in the Conjugation of Spanish Verbs section:

abnegarse {49} *vr* . . .

volver {89} *vi* . . .

Entries for Spanish verbs with regular conjugations are not cross-referenced; however, model conjugations for regular Spanish verbs are included in the Conjugation of Spanish Verbs section beginning on page 38a.

Adverbs and Adjectives

The comparative and superlative forms of English adjective and adverb main entries are shown when suffixation brings about a change in spelling of the root word, when the inflection is irregular, and when there are variant inflected forms:

wet[2] *adj* **wetter; wettest** . . .

good[2] *adj* **better** . . . ; **best** . . .

evil[1] . . . *adj* **eviler** *or* **eviller; evilest** *or* **evillest** . . .

The superlative forms of adjectives and adverbs of two or more syllables are usually cut back; the superlative is shown in full, however, when it is desirable to indicate the pronunciation of the inflected form:

early[1] . . . *adv* **earlier; -est** . . .

gaudy . . . *adj* **gaudier; -est** . . .

secure[2] *adj* **-curer; -est** . . .

but

young[1] . . . *adj* **younger** [ˈjʌŋgər]; **youngest** [-gəst] . . .

At a few entries only the superlative form is shown:

mere *adj, superlative* **merest** . . .

The absence of the comparative form indicates that there is no evidence of its use.

The comparative and superlative forms of adjectives and adverbs are usually not shown when the base word is unchanged by suffixation:

quiet³ *adj* **1** . . .

Usage

1. Usage Labels

Two types of usage labels are used in this dictionary—regional and stylistic. Spanish words that are limited in use to a specific area or areas of Latin America, or to Spain, are given labels indicating the countries in which they are most commonly used:

guarachear *vi Cuba, PRi fam* . . .

bucket . . . *n* : . . . cubeta *f Mex*

The following regional labels are used in this book: *Arg* (Argentina), *Bol* (Bolivia), *CA* (Central America), *Car* (Caribbean), *Chile* (Chile), *Col* (Colombia), *CoRi* (Costa Rica), *Cuba* (Cuba), *DomRep* (Dominican Republic), *Ecua* (Ecuador), *Sal* (El Salvador), *Guat* (Guatemala), *Hond* (Honduras), *Mex* (Mexico), *Nic* (Nicaragua), *Pan* (Panama), *Par* (Paraguay), *Peru* (Peru), *PRi* (Puerto Rico), *Spain* (Spain), *Uru* (Uruguay), *Ven* (Venezuela).

Since this book focuses on the Spanish spoken in Latin America, only the most common regionalisms from Spain have been included in order to allow for more thorough coverage of Latin-American forms.

A number of Spanish words are given a *fam* (familiar) label as well, indicating that these words are suitable for informal contexts but would not normally be used in formal writing or speaking. The stylistic label *usu considered vulgar* is added for a word which is usually considered vulgar or offensive but whose widespread use justifies its inclusion in this book. The label is intended to warn the reader that the word in question may be inappropriate in polite conversation.

2. Usage Notes

Definitions are sometimes preceded by parenthetical usage notes that give supplementary semantic information:

not . . . *adv* **1** (*used to form a negative*) : no . . .

within[2] *prep* . . . **2** (*in expressions of distance*) : . . . **3** (*in expressions of time*) : . . .

e[2] *conj* (*used instead of* **y** *before words beginning with i or hi*) : . . .

poder[1] . . . *v aux* . . . **2** (*expressing possibility*) : . . . **3** (*expressing permission*) : . . .

Additional semantic orientation is also sometimes given in the form of parenthetical notes appearing within the definition:

calibrate . . . *vt* . . . : calibrar (armas), graduar (termómetros)

palco *nm* : box (in a theater or stadium)

Occasionally a usage note is used in place of a definition. This is usually done when the entry word has no single foreign-language equivalent. This type of usage note will be accompanied by examples of common use:

shall . . . *v aux* . . . **1** (*used to express a command*) ⟨you shall do as I say : harás lo que te digo⟩ . . .

3. Illustrations of Usage

Definitions are sometimes followed by verbal illustrations that show a typical use of the word in context or a common idiomatic usage. These verbal illustrations include a translation and are enclosed in angle brackets:

lejos *adv* **1 :** far away, distant ⟨a lo lejos : in the distance, far off⟩ . . .

make[1] . . . **9** . . . **:** ganar ⟨to make a living : ganarse la vida⟩ . . .

Sense Division

A boldface colon is used to introduce a definition:

fable . . . *n* **:** fábula *f*

Boldface Arabic numerals separate the senses of a word that has more than one sense:

laguna *nf* **1 :** lagoon **2 :** lacuna, gap

Whenever some information (such as a synonym, a boldface word or phrase, a usage note, a cross-reference, or a label) follows a sense number, it applies only to that specific numbered sense and not to any other boldface numbered senses:

abanico *nm* . . . **2** GAMA **:** . . .

tonic[2] *n* . . . **2** *or* **tonic water :** . . .

grillo *nm* . . . **2 grillos** *nmpl* **:** . . .

fairy . . . *n, pl* **fairies** . . . **2 fairy tale :** . . .

myself . . . *pron* **1** (*used reflexively*) **:** . . .

pike . . . *n* . . . **3** → **turnpike**

atado[2] *nm* . . . **2** *Arg* **:** . . .

Cross-References

Three different kinds of cross-references are used in this dictionary: synonymous, cognate, and inflectional. In each instance the cross-reference is readily recognized by the boldface arrow following the entry word.

Synonymous and cognate cross-references indicate that a definition at the entry cross-referred to can be substituted for the entry word:

scapula . . . → shoulder blade

amuck . . . → amok

An inflectional cross-reference is used to identify the entry word as an inflected form of another word (as a noun or verb):

fue, etc. → ir, ser

mice → mouse

Synonyms

At many entries or senses in this book, a synonym in small capital letters is provided before the boldface colon and the following defining text. These synonyms are all main entries or bold notes elsewhere in the book. They serve as a helpful guide to the meaning of the entry or sense and also give the reader an additional term that might be substituted in a similar context. On the English-to-Spanish side synonyms are particularly abundant, since special care has been taken to guide the English speaker—by means of synonyms, verbal illustrations, or usage notes—to the meaning of the Spanish terms at each sense of a multisense entry.

Spanish Grammar

Accentuation

Spanish word stress is generally determined according to the following rules:

- Words ending in a vowel, or in *-n* or *-s,* are stressed on the penultimate syllable (*zapato*, ***lla**man*).
- Words ending in a consonant other than *-n* or *-s* are stressed on the last syllable (*per**diz**, curiosi**dad***).

Exceptions to these rules have a written accent mark over the stressed vowel (***fá**cil*, *habla**rá***, ***úl**timo*). There are also a few words which take accent marks in order to distinguish them from homonyms (*si*, *sí*; *que*, *qué*; *el*, *él*; *etc.)*.

Adverbs ending in *-mente* have two stressed syllables since they retain both the stress of the root word and of the *-mente* suffix (***len**ta**men**te*, *di**fí**cil**men**te*). Many compounds also have two stressed syllables (***lim**piapara**bri**sas*).

Punctuation and Capitalization

Questions and exclamations in Spanish are preceded by an inverted question mark ¿ and an inverted exclamation mark ¡, respectively:

¿Cuándo llamó Ana?
Y tú, ¿qué piensas?

¡No hagas eso!
Pero, ¡qué lástima!

In Spanish, unlike English, the following words are not capitalized:

- Names of days, months, and languages (*jueves, octubre, español*).

- Spanish adjectives or nouns derived from proper nouns (*los nicaragüenses, una teoría marxista*).

Articles

1. Definite Article

Spanish has five forms of the definite article: *el* (masculine singular), *la* (feminine singular), *los* (masculine plural), *las* (feminine plural), and *lo* (neuter). The first four agree in gender and number with the nouns they limit (*el carro,* the car; *las tijeras,* the scissors), although the form *el* is used with feminine singular nouns beginning with a stressed *a-* or *ha-* (*el águila, el hambre*).

The neuter article *lo* is used with the masculine singular form of an adjective to express an abstract concept (*lo mejor de este método,* the best thing about this method; *lo meticuloso de su trabajo,* the meticulousness of her work; *lo mismo para mí,* the same for me).

Whenever the masculine article *el* immediately follows the words *de* or *a,* it combines with them to form the contractions *del* and *al,* respectively (*viene* **del** campo, vi **al** hermano de Roberto).

The use of *el, la, los,* and *las* in Spanish corresponds largely to the use of *the* in English; some exceptions are noted below.

The definite article is used:

- When referring to something as a class (*los gatos son ágiles,* cats are agile; *me gusta el café,* I like coffee).

- In references to meals and in most expressions of time (*¿comiste el almuerzo?,* did you eat lunch?; *vino el año pasado,* he came last year; *son las dos,* it's two o'clock; *prefiero el verano,* I prefer summer; *la reunión es el lunes,* the meeting is on Monday; but: *hoy es lunes,* today is Monday).

- Before titles (except *don, doña, san, santo, santa, fray,* and *sor*) in third-person references to people (*la señora Rivera llamó,* Mrs. Rivera called; but: *hola, señora Rivera,* hello, Mrs. Rivera).

- In references to body parts and personal possessions (*me duele la cabeza,* my head hurts; *dejó el sombrero,* he left his hat).
- To mean "the one" or "the ones" when the subject is already understood (*la de madera,* the wooden one; *los que vi ayer,* the ones I saw yesterday).

The definite article is omitted:

- Before a noun in apposition, if the noun is not modified (*Caracas, capital de Venezuela;* but: *Pico Bolívar, la montaña más alta de Venezuela*).
- Before a number in a royal title (*Carlos Quinto,* Charles the Fifth).

2. Indefinite Article

The forms of the indefinite article in Spanish are *un* (masculine singular), *una* (feminine singular), *unos* (masculine plural), and *unas* (feminine plural). They agree in number and gender with the nouns they limit (*una mesa,* a table; *unos platos,* some plates), although the form *un* is used with feminine singular nouns beginning with a stressed *a-* or *ha-* (*un ala, un hacha*).

The use of *un, una, unos,* and *unas* in Spanish corresponds largely to the use of *a, an,* and *some* in English, with some exceptions:

- Indefinite articles are generally omitted before nouns identifying someone or something as a member of a class or category (*Paco es profesor/católico,* Paco is a professor/Catholic; *se llama páncreas,* it's called a pancreas).
- They are also often omitted in instances where quantity is understood from context (*vine sin chaqueta,* I came without a jacket; *no tengo carro,* I don't have a car).

Nouns

1. Gender

Nouns in Spanish are either masculine or feminine. A noun's gender can often be determined according to the following guidelines:

- Nouns ending in *-aje, -o,* or *-or* are usually masculine (*el traje, el libro, el sabor*), with some exceptions (*la mano, la foto, la labor,* etc.).

- Nouns ending in *-a, -dad, -ión, -tud,* or *-umbre* are usually feminine (*la alfombra, la capacidad, la excepción, la juventud, la certidumbre*). Exceptions include: *el día, el mapa,* and many learned borrowings ending in *-ma* (*el idioma, el tema*).

Most nouns referring to people or animals agree in gender with the subject (*el hombre, la mujer; el hermano, la hermana; el perro, la perra*). However, some nouns referring to people, including those ending in *-ista,* use the same form for both sexes (*el artista, la artista; el modelo, la modelo;* etc.).

A few names of animals exist in only one gender form (*la jirafa, el sapo,* etc.). In these instances, the adjectives *macho* and *hembra* are sometimes used to distinguish males and females (*una jirafa macho,* a male giraffe).

2. Pluralization

Plurals of Spanish nouns are formed as follows:

- Nouns ending in an unstressed vowel or an accented *-é* are pluralized by adding *-s* (*la vaca, las vacas; el café, los cafés*).

- Nouns ending in a consonant other than *-s,* or in a stressed vowel other than *-é,* are generally pluralized by adding *-es* (*el papel, los papeles; el rubí, los rubíes*). Exceptions include *papá* (*papás*) and *mamá* (*mamás*).

- Nouns with an unstressed final syllable ending in *-s* usually have a zero plural (*la crisis, las crisis; el jueves, los jueves*). Other nouns ending in *-s* add *-es* to form the plural (*el mes, los meses; el país, los países*).

- Nouns ending in *-z* are pluralized by changing the *-z* to *-c* and adding *-es* (*el lápiz, los lápices; la vez, las veces*).

- Many compound nouns have a zero plural (*el paraguas, los paraguas; el aguafiestas, los aguafiestas*).

- The plurals of *cualquiera* and *quienquiera* are *cualesquiera* and *quienesquiera,* respectively.

Adjectives

1. Gender and Number

Most adjectives agree in gender and number with the nouns they modify (un chico *alto,* una chica *alta,* unos chicos *altos,* unas chicas *altas*). Some adjectives, including those ending in *-e* and *-ista* (*fuerte, altruista*) and comparative adjectives ending in *-or* (*mayor, mejor*), vary only for number.

Adjectives whose masculine singular forms end in *-o* generally change the *-o* to *-a* to form the feminine (*pequeño → pequeña*). Masculine adjectives ending in *-án, -ón,* or *-dor,* and masculine adjectives of nationality which end in a consonant, usually add *-a* to form the feminine (*holgazán → holgazana*; *llorón → llorona*; *trabajador → trabajadora*; *irlandés → irlandesa*).

Adjectives are pluralized in much the same manner as nouns:

- The plurals of adjectives ending in an unstressed vowel or an accented *-é* are formed by adding an *-s* (un postre *rico,* unos postres *ricos;* una camisa *café,* unas camisas *cafés*).
- Adjectives ending in a consonant, or in a stressed vowel other than *-é,* are generally pluralized by adding *-es* (un niño *cortés,* unos niños *corteses;* una persona *iraní,* unas personas *iraníes*).
- Adjectives ending in *-z* are pluralized by changing the *-z* to *-c* and adding *-es* (una respuesta *sagaz*, unas respuestas *sagaces*).

2. Shortening

- The following masculine singular adjectives drop their final *-o* when they occur before a masculine singular noun: *bueno* (*buen*), *malo* (*mal*), *uno* (*un*), *alguno* (*algún*), *ninguno* (*ningún*), *primero* (*primer*), *tercero* (*tercer*).
- *Grande* shortens to *gran* before any singular noun.
- *Ciento* shortens to *cien* before any noun.
- The title *Santo* shortens to *San* before all masculine names except those beginning with *To-* or *Do-* (*San Juan, Santo Tomás*).

3. Position

Descriptive adjectives generally follow the nouns they modify (*una cosa útil, un actor famoso*). However, adjectives that express an inherent quality often precede the noun (*la blanca nieve*).

Some adjectives change meaning depending on whether they occur before or after the noun: *un pobre niño,* a poor (pitiable) child; *un niño pobre,* a poor (not rich) child; *un gran hombre,* a great man; *un hombre grande,* a big man; *el único libro,* the only book; *el libro único,* the unique book, etc.

4. Comparative and Superlative Forms

The comparative of Spanish adjectives is generally rendered as *más . . . que* (more . . . than) or *menos . . . que* (less . . . than): *soy más alta que él,* I'm taller than he; *son menos inteligentes que tú,* they're less intelligent than you.

The superlative of Spanish adjectives usually follows the formula *definite article* + (*noun* +) *más/menos* + *adjective: ella es la estudiante más trabajadora,* she is the hardest-working student; *él es el menos conocido,* he's the least known.

A few Spanish adjectives have irregular comparative and superlative forms:

Adjective	Comparative/Superlative
bueno (good)	**mejor** (better, best)
malo (bad)	**peor** (worse, worst)
grande[1] (big, great), **viejo** (old)	**mayor** (greater, older; greatest, oldest)
pequeño[1] (little), **joven** (young)	**menor** (lesser, younger; least, youngest)
mucho (much), **muchos** (many)	**más** (more, most)
poco (little), **pocos** (few)	**menos** (less, least)

[1] These words have regular comparative and superlative forms when used in reference to physical size: *él es más grande que yo; nuestra casa es la más pequeña.*

ABSOLUTE SUPERLATIVE

The absolute superlative is formed by placing *muy* before the adjective, or by adding the suffix *-ísimo* (*ella es muy simpática* or *ella es simpatiquísima,* she is very nice). The absolute superlative using *-ísimo* is formed according to the following rules:

- Adjectives ending in a consonant other than *-z* simply add the *-ísimo* ending (*fácil* → *facilísimo*).
- Adjectives ending in *-z* change this consonant to *-c* and add *-ísimo* (*feliz* → *felicísimo*).
- Adjectives ending in a vowel or diphthong drop the vowel or diphthong and add *-ísimo* (*claro* → *clarísimo; amplio* → *amplísimo*).
- Adjectives ending in *-co* or *-go* change these endings to *qu* and *gu,* respectively, and add *-ísimo* (*rico* → *riquísimo; largo* → *larguísimo*).
- Adjectives ending in *-ble* change this ending to *-bil* and add *-ísimo* (*notable* → *notabilísimo*).
- Adjectives containing the stressed diphthong *ie* or *ue* will sometimes change these to *e* and *o,* respectively (*ferviente* → *fervientísimo* or *ferventísimo; bueno* → *buenísimo* or *bonísimo*).

Adverbs

Adverbs can be formed by adding the adverbial suffix *-mente* to virtually any adjective (*fácil* → *fácilmente*). If the adjective varies for gender, the feminine form is used as the basis for forming the adverb (*rápido* → *rápidamente*).

Pronouns

1. Personal Pronouns

The personal pronouns in Spanish are:

Person		Singular	Plural	
FIRST	**yo**	I	**nosotros, nosotras**	we
SECOND	**tú**	you (familiar)	**vosotros**[2], **vosotras**[2]	you, all of you
	vos[1]	you		
	usted	you (formal)	**ustedes**[3]	you, all of you
THIRD	**él**	he	**ellos, ellas**	they
	ella	she		
	ello	it (neuter)		

[1] Familiar form used in addition to *tú* in South and Central America.

[2] Familiar form used in Spain.

[3] Formal form used in Spain; familiar and formal form used in Latin America.

FAMILIAR VS. FORMAL

The second person personal pronouns exist in both familiar and formal forms. The familiar forms are generally used when addressing relatives, friends, and children, although usage varies considerably from region to region; the formal forms are used in other contexts to show courtesy, respect, or emotional distance.

In Spain and in the Caribbean, *tú* is used exclusively as the familiar singular "you." In South and Central America, however, *vos* either competes with *tú* to varying degrees or replaces it entirely. (For a more detailed explanation of *vos* and its corresponding verb forms, refer to the Conjugation of Spanish Verbs section.)

The plural familiar form *vosotros, -as* is used only in Spain, where *ustedes* is reserved for formal contexts. In Latin America, *vosotros, -as* is not used, and *ustedes* serves as the all-purpose plural "you."

It should be noted that while *usted* and *ustedes* are regarded as second person pronouns, they take the third person form of the verb.

USAGE

In Spanish, personal pronouns are generally omitted (*voy al cine,* I'm going to the movies; *¿llamaron?,* did they call?), although they are sometimes used for purposes of emphasis or clarity (*se* *lo diré yo,* I will tell them; *vino ella, pero él se quedó,* she came, but he stayed behind). The forms *usted* and *ustedes* are usually included out of courtesy (*¿cómo está usted?,* how are you?).

Personal pronouns are not generally used in reference to inanimate objects or living creatures other than humans; in these instances, the pronoun is most often omitted (*¿es nuevo? no, es viejo,* is it new? no, it's old).

The neuter third person pronoun *ello* is reserved for indefinite subjects (as abstract concepts): *todo ello implica* . . . , all of this implies . . . ; *por si ello fuera poco* . . . , as if that weren't enough . . . . It most commonly appears in formal writing and speech. In less formal contexts, *ello* is often either omitted or replaced with *esto, eso,* or *aquello*.

2. Prepositional Pronouns

Prepositional pronouns are used as the objects of prepositions (*¿es para mí?,* is it for me?; *se lo dio a ellos,* he gave it to them).

The prepositional pronouns in Spanish are:

Singular		Plural	
mí	me	**nosotros, nosotras**	us
ti	you	**vosotros[1], vosotras[1]**	you
usted	you (formal)	**ustedes**	you
él	him	**ellos, ellas**	them
ella	her		
ello	it (neuter)		
sí	yourself, himself, herself, itself, oneself	**sí**	yourselves, themselves

1 Used primarily in Spain.

When the preposition *con* is followed by *mí, ti,* or *sí,* both words are replaced by *conmigo, contigo,* and *consigo,* respectively (*¿vienes conmigo?,* are you coming with me?; *habló contigo,* he spoke with you; *no lo trajo consigo,* she didn't bring it with her).

3. Object Pronouns

DIRECT OBJECT PRONOUNS

Direct object pronouns represent the primary goal or result of the action of a verb. The direct object pronouns in Spanish are:

Singular		**Plural**	
me	me	**nos**	us
te	you	**os**[1]	you
le[2]	you, him	**les**[2]	you, them
lo	you, him, it	**los**	you, them
la	you, her, it	**las**	you, them

[1] Used only in Spain.
[2] Used mainly in Spain.

Agreement

The third person forms agree in both gender and number with the nouns they replace or the people they refer to (*pintó las paredes,* she painted the walls → *las pintó,* she painted them; *visitaron al señor Juárez*, they visited Mr. Juárez → *lo visitaron*, they visited him). The remaining forms vary only for number.

Position

Direct object pronouns are normally affixed to the end of an affirmative command, a simple infinitive, or a present participle (*¡hazlo!,* do it!; *es difícil hacerlo,* it's difficult to do it; *haciéndolo, aprenderás,* you'll learn by doing it). With constructions involving an auxiliary verb and an infinitive or present participle, the pronoun may occur either immediately before the construction or suffixed to it (*lo voy a hacer* or *voy a hacerlo,* I'm going to do it; *estoy haciéndolo* or *lo estoy haciendo,* I'm doing it). In all other cases, the pronoun immediately precedes the conjugated verb (*no lo haré,* I won't do it).

Regional Variation

In Spain and in a few areas of Latin America, *le* and *les* are used in place of *lo* and *los* when referring to or addressing people (*le vieron,* they saw him; *les vistió,* she dressed them). In most parts of Latin America, however, *los* and *las* are used for the second person plural in both formal and familiar contexts.

The second person plural familiar form *os* is restricted to Spain.

INDIRECT OBJECT PRONOUNS

Indirect object pronouns represent the secondary goal of the action of a verb (*me dio el regalo,* he gave me the gift; *les dije que no,* I told them no). The indirect object pronouns in Spanish are:

Singular		Plural	
me	(to, for, from) me	**nos**	(to, for, from) us
te	(to, for, from) you	**os**[1]	(to, for, from) you
le	(to, for, from) you, him, her, it	**les**	(to, for, from) you, them
se[2]		**se**[2]	

[1]Used only in Spain.
[2]See explanation below.

Position

Indirect object pronouns follow the same rules as direct object pronouns with regard to their position in relation to verbs. When they occur with direct object pronouns, the indirect object pronoun always precedes (*nos lo dio,* she gave it to us; *estoy trayéndotela,* I'm bringing it to you).

Use of *Se*

When the indirect object pronouns *le* or *les* occur before any direct object pronoun beginning with an *l-*, the indirect object pronouns *le* and *les* convert to *se* (*les mandé la carta,* I sent them the letter → *se la mandé,* I sent it to them; *vamos a comprarle los aretes,* let's buy her the earrings → *vamos a comprárselos,* let's buy them for her).

4. Reflexive Pronouns

Reflexive pronouns are used to refer back to the subject of the verb (*me hice daño,* I hurt myself; *se vistieron,* they got dressed, they dressed themselves; *nos lo compramos,* we bought it for ourselves).

The reflexive pronouns in Spanish are:

Singular		Plural	
me	myself	**nos**	ourselves
te	yourself	**os**[1]	yourselves
se	yourself, himself, herself, itself	**se**	yourselves, themselves

[1]Used only in Spain.

Reflexive pronouns are also used:

- When the verb describes an action performed to one's own body, clothing, etc. (*me quité los zapatos,* I took off my shoes; *se arregló el pelo,* he fixed his hair).
- In the plural, to indicate reciprocal action (*se hablan con frecuencia,* they speak with each other frequently).
- In the third person singular and plural, as an indefinite subject reference (*se dice que es verdad,* they say it's true; *nunca se sabe,* one never knows; *se escribieron miles de páginas,* thousands of pages were written).

It should be noted that many verbs which take reflexive pronouns in Spanish have intransitive equivalents in English (*ducharse,* to shower; *quejarse,* to complain; etc.).

5. Relative Pronouns

Relative pronouns introduce subordinate clauses acting as nouns or modifiers (*el libro que escribió* . . . , the book that he wrote . . . ; *las chicas a quienes conociste* . . . , the girls whom you met . . .). In Spanish, the relative pronouns are:

que (that, which, who, whom)

quien, quienes (who, whom, that, whoever, whomever)

el cual, la cual, los cuales, las cuales (which, who)

el que, la que, los que, las que (which, who, whoever)

lo cual (which)

lo que (what, which, whatever)

cuanto, cuanta, cuantos, cuantas (all those that, all that, whatever, whoever, as much as, as many as)

Relative pronouns are not omitted in Spanish as they often are in English: *el carro que vi ayer,* the car (that) I saw yesterday. When relative pronouns are used with prepositions, the preposition precedes the clause (*la película sobre la cual le hablé,* the film I spoke to you about).

The relative pronoun *que* can be used in reference to both people and things. Unlike other relative pronouns, *que* does not take the personal *a* when used as a direct object referring to a person (*el hombre que llamé,* the man that I called; but: *el hombre a quien llamé,* the man whom I called).

Quien is used only in reference to people. It varies in number with the explicit or implied antecedent (*las mujeres con quienes charlamos . . . ,* the women we chatted with; *quien lo hizo pagará,* whoever did it will pay).

El cual and *el que* vary for both number and gender, and are therefore often used in situations where *que* or *quien(es)* might create ambiguity: *nos contó algunas cosas sobre los libros, las cuales eran interesantes,* he told us some things about the books which (the things) were interesting.

Lo cual and *lo que* are used to refer back to a whole clause, or to something indefinite (*dijo que iría, lo cual me alegró,* he said he would go, which made me happy; *pide lo que quieras,* ask for whatever you want).

Cuanto varies for both number and gender with the implied antecedent: *conté a cuantas (personas) pude,* I counted as many (people) as I could. If an indefinite mass quantity is referred to, the masculine singular form is used (*anoté cuanto decía,* I jotted down whatever he said).

Possessives

1. Possessive Adjectives

UNSTRESSED FORMS

Singular		Plural	
mi(s)	my	**nuestro(s), nuestra(s)**	our
tu(s)	your	**vuestro(s)**[1], **vuestra(s)**[1]	your
su(s)	your, his, her, its	**su(s)**	your, their

[1] Used only in Spain.

STRESSED FORMS

Singular		Plural	
mío(s), mía(s)	my, mine, of mine	**nuestro(s), nuestra(s)**	our, ours, of ours
tuyo(s), tuya(s)	your, yours, of yours	**vuestro(s)**[1], **vuestra(s)**[1]	your, yours, of yours
suyo(s), suya(s)	your, yours, of yours; his, of his; her, hers, of hers; its, of its	**suyo(s), suya(s)**	your, yours, of yours; their, theirs, of theirs

[1]Used only in Spain.

The unstressed forms of possessive adjectives precede the nouns they modify (*mis zapatos,* my shoes; *nuestra escuela,* our school).

The stressed forms occur after the noun and are often used for purposes of emphasis (*el carro tuyo,* your car; *la pluma es mía,* the pen is mine; *unos amigos nuestros,* some friends of ours).

All possessive adjectives agree with the noun in number. The stressed forms, as well as the unstressed forms *nuestro* and *vuestro,* also vary for gender.

2. Possessive Pronouns

The possessive pronouns have the same forms as the stressed possessive adjectives (see table above). They are always preceded by the definite article, and they agree in number and gender with the nouns they replace (*las llaves mías,* my keys → *las mías,* mine; *los guantes nuestros,* our gloves → *los nuestros,* ours).

Demonstratives

1. Demonstrative Adjectives

The demonstrative adjectives in Spanish are:

Singular		Plural	
este, esta	this	**estos, estas**	these
ese, esa	that	**esos, esas**	those
aquel, aquella	that	**aquellos, aquellas**	those

Demonstrative adjectives agree with the nouns they modify in gender and number (*esta chica, aquellos árboles*). They normally precede the noun, but may occasionally occur after for purposes of emphasis or to express contempt: *en la época aquella de cambio,* in that era of change; *el perro ese ha ladrado toda la noche,* that (awful, annoying, etc.) dog barked all night long.

The forms *aquel, aquella, aquellos,* and *aquellas* are generally used in reference to people and things that are relatively distant from the speaker in space or time: *ese libro,* that book (a few feet away); *aquel libro,* that book (way over there).

2. Demonstrative Pronouns

The demonstrative pronouns in Spanish are orthographically identical to the demonstrative adjectives except that they take an accent mark over the stressed vowel (*éste, ése, aquél,* etc.). In addition, there are three neuter forms—*esto, eso,* and *aquello*—which are used when referring to abstract ideas or unidentified things (*¿te dijo eso?,* he said that to you?; *¿qué es esto?,* what is this?; *tráeme todo aquello,* bring me all that stuff).

Except for the neuter forms, demonstrative pronouns agree in gender and number with the nouns they replace (*esta silla,* this chair → *ésta,* this one; *aquellos vasos,* those glasses → *aquéllos,* those ones).

Abbreviations in This Work

adj adjective
adv adverb
Arg Argentina
Bol Bolivia
Brit British
CA Central America
Car Caribbean region
Col Colombia
conj conjunction
CoRi Costa Rica
DomRep Dominican Republic
Ecua Ecuador
esp especially
f feminine
fam familiar or colloquial
fpl feminine plural
Guat Guatemala
Hond Honduras
interj interjection
m masculine
Mex Mexico
mf masculine or feminine
mfpl masculine or feminine plural
mpl masculine plural
n noun
nf feminine noun
nfpl feminine plural noun
nfs & pl invariable singular or plural feminine noun
Nic Nicaragua
nm masculine noun
nmf masculine or feminine noun
nmfpl plural noun invariable for gender
nmfs & pl noun invariable for both gender and number
nmpl masculine plural noun
nms & pl invariable singular or plural masculine noun
npl plural noun
ns & pl noun invariable for plural
Pan Panama
Par Paraguay
pl plural
pp past participle
prep preposition
PRi Puerto Rico
pron pronoun
s singular
Sal El Salvador
Uru Uruguay
usu usually
v verb (transitive and intransitive)
v aux auxiliary verb
Ven Venezuela
vi intransitive verb
v impers impersonal verb
vr reflexive verb
vt transitive verb

Conjugation of Spanish Verbs

Simple Tenses

Tense	Regular Verbs Ending in -AR hablar	
PRESENT INDICATIVE	hablo hablas habla	hablamos habláis hablan
PRESENT SUBJUNCTIVE	hable hables hable	hablemos habléis hablen
PRETERIT INDICATIVE	hablé hablaste habló	hablamos hablasteis hablaron
IMPERFECT INDICATIVE	hablaba hablabas hablaba	hablábamos hablabais hablaban
IMPERFECT SUBJUNCTIVE	hablara hablaras hablara	habláramos hablarais hablaran
	or	
	hablase hablases hablase	hablásemos hablaseis hablasen
FUTURE INDICATIVE	hablaré hablarás hablará	hablaremos hablaréis hablarán
FUTURE SUBJUNCTIVE	hablare hablares hablare	habláremos hablareis hablaren
CONDITIONAL	hablaría hablarías hablaría	hablaríamos hablaríais hablarían
IMPERATIVE	 habla hable	hablemos hablad hablen
PRESENT PARTICIPLE (GERUND)	hablando	
PAST PARTICIPLE	hablado	

Regular Verbs Ending in -ER comer		**Regular Verbs Ending in -IR** vivir	
como	comemos	vivo	vivimos
comes	coméis	vives	vivís
come	comen	vive	viven
coma	comamos	viva	vivamos
comas	comáis	vivas	viváis
coma	coman	viva	vivan
comí	comimos	viví	vivimos
comiste	comisteis	viviste	vivisteis
comió	comieron	vivió	vivieron
comía	comíamos	vivía	vivíamos
comías	comíais	vivías	vivíais
comía	comían	vivía	vivían
comiera	comiéramos	viviera	viviéramos
comieras	comierais	vivieras	vivierais
comiera	comieran	viviera	vivieran
or		*or*	
comiese	comiésemos	viviese	viviésemos
comieses	comieseis	vivieses	vivieseis
comiese	comiesen	viviese	viviesen
comeré	comeremos	viviré	viviremos
comerás	comeréis	vivirás	viviréis
comerá	comerán	vivirá	vivirán
comiere	comiéremos	viviere	viviéremos
comieres	comiereis	vivieres	viviereis
comiere	comieren	viviere	vivieren
comería	comeríamos	viviría	viviríamos
comerías	comeríais	vivirías	viviríais
comería	comerían	viviría	vivirían
	comamos		vivamos
come	comed	vive	vivid
coma	coman	viva	vivan
comiendo		viviendo	
comido		vivido	

Compound Tenses

1. Perfect Tenses

The perfect tenses are formed with *haber* and the past participle:

PRESENT PERFECT

he hablado, etc. (*indicative*);
haya hablado, etc. (*subjunctive*)

PAST PERFECT

había hablado, etc. (*indicative*);
hubiera hablado, etc. (*subjunctive*)
or
hubiese hablado, etc. (*subjunctive*)

PRETERIT PERFECT

hube hablado, etc. (*indicative*)

FUTURE PERFECT

habré hablado, etc. (*indicative*)

CONDITIONAL PERFECT

habría hablado, etc. (*indicative*)

2. Progressive Tenses

The progressive tenses are formed with *estar* and the present participle:

PRESENT PROGRESSIVE

estoy llamando, etc. (*indicative*);
esté llamando, etc. (*subjunctive*)

IMPERFECT PROGRESSIVE

estaba llamando, etc. (*indicative*);
estuviera llamando, etc. (*subjunctive*)
or
estuviese llamando, etc. (*subjunctive*)

PRETERIT PROGRESSIVE

estuve llamando, etc. (*indicative*)

FUTURE PROGRESSIVE

estaré llamando, etc. (*indicative*)

CONDITIONAL PROGRESSIVE

estaría llamando, etc. (*indicative*)

PRESENT PERFECT PROGRESSIVE

he estado llamando, etc. (*indicative*);
haya estado llamando, etc. (*subjunctive*)

PAST PERFECT PROGRESSIVE

había estado llamando, etc. (*indicative*);
hubiera estado llamando, etc. (*subjunctive*)
or
hubiese estado llamando, etc. (*subjunctive*)

Use of *Vos*

In parts of South and Central America, *vos* often replaces or competes with *tú* as the second person familiar personal pronoun. It is particularly well established in the Río de la Plata region and much of Central America.

The pronoun *vos* often takes a distinct set of verb forms, usually in the present tense and the imperative. These vary widely from region to region; examples of the most common forms are shown below.

INFINITIVE FORM	hablar	comer	vivir
PRESENT INDICATIVE	vos hablás	vos comés	vos vivís
PRESENT SUBJUNCTIVE	vos hablés	vos comás	vos vivás
IMPERATIVE	hablá	comé	viví

In some areas, *vos* may take the *tú* or *vosotros* forms of the verb, while in others (as Uruguay), *tú* is combined with the *vos* verb forms.

Irregular Verbs

The *imperfect subjunctive*, the *future subjunctive*, the *conditional*, and most forms of the *imperative* are not included in the model conjugations list, but can be derived as follows:

The *imperfect subjunctive* and the *future subjunctive* are formed from the third person plural form of the preterit tense by removing the last syllable (*-ron*) and adding the appropriate suffix:

PRETERIT INDICATIVE, THIRD PERSON PLURAL (querer)	quisieron
IMPERFECT SUBJUNCTIVE (querer)	quisiera, quisieras, etc. *or* quisiese, quisieses, etc.
FUTURE SUBJUNCTIVE (querer)	quisiere, quisieres, etc.

The conditional uses the same stem as the future indicative:

FUTURE INDICATIVE (poner)	pondré, pondrás, etc.
CONDITIONAL (poner)	pondría, pondrías, etc.

The third person singular, first person plural, and third person plural forms of the *imperative* are the same as the corresponding forms of the present subjunctive.

The second person plural *(vosotros)* form of the *imperative* is formed by removing the final *-r* of the infinitive form and adding a *-d* (ex.: *oír* → *oíd)*.

Model Conjugations of Irregular Verbs

The model conjugations below include the following simple tenses: the *present indicative* (IND), the *present subjunctive* (SUBJ), the *preterit indicative* (PRET), the *imperfect indicative* (IMPF), the *future indicative* (*FUT*), the second person singular form of the *imperative* (*IMPER*), the *present participle* or *gerund* (*PRP*), and the *past participle* (*PP*). Each set of conjugations is preceded by the corresponding infinitive form of the verb, shown in bold type. Only tenses containing irregularities are listed, and the irregular verb forms within each tense are displayed in bold type.

Each irregular verb entry in the Spanish-English section of this dictionary is cross-referred by number to one of the following model conjugations. These cross-reference numbers are shown in curly braces { } immediately following the entry's functional label.

1 **abolir** *(defective verb)* : *IND* abolimos, abolís *(other forms not used); SUBJ (not used); IMPER (only second person plural is used)*

2 **abrir** : *PP* abierto

3 **actuar** : *IND* **actúo, actúas, actúa**, actuamos, actuáis, **actúan**; *SUBJ* **actúe, actúes, actúe**, actuemos, actuéis, **actúen**; *IMPER* **actúa**

4 **adquirir** : *IND* **adquiero, adquieres, adquiere**, adquirimos, adquirís, **adquieren**; *SUBJ* **adquiera, adquieras, adquiera**, adquiramos, adquiráis, **adquieran**; *IMPER* **adquiere**

5 **airar** : *IND* **aíro, aíras, aíra**, airamos, airáis, **aíran**; *SUBJ* **aíre, aíres, aíre**, airemos, airéis, **aíren**; *IMPER* **aíra**

6 **andar** : *PRET* **anduve, anduviste, anduvo, anduvimos, anduvisteis, anduvieron**

7 **asir** : *IND* **asgo**, ases, ase, asimos, asís, asen; *SUBJ* **asga, asgas, asga, asgamos, asgáis, asgan**

8 **aunar** : *IND* **aúno, aúnas, aúna**, aunamos, aunáis, **aúnan**; *SUBJ* **aúne, aúnes, aúne**, aunemos, aunéis, **aúnen**; *IMPER* **aúna**

9 **avergonzar** : *IND* **avergüenzo, avergüenzas, avergüenza**, avergonzamos, avergonzáis, **avergüenzan**; *SUBJ* **avergüence, avergüences, avergüence, avergoncemos, avergoncéis, avergüencen**; *PRET* **avergoncé**; *IMPER* **avergüenza**

10 **averiguar** : *SUBJ* **averigüe, averigües, averigüe, averigüemos, averigüéis, averigüen**; *PRET* **averigüé**, averiguaste, averiguó, averiguamos, averiguasteis, averiguaron

11 **bendecir** : *IND* **bendigo, bendices, bendice**, bendecimos, bendecís, **bendicen**; *SUBJ* **bendiga, bendigas, bendiga, bendigamos, bendigáis, bendigan**; *PRET* **bendije, bendijiste, bendijo, bendijimos, bendijisteis, bendijeron**; *IMPER* **bendice**

12 **caber** : *IND* **quepo**, cabes, cabe, cabemos, cabéis, caben; *SUBJ* **quepa, quepas, quepa, quepamos, quepáis, quepan**; *PRET* **cupe, cupiste, cupo, cupimos, cupisteis, cupieron**; *FUT* **cabré, cabrás, cabrá, cabremos, cabréis, cabrán**

13 **caer** : *IND* **caigo**, caes, cae, caemos, caéis, caen; *SUBJ* **caiga, caigas, caiga, caigamos, caigáis, caigan**; *PRET* caí, **caíste, cayó, caímos, caísteis, cayeron**; *PRP* **cayendo**; *PP* **caído**

14 **cocer** : *IND* **cuezo, cueces, cuece**, cocemos, cocéis, **cuecen**; *SUBJ* **cueza, cuezas, cueza, cozamos, cozáis, cuezan**; *IMPER* **cuece**

15 **coger** : *IND* **cojo**, coges, coge, cogemos, cogéis, cogen; *SUBJ* **coja, cojas, coja, cojamos, cojáis, cojan**

16 **colgar** : *IND* **cuelgo, cuelgas, cuelga**, colgamos, colgáis, **cuelgan**; *SUBJ* **cuelgue, cuelgues, cuelgue, colguemos, colguéis, cuelguen**; *PRET* **colgué**, colgaste, colgó, colgamos, colgasteis, colgaron; *IMPER* **cuelga**

17 **concernir** *(defective verb; used only in the third person singular and plural of the present indicative, present subjunctive, and imperfect subjunctive) see* 25 **discernir**

18 **conocer** : *IND* **conozco**, conoces, conoce, conocemos, conocéis, conocen; *SUBJ* **conozca, conozcas, conozca, conozcamos, conozcáis, conozcan**

19 **contar** : *IND* **cuento, cuentas, cuenta**, contamos, contáis, **cuentan**; *SUBJ* **cuente, cuentes, cuente**, contemos, contéis, **cuenten**; *IMPER* **cuenta**

20 **creer** : *PRET* creí, **creíste, creyó, creímos, creísteis, creyeron**; *PRP* **creyendo**; *PP* **creído**

21 **cruzar** : *SUBJ* **cruce, cruces, cruce, crucemos, crucéis, crucen**; *PRET* **crucé**, cruzaste, cruzó, cruzamos, cruzasteis, cruzaron

22 **dar** : *IND* **doy**, das, da, damos, **dais**, dan; *SUBJ* **dé**, des, **dé**, demos, **deis**, den; *PRET* **di, diste, dio, dimos, disteis, dieron**

23 **decir** : *IND* **digo, dices, dice**, decimos, decís, **dicen**; *SUBJ* **diga, digas, diga, digamos, digáis, digan**; *PRET* **dije, dijiste, dijo, dijimos, dijisteis, dijeron**; *FUT* **diré, dirás, dirá, diremos, diréis, dirán**; *IMPER* **di**; *PRP* **diciendo**; *PP* **dicho**

24 **delinquir** : *IND* **delinco**, delinques, delinque, delinquimos, delinquís, delinquen; *SUBJ* **delinca, delincas, delinca, delincamos, delincáis, delincan**

25 **discernir** : *IND* **discierno, disciernes, discierne**, discernimos, discernís, **disciernen**; *SUBJ* **discierna, disciernas, discierna**, discernamos, discernáis, **disciernan**; *IMPER* **discierne**

26 **distinguir** : *IND* **distingo**, distingues, distingue, distinguimos, distinguís, distinguen; *SUBJ* **distinga, distingas, distinga, distingamos, distingáis, distingan**

27 **dormir** : *IND* **duermo, duermes, duerme**, dormimos, dormís, **duermen**; *SUBJ* **duerma, duermas, duerma, durmamos, durmáis, duerman**; *PRET* dormí, dormiste, **durmió**, dormimos, dormisteis, **durmieron**; *IMPER* **duerme**; *PRP* **durmiendo**

28 **elegir** : *IND* **elijo, eliges, elige**, elegimos, elegís, **eligen**; *SUBJ* **elija, elijas, elija, elijamos, elijáis, elijan**; *PRET* elegí, elegiste, **eligió**, elegimos, elegisteis, **eligieron**; *IMPER* **elige**; *PRP* **eligiendo**

29 **empezar** : *IND* **empiezo, empiezas, empieza**, empezamos, empezáis, **empiezan**; *SUBJ* **empiece, empieces, empiece, empecemos, empecéis, empiecen**; *PRET* **empecé**, empezaste, empezó, empezamos, empezasteis, empezaron; *IMPER* **empieza**

30 **enraizar** : *IND* **enraízo, enraízas, enraíza**, enraizamos, enraizáis, **enraízan**; *SUBJ* **enraíce, enraíces, enraíce, enraicemos, enraicéis, enraícen**; *PRET* **enraicé**, enraizaste, enraizó, enraizamos, enraizasteis, enraizaron; *IMPER* **enraíza**

31 **erguir** : *IND* **irgo** *or* **yergo, irgues** *or* **yergues, irgue** *or* **yergue**, erguimos, erguís, **irguen** *or* **yerguen**; *SUBJ* **irga** *or* **yerga, irgas** *or* **yergas, irga** *or* **yerga, irgamos, irgáis, irgan** *or* **yergan**; *PRET* erguí, erguiste, **irguió**, erguimos, erguisteis, **irguieron**; *IMPER* **irgue** *or* **yergue**; *PRP* **irguiendo**

32 **errar** : *IND* **yerro, yerras, yerra,** erramos, erráis, **yerran;** *SUBJ* **yerre, yerres, yerre,** erremos, erréis, **yerren;** *IMPER* **yerra**

33 **escribir** : *PP* **escrito**

34 **estar** : *IND* **estoy, estás, está,** estamos, estáis, **están;** *SUBJ* **esté, estés, esté,** estemos, estéis, **estén;** *PRET* **estuve, estuviste, estuvo, estuvimos, estuvisteis, estuvieron;** *IMPER* **está**

35 **exigir** : *IND* **exijo,** exiges, exige, exigimos, exigís, exigen; *SUBJ* **exija, exijas, exija, exijamos, exijáis, exijan**

36 **forzar** : *IND* **fuerzo, fuerzas, fuerza,** forzamos, forzáis, **fuerzan;** *SUBJ* **fuerce, fuerces, fuerce, forcemos, forcéis, fuercen;** *PRET* **forcé,** forzaste, forzó, forzamos, forzasteis, forzaron; *IMPER* **fuerza**

37 **freír** : *IND* **frío, fríes, fríe, freímos,** freís, **fríen;** *SUBJ* **fría, frías, fría, friamos, friáis, frían;** *PRET* freí, **freíste, frió, freímos, freísteis, frieron;** *IMPER* **fríe;** *PRP* **friendo;** *PP* **frito**

38 **gruñir** : *PRET* gruñí, gruñiste, **gruñó,** gruñimos, gruñisteis, **gruñeron;** *PRP* **gruñendo**

39 **haber** : *IND* **he, has, ha, hemos,** habéis, **han;** *SUBJ* **haya, hayas, haya, hayamos, hayáis, hayan;** *PRET* **hube, hubiste, hubo, hubimos, hubisteis, hubieron;** *FUT* **habré, habrás, habrá, habremos, habréis, habrán;** *IMPER* **he**

40 **hacer** : *IND* **hago,** haces, hace, hacemos, hacéis, hacen; *SUBJ* **haga, hagas, haga, hagamos, hagáis, hagan;** *PRET* **hice, hiciste, hizo, hicimos, hicisteis, hicieron;** *FUT* **haré, harás, hará, haremos, haréis, harán;** *IMPER* **haz;** *PP* **hecho**

41 **huir** : *IND* **huyo, huyes, huye,** huimos, huís, **huyen;** *SUBJ* **huya, huyas, huya, huyamos, huyáis, huyan;** *PRET* huí, huiste, **huyó,** huimos, huisteis, **huyeron;** *IMPER* **huye;** *PRP* **huyendo**

42 **imprimir** : *PP* **impreso**

43 **ir** : *IND* **voy, vas, va, vamos, vais, van;** *SUBJ* **vaya, vayas, vaya, vayamos, vayáis, vayan;** *PRET* **fui, fuiste, fue, fuimos, fuisteis, fueron;** *IMPF* **iba, ibas, iba, íbamos, ibais, iban;** *IMPER* **ve;** *PRP* **yendo;** *PP* **ido**

44 **jugar** : *IND* **juego, juegas, juega,** jugamos, jugáis, **juegan;** *SUBJ* **juegue, juegues, juegue, juguemos, juguéis, jueguen;** *PRET*

jugué, jugaste, jugó, jugamos, jugasteis, jugaron; *IMPER* **juega**

45 **lucir** : *IND* **luzco**, luces, luce, lucimos, lucís, lucen; *SUBJ* **luzca, luzcas, luzca, luzcamos, luzcáis, luzcan**

46 **morir** : *IND* **muero, mueres, muere**, morimos, morís, **mueren**; *SUBJ* **muera, mueras, muera, muramos, muráis, mueran**; *PRET* morí, moriste, **murió**, morimos, moristeis, **murieron**; *IMPER* **muere**; *PRP* **muriendo**; *PP* **muerto**

47 **mover** : *IND* **muevo, mueves, mueve**, movemos, movéis, **mueven**; *SUBJ* **mueva, muevas, mueva**, movamos, mováis, **muevan**; *IMPER* **mueve**

48 **nacer** : *IND* **nazco**, naces, nace, nacemos, nacéis, nacen; *SUBJ* **nazca, nazcas, nazca, nazcamos, nazcáis, nazcan**

49 **negar** : *IND* **niego, niegas, niega**, negamos, negáis, **niegan**; *SUBJ* **niegue, niegues, niegue, neguemos, neguéis, nieguen**; *PRET* **negué**, negaste, negó, negamos, negasteis, negaron; *IMPER* **niega**

50 **oír** : *IND* **oigo, oyes, oye, oímos**, oís, **oyen**; *SUBJ* **oiga, oigas, oiga, oigamos, oigáis, oigan**; *PRET* oí, **oíste, oyó, oímos, oísteis, oyeron**; *IMPER* **oye**; *PRP* **oyendo**; *PP* **oído**

51 **oler** : *IND* **huelo, hueles, huele**, olemos, oléis, **huelen**; *SUBJ* **huela, huelas, huela**, olamos, oláis, **huelan**; *IMPER* **huele**

52 **pagar** : *SUBJ* **pague, pagues, pague, paguemos, paguéis, paguen**; *PRET* **pagué**, pagaste, pagó, pagamos, pagasteis, pagaron

53 **parecer** : *IND* **parezco**, pareces, parece, parecemos, parecéis, parecen; *SUBJ* **parezca, parezcas, parezca, parezcamos, parezcáis, parezcan**

54 **pedir** : *IND* **pido, pides, pide**, pedimos, pedís, **piden**; *SUBJ* **pida, pidas, pida, pidamos, pidáis, pidan**; *PRET* pedí, pediste, **pidió**, pedimos, pedisteis, **pidieron**; *IMPER* **pide**; *PRP* **pidiendo**

55 **pensar** : *IND* **pienso, piensas, piensa**, pensamos, pensáis, **piensan**; *SUBJ* **piense, pienses, piense**, pensemos, penséis, **piensen**; *IMPER* **piensa**

56 **perder** : *IND* **pierdo, pierdes, pierde,** perdemos, perdéis, **pierden;** *SUBJ* **pierda, pierdas, pierda,** perdamos, perdáis, **pierdan;** *IMPER* **pierde**

57 **placer** : *IND* **plazco,** places, place, placemos, placéis, placen; *SUBJ* **plazca, plazcas, plazca, plazcamos, plazcáis, plazcan;** *PRET* plací, placiste, plació *or* **plugo,** placimos, placisteis, placieron *or* **pluguieron**

58 **poder** : *IND* **puedo, puedes, puede,** podemos, podéis, **pueden;** *SUBJ* **pueda, puedas, pueda,** podamos, podáis, **puedan;** *PRET* **pude, pudiste, pudo, pudimos, pudisteis, pudieron;** *FUT* **podré, podrás, podrá, podremos, podréis, podrán;** *IMPER* **puede;** *PRP* **pudiendo**

59 **podrir** *or* **pudrir** : *PP* **podrido** *(all other forms based on* pudrir*)*

60 **poner** : *IND* **pongo,** pones, pone, ponemos, ponéis, ponen; *SUBJ* **ponga, pongas, ponga, pongamos, pongáis, pongan;** *PRET* **puse, pusiste, puso, pusimos, pusisteis, pusieron;** *FUT* **pondré, pondrás, pondrá, pondremos, pondréis, pondrán;** *IMPER* **pon;** *PP* **puesto**

61 **producir** : *IND* **produzco,** produces, produce, producimos, producís, producen; *SUBJ* **produzca, produzcas, produzca, produzcamos, produzcáis, produzcan;** *PRET* **produje, produjiste, produjo, produjimos, produjisteis, produjeron**

62 **prohibir** : *IND* **prohíbo, prohíbes, prohíbe,** prohibimos, prohibís, **prohíben;** *SUBJ* **prohíba, prohíbas, prohíba,** prohibamos, prohibáis, **prohíban;** *IMPER* **prohíbe**

63 **proveer** : *PRET* proveí, **proveíste, proveyó, proveímos, proveísteis, proveyeron;** *PRP* **proveyendo;** *PP* **provisto**

64 **querer** : *IND* **quiero, quieres, quiere,** queremos, queréis, **quieren;** *SUBJ* **quiera, quieras, quiera,** queramos, queráis, **quieran;** *PRET* **quise, quisiste, quiso, quisimos, quisisteis, quisieron;** *FUT* **querré, querrás, querrá, querremos, querréis, querrán;** *IMPER* **quiere**

65 **raer** : *IND* rao *or* **raigo** *or* **rayo,** raes, rae, raemos, raéis, raen; *SUBJ* **raiga** *or* **raya, raigas** *or* **rayas, raiga** *or* **raya, raigamos** *or* **rayamos, raigáis** *or* **rayáis, raigan** *or* **rayan;** *PRET* **raí, raíste, rayó, raímos, raísteis, rayeron;** *PRP* **rayendo;** *PP* **raído**

66 **reír** : *IND* **río, ríes, ríe, reímos**, reís, **ríen**; *SUBJ* **ría, rías, ría, riamos, riáis, rían**; *PRET* reí, **reíste, rió, reímos, reísteis, rieron**; *IMPER* **ríe**; *PRP* **riendo**; *PP* **reído**

67 **reñir** : *IND* **riño, riñes, riñe**, reñimos, reñís, **riñen**; *SUBJ* **riña, riñas, riña, riñamos, riñáis, riñan**; *PRET* reñí, reñiste, **riñó**, reñimos, reñisteis, **riñeron**; *IMPER* riñe; *PRP* riñendo

68 **reunir** : *IND* **reúno, reúnes, reúne**, reunimos, reunís, **reúnen**; *SUBJ* **reúna, reúnas, reúna**, reunamos, reunáis, **reúnan**; *IMPER* **reúne**

69 **roer** : *IND* roo *or* **roigo** *or* **royo**, roes, roe, roemos, roéis, roen; *SUBJ* roa *or* **roiga** *or* **roya**, roas *or* **roigas** *or* **royas**, roa *or* **roiga** *or* **roya**, roamos *or* **roigamos** *or* **royamos**, roáis *or* **roigáis** *or* **royáis**, roan *or* **roigan** *or* **royan**; *PRET* roí, **roíste, royó, roímos, roísteis, royeron**; *PRP* **royendo**; *PP* **roído**

70 **romper** : *PP* **roto**

71 **saber** : *IND* **sé**, sabes, sabe, sabemos, sabéis, saben; *SUBJ* **sepa, sepas, sepa, sepamos, sepáis, sepan**; *PRET* **supe, supiste, supo, supimos, supisteis, supieron**; *FUT* **sabré, sabrás, sabrá, sabremos, sabréis, sabrán**

72 **sacar** : *SUBJ* **saque, saques, saque, saquemos, saquéis, saquen**; *PRET* **saqué**, sacaste, sacó, sacamos, sacasteis, sacaron

73 **salir** : *IND* **salgo**, sales, sale, salimos, salís, salen; *SUBJ* **salga, salgas, salga, salgamos, salgáis, salgan**; *FUT* **saldré, saldrás, saldrá, saldremos, saldréis, saldrán**; *IMPER* **sal**

74 **satisfacer** : *IND* **satisfago**, satisfaces, satisface, satisfacemos, satisfacéis, satisfacen; *SUBJ* **satisfaga, satisfagas, satisfaga, satisfagamos, satisfagáis, satisfagan**; *PRET* **satisfice, satisficiste, satisfizo, satisficimos, satisficisteis, satisficieron**; *FUT* **satisfaré, satisfarás, satisfará, satisfaremos, satisfaréis, satisfarán**; *IMPER* **satisfaz** *or* satisface; *PP* **satisfecho**

75 **seguir** : *IND* **sigo, sigues, sigue**, seguimos, seguís, **siguen**; *SUBJ* **siga, sigas, siga, sigamos, sigáis, sigan**; *PRET* seguí, seguiste, **siguió**, seguimos, seguisteis, **siguieron**; *IMPER* **sigue**; *PRP* **siguiendo**

76 **sentir** : *IND* **siento, sientes, siente**, sentimos, sentís, **sienten**; *SUBJ* **sienta, sientas, sienta, sintamos, sintáis, sientan**; *PRET*

sentí, sentiste, **sintió**, sentimos, sentisteis, **sintieron**; *IMPER* **siente**; *PRP* **sintiendo**

77 **ser** : *IND* **soy, eres, es, somos, sois, son**; *SUBJ* **sea, seas, sea, seamos, seáis, sean**; *PRET* **fui, fuiste, fue, fuimos, fuisteis, fueron**; *IMPF* **era, eras, era, éramos, erais, eran**; *IMPER* **sé**; *PRP* **siendo**; *PP* **sido**

78 **soler** *(defective verb; used only in the present, preterit, and imperfect indicative, and the present and imperfect subjunctive) see* 47 **mover**

79 **tañer** : *PRET* tañí, tañiste, **tañó**, tañimos, tañisteis, **tañeron**; *PRP* **tañendo**

80 **tener** : *IND* **tengo, tienes, tiene**, tenemos, tenéis, **tienen**; *SUBJ* **tenga, tengas, tenga, tengamos, tengáis, tengan**; *PRET* **tuve, tuviste, tuvo, tuvimos, tuvisteis, tuvieron**; *FUT* **tendré, tendrás, tendrá, tendremos, tendréis, tendrán**; *IMPER* **ten**

81 **traer** : *IND* **traigo**, traes, trae, traemos, traéis, traen; *SUBJ* **traiga, traigas, traiga, traigamos, traigáis, traigan**; *PRET* **traje, trajiste, trajo, trajimos, trajisteis, trajeron**; *PRP* **trayendo**; *PP* **traído**

82 **trocar** : *IND* **trueco, truecas, trueca**, trocamos, trocáis, **truecan**; *SUBJ* **trueque, trueques, trueque, troquemos, troquéis, truequen**; *PRET* **troqué**, trocaste, trocó, trocamos, trocasteis, trocaron; *IMPER* **trueca**

83 **uncir** : *IND* **unzo**, unces, unce, uncimos, uncís, uncen; *SUBJ* **unza, unzas, unza, unzamos, unzáis, unzan**

84 **valer** : *IND* **valgo**, vales, vale, valemos, valéis, valen; *SUBJ* **valga, valgas, valga, valgamos, valgáis, valgan**; *FUT* **valdré, valdrás, valdrá, valdremos, valdréis, valdrán**

85 **variar** : *IND* **varío, varías, varía**, variamos, variáis, **varían**; *SUBJ* **varíe, varíes, varíe**, variemos, variéis, **varíen**; *IMPER* **varía**

86 **vencer** : *IND* **venzo**, vences, vence, vencemos, vencéis, vencen; *SUBJ* **venza, venzas, venza, venzamos, venzáis, venzan**

87 **venir** : *IND* **vengo, vienes, viene**, venimos, venís, **vienen**; *SUBJ* **venga, vengas, venga, vengamos, vengáis, vengan**; *PRET* **vine, viniste, vino, vinimos, vinisteis, vinieron**; *FUT* **vendré,**

vendrás, vendrá, vendremos, vendréis, vendrán; *IMPER* **ven**; *PRP* **viniendo**

88 **ver** : *IND* veo, **ves, ve, vemos, veis, ven**; *PRET* **vi, viste, vio, vimos, visteis, vieron**; *IMPER* **ve**; *PRP* **viendo**; *PP* **visto**

89 **volver** : *IND* **vuelvo, vuelves, vuelve**, volvemos, volvéis, **vuelven**; *SUBJ* **vuelva, vuelvas, vuelva**, volvamos, volváis, **vuelvan**; *IMPER* **vuelve**; *PP* **vuelto**

90 **yacer** : *IND* **yazco** *or* **yazgo** *or* **yago**, yaces, yace, yacemos, yacéis, yacen; *SUBJ* **yazca** *or* **yazga** *or* **yaga, yazcas** *or* **yazgas** *or* **yagas, yazca** *or* **yazga** *or* **yaga, yazcamos** *or* **yazgamos** *or* **yagamos, yazcáis** *or* **yazgáis** *or* **yagáis, yazcan** *or* **yazgan** *or* **yagan**; *IMPER* yace *or* **yaz**

Irregular English Verbs

INFINITIVE	PAST	PAST PARTICIPLE
arise	arose	arisen
awake	awoke	awoken *or* awaked
be	was, were	been
bear	bore	borne
beat	beat	beaten *or* beat
become	became	become
befall	befell	befallen
begin	began	begun
behold	beheld	beheld
bend	bent	bent
beseech	beseeched *or* besought	beseeched *or* besought
beset	beset	beset
bet	bet	bet
bid	bade *or* bid	bidden *or* bid
bind	bound	bound
bite	bit	bitten
bleed	bled	bled
blow	blew	blown
break	broke	broken
breed	bred	bred
bring	brought	brought
build	built	built
burn	burned *or* burnt	burned *or* burnt
burst	burst	burst
buy	bought	bought
can	could	—
cast	cast	cast
catch	caught	caught
choose	chose	chosen
cling	clung	clung
come	came	come
cost	cost	cost
creep	crept	crept
cut	cut	cut
deal	dealt	dealt
dig	dug	dug
do	did	done
draw	drew	drawn
dream	dreamed *or* dreamt	dreamed *or* dreamt
drink	drank	drunk *or* drank
drive	drove	driven
dwell	dwelled *or* dwelt	dwelled *or* dwelt

INFINITIVE	PAST	PAST PARTICIPLE
eat	ate	eaten
fall	fell	fallen
feed	fed	fed
feel	felt	felt
fight	fought	fought
find	found	found
flee	fled	fled
fling	flung	flung
fly	flew	flown
forbid	forbade	forbidden
forecast	forecast	forecast
forego	forewent	foregone
foresee	foresaw	foreseen
foretell	foretold	foretold
forget	forgot	forgotten *or* forgot
forgive	forgave	forgiven
forsake	forsook	forsaken
freeze	froze	frozen
get	got	got *or* gotten
give	gave	given
go	went	gone
grind	ground	ground
grow	grew	grown
hang	hung	hung
have	had	had
hear	heard	heard
hide	hid	hidden *or* hid
hit	hit	hit
hold	held	held
hurt	hurt	hurt
keep	kept	kept
kneel	knelt *or* kneeled	knelt *or* kneeled
know	knew	known
lay	laid	laid
lead	led	led
lean	leaned	leaned
leap	leaped *or* leapt	leaped *or* leapt
learn	learned	learned
leave	left	left
lend	lent	lent
let	let	let
lie	lay	lain
light	lit *or* lighted	lit *or* lighted
lose	lost	lost
make	made	made
may	might	—

INFINITIVE	PAST	PAST PARTICIPLE
mean	meant	meant
meet	met	met
mow	mowed	mowed *or* mown
pay	paid	paid
put	put	put
quit	quit	quit
read	read	read
rend	rent	rent
rid	rid	rid
ride	rode	ridden
ring	rang	rung
rise	rose	risen
run	ran	run
saw	sawed	sawed *or* sawn
say	said	said
see	saw	seen
seek	sought	sought
sell	sold	sold
send	sent	sent
set	set	set
shake	shook	shaken
shall	should	—
shear	sheared	sheared *or* shorn
shed	shed	shed
shine	shone *or* shined	shone *or* shined
shoot	shot	shot
show	showed	shown *or* showed
shrink	shrank *or* shrunk	shrunk *or* shrunken
shut	shut	shut
sing	sang *or* sung	sung
sink	sank *or* sunk	sunk
sit	sat	sat
slay	slew	slain
sleep	slept	slept
slide	slid	slid
sling	slung	slung
smell	smelled *or* smelt	smelled *or* smelt
sow	sowed	sown *or* sowed
speak	spoke	spoken
speed	sped *or* speeded	sped *or* speeded
spell	spelled	spelled
spend	spent	spent
spill	spilled	spilled
spin	spun	spun
spit	spit *or* spat	spit *or* spat
split	split	split

INFINITIVE	PAST	PAST PARTICIPLE
spoil	spoiled	spoiled
spread	spread	spread
spring	sprang *or* sprung	sprung
stand	stood	stood
steal	stole	stolen
stick	stuck	stuck
sting	stung	stung
stink	stank *or* stunk	stunk
stride	strode	stridden
strike	struck	struck
swear	swore	sworn
sweep	swept	swept
swell	swelled	swelled *or* swollen
swim	swam	swum
swing	swung	swung
take	took	taken
teach	taught	taught
tear	tore	torn
tell	told	told
think	thought	thought
throw	threw	thrown
thrust	thrust	thrust
tread	trod	trodden *or* trod
wake	woke	woken *or* waked
waylay	waylaid	waylaid
wear	wore	worn
weave	wove *or* weaved	woven *or* weaved
wed	wedded	wedded
weep	wept	wept
will	would	—
win	won	won
wind	wound	wound
withdraw	withdrew	withdrawn
withhold	withheld	withheld
withstand	withstood	withstood
wring	wrung	wrung
write	wrote	written

Spelling-to-Sound Correspondences in Spanish

For example words for the phonetic symbols below, see Pronunciation Symbols on page 58a.

VOWELS

a [a]

e [e] in open syllables (syllables ending with a vowel); [ɛ] in closed syllables (syllables ending with a consonant)

i [i]; before another vowel in the same syllable pronounced as [j] ([ʒ] or [ʃ] in Argentina and Uruguay; [ʤ] when at the beginning of a word in the Caribbean)

o [o] in open syllables (syllables ending with a vowel); [ɔ] in closed syllables (syllables ending with a consonant)

u [u]; before another vowel in the same syllable pronounced as [w]

y [i]; before another vowel in the same syllable pronounced as [j] ([ʒ] or [ʃ] in Argentina and Uruguay; [ʤ] when at the beginning of a word in the Caribbean)

CONSONANTS

b [b] at the beginning of a word or after *m* or *n*; [β] elsewhere

c [s] before *i* or *e* in Latin America and parts of southern Spain, [θ] in northern Spain; [k] elsewhere

ch [ʧ]; frequently [ʃ] in Chile and Panama; sometimes [ts] in Chile

d [d] at the beginning of a word or after *n* or *l*; [ð] elsewhere, frequently silent between vowels

f [f]; [Φ] in Honduras (no English equivalent for this sound; like [f] but made with both lips)

g [x] before *i* or *e* ([h] in the Caribbean and Central America); [g] at the beginning of a word or after *n* and not before *i* or *e*; [ɣ] elsewhere, frequently silent between vowels

gu [gw] at the beginning of a word before *a*, *o;* [ɣw] elsewhere before *a*, *o*; frequently just [w] between vowels; [g] at the beginning of a word before *i*, *e*; [ɣ] elsewhere before *i*, *e*; frequently silent between vowels

gü [gw] at the beginning of a word, [ɣw] elsewhere; frequently just [w] between vowels

h silent

j [x] ([h] in the Caribbean and Central America)

k [k]

l [l]

ll [j]; [ʒ] or [ʃ] in Argentina and Uruguay; [ʤ] when at the beginning of a word in the Caribbean;

	[lʲ] in Bolivia, Paraguay, Peru, and parts of northern Spain (no English equivalent; like "lli" in *million*)
m	[m]
n	[n]; frequently [ŋ] at the end of a word when next word begins with a vowel
ñ	[ɲ]
p	[p]
qu	[k]
r	[r] (no English equivalent; a trilled sound) at the beginning of words; [ɾ̥]/[ɾ] elsewhere
rr	[r] (no English equivalent; a trilled sound)
s	[s]; frequently [z] before *b*, *d*, *g*, *m*, *n*, *l*, *r*; at the end of a word [h] or silent in many parts of Latin America and some parts of Spain
t	[t]
v	[b] at the beginning of a word or after *m* or *n*; [β] elsewhere
x	[ks] or [gz] between vowels; [s] before consonants
z	[s] in Latin America and parts of southern Spain, [θ] in northern Spain; at the end of a word [h] or silent in many parts of Latin America and some parts of Spain

Pronunciation Symbols

VOWELS

æ	**a**sk, b**a**t, gl**a**d
ɑ	c**o**t, b**o**mb
a	*New England* **au**nt, *British* **a**sk, gl**a**ss, *Spanish* c**a**sa
e	*Spanish* p**e**so, j**e**fe
ɛ	**e**gg, b**e**t, f**e**d
ə	**a**bout, jav**e**lin, Al**a**bam**a**
ə	when italicized as in *ə*l, *ə*m, *ə*n, indicates a syllabic pronunciation of the consonant as in bott**le**, pris**m**, butt**on**
i	ver**y**, an**y**, thirt**y**, *Spanish* piñ**a**
iː	**ea**t, b**ea**d, b**ee**
ɪ	**i**d, b**i**d, p**i**t
o	**O**hio, yell**o**wer, potat**o**, *Spanish* **ó**valo
oː	**oa**ts, **ow**n, z**o**ne, bl**ow**
ɔ	**aw**l, m**au**l, c**au**ght, p**aw**
ʊ	s**u**re, sh**ou**ld, c**ou**ld
u	*Spanish* **u**va, c**u**lpa
uː	b**oo**t, f**ew**, c**oo**
ʌ	**u**nder, p**u**tt, b**u**d
eɪ	**ei**ght, w**a**de, b**ay**
aɪ	**i**ce, b**i**te, t**ie**
aʊ	**ou**t, g**ow**n, pl**ow**
ɔɪ	**oy**ster, c**oi**l, b**oy**
ər	f**ur**th**er**, st**ir**
ɒ	*British* b**o**nd, g**o**d
ː	indicates that the preceding vowel is long. Long vowels are almost always diphthongs in English, but not in Spanish.

CONSONANTS

b	**b**a**b**y, la**b**or, ca**b**
β	*Spanish* ca**b**o, ó**v**alo
d	**d**ay, rea**d**y, ki**d**
ʤ	**j**ust, ba**dg**er, fu**dg**e
ð	**th**en, ei**th**er, ba**th**e
f	**f**oe, tou**gh**, bu**ff**
g	**g**o, bi**gg**er, ba**g**
ɣ	*Spanish* tra**g**ar, da**g**a
h	**h**ot, a**h**a
j	**y**es, vine**y**ard
k	**c**at, **k**eep, la**cqu**er, flo**ck**
l	**l**aw, ho**ll**ow, boi**l**
m	**m**at, he**m**p, ha**mm**er, ri**m**
n	**n**ew, te**n**t, te**n**or, ru**n**
ŋ	ru**ng**, ha**ng**, swi**ng**er
ɲ	*Spanish* caba**ñ**a, pi**ñ**a
p	**p**ay, la**p**se, to**p**
r	**r**ope, bu**r**n, ta**r**
s	**s**ad, mi**s**t, ki**ss**
ʃ	**sh**oe, mi**ss**ion, slu**sh**
t	**t**oe, bu**tt**on, ma**t**
t̬	indicates that some speakers of English pronounce this as a voiced alveolar flap [ɾ], as in la**t**er, ca**tt**y, ba**tt**le
ʧ	**ch**oose, ba**tch**
θ	**th**in, e**th**er, ba**th**
v	**v**at, ne**v**er, ca**v**e
w	**w**et, soft**w**are
x	*German* Ba**ch**, *Scots* lo**ch**, *Spanish* **g**ente, **j**efe
z	**z**oo, ea**s**y, bu**zz**
ʒ	**j**aborandi, a**z**ure, bei**g**e
h, k, p, t	when italicized indicate sounds which are present in the pronunciation of some speakers of English but absent in that of others, so that *whence* [ˈ*h*wɛn*t*s] can be pronounced as [ˈwɛns], [ˈhwɛns], [ˈwɛnts], or [ˈhwɛnts]

STRESS MARKS

ˈ	high stress	**pen**manship
ˌ	low stress	penman**ship**

Spanish–English Dictionary

A

a¹ *nf* : first letter of the Spanish alphabet

a² *prep* **1** : to ⟨nos vamos a México : we're going to Mexico⟩ **2** (*used before direct or indirect objects referring to persons*) ⟨¿llamaste a tu papá? : did you call your dad?⟩ ⟨como a usted le guste : as you wish⟩ **3** : in the manner of ⟨papas a la francesa : french fries⟩ **4** : on, by means of ⟨a pie : on foot⟩ **5** : per, each ⟨tres pastillas al día : three pills per day⟩ **6** : at ⟨a las dos : at two o'clock⟩ ⟨al principio : at first⟩ **7** (*with infinitive*) ⟨enséñales a leer : teach them to read⟩ ⟨problemas a resolver : problems to be solved⟩

ábaco *nm* : abacus

abad *nm* : abbot

abadesa *nf* : abbess

abadía *nf* : abbey

abajo *adv* **1** : down ⟨póngalo más abajo : put it further down⟩ ⟨arriba y abajo : up and down⟩ **2** : downstairs **3** : under, beneath ⟨el abajo firmante : the undersigned⟩ **4** : down with ⟨¡abajo la inflación! : down with inflation!⟩ **5 ~ de** : under, beneath **6 de ~** : bottom ⟨el cajón de abajo : the bottom drawer⟩ **7 hacia ~** *or* **para ~** : downwards **8 cuesta abajo** : downhill **9 río abajo** : downstream

abalanzarse {21} *vr* : to hurl oneself, to rush

abanderado, -da *n* : standard-bearer

abandonado, -da *adj* **1** : abandoned, deserted **2** : neglected **3** : slovenly, unkempt

abandonar *vt* **1** DEJAR : to abandon, to leave **2** : to give up, to quit ⟨abandonaron la búsqueda : they gave up the search⟩ — **abandonarse** *vr* **1** : to neglect oneself **2 ~ a** : to succumb to, to give oneself over to

abandono *nm* **1** : abandonment **2** : neglect **3** : withdrawal ⟨ganar por abandono : to win by default⟩

abanicar {72} *vt* : to fan — **abanicarse** *vr*

abanico *nm* **1** : fan **2** GAMA : range, gamut

abaratamiento *nm* : price reduction

abaratar *vt* : to lower the price of — **abaratarse** *vr* : to go down in price

abarcar {72} *vt* **1** : to cover, to include, to embrace **2** : to undertake **3** : to monopolize

abaritonado, -da *adj* : baritone

abarrotado, -da *adj* : packed, crammed

abarrotar *vt* : to fill up, to pack

abarrotería *nf CA, Mex* : grocery store

abarrotero, -ra *n Col, Mex* : grocer

abarrotes *nmpl* **1** : groceries, supplies **2 tienda de abarrotes** : general store, grocery store

abastecedor, -dora *n* : supplier

abastecer {53} *vt* : to supply, to stock — **abastecerse** *vr* : to stock up

abastecimiento → **abasto**

abasto *nm* : supply, supplying ⟨no da abasto : there isn't enough for all⟩

abatido, -da *adj* : dejected, depressed

abatimiento *nm* **1** : drop, reduction **2** : dejection, depression

abatir *vt* **1** DERRIBAR : to demolish, to knock down **2** : to shoot down **3** DEPRIMIR : to depress, to bring low — **abatirse** *vr* **1** DEPRIMIRSE : to get depressed **2 ~ sobre** : to swoop down on

abdicación *nf, pl* **-ciones** : abdication

abdicar {72} *vt* : to relinquish, to abdicate

abdomen *nm, pl* **-dómenes** : abdomen

abdominal *adj* : abdominal

abecé *nm* : ABC's *pl*

abecedario *nm* ALFABETO : alphabet

abedul *nm* : birch (tree)

abeja *nf* : bee

abejorro *nm* : bumblebee

aberración *nf, pl* **-ciones** : aberration

aberrante *adj* : aberrant, perverse

abertura *nf* **1** : aperture, opening **2** AGUJERO : hole **3** : slit (in a skirt, etc.) **4** GRIETA : crack

abeto *nm* : fir (tree)

abierto¹ *pp* → **abrir**

abierto², -ta *adj* **1** : open **2** : candid, frank **3** : generous — **abiertamente** *adv*

abigarrado, -da *adj* : multicolored, variegated

abigeato *nm* : rustling (of livestock)

abismal *adj* : abysmal, vast

abismo *nm* : abyss, chasm ⟨al borde del abismo : on the brink of ruin⟩

abjurar *vi* **~ de** : to abjure — **abjuración** *nf*

ablandamiento *nm* : softening, moderation

ablandar *vt* **1** SUAVIZAR : to soften **2** CALMAR : to soothe, to appease — *vi* : to moderate, to get milder — **ablandarse** *vr* **1** : to become soft, to soften **2** CEDER : to yield, to relent

ablución *nf, pl* **-ciones** : ablution

abnegación *nf, pl* **-ciones** : abnegation, self-denial

abnegado, -da *adj* : self-sacrificing, selfless

abnegarse {49} *vr* : to deny oneself

abobado, -da *adj* **1** : silly, stupid **2** : bewildered

abocarse {72} *vr* **1** DIRIGIRSE : to head, to direct oneself **2** DEDICARSE : to dedicate oneself

abochornar *vt* AVERGONZAR : to embarrass, to shame — **abochornarse** *vr*

abofetear *vt* : to slap

abogacía *nf* : law, legal profession

abogado, -da *n* : lawyer, attorney

abogar {52} *vi* **~ por** : to plead for, to defend, to advocate

abolengo *nm* LINAJE : lineage, ancestry
abolición *nf, pl* **-ciones** : abolition
abolir {1} *vt* DEROGAR : to abolish, to repeal
abolladura *nf* : dent
abollar *vt* : to dent
abombar *vt* : to warp, to cause to bulge — **abombarse** *vr* : to decompose, to go bad
abominable *adj* ABORRECIBLE : abominable
abominación *nf, pl* **-ciones** : abomination
abominar *vt* ABORRECER : to abominate, to abhor
abonado, -da *n* : subscriber
abonar *vt* **1** : to pay **2** FERTILIZAR : to fertilize — **abonarse** *vr* : to subscribe
abono *nm* **1** : payment, installment **2** FERTILIZANTE : fertilizer **3** : season ticket
abordaje *nm* : boarding
abordar *vt* **1** : to address, to broach **2** : to accost, to waylay **3** : to come on board
aborigen[1] *adj, pl* **-rígenes** : aboriginal, native
aborigen[2] *nmf, pl* **-rígenes** : aborigine, indigenous inhabitant
aborrecer {53} *vt* ABOMINAR, ODIAR : to abhor, to detest, to hate
aborrecible *adj* ABOMINABLE, ODIOSO : abominable, detestable
aborrecimiento *nm* : abhorrence, loathing
abortar *vi* : to have an abortion — *vt* **1** : to abort **2** : to quash, to suppress
abortista *nmf* : abortionist
abortivo, -va *adj* : abortive
aborto *nm* **1** : abortion **2** : miscarriage
abotonar *vt* : to button — **abotonarse** *vr* : to button up
abovedado, -da *adj* : vaulted
abrasador, -dora *adj* : burning, scorching
abrasar *vt* QUEMAR : to burn, to sear, to scorch
abrasivo[1], **-va** *adj* : abrasive
abrasivo[2] *nm* : abrasive
abrazadera *nf* : clamp, brace
abrazar {21} *vt* : to hug, to embrace — **abrazarse** *vr*
abrazo *nm* : hug, embrace
abrebotellas *nms & pl* : bottle opener
abrelatas *nms & pl* : can opener
abrevadero *nm* BEBEDERO : watering trough
abreviación *nf, pl* **-ciones** : abbreviation
abreviar *vt* **1** : to abbreviate **2** : to shorten, to cut short
abreviatura → **abreviación**
abridor *nm* : bottle opener, can opener
abrigadero *nm* : shelter, windbreak
abrigado, -da *adj* **1** : sheltered **2** : warm, wrapped up (with clothing)
abrigar {52} *vt* **1** : to shelter, to protect **2** : to keep warm, to dress warmly **3** : to cherish, to harbor ‹abrigar esperanzas : to cherish hopes› — **abrigarse** *vr* : to dress warmly
abrigo *nm* **1** : coat, overcoat **2** : shelter, refuge
abril *nm* : April
abrillantador *nm* : polish
abrillantar *vt* : to polish, to shine
abrir {2} *vt* **1** : to open **2** : to unlock, to undo **3** : to turn on (a tap or faucet) — *vi* : to open, to open up — **abrirse** *vr* **1** : to open up **2** : to clear (of the skies)
abrochar *vt* : to button, to fasten — **abrocharse** *vr* : to fasten, to hook up
abrogación *nf, pl* **-ciones** : abrogation, annulment, repeal
abrogar {52} *vt* : to abrogate, to annul, to repeal
abrojo *nm* : bur (of a plant)
abrumador, -dora *adj* : crushing, overwhelming
abrumar *vt* **1** AGOBIAR : to overwhelm **2** OPRIMIR : to oppress, to burden
abrupto, -ta *adj* **1** : abrupt **2** ESCARPADO : steep — **abruptamente** *adv*
absceso *nm* : abscess
absolución *nf, pl* **-ciones** **1** : absolution **2** : acquittal
absolutismo *nm* : absolutism
absoluto, -ta *adj* **1** : absolute, unconditional **2 en ~** : not at all ‹no me gustó en absoluto : I did not like it at all› — **absolutamente** *adv*
absolver {89} *vt* **1** : to absolve **2** : to acquit
absorbente *adj* **1** : absorbent **2** : absorbing, engrossing
absorber *vt* **1** : to absorb, to soak up **2** : to occupy, to take up, to engross
absorción *nf, pl* **-ciones** : absorption
absorto, -ta *adj* : absorbed, engrossed
abstemio[1], **-mia** *adj* : abstemious, teetotal
abstemio[2], **-mia** *n* : teetotaler
abstención *nf, pl* **-ciones** : abstention
abstenerse {80} *vr* : to abstain, to refrain
abstinencia *nf* : abstinence
abstracción *nf, pl* **-ciones** : abstraction
abstracto, -ta *adj* : abstract
abstraer {81} *vt* : to abstract — **abstraerse** *vr* : to lose oneself in thought
abstraído, -da *adj* : preoccupied, withdrawn
abstruso, -sa *adj* : abstruse
abstuvo, etc. → **abstenerse**
absuelto *pp* → **absolver**
absurdo[1], **-da** *adj* DISPARATADO, RIDÍCULO : absurd, ridiculous — **absurdamente** *adv*
absurdo[2] *nm* : absurdity
abuchear *vt* : to boo, to jeer
abucheo *nm* : booing, jeering
abuela *nf* **1** : grandmother **2** : old woman **3 ¡tu abuela!** *fam* : no way!, forget about it!
abuelo *nm* **1** : grandfather **2** : old man **3 abuelos** *nmpl* : grandparents, ancestors

abulia *nf* : apathy, lethargy
abúlico, -ca *adj* : lethargic, apathetic
abultado, -da *adj* : bulging, bulky
abultar *vi* : to bulge — *vt* : to enlarge, to expand
abundancia *nf* : abundance
abundante *adj* : abundant, plentiful — **abundantemente** *adv*
abundar *vi* **1** : to abound, to be plentiful **2 ~ en** : to be in agreement with
aburrido, -da *adj* **1** : bored, tired, fed up **2** TEDIOSO : boring, tedious
aburrimiento *nm* : boredom, weariness
aburrir *vt* : to bore, to tire — **aburrirse** *vr* : to get bored
abusado, -da *adj Mex fam* : sharp, on the ball
abusador, -dora *n* : abuser
abusar *vi* **1** : to go too far, to do something to excess **2 ~ de** : to abuse (as drugs) **3 ~ de** : to take unfair advantage of
abusivo, -va *adj* **1** : abusive **2** : outrageous, excessive
abuso *nm* **1** : abuse **2** : injustice, outrage
abyecto, -ta *adj* : despicable, contemptible
acá *adv* AQUÍ : here, over here ⟨¡ven acá! : come here!⟩
acabado[1], **-da** *adj* **1** : finished, done, completed **2** : old, worn-out
acabado[2] *nm* : finish ⟨un acabado brillante : a glossy finish⟩
acabar *vi* **1** TERMINAR : to finish, to end **2 ~ de** : to have just (done something) ⟨acabo de ver a tu hermano : I just saw your brother⟩ **3 ~ con** : to put an end to, to stamp out — *vt* TERMINAR : to finish — **acabarse** *vr* TERMINARSE : to come to an end, to run out ⟨se me acabó el dinero : I ran out of money⟩
acacia *nf* : acacia
academia *nf* : academy
académico[1], **-ca** *adj* : academic, scholastic — **académicamente** *adv*
académico[2], **-ca** *n* : academic, academician
acaecer {53} *vt* (*3rd person only*) : to happen, to take place
acalambrarse *vr* : to cramp up, to get a cramp
acallar *vt* : to quiet, to silence
acalorado, -da *adj* : emotional, heated
acaloramiento *nm* **1** : heat **2** : ardor, passion
acalorar *vt* : to heat up, to inflame — **acalorarse** *vr* : to get upset, to get worked up
acampada *nf* : camp, camping ⟨ir de acampada : to go camping⟩
acampar *vi* : to camp
acanalar *vt* **1** : to groove, to furrow **2** : to corrugate
acantilado *nm* : cliff
acanto *nm* : acanthus
acantonar *vt* : to station, to quarter
acaparador, -dora *adj* : greedy, selfish
acaparar *vt* **1** : to stockpile, to hoard **2** : to monopolize
acápite *nm* : paragraph
acariciar *vt* : to caress, to stroke, to pet
ácaro *nm* : mite
acarrear *vt* **1** : to haul, to carry **2** : to bring, to give rise to ⟨los problemas que acarrea : the problems that come along with it⟩
acarreo *nm* : transport, haulage
acartonarse *vr* **1** : to stiffen **2** : to become wizened
acaso *adv* **1** : perhaps, by any chance **2 por si acaso** : just in case
acatamiento *nm* : compliance, observance
acatar *vt* : to comply with, to respect
acaudalado, -da *adj* RICO : wealthy, rich
acaudillar *vt* : to lead, to command
acceder *vi* **~ a** **1** : to accede to, to agree to **2** : to assume (a position) **3** : to gain access to
accesar *vt* : to access (on a computer)
accesibilidad *nf* : accessibility
accesible *adj* ASEQUIBLE : accessible, attainable
acceso *nm* **1** : access **2** : admittance, entrance
accesorio[1], **-ria** *adj* **1** : accessory **2** : incidental
accesorio[2] *nm* **1** : accessory **2** : prop (in the theater)
accidentado[1], **-da** *adj* **1** : eventful, turbulent **2** : rough, uneven **3** : injured
accidentado[2], **-da** *n* : accident victim
accidental *adj* : accidental, unintentional — **accidentalmente** *adv*
accidentarse *vr* : to have an accident
accidente *nm* **1** : accident **2** : unevenness **3 accidente geográfico** : geographical feature
acción *nf, pl* **acciones** **1** : action **2** ACTO : act, deed **3** : share, stock
accionamiento *nm* : activation
accionar *vt* : to put into motion, to activate — *vi* : to gesticulate
accionario, -ria *adj* : stock ⟨mercado accionario : stock market⟩
accionista *nmf* : stockholder, shareholder
acebo *nm* : holly
acechar *vt* **1** : to watch, to spy on **2** : to stalk, to lie in wait for
acecho *nm* **al acecho** : lying in wait
acedera *nf* : sorrel (herb)
acéfalo, -la *adj* : leaderless
aceitar *vt* : to oil
aceite *nm* **1** : oil **2 aceite de ricino** : castor oil **3 aceite de oliva** : olive oil
aceitera *nf* **1** : cruet (for oil) **2** : oilcan **3** *Mex* : oil refinery
aceitoso, -sa *adj* : oily
aceituna *nf* OLIVA : olive
aceituno *nm* OLIVO : olive tree
aceleración *nf, pl* **-ciones** : acceleration, speeding up
acelerado, -da *adj* : accelerated, speedy
acelerador *nm* : accelerator

aceleramiento *nm* → **aceleración**
acelerar *vt* **1** : to accelerate, to speed up **2** AGILIZAR : to expedite — *vi* : to accelerate (of an automobile) — **acelerarse** *vr* : to hasten, to hurry up
acelga *nf* : chard, Swiss chard
acendrado, -da *adj* : pure, unblemished
acendrar *vt* : to purify, to refine
acento *nm* **1** : accent **2** : stress, emphasis
acentuación *nf, pl* **-ciones** : accentuation
acentuado, -da *adj* : marked, pronounced
acentuar {3} *vt* **1** : to accent **2** : to emphasize, to stress — **acentuarse** *vr* : to become more pronounced
acepción *nf, pl* **-ciones** SIGNIFICADO : sense, meaning
aceptabilidad *nf* : acceptability
aceptable *adj* : acceptable
aceptación *nf, pl* **-ciones** **1** : acceptance **2** APROBACIÓN : approval
aceptar *vt* **1** : to accept **2** : to approve
acequia *nf* **1** : irrigation ditch **2** *Mex* : sewer
acera *nf* : sidewalk
acerado, -da *adj* **1** : made of steel **2** : steely, tough
acerbo, -ba *adj* **1** : harsh, cutting ⟨comentarios acerbos : cutting remarks⟩ **2** : bitter — **acerbamente** *adv*
acerca *prep* **∼ de** : about, concerning
acercamiento *nm* : rapprochement, reconciliation
acercar {72} *vt* APROXIMAR, ARRIMAR : to bring near, to bring closer — **acercarse** *vr* APROXIMARSE, ARRIMARSE : to approach, to draw near
acería *nf* : steel mill
acerico *nm* : pincushion
acero *nm* : steel ⟨acero inoxidable : stainless steel⟩
acérrimo, -ma *adj* **1** : staunch, steadfast **2** : bitter ⟨un acérrimo enemigo : a bitter enemy⟩
acertado, -da *adj* CORRECTO : accurate, correct, on target — **acertadamente** *adv*
acertante[1] *adj* : winning
acertante[2] *nmf* : winner
acertar {55} *vt* : to guess correctly — *vi* **1** ATINAR : to be correct, to be on target **2 ∼ a** : to manage to
acertijo *nm* ADIVINANZA : riddle
acervo *nm* **1** : pile, heap **2** : wealth, heritage ⟨el acervo artístico del instituto : the artistic treasures of the institute⟩
acetato *nm* : acetate
acético, -ca *adj* : acetic ⟨ácido acético : acetic acid⟩
acetileno *nm* : acetylene
acetona *nf* **1** : acetone **2** : nail-polish remover
achacar {72} *vt* : to attribute, to impute ⟨te achaca todos sus problemas : he blames all his problems on you⟩
achacoso, -sa *adj* : frail, sickly
achaparrado, -da *adj* : stunted, scrubby ⟨árboles achaparrados : scrubby trees⟩
achaques *nmpl* : aches and pains
achatar *vt* : to flatten
achicar {72} *vt* **1** REDUCIR : to make smaller, to reduce **2** : to intimidate **3** : to bail out (water) — **achicarse** *vr* : to become intimidated
achicharrar *vt* : to scorch, to burn to a crisp
achicoria *nf* : chicory
achispado, -da *adj fam* : tipsy
achote *or* **achiote** *nm* : annatto seed
achuchón *nm, pl* **-chones** **1** : push, shove **2** *fam* : squeeze, hug **3** *fam* : mild illness
aciago, -ga *adj* : fateful, unlucky
acicalar *vt* **1** PULIR : to polish **2** : to dress up, to adorn — **acicalarse** *vr* : to get dressed up
acicate *nm* **1** : spur **2** INCENTIVO : incentive, stimulus
acidez *nf, pl* **-deces** **1** : acidity **2** : sourness **3 acidez estomacal** : heartburn
acidificar {72} *vt* : to acidify
ácido[1], **-da** *adj* AGRIO : acid, sour
ácido[2] *nm* : acid
acierto *nm* **1** : correct answer, right choice **2** : accuracy, skill, deftness
acimut *nm* : azimuth
acitronar *vt Mex* : to fry until crisp
aclamación *nf, pl* **-ciones** : acclaim, acclamation
aclamar *vt* : to acclaim, to cheer, to applaud
aclaración *nf, pl* **-ciones** CLARIFICACIÓN : clarification, explanation
aclarar *vt* **1** CLARIFICAR : to clarify, to explain, to resolve **2** : to lighten **3 aclarar la voz** : to clear one's throat — *vi* **1** : to get light, to dawn **2** : to clear up — **aclararse** *vr* : to become clear
aclaratorio, -ria *adj* : explanatory
aclimatar *vt* : to acclimatize — **aclimatarse** *vr* **∼ a** : to get used to — **aclimatación** *nf*
acné *nm* : acne
acobardar *vt* INTIMIDAR : to frighten, to intimidate — **acobardarse** *vr* : to be frightened, to cower
acodarse *vr* **∼ en** : to lean (one's elbows) on
acogedor, -dora *adj* : cozy, warm, friendly
acoger {15} *vt* **1** REFUGIAR : to take in, to shelter **2** : to receive, to welcome — **acogerse** *vr* **1** REFUGIARSE : to take refuge **2 ∼ a** : to resort to, to avail oneself of
acogida *nf* **1** AMPARO, REFUGIO : refuge, protection **2** RECIBIMIENTO : reception, welcome
acolchar *vt* **1** : to pad (a wall, etc.) **2** : to quilt
acólito *nm* **1** MONAGUILLO : altar boy **2** : follower, helper, acolyte
acomedido, -da *adj* : helpful, obliging

acometer *vt* **1** ATACAR : to attack, to assail **2** EMPRENDER : to undertake, to begin — *vi* ~ **contra** : to rush against
acometida *nf* ATAQUE : attack, assault
acomodado, -da *adj* **1** : suitable, appropriate **2** : well-to-do, prosperous
acomodador, -dora *n* : usher, usherette *f*
acomodar *vt* **1** : to accommodate, to make room for **2** : to adjust, to adapt — **acomodarse** *vr* **1** : to settle in **2** ~ **a** : to adapt to
acomodaticio, -cia *adj* : accommodating, obliging
acomodo *nm* **1** : job, position **2** : arrangement, placement **3** : accommodation, lodging
acompañamiento *nm* : accompaniment
acompañante *nmf* **1** COMPAÑERO : companion **2** : accompanist
acompañar *vt* : to accompany, to go with
acompasado, -da *adj* : rhythmic, regular, measured
acomplejado, -da *adj* : full of complexes, neurotic
acondicionado, -da *adj* **1** : equipped, fitted-out **2 bien acondicionado** : in good shape, in a fit state
acondicionador *nm* **1** : conditioner **2 acondicionador de aire** : air conditioner
acondicionar *vt* **1** : to condition **2** : to fit out, to furnish
acongojado, -da *adj* : distressed, upset
acongojarse *vr* : to grieve, to become distressed
aconsejable *adj* : advisable
aconsejar *vt* : to advise, to counsel
acontecer {53} *vt* (*3rd person only*) : to occur, to happen
acontecimiento *nm* SUCESO : event
acopiar *vt* : to gather, to collect, to stockpile
acopio *nm* : collection, stock
acoplamiento *nm* : connection, coupling
acoplar *vt* : to couple, to connect — **acoplarse** *vr* : to fit together
acoquinar *vt* : to intimidate
acorazado¹, -da *adj* BLINDADO : armored
acorazado² *nm* : battleship
acordado, -da *adj* : agreed upon
acordar {19} *vt* **1** : to agree on **2** OTORGAR : to award, to bestow — **acordarse** *vr* RECORDAR : to remember, to recall
acorde¹ *adj* **1** : in agreement, in accordance **2** ~ **con** : in keeping with
acorde² *nm* : chord
acordeón *nm, pl* **-deones** : accordion — **acordeonista** *nmf*
acordonar *vt* **1** : to cordon off **2** : to lace up **3** : to mill (coins)
acorralar *vt* ARRINCONAR : to corner, to hem in, to corral
acortar *vt* : to shorten, to cut short — **acortarse** *vr* **1** : to become shorter **2** : to end early
acosar *vt* PERSEGUIR : to pursue, to hound, to harass
acoso *nm* ASEDIO : harassment ⟨acoso sexual : sexual harassment⟩
acostar {19} *vt* **1** : to lay (something) down **2** : to put to bed — **acostarse** *vr* **1** : to lie down **2** : to go to bed
acostumbrado, -da *adj* **1** HABITUADO : accustomed **2** HABITUAL : usual, customary
acostumbrar *vt* : to accustom — *vi* : to be accustomed, to be in the habit — **acostumbrarse** *vr*
acotación *nf, pl* **-ciones** **1** : marginal note **2** : stage direction
acotado, -da *adj* : enclosed
acotamiento *nm Mex* : shoulder (of a road)
acotar *vt* **1** ANOTAR : to note, to annotate **2** DELIMITAR : to mark off (land), to demarcate
acre¹ *adj* **1** : acrid, pungent **2** MORDAZ : caustic, biting
acre² *nm* : acre
acrecentamiento *nm* : growth, increase
acrecentar {55} *vt* AUMENTAR : to increase, to augment
acreditación *nf, pl* **-ciones** : accreditation
acreditado, -da *adj* **1** : accredited, authorized **2** : reputable
acreditar *vt* **1** : to accredit, to authorize **2** : to credit **3** : to prove, to verify — **acreditarse** *vr* : to gain a reputation
acreedor¹, -dora *adj* : deserving, worthy
acreedor², -dora *n* : creditor
acribillar *vt* **1** : to riddle, to pepper (with bullets, etc.) **2** : to hound, to harass
acrílico *nm* : acrylic
acrimonia *nf* **1** : pungency **2** : acrimony
acrimonioso, -sa *adj* : acrimonious
acriollarse *vr* : to adopt local customs, to go native
acritud *nf* **1** : pungency, bitterness **2** : intensity, sharpness **3** : harshness, asperity
acrobacia *nf* : acrobatics
acróbata *nmf* : acrobat
acrobático, -ca *adj* : acrobatic
acrónimo *nm* : acronym
acta *nf* **1** : document, certificate ⟨acta de nacimiento : birth certificate⟩ **2 actas** *nfpl* : minutes (of a meeting)
actitud *nf* **1** : attitude **2** : posture, position
activación *nf, pl* **-ciones** **1** : activation, stimulation **2** ACELERACIÓN : acceleration, speeding up
activar *vt* **1** : to activate **2** : to stimulate, to energize **3** : to speed up
actividad *nf* : activity
activista *nmf* : activist
activo¹, -va *adj* : active — **activamente** *adv*
activo² *nm* : assets *pl* ⟨activo y pasivo : assets and liabilities⟩

acto *nm* **1** ACCIÓN : act, deed **2** : act (in a play) **3 el acto sexual** : sexual intercourse **4 en el acto** : right away, on the spot **5 acto seguido** : immediately after
actor *nm* ARTISTA : actor
actriz *nf, pl* **actrices** ARTISTA : actress
actuación *nf, pl* **-ciones 1** : performance **2 actuaciones** *nfpl* DILIGENCIAS : proceedings
actual *adj* PRESENTE : present, current
actualidad *nf* **1** : present time ⟨en la actualidad : at present⟩ **2 actualidades** *nfpl* : current affairs
actualización *nf, pl* **-ciones** : updating, modernization
actualizar {21} *vt* : to modernize, to bring up to date
actualmente *adv* : at present, nowadays
actuar {3} *vi* : to act, to perform
actuarial *adj* : actuarial
actuario, -ria *n* : actuary
acuarela *nf* : watercolor
acuario *nm* : aquarium
Acuario *nmf* : Aquarius, Aquarian
acuartelar *vt* : to quarter (troops)
acuático, -ca *adj* : aquatic, water
acuchillar *vt* APUÑALAR : to knife, to stab
acuciante *adj* : pressing, urgent
acucioso, -sa → **acuciante**
acudir *vi* **1** : to go, to come (someplace for a specific purpose) ⟨acudió a la puerta : he went to the door⟩ ⟨acudimos en su ayuda : we came to her aid⟩ **2** : to be present, to show up ⟨acudí a la cita : I showed up for the appointment⟩ **3 ~ a** : to turn to, to have recourse to ⟨hay que acudir al médico : you must consult the doctor⟩
acueducto *nm* : aqueduct
acuerdo *nm* **1** : agreement **2 estar de acuerdo** : to agree **3 de acuerdo con** : in accordance with **4 de ~** : OK, all right
acuicultura *nf* : aquaculture
acullá *adv* : yonder, over there
acumulación *nf, pl* **-ciones** : accumulation
acumulador *nm* : storage battery
acumular *vt* : to accumulate, to amass — **acumularse** *vr* : to build up, to pile up
acumulativo, -va *adj* : cumulative — **acumulativamente** *adv*
acunar *vt* : to rock, to cradle
acuñar *vt* : to coin, to mint
acuoso, -sa *adj* : aqueous, watery
acupuntura *nf* : acupuncture
acurrucarse {72} *vr* : to cuddle, to nestle, to curl up
acusación *nf, pl* **-ciones 1** : accusation, charge **2 la acusación** : the prosecution
acusado¹, -da *adj* : prominent, marked
acusado², -da *n* : defendant
acusador, -dora *n* **1** : accuser **2** FISCAL : prosecutor
acusar *vt* **1** : to accuse, to charge **2** : to reveal, to betray ⟨sus ojos acusaban la desconfianza : his eyes revealed distrust⟩ — **acusarse** *vr* : to confess
acusativo *nm* : objective (in grammar)
acusatorio, -ria *adj* : accusatory
acuse *nm* **acuse de recibo** : acknowledgment of receipt
acústica *nf* : acoustics
acústico, -ca *adj* : acoustic
adagio *nm* **1** REFRÁN : adage, proverb **2** : adagio
adalid *nm* : leader, champion
adaptable *adj* : adaptable — **adaptabilidad** *nf*
adaptación *nf, pl* **-ciones** : adaptation, adjustment
adaptado, -da *adj* : suited, adapted
adaptador *nm* : adapter (in electricity)
adaptar *vt* **1** MODIFICAR : to adapt **2** : to adjust, to fit — **adaptarse** *vr* : to adapt oneself, to conform
adecentar *vt* : to tidy up
adecuación *nf, pl* **-ciones** ADAPTACIÓN : adaptation
adecuadamente *adv* : adequately
adecuado, -da *adj* **1** IDÓNEO : suitable, appropriate **2** : adequate
adecuar {8} *vt* : to adapt, to make suitable — **adecuarse** *vr* **~ a** : to be appropriate for, to fit in with
adefesio *nm* : eyesore, monstrosity
adelantado, -da *adj* **1** : advanced, ahead **2** : fast (of a clock or watch) **3 por ~** : in advance
adelantamiento *nm* **1** : advancement **2** : speeding up
adelantar *vt* **1** : to advance, to move forward **2** : to overtake, to pass **3** : to reveal (information) in advance **4** : to advance, to lend (money) — **adelantarse** *vr* **1** : to advance, to get in front **2 ~ a** : to forestall, to preempt
adelante *adv* **1** : ahead, in front, forward **2 más adelante** : further on, later on **3 ¡adelante!** : come in!
adelanto *nm* **1** : advance, progress **2** : advance payment **3** : earliness ⟨llevamos una hora de adelanto : we're running an hour ahead of time⟩
adelfa *nf* : oleander
adelgazar {21} *vt* : to thin, to reduce — *vi* : to lose weight
ademán *nm, pl* **-manes 1** GESTO : gesture **2 ademanes** *nmpl* : manners
además *adv* **1** : besides, furthermore **2 ~ de** : in addition to, as well as
adenoides *nfpl* : adenoids
adentrarse *vr* **~ en** : to go into, to penetrate
adentro *adv* : inside, within
adentros *nmpl* **decirse para sus adentros** : to say to oneself ⟨me dije para mis adentros que nunca regresaría : I told myself that I'd never go back⟩
adepto¹, -ta *adj* : supportive ⟨ser adepto a : to be a follower of⟩
adepto², -ta *n* PARTIDARIO : follower, supporter

aderezar {21} *vt* **1** SAZONAR : to season, to dress (salad) **2** : to embellish, to adorn

aderezo *nm* **1** : dressing, seasoning **2** : adornment, embellishment

adeudar *vt* **1** : to debit **2** DEBER : to owe

adeudo *nm* **1** DÉBITO : debit **2** *Mex* : debt, indebtedness

adherencia *nf* **1** : adherence, adhesiveness **2** : appendage, accretion

adherente *adj* : adhesive, sticky

adherirse {76} *vr* : to adhere, to stick

adhesión *nf, pl* **-siones 1** : adhesion **2** : attachment, commitment (to a cause, etc.)

adhesivo[1], **-va** *adj* : adhesive

adhesivo[2] *nm* : adhesive

adicción *nf, pl* **-ciones** : addiction

adición *nf, pl* **-ciones** : addition

adicional *adj* : additional — **adicionalmente** *adv*

adicionar *vt* : to add

adictivo, -va *adj* : addictive

adicto[1], **-ta** *adj* **1** : addicted **2** : devoted, dedicated

adicto[2], **-ta** *n* **1** : addict **2** PARTIDARIO : supporter, advocate

adiestrador, -dora *n* : trainer

adiestramiento *nm* : training

adiestrar *vt* : to train

adinerado, -da *adj* : moneyed, wealthy

adiós *nm, pl* **adioses 1** DESPEDIDA : farewell, good-bye **2 ¡adiós!** : good-bye!

aditamento *nm* : attachment, accessory

aditivo *nm* : additive

adivinación *nf, pl* **-ciones 1** : guess **2** : divination, prediction

adivinanza *nf* ACERTIJO : riddle

adivinar *vt* **1** : to guess **2** : to foretell, to predict

adivino, -na *n* : fortune-teller

adjetivo[1], **-va** *adj* : adjectival

adjetivo[2] *nm* : adjective

adjudicación *nf, pl* **-ciones 1** : adjudication **2** : allocation, awarding, granting

adjudicar {72} *vt* **1** : to adjudge, to adjudicate **2** : to assign, to allocate ⟨adjudicar la culpa : to assign the blame⟩ **3** : to award, to grant

adjuntar *vt* : to enclose, to attach

adjunto[1], **-ta** *adj* : enclosed, attached

adjunto[2], **-ta** *n* : deputy, assistant

adjunto[3] *nm* : adjunct

administración *nf, pl* **-ciones 1** : administration, management **2 administración de empresas** : business administration

administrador, -dora *n* : administrator, manager

administrar *vt* : to administer, to manage, to run

administrativo, -va *adj* : administrative

admirable *adj* : admirable, impressive — **admirablemente** *adv*

admiración *nf, pl* **-ciones** : admiration

admirador, -dora *n* : admirer

admirar *vt* **1** : to admire **2** : to amaze, to astonish — **admirarse** *vr* : to be amazed

admirativo, -va *adj* : admiring

admisibilidad *nf* : admissibility

admisible *adj* : admissible, allowable

admisión *nf, pl* **-siones** : admission, admittance

admitir *vt* **1** : to admit, to let in **2** : to acknowledge, to concede **3** : to allow, to make room for ⟨la ley no admite cambios : the law doesn't allow for changes⟩

admonición *nf, pl* **-ciones** : admonition, warning

admonitorio, -ria *adj* : admonitory

ADN *nm* (*á*cido *d*esoxirribo*n*ucleico) : DNA

adobar *vt* : to marinate

adobe *nm* : adobe

adobo *nm* **1** : marinade, seasoning **2** *Mex* : spicy marinade used for cooking pork

adoctrinamiento *nm* : indoctrination

adoctrinar *vt* : to indoctrinate

adolecer {53} *vi* PADECER : to suffer ⟨adolece de timidez : he suffers from shyness⟩

adolescencia *nf* : adolescence

adolescente[1] *adj* : adolescent, teenage

adolescente[2] *nmf* : adolescent, teenager

adonde *conj* : where ⟨el lugar adonde vamos es bello : the place where we're going is beautiful⟩

adónde *adv* : where ⟨¿adónde vamos? : where are we going?⟩

adondequiera *adv* : wherever, anywhere ⟨adondequiera que vayas : anywhere you go⟩

adopción *nf, pl* **-ciones** : adoption

adoptar *vt* **1** : to adopt (a measure), to take (a decision) **2** : to adopt (children)

adoptivo, -va *adj* **1** : adopted (children, country) **2** : adoptive (parents)

adoquín *nm, pl* **-quines** : paving stone, cobblestone

adorable *adj* : adorable, lovable

adoración *nf, pl* **-ciones** : adoration, worship

adorador[1], **-dora** *adj* : adoring, worshipping

adorador[2], **-dora** *n* : worshipper

adorar *vt* : to adore, to worship

adormecer {53} *vt* **1** : to make sleepy, to lull to sleep **2** : to numb — **adormecerse** *vr* **1** : to doze off **2** : to go numb

adormecimiento *nm* **1** SUEÑO : drowsiness, sleepiness **2** INSENSIBILIDAD : numbness

adormilarse *vr* : to doze, to drowse

adornar *vt* DECORAR : to decorate, to adorn

adorno *nm* : ornament, decoration

adquirido, -da *adj* **1** : acquired **2 mal adquirido** : ill-gotten

adquirir {4} *vt* **1** : to acquire, to gain **2** COMPRAR : to purchase

adquisición *nf, pl* **-ciones 1** : acquisition **2** COMPRA : purchase
adquisitivo, -va *adj* **poder adquisitivo** : purchasing power
adrede *adv* : intentionally, on purpose
adrenalina *nf* : adrenaline
adscribir {33} *vt* : to assign, to appoint — **adscribirse** *vr* **~ a** : to become a member of
adscripción *nf, pl* **-ciones** : assignment, appointment
adscrito *pp* → **adscribir**
aduana *nf* : customs, customs office
aduanero[1], **-ra** *adj* : customs
aduanero[2], **-ra** *n* : customs officer
aducir {61} *vt* : to adduce, to offer as proof
adueñarse *vr* **~ de** : to take possession of, to take over
adulación *nf, pl* **-ciones** : adulation, flattery
adulador[1], **-dora** *adj* : flattering
adulador[2], **-dora** *n* : flatterer, toady
adular *vt* LISONJEAR : to flatter
adulteración *nf, pl* **-ciones** : adulteration
adulterar *vt* : to adulterate
adulterio *nm* : adultery
adúltero[1], **-ra** *adj* : adulterous
adúltero[2], **-ra** *n* : adulterer
adultez *nf* : adulthood
adulto, -ta *adj & n* : adult
adusto, -ta *adj* : harsh, severe
advenedizo, -za *n* **1** : upstart, parvenu **2** : newcomer
advenimiento *nm* : advent
adverbio *nm* : adverb — **adverbial** *adj*
adversario[1], **-ria** *adj* : opposing, contrary
adversario[2], **-ria** *n* OPOSITOR : adversary, opponent
adversidad *nf* : adversity
adverso, -sa *adj* DESFAVORABLE : adverse, unfavorable — **adversamente** *adv*
advertencia *nf* AVISO : warning
advertir {76} *vt* **1** AVISAR : to warn **2** : to notice, to tell ⟨no advertí que estuviera enojada : I couldn't tell she was angry⟩
Adviento *nm* : Advent
adyacente *adj* : adjacent
aéreo, -rea *adj* **1** : aerial, air **2 correo aéreo** : airmail
aeróbic *nm* : aerobics
aeróbico, -ca *adj* : aerobic
aerobio, -bia *adj* : aerobic
aerodinámica *nf* : aerodynamics
aerodinámico, -ca *adj* : aerodynamic, streamlined
aeródromo *nm* : airfield
aeroespacial *adj* : aerospace
aerolínea *nf* : airline
aeromozo, -za *n* : flight attendant, steward *m,* stewardess *f*
aeronáutica *nf* : aeronautics
aeronáutico, -ca *adj* : aeronautical
aeronave *nf* : aircraft
aeropostal *adj* : airmail
aeropuerto *nm* : airport
aerosol *nm* : aerosol, aerosol spray
aeróstata *nmf* : balloonist
aerotransportado, -da *adj* : airborne
aerotransportar *vt* : to airlift
afabilidad *nf* : affability
afable *adj* : affable — **afablemente** *adv*
afamado, -da *adj* : well-known, famous
afán *nm, pl* **afanes 1** ANHELO : eagerness, desire **2** EMPEÑO : effort, determination
afanador, -dora *n Mex* : cleaning person, cleaner
afanarse *vr* : to toil, to strive
afanosamente *adv* : zealously, industriously, busily
afanoso, -sa *adj* **1** : eager, industrious **2** : arduous, hard
afear *vt* : to make ugly, to disfigure
afección *nf, pl* **-ciones 1** : fondness, affection **2** : illness, complaint
afectación *nf, pl* **-ciones** : affectation
afectado, -da *adj* **1** : affected, mannered **2** : influenced **3** : afflicted **4** : feigned
afectar *vt* **1** : to affect **2** : to upset **3** : to feign, to pretend
afectísimo, -ma *adj* **suyo afectísimo** : yours truly
afectivo, -va *adj* : emotional
afecto[1], **-ta** *adj* **1** : affected, afflicted **2** : fond, affectionate
afecto[2] *nm* CARIÑO : affection
afectuoso, -sa *adj* CARIÑOSO : affectionate, caring
afeitadora *nf* : shaver, electric razor
afeitar *vt* RASURAR : to shave — **afeitarse** *vr*
afelpado, -da *adj* : plush
afeminado, -da *adj* : effeminate
aferrado, -da *adj* : obstinate, stubborn
aferrarse {55} *vr* : to cling, to hold on
affidávit *nm, pl* **-dávits** : affidavit
afgano, -na *adj & n* : Afghan
AFI *nm* (*A*lfabeto *F*onético *I*nternacional) : IPA
afianzar {21} *vt* **1** : to secure, to strengthen **2** : to guarantee, to vouch for — **afianzarse** *vr* ESTABLECERSE : to establish oneself
afiche *nm* : poster
afición *nf, pl* **-ciones 1** : enthusiasm, penchant, fondness ⟨afición al deporte : love of sports⟩ **2** PASATIEMPO : hobby
aficionado[1], **-da** *adj* ENTUSIASTA : enthusiastic, keen
aficionado[2], **-da** *n* **1** ENTUSIASTA : enthusiast, fan **2** : amateur
áfido *nm* : aphid
afiebrado, -da *adj* : feverish
afilado, -da *adj* **1** : sharp **2** : long, pointed ⟨una nariz afilada : a sharp nose⟩
afilador *nm* : sharpener
afilalápices *nms & pl* : pencil sharpener
afilar *vt* : to sharpen
afiliación *nf, pl* **-ciones** : affiliation

afiliado[1], **-da** *adj* : affiliated
afiliado[2], **-da** *n* : member
afiliarse *vr* : to become a member, to join, to affiliate
afín *adj, pl* **afines** **1** PARECIDO : related, similar ⟨la biología y disciplinas afines : biology and related disciplines⟩ **2** PRÓXIMO : adjacent, nearby
afinación *nf, pl* **-ciones** **1** : tune-up **2** : tuning (of an instrument)
afinador, **-dora** *n* : tuner (of musical instruments)
afinar *vt* **1** : to perfect, to refine **2** : to tune (an instrument) — *vi* : to sing or play in tune
afincarse {72} *vr* : to establish oneself, to settle in
afinidad *nf* : affinity, similarity
afirmación *nf, pl* **-ciones** **1** : statement **2** : affirmation
afirmar *vt* **1** : to state, to affirm **2** REFORZAR : to make firm, to strengthen
afirmativo, **-va** *adj* : affirmative — **afirmativamente** *adj*
aflicción *nf, pl* **-ciones** DESCONSUELO, PESAR : grief, sorrow
afligido, **-da** *adj* : grief-stricken, sorrowful
afligir {35} *vt* **1** : to distress, to upset **2** : to afflict — **afligirse** *vr* : to grieve
aflojar *vt* **1** : to loosen, to slacken **2** *fam* : to pay up, to fork over — *vi* : to slacken, to ease up — **aflojarse** *vr* : to become loose, to slacken
afloramiento *nm* : outcropping, emergence
aflorar *vi* : to come to the surface, to emerge
afluencia *nf* **1** : flow, influx **2** : abundance, plenty
afluente *nm* : tributary
afluir {41} *vi* **1** : to flock ⟨la gente afluía a la frontera : people were flocking to the border⟩ **2** : to flow
aforismo *nm* : aphorism
aforo *nm* **1** : appraisal, assessment **2** : maximum capacity (of a theater, highway, etc.)
afortunado, **-da** *adj* : fortunate, lucky — **afortunadamente** *adv*
afrecho *nm* : bran, mash
afrenta *nf* : affront, insult
afrentar *vt* : to affront, to dishonor, to insult
africano, **-na** *adj & n* : African
afroamericano, **-na** *adj & n* : Afro-American
afrodisiaco *or* **afrodisíaco** *nm* : aphrodisiac
afrontamiento *nm* : confrontation
afrontar *vt* : to confront, to face up to
afrutado, **-da** *adj* : fruity
afuera *adv* **1** : out ⟨¡afuera! : get out!⟩ **2** : outside, outdoors
afueras *nfpl* ALEDAÑOS : outskirts
agachadiza *nf* : snipe (bird)
agachar *vt* : to lower (a part of the body) ⟨agachar la cabeza : to bow one's head⟩ — **agacharse** *vr* : to crouch, to stoop, to bend down
agalla *nf* **1** BRANQUIA : gill **2** **tener agallas** *fam* : to have guts, to have courage
agarradera *nf* ASA, ASIDERO : handle, grip
agarrado, **-da** *adj fam* : cheap, stingy
agarrar *vt* **1** : to grab, to grasp **2** : to catch, to take — *vi* **agarrar y** *fam* : to do (something) abruptly ⟨el día siguiente agarró y se fue : the next day he up and left⟩ — **agarrarse** *vr* **1** : to hold on, to cling **2** *fam* : to get into a fight ⟨se agarraron a golpes : they came to blows⟩
agarre *nm* : grip, grasp
agarrotarse *vr* **1** : to stiffen up **2** : to seize up
agasajar *vt* : to fête, to wine and dine
agasajo *nm* : lavish attention
ágata *nf* : agate
agave *nm* : agave
agazaparse *vr* **1** AGACHARSE : to crouch **2** : to hide
agencia *nf* : agency, office
agenciar *vt* : to obtain, to procure — **agenciarse** *vr* : to manage, to get by
agenda *nf* **1** : agenda **2** : appointment book
agente *nmf* **1** : agent **2** **agente de viajes** : travel agent **3** **agente de bolsa** : stockbroker **4** **agente de tráfico** : traffic officer
agigantado, **-da** *adj* GIGANTESCO : gigantic
agigantar *vt* **1** : to increase greatly, to enlarge **2** : to exaggerate
ágil *adj* **1** : agile, nimble **2** : sharp, lively (of a response, etc.) — **ágilmente** *adv*
agilidad *nf* : agility, nimbleness
agilizar {21} *vt* ACELERAR : to expedite, to speed up
agitación *nf, pl* **-ciones** **1** : agitation **2** NERVIOSISMO : nervousness
agitado, **-da** *adj* **1** : agitated, excited **2** : choppy, rough, turbulent
agitador, **-dora** *n* PROVOCADOR : agitator
agitar *vt* **1** : to agitate, to shake **2** : to wave, to flap **3** : to stir up — **agitarse** *vr* **1** : to toss about, to flap around **2** : to get upset
aglomeración *nf, pl* **-ciones** **1** : conglomeration, mass **2** GENTÍO : crowd
aglomerar *vt* : to cluster, to amass — **aglomerarse** *vr* : to crowd together
aglutinar *vt* : to bring together, to bind
agnóstico, **-ca** *adj & n* : agnostic
agobiado, **-da** *adj* : weary, worn-out, weighted-down
agobiante *adj* **1** : exhausting, overwhelming **2** : stifling, oppressive
agobiar *vt* **1** OPRIMIR : to oppress, to burden **2** ABRUMAR : to overwhelm **3** : to wear out, to exhaust
agonía *nf* : agony, death throes
agonizante *adj* : dying

agonizar {21} *vi* **1** : to be dying **2** : to be in agony **3** : to dim, to fade
agorero, -ra *adj* : ominous
agostar *vt* **1** : to parch **2** : to wither — **agostarse** *vr*
agosto *nm* **1** : August **2 hacer uno su agosto** : to make a fortune, to make a killing
agotado, -da *adj* **1** : exhausted, used up **2** : sold out **3** FATIGADO : worn-out, tired
agotador, -dora *adj* : exhausting
agotamiento *nm* FATIGA : exhaustion
agotar *vt* **1** : to exhaust, to use up **2** : to weary, to wear out — **agotarse** *vr*
agraciado[1], **-da** *adj* **1** : attractive **2** : fortunate
agraciado[2], **-da** *n* : winner
agradable *adj* GRATO, PLACENTERO : pleasant, agreeable — **agradablemente** *adv*
agradar *vi* : to be pleasing ⟨nos agradó mucho el resultado : we were very pleased with the result⟩
agradecer {53} *vt* **1** : to be grateful for **2** : to thank
agradecido, -da *adj* : grateful, thankful
agradecimiento *nm* : gratitude, thankfulness
agrado *nm* **1** GUSTO : taste, liking ⟨no es de su agrado : it's not to his liking⟩ **2** : graciousness, agreeableness **3 con ~** : with pleasure, willingly ⟨lo haré con agrado : I will be happy to do it⟩
agrandar *vt* **1** : to exaggerate **2** : to enlarge — **agrandarse** *vr*
agrario, -ria *adj* : agrarian, agricultural
agravación *nf, pl* **-ciones** : aggravation, worsening
agravante *adj* : aggravating
agravar *vt* **1** : to increase (weight), to make heavier **2** EMPEORAR : to aggravate, to worsen — **agravarse** *vr*
agraviar *vt* INJURIAR, OFENDER : to offend, to insult
agravio *nm* INJURIA : affront, offense, insult
agredir {1} *vt* : to assail, to attack
agregado[1], **-da** *n* **1** : attaché **2** : assistant professor
agregado[2] *nm* **1** : aggregate **2** AÑADIDURA : addition, something added
agregar {52} *vt* **1** AÑADIR : to add, to attach **2** : to appoint — **agregarse** *vr* : to join
agresión *nf, pl* **-siones 1** : aggression **2** ATAQUE : attack
agresividad *nf* : aggressiveness, aggression
agresivo, -va *adj* : aggressive — **agresivamente** *adv*
agresor[1], **-sora** *adj* : hostile, attacking
agresor[2], **-sora** *n* **1** : aggressor **2** : assailant, attacker
agreste *adj* **1** CAMPESTRE : rural **2** : wild, untamed
agriar *vt* **1** : to sour, to make sour **2** : to embitter — **agriarse** *vr* : to turn sour
agrícola *adj* : agricultural
agricultor, -tora *n* : farmer, grower
agricultura *nf* : agriculture, farming
agridulce *adj* **1** : bittersweet **2** : sweet-and-sour
agrietar *vt* : to crack — **agrietarse** *vr* **1** : to crack **2** : to chap
agrimensor, -sora *n* : surveyor
agrimensura *nf* : surveying
agrio, agria *adj* **1** ÁCIDO : sour **2** : caustic, acrimonious
agriparse *vr* : to catch the flu
agroindustria *nf* : agribusiness
agronomía *nf* : agronomy
agropecuario, -ria *adj* : pertaining to livestock and agriculture
agrupación *nf, pl* **-ciones** GRUPO : group, association
agrupamiento *nm* : grouping, concentration
agrupar *vt* : to group together
agua *nf* **1** : water **2 agua oxigenada** : hydrogen peroxide **3 aguas negras** *or* **aguas residuales** : sewage **4 como agua para chocolate** *Mex fam* : furious **5 echar aguas** *Mex fam* : to keep an eye out, to be on the lookout
aguacate *nm* : avocado
aguacero *nm* : shower, downpour
aguado, -da *adj* **1** DILUIDO : watered-down, diluted **2** *CA, Col, Mex fam* : soft, flabby **3** *Mex, Peru fam* : dull, boring
aguafiestas *nmfs & pl* : killjoy, stick-in-the-mud, spoilsport
aguafuerte *nm* : etching
aguamanil *nm* : ewer, pitcher
aguanieve *nf* : sleet ⟨caer aguanieve : to be sleeting⟩
aguantar *vt* **1** SOPORTAR : to bear, to tolerate, to withstand **2** : to hold **3 aguantar las ganas** : to resist an urge ⟨no pude aguantar las ganas de reír : I couldn't keep myself from laughing⟩ — *vi* : to hold out, to last — **aguantarse** *vr* **1** : to resign oneself **2** : to restrain oneself
aguante *nm* **1** TOLERANCIA : tolerance, patience **2** RESISTENCIA : endurance, strength
aguar {10} *vt* **1** : to water down, to dilute **2 aguar la fiesta** *fam* : to spoil the party
aguardar *vt* ESPERAR : to wait for, to await — *vi* : to be in store
aguardiente *nm* : clear brandy
aguarrás *nm* : turpentine
agudeza *nf* **1** : keenness, sharpness **2** : shrillness **3** : witticism
agudizar {21} *vt* : to intensify, to heighten
agudo, -da *adj* **1** : acute, sharp **2** : shrill, high-pitched **3** PERSPICAZ : clever, shrewd
agüero *nm* AUGURIO, PRESAGIO : augury, omen
aguijón *nm, pl* **-jones 1** : stinger (of a bee, etc.) **2** : goad

aguijonear *vt* : to goad
águila *nf* **1** : eagle **2 águila o sol** *Mex* : heads or tails
aguileño, -ña *adj* : aquiline
aguilera *nf* : aerie, eagle's nest
aguilón *nm, pl* **-lones** : gable
aguinaldo *nm* **1** : Christmas bonus, year-end bonus **2** *PRi, Ven* : Christmas carol
agüitarse *vr Mex fam* : to have the blues, to feel discouraged
aguja *nf* **1** : needle **2** : steeple, spire
agujerear *vt* : to make a hole in, to pierce
agujero *nm* **1** : hole **2 agujero negro** : black hole (in astronomy)
agujeta *nf* **1** *Mex* : shoelace **2 agujetas** *nfpl* : muscular soreness or stiffness
agusanado, -da *adj* : worm-eaten
aguzar {21} *vt* **1** : to sharpen ⟨aguzar el ingenio : to sharpen one's wits⟩ **2 aguzar el oído** : to prick up one's ears
ah *interj* : oh!
ahí *adv* **1** : there ⟨ahí está : there it is⟩ **2 por ~** : somewhere, thereabouts **3 de ahí que** : with the result that, so that
ahijado, -da *n* : godchild, godson *m*, goddaughter *f*
ahijar {5} *vt* : to adopt (a child)
ahínco *nm* : eagerness, zeal
ahogar {52} *vt* **1** : to drown **2** : to smother **3** : to choke back, to stifle — **ahogarse** *vr*
ahogo *nm* : breathlessness, suffocation
ahondar *vt* : to deepen — *vi* : to elaborate, to go into detail
ahora *adv* **1** : now **2 ahora mismo** : right now **3 hasta ~** : so far **4 por ~** : for the time being
ahorcar {72} *vt* : to hang, to kill by hanging — **ahorcarse** *vr*
ahorita *adv fam* : right now, right away
ahorquillado, -da *adj* : forked
ahorrador, -dora *adj* : thrifty
ahorrar *vt* **1** : to save (money) **2** : to spare, to conserve — *vi* : to save up — **ahorrarse** *vr* : to spare oneself
ahorrativo, -va *adj* : thrifty, frugal
ahorro *nm* : saving ⟨cuenta de ahorros : savings account⟩
ahuecar {72} *vt* **1** : to hollow out **2** : to cup (one's hands) **3** : to plump up, to fluff up
ahuizote *nm Mex fam* : annoying person, pain in the neck
ahumar {8} *vt* : to smoke, to cure
ahuyentar *vt* **1** : to scare away, to chase away **2** : to banish, to dispel ⟨ahuyentar las dudas : to dispel doubts⟩
airado, -da *adj* FURIOSO : angry, irate
airar {5} *vt* : to make angry, to anger
aire *nm* **1** : air **2 aire acondicionado** : air-conditioning **3 darse aires** : to give oneself airs
airear *vt* : to air, to air out — **airearse** *vr* : to get some fresh air
airoso, -sa *adj* **1** : elegant, graceful **2 salir airoso** : to come out winning
aislacionismo *nm* : isolationism
aislacionista *adj & nmf* : isolationist
aislado, -da *adj* : isolated, alone
aislador *nm* : insulator (part)
aislamiento *nm* **1** : isolation **2** : insulation
aislante *nm* : insulator, nonconductor
aislar {5} *vt* **1** : to isolate **2** : to insulate
ajado, -da *adj* **1** : worn, shabby **2** : wrinkled, crumpled
ajar *vt* : to wear out, to spoil
ajardinado, -da *adj* : landscaped
ajedrecista *nmf* : chess player
ajedrez *nm, pl* **-dreces 1** : chess **2** : chess set
ajeno, -na *adj* **1** : alien **2** : of another, of others ⟨propiedad ajena : somebody else's property⟩ **3 ~ a** : foreign to **4 ~ de** : devoid of, free from
ajetreado, -da *adj* : hectic, busy
ajetrearse *vr* : to bustle about, to rush around
ajetreo *nm* : hustle and bustle, fuss
ají *nm, pl* **ajíes** : chili pepper
ajo *nm* : garlic
ajonjolí *nm, pl* **-líes** : sesame
ajuar *nm* : trousseau
ajustable *adj* : adjustable
ajustado, -da *adj* **1** CEÑIDO : tight, tight-fitting **2** : close, tight ⟨una ajustada victoria : a close victory⟩
ajustar *vt* **1** : to adjust, to adapt **2** : to take in (clothing) **3** : to settle, to resolve — **ajustarse** *vr* : to fit, to conform
ajuste *nm* **1** : adjustment **2** : tightening
ajusticiar *vt* EJECUTAR : to execute, to put to death
al *prep* (contraction of a and el) → **a²**
ala *nf* **1** : wing **2** : brim (of a hat)
Alá *nm* : Allah
alabanza *nf* ELOGIO : praise
alabar *vt* : to praise — **alabarse** *vr* : to boast
alabastro *nm* : alabaster
alabear *vt* : to warp — **alabearse** *vr*
alabeo *nm* : warp, warping
alacena *nf* : cupboard, larder
alacrán *nm, pl* **-cranes** ESCORPIÓN : scorpion
alado, -da *adj* : winged
alambique *nm* : still (to distill alcohol)
alambre *nm* **1** : wire **2 alambre de púas** : barbed wire
alameda *nf* **1** : poplar grove **2** : tree-lined avenue
álamo *nm* **1** : poplar **2 álamo temblón** : aspen
alar *nm* : eaves *pl*
alarde *nm* **1** : show, display **2 hacer alarde de** : to make show of, to boast about
alardear *vi* PRESUMIR : to boast, to brag
alargado, -da *adj* : elongated, slender
alargamiento *nm* : lengthening, extension, elongation
alargar {52} *vt* **1** : to extend, to lengthen **2** PROLONGAR : to prolong — **alargarse** *vr*

alarido *nm* : howl, shriek
alarma *nf* : alarm
alarmante *adj* : alarming — **alarmantemente** *adv*
alarmar *vt* : to alarm
alazán *nm, pl* **-zanes** : sorrel (color or animal)
alba *nf* AMANECER : dawn, daybreak
albacea *nmf* TESTAMENTARIO : executor, executrix *f*
albahaca *nf* : basil
albanés, -nesa *adj & n, mpl* **-neses** : Albanian
albañil *nmf* : bricklayer, mason
albañilería *nf* : bricklaying, masonry
albaricoque *nm* : apricot
albatros *nm* : albatross
albedrío *nm* : will ‹libre albedrío : free will›
alberca *nf* **1** : reservoir, tank **2** *Mex* : swimming pool
albergar {52} *vt* ALOJAR : to house, to lodge, to shelter
albergue *nm* **1** : shelter, refuge **2** : hostel
albino, -na *adj & n* : albino — **albinismo** *nm*
albóndiga *nf* : meatball
albor *nm* **1** : dawning, beginning **2** BLANCURA : whiteness
alborada *nf* : dawn
alborear *v impers* : to dawn
alborotado, -da *adj* **1** : excited, agitated **2** : rowdy, unruly
alborotador¹, -dora *adj* **1** : noisy, boisterous **2** : rowdy, unruly
alborotador², -dora *n* : agitator, troublemaker, rioter
alborotar *vt* **1** : to excite, to agitate **2** : to incite, to stir up — **alborotarse** *vr* **1** : to get excited **2** : to riot
alboroto *nm* **1** : disturbance, ruckus **2** MOTÍN : riot
alborozado, -da *adj* : jubilant
alborozar {21} *vt* : to gladden, to cheer
alborozo *nm* : joy, elation
álbum *nm* : album ‹álbum de recortes : scrapbook›
albúmina *nf* : albumin
albur *nm* **1** : chance, risk **2** *Mex* : pun
alca *nf* : auk
alcachofa *nf* : artichoke
alcahuete, -ta *n* CHISMOSO : gossip
alcaide *nm* : warden (in a prison)
alcalde, -desa *n* : mayor
alcaldía *nf* **1** : mayoralty **2** AYUNTAMIENTO : city hall
álcali *nm* : alkali
alcalino, -na *adj* : alkaline — **alcalinidad** *nf*
alcance *nm* **1** : reach **2** : range, scope
alcancía *nf* **1** : piggy bank, money box **2** : collection box (for alms, etc.)
alcanfor *nm* : camphor
alcantarilla *nf* CLOACA : sewer, drain
alcanzar {21} *vt* **1** : to reach **2** : to catch up with **3** LOGRAR : to achieve, to attain — *vi* **1** DAR : to suffice, to be enough **2** ~ **a** : to manage to
alcaparra *nf* : caper
alcapurria *nf PRi* : stuffed fritter made with taro and green banana
alcaravea *nf* : caraway
alcatraz *nm, pl* **-traces** : gannet
alcázar *nm* : fortress, castle
alce¹, etc. → **alzar**
alce² *nm* : moose, European elk
alcoba *nf* : bedroom
alcohol *nm* : alcohol
alcohólico, -ca *adj & n* : alcoholic
alcoholismo *nm* : alcoholism
alcoholizarse {21} *vr* : to become an alcoholic
alcornoque *nm* **1** : cork oak **2** *fam* : idiot, fool
alcurnia *nf* : ancestry, lineage
aldaba *nf* : door knocker
aldea *nf* : village
aldeano¹, -na *adj* : village, rustic
aldeano², -na *n* : villager
aleación *nf, pl* **-ciones** : alloy
alear *vt* : to alloy
aleatorio, -ria *adj* : random, fortuitous — **aleatoriamente** *adv*
alebrestar *vt* : to excite, to make nervous — **alebrestarse** *vr*
aledaño, -ña *adj* : bordering, neighboring
aledaños *nmpl* AFUERAS : outskirts, surrounding area
alegar {52} *vt* : to assert, to allege — *vi* DISCUTIR : to argue
alegato *nm* **1** : allegation, claim **2** *Mex* : argument, summation (in law) **3** : argument, dispute
alegoría *nf* : allegory
alegórico, -ca *adj* : allegorical
alegrar *vt* : to make happy, to cheer up — **alegrarse** *vr* : to be glad, to rejoice
alegre *adj* **1** : glad, cheerful **2** : colorful, bright **3** *fam* : tipsy
alegremente *adv* : happily, cheerfully
alegría *nf* : joy, cheer, happiness
alejado, -da *adj* : remote
alejamiento *nm* **1** : removal, separation **2** : estrangement
alejar *vt* **1** : to remove, to move away **2** : to estrange, to alienate — **alejarse** *vr* **1** : to move away, to stray **2** : to drift apart
alelado, -da *adj* **1** : bewildered, stupefied **2** : foolish, stupid
aleluya *interj* : hallelujah!, alleluia!
alemán¹, -mana *adj & n, mpl* **-manes** : German
alemán² *nm* : German (language)
alentador, -dora *adj* : encouraging
alentar {55} *vt* : to encourage, to inspire — *vi* : to breathe
alerce *nm* : larch
alérgeno *nm* : allergen
alergia *nf* : allergy
alérgico, -ca *adj* : allergic
alero *nm* **1** : eaves *pl* **2** : forward (in basketball)

alerón *nm, pl* **-rones** : aileron
alerta[1] *adv* : on the alert
alerta[2] *adj & nf* : alert
alertar *vt* : to alert
aleta *nf* **1** : fin **2** : flipper **3** : small wing
aletargado, -da *adj* : lethargic, sluggish, torpid
aletargarse {52} *vr* : to feel drowsy, to become lethargic
aletear *vi* : to flutter, to flap one's wings
aleteo *nm* : flapping, flutter
alevín *nm, pl* **-vines 1** : fry, young fish **2** PRINCIPIANTE : beginner
alevosía *nf* **1** : treachery **2** : premeditation
alevoso, -sa *adj* : treacherous
alfabético, -ca *adj* : alphabetical — **alfabéticamente** *adv*
alfabetismo *nm* : literacy
alfabetizado, -da *adj* : literate
alfabetizar {21} *vt* : to alphabetize
alfabeto *nm* : alphabet
alfalfa *nf* : alfalfa
alfanje *nm* : cutlass, scimitar
alfarería *nf* : pottery
alfarero, -ra *n* : potter
alféizar *nm* : sill, windowsill
alfeñique *nm fam* : wimp, weakling
alférez *nmf, pl* **-reces 1** : second lieutenant **2** : ensign
alfil *nm* : bishop (in chess)
alfiler *nm* **1** : pin **2** BROCHE : brooch
alfiletero *nm* : pincushion
alfombra *nf* : carpet, rug
alfombrado *nm* : carpeting
alfombrar *vt* : to carpet
alfombrilla *nf* : small rug, mat
alforfón *nm, pl* **-fones** : buckwheat
alforja *nf* : saddlebag
alforza *nf* : pleat, tuck
alga *nf* **1** : aquatic plant, alga **2** : seaweed
algarabía *nf* **1** : gibberish, babble **2** : hubbub, uproar
álgebra *nf* : algebra
algebraico, -ca *adj* : algebraic
álgido, -da *adj* **1** : critical, decisive **2** : icy cold
algo[1] *adv* : somewhat, rather <es simpático, pero algo tacaño : he's nice but rather stingy>
algo[2] *pron* **1** : something **2 ~ de** : some, a little <tengo algo de dinero : I've got some money>
algodón *nm, pl* **-dones** : cotton
algoritmo *nm* : algorithm
alguacil *nm* : constable
alguien *pron* : somebody, someone
alguno[1], **-na** *adj* (**algún** *before masculine singular nouns*) **1** : some, any <algún día : someday, one day> **2** (*in negative constructions*) : not any, not at all <no tengo noticia alguna : I have no news at all> **3 algunas veces** : sometimes
alguno[2], **-na** *pron* **1** : one, someone, somebody <alguno de ellos : one of them> **2 algunos, -nas** *pron pl* : some, a few <algunos quieren trabajar : some want to work>
alhaja *nf* : jewel, gem
alhajar *vt* : to adorn with jewels
alharaca *nf* : fuss
alhelí *nm* : wallflower
aliado[1], **-da** *adj* : allied
aliado[2], **-da** *n* : ally
alianza *nf* : alliance
aliarse {85} *vr* : to form an alliance, to ally oneself
alias *adv & nm* : alias
alicaído, -da *adj* : depressed, discouraged
alicates *nmpl* PINZAS : pliers
aliciente *nm* **1** INCENTIVO : incentive **2** ATRACCIÓN : attraction
alienación *nf, pl* **-ciones** : alienation, derangement
alienar *vt* ENAJENAR : to alienate
aliento *nm* **1** : breath **2** : courage, strength **3 dar aliento a** : to encourage
aligerar *vt* **1** : to lighten **2** ACELERAR : to hasten, to quicken
alijo *nm* : cache, consignment (of contraband)
alimaña *nf* : pest, vermin
alimentación *nf, pl* **-ciones** NUTRICIÓN : nutrition, nourishment
alimentar *vt* **1** NUTRIR : to feed, to nourish **2** MANTENER : to support (a family) **3** FOMENTAR : to nurture, to foster — **alimentarse** *vr* **~ con** : to live on
alimentario, -ria → **alimenticio**
alimenticio, -cia *adj* **1** : nutritional, food, dietary **2** : nutritious, nourishing
alimento *nm* : food, nourishment
aliñar *vt* **1** : to dress (salad) **2** CONDIMENTAR : to season
alineación *nf, pl* **-ciones 1** : alignment **2** : lineup (in sports)
alineamiento *nm* : alignment
alinear *vt* **1** : to align **2** : to line up — **alinearse** *vr* **1** : to fall in, to line up **2 ~ con** : to align oneself with
aliño *nm* : seasoning, dressing
alipús *nm, pl* **-puses** *Mex fam* : booze, drink
alisar *vt* : to smooth
aliso *nm* : alder
alistamiento *nm* : enlistment, recruitment
alistar *vt* **1** : to recruit **2** : to make ready — **alistarse** *vr* : to join up, to enlist
aliteración *nf, pl* **-ciones** : alliteration
aliviar *vt* MITIGAR : to relieve, to alleviate, to soothe — **aliviarse** *vr* : to recover, to get better
alivio *nm* : relief
aljaba *nf* : quiver (for arrows)
aljibe *nm* : cistern, well
allá *adv* **1** : there, over there **2 más allá** : farther away **3 más allá de** : beyond **4 allá tú** : that's up to you

allanamiento *nm* **1** : (police) raid **2 allanamiento de morada** : breaking and entering
allanar *vt* **1** : to raid, to search **2** : to resolve, to solve **3** : to smooth, to level out
allegado[1], **-da** *adj* : close, intimate
allegado[2], **-da** *n* : close friend, relation ⟨parientes y allegados : friends and relations⟩
allegar {52} *vt* : to gather, to collect
allende[1] *adv* : beyond, on the other side
allende[2] *prep* : beyond ⟨allende las montañas : beyond the mountains⟩
allí *adv* : there, over there ⟨allí mismo : right there⟩ ⟨hasta allí : up to that point⟩
alma *nf* **1** : soul **2** : person, human being **3 no tener alma** : to be pitiless **4 tener el alma en un hilo** : to have one's heart in one's mouth
almacén *nm, pl* **-cenes** **1** BODEGA : warehouse, storehouse **2** TIENDA : shop, store **3 gran almacén** *Spain* : department store
almacenaje → **almacenamiento**
almacenamiento *nm* : storage ⟨almacenamiento de datos : data storage⟩
almacenar *vt* : to store, to put in storage
almacenero, -ra *n* : shopkeeper
almacenista *nm* MAYORISTA : wholesaler
almádena *nf* : sledgehammer
almanaque *nm* : almanac
almeja *nf* : clam
almendra *nf* **1** : almond **2** : kernel
almendro *nm* : almond tree
almiar *nm* : haystack
almíbar *nm* : syrup
almidón *nm, pl* **-dones** : starch
almidonar *vt* : to starch
alminar *nm* MINARETE : minaret
almirante *nm* : admiral
almizcle *nm* : musk
almohada *nf* : pillow
almohadilla *nf* **1** : small pillow, cushion **2** : bag, base (in baseball)
almohadón *nm, pl* **-dones** : bolster, cushion
almohazar {21} *vt* : to curry (a horse)
almoneda *nf* SUBASTA : auction
almorranas *nfpl* HEMORROIDES : hemorrhoids, piles
almorzar {36} *vi* : to have lunch — *vt* : to have for lunch
almuerzo *nm* : lunch
alocado, -da *adj* **1** : crazy **2** : wild, reckless **3** : silly, scatterbrained
alocución *nf, pl* **-ciones** : speech, address
áloe *or* **aloe** *nm* : aloe
alojamiento *nm* : lodging, accommodations *pl*
alojar *vt* ALBERGAR : to house, to lodge — **alojarse** *vr* : to lodge, to room
alondra *nf* : lark, skylark
alpaca *nf* : alpaca
alpinismo *nm* : mountain climbing, mountaineering
alpinista *nmf* : mountain climber
alpino, -na *adj* : Alpine, alpine
alpiste *nm* : birdseed
alquilar *vt* ARRENDAR : to rent, to lease
alquiler *nm* ARRENDAMIENTO : rent, rental
alquimia *nf* : alchemy
alquimista *nmf* : alchemist
alquitrán *nm, pl* **-tranes** BREA : tar
alquitranar *vt* : to tar, to cover with tar
alrededor[1] *adv* **1** : around, about ⟨todo temblaba alrededor : all around things were shaking⟩ **2 ~ de** : around, approximately ⟨alrededor de quince personas : around fifteen people⟩
alrededor[2] *prep* **~ de** : around, about ⟨corrió alrededor de la casa : she ran around the house⟩ ⟨llegaré alrededor de diciembre : I will get there around December⟩
alrededores *nmpl* ALEDAÑOS : surroundings, outskirts
alta *nf* **1** : admission, entry, enrollment **2 dar de alta** : to release, to discharge (a patient)
altanería *nf* ALTIVEZ, ARROGANCIA : arrogance, haughtiness
altanero, -ra *adj* ALTIVO, ARROGANTE : arrogant, haughty — **altaneramente** *adv*
altar *nm* : altar
altavoz *nm, pl* **-voces** ALTOPARLANTE : loudspeaker
alteración *nf, pl* **-ciones** **1** MODIFICACIÓN : alteration, modification **2** PERTURBACIÓN : disturbance, disruption
alterado, -da *adj* : upset
alterar *vt* **1** MODIFICAR : to alter, to modify **2** PERTURBAR : to disturb, to disrupt — **alterarse** *vr* : to get upset, to get worked up
altercado *nm* DISCUSIÓN, DISPUTA : altercation, argument, dispute
alternador *nm* : alternator
alternancia *nf* : alternation, rotation
alternar *vi* **1** : to alternate **2** : to mix, to socialize — *vt* : to alternate — **alternarse** *vr* : to take turns
alternativa *nf* OPCIÓN : alternative, option
alternativo, -va *adj* **1** : alternating **2** : alternative — **alternativamente** *adv*
alterno, -na *adj* : alternate ⟨corriente alterna : alternating current⟩
alteza *nf* **1** : loftiness, lofty height **2 Alteza** : Highness
altibajos *nmpl* **1** : unevenness (of terrain) **2** : ups and downs
altímetro *nm* : altimeter
altiplanicie *nf* → **altiplano**
altiplano *nm* : high plateau, upland
altisonante *adj* **1** : pompous, affected (of language) **2** *Mex* : rude, obscene (of language)
altitud *nf* : altitude

altivez *nf, pl* **-veces** ALTANERÍA, ARROGANCIA : arrogance, haughtiness
altivo, -va *adj* ALTANERO, ARROGANTE : arrogant, haughty
alto[1] *adv* **1** : high **2** : loud, loudly
alto[2], **-ta** *adj* **1** : tall, high **2** : loud ⟨en voz alta : aloud, out loud⟩
alto[3] *nm* **1** ALTURA : height, elevation **2** : stop, halt **3 altos** *nmpl* : upper floors
alto[4] *interj* : halt!, stop!
altoparlante *nm* ALTAVOZ : loudspeaker
altozano *nm* : hillock
altruismo *nm* : altruism
altruista[1] *adj* : altruistic
altruista[2] *nmf* : altruist
altura *nf* **1** : height **2** : altitude **3** : loftiness, nobleness **4 a la altura de** : near, up by ⟨en la avenida San Antonio a la altura de la Calle Tres : on San Antonio Avenue up near Third Street⟩ **5 a estas alturas** : at this point, at this stage of the game
alubia *nf* : kidney bean
alucinación *nf, pl* **-ciones** : hallucination
alucinante *adj* : hallucinatory
alucinar *vi* : to hallucinate
alucinógeno[1], **-na** *adj* : hallucinogenic
alucinógeno[2] *nm* : hallucinogen
alud *nm* AVALANCHA : avalanche, landslide
aludido, -da *n* **1** : person in question ⟨el aludido : the aforesaid⟩ **2 darse por aludido** : to take it personally
aludir *vi* : to allude, to refer
alumbrado *nm* ILUMINACIÓN : lighting
alumbramiento *nm* **1** : lighting **2** : childbirth
alumbrar *vt* **1** ILUMINAR : to light, to illuminate **2** : to give birth to
alumbre *nm* : alum
aluminio *nm* : aluminum
alumnado *nm* : student body
alumno, -na *n* **1** : pupil, student **2 ex–alumno, -na** : alumnus, alumna *f* **3 ex–alumnos, -nas** *npl* : alumni, alumnae *f*
alusión *nf, pl* **-siones** : allusion, reference
alusivo, -va *adj* **1** : allusive **2 ~ a** : in reference to, regarding
aluvión *nm, pl* **-viones** : flood, barrage
alza *nf* SUBIDA : rise ⟨precios en alza : rising prices⟩
alzamiento *nm* LEVANTAMIENTO : uprising, insurrection
alzar {21} *vt* **1** ELEVAR, LEVANTAR : to lift, to raise **2** : to erect — **alzarse** *vr* LEVANTARSE : to rise up
ama *nf* → **amo**
amabilidad *nf* : kindness
amable *adj* : kind, nice — **amablemente** *adv*
amado[1], **-da** *adj* : beloved, darling
amado[2], **-da** *n* : sweetheart, loved one
amaestrar *vt* : to train (animals)
amafiarse *vr Mex fam* : to conspire, to be in cahoots
amagar {52} *vt* **1** : to show signs of (an illness, etc.) **2** : to threaten — *vi* **1** : to be imminent, to threaten **2** : to feint, to dissemble
amago *nm* **1** AMENAZA : threat **2** : sign, hint
amainar *vi* : to abate, to ease up, to die down
amalgama *nf* : amalgam
amalgamar *vt* : to amalgamate, to unite
amamantar *v* : to breast-feed, to nurse, to suckle
amanecer[1] {53} *v impers* **1** : to dawn **2** : to begin to show, to appear **3** : to wake up (in the morning)
amanecer[2] *nm* ALBA : dawn, daybreak
amanerado, -da *adj* : affected, mannered
amansar *vt* **1** : to tame **2** : to soothe, to calm down — **amansarse** *vr*
amante[1] *adj* : loving, fond
amante[2] *nmf* : lover
amañar *vt* : to rig, to fix, to tamper with — **amañarse** *vr* **amañárselas** : to manage
amaño *nm* **1** : skill, dexterity **2** : trick, ruse
amapola *nf* : poppy
amar *vt* : to love — **amarse** *vr*
amargado, -da *adj* : embittered, bitter
amargar {52} *vt* : to make bitter, to embitter — *vi* : to taste bitter
amargo[1], **-ga** *adj* : bitter — **amargamente** *adv*
amargo[2] *nm* : bitterness, tartness
amargura *nf* **1** : bitterness **2** : grief, sorrow
amarilis *nf* : amaryllis
amarillear *vi* : to yellow, to turn yellow
amarillento, -ta *adj* : yellowish
amarillismo *nm* : yellow journalism, sensationalism
amarillo[1], **-lla** *adj* : yellow
amarillo[2] *nm* : yellow
amarra *nf* **1** : mooring, mooring line **2 soltar las amarras de** : to loosen one's grip on
amarrar *vt* **1** : to moor (a boat) **2** ATAR : to fasten, to tie up, to tie down
amartillar *vt* : to cock (a gun)
amasar *vt* **1** : to amass **2** : to knead **3** : to mix, to prepare
amasijo *nm* : jumble, hodgepodge
amasio, -sia *n* : lover, paramour
amateur *adj & nmf* : amateur — **amateurismo** *nm*
amatista *nf* : amethyst
amatorio, -ria *adj* : amatory, sexual ⟨poesía amatoria : love poems⟩
amazona *nf* **1** : Amazon (in mythology) **2** : horsewoman
amazónico, -ca *adj* : amazonian
ambages *nmpl* **sin ~** : without hesitation, straight to the point
ámbar *nm* **1** : amber **2 ámbar gris** : ambergris
ambición *nf, pl* **-ciones** : ambition
ambicionar *vt* : to aspire to, to seek

ambicioso, -sa *adj* : ambitious — **ambiciosamente** *adv*
ambidextro, -tra *adj* : ambidextrous
ambientación *nf, pl* **-ciones** : setting, atmosphere
ambiental *adj* : environmental — **ambientalmente** *adv*
ambientalista *nmf* : environmentalist
ambientar *vt* : to give atmosphere to, to set (in literature and drama) — **ambientarse** *vr* : to adjust, to get one's bearings
ambiente *nm* **1** : atmosphere **2** : environment **3** : surroundings *pl*
ambigüedad *nf* : ambiguity
ambiguo, -gua *adj* : ambiguous
ámbito *nm* : domain, field, area
ambivalencia *nf* : ambivalence
ambivalente *adj* : ambivalent
ambos, -bas *adj & pron* : both
ambulancia *nf* : ambulance
ambulante *adj* **1** : traveling, itinerant **2 vendedor ambulante** : street vendor
ameba *nf* : amoeba
amedrentar *vt* : to frighten, to intimidate — **amedrentarse** *vr*
amén *nm* **1** : amen **2 ~ de** : in addition to, besides **3 en un decir amén** : in an instant
amenaza *nf* : threat, menace
amenazador, -dora *adj* : threatening, menacing
amenazante → **amenazador**
amenazar {21} *v* : to threaten
amenguar {10} *vt* **1** : to diminish **2** : to belittle, to dishonor
amenidad *nf* : pleasantness, amenity
amenizar {21} *vt* **1** : to make pleasant **2** : to brighten up, to add life to
ameno, -na *adj* : agreeable, pleasant
amento *nm* : catkin
americano, -na *adj & n* : American
amerindio, -dia *adj & n* : Amerindian
ameritar *vt* MERECER : to deserve
ametralladora *nf* : machine gun
amianto *nm* : asbestos
amiba → **ameba**
amigable *adj* : friendly, amicable — **amigablemente** *adv*
amígdala *nf* : tonsil
amigdalitis *nf* : tonsilitis
amigo[1], **-ga** *adj* : friendly, close
amigo[2], **-ga** *n* : friend
amigote *nm* : crony, pal
amilanar *vt* **1** : to frighten **2** : to daunt, to discourage — **amilanarse** *vr* : to lose heart
aminoácido *nm* : amino acid
aminorar *vt* : to reduce, to lessen — *vi* : to diminish
amistad *nf* : friendship
amistoso, -sa *adj* : friendly — **amistosamente** *adv*
amnesia *nf* : amnesia
amnésico, -ca *adj & n* : amnesiac, amnesic
amnistía *nf* : amnesty
amnistiar {85} *vt* : to grant amnesty to
amo, ama *n* **1** : master *m*, mistress *f* **2** : owner, keeper (of an animal) **3 ama de casa** : housewife **4 ama de llaves** : housekeeper
amodorrado, -da *adj* : drowsy
amolar {19} *vt* **1** : to grind, to sharpen **2** : to pester, to annoy
amoldable *adj* : adaptable
amoldar *vt* **1** : to mold **2** : to adapt, to adjust — **amoldarse** *vr*
amonestación *nf, pl* **-ciones 1** APERCIBIMIENTO : admonition, warning **2 amonestaciones** *nfpl* : banns
amonestar *vt* APERCIBIR : to admonish, to warn
amoníaco *or* **amoniaco** *nm* : ammonia
amontonamiento *nm* : accumulation, piling up
amontonar *vt* **1** APILAR : to pile up, to heap up **2** : to collect, to gather **3** : to hoard — **amontonarse** *vr*
amor *nm* **1** : love **2** : loved one, beloved **3 amor propio** : self-esteem **4 hacer el amor** : to make love
amoral *adj* : amoral
amoratado, -da *adj* : black-and-blue, bruised, livid
amordazar {21} *vt* **1** : to gag, to muzzle **2** : to silence
amorfo, -fa *adj* : shapeless, amorphous
amorío *nm* : love affair, fling
amoroso, -sa *adj* **1** : loving, affectionate **2** : amorous ⟨una mirada amorosa : an amorous glance⟩ **3** : charming, cute — **amorosamente** *adv*
amortiguación *nf* : cushioning, absorption
amortiguador *nm* : shock absorber
amortiguar {10} *vt* : to soften (an impact)
amortizar {21} *vt* : to amortize, to pay off — **amortización** *nf*
amotinado[1], **-da** *adj* : rebellious, insurgent, mutinous
amotinado[2], **-da** *n* : rebel, insurgent, mutineer
amotinamiento *nm* : uprising, rebellion
amotinar *vt* : to incite (to riot), to agitate — **amotinarse** *vr* **1** : to riot, to rebel **2** : to mutiny
amparar *vt* : to safeguard, to protect — **ampararse** *vr* **1 ~ de** : to take shelter from **2 ~ en** : to have recourse to
amparo *nm* ACOGIDA, REFUGIO : protection, refuge
amperímetro *nm* : ammeter
amperio *nm* : ampere
ampliable *adj* : expandable, enlargeable, extendible
ampliación *nf, pl* **-ciones** : expansion, extension
ampliar {85} *vt* **1** : to expand, to extend **2** : to widen **3** : to enlarge (photographs) **4** : to elaborate on, to develop (ideas)
amplificador *nm* : amplifier
amplificar {72} *vt* : to amplify — **amplificación** *nf*

amplio, **-plia** *adj* : broad, wide, ample — **ampliamente** *adj*
amplitud *nf* **1** : breadth, extent **2** : spaciousness
ampolla *nf* **1** : blister **2** : vial, ampoule
ampollar *vt* : to blister — **ampollarse** *vr*
ampolleta *nf* **1** : small vial **2** : hourglass **3** *Chile* : light bulb
ampulosidad *nf* : pompousness, bombast
ampuloso, **-sa** *adj* GRANDILOCUENTE : pompous, bombastic — **ampulosamente** *adv*
amputar *vt* : to amputate — **amputación** *nf*
amueblar *vt* : to furnish
amuleto *nm* TALISMÁN : amulet, charm
amurallar *vt* : to wall in, to fortify
anacardo *nm* : cashew nut
anaconda *nf* : anaconda
anacrónico, **-ca** *adj* : anachronistic
anacronismo *nm* : anachronism
ánade *nmf* **1** : duck **2 ánade real** : mallard
anagrama *nm* : anagram
anal *adj* : anal
anales *nmpl* : annals
analfabetismo *nm* : illiteracy
analfabeto, **-ta** *adj & n* : illiterate
analgésico[1], **-ca** *adj* : analgesic, painkilling
analgésico[2] *nm* : painkiller, analgesic
análisis *nm* : analysis
analista *nmf* **1** : analyst **2** : annalist
analítico, **-ca** *adj* : analytical, analytic — **analíticamente** *adv*
analizar {21} *vt* : to analyze
analogía *nf* : analogy
analógico, **-ca** *adj* **1** : analogical **2** : analog ⟨computadora analógica : analog computer⟩
análogo, **-ga** *adj* : analogous, similar
ananá *or* **ananás** *nm, pl* **-nás** : pineapple
anaquel *nm* REPISA : shelf
anaranjado[1], **-da** *adj* NARANJA : orange-colored
anaranjado[2] *nm* NARANJA : orange (color)
anarquía *nf* : anarchy
anárquico, **-ca** *adj* : anarchic
anarquismo *nm* : anarchism
anarquista *adj & nmf* : anarchist
anatema *nm* : anathema
anatomía *nf* : anatomy — **anatomista** *nmf*
anatómico, **-ca** *adj* : anatomical — **anatómicamente** *adv*
anca *nf* **1** : haunch, hindquarter **2 ancas de rana** : frogs' legs
ancestral *adj* **1** : ancient, traditional **2** : ancestral
ancestro *nm* ASCENDIENTE : ancestor, forefather *m*
ancho[1], **-cha** *adj* **1** : wide, broad **2** : ample, loose-fitting
ancho[2] *nm* : width, breadth
anchoa *nf* : anchovy
anchura *nf* : width, breadth
ancianidad *nf* SENECTUD : old age
anciano[1], **-na** *adj* : aged, old, elderly
anciano[2], **-na** *n* : elderly person
ancla *nf* : anchor
ancladero → **anclaje**
anclaje *nm* : anchorage
anclar *v* FONDEAR : to anchor
andadas *nfpl* **1** : tracks **2 volver a las andadas** : to go back to one's old ways, to backslide
andador[1] *nm* **1** : walker, baby walker **2** *Mex* : walkway
andador[2], **-dora** *n* : walker, one who walks
andadura *nf* : course, journey ⟨su agotadora andadura al campeonato : his exhausting journey to the championship⟩
andaluz, **-luza** *adj & n, mpl* **-luces** : Andalusian
andamiaje *nm* **1** : scaffolding **2** ESTRUCTURA : structure, framework
andamio *nm* : scaffold
andanada *nf* **1** : volley, broadside **2 soltar una andanada a** : to reprimand
andanzas *nfpl* : adventures
andar[1] {6} *vi* **1** CAMINAR : to walk **2** IR : to go, to travel **3** FUNCIONAR : to run, to function ⟨el auto anda bien : the car runs well⟩ **4** : to ride ⟨andar a caballo : to ride on horseback⟩ **5** : to be ⟨anda sin dinero : he's broke⟩ — *vt* : to walk, to travel
andar[2] *nm* : walk, gait
andas *nfpl* : stand (for a coffin), bier
andén *nm, pl* **andenes** **1** : (train) platform **2** *CA, Col* : sidewalk
andino, **-na** *adj* : Andean
andorrano, **-na** *adj & n* : Andorran
andrajos *nmpl* : rags, tatters
andrajoso, **-sa** *adj* : ragged, tattered
andrógino, **-na** *adj* : androgynous
andurriales *nmpl* : remote place
anea *nf* : cattail
anduvo, etc. → **andar**
anécdota *nf* : anecdote
anecdótico, **-ca** *adj* : anecdotal
anegar {52} *vt* **1** INUNDAR : to flood **2** AHOGAR : to drown **3** : to overwhelm — **anegarse** *vr* : to be flooded
anejo *nm* → **anexo**[2]
anemia *nf* : anemia
anémico, **-ca** *adj* : anemic
anémona *nf* : anemone
anestesia *nf* : anesthesia
anestesiar *vt* : to anesthetize
anestésico[1], **-ca** *adj* : anesthetic
anestésico[2] *nm* : anesthetic
anestesista *nmf* : anesthetist
aneurisma *nmf* : aneurysm
anexar *vt* : to annex, to attach
anexión *nf, pl* **-xiones** : annexation
anexo[1], **-xa** *adj* : attached, joined, annexed
anexo[2] *nm* **1** : annex **2** : supplement (to a book), appendix
anfetamina *nf* : amphetamine

anfibio[1], **-bia** *adj* : amphibious
anfibio[2] *nm* : amphibian
anfiteatro *nm* **1** : amphitheater **2** : lecture hall
anfitrión, -triona *n, mpl* **-triones** : host, hostess *f*
ánfora *nf* **1** : amphora **2** *Mex, Peru* : ballot box
ángel *nm* : angel
angelical *adj* : angelic, angelical
angélico, -ca *adj* → **angelical**
angina *nf* **1** *or* **angina de pecho** : angina **2** *Mex* : tonsil
anglicano, -na *adj & n* : Anglican
angloparlante[1] *adj* : English-speaking
angloparlante[2] *nmf* : English speaker
anglosajón, -jona *adj & n, mpl* **-jones** : Anglo-Saxon
angoleño, -ña *adj & n* : Angolan
angora *nf* : angora
angostar *vt* : to narrow — **angostarse** *vr*
angosto, -ta *adj* : narrow
angostura *nf* : narrowness
anguila *nf* : eel
angular *adj* : angular — **angularidad** *nf*
ángulo *nm* **1** : angle **2** : corner **3 ángulo muerto** : blind spot
anguloso, -sa *adj* : angular, sharp ⟨una cara angulosa : an angular face⟩ — **angulosidad** *nf*
angustia *nf* **1** CONGOJA : anguish, distress **2** : anxiety, worry
angustiar *vt* **1** : to anguish, to distress **2** : to worry — **angustiarse** *vr*
angustioso, -sa *adj* **1** : anguished, distressed **2** : distressing, worrisome
anhelante *adj* : yearning, longing
anhelar *vt* : to yearn for, to crave
anhelo *nm* : longing, yearning
anidar *vi* **1** : to nest **2** : to make one's home, to dwell — *vt* : to shelter
anillo *nm* SORTIJA : ring
ánima *n* ALMA : soul
animación *nf, pl* **-ciones 1** : animation **2** VIVEZA : liveliness
animado, -da *adj* **1** : animated, lively **2** : cheerful — **animadamente** *adv*
animador, -dora *n* **1** : (television) host **2** : cheerleader
animadversión *nf, pl* **-siones** ANIMOSIDAD : animosity, antagonism
animal[1] *adj* **1** : animal **2** ESTÚPIDO : stupid, idiotic **3** : rough, brutish
animal[2] *nm* : animal
animal[3] *nmf* **1** IDIOTA : idiot, fool **2** : brute, beastly person
animar *vt* **1** ALENTAR : to encourage, to inspire **2** : to animate, to enliven **3** : to brighten up, to cheer up — **animarse** *vr*
anímico, -ca *adj* : mental ⟨estado anímico : state of mind⟩
ánimo *nm* **1** ALMA : spirit, soul **2** : mood, spirits *pl* **3** : encouragement **4** PROPÓSITO : intention, purpose ⟨sociedad sin ánimo de lucro : nonprofit organization⟩ **5** : energy, vitality
animosidad *nf* ANIMADVERSIÓN : animosity, ill will
animoso, -sa *adj* : brave, spirited
aniñado, -da *adj* : childlike
aniquilación *nf* → **aniquilamiento**
aniquilamiento *nm* : annihilation, extermination
aniquilar *vt* **1** : to annihilate, to wipe out **2** : to overwhelm, to bring to one's knees — **aniquilarse** *vr*
anís *nm* **1** : anise **2 semilla de anís** : aniseed
aniversario *nm* : anniversary
ano *nm* : anus
anoche *adv* : last night
anochecer[1] {53} *v impers* : to get dark
anochecer[2] *nm* : dusk, nightfall
anodino, -na *adj* : insipid, dull
ánodo *nm* : anode
anomalía *nf* : anomaly
anómalo, -la *adj* : anomalous
anonadado, -da *adj* : dumbfounded, speechless
anonadar *vt* : to dumbfound, to stun
anonimato *nm* : anonymity
anónimo, -ma *adj* : anonymous — **anónimamente** *adv*
anorexia *nf* : anorexia
anoréxico, -ca *adj* : anorexic
anormal *adj* : abnormal — **anormalmente** *adv*
anormalidad *nf* : abnormality
anotación *nf, pl* **-ciones 1** : annotation, note **2** : scoring (in sports) ⟨lograron una anotación : they managed to score a goal⟩
anotar *vt* **1** : to annotate **2** APUNTAR, ESCRIBIR : to write down, to jot down **3** : to score (in sports) — *vi* : to score
anquilosado, -da *adj* **1** : stiff-jointed **2** : stagnated, stale
anquilosamiento *nm* **1** : stiffness (of joints) **2** : stagnation, paralysis
anquilosarse *vr* **1** : to stagnate **2** : to become stiff or paralyzed
anquilostoma *nm* : hookworm
ánsar *nm* : goose
ansarino *nm* : gosling
ansia *nf* **1** INQUIETUD : apprehensiveness, uneasiness **2** ANGUSTIA : anguish, distress **3** ANHELO : longing, yearning
ansiar {85} *vt* : to long for, to yearn for
ansiedad *nf* : anxiety
ansioso, -sa *adj* **1** : anxious, worried **2** : eager — **ansiosamente** *adv*
antagónico, -ca *adj* : conflicting, opposing
antagonismo *nm* : antagonism
antagonista[1] *adj* : antagonistic
antagonista[2] *nmf* : antagonist, opponent
antagonizar {21} *vt* : to antagonize
antaño *adv* : yesteryear, long ago
antártico, -ca *adj* **1** : antarctic **2 círculo antártico** : antarctic circle
ante[1] *nm* **1** : elk, moose **2** : suede
ante[2] *prep* **1** : before, in front of **2** : considering, in view of **3 ante todo** : first and foremost, above all

anteanoche *adv* : the night before last

anteayer *adv* : the day before yesterday

antebrazo *nm* : forearm

antecedente[1] *adj* : previous, prior

antecedente[2] *nm* **1** : precedent **2 antecedentes** *nmpl* : record, background

anteceder *v* : to precede

antecesor, -sora *n* **1** ANTEPASADO : ancestor **2** PREDECESOR : predecessor

antedicho, -cha *adj* : aforesaid, above

antelación *nf, pl* **-ciones 1** : advance notice **2 con ~** : in advance, beforehand

antemano *adv* **de ~** : in advance ⟨se lo agradezco de antemano : I thank you in advance⟩

antena *nf* : antenna

antenoche → **anteanoche**

anteojera *nf* **1** : eyeglass case **2 anteojeras** *nfpl* : blinders

anteojos *nmpl* GAFAS : glasses, eyeglasses

antepasado[1], **-da** *adj* : before last ⟨el domingo antepasado : the Sunday before last⟩

antepasado[2], **-da** *n* ANTECESOR : ancestor

antepecho *nm* **1** : guardrail **2** : ledge, sill

antepenúltimo, -ma *adj* : third from last

anteponer {60} *vt* **1** : to place before ⟨anteponer al interés de la nación el interés de la comunidad : to place the interests of the community before national interest⟩ **2** : to prefer

anteproyecto *nm* **1** : draft, proposal **2 anteproyecto de ley** : bill

antera *nf* : anther

anterior *adj* **1** : previous **2** : earlier ⟨tiempos anteriores : earlier times⟩ **3** : anterior, forward, front

anterioridad *nf* **1** : priority **2 con ~** : beforehand, in advance

anteriormente *adv* : previously, beforehand

antes *adv* **1** : before, earlier **2** : formerly, previously **3** : rather, sooner ⟨antes prefiero morir : I'd rather die⟩ **4 ~ de** : before, previous to ⟨antes de hoy : before today⟩ **5 antes que** : before ⟨antes que llegue Luis : before Luis arrives⟩ **6 cuanto antes** : as soon as possible **7 antes bien** : on the contrary

antesala *nf* **1** : anteroom, waiting room, lobby **2** : prelude, prologue

antiaborto, -ta *adj* : antiabortion

antiácido *nm* : antacid

antiadherente *adj* : nonstick

antiaéreo, -rea *adj* : antiaircraft

antiamericano, -na *adj* : anti-American

antibalas *adj* : bulletproof

antibiótico[1], **-ca** *adj* : antibiotic

antibiótico[2] *nm* : antibiotic

antichoque *adj* : shockproof

anticipación *nf, pl* **-ciones 1** : expectation, anticipation **2 con ~** : in advance

anticipado, -da *adj* **1** : advance, early **2 por ~** : in advance

anticipar *vt* **1** : to anticipate, to forestall, to deal with in advance **2** : to pay in advance — **anticiparse** *vr* **1** : to be early **2** ADELANTARSE : to get ahead

anticipo *nm* **1** : advance (payment) **2** : foretaste, preview

anticlerical *adj* : anticlerical

anticlimático, -ca : anticlimactic

anticlímax *nm* : anticlimax

anticomunismo *nm* : anticommunism

anticomunista *adj & nmf* : anticommunist

anticoncepción *nf, pl* **-ciones** : birth control, contraception

anticonceptivo *nm* : contraceptive

anticongelante *nm* : antifreeze

anticuado, -da *adj* : antiquated, outdated

anticuario[1], **-ria** *adj* : antique, antiquarian

anticuario[2], **-ria** *n* : antiquarian, antiquary

anticuario[3] *nm* : antique shop

anticuerpo *nm* : antibody

antidemocrático, -ca *adj* : antidemocratic

antideportivo, -va *adj* : unsportsmanlike

antidepresivo *nm* : antidepressant

antídoto *nm* : antidote

antidrogas *adj* : antidrug

antier → **anteayer**

antiestético, -ca *adj* : unsightly, unattractive

antifascista *adj & nmf* : antifascist

antifaz *nm, pl* **-faces** : mask

antifeminista *adj & nmf* : antifeminist

antífona *nf* : anthem

antígeno *nm* : antigen

antigualla *nf* **1** : antique **2** : relic, old thing

antiguamente *adv* **1** : formerly, once **2** : long ago

antigüedad *nf* **1** : antiquity **2** : seniority **3** : age ⟨con siglos de antigüedad : centuries-old⟩ **4 antigüedades** *nfpl* : antiques

antiguo, -gua *adj* **1** : ancient, old **2** : former **3** : old-fashioned ⟨a la antigua : in the old-fashioned way⟩ **4 Antiguo Testamento** : Old Testament

antihigiénico, -ca *adj* INSALUBRE : unhygienic, unsanitary

antihistamínico *nm* : antihistamine

antiimperialismo *nm* : anti-imperialism

antiimperialista *adj & nmf* : anti-imperialist

antiinflacionario, -ria *adj* : anti-inflationary

antiinflamatorio, -ria *adj* : anti-inflammatory

antillano[1], **-na** *adj* CARIBEÑO : Caribbean, West Indian

antillano[2], **-na** *n* : West Indian

antílope *nm* : antelope

antimilitarismo *nm* : antimilitarism

antimilitarista *adj & nmf* : antimilitarist

antimonio *nm* : antimony

antimonopolista *adj* : antimonopoly, antitrust

antinatural *adj* : unnatural, perverse

antipatía *nf* : aversion, dislike

antipático, -ca *adj* : obnoxious, unpleasant

antipatriótico, -ca *adj* : unpatriotic

antirrábico, -ca *adj* : antirabies ⟨vacuna antirrábica : rabies vaccine⟩

antirreglamentario, -ria *adj* **1** : unlawful, illegal **2** : foul (in sports)

antirrevolucionario, -ria *adj & n* : antirevolutionary

antirrobo, -ba *adj* : antitheft

antisemita *adj* : anti-Semitic

antisemitismo *nm* : anti-Semitism

antiséptico[1], **-ca** *adj* : antiseptic

antiséptico[2] *nm* : antiseptic

antisocial *adj* : antisocial

antitabaco *adj* : antismoking

antiterrorista *adj* : antiterrorist

antítesis *nf* : antithesis

antitoxina *nf* : antitoxin

antitranspirante *nm* : antiperspirant

antojadizo, -za *adj* CAPRICHOSO : capricious

antojarse *vr* **1** APETECER : to be appealing, to be desirable ⟨se me antoja un helado : I feel like having ice cream⟩ **2** : to seem, to appear ⟨los árboles se antojaban fantasmas : the trees seemed like ghosts⟩

antojitos *nmpl Mex* : traditional Mexican snack foods

antojo *nm* **1** CAPRICHO : whim **2** : craving

antología *nf* **1** : anthology **2 de ~** *fam* : fantastic, incredible

antónimo *nm* : antonym

antonomasia *nf* **por ~** : par excellence

antorcha *nf* : torch

antracita *nf* : anthracite

antro *nm* **1** : cave, den **2** : dive, seedy nightclub

antropofagia *nf* CANIBALISMO : cannibalism

antropófago[1], **-ga** *adj* : cannibalistic

antropófago[2], **-ga** *n* CANÍBAL : cannibal

antropoide *adj & nmf* : anthropoid

antropología *nf* : anthropology

antropológico, -ca *adj* : anthropological

antropólogo, -ga *n* : anthropologist

anual *adj* : annual, yearly — **anualmente** *adv*

anualidad *nf* : annuity

anuario *nm* : yearbook, annual

anudar *vt* : to knot, to tie in a knot — **anudarse** *vr*

anuencia *nf* : consent

anulación *nf, pl* **-ciones** : annulment, nullification

anular *vt* : to annul, to cancel

anunciador, -dora *n* → **anunciante**

anunciante *nmf* : advertiser

anunciar *vt* **1** : to announce **2** : to advertise

anuncio *nm* **1** : announcement **2** : advertisement, commercial

anzuelo *nm* **1** : fishhook **2 morder el anzuelo** : to take the bait

añadido *nm* : addition

añadidura *nf* **1** : additive, addition **2 por ~** : in addition, furthermore

añadir *vt* **1** AGREGAR : to add **2** AUMENTAR : to increase

añejar *vt* : to age, to ripen

añejo, -ja *adj* **1** : aged, vintage **2** : age-old, musty, stale

añicos *nmpl* : smithereens, bits ⟨hacer(se) añicos : to shatter⟩

añil *nm* **1** : indigo **2** : bluing

año *nm* **1** : year ⟨en el año 1990 : in (the year) 1990⟩ ⟨tiene diez años : she is ten years old⟩ **2** : grade ⟨cuarto año : fourth grade⟩ **3 año bisiesto** : leap year **4 año luz** : light-year **5 Año Nuevo** : New Year

añoranza *nf* : longing, yearning

añorar *vt* **1** DESEAR : to long for **2** : to grieve for, to miss — *vi* : to mourn, to grieve

añoso, -sa *adj* : aged, old

aorta *nf* : aorta

apabullante *adj* : overwhelming, crushing

apabullar *vt* : to overwhelm

apacentar {55} *vt* : to pasture, to put to pasture

apache *adj & nmf* : Apache

apachurrado, -da *adj fam* : depressed, down

apachurrar *vt* : to crush, to squash

apacible *adj* : gentle, mild, calm — **apaciblemente** *adv*

apaciguador, -dora *adj* : calming

apaciguamiento *nm* : appeasement

apaciguar {10} *vt* APLACAR : to appease, to pacify — **apaciguarse** *vr* : to calm down

apadrinar *vt* **1** : to be a godparent to **2** : to sponsor, to support

apagado, -da *adj* **1** : off, out ⟨la luz está apagada : the light is off⟩ **2** : dull, subdued

apagador *nm Mex* : switch

apagar {52} *vt* **1** : to turn off, to shut off **2** : to extinguish, to put out — **apagarse** *vr* **1** : to go out, to fade **2** : to wane, to die down

apagón *nm, pl* **-gones** : blackout (of power)

apalancamiento *nm* : leverage

apalancar {72} *vt* **1** : to jack up **2** : to pry open

apalear *vt* : to beat up, to thrash

apantallar *vt Mex* : to dazzle, to impress

apañar *vt* **1** : to seize, to grasp **2** : to repair, to mend — **apañarse** *vr* : to manage, to get along

apaño *nm fam* **1** : patch **2** HABILIDAD : skill, knack

apapachar *vt Mex fam* : to cuddle, to caress — **apapacharse** *vr*

aparador *nm* **1** : sideboard, cupboard **2** ESCAPARATE, VITRINA : shop window

aparato *nm* **1** : machine, appliance, apparatus ⟨aparato auditivo : hearing aid⟩ ⟨aparato de televisión : television set⟩ **2** : system ⟨aparato digestivo : digestive system⟩ **3** : display, ostentation ⟨sin aparato : without ceremony⟩ **4 aparatos** *nmpl* : braces (for the teeth)

aparatoso, -sa *adj* **1** : ostentatious **2** : spectacular

aparcamiento *nm Spain* **1** : parking **2** : parking lot

aparcar {72} *v Spain* : to park

aparcero, -ra *n* : sharecropper

aparear *vt* **1** : to mate (animals) **2** : to match up — **aparearse** *vr* : to mate

aparecer {53} *vi* **1** : to appear **2** PRESENTARSE : to show up **3** : to turn up, to be found — **aparecerse** *vr* : to appear

aparejado, -da *adj* **1 ir aparejado con** : to go hand in hand with **2 llevar aparejado** : to entail

aparejar *vt* **1** PREPARAR : to prepare, to make ready **2** : to harness (a horse) **3** : to fit out (a ship)

aparejo *nm* **1** : equipment, gear **2** : harness, saddle **3** : rig, rigging (of a ship)

aparentar *vt* **1** : to seem, to appear ⟨no aparentas tu edad : you don't look your age⟩ **2** FINGIR : to feign, to pretend

aparente *adj* **1** : apparent **2** : showy, striking — **aparentemente** *adv*

aparición *nf, pl* **-ciones** **1** : appearance **2** PUBLICACIÓN : publication, release **3** FANTASMA : apparition, vision

apariencia *nf* **1** ASPECTO : appearance, look **2 en ~** : seemingly, apparently

apartado *nm* **1** : section, paragraph **2 apartado postal** : post office box

apartamento *nm* DEPARTAMENTO : apartment

apartar *vt* **1** ALEJAR : to move away, to put at a distance **2** : to put aside, to set aside, to separate — **apartarse** *vr* **1** : to step aside, to move away **2** DESVIARSE : to stray

aparte[1] *adv* **1** : apart, aside ⟨modestia aparte : if I say so myself⟩ **2** : separately **3 ~ de** : apart from, besides

aparte[2] *adj* : separate, special

aparte[3] *nm* : aside (in theater)

apartheid *nm* : apartheid

apasionado, -da *adj* : passionate, enthusiastic — **apasionadamente** *adv*

apasionante *adj* : fascinating, exciting

apasionar *vt* : to enthuse, to excite — **apasionarse** *vr*

apatía *nf* : apathy

apático, -ca *adj* : apathetic

apearse *vr* **1** DESMONTAR : to dismount **2** : to get out of or off (a vehicle)

apedrear *vt* : to stone, to throw stones at

apegado, -da *adj* : attached, close, devoted ⟨es muy apegado a su familia : he is very devoted to his family⟩

apegarse {52} *vr* **~ a** : to become attached to, to grow fond of

apego *nm* AFICIÓN : attachment, fondness, inclination

apelación *nf, pl* **-ciones** : appeal (in court)

apelar *vi* **1** : to appeal **2 ~ a** : to resort to

apelativo *nm* APELLIDO : last name, surname

apellidarse *vr* : to have for a last name ⟨¿cómo se apellida? : what is your last name?⟩

apellido *nm* : last name, surname

apelotonar *vt* : to roll into a ball, to bundle up

apenar *vt* : to aggrieve, to sadden — **apenarse** *vr* **1** : to be saddened **2** : to become embarrassed

apenas[1] *adv* : hardly, scarcely

apenas[2] *conj* : as soon as

apéndice *nm* **1** : appendix **2** : appendage

apendicectomía *nf* : appendectomy

apendicitis *nf* : appendicitis

apercibimiento *nm* **1** : preparation **2** AMONESTACIÓN : warning

apercibir *vt* **1** DISPONER : to prepare, to make ready **2** AMONESTAR : to warn **3** OBSERVAR : to observe, to perceive — **apercibirse** *vr* **1** : to get ready **2 ~ de** : to notice

aperitivo *nm* **1** : appetizer **2** : aperitif

apero *nm* : tool, implement

apertura *nf* **1** : opening, aperture **2** : commencement, beginning **3** : openness

apesadumbrar *vt* : to distress, to sadden — **apesadumbrarse** *vr* : to be weighed down

apestar *vt* **1** : to infect with the plague **2** : to corrupt — *vi* : to stink

apestoso, -sa *adj* : stinking, foul

apetecer {53} *vt* **1** : to crave, to long for ⟨apeteció la fama : he longed for fame⟩ **2** : to appeal to ⟨me apetece un bistec : I feel like having a steak⟩ ⟨¿cuándo te apetece ir? : when do you want to go?⟩ — *vi* : to be appealing

apetecible *adj* : appetizing, appealing

apetito *nm* : appetite

apetitoso, -sa *adj* : appetizing

apiario *nm* : apiary

ápice *nm* **1** : apex, summit **2** PIZCA : bit, smidgen

apicultor, -tora *n* : beekeeper

apicultura *nf* : beekeeping

apilar *vt* AMONTONAR : to heap up, to pile up — **apilarse** *vr*

apiñado, -da *adj* : jammed, crowded

apiñar *vt* : to pack, to cram — **apiñarse** *vr* : to crowd together, to huddle

apio *nm* : celery

apisonadora *nf* : steamroller

apisonar *vt* : to pack down, to tamp

aplacamiento *nm* : appeasement

aplacar {72} *vt* APACIGUAR : to appease, to placate — **aplacarse** *vr* : to calm down

aplanadora *nf* : steamroller
aplanar *vt* : to flatten, to level
aplastante *adj* : crushing, overwhelming
aplastar *vt* : to crush, to squash
aplaudir *v* : to applaud
aplauso *nm* **1** : applause, clapping **2** : praise, acclaim
aplazamiento *nm* : postponement
aplazar {21} *vt* : to postpone, to defer
aplicable *adj* : applicable — **aplicabilidad** *nf*
aplicación *nf, pl* **-ciones** **1** : application **2** : diligence, dedication
aplicado, -da *adj* : diligent, industrious
aplicador *nm* : applicator
aplicar {72} *vt* : to apply — **aplicarse** *vr* : to apply oneself
aplique *or* **apliqué** *nm* : appliqué
aplomar *vt* : to plumb, to make vertical
aplomo *nm* : aplomb, composure
apocado, -da *adj* : timid
apocalipsis *nms & pl* : apocalypse ⟨el Libro del Apocalipsis : the Book of Revelation⟩
apocalíptico, -ca *adj* : apocalyptic
apocamiento *nm* : timidity
apocarse {72} *vr* **1** : to shy away, to be intimidated **2** : to humble oneself, to sell oneself short
apócrifo, -fa *adj* : apocryphal
apodar *vt* : to nickname, to call — **apodarse** *vr*
apoderado, -da *n* : proxy, agent
apoderar *vt* : to authorize, to empower — **apoderarse** *vr* **~ de** : to seize, to take over
apodo *nm* SOBRENOMBRE : nickname
apogeo *nm* : acme, peak, zenith
apología *nf* : defense, apology
apoplejía *nf* : apoplexy, stroke
apoplético, -ca *adj* : apoplectic
aporrear *vt* : to bang on, to beat, to bludgeon
aportación *nf, pl* **-ciones** : contribution
aportar *vt* CONTRIBUIR : to contribute, to provide
aporte *nm* → **aportación**
apostador, -dora *n* : bettor, better
apostar {19} *v* : to bet, to wager ⟨apuesto que no viene : I bet he's not coming⟩
apostasía *nf* : apostasy
apóstata *nmf* : apostate
apostilla *nf* : note
apostillar *vt* : to annotate
apóstol *nm* : apostle
apostólico, -ca *adj* : apostolic
apóstrofe *nmf* : apostrophe
apostura *nf* : elegance, gracefulness
apoyacabezas *nms & pl* : headrest
apoyapiés *nms & pl* : footrest
apoyar *vt* **1** : to support, to back **2** : to lean, to rest — **apoyarse** *vr* **1 ~ en** : to lean on **2 ~ en** : to be based on, to rest on
apoyo *nm* : support, backing
apreciable *adj* : appreciable, substantial, considerable
apreciación *nf, pl* **-ciones** **1** : appreciation **2** : appraisal, evaluation
apreciar *vt* **1** ESTIMAR : to appreciate, to value **2** EVALUAR : to appraise, to assess — **apreciarse** *vr* : to appreciate, to increase in value
aprecio *nm* **1** ESTIMO : esteem, appreciation **2** EVALUACIÓN : appraisal, assessment
aprehender *vt* **1** : to apprehend, to capture **2** : to conceive of, to grasp
aprehensión *nf, pl* **-siones** : apprehension, capture, arrest
apremiante *adj* : pressing, urgent
apremiar *vt* INSTAR : to pressure, to urge — *vi* URGIR : to be urgent ⟨el tiempo apremia : time is of the essence⟩
apremio *nm* : pressure, urgency
aprender *v* : to learn — **aprenderse** *vr*
aprendiz, -diza *n, mpl* **-dices** : apprentice, trainee
aprendizaje *nm* : apprenticeship
aprensión *nf, pl* **-siones** : apprehension, dread
aprensivo, -va *adj* : apprehensive, worried
apresamiento *nm* : seizure, capture
apresar *vt* : to capture, to seize
aprestar *vt* : to make ready, to prepare — **aprestarse** *vr* : to get ready
apresuradamente *adv* **1** : hurriedly **2** : hastily, too fast
apresurado, -da *adj* : hurried, in a rush
apresuramiento *nm* : hurry, haste
apresurar *vt* : to quicken, to speed up — **apresurarse** *vr* : to hurry up, to make haste
apretado, -da *adj* **1** : tight **2** *fam* : cheap, tightfisted — **apretadamente** *adv*
apretar {55} *vt* **1** : to press, to push (a button) **2** : to tighten **3** : to squeeze — *vi* **1** : to press, to push **2** : to fit tightly, to be too tight ⟨los zapatos me aprietan : my shoes are tight⟩
apretón *nm, pl* **-tones** **1** : squeeze **2** **apretón de manos** : handshake
apretujar *vt* : to squash, to squeeze — **apretujarse** *vr*
aprieto *nm* APURO : predicament, difficulty ⟨estar en un aprieto : to be in a fix⟩
aprisa *adv* : quickly, hurriedly
aprisionar *vt* **1** : to imprison **2** : to trap, to box in
aprobación *nf, pl* **-ciones** : approval, endorsement
aprobar {19} *vt* **1** : to approve of **2** : to pass (a law, an exam) — *vi* : to pass (in school)
aprobatorio, -ria *adj* : approving
apropiación *nf, pl* **-ciones** : appropriation
apropiado, -da *adj* : appropriate, proper, suitable — **apropiadamente** *adv*
apropiarse *vr* **~ de** : to take possession of, to appropriate
aprovechable *adj* : usable

aprovechado[1], **-da** *adj* **1** : diligent, hardworking **2** : pushy, opportunistic
aprovechado[2], **-da** *n* : pushy person, opportunist
aprovechamiento *nm* : use, exploitation
aprovechar *vt* : to take advantage of, to make good use of — *vi* **1** : to be of use **2** : to progress, to improve — **aprovecharse** *vr* ~ **de** : to take advantage of, to exploit
aprovisionamiento *nm* : provisions *pl*, supplies *pl*
aprovisionar *vt* : to provide, to supply (with provisions)
aproximación *nf, pl* **-ciones** **1** : approximation, estimate **2** : rapprochement
aproximado, **-da** *adj* : approximate, estimated — **aproximadamente** *adv*
aproximar *vt* ACERCAR, ARRIMAR : to approximate, to bring closer — **aproximarse** *vr* ACERCARSE, ARRIMARSE : to approach, to move closer
aptitud *nf* : aptitude, capability
apto, **-ta** *adj* **1** : suitable, suited, fit **2** HÁBIL : capable, competent
apuesta *nf* : bet, wager
apuesto, **-ta** *adj* : elegant, good-looking
apuntador, **-dora** *n* : prompter
apuntalar *vt* : to prop up, to shore up
apuntar *vt* **1** : to aim, to point **2** ANOTAR : to write down, to jot down **3** INDICAR, SEÑALAR : to point to, to point out **4** : to prompt (in the theater) — *vi* **1** : to take aim **2** : to become evident — **apuntarse** *vr* **1** : to sign up, to enroll **2** : to score
apunte *nm* : note
apuñalar *vt* : to stab
apuradamente *adv* **1** : with difficulty **2** : hurriedly, hastily
apurado, **-da** *adj* **1** APRESURADO : rushed, pressured **2** : poor, needy **3** : difficult, awkward **4** : embarrassed
apurar *vt* **1** APRESURAR : to hurry, to rush **2** : to use up, to exhaust **3** : to trouble — **apurarse** *vr* **1** APRESURARSE : to hurry up **2** PREOCUPARSE : to worry
apuro *nm* **1** APRIETO : predicament, jam **2** : rush, hurry **3** : embarrassment
aquejar *vt* : to afflict
aquel, **aquella** *adj, mpl* **aquellos** : that, those
aquél, **aquélla** *pron, mpl* **aquéllos** **1** : that (one), those (ones) **2** : the former
aquello *pron* (*neuter*) : that, that matter, that business ⟨aquello fue algo serio : that was something serious⟩
aquí *adv* **1** : here **2** : now ⟨de aquí en adelante : from now on⟩ **3** **por** ~ : around here, hereabouts
aquiescencia *nf* : acquiescence, approval
aquietar *vt* : to allay, to calm — **aquietarse** *vr* : to calm down
aquilatar *vt* **1** : to assay **2** : to assess, to size up
ara *nf* **1** : altar **2** **en aras de** : in the interests of, for the sake of
árabe[1] *adj & nmf* : Arab, Arabian
árabe[2] *nm* : Arabic (language)
arabesco *nm* : arabesque — **arabesco**, **-ca** *adj*
arábigo, **-ga** *adj* **1** : Arabic, Arabian **2** **número arábigo** : Arabic numeral
arable *adj* : arable
arado *nm* : plow
aragonés, **-nesa** *adj & n, mpl* **-neses** : Aragonese
arancel *nm* : tariff, duty
arándano *nm* : blueberry
arandela *nf* : washer (for a faucet, etc.)
araña *nf* **1** : spider **2** : chandelier
arañar *v* : to scratch, to claw
arañazo *nm* : scratch
arar *v* : to plow
arbitraje *nm* **1** : arbitration **2** : refereeing (in sports)
arbitrar *v* **1** : to arbitrate **2** : to referee, to umpire
arbitrariedad *nf* **1** : arbitrariness **2** INJUSTICIA : injustice, wrong
arbitrario, **-ria** *adj* **1** : arbitrary **2** : unfair, unjust — **arbitrariamente** *adv*
arbitrio *nm* **1** ALBEDRÍO : will **2** JUICIO : judgment
árbitro, **-tra** *n* **1** : arbitrator, arbiter **2** : referee, umpire
árbol *nm* **1** : tree **2** **árbol genealógico** : family tree
arbolado[1], **-da** *adj* : wooded
arbolado[2] *nm* : woodland
arboleda *nf* : grove, wood
arbóreo, **-rea** *adj* : arboreal
arbusto *nm* : shrub, bush, hedge
arca *nf* **1** : ark **2** : coffer, chest
arcada *nf* **1** : arcade, series of arches **2** **arcadas** *nfpl* : retching ⟨hacer arcadas : to retch⟩
arcaico, **-ca** *adj* : archaic
arcángel *nm* : archangel
arcano, **-na** *adj* : arcane
arce *nm* : maple tree
arcén *nm, pl* **arcenes** : hard shoulder, berm
archidiócesis *nfs & pl* : archdiocese
archipiélago *nm* : archipelago
archivador *nm* : filing cabinet
archivar *vt* **1** : to file **2** : to archive
archivero, **-ra** *n* : archivist
archivista *nmf* : archivist
archivo *nm* **1** : file **2** : archive, archives *pl*
arcilla *nf* : clay
arco *nm* **1** : arch, archway **2** : bow (in archery) **3** : arc **4** : wicket (in croquet) **5** PORTERÍA : goal, goalposts *pl* **6** **arco iris** : rainbow
arder *vi* **1** : to burn ⟨el bosque está ardiendo : the forest is in flames⟩ ⟨arder de ira : to burn with anger, to be seething⟩ **2** : to smart, to sting, to burn ⟨le ardía el estómago : he had heartburn⟩
ardid *nm* : scheme, ruse

ardiente *adj* **1** : burning **2** : ardent, passionate — **ardientemente** *adv*
ardilla *nf* **1** : squirrel **2** *or* **ardilla listada** : chipmunk
ardor *nm* **1** : heat **2** : passion, ardor
ardoroso, -sa *adj* : heated, impassioned
arduo, -dua *adj* : arduous, grueling — **arduamente** *adv*
área *nf* : area
arena *nf* **1** : sand ‹arena movediza : quicksand› **2** : arena
arenga *nf* : harangue, lecture
arengar {52} *vt* : to harangue, to lecture
arenilla *nf* **1** : fine sand **2 arenillas** *nfpl* : kidney stones
arenisca *nf* : sandstone
arenoso, -sa *adj* : sandy, gritty
arenque *nm* : herring
arepa *nf* : cornmeal bread
arete *nm* : earring
argamasa *nf* : mortar (cement)
argelino, -na *adj & n* : Algerian
argentino, -na *adj & n* : Argentinian, Argentine
argolla *nf* : hoop, ring
argón *nm* : argon
argot *nm* : slang
argucia *nf* : sophistry, subtlety
argüir {41} *vi* : to argue — *vt* **1** ARGUMENTAR : to contend, to argue **2** INFERIR : to deduce **3** PROBAR : to prove
argumentación *nf, pl* **-ciones** : line of reasoning, argument
argumentar *vt* : to argue, to contend
argumento *nm* **1** : argument, reasoning **2** : plot, story line
aria *nf* : aria
aridez *nf, pl* **-deces** : aridity, dryness
árido, -da *adj* : arid, dry
Aries *nmf* : Aries
ariete *nm* : battering ram
arisco, -ca *adj* : surly, sullen, unsociable
arista *nf* **1** : ridge, edge **2** : beard (of a plant) **3 aristas** *nfpl* : rough edges, complications, problems
aristocracia *nf* : aristocracy
aristócrata *nmf* : aristocrat
aristocrático, -ca *adj* : aristocratic
aritmética *nf* : arithmetic
aritmético, -ca *adj* : arithmetic, arithmetical — **aritméticamente** *adv*
arlequín *nm, pl* **-quines** : harlequin
arma *nf* **1** : weapon **2 armas** *nfpl* : armed forces **3 arma de fuego** : firearm
armada *nf* : navy, fleet
armadillo *nm* : armadillo
armado, -da *adj* **1** : armed **2** : assembled, put together **3** *PRi* : obstinate, stubborn
armador, -dora *n* : shipowner
armadura *nf* **1** : armor **2** ARMAZÓN : skeleton, framework
armamento *nm* : armament, arms *pl*, weaponry
armar *vt* **1** : to assemble, to put together **2** : to create, to cause ‹armar un escándalo : to cause a scene› **3** : to arm — **armarse** *vr* **armarse de valor** : to steel oneself
armario *nm* **1** CLÓSET, ROPERO : closet **2** ALACENA : cupboard
armatoste *nm fam* : monstrosity, contraption
armazón *nmf, pl* **-zones 1** ESQUELETO : framework, skeleton ‹armazón de acero : steel framework› **2** : frames *pl* (of eyeglasses)
armenio, -nia *adj & n* : Armenian
armería *nf* **1** : armory **2** : arms museum **3** : gunsmith's shop **4** : gunsmith's craft
armiño *nm* : ermine
armisticio *nm* : armistice
armonía *nf* : harmony
armónica *nf* : harmonica
armónico, -ca *adj* **1** : harmonic **2** : harmonious — **armónicamente** *adv*
armonioso, -sa *adj* : harmonious — **armoniosamente** *adv*
armonizar {21} *vt* **1** : to harmonize **2** : to reconcile — *vi* : to harmonize, to blend together
arnés *nm, pl* **arneses** : harness
aro *nm* **1** : hoop **2** : napkin ring **3** *Arg, Chile, Uru* : earring
aroma *nm* : aroma, scent
aromático, -ca *adj* : aromatic
arpa *nf* : harp
arpegio *nm* : arpeggio
arpía *nf* : shrew, harpy
arpillera *nf* : burlap
arpista *nmf* : harpist
arpón *nm, pl* **arpones** : harpoon — **arponear** *vt*
arquear *vt* : to arch, to bend — **arquearse** *vr* : to bend, to bow
arqueología *nf* : archaeology
arqueológico, -ca *adj* : archaeological
arqueólogo, -ga *n* : archaeologist
arquero, -ra *n* **1** : archer **2** PORTERO : goalkeeper, goalie
arquetípico, -ca *adj* : archetypal
arquetipo *nm* : archetype
arquitecto, -ta *n* : architect
arquitectónico, -ca *adj* : architectural — **aquitectónicamente** *adv*
arquitectura *nf* : architecture
arrabal *nm* **1** : slum **2 arrabales** *nmpl* : outskirts, outlying area
arracada *nf* : hoop earring
arracimarse *vr* : to cluster together
arraigado, -da *adj* : deep-seated, ingrained
arraigar {52} *vi* : to take root, to become established — **arraigarse** *vr*
arraigo *nm* : roots *pl* ‹con mucho arraigo : deep-rooted›
arrancar {72} *vt* **1** : to pull out, to tear out **2** : to pick, to pluck (a flower) **3** : to start (an engine) **4** : to boot (a computer) — *vi* **1** : to start an engine **2** : to get going — **arrancarse** *vr* : to pull out, to pull off

arrancón *nm, pl* **-cones** *Mex* **1** : sudden loud start (of a car) **2 carrera de arrancones** : drag race
arranque *nm* **1** : starter (of a car) **2** ARREBATO : outburst, fit **3 punto de arranque** : beginning, starting point
arrasar *vt* **1** : to level, to smooth **2** : to devastate, to destroy **3** : to fill to the brim
arrastrar *vt* **1** : to drag, to tow **2** : to draw, to attract — *vi* : to hang down, to trail — **arrastrarse** *vr* **1** : to crawl **2** : to grovel
arrastre *nm* **1** : dragging **2** : pull, attraction **3 red de arrastre** : dragnet, trawling net
arrayán *nm, pl* **-yanes** **1** MIRTO : myrtle **2 arrayán brabántico** : bayberry, wax myrtle
arrear *vt* : to urge on, to drive — *vi* : to hurry along
arrebatado, -da *adj* **1** PRECIPITADO : impetuous, hotheaded, rash **2** : flushed, blushing
arrebatar *vt* **1** : to snatch, to seize **2** CAUTIVAR : to captivate — **arrebatarse** *vr* : to get carried away (with anger, etc.)
arrebato *nm* ARRANQUE : fit, outburst
arreciar *vi* : to intensify, to worsen
arrecife *nm* : reef
arreglado, -da *adj* **1** : fixed, repaired **2** : settled, sorted out **3** : neat, tidy **4** : smart, dressed-up
arreglar *vt* **1** COMPONER : to repair, to fix **2** : to tidy up ⟨arregla tu cuarto : pick up your room⟩ **3** : to solve, to work out ⟨quiero arreglar este asunto : I want to settle this matter⟩ — **arreglarse** *vr* **1** : to get dressed (up) ⟨arreglarse el pelo : to get one's hair done⟩ **2 arreglárselas** *fam* : to get by, to manage
arreglo *nm* **1** : repair **2** : arrangement **3** : agreement, understanding
arrellanarse *vr* : to settle (in a chair)
arremangarse {52} *vr* : to roll up one's sleeves
arremeter *vi* EMBESTIR : to attack, to charge
arremetida *nf* EMBESTIDA : attack, onslaught
arremolinarse *vr* **1** : to crowd around, to mill about **2** : to swirl (about)
arrendador, -dora *n* **1** : landlord, landlady *f* **2** : tenant, lessee
arrendajo *nm* : jay
arrendamiento *nm* **1** ALQUILER : rental, leasing **2 contrato de arrendamiento** : lease
arrendar {55} *vt* ALQUILAR : to rent, to lease
arrendatario, -ria *n* : tenant, lessee, renter
arreos *nmpl* GUARNICIONES : tack, harness, trappings
arrepentido, -da *adj* : repentant, remorseful
arrepentimiento *nm* : regret, remorse, repentance
arrepentirse {76} *vr* **1** : to regret, to be sorry **2** : to repent
arrestar *vt* DETENER : to arrest, to detain
arresto *nm* **1** DETENCIÓN : arrest **2 arrestos** *nmpl* : boldness, daring
arriar {85} *vt* **1** : to lower (a flag, etc.) **2** : to slacken (a rope, etc.)
arriate *nm Mex, Spain* : bed (for plants), border
arriba *adv* **1** : up, upwards **2** : above, overhead **3** : upstairs **4 ~ de** : more than **5 de arriba abajo** : from top to bottom, from head to foot
arribar *vi* **1** : to arrive **2** : to dock, to put into port
arribista *nmf* : parvenu, upstart
arribo *nm* : arrival
arriendo *nm* ARRENDAMIENTO : rent, rental
arriero, -ra *n* : mule driver, muleteer
arriesgado, -da *adj* **1** : risky **2** : bold, daring
arriesgar {52} *vt* : to risk, to venture — **arriesgarse** *vr* : to take a chance
arrimado, -da *n Mex fam* : sponger, freeloader
arrimar *vt* ACERCAR, APROXIMAR : to bring closer, to draw near — **arrimarse** *vr* ACERCARSE, APROXIMARSE : to approach, to get close
arrinconar *vt* **1** ACORRALAR : to corner, to box in **2** : to push aside, to abandon
arroba *nf* : arroba (Spanish unit of measurement)
arrobamiento *nm* : rapture, ecstasy
arrobar *vt* : to enrapture, to enchant — **arrobarse** *vr*
arrocero[1], **-ra** *adj* : rice
arrocero[2], **-ra** *n* : rice grower
arrodillarse *vr* : to kneel (down)
arrogancia *nf* ALTANERÍA, ALTIVEZ : arrogance, haughtiness
arrogante *adj* ALTANERO, ALTIVO : arrogant, haughty
arrogarse {52} *vr* : to usurp, to arrogate
arrojado, -da *adj* : daring, fearless
arrojar *vt* **1** : to hurl, to cast, to throw **2** : to give off, to spew out **3** : to yield, to produce **4** *fam* : to vomit — **arrojarse** *vr* PRECIPITARSE : to throw oneself, to leap
arrojo *nm* : boldness, fearlessness
arrollador, -dora *adj* : sweeping, overwhelming
arrollar *vt* **1** : to sweep away, to carry away **2** : to crush, to overwhelm **3** : to run over (with a vehicle)
arropar *vt* : to clothe, to cover (up) — **arroparse** *vr*
arrostrar *vt* : to confront, to face (up to)
arroyo *nm* **1** RIACHUELO : brook, creek, stream **2** : gutter
arroz *nm, pl* **arroces** : rice
arrozal *nm* : rice field, rice paddy
arruga *nf* : wrinkle, fold, crease

arrugado, -da *adj* : wrinkled, creased, lined
arrugar {52} *vt* : to wrinkle, to crease, to pucker — **arrugarse** *vr*
arruinar *vt* : to ruin, to wreck — **arruinarse** *vr* **1** : to be ruined **2** : to fall into ruin, to go bankrupt
arrullar *vt* : to lull to sleep — *vi* : to coo
arrullo *nm* **1** : lullaby **2** : coo (of a dove)
arrumaco *nm fam* : kissing, cuddling
arrumbar *vt* **1** : to lay aside, to put away **2** : to floor, to leave speechless
arsenal *nm* : arsenal
arsénico *nm* : arsenic
arte *nmf* (*usually m in singular, f in plural*) **1** : art ⟨artes y oficios : arts and crafts⟩ ⟨bellas artes : fine arts⟩ **2** HABILIDAD : skill **3** : cunning, cleverness
artefacto *nm* **1** : artifact **2** DISPOSITIVO : device
artemisa *nf* : sagebrush
arteria *nf* : artery — **arterial** *adj*
arteriosclerosis *nf* : arteriosclerosis, hardening of the arteries
artero, -ra *adj* : wily, crafty
artesanal *adj* : pertaining to crafts or craftsmanship, handmade
artesanía *nf* **1** : craftsmanship **2** : handicrafts *pl*
artesano, -na *n* : artisan, craftsman *m*, craftsperson
artesiano, -na *adj* : artesian ⟨pozo artesiano : artesian well⟩
ártico, -ca *adj* : arctic
articulación *nf, pl* **-ciones 1** : articulation, pronunciation **2** COYUNTURA : joint
articular *vt* **1** : to articulate, to utter **2** : to connect with a joint **3** : to coordinate, to orchestrate
articulista *nmf* : columnist
artículo *nm* **1** : article, thing **2** : item, feature, report **3 artículo de comercio** : commodity **4 artículos de primera necesidad** : essentials **5 artículos de tocador** : toiletries
artífice *nmf* **1** ARTESANO : artisan **2** : mastermind, architect
artificial *adj* **1** : artificial, man-made **2** : feigned, false — **artificialmente** *adv*
artificio *nm* **1** HABILIDAD : skill **2** APARATO : device, appliance **3** ARDID : artifice, ruse
artificioso, -sa *adj* **1** : skillful **2** : cunning, deceptive
artillería *nf* : artillery
artillero, -ra *n* : artilleryman *m*, gunner
artilugio *nm* : gadget, contraption
artimaña *nf* : ruse, trick
artista *nmf* **1** : artist **2** ACTOR, ACTRIZ : actor, actress *f*
artístico, -ca *adj* : artistic — **artísticamente** *adv*
artrítico, -ca *adj* : arthritic
artritis *nfs & pl* : arthritis
artrópodo *nm* : arthropod
arveja *nf* GUISANTE : pea
arzobispado *nm* : archbishopric
arzobispo *nm* : archbishop
as *nm* : ace
asa *nf* AGARRADERA, ASIDERO : handle, grip
asado¹, -da *adj* : roasted, grilled, broiled
asado² *nm* **1** : roast **2** : barbecued meat **3** : barbecue, cookout
asador *nm* : spit, rotisserie
asaduras *nfpl* : entrails, offal
asalariado¹, -da *adj* : wage-earning, salaried
asalariado², -da *n* : wage earner
asaltante *nmf* **1** : mugger, robber **2** : assailant
asaltar *vt* **1** : to assault **2** : to mug, to rob **3 asaltar al poder** : to seize power
asalto *nm* **1** : assault **2** : mugging, robbery **3** : round (in boxing) **4 asalto al poder** : coup d'etat
asamblea *nf* : assembly, meeting
asambleísta *nmf* : assemblyman *m*, assemblywoman *f*
asar *vt* : to roast, to grill — **asarse** *vr fam* : to roast, to be dying from heat
asbesto *nm* : asbestos
ascendencia *nf* **1** : ancestry, descent **2 ~ sobre** : influence over
ascendente *adj* : ascending, upward ⟨un curso ascendente : an upward trend⟩
ascender {56} *vt* **1** : to ascend, to rise up **2** : to be promoted ⟨ascendió a gerente : she was promoted to manager⟩ **3 ~ a** : to amount to, to reach ⟨las deudas ascienden a 20 millones de pesos : the debt amounts to 20 million pesos⟩ — *vt* : to promote
ascendiente¹ *nmf* ANCESTRO : ancestor
ascendiente² *nm* INFLUENCIA : influence, ascendancy
ascensión *nf, pl* **-siones 1** : ascent, rise **2 Fiesta de la Ascensión** : Ascension Day
ascenso *nm* **1** : ascent, rise **2** : promotion
ascensor *nm* ELEVADOR : elevator
asceta *nmf* : ascetic
ascético, -ca *adj* : ascetic
ascetismo *nm* : asceticism
asco *nm* **1** : disgust ⟨¡qué asco! : that's disgusting!, how revolting!⟩ **2 darle asco (a alguien)** : to sicken, to revolt **3 estar hecho un asco** : to be filthy **4 hacerle ascos a** : to turn up one's nose at
ascua *nf* **1** BRASA : ember **2 estar en ascuas** *fam* : to be on edge
asear *vt* **1** : to wash, to clean **2** : to tidy up — **asearse** *vr*
asechanza *nf* : snare, trap
asechar *vt* : to set a trap for
asediar *vt* **1** SITIAR : to besiege **2** ACOSAR : to harass
asedio *nm* **1** : siege **2** ACOSO : harassment
asegurador¹, -dora *adj* **1** : insuring, assuring **2** : pertaining to insurance

asegurador[2], **-dora** *n* : insurer, underwriter
aseguradora *nf* : insurance company
asegurar *vt* **1** : to assure **2** : to secure **3** : to insure — **asegurarse** *vr* **1** CERCIORARSE : to make sure **2** : to take out insurance, to insure oneself
asemejar *vt* **1** : to make similar ⟨ese bigote te asemeja a tu abuelo : that mustache makes you look like your grandfather⟩ **2** *Mex* : to be similar to, to resemble — **asemejarse** *vr* **~ a** : to look like, to resemble
asentaderas *nfpl fam* : bottom, buttocks *pl*
asentado, **-da** *adj* : settled, established
asentamiento *nm* : settlement
asentar {55} *vt* **1** : to lay down, to set down, to place **2** : to settle, to establish **3** *Mex* : to state, to affirm — **asentarse** *vr* **1** : to settle **2** ESTABLECERSE : to settle down, to establish oneself
asentimiento *nm* : assent, consent
asentir {76} *vt* : to consent, to agree
aseo *nm* : cleanliness
aséptico, **-ca** *adj* : aseptic, germ-free
asequible *adj* ACCESIBLE : accessible, attainable
aserción *nf* → **aserto**
aserradero *nm* : sawmill
aserrar {55} *vt* : to saw
aserrín *nm, pl* **-rrines** : sawdust
aserto *nm* : assertion, affirmation
asesinar *vt* **1** : to murder **2** : to assassinate
asesinato *nm* **1** : murder **2** : assassination
asesino[1], **-na** *adj* : murderous, homicidal
asesino[2], **-na** *n* **1** : murderer, killer **2** : assassin
asesor, **-sora** *n* : advisor, consultant
asesoramiento *nm* : advice, counsel
asesorar *vt* : to advise, to counsel — **asesorarse** *vr* **~ de** : to consult
asesoría *nf* **1** : consulting, advising **2** : consultant's office
asestar {55} *vt* **1** : to aim, to point (a weapon) **2** : to deliver, to deal (a blow)
aseveración *nf, pl* **-ciones** : assertion, statement
aseverar *vt* : to assert, to state
asexual *adj* : asexual — **asexualmente** *adv*
asfaltado[1], **-da** *adj* : asphalted, paved
asfaltado[2] *nm* PAVIMENTO : pavement, asphalt
asfaltar *vt* : to pave, to blacktop
asfalto *nm* : asphalt
asfixia *nf* : asphyxia, asphyxiation, suffocation
asfixiar *vt* : to asphyxiate, to suffocate, to smother — **asfixiarse** *vr*
asga, etc. → **asir**
así[1] *adv* **1** : like this, like that **2** : so, thus ⟨así sea : so be it⟩ **3 ~ de** : so, about so ⟨una caja así de grande : a box about so big⟩ **4 así que** : so, therefore **5 ~ como** : as well as **6 así así** : so-so, fair
así[2] *adj* : such, such a ⟨un talento así es inestimable : a talent like that is priceless⟩
así[3] *conj* AUNQUE : even if, even though ⟨no irá, así le paguen : he won't go, even if they pay him⟩
asiático[1], **-ca** *adj* : Asian, Asiatic
asiático[2], **-ca** *n* : Asian
asidero *nm* **1** AGARRADERA, ASA : grip, handle **2** AGARRE : grip, hold
asiduamente *adv* : regularly, frequently
asiduidad *nf* **1** : assiduousness **2** : regularity, frequency
asiduo, **-dua** *adj* **1** : assiduous **2** : frequent, regular
asiento *nm* **1** : seat, chair ⟨asiento trasero : back seat⟩ **2** : location, site
asignación *nf, pl* **-ciones** **1** : allocation **2** : appointment, designation **3** : allowance, pay **4** *PRi* : homework, assignment
asignar *vt* **1** : to assign, to allocate **2** : to appoint
asignatura *nf* MATERIA : subject, course
asilado, **-da** *n* : exile, refugee
asilo *nm* : asylum, refuge, shelter
asimetría *nf* : asymmetry
asimétrico, **-ca** *adj* : asymmetrical, asymmetric
asimilación *nf, pl* **-ciones** : assimilation
asimilar *vt* : to assimilate — **asimilarse** *vr* **~ a** : to be similar to, to resemble
asimismo *adv* **1** IGUALMENTE : similarly, likewise **2** TAMBIÉN : as well, also
asir {7} *vt* : to seize, to grasp — **asirse** *vr* **~ a** : to cling to
asistencia *nf* **1** : attendance **2** : assistance **3** : assist (in sports)
asistente[1] *adj* : attending, in attendance
asistente[2] *nmf* **1** : assistant **2 los asistentes** : those present, those in attendance
asistir *vi* : to attend, to be present ⟨asistir a clase : to attend class⟩ — *vt* : to aid, to assist
asma *nf* : asthma
asmático, **-ca** *adj* : asthmatic
asno *nm* BURRO : ass, donkey
asociación *nf, pl* **-ciones** **1** : association, relationship **2** : society, group, association
asociado[1], **-da** *adj* : associate, associated
asociado[2], **-da** *n* : associate, partner
asociar *vt* **1** : to associate, to connect **2** : to pool (resources) **3** : to take into partnership — **asociarse** *vr* **1** : to become partners **2 ~ a** : to join, to become a member of
asolar {19} *vt* : to devastate, to destroy
asoleado, **-da** *adj* : sunny
asolear *vt* : to put in the sun — **asolearse** *vr* : to sunbathe
asomar *vt* : to show, to stick out — *vi* : to appear, to become visible — **aso-**

marse *vr* **1** : to show, to appear **2** : to lean out, to look out ⟨se asomó por la ventana : he leaned out the window⟩
asombrar *vt* MARAVILLAR : to amaze, to astonish — **asombrarse** *vr* : to marvel, to be amazed
asombro *nm* : amazement, astonishment
asombroso, -sa *adj* : amazing, astonishing — **asombrosamente** *adv*
asomo *nm* **1** : hint, trace **2 ni por asomo** : by no means
aspa *nf* : blade (of a fan or propeller)
aspaviento *nm* : exaggerated movement, fuss, flounce
aspecto *nm* **1** : aspect **2** APARIENCIA : appearance, look
aspereza *nf* RUDEZA : roughness, coarseness
áspero, -ra *adj* : rough, coarse, abrasive — **ásperamente** *adv*
aspersión *nf, pl* **-siones** : sprinkling
aspersor *nm* : sprinkler
aspiración *nf, pl* **-ciones 1** : inhalation, breathing in **2** ANHELO : aspiration, desire
aspiradora *nf* : vacuum cleaner
aspirante *nmf* : applicant, candidate
aspirar *vi* **~ a** : to aspire to — *vt* : to inhale, to breathe in
aspirina *nf* : aspirin
asquear *vt* : to sicken, to disgust
asquerosidad *nf* : filth, foulness
asqueroso, -sa *adj* : disgusting, sickening, repulsive — **asquerosamente** *adv*
asta *nf* **1** : flagpole ⟨a media asta : at half-mast⟩ **2** : horn, antler **3** : shaft (of a weapon)
ástaco *nm* : crayfish
astado, -da *adj* : horned
aster *nm* : aster
asterisco *nm* : asterisk
asteroide *nm* : asteroid
astigmatismo *nm* : astigmatism
astil *nm* : shaft (of an arrow or feather)
astilla *nf* **1** : splinter, chip **2 de tal palo, tal astilla** : like father, like son
astillar *vt* : to splinter — **astillarse** *vr*
astillero *nm* : dry dock, shipyard
astral *adj* : astral
astringente *adj & nm* : astringent — **astringencia** *nf*
astro *nm* **1** : heavenly body **2** : star
astrología *nf* : astrology
astrológico, -ca *adj* : astrological
astrólogo, -ga *n* : astrologer
astronauta *nmf* : astronaut
astronáutica *nf* : astronautics
astronáutico, -ca *adj* : astronautic, astronautical
astronave *nf* : spaceship
astronomía *nf* : astronomy
astronómico, -ca *adj* : astronomical — **astronómicamente** *adv*
astrónomo, -ma *n* : astronomer
astroso, -sa *adj* DESALIÑADO : slovenly, untidy
astucia *nf* **1** : astuteness, shrewdness **2** : cunning, guile
astuto, -ta *adj* **1** : astute, shrewd **2** : crafty, tricky — **astutamente** *adv*
asueto *nm* : time off, break
asumir *vt* **1** : to assume, to take on ⟨asumir el cargo : to take office⟩ **2** SUPONER : to assume, to suppose
asunción *nf, pl* **-ciones** : assumption
asunto *nm* **1** CUESTIÓN, TEMA : affair, matter, subject **2 asuntos** *nmpl* : affairs, business
asustadizo, -za *adj* : nervous, jumpy, skittish
asustado, -da *adj* : frightened, afraid
asustar *vt* ESPANTAR : to scare, to frighten — **asustarse** *vr*
atacante *nmf* : assailant, attacker
atacar {72} *v* : to attack
atado[1]**, -da** *adj* : shy, inhibited
atado[2] *nm* **1** : bundle, bunch **2** *Arg* : pack (of cigarettes)
atadura *nf* LIGADURA : tie, bond
atajar *vt* **1** IMPEDIR : to block, to stop **2** INTERRUMPIR : to interrupt, to cut off **3** CONTENER : to hold back, to restrain — *vi* **~ por** : to take a shortcut through
atajo *nm* : shortcut
atalaya *nf* **1** : watchtower **2** : vantage point
atañer {79} *vt* **~ a** (*3rd person only*) : to concern, to have to do with ⟨eso no me atañe : that does not concern me⟩
ataque *nm* **1** : attack, assault **2** : fit ⟨ataque de risa : fit of laughter⟩ **3 ataque de nervios** : nervous breakdown **4 ataque cardíaco** *or* **ataque al corazón** : heart attack
atar *vt* AMARRAR : to tie, to tie up, to tie down — **atarse** *vr*
atarantado, -da *adj fam* **1** : restless **2** : dazed, stunned
atarantar *vt fam* : to daze, to stun
atarazana *nf* : shipyard
atardecer[1] {53} *v impers* : to get dark
atardecer[2] *nm* : late afternoon, dusk
atareado, -da *adj* : busy, overworked
atascar {72} *vt* **1** ATORAR : to block, to clog, to stop up **2** : to hinder — **atascarse** *vr* **1** : to become obstructed **2** : to get bogged down **3** PARARSE : to stall
atasco *nm* **1** : blockage **2** EMBOTELLAMIENTO : traffic jam
ataúd *nm* : coffin, casket
ataviar {85} *vt* : to dress, to clothe — **ataviarse** *vr* : to dress up
atavío *nm* ATUENDO : dress, attire
ateísmo *nm* : atheism
atemorizar {21} *vt* : to frighten, to intimidate — **atemorizarse** *vr*
atemperar *vt* : to temper, to moderate
atención[1] *nf, pl* **-ciones 1** : attention **2 poner atención** *or* **prestar atención** : to pay attention **3 llamar la atención** : to attract attention **4 en atención a** : in view of
atención[2] *interj* **1** : attention! **2** : watch out!

atender {56} *vt* **1** : to help, to wait on **2** : to look after, to take care of **3** : to heed, to listen to — *vi* : to pay attention
atenerse {80} *vr* : to abide ⟨tendrás que atenerte a las reglas : you will have to abide by the rules⟩
atentado *nm* : attack, assault
atentamente *adv* **1** : attentively, carefully **2** (*used in correspondence*) : sincerely, sincerely yours
atentar {55} *vi* ~ **contra** : to make an attempt on, to threaten ⟨atentaron contra su vida : they made an attempt on his life⟩
atento, -ta *adj* **1** : attentive, mindful **2** CORTÉS : courteous
atenuación *nf, pl* **-ciones** **1** : lessening **2** : understatement
atenuante[1] *adj* : extenuating, mitigating
atenuante[2] *nmf* : extenuating circumstance, excuse
atenuar {3} *vt* **1** MITIGAR : to extenuate, to mitigate **2** : to dim (light), to tone down (colors) **3** : to minimize, to lessen
ateo[1], **atea** *adj* : atheistic
ateo[2], **atea** *n* : atheist
aterciopelado, -da *adj* : velvety, downy
aterido, -da *adj* : freezing, frozen
aterrador, -dora *adj* : terrifying
aterrar {55} *vt* : to terrify, to frighten
aterrizaje *nm* : landing (of a plane)
aterrizar {21} *vt* : to land, to touch down
aterrorizar {21} *vt* **1** : to terrify **2** : to terrorize — **aterrorizarse** *vr* : to be terrified
atesorar *vt* : to hoard, to amass
atestado, -da *adj* : crowded, packed
atestar {55} *vt* **1** ATIBORRAR : to crowd, to pack **2** : to witness, to testify to — *vi* : to testify
atestiguar {10} *vt* : to testify to, to bear witness to — *vi* DECLARAR : to testify
atiborrar *vt* : to pack, to crowd — **atiborrarse** *vr* : to stuff oneself
ático *nm* **1** : penthouse **2** BUHARDILLA, DESVÁN : attic
atigrado, -da *adj* : tabby (of cats), striped (of fur)
atildado, -da *adj* : smart, neat, dapper
atildar *vt* **1** : to put a tilde over **2** : to clean up, to smarten up — **atildarse** *vr* : to get spruced up
atinar *vi* ACERTAR : to be accurate, to be on target
atingencia *nf* : bearing, relevance
atípico, -ca *adj* : atypical
atiplado, -da *adj* : shrill, high-pitched
atirantar *vt* : to make taut, to tighten
atisbar *vt* **1** : to spy on, to watch **2** : to catch a glimpse of, to make out
atisbo *nm* : glimpse, sign, hint
atizador *nm* : poker (for a fire)
atizar {21} *vt* **1** : to poke, to stir, to stoke (a fire) **2** : to stir up, to rouse **3** *fam* : to give, to land (a blow)
atlántico, -ca *adj* : Atlantic
atlas *nm* : atlas
atleta *nmf* : athlete
atlético, -ca *adj* : athletic
atletismo *nm* : athletics
atmósfera *nf* : atmosphere
atmosférico, -ca *adj* : atmospheric
atole *nm Mex* **1** : thick hot beverage prepared with corn flour **2 darle atole con el dedo (a alguien)** : to string (someone) along
atollarse *vr* : to get stuck, to get bogged down
atolón *nm, pl* **-lones** : atoll
atolondrado, -da *adj* **1** ATURDIDO : bewildered, dazed **2** DESPISTADO : scatterbrained, absentminded
atómico, -ca *adj* : atomic
atomizador *nm* : atomizer
atomizar {21} *vt* FRAGMENTAR : to fragment, to break into bits
átomo *nm* : atom
atónito, -ta *adj* : astonished, amazed
atontar *vt* **1** : to stupefy **2** : to bewilder, to confuse
atorar *vt* ATASCAR : to block, to clog — **atorarse** *vr* **1** ATASCARSE : to get stuck **2** ATRAGANTARSE : to choke
atormentador, -dora *n* : tormenter
atormentar *vt* : to torment, to torture — **atormentarse** *vr* : to torment oneself, to agonize
atornillar *vt* : to screw (in, on, down)
atorrante *nmf Arg* : bum, loafer
atosigar {52} *vt* : to harass, to annoy
atracadero *nm* : dock, pier
atracador, -dora *n* : robber, mugger
atracar {72} *vt* : to dock, to land — *vt* : to hold up, to rob, to mug — **atracarse** *vr fam* ~ **de** : to gorge oneself with
atracción *nf, pl* **-ciones** : attraction
atraco *nm* : holdup, robbery
atractivo[1], **-va** *adj* : attractive
atractivo[2] *nm* : attraction, appeal, charm
atraer {81} *vt* : to attract — **atraerse** *vr* **1** : to attract (each other) **2** GANARSE : to gain, to win
atragantarse *vr* : to choke (on food)
atrancar {72} *vt* : to block, to bar — **atrancarse** *vr*
atrapada *nf* : catch
atrapar *vt* : to trap, to capture
atrás *adv* **1** DETRÁS : back, behind ⟨se quedó atrás : he stayed behind⟩ **2** ANTES : ago ⟨mucho tiempo atrás : long ago⟩ **3 para** ~ *or* **hacia** ~ : backwards, toward the rear **4** ~ **de** : in back of, behind
atrasado, -da *adj* **1** : late, overdue **2** : backward **3** : old-fashioned **4** : slow (of a clock or watch)
atrasar *vt* : to delay, to put off — *vi* : to lose time — **atrasarse** *vr* : to fall behind
atraso *nm* **1** RETRASO : lateness, delay ⟨llegó con 20 minutos de atraso : he was 20 minutes late⟩ **2** : backwardness **3 atrasos** *nmpl* : arrears

atravesar {55} *vt* **1** CRUZAR : to cross, to go across **2** : to pierce **3** : to lay across **4** : to go through (a situation or crisis) — **atravesarse** *vr* **1** : to be in the way ⟨se me atravesó : it blocked my path⟩ **2** : to interfere, to meddle
atrayente *adj* : attractive
atreverse *vr* **1** : to dare **2** : to be insolent
atrevido, -da *adj* **1** : bold, daring **2** : insolent
atrevimiento *nm* **1** : daring, boldness **2** : insolence
atribución *nf, pl* **-ciones** : attribution
atribuible *adj* IMPUTABLE : attributable, ascribable
atribuir {41} *vt* **1** : to attribute, to ascribe **2** : to grant, to confer — **atribuirse** *vr* : to take credit for
atribular *vt* : to afflict, to trouble — **atribularse** *vr*
atributo *nm* : attribute
atril *nm* : lectern, stand
atrincherar *vt* : to entrench — **atrincherarse** *vr* **1** : to dig in, to entrench oneself **2 ~ en** : to hide behind
atrio *nm* **1** : atrium **2** : portico
atrocidad *nf* : atrocity
atrofia *nf* : atrophy
atrofiar *v* : to atrophy
atronador, -dora *adj* : thunderous, deafening
atropellado, -da *adj* **1** : rash, hasty **2** : brusque, abrupt
atropellamiento → **atropello**
atropellar *vt* **1** : to knock down, to run over **2** : to violate, to abuse — **atropellarse** *vr* : to rush through (a task), to trip over one's words
atropello *nm* : abuse, violation, outrage
atroz *adj, pl* **atroces** : atrocious, appalling — **atrozmente** *adv*
atuendo *nm* ATAVÍO : attire, costume
atufar *vt* : to vex, to irritate — **atufarse** *vr* **1** : to get angry **2** : to smell bad, to stink
atún *nm, pl* **atunes** : tuna fish, tuna
aturdimiento *nm* : bewilderment, confusion
aturdir *vt* **1** : to stun, to shock **2** : to bewilder, to confuse, to stupefy
atuvo, etc. → **atenerse**
audacia *nf* OSADÍA : boldness, audacity
audaz *adj, pl* **audaces** : bold, audacious, daring — **audazmente** *adv*
audible *adj* : audible
audición *nf, pl* **-ciones** **1** : hearing **2** : audition
audiencia *nf* : audience
audífono *nm* **1** : hearing aid **2 audífonos** *nmpl* : headphones, earphones
audio *nm* : audio
audiovisual *adj* : audiovisual
auditar *vt* : to audit
auditivo, -va *adj* : auditory, hearing, aural ⟨aparato auditivo : hearing aid⟩
auditor, -tora *n* : auditor
auditoría *nf* : audit
auditorio *nm* **1** : auditorium **2** : audience
auge *nm* **1** : peak, height **2** : boom, upturn
augur *nm* : augur
augurar *vt* : to predict, to foretell
augurio *nm* AGÜERO, PRESAGIO : augury, omen
augusto, -ta *adj* : august
aula *nf* : classroom
aullar {8} *vt* : to howl, to wail
aullido *nm* : howl, wail
aumentar *vt* ACRECENTAR : to increase, to raise — *vi* : to rise, to increase, to grow
aumento *nm* INCREMENTO : increase, rise
aun *adv* **1** : even ⟨ni aun en coche llegaría a tiempo : I wouldn't arrive on time even if I drove⟩ **2 aun así** : even so **3 aun más** : even more
aún *adv* **1** TODAVÍA : still, yet ⟨¿aún no ha llegado el correo? : the mail still hasn't come?⟩ **2 más aún** : furthermore
aunar {8} *vt* : to join, to combine — **aunarse** *vr* : to unite
aunque *conj* **1** : though, although, even if, even though **2 aunque sea** : at least
aura *nf* **1** : aura **2** : turkey buzzard
áureo, -rea *adj* : golden
aureola *nf* **1** : halo **2** : aura (of power, fame, etc.)
aurícula *nf* : auricle
auricular *nm* : telephone receiver
aurora *nf* **1** : dawn **2 aurora boreal** : aurora borealis
ausencia *nf* : absence
ausentarse *vr* **1** : to leave, to go away **2 ~ de** : to stay away from
ausente[1] *adj* : absent, missing
ausente[2] *nmf* **1** : absentee **2** : missing person
auspiciar *vt* **1** PATROCINAR : to sponsor **2** FOMENTAR : to foster, to promote
auspicios *nmpl* : sponsorship, auspices
austeridad *nf* : austerity
austero, -ra *adj* : austere
austral[1] *adj* : southern
austral[2] *nm* : former monetary unit of Argentina
australiano, -na *adj & n* : Australian
austriaco *or* **austríaco, -ca** *adj & n* : Austrian
autenticar {72} *vt* : to authenticate — **autenticación** *nf*
autenticidad *nf* : authenticity
auténtico, -ca *adj* : authentic — **auténticamente** *adv*
autentificar {72} *vt* : to authenticate — **autentificación** *nf*
autismo *nm* : autism
autista *adj* : autistic
auto *nm* : auto, car
autoayuda *nf* : self-help
autobiografía *nf* : autobiography
autobiográfico, -ca *adj* : autobiographical
autobús *nm, pl* **-buses** : bus

autocompasión *nf* : self-pity
autocontrol *nm* : self-control
autocracia *nf* : autocracy
autócrata *nmf* : autocrat
autocrático, -ca *adj* : autocratic
autóctono, -na *adj* : indigenous, native ⟨arte autóctono : indigenous art⟩
autodefensa *nf* : self-defense
autodestrucción *nf* : self-destruction — **autodestructivo, -va** *adj*
autodeterminación *nf* : self-determination
autodidacta[1] *adj* : self-taught
autodidacta[2] *nmf* : self-taught person, autodidact
autodidacto[1], **-ta** *adj* → **autodidacta**[1]
autodidacto[2], **-ta** *n* → **autodidacta**[2]
autodisciplina *nf* : self-discipline
autoestima *nf* : self-esteem
autogobierno *nm* : self-government
autografiar *vt* : to autograph
autógrafo *nm* : autograph
autoinfligido, -da *adj* : self-inflicted
automación → **automatización**
autómata *nm* : automaton
automático, -ca *adj* : automatic — **automáticamente** *adv*
automatización *nf* : automation
automatizar {21} *vt* : to automate
automotor, -tora *adj* **1** : self-propelled **2** : automotive, car
automotriz[1] *adj, pl* **-trices** : automotive, car
automotriz[2] *nf, pl* **-trices** : automaker
automóvil *nm* : automobile
automovilista *nmf* : motorist
automovilístico, -ca *adj* : automobile, car ⟨accidente automovilístico : automobile accident⟩
autonombrado, -da *adj* : self-appointed
autonomía *nf* : autonomy
autónomo, -ma *adj* : autonomous — **autónomamente** *adv*
autopista *nf* : expressway, highway
autoproclamado, -da *adj* : self-proclaimed, self-appointed
autopropulsado, -da *adj* : self-propelled
autopsia *nf* : autopsy
autor, -tora *n* **1** : author **2** : perpetrator
autoría *nf* : authorship
autoridad *nf* : authority
autoritario, -ria *adj* : authoritarian
autorización *nf, pl* **-ciones** : authorization
autorizado, -da *adj* **1** : authorized **2** : authoritative
autorizar {21} *vt* : to authorize, to approve
autorretrato *nm* : self-portrait
autoservicio *nm* **1** : self-service restaurant **2** SUPERMERCADO : supermarket
autostop *nm* **1** : hitchhiking **2 hacer autostop** : to hitchhike
autostopista *nmf* : hitchhiker
autosuficiencia *nf* : self-sufficiency — **autosuficiente** *adj*
auxiliar[1] *vt* : to aid, to assist
auxiliar[2] *adj* : assistant, auxiliary
auxiliar[3] *nmf* **1** : assistant, helper **2 auxiliar de vuelo** : flight attendant
auxilio *nm* **1** : aid, assistance **2 primeros auxilios** : first aid
aval *nm* : guarantee, endorsement
avalancha *nf* ALUD : avalanche
avalar *vt* : to guarantee, to endorse
avaluar {3} *vt* : to evaluate, to appraise
avalúo *nm* : appraisal, evaluation
avance *nm* ADELANTO : advance
avanzado, -da *adj* **1** : advanced **2** : progressive
avanzar {21} *v* : to advance, to move forward
avaricia *nf* CODICIA : greed, avarice
avaricioso, -sa *adj* : avaricious, greedy
avaro[1], **-ra** *adj* : miserly, greedy
avaro[2], **-ra** *n* : miser
avasallador, -dora *adj* : overwhelming
avasallamiento *nm* : subjugation, domination
avasallar *vt* : to overpower, to subjugate
ave *nf* **1** : bird **2 aves de corral** : poultry **3 ave rapaz** *or* **ave de presa** : bird of prey
avecinarse *vr* : to approach, to come near
avecindarse *vr* : to settle, to take up residence
avellana *nf* : hazelnut, filbert
avellano *nm* : hazel
avena *nf* **1** : oat, oats *pl* **2** : oatmeal
avenencia *nf* : agreement, pact
avenida *nf* : avenue
avenir {87} *vt* : to reconcile, to harmonize — **avenirse** *vr* **1** : to agree, to come to terms **2** : to get along
aventajado, -da *adj* : outstanding
aventajar *vt* **1** : to be ahead of, to lead **2** : to surpass, to outdo
aventar {55} *vt* **1** : to fan **2** : to winnow **3** *Col, Mex* : to throw, to toss — **aventarse** *vr* **1** *Col, Mex* : to hurl oneself **2** *Mex fam* : to dare, to take a chance
aventón *nm, pl* **-tones** *Col, Mex fam* : ride, lift
aventura *nf* **1** : adventure **2** RIESGO : venture, risk **3** : love affair
aventurado, -da *adj* : hazardous, risky
aventurar *vt* : to venture, to risk — **aventurarse** *vr* : to take a risk
aventurero[1], **-ra** *adj* : adventurous
aventurero[2], **-ra** *n* : adventurer
avergonzado, -da *adj* **1** : ashamed **2** : embarrassed
avergonzar {9} *vt* APENAR : to shame, to embarrass — **avergonzarse** *vr* APENARSE : to be ashamed, to be embarrassed
avería *nf* **1** : damage **2** : breakdown, malfunction
averiado, -da *adj* **1** : damaged, faulty **2** : broken down
averiar {85} *vt* : to damage — **averiarse** *vr* : to break down
averiguación *nf, pl* **-ciones** : investigation, inquiry

averiguar {10} *vt* **1** : to find out, to ascertain **2** : to investigate
aversión *nf, pl* **-siones** : aversion, dislike
avestruz *nm, pl* **-truces** : ostrich
avezado, -da *adj* : seasoned, experienced
aviación *nf, pl* **-ciones** : aviation
aviador, -dora *n* : aviator, flyer
aviar {85} *vt* **1** : to prepare, to make ready **2** : to tidy up **3** : to equip, to supply
avicultor, -tora *n* : poultry farmer
avicultura *nf* : poultry farming
avidez *nf, pl* **-deces** : eagerness
ávido, -da *adj* : eager, avid — **ávidamente** *adv*
avieso, -sa *adj* **1** : twisted, distorted **2** : wicked, depraved
avinagrado, -da *adj* : vinegary, sour
avío *nm* **1** : preparation, provision **2** : loan (for agriculture or mining) **3 avíos** *nmpl* : gear, equipment
avión *nm, pl* **aviones** : airplane
avioneta *nf* : light airplane
avisar *vt* **1** : to notify, to inform **2** : to advise, to warn
aviso *nm* **1** : notice **2** : advertisement, ad **3** ADVERTENCIA : warning **4 estar sobre aviso** : to be on the alert
avispa *nf* : wasp
avispado, -da *adj fam* : clever, sharp
avispero *nm* : wasps' nest
avispón *nm, pl* **-pones** : hornet
avistar *vt* : to sight, to catch sight of
avituallar *vt* : to suppy with food, to provision
avivar *vt* **1** : to enliven, to brighten **2** : to strengthen, to intensify
avizorar *vt* **1** ACECHAR : to spy on, to watch **2** : to observe, to perceive ⟨se avizoran dificultades : difficulties are expected⟩
axila *nf* : underarm, armpit
axioma *nm* : axiom
axiomático, -ca *adj* : axiomatic
ay *interj* **1** : oh! **2** : ouch!, ow!
ayer¹ *adv* : yesterday
ayer² *nm* ANTAÑO : yesteryear, days gone by
ayote *nm CA, Mex* : squash, pumpkin
ayuda *nf* **1** : help, assistance **2 ayuda de cámara** : valet
ayudante *nmf* : helper, assistant
ayudar *vt* : to help, to assist — **ayudarse** *vr* ~ **de** : to make use of
ayunar *vi* : to fast
ayunas *nfpl* **en ~** : fasting ⟨este medicamento ha de tomarse en ayunas : this medication should be taken on an empty stomach⟩
ayuno *nm* : fast
ayuntamiento *nm* **1** : town hall, city hall **2** : town or city council
azabache *nm* : jet ⟨negro azabache : jet black⟩
azada *nf* : hoe
azafata *nf* **1** : stewardess *f* **2** : hostess *f* (on a TV show)
azafrán *nm, pl* **-franes** **1** : saffron **2** : crocus
azahar *nm* : orange blossom
azalea *nf* : azalea
azar *nm* **1** : chance ⟨juegos de azar : games of chance⟩ **2** : accident, misfortune **3 al azar** : at random, randomly
azaroso, -sa *adj* **1** : perilous, hazardous **2** : turbulent, eventful
azimut *nm* : azimuth
azogue *nm* : mercury, quicksilver
azorar *vt* **1** : to alarm, to startle **2** : to fluster, to embarrass — **azorarse** *vr* : to get embarrassed
azotar *vt* **1** : to whip, to flog **2** : to lash, to batter **3** : to devastate, to afflict
azote *nm* **1** LÁTIGO : whip, lash **2** *fam* : spanking, licking **3** : calamity, scourge
azotea *nf* : flat roof, terraced roof
azteca *adj & nmf* : Aztec
azúcar *nmf* : sugar — **azucarar** *vt*
azucarado, -da *adj* : sweetened, sugary
azucarera *nf* : sugar bowl
azucarero, -ra *adj* : sugar ⟨industria azucarera : sugar industry⟩
azucena *nf* : white lily
azuela *nf* : adze
azufre *nm* : sulphur — **azufroso, -sa** *adj*
azul *adj & nm* : blue
azulado, -da *adj* : bluish
azulejo *nm* : ceramic tile, floor tile
azuloso, -sa *adj* : bluish
azulete *nm* : bluing
azur¹ *adj* CELESTE : azure
azur² *n* CELESTE : azure, sky blue
azuzar {21} *vt* : to incite, to egg on

B

b *nf* : second letter of the Spanish alphabet
baba *nf* **1** : spittle, saliva **2** : dribble, drool (of a baby) **3** : slime, ooze
babear *vi* **1** : to drool, to slobber **2** : to ooze
babel *nmf* : babel, chaos, bedlam
babero *nm* : bib
babor *nm* : port, port side
babosa *nf* : slug (mollusk)
babosada *nf CA, Mex* : silly act or remark
baboso, -sa *adj* **1** : drooling, slobbering **2** : slimy **3** *CA, Mex fam* : silly, dumb
babucha *nf* : slipper
babuino *nm* : baboon
bacalao *nm* : cod (fish)

bache *nm* **1** : pothole **2** *PRi* : deep puddle **3** : bad period, rough time ⟨bache económico : economic slump⟩
bachiller *nmf* : high school graduate
bachillerato *nm* : high school diploma
bacilo *nm* : bacillus
bacon *nm Spain* : bacon
bacteria *nf* : bacterium
bacteriano, -na *adj* : bacterial
bacteriología *nf* : bacteriology
bacteriológico, -ca *adj* : bacteriologic, bacteriological
bacteriólogo, -ga *n* : bacteriologist
báculo *nm* **1** : staff, stick **2** : comfort, support
badajo *nm* : clapper (of a bell)
badén *nm, pl* **badenes** **1** : (paved) ford, channel **2** : dip, ditch (in a road) **3** : speed bump
bádminton *nm* : badminton
bafle *or* **baffle** *nm* **1** : baffle **2** : speaker, loudspeaker
bagaje *nm* **1** EQUIPAJE : baggage, luggage **2** : background ⟨bagaje cultural : cultural baggage⟩
bagatela *nf* : trifle, trinket
bagre *nm* : catfish
bahía *nf* : bay
bailar *vt* : to dance — *vi* **1** : to dance **2** : to spin **3** : to be loose, to be too big
bailarín[1], -rina *adj, mpl* **-rines** **1** : dancing **2** : fond of dancing
bailarín[2], -rina *n, mpl* **-rines** **1** : dancer **2** : ballet dancer, ballerina *f*
baile *nm* **1** : dance **2** : dance party, ball **3 llevarse al baile a** *Mex fam* : to take for a ride, to take advantage of
baja *nf* **1** DESCENSO : fall, drop **2** : slump, recession **3** : loss, casualty **4 dar de baja** : to discharge, to dismiss **5 darse de baja** : to withdraw, to drop out
bajada *nf* **1** : descent **2** : dip, slope **3** : decrease, drop
bajar *vt* **1** DESCENDER : to lower, to let down, to take down **2** REDUCIR : to reduce (prices) **3** INCLINAR : to lower, to bow (the head) **4** : to go down, to descend **5 bajar de categoría** : to downgrade — *vi* **1** : to drop, to fall **2** : to come down, to go down **3** : to ebb (of tides) — **bajarse** *vr* **~ de** : to get off, to get out of (a vehicle)
bajeza *nf* **1** : low or despicable act **2** : baseness
bajío *nm* **1** : lowland **2** : shoal, sandbank, shallows
bajista *nmf* : bass player, bassist
bajo[1] *adv* **1** : down, low **2** : softly, quietly ⟨habla más bajo : speak more softly⟩
bajo[2], -ja *adj* **1** : low **2** : short (of stature) **3** : soft, faint, deep (of sounds) **4** : lower ⟨el bajo Amazonas : the lower Amazon⟩ **5** : lowered ⟨con la mirada baja : with lowered eyes⟩ **6** : base, vile **7 los bajos fondos** : the underworld
bajo[3] *nm* **1** : bass (musical instrument) **2** : first floor, ground floor **3** : hemline
bajo[4] *prep* : under, beneath, below
bajón *nm, pl* **bajones** : sharp drop, slump
bajorrelieve *nm* : bas-relief
bala *nf* **1** : bullet **2** : bale
balacera *nf* TIROTEO : shoot-out, gunfight
balada *nf* : ballad
balance *nm* **1** : balance **2** : balance sheet
balancear *vt* **1** : to balance **2** : to swing (one's arms, etc.) **3** : to rock (a boat) — **balancearse** *vr* **1** OSCILAR : to swing, to sway, to rock **2** VACILAR : to hesitate, to vacillate
balanceo *nm* **1** : swaying, rocking **2** : vacillation
balancín *nm, pl* **-cines** **1** : rocking chair **2** SUBIBAJA : seesaw
balandra *nf* : sloop
balanza *nf* BÁSCULA : scales *pl,* balance
balar *vi* : to bleat
balaustrada *nf* : balustrade
balaustre *nm* : baluster
balazo *nm* **1** TIRO : shot, gunshot **2** : bullet wound
balboa *nf* : balboa (monetary unit of Panama)
balbucear *vi* **1** : to mutter, to stammer **2** : to prattle, to babble ⟨los niños están balbuceando : the children are prattling away⟩
balbuceo *nm* : mumbling, stammering
balbucir → **balbucear**
balcánico, -ca *adj* : Balkan
balcón *nm, pl* **balcones** : balcony
balde *nm* **1** CUBO : bucket, pail **2 en ~** : in vain, to no avail
baldío[1], -día *adj* **1** : fallow, uncultivated **2** : useless, vain
baldío[2] *nm* **1** : wasteland **2** *Mex* : vacant lot
baldosa *nf* LOSETA : floor tile
balear *vt* : to shoot, to shoot at
balero *nm* **1** *Mex* : ball bearing **2** *Mex, PRi* : cup-and-ball toy
balido *nm* : bleat
balín *nm, pl* **balines** : pellet
balística *nf* : ballistics
balístico, -ca *adj* : ballistic
baliza *nf* **1** : buoy **2** : beacon (for aircraft)
ballena *nf* : whale
ballenero[1], -ra *adj* : whaling
ballenero[2], -ra *n* : whaler
ballenero[3] *nm* : whaleboat, whaler
ballesta *nf* **1** : crossbow **2** : spring (of an automobile)
ballet *nm* : ballet
balneario *nm* : spa, bathing resort
balompié *nm* FUTBOL : soccer
balón *nm, pl* **balones** : ball
baloncesto *nm* BASQUETBOL : basketball
balsa *nf* **1** : raft **2** : balsa **3** : pond, pool
balsámico, -ca *adj* : soothing

bálsamo *nm* : balsam, balm

báltico, -ca *adj* : Baltic

baluarte *nm* BASTIÓN : bulwark, bastion

bambolear *vi* **1** : to sway, to swing **2** : to wobble — **bambolearse** *vr*

bamboleo *nm* **1** : swaying, swinging **2** : wobbling

bambú *nm, pl* **bambúes** *or* **bambús** : bamboo

banal *adj* : banal, trivial

banalidad *nf* : banality

banana *nf* : banana

bananero[1], **-ra** *adj* : banana

bananero[2] *nm* : banana tree

banano *nm* **1** : banana tree **2** *CA, Col* : banana

banca *nf* **1** : banking **2** BANCO : bench

bancada *nf* **1** : group, faction **2** : workbench

bancal *nm* **1** : terrace (in agriculture) **2** : plot (of land)

bancario, -ria *adj* : bank, banking

bancarrota *nf* QUIEBRA : bankruptcy

banco *nm* **1** : bank ⟨banco central : central bank⟩ ⟨banco de datos : data bank⟩ ⟨banco de arena : sandbank⟩ ⟨banco de sangre : blood bank⟩ **2** BANCA : stool, bench **3** : pew **4** : school (of fish)

banda *nf* **1** : band, strip **2** *Mex* : belt ⟨banda transportadora : conveyor belt⟩ **3** : band (of musicians) **4** : gang (of persons), flock (of birds) **5 banda de rodadura** : tread (of a tire, etc.) **6 banda sonora** *or* **banda de sonido** : sound track

bandada *nf* : flock (of birds), school (of fish)

bandazo *nm* : swerving, lurch

bandearse *vr* : to look after oneself, to cope

bandeja *nf* : tray, platter

bandera *nf* : flag, banner

banderazo *nm* : starting signal (in sports)

banderilla *nf* : banderilla, dart (in bullfighting)

banderín *nm, pl* **-rines** : pennant, small flag

bandidaje *nm* : banditry

bandido, -da *n* BANDOLERO : bandit, outlaw

bando *nm* **1** FACCIÓN : faction, side **2** EDICTO : proclamation

bandolerismo *nm* : banditry

bandolero, -ra *n* BANDIDO : bandit, outlaw

bangladesí *adj & nmf* : Bangladeshi

banjo *nm* : banjo

banquero, -ra *n* : banker

banqueta *nf* **1** : footstool, stool, bench **2** *Mex* : sidewalk

banquete *nm* : banquet

banquetear *v* : to feast

banquillo *nm* **1** : bench (in sports) **2** : dock, defendant's seat

bañadera *nf* → **bañera**

bañar *vt* **1** : to bathe, to wash **2** : to immerse, to dip **3** : to coat, to cover ⟨bañado en lágrimas : bathed in tears⟩ — **bañarse** *vr* **1** : to take a bath, to bathe **2** : to go for a swim

bañera *nf* TINA : bathtub

bañista *nmf* : bather

baño *nm* **1** : bath **2** : swim, dip **3** : bathroom **4 baño María** : double boiler

baqueta *nf* **1** : ramrod **2 baquetas** *nfpl* : drumsticks

bar *nm* : bar, tavern

baraja *nf* : deck of cards

barajar *vt* **1** : to shuffle (cards) **2** : to consider, to toy with

baranda *nf* : rail, railing

barandal *nm* **1** : rail, railing **2** : bannister, handrail

barandilla *nf Spain* : bannister, handrail, railing

barata *nf* **1** *Mex* : sale, bargain **2** *Chile* : cockroach

baratija *nf* : bauble, trinket

baratillo *nm* : rummage sale, flea market

barato[1] *adv* : cheap, cheaply ⟨te lo vendo barato : I'll sell it to you cheap⟩

barato[2], **-ta** *adj* : cheap, inexpensive

baratura *nf* **1** : cheapness **2** : cheap thing

barba *nf* **1** : beard, stubble **2** : chin

barbacoa *nf* : barbecue

bárbaramente *adv* : barbarously

barbaridad *nf* **1** : barbarity, atrocity **2 ¡qué barbaridad!** : that's outrageous!

barbarie *nf* : barbarism, savagery

bárbaro[1] *adv fam* : wildly ⟨anoche lo pasamos bárbaro : we had a wild time last night⟩

bárbaro[2], **-ra** *adj* **1** : barbarous, wild, uncivilized **2** *fam* : great, fantastic

bárbaro[3], **-ra** *n* : barbarian

barbecho *nm* : fallow land ⟨dejar en barbecho : to leave fallow⟩

barbero, -ra *n* : barber

barbilla *nf* MENTÓN : chin

barbitúrico *nm* : barbiturate

barbudo[1], **-da** *adj* : bearded

barbudo[2] *nm* : bearded man

barca *nf* **1** : boat **2 barca de pasaje** : ferryboat

barcaza *nf* : barge

barcia *nf* : chaff

barco *nm* **1** BARCA : boat **2** BUQUE, NAVE : ship

bardo *nm* : bard

bario *nm* : barium

barítono *nm* : baritone

barlovento *nm* : windward

barman *nm* : bartender

barniz *nm, pl* **barnices** **1** LACA : varnish, lacquer **2** : glaze (on ceramics, etc.)

barnizar {21} *vt* **1** : to varnish **2** : to glaze

barométrico, -ca *adj* : barometric

barómetro *nm* : barometer

barón *nm, pl* **barones** : baron

baronesa *nf* : baroness
baronet *nm* : baronet
barquero, -ra : boatman *m,* boatwoman *f*
barquillo *nm* : wafer, thin cookie or cracker
barra *nf* : bar
barraca *nf* **1** CABAÑA, CHOZA : hut, cabin **2** : booth, stall
barracuda *nf* : barracuda
barranca *nf* **1** : hillside, slope **2** → **barranco**
barranco *nm* : ravine, gorge
barredora *nf* : street sweeper (machine)
barrena *nf* **1** TALADRO : drill, auger, gimlet **2** : tailspin
barrenar *vt* **1** : to drill **2** : to undermine
barrendero, -ra *n* : sweeper, street cleaner
barrer *v* : to sweep — **barrerse** *vr* : to slide (in sports)
barrera *nf* OBSTÁCULO : barrier, obstacle ⟨barrera de sonido : sound barrier⟩
barreta *nf* : crowbar
barriada *nf* **1** : district, quarter **2** : slums *pl*
barrica *nf* BARRIL, TONEL : barrel, cask, keg
barricada *nf* : barricade
barrida *nf* **1** : sweep **2** : slide (in sports)
barrido *nm* : sweeping
barriga *nf* PANZA : belly, paunch
barrigón, -gona *adj, mpl* **-gones** *fam* : potbellied, paunchy
barril *nm* **1** BARRICA : barrel, keg **2** **cerveza de barril** : draft beer
barrio *nm* **1** : neighborhood, district **2** **barrios bajos** : slums *pl*
barro *nm* **1** LODO : mud **2** ARCILLA : clay **3** ESPINILLA, GRANO : pimple, blackhead
barroco, -ca *adj* : baroque
barroso, -sa *adj* ENLODADO : muddy
barrote *nm* : bar (on a window)
barrunto *nm* **1** SOSPECHA : suspicion **2** INDICIO : sign, indication, hint
bártulos *nmpl* : things, belongings ⟨liar los bártulos : to pack one's things⟩
barullo *nm* BULLA : racket, ruckus
basa *nf* : base, pedestal
basalto *nm* : basalt
basar *vt* FUNDAR : to base — **basarse** *vr* FUNDARSE ~ **en** : to be based on
báscula *nf* BALANZA : balance, scales *pl*
base *nf* **1** : base, bottom **2** : base (in baseball) **3** FUNDAMENTO : basis, foundation **4** **base de datos** : database **5** **a base de** : based on, by means of **6** **en base a** : based on, on the basis of
básico, -ca *adj* FUNDAMENTAL : basic — **básicamente** *adv*
basílica *nf* : basilica
basquetbol *or* **básquetbol** *nm* BALONCESTO : basketball
basset *nm* : basset hound
bastante[1] *adv* **1** : enough, sufficiently ⟨he trabajado bastante : I have worked enough⟩ **2** : fairly, rather, quite ⟨llegaron bastante temprano : they arrived quite early⟩
bastante[2] *adj* : enough, sufficient
bastante[3] *pron* : enough ⟨hemos visto bastante : we have seen enough⟩
bastar *vi* : to be enough, to suffice
bastardilla *nf* CURSIVA : italic type, italics *pl*
bastardo, -da *adj & n* : bastard
bastidor *nm* **1** : framework, frame **2** : wing (in theater) ⟨entre bastidores : backstage, behind the scenes⟩
bastilla *nf* : hem
bastión *nf, pl* **bastiones** BALUARTE : bastion, bulwark
basto, -ta *adj* : coarse, rough
bastón *nm, pl* **bastones** **1** : cane, walking stick **2** : baton **3** **bastón de mando** : staff (of authority)
basura *nf* DESECHOS : garbage, waste, refuse
basurero[1], **-ra** *n* : garbage collector
basurero[2] *nm Mex* : garbage can
bata *nf* **1** : bathrobe, housecoat **2** : smock, coverall, lab coat
batalla *nf* **1** : battle **2** : fight, struggle **3** **de** ~ : ordinary, everyday ⟨mis zapatos de batalla : my everyday shoes⟩
batallar *vi* LIDIAR, LUCHAR : to battle, to fight
batallón *nm, pl* **-llones** : battalion
batata *nf* : yam, sweet potato
batazo *nm* HIT : hit (in baseball)
bate *nm* : baseball bat
batea *nf* **1** : tray, pan **2** : flat-bottomed boat, punt
bateador, -dora *n* : batter, hitter
batear *vi* : to bat — *vt* : to hit
bateo *nm* : batting (in baseball)
batería *nf* **1** PILA : battery **2** : drum kit, drums *pl* **3** **batería de cocina** : kitchen utensils *pl*
baterista *nmf* : drummer
batido *nm* LICUADO : milk shake
batidor *nm* : eggbeater, whisk, mixer
batidora *nf* : (electric) mixer
batir *vt* **1** GOLPEAR : to beat, to hit **2** VENCER : to defeat **3** REVOLVER : to mix, to beat **4** : to break (a record) — **batirse** *vr* : to fight
batista *nf* : batiste, cambric
batuta *nf* **1** : baton **2** **llevar la batuta** : to be the leader, to call the tune
baúl *nm* : trunk, chest
bautismal *adj* : baptismal
bautismo *nm* : baptism, christening
bautista *adj & nmf* : Baptist
bautizar {21} *vt* : to baptize, to christen
bautizo → **bautismo**
bávaro, -ra *adj & n* : Bavarian
baya *nf* **1** : berry **2** **baya de saúco** : elderberry
bayeta *nf* : cleaning cloth
bayoneta *nf* : bayonet
baza *nf* **1** : trick (in card games) **2** **meter baza en** : to butt in on
bazar *nm* : bazaar
bazo *nm* : spleen

bazofia *nf* **1** : table scraps *pl* **2** : slop, swill **3** : hogwash, rubbish
bazuca *nf* : bazooka
beagle *nm* : beagle
beatificar {72} *vt* : to beatify — **beatificación** *nf*
beatífico, -ca *adj* : beatific
beatitud *nf* : beatitude
beato, -ta *adj* **1** : blessed **2** : pious, devout **3** : sanctimonious, overly devout
bebé *nm* : baby
bebedero *nm* **1** ABREVADERO : watering trough **2** *Mex* : drinking fountain
bebedor, -dora *n* : drinker
beber *v* TOMAR : to drink
bebida *nf* : drink, beverage
beca *nf* : grant, scholarship
becado, -da *n* : scholar, scholarship holder
becerro, -rra *n* : calf
begonia *nf* : begonia
beige *adj & nm* : beige
beisbol *or* **béisbol** *nm* : baseball
beisbolista *nmf* : baseball player
beldad *nf* BELLEZA, HERMOSURA : beauty
belén *nf, pl* **belenes** NACIMIENTO : Nativity scene
belga *adj & nmf* : Belgian
beliceño, -ña *adj & n* : Belizean
belicista[1] *adj* : militaristic
belicista[2] *nmf* : warmonger
bélico, -ca *adj* GUERRERO : war, fighting <esfuerzos bélicos : war efforts>
belicosidad *nf* : bellicosity
belicoso, -sa *adj* **1** : warlike, martial **2** : aggressive, belligerent
beligerancia *nf* : belligerence
beligerante *adj & nmf* : belligerent
bellaco[1], **-ca** *adj* : sly, cunning
bellaco[2], **-ca** *n* : rogue, scoundrel
belleza *nf* BELDAD, HERMOSURA : beauty
bello, -lla *adj* **1** HERMOSO : beautiful **2 bellas artes** : fine arts
bellota *nf* : acorn
bemol *nm* : flat (in music) — **bemol** *adj*
benceno *nm* : benzene
bendecir {11} *vt* **1** CONSAGRAR : to bless, to consecrate **2** ALABAR : to praise, to extol **3 bendecir la mesa** : to say grace
bendición *nf, pl* **-ciones** : benediction, blessing
bendiga, bendijo etc. → **bendecir**
bendito, -ta *adj* **1** : blessed, holy **2** : fortunate **3** : silly, simple-minded
benedictino, -na *adj & n* : Benedictine
benefactor[1], **-tora** *adj* : beneficent
benefactor[2], **-tora** *n* : benefactor, benefactress *f*
beneficencia *nf* : beneficence, charity
beneficiar *vt* : to benefit, to be of assistance to — **beneficiarse** *vr* : to benefit, to profit
beneficiario, -ria *n* : beneficiary
beneficio *nm* **1** GANANCIA, PROVECHO : gain, profit **2** : benefit
beneficioso, -sa *adj* PROVECHOSO : beneficial
benéfico, -ca *adj* : charitable, beneficent
benemérito, -ta *adj* : meritorious, worthy
beneplácito *nm* : approval, consent
benevolencia *nf* BONDAD : benevolence, kindness
benévolo, -la *adj* BONDADOSO : benevolent, kind, good
bengala *nf* **luz de bengala 1** : flare (signal) **2** : sparkler
bengalí[1] *adj & nmf* : Bengali
bengalí[2] *nm* : Bengali (language)
benignidad *nf* : mildness, kindness
benigno, -na *adj* : benign, mild
beninés, -nesa *adj & n* : Beninese
benjamín, -mina *n, mpl* **-mines** : youngest child
beodo[1], **-da** *adj* : drunk, inebriated
beodo[2], **-da** *n* : drunkard
berberecho *nm* : cockle
berbiquí *nm* : brace (in carpentry)
berenjena *nf* : eggplant
bergantín *nm, pl* **-tines** : brig (ship)
berilo *nm* : beryl
bermudas *nfpl* : Bermuda shorts
berrear *vi* **1** : to bellow, to low **2** : to bawl, to howl
berrido *nm* **1** : bellowing **2** : howl, scream
berrinche *nm fam* : tantrum, conniption
berro *nm* : watercress
berza *nf* : cabbage
besar *vt* : to kiss
beso *nm* : kiss
bestia[1] *adj* **1** : ignorant, stupid **2** : boorish, rude
bestia[2] *nf* : beast, animal
bestia[3] *nmf* **1** IGNORANTE : ignoramus **2** : brute
bestial *adj* **1** : bestial, beastly **2** *fam* : huge, enormous <hace un frío bestial : it's terribly cold> **3** *fam* : great, fantastic
besuquear *vt fam* : to cover with kisses — **besuquearse** *vr fam* : to neck, to smooch
betabel *nm Mex* : beet
betún *nm, pl* **betunes 1** : shoe polish **2** *Mex* : icing
bianual *adj* : biannual
biatlón *nm, pl* **-lones** : biathlon
biberón *nm, pl* **-rones** : baby's bottle
biblia *nf* **1** : bible **2 la Biblia** : the Bible
bíblico, -ca *adj* : biblical
bibliografía *nf* : bibliography
bibliográfico, -ca *adj* : bibliographic, bibliographical
bibliógrafo, -fa *n* : bibliographer
biblioteca *nf* : library
bibliotecario, -ria *n* : librarian
bicameral *adj* : bicameral
bicarbonato *nm* **1** : bicarbonate **2 bicarbonato de soda** : sodium bicarbonate, baking soda
bicentenario *nm* : bicentennial

bíceps *nms & pl* : biceps
bicho *nm* : small animal, bug, insect
bici *nf fam* : bike
bicicleta *nf* : bicycle
bicolor *adj* : two-tone
bicúspide *adj* : bicuspid
bidón *nm, pl* **bidones** : large can, (oil) drum
bien[1] *adv* **1** : well ⟨¿dormiste bien? : did you sleep well?⟩ **2** CORRECTAMENTE : correctly, properly, right ⟨hay que hacerlo bien : it must be done correctly⟩ **3** : very, quite ⟨el libro era bien divertido : the book was very amusing⟩ **4** : easily ⟨bien puede acabarlo en un día : he can easily finish it in a day⟩ **5** : willingly, readily ⟨bien lo aceptaré : I'll gladly accept it⟩ **6 bien que** : although **7 más bien** : rather
bien[2] *adj* **1** : well, OK, all right ⟨¿te sientes bien? : are you feeling all right?⟩ **2** : pleasant, agreeable ⟨las flores huelen bien : the flowers smell very nice⟩ **3** : satisfactory **4** : correct, right
bien[3] *nm* **1** : good ⟨el bien y el mal : good and evil⟩ **2 bienes** *nmpl* : property, goods, possessions
bienal *adj & nf* : biennial — **bienalmente** *adv*
bienaventurado, -da *adj* **1** : blessed **2** : fortunate, happy
bienaventuranzas *nfpl* : Beatitudes
bienestar *nm* **1** : welfare, well-being **2** CONFORT : comfort
bienhechor[1], **-chora** *adj* : beneficent, benevolent
bienhechor[2], **-chora** *n* : benefactor, benefactress *f*
bienintencionado, -da *adj* : well-meaning
bienvenida *nf* **1** : welcome **2 dar la bienvenida a** : to welcome
bienvenido, -da *adj* : welcome
bies *nm* : bias (in sewing)
bife *nm Arg, Chile, Uru* : steak
bífido, -da *adj* : forked
bifocal *adj* : bifocal
bifocales *nmpl* : bifocals
bifurcación *nf, pl* **-ciones** : fork (in a river or road)
bifurcarse {72} *vr* : to fork
bigamia *nf* : bigamy
bígamo, -ma *n* : bigamist
bigote *nm* **1** : mustache **2** : whisker (of an animal)
bigotudo, -da *adj* : mustached, having a big mustache
bikini *nm* : bikini
bilateral *adj* : bilateral — **bilateralmente** *adv*
bilingüe *adj* : bilingual
bilioso, -sa *adj* **1** : bilious **2** : irritable
bilis *nf* : bile
billar *nm* : pool, billiards
billete *nm* **1** : bill ⟨un billete de cinco dólares : a five-dollar bill⟩ **2** BOLETO : ticket ⟨billete de ida y vuelta : round-trip ticket⟩
billetera *nf* : billfold, wallet
billón *nm, pl* **billones 1** : billion (Great Britain) **2** : trillion (U.S.A.)
bimestral *adj* : bimonthly — **bimestralmente** *adv*
bimotor *adj* : twin-engined
binacional *adj* : binational
binario, -ria *adj* : binary
bingo *nm* : bingo
binocular *adj* : binocular
binoculares *nmpl* : binoculars
binomio *nm* **1** : binomial **2** PAREJA : pair, duo
biodegradable *adj* : biodegradable
biodegradarse *vr* : to biodegrade
biodiversidad *nf* : biodiversity
biofísica *nf* : biophysics
biofísico[1], **-ca** *adj* : biophysical
biofísico[2], **-ca** *n* : biophysicist
biografía *nf* : biography
biográfico, -ca *adj* : biographical
biógrafo, -fa *n* : biographer
biología *nf* : biology
biológico, -ca *adj* : biological, biologic — **biológicamente** *adv*
biólogo, -ga *n* : biologist
biombo *nm* MAMPARA : folding screen, room divider
biomecánica *nf* : biomechanics
biopsia *nf* : biopsy
bioquímica *nf* : biochemistry
bioquímico[1], **-ca** *adj* : biochemical
bioquímico[2], **-ca** *n* : biochemist
biosfera *or* **biósfera** *nf* : biosphere
biotecnología *nf* : biotechnology
biótico, -ca *adj* : biotic
bipartidismo *nm* : two-party system
bipartidista *adj* : bipartisan
bípedo *nm* : biped
birlar *vt fam* : to swipe, to pinch
birmano, -na *adj & n* : Burmese
bis[1] *adv* **1** : twice, again (in music) **2** : a, A ⟨artículo 47 bis : Article 47A⟩ ⟨calle Bolívar, número 70 bis : Bolívar Street, number 70A⟩
bis[2] *nm* : encore
bisabuelo, -la *n* : great-grandfather *m,* great-grandmother *f,* great-grandparent
bisagra *nf* : hinge
bisecar {72} *vt* : bisect — **bisección** *nf*
bisel *nm* : bevel
biselar *vt* : to bevel
bisexual *adj* : bisexual
bisiesto *adj* **año bisiesto** : leap year
bismuto *nm* : bismuth
bisnieto, -ta *n* : great-grandson *m,* great-granddaughter *f,* great-grandchild
bisonte *nm* : bison, buffalo
bisoñé *nm* : hairpiece, toupee
bisoño[1], **-ña** *adj* : inexperienced, green
bisoño[2], **-ña** *n* : rookie, greenhorn
bistec *nm* : steak, beefsteak
bisturí *nm* ESCALPELO : scalpel
bisutería *nf* : costume jewelry
bit *nm* : bit (unit of information)
bivalvo *nm* : bivalve
bizarría *nf* **1** : courage, gallantry **2** : generosity

bizarro, -rra *adj* **1** VALIENTE : courageous, valiant **2** GENEROSO : generous
bizco, -ca *adj* : cross-eyed
bizcocho *nm* **1** : sponge cake **2** : biscuit **3** *Mex* : breadstick
bizquera *nf* : crossed eyes, squint
blanco[1], -ca *adj* : white
blanco[2], -ca *n* : white person
blanco[3] *nm* **1** : white **2** : target, bull's-eye ⟨dar en el blanco : to hit the target, to hit the nail on the head⟩ **3** : blank space, blank ⟨un cheque en blanco : a blank check⟩
blancura *nf* : whiteness
blancuzco, -ca *adj* **1** : whitish, off-white **2** PÁLIDO : pale
blandir {1} *vt* : to wave, to brandish
blando, -da *adj* **1** SUAVE : soft, tender **2** : weak (in character) **3** : lenient
blandura *nf* **1** : softness, tenderness **2** : leniency
blanqueador *nm* : bleach, whitener
blanquear *vt* **1** : to whiten, to bleach **2** : to shut out (in sports) **3** : to launder (money) — *vi* : to turn white
blanquillo *nm CA, Mex* : egg
blasfemar *vi* : to blaspheme
blasfemia *nf* : blasphemy
blasfemo, -ma *adj* : blasphemous
blazer *nm* : blazer
bledo *nm* **no me importa un bledo** *fam* : I couldn't care less, I don't give a damn
blindado, -da *adj* ACORAZADO : armored
blindaje *nm* **1** : armor, armor plating **2** : shield (for cables, machinery, etc.)
bloc *nm, pl* **blocs** : writing pad, pad of paper
blof *nm Col, Mex* : bluff
blofear *vi Col, Mex* : to bluff
blondo, -da *adj* : blond, flaxen
bloque *nm* **1** : block **2** GRUPO : bloc ⟨el bloque comunista : the Communist bloc⟩
bloquear *vt* **1** OBSTRUIR : to block, to obstruct **2** : to blockade
bloqueo *nm* **1** OBSTRUCCIÓN : blockage, obstruction **2** : blockade
blusa *nf* : blouse
blusón *nm, pl* **blusones** : loose shirt, smock
boa *nf* : boa
boato *nm* : ostentation, show
bobada *nf* **1** : stupid remark or action **2 decir bobadas** : to talk nonsense
bobalicón, -cona *adj, mpl* **-cones** *fam* : silly, stupid
bobina *nf* CARRETE : bobbin, reel
bobo[1], -ba *adj* : silly, stupid
bobo[2], -ba *n* : fool, simpleton
boca *nf* **1** : mouth **2 boca arriba** : face up, on one's back **3 boca abajo** : face down, prone **4 boca de riego** : hydrant **5 en boca de** : according to
bocacalle *nf* : entrance to a street ⟨gire a la última bocacalle : take the last turning⟩
bocadillo *nm Spain* : sandwich
bocado *nm* **1** : bite, mouthful **2** FRENO : bit (of a bridle)
bocajarro *nm* **a ~** : point-blank, directly
bocallave *nf* : keyhole
bocanada *nf* **1** : swig, swallow **2** : puff, mouthful (of smoke) **3** : gust (of air) **4** : stream (of people)
boceto *nm* : sketch, outline
bochinche *nm fam* : ruckus, uproar
bochorno *nm* **1** VERGÜENZA : embarrassment **2** : hot and humid weather **3** : hot flash
bochornoso, -sa *adj* **1** EMBARAZOSO : embarrassing **2** : hot and muggy
bocina *nf* **1** : horn, trumpet **2** : automobile horn **3** : mouthpiece (of a telephone) **4** *Mex* : loudspeaker
bocinazo *nm* : honk (of a horn)
bocio *nm* : goiter
bocón, -cona *n, mpl* **bocones** *fam* : blabbermouth, loudmouth
boda *nf* : wedding
bodega *nf* **1** : wine cellar **2** *Chile, Col, Mex* : storeroom, warehouse **3** (*in various countries*) : grocery store
bofetada *nf* CACHETADA : slap on the face
bofetear *vt* CACHETEAR : to slap
bofetón *nm* → **bofetada**
bofo, -fa *adj* : flabby
boga *nf* : fashion, vogue ⟨estar en boga : to be in style⟩
bogotano[1], -na *adj* : of or from Bogotá
bogotano[2], -na *n* : person from Bogotá
bohemio, -mia *adj & n* : bohemian, Bohemian
boicot *nm, pl* **boicots** : boycott
boicotear *vt* : to boycott
boina *nf* : beret
boiserie *nf* : wood paneling, wainscoting
boj *nm, pl* **bojes** : box (plant), boxwood
bola *nf* **1** : ball ⟨bola de nieve : snowball⟩ **2** *fam* : lie, fib **3** *Mex fam* : bunch, group ⟨una bola de rateros : a bunch of thieves⟩ **4** *Mex* : uproar, tumult
bolear *vt Mex* : to polish (shoes)
bolera *nf* : bowling alley
bolero *nm* : bolero
boleta *nf* **1** : ballot **2** : ticket **3** : receipt
boletería *nf* TAQUILLA : box office, ticket office
boletín *nm, pl* **-tines** **1** : bulletin **2** : journal, review **3 boletín de prensa** : press release
boleto *nm* BILLETE : ticket
boliche *nm* **1** BOLOS : bowling **2** *Arg* : bar, tavern
bólido *nm* **1** : race car **2** METEORO : meteor
bolígrafo *nm* : ballpoint pen
bolillo *nm* **1** : bobbin **2** *Mex* : roll, bun
bolívar *nm* : bolivar (monetary unit of Venezuela)
boliviano[1], -na *adj & n* : Bolivian
boliviano[2] *nm* : boliviano (monetary unit of Bolivia)

bollo *nm* : bun, sweet roll
bolo *nm* : bowling pin, tenpin
bolos *nmpl* BOLICHE : bowling
bolsa *nf* **1** : bag, sack **2** *Mex* : pocketbook, purse **3** *Mex* : pocket **4 la Bolsa** : the stock market, the stock exchange **5 bolsa de trabajo** : employment agency
bolsear *vi Mex* : to pick pockets
bolsillo *nm* **1** : pocket **2 dinero de bolsillo** : pocket change, loose change
bolso *nm* : pocketbook, handbag
bomba *nf* **1** : bomb **2** : bubble **3** : pump ⟨bomba de gasolina : gas pump⟩
bombachos *nmpl* : baggy pants, bloomers
bombardear *vt* **1** : to bomb **2** : to bombard
bombardeo *nm* **1** : bombing, shelling **2** : bombardment
bombardero *nm* : bomber (airplane)
bombástico, -ca *adj* : bombastic
bombear *vt* : to pump
bombero, -ra *n* : firefighter, fireman *m*
bombilla *nf* : lightbulb
bombillo *nm CA, Col, Ven* : lightbulb
bombo *nm* **1** : bass drum **2** *fam* : exaggerated praise, hype ⟨con bombos y platillos : with great fanfare⟩
bombón *nm, pl* **bombones 1** : bonbon, chocolate **2** *Mex* : marshmallow
bonachón[1], **-chona** *adj, mpl* **-chones** *fam* : good-natured, kindhearted
bonachón[2], **-chona** *n, mpl* **-chones** *fam* BUENAZO : kindhearted person
bonaerense[1] *adj* : of or from Buenos Aires
bonaerense[2] *nmf* : person from Buenos Aires
bonanza *nf* **1** PROSPERIDAD : prosperity ⟨bonanza económica : economic boom⟩ **2** : calm weather **3** : rich ore deposit, bonanza
bondad *nf* BENEVOLENCIA : goodness, kindness ⟨tener la bondad de hacer algo : to be kind enough to do something⟩
bondadoso, -sa *adj* BENÉVOLO : kind, kindly, good — **bondadosamente** *adv*
bonete *nm* : cap, mortarboard
boniato *nm* : sweet potato
bonificación *nf, pl* **-ciones 1** : discount **2** : bonus, extra
bonito[1] *adv* : nicely, well ⟨¡qué bonito canta tu hermana! : your sister sings wonderfully!⟩
bonito[2], **-ta** *adj* LINDO : pretty, lovely ⟨tiene un apartamento bonito : she has a nice apartment⟩
bonito[3] *nm* : bonito (tuna)
bono *nm* **1** : bond ⟨bono bancario : bank bond⟩ **2** : voucher
boqueada *nf* : gasp ⟨dar la última boqueada : to give one's last gasp⟩
boquear *vi* **1** : to gasp **2** : to be dying
boquete *nm* : gap, opening, breach
boquiabierto, -ta *adj* : open-mouthed, speechless, agape
boquilla *nf* : mouthpiece (of a musical instrument)
borbollar *vi* : to bubble
borbotar *or* **borbotear** *vi* : to boil, to bubble, to gurgle
borboteo *nm* : bubbling, gurgling
borda *nf* : gunwale
bordado *nm* : embroidery, needlework
bordar *v* : to embroider
borde *nm* **1** : border, edge **2 al borde de** : on the verge of ⟨estoy al borde de la locura : I'm about to go crazy⟩
bordear *vt* **1** : to border, to skirt ⟨el Río Este bordea Manhattan : the East River borders Manhattan⟩ **2** : to border on ⟨bordea la irrealidad : it borders on unreality⟩ **3** : to line ⟨una calle bordeada de árboles : a street lined with trees⟩
bordillo *nm* : curb
bordo *nm* **a ~** : aboard, on board
boreal *adj* : northern
borgoña *nf* : burgundy
bórico, -ca *adj* : boric ⟨ácido bórico : boric acid⟩
boricua *adj & nmf fam* : Puerto Rican
borinqueño, -ña → **boricua**
borla *nf* **1** : pom-pom, tassel **2** : powder puff
boro *nm* : boron
borrachera *nf* : drunkenness ⟨agarró una borrachera : he got drunk⟩
borrachín, -china *n, mpl* **-chines** *fam* : lush, drunk
borracho[1], **-cha** *adj* EBRIO : drunk, intoxicated
borracho[2], **-cha** *n* : drunk, drunkard
borrador *nm* **1** : rough copy, first draft ⟨en borrador : in the rough⟩ **2** : eraser
borrar *vt* : to erase, to blot out — **borrarse** *vr* **1** : to fade, to fade away **2** : to resign, to drop out **3** *Mex fam* : to split, to leave ⟨me borro : I'm out of here⟩
borrascoso, -sa *adj* : gusty, blustery
borrego, -ga *n* **1** : lamb, sheep **2** : simpleton, fool
borrico → **burro**
borrón *nm, pl* **borrones** : smudge, blot ⟨borrón y cuenta nueva : let's start on a clean slate, let's start over again⟩
borronear *vt* : to smudge, to blot
borroso, -sa *adj* **1** : blurry, smudgy **2** CONFUSO : unclear, confused
boscoso, -sa *adj* : wooded
bosnio, -nia *adj & n* : Bosnian
bosque *nm* : woods, forest
bosquecillo *nm* : grove, copse, thicket
bosquejar *vt* ESBOZAR : to outline, to sketch
bosquejo *nm* **1** TRAZADO : outline, sketch **2** : draft
bostezar {21} *vi* : to yawn
bostezo *nm* : yawn
bota *nf* **1** : boot **2** : wineskin
botana *nf Mex* : snack, appetizer
botanear *vi Mex* : to have a snack
botánica *nf* : botany

botánico[1], **-ca** *adj* : botanical
botánico[2], **-ca** *n* : botanist
botar *vt* **1** ARROJAR : to throw, to fling, to hurl **2** TIRAR : to throw out, to throw away **3** : to launch (a ship)
bote *nm* **1** : small boat ⟨bote de remos : rowboat⟩ **2** : can, jar **3** : jump, bounce **4** *Mex fam* : jail
botella *nf* : bottle
botica *nf* FARMACIA : drugstore, pharmacy
boticario, -ria *n* FARMACÉUTICO : pharmacist, druggist
botín *nm, pl* **botines 1** : baby's bootee **2** : ankle boot **3** : booty, plunder
botiquín *nm, pl* **-quines 1** : medicine cabinet **2** : first-aid kit
botón *nm, pl* **botones 1** : button **2** : bud **3** INSIGNIA : badge
botones *nmfs & pl* : bellhop
botulismo *nm* : botulism
boulevard [ˌbuleˈvar] → **bulevar**
bouquet *nm* **1** : fragrance, bouquet (of wine) **2** RAMILLETE : bouquet (of flowers)
boutique *nf* : boutique
bóveda *nf* **1** : vault, dome **2** CRIPTA : crypt
bovino, -na *adj* : bovine
box *nm, pl* **boxes 1** : pit (in auto racing) **2** *Mex* : boxing
boxeador, -dora *n* : boxer
boxear *vi* : to box
boxeo *nm* : boxing
boya *nf* : buoy
boyante *adj* **1** : buoyant **2** : prosperous, thriving
bozal *nm* **1** : muzzle **2** : halter (for a horse)
bracear *vi* **1** : to wave one's arms **2** : to make strokes (in swimming)
bracero, -ra *n* : migrant worker, day laborer
braguero *nm* : truss (in medicine)
bragueta *nf* : fly, pants zipper
braille *adj & nm* : braille
bramante *nm* : twine, string
bramar *vi* **1** RUGIR : to roar, to bellow **2** : to howl (of the wind)
bramido *nm* : bellowing, roar
brandy *nm* : brandy
branquia *nf* AGALLA : gill
brasa *nf* ASCUA : ember, live coal
brasero *nm* : brazier
brasier *nm Col, Mex* : brassiere, bra
brasileño, -ña *adj & n* : Brazilian
bravata *nf* **1** JACTANCIA : boast, bravado **2** AMENAZA : threat
bravo, -va *adj* **1** FEROZ : ferocious, fierce ⟨un perro bravo : a ferocious dog⟩ **2** EXCELENTE : excellent, great ⟨¡bravo! : bravo!, well done!⟩ **3** : rough, rugged, wild **4** : annoyed, angry
bravucón, -cona *n, mpl* **-cones** : bully
bravuconadas *nfpl* : bravado
bravura *nf* **1** FEROCIDAD : fierceness, ferocity **2** VALENTÍA : bravery
braza *nf* **1** : breaststroke **2** : fathom (unit of length)
brazada *nf* : stroke (in swimming)
brazalete *nm* PULSERA : bracelet, bangle
brazo *nm* **1** : arm **2 brazo derecho** : right-hand man **3 brazos** *nmpl* : hands, laborers
brea *nf* ALQUITRÁN : tar, pitch
brebaje *nm* : potion, brew
brecha *nf* **1** : gap, breach ⟨estar siempre en la brecha : to be always there when needed, to stay in the thick of things⟩ **2** : gash
brécol *nm* : broccoli
brega *nf* **1** LUCHA : struggle, fight **2** : hard work
bregar {52} *vi* **1** LUCHAR : to struggle **2** : to toil, to work hard **3 ~ con** : to deal with
brete *nm* : jam, tight spot
breve *adj* **1** CORTO : brief, short **2 en ~** : shortly, in short — **brevemente** *adv*
brevedad *nf* : brevity, shortness
breviario *nm* : breviary
brezal *nm* : heath, moor
brezo *nm* : heather
bribón, -bona *n, mpl* **bribones** : rascal, scamp
bricolaje *or* **bricolage** *nm* : do-it-yourself
brida *nf* : bridle
brigada *nf* **1** : brigade **2** : gang, team, squad
brigadier *nm* : brigadier
brillante[1] *adj* : brilliant, bright — **brillantemente** *adv*
brillante[2] *nm* DIAMANTE : diamond
brillantez *nf* : brilliance, brightness
brillar *vi* : to shine, to sparkle
brillo *nm* **1** LUSTRE : luster, shine **2** : brilliance
brilloso, -sa *adj* LUSTROSO : lustrous, shiny
brincar {72} *vi* **1** SALTAR : to jump around, to leap about **2** : to frolic, to gambol
brinco *nm* **1** SALTO : jump, leap, skip **2 pegar un brinco** : to give a start, to jump
brindar *vi* : to drink a toast ⟨brindó por los vencedores : he toasted the victors⟩ — *vt* OFRECER, PROPORCIONAR : to offer, to provide — **brindarse** *vr* : to offer one's assistance, to volunteer
brindis *nm* : toast, drink ⟨hacer un brindis : to drink a toast⟩
brinque, etc. → **brincar**
brío *nm* **1** : force, determination **2** : spirit, verve
brioso, -sa *adj* : spirited, lively
briqueta *nf* : briquette
brisa *nf* : breeze
británico[1], **-ca** *adj* : British
británico[2], **-ca** *n* **1** : British person **2 los británicos** : the British
brizna *nf* **1** : strand, thread **2** : blade (of grass)

broca *nf* : drill bit
brocado *nm* : brocade
brocha *nf* : paintbrush
broche *nm* **1** ALFILER : brooch **2** : fastener, clasp **3 broche de oro** : finishing touch
brocheta *nf* : skewer
brócoli *nm* : broccoli
broma *nf* **1** CHISTE : joke, prank **2** : fun, merriment **3 en ~** : in jest, jokingly
bromear *vi* : to joke, to fool around ⟨sólo estaba bromeando : I was only kidding⟩
bromista[1] *adj* : fun-loving, joking
bromista[2] *nmf* : joker, prankster
bromo *nm* : bromine
bronca *nf fam* : fight, quarrel, fuss
bronce *nm* : bronze
bronceado[1], **-da** *adj* **1** : tanned, suntanned **2** : bronze
bronceado[2] *nm* **1** : suntan, tan **2** : bronzing
broncearse *vr* : to get a suntan
bronco, -ca *adj* **1** : harsh, rough **2** : untamed, wild
bronquial *adj* : bronchial
bronquio *nm* : bronchial tube, bronchus
bronquitis *nf* : bronchitis
broqueta *nf* : skewer
brotar *vi* **1** : to bud, to sprout **2** : to spring up, to stream, to gush forth **3** : to break out, to appear
brote *nm* **1** : outbreak **2** : sprout, bud, shoot
broza *nf* **1** : brushwood **2** MALEZA : scrub, undergrowth
brujería *nf* HECHICERÍA : witchcraft, sorcery
brujo[1], **-ja** *adj* : bewitching
brujo[2], **-ja** *n* : warlock *m,* witch *f,* sorcerer
brújula *nf* : compass
bruma *nf* : haze, mist
brumoso, -sa *adj* : hazy, misty
bruñir {38} *vt* : to burnish, to polish (metals)
brusco, -ca *adj* **1** SÚBITO : sudden, abrupt **2** : curt, brusque — **bruscamente** *adv*
brusquedad *nf* **1** : abruptness, suddenness **2** : brusqueness
brutal *adj* **1** : brutal **2** *fam* : incredible, terrific — **brutalmente** *adv*
brutalidad *nf* CRUELDAD : brutality
brutalizar {21} *vt* : to brutalize, to maltreat
bruto[1], **-ta** *adj* **1** : gross ⟨peso bruto : gross weight⟩ ⟨ingresos brutos : gross income⟩ **2** : unrefined ⟨petróleo bruto : crude oil⟩ **3** : brutish, stupid
bruto[2], **-ta** *n* **1** : brute **2** : dunce, blockhead
bubónico, -ca *adj* : bubonic
bucal *adj* : oral
bucanero *nm* : buccaneer, pirate
buccino *nm* : whelk
buceador, -dora *n* : diver, scuba diver
bucear *vi* **1** : to dive, to swim underwater **2** : to explore, to delve
buceo *nm* **1** : diving, scuba diving **2** : exploration, searching
buche *nm* **1** : crop (of a bird) **2** *fam* : belly, gut **3** : mouthful ⟨hacer buches : to rinse one's mouth⟩
bucle *nm* **1** : curl, ringlet **2** : loop
bucólico, -ca *adj* : bucolic
budín *nm, pl* **budines** : pudding
budismo *nm* : Buddhism
budista *adj & nmf* : Buddhist
buen *adj* → **bueno**[1]
buenamente *adv* **1** : easily **2** : willingly
buenaventura *nf* **1** : good luck **2** : fortune, future ⟨le dijo la buenaventura : she told his fortune⟩
buenazo, -za *n fam* BONACHÓN : kindhearted person
bueno[1], **-na** *adj* (**buen** *before masculine singular nouns*) **1** : good ⟨una buena idea : a good idea⟩ **2** BONDADOSO : nice, kind **3** APROPIADO : proper, appropriate **4** SANO : well, healthy **5** : considerable, goodly ⟨una buena cantidad : a lot⟩ **6 buenos días** : hello, good day **7 buenas tardes** : good afternoon **8 buenas noches** : good evening, good night
bueno[2] *interj* **1** : OK!, all right! **2** *Mex* : hello! (on the telephone)
buey *nm* : ox, steer
búfalo *nm* **1** : buffalo **2 búfalo de agua** : water buffalo
bufanda *nf* : scarf, muffler
bufar *vi* : to snort
bufet *or* **bufé** *nm* : buffet-style meal
bufete *nm* **1** : law firm, law office **2** : writing desk
bufido *nm* : snort
bufo, -fa *adj* : comic
bufón, -fona *n, mpl* **bufones** : clown, buffoon, jester
bufonada *nf* **1** : jest, buffoonery **2** : sarcasm
buhardilla *nf* **1** ÁTICO, DESVÁN : attic **2** : dormer window
búho *nm* **1** : owl **2** *fam* : hermit, recluse
buhonero, -ra *n* MERCACHIFLE : peddler
buitre *nm* : vulture
bujía *nf* : spark plug
bula *nf* : papal bull
bulbo *nm* : bulb
bulboso, -sa *adj* : bulbous
bulevar *nm* : boulevard
búlgaro, -ra *adj & n* : Bulgarian
bulla *nf* BARULLO : racket, rowdiness
bullicio *nm* **1** : ruckus, uproar **2** : hustle and bustle
bullicioso, -sa *adj* : noisy, busy, turbulent
bullir {38} *vi* **1** HERVIR : to boil **2** MOVERSE : to stir, to bustle about
bulto *nm* **1** : package, bundle **2** : piece of luggage, bag **3** : size, bulk, volume **4** : form, shape **5** : lump (on the body), swelling, bulge

bumerán *nm, pl* **-ranes** : boomerang

búnker *nm, pl* **búnkers** : bunker

búnquer → **búnker**

buñuelo *nm* : fried pastry

buque *nm* BARCO : ship, vessel

burbuja *nf* : bubble, blister (on a surface)

burbujear *vi* **1** : to bubble **2** : to fizz

burbujeo *nm* : bubbling

burdel *nm* : brothel, whorehouse

burdo, -da *adj* **1** : coarse, rough **2** : crude, clumsy ⟨una burda mentira : a clumsy lie⟩ — **burdamente** *adj*

burgués, -guesa *adj & n, mpl* **burgueses** : bourgeois

burguesía *nf* : bourgeoisie, middle class

burla *nf* **1** : mockery, ridicule **2** : joke, trick **3 hacer burla de** : to make fun of, to mock

burlar *vt* ENGAÑAR : to trick, to deceive — **burlarse** *vr* ~ **de** : to make fun of, to ridicule

burlesco, -ca *adj* : burlesque, comic

burlón[1], -lona *adj, mpl* **burlones** : joking, mocking

burlón[2], -lona *n, mpl* **burlones** : joker

burocracia *nf* : bureaucracy

burócrata *nmf* : bureaucrat

burocrático, -ca *adj* : bureaucratic

burrada *nf fam* : stupid act, nonsense

burrito *nm* : burrito

burro[1], -rra *adj fam* : dumb, stupid

burro[2], -rra *n* **1** ASNO : donkey, ass **2** *fam* : dunce, poor student

burro[3] *nm* **1** : sawhorse **2** *Mex* : ironing board **3** *Mex* : stepladder

bursátil *adj* : stock-market

bursitis *nf* : bursitis

burundés, -desa *adj & n* : Burundian

bus *nm* : bus

busca *nf* : search

buscador, -dora *n* : hunter (for treasure, etc.), prospector

buscapersonas *nms & pl* : beeper, pager

buscapleitos *nmfs & pl* : troublemaker

buscar {72} *vt* **1** : to look for, to seek **2** : to pick up, to collect **3** : to provoke — *vi* : to look, to search ⟨buscó en los bolsillos : he searched through his pockets⟩

buscavidas *nmf & pl* **1** : busybody **2** : go-getter

busque, etc. → **buscar**

búsqueda *nf* : search

busto *nm* : bust

butaca *nf* **1** SILLÓN : armchair **2** : seat (in a theatre) **3** *Mex* : pupil's desk

butano *nm* : butane

buzo[1], -za *adj Mex fam* : smart, astute ⟨¡ponte buzo! : get with it!, get on the ball!⟩

buzo[2] *nm* : diver, scuba diver

buzón *nm, pl* **buzones** : mailbox

byte *nm* : byte

C

c *nf* : third letter of the Spanish alphabet

cabal *adj* **1** : exact, correct **2** : complete **3** : upright, honest

cabales *nmpl* **no estar en sus cabales** : not to be in one's right mind

cabalgar {52} *vi* : to ride (on horseback)

cabalgata *nf* : cavalcade, procession

cabalidad *nf* **a** ~ : thoroughly, conscientiously

caballa *nf* : mackerel

caballada *nf* **1** : herd of horses **2** *fam* : nonsense, stupidity, outrageousness

caballar *adj* EQUINO : horse, equine

caballeresco, -ca *adj* : gallant, chivalrous

caballería *nf* **1** : cavalry **2** : horse, mount **3** : knighthood, chivalry

caballeriza *nf* : stable

caballero[1] → **caballeroso**

caballero[2] *nm* **1** : gentleman **2** : knight

caballerosidad *nf* : chivalry, gallantry

caballeroso, -sa *adj* : gentlemanly, chivalrous

caballete *nm* **1** : ridge **2** : easel **3** : trestle (for a table, etc.) **4** : bridge (of the nose) **5** : sawhorse

caballista *nmf* : horseman *m*, horsewoman *f*

caballito *nm* **1** : rocking horse **2 caballito de mar** : seahorse **3 caballitos** *nmpl* : merry-go-round

caballo *nm* **1** : horse **2** : knight (in chess) **3 caballo de fuerza** *or* **caballo de vapor** : horsepower

cabalmente *adv* : fully, exactly

cabaña *nf* CHOZA : cabin, hut

cabaret *nm, pl* **-rets** : nightclub, cabaret

cabecear *vt* : to head (in soccer) — *vi* **1** : to nod one's head **2** : to lurch, to pitch

cabecera *nf* **1** : headboard **2** : head ⟨cabecera de la mesa : head of the table⟩ **3** : heading, headline **4** : headwaters *pl* **5 médico de cabecera** : family doctor **6 cabecera municipal** *CA, Mex* : downtown area

cabecilla *nmf* : ringleader, kingpin

cabellera *nf* : head of hair, mane

cabello *nm* : hair

cabelludo, -da *adj* **1** : hairy **2 cuero cabelludo** : scalp

caber {12} *vi* **1** : to fit, to go ⟨no sé si cabremos todos en el coche : I don't know if we'll all fit in the car⟩ **2** : to be possible ⟨no cabe duda alguna : there's no doubt about it⟩ ⟨cabe que llegue mañana : he may come tomorrow⟩

cabestrillo *nm* : sling ⟨llevo el brazo en cabestrillo : my arm is in a sling⟩

cabestro *nm* : halter (for an animal)

cabeza *nf* **1** : head **2 cabeza hueca** : scatterbrain **3 de** ~ : head first **4 dolor de cabeza** : headache

cabezada *nf* **1** : butt, blow with the head **2** : nod ⟨echar una cabezada : to take a nap, to doze off⟩
cabezal *nm* : bolster
cabezazo *nm* : butt, blow with the head
cabezón, -zona *adj, mpl* **-zones** *fam* **1** : having a big head **2** : pigheaded, stubborn
cabida *nf* **1** : room, space, capacity **2** **dar cabida a** : to accommodate, to hold
cabildear *vi* : to lobby
cabildeo *nm* : lobbying
cabildero, -ra *n* : lobbyist
cabildo *nm* AYUNTAMIENTO **1** : town or city hall **2** : town or city council
cabina *nf* **1** : cabin **2** : booth **3** : cab (of a truck), cockpit (of an airplane)
cabizbajo, -ja *adj* : dejected, downcast
cable *nm* : cable
cableado *nm* : wiring
cabo *nm* **1** : end ⟨al cabo de dos semanas : at the end of two weeks⟩ **2** : stub, end piece **3** : corporal **4** : cape, headland ⟨el Cabo Cañaveral : Cape Canaveral⟩ **5** **al fin y al cabo** : after all, in the end **6** **llevar a cabo** : to carry out, to do
caboverdiano, -na *adj & n* : Cape Verdean
cabrá, etc. → **caber**
cabra *nf* : goat
cabrestante *nm* : windlass
cabrío, -ría *adj* : goat, caprine
cabriola *nf* **1** : skip, jump **2** **hacer cabriolas** : to prance
cabriolar *vi* : to prance
cabrito *nm* : kid, baby goat
cabús *nm, pl* **cabuses** *Mex* : caboose
cacahuate *or* **cacahuete** *nm* : peanut
cacalote *nm Mex* : crow
cacao *nm* : cacao, cocoa bean
cacarear *vi* : to crow, to cackle, to cluck — *vt fam* : to boast about, to crow about ⟨cacarear un huevo : to brag about an accomplishment⟩
cacareo *nm* **1** : clucking (of a hen), crowing (of a rooster) **2** : boasting
cacatúa *nf* : cockatoo
cace, etc. → **cazar**
cacería *nf* **1** CAZA : hunt, hunting **2** : hunting party
cacerola *nf* : pan, saucepan
cacha *nf* : butt (of a gun)
cachar *vt fam* : to catch
cacharro *nm* **1** *fam* : thing, piece of junk **2** *fam* : jalopy **3** **cacharros** *nmpl* : pots and pans
cache *nm* : cache, cache memory
caché *nm* : cachet
cachear *vt* : to search, to frisk
cachemir *nm* : cashmere
cachetada *nf* BOFETADA : slap on the face
cachete *nm* : cheek
cachetear *vt* BOFETEAR : to slap
cachiporra *nf* : bludgeon, club, blackjack
cachirul *nm Mex fam* : cheating ⟨hacer cachirul : to cheat⟩
cachivache *nm fam* : thing ⟨mete tus cachivaches en el maletero : put your stuff in the trunk⟩
cacho *nm fam* : piece, bit
cachorro, -rra *n* **1** : cub **2** PERRITO : puppy
cachucha *nf Mex* : cap, baseball cap
cacique *nm* **1** : chief (of a tribe) **2** : boss (in politics)
cacofonía *nf* : cacophony
cacofónico, -ca *adj* : cacophonous
cacto *nm* : cactus
cactus → **cacto**
cada *adj* **1** : each ⟨cuestan diez pesos cada una : they cost ten pesos each⟩ **2** : every ⟨cada vez : every time⟩ **3** : such, some ⟨sales con cada historia : you come up with such crazy stories⟩ **4** **cada vez más** : more and more, increasingly **5** **cada vez menos** : less and less
cadalso *nm* : scaffold, gallows
cadáver *nm* : corpse, cadaver
cadavérico, -ca *adj* **1** : cadaverous **2** PÁLIDO : deathly pale
caddie *or* **caddy** *nmf, pl* **caddies** : caddy
cadena *nf* **1** : chain **2** : network, channel **3** **cadena de montaje** : assembly line **4** **cadena perpetua** : life sentence
cadencia *nf* : cadence, rhythm
cadencioso, -sa *adj* : rhythmic, rhythmical
cadera *nf* : hip
cadete *nmf* : cadet
cadmio *nm* : cadmium
caducar {72} *vi* : to expire
caducidad *nf* : expiration
caduco, -ca *adj* **1** : outdated, obsolete **2** : deciduous
caer {13} *vi* **1** : to fall, to drop **2** : to collapse **3** : to hang (down) **4** **caer bien** *fam* : to be pleasant, to be likeable ⟨me caes bien : I like you⟩ **5** **caer mal** *or* **caer gordo** *fam* : to be unpleasant, to be unlikeable — **caerse** *vr* : to fall down
café[1] *adj* : brown ⟨ojos cafés : brown eyes⟩
café[2] *nm* **1** : coffee **2** : café
cafeína *nf* : caffeine
cafetal *nm* : coffee plantation
cafetalero[1], **-ra** *adj* : coffee ⟨cosecha cafetalera : coffee harvest⟩
cafetalero[2], **-ra** *n* : coffee grower
cafetera *nf* : coffeepot, coffeemaker
cafetería *nf* **1** : coffee shop, café **2** : lunchroom, cafeteria
cafetero[1], **-ra** *adj* : coffee-producing
cafetero[2], **-ra** *n* : coffee grower
cafeticultura *nf Mex* : coffee industry
caguama *nf* **1** : large Caribbean turtle **2** *Mex* : large bottle of beer
caída *nf* **1** BAJA, DESCENSO : fall, drop **2** : collapse, downfall
caiga, etc. → **caer**
caimán *nm, pl* **caimanes** : alligator, caiman

caimito *nm* : star apple
caja *nf* **1** : box, case **2** : cash register, checkout counter **3** : bed (of a truck) **4** *fam* : coffin **5 caja fuerte** *or* **caja de caudales** : safe **6 caja de seguridad** : safe-deposit box **7 caja torácica** : rib cage
cajero, -ra *n* **1** : cashier **2** : teller **3 cajero automático** : automated teller machine, ATM
cajeta *nf Mex* : a sweet caramel-flavored spread
cajetilla *nf* : pack (of cigarettes)
cajón *nm, pl* **cajones 1** : drawer, till **2** : crate, case **3 cajón de estacionamiento** *Mex* : parking space
cajuela *nf Mex* : trunk (of a car)
cal *nf* : lime, quicklime
cala *nf* : cove, inlet
calabacín *nm, pl* **-cines** : zucchini
calabacita *nf Mex* : zucchini
calabaza *nf* **1** : pumpkin, squash **2** : gourd **3 dar calabazas a** : to give the brush-off to, to jilt
calabozo *nm* **1** : prison **2** : jail cell
calado[1], -da *adj* **1** : drenched **2** : openworked
calado[2] *nm* **1** : draft (of a ship) **2** : openwork
calafatear *vt* : to caulk
calamar *nm* **1** : squid **2 calamares** *nmpl* : calamari
calambre *nm* **1** ESPASMO : cramp **2** : electric shock, jolt
calamidad *nf* DESASTRE : calamity, disaster
calamina *nf* : calamine
calamitoso, -sa *adj* : calamitous, disastrous
calaña *nf* : ilk, kind, sort ⟨una persona de mala calaña : a bad sort⟩
calar *vt* **1** : to soak through **2** : to pierce, to penetrate — *vi* : to catch on — **calarse** *vr* : to get drenched
calavera[1] *nf* **1** : skull **2** *Mex* : taillight
calavera[2] *nm* : rake, rogue
calcar {72} *vt* **1** : to trace **2** : to copy, to imitate
calce, etc. → **calzar**
calceta *nf* : knee-high stocking
calcetería *nf* : hosiery
calcetín *nm, pl* **-tines** : sock
calcificar {72} *v* : to calcify — **calcificarse** *vr*
calcinar *vt* : to char, to burn
calcio *nm* : calcium
calco *nm* **1** : transfer, tracing **2** : copy, image
calcomanía *nf* : decal, transfer
calculador, -dora *adj* : calculating
calculadora *nf* : calculator
calcular *vt* **1** : to calculate, to estimate **2** : to plan, to scheme
cálculo *nm* **1** : calculation, estimation **2** : calculus **3** : plan, scheme **4 cálculo biliar** : gallstone **5 hoja de cálculo** : spreadsheet
caldas *nfpl* : hot springs
caldear *vt* : to heat, to warm — **caldearse** *vr* **1** : to heat up **2** : to become heated, to get tense
caldera *nf* **1** : cauldron **2** : boiler
caldo *nm* **1** CONSOMÉ : broth, stock **2 caldo de cultivo** : culture medium, breeding ground
caldoso, -sa *adj* : watery
calefacción *nf, pl* **-ciones** : heating, heat
calefactor *nm* : heater
caleidoscopio → **calidoscopio**
calendario *nm* **1** : calendar **2** : timetable, schedule
caléndula *nf* : marigold
calentador *nm* : heater
calentamiento *nm* **1** : heating, warming **2** : warm-up (in sports)
calentar {55} *vt* **1** : to heat, to warm **2** *fam* : to annoy, to anger **3** *fam* : to excite, to turn on — **calentarse** *vr* **1** : to get warm, to heat up **2** : to warm up (in sports) **3** *fam* : to become sexually aroused **4** *fam* : to get mad
calentura *nf* **1** FIEBRE : temperature, fever **2** : cold sore
calibrador *nm* : gauge, calipers *pl*
calibrar *vt* : to calibrate — **calibración** *nf*
calibre *nm* **1** : caliber, gauge **2** : importance, excellence **3** : kind, sort ⟨un problema de grueso calibre : a serious problem⟩
calidad *nf* **1** : quality, grade **2** : position, status **3 en calidad de** : as, in the capacity of
cálido, -da *adj* **1** : hot ⟨un clima cálido : a hot climate⟩ **2** : warm ⟨una cálida bienvenida : a warm welcome⟩
calidoscopio *nm* : kaleidoscope
caliente *adj* **1** : hot, warm ⟨mantenerse caliente : to stay warm⟩ **2** : heated, fiery ⟨una disputa caliente : a heated argument⟩ **3** *fam* : sexually excited, horny
califa *nm* : caliph
calificación *nf, pl* **-ciones 1** NOTA : grade (for a course) **2** : rating, score **3** CLASIFICACIÓN : qualification, qualifying ⟨ronda de calificación : qualifying round⟩
calificar {72} *vt* **1** : to grade **2** : to describe, to rate ⟨la calificaron de buena alumna : they described her as a good student⟩ **3** : to qualify, to modify (in grammar)
calificativo[1], -va *adj* : qualifying
calificativo[2] *nm* : qualifier, epithet
caligrafía *nf* **1** ESCRITURA : handwriting **2** : calligraphy
calipso *nm* : calypso
calistenia *nf* : calisthenics
cáliz *nm, pl* **cálices 1** : chalice, goblet **2** : calyx
caliza *nf* : limestone
callado, -da *adj* : quiet, silent — **calladamente** *adv*
callar *vi* : to keep quiet, to be silent — *vt* **1** : to silence, to hush ⟨¡calla a los

niños! : keep the children quiet!⟩ **2** : to keep secret — **callarse** *vr* : to remain silent ⟨¡cállate! : be quiet!, shut up!⟩
calle *nf* : street, road
callejear *vi* : to wander about the streets, to hang out
callejero, -ra *adj* : street ⟨perro callejero : stray dog⟩
callejón *nm, pl* **-jones** **1** : alley **2 callejón sin salida** : dead-end street
callo *nm* **1** : callus, corn **2 callos** *nmpl* : tripe
calloso, -sa *adj* : callous
calma *nf* : calm, quiet
calmante[1] *adj* : calming, soothing
calmante[2] *nm* : tranquilizer, sedative
calmar *vt* TRANQUILIZAR : to calm, to soothe — **calmarse** *vr* : to calm down
calmo, -ma *adj* TRANQUILO : calm, tranquil
calmoso, -sa *adj* **1** TRANQUILO : calm, quiet **2** LENTO : slow, sluggish
calor *nm* **1** : heat ⟨hace calor : it's hot outside⟩ ⟨tener calor : to feel hot⟩ **2** : warmth, affection **3** : ardor, passion
caloría *nf* : calorie
calórico, -ca *adj* : caloric
calorífico, -ca *adj* : caloric
calque, etc. → **calcar**
calumnia *nf* : slander, libel — **calumnioso, -sa** *adj*
calumniar *vt* : to slander, to libel
caluroso, -sa *adj* **1** : hot **2** : warm, enthusiastic
calva *nf* : bald spot, bald head
calvario *nm* **1** : Calvary **2** : Stations of the Cross *pl* **3 vivir un calvario** : to suffer great adversity
calvicie *nf* : baldness
calvo[1], **-va** *adj* : bald
calvo[2], **-va** *n* : bald person
calza *nf* : block, wedge
calzada *nf* : roadway, avenue
calzado *nm* : footwear
calzador *nm* : shoehorn
calzar {21} *vt* **1** : to wear (shoes) ⟨¿de cuál calza? : what is your shoe size?⟩ ⟨siempre calzaban tenis : they always wore sneakers⟩ **2** : to provide with shoes
calzo *nm* : chock, wedge
calzoncillos *nmpl* : underpants, briefs
calzones *nmpl* : underpants, panties
cama *nf* **1** : bed **2 cama elástica** : trampoline
camada *nf* : litter, brood
camafeo *nm* : cameo
camaleón *nm, pl* **-leones** : chameleon
cámara *nf* **1** : camera **2** : chamber, room **3** : house (in government) **4** : inner tube
camarada *nmf* **1** : comrade, companion **2** : colleague
camaradería *nf* : camaraderie
camarero, -ra *n* **1** MESERO : waiter, waitress *f* **2** : bellhop *m*, chambermaid *f* (in a hotel) **3** : steward *m*, stewardess *f* (on a ship, etc.)
camarilla *nf* : political clique
camarógrafo, -fa *n* : cameraman *m*, camerawoman *f*
camarón *nm, pl* **-rones** **1** : shrimp **2** : prawn
camarote *nm* : cabin, stateroom
camastro *nm* : small hard bed, pallet
cambalache *nm fam* : swap
cambiante *adj* **1** : changing **2** VARIABLE : changeable, variable
cambiar *vt* **1** ALTERAR, MODIFICAR : to change **2** : to exchange, to trade — *vi* **1** : to change **2 cambiar de velocidad** : to shift gears — **cambiarse** *vr* **1** : to change (clothing) **2** MUDARSE : to move (to a new address)
cambio *nm* **1** : change, alteration **2** : exchange **3** : change (money) **4 en cambio** : instead **5 en cambio** : however, on the other hand
cambista *nmf* : exchange broker
camboyano, -na *adj & n* : Cambodian
cambur *nm Ven* : banana
camelia *nf* : camellia
camello *nm* : camel
camellón *nm, pl* **-llones** *Mex* : traffic island
camerino *nm* : dressing room
camerunés, -nesa *adj, mpl* **-neses** : Cameroonian
camilla *nf* : stretcher
camillero, -ra *n* : orderly (in a hospital)
caminante *nmf* : wayfarer, walker
caminar *vi* ANDAR : to walk, to move — *vt* : to walk, to cover (a distance)
caminata *nf* : hike, long walk
camino *nm* **1** : path, road **2** : journey ⟨ponerse en camino : to set off⟩ **3** : way ⟨a medio camino : halfway there⟩
camión *nm, pl* **camiones** **1** : truck **2** *Mex* : bus
camionero, -ra *n* **1** : truck driver **2** *Mex* : bus driver
camioneta *nf* : light truck, van
camisa *nf* **1** : shirt **2 camisa de fuerza** : straitjacket
camiseta *nf* **1** : T-shirt **2** : undershirt
camisón *nm, pl* **-sones** : nightshirt, nightgown
camorra *nf fam* : fight, trouble ⟨buscar camorra : to pick a fight⟩
camote *nm* **1** : root vegetable similar to the sweet potato **2 hacerse camote** *Mex fam* : to get mixed up
campal *adj* : pitched, fierce ⟨batalla campal : pitched battle⟩
campamento *nm* : camp
campana *nf* : bell
campanada *nf* TAÑIDO : stroke (of a bell), peal
campanario *nm* : bell tower, belfry
campanilla *nf* **1** : small bell, handbell **2** : uvula
campante *adj* : nonchalant, smug ⟨seguir tan campante : to go on as if nothing had happened⟩

campaña *nf* **1** CAMPO : countryside, country **2** : campaign **3 tienda de campaña** : tent
campañol *nm* : vole
campechana *nf Mex* : puff pastry
campechanía *nf* : geniality
campechano, -na *adj* : open, cordial, friendly
campeón, -peona *n, mpl* **-peones** : champion
campeonato *nm* : championship
cámper *nm* : camper (vehicle)
campero, -ra *adj* : country, rural
campesino, -na *n* : peasant, farm laborer
campestre *adj* : rural, rustic
camping *nm* **1** : camping **2** : campsite
campiña *nf* CAMPO : countryside, country
campista *nmf* : camper
campo *nm* **1** CAMPAÑA : countryside, country **2** : field ‹campo de aviación : airfield› ‹su campo de responsabilidad : her field of responsibility›
camposanto *nm* : graveyard, cemetery
campus *nms & pl* : campus
camuflaje *nm* : camouflage
camuflajear *vt* : to camouflage
camuflar → **camuflajear**
can *nm* : hound, dog
cana *nf* **1** : gray hair **2 salirle canas** : to go gray, to get gray hair **3 echar una cana al aire** : to let one's hair down
canadiense *adj & nmf* : Canadian
canal[1] *nm* **1** : canal **2** : channel
canal[2] *nmf* : gutter, groove
canalé *nm* : rib, ribbing (in fabric)
canaleta *nf* : gutter
canalete *nm* : paddle
canalizar {21} *vt* : to channel
canalla[1] *adj fam* : low, rotten
canalla[2] *nmf fam* : bastard, swine
canapé *nm* **1** : hors d'oeuvre, canapé **2** SOFÁ : couch, sofa
canario[1], **-ria** *adj* : of or from the Canary Islands
canario[2], **-ria** *n* : Canarian, Canary Islander
canario[3] *nm* : canary
canasta *nf* **1** : basket **2** : canasta (card game)
cancel *nm* **1** : sliding door **2** : partition
cancelación *nf, pl* **-ciones 1** : cancellation **2** : payment in full
cancelar *vt* **1** : to cancel **2** : to pay off, to settle
cáncer *nm* : cancer
Cáncer *nmf* : Cancer
cancerígeno[1], **-na** *adj* : carcinogenic
cancerígeno[2] *nm* : carcinogen
canceroso, -sa *adj* : cancerous
cancha *nf* : court, field (for sports)
canciller *nm* : chancellor
cancillería *nf* : chancellery, ministry
canción *nf, pl* **canciones 1** : song **2 canción de cuna** : lullaby
cancionero[1] *nm* : songbook
cancionero[2], **-ra** *n Mex* : songster, songstress *f*
candado *nm* : padlock
candela *nf* **1** : flame, fire **2** : candle
candelabro *nm* : candelabra
candelero *nm* **1** : candlestick **2 estar en el candelero** : to be the center of attention
candente *adj* : red-hot
candidato, -ta *n* : candidate, applicant
candidatura *nf* : candidacy
candidez *nf* **1** : simplicity **2** INGENUIDAD : naïveté, ingenuousness
cándido, -da *adj* **1** : simple, unassuming **2** INGENUO : naive, ingenuous
candil *nm* : oil lamp
candilejas *nfpl* : footlights
candor *nm* : naïveté, innocence
candoroso, -sa *adj* : naive, innocent
canela *nf* : cinnamon
canesú *nm* : yoke (of clothing)
cangrejo *nm* JAIBA : crab
canguro *nm* **1** : kangaroo **2 hacer de canguro** *Spain* : to baby-sit
caníbal[1] *adj* : cannibalistic
caníbal[2] *nmf* ANTROPÓFAGO : cannibal
canibalismo *nm* ANTROPOFAGIA : cannibalism
canibalizar {21} *vt* : to cannibalize
canica *nf* : marble ‹jugar a las canicas : to play marbles›
caniche *nm* : poodle
canijo, -ja *adj* **1** *fam* : puny, weak **2** *Mex fam* : tough, hard ‹un examen muy canijo : a very tough exam›
canilla *nf* **1** : shin, shinbone **2** *Arg, Uru* : faucet
canino[1], **-na** *adj* : canine
canino[2] *nm* **1** COLMILLO : canine (tooth) **2** : dog, canine
canje *nm* INTERCAMBIO : exchange, trade
canjear *vt* INTERCAMBIAR : to exchange, to trade
cannabis *nm* : cannabis
cano, -na *adj* : gray ‹un hombre de pelo cano : a gray-haired man›
canoa *nf* : canoe
canon *nm, pl* **cánones** : canon
canónico, -ca *adj* **1** : canonical **2 derecho canónico** : canon law
canónigo *nm* : canon (of a church)
canonizar {21} *vt* : to canonize — **canonización** *nf*
canoso, -sa → **cano**
cansado, -da *adj* **1** : tired ‹estar cansado : to be tired› **2** : tiresome, wearying ‹ser cansado : to be tiring›
cansancio *nm* FATIGA : fatigue, weariness
cansar *vt* FATIGAR : to wear out, to tire — *vi* : to be tiresome — **cansarse** *vr* **1** : to wear oneself out **2** : to get bored
cansino, -na *adj* : slow, weary, lethargic
cantaleta *nf fam* : nagging ‹la misma cantaleta : the same old story›
cantalupo *nm* : cantaloupe
cantante *nmf* : singer
cantar[1] *v* : to sing

cantar[2] *nm* : song, ballad

cántaro *nm* **1** : pitcher, jug **2 llover a cántaros** *fam* : to rain cats and dogs

cantata *nf* : cantata

cantera *nf* : quarry ⟨cantera de piedra : stone quarry⟩

cántico *nm* : canticle, chant

cantidad[1] *adv fam* : really ⟨ese carro me costó cantidad : that car cost me plenty⟩

cantidad[2] *nf* **1** : quantity **2** : sum, amount (of money) **3** *fam* : a lot, a great many ⟨había cantidad de niños en el parque : there were tons of kids in the park⟩

cantimplora *nf* : canteen, water bottle

cantina *nf* **1** : tavern, bar **2** : canteen, mess, dining quarters *pl*

cantinero, -ra *n* : bartender

canto *nm* **1** : singing **2** : chant ⟨canto gregoriano : Gregorian chant⟩ **3** : song (of a bird) **4** : edge, end ⟨de canto : on end, sideways⟩ **5 canto rodado** : boulder

cantón *nm, pl* **cantones 1** : canton **2** *Mex fam* : place, home

cantonés[1], **-nesa** *adj & n, mpl* **-neses** : Cantonese

cantonés[2] *nm, pl* **-neses** : Cantonese (language)

cantor[1], **-tora** *adj* **1** : singing **2 pájaro cantor** : songbird

cantor[2], **-tora** *n* **1** : singer **2** : cantor

caña *nf* **1** : cane ⟨caña de azúcar : sugarcane⟩ **2** : reed **3 caña de pescar** : fishing rod **4 caña del timón** : tiller (of a boat)

cañada *nf* : ravine, gully

cáñamo *nm* : hemp

cañaveral *nm* : sugarcane field

cañería *nf* TUBERÍA : pipes *pl*, piping

caño *nm* **1** : pipe **2** : spout **3** : channel (for navigation)

cañón *nm, pl* **cañones 1** : cannon **2** : barrel (of a gun) **3** : canyon

cañonear *vt* : to shell, to bombard

cañoneo *nm* : shelling, bombardment

cañonero *nm* : gunboat

caoba *nf* : mahogany

caolín *nm* : kaolin

caos *nm* : chaos

caótico, -ca *adj* : chaotic

capa *nf* **1** : cape, cloak **2** : coating **3** : layer, stratum **4** : (social) class, stratum

capacidad *nf* **1** : capacity **2** : capability, ability

capacitación *nf, pl* **-ciones** : training

capacitar *vt* : to train, to qualify

caparazón *nm, pl* **-zones** : shell, carapace

capataz *nmf, pl* **-taces** : foreman *m*, forewoman *f*

capaz *adj, pl* **capaces 1** APTO : capable, able **2** COMPETENTE : competent **3** : spacious ⟨capaz para : with room for⟩

capcioso, -sa *adj* : cunning, deceptive ⟨pregunta capciosa : trick question⟩

capea *nf* : amateur bullfight

capear *vt* **1** : to make a pass with the cape (in bullfighting) **2** : to dodge, to weather ⟨capear el temporal : to ride out the storm⟩

capellán *nm, pl* **-llanes** : chaplain

capilar *nm* : capillary — **capilar** *adj*

capilla *nf* : chapel

capirotada *nf Mex* : traditional bread pudding

capirotazo *nm* : flip, flick

capital[1] *adj* **1** : capital **2** : chief, principal

capital[2] *nm* : capital ⟨capital de riesgo : venture capital⟩

capital[3] *nf* : capital, capital city

capitalino[1], **-na** *adj* : of or from a capital city

capitalino[2], **-na** *n* : inhabitant of a capital city

capitalismo *nm* : capitalism

capitalista *adj & nmf* : capitalist

capitalizar {21} *vt* : to capitalize — **capitalización** *nf*

capitán, -tana *n, mpl* **-tanes** : captain

capitanear *vt* : to captain, to command

capitanía *nf* : captaincy

capitel *nm* : capital (of a column)

capitolio *nm* : capitol

capitulación *nf, pl* **-ciones** : capitulation

capitular *vi* : to capitulate, to surrender

capítulo *nm* **1** : chapter, section **2** : matter, subject

capó *nm* : hood (of a car)

capón *nm, pl* **capones** : capon

caporal *nm* **1** : chief, leader **2** : foreman (on a ranch)

capota *nf* : top (of a convertible)

capote *nm* **1** : cloak, overcoat **2** : bullfighter's cape **3** *Mex* COFRE : hood (of a car)

capricho *nm* ANTOJO : whim, caprice

caprichoso, -sa *adj* ANTOJADIZO : capricious, fickle

Capricornio *nmf* : Capricorn

cápsula *nf* : capsule

captar *vt* **1** : to catch, to grasp **2** : to gain, to attract **3** : to harness, to collect (waters)

captor, -tora *n* : captor

captura *nf* : capture, seizure

capturar *vt* : to capture, to seize

capucha *nf* : hood, cowl

capuchina *nf* : nasturtium

capuchino *nm* **1** : Capuchin (monk) **2** : capuchin (monkey) **3** : cappuccino

capullo *nm* **1** : cocoon **2** : bud (of a flower)

caqui *adj & nm* : khaki

cara *nf* **1** : face **2** ASPECTO : look, appearance ⟨¡qué buena cara tiene ese pastel! : that cake looks delicious!⟩ **3** *fam* : nerve, gall **4 ~ a** *or* **de cara a** : facing **5 de cara a** : in view of, in the light of

carabina *nf* : carbine

caracol *nm* **1** : snail **2** CONCHA : conch, seashell **3** : cochlea **4** : ringlet

caracola *nf* : conch

carácter *nm, pl* **caracteres** **1** ÍNDOLE : character, kind, nature **2** TEMPERAMENTO : disposition, temperament **3** : letter, symbol ⟨caracteres chinos : Chinese characters⟩

característica *nf* RASGO : trait, feature, characteristic

característico, -ca *adj* : characteristic — **característicamente** *adv*

caracterizar {21} *vt* : to characterize — **caracterización** *nf*

caramba *interj* **1** (*expressing annoyance*) : darn!, heck! **2** (*expressing disgust or surprise*) : jeez!

carámbano *nm* : icicle

carambola *nf* **1** : carom **2** : ruse, trick ⟨por carambola : by a lucky chance⟩

caramelo *nm* **1** : caramel **2** DULCE : candy

caramillo *nm* **1** : pipe, small flute **2** : heap, pile

caraqueño[1], **-ña** *adj* : of or from Caracas

caraqueño[2], **-ña** *n* : person from Caracas

carátula *nf* **1** : title page **2** : cover, dust jacket **3** CARETA : mask **4** *Mex* : face, dial (of a clock or watch)

caravana *nf* **1** : caravan **2** : convoy, motorcade **3** REMOLQUE : trailer

caray → **caramba**

carbohidrato *nm* : carbohydrate

carbón *nm, pl* **carbones** **1** : coal **2** : charcoal

carbonatado, -da *adj* : carbonated

carbonato *nm* : carbonate

carboncillo *nm* : charcoal

carbonera *nf* : coal cellar, coal bunker (on a ship)

carbonero, -ra *adj* : coal

carbonizar {21} *vt* : to carbonize, to char

carbono *nm* : carbon

carbunco *or* **carbunclo** *nm* : carbuncle

carburador *nm* : carburetor

carburante *nm* : fuel

carca *nmf fam* : old fogy

carcacha *nf fam* : jalopy, wreck

carcaj *nm* : quiver (for arrows)

carcajada *nf* : loud laugh, guffaw ⟨reírse a carcajadas : to roar with laughter⟩

carcajearse *vr* : to roar with laughter, to be in stitches

cárcel *nf* PRISIÓN : jail, prison

carcelero, -ra *n* : jailer

carcinogénico, -ca *adj* : carcinogenic

carcinógeno *nm* CANCERÍGENO : carcinogen

carcinoma *nm* : carcinoma

carcomer *vt* : to eat away at, to consume

carcomido, -da *adj* **1** : worm-eaten **2** : decayed, rotten

cardán *nm, pl* **cardanes** : universal joint

cardar *vt* : to card, to comb

cardenal *nm* **1** : cardinal (in religion) **2** : bruise

cardíaco *or* **cardiaco, -ca** *adj* : cardiac, heart

cárdigan *nm, pl* **-gans** : cardigan

cardinal *adj* : cardinal

cardiología *nf* : cardiology

cardiólogo, -ga *n* : cardiologist

cardiovascular *adj* : cardiovascular

cardo *nm* : thistle

cardumen *nm* : school of fish

carear *vt* : to bring face-to-face

carecer {53} *vi* **~ de** : to lack ⟨el cheque carecía de fondos : the check lacked funds⟩

carencia *nf* **1** FALTA : lack **2** ESCASEZ : shortage **3** DEFICIENCIA : deficiency

carente *adj* **~ de** : lacking (in)

carero, -ra *adj fam* : pricey

carestía *nf* **1** : rise in cost ⟨la carestía de la vida : the high cost of living⟩ **2** : dearth, scarcity

careta *nf* MÁSCARA : mask

carey *nm* **1** : hawksbill turtle, sea turtle **2** : tortoiseshell

carga *nf* **1** : loading **2** : freight, load, cargo **3** : burden, responsibility **4** : charge ⟨carga eléctrica : electrical charge⟩ **5** : attack, charge

cargado, -da *adj* **1** : loaded **2** : bogged down, weighted down **3** : close, stuffy **4** : charged ⟨cargado de tensión : charged with tension⟩ **5** FUERTE : strong ⟨café cargado : strong coffee⟩ **6 cargado de hombros** : stoop-shouldered

cargador[1], **-dora** *n* : longshoreman *m*, longshorewoman *f*

cargador[2] *nm* **1** : magazine (for a firearm) **2** : charger (for batteries)

cargamento *nm* : cargo, load

cargar {52} *vt* **1** : to carry **2** : to load, to fill **3** : to charge — *vi* **1** : to load **2** : to rest (in architecture) **3 ~ sobre** : to fall upon

cargo *nm* **1** : burden, load **2** : charge ⟨a cargo de : in charge of⟩ **3** : position, office

cargue, etc. → **cargar**

carguero[1], **-ra** *adj* : freight, cargo ⟨tren carguero : freight train⟩

carguero[2] *nm* : freighter, cargo ship

cariarse *vr* : to decay (of teeth)

caribe *adj* : Caribbean ⟨el mar Caribe : the Caribbean Sea⟩

caribeño, -ña *adj* : Caribbean

caribú *nm* : caribou

caricatura *nf* **1** : caricature **2** : cartoon

caricaturista *nmf* : caricaturist, cartoonist

caricaturizar {21} *vt* : to caricature

caricia *nf* **1** : caress **2 hacer caricias** : to pet, to stroke

caridad *nf* **1** : charity **2** LIMOSNA : alms *pl*

caries *nfs & pl* : cavity (in a tooth)

carillón *nm, pl* **-llones** **1** : carillon **2** : glockenspiel

cariño *nm* AFECTO : affection, love

cariñoso, -sa *adj* AFECTUOSO : affectionate, loving — **cariñosamente** *adv*

carioca[1] *adj* : of or from Rio de Janeiro

carioca[2] *nmf* : person from Rio de Janeiro
carisma *nf* : charisma
carismático, -ca *adj* : charismatic
carita *adj Mex fam* : cute (said of a man) ⟨tu primo se cree muy carita : your cousin thinks he's gorgeous⟩
caritativo, -va *adj* : charitable
cariz *nm, pl* **carices** : appearance, aspect
carmesí *adj & nm* : crimson
carmín *nm, pl* **carmines** **1** : carmine **2** **carmín de labios** : lipstick
carnada *nf* CEBO : bait
carnal *adj* **1** : carnal **2** **primo carnal** : first cousin
carnaval *nm* : carnival
carnaza *nf* : bait
carne *nf* **1** : meat ⟨carne molida : ground beef⟩ **2** : flesh ⟨carne de gallina : goose bumps⟩
carné → **carnet**
carnero *nm* **1** : ram, sheep **2** : mutton
carnet *nm* **1** : identification card, ID **2** : membership card **3** **carnet de conducir** *Spain* : driver's license
carnicería *nf* **1** : butcher shop **2** MATANZA : slaughter, carnage
carnicero, -ra *n* : butcher
carnívoro[1], **-ra** *adj* : carnivorous
carnívoro[2] *nm* : carnivore
carnoso, -sa *adj* : fleshy, meaty
caro[1] *adv* : dearly, a lot ⟨pagué caro : I paid a high price⟩
caro[2], **-ra** *adj* **1** : expensive, dear **2** QUERIDO : dear, beloved
carpa *nf* **1** : carp **2** : big top (of a circus) **3** : tent
carpelo *nm* : carpel
carpeta *nf* : folder, binder, portfolio (of drawings, etc.)
carpetazo *nm* **dar carpetazo a** : to shelve, to defer
carpintería *nf* **1** : carpentry **2** : carpenter's workshop
carpintero, -ra *n* : carpenter
carraspear *vi* : to clear one's throat
carraspera *nf* : hoarseness ⟨tener carraspera : to have a frog in one's throat⟩
carrera *nf* **1** : run, running ⟨a la carrera : at full speed⟩ ⟨de carrera : hastily⟩ **2** : race **3** : course of study **4** : career, profession **5** : run (in baseball)
carreta *nf* : cart, wagon
carrete *nm* **1** BOBINA : reel, spool **2** : roll of film
carretel → **carrete**
carretera *nf* : highway, road ⟨carretera de peaje : turnpike⟩
carretero, -ra *adj* : highway ⟨el sistema carretero nacional : the national highway system⟩
carretilla *nf* **1** : wheelbarrow **2** **carretilla elevadora** : forklift
carril *nm* **1** : lane ⟨carretera de doble carril : two-lane highway⟩ **2** : rail (on a railroad track)
carrillo *nm* : cheek, jowl
carrito *nm* : cart ⟨carrito de compras : shopping cart⟩
carrizo *nm* JUNCO : reed
carro *nm* **1** COCHE : car **2** : cart **3** *Chile, Mex* : coach (of a train) **4** **carro alegórico** : float (in a parade)
carrocería *nf* : bodywork, body (of a vehicle)
carroña *nf* : carrion
carroñero, -ra *n* : scavenger (animal)
carroza *nf* **1** : carriage **2** : float (in a parade)
carruaje *nm* : carriage
carrusel *nm* **1** : merry-go-round **2** : carousel ⟨carrusel de equipaje : luggage carousel⟩
carta *nf* **1** : letter **2** NAIPE : playing card **3** : charter, constitution **4** MENÚ : menu **5** : map, chart **6** **tomar cartas en** : to intervene in
cártamo *nm* : safflower
cartearse *vr* ESCRIBIRSE : to write to one another, to correspond
cartel *nm* : sign, poster
cártel *or* **cartel** *nm* : cartel
cartelera *nf* **1** : billboard **2** : marquee
cartera *nf* **1** BILLETERA : wallet, billfold **2** BOLSO : pocketbook, purse **3** : portfolio ⟨cartera de acciones : stock portfolio⟩
carterista *nmf* : pickpocket
cartero, -ra *n* : letter carrier, mailman *m*
cartilaginoso, -sa *adj* : cartilaginous, gristly
cartílago *nm* : cartilage
cartilla *nf* **1** : primer, reader **2** : booklet ⟨cartilla de ahorros : bankbook⟩
cartografía *nf* : cartography
cartógrafo, -fa *n* : cartographer
cartón *nm, pl* **cartones** **1** : cardboard ⟨cartón madera : fiberboard⟩ **2** : carton
cartucho *nm* : cartridge
cartulina *nf* : poster board, cardboard
carúncula *nf* : wattle (of a bird)
casa *nf* **1** : house, building **2** HOGAR : home **3** : household, family **4** : company, firm **5** **echar la casa por la ventana** : to spare no expense
casaca *nf* : jacket
casado[1], **-da** *adj* : married
casado[2], **-da** *n* : married person
casamentero, -ra *n* : matchmaker
casamiento *nm* **1** : marriage **2** BODA : wedding
casar *vt* : to marry — *vi* : to go together, to match up — **casarse** *vr* **1** : to get married **2** **~ con** : to marry
casateniente *nmf Mex* : landlord, landlady *f*
cascabel[1] *nm* : small bell
cascabel[2] *nf* : rattlesnake
cascada *nf* CATARATA, SALTO : waterfall, cascade
cascajo *nm* **1** : pebble, rock fragment **2** *fam* : piece of junk
cascanueces *nms & pl* : nutcracker

cascar {72} *vt* : to crack (a shell) — **cascarse** *vr* : to crack, to chip

cáscara *nf* **1** : skin, peel, rind, husk **2** : shell (of a nut or egg)

cascarón *nm, pl* **-rones 1** : eggshell **2** *Mex* : shell filled with confetti

cascarrabias *nmfs & pl fam* : grouch, crab

casco *nm* **1** : helmet **2** : hull **3** : hoof **4** : fragment, shard **5** : center (of a town) **6** *Mex* : empty bottle **7 cascos** *nmpl* : headphones

caserío *nm* **1** : country house **2** : hamlet

casero[1], **-ra** *adj* **1** : domestic, household **2** : homemade

casero[2], **-ra** *n* DUEÑO : landlord *m*, landlady *f*

caseta *nf* : booth, stand, stall ⟨caseta telefónica : telephone booth⟩

casete → **cassette**

casi *adv* **1** : almost, nearly, virtually **2** (*in negative phrases*) : hardly ⟨casi nunca : hardly ever⟩

casilla *nf* **1** : booth **2** : pigeonhole **3** : box (on a form)

casino *nm* **1** : casino **2** : (social) club

caso *nm* **1** : case **2 en caso de** : in case of, in the event of **3 hacer caso de** : to pay attention to, to notice **4 hacer caso omiso de** : to ignore, to take no notice of **5 no venir al caso** : to be beside the point

caspa *nf* : dandruff

casque, etc. → **cascar**

casquete *nm* **1** : skullcap **2 casquete glaciar** : ice cap **3 casquete corto** *Mex* : crew cut

casquillo *nm* : case, casing (of a bullet)

cassette *nmf* : cassette

casta *nf* **1** : caste **2** : lineage, stock ⟨de casta : thoroughbred, purebred⟩ **3 sacar la casta** *Mex* : to come out ahead

castaña *nf* : chestnut

castañetear *vi* : to chatter (of teeth)

castaño[1], **-ña** *adj* : chestnut, brown

castaño[2] *nm* **1** : chestnut tree **2** : chestnut, brown

castañuela *nf* : castanet

castellano[1], **-na** *adj & n* : Castilian

castellano[2] *nm* ESPAÑOL : Spanish, Castilian (language)

castidad *nf* : chastity

castigar {52} *vt* : to punish

castigo *nm* : punishment

castillo *nm* **1** : castle **2 castillo de proa** : forecastle

casto, -ta *adj* : chaste, pure — **castamente** *adv*

castor *nm* : beaver

castración *nf, pl* **-ciones** : castration

castrar *vt* **1** : to castrate, to spay, to neuter, to geld **2** DEBILITAR : to weaken, to debilitate

castrense *adj* : military

casual *adj* **1** FORTUITO : fortuitous, accidental **2** *Mex* : casual (of clothing)

casualidad *nf* **1** : chance **2 por ~** *or* **de ~** : by chance, by any chance

casualmente *adv* : accidentally, by chance

casucha *or* **casuca** *nf* : shanty, hovel

cataclismo *nm* : cataclysm

catacumbas *nfpl* : catacombs

catador, -dora *n* : wine taster

catalán[1], **-lana** *adj & n, mpl* **-lanes** : Catalan

catalán[2] *nm* : Catalan (language)

catálisis *nf* : catalysis

catalítico, -ca *adj* : catalytic

catalizador *nm* **1** : catalyst **2** : catalytic converter

catalogar {52} *vt* : to catalog, to classify

catálogo *nm* : catalog

catamarán *nm, pl* **-ranes** : catamaran

cataplasma *nf* : poultice

catapulta *nf* : catapult

catapultar *vt* : to catapult

catar *vt* **1** : to taste, to sample **2** : to look at, to examine

catarata *nf* **1** CASCADA, SALTO : waterfall **2** : cataract

catarro *nm* RESFRIADO : cold, catarrh

catarsis *nf* : catharsis

catártico, -ca *adj* : cathartic

catástrofe *nf* DESASTRE : catastrophe, disaster

catastrófico, -ca *adj* DESASTROSO : catastrophic, disastrous

catcher *nmf* : catcher (in baseball)

catecismo *nm* : catechism

cátedra *nf* **1** : chair, professorship **2** : subject, class **3 libertad de cátedra** : academic freedom

catedral *nf* : cathedral

catedrático, -ca *n* PROFESOR : professor

categoría *nf* **1** CLASE : category **2** RANGO : rank, standing **3 categoría gramatical** : part of speech **4 de ~** : first-rate, outstanding

categórico, -ca *adj* : categorical, unequivocal — **categóricamente** *adv*

catéter *nm* : catheter

cátodo *nm* : cathode

catolicismo *nm* : Catholicism

católico, -ca *adj & n* : Catholic

catorce *adj & nm* : fourteen

catorceavo *nm* : fourteenth

catre *nm* : cot

catsup *nm* : ketchup

caucásico, -ca *adj & n* : Caucasian

cauce *nm* **1** LECHO : riverbed **2** : means *pl*, channel

caucho *nm* **1** GOMA : rubber **2** : rubber tree **3** *Ven* : tire

caución *nf, pl* **cauciones** FIANZA : bail, security

caudal *nm* **1** : volume of water **2** RIQUEZA : capital, wealth **3** ABUNDANCIA : abundance

caudillaje *nm* : leadership

caudillo *nm* : leader, commander

causa *nf* **1** MOTIVO : cause, reason, motive ⟨a causa de : because of⟩ **2** IDEAL : cause ⟨morir por una causa : to die for a cause⟩ **3** : lawsuit
causal[1] *adj* : causal
causal[2] *nm* : cause, grounds *pl*
causalidad *nf* : causality
causante[1] *adj* **~ de** : causing, responsible for
causante[2] *nmf Mex* : taxpayer
causar *vt* **1** : to cause **2** : to provoke, to arouse ⟨eso me causa gracia : that strikes me as being funny⟩
cáustico, -ca *adj* : caustic
cautela *nf* : caution, prudence
cautelar *adj* : precautionary, preventive
cauteloso, -sa *adj* : cautious, prudent — **cautelosamente** *adv*
cauterizar {21} *vt* : to cauterize
cautivador, -dora *adj* : captivating
cautivar *vt* HECHIZAR : to captivate, to charm
cautiverio *nm* : captivity
cautivo, -va *adj & n* : captive
cauto, -ta *adj* : cautious, careful
cavar *vt* : to dig — *vi* **~ en** : to delve into, to probe
caverna *nf* : cavern, cave
cavernoso, -sa *adj* **1** : cavernous **2** : deep, resounding
caviar *nm* : caviar
cavidad *nf* : cavity
cavilar *vi* : to ponder, to deliberate
cayado *nm* : crook, staff, crosier
cayena *nf* : cayenne pepper
cayó, etc. → **caer**
caza[1] *nf* **1** CACERÍA : hunt, hunting **2** : game
caza[2] *nm* : fighter plane
cazador, -dora *n* **1** : hunter **2 cazador furtivo** : poacher
cazar {21} *vt* **1** : to hunt **2** : to catch, to bag **3** *fam* : to land (a job, a spouse) — *vi* : to go hunting
cazatalentos *nmfs & pl* : talent scout
cazo *nm* **1** : saucepan, pot **2** CUCHARÓN : ladle
cazuela *nf* **1** : pan, saucepan **2** : casserole
cazurro, -ra *adj* : sullen, surly
CD *nm* : CD, compact disk
cebada *nf* : barley
cebar *vt* **1** : to bait **2** : to feed, to fatten **3** : to prime (a pump, etc.) — **cebarse** *vr* **~ en** : to take it out on
cebo *nm* **1** CARNADA : bait **2** : feed **3** : primer (for firearms)
cebolla *nf* : onion
cebolleta *nf* : scallion, green onion
cebollino *nm* **1** : chive **2** : scallion
cebra *nf* : zebra
cebú *nm, pl* **cebús** *or* **cebúes** : zebu (cattle)
cecear *vi* : to lisp
ceceo *nm* : lisp
cecina *nf* : dried beef, beef jerky
cedazo *nm* : sieve
ceder *vi* **1** : to yield, to give way **2** : to diminish, to abate **3** : to give in, to relent — *vt* : to cede, to hand over
cedro *nm* : cedar
cédula *nf* : document, certificate
céfiro *nm* : zephyr
cegador, -dora *adj* : blinding
cegar {49} *vt* **1** : to blind **2** : to block, to stop up — *vi* : to be blinded, to go blind
cegatón, -tona *adj, mpl* **-tones** *fam* : blind as a bat
ceguera *nf* : blindness
ceiba *nf* : ceiba, silk-cotton tree
ceja *nf* **1** : eyebrow ⟨fruncir las cejas : to knit one's brows⟩ **2** : flange, rim
cejar *vi* : to give in, to back down
celada *nf* : trap, ambush
celador, -dora *n* GUARDIA : guard, warden
celda *nf* : cell (of a jail)
celebración *nf, pl* **-ciones** : celebration
celebrado, -da *adj* CÉLEBRE, FAMOSO : famous, celebrated
celebrante *nmf* OFICIANTE : celebrant
celebrar *vt* **1** FESTEJAR : to celebrate **2** : to hold (a meeting) **3** : to say (Mass) **4** : to welcome, to be happy about — *vi* : to be glad — **celebrarse** *vr* **1** : to be celebrated, to fall **2** : to be held, to take place
célebre *adj* CELEBRADO, FAMOSO : celebrated, famous
celebridad *nf* **1** : celebrity **2** FAMA : fame, renown
celeridad *nf* : celerity, swiftness
celeste[1] *adj* **1** : celestial **2** : sky blue, azure
celeste[2] *nm* : sky blue
celestial *adj* : heavenly, celestial
celibato *nm* : celibacy
célibe *adj & nmf* : celibate
cello *nm* : cello
celo *nm* **1** : zeal, fervor **2** : heat (of females), rut (of males) **3 celos** *nmpl* : jealousy ⟨tenerle celos a alguien : to be jealous of someone⟩
celofán *nm, pl* **-fanes** : cellophane
celosía *nf* **1** : lattice window **2** : latticework, trellis
celoso, -sa *adj* **1** : jealous **2** : zealous — **celosamente** *adv*
celta[1] *adj* : Celtic
celta[2] *nmf* : Celt
célula *nf* : cell
celular *adj* : cellular
celuloide *nm* **1** : celluloid **2** : film, cinema
celulosa *nf* : cellulose
cementar *vt* : to cement
cementerio *nm* : cemetery
cemento *nm* : cement
cena *nf* : supper, dinner
cenador *nm* : arbor
cenagal *nm* : bog, quagmire
cenagoso, -sa *adj* : swampy
cenar *vi* : to have dinner, to have supper — *vt* : to have for dinner or supper

⟨anoche cenamos tamales : we had tamales for supper last night⟩
cencerro *nm* : cowbell
cenicero *nm* : ashtray
ceniciento, -ta *adj* : ashen
cenit *nm* : zenith, peak
ceniza *nf* **1** : ash **2 cenizas** *nfpl* : ashes (of a deceased person)
cenizo, -za *n* : jinx
cenote *nm Mex* : natural deposit of spring water
censar *vt* : to take a census of
censo *nm* : census
censor, -sora *n* : censor, critic
censura *nf* **1** : censorship **2** : censure, criticism
censurable *adj* : reprehensible, blameworthy
censurar *vt* **1** : to censor **2** : to censure, to criticize
centauro *nm* : centaur
centavo *nm* **1** : cent (in English-speaking countries) **2** : unit of currency in various Latin-American countries
centella *nf* **1** : lightning flash **2** : spark
centellear *vi* **1** : to twinkle **2** : to gleam, to sparkle
centelleo *nm* : twinkling, sparkle
centenar *nm* **1** : hundred **2 a centenares** : by the hundreds
centenario[1], **-ria** *adj & n* : centenarian
centenario[2] *nm* : centennial
centeno *nm* : rye
centésimo[1], **-ma** *adj* : hundredth
centésimo[2] *nm* : hundredth
centígrado *adj* : centigrade, Celsius
centigramo *nm* : centigram
centímetro *nm* : centimeter
centinela *nmf* : sentinel, sentry
central[1] *adj* **1** : central **2** PRINCIPAL : main, principal
central[2] *nf* **1** : main office, headquarters **2 central camionera** *Mex* : bus terminal
centralita *nf* : switchboard
centralizar {21} *vt* : to centralize — **centralización** *nf*
centrar *vt* **1** : to center **2** : to focus — **centrarse** *vr* **~ en** : to focus on, to concentrate on
céntrico, -ca *adj* : central
centrífugo, -ga *adj* : centrifugal
centrípeto, -ta *adj* : centripetal
centro[1] *nmf* : center (in sports)
centro[2] *nm* **1** MEDIO : center ⟨centro de atención : center of attention⟩ ⟨centro de gravedad : center of gravity⟩ **2** : downtown **3 centro de mesa** : centerpiece
centroamericano, -na *adj & n* : Central American
ceñido, -da *adj* AJUSTADO : tight, tight-fitting
ceñir {67} *vt* **1** : to encircle, to surround **2** : to hug, to cling to ⟨me ciñe demasiado : it's too tight on me⟩ — **ceñirse** *vr* **~ a** : to restrict oneself to, to stick to
ceño *nm* **1** : frown, scowl **2 fruncir el ceño** : to frown, to knit one's brows
cepa *nf* **1** : stump (of a tree) **2** : stock (of a vine) **3** LINAJE : ancestry, stock
cepillar *vt* **1** : to brush **2** : to plane (wood) — **cepillarse** *vr*
cepillo *nm* **1** : brush ⟨cepillo de dientes : toothbrush⟩ **2** : plane (for woodworking)
cepo *nm* : trap (for animals)
cera *nf* **1** : wax ⟨cera de abejas : beeswax⟩ **2** : polish
cerámica *nf* **1** : ceramics *pl* **2** : pottery
cerámico, -ca *adj* : ceramic
ceramista *nmf* ALFARERO : potter
cerca[1] *adv* **1** : close, near, nearby **2 ~ de** : nearly, almost
cerca[2] *nf* **1** : fence **2** : (stone) wall
cercado *nm* : enclosure
cercanía *nf* **1** PROXIMIDAD : proximity, closeness **2 cercanías** *nfpl* : outskirts, suburbs
cercano, -na *adj* : near, close
cercar {72} *vt* **1** : to fence in, to enclose **2** : to surround
cercenar *vt* **1** : to cut off, to amputate **2** : to diminish, to curtail
cerceta *nf* : teal (duck)
cerciorarse *vr* ASEGURARSE **~ de** : to make sure of, to verify
cerco *nm* **1** : siege **2** : cordon, circle **3** : fence
cerda *nf* **1** : bristle **2** : sow
cerdo *nm* **1** : pig, hog **2 carne de cerdo** : pork
cereal *nm* : cereal — **cereal** *adj*
cerebelo *nm* : cerebellum
cerebral *adj* : cerebral
cerebro *nm* : brain
ceremonia *nf* : ceremony — **ceremonial** *adj*
ceremonioso, -sa *adj* : ceremonious
cereza *nf* : cherry
cerezo *nm* : cherry tree
cerilla *nf* **1** : match **2** : earwax
cerillo *nm* (*in various countries*) : match
cerner {56} *vt* : to sift — **cernerse** *vr* **1** : to hover **2 ~ sobre** : to loom over, to threaten
cernidor *nm* : sieve
cernir → **cerner**
cero *nm* : zero
ceroso, -sa *adj* : waxy
cerque, etc. → **cercar**
cerquita *adv fam* : very close, very near
cerrado, -da *adj* **1** : closed, shut **2** : thick, broad ⟨tiene un acento cerrado : she has a thick accent⟩ **3** : cloudy, overcast **4** : quiet, reserved **5** : dense, stupid
cerradura *nf* : lock
cerrajería *nf* : locksmith's shop
cerrajero, -ra *n* : locksmith
cerrar {55} *vt* **1** : to close, to shut **2** : to turn off **3** : to bring to an end — *vi* **1** : to close up, to lock up **2** : to close down — **cerrarse** *vr* **1** : to close **2** : to fasten, to button up **3** : to conclude, to end

cerrazón *nf, pl* **-zones** : obstinacy, stubbornness
cerro *nm* COLINA, LOMA : hill
cerrojo *nm* PESTILLO : bolt, latch
certamen *nm, pl* **-támenes** : competition, contest
certero, -ra *adj* : accurate, precise — **certeramente** *adv*
certeza *nf* : certainty
certidumbre *nf* : certainty
certificable *adj* : certifiable
certificación *nf, pl* **-ciones** : certification
certificado[1], **-da** *adj* **1** : certified **2** : registered (of mail)
certificado[2] *nm* **1** : certificate **2** : registered letter
certificar {72} *vt* **1** : to certify **2** : to register (mail)
cervato *nm* : fawn
cervecera *nf* : brewery
cervecería *nf* **1** : brewery **2** : beer hall, bar
cerveza *nf* : beer ⟨cerveza de barril : draft beer⟩
cervical *adj* : cervical
cerviz *nf, pl* **cervices** : nape of the neck, cervix
cesación *nf, pl* **-ciones** : cessation, suspension
cesante *adj* : laid off, unemployed
cesantía *nf* : unemployment
cesar *vi* : to cease, to stop — *vt* : to dismiss, to lay off
cesárea *nf* : cesarean, C-section
cese *nm* **1** : cessation, stop ⟨cese del fuego : cease-fire⟩ **2** : dismissal
cesio *nm* : cesium
cesión *nf, pl* **cesiones** : transfer, assignment ⟨cesión de bienes : transfer of property⟩
césped *nm* : lawn, grass
cesta *nf* **1** : basket **2** : jai alai racket
cesto *nm* **1** : hamper **2** : basket (in basketball) **3 cesto de (la) basura** : wastebasket
cetrería *nf* : falconry
cetrino, -na *adj* : sallow
cetro *nm* : scepter
chabacano[1], **-na** *adj* : tacky, tasteless
chabacano[2] *nm Mex* : apricot
chacal *nm* : jackal
cháchara *nf fam* **1** : small talk, chatter **2 cháchacharas** *nfpl* : trinkets, junk
chacharear *vi fam* : to chatter, to gab
chacra *nf Arg, Chile, Peru* : small farm
chadiano, -na *adj & n* : Chadian
chal *nm* MANTÓN : shawl
chalado[1], **-da** *adj fam* : crazy, nuts
chalado[2], **-da** *n* : nut, crazy person
chalán *nm, pl* **chalanes** *Mex* : barge
chalé → **chalet**
chaleco *nm* : vest
chalet *nm Spain* : house
chalupa *nf* **1** : small boat **2** *Mex* : small stuffed tortilla
chamaco, -ca *n Mex fam* : kid, boy *m*, girl *f*
chamarra *nf* **1** : sheepskin jacket **2** : poncho, blanket
chamba *nf Mex, Peru fam* : job, work
chambear *vi Mex, Peru fam* : to work
chamo, -ma *n Ven fam* **1** : kid, boy *m*, girl *f* **2** : buddy, pal
champaña *or* **champán** *nm* : champagne
champiñón *nm, pl* **-ñones** : mushroom
champú *nm, pl* **-pus** *or* **-púes** : shampoo
champurrado *nm Mex* : hot chocolate thickened with cornstarch
chamuco *nm Mex fam* : devil
chamuscar {72} *vt* : to singe, to scorch — **chamuscarse** *vr*
chamusquina *nf* : scorch
chance *nm* OPORTUNIDAD : chance, opportunity
chancho[1], **-cha** *adj fam* : dirty, filthy, gross
chancho[2], **-cha** *n* **1** : pig, hog **2** *fam* : slob
chanchullero, -ra *adj fam* : shady, crooked
chanchullo *nm fam* : shady deal, scam
chancla *nf* **1** : thong sandal, slipper **2** : old shoe
chancleta → **chancla**
chanclo *nm* **1** : clog **2 chanclos** *nmpl* : overshoes, galoshes, rubbers
chancro *nm* : chancre
changarro *nm Mex* : small shop, stall
chango, -ga *n Mex* : monkey
chantaje *nm* : blackmail
chantajear *vt* : to blackmail
chantajista *nmf* : blackmailer
chanza *nf* **1** : joke, jest **2** *Mex fam* : chance, opportunity
chapa *nf* **1** : sheet, panel, veneer **2** : lock **3** : badge
chapado, -da *adj* **1** : plated **2 chapado a la antigua** : old-fashioned
chapar *vt* **1** : to veneer **2** : to plate (metals)
chaparrón *nm, pl* **-rrones** **1** : downpour **2** : great quantity, torrent
chapeado, -da *adj Col, Mex* : flushed
chapopote *nm Mex* : tar, blacktop
chapotear *vi* : to splash about
chapucero[1], **-ra** *adj* **1** : crude, shoddy **2** *Mex fam* : dishonest
chapucero[2], **-ra** *n* **1** : sloppy worke[r] bungler **2** *Mex fam* : cheat, swind[ler]
chapulín *nm, pl* **-lines** *CA, [Mex]* : grasshopper, locust
chapuza *nf* **1** : botched job **2** *Me[x]* : fraud, trick ⟨hacer chapuza[s] ... cheat⟩
chapuzón *nm, pl* **-zones** : di[p] ⟨darse un chapuzón : to go fo[r a] dip⟩
chaqueta *nf* : jacket
charada *nf* : charades (gam[e])
charango *nm* : traditio[nal] ... stringed instrument
charca *nf* : pond, pool
charco *nm* : puddle, poo[l]

charcutería *nf* : delicatessen
charla *nf* : chat, talk
charlar *vi* : to chat, to talk
charlatán[1], **-tana** *adj* : talkative, chatty
charlatán[2], **-tana** *n, mpl* **-tanes 1** : chatterbox **2** FARSANTE : charlatan, phony
charlatanear *vi* : to chatter away
charol *nm* **1** : lacquer, varnish **2** : patent leather **3** : tray
charola *nf Bol, Mex, Peru* : tray
charreada *nf Mex* : charro show, rodeo
charretera *nf* : epaulet
charro[1], **-rra** *adj* **1** : gaudy, tacky **2** *Mex* : pertaining to charros
charro[2], **-rra** *n Mex* : charro (Mexican cowboy or cowgirl)
chascarrillo *nm fam* : joke, funny story
chasco *nm* **1** BROMA : trick, joke **2** DECEPCIÓN, DESILUSIÓN : disillusionment, disappointment
chasis *or* **chasís** *nm* : chassis
chasquear *vt* **1** : to click (the tongue, fingers, etc.) **2** : to snap (a whip)
chasquido *nm* **1** : click (of the tongue or fingers) **2** : snap, crack
chatarra *nf* : scrap metal
chato, -ta *adj* **1** : pug-nosed **2** : flat
chauvinismo *nm* : chauvinism
chauvinista[1] *adj* : chauvinistic
chauvinista[2] *nmf* : chauvinist
chaval, **-vala** *n fam* : kid, boy *m,* girl *f*
chavo[1], **-va** *adj Mex fam* : young
chavo[2], **-va** *n Mex fam* : kid, boy *m,* girl *f*
chavo[3] *nm fam* : cent, buck ⟨no tengo un chavo : I'm broke⟩
chayote *nm* : chayote (plant, fruit)
checar {72} *vt Mex* : to check, to verify
checo[1], **-ca** *adj & n* : Czech
checo[2] *nm* : Czech (language)
checoslovaco, -ca *adj & n* : Czechoslovakian
chef *nm* : chef
chelín *nm, pl* **chelines** : shilling
cheque[1], **etc.** → **checar**
cheque[2] *nm* **1** : check **2 cheque de viajero** : traveler's check
chequear *vt* **1** : to check, to verify **2** : to check in (baggage)
chequeo *nm* **1** INSPECCIÓN : check, inspection **2** : checkup, examination
chequera *nf* : checkbook
chévere *adj fam* : great, fantastic
chic *adj & nm* : chic
chica → **chico**
chicano, -na *adj & n* : Chicano *m,* Chicana *f*
chicha *nf* : fermented alcoholic beverage made from corn
chícharo *nm* : pea
chicharra *nf* **1** CIGARRA : cicada **2** : buzzer
chicharrón *nm, pl* **-rrones 1** : pork rind **2 darle chicharrón a** *Mex fam* : to get rid of
chichón *nm, pl* **chichones** : bump, swelling
chicle *nm* : chewing gum
chicloso *nm Mex* : taffy
chico[1], **-ca** *adj* **1** : little, small **2** : young
chico[2], **-ca** *n* **1** : child, boy *m,* girl *f* **2** : young man *m,* young woman *f*
chicote *nm* LÁTIGO : whip, lash
chiffon → **chifón**
chiflado[1], **-da** *adj fam* : nuts, crazy
chiflado[2], **-da** *n fam* : crazy person, lunatic
chiflar *vi* : to whistle — *vt* : to whistle at, to boo — **chiflarse** *vr fam* **~ por** : to be crazy about
chiflido *nm* : whistle, whistling
chiflón *nm, pl* **chiflones** : draft (of air)
chifón *nm, pl* **chifones** : chiffon
chilango[1], **-ga** *adj Mex fam* : of or from Mexico City
chilango[2], **-ga** *n Mex fam* : person from Mexico City
chilaquiles *nmpl Mex* : shredded tortillas in sauce
chile *nm* : chili pepper
chileno, -na *adj & n* : Chilean
chillar *vi* **1** : to squeal, to screech **2** : to scream, to yell **3** : to be gaudy, to clash
chillido *nm* **1** : scream, shout **2** : squeal, screech, cry (of an animal)
chillo *nm PRi* : red snapper
chillón, **-llona** *adj, mpl* **chillones 1** : piercing, shrill **2** : loud, gaudy
chilpayate *nmf Mex fam* : child, little kid
chimenea *nf* **1** : chimney **2** : fireplace
chimichurri *nm Arg* : traditional hot sauce
chimpancé *nm* : chimpanzee
china *nf* **1** : pebble, small stone **2** *PRi* : orange
chinchar *vt fam* : to annoy, to pester — **chincharse** *vr fam* : to put up with something, to grin and bear it
chinchayote *nm Mex* : chayote root
chinche[1] *nf* **1** : bedbug **2** *Ven* : ladybug **3** : thumbtack
chinche[2] *nmf fam* : nuisance, pain in the neck
chinchilla *nf* : chinchilla
chino[1], **-na** *adj* **1** : Chinese **2** *Mex* : curly, kinky
chino[2], **-na** *n* : Chinese person
chino[3] *nm* : Chinese (language)
chip *nm, pl* **chips** : chip ⟨chip de memoria : memory chip⟩
chipote *nm Mex fam* : bump (on the head)
chipotle *nm Mex* : type of chili pepper
chipriota *adj & nmf* : Cypriot
chiquear *vt Mex* : to spoil, to indulge
chiquero *nm* POCILGA : pigpen, pigsty
chiquillada *nf* : childish prank
chiquillo[1], **-lla** *adj* : very young, little
chiquillo[2], **-lla** *n* : kid, youngster
chiquito[1], **-ta** *adj* : tiny
chiquito[2], **-ta** *n* : little one, baby
chiribita *nf* **1** : spark **2 chiribitas** *nfpl* : spots before the eyes
chiribitil *nm* **1** DESVÁN : attic, garret **2** : cubbyhole

chirigota *nf fam* : joke
chirimía *nf* : traditional reed pipe
chirimoya *nf* : cherimoya, custard apple
chiripa *nf* **1** : fluke **2 de ~** : by sheer luck
chirivía *nf* : parsnip
chirona *nf fam* : slammer, jail
chirriar {85} *vi* **1** : to squeak, to creak **2** : to screech — **chirriante** *adj*
chirrido *nm* **1** : squeak, squeaking **2** : screech, screeching
chirrión *nm, pl* **chirriones** *Mex* : whip, lash
chisme *nm* **1** : gossip, tale **2** *Spain fam* : gadget, thingamajig
chismear *vi* : to gossip
chismoso[1], **-sa** *adj* : gossipy, gossiping
chismoso[2], **-sa** *n* **1** : gossiper, gossip **2** *Mex fam* : tattletale
chispa[1] *adj* **1** *Mex fam* : lively, vivacious ⟨un perrito chispa : a frisky puppy⟩ **2** *Spain fam* : tipsy
chispa[2] *nf* **1** : spark **2 echar chispas** : to be furious
chispeante *adj* : sparkling, scintillating
chispear *vi* **1** : to give off sparks **2** : to sparkle
chisporrotear *vi* : to crackle, to sizzle
chiste *nm* **1** : joke, funny story **2 tener chiste** : to be funny **3 tener su chiste** *Mex* : to be tricky
chistoso[1], **-sa** *adj* **1** : funny, humorous **2** : witty
chistoso[2], **-sa** *n* : wit, joker
chivas *nfpl Mex fam* : stuff, odds and ends
chivo[1], **-va** *n* **1** : kid, young goat **2 chivo expiatorio** : scapegoat
chivo[2] *nm* **1** : billy goat **2** : fit of anger
chocante *adj* **1** : shocking **2** : unpleasant, rude
chocar {72} *vi* **1** : to crash, to collide **2** : to clash, to conflict **3** : to be shocking ⟨le chocó : he was shocked⟩ **4** *Mex, Ven fam* : to be unpleasant or obnoxious ⟨me choca tu jefe : I can't stand your boss⟩ — *vt* **1** : to shake (hands) **2** : to clink glasses
chochear *vi* **1** : to be senile **2 ~ por** : to dote on, to be soft on
chochín *nm, pl* **-chines** : wren
chocho, -cha *adj* **1** : senile **2** : doting
choclo *nm* **1** : ear of corn, corncob **2** : corn **3 meter el choclo** *Mex fam* : to make a mistake
chocolate *nm* **1** : chocolate **2** : hot chocolate, cocoa
chofer *or* **chófer** *nm* **1** : chauffeur **2** : driver
choke *nm* : choke (of an automobile)
chole *interj Mex fam* **¡ya chole!** : enough!, cut it out!
cholo, -la *adj & n* : mestizo
cholla *nf fam* : head
chollo *nm Spain fam* : bargain
chongo *nm* **1** *Mex* : bun (chignon) **2 chongos** *nmpl Mex* : dessert made with fried bread
choque[1], **etc.** → **chocar**
choque[2] *nm* **1** : crash, collision **2** : clash, conflict **3** : shock
chorizo *nm* : chorizo, sausage
chorrear *vi* **1** : to drip **2** : to pour out, to gush out
chorrito *nm* : squirt, splash
chorro *nm* **1** : flow, stream, jet **2** *Mex fam* : heap, ton
choteado, -da *adj Mex fam* : worn-out, stale ⟨esa canción está bien choteada : that song's been played to death⟩
chotear *vt* : to make fun of
choteo *nm* : joking around, kidding
chovinismo, chovinista → **chauvinismo, chauvinista**
choza *nf* BARRACA, CABAÑA : hut, shack
chubasco *nm* : downpour, storm
chuchería *nf* : knickknack, trinket
chueco, -ca *adj* **1** : crooked, bent **2** *Chile, Mex fam* : dishonest, shady
chulada *nf Mex, Spain fam* : cute or pretty thing ⟨¡qué chulada de vestido! : what a lovely dress!⟩
chulear *vt Mex fam* : to compliment
chuleta *nf* : cutlet, chop
chulo[1], **-la** *adj* **1** *fam* : cute, pretty **2** *Spain fam* : cocky, arrogant
chulo[2] *nm Spain* : pimp
chupada *nf* **1** : suck, sucking **2** : puff, drag (on a cigarette)
chupado, -da *adj fam* **1** : gaunt, skinny **2** : plastered, drunk
chupaflor *nm* COLIBRÍ : hummingbird
chupamirto *nm Mex* : hummingbird
chupar *vt* **1** : to suck **2** : to absorb **3** : to puff on **4** *fam* : to drink, to guzzle — *vi* : to suckle — **chuparse** *vr* **1** : to waste away **2** *fam* : to put up with **3 ¡chúpate esa!** *fam* : take that!
chupete *nm* **1** : pacifier **2** *Chile, Peru* : lollipop
chupetear *vt* : to suck (at)
chupón *nm, pl* **chupones** **1** : sucker (of a plant) **2** : baby bottle, pacifier
churrasco *nm* **1** : steak **2** : barbecued meat
churro *nm* **1** : fried dough **2** *fam* : botch, mess **3** *fam* : attractive person, looker
chusco, -ca *adj* : funny, amusing
chusma *nf* GENTUZA : riffraff, rabble
chutar *vi* : to shoot (in soccer)
chute *nm* : shot (in soccer)
cianuro *nm* : cyanide
cibernética *nf* : cybernetics
cicatriz *nf, pl* **-trices** : scar
cicatrizarse {21} *vr* : to form a scar, to heal
cíclico, -ca *adj* : cyclical
ciclismo *nm* : bicycling
ciclista *nmf* : bicyclist
ciclo *nm* : cycle
ciclomotor *nm* : moped
ciclón *nm, pl* **ciclones** : cyclone
cicuta *nf* : hemlock
cidra *nf* : citron (fruit)
ciega, ciegue etc. → **cegar**

ciego[1], **-ga** *adj* **1** INVIDENTE : blind **2 a ciegas** : blindly **3 quedarse ciego** : to go blind — **ciegamente** *adv*
ciego[2], **-ga** *n* INVIDENTE : blind person
cielo *nm* **1** : sky **2** : heaven **3** : ceiling
ciempiés *nms & pl* : centipede
cien[1] *adj* **1** : a hundred, hundred ⟨las primeras cien páginas : the first hundred pages⟩ **2 cien por cien** *or* **cien por ciento** : a hundred percent, through and through, wholeheartedly
cien[2] *nm* : one hundred
ciénaga *nf* : swamp, bog
ciencia *nf* **1** : science **2** : learning, knowledge **3 a ciencia cierta** : for a fact, for certain
cieno *nm* : mire, mud, silt
científico[1], **-ca** *adj* : scientific — **científicamente** *adv*
científico[2], **-ca** *n* : scientist
ciento[1] *adj* (*used in compound numbers*) : one hundred ⟨ciento uno : one hundred and one⟩
ciento[2] *nm* **1** : hundred, group of a hundred **2 por ~** : percent
cierne, etc. → **cerner**
cierra, etc. → **cerrar**
cierre *nm* **1** : closing, closure **2** : fastener, clasp, zipper
cierto, -ta *adj* **1** : true, certain, definite ⟨lo cierto es que . . . : the fact is that . . . ⟩ **2** : certain, one ⟨cierto día de verano : one summer day⟩ ⟨bajo ciertas circunstancias : under certain circumstances⟩ **3 por ~** : in fact, as a matter of fact — **ciertamente** *adv*
ciervo, -va *n* : deer, stag *m,* hind *f*
cifra *nf* **1** : figure, number **2** : quantity, amount **3** CLAVE : code, cipher
cifrar *vt* **1** : to write in code **2** : to place, to pin ⟨cifró su esperanza en la lotería : he pinned his hopes on the lottery⟩ — **cifrarse** *vr* : to amount ⟨la multa se cifra en millares : the fine amounts to thousands⟩
cigarra *nf* CHICHARRA : cicada
cigarrera *nf* : cigarette case
cigarrillo *nm* : cigarette
cigarro *nm* **1** : cigarette **2** PURO : cigar
cigoto *nm* : zygote
cigüeña *nf* : stork
cilantro *nm* : cilantro, coriander
cilíndrico, -ca *adj* : cylindrical
cilindro *nm* : cylinder
cima *nf* CUMBRE : peak, summit, top
cimarrón, -rrona *adj, mpl* **-rrones** : untamed, wild
címbalo *nm* : cymbal
cimbel *nm* : decoy
cimbrar *vt* : to shake, to rock — **cimbrarse** *vr* : to sway, to swing
cimentar {55} *vt* **1** : to lay the foundation of, to establish **2** : to strengthen, to cement
cimientos *nmpl* : base, foundation(s)
cinc *nm* : zinc
cincel *nm* : chisel
cincelar *vt* **1** : to chisel **2** : to engrave
cincha *nf* : cinch, girth
cinchar *vt* : to cinch (a horse)
cinco *adj & nm* : five
cincuenta *adj & nm* : fifty
cincuentavo[1], **-va** *adj* : fiftieth
cincuentavo[2] *nm* : fiftieth (fraction)
cine *nm* **1** : cinema, movies *pl* **2** : movie theater
cineasta *nmf* : filmmaker
cinematográfico, -ca *adj* : movie, film, cinematic ⟨la industria cinematográfica : the film industry⟩
cingalés[1], **-lesa** *adj & n* : Sinhalese
cingalés[2] *nm* : Sinhalese (language)
cínico[1], **-ca** *adj* **1** : cynical **2** : shameless, brazen — **cínicamente** *adv*
cínico[2], **-ca** *n* : cynic
cinismo *nm* : cynicism
cinta *nf* **1** : ribbon **2** : tape ⟨cinta métrica : tape measure⟩ **3** : strap, belt ⟨cinta transportadora : conveyor belt⟩
cinto *nm* : strap, belt
cintura *nf* **1** : waist, waistline **2 meter en cintura** *fam* : to bring into line, to discipline
cinturón *nm, pl* **-rones** **1** : belt **2 cinturón de seguridad** : seat belt
ciñe, etc. → **ceñir**
ciprés *nm, pl* **cipreses** : cypress
circo *nm* : circus
circón *nm, pl* **circones** : zircon
circonio *nm* : zirconium
circuitería *nf* : circuitry
circuito *nm* : circuit
circulación *nf, pl* **-ciones** **1** : circulation **2** : movement **3** : traffic
circular[1] *vi* **1** : to circulate **2** : to move along **3** : to drive
circular[2] *adj* : circular
circular[3] *nf* : circular, flier
circulatorio, -ria *adj* : circulatory
círculo *nm* **1** : circle **2** : club, group
circuncidar *vt* : to circumcise
circuncisión *nf, pl* **-siones** : circumcision
circundar *vt* : to surround — **circundante** *adj*
circunferencia *nf* : circumference
circunflejo, -ja *adj* **acento circunflejo** : circumflex
circunlocución *nf, pl* **-ciones** : circumlocution
circunloquio *nm* → **circunlocución**
circunnavegar {52} *vt* : to circumnavigate — **circunnavegación** *nf*
circunscribir {33} *vt* : to circumscribe, to constrict, to limit — **circunscribirse** *vr*
circunscripción *nf, pl* **-ciones** **1** : limitation, restriction **2** : constituency
circunscrito *pp* → **circunscribir**
circunspección *nf, pl* **-ciones** : circumspection, prudence
circunspecto, -ta *adj* : circumspect, prudent
circunstancia *nf* : circumstance
circunstancial *adj* : circumstantial, incidental

circunstante *nmf* **1** : onlooker, bystander **2 los circunstantes** : those present

circunvalación *nf, pl* **-ciones** : surrounding, encircling ⟨carretera de circunvalación : bypass, beltway⟩

circunvecino, -na *adj* : surrounding, neighboring

cirio *nm* : large candle

cirro *nm* : cirrus (cloud)

cirrosis *nf* : cirrhosis

ciruela *nf* **1** : plum **2 ciruela pasa** : prune

cirugía *nf* : surgery

cirujano, -na *n* : surgeon

cisma *nm* : schism, rift

cisne *nm* : swan

cisterna *nf* : cistern, tank

cita *nf* **1** : quote, quotation **2** : appointment, date

citable *adj* : quotable

citación *nf, pl* **-ciones** EMPLAZAMIENTO : summons, subpoena

citadino[1]**, -na** *adj* : of the city, urban

citadino[2]**, -na** *n* : city dweller

citado, -da *adj* : said, aforementioned

citar *vt* **1** : to quote, to cite **2** : to make an appointment with **3** : to summon (to court), to subpoena — **citarse** *vr* ~ **con** : to arrange to meet (someone)

cítara *nf* : zither

citatorio *nm* : subpoena

citoplasma *nm* : cytoplasm

cítrico[1]**, -ca** *adj* : citric

cítrico[2] *nm* : citrus fruit

ciudad *nf* **1** : city, town **2 ciudad universitaria** : college or university campus **3 ciudad perdida** *Mex* : shantytown

ciudadanía *nf* **1** : citizenship **2** : citizenry, citizens *pl*

ciudadano[1]**, -na** *adj* : civic, city

ciudadano[2]**, -na** *n* **1** NACIONAL : citizen **2** HABITANTE : resident, city dweller

ciudadela *nf* : citadel, fortress

cívico, -ca *adj* **1** : civic **2** : public-spirited

civil[1] *adj* **1** : civil **2** : civilian

civil[2] *nmf* : civilian

civilidad *nf* : civility, courtesy

civilización *nf, pl* **-ciones** : civilization

civilizar {21} *vt* : to civilize

civismo *nm* : community spirit, civicmindedness, civics

cizaña *nf* : discord, rift

clamar *vi* : to clamor, to raise a protest — *vt* : to cry out for

clamor *nm* : clamor, outcry

clamoroso, -sa *adj* : clamorous, resounding, thunderous

clan *nm* : clan

clandestinidad *nf* : secrecy ⟨en la clandestinidad : underground⟩

clandestino, -na *adj* : clandestine, secret

clara *nf* : egg white

claraboya *nf* : skylight

claramente *adv* : clearly

clarear *v impers* **1** : to clear, to clear up **2** : to get light, to dawn — *vi* : to go gray, to turn white

claridad *nf* **1** NITIDEZ : clarity, clearness **2** : brightness, light

clarificación *nf, pl* **-ciones** ACLARACIÓN : clarification, explanation

clarificar {72} *vt* ACLARAR : to clarify, to explain

clarín *nm, pl* **clarines** : bugle

clarinete *nm* : clarinet

clarividencia *nf* **1** : clairvoyance **2** : perspicacity, discernment

clarividente[1] *adj* **1** : clairvoyant **2** : perspicacious, discerning

clarividente[2] *nmf* : clairvoyant

claro[1] *adv* **1** : clearly ⟨habla más claro : speak more clearly⟩ **2** : of course, surely ⟨¡claro!, ¡claro que sí! : absolutely!, of course!⟩ ⟨claro que entendió : of course she understood⟩

claro[2]**, -ra** *adj* **1** : bright, clear **2** : pale, fair, light **3** : clear, evident

claro[3] *nm* **1** : clearing **2 claro de luna** : moonlight

clase *nf* **1** : class **2** ÍNDOLE, TIPO : sort, kind, type

clasicismo *nm* : classicism

clásico[1]**, -ca** *adj* **1** : classic **2** : classical

clásico[2] *nm* : classic

clasificación *nf, pl* **-ciones** **1** : classification, sorting out **2** : rating **3** CALIFICACIÓN : qualification (in competitions)

clasificado, -da *adj* : classified ⟨aviso clasificado : classified ad⟩

clasificar {72} *vt* **1** : to classify, to sort out **2** : to rate, to rank — *vi* CALIFICAR : to qualify (in competitions) — **clasificarse** *vr*

claudicación *nf, pl* **-ciones** : surrender, abandonment of one's principles

claudicar {72} *vi* : to back down, to abandon one's principles

claustro *nm* : cloister

claustrofobia *nf* : claustrophobia

claustrofóbico, -ca *adj* : claustrophobic

cláusula *nf* : clause

clausura *nf* **1** : closure, closing **2** : closing ceremony **3** : cloister

clausurar *vt* **1** : to close, to bring to a close **2** : to close down

clavadista *nmf* : diver

clavado[1]**, -da** *adj* **1** : nailed, fixed, stuck **2** *fam* : punctual, on the dot **3** *fam* : identical ⟨es clavado a su padre : he's the image of his father⟩

clavado[2] *nm* : dive

clavar *vt* **1** : to nail, to hammer **2** HINCAR : to plunge, to stick **3** : to fix (one's eyes) on — **clavarse** *vr* : to stick oneself (with a sharp object)

clave[1] *adj* : key, essential

clave[2] *nf* **1** CIFRA : code **2** : key ⟨la clave del misterio : the key to the mystery⟩ **3** : clef **4** : keystone

clavel *nm* : carnation

clavelito *nm* : pink (flower)

clavicémbalo *nm* : harpsichord
clavícula *nf* : collarbone
clavija *nf* **1** : plug **2** : peg, pin
clavo *nm* **1** : nail ⟨clavo grande : spike⟩ **2** : clove **3 dar en el clavo** : to hit the nail on the head
claxon *nm, pl* **cláxones** : horn (of an automobile)
clemencia *nf* : clemency, mercy
clemente *adj* : merciful
cleptomanía *nf* : kleptomania
cleptómano, -na *n* : kleptomaniac
clerecía *nf* : ministry, ministers *pl*
clerical *adj* : clerical
clérigo, -ga *n* : cleric, member of the clergy
clero *nm* : clergy
cliché *nm* **1** : cliché **2** : stencil **3** : negative (of a photograph)
cliente, -ta *n* : customer, client
clientela *nf* : clientele, customers *pl*
clima *nm* **1** : climate **2** AMBIENTE : atmosphere, ambience
climático, -ca *adj* : climatic
climatización *nf, pl* **-ciones** : air-conditioning
climatizar {21} *vt* : to air-condition — **climatizado, -da** *adj*
clímax *nm* : climax
clínica *nf* : clinic
clínico, -ca *adj* : clinical — **clínicamente** *adv*
clip *nm, pl* **clips** **1** : clip **2** : paper clip
clítoris *nms & pl* : clitoris
cloaca *nf* ALCANTARILLA : sewer
clocar {82} *vi* : to cluck
cloche *nm CA, Car, Col, Ven* : clutch (of an automobile)
clon *nm* : clone
cloqué, etc. → **clocar**
cloquear *vi* : to cluck
clorar *vt* : to chlorinate — **cloración** *nf*
cloro *nm* : chlorine
clorofila *nf* : chlorophyll
cloroformo *nm* : chloroform
cloruro *nm* : chloride
clóset *nm, pl* **clósets** **1** : closet **2** : cupboard
club *nm* : club
clueca, clueque etc. → **clocar**
coa *nf Mex* : hoe
coacción *nf, pl* **-ciones** : coercion, duress
coaccionar *vt* : to coerce
coactivo, -va *adj* : coercive
coagular *v* : to clot, to coagulate — **coagulación** *nf*
coágulo *nm* : clot
coalición *nf, pl* **-ciones** : coalition
coartada *nf* : alibi
coartar *vt* : to restrict, to limit
cobalto *nm* : cobalt
cobarde¹ *adj* : cowardly
cobarde² *nmf* : coward
cobardía *nf* : cowardice
cobaya *nf* : guinea pig
cobertizo *nm* : shed, shelter
cobertor *nm* COLCHA : bedspread, quilt
cobertura *nf* **1** : coverage **2** : cover, collateral
cobija *nf* FRAZADA, MANTA : blanket
cobijar *vt* : to shelter — **cobijarse** *vr* : to take shelter
cobra *nf* : cobra
cobrador, -dora *n* **1** : collector **2** : conductor (of a bus or train)
cobrar *vt* **1** : to charge **2** : to collect, to draw, to earn **3** : to acquire, to gain **4** : to recover, to retrieve **5** : to cash (a check) **6** : to claim, to take (a life) **7** : to shoot (game), to bag — *vi* **1** : to be paid **2 llamar por cobrar** *Mex* : to call collect
cobre *nm* : copper
cobrizo, -za *adj* : coppery
cobro *nm* : collection (of money), cashing (of a check)
coca *nf* **1** : coca **2** *fam* : coke, cocaine
cocaína *nf* : cocaine
cocal *nm* : coca plantation
cocción *nf, pl* **cocciones** : cooking
cocear *vi* : to kick (of an animal)
cocer {14} *vt* **1** COCINAR : to cook **2** HERVIR : to boil
cochambre *nmf fam* : filth, grime
cochambroso, -sa *adj* : filthy, grimy
coche *nm* **1** : car, automobile **2** : coach, carriage **3 coche cama** : sleeping car **4 coche fúnebre** : hearse
cochecito *nm* : baby carriage, stroller
cochera *nf* : garage, carport
cochinada *nf fam* **1** : filthy language **2** : disgusting behavior **3** : dirty trick
cochinillo *nm* : suckling pig, piglet
cochino¹, -na *adj* **1** : dirty, filthy, disgusting **2** *fam* : rotten, lousy
cochino², -na *n* : pig, hog
cocido¹, -da *adj* **1** : boiled, cooked **2 bien cocido** : well-done
cocido² *nm* ESTOFADO, GUISADO : stew
cociente *nm* : quotient
cocimiento *nm* : cooking, baking
cocina *nf* **1** : kitchen **2** : stove **3** : cuisine, cooking
cocinar *v* : to cook
cocinero, -ra *n* : cook, chef
cocineta *nf Mex* : kitchenette
coco *nm* **1** : coconut **2** *fam* : head **3** *fam* : bogeyman
cocoa *nf* : cocoa, hot chocolate
cocodrilo *nm* : crocodile
cocotero *nm* : coconut palm
coctel *or* **cóctel** *nm* **1** : cocktail **2** : cocktail party
coctelera *nf* : cocktail shaker
codazo *nm* **1 darle un codazo a** : to elbow, to nudge **2 abrirse paso a codazos** : to elbow one's way through
codearse *vr* : to rub elbows, to hobnob
códice *nm* : codex, manuscript
codicia *nf* AVARICIA : avarice, covetousness
codiciar *vt* : to covet
codicilo *nm* : codicil
codicioso, -sa *adj* : avaricious, covetous

codificación *nf, pl* **-ciones** **1** : codification **2** : coding, encoding

codificar {72} *vt* **1** : to codify **2** : to code, to encode

código *nm* **1** : code **2 código postal** : zip code **3 código morse** : Morse code

codo[1], **-da** *adj Mex* : cheap, stingy

codo[2], **-da** *n Mex* : tightwad, cheapskate

codo[3] *nm* : elbow

codorniz *nf, pl* **-nices** : quail

coeficiente *nm* **1** : coefficient **2 coeficiente intelectual** : IQ, intelligence quotient

coexistir *vi* : to coexist — **coexistencia** *nf*

cofa *nf* : crow's nest

cofre *nm* **1** BAÚL : trunk, chest **2** *Mex* CAPOTE : hood (of a car)

coger {15} *vt* **1** : to seize, to take hold of **2** : to catch **3** : to pick up **4** : to gather, to pick **5** : to gore — **cogerse** *vr* AGARRARSE : to hold on

cogida *nf* **1** : gathering, harvest **2** : goring

cognición *nf, pl* **-ciones** : cognition

cognitivo, -va *adj* : cognitive

cogollo *nm* **1** : heart (of a vegetable) **2** : bud, bulb **3** : core, crux ⟨el cogollo de la cuestión : the heart of the matter⟩

cogote *nm* : scruff, nape

cohabitar *vi* : to cohabit — **cohabitación** *nf*

cohechar *vt* SOBORNAR : to bribe

cohecho *nm* SOBORNO : bribe, bribery

coherencia *nf* : coherence — **coherente** *adj*

cohesión *nf, pl* **-siones** : cohesion

cohesivo, -va *adj* : cohesive

cohete *nm* : rocket

cohibición *nf, pl* **-ciones** **1** : (legal) restraint **2** INHIBICIÓN : inhibition

cohibido, -da *adj* : inhibited, shy

cohibir {62} *vt* : to inhibit, to make self-conscious — **cohibirse** *vr* : to feel shy or embarrassed

cohorte *nf* : cohort

coima *nf Arg, Chile, Peru* : bribe

coimear *vt Arg, Chile, Peru* : to bribe

coincidencia *nf* : coincidence

coincidente *adj* **1** : coincident **2** ACORDE : coinciding

coincidir *vi* **1** : to coincide **2** : to agree

coito *nm* : sexual intercourse, coitus

coja, etc. → **coger**

cojear *vi* **1** : to limp **2** : to wobble, to rock **3 cojear del mismo pie** : to be two of a kind

cojera *nf* : limp

cojín *nm, pl* **cojines** : cushion, throw pillow

cojinete *nm* **1** : bearing, bushing **2 cojinete de bola** : ball bearing

cojo[1], **-ja** *adj* **1** : limping, lame **2** : wobbly **3** : weak, ineffectual

cojo[2], **-ja** *n* : lame person

cojones *nmpl usu considered vulgar* **1** : testicles *pl* **2** : guts *pl,* courage

col *nf* **1** REPOLLO : cabbage **2 col de Bruselas** : Brussels sprout **3 col rizada** : kale

cola *nf* **1** RABO : tail ⟨cola de caballo : ponytail⟩ **2** FILA : line (of people) ⟨hacer cola : to wait in line⟩ **3** : cola, drink **4** : train (of a dress) **5** : tails *pl* (of a tuxedo) **6** PEGAMENTO : glue **7** *fam* : buttocks *pl,* rear end

colaboracionista *nmf* : collaborator, traitor

colaborador, -dora *n* **1** : contributor (to a periodical) **2** : collaborator

colaborar *vi* : to collaborate — **colaboración** *nf*

colación *nf, pl* **-ciones** **1** : light meal **2** : comparison, collation ⟨sacar a colación : to bring up, to broach⟩ **3** : conferral (of a degree)

colador *nm* **1** : colander, strainer **2** *PRi* : small coffeepot

colapso *nm* **1** : collapse **2** : standstill

colar {19} *vt* : to strain, to filter — **colarse** *vr* **1** : to sneak in, to cut in line, to gate-crash **2** : to slip up, to make a mistake

colateral[1] *adj* : collateral — **colateralmente** *adv*

colateral[2] *nm* : collateral

colcha *nf* COBERTOR : bedspread, quilt

colchón *nm, pl* **colchones** **1** : mattress **2** : cushion, padding, buffer

colchoneta *nf* : mat (for gymnastic sports)

colear *vi* **1** : to wag its tail **2 vivito y coleando** *fam* : alive and kicking

colección *nf, pl* **-ciones** : collection

coleccionar *vt* : to collect, to keep a collection of

coleccionista *nmf* : collector

colecta *nf* : collection (of donations)

colectar *vt* : to collect

colectividad *nf* : community, group

colectivo[1], **-va** *adj* : collective — **colectivamente** *adv*

colectivo[2] *nm* **1** : collective **2** *Arg, Bol, Peru* : city bus

colector[1], **-tora** *n* : collector ⟨colector de impuestos : tax collector⟩

colector[2] *nm* **1** : sewer **2** : manifold (of an engine)

colega *nmf* **1** : colleague **2** HOMÓLOGO : counterpart **3** *fam* : buddy

colegiado[1], **-da** *adj* : collegiate

colegiado[2], **-da** *n* **1** ÁRBITRO : referee **2** : member (of a professional association)

colegial[1], **-giala** *adj* **1** : school, collegiate **2** *Mex fam* : green, inexperienced

colegial[2], **-giala** *n* : schoolboy *m,* schoolgirl *f*

colegiatura *nf Mex* : tuition

colegio *nm* **1** : school **2** : college ⟨colegio electoral : electoral college⟩ **3** : professional association

colegir {28} *vt* **1** JUNTAR : to collect, to gather **2** INFERIR : to infer, to deduce
cólera[1] *nm* : cholera
cólera[2] *nf* FURIA, IRA : anger, rage
colérico, -ca *adj* **1** FURIOSO : angry **2** IRRITABLE : irritable
colesterol *nm* : cholesterol
coleta *nf* **1** : ponytail **2** : pigtail
coletazo *nm* : lash, flick (of a tail)
colgado, -da *adj* **1** : hanging, hanged **2** : pending **3 dejar colgado a** : to disappoint, to let down
colgante[1] *adj* : hanging, dangling
colgante[2] *nm* : pendant, charm (on a bracelet)
colgar {16} *vt* **1** : to hang (up), to put up **2** AHORCAR : to hang (someone) **3** : to hang up (a telephone) **4** *fam* : to fail (an exam) — **colgarse** *vr* **1** : to hang, to be suspended **2** AHORCARSE : to hang oneself **3** : to hang up a telephone
colibrí *nm* CHUPAFLOR : hummingbird
cólico *nm* : colic
coliflor *nf* : cauliflower
colilla *nf* : butt (of a cigarette)
colina *nf* CERRO, LOMA : hill
colindante *adj* CONTIGUO : adjacent, neighboring
colindar *vi* : to adjoin, to be adjacent
coliseo *nm* : coliseum
colisión *nf, pl* **-siones** : collision
colisionar *vi* : to collide
collage *nm* : collage
collar *nm* **1** : collar (for an animal) **2** : necklace ‹collar de perlas : string of pearls›
colmado, -da *adj* : heaping
colmar *vt* **1** : to fill to the brim **2** : to fulfill, to satisfy **3** : to heap, to shower ‹me colmaron de regalos : they showered me with gifts›
colmena *nf* : beehive
colmenar *nm* APIARIO : apiary
colmillo *nm* **1** CANINO : canine (tooth), fang **2** : tusk
colmilludo, -da *adj Mex, PRi* : astute, shrewd, crafty
colmo *nm* : height, extreme, limit ‹el colmo de la locura : the height of folly› ‹¡eso es el colmo! : that's the last straw!›
colocación *nf, pl* **-ciones** **1** : placement, placing **2** : position, job **3** : investment
colocar {72} *vt* **1** PONER : to place, to put **2** : to find a job for **3** : to invest — **colocarse** *vr* **1** SITUARSE : to position oneself **2** : to get a job
colofón *nm, pl* **-fones** **1** : ending, finale **2** : colophon
colofonia *nf* : rosin
colombiano, -na *adj & n* : Colombian
colon *nm* : (intestinal) colon
colón *nm, pl* **colones** : Costa Rican and Salvadoran unit of currency
colonia *nf* **1** : colony **2** : cologne **3** *Mex* : residential area, neighborhood
colonial *adj* : colonial
colonización *nf, pl* **-ciones** : colonization
colonizador[1], **-dora** *adj* : colonizing
colonizador[2], **-dora** *n* : colonizer, colonist
colonizar {21} *vt* : to colonize, to settle
colono, -na *n* **1** : settler, colonist **2** : tenant farmer
coloquial *adj* : colloquial
coloquio *nm* **1** : discussion, talk **2** : conference, symposium
color *nm* **1** : color **2** : paint, dye **3 colores** *nmpl* : colored pencils
coloración *nf, pl* **-ciones** : coloring, coloration
colorado[1], **-da** *adj* **1** ROJO : red **2 ponerse colorado** : to blush **3 chiste colorado** *Mex* : off-color joke
colorado[2] *nm* ROJO : red
colorante *nm* : coloring ‹colorante de alimentos : food coloring›
colorear *vt* : to color — *vi* **1** : to redden **2** : to ripen
colorete *nm* : rouge, blusher
colorido *nm* : color, coloring
colorín *nm, pl* **-rines** **1** : bright color **2** : goldfinch
colosal *adj* : colossal
coloso *nm* : colossus
coludir *vi* : to be in collusion, to conspire
columna *nf* **1** : column **2 columna vertebral** : spine, backbone
columnata *nf* : colonnade
columnista *nmf* : columnist
columpiar *vt* : to push (on a swing) — **columpiarse** *vr* : to swing
columpio *nm* : swing
colusión *nf, pl* **-siones** : collusion
colza *nf* : rape (plant)
coma[1] *nm* : coma
coma[2] *nf* : comma
comadre *nf* **1** : godmother of one's child **2** : mother of one's godchild **3** *fam* : neighbor, female friend **4** *fam* : gossip
comadrear *vi fam* : to gossip
comadreja *nf* : weasel
comadrona *nf* : midwife
comanche *nmf* : Comanche
comandancia *nf* **1** : command headquarters **2** : command
comandante *nmf* **1** : commander, commanding officer **2** : major
comandar *vt* : to command, to lead
comando *nm* **1** : commando **2** : command (for computers)
comarca *nf* REGIÓN : region
comarcal *adj* REGIONAL : regional, local
comatoso, -sa *adj* : comatose
combar *vt* : to bend, to curve — **combarse** *vr* **1** : to bend, to buckle **2** : to warp, to bulge, to sag
combate *nm* **1** : combat **2** : fight, boxing match
combatiente *nmf* : combatant, fighter
combatir *vt* : to combat, to fight against — *vi* : to fight

combatividad *nf* : fighting spirit
combativo, -va *adj* : combative, spirited
combinación *nf, pl* **-ciones 1** : combination **2** : connection (in travel)
combinar *vt* **1** UNIR : to combine, to mix together **2** : to match, to put together — **combinarse** *vr* : to get together, to conspire
combo *nm* **1** : (musical) band **2** *Chile, Peru* : sledgehammer **3** *Chile, Peru* : punch
combustible[1] *adj* : combustible
combustible[2] *nm* : fuel
combustión *nf, pl* **-tiones** : combustion
comedero *nm* : trough, feeder
comedia *nf* : comedy
comediante *nmf* : actor, actress *f*
comedido, -da *adj* MESURADO : moderate, restrained
comediógrafo, -fa *n* : playwright
comedor *nm* : dining room
comején *nm, pl* **-jenes** : termite
comelón[1], **-lona** *adj, mpl* **-lones** *fam* : gluttonous
comelón[2], **-lona** *n, pl* **-lones** *fam* : big eater, glutton
comensal *nmf* : dinner guest
comentador, -dora *n* → **comentarista**
comentar *vt* **1** : to comment on, to discuss **2** : to mention, to remark
comentario *nm* **1** : comment, remark ⟨sin comentarios : no comment⟩ **2** : commentary
comentarista *nmf* : commentator
comenzar {29} *v* EMPEZAR : to begin, to start
comer[1] *vt* **1** : to eat **2** : to consume, to eat up, to eat into — *vi* **1** : to eat **2** CENAR : to have a meal **3 dar de comer** : to feed — **comerse** *vr* : to eat up
comer[2] *nm* : eating, dining
comercial *adj & nm* : commercial — **comercialmente** *adv*
comercializar {21} *vt* **1** : to commercialize **2** : to market
comerciante *nmf* : merchant, dealer
comerciar *vi* : to do business, to trade
comercio *nm* **1** : commerce, trade **2** NEGOCIO : business, place of business
comestible *adj* : edible
comestibles *nmpl* VÍVERES : groceries, food
cometa[1] *nm* : comet
cometa[2] *nf* : kite
cometer *vt* **1** : to commit **2 cometer un error** : to make a mistake
cometido *nm* : assignment, task
comezón *nf, pl* **-zones** PICAZÓN : itchiness, itching
comible *adj fam* : eatable, edible
comic *or* **cómic** *nm* : comic strip, comic book
comicastro, -tra *n* : second-rate actor, ham
comicidad *nf* HUMOR : humor, wit
comicios *nmpl* : elections, voting
cómico[1], **-ca** *adj* : comic, comical
cómico[2], **-ca** *n* HUMORISTA : comic, comedian, comedienne *f*
comida *nf* **1** : food **2** : meal **3** : dinner **4 comida basura** : junk food **5 comida rápida** : fast food
comidilla *nf* : talk, gossip
comienzo *nm* **1** : start, beginning **2 al comienzo** : at first **3 dar comienzo** : to begin
comillas *nfpl* : quotation marks ⟨entre comillas : in quotes⟩
comilón, -lona → **comelón, -lona**
comilona *nf fam* : feast
comino *nm* **1** : cumin **2 me vale un comino** *fam* : not to matter to someone ⟨no me importa un comino : I couldn't care less⟩
comisaría *nf* : police station
comisario, -ria *n* : commissioner
comisión *nf, pl* **-siones 1** : commission, committing **2** : committee **3** : percentage, commission ⟨comisión sobre las ventas : sales commission⟩
comisionado[1], **-da** *adj* : commissioned, entrusted
comisionado[2], **-da** *n* → **comisario**
comisionar *vt* : to commission
comité *nm* : committee
comitiva *nf* : retinue, entourage
como[1] *adv* **1** : around, about ⟨cuesta como 500 pesos : it costs around 500 pesos⟩ **2** : kind of, like ⟨tengo como mareos : I'm kind of dizzy⟩
como[2] *conj* **1** : how, as ⟨hazlo como dijiste que lo harías : do it the way you said you would⟩ **2** : since, given that ⟨como estaba lloviendo, no salí : since it was raining, I didn't go out⟩ **3** : if ⟨como lo vuelva a hacer lo arrestarán : if he does that again he'll be arrested⟩ **4 como quiera** : in any way
como[3] *prep* **1** : like, as ⟨ligero como una pluma : light as a feather⟩ **2 así como** : as well as
cómo *adv* : how ⟨¿cómo estás? : how are you?⟩ ⟨¿a cómo están las manzanas? : how much are the apples?⟩ ⟨¿cómo? : excuse me?, what was that?⟩ ⟨¿se puede? ¡cómo no! : may I? please do!⟩
cómoda *nf* : bureau, chest of drawers
comodidad *nf* **1** : comfort **2** : convenience
comodín *nm, pl* **-dines 1** : joker, wild card **2** : all-purpose word or thing **3** : pretext, excuse
cómodo, -da *adj* **1** CONFORTABLE : comfortable **2** : convenient — **cómodamente** *adv*
comodoro *nm* : commodore
comoquiera *adv* **1** : in any way **2 comoquiera que** : in whatever way, however ⟨comoquiera que sea eso : however that may be⟩
compa *nm fam* : buddy, pal
compactar *vt* : to compact, to compress
compacto, -ta *adj* : compact

compadecer {53} *vt* : to sympathize with, to feel sorry for — **compadecerse** *vr* **1 ~ de** : to take pity on, to commiserate with **2 ~ con** : to fit, to accord (with)
compadre *nm* **1** : godfather of one's child **2** : father of one's godchild **3** *fam* : buddy, pal
compaginar *vt* **1** COORDINAR : to combine, to coordinate **2** : to collate
compañerismo *nm* : comradeship, camaraderie
compañero, -ra *n* : companion, mate, partner
compañía *nf* **1** : company ⟨llegó en compañía de su madre : he arrived with his mother⟩ **2** EMPRESA, FIRMA : firm, company
comparable *adj* : comparable
comparación *nf, pl* **-ciones** : comparison
comparado, -da *adj* : comparative ⟨literatura comparada : comparative literature⟩
comparar *vt* : to compare
comparativo[1], **-va** *adj* : comparative, relative — **comparativamente** *adv*
comparativo[2] *nm* : comparative degree or form
comparecencia *nf* **1** : appearance (in court) **2 orden de comparecencia** : subpoena, summons
comparecer {53} *vi* : to appear (in court)
compartimiento *or* **compartimento** *nm* : compartment
compartir *vt* : to share
compás *nm, pl* **-pases 1** : beat, rhythm, time **2** : compass
compasión *nf, pl* **-siones** : compassion, pity
compasivo, -va *adj* : compassionate, sympathetic
compatibilidad *nf* : compatibility
compatible *adj* : compatible
compatriota *nmf* PAISANO : compatriot, fellow countryman
compeler *vt* : to compel
compendiar *vt* : to summarize, to condense
compendio *nm* : summary
compenetración *nf, pl* **-ciones** : rapport, mutual understanding
compenetrarse *vr* **1** : to understand each other **2 ~ con** : to identify oneself with
compensación *nf, pl* **-ciones** : compensation
compensar *vt* : to compensate for, to make up for — *vi* : to be worth one's while
compensatorio, -ria *adj* : compensatory
competencia *nf* **1** : competition, rivalry **2** : competence
competente *adj* : competent, able — **competentemente** *adv*
competición *nf, pl* **-ciones** : competition
competidor[1], **-dora** *adj* RIVAL : competing, rival
competidor[2], **-dora** *n* RIVAL : competitor, rival
competir {54} *vi* : to compete
competitividad *nf* : competitiveness
competitivo, -va *adj* : competitive — **competitivamente** *adv*
compilar *vt* : to compile — **compilación** *nf*
compinche *nmf fam* **1** : buddy, pal **2** : partner in crime, accomplice
complacencia *nf* : pleasure, satisfaction
complacer {57} *vt* : to please — **complacerse** *vr* **~ en** : to take pleasure in
complaciente *adj* : obliging, eager to please
complejidad *nf* : complexity
complejo[1], **-ja** *adj* : complex
complejo[2] *nm* : complex
complementar *vt* : to complement, to supplement — **complementarse** *vr*
complementario, -ria *adj* : complementary
complemento *nm* **1** : complement, supplement **2** : supplementary pay, allowance
completamente *adv* : completely, totally
completar *vt* TERMINAR : to complete, to finish
completo, -ta *adj* **1** : complete **2** : perfect, absolute **3** : full, detailed
complexión *nf, pl* **-xiones** : (physical) constitution
complicación *nf, pl* **-ciones** : complication
complicado, -da *adj* : complicated
complicar {72} *vt* **1** : to complicate **2** : to involve — **complicarse** *vr*
cómplice *nmf* : accomplice
complicidad *nf* : complicity
complot *nm, pl* **complots** CONFABULACIÓN, CONSPIRACIÓN : conspiracy, plot
componenda *nf* : shady deal, scam
componente *adj & nm* : component, constituent
componer {60} *vt* **1** ARREGLAR : to fix, to repair **2** CONSTITUIR : to make up, to compose **3** : to compose, to write **4** : to set (a bone) — **componerse** *vr* **1** : to improve, to get better **2 ~ de** : to consist of
comportamiento *nm* CONDUCTA : behavior, conduct
comportarse *vr* : to behave, to conduct oneself
composición *nf, pl* **-ciones 1** OBRA : composition, work **2** : makeup, arrangement
compositor, -tora *n* : composer, songwriter
compostura *nf* **1** : composure **2** : mending, repair
compra *nf* **1** : purchase **2 ir de compras** : to go shopping **3 orden de compra** : purchase order

comprador, -dora *n* : buyer, shopper
comprar *vt* : to buy, to purchase
compraventa *nf* : buying and selling
comprender *vt* **1** ENTENDER : to comprehend, to understand **2** ABARCAR : to cover, to include — *vi* : to understand ⟨¡ya comprendo! : now I understand!⟩
comprensible *adj* : understandable — **comprensiblemente** *adv*
comprensión *nf, pl* **-siones 1** : comprehension, understanding, grasp **2** : understanding, sympathy
comprensivo, -va *adj* : understanding
compresa *nf* **1** : compress **2** *or* **compresa higiénica** : sanitary napkin
compresión *nf, pl* **-siones** : compression
compresor *nm* : compressor
comprimido *nm* PÍLDORA, TABLETA : pill, tablet
comprimir *vt* : to compress
comprobable *adj* : verifiable, provable
comprobación *nf, pl* **-ciones** : verification, confirmation
comprobante *nm* **1** : proof ⟨comprobante de identidad : proof of identity⟩ **2** : voucher, receipt ⟨comprobante de ventas : sales slip⟩
comprobar {19} *vt* **1** : to verify, to check **2** : to prove
comprometedor, -dora *adj* : compromising
comprometer *vt* **1** : to compromise **2** : to jeopardize **3** : to commit, to put under obligation — **comprometerse** *vr* **1** : to commit oneself **2** ~ **con** : to get engaged to
comprometido, -da *adj* **1** : compromising, awkward **2** : committed, obliged **3** : engaged (to be married)
compromiso *nm* **1** : obligation, commitment **2** : engagement ⟨anillo de compromiso : engagement ring⟩ **3** : agreement **4** : awkward situation, fix
compuerta *nf* : floodgate
compuesto[1] *pp* → **componer**
compuesto[2], **-ta** *adj* **1** : fixed, repaired **2** : compound, composite **3** : decked out, spruced up **4** ~ **de** : made up of, consisting of
compuesto[3] *nm* : compound
compulsión *nf, pl* **-siones** : compulsion
compulsivo, -va *adj* **1** : compelling, urgent **2** : compulsive — **compulsivamente** *adv*
compungido, -da *adj* : contrite, remorseful
compungirse {35} *vr* : to feel remorse
compuso, etc. → **componer**
computable *adj* : countable ⟨años computables : years accrued⟩ ⟨ingresos computables : qualifying income⟩
computación *nf, pl* **-ciones** : computing, computers *pl*
computador *nm* → **computadora**
computadora *nf* **1** : computer **2 computadora portátil** : laptop computer
computar *vt* : to compute, to calculate
computarizar {21} *vt* : to computerize
cómputo *nm* : computation, calculation
comulgar {52} *vi* : to receive Communion
común *adj, pl* **comunes 1** : common **2 común y corriente** : ordinary, regular **3 por lo común** : generally, as a rule
comuna *nf* : commune
comunal *adj* : communal
comunicación *nf, pl* **-ciones 1** : communication **2** : access, link **3** : message, report
comunicado *nm* **1** : communiqué **2 comunicado de prensa** : press release
comunicar {72} *vt* **1** : to communicate, to convey **2** : to notify — **comunicarse** *vr* ~ **con 1** : to contact, to get in touch with **2** : to be connected to
comunicativo, -va *adj* : communicative, talkative
comunidad *nf* : community
comunión *nf, pl* **-niones 1** : communion, sharing **2** : Communion
comunismo *nm* : communism, Communism
comunista *adj & nmf* : communist
comúnmente *adv* : commonly
con *prep* **1** : with ⟨vengo con mi padre : I'm going with my father⟩ ⟨¡con quién hablas? : who are you speaking to?⟩ **2** : in spite of ⟨con todo : in spite of it all⟩ **3** : to, towards ⟨ella es amable con los niños : she is kind to the children⟩ **4** : by ⟨con llegar temprano : by arriving early⟩ **5 con (tal) que** : as long as, so long as
conato *nm* : attempt, effort ⟨conato de robo : attempted robbery⟩
cóncavo, -va *adj* : concave
concebible *adj* : conceivable
concebir {54} *vt* **1** : to conceive **2** : to conceive of, to imagine — *vi* : to conceive, to become pregnant
conceder *vt* **1** : to grant, to bestow **2** : to concede, to admit
concejal, -jala *n* : councilman *m,* councilwoman *f,* alderman *m,* alderwoman *f*
concejo *nm* : council ⟨concejo municipal : town council⟩
concentración *nf, pl* **-ciones** : concentration
concentrado *nm* : concentrate
concentrar *vt* : to concentrate — **concentrarse** *vr*
concéntrico, -ca *adj* : concentric
concepción *nf, pl* **-ciones** : conception
concepto *nm* NOCIÓN : concept, idea, opinion
conceptuar {3} *vt* : to regard, to judge
concernir {17} *vi* : to be of concern
concertar {55} *vt* **1** : to arrange, to set up **2** : to agree on, to settle **3** : to harmonize — *vi* : to be in harmony
concesión *nf, pl* **-siones 1** : concession **2** : awarding, granting
concha *nf* : conch, seashell

conciencia *nf* **1** : conscience **2** : consciousness, awareness
concientizar {21} *vt* : to make aware — **concientizarse** *vr* **~ de** : to realize, to become aware of
concienzudo, -da *adj* : conscientious
concierto *nm* **1** : concert **2** : agreement **3** : concerto
conciliador¹, -dora *adj* : conciliatory
conciliador², -dora *n* : arbitrator, peacemaker
conciliar *vt* : to conciliate, to reconcile — **conciliación** *nf*
conciliatorio, -ria *adj* → **conciliador¹**
concilio *nm* : (church) council
conciso, -sa *adj* : concise — **concisión** *nf*
conciudadano, -na *n* : fellow citizen
cónclave *nm* : conclave, private meeting
concluir {41} *vt* **1** TERMINAR : to conclude, to finish **2** DEDUCIR : to deduce, to infer — *vi* : to end, to conclude
conclusión *nf, pl* **-siones** : conclusion
concluyente *adj* : conclusive
concomitante *adj* : concomitant
concordancia *nf* : agreement, accordance
concordar {19} *vi* : to agree, to coincide — *vt* : to reconcile
concordia *nf* : concord, harmony
concretar *vt* **1** : to pinpoint, to specify **2** : to fulfill, to realize — **concretarse** *vr* : to become real, to take shape
concretizar → **concretar**
concreto¹, -ta *adj* **1** : concrete, actual **2** : definite, specific ‹en concreto : specifically› — **concretamente** *adv*
concreto² *nm* HORMIGÓN : concrete
concubina *nf* : concubine
concurrencia *nf* **1** : audience, turnout **2** : concurrence
concurrente *adj* : concurrent — **concurrentemente** *adv*
concurrido, -da *adj* : busy, crowded
concurrir *vi* **1** : to converge, to come together **2** : to concur, to agree **3** : to take part, to participate **4** : to attend, to be present ‹concurrir a una reunión : to attend a meeting› **5 ~ a** : to contribute to
concursante *nmf* : contestant, competitor
concursar *vt* : to compete in — *vi* : to compete, to participate
concurso *nm* **1** : contest, competition **2** : concurrence, coincidence **3** : crowd, gathering **4** : cooperation, assistance
condado *nm* **1** : county **2** : earldom
conde, -desa *n* : count *m*, earl *m*, countess *f*
condecoración *nf, pl* **-ciones** : decoration, medal
condecorar *vt* : to decorate, to award (a medal)
condena *nf* **1** REPROBACIÓN : disapproval, condemnation **2** SENTENCIA : sentence, conviction
condenable *adj* : reprehensible
condenación *nf, pl* **-ciones** **1** : condemnation **2** : damnation
condenado¹, -da *adj* **1** : fated, doomed **2** : convicted, sentenced **3** *fam* : darn, damned
condenado², -da *n* : convict
condenar *vt* **1** : to condemn **2** : to sentence **3** : to board up, to wall up — **condenarse** *vr* : to be damned
condensación *nf, pl* **-ciones** : condensation
condensar *vt* : to condense
condesa *nf* → **conde**
condescendencia *nf* : condescension
condescender {56} *vi* **1** : to condescend **2** : to agree, to acquiesce
condición *nf, pl* **-ciones** **1** : condition, state **2** : capacity, position **3 condiciones** *nfpl* : conditions, circumstances ‹condiciones de vida : living conditions›
condicional *adj* : conditional — **condicionalmente** *adv*
condicionamiento *nm* : conditioning
condicionar *vt* **1** : to condition, to determine **2 ~ a** : to be contingent on, to depend on
condimentar *vt* SAZONAR : to season, to spice
condimento *nm* : condiment, seasoning, spice
condiscípulo, -la *n* : classmate
condolencia *nf* : condolence, sympathy
condolerse {47} *vr* : to sympathize
condominio *nm* : condominium, condo
condón *nm, pl* **condones** : condom
cóndor *nm* : condor
conducción *nf, pl* **-ciones** **1** : conduction (of electricity, etc.) **2** DIRECCIÓN : management, direction
conducir {61} *vt* **1** DIRIGIR, GUIAR : to direct, to lead **2** MANEJAR : to drive (a vehicle) — *vi* **1** : to drive a vehicle **2 ~ a** : to lead to — **conducirse** *vr* PORTARSE : to behave, to conduct oneself
conducta *nf* COMPORTAMIENTO : conduct, behavior
conducto *nm* : conduit, channel, duct
conductor¹, -tora *adj* : conducting, leading
conductor², -tora *n* : driver
conductor³ *nm* : conductor (of electricity, etc.)
conectar *vt* : to connect — *vi* **~ con** : to link up with, to communicate with
conector *nm* : connector
conejera *nf* : rabbit hutch
conejillo *nm* **conejillo de Indias** : guinea pig
conejo, -ja *n* : rabbit
conexión *nf, pl* **-xiones** : connection
confabulación *nf, pl* **-ciones** COMPLOT, CONSPIRACIÓN : plot, conspiracy
confabularse *vr* : to plot, to conspire
confección *nf, pl* **-ciones** **1** : preparation **2** : tailoring, dressmaking
confeccionar *vt* : to make, to produce, to prepare

confederación *nf, pl* **-ciones** : confederation
confederarse *vr* : to confederate, to form a confederation
conferencia *nf* **1** REUNIÓN : conference, meeting **2** : lecture
conferenciante *nmf* : lecturer
conferencista → **conferenciante**
conferir {76} *vt* : to confer, to bestow
confesar {55} *v* : to confess — **confesarse** *vr* : to go to confession
confesión *nf, pl* **-siones** **1** : confession **2** : creed, denomination
confesionario *nm* : confessional
confesor *nm* : confessor
confeti *nm* : confetti
confiable *adj* : trustworthy, reliable
confiado, -da *adj* **1** : confident, self-confident **2** : trusting — **confiadamente** *adv*
confianza *nf* **1** : trust ⟨de poca confianza : untrustworthy⟩ **2** : confidence, self-confidence
confianzudo, -da *adj* : forward, presumptuous
confiar {85} *vi* : to have trust, to be trusting — *vt* **1** : to confide **2** : to entrust — **confiarse** *vr* **1** : to be overconfident **2** ~ **a** : to confide in
confidencia *nf* : confidence, secret
confidencial *adj* : confidential — **confidencialmente** *adv*
confidencialidad *nf* : confidentiality
confidente *nmf* **1** : confidant, confidante *f* **2** : informer
configuración *nf, pl* **-ciones** : configuration, shape
configurar *vt* : to shape, to form
confín *nm, pl* **confines** : boundary, limit
confinamiento *nm* : confinement
confinar *vt* **1** : to confine, to limit **2** : to exile — *vi* ~ **con** : to border on
confirmación *nf, pl* **-ciones** : confirmation
confirmar *vt* : to confirm, to substantiate
confiscación *nf, pl* **-ciones** : confiscation
confiscar {72} *vt* DECOMISAR : to confiscate, to seize
confitado, -da *adj* : candied
confite *nm* : comfit, candy
confitería *nf* **1** DULCERÍA : candy store, confectionery **2** : tearoom, café
confitero, -ra *n* : confectioner
confitura *nf* : preserves, jam
conflagración *nf, pl* **-ciones** **1** : conflagration, fire **2** : war
conflictivo, -va *adj* **1** : troubled **2** : controversial
conflicto *nm* : conflict
confluencia *nf* : junction, confluence
confluir {41} *vi* **1** : to converge, to join **2** : to gather, to assemble
conformar *vt* **1** : to form, to create **2** : to constitute, to make up — **conformarse** *vr* **1** RESIGNARSE : to resign oneself **2** : to comply, to conform **3** ~ **con** : to content oneself with, to be satisfied with
conforme[1] *adj* **1** : content, satisfied **2** ~ **a** : in accordance with
conforme[2] *conj* : as ⟨entreguen sus tareas conforme vayan saliendo : hand in your homework as you leave⟩
conformidad *nf* **1** : agreement, consent **2** : resignation
confort *nm* : comfort
confortable *adj* CÓMODO : comfortable
confortar *vt* CONSOLAR : to comfort, to console
confraternidad *nf* : brotherhood, fraternity
confraternización *nf, pl* **-ciones** : fraternization
confraternizar *vi* : to fraternize
confrontación *nf, pl* **-ciones** : confrontation
confrontar *vt* **1** ENCARAR : to confront **2** : to compare **3** : to bring face-to-face — *vi* : to border — **confrontarse** *vr* ~ **con** : to face up to
confundir *vt* : to confuse, to mix up — **confundirse** *vr* : to make a mistake, to be confused ⟨confundirse de número : to get the wrong number⟩
confusión *nf, pl* **-siones** : confusion
confuso, -sa *adj* **1** : confused, mixed-up **2** : obscure, indistinct
congelación *nf, pl* **-ciones** **1** : freezing **2** : frostbite
congelado, -da *adj* HELADO : frozen
congelador *nm* HELADORA : freezer
congelamiento *nm* → **congelación**
congelar *vt* : to freeze — **congelarse** *vr*
congeniar *vi* : to get along (with someone)
congénito, -ta *adj* : congenital
congestión *nf, pl* **-tiones** : congestion
congestionado, -da *adj* : congested
congestionamiento *nm* → **congestión**
congestionarse *vr* **1** : to become flushed **2** : to become congested
conglomerado[1], **-da** *adj* : conglomerate, mixed
conglomerado[2] *nm* : conglomerate, conglomeration
congoja *nf* ANGUSTIA : anguish, grief
congoleño, -ña *adj & n* : Congolese
congraciarse *vr* : to ingratiate oneself
congratular *vt* FELICITAR : to congratulate
congregación *nf, pl* **-ciones** : congregation, gathering
congregar {52} *vt* : to bring together — **congregarse** *vr* : to congregate, to assemble
congresista *nmf* : congressman *m,* congresswoman *f*
congreso *nm* : congress, conference
congruencia *nf* **1** : congruence **2** COHERENCIA : coherence — **congruente** *adj*
cónico, -ca *adj* : conical, conic
conífera *nf* : conifer

conífero, -ra *adj* : coniferous
conjetura *nf* : conjecture, guess
conjeturar *vt* : to guess, to conjecture
conjugación *nf, pl* **-ciones** : conjugation
conjugar {52} *vt* **1** : to conjugate **2** : to combine
conjunción *nf, pl* **-ciones** : conjunction
conjuntivo, -va *adj* : connective ⟨tejido conjuntivo : connective tissue⟩
conjunto¹, -ta *adj* : joint
conjunto² *nm* **1** : collection, group **2** : ensemble, outfit ⟨conjunto musical : musical ensemble⟩ **3** : whole, entirety ⟨en conjunto : as a whole, altogether⟩
conjurar *vt* **1** : to exorcise **2** : to avert, to ward off — *vi* CONSPIRAR : to conspire, to plot
conjuro *nm* **1** : exorcism **2** : spell
conllevar *vt* **1** : to bear, to suffer **2** IMPLICAR : to entail, to involve
conmemorar *vt* : to commemorate — **conmemoración** *nf*
conmemorativo, -va *adj* : commemorative, memorial
conmigo *pron* : with me ⟨habló conmigo : he talked with me⟩
conminar *vt* AMENAZAR : to threaten, to warn
conmiseración *nf, pl* **-ciones** : pity, commiseration
conmoción *nf, pl* **-ciones** **1** : shock, upheaval **2** *or* **conmoción cerebral** : concussion
conmocionar *vt* : to shake, to shock
conmovedor, -dora *adj* EMOCIONANTE : moving, touching
conmover {47} *vt* **1** EMOCIONAR : to move, to touch **2** : to shake up — **conmoverse** *vr*
conmutador *nm* **1** : switch **2** : switchboard
conmutar *vt* **1** : to commute (a sentence) **2** : to switch, to exchange
connivencia *nf* : connivance
connotación *nf, pl* **-ciones** : connotation
connotar *vt* : to connote, to imply
cono *nm* : cone
conocedor¹, -dora *adj* : knowledgeable
conocedor², -dora *n* : connoisseur, expert
conocer {18} *vt* **1** : to know, to be acquainted with ⟨ya lo conocí : I've already met him⟩ **2** : to meet **3** RECONOCER : to recognize — **conocerse** *vr* **1** : to know each other **2** : to meet **3** : to know oneself
conocido¹, -da *adj* **1** : familiar **2** : well-known, famous
conocido², -da *n* : acquaintance
conocimiento *nm* **1** : knowledge **2** SENTIDO : consciousness
conque *conj* : so, so then, and so ⟨¡ah, conque esas tenemos! : oh, so that's what's going on!⟩
conquista *nf* : conquest
conquistador¹, -dora *adj* : conquering
conquistador², -dora *n* : conqueror
conquistar *vt* : to conquer
consabido, -da *adj* : usual, typical
consagración *nf, pl* **-ciones** : consecration
consagrar *vt* **1** : to consecrate **2** DEDICAR : to dedicate, to devote
consciencia → **conciencia**
consciente *adj* : conscious, aware — **conscientemente** *adv*
conscripción *nf, pl* **-ciones** : conscription, draft
conscripto, -ta *n* : conscript, inductee
consecución *nf, pl* **-ciones** : attainment
consecuencia *nf* **1** : consequence, result ⟨a consecuencia de : as a result of⟩ **2 en ~** : accordingly
consecuente *adj* : consistent — **consecuentemente** *adv*
consecutivo, -va *adj* : consecutive, successive — **consecutivamente** *adv*
conseguir {75} *vt* **1** : to get, to obtain **2** : to achieve, to attain **3** : to manage to ⟨consiguió acabar el trabajo : she managed to finish the job⟩
consejero, -ra *n* : adviser, counselor
consejo *nm* **1** : advice, counsel **2** : council ⟨consejo de guerra : court-martial⟩
consenso *nm* : consensus
consentido, -da *adj* : spoiled, pampered
consentimiento *nm* : consent, permission
consentir {76} *vt* **1** PERMITIR : to consent to, to allow **2** MIMAR : to pamper, to spoil — *vi* **~ en** : to agree to, to approve of
conserje *nmf* : custodian, janitor, caretaker
conserva *nf* **1** : preserve(s), jam **2 conservas** *nfpl* : canned goods
conservación *nf, pl* **-ciones** : conservation, preservation
conservacionista *nmf* : conservationist
conservador¹, -dora *adj & n* : conservative
conservador² *nm* : preservative
conservadurismo *nf* : conservatism
conservante *nm* : preservative
conservar *vt* **1** : to preserve **2** GUARDAR : to keep, to conserve
conservatorio *nm* : conservatory
considerable *adj* : considerable — **considerablemente** *adv*
consideración *nf, pl* **-ciones** **1** : consideration **2** : respect **3 de ~** : considerable, important
considerado, -da *adj* **1** : considerate, thoughtful **2** : respected
considerar *vt* **1** : to consider, to think over **2** : to judge, to deem **3** : to treat with respect
consigna *nf* **1** ESLOGAN : slogan **2** : assignment, orders *pl* **3** : checkroom
consignación *nf, pl* **-ciones** **1** : consignment **2** ASIGNACIÓN : allocation
consignar *vt* **1** : to consign **2** : to record, to write down **3** : to assign, to allocate

consigo *pron* : with her, with him, with you, with oneself ⟨se llevó las llaves consigo : she took the keys with her⟩
consiguiente *adj* **1** : resulting, consequent **2 por ~** : consequently, as a result
consistencia *nf* : consistency
consistente *adj* **1** : firm, strong, sound **2** : consistent — **consistentemente** *adv*
consistir *vi* **1 ~ en** : to consist of **2 ~ en** : to lie in, to consist in
consola *nf* : console
consolación *nf, pl* **-ciones** : consolation ⟨premio de consolación : consolation prize⟩
consolar {19} *vt* CONFORTAR : to console, to comfort
consolidar *vt* : to consolidate — **consolidación** *nf*
consomé *nm* CALDO : consommé, clear soup
consonancia *nf* **1** : consonance, harmony **2 en consonancia con** : in accordance with
consonante[1] *adj* : consonant, harmonious
consonante[2] *nf* : consonant
consorcio *nm* : consortium
consorte *nmf* : consort, spouse
conspicuo, -cua *adj* : eminent, famous
conspiración *nf, pl* **-ciones** COMPLOT, CONFABULACIÓN : conspiracy, plot
conspirador, -dora *n* : conspirator
conspirar *vi* CONJURAR : to conspire, to plot
constancia *nf* **1** PRUEBA : proof, certainty **2** : record, evidence ⟨que quede constancia : for the record⟩ **3** : perseverance, constancy
constante[1] *adj* : constant — **constantemente** *adv*
constante[2] *nf* : constant
constar *vi* **1** : to be evident, to be on record ⟨que conste : believe me, have no doubt⟩ **2 ~ de** : to consist of
constatación *nf, pl* **-ciones** : confirmation, proof
constatar *vt* **1** : to verify **2** : to state
constelación *nf, pl* **-ciones** : constellation
consternación *nf, pl* **-ciones** : consternation, dismay
consternar *vt* : to dismay, to appall
constipación *nf, pl* **-ciones** : constipation
constipado[1], **-da** *adj* **estar constipado** : to have a cold
constipado[2] *nm* RESFRIADO : cold
constiparse *vr* : to catch a cold
constitución *nf, pl* **-ciones** : constitution — **constitucional** *adj* — **constitucionalmente** *adv*
constitucionalidad *nf* : constitutionality
constituir {41} *vt* **1** FORMAR : to constitute, to make up, to form **2** FUNDAR : to establish, to set up — **constituirse** *vr* **~ en** : to set oneself up as, to become
constitutivo, -va *adj* : constituent, component
constituyente *adj & nmf* : constituent
constreñir {67} *vt* **1** FORZAR, OBLIGAR : to constrain, to oblige **2** LIMITAR : to restrict, to limit
construcción *nf, pl* **-ciones** : construction, building
constructivo, -va *adj* : constructive — **constructivamente** *adv*
constructor, -tora *n* : builder
constructora *nf* : construction company
construir {41} *vt* : to build, to construct
consuelo *nm* : consolation, comfort
consuetudinario, -ria *adj* **1** : customary, habitual **2 derecho consuetudinario** : common law
cónsul *nmf* : consul — **consular** *adj*
consulado *nm* : consulate
consulta *nf* **1** : consultation **2** : inquiry
consultar *vt* : to consult
consultor[1], **-tora** *adj* : consulting ⟨firma consultora : consulting firm⟩
consultor[2], **-tora** *n* : consultant
consultorio *nm* : office (of a doctor or dentist)
consumación *nf, pl* **-ciones** : consummation
consumado, -da *adj* : consummate, perfect
consumar *vt* **1** : to consummate, to complete **2** : to commit, to carry out
consumible *adj* : consumable
consumición *nf, pl* **-ciones** **1** : consumption **2** : drink (in a restaurant)
consumido, -da *adj* : thin, emaciated
consumidor, -dora *n* : consumer
consumir *vt* : to consume — **consumirse** *vr* : to waste away
consumo *nm* : consumption
contabilidad *nf* **1** : accounting, bookkeeping **2** : accountancy
contabilizar {21} *vt* : to enter, to record (in accounting)
contable[1] *adj* : countable
contable[2] *nmf Spain* : accountant, bookkeeper
contactar *vt* : to contact — *vi* **~ con** : to get in touch with, to contact
contacto *nm* : contact
contado[1], **-da** *adj* **1** : counted ⟨tenía los días contados : his days were numbered⟩ **2** : rare, scarce ⟨en contadas ocasiones : on rare occasions⟩
contado[2] *nm* **al contado** : cash ⟨pagar al contado : to pay in cash⟩
contador[1], **-dora** *n* : accountant
contador[2] *nm* : meter ⟨contador de agua : water meter⟩
contaduría *nf* **1** : accounting office **2** CONTABILIDAD : accountancy
contagiar *vt* **1** : to infect **2** : to transmit (a disease) — **contagiarse** *vr* **1** : to be contagious **2** : to become infected
contagio *nm* : contagion, infection

contagioso, -sa *adj* : contagious, catching
contaminación *nf, pl* **-ciones** : contamination, pollution
contaminante *nm* : pollutant, contaminant
contaminar *vt* : to contaminate, to pollute
contar {19} *vt* **1** : to count **2** : to tell **3** : to include — *vi* **1** : to count (up) **2** : to matter, to be of concern ⟨eso no cuenta : that doesn't matter⟩ **3** ~ **con** : to rely on, to count on — **contarse** *vr* ~ **entre** : to be numbered among
contemplación *nf, pl* **-ciones** : contemplation — **contemplativo, -va** *adj*
contemplar *vt* **1** : to contemplate, to ponder **2** : to gaze at, to look at
contemporáneo, -nea *adj & n* : contemporary
contención *nf, pl* **-ciones** : containment, holding
contencioso, -sa *adj* : contentious
contender {56} *vi* **1** : to contend, to compete **2** : to fight
contendiente *nmf* : contender
contenedor *nm* **1** : container, receptacle **2** : Dumpster™
contener {80} *vt* **1** : to contain, to hold **2** ATAJAR : to restrain, to hold back — **contenerse** *vr* : to restrain oneself
contenido¹, -da *adj* : restrained, reserved
contenido² *nm* : contents *pl,* content
contentar *vt* : to please, to make happy — **contentarse** *vr* : to be satisfied, to be pleased
contento¹, -ta *adj* : contented, glad, happy
contento² *nm* : joy, happiness
contestación *nf, pl* **-ciones** **1** : answer, reply **2** : protest
contestar *vt* RESPONDER : to answer — *vi* **1** RESPONDER : to answer, to reply **2** REPLICAR : to answer back
contexto *nm* : context
contienda *nf* **1** : dispute, conflict **2** : contest, competition
contigo *pron* : with you ⟨voy contigo : I'm going with you⟩
contiguo, -gua *adj* COLINDANTE : contiguous, adjacent
continencia *nf* : continence
continente *nm* : continent — **continental** *adj*
contingencia *nf* : contingency, eventuality
contingente *adj & nm* : contingent
continuación *nf, pl* **-ciones** **1** : continuation **2 a** ~ : next ⟨lo demás sigue a continuación : the rest follows⟩ **3 a continuación de** : after, following
continuar {3} *v* : to continue
continuidad *nf* : continuity
continuo, -nua *adj* : continuous, steady, constant — **continuamente** *adv*
contonearse *vr* : to sway one's hips
contoneo *nm* : swaying, wiggling (of the hips)
contorno *nm* **1** : outline **2 contornos** *nmpl* : outskirts
contorsión *nf, pl* **-siones** : contortion
contra¹ *nf* **1** *fam* : difficulty, snag **2 llevar la contra a** : to oppose, to contradict
contra² *nm* : con ⟨los pros y los contras : the pros and cons⟩
contra³ *prep* : against
contraalmirante *nm* : rear admiral
contraatacar {72} *v* : to counterattack — **contraataque** *nm*
contrabajo *nm* : double bass
contrabalancear *vt* : to counterbalance — **contrabalanza** *nf*
contrabandear *v* : to smuggle
contrabandista *nmf* : smuggler, black marketeer
contrabando *nm* **1** : smuggling **2** : contraband
contracción *nf, pl* **-ciones** : contraction
contracepción *nf, pl* **-ciones** : contraception
contraceptivo *nm* ANTICONCEPTIVO : contraceptive
contrachapado *nm* : plywood
contracorriente *nf* **1** : crosscurrent **2 ir a contracorriente** : to go against the tide
contractual *adj* : contractual
contradecir {11} *vt* DESMENTIR : to contradict — **contradecirse** *vr* DESDECIRSE : to contradict oneself
contradicción *nf, pl* **-ciones** : contradiction
contradictorio, -ria *adj* : contradictory
contraer {81} *vt* **1** : to contract (a disease) **2** : to establish by contract ⟨contraer matrimonio : to get married⟩ **3** : to tighten, to contract — **contraerse** *vr* : to contract, to tighten up
contrafuerte *nm* : buttress
contragolpe *nm* **1** : counterblow **2** : backlash
contrahecho, -cha *adj* : deformed, hunchbacked
contraindicado, -da *adj* : contraindicated — **contraindicación** *nf*
contralor, -lora *n* : comptroller
contralto *nmf* : contralto
contramaestre *nm* **1** : boatswain **2** : foreman
contramandar *vt* : to countermand
contramano *nm* **a** ~ : the wrong way (on a street)
contramedida *nf* : countermeasure
contraorden *nf* : countermand
contraparte *nf* **1** : counterpart **2 en** ~ : on the other hand
contrapartida *nf* : compensation
contrapelo *nm* **a** ~ : in the wrong direction, against the grain
contrapeso *nm* : counterbalance
contraponer {60} *vt* **1** : to counter, to oppose **2** : to contrast, to compare
contraposición *nf, pl* **-ciones** : comparison
contraproducente *adj* : counterproductive

contrapunto *nm* : counterpoint
contrariar {85} *vt* **1** : to contradict, to oppose **2** : to vex, to annoy
contrariedad *nf* **1** : setback, obstacle **2** : vexation, annoyance
contrario, -ria *adj* **1** : contrary, opposite ⟨al contrario : on the contrary⟩ **2** : conflicting, opposed
contrarrestar *vt* : to counteract
contrarrevolución *nf, pl* **-ciones** : counterrevolution — **contrarrevolucionario, -ria** *adj & n*
contrasentido *nm* : contradiction
contraseña *nf* : password
contrastante *adj* : contrasting
contrastar *vt* **1** : to resist **2** : to check, to confirm — *vi* : to contrast
contraste *nm* : contrast
contratar *vt* **1** : to contract for **2** : to hire, to engage
contratiempo *nm* **1** PERCANCE : mishap, accident **2** DIFICULTAD : setback, difficulty
contratista *nmf* : contractor
contrato *nm* : contract
contravenir {87} *vt* : to contravene, to infringe
contraventana *nf* : shutter
contribución *nf, pl* **-ciones** : contribution
contribuidor, -dora *n* : contributor
contribuir {41} *vt* **1** APORTAR : to contribute **2** : to pay (in taxes) — *vi* **1** : contribute, to help out **2** : to pay taxes
contribuyente[1] *adj* : contributing
contribuyente[2] *nmf* : taxpayer
contrición *nf, pl* **-ciones** : contrition
contrincante *nmf* : rival, opponent
contrito, -ta *adj* : contrite, repentant
control *nm* **1** : control **2** : inspection, check **3** : checkpoint, roadblock
controlador, -dora *n* : controller ⟨controlador aéreo : air traffic controller⟩
controlar *vt* **1** : to control **2** : to monitor, to check
controversia *nf* : controversy
controversial → **controvertido**
controvertido, -da *adj* : controversial
controvertir {76} *vt* : to dispute, to argue about — *vi* : to argue, to debate
contubernio *nm* : conspiracy
contumacia *nf* : obstinacy, stubbornness
contumaz *adj, pl* **-maces** : obstinate, stubbornly disobedient
contundencia *nf* **1** : forcefulness, weight **2** : severity
contundente *adj* **1** : blunt ⟨un objeto contundente : a blunt instrument⟩ **2** : forceful, convincing — **contundentemente** *adv*
contusión *nf, pl* **-siones** : bruise, contusion
contuvo, etc. → **contener**
convalecencia *nf* : convalescence
convalecer {53} *vi* : to convalesce, to recover
convaleciente *adj & nmf* : convalescent
convección *nf, pl* **-ciones** : convection
convencer {86} *vt* : to convince, to persuade — **convencerse** *vr*
convencimiento *nm* : belief, conviction
convención *nf, pl* **-ciones** **1** : convention, conference **2** : pact, agreement **3** : convention, custom
convencional *adj* : conventional — **convencionalmente** *adv*
convencionalismo *nm* : conventionality
conveniencia *nf* **1** : convenience **2** : fitness, suitability, advisability
conveniente *adj* **1** : convenient **2** : suitable, advisable
convenio *nm* PACTO : agreement, pact
convenir {87} *vi* **1** : to be suitable, to be advisable **2** : to agree
convento *nm* **1** : convent **2** : monastery
convergencia *nf* : convergence
convergente *adj* : convergent, converging
converger {15} *vi* **1** : to converge **2** ~ **en** : to concur on
conversación *nf, pl* **-ciones** : conversation
conversador, -dora *n* : conversationalist, talker
conversar *vi* : to converse, to talk
conversión *nf, pl* **-siones** : conversion
converso, -sa *n* : convert
convertible *adj & nm* : convertible
convertidor *nm* : converter
convertir {76} *vt* **1** : to convert **2** : to transform, to change **3** : to exchange (money) — **convertirse** *vr* ~ **en** : to turn into
convexo, -xa *adj* : convex
convicción *nf, pl* **-ciones** : conviction
convicto[1], **-ta** *adj* : convicted
convicto[2], **-ta** *n* : convict, prisoner
convidado, -da *n* : guest
convidar *vt* **1** INVITAR : to invite **2** : to offer
convincente *adj* : convincing — **convincentemente** *adv*
convivencia *nf* **1** : coexistence **2** : cohabitation
convivir *vi* **1** : to coexist **2** : to live together
convocación *nf, pl* **-ciones** : convocation
convocar {72} *vt* : to convoke, to call together
convocatoria *nf* : summons, call
convoy *nm* : convoy
convulsión *nf, pl* **-siones** **1** : convulsion **2** : agitation, upheaval
convulsionar *vt* : to shake, to convulse — **convulsionarse** *vr*
convulsivo, -va *adj* : convulsive
conyugal *adj* : conjugal
cónyuge *nmf* : spouse, partner
coñac *nm* : cognac, brandy
cooperación *nf, pl* **-ciones** : cooperation
cooperador, -dora *adj* : cooperative

cooperar *vi* : to cooperate
cooperativa *nf* : cooperative, co-op
cooperativo, -va *adj* : cooperative
cooptar *vt* : to co-opt
coordenada *nf* : coordinate
coordinación *nf, pl* **-ciones** : coordination
coordinador, -dora *n* : coordinator
coordinar *vt* COMPAGINAR : to coordinate, to combine
copa *nf* **1** : wineglass, goblet **2** : drink ⟨irse de copas : to go out drinking⟩ **3** : cup, trophy
copar *vt* **1** : to take ⟨ya está copado el puesto : the job is already taken⟩ **2** : to fill, to crowd
copartícipe *nmf* : joint partner
copete *nm* **1** : tuft (of hair) **2 estar hasta el copete** : to be completely fed up
copia *nf* **1** : copy **2** : imitation, replica
copiadora *nf* : photocopier
copiar *vt* : to copy
copiloto *nmf* : copilot
copioso, -sa *adj* : copious, abundant
copla *nf* **1** : popular song or ballad **2** : couplet, stanza
copo *nm* **1** : snowflake **2 copos de avena** : rolled oats **3 copos de maíz** : cornflakes
copra *nf* : copra
cópula *nf* : copulation
copular *vi* : to copulate
coque *nm* : coke (fuel)
coqueta *nf* : dressing table
coquetear *vi* : to flirt
coqueteo *nm* : flirting, coquetry
coqueto¹, -ta *adj* : flirtatious, coquettish
coqueto², -ta *n* : flirt
coraje *nm* **1** VALOR : valor, courage **2** IRA : anger ⟨darle coraje a alguien : to make someone angry⟩
corajudo, -da *adj* : brave
coral¹ *nm* **1** : coral **2** : chorale
coral² *nf* : choir
Corán *nm* **el Corán** : the Koran
coraza *nf* **1** : armor, armor plating **2** : shell (of an animal)
corazón *nm, pl* **-zones** **1** : heart ⟨de todo corazón : wholeheartedly⟩ ⟨de buen corazón : kindhearted⟩ **2** : core **3** : darling, sweetheart
corazonada *nf* : hunch, impulse
corbata *nf* : tie, necktie
corcel *nm* : steed, charger
corchete *nm* **1** : hook and eye, clasp **2** : square bracket
corcho *nm* : cork
corcholata *nf Mex* : cap, bottle top
corcovear *vi* : to buck
cordel *nm* : cord, string
cordero *nm* : lamb
cordial¹ *adj* : cordial, affable — **cordialmente** *adv*
cordial² *nm* : cordial (liqueur)
cordialidad *nf* : cordiality, warmth
cordillera *nf* : mountain range
córdoba *nf* : Nicaraguan unit of currency
cordón *nm, pl* **cordones** **1** : cord ⟨cordón umbilical : umbilical cord⟩ **2** : cordon
cordura *nf* **1** : sanity **2** : prudence, good judgment
coreano¹, -na *adj & n* : Korean
coreano² *nm* : Korean (language)
corear *vt* : to chant, to chorus
coreografía *nf* : choreography
coreografiar {85} *vt* : to choreograph
coreográfico, -ca *adj* : choreographic
coreógrafo, -fa *n* : choreographer
corista *nmf* **1** : chorister **2** : chorus girl *f*
cormorán *nm, pl* **-ranes** : cormorant
cornada *nf* : goring, butt (with thehorns)
córnea *nf* : cornea
cornear *vt* : to gore
cornejo *nm* : dogwood (tree)
corneta *nf* : bugle, horn, cornet
cornisa *nf* : cornice
cornudo, -da *adj* : horned
coro *nm* **1** : choir **2** : chorus
corola *nf* : corolla
corolario *nm* : corollary
corona *nf* **1** : crown **2** : wreath, garland **3** : corona (in astronomy)
coronación *nf, pl* **-ciones** : coronation
coronar *vt* **1** : to crown **2** : to reach the top of, to culminate
coronario, -ria *adj* : coronary
coronel, -nela *n* : colonel
coronilla *nf* **1** : crown (of the head) **2 estar hasta la coronilla** : to be completely fed up
corpiño *nm* **1** : bodice **2** *Arg* : brassiere, bra
corporación *nf, pl* **-ciones** : corporation
corporal *adj* : corporal, bodily
corporativo, -va *adj* : corporate
corpóreo, -rea *adj* : corporeal, physical
corpulencia *nf* : corpulence, stoutness, sturdiness
corpulento, -ta *adj* ROBUSTO : robust, stout, sturdy
corpúsculo *nm* : corpuscle
corral *nm* **1** : farmyard **2** : corral, pen, stockyard **3** *or* **corralito** : playpen
correa *nf* : strap, belt
correcaminos *nms & pl* : roadrunner
corrección *nf, pl* **-ciones** **1** : correction **2** : correctness, propriety **3** : rebuke, reprimand **4 corrección de pruebas** : proofreading
correccional *nm* REFORMATORIO : reformatory
correctivo, -va *adj* : corrective ⟨lentes correctivos : corrective lenses⟩
correcto, -ta *adj* **1** : correct, right **2** : courteous, polite — **correctamente** *adv*
corrector, -tora *n* : proofreader
corredizo, -za *adj* : sliding ⟨puerta corrediza : sliding door⟩
corredor¹, -dora *n* **1** : runner, racer **2** : agent, broker ⟨corredor de bolsa : stockbroker⟩
corredor² *nm* PASILLO : corridor, hallway

correduría *nf* → **corretaje**
corregir {28} *vt* **1** ENMENDAR : to correct, to emend **2** : to reprimand **3 corregir pruebas** : to proofread — **corregirse** *vr* : to reform, to mend one's ways
correlación *nf, pl* **-ciones** : correlation
correo *nm* **1** : mail ⟨correo aéreo : airmail⟩ **2** : post office
correoso, -sa *adj* : leathery, rough
correr *vi* **1** : to run, to race **2** : to rush **3** : to flow — *vt* **1** : to travel over, to cover **2** : to move, to slide, to roll, to draw (curtains) **3 correr un riesgo** : to run a risk — **correrse** *vr* **1** : to move along **2** : to run, to spill over
correspondencia *nf* **1** : correspondence, mail **2** : equivalence **3** : connection, interchange
corresponder *vi* **1** : to correspond **2** : to pertain, to belong **3** : to be appropriate, to fit **4** : to reciprocate — **corresponderse** *vr* : to write to each other
correspondiente *adj* : corresponding, respective
corresponsal *nmf* : correspondent
corretaje *nm* : brokerage
corretear *vi* **1** VAGAR : to loiter, to wander about **2** : to run around, to scamper about — *vt* : to pursue, to chase
corrida *nf* **1** : run, dash **2** : bullfight
corrido[1], **-da** *adj* **1** : straight, continuous **2** : worldly, experienced
corrido[2] *nm* : Mexican narrative folk song
corriente[1] *adj* **1** : common, everyday **2** : current, present **3** *Mex* : cheap, trashy **4 perro corriente** *Mex* : mutt
corriente[2] *nf* **1** : current ⟨corriente alterna : alternating current⟩ ⟨direct current : corriente continua⟩ **2** : draft **3** TENDENCIA : tendency, trend
corrillo *nm* : small group, clique
corro *nm* : ring, circle (of people)
corroboración *nf, pl* **-ciones** : corroboration
corroborar *vt* : to corroborate
corroer {69} *vt* **1** : to corrode **2** : to erode, to wear away
corromper *vt* **1** : to corrupt **2** : to rot — **corromperse** *vr*
corrompido, -da *adj* CORRUPTO : corrupt, rotten
corrosión *nf, pl* **-siones** : corrosion
corrosivo, -va *adj* : corrosive
corrugar {52} *vt* : to corrugate — **corrugación** *nf*
corrupción *nf, pl* **-ciones** **1** : decay **2** : corruption
corruptela *nf* : corruption, abuse of power
corrupto, -ta *adj* CORROMPIDO : corrupt
corsario *nm* : privateer
corsé *nm* : corset
cortada *nf* : cut, gash
cortador, -dora *n* : cutter
cortadora *nf* : cutter, slicer
cortadura *nf* : cut, slash
cortafuegos *nms & pl* **1** : firebreak **2** : firewall (program)
cortante *adj* : cutting, sharp
cortar *vt* **1** : to cut, to slice, to trim **2** : to cut out, to omit **3** : to cut off, to interrupt **4** : to block, to close off **5** : to curdle (milk) — *vi* **1** : to cut **2** : to break up **3** : to hang up (the telephone) — **cortarse** *vr* **1** : to cut oneself ⟨cortarse el pelo : to cut one's hair⟩ **2** : to be cut off **3** : to sour (of milk)
cortauñas *nms & pl* : nail clippers
corte[1] *nm* **1** : cut, cutting ⟨corte de pelo : haircut⟩ **2** : style, fit
corte[2] *nf* **1** : court ⟨corte suprema : supreme court⟩ **2 hacer la corte a** : to court, to woo
cortejar *vt* GALANTEAR : to court, to woo
cortejo *nm* **1** GALANTEO : courtship **2** : retinue, entourage
cortés *adj* : courteous, polite — **cortésmente** *adv*
cortesano[1], **-na** *adj* : courtly
cortesano[2], **-na** *n* : courtier
cortesía *nf* **1** : courtesy, politeness **2 de ~** : complimentary, free
corteza *nf* **1** : bark **2** : crust **3** : peel, rind **4** : cortex ⟨corteza cerebral : cerebral cortex⟩
cortijo *nm* : farmhouse
cortina *nf* : curtain
cortisona *nf* : cortisone
corto, -ta *adj* **1** : short (in length or duration) **2** : scarce **3** : timid, shy **4 corto de vista** : nearsighted
cortocircuito *nm* : short circuit
corvejón *nm, pl* **-jones** JARRETTE : hock
corvo, -va *adj* : curved, bent
cosa *nf* **1** : thing, object **2** : matter, affair **3 otra cosa** : anything else, something else
cosecha *nf* : harvest, crop
cosechador, -dora *n* : harvester, reaper
cosechadora *nf* : harvester (machine)
cosechar *vt* **1** : to harvest, to reap **2** : to win, to earn, to garner — *vi* : to harvest
coser *vt* **1** : to sew **2** : to stitch up — *vi* : to sew
cosmético[1], **-ca** *adj* : cosmetic
cosmético[2] *nm* : cosmetic
cósmico, -ca *adj* : cosmic
cosmonauta *nmf* : cosmonaut
cosmopolita *adj & nmf* : cosmopolitan
cosmos *nm* : cosmos
cosquillas *nfpl* **1** : tickling **2 hacer cosquillas** : to tickle
cosquilleo *nm* : tickling sensation, tingle
cosquilloso, -sa *adj* : ticklish
costa *nf* **1** : coast, shore **2** : cost ⟨a toda costa : at all costs⟩
costado *nm* **1** : side **2 al costado** : alongside
costar {19} *v* : to cost ⟨¿cuánto cuesta? : how much does it cost?⟩
costarricense *adj & nmf* : Costa Rican
costarriqueño, -ña → **costarricense**
coste → **costo**
costear *vt* : to pay for, to finance

costero, -ra *adj* : coastal, coast
costilla *nf* **1** : rib **2** : chop, cutlet **3** *fam* : better half, wife
costo *nm* **1** : cost, price **2 costo de vida** : cost of living
costoso, -sa *adj* : costly, expensive
costra *nf* **1** : crust **2** POSTILLA : scab
costumbre *nf* **1** : custom **2** HÁBITO : habit
costura *nf* **1** : seam **2** : sewing, dressmaking **3 alta costura** : haute couture
costurera *nf* : seamstress *f*
cotejar *vt* : to compare, to collate
cotejo *nm* : comparison, collation
cotidiano, -na *adj* : daily, everyday ⟨la vida cotidiana : daily life⟩
cotización *nf, pl* **-ciones** **1** : market price **2** : quote, estimate
cotizado, -da *adj* : in demand, sought after
cotizar {21} *vt* : to quote, to value — **cotizarse** *vr* : to be worth
coto *nm* **1** : enclosure, reserve **2 poner coto a** : to put a stop to
cotorra *nf* **1** : small parrot **2** *fam* : chatterbox, windbag
cotorrear *vi fam* : to chatter, to gab, to blab
cotorreo *nm fam* : chatter, prattle
coyote *nm* **1** : coyote **2** *Mex fam* : smuggler (of illegal immigrants)
coyuntura *nf* **1** ARTICULACIÓN : joint **2** : occasion, moment
coz *nf, pl* **coces** : kick (of an animal)
crac *nm, pl* **cracs** : crash (of the stock market)
cozamos, etc. → **cocer**
craneal *adj* : cranial
cráneo *nf* : cranium, skull — **craneano, -na** *adj*
cráter *nm* : crater
crayón *nm, pl* **-yones** : crayon
creación *nf, pl* **-ciones** : creation
creador¹, -dora *adj* : creative, creating
creador², -dora *n* : creator
crear *vt* **1** : to create, to cause **2** : to originate
creatividad *nf* : creativity
creativo, -va *adj* : creative
crecer {53} *vi* **1** : to grow **2** : to increase
crecida *nf* : flooding, floodwater
crecido, -da *adj* **1** : grown, grown-up **2** : large (of numbers)
creciente *adj* **1** : growing, increasing **2 luna creciente** : waxing moon
crecientemente *adv* : increasingly
crecimiento *nm* **1** : growth **2** : increase
credencial *adj* **cartas credenciales** : credentials
credenciales *nfpl* : documents, documentation, credentials
credibilidad *nf* : credibility
crédito *nm* : credit
credo *nm* : creed, credo
credulidad *nf* : credulity
crédulo, -la *adj* : credulous, gullible
creencia *nf* : belief
creer {20} *v* **1** : to believe **2** : to suppose, to think ⟨creo que sí : I think so⟩ — **creerse** *vr* **1** : to believe, to think **2** : to regard oneself as ⟨se cree guapísimo : he thinks he's so handsome⟩
creíble *adj* : believable, credible
creído, -da *adj* **1** *fam* : conceited **2** : confident, sure
crema *nf* **1** : cream **2 la crema y nata** : the pick of the crop
cremación *nf, pl* **-ciones** : cremation
cremallera *nf* : zipper
cremar *vt* : to cremate
cremoso, -sa *adj* : creamy
crepa *nf Mex* : crepe (pancake)
crepe *or* **crep** *nmf* : crepe (pancake)
crepé *nm* **1** → **crespón** **2 papel crepé** : crepe paper
crepitar *vi* : to crackle
crepúsculo *nm* : twilight
crescendo *nm* : crescendo
crespo, -pa *adj* : curly, frizzy
crespón *nm, pl* **crespones** : crepe (fabric)
cresta *nf* **1** : crest **2** : comb (of a rooster)
creta *nf* : chalk (mineral)
cretino, -na *n* : cretin
creyente *nmf* : believer
creyó, etc. → **creer**
crezca, etc. → **crecer**
cría *nf* **1** : breeding, rearing **2** : young **3** : litter
criadero *nm* : hatchery
criado¹, -da *adj* **1** : raised, brought up **2 bien criado** : well-bred
criado², -da *n* : servant, maid *f*
criador, -dora *n* : breeder
crianza *nf* : upbringing, rearing
criar {85} *vt* **1** : to breed **2** : to bring up, to raise
criatura *nf* **1** : baby, child **2** : creature
criba *nf* : sieve, screen
cribar *vt* : to sift
cric *nm, pl* **crics** : jack
crimen *nm, pl* **crímenes** : crime
criminal *adj & nmf* : criminal
crin *nf* **1** : mane **2** : horsehair
criollo¹, -lla *adj* **1** : Creole **2** : native, national ⟨comida criolla : native cuisine⟩
criollo², -lla *n* : Creole
criollo³ *nm* : Creole (language)
cripta *nf* : crypt
críptico, -ca *adj* **1** : cryptic, coded **2** : enigmatic, cryptic
criptón *nm* : krypton
críquet *nm* : cricket (game)
crisálida *nf* : chrysalis, pupa
crisantemo *nm* : chrysanthemum
crisis *nf* **1** : crisis **2 crisis nerviosa** : nervous breakdown
crisma *nf fam* : head ⟨romperle la crisma a alguien : to knock someone's block off⟩
crisol *nm* **1** : crucible **2** : melting pot
crispar *vt* **1** : to cause to contract **2** : to irritate, to set on edge ⟨eso me crispa : that gets on my nerves⟩ — **crisparse** *vr* : to tense up

cristal *nm* **1** VIDRIO : glass, piece of glass **2** : crystal
cristalería *nf* **1** : glassware shop ⟨como chivo en cristalería : like a bull in a china shop⟩ **2** : glassware, crystal
cristalino[1], **-na** *adj* : crystalline, clear
cristalino[2] *nm* : lens (of the eye)
cristalizar {21} *vi* : to crystallize — **cristalización** *nf*
cristiandad *nf* : Christendom
cristianismo *nm* : Christianity
cristiano, -na *adj & n* : Christian
Cristo *nm* : Christ
criterio *nm* **1** : criterion **2** : judgment, sense
crítica *nf* **1** : criticism **2** : review, critique
criticar {72} *vt* : to criticize
crítico[1], **-ca** *adj* : critical — **críticamente** *adv*
crítico[2], **-ca** *n* : critic
criticón[1], **-cona** *adj, mpl* **-cones** *fam* : hypercritical, captious
criticón[2], **-cona** *n, mpl* **-cones** *fam* : faultfinder, critic
croar *vi* : to croak
croata *adj & nmf* : Croatian
crocante *adj* : crunchy
croché *or* **crochet** *nm* : crochet
cromático, -ca *adj* : chromatic
cromo *nm* **1** : chromium, chrome **2** : picture card, sports card
cromosoma *nm* : chromosome
crónica *nf* **1** : news report **2** : chronicle, history
crónico, -ca *adj* : chronic
cronista *nmf* **1** : reporter, newscaster **2** HISTORIADOR : chronicler, historian
cronología *nf* : chronology
cronológico, -ca *adj* : chronological — **cronológicamente** *adv*
cronometrador, -dora *n* : timekeeper
cronometrar *vt* : to time, to clock
cronómetro *nm* : chronometer
croquet *nm* : croquet
croqueta *nf* : croquette
croquis *nm* : rough sketch
cruce[1], **etc.** → **cruzar**
cruce[2] *nm* **1** : crossing, cross **2** : crossroads, intersection ⟨cruce peatonal : crosswalk⟩
crucero *nm* **1** : cruise **2** : cruiser, warship **3** *Mex* : intersection
crucial *adj* : crucial — **crucialmente** *adv*
crucificar {72} *vt* : to crucify
crucifijo *nm* : crucifix
crucifixión *nf, pl* **-fixiones** : crucifixion
crucigrama *nm* : crossword puzzle
crudo[1], **-da** *adj* **1** : raw **2** : crude, harsh
crudo[2] *nm* : crude oil
cruel *adj* : cruel — **cruelmente** *adv*
crueldad *nf* : cruelty
cruento, -ta *adj* : bloody
crujido *nm* **1** : rustling **2** : creaking **3** : crackling (of a fire) **4** : crunching
crujiente *adj* : crunchy, crisp
crujir *vi* **1** : to rustle **2** : to creak, to crack **3** : to crunch
crup *nm* : croup
crustáceo *nm* : crustacean
crutón *nm, pl* **crutones** : crouton
cruz *nf, pl* **cruces** : cross
cruza *nf* : cross (hybrid)
cruzada *nf* : crusade
cruzado[1], **-da** *adj* : crossed ⟨espadas cruzadas : crossed swords⟩
cruzado[2] *nm* **1** : crusader **2** : Brazilian unit of currency
cruzar {21} *vt* **1** : to cross **2** : to exchange (words, greetings) **3** : to cross, to interbreed — **cruzarse** *vr* **1** : to intersect **2** : to meet, to pass each other
cuaderno *nm* LIBRETA : notebook
cuadra *nf* **1** : city block **2** : stable
cuadrado[1], **-da** *adj* : square
cuadrado[2] *nm* : square ⟨elevar al cuadrado : to square (a number)⟩
cuadragésimo[1] *adj* : fortieth, forty-
cuadragésimo[2], **-ma** *n* : fortieth, forty- (in a series)
cuadrante *nm* **1** : quadrant **2** : dial
cuadrar *vi* : to conform, to agree — *vt* : to square — **cuadrarse** *vr* : to stand at attention
cuadriculado *nm* : grid (on a map, etc.)
cuadrilátero *nm* **1** : quadrilateral **2** : ring (in sports)
cuadrilla *nf* : gang, team, group
cuadro *nm* **1** : square ⟨una blusa a cuadros : a checkered blouse⟩ **2** : painting, picture **3** : baseball diamond, infield **4** : panel, board, cadre
cuadrúpedo *nm* : quadruped
cuadruple *adj* : quadruple
cuadruplicar {72} *vt* : to quadruple — **cuadruplicarse** *vr*
cuajada *nf* : curd
cuajar *vi* **1** : to curdle **2** COAGULAR : to clot, to coagulate **3** : to set, to jell **4** : to be accepted ⟨su idea no cuajó : his idea didn't catch on⟩ — *vt* **1** : to curdle **2 ~ de** : to fill with
cual[1] *prep* : like, as
cual[2] *pron* **1 el cual, la cual, los cuales, las cuales** : who, whom, which ⟨la razón por la cual lo dije : the reason I said it⟩ **2 lo cual** : which ⟨se rió, lo cual me dio rabia : he laughed, which made me mad⟩ **3 cada cual** : everyone, everybody
cuál[1] *adj* : which, what ⟨¿cuáles libros? : which books?⟩
cuál[2] *pron* **1** (*in questions*) : which (one), what (one) ⟨¿cuál es el mejor? : which one is the best?⟩ ⟨¿cuál es tu apellido? : what is your last name?⟩ **2 cuál más, cuál menos** : some more, some less
cualidad *nf* : quality, trait
cualitativo, -va *adj* : qualitative — **cualitativamente** *adv*
cualquier *adj* → **cualquiera**[1]
cualquiera[1] (**cualquier** *before nouns*) *adj, pl* **cualesquiera** **1** : any, whichever ⟨cualquier persona : any person⟩ **2** : everyday, ordinary ⟨un hombre cualquiera : an ordinary man⟩

cualquiera[2] *pron, pl* **cualesquiera** **1** : anyone, anybody, whoever **2** : whatever, whichever

cuán *adv* : how ⟨¡cuán risible fue todo eso! : how funny it all was!⟩

cuando[1] *conj* **1** : when ⟨cuando llegó : when he arrived⟩ **2** : since, if ⟨cuando lo dices : if you say so⟩ **3 cuando más** : at the most **4 de vez en cuando** : from time to time

cuando[2] *prep* : during, at the time of ⟨cuando la guerra : during the war⟩

cuándo *adv & conj* **1** : when ⟨¿cuándo llegará? : when will she arrive?⟩ ⟨no sabemos cuándo será : we don't know when it will be⟩ **2 ¿de cuándo acá?** : since when?, how come?

cuantía *nf* **1** : quantity, extent **2** : significance, import

cuántico, -ca *adj* : quantum ⟨teoría cuántica : quantum theory⟩

cuantioso, -sa *adj* **1** : abundant, considerable **2** : heavy, grave ⟨cuantiosos daños : heavy damage⟩

cuantitativo, -va *adj* : quantitative — **cuantitativamente** *adv*

cuanto[1] *adv* **1** : as much as ⟨come cuanto puedas : eat as much as you can⟩ **2 cuanto antes** : as soon as possible **3 en ~** : as soon as **4 en cuanto a** : as for, as regards

cuanto[2], **-ta** *adj* : as many, whatever ⟨llévate cuantas flores quieras : take as many flowers as you wish⟩

cuanto[3], **-ta** *pron* **1** : as much as, all that, everything ⟨tengo cuanto deseo : I have all that I want⟩ **2 unos cuantos, unas cuantas** : a few

cuánto[1] *adv* : how much, how many ⟨¿a cuánto están las manzanas? : how much are the apples?⟩ ⟨no sé cuánto desean : I don't know how much they want⟩

cuánto[2], **-ta** *adj* : how much, how many ⟨¿cuántos niños tiene? : how many children do you have?⟩

cuánto[3] *pron* : how much, how many ⟨¿cuántos quieren participar? : how many want to take part?⟩ ⟨¿cuánto cuesta? : how much does it cost?⟩

cuarenta *adj & nm* : forty

cuarentavo[1], **-va** *adj* : fortieth

cuarentavo[2] *nm* : fortieth (fraction)

cuarentena *nf* **1** : group of forty **2** : quarantine

Cuaresma *nf* : Lent

cuartear *vt* **1** : to quarter **2** : to divide up — **cuartearse** *vr* AGRIETARSE : to crack, to split

cuartel *nm* **1** : barracks, headquarters **2** : mercy ⟨una guerra sin cuartel : a merciless war⟩

cuartelazo *nm* : coup d'état

cuarteto *nm* : quartet

cuartilla *nf* : sheet (of paper)

cuarto[1], **-ta** *adj* : fourth

cuarto[2], **-ta** *n* : fourth (in a series)

cuarto[3] *nm* **1** : quarter, fourth ⟨cuarto de galón : quart⟩ **2** HABITACIÓN : room

cuarzo *nm* : quartz

cuate, -ta *n Mex* **1** : twin **2** *fam* : buddy, pal

cuatrero, -ra *n* : rustler

cuatrillizo, -za *n* : quadruplet

cuatro *adj & nm* : four

cuatrocientos[1], **-tas** *adj* : four hundred

cuatrocientos[2] *nms & pl* : four hundred

cuba *nf* BARRIL : cask, barrel

cubano, -na *adj & n* : Cuban

cubertería *nf* : flatware, silverware

cubeta *nf* **1** : keg, cask **2** : bulb (of a thermometer) **3** *Mex* : bucket, pail

cúbico, -ca *adj* : cubic, cubed

cubículo *nm* : cubicle

cubierta *nf* **1** : covering **2** FORRO : cover, jacket (of a book) **3** : deck

cubierto[1] *pp* → **cubrir**

cubierto[2] *nm* **1** : cover, shelter ⟨bajo cubierto : under cover⟩ **2** : table setting **3** : utensil, piece of silverware

cubil *nm* : den, lair

cúbito *nm* : ulna

cubo *nm* **1** : cube **2** BALDE : pail, bucket, can ⟨cubo de basura : garbage can⟩ **3** : hub (of a wheel)

cubrecama *nm* COLCHA : bedspread

cubrir {2} *vt* : to cover — **cubrirse** *vr*

cucaracha *nf* : cockroach, roach

cuchara *nf* : spoon

cucharada *nf* : spoonful

cucharilla *or* **cucharita** *nf* : teaspoon

cucharón *nm, pl* **-rones** : ladle

cuchichear *vi* : to whisper

cuchicheo *nm* : whisper

cuchilla *nf* **1** : kitchen knife, cleaver **2** : blade ⟨cuchilla de afeitar : razor blade⟩ **3** : crest, ridge

cuchillada *nf* : stab, knife wound

cuchillo *nm* : knife

cuclillas *nfpl* **en ~** : squatting, crouching

cuco[1], **-ca** *adj fam* : pretty, cute

cuco[2] *nm* : cuckoo

cucurucho *nm* : ice-cream cone

cuece, cueza etc. → **cocer**

cuela, etc. → **colar**

cuelga, cuelgue etc. → **colgar**

cuello *nm* **1** : neck **2** : collar (of a shirt) **3 cuello del útero** : cervix

cuenca *nf* **1** : river basin **2** : eye socket

cuenco *nm* : bowl, basin

cuenta[1], **etc.** → **contar**

cuenta[2] *nf* **1** : calculation, count **2** : account **3** : check, bill **4 darse cuenta** : to realize **5 tener en cuenta** : to bear in mind

cuentagotas *nfs & pl* **1** : dropper **2 con ~** : little by little

cuentista *nmf* **1** : short story writer **2** *fam* : liar, fibber

cuento *nm* **1** : story, tale **2 cuento de hadas** : fairy tale **3 sin ~** : countless

cuerda *nf* **1** : cord, rope, string **2 cuerdas vocales** : vocal cords **3 darle cuerda a** : to wind up (a clock, a toy, etc.)

cuerdo, -da *adj* : sane, sensible
cuerno *nm* **1** : horn, antler **2** : cusp (of the moon) **3** : horn (musical instrument)
cuero *nm* **1** : leather, hide **2 cuero cabelludo** : scalp
cuerpo *nm* **1** : body **2** : corps
cuervo *nm* : crow, raven
cuesta[1], **etc.** → **costar**
cuesta[2] *nf* **1** : slope ⟨cuesta arriba : uphill⟩ **2 a cuestas** : on one's back
cuestión *nf, pl* **-tiones** ASUNTO, TEMA : matter, affair
cuestionable *adj* : questionable, dubious
cuestionar *vt* : to question
cuestionario *nm* **1** : questionnaire **2** : quiz
cueva *nf* : cave
cuidado *nm* **1** : care **2** : worry, concern **3 tener cuidado** : to be careful **4 ¡cuidado!** : watch out!, be careful!
cuidador, -dora *n* : caretaker
cuidadoso, -sa *adj* : careful, attentive — **cuidadosamente** *adv*
cuidar *vt* **1** : to take care of, to look after **2** : to pay attention to — *vi* **1 ~ de** : to look after **2 cuidar de que** : to make sure that — **cuidarse** *vr* : to take care of oneself
culata *nf* : butt (of a gun)
culatazo *nf* : kick, recoil
culebra *nf* SERPIENTE : snake
culi *nmf* : coolie
culinario, -ria *adj* : culinary
culminante *adj* **punto culminante** : peak, high point, climax
culminar *vi* : to culminate — **culminación** *nf*
culo *nm* **1** *fam* : backside, behind **2** : bottom (of a glass)
culpa *nf* **1** : fault, blame ⟨echarle la culpa a alguien : to blame someone⟩ **2** : sin
culpabilidad *nf* : guilt
culpable[1] *adj* : guilty
culpable[2] *nmf* : culprit, guilty party
culpar *vt* : to blame
cultivado, -da *adj* **1** : cultivated, farmed **2** : cultured
cultivador, -dora *n* : cultivator
cultivar *vt* **1** : to cultivate **2** : to foster
cultivo *nm* **1** : cultivation, farming **2** : crop
culto[1], **-ta** *adj* : cultured, educated
culto[2] *nm* **1** : worship **2** : cult
cultura *nf* : culture
cultural *adj* : cultural — **culturalmente** *adv*
cumbre *nf* CIMA : top, peak, summit
cumpleaños *nms & pl* : birthday
cumplido[1], **-da** *adj* **1** : complete, full **2** : courteous, correct
cumplido[2] *nm* : compliment, courtesy ⟨por cumplido : out of courtesy⟩ ⟨andarse con cumplidos : to stand on ceremony, to be formal⟩
cumplimentar *vt* **1** : to congratulate **2** : to carry out, to perform
cumplimiento *nm* **1** : completion, fulfillment **2** : performance
cumplir *vt* **1** : to accomplish, to carry out **2** : to comply with, to fulfill **3** : to attain, to reach ⟨su hermana cumple los 21 el viernes : her sister will be 21 on Friday⟩ — *vi* **1** : to expire, to fall due **2** : to fulfill one's obligations ⟨cumplir con el deber : to do one's duty⟩ ⟨cumplir con la palabra : to keep one's word⟩ — **cumplirse** *vr* **1** : to come true, to be fulfilled ⟨se cumplieron sus sueños : her dreams came true⟩ **2** : to run out, to expire
cúmulo *nm* **1** MONTÓN : heap, pile **2** : cumulus
cuna *nf* **1** : cradle **2** : birthplace ⟨Puerto Rico es la cuna de la música salsa : Puerto Rico is the birthplace of salsa music⟩
cundir *vi* **1** : to propagate, to spread ⟨cundió el pánico en el vecindario : panic spread throughout the neighborhood⟩ **2** : to progress, to make headway
cuneta *nf* : ditch (in a road), gutter
cuña *nf* : wedge
cuñado, -da *n* : brother-in-law *m*, sister-in-law *f*
cuño *nm* : die (for stamping)
cuota *nf* **1** : fee, dues **2** : quota, share **3** : installment, payment
cupé *nm* : coupe
cupo[1], **etc.** → **caber**
cupo[2] *nm* **1** : quota, share **2** : capacity, room
cupón *nm, pl* **cupones** **1** : coupon, voucher **2 cupón federal** : food stamp
cúpula *nf* : dome, cupola
cura[1] *nm* : priest
cura[2] *nf* **1** CURACIÓN, TRATAMIENTO : cure, treatment **2** : dressing, bandage
curación *nf, pl* **-ciones** CURA, TRATAMIENTO : cure, treatment
curandero, -ra *nm* **1** : witch doctor **2** : quack, charlatan
curar *vt* **1** : to cure, to heal **2** : to treat, to dress **3** CURTIR : to tan **4** : to cure (meat) — *vi* : to get well, to recover — **curarse** *vr*
curativo, -va *adj* : curative, healing
curiosear *vi* **1** : to snoop, to pry **2** : to browse — *vt* : to look over, to check
curiosidad *nf* **1** : curiosity **2** : curio
curioso, -sa *adj* **1** : curious, inquisitive **2** : strange, unusual, odd — **curiosamente** *adv*
currículo → **currículum**
currículum *nm, pl* **-lums** **1** : résumé, curriculum vitae **2** : curriculum, course of study
curry ['kurri] *nm, pl* **-rries** **1** : curry powder **2** : curry (dish)
cursar *vt* **1** : to attend (school), to take (a course) **2** : to dispatch, to pass on
cursi *adj fam* : affected, pretentious
cursilería *nf* **1** : vulgarity, poor taste **2** : pretentiousness

cursiva *nf* BASTARDILLA : italic type, italics *pl*
curso *nm* **1** : course, direction **2** : school year **3** : course, subject (in school)
cursor *nm* : cursor
curtido, -da *adj* : weather-beaten, leathery (of skin)
curtidor, -dora *n* : tanner
curtiduría *nf* : tannery
curtir *vt* **1** : to tan **2** : to harden, to weather — **curtirse** *vr*
curva *nf* : curve, bend
curvar *vt* : to bend
curvatura *nf* : curvature
curvilíneo, -nea *adj* : curvaceous, shapely
curvo, -va *adj* : curved, bent
cúspide *nf* : zenith, apex, peak
custodia *nf* : custody
custodiar *vt* : to guard, to look after
custodio, -dia *n* : keeper, guardian
cúter *nm* : cutter (boat)
cutícula *nf* : cuticle
cutis *nms & pl* : skin, complexion
cuyo, -ya *adj* **1** : whose, of whom, of which **2 en cuyo caso** : in which case

D

d *nf* : fourth letter of the Spanish alphabet
dable *adj* : feasible, possible
dactilar *adj* **huellas dactilares** : fingerprints
dádiva *nf* : gift, handout
dadivoso, -sa *adj* : generous
dado, -da *adj* **1** : given **2 dado que** : given that, since
dador, -dora *n* : giver, donor
dados *nmpl* : dice
daga *nf* : dagger
dalia *nf* : dahlia
dálmata *nm* : dalmatian
daltónico, -ca *adj* : color-blind
daltonismo *nm* : color blindness
dama *nf* **1** : lady **2 damas** *nfpl* : checkers
damasco *nm* : damask
damisela *nf* : damsel
damnificado, -da *n* : victim (of a disaster)
damnificar {72} *vt* : to damage, to injure
dance, etc. → **danzar**
dandi *nm* : dandy, fop
danés[1], **-nesa** *adj* : Danish
danés[2], **-nesa** *n, mpl* **daneses** : Dane, Danish person
danza *nf* : dance, dancing ⟨danza folklórica : folk dance⟩
danzante, -ta *n* BAILARÍN : dancer
danzar {21} *v* BAILAR : to dance
dañar *vt* **1** : to damage, to spoil **2** : to harm, to hurt — **dañarse** *vr*
dañino, -na *adj* : harmful
daño *nm* **1** : damage **2** : harm, injury **3 hacer daño a** : to harm, to damage **4 daños y perjuicios** : damages
dar {22} *vt* **1** : to give **2** ENTREGAR : to deliver, to hand over **3** : to hit, to strike **4** : to yield, to produce **5** : to perform **6** : to give off, to emit **7 ~ como** *or* **~ por** : to regard as, to consider — *vi* **1** ALCANZAR : to suffice, to be enough ⟨no me da para dos pasajes : I don't have enough for two fares⟩ **2 ~ a** *or* **~ sobre** : to overlook, to look out on **3 ~ con** : to run into **4 ~ con** : to hit upon (an idea) **5 dar de sí** : to give, to stretch — **darse** *vr* **1** : to give in, to surrender **2** : to occur, to arise **3** : to grow, to come up **4 ~ con** *or* **~ contra** : to hit oneself against **5 dárselas de** : to boast about ⟨se las da de muy listo : he thinks he's very smart⟩
dardo *nm* : dart
datar *vt* : to date — *vi* **~ de** : to date from, to date back to
dátil *nm* : date (fruit)
dato *nm* **1** : fact, piece of information **2 datos** *nmpl* : data, information
dé → **dar**
de *prep* **1** : of ⟨la casa de Pepe : Pepe's house⟩ ⟨un niño de tres años : a three-year-old boy⟩ **2** : from ⟨es de Managua : she's from Managua⟩ ⟨salió del edificio : he left the building⟩ **3** : in, at ⟨a las tres de la mañana : at three in the morning⟩ ⟨salen de noche : they go out at night⟩ **4** : than ⟨más de tres : more than three⟩
deambular *vi* : to wander, to roam
debacle *nf* : debacle
debajo *adv* **1** : underneath, below, on the bottom **2 ~ de** : under, underneath **3 por ~** : below, beneath
debate *nm* : debate
debatir *vt* : to debate, to discuss — **debatirse** *vr* : to struggle
debe *nm* : debit column, debit
deber[1] *vt* : to owe — *v aux* **1** : must, have to ⟨debo ir a la oficina : I must go to the office⟩ **2** : should, ought to ⟨deberías buscar trabajo : you ought to look for work⟩ **3** (*expressing probability*) : must ⟨debe ser mexicano : he must be Mexican⟩ — **deberse** *vr* **~ a** : to be due to
deber[2] *nm* **1** OBLIGACIÓN : duty, obligation **2 deberes** *nmpl, Spain* : homework
debidamente *adv* : properly, duly
debido, -da *adj* **1** : right, proper, due **2 ~ a** : due to, owing to
débil *adj* : weak, feeble — **débilmente** *adv*
debilidad *nf* : weakness, debility, feebleness
debilitamiento *nm* : debilitation, weakening

debilitar *vt* : to debilitate, to weaken — **debilitarse** *vr*
debilucho[1], **-cha** *adj* : weak, frail
debilucho[2], **-cha** *n* : weakling
debitar *vt* : to debit
débito *nm* **1** DEUDA : debt **2** : debit
debut [de'but] *nm, pl* **debuts** : debut
debutante[1] *nmf* : beginner, newcomer
debutante[2] *nf* : debutante *f*
debutar *vi* : to debut, to make a debut
década *nf* DECENIO : decade
decadencia *nf* **1** : decadence **2** : decline
decadente *adj* **1** : decadent **2** : declining
decaer {13} *vi* **1** : to decline, to decay, to deteriorate **2** FLAQUEAR : to weaken, to flag
decaiga, etc. → **decaer**
decano, -na *n* **1** : dean **2** : senior member
decantar *vt* : to decant
decapitar *vt* : to decapitate, to behead
decayó, etc. → **decaer**
decena *nf* : group of ten
decencia *nf* : decency
decenio *nm* DÉCADA : decade
decente *adj* : decent — **decentemente** *adv*
decepción *nf, pl* **-ciones** : disappointment, letdown
decepcionante *adj* : disappointing
decepcionar *vt* : to disappoint, to let down — **decepcionarse** *vr*
deceso *nm* DEFUNCIÓN : death, passing
dechado *nm* **1** : sampler (of embroidery) **2** : model, paragon
decibelio *or* **decibel** *nm* : decibel
decidido, -da *adj* : decisive, determined, resolute — **decididamente** *adv*
decidir *vt* **1** : to decide, to determine ⟨no he decidido nada : I haven't made a decision⟩ **2** : to persuade, to decide ⟨su padre lo decidió a estudiar : his father persuaded him to study⟩ — *vi* : to decide — **decidirse** *vr* : to make up one's mind
decimal *adj* : decimal
décimo, -ma *adj* : tenth — **décimo, -ma** *n*
decimoctavo[1], **-va** *adj* : eighteenth
decimoctavo[2], **-va** *n* : eighteenth (in a series)
decimocuarto[1], **-ta** *adj* : fourteenth
decimocuarto[2], **-ta** *n* : fourteenth (in a series)
decimonoveno[1], **-na** *or* **decimonono, -na** *adj* : nineteenth
decimonoveno[2], **-na** *or* **decimonono, -na** *n* : nineteenth (in a series)
decimoquinto[1], **-ta** *adj* : fifteenth
decimoquinto[2], **-ta** *n* : fifteenth (in a series)
decimoséptimo[1], **-ma** *adj* : seventeenth
decimoséptimo[2], **-ma** *n* : seventeenth (in a series)
decimosexto[1], **-ta** *adj* : sixteenth
decimosexto[2], **-ta** *n* : sixteenth (in a series)
decimotercero[1], **-ra** *adj* : thirteenth
decimotercero[2], **-ra** *n* : thirteenth (in a series)
decir[1] {23} *vt* **1** : to say ⟨dice que no quiere ir : she says she doesn't want to go⟩ **2** : to tell ⟨dime lo que estás pensando : tell me what you're thinking⟩ **3** : to speak, to talk ⟨no digas tonterías : don't talk nonsense⟩ **4** : to call ⟨me dicen Rosy : they call me Rosy⟩ **5 es decir** : that is to say **6 querer decir** : to mean — **decirse** *vr* **1** : to say to oneself **2** : to be said ⟨¿cómo se dice "lápiz" en francés? : how do you say "pencil" in French?⟩
decir[2] *nm* DICHO : saying, expression
decisión *nf, pl* **-siones** : decision, choice
decisivo, -va *adj* : decisive, conclusive — **decisivamente** *adv*
declamar *vi* : to declaim — *vt* : to recite
declaración *nf, pl* **-ciones** **1** : declaration, statement **2** TESTIMONIO : deposition, testimony **3 declaración de derechos** : bill of rights **4 declaración jurada** : affidavit
declarado, -da *adj* : professed, open — **declaradamente** *adv*
declarar *vt* : to declare, to state — *vi* ATESTIGUAR : to testify — **declararse** *vr* **1** : to declare oneself, to make a statement **2** : to confess one's love **3** : to plead (in court) ⟨declararse inocente : to plead not guilty⟩
declinación *nf, pl* **-ciones** **1** : drop, downward trend **2** : declination **3** : declension (in grammar)
declinar *vt* : to decline, to turn down — *vi* **1** : to draw to a close **2** : to diminish, to decline
declive *nm* **1** DECADENCIA : decline **2** : slope, incline
decodificador *nm* : decoder
decolar *vi Chile, Col, Ecua* : to take off (of an airplane)
decolorar *vt* : to bleach — **decolorarse** *vr* : to fade
decomisar *vt* CONFISCAR : to seize, to confiscate
decomiso *nm* : seizure, confiscation
decoración *nf, pl* **-ciones** **1** : decoration **2** : decor **3** : stage set, scenery
decorado *nm* : stage set, scenery
decorador, -dora *n* : decorator
decorar *vt* ADORNAR : to decorate, to adorn
decorativo, -va *adj* : decorative, ornamental
decoro *nm* : decorum, propriety
decoroso, -sa *adj* : decent, proper, respectable
decrecer {53} *vi* : to decrease, to wane, to diminish — **decreciente** *adj*
decrecimiento *nm* : decrease, decline
decrépito, -ta *adj* : decrepit
decretar *vt* : to decree, to order
decreto *nm* : decree
decúbito *nm* : horizontal position ⟨en decúbito prono : prone⟩ ⟨en decúbito supino : supine⟩

dedal *nm* : thimble
dedalera *nf* DIGITAL : foxglove
dedicación *nf, pl* **-ciones** : dedication, devotion
dedicar {72} *vt* CONSAGRAR : to dedicate, to devote — **dedicarse** *vr* **~ a** : to devote oneself to, to engage in
dedicatoria *nf* : dedication (of a book, song, etc.)
dedo *nm* **1** : finger ⟨dedo meñique : little finger⟩ **2 dedo del pie** : toe
deducción *nf, pl* **-ciones** : deduction
deducible *adj* **1** : deducible, inferable **2** : deductible
deducir {61} *vt* **1** INFERIR : to deduce **2** DESCONTAR : to deduct
defecar {72} *vi* : to defecate — **defecación** *nf*
defecto *nm* **1** : defect, flaw, shortcoming **2 en su defecto** : lacking that, in the absence of that
defectuoso, -sa *adj* : defective, faulty
defender {56} *vt* : to defend, to protect — **defenderse** *vr* **1** : to defend oneself **2** : to get by, to know the basics ⟨su inglés no es perfecto pero se defiende : his English isn't perfect but he gets by⟩
defendible *adj* : defensible, tenable
defensa¹ *nf* : defense
defensa² *nmf* : defender, back (in sports)
defensiva *nf* : defensive, defense
defensivo, -va *adj* : defensive — **defensivamente** *adv*
defensor¹, -sora *adj* : defending, defense
defensor², -sora *n* **1** : defender, advocate **2** : defense counsel
defeño, -ña *n* : person from the Federal District (Mexico City)
deferencia *nf* : deference
deficiencia *nf* : deficiency, flaw
deficiente *adj* : deficient
déficit *nm, pl* **-cits** **1** : deficit **2** : shortage, lack
definición *nf, pl* **-ciones** : definition
definido, -da *adj* : definite, well-defined
definir *vt* **1** : to define **2** : to determine
definitivamente *adv* **1** : finally **2** : permanently, for good **3** : definitely, absolutely
definitivo, -va *adj* **1** : definitive, conclusive **2 en definitiva** : all in all, on the whole **3 en definitiva** *Mex* : permanently, for good
deflación *nf, pl* **-ciones** : deflation
deforestación *nf, pl* **-ciones** : deforestation
deformación *nf, pl* **-ciones** **1** : deformation **2** : distortion
deformar *vt* **1** : to deform, to disfigure **2** : to distort — **deformarse** *vr*
deforme *adj* : deformed, misshapen
deformidad *nf* : deformity
defraudación *nf, pl* **-ciones** : fraud
defraudar *vt* **1** ESTAFAR : to defraud, to cheat **2** : to disappoint
defunción *nf, pl* **-ciones** DECESO : death, passing
degeneración *nf, pl* **-ciones** **1** : degeneration **2** : degeneracy, depravity
degenerado, -da *adj* DEPRAVADO : degenerate
degenerar *vi* : to degenerate
degenerativo, -va *adj* : degenerative
degollar {19} *vt* **1** : to slit the throat of, to slaughter **2** DECAPITAR : to behead **3** : to ruin, to destroy
degradación *nf, pl* **-ciones** **1** : degradation **2** : demotion
degradar *vt* **1** : to degrade, to debase **2** : to demote
degustación *nf, pl* **-ciones** : tasting, sampling
degustar *vt* : to taste
deidad *nf* : deity
deificar {72} *vt* : to idolize, to deify
dejado, -da *adj* **1** : slovenly **2** : careless, lazy
dejar *vt* **1** : to leave **2** ABANDONAR : to abandon, to forsake **3** : to let be, to let go **4** PERMITIR : to allow, to permit — *vi* **~ de** : to stop, to quit ⟨dejar de fumar : to quit smoking⟩ — **dejarse** *vr* **1** : to let oneself be ⟨se deja insultar : he lets himself be insulted⟩ **2** : to forget, to leave ⟨me dejé las llaves en el carro : I left the keys in the car⟩ **3** : to neglect oneself, to let oneself go **4** : to grow ⟨nos estamos dejando el pelo largo : we're growing our hair long⟩
dejo *nm* **1** : aftertaste **2** : touch, hint **3** : (regional) accent
del (*contraction of* **de** *and* **el**) → **de**
delación *nf, pl* **-ciones** : denunciation, betrayal
delantal *nm* **1** : apron **2** : pinafore
delante *adv* **1** ENFRENTE : ahead, in front **2 ~ de** : before, in front of
delantera *nf* **1** : front, front part, front row ⟨tomar la delantera : to take the lead⟩ **2** : forward line (in sports)
delantero¹, -ra *adj* **1** : front, forward **2 tracción delantera** : front-wheel drive
delantero², -ra *n* : forward (in sports)
delatar *vt* **1** : to betray, to reveal **2** : to denounce, to inform against
delegación *nf, pl* **-ciones** : delegation
delegado, -da *n* : delegate, representative
delegar {52} *vt* : to delegate
deleitar *vt* : to delight, to please — **deleitarse** *vr*
deleite *nm* : delight, pleasure
deletrear *vi* : to spell ⟨¿como se deletrea? : how do you spell it?⟩
deleznable *adj* **1** : brittle, crumbly **2** : slippery **3** : weak, fragile ⟨una excusa deleznable : a weak excuse⟩
delfín *nm, pl* **delfines** **1** : dolphin **2** : dauphin, heir apparent
delgadez *nf* : thinness, skinniness
delgado, -da *adj* **1** FLACO : thin, skinny **2** ESBELTO : slender, slim **3** DELICADO : delicate, fine **4** AGUDO : sharp, clever
deliberación *nf, pl* **-ciones** : deliberation

deliberado, -da *adj* : deliberate, intentional — **deliberadamente** *adv*
deliberar *vi* : to deliberate
deliberativo, -va *adj* : deliberative
delicadeza *nf* **1** : delicacy, fineness **2** : gentleness, softness **3** : tact, discretion, consideration
delicado, -da *adj* **1** : delicate, fine **2** : sensitive, frail **3** : difficult, tricky **4** : fussy, hard to please **5** : tactful, considerate
delicia *nf* : delight
delicioso, -sa *adj* **1** RICO : delicious **2** : delightful
delictivo, -va *adj* : criminal
delictuoso, -sa → **delictivo**
delimitación *nf, pl* **-ciones** **1** : demarcation **2** : defining, specifying
delimitar *vt* **1** : to demarcate **2** : to define, to specify
delincuencia *nf* : delinquency, crime
delincuente¹ *adj* : delinquent
delincuente² *nmf* CRIMINAL : delinquent, criminal
delinear *vt* **1** : to delineate, to outline **2** : to draft, to draw up
delinquir {24} *vi* : to break the law
delirante *adj* : delirious
delirar *vi* **1** DESVARIAR : to be delirious **2** : to rave, to talk nonsense
delirio *nm* **1** DESVARÍO : delirium **2** DISPARATE : nonsense, ravings *pl* ‹delirios de grandeza : delusions of grandeur› **3** FRENESÍ : mania, frenzy ‹¡fue el delirio! : it was wild!›
delito *nm* : crime, offense
delta *nm* : delta
demacrado, -da *adj* : emaciated, gaunt
demagogia *nf* : demagogy
demagógico, -ca *adj* : demagogic, demagogical
demagogo, -ga *n* : demagogue
demanda *nf* **1** : demand ‹la oferta y la demanda : supply and demand› **2** : petition, request **3** : lawsuit
demandado, -da *n* : defendant
demandante *nmf* : plaintiff
demandar *vt* **1** : to demand **2** REQUERIR : to call for, to require **3** : to sue, to file a lawsuit against
demarcar {72} *vt* : to demarcate — **demarcación** *nf*
demás¹ *adj* : remaining ‹acabó las demás tareas : she finished the rest of the chores›
demás² *pron* **1 lo (la, los, las) demás** : the rest, everyone else, everything else ‹Pepe, Rosa, y los demás : Pepe, Rosa, and everybody else› **2 estar por demás** : to be of no use, to be pointless ‹no estaría por demás : it couldn't hurt, it's worth a try› **3 por demás** : extremely **4 por lo demás** : otherwise **5 y demás** : and so on, et cetera
demasía *nf* **en ~** : excessively, in excess
demasiado¹ *adv* **1** : too ‹vas demasiado aprisa : you're going too fast› **2** : too much ‹estoy comiendo demasiado : I'm eating too much›
demasiado², -da *adj* : too much, too many, excessive
demencia *nf* **1** : dementia **2** LOCURA : madness, insanity
demente¹ *adj* : insane, mad
demente² *nmf* : insane person
demeritar *vt* **1** : to detract from **2** : to discredit
demérito *nm* **1** : fault **2** : discredit, disrepute
democracia *nf* : democracy
demócrata¹ *adj* : democratic
demócrata² *nmf* : democrat
democrático, -ca *adj* : democratic — **democráticamente** *adv*
democratizar {21} *vt* : to democratize, to make democratic
demografía *nf* : demography
demográfico, -ca *adj* : demographic
demoledor, -dora *adj* : devastating
demoler {47} *vt* DERRIBAR, DERRUMBAR : to demolish, to destroy
demolición *nf, pl* **-ciones** : demolition
demonio *nm* DIABLO : devil, demon
demora *nf* : delay
demorar *vt* **1** RETRASAR : to delay **2** TARDAR : to take, to last ‹la reparación demorará varios días : the repair will take several days› — *vi* : to delay, to linger — **demorarse** *vr* **1** : to be slow, to take a long time **2** : to take too long
demostración *nf, pl* **-ciones** : demonstration
demostrar {19} *vt* : to demonstrate, to show
demostrativo, -va *adj* : demonstrative
demudar *vt* : to change, to alter — **demudarse** *vr* : to change one's expression
denegación *nf, pl* **-ciones** : denial, refusal
denegar {49} *vt* : to deny, to turn down
denigrante *adj* : degrading, humiliating
denigrar *vt* **1** DIFAMAR : to denigrate, to disparage **2** : to degrade, to humiliate
denodado, -da *adj* : bold, dauntless
denominación *nf, pl* **-ciones** **1** : name, designation **2** : denomination (of money)
denominador *nm* : denominator
denominar *vt* : to designate, to name
denostar {19} *vt* : to revile
denotar *vt* : to denote, to show
densidad *nf* : density, thickness
denso, -sa *adj* : dense, thick — **densamente** *adv*
dentado, -da *adj* SERRADO : serrated, jagged
dentadura *nf* **1** : teeth *pl* **2 dentadura postiza** : dentures *pl*
dental *adj* : dental
dentellada *nf* **1** : bite **2** : tooth mark
dentera *nf* **1** : envy, jealousy **2 dar dentera** : to set one's teeth on edge
dentición *nf, pl* **-ciones** **1** : teething **2** : dentition, set of teeth

dentífrico *nm* : toothpaste
dentista *nmf* : dentist
dentro *adv* **1** : in, inside **2** : indoors **3** **~ de** : within, inside, in **4** **dentro de poco** : soon, shortly **5** **dentro de todo** : all in all, all things considered **6** **por ~** : inwardly, inside
denuedo *nm* : valor, courage
denuesto *nm* : insult
denuncia *nf* **1** : denunciation, condemnation **2** : police report
denunciante *nmf* : accuser (of a crime)
denunciar *vt* **1** : to denounce, to condemn **2** : to report (to the authorities)
deparar *vt* : to have in store for, to provide with ⟨no sabemos lo que nos depara el destino : we don't know what fate has in store for us⟩
departamental *adj* **1** : departmental **2** **tienda departamental** *Mex* : department store
departamento *nm* **1** : department **2** APARTAMENTO : apartment
departir *vi* : to converse
dependencia *nf* **1** : dependence, dependency ⟨dependencia emocional : emotional dependence⟩ ⟨dependencia del alcohol : dependence on alcohol⟩ **2** : agency, branch office
depender *vi* **1** : to depend **2** **~ de** : to depend on **3** **~ de** : to be subordinate to
dependiente[1] *adj* : dependent
dependiente[2], **-ta** *n* : clerk, salesperson
deplorable *adj* : deplorable
deplorar *vt* **1** : to deplore **2** LAMENTAR : to regret
deponer {60} *vt* **1** : to depose, to overthrow **2** : to abandon (an attitude or stance) **3** **deponer las armas** : to lay down one's arms — *vi* **1** TESTIFICAR : to testify, to make a statement **2** EVACUAR : to defecate
deportación *nf, pl* **-ciones** : deportation
deportar *vt* : to deport
deporte *nm* : sport, sports *pl* ⟨hacer deporte : to engage in sports⟩
deportista[1] *adj* **1** : fond of sports **2** : sporty
deportista[2] *nmf* **1** : sports fan **2** : athlete, sportsman *m*, sportswoman *f*
deportividad *nf Spain* : sportsmanship
deportivo, -va *adj* **1** : sports, sporting ⟨artículos deportivos : sporting goods⟩ **2** : sporty
deposición *nf, pl* **-ciones** **1** : statement, testimony **2** : removal from office
depositante *nmf* : depositor
depositar *vt* **1** : to deposit, to place **2** : to store — **depositarse** *vr* : to settle
depósito *nm* **1** : deposit **2** : warehouse, storehouse
depravación *nf, pl* **-ciones** : depravity
depravado, -da *adj* DEGENERADO : depraved, degenerate
depravar *vt* : to deprave, to corrupt
depreciación *nf, pl* **-ciones** : depreciation
depreciar *vt* : to depreciate, to reduce the value of — **depreciarse** *vr* : to lose value
depredación *nf* SAQUEO : depredation, plunder
depredador[1], **-dora** *adj* : predatory
depredador[2] *nm* **1** : predator **2** SAQUEADOR : plunderer
depresión *nf, pl* **-siones** **1** : depression **2** : hollow, recess **3** : drop, fall **4** : slump, recession
depresivo[1], **-va** *adj* **1** : depressive **2** : depressant
depresivo[2] *nm* : depressant
deprimente *adj* : depressing
deprimir *vt* **1** : to depress **2** : to lower — **deprimirse** *vr* ABATIRSE : to get depressed
depuesto *pp* → **deponer**
depuración *nf, pl* **-ciones** **1** PURIFICACIÓN : purification **2** PURGA : purge **3** : refinement, polish
depurar *vt* **1** PURIFICAR : to purify **2** PURGAR : to purge
depuso, etc. → **deponer**
derecha *nf* **1** : right **2** : right hand, right side **3** : right wing, right (in politics)
derechazo *nm* **1** : pass with the cape on the right hand (in bullfighting) **2** : right (in boxing) **3** : forehand (in tennis)
derechista[1] *adj* : rightist, right-wing
derechista[2] *nmf* : right-winger
derecho[1] *adv* **1** : straight **2** : upright **3** : directly
derecho[2], **-cha** *adj* **1** : right **2** : right-hand **3** RECTO : straight, upright, erect
derecho[3] *nm* **1** : right ⟨derechos humanos : human rights⟩ **2** : law ⟨derecho civil : civil law⟩ **3** : right side (of cloth or clothing)
deriva *nf* **1** : drift **2** **a la deriva** : adrift
derivación *nf, pl* **-ciones** **1** : derivation **2** RAMIFICACIÓN : ramification, consequence
derivar *vi* **1** : to drift **2** **~ de** : to come from, to derive from **3** **~ en** : to result in — *vt* : to steer, to direct ⟨derivó la discusión hacia la política : he steered the discussion over to politics⟩ — **derivarse** *vr* : to be derived from, to arise from
dermatología *nf* : dermatology
dermatológico, -ca *adj* : dermatological
dermatólogo, -ga *n* : dermatologist
derogación *nf, pl* **-ciones** : abolition, repeal
derogar {52} *vt* ABOLIR : to abolish, to repeal
derramamiento *nm* **1** : spilling, overflowing **2** **derramamiento de sangre** : bloodshed
derramar *vt* **1** : to spill **2** : to shed (tears, blood) — **derramarse** *vr* **1** : to spill over **2** : to scatter
derrame *nm* **1** : spilling, shedding **2** : leakage, overflow **3** : discharge, hemorrhage
derrapar *vi* : to skid

derrape *nm* : skid
derredor *nm* **al derredor** *or* **en derredor** : around, round about
derrengado, -da *adj* **1** : bent, twisted **2** : exhausted
derretir {54} *vt* : to melt, to thaw — **derretirse** *vr* **1** : to melt, to thaw **2** ~ **por** *fam* : to be crazy about
derribar *vt* **1** DEMOLER, DERRUMBAR : to demolish, to knock down **2** : to shoot down, to bring down (an airplane) **3** DERROCAR : to overthrow
derribo *nm* **1** : demolition, razing **2** : shooting down **3** : overthrow
derrocamiento *nm* : overthrow
derrocar {72} *vt* DERRIBAR : to overthrow, to topple
derrochador[1], **-dora** *adj* : extravagant, wasteful
derrochador[2], **-dora** *n* : spendthrift
derrochar *vt* : to waste, to squander
derroche *nm* : extravagance, waste
derrota *nf* **1** : defeat, rout **2** : course (at sea)
derrotar *vt* : to defeat
derrotero *nm* RUTA : course
derrotista *adj & nmf* : defeatist
derruir {41} *vt* : to demolish, to tear down
derrumbamiento *nm* : collapse
derrumbar *vt* **1** DEMOLER, DERRIBAR : to demolish, to knock down **2** DESPEÑAR : to cast down, to topple — **derrumbarse** *vr* DESPLOMARSE : to collapse, to break down
derrumbe *nm* **1** DESPLOME : collapse, fall ⟨el derrumbe del comunismo : the fall of Communism⟩ **2** : landslide
desabastecimiento *nm* : shortage, scarcity
desabasto *nm Mex* : shortage, scarcity
desabrido, -da *adj* : tasteless, bland
desabrigar {52} *vt* **1** : to undress **2** : to uncover **3** : to deprive of shelter
desabrochar *vt* : to unbutton, to undo — **desabrocharse** *vr* : to come undone
desacatar *vt* **1** DESAFIAR : to defy **2** DESOBEDECER : to disobey
desacato *nm* **1** : disrespect **2** : contempt (of court)
desacelerar *vi* : to decelerate, to slow down
desacertado, -da *adj* **1** : mistaken **2** : unwise
desacertar {55} *vi* ERRAR : to err, to be mistaken
desacierto *nm* ERROR : error, mistake
desaconsejable *adj* : inadvisable
desaconsejado, -da *adj* : ill-advised, unwise
desacorde *adj* **1** : conflicting **2** : discordant
desacostumbrado, -da *adj* : unaccustomed, unusual
desacreditar *vt* DESPRESTIGIAR : to discredit, to disgrace
desactivar *vt* : to deactivate, to defuse
desacuerdo *nm* : disagreement
desafiante *adj* : defiant
desafiar {85} *vt* RETAR : to defy, to challenge
desafilado, -da *adj* : blunt
desafinado, -da *adj* : out-of-tune, off-key
desafinarse *vr* : to go out of tune
desafío *nm* **1** RETO : challenge **2** RESISTENCIA : defiance
desafortunado, -da *adj* : unfortunate, unlucky — **desafortunadamente** *adv*
desafuero *nm* ABUSO : injustice, outrage
desagradable *adj* : unpleasant, disagreeable — **desagradablemente** *adv*
desagradar *vi* : to be unpleasant, to be disagreeable
desagradecido, -da *adj* : ungrateful
desagrado *nm* **1** : displeasure **2 con** ~ : reluctantly
desagravio *nm* **1** : apology **2** : amends, reparation
desagregarse {52} *vr* : to break up, to disintegrate
desaguar {10} *vi* : to drain, to empty
desagüe *nm* **1** : drain **2** : drainage
desahogado, -da *adj* **1** : well-off, comfortable **2** : spacious, roomy
desahogar {52} *vt* **1** : to relieve, to ease **2** : to give vent to — **desahogarse** *vr* **1** : to recover, to feel better **2** : to unburden oneself, to let off steam
desahogo *nm* **1** : relief, outlet **2 con** ~ : comfortably
desahuciar *vt* **1** : to deprive of hope **2** : to evict — **desahuciarse** *vr* : to lose all hope
desahucio *nm* : eviction
desairar {5} *vt* : to snub, to rebuff
desaire *nm* : rebuff, snub, slight
desajustar *vt* **1** : to disarrange, to put out of order **2** : to upset (plans)
desajuste *nm* **1** : maladjustment **2** : imbalance **3** : upset, disruption
desalentador, -dora *adj* : discouraging, disheartening
desalentar {55} *vt* DESANIMAR : to discourage, to dishearten — **desalentarse** *vr*
desaliento *nm* : discouragement
desaliñado, -da *adj* : slovenly, untidy
desalmado, -da *adj* : heartless, callous
desalojar *vt* **1** : to remove, to clear **2** EVACUAR : to evacuate, to vacate **3** : to evict
desalojo *nm* **1** : removal, expulsion **2** : evacuation **3** : eviction
desamor *nm* **1** FRIALDAD : indifference **2** ENEMISTAD : dislike, enmity
desamparado, -da *adj* DESVALIDO : helpless, destitute
desamparar *vt* : to abandon, to forsake
desamparo *nm* **1** : abandonment, neglect **2** : helplessness
desamueblado, -da *adj* : unfurnished
desandar {6} *vt* : to go back, to return to the starting point
desangelado, -da *adj* : dull, lifeless
desangrar *vt* : to bleed, to bleed dry — **desangrarse** *vr* **1** : to be bleeding **2** : to bleed to death

desanimar *vt* DESALENTAR : to discourage, to dishearten — **desanimarse** *vr*
desánimo *nm* DESALIENTO : discouragement, dejection
desanudar *vt* : to untie, to disentangle
desapacible *adj* : unpleasant, disagreeable
desaparecer {53} *vt* : to cause to disappear — *vi* : to disappear, to vanish
desaparecido[1], **-da** *adj* **1** : late, deceased **2** : missing
desaparecido[2], **-da** *n* : missing person
desaparición *nf, pl* **-ciones** : disappearance
desapasionado, -da *adj* : dispassionate, impartial — **desapasionadamente** *adv*
desapego *nm* : coolness, indifference
desapercibido, -da *adj* **1** : unnoticed **2** DESPREVENIDO : unprepared, off guard
desaprobación *nf, pl* **-ciones** : disapproval
desaprobar {19} *vt* REPROBAR : to disapprove of
desaprovechar *vt* MALGASTAR : to waste, to misuse — *vi* : to lose ground, to slip back
desarmador *nm Mex* : screwdriver
desarmar *vt* **1** : to disarm **2** DESMONTAR : to disassemble, to take apart
desarme *nm* : disarmament
desarraigado, -da *adj* : rootless
desarraigar {52} *vt* : to uproot, to root out
desarreglado, -da *adj* : untidy, disorganized
desarreglar *vt* **1** : to mess up **2** : to upset, to disrupt
desarreglo *nm* **1** : untidiness **2** : disorder, confusion
desarrollar *vt* : to develop — **desarrollarse** *vr* : to take place
desarrollo *nm* : development
desarticulación *nf, pl* **-ciones** **1** : dislocation **2** : breaking up, dismantling
desarticular *vt* **1** DISLOCAR : to dislocate **2** : to break up, to dismantle
desaseado, -da *adj* **1** : dirty **2** : messy, untidy
desastre *nm* CATÁSTROFE : disaster
desastroso, -sa *adj* : disastrous, catastrophic
desatar *vt* **1** : to undo, to untie **2** : to unleash **3** : to trigger, to precipitate — **desatarse** *vr* : to break out, to erupt
desatascar {72} *vt* : to unblock, to clear
desatención *nf, pl* **-ciones** **1** : absentmindedness, distraction **2** : discourtesy
desatender {56} *vt* **1** : to disregard **2** : to neglect
desatento, -ta *adj* **1** DISTRAÍDO : absentminded **2** GROSERO : discourteous, rude
desatinado, -da *adj* : foolish, silly
desatino *nm* : folly, mistake
desautorizar {21} *vt* : to deprive of authority, to discredit
desavenencia *nf* DISCORDANCIA : disagreement, dispute
desayunar *vi* : to have breakfast — *vt* : to have for breakfast
desayuno *nm* : breakfast
desazón *nf, pl* **-zones** INQUIETUD : uneasiness, anxiety
desbalance *nm* : imbalance
desbancar {72} *vt* : to displace, to oust
desbandada *nf* : scattering, dispersal
desbarajuste *nm* DESORDEN : disarray, disorder, mess
desbaratar *vt* **1** ARRUINAR : to destroy, to ruin **2** DESCOMPONER : to break, to break down — **desbaratarse** *vr* : to fall apart
desbloquear *vt* **1** : to open up, to clear, to break through **2** : to free, to release
desbocado, -da *adj* : unbridled, rampant
desbocarse {72} *vr* : to run away, to bolt
desbordamiento *nm* : overflowing
desbordante *adj* : overflowing, bursting ⟨desbordante de energía : bursting with energy⟩
desbordar *vt* **1** : to overflow, to spill over **2** : to surpass, to exceed — **desbordarse** *vr*
descabellado, -da *adj* : outlandish, ridiculous
descafeinado, -da *adj* : decaffeinated
descalabrar *vt* : to hit on the head — **descalabrarse** *vr*
descalabro *nm* : setback, misfortune, loss
descalificación *nf, pl* **-ciones** **1** : disqualification **2** : disparaging remark
descalificar {72} *vt* **1** : to disqualify **2** DESACREDITAR : to discredit — **descalificarse** *vr*
descalzarse {21} *vr* : take off one's shoes
descalzo, -za *adj* : barefoot
descansado, -da *adj* **1** : rested, refreshed **2** : restful, peaceful
descansar *vi* : to rest, to relax — *vt* : to rest ⟨descansar la vista : to rest one's eyes⟩
descansillo *nm* : landing (of a staircase)
descanso *nm* **1** : rest, relaxation **2** : break **3** : landing (of a staircase) **4** : intermission
descapotable *adj & nm* : convertible
descarado, -da *adj* : brazen, impudent — **descaradamente** *adv*
descarga *nf* **1** : discharge **2** : unloading
descargar {52} *vt* **1** : to discharge **2** : to unload **3** : to release, to free **4** : to take out, to vent (anger, etc.) — **descargarse** *vr* **1** : to unburden oneself **2** : to quit **3** : to lose power
descargo *nm* **1** : unloading **2** : defense ⟨testigo de descargo : witness for the defense⟩
descarnado, -da *adj* : scrawny, gaunt
descaro *nm* : audacity, nerve

descarriado, -da *adj* : lost, gone astray
descarrilar *vi* : to derail — **descarrilarse** *vr*
descartar *vt* : to rule out, to reject — **descartarse** *vr* : to discard
descascarar *vt* : to peel, to shell, to husk — **descascararse** *vr* : to peel off, to chip
descendencia *nf* **1** : descendants *pl* **2** LINAJE : descent, lineage
descendente *adj* : downward, descending
descender {56} *vt* **1** : to descend, to go down **2** BAJAR : to lower, to take down, to let down — *vi* **1** : to descend, to come down **2** : to drop, to fall **3 ~ de** : to be a descendant of
descendiente *adj & nm* : descendant
descenso *nm* **1** : descent **2** BAJA, CAÍDA : drop, fall
descentralizar {21} *vt* : to decentralize — **descentralizarse** *vr* — **descentralización** *nf*
descifrable *adj* : decipherable
descifrar *vt* : to decipher, to decode
descodificar {72} *vt* : to decode
descolgar {16} *vt* **1** : to take down, to let down **2** : to pick up, to answer (the telephone)
descollar {19} *vi* SOBRESALIR : to stand out, to be outstanding, to excel
descolorarse *vr* : to fade
descolorido, -da *adj* : discolored, faded
descomponer {60} *vt* **1** : to rot, to decompose **2** DESBARATAR : to break, to break down — **descomponerse** *vr* **1** : to break down **2** : to decompose
descomposición *nf, pl* **-ciones** **1** : breakdown, decomposition **2** : decay
descompresión *nf* : decompression
descompuesto[1] *pp* → **descomponer**
descompuesto[2], **-ta** *adj* **1** : broken down, out of order **2** : rotten, decomposed
descomunal *adj* **1** ENORME : enormous, huge **2** EXTRAORDINARIO : extraordinary
desconcertante *adj* : disconcerting
desconcertar {55} *vt* : to disconcert — **desconcertarse** *vr*
desconchar *vt* : to chip — **desconcharse** *vr* : to chip off, to peel
desconcierto *nm* : uncertainty, confusion
desconectar *vt* **1** : to disconnect, to switch off **2** : to unplug
desconfiado, -da *adj* : distrustful, suspicious
desconfianza *nf* RECELO : distrust, suspicion
desconfiar {85} *vi* **~ de** : to distrust, to be suspicious of
descongelar *vt* **1** : to thaw **2** : to defrost **3** : to unfreeze (assets — **descongelarse** *vr*
descongestionante *adj & nm* : decongestant
desconocer {18} *vt* **1** IGNORAR : to be unaware of **2** : to fail to recognize
desconocido[1], **-da** *adj* : unknown, unfamiliar
desconocido[2], **-da** *n* EXTRAÑO : stranger
desconocimiento *nm* : ignorance
desconsiderado, -da *adj* : inconsiderate, thoughtless — **desconsideradamente** *adj*
desconsolado, -da *adj* : disconsolate, heartbroken
desconsuelo *nm* AFLICCIÓN : grief, distress, despair
descontaminar *vt* : to decontaminate — **descontaminación** *nf*
descontar {19} *vt* **1** : to discount, to deduct **2** EXCEPTUAR : to except, to exclude
descontento[1], **-ta** *adj* : discontented, dissatisfied
descontento[2] *nm* : discontent, dissatisfaction
descontrol *nm* : lack of control, disorder, chaos
descontrolarse *vr* : to get out of control, to be out of hand
descorazonado, -da *adj* : disheartened, discouraged
descorazonador, -dora *adj* : disheartening, discouraging
descorrer *vt* : to draw back
descortés *adj, pl* **-teses** : discourteous, rude
descortesía *nf* : discourtesy, rudeness
descrédito *nm* DESPRESTIGIO : discredit
descremado, -da *adj* : nonfat, skim
describir {33} *vt* : to describe
descripción *nf, pl* **-ciones** : description
descriptivo, -va *adj* : descriptive
descrito *pp* → **describir**
descuartizar {21} *vt* **1** : to cut up, to quarter **2** : to tear to pieces
descubierto[1] *pp* → **descubrir**
descubierto[2], **-ta** *adj* **1** : exposed, revealed **2 al descubierto** : out in the open
descubridor, -dora *n* : discoverer, explorer
descubrimiento *nm* : discovery
descubrir {2} *vt* **1** HALLAR : to discover, to find out **2** REVELAR : to uncover, to reveal — **descubrirse** *vr*
descuento *nm* REBAJA : discount
descuidado, -da *adj* **1** : neglectful, careless **2** : neglected, unkempt
descuidar *vt* : to neglect, to overlook — *vi* : to be careless — **descuidarse** *vr* **1** : to be careless, to drop one's guard **2** : to let oneself go
descuido *nm* **1** : carelessness, negligence **2** : slip, oversight
desde *prep* **1** : from **2** : since **3 desde ahora** : from now on **4 desde entonces** : since then **5 desde hace** : for, since (a time) ⟨ha estado nevando desde hace dos días : it's been snowing for

two days⟩ **6 desde luego** : of course **7 desde que** : since, ever since **8 desde ya** : right now, immediately
desdecir {11} *vi* **1 ~ de** : to be unworthy of **2 ~ de** : to clash with — **desdecirse** *vr* **1** CONTRADECIRSE : to contradict oneself **2** RETRACTARSE : to go back on one's word
desdén *nm, pl* **desdenes** DESPRECIO : disdain, scorn
desdentado, -da *adj* : toothless
desdeñar *vt* DESPRECIAR : to disdain, to scorn, to despise
desdeñoso, -sa *adj* : disdainful, scornful — **desdeñosamente** *adv*
desdibujar *vt* : to blur — **desdibujarse** *vr*
desdicha *nf* **1** : misery **2** : misfortune
desdichado¹, -da *adj* **1** : unfortunate **2** : miserable, unhappy
desdichado², -da *n* : wretch
desdicho *pp* → **desdecir**
desdiga, desdijo etc. → **desdecir**
desdoblar *vt* DESPLEGAR : to unfold
deseable *adj* : desirable
desear *vt* **1** : to wish ⟨te deseo buena suerte : I wish you good luck⟩ **2** QUERER : to want, to desire
desecar {72} *vt* : to dry (flowers, etc.)
desechable *adj* : disposable
desechar *vt* **1** : to discard, to throw away **2** RECHAZAR : to reject
desecho *nm* **1** : reject **2 desechos** *nmpl* RESIDUOS : rubbish, waste
desembarazarse {21} *vr* **~ de** : to get rid of
desembarcadero *nm* : jetty, landing pier
desembarcar {72} *vi* : to disembark — *vt* : to unload
desembarco *nm* **1** : landing, arrival **2** : unloading
desembarque → **desembarco**
desembocadura *nf* **1** : mouth (of a river) **2** : opening, end (of a street)
desembocar {72} *vi* **~ en** *or* **~ a 1** : to flow into, to join **2** : to lead to, to result in
desembolsar *vt* PAGAR : to disburse, to pay out
desembolso *nm* PAGO : disbursement, payment
desempacar {72} *v* : to unpack
desempate *nm* : tiebreaker, play-off
desempeñar *vt* **1** : to play (a role) **2** : to fulfill, to carry out **3** : to redeem (from a pawnshop) — **desempeñarse** *vr* : to function, to act
desempeño *nm* **1** : fulfillment, carrying out **2** : performance
desempleado¹, -da *adj* : unemployed
desempleado², -da *n* : unemployed person
desempleo *nm* : unemployment
desempolvar *vt* **1** : to dust off **2** : to resurrect, to revive
desencadenar *vt* **1** : to unchain **2** : to trigger, to unleash — **desencadenarse** *vr*
desencajar *vt* **1** : to dislocate **2** : to disconnect, to disengage
desencantar *vt* : to disenchant, to disillusion — **desencantarse** *vr*
desencanto *nm* : disenchantment, disillusionment
desenchufar *vt* : to disconnect, to unplug
desenfadado, -da *adj* **1** : uninhibited, carefree **2** : confident, self-assured
desenfado *nm* **1** DESENVOLTURA : self-assurance, confidence **2** : naturalness, ease
desenfrenadamente *adv* : wildly, with abandon
desenfrenado, -da *adj* : unbridled, unrestrained
desenfreno *nm* : abandon, unrestraint
desenganchar *vt* : to unhitch, to uncouple
desengañar *vt* : to disillusion, to disenchant — **desengañarse** *vr*
desengaño *nm* : disenchantment, disillusionment
desenlace *nm* : ending, outcome
desenlazar {21} *vt* **1** : to untie **2** : to clear up, to resolve
desenmarañar *vt* : to disentangle, to unravel
desenmascarar *vt* : to unmask, to expose
desenredar *vt* : to untangle, to disentangle
desenrollar *vt* : to unroll, to unwind
desentenderse {56} *vr* **1 ~ de** : to want nothing to do with, to be uninterested in **2 ~ de** : to pretend ignorance of
desenterrar {55} *vt* **1** EXHUMAR : to exhume **2** : to unearth, to dig up
desentonar *vi* **1** : to clash, to conflict **2** : to be out of tune, to sing off-key
desentrañar *vt* : to get to the bottom of, to unravel
desenvainar *vt* : to draw, to unsheathe (a sword)
desenvoltura *nf* **1** DESENFADO : confidence, self-assurance **2** ELOCUENCIA : eloquence, fluency
desenvolver {89} *vt* : to unwrap, to open — **desenvolverse** *vr* **1** : to unfold, to develop **2** : to manage, to cope
desenvuelto¹ *pp* → **desenvolver**
desenvuelto², -ta *adj* : confident, relaxed, self-assured
deseo *nm* : wish, desire
deseoso, -sa *adj* : eager, anxious
desequilibrar *vt* : to unbalance, to throw off balance — **desequilibrarse** *vr*
desequilibrio *nm* : imbalance
deserción *nf, pl* **-ciones** : desertion, defection
desertar *vi* **1** : to desert, to defect **2 ~ de** : to abandon, to neglect
desertor, -tora *n* : deserter, defector
desesperación *nf, pl* **-ciones** : desperation, despair

desesperado, -da *adj* : desperate, despairing, hopeless — **desesperadamente** *adv*
desesperanza *nf* : despair, hopelessness
desesperar *vt* : to exasperate — *vi* : to despair, to lose hope — **desesperarse** *vr* : to become exasperated
desestimar *vt* **1** : to reject, to disallow **2** : to have a low opinion of
desfachatez *nf, pl* **-teces** : audacity, nerve, cheek
desfalcador, -dora *n* : embezzler
desfalcar {72} *vt* : to embezzle
desfalco *nm* : embezzlement
desfallecer {53} *vi* **1** : to weaken **2** : to faint
desfallecimiento *nm* **1** : weakness **2** : fainting
desfasado, -da *adj* **1** : out of sync **2** : out of step, behind the times
desfase *nm* : gap, lag ⟨desfase horario : jet lag⟩
desfavorable *adj* : unfavorable, adverse — **desfavorablemente** *adv*
desfavorecido, -da *adj* : underprivileged
desfigurar *vt* **1** : to disfigure, to mar **2** : to distort, to misrepresent
desfiladero *nm* : narrow gorge, defile
desfilar *vi* : to parade, to march
desfile *nm* : parade, procession
desfogar {52} *vt* **1** : to vent **2** *Mex* : to unclog, to unblock — **desfogarse** *vr* : to vent one's feelings, to let off steam
desforestación *nf, pl* **-ciones** : deforestation
desgajar *vt* **1** : to tear off **2** : to break apart — **desgajarse** *vr* : to come apart
desgana *nf* **1** INAPETENCIA : lack of appetite **2** APATÍA : apathy, unwillingness, reluctance
desgano *nm* → **desgana**
desgarbado, -da *adj* : ungainly
desgarrador, -dora *adj* : heartrending, heartbreaking
desgarradura *nf* : tear, rip
desgarrar *vt* **1** : to tear, to rip **2** : to break (one's heart) — **desgarrarse** *vr*
desgarre → **desgarro**
desgarro *nm* : tear
desgarrón *nm, pl* **-rrones** : rip, tear
desgastar *vt* **1** : to use up **2** : to wear away, to wear down
desgaste *nm* : deterioration, wear and tear
desglosar *vt* : to break down, to itemize
desglose *nm* : breakdown, itemization
desgobierno *nm* : anarchy, disorder
desgracia *nf* **1** : misfortune **2** : disgrace **3 por ~** : unfortunately
desgraciadamente *adv* : unfortunately
desgraciado¹, -da *adj* **1** : unfortunate, unlucky **2** : vile, wretched
desgraciado², -da *n* : unfortunate person, wretch
desgranar *vt* : to shuck, to shell
deshabitado, -da *adj* : unoccupied, uninhabited
deshacer {40} *vt* **1** : to destroy, to ruin **2** DESATAR : to undo, to untie **3** : to break apart, to crumble **4** : to dissolve, to melt **5** : to break, to cancel — **deshacerse** *vr* **1** : to fall apart, to come undone **2 ~ de** : to get rid of
deshecho¹ *pp* → **deshacer**
deshecho², -cha *adj* **1** : destroyed, ruined **2** : devastated, shattered **3** : undone, untied
desheredado, -da *adj* MARGINADO : dispossessed, destitute
desheredar *vt* : to disinherit
deshicieron, etc. → **deshacer**
deshidratar *vt* : to dehydrate — **deshidratación** *nf*
deshielo *nm* : thaw, thawing
deshilachar *vt* : to fray — **deshilacharse** *vr*
deshizo → **deshacer**
deshonestidad *nf* : dishonesty
deshonesto, -ta *adj* : dishonest
deshonra *nf* : dishonor, disgrace
deshonrar *vt* : to dishonor, to disgrace
deshonroso, -sa *adj* : dishonorable, disgraceful
deshuesar *vt* **1** : to pit (a fruit, etc.) **2** : to bone, to debone
deshumanizar {21} *vt* : to dehumanize — **deshumanización** *nf*
desidia *nf* **1** APATÍA : apathy, indolence **2** NEGLIGENCIA : negligence, sloppiness
desierto¹, -ta *adj* : deserted, uninhabited
desierto² *nm* : desert
designación *nf, pl* **-ciones** NOMBRAMIENTO : appointment, naming (to an office, etc.)
designar *vt* NOMBRAR : to designate, to appoint, to name
designio *nm* : plan
desigual *adj* **1** : unequal **2** DISPAREJO : uneven
desigualdad *nf* **1** : inequality **2** : unevenness
desilusión *nf, pl* **-siones** DESENCANTO, DESENGAÑO : disillusionment, disenchantment
desilusionar *vt* DESENCANTAR, DESENGAÑAR : to disillusion, to disenchant — **desilusionarse** *vr*
desinfectante *adj & nm* : disinfectant
desinfectar *vt* : to disinfect — **desinfección** *nf*
desinflar *vt* : to deflate — **desinflarse** *vr*
desinhibido, -da *adj* : uninhibited, unrestrained
desintegración *nf, pl* **-ciones** : disintegration
desintegrar *vt* : to disintegrate, to break up — **desintegrarse** *vr*
desinterés *nm* **1** : lack of interest, indifference **2** : unselfishness
desinteresado, -da *adj* GENEROSO : unselfish
desintoxicar {72} *vt* : to detoxify, to detox

desistir *vi* **1** : to desist, to stop **2 ~ de** : to give up, to relinquish
deslave *nm Mex* : landslide
desleal *adj* INFIEL : disloyal — **deslealmente** *adv*
deslealtad *nf* : disloyalty
desleír {66} *vt* : to dilute, to dissolve
desligar {52} *vt* **1** : to separate, to undo **2** : to free (from an obligation) — **desligarse** *vr* **~ de** : to extricate oneself from
deslindar *vt* **1** : to mark the limits of, to demarcate **2** : to define, to clarify
deslinde *nm* : demarcation
desliz *nm, pl* **deslices** : error, mistake, slip ⟨desliz de la lengua : slip of the tongue⟩
deslizar {21} *vt* **1** : to slide, to slip **2** : to slip in — **deslizarse** *vr* **1** : to slide, to glide **2** : to slip away
deslucido, -da *adj* **1** : unimpressive, dull **2** : faded, dingy, tarnished
deslucir {45} *vt* **1** : to spoil **2** : to fade, to dull, to tarnish **3** : to discredit
deslumbrar *vt* : to dazzle — **deslumbrante** *adj*
deslustrado, -da *adj* : dull, lusterless
deslustrar *vt* : to tarnish, to dull
deslustre *nm* : tarnish
desmán *nm, pl* **desmanes** **1** : outrage, abuse **2** : misfortune
desmandarse *vr* : to behave badly, to get out of hand
desmantelar *vt* DESMONTAR : to dismantle
desmañado, -da *adj* : clumsy, awkward
desmayado, -da *adj* **1** : fainting, weak **2** : dull, pale
desmayar *vi* : to lose heart, to falter — **desmayarse** *vr* DESVANECERSE : to faint, to swoon
desmayo *nm* **1** : faint, fainting **2 sufrir un desmayo** : to faint
desmedido, -da *adj* DESMESURADO : excessive, undue
desmejorar *vt* : to weaken, to make worse — *vi* : to decline (in health), to get worse
desmembramiento *nm* : dismemberment
desmembrar {55} *vt* **1** : to dismember **2** : to break up
desmemoriado, -da *adj* : absentminded, forgetful
desmentido *nm* : denial
desmentir {76} *vt* **1** NEGAR : to deny, to refute **2** CONTRADECIR : to contradict
desmenuzar {21} *vt* **1** : to break down, to scrutinize **2** : to crumble, to shred — **desmenuzarse** *vr*
desmerecer {53} *vt* : to be unworthy of — *vi* **1** : to decline in value **2 ~ de** : to compare unfavorably with
desmesurado, -da *adj* DESMEDIDO : excessive, inordinate — **desmesuradamente** *adv*
desmigajar *vt* : to crumble — **desmigajarse** *vr*
desmilitarizado, -da *adj* : demilitarized
desmontar *vt* **1** : to clear, to level off **2** DESMANTELAR : to dismantle, to take apart — *vi* : to dismount
desmonte *nm* : clearing, leveling
desmoralizador, -dora *adj* : demoralizing
desmoralizar {21} *vt* DESALENTAR : to demoralize, to discourage
desmoronamiento *nm* : crumbling, falling apart
desmoronar *vt* : to wear away, to erode — **desmoronarse** *vr* : to crumble, to deteriorate, to fall apart
desmotadora *nf* : gin, cotton gin
desmovilizar {21} *vt* : to demobilize — **desmovilización** *nf*
desnaturalizar {21} *vt* **1** : to denature **2** : to distort, to alter
desnivel *nm* **1** : disparity, difference **2** : unevenness (of a surface)
desnivelado, -da *adj* **1** : uneven **2** : unbalanced
desnudar *vt* **1** : to undress **2** : to strip, to lay bare — **desnudarse** *vr* : to undress, to strip off one's clothing
desnudez *nf, pl* **-deces** : nudity, nakedness
desnudismo → **nudismo**
desnudista → **nudista**
desnudo[1], **-da** *adj* : nude, naked, bare
desnudo[2] *nm* : nude
desnutrición *nf, pl* **-ciones** MALNUTRICIÓN : malnutrition, undernourishment
desnutrido, -da *adj* MALNUTRIDO : malnourished, undernourished
desobedecer {53} *v* : to disobey
desobediencia *nf* : disobedience — **desobediente** *adj*
desocupación *nf, pl* **-ciones** : unemployment
desocupado, -da *adj* **1** : vacant, empty **2** : free, unoccupied **3** : unemployed
desocupar *vt* **1** : to empty **2** : to vacate, to move out of — **desocuparse** *vr* : to leave, to quit (a job)
desodorante *adj & nm* : deodorant
desolación *nf, pl* **-ciones** : desolation
desolado, -da *adj* **1** : desolate **2** : devastated, distressed
desolador, -dora *adj* **1** : devastating **2** : bleak, desolate
desollar *vt* : to skin, to flay
desorbitado, -da *adj* **1** : excessive, exorbitant **2 con los ojos desorbitados** : with eyes popping out of one's head
desorden *nm, pl* **desórdenes** **1** DESBARAJUSTE : disorder, mess **2** : disorder, disturbance, upset
desordenado, -da *adj* **1** : untidy, messy **2** : disorderly, unruly
desordenar *vt* : to mess up — **desordenarse** *vr* : to get messed up
desorganización *nf, pl* **-ciones** : disorganization
desorganizar {21} *vt* : to disrupt, to disorganize

desorientación *nf, pl* **-ciones** : disorientation, confusion
desorientar *vt* : to disorient, to mislead, to confuse — **desorientarse** *vr* : to become disoriented, to lose one's way
desovar *vi* : to spawn
despachar *vt* **1** : to complete, to conclude **2** : to deal with, to take care of, to handle **3** : to dispatch, to send off **4** *fam* : to finish off, to kill — **despacharse** *vr fam* : to gulp down, to polish off
despacho *nm* **1** : dispatch, shipment **2** OFICINA : office, study
despacio *adv* LENTAMENTE, LENTO : slowly, slow ⟨¡despacio! : take it easy!, easy does it!⟩
desparasitar *vt* : to worm (an animal), to delouse
desparpajo *nm fam* **1** : self-confidence, nerve **2** *CA* : confusion, muddle
desparramar *vt* **1** : to spill, to splatter **2** : to spread, to scatter
despatarrarse *vr* : to sprawl (out)
despavorido, -da *adj* : terrified, horrified
despecho *nm* **1** : spite **2 a despecho de** : despite, in spite of
despectivo, -va *adj* **1** : contemptuous, disparaging **2** : derogatory, pejorative
despedazar {21} *vt* : to cut to pieces, to tear apart
despedida *nf* **1** : farewell, good-bye **2 despedida de soltera** : bridal shower
despedir {54} *vt* **1** : to see off, to show out **2** : to dismiss, to fire **3** EMITIR : to give off, to emit ⟨despedir un olor : to give off an odor⟩ — **despedirse** *vr* : to take one's leave, to say good-bye
despegado, -da *adj* **1** : separated, detached **2** : cold, distant
despegar {52} *vt* : to remove, to detach — *vi* : to take off, to lift off, to blast off
despegue *nm* : takeoff, liftoff
despeinado, -da *adj* : disheveled, tousled ⟨estoy despeinada : my hair's a mess⟩
despeinarse *vr* **1** : to mess up one's hair **2** : to become disheveled ⟨me despeiné : my hair got messed up⟩
despejado, -da *adj* **1** : clear, fair **2** : alert, clear-headed **3** : uncluttered, unobstructed
despejar *vt* **1** : to clear, to free **2** : to clarify — *vi* **1** : to clear up **2** : to punt (in sports)
despeje *nm* **1** : clearing **2** : punt (in sports)
despellejar *vt* : to skin (an animal)
despenalizar {21} *vt* : to legalize — **despenalización** *nf*
despensa *nf* **1** : pantry, larder **2** PROVISIONES : provisions *pl,* supplies *pl*
despeñar *vt* : to hurl down
despepitar *vt* : to seed, to remove the seeds from
desperdiciar *vt* **1** DESAPROVECHAR, MALGASTAR : to waste **2** : to miss, to miss out on
desperdicio *nm* **1** : waste **2 desperdicios** *nmpl* RESIDUOS : refuse, scraps, rubbish
desperdigar {52} *vt* DISPERSAR : to disperse, to scatter
desperfecto *nm* **1** DEFECTO : flaw, defect **2** : damage
despertador *nm* : alarm clock
despertar {55} *vi* : to awaken, to wake up — *vt* **1** : to arouse, to wake **2** EVOCAR : to elicit, to evoke — **despertarse** *vr* : to wake (oneself) up
despiadado, -da *adj* CRUEL : cruel, merciless, pitiless — **despiadadamente** *adv*
despido *nm* : dismissal, layoff
despierto, -ta *adj* **1** : awake, alert **2** LISTO : clever, sharp ⟨con la mente despierta : with a sharp mind⟩
despilfarrador¹, -dora *adj* : extravagant, wasteful
despilfarrador², -dora *n* : spendthrift, prodigal
despilfarrar *vt* MALGASTAR : to squander, to waste
despilfarro *nm* : extravagance, wastefulness
despintar *vt* : to strip the paint from — **despintarse** *vr* : to fade, to wash off, to peel off
despistado¹, -da *adj* **1** DISTRAÍDO : absentminded, forgetful **2** CONFUSO : confused, bewildered
despistado², -da *n* : scatterbrain, absentminded person
despistar *vt* : to throw off the track, to confuse — **despistarse** *vr*
despiste *nm* **1** : absentmindedness **2** : mistake, slip
desplantador *nm* : garden trowel
desplante *nm* : insolence, rudeness
desplazamiento *nm* **1** : movement, displacement **2** : journey
desplazar {21} *vt* **1** : to replace, to displace **2** TRASLADAR : to move, to shift
desplegar {49} *vt* **1** : to display, to show, to manifest **2** DESDOBLAR : to unfold, to unfurl **3** : to spread (out) **4** : to deploy
despliegue *nm* **1** : display **2** : deployment
desplomarse *vr* **1** : to plummet, to fall **2** DERRUMBARSE : to collapse, to break down
desplome *nm* **1** : fall, drop **2** : collapse
desplumar *vt* : to pluck (a chicken, etc.)
despoblado¹, -da *adj* : uninhabited, deserted
despoblado² *nm* : open country, deserted area
despoblar {19} *vt* : to depopulate
despojar *vt* **1** : to strip, to clear **2** : to divest, to deprive — **despojarse** *vr* **1 ~ de** : to remove (clothing) **2 ~ de** : to relinquish, to renounce

despojos *nmpl* **1** : remains, scraps **2** : plunder, spoils
desportilladura *nf* : chip, nick
desportillar *vt* : to chip — **desportillarse** *vr*
desposeer {20} *vt* : to dispossess
déspota *nmf* : despot, tyrant
despotismo *nm* : despotism — **despótico, -ca** *adj*
despotricar {72} *vi* : to rant and rave, to complain excessively
despreciable *adj* **1** : despicable, contemptible **2** : negligible ‹nada despreciable : not inconsiderable, significant›
despreciar *vt* DESDEÑAR, MENOSPRECIAR : to despise, to scorn, to disdain
despreciativo, -va *adj* : scornful, disdainful
desprecio *nm* DESDÉN, MENOSPRECIO : disdain, contempt, scorn
desprender *vt* **1** SOLTAR : to detach, to loosen, to unfasten **2** EMITIR : to emit, to give off — **desprenderse** *vr* **1** : to come off, to come undone **2** : to be inferred, to follow **3** ~ **de** : to part with, to get rid of
desprendido, -da *adj* : generous, unselfish, disinterested
desprendimiento *nm* **1** : detachment **2** GENEROSIDAD : generosity **3 desprendimiento de tierras** : landslide
despreocupación *nf, pl* **-ciones** : indifference, lack of concern
despreocupado, -da *adj* : carefree, easygoing, unconcerned
desprestigiar *vt* DESACREDITAR : to discredit, to disgrace — **desprestigiarse** *vr* : to lose prestige
desprestigio *nm* DESCRÉDITO : discredit, disrepute
desprevenido, -da *adj* DESAPERCIBIDO : unprepared, off guard, unsuspecting
desproporción *nf, pl* **-ciones** : disproportion, disparity
desproporcionado, -da : out of proportion
despropósito *nm* : piece of nonsense, absurdity
desprotegido, -da *adj* : unprotected, vulnerable
desprovisto, -ta *adj* ~ **de** : devoid of, lacking in
después *adv* **1** : afterward, later **2** : then, next **3** ~ **de** : after, next after ‹después de comer : after eating› **4 después (de) que** : after ‹después que lo acabé : after I finished it› **5 después de todo** : after all **6 poco después** : shortly after, soon thereafter
despuntado, -da *adj* : blunt, dull
despuntar *vt* : to blunt — *vi* **1** : to dawn **2** : to sprout **3** : to excel, to stand out
desquiciar *vt* **1** : to unhinge (a door) **2** : to drive crazy — **desquiciarse** *vr* : to go crazy
desquitarse *vr* **1** : to get even, to retaliate **2** ~ **con** : to take it out on
desquite *nm* : revenge
desregulación *nf, pl* **-ciones** : deregulation
desregular *vt* : to deregulate
desregularización *nf* → **desregulación**
destacadamente *adv* : outstandingly, prominently
destacado, -da *adj* **1** : outstanding, prominent **2** : stationed, posted
destacamento *nm* : detachment (of troops)
destacar {72} *vt* **1** ENFATIZAR, SUBRAYAR : to emphasize, to highlight, to stress **2** : to station, to post — *vi* : to stand out
destajo *nm* **1** : piecework **2 a** ~ : by the item, by the job
destapador *nm* : bottle opener
destapar *vt* **1** : to open, to take the top off **2** DESCUBRIR : to reveal, to uncover **3** : to unblock, to unclog
destape *nm* : uncovering, revealing
destartalado, -da *adj* : dilapidated, tumbledown
destellar *vi* **1** : to sparkle, to flash, to glint **2** : to twinkle
destello *nm* **1** : flash, sparkle, twinkle **2** : glimmer, hint
destemplado, -da *adj* **1** : out of tune **2** : irritable, out of sorts **3** : unpleasant (of weather)
desteñir {67} *vi* : to run, to fade — **desteñirse** *vr* DESCOLORARSE : to fade
desterrado[1], **-da** *adj* : banished, exiled
desterrado[2], **-da** *n* : exile
desterrar {55} *vt* **1** EXILIAR : to banish, to exile **2** ERRADICAR : to eradicate, to do away with
destetar *vt* : to wean
destiempo *adv* **a** ~ : at the wrong time
destierro *nm* EXILIO : exile
destilación *nf, pl* **-ciones** : distillation
destilador, -dora *n* : distiller
destilar *vt* **1** : to exude **2** : to distill
destilería *nf* : distillery
destinación *nf, pl* **-ciones** DESTINO : destination
destinado, -da *adj* : destined, bound
destinar *vt* **1** : to appoint, to assign **2** ASIGNAR : to earmark, to allot
destinatario, -ria *n* **1** : addressee **2** : payee
destino *nm* **1** : destiny, fate **2** DESTINACIÓN : destination **3** : use **4** : assignment, post
destitución *nf, pl* **-ciones** : dismissal, removal from office
destituir {41} *vt* : to dismiss, to remove from office
destorcer {14} *vt* : to untwist
destornillador *nm* : screwdriver
destornillar *vt* : to unscrew
destrabar *vt* **1** : to untie, to undo, to ease up **2** : to separate
destreza *nf* HABILIDAD : dexterity, skill
destronar *vt* : to depose, to dethrone
destrozado, -da *adj* **1** : ruined, destroyed **2** : devastated, brokenhearted

destrozar {21} *vt* **1** : to smash, to shatter **2** : to destroy, to wreck — **destrozarse** *vr*
destrozo *nm* **1** DAÑO : damage **2** : havoc, destruction
destrucción *nf, pl* **-ciones** : destruction
destructivo, -va *adj* : destructive
destructor[1], **-tora** *adj* : destructive
destructor[2] *nm* : destroyer (ship)
destruir {41} *vt* : to destroy — **destruirse** *vr*
desubicado, -da *adj* **1** : out of place **2** : confused, disoriented
desunión *nf, pl* **-niones** : disunity
desunir *vt* : to split, to divide
desusado, -da *adj* **1** INSÓLITO : unusual **2** OBSOLETO : obsolete, disused, antiquated
desuso *nm* : disuse, obsolescence ⟨caer en desuso : to fall into disuse⟩
desvaído, -da *adj* **1** : pale, washed-out **2** : vague, blurred
desvainar *vt* : to shell
desvalido, -da *adj* DESAMPARADO : destitute, helpless
desvalijar *vt* **1** : to ransack **2** : to rob
desvalorización *nf, pl* **-ciones** **1** DEVALUACIÓN : devaluation **2** : depreciation
desvalorizar {21} *vt* : to devalue
desván *nm, pl* **desvanes** ÁTICO, BUHARDILLA : attic
desvanecer {53} *vt* **1** DISIPAR : to make disappear, to dispel **2** : to fade, to blur — **desvanecerse** *vr* **1** : to vanish, to disappear **2** : to fade **3** DESMAYARSE : to faint, to swoon
desvanecimiento *nm* **1** : disappearance **2** DESMAYO : faint **3** : fading
desvariar {85} *vi* **1** DELIRAR : to be delirious **2** : to rave, to talk nonsense
desvarío *nm* DELIRIO : delirium
desvelado, -da *adj* : sleepless
desvelar *vt* **1** : to keep awake **2** REVELAR : to reveal, to disclose — **desvelarse** *vr* **1** : to stay awake **2** : to do one's utmost
desvelo *nm* **1** : sleeplessness **2 desvelos** *nmpl* : efforts, pains
desvencijado, -da *adj* : dilapidated, rickety
desventaja *nf* : disadvantage, drawback
desventajoso, -sa *adj* : disadvantageous, unfavorable
desventura *nf* INFORTUNIO : misfortune
desventurado, -da *adj* : unfortunate, ill-fated
desvergonzado, -da *adj* : shameless, impudent
desvergüenza *nf* : shamelessness, impudence
desvestir {54} *vt* : to undress — **desvestirse** *vr* : to get undressed
desviación *nf, pl* **-ciones** **1** : deviation, departure **2** : detour, diversion
desviar {85} *vt* **1** : to change the course of, to divert **2** : to turn away, to deflect — **desviarse** *vr* **1** : to branch off **2** APARTARSE : to stray
desvinculación *nf, pl* **-ciones** : dissociation
desvincular *vt* **~ de** : to separate from, to dissociate from — **desvincularse** *vr*
desvío *nm* **1** : diversion, detour **2** : deviation
desvirtuar {3} *vt* **1** : to impair, to spoil **2** : to detract from **3** : to distort, to misrepresent
detalladamente *adv* : in detail, at great length
detallar *vt* : to detail
detalle *nm* **1** : detail **2 al detalle** : retail
detallista[1] *adj* **1** : meticulous **2** : retail
detallista[2] *nmf* **1** : perfectionist **2** : retailer
detección *nf, pl* **-ciones** : detection
detectar *vt* : to detect — **detectable** *adj*
detective *nmf* : detective
detector *nm* : detector ⟨detector de mentiras : lie detector⟩
detención *nf, pl* **-ciones** **1** ARRESTO : detention, arrest **2** : stop, halt **3** : delay, holdup
detener {80} *vt* **1** ARRESTAR : to arrest, to detain **2** PARAR : to stop, to halt **3** : to keep, to hold back — **detenerse** *vr* **1** : to stop **2** : to delay, to linger
detenidamente *adv* : thoroughly, at length
detenimiento *nm* **con ~** : carefully, in detail
detentar *vt* : to hold, to retain
detergente *nm* : detergent
deteriorado, -da *adj* : damaged, worn
deteriorar *vt* ESTROPEAR : to damage, to spoil — **deteriorarse** *vr* **1** : to get damaged, to wear out **2** : to deteriorate, to worsen
deterioro *nm* **1** : deterioration, wear **2** : worsening, decline
determinación *nf, pl* **-ciones** **1** : determination, resolve **2 tomar una determinación** : to make a decision
determinado, -da *adj* **1** : certain, particular **2** : determined, resolute
determinante[1] *adj* : determining, deciding
determinante[2] *nm* : determinant
determinar *vt* **1** : to determine **2** : to cause, to bring about — **determinarse** *vr* : to make up one's mind, to decide
detestar *vt* : to detest — **detestable** *adj*
detonación *nf, pl* **-ciones** : detonation
detonador *nm* : detonator
detonante[1] *adj* : detonating, explosive
detonante[2] *nm* **1** → **detonador** **2** : catalyst, cause
detonar *vi* : to detonate, to explode
detractor, -tora *n* : detractor, critic
detrás *adv* **1** : behind **2 ~ de** : in back of **3 por ~** : from behind
detrimento *nm* : detriment ⟨en detrimento de : to the detriment of⟩
detuvo, etc. → **detener**

deuda *nf* **1** DÉBITO : debt **2 en deuda con** : indebted to
deudo, -da *n* : relative
deudor¹, -dora *adj* : indebted
deudor², -dora *n* : debtor
devaluación *nf, pl* **-ciones** DESVALORIZACIÓN : devaluation
devaluar {3} *vt* : to devalue — **devaluarse** *vr* : to depreciate
devanarse *vr* **devanarse los sesos** : to rack one's brains
devaneo *nm* **1** : flirtation, fling **2** : idle pursuit
devastador, -dora *adj* : devastating
devastar *vt* : to devastate — **devastación** *nf*
devenir {87} *vi* **1** : to come about **2 ~ en** : to become, to turn into
devoción *nf, pl* **-ciones** : devotion
devolución *nf, pl* **-ciones** REEMBOLSO : return, refund
devolver {89} *vt* **1** : to return, to give back **2** REEMBOLSAR : to refund, to pay back **3** : to vomit, to bring up — *vi* : to vomit, to throw up — **devolverse** *vr* : to return, to come back, to go back
devorar *vt* **1** : to devour **2** : to consume
devoto¹, -ta *adj* : devout — **devotamente** *adv*
devoto², -ta *n* : devotee, admirer
di → **dar, decir**
día *nm* **1** : day ⟨todos los días : every day⟩ **2** : daytime, daylight ⟨de día : by day, in the daytime⟩ ⟨en pleno día : in broad daylight⟩ **3 al día** : up-to-date **4 en su día** : in due time
diabetes *nf* : diabetes
diabético, -ca *adj & n* : diabetic
diablillo *nm* : little devil, imp
diablo *nm* DEMONIO : devil
diablura *nf* **1** : prank **2 diabluras** *nfpl* : mischief
diabólico, -ca *adj* : diabolical, diabolic, devilish
diaconisa *nf* : deaconess
diácono *nm* : deacon
diacrítico, -ca *adj* : diacritic, diacritical
diadema *nf* : diadem, crown
diáfano, -na *adj* : diaphanous
diafragma *nm* : diaphragm
diagnosticar {72} *vt* : to diagnose
diagnóstico¹, -ca *adj* : diagnostic
diagnóstico² *nm* : diagnosis
diagonal *adj & nf* : diagonal — **diagonalmente** *adv*
diagrama *nm* **1** : diagram **2 diagrama de flujo** ORGANIGRAMA : flowchart
dial *nm* : dial (on a radio, etc.)
dialecto *nm* : dialect
dialogar {52} *vi* : to have a talk, to converse
diálogo *nm* : dialogue
diamante *nm* : diamond
diametral *adj* : diametric, diametrical — **diametralmente** *adv*
diámetro *nm* : diameter
diana *nf* **1** : target, bull's-eye **2** *or* **toque de diana** : reveille
diapositiva *nf* : slide, transparency
diario¹ *adv Mex* : every day, daily
diario², -ria *adj* : daily, everyday — **diariamente** *adv*
diario³ *nm* **1** : diary **2** PERIÓDICO : newspaper
diarrea *nf* : diarrhea
diatriba *nf* : diatribe, tirade
dibujante *nmf* **1** : draftsman *m*, draftswoman *f* **2** CARICATURISTA : cartoonist
dibujar *vt* **1** : to draw, to sketch **2** : to portray, to depict
dibujo *nm* **1** : drawing **2** : design, pattern **3 dibujos animados** : (animated) cartoons
dicción *nf, pl* **-ciones** : diction
diccionario *nm* : dictionary
dícese → **decir**
dicha *nf* **1** SUERTE : good luck **2** FELICIDAD : happiness, joy
dicho¹ *pp* → **decir**
dicho², -cha *adj* : said, aforementioned
dicho³ *nm* DECIR : saying, proverb
dichoso, -sa *adj* **1** : blessed **2** FELIZ : happy **3** AFORTUNADO : fortunate, lucky
diciembre *nm* : December
diciendo → **decir**
dictado *nm* : dictation
dictador, -dora *n* : dictator
dictadura *nf* : dictatorship
dictamen *nm, pl* **dictámenes 1** : report **2** : judgment, opinion
dictaminar *vt* : to report — *vi* : to give an opinion, to pass judgment
dictar *vt* **1** : to dictate **2** : to pronounce (a judgment) **3** : to give, to deliver ⟨dictar una conferencia : to give a lecture⟩
dictatorial *adj* : dictatorial
didáctico, -ca *adj* : didactic
diecinueve *adj & nm* : nineteen
diecinueveavo¹, -va *adj* : nineteenth
diecinueveavo² *nm* : nineteenth (fraction)
dieciocho *adj & nm* : eighteen
dieciochoavo¹, -va *or* **dieciochavo, -va** *adj* : eighteenth
dieciochoavo² *or* **dieciochavo** *nm* : eighteenth (fraction)
dieciséis *adj & nm* : sixteen
dieciseisavo¹, -va *adj* : sixteenth
dieciseisavo² *nm* : sixteenth (fraction)
diecisiete *adj & nm* : seventeen
diecisieteavo¹, -va *adj* : seventeenth
diecisieteavo² *nm* : seventeenth
diente *nm* **1** : tooth ⟨diente canino : eyetooth, canine tooth⟩ **2** : tusk, fang **3** : prong, tine **4 diente de león** : dandelion
dieron, etc. → **dar**
diesel ['disɛl] *nm* : diesel
diestra *nf* : right hand
diestramente *adv* : skillfully, adroitly
diestro¹, -tra *adj* **1** : right **2** : skillful, accomplished
diestro² *nm* : bullfighter, matador
dieta *nf* : diet

dietética *nf* : dietetics
dietético, -ca *adj* : dietetic
dietista *nmf* : dietitian
diez *adj & nm, pl* **dieces** : ten
difamación *nf, pl* **-ciones** : defamation, slander
difamar *vt* : to defame, to slander
difamatorio, -ria *adj* : slanderous, defamatory, libelous
diferencia *nf* **1** : difference **2 a diferencia de** : unlike, in contrast to
diferenciación *nf, pl* **-ciones** : differentiation
diferenciar *vt* : to differentiate between, to distinguish — **diferenciarse** *vr* : to differ
diferendo *nm* : dispute, conflict
diferente *adj* DISTINTO : different — **diferentemente** *adv*
diferir {76} *vt* DILATAR, POSPONER : to postpone, to put off — *vi* : to differ
difícil *adj* : difficult, hard
difícilmente *adv* **1** : with difficulty **2** : hardly
dificultad *nf* : difficulty
dificultar *vt* : to make difficult, to obstruct
dificultoso, -sa *adj* : difficult, hard
difteria *nf* : diphtheria
difundir *vt* **1** : to diffuse, to spread out **2** : to broadcast, to spread
difunto, -ta *adj & n* FALLECIDO : deceased
difusión *nf, pl* **-siones 1** : spreading **2** : diffusion (of heat, etc.) **3** : broadcast, broadcasting ⟨los medios de difusión : the media⟩
difuso, -sa *adj* : diffuse, widespread
diga, etc. → **decir**
digerir {76} *vt* : to digest — **digerible** *adj*
digestión *nf, pl* **-tiones** : digestion
digestivo, -va *adj* : digestive
digital[1] *adj* : digital — **digitalmente** *adv*
digital[2] *nf* **1** DEDALERA : foxglove **2** : digitalis
dígito *nm* : digit
dignarse *vr* : to deign, to condescend ⟨no se dignó contestar : he didn't deign to answer⟩
dignatario, -ria *n* : dignitary
dignidad *nf* **1** : dignity **2** : dignitary
dignificar {72} *vt* : to dignify
digno, -na *adj* **1** HONORABLE : honorable **2** : worthy — **dignamente** *adv*
digresión *nf, pl* **-ciones** : digression
dije *nm* : charm (on a bracelet)
dijo, etc. → **decir**
dilación *nf, pl* **-ciones** : delay
dilapidar *vt* : to waste, to squander
dilatar *vt* **1** : to dilate, to widen, to expand **2** DIFERIR, POSPONER : to put off, to postpone — **dilatarse** *vr* **1** : to expand (of gases, metals, etc.) **2** *Mex* : to take long, to be long
dilatorio, -ria *adj* : dilatory, delaying
dilema *nm* : dilemma
diletante *nmf* : dilettante
diligencia *nf* **1** : diligence, care **2** : promptness, speed **3** : action, step **4** : task, errand **5** : stagecoach **6 diligencias** *nfpl* : judicial procedures, formalities
diligente *adj* : diligent — **diligentemente** *adv*
dilucidar *vt* : to elucidate, to clarify
dilución *nf, pl* **-ciones** : dilution
diluir {41} *vt* : to dilute
diluviar *v impers* : to pour (with rain), to pour down
diluvio *nm* **1** : flood **2** : downpour
dimensión *nf, pl* **-siones** : dimension — **dimensional** *adj*
dimensionar *vt* : to measure, to gauge
diminutivo[1]**, -va** *adj* : diminutive
diminutivo[2] *nm* : diminutive
diminuto, -ta *adj* : minute, tiny
dimisión *nf, pl* **-siones** : resignation
dimitir *vi* : to resign, to step down
dimos → **dar**
dinámica *nf* : dynamics
dinámico, -ca *adj* : dynamic — **dinámicamente** *adv*
dinamismo *nm* : energy, vigor
dinamita *nf* : dynamite
dinamitar *vt* : to dynamite
dínamo *or* **dinamo** *nm* : dynamo
dinastía *nf* : dynasty
dineral *nm* : fortune, large sum of money
dinero *nm* : money
dinosaurio *nm* : dinosaur
dintel *nm* : lintel
dio, etc. → **dar**
diocesano, -na *adj* : diocesan
diócesis *nfs & pl* : diocese
dios, diosa *n* : god, goddess *f*
Dios *nm* : God
diploma *nm* : diploma
diplomacia *nf* : diplomacy
diplomado[1]**, -da** *adj* : qualified, trained
diplomado[2] *nm Mex* : seminar
diplomático[1]**, -ca** *adj* : diplomatic — **diplomáticamente** *adv*
diplomático[2]**, -ca** *n* : diplomat
diptongo *nm* : diphthong
diputación *nf, pl* **-ciones** : deputation, delegation
diputado, -da *n* : delegate, representative
dique *nm* : dike
dirá, etc. → **decir**
dirección *nf, pl* **-ciones 1** : address **2** : direction **3** : management, leadership **4** : steering (of an automobile)
direccional[1] *adj* : directional
direccional[2] *nf* : directional, turn signal
directa *nf* : high gear
directamente *adv* : straight, directly
directiva *nf* **1** ORDEN : directive **2** DIRECTORIO, JUNTA : board of directors
directivo[1]**, -va** *adj* : executive, managerial
directivo[2]**, -va** *n* : executive, director
directo, -ta *adj* **1** : direct, straight, immediate **2 en ~** : live (in broadcasting)

director, -tora *n* **1** : director, manager, head **2** : conductor (of an orchestra)
directorial *adj* : managing, executive
directorio *nm* **1** : directory **2** DIRECTIVA, JUNTA : board of directors
directriz *nf, pl* **-trices** : guideline
dirigencia *nf* : leaders *pl,* leadership
dirigente[1] *adj* : directing, leading
dirigente[2] *nmf* : director, leader
dirigible *nm* : dirigible, blimp
dirigir {35} *vt* **1** : to direct, to lead **2** : to address **3** : to aim, to point **4** : to conduct (music) — **dirigirse** *vr* **~ a 1** : to go towards **2** : to speak to, to address
dirimir *vt* **1** : to resolve, to settle **2** : to annul, to dissolve (a marriage)
discapacidad *nf* MINUSVALÍA : disability, handicap
discapacitado[1], **-da** *adj* : disabled, handicapped
discapacitado[2], **-da** *n* : disabled person, handicapped person
discar {72} *v* : to dial
discernimiento *nm* : discernment
discernir {25} *v* : to discern, to distinguish
disciplina *nf* : discipline
disciplinar *vt* : to discipline — **disciplinario, -ria** *adj*
discípulo, -la *n* : disciple, follower
disc jockey [ˌdiskˈjoke, -ˈʤo-] *nmf* : disc jockey
disco *nm* **1** : phonograph record **2** : disc, disk 〈disco compacto : compact disc〉 **3** : discus
díscolo, -la *adj* : unruly, disobedient
disconforme *adj* : in disagreement
discontinuidad *nf* : discontinuity
discontinuo, -nua *adj* : discontinuous
discordancia *nf* DESAVENENCIA : conflict, disagreement
discordante *adj* **1** : discordant **2** : conflicting
discordia *nf* : discord
discoteca *nf* **1** : disco, discotheque **2** *CA, Mex* : record store
discreción *nf, pl* **-ciones** : discretion
discrecional *adj* : discretionary
discrepancia *nf* : discrepancy
discrepar *vi* **1** : to disagree **2** : to differ
discreto, -ta *adj* : discreet — **discretamente** *adv*
discriminación *nf, pl* **-ciones** : discrimination
discriminar *vt* **1** : to discriminate against **2** : to distinguish, to differentiate
discriminatorio, -ria *adj* : discriminatory
disculpa *nf* **1** : apology **2** : excuse
disculpable *adj* : excusable
disculpar *vt* : to excuse, to pardon — **disculparse** *vr* : to apologize
discurrir *vi* **1** : to flow **2** : to pass, to go by **3** : to ponder, to reflect
discurso *nm* **1** ORACIÓN : speech, address **2** : discourse, treatise
discusión *nf, pl* **-siones** **1** : discussion **2** ALTERCADO, DISPUTA : argument
discutible *adj* : arguable, debatable
discutidor, -dora *adj* : argumentative
discutir *vt* **1** : to discuss **2** : to dispute — *vi* ALTERCAR : to argue, to quarrel
disecar {72} *vt* **1** : to dissect **2** : to stuff (for preservation)
disección *nf, pl* **-ciones** : dissection
diseminación *nf, pl* **-ciones** : dissemination, spreading
diseminar *vt* : to disseminate, to spread
disensión *nf, pl* **-siones** : dissension, disagreement
disentería *nf* : dysentery
disentir {76} *vi* : to dissent, to disagree
diseñador, -dora *n* : designer
diseñar *vt* **1** : to design, to plan **2** : to lay out, to outline
diseño *nm* : design
disentimiento *nm* : dissent
disertación *nf, pl* **-ciones** **1** : lecture, talk **2** : dissertation
disertar *vi* : to lecture, to give a talk
disfraz *nm, pl* **disfraces** **1** : disguise **2** : costume **3** : front, pretense
disfrazar {21} *vt* **1** : to disguise **2** : to mask, to conceal — **disfrazarse** *vr* : to wear a costume, to be in disguise
disfrutar *vt* : to enjoy — *vi* : to enjoy oneself, to have a good time
disfrute *nm* : enjoyment
disfunción *nf, pl* **-ciones** : dysfunction — **disfuncional** *adj*
disgresión → **digresión**
disgustar *vt* : to upset, to displease, to make angry — **disgustarse** *vr*
disgusto *nm* **1** : annoyance, displeasure **2** : argument, quarrel **3** : trouble, misfortune
disidencia *nf* : dissidence, dissent
disidente *adj & nmf* : dissident
disímbolo, -la *adj Mex* : dissimilar
disímil *adj* : dissimilar
disimulado, -da *adj* **1** : concealed, disguised **2** : furtive, sly
disimular *vi* : to dissemble, to pretend — *vt* : to conceal, to hide
disimulo *nm* **1** : dissembling, pretense **2** : slyness, furtiveness **3** : tolerance
disipar *vt* **1** : to dissipate, to dispel **2** : to squander — **disiparse** *vr*
diskette [diˈskɛt] *nm* : floppy disk, diskette
dislocar {72} *vt* : to dislocate — **dislocación** *nf*
disminución *nf, pl* **-ciones** : decrease, drop, fall
disminuir {41} *vt* REDUCIR : to reduce, to decrease, to lower — *vi* **1** : to lower **2** : to drop, to fall
disociación *nf, pl* **-ciones** : dissociation
disociar *vt* : to dissociate, to separate
disolución *nf, pl* **-ciones** **1** : dissolution, dissolving **2** : breaking up **3** : dissipation
disoluto, -ta *adj* : dissolute, dissipated

disolver {89} *vt* **1** : to dissolve **2** : to break up — **disolverse** *vr*
disonancia *nf* : dissonance — **disonante** *adj*
dispar *adj* **1** : different, disparate **2** DIVERSO : diverse **3** DESIGUAL : inconsistent
disparado, -da *adj* **salir disparado** *fam* : to take off in a hurry, to rush away
disparar *vi* **1** : to shoot, to fire **2** *Mex fam* : to pay — *vt* **1** : to shoot **2** *Mex fam* : to treat to, to buy — **dispararse** *vr* : to shoot up, to skyrocket
disparatado, -da *adj* ABSURDO, RIDÍCULO : absurd, ridiculous, crazy
disparate *nm* : silliness, stupidity 〈decir disparates : to talk nonsense〉
disparejo, -ja *adj* DESIGUAL : uneven
disparidad *nf* : disparity
disparo *nm* TIRO : shot
dispendio *nm* : wastefulness, extravagance
dispendioso, -sa *adj* : wasteful, extravagant
dispensa *nf* : dispensation
dispensable *adj* **1** : dispensable **2** : excusable
dispensar *vt* **1** : to dispense, to give, to grant **2** EXCUSAR : to excuse, to forgive **3** EXIMIR : to exempt
dispensario *nm* **1** : dispensary, clinic **2** *Mex* : dispenser
dispersar *vt* DESPERDIGAR : to disperse, to scatter
dispersión *nf, pl* **-siones** : dispersion
disperso, -sa *adj* : dispersed, scattered
displicencia *nf* : indifference, coldness, disdain
displicente *adj* : indifferent, cold, disdainful
disponer {60} *vt* **1** : to arrange, to lay out **2** : to stipulate, to order **3** : to prepare — *vi* ~ **de** : to have at one's disposal — **disponerse** *vr* ~ **a** : to prepare to, to be about to
disponibilidad *nf* : availability
disponible *adj* : available
disposición *nf, pl* **-ciones** **1** : disposition **2** : aptitude, talent **3** : order, arrangement **4** : willingness, readiness **5 última disposición** : last will and testament
dispositivo *nm* **1** APARATO, MECANISMO : device, mechanism **2** : force, detachment
dispuesto[1] *pp* → **disponer**
dispuesto[2], **-ta** *adj* PREPARADO : ready, prepared, disposed
dispuso, etc. → **disponer**
disputa *nf* ALTERCADO, DISCUSIÓN : dispute, argument
disputar *vi* : to argue, to contend, to vie — *vt* : to dispute, to question — **disputarse** *vr* : to be in competition for 〈se disputan la corona : they're fighting for the crown〉
disquera *nf* : record label, recording company
disquete → **diskette**
disquisición *nf, pl* **-ciones** **1** : formal discourse **2 disquisiciones** *nfpl* : digressions
distancia *nf* : distance
distanciamiento *nm* **1** : distancing **2** : rift, estrangement
distanciar *vt* **1** : to space out **2** : to draw apart — **distanciarse** *vr* : to grow apart, to become estranged
distante *adj* **1** : distant, far-off **2** : aloof
distar *vi* ~ **de** : to be far from 〈dista de ser perfecto : he is far from perfect〉
diste → **dar**
distender {56} *vt* : to distend, to stretch
distensión *nf, pl* **-siones** : distension
distinción *nf, pl* **-ciones** : distinction
distinguible *adj* : distinguishable
distinguido, -da *adj* : distinguished, refined
distinguir {26} *vt* **1** : to distinguish **2** : to honor — **distinguirse** *vr*
distintivo, -va *adj* : distinctive, distinguishing
distinto, -ta *adj* **1** DIFERENTE : different **2** CLARO : distinct, clear, evident
distorsión *nf, pl* **-siones** : distortion
distorsionar *vt* : to distort
distracción *nf, pl* **-ciones** **1** : distraction, amusement **2** : forgetfulness **3** : oversight
distraer {81} *vt* **1** : to distract **2** ENTRETENER : to entertain, to amuse — **distraerse** *vr* **1** : to get distracted **2** : to amuse oneself
distraídamente *adv* : absentmindedly
distraído[1] *pp* → **distraer**
distraído[2], **-da** *adj* **1** : distracted, preoccupied **2** DESPISTADO : absent-minded
distribución *nf, pl* **-ciones** : distribution
distribuidor, -dora *n* : distributor
distribuir {41} *vt* : to distribute
distributivo, -va *adj* : distributive
distrital *adj* : district, of the district
distrito *nm* : district
distrofia *nf* : dystrophy 〈distrofia muscular : muscular dystrophy〉
disturbio *nm* : disturbance
disuadir *vt* : to dissuade, to discourage
disuasión *nf, pl* **-siones** : dissuasion
disuasivo, -va *adj* : deterrent, discouraging
disuasorio, -ria *adj* : discouraging
disuelto *pp* → **disolver**
disyuntiva *nf* : dilemma
DIU ['diu] *nm* (*d*ispositivo *i*ntra*u*terino) : IUD, intrauterine device
diurético[1], **-ca** *adj* : diuretic
diurético[2] *nm* : diuretic
diurno, -na *adj* : day, daytime
diva *nf* → **divo**
divagar {52} *vi* : to digress
diván *nm, pl* **divanes** : divan
divergencia *nf* : divergence, difference
divergente *adj* : divergent, differing
divergir {35} *vi* **1** : to diverge **2** : to differ, to disagree

diversidad *nf* : diversity, variety
diversificación *nf, pl* **-ciones** : diversification
diversificar {72} *vt* : to diversify
diversión *nf, pl* **-siones** ENTRETENIMIENTO : fun, amusement, diversion
diverso, -sa *adj* : diverse, various
divertido, -da *adj* **1** : amusing, funny **2** : entertaining, enjoyable
divertir {76} *vt* ENTRETENER : to amuse, to entertain — **divertirse** *vr* : to have fun, to have a good time
dividendo *nm* : dividend
dividir *vt* **1** : to divide, to split **2** : to distribute, to share out — **dividirse** *vr*
divieso *nm* : boil
divinidad *nf* : divinity
divino, -na *adj* : divine
divisa *nf* **1** : currency **2** LEMA : motto **3** : emblem, insignia
divisar *vt* : to discern, to make out
divisible *adj* : divisible
división *nf, pl* **-siones** : division
divisionismo *nm* : factionalism
divisivo, -va *adj* : divisive
divisor *nm* : denominator
divisorio, -ria *adj* : dividing
divo, -va *n* **1** : prima donna **2** : celebrity, star
divorciado[1]**, -da** *adj* **1** : divorced **2** : split, divided
divorciado[2]**, -da** *n* : divorcé *m*, divorcée *f*
divorciar *vt* : to divorce — **divorciarse** *vr* : to get a divorce
divorcio *nm* : divorce
divulgación *nf, pl* **-ciones** **1** : spreading, dissemination **2** : popularization
divulgar {52} *vt* **1** : to spread, to circulate **2** REVELAR : to divulge, to reveal **3** : to popularize — **divulgarse** *vr*
dizque *adv* : supposedly, apparently
dobladillar *vt* : to hem
dobladillo *nm* : hem
doblar *vt* **1** : to double **2** PLEGAR : to fold, to bend **3** : to turn ⟨doblar la esquina : to turn the corner⟩ **4** : to dub — *vi* **1** : to turn **2** : to toll, to ring — **doblarse** *vr* **1** : to fold up, to double over **2** : to give in, to yield
doble[1] *adj* : double — **doblemente** *adv*
doble[2] *nm* **1** : double **2** : toll (of a bell), knell
doble[3] *nmf* : stand-in, double
doblegar {52} *vt* **1** : to fold, to crease **2** : to force to yield — **doblegarse** *vr* : to yield, to bow
doblez[1] *nm, pl* **dobleces** : fold, crease
doblez[2] *nmf* : duplicity, deceitfulness
doce *adj & nm* : twelve
doceavo[1]**, -va** *adj* : twelfth
doceavo[2] *nm* : twelfth (fraction)
docena *nf* **1** : dozen **2 docena de fraile** : baker's dozen
docencia *nf* : teaching
docente[1] *adj* : educational, teaching
docente[2] *n* : teacher, lecturer
dócil *adj* : docile — **dócilmente** *adv*
docilidad *nf* : docility
docto, -ta *adj* : learned, erudite
doctor, -tora *n* : doctor
doctorado *nm* : doctorate
doctrina *nf* : doctrine — **doctrinal** *adj*
documentación *nf, pl* **-ciones** : documentation
documental *adj & nm* : documentary
documentar *vt* : to document
documento *nm* : document
dogma *nm* : dogma
dogmático, -ca *adj* : dogmatic
dogmatismo *nm* : dogmatism
dólar *nm* : dollar
dolencia *nf* : ailment, malaise
doler {47} *vi* **1** : to hurt, to ache **2** : to grieve — **dolerse** *vr* **1** : to be distressed **2** : to complain
doliente *nmf* : mourner, bereaved
dolor *nm* **1** : pain, ache ⟨dolor de cabeza : headache⟩ **2** PENA, TRISTEZA : grief, sorrow
dolorido, -da *adj* **1** : sore, aching **2** : hurt, upset
doloroso, -sa *adj* **1** : painful **2** : distressing — **dolorosamente** *adv*
doloso, -sa *adj* : fraudulent — **dolosamente** *adv*
domador, -dora *n* : tamer
domar *vt* : to tame, to break in
domesticado, -da *adj* : domesticated, tame
domesticar {72} *vt* : to domesticate, to tame
doméstico, -ca *adj* : domestic, household
domiciliado, -da *adj* : residing
domiciliario, -ria *adj* **1** : home **2 arresto domiciliario** : house arrest
domiciliarse *vr* RESIDIR : to reside
domicilio *nm* : home, residence ⟨cambio de domicilio : change of address⟩
dominación *nf, pl* **-ciones** : domination
dominancia *nf* : dominance
dominante *adj* **1** : dominant **2** : domineering
dominar *vt* **1** : to dominate **2** : to master, to be proficient at — *vi* : to predominate, to prevail — **dominarse** *vr* : to control oneself
domingo *nm* : Sunday
dominical *adj* : Sunday ⟨periódico dominical : Sunday newspaper⟩
dominicano, -na *adj & n* : Dominican
dominio *nm* **1** : dominion, power **2** : mastery **3** : domain, field
dominó *nm, pl* **-nós** **1** : domino (tile) **2** : dominoes *pl* (game)
domo *nm* : dome
don[1] *nm* **1** : gift, present **2** : talent
don[2] *nm* **1** : title of courtesy preceding a man's first name **2 don nadie** : nobody, insignificant person
dona *nf Mex* : doughnut, donut
donación *nf, pl* **-ciones** : donation
donador, -dora *n* : donor
donaire *nm* **1** GARBO : grace, poise **2** : witticism

donante *nf* → **donador**
donar *vt* : to donate
donativo *nm* : donation
doncella *nf* : maiden, damsel
doncellez *nf* : maidenhood
donde[1] *conj* : where, in which ⟨el pueblo donde vivo : the town where I live⟩
donde[2] *prep* : over by ⟨lo encontré donde la silla : I found it over by the chair⟩
dónde *adv* : where ⟨¿dónde está su casa? : where is your house?⟩
dondequiera *adv* **1** : anywhere, no matter where **2 dondequiera que** : wherever, everywhere
doña *nf* : title of courtesy preceding a woman's first name
doquier *adv* **por ~** : everywhere, all over
dorado[1], **-da** *adj* : gold, golden
dorado[2], **-da** *nm* : gilt
dorar *vt* **1** : to gild **2** : to brown (food)
dormido, -da *adj* **1** : asleep **2** : numb ⟨tiene el pie dormido : her foot's numb, her foot's gone to sleep⟩
dormilón, -lona *n* : sleepyhead, late riser
dormir {27} *vt* : to put to sleep — *vi* : to sleep — **dormirse** *vr* : to fall asleep
dormitar *vi* : to snooze, to doze
dormitorio *nm* **1** : bedroom **2** : dormitory
dorsal[1] *adj* : dorsal
dorsal[2] *nm* : number (worn in sports)
dorso *nm* **1** : back ⟨el dorso de la mano : the back of the hand⟩ **2** *Mex* : backstroke
dos *adj & nm* : two
doscientos[1], **-tas** *adj* : two hundred
doscientos[2] *nms & pl* : two hundred
dosel *nm* : canopy
dosificación *nf, pl* **-ciones** : dosage
dosis *nfs & pl* **1** : dose **2** : amount, quantity
dossier *nm* : dossier
dotación *nf, pl* **-ciones 1** : endowment, funding **2** : staff, personnel
dotado, -da *adj* **1** : gifted **2 ~ de** : endowed with, equipped with
dotar *vt* **1** : to provide, to equip **2** : to endow
dote *nf* **1** : dowry **2 dotes** *nfpl* : talent, gift
doy → **dar**
draga *nf* : dredge
dragado *nm* : dredging
dragar {52} *vt* : to dredge
dragón *nm, pl* **dragones 1** : dragon **2** : snapdragon
drague, etc. → **dragar**
drama *nm* : drama
dramático, -ca *adj* : dramatic — **dramáticamente** *adv*
dramatizar {21} *vt* : to dramatize — **dramatización** *nf*
dramaturgo, -ga *n* : dramatist, playwright
drástico, -ca *adj* : drastic — **drásticamente** *adv*
drenaje *nm* : drainage
drenar *vt* : to drain
drene *nm Mex* : drain
driblar *vi* : to dribble (in basketball)
drible *nm* : dribble (in basketball)
droga *nf* : drug
drogadicción *nf, pl* **-ciones** : drug addiction
drogadicto, -ta *n* : drug addict
drogar {52} *vt* : to drug — **drogarse** *vr* : to take drugs
drogue, etc. → **drogar**
droguería *nf* FARMACIA : drugstore
dromedario *nm* : dromedary
dual *adj* : dual
dualidad *nf* : duality
dualismo *nm* : dualism
ducha *nf* : shower ⟨darse una ducha : to take a shower⟩
ducharse *vr* : to take a shower
ducho, -cha *adj* : experienced, skilled, expert
dúctil *adj* : ductile
ducto *nm* **1** : duct, shaft **2** : pipeline
duda *nf* : doubt ⟨no cabe duda : there's no doubt about it⟩
dudar *vt* : to doubt — *vi* **~ en** : to hesitate to ⟨no dudes en pedirme ayuda : don't hesitate to ask me for help⟩
dudoso, -sa *adj* **1** : doubtful **2** : dubious, questionable — **dudosamente** *adv*
duele, etc. → **doler**
duelo *nm* **1** : duel **2** LUTO : mourning
duende *nm* **1** : elf, goblin **2** ENCANTO : magic, charm ⟨una bailarina que tiene duende : a dancer with a certain magic⟩
dueño, -ña *n* **1** : owner, proprietor, proprietress *f* **2** : landlord, landlady *f*
duerme, etc. → **dormir**
dueto *nm* : duet
dulce[1] *adv* : sweetly, softly
dulce[2] *adj* **1** : sweet **2** : mild, gentle, mellow — **dulcemente** *adv*
dulce[3] *nm* : candy, sweet
dulcería *nf* : candy store
dulcificante *nm* : sweetener
dulzura *nf* **1** : sweetness **2** : gentleness, mellowness
duna *nf* : dune
dúo *nm* : duo, duet
duodécimo[1], **-ma** *adj* : twelfth
duodécimo[2], **-ma** *nm* : twelfth (in a series)
dúplex *nms & pl* : duplex apartment
duplicación *nf, pl* **-ciones** : duplication, copying
duplicado *nm* : duplicate, copy
duplicar {72} *vt* **1** : to double **2** : to duplicate, to copy
duplicidad *nf* : duplicity
duque *nm* : duke
duquesa *nf* : duchess
durabilidad *nf* : durability
durable → **duradero**

duración *nf, pl* **-ciones** : duration, length
duradero, -ra *adj* : durable, lasting
duramente *adv* **1** : harshly, severely **2** : hard
durante *prep* : during ⟨durante todo el día : all day long⟩ ⟨trabajó durante tres horas : he worked for three hours⟩
durar *vi* : to last, to endure
durazno *nm* **1** : peach **2** : peach tree
dureza *nf* **1** : hardness, toughness **2** : severity, harshness
durmiente[1] *adj* : sleeping
durmiente[2] *nmf* : sleeper
durmió, etc. → **dormir**
duro[1] *adv* : hard ⟨trabajé tan duro : I worked so hard⟩
duro[2], **-ra** *adj* **1** : hard, tough **2** : harsh, severe

E

e[1] *nf* : fifth letter of the Spanish alphabet
e[2] *conj* (*used instead of* **y** *before words beginning with i- or hi-*) : and
ebanista *nmf* : cabinetmaker
ebanistería *nf* : cabinetmaking
ébano *nm* : ebony
ebriedad *nf* EMBRIAGUEZ : inebriation, drunkenness
ebrio, -bria *adj* EMBRIAGADO : inebriated, drunk
ebullición *nf, pl* **-ciones** : boiling
eccéntrico → **excéntrico**
echar *vt* **1** LANZAR : to throw, to cast, to hurl **2** EXPULSAR : to throw out, to expel **3** EMITIR : to emit, give off **4** BROTAR : to sprout, to put forth **5** DESPEDIR : to fire, to dismiss **6** : to put in, to add **7 echar a perder** : to spoil, to ruin **8 echar de menos** : to miss ⟨echan de menos a su madre : they miss their mother⟩ — *vi* **1** : to start off **2** **~ a** : to begin to — **echarse** *vr* **1** : to throw oneself **2** : to lie down **3** : to put on **4** **~ a** : to start to **5 echarse a perder** : to go bad, to spoil **6 echárselas de** : to pose as
ecléctico, -ca *adj* : eclectic
eclesiástico[1], **-ca** *adj* : ecclesiastical, ecclesiastic
eclesiástico[2] *nm* CLÉRIGO : cleric, clergyman
eclipsar *vt* **1** : to eclipse **2** : to outshine, to surpass
eclipse *nm* : eclipse
eco *nm* : echo
ecografía *nf* : ultrasound scanning
ecología *nf* : ecology
ecológico, -ca *adj* : ecological — **ecológicamente** *adv*
ecologista *nmf* : ecologist, environmentalist
ecólogo, -ga *n* : ecologist
economía *nf* **1** : economy **2** : economics
económicamente *adv* : financially
económico, -ca *adj* : economic, economical
economista *nmf* : economist
economizar {21} *vt* : to save, to economize on — *vi* : to save up, to be frugal
ecosistema *nm* : ecosystem
ecuación *nf, pl* **-ciones** : equation
ecuador *nm* : equator
ecuánime *adj* **1** : even-tempered **2** : impartial
ecuanimidad *nf* **1** : equanimity **2** : impartiality
ecuatorial *adj* : equatorial
ecuatoriano, -na *adj & n* : Ecuadorian
ecuestre *adj* : equestrian
ecuménico, -ca *adj* : ecumenical
eczema *nm* : eczema
edad *nf* **1** : age ⟨¿qué edad tiene? : how old is she?⟩ **2** ÉPOCA, ERA : epoch, era
edema *nm* : edema
Edén *nm, pl* **Edenes** : Eden, paradise
edición *nf, pl* **-ciones** **1** : edition **2** : publication, publishing
edicto *nm* : edict, proclamation
edificación *nf, pl* **-ciones** **1** : edification **2** : construction, building
edificante *adj* : edifying
edificar {72} *vt* **1** : to edify **2** CONSTRUIR : to build, to construct
edificio *nm* : building, edifice
editar *vt* **1** : to edit **2** PUBLICAR : to publish
editor[1], **-tora** *adj* : publishing ⟨casa editora : publishing house⟩
editor[2], **-tora** *n* **1** : editor **2** : publisher
editora *nf* : publisher, publishing company
editorial[1] *adj* **1** : publishing **2** : editorial
editorial[2] *nm* : editorial
editorial[3] *nf* : publishing house
editorializar {21} *vi* : to editorialize
edredón *nm, pl* **-dones** COBERTOR, COLCHA : comforter, eiderdown, quilt
educable *adj* : educable, teachable
educación *nf, pl* **-ciones** **1** ENSEÑANZA : education **2** : manners *pl* — **educacional** *adj*
educado, -da *adj* : polite, well-mannered
educador, -dora *n* : educator
educando, -da *n* ALUMNO, PUPILO : pupil, student
educar {72} *vt* **1** : to educate **2** CRIAR : to bring up, to raise **3** : to train — **educarse** *vr* : to be educated
educativo, -va *adj* : educational
efectista *adj* : dramatic, sensational
efectivamente *adv* : really, actually
efectividad *nf* : effectiveness

efectivo[1], **-va** *adj* **1** : effective **2** : real, actual **3** : permanent, regular (of employment)
efectivo[2] *nm* : cash
efecto *nm* **1** : effect **2 en ~** : actually, in fact **3 efectos** *nmpl* : goods, property ‹efectos personales : personal effects›
efectuar {3} *vt* : to carry out, to bring about
efervescencia *nf* **1** : effervescence **2** : vivacity, high spirits *pl*
efervescente *adj* **1** : effervescent **2** : vivacious
eficacia *nf* **1** : effectiveness, efficacy **2** : efficiency
eficaz *adj, pl* **-caces 1** : effective **2** EFICIENTE : efficient — **eficazmente** *adv*
eficiencia *nf* : efficiency
eficiente *adj* EFICAZ : efficient — **eficientemente** *adv*
eficientizar {21} *vt Mex* : to streamline, to make more efficient
efigie *nf* : effigy
efímera *nf* : mayfly
efímero, -ra *adj* : ephemeral
efusión *nf, pl* **-siones 1** : effusion **2** : warmth, effusiveness **3 con ~** : effusively
efusivo, -va *adj* : effusive — **efusivamente** *adv*
egipcio, -cia *adj & n* : Egyptian
eglefino *nm* : haddock
ego *nm* : ego
egocéntrico, -ca *adj* : egocentric, self-centered
egoísmo *nm* : selfishness, egoism
egoísta[1] *adj* : selfish, egoistic
egoísta[2] *nmf* : egoist, selfish person
egotismo *nm* : egotism, conceit
egotista[1] *adj* : egotistic, egotistical, conceited
egotista[2] *nmf* : egotist, conceited person
egresado, -da *n* : graduate
egresar *vi* : to graduate
egreso *nm* **1** : graduation **2 ingresos y egresos** : income and expenditure
eh *interj* **1** : hey! **2** : eh?, huh?
eje *nm* **1** : axle **2** : axis
ejecución *nf, pl* **-ciones** : execution
ejecutante *nmf* : performer
ejecutar *vt* **1** : to execute, to put to death **2** : to carry out, to perform
ejecutivo, -va *adj & n* : executive
ejecutor, -tora *n* : executor
ejemplar[1] *adj* : exemplary, model
ejemplar[2] *nm* **1** : copy (of a book, magazine, etc.) **2** : specimen, example
ejemplificar {72} *vt* : to exemplify, to illustrate
ejemplo *nm* **1** : example **2 por ~** : for example **3 dar ejemplo** : to set an example
ejercer {86} *vi* **~ de** : to practice as, to work as — *vt* **1** : to practice **2** : exercise (a right) **3** : to exert
ejercicio *nm* **1** : exercise **2** : practice
ejercitar *vt* **1** : to exercise **2** ADIESTRAR : to drill, to train
ejército *nm* : army
ejidal *adj Mex* : cooperative
ejido *nm* **1** : common land **2** *Mex* : cooperative
ejote *nm Mex* : green bean
el[1] *pron* (*referring to masculine nouns*) **1** : the one ‹tengo mi libro y el tuyo : I have my book and yours› ‹de los cantantes me gusta el de México : I prefer the singer from México› **2 el que** : he who, whoever, the one that ‹el que vino ayer : the one who came yesterday› ‹el que trabaja duro estará contento : he who works hard will be happy›
el[2], **la** *art, pl* **los, las** : the ‹los niños están en la casa : the boys are in the house› ‹me duele el pie : my foot hurts›
él *pron* : he, him ‹él es mi amigo : he's my friend› ‹hablaremos con él : we will speak with him›
elaboración *nf, pl* **-ciones 1** PRODUCCIÓN : production, making **2** : preparation, devising
elaborado, -da *adj* : elaborate
elaborar *vt* **1** : to make, to produce **2** : to devise, to draw up
elasticidad *nf* : elasticity
elástico[1], **-ca** *adj* **1** FLEXIBLE : flexible **2** : elastic
elástico[2] *nm* **1** : elastic (material) **2** : rubber band
elección *nf, pl* **-ciones 1** SELECCIÓN : choice, selection **2** : election
electivo, -va *adj* : elective
electo, -ta *adj* : elect ‹el presidente electo : the president-elect›
elector, -tora *n* : elector, voter
electorado *nm* : electorate
electoral *adj* : electoral, election
electricidad *nf* : electricity
electricista *nmf* : electrician
eléctrico, -ca *adj* : electric, electrical
electrificar {72} *vt* : to electrify — **electrificación** *nf*
electrizar {21} *vt* : to electrify, to thrill — **electrizante** *adj*
electrocardiógrafo *nm* : electrocardiograph
electrocardiograma *nm* : electrocardiogram
electrocutar *vt* : to electrocute — **electrocución** *nf*
electrodo *nm* : electrode
electrodoméstico *nm* : electric appliance
electroimán *nm, pl* **-manes** : electromagnet
electrólisis *nfs & pl* : electrolysis
electrolito *nm* : electrolyte
electromagnético, -ca *adj* : electromagnetic
electromagnetismo *nm* : electromagnetism
electrón *nm, pl* **-trones** : electron
electrónica *nf* : electronics
electrónico, -ca *adj* : electronic — **electrónicamente** *adv*

elefante, -ta *n* : elephant

elegancia *nf* : elegance

elegante *adj* : elegant, smart — **elegantemente** *adv*

elegía *nf* : elegy

elegíaco, -ca *adj* : elegiac

elegibilidad *nf* : eligibility

elegible *adj* : eligible

elegido, -da *adj* **1** : chosen, selected **2** : elected

elegir {28} *vt* **1** ESCOGER, SELECCIONAR : to choose, to select **2** : to elect

elemental *adj* **1** : elementary, basic **2** : fundamental, essential

elemento *nm* : element

elenco *nm* : cast (of actors)

elepé *nm* : long-playing record

elevación *nf, pl* **-ciones** : elevation, height

elevado, -da *adj* **1** : elevated, lofty **2** : high

elevador *nm* ASCENSOR : elevator

elevar *vt* **1** ALZAR : to raise, to lift **2** AUMENTAR : to raise, to increase **3** : to elevate (in a hierarchy), to promote **4** : to present, to submit — **elevarse** *vr* : to rise

elfo *nm* : elf

eliminación *nf, pl* **-ciones** : elimination, removal

eliminar *vt* **1** : to eliminate, to remove **2** : to do in, to kill

elipse *nf* : ellipse

elipsis *nf* : ellipsis

elíptico, -ca *adj* : elliptical, elliptic

elite *or* **élite** *nf* : elite

elixir *or* **elíxir** *nm* : elixir

ella *pron* : she, her ⟨ella es mi amiga : she is my friend⟩ ⟨nos fuimos con ella : we left with her⟩

ello *pron* : it ⟨es por ello que me voy : that's why I'm going⟩

ellos, ellas *pron pl* **1** : they, them **2 de ellos, de ellas** : theirs

elocución *nf, pl* **-ciones** : elocution

elocuencia *nf* : eloquence

elocuente *adj* : eloquent — **elocuentemente** *adv*

elogiar *vt* ENCOMIAR : to praise

elogio *nm* : praise

elote *nm* **1** *Mex* : corn, maize **2** *CA, Mex* : corncob

elucidación *nf, pl* **-ciones** ESCLARECIMIENTO : elucidation

elucidar *vt* ESCLARECER : to elucidate

eludir *vt* EVADIR : to evade, to avoid, to elude

emanación *nf, pl* **-ciones** : emanation

emanar *vi* **~ de** : to emanate from — *vt* : to exude

emancipar *vt* : to emancipate — **emancipación** *nf*

embadurnar *vt* EMBARRAR : to smear, to daub

embajada *nf* : embassy

embajador, -dora *n* : ambassador

embalaje *nm* : packing, packaging

embalar *vt* EMPAQUETAR : to pack

embaldosar *vt* : to tile, to pave with tiles

embalsamar *vt* : to embalm

embalsar *vt* : to dam, to dam up

embalse *nm* : dam, reservoir

embarazada *adj* ENCINTA, PREÑADA : pregnant, expecting

embarazar {21} *vt* **1** : to obstruct, to hamper **2** PREÑAR : to make pregnant

embarazo *nm* : pregnancy

embarazoso, -sa *adj* : embarrassing, awkward

embarcación *nf, pl* **-ciones** : boat, craft

embarcadero *nm* : wharf, pier, jetty

embarcar {72} *vi* : to embark, to board — *vt* : to load

embarco *nm* : embarkation

embargar {52} *vt* **1** : to seize, to impound **2** : to overwhelm

embargo *nm* **1** : seizure **2** : embargo **3 sin ~** : however, nevertheless

embarque *nm* **1** : embarkation **2** : shipment

embarrancar {72} *vi* **1** : to run aground **2** : to get bogged down

embarrar *vt* **1** : to cover with mud **2** EMBADURNAR : to smear

embarullar *vt fam* : to muddle, to confuse — **embarullarse** *vr fam* : to get mixed up

embate *nm* **1** : onslaught **2** : battering (of waves or wind)

embaucador, -dora *n* : swindler, deceiver

embaucar {72} *vt* : to trick, to swindle

embeber *vt* : to absorb, to soak up — *vi* : to shrink

embelesado, -da *adj* : spellbound

embelesar *vt* : to enchant, to captivate

embellecer {53} *vt* : to embellish, to beautify

embellecimiento *nm* : beautification, embellishment

embestida *nf* **1** : charge (of a bull) **2** ARREMETIDA : attack, onslaught

embestir {54} *vt* : to hit, to run into, to charge at — *vi* ARREMETER : to charge, to attack

emblanquecer {53} *vt* BLANQUEAR : to bleach, to whiten — **emblanquecerse** *vr* : to turn white

emblema *nm* : emblem

emblemático, -ca *adj* : emblematic

embolia *nf* : embolism

émbolo *nm* : piston

embolsarse *vr* **1** : to pocket (money) **2** : to collect (payment)

emborracharse *vr* EMBRIAGARSE : to get drunk

emborronar *vt* **1** : to blot, to smudge **2** GARABATEAR : to scribble

emboscada *nf* : ambush

emboscar {72} *vt* : to ambush — **emboscarse** *vr* : to lie in ambush

embotadura *nf* : bluntness, dullness

embotar *vt* **1** : to dull, to blunt **2** : to weaken, to enervate

embotellamiento *nm* ATASCO : traffic jam

embotellar *vt* ENVASAR : to bottle
embragar {52} *vi* : to engage the clutch
embrague *nm* : clutch
embravecerse {53} *vr* **1** : to get furious **2** : to get rough ‹el mar se embraveció : the sea became tempestuous›
embriagado, -da *adj* : inebriated, drunk
embriagador, -dora *adj* : intoxicating
embriagarse {52} *vr* EMBORRACHARSE : to get drunk
embriaguez *nf* EBRIEDAD : drunkenness, inebriation
embrión *nm, pl* **embriones** : embryo
embrionario, -ria *adj* : embryonic
embrollo *nm* ENREDO : imbroglio, confusion
embrujar *vt* HECHIZAR : to bewitch
embrujo *nm* : spell, curse
embudo *nm* : funnel
embuste *nm* **1** MENTIRA : lie, fib **2** ENGAÑO : trick, hoax
embustero[1], **-ra** *adj* : lying, deceitful
embustero[2], **-ra** *n* : liar, cheat
embutido *nm* **1** : sausage **2** : inlaid work
embutir *vt* **1** : to cram, to stuff, to jam **2** : to inlay
emergencia *nf* **1** : emergency **2** : emergence
emergente *adj* **1** : emergent **2** : consequent, resultant
emerger {15} *vi* : to emerge, to surface
emético[1], **-ca** *adj* : emetic
emético[2] *nm* : emetic
emigración *nf, pl* **-ciones** **1** : emigration **2** : migration
emigrante *adj & nmf* : emigrant
emigrar *vi* **1** : to emigrate **2** : to migrate
eminencia *nf* : eminence
eminente *adj* : eminent, distinguished
eminentemente *adv* : basically, essentially
emisario[1], **-ria** *n* : emissary
emisario[2] *nm* : outlet (of a body of water)
emisión *nf, pl* **-siones** **1** : emission **2** : broadcast **3** : issue ‹emisión de acciones : stock issue›
emisor *nm* TRANSMISOR : television or radio transmitter
emisora *nf* : radio station
emitir *vt* **1** : to emit, to give off **2** : to broadcast **3** : to issue **4** : to cast (a vote)
emoción *nf, pl* **-ciones** : emotion — **emocional** *adj* — **emocionalmente** *adv*
emocionado, -da *adj* **1** : moved, affected by emotion **2** ENTUSIASMADO : excited
emocionante *adj* **1** CONMOVEDOR : moving, touching **2** EXCITANTE : exciting, thrilling
emocionar *vt* **1** CONMOVER : to move, to touch **2** : to excite, to thrill — **emocionarse** *vr*
emotivo, -va *adj* : emotional, moving
empacador, -dora *n* : packer
empacar {72} *vt* **1** EMPAQUETAR : to pack **2** : to bale — *vi* : to pack — **empacarse** *vr* **1** : to balk, to refuse to budge **2** *Col, Mex fam* : to eat ravenously, to devour
empachar *vt* **1** ESTORBAR : to obstruct **2** : to give indigestion to **3** DISFRAZAR : to disguise, to mask — **empacharse** *vr* **1** INDIGESTARSE : to get indigestion **2** AVERGONZARSE : to be embarrassed
empacho *nm* **1** INDIGESTIÓN : indigestion **2** VERGÜENZA : embarrassment **3** **no tener empacho en** : to have no qualms about
empadronarse *vr* : to register to vote
empalagar {52} *vt* **1** : to cloy, to surfeit **2** FASTIDIAR : to annoy, to bother
empalagoso, -sa *adj* MELOSO : cloying, excessively sweet
empalar *vt* : to impale
empalizada *nf* : palisade (fence)
empalmar *vt* **1** : to splice, to link **2** : to combine — *vi* : to meet, to converge
empalme *nm* **1** CONEXIÓN : connection, link **2** : junction
empanada *nf* : pie, turnover
empanadilla *nf* : meat or seafood pie
empanar *vt* : to bread
empantanado, -da *adj* : bogged down, delayed
empañar *vt* **1** : to steam up **2** : to tarnish, to sully
empapado, -da *adj* : soggy, sodden
empapar *vt* MOJAR : to soak, to drench — **empaparse** *vr* **1** : to get soaking wet **2** **~ de** : to absorb, to be imbued with
empapelar *vt* : to wallpaper
empaque *nm fam* **1** : presence, bearing **2** : pomposity **3** DESCARO : impudence, nerve
empaquetar *vt* EMBALAR : to pack, to package — **empaquetarse** *vr fam* : to dress up
emparedado *nm* : sandwich
emparedar *vt* : to wall in, to confine
emparejar *vt* **1** : to pair, to match up **2** : to make even — *vi* : to catch up — **emparejarse** *vr* : to pair up
emparentado, -da *adj* : related
emparentar {55} *vi* : to become related by marriage
emparrillado *nm Mex* : gridiron (in football)
empastar *vt* **1** : to fill (a tooth) **2** : to bind (a book)
empaste *nm* : filling (of a tooth)
empatar *vt* : to tie, to connect — *vi* : to result in a draw, to be tied — **empatarse** *vr Ven* : to hook up, to link together
empate *nm* : draw, tie
empatía *nf* : empathy
empecinado, -da *adj* TERCO : stubborn
empecinarse *vr* OBSTINARSE : to be stubborn, to persist
empedernido, -da *adj* INCORREGIBLE : hardened, inveterate
empedrado *nm* : paving, pavement

empedrar {55} *vt* : to pave (with stones)
empeine *nm* : instep
empellón *nm, pl* **-llones** : shove, push
empelotado, -da *adj* **1** *Mex fam* : madly in love **2** *fam* : stark naked
empeñado, -da *adj* : determined, committed
empeñar *vt* **1** : to pawn **2** : to pledge, to give (one's word) — **empeñarse** *vr* **1** : to insist stubbornly **2** : to make an effort
empeño *nm* **1** : pledge, commitment **2** : insistence **3** ESFUERZO : effort, determination **4** : pawning ⟨casa de empeños : pawnshop⟩
empeoramiento *nm* : worsening, deterioration
empeorar *vi* : to deteriorate, to get worse — *vt* : to make worse
empequeñecer {53} *vi* : to diminish, to become smaller — *vt* : to minimize, to make smaller
emperador *nm* : emperor
emperatriz *nf, pl* **-trices** : empress
empero *conj* : however, nevertheless
empezar {29} *v* COMENZAR : to start, to begin
empinado, -da *adj* : steep
empinar *vt* ELEVAR : to lift, to raise — **empinarse** *vr* : to stand on tiptoe
empírico, -ca *adj* : empirical — **empíricamente** *adv*
emplasto *nm* : poultice, dressing
emplazamiento *nm* **1** : location, site **2** CITACIÓN : summons, subpoena
emplazar {21} *vt* **1** CONVOCAR : to convene, to summon **2** : to subpoena **3** UBICAR : to place, to position
empleado, -da *n* : employee
empleador, -dora *n* PATRÓN : employer
emplear *vt* **1** : to employ **2** USAR : to use — **emplearse** *vr* **1** : to get a job **2** : to occupy oneself
empleo *nm* **1** OCUPACIÓN : employment, occupation, job **2** : use, usage
empobrecer {53} *vt* : to impoverish — *vi* : to become poor — **empobrecerse** *vr*
empobrecimiento *nm* : impoverishment
empollar *vi* : to brood eggs — *vt* : to incubate
empolvado, -da *adj* **1** : dusty **2** : powdered, powdery
empolvar *vt* **1** : to cover with dust **2** : to powder — **empolvarse** *vr* **1** : to gather dust **2** : to powder one's face
emporio *nm* **1** : center, capital, empire ⟨un emporio cultural : a cultural center⟩ ⟨un emporio financiero : a financial empire⟩ **2** : department store
empotrado, -da *adj* : built-in ⟨armarios empotrados : built-in cabinets⟩
empotrar *vt* : to build into, to embed
emprendedor, -dora *adj* : enterprising
emprender *vt* : to undertake, to begin
empresa *nf* **1** COMPAÑÍA, FIRMA : company, corporation, firm **2** : undertaking, venture
empresariado *nm* **1** : business world **2** : management, managers *pl*
empresarial *adj* : business, managerial, corporate
empresario, -ria *n* **1** : manager **2** : businessman *m*, businesswoman *f* **3** : impresario
empréstito *nm* : loan
empujar *vi* : to push, to shove — *vt* **1** : to push **2** PRESIONAR : to spur on, to press
empuje *nm* : impetus, drive
empujón *nm, pl* **-jones** : push, shove
empuñadura *nf* MANGO : hilt, handle
empuñar *vt* **1** ASIR : to grasp **2 empuñar las armas** : to take up arms
emú *nm* : emu
emular *vt* IMITAR : to emulate — **emulación** *nf*
emulsión *nf, pl* **-siones** : emulsion
emulsionante *nm* : emulsifier
emulsionar *vt* : to emulsify
en *prep* **1** : in ⟨en el bolsillo : in one's pocket⟩ ⟨en una semana : in a week⟩ **2** : on ⟨en la mesa : on the table⟩ **3** : at ⟨en casa : at home⟩ ⟨en el trabajo : at work⟩ ⟨en ese momento : at that moment⟩
enagua *nf* : petticoat, slip
enajenación *nf, pl* **-ciones** **1** : transfer (of property) **2** : alienation **3** : absentmindedness
enajenado, -da *adj* : out of one's mind
enajenar *vt* **1** : to transfer (property) **2** : to alienate **3** : to enrapture — **enajenarse** *vr* **1** : to become estranged **2** : to go mad
enaltecer {53} *vt* : to praise, to extol
enamorado¹, -da *adj* : in love
enamorado², -da *n* : lover, sweetheart
enamoramiento *nm* : infatuation, crush
enamorar *vt* : to enamor, to win the love of — **enamorarse** *vr* : to fall in love
enamoriscarse {72} *vr fam* : to have a crush, to be infatuated
enamorizado, -da *adj* : amorous, passionate
enano¹, -na *adj* : tiny, minute
enano², -na *n* : dwarf, midget
enarbolar *vt* **1** : to hoist, to raise **2** : to brandish
enarcar {72} *vt* : to arch, to raise
enardecer {53} *vt* **1** : to arouse (anger, passions) **2** : to stir up, to excite — **enardecerse** *vr*
encabezado *nm Mex* : headline
encabezamiento *nm* **1** : heading **2** : salutation, opening
encabezar {21} *vt* **1** : to head, to lead **2** : to put a heading on
encabritarse *vr* **1** : to rear up **2** *fam* : to get angry
encadenar *vt* **1** : to chain **2** : to connect, to link **3** INMOVILIZAR : to immobilize

encajar *vi* : to fit, to fit together, to fit in — *vt* **1** : to insert, to stick **2** : to take, to cope with ⟨encajó el golpe : he withstood the blow⟩
encaje *nm* **1** : lace **2** : financial reserve
encajonar *vt* **1** : to box, to crate **2** : to cram in
encalar *vt* : to whitewash
encallar *vi* **1** : to run aground **2** : to get stuck
encallecido, -da *adj* : callused
encamar *vt* : to confine to a bed
encaminado, -da *adj* **1** : on the right track **2 ~ a** : aimed at, designed to
encaminar *vt* **1** : to direct, to channel **2** : to head in the right direction — **encaminarse** *vr* **~ a** : to head for, to aim at
encandilar *vt* : to dazzle
encanecer {53} *vi* : to gray, to go gray
encantado, -da *adj* **1** : charmed, bewitched **2** : delighted
encantador[1], **-dora** *adj* : charming, delightful
encantador[2], **-dora** *n* : magician
encantamiento *nm* : enchantment, spell
encantar *vt* **1** : to enchant, to bewitch **2** : to charm, to delight ⟨me encanta esta canción : I love this song⟩
encanto *nm* **1** : charm, fascination **2** HECHIZO : spell **3** : delightful person or thing
encañonar *vt* : to point (a gun) at, to hold up
encapotado, -da *adj* : cloudy, overcast
encapotarse *vr* : to cloud over, to become overcast
encaprichado, -da *adj* : infatuated
encaprichamiento *nm* : infatuation
encapuchado, -da *adj* : hooded
encarado, -da *adj* **estar mal encarado** *fam* : to be ugly-looking, to look mean
encaramar *vt* : to raise, to lift up — **encaramarse** *vr* : to perch
encarar *vt* CONFRONTAR : to face, to confront
encarcelación *nf* → **encarcelamiento**
encarcelamiento *nm* : incarceration, imprisonment
encarcelar *vt* : to incarcerate, to imprison
encarecer {53} *vt* **1** : to increase, to raise (price, value) **2** : to beseech, to entreat — **encarecerse** *vr* : to become more expensive
encarecidamente *adv* : insistently, urgently
encarecimiento *nm* : increase, rise (in price)
encargado[1], **-da** *adj* : in charge
encargado[2], **-da** *n* : manager, person in charge
encargar {52} *vt* **1** : to put in charge of **2** : to recommend, to advise **3** : to order, to request — **encargarse** *vr* **~ de** : to take charge of
encargo *nm* **1** : errand **2** : job assignment **3** : order ⟨hecho de encargo : custom-made, made to order⟩
encariñarse *vr* **~ con** : to become fond of, to grow attached to
encarnación *nf, pl* **-ciones** : incarnation, embodiment
encarnado[1], **-da** *adj* **1** : incarnate **2** : flesh-colored **3** : red **4** : ingrown
encarnado[2] *nm* : red
encarnar *vt* : to incarnate, to embody — **encarnarse** *vr* **encarnarse una uña** : to have an ingrown nail
encarnizado, -da *adj* **1** : bloodshot, inflamed **2** : fierce, bloody
encarnizar {21} *vt* : to enrage, to infuriate — **encarnizarse** *vr* : to be brutal, to attack viciously
encarrilar *vt* : to guide, to put on the right track
encasillar *vt* CLASIFICAR : to classify, to pigeonhole, to categorize
encausar *vt* : to prosecute, to charge
encauzar {21} *vt* : to channel, to guide — **encauzarse** *vr*
encebollado, -da *adj* : cooked with onions
encefalitis *nms & pl* : encephalitis
enceguecedor, -dora *n* : blinding
encendedor *nm* : lighter
encender {56} *vi* : to light — *vt* **1** : to light, to set fire to **2** PRENDER : to switch on **3** : to start (a motor) **4** : to arouse, to kindle — **encenderse** *vr* **1** : to get excited **2** : to blush
encendido[1], **-da** *adj* **1** : burning **2** : flushed **3** : fiery, passionate
encendido[2] *nm* : ignition
encerado *nm* **1** : waxing, polishing **2** : blackboard
encerar *vt* : to wax, to polish
encerrar {55} *vt* **1** : to lock up, to shut away **2** : to contain, to include **3** : to involve, to entail
encerrona *nf* **1** TRAMPA : trap, setup **2** **prepararle una encerrona a alguien** : to set a trap for someone, to set someone up
encestar *vi* : to make a basket (in basketball)
enchapado *nm* : plating, coating (of metal)
encharcamiento *nm* : flood, flooding
encharcar {72} *vt* : to flood, to swamp — **encharcarse** *vr*
enchilada *nf* : enchilada
enchilar *vt Mex* : to season with chili
enchuecar {72} *vt Chile, Mex fam* : to make crooked, to twist
enchufar *vt* **1** : to plug in **2** : to connect, to fit together
enchufe *nm* **1** : connection **2** : plug, socket
encía *nf* : gum (tissue)
encíclica *nf* : encyclical
enciclopedia *nf* : encyclopedia
enciclopédico, -ca *adj* : encyclopedic
encierro *nm* **1** : confinement **2** : enclosure
encima *adv* **1** : on top, above **2** ADEMÁS : as well, besides **3 ~ de** : on, on top

of, over **4 por encima de** : above, beyond <por encima de la ley : above the law> **5 echarse encima** : to take upon oneself **6 estar encima de** *fam* : to nag, to criticize **7 quitarse de encima** : to get rid of
encina *nf* : evergreen oak
encinta *adj* EMBARAZADA, PREÑADA : pregnant, expecting
enclaustrado, -da *adj* : cloistered, shut away
enclavado, -da *adj* : buried
enclenque *adj* : weak, sickly
encoger {15} *vt* **1** : to shrink, to make smaller **2** : to intimidate — *vi* : to shrink, to contract — **encogerse** *vr* **1** : to shrink **2** : to be intimidated, to cower, to cringe **3 encogerse de hombros** : to shrug (one's shoulders)
encogido, -da *adj* **1** : shriveled, shrunken **2** TÍMIDO : shy, inhibited
encogimiento *nm* **1** : shrinking, shrinkage **2** : shrug **3** TIMIDEZ : shyness
encolar *vt* : to paste, to glue
encolerizar {21} *vt* ENFURECER : to enrage, to infuriate — **encolerizarse** *vr*
encomendar {55} *vt* CONFIAR : to entrust, to commend — **encomendarse** *vr*
encomiable *adj* : commendable, praiseworthy
encomiar *vt* ELOGIAR : to praise, to pay tribute to
encomienda *nf* **1** : charge, mission **2** : royal land grant **3** : parcel
encomio *nm* : praise, eulogy
encomioso, -sa *adj* : eulogistic, laudatory
enconar *vt* **1** : to irritate, to anger **2** : to inflame — **enconarse** *vr* **1** : to become heated **2** : to fester
encono *nm* **1** RENCOR : animosity, rancor **2** : inflammation, infection
encontrado, -da *adj* : contrary, opposing
encontrar {19} *vt* **1** HALLAR : to find **2** : to encounter, to meet — **encontrarse** *vr* **1** REUNIRSE : to meet **2** : to clash, to conflict **3** : to be <su abuelo se encuentra mejor : her grandfather is doing better>
encorvar *vt* : to bend, to curve — **encorvarse** *vr* : to hunch over, to stoop
encrespar *vt* **1** : to curl, to ruffle, to ripple **2** : to annoy, to irritate — **encresparse** *vr* **1** : to curl one's hair **2** : to become choppy **3** : to get annoyed
encrucijada *nf* : crossroads
encuadernación *nf, pl* **-ciones** : bookbinding
encuadernar *vt* EMPASTAR : to bind (a book)
encuadrar *vt* **1** ENMARCAR : to frame **2** ENCAJAR : to fit, to insert **3** COMPRENDER : to contain, to include
encubierto *pp* → **encubrir**
encubrimiento *nm* : cover-up
encubrir {2} *vt* : to cover up, to conceal
encuentro *nm* **1** : meeting, encounter **2** : conference, congress
encuerado, -da *adj fam* : naked
encuerar *vt fam* : to undress
encuesta *nf* **1** INVESTIGACIÓN, PESQUISA : inquiry, investigation **2** SONDEO : survey
encuestador, -dora *n* : pollster
encuestar *vt* : to poll, to take a survey of
encumbrado, -da *adj* **1** : lofty, high **2** : eminent, distinguished
encumbrar *vt* **1** : to exalt, to elevate **2** : to extol — **encumbrarse** *vr* : to reach the top
encurtir *vt* ESCABECHAR : to pickle
ende *adv* **por ~** : therefore, consequently
endeble *adj* : feeble, weak
endeblez *nf* : weakness, frailty
endémico, -ca *adj* : endemic
endemoniado, -da *adj* : fiendish, diabolical
endentecer {53} *vi* : to teethe
enderezar {21} *vt* **1** : to straighten (out) **2** : to stand on end, to put upright
endeudado, -da *adj* : in debt, indebted
endeudamiento *nm* : indebtedness
endeudarse *vr* **1** : to go into debt **2** : to feel obliged
endiabladamente *adv* : extremely, diabolically
endiablado, -da *adj* **1** : devilish, diabolical **2** : complicated, difficult
endibia *or* **endivia** *nf* : endive
endilgar {52} *vt fam* : to spring, to foist <me endilgó la responsabilidad : he saddled me with the responsibility>
endocrino, -na *adj* : endocrine
endogamia *nf* : inbreeding
endosar *vt* : to endorse
endoso *nm* : endorsement
endulzante *nm* : sweetener
endulzar {21} *vt* **1** : to sweeten **2** : to soften, to mellow — **endulzarse** *vr*
endurecer {53} *vt* : to harden, to toughen — **endurecerse** *vr*
enebro *nm* : juniper
eneldo *nm* : dill
enema *nm* : enema
enemigo, -ga *adj & n* : enemy
enemistad *nf* : enmity, hostility
enemistar *vt* : to make enemies of — **enemistarse** *vr* **~ con** : to fall out with
energía *nf* : energy
enérgico, -ca *adj* **1** : energetic, vigorous **2** : forceful, emphatic — **enérgicamente** *adv*
energúmeno, -na *n fam* : lunatic, crazy person
enero *nm* : January
enervar *vt* **1** : to enervate **2** *fam* : to annoy, to get on one's nerves — **enervante** *adj*
enésimo, -ma *adj* : umpteenth, nth
enfadar *vt* **1** : to annoy, to make angry **2** *Mex fam* : to bore — **enfadarse** *vr* : to get angry, to get annoyed

enfado *nm* : anger, annoyance
enfadoso, -sa *adj* : irritating, annoying
enfardar *vt* : to bale
énfasis *nms & pl* : emphasis
enfático, -ca *adj* : emphatic — **enfáticamente** *adv*
enfatizar {21} *vt* DESTACAR, SUBRAYAR : to emphasize
enfermar *vt* : to make sick — *vi* : to fall ill, to get sick — **enfermarse** *vr*
enfermedad *nf* **1** INDISPOSICIÓN : sickness, illness **2** : disease
enfermería *nf* : infirmary
enfermero, -ra *n* : nurse
enfermizo, -za *adj* : sickly
enfermo[1], **-ma** *adj* : sick, ill
enfermo[2], **-ma** *n* **1** : sick person, invalid **2** PACIENTE : patient
enfilar *vt* **1** : to take, to go along <enfiló la carretera de Montevideo : she went up the road to Montevideo> **2** : to line up, to put in a row **3** : to string, to thread **4** : to aim, to direct — *vi* : to make one's way
enflaquecer {53} *vi* : to lose weight, to become thin — *vt* : to emaciate
enfocar {72} *vt* **1** : to focus (on) **2** : to consider, to look at
enfoque *nm* : focus
enfrascamiento *nm* : immersion, absorption
enfrascarse {72} *vr* **~ en** : to immerse oneself in, to get caught up in
enfrentamiento *nm* : clash, confrontation
enfrentar *vt* : to confront, to face — **enfrentarse** *vr* **1 ~ con** : to clash with **2 ~ a** : to face up to
enfrente *adv* **1** DELANTE : in front **2** : opposite
enfriamiento *nm* **1** CATARRO : chill, cold **2** : cooling off, damper
enfriar {85} *vt* **1** : to chill, to cool **2** : to cool down, to dampen — *vi* : to get cold — **enfriarse** *vr* : to get chilled, to catch a cold
enfundar *vt* : to sheathe, to encase
enfurecer {53} *vt* ENCOLERIZAR : to infuriate — **enfurecerse** *vr* : to fly into a rage
enfurecido, -da *adj* : furious, raging
enfurruñarse *vr fam* : to sulk
engalanar *vt* : to decorate, to deck out — **engalanarse** *vr* : to dress up
enganchar *vt* **1** : to hook, to snag **2** : to attach, to hitch up — **engancharse** *vr* **1** : to get snagged, to get hooked **2** : to enlist
enganche *nm* **1** : hook **2** : coupling, hitch **3** *Mex* : down payment
engañar *vt* **1** EMBAUCAR : to trick, to deceive, to mislead **2** : to cheat on, to be unfaithful to — **engañarse** *vr* **1** : to be mistaken **2** : to deceive oneself
engaño *nm* **1** : deception, trick **2** : fake, feint (in sports)
engañoso, -sa *adj* **1** : deceitful **2** : misleading, deceptive
engarrotarse *vr* : to stiffen up, to go numb
engatusamiento *nm* : cajolery
engatusar *vt* : to coax, to cajole
engendrar *vt* **1** : to beget, to father **2** : to give rise to, to engender
engentarse *vr Mex* : to be in a daze
englobar *vt* : to include, to embrace
engomar *vt* : to glue
engordar *vt* : to fatten, to fatten up — *vi* : to gain weight
engorro *nm* : nuisance, bother
engorroso, -sa *adj* : bothersome
engranaje *nm* : gears *pl*, cogs *pl*
engranar *vt* : to mesh, to engage — *vi* : to mesh gears
engrandecer {53} *vt* **1** : to enlarge **2** : to exaggerate **3** : to exalt
engrandecimiento *nm* **1** : enlargement **2** : exaggeration **3** : exaltation
engrane *nm Mex* : cogwheel
engrapadora *nf* : stapler
engrapar *vt* : to staple
engrasar *vt* : to grease, to lubricate
engrase *nm* : greasing, lubrication
engreído, -da *adj* PRESUMIDO, VANIDOSO : vain, conceited, stuck-up
engreimiento *nm* ARROGANCIA : arrogance, conceit
engreír {66} *vt* ENVANECER : to make vain — **engreírse** *vr* : to become conceited
engrosar {19} *vt* : to enlarge, to increase, to swell — *vi* ENGORDAR : to gain weight
engrudo *nm* : paste
engullir {38} *vt* : to gulp down, to gobble up — **engullirse** *vr*
enharinar *vt* : to flour
enhebrar *vt* ENSARTAR : to string, to thread
enhiesto, -ta *adj* **1** : erect, upright **2** : lofty, towering
enhilar *vt* : to thread (a needle, etc.)
enhorabuena *nf* FELICIDADES : congratulations *pl*
enigma *nm* : enigma, mystery
enigmático, -ca *adj* : enigmatic — **enigmáticamente** *adv*
enjabonar *vt* : to soap up, to lather — **enjabonarse** *vr*
enjaezar {21} *vt* : to harness
enjalbegar {52} *vt* : to whitewash
enjambrar *vi* : to swarm
enjambre *nm* **1** : swarm **2** MUCHEDUMBRE : crowd, mob
enjaular *vt* **1** : to cage **2** *fam* : to jail, to lock up
enjuagar {52} *vt* : to rinse — **enjuagarse** *vr* : to rinse out
enjuague *nm* **1** : rinse **2 enjuague bucal** : mouthwash
enjugar {52} *vt* : to wipe away (tears)
enjuiciar *vt* **1** : to indict, to prosecute **2** JUZGAR : to try
enjundioso, -sa *adj* : substantial, weighty
enjuto, -ta *adj* : lean, gaunt

enlace *nm* **1** : bond, link, connection **2** : liaison
enladrillado *nm* : brick paving
enladrillar *vt* : to pave with bricks
enlatar *vt* ENVASAR : to can
enlazar {21} *v* : to join, to link, to fit together
enlistar *vt* : to list — **enlistarse** *vr* : to enlist
enlodado, -da *adj* BARROSO : muddy
enlodar *vt* **1** : to cover with mud **2** : to stain, to sully — **enlodarse** *vr*
enlodazar → **enlodar**
enloquecedor, -dora *adj* : maddening
enloquecer {53} *vt* ALOCAR : to drive crazy — **enloquecerse** *vr* : to go crazy
enlosado *nm* : flagstone pavement
enlosar *vt* : to pave with flagstone
enlutarse *vr* : to go into mourning
enmaderado *nm* **1** : wood paneling **2** : hardwood floor
enmarañar *vt* **1** : to tangle **2** : to complicate **3** : to confuse, to mix up — **enmarañarse** *vr*
enmarcar {72} *vt* **1** ENCUADRAR : to frame **2** : to provide the setting for
enmascarar *vt* : to mask, to disguise
enmasillar *vt* : to putty, to caulk
enmendar {55} *vt* **1** : to amend **2** CORREGIR : to emend, to correct **3** COMPENSAR : to compensate for — **enmendarse** *vr* : to mend one's ways
enmienda *nf* **1** : amendment **2** : correction, emendation
enmohecerse {53} *vr* **1** : to become moldy **2** OXIDARSE : to rust, to become rusty
enmudecer {53} *vt* : to mute, to silence — *vi* : to fall silent
enmugrar *vt* : to soil, to make dirty — **enmugrarse** *vr* : to get dirty
ennegrecer {53} *vt* : to blacken, to darken — **ennegrecerse** *vr*
ennoblecer {53} *vt* **1** : to ennoble **2** : to embellish
enojadizo, -za *adj* IRRITABLE : irritable, cranky
enojado, -da *adj* **1** : annoyed **2** : angry, mad
enojar *vt* **1** : to anger **2** : to annoy, to upset — **enojarse** *vr*
enojo *nm* **1** CÓLERA : anger **2** : annoyance
enojón, -jona *adj, pl* **-jones** *Chile, Mex fam* : irritable, cranky
enojoso, -sa *adj* FASTIDIOSO, MOLESTOSO : annoying, irritating
enorgullecer {53} *vt* : to make proud — **enorgullecerse** *vr* : to pride oneself
enorme *adj* INMENSO : enormous, huge — **enormemente** *adv*
enormidad *nf* **1** : enormity, seriousness **2** : immensity, hugeness
enraizado, -da *adj* : deep-seated, deeply rooted
enraizar {30} *vi* : to take root
enramada *nf* : arbor, bower
enramar *vt* : to cover with branches
enrarecer {53} *vt* : to rarefy — **enrarecerse** *vr*
enredadera *nf* : climbing plant, vine
enredar *vt* **1** : to tangle up, to entangle **2** : to confuse, to complicate **3** : to involve, to implicate — **enredarse** *vr*
enredo *nm* **1** EMBROLLO : muddle, confusion **2** MARAÑA : tangle
enredoso, -sa *adj* : complicated, tricky
enrejado *nm* **1** : railing **2** : grating, grille **3** : trellis, lattice
enrevesado, -da *adj* : complicated, involved
enriquecer {53} *vt* : to enrich — **enriquecerse** *vr* : to get rich
enriquecido, -da *adj* : enriched
enriquecimiento *nm* : enrichment
enrojecer {53} *vt* : to make red, to redden — **enrojecerse** *vr* : to blush
enrolar *vt* RECLUTAR : to recruit — **enrolarse** *vr* INSCRIBIRSE : to enlist, to sign up
enrollar *vt* : to roll up, to coil — **enrollarse** *vr*
enronquecerse {53} *vr* : to become hoarse
enroscar {72} *vt* TORCER : to twist — **enroscarse** *vr* : to coil, to twine
ensacar {72} *vt* : to bag (up)
ensalada *nf* : salad
ensaladera *nf* : salad bowl
ensalmo *nm* : incantation, spell
ensalzar {21} *vt* **1** : to praise, to extol **2** EXALTAR : to exalt
ensamblaje *nm* : assembly
ensamblar *vt* **1** : to assemble **2** : to join, to fit together
ensanchar *vt* **1** : to widen **2** : to expand, to extend — **ensancharse** *vr*
ensanche *nm* **1** : widening **2** : expansion, development
ensangrentado, -da *adj* : bloody, bloodstained
ensañarse *vr* : to act cruelly, to be merciless
ensartar *vt* **1** ENHEBRAR : to string, to thread **2** : to skewer, to pierce
ensayar *vi* : to rehearse — *vt* **1** : to try out, to test **2** : to assay
ensayista *nmf* : essayist
ensayo *nm* **1** : essay **2** : trial, test **3** : rehearsal **4** : assay (of metals)
enseguida *adv* INMEDIATAMENTE : right away, immediately, at once
ensenada *nf* : cove, inlet
enseña *nf* **1** INSIGNIA : emblem, insignia **2** : standard, banner
enseñanza *nf* **1** EDUCACIÓN : education **2** : teaching
enseñar *vt* **1** : to teach **2** MOSTRAR : to show, to display — **enseñarse** *vr* **~ a** : to learn to, to get used to
enseres *nmpl* : equipment, furnishings *pl* ⟨enseres domésticos : household goods⟩
ensillar *vt* : to saddle (up)
ensimismado, -da *adj* : absorbed, engrossed

ensimismarse *vr* : to lose oneself in thought
ensoberbecerse {53} *vr* : to become haughty
ensombrecer {53} *vt* : to cast a shadow over, to darken — **ensombrecerse** *vr*
ensoñación *nf, pl* **-ciones** : fantasy
ensopar *vt* **1** : to drench **2** : to dunk, to dip
ensordecedor, -dora *adj* : deafening, thunderous
ensordecer {53} *vt* : to deafen — *vi* : to go deaf
ensuciar *vt* : to soil, to dirty — **ensuciarse** *vr*
ensueño *nm* **1** : daydream, revery **2** FANTASÍA : illusion, fantasy
entablar *vt* **1** : to cover with boards **2** : to initiate, to enter into, to start
entallar *vt* AJUSTAR : to tailor, to fit, to take in — *vi* QUEDAR : to fit
ente *nm* **1** : being, entity **2** : body, organization ⟨ente rector : ruling body⟩ **3** *fam* : eccentric, crackpot
enteco, -ca *adj* : gaunt, frail
entenado, -da *n Mex* : stepchild, stepson *m,* stepdaughter *f*
entender[1] {56} *vt* **1** COMPRENDER : to understand **2** OPINAR : to think, to believe **3** : to mean, to intend **4** DEDUCIR : to infer, to deduce — *vi* **1** : to understand ⟨¡ya entiendo! : now I understand!⟩ **2** **~ de** : to know about, to be good at **3** **~ en** : to be in charge of — **entenderse** *vr* **1** : to be understood **2** : to get along well, to understand each other **3** **~ con** : to deal with
entender[2] *nm* **a mi entender** : in my opinion
entendible *adj* : understandable
entendido[1]**, -da** *adj* **1** : skilled, expert **2 tener entendido** : to understand, to be under the impression ⟨teníamos entendido que vendrías : we were under the impression you would come⟩ **3 darse por entendido** : to go without saying
entendido[2] *nm* : expert, authority, connoisseur
entendimiento *nm* **1** : intellect, mind **2** : understanding, agreement
enterado, -da *adj* : aware, well-informed ⟨estar enterado de : to be privy to⟩
enteramente *adv* : entirely, completely
enterar *vt* INFORMAR : to inform — **enterarse** *vr* INFORMARSE : to find out, to learn
entereza *nf* **1** INTEGRIDAD : integrity **2** FORTALEZA : fortitude **3** FIRMEZA : resolve
enternecedor, -dora *adj* CONMOVEDOR : touching, moving
enternecer {53} *vt* CONMOVER : to move, to touch
entero[1]**, -ra** *adj* **1** : entire, whole **2** : complete, absolute **3** : intact — **enteramente** *adv*
entero[2] *nm* **1** : integer, whole number **2** : point (in finance)
enterramiento *nm* : burial
enterrar {55} *vt* : to bury
entibiar *vt* : to cool (down) — **entibiarse** *vr* : to become lukewarm
entidad *nf* **1** ENTE : entity **2** : body, organization **3** : firm, company **4** : importance, significance
entierro *nm* **1** : burial **2** : funeral
entintar *vt* : to ink
entoldado *nm* : awning
entomología *nf* : entomology
entomólogo, -ga *n* : entomologist
entonación *nf, pl* **-ciones** : intonation
entonar *vi* : to be in tune — *vt* **1** : to intone **2** : to tone up
entonces *adv* **1** : then **2 desde ~** : since then **3 en aquel entonces** : in those days
entornado, -da *adj* ENTREABIERTO : half-closed, ajar
entornar *vt* ENTREABRIR : to leave ajar
entorno *nm* : surroundings *pl,* environment
entorpecer {53} *vt* **1** : to hinder, to obstruct **2** : to dull — **entorpecerse** *vr* : to dull the senses
entrada *nf* **1** : entrance, entry **2** : ticket, admission **3** : beginning, onset **4** : entrée **5** : cue (in music) **6 entradas** *nfpl* : income ⟨entradas y salidas : income and expenditures⟩ **7 tener entradas** : to have a receding hairline
entrado, -da *adj* **entrado en años** : elderly
entramado *nm* : framework
entrampar *vt* **1** ATRAPAR : to entrap, to ensnare **2** ENGAÑAR : to deceive, to trick
entrante *adj* **1** : next, upcoming ⟨el año entrante : next year⟩ **2** : incoming, new ⟨el presidente entrante : the president elect⟩
entraña *nf* **1** MEOLLO : core, heart, crux **2 entrañas** *nfpl* VÍSCERAS : entrails
entrañable *adj* : close, intimate
entrañar *vt* : to entail, to involve
entrar *vi* **1** : to enter, to go in, to come in **2** : to begin — *vt* **1** : to bring in, to introduce **2** : to access
entre *prep* **1** : between **2** : among
entreabierto[1] *pp* → **entreabrir**
entreabierto[2]**, -ta** *adj* ENTORNADO : half-open, ajar
entreabrir {2} *vt* ENTORNAR : to leave ajar
entreacto *nm* : intermission, interval
entrecano, -na *adj* : grayish, graying
entrecejo *nm* **fruncir el entrecejo** : to knit one's brows
entrecomillar *vt* : to place in quotation marks
entrecortado, -da *adj* **1** : labored, difficult ⟨respiración entrecortada : shortness of breath⟩ **2** : faltering, hesitant ⟨con la voz entrecortada : with a catch in his voice⟩

entrecruzar {21} *vt* ENTRELAZAR : to interweave, to intertwine — **entrecruzarse** *vr*
entredicho *nm* **1** DUDA : doubt, question **2** : prohibition
entrega *nf* **1** : delivery **2** : handing over, surrender **3** : installment 〈entrega inicial : down payment〉
entregar {52} *vt* **1** : to deliver **2** DAR : to give, to present **3** : to hand in, to hand over — **entregarse** *vr* **1** : to surrender, to give in **2** : to devote oneself
entrelazar {21} *vt* ENTRECRUZAR : to interweave, to intertwine
entremedias *adv* **1** : in between, halfway **2** : in the meantime
entremés *nm, pl* **-meses** **1** APERITIVO : appetizer, hors d'oeuvre **2** : interlude, short play
entremeterse → **entrometerse**
entremetido *nm* → **entrometido**
entremezclar *vt* : to intermingle
entrenador, -dora *n* : trainer, coach
entrenamiento *nm* : training, drill, practice
entrenar *vt* : to train, to drill, to practice — **entrenarse** *vr* : to train, to spar (in boxing)
entreoír {50} *vt* : to hear indistinctly
entrepierna *nf* **1** : inner thigh **2** : crotch **3** : inseam
entrepiso *nm* ENTRESUELO : mezzanine
entresacar {72} *vt* **1** SELECCIONAR : to pick out, to select **2** : to thin out
entresuelo *nm* ENTREPISO : mezzanine
entretanto¹ *adv* : meanwhile
entretanto² *nm* **en el entretanto** : in the meantime
entretejer *vt* : to interweave
entretela *nf* : facing (of a garment)
entretener {80} *vt* **1** DIVERTIR : to entertain, to amuse **2** DISTRAER : to distract **3** DEMORAR : to delay, to hold up — **entretenerse** *vr* **1** : to amuse oneself **2** : to dally
entretenido, -da *adj* DIVERTIDO : entertaining, amusing
entretenimiento *nm* **1** : entertainment, pastime **2** DIVERSIÓN : fun, amusement
entrever {88} *vt* **1** : to catch a glimpse of **2** : to make out, to see indistinctly
entreverar *vt* : to mix, to intermingle
entrevero *nm* : confusion, disorder
entrevista *nf* : interview
entrevistador, -dora *n* : interviewer
entrevistar *vt* : to interview — **entrevistarse** *vr* REUNIRSE **~ con** : to meet with
entristecer {53} *vt* : to sadden
entrometerse *vr* : to interfere, to meddle
entrometido, -da *n* : meddler, busybody
entroncar {72} *vt* RELACIONAR : to establish a relationship between, to connect — *vi* **1** : to be related **2** : to link up, to be connected
entronque *nm* **1** : kinship **2** VÍNCULO : link, connection
entuerto *nm* : wrong, injustice
entumecer {53} *vt* : to make numb, to be numb — **entumecerse** *vr* : to go numb, to fall asleep
entumecido, -da *adj* **1** : numb **2** : stiff (of muscles, joints, etc.)
entumecimiento *nm* : numbness
enturbiar *vt* **1** : to cloud **2** : to confuse — **enturbiarse** *vr*
entusiasmar *vt* : to excite, to fill with enthusiasm — **entusiasmarse** *vr* : to get excited
entusiasmo *nm* : enthusiasm
entusiasta¹ *adj* : enthusiastic
entusiasta² *nmf* AFICIONADO : enthusiast
enumerar *vt* : to enumerate — **enumeración** *nf*
enunciación *nf, pl* **-ciones** : enunciation, statement
enunciar *vt* : to enunciate, to state
envainar *vt* : to sheathe
envalentonar *vt* : to make bold, to encourage — **envalentonarse** *vr*
envanecer {53} *vt* ENGREÍR : to make vain — **envanecerse** *vr*
envasar *vt* **1** EMBOTELLAR : to bottle **2** ENLATAR : to can **3** : to pack in a container
envase *nm* **1** : packaging, packing **2** : container **3** LATA : can **4** : empty bottle
envejecer {53} *vt* : to age, to make look old — *vi* : to age, to grow old
envejecido, -da *adj* : aged, old-looking
envejecimiento *nm* : aging
envenenamiento *nm* : poisoning
envenenar *vt* **1** : to poison **2** : to embitter
envergadura *nf* **1** : span, breadth, spread **2** : importance, scope
envés *nm, pl* **enveses** : reverse, opposite side
enviado, -da *n* : envoy, correspondent
enviar {85} *vt* **1** : to send **2** : to ship
envidia *nf* : envy, jealousy
envidiar *vt* : to envy — **envidiable** *adj*
envidioso, -sa *adj* : envious, jealous
envilecer {53} *vt* : to degrade, to debase
envilecimiento *nm* : degradation, debasement
envío *nm* **1** : shipment **2** : remittance
enviudar *vi* : to be widowed, to become a widower
envoltorio *nm* **1** : bundle, package **2** : wrapping, wrapper
envoltura *nf* : wrapper, wrapping
envolver {89} *vt* **1** : to wrap **2** : to envelop, to surround **3** : to entangle, to involve — **envolverse** *vr* **1** : to become involved **2** : to wrap oneself (up)
envuelto *pp* → **envolver**
enyerbar *vt Mex* : to bewitch
enyesar *vt* **1** : to plaster **2** ESCAYOLAR : to put in a plaster cast
enzima *nf* : enzyme
éon *nm, pl* **eones** : aeon
eperlano *nm* : smelt (fish)

épico, **-ca** *adj* : epic
epicúreo[1], **-rea** *adj* : epicurean
epicúreo[2], **-rea** *n* : epicure
epidemia *nf* : epidemic
epidémico, **-ca** *adj* : epidemic
epidermis *nf* : epidermis
epifanía *nf* : feast of the Epiphany (January 6th)
epigrama *nm* : epigram
epilepsia *nf* : epilepsy
epiléptico, **-ca** *adj & n* : epileptic
epílogo *nm* : epilogue
episcopal *adj* : episcopal
episcopaliano, **-na** *adj & n* : Episcopalian
episódico, **-ca** *adj* : episodic
episodio *nm* : episode
epístola *nf* : epistle
epitafio *nm* : epitaph
epíteto *nm* : epithet, name
epítome *nm* : summary, abstract
época *nf* **1** EDAD, ERA, PERÍODO : epoch, age, period **2** : time of year, season **3 de ~** : vintage, antique
epopeya *nf* : epic poem
equidad *nf* JUSTICIA : equity, justice, fairness
equilátero, **-ra** *adj* : equilateral
equilibrado, **-da** *adj* : well-balanced
equilibrar *vt* : to balance — **equilibrarse** *vr*
equilibrio *nm* **1** : balance, equilibrium ⟨perder el equilibrio : to lose one's balance⟩ ⟨equilibrio político : balance of power⟩ **2** : poise, aplomb
equilibrista *nmf* ACRÓBATA, FUNÁMBULO : acrobat, tightrope walker
equino, **-na** *adj* : equine
equinoccio *nm* : equinox
equipaje *nm* BAGAJE : baggage, luggage
equipamiento *nm* : equipping, equipment
equipar *vt* : to equip — **equiparse** *vr*
equiparable *adj* : comparable
equiparar *vt* **1** IGUALAR : to put on a same level, to make equal **2** COMPARAR : to compare
equipo *nm* **1** : team, crew **2** : gear, equipment
equitación *nf, pl* **-ciones** : horseback riding, horsemanship
equitativo, **-va** *adj* JUSTO : equitable, fair, just — **equitativamente** *adv*
equivalencia *nf* : equivalence
equivalente *adj & nm* : equivalent
equivaler {84} *vi* : to be equivalent
equivocación *nf, pl* **-ciones** ERROR : error, mistake
equivocado, **-da** *adj* : mistaken, wrong — **equivocadamente** *adv*
equivocar {72} *vt* : to mistake, to confuse — **equivocarse** *vr* : to make a mistake, to be wrong
equívoco[1], **-ca** *adj* AMBIGUO : ambiguous, equivocal
equívoco[2] *nm* : misunderstanding
era[1], **etc.** → **ser**
era[2] *nf* EDAD, ÉPOCA : era, age
erario *nm* : public treasury
erección *nf, pl* **-ciones** : erection, raising
eremita *nmf* ERMITAÑO : hermit
ergonomía *nf* : ergonomics
erguido, **-da** *adj* : erect, upright
erguir {31} *vt* : to raise, to lift up — **erguirse** *vr* : to straighten up
erial *nm* : uncultivated land
erigir {35} *vt* : to build, to erect — **erigirse** *vr* **~ en** : to set oneself up as
erizado, **-da** *adj* : bristly
erizarse {21} *vr* : to bristle, to stand on end
erizo *nm* **1** : hedgehog **2 erizo de mar** : sea urchin
ermitaño[1], **-ña** *n* EREMITA : hermit, recluse
ermitaño[2] *nm* : hermit crab
erogación *nf, pl* **-ciones** : expenditure
erogar {52} *vt* **1** : to pay out **2** : to distribute
erosión *nf, pl* **-siones** : erosion
erosionar *vt* : to erode
erótico, **-ca** *adj* : erotic
erotismo *nm* : eroticism
errabundo, **-da** *adj* ERRANTE, VAGABUNDO : wandering
erradicar {72} *vt* : to eradicate — **erradicación** *nf*
errado, **-da** *adj* : wrong, mistaken
errante *adj* ERRABUNDO, VAGABUNDO : errant, wandering
errar {32} *vt* FALLAR : to miss — *vi* **1** DESACERTAR : to be wrong, to be mistaken **2** VAGAR : to wander
errata *nf* : misprint, error
errático, **-ca** *adj* : erratic — **erráticamente** *adv*
erróneo, **-nea** *adj* EQUIVOCADO : erroneous, wrong — **erróneamente** *adv*
error *nm* EQUIVOCACIÓN : error, mistake
eructar *vi* : to belch, to burp
eructo *nm* : belch, burp
erudición *nf, pl* **-ciones** : erudition, learning
erudito[1], **-ta** *adj* LETRADO : erudite, learned
erudito[2], **-ta** *n* : scholar
erupción *nf, pl* **-ciones** **1** : eruption **2** SARPULLIDO : rash
eruptivo, **-va** *adj* : eruptive
es → **ser**
esbelto, **-ta** *adj* DELGADO : slender, slim
esbirro *nm* : henchman
esbozar {21} *vt* BOSQUEJAR : to sketch, to outline
esbozo *nm* **1** : sketch **2** : rough draft
escabechar *vt* **1** ENCURTIR : to pickle **2** *fam* : to kill, to rub out
escabeche *nm* : brine (for pickling)
escabechina *nf* MASACRE : massacre, bloodbath
escabel *nm* : footstool
escabroso, **-sa** *adj* **1** : rugged, rough **2** : difficult, tough **3** : risqué
escabullirse {38} *vr* : to slip away, to escape

escala *nf* **1** : scale **2** ESCALERA : ladder **3** : stopover
escalada *nf* : ascent, climb
escalador, -dora *n* ALPINISTA : mountain climber
escalafón *nm, pl* **-fones 1** : list of personnel **2** : salary scale, rank
escalar *vt* : to climb, to scale — *vi* **1** : to go climbing **2** : to escalate
escaldar *vt* : to scald
escalera *nf* **1** : ladder ⟨escalera de tijera : stepladder⟩ **2** : stairs *pl*, staircase **3 escalera mecánica** : escalator
escalfador *nm* : chafing dish
escalfar *vt* : to poach (eggs)
escalinata *nf* : flight of stairs
escalofriante *adj* : horrifying, bloodcurdling
escalofrío *nm* : shiver, chill, shudder
escalón *nm, pl* **-lones 1** : echelon **2** : step, rung
escalonado, -da *adj* GRADUAL : gradual, staggered
escalonar *vt* **1** : to terrace **2** : to stagger, to alternate
escalpelo *nm* BISTURÍ : scalpel
escama *nf* **1** : scale (of fish or reptiles) **2** : flake (of skin)
escamar *vt* **1** : to scale (fish) **2** : to make suspicious
escamocha *nf Mex* : fruit salad
escamoso, -sa *adj* : scaly
escamotear *vt* **1** : to palm, to conceal **2** *fam* : to lift, to swipe **3** : to hide, to cover up
escandalizar {21} *vt* : to shock, to scandalize — *vi* : to make a fuss — **escandalizarse** *vr* : to be shocked
escándalo *nm* **1** : scandal **2** : scene, commotion
escandaloso, -sa *adj* **1** : shocking, scandalous **2** RUIDOSO : noisy, rowdy **3** : flagrant, outrageous — **escandalosamente** *adv*
escandinavo, -va *adj & n* : Scandinavian
escandir *vt* : to scan (poetry)
escanear *vt* : to scan
escáner *nm* : scanner, scan
escaño *nm* **1** : seat (in a legislative body) **2** BANCO : bench
escapada *nf* HUIDA : flight, escape
escapar *vi* HUIR : to escape, to flee, to run away — **escaparse** *vr* : to escape notice, to leak out
escaparate *nm* **1** : shop window **2** : showcase
escapatoria *nf* **1** : loophole, excuse, pretext ⟨no tener escapatoria : to have no way out⟩ **2** ESCAPADA : escape, flight
escape *nm* **1** FUGA : escape **2** : exhaust (from a vehicle)
escapismo *nm* : escapism
escápula *nf* OMÓPLATO : scapula, shoulder blade
escapulario *nm* : scapular
escarabajo *nm* : beetle
escaramuza *nf* **1** : skirmish **2** : scrimmage
escaramuzar {21} *vi* : to skirmish
escarapela *nf* : rosette (ornament)
escarbar *vt* **1** : to dig, to scratch up **2** : to poke, to pick **3 ~ en** : to investigate, to pry into
escarcha *nf* **1** : frost **2** *Mex, PRi* : glitter
escarchar *vt* **1** : to frost (a cake) **2** : to candy (fruit)
escardar *vt* **1** : to weed, to hoe **2** : to weed out
escariar *vt* : to ream
escarlata *adj & nf* : scarlet
escarlatina *nf* : scarlet fever
escarmentar {55} *vt* : to punish, to teach a lesson to — *vi* : to learn one's lesson
escarmiento *nm* **1** : lesson, warning **2** CASTIGO : punishment
escarnecer {53} *vt* RIDICULIZAR : to ridicule, to mock
escarnio *nm* : ridicule, mockery
escarola *nf* : escarole
escarpa *nf* : escarpment, steep slope
escarpado, -da *adj* : steep, sheer
escarpia *nf* : hook, spike
escasamente *adv* : scarcely, barely
escasear *vi* : to be scarce, to run short
escasez *nf, pl* **-seces** : shortage, scarcity
escaso, -sa *adj* **1** : scarce, scant **2 ~ de** : short of
escatimar *vt* : to skimp on, to be sparing with ⟨no escatimar esfuerzos : to spare no effort⟩
escayola *nf* **1** : plaster (for casts) **2** : plaster cast
escayolar *vt* : to put in a plaster cast
escena *nf* **1** : scene **2** : stage
escenario *nm* **1** ESCENA : stage **2** : setting, scene ⟨el escenario del crimen : the scene of the crime⟩
escénico, -ca *adj* **1** : scenic **2** : stage
escenificar {72} *vt* : to stage, to dramatize
escepticismo *nm* : skepticism
escéptico[1], **-ca** *adj* : skeptical
escéptico[2], **-ca** *n* : skeptic
escindirse *vr* **1** : to split **2** : to break away
escisión *nf, pl* **-siones 1** : split, division **2** : excision
esclarecer {53} *vt* **1** ELUCIDAR : to elucidate, to clarify **2** ILUMINAR : to illuminate, to light up
esclarecimiento *nm* ELUCIDACIÓN : elucidation, clarification
esclavitud *nf* : slavery
esclavización *nf, pl* **-ciones** : enslavement
esclavizar {21} *vt* : to enslave
esclavo, -va *n* : slave
esclerosis *nf* **esclerosis múltiple** : multiple sclerosis
esclusa *nf* : floodgate, lock (of a canal)
escoba *nf* : broom
escobilla *nf* : small broom, brush, whisk broom
escobillón *nm, pl* **-llones** : swab

escocer {14} *vi* ARDER : to smart, to sting — **escocerse** *vr* : to be sore
escocés[1], **-cesa** *adj, mpl* **-ceses 1** : Scottish **2** : tartan, plaid
escocés[2], **-cesa** *n, mpl* **-ceses** : Scottish person, Scot
escocés[3] *nm* **1** : Scots (language) **2** *pl* **-ceses** : Scotch (whiskey)
escofina *nf* : file, rasp
escoger {15} *vt* ELEGIR, SELECCIONAR : to choose, to select
escogido, -da *adj* : choice, select
escolar[1] *adj* : school
escolar[2] *nmf* : student, pupil
escolaridad *nf* : schooling ⟨escolaridad obligatoria : compulsory education⟩
escolarización *nf, pl* **-ciones** : education, schooling
escollo *nm* **1** : reef **2** OBSTÁCULO : obstacle
escolta *nmf* : escort
escoltar *vt* : to escort, to accompany
escombro *nm* **1** : debris, rubbish **2 escombros** *nmpl* : ruins, rubble
esconder *vt* OCULTAR : to hide, to conceal
escondidas *nfpl* **1** : hide-and-seek **2 a ~** : secretly, in secret
escondimiento *nm* : concealment
escondite *nm* **1** ENCONDRIJO : hiding place **2** ESCONDIDAS : hide-and-seek
escondrijo *nm* ESCONDITE : hiding place
escopeta *nf* : shotgun
escoplear *vt* : to chisel (out)
escoplo *nm* : chisel
escora *nf* : list, heeling
escorar *vi* : to list, to heel (of a boat)
escorbuto *nm* : scurvy
escoria *nf* **1** : slag, dross **2** HEZ : dregs *pl*, scum ⟨la escoria de la sociedad : the dregs of society⟩
Escorpio *or* **Escorpión** *nmf* : Scorpio
escorpión *nm, pl* **-piones** ALACRÁN : scorpion
escote *nm* **1** : low neckline **2 pagar a escote** : to go dutch
escotilla *nf* : hatch, hatchway
escotillón *nf, pl* **-llones** : trapdoor
escozor *nm* : smarting, stinging
escriba *nm* : scribe
escribano, -na *n* **1** : court clerk **2** NOTARIO : notary public
escribir {33} *v* **1** : to write **2** : to spell — **escribirse** *vr* CARTEARSE : to write to one another, to correspond
escrito[1] *pp* → **escribir**
escrito[2], **-ta** *adj* : written
escrito[3] *nm* **1** : written document **2 escritos** *nmpl* : writings, works
escritor, -tora *n* : writer
escritorio *nm* : desk
escritorzuelo, -la *n* : hack (writer)
escritura *nf* **1** : writing, handwriting **2** : deed **3 las Escrituras** : the Scriptures
escroto *nm* : scrotum
escrúpulo *nm* : scruple
escrupuloso, -sa *adj* **1** : scrupulous **2** METICULOSO : exact, meticulous — **escrupulosamente** *adv*
escrutador, -dora *adj* : penetrating, searching
escrutar *vt* ESCUDRIÑAR : to scrutinize, to examine closely
escrutinio *nm* : scrutiny
escuadra *nf* **1** : square (instrument) **2** : fleet, squadron
escuadrilla *nf* : squadron, formation, flight
escuadrón *nm, pl* **-drones** : squadron
escuálido, -da *adj* **1** : skinny, scrawny **2** INMUNDO : filthy, squalid
escuchar *vt* **1** : to listen to **2** : to hear — *vi* : to listen — **escucharse** *vr*
escudar *vt* : to shield — **escudarse** *vr* **~ en** : to hide behind
escudero *nm* : squire
escudo *nm* **1** : shield **2 escudo de armas** : coat of arms
escudriñar *vt* **1** ESCRUTAR : to scrutinize **2** : to inquire into, to investigate
escuela *nf* : school
escueto, -ta *adj* **1** : plain, simple **2** : succinct, concise — **escuetamente** *adv*
escuincle, -cla *n Mex fam* : child, kid
esculcar {72} *vt* : to search
esculpir *vt* **1** : to sculpt **2** : to carve, to engrave — *vi* : to sculpt
escultor, -tora *n* : sculptor
escultórico, -ca *adj* : sculptural
escultura *nf* : sculpture
escultural *adj* : statuesque
escupidera *nf* : spittoon, cuspidor
escupir *v* : to spit
escupitajo *nm* : spit
escurridizo, -za *adj* : slippery, elusive
escurridor *nm* **1** : dish rack **2** : colander
escurrir *vt* **1** : to wring out **2** : to drain — *vi* **1** : to drain **2** : to drip, to drip-dry — **escurrirse** *vr* : to slip away
ese, esa *adj, mpl* **esos** : that, those
ése, ésa *pron, mpl* **ésos** : that one, those ones *pl*
esencia *nf* : essence
esencial *adj* : essential — **esencialmente** *adv*
esfera *nf* **1** : sphere **2** : face, dial (of a watch)
esférico[1], **-ca** *adj* : spherical
esférico[2] *nm* : ball (in sports)
esfinge *nf* : sphinx
esforzado, -da *adj* **1** : energetic, vigorous **2** VALIENTE : courageous, brave
esforzar {36} *vt* : to strain — **esforzarse** *vr* : to make an effort
esfuerzo *nm* **1** : effort **2** ÁNIMO, VIGOR : spirit, vigor **3 sin ~** : effortlessly
esfumar *vt* : to tone down, to soften — **esfumarse** *vr* **1** : to fade away, to vanish **2** *fam* : to take off, to leave
esgrima *nf* : fencing (sport)
esgrimidor, -dora *n* : fencer
esgrimir *vt* **1** : to brandish, to wield **2** : to use, to resort to — *vi* : to fence

esguince *nm* : sprain, strain (of a muscle)
eslabón *nm, pl* **-bones** : link
eslabonar *vt* : to link, to connect, to join
eslavo[1], **-va** *adj* : Slavic
eslavo[2], **-va** *n* : Slav
eslogan *nm, pl* **-lóganes** : slogan
eslovaco, -ca *adj & n* : Slovakian, Slovak
esloveno, -na *adj & nm* : Slovene, Slovenian
esmaltar *vt* : to enamel
esmalte *nm* **1** : enamel **2 esmalte de uñas** : nail polish
esmerado, -da *adj* : careful, painstaking
esmeralda *nf* : emerald
esmerarse *vr* : to take great pains, to do one's utmost
esmeril *nm* : emery
esmero *nm* : meticulousness, great care
esmoquin *nm, pl* **-quins** : tuxedo
esnob[1] *adj, pl* **esnobs** : snobbish
esnob[2] *nmf, pl* **esnobs** : snob
esnobismo *nm* : snobbery, snobbishness
eso *pron* (*neuter*) **1** : that ⟨eso no me gusta : I don't like that⟩ **2 ¡eso es!** : that's it!, that's right! **3 a eso de** : around ⟨a eso de las tres : around three o'clock⟩ **4 en ~** : at that point, just then
esófago *nm* : esophagus
esos → **ese**
ésos → **ése**
esotérico, -ca *adj* : esoteric — **esotéricamente** *adv*
espabilado, -da *adj* : bright, smart
espabilarse *vr* **1** : to awaken **2** : to get a move on **3** : to get smart, to wise up
espacial *adj* **1** : space **2** : spatial
espaciar *vt* DISTANCIAR : to space out, to spread out
espacio *nm* **1** : space, room **2** : period, length (of time) **3 espacio exterior** : outer space
espacioso, -sa *adj* : spacious, roomy
espada[1] *nf* **1** : sword **2 espadas** *nfpl* : spades (in playing cards)
espada[2] *nm* MATADOR, TORERO : bullfighter, matador
espadaña *nf* **1** : belfry **2** : cattail
espadilla *nf* : scull, oar
espagueti *nm or* **espaguetis** *nmpl* : spaghetti
espalda *nf* **1** : back **2 espaldas** *nfpl* : shoulders, back **3 por la espalda** : from behind
espaldarazo *nm* **1** : recognition, support **2** : slap on the back
espaldera *nf* : trellis
espantajo *nm* : scarecrow
espantapájaros *nms & pl* : scarecrow
espantar *vt* ASUSTAR : to scare, to frighten — **espantarse** *vr*
espanto *nm* : fright, fear, horror
espantoso, -sa *adj* **1** : frightening, terrifying **2** : frightful, dreadful
español[1], **-ñola** *adj* : Spanish
español[2], **-ñola** *n* : Spaniard
español[3] *nm* CASTELLANO : Spanish (language)
esparadrapo *nm* : adhesive bandage, Band-Aid™
esparcimiento *nm* **1** DIVERSIÓN, RECREO : entertainment, recreation **2** DESCANSO : relaxation **3** DISEMINACIÓN : dissemination, spreading
esparcir {83} *vt* DISPERSAR : to scatter, to spread — **esparcirse** *vr* **1** : to spread out **2** DESCANSARSE : to take it easy **3** DIVERTIRSE : to amuse oneself
espárrago *nm* : asparagus
espartano, -na *adj* : severe, austere
espasmo *nm* : spasm
espasmódico, -ca *adj* : spasmodic
espástico, -ca *adj* : spastic
espátula *nf* : spatula
especia *nf* : spice
especial *adj & nm* : special
especialidad *nf* : specialty
especialista *nmf* : specialist, expert
especialización *nf, pl* **-ciones** : specialization
especializarse {21} *vr* : to specialize
especialmente *adv* : especially, particularly
especie *nf* **1** : species **2** CLASE, TIPO : type, kind, sort
especificación *nf, pl* **-ciones** : specification
especificar {72} *vt* : to specify
específico, -ca *adj* : specific — **específicamente** *adv*
espécimen *nm, pl* **especímenes** : specimen
especioso, -sa *adj* : specious
espectacular *adj* : spectacular — **espectacularmente** *adv*
espectáculo *nm* **1** : spectacle, sight **2** : show, performance
espectador, -dora *n* : spectator, onlooker
espectro *nm* **1** : ghost, specter **2** : spectrum
especulación *nf, pl* **-ciones** : speculation
especulador, -dora *n* : speculator
especular *vi* : to speculate
especulativo, -va *adj* : speculative
espejismo *nm* **1** : mirage **2** : illusion
espejo *nm* : mirror
espejuelos *nmpl* ANTEOJOS : spectacles, glasses
espeluznante *adj* : hair-raising, terrifying
espera *nf* : wait
esperado, -da *adj* : anticipated
esperanza *nf* : hope, expectation
esperanzado, -da *adj* : hopeful
esperanzador, -dora *adj* : encouraging, promising
esperanzar {21} *vt* : to give hope to
esperar *vt* **1** AGUARDAR : to wait for, to await **2** : to expect **3** : to hope ⟨espero poder trabajar : I hope to be able to work⟩ ⟨espero que sí : I hope so⟩ — *vi*

: to wait — **esperarse** *vr* **1** : to expect, to be hoped ⟨como podría esperarse : as would be expected⟩ **2** : to hold on, to hang on ⟨espérate un momento : hold on a minute⟩

esperma *nmf* : sperm

esperpéntico, -ca *adj* GROTESCO : grotesque

esperpento *nm fam* MAMARRACHO : sight, fright ⟨voy hecha un esperpento : I really look a sight⟩

espesante *nm* : thickener

espesar *vt* : to thicken — **espesarse** *vr*

espeso, -sa *adj* : thick, heavy, dense

espesor *nm* : thickness, density

espesura *nf* **1** : thickness **2** : thicket

espetar *vt* **1** : to blurt out **2** : to skewer

espía *nmf* : spy

espiar {85} *vt* : to spy on, to observe — *vi* : to spy

espiga *nf* **1** : ear (of wheat) **2** : spike (of flowers)

espigado, -da *adj* : willowy, slender

espigar {52} *vt* : to glean, to gather — **espigarse** *vr* : to grow quickly, to shoot up

espigón *nm, pl* **-gones** : breakwater

espina *nf* **1** : thorn **2** : spine ⟨espina dorsal : spinal column⟩ **3** : fish bone

espinaca *nf* **1** : spinach (plant) **2 espinacas** *nfpl* : spinach (food)

espinal *adj* : spinal

espinazo *nm* : backbone

espineta *nf* : spinet

espinilla *nf* **1** BARRO, GRANO : pimple **2** : shin

espino *nm* : hawthorn

espinoso, -sa *adj* **1** : thorny, prickly **2** : bony (of fish) **3** : knotty, difficult

espionaje *nm* : espionage

espiración *nf, pl* **-ciones** : exhalation

espiral *adj & nf* : spiral

espirar *vt* EXHALAR : to breathe out, to give off — *vi* : to exhale

espiritismo *nm* : spiritualism

espiritista *nmf* : spiritualist

espíritu *nm* **1** : spirit **2** ÁNIMO : state of mind, spirits *pl* **3 el Espíritu Santo** : the Holy Ghost

espiritual *adj* : spiritual — **espiritualmente** *adv*

espiritualidad *nf* : spirituality

espita *nf* : spigot, tap

esplendidez *nf, pl* **-deces** ESPLENDOR : magnificence, splendor

espléndido, -da *adj* **1** : splendid, magnificent **2** : generous, lavish — **espléndidamente** *adv*

esplendor *nm* ESPLENDIDEZ : splendor

esplendoroso, -sa *adj* MAGNÍFICO : magnificent, grand

espliego *nm* LAVANDA : lavender

espolear *vt* : to spur on

espoleta *nf* **1** DETONADOR : detonator, fuse **2** : wishbone

espolón *nm, pl* **-lones** : spur (of poultry), fetlock (of a horse)

espolvorear *vt* : to sprinkle, to dust

esponja *nf* **1** : sponge **2 tirar la esponja** : to throw in the towel

esponjado, -da *adj* : spongy

esponjoso, -sa *adj* **1** : spongy **2** : soft, fluffy

esponsales *nmpl* : betrothal, engagement

espontaneidad *nf* : spontaneity

espontáneo, -nea *adj* : spontaneous — **espontáneamente** *adv*

espora *nf* : spore

esporádico, -ca *adj* : sporadic — **esporádicamente** *adv*

esposar *vt* : to handcuff

esposas *nfpl* : handcuffs

esposo, -sa *n* : spouse, wife *f*, husband *m*

esprint *nm* : sprint

esprintar *vi* : to sprint

esprínter *nmf* : sprinter

espuela *nf* : spur

espuerta *nf* : two-handled basket

espulgar {52} *vt* **1** : to delouse **2** : to scrutinize

espuma *nf* **1** : foam **2** : lather **3** : froth, head (on beer)

espumar *vi* : to foam, to froth — *vt* : to skim off

espumoso, -sa *adj* : foamy, frothy

espurio, -ria *adj* : spurious

esputar *v* : to expectorate, to spit

esputo *nm* : spit, sputum

esqueje *nm* : cutting (from a plant)

esquela *nf* **1** : note **2** : notice, announcement

esquelético, -ca *adj* : emaciated, skeletal

esqueleto *nm* **1** : skeleton **2** ARMAZÓN : framework

esquema *nf* BOSQUEJO : outline, sketch, plan

esquemático, -ca *adj* : schematic

esquí *nm* **1** : ski **2 esquí acuático** : water ski, waterskiing

esquiador, -dora *n* : skier

esquiar {85} *vi* : to ski

esquife *nm* : skiff

esquila *nf* **1** CENCERRO : cowbell **2** : shearing

esquilar *vt* TRASQUILAR : to shear

esquimal *adj & nmf* : Eskimo

esquina *nf* : corner

esquinazo *nm* **1** : corner **2 dar esquinazo a** *fam* : to stand up, to give the slip to

esquirla *nf* : splinter (of bone, glass, etc.)

esquirol *nm* ROMPEHUELGAS : strikebreaker, scab

esquisto *nm* : shale

esquivar *vt* **1** EVADIR : to dodge, to evade **2** EVITAR : to avoid

esquivez *nf, pl* **-veces** **1** : aloofness **2** TIMIDEZ : shyness

esquivo, -va *adj* **1** HURAÑO : aloof, unsociable **2** : shy **3** : elusive, evasive

esquizofrenia *nf* : schizophrenia

esquizofrénico, -ca *adj & n* : schizophrenic

esta *adj* → **este**[1]
ésta → **éste**
estabilidad *nf* : stability
estabilización *nf, pl* **-ciones** : stabilization
estabilizador *nm* : stabilizer
estabilizar {21} *vt* : to stabilize — **estabilizarse** *vr*
estable *adj* : stable, steady
establecer {53} *vt* FUNDAR, INSTITUIR : to establish, to found, to set up — **establecerse** *vr* INSTALARSE : to settle, to establish oneself
establecimiento *nm* **1** : establishing **2** : establishment, institution, office
establo *nm* : stable
estaca *nf* : stake, picket, post
estacada *nf* **1** : picket fence **2** : stockade
estacar {72} *vt* **1** : to stake out **2** : to fasten down with stakes — **estacarse** *vr* : to remain rigid
estación *nf, pl* **-ciones** **1** : station ⟨estación de servicio : service station, gas station⟩ **2** : season
estacional *adj* : seasonal
estacionamiento *nm* **1** : parking **2** : parking lot
estacionar *vt* **1** : to place, to station **2** : to park — **estacionarse** *vr* **1** : to park **2** : to remain stationary
estacionario, -ria *adj* **1** : stationary **2** : stable
estada *nf* : stay
estadía *nf* ESTANCIA : stay, sojourn
estadio *nm* **1** : stadium **2** : phase, stage
estadista *nmf* : statesman
estadística *nf* **1** : statistic, figure **2** : statistics
estadístico[1], **-ca** *adj* : statistical — **estadísticamente** *adv*
estadístico[2], **-ca** *n* : statistician
estado *nm* **1** : state **2** : status ⟨estado civil : marital status⟩ **3** CONDICIÓN : condition
estadounidense *adj & nmf* AMERICANO, NORTEAMERICANO : American
estafa *nf* : swindle, fraud
estafador, -dora *n* : cheat, swindler
estafar *vt* DEFRAUDAR : to swindle, to defraud
estalactita *nf* : stalactite
estalagmita *nf* : stalagmite
estallar *vi* **1** REVENTAR : to burst, to explode, to erupt **2** : to break out
estallido *nm* **1** EXPLOSIÓN : explosion **2** : report (of a gun) **3** : outbreak, outburst
estambre *nm* **1** : worsted (fabric) **2** : stamen
estampa *nf* **1** ILUSTRACIÓN, IMAGEN : printed image, illustration **2** ASPECTO : appearance, demeanor
estampado[1], **-da** *adj* : patterned, printed
estampado[2] *nm* : print, pattern
estampar *vt* : to stamp, to print, to engrave
estampida *nf* : stampede
estampilla *nf* **1** : rubber stamp **2** SELLO, TIMBRE : postage stamp
estancado, -da *adj* : stagnant
estancamiento *nm* : stagnation
estancar {72} *vt* **1** : to dam up, to hold back **2** : to bring to a halt, to deadlock — **estancarse** *vr* **1** : to stagnate **2** : to be brought to a standstill, to be deadlocked
estancia *nf* **1** ESTADÍA : stay, sojourn **2** : ranch, farm
estanciero, -ra *n* : rancher, farmer
estanco, -ca *adj* : watertight
estándar *adj & nm* : standard
estandarización *nf, pl* **-ciones** : standardization
estandarizar {21} *vt* : to standardize
estandarte *nm* : standard, banner
estanque *nm* **1** : pool, pond **2** : tank, reservoir
estante *nm* REPISA : shelf
estantería *nf* : shelves *pl,* bookcase
estaño *nm* : tin
estaquilla *nf* **1** : peg **2** ESPIGA : spike
estar {34} *v aux* : to be ⟨estoy aprendiendo inglés : I'm learning English⟩ ⟨está terminado : it's finished⟩ — *vi* **1** (*indicating a state or condition*) : to be ⟨está muy alto : he's so tall, he's gotten very tall⟩ ⟨¿ya estás mejor? : are you feeling better now?⟩ ⟨estoy casado : I'm married⟩ **2** (*indicating location*) : to be ⟨están en la mesa : they're on the table⟩ ⟨estamos en la página 2 : we're on page 2⟩ **3** : to be at home ⟨¿está María? : is Maria in?⟩ **4** : to remain ⟨estaré aquí 5 días : I'll be here for 5 days⟩ **5** : to be ready, to be done ⟨estará para las diez : it will be ready by ten o'clock⟩ **6** : to agree ⟨¿estamos? : are we in agreement?⟩ ⟨estoy contigo : I'm with you⟩ **7 ¿cómo estás?** : how are you? **8 ¡está bien!** : all right!, that's fine! **9 ~ a** : to cost **10 ~ a** : to be ⟨¿a qué día estamos? : what's today's date?⟩ **11 ~ con** : to have ⟨está con fiebre : she has a fever⟩ **12 ~ de** : to be ⟨estoy de vacaciones : I'm on vacation⟩ ⟨está de director hoy : he's acting as director today⟩ **13 estar bien (mal)** : to be well (sick) **14 ~ para** : to be in the mood for **15 ~ por** : to be in favor of **16 ~ por** : to be about to ⟨está por cerrar : it's on the verge of closing⟩ **17 estar de más** : to be unnecessary **18 estar que** : to be (in a state or condition) ⟨está que echa chispas : he's hopping mad⟩ — **estarse** *vr* QUEDARSE : to stay, to remain ⟨¡estáte quieto! : be still!⟩
estarcir {83} *vt* : to stencil
estatal *adj* : state, national
estática *nf* : static
estático, -ca *adj* : static
estatizar {21} *vt* : to nationalize — **estatización** *nf*
estatua *nf* : statue

estatuilla *nf* : statuette, figurine
estatura *nf* : height, stature ⟨de mediana estatura : of medium height⟩
estatus *nm* : status, prestige
estatutario, -ria *adj* : statutory
estatuto *nm* : statute
este[1], **esta** *adj, mpl* **estos** : this, these
este[2] *adj* : eastern, east
este[3] *nm* **1** ORIENTE : east **2** : east wind **3 el Este** : the East, the Orient
éste, ésta *pron, mpl* **éstos** **1** : this one, these ones *pl* **2** : the latter
estela *nf* **1** : wake (of a ship) **2** RASTRO : trail (of dust, smoke, etc.)
estelar *adj* : stellar
estelarizar {21} *vt Mex* : to star in, to be the star of
esténcil *nm* : stencil
estentóreo, -rea *adj* : loud, thundering
estepa *nf* : steppe
éster *nf* : ester
estera *nf* : mat
estercolero *nm* : dunghill
estéreo *adj & nm* : stereo
estereofónico, -ca *adj* : stereophonic
estereotipado, -da *adj* : stereotyped
estereotipar *vt* : to stereotype
estereotipo *nm* : stereotype
estéril *adj* **1** : sterile, germ-free **2** : infertile, barren **3** : futile, vain
esterilidad *nf* **1** : sterility **2** : infertility
esterilizar {21} *vt* **1** : to sterilize, to disinfect **2** : to sterilize (a person), to spay (an animal) — **esterilización** *nf*
esterlina *adj* : sterling
esternón *nm, pl* **-nones** : sternum
estero *nm* : estuary
estertor *nm* : death rattle
estética *nf* : aesthetics
estético, -ca *adj* : aesthetic — **estéticamente** *adv*
estetoscopio *nm* : stethoscope
estibador, -dora *n* : longshoreman, stevedore
estibar *vt* : to load (freight)
estiércol *nm* : dung, manure
estigma *nm* : stigma
estigmatizar {21} *vt* : to stigmatize, to brand
estilarse *vr* : to be in fashion
estilete *nm* : stiletto
estilista *nmf* : stylist
estilizar {21} *vt* : to stylize
estilo *nm* **1** : style **2** : fashion, manner **3** : stylus
estima *nf* ESTIMACIÓN : esteem, regard
estimable *adj* **1** : considerable **2** : estimable, esteemed
estimación *nf, pl* **-ciones** **1** ESTIMA : esteem, regard **2** : estimate
estimado, -da *adj* : esteemed, dear ⟨Estimado señor Ortiz : Dear Mr. Ortiz⟩
estimar *vt* **1** APRECIAR : to esteem, to respect **2** EVALUAR : to estimate, to appraise **3** OPINAR : to consider, to deem
estimulación *nf, pl* **-ciones** : stimulation
estimulante[1] *adj* : stimulating
estimulante[2] *nm* : stimulant
estimular *vt* **1** : to stimulate **2** : to encourage
estímulo *nm* **1** : stimulus **2** INCENTIVO : incentive, encouragement
estío *nm* : summertime
estipendio *nm* **1** : salary **2** : stipend, remuneration
estipular *vt* : to stipulate — **estipulación** *nf*
estirado, -da *adj* **1** : stretched, extended **2** PRESUMIDO : stuck-up, conceited
estiramiento *nm* **1** : stretching **2 estiramiento facial** : face-lift
estirar *vt* : to stretch (out), to extend — **estirarse** *vr*
estirón *nm, pl* **-rones** **1** : pull, tug **2 dar un estirón** : to grow quickly, to shoot up
estirpe *nf* LINAJE : lineage, stock
estival *adj* VERANIEGO : summer
esto *pron* (*neuter*) **1** : this ⟨¿qué es esto? : what is this?⟩ **2 en ~** : at this point **3 por ~** : for this reason
estocada *nf* **1** : final thrust (in bullfighting) **2** : thrust, lunge (in fencing)
estofa *nf* CLASE : class, quality ⟨de baja estofa : low-class, poor-quality⟩
estofado *nm* COCIDO, GUISADO : stew
estofar *vt* GUISAR : to stew
estoicismo *nm* : stoicism
estoico[1], **-ca** *adj* : stoic, stoical
estoico[2], **-ca** *n* : stoic
estola *nf* : stole
estomacal *adj* GÁSTRICO : stomach, gastric
estómago *nm* : stomach
estoniano, -na *adj & n* : Estonian
estonio, -nia *adj & n* : Estonian
estopa *nf* **1** : tow (yarn or cloth) **2** : burlap
estopilla *nf* : cheesecloth
estoque *nm* : rapier, sword
estorbar *vt* OBSTRUIR : to obstruct, to hinder — *vi* : to get in the way
estorbo *nm* **1** : obstacle, hindrance **2** : nuisance
estornino *nm* : starling
estornudar *vi* : to sneeze
estornudo *nm* : sneeze
estos *adj* → **este**[1]
éstos → **éste**
estoy → **estar**
estrabismo *nm* : squint
estrado *nm* **1** : dais, platform, bench (of a judge) **2 estrados** *nmpl* : courts of law
estrafalario, -ria *adj* ESTRAMBÓTICO, EXCÉNTRICO : eccentric, bizarre
estragar {52} *vt* DEVASTAR : to ruin, to devastate
estragón *nm* : tarragon
estragos *nmpl* **1** : ravages, destruction, devastation ⟨los estragos de la guerra : the ravages of war⟩ **2 hacer estragos en** *or* **causar estragos entre** : to play havoc with
estrambótico, -ca *adj* ESTRAFALARIO, EXCÉNTRICO : eccentric, bizarre

estrangulamiento *nm* : strangling, strangulation
estrangular *vt* AHOGAR : to strangle — **estrangulación** *nf*
estratagema *nf* ARTIMAÑA : stratagem, ruse
estratega *nmf* : strategist
estrategia *nf* : strategy
estratégico, -ca *adj* : strategic, tactical — **estratégicamente** *adv*
estratificación *nf, pl* **-ciones** : stratification
estratificado, -da *adj* : stratified
estrato *nm* : stratum, layer
estratosfera *nf* : stratosphere
estratosférico, -ca *adj* **1** : stratospheric **2** : astronomical, exorbitant
estrechamiento *nm* **1** : narrowing **2** : narrow point **3** : tightening, strengthening (of relations)
estrechar *vt* **1** : to narrow **2** : to tighten, to strengthen (a bond) **3** : to hug, to embrace **4 estrechar la mano de** : to shake hands with — **estrecharse** *vr*
estrechez *nf, pl* **-checes** **1** : tightness, narrowness **2 estrecheces** *nfpl* : financial problems
estrecho[1], **-cha** *adj* **1** : tight, narrow **2** ÍNTIMO : close — **estrechamente** *adv*
estrecho[2] *nm* : strait, narrows
estrella *nf* **1** ASTRO : star ⟨estrella fugaz : shooting star⟩ **2** : destiny ⟨tener buena estrella : to be born lucky⟩ **3** : movie star **4 estrella de mar** : starfish
estrellado, -da *adj* **1** : starry **2** : star-shaped **3 huevos estrellados** : fried eggs
estrellamiento *nm* : crash, collision
estrellar *vt* : to smash, to crash — **estrellarse** *vr* : to crash, to collide
estrellato *nm* : stardom
estremecedor, -dora *adj* : horrifying
estremecer {53} *vt* : to cause to shake — *vi* : to tremble, to shake — **estremecerse** *vr* : to shudder, to shiver (with emotion)
estremecimiento *nm* : trembling, shaking, shivering
estrenar *vt* **1** : to use for the first time **2** : to premiere, to open — **estrenarse** *vr* : to make one's debut
estreno *nm* DEBUT : debut, premiere
estreñimiento *nm* : constipation
estreñirse {67} *vr* : to be constipated
estrépito *nm* ESTRUENDO : clamor, din
estrepitoso, -sa *adj* : clamorous, noisy — **estrepitosamente** *adv*
estrés *nm, pl* **estreses** : stress
estresante *adj* : stressful
estresar *vt* : to stress, to stress out
estría *nf* : fluting, groove
estribación *nf, pl* **-ciones** **1** : spur, ridge **2 estribaciones** *nfpl* : foothills
estribar *vi* FUNDARSE **~ en** : to be due to, to stem from
estribillo *nm* : refrain, chorus
estribo *nm* **1** : stirrup **2** : abutment, buttress **3 perder los estribos** : to lose one's temper
estribor *nm* : starboard
estricnina *nf* : strychnine
estricto, -ta *adj* SEVERO : strict, severe — **estrictamente** *adv*
estridente *adj* : strident, shrill, loud — **estridentemente** *adv*
estrofa *nf* : stanza, verse
estrógeno *nm* : estrogen
estropajo *nm* : scouring pad
estropear *vt* **1** ARRUINAR : to ruin, to spoil **2** : to break, to damage — **estropearse** *vr* **1** : to spoil, to go bad **2** : to break down
estropicio *nm* DAÑO : damage, breakage
estructura *nf* : structure, framework
estructuración *nf, pl* **-ciones** : structuring, structure
estructural *adj* : structural — **estructuralmente** *adv*
estructurar *vt* : to structure, to organize
estruendo *nm* ESTRÉPITO : racket, din, roar
estruendoso, -sa *adj* : resounding, thunderous
estrujar *vt* APRETAR : to press, to squeeze
estuario *nm* : estuary
estuche *nm* : kit, case
estuco *nm* : stucco
estudiado, -da *adj* : affected, mannered
estudiantado *nm* : student body, students *pl*
estudiante *nmf* : student
estudiantil *adj* : student ⟨la vida estudiantil : student life⟩
estudiar *v* : to study
estudio *nm* **1** : study **2** : studio **3 estudios** *nmpl* : studies, education
estudioso, -sa *adj* : studious
estufa *nf* **1** : stove, heater **2** *Col, Mex* : cooking stove, range
estupefacción *nf, pl* **-ciones** : stupefaction, astonishment
estupefaciente[1] *adj* : narcotic
estupefaciente[2] *nm* DROGA, NARCÓTICO : drug, narcotic
estupefacto, -ta *adj* : astonished, stunned
estupendo, -da *adj* MARAVILLOSO : stupendous, marvelous — **estupendamente** *adv*
estupidez *nf, pl* **-deces** **1** : stupidity **2** : nonsense
estúpido[1], **-da** *adj* : stupid — **estúpidamente** *adj*
estúpido[2], **-da** *n* IDIOTA : idiot, fool
estupor *nm* **1** : stupor **2** : amazement
esturión *nm, pl* **-riones** : sturgeon
estuvo, etc. → **estar**
etano *nm* : ethane
etanol *nm* : ethanol
etapa *nf* FASE : stage, phase
etcétera[1] : et cetera, and so on
etcétera[2] *nmf* : et cetera
éter *nm* : ether

etéreo, -rea *adj* : ethereal, heavenly
eternidad *nf* : eternity
eternizar {21} *vt* PERPETUAR : to make eternal, to perpetuate — **eternizarse** *vr fam* : to take forever
eterno, -na *adj* : eternal, endless — **eternamente** *adv*
ética *nf* : ethics
ético, -ca *adj* : ethical — **éticamente** *adv*
etimología *nf* : etymology
etimológico, -ca *adj* : etymological
etimólogo, -ga *n* : etymologist
etíope *adj & nmf* : Ethiopian
etiqueta *nf* **1** : etiquette **2** : tag, label **3 de** ~ : formal, dressy
etiquetar *vt* : to label
étnico, -ca *adj* : ethnic
etnología *nf* : ethnology
etnólogo, -ga *n* : ethnologist
eucalipto *nm* : eucalyptus
Eucaristía *nf* : Eucharist, communion
eucarístico, -ca *adj* : eucharistic
eufemismo *nm* : euphemism
eufemístico, -ca *adj* : euphemistic
eufonía *nf* : euphony
eufónico, -ca *adj* : euphonious
euforia *nf* : euphoria, joyousness
eufórico, -ca *adj* : euphoric, exuberant, joyous — **eufóricamente** *adv*
eunuco *nm* : eunuch
europeo, -pea *adj & n* : European
euskera *nm* : Basque (language)
eutanasia *nf* : euthanasia
evacuación *nf, pl* **-ciones** : evacuation
evacuar *vt* **1** : to evacuate, to vacate **2** : to carry out — *vi* : to have a bowel movement
evadir *vt* ELUDIR : to evade, to avoid — **evadirse** *vr* : to escape, to slip away
evaluación *nf, pl* **-ciones** : assessment, evaluation
evaluador, -dora *n* : assessor
evaluar {3} *vt* : to evaluate, to assess, to appraise
evangélico, -ca *adj* : evangelical — **evangélicamente** *adv*
evangelio *nm* : gospel
evangelismo *nm* : evangelism
evangelista *nm* : evangelist
evangelizador, -dora *n* : evangelist, missionary
evaporación *nf, pl* **-ciones** : evaporation
evaporar *vt* : to evaporate — **evaporarse** *vr* ESFUMARSE : to disappear, to vanish
evasión *nf, pl* **-siones** **1** : escape, flight **2** : evasion, dodge
evasiva *nf* : excuse, pretext
evasivo, -va *adj* : evasive
evento *nm* : event
eventual *adj* **1** : possible **2** : temporary ⟨trabajadores eventuales : temporary workers⟩ — **eventualmente** *adv*
eventualidad *nf* : possibility, eventuality
evidencia *nf* **1** : evidence, proof **2 poner en evidencia** : to demonstrate, to make clear
evidenciar *vt* : to demonstrate, to show — **evidenciarse** *vr* : to be evident
evidente *adj* : evident, obvious, clear — **evidentemente** *adv*
eviscerar *vt* : to eviscerate
evitable *adj* : avoidable, preventable
evitar *vt* **1** : to avoid **2** PREVENIR : to prevent **3** ELUDIR : to escape, to elude
evocación *nf, pl* **-ciones** : evocation
evocador, -dora *adj* : evocative
evocar {72} *vt* **1** : to evoke **2** RECORDAR : to recall
evolución *nf, pl* **-ciones** **1** : evolution **2** : development, progress
evolucionar *vi* **1** : to evolve **2** : to change, to develop
evolutivo, -va *adj* : evolutionary
exabrupto *nm* : pointed remark
exacción *nf, pl* **-ciones** : levying, exaction
exacerbar *vt* **1** : to exacerbate, to aggravate **2** : to irritate, to exasperate
exactamente *adv* : exactly
exactitud *nf* PRECISIÓN : accuracy, precision, exactitude
exacto, -ta *adj* PRECISO : accurate, precise, exact
exageración *nf, pl* **-ciones** : exaggeration
exagerado, -da *adj* **1** : exaggerated **2** : excessive — **exageradamente** *adv*
exagerar *v* : to exaggerate
exaltación *nf, pl* **-ciones** **1** : exaltation **2** : excitement, agitation
exaltado¹, -da *adj* : excitable, hotheaded
exaltado², -da *n* : hothead
exaltar *vt* **1** ENSALZAR : to exalt, to extol **2** : to excite, to agitate — **exaltarse** *vr* ACALORARSE : to get overexcited
ex–alumno → **alumno**
examen *nm, pl* **exámenes** **1** : examination, test **2** : consideration, investigation
examinar *vt* **1** : to examine **2** INSPECCIONAR : to inspect — **examinarse** *vr* : to take an exam
exánime *adj* **1** : lifeless **2** : exhausted
exasperante *adj* : exasperating
exasperar *vt* IRRITAR : to exasperate, to irritate — **exasperación** *nf*
excavación *nf, pl* **-ciones** : excavation
excavadora *nf* : excavator
excavar *v* : to excavate, to dig
excedente¹ *adj* **1** : excessive **2** : excess, surplus
excedente² *nm* : surplus, excess
exceder *vt* : to exceed, to surpass — **excederse** *vr* : to go too far
excelencia *nf* **1** : excellence **2** : excellency ⟨Su Excelencia : His Excellency⟩
excelente *adj* : excellent — **excelentemente** *adv*
excelso, -sa *adj* : lofty, sublime
excentricidad *nf* : eccentricity
excéntrico, -ca *adj & n* : eccentric
excepción *nf, pl* **-ciones** : exception
excepcional *adj* EXTRAORDINARIO : exceptional, extraordinary, rare

excepto *prep* SALVO : except
exceptuar {3} *vt* EXCLUIR : to except, to exclude
excesivo, -va *adj* : excessive — **excesivamente** *adv*
exceso *nm* **1** : excess **2 excesos** *nmpl* : excesses, abuses **3 exceso de velocidad** : speeding
excitabilidad *nf* : excitability
excitación *nf, pl* **-ciones** : excitement
excitante *adj* : exciting
excitar *vt* : to excite, to arouse — **excitarse** *vr*
exclamación *nf, pl* **-ciones** : exclamation
exclamar *v* : to exclaim
excluir {41} *vt* EXCEPTUAR : to exclude, to leave out
exclusión *nf, pl* **-siones** : exclusion
exclusividad *nf* **1** : exclusiveness **2** : exclusive rights *pl*
exclusivista *adj & nmf* : exclusivist
exclusivo, -va *adj* : exclusive — **exclusivamente** *adv*
excomulgar {52} *vt* : to excommunicate
excomunión *nf, pl* **-niones** : excommunication
excreción *nf, pl* **-ciones** : excretion
excremento *nm* : excrement
excretar *vt* : to excrete
exculpar *vt* : to exonerate, to exculpate — **exculpación** *nf*
excursión *nf, pl* **-siones** : excursion, outing
excursionista *nmf* **1** : sightseer, tourist **2** : hiker
excusa *nf* **1** PRETEXTO : excuse **2** DISCULPA : apology
excusado *nm Mex* : toilet
excusar *vt* **1** : to excuse **2** : to exempt — **excusarse** *vr* : to apologize, to send one's regrets
execrable *adj* : detestable, abominable
exención *nf, pl* **-ciones** : exemption
exento, -ta *adj* **1** : exempt, free **2 exento de impuestos** : tax-exempt
exequias *nfpl* FUNERALES : funeral rites
exhalación *nf, pl* **-ciones** **1** : exhalation **2** : shooting star ⟨salió como una exhalación : he took off like a shot⟩
exhalar *vt* ESPIRAR : to exhale, to give off
exhaustivo, -va *adj* : exhaustive — **exhaustivamente** *adv*
exhausto, -ta *adj* AGOTADO : exhausted, worn-out
exhibición *nf, pl* **-ciones** **1** : exhibition, show **2** : showing
exhibir *vt* : to exhibit, to show, to display — **exhibirse** *vr*
exhortación *nf, pl* **-ciones** : exhortation
exhortar *vt* : to exhort
exhumar *vt* DESENTERRAR : to exhume — **exhumación** *nf*
exigencia *nf* : demand, requirement
exigente *adj* : demanding, exacting
exigir {35} *vt* **1** : to demand, to require **2** : to exact, to levy
exiguo, -gua *adj* : meager
exiliado[1], **-da** *adj* : exiled, in exile
exiliado[2], **-da** *n* : exile
exiliar *vt* DESTERRAR : to exile, to banish — **exiliarse** *vr* : to go into exile
exilio *nm* DESTIERRO : exile
eximio, -mia *adj* : distinguished, eminent
eximir *vt* EXONERAR : to exempt
existencia *nf* **1** : existence **2 existencias** *nfpl* MERCANCÍA : goods, stock
existente *adj* **1** : existing, in existence **2** : in stock
existir *vi* : to exist
éxito *nm* **1** TRIUNFO : success, hit **2 tener éxito** : to be successful
exitoso, -sa *adj* : successful — **exitosamente** *adv*
éxodo *nm* : exodus
exoneración *nf, pl* **-ciones** EXENCIÓN : exoneration, exemption
exonerar *vt* **1** EXIMIR : to exempt, to exonerate **2** DESPEDIR : to dismiss
exorbitante *adj* : exorbitant
exorcismo *nm* : exorcism — **exorcista** *nmf*
exorcizar {21} *vt* : to exorcise
exótico, -ca *adj* : exotic
expandir *vt* EXPANSIONAR : to expand — **expandirse** *vr* : to spread
expansión *nf, pl* **-siones** **1** : expansion, spread **2** DIVERSIÓN : recreation, relaxation
expansionar *vt* EXPANDIR : to expand — **expansionarse** *vr* **1** : to expand **2** DIVERTIRSE : to amuse oneself, to relax
expansivo, -va *adj* : expansive
expatriado, -da *adj & n* : expatriate
expatriarse {85} *vr* **1** EMIGRAR : to emigrate **2** : to go into exile
expectación *nf, pl* **-ciones** : expectation, anticipation
expectante *adj* : expectant
expectativa *nf* **1** : expectation, hope **2 expectativas** *nfpl* : prospects
expedición *nf, pl* **-ciones** : expedition
expediente *nm* **1** : expedient, means **2** ARCHIVO : file, dossier, record
expedir {54} *vt* **1** EMITIR : to issue **2** DESPACHAR : to dispatch, to send
expedito, -ta *adj* **1** : free, clear **2** : quick, easy
expeler *vt* : to expel, to eject
expendedor, -dora *n* : dealer, seller
expendio *nm* TIENDA : store, shop
expensas *nfpl* **1** : expenses, costs **2 a expensas de** : at the expense of
experiencia *nf* **1** : experience **2** EXPERIMENTO : experiment
experimentación *nf, pl* **-ciones** : experimentation
experimental *adj* : experimental
experimentar *vi* : to experiment — *vt* **1** : to experiment with, to test out **2** : to experience
experimento *nm* EXPERIENCIA : experiment

experto, -ta *adj & n* : expert
expiación *nf, pl* **-ciones** : expiation, atonement
expiar {85} *vt* : to expiate, to atone for
expiración *nf, pl* **-ciones** VENCIMIENTO : expiration
expirar *vi* **1** FALLECER, MORIR : to pass away, to die **2** : to expire
explanada *nf* : esplanade, promenade
explayar *vt* : to extend — **explayarse** *vr* : to expound, to speak at length
explicable *adj* : explicable, explainable
explicación *nf, pl* **-ciones** : explanation
explicar {72} *vt* : to explain — **explicarse** *vr* : to understand
explicativo, -va *adj* : explanatory
explicitar *vt* : to state explicitly, to specify
explícito, -ta *adj* : explicit — **explícitamente** *adv*
exploración *nf, pl* **-ciones** : exploration
explorador, -dora *n* : explorer, scout
explorar *vt* : to explore — **exploratorio, -ria** *adj*
explosión *nf, pl* **-siones** **1** ESTALLIDO : explosion **2** : outburst ⟨una explosión de ira : an outburst of anger⟩
explosionar *vi* : to explode
explosivo, -va *adj* : explosive
explotación *nf, pl* **-ciones** **1** : exploitation **2** : operation, running
explotar *vt* **1** : to exploit **2** : to operate, to run — *vi* ESTALLAR, REVENTAR : to explode — **explotable** *adj*
exponencial *adj* : exponential — **exponencialmente** *adv*
exponente *nm* : exponent
exponer {60} *vt* **1** : to exhibit, to show, to display **2** : to explain, to present, to set forth **3** : to expose, to risk — *vi* : to exhibit
exportación *nf, pl* **-ciones** **1** : exportation **2 exportaciones** *nfpl* : exports
exportador, -dora *n* : exporter
exportar *vt* : to export — **exportable** *adj*
exposición *nf, pl* **-ciones** **1** EXHIBICIÓN : exposition, exhibition **2** : exposure **3** : presentation, statement
expositor, -tora *n* **1** : exhibitor **2** : exponent
exprés *nms & pl* **1** : express, express train **2** : espresso
expresamente *adv* : expressly, on purpose
expresar *vt* : to express — **expresarse** *vr*
expresión *nf, pl* **-siones** : expression
expresivo, -va *adj* **1** : expressive **2** CARIÑOSO : affectionate — **expresivamente** *adv*
expreso¹, -sa *adj* : express, specific
expreso² *nm* : express train, express
exprimidor *nm* : squeezer, juicer
exprimir *vt* **1** : to squeeze **2** : to exploit
expropiar *vt* : to expropriate, to commandeer — **expropiación** *nf*
expuesto¹ *pp* → **exponer**
expuesto², -ta *adj* **1** : exposed **2** : hazardous, risky
expulsar *vt* : to expel, to eject
expulsión *nf, pl* **-siones** : expulsion
expurgar {52} *vt* : to expurgate
expuso, etc. → **exponer**
exquisitez *nf, pl* **-teces** **1** : exquisiteness, refinement **2** : delicacy, special dish
exquisito, -ta *adj* **1** : exquisite **2** : delicious
extasiarse {85} *vr* : to be in ecstasy, to be enraptured
éxtasis *nms & pl* : ecstasy, rapture
extático, -ca *adj* : ecstatic
extemporáneo, -nea *adj* **1** : unseasonable **2** : untimely
extender {56} *vt* **1** : to spread out, to stretch out **2** : to broaden, to expand ⟨extender la influencia : to broaden one's influence⟩ **3** : to draw up (a document), to write out (a check) — **extenderse** *vr* **1** : to spread **2** : to last
extendido, -da *adj* **1** : outstretched **2** : widespread
extensamente *adv* : extensively, at length
extensible *adj* : extensible, extendable
extensión *nf, pl* **-siones** **1** : extension, stretching **2** : expanse, spread **3** : extent, range **4** : length, duration
extensivo, -va *adj* **1** : extensive **2 hacer extensivo** : to extend
extenso, -sa *adj* **1** : extensive, detailed **2** : spacious, vast
extenuar {3} *vt* : to exhaust, to tire out — **extenuarse** *vr* — **extenuante** *adj*
exterior¹ *adj* **1** : exterior, external **2** : foreign ⟨asuntos exteriores : foreign affairs⟩
exterior² *nm* **1** : outside **2** : abroad
exteriorizar {21} *vt* : to express, to reveal
exteriormente *adv* : outwardly
exterminar *vt* : to exterminate — **exterminación** *nf*
exterminio *nm* : extermination
externar *vt Mex* : to express, to display
externo, -na *adj* : external, outward
extinción *nf, pl* **-ciones** : extinction
extinguidor *nm* : fire extinguisher
extinguir {26} *vt* **1** APAGAR : to extinguish, to put out **2** : to wipe out — **extinguirse** *vr* **1** APAGARSE : to go out, to fade out **2** : to die out, to become extinct
extinto, -ta *adj* : extinct
extintor *nm* : extinguisher
extirpación *n, pl* **-ciones** : removal, excision
extirpar *vt* : to eradicate, to remove, to excise — **extirparse** *vr*
extorsión *nf, pl* **-siones** **1** : extortion **2** : harm, trouble
extorsionar *vt* : to extort
extra¹ *adv* : extra
extra² *adj* **1** : additional, extra **2** : superior, top-quality
extra³ *nmf* : extra (in movies)

extra[4] *nm* : extra expense ⟨paga extra : bonus⟩
extracción *nf, pl* **-ciones** : extraction
extracto *nm* **1** : extract ⟨extracto de vainilla : vanilla extract⟩ **2** : abstract, summary
extractor *nm* : extractor
extracurricular *adj* : extracurricular
extradición *nf, pl* **-ciones** : extradition
extraditar *vt* : to extradite
extraer {81} *vt* : to extract
extraído *pp* → **extraer**
extrajudicial *adj* : out-of-court
extramatrimonial *adj* : extramarital
extranjerizante *adj* : foreign-sounding, foreign-looking
extranjero[1], **-ra** *adj* : foreign
extranjero[2], **-ra** *n* : foreigner
extranjero[3] *nm* : foreign countries *pl* ⟨viajó al extranjero : he traveled abroad⟩ ⟨trabajan en el extranjero : they work overseas⟩
extrañamente *adv* : strangely, oddly
extrañamiento *nm* ASOMBRO : amazement, surprise, wonder
extrañar *vt* : to miss (someone) — **extrañarse** *vr* : to be surprised
extrañeza *nf* **1** : strangeness, oddness **2** : surprise
extraño[1], **-ña** *adj* **1** RARO : strange, odd **2** EXTRANJERO : foreign
extraño[2], **-ña** *n* DESCONOCIDO : stranger
extraoficial *adj* OFICIOSO : unofficial — **extraoficialmente** *adv*
extraordinario, -ria *adj* EXCEPCIONAL : extraordinary — **extraordinariamente** *adv*
extrasensorial *adj* : extrasensory ⟨percepción extrasensorial : extrasensory perception⟩
extraterrestre *adj & nmf* : extraterrestrial, alien
extravagancia *nf* : extravagance, outlandishness, flamboyance
extravagante *adj* : extravagant, outrageous, flamboyant
extraviar {85} *vt* **1** : to mislead, to lead astray **2** : to misplace, to lose — **extraviarse** *vr* : to get lost, to go astray
extravío *nm* **1** PÉRDIDA : loss, misplacement **2** : misconduct
extremado, -da *adj* : extreme — **extremadamente** *adv*
extremar *vt* : to carry to extremes — **extremarse** *vr* : to do one's utmost
extremidad *nf* **1** : extremity, tip, edge **2 extremidades** *nfpl* : extremities
extremista *adj & nmf* : extremist
extremo[1], **-ma** *adj* **1** : extreme, utmost **2** EXCESIVO : excessive **3 en caso extremo** : as a last resort
extremo[2] *nm* **1** : extreme, end **2 al extremo de** : to the point of **3 en ~** : in the extreme
extrovertido[1], **-da** *adj* : extroverted, outgoing
extrovertido[2], **-da** *n* : extrovert
extrudir *vt* : to extrude
exuberancia *nf* **1** : exuberance **2** : luxuriance, lushness
exuberante *adj* : exuberant, luxuriant — **exuberantemente** *adv*
exudar *vt* : to exude
exultación *nf, pl* **-ciones** : exultation, elation
exultante *adj* : exultant, elated — **exultantemente** *adv*
exultar *vi* : to exult, to rejoice
eyacular *vi* : to ejaculate — **eyaculación** *nf*
eyección *nf, pl* **-ciones** : ejection, expulsion
eyectar *vt* : to eject, to expel — **eyectarse** *vr*

F

f *nf* : sixth letter of the Spanish alphabet
fábrica *nf* FACTORÍA : factory
fabricación *nf, pl* **-ciones** : manufacture
fabricante *nmf* : manufacturer
fabricar {72} *vt* MANUFACTURAR : to manufacture, to make
fabril *adj* INDUSTRIAL : industrial, manufacturing
fábula *nf* **1** : fable **2** : fabrication, fib
fabuloso, -sa *adj* **1** : fabulous, fantastic **2** : mythical, fabled
facción *nf, pl* **facciones 1** : faction **2 facciones** *nfpl* RASGOS : features
faccioso, -sa *adj* : factious
faceta *nf* : facet
facha *nf* : appearance, look ⟨estar hecho una facha : to look a sight⟩
fachada *nf* : facade
facial *adj* : facial
fácil *adj* **1** : easy **2** : likely, probable ⟨es fácil que no pase : it probably won't happen⟩
facilidad *nf* **1** : facility, ease **2 facilidades** *nfpl* : facilities, services **3 facilidades** *nfpl* : opportunities
facilitar *vt* **1** : to facilitate **2** : to provide, to supply
fácilmente *adv* : easily, readily
facsímil *or* **facsímile** *nm* **1** : facsimile, copy **2** : fax
facsimilar *adj* : facsimile
factibilidad *nf* : feasibility
factible *adj* : feasible, practicable
facticio, -cia *adj* : artificial, factitious
factor[1], **-tora** *n* **1** : agent, factor **2** : baggage clerk
factor[2] *nm* ELEMENTO : factor, element
factoría *nf* FÁBRICA : factory
factótum *nm* : factotum

factura *nf* **1** : making, manufacturing **2** : bill, invoice
facturación *nf, pl* **-ciones** **1** : invoicing, billing **2** : check-in
facturar *vt* **1** : to bill, to invoice **2** : to register, to check in
facultad *nf* **1** : faculty, ability ⟨facultades mentales : mental faculties⟩ **2** : authority, power **3** : school (of a university) ⟨facultad de derecho : law school⟩
facultar *vt* : to authorize, to empower
facultativo, -va *adj* **1** OPTATIVO : voluntary, optional **2** : medical ⟨informe facultativo : medical report⟩
faena *nf* : task, job, work ⟨faenas domésticas : housework⟩
faenar *vi* **1** : to work, to labor **2** PESCAR : to fish
fagot *nm* : bassoon
faisán *nm, pl* **faisanes** : pheasant
faja *nf* **1** : sash, belt **2** : girdle **3** : strip (of land)
fajar *vt* **1** : to wrap (a sash or girdle) around **2** : to hit, to thrash — **fajarse** *vr* **1** : to put on a sash or girdle **2** : to come to blows
fajín *nm, pl* **-jines** : sash, belt
fajo *nm* : bundle, sheaf ⟨un fajo de billetes : a wad of cash⟩
falacia *nf* : fallacy
falaz, -laza *adj, mpl* **falaces** FALSO : fallacious, false
falda *nf* **1** : skirt ⟨falda escocesa : kilt⟩ **2** REGAZO : lap (of the body) **3** VERTIENTE : side, slope
faldón *nm, pl* **-dones** **1** : tail (of a shirt, etc.) **2** : full skirt **3 faldón bautismal** : christening gown
falible *adj* : fallible
fálico, -ca *adj* : phallic
falla *nf* **1** : flaw, defect **2** : (geological) fault **3** : fault, failing
fallar *vi* **1** FRACASAR : to fail, to go wrong **2** : to rule (in a court of law) — *vt* **1** ERRAR : to miss (a target) **2** : to pronounce judgment on
fallecer {53} *vi* MORIR : to pass away, to die
fallecido, -da *adj & n* DIFUNTO : deceased
fallecimiento *nm* : demise, death
fallido, -da *adj* : failed, unsuccessful
fallo *nm* **1** SENTENCIA : sentence, judgment, verdict **2** : error, fault
falo *nm* : phallus, penis
falsamente *adv* : falsely
falsear *vt* **1** : to falsify, to fake **2** : to distort — *vi* **1** CEDER : to give way **2** : to be out of tune
falsedad *nf* **1** : falseness, hypocrisy **2** MENTIRA : falsehood, lie
falsete *nm* : falsetto
falsificación *nf, pl* **-ciones** **1** : counterfeit, forgery **2** : falsification
falsificador, -dora *n* : counterfeiter, forger
falsificar {72} *vt* **1** : to counterfeit, to forge **2** : to falsify
falso, -sa *adj* **1** FALAZ : false, untrue **2** : counterfeit, forged
falta *nf* **1** CARENCIA : lack ⟨hacer falta : to be lacking, to be needed⟩ **2** DEFECTO : defect, fault, error **3** : offense, misdemeanor **4** : foul (in basketball), fault (in tennis)
faltar *vi* **1** : to be lacking, to be needed ⟨me falta tiempo : I don't have enough time⟩ **2** : to be absent, to be missing **3** QUEDAR : to remain, to be left ⟨faltan pocos días para la fiesta : the party is just a few days away⟩ **4 ¡no faltaba más!** : don't mention it!, you're welcome!
falto, -ta *adj* **~ de** : lacking (in), short of
fama *nf* **1** : fame **2** REPUTACIÓN : reputation **3 de mala fama** : disreputable
famélico, -ca *adj* HAMBRIENTO : starving, famished
familia *nf* **1** : family **2 familia política** : in-laws
familiar[1] *adj* **1** CONOCIDO : familiar **2** : familial, family **3** INFORMAL : informal
familiar[2] *nmf* PARIENTE : relation, relative
familiaridad *nf* **1** : familiarity **2** : informality
familiarizarse {21} *vr* **~ con** : to familiarize oneself with
famoso[1]**, -sa** *adj* CÉLEBRE : famous
famoso[2]**, -sa** *n* : celebrity
fanal *nm* **1** : beacon, signal light **2** *Mex* : headlight
fanático, -ca *adj & n* : fanatic
fanatismo *nm* : fanaticism
fandango *nm* : fandango
fanfarria *nf* **1** : (musical) fanfare **2** : pomp, ceremony
fanfarrón[1]**, -rrona** *adj, mpl* **-rrones** *fam* : bragging, boastful
fanfarrón[2]**, -rrona** *n, mpl* **-rrones** *fam* : braggart
fanfarronada *nf* : boast, bluster
fanfarronear *vi* : to brag, to boast
fango *nm* LODO : mud, mire
fangosidad *nf* : muddiness
fangoso, -sa *adj* LODOSO : muddy
fantasear *vi* : to fantasize, to daydream
fantasía *nf* **1** : fantasy **2** : imagination
fantasioso, -sa *adj* : fanciful
fantasma *nm* : ghost, phantom
fantasmagórico, -ca *adj* : phantasmagoric
fantasmal *adj* : ghostly
fantástico, -ca *adj* **1** : fantastic, imaginary, unreal **2** *fam* : great, fantastic
faquir *nm* : fakir
farándula *nf* : show business, theater
faraón *nm, pl* **faraones** : pharaoh
fardo *nm* **1** : bale **2** : bundle
farfulla *nf* : jabbering
farfullar *v* : to jabber, to gabble
faringe *nf* : pharynx

faríngeo, -gea *adj* : pharyngeal
fariña *nf* : coarse manioc flour
farmacéutico¹, **-ca** *adj* : pharmaceutical
farmacéutico², **-ca** *n* : pharmacist
farmacia *nf* : drugstore, pharmacy
fármaco *nm* : medicine, drug
farmacodependencia *nf* : drug addiction
farmacología *nf* : pharmacology
faro *nm* **1** : lighthouse **2** : headlight
farol *nm* **1** : streetlight **2** : lantern, lamp **3** *fam* : bluff **4** *Mex* : headlight
farola *nf* **1** : lamppost **2** : streetlight
farolero, -ra *n fam* : bluffer
farra *nf* : spree, revelry
fárrago *nm* REVOLTIJO : hodgepodge, jumble
farsa *nf* **1** : farce **2** : fake, sham
farsante *nmf* CHARLATÁN : charlatan, fraud, phony
fascículo *nm* : fascicle, part (of a publication)
fascinación *nf, pl* **-ciones** : fascination
fascinante *adj* : fascinating
fascinar *vt* **1** : to fascinate **2** : to charm, to captivate
fascismo *nm* : fascism
fascista *adj & nmf* : fascist
fase *nf* : phase, stage
fastidiar *vt* **1** MOLESTAR : to annoy, to bother, to hassle **2** ABURRIR : to bore — *vi* : to be annoying or bothersome
fastidio *nm* **1** MOLESTIA : annoyance, nuisance, hassle **2** ABURRIMIENTO : boredom
fastidioso, -sa *adj* **1** MOLESTO : annoying, bothersome **2** ABURRIDO : boring
fatal *adj* **1** MORTAL : fatal **2** *fam* : awful, terrible **3** : fateful, unavoidable
fatalidad *nf* **1** : fatality **2** DESGRACIA : misfortune, bad luck
fatalismo *nm* : fatalism
fatalista¹ *adj* : fatalistic
fatalista² *nmf* : fatalist
fatalmente *adv* **1** : unavoidably **2** : unfortunately
fatídico, -ca *adj* : fateful, momentous
fatiga *nf* CANSANCIO : fatigue
fatigado, -da *adj* AGOTADO : weary, tired
fatigar {52} *vt* CANSAR : to fatigue, to tire — **fatigarse** *vr* : to wear oneself out
fatigoso, -sa *adj* : fatiguing, tiring
fatuidad *nf* **1** : fatuousness **2** VANIDAD : vanity, conceit
fatuo, -tua *adj* **1** : fatuous **2** PRESUMIDO : vain
fauces *nfpl* : jaws *pl,* maw
faul *nm, pl* **fauls** : foul, foul ball
fauna *nf* : fauna
fausto *nm* : splendor, magnificence
favor *nm* **1** : favor **2 a favor de** : in favor of **3 por ~** : please
favorable *adj* : favorable — **favorablemente** *adv*
favorecedor, -dora *adj* : becoming, flattering
favorecer {53} *vt* **1** : to favor **2** : to look well on, to suit
favorecido, -da *adj* **1** : flattering **2** : fortunate
favoritismo *nm* : favoritism
favorito, -ta *adj & n* : favorite
fax *nm* : fax, facsimile
fayuca *nf Mex* **1** : contraband **2** : black market
fayuquero *nm Mex* : smuggler, black marketeer
faz *nf* **1** : face, countenance ⟨la faz de la tierra : the face of the earth⟩ **2** : side (of coins, fabric, etc.)
fe *nf* **1** : faith **2** : assurance, testimony ⟨dar fe de : to bear witness to⟩ **3** : intention, will ⟨de buena fe : bona fide, in good faith⟩
fealdad *nf* : ugliness
febrero *nm* : February
febril *adj* : feverish — **febrilmente** *adv*
fecal *adj* : fecal
fecha *nf* **1** : date **2 fecha de caducidad** *or* **fecha de vencimiento** : expiration date **3 fecha límite** : deadline
fechar *vt* : to date, to put a date on
fechoría *nf* : misdeed
fécula *nf* : starch
fecundar *vt* : to fertilize (an egg) — **fecundación** *nf*
fecundidad *nf* **1** : fecundity, fertility **2** : productiveness
fecundo, -da *adj* FÉRTIL : fertile, fecund
federación *nf, pl* **-ciones** : federation
federal *adj* : federal
federalismo *nm* : federalism
federalista *adj & nmf* : federalist
federar *vt* : to federate
fehaciente *adj* : reliable, irrefutable — **fehacientemente** *adv*
feldespato *nm* : feldspar
felicidad *nf* **1** : happiness **2 ¡felicidades!** : best wishes!, congratulations!, happy birthday!
felicitación *nf, pl* **-ciones 1** : congratulation ⟨¡felicitaciones! : congratulations!⟩ **2** : greeting card
felicitar *vt* CONGRATULAR : to congratulate — **felicitarse** *vr* **~ de** : to be glad about
feligrés, -gresa *n, mpl* **-greses** : parishioner
feligresía *nf* : parish
felino, -na *adj & n* : feline
feliz *adj, pl* **felices 1** : happy **2 Feliz Navidad** : Merry Christmas
felizmente *adv* **1** : happily **2** : fortunately, luckily
felonía *nf* : felony
felpa *nf* **1** : terry cloth **2** : plush
felpudo *nm* : doormat
femenil *adj* : women's, girls' ⟨futbol femenil : women's soccer⟩
femenino, -na *adj* **1** : feminine **2** : women's ⟨derechos femeninos : women's rights⟩ **3** : female
femineidad *nf* : femininity
feminidad *nf* : femininity
feminismo *nm* : feminism
feminista *adj & nmf* : feminist

femoral *adj* : femoral
fémur *nm* : femur, thighbone
fenecer {53} *vi* **1** : to die, to pass away **2** : to come to an end, to cease
fénix *nm* : phoenix
fenomenal *adj* **1** : phenomenal **2** *fam* : fantastic, terrific — **fenomenalmente** *adv*
fenómeno *nm* **1** : phenomenon **2** : prodigy, genius
feo[1] *adv* : badly, bad
feo[2], **fea** *adj* **1** : ugly **2** : unpleasant, nasty
féretro *nm* ATAÚD : coffin, casket
feria *nf* **1** : fair, market **2** : festival, holiday **3** *Mex* : change (money)
feriado, **-da** *adj* **día feriado** : public holiday
ferial *nm* : fairground
fermentar *v* : to ferment — **fermentación** *nf*
fermento *nm* : ferment
ferocidad *nf* : ferocity, fierceness
feroz *adj, pl* **feroces** FIERO : ferocious, fierce — **ferozmente** *adv*
férreo, **-rrea** *adj* **1** : iron **2** : strong, steely ⟨una voluntad férrea : an iron will⟩ **3** : strict, severe **4** **vía férrea** : railroad track
ferretería *nf* **1** : hardware store **2** : hardware **3** : foundry, ironworks
férrico, **-ca** *adj* : ferric
ferrocarril *nm* : railroad, railway
ferrocarrilero → **ferroviario**
ferroso, **-sa** *adj* : ferrous
ferroviario, **-ria** *adj* : rail, railroad
ferry *nm, pl* **ferrys** : ferry
fértil *adj* FECUNDO : fertile, fruitful
fertilidad *nf* : fertility
fertilizante[1] *adj* : fertilizing ⟨droga fertilizante : fertility drug⟩
fertilizante[2] *nm* ABONO : fertilizer
fertilizar *vt* ABONAR : to fertilize — **fertilización** *nf*
ferviente *adj* FERVOROSO : fervent
fervor *nm* : fervor, zeal
fervoroso, **-sa** *adj* FERVIENTE : fervent, zealous
festejar *vt* **1** CELEBRAR : to celebrate **2** AGASAJAR : to entertain, to wine and dine **3** *Mex fam* : to thrash, to beat
festejo *nm* : celebration, festivity
festín *nm, pl* **festines** : banquet, feast
festinar *vt* : to hasten, to hurry up
festival *nm* : festival
festividad *nf* **1** : festivity **2** : (religious) feast, holiday
festivo, **-va** *adj* **1** : festive **2** **día festivo** : holiday — **festivamente** *adv*
fetal *adj* : fetal
fetiche *nm* : fetish
fétido, **-da** *adj* : fetid, foul
feto *nm* : fetus
feudal *adj* : feudal — **feudalismo** *nm*
feudo *nm* **1** : fief **2** : domain, territory
fiabilidad *nf* : reliability, trustworthiness
fiable *adj* : trustworthy, reliable
fiado, **-da** *adj* : on credit
fiador, **-dora** *n* : bondsman, guarantor
fiambrería *nf* : delicatessen
fiambres *nfpl* : cold cuts
fianza *nf* **1** CAUCIÓN : bail, bond **2** : surety, deposit
fiar {85} *vt* **1** : to sell on credit **2** : to guarantee — **fiarse** *vr* ~ **de** : to place trust in
fiasco *nm* FRACASO : fiasco, failure
fibra *nf* **1** : fiber **2** **fibra de vidrio** : fiberglass
fibrilar *vi* : to fibrillate — **fibrilación** *nf*
fibroso, **-sa** *adj* : fibrous
ficción *nf, pl* **ficciones** **1** : fiction **2** : fabrication, lie
ficha *nf* **1** : index card **2** : file, record **3** : token **4** : domino, checker, counter, poker chip
fichar *vt* **1** : to open a file on **2** : to sign up — *vi* : to punch in, to punch out
fichero *nm* **1** : card file **2** : filing cabinet
ficticio, **-cia** *adj* : fictitious
fidedigno, **-na** *adj* FIABLE : reliable, trustworthy
fideicomisario, **-ria** *n* : trustee
fideicomiso *nm* : trusteeship, trust ⟨guardar en fideicomiso : to hold in trust⟩
fidelidad *nf* : fidelity, faithfulness
fideo *nm* : noodle
fiduciario[1], **-ria** *adj* : fiduciary
fiduciario[2], **-ria** *n* : trustee
fiebre *nf* **1** CALENTURA : fever, temperature ⟨fiebre amarilla : yellow fever⟩ ⟨fiebre palúdica : malaria⟩ **2** : fever, excitement
fiel[1] *adj* **1** : faithful, loyal **2** : accurate — **fielmente** *adv*
fiel[2] *nm* **1** : pointer (of a scale) **2** **los fieles** : the faithful
fieltro *nm* : felt
fiera *nf* **1** : wild animal, beast **2** : fiend, demon ⟨una fiera para el trabajo : a demon for work⟩
fiereza *nf* : fierceness, ferocity
fiero, **-ra** *adj* FEROZ : fierce, ferocious
fierro *nm* HIERRO : iron
fiesta *nf* **1** : party, fiesta **2** : holiday, feast day
figura *nf* **1** : figure **2** : shape, form **3** **figura retórica** : figure of speech
figurado, **-da** *adj* : figurative — **figuradamente** *adv*
figurar *vi* **1** : to figure, to be included ⟨Rivera figura entre los más grandes pintores de México : Rivera is among Mexico's greatest painters⟩ **2** : to be prominent, to stand out — *vt* : to represent ⟨esta línea figura el horizonte : this line represents the horizon⟩ — **figurarse** *vr* : to imagine, to think ⟨¡figúrate el lío en que se metió! : imagine the mess she got into!⟩
fijación *nf, pl* **-ciones** **1** : fixation, obsession **2** : fixing, establishing **3** : fastening, securing
fijador *nm* **1** : fixative **2** : hair spray

fijamente *adv* : fixedly

fijar *vt* **1** : to fasten, to affix **2** ESTABLECER : to establish, to set up **3** CONCRETAR : to set, to fix ⟨fijar la fecha : to set the date⟩ — **fijarse** *vr* **1** : to settle, to become fixed **2 ~ en** : to notice, to pay attention to

fijeza *nf* **1** : firmness (of convictions) **2** : persistence, constancy ⟨mirar con fijeza a : to stare at⟩

fijiano, -na *adj & n* : Fijian

fijo, -ja *adj* **1** : fixed, firm, steady **2** PERMANENTE : permanent

fila *nf* **1** HILERA : line, file ⟨ponerse en fila : to get in line⟩ **2** : rank, row **3 filas** *nfpl* : ranks ⟨cerrar filas : to close ranks⟩

filamento *nm* : filament

filantropía *nf* : philanthropy

filantrópico, -ca *adj* : philanthropic

filántropo, -pa *n* : philanthropist

filatelia *nf* : philately, stamp collecting

filatelista *nmf* : stamp collector, philatelist

fildeador, -dora *n* : fielder

filete *nm* **1** : fillet **2** SOLOMILLO : sirloin **3** : thread (of a screw)

filiación *nf, pl* **-ciones** **1** : affiliation, connection **2** : particulars *pl,* (police) description

filial[1] *adj* : filial

filial[2] *nf* : affiliate, subsidiary

filibustero *nm* : freebooter, pirate

filigrana *nf* **1** : filigree **2** : watermark (on paper)

filipino, -na *adj & n* : Filipino

filmación *nf, pl* **-ciones** : filming, shooting

filmar *vt* : to film, to shoot

filme *or* **film** *nm* PELÍCULA : film, movie

filmina *nf* : slide, transparency

filo *nm* **1** : cutting edge, blade **2** : edge ⟨al filo del escritorio : at the edge of the desk⟩ ⟨al filo de la medianoche : at the stroke of midnight⟩

filología *nf* : philology

filólogo, -ga *n* : philologist

filón *nm, pl* **filones** **1** : seam, vein (of minerals) **2** *fam* : successful business, gold mine

filoso, -sa *adj* : sharp

filosofar *vi* : to philosophize

filosofía *nf* : philosophy

filosófico, -ca *adj* : philosophic, philosophical — **filosóficamente** *adv*

filósofo, -fa *n* : philosopher

filtración *nf* : seepage, leaking

filtrar *v* : to filter — **filtrarse** *vr* : to seep through, to leak

filtro *nm* : filter

filudo, -da *adj* : sharp

fin *nm* **1** : end **2** : purpose, aim, objective **3 en ~** : in short **4 fin de semana** : weekend **5 por ~** : finally, at last

finado, -da *adj & n* DIFUNTO : deceased

final[1] *adj* : final, ultimate — **finalmente** *adv*

final[2] *nm* : end, conclusion, finale

final[3] *nf* : final, play-off

finalidad *nf* **1** : purpose, aim **2** : finality

finalista *nmf* : finalist

finalización *nf* : completion, end

finalizar {21} *v* : to finish, to end

financiación *nf, pl* **-ciones** : financing, funding

financiamiento *nm* → **financiación**

financiar *vt* : to finance, to fund

financiero[1], **-ra** *adj* : financial

financiero[2], **-ra** *n* : financier

financista *nmf* : financier

finanzas *nfpl* : finances, finance ⟨altas finanzas : high finance⟩

finca *nf* **1** : farm, ranch **2** : country house

fineza *nf* FINURA, REFINAMIENTO : refinement

fingido, -da *adj* : false, feigned

fingimiento *nm* : pretense

fingir {35} *v* : to feign, to pretend

finiquitar *vt* **1** : to settle (an account) **2** : to conclude, to bring to an end

finiquito *nm* : settlement (of an account)

finito, -ta *adj* : finite

finja, etc. → **fingir**

finlandés, -desa *adj & n* : Finnish

fino, -na *adj* **1** : fine, excellent **2** : delicate, slender **3** REFINADO : refined **4** : sharp, acute ⟨olfato fino : keen sense of smell⟩ **5** : subtle

finta *nf* : feint

fintar *or* **fintear** *vi* : to feint

finura *nf* **1** : fineness, high quality **2** FINEZA, REFINAMIENTO : refinement

fiordo *nm* : fjord

fique *nm* : sisal

firma *nf* **1** : signature **2** : signing **3** EMPRESA : firm, company

firmamento *nm* : firmament, sky

firmante *nmf* : signer, signatory

firmar *v* : to sign

firme *adj* **1** : firm, resolute **2** : steady, stable

firmemente *adv* : firmly

firmeza *nf* **1** : firmness, stability **2** : strength, resolve

firuletes *nmpl* : frills, adornments

fiscal[1] *adj* : fiscal — **fiscalmente** *adv*

fiscal[2] *nmf* : district attorney, prosecutor

fiscalizar {21} *vt* **1** : to audit, to inspect **2** : to oversee **3** : to criticize

fisco *nm* : national treasury, exchequer

fisgar {52} *vt* HUSMEAR : to pry into, to snoop on

fisgón, -gona *n, mpl* **fisgones** : snoop, busybody

fisgonear *vi* : to snoop, to pry

fisgue, etc. → **fisgar**

física *nf* : physics

físico[1], **-ca** *adj* : physical — **físicamente** *adv*

físico[2], **-ca** *n* : physicist

físico[3] *nm* : physique, figure

fisiología *nf* : physiology

fisiológico, -ca *adj* : physiological, physiologic
fisiólogo, -ga *n* : physiologist
fisión *nf, pl* **fisiones** : fission — **fisionable** *adj*
fisionomía → **fisonomía**
fisioterapeuta *nmf* : physical therapist
fisioterapia *nf* : physical therapy
fisonomía *nf* : physiognomy, features *pl*
fistol *nm Mex* : tie clip
fisura *nf* : fissure, crevasse
fláccido, -da *or* **flácido, -da** *adj* : flaccid, flabby
flaco, -ca *adj* **1** DELGADO : thin, skinny **2** : feeble, weak ⟨una flaca excusa : a feeble excuse⟩
flagelar *vt* : to flagellate — **flagelación** *nf*
flagelo *nm* **1** : scourge, whip **2** : calamity
flagrante *adj* : flagrant, glaring, blatant — **flagrantemente** *adv*
flama *nf* LLAMA : flame
flamante *adj* **1** : bright, brilliant **2** : brand-new
flamear *vi* **1** LLAMEAR : to flame, to blaze **2** ONDEAR : to flap, to flutter
flamenco[1], -ca *adj* **1** : flamenco **2** : Flemish
flamenco[2], -ca *n* : Fleming, Flemish person
flamenco[3] *nm* **1** : Flemish (language) **2** : flamingo **3** : flamenco (music or dance)
flanco *nm* : flank, side
flanquear *vt* : to flank
flaquear *vi* DECAER : to flag, to weaken
flaqueza *nf* **1** DEBILIDAD : frailty, feebleness **2** : thinness **3** : weakness, failing
flato *nm* : gloom, melancholy
flatulento, -ta *adj* : flatulent — **flatulencia** *nf*
flauta *nf* **1** : flute **2 flauta dulce** : recorder
flautín *nm, pl* **flautines** : piccolo
flautista *nmf* : flute player, flutist
flebitis *nf* : phlebitis
flecha *nf* : arrow
fleco *nm* **1** : bangs *pl* **2** : fringe
flema *nf* : phlegm
flemático, -ca *adj* : phlegmatic, stolid, impassive
flequillo *nm* : bangs *pl*
fletar *vt* **1** : to charter, to hire **2** : to load (freight)
flete *nm* **1** : charter fee **2** : shipping cost **3** : freight, cargo
fletero *nm* : shipper, carrier
flexibilidad *nf* : flexibility
flexibilizar {21} *vt* : to make more flexible
flexible[1] *adj* : flexible
flexible[2] *nm* **1** : flexible electrical cord **2** : soft hat
flirtear *vi* : to flirt
flojear *vi* **1** DEBILITARSE : to weaken, to flag **2** : to idle, to loaf around
flojedad *nf* : weakness
flojera *nf fam* **1** : lethargy, feeling of weakness **2** : laziness
flojo, -ja *adj* **1** SUELTO : loose, slack **2** : weak, poor ⟨está flojo en las ciencias : he's weak in science⟩ **3** PEREZOSO : lazy
flor *nf* **1** : flower **2 flor de Pascua** : poinsettia
flora *nf* : flora
floración *nf* : flowering ⟨en plena floración : in full bloom⟩
floral *adj* : floral
floreado, -da *adj* : flowered, flowery
florear *vi* FLORECER : to flower, to bloom — *vt* **1** : to adorn with flowers **2** *Mex* : to flatter, to compliment
florecer {53} *vi* **1** : to bloom, to blossom **2** : to flourish, to thrive
floreciente *adj* **1** : flowering **2** PRÓSPERO : flourishing, thriving
florecimiento *nm* : flowering
floreo *nm* : flourish
florería *nf* : flower shop, florist's
florero[1], -ra *n* : florist
florero[2] *nm* JARRÓN : vase
floresta *nf* **1** : glade, grove **2** BOSQUE : woods
florido, -da *adj* **1** : full of flowers **2** : florid, flowery ⟨escritos floridos : flowery prose⟩
florista *nmf* : florist
floritura *nf* : frill, embellishment
flota *nf* : fleet
flotabilidad *nf* : buoyancy
flotación *nf, pl* **-ciones** : flotation
flotador *nm* **1** : float **2** : life preserver
flotante *adj* : floating, buoyant
flotar *vi* : to float
flote *nm* **a ~** : afloat
flotilla *nf* : flotilla, fleet
fluctuar {3} *vi* **1** : to fluctuate **2** VACILAR : to vacillate — **fluctuación** *nf* — **fluctuante** *adj*
fluidez *nf* **1** : fluency **2** : fluidity
fluido[1], -da *adj* **1** : flowing **2** : fluent **3** : fluid
fluido[2] *nm* : fluid
fluir {41} *vi* : to flow
flujo *nm* **1** : flow **2** : discharge
flúor *nm* : fluorine
fluoración *nf, pl* **-ciones** : fluoridation
fluorescencia *nf* : fluorescence — **fluorescente** *adj*
fluorizar {21} *vt* : to fluoridate
fluoruro *nm* : fluoride
fluvial *adj* : fluvial, river
fluye, etc. → **fluir**
fobia *nf* : phobia
foca *nf* : seal (animal)
focal *adj* : focal
focha *nf* : coot
foco *nm* **1** : focus **2** : center, pocket **3** : lightbulb **4** : spotlight **5** : headlight
fofo, -fa *adj* **1** ESPONJOSO : soft, spongy **2** : flabby
fogaje *nm* **1** FUEGO : skin eruption, cold sore **2** BOCHORNO : hot and humid weather

fogata *nf* : bonfire
fogón *nm, pl* **fogones** : bonfire
fogonazo *nm* : flash, explosion
fogonero, -ra *n* : stoker (of a furnace), fireman
fogoso, -sa *adj* ARDIENTE : ardent
foguear *vt* : to inure, to accustom
foja *nf* : sheet (of paper)
folículo *nm* : follicle
folio *nm* : folio, leaf
folklore *nm* : folklore
folklórico, -ca *adj* : folk, traditional
follaje *nm* : foliage
folleto *nm* : pamphlet, leaflet, circular
fomentar *vt* **1** : to foment, to stir up **2** PROMOVER : to promote, to foster
fomento *nm* : promotion, encouragement
fonda *nf* **1** POSADA : inn **2** : small restaurant
fondeado, -da *adj fam* : rich, in the money
fondear *vt* **1** : to sound **2** : to sound out, to examine **3** *Mex* : to fund, to finance — *vi* ANCLAR : to anchor — **fondearse** *vr fam* : to get rich
fondeo *nm* **1** : anchoring **2** *Mex* : funding, financing
fondillos *mpl* : seat, bottom (of clothing)
fondo *nm* **1** : bottom **2** : rear, back, end **3** : depth **4** : background **5** : sea bed **6** : fund <fondo de inversiones : investment fund> **7** *Mex* : slip, petticoat **8 fondos** *nmpl* : funds, resources <cheque sin fondos : bounced check> **9 a ~** : thoroughly, in depth **10 en ~** : abreast
fonema *nm* : phoneme
fonética *nf* : phonetics
fonético, -ca *adj* : phonetic
fontanería *nf* PLOMERÍA : plumbing
fontanero, -ra *n* PLOMERO : plumber
footing [ˈfuˌtɪŋ] *nm* : jogging <hacer footing : to jog>
foque *nm* : jib
forajido, -da *n* : bandit, fugitive, outlaw
foráneo, -nea *adj* : foreign, strange
forastero, -ra *n* : stranger, outsider
forcejear *vi* : to struggle
forcejeo *nm* : struggle
fórceps *nms & pl* : forceps *pl*
forense *adj* : forensic, legal
forestal *adj* : forest
forja *nf* FRAGUA : forge
forjar *vt* **1** : to forge **2** : to shape, to create <forjar un compromiso : to hammer out a compromise> **3** : to invent, to concoct
forma *nf* **1** : form, shape **2** MANERA, MODO : manner, way **3** : fitness <estar en forma : to be fit, to be in shape> **4 formas** *nfpl* : appearances, conventions
formación *nf, pl* **-ciones 1** : formation **2** : training <formación profesional : vocational training>
formal *adj* **1** : formal **2** : serious, dignified **3** : dependable, reliable
formaldehído *nm* : formaldehyde
formalidad *nf* **1** : formality **2** : seriousness, dignity **3** : dependability, reliability
formalizar {21} *vt* : to formalize, to make official
formalmente *adv* : formally
formar *vt* **1** : to form, to make **2** CONSTITUIR : to constitute, to make up **3** : to train, to educate — **formarse** *vr* **1** DESARROLLARSE : to develop, to take shape **2** EDUCARSE : to be educated
formatear *vt* : to format
formativo, -va *adj* : formative
formato *nm* : format
formidable *adj* **1** : formidable, tremendous **2** *fam* : fantastic, terrific
formón *nm, pl* **formones** : chisel
fórmula *nf* : formula
formulación *nf, pl* **-ciones** : formulation
formular *vt* **1** : to formulate, to draw up **2** : to make, to lodge (a protest or complaint)
formulario *nm* : form <rellenar un formulario : to fill out a form>
fornicar {72} *vi* : to fornicate — **fornicación** *nf*
fornido, -da *adj* : well-built, burly, hefty
foro *nm* **1** : forum **2** : public assembly, open discussion
forraje *nm* **1** : forage, fodder **2** : foraging **3** *fam* : hodgepodge
forrajear *vi* : to forage
forrar *vt* **1** : to line (a garment) **2** : to cover (a book)
forro *nm* **1** : lining **2** CUBIERTA : book cover
forsitia *nf* : forsythia
fortachón, -chona *adj, pl* **-chones** *fam* : brawny, strong, tough
fortalecer {53} *vt* : to strengthen, to fortify — **fortalecerse** *vr*
fortalecimiento *nm* **1** : strengthening, fortifying **2** : fortifications
fortaleza *nf* **1** : fortress **2** FUERZA : strength **3** : resolution, fortitude
fortificación *nf, pl* **-ciones** : fortification
fortificar {72} *vt* **1** : to fortify **2** : to strengthen
fortín *nm, pl* **fortines** : small fort
fortuito, -ta *adj* : fortuitous
fortuna *nf* **1** SUERTE : fortune, luck **2** RIQUEZA : wealth, fortune
forzar {36} *vt* **1** OBLIGAR : to force, to compel **2** : to force open **3** : to strain <forzar los ojos : to strain one's eyes>
forzosamente *adv* **1** : forcibly, by force **2** : necessarily, inevitably <forzosamente tendrán que pagar : they'll have no choice but to pay>
forzoso, -sa *adj* **1** : forced, compulsory **2** : necessary, inevitable
fosa *nf* **1** : ditch, pit <fosa séptica : septic tank> **2** TUMBA : grave **3** : cavity <fosas nasales : nasal cavities, nostrils>
fosfato *nm* : phosphate

fosforescencia *nf* : phosphorescence — **fosforescente** *adj*
fósforo *nm* **1** CERILLA : match **2** : phosphorus
fósil[1] *adj* : fossilized, fossil
fósil[2] *nm* : fossil
fosilizarse {21} *vr* : to fossilize, to become fossilized
foso *nm* **1** FOSA, ZANJA : ditch **2** : pit (of a theater) **3** : moat
foto *nf* : photo, picture
fotocopia *nf* : photocopy — **fotocopiar** *vt*
fotocopiadora *nf* COPIADORA : photocopier
fotoeléctrico, -ca *adj* : photoelectric
fotogénico, -ca *adj* : photogenic
fotografía *nf* **1** : photograph **2** : photography
fotografiar {85} *vt* : to photograph
fotográfico, -ca *adj* : photographic — **fotográficamente** *adv*
fotógrafo, -fa *n* : photographer
fotosíntesis *nf* : photosynthesis
fotosintético, -ca *adj* : photosynthetic
fracasado[1], **-da** *adj* : unsuccessful, failed
fracasado[2], **-da** *n* : failure
fracasar *vi* **1** FALLAR : to fail **2** : to fall through
fracaso *nm* FIASCO : failure
fracción *nf, pl* **fracciones** **1** : fraction **2** : part, fragment **3** : faction, splinter group
fraccionamiento *nm* **1** : division, breaking up **2** *Mex* : residential area, housing development
fraccionar *vt* : to divide, to break up
fraccionario, -ria *adj* : fractional
fractura *nf* **1** : fracture **2 fractura complicada** : compound fracture
fracturarse *vr* QUEBRARSE, ROMPERSE : to fracture, to break ⟨fracturarse el brazo : to break one's arm⟩
fragancia *nf* : fragrance, scent
fragante *adj* : fragrant
fragata *nf* : frigate
frágil *adj* **1** : fragile **2** : frail, delicate
fragilidad *nf* **1** : fragility **2** : frailty, delicacy
fragmentar *vt* : to fragment — **fragmentación** *nf*
fragmentario, -ria *adj* : fragmentary, sketchy
fragmento *nm* **1** : fragment, shard **2** : bit, snippet **3** : excerpt, passage
fragor *nm* : clamor, din, roar
fragoroso, -sa *adj* : thunderous, deafening
fragoso, -sa *adj* **1** : rough, uneven **2** : thick, dense
fragua *nf* FORJA : forge
fraguar {10} *vt* **1** : to forge **2** : to conceive, to concoct, to hatch — *vi* : to set, to solidify
fraile *nm* : friar, monk
frambuesa *nf* : raspberry
francamente *adv* **1** : frankly, candidly **2** REALMENTE : really ⟨es francamente admirable : it's really impressive⟩
francés[1], **-cesa** *adj, mpl* **franceses** : French
francés[2], **-cesa** *n, mpl* **franceses** : French person, Frenchman *m*, Frenchwoman *f*
francés[3] *nm* : French (language)
franciscano, -na *adj & n* : Franciscan
francmasón, -sona *n, mpl* **-sones** : Freemason — **francmasonería** *nf*
franco[1], **-ca** *adj* **1** CÁNDIDO : frank, candid **2** PATENTE : clear, obvious **3** : free ⟨franco a bordo : free on board⟩
franco[2] *nm* : franc
francotirador, -dora *n* : sniper
franela *nf* : flannel
franja *nf* **1** : stripe, band **2** : border, fringe
franquear *vt* **1** : to clear **2** ATRAVESAR : to cross, to go through **3** : to pay the postage on
franqueo *nm* : postage
franqueza *nf* : frankness
franquicia *nf* **1** EXENCIÓN : exemption **2** : franchise
frasco *nm* : small bottle, flask, vial
frase *nf* **1** : phrase **2** ORACIÓN : sentence
frasear *vt* : to phrase
fraternal *adj* : fraternal, brotherly
fraternidad *nf* **1** : brotherhood **2** : fraternity
fraternizar {21} *vi* : to fraternize — **fraternización** *nf*
fraterno, -na *adj* : fraternal, brotherly
fratricida *adj* : fratricidal
fratricidio *nm* : fratricide
fraude *nm* : fraud
fraudulento, -ta *adj* : fraudulent — **fraudulentamente** *adv*
fray *nm* : brother (title of a friar) ⟨Fray Bartolomé : Brother Bartholomew⟩
frazada *nf* COBIJA, MANTA : blanket
frecuencia *nf* : frequency
frecuentar *vt* : to frequent, to haunt
frecuente *adj* : frequent — **frecuentemente** *adv*
fregadera *nf fam* : hassle, pain in the neck
fregadero *nm* : kitchen sink
fregado[1], **-da** *adj fam* : annoying, bothersome
fregado[2] *nm* **1** : scrubbing, scouring **2** *fam* : mess, muddle
fregar {49} *vt* **1** : to scrub, to scour, to wash ⟨fregar los trastes : to do the dishes⟩ ⟨fregar el suelo : to scrub the floor⟩ **2** *fam* : to annoy — *vi* **1** : to wash the dishes **2** : to clean, to scrub **3** *fam* : to be annoying
freidera *nf Mex* : frying pan
freír {37} *vt* : to fry — **freírse** *vr*
frenar *vt* **1** : to brake **2** DETENER : to curb, to check — *vi* : to apply the brakes — **frenarse** *vr* : to restrain oneself

frenesí *nm* : frenzy
frenético, -ca *adj* : frantic, frenzied — **frenéticamente** *adv*
freno *nm* **1** : brake **2** : bit (of a bridle) **3** : check, restraint **4 frenos** *nmpl Mex* : braces (for teeth)
frente[1] *nm* **1** : front ⟨al frente de : at the head of⟩ ⟨en frente : in front, opposite⟩ **2** : facade **3** : front line, sphere of activity **4** : front (in meteorology) ⟨frente frío : cold front⟩ **5 hacer frente a** : to face up to, to brave
frente[2] *nf* **1** : forehead, brow **2 frente a frente** : face to face
fresa *nf* **1** : strawberry **2** : drill (in dentistry)
fresco[1], **-ca** *adj* **1** : fresh **2** : cool **3** *fam* : insolent, nervy
fresco[2] *nm* **1** : coolness **2** : fresh air ⟨al fresco : in the open air, outdoors⟩ **3** : fresco
frescor *nm* : cool air ⟨el frescor de la noche : the cool of the evening⟩
frescura *nf* **1** : freshness **2** : coolness **3** : calmness **4** DESCARO : nerve, audacity
fresno *nm* : ash (tree)
freza *nf* : spawn, roe
frezar {21} *vi* DESOVAR : to spawn
friable *adj* : friable
frialdad *nf* **1** : coldness **2** INDIFERENCIA : indifference, unconcern
fríamente *adv* : coldly, indifferently
fricasé *nm* : fricassee
fricción *nf, pl* **fricciones 1** : friction **2** : rubbing, massage **3** : discord, disagreement ⟨fricción entre los hermanos : friction between the brothers⟩
friccionar *vt* **1** FROTAR : to rub **2** : to massage
friega[1], **friegue, etc.** → **fregar**
friega[2] *nf* **1** FRICCIÓN : rubdown, massage **2** : annoyance, bother
frigidez *nf* : (sexual) frigidity
frigorífico *nm Spain* : refrigerator
frijol *nm* : bean ⟨frijoles refritos : refried beans⟩
frío[1], **fría** *adj* **1** : cold **2** INDIFERENTE : cool, indifferent
frío[2] *nm* **1** : cold ⟨hace mucho frío esta noche : it's very cold tonight⟩ **2** INDIFERENCIA : coldness, indifference **3 tener frío** : to feel cold ⟨tengo frío : I'm cold⟩ **4 tomar frío** RESFRIARSE : to catch a cold
friolento, -ta *adj* : sensitive to cold
friolera *nf* (*used ironically or humorously*) : trifling amount ⟨una friolera de mil dólares : a mere thousand dollars⟩
friso *nm* : frieze
fritar *vt* : to fry
frito[1] *pp* → **freír**
frito[2], **-ta** *adj* **1** : fried **2** *fam* : worn-out, fed up ⟨tener frito a alguien : to get on someone's nerves⟩ **3** *fam* : fast asleep ⟨se quedó frito en el sofá : she fell asleep on the couch⟩
fritura *nf* **1** : frying **2** : fried food
frivolidad *nf* : frivolity
frívolo, -la *adj* : frivolous — **frívolamente** *adv*
fronda *nf* **1** : frond **2 frondas** *nfpl* : foliage
frondoso, -sa *adj* : leafy, luxuriant
frontal *adj* : frontal, head-on ⟨un choque frontal : a head-on collision⟩
frontalmente *adv* : head-on
frontera *nf* : border, frontier
fronterizo, -za *adj* : border, on the border ⟨estados fronterizos : neighboring states⟩
frontispicio *nm* : frontispiece
frotar *vt* **1** : to rub **2** : to strike (a match) — **frotarse** *vr* : to rub (together)
frote *nm* : rubbing, rub
fructífero, -ra *adj* : fruitful, productive
fructificar {72} *vi* **1** : to bear or produce fruit **2** : to be productive
fructuoso, -sa *adj* : fruitful
frugal *adj* : frugal, thrifty — **frugalmente** *adv*
frugalidad *adj* : frugality
frunce *nm* : gather (in cloth), pucker
fruncido *nm* : gathering, shirring
fruncir {83} *vt* **1** : to gather, to shirr **2 fruncir el ceño** : to knit one's brow, to frown **3 fruncir la boca** : to pucker up, to purse one's lips
frunza, etc. → **fruncir**
frustración *nf, pl* **-ciones** : frustration
frustrado, -da *adj* **1** : frustrated **2** : failed, unsuccessful
frustrante *adj* : frustrating
frustrar *vt* : to frustrate, to thwart — **frustrarse** *vr* FRACASAR : to fail, to come to nothing ⟨se frustraron sus esperanzas : his hopes were dashed⟩
fruta *nf* : fruit
frutal[1] *adj* : fruit, fruit-bearing
frutal[2] *nm* : fruit tree
frutilla *nf* : South American strawberry
fruto *nm* **1** : fruit, agricultural product ⟨los frutos de la tierra : the fruits of the earth⟩ **2** : result, consequence ⟨los frutos de su trabajo : the fruits of his labor⟩
fucsia *adj & nm* : fuchsia
fue, etc. → **ir, ser**
fuego *nm* **1** : fire **2** : light ⟨¿tienes fuego? : have you got a light?⟩ **3** : flame, burner (on a stove) **4** : ardor, passion **5** FOGAJE : skin eruption, cold sore **6 fuegos artificiales** *nmpl* : fireworks
fuelle *nm* : bellows
fuente *nf* **1** MANANTIAL : spring **2** : fountain **3** ORIGEN : source ⟨fuentes informativas : sources of information⟩ **4** : platter, serving dish
fuera *adv* **1** : outside, out **2** : abroad, away **3 ~ de** : outside of, out of, beyond **4 ~ de** : besides, in addition to ⟨fuera de eso : aside from that⟩ **5 fuera de lugar** : out of place, amiss
fuerce, fuerza etc. → **forzar**

fuero *nm* **1** JURISDICCIÓN : jurisdiction **2** : privilege, exemption **3 fuero interno** : conscience, heart of hearts
fuerte[1] *adv* **1** : strongly, tightly, hard **2** : loudly **3** : abundantly
fuerte[2] *adj* **1** : strong **2** : intense ⟨un fuerte dolor : an intense pain⟩ **3** : loud **4** : extreme, excessive
fuerte[3] *nm* **1** : fort, stronghold **2** : forte, strong point
fuerza *nf* **1** : strength, vigor ⟨fuerza de voluntad : willpower⟩ **2** : force ⟨fuerza bruta : brute force⟩ **3** : power, might ⟨fuerza de brazos : manpower⟩ **4 fuerzas** *nfpl* : forces ⟨fuerzas armadas : armed forces⟩ **5 a fuerza de** : by, by dint of
fuetazo *nm* : lash
fuga *nf* **1** HUIDA : flight, escape **2** : fugue **3** : leak ⟨fuga de gas : gas leak⟩
fugarse {52} *vr* **1** : to escape **2** HUIR : to flee, to run away **3** : to elope
fugaz *adj, pl* **fugaces** : brief, fleeting
fugitivo, -va *adj & n* : fugitive
fulana *nf* : hooker, slut
fulano, -na *n* : so-and-so, what's-his-name, what's-her-name ⟨fulano, mengano, y zutano : Tom, Dick, and Harry⟩ ⟨señora fulana de tal : Mrs. so-and-so⟩
fulcro *nm* : fulcrum
fulgor *nm* : brilliance, splendor
fulgurar *vi* : to shine brightly, to gleam, to glow
fulminante *adj* **1** : fulminating, explosive **2** : devastating, terrible ⟨una mirada fulminante : a withering look⟩
fulminar *vt* **1** : to strike with lightning **2** : to strike down ⟨fulminar a alguien con la mirada : to look daggers at someone⟩
fumador, -dora *n* : smoker
fumar *v* : to smoke
fumble *nm* : fumble (in football)
fumblear *vt* : to fumble (in football)
fumigante *nm* : fumigant
fumigar {52} *vt* : to fumigate — **fumigación** *nf*
funámbulo, -la *n* EQUILIBRISTA : tightrope walker
función *nf, pl* **funciones** **1** : function **2** : duty **3** : performance, show
funcional *adj* : functional — **funcionalmente** *adv*
funcionamiento *nm* **1** : functioning **2 en ~** : in operation
funcionar *vi* **1** : to function **2** : to run, to work
funcionario, -ria *n* : civil servant, official
funda *nf* **1** : case, cover, sheath **2** : pillowcase
fundación *nf, pl* **-ciones** : foundation, establishment
fundado, -da *adj* : well-founded, justified
fundador, -dora *n* : founder
fundamental *adj* BÁSICO : fundamental, basic — **fundamentalmente** *adv*
fundamentalismo *nm* : fundamentalism
fundamentalista *nmf* : fundamentalist
fundamentar *vt* **1** : to lay the foundations for **2** : to support, to back up **3** : to base, to found
fundamento *nm* : basis, foundation, groundwork
fundar *vt* **1** ESTABLECER, INSTITUIR : to found, to establish **2** BASAR : to base — **fundarse** *vr* **~ en** : to be based on, to stem from
fundición *nf, pl* **-ciones** **1** : founding, smelting **2** : foundry
fundir *vt* **1** : to melt down, to smelt **2** : to fuse, to merge **3** : to burn out (a lightbulb) — **fundirse** *vr* **1** : to fuse together, to blend, to merge **2** : to melt, to thaw **3** : to fade (in television or movies)
fúnebre *adj* **1** : funeral, funereal **2** LÚGUBRE : gloomy, mournful
funeral[1] *adj* : funeral, funerary
funeral[2] *nm* **1** : funeral **2 funerales** *nmpl* EXEQUIAS : funeral rites
funeraria *nf* **1** : funeral home, funeral parlor **2 director de funeraria** : funeral director, undertaker
funerario, -ria *adj* : funeral
funesto, -ta *adj* : terrible, disastrous ⟨consecuencias funestas : disastrous consequences⟩
fungicida[1] *adj* : fungicidal
fungicida[2] *nm* : fungicide
fungir {35} *vi* : to act, to function ⟨fungir de asesor : to act as a consultant⟩
fungoso, -sa *adj* : fungous
funja, etc. → **fungir**
furgón *nm, pl* **furgones** **1** : van, truck **2** : freight car, boxcar **3 furgón de cola** : caboose
furgoneta *nf* : van
furia *nf* **1** CÓLERA, IRA : fury, rage **2** : violence, fury ⟨la furia de la tormenta : the fury of the storm⟩
furibundo, -da *adj* : furious
furiosamente *adv* : furiously, frantically
furioso, -sa *adj* **1** AIRADO : furious, irate **2** : intense, violent
furor *nm* **1** : fury, rage **2** : violence (of the elements) **3** : passion, frenzy **4** : enthusiasm ⟨hacer furor : to be all the rage⟩
furtivo, -va *adj* : furtive — **furtivamente** *adv*
furúnculo *nm* DIVIESO : boil
fuselaje *nm* : fuselage
fusible *nm* : (electrical) fuse
fusil *nm* : rifle
fusilar *vt* **1** : to shoot, to execute (by firing squad) **2** *fam* : to plagiarize, to pirate
fusilería *nf* **1** : rifles *pl*, rifle fire **2 descarga de fusilería** : fusillade
fusión *nf, pl* **fusiones** **1** : fusion **2** : union, merger

fusionar *vt* **1** : to fuse **2** : to merge, to amalgamate — **fusionarse** *vr*
fusta *nf* : riding crop
fustigar {52} *vt* **1** AZOTAR : to whip, to lash **2** : to upbraid, to berate
futbol *or* **fútbol** *nm* **1** : soccer **2 futbol americano** : football
futbolista *nmf* : soccer player
futesa *nf* **1** : small thing, trifle **2 futesas** *nfpl* : small talk
fútil *adj* : trifling, trivial
futurista *adj* : futuristic
futuro[1], **-ra** *adj* : future
futuro[2] *nm* PORVENIR : future

G

g *nf* : seventh letter of the Spanish alphabet
gabán *nm, pl* **gabanes** : topcoat, overcoat
gabardina *nf* **1** : gabardine **2** : trench coat, raincoat
gabarra *nf* : barge
gabinete *nm* **1** : cabinet (in government) **2** : study, office (in the home) **3** : (professional) office
gablete *nm* : gable
gabonés, -nesa *adj & n, mpl* **-neses** : Gabonese
gacela *nf* : gazelle
gaceta *nf* : gazette, newspaper
gachas *nfpl* : porridge
gacho, -cha *adj* **1** : drooping, turned downward **2** *Mex fam* : nasty, awful **3 ir a gachas** *fam* : to go on all fours
gaélico[1], **-ca** *adj* : Gaelic
gaélico[2] *nm* : Gaelic (language)
gafas *nfpl* ANTEOJOS : eyeglasses, glasses
gaita *nf* : bagpipes *pl*
gajes *nmpl* **gajes del oficio** : occupational hazards
gajo *nm* **1** : broken branch (of a tree) **2** : cluster, bunch (of fruit) **3** : segment (of citrus fruit)
gala *nf* **1** : gala ⟨vestido de gala : formal dress⟩ ⟨tener algo a gala : to be proud of something⟩ **2 galas** *nfpl* : finery, attire
galáctico, -ca *adj* : galactic
galán *nm, pl* **galanes** **1** : ladies' man, gallant **2** : leading man, hero **3** : boyfriend, suitor
galano, -na *adj* **1** : elegant **2** *Mex* : mottled
galante *adj* : gallant, attentive — **galantemente** *adv*
galantear *vt* **1** CORTEJAR : to court, to woo **2** : to flirt with
galanteo *nm* **1** CORTEJO : courtship **2** : flirtation, flirting
galantería *nf* **1** : gallantry, attentiveness **2** : compliment
galápago *nm* : aquatic turtle
galardón *nm, pl* **-dones** : award, prize
galardonado, -da *adj* : prize-winning
galardonar *vt* : to give an award to
galaxia *nf* : galaxy
galeno *nm fam* : physician, doctor
galeón *nm, pl* **galeones** : galleon
galera *nf* : galley
galería *nf* **1** : gallery, balcony (in a theater) ⟨galería comercial : shopping mall⟩ **2** : corridor, passage
galerón *n, mpl* **-rones** *Mex* : large hall
galés[1], **-lesa** *adj* : Welsh
galés[2], **-lesa** *n, mpl* **galeses** **1** : Welshman *m,* Welshwoman *f* **2 los galeses** : the Welsh
galés[3] *nm* : Welsh (language)
galgo *nm* : greyhound
galimatías *nms & pl* : gibberish, nonsense
galio *nm* : gallium
gallardete *nm* : pennant, streamer
gallardía *nf* **1** VALENTÍA : bravery **2** APOSTURA : elegance, gracefulness
gallardo, -da *adj* **1** VALIENTE : brave **2** APUESTO : elegant, graceful
gallear *vi* : to show off, to strut around
gallego[1], **-ga** *adj* **1** : Galician **2** *fam* : Spanish
gallego[2], **-ga** *n* **1** : Galician **2** *fam* : Spaniard
galleta *nf* **1** : cookie **2** : cracker
gallina *nf* **1** : hen **2 gallina de Guinea** : guinea fowl
gallinazo *nm* : vulture, buzzard
gallinero *nm* : chicken coop, henhouse
gallito, -ta *adj fam* : cocky, belligerent
gallo *nm* **1** : rooster, cock **2** *fam* : squeak or crack in the voice **3** *Mex* : serenade **4 gallo de pelea** : gamecock
galo[1], **-la** *adj* **1** : Gaulish **2** : French
galo[2], **-la** *n* : Frenchman *m,* Frenchwoman *f*
galocha *nf* : galosh
galón *nm, pl* **galones** **1** : gallon **2** : stripe (military insignia)
galopada *nf* : gallop
galopante *adj* : galloping ⟨inflación galopante : galloping inflation⟩
galopar *vi* : to gallop
galope *nm* : gallop
galpón *nm, pl* **galpones** : shed, storehouse
galvanizar {21} *vt* : to galvanize — **galvanización** *nf*
gama *nf* **1** : range, spectrum, gamut **2** → **gamo**
gamba *nf* : large shrimp, prawn
gamberro, -rra *n Spain* : hooligan, troublemaker
gambiano, -na *adj & n* : Gambian
gambito *nm* : gambit (in chess)
gameto *nm* : gamete

gamo, -ma *n* : fallow deer

gamuza *nf* **1** : suede **2** : chamois

gana *nf* **1** : desire, inclination **2 de buena gana** : willingly, readily, gladly **3 de mala gana** : reluctantly, halfheartedly **4 tener ganas de** : to feel like, to be in the mood for ⟨tengo ganas de bailar : I feel like dancing⟩ **5 ponerle ganas a algo** : to put effort into something

ganadería *nf* **1** : cattle raising, stockbreeding **2** : cattle ranch **3** GANADO : cattle *pl,* livestock

ganadero[1]**, -ra** *adj* : cattle, ranching

ganadero[2]**, -ra** *n* : rancher, stockbreeder

ganado *nm* **1** : cattle *pl,* livestock **2 ganado ovino** : sheep *pl* **3 ganado porcino** : swine *pl*

ganador[1]**, -dora** *adj* : winning

ganador[2]**, -dora** *n* : winner

ganancia *nf* **1** : profit **2 ganancias** *nfpl* : winnings, gains

ganancioso, -sa *adj* : profitable

ganar *vt* **1** : to win **2** : to gain ⟨ganar tiempo : to buy time⟩ **3** : to earn ⟨ganar dinero : to make money⟩ **4** : to acquire, to obtain — *vi* **1** : to win **2** : to profit ⟨salir ganando : to come out ahead⟩ — **ganarse** *vr* **1** : to gain, to win ⟨ganarse a alguien : to win someone over⟩ **2** : to earn ⟨ganarse la vida : to make a living⟩ **3** : to deserve

gancho *nm* **1** : hook **2** : clothes hanger **3** : hairpin, bobby pin **4** *Col* : safety pin

gandul[1] *nm CA, Car, Col* : pigeon pea

gandul[2]**, -dula** *n fam* : idler, lazybones

gandulear *vi* : to idle, to loaf, to lounge about

ganga *nf* : bargain

ganglio *nm* **1** : ganglion **2** : gland

gangrena *nf* : gangrene — **gangrenoso, -sa** *adj*

gángster *nmf, pl* **gángsters** : gangster

gansada *nf* : silly thing, nonsense

ganso, -sa *n* **1** : goose, gander *m* **2** : idiot, fool

gañido *nm* : yelp (of a dog)

gañir {38} *vi* : to yelp

garabatear *v* : to scribble, to scrawl, to doodle

garabato *nm* **1** : doodle **2 garabatos** *nmpl* : scribble, scrawl

garaje *nm* : garage

garante *nmf* : guarantor

garantía *nf* **1** : guarantee, warranty **2** : security ⟨garantía de trabajo : job security⟩

garantizar {21} *vt* : to guarantee

garapiña *nf* : pineapple drink

garapiñar *vt* : to candy

garbanzo *nm* : chickpea, garbanzo

garbo *nm* **1** DONAIRE : grace, poise **2** : jauntiness

garboso, -sa *adj* **1** : graceful **2** : elegant, stylish

garceta *nf* : egret

gardenia *nf* : gardenia

garfio *nm* : hook, gaff, grapnel

gargajo *nm fam* : phlegm

garganta *nf* **1** : throat **2** : neck (of a person or a bottle) **3** : ravine, narrow pass

gargantilla *nf* : choker, necklace

gárgara *nf* **1** : gargle, gargling **2 hacer gárgaras** : to gargle

gargarizar *vi* : to gargle

gárgola *nf* : gargoyle

garita *nf* **1** : cabin, hut **2** : sentry box, lookout post

garoso, -sa *adj Col, Ven* : gluttonous, greedy

garra *nf* **1** : claw **2** : hand, paw **3 garras** *nfpl* : claws, clutches ⟨caer en las garras de alguien : to fall into someone's clutches⟩

garrafa *nf* : decanter, carafe

garrafal *adj* : terrible, monstrous

garrafón *nm, pl* **-fones** : large decanter, large bottle

garrapata *nf* : tick

garrobo *nm CA* : large lizard, iguana

garrocha *nf* **1** PICA : lance, pike **2** : pole ⟨salto con garrocha : pole vault⟩

garrotazo *nm* : blow (with a club)

garrote *nm* **1** : club, stick **2** *Mex* : brake

garúa *nf* : drizzle

garuar {3} *v impers* LLOVIZNAR : to drizzle

garza *nf* : heron

gas *nm* : gas, vapor, fumes *pl* ⟨gas lacrimógeno : tear gas⟩

gasa *nf* : gauze

gasear *vt* **1** : to gas **2** : to aerate (a liquid)

gaseosa *nf* REFRESCO : soda, soft drink

gaseoso, -sa *adj* **1** : gaseous **2** : carbonated, fizzy

gasoducto *nm* : gas pipeline

gasolina *nf* : gasoline, gas

gasolinera *nf* : gas station, service station

gastado, -da *adj* **1** : spent **2** : worn, worn-out

gastador[1]**, -dora** *adj* : extravagant, spendthrift

gastador[2]**, -dora** *n* : spendthrift

gastar *vt* **1** : to spend **2** CONSUMIR : to consume, to use up **3** : to squander, to waste **4** : to wear ⟨gasta un bigote : he sports a mustache⟩ — **gastarse** *vr* **1** : to spend, to expend **2** : to run down, to wear out

gasto *nm* **1** : expense, expenditure **2** DETERIORO : wear **3 gastos generales** *or* **gastos indirectos** : overhead

gástrico, -ca *adj* : gastric

gastritis *nf* : gastritis

gastronomía *nf* : gastronomy

gastronómico, -ca *adj* : gastronomic

gastrónomo, -ma *n* : gourmet

gatas *adv* **andar a gatas** : to crawl, to go on all fours

gatear *vi* **1** : to crawl **2** : to climb, to clamber (up)

gatillero *nm Mex* : gunman
gatillo *nm* : trigger
gatito, -ta *n* : kitten
gato[1], **-ta** *n* : cat
gato[2] *nm* : jack (for an automobile)
gauchada *nf Arg, Uru* : favor, kindness
gaucho *nm* : gaucho
gaveta *nf* **1** CAJÓN : drawer **2** : till
gavilla *nf* **1** : gang, band **2** : sheaf
gaviota *nf* : gull, seagull
gay ['ge, 'gai] *adj* : gay (homosexual)
gaza *nf* : loop
gazapo *nm* **1** : young rabbit **2** : misprint, error
gazmoñería *nf* MOJIGATERÍA : prudery, primness
gazmoño[1], **-ña** *adj* : prudish, prim
gazmoño[2], **-ña** *n* MOJIGATO : prude, prig
gaznate *nm* : throat, gullet
gazpacho *nm* : gazpacho
géiser *or* **géyser** *nm* : geyser
gel *nm* : gel
gelatina *nf* : gelatin
gélido, -da *adj* : icy, freezing cold
gelificarse *vr* : to jell
gema *nf* : gem
gemelo[1], **-la** *adj & n* MELLIZO : twin
gemelo[2] *nm* **1** : cuff link **2 gemelos** *nmpl* BINOCULARES : binoculars
gemido *nm* : moan, groan, wail
Géminis *nmf* : Gemini
gemir {54} *vi* : to moan, to groan, to wail
gen *or* **gene** *nm* : gene
gendarme *nmf* POLICÍA : police officer, policeman *m*, policewoman *f*
gendarmería *nf* : police
genealogía *nf* : genealogy
genealógico, -ca *adj* : genealogical
generación *nf, pl* **-ciones 1** : generation ⟨tercera generación : third generation⟩ **2** : generating, creating **3** : class ⟨la generación del '97 : the class of '97⟩
generacional *adj* : generation, generational
generador *nm* : generator
general[1] *adj* **1** : general **2 en ~** *or* **por lo general** : in general, generally
general[2] *nmf* **1** : general **2 general de división** : major general
generalidad *nf* **1** : generality, generalization **2** : majority
generalización *nf, pl* **-ciones 1** : generalization **2** : escalation, spread
generalizado, -da *adj* : generalized, widespread
generalizar {21} *vi* : to generalize — *vt* : to spread, to spread out — **generalizarse** *vr* : to become widespread
generalmente *adv* : usually, generally
generar *vt* : to generate — **generarse** *vr*
genérico, -ca *adj* : generic
género *nm* **1** : genre, class, kind ⟨el género humano : the human race, mankind⟩ **2** : gender (in grammar) **3 géneros** *nmpl* : goods, commodities
generosidad *nf* : generosity
generoso, -sa *adj* **1** : generous, unselfish **2** : ample — **generosamente** *adv*
genética *nf* : genetics
genético, -ca *adj* : genetic — **genéticamente** *adv*
genetista *nmf* : geneticist
genial *adj* **1** AGRADABLE : genial, pleasant **2** : brilliant ⟨una obra genial : a work of genius⟩ **3** *fam* FORMIDABLE : fantastic, terrific
genialidad *nf* **1** : genius **2** : stroke of genius **3** : eccentricity
genio *nm* **1** : genius **2** : temper, disposition ⟨de mal genio : bad-tempered⟩ **3** : genie
genital *adj* : genital
genitales *nmpl* : genitals, genitalia
genocidio *nm* : genocide
genotipo *nm* : genotype
gente *nf* **1** : people **2** : relatives *pl*, folks *pl* **3 gente menuda** *fam* : children, kids *pl* **4 ser buena gente** : to be nice, to be kind
gentil[1] *adj* **1** AMABLE : kind **2** : gentile
gentil[2] *nmf* : gentile
gentileza *nf* **1** AMABILIDAD : kindness **2** CORTESÍA : courtesy
gentilicio, -cia *adj* **1** : national, tribal **2** : family
gentío *nm* MUCHEDUMBRE, MULTITUD : crowd, mob
gentuza *nf* CHUSMA : riffraff, rabble
genuflexión *nf, pl* **-xiones 1** : genuflection **2 hacer una genuflexión** : to genuflect
genuino, -na *adj* : genuine — **genuinamente** *adv*
geofísica *nf* : geophysics
geofísico, -ca *adj* : geophysical
geografía *nf* : geography
geográfico, -ca *adj* : geographic, geographical — **geográficamente** *adv*
geógrafo, -fa *n* : geographer
geología *nf* : geology
geológico, -ca *adj* : geologic, geological — **geológicamente** *adv*
geólogo, -ga *n* : geologist
geometría *nf* : geometry
geométrico, -ca *adj* : geometric, geometrical — **geométricamente** *adv*
geopolítica *nf* : geopolitics
geopolítico, -ca *adj* : geopolitical
georgiano, -na *adj & n* : Georgian
geranio *nm* : geranium
gerbo *nm* : gerbil
gerencia *nf* : management, administration
gerencial *adj* : managerial
gerente *nmf* : manager, director
geriatría *nf* : geriatrics
geriátrico, -ca *adj* : geriatric
germanio *nm* : germanium
germano, -na *adj* : Germanic, German
germen *nm, pl* **gérmenes** : germ
germicida *nf* : germicide
germinación *nf, pl* **-ciones** : germination
germinar *vi* : to germinate, to sprout
gerontología *nf* : gerontology
gerundio *nm* : gerund

gesta *nf* : deed, exploit
gestación *nf, pl* **-ciones** : gestation
gesticulación *nf, pl* **-ciones** : gesturing, gesticulation
gesticular *vi* : to gesticulate, to gesture
gestión *nf, pl* **gestiones** **1** TRÁMITE : procedure, step **2** ADMINISTRACIÓN : management **3 gestiones** *nfpl* : negotiations
gestionar *vt* **1** : to negotiate, to work towards **2** ADMINISTRAR : to manage, to handle
gesto *nm* **1** ADEMÁN : gesture **2** : facial expression **3** MUECA : grimace
gestor[1], **-tora** *adj* : facilitating, negotiating, managing
gestor[2], **-tora** *n* : facilitator, manager
géyser → **géiser**
ghanés, -nesa *adj & n, mpl* **ghaneses** : Ghanaian
ghetto → **gueto**
giba *nf* **1** : hump (of an animal) **2** : hunchback (of a person)
gibón *nm, pl* **gibones** : gibbon
giboso[1], **-sa** *adj* : hunchbacked, humpbacked
giboso[2], **-sa** *n* : hunchback, humpback
gigabyte *nm* : gigabyte
gigante[1] *adj* : giant, gigantic
gigante[2], **-ta** *n* : giant
gigantesco, -ca *adj* : gigantic, huge
gime, etc. → **gemir**
gimnasia *nf* : gymnastics
gimnasio *nm* : gymnasium, gym
gimnasta *nmf* : gymnast
gimnástico, -ca *adj* : gymnastic
gimotear *vi* LLORIQUEAR : to whine, to whimper
gimoteo *nm* : whimpering
ginebra *nf* : gin
ginecología *nf* : gynecology
ginecológico, -ca *adj* : gynecologic, gynecological
ginecólogo, -ga *n* : gynecologist
ginseng *nm* : ginseng
gira *nf* : tour
giralda *nf* : weather vane
girar *vi* **1** : to turn around, to revolve **2** : to swing around, to swivel — *vt* **1** : to turn, to twist, to rotate **2** : to draft (checks) **3** : to transfer (funds)
girasol *nm* MIRASOL : sunflower
giratorio, -ria *adj* : revolving
giro *nm* **1** VUELTA : turn, rotation **2** : change of direction ⟨giro de 180 grados : U-turn, about-face⟩ **3 giro bancario** : bank draft **4 giro postal** : money order
giroscopio *or* **giróscopo** *nm* : gyroscope
gis *nm Mex* : chalk
gitano, -na *adj & n* : Gypsy
glacial *adj* : glacial, icy — **glacialmente** *adv*
glaciar *nm* : glacier
gladiador *nm* : gladiator
gladiolo *or* **gladíolo** *nm* : gladiolus
glándula *nf* : gland — **glandular** *adj*
glaseado *nm* : glaze, icing
glasear *vt* : to glaze
glaucoma *nm* : glaucoma
glicerina *nf* : glycerin, glycerol
glicinia *nf* : wisteria
global *adj* **1** : global, worldwide **2** : full, comprehensive **3** : total, overall
globalizar {21} *vt* **1** ABARCAR : to include, to encompass **2** : to extend worldwide
globalmente *adv* : globally, as a whole
globo *nm* **1** : globe, sphere **2** : balloon **3 globo ocular** : eyeball
glóbulo *nm* **1** : globule **2** : blood cell, corpuscle
gloria *nf* **1** : glory **2** : fame, renown **3** : delight, enjoyment **4** : star, legend ⟨las glorias del cine : the great names in motion pictures⟩
glorieta *nf* **1** : rotary, traffic circle **2** : bower, arbor
glorificar {72} *vt* ALABAR : to glorify — **glorificación** *nf*
glorioso, -sa *adj* : glorious — **gloriosamente** *adv*
glosa *nf* **1** : gloss **2** : annotation, commentary
glosar *vt* **1** : to gloss **2** : to annotate, to comment on (a text)
glosario *nm* : glossary
glotis *nf* : glottis
glotón[1], **-tona** *adj, mpl* **glotones** : gluttonous
glotón[2], **-tona** *n, mpl* **glotones** : glutton
glotón[3] *nm, pl* **glotones** : wolverine
glotonería *nf* GULA : gluttony
glucosa *nf* : glucose
glutinoso, -sa *adj* : glutinous
gnomo ['nomo] *nm* : gnome
gobernación *nf, pl* **-ciones** : governing, government
gobernador, -dora *n* : governor
gobernante[1] *adj* : ruling, governing
gobernante[2] *nmf* : ruler, leader, governor
gobernar {55} *vt* **1** : to govern, to rule **2** : to steer, to sail (a ship) — *vi* **1** : to govern **2** : to steer
gobierno *nm* : government
goce[1], **etc.** → **gozar**
goce[2] *nm* **1** PLACER : enjoyment, pleasure **2** : use, possession
gol *nm* : goal (in soccer)
golear *vt* : to rout, to score many goals against (in soccer)
goleta *nf* : schooner
golf *nm* : golf
golfista *nmf* : golfer
golfo *nm* : gulf, bay
golondrina *nf* **1** : swallow (bird) **2 golondrina de mar** : tern
golosina *nf* : sweet, snack
goloso, -sa *adj* : fond of sweets ⟨ser goloso : to have a sweet tooth⟩
golpazo *nm* : heavy blow, bang, thump
golpe *nm* **1** : blow ⟨caerle a golpes a alguien : to give someone a beating⟩ **2** : knock **3 de ~** : suddenly **4 de un**

golpe : all at once, in one fell swoop **5** **golpe de estado** : coup, coup d'etat **6** **golpe de suerte** : stroke of luck

golpeado, -da *adj* **1** : beaten, hit **2** : bruised (of fruit) **3** : dented

golpear *vt* **1** : to beat (up), to hit **2** : to slam, to bang, to strike — *vi* **1** : to knock (at a door) **2** : to beat ⟨la lluvia golpeaba contra el tejado : the rain beat against the roof⟩ — **golpearse** *vr*

golpetear *v* : to knock, to rattle, to tap

golpeteo *nm* : banging, knocking, tapping

goma *nf* **1** : gum ⟨goma de mascar : chewing gum⟩ **2** CAUCHO : rubber ⟨goma espuma : foam rubber⟩ **3** PEGAMENTO : glue **4** : rubber band **5** *Arg* : tire **6** *or* **goma de borrar** : eraser

gomita *nf* : rubber band

gomoso, -sa *adj* : gummy, sticky

góndola *nf* : gondola

gong *nm* : gong

gonorrea *nf* : gonorrhea

gorda *nf Mex* : thick corn tortilla

gordinflón[1], -flona *adj, mpl* **-flones** *fam* : chubby, pudgy

gordinflón[2], -flona *n, mpl* **-flones** *fam* : chubby person

gordo[1], -da *adj* **1** : fat **2** : thick **3** : fatty, greasy, oily **4** : unpleasant ⟨me cae gorda tu tía : I can't stand your aunt⟩

gordo[2], -da *n* : fat person

gordo[3] *nm* **1** GRASA : fat **2** : jackpot

gordura *nf* : fatness, flab

gorgojo *nm* : weevil

gorgotear *vi* : to gurgle, to bubble

gorgoteo *nm* : gurgle

gorila *nm* : gorilla

gorjear *vi* **1** : to chirp, to tweet, to warble **2** : to gurgle

gorjeo *nm* **1** : chirping, warbling **2** : gurgling

gorra *nf* **1** : bonnet **2** : cap **3** **de ~** *fam* : for free, at someone else's expense ⟨vivir de gorra : to sponge, to freeload⟩

gorrear *vt fam* : to bum, to scrounge — *vi fam* : to freeload

gorrero, -ra *n fam* : freeloader, sponger

gorrión *nm, pl* **gorriones** : sparrow

gorro *nm* **1** : cap **2** **estar hasta el gorro** : to be fed up

gorrón, -rrona *n, mpl* **gorrones** *fam* : freeloader, scrounger

gorronear *vt fam* : to bum, to scrounge — *vi fam* : to freeload

gota *nf* **1** : drop ⟨una gota de sudor : a bead of sweat⟩ ⟨como dos gotas de agua : like two peas in a pod⟩ ⟨sudar la gota gorda : to sweat buckets, to work very hard⟩ **2** : gout

gotear *v* **1** : to drip **2** : to leak — *v impers* LLOVIZNAR : to drizzle

goteo *nm* : drip, dripping

gotera *nf* **1** : leak **2** : stain (from dripping water)

gotero *nm* : (medicine) dropper

gótico, -ca *adj* : Gothic

gourmet *nmf* : gourmet

gozar {21} *vi* **1** : to enjoy oneself, to have a good time **2** **~ de** : to enjoy, to have, to possess ⟨gozar de buena salud : to enjoy good health⟩ **3** **~ con** : to take delight in

gozne *nm* BISAGRA : hinge

gozo *nm* **1** : joy **2** PLACER : enjoyment, pleasure

gozoso, -sa *adj* : joyful

grabación *nf, pl* **-ciones** : recording

grabado *nm* **1** : engraving **2** **grabado al aguafuerte** : etching

grabador, -dora *n* : engraver

grabadora *nf* : tape recorder

grabar *vt* **1** : to engrave **2** : to record, to tape — *vi* **grabar al aguafuerte** : to etch — **grabarse** *vr* **grabársele a alguien en la memoria** : to become engraved on someone's mind

gracia *nf* **1** : grace **2** : favor, kindness **3** : humor, wit ⟨su comentario no me hizo gracia : I wasn't amused by his remark⟩ **4** **gracias** *nfpl* : thanks ⟨¡gracias! : thank you!⟩ ⟨dar gracias : to give thanks⟩

grácil *adj* **1** : graceful **2** : delicate, slender, fine

gracilidad *nm* : gracefulness

gracioso, -sa *adj* **1** CHISTOSO : funny, amusing **2** : cute, attractive

grada *nf* **1** : harrow **2** PELDAÑO : step, stair **3** **gradas** *nfpl* : bleachers, grandstand

gradación *nf, pl* **-ciones** : gradation, scale

gradar *vt* : to harrow, to hoe

gradería *nf* : tiers *pl*, stands *pl*, rows *pl* (in a theater)

gradiente *nf* : gradient, slope

grado *nm* **1** : degree (in meteorology and mathematics) ⟨grado centígrado : degree centigrade⟩ **2** : extent, level, degree ⟨en grado sumo : greatly, to the highest degree⟩ **3** RANGO : rank **4** : year, class (in education) **5** **de buen grado** : willingly, readily

graduable *adj* : adjustable

graduación *nf, pl* **-ciones** **1** : graduation (from a school) **2** GRADO : rank **3** : alcohol content, proof

graduado[1], -da *adj* **1** : graduated **2** **lentes graduados** : prescription lenses

graduado[2], -da *n* : graduate

gradual *adj* : gradual — **gradualmente** *adv*

graduar {3} *v* **1** : to regulate, to adjust **2** CALIBRAR : to calibrate, to gauge — **graduarse** *vr* : to graduate (from a school)

graffiti *or* **grafiti** *nmpl* : graffiti *pl*

gráfica *nf* → **gráfico[2]**

gráfico[1], -ca *adj* : graphic — **gráficamente** *adv*

gráfico[2] *nm* **1** : graph, chart **2** : graphic (for a computer, etc.) **3** **gráfico de barras** : bar graph

grafismo *nm* : graphics *pl*

grafito *nm* : graphite
gragea *nf* **1** : coated pill or tablet **2 grageas** *nfpl* : sprinkles, jimmies
grajo *nm* : rook (bird)
grama *nf* : grass
gramática *nf* : grammar
gramatical *adj* : grammatical — **gramaticalmente** *adv*
gramo *nm* : gram
gran → **grande**
grana *nf* : scarlet, deep red
granada *nf* **1** : pomegranate **2** : grenade ⟨granada de mano : hand grenade⟩
granadero *nm* **1** : grenadier **2 granaderos** *nmpl Mex* : riot squad
granadino, -na *adj & n* : Grenadian
granado, -da *adj* **1** DISTINGUIDO : distinguished **2** : choice, select
granate *nm* **1** : garnet **2** : deep red, maroon
grande *adj* (**gran** *before singular nouns*) **1** : large, big ⟨un libro grande : a big book⟩ **2** ALTO : tall **3** NOTABLE : great ⟨un gran autor : a great writer⟩ **4** (*indicating intensity*) : great ⟨con gran placer : with great pleasure⟩ **5** : old, grown-up ⟨hijos grandes : grown children⟩
grandeza *nf* **1** MAGNITUD : greatness, size **2** : nobility **3** : generosity, graciousness **4** : grandeur, magnificence
grandilocuencia *nf* : grandiloquence — **grandilocuente** *adj*
grandiosidad *nf* : grandeur
grandioso, -sa *adj* **1** MAGNÍFICO : grand, magnificent **2** : grandiose
granel *adv* **1 a ~** : galore, in great quantities **2 a ~** : in bulk ⟨vender a granel : to sell in bulk⟩
granero *nm* : barn, granary
granito *nm* : granite
granizada *nf* : hailstorm
granizar {21} *v impers* : to hail
granizo *nm* : hail
granja *nf* : farm
granjear *vt* : to earn, to win — **granjearse** *vr* : to gain, to earn
granjero, -ra *n* : farmer
grano *nm* **1** PARTÍCULA : grain, particle ⟨un grano de arena : a grain of sand⟩ **2** : grain (of rice, etc.), bean (of coffee), seed **3** : grain (of wood or rock) **4** BARRO, ESPINILLA : pimple **5 ir al grano** : to get to the point
granuja *nmf* PILLUELO : rascal, urchin
granular[1] *vt* : to granulate — **granularse** *vr* : to break out in spots
granular[2] *adj* : granular, grainy
granza *nf* : chaff
grapa *nf* **1** : staple **2** : clamp
grapadora *nf* ENGRAPADORA : stapler
grapar *vt* ENGRAPAR : to staple
grasa *nf* **1** : grease **2** : fat **3** *Mex* : shoe polish
grasiento, -ta *adj* : greasy, oily
graso, -sa *adj* **1** : fatty **2** : greasy, oily
grasoso, -sa *adj* GRASIENTO : greasy, oily
gratificación *nf, pl* **-ciones 1** SATISFACCIÓN : gratification **2** : bonus **3** RECOMPENSA : recompense, reward
gratificar {72} *vt* **1** SATISFACER : to satisfy, to gratify **2** RECOMPENSAR : to reward **3** : to give a bonus to
gratinado, -da *adj* : au gratin
gratis[1] *adv* GRATUITAMENTE : free, for free, gratis
gratis[2] *adj* GRATUITO : free, gratis
gratitud *nf* : gratitude
grato, -ta *adj* AGRADABLE, PLACENTERO : pleasant, agreeable — **gratamente** *adv*
gratuitamente *adv* **1** : gratuitously **2** GRATIS : free, for free, gratis
gratuito, -ta *adj* **1** : gratuitous, unwarranted **2** GRATIS : free, gratis
grava *nf* : gravel
gravamen *nm, pl* **-vámenes 1** : burden, obligation **2** : (property) tax
gravar *vt* **1** : to burden, to encumber **2** : to levy (a tax)
grave *adj* **1** : grave, important **2** : serious, somber **3** : serious (of an illness)
gravedad *nf* **1** : gravity ⟨centro de gravedad : center of gravity⟩ **2** : seriousness, severity
gravemente *adv* : gravely, seriously
gravilla *nf* : (fine) gravel
gravitación *nf, pl* **-ciones** : gravitation
gravitacional *adj* : gravitational
gravitar *vi* **1** : to gravitate **2 ~ sobre** : to rest on **3 ~ sobre** : to loom over
gravoso, -sa *adj* **1** ONEROSO : burdensome, onerous **2** : costly
graznar *vi* : to caw, to honk, to quack, to squawk
graznido *nm* : cawing, honking, quacking, squawking
gregario, -ria *adj* : gregarious
gregoriano, -na *adj* : Gregorian
gremial *adj* SINDICAL : union, labor
gremio *nm* SINDICATO : union, guild
greña *nf* **1** : mat, tangle **2 greñas** *nfpl* MELENAS : shaggy hair, mop
greñudo, -da *n* HIPPIE, MELENUDO : longhair, hippie
grey *nf* : congregation, flock
griego[1], **-ga** *adj & n* : Greek
griego[2] *nm* : Greek (language)
grieta *nf* : crack, crevice
grifo *nm* **1** : faucet ⟨agua del grifo : tap water⟩ **2** : griffin
grillete *nm* : shackle
grillo *nm* **1** : cricket **2 grillos** *nmpl* : fetters, shackles
grima *nf* **1** : disgust, uneasiness **2 darle grima a alguien** : to get on someone's nerves
gringo, -ga *adj & n* YANQUI : Yankee, gringo
gripa *nf Col, Mex* : flu
gripe *nf* : flu
gris *adj* **1** : gray **2** : overcast, cloudy
grisáceo, -cea *adj* : grayish
gritar *v* : to shout, to scream, to cry
gritería *nf* : shouting, clamor

grito *nm* : shout, scream, cry ‹a grito pelado : at the top of one's voice›
groenlandés, -desa *adj & n* : Greenlander
grogui *adj fam* : dazed, groggy
grosella *nf* **1** : currant **2 grosella espinosa** : gooseberry
grosería *nf* **1** : insult, coarse language **2** : rudeness, discourtesy
grosero¹, **-ra** *adj* **1** : rude, fresh **2** : coarse, vulgar
grosero², **-ra** *n* : rude person
grosor *nm* : thickness
grosso *adj* **a grosso modo** : roughly, broadly, approximately
grotesco, -ca *adj* : grotesque, hideous
grúa *nf* **1** : crane (machine) **2** : tow truck
gruesa *nf* : gross
grueso¹, **-sa** *adj* **1** : thick, bulky **2** : heavy, big **3** : heavyset, stout
grueso² *nm* **1** : thickness **2** : main body, mass **3 en ~** : in bulk
grulla *nf* : crane (bird)
grumo *nm* : lump, glob
gruñido *nm* : growl, grunt
gruñir {38} *vi* **1** : to growl, to grunt **2** : to grumble
gruñón¹, **-ñona** *adj, mpl* **gruñones** *fam* : grumpy, crabby
gruñón², **-ñona** *n, mpl* **gruñones** *fam* : grumpy person, nag
grupa *nf* : rump, hindquarters *pl*
grupo *nm* : group
gruta *nf* : grotto, cave
guacal *nm Col, Mex, Ven* : crate
guacamayo *nm* : macaw
guacamole *or* **guacamol** *nm* : guacamole
guacamote *nm Mex* : yuca, cassava
guachinango → **huachinango**
guacho, -cha *adj* **1** *Arg, Col, Chile, Peru* : orphaned **2** *Chile, Peru* : odd, unmatched
guadaña *nf* : scythe
guagua *nf* **1** *Arg, Col, Chile, Peru* : baby **2** *Cuba, PRi* : bus
guaira *nf* **1** *CA* : traditional flute **2** *Peru* : smelting furnace
guajiro, -ra *n Cuba* : peasant
guajolote *nm Mex* : turkey
guanábana *nf* : guanabana, soursop (fruit)
guanaco *nm* : guanaco
guandú *nm CA, Car, Col* : pigeon pea
guango, -ga *adj Mex* **1** : loose-fitting, baggy **2** : slack, loose
guano *nm* : guano
guante *nm* **1** : glove ‹guante de boxeo : boxing glove› **2 arrojarle el guante (a alguien)** : to throw down the gauntlet (to someone)
guantelete *nm* : gauntlet
guapo, -pa *adj* **1** : handsome, good-looking, attractive **2** : elegant, smart **3** *fam* : bold, dashing
guapura *nf fam* : handsomeness, attractiveness, good looks *pl* ‹¡qué guapura! : what a vision!›
guarache → **huarache**
guarachear *vi Cuba, PRi fam* : to go on a spree, to go out on the town
guaraní¹ *adj & nmf* : Guarani
guaraní² *nm* : Guarani (language of Paraguay)
guarda *nmf* **1** GUARDIÁN : security guard **2** : keeper, custodian
guardabarros *nms & pl* : fender, mudguard
guardabosque *nmf* : forest ranger, gamekeeper
guardacostas¹ *nmfs & pl* : coastguardsman
guardacostas² *nms & pl* : coast guard vessel
guardaespaldas *nmfs & pl* : bodyguard
guardafangos *nms & pl* : fender, mudguard
guardameta *nmf* ARQUERO, PORTERO : goalkeeper, goalie
guardapelo *nm* : locket
guardapolvo *nm* **1** : dustcover **2** : duster, housecoat
guardar *vt* **1** : to guard **2** : to maintain, to preserve **3** CONSERVAR : to put away **4** RESERVAR : to save **5** : to keep (a secret or promise) — **guardarse** *vr* **1 ~ de** : to refrain from **2 ~ de** : to guard against, to be careful not to
guardarropa *nm* **1** : cloakroom, checkroom **2** ARMARIO : closet, wardrobe
guardería *nf* : nursery, day-care center
guardia¹ *nf* **1** : guard, defense **2** : guard duty, watch **3 en ~** : on guard
guardia² *nmf* **1** : sentry, guardsman, guard **2** : police officer, policeman *m*, policewoman *f*
guardiamarina *nmf* : midshipman
guardián, -diana *n, mpl* **guardianes** **1** GUARDA : security guard, watchman **2** : guardian, keeper **3 perro guardián** : watchdog
guarecer {53} *vt* : to shelter, to protect — **guarecerse** *vr* : to take shelter
guarida *nf* **1** : den, lair **2** : hideout
guarismo *nm* : figure, numeral
guarnecer {53} *vt* **1** : to adorn **2** : to garnish **3** : to garrison
guarnición *nf, pl* **-ciones** **1** : garnish **2** : garrison **3** : decoration, trimming, setting (of a jewel)
guaro *nm CA* : liquor distilled from sugarcane
guasa *nf fam* **1** : joking, fooling around **2 de ~** : in jest, as a joke
guasón¹, **-sona** *adj, mpl* **guasones** *fam* : funny, witty
guasón², **-sona** *n, mpl* **guasones** *fam* : joker, clown
guatemalteco, -ca *adj & n* : Guatemalan
guau *interj* : wow!
guayaba *nf* : guava (fruit)
gubernamental *adj* : governmental
gubernativo, -va → **gubernamental**
gubernatura *nf Mex* : governing body
guepardo *nm* : cheetah
güero, -ra *adj Mex* : blond, fair

guerra *nf* **1** : war ⟨declarar la guerra : to declare war⟩ ⟨guerra sin cuartel : all-out war⟩ **2** : warfare **3** LUCHA : conflict, struggle
guerrear *vi* : to wage war
guerrero[1], **-ra** *adj* **1** : war, fighting **2** : warlike
guerrero[2], **-ra** *n* : warrior
guerrilla *nf* : guerrilla warfare
guerrillero, -ra *adj & n* : guerrilla
gueto *nm* : ghetto
guía[1] *nf* **1** : directory, guidebook **2** ORIENTACIÓN : guidance, direction ⟨la conciencia me sirve como guía : conscience is my guide⟩
guía[2] *nmf* : guide, leader ⟨guía de turismo : tour guide⟩
guiar {85} *vt* **1** : to guide, to lead **2** CONDUCIR : to manage — **guiarse** *vr* : to be guided by, to go by
guija *nf* : pebble
guijarro *nm* : pebble
guillotina *nf* : guillotine — **guillotinar** *vt*
guinda[1] *adj & nm Mex* : burgundy (color)
guinda[2] *nf* : morello (cherry)
guineo *nm Car* : banana
guinga *nf* : gingham
guiñada → **guiño**
guiñar *vi* : to wink
guiño *nm* : wink
guión *nm, pl* **guiones** **1** : script, screenplay **2** : hyphen, dash **3** ESTANDARTE : standard, banner
guirnalda *nf* : garland
guisa *nf* **1** : manner, fashion **2 a guisa de** : like, by way of **3 de tal guisa** : in such a way
guisado ESTOFADO *nm* : stew
guisante *nm* : pea
guisar *vt* **1** ESTOFAR : to stew **2** *Spain* : to cook
guiso *nm* **1** : stew **2** : casserole
güisqui → **whisky**
guita *nf* : string, twine
guitarra *nf* : guitar
guitarrista *nmf* : guitarist
gula *nf* GLOTONERÍA : gluttony, greed
gusano *nm* **1** LOMBRIZ : worm, earthworm ⟨gusano de seda : silkworm⟩ **2** : caterpillar, maggot, grub
gustar *vt* **1** : to taste **2** : to like ⟨¿gustan pasar? : would you like to come in?⟩ — *vi* **1** : to be pleasing ⟨me gustan los dulces : I like sweets⟩ ⟨a María le gusta Carlos : Maria is attracted to Carlos⟩ ⟨no me gusta que me griten : I don't like to be yelled at⟩ **2 ~ de** : to like, to enjoy ⟨no gusta de chismes : she doesn't like gossip⟩ **3 como guste** : as you wish, as you like
gustativo, -va *adj* : taste ⟨papilas gustativas : taste buds⟩
gusto *nm* **1** : flavor, taste **2** : taste, style **3** : pleasure, liking **4** : whim, fancy ⟨a gusto : at will⟩ **5 a ~** : comfortable, at ease **6 al gusto** : to taste, as one likes **7 mucho gusto** : pleased to meet you
gustosamente *adv* : gladly
gustoso, -sa *adj* **1** : willing, glad ⟨nuestra empresa participará gustosa : our company will be pleased to participate⟩ **2** : zesty, tasty
gutural *adj* : guttural

H

h *nf* : eighth letter of the Spanish alphabet
ha → **haber**
haba *nf* : broad bean
habanero[1], **-ra** *adj* : of or from Havana
habanero[2], **-ra** *n* : native or resident of Havana
haber[1] {39} *v aux* **1** : have, has ⟨no ha llegado el envío : the shipment hasn't arrived⟩ **2 ~ de** : must ⟨ha de ser tarde : it must be late⟩ — *v impers* **1 hay** : there is, there are ⟨hay dos mensajes : there are two messages⟩ ⟨¿qué hay de nuevo? : what's new?⟩ **2 hay que** : it is necessary ⟨hay que trabajar más rápido : you have to work faster⟩
haber[2] *nm* **1** : assets *pl* **2** : credit, credit side **3 haberes** *nmpl* : salary, income, remuneration
habichuela *nf* **1** : bean, kidney bean **2** : green bean
hábil *adj* **1** : able, skillful **2** : working ⟨días hábiles : working days⟩
habilidad *nf* CAPACIDAD : ability, skill
habilidoso, -sa *adj* : skillful, clever
habilitación *nf, pl* **-ciones** **1** : authorization **2** : furnishing, equipping
habilitar *vt* **1** : to enable, to authorize, to empower **2** : to equip, to furnish
hábilmente *adv* : skillfully, expertly
habitable *adj* : habitable, inhabitable
habitación *nf, pl* **-ciones** **1** CUARTO : room **2** DORMITORIO : bedroom **3** : habitation, occupancy
habitante *nmf* : inhabitant, resident
habitar *vt* : to inhabit — *vi* : to reside, to dwell
hábitat *nm, pl* **-tats** : habitat
hábito *nm* **1** : habit, custom **2** : habit (of a monk or nun)
habitual *adj* : habitual, customary — **habitualmente** *adv*
habituar {3} *vt* : to accustom, to habituate — **habituarse** *vr* **~ a** : to get used to, to grow accustomed to
habla *nf* **1** : speech **2** : language, dialect **3 de ~** : speaking ⟨de habla inglesa : English-speaking⟩
hablado, -da *adj* **1** : spoken **2 mal hablado** : foulmouthed

hablador[1], **-dora** *adj* : talkative
hablador[2], **-dora** *n* : chatterbox
habladuría *nf* **1** : rumor **2 habladurías** *nfpl* : gossip, scandal
hablante *nmf* : speaker
hablar *vi* **1** : to speak, to talk ⟨hablar en broma : to be joking⟩ **2 ~ de** : to mention, to talk about **3 dar que hablar** : to make people talk — *vt* **1** : to speak (a language) **2** : to talk about, to discuss ⟨háblalo con tu jefe : discuss it with your boss⟩ — **hablarse** *vr* **1** : to speak to each other, to be on speaking terms **2 se habla inglés (etc.)** : English (etc.) spoken
habrá, etc. → **haber**
hacedor, -dora *n* : creator, maker, doer
hacendado, -da *n* : landowner
hacer {40} *vt* **1** : to make **2** : to do, to perform **3** : to force, to oblige ⟨los hice esperar : I made them wait⟩ — *vi* : to act ⟨haces bien : you're doing the right thing⟩ — *v impers* **1** (*referring to weather*) ⟨hacer frío : to be cold⟩ ⟨hace viento : it's windy⟩ **2 hace** : ago ⟨hace mucho tiempo : a long time ago, for a long time⟩ **3 no le hace** : it doesn't matter, it makes no difference **4 hacer falta** : to be necessary, to be needed — **hacerse** *vr* **1** : to become **2** : to pretend, to act, to play ⟨hacerse el tonto : to play dumb⟩ **3** : to seem ⟨el examen se me hizo difícil : the exam seemed difficult to me⟩ **4** : to get, to grow ⟨se hace tarde : it's growing late⟩
hacha *nf* : hatchet, ax
hachazo *nm* : blow, chop (with an ax)
hachís *nm* : hashish
hacia *prep* **1** : toward, towards ⟨hacia abajo : downward⟩ ⟨hacia adelante : forward⟩ **2** : near, around, about ⟨hacia las seis : about six o'clock⟩
hacienda *nf* **1** : estate, ranch, farm **2** : property **3** : livestock **4 la Hacienda** : department of revenue, tax office
hacinar *vt* **1** : to pile up, to stack **2** : to overcrowd — **hacinarse** *vr* : to crowd together
hada *nf* : fairy
hado *nm* : destiny, fate
haga, etc. → **hacer**
haitiano, -na *adj & n* : Haitian
hala *interj Spain* **1** (*expressing encouragement or disbelief*) : come on! **2** (*expressing surprise*) : wow! **3** (*expressing protest*) : hey!
halagador[1], **-dora** *adj* : flattering
halagador[2], **-dora** *n* : flatterer
halagar {52} *vt* : to flatter, to compliment
halago *nm* : flattery, praise
halagüeño, -ña *adj* **1** : flattering **2** : encouraging, promising
halar *vt CA, Car* → **jalar**
halcón *nm, pl* **halcones** : hawk, falcon
halibut *nm, pl* **-buts** : halibut
hálito *nm* **1** : breath **2** : gentle breeze
hallar *vt* **1** ENCONTRAR : to find **2** DESCUBRIR : to discover, to find out — **hallarse** *vr* **1** : to be situated, to find oneself **2** : to feel ⟨no se halla bien : he doesn't feel comfortable, he feels out of place⟩
hallazgo *nm* **1** : discovery **2** : find ⟨¡es un verdadero hallazgo! : it's a real find!⟩
halo *nm* **1** : halo **2** : aura
halógeno *nm* : halogen
hamaca *nf* : hammock
hambre *nf* **1** : hunger **2** : starvation **3 tener hambre** : to be hungry **4 dar hambre** : to make hungry
hambriento, -ta *adj* : hungry, starving
hambruna *nf* : famine
hamburguesa *nf* : hamburger
hampa *nf* : criminal underworld
hampón, -pona *n, mpl* **hampones** : criminal, thug
hámster [ˈxamster] *nm, pl* **hámsters** : hamster
han → **haber**
handicap *or* **hándicap** [ˈhandiˌkap] *nm, pl* **-caps** : handicap (in sports)
hangar *nm* : hangar
hará, etc. → **hacer**
haragán[1], **-gana** *adj, mpl* **-ganes** : lazy, idle
haragán[2], **-gana** *n, mpl* **-ganes** HOLGAZÁN : slacker, good-for-nothing
haraganear *vi* : to be lazy, to waste one's time
haraganería *nf* : laziness
harapiento, -ta *adj* : ragged, tattered
harapos *nmpl* ANDRAJOS : rags, tatters
hardware [ˈhardˌwɛr] *nm* : computer hardware
harén *nm, pl* **harenes** : harem
harina *nf* **1** : flour **2 harina de maíz** : cornmeal
hartar *vt* **1** : to glut, to satiate **2** FASTIDIAR : to tire, to irritate, to annoy — **hartarse** *vr* : to be weary, to get fed up
harto[1] *adv* : most, extremely, very
harto[2], **-ta** *adj* **1** : full, satiated **2** : fed up
hartura *nf* **1** : surfeit **2** : abundance, plenty
has → **haber**
hasta[1] *adv* : even
hasta[2] *prep* **1** : until, up until ⟨hasta entonces : until then⟩ ⟨¡hasta luego! : see you later!⟩ **2** : as far as ⟨nos fuimos hasta Managua : we went all the way to Managua⟩ **3** : up to ⟨hasta cierto punto : up to a certain point⟩ **4 hasta que** : until
hastiar {85} *vt* **1** : to make weary, to bore **2** : to disgust, to sicken — **hastiarse** *vr* **~ de** : to get tired of
hastío *nm* **1** TEDIO : tedium **2** REPUGNANCIA : disgust
hato *nm* **1** : flock, herd **2** : bundle (of possessions)
hawaiano, -na *adj & n* : Hawaiian
hay → **haber**[1]

haya[1], etc. → **haber**
haya[2] *nf* : beech (tree and wood)
hayuco *nm* : beechnut
haz[1] → **hacer**
haz[2] *nm, pl* **haces** **1** FARDO : bundle **2** : beam (of light)
haz[3] *nf, pl* **haces** **1** : face **2 haz de la tierra** : surface of the earth
hazaña *nf* PROEZA : feat, exploit
hazmerreír *nm fam* : laughingstock
he[1] {39} → **haber**
he[2] *v impers* **he aquí** : here is, here are, behold
hebilla *nf* : buckle, clasp
hebra *nf* : strand, thread
hebreo[1], **-brea** *adj & n* : Hebrew
hebreo[2] *nm* : Hebrew (language)
hecatombe *nf* **1** MATANZA : massacre **2** : disaster
heces → **hez**
hechicería *nf* **1** BRUJERÍA : sorcery, witchcraft **2** : curse, spell
hechicero[1], **-ra** *adj* : bewitching, enchanting
hechicero[2], **-ra** *n* : sorcerer, sorceress *f*
hechizar {21} *vt* **1** EMBRUJAR : to bewitch **2** CAUTIVAR : to charm
hechizo *nm* **1** SORTILEGIO : spell, enchantment **2** ENCANTO : charm, fascination
hecho[1] *pp* → **hacer**
hecho[2], **-cha** *adj* **1** : made, done **2** : ready-to-wear **3** : complete, finished ⟨hecho y derecho : full-fledged⟩
hecho[3] *nm* **1** : fact **2** : event ⟨hechos históricos : historic events⟩ **3** : act, action **4 de ～** : in fact, in reality
hechura *nf* **1** : style **2** : craftsmanship, workmanship **3** : product, creation
hectárea *nf* : hectare
heder {56} *vi* : to stink, to reek
hediondez *nf, pl* **-deces** : stink, stench
hediondo, -da *adj* MALOLIENTE : foul-smelling, stinking
hedor *nm* : stench, stink
hegemonía *nf* **1** : dominance **2** : hegemony (in politics)
helada *nf* : frost (in meteorology)
heladería *nf* : ice-cream parlor, ice-cream stand
helado[1], **-da** *adj* **1** GÉLIDO : icy, freezing cold **2** CONGELADO : frozen
helado[2] *nm* : ice cream
heladora *nf* CONGELADOR : freezer
helar {55} *v* CONGELAR : to freeze — *v impers* : to produce frost ⟨anoche heló : there was frost last night⟩ — **helarse** *vr*
helecho *nm* : fern, bracken
hélice *nf* **1** : spiral, helix **2** : propeller
helicóptero *nm* : helicopter
helio *nm* : helium
helipuerto *nm* : heliport
hembra *adj & nf* : female
hemisférico, -ca *adj* : hemispheric, hemispherical
hemisferio *nm* : hemisphere
hemofilia *nf* : hemophilia
hemofílico, -ca *adj & n* : hemophiliac
hemoglobina *nf* : hemoglobin
hemorragia *nf* **1** : hemorrhage **2 hemorragia nasal** : nosebleed
hemorroides *nfpl* ALMORRANAS : hemorrhoids, piles
hemos → **haber**
henchido, -da *adj* : swollen, bloated
henchir {54} *vt* **1** : to stuff, to fill **2** : to swell, to swell up — **henchirse** *vr* **1** : to stuff oneself **2** LLENARSE : to fill up, to be full
hender {56} *vt* : to cleave, to split
hendidura *nf* : crack, crevice, fissure
henequén *nm, pl* **-quenes** : sisal hemp
heno *nm* : hay
hepatitis *nf* : hepatitis
heráldica *nf* : heraldry
heráldico, -ca *adj* : heraldic
heraldo *nm* : herald
herbario, -ria *adj* : herbal
herbicida *nm* : herbicide, weed killer
herbívoro[1], **-ra** *adj* : herbivorous
herbívoro[2] *nm* : herbivore
herbolario, -ria *n* : herbalist
hercio *nm* : hertz
hercúleo, -lea *adj* : herculean
heredar *vt* : to inherit
heredero, -ra *n* : heir, heiress *f*
hereditario, -ria *adj* : hereditary
hereje *nmf* : heretic
herejía *nf* : heresy
herencia *nf* **1** : inheritance **2** : heritage **3** : heredity
herético, -ca *adj* : heretical
herida *nf* : injury, wound
herido[1], **-da** *adj* **1** : injured, wounded **2** : hurt, offended
herido[2], **-da** *n* : injured person, casualty
herir {76} *vt* **1** : to injure, to wound **2** : to hurt, to offend
hermafrodita *nmf* : hermaphrodite
hermanar *vt* **1** : to unite, to bring together **2** : to match up, to twin (cities)
hermanastro, -tra *n* : half brother *m*, half sister *f*
hermandad *nf* **1** FRATERNIDAD : brotherhood ⟨hermandad de mujeres : sisterhood, sorority⟩ **2** : association
hermano, -na *n* : sibling, brother *m*, sister *f*
hermético, -ca *adj* : hermetic, watertight — **herméticamente** *adv*
hermoso, -sa *adj* BELLO : beautiful, lovely — **hermosamente** *adv*
hermosura *nf* BELLEZA : beauty, loveliness
hernia *nf* : hernia
héroe *nm* : hero
heroicidad *nf* : heroism, heroic deed
heroico, -ca *adj* : heroic — **heroicamente** *adv*
heroína *nf* **1** : heroine **2** : heroin
heroísmo *nm* : heroism
herpes *nms & pl* **1** : herpes **2** : shingles
herradura *nf* : horseshoe
herraje *nm* : ironwork

herramienta *nf* : tool
herrar {55} *vt* : to shoe (a horse)
herrería *nf* : blacksmith's shop
herrero, -ra *n* : blacksmith
herrumbre *nf* ORÍN : rust
herrumbroso, -sa *adj* OXIDADO : rusty
hertzio *nm* : hertz
hervidero *nm* **1** : mass, swarm **2** : hotbed (of crime, etc.)
hervidor *nm* : kettle
hervir {76} *vi* **1** BULLIR : to boil, to bubble **2 ~ de** : to teem with, to be swarming with — *vt* : to boil
hervor *nm* **1** : boiling **2** : fervor, ardor
heterogeneidad *nf* : heterogeneity
heterogéneo, -nea *adj* : heterogeneous
heterosexual *adj & nmf* : heterosexual
heterosexualidad *nf* : heterosexuality
hexágono *nm* : hexagon — **hexagonal** *adj*
hez *nf, pl* **heces 1** ESCORIA : scum, dregs *pl* **2** : sediment, lees *pl* **3 heces** *nfpl* : feces, excrement
hiato *nm* : hiatus
hibernar *vi* : to hibernate — **hibernación** *nf*
híbrido¹, -da *adj* : hybrid
híbrido² *nm* : hybrid
hicieron, etc. → **hacer**
hidalgo, -ga *n* : nobleman *m,* noblewoman *f*
hidrante *nm CA, Col* : hydrant
hidratar *vt* : to moisturize — **hidratante** *adj*
hidrato *nm* **1** : hydrate **2 hidrato de carbono** : carbohydrate
hidráulico, -ca *adj* : hydraulic
hidroavión *nm, pl* **-viones** : seaplane
hidrocarburo *nm* : hydrocarbon
hidroeléctrico, -ca *adj* : hydroelectric
hidrofobia *nf* RABIA : hydrophobia, rabies
hidrófugo, -ga *adj* : water-repellent
hidrógeno *nm* : hydrogen
hidroplano *nm* : hydroplane
hiede, etc. → **heder**
hiedra *nf* **1** : ivy **2 hiedra venenosa** : poison ivy
hiel *nf* **1** BILIS : bile **2** : bitterness
hiela, etc. → **helar**
hielo *nm* **1** : ice **2** : coldness, reserve ⟨romper el hielo : to break the ice⟩
hiena *nf* : hyena
hiende, etc. → **hender**
hierba *nf* **1** : herb **2** : grass **3 mala hierba** : weed
hierbabuena *nf* : mint, spearmint
hiere, etc. → **herir**
hierra, etc. → **herrar**
hierro *nm* **1** : iron ⟨hierro fundido : cast iron⟩ **2** : branding iron
hierve, etc. → **hervir**
hígado *nm* : liver
higiene *nf* : hygiene
higiénico, -ca *adj* : hygienic — **higiénicamente** *adv*
higienista *nmf* : hygienist
higo *nm* **1** : fig **2 higo chumbo** : prickly pear (fruit)
higrómetro *nm* : hygrometer
higuera *nf* : fig tree
hijastro, -tra *n* : stepson *m,* stepdaughter *f*
hijo, -ja *n* **1** : son *m,* daughter *f* **2 hijos** *nmpl* : children, offspring
híjole *interj Mex* : wow!, good grief!
hilacha *nf* **1** : ravel, loose thread **2 mostrar la hilacha** : to show one's true colors
hilado *nm* **1** : spinning **2** HILO : yarn, thread
hilar *vt* **1** : to spin (thread) **2** : to consider, to string together (ideas) — *vi* **1** : to spin **2 hilar delgado** : to split hairs
hilarante *adj* **1** : humorous, hilarious **2 gas hilarante** : laughing gas
hilaridad *nf* : hilarity
hilera *nf* FILA : file, row, line
hilo *nm* **1** : thread ⟨colgar de un hilo : to hang by a thread⟩ ⟨hilo dental : dental floss⟩ **2** LINO : linen **3** : (electric) wire **4** : theme, thread (of a discourse) **5** : trickle (of water, etc.)
hilvanar *vt* **1** : to baste, to tack **2** : to piece together
himnario *nm* : hymnal
himno *nm* **1** : hymn **2 himno nacional** : national anthem
hincapié *nm* **hacer hincapié en** : to emphasize, to stress
hincar {72} *vt* CLAVAR : to stick, to plunge — **hincarse** *vr* **hincarse de rodillas** : to kneel down, to fall to one's knees
hinchado, -da *adj* **1** : swollen, inflated **2** : pompous, overblown
hinchar *vt* **1** INFLAR : to inflate **2** : to exaggerate — **hincharse** *vr* **1** : to swell up **2** : to become conceited, to swell with pride
hinchazón *nf, pl* **-zones** : swelling
hinche, etc. → **henchir**
hindi *nm* : Hindi
hindú *adj & nmf* : Hindu
hinduismo *nm* : Hinduism
hiniesta *nf* : broom (plant)
hinojo *nm* **1** : fennel **2 de hinojos** : on bended knee
hinque, etc. → **hincar**
hipar *vi* : to hiccup
hiperactividad *nf* : hyperactivity
hiperactivo, -va *adj* : hyperactive, overactive
hipérbole *nf* : hyperbole
hiperbólico, -ca *adj* : hyperbolic, exaggerated
hipercrítico, -ca *adj* : hypercritical
hipermetropía *nf* : farsightedness
hipersensibilidad *nf* : hypersensitivity
hipersensible *adj* : hypersensitive
hipertensión *nf, pl* **-siones** : hypertension, high blood pressure
hip–hop [ˌxipˈxop] *nm* : hip-hop (music)
hípico, -ca *adj* : equestrian ⟨concurso hípico : horse show⟩
hipil → **huipil**
hipnosis *nfs & pl* : hypnosis

hipnótico, -ca *adj* : hypnotic

hipnotismo *nm* : hypnotism

hipnotizador[1], **-dora** *adj* **1** : hypnotic **2** : spellbinding, mesmerizing

hipnotizador[2], **-dora** *n* : hypnotist

hipnotizar {21} *vt* : to hypnotize

hipo *nm* : hiccup, hiccups *pl*

hipocampo *nm* : sea horse

hipocondría *nf* : hypochondria

hipocondríaco, -ca *adj & n* : hypochondriac

hipocresía *nf* : hypocrisy

hipócrita[1] *adj* : hypocritical — **hipócritamente** *adv*

hipócrita[2] *nmf* : hypocrite

hipodérmico, -ca *adj* **aguja hipodérmica** : hypodermic needle

hipódromo *nm* : racetrack

hipopótamo *nm* : hippopotamus

hipoteca *nf* : mortgage

hipotecar {72} *vt* **1** : to mortgage **2** : to compromise, to jeopardize

hipotecario, -ria *adj* : mortgage

hipotensión *nf* : low blood pressure

hipotenusa *nf* : hypotenuse

hipótesis *nfs & pl* : hypothesis

hipotético, -ca *adj* : hypothetical — **hipotéticamente** *adv*

hippie *or* **hippy** [ˈhipi] *nmf, pl* **hippies** [-pis] : hippie

hiriente *adj* : hurtful, offensive

hirió, etc. → **herir**

hirsuto, -ta *adj* **1** : hirsute, hairy **2** : bristly, wiry

hirviente *adj* : boiling

hirvió, etc. → **hervir**

hisopo *nm* **1** : hyssop **2** : cotton swab

hispánico, -ca *adj & n* : Hispanic

hispano[1], **-na** *adj* : Hispanic ⟨de habla hispana : Spanish-speaking⟩

hispano[2], **-na** *n* : Hispanic (person)

hispanoamericano[1], **-na** *adj* LATINOAMERICANO : Latin-American

hispanoamericano[2], **-na** *n* LATINOAMERICANO : Latin American

hispanohablante[1] *adj* : Spanish-speaking

hispanohablante[2] *nmf* : Spanish speaker

histerectomía *nf* : hysterectomy

histeria *nf* **1** : hysteria **2** : hysterics

histérico, -ca *adj* : hysterical — **histéricamente** *adv*

histerismo *nm* **1** : hysteria **2** : hysterics

historia *nf* **1** : history **2** NARRACIÓN, RELATO : story

historiador, -dora *n* : historian

historial *nm* **1** : record, document **2** CURRÍCULUM : résumé, curriculum vitae

histórico, -ca *adj* **1** : historical **2** : historic, important — **históricamente** *adv*

historieta *nf* : comic strip

histrionismo *nm* : histrionics, acting

hit [ˈhit] *nm, pl* **hits** **1** ÉXITO : hit, popular song **2** : hit (in baseball)

hito *nm* : milestone, landmark

hizo → **hacer**

hobby [ˈhɔbi] *nm, pl* **hobbies** [-bis] : hobby

hocico *nm* : snout, muzzle

hockey [ˈhɔke, -ki] *nm* : hockey

hogar *nm* **1** : home **2** : hearth, fireplace

hogareño, -ña *adj* **1** : home-loving **2** : domestic, homelike

hogaza *nf* : large loaf (of bread)

hoguera *nf* **1** FOGATA : bonfire **2** **morir en la hoguera** : to burn at the stake

hoja *nf* **1** : leaf, petal, blade (of grass) **2** : sheet (of paper), page (of a book) ⟨hoja de cálculo : spreadsheet⟩ **3** FORMULARIO : form ⟨hoja de pedido : order form⟩ **4** : blade (of a knife) ⟨hoja de afeitar : razor blade⟩

hojalata *nf* : tinplate

hojaldre *nm* : puff pastry

hojarasca *nf* : fallen leaves *pl*

hojear *vt* : to leaf through (a book or magazine)

hojuela *nf* **1** : leaflet, young leaf **2** : flake

hola *interj* : hello!, hi!

holandés[1], **-desa** *adj, mpl* **-deses** : Dutch

holandés[2], **-desa** *n, mpl* **-deses** : Dutch person, Dutchman *m*, Dutchwoman *f* ⟨los holandeses : the Dutch⟩

holandés[3] *nm* : Dutch (language)

holgadamente *adv* : comfortably, easily ⟨vivir holgadamente : to be well-off⟩

holgado, -da *adj* **1** : loose, baggy **2** : at ease, comfortable

holganza *nf* : leisure, idleness

holgazán[1], **-zana** *adj, mpl* **-zanes** : lazy

holgazán[2], **-zana** *n, mpl* **-zanes** HARAGÁN : slacker, idler

holgazanear *vi* HARAGANEAR : to laze around, to loaf

holgazanería *nf* PEREZA : idleness, laziness

holgura *nf* **1** : looseness **2** COMODIDAD : comfort, ease

holístico, -ca *adj* : holistic

hollar {19} *vt* : to tread on, to trample

hollín *nm, pl* **hollines** TIZNE : soot

holocausto *nm* : holocaust

holograma *nm* : hologram

hombre *nm* **1** : man ⟨el hombre : man, mankind⟩ **2** **hombre de estado** : statesman **3** **hombre de negocios** : businessman **4** **hombre lobo** : werewolf

hombrera *nf* **1** : shoulder pad **2** : epaulet

hombría *nf* : manliness

hombro *nm* : shoulder ⟨encogerse de hombros : to shrug one's shoulders⟩

hombruno, -na *adj* : mannish

homenaje *nm* : homage, tribute ⟨rendir homenaje a : to pay tribute to⟩

homenajear *vt* : to pay homage to, to honor

homeopatía *nf* : homeopathy

homicida[1] *adj* : homicidal, murderous

homicida[2] *nmf* ASESINO : murderer

homicidio *nm* ASESINATO : homicide, murder

homilía *nf* : homily, sermon
homófono *nm* : homophone
homogeneidad *nf* : homogeneity
homogeneización *nf* : homogenization
homogeneizar {21} *vt* : to homogenize
homogéneo, -nea *adj* : homogeneous
homógrafo *nm* : homograph
homologación *nf, pl* **-ciones** **1** : sanctioning, approval **2** : parity
homologar {52} *vt* **1** : to sanction **2** : to bring into line
homólogo[1], **-ga** *adj* : homologous, equivalent
homólogo[2], **-ga** *n* : counterpart
homónimo[1], **-ma** *n* TOCAYO : namesake
homónimo[2] *nm* : homonym
homosexual *adj & nmf* : homosexual
homosexualidad *nf* : homosexuality
honda *nf* : sling
hondo[1] *adv* : deeply
hondo[2], **-da** *adj* PROFUNDO : deep ⟨en lo más hondo de : in the depths of⟩ — **hondamente** *adv*
hondonada *nf* **1** : hollow, depression **2** : ravine, gorge
hondura *nf* : depth
hondureño, -ña *adj & n* : Honduran
honestidad *nf* **1** : decency, modesty **2** : honesty, uprightness
honesto, -ta *adj* **1** : decent, virtuous **2** : honest, honorable — **honestamente** *adv*
hongo *nm* **1** : fungus **2** : mushroom
honor *nm* **1** : honor ⟨en honor a la verdad : to be quite honest⟩ **2 honores** *nmpl* : honors ⟨hacer los honores : to do the honors⟩
honorable *adj* HONROSO : honorable — **honorablemente** *adv*
honorario, -ria *adj* : honorary
honorarios *nmpl* : payment, fees (for professional services)
honorífico, -ca *adj* : honorary ⟨mención honorífica : honorable mention⟩
honra *nf* **1** : dignity, self-respect ⟨tener a mucha honra : to take great pride in⟩ **2** : good name, reputation
honradamente *adv* : honestly, decently
honradez *nf, pl* **-deces** : honesty, integrity, probity
honrado, -da *adj* **1** HONESTO : honest, upright **2** : honored
honrar *vt* **1** : to honor **2** : to be a credit to ⟨su generosidad lo honra : his generosity does him credit⟩
honroso, -sa *adj* HONORABLE : honorable — **honrosamente** *adv*
hora *nf* **1** : hour ⟨media hora : half an hour⟩ ⟨a la última hora : at the last minute⟩ ⟨a la hora en punto : on the dot⟩ ⟨horas de oficina : office hours⟩ **2** : time ⟨¿qué hora es? : what time is it?⟩ **3** CITA : appointment
horario *nm* : schedule, timetable, hours *pl* ⟨horario de visita : visiting hours⟩
horca *nf* **1** : gallows *pl* **2** : pitchfork
horcajadas *nfpl* **a ~** : astride, astraddle
horcón *nm, pl* **horcones** : wooden post, prop
horda *nf* : horde
horizontal *adj* : horizontal — **horizontalmente** *adv*
horizonte *nm* : horizon, skyline
horma *nf* **1** : shoe tree **2** : shoemaker's last
hormiga *nf* : ant
hormigón *nm, pl* **-gones** CONCRETO : concrete
hormigonera *nf* : cement mixer
hormigueo *nm* **1** : tingling, pins and needles *pl* **2** : uneasiness
hormiguero *nm* **1** : anthill **2** : swarm (of people)
hormona *nf* : hormone — **hormonal** *adj*
hornacina *nf* : niche, recess
hornada *nf* : batch
hornear *vt* : to bake
hornilla *nf* : burner (of a stove)
horno *nm* **1** : oven ⟨horno crematorio : crematorium⟩ ⟨horno de microondas : microwave oven⟩ **2** : kiln
horóscopo *nm* : horoscope
horqueta *nf* **1** : fork (in a river or road) **2** : crotch (in a tree) **3** : small pitchfork
horquilla *nf* **1** : hairpin, bobby pin **2** : pitchfork
horrendo, -da *adj* : horrendous, horrible
horrible *adj* : horrible, dreadful — **horriblemente** *adv*
horripilante *adj* : horrifying, hair-raising
horripilar *vt* : to horrify, to terrify
horror *nm* : horror, dread
horrorizado, -da *adj* : terrified
horrorizar {21} *vt* : to horrify, to terrify — **horrorizarse** *vr*
horroroso, -sa *adj* **1** : horrifying, terrifying **2** : dreadful, bad
hortaliza *nf* **1** : vegetable **2 hortalizas** *nfpl* : garden produce
hortera *adj Spain fam* : tacky, gaudy
hortícola *adj* : horticultural
horticultor, -ra *n* : horticulturist
horticultura *nf* : horticulture
hosco, -ca *adj* : sullen, gloomy
hospedaje *nm* : lodging, accommodations *pl*
hospedar *vt* : to provide with lodging, to put up — **hospedarse** *vr* : to stay, to lodge
hospicio *nm* : orphanage
hospital *nm* : hospital
hospitalario, -ria *adj* : hospitable
hospitalidad *nf* : hospitality
hospitalización *nf, pl* **-ciones** : hospitalization
hospitalizar {21} *vt* : to hospitalize — **hospitalizarse** *vr*
hostería *nf* POSADA : inn
hostia *nf* : host, Eucharist
hostigamiento *nm* : harassment
hostigar {52} *vt* ACOSAR, ASEDIAR : to harass, to pester
hostil *adj* : hostile

hostilidad *nf* **1** : hostility, antagonism **2 hostilidades** *nfpl* : (military) hostilities

hostilizar {21} *vt* : to harass

hotel *nm* : hotel

hotelero[1], **-ra** *adj* : hotel ⟨la industria hotelera : the hotel business⟩

hotelero[2], **-ra** *n* : hotel manager, hotelier

hoy *adv* **1** : today ⟨hoy mismo : right now, this very day⟩ **2** : now, nowadays ⟨de hoy en adelante : from now on⟩

hoyo *nm* AGUJERO : hole

hoyuelo *nm* : dimple

hoz *nf, pl* **hoces** : sickle

hozar {21} *vi* : to root (of a pig)

huachinango *nm Mex* : red snapper

huarache *nm* : huarache sandal

hubo, etc. → **haber**

hueco[1], **-ca** *adj* **1** : hollow, empty **2** : soft, spongy **3** : hollow-sounding, resonant **4** : proud, conceited **5** : superficial

hueco[2] *nm* **1** : hole, hollow, cavity **2** : gap, space **3** : recess, alcove

huele, etc. → **oler**

huelga *nf* **1** PARO : strike **2 hacer huelga** : to strike, to go on strike

huelguista *nmf* : striker

huella[1], **etc.** → **hollar**

huella[2] *nf* **1** : footprint ⟨seguir las huellas de alguien : to follow in someone's footsteps⟩ **2** : mark, impact ⟨dejar huella : to leave one's mark⟩ ⟨sin dejar huella : without a trace⟩ **3 huella digital** *or* **huella dactilar** : fingerprint

huérfano[1], **-na** *adj* **1** : orphan, orphaned **2** : defenseless **3 ~ de** : lacking, devoid of

huérfano[2], **-na** *n* : orphan

huerta *nf* **1** : large vegetable garden, truck farm **2** : orchard **3** : irrigated land

huerto *nm* **1** : vegetable garden **2** : orchard

hueso *nm* **1** : bone **2** : pit, stone (of a fruit)

huésped[1], **-peda** *n* INVITADO : guest

huésped[2] *nm* : host ⟨organismo huésped : host organism⟩

huestes *nfpl* **1** : followers **2** : troops, army

huesudo, -da *adj* : bony

hueva *nf* : roe, spawn

huevo *nm* : egg ⟨huevos revueltos : scrambled eggs⟩

huida *nf* : flight, escape

huidizo, -za *adj* **1** ESCURRIDIZO : elusive, slippery **2** : shy, evasive

huipil *nm CA, Mex* : traditional sleeveless blouse or dress

huir {41} *vi* **1** ESCAPAR : to escape, to flee **2 ~ de** : to avoid

huiro *nm Chile, Peru* : seaweed

huizache *nm* : huisache, acacia

hule *nm* **1** : oilcloth, oilskin **2** *Mex* : rubber **3 hule espuma** *Mex* : foam rubber

humanidad *nf* **1** : humanity, mankind **2** : humaneness **3 humanidades** *nfpl* : humanities *pl*

humanismo *nm* : humanism

humanista *nmf* : humanist

humanístico, -ca *adj* : humanistic

humanitario, -ria *adj & n* : humanitarian

humano[1], **-na** *adj* **1** : human **2** BENÉVOLO : humane, benevolent — **humanamente** *adv*

humano[2] *nm* : human being, human

humareda *nf* : cloud of smoke

humeante *adj* **1** : smoky **2** : smoking, steaming

humear *vi* **1** : to smoke **2** : to steam

humectante[1] *adj* : moisturizing

humectante[2] *nm* : moisturizer

humedad *nf* **1** : humidity **2** : dampness, moistness

humedecer {53} *vt* **1** : to humidify **2** : to moisten, to dampen

húmedo, -da *adj* **1** : humid **2** : moist, damp

humidificador *nm* : humidifier

humidificar {72} *vt* : to humidify

humildad *nf* **1** : humility **2** : lowliness

humilde *adj* **1** : humble **2** : lowly ⟨gente humilde : poor people⟩

humildemente *adv* : meekly, humbly

humillación *nf, pl* **-ciones** : humiliation

humillante *adj* : humiliating

humillar *vt* : to humiliate — **humillarse** *vr* : to humble oneself ⟨humillarse a hacer algo : to stoop to doing something⟩

humo *nm* **1** : smoke, steam, fumes **2 humos** *nmpl* : airs *pl,* conceit

humor *nm* **1** : humor **2** : mood, temper ⟨está de buen humor : she's in a good mood⟩

humorada *nf* **1** BROMA : joke, witticism **2** : whim, caprice

humorismo *nm* : humor, wit

humorista *nmf* : humorist, comedian, comedienne *f*

humorístico, -ca *adj* : humorous — **humorísticamente** *adv*

humoso, -sa *adj* : smoky, steamy

humus *nm* : humus

hundido, -da *adj* **1** : sunken **2** : depressed

hundimiento *nm* **1** : sinking **2** : collapse, ruin

hundir *vt* **1** : to sink **2** : to destroy, to ruin — **hundirse** *vr* **1** : to sink down **2** : to cave in **3** : to break down, to go to pieces

húngaro[1], **-ra** *adj & n* : Hungarian

húngaro[2] *nm* : Hungarian (language)

huracán *nm, pl* **-canes** : hurricane

huraño, -ña *adj* **1** : unsociable, aloof **2** : timid, skittish (of an animal)

hurgar {52} *vt* : to poke, to jab, to rake (a fire) — *vi* **~ en** : to rummage in, to poke through

hurgue, etc. → **hurgar**

hurón *nm, pl* **hurones** : ferret

huronear *vi* : to pry, to snoop

hurra *interj* : hurrah!, hooray!
hurtadillas *nfpl* **a ~** : stealthily, on the sly
hurtar *vt* ROBAR : to steal
hurto *nm* **1** : theft, robbery **2** : stolen property, loot
husmear *vt* **1** : to follow the scent of, to track **2** : to sniff out, to pry into — *vi* **1** : to pry, to snoop **2** : to sniff around (of an animal)
huso *nm* **1** : spindle **2 huso horario** : time zone
huy *interj* : ow!, ouch!
huye, etc. → **huir**

I

i *nf* : ninth letter of the Spanish alphabet
iba, etc. → **ir**
ibérico, -ca *adj* : Iberian
ibero, -ra *or* **íbero, -ra** *adj & n* : Iberian
iberoamericano, -na *adj* HISPANOAMERICANO, LATINOAMERICANO : Latin-American
ibis *nfs & pl* : ibis
ice, etc. → **izar**
iceberg *nm, pl* **icebergs** : iceberg
icono *nm* : icon
iconoclasia *nf* : iconoclasm
iconoclasta *nmf* : iconoclast
ictericia *nf* : jaundice
ida *nf* **1** : going, departure **2 ida y vuelta** : round-trip **3 idas y venidas** : comings and goings
idea *nf* **1** : idea, notion **2** : opinion, belief **3** PROPÓSITO : intention
ideal *adj & nm* : ideal — **idealmente** *adv*
idealismo *nm* : idealism
idealista¹ *adj* : idealistic
idealista² *nmf* : idealist
idealizar {21} *vt* : to idealize — **idealización** *nf*
idear *vt* : to devise, to think up
ideario *nm* : ideology
ídem *nm* : idem, the same, ditto
idéntico, -ca *adj* : identical, alike — **idénticamente** *adv*
identidad *nf* : identity
identificable *adj* : identifiable
identificación *nf, pl* **-ciones** **1** : identification, identifying **2** : identification document, ID
identificar {72} *vt* : to identify — **identificarse** *vr* **1** : to identify oneself **2 ~ con** : to identify with
ideología *nf* : ideology — **ideológicamente** *adv*
ideológico, -ca *adj* : ideological
idílico, -ca *adj* : idyllic
idilio *nm* : idyll
idioma *nm* : language ⟨el idioma inglés : the English language⟩
idiomático, -ca *adj* : idiomatic — **idiomáticamente** *adv*
idiosincrasia *nf* : idiosyncrasy
idiosincrásico, -ca *adj* : idiosyncratic
idiota¹ *adj* : idiotic, stupid, foolish
idiota² *nmf* : idiot, foolish person
idiotez *nf, pl* **-teces** **1** : idiocy **2** : idiotic act or remark ⟨¡no digas idioteces! : don't talk nonsense!⟩
ido *pp* → **ir**
idólatra¹ *adj* : idolatrous
idólatra² *nmf* : idolater
idolatrar *vt* : to idolize
idolatría *nf* : idolatry
ídolo *nm* : idol
idoneidad *nf* : suitability
idóneo, -nea *adj* ADECUADO : suitable, fitting
iglesia *nf* : church
iglú *nm* : igloo
ignición *nf, pl* **-ciones** : ignition
ignífugo, -ga *adj* : fire-resistant, fireproof
ignominia *nf* : ignominy, disgrace
ignominioso, -sa *adj* : ignominious, shameful
ignorancia *nf* : ignorance
ignorante¹ *adj* : ignorant
ignorante² *nmf* : ignorant person, ignoramus
ignorar *vt* **1** : to ignore **2** DESCONOCER : to be unaware of ⟨lo ignoramos por absoluto : we have no idea⟩
ignoto, -ta *adj* : unknown
igual¹ *adv* **1** : in the same way **2 por ~** : equally
igual² *adj* **1** : equal **2** IDÉNTICO : the same, alike **3** : even, smooth **4** SEMEJANTE : similar **5** CONSTANTE : constant
igual³ *nmf* : equal, peer
igualación *nf* **1** : equalization **2** : leveling, smoothing **3** : equating (in mathematics)
igualado, -da *adj* **1** : even (of a score) **2** : level **3** *Mex* : disrespectful
igualar *vt* **1** : to equalize **2** : to tie ⟨igualar el marcador : to even the score⟩
igualdad *nf* **1** : equality **2** UNIFORMIDAD : evenness, uniformity
igualmente *adv* **1** : equally **2** ASIMISMO : likewise
iguana *nf* : iguana
ijada *nf* : flank, loin, side
ijar *nm* → **ijada**
ilegal¹ *adj* : illegal, unlawful — **ilegalmente** *adv*
ilegal² *nmf CA, Mex* : illegal alien
ilegalidad *nf* : illegality, unlawfulness
ilegibilidad *nf* : illegibility
ilegible *adj* : illegible — **ilegiblemente** *adv*
ilegitimidad *nf* : illegitimacy
ilegítimo, -ma *adj* : illegitimate, unlawful

ileso, -sa *adj* : uninjured, unharmed
ilícito, -ta *adj* : illicit — **ilícitamente** *adv*
ilimitado, -da *adj* : unlimited
ilógico, -ca *adj* : illogical — **ilógicamente** *adv*
iluminación *nf, pl* **-ciones** **1** : illumination **2** ALUMBRADO : lighting
iluminado, -da *adj* : illuminated, lighted
iluminar *vt* **1** : to illuminate, to light (up) **2** : to enlighten
ilusión *nf, pl* **-siones** **1** : illusion, delusion **2** ESPERANZA : hope ⟨hacerse ilusiones : to get one's hopes up⟩
ilusionado, -da *adj* ESPERANZADO : hopeful, eager
ilusionar *vt* : to build up hope, to excite — **ilusionarse** *vr* : to get one's hopes up
iluso¹, -sa *adj* : naive, gullible
iluso², -sa *n* SOÑADOR : dreamer, visionary
ilusorio, -ria *adj* ENGAÑOSO : illusory, misleading
ilustración *nf, pl* **-ciones** **1** : illustration **2** : erudition, learning ⟨la Ilustración : the Enlightenment⟩
ilustrado, -da *adj* **1** : illustrated **2** DOCTO : learned, erudite
ilustrador, -dora *n* : illustrator
ilustrar *vt* **1** : to illustrate **2** ACLARAR, CLARIFICAR : to explain
ilustrativo, -va *adj* : illustrative
ilustre *adj* : illustrious, eminent
imagen *nf, pl* **imágenes** : image, picture
imaginable *adj* : imaginable, conceivable
imaginación *nf, pl* **-ciones** : imagination
imaginar *vt* : to imagine — **imaginarse** *vr* **1** : to suppose, to imagine **2** : to picture
imaginario, -ria *adj* : imaginary
imaginativo, -va *adj* : imaginative — **imaginativamente** *adv*
imaginería *nf* **1** : imagery **2** : image making (in religion)
imán *nm, pl* **imanes** : magnet
imantar *vt* : to magnetize
imbatible *adj* : unbeatable
imbécil¹ *adj* : stupid, idiotic
imbécil² *nmf* **1** : imbecile **2** *fam* : idiot, dope
imborrable *adj* : indelible
imbuir {41} *vt* : to imbue — **imbuirse** *vr*
imitación *nf, pl* **-ciones** **1** : imitation **2** : mimicry, impersonation
imitador¹, -dora *adj* : imitative
imitador², -dora *n* **1** : imitator **2** : mimic
imitar *vt* **1** : to imitate, to copy **2** : to mimic, to impersonate
imitativo, -va *adj* → **imitador¹**
impaciencia *nf* : impatience
impacientar *vt* : to make impatient, to exasperate — **impacientarse** *vr*
impaciente *adj* : impatient — **impacientemente** *adv*
impactado, -da *adj* : shocked, stunned
impactante *adj* **1** : shocking **2** : impressive, powerful
impactar *vt* **1** GOLPEAR : to hit **2** IMPRESIONAR : to impact, to affect — **impactarse** *vr*
impacto *nm* **1** : impact, effect **2** : shock, collision
impagable *adj* **1** : unpayable **2** : priceless
impago *nm* : nonpayment
impalpable *adj* INTANGIBLE : impalpable, intangible
impar¹ *adj* : odd ⟨números impares : odd numbers⟩
impar² *nm* : odd number
imparable *adj* : unstoppable
imparcial *adj* : impartial — **imparcialmente** *adv*
imparcialidad *nf* : impartiality
impartir *vt* : to impart, to give
impasible *adj* : impassive, unmoved — **impasiblemente** *adv*
impasse *nm* : impasse
impávido, -da *adj* : undaunted, unperturbed
impecable *adj* INTACHABLE : impeccable, faultless — **impecablemente** *adv*
impedido, -da *adj* : disabled, crippled
impedimento *nm* **1** : impediment, obstacle **2** : disability
impedir {54} *vt* **1** : to prevent, to block **2** : to impede, to hinder
impeler *vt* **1** : to drive, to propel **2** : to impel
impenetrable *adj* : impenetrable — **impenetrabilidad** *nf*
impenitente *adj* : unrepentant, impenitent
impensable *adj* : unthinkable
impensado, -da *adj* : unforeseen, unexpected
imperante *adj* : prevailing
imperar *vi* **1** : to reign, to rule **2** PREDOMINAR : to prevail
imperativo¹, -va *adj* : imperative
imperativo² *nm* : imperative
imperceptible *adj* : imperceptible — **imperceptiblemente** *adv*
imperdible *nm Spain* : safety pin
imperdonable *adj* : unpardonable, unforgivable
imperecedero, -ra *adj* **1** : imperishable **2** INMORTAL : immortal, everlasting
imperfección *nf, pl* **-ciones** **1** : imperfection **2** DEFECTO : defect, flaw
imperfecto¹, -ta *adj* : imperfect, flawed
imperfecto² *nm* : imperfect tense
imperial *adj* : imperial
imperialismo *nm* : imperialism
imperialista *adj & nmf* : imperialist
impericia *nf* : lack of skill, incompetence
imperio *nm* : empire
imperioso, -sa *adj* **1** : imperious **2** : pressing, urgent — **imperiosamente** *adv*
impermeabilizante *adj* : water-repellent
impermeabilizar {21} *vt* : to waterproof
impermeable¹ *adj* **1** : impervious **2** : impermeable, waterproof
impermeable² *nm* : raincoat

impersonal *adj* : impersonal — **impersonalmente** *adv*

impertinencia *nf* INSOLENCIA : impertinence, insolence

impertinente *adj* **1** INSOLENTE : impertinent, insolent **2** INOPORTUNO : inappropriate, uncalled-for **3** IRRELEVANTE : irrelevant

imperturbable *adj* : imperturbable, impassive, stolid

ímpetu *nm* **1** : impetus, momentum **2** : vigor, energy **3** : force, violence

impetuoso, -sa *adj* : impetuous, impulsive — **impetuosamente** *adv*

impiedad *nf* : impiety

impío, -pía *adj* : impious, ungodly

implacable *adj* : implacable, relentless — **implacablemente** *adv*

implantación *nf, pl* **-ciones** **1** : implantation **2** ESTABLECIMIENTO : establishment, introduction

implantado, -da *adj* : well-established

implantar *vt* **1** : to implant **2** ESTABLECER : to establish, to introduce — **implantarse** *vr*

implante *nm* : implant

implementar *vt* : to implement — **implementarse** *vr* — **implementación** *nf*

implemento *nm* : implement, tool

implicación *nf, pl* **-ciones** : implication

implicar {72} *vt* **1** ENREDAR, ENVOLVER : to involve, to implicate **2** : to imply

implícito, -ta *adj* : implied, implicit — **implícitamente** *adv*

implorar *vt* : to implore

implosión *nf, pl* **-siones** : implosion — **implosivo, -va** *adj*

implosionar *vi* : to implode

imponderable *adj & nm* : imponderable

imponente *adj* : imposing, impressive

imponer {60} *vt* **1** : to impose **2** : to confer — *vi* : to be impressive, to command respect — **imponerse** *vr* **1** : to take on (a duty) **2** : to assert oneself **3** : to prevail

imponible *adj* : taxable

impopular *adj* : unpopular — **impopularidad** *nf*

importación *nf, pl* **-ciones** **1** : importation **2** **importaciones** *nfpl* : imports

importado, -da *adj* : imported

importador[1], **-dora** *adj* : importing

importador[2], **-dora** *n* : importer

importancia *nf* : importance

importante *adj* : important — **importantemente** *adv*

importar *vi* : to matter, to be important ⟨no le importa lo que piensen : she doesn't care what they think⟩ — *vt* : to import

importe *nm* **1** : price, cost **2** : sum, amount

importunar *vt* : to bother, to inconvenience — *vi* : to be inconvenient

importuno, -na *adj* **1** : inopportune, inconvenient **2** : bothersome, annoying

imposibilidad *nf* : impossibility

imposibilitado, -da *adj* **1** : disabled, crippled **2** **verse imposibilitado** : to be unable (to do something)

imposibilitar *vt* **1** : to make impossible **2** : to disable, to incapacitate — **imposibilitarse** *vr* : to become disabled

imposible *adj* : impossible

imposición *nf, pl* **-ciones** **1** : imposition **2** EXIGENCIA : demand, requirement **3** : tax **4** : deposit

impositivo, -va *adj* : tax ⟨tasa impositiva : tax rate⟩

impostor, -tora *n* : impostor

impostura *nf* **1** : fraud, imposture **2** CALUMNIA : slander

impotencia *nf* **1** : impotence, powerlessness **2** : impotence (in medicine)

impotente *adj* **1** : powerless **2** : impotent

impracticable *adj* : impracticable

imprecisión *nf, pl* **-siones** **1** : imprecision, vagueness **2** : inaccuracy

impreciso, -sa *adj* **1** : imprecise, vague **2** : inaccurate

impredecible *adj* : unpredictable

impregnar *vt* : to impregnate

imprenta *nf* **1** : printing **2** : printing shop, press

imprescindible *adj* : essential, indispensable

impresentable *adj* : unpresentable, unfit

impresión *nf, pl* **-siones** **1** : print, printing **2** : impression, feeling

impresionable *adj* : impressionable

impresionante *adj* : impressive, incredible, amazing — **impresionantemente** *adv*

impresionar *vt* **1** : to impress, to strike **2** : to affect, to move — *vi* : to make an impression — **impresionarse** *vr* : to be affected, to be removed

impresionismo *nm* : impressionism

impresionista[1] *adj* : impressionist, impressionistic

impresionista[2] *nmf* : impressionist

impreso[1] *pp* → **imprimir**

impreso[2], **-sa** *adj* : printed

impreso[3] *nm* PUBLICACIÓN : printed matter, publication

impresor, -sora *n* : printer

impresora *nf* : (computer) printer

imprevisible *adj* : unforeseeable

imprevisión *nf, pl* **-siones** : lack of foresight, thoughtlessness

imprevisto[1], **-ta** *adj* : unexpected, unforeseen

imprevisto[2] *nm* : unexpected occurrence, contingency

imprimir {42} *vt* **1** : to print **2** : to imprint, to stamp, to impress

improbabilidad *nf* : improbability

improbable *adj* : improbable, unlikely

improcedente *adj* **1** : inadmissible **2** : inappropriate, improper

improductivo, -va *adj* : unproductive

improperio *nm* : affront, insult

impropiedad *nf* : impropriety

impropio, **-pia** *adj* **1** : improper, incorrect **2** INADECUADO : unsuitable, inappropriate
improvisación *nf, pl* **-ciones** : improvisation, ad-lib
improvisado, **-da** *adj* : improvised, ad-lib
improvisar *v* : to improvise, to ad-lib
improviso *adj* **de ~** : all of a sudden, unexpectedly
imprudencia *nf* INDISCRECIÓN : imprudence, indiscretion
imprudente *adj* INDISCRETO : imprudent, indiscreet — **imprudentemente** *adv*
impúdico, **-ca** *adj* : shameless, indecent
impuesto[1] *pp* → **imponer**
impuesto[2] *nm* : tax
impugnar *vt* : to challenge, to contest
impulsar *vt* : to propel, to drive
impulsividad *nf* : impulsiveness
impulsivo, **-va** *adj* : impulsive — **impulsivamente** *adv*
impulso *nm* **1** : drive, thrust **2** : impulse, urge
impune *adj* : unpunished
impunemente *adv* : with impunity
impunidad *nf* : impunity
impureza *nf* : impurity
impuro, **-ra** *adj* : impure
impuso, **etc.** → **imponer**
imputable *adj* ATRIBUIBLE : attributable
imputación *nf, pl* **-ciones** **1** : attribution, imputation **2** : accusation
imputar *vt* ATRIBUIR : to impute, to attribute
inacabable *adj* : endless
inacabado, **-da** *adj* INCONCLUSO : unfinished
inaccesibilidad *nf* : inaccessibility
inaccesible *adj* **1** : inaccessible **2** : unattainable
inacción *nf, pl* **-ciones** : inactivity, inaction
inaceptable *adj* : unacceptable
inactividad *nf* : inactivity, idleness
inactivo, **-va** *adj* : inactive, idle
inadaptado[1], **-da** *adj* : maladjusted
inadaptado[2], **-da** *n* : misfit
inadecuación *nf, pl* **-ciones** : inadequacy
inadecuado, **-da** *adj* **1** : inadequate **2** IMPROPIO : inappropriate — **inadecuadamente** *adv*
inadmisible *adj* **1** : inadmissible **2** : unacceptable
inadvertencia *nf* : oversight
inadvertidamente *adv* : inadvertently
inadvertido, **-da** *adj* **1** : unnoticed ⟨pasar inadvertido : to go unnoticed⟩ **2** DESPISTADO, DISTRAÍDO : inattentive, distracted
inagotable *adj* : inexhaustible
inaguantable *adj* INSOPORTABLE : insufferable, unbearable
inalámbrico, **-ca** *adj* : wireless, cordless
inalcanzable *adj* : unreachable, unattainable
inalienable *adj* : inalienable
inalterable *adj* **1** : unalterable, unchangeable **2** : impassive **3** : colorfast
inamovible *adj* : immovable, fixed
inanición *nf, pl* **-ciones** : starvation
inanimado, **-da** *adj* : inanimate
inapelable *adj* : indisputable
inapetencia *nf* : lack of appetite
inaplicable *adj* : inapplicable
inapreciable *adj* **1** : imperceptible, negligible **2** : invaluable
inapropiado, **-da** *adj* : inappropriate, unsuitable
inarticulado, **-da** *adj* : inarticulate, unintelligible — **inarticuladamente** *adv*
inasequible *adj* : unattainable, inaccessible
inasistencia *nf* AUSENCIA : absence
inatacable *adj* : unassailable, indisputable
inaudible *adj* : inaudible
inaudito, **-ta** *adj* : unheard-of, unprecedented
inauguración *nf, pl* **-ciones** : inauguration
inaugural *adj* : inaugural, opening
inaugurar *vt* **1** : to inaugurate **2** : to open
inca *adj & nmf* : Inca
incalculable *adj* : incalculable
incalificable *adj* : indescribable
incandescencia *nf* : incandescence — **incandescente** *adj*
incansable *adj* INFATIGABLE : tireless — **incansablemente** *adv*
incapacidad *nf* **1** : inability, incapacity **2** : disability, handicap
incapacitado, **-da** *adj* **1** : disqualified **2** : disabled, handicapped
incapacitar *vt* **1** : to incapacitate, to disable **2** : to disqualify
incapaz *adj, pl* **-paces** **1** : incapable, unable **2** : incompetent, inept
incautación *nf, pl* **-ciones** : seizure, confiscation
incautar *vt* CONFISCAR : to confiscate, to seize — **incautarse** *vr*
incauto, **-ta** *adj* : unwary, unsuspecting
incendiar *vt* : to set fire to, to burn (down) — **incendiarse** *vr* : to catch fire
incendiario[1], **-ria** *adj* : incendiary, inflammatory
incendiario[2], **-ria** *n* : arsonist
incendio *nm* **1** : fire **2 incendio premeditado** : arson
incensario *nm* : censer
incentivar *vt* : to encourage, to stimulate
incentivo *nm* : incentive
incertidumbre *nf* : uncertainty, suspense
incesante *adj* : incessant — **incesantemente** *adv*
incesto *nm* : incest
incestuoso, **-sa** *adj* : incestuous
incidencia *nf* **1** : incident **2** : effect, impact **3 por ~** : by chance, accidentally

incidental *adj* : incidental
incidentalmente *adv* : by chance
incidente *nm* : incident, occurrence
incidir *vi* **1 ~ en** : to fall into, to enter into ⟨incidimos en el mismo error : we fell into the same mistake⟩ **2 ~ en** : to affect, to influence, to have a bearing on
incienso *nm* : incense
incierto, -ta *adj* **1** : uncertain **2** : untrue **3** : unsteady, insecure
incineración *nf, pl* **-ciones** **1** : incineration **2** : cremation
incinerador *nm* : incinerator
incinerar *vt* **1** : to incinerate **2** : to cremate
incipiente *adj* : incipient
incisión *nf, pl* **-siones** : incision
incisivo¹, -va *adj* : incisive
incisivo² *nm* : incisor
inciso *nm* : digression, aside
incitación *nf, pl* **-ciones** : incitement
incitador¹, -dora *n* : instigator, agitator
incitador², -dora *adj* : provocative
incitante *adj* : provocative
incitar *vt* : to incite, to rouse
incivilizado, -da *adj* : uncivilized
inclemencia *nf* : inclemency, severity
inclemente *adj* : inclement
inclinación *nf, pl* **-ciones** **1** PROPENSIÓN : inclination, tendency **2** : incline, slope
inclinado, -da *adj* **1** : sloping **2** : inclined, apt
inclinar *vt* : to tilt, to lean, to incline ⟨inclinar la cabeza : to bow one's head⟩ — **inclinarse** *vr* **1** : to lean, to lean over **2 ~ a** : to be inclined to
incluir {41} *vt* : to include
inclusión *nf, pl* **-siones** : inclusion
inclusive *adv* : inclusively, up to and including
inclusivo, -va *adj* : inclusive
incluso *adv* **1** AUN : even, in fact ⟨es importante e incluso crucial : it is important and even crucial⟩ **2** : inclusively
incógnita *nf* **1** : unknown quantity (in mathematics) **2** : mystery
incógnito, -ta *adj* **1** : unknown **2 de incógnito** : incognito
incoherencia *nf* : incoherence
incoherente *adj* : incoherent — **incoherentemente** *adv*
incoloro, -ra *adj* : colorless
incombustible *adj* : fireproof
incomible *adj* : inedible
incomodar *vt* **1** : to make uncomfortable **2** : to inconvenience — **incomodarse** *vr* : to put oneself out, to take the trouble
incomodidad *nf* **1** : discomfort, awkwardness **2** MOLESTIA : inconvenience, bother
incómodo, -da *adj* **1** : uncomfortable, awkward **2** INCONVENIENTE : inconvenient
incomparable *adj* : incomparable
incompatibilidad *nf* : incompatibility
incompatible *adj* : incompatible, uncongenial
incompetencia *nf* : incompetence
incompetente *adj & nmf* : incompetent
incompleto, -ta *adj* : incomplete
incomprendido, -da *adj* : misunderstood
incomprensible *adj* : incomprehensible
incomprensión *nf, pl* **-siones** : lack of understanding, incomprehension
incomunicación *nf, pl* **-ciones** : lack of communication
incomunicado, -da *adj* **1** : cut off, isolated **2** : in solitary confinement
inconcebible *adj* : inconceivable, unthinkable — **inconcebiblemente** *adv*
inconcluso, -sa *adj* INACABADO : unfinished
incondicional *adj* : unconditional — **incondicionalmente** *adv*
inconexo, -xa *adj* : unconnected, disconnected
inconfesable *adj* : unspeakable, shameful
inconforme *adj & nmf* : nonconformist
inconformidad *nf* : nonconformity
inconformista *adj & nmf* : nonconformist
inconfundible *adj* : unmistakable, obvious — **inconfundiblemente** *adv*
incongruencia *nf* : incongruity
incongruente *adj* : incongruous
inconmensurable *adj* : vast, immeasurable
inconquistable *adj* : unyielding
inconsciencia *nf* **1** : unconsciousness, unawareness **2** : irresponsibility
inconsciente¹ *adj* **1** : unconscious, unaware **2** : reckless, needless — **inconscientemente** *adv*
inconsciente² *nm* **el inconsciente** : the unconscious
inconsecuente *adj* : inconsistent — **inconsecuencia** *nf*
inconsiderado, -da *adj* : inconsiderate, thoughtless
inconsistencia *nf* : inconsistency
inconsistente *adj* **1** : weak, flimsy **2** : inconsistent, weak (of an argument)
inconsolable *adj* : inconsolable — **inconsolablemente** *adv*
inconstancia *nf* : inconstancy
inconstante *adj* : inconstant, fickle, changeable
inconstitucional *adj* : unconstitutional
inconstitucionalidad *nf* : unconstitutionality
incontable *adj* INNUMERABLE : countless, innumerable
incontenible *adj* : uncontrollable, unstoppable
incontestable *adj* INCUESTIONABLE, INDISCUTIBLE : irrefutable, indisputable
incontinencia *nf* : incontinence — **incontinente** *adj*
incontrolable *adj* : uncontrollable
incontrolado, -da *adj* : uncontrolled, out of control

incontrovertible *adj* : indisputable
inconveniencia *nf* **1** : inconvenience, trouble **2** : unsuitability, inappropriateness **3** : tactless remark
inconveniente[1] *adj* **1** INCÓMODO : inconvenient **2** INAPROPIADO : improper, unsuitable
inconveniente[2] *nm* : obstacle, problem, snag ⟨no tengo inconveniente en hacerlo : I don't mind doing it⟩
incorporación *nf, pl* **-ciones** : incorporation
incorporar *vt* **1** : to incorporate **2** : to add, to include — **incorporarse** *vr* **1** : to sit up **2** ~ **a** : to join
incorpóreo, -rea *adj* : incorporeal, bodiless
incorrección *n, pl* **-ciones** : impropriety, improper word or action
incorrecto, -ta *adj* : incorrect — **incorrectamente** *adv*
incorregible *adj* : incorrigible — **incorregibilidad** *nf*
incorruptible *adj* : incorruptible
incredulidad *nf* : incredulity, skepticism
incrédulo[1], **-la** *adj* : incredulous, skeptical
incrédulo[2], **-la** *n* : skeptic
increíble *adj* : incredible, unbelievable — **increíblemente** *adv*
incrementar *vt* : to increase — **incrementarse** *vr*
incremento *nm* AUMENTO : increase
incriminar *vt* : to incriminate — **incriminación** *nf*
incriminatorio, -ria *adj* : incriminating, incriminatory
incruento, -ta *adj* : bloodless
incrustación *nf, pl* **-ciones** : inlay
incrustar *vt* **1** : to embed **2** : to inlay — **incrustarse** *vr* : to become embedded
incubación *nf, pl* **-ciones** : incubation
incubadora *nf* : incubator
incubar *v* : to incubate
incuestionable *adj* INCONTESTABLE, INDISCUTIBLE : unquestionable, indisputable — **incuestionablemente** *adv*
inculcar {72} *vt* : to inculcate, to instill
inculpar *vt* ACUSAR : to accuse, to charge
inculto, -ta *adj* **1** : uncultured, ignorant **2** : uncultivated, fallow
incumbencia *nf* : obligation, responsibility
incumbir *vi* (*3rd person only*) ~ **a** : to be incumbent upon, to be of concern to ⟨a mí no me incumbe : it's not my concern⟩
incumplido, -da *adj* : irresponsible, unreliable
incumplimiento *nm* **1** : nonfulfillment, neglect **2 incumplimiento de contrato** : breach of contract
incumplir *vt* : to fail to carry out, to break (a promise, a contract)
incurable *adj* : incurable
incurrir *vi* **1** ~ **en** : to incur ⟨incurrir en gastos : to incur expenses⟩ **2** ~ **en** : to fall into, to commit ⟨incurrió en un error : he made a mistake⟩
incursión *nf, pl* **-siones** : incursion, raid
incursionar *vi* **1** : to raid **2** ~ **en** : to go into, to enter ⟨el actor incursionó en el baile : the actor worked in dance for awhile⟩
indagación *nf, pl* **-ciones** : investigation, inquiry
indagar {52} *vt* : to inquire into, to investigate
indebido, -da *adj* : improper, undue — **indebidamente** *adv*
indecencia *nf* : indecency, obscenity
indecente *adj* : indecent, obscene
indecible *adj* : indescribable, inexpressible
indecisión *nf, pl* **-siones** : indecision
indeciso, -sa *adj* **1** IRRESOLUTO : indecisive **2** : undecided
indeclinable *adj* : unavoidable
indecoro *nm* : impropriety, indecorousness
indecoroso, -sa *adj* : indecorous, unseemly
indefectible *adj* : unfailing, sure
indefendible *adj* : indefensible
indefenso, -sa *adj* : defenseless, helpless
indefinible *adj* : indefinable
indefinido, -da *adj* **1** : undefined, vague **2** INDETERMINADO : indefinite — **indefinidamente** *adv*
indeleble *adj* : indelible — **indeleblemente** *adv*
indelicado, -da *adj* : indelicate, tactless
indemnización *nf, pl* **-ciones** **1** : indemnity **2 indemnización por despido** : severance pay
indemnizar {21} *vt* : to indemnify, to compensate
independencia *nf* : independence
independiente *adj* : independent — **independientemente** *adv*
independizarse {21} *vr* : to become independent, to gain independence
indescifrable *adj* : indecipherable
indescriptible *adj* : indescribable — **indescriptiblemente** *adv*
indeseable *adj & nmf* : undesirable
indestructible *adj* : indestructible
indeterminación *nf, pl* **-ciones** : indeterminacy
indeterminado, -da *adj* **1** INDEFINIDO : indefinite **2** : indeterminate
indexar *vt* INDICIAR : to index (wages, prices, etc.)
indicación *nf, pl* **-ciones** **1** : sign, signal **2** : direction, instruction **3** : suggestion, hint
indicado, -da *adj* **1** APROPIADO : appropriate, suitable **2** : specified, indicated ⟨al día indicado : on the specified day⟩
indicador *nm* **1** : gauge, dial, meter **2** : indicator ⟨indicadores económicos : economic indicators⟩
indicar {72} *vt* **1** SEÑALAR : to indicate **2** ENSEÑAR, MOSTRAR : to show
indicativo[1], **-va** *adj* : indicative
indicativo[2] *nm* : indicative (mood)

índice *nm* **1** : index **2** : index finger, forefinger **3** INDICIO : indication
indiciar *vt* : to index (prices, wages, etc.)
indicio *nm* : indication, sign
indiferencia *nf* : indifference
indiferente *adj* **1** : indifferent, unconcerned **2 ser indiferente** : to be of no concern <me es indiferente : it doesn't matter to me>
indígena[1] *adj* : indigenous, native
indígena[2] *nmf* : native
indigencia *nf* MISERIA : poverty, destitution
indigente *adj & nmf* : indigent
indigestarse *vr* **1** EMPACHARSE : to have indigestion **2** *fam* : to nauseate, to disgust <ese tipo se me indigesta : that guy makes me sick>
indigestión *nf, pl* **-tiones** EMPACHO : indigestion
indigesto, -ta *adj* : indigestible, difficult to digest
indignación *nf, pl* **-ciones** : indignation
indignado, -da *adj* : indignant
indignante *adj* : outrageous, infuriating
indignar *vt* : to outrage, to infuriate — **indignarse** *vr*
indignidad *nf* : indignity
indigno, -na *adj* : unworthy
índigo *nm* : indigo
indio[1], **-dia** *adj* **1** : American Indian, Indian, Amerindian **2** : Indian (from India)
indio[2], **-dia** *n* **1** : American Indian **2** : Indian (from India)
indirecta *nf* **1** : hint, innuendo **2 echar indirectas** *or* **lanzar indirectas** : to drop a hint, to insinuate
indirecto, -ta *adj* : indirect — **indirectamente** *adv*
indisciplina *nf* : indiscipline, unruliness
indisciplinado, -da *adj* : undisciplined, unruly
indiscreción *nf, pl* **-ciones** **1** IMPRUDENCIA : indiscretion **2** : tactless remark
indiscreto, -ta *adj* IMPRUDENTE : indiscreet, imprudent — **indiscretamente** *adv*
indiscriminado, -da *adj* : indiscriminate — **indiscriminadamente** *adv*
indiscutible *adj* INCONTESTABLE, INCUESTIONABLE : indisputable, unquestionable — **indiscutiblemente** *adv*
indispensable *adj* : indispensable — **indispensablemente** *adv*
indisponer {60} *vt* **1** : to spoil, to upset **2** : to make ill — **indisponerse** *vr* **1** : to become ill **2 ~ con** : to fall out with
indisposición *nf, pl* **-ciones** : indisposition, illness
indispuesto, -ta *adj* : unwell, indisposed
indistinguible *adj* : indistinguishable
indistintamente *adv* **1** : indistinctly **2** : indiscriminately
indistinto, -ta *adj* : indistinct, vague, faint
individual *adj* : individual — **individualmente** *adv*
individualidad *nf* : individuality
individualismo *nm* : individualism
individualista[1] *adj* : individualistic
individualista[2] *nmf* : individualist
individualizar {21} *vt* : to individualize
individuo *nm* : individual, person
indivisible *adj* : indivisible — **indivisibilidad** *nf*
indocumentado, -da *n* : illegal immigrant
índole *nf* **1** : nature, character **2** CLASE, TIPO : sort, kind
indolencia *nf* : indolence, laziness
indolente *adj* : indolent, lazy
indoloro, -ra *adj* : painless
indomable *adj* **1** : indomitable **2** : unruly, unmanageable
indómito, -ta *adj* : indomitable
indonesio, -sia *adj & n* : Indonesian
inducción *nf, pl* **-ciones** : induction
inducir {61} *vt* **1** : to induce, to cause **2** : to infer, to deduce
inductivo, -va *adj* : inductive
indudable *adj* : unquestionable, beyond doubt
indudablemente *adv* : undoubtedly, unquestionably
indulgencia *nf* **1** : indulgence, leniency **2** : indulgence (in religion)
indulgente *adj* : indulgent, lenient
indultar *vt* : to pardon, to reprieve
indulto *nm* : pardon, reprieve
indumentaria *nf* : clothing, attire
industria *nf* : industry
industrial[1] *adj* : industrial
industrial[2] *nmf* : industrialist, manufacturer
industrialización *nf, pl* **-ciones** : industrialization
industrializar {21} *vt* : to industrialize
industrioso, -sa *adj* : industrious
inédito, -ta *adj* **1** : unpublished **2** : unprecedented
inefable *adj* : ineffable
ineficacia *nf* **1** : inefficiency **2** : ineffectiveness
ineficaz *adj, pl* **-caces** **1** : inefficient **2** : ineffective — **ineficazmente** *adv*
ineficiencia *nf* : inefficiency
ineficiente *adj* : inefficient — **ineficientemente** *adv*
inelegancia *nf* : inelegance — **inelegante** *adj*
inelegible *adj* : ineligible — **inelegibilidad** *nf*
ineludible *adj* : inescapable, unavoidable — **ineludiblemente** *adv*
ineptitud *nf* : ineptitude, incompetence
inepto, -ta *adj* : inept, incompetent
inequidad *nf* : inequity
inequitativo, -va *adj* : inequitable
inequívoco, -ca *adj* : unequivocal, unmistakable — **inequívocamente** *adv*
inercia *nf* **1** : inertia **2** : apathy, passivity **3 por ~** : out of habit
inerme *adj* : unarmed, defenseless

inerte *adj* : inert
inescrupuloso, -sa *adj* : unscrupulous
inescrutable *adj* : inscrutable
inesperado, -da *adj* : unexpected — **inesperadamente** *adv*
inestabilidad *nf* : instability, unsteadiness
inestable *adj* : unstable, unsteady
inestimable *adj* : inestimable, invaluable
inevitabilidad *nf* : inevitability
inevitable *adj* : inevitable, unavoidable — **inevitablemente** *adv*
inexactitud *nf* : inaccuracy
inexacto, -ta *adj* : inexact, inaccurate
inexcusable *adj* : inexcusable, unforgivable
inexistencia *nf* : lack, nonexistence
inexistente *adj* : nonexistent
inexorable *adj* : inexorable — **inexorablemente** *adv*
inexperiencia *nf* : inexperience
inexperto, -ta *adj* : inexperienced, unskilled
inexplicable *adj* : inexplicable — **inexplicablemente** *adv*
inexplorado, -da *adj* : unexplored
inexpresable *adj* : inexpressible
inexpresivo, -va *adj* : inexpressive, expressionless
inexpugnable *adj* : impregnable
inextinguible *adj* **1** : inextinguishable **2** : unquenchable
inextricable *adj* : inextricable — **inextricablemente** *adv*
infalibilidad *nf* : infallibility
infalible *adj* : infallible — **infaliblemente** *adv*
infame *adj* **1** : infamous **2** : loathsome, vile ⟨tiempo infame : terrible weather⟩
infamia *nf* : infamy, disgrace
infancia *nf* **1** NIÑEZ : infancy, childhood **2** : children *pl* **3** : beginnings *pl*
infante *nm* **1** : infante, prince **2** : infantryman
infantería *nf* : infantry
infantil *adj* **1** : childish, infantile **2** : child's, children's
infantilismo *nm* **1** : infantilism **2** INMADUREZ : childishness
infarto *nm* : heart attack
infatigable *adj* : indefatigable, tireless — **infatigablemente** *adv*
infección *nf, pl* **-ciones** : infection
infeccioso, -sa *adj* : infectious
infectar *vt* : to infect — **infectarse** *vr*
infecto, -ta *adj* **1** : infected **2** : repulsive, sickening
infecundidad *nf* : infertility
infecundo, -da *adj* : infertile, barren
infelicidad *nf* : unhappiness
infeliz[1] *adj, pl* **-lices** **1** : unhappy **2** : hapless, unfortunate, wretched
infeliz[2] *nmf, pl* **-lices** : wretch
inferencia *nf* : inference
inferior[1] *adj* : inferior, lower
inferior[2] *nmf* : inferior, underling
inferioridad *nf* : inferiority
inferir {76} *vt* **1** DEDUCIR : to infer, to deduce **2** : to cause (harm or injury), to inflict
infernal *adj* : infernal, hellish
infestación *n, pl* **-ciones** : infestation
infestar *vt* **1** : to infest **2** : to overrun, to invade
infición *nf, pl* **-ciones** *Mex* : pollution
infidelidad *nf* : unfaithfulness, infidelity
infiel[1] *adj* : unfaithful, disloyal
infiel[2] *nmf* : infidel, heathen
infierno *nm* **1** : hell **2 el quinto infierno** : the middle of nowhere
infiltrar *vt* : to infiltrate — **infiltrarse** *vr* — **infiltración** *nf*
infinidad *nf* **1** : infinity **2** SINFÍN : great number, huge quantity ⟨una infinidad de veces : countless times⟩
infinitesimal *adj* : infinitesimal
infinitivo *nm* : infinitive
infinito[1] *adv* : infinitely, vastly
infinito[2], **-ta** *adj* **1** : infinite **2** : limitless, endless **3 hasta lo infinito** : ad infinitum — **infinitamente** *adv*
infinito[3] *nm* : infinity
inflable *adj* : inflatable
inflación *nf, pl* **-ciones** : inflation
inflacionario, -ria *adj* : inflationary
inflacionista → **inflacionario**
inflamable *adj* : flammable
inflamación *nf, pl* **-ciones** : inflammation
inflamar *vt* : to inflame
inflamatorio, -ria *adj* : inflammatory
inflar *vt* HINCHAR : to inflate — **inflarse** *vr* **1** : to swell **2** : to become conceited
inflexibilidad *nf* : inflexibility
inflexible *adj* : inflexible, unyielding
inflexión *nf, pl* **-xiones** : inflection
infligir {35} *vt* : to inflict
influencia *nf* INFLUJO : influence
influenciable *adj* : easily influenced, suggestible
influenciar *vt* : to influence
influenza *nf* : influenza
influir {41} *vt* : to influence — *vi* **~ en** *or* **~ sobre** : to have an influence on, to affect
influjo *nm* INFLUENCIA : influence
influyente *adj* : influential
información *nf, pl* **-ciones** **1** : information **2** INFORME : report, inquiry **3** NOTICIAS : news
informado, -da *adj* : informed ⟨bien informado : well-informed⟩
informador, -dora *n* : informer, informant
informal *adj* **1** : unreliable (of persons) **2** : informal, casual — **informalmente** *adv*
informalidad *nf* : informality
informante *nmf* : informant
informar *vt* ENTERAR : to inform — *vi* : to report — **informarse** *vr* ENTERARSE : to get information, to find out
informática *nf* : computer science, computing

informativo[1], **-va** *adj* : informative
informativo[2] *nm* : news program, news
informatización *nf, pl* **-ciones** : computerization
informatizar {21} *vt* : to computerize
informe[1] *adj* AMORFO : shapeless, formless
informe[2] *nm* **1** : report **2** : reference (for employment) **3 informes** *nmpl* : information, data
infortunado, -da *adj* : unfortunate, unlucky
infortunio *nm* **1** DESGRACIA : misfortune **2** CONTRATIEMPO : mishap
infracción *nf, pl* **-ciones** : violation, offense, infraction
infractor, -tora *n* : offender
infraestructura *nf* : infrastructure
infrahumano, -na *adj* : subhuman
infranqueable *adj* **1** : impassable **2** : insurmountable
infrarrojo, -ja *adj* : infrared
infrecuente *adj* : infrequent
infringir {35} *vt* : to infringe, to breach
infructuoso, -sa *adj* : fruitless — **infructuosamente** *adv*
ínfulas *nfpl* **1** : conceit **2 darse ínfulas** : to put on airs
infundado, -da *adj* : unfounded, baseless
infundio *nm* : false story, lie, tall tale <todo eso son infundios : that's a pack of lies>
infundir *vt* **1** : to instill **2 infundir ánimo a** : to encourage **3 infundir miedo a** : to intimidate
infusión *nf, pl* **-siones** : infusion
ingeniar *vt* : to devise, to think up — **ingeniarse** *vr* : to manage, to find a way
ingeniería *nf* : engineering
ingeniero, -ra *n* : engineer
ingenio *nm* **1** : ingenuity **2** CHISPA : wit, wits **3** : device, apparatus **4 ingenio azucarero** : sugar refinery
ingenioso, -sa *adj* **1** : ingenious **2** : clever, witty — **ingeniosamente** *adv*
ingente *adj* : huge, enormous
ingenuidad *nf* : naïveté, ingenuousness
ingenuo[1], **-nua** *adj* CÁNDIDO : naive — **ingenuamente** *adv*
ingenuo[2], **-nua** *n* : naive person
ingerencia → **injerencia**
ingerir {76} *vt* : to ingest, to consume
ingestión *nf, pl* **-tiones** : ingestion
ingle *nf* : groin
inglés[1], **-glesa** *adj, mpl* **ingleses** : English
inglés[2], **-glesa** *n, mpl* **ingleses** : Englishman *m,* Englishwoman *f*
inglés[3] *nm* : English (language)
inglete *nm* : miter joint
ingobernable *adj* : ungovernable, lawless
ingratitud *nf* : ingratitude
ingrato[1], **-ta** *adj* **1** : ungrateful **2** : thankless
ingrato[2], **-ta** *n* : ingrate
ingrediente *nm* : ingredient
ingresar *vt* **1** : to admit <ingresaron a Luis al hospital : Luis was admitted into the hospital> **2** : to deposit — *vi* **1** : to enter, to go in **2 ~ en** : to join, to enroll in
ingreso *nm* **1** : entrance, entry **2** : admission **3 ingresos** *nmpl* : income, earnings *pl*
íngrimo, -ma *adj* : all alone, all by oneself
inhábil *adj* : unskillful, clumsy
inhabilidad *nf* **1** : unskillfulness **2** : unfitness
inhabilitar *vt* **1** : to disqualify, to bar **2** : to disable
inhabitable *adj* : uninhabitable
inhabituado, -da *adj* **~ a** : unaccustomed to
inhalador *nm* : inhaler
inhalante *nm* : inhalant
inhalar *vt* : to inhale — **inhalación** *nf*
inherente *adj* : inherent
inhibición *nf, pl* **-ciones** COHIBICIÓN : inhibition
inhibir *vt* : to inhibit — **inhibirse** *vr*
inhóspito, -ta *adj* : inhospitable
inhumación *nf, pl* **-ciones** : interment, burial
inhumanidad *nf* : inhumanity
inhumano, -na *adj* : inhuman, cruel, inhumane
inhumar *vt* : to inter, to bury
iniciación *nf, pl* **-ciones 1** : initiation **2** : introduction
iniciado, -da *n* : initiate
iniciador[1], **-dora** *adj* : initiatory
iniciador[2], **-dora** *n* : initiator, originator
inicial[1] *adj* : initial, original — **inicialmente** *adv*
inicial[2] *nf* : initial (letter)
iniciar *vt* COMENZAR : to initiate, to begin — **iniciarse** *vr*
iniciativa *nf* : initiative
inicio *nm* COMIENZO : beginning
inicuo, -cua *adj* : iniquitous, wicked
inigualado, -da *adj* : unequaled
inimaginable *adj* : unimaginable
inimitable *adj* : inimitable
ininteligible *adj* : unintelligible
ininterrumpido, -da *adj* : uninterrupted, continuous — **ininterrumpidamente** *adv*
iniquidad *nf* : iniquity, wickedness
injerencia *nf* : interference
injerirse {76} *vr* ENTROMETERSE, INMISCUIRSE : to meddle, to interfere
injertar *vt* : to graft
injerto *nm* : graft <injerto de piel : skin graft>
injuria *nf* AGRAVIO : affront, insult
injuriar *vt* INSULTAR : to insult, to revile
injurioso, -sa *adj* : insulting, abusive
injusticia *nf* : injustice, unfairness
injustificable *adj* : unjustifiable
injustificadamente *adv* : unjustifiably, unfairly
injustificado, -da *adj* : unjustified, unwarranted

injusto, -ta *adj* : unfair, unjust — **injustamente** *adv*
inmaculado, -da *adj* : immaculate, spotless
inmadurez *nf, pl* **-reces** : immaturity
inmaduro, -ra *adj* **1** : immature **2** : unripe
inmediaciones *nfpl* : environs, surrounding area
inmediatamente *adv* ENSEGUIDA : immediately
inmediatez *nf, pl* **-teces** : immediacy
inmediato, -ta *adj* **1** : immediate **2** CONTIGUO : adjoining **3 de ~** : immediately, right away **4 ~ a** : next to, close to
inmejorable *adj* : excellent, unbeatable
inmemorial *adj* : immemorial ⟨tiempos inmemoriales : time immemorial⟩
inmensidad *nf* : immensity, vastness
inmenso, -sa *adj* ENORME : immense, huge, vast — **inmensamente** *adv*
inmensurable *adj* : boundless, immeasurable
inmerecido, -da *adj* : undeserved — **inmerecidamente** *adv*
inmersión *nf, pl* **-siones** : immersion
inmerso, -sa *adj* **1** : immersed **2** : involved, absorbed
inmigración *nf, pl* **-ciones** : immigration
inmigrado, -da *adj & n* : immigrant
inmigrante *adj & nmf* : immigrant
inmigrar *vi* : to immigrate
inminencia *nf* : imminence
inminente *adj* : imminent — **inminentemente** *adv*
inmiscuirse {41} *vr* ENTROMETERSE, INJERIRSE : to meddle, to interfere
inmobiliario, -ria *adj* : real estate, property
inmoderación *n, pl* **-ciones** : immoderation, intemperance
inmoderado, -da *adj* : immoderate, excessive — **inmoderamente** *adv*
inmodestia *nf* : immodesty — **inmodesto, -ta** *adj*
inmolar *vt* : to immolate — **inmolación** *nf*
inmoral *adj* : immoral
inmoralidad *nf* : immorality
inmortal *adj & nmf* : immortal
inmortalidad *nf* : immortality
inmortalizar {21} *vt* : to immortalize
inmotivado, -da *adj* **1** : unmotivated **2** : groundless
inmovible *adj* : immovable, fixed
inmóvil *adj* **1** : still, motionless **2** : steadfast
inmovilidad *nf* : immobility
inmovilizar {21} *vt* : to immobilize
inmueble *nm* : building, property
inmundicia *nf* : dirt, filth, trash
inmundo, -da *adj* : dirty, filthy, nasty
inmune *adj* : immune
inmunidad *nf* : immunity
inmunizar {21} *vt* : to immunize — **inmunización** *nf*
inmunología *nf* : immunology
inmunológico, -ca *adj* : immune ⟨sistema inmunológico : immune system⟩
inmutabilidad *nf* : immutability
inmutable *adj* : immutable, unchangeable
innato, -ta *adj* : innate, inborn
innecesario, -ria *adj* : unnecessary — **innecesariamente** *adv*
innegable *adj* : undeniable
innoble *adj* : ignoble — **innoblemente** *adv*
innovación *nf, pl* **-ciones** : innovation
innovador, -dora *adj* : innovative
innovar *vt* : to introduce — *vi* : to innovate
innumerable *adj* INCONTABLE : innumerable, countless
inobjetable *adj* : indisputable, unobjectionable
inocencia *nf* : innocence
inocente[1] *adj* **1** : innocent **2** INGENUO : naive — **inocentemente** *adv*
inocente[2] *nmf* : innocent person
inocentón[1], **-tona** *adj, mpl* **-tones** : naive, gullible
inocentón[2], **-tona** *n, mpl* **-tones** : simpleton, dupe
inocuidad *nf* : harmlessness
inocular *vt* : to inoculate, to vaccinate — **inoculación** *nf*
inocuo, -cua *adj* : innocuous, harmless
inodoro[1], **-ra** *adj* : odorless
inodoro[2] *nm* : toilet
inofensivo, -va *adj* : inoffensive, harmless
inolvidable *adj* : unforgettable
inoperable *adj* : inoperable
inoperante *adj* : ineffective, inoperative
inopinado, -da *adj* : unexpected — **inopinadamente** *adv*
inoportuno, -na *adj* : untimely, inopportune, inappropriate
inorgánico, -ca *adj* : inorganic
inoxidable *adj* **1** : rustproof **2 acero inoxidable** : stainless steel
inquebrantable *adj* : unshakable, unwavering
inquietante *adj* : disturbing, worrisome
inquietar *vt* PREOCUPAR : to disturb, to upset, to worry — **inquietarse** *vr*
inquieto, -ta *adj* **1** : anxious, uneasy, worried **2** : restless
inquietud *nf* **1** : anxiety, uneasiness, worry **2** AGITACIÓN : restlessness
inquilinato *nm* : tenancy
inquilino, -na *n* : tenant, occupant
inquina *nf* **1** : aversion, dislike **2** : ill will ⟨tener inquina a alguien : to have a grudge against someone⟩
inquirir {4} *vi* : to make inquiries — *vt* : to investigate
inquisición *nf, pl* **-ciones** : investigation, inquiry
inquisidor, -dora *adj* : inquisitive
inquisitivo, -va *adj* : inquisitive, curious — **inquisitivamente** *adv*
insaciable *adj* : insatiable
insalubre *adj* **1** : unhealthy **2** ANTIHIGIÉNICO : unsanitary

insalubridad *nf* : unhealthiness
insalvable *adj* : insuperable, insurmountable
insano, -na *adj* **1** LOCO : insane, mad **2** INSALUBRE : unhealthy
insatisfacción *nf, pl* **-ciones** : dissatisfaction
insatisfactorio *nm* : unsatisfactory
insatisfecho, -cha *adj* **1** : dissatisfied **2** : unsatisfied
inscribir {33} *vt* **1** MATRICULAR : to enroll, to register **2** GRABAR : to engrave — **inscribirse** *vr* : to register, to sign up
inscripción *nf, pl* **-ciones 1** MATRÍCULA : enrollment, registration **2** : inscription
inscrito *pp* → **inscribir**
insecticida¹ *adj* : insecticidal
insecticida² *nm* : insecticide
insecto *nm* : insect
inseguridad *nf* **1** : insecurity **2** : lack of safety **3** : uncertainty
inseguro, -ra *adj* **1** : insecure **2** : unsafe **3** : uncertain
inseminar *vt* : to inseminate — **inseminación** *nf*
insensatez *nf, pl* **-teces** : foolishness, stupidity
insensato¹, **-ta** *adj* : foolish, senseless
insensato², **-ta** *n* : fool
insensibilidad *nf* : insensitivity
insensible *adj* : insensitive, unfeeling
inseparable *adj* : inseparable — **inseparablemente** *adv*
inserción *nf, pl* **-ciones** : insertion
insertar *vt* : to insert
inservible *adj* INÚTIL : useless, unusable
insidia *nf* **1** : snare, trap **2** : malice
insidioso, -sa *adj* : insidious
insigne *adj* : noted, famous
insignia *nf* ENSEÑA : insignia, emblem, badge
insignificancia *nf* **1** : insignificance **2** NIMIEDAD : trifle, triviality
insignificante *adj* : insignificant
insincero, -ra *adj* : insincere — **insinceridad** *nf*
insinuación *nf, pl* **-ciones** : insinuation, hint
insinuante *adj* : suggestive
insinuar {3} *vt* : to insinuate, to hint at — **insinuarse** *vr* **1 ~ a** : to make advances to **2 ~ en** : to worm one's way into
insipidez *nf, pl* **-deces** : insipidness, blandness
insípido, -da *adj* : insipid, bland
insistencia *nf* : insistence
insistente *adj* : insistent — **insistentemente** *adv*
insistir *v* : to insist
insociable *adj* : unsociable
insolación *nf, pl* **-ciones** : sunstroke
insolencia *nf* IMPERTINENCIA : insolence
insolente *adj* IMPERTINENTE : insolent
insólito, -ta *adj* : rare, unusual
insoluble *adj* : insoluble — **insolubilidad** *nf*
insolvencia *nf* : insolvency, bankruptcy
insolvente *adj* : insolvent, bankrupt
insomne *adj & nmf* : insomniac
insomnio *nm* : insomnia
insondable *adj* : fathomless, deep
insonorizado, -da *adj* : soundproof
insoportable *adj* INAGUANTABLE : unbearable, intolerable
insoslayable *adj* : unavoidable, inescapable
insospechado, -da *adj* : unexpected, unforeseen
insostenible *adj* : untenable
inspección *nf, pl* **-ciones** : inspection
inspeccionar *vt* : to inspect
inspector, -tora *n* : inspector
inspiración *nf, pl* **-ciones 1** : inspiration **2** INHALACIÓN : inhalation
inspirador, -dora *adj* : inspiring
inspirar *vt* : to inspire — *vi* INHALAR : to inhale
instalación *nf, pl* **-ciones** : installation
instalar *vt* **1** : to install **2** : to instate — **instalarse** *vr* ESTABLECERSE : to settle, to establish oneself
instancia *nf* **1** : petition, request **2 en última instancia** : as a last resort
instantánea *nf* : snapshot
instantáneo, -nea *adj* : instantaneous — **instantáneamente** *adv*
instante *nm* **1** : instant, moment **2 al instante** : immediately **3 a cada instante** : frequently, all the time **4 por instantes** : constantly, incessantly
instar *vt* APREMIAR : to urge, to press — *vi* URGIR : to be urgent or pressing ⟨insta que vayamos pronto : it is imperative that we leave soon⟩
instauración *nf, pl* **-ciones** : establishment
instaurar *vt* : to establish
instigador, -dora *n* : instigator
instigar {52} *vt* : to instigate, to incite
instintivo, -va *adj* : instinctive — **instintivamente** *adv*
instinto *nm* : instinct
institución *nf, pl* **-ciones** : institution
institucional *adj* : institutional — **institucionalmente** *adv*
institucionalización *nf, pl* **-ciones** : institutionalization
institucionalizar {21} *vt* : to institutionalize
instituir {41} *vt* ESTABLECER, FUNDAR : to institute, to establish, to found
instituto *nm* : institute
institutriz *nf, pl* **-trices** : governess *f*
instrucción *nf, pl* **-ciones 1** EDUCACIÓN : education **2 instrucciones** *nfpl* : instructions, directions
instructivo, -va *adj* : instructive, educational
instructor, -tora *n* : instructor
instruir {41} *vt* **1** ADIESTRAR : to instruct, to train **2** ENSEÑAR : to educate, to teach

instrumentación *nf, pl* **-ciones** : orchestration
instrumental *adj* : instrumental
instrumentar *vt* : to orchestrate
instrumentista *nmf* : instrumentalist
instrumento *nm* : instrument
insubordinado, -da *adj* : insubordinate — **insubordinación** *nf*
insubordinarse *vr* : to rebel
insuficiencia *nf* **1** : insufficiency, inadequacy **2 insuficiencia cardíaca** : heart failure
insuficiente *adj* : insufficient, inadequate — **insuficientemente** *adv*
insufrible *adj* : insufferable
insular *adj* : insular
insularidad *nf* : insularity
insulina *nf* : insulin
insulso, -sa *adj* **1** INSÍPIDO : insipid, bland **2** : dull
insultante *adj* : insulting
insultar *vt* : to insult
insulto *nm* : insult
insumos *nmpl* : supplies ⟨insumos agrícolas : agricultural supplies⟩
insuperable *adj* : insuperable, insurmountable
insurgente *adj & nmf* : insurgent — **insurgencia** *nf*
insurrección *nf, pl* **-ciones** : insurrection, uprising
insustancial *adj* : insubstantial, flimsy
insustituible *adj* : irreplaceable
intachable *adj* : irreproachable, faultless
intacto, -ta *adj* : intact
intangible *adj* IMPALPABLE : intangible, impalpable
integración *nf, pl* **-ciones** : integration
integral *adj* **1** : integral, essential **2 pan integral** : whole grain bread
integrante[1] *adj* : integrating, integral
integrante[2] *nmf* : member
integrar *vt* : to make up, to compose — **integrarse** *vr* : to integrate, to fit in
integridad *nf* **1** RECTITUD : integrity, honesty **2** : wholeness, completeness
integrismo *nm* : fundamentalism
integrista *adj & nmf* : fundamentalist
íntegro, -gra *adj* **1** : honest, upright **2** ENTERO : whole, complete **3** : unabridged
intelecto *nm* : intellect
intelectual *adj & nmf* : intellectual — **intelectualmente** *adv*
intelectualidad *nf* : intelligentsia
inteligencia *nf* : intelligence
inteligente *adj* : intelligent — **inteligentemente** *adv*
inteligible *adj* : intelligible — **inteligibilidad** *nf*
intemperancia *adj* : intemperance, excess
intemperie *nf* **1** : bad weather, elements *pl* **2 a la intemperie** : in the open air, outside
intempestivo, -va *adj* : inopportune, untimely — **intempestivamente** *adv*
intención *nf, pl* **-ciones** : intention, plan
intencionado, -da → **intencional**
intencional *adj* : intentional — **intencionalmente** *adv*
intendencia *nf* : management, administration
intendente *nmf* : quartermaster
intensidad *nf* : intensity
intensificación *nf, pl* **-ciones** : intensification
intensificar {72} *vt* : to intensify — **intensificarse** *vr*
intensivo, -va *adj* : intensive — **intensivamente** *adv*
intenso, -sa *adj* : intense — **intensamente** *adv*
intentar *vt* : to attempt, to try
intento *nm* **1** PROPÓSITO : intent, intention **2** TENTATIVA : attempt, try
interacción *nf, pl* **-ciones** : interaction
interactivo, -va *adj* : interactive
interactuar {3} *vi* : to interact
intercalar *vt* : to intersperse, to insert
intercambiable *adj* : interchangeable
intercambiar *vt* CANJEAR : to exchange, to trade
intercambio *nm* CANJE : exchange, trade
interceder *vi* : to intercede
intercepción *nf, pl* **-ciones** : interception
interceptar *vt* **1** : to intercept, to block **2 interceptar las líneas** : to wiretap
intercesión *nf, pl* **-siones** : intercession
intercomunicación *nf, pl* **-ciones** : intercommunication
interconexión *nf, pl* **-xiones** : interconnection
interconfesional *adj* : interdenominational
interdepartamental *adj* : interdepartmental
interdependencia *nf* : interdependence — **interdependiente** *adj*
interdicción *nf, pl* **-ciones** : interdiction, prohibition
interés *nm, pl* **-reses** : interest
interesado, -da *adj* **1** : interested **2** : selfish, self-seeking
interesante *adj* : interesting
interesar *vt* : to interest — *vi* : to be of interest, to be interesting — **interesarse** *vr*
interestatal *adj* : interstate ⟨autopista interestatal : interstate highway⟩
interestelar *adj* : interstellar
interfase → **interfaz**
interfaz *nf, pl* **-faces** : interface
interferencia *nf* : interference, static
interferir {76} *vi* : to interfere, to meddle — *vt* : to interfere with, to obstruct
intergaláctico, -ca *adj* : intergalactic
intergubernamental *adj* : intergovernmental
interín[1] *or* **ínterin** *adv* : meanwhile
interín[2] *or* **ínterin** *nm, pl* **-rines** : meantime, interim ⟨en el interín : in the meantime⟩

interinamente *adv* : temporarily
interino, -na *adj* : acting, temporary, interim
interior[1] *adj* : interior, inner
interior[2] *nm* **1** : interior, inside **2** : inland region
interiormente *adv* : inwardly
interjección *nf, pl* **-ciones** : interjection
interlocutor, -tora *n* : interlocutor, speaker
interludio *nm* : interlude
intermediario, -ria *adj & n* : intermediary, go-between
intermedio[1], **-dia** *adj* : intermediate
intermedio[2] *nm* **1** : intermission **2 por intermedio de** : by means of
interminable *adj* : interminable, endless — **interminablemente** *adv*
intermisión *nf, pl* **-siones** : intermission, pause
intermitente[1] *adj* **1** : intermittent **2** : flashing, blinking (of a light) — **intermitentemente** *adv*
intermitente[2] *nm* : blinker, turn signal
internacional *adj* : international — **internacionalmente** *adv*
internacionalismo *nm* : internationalism
internacionalizar {21} *vt* : to internationalize
internado *nm* : boarding school
internar *vt* : to commit, to confine — **internarse** *vr* **1** : to penetrate, to advance into **2 ~ en** : to go into, to enter
internista *nmf* : internist
interno[1], **-na** *adj* : internal — **internamente** *adv*
interno[2], **-na** *n* **1** : intern **2** : inmate, internee
interpelación *nf, pl* **-ciones** : appeal, plea
interpelar *vt* : to question (formally)
interpersonal *adj* : interpersonal
interpolar *vt* : to insert, to interpolate
interponer {60} *vt* : to interpose — **interponerse** *vr* : to intervene
interpretación *nf, pl* **-ciones** : interpretation
interpretar *vt* **1** : to interpret **2** : to play, to perform
interpretativo, -va *adj* : interpretive
intérprete *nmf* **1** TRADUCTOR : interpreter **2** : performer
interpuesto *pp* → **interponer**
interracial *adj* : interracial
interrelación *nf, pl* **-ciones** : interrelationship
interrelacionar *vi* : to interrelate
interrogación *nf, pl* **-ciones** **1** : interrogation, questioning **2 signo de interrogación** : question mark
interrogador, -dora *n* : interrogator, questioner
interrogante[1] *adj* : questioning
interrogante[2] *nm* **1** : question mark **2** : query
interrogar {52} *vt* : to interrogate, to question
interrogativo, -va *adj* : interrogative
interrogatorio *nm* : interrogation, questioning
interrumpir *v* : to interrupt
interrupción *nf, pl* **-ciones** : interruption
interruptor *nm* **1** : (electrical) switch **2** : circuit breaker
intersección *nf, pl* **-ciones** : intersection
intersticio *nm* : interstice — **intersticial** *adj*
interuniversitario, -ria *adj* : intercollegiate
interurbano, -na *adj* **1** : intercity **2** : long-distance ⟨llamadas interurbanas : long-distance calls⟩
intervalo *nm* : interval
intervención *nf, pl* **-ciones** **1** : intervention **2** : audit **3 intervención quirúrgica** : operation
intervencionista *adj & nmf* : interventionist
intervenir {87} *vi* **1** : to take part **2** INTERCEDER : to intervene, to intercede — *vt* **1** : to control, to supervise **2** : to audit **3** : to operate on **4** : to tap (a telephone)
interventor, -tora *n* **1** : inspector **2** : auditor, comptroller
intestado, -da *adj* : intestate
intestinal *adj* : intestinal
intestino *nm* : intestine
intimar *vi* **~ con** : to become friendly with — *vt* : to require, to call on
intimidación *nf, pl* **-ciones** : intimidation
intimidad *nf* **1** : intimacy **2** : privacy, private life
intimidar *vt* ACOBARDAR : to intimidate
íntimo, -ma *adj* **1** : intimate, close **2** PRIVADO : private — **íntimamente** *adv*
intitular *vt* : to entitle, to title
intocable *adj* : untouchable
intolerable *adj* : intolerable, unbearable
intolerancia *nf* : intolerance
intolerante[1] *adj* : intolerant
intolerante[2] *nmf* : intolerant person, bigot
intoxicación *nf, pl* **-ciones** : poisoning
intoxicante *nm* : poison
intoxicar {72} *vt* : to poison
intranquilidad *nf* PREOCUPACIÓN : worry, anxiety
intranquilizar {21} *vt* : to upset, to make uneasy — **intranquilizarse** *vr* : to get worried, to be anxious
intranquilo, -la *adj* PREOCUPADO : uneasy, worried
intransigencia *nf* : intransigence
intransigente *adj* : intransigent, unyielding
intransitable *adj* : impassable
intransitivo, -va *adj* : intransitive
intrascendente *adj* : unimportant, insignificant
intratable *adj* **1** : intractable **2** : awkward **3** : unsociable
intravenoso, -sa *adj* : intravenous

intrepidez *nf* : fearlessness
intrépido, -da *adj* : intrepid, fearless
intriga *nf* : intrigue
intrigante *nmf* : schemer
intrigar {52} *v* : to intrigue — **intrigante** *adj*
intrincado, -da *adj* : intricate, involved
intrínseco, -ca *adj* : intrinsic — **intrínsecamente** *adv*
introducción *nf, pl* **-ciones** : introduction
introducir {61} *vt* **1** : to introduce **2** : to bring in **3** : to insert **4** : to input, to enter — **introducirse** *vr* : to penetrate, to get into
introductorio, -ria *adj* : introductory
intromisión *nf, pl* **-siones** : interference, meddling
introspección *nf, pl* **-ciones** : introspection
introspectivo, -va *adj* : introspective
introvertido[1], **-da** *adj* : introverted
introvertido[2], **-da** *n* : introvert
intrusión *nf, pl* **-siones** : intrusion
intruso[1], **-sa** *adj* : intrusive
intruso[2], **-sa** *n* : intruder
intuición *nf, pl* **-ciones** : intuition
intuir {41} *vt* : to intuit, to sense
intuitivo, -va *adj* : intuitive — **intuitivamente** *adv*
inundación *nf, pl* **-ciones** : flood, inundation
inundar *vt* : to flood, to inundate
inusitado, -da *adj* : unusual, uncommon — **inusitadamente** *adv*
inusual *adj* : unusual, uncommon — **inusualmente** *adv*
inútil[1] *adj* INSERVIBLE : useless — **inútilmente** *adv*
inútil[2] *nmf* : good-for-nothing
inutilidad *nf* : uselessness
inutilizar {21} *vt* **1** : to make useless **2** INCAPACITAR : to disable, to put out of commission
invadir *vt* : to invade
invalidar *vt* : to nullify, to invalidate
invalidez *nf, pl* **-deces** **1** : invalidity **2** : disablement
inválido, -da *adj & n* : invalid
invalorable *adj* : invaluable
invariable *adj* : invariable — **invariablemente** *adv*
invasión *nf, pl* **-siones** : invasion
invasivo, -va *adj* : invasive
invasor[1], **-sora** *adj* : invading
invasor[2], **-sora** *n* : invader
invectiva *nf* : invective, abuse
invencibilidad *nf* : invincibility
invencible *adj* **1** : invincible **2** : insurmountable
invención *nf, pl* **-ciones** **1** INVENTO : invention **2** MENTIRA : fabrication, lie
inventar *vt* **1** : to invent **2** : to fabricate, to make up
inventariar {85} *vt* : to inventory
inventario *nm* : inventory
inventiva *nf* : ingenuity, inventiveness
inventivo, -va *adj* : inventive
invento *nm* INVENCIÓN : invention
inventor, -tora *n* : inventor
invernadero *nm* : greenhouse, hothouse
invernal *adj* : winter, wintry
invernar {55} *vi* **1** : to spend the winter **2** HIBERNAR : to hibernate
inverosímil *adj* : unlikely, far-fetched
inversión *nf, pl* **-siones** **1** : inversion **2** : investment
inversionista *nmf* : investor
inverso[1], **-sa** *adj* **1** : inverse, inverted **2** CONTRARIO : opposite **3 a la inversa** : on the contrary, vice versa **4 en orden inverso** : in reverse order — **inversamente** *adv*
inverso[2] *n* : inverse
inversor, -sora *n* : investor
invertebrado[1], **-da** *adj* : invertebrate
invertebrado[2] *nm* : invertebrate
invertir {76} *vt* **1** : to invert, to reverse **2** : to invest — *vi* : to make an investment — **invertirse** *vr* : to be reversed
investidura *nf* : investiture, inauguration
investigación *nf, pl* **-ciones** **1** ENCUESTA, INDAGACIÓN : investigation, inquiry **2** : research
investigador[1], **-dora** *adj* : investigative
investigador[2], **-dora** *n* **1** : investigator **2** : researcher
investigar {52} *vt* **1** INDAGAR : to investigate **2** : to research — *vi* **~ sobre** : to do research into
investir {54} *vt* **1** : to empower **2** : to swear in, to inaugurate
inveterado, -da *adj* : inveterate, deep-seated
invicto, -ta *adj* : undefeated
invidente[1] *adj* CIEGO : blind, sightless
invidente[2] *nmf* CIEGO : blind person
invierno *nm* : winter, wintertime
inviolable *adj* : inviolable — **inviolabilidad** *nf*
inviolado, -da *adj* : inviolate, pure
invisibilidad *nf* : invisibility
invisible *adj* : invisible — **invisiblemente** *adv*
invitación *nf, pl* **-ciones** : invitation
invitado, -da *n* : guest
invitar *vt* : to invite
invocación *nf, pl* **-ciones** : invocation
invocar {72} *vt* : to invoke, to call on
involucramiento *nm* : involvement
involucrar *vt* : to implicate, to involve — **involucrarse** *vr* : to get involved
involuntario, -ria *adj* : involuntary — **involuntariamente** *adv*
invulnerable *adj* : invulnerable
inyección *nf, pl* **-ciones** : injection, shot
inyectado, -da *adj* **ojos inyectados** : bloodshot eyes
inyectar *vt* : to inject
ion *nm* : ion
iónico, -ca *adj* : ionic
ionizar {21} *vt* : to ionize — **ionización** *nf*
ionosfera *nf* : ionosphere
ir {43} *vi* **1** : to go ⟨ir a pie : to go on foot, to walk⟩ ⟨ir a caballo : to ride

horseback⟩ ⟨ir a casa : to go home⟩ **2** : to lead, to extend, to stretch ⟨el camino va de Cali a Bogotá : the road goes from Cali to Bogotá⟩ **3** FUNCIONAR : to work, to function ⟨esta computadora ya no va : this computer doesn't work anymore⟩ **4** : to get on, to get along ⟨¿cómo te va? : how are you?, how's it going?⟩ ⟨el negocio no va bien : the business isn't doing well⟩ **5** : to suit ⟨ese vestido te va bien : that dress really suits you⟩ **6 ~ con** : to be ⟨ir con prisa : to be in a hurry⟩ **7 ~ por** : to follow, to go along ⟨fueron por la costa : they followed the shoreline⟩ **8 dejarse ir** : to let oneself go **9 ir a parar** : to end up **10 vamos a ver** : let's see — *v aux* **1** (*with present participle*) ⟨ir caminando : to walk⟩ ⟨¡voy corriendo! : I'll be right there!⟩ **2 ~ a** : to be going to ⟨voy a hacerlo : I'm going to do it⟩ ⟨el avión va a despegar : the plane is about to take off⟩ — **irse** *vr* **1** : to leave, to go ⟨¡vámonos! : let's go!⟩ ⟨todo el mundo se fue : everyone left⟩ **2** ESCAPARSE : to leak **3** GASTARSE : to be used up, to be gone

ira *nf* CÓLERA, FURIA : wrath, anger

iracundo, -da *adj* : irate, angry

iraní *adj & nmf* : Iranian

iraquí *adj & nmf* : Iraqi

irascible *adj* : irascible, irritable — **irascibilidad** *nf*

irga, irgue etc. → **erguir**

iridio *nm* : iridium

iridiscencia *nf* : iridescence — **iridiscente** *adj*

iris *nms & pl* **1** : iris **2 arco iris** : rainbow

irlandés¹, -desa *adj, mpl* **-deses** : Irish

irlandés², -desa *n, pl* **-deses** : Irish person, Irishman *m*, Irishwoman *f*

irlandés³ *nm* : Irish (language)

ironía *nf* : irony

irónico, -ca *adj* : ironic, ironical — **irónicamente** *adv*

irracional *adj* : irrational — **irracionalmente** *adv*

irracionalidad *nf* : irrationality

irradiación *nf, pl* **-ciones** : irradiation

irradiar *vt* : to radiate, to irradiate

irrazonable *adj* : unreasonable

irreal *adj* : unreal

irrebatible *adj* : unanswerable, irrefutable

irreconciliable *adj* : irreconcilable

irreconocible *adj* : unrecognizable

irrecuperable *adj* : irrecoverable, irretrievable

irredimible *adj* : irredeemable

irreductible *adj* : unyielding

irreemplazable *adj* : irreplaceable

irreflexión *nf, pl* **-xiones** : thoughtlessness, impetuosity

irreflexivo, -va *adj* : rash, unthinking — **irreflexivamente** *adv*

irrefrenable *adj* : uncontrollable, unstoppable ⟨un impulso irrefrenable : an irresistible urge⟩

irrefutable *adj* : irrefutable

irregular *adj* : irregular — **irregularmente** *adv*

irregularidad *nf* : irregularity

irrelevante *adj* : irrelevant — **irrelevancia** *nf*

irreligioso, -sa *adj* : irreligious

irremediable *adj* : incurable — **irremediablemente** *adv*

irreparable *adj* : irreparable

irreprimible *adj* : irrepressible

irreprochable *adj* : irreproachable

irresistible *adj* : irresistible — **irresistiblemente** *adv*

irresolución *nf, pl* **-ciones** : indecision, hesitation

irresoluto, -ta *adj* INDECISO : undecided

irrespeto *nm* : disrespect

irrespetuoso, -sa *adj* : disrespectful — **irrespetuosamente** *adv*

irresponsabilidad *nf* : irresponsibility

irresponsable *adj* : irresponsible — **irresponsablemente** *adv*

irrestricto, -ta *adj* : unrestricted, unconditional

irreverencia *nf* : disrespect

irreverente *adj* : disrespectful

irreversible *adj* : irreversible

irrevocable *adj* : irrevocable — **irrevocablemente** *adv*

irrigar {52} *vt* : to irrigate — **irrigación** *nf*

irrisible *adj* : laughable

irrisión *nf, pl* **-siones** : derision, ridicule

irrisorio, -ria *adj* RISIBLE : ridiculous, ludicrous

irritabilidad *nf* : irritability

irritable *adj* : irritable

irritación *nf, pl* **-ciones** : irritation

irritante *adj* : irritating

irritar *vt* : to irritate — **irritación** *nf*

irrompible *adj* : unbreakable

irrumpir *vi* **~ en** : to burst into

irrupción *nf, pl* **-ciones** **1** : irruption **2** : invasion

isla *nf* : island

islámico, -ca *adj* : Islamic, Muslim

islandés¹, -desa *adj, mpl* **-deses** : Icelandic

islandés², -desa *n, mpl* **-deses** : Icelander

islandés³ *nm* : Icelandic (language)

isleño, -ña *n* : islander

islote *nm* : islet

isometría *nfs & pl* : isometrics

isométrico, -ca *adj* : isometric

isósceles *adj* : isosceles ⟨triángulo isósceles : isosceles triangle⟩

isótopo *nm* : isotope

israelí *adj & nmf* : Israeli

istmo *nm* : isthmus

itacate *nm Mex* : pack, provisions *pl*

italiano¹, -na *adj & n* : Italian

italiano² *nm* : Italian (language)

iterbio *nm* : ytterbium

itinerante *adj* AMBULANTE : traveling, itinerant

itinerario *nm* : itinerary, route

itrio *nm* : yttrium
izar {21} *vt* : to hoist, to raise ⟨izar la bandera : to raise the flag⟩
izquierda *nf* : left
izqulerdista *adj & nmf* : leftist
izquierdo, -da *adj* : left

J

j *nf* : tenth letter of the Spanish alphabet
ja *interj* **1** : ha! **2 ja, ja** : ha-ha!
jabalí *nm* : wild boar
jabalina *nf* : javelin
jabón *nm, pl* **jabones** : soap
jabonar *vt* ENJABONAR : to soap up, to lather — **jabonarse** *vr*
jabonera *nf* : soap dish
jabonoso, -sa *adj* : soapy
jaca *nf* **1** : pony **2** YEGUA : mare
jacal *nm Mex* : shack, hut
jacinto *nm* : hyacinth
jactancia *nf* **1** : boastfulness **2** : boasting, bragging
jactancioso[1], **-sa** *adj* : boastful
jactancioso[2], **-sa** *n* : boaster, braggart
jactarse *vr* : to boast, to brag
jade *nm* : jade
jadear *vi* : to pant, to gasp, to puff — **jadeante** *adj*
jadeo *nm* : panting, gasping, puffing
jaez *nm, pl* **jaeces** **1** : harness **2** : kind, sort, ilk **3 jaeces** *nmpl* : trappings
jaguar *nm* : jaguar
jai alai *nm* : jai alai
jaiba *nf* CANGREJO : crab
jalapeño *nm Mex* : jalapeño pepper
jalar *vt* **1** : to pull, to tug **2** *fam* : to attract, to draw in ⟨las ideas nuevas lo jalan : new ideas appeal to him⟩ — *vi* **1** : to pull, to pull together **2** *fam* : to hurry up, to get going **3** *Mex fam* : to be in working order ⟨esta máquina no jala : this machine doesn't work⟩
jalbegue *nm* : whitewash
jalea *nf* : jelly
jalear *vt* : to encourage, to urge on
jaleo *nm* **1** *fam* : uproar, ruckus, racket **2** *fam* : confusion, hassle **3** : cheering and clapping (for a dance)
jalón *nm, pl* **jalones** **1** : milestone, landmark **2** TIRÓN : pull, tug
jalonar *vt* : to mark, to stake out
jalonear *vt Mex, Peru fam* : to tug at — *vi* **1** *fam* : to pull, to tug **2** *CA fam* : to haggle
jamaica *nf* : hibiscus
jamaicano, -na → **jamaiquino**
jamaiquino, -na *adj & n* : Jamaican
jamás *adv* **1** NUNCA : never **2 nunca jamás** *or* **jamás de los jamases** : never ever **3 para siempre jamás** : for ever and ever
jamba *nf* : jamb
jamelgo *nm* : nag (horse)
jamón *nm, pl* **jamones** : ham
Janucá *nmf* : Hanukkah
japonés[1], **-nesa** *adj & n, mpl* **-neses** : Japanese
japonés[2] *nm, pl* **-neses** : Japanese (language)
jaque *nm* **1** : check (in chess) ⟨jaque mate : checkmate⟩ **2 tener en jaque** : to intimidate, to bully
jaqueca *nf* : headache, migraine
jarabe *nm* **1** : syrup **2** : Mexican folk dance
jarana *nf* **1** *fam* : revelry, partying, spree **2** *fam* : joking, fooling around **3** : small guitar
jaranear *vi fam* : to go on a spree, to party
jarcia *nf* **1** : rigging **2** : fishing tackle
jardín *nm, pl* **jardines** **1** : garden **2 jardín de niños** : kindergarten **3 los jardines** *nmpl* : the outfield
jardinería *nf* : gardening
jardinero, -ra *n* **1** : gardener **2** : outfielder (in baseball)
jarra *nf* **1** : pitcher, jug **2** : stein, mug **3 de jarras** *or* **en jarras** : akimbo
jarrete *nm* **1** : back of the knee **2** CORVEJÓN : hock
jarro *nm* **1** : pitcher, jug **2** : mug
jarrón *nm, pl* **jarrones** FLORERO : vase
jaspe *nm* : jasper
jaspeado, -da *adj* **1** VETEADO : streaked, veined **2** : speckled, mottled
jaula *nf* : cage
jauría *nf* : pack of hounds
javanés, -nesa *adj & n* : Javanese
jazmín *nm, pl* **jazmines** : jasmine
jazz ['jas, 'ʤas] *nm* : jazz
jeans ['jins, 'ʤins] *nmpl* : jeans
jeep ['jip, 'ʤip] *nm, pl* **jeeps** : jeep
jefatura *nf* **1** : leadership **2** : headquarters ⟨jefatura de policía : police headquarters⟩
jefe, -fa *n* **1** : chief, head, leader ⟨jefe de bomberos : fire chief⟩ **2** : boss
Jehová *nm* : Jehovah
jején *nm, pl* **jejenes** : gnat, small mosquito
jengibre *nm* : ginger
jeque *nm* : sheikh, sheik
jerarca *nmf* : leader, chief
jerarquía *nf* **1** : hierarchy **2** RANGO : rank
jerárquico, -ca *adj* : hierarchical
jerbo *nm* : gerbil
jerez *nm, pl* **jereces** : sherry
jerga *nf* **1** : jargon, slang **2** : coarse cloth
jerigonza *nf* GALIMATÍAS : mumbo jumbo, gibberish
jeringa *nf* : syringe
jeringar {52} *vt* **1** : to inject **2** *fam* JOROBAR : to annoy, to pester — *vi fam*

JOROBAR : to be annoying, to be a nuisance
jeringuear → **jeringar**
jeringuilla → **jeringa**
jeroglífico *nm* : hieroglyphic
jersey *nm, pl* **jerseys** **1** : jersey (fabric) **2** *Spain* : sweater
Jesucristo *nm* : Jesus Christ
jesuita *adj & nm* : Jesuit
Jesús *nm* **1** : Jesus **2** **¡Jesús!** : goodness!, good heavens!
jeta *nf* **1** : snout **2** *fam* : face, mug
jíbaro, -ra *adj* **1** : Jivaro **2** : rustic, rural
jibia *nf* : cuttlefish
jícama *nf* : jicama
jícara *nf Mex* : calabash
jilguero *nm* : European goldfinch
jinete *nmf* : horseman, horsewoman *f*, rider
jinetear *vt* **1** : to ride, to perform (on horseback) **2** DOMAR : to break in (a horse) — *vi* CABALGAR : to ride horseback
jingoísmo [ˌʤɪŋgoˈizmo, ˌʤɪŋ-] *nm* : jingoism
jingoísta *adj* : jingoist, jingoistic
jiote *nm Mex* : rash
jira *nf* : outing, picnic
jirafa *nf* **1** : giraffe **2** : boom microphone
jirón *nm, pl* **jirones** : shred, rag ⟨hecho jirones : in tatters⟩
jitomate *nm Mex* : tomato
jockey [ˈjɔki, ˈʤɔ-] *nmf, pl* **jockeys** [-kis] : jockey
jocosidad *nf* : humor, jocularity
jocoso, -sa *adj* : playful, jocular — **jocosamente** *adv*
jofaina *nf* : washbowl
jogging [ˈjɔgɪŋ, ˈʤɔ-] *nm* : jogging
jolgorio *nm* : merrymaking, fun
jonrón *nm, pl* **jonrones** : home run
jordano, -na *adj & n* : Jordanian
jornada *nf* **1** : expedition, day's journey **2** **jornada de trabajo** : working day **3** **jornadas** *nfpl* : conference, congress
jornal *nm* **1** : day's pay **2** **a ~** : by the day
jornalero, -ra *n* : day laborer
joroba *nf* **1** GIBA : hump **2** *fam* : nuisance, pain in the neck
jorobado¹, -da *adj* GIBOSO : hunchbacked, humpbacked
jorobado², -da *n* GIBOSO : hunchback, humpback
jorobar *vt fam* JERINGAR : to bother, to annoy — *vi fam* JERINGAR : to be annoying, to be a nuisance
jorongo *nm Mex* : full-length poncho
jota *nf* **1** : jot, bit ⟨no entiendo ni jota : I don't understand a word of it⟩ ⟨no se ve ni jota : you can't see a thing⟩ **2** : jack (in playing cards)
joven¹ *adj, pl* **jóvenes** **1** : young **2** : youthful
joven² *nmf, pl* **jóvenes** : young man *m*, young woman *f*, young person
jovial *adj* : jovial, cheerful — **jovialmente** *adv*
jovialidad *nf* : joviality, cheerfulness
joya *nf* **1** : jewel, piece of jewelry **2** : treasure, gem ⟨la nueva empleada es una joya : the new employee is a real gem⟩
joyería *nf* **1** : jewelry store **2** : jewelry **3** **joyería de fantasía** : costume jewelry
joyero, -ra *n* : jeweler
juanete *nm* : bunion
jubilación *nf, pl* **-ciones** **1** : retirement **2** PENSIÓN : pension
jubilado¹, -da *adj* : retired, in retirement
jubilado², -da *nmf* : retired person, retiree
jubilar *vt* **1** : to retire, to pension off **2** *fam* : to get rid of, to discard — **jubilarse** *vr* : to retire
jubileo *nm* : jubilee
júbilo *nm* : jubilation, joy
jubiloso, -sa *adj* : jubilant, joyous
judaico, -ca *adj* : Judaic, Jewish
judaísmo *nm* : Judaism
judía *nf* **1** : bean **2** *or* **judía verde** : green bean, string bean
judicatura *nf* **1** : judiciary, judges *pl* **2** : office of judge
judicial *adj* : judicial — **judicialmente** *adv*
judío¹, -día *adj* : Jewish
judío², -día *n* : Jewish person, Jew
judo [ˈjuðo, ˈʤu-] *nm* : judo
juega, juegue, etc. → **jugar**
juego *nm* **1** : play, playing ⟨poner en juego : to bring into play⟩ **2** : game, sport ⟨juego de cartas : card game⟩ ⟨Juegos Olímpicos : Olympic Games⟩ **3** : gaming, gambling ⟨estar en juego : to be at stake⟩ **4** : set ⟨un juego de llaves : a set of keys⟩ **5** **hacer juego** : to go together, to match **6** **juego de manos** : conjuring trick, sleight of hand
juerga *nf* : partying, binge ⟨irse de juerga : to go on a spree⟩
juerguista *nmf* : reveler, carouser
jueves *nms & pl* : Thursday
juez¹ *nmf, pl* **jueces** **1** : judge **2** ÁRBITRO : umpire, referee
juez², jueza *n* → **juez¹**
jugada *nf* **1** : play, move **2** : trick ⟨hacer una mala jugada : to play a dirty trick⟩
jugador, -dora *n* **1** : player **2** : gambler
jugar {44} *vi* **1** : to play ⟨jugar a la pelota : to play ball⟩ **2** APOSTAR : to gamble, to bet **3** : to joke, to kid — *vt* **1** : to play ⟨jugar un papel : to play a role⟩ ⟨jugar una carta : to play a card⟩ **2** : to bet — **jugarse** *vr* **1** : to risk, to gamble away ⟨jugarse la vida : to risk one's life⟩ **2** **jugarse el todo por el todo** : to risk everything
jugarreta *nf fam* : prank, dirty trick
juglar *nm* : minstrel

jugo *nm* **1** : juice **2** : substance, essence ⟨sacarle el jugo a algo : to get the most out of something⟩
jugosidad *nf* : juiciness, succulence
jugoso, -sa *adj* : juicy
juguete *nm* : toy
juguetear *vi* **1** : to play, to cavort, to frolic **2** : to toy, to fiddle
juguetería *nf* : toy store
juguetón, -tona *adj, mpl* **-tones** : playful — **juguetonamente** *adv*
juicio *nm* **1** : good judgment, reason, sense **2** : opinion ⟨a mi juicio : in my opinion⟩ **3** : trial ⟨llevar a juicio : to take to court⟩
juicioso, -sa *adj* : judicious, wise — **juiciosamente** *adv*
julio *nm* : July
juncia *nf* : sedge
junco *nm* **1** : reed, rush **2** : junk (boat)
jungla *nf* : jungle
junio *nm* : June
junquillo *nm* : jonquil
junta *nf* **1** : board, committee ⟨junta directiva : board of directors⟩ **2** REUNIÓN : meeting, session **3** : junta **4** : joint, gasket
juntamente *adv* **1** : jointly, together ⟨juntamente con : together with⟩ **2** : at the same time
juntar *vt* **1** UNIR : to unite, to combine, to put together **2** REUNIR : to collect, to gather together, to assemble **3** : to close partway ⟨juntar la puerta : to leave the door ajar⟩ — **juntarse** *vr* **1** : to join together **2** : to socialize, to get together
junto, -ta *adj* **1** UNIDO : joined, united **2** : close, adjacent ⟨colgaron los dos retratos juntos : they hung the two paintings side by side⟩ **3** (*used adverbially*) : together ⟨llegamos juntos : we arrived together⟩ **4 ~ a** : next to, alongside of **5 ~ con** : together with, along with
juntura *nf* : joint, coupling
Júpiter *nm* : Jupiter
jura *nf* : oath, pledge ⟨jura de bandera : pledge of allegiance⟩
jurado[1] *nm* : jury
jurado[2], **-da** *n* : juror
juramento *nm* **1** : oath ⟨juramento hipocrático : Hippocratic oath⟩ **2** : swearword, oath
jurar *vt* **1** : to swear ⟨jurar lealtad : to swear loyalty⟩ **2** : to take an oath ⟨el alcalde juró su cargo : the mayor took the oath of office⟩ — *vi* : to curse, to swear
jurídico, -ca *adj* : legal
jurisdicción *nf, pl* **-ciones** : jurisdiction
jurisdiccional *adj* : jurisdictional, territorial
jurisprudencia *nf* : jurisprudence, law
jurista *nmf* : jurist
justa *nf* **1** : joust **2** TORNEO : tournament, competition
justamente *adv* **1** PRECISAMENTE : precisely, exactly **2** : justly, fairly
justar *vi* : to joust
justicia *nf* **1** : justice, fairness ⟨hacerle justicia a : to do justice to⟩ ⟨ser de justicia : to be only fair⟩ **2 la justicia** : the law ⟨tomarse la justicia por su mano : to take the law into one's own hands⟩
justiciero, -ra *adj* : righteous, avenging
justificable *adj* : justifiable
justificación *nf, pl* **-ciones** : justification
justificante *nm* **1** : justification **2** : proof, voucher
justificar {72} *vt* **1** : to justify **2** : to excuse, to vindicate
justo[1] *adv* **1** : justly **2** : right, exactly ⟨justo a tiempo : just in time⟩ **3** : tightly
justo[2], **-ta** *adj* **1** : just, fair **2** : right, exact **3** : tight ⟨estos zapatos me quedan muy justos : these shoes are too tight⟩
justo[3], **-ta** *n* : just person ⟨los justos : the just⟩
juvenil *adj* **1** : juvenile, young, youthful **2** ADOLESCENTE : teenage
juventud *nf* **1** : youth **2** : young people
juzgado *nm* TRIBUNAL : court, tribunal
juzgar {52} *vt* **1** : to try, to judge (a case in court) **2** : to pass judgment on **3** CONSIDERAR : to consider, to deem
juzgue, etc. → **juzgar**

K

k *nf* : eleventh letter of the Spanish alphabet
káiser *nm* : kaiser
kaki → **caqui**
kaleidoscopio → **caleidoscopio**
kamikaze *adj & nm* : kamikaze
kampucheano, -na *adj & n* : Kampuchean
kan *nm* : khan
karaoke *nm* : karaoke
karate *or* **kárate** *nm* : karate
kayac *or* **kayak** *nm, pl* **kayacs** *or* **kayaks** : kayak
keniano, -na *adj & n* : Kenyan
kepí *nm* : kepi
kermesse *or* **kermés** [kɛrˈmɛs] *nf, pl* **kermesses** *or* **kermeses** [-ˈmɛsɛs] : charity fair, bazaar
kerosene *or* **kerosén** *or* **keroseno** *nm* : kerosene, paraffin
kibutz *or* **kibbutz** *nms & pl* : kibbutz
kilo *nm* **1** : kilo, kilogram **2** *fam* : large amount
kilobyte [ˌkiloˈbait] *nm* : kilobyte
kilociclo *nm* : kilocycle
kilogramo *nm* : kilogram

kilohertzio *nm* : kilohertz
kilometraje *nm* : distance in kilometers, mileage
kilométrico, -ca *adj fam* : endless, very long
kilómetro *nm* : kilometer
kilovatio *nm* : kilowatt
kimono *nm* : kimono
kinder ['kɪndɛr] → **kindergarten**
kindergarten [ˌkɪndɛr'gartɛn] *nm, pl* **kindergartens** [-tɛns] : kindergarten, nursery school
kinesiología *nf* : physical therapy
kinesiólogo, -ga *n* : physical therapist
kiosco → **quiosco**
kit *nm, pl* **kits** : kit
kiwi ['kiwi] *nm* **1** : kiwi (bird) **2** : kiwifruit
klaxon → **claxon**
knockout [nɔ'kaut] → **nocaut**
koala *nm* : koala bear
kriptón *nm* : krypton
kurdo[1], -da *adj* : Kurdish
kurdo[2], -da *n* : Kurd
kuwaití [kuˌwai'ti] *adj & nmf* : Kuwaiti

L

l *nf* : twelfth letter of the Spanish alphabet
la[1] *pron* **1** : her, it ⟨llámala hoy : call her today⟩ ⟨sacó la botella y la abrió : he took out the bottle and opened it⟩ **2** (*formal*) : you ⟨no la vi a usted, Señora Díaz : I didn't see you, Mrs. Díaz⟩ **3** : the one ⟨mi casa y la de la puerta roja : my house and the one with the red door⟩ **4 la que** : the one who
la[2] *art* → **el[2]**
laberíntico, -ca *adj* : labyrinthine
laberinto *nm* : labyrinth, maze
labia *nf fam* : gift of gab ⟨tu amigo tiene labia : your friend has a way with words⟩
labial *adj* : labial, lip ⟨lápiz labial : lipstick⟩
labio *nm* **1** : lip **2 labio leporino** : harelip
labor *nf* : work, labor
laborable *adj* **1** : arable **2 día laborable** : workday, business day
laboral *adj* : work, labor ⟨costos laborales : labor costs⟩
laborar *vi* : to work
laboratorio *nm* : laboratory, lab
laboriosidad *nf* : industriousness, diligence
laborioso, -sa *adj* **1** : laborious, hard **2** : industrious, hardworking
labrado[1], -da *adj* **1** : cultivated, tilled **2** : carved, wrought
labrado[2] *nm* : cultivated field
labrador, -dora *n* : farmer
labranza *nf* : farming
labrar *vt* **1** : to carve, to work (metal) **2** : to cultivate, to till **3** : to cause, to bring about
laca *nf* **1** : lacquer, shellac **2** : hair spray **3 laca de uñas** : nail polish
lacayo *nm* : lackey
lace, etc. → **lazar**
lacear *vt* : to lasso
laceración *nf, pl* **-ciones** : laceration
lacerante *adj* : hurtful, wounding
lacerar *vt* **1** : to lacerate, to cut **2** : to hurt, to wound (one's feelings)
lacio, -cia *adj* **1** : limp, lank **2 pelo lacio** : straight hair
lacónico, -ca *adj* : laconic — **lacónicamente** *adv*
lacra *nf* **1** : scar, mark (on the skin) **2** : stigma, blemish
lacrar *vt* : to seal (with wax)
lacrimógeno, -na *adj* **gas lacrimógeno** : tear gas
lacrimoso, -sa *adj* : tearful, moving
lactancia *nf* **1** : lactation **2** : breastfeeding
lactante *nmf* : nursing infant, suckling
lactar *v* : to breast-feed
lácteo, -tea *adj* **1** : dairy **2 Vía Láctea** : Milky Way
láctico, -ca *adj* : lactic
lactosa *nf* : lactose
ladeado, -da *adj* : crooked, tilted, lopsided
ladear *vt* : to tilt, to tip — **ladearse** *vr* : to bend (over)
ladera *nf* : slope, hillside
ladino[1], -na *adj* **1** : cunning, shrewd **2** *CA, Mex* : mestizo
ladino[2], -na *n* **1** : trickster **2** *CA, Mex* : Spanish-speaking Indian **3** *CA, Mex* : mestizo
lado *nm* **1** : side **2** PARTE : place ⟨miró por todos lados : he looked everywhere⟩ **3 al lado de** : next to, beside **4 de ~** : tilted, sideways ⟨está de lado : it's lying on its side⟩ **5 hacerse a un lado** : to step aside **6 lado a lado** : side by side **7 por otro lado** : on the other hand
ladrar *vi* : to bark
ladrido *nm* : bark (of a dog), barking
ladrillo *nm* **1** : brick **2** AZULEJO : tile
ladrón, -drona *n, mpl* **ladrones** : robber, thief, burglar
lagartija *nf* : small lizard
lagarto *nm* **1** : lizard **2 lagarto de Indias** : alligator
lago *nm* : lake
lágrima *nf* : tear, teardrop
lagrimear *vi* **1** : to water (of eyes) **2** : to weep easily
laguna *nf* **1** : lagoon **2** : lacuna, gap
laicado *nm* : laity
laico[1], -ca *adj* : lay, secular
laico[2], -ca *n* : layman *m,* laywoman *f*

laja *nf* : slab
lama[1] *nf* : slime, ooze
lama[2] *nm* : lama
lamber *vt* : to lick
lamé *nm* : lamé
lamentable *adj* **1** : unfortunate, lamentable **2** : pitiful, sad
lamentablemente *adv* : unfortunately, regrettably
lamentación *nf, pl* **-ciones** : lamentation, groaning, moaning
lamentar *vt* **1** : to lament **2** : to regret ⟨lo lamento : I'm sorry⟩ — **lamentarse** *vr* : to grumble, to complain
lamento *nm* : lament, groan, cry
lamer *vt* **1** : to lick **2** : to lap against
lamida *nf* : lick
lámina *nf* **1** PLANCHA : sheet, plate **2** : plate, illustration
laminado[1], **-da** *adj* : laminated
laminado[2] *nm* : laminate
laminar *vt* : to laminate — **laminación** *nf*
lámpara *nf* : lamp
lampiño, **-ña** *adj* : hairless
lamprea *nf* : lamprey
lana *nf* **1** : wool ⟨lana de acero : steel wool⟩ **2** *Mex fam* : money, dough
lance[1], **etc.** → **lanzar**
lance[2] *nm* **1** INCIDENTE : event, incident **2** RIÑA : quarrel **3** : throw, cast (of a net, etc.) **4** : move, play (in a game), throw (of dice)
lancear *vt* : to spear
lanceta *nf* : lancet
lancha *nf* **1** : small boat, launch **2 lancha motora** : motorboat, speedboat
langosta *nf* **1** : lobster **2** : locust
langostino *nm* : prawn, crayfish
languidecer {53} *vi* : to languish
languidez *nf, pl* **-deces** : languor, listlessness
lánguido, **-da** *adj* : languid, listless — **lánguidamente** *adv*
lanolina *nf* : lanolin
lanudo, **-da** *adj* : woolly
lanza *nf* : spear, lance
lanzadera *nf* **1** : shuttle (for weaving) **2 lanzadera espacial** : space shuttle
lanzado, **-da** *adj* **1** : impulsive, brazen **2** : forward, determined ⟨ir lanzado : to hurtle along⟩
lanzador, **-dora** *n* : thrower, pitcher
lanzallamas *nms & pl* : flamethrower
lanzamiento *nm* **1** : throw **2** : pitch (in baseball) **3** : launching, launch
lanzar {21} *vt* **1** : to throw, to hurl **2** : to pitch **3** : to launch — **lanzarse** *vr* **1** : to throw oneself (at, into) **2 ~ a** : to embark upon, to undertake
laosiano, **-na** *adj & n* : Laotian
lapicero *nm* **1** : mechanical pencil **2** *CA, Peru* : ballpoint pen
lápida *nf* : marker, tombstone
lapidar *vt* APEDREAR : to stone
lapidario, **-ria** *adj & n* : lapidary
lápiz *nm, pl* **lápices** **1** : pencil **2 lápiz de labios** *or* **lápiz labial** : lipstick
lapón, **-pona** *adj & n, mpl* **lapones** : Lapp
lapso *nm* : lapse, space (of time)
lapsus *nms & pl* : error, slip
laptop *nm, pl* **laptops** : laptop
laquear *vt* : to lacquer, to varnish, to shellac
largamente *adv* **1** : at length, extensively **2** : easily, comfortably **3** : generously
largar {52} *vt* **1** SOLTAR : to let loose, to release **2** AFLOJAR : to loosen, to slacken **3** *fam* : to give, to hand over **4** *fam* : to hurl, to let fly (insults, etc.) — **largarse** *vr fam* : to scram, to beat it
largo[1], **-ga** *adj* **1** : long **2 a lo largo** : lengthwise **3 a lo largo de** : along **4 a la larga** : in the long run
largo[2] *nm* : length ⟨tres metros de largo : three meters long⟩
largometraje *nm* : feature film
largue, **etc.** → **largar**
larguero *nm* : crossbeam
largueza *nf* : generosity, largesse
larguirucho, **-cha** *adj fam* : lanky
largura *nf* : length
laringe *nf* : larynx
laringitis *nfs & pl* : laryngitis
larva *nf* : larva — **larval** *adj*
las → **el[2]**, **los[1]**
lasaña *nf* : lasagna
lasca *nf* : chip, chipping
lascivia *nf* : lasciviousness, lewdness
lascivo, **-va** *adj* : lascivious, lewd — **lascivamente** *adv*
láser *nm* : laser
lasitud *nf* : lassitude, weariness
laso, **-sa** *adj* : languid, weary
lástima *nf* **1** : compassion, pity **2** PENA : shame, pity ⟨¡qué lástima! : what a shame!⟩
lastimadura *nf* : injury, wound
lastimar *vt* **1** DAÑAR, HERIR : to hurt, to injure **2** AGRAVIAR : to offend — **lastimarse** *vr* : to hurt oneself
lastimero, **-ra** *adj* : pitiful, wretched
lastimoso, **-sa** *adj* **1** : shameful **2** : pitiful, terrible
lastrar *vt* **1** : to ballast **2** : to burden, to encumber
lastre *nm* **1** : burden **2** : ballast
lata *nf* **1** : tinplate **2** : tin can **3** *fam* : pest, bother, nuisance **4 dar lata** *fam* : to bother, to annoy
latencia *nf* : latency
latente *adj* : latent
lateral[1] *adj* **1** : lateral, side **2** : indirect — **lateralmente** *adv*
lateral[2] *nm* : end piece, side
látex *nms & pl* : latex
latido *nm* : beat, throb ⟨latido del corazón : heartbeat⟩
latifundio *nm* : large estate
latigazo *nm* : lash (with a whip)
látigo *nm* AZOTE : whip
latín *nm* : Latin (language)
latino[1], **-na** *adj* **1** : Latin **2** *fam* : Latin-American

latino², **-na** *n fam* : Latin American
latinoamericano¹, **-na** *adj* HISPANOAMERICANO : Latin American
latinoamericano, **-na** *n* : Latin American
latir *vi* **1** : to beat, to throb **2 latirle a uno** *Mex fam* : to have a hunch ⟨me late que no va a venir : I have a feeling he's not going to come⟩
latitud *nf* **1** : latitude **2** : breadth
lato, **-ta** *adj* **1** : extended, lengthy **2** : broad (in meaning)
latón *nm, pl* **latones** : brass
latoso¹, **-sa** *adj fam* : annoying, bothersome
latoso², **-sa** *n fam* : pest, nuisance
latrocinio *nm* : larceny
laúd *nm* : lute
laudable *adj* : laudable, praiseworthy
laudo *nm* : findings, decision
laureado, **-da** *adj & n* : laureate
laurear *vt* : to award, to honor
laurel *nm* **1** : laurel **2** : bay leaf **3 dormirse en sus laureles** : to rest on one's laurels
lava *nf* : lava
lavable *adj* : washable
lavabo *nm* **1** LAVAMANOS : sink, washbowl **2** : lavatory, toilet
lavadero *nm* : laundry room
lavado *nm* **1** : laundry, wash **2** : laundering ⟨lavado de dinero : money laundering⟩
lavadora *nf* : washing machine
lavamanos *nms & pl* LAVABO : sink, washbowl
lavanda *nf* ESPLIEGO : lavender
lavandería *nf* : laundry (service)
lavandero, **-ra** *n* : launderer, laundress *f*
lavaplatos *nms & pl* **1** : dishwasher **2** *Chile, Col, Mex* : kitchen sink
lavar *vt* **1** : to wash, to clean **2** : to launder (money) **3 lavar en seco** : to dry-clean — **lavarse** *vr* **1** : to wash oneself **2 lavarse las manos de** : to wash one's hands of
lavativa *nf* : enema
lavatorio *nm* : lavatory, washroom
lavavajillas *nms & pl* : dishwasher
laxante *adj & nm* : laxative
laxitud *nf* : laxity, slackness
laxo, **-xa** *adj* : lax, slack
lazada *nf* : bow, loop
lazar {21} *vt* : to rope, to lasso
lazo *nm* **1** VÍNCULO : link, bond **2** : bow, ribbon **3** : lasso, lariat
le *pron* **1** : to her, to him, to it ⟨¿qué le dijiste? : what did you tell him?⟩ **2** : from her, from him, from it ⟨el ladrón le robó la cartera : the thief stole his wallet⟩ **3** : for her, for him, for it ⟨cómprale flores a tu mamá : buy your mom some flowers⟩ **4** (*formal*) : to you, for you ⟨le traje un regalo : I brought you a gift⟩
leal *adj* : loyal, faithful — **lealmente** *adv*
lealtad *nf* : loyalty, allegiance
lebrel *nm* : hound
lección *nf, pl* **lecciones** : lesson
lechada *nf* **1** : whitewash **2** : grout
lechal *adj* : suckling, unweaned ⟨cordero lechal : suckling lamb⟩
leche *nf* **1** : milk ⟨leche en polvo : powdered milk⟩ ⟨leche de magnesia : milk of magnesia⟩ **2** : milky sap
lechera *nf* **1** : milk jug **2** : dairymaid *f*
lechería *nf* : dairy store
lechero¹, **-ra** *adj* : dairy
lechero², **-ra** *n* : milkman *m*, milk dealer
lecho *nm* **1** : bed ⟨un lecho de rosas : a bed of roses⟩ ⟨lecho de muerte : deathbed⟩ **2** : riverbed **3** : layer, stratum (in geology)
lechón, **-chona** *n, mpl* **lechones** : suckling pig
lechoso, **-sa** *adj* : milky
lechuga *nf* : lettuce
lechuza *nf* BÚHO : owl, barn owl
lectivo, **-va** *adj* : school ⟨año lectivo : school year⟩
lector¹, **-tora** *adj* : reading ⟨nivel lector : reading level⟩
lector², **-tora** *n* : reader
lector³ *nm* : scanner, reader ⟨lector óptico : optical scanner⟩
lectura *nf* **1** : reading **2** : reading matter
leer {20} *v* : to read
legación *nf, pl* **-ciones** : legation
legado *nm* **1** : legacy, bequest **2** : legate, emissary
legajo *nm* : dossier, file
legal *adj* : legal, lawful — **legalmente** *adv*
legalidad *nf* : legality, lawfulness
legalista *adj* : legalistic
legalizar {21} *vt* : to legalize — **legalización** *nf*
legar {52} *vt* **1** : to bequeath, to hand down **2** DELEGAR : to delegate
legendario, **-ria** *adj* : legendary
legible *adj* : legible
legión *nf, pl* **legiones** : legion
legionario, **-ria** *n* : legionnaire
legislación *nf* **1** : legislation, lawmaking **2** : laws *pl*, legislation
legislador¹, **-dora** *adj* : legislative
legislador², **-dora** *n* : legislator
legislar *vi* : to legislate
legislativo, **-va** *adj* : legislative
legislatura *nf* **1** : legislature **2** : term of office
legitimar *vt* **1** : to legitimize **2** : to authenticate — **legitimación** *nf*
legitimidad *nf* : legitimacy
legítimo, **-ma** *adj* **1** : legitimate **2** : genuine, authentic — **legítimamente** *adv*
lego¹, **-ga** *adj* **1** : secular, lay **2** : uninformed, ignorant
lego², **-ga** *n* : layperson, layman *m*, laywoman *f*
legua *nf* **1** : league **2 notarse a leguas** : to be very obvious ⟨se notaba a leguas : you could tell from a mile away⟩

legue, etc. → **legar**
legumbre *nf* **1** HORTALIZA : vegetable **2** : legume
leíble *adj* : readable
leída *nf* : reading, read ⟨de una leída : in one reading, at one go⟩
leído[1] *pp* → **leer**
leído[2], **-da** *adj* : well-read
lejanía *nf* : remoteness, distance
lejano, -na *adj* : remote, distant, far away
lejía *nf* **1** : lye **2** : bleach
lejos *adv* **1** : far away, distant ⟨a lo lejos : in the distance, far off⟩ ⟨desde lejos : from a distance⟩ **2** : long ago, a long way off ⟨está lejos de los 50 años : he's a long way from 50 years old⟩ **3 de ~** : by far ⟨esta decisión fue de lejos la más fácil : this decision was by far the easiest⟩ **4 ~ de** : far from ⟨lejos de ser reprobado, recibió una nota de B : far from failing, he got a B⟩
lelo, -la *adj* : silly, stupid
lema *nm* : motto, slogan
lencería *nf* : lingerie
lengua *nf* **1** : tongue ⟨morderse la lengua : to bite one's tongue⟩ **2** IDIOMA : language ⟨lengua materna : mother tongue, native language⟩ ⟨lengua muerta : dead language⟩
lenguado *nm* : sole, flounder
lenguaje *nm* **1** : language, speech **2 lenguaje gestual** *or* **lenguaje de gestos** : sign language **3 lenguaje de programación** : programming language
lengüeta *nf* **1** : tongue (of a shoe), tab, flap **2** : reed (of a musical instrument) **3** : barb, point
lengüetada *nf* **beber a lengüetadas** : to lap (up)
lenidad *nf* : leniency
lenitivo, -va *adj* : soothing
lente *nmf* **1** : lens ⟨lentes de contacto : contact lenses⟩ **2 lentes** *nmpl* ANTEOJOS : eyeglasses ⟨lentes de sol : sunglasses⟩
lenteja *nf* : lentil
lentejuela *nf* : sequin, spangle
lentitud *nf* : slowness
lento[1] *adv* DESPACIO : slowly
lento[2], **-ta** *adj* **1** : slow **2** : slow-witted, dull — **lentamente** *adv*
leña *nf* : wood, firewood
leñador, -dora *n* : lumberjack, woodcutter
leñera *nf* : woodshed
leño *nm* : log
leñoso, -sa *adj* : woody
Leo *nmf* : Leo
león, -ona *n, mpl* **leones** **1** : lion, lioness *f* **2** (*in various countries*) : puma, cougar
leonado, -da *adj* : tawny
leonino, -na *adj* **1** : leonine **2** : one-sided, unfair
leopardo *nm* : leopard
leotardo *nm* MALLA : leotard, tights *pl*
leperada *nf Mex* : obscenity
lépero, -ra *adj Mex* : vulgar, coarse
lepra *nf* : leprosy
leproso[1], **-sa** *adj* : leprous
leproso[2], **-sa** *n* : leper
lerdo, -da *adj* **1** : clumsy **2** : dull, oafish, slow-witted
les *pron* **1** : to them ⟨dales una propina : give them a tip⟩ **2** : from them ⟨se les privó de su herencia : they were deprived of their inheritance⟩ **3** : for them ⟨les hice sus tareas : I did their homework for them⟩ **4** : to you *pl*, for you *pl* ⟨les compré un regalo : I bought you all a present⟩
lesbiana *nf* : lesbian — **lesbiano, -na** *adj*
lesbianismo *nm* : lesbianism
lesión *nf, pl* **lesiones** HERIDA : lesion, wound, injury ⟨una lesión grave : a serious injury⟩
lesionado, -da *adj* HERIDO : injured, wounded
lesionar *vt* : to injure, to wound — **lesionarse** *vr* : to hurt oneself
lesivo, -va *adj* : harmful, damaging
letal *adj* MORTÍFERO : deadly, lethal — **letalmente** *adv*
letanía *nf* **1** : litany **2** *fam* : spiel, song and dance
letárgico, -ca *adj* : lethargic
letargo *nm* : lethargy, torpor
letón[1], **-tona** *adj & n, mpl* **letones** : Latvian
letón[2] *nm* : Latvian (language)
letra *nf* **1** : letter **2** CALIGRAFÍA : handwriting, lettering **3** : lyrics *pl* **4 al pie de la letra** : word for word, by the book **5 letras** *nfpl* : arts (in education)
letrado[1], **-da** *adj* ERUDITO : learned, erudite
letrado[2], **-da** *n* : attorney-at-law, lawyer
letrero *nm* RÓTULO : sign, notice
letrina *nf* : latrine
letrista *nmf* : lyricist, songwriter
leucemia *nf* : leukemia
leva *nf* : cam
levadizo, -za *adj* **1** : liftable **2 puente levadizo** : drawbridge
levadura *nf* **1** : yeast, leavening **2 levadura en polvo** : baking powder
levantamiento *nm* **1** ALZAMIENTO : uprising **2** : raising, lifting ⟨levantamiento de pesas : weight lifting⟩
levantar *vt* **1** ALZAR : to lift, to raise **2** : to put up, to erect **3** : to call off, to adjourn **4** : to give rise to, to arouse ⟨levantar sospechas : to arouse suspicion⟩ — **levantarse** *vr* **1** : to rise, to stand up **2** : to get out of bed
levar *vt* **levar anclas** : to weigh anchor
leve *adj* **1** : light, slight **2** : trivial, unimportant — **levemente** *adv*
levedad *nf* : lightness
levemente *adv* LIGERAMENTE : lightly, softly
leviatán *nm, pl* **-tanes** : leviathan
léxico[1], **-ca** *adj* : lexical
léxico[2] *nm* : lexicon, glossary
lexicografía *nf* : lexicography

lexicográfico, -ca *adj* : lexicographical, lexicographic
lexicógrafo, -fa *n* : lexicographer
ley *nf* **1** : law ⟨fuera de la ley : outside the law⟩ ⟨la ley de gravedad : the law of gravity⟩ **2** : purity (of metals) ⟨oro de ley : pure gold⟩
leyenda *nf* **1** : legend **2** : caption, inscription
leyó, etc. → **leer**
liar {85} *vt* **1** ATAR : to bind, to tie (up) **2** : to roll (a cigarette) **3** : to confuse — **liarse** *vr* : to get mixed up
libanés, -nesa *adj & n, mpl* **-neses** : Lebanese
libar *vt* **1** : to suck (nectar) **2** : to sip, to swig (liquor, etc.)
libelo *nm* **1** : libel, lampoon **2** : petition (in court)
libélula *nf* : dragonfly
liberación *nf, pl* **-ciones** : liberation, deliverance ⟨liberación de la mujer : women's liberation⟩
liberado, -da *adj* **1** : liberated ⟨una mujer liberada : a liberated woman⟩ **2** : freed, delivered
liberal *adj & nmf* : liberal
liberalidad *nf* : generosity, liberality
liberalismo *nm* : liberalism
liberalizar {21} *vt* : to liberalize — **liberalización** *nf*
liberar *vt* : to liberate, to free — **liberarse** *vr* : to get free of
liberiano, -na *adj & n* : Liberian
libertad *nf* **1** : freedom, liberty ⟨tomarse la libertad de : to take the liberty of⟩ **2 libertad bajo fianza** : bail **3 libertad condicional** : parole
libertador[1], -dora *adj* : liberating
libertador[2], -dora *n* : liberator
libertar *vt* LIBRAR : to set free
libertario, -ria *adj & n* : libertarian
libertinaje *nm* : licentiousness, dissipation
libertino[1], -na *adj* : licentious, dissolute
libertino[2], -na *n* : libertine
libidinoso, -sa *adj* : lustful, lewd
libido *nf* : libido
libio, -bia *adj & n* : Libyan
libra *nf* **1** : pound **2 libra esterlina** : pound sterling
Libra *nmf* : Libra
libramiento *nm* **1** : liberating, freeing **2** LIBRANZA : order of payment **3** *Mex* : beltway
libranza *nf* : order of payment
librar *vt* **1** LIBERTAR : to deliver, to set free **2** : to wage ⟨librar batalla : to do battle⟩ **3** : to issue ⟨librar una orden : to issue an order⟩ — **librarse** *vr* **~ de** : to free oneself from, to get out of
libre[1] *adj* **1** : free ⟨un país libre : a free country⟩ ⟨libre de : free from, exempt from⟩ ⟨libre albedrío : free will⟩ **2** DESOCUPADO : vacant **3 día libre** : day off
libre[2] *nm Mex* : taxi
librea *nf* : livery
librecambio *nm* : free trade
libremente *adv* : freely
librería *nf* : bookstore
librero[1], -ra *n* : bookseller
librero[2] *nm Mex* : bookcase
libresco, -ca *adj* : bookish
libreta *nf* CUADERNO : notebook
libretista *nmf* **1** : librettist **2** : scriptwriter
libreto *nm* : libretto, script
libro *nm* **1** : book ⟨libro de texto : textbook⟩ **2 libros** *nmpl* : books (in bookkeeping), accounts ⟨llevar los libros : to keep the books⟩
licencia *nf* **1** : permission **2** : leave, leave of absence **3** : permit, license ⟨licencia de conducir : driver's license⟩
licenciado, -da *n* **1** : university graduate **2** ABOGADO : lawyer
licenciar *vt* **1** : to license, to permit, to allow **2** : to discharge **3** : to grant a university degree to — **licenciarse** *vr* : to graduate
licenciatura *nf* **1** : college degree **2** : course of study (at a college or university)
licencioso, -sa *adj* : licentious, lewd
liceo *nm* : secondary school, high school
licitación *nf, pl* **-ciones** : bid, bidding
licitar *vt* : to bid on
lícito, -ta *adj* **1** : lawful, licit **2** JUSTO : just, fair
licor *nm* **1** : liquor **2** : liqueur
licorera *nf* : decanter
licuado *nm* BATIDO : milk shake
licuadora *nf* : blender
licuar {3} *vt* : to liquefy — **licuarse** *vr*
lid *nf* **1** : fight, combat **2** : argument, dispute **3 lides** *nfpl* : matters, affairs **4 en buena lid** : fair and square
líder[1] *adj* : leading, foremost
líder[2] *nmf* : leader
liderar *vt* DIRIGIR : to lead, to head
liderato *nm* : leadership, leading
liderazgo → **liderato**
lidiar *vt* : to fight — *vi* BATALLAR, LUCHAR : to struggle, to battle, to wrestle
liebre *nf* : hare
liendre *nf* : nit
lienzo *nm* **1** : linen **2** : canvas, painting **3** : stretch of wall or fencing
liga *nf* **1** ASOCIACIÓN : league **2** GOMITA : rubber band **3** : garter
ligado, -da *adj* : linked, connected
ligadura *nf* **1** ATADURA : tie, bond **2** : ligature
ligamento *nm* : ligament
ligar {52} *vt* : to bind, to tie (up)
ligeramente *adv* **1** : slightly **2** LEVEMENTE : lightly, gently **3** : casually, flippantly
ligereza *nf* **1** : lightness **2** : flippancy **3** : agility
ligero, -ra *adj* **1** : light, lightweight **2** : slight, minor **3** : agile, quick **4** : lighthearted, superficial
lignito *nm* : lignite

ligue, etc. → **ligar**
lija *nf or* **papel de lija** : sandpaper
lijar *vt* : to sand
lila[1] *adj* : lilac, light purple
lila[2] *nf* : lilac
lima *nf* **1** : lime (fruit) **2** : file ⟨lima de uñas : nail file⟩
limadora *nf* : polisher
limar *vt* **1** : to file **2** : to polish, to put the final touch on **3** : to smooth over ⟨limar las diferencias : to iron out differences⟩
limbo *nm* **1** : limbo **2** : limb (in botany and astronomy)
limeño[1], **-ña** *adj* : of or from Lima, Peru
limeño[2], **-ña** *n* : person from Lima, Peru
limero *nm* : lime tree
limitación *nf, pl* **-ciones** **1** : limitation **2** : limit, restriction ⟨sin limitación : unlimited⟩
limitado, **-da** *adj* **1** RESTRINGIDO : limited **2** : dull, slow-witted
limitar *vt* RESTRINGIR : to limit, to restrict — *vi* **~ con** : to border on — **limitarse** *vr* **~ a** : to limit oneself to
límite *nm* **1** : boundary, border **2** : limit ⟨el límite de mi paciencia : the limit of my patience⟩ ⟨límite de velocidad : speed limit⟩ **3 fecha límite** : deadline
limítrofe *adj* LINDANTE, LINDERO : bordering, adjoining
limo *nm* : slime, mud
limón *nm, pl* **limones** **1** : lemon **2** : lemon tree **3 limón verde** *Mex* : lime
limonada *nf* : lemonade
limosna *nf* : alms, charity
limosnear *vi* : to beg (for alms)
limosnero, **-ra** *n* MENDIGO : beggar
limoso, **-sa** *adj* : slimy
limpiabotas *nmfs & pl* : bootblack
limpiador[1], **-dora** *adj* : cleaning
limpiador[2], **-dora** *n* : cleaning person, cleaner
limpiamente *adv* : cleanly, honestly, fairly
limpiaparabrisas *nms & pl* : windshield wiper
limpiar *vt* **1** : to clean, to cleanse **2** : to clean up, to remove defects **3** *fam* : to clean out (in a game) **4** *fam* : to swipe, to pinch — *vi* : to clean — **limpiarse** *vr*
limpiavidrios *nmfs & pl Mex* : windshield wiper
límpido, **-da** *adj* : limpid
limpieza *nf* **1** : cleanliness, tidiness **2** : cleaning **3** HONRADEZ : integrity, honesty **4** DESTREZA : skill, dexterity
limpio[1] *adv* : fairly
limpio[2], **-pia** *adj* **1** : clean, neat **2** : honest ⟨un juego limpio : a fair game⟩ **3** : free ⟨limpio de impurezas : pure, free from impurities⟩ **4** : clear, net ⟨ganancia limpia : clear profit⟩
limusina *nf* : limousine
linaje *nm* ABOLENGO : lineage, ancestry
linaza *nf* : linseed
lince *nm* : lynx
linchamiento *nm* : lynching
linchar *vt* : to lynch
lindante *adj* LIMÍTROFE, LINDERO : bordering, adjoining
lindar *vi* **1 ~ con** : to border, to skirt **2 ~ con** BORDEAR : to border on, to verge on
linde *nmf* : boundary, limit
lindero[1], **-ra** *adj* LIMÍTROFE, LINDANTE : bordering, adjoining
lindero[2] *nm* : boundary, limit
lindeza *nf* **1** : prettiness **2** : clever remark **3 lindezas** *nfpl, (used ironically)* : insults
lindo[1] *adv* **1** : beautifully, wonderfully ⟨canta lindo tu mujer : your wife sings beautifully⟩ **2 de lo lindo** : a lot, a great deal ⟨los zancudos nos picaban de lo lindo : the mosquitoes were biting away at us⟩
lindo[2], **-da** *adj* **1** BONITO : pretty, lovely **2** MONO : cute
línea *nf* **1** : line ⟨línea divisoria : dividing line⟩ ⟨línea de banda : sideline⟩ **2** : line, course, position ⟨línea de conducta : course of action⟩ ⟨en líneas generales : in general terms, along general lines⟩ **3** : line, service ⟨línea aérea : airline⟩ ⟨línea telefónica : telephone line⟩
lineal *adj* : linear
linfa *nf* : lymph
linfático, **-ca** *adj* : lymphatic
lingote *nm* : ingot
lingüista *nmf* : linguist
lingüística *nf* : linguistics
lingüístico, **-ca** *adj* : linguistic
linimento *nm* : liniment
lino *nm* **1** : linen **2** : flax
linóleo *nm* : linoleum
linterna *nf* **1** : lantern **2** : flashlight
lío *nm fam* **1** : confusion, mess **2** : hassle, trouble, jam ⟨meterse en un lío : to get into a jam⟩ **3** : affair, liaison
liofilizar {21} *vt* : to freeze-dry
lioso, **-sa** *adj fam* **1** : confusing, muddled **2** : troublemaking
liquen *nm* : lichen
liquidación *nf, pl* **-ciones** **1** : liquidation **2** : clearance sale **3** : settlement, payment
liquidar *vt* **1** : to liquefy **2** : to liquidate **3** : to settle, to pay off **4** *fam* : to rub out, to kill
liquidez *nf, pl* **-deces** : liquidity
líquido[1], **-da** *adj* **1** : liquid, fluid **2** : net ⟨ingresos líquidos : net income⟩
líquido[2] *nm* **1** : liquid, fluid ⟨líquido de frenos : brake fluid⟩ **2** : ready cash, liquid assets
lira *nf* : lyre
lírica *nf* : lyric poetry
lírico, **-ca** *adj* : lyric, lyrical
lirio *nm* **1** : iris **2 lirio de los valles** MUGUETE : lily of the valley
lirismo *nm* : lyricism
lirón *nm, pl* **lirones** : dormouse
lisiado[1], **-da** *adj* : disabled, crippled

lisiado[2], **-da** *n* : disabled person, cripple

lisiar *vt* : to cripple, to disable — **lisiarse** *vr*

liso, -sa *adj* **1** : smooth **2** : flat **3** : straight ‹pelo liso : straight hair› **4** : plain, unadorned ‹liso y llano : plain and simple›

lisonja *nf* : flattery

lisonjear *vt* ADULAR : to flatter

lista *nf* **1** : list **2** : roster, roll ‹pasar lista : to take attendance› **3** : stripe, strip **4** : menu

listado[1], **-da** *adj* : striped

listado[2] *nm* : listing

listar *vt* : to list

listeza *nf* : smartness, alertness

listo, -ta *adj* **1** DISPUESTO, PREPARADO : ready ‹¿estás listo? : are you ready?› **2** : clever, smart

listón *nm, pl* **listones** **1** : ribbon **2** : strip (of wood), lath **3** : high bar (in sports)

lisura *nf* : smoothness

litera *nf* : bunk bed, berth

literal *adj* : literal — **literalmente** *adv*

literario, -ria *adj* : literary

literato, -ta *n* : writer, author

literatura *nf* : literature

litigante *adj & nmf* : litigant

litigar {52} *vi* : to litigate, to be in litigation

litigio *nm* **1** : litigation, lawsuit **2 en ~** : in dispute

litigioso, -sa *adj* : litigious

litio *nm* : lithium

litografía *nf* **1** : lithography **2** : lithograph

litógrafo, -fa *n* : lithographer

litoral[1] *adj* : coastal

litoral[2] *nm* : shore, seaboard

litosfera *nf* : lithosphere

litro *nm* : liter

lituano[1], **-na** *adj & n* : Lithuanian

lituano[2] *nm* : Lithuanian (language)

liturgia *nf* : liturgy

litúrgico, -ca *adj* : liturgical — **litúrgicamente** *adv*

liviandad *nf* LIGEREZA : lightness

liviano, -na *adj* **1** : light, slight **2** INCONSTANTE : fickle

lividez *nf* PALIDEZ : pallor

lívido, -da *adj* **1** AMORATADO : livid **2** PÁLIDO : pallid, extremely pale

living *nm* : living room

llaga *nf* : sore, wound

llama *nf* **1** : flame **2** : llama

llamada *nf* : call ‹llamada a larga distancia : long-distance call› ‹llamada al orden : call to order›

llamado[1], **-da** *adj* : named, called ‹una mujer llamada Rosa : a woman called Rosa›

llamado[2] → **llamamiento**

llamador *nm* : door knocker

llamamiento *nm* : call, appeal

llamar *vt* **1** : to name, to call **2** : to call, to summon **3** : to phone, to call up — **llamarse** *vr* : to be called, to be named ‹¿cómo te llamas? : what's your name?›

llamarada *nf* **1** : flare-up, sudden blaze **2** : flushing (of the face)

llamativo, -va *adj* : flashy, showy, striking

llameante *adj* : flaming, blazing

llamear *vi* : to flame, to blaze

llana *nf* **1** : trowel **2** → **llano**[2]

llanamente *adv* : simply, plainly, straightforwardly

llaneza *nf* : simplicity, naturalness

llano[1], **-na** *adj* **1** : even, flat **2** : frank, open **3** LISO : plain, simple

llano[2] *nm* : plain

llanta *nf* **1** NEUMÁTICO : tire **2** : rim

llantén *nm, pl* **llantenes** : plantain (weed)

llanto *nm* : crying, weeping

llanura *nf* : plain, prairie

llave *nf* **1** : key **2** : faucet **3** INTERRUPTOR : switch **4** : brace (punctuation mark) **5 llave inglesa** : monkey wrench

llavero *nm* : key chain, key ring

llegada *nf* : arrival

llegar {52} *vi* **1** : to arrive, to come **2 ~ a** : to arrive at, to reach, to amount to **3 ~ a** : to manage to ‹llegó a terminar la novela : she managed to finish the novel› **4 llegar a ser** : to become ‹llegó a ser un miembro permanente : he became a permanent member›

llegue, etc. → **llegar**

llenar *vt* **1** : to fill, to fill up, to fill in **2** : to meet, to fulfill ‹los regalos no llenaron sus expectativas : the gifts did not meet her expectations› — **llenarse** *vr* : to fill up, to become full

llenito, -ta *adj fam* REGORDETE : chubby, plump

lleno[1], **-na** *adj* **1** : full, filled **2 de ~** : completely, fully **3 estar lleno de sí mismo** : to be full of oneself

lleno[2] *nm* **1** *fam* : plenty, abundance **2** : full house, sellout

llevadero, -ra *adj* : bearable

llevar *vt* **1** : to take away, to carry ‹me gusta, me lo llevo : I like it, I'll take it› **2** : to wear **3** : to take, to lead ‹llevamos a Pedro al cine : we took Pedro to the movies› **4 llevar a cabo** : to carry out **5 llevar adelante** : to carry on, to keep going — *vi* : to lead ‹un problema lleva al otro : one problem leads to another› — *v aux* : to have ‹llevo mucho tiempo buscándolo : I've been looking for it for a long time› ‹lleva leído medio libro : he's halfway through the book› — **llevarse** *vr* **1** : to take away, to carry off **2** : to get along ‹siempre nos llevábamos bien : we always got along well›

llorar *vi* : to cry, to weep — *vt* : to mourn, to bewail

lloriquear *vi* : to whimper, to whine

lloriqueo *nm* : whimpering, whining

llorón, -rona *n, mpl* **llorones** : crybaby, whiner

lloroso, -sa *adj* : tearful, sad

llovedizo, -za *adj* : rain ⟨agua llovediza : rainwater⟩
llover {47} *v impers* : to rain ⟨está lloviendo : it's raining⟩ ⟨llover a cántaros : to rain cats and dogs⟩ — *vi* : to rain down, to shower ⟨le llovieron regalos : he was showered with gifts⟩
llovizna *nf* : drizzle, sprinkle
lloviznar *v impers* : to drizzle, to sprinkle
llueve, etc. → **llover**
lluvia *nf* **1** : rain, rainfall **2** : barrage, shower
lluvioso, -sa *adj* : rainy
lo[1] *pron* **1** : him, it ⟨lo vi ayer : I saw him yesterday⟩ ⟨lo entiendo : I understand it⟩ ⟨no lo creo : I don't believe so⟩ **2** (*formal, masculine*) : you ⟨disculpe, señor, no lo oí : excuse me sir, I didn't hear you⟩ **3 lo que** : what, that which ⟨eso es lo que más le gusta : that's what he likes the most⟩
lo[2] *art* **1** : the ⟨lo mejor : the best, the best thing⟩ **2** : how ⟨sé lo bueno que eres : I know how good you are⟩
loa *nf* : praise
loable *adj* : laudable, praiseworthy — **loablemente** *adv*
loar *vt* : to praise, to laud
lobato, -ta *n* : wolf cub
lobby *nm* : lobby, pressure group
lobo, -ba *n* : wolf
lóbrego, -ga *adj* SOMBRÍO : gloomy, dark
lobulado, -da *adj* : lobed
lóbulo *nm* : lobe ⟨lóbulo de la oreja : earlobe⟩
locación *nf, pl* **-ciones 1** : location (in moviemaking) **2** *Mex* : place
local[1] *adj* : local — **localmente** *adv*
local[2] *nm* : premises *pl*
localidad *nf* : town, locality
localización *nf, pl* **-ciones 1** : locating, localization **2** : location
localizar {21} *vt* **1** UBICAR : to locate, to find **2** : to localize — **localizarse** *vr* UBICARSE : to be located ⟨se localiza en el séptimo piso : it is located on the seventh floor⟩
locatario, -ria *n* : tenant
loción *nf, pl* **lociones** : lotion
lócker *nm, pl* **lóckers** : locker
loco[1], **-ca** *adj* **1** DEMENTE : crazy, insane, mad **2 a lo loco** : wildly, recklessly **3 volverse loco** : to go mad
loco[2], **-ca** *n* **1** : crazy person, lunatic **2 hacerse el loco** : to act the fool
locomoción *nf, pl* **-ciones** : locomotion
locomotor, -tora *adj* : locomotive
locomotora *nf* **1** : locomotive **2** : driving force
locuacidad *nf* : loquacity, talkativeness
locuaz *adj, pl* **locuaces** : loquacious, talkative
locución *nf, pl* **-ciones** : locution, phrase ⟨locución adverbial : adverbial phrase⟩
locura *nf* **1** : insanity, madness **2** : crazy thing, folly
locutor, -tora *n* : announcer
lodazal *nm* : bog, quagmire
lodo *nm* BARRO : mud, mire
lodoso, -sa *adj* : muddy
logaritmo *nm* : logarithm
logia *nf* : lodge ⟨logia masónica : Masonic lodge⟩
lógica *nf* : logic
lógico, -ca *adj* : logical — **lógicamente** *adv*
logística *nf* : logistics *pl*
logístico, -ca *adj* : logistic, logistical
logo → **logotipo**
logotipo *nm* : logo
logrado, -da *adj* : successful, well done
lograr *vt* **1** : to get, to obtain **2** : to achieve, to attain — **lograrse** *vr* : to be successful
logro *nm* : achievement, attainment
loma *nf* : hill, hillock
lombriz *nf, pl* **lombrices** : worm ⟨lombriz de tierra : earthworm, night crawler⟩ ⟨lombriz solitaria : tapeworm⟩ ⟨tener lombrices : to have worms⟩
lomo *nm* **1** : back (of an animal) **2** : loin ⟨lomo de cerdo : pork loin⟩ **3** : spine (of a book) **4** : blunt edge (of a knife)
lona *nf* : canvas
loncha *nf* LONJA, REBANADA : slice
lonche *nm* **1** ALMUERZO : lunch **2** *Mex* : submarine sandwich
lonchería *nf Mex* : luncheonette
londinense[1] *adj* : of or from London
londinense[2] *nmf* : Londoner
longaniza *nf* : spicy pork sausage
longevidad *nf* : longevity
longevo, -va *adj* : long-lived
longitud *nf* **1** LARGO : length ⟨longitud de onda : wavelength⟩ **2** : longitude
longitudinal *adj* : longitudinal
lonja *nf* LONCHA, REBANADA : slice
lontananza *nf* : background ⟨en lontananza : in the distance, far away⟩
lord *nm, pl* **lores** (*title in England*) : lord
loro *nm* : parrot
los[1], **las** *pron* **1** : them ⟨hice galletas y se las di a los nuevos vecinos : I made cookies and gave them to the new neighbors⟩ **2** : you ⟨voy a llevarlos a los dos : I am going to take both of you⟩ **3 los que, las que** : those, who, the ones ⟨los que van a cantar deben venir temprano : those who are singing must come early⟩ **4** (*used with* **haber**) ⟨los hay en varios colores : they come in various colors⟩
los[2] *art* → **el**[2]
losa *nf* : flagstone, paving stone
loseta *nf* BALDOSA : floor tile
lote *nm* **1** : part, share **2** : batch, lot **3** : plot of land, lot
lotería *nf* : lottery
loto *nm* : lotus
loza *nf* **1** : crockery, earthenware **2** : china
lozanía *nf* **1** : healthiness, robustness **2** : luxuriance, lushness

lozano, -na *adj* **1** : robust, healthy-looking ⟨un rostro lozano : a smooth, fresh face⟩ **2** : lush, luxuriant
LSD *nm* : LSD
lubricante[1] *adj* : lubricating
lubricante[2] *nm* : lubricant
lubricar {72} *vt* : to lubricate, to oil — **lubricación** *nf*
lucero *nm* : bright star ⟨lucero del alba : morning star⟩
lucha *nf* **1** : struggle, fight **2** : wrestling
luchador, -dora *n* **1** : fighter **2** : wrestler
luchar *vi* **1** : to fight, to struggle **2** : to wrestle
luchón, -chona *adj, mpl* **luchones** *Mex* : industrious, hardworking
lucidez *nf, pl* **-deces** : lucidity, clarity
lucido, -da *adj* MAGNÍFICO : magnificent, splendid
lúcido, -da *adj* : lucid
luciérnaga *nf* : firefly, glowworm
lucimiento *nm* **1** : brilliance, splendor, sparkle **2** : triumph, success ⟨salir con lucimiento : to succeed with flying colors⟩
lucio *nm* : pike (fish)
lucir {45} *vi* **1** : to shine **2** : to look good, to stand out **3** : to seem, to appear ⟨ahora luce contento : he looks happy now⟩ — *vt* **1** : to wear, to sport **2** : to flaunt, to show off — **lucirse** *vr* **1** : to distinguish oneself, to excel **2** : to show off
lucrarse *vr* : to make a profit
lucrativo, -va *adj* : lucrative, profitable — **lucrativamente** *adv*
lucro *nm* GANANCIA : profit, gain
luctuoso, -sa *adj* : mournful, tragic
luego[1] *adv* **1** DESPUÉS : then, afterwards **2** : later (on) **3 desde ~** : of course **4 ¡hasta luego!** : see you later! **5 luego que** : as soon as **6 luego luego** *Mex fam* : right away, immediately
luego[2] *conj* : therefore ⟨pienso, luego existo : I think, therefore I am⟩
lugar *nm* **1** : place, position ⟨se llevó el primer lugar en su división : she took first place in her division⟩ **2** ESPACIO : space, room **3 dar lugar a** : to give rise to, to lead to **4 en lugar de** : instead of **5 lugar común** : cliché, platitude **6 tener lugar** : to take place
lugareño[1], **-ña** *adj* : village, rural
lugareño[2], **-ña** *n* : villager
lugarteniente *nmf* : lieutenant, deputy
lúgubre *adj* : gloomy, lugubrious
lujo *nm* **1** : luxury **2 de ~** : deluxe
lujoso, -sa *adj* : luxurious
lujuria *nf* : lust, lechery
lujurioso, -sa *adj* : lustful, lecherous
lumbago *nm* : lumbago
lumbar *adj* : lumbar
lumbre *nf* **1** FUEGO : fire **2** : brilliance, splendor **3 poner en la lumbre** : to put on the stove, to warm up
lumbrera *nf* **1** : skylight **2** : vent, port **3** : brilliant person, luminary
luminaria *nf* **1** : altar lamp **2** LUMBRERA : luminary, celebrity
luminiscencia *nf* : luminescence — **luminiscente** *adj*
luminosidad *nf* : luminosity, brightness
luminoso, -sa *adj* : shining, luminous
luna *nf* **1** : moon **2 luna de miel** : honeymoon
lunar[1] *adj* : lunar
lunar[2] *nm* **1** : mole, beauty spot **2** : defect, blemish **3** : polka dot
lunático, -ca *adj & n* : lunatic
lunes *nms & pl* : Monday
luneta *nf* **1** : lens (of eyeglasses) **2** : windshield (of an automobile) **3** : crescent
lupa *nf* : magnifying glass
lúpulo *nm* : hops (plant)
lustrar *vt* : to shine, to polish
lustre *nm* **1** BRILLO : luster, shine **2** : glory, distinction
lustroso, -sa *adj* BRILLOSO : lustrous, shiny
luto *nm* : mourning ⟨estar de luto : to be in mourning⟩
luz *nf, pl* **luces** **1** : light **2** : lighting **3** *fam* : electricity **4** : window, opening **5** : light, lamp **6** : span, spread (between supports) **7 a la luz de** : in light of **8 dar a luz** : to give birth **9 traje de luces** : matador's costume
luzca, etc. → **lucir**

M

m *nf* : thirteenth letter of the Spanish alphabet
macabro, -bra *adj* : macabre
macaco[1], **-ca** *adj* : ugly, misshapen
macaco[2], **-ca** *n* : macaque
macadán *nm, pl* **-danes** : macadam
macana *nf* **1** : club, cudgel **2** *fam* : nonsense, silliness **3** *fam* : lie, fib
macanudo, -da *adj fam* : great, fantastic
macarrón *nm, pl* **-rrones** **1** : macaroon **2 macarrones** *nmpl* : macaroni
maceta *nf* **1** : flowerpot **2** : mallet **3** *Mex fam* : head
macetero *nm* **1** : plant stand **2** TIESTO : flowerpot, planter
machacar {72} *vt* **1** : to crush, to grind **2** : to beat, to pound — *vi* : to insist, to go on (about)
machacón, -cona *adj, mpl* **-cones** : insistent, tiresome
machete *nm* : machete
machetear *vt* : to hack with a machete — *vi Mex fam* : to plod, to work tirelessly
machismo *nm* **1** : machismo **2** : male chauvinism
machista *nm* : male chauvinist

macho[1] *adj* **1** : male **2** : macho, virile, tough

macho[2] *nm* **1** : male **2** : he-man

machote *nm* **1** *fam* : tough guy, he-man **2** *CA, Mex* : rough draft, model **3** *Mex* : blank form

machucar {72} *vt* **1** : to pound, to beat, to crush **2** : to bruise

machucón *nm, pl* **-cones** **1** MORETÓN : bruise **2** : smashing, pounding

macilento, -ta *adj* : gaunt, wan

macis *nm* : mace (spice)

macizo, -za *adj* **1** : solid ⟨oro macizo : solid gold⟩ **2** : strong, strapping **3** : massive

macrocosmo *nm* : macrocosm

mácula *nf* : blemish, stain

madeja *nf* **1** : skein, hank **2** : tangle (of hair)

madera *nf* **1** : wood **2** : lumber, timber **3 madera dura** *or* **madera noble** : hardwood

maderero, -ra *adj* : timber, lumber

madero *nm* : piece of lumber, plank

madrastra *nf* : stepmother

madrazo *nm Mex fam* : punch, blow ⟨se agarraron a madrazos : they beat each other up⟩

madre *nf* **1** : mother **2 madre política** : mother-in-law **3 la Madre Patria** : the mother country (said of Spain)

madrear *vt Mex fam* : to beat up

madreperla *nf* NÁCAR : mother-of-pearl

madreselva *nf* : honeysuckle

madriguera *nf* : burrow, den, lair

madrileño[1], **-ña** *adj* : of or from Madrid

madrileño[2], **-ña** *n* : person from Madrid

madrina *nf* **1** : godmother **2** : bridesmaid **3** : sponsor

madrugada *nf* **1** : early morning, wee hours **2** ALBA : dawn, daybreak

madrugador, -dora *n* : early riser

madrugar {52} *vi* **1** : to get up early **2** : to get a head start

madurar *v* **1** : to ripen **2** : to mature

madurez *nf, pl* **-reces** **1** : maturity **2** : ripeness

maduro, -ra *adj* **1** : mature **2** : ripe

maestría *nf* **1** : mastery, skill **2** : master's degree

maestro[1], **-tra** *adj* **1** : masterly, skilled **2** : chief, main **3** : trained ⟨un elefante maestro : a trained elephant⟩

maestro[2], **-tra** *n* **1** : teacher (in grammar school) **2** : expert, master **3** : maestro

Mafia *nf* : Mafia

mafioso, -sa *n* : mafioso, gangster

magdalena *nf* : bun, muffin

magenta *adj & n* : magenta

magia *nf* : magic

mágico, -ca *adj* : magic, magical — **mágicamente** *adv*

magisterio *nm* **1** : teaching **2** : teachers *pl,* teaching profession

magistrado, -da *n* : magistrate, judge

magistral *adj* **1** : masterful, skillful **2** : magisterial

magistralmente *adv* : masterfully, brilliantly

magistratura *nf* : judgeship, magistracy

magma *nm* : magma

magnanimidad *nf* : magnanimity

magnánimo, -ma *adj* GENEROSO : magnanimous — **magnánimamente** *adv*

magnate *nmf* : magnate, tycoon

magnesia *nf* : magnesia

magnesio *nm* : magnesium

magnético, -ca *adj* : magnetic

magnetismo *nm* : magnetism

magnetizar {21} *vt* : to magnetize

magnetófono *nm* : tape recorder

magnetofónico, -ca *adj* **cinta magnetofónica** : magnetic tape

magnificar {72} *vt* **1** : to magnify **2** EXAGERAR : to exaggerate **3** ENSALZAR : to exalt, to extol, to praise highly

magnificencia *nf* : magnificence, splendor

magnífico, -ca *adj* ESPLENDOROSO : magnificent, splendid — **magníficamente** *adv*

magnitud *nf* : magnitude

magnolia *nf* : magnolia (flower)

magnolio *nm* : magnolia (tree)

mago, -ga *n* **1** : magician **2** : wizard (in folk tales, etc.) **3 los Reyes Magos** : the Magi

magro, -gra *adj* **1** : lean (of meat) **2** : meager

maguey *nm* : maguey

magulladura *nf* MORETÓN : bruise

magullar *vt* : to bruise — **magullarse** *vr*

mahometano[1], **-na** *adj* ISLÁMICO : Islamic, Muslim

mahometano[2], **-na** *n* : Muslim

mahonesa → **mayonesa**

maicena *nf* : cornstarch

mainframe [ˈmein,freim] *nm* : mainframe

maíz *nm* : corn, maize

maizal *nm* : cornfield

maja *nf* : pestle

majadería *nf* **1** TONTERÍA : stupidity, foolishness **2** *Mex* LEPERADA : insult, obscenity

majadero[1], **-ra** *adj* **1** : foolish, silly **2** *Mex* LÉPERO : crude, vulgar

majadero[2], **-ra** *n* **1** TONTO : fool **2** *Mex* : rude person, boor

majar *vt* : to crush, to mash

majestad *nf* : majesty ⟨Su Majestad : Your Majesty⟩

majestuosamente *adv* : majestically

majestuosidad *nf* : majesty, grandeur

majestuoso, -sa *adj* : majestic, stately

majo, -ja *adj Spain* **1** : nice, likeable **2** GUAPO : attractive, good-looking

mal[1] *adv* **1** : badly, poorly ⟨baila muy mal : he dances very badly⟩ **2** : wrong, incorrectly ⟨me entendió mal : she misunderstood me⟩ **3** : with difficulty, hardly ⟨mal puedo oírte : I can hardly hear you⟩ **4 de mal en peor** : from bad to worse **5 menos mal** : it could have been worse

mal[2] *adj* → **malo**
mal[3] *nm* **1** : evil, wrong **2** DAÑO : harm, damage **3** DESGRACIA : misfortune **4** ENFERMEDAD : illness, sickness
malabar *adj* **juegos malabares** : juggling
malabarista *nmf* : juggler
malaconsejado, -da *adj* : ill-advised
malacostumbrado, -da *adj* CONSENTIDO : spoiled, pampered
malacostumbrar *vt* : to spoil
malagradecido, -da *adj* INGRATO : ungrateful
malaisio → **malasio**
malaquita *nf* : malachite
malaria *nf* PALUDISMO : malaria
malasio, -sia *adj & n* : Malaysian
malauiano, -na *adj & n* : Malawian
malaventura *nf* : misadventure, misfortune
malaventurado, -da *adj* MALHADADO : ill-fated, unfortunate
malayo, -ya *adj & n* : Malay, Malayan
malbaratar *vt* **1** MALGASTAR : to squander **2** : to undersell
malcriado[1], **-da** *adj* **1** : ill-bred, ill-mannered **2** : spoiled, pampered
malcriado[2], **-da** *n* : spoiled brat
maldad *nf* **1** : evil, wickedness **2** : evil deed
maldecir {11} *vt* : to curse, to damn — *vi* **1** : to curse, to swear **2 ~ de** : to speak ill of, to slander, to defame
maldición *nf, pl* **-ciones** : curse
maldiga, maldijo etc. → **maldecir**
maldito, -ta *adj* **1** : cursed, damned ⟨¡maldita sea! : damn it all!⟩ **2** : wicked
maldoso, -sa *adj Mex* : mischievous
maleable *adj* : malleable
maleante *nmf* : crook, thug
malecón *nm, pl* **-cones** : jetty, breakwater
maleducado, -da *adj* : ill-mannered, rude
maleficio *nm* : curse, hex
maléfico, -ca *adj* : evil, harmful
malentender {56} *vt* : to misunderstand
malentendido *nm* : misunderstanding
malestar *nm* **1** : discomfort **2** IRRITACIÓN : annoyance **3** INQUIETUD : uneasiness, unrest
maleta *nf* : suitcase, bag ⟨haz tus maletas : pack your bags⟩
maletero[1], **-ra** *n* : porter
maletero[2] *nm* : trunk (of an automobile)
maletín *nm, pl* **-tines 1** PORTAFOLIO : briefcase **2** : overnight bag, satchel
malevolencia *nf* : malevolence, wickedness
malévolo, -la *adj* : malevolent, wicked
maleza *nf* **1** : thicket, underbrush **2** : weeds *pl*
malformación *nf, pl* **-ciones** : malformation
malgache *adj & nmf* : Madagascan
malgastar *vt* : to squander (resources), to waste (time, effort)
malhablado, -da *adj* : foul-mouthed
malhadado, -da *adj* MALAVENTURADO : ill-fated
malhechor, -chora *n* : criminal, delinquent, wrongdoer
malherir {76} *vt* : to injure seriously
malhumor *nm* : bad mood, sullenness
malhumorado, -da *adj* : bad-tempered, cross
malicia *nf* **1** : wickedness, malice **2** : mischief, naughtiness **3** : cunning, craftiness
malicioso, -sa *adj* **1** : malicious **2** PÍCARO : mischievous
malignidad *nf* **1** : malignancy **2** MALDAD : evil
maligno, -na *adj* **1** : malignant ⟨un tumor maligno : a malignant tumor⟩ **2** : evil, harmful, malign
malinchismo *nm Mex* : preference for foreign goods or people — **malinchista** *adj*
malintencionado, -da *adj* : malicious, spiteful
malinterpretar *vt* : to misinterpret
malla *nf* **1** : mesh **2** LEOTARDO : leotard, tights *pl* **3 malla de baño** : bathing suit
mallorquín, -quina *adj & n* : Majorcan
malnutrición *nf, pl* **-ciones** DESNUTRICIÓN : malnutrition
malnutrido, -da *adj* DESNUTRIDO : malnourished, undernourished
malo[1], **-la** *adj* (**mal** *before masculine singular nouns*) **1** : bad ⟨mala suerte : bad luck⟩ **2** : wicked, naughty **3** : cheap, poor (quality) **4** : harmful ⟨malo para la salud : bad for one's health⟩ **5** (*using the form* **mal**) : unwell ⟨estar mal del corazón : to have heart trouble⟩ **6 estar de malas** : to be in a bad mood
malo[2], **-la** *n* : villain, bad guy (in novels, movies, etc.)
malogrado, -da *adj* : failed, unsuccessful
malograr *vt* **1** : to spoil, to ruin **2** : to waste (an opportunity, time) — **malograrse** *vr* **1** FRACASAR : to fail **2** : to die young
malogro *nm* **1** : untimely death **2** FRACASO : failure
maloliente *adj* HEDIONDO : foul-smelling, smelly
malparado, -da *adj* **salir malparado** *or* **quedar malparado** : to come out of (something) badly, to end up in a bad state
malpensado, -da *adj* : distrustful, suspicious, nasty-minded
malquerencia *nf* AVERSIÓN : ill will, dislike
malquerer {64} *vt* : to dislike
malquiso, etc. → **malquerer**
malsano, -na *adj* : unhealthy
malsonante *adj* : rude, offensive ⟨palabras malsonantes : foul language⟩
malta *nf* : malt
malteada *nf* : malted milk ⟨malteada de chocolate : chocolate malt⟩

maltés, **-tesa** *adj & n, mpl* **malteses** : Maltese
maltratar *vt* **1** : to mistreat, to abuse **2** : to damage, to spoil
maltrato *nm* : mistreatment, abuse
maltrecho, -cha *adj* : battered, damaged
malucho, -cha *adj fam* : sick, under the weather
malva *adj & nm* : mauve
malvado[1], **-da** *adj* : evil, wicked
malvado[2], **-da** *n* : evildoer, wicked person
malvavisco *nm* : marshmallow
malvender *vt* : to sell at a loss
malversación *nf, pl* **-ciones** : misappropriation (of funds), embezzlement
malversador, **-dora** *n* : embezzler
malversar *vt* : to embezzle
malvivir *vi* : to live badly, to just scrape by
mamá *nf fam* : mom, mama
mamar *vi* **1** : to suckle **2 darle de mamar a** : to breast-feed — *vt* **1** : to suckle, to nurse **2** : to learn from childhood, to grow up with — **mamarse** *vr fam* : to get drunk
mamario, **-ria** *adj* : mammary
mamarracho *nm fam* **1** ESPERPENTO : mess, sight **2** : laughingstock, fool **3** : rubbish, junk
mambo *nm* : mambo
mami *nf fam* : mommy
mamífero[1], **-ra** *adj* : mammalian
mamífero[2] *nm* : mammal
mamila *nf* **1** : nipple **2** *Mex* : baby bottle, pacifier
mamografía *nf* : mammogram
mamola *nf* : pat, chuck under the chin
mamotreto *nm fam* **1** : huge book, tome **2** ARMATOSTE : hulk, monstrosity
mampara *nf* BIOMBO : screen, room divider
mamparo *nm* : bulkhead
mampostería *nf* : masonry, stonemasonry
mampostero *nm* : mason, stonemason
mamut *nm, pl* **mamuts** : mammoth
maná *nm* : manna
manada *nf* **1** : flock, herd, pack **2** *fam* : horde, mob ⟨llegaron en manada : they came in droves⟩
manantial *nm* **1** FUENTE : spring **2** : source
manar *vi* **1** : to flow **2** : to abound
manatí *nm* : manatee
mancha *nf* **1** : stain, spot, mark ⟨mancha de sangre : bloodstain⟩ **2** : blemish, blot ⟨una mancha en su reputación : a blemish on his reputation⟩ **3** : patch
manchado, **-da** *adj* : stained
manchar *vt* **1** ENSUCIAR : to stain, to soil **2** DESHONRAR : to sully, to tarnish — **mancharse** *vr* : to get dirty
mancillar *vt* : to sully, to besmirch
manco, **-ca** *adj* : one-armed, one-handed
mancomunar *vt* : to combine, to pool — **mancomunarse** *vr* : to unite, to join together
mancomunidad *nf* **1** : commonwealth **2** : association, confederation
mancuernas *nfpl* : cuff links
mancuernillas *nf Mex* : cuff links
mandadero, **-ra** *n* : errand boy *m*, errand girl *f*, messenger
mandado *nm* **1** : order, command **2** : errand ⟨hacer los mandados : to run errands, to go shopping⟩
mandamás *nmf, pl* **-mases** *fam* : boss, bigwig, honcho
mandamiento *nm* **1** : commandment **2** : command, order, warrant ⟨mandamiento judicial : warrant, court order⟩
mandar *vt* **1** ORDENAR : to command, to order **2** ENVIAR : to send ⟨te manda saludos : he sends you his regards⟩ **3** ECHAR : to hurl, to throw **4 ¿mande?** *Mex* : yes?, pardon? — *vi* : to be the boss, to be in charge — **mandarse** *vr Mex* : to take liberties, to take advantage
mandarín *nm* : Mandarin
mandarina *nf* : mandarin orange, tangerine
mandatario, **-ria** *n* **1** : leader (in politics) ⟨primer mandatario : head of state⟩ **2** : agent (in law)
mandato *nm* **1** : term of office **2** : mandate
mandíbula *nf* **1** : jaw **2** : mandible
mandil *nm* **1** DELANTAL : apron **2** : horse blanket
mandilón *nm, pl* **-lones** *fam* : wimp, coward
mandioca *nf* **1** : manioc, cassava **2** : tapioca
mando *nm* **1** : command, leadership **2** : control (for a device) ⟨mando a distancia : remote control⟩ **3 al mando de** : in charge of **4 al mando de** : under the command of
mandolina *nf* : mandolin
mandón, **-dona** *adj, mpl* **mandones** : bossy, domineering
mandonear *vt fam* MANGONEAR : to boss around
mandrágora *nf* : mandrake
manecilla *nf* : hand (of a clock), pointer
manejable *adj* **1** : manageable **2** : docile, easily led
manejar *vt* **1** CONDUCIR : to drive (a car) **2** OPERAR : to handle, to operate **3** : to manage **4** : to manipulate (a person) — *vi* : to drive — **manejarse** *vr* **1** COMPORTARSE : to behave **2** : to get along, to manage
manejo *nm* **1** : handling, operation **2** : management
manera *nf* **1** MODO : way, manner, fashion **2 de cualquier manera** *or* **de todas maneras** : anyway, anyhow **3 de manera que** : so, in order that **4 de ninguna manera** : by no means, absolutely not **5 manera de ser** : personality, demeanor

manga *nf* **1** : sleeve **2** MANGUERA : hose
manganeso *nm* : manganese
mangle *nm* : mangrove
mango *nm* **1** : hilt, handle **2** : mango
mangonear *vt fam* : to boss around, to bully — *vi* **1** : to be bossy **2** : to loaf, to fool around
mangosta *nf* : mongoose
manguera *nf* : hose
manguito *nm* **1** : muff **2** : sleeve (of a pipe, etc.), hose (of a car)
maní *nm, pl* **maníes** : peanut
manía *nf* **1** OBSESIÓN : mania, obsession **2** : craze, fad **3** : odd habit, peculiarity **4** : dislike, aversion
maníaco¹, -ca *adj* : maniacal
maníaco², -ca *n* : maniac
maniatar *vt* : to tie the hands of, to manacle
maniático¹, -ca *adj* **1** MANÍACO : maniacal **2** : obsessive **3** : fussy, finicky
maniático², -ca *n* **1** MANÍACO : maniac, lunatic **2** : obsessive person, fanatic **3** : eccentric, crank
manicomio *nm* : insane asylum, madhouse
manicura *nf* : manicure
manicuro, -ra *n* : manicurist
manido, -da *adj* : hackneyed, stale, trite
manifestación *nf, pl* **-ciones** **1** : manifestation, sign **2** : demonstration, rally
manifestante *nmf* : demonstrator
manifestar {55} *vt* **1** : to demonstrate, to show **2** : to declare — **manifestarse** *vr* **1** : to be or become evident **2** : to state one's position ⟨se han manifestado a favor del acuerdo : they have declared their support for the agreement⟩ **3** : to demonstrate, to rally
manifiesto¹, -ta *adj* : manifest, evident, clear — **manifiestamente** *adv*
manifiesto² *nm* : manifesto
manija *nf* MANGO : handle
manilla → **manecilla**
manillar *nm* : handlebars *pl*
maniobra *nf* : maneuver, stratagem
maniobrar *v* : to maneuver
manipulación *nf, pl* **-ciones** : manipulation
manipulador¹, -dora *adj* : manipulating, manipulative
manipulador², -dora *n* : manipulator
manipular *vt* **1** : to manipulate **2** MANEJAR : to handle
maniquí¹ *nmf, pl* **-quíes** : mannequin, model
maniquí² *nm, pl* **-quíes** : mannequin, dummy
manirroto¹, -ta *adj* : extravagant
manirroto², -ta *n* : spendthrift
manivela *nf* : crank
manjar *nm* : delicacy, special dish
mano¹ *nf* **1** : hand **2** : coat (of paint or varnish) **3 a ~** : by hand **4 a ~** *or* **a la mano** : handy, at hand, nearby **5 darse la mano** : to shake hands **6 de la mano** : hand in hand ⟨la política y la economía van de la mano : politics and economics go hand in hand⟩ **7 de primera mano** : firsthand, at firsthand **8 de segunda mano** : secondhand ⟨ropa de segunda mano : secondhand clothing⟩ **9 mano a mano** : one-on-one **10 mano de obra** : labor, manpower **11 mano de mortero** : pestle **12 echar una mano** : to lend a hand **13 mano negra** *Mex fam* : shady dealings *pl*
mano², -na *n Mex fam* : buddy, pal ⟨¡oye, mano! : hey man!⟩
manojo *nm* PUÑADO : handful, bunch
manopla *nf* **1** : mitten, mitt **2** : brass knuckles *pl*
manosear *vt* **1** : to handle or touch excessively **2** ACARICIAR : to fondle, to caress
manotazo *nm* : slap, smack, swipe
manotear *vi* : to wave one's hands, to gesticulate
mansalva *adv* **a ~** : at close range
mansarda *nf* BUHARDILLA : attic
mansedumbre *nf* **1** : gentleness, meekness **2** : tameness
mansión *nf, pl* **-siones** : mansion
manso, -sa *adj* **1** : gentle, meek **2** : tame — **mansamente** *adv*
manta *nf* **1** COBIJA, FRAZADA : blanket **2** : poncho **3** *Mex* : coarse cotton fabric
manteca *nf* **1** GRASA : lard, fat **2** : butter
mantecoso, -sa *adj* : buttery
mantel *nm* **1** : tablecloth **2** : altar cloth
mantelería *nf* : table linen
mantener {80} *vt* **1** SUSTENTAR : to support, to feed ⟨mantener uno su familia : to support one's family⟩ **2** CONSERVAR : to keep, to preserve **3** CONTINUAR : to keep up, to sustain ⟨mantener una correspondencia : to keep up a correspondence⟩ **4** AFIRMAR : to maintain, to affirm — **mantenerse** *vr* **1** : to support oneself, to subsist **2** **mantenerse firme** : to hold one's ground
mantenimiento *nm* **1** : maintenance, upkeep **2** : sustenance, food **3** : preservation
mantequera *nf* **1** : churn **2** : butter dish
mantequería *nf* **1** : creamery, dairy **2** : grocery store
mantequilla *nf* : butter
mantilla *nf* : mantilla
mantis *nf* **mantis religiosa** : praying mantis
manto *nm* **1** : cloak **2** : mantle (in geology)
mantón *nm, pl* **-tones** CHAL : shawl
mantuvo, etc. → **mantener**
manual¹ *adj* **1** : manual ⟨trabajo manual : manual labor⟩ **2** : handy, manageable — **manualmente** *adv*
manual² *nm* : manual, handbook
manualidades *nfpl* : handicrafts (in schools)
manubrio *nm* **1** : handle, crank **2** : handlebars *pl*

manufactura *nf* **1** FABRICACIÓN : manufacture **2** : manufactured item, product **3** FÁBRICA : factory
manufacturar *vt* FABRICAR : to manufacture
manufacturero[1], **-ra** *adj* : manufacturing
manufacturero[2], **-ra** *n* FABRICANTE : manufacturer
manuscrito[1], **-ta** *adj* : handwritten
manuscrito[2] *nm* : manuscript
manutención *nf, pl* **-ciones** : maintenance, support
manzana *nf* **1** : apple **2** CUADRA : block (enclosed by streets or buildings) **3** *or* **manzana de Adán** : Adam's apple
manzanal *nm* **1** : apple orchard **2** MANZANO : apple tree
manzanar *nm* : apple orchard
manzanilla *nf* **1** : chamomile **2** : chamomile tea
manzano *nm* : apple tree
maña *nf* **1** : dexterity, skill **2** : cunning, guile **3 mañas** *or* **malas mañas** *nfpl* : bad habits, vices
mañana *nf* **1** : morning **2** : tomorrow
mañanero, -ra *adj* MATUTINO : morning ⟨rocío mañanero : morning dew⟩
mañanitas *nfpl Mex* : birthday serenade
mañoso, -sa *adj* **1** HÁBIL : skillful **2** ASTUTO : cunning, crafty **3** : fussy, finicky
mapa *nm* CARTA : map
mapache *nm* : raccoon
mapamundi *nm* : map of the world
maqueta *nf* : model, mock-up
maquillador, -dora *n* : makeup artist
maquillaje *nm* : makeup
maquillarse *vr* : to put on makeup, to make oneself up
máquina *nf* **1** : machine ⟨máquina de coser : sewing machine⟩ ⟨máquina de escribir : typewriter⟩ **2** LOCOMOTORA : engine, locomotive **3** : machine (in politics) **4 a toda máquina** : at full speed
maquinación *nf, pl* **-ciones** : machination, scheme, plot
maquinal *adj* : mechanical, automatic — **maquinalmente** *adv*
maquinar *vt* : to plot, to scheme
maquinaria *nf* **1** : machinery **2** : mechanism, works *pl*
maquinilla *nf* **1** : small machine or device **2** *CA, Car* : typewriter
maquinista *nmf* **1** : machinist **2** : railroad engineer
mar *nmf* **1** : sea ⟨un mar agitado : a rough sea⟩ ⟨hacerse a la mar : to set sail⟩ **2 alta mar** : high seas
maraca *nf* : maraca
maraña *nf* **1** : thicket **2** ENREDO : tangle, mess
marasmo *nm* : paralysis, stagnation
maratón *nm, pl* **-tones** : marathon
maravilla *nf* **1** : wonder, marvel ⟨a las mil maravillas : wonderfully, marvelously⟩ ⟨hacer maravillas : to work wonders⟩ **2** : marigold
maravillar *vt* ASOMBRAR : to astonish, to amaze — **maravillarse** *vr* : to be amazed, to marvel
maravilloso, -sa *adj* ESTUPENDO : wonderful, marvelous — **maravillosamente** *adv*
marbete *nm* **1** ETIQUETA : label, tag **2** *PRi* : registration sticker (of a car)
marca *nf* **1** : mark **2** : brand, make **3** : trademark ⟨marca registrada : registered trademark⟩ **4** : record (in sports) ⟨batir la marca : to beat the record⟩
marcado, -da *adj* : marked ⟨un marcado contraste : a marked contrast⟩
marcador *nm* **1** TANTEADOR : scoreboard **2** : marker, felt-tipped pen **3 marcador de libros** : bookmark
marcaje *nm* **1** : scoring (in sports) **2** : guarding (in sports)
marcapasos *nms & pl* : pacemaker
marcar {72} *vt* **1** : to mark **2** : to brand (livestock) **3** : to indicate, to show **4** RESALTAR : to emphasize **5** : to dial (a telephone) **6** : to guard (an opponent) **7** ANOTAR : to score (a goal, a point) — *vi* **1** ANOTAR : to score **2** : to dial
marcha *nf* **1** : march **2** : hike, walk ⟨ir de marcha : to go hiking⟩ **3** : pace, speed ⟨a toda marcha : at top speed⟩ **4** : gear (of an automobile) ⟨marcha atrás : reverse, reverse gear⟩ **5 en ~** : in motion, in gear, under way
marchar *vi* **1** IR : to go, to travel **2** ANDAR : to walk **3** FUNCIONAR : to work, to go **4** : to march — **marcharse** *vr* : to leave
marchitar *vi* : to make wither, to wilt — **marchitarse** *vr* **1** : to wither, to shrivel up, to wilt **2** : to languish, to fade away
marchito, -ta *adj* : withered, faded
marcial *adj* : martial, military
marco *nm* **1** : frame, framework **2** : goalposts *pl* **3** AMBIENTE : setting, atmosphere **4** : mark (unit of currency)
marea *nf* : tide
mareado, -da *adj* **1** : dizzy, lightheaded **2** : queasy, nauseous **3** : seasick
marear *vt* **1** : to make sick ⟨los gases me marearon : the fumes made me sick⟩ **2** : to bother, to annoy — **marearse** *vr* **1** : to get sick, to become nauseated **2** : to feel dizzy **3** : to get tipsy
marejada *nf* **1** : surge, swell (of the sea) **2** : undercurrent, ferment, unrest
maremoto *nm* : tidal wave
mareo *nm* **1** : dizzy spell **2** : nausea **3** : seasickness, motion sickness **4** : annoyance, vexation
marfil *nm* : ivory
margarina *nf* : margarine
margarita *nf* **1** : daisy **2** : margarita (cocktail)
margen[1] *nf, pl* **márgenes** : bank (of a river), side (of a street)

margen[2] *nm, pl* **márgenes** **1** : edge, border **2** : margin ⟨margen de ganancia : profit margin⟩
marginación *nf, pl* **-ciones** : marginalization, exclusion
marginado[1], **-da** *adj* **1** DESHEREDADO : outcast, alienated, dispossessed **2** **clases marginadas** : underclass
marginado[2], **-da** *n* : outcast, misfit
marginal *adj* : marginal, fringe
marginalidad *nf* : marginality
marginar *vt* : to ostracize, to exclude
mariachi *nm* : mariachi musician or band
maridaje *nm* : marriage, union
maridar *vt* UNIR : to marry, to unite
marido *nm* ESPOSO : husband
marihuana *or* **mariguana** *or* **marijuana** *nf* : marihuana
marimacho *nmf fam* **1** : mannish woman **2** : tomboy
marimba *nf* : marimba
marina *nf* **1** : coast, coastal area **2** : navy, fleet ⟨marina mercante : merchant marine⟩
marinada *nf* : marinade
marinar *vt* : to marinate
marinero[1], **-ra** *adj* **1** : seaworthy **2** : sea, marine
marinero[2] *nm* : sailor
marino[1], **-na** *adj* : marine, sea
marino[2] *nm* : sailor, seaman
marioneta *nf* TÍTERE : puppet, marionette
mariposa *nf* **1** : butterfly **2** **mariposa nocturna** : moth
mariquita[1] *nf* : ladybug
mariquita[2] *nm fam* : sissy, wimp
mariscal *nm* **1** : marshal **2** **mariscal de campo** : field marshal (in the military), quarterback (in football)
marisco *nm* **1** : shellfish **2** **mariscos** *nmpl* : seafood
marisma *nf* : marsh, salt marsh
marital *adj* : marital, married ⟨la vida marital : married life⟩
marítimo, -ma *adj* : maritime, shipping ⟨la industria marítima : the shipping industry⟩
marmita *nf* : (cooking) pot
mármol *nm* : marble
marmóreo, -rea *adj* : marble, marmoreal
marmota *nf* **1** : marmot **2** **marmota de América** : woodchuck, groundhog
maroma *nf* **1** : rope **2** : acrobatic stunt **3** *Mex* : somersault
marque, etc. → **marcar**
marqués, -quesa *n, mpl* **marqueses** : marquis *m,* marquess *m,* marquise *f,* marchioness *f*
marquesina *nf* : marquee, canopy
marqueta *nf Mex* : block (of chocolate), lump (of sugar or salt)
marranada *nf* **1** : disgusting thing **2** : dirty trick
marrano[1], **-na** *adj* : filthy, disgusting
marrano[2], **-na** *n* **1** CERDO : pig, hog **2** : dirty pig, slob
marrar *vt* : to miss (a target) — *vi* : to fail, to go wrong
marras *adv* **1** : long ago **2** **de ~** : said, aforementioned ⟨el individuo de marras : the individual in question⟩
marrasquino *nm* : maraschino
marrón *adj & nm, pl* **marrones** CASTAÑO : brown
marroquí *adj & nmf, pl* **-quíes** : Moroccan
marsopa *nf* : porpoise
marsupial *nm* : marsupial
marta *nf* **1** : marten **2** **marta cebellina** : sable (animal)
Marte *nm* : Mars
martes *nms & pl* : Tuesday
martillar *v* : to hammer
martillazo *nm* : blow with a hammer
martillo *nm* **1** : hammer **2** **martillo neumático** : jackhammer
martinete *nm* **1** : heron **2** : pile driver
mártir *nmf* : martyr
martirio *nm* **1** : martyrdom **2** : ordeal, torment
martirizar {21} *vt* **1** : to martyr **2** ATORMENTAR : to torment
marxismo *nm* : Marxism
marxista *adj & nmf* : Marxist
marzo *nm* : March
mas *conj* PERO : but
más[1] *adv* **1** : more ⟨¿hay algo más grande? : is there anything bigger?⟩ **2** : most ⟨Luis es el más alto : Luis is the tallest⟩ **3** : longer ⟨el sabor dura más : the flavor lasts longer⟩ **4** : rather ⟨más querría andar : I would rather walk⟩ **5** **a ~** : besides, in addition **6** **más allá** : further **7** **qué . . . más . . .** : what . . ., what a . . . ⟨¡qué día más bonito! : what a beautiful day!⟩
más[2] *adj* **1** : more ⟨dáme dos kilos más : give me two more kilos⟩ **2** : most ⟨la que ganó más dinero : the one who earned the most money⟩ **3** : else ⟨¿quién más quiere vino? : who else wants wine?⟩
más[3] *n* : plus sign
más[4] *prep* : plus ⟨tres más dos es igual a cinco : three plus two equals five⟩
más[5] *pron* **1** : more ⟨¿tienes más? : do you have more?⟩ **2** **a lo más** : at most **3** **de ~** : extra, excess **4** **más o menos** : more or less, approximately **5** **por más que** : no matter how much ⟨por más que corras no llegarás a tiempo : no matter how fast you run you won't arrive on time⟩
masa *nf* **1** : mass, volume ⟨masa atómica : atomic mass⟩ ⟨producción en masa : mass production⟩ **2** : dough, batter **3** **masas** *nfpl* : people, masses ⟨las masas populares : the common people⟩ **4** **masa harina** *Mex* : corn flour (for tortillas, etc.)
masacrar *vt* : to massacre
masacre *nf* : massacre
masaje *nm* : massage
masajear *vt* : to massage

masajista *nmf* : masseur *m,* masseuse *f*
mascar {72} *v* MASTICAR : to chew
máscara *nf* **1** CARETA : mask **2** : appearance, pretense **3 máscara antigás** : gas mask
mascarada *nf* : masquerade
mascarilla *nf* **1** : mask (in medicine) ⟨mascarilla de oxígeno : oxygen mask⟩ **2** : facial mask (in cosmetology)
mascota *nf* : mascot
masculinidad *nf* : masculinity
masculino, -na *adj* **1** : masculine, male **2** : manly **3** : masculine (in grammar)
mascullar *v* : to mumble, to mutter
masificado, -da *adj* : overcrowded
masilla *nf* : putty
masivamente *adv* : en masse
masivo, -va *adj* : mass ⟨comunicación masiva : mass communication⟩
masón *nm, pl* **masones** FRANCMASÓN : Mason, Freemason
masonería *nf* FRANCMASONERÍA : Masonry, Freemasonry
masónico, -ca *adj* : Masonic
masoquismo *nm* : masochism
masoquista[1] *adj* : masochistic
masoquista[2] *nmf* : masochist
masque, etc. → **mascar**
masticar {72} *v* MASCAR : to chew, to masticate
mástil *nm* **1** : mast **2** ASTA : flagpole **3** : neck (of a stringed instrument)
mastín *nm, pl* **mastines** : mastiff
mástique *nm* : putty, filler
mastodonte *nm* : mastodon
masturbación *nf, pl* **-ciones** : masturbation
masturbarse *vr* : to masturbate
mata *nf* **1** ARBUSTO : bush, shrub **2** : plant ⟨mata de tomate : tomato plant⟩ **3** : sprig, tuft **4 mata de pelo** : mop of hair
matadero *nm* : slaughterhouse, abattoir
matado, -da *adj Mex* : strenuous, exhausting
matador *nm* TORERO : matador, bullfighter
matamoscas *nms & pl* : flyswatter
matanza *nf* MASACRE : slaughter, butchering
matar *vt* **1** : to kill **2** : to slaughter, to butcher **3** APAGAR : to extinguish, to put out (fire, light) **4** : to tone down (colors) **5** : to pass, to waste (time) **6** : to trump (in card games) — *vi* : to kill — **matarse** *vr* **1** : to be killed **2** SUICIDARSE : to commit suicide **3** *fam* : to exhaust oneself ⟨se mató tratando de terminarlo : he knocked himself out trying to finish it⟩
matasanos *nms & pl fam* : quack
matasellar *vt* : to cancel (a stamp), to postmark
matasellos *nms & pl* : postmark
matatena *nf Mex* : jacks
mate[1] *adj* : matte, dull
mate[2] *nm* **1** : maté **2 jaque mate** : checkmate ⟨darle mate a *or* darle jaque mate a : to checkmate⟩
matemática → **matemáticas**
matemáticas *nfpl* : mathematics, math
matemático[1], **-ca** *adj* : mathematical — **matemáticamente** *adv*
matemático[2], **-ca** *n* : mathematician
materia *nf* **1** : matter ⟨materia gris : gray matter⟩ **2** : material ⟨materia prima : raw material⟩ **3** : (academic) subject **4 en materia de** : on the subject of, concerning
material[1] *adj* **1** : material, physical, real **2 daños materiales** : property damage
material[2] *nm* **1** : material ⟨material de construcción : building material⟩ **2** EQUIPO : equipment, gear
materialismo *nm* : materialism
materialista[1] *adj* : materialistic
materialista[2] *nmf* **1** : materialist **2** *Mex* : truck driver
materializar {21} *vt* : to bring to fruition, to realize — **materializarse** *vr* : to materialize, to come into being
materialmente *adv* **1** : materially, physically ⟨materialmente imposible : physically impossible⟩ **2** : really, absolutely
maternal *adj* : maternal, motherly
maternidad *nf* **1** : maternity, motherhood **2** : maternity hospital, maternity ward
materno, -na *adj* : maternal
matinal *adj* MATUTINO : morning ⟨la pálida luz matinal : the pale morning light⟩
matinée *or* **matiné** *nf* : matinee
matiz *nm, pl* **matices** **1** : hue, shade **2** : nuance
matización *nf, pl* **-ciones** **1** : tinting, toning, shading **2** : clarification (of a statement)
matizar {21} *vt* **1** : to tinge, to tint (colors) **2** : to vary, to modulate (sounds) **3** : to qualify (statements)
matón *nm, pl* **matones** : thug, bully
matorral *nm* **1** : thicket **2** : scrub, scrubland
matraca *nf* **1** : rattle, noisemaker **2 dar la matraca a** : to pester, to nag
matriarca *nf* : matriarch
matriarcado *nm* : matriarchy
matrícula *nf* **1** : list, roll, register **2** INSCRIPCIÓN : registration, enrollment **3** : license plate, registration number
matriculación *nf, pl* **-ciones** : matriculation, registration
matricular *vt* **1** INSCRIBIR : to enroll, to register (a person) **2** : to register (a vehicle) — **matricularse** *vr* : to matriculate
matrimonial *adj* : marital, matrimonial ⟨la vida matrimonial : married life⟩
matrimonio *nm* **1** : marriage, matrimony **2** : married couple
matriz *nf, pl* **matrices** **1** : uterus, womb **2** : original, master copy **3** : main office, headquarters **4** : stub (of a check) **5** : matrix ⟨matriz de puntos : dot matrix⟩

matrona *nf* : matron
matronal *adj* : matronly
matutino[1], **-na** *adj* : morning ⟨la edición matutina : the morning edition⟩
matutino[2] *nm* : morning paper
maullar {8} *vi* : to meow
maullido *nm* : meow
mauritano, -na *adj & n* : Mauritanian
mausoleo *nm* : mausoleum
maxilar *nm* : jaw, jawbone
máxima *nf* : maxim
máxime *adv* ESPECIALMENTE : especially, principally
maximizar {21} *vt* : to maximize
máximo[1], **-ma** *adj* : maximum, greatest, highest
máximo[2] *nm* **1** : maximum **2 al máximo** : to the utmost **3 como ~** : at the most, at the latest
maya[1] *adj & nmf* : Mayan
maya[2] *nmf* : Maya, Mayan
mayo *nm* : May
mayonesa *nf* : mayonnaise
mayor[1] *adj* **1** (*comparative of* **grande**) : bigger, larger, greater, elder, older **2** (*superlative of* **grande**) : biggest, largest, greatest, eldest, oldest **3** : grown-up, mature **4** : main, major **5 mayor de edad** : of (legal) age **6 al por mayor** *or* **por ~** : wholesale
mayor[2] *nmf* **1** : major (in the military) **2** : adult
mayoral *nm* CAPATAZ : foreman, overseer
mayordomo *nm* : butler, majordomo
mayoreo *nm* : wholesale
mayores *nmpl* : grown-ups, elders
mayoría *nf* **1** : majority **2 en su mayoría** : on the whole
mayorista[1] *adj* ALMACENISTA : wholesale
mayorista[2] *nmf* : wholesaler
mayoritariamente *adv* : primarily, chiefly
mayoritario, -ria *adj & n* : majority ⟨un consenso mayoritario : a majority consensus⟩
mayormente *adv* : primarily, chiefly
mayúscula *nf* : capital letter
mayúsculo, -la *adj* **1** : capital, uppercase **2** : huge, terrible ⟨un problema mayúsculo : a huge problem⟩
maza *nf* **1** : mace (weapon) **2** : drumstick **3** *fam* : bore, pest
mazacote *nm* **1** : concrete **2** : lumpy mess (of food) **3** : eyesore, crude work of art
mazapán *nm, pl* **-panes** : marzipan
mazmorra *nf* CALABOZO : dungeon
mazo *nm* **1** : mallet **2** : pestle **3** MANOJO : handful, bunch
mazorca *nf* **1** CHOCLO : cob, ear of corn **2 pelar la mazorca** *Mex fam* : to smile from ear to ear
me *pron* **1** : me ⟨me vieron : they saw me⟩ **2** : to me, for me, from me ⟨dame el libro : give me the book⟩ ⟨me lo compró : he bought it for me⟩ ⟨me robaron la cartera : they stole my pocketbook⟩ **3** : myself, to myself, for myself, from myself ⟨me preparé una buena comida : I cooked myself a good dinner⟩ ⟨me equivoqué : I made a mistake⟩
mecánica *nf* : mechanics
mecánico[1], **-ca** *adj* : mechanical — **mecánicamente** *adv*
mecánico[2], **-ca** *n* **1** : mechanic **2** : technician ⟨mecánico dental : dental technician⟩
mecanismo *nm* : mechanism
mecanización *nf, pl* **-ciones** : mechanization
mecanizar {21} *vt* : to mechanize
mecanografía *nf* : typing
mecanografiar {85} *vt* : to type
mecanógrafo, -fa *n* : typist
mecate *nm CA, Mex, Ven* : rope, twine, cord
mecedor *nm* : glider (seat)
mecedora *nf* : rocking chair
mecenas *nmfs & pl* : patron (of the arts), sponsor
mecenazgo *nm* PATROCINIO : sponsorship, patronage
mecer {86} *vt* **1** : to rock **2** COLUMPIAR : to push (on a swing) — **mecerse** *vr* : to rock, to swing, to sway
mecha *nf* **1** : fuse **2** : wick **3 mechas** *nfpl* : highlights (in hair)
mechero *nm* **1** : burner **2** *Spain* : lighter
mechón *nm, pl* **mechones** : lock (of hair)
medalla *nf* : medal, medallion
medallista *nmf* : medalist
medallón *nm, pl* **-llones** **1** : medallion **2** : locket
media *nf* **1** CALCETÍN : sock **2** : average, mean **3 medias** *nfpl* : stockings, hose, tights **4 a medias** : by halves, half and half, halfway ⟨ir a medias : to go halves⟩ ⟨verdad a medias : half-truth⟩
mediación *nf, pl* **-ciones** : mediation
mediado, -da *adj* **1** : half full, half empty, half over **2** : halfway through ⟨mediada la tarea : halfway through the job⟩
mediador, -dora *n* : mediator
mediados *nmpl* **a mediados de** : halfway through, in the middle of ⟨a mediados del mes : towards the middle of the month, mid-month⟩
medialuna *nf* **1** : crescent **2** : croissant, crescent roll
medianamente *adv* : fairly, moderately
medianero, -ra *adj* **1** : dividing **2** : mediating
medianía *nf* **1** : middle position **2** : mediocre person, mediocrity
mediano, -na *adj* **1** : medium, average ⟨la mediana edad : middle age⟩ **2** : mediocre
medianoche *nf* : midnight
mediante *prep* : through, by means of ⟨Dios mediante : God willing⟩
mediar *vi* **1** : to mediate **2** : to be in the middle, to be halfway through **3** : to elapse, to pass ⟨mediaron cinco años entre el inicio de la guerra y el armisti-

cio : five years passed between the start of the war and the armistice⟩ **4** : to be a consideration ⟨media el hecho de que cuesta mucho : one must take into account that it is costly⟩ **5** : to come up, to happen ⟨medió algo urgente : something pressing came up⟩

mediatizar {21} *vt* : to influence, to interfere with

medicación *nf, pl* **-ciones** : medication, treatment

medicamento *nm* : medication, medicine, drug

medicar {72} *vt* : to medicate — **medicarse** *vr* : to take medicine

medicina *nf* : medicine

medicinal *adj* **1** : medicinal **2** : medicated

medicinar *vt* : to give medication to, to dose

medición *nf, pl* **-ciones** : measuring, measurement

médico[1], **-ca** *adj* : medical ⟨una receta médica : a doctor's prescription⟩

médico[2], **-ca** *n* DOCTOR : doctor, physician

medida *nf* **1** : measurement, measure ⟨hecho a medida : custom-made⟩ **2** : measure, step ⟨tomar medidas : to take steps⟩ **3** : moderation, prudence ⟨sin medida : immoderately⟩ **4** : extent, degree ⟨en gran medida : to a great extent⟩

medidor *nm* : meter, gauge

medieval *adj* : medieval — **medievalista** *nmf*

medievo → **medioevo**

medio[1] *adv* **1** : half ⟨está medio dormida : she's half asleep⟩ **2** : rather, kind of ⟨está medio aburrida esta fiesta : this party is rather boring⟩

medio[2], **-dia** *adj* **1** : half ⟨una media hora : half an hour⟩ ⟨medio hermano : half brother⟩ ⟨a media luz : in the half-light⟩ ⟨son las tres y media : it's half past three, it's three-thirty⟩ **2** : midway, halfway ⟨a medio camino : halfway there⟩ **3** : middle ⟨la clase media : the middle class⟩ **4** : average ⟨la temperatura media : the average temperature⟩

medio[3] *nm* **1** CENTRO : middle, center ⟨en medio de : in the middle of, amid⟩ **2** AMBIENTE : milieu, environment **3** : medium, spiritualist **4** : means *pl*, way ⟨por medio de : by means of⟩ ⟨los medios de comunicación : the media⟩ **5 medios** *nmpl* : means, resources

mediocampista *nmf* : midfielder

mediocre *adj* : mediocre, average

mediocridad *nf* : mediocrity

mediodía *nm* : noon, midday

medioevo *nm* : Middle Ages

medir {54} *vt* **1** : to measure **2** : to weigh, to consider ⟨medir los riesgos : to weigh the risks⟩ — *vi* : to measure — **medirse** *vr* : to be moderate, to exercise restraint

meditabundo, **-da** *adj* PENSATIVO : pensive, thoughtful

meditación *nf, pl* **-ciones** : meditation, thought

meditar *vi* : to meditate, to think ⟨meditar sobre la vida : to contemplate life⟩ — *vt* **1** : to think over, to consider **2** : to plan, to work out

meditativo, **-va** *adj* : pensive

mediterráneo, **-nea** *adj* : Mediterranean

medrar *vi* **1** PROSPERAR : to prosper, to thrive **2** AUMENTAR : to increase, to grow

medro *nm* PROSPERIDAD : prosperity, growth

medroso, **-sa** *adj* : fainthearted, fearful

médula *nf* **1** : marrow, pith **2 médula espinal** : spinal cord

medular *adj* : fundamental, core ⟨el punto medular : the crux of the matter⟩

medusa *nf* : jellyfish, medusa

megabyte *nm* : megabyte

megáfono *nm* : megaphone

megahercio *nm* : megahertz

megahertzio *nm* : megahertz

megatón *nm, pl* **-tones** : megaton

megavatio *nm* : megawatt

mejicano → **mexicano**

mejilla *nf* : cheek

mejillón *nm, pl* **-llones** : mussel

mejor[1] *adv* **1** : better ⟨Carla cocina mejor que Ana : Carla cooks better than Ann⟩ **2** : best ⟨ella es la que lo hace mejor : she's the one who does it best⟩ **3** : rather ⟨mejor morir que rendirme : I'd rather die than give up⟩ **4** : it's better that . . . ⟨mejor te vas : you'd better go⟩ **5 a lo mejor** : maybe, perhaps

mejor[2] *adj* **1** (*comparative of* **bueno**) : better ⟨a falta de algo mejor : for lack of something better⟩ **2** (*comparative of* **bien**) : better ⟨está mucho mejor : he's much better⟩ **3** (*superlative of* **bueno**) : best, the better ⟨mi mejor amigo : my best friend⟩ **4** (*superlative of* **bien**) : best, the better ⟨duermo mejor en un clima seco : I sleep best in a dry climate⟩ **5** PREFERIBLE : preferable, better **6 lo mejor** : the best thing, the best part

mejor[3] *nmf* (*with definite article*) : the better (one), the best (one)

mejora *nf* : improvement

mejoramiento *nm* : improvement

mejorana *nf* : marjoram

mejorar *vt* : to improve, to make better — *vi* : to improve, to get better — **mejorarse** *vr*

mejoría *nf* : improvement, betterment

mejunje *nm* : concoction, brew

melancolía *nf* : melancholy, sadness

melancólico, **-ca** *adj* : melancholy, sad

melanoma *nm* : melanoma

melaza *nf* : molasses

melena *nf* **1** : mane **2** : long hair **3 melenas** *nfpl* GREÑAS : shaggy hair, mop

melenudo[1], **-da** *adj fam* : longhaired
melenudo[2], **-da** *n* GREÑUDO : longhair, hippie
melindres *nmpl* **1** : affectation, airs *pl* **2** : finickiness
melindroso[1], **-sa** *adj* **1** : affected **2** : fussy, finicky
melindroso[2], **-sa** *n* : finicky person, fussbudget
melisa *nf* : lemon balm
mella *nf* **1** : dent, nick **2 hacer mella en** : to have an effect on, to make an impression on
mellado, -da *adj* **1** : chipped, dented **2** : gap-toothed
mellar *vt* : to dent, to nick
mellizo, -za *adj & n* GEMELO : twin
melocotón *nm, pl* **-tones** : peach
melodía *nf* : melody, tune
melódico, -ca *adj* : melodic
melodioso, -sa *adj* : melodious
melodrama *nm* : melodrama
melodramático, -ca *adj* : melodramatic
melón *nm, pl* **melones** : melon, cantaloupe
meloso, -sa *adj* **1** : honeyed, sweet **2** EMPALAGOSO : cloying, saccharine
membrana *nf* **1** : membrane **2 membrana interdigital** : web, webbing (of a bird's foot) — **membranoso, -sa** *adj*
membresía *nf* : membership, members *pl*
membrete *nm* : letterhead, heading
membrillo *nm* : quince
membrudo, -da *adj* FORNIDO : muscular, well-built
memez *nf, pl* **memeces** : stupid thing
memo, -ma *adj* : silly, stupid
memorabilia *nf* : memorabilia
memorable *adj* : memorable
memorándum *or* **memorando** *nm, pl* **-dums** *or* **-dos** **1** : memorandum, memo **2** : memo book, appointment book
memoria *nf* **1** : memory ⟨de memoria : by heart⟩ ⟨hacer memoria : to try to remember⟩ ⟨traer a la memoria : to call to mind⟩ **2** RECUERDO : remembrance, memory ⟨su memoria perdurará para siempre : his memory will live forever⟩ **3** : report ⟨memoria annual : annual report⟩ **4 memorias** *nfpl* : memoirs
memorizar {21} *vt* : to memorize — **memorización** *nf*
mena *nf* : ore
menaje *nm* : household goods *pl*, furnishings *pl*
mención *nf, pl* **-ciones** : mention
mencionar *vt* : to mention, to refer to
mendaz *adj, pl* **mendaces** : mendacious, lying
mendicidad *nf* : begging
mendigar {52} *vi* : to beg — *vt* : to beg for
mendigo, -ga *n* LIMOSNERO : beggar
mendrugo *nm* : crust (of bread)
menear *vt* **1** : to shake (one's head) **2** : to sway, to wiggle (one's hips) **3** : to wag (a tail) **4** : to stir (a liquid) — **menearse** *vr* **1** : to wiggle one's hips **2** : to fidget
meneo *nm* **1** : movement **2** : shake, toss **3** : swaying, wagging, wiggling **4** : stir, stirring
menester *nm* **1** : activity, occupation, duties *pl* **2 ser menester** : to be necessary ⟨es menester que vengas : you must come⟩
mengano, -na → **fulano**
mengua *nf* **1** : decrease, decline **2** : lack, want **3** : discredit, dishonor
menguar *vt* : to diminish, to lessen — *vi* **1** : to decline, to decrease **2** : to wane — **menguante** *adj*
meningitis *nf* : meningitis
menisco *nm* : meniscus, cartilage
menjurje → **mejunje**
menopausia *nf* : menopause
menor[1] *adj* **1** (*comparative of* **pequeño**) : smaller, lesser, younger **2** (*superlative of* **pequeño**) : smallest, least, youngest **3** : minor **4 al por menor** : retail **5 ser menor de edad** : to be a minor, to be underage
menor[2] *nmf* : minor, juvenile
menos[1] *adv* **1** : less ⟨llueve menos en agosto : it rains less in August⟩ **2** : least ⟨el coche menos caro : the least expensive car⟩ **3 ~ de** : less than, fewer than
menos[2] *adj* **1** : less, fewer ⟨tengo más trabajo y menos tiempo : I have more work and less time⟩ **2** : least, fewest ⟨la clase que tiene menos estudiantes : the class that has the fewest students⟩
menos[3] *prep* **1** SALVO, EXCEPTO : except **2** : minus ⟨quince menos cuatro son once : fifteen minus four is eleven⟩
menos[4] *pron* **1** : less, fewer ⟨no deberías aceptar menos : you shouldn't accept less⟩ **2 al menos** *or* **por lo menos** : at least **3 a menos que** : unless
menoscabar *vt* **1** : to lessen, to diminish **2** : to disgrace, to discredit **3** PERJUDICAR : to harm, to damage
menoscabo *nm* **1** : lessening, diminishing **2** : disgrace, discredit **3** : harm, damage
menospreciar *vt* **1** DESPRECIAR : to scorn, to look down on **2** : to underestimate, to undervalue
menosprecio *nm* DESPRECIO : contempt, scorn
mensaje *nm* : message
mensajero, -ra *n* : messenger
menso, -sa *adj Mex fam* : foolish, stupid
menstrual *adj* : menstrual
menstruar {3} *vi* : to menstruate — **menstruación** *nf*
mensual *adj* : monthly
mensualidad *nf* **1** : monthly payment, installment **2** : monthly salary
mensualmente *adv* : every month, monthly

mensurable *adj* : measurable
menta *nf* **1** : mint, peppermint **2 menta verde** : spearmint
mentado, -da *adj* **1** : aforementioned **2** FAMOSO : renowned, famous
mental *adj* : mental, intellectual — **mentalmente** *adv*
mentalidad *nf* : mentality
mentar {55} *vt* **1** : to mention, to name **2 mentar la madre a** *fam* : to insult, to swear at
mente *nf* : mind ⟨tener en mente : to have in mind⟩
mentecato¹, -ta *adj* : foolish, simple
mentecato², -ta *n* : fool, idiot
mentir {76} *vi* : to lie
mentira *nf* : lie
mentiroso¹, -sa *adj* EMBUSTERO : lying, untruthful
mentiroso², -sa *n* EMBUSTERO : liar
mentís *nm, pl* **mentises** : denial, repudiation ⟨dar el mentís a : to deny, to refute⟩
mentol *nm* : menthol
mentón *nm, pl* **mentones** BARBILLA : chin
mentor *nm* : mentor, counselor
menú *nm, pl* **menús** : menu
menudear *vi* : to occur frequently — *vt* : to do repeatedly
menudencia *nf* **1** : trifle **2 menudencias** *nfpl* : giblets
menudeo *nm* : retail, retailing
menudillos *nmpl* : giblets
menudo¹, -da *adj* **1** : minute, small **2 a ~** FRECUENTEMENTE : often, frequently
menudo² *nm* **1** *Mex* : tripe stew **2 menudos** *nmpl* : giblets
meñique *nm or* **dedo meñique** : little finger, pinkie
meollo *nm* **1** MÉDULA : marrow **2** SESO : brains *pl* **3** ENTRAÑA : essence, core ⟨el meollo del asunto : the heart of the matter⟩
mequetrefe *nm fam* : good-for-nothing
mercachifle *nm* : peddler, hawker
mercadeo *nm* : marketing
mercadería *nf* : merchandise, goods *pl*
mercado *nm* : market ⟨mercado de trabajo *or* mercado laboral : labor market⟩ ⟨mercado de valores *or* mercado bursátil : stock market⟩
mercadotecnia *nf* : marketing
mercancía *nf* : merchandise, goods *pl*
mercante *nmf* : merchant, dealer
mercantil *adj* COMERCIAL : commercial, mercantile
merced *nf* **1** : favor **2 ~ a** : thanks to, due to **3 a merced de** : at the mercy of
mercenario, -ria *adj & n* : mercenary
mercería *nf* : notions store
Mercosur *nm* : economic community consisting of Argentina, Brazil, Paraguay, and Uruguay
mercurio *nm* : mercury
Mercurio *nm* : Mercury (planet)
merecedor, -dora *adj* : deserving, worthy
merecer {53} *vt* : to deserve, to merit — *vi* : to be worthy
merecidamente *adv* : rightfully, deservedly
merecido *nm* : something merited, due ⟨recibieron su merecido : they got their just deserts⟩
merecimiento *nm* : merit, worth
merendar {55} *vi* : to have an afternoon snack — *vt* : to have as an afternoon snack
merendero *nm* **1** : lunchroom, snack bar **2** : picnic area
merengue *nm* **1** : meringue **2** : merengue (dance)
meridiano¹, -na *adj* **1** : midday **2** : crystal clear
meridiano² *nm* : meridian
meridional *adj* SUREÑO : southern
merienda *nf* : afternoon snack, tea
mérito *nm* : merit
meritorio¹, -ria *adj* : deserving, meritorious
meritorio², -ria *n* : intern, trainee
merluza *nf* : hake
merma *nf* **1** : decrease, cut **2** : waste, loss
mermar *vi* : to decrease, to diminish — *vt* : to reduce, to cut down
mermelada *nf* : marmalade, jam
mero¹, -ra *adv Mex fam* **1** : nearly, almost ⟨ya mero me caí : I almost fell⟩ **2** : just, exactly ⟨aquí mero : right here⟩
mero², -ra *adj* **1** : mere, simple **2** *Mex fam* (*used as an intensifier*) : very ⟨en el mero centro : in the very center of town⟩
mero³ *nm* : grouper
merodeador, -dora *n* **1** : marauder **2** : prowler
merodear *vi* **1** : to maraud, to pillage **2** : to prowl around, to skulk
mes *nm* : month
mesa *nf* **1** : table **2** : committee, board
mesada *nf* : allowance, pocket money
mesarse *vr* : to pull at ⟨mesarse los cabellos : to tear one's hair⟩
mesero, -ra *n* CAMARERO : waiter, waitress *f*
meseta *nf* : plateau, tableland
Mesías *nm* : Messiah
mesón *nm, pl* **mesones** : inn
mesonero, -ra *nm* : innkeeper
mestizo¹, -za *adj* **1** : of mixed ancestry **2** HÍBRIDO : hybrid
mestizo², -za *n* : person of mixed ancestry
mesura *nf* **1** MODERACIÓN : moderation, discretion **2** CORTESÍA : courtesy **3** GRAVEDAD : seriousness, dignity
mesurado, -da *adj* COMEDIDO : moderate, restrained
mesurar *vt* : to moderate, to restrain, to temper — **mesurarse** *vr* : to restrain oneself
meta *nf* : goal, objective

metabólico, -ca *adj* : metabolic
metabolismo *nm* : metabolism
metabolizar {21} *vt* : to metabolize
metafísica *nf* : metaphysics
metafísico, -ca *adj* : metaphysical
metáfora *nf* : metaphor
metafórico, -ca *adj* : metaphoric, metaphorical
metal *nm* **1** : metal **2** : brass section (in an orchestra)
metálico, -ca *adj* : metallic, metal
metalistería *nf* : metalworking
metalurgia *nf* : metallurgy
metalúrgico[1], **-ca** *adj* : metallurgical
metalúrgico[2], **-ca** *n* : metallurgist
metamorfosis *nfs & pl* : metamorphosis
metano *nm* : methane
metedura *nf* **metedura de pata** : blunder, faux pas
meteórico, -ca *adj* : meteoric
meteorito *nm* : meteorite
meteoro *nm* : meteor
meteorología *nf* : meteorology
meteorológico, -ca *adj* : meteorologic, meteorological
meteorólogo, -ga *n* : meteorologist
meter *vt* **1** : to put (in) ⟨metieron su dinero en el banco : they put their money in the bank⟩ **2** : to fit, to squeeze ⟨puedes meter dos líneas más en esa página : you can fit two more lines on that page⟩ **3** : to place (in a job) ⟨lo metieron de barrendero : they got him a job as a street sweeper⟩ **4** : to involve ⟨lo metió en un buen lío : she got him in an awful mess⟩ **5** : to make, to cause ⟨meten demasiado ruido : they make too much noise⟩ **6** : to spread (a rumor) **7** : to strike (a blow) **8** : to take up, to take in (clothing) **9 a todo meter** : at top speed — **meterse** *vr* **1** : to get into, to enter **2** *fam* : to meddle ⟨no te metas en lo que no te importa : mind your own business⟩ **3 ~ con** *fam* : to pick a fight with, to provoke ⟨no te metas conmigo : don't mess with me⟩
metiche[1] *adj Mex fam* : nosy
metiche[2] *nmf Mex fam* : busybody
meticulosidad *nf* : thoroughness, meticulousness
meticuloso, -sa *adj* : meticulous, thorough — **meticulosamente** *adv*
metida *nf* **metida de pata** *fam* : blunder, gaffe, blooper
metódico, -ca *adj* : methodical — **metódicamente** *adv*
metodista *adj & nmf* : Methodist
método *nm* : method
metodología *nf* : methodology
metomentodo *nmf fam* : busybody
metraje *nm* : length (of a film) ⟨de largo metraje : feature-length⟩
metralla *nf* : shrapnel
metralleta *nf* : submachine gun
métrico, -ca *adj* **1** : metric **2 cinta métrica** : tape measure
metro *nm* **1** : meter **2** : subway
metrónomo *nm* : metronome
metrópoli *nf or* **metrópolis** *nfs & pl* : metropolis
metropolitano, -na *adj* : metropolitan
mexicanismo *nm* : Mexican word or expression
mexicano, -na *adj & n* : Mexican
mexicoamericano, -na *adj & n* : Mexican-American
meza, etc. → **mecer**
mezcla *nf* **1** : mixing **2** : mixture, blend **3** : mortar (masonry material)
mezclar *vt* **1** : to mix, to blend **2** : to mix up, to muddle **3** INVOLUCRAR : to involve — **mezclarse** *vr* **1** : to get mixed up (in) **2** : to mix, to mingle (socially)
mezclilla *nf Chile, Mex* : denim ⟨pantalones de mezclilla : jeans⟩
mezcolanza *nf* : jumble, hodgepodge
mezquindad *nf* **1** : meanness, stinginess **2** : petty deed, mean action
mezquino[1], **-na** *adj* **1** : mean, petty **2** : stingy **3** : paltry
mezquino[2] *nm Mex* : wart
mezquita *nf* : mosque
mezquite *nm* : mesquite
mi *adj* : my
mí *pron* **1** : me ⟨es para mí : it's for me⟩ ⟨a mí no me importa : it doesn't matter to me⟩ **2 mí mismo, mí misma** : myself
miasma *nm* : miasma
miau *nm* : meow
mica *nf* : mica
mico *nm* : monkey, long-tailed monkey
micra *nf* : micron
microbio *nm* : microbe, germ
microbiología *nf* : microbiology
microbiológico, -ca *adj* : microbiological
microbús *nm, pl* **-buses** : minibus
microcomputadora *nf* : microcomputer
microcosmos *nms & pl* : microcosm
microficha *nf* : microfiche
microfilm *nm, pl* **-films** : microfilm
micrófono *nm* : microphone
micrómetro *nm* : micrometer
microonda *nf* : microwave
microondas *nms & pl* : microwave, microwave oven
microordenador *nm Spain* : microcomputer
microorganismo *nm* : microorganism
microprocesador *nm* : microprocessor
microscópico, -ca *adj* : microscopic
microscopio *nm* : microscope
mide, etc. → **medir**
miedo *nm* **1** TEMOR : fear ⟨le tiene miedo al perro : he's scared of the dog⟩ ⟨tenían miedo de hablar : they were afraid to speak⟩ **2 dar miedo** : to frighten
miedoso, -sa *adj* TEMEROSO : fearful
miel *nf* : honey
miembro *nm* **1** : member **2** EXTREMIDAD : limb, extremity
mienta, etc. → **mentar**
miente, etc. → **mentir**

mientras[1] *adv* **1** *or* **mientras tanto** : meanwhile, in the meantime **2 mientras más** : the more ⟨mientras más como, más quiero : the more I eat, the more I want⟩
mientras[2] *conj* **1** : while, as ⟨roncaba mientras dormía : he snored while he was sleeping⟩ **2** : as long as ⟨luchará mientras pueda : he will fight as long as he is able⟩ **3 mientras que** : while, whereas ⟨él es alto mientras que ella es muy baja : he is tall, whereas she is very short⟩
miércoles *nms & pl* : Wednesday
miga *nf* **1** : crumb **2 hacer buenas (malas) migas con** : to get along well (poorly) with
migaja *nf* **1** : crumb **2 migajas** *nfpl* SOBRAS : leftovers, scraps
migración *nf, pl* **-ciones** : migration
migrante *nmf* : migrant
migraña *nf* : migraine
migratorio, -ria *adj* : migratory
mijo *nm* : millet
mil[1] *adj* : thousand
mil[2] *nm* : one thousand, a thousand
milagro *nm* : miracle ⟨de milagro : miraculously⟩
milagroso, -sa *adj* : miraculous, marvelous — **milagrosamente** *adv*
milenio *nm* : millennium
milésimo, -ma *adj* : thousandth — **milésimo** *nm*
milicia *nf* **1** : militia **2** : military service
miligramo *nm* : milligram
mililitro *nm* : milliliter
milímetro *nm* : millimeter
militancia *nf* : militancy
militante[1] *adj* : militant
militante[2] *nmf* : militant, activist
militar[1] *vi* **1** : to serve (in the military) **2** : to be active (in politics)
militar[2] *adj* : military
militar[3] *nmf* SOLDADO : soldier
militarismo *nm* : militarism
militarista *adj & nmf* : militarist
militarizar {21} *vt* : to militarize
milla *nf* : mile
millar *nm* : thousand
millón *nm, pl* **millones** : million
millonario, -ria *n* : millionaire
millonésimo[1], **-ma** *adj* : millionth
millonésimo[2] *nm* : millionth
mil millones *nms & pl* : billion
milpa *nf CA, Mex* : cornfield
milpiés *nms & pl* : millipede
mimar *vt* CONSENTIR : to pamper, to spoil
mimbre *nm* : wicker
mimeógrafo *nm* : mimeograph
mímica *nf* **1** : mime, sign language **2** IMITACIÓN : mimicry
mimo *nm* **1** : pampering, indulgence ⟨hacerle mimos a alguien : to pamper someone⟩ **2** : mime
mimoso, -sa *adj* **1** : fussy, finicky **2** : affectionate, clinging
mina *nf* **1** : mine **2** : lead (for pencils)
minar *vt* **1** : to mine **2** DEBILITAR : to undermine
minarete *nm* ALMINAR : minaret
mineral *adj & nm* : mineral
minería *nf* : mining
minero[1], **-ra** *adj* : mining
minero[2], **-ra** *n* : miner, mine worker
miniatura *nf* : miniature
minicomputadora *nf* : minicomputer
minifalda *nf* : miniskirt
minifundio *nm* : small farm
minimizar {21} *vt* : to minimize
mínimo[1], **-ma** *adj* **1** : minimum ⟨salario mínimo : minimum wage⟩ **2** : least, smallest **3** : very small, minute
mínimo[2] *nm* **1** : minimum, least amount **2** : modicum, small amount **3 como ~** : at least
minino, -na *n fam* : pussy, pussycat
miniserie *nf* : miniseries
ministerial *adj* : ministerial
ministerio *nm* : ministry, department
ministro, -tra *n* : minister, secretary ⟨primer ministro : prime minister⟩ ⟨Ministro de Defensa : Secretary of Defense⟩
minivan [ˌmini'ban, -'van] *nf, pl* **-vanes** : minivan
minoría *nf* : minority
minorista[1] *adj* : retail
minorista[2] *nmf* : retailer
minoritario, -ria *adj* : minority
mintió, etc. → **mentir**
minuciosamente *adv* **1** : minutely **2** : in great detail **3** : thoroughly, meticulously
minucioso, -sa *adj* **1** : minute **2** DETALLADO : detailed **3** : thorough, meticulous
minué *nm* : minuet
minúsculo, -la *adj* DIMINUTO : tiny, miniscule
minusvalía *nf* : disability, handicap
minusválido[1], **-da** *adj* : handicapped, disabled
minusválido[2], **-da** *n* : handicapped person
minuta *nf* **1** BORRADOR : rough draft **2** : bill, fee
minutero *nm* : minute hand
minuto *nm* : minute
mío[1], **mía** *adj* **1** : my, of mine ⟨¡Dios mío! : my God!, good heavens!⟩ ⟨una amiga mía : a friend of mine⟩ **2** : mine ⟨es mío : it's mine⟩
mío[2], **mía** *pron* (*with definite article*) : mine, my own ⟨tus zapatos son iguales a los míos : your shoes are just like mine⟩
miope *adj* : nearsighted, myopic
miopía *nf* : myopia, nearsightedness
mira *nf* **1** : sight (of a firearm or instrument) **2** : aim, objective ⟨con miras a : with the intention of, with a view to⟩ ⟨de amplias miras : broad-minded⟩ ⟨poner la mira en : to aim at, to aspire to⟩

mirada *nf* **1** : look, glance, gaze **2** EXPRESIÓN : look, expression ⟨una mirada de sorpresa : a look of surprise⟩

mirado, -da *adj* **1** : cautious, careful **2** : considerate **3 bien mirado** : well thought of **4 mal mirado** : disliked, disapproved of

mirador *nm* : balcony, lookout, vantage point

miramiento *nm* **1** CONSIDERACIÓN : consideration, respect **2 sin miramientos** : without due consideration, carelessly

mirar *vt* **1** : to look at **2** OBSERVAR : to watch **3** REFLEXIONAR : to consider, to think over — *vi* **1** : to look **2** : to face, to overlook **3 ~ por** : to look after, to look out for — **mirarse** *vr* **1** : to look at oneself **2** : to look at each other

mirasol *nm* GIRASOL : sunflower

miríada *nf* : myriad

mirlo *nm* : blackbird

mirra *nf* : myrrh

mirto *nm* ARRAYÁN : myrtle

misa *nf* : Mass

misantropía *nf* : misanthropy

misantrópico, -ca *adj* : misanthropic

misántropo, -pa *n* : misanthrope

miscelánea *nf* : miscellany

misceláneo, -nea *adj* : miscellaneous

miserable *adj* **1** LASTIMOSO : miserable, wretched **2** : paltry, meager **3** MEZQUINO : stingy, miserly **4** : despicable, vile

miseria *nf* **1** POBREZA : poverty **2** : misery, suffering **3** : pittance, meager amount

misericordia *nf* COMPASIÓN : mercy, compassion

misericordioso, -sa *adj* : merciful

mísero, -ra *adj* **1** : wretched, miserable **2** : stingy **3** : paltry, meager

misil *nm* : missile

misión *nf, pl* **misiones** : mission

misionero, -ra *adj & n* : missionary

misiva *nf* : missive, letter

mismísimo, -ma *adj* (*used as an intensifier*) : very, selfsame ⟨el mismísimo día : that very same day⟩

mismo[1] *adv* (*used as an intensifier*) : right, exactly ⟨hazlo ahora mismo : do it right now⟩ ⟨te llamará hoy mismo : he'll definitely call you today⟩

mismo[2], **-ma** *adj* **1** : same **2** (*used as an intensifier*) : very ⟨en ese mismo momento : at that very moment⟩ **3** : oneself ⟨lo hizo ella misma : she made it herself⟩ **4 por lo mismo** : for that reason

misoginia *nf* : misogyny

misógino *nm* : misogynist

misterio *nm* : mystery

misterioso, -sa *adj* : mysterious — **misteriosamente** *adv*

misticismo *nm* : mysticism

místico[1], **-ca** *adj* : mystic, mystical

místico[2], **-ca** *n* : mystic

mitad *nf* **1** : half ⟨mitad y mitad : half and half⟩ **2** MEDIO : middle ⟨a mitad de : halfway through⟩ ⟨por la mitad : in half⟩

mítico, -ca *adj* : mythical, mythic

mitigar {52} *vt* ALIVIAR : to mitigate, to alleviate — **mitigación** *nf*

mitin *nm, pl* **mítines** : (political) meeting, rally

mito *nm* LEYENDA : myth, legend

mitología *nf* : mythology

mitológico, -ca *adj* : mythological

mitosis *nfs & pl* : mitosis

mitra *nf* : miter (bishop's hat)

mixto, -ta *adj* **1** : mixed, joint **2** : coeducational

mixtura *nf* : mixture, blend

mnemónico, -ca *adj* : mnemonic

mobiliario *nm* : furniture

mocasín *nm, pl* **-sines** : moccasin

mocedad *nf* **1** JUVENTUD : youth **2** : youthful prank

mochila *nf* MORRAL : backpack, knapsack

moción *nf, pl* **-ciones** **1** MOVIMIENTO : motion, movement **2** : motion (to a court or assembly)

moco *nm* **1** : mucus **2** *fam* : snot ⟨limpiarse los mocos : to wipe one's (runny) nose⟩

mocoso, -sa *n* : kid, brat

moda *nf* **1** : fashion, style **2 a la moda** *or* **de ~** : in style, fashionable **3 moda pasajera** : fad

modales *nmpl* : manners

modalidad *nf* **1** CLASE : kind, type **2** MANERA : way, manner

modelar *vt* : to model, to mold — **modelarse** *vr* : to model oneself after, to emulate

modelo[1] *adj* : model ⟨una casa modelo : a model home⟩

modelo[2] *nm* : model, example, pattern

modelo[3] *nmf* : model, mannequin

módem *or* **modem** [ˈmoðɛm] *nm* : modem

moderación *nf, pl* **-ciones** MESURA : moderation

moderado, -da *adj & n* : moderate — **moderadamente** *adv*

moderador, -dora *n* : moderator, chair

moderar *vt* **1** TEMPERAR : to temper, to moderate **2** : to curb, to reduce ⟨moderar gastos : to curb spending⟩ **3** PRESIDIR : to chair (a meeting) — **moderarse** *vr* **1** : to restrain oneself **2** : to diminish, to calm down

modernidad *nf* **1** : modernity, modernness **2** : modern age

modernismo *nm* : modernism

modernista[1] *adj* : modernist, modernistic

modernista[2] *nmf* : modernist

modernizar {21} *vt* : to modernize — **modernización** *nf*

moderno, -na *adj* : modern, up-to-date

modestia *nf* : modesty

modesto, **-ta** *adj* : modest — **modestamente** *adv*
modificación *nf, pl* **-ciones** : alteration
modificador[1], **-dora** *adj* : modifying, moderating
modificador[2] → **modificante**
modificante *nm* : modifier
modificar {72} *vt* ALTERAR : to modify, to alter, to adapt
modismo *nm* : idiom
modista *nmf* **1** : dressmaker **2** : fashion designer
modo *nm* **1** MANERA : way, manner, mode ⟨de un modo u otro : one way or another⟩ ⟨a mi modo de ver : to my way of thinking⟩ **2** : mood (in grammar) **3** : mode (in music) **4 a modo de** : by way of, in the manner of, like ⟨a modo de ejemplo : by way of example⟩ **5 de cualquier modo** : in any case, anyway **6 de modo que** : so, in such a way that **7 de todos modos** : in any case, anyway **8 en cierto modo** : in a way, to a certain extent
modorra *nf* : drowsiness, lethargy
modular[1] *v* : to modulate — **modulación** *nf*
modular[2] *adj* : modular
módulo *nm* : module, unit
mofa *nf* **1** : mockery, ridicule **2 hacer mofa de** : to make fun of, to ridicule
mofarse *vr* **~ de** : to scoff at, to make fun of
mofeta *nf* ZORRILLO : skunk
mofle *nm CA, Mex* : muffler (of a car)
moflete *nm fam* : fat cheek
mofletudo, **-da** *adj fam* : fat-cheeked, chubby
mohín *nm, pl* **mohines** : grimace, face
mohino, **-na** *adj* : gloomy, melancholy
moho *nm* **1** : mold, mildew **2** : rust
mohoso, **-sa** *adj* **1** : moldy **2** : rusty
moisés *nm, pl* **moiseses** : bassinet, cradle
mojado[1], **-da** *adj* : wet
mojado[2], **-da** *n Mex fam* : illegal immigrant
mojar *vt* **1** : to wet, to moisten **2** : to dunk — **mojarse** *vr* : to get wet
mojigatería *nf* **1** : hypocrisy **2** GAZMOÑERÍA : primness, prudery
mojigato[1], **-ta** *adj* : prudish, prim — **mojigatamente** *adv*
mojigato[2], **-ta** *n* : prude, prig
mojón *nm, pl* **mojones** : boundary stone, marker
molar *nm* MUELA : molar
molcajete *nm Mex* : mortar
molde *nm* **1** : mold, form **2 letras de molde** : printing, block lettering
moldear *vt* **1** FORMAR : to mold, to shape **2** : to cast
moldura *nf* : molding
mole[1] *nm Mex* **1** : spicy sauce made with chilies and usually chocolate **2** : meat served with mole sauce
mole[2] *nf* : mass, bulk
molécula *nf* : molecule — **molecular** *adj*
moler {47} *vt* **1** : to grind, to crush **2** CANSAR : to exhaust, to wear out
molestar *vt* **1** FASTIDIAR : to annoy, to bother **2** : to disturb, to disrupt — *vi* : to be a nuisance — **molestarse** *vr* **~ en** : to take the trouble to
molestia *nf* **1** FASTIDIO : annoyance, bother, nuisance **2** : trouble ⟨se tomó la molestia de investigar : she took the trouble to investigate⟩ **3** MALESTAR : discomfort
molesto, **-ta** *adj* **1** ENOJADO : bothered, annoyed **2** FASTIDIOSO : bothersome, annoying
molestoso, **-sa** *adj* : bothersome, annoying
molido, **-da** *adj* **1** MACHACADO : ground, crushed **2 estar molido** : to be exhausted
molienda *nf* : milling, grinding
molinero, **-ra** *n* : miller
molinillo *nm* : grinder, mill ⟨molinillo de café : coffee grinder⟩
molino *nm* **1** : mill **2 molino de viento** : windmill
molla *nf* : soft fleshy part, flesh (of fruit), lean part (of meat)
molleja *nf* : gizzard
molusco *nm* : mollusk
momentáneamente *adv* : momentarily
momentáneo, **-nea** *adj* **1** : momentary **2** TEMPORARIO : temporary
momento *nm* **1** : moment, instant ⟨espera un momentito : wait just a moment⟩ **2** : time, period of time ⟨momentos difíciles : hard times⟩ **3** : present, moment ⟨los atletas del momento : the athletes of the moment, today's popular athletes⟩ **4** : momentum **5 al momento** : right away, at once **6 de ~** : at the moment, for the moment **7 de un momento a otro** : any time now **8 por momentos** : at times
momia *nf* : mummy
monaguillo *nm* ACÓLITO : altar boy
monarca *nmf* : monarch
monarquía *nf* : monarchy
monárquico, **-ca** *n* : monarchist
monasterio *nm* : monastery
monástico, **-ca** *adj* : monastic
mondadientes *nms & pl* PALILLO : toothpick
mondar *vt* : to peel
mondongo *nm* ENTRAÑAS : innards *pl*, insides *pl*, guts *pl*
moneda *nf* **1** : coin **2** : money, currency
monedero *nm* : change purse
monetario, **-ria** *adj* : monetary, financial
mongol, **-gola** *adj & n* : Mongol, Mongolian
monitor[1], **-tora** *n* : instructor (in sports)
monitor[2] *nm* : monitor ⟨monitor de televisión : television monitor⟩
monitorear *vt* : to monitor
monja *nf* : nun
monje *nm* : monk
mono[1], **-na** *adj fam* : lovely, pretty, cute, darling

mono[2], **-na** *n* : monkey
monóculo *nm* : monocle
monogamia *nf* : monogamy
monógamo, -ma *adj* : monogamous
monografía *nf* : monograph
monograma *nm* : monogram
monolingüe *adj* : monolingual
monolítico, -ca *adj* : monolithic
monolito *nm* : monolith
monólogo *nm* : monologue
monomanía *nf* : obsession
monopatín *nm, pl* **-tines** **1** : scooter **2** : skateboard
monopolio *nm* : monopoly
monopolizar {21} *vt* : to monopolize — **monopolización** *nf*
monosilábico, -ca *adj* : monosyllabic
monosílabo *nm* : monosyllable
monoteísmo *nm* : monotheism
monoteísta[1] *adj* : monotheistic
monoteísta[2] *nmf* : monotheist
monotonía *nf* **1** : monotony **2** : monotone
monótono, -na *adj* : monotonous — **monótonamente** *adv*
monóxido *nm* : monoxide ⟨monóxido de carbono : carbon monoxide⟩
monserga *nf* : gibberish, drivel
monstruo *nm* : monster
monstruosidad *nf* : monstrosity
monstruoso, -sa *adj* : monstrous — **monstruosamente** *adv*
monta *nf* **1** : sum, total **2** : importance, value ⟨de poca monta : unimportant, insignificant⟩
montaje *nm* **1** : assembling, assembly **2** : montage
montante *nm* : transom, fanlight
montaña *nf* **1** MONTE : mountain **2** **montaña rusa** : roller coaster
montañero, -ra *n* : mountaineer, mountain climber
montañoso, -sa *adj* : mountainous
montar *vt* **1** : to mount **2** ESTABLECER : to set up, to establish **3** ARMAR : to assemble, to put together **4** : to edit (a film) **5** : to stage, to put on (a show) **6** : to cock (a gun) **7** **montar en bicicleta** : to get on a bicycle **8** **montar a caballo** CABALGAR : to ride horseback
monte *nm* **1** MONTAÑA : mountain, mount **2** : woodland, scrubland ⟨monte bajo : underbrush⟩ **3** : outskirts (of a town), surrounding country **4** **monte de piedad** : pawnshop
montés *adj, pl* **monteses** : wild (of animals or plants)
montículo *nm* **1** : mound, heap **2** : hillock, knoll
monto *nm* : amount, total
montón *nm, pl* **-tones** **1** : heap, pile **2** *fam* : ton, load ⟨un montón de preguntas : a ton of questions⟩ ⟨montones de gente : loads of people⟩
montura *nf* **1** : mount (horse) **2** : saddle, tack **3** : setting, mounting (of jewelry) **4** : frame (of glasses)
monumental *adj fam* **1** : tremendous, terrific **2** : massive, huge
monumento *nm* : monument
monzón *nm, pl* **monzones** : monsoon
moño *nm* **1** : bun (chignon) **2** LAZO : bow, knot ⟨corbata de moño : bow tie⟩
moquear *vi* : to snivel
moquillo *nm* : distemper
mora *nf* **1** : blackberry **2** : mulberry
morada *nf* RESIDENCIA : dwelling, abode
morado[1], **-da** *adj* : purple
morado[2] *nm* : purple
morador, -dora *n* : dweller, inhabitant
moral[1] *adj* : moral — **moralmente** *adv*
moral[2] *nf* **1** MORALIDAD : ethics, morality, morals *pl* **2** ÁNIMO : morale, spirits *pl*
moraleja *nf* : moral (of a story)
moralidad *nf* : morality
moralista[1] *adj* : moralistic
moralista[2] *nmf* : moralist
morar *vi* : to dwell, to reside
moratoria *nf* : moratorium
mórbido, -da *adj* : morbid
morboso, -sa *adj* : morbid — **morbosidad** *nf*
morcilla *nf* : blood sausage, blood pudding
mordacidad *nf* : bite, sharpness
mordaz *adj* : caustic, scathing
mordaza *nf* **1** : gag **2** : clamp
mordedura *nf* : bite (of an animal)
morder {47} *v* : to bite
mordida *nf* **1** : bite **2** *CA, Mex* : bribe, payoff
mordisco *nm* : bite, nibble
mordisquear *vt* : to nibble (on), to bite
morena *nf* **1** : moraine **2** : moray (eel)
moreno[1], **-na** *adj* **1** : brunette **2** : dark, dark-skinned
moreno[2], **-na** *n* **1** : brunette **2** : dark-skinned person
moretón *nm, pl* **-tones** : bruise
morfina *nf* : morphine
morfología *nf* : morphology
morgue *nf* : morgue
moribundo[1], **-da** *adj* : dying, moribund
moribundo[2], **-da** *n* : dying person
morillo *nm* : andiron
morir {46} *vi* **1** FALLECER : to die **2** APAGARSE : to die out, to go out
mormón, -mona *adj & n, pl* **mormones** : Mormon
moro[1], **-ra** *adj* : Moorish
moro[2], **-ra** *n* **1** : Moor **2** : Muslim
morosidad *nf* **1** : delinquency (in payment) **2** : slowness
moroso, -sa *adj* **1** : delinquent, in arrears ⟨cuentas morosas : delinquent accounts⟩ **2** : slow, sluggish
morral *nm* MOCHILA : backpack, knapsack
morralla *nf* **1** : small fish **2** : trash, riffraff **3** *Mex* : small change
morriña *nf* : homesickness
morro *nm* HOCICO : snout

morsa *nf* : walrus

morse *nm* : Morse code

mortaja *nf* SUDARIO : shroud

mortal[1] *adj* **1** : mortal **2** FATAL : fatal, deadly — **mortalmente** *adv*

mortal[2] *nmf* : mortal

mortalidad *nf* : mortality

mortandad *nf* **1** : loss of life, death toll **2** : carnage, slaughter

mortero *nm* : mortar (bowl, cannon, or building material)

mortífero, -ra *adj* LETAL : deadly, fatal

mortificación *nf, pl* **-ciones** **1** : mortification **2** TORMENTO : anguish, torment

mortificar {72} *vt* **1** : to mortify **2** TORTURAR : to trouble, to torment — **mortificarse** *vr* : to be mortified, to feel embarrassed

mosaico *nm* : mosaic

mosca *nf* **1** : fly **2** **mosca común** : housefly

moscada *adj* **nuez moscada** : nutmeg

moscovita *adj & nmf* : Muscovite

mosquearse *vr* **1** : to become suspicious **2** : to take offense

mosquete *nm* : musket

mosquetero *nm* : musketeer

mosquitero *nm* : mosquito net

mosquito *nm* ZANCUDO : mosquito

mostachón *nm, pl* **-chones** : macaroon

mostaza *nf* : mustard

mostrador *nm* : counter (in a store)

mostrar {19} *vt* **1** : to show **2** EXHIBIR : to exhibit, to display — **mostrarse** *vr* : to show oneself, to appear

mota *nf* **1** : fleck, speck **2** : defect, blemish

mote *nm* SOBRENOMBRE : nickname

moteado, -da *adj* : dotted, spotted, dappled

motel *nm* : motel

motín *nm, pl* **motines** **1** : riot **2** : rebellion, mutiny

motivación *nf, pl* **-ciones** : motivation — **motivacional** *adj*

motivar *vt* **1** CAUSAR : to cause **2** IMPULSAR : to motivate

motivo *nm* **1** MÓVIL : motive **2** CAUSA : cause, reason **3** TEMA : theme, motif

moto *nf* : motorcycle, motorbike

motocicleta *nf* : motorcycle

motociclismo *nm* : motorcycling

motociclista *nmf* : motorcyclist

motor[1], **-ra** *adj* MOTRIZ : motor

motor[2] *nm* **1** : motor, engine **2** : driving force, cause

motorista *nmf* : motorist

motriz *adj, pl* **motrices** : driving

motu proprio *adv* **de motu proprio** [de ˈmotuˈproprio] : voluntarily, of one's own accord

mousse [ˈmus] *nmf* : mousse

mover {47} *vt* **1** TRASLADAR : to move, to shift **2** AGITAR : to shake, to nod (the head) **3** ACCIONAR : to power, to drive **4** INDUCIR : to provoke, to cause **5** : to excite, to stir — **moverse** *vr* **1** : to move, to move over **2** : to hurry, to get a move on **3** : to get moving, to make an effort

movible *adj* : movable

movida *nf* : move (in a game)

móvil[1] *adj* : mobile

móvil[2] *nm* **1** MOTIVO : motive **2** : mobile

movilidad *nf* : mobility

movilizar {21} *vt* : to mobilize — **movilización** *nf*

movimiento *nm* : movement, motion ⟨movimiento del cuerpo : bodily movement⟩ ⟨movimiento sindicalista : labor movement⟩

mozo[1], **-za** *adj* : young, youthful

mozo[2], **-za** *n* **1** JOVEN : young man *m,* young woman *f,* youth **2** : helper, servant **3** *Arg, Chile, Col, Peru* : waiter *m,* waitress *f*

mucamo, -ma *n* : servant, maid *f*

muchacha *nf* : maid

muchacho, -cha *n* **1** : kid, boy *m,* girl *f* **2** JOVEN : young man *m,* young woman *f*

muchedumbre *nf* MULTITUD : crowd, multitude

mucho[1] *adv* **1** : much, a lot ⟨mucho más : much more⟩ ⟨le gusta mucho : he likes it a lot⟩ **2** : long, a long time ⟨tardó mucho en venir : he was a long time getting here⟩ **3** **por mucho que** : no matter how much

mucho[2], **-cha** *adj* **1** : a lot of, many, much ⟨mucha gente : a lot of people⟩ ⟨hace mucho tiempo que no lo veo : I haven't seen him in ages⟩ **2** **muchas veces** : often

mucho[3], **-cha** *pron* **1** : a lot, many, much ⟨hay mucho que hacer : there is a lot to do⟩ ⟨muchas no vinieron : many didn't come⟩ **2** **cuando ~** *or* **como ~** : at most **3** **con ~** : by far **4** **ni mucho menos** : not at all, far from it

mucílago *nm* : mucilage

mucosidad *nf* : mucus

mucoso, -sa *adj* : mucous, slimy

muda *nf* **1** : change ⟨muda de ropa : change of clothes⟩ **2** : molt, molting

mudanza *nf* **1** CAMBIO : change **2** TRASLADO : move, moving

mudar *v* **1** CAMBIAR : to change **2** : to molt, to shed — **mudarse** *vr* **1** TRASLADARSE : to move (one's residence) **2** : to change (clothes)

mudo[1], **-da** *adj* **1** SILENCIOSO : silent ⟨el cine mudo : silent films⟩ **2** : mute, dumb

mudo[2], **-da** *n* : mute

mueble *nm* **1** : piece of furniture **2** **muebles** *nmpl* : furniture, furnishings

mueblería *nf* : furniture store

mueca *nf* : grimace, face

muela *nf* **1** : tooth, molar ⟨dolor de muelas : toothache⟩ ⟨muela de juicio : wisdom tooth⟩ **2** : millstone **3** : whetstone

muele, etc. → **moler**

muelle[1] *adj* : soft, comfortable, easy
muelle[2] *nm* **1** : wharf, dock **2** RESORTE : spring
muérdago *nm* : mistletoe
muerde, etc. → **morder**
muere, etc. → **morir**
muerte *nf* : death
muerto[1] *pp* → **morir**
muerto[2], **-ta** *adj* **1** : dead **2** : lifeless, flat, dull **3 ∼ de** : dying of ⟨estoy muerto de hambre : I'm dying of hunger⟩
muerto[3], **-ta** *nm* DIFUNTO : dead person, deceased
muesca *nf* : nick, notch
muestra[1], **etc.** → **mostrar**
muestra[2] *nf* **1** : sample **2** SEÑAL : sign, show ⟨una muestra de respeto : a show of respect⟩ **3** EXPOSICIÓN : exhibition, exposition **4** : pattern, model
mueve, etc. → **mover**
mugido *nm* : moo, lowing, bellow
mugir {35} *vi* : to moo, to low, to bellow
mugre *nf* SUCIEDAD : grime, filth
mugriento, -ta *adj* : filthy
muguete *nm* : lily of the valley
muja, etc. → **mugir**
mujer *nf* **1** : woman **2** ESPOSA : wife
mulato, -ta *adj & n* : mulatto
muleta *nf* : crutch
mullido, -da *adj* **1** : soft, fluffy **2** : spongy, springy
mulo, -la *n* : mule
multa *nf* : fine
multar *vt* : to fine
multicolor *adj* : multicolored
multicultural *adj* : multicultural
multidisciplinario, -ria *adj* : multidisciplinary
multifacético, -ca *adj* : multifaceted
multifamiliar *adj* : multifamily
multilateral *adj* : multilateral
multimedia *nf* : multimedia
multimillonario, -ria *n* : multimillionaire
multinacional *adj* : multinational
múltiple *adj* : multiple
multiplicación *nf, pl* **-ciones** : multiplication
multiplicar {72} *v* **1** : to multiply **2** : to increase — **multiplicarse** *vr* : to multiply, to reproduce
multiplicidad *nf* : multiplicity
múltiplo *nm* : multiple
multitud *nf* MUCHEDUMBRE : crowd, multitude
multiuso, -sa *adj* : multipurpose
multivitamínico, -ca *adj* : multivitamin
mundano, -na *adj* : worldly, earthly
mundial *adj* : world, worldwide
mundialmente *adv* : worldwide, all over the world
mundo *nm* **1** : world **2 todo el mundo** : everyone, everybody
municiones *nfpl* : ammunition, munitions
municipal *adj* : municipal
municipio *nm* **1** : municipality **2** AYUNTAMIENTO : town council
muñeca *nf* **1** : doll **2** MANIQUÍ : mannequin **3** : wrist
muñeco *nm* **1** : doll, boy doll **2** MARIONETA : puppet
muñón *nm, pl* **muñones** : stump (of an arm or leg)
mural *adj & nm* : mural
muralista *nmf* : muralist
muralla *nf* : rampart, wall
murciélago *nm* : bat (animal)
murga *nf* : band of street musicians
murió, etc. → **morir**
murmullo *nm* **1** : murmur, murmuring **2** : rustling, rustle ⟨el murmullo de las hojas : the rustling of the leaves⟩
murmurar *vt* **1** : to murmur, to mutter **2** : to whisper (gossip) — *vi* **1** : to murmur **2** CHISMEAR : to gossip
muro *nm* : wall
musa *nf* : muse
musaraña *nf* : shrew
muscular *adj* : muscular
musculatura *nf* : muscles *pl*, musculature
músculo *nm* : muscle
musculoso, -sa *adj* : muscular, brawny
muselina *nf* : muslin
museo *nm* : museum
musgo *nm* : moss
musgoso, -sa *adj* : mossy
música *nf* : music
musical *adj* : musical — **musicalmente** *adv*
músico[1], **-ca** *adj* : musical
músico[2], **-ca** *n* : musician
musitar *vt* : to mumble, to murmur
muslo *nm* : thigh
musulmán, -mana *adj & n, mpl* **-manes** : Muslim
mutación *nf, pl* **-ciones** : mutation
mutante *adj & nm* : mutant
mutar *v* : to mutate
mutilar *vt* : to mutilate — **mutilación** *nf*
mutis *nm* **1** : exit (in theater) **2** : silence
mutual *adj* : mutual
mutuo, -tua *adj* : mutual, reciprocal — **mutuamente** *adv*
muy *adv* **1** : very, quite ⟨es muy inteligente : she's very intelligent⟩ ⟨muy bien : very well, fine⟩ ⟨eso es muy americano : that's typically American⟩ **2** : too ⟨es muy grande para él : it's too big for him⟩

N

n *nf* : fourteenth letter of the Spanish alphabet
nabo *nm* : turnip
nácar *nm* MADREPERLA : nacre, mother-of-pearl
nacarado, -da *adj* : pearly
nacer {48} *vi* **1** : to be born ⟨nací en Guatemala : I was born in Guatemala⟩ ⟨no nació ayer : he wasn't born yesterday⟩ **2** : to hatch **3** : to bud, to sprout **4** : to rise, to originate **5 nacer para algo** : to be born to be something **6 volver a nacer** : to have a lucky escape
nacido[1], -da *adj* **1** : born **2 recién nacido** : newborn
nacido[2], -da *n* **1 los nacidos** : those born (at a particular time) **2 recién nacido** : newborn baby
naciente *adj* **1** : newfound, growing **2** : rising ⟨el sol naciente : the rising sun⟩
nacimiento *nm* **1** : birth **2** : source (of a river) **3** : beginning, origin **4** BELÉN : Nativity scene, crèche
nación *nf, pl* **naciones** : nation, country, people (of a country)
nacional[1] *adj* : national
nacional[2] *nmf* CIUDADANO : national, citizen
nacionalidad *nf* : nationality
nacionalismo *nm* : nationalism
nacionalista[1] *adj* : nationalist, nationalistic
nacionalista[2] *nmf* : nationalist
nacionalización *nf, pl* **-ciones 1** : nationalization **2** : naturalization
nacionalizar {21} *vt* **1** : to nationalize **2** : to naturalize (as a citizen) — **nacionalizarse** *vr*
naco, -ca *adj Mex* : trashy, vulgar, common
nada[1] *adv* : not at all, not in the least ⟨no estamos nada cansados : we are not at all tired⟩
nada[2] *nf* **1** : nothingness **2** : smidgen, bit ⟨una nada le disgusta : the slightest thing upsets him⟩
nada[3] *pron* **1** : nothing ⟨no estoy haciendo nada : I'm not doing anything⟩ **2 casi nada** : next to nothing **3 de ~** : you're welcome **4 dentro de nada** : very soon, in no time **5 nada más** : nothing else, nothing more
nadador, -dora *n* : swimmer
nadar *vi* **1** : to swim **2 ~ en** : to be swimming in, to be rolling in — *vt* : to swim
nadería *nf* : small thing, trifle
nadie *pron* : nobody, no one ⟨no vi a nadie : I didn't see anyone⟩
nadir *nm* : nadir
nado *nm* **1** *Mex* : swimming **2 a ~** : swimming ⟨cruzó el río a nado : he swam across the river⟩
nafta *nf* **1** : naphtha **2** (*in various countries*) : gasoline
naftalina *nf* : naphthalene, mothballs *pl*
náhuatl[1] *adj & nmf, pl* **nahuas** : Nahuatl
náhuatl[2] *nm* : Nahuatl (language)
nailon → **nilón**
naipe *nm* : playing card
nalga *nf* **1** : buttock **2 nalgas** *nfpl* : buttocks, bottom
nalgada *nf* : smack on the bottom, spanking
namibio, -bia *adj & n* : Namibian
nana *nf* **1** : lullaby **2** *fam* : grandma **3** *CA, Col, Mex, Ven* : nanny
nanay *interj fam* : no way!, not likely!
naranja[1] *adj & nm* : orange (color)
naranja[2] *nf* : orange (fruit)
naranjal *nm* : orange grove
naranjo *nm* : orange tree
narcisismo *nm* : narcissism
narcisista[1] *adj* : narcissistic
narcisista[2] *nmf* : narcissist
narciso *nm* : narcissus, daffodil
narcótico[1], -ca *adj* : narcotic
narcótico[2] *nm* : narcotic
narcotizar {21} *vt* : to drug, to dope
narcotraficante *nmf* : drug trafficker
narcotráfico *nm* : drug trafficking
narigón, -gona *adj, mpl* **-gones** : big-nosed
narigudo → **narigón**
nariz *nf, pl* **narices 1** : nose ⟨sonar(se) la nariz : to blow one's nose⟩ **2** : sense of smell
narración *nf, pl* **-ciones** : narration, account
narrador, -dora *n* : narrator
narrar *vt* : to narrate, to tell
narrativa *nf* : narrative, story
narrativo, -va *adj* : narrative
narval *nm* : narwhal
nasa *nf* : creel
nasal *adj* : nasal
nata *nf* **1** : cream ⟨nata batida : whipped cream⟩ **2** : skin (on boiled milk)
natación *nf, pl* **-ciones** : swimming
natal *adj* : native, natal
natalicio *nm* : birthday ⟨el natalicio de George Washington : George Washington's birthday⟩
natalidad *nf* : birthrate
natillas *nfpl* : custard
natividad *nf* : birth, nativity
nativo, -va *adj & n* : native
nato, -ta *adj* : born, natural
natural[1] *adj* **1** : natural **2** : normal ⟨como es natural : naturally, as expected⟩ **3 ~ de** : native of, from **4 de tamaño natural** : life-size
natural[2] *nm* **1** CARÁCTER : disposition, temperament **2** : native ⟨un natural de Venezuela : a native of Venezuela⟩
naturaleza *nf* **1** : nature ⟨la madre naturaleza : mother nature⟩ **2** ÍNDOLE : nature, disposition, constitution ⟨la naturaleza humana : human nature⟩ **3 naturaleza muerta** : still life

naturalidad *nf* : simplicity, naturalness
naturalismo *nm* : naturalism
naturalista[1] *adj* : naturalistic
naturalista[2] *nmf* : naturalist
naturalización *nf, pl* **-ciones** : naturalization
naturalizar {21} *vt* : to naturalize — **naturalizarse** *vr* NACIONALIZARSE : to become naturalized
naturalmente *adv* **1** : naturally, inherently **2** : of course
naufragar {52} *vi* **1** : to be shipwrecked **2** FRACASAR : to fail, to collapse
naufragio *nm* **1** : shipwreck **2** FRACASO : failure, collapse
náufrago[1], **-ga** *adj* : shipwrecked, castaway
náufrago[2], **-ga** *n* : shipwrecked person, castaway
náusea *nf* **1** : nausea **2 dar náuseas** : to nauseate, to disgust **3 náuseas matutinas** : morning sickness
nauseabundo, **-da** *adj* : nauseating, sickening
náutica *nf* : navigation
náutico, **-ca** *adj* : nautical
nautilo *nm* : nautilus
navaja *nf* **1** : pocketknife, penknife ⟨navaja de muelle : switchblade⟩ **2 navaja de afeitar** : straight razor, razor blade
navajo, **-ja** *adj & n* : Navajo
naval *adj* : naval
nave *nf* **1** : ship ⟨nave capitana : flagship⟩ ⟨nave espacial : spaceship⟩ **2** : nave ⟨nave lateral : aisle⟩ **3 quemar uno sus naves** : to burn one's bridges
navegabilidad *nf* : navigability
navegable *adj* : navigable
navegación *nf, pl* **-ciones** : navigation
navegante[1] *adj* : sailing, seafaring
navegante[2] *nmf* : navigator
navegar {52} *v* : to navigate, to sail
Navidad *nf* : Christmas, Christmastime ⟨Feliz Navidad : Merry Christmas⟩
navideño, **-ña** *adj* : Christmas
naviero, **-ra** *adj* : shipping
náyade *nf* : naiad
nazca, etc. → **nacer**
nazi *adj & nmf* : Nazi
nazismo *nm* : Nazism
nébeda *nf* : catnip
neblina *nf* : light fog, mist
neblinoso, **-sa** *adj* : misty, foggy
nebulosa *nf* : nebula
nebulosidad *nf* : mistiness, haziness
nebuloso, **-sa** *adj* **1** : hazy, misty **2** : nebulous, vague
necedad *nf* : stupidity, foolishness ⟨decir necedades : to talk nonsense⟩
necesariamente *adv* : necessarily
necesario, **-ria** *adj* **1** : necessary **2 si es necesario** : if need be **3 hacerse necesario** : to be required
neceser *nm* : toilet kit, vanity case
necesidad *nf* **1** : need, necessity **2** : poverty, want **3 necesidades** *nfpl* : hardships **4 hacer sus necesidades** : to relieve oneself
necesitado, **-da** *adj* : needy
necesitar *vt* **1** : to need **2** : to necessitate, to require — *vi* **~ de** : to have need of
necio[1], **-cia** *adj* **1** : foolish, silly, dumb **2** *fam* : naughty
necio[2], **-cia** *n* ESTÚPIDO : fool, idiot
necrología *nf* : obituary
necrópolis *nfs & pl* : cemetery
néctar *nm* : nectar
nectarina *nf* : nectarine
neerlandés[1], **-desa** *adj, mpl* **-deses** HOLANDÉS : Dutch
neerlandés[2], **-desa** *n, mpl* **-deses** HOLANDÉS : Dutch person, Dutchman *m*
nefando, **-da** *adj* : unspeakable, heinous
nefario, **-ria** *adj* : nefarious
nefasto, **-ta** *adj* **1** : ill-fated, unlucky **2** : disastrous, terrible
negación *nf, pl* **-ciones** **1** : negation, denial **2** : negative (in grammar)
negar {49} *vt* **1** : to deny **2** REHUSAR : to refuse **3** : to disown — **negarse** *vr* **1** : to refuse **2** : to deny oneself
negativa *nf* **1** : denial **2** : refusal
negativo[1], **-va** *adj* : negative
negativo[2] *nm* : negative (of a photograph)
negligé *nm* : negligee
negligencia *nf* : negligence
negligente *adj* : neglectful, negligent — **negligentemente** *adv*
negociable *adj* : negotiable
negociación *nf, pl* **-ciones** **1** : negotiation **2 negociación colectiva** : collective bargaining
negociador, **-dora** *n* : negotiator
negociante *nmf* : businessman *m*, businesswoman *f*
negociar *vt* : to negotiate — *vi* : to deal, to do business
negocio *nm* **1** : business, place of business **2** : deal, transaction **3 negocios** *nmpl* : commerce, trade, business
negrero, **-ra** *n* **1** : slave trader **2** *fam* : slave driver, brutal boss
negrita *nf* : boldface (type)
negro[1], **-gra** *adj* **1** : black, dark **2** BRONCEADO : suntanned **3** : gloomy, awful, desperate ⟨la cosa se está poniendo negra : things are looking bad⟩ **4 mercado negro** : black market
negro[2], **-gra** *n* **1** : dark-skinned person, black person **2** *fam* : darling, dear
negro[3] *nm* : black (color)
negrura *nf* : blackness
negruzco, **-ca** *adj* : blackish
nene, **-na** *n* : baby, small child
nenúfar *nm* : water lily
neocelandés → **neozelandés**
neoclasicismo *nm* : neoclassicism
neoclásico, **-ca** *adj* : neoclassical
neófito, **-ta** *n* : neophyte, novice
neologismo *nm* : neologism
neón *nm, pl* **neones** : neon
neoyorquino[1], **-na** *adj* : of or from New York

neoyorquino[2], **-na** *n* : New Yorker
neozelandés[1], **-desa** *adj, mpl* **-deses** : of or from New Zealand
neozelandés[2], **-desa** *n, mpl* **-deses** : New Zealander
nepalés, **-lesa** *adj & n, mpl* **-leses** : Nepali
nepotismo *nm* : nepotism
neptunio *nm* : neptunium
Neptuno *nm* : Neptune
nervio *nm* **1** : nerve **2** : tendon, sinew, gristle (in meat) **3** : energy, drive **4** : rib (of a vault) **5 nervios** *nmpl* : nerves ⟨estar mal de los nervios : to be a bundle of nerves⟩ ⟨ataque de nervios : nervous breakdown⟩
nerviosamente *adv* : nervously
nerviosidad → **nerviosismo**
nerviosismo *nf* : nervousness, anxiety
nervioso, -sa *adj* **1** : nervous, nerve ⟨sistema nervioso : nervous system⟩ **2** : high-strung, restless, anxious ⟨ponerse nervioso : to get nervous⟩ **3** : vigorous, energetic
nervudo, **-da** *adj* : sinewy, wiry
neta *nf Mex fam* : truth ⟨la neta es que me cae mal : the truth is, I don't like her⟩
netamente *adv* : clearly, obviously
neto, **-ta** *adj* **1** : net ⟨peso neto : net weight⟩ **2** : clear, distinct
neumático[1], **-ca** *adj* : pneumatic
neumático[2] *nm* LLANTA : tire
neumonía *nf* PULMONÍA : pneumonia
neural *adj* : neural
neuralgia *nf* : neuralgia
neuritis *nf* : neuritis
neurología *nf* : neurology
neurológico, **-ca** *adj* : neurological, neurologic
neurólogo, **-ga** *n* : neurologist
neurosis *nfs & pl* : neurosis
neurótico, **-ca** *adj & n* : neurotic
neutral *adj* : neutral
neutralidad *nf* : neutrality
neutralizar {21} *vt* : to neutralize — **neutralización** *nf*
neutro, **-tra** *adj* **1** : neutral **2** : neuter
neutrón *nm, pl* **neutrones** : neutron
nevada *nf* : snowfall
nevado, **-da** *adj* **1** : snowcapped **2** : snow-white
nevar {55} *v impers* : to snow
nevasca *nf* : snowstorm, blizzard
nevera *nf* REFRIGERADOR : refrigerator
nevería *nf Mex* : ice cream parlor
nevisca *nf* : light snowfall, flurry
nevoso, **-sa** *adj* : snowy
nexo *nm* VÍNCULO : link, connection, nexus
ni *conj* **1** : neither, nor ⟨afuera no hace ni frío ni calor : it's neither cold nor hot outside⟩ **2 ni que** : not even if, not as if ⟨ni que me pagaran : not even if they paid me⟩ ⟨ni que fuera (yo) su madre : it's not as if I were his mother⟩ **3 ni siquiera** : not even ⟨ni siquiera nos llamaron : they didn't even call us⟩
nicaragüense *adj & nmf* : Nicaraguan
nicho *nm* : niche
nicotina *nf* : nicotine
nido *nm* **1** : nest **2** : hiding place, den
niebla *nf* : fog, mist
niega, niegue etc. → **negar**
nieto, **-ta** *n* **1** : grandson *m*, granddaughter *f* **2 nietos** *nmpl* : grandchildren
nieva, etc. → **nevar**
nieve *nf* **1** : snow **2** *Cuba, Mex, PRi* : sherbet
nigeriano, **-na** *adj & n* : Nigerian
nigua *nf* : sand flea, chigger
nihilismo *nm* : nihilism
nilón *or* **nilon** *nm, pl* **nilones** : nylon
nimbo *nm* **1** : halo **2** : nimbus
nimiedad *nf* INSIGNIFICANCIA : trifle, triviality
nimio, **-mia** *adj* INSIGNIFICANTE : insignificant, trivial
ninfa *nf* : nymph
ningunear *vt Mex fam* : to disrespect
ninguno[1], **-na** (**ningún** *before masculine singular nouns*) *adj, mpl* **ningunos** : no, none ⟨no es ninguna tonta : she's no fool⟩ ⟨no debe hacerse en ningún momento : that should never be done⟩
ninguno[2], **-na** *pron* **1** : neither, none ⟨ninguno de los dos ha vuelto aún : neither one has returned yet⟩ **2** : no one, no other ⟨te quiero más que a ninguna : I love you more than any other⟩
niña *nf* **1** PUPILA : pupil (of the eye) **2 la niña de los ojos** : the apple of one's eye
niñada *nf* **1** : childishness **2** : trifle, silly thing
niñería → **niñada**
niñero, **-ra** *n* : baby-sitter, nanny
niñez *nf, pl* **niñeces** INFANCIA : childhood
niño, **-ña** *n* : child, boy *m*, girl *f*
niobio *nm* : niobium
nipón, **-pona** *adj & n, mpl* **nipones** JAPONÉS : Japanese
níquel *nm* : nickel
nitidez *nf, pl* **-deces** CLARIDAD : clarity, vividness, sharpness
nítido, -da *adj* CLARO : clear, vivid, sharp
nitrato *nm* : nitrate
nítrico, -ca *adj* **ácido nítrico** : nitric acid
nitrito *nm* : nitrite
nitrógeno *nm* : nitrogen
nitroglicerina *nf* : nitroglycerin
nivel *nm* **1** : level, height ⟨nivel del mar : sea level⟩ **2** : level, standard ⟨nivel de vida : standard of living⟩
nivelar *vt* : to level (out)
nixtamal *nm Mex* : limed corn used for tortillas
no *adv* **1** : no ⟨¿quieres ir al mercado? no, voy más tarde : do you want to go shopping? no, I'm going later⟩ **2** : not ⟨¡no hagas eso! : don't do that!⟩ ⟨creo que no : I don't think so⟩ **3** : non- ⟨no fumador : non-smoker⟩ **4 ¡como no!** : of course! **5 no bien** : as soon as, no sooner

nobelio *nm* : nobelium
noble[1] *adj* : noble — **noblemente** *adv*
noble[2] *nmf* : nobleman *m*, noblewoman *f*
nobleza *nf* **1** : nobility **2** HONRADEZ : honesty, integrity
nocaut *nm* : knockout, KO
noche *nf* **1** : night, nighttime, evening **2 buenas noches** : good evening, good night **3 de noche** *or* **por la noche** : at night **4 hacerse de noche** : to get dark
Nochebuena *nf* : Christmas Eve
nochecita *nf* : dusk
Nochevieja *nf* : New Year's Eve
noción *nf, pl* **nociones** **1** CONCEPTO : notion, concept **2 nociones** *nfpl* : smattering, rudiments *pl*
nocivo, -va *adj* DAÑINO : harmful, noxious
noctámbulo, -la *n* **1** : sleepwalker **2** : night owl
nocturno[1], **-na** *adj* : night, nocturnal
nocturno[2] *nm* : nocturne
nodriza *nf* : wet nurse
nódulo *nm* : nodule
nogal *nm* **1** : walnut tree **2** *Mex* : pecan tree **3 nogal americano** : hickory
nómada[1] *adj* : nomadic
nómada[2] *nmf* : nomad
nomás *adv* : only, just ⟨lo hice nomás porque sí : I did it just because⟩ ⟨nomás de recordarlo me enojo : I get angry just remembering it⟩ ⟨nomás faltan dos semanas para Navidad : there are only two weeks left till Christmas⟩
nombradía *nf* RENOMBRE : fame, renown
nombrado, -da *adj* : famous, well-known
nombramiento *nm* : appointment, nomination
nombrar *vt* **1** : to appoint **2** : to mention, to name
nombre *nm* **1** : name ⟨nombre de pluma : pseudonym, pen name⟩ ⟨en nombre : on behalf of⟩ ⟨sin nombre : nameless⟩ **2** : noun ⟨nombre propio : proper noun⟩ **3** : fame, renown
nomenclatura *nf* : nomenclature
nomeolvides *nmfs & pl* : forget-me-not
nómina *nf* : payroll
nominación *nf, pl* **-ciones** : nomination
nominal *adj* : nominal — **nominalmente** *adv*
nominar *vt* : to nominate
nominativo[1], **-va** *adj* : nominative
nominativo[2] *nm* : nominative (case)
nomo *nm* : gnome
non[1] *adj* IMPAR : odd, not even
non[2] *nm* : odd number
nonagésimo[1], **-ma** *adj* : ninetieth, ninety-
nonagésimo[2], **-ma** *n* : ninetieth, ninety- (in a series)
nono, -na *adj* : ninth — **nono** *nm*
nopal *nm* : nopal, cactus
nopalitos *nmpl Mex* : pickled cactus leaves
noquear *vt* : to knock out, to KO
norcoreano, -na *adj & n* : North Korean
nordeste[1] *or* **noreste** *adj* **1** : northeastern **2** : northeasterly
nordeste[2] *or* **noreste** *nm* : northeast
nórdico, -ca *adj & n* **1** ESCANDINAVO : Scandinavian **2** : Norse
noreste → **nordeste**
noria *nf* **1** : waterwheel **2** : Ferris wheel
norirlandés[1], **-desa** *adj, mpl* **-deses** : Northern Irish
norirlandés[2], **-desa** *n, mpl* **-deses** : person from Northern Ireland
norma *nf* **1** : rule, regulation **2** : norm, standard
normal *adj* **1** : normal, usual **2** : standard **3 escuela normal** : teacher-training college
normalidad *nf* : normality, normalcy
normalización *nf, pl* **-ciones** *nf* **1** REGULARIZACIÓN : normalization **2** ESTANDARIZACIÓN : standardization
normalizar {21} *vt* **1** REGULARIZAR : to normalize **2** ESTANDARIZAR : to standardize — **normalizarse** *vr* : to return to normal
normalmente *adv* GENERALMENTE : ordinarily, generally
noroeste[1] *adj* **1** : northwestern **2** : northwesterly
noroeste[2] *nm* : northwest
norte[1] *adj* : north, northern
norte[2] *nm* **1** : north **2** : north wind **3** META : aim, objective
norteamericano, -na *adj & n* **1** : North American **2** AMERICANO, ESTADOUNIDENSE : American, native or inhabitant of the United States
norteño[1], **-ña** *adj* : northern
norteño[2], **-ña** *n* : Northerner
noruego[1], **-ga** *adj & n* : Norwegian
noruego[2] *nm* : Norwegian (language)
nos *pron* **1** : us ⟨nos enviaron a la frontera : they sent us to the border⟩ **2** : ourselves ⟨nos divertimos muchísimo : we enjoyed ourselves a great deal⟩ **3** : each other, one another ⟨nos vimos desde lejos : we saw each other from far away⟩ **4** : to us, for us, from us ⟨nos lo dio : he gave it to us⟩ ⟨nos lo compraron : they bought it from us⟩
nosotros, -tras *pron* **1** : we ⟨nosotros llegamos ayer : we arrived yesterday⟩ **2** : us ⟨ven con nosotros : come with us⟩ **3 nosotros mismos** : ourselves ⟨lo arreglamos nosotros mismos : we fixed it ourselves⟩
nostalgia *nf* **1** : nostalgia, longing **2** : homesickness
nostálgico, -ca *adj* **1** : nostalgic **2** : homesick
nota *nf* **1** : note, message **2** : announcement ⟨nota de prensa : press release⟩ **3** : grade, mark (in school) **4** : characteristic, feature, touch **5** : note (in music) **6** : bill, check (in a restaurant)

notable *adj* **1** : notable, noteworthy **2** : outstanding
notación *nf, pl* **-ciones** : notation
notar *vt* **1** : to notice ⟨hacer notar algo : to point out something⟩ **2** : to tell ⟨la diferencia se nota inmediatamente : you can tell the difference right away⟩ — **notarse** *vr* **1** : to be evident, to show **2** : to feel, to seem
notario, -ria *n* : notary, notary public
noticia *nf* **1** : news item, piece of news **2 noticias** *nfpl* : news
noticiero *nm* : news program, newscast
noticioso, -sa *adj* : news ⟨agencia noticiosa : news agency⟩
notificación *nf, pl* **-ciones** : notification
notificar {72} *vt* : to notify, to inform
notoriedad *nf* **1** : knowledge, obviousness **2** : fame, notoriety
notorio, -ria *adj* **1** OBVIO : obvious, evident **2** CONOCIDO : well-known
novato[1], **-ta** *adj* : inexperienced, new
novato[2], **-ta** *n* : beginner, novice
novecientos[1], **-tas** *adj* : nine hundred
novecientos[2] *nms & pl* : nine hundred
novedad *nf* **1** : newness, novelty **2** : innovation
novedoso, -sa *adj* : original, novel
novel *adj* NOVATO : inexperienced, new
novela *nf* **1** : novel **2** : soap opera
novelar *vt* : to fictionalize, to make a novel out of
novelesco, -ca *adj* **1** : fictional **2** : fantastic, fabulous
novelista *nmf* : novelist
novena *nf* : novena
noveno, -na *adj* : ninth — **noveno, -na** *n*
noventa *adj & nm* : ninety
noventavo[1], **-va** *adj* : ninetieth
noventavo[2] *nm* : ninetieth (fraction)
noviazgo *nm* **1** : courtship, relationship **2** : engagement, betrothal
novicio, -cia *n* **1** : novice (in religion) **2** PRINCIPIANTE : novice, beginner
noviembre *nm* : November
novilla *nf* : heifer
novillada *nf* : bullfight featuring young bulls
novillero, -ra *n* : apprentice bullfighter
novillo *nm* : young bull
novio, -via *n* **1** : boyfriend *m*, girlfriend *f* **2** PROMETIDO : fiancé *m*, fiancée *f* **3** : bridegroom *m*, bride *f*
novocaína *nf* : novocaine
nubarrón *nm, pl* **-rrones** : storm cloud
nube *nf* **1** : cloud ⟨andar en las nubes : to have one's head in the clouds⟩ ⟨por las nubes : sky-high⟩ **2** : cloud (of dust), swarm (of insects, etc.)
nublado[1], **-da** *adj* **1** NUBOSO : cloudy, overcast **2** : clouded, dim
nublado[2] *nm* **1** : storm cloud **2** AMENAZA : menace, threat
nublar *vt* **1** : to cloud **2** OSCURECER : to obscure — **nublarse** *vr* : to get cloudy
nubosidad *nf* : cloudiness
nuboso, -sa *adj* NUBLADO : cloudy
nuca *nf* : nape, back of the neck
nuclear *adj* : nuclear
núcleo *nm* **1** : nucleus **2** : center, heart, core
nudillo *nm* : knuckle
nudismo *nm* : nudism
nudista *adj & nmf* : nudist
nudo *nm* **1** : knot ⟨nudo de rizo : square knot⟩ ⟨un nudo en la garganta : a lump in one's throat⟩ **2** : node **3** : junction, hub ⟨nudo de comunicaciones : communication center⟩ **4** : crux, heart (of a problem, etc.)
nudoso, -sa *adj* : knotty, gnarled
nuera *nf* : daughter-in-law
nuestro[1], **-tra** *adj* : our
nuestro[2], **-tra** *pron* (*with definite article*) : ours, our own ⟨el nuestro es más grande : ours is bigger⟩ ⟨es de los nuestros : it's one of ours⟩
nuevamente *adv* : again, anew
nuevas *nfpl* : tidings *pl*
nueve *adj & nm* : nine
nuevecito, -ta *adj* : brand-new
nuevo, -va *adj* **1** : new ⟨una casa nueva : a new house⟩ ⟨¿qué hay de nuevo? : what's new?⟩ **2 de ~** : again, once more **3 Nuevo Testamento** : New Testament
nuez *nf, pl* **nueces** **1** : nut **2** : walnut **3** *Mex* : pecan **4 nuez de Adán** : Adam's apple **5 nuez moscada** : nutmeg
nulidad *nf* **1** : nullity **2** : incompetent person ⟨¡es una nulidad! : he's hopeless!⟩
nulo, -la *adj* **1** : null, null and void **2** INEPTO : useless, inept ⟨es nula para la cocina : she's hopeless at cooking⟩
numen *nm* : poetic muse, inspiration
numerable *adj* : countable
numeración *nf, pl* **-ciones** **1** : numbering **2** : numbers *pl*, numerals *pl* ⟨numeración romana : Roman numerals⟩
numerador *nm* : numerator
numeral *adj* : numeral
numerar *vt* : to number
numerario, -ria *adj* : long-standing, permanent ⟨profesor numerario : tenured professor⟩
numérico, -ca *adj* : numerical — **numéricamente** *adv*
número *nm* **1** : number ⟨número impar : odd number⟩ ⟨número ordinal : ordinal number⟩ ⟨número arábico : Arabic numeral⟩ ⟨número quebrado : fraction⟩ **2** : issue (of a publication) **3 sin ~** : countless
numeroso, -sa *adj* : numerous
numismática *nf* : numismatics
nunca *adv* **1** : never, ever ⟨nunca es tarde : it's never too late⟩ ⟨no trabaja casi nunca : he hardly ever works⟩ **2 nunca más** : never again **3 nunca jamás** : never ever
nuncio *nm* : harbinger, herald
nupcial *adj* : nuptial, wedding
nupcias *nfpl* : nuptials *pl*, wedding

nutria *nf* **1** : otter **2** : nutria
nutrición *nf, pl* **-ciones** : nutrition, nourishment
nutrido, -da *adj* **1** : nourished ⟨mal nutrido : undernourished, malnourished⟩ **2** : considerable, abundant ⟨de nutrido : full of, abounding in⟩
nutriente *nm* : nutrient
nutrimento *nm* : nutriment
nutrir *vt* **1** ALIMENTAR : to feed, to nourish **2** : to foster, to provide
nutritivo, -va *adj* : nourishing, nutritious
nylon → **nilón**
ñ *nf* : fifteenth letter of the Spanish alphabet
ñame *nm* : yam
ñandú *nm* : rhea
ñapa *nf* : extra amount ⟨de ñapa : for good measure⟩
ñoñear *vi fam* : to whine
ñoño, -ña *adj fam* : whiny, fussy ⟨no seas tan ñoño : don't be such a wimp⟩
ñoquis *nmpl* : gnocchi *pl*
ñu *nm* : gnu, wildebeest

O

o[1] *nf* : sixteenth letter of the Spanish alphabet
o[2] *conj* (**u** *before words beginning with o- or ho-*) **1** : or ⟨¿vienes con nosotros o te quedas? : are you coming with us or staying?⟩ **2** : either ⟨o vienes con nosotros o te quedas : either you come with us or you stay⟩ **3 o sea** : that is to say, in other words
oasis *nms & pl* : oasis
obcecado, -da *adj* **1** : blinded ⟨obcecado por la ira : blinded by rage⟩ **2** : stubborn, obstinate
obcecar {72} *vt* : to blind (by emotions) — **obcecarse** *vr* : to become stubborn
obedecer {53} *vt* : to obey ⟨obedecer órdenes : to obey orders⟩ ⟨obedece a tus padres : obey your parents⟩ — *vi* **1** : to obey **2 ~ a** : to respond to **3 ~ a** : to be due to, to result from
obediencia *nf* : obedience
obediente *adj* : obedient — **obedientemente** *adv*
obelisco *nm* : obelisk
obertura *nf* : overture
obesidad *nf* : obesity
obeso, -sa *adj* : obese
óbice *nm* : obstacle, impediment
obispado *nm* DIÓCESIS : bishopric, diocese
obispo *nm* : bishop
obituario *nm* : obituary
objeción *nf, pl* **-ciones** : objection ⟨ponerle objeciones a algo : to object to something⟩
objetar *v* : to object ⟨no tengo nada que objetar : I have no objections⟩
objetividad *nf* : objectivity
objetivo[1], **-va** *adj* : objective — **objetivamente** *adv*
objetivo[2] *nm* **1** META : objective, goal, target **2** : lens
objeto *nm* **1** COSA : object, thing **2** OBJETIVO : objective, purpose ⟨con objeto de : in order to, with the aim of⟩ **3 objeto volador no identificado** : unidentified flying object
objetor, -tora *n* : objector ⟨objetor de conciencia : conscientious objector⟩
oblea *nf* **1** : wafer **2 hecho una oblea** *fam* : skinny as a rail
oblicuo, -cua *adj* : oblique — **oblicuamente** *adv*
obligación *nf, pl* **-ciones** **1** DEBER : obligation, duty **2** : bond, debenture
obligado, -da *adj* **1** : obliged **2** : obligatory, compulsory **3** : customary
obligar {52} *vt* : to force, to require, to oblige — **obligarse** *vr* : to commit oneself, to undertake (to do something)
obligatorio, -ria *adj* : mandatory, required, compulsory
obliterar *vt* : to obliterate, to destroy — **obliteración** *nf*
oblongo, -ga *adj* : oblong
obnubilación *nf, pl* **-ciones** : bewilderment, confusion
obnubilar *vt* : to daze, to bewilder
oboe[1] *nm* : oboe
oboe[2] *nmf* : oboist
obra *nf* **1** : work ⟨obra de arte : work of art⟩ ⟨obra de teatro : play⟩ ⟨obra de consulta : reference work⟩ **2** : deed ⟨una buena obra : a good deed⟩ **3** : construction work **4 obra maestra** : masterpiece **5 obras públicas** : public works **6 por obra de** : thanks to, because of
obrar *vt* : to work, to produce ⟨obrar milagros : to work miracles⟩ — *vi* **1** : to act, to behave ⟨obrar con cautela : to act with caution⟩ **2 obrar en poder de** : to be in possession of
obrero[1], **-ra** *adj* : working ⟨la clase obrera : the working class⟩
obrero[2], **-ra** *n* : worker, laborer
obscenidad *nf* : obscenity
obsceno, -na *adj* : obscene
obscurecer, obscuridad, obscuro → **oscurecer, oscuridad, oscuro**
obsequiar *vt* REGALAR : to give, to present ⟨lo obsequiaron con una placa : they presented him with a plaque⟩
obsequio *nm* REGALO : gift, present
obsequiosidad *nf* : attentiveness, deference
obsequioso, -sa *adj* : obliging, attentive
observable *adj* : observable
observación *nf, pl* **-ciones** **1** : observation, watching **2** : remark, comment
observador[1], **-dora** *adj* : observant

observador[2], **-dora** *n* : observer, watcher
observancia *nf* : observance
observante *adj* : observant ⟨los judíos observantes : observant Jews⟩
observar *vt* **1** : to observe, to watch ⟨estábamos observando a los niños : we were watching the children⟩ **2** NOTAR : to notice **3** ACATAR : to obey, to abide by **4** COMENTAR : to remark, to comment
observatorio *nm* : observatory
obsesión *nf, pl* **-siones** : obsession
obsesionar *vt* : to obsess, to preoccupy excessively — **obsesionarse** *vr*
obsesivo, **-va** *adj* : obsessive
obseso, **-sa** *adj* : obsessed
obsolescencia *nf* DESUSO : obsolescence — **obsolescente** *adj*
obsoleto, **-ta** *adj* DESUSADO : obsolete
obstaculizar {21} *vt* IMPEDIR : to obstruct, to hinder
obstáculo *nm* IMPEDIMENTO : obstacle
obstante[1] *conj* **no obstante** : nevertheless, however
obstante[2] *prep* **no obstante** : in spite of, despite ⟨mantuvo su inocencia no obstante la evidencia : he maintained his innocence in spite of the evidence⟩
obstar *v impers* **~ a** *or* **~ para** : to hinder, to prevent ⟨eso no obsta para que me vaya : that doesn't prevent me from leaving⟩
obstetra *nmf* TOCÓLOGO : obstetrician
obstetricia *nf* : obstetrics
obstétrico, **-ca** *adj* : obstetric, obstetrical
obstinación *nf, pl* **-ciones** **1** TERQUEDAD : obstinacy, stubbornness **2** : perseverance, tenacity
obstinado, **-da** *adj* **1** TERCO : obstinate, stubborn **2** : persistent — **obstinadamente** *adv*
obstinarse *vr* EMPECINARSE : to be obstinate, to be stubborn
obstrucción *nf, pl* **-ciones** : obstruction, blockage
obstruccionismo *nm* : obstructionism, filibustering
obstruccionista *adj* : obstructionist, filibustering
obstructor, **-tora** *adj* : obstructive
obstruir {41} *vt* BLOQUEAR : to obstruct, to block, to clog — **obstruirse** *vr*
obtención *nf* : obtaining, procurement
obtener {80} *vt* : to obtain, to secure, to get — **obtenible** *adj*
obturador *nm* : shutter (of a camera)
obtuso, **-sa** *adj* : obtuse
obtuvo, etc. → **obtener**
obús *nm, pl* **obuses** **1** : mortar (weapon) **2** : mortar shell
obviar *vt* : to get around (a difficulty), to avoid
obvio, **-via** *adj* : obvious — **obviamente** *adv*
oca *nf* : goose
ocasión *nf, pl* **-siones** **1** : occasion, time **2** : opportunity, chance **3** : bargain **4 de ~** : secondhand **5 aviso de ocasión** *Mex* : classified ad
ocasional *adj* **1** : occasional **2** : chance, fortuitous
ocasionalmente *adv* **1** : occasionally **2** : by chance
ocasionar *vt* CAUSAR : to cause, to occasion
ocaso *nm* **1** ANOCHECER : sunset, sundown **2** DECADENCIA : decline, fall
occidental *adj* : western, occidental
occidente *nm* **1** OESTE, PONIENTE : west **2 el Occidente** : the West
oceánico, **-ca** *adj* : oceanic
océano *nm* : ocean
oceanografía *nf* : oceanography
oceanográfico, **-ca** *adj* : oceanographic
ocelote *nm* : ocelot
ochenta *adj & nm* : eighty
ochentavo[1], **-va** *adj* : eightieth
ochentavo[2] *nm* : eightieth (fraction)
ocho *adj & nm* : eight
ochocientos[1], **-tas** *adj* : eight hundred
ochocientos[2] *ms & pl* : eight hundred
ocio *nm* **1** : free time, leisure **2** : idleness
ociosidad *nf* : idleness, inactivity
ocioso, **-sa** *adj* **1** INACTIVO : idle, inactive **2** INÚTIL : pointless, useless
ocre *nm* : ocher
octágono *nm* : octagon — **octagonal** *adj*
octava *nf* : octave
octavo, **-va** *adj* : eighth — **octavo**, **-va** *n*
octeto *nm* **1** : octet **2** : byte
octogésimo[1], **-ma** *adj* : eightieth, eighty-
octogésimo[2], **-ma** *n* : eightieth, eighty- (in a series)
octubre *nm* : October
ocular *adj* **1** : ocular, eye ⟨músculos oculares : eye muscles⟩ **2 testigo ocular** : eyewitness
oculista *nmf* : oculist, ophthalmologist
ocultación *nf, pl* **-ciones** : concealment
ocultar *vt* ESCONDER : to conceal, to hide — **ocultarse** *vr*
oculto, **-ta** *adj* **1** ESCONDIDO : hidden, concealed **2** : occult
ocupación *nf, pl* **-ciones** **1** : occupation, activity **2** : occupancy **3** EMPLEO : employment, job
ocupacional *adj* : occupational, job-related
ocupado, **-da** *adj* **1** : busy **2** : taken ⟨este asiento está ocupado : this seat is taken⟩ **3** : occupied ⟨territorios ocupados : occupied territories⟩ **4 señal de ocupado** : busy signal
ocupante *nmf* : occupant
ocupar *vt* **1** : to occupy, to take possession of **2** : to hold (a position) **3** : to employ, to keep busy **4** : to fill (space, time) **5** : to inhabit (a dwelling) **6** : to bother, to concern — **ocuparse** *vr* **~ de 1** : to be concerned with **2** : to take care of

ocurrencia *nf* **1** : occurrence, event **2** : witticism **3** : bright idea

ocurrente *adj* **1** : witty **2** : clever, sharp

ocurrir *vi* : to occur, to happen — **ocurrirse** *vr* **~ a** : to occur to, to strike ⟨se me ocurrió una mejor idea : a better idea occurred to me⟩

oda *nf* : ode

odiar *vt* ABOMINAR, ABORRECER : to hate

odio *nm* : hate, hatred

odioso, -sa *adj* ABOMINABLE, ABORRECIBLE : hateful, detestable

odisea *nf* : odyssey

odontología *nf* : dentistry, dental surgery

odontólogo, -ga *n* : dentist, dental surgeon

oeste[1] *adj* **1** : west, western ⟨la región oeste : the western region⟩ **2** : westerly

oeste[2] *nm* **1** : west, West **2** : west wind

ofender *vt* AGRAVIAR : to offend, to insult — *vi* : to offend, to be insulting — **ofenderse** *vr* : to take offense

ofensa *nf* : offense, insult

ofensiva *nf* : offensive ⟨pasar a la ofensiva : to go on the offensive⟩

ofensivo, -va *adj* : offensive, insulting

ofensor, -sora *n* : offender

oferente *nmf* **1** : supplier **2** FUENTE : source ⟨un oferente no identificado : an unidentified source⟩

oferta *nf* **1** : offer **2** : sale, bargain ⟨las camisas están en oferta : the shirts are on sale⟩ **3 oferta y demanda** : supply and demand

ofertar *vt* OFRECER : to offer

oficial[1] *adj* : official — **oficialmente** *adv*

oficial[2] *nmf* **1** : officer, police officer, commissioned officer (in the military) **2** : skilled worker

oficializar {21} *vt* : to make official

oficiante *nmf* : celebrant

oficiar *vt* **1** : to inform officially **2** : to officiate at, to celebrate (Mass) — *vi* **~ de** : to act as

oficina *nf* : office

oficinista *nmf* : office worker

oficio *nm* **1** : trade, profession ⟨es electricista de oficio : he's an electrician by trade⟩ **2** : function, role **3** : official communication **4** : experience ⟨tener oficio : to be experienced⟩ **5** : religious ceremony

oficioso, -sa *adj* **1** EXTRAOFICIAL : unofficial **2** : officious — **oficiosamente** *adv*

ofrecer {53} *vt* **1** : to offer **2** : to provide, to give **3** : to present (an appearance, etc.) — **ofrecerse** *vr* **1** : to offer oneself, to volunteer **2** : to open up, to present itself

ofrecimiento *nm* : offer, offering

ofrenda *nf* : offering

oftalmología *nf* : ophthalmology

oftalmólogo, -ga *n* : ophthalmologist

ofuscación *nf, pl* **-ciones** : blindness, confusion

ofuscar {72} *vt* **1** : to blind, to dazzle **2** CONFUNDIR : to bewilder, to confuse — **ofuscarse** *vr* **~ con** : to be blinded by

ogro *nm* : ogre

ohm *nm, pl* **ohms** : ohm

ohmio → **ohm**

oídas *nfpl* **de ~** : by hearsay

oído *nm* **1** : ear ⟨oído interno : inner ear⟩ **2** : hearing ⟨duro de oído : hard of hearing⟩ **3 tocar de oído** : to play by ear

oiga, etc. → **oír**

oír {50} *vi* : to hear — *vt* **1** : to hear **2** ESCUCHAR : to listen to **3** : to pay attention to, to heed **4 ¡oye!** *or* **¡oiga!** : listen!, excuse me!, look here!

ojal *nm* : buttonhole

ojalá *interj* **1** : I hope so!, if only!, God willing! **2** : I hope, I wish, hopefully ⟨¡ojalá que le vaya bien! : I hope things go well for her!⟩ ⟨¡ojalá no llueva! : hopefully it won't rain!⟩

ojeada *nf* : glimpse, glance ⟨echar una ojeada : to have a quick look⟩

ojear *vt* : to eye, to have a look at

ojete *nm* : eyelet

ojiva *nf* : warhead

ojo *nm* **1** : eye **2** : judgment, sharpness ⟨tener buen ojo para : to be a good judge of, to have a good eye for⟩ **3** : hole (in cheese), eye (in a needle), center (of a storm) **4** : span (of a bridge) **5 a ojos vistas** : openly, publicly **6 andar con ojo** : to be careful **7 ojo de agua** *Mex* : spring, source **8 ¡ojo!** : look out!, pay attention!

ola *nf* **1** : wave **2 ola de calor** : heat wave

oleada *nf* : swell, wave ⟨una oleada de protestas : a wave of protests⟩

oleaje *nm* : waves *pl*, surf

óleo *nm* **1** : oil **2** : oil painting

oleoducto *nm* : oil pipeline

oleoso, -sa *adj* : oily

oler {51} *vt* **1** : to smell **2** INQUIRIR : to pry into, to investigate **3** AVERIGUAR : to smell out, to uncover — *vi* **1** : to smell ⟨huele mal : it smells bad⟩ **2 ~ a** : to smell like, to smell of ⟨huele a pino : it smells like pine⟩ — **olerse** *vr* : to have a hunch, to suspect

olfatear *vt* **1** : to sniff **2** : to sense, to sniff out

olfativo, -va *adj* : olfactory

olfato *nm* **1** : sense of smell **2** : nose, instinct

oligarquía *nf* : oligarchy

olimpiada *or* **olimpíada** *nf* **1** : Olympiad **2** *or* **olympiadas** *nfpl* : Olympics *pl*

olímpico, -ca *adj* : Olympic

olisquear *vt* : to sniff at

oliva *nf* ACEITUNA : olive ⟨aceite de oliva : olive oil⟩

olivo *nm* : olive tree

olla *nf* **1** : pot ⟨olla de presión : pressure cooker⟩ **2 olla podrida** : Spanish stew

olmeca *adj & nmf* : Olmec
olmo *nm* : elm
olor *nm* : smell, odor
oloroso, -sa *adj* : scented, fragrant
olote *nm Mex* : cob, corncob
olvidadizo, -za *adj* : forgetful, absent-minded
olvidar *vt* **1** : to forget, to forget about ⟨olvida lo que pasó : forget about what happened⟩ **2** : to leave behind ⟨olvidé mi chequera en la casa : I left my checkbook at home⟩ — **olvidarse** *vr* : to forget ⟨se me olvidó mi cuaderno : I forgot my notebook⟩ ⟨se le olvidó llamarme : he forgot to call me⟩
olvido *nm* **1** : forgetfulness **2** : oblivion **3** DESCUIDO : oversight
omaní *adj & nmf* : Omani
ombligo *nm* : navel, belly button
ombudsman *nmfs & pl* : ombudsman
omelette *nmf* : omelet
ominoso, -sa *adj* : ominous — **ominosamente** *adv*
omisión *nf, pl* **-siones** : omission, neglect
omiso, -sa *adj* **1** NEGLIGENTE : neglectful **2 hacer caso omiso de** : to ignore
omitir *vt* **1** : to omit, to leave out **2** : to fail to ⟨omitió dar su nombre : he failed to give his name⟩
ómnibus *n, pl* **-bus** *or* **-buses** : bus, coach
omnipotencia *nf* : omnipotence
omnipotente *adj* TODOPODEROSO : omnipotent, almighty
omnipresencia *nf* : ubiquity, omnipresence
omnipresente *adj* : ubiquitous, omnipresent
omnisciente *adj* : omniscient — **omnisciencia** *nf*
omnívoro, -ra *adj* : omnivorous
omóplato *or* **omoplato** *nm* : shoulder blade
once *adj & nm* : eleven
onceavo[1], **-va** *adj* : eleventh
onceavo[2] *nm* : eleventh (fraction)
onda *nf* **1** : wave, ripple, undulation ⟨onda sonora : sound wave⟩ **2** : wave (in hair) **3** : scallop (on clothing) **4** *fam* : wavelength, understanding ⟨agarrar la onda : to get the point⟩ ⟨en la onda : on the ball, with it⟩ **5 ¿qué onda?** *fam* : what's happening?, what's up?
ondear *vi* : to ripple, to undulate, to flutter
ondulación *nf, pl* **-ciones** : undulation
ondulado, -da *adj* **1** : wavy ⟨pelo ondulado : wavy hair⟩ **2** : undulating
ondulante *adj* : undulating
ondular *vt* : to wave (hair) — *vi* : to undulate, to ripple
oneroso, -sa *adj* GRAVOSO : onerous, burdensome
ónix *nm* : onyx
onza *nf* : ounce
opacar {72} *vt* **1** : to make opaque or dull **2** : to outshine, to overshadow
opacidad *nf* **1** : opacity **2** : dullness
opaco, -ca *adj* **1** : opaque **2** : dull
ópalo *nm* : opal
opción *nf, pl* **opciones 1** ALTERNATIVA : option, choice **2** : right, chance ⟨tener opción a : to be eligible for⟩
opcional *adj* : optional — **opcionalmente** *adv*
ópera *nf* : opera
operación *nf, pl* **-ciones 1** : operation **2** : transaction, deal
operacional *adj* : operational
operador, -dora *n* **1** : operator **2** : cameraman, projectionist
operante *adj* : operating, working
operar *vt* **1** : to produce, to bring about **2** INTERVENIR : to operate on **3** *Mex* : to operate, to run (a machine) — *vi* **1** : to operate, to function **2** : to deal, to do business — **operarse** *vr* **1** : to come about, to take place **2** : to have an operation
operario, -ria *n* : laborer, worker
operático, -ca → **operístico**
operativo[1], **-va** *adj* **1** : operating ⟨capacidad operativa : operating capacity⟩ **2** : operative
operativo[2] *nm* : operation ⟨operativo militar : military operation⟩
opereta *nf* : operetta
operístico, -ca *adj* : operatic
opiato *nm* : opiate
opinable *adj* : arguable
opinar *vi* **1** : to think, to have an opinion **2** : to express an opinion **3 opinar bien de** : to think highly of — *vt* : to think ⟨opinamos lo mismo : we're of the same opinion, we're in agreement⟩
opinión *nf, pl* **-niones** : opinion, belief
opio *nm* : opium
oponente *nmf* : opponent
oponer {60} *vt* **1** CONTRAPONER : to oppose, to place against **2 oponer resistencia** : to resist, to put up a fight — **oponerse** *vr* ~ **a** : to object to, to be against
oporto *nm* : port (wine)
oportunamente *adv* **1** : at the right time, opportunely **2** : appropriately
oportunidad *nf* : opportunity, chance
oportunismo *nm* : opportunism
oportunista[1] *adj* : opportunistic
oportunista[2] *nmf* : opportunist
oportuno, -na *adj* **1** : opportune, timely **2** : suitable, appropriate
oposición *nf, pl* **-ciones** : opposition
opositor, -tora *n* ADVERSARIO : opponent
oposum *nm* ZARIGÜEYA : opossum
opresión *nf, pl* **-siones 1** : oppression **2 opresión de pecho** : tightness in the chest
opresivo, -va *adj* : oppressive
opresor[1], **-sora** *adj* : oppressive
opresor[2], **-sora** *n* : oppressor

oprimir *vt* **1** : to oppress **2** : to press, to squeeze ⟨oprima el botón : push the button⟩
oprobio *nm* : opprobrium, shame
optar *vi* **1 ~ por** : to opt for, to choose **2 ~ a** : to aspire to, to apply for ⟨dos candidatos optan a la presidencia : two candidates are running for president⟩
optativo, -va *adj* FACULTATIVO : optional
óptica *nf* **1** : optics **2** : optician's shop **3** : viewpoint
óptico[1], **-ca** *adj* : optical, optic
óptico[2], **-ca** *n* : optician
optimismo *nm* : optimism
optimista[1] *adj* : optimistic
optimista[2] *nmf* : optimist
óptimo, -ma *adj* : optimum, optimal
optometría *nf* : optometry — **optometrista** *nmf*
opuesto[1] *pp* → **oponer**
opuesto[2] *adj* **1** : opposite, contrary **2** : opposed
opulencia *nf* : opulence — **opulento, -ta** *adj*
opus *nm* : opus
opuso, etc. → **oponer**
ora *conj* : now ⟨los matices eran variados, ora verdes, ora ocres : the hues were varied, now green, now ocher⟩
oración *nf, pl* **-ciones** **1** DISCURSO : oration, speech **2** PLEGARIA : prayer **3** FRASE : sentence, clause
oráculo *nm* : oracle
orador, -dora *n* : speaker, orator
oral *adj* : oral — **oralmente** *adv*
órale *interj Mex fam* **1** : sure!, OK! ⟨¿los dos por cinco pesos? ¡órale! : both for five pesos? you've got a deal!⟩ **2** : come on! ⟨¡órale, vámonos! : come on, let's go!⟩
orangután *nm, pl* **-tanes** : orangutan
orar *vi* REZAR : to pray
oratoria *nf* : oratory
oratorio *nm* **1** CAPILLA : oratory, chapel **2** : oratorio
orbe *nm* **1** : orb, sphere **2** GLOBO : globe, world
órbita *nf* **1** : orbit **2** : eye socket **3** ÁMBITO : sphere, field
orbitador *nm* : space shuttle, orbiter
orbital *adj* : orbital
orbitar *v* : to orbit
orden[1] *nm, pl* **órdenes** **1** : order ⟨todo está en orden : everything's in order⟩ ⟨por orden cronológico : in chronological order⟩ **2 orden del día** : agenda (at a meeting) **3 orden público** : law and order
orden[2] *nf, pl* **órdenes** **1** : order ⟨una orden religiosa : a religious order⟩ ⟨una orden de tacos : an order of tacos⟩ **2 orden de compra** : purchase order **3 estar a la orden del día** : to be the order of the day, to be prevalent
ordenación *nf, pl* **-ciones** **1** : ordination **2** : ordering, organizing
ordenadamente *adv* : in an orderly fashion, neatly
ordenado, -da *adj* : orderly, neat
ordenador *nm Spain* : computer
ordenamiento *nm* **1** : ordering, organizing **2** : code (of laws)
ordenanza[1] *nf* REGLAMENTO : ordinance, regulation
ordenanza[2] *nm* : orderly (in the armed forces)
ordenar *vt* **1** MANDAR : to order, to command **2** ARREGLAR : to put in order, to arrange **3** : to ordain (a priest)
ordeñar *vt* : to milk
ordeño *nm* : milking
ordinal *nm* : ordinal (number)
ordinariamente *adv* **1** : usually **2** : coarsely
ordinariez *nf* : coarseness, vulgarity
ordinario, -ria *adj* **1** : ordinary **2** : coarse, common, vulgar **3 de ~** : usually
orear *vt* : to air
orégano *nm* : oregano
oreja *nf* : ear
orfanato *nm* : orphanage
orfanatorio *nm Mex* : orphanage
orfebre *nmf* : goldsmith, silversmith
orfebrería *nf* : articles of gold or silver
orfelinato *nm* : orphanage
orgánico, -ca *adj* : organic — **orgánicamente** *adv*
organigrama *nm* : organization chart, flowchart
organismo *nm* **1** : organism **2** : agency, organization
organista *nmf* : organist
organización *nf, pl* **-ciones** : organization
organizador[1], **-dora** *adj* : organizing
organizador[2], **-dora** *n* : organizer
organizar {21} *vt* : to organize, to arrange — **organizarse** *vr* : to get organized
organizativo, -va *adj* : organizational
órgano *nm* : organ
orgasmo *nm* : orgasm
orgía *nf* : orgy
orgullo *nm* : pride
orgulloso, -sa *adj* : proud — **orgullosamente** *adv*
orientación *nf, pl* **-ciones** **1** : orientation **2** DIRECCIÓN : direction, course **3** GUÍA : guidance, direction
oriental[1] *adj* **1** : eastern **2** : oriental **3** *Arg, Uru* : Uruguayan
oriental[2] *nmf* **1** : Easterner **2** : Oriental **3** *Arg, Uru* : Uruguayan
orientar *vt* **1** : to orient, to position **2** : to guide, to direct — **orientarse** *vr* **1** : to orient oneself, to get one's bearings **2 ~ hacia** : to turn towards, to lean towards
oriente *nm* **1** : east, East **2 el Oriente** : the Orient
orífice *nmf* : goldsmith
orificio *nm* : orifice, opening
origen *nm, pl* **orígenes** **1** : origin **2** : lineage, birth **3 dar origen a** : to give rise to **4 en su origen** : originally

original *adj & nm* : original — **originalmente** *adv*
originalidad *nf* : originality
originar *vt* : to originate, to give rise to — **originarse** *vr* : to originate, to begin
originario, -ria *adj* ~ **de** : native of
originariamente *adv* : originally
orilla *nf* **1** BORDE : border, edge **2** : bank (of a river) **3** : shore
orillar *vt* **1** : to skirt, to go around **2** : to trim, to edge (cloth) **3** : to settle, to wind up **4** *Mex* : to pull over (a vehicle)
orín *nm* **1** HERRUMBRE : rust **2 orines** *nmpl* : urine
orina *nf* : urine
orinación *nf* : urination
orinal *nm* : urinal (vessel)
orinar *vi* : to urinate — **orinarse** *vr* : to wet oneself
oriol *nm* OROPÉNDOLA : oriole
oriundo, -da *adj* ~ **de** : native of
orla *nf* : border, edging
orlar *vt* : to edge, to trim
ornamentación *nf, pl* **-ciones** : ornamentation
ornamental *adj* : ornamental
ornamentar *vt* ADORNAR : to ornament, to adorn
ornamento *nm* : ornament, adornment
ornar *vt* : to adorn, to decorate
ornitología *nf* : ornithology
ornitólogo, -ga *n* : ornithologist
ornitorrinco *nm* : platypus
oro *nm* : gold
orondo, -da *adj* **1** : rounded, potbellied (of a container) **2** *fam* : smug, self-satisfied
oropel *nm* : glitz, glitter, tinsel
oropéndola *nf* : oriole
orquesta *nf* : orchestra — **orquestal** *adj*
orquestar *vt* : to orchestrate — **orquestación** *nf*
orquídea *nf* : orchid
ortiga *nf* : nettle
ortodoncia *nf* : orthodontics
ortodoncista *nmf* : orthodontist
ortodoxia *nf* : orthodoxy
ortodoxo, -xa *adj* : orthodox
ortografía *nf* : orthography, spelling
ortográfico, -ca *adj* : orthographic, spelling
ortopedia *nf* : orthopedics
ortopédico, -ca *adj* : orthopedic
ortopedista *nmf* : orthopedist
oruga *nf* **1** : caterpillar **2** : track (of a tank, etc.)
orzuelo *nm* : sty, stye (in the eye)
os *pron pl* (*objective form of* **vosotros**) *Spain* **1** : you, to you **2** : yourselves, to yourselves **3** : each other, to each other
osa *nf* → **oso**
osadía *nf* **1** VALOR : boldness, daring **2** AUDACIA : audacity, nerve
osado, -da *adj* **1** : bold, daring **2** : audacious, impudent — **osadamente** *adv*
osamenta *nf* : skeletal remains *pl*, bones *pl*
osar *vi* : to dare
oscilación *nf, pl* **-ciones 1** : oscillation **2** : fluctuation **3** : vacillation, wavering
oscilar *vi* **1** BALANCEARSE : to swing, to sway, to oscillate **2** FLUCTUAR : to fluctuate **3** : to vacillate, to waver
oscuramente *adv* : obscurely
oscurecer {53} *vt* **1** : to darken **2** : to obscure, to confuse, to cloud **3 al oscurecer** : at dusk, at nightfall — *v impers* : to grow dark, to get dark — **oscurecerse** *vr* : to darken, to dim
oscuridad *nf* **1** : darkness **2** : obscurity
oscuro, -ra *adj* **1** : dark **2** : obscure **3 a oscuras** : in the dark, in darkness
óseo, ósea *adj* : skeletal, bony
ósmosis *or* **osmosis** *nf* : osmosis
oso, osa *n* **1** : bear **2 Osa Mayor** : Big Dipper **3 Osa Menor** : Little Dipper **4 oso blanco** : polar bear **5 oso hormiguero** : anteater **6 oso de peluche** : teddy bear
ostensible *adj* : ostensible, apparent — **ostensiblemente** *adv*
ostentación *nf, pl* **-ciones** : ostentation, display
ostentar *vt* **1** : to display, to flaunt **2** POSEER : to have, to hold ‹ostenta el récord mundial : he holds the world record›
ostentoso, -sa *adj* : ostentatious, showy — **ostentosamente** *adv*
osteópata *nmf* : osteopath
osteopatía *n* : osteopathy
osteoporosis *nf* : osteoporosis
ostión *nm, pl* **ostiones 1** *Mex* : oyster **2** *Chile* : scallop
ostra *nf* : oyster
ostracismo *nm* : ostracism
otear *vt* : to scan, to survey, to look over
otero *nm* : knoll, hillock
otomana *nf* : ottoman (mueble)
otomano, -na *adj & n* : Ottoman
otoñal *adj* : autumn, autumnal
otoño *nm* : autumn, fall
otorgamiento *nm* : granting, awarding
otorgar {52} *vt* **1** : to grant, to award **2** : to draw up, to frame (a legal document)
otro[1], **otra** *adj* **1** : other **2** : another ‹en otro juego, ellos ganaron : in another game, they won› **3 otra vez** : again **4 de otra manera** : otherwise **5 otra parte** : elsewhere **6 en otro tiempo** : once, formerly
otro[2], **otra** *pron* **1** : another one ‹dame otro : give me another› **2** : other one ‹el uno o el otro : one or the other› **3 los otros, las otras** : the others, the rest ‹me dio una y se quedó con las otras : he gave me one and kept the rest›
ovación *nf, pl* **-ciones** : ovation
ovacionar *vt* : to cheer, to applaud

oval → **ovalado**
ovalado, -da *adj* : oval
óvalo *nm* : oval
ovárico, -ca *adj* : ovarian
ovario *nm* : ovary
oveja *nf* **1** : sheep, ewe **2 oveja negra** : black sheep
overol *nm* : overalls *pl*
ovillar *vt* : to roll into a ball
ovillo *nm* **1** : ball (of yarn) **2** : tangle
ovni *or* **OVNI** *nm* (*o*bjeto *v*olador *no* *i*dentificado) : UFO
ovoide *adj* : ovoid, ovoidal
ovulación *nf, pl* **-ciones** : ovulation
ovular *vi* : to ovulate
óvulo *nm* : ovum
oxidación *nf, pl* **-ciones 1** : oxidation **2** : rusting
oxidado, -da *adj* : rusty
oxidar *vt* **1** : to cause to rust **2** : to oxidize — **oxidarse** *vr* : to rust, to become rusty
óxido *nm* **1** HERRUMBRE, ORÍN : rust **2** : oxide
oxigenar *vt* **1** : to oxygenate **2** : to bleach (hair)
oxígeno *nm* : oxygen
oxiuro *nm* : pinworm
oye, etc. → **oír**
oyente *nmf* **1** : listener **2** : auditor, auditing student
ozono *nm* : ozone

P

p *nf* : seventeenth letter of the Spanish alphabet
pabellón *nm, pl* **-llones 1** : pavilion **2** : summerhouse, lodge **3** : flag (of a vessel)
pabilo *nm* MECHA : wick
paca *nf* FARDO : bale
pacana *nf* : pecan
pacer {48} *v* : to graze, to pasture
paces → **paz**
pachanga *nf fam* : party, bash
paciencia *nf* : patience
paciente *adj & nmf* : patient — **pacientemente** *adv*
pacificación *nf, pl* **-ciones** : pacification
pacíficamente *adv* : peacefully, peaceably
pacificar {72} *vt* : to pacify, to calm — **pacificarse** *vr* : to calm down, to abate
pacífico, -ca *adj* : peaceful, pacific
pacifismo *nm* : pacifism
pacifista *adj & nmf* : pacifist
pacotilla *nf* **de ~** : shoddy, trashy
pactar *vt* : to agree on — *vi* : to come to an agreement
pacto *nm* CONVENIO : pact, agreement
padecer {53} *vt* : to suffer, to endure — *vi* ADOLECER **~ de** : to suffer from
padecimiento *nm* **1** : suffering **2** : ailment, condition
padrastro *nm* **1** : stepfather **2** : hangnail
padre[1] *adj Mex fam* : fantastic, great
padre[2] *nm* **1** : father **2 padres** *nmpl* : parents
padrenuestro *nm* : Lord's Prayer, paternoster
padrino *nm* **1** : godfather **2** : best man **3** : sponsor, patron
padrón *nm, pl* **padrones** : register, roll ⟨padrón municipal : city register⟩
paella *nf* : paella
paga *nf* **1** : payment **2** : pay, wages *pl*
pagadero, -ra *adj* : payable
pagado, -da *adj* **1** : paid **2 pagado de sí mismo** : self-satisfied, smug
pagador, -dora *n* : payer
paganismo *nm* : paganism
pagano, -na *adj & n* : pagan
pagar {52} *vt* : to pay, to pay for, to repay — *vi* : to pay
pagaré *nm* VALE : promissory note, IOU
página *nf* : page
pago *nm* **1** : payment **2 en pago de** : in return for
pagoda *nf* : pagoda
pague, etc. → **pagar**
país *nm* **1** NACIÓN : country, nation **2** REGIÓN : region, territory
paisaje *nm* : scenery, landscape
paisano, -na *n* COMPATRIOTA : compatriot, fellow countryman
paja *nf* **1** : straw **2** *fam* : trash, tripe
pajar *nm* : hayloft, haystack
pajarera *nf* : aviary
pájaro *nm* : bird ⟨pájaro cantor : songbird⟩ ⟨pájaro bobo : penguin⟩ ⟨pájaro carpintero : woodpecker⟩
pajita *nf* : (drinking) straw
pajote *nm* : straw, mulch
pala *nf* **1** : shovel, spade **2** : blade (of an oar or a rotor) **3** : paddle, racket
palabra *nf* **1** VOCABLO : word **2** PROMESA : word, promise ⟨un hombre de palabra : a man of his word⟩ **3** HABLA : speech **4** : right to speak ⟨tener la palabra : to have the floor⟩
palabrería *nf* : empty talk
palabrota *nf* : swearword
palacio *nm* **1** : palace, mansion **2 palacio de justicia** : courthouse
paladar *nm* **1** : palate **2** GUSTO : taste
paladear *vt* SABOREAR : to savor
paladín *nm, pl* **-dines** : champion, defender
palanca *nf* **1** : lever, crowbar **2** *fam* : leverage, influence **3 palanca de cambio** *or* **palanca de velocidad** : gearshift
palangana *nf* : washbowl
palanqueta *nf* : jimmy, small crowbar
palco *nm* : box (in a theater or stadium)
palear *vt* **1** : to shovel **2** : to paddle
palenque *nm* **1** ESTACADA : stockade, palisade **2** : arena, ring

paleontología *nf* : paleontology
paleontólogo, -ga *n* : paleontologist
palestino, -na *adj & n* : Palestinian
palestra *nf* : arena ‹salir a la palestra : to join the fray›
paleta *nf* **1** : palette **2** : trowel **3** : spatula **4** : blade, vane **5** : paddle **6** *CA, Mex* : lollipop, Popsicle
paletilla *nf* : shoulder blade
paliar *vt* MITIGAR : to alleviate, to palliate
paliativo[1], **-va** *adj* : palliative
paliativo[2] *nm* : palliative
palidecer {53} *vi* : to turn pale
palidez *nf, pl* **-deces** : paleness, pallor
pálido, -da *adj* : pale
palillo *nm* **1** MONDADIENTES : toothpick **2 palillos** *nmpl* : chopsticks **3 palillo de tambor** : drumstick
paliza *nf* : beating, pummeling ‹darle una paliza a : to beat, to thrash›
palma *nf* **1** : palm (of the hand) **2** : palm (tree or leaf) **3 batir palmas** : to clap, to applaud **4 llevarse la palma** *fam* : to take the cake
palmada *nf* **1** : pat **2** : slap **3** : clap
palmarés *nm* : record (of achievements)
palmario, -ria *adj* MANIFIESTO : clear, manifest
palmeado, -da *adj* : webbed
palmear *vt* : to slap on the back — *vi* : to clap, to applaud
palmera *nf* : palm tree
palmo *nm* **1** : span, small amount **2 palmo a palmo** : bit by bit, inch by inch **3 dejar con un palmo de narices** : to disappoint
palmotear *vi* : to applaud
palmoteo *nm* : clapping, applause
palo *nm* **1** : stick, pole, post **2** : shaft, handle ‹palo de escoba : broomstick› **3** : mast, spar **4** : wood **5** : blow (with a stick) **6** : suit (of cards)
paloma *nf* **1** : pigeon, dove **2 paloma mensajera** : carrier pigeon
palomilla *nf* : moth
palomitas *nfpl* : popcorn
palpable *adj* : palpable, tangible
palpar *vt* : to feel, to touch
palpitación *nf, pl* **-ciones** : palpitation
palpitar *vi* : to palpitate, to throb — **palpitante** *adj*
palta *nf* : avocado
paludismo *nm* MALARIA : malaria
palurdo, -da *n* : boor, yokel, bumpkin
pampa *nf* : pampa
pampeano, -na *adj* : pampean, pampas
pampero → **pampeano**
pan *nm* **1** : bread **2** : loaf of bread **3** : cake, bar ‹pan de jabón : bar of soap› **4 pan dulce** *CA, Mex* : traditional pastry **5 pan tostado** : toast **6 ser pan comido** *fam* : to be a piece of cake, to be a cinch
pana *nf* : corduroy
panacea *nf* : panacea
panadería *nf* : bakery, bread shop
panadero, -ra *n* : baker
panal *nm* : honeycomb
panameño, -ña *adj & n* : Panamanian
pancarta *nf* : placard, sign
pancita *nf Mex* : tripe
páncreas *nms & pl* : pancreas
panda *nmf* : panda
pandeado, -da *adj* : warped
pandearse *vr* **1** : to warp **2** : to bulge, to sag
pandemonio *or* **pandemónium** *nm* : pandemonium
pandereta *nf* : tambourine
pandero *nm* : tambourine
pandilla *nf* **1** : group, clique **2** : gang
panecito *nm* : roll, bread roll
panegírico[1], **-ca** *adj* : eulogistic, panegyrical
panegírico[2] *nm* : eulogy, panegyric
panel *nm* : panel — **panelista** *nmf*
panera *nf* : bread box
panfleto *nm* : pamphlet
pánico *nm* : panic
panorama *nm* **1** VISTA : panorama, view **2** : scene, situation ‹el panorama nacional : the national scene› **3** PERSPECTIVA : outlook
panorámico, -ca *adj* : panoramic
panqueque *nm* : pancake
pantaletas *nfpl* : panties
pantalla *nf* **1** : screen, monitor **2** : lampshade **3** : fan
pantalón *nm, pl* **-lones** **1** : pants *pl,* trousers *pl* **2 pantalones vaqueros** : jeans **3 pantalones de mezclilla** *Chile, Mex* : jeans **4 pantalones de montar** : jodhpurs
pantano *nm* **1** : swamp, marsh, bayou **2** : reservoir **3** : obstacle, difficulty
pantanoso, -sa *adj* **1** : marshy, swampy **2** : difficult, thorny
panteón *nm, pl* **-teones** **1** CEMENTERIO : cemetery **2** : pantheon, mausoleum
pantera *nf* : panther
pantimedias *nfpl Mex* : panty hose
pantomima *nf* : pantomime
pantorrilla *nf* : calf (of the leg)
pantufla *nf* ZAPATILLA : slipper
panza *nf* BARRIGA : belly, paunch
panzón, -zona *adj, mpl* **panzones** : potbellied, paunchy
pañal *nm* : diaper
pañería *nf* **1** : cloth, material **2** : fabric store
pañito *nm* : doily
paño *nm* **1** : cloth **2** : rag, dust cloth **3 paño de cocina** : dishcloth **4 paño higiénico** : sanitary napkin
pañuelo *nm* **1** : handkerchief **2** : scarf
papa[1] *nm* : pope
papa[2] *nf* **1** : potato **2 papa dulce** : sweet potato **3 papas fritas** : potato chips, french fries **4 papas a la francesa** *Mex* : french fries
papá *nm fam* **1** : dad, pop **2 papás** *nmpl* : parents, folks
papada *nf* **1** : double chin, jowl **2** : dewlap
papagayo *nm* LORO : parrot

papal *adj* : papal

papalote *nm Mex* : kite

papaya *nf* : papaya

papel *nm* **1** : paper, piece of paper **2** : role, part **3 papel de estaño** : tinfoil **4 papel de empapelar** *or* **papel pintado** : wallpaper **5 papel higiénico** : toilet paper **6 papel de lija** : sandpaper

papeleo *nm* : paperwork, red tape

papelera *nf* : wastebasket

papelería *nf* : stationery store

papelero, -ra *adj* : paper

papeleta *nf* **1** : ballot **2** : ticket, slip

paperas *nfpl* : mumps

papi *nm fam* : daddy, papa

papilla *nf* **1** : pap, mash **2 hacer papilla** : to beat to a pulp

papiro *nm* : papyrus

paquete *nm* BULTO : package, parcel

paquistaní *adj & nmf* : Pakistani

par[1] *adj* : even (in number)

par[2] *nm* **1** : pair, couple **2** : equal, peer ⟨sin par : matchless, peerless⟩ **3** : par (in golf) **4** : rafter **5 de par en par** : wide open

par[3] *nf* **1** : par ⟨por encima de la par : above par⟩ **2 a la par que** : at the same time as, as well as ⟨interesante a la par que instructivo : both interesting and informative⟩

para *prep* **1** : for ⟨para ti : for you⟩ ⟨alta para su edad : tall for her age⟩ ⟨una cita para el lunes : an appointment for Monday⟩ **2** : to, towards ⟨para la derecha : to the right⟩ ⟨van para el río : they're heading towards the river⟩ **3** : to, in order to ⟨lo hace para molestarte : he does it to annoy you⟩ **4** : around, by (a time) ⟨para mañana estarán listos : they'll be ready by tomorrow⟩ **5 para adelante** : forwards **6 para atrás** : backwards **7 para que** : so, so that, in order that ⟨te lo digo para que sepas : I'm telling you so you'll know⟩

parabién *nm, pl* **-bienes** : congratulations *pl*

parábola *nf* **1** : parable **2** : parabola

parabrisas *nms & pl* : windshield

paracaídas *nms & pl* : parachute

paracaidista *nmf* **1** : parachutist **2** : paratrooper

parachoques *nms & pl* : bumper

parada *nf* **1** : stop ⟨parada de autobús : bus stop⟩ **2** : catch, save, parry (in sports) **3** DESFILE : parade

paradero *nm* : whereabouts

paradigma *nm* : paradigm

paradisíaco, -ca *or* **paradisiaco, -ca** *adj* : heavenly

parado, -da *adj* **1** : motionless, idle, stopped **2** : standing (up) **3** : confused, bewildered **4 bien (mal) parado** : in good (bad) shape ⟨salió bien parado : it turned out well for him⟩

paradoja *nf* : paradox

paradójico, -ca *adj* : paradoxical

parafernalia *nf* : paraphernalia

parafina *nf* : paraffin

parafrasear *vt* : to paraphrase

paráfrasis *nfs & pl* : paraphrase

paraguas *nms & pl* : umbrella

paraguayo, -ya *adj & n* : Paraguayan

paraíso *nm* **1** : paradise, heaven **2 paraíso fiscal** : tax shelter

paraje *nm* : spot, place

paralelismo *nm* : parallelism, similarity

paralelo[1], **-la** *adj* : parallel

paralelo[2] *nm* : parallel

paralelogramo *nm* : parallelogram

parálisis *nfs & pl* **1** : paralysis **2** : standstill **3 parálisis cerebral** : cerebral palsy

paralítico, -ca *adj & n* : paralytic

paralizar {21} *vt* **1** : to paralyze **2** : to bring to a standstill — **paralizarse** *vr*

parámetro *nm* : parameter

páramo *nm* : barren plateau, moor

parangón *nm, pl* **-gones** **1** : comparison **2 sin ~** : incomparable

paraninfo *nm* : auditorium, assembly hall

paranoia *nf* : paranoia

paranoico, -ca *adj & n* : paranoid

parapeto *nm* : parapet, rampart

parapléjico, -ca *adj & n* : paraplegic

parar *vt* **1** DETENER : to stop **2** : to stand, to prop — *vi* **1** CESAR : to stop **2** : to stay, to put up **3 ir a parar** : to end up, to wind up — **pararse** *vr* **1** : to stop **2** ATASCARSE : to stall (out) **3** : to stand up, to get up

pararrayos *nms & pl* : lightning rod

parasitario, -ria *adj* : parasitic

parasitismo *nm* : parasitism

parásito *nm* : parasite

parasol *nm* SOMBRILLA : parasol

parcela *nf* : parcel, tract of land

parcelar *vt* : to parcel (land)

parchar *vt* : to patch, to patch up

parche *nm* : patch

parcial *adj* : partial — **parcialmente** *adv*

parcialidad *nf* : partiality, bias

parco, -ca *adj* **1** : sparing, frugal **2** : moderate, temperate

pardo, -da *adj* : brownish grey

pardusco → **pardo**

parecer[1] {53} *vi* **1** : to seem, to look, to appear to be ⟨parece bien fácil : it looks very easy⟩ ⟨así parece : so it seems⟩ ⟨pareces una princesa : you look like a princess⟩ **2** : to think, to have an opinion ⟨me parece que sí : I think so⟩ **3** : to like, to be in agreement ⟨si te parece : if you like, if it's all right with you⟩ — **parecerse** *vr* **~ a** : to resemble

parecer[2] *nm* **1** OPINIÓN : opinion **2** ASPECTO : appearance ⟨al parecer : apparently⟩

parecido[1], **-da** *adj* **1** : similar, alike **2 bien parecido** : good-looking

parecido[2] *nm* : resemblance, similarity

pared *nf* : wall

pareja *nf* **1** : couple, pair **2** : partner, mate

parejo, -ja *adj* **1** : even, smooth, level **2** : equal, similar
parentela *nf* : relations *pl,* kinfolk
parentesco *nm* : relationship, kinship
paréntesis *nms & pl* **1** : parenthesis **2** : digression
parentético, -ca *adj* : parenthetic, parenthetical
paria *nmf* : pariah, outcast
paridad *nf* : parity, equality
pariente *nmf* : relative, relation
parir *vi* : to give birth — *vt* : to give birth to, to bear
parking *nm* : parking lot
parlamentar *vi* : to talk, to parley
parlamentario[1], -ria *adj* : parliamentary
parlamentario[2], -ria *n* : member of parliament
parlamento *nm* **1** : parliament **2** : negotiations *pl,* talks *pl*
parlanchín[1], -china *adj, mpl* **-chines** : chatty, talkative
parlanchín[2], -china *n, mpl* **-chines** : chatterbox
parlante *nm* ALTOPARLANTE : loudspeaker
parlotear *vi fam* : to gab, to chat, to prattle
parloteo *nm fam* : prattle, chatter
paro *nm* **1** HUELGA : strike **2** : stoppage, stopping **3 paro forzoso** : layoff
parodia *nf* : parody
parodiar *vt* : to parody
paroxismo *nm* **1** : fit, paroxysm **2** : peak, height ⟨llevaral paroxismo : to carry to the extreme⟩
parpadear *vi* **1** : to blink **2** : to flicker
parpadeo *nm* **1** : blink, blinking **2** : flickering
párpado *nm* : eyelid
parque *nm* **1** : park **2 parque de atracciones** : amusement park
parquear *vt* : to park — **parquearse** *vr*
parqueo *nm* : parking
parquet *or* **parqué** *nm* : parquet
parquímetro *nm* : parking meter
parra *nf* : vine, grapevine
párrafo *nm* : paragraph
parranda *nf fam* : party, spree
parrilla *nf* **1** : broiler, grill **2** : grate
parrillada *nf* BARBACOA : barbecue
párroco *nm* : parish priest
parroquia *nf* **1** : parish **2** : parish church **3** : customers *pl,* clientele
parroquial *adj* : parochial
parroquiano, -na *nm* **1** : parishioner **2** : customer, patron
parsimonia *nf* **1** : calm **2** : parsimony, thrift
parsimonioso, -sa *adj* **1** : calm, unhurried **2** : parsimonious, thrifty
parte[1] *nm* : report, dispatch
parte[2] *nf* **1** : part, share **2** : part, place ⟨en alguna parte : somewhere⟩ ⟨por todas partes : everywhere⟩ **3** : party (in negotiations, etc.) **4 de parte de** : on behalf of **5 ¿de parte de quién?** : may I ask who's calling? **6 tomar parte** : to take part
partero, -ra *n* : midwife
partición *nf, pl* **-ciones** : division, sharing
participación *nf, pl* **-ciones** **1** : participation **2** : share, interest **3** : announcement, notice
participante *nmf* **1** : participant **2** : competitor, entrant
participar *vi* **1** : to participate, to take part **2 ~ en** : to have a share in — *vt* : to announce, to notify
partícipe *nmf* : participant
participio *nm* : participle
partícula *nf* : particle
particular[1] *adj* **1** : particular, specific **2** : private, personal **3** : special, unique
particular[2] *nm* **1** : matter, detail **2** : individual
particularidad *nf* : characteristic, peculiarity
particularizar {21} *vt* **1** : to distinguish, to characterize **2** : to specify
partida *nf* **1** : departure **2** : item, entry **3** : certificate ⟨partida de nacimiento : birth certificate⟩ **4** : game, match, hand **5** : party, group
partidario, -ria *n* : follower, supporter
partido *nm* **1** : (political) party **2** : game, match ⟨partido de futbol : soccer game⟩ **3** APOYO : support, following **4** PROVECHO : profit, advantage ⟨sacar partido de : to profit from⟩
partir *vt* **1** : to cut, to split **2** : to break, to crack **3** : to share (out), to divide — *vi* **1** : to leave, to depart **2 ~ de** : to start from **3 a partir de** : as of, from ⟨a partir de hoy : as of today⟩ — **partirse** *vr* **1** : to smash, to split open **2** : to chap
partisano, -na *adj & n* : partisan
partitura *nf* : (musical) score
parto *nm* **1** : childbirth, delivery, labor ⟨estar de parto : to be in labor⟩ **2** : product, creation, brainchild
parvulario *nm* : nursery school
párvulo, -la *n* : toddler, preschooler
pasa *nf* **1** : raisin **2 pasa de Corinto** : currant
pasable *adj* : passable, tolerable — **pasablemente** *adv*
pasada *nf* **1** : passage, passing **2** : pass, wipe, coat (of paint) **3 de ~** : in passing **4 mala pasada** : dirty trick
pasadizo *nm* : passageway, corridor
pasado[1], -da *adj* **1** : past ⟨el año pasado : last year⟩ ⟨pasado mañana : the day after tomorrow⟩ ⟨pasadas las siete : after seven o'clock⟩ **2** : stale, bad, overripe **3** : old-fashioned, out-of-date **4** : overripe, slightly spoiled
pasado[2] *nm* : past
pasador *nm* **1** : bolt, latch **2** : barrette **3** *Mex* : bobby pin
pasaje *nm* **1** : ticket (for travel) **2** TARIFA : fare **3** : passageway **4** : passengers *pl*
pasajero[1], -ra *adj* : passing, fleeting
pasajero[2], -ra *n* : passenger

pasamanos *nms & pl* **1** : handrail **2** : bannister

pasante *nmf* : assistant

pasaporte *nm* : passport

pasar *vi* **1** : to pass, to go by, to come by **2** : to come in, to enter ⟨¿se puede pasar? : may we come in?⟩ **3** : to happen ⟨¿qué pasa? : what's happening?, what's going on?⟩ **4** : to manage, to get by **5** : to be over, to end **6 ~ de** : to exceed, to go beyond **7 ~ por** : to pretend to be — *vt* **1** : to pass, to give ⟨¿me pasas la sal? : would you pass me the salt?⟩ **2** : to pass (a test) **3** : to go over, to cross **4** : to spend (time) **5** : to tolerate **6** : to go through, to suffer **7** : to show (a movie, etc.) **8** : to overtake, to pass, to surpass **9** : to pass over, to wipe up **10 pasarlo bien** *or* **pasarla bien** : to have a good time **11 pasarlo mal** *or* **pasarla mal** : to have a bad time, to have a hard time **12 pasar por alto** : to overlook, to omit — **pasarse** *vr* **1** : to move, to pass, to go away **2** : to slip one's mind, to forget **3** : to go too far

pasarela *nf* **1** : gangplank **2** : footbridge **3** : runway, catwalk

pasatiempo *nm* : pastime, hobby

Pascua *nf* **1** : Easter **2** : Passover **3** : Christmas **4 Pascuas** *nfpl* : Christmas season

pase *nm* **1** PERMISO : pass, permit **2 pase de abordar** *Mex* : boarding pass

pasear *vi* : to take a walk, to go for a ride — *vt* **1** : to take for a walk **2** : to parade around, to show off — **pasearse** *vr* : to walk around

paseo *nm* **1** : walk, stroll **2** : ride **3** EXCURSIÓN : outing, trip **4** : avenue, walk **5** *or* **paseo marítimo** : boardwalk

pasiflora *nf* : passionflower

pasillo *nm* CORREDOR : hallway, corridor, aisle

pasión *nf, pl* **pasiones** : passion

pasional *adj* : passionate ⟨crimen pasional : crime of passion⟩

pasionaria → **pasiflora**

pasivo[1], **-va** *adj* : passive — **pasivamente** *adv*

pasivo[2] *nm* **1** : liability ⟨activos y pasivos : assets and liabilities⟩ **2** : debit side (of an account)

pasmado, -da *adj* : stunned, flabbergasted

pasmar *vt* : to amaze, to stun — **pasmarse** *vr*

pasmo *nm* **1** : shock, astonishment **2** : wonder, marvel

pasmoso, -sa *adj* : incredible, amazing — **pasmosamente** *adv*

paso[1], **-sa** *adj* : dried ⟨ciruela pasa : prune⟩

paso[2] *nm* **1** : passage, passing ⟨de paso : in passing, on the way⟩ **2** : way, path ⟨abrirse paso : to make one's way⟩ **3** : crossing ⟨paso de peatones : crosswalk⟩ ⟨paso a desnivel : underpass⟩ ⟨paso elevado : overpass⟩ **4** : step ⟨paso a paso : step by step⟩ **5** : pace, gait ⟨a buen paso : quickly, at a good rate⟩

pasta *nf* **1** : paste ⟨pasta de dientes *or* pasta dental : toothpaste⟩ **2** : pasta **3** : pastry dough **4 libro en pasta dura** : hardcover book **5 tener pasta de** : to have the makings of

pastar *vi* : to graze — *vt* : to put to pasture

pastel[1] *adj* : pastel

pastel[2] *nm* **1** : cake ⟨pastel de cumpleaños : birthday cake⟩ **2** : pie, turnover **3** : pastel

pastelería *nf* : pastry shop

pasteurización *nf, pl* **-ciones** : pasteurization

pasteurizar {21} *vt* : to pasteurize

pastilla *nf* **1** COMPRIMIDO, PÍLDORA : pill, tablet **2** : lozenge ⟨pastilla para la tos : cough drop⟩ **3** : cake (of soap), bar (of chocolate)

pastizal *nm* : pasture, grazing land

pasto *nm* **1** : pasture **2** HIERBA : grass, lawn

pastor, -tora *n* **1** : shepherd, shepherdess *f* **2** : minister, pastor

pastoral *adj & nf* : pastoral

pastorear *vt* : to shepherd, to tend

pastorela *nf* **1** : pastoral, pastourelle **2** *Mex* : a traditional Christmas play

pastoso, -sa *adj* **1** : pasty, doughy **2** : smooth, mellow (of sounds)

pata *nf* **1** : paw, leg (of an animal) **2** : foot, leg (of furniture) **3 patas de gallo** : crow's-feet **4 meter la pata** *fam* : to put one's foot in it, to make a blunder

patada *nf* **1** PUNTAPIÉ : kick **2** : stamp (of the foot)

patalear *vi* **1** : to kick **2** : to stamp one's feet

pataleta *nf fam* : tantrum

patán[1] *adj, pl* **patanes** : boorish, crude

patán[2] *nm, pl* **patanes** : boor, lout

patata *nf Spain* : potato

pateador, -dora *n* : kicker (in sports)

patear *vt* : to kick — *vi* : to stamp one's foot

patentar *vt* : to patent

patente[1] *adj* EVIDENTE : obvious, patent — **patentemente** *adv*

patente[2] *nf* : patent

paternal *adj* : fatherly, paternal

paternidad *nf* **1** : fatherhood, paternity **2** : parenthood **3** : authorship

paterno, -na *adj* : paternal ⟨abuela paterna : paternal grandmother⟩

patético, -ca *adj* : pathetic, moving

patetismo *nm* : pathos

patíbulo *nm* : gallows, scaffold

patillas *nfpl* : sideburns

patín *nm, pl* **patines** : skate ⟨patín de ruedas : roller skate⟩

patinador, -dora *n* : skater

patinaje *nm* : skating

patinar *vi* **1** : to skate **2** : to skid, to slip **3** *fam* : to slip up, to blunder

patinazo *nm* **1** : skid **2** *fam* : blunder, slipup

patineta *nf* **1** : scooter **2** : skateboard
patinete *nm* : scooter
patio *nm* **1** : courtyard, patio **2 patio de recreo** : playground
patito, -ta *n* : duckling
pato, -ta *n* **1** : duck **2 pato real** : mallard **3 pagar el pato** *fam* : to take the blame
patología *nf* : pathology
patológico, -ca *adj* : pathological
patólogo, -ga *n* : pathologist
patraña *nf* : tall tale, humbug, nonsense
patria *nf* : native land
patriarca *nm* : patriarch — **patriarcal** *adj*
patriarcado *nm* : patriarchy
patrimonio *nm* : patrimony, legacy
patrio, -tria *adj* **1** : native, home ⟨suelo patrio : native soil⟩ **2** : paternal
patriota[1] *adj* : patriotic
patriota[2] *nmf* : patriot
patriotería *nf* : jingoism, chauvinism
patriotero[1], **-ra** *adj* : jingoistic, chauvinistic
patriotero[2], **-ra** *n* : jingoist, chauvinist
patriótico, -ca *adj* : patriotic
patriotismo *nm* : patriotism
patrocinador, -dora *n* : sponsor, patron
patrocinar *vt* : to sponsor
patrocinio *nm* : sponsorship, patronage
patrón[1], **-trona** *n, mpl* **patrones 1** JEFE : boss **2** : patron saint
patrón[2] *nm, pl* **patrones 1** : standard **2** : pattern (in sewing)
patronal *adj* **1** : management, employers' ⟨sindicato patronal : employers' association⟩ **2** : pertaining to a patron saint ⟨fiesta patronal : patron saint's day⟩
patronato *nm* **1** : board, council **2** : foundation, trust
patrono, -na *n* **1** : employer **2** : patron saint
patrulla *nf* **1** : patrol **2** : police car, cruiser
patrullar *v* : to patrol
patrullero *nm* **1** : police car **2** : patrol boat
paulatino, -na *adj* : gradual
paupérrimo, -ma *adj* : destitute, poverty-stricken
pausa *nf* : pause, break
pausado[1] *adv* : slowly, deliberately ⟨habla más pausado : speak more slowly⟩
pausado[2], **-da** *adj* : slow, deliberate — **pausadamente** *adv*
pauta *nf* **1** : rule, guideline **2** : lines *pl* (on paper)
pava *nf Arg, Bol, Chile* : kettle
pavimentar *vt* : pave
pavimento *nm* : pavement
pavo, -va *n* **1** : turkey **2 pavo real** : peacock **3 comer pavo** : to be a wallflower
pavón *nm, pl* **pavones** : peacock
pavonearse *vr* : to strut, to swagger
pavoneo *nm* : strut, swagger
pavor *nm* TERROR : dread, terror
pavoroso, -sa *adj* ATERRADOR : dreadful, terrifying
payasada *nf* BUFONADA : antic, buffoonery
payasear *vi* : to clown around
payaso, -sa *n* : clown
paz *nf, pl* **paces 1** : peace **2 dejar en paz** : to leave alone **3 hacer las paces** : to make up, to reconcile
pazca, etc. → **pacer**
PC *nmf* : PC, personal computer
peaje *nm* : toll
peatón *nm, pl* **-tones** : pedestrian
peatonal *adj* : pedestrian
peca *nf* : freckle
pecado *nm* : sin
pecador[1], **-dora** *adj* : sinful, sinning
pecador[2], **-dora** *n* : sinner
pecaminoso, -sa *adj* : sinful
pecar {72} *vi* **1** : to sin **2 ~ de** : to be too much (something) ⟨no pecan de amabilidad : they're not overly friendly⟩
pécari *or* **pecarí** *nm* : peccary
pececillo *nm* : small fish
pecera *nf* : fishbowl, fish tank
pecho *nm* **1** : chest **2** SENO : breast, bosom **3** : heart, courage **4 dar el pecho** : to breast-feed **5 tomar a pecho** : to take to heart
pechuga *nf* : breast (of fowl)
pecoso, -sa *adj* : freckled
pectoral *adj* : pectoral
peculado *nm* : embezzlement
peculiar *adj* **1** CARACTERÍSTICO : particular, characteristic **2** RARO : peculiar, uncommon
peculiaridad *nf* : peculiarity
pecuniario, -ria *adj* : pecuniary
pedagogía *nf* : pedagogy
pedagógico, -ca *adj* : pedagogic, pedagogical
pedagogo, -ga *n* : educator, pedagogue
pedal *nm* : pedal
pedalear *vi* : to pedal
pedante[1] *adj* : pedantic
pedante[2] *nmf* : pedant
pedantería *nf* : pedantry
pedazo *nm* TROZO : piece, bit, chunk ⟨caerse a pedazos : to fall to pieces⟩ ⟨hacer pedazos : to tear into shreds, to smash to pieces⟩
pedernal *nm* : flint
pedestal *nm* : pedestal
pedestre *adj* : commonplace, pedestrian
pediatra *nmf* : pediatrician
pediatría *nf* : pediatrics
pediátrico, -ca *adj* : pediatric
pedido *nm* **1** : order (of merchandise) **2** : request
pedigrí *nm* : pedigree
pedir {54} *vt* **1** : to ask for, to request ⟨le pedí un préstamo a Claudia : I asked Claudia for a loan⟩ **2** : to order (food, merchandise) **3 pedir disculpas** *or* **pedir perdón** : to apologize — *vi* **1** : to order **2** : to beg

pedrada *nf* **1** : blow (with a rock or stone) ⟨la ventana se quebró de una pedrada : the window was broken by a rock⟩ **2** *fam* : cutting remark, dig
pedregal *nm* : rocky ground
pedregoso, -sa *adj* : rocky, stony
pedrera *nf* CANTERA : quarry
pedrería *nf* : precious stones *pl*, gems *pl*
pegado, -da *adj* **1** : glued, stuck, stuck together **2 ~ a** : right next to
pegajoso, -sa *adj* **1** : sticky, gluey **2** : catchy ⟨una tonada pegajosa : a catchy tune⟩
pegamento *nm* : adhesive, glue
pegar {52} *vt* **1** : to glue, to stick, to paste **2** : to attach, to sew on **3** : to infect with, to give ⟨me pegó el resfriado : he gave me his cold⟩ **4** GOLPEAR : to hit, to deal, to strike ⟨me pegaron un puntapié : they gave me a kick⟩ **5** : to give (out with) ⟨pegó un grito : she let out a yell⟩ — *vi* **1** : to adhere, to stick **2 ~ en** : to hit, to strike (against) **3 ~ con** : to match, to go with — **pegarse** *vr* **1** GOLPEARSE : to hit oneself, to hit each other **2** : to stick, to take hold **3** : to be contagious **4** *fam* : to tag along, to stick around
pegote *nm* **1** : sticky mess **2** *Mex* : sticker, adhesive label
pegue, etc. → **pegar**
peinado *nm* : hairstyle, hairdo
peinador, -dora *n* : hairdresser
peinar *vt* : to comb — **peinarse** *vr*
peine *nm* : comb
peineta *nf* : ornamental comb
peladez *nf, pl* **-deces** *Mex fam* : obscenity, bad language
pelado, -da *adj* **1** : bald, hairless **2** : peeled **3** : bare, barren **4** : broke, penniless **5** *Mex fam* : coarse, crude
pelador *nm* : peeler
pelagra *nf* : pellagra
pelaje *nm* : coat (of an animal), fur
pelar *vt* **1** : to peel, to shell **2** : to skin **3** : to pluck **4** : to remove hair from **5** *fam* : to clean out (of money) — **pelarse** *vr* **1** : to peel **2** *fam* : to get a haircut **3** *Mex fam* : to split, to leave
peldaño *nm* **1** : step, stair **2** : rung
pelea *nf* **1** LUCHA : fight **2** : quarrel
pelear *vi* **1** LUCHAR : to fight **2** DISPUTAR : to quarrel — **pelearse** *vr*
peleón, -ona *adj, mpl* **-ones** *Spain* : quarrelsome, argumentative
peleonero, -ra *adj Mex* : quarrelsome
peletería *nf* **1** : fur shop **2** : fur trade
peletero, -ra *n* : furrier
peliagudo, -da *adj* : tricky, difficult, ticklish
pelícano *nm* : pelican
película *nf* **1** : movie, film **2** : (photographic) film **3** : thin covering, layer
peligrar *vi* : to be in danger
peligro *nm* **1** : danger, peril **2** : risk ⟨correr peligro de : to run the risk of⟩
peligroso, -sa *adj* : dangerous, hazardous
pelirrojo¹, -ja *adj* : red-haired, redheaded
pelirrojo², -ja *n* : redhead
pellejo *nm* **1** : hide, skin **2 salvar el pellejo** : to save one's neck
pellizcar {72} *vt* **1** : to pinch **2** : to nibble on
pellizco *nm* : pinch
pelo *nm* **1** : hair **2** : fur **3** : pile, nap **4 a pelo** : bareback **5 con pelos y señales** : in great detail **6 no tener pelos en la lengua** : to not mince words, to be blunt **7 tomarle el pelo a alguien** : to tease someone, to pull someone's leg
pelón, -lona *adj, mpl* **pelones** **1** : bald **2** *fam* : broke **3** *Mex fam* : tough, difficult
pelota *nf* **1** : ball **2** *fam* : head **3 en pelotas** *fam* : naked **4 pelota vasca** : jai alai **5 pasar la pelota** *fam* : to pass the buck
pelotón *nm, pl* **-tones** : squad, detachment
peltre *nm* : pewter
peluca *nf* : wig
peluche *nm* : plush (fabric)
peludo, -da *adj* : hairy, shaggy, bushy
peluquería *nf* **1** : hairdresser's, barber shop **2** : hairdressing
peluquero, -ra *n* : barber, hairdresser
peluquín *nm, pl* **-quines** TUPÉ : hairpiece, toupee
pelusa *nf* : lint, fuzz
pélvico, -ca *adj* : pelvic
pelvis *nfs & pl* : pelvis
pena *nf* **1** CASTIGO : punishment, penalty ⟨pena de muerte : death penalty⟩ **2** AFLICCIÓN : sorrow, grief ⟨morir de pena : to die of a broken heart⟩ ⟨¡qué pena! : what a shame!, how sad!⟩ **3** DOLOR : pain, suffering **4** DIFICULTAD : difficulty, trouble ⟨a duras penas : with great difficulty⟩ **5** VERGÜENZA : shame, embarrassment **6 valer la pena** : to be worthwhile
penacho *nm* **1** : crest, tuft **2** : plume (of feathers)
penal¹ *adj* : penal
penal² *nm* CÁRCEL : prison, penitentiary
penalidad *nf* **1** : hardship **2** : penalty, punishment
penalizar {21} *vt* : to penalize
penalty *nm* : penalty (in sports)
penar *vt* : to punish, to penalize — *vi* : to suffer, to grieve
pendenciero, -ra *adj* : argumentative, quarrelsome
pender *vi* **1** : to hang **2** : to be pending
pendiente¹ *adj* **1** : pending **2 estar pendiente de** : to be watchful of, to be on the lookout for
pendiente² *nm Spain* : earring
pendiente³ *nf* : slope, incline
pendón *nm, pl* **pendones** : banner
péndulo *nm* : pendulum
pene *nm* : penis

penetración *nf, pl* **-ciones 1** : penetration **2** : insight

penetrante *adj* **1** : penetrating, piercing **2** : sharp, acute **3** : deep (of a wound)

penetrar *vi* **1** : to penetrate, to sink in **2 ~ por** *or* **~ en** : to pierce, to go in, to enter into ⟨el frío penetra por la ventana : the cold comes right in through the window⟩ — *vt* **1** : to penetrate, to permeate **2** : to pierce ⟨el dolor penetró su corazón : sorrow pierced her heart⟩ **3** : to fathom, to understand

penicilina *nf* : penicillin

península *nf* : peninsula — **peninsular** *adj*

penitencia *nf* : penance, penitence

penitenciaría *nf* : penitentiary

penitente *adj & nmf* : penitent

penol *nm* : yardarm

penoso, -sa *adj* **1** : painful, distressing **2** : difficult, arduous **3** : shy, bashful

pensado, -da *adj* **1 bien pensado** : well thought-out **2 en el momento menos pensado** : when least expected **3 poco pensado** : badly thought-out **4 mal pensado** : evil-minded

pensador, -dora *n* : thinker

pensamiento *nm* **1** : thought **2** : thinking **3** : pansy

pensar {55} *vi* **1** : to think **2 ~ en** : to think about — *vt* **1** : to think **2** : to think about **3** : to intend, to plan on — **pensarse** *vr* : to think over

pensativo, -va *adj* : pensive, thoughtful

pensión *nf, pl* **pensiones 1** JUBILACIÓN : pension **2** : boarding house **3 pensión alimenticia** : alimony

pensionado, -da *n* → **pensionista**

pensionista *nmf* **1** JUBILADO : pensioner, retiree **2** : boarder, lodger

pentágono *nm* : pentagon — **pentagonal** *adj*

pentagrama *nm* : staff (in music)

penúltimo, -ma *adj* : next to last, penultimate

penumbra *nf* : semidarkness

penuria *nf* **1** ESCASEZ : shortage, scarcity **2** : poverty

peña *nf* : rock, crag

peñasco *nm* : crag, large rock

peñón → **peñasco**

peón *nm, pl* **peones 1** : laborer, peon **2** : pawn (in chess)

peonía *nf* : peony

peor[1] *adv* **1** (*comparative of* **mal**) : worse ⟨se llevan peor que antes : they get along worse than before⟩ **2** (*superlative of* **mal**) : worst ⟨me fue peor que a nadie : I did the worst of all⟩

peor[2] *adj* **1** (*comparative of* **malo**) : worse ⟨es peor que el original : it's worse than the original⟩ **2** (*superlative of* **malo**) : worst ⟨el peor de todos : the worst of all⟩

pepa *nf* : seed, pit (of a fruit)

pepenador, -dora *n CA, Mex* : scavenger

pepenar *vt CA, Mex* : to scavenge, to scrounge

pepinillo *nm* : pickle, gherkin

pepino *nm* : cucumber

pepita *nf* **1** : seed, pip **2** : nugget **3** *Mex* : dried pumpkin seed

peque, etc. → **pecar**

pequeñez *nf, pl* **-ñeces 1** : smallness **2** : trifle, triviality **3 pequeñez de espíritu** : pettiness

pequeño[1], -ña *adj* **1** : small, little ⟨un libro pequeño : a small book⟩ **2** : young **3** BAJO : short

pequeño[2], -ña *n* : child, little one

pera *nf* : pear

peraltar *vt* : to bank (a road)

perca *nf* : perch (fish)

percal *nm* : percale

percance *nm* : mishap, misfortune

percatarse *vr* **~ de** : to notice, to become aware of

percebe *nm* : barnacle

percepción *nf, pl* **-ciones 1** : perception **2** : idea, notion **3** COBRO : receipt (of payment), collection

perceptible *adj* : perceptible, noticeable — **perceptiblemente** *adv*

percha *nf* **1** : perch **2** : coat hanger **3** : coatrack, coat hook

perchero *nm* : coatrack

percibir *vt* **1** : to perceive, to notice, to sense **2** : to earn, to draw (a salary)

percudido, -da *adj* : grimy

percudir *vt* : to make grimy — **percudirse** *vr*

percusión *nf, pl* **-siones** : percussion

percusor *or* **percutor** *nm* : hammer (of a firearm)

perdedor[1], -dora *adj* : losing

perdedor[2], -dora *n* : loser

perder {56} *vt* **1** : to lose **2** : to miss ⟨perdimos la oportunidad : we missed the opportunity⟩ **3** : to waste (time) — *vi* : to lose — **perderse** *vr* EXTRAVIARSE : to get lost, to stray

perdición *nf, pl* **-ciones** : perdition, damnation

pérdida *nf* **1** : loss **2 pérdida de tiempo** : waste of time

perdidamente *adv* : hopelessly

perdido, -da *adj* **1** : lost **2** : inveterate, incorrigible ⟨es un caso perdido : he's a hopeless case⟩ **3** : in trouble, done for **4 de ~** *Mex fam* : at least

perdigón *nm, pl* **-gones** : shot, pellet

perdiz *nf, pl* **perdices** : partridge

perdón[1] *nm, pl* **perdones** : forgiveness, pardon

perdón[2] *interj* : excuse me!, sorry!

perdonable *adj* : forgivable

perdonar *vt* **1** DISCULPAR : to forgive, to pardon **2** : to exempt, to excuse

perdurable *adj* : lasting

perdurar *vi* : to last, to endure, to survive

perecedero, -ra *adj* : perishable

perecer {53} *vi* : to perish, to die

peregrinación *nf, pl* **-ciones** : pilgrimage

peregrinaje *nm* → **peregrinación**

peregrino[1], **-na** *adj* **1** : unusual, odd **2** MIGRATORIO : migratory
peregrino[2], **-na** *n* : pilgrim
perejil *nm* : parsley
perenne *adj* : perennial
perentorio, -ria *adj* **1** : peremptory **2** URGENTE : urgent **3** FIJO : fixed, set
pereza *nf* FLOJERA, HOLGAZANERÍA : laziness, idleness
perezoso[1], **-sa** *adj* FLOJO, HOLGAZÁN : lazy
perezoso[2] *nm* : sloth (animal)
perfección *nf, pl* **-ciones** : perfection
perfeccionamiento *nm* : perfecting, refinement
perfeccionar *vt* : to perfect, to refine
perfeccionismo *nm* : perfectionism
perfeccionista *nmf* : perfectionist
perfecto, -ta *adj* : perfect — **perfectamente** *adv*
perfidia *nf* : perfidy, treachery
pérfido, -da *adj* : perfidious
perfil *nm* **1** : profile **2 de ~** : sideways, from the side **3 perfiles** *nmpl* RASGOS : features, characteristics
perfilar *vt* : to outline, to define — **perfilarse** *vr* **1** : to be outlined, to be silhouetted **2** : to take shape
perforación *nf, pl* **-ciones 1** : perforation **2** : drilling
perforadora *nf* **1** : hole punch (for paper) **2** : drill (in mining, etc.)
perforar *vt* **1** : to perforate, to pierce **2** : to drill, to bore
perfumar *vt* : to perfume, to scent — **perfumarse** *vr*
perfume *nm* : perfume, scent
pergamino *nm* : parchment
pérgola *nf* : pergola, arbor
pericia *nf* : skill, expertise
pericial *adj* : expert ⟨testigo pericial : expert witness⟩
perico *nm* COTORRA : small parrot
periferia *nf* : periphery
periférico[1], **-ca** *adj* : peripheral
periférico[2] *nm* **1** *CA, Mex* : beltway **2** : peripheral
perilla *nf* **1** : goatee **2** : pommel (on a saddle) **3** *Col, Mex* : knob, handle **4 perilla de la oreja** : earlobe **5 de perillas** *fam* : handy, just right
perímetro *nm* : perimeter
periódico[1], **-ca** *adj* : periodic — **periódicamente** *adv*
periódico[2] *nm* DIARIO : newspaper
periodismo *nm* : journalism
periodista *nmf* : journalist
periodístico, -ca *adj* : journalistic, news
período *or* **periodo** *nm* : period
peripecia *nf* VICISITUD : vicissitude, reversal ⟨las peripecias de su carrera : the ups and downs of her career⟩
periquito *nm* **1** : parakeet **2 periquito australiano** : budgerigar
periscopio *nm* : periscope
perito, -ta *adj & n* : expert
perjudicar {72} *vt* : to harm, to be detrimental to
perjudicial *adj* : harmful, detrimental
perjuicio *nm* **1** : harm, damage **2 en perjuicio de** : to the detriment of
perjurar *vi* : to perjure oneself
perjurio *nm* : perjury
perjuro, -ra *n* : perjurer
perla *nf* **1** : pearl **2 de perlas** *fam* : wonderfully ⟨me viene de perlas : it suits me just fine⟩
permanecer {53} *vi* **1** QUEDARSE : to remain, to stay **2** SEGUIR : to remain, to continue to be
permanencia *nf* **1** : permanence, continuance **2** ESTANCIA : stay
permanente[1] *adj* **1** : permanent **2** : constant — **permanentemente** *adv*
permanente[2] *nf* : permanent (wave)
permeabilidad *nf* : permeability
permeable *adj* : permeable
permisible *adj* : permissible, allowable
permisividad *nf* : permissiveness
permisivo, -va *adv* : permissive
permiso *nm* **1** : permission **2** : permit, license **3** : leave, furlough **4 con ~** : excuse me, pardon me
permitir *vt* : to permit, to allow — **permitirse** *vr*
permuta *nf* : exchange
permutar *vt* INTERCAMBIAR : to exchange
pernicioso, -sa *adj* : pernicious, destructive
pernil *nm* **1** : haunch (of an animal) **2** : leg (of meat), ham **3** : trouser leg
perno *nm* : bolt, pin
pernoctar *vi* : to stay overnight, to spend the night
pero[1] *nm* **1** : fault, defect ⟨ponerle peros a : to find fault with⟩ **2** : objection
pero[2] *conj* : but
perogrullada *nf* : truism, platitude, cliché
peroné *nm* : fibula
perorar *vi* : to deliver a speech
perorata *nf* : oration, long-winded speech
peróxido *nm* : peroxide
perpendicular *adj & nf* : perpendicular
perpetrar *vt* : to perpetrate
perpetuar {3} *vt* ETERNIZAR : to perpetuate
perpetuidad *nf* : perpetuity
perpetuo, -tua *adj* : perpetual — **perpetuamente** *adv*
perplejidad *nf* : perplexity
perplejo, -ja *adj* : perplexed, puzzled
perrada *nf fam* : dirty trick
perrera *nf* : kennel, dog pound
perrero, -ra *n* : dogcatcher
perrito, -ta *n* CACHORRO : puppy, small dog
perro, -rra *n* **1** : dog, bitch *f* **2 perro caliente** : hot dog **3 perro salchicha** : dachshund **4 perro faldero** : lapdog **5 perro cobrador** : retriever
persa[1] *adj & nmf* : Persian
persa[2] *nm* : Persian (language)

persecución *nf, pl* **-ciones** 1 : pursuit, chase 2 : persecution
perseguidor, -dora *n* 1 : pursuer 2 : persecutor
perseguir {75} *vt* 1 : to pursue, to chase 2 : to persecute 3 : to pester, to annoy
perseverancia *nf* : perseverance
perseverar *vi* : to persevere
persiana *nf* : blind, venetian blind
persignarse *vr* SANTIGUARSE : to cross oneself, to make the sign of the cross
persistir *vi* : to persist — **persistencia** *nf* — **persistente** *adj*
persona *nf* : person
personaje *nm* 1 : character (in drama or literature) 2 : personage, celebrity
personal[1] *adj* : personal — **personalmente** *adv*
personal[2] *nm* : personnel, staff
personalidad *nf* : personality
personalizar {21} *vt* : to personalize
personificar {72} *vi* : to personify — **personificación** *nf*
perspectiva *nf* 1 : perspective, view 2 : prospect, outlook
perspicacia *nf* : shrewdness, perspicacity, insight
perspicaz *adj, pl* **-caces** : shrewd, perspicacious
persuadir *vt* : to persuade — **persuadirse** *vr* : to become convinced
persuasión *nf, pl* **-siones** : persuasion
persuasivo, -va *adj* : persuasive
pertenecer {53} *vi* : to belong
perteneciente *adj* ~ **a** : belonging to
pertenencia *nf* 1 : membership 2 : ownership 3 **pertenencias** *nfpl* : belongings, possessions
pértiga *nf* GARROCHA : pole ⟨salto de pértiga : pole vault⟩
pertinaz *adj, pl* **-naces** 1 OBSTINADO : obstinate 2 PERSISTENTE : persistent
pertinencia *nf* : pertinence, relevance — **pertinente** *adj*
pertrechos *nmpl* : equipment, gear
perturbación *nf, pl* **-ciones** : disturbance, disruption
perturbador, -dora *adj* 1 INQUIETANTE : disturbing, troubling 2 : disruptive
perturbar *vt* 1 : to disturb, to trouble 2 : to disrupt
peruano, -na *adj & n* : Peruvian
perversidad *nf* : perversity, depravity
perversión *nf, pl* **-siones** : perversion
perverso, -sa *adj* : wicked, depraved
pervertido[1], **-da** *adj* DEPRAVADO : perverted, depraved
pervertido[2], **-da** *n* : pervert
pervertir {76} *vt* : to pervert, to corrupt
pesa *nf* 1 : weight 2 **levantamiento de pesas** : weightlifting
pesadamente *adv* 1 : heavily 2 : slowly, clumsily
pesadez *nf, pl* **-deces** 1 : heaviness 2 : slowness 3 : tediousness
pesadilla *nf* : nightmare
pesado[1], **-da** *adj* 1 : heavy 2 : slow 3 : irritating, annoying 4 : tedious, boring 5 : tough, difficult
pesado[2], **-da** *n fam* : bore, pest
pesadumbre *nf* AFLICCIÓN : grief, sorrow, sadness
pésame *nm* : condolences *pl* ⟨mi más sentido pésame : my heartfelt condolences⟩
pesar[1] *vt* 1 : to weigh 2 EXAMINAR : to consider, to think over — *vi* 1 : to weigh ⟨¿cuánto pesa? : how much does it weigh?⟩ 2 : to be heavy 3 : to weigh heavily, to be a burden ⟨no le pesa : it's not a burden on him⟩ ⟨pesa sobre mi corazón : it weighs upon my heart⟩ 4 INFLUIR : to carry weight, to have bearing 5 (*with personal pronouns*) : to grieve, to sadden ⟨me pesa mucho : I'm very sorry⟩ 6 **pese a** : in spite of, despite
pesar[2] *nm* 1 AFLICCIÓN, PENA : sorrow, grief 2 REMORDIMIENTO : remorse 3 **a pesar de** : in spite of, despite
pesaroso, -sa *adj* 1 : sad, mournful 2 ARREPENTIDO : sorry, regretful
pesca *nf* : fishing
pescadería *nf* : fish market
pescado *nm* : fish (as food)
pescador, -dora *n* : fisherman *m*, fisherwoman *f*
pescar {72} *vt* 1 : to fish for 2 : to catch 3 *fam* : to get a hold of, to land — *vi* : to fish, to go fishing
pescuezo *nm* : neck
pesebre *nm* : manger
pesero *nm Mex* : minibus
peseta *nf* : peseta (Spanish unit of currency)
pesimismo *nm* : pessimism
pesimista[1] *adj* : pessimistic
pesimista[2] *nmf* : pessimist
pésimo, -ma *adj* : dreadful, abominable
peso *nm* 1 : weight, heaviness 2 : burden, responsibility 3 : weight (in sports) 4 BÁSCULA : scales *pl* 5 : peso
pesque, etc. → **pescar**
pesquería *nf* : fishery
pesquero[1], **-ra** *adj* : fishing ⟨pueblo pesquero : fishing village⟩
pesquero[2] *nm* : fishing boat
pesquisa *nf* INVESTIGACIÓN : inquiry, investigation
pestaña *nf* 1 : eyelash 2 : flange, rim
pestañear *vi* : to blink
pestañeo *nm* : blink
peste *nf* 1 : plague, pestilence 2 : stench, stink 3 : nuisance, pest
pesticida *nm* : pesticide
pestilencia *nf* 1 : stench, foul odor 2 : pestilence
pestilente *adj* 1 : foul, smelly 2 : pestilent
pestillo *nm* CERROJO : bolt, latch
petaca *nf* 1 *Mex* : suitcase 2 **petacas** *nfpl Mex fam* : bottom, behind
pétalo *nm* : petal
petardear *vi* : to backfire

petardeo *nm* : backfiring
petardo *nm* : firecracker
petate *nm Mex* : mat
petición *nf, pl* **-ciones** : petition, request
peticionar *vt* : to petition
peticionario, -ria *n* : petitioner
petirrojo *nm* : robin
peto *nm* : bib (of clothing)
pétreo, -trea *adj* : stone, stony
petrificar {72} *vt* : to petrify
petróleo *nm* : oil, petroleum
petrolero[1], **-ra** *adj* : oil ⟨industria petrolera : oil industry⟩
petrolero[2] *nm* : oil tanker
petrolífero, -ra *adj* → **petrolero**[1]
petulancia *nf* INSOLENCIA : insolence, petulance
petulante *adj* INSOLENTE : insolent, petulant — **petulantemente** *adv*
petunia *nf* : petunia
peyorativo, -va *adj* : pejorative
pez[1] *nm, pl* **peces 1** : fish **2 pez de colores** : goldfish **3 pez espada** : swordfish **4 pez gordo** : big shot
pez[2] *nf, pl* **peces** : pitch, tar
pezón *nm, pl* **pezones** : nipple
pezuña *nf* : hoof ⟨pezuña hendida : cloven hoof⟩
pi *nf* : pi
piadoso, -sa *adj* **1** : compassionate, merciful **2** DEVOTO : pious, devout
pianista *nmf* : pianist, piano player
piano *nm* : piano
piar {85} *vi* : to chirp, to cheep, to tweet
pibe, -ba *n Arg, Uru fam* : kid, child
pica *nf* **1** : pike, lance **2** : goad (in bullfighting) **3** : spade (in playing cards)
picada *nf* **1** : bite, sting (of an insect) **2** : sharp descent
picadillo *nm* **1** : minced meat, hash **2 hacer picadillo a** : to beat to a pulp
picado, -da *adj* **1** : perforated **2** : minced, chopped **3** : decayed (of teeth) **4** : choppy, rough **5** *fam* : annoyed, miffed
picador *nm* : picador
picadura *nf* **1** : sting, bite **2** : prick, puncture **3** : decay, cavity
picaflor *nm* COLIBRÍ : hummingbird
picana *nf* : goad, prod
picante[1] *adj* **1** : hot, spicy **2** : sharp, cutting **3** : racy, risqué
picante[2] *nm* **1** : spiciness **2** : hot spices *pl*, hot sauce
picaporte *nm* **1** : latch **2** : door handle **3** ALDABA : door knocker
picar {72} *vt* **1** : to sting, to bite **2** : to peck at **3** : to nibble on **4** : to prick, to puncture, to punch (a ticket) **5** : to grind, to chop **6** : to goad, to incite **7** : to pique, to provoke — *vi* **1** : to itch **2** : to sting **3** : to be spicy **4** : to nibble **5** : to take the bait **6 ~ en** : to dabble in **7 picar muy alto** : to aim too high — **picarse** *vr* **1** : to get a cavity, to decay **2** : to get annoyed, to take offense
picardía *nf* **1** : cunning, craftiness **2** : prank, dirty trick
picaresco, -ca *adj* **1** : picaresque **2** : rascally, roguish
pícaro[1], **-ra** *adj* **1** : mischievous **2** : cunning, sly **3** : off-color, risqué
pícaro[2], **-ra** *n* **1** : rogue, scoundrel **2** : rascal
picazón *nf, pl* **-zones** COMEZÓN : itch
picea *nf* : spruce (tree)
pichel *nm* : pitcher, jug
pichón, -chona *n, mpl* **pichones 1** : young pigeon, squab **2** *Mex fam* : novice, greenhorn
picnic *nm* : picnic
pico *nm* **1** : peak **2** : point, spike **3** : beak, bill **4** : pick, pickax **5 y pico** : and a little, and a bit ⟨las siete y pico : a little after seven⟩ ⟨dos metros y pico : a bit over two meters⟩
picor *nm* : itch, irritation
picoso, -sa *adj Mex* : very hot, spicy
picota *nf* **1** : pillory, stock **2 poner a alguien en la picota** : to put someone on the spot
picotada *nf* → **picotazo**
picotazo *nm* : peck (of a bird)
picotear *vt* : to peck — *vi* : to nibble, to pick
pictórico, -ca *adj* : pictorial
picudo, -da *adj* **1** : pointy, sharp **2 ~ para** *Mex fam* : clever at, good at
pide, etc. → **pedir**
pie *nm* **1** : foot ⟨a pie : on foot⟩ ⟨de pie : on one's feet, standing⟩ **2** : base, bottom, stem, foot ⟨pie de la cama : foot of the bed⟩ ⟨pie de una lámpara : base of a lamp⟩ ⟨pie de la escalera : bottom of the stairs⟩ ⟨pie de una copa : stem of a glass⟩ **3** : foot (in measurement) ⟨pie cuadrado : square foot⟩ **4** : cue (in theater) **5 dar pie a** : to give cause for, to give rise to **6 en pie de igualdad** : on equal footing
piedad *nf* **1** COMPASIÓN : mercy, pity **2** DEVOCIÓN : piety, devotion
piedra *nf* **1** : stone **2** : flint (of a lighter) **3** : hailstone **4 piedra de afilar** : whetstone, grindstone **5 piedra angular** : cornerstone **6 piedra arenisca** : sandstone **7 piedra caliza** : limestone **8 piedra imán** : lodestone **9 piedra de molino** : millstone **10 piedra de toque** : touchstone
piel *nf* **1** : skin **2** CUERO : leather, hide ⟨piel de venado : deerskin⟩ **3** : fur, pelt **4** CÁSCARA : peel, skin **5 piel de gallina** : goose bumps *pl* ⟨me pone la piel de gallina : it gives me goose bumps⟩
piélago *nm* **el piélago** : the deep, the ocean
piensa, etc. → **pensar**
pienso *nm* : feed, fodder
pierde, etc. → **perder**
pierna *nf* : leg
pieza *nf* **1** ELEMENTO : piece, part, component ⟨vestido de dos piezas : two-piece dress⟩ ⟨pieza de recambio : spare part⟩ ⟨pieza clave : key element⟩ **2** : piece (in chess) **3** OBRA : piece, work

⟨pieza de teatro : play⟩ **4** : room, bedroom

pifia *nf fam* : goof, blunder

pigargo *nm* : osprey

pigmentación *nf, pl* **-ciones** : pigmentation

pigmento *nm* : pigment

pigmeo, -mea *adj & n* : pygmy, Pygmy

pijama *nm* : pajamas *pl*

pila *nf* **1** BATERÍA : battery ⟨pila de linterna : flashlight battery⟩ **2** MONTÓN : pile, heap **3** : sink, basin, font ⟨pila bautismal : baptismal font⟩ ⟨pila para pájaros : birdbath⟩

pilar *nm* **1** : pillar, column **2** : support, mainstay

píldora *nf* PASTILLA : pill

pillaje *nm* : pillage, plunder

pillar *vt* **1** *fam* : to catch ⟨¡cuidado! ¡nos pillarán! : watch out! they'll catch us!⟩ **2** *fam* : to grasp, to catch on ⟨¿no lo pillas? : don't you get it?⟩

pillo[1], -lla *adj* : cunning, crafty

pillo[2], -lla *n* **1** : rascal, brat **2** : rogue, scoundrel

pilluelo, -la *n* : urchin

pilón *nm, pl* **pilones** **1** PILA : basin **2** : pillar, tower (for cables), pylon (of a bridge) **3** *Mex* : extra, lagniappe

pilotar *vt* : to pilot, to drive

pilote *nm* : pile (stake)

pilotear → **pilotar**

piloto *nm* **1** : pilot, driver **2** : pilot light

piltrafa *nf* **1** : poor quality meat **2** : wretch **3 piltrafas** *nfpl* : food scraps

pimentero *nm* : pepper shaker

pimentón *nm, pl* **-tones** **1** : paprika **2** : cayenne pepper

pimienta *nf* **1** : pepper (condiment) **2 pimienta de Jamaica** : allspice

pimiento *nm* : pepper (fruit) ⟨pimiento verde : green pepper⟩

pináculo *nm* **1** : pinnacle (of a building) **2** : peak, acme

pincel *nm* : paintbrush

pincelada *nf* **1** : brushstroke **2 últimas pinceladas** : final touches

pinchar *vt* **1** PICAR : to puncture (a tire) **2** : to prick, to stick **3** : to goad, to tease, to needle — *vi* **1** : to be prickly **2** : to get a flat tire **3** *fam* : to get beaten, to lose out — **pincharse** *vr* : to give oneself an injection

pinchazo *nm* **1** : prick, jab **2** : puncture, flat tire

pingüe *adj* **1** : rich, huge (of profits) **2** : lucrative

pingüino *nm* : penguin

pininos *or* **pinitos** *nmpl* : first steps ⟨hacer pininos : to take one's first steps, to toddle⟩

pino *nm* : pine, pine tree

pinta *nf* **1** : dot, spot **2** : pint **3** *fam* : aspect, appearance ⟨las peras tienen buena pinta : the pears look good⟩ **4 pintas** *nfpl Mex* : graffiti

pintadas *nfpl* : graffiti

pintar *vt* **1** : to paint **2** : to draw, to mark **3** : to describe, to depict — *vi* **1** : to paint, to draw **2** : to look ⟨no pinta bien : it doesn't look good⟩ **3** *fam* : to count ⟨aquí no pinta nada : he has no say here⟩ — **pintarse** *vr* **1** MAQUILLARSE : to put on makeup **2 pintárselas solo** *fam* : to manage by oneself, to know it all

pintarrajear *vt* : to daub (with paint)

pinto, -ta *adj* : speckled, spotted

pintor, -tora *n* **1** : painter **2 pintor de brocha gorda** : housepainter, dauber

pintoresco, -ca *adj* : picturesque, quaint

pintura *nf* **1** : paint **2** : painting (art, work of art)

pinza *nf* **1** : clothespin **2** : claw, pincer **3** : pleat, dart **4 pinzas** *nfpl* : tweezers **5 pinzas** *nfpl* ALICATES : pliers, pincers

pinzón *nm, pl* **pinzones** : finch

piña *nf* **1** : pineapple **2** : pine cone

piñata *nf* : piñata

piñón *nm, pl* **piñones** **1** : pine nut **2** : pinion

pío[1], pía *adj* **1** DEVOTO : pious, devout **2** : piebald, pied, dappled

pío[2] *nm* : peep, tweet, cheep

piocha *nf* **1** : pickax **2** *Mex* : goatee

piojo *nm* : louse

piojoso, -sa *adj* **1** : lousy **2** : filthy

pionero[1], -ra *adj* : pioneering

pionero[2], -ra *n* : pioneer

pipa *nf* : pipe (for smoking)

pipián *nm, pl* **pipianes** *Mex* : a spicy sauce or stew

pipiolo, -la *n fam* **1** : greenhorn, novice **2** : kid, youngster

pique[1], etc. → **picar**

pique[2] *nm* **1** : pique, resentment **2** : rivalry, competition **3 a pique de** : about to, on the verge of **4 irse a pique** : to sink, to founder

piqueta *nf* : pickax

piquete *nm* **1** : picketers *pl*, picket line **2** : squad, detachment **3** *Mex* : prick, jab

piquetear *vt* **1** : to picket **2** *Mex* : to prick, to jab

pira *nf* : pyre

piragua *nf* : canoe — **piragüista** *nmf*

pirámide *nf* : pyramid

piraña *nf* : piranha

pirata[1] *adj* : bootleg, pirated

pirata[2] *nmf* **1** : pirate **2** : bootlegger **3 pirata aéreo** : hijacker

piratear *vt* **1** : to hijack, to commandeer **2** : to bootleg, to pirate

piratería *nf* : piracy, bootlegging

piromanía *nf* : pyromania

pirómano, -na *n* : pyromaniac

piropo *nm* : flirtatious compliment

pirotecnia *nf* : fireworks *pl*, pyrotechnics *pl*

pirotécnico, -ca *adj* : fireworks, pyrotechnic

pírrico, -ca *adj* : Pyrrhic

pirueta *nf* : pirouette

pirulí *nm* : cone-shaped lollipop

pisada *nf* **1** : footstep **2** HUELLA : footprint
pisapapeles *nms & pl* : paperweight
pisar *vt* **1** : to step on, to set foot in **2** : to walk all over, to mistreat — *vi* : to step, to walk, to tread
piscina *nf* **1** : swimming pool **2** : fish pond
Piscis *nmf* : Pisces
piso *nm* **1** PLANTA : floor, story **2** SUELO : floor **3** *Spain* : apartment
pisotear *vt* **1** : to stamp on, to trample **2** PISAR : to walk all over **3** : to flout, to disregard
pisotón *nm, pl* **-tones** : stamp, step ⟨sufrieron empujones y pisotones : they were pushed and stepped on⟩
pista *nf* **1** RASTRO : trail, track ⟨siguen la pista de los sospechosos : they're on the trail of the suspects⟩ **2** : clue **3** CAMINO : road, trail **4** : track, racetrack **5** : ring, arena, rink **6 pista de aterrizaje** : runway, airstrip **7 pista de baile** : dance floor
pistacho *nm* : pistachio
pistilo *nm* : pistil
pistola *nf* **1** : pistol, handgun **2** : spray gun
pistolera *nf* : holster
pistolero *nm* : gunman
pistón *nm, pl* **pistones** : piston
pita *nf* **1** : agave **2** : pita fiber **3** : twine
pitar *vi* **1** : to blow a whistle **2** : to whistle, to boo **3** : to beep, to honk, to toot — *vt* : to whistle at, to boo
pitido *nm* **1** : whistle, whistling **2** : beep, honk, toot
pito *nm* **1** SILBATO : whistle **2 no me importa un pito** *fam* : I don't give a damn
pitón *nm, pl* **pitones** **1** : python **2** : point of a bull's horn
pituitario, -ria *adj* : pituitary
pívot *nmf, pl* **pívots** : center (in basketball)
pivote *nm* : pivot
piyama *nmf* : pajamas *pl*
pizarra *nf* **1** : slate **2** : blackboard **3** : scoreboard
pizarrón *nm, pl* **-rrones** : blackboard, chalkboard
pizca *nf* **1** : pinch ⟨una pizca de canela : a pinch of cinnamon⟩ **2** : speck, trace ⟨ni pizca : not a bit⟩ **3** *Mex* : harvest
pizcar {72} *vt Mex* : to harvest
pizque, etc. → **pizcar**
pizza ['pitsa, 'pisa] *nf* : pizza
pizzería *nf* : pizzeria, pizza parlor
placa *nf* **1** : sheet, plate **2** : plaque, nameplate **3** : plate (in photography) **4** : badge, insignia **5 placa de matrícula** : license plate, tag **6 placa dental** : plaque, tartar
placebo *nm* : placebo
placenta *nf* : placenta, afterbirth
placentero, -ra *adj* AGRADABLE, GRATO : pleasant, agreeable
placer¹ {57} *vi* GUSTAR : to be pleasing ⟨hazlo como te plazca : do it however you please⟩
placer² *nm* **1** : pleasure, enjoyment **2 a ~** : as much as one wants
plácido, -da *adj* TRANQUILO : placid, calm
plaga *nf* **1** : plague, infestation, blight **2** CALAMIDAD : disaster, scourge
plagado, -da *adj* **~ de** : filled with, covered with
plagar {52} *vt* : to plague
plagiar *vt* **1** : to plagiarize **2** SECUESTRAR : to kidnap, to abduct
plagiario, -ria *n* **1** : plagiarist **2** SECUESTRADOR : kidnapper, abductor
plagio *nm* **1** : plagiarism **2** SECUESTRO : kidnapping, abduction
plague, etc. → **plagar**
plan *nm* **1** : plan, strategy, program ⟨plan de inversiones : investment plan⟩ ⟨plan de estudios : curriculum⟩ **2** PLANO : plan, diagram **3** : attitude, intent, purpose ⟨ponte en plan serio : be serious⟩ ⟨estamos en plan de divertirnos : we're looking to have some fun⟩
plana *nf* **1** : page ⟨noticias en primera plana : front-page news⟩ **2 plana mayor** : staff (in the military)
plancha *nf* **1** : iron, ironing **2** : grill, griddle ⟨a la plancha : grilled⟩ **3** : sheet, plate ⟨plancha para hornear : baking sheet⟩ **4** *fam* : blunder, blooper
planchada *nf* : ironing, pressing
planchado *nm* → **planchada**
planchar *v* : to iron
planchazo *nm fam* : goof, blunder
plancton *nm* : plankton
planeación *nf* → **planeamiento**
planeador *nm* : glider (aircraft)
planeamiento *nm* : plan, planning
planear *vt* : to plan — *vi* : to glide (in the air)
planeo *nm* : gliding, soaring
planeta *nm* : planet
planetario¹, -ria *adj* **1** : planetary **2** : global, worldwide
planetario² *nm* : planetarium
planicie *nf* : plain
planificación *nf* : planning ⟨planificación familiar : family planning⟩
planificar {72} *vt* : to plan
planilla *nf* **1** LISTA : list **2** NÓMINA : payroll **3** TABLA : chart, table **4** *Mex* : slate, ticket (of candidates) **5 planilla de cálculo** *Arg, Chile* : spreadsheet
plano¹, -na *adj* : flat, level, plane
plano² *nm* **1** PLAN : map, plan **2** : plane (surface) **3** NIVEL : level ⟨en un plano personal : on a personal level⟩ **4** : shot (in photography) **5 de ~** : flatly, outright, directly ⟨se negó de plano : he flatly refused⟩
planta *nf* **1** : plant ⟨planta de interior : houseplant⟩ **2** FÁBRICA : plant, factory **3** PISO : floor, story **4** : staff, employees *pl* **5** : sole (of the foot)

plantación *nf, pl* **-ciones** **1** : plantation **2** : planting

plantado, -da *adj* **1** : planted **2 dejar plantado** : to stand up (a date), to dump (a lover)

plantar *vt* **1** : to plant, to sow ⟨plantar de flores : to plant with flowers⟩ **2** : to put in, to place **3** *fam* : to plant, to land ⟨plantar un beso : to plant a kiss⟩ **4** *fam* : to leave, to jilt — **plantarse** *vr* **1** : to stand firm **2** *fam* : to arrive, to show up **3** *fam* : to balk

planteamiento *nm* **1** : approach, position ⟨el planteamiento feminista : the feminist viewpoint⟩ **2** : explanation, exposition **3** : proposal, suggestion, plan

plantear *vt* **1** : to set forth, to bring up, to suggest **2** : to establish, to set up **3** : to create, to pose (a problem) — **plantearse** *vr* **1** : to think about **2** : to arise

plantel *nm* **1** : educational institution **2** : staff, team

planteo → **planteamiento**

plantilla *nf* **1** : insole **2** : pattern, template, stencil **3** *Mex, Spain* : staff, roster of employees

plantío *nm* : field (planted with a crop)

plantón *nm, pl* **plantones** **1** : seedling **2** : long wait ⟨darle a alguien un plantón : to stand someone up⟩

plañidero¹, -ra *adj* : mournful

plañidero², -ra *nf* : hired mourner

plañir {38} *v* : to mourn, to lament

plasma *nm* : plasma

plasmar *vt* : to express, to give form to — **plasmarse** *vr*

plasta *nf* : soft mass, lump

plástica *nf* : modeling, sculpture

plasticidad *nf* : plasticity

plástico¹, -ca *adj* : plastic

plástico² *nm* : plastic

plastificar {72} *vt* : to laminate

plata *nf* **1** : silver **2** : money

plataforma *nf* **1** ESTRADO, TARIMA : platform, dais **2** : platform (in politics) **3** : springboard, stepping stone **4 plataforma continental** : continental shelf **5 plataforma de lanzamiento** : launchpad **6 plataforma petrolífera** : oil rig (at sea)

platal *nm* : large sum of money, fortune

platanal *nm* : banana plantation

platanero¹, -ra *adj* : banana, banana-producing

platanero², -ra *n* : banana grower

plátano *nm* **1** : banana **2** : plantain **3 plátano macho** *Mex* : plantain

platea *nf* : orchestra, pit (in a theater)

plateado, -da *adj* **1** : silver, silvery **2** : silver-plated

plática *nf* **1** : talk, lecture **2** : chat, conversation

platicar {72} *vi* : to talk, to chat — *vt Mex* : to tell, to say

platija *nf* : flatfish, flounder

platillo *nm* **1** : saucer ⟨platillo volador : flying saucer⟩ **2** : cymbal **3** *Mex* : dish ⟨platillos típicos : local dishes⟩

platino *nm* : platinum

plato *nm* **1** : plate, dish ⟨lavar los platos : to do the dishes⟩ **2** : serving, helping **3** : course (of a meal) **4** : dish ⟨plato típico : typical dish⟩ **5** : home plate (in baseball) **6 plato hondo** : soup bowl

plató *nm* : set (in the movies)

platónico, -ca *adj* : platonic

playa *nf* : beach, seashore

playera *nf* **1** : canvas sneaker **2** *CA, Mex* : T-shirt

plaza *nf* **1** : square, plaza **2** : marketplace **3** : room, space, seat (in a vehicle) **4** : post, position **5 plaza fuerte** : stronghold, fortified city **6 plaza de toros** : bullring

plazca, etc. → **placer**

plazo *nm* **1** : period, term ⟨un plazo de cinco días : a period of five days⟩ ⟨a largo plazo : long-term⟩ **2** ABONO : installment ⟨pagar a plazos : to pay in installments⟩

pleamar *nf* : high tide

plebe *nf* : common people, masses *pl*

plebeyo¹, -ya *adj* : plebeian

plebeyo², -ya *n* : plebeian, commoner

plegable *adj* : folding, collapsible

plegadizo → **plegable**

plegar {49} *vt* DOBLAR : to fold, to bend — **plegarse** *vr* : to give in, to yield

plegaria *nf* ORACIÓN : prayer

pleito *nm* **1** : lawsuit **2** : fight, argument, dispute

plenamente *adv* COMPLETAMENTE : fully, completely

plenario, -ria *adj* : plenary, full

plenilunio *nm* : full moon

plenipotenciario, -ria *n* : plenipotentiary

plenitud *nf* : fullness, abundance

pleno, -na *adj* COMPLETO ((*often used as an intensifier*)) : full, complete ⟨en pleno uso de sus facultades : in full command of his faculties⟩ ⟨en plena noche : in the middle of the night⟩ ⟨en pleno corazón de la ciudad : right in the heart of the city⟩

plétora *nf* : plethora

pleuresía *nf* : pleurisy

pliega, pliegue etc. → **plegar**

pliego *nm* **1** HOJA : sheet of paper **2** : sealed document

pliegue *nm* **1** DOBLEZ : crease, fold **2** : pleat

plisar *vt* : to pleat

plomada *nf* **1** : plumb line **2** : sinker

plomería *nf* FONTANERÍA : plumbing

plomero, -ra *n* FONTANERO : plumber

plomizo, -za *adj* : leaden

plomo *nm* **1** : lead **2** : plumb line **3** : fuse **4** *fam* : bore, drag **5 a ~** : plumb, straight

plugo, etc. → **placer**

pluma *nf* **1** : feather **2** : pen **3 pluma fuente** : fountain pen

plumaje *nm* : plumage
plumero *nm* : feather duster
plumilla *nf* : nib
plumón *nm, pl* **plumones** : down
plumoso, -sa *adj* : feathery, downy
plural *adj & nm* : plural
pluralidad *nf* : plurality
pluralizar {21} *vt* : to pluralize
pluriempleado, -da *adj* : holding more than one job
pluriempleo *nm* : moonlighting
plus *nm* : bonus
plusvalía *nf* : appreciation, capital gain
Plutón *nm* : Pluto
plutocracia *nf* : plutocracy
plutonio *nm* : plutonium
población *nf, pl* **-ciones 1** : population **2** : city, town, village
poblado¹, -da *adj* **1** : inhabited, populated **2** : full, thick ⟨cejas pobladas : bushy eyebrows⟩
poblado² *nm* : village, settlement
poblador, -dora *n* : settler
poblar {19} *vt* **1** : to populate, to inhabit **2** : to settle, to colonize **3 ~ de** : to stock with, to plant with — **poblarse** *vr* : to fill up, to become crowded
pobre¹ *adj* **1** : poor, impoverished **2** : unfortunate ⟨¡pobre de mí! : poor me!⟩ **3** : weak, deficient ⟨una dieta pobre : a poor diet⟩
pobre² *nmf* : poor person ⟨los pobres : the poor⟩ ⟨¡pobre! : poor thing!⟩
pobremente *adv* : poorly
pobreza *nf* : poverty
pocilga *nf* CHIQUERO : pigsty, pigpen
pocillo *nm* : small coffee cup, demitasse
poción *nf, pl* **pociones** : potion
poco¹ *adv* **1** : little, not much ⟨poco probable : not very likely⟩ ⟨come poco : he doesn't eat much⟩ **2** : a short time, a while ⟨tardaremos poco : we won't be very long⟩ **3 poco antes** : shortly before **4 poco después** : shortly after
poco², -ca *adj* **1** : little, not much, (a) few ⟨tengo poco dinero : I don't have much money⟩ ⟨en no pocas ocasiones : on more than a few occasions⟩ ⟨poca gente : few people⟩ **2 pocas veces** : rarely
poco³, -ca *pron* **1** : little, few ⟨le falta poco para terminar : he's almost finished⟩ ⟨uno de los pocos que quedan : one of the remaining few⟩ **2 un poco** : a little, a bit ⟨un poco de vino : a little wine⟩ ⟨un poco extraño : a bit strange⟩ **3 a ~** *Mex* (*used to express disbelief*) ⟨¿a poco no se te hizo difícil? : you mean you didn't find it difficult?⟩ **4 de a poco** : little by little **5 hace poco** : not long ago **6 poco a poco** : little by little **7 dentro de poco** : shortly, in a little while **8 por ~** : nearly, almost
podar *vt* : to prune, to trim
poder¹ {58} *v aux* **1** : to be able to, can ⟨no puede hablar : he can't speak⟩ **2** (*expressing possibility*) : might, may ⟨puede llover : it may rain at any moment⟩ ⟨¿cómo puede ser? : how can that be?⟩ **3** (*expressing permission*) : can, may ⟨¿puedo ir a la fiesta? : can I go to the party?⟩ ⟨¿se puede? : may I come in?⟩ — *vi* **1** : to beat, to defeat ⟨cree que le puede a cualquiera : he thinks he can beat anyone⟩ **2** : to be possible ⟨¿crees que vendrán? — puede (que sí) : do you think they'll come? — maybe⟩ **3 ~ con** : to cope with, to manage ⟨¡no puedo con estos niños! : I can't handle these children!⟩ **4 no poder más** : to have had enough ⟨no puede más : she can't take anymore⟩ **5 no poder menos que** : to not be able to help ⟨no pudo menos que asombrarse : she couldn't help but be amazed⟩
poder² *nm* **1** : control, power ⟨poder adquisitivo : purchasing power⟩ **2** : authority ⟨el poder legislativo : the legislature⟩ **3** : possession ⟨está en mi poder : it's in my hands⟩ **4** : strength, force ⟨poder militar : military might⟩
poderío *nm* **1** : power **2** : wealth, influence
poderoso, -sa *adj* **1** : powerful **2** : wealthy, influential **3** : effective
podiatría *nf* : podiatry
podio *nm* : podium
pódium → **podio**
podología *nf* : podiatry, chiropody
podólogo, -ga *n* : podiatrist, chiropodist
podrá, etc. → **poder**
podredumbre *nf* **1** : decay, rottenness **2** : corruption
podrido, -da *adj* **1** : rotten, decayed **2** : corrupt
podrir → **pudrir**
poema *nm* : poem
poesía *nf* **1** : poetry **2** POEMA : poem
poeta *nmf* : poet
poético, -ca *adj* : poetic, poetical
pogrom *nm* : pogrom
póker *or* **poker** *nm* : poker (card game)
polaco¹, -ca *adj* : Polish
polaco², -ca *n* : Pole, Polish person
polaco³ *nm* : Polish (language)
polar *adj* : polar
polarizar {21} *vt* : to polarize — **polarizarse** *vr* — **polarización** *nf*
polea *nf* : pulley
polémica *nf* CONTROVERSIA : controversy, polemics
polémico, -ca *adj* CONTROVERTIDO : controversial, polemical
polen *nm, pl* **pólenes** : pollen
policía¹ *nf* : police
policía² *nmf* : police officer, policeman *m,* policewoman *f*
policíaco, -ca *or* **policiaco, -ca** *adj* : police ⟨novela policíaca : detective story⟩
policial *adj* : police
poliéster *nm* : polyester
poligamia *nf* : polygamy
polígamo¹, -ma *adj* : polygamous
polígamo², -ma *n* : polygamist
polígono *nm* : polygon — **poligonal** *adj*

poliinsaturado, -da *adj* : polyunsaturated
polilla *nf* : moth
polimerizar {21} *vt* : to polymerize
polímero *nm* : polymer
polinesio, -sia *adj & n* : Polynesian
polinizar {21} *vt* : to pollinate — **polinización** *nf*
polio *nf* : polio
poliomielitis *nf* : poliomyelitis, polio
polisón *nm, pl* **-sones** : bustle (on clothing)
politécnico, -ca *adj* : polytechnic
politeísmo *nm* : polytheism — **politeísta** *adj & nmf*
política *nf* **1** : politics **2** : policy
políticamente *adv* : politically
político[1], **-ca** *adj* **1** : political **2** : tactful, politic **3** : by marriage ⟨padre político : father-in-law⟩
político[2], **-ca** *n* : politician
póliza *nf* : policy ⟨póliza de seguros : insurance policy⟩
polizón *nm, pl* **-zones** : stowaway ⟨viajar de polizón : to stow away⟩
polka *nf* : polka
polla *nf* APUESTA : bet
pollera *nf* **1** : chicken coop **2** : skirt
pollero, -ra *n* **1** : poulterer **2** : poultry farm **3** *Mex fam* COYOTE : smuggler of illegal immigrants
pollito, -ta *n* : chick, young bird, fledgling
pollo, -lla *n* **1** : chicken **2** POLLITO : chick **3** JOVEN : young man *m*, young lady *f*
polluelo *nm* → **pollito**
polo *nm* **1** : pole ⟨el Polo Norte : the North Pole⟩ ⟨polo negativo : negative pole⟩ **2** : polo (sport) **3** : polo shirt **4** : focal point, center **5 polo opuesto** : exact opposite
polución *nf, pl* **-ciones** CONTAMINACIÓN : pollution
polvareda *nf* **1** : cloud of dust **2** : uproar, fuss
polvera *nf* : compact (for face powder)
polvo *nm* **1** : dust **2** : powder **3 polvos** *nmpl* : face powder **4 polvos de hornear** : baking powder **5 hacer polvo** *fam* : to crush, to shatter ⟨vas a hacer polvo el reloj : you're going to destroy your watch⟩
pólvora *nf* **1** : gunpowder **2** : fireworks *pl*
polvoriento, -ta *adj* : dusty, powdery
polvorín *nm, pl* **-rines** : magazine, storehouse (for explosives)
pomada *nf* : ointment, cream
pomelo *nm* : grapefruit
pómez *nf or* **piedra pómez** : pumice
pomo *nm* **1** : pommel (on a sword) **2** : knob, handle **3** : perfume bottle
pompa *nf* **1** : bubble **2** : pomp, splendor **3 pompas fúnebres** : funeral
pompón *nm, pl* **pompones** BORLA : pom-pom
pomposidad *nf* **1** : pomp, splendor **2** : pomposity, ostentation
pomposo, -sa *adj* : pompous — **pomposamente** *adv*
pómulo *nm* : cheekbone
pon → **poner**
ponchadura *nf Mex* : puncture, flat (tire)
ponchar *vt* **1** : to strike out (in baseball) **2** *Mex* : to puncture — **poncharse** *vr* **1** *Col, Ven* : to strike out (in baseball) **2** *Mex* : to blow out (of a tire)
ponche *nm* **1** : punch (drink) **2 ponche de huevo** : eggnog
poncho *nm* : poncho
ponderación *nf, pl* **-ciones** **1** : consideration, deliberation **2** : high praise
ponderar *vt* **1** : to weigh, to consider **2** : to speak highly of
pondrá, etc. → **poner**
ponencia *nf* **1** DISCURSO : paper, presentation, address **2** INFORME : report
ponente *nmf* : speaker, presenter
poner {60} *vt* **1** COLOCAR : to put, to place ⟨pon el libro en la mesa : put the book on the table⟩ **2** AGREGAR, AÑADIR : to put in, to add **3** : to put on (clothes) **4** CONTRIBUIR : to contribute **5** ESCRIBIR : to put in writing ⟨no le puso su nombre : he didn't put his name on it⟩ **6** IMPONER : to set, to impose **7** EXPONER : to put, to expose ⟨lo puso en peligro : she put him in danger⟩ **8** : to prepare, to arrange ⟨poner la mesa : to set the table⟩ **9** : to name ⟨le pusimos Ana : we called her Ana⟩ **10** ESTABLECER : to set up, to establish ⟨puso un restaurante : he opened up a restaurant⟩ **11** INSTALAR : to install, to put in **12** (*with an adjective or adverb*) : to make ⟨siempre lo pones de mal humor : you always put him in a bad mood⟩ **13** : to turn on, to switch on **14** SUPONER : to suppose ⟨pongamos que no viene : supposing he doesn't come⟩ **15** : to lay (eggs) **16 ~ a** : to start (someone doing something) ⟨lo puse a trabajar : I put him to work⟩ **17 ~ de** : to place as ⟨la pusieron de directora : they made her director⟩ **18 ~ en** : to put in (a state or condition) ⟨poner en duda : to call into question⟩ — *vi* **1** : to contribute **2** : to lay eggs — **ponerse** *vr* **1** : to move (into a position) ⟨ponerse de pie : to stand up⟩ **2** : to put on, to wear **3** : to become, to turn ⟨se puso colorado : he turned red⟩ **4** : to set (of the sun or moon)
poni *or* **poney** *nm* : pony
ponga, etc. → **poner**
poniente *nm* **1** OCCIDENTE : west **2** : west wind
ponqué *nm Col, Ven* : cake
pontifical *adj* : pontifical
pontificar {72} *vi* : to pontificate
pontífice *nm* : pontiff, pope
pontón *nm, pl* **pontones** : pontoon
ponzoña *nf* VENENO : poison — **ponzoñoso, -sa** *adj*

popa *nf* **1** : stern **2 a ~** : astern, abaft, aft
popelín *nm, pl* **-lines** : poplin
popelina *nf* : poplin
popote *nm Mex* : (drinking) straw
populachero, -ra *adj* : common, popular, vulgar
populacho *nm* : rabble, masses *pl*
popular *adj* **1** : popular **2** : traditional **3** : colloquial
popularidad *nf* : popularity
popularizar {21} *vt* : to popularize — **popularizarse** *vr*
populista *adj & nmf* : populist — **populismo** *nm*
populoso, -sa *adj* : populous
popurrí *nm* : potpourri
por *prep* **1** : for, during ‹se quedaron allí por la semana : they stayed there during the week› ‹por el momento : for now, at the moment› **2** : around, during ‹por noviembre empieza a nevar : around November it starts to snow› ‹por la mañana : in the morning› **3** : around (a place) ‹debe estar por allí : it must be over there› ‹por todas partes : everywhere› **4** : by, through, along ‹por la puerta : through the door› ‹pasé por tu casa : I stopped by your house› ‹por la costa : along the coast› **5** : for, for the sake of ‹lo hizo por su madre : he did it for his mother› ‹¡por Dios! : for heaven's sake!› **6** : because of, on account of ‹llegué tarde por el tráfico : I arrived late because of the traffic› ‹dejar por imposible : to give up as impossible› **7** : per ‹60 millas por hora : 60 miles per hour› ‹por docena : by the dozen› **8** : for, in exchange for, instead of ‹su hermana habló por él : his sister spoke on his behalf› **9** : by means of ‹hablar por teléfono : to talk on the phone› ‹por escrito : in writing› **10** : as for ‹por mí : as far as I'm concerned› **11** : times ‹tres por dos son seis : three times two is six› **12** SEGÚN : from, according to ‹por lo que dices : judging from what you're telling me› **13** : as, for ‹por ejemplo : for example› **14** : by ‹hecho por mi abuela : made by my grandmother› ‹por correo : by mail› **15** : for, in order to ‹lucha por ganar su respeto : he struggles to win her respect› **16 estar por** : to be about to **17 por ciento** : percent **18 por favor** : please **19 por lo tanto** : therefore, consequently **20 ¿por qué?** : why? **21 por que** → **porque 22 por . . . que** : no matter how ‹por mucho que intente : no matter how hard I try› **23 por si** *or* **por si acaso** : just in case
porcelana *nf* : china, porcelain
porcentaje *nm* : percentage
porche *nm* : porch
porción *nf, pl* **porciones 1** : portion **2** PARTE : part, share **3** RACIÓN : serving, helping
pordiosear *vi* MENDIGAR : beg
pordiosero, -ra *n* MENDIGO : beggar
porfiado, -da *adj* OBSTINADO, TERCO : obstinate, stubborn — **porfiadamente** *adv*
porfiar {85} *vi* : to insist, to persist
pormenor *nm* DETALLE : detail
pormenorizar {21} *vi* : to go into detail — *vt* : to tell in detail
pornografía *nf* : pornography
pornográfico, -ca *adj* : pornographic
poro *nm* : pore
poroso, -sa *adj* : porous — **porosidad** *nf*
poroto *nm Arg, Chile, Uru* : bean
porque *conj* **1** : because **2** *or* **por que** : in order that
porqué *nm* : reason, cause
porquería *nf* **1** SUCIEDAD : dirt, filth **2** : nastiness, vulgarity **3** : worthless thing, trifle **4** : junk food
porra *nf* **1** : nightstick, club **2** *Mex* : cheer, yell ‹los aficionados le echaban porras : the fans cheered him on›
porrazo *nm* **1** : blow, whack **2 de golpe y porrazo** : suddenly
porrista *nmf* **1** : cheerleader **2** : fan, supporter
portaaviones *nms & pl* : aircraft carrier
portada *nf* **1** : title page **2** : cover **3** : facade, front
portador, -dora *n* : carrier, bearer
portafolio *or* **portafolios** *nm, pl* **-lios 1** MALETÍN : briefcase **2** : portfolio (of investments)
portal *nm* **1** : portal, doorway **2** VESTÍBULO : vestibule, hall
portar *vt* **1** : to carry, to bear **2** : to wear — **portarse** *vr* CONDUCIRSE : to behave ‹pórtate bien : behave yourself›
portátil *adj* : portable
portaviandas *nms & pl* : lunch box
portaviones *nm* → **portaaviones**
portavoz *nmf, pl* **-voces** : spokesperson, spokesman *m*, spokeswoman *f*
portazo *nm* : slam (of a door)
porte *nm* **1** ASPECTO : bearing, demeanor **2** TRANSPORTE : transport, carrying ‹porte pagado : postage paid›
portento *nm* MARAVILLA : marvel, wonder
portentoso, -sa *adj* MARAVILLOSO : marvelous, wonderful
porteño, -ña *adj* : of or from Buenos Aires
portería *nf* **1** ARCO : goal, goalposts *pl* **2** : superintendent's office
portero, -ra *n* **1** ARQUERO : goalkeeper, goalie **2** : doorman *m* **3** : janitor, superintendent
pórtico *nm* : portico
portilla *nf* : porthole
portón *nm, pl* **portones 1** : main door **2** : gate
portugués¹, -guesa *adj & n, mpl* **-gueses** : Portuguese
portugués² *nm* : Portuguese (language)

porvenir *nm* FUTURO : future
pos *adv* **en pos de** : in pursuit of
posada *nf* **1** : inn **2** *Mex* : Advent celebration
posadero, -ra *n* : innkeeper
posar *vi* : to pose — *vt* : to place, to lay — **posarse** *vr* **1** : to land, to light, to perch **2** : to settle, to rest
posavasos *nms & pl* : coaster (for drinks)
posdata → **postdata**
pose *nf* : pose
poseedor, -dora *n* : possessor, holder
poseer {20} *vt* : to possess, to hold, to have
poseído, -da *adj* : possessed
posesión *nf, pl* **-siones** : possession
posesionarse *vr* **~ de** : to take possession of, to take over
posesivo[1]**, -va** *adj* : possessive
posesivo[2] *nm* : possessive case
posguerra *nf* : postwar period
posibilidad *nf* **1** : possibility **2 posibilidades** *nfpl* : means, income
posibilitar *vt* : to make possible, to permit
posible *adj* : possible — **posiblemente** *adv*
posición *nf, pl* **-ciones** **1** : position, place **2** : status, standing **3** : attitude, stance
posicionar *vt* **1** : to position, to place **2** : to establish — **posicionarse** *vr*
positivo[1]**, -va** *adj* : positive
positivo[2] *nm* : print (in photography)
poso *nm* **1** : sediment, dregs *pl* **2** : grounds *pl* (of coffee)
posoperatorio, -ria *adj* : postoperative
posponer {60} *vt* **1** : to postpone **2** : to put behind, to subordinate
pospuso, etc. → **posponer**
posta *nf* : relay race
postal[1] *adj* : postal
postal[2] *nf* : postcard
postdata *nf* : postscript
poste *nm* : post, pole ⟨poste de teléfonos : telephone pole⟩
póster *or* **poster** *nm, pl* **pósters** *or* **posters** : poster, placard
postergación *nf, pl* **-ciones** : postponement, deferring
postergar {52} *vt* **1** : to delay, to postpone **2** : to pass over (an employee)
posteridad *nf* : posterity
posterior *adj* **1** ULTERIOR : later, subsequent **2** TRASERO : back, rear
postgrado *nm* : graduate course
postgraduado, -da *n* : graduate student, postgraduate
postigo *nm* **1** CONTRAVENTANA : shutter **2** : small door, wicket gate
postilla *nf* : scab
postizo, -za *adj* : artificial, false ⟨dentadura postiza : dentures⟩
postnatal *adj* : postnatal
postor, -tora *n* : bidder ⟨mejor postor : highest bidder⟩
postración *nf, pl* **-ciones** **1** : prostration **2** ABATIMIENTO : depression
postrado, -da *adj* **1** : prostrate **2 postrado en cama** : bedridden
potranco, -ca *n* → **potro**[1]
postrar *vt* DEBILITAR : to debilitate, to weaken — **postrarse** *vr* : to prostrate oneself
postre *nm* : dessert
postrero, -ra *adj* (**postrer** *before masculine singular nouns*) ÚLTIMO : last
postulación *nf, pl* **-ciones** **1** : collection **2** : nomination (of a candidate)
postulado *nm* : postulate, assumption
postulante, -ta *n* **1** : postulant **2** : candidate, applicant
postular *vt* **1** : to postulate **2** : to nominate **3** : to propose — **postularse** *vr* : to run, to be a candidate
póstumo, -ma *adj* : posthumous — **póstumamente** *adv*
postura *nf* **1** : posture, position (of the body) **2** ACTITUD, POSICIÓN : position, stance
potable *adj* : drinkable, potable
potaje *nm* : thick vegetable soup, pottage
potasa *nf* : potash
potasio *nm* : potassium
pote *nm* **1** OLLA : pot **2** : jar, container
potencia *nf* **1** : power ⟨potencias extranjeras : foreign powers⟩ ⟨elevado a la tercera potencia : raised to the third power⟩ **2** : capacity, potency
potencial *adj & nm* : potential
potenciar *vt* : to promote, to foster
potenciómetro *nm* : dimmer, dimmer switch
potentado, -da *n* **1** SOBERANO : potentate, sovereign **2** MAGNATE : tycoon, magnate
potente *adj* **1** : powerful, strong **2** : potent, virile
potestad *nf* **1** AUTORIDAD : authority, jurisdiction **2 patria potestad** : custody, guardianship
potrero *nm* **1** : field, pasture **2** : cattle ranch
potro[1]**, -tra** *n* : colt *m,* filly *f*
potro[2] *nm* **1** : rack (for torture) **2** : horse (in gymnastics)
pozo *nm* **1** : well ⟨pozo de petróleo : oil well⟩ **2** : deep pool (in a river) **3** : mine shaft **4** *Arg, Par, Uru* : pothole **5 pozo séptico** : cesspool
pozole *nm Mex* : spicy stew made with pork and hominy
práctica *nf* **1** : practice, experience **2** EJERCICIO : exercising ⟨la práctica de la medicina : the practice of medicine⟩ **3** APLICACIÓN : application, practice ⟨poner en práctica : to put into practice⟩ **4 prácticas** *nfpl* : training
practicable *adj* : practicable, feasible
prácticamente *adv* : practically
practicante[1] *adj* : practicing ⟨católicos practicantes : practicing Catholics⟩

practicante[2] *nmf* : practicer, practitioner
practicar {72} *vt* **1** : to practice **2** : to perform, to carry out **3** : to exercise (a profession) — *vi* : to practice
práctico, -ca *adj* : practical, useful
pradera *nf* : grassland, prairie
prado *nm* **1** CAMPO : field, meadow **2** : park
pragmático, -ca *adj* : pragmatic — **pragmáticamente** *adv*
pragmatismo *nm* : pragmatism
preámbulo *nm* **1** INTRODUCCIÓN : preamble, introduction **2** RODEO : evasion ⟨gastar preámbulos : to beat around the bush⟩
prebélico, -ca *adj* : antebellum
prebenda *nf* : privilege, perquisite
precalentar {55} *vt* : to preheat
precariedad *nf* : precariousness
precario, -ria *adj* : precarious — **precariamente** *adv*
precaución *nf, pl* **-ciones** **1** : precaution ⟨medidas de precaución : precautionary measures⟩ **2** PRUDENCIA : caution, care ⟨con precaución : cautiously⟩
precautorio, -ria *adj* : precautionary
precaver *vt* PREVENIR : to prevent, to guard against — **precaverse** *vr* PREVENIRSE : to take precautions, to be on guard
precavido, -da *adj* CAUTELOSO : cautious, prudent
precedencia *nf* : precedence, priority
precedente[1] *adj* : preceding, previous
precedente[2] *nm* : precedent
preceder *v* : to precede
precepto *nm* : rule, precept
preciado, -da *adj* : esteemed, prized, valuable
preciarse *vr* **1** JACTARSE : to boast, to brag **2** **~ de** : to pride oneself on
precinto *nm* : seal
precio *nm* **1** : price **2** : cost, sacrifice ⟨a cualquier precio : whatever the cost⟩
preciosidad *nf* : beautiful thing ⟨este vestido es una preciosidad : this dress is lovely⟩
precioso, -sa *adj* **1** HERMOSO : beautiful, exquisite **2** VALIOSO : precious, valuable
precipicio *nm* **1** : precipice **2** RUINA : ruin
precipitación *nf, pl* **-ciones** **1** PRISA : haste, hurry, rush **2** : precipitation, rain, snow
precipitado, -da *adj* **1** : hasty, sudden **2** : rash — **precipitadamente** *adv*
precipitar *vt* **1** APRESURAR : to hasten, to speed up **2** ARROJAR : to hurl, to throw — **precipitarse** *vr* **1** APRESURARSE : to rush **2** : to act rashly **3** ARROJARSE : to throw oneself
precisamente *adv* JUSTAMENTE : precisely, exactly
precisar *vt* **1** : to specify, to determine exactly **2** NECESITAR : to need, to require — *vi* : to be necessary
precisión *nf, pl* **-siones** **1** EXACTITUD : precision, accuracy **2** CLARIDAD : clarity (of style, etc.) **3** NECESIDAD : necessity ⟨tener precisión de : to have need of⟩
preciso, -sa *adj* **1** EXACTO : precise **2** : very, exact ⟨en ese preciso instante : at that very instant⟩ **3** NECESARIO : necessary
precocidad *nf* : precocity
precocinar *vt* : to precook
preconcebir {54} *vt* : to preconceive
precondición *nf, pl* **-ciones** : precondition
preconizar {21} *vt* **1** : to recommend, to advocate **2** : to extol
precoz *adj, pl* **precoces** **1** : precocious **2** : early, premature — **precozmente** *adv*
precursor, -sora *n* : forerunner, precursor
predecesor, -sora *n* ANTECESOR : predecessor
predecir {11} *vt* : to foretell, to predict
predestinado, -da *adj* : predestined, fated
predestinar *vt* : to predestine — **predestinación** *nf*
predeterminar *vt* : to predetermine
prédica *nf* SERMÓN : sermon
predicado *nm* : predicate
predicador, -dora *n* : preacher
predicar {72} *v* : to preach
predicción *nf, pl* **-ciones** **1** : prediction **2** PRONÓSTICO : forecast ⟨predicción del tiempo : weather forecast⟩
prediga, predijo etc. → **predecir**
predilección *nf, pl* **-ciones** : predilection, preference
predilecto, -ta *adj* : favorite
predio *nm* : property, piece of land
predisponer {60} *vt* **1** : to predispose, to incline **2** : to prejudice, to bias
predisposición *nf, pl* **-ciones** **1** : predisposition, tendency **2** : prejudice, bias
predominante *adj* : predominant — **predominantemente** *adv*
predominar *vi* PREVALECER : to predominate, to prevail
predominio *nm* : predominance, prevalence
preeminente *adj* : preeminent — **preeminencia** *nf*
preescolar *adj & nm* : preschool
preestreno *nm* : preview
prefabricado, -da *adj* : prefabricated
prefacio *nm* : preface
prefecto *nm* : prefect
preferencia *nf* **1** : preference **2** PRIORIDAD : priority **3 de ~** : preferably
preferencial *adj* : preferential
preferente *adj* : preferential, special ⟨trato preferente : special treatment⟩
preferentemente *adv* : preferably

preferible *adj* : preferable
preferido, -da *adj & n* : favorite
preferir {76} *vt* : to prefer
prefigurar *vt* : foreshadow, prefigure
prefijo *nm* : prefix
pregonar *vt* **1** : to proclaim, to announce **2** : to hawk (merchandise) **3** : to extol **4** : to reveal, to disclose
pregunta *nf* **1** : question **2 hacer una pregunta** : to ask a question
preguntar *vt* : to ask, to question — *vi* : to ask, to inquire — **preguntarse** *vr* : to wonder
preguntón, -tona *adj, mpl* **-tones** : inquisitive
prehistórico, -ca *adj* : prehistoric
prejuiciado, -da *adj* : prejudiced
prejuicio *nm* : prejudice
prejuzgar {52} *vt* : to prejudge
prelado *nm* : prelate
preliminar *adj & nm* : preliminary
preludio *nm* : prelude
prematrimonial *adj* : premarital
prematuro, -ra *adj* : premature
premeditación *nf, pl* **-ciones** : premeditation
premeditar *vt* : to premeditate, to plan
premenstrual *adj* : premenstrual
premiado, -da *adj* : winning, prizewinning
premiar *vt* **1** : to award a prize to **2** : to reward
premier *nmf* : premier, prime minister
premio *nm* **1** : prize ⟨premio gordo : grand prize, jackpot⟩ **2** : reward **3** : premium
premisa *nf* : premise, basis
premolar *nm* : bicuspid (tooth)
premonición *nf, pl* **-ciones** : premonition
premura *nf* : haste, urgency
prenatal *adj* : prenatal
prenda *nf* **1** : piece of clothing **2** : security, pledge
prendar *vt* **1** : to charm, to captivate **2** : to pawn, to pledge — **prendarse** *vr* **~ de** : to fall in love with
prendedor *nm* : brooch, pin
prender *vt* **1** SUJETAR : to pin, to fasten **2** APRESAR : to catch, to apprehend **3** : to light (a cigarette, a match) **4** : to turn on ⟨prende la luz : turn on the light⟩ **5 prender fuego a** : to set fire to — *vi* **1** : to take root **2** : to catch fire **3** : to catch on
prensa *nf* **1** : printing press **2** : press ⟨conferencia de prensa : press conference⟩
prensar *vt* : to press
prensil *adj* : prehensile
preñado, -da *adj* **1** : pregnant **2 ~ de** : filled with
preñar *vt* EMBARAZAR : to make pregnant
preñez *nf, pl* **preñeces** : pregnancy
preocupación *nf, pl* **-ciones** INQUIETUD : worry, concern
preocupante *adj* : worrisome
preocupar *vt* INQUIETAR : to worry, to concern — **preocuparse** *vr* APURARSE : to worry, to be concerned
preparación *nf, pl* **-ciones** **1** : preparation, readiness **2** : education, training **3** : (medicinal) preparation
preparado¹, -da *adj* **1** : ready, prepared **2** : trained
preparado² *nm* : preparation, mixture
preparar *vt* **1** : to prepare, to make ready **2** : to teach, to train, to coach — **prepararse** *vr*
preparativos *nmpl* : preparations
preparatoria *nf Mex* : high school
preparatorio, -ria *adj* : preparatory
preponderante *adj* : preponderant, predominant — **preponderancia** *nf* — **preponderantemente** *adv*
preposición *nf, pl* **-ciones** : preposition — **preposicional** *adj*
prepotente *adj* : arrogant, domineering, overbearing — **prepotencia** *nf*
prerrogativa *nf* : prerogative, privilege
presa *nf* **1** : capture, seizure ⟨hacer presa de : to seize⟩ **2** : catch, prey ⟨presa de : prey to, seized with⟩ **3** : claw, fang **4** DIQUE : dam **5** : morsel, piece (of food)
presagiar *vt* : to presage, to portend
presagio *nm* : omen, portent
presbiterio *nm* : presbytery, sanctuary (of a church)
presbítero *nm* : presbyter
presciencia *nf* : prescience
prescindible *adj* : expendable, dispensable
prescindir *vi* **1 ~ de** : to do without, to dispense with **2** DESATENDER : to ignore, to disregard **3** OMITIR : to omit, to skip
prescribir {33} *vt* : to prescribe
prescripción *nf, pl* **-ciones** : prescription
prescrito *pp* → **prescribir**
presencia *nf* **1** : presence **2** ASPECTO : appearance
presenciar *vt* : to be present at, to witness
presentable *adj* : presentable
presentación *nf, pl* **-ciones** **1** : presentation **2** : introduction **3** : appearance
presentador, -dora *n* : newscaster, anchorman *m*, anchorwoman *f*
presentar *vt* **1** : to present, to show **2** : to offer, to give **3** : to submit (a document), to launch (a product) **4** : to introduce (a person) — **presentarse** *vr* **1** : to show up, to appear **2** : to arise, to come up **3** : to introduce oneself
presente¹ *adj* **1** : present, in attendance **2** : present, current **3 tener presente** : to keep in mind
presente² *nm* **1** : present (time, tense) **2** : one present ⟨entre los presentes se encontraban . . . : those present included . . .⟩
presentimiento *nm* : premonition, hunch, feeling

presentir {76} *vt* : to sense, to intuit <presentía lo que iba a pasar : he sensed what was going to happen>
preservación *nf, pl* **-ciones** : preservation
preservar *vt* **1** : to preserve **2** : to protect
preservativo *nm* CONDÓN : condom
presidencia *nf* **1** : presidency **2** : chairmanship
presidencial *adj* : presidential
presidente, -ta *n* **1** : president **2** : chair, chairperson **3** : presiding judge
presidiario, -ria *n* : convict, prisoner
presidio *nm* : prison, penitentiary
presidir *vt* **1** MODERAR : to preside over, to chair **2** : to dominate, to rule over
presilla *nf* : eye, loop, fastener
presión *nf, pl* **presiones** **1** : pressure **2 presión arterial** : blood pressure
presionar *vt* **1** : to pressure **2** : to press, to push — *vi* : to put on the pressure
preso[1], **-sa** *adj* : imprisoned
preso[2], **-sa** *n* : prisoner
prestado, -da *adj* **1** : borrowed, on loan **2 pedir prestado** : to borrow
prestamista *nmf* : moneylender, pawnbroker
préstamo *nm* : loan
prestar *vt* **1** : to lend, to loan **2** : to render (a service), to give (aid) **3 prestar atención** : to pay attention **4 prestar juramento** : to take an oath — **prestarse** *vr* : to lend oneself <se presta a confusiones : it lends itself to confusion>
prestatario, -ria *n* : borrower
presteza *nf* : promptness, speed
prestidigitación *nf, pl* **-ciones** : sleight of hand, prestidigitation
prestidigitador, -dora *n* : conjurer, magician
prestigio *nm* : prestige — **prestigioso, -sa** *adj*
presto[1] *adv* : promptly, at once
presto[2], **-ta** *adj* **1** : quick, prompt **2** DISPUESTO, PREPARADO : ready
presumido, -da *adj* VANIDOSO : conceited, vain
presumir *vt* SUPONER : to presume, to suppose — *vi* **1** ALARDEAR : to boast, to show off **2 ~ de** : to consider oneself <presume de inteligente : he thinks he's intelligent>
presunción *nf, pl* **-ciones** **1** SUPOSICIÓN : presumption, supposition **2** VANIDAD : conceit, vanity
presunto, -ta *adj* : presumed, supposed, alleged — **presuntamente** *adv*
presuntuoso, -sa *adj* : conceited
presuponer {60} *vt* : to presuppose
presupuestal *adj* : budget, budgetary
presupuestar *vi* : to budget — *vt* : to budget for
presupuestario, -ria *adj* : budget, budgetary
presupuesto *nm* **1** : budget, estimate **2** : assumption, supposition
presurizar {21} *vt* : to pressurize
presuroso, -sa *adj* : hasty, quick
pretencioso, -sa *adj* : pretentious
pretender *vt* **1** INTENTAR : to attempt, to try <pretendo estudiar : I'm trying to study> **2** AFIRMAR : to claim <pretende ser pobre : he claims he's poor> **3** : to seek, to aspire to <¿qué pretendes tú? : what are you after?> **4** CORTEJAR : to court **5 pretender que** : to expect <¿pretendes que lo crea? : do you expect me to believe you?>
pretendiente[1] *nmf* **1** : candidate, applicant **2** : pretender, claimant (to a throne, etc.)
pretendiente[2] *nm* : suitor
pretensión *nf, pl* **-siones** **1** : intention, hope, plan **2** : pretension <sin pretensiones : unpretentious>
pretexto *nm* EXCUSA : pretext, excuse
pretil *nm* : parapet, railing
prevalecer {53} *vi* : to prevail, to triumph
prevaleciente *adj* : prevailing, prevalent
prevalerse {84} *vr* **~ de** : to avail oneself of, to take advantage of
prevención *nf, pl* **-ciones** **1** : prevention **2** : preparation, readiness **3** : precautionary measure **4** : prejudice, bias
prevenido, -da *adj* **1** PREPARADO : prepared, ready **2** ADVERTIDO : forewarned **3** CAUTELOSO : cautious
prevenir {87} *vt* **1** : to prevent **2** : to warn — **prevenirse** *vr* **~ contra** *or* **~ de** : to take precautions against
preventivo, -va *adj* : preventive, precautionary
prever {88} *vt* ANTICIPAR : to foresee, to anticipate
previo, -via *adj* **1** : previous, prior **2** : after, upon <previo pago : after paying, upon payment>
previsible *adj* : foreseeable
previsión *nf, pl* **-siones** **1** : foresight **2** : prediction, forecast **3** : precaution
previsor, -sora *adj* : farsighted, prudent
prieto, -ta *adj* **1** : blackish, dark **2** : dark-skinned, swarthy **3** : tight, compressed
prima *nf* **1** : premium **2** : bonus **3** → **primo**
primacía *nf* **1** : precedence, priority **2** : superiority, supremacy
primado *nm* : primate (bishop)
primario, -ria *adj* : primary
primate *nm* : primate
primavera *nf* **1** : spring (season) **2** PRÍMULA : primrose
primaveral *adj* : spring, springlike
primero[1] *adv* **1** : first **2** : rather, sooner
primero[2], **-ra** *adj* (**primer** *before masculine singular nouns*) **1** : first **2** : top, leading **3** : fundamental, basic **4 de primera** : first-rate
primero[3], **-ra** *n* : first
primicia *nf* **1** : first fruits **2** : scoop, exclusive

primigenio, -nia *adj* : original, primary
primitivo, -va *adj* **1** : primitive **2** ORIGINAL : original
primo, -ma *n* : cousin
primogénito, -ta *adj & n* : firstborn
primor *nm* **1** : skill, care **2** : beauty, elegance
primordial *adj* **1** : primordial **2** : basic, fundamental
primoroso, -sa *adj* **1** : exquisite, fine, delicate **2** : skillful
prímula *nf* : primrose
princesa *nf* : princess
principado *nm* : principality
principal¹ *adj* **1** : main, principal **2** : foremost, leading
principal² *nm* : capital, principal
príncipe *nm* : prince
principesco, -ca *adj* : princely
principiante¹ *adj* : beginning
principiante² *nmf* : beginner, novice
principiar *vt* EMPEZAR : to begin
principio *nm* **1** COMIENZO : beginning **2** : principle **3 al principio** : at first **4 a principios de** : at the beginning of ⟨a principios de agosto : at the beginning of August⟩ **5 en ~** : in principle
pringar {52} *vt* **1** : to dip (in grease) **2** : to soil, to spatter (with grease) — **pringarse** *vr*
pringoso, -sa *adj* : greasy
pringue¹, etc. → **pringar**
pringue² *nm* : grease, drippings *pl*
prior, priora *n* : prior *m,* prioress *f*
priorato *nm* : priory
prioridad *nf* : priority, precedence
prisa *nf* **1** : hurry, rush **2 a ~** *or* **de ~** : quickly, fast **3 a toda prisa** : as fast as possible **4 darse prisa** : to hurry **5 tener prisa** : to be in a hurry
prisión *nf, pl* **prisiones 1** CÁRCEL : prison, jail **2** ENCARCELAMIENTO : imprisonment
prisionero, -ra *n* : prisoner
prisma *nm* : prism
prismáticos *nmpl* : binoculars
prístino, -na *adj* : pristine
privacidad *nf* : privacy
privación *nf, pl* **-ciones 1** : deprivation **2** : privation, want
privado, -da *adj* : private — **privadamente** *adv*
privar *vt* **1** DESPOJAR : to deprive **2** : to stun, to knock out — **privarse** *vr* : to deprive oneself
privativo, -va *adj* : exclusive, particular
privilegiado, -da *adj* : privileged
privilegiar *vt* : to grant a privilege to, to favor
privilegio *nm* : privilege
pro¹ *nm* **1** : pro, advantage ⟨los pros y contras : the pros and cons⟩ **2 en pro de** : for, in favor of
pro² *prep* : for, in favor of ⟨grupos pro derechos humanos : groups supporting human rights⟩
proa *nf* : bow, prow
probabilidad *nf* : probability
probable *adj* : probable, likely
probablemente *adv* : probably
probar {19} *vt* **1** : to demonstrate, to prove **2** : to test, to try out **3** : to try on (clothing) **4** : to taste, to sample — *vi* : to try — **probarse** *vr* : to try on (clothing)
probeta *nf* : test tube
probidad *nf* : probity
problema *nm* : problem
problemática *nf* : set of problems ⟨la problemática que debemos enfrentar : the problems we must face⟩
probóscide *nf* : proboscis
problemático, -ca *adj* : problematic
procaz *adj, pl* **procaces 1** : insolent, impudent **2** : indecent
procedencia *nf* : origin, source
procedente *adj* **1** : proper, fitting **2 ~ de** : coming from
proceder *vi* **1** AVANZAR : to proceed **2** : to act, to behave **3** : to be appropriate, to be fitting **4 ~ de** : to originate from, to come from
procedimiento *nm* : procedure, process
prócer *nmf* : eminent person, leader
procesado, -da *n* : accused, defendant
procesador *nm* : processor ⟨procesador de textos : word processor⟩
procesamiento *nm* : processing ⟨procesamiento de datos : data processing⟩
procesar *vt* **1** : to prosecute, to try **2** : to process
procesión *nf, pl* **-siones** : procession
proceso *nm* **1** : process **2** : trial, proceedings *pl*
proclama *nf* : proclamation
proclamación *nf, pl* **-ciones** : proclamation
proclamar *vt* : to proclaim — **proclamarse** *vr*
proclive *adj* **~ a** : inclined to, prone to
proclividad *nf* : proclivity, inclination
procrear *vi* : to procreate — **procreación** *nf*
procurador, -dora *n* ABOGADO : attorney
procurar *vt* **1** INTENTAR : to try, to endeavor **2** CONSEGUIR : to obtain, to procure **3 procurar hacer** : to manage to do
prodigar {52} *vt* : to lavish, to be generous with
prodigio *nm* : wonder, marvel
prodigioso, -sa *adj* : prodigious, marvelous
pródigo¹, -ga *adj* **1** : generous, lavish **2** : wasteful, prodigal
pródigo², -ga *n* : spendthrift, prodigal
producción *nf, pl* **-ciones 1** : production **2 producción en serie** : mass production
producir {61} *vt* **1** : to produce, to make, to manufacture **2** : to cause, to bring about **3** : to bear (interest) — **producirse** *vr* : to take place, to occur
productividad *nf* : productivity
productivo, -va *adj* **1** : productive **2** LUCRATIVO : profitable

producto *nm* **1** : product **2** : proceeds *pl*, yield
productor, -tora *n* : producer
proeza *nf* HAZAÑA : feat, exploit
profanar *vt* : to profane, to desecrate — **profanación** *nf*
profano¹, **-na** *adj* **1** : profane **2** : worldly, secular
profano², **-na** *n* : nonspecialist
profecía *nf* : prophecy
proferir {76} *vt* **1** : to utter **2** : to hurl (insults)
profesar *vt* **1** : to profess, to declare **2** : to practice, to exercise
profesión *nf, pl* **-siones** : profession
profesional *adj & nmf* : professional — **profesionalmente** *adv*
profesionalismo *nm* : professionalism
profesionalizar {21} *vt* : to professionalize
profesionista *nmf Mex* : professional
profesor, -sora *n* **1** MAESTRO : teacher **2** : professor
profesorado *nm* **1** : faculty **2** : teaching profession
profeta *nm* : prophet
profético, -ca *adj* : prophetic
profetisa *nf* : prophetess, prophet
profetizar {21} *vt* : to prophesy
prófugo, -ga *adj & n* : fugitive
profundidad *nf* : depth, profundity
profundizar {21} *vt* **1** : to deepen **2** : to study in depth — *vi* **~ en** : to go deeply into, to study in depth
profundo, -da *adj* **1** HONDO : deep **2** : profound — **profundamente** *adv*
profusión *nf, pl* **-siones** : abundance, profusion
profuso, -sa *adj* : profuse, abundant, extensive
progenie *nf* : progeny, offspring
progenitor, -tora *n* ANTEPASADO : ancestor, progenitor
progesterona *nf* : progesterone
prognóstico *nm* : prognosis
programa *nm* **1** : program **2** : plan **3 programa de estudios** : curriculum
programable *adj* : programmable
programación *nf, pl* **-ciones 1** : programming **2** : planning
programador, -dora *n* : programmer
programar *vt* **1** : to schedule, to plan **2** : to program (a computer, etc.)
progresar *vi* : to progress, to make progress
progresista *adj & nmf* : progressive
progresivo, -va *adj* : progressive, gradual
progreso *nm* : progress
prohibición *nf, pl* **-ciones** : ban, prohibition
prohibir {62} *vt* : to prohibit, to ban, to forbid
prohibitivo, -va *adj* : prohibitive
prohijar {5} *vt* ADOPTAR : to adopt
prójimo *nm* : neighbor, fellow man
prole *nf* : offspring, progeny
proletariado *nm* : proletariat, working class
proletario, -ria *adj & n* : proletarian
proliferar *vi* : to proliferate — **proliferación** *nf*
prolífico, -ca *adj* : prolific
prolijo, -ja *adj* : wordy, long-winded
prólogo *nm* : prologue, preface, foreword
prolongación *nf, pl* **-ciones** : extension, lengthening
prolongar {52} *vt* **1** : to prolong **2** : to extend, to lengthen — **prolongarse** *vr* CONTINUAR : to last, to continue
promediar *vt* **1** : to average **2** : to divide in half — *vi* : to be half over
promedio *nm* **1** : average **2** : middle, midpoint
promesa *nf* : promise
prometedor, -dora *adj* : promising, hopeful
prometer *vt* : to promise — *vi* : to show promise — **prometerse** *vr* COMPROMETERSE : to get engaged
prometido¹, **-da** *adj* : engaged
prometido², **-da** *n* NOVIO : fiancé *m*, fiancée *f*
prominente *adj* : prominent — **prominencia** *nf*
promiscuo, -cua *adj* : promiscuous — **promiscuidad** *nf*
promisorio, -ria *adj* **1** : promising **2** : promissory
promoción *nf, pl* **-ciones 1** : promotion **2** : class, year **3** : play-off (in soccer)
promocionar *vt* : to promote — **promocional** *adj*
promontorio *nm* : promontory, headland
promotor, -tora *n* : promoter
promover {47} *vt* **1** : to promote, to advance **2** FOMENTAR : to foster, to encourage **3** PROVOCAR : to provoke, to cause
promulgación *nf, pl* **-ciones 1** : enactment **2** : proclamation, enactment
promulgar {52} *vt* **1** : to promulgate, to proclaim **2** : to enact (a law or decree)
prono, -na *adj* : prone
pronombre *nm* : pronoun
pronosticar {72} *vt* : to predict, to forecast
pronóstico *nm* **1** PREDICCIÓN : forecast, prediction **2** : prognosis
prontitud *nf* **1** PRESTEZA : promptness, speed **2 con ~** : promptly, quickly
pronto¹ *adv* **1** : quickly, promptly **2** : soon **3 de ~** : suddenly **4 lo más pronto posible** : as soon as possible **5 tan pronto como** : as soon as
pronto², **-ta** *adj* **1** RÁPIDO : quick, speedy, prompt **2** PREPARADO : ready
pronunciación *nf, pl* **-ciones** : pronunciation
pronunciado, -da *adj* **1** : pronounced, sharp, steep **2** : marked, noticeable
pronunciamiento *nm* **1** : pronouncement **2** : military uprising
pronunciar *vt* **1** : to pronounce, to say **2** : to give, to deliver (a speech) **3 pro-**

nunciar un fallo : to pronounce sentence — **pronunciarse** *vr* : to declare oneself
propagación *nf, pl* **-ciones** : propagation, spreading
propaganda *nf* **1** : propaganda **2** PUBLICIDAD : advertising
propagar {52} *vt* **1** : to propagate **2** : to spread, to disseminate — **propagarse** *vr*
propalar *vt* **1** : to divulge **2** : to spread
propano *nm* : propane
propasarse *vr* : to go too far, to overstep one's bounds
propensión *nf, pl* **-siones** INCLINACIÓN : inclination, propensity
propenso, -sa *adj* : prone, susceptible
propiamente *adv* **1** : properly, correctly **2** : exactly, precisely ⟨propiamente dicho : strictly speaking⟩
propiciar *vt* **1** : to propitiate **2** : to favor, to foster
propicio, -cia *adj* : favorable, propitious
propiedad *nf* **1** : property ⟨propiedad privada : private property⟩ **2** : ownership **3** CUALIDAD : property, quality **4** : suitability, appropriateness
propietario[1], **-ria** *adj* : proprietary
propietario[2], **-ria** *n* DUEÑO : owner, proprietor
propina *nf* : tip, gratuity
propinar *vt* : to give, to strike ⟨propinar una paliza : to give a beating⟩
propio, -pia *adj* **1** : own ⟨su propia casa : his own house⟩ ⟨sus recursos propios : their own resources⟩ **2** APROPIADO : appropriate, suitable **3** CARACTERÍSTICO : characteristic, typical **4** MISMO : oneself ⟨el propio director : the director himself⟩
proponer {60} *vt* **1** : to propose, to suggest **2** : to nominate — **proponerse** *vr* : to intend, to plan, to set out ⟨lo que se propone lo cumple : he does what he sets out to do⟩
proporción *nf, pl* **-ciones** **1** : proportion **2** : ratio (in mathematics) **3 proporciones** *nfpl* : proportions, size ⟨de grandes proporciones : very large⟩
proporcionado, -da *adj* **1** : proportionate **2** : proportioned ⟨bien proporcionado : well-proportioned⟩ — **proporcionadamente** *adv*
proporcional *adj* : proportional — **proporcionalmente** *adv*
proporcionar *vt* **1** : to provide, to give **2** : to proportion, to adapt
proposición *nf, pl* **-ciones** : proposal, proposition
propósito *nm* **1** INTENCIÓN : purpose, intention **2 a ~** : by the way **3 a ~** : on purpose, intentionally
propuesta *nf* PROPOSICIÓN : proposal
propulsar *vt* **1** IMPULSAR : to propel, to drive **2** PROMOVER : to promote, to encourage
propulsión *nf, pl* **-siones** : propulsion
propulsor *nm* : propellant
propuso, etc. → **proponer**
prorrata *nf* **1** : share, quota **2 a ~** : pro rata, proportionately
prórroga *nf* **1** : extension, deferment **2** : overtime (in sports)
prorrogar {52} *vt* **1** : to extend (a deadline) **2** : to postpone
prorrumpir *vi* : to burst forth, to break out ⟨prorrumpí en lágrimas : I burst into tears⟩
prosa *nf* : prose
prosaico, -ca *adj* : prosaic, mundane
proscribir {33} *v* **1** PROHIBIR : to prohibit, to ban, to proscribe **2** DESTERRAR : to banish, to exile
proscripción *nf, pl* **-ciones** **1** PROHIBICIÓN : ban, proscription **2** DESTIERRO : banishment
proscrito[1] *pp* → **proscribir**
proscrito[2], **-ta** *n* **1** DESTERRADO : exile **2** : outlaw
prosecución *nf, pl* **-ciones** **1** : continuation **2** : pursuit
proseguir {75} *vt* **1** CONTINUAR : to continue **2** : to pursue (studies, goals) — *vi* : to continue, to go on
prosélito, -ta *n* : proselyte
prospección *nf, pl* **-ciones** : prospecting, exploration
prospectar *vi* : to prospect
prospecto *nm* : prospectus, leaflet, brochure
prosperar *vi* : to prosper, to thrive
prosperidad *nf* : prosperity
próspero, -ra *adj* : prosperous, flourishing
próstata *nf* : prostate
prostitución *nf, pl* **-ciones** : prostitution
prostituir {41} *vt* : to prostitute — **prostituirse** *vr* : to prostitute oneself
prostituto, -ta *n* : prostitute
protagonista *nmf* **1** : protagonist, main character **2** : leader
protagonizar {21} *vt* : to star in
protección *nf, pl* **-ciones** : protection
protector[1], **-tora** *adj* : protective
protector[2], **-tora** *n* **1** : protector, guardian **2** : patron
protector[3] *nm* : protector, guard ⟨chaleco protector : chest protector⟩
protectorado *nm* : protectorate
proteger {15} *vt* : to protect, to defend — **protegerse** *vr*
protegido, -da *n* : protégé
proteína *nf* : protein
prótesis *nfs & pl* : prosthesis
protesta *nf* **1** : protest **2** *Mex* : promise, oath
protestante *adj & nmf* : Protestant
protestantismo *nm* : Protestantism
protestar *vi* : to protest, to object — *vt* **1** : to protest, to object to **2** : to declare, to profess
protocolo *nm* : protocol
protón *nm, pl* **protones** : proton
protoplasma *nm* : protoplasm
prototipo *nm* : prototype
protozoario *or* **protozoo** *nm* : protozoan

protuberancia *nf* : protuberance — **protuberante** *adj*

provecho *nm* : benefit, advantage

provechoso, -sa *adj* BENEFICIOSO : beneficial, profitable, useful — **provechosamente** *adv*

proveedor, -dora *n* : provider, supplier

proveer {63} *vt* : to provide, to supply — **proveerse** *vr* **~ de** : to obtain, to supply oneself with

provenir {87} *vi* **~ de** : to come from

provenzal[1] *adj* : Provençal

provenzal[2] *nmf* : Provençal

provenzal[3] *nm* : Provençal (language)

proverbio *nm* REFRÁN : proverb — **proverbial** *adj*

providencia *nf* **1** : providence, foresight **2** : Providence, God **3 providencias** *nfpl* : steps, measures

providencial *adj* : providential

provincia *nf* : province — **provincial** *adj*

provinciano, -na *adj* : provincial, unsophisticated

provisión *nf, pl* **-siones** : provision

provisional *adj* : provisional, temporary

provisionalmente *adv* : provisionally, tentatively

provisorio, -ria *adj* : provisional, temporary

provisto *pp* → **proveer**

provocación *nf, pl* **-ciones** : provocation

provocador[1], **-dora** *adj* : provocative, provoking

provocador[2], **-dora** *n* AGITADOR : agitator

provocar {72} *vt* **1** CAUSAR : to provoke, to cause **2** IRRITAR : to provoke, to pique

provocativo, -va *adj* : provocative

proxeneta *nmf* : pimp *m*

próximamente *adv* : shortly, soon

proximidad *nf* **1** : nearness, proximity **2 proximidades** *nfpl* : vicinity

próximo, -ma *adj* **1** : near, close ⟨la Navidad está próxima : Christmas is almost here⟩ **2** SIGUIENTE : next, following ⟨la próxima semana : the following week⟩

proyección *nf, pl* **-ciones 1** : projection **2** : showing, screening (of a film) **3** : range, influence, diffusion

proyectar *vt* **1** : to plan **2** LANZAR : to throw, to hurl **3** : to project, to cast (light or shadow) **4** : to show, to screen (a film)

proyectil *nm* : projectile, missile

proyecto *nm* **1** : plan, project **2 proyecto de ley** : bill

proyector *nm* **1** : projector **2** : spotlight

prudencia *nf* : prudence, care, discretion

prudente *adj* : prudent, sensible, reasonable

prueba[1], **etc.** → **probar**

prueba[2] *nf* **1** : proof, evidence **2** : trial, test **3** : proof (in printing or photography) **4** : event, qualifying round (in sports) **5 a prueba de agua** : waterproof **6 prueba de fuego** : acid test **7 poner a prueba** : to put to the test

prurito *nm* **1** : itching **2** : desire, urge

psicoanálisis *nm* : psychoanalysis — **psicoanalista** *nmf*

psicoanalítico, -ca *adj* : psychoanalytic

psicoanalizar {21} *vt* : to psychoanalyze

psicología *nf* : psychology

psicológico, -ca *adj* : psychological — **psicológicamente** *adv*

psicólogo, -ga *n* : psychologist

psicópata *nmf* : psychopath

psicopático, -ca *adj* : psycopathic

psicosis *nfs & pl* : psychosis

psicosomático, -ca *adj* : psychosomatic

psicoterapeuta *nmf* : psychotherapist

psicoterapia *nf* : psychotherapy

psicótico, -ca *adj & n* : psychotic

psique *nf* : psyche

psiquiatra *nmf* : psychiatrist

psiquiatría *nf* : psychiatry

psiquiátrico[1], **-ca** *adj* : psychiatric

psiquiátrico[2] *nm* : mental hospital

psíquico, -ca *adj* : psychic

psiquis *nfs & pl* : psyche

psoriasis *nf* : psoriasis

ptomaína *nf* : ptomaine

púa *nf* **1** : barb ⟨alambre de púas : barbed wire⟩ **2** : tooth (of a comb) **3** : quill, spine

pubertad *nf* : puberty

pubiano → **púbico**

púbico, -ca *adj* : pubic

publicación *nf, pl* **-ciones** : publication

publicar {72} *vt* **1** : to publish **2** DIVULGAR : to divulge, to disclose

publicidad *nf* **1** : publicity **2** : advertising

publicista *nmf* : publicist

publicitar *vt* **1** : to publicize **2** : to advertise

publicitario, -ria *adj* : advertising, publicity ⟨agencia publicitaria : advertising agency⟩

público[1], **-ca** *adj* : public — **públicamente** *adv*

público[2] *nm* **1** : public **2** : audience, spectators *pl*

puchero *nm* **1** : pot **2** : stew **3** : pout ⟨hacer pucheros : to pout⟩

pucho *nm* **1** : waste, residue **2** : cigarette butt **3 a puchos** : little by little, bit by bit

púdico, -ca *adj* : chaste, modest

pudiente *adj* **1** : powerful **2** : rich, wealthy

pudín *nm, pl* **pudines** BUDÍN : pudding

pudo, etc. → **poder**

pudor *nm* : modesty, reserve

pudoroso, -sa *adj* : modest, reserved, shy

pudrir {59} *vt* **1** : to rot **2** *fam* : to annoy, to upset — **pudrirse** *vr* **1** : to rot **2** : to languish

pueblerino, -na *adj* : provincial, countrified

puebla, etc. → **poblar**

pueblo *nm* **1** NACIÓN : people **2** : common people **3** ALDEA, POBLADO : town, village

puede, etc. → **poder**

puente *nm* **1** : bridge ⟨puente levadizo : drawbridge⟩ **2** : denture, bridge **3 puente aéreo** : airlift

puerco[1], **-ca** *adj* : dirty, filthy

puerco[2], **-ca** *n* **1** CERDO, MARRANO : pig, hog **2** : pig, dirty or greedy person **3 puerco espín** : porcupine

pueril *adj* : childish, puerile

puerro *nm* : leek

puerta *nf* **1** : door, entrance, gate **2 a puerta cerrada** : behind closed doors

puerto *nm* **1** : port, harbor **2** : mountain pass **3 puerto marítimo** : seaport

puertorriqueño, -ña *adj & n* : Puerto Rican

pues *conj* **1** : since, because, for ⟨no puedo ir, pues no tengo plata : I can't go, since I don't have any money⟩ ⟨lo hace, pues a él le gusta : he does it because he likes to⟩ **2** (*used interjectionally*) : well, then ⟨¡pues claro que sí! : well, of course!⟩ ⟨¡pues no voy! : well then, I'm not going!⟩

puesta *nf* **1** : setting ⟨puesta del sol : sunset⟩ **2** : laying (of eggs) **3 puesta a punto** : tune-up **4 puesta en marcha** : start, starting up

puestero, -ra *n* : seller, vendor

puesto[1] *pp* → **poner**

puesto[2], **-ta** *adj* : dressed ⟨bien puesto : well-dressed⟩

puesto[3] *nm* **1** LUGAR, SITIO : place, position **2** : position, job **3** : kiosk, stand, stall **4 puesto que** : since, given that

pugilato *nm* BOXEO : boxing, pugilism

pugilista *nm* BOXEADOR : boxer, pugilist

pugna *nf* **1** CONFLICTO, LUCHA : conflict, struggle **2 en ~** : at odds, in conflict

pugnar *vi* LUCHAR : to fight, to strive, to struggle

pugnaz *adj* : pugnacious

pujante *adj* : mighty, powerful

pujanza *nf* : strength, vigor ⟨pujanza económica : economic strength⟩

pulcritud *nf* **1** : neatness, tidiness **2** ESMERO : meticulousness

pulcro, -cra *adj* **1** : clean, neat **2** : exquisite, delicate, refined

pulga *nf* **1** : flea **2 tener malas pulgas** : to be bad-tempered

pulgada *nf* : inch

pulgar *nm* **1** : thumb **2** : big toe

pulir *vt* **1** : to polish, to shine **2** REFINAR : to refine, to perfect

pulla *nf* **1** : cutting remark, dig, gibe **2** : obscenity

pulmón *nm, pl* **pulmones** : lung

pulmonar *adj* : pulmonary

pulmonía *nf* NEUMONÍA : pneumonia

pulpa *nf* : pulp, flesh

pulpería *nf* : small grocery store

púlpito *nm* : pulpit

pulpo *nm* : octopus

pulsación *nf, pl* **-ciones 1** : beat, pulsation, throb **2** : keystroke

pulsar *vt* **1** APRETAR : to press, to push **2** : to strike (a key) **3** : to assess — *vi* : to beat, to throb

pulsera *nf* : bracelet

pulso *nm* **1** : pulse ⟨tomarle el pulso a alguien : to take someone's pulse⟩ ⟨tomarle el pulso a la opinión : to sound out opinion⟩ **2** : steadiness (of hand) ⟨dibujo a pulso : freehand sketch⟩

pulular *vi* ABUNDAR : to abound, to swarm ⟨en el río pululan los peces : the river is teeming with fish⟩

pulverizador *nm* **1** : atomizer, spray **2** : spray gun

pulverizar {21} *vt* **1** : to pulverize, to crush **2** : to spray

puma *nf* : cougar, puma

puna *nf* : bleak Andean tableland

punción *nf, pl* **punciones** : puncture

punible *adj* : punishable

punitivo, -va *adj* : punitive

punce, etc. → **punzar**

punta *nf* **1** : tip, end ⟨punta del dedo : fingertip⟩ ⟨en la punta de la lengua : at the tip of one's tongue⟩ **2** : point (of a weapon or pencil) ⟨punta de lanza : spearhead⟩ **3** : point, headland **4** : bunch, lot ⟨una punta de ladrones : a bunch of thieves⟩ **5 a punta de** : by, by dint of

puntada *nf* **1** : stitch (in sewing) **2** PUNZADA : sharp pain, stitch, twinge **3** *Mex* : witticism, quip

puntal *nm* **1** : prop, support **2** : stanchion

puntapié *nm* PATADA : kick

puntazo *nm* CORNADA : wound (from a goring)

puntear *vt* **1** : to pluck (a guitar) **2** : to lead (in sports)

puntería *nf* : aim, marksmanship

puntero *nm* **1** : pointer **2** : leader

puntiagudo, -da *adj* : sharp, pointed

puntilla *nf* **1** : lace edging **2** : dagger (in bullfighting) **3 de puntillas** : on tiptoe

puntilloso, -sa *adj* : punctilious

punto *nm* **1** : dot, point **2** : period (in punctuation) **3** : item, question **4** : spot, place **5** : moment, stage, degree **6** : point (in a score) **7** : stitch **8 en ~** : on the dot, sharp ⟨a las dos en punto : at two o'clock sharp⟩ **9 al punto** : at once **10 a punto fijo** : exactly, certainly **11 dos puntos** : colon **12 hasta cierto punto** : up to a point **13 punto decimal** : decimal point **14 punto de vista** : point of view **15 punto y coma** : semicolon **16 y punto** : period ⟨es el mejor que hay y punto : it's the best there is, period⟩ **17 puntos cardinales** : points of the compass

puntuación *nf, pl* **-ciones 1** : punctuation **2** : scoring, score, grade
puntual *adj* **1** : prompt, punctual **2** : exact, accurate — **puntualmente** *adv*
puntualidad *nf* **1** : promptness, punctuality **2** : exactness, accuracy
puntualizar {21} *vt* **1** : to specify, to state **2** : to point out
puntuar {3} *vt* : to punctuate — *vi* : to score points
punzada *nf* : sharp pain, twinge, stitch
punzante *adj* **1** : sharp **2** CÁUSTICO : biting, caustic
punzar {21} *vt* : to pierce, to puncture
punzón *nm, pl* **punzones 1** : awl **2** : hole punch
puñado *nm* **1** : handful **2 a puñados** : lots of, by the handful
puñal *nm* DAGA : dagger
puñalada *nf* : stab, stab wound
puñetazo *nm* : punch (with the fist)
puño *nm* **1** : fist **2** : handful, fistful **3** : cuff (of a shirt) **4** : handle, hilt
pupila *nf* : pupil (of the eye)
pupilo, -la *n* **1** : pupil, student **2** : ward, charge
pupitre *nm* : writing desk
puré *nm* : purée ⟨puré de papas : mashed potatoes⟩
pureza *nf* : purity
purga *nf* **1** : laxative **2** : purge
purgante *adj & nm* : laxative, purgative
purgar {52} *vt* **1** : to purge, to cleanse **2** : to liquidate (in politics) **3** : to give a laxative to — **purgarse** *vr* **1** : to take a laxative **2 ~ de** : to purge oneself of
purgatorio *nm* : purgatory
purgue, etc. → **purgar**
purificador *nm* : purifier
purificar {72} *vt* : to purify — **purificación** *nf*
puritano[1], -na *adj* : puritanical, puritan
puritano[2], -na *n* **1** : Puritan **2** : puritan
puro[1] *adv* : sheer, much ⟨de puro terco : out of sheer stubbornness⟩
puro[2], -ra *adj* **1** : pure ⟨aire puro : fresh air⟩ **2** : plain, simple, sheer ⟨por pura curiosidad : from sheer curiosity⟩ **3** : only, just ⟨emplean puras mujeres : they only employ women⟩ **4 pura sangre** : Thoroughbred horse
puro[3] *nm* : cigar
púrpura *nf* : purple
purpúreo, -rea *adj* : purple
purpurina *nf* : glitter (for decoration)
pus *nm* : pus
pusilánime *adj* COBARDE : pusillanimous, cowardly
puso, etc. → **poner**
pústula *nf* : pustule, pimple
puta *nf* : whore, slut
putrefacción *nf, pl* **-ciones** : putrefaction
putrefacto, -ta *adj* **1** PODRIDO : putrid, rotten **2** : decayed
pútrido, -da *adj* : putrid, rotten
puya *nf* **1** : point (of a lance) **2 lanzar una puya** : to gibe, to taunt

Q

q *nf* : eighteenth letter of the Spanish alphabet
que[1] *conj* **1** : that ⟨dice que está listo : he says that he's ready⟩ ⟨espero que lo haga : I hope that he does it⟩ **2** : than ⟨más que nada : more than anything⟩ **3** (*implying permission or desire*) ⟨¡que entre! : send him in!⟩ ⟨¡que te vaya bien! : I wish you well!⟩ **4** (*indicating a reason or cause*) ⟨¡cuidado, que te caes! : be careful, you're about to fall!⟩ ⟨no provoques al perro, que te va a morder : don't provoke the dog or (else) he'll bite⟩ **5 es que** : the thing is that, I'm afraid that **6 yo que tú** : if I were you
que[2] *pron* **1** : who, that ⟨la niña que viene : the girl who is coming⟩ **2** : whom, that ⟨los alumnos que enseñé : the students that I taught⟩ **3** : that, which ⟨el carro que me gusta : the car that I like⟩ **4 el (la, lo, las, los) que** → **el[1], la[1], lo[1], los[1]**
qué[1] *adv* : how, what ⟨¡qué bonito! : how pretty!⟩
qué[2] *adj* : what, which ⟨¿qué hora es? : what time is it?⟩
qué[3] *pron* : what ⟨¿qué quieres? : what do you want?⟩
quebracho *nm* : quebracho (tree)
quebrada *nf* DESFILADERO : ravine, gorge
quebradizo, -za *adj* FRÁGIL : breakable, delicate, fragile
quebrado[1], -da *adj* **1** : bankrupt **2** : rough, uneven **3** ROTO : broken
quebrado[2] *nm* : fraction
quebrantamiento *nm* **1** : breaking **2** : deterioration, weakening
quebrantar *vt* **1** : to break, to split, to crack **2** : to weaken **3** : to violate (a law or contract)
quebranto *nm* **1** : break, breaking **2** AFLICCIÓN : affliction, grief **3** PÉRDIDA : loss
quebrar {55} *vt* **1** ROMPER : to break **2** DOBLAR : to bend, to twist — *vi* **1** : to go bankrupt **2** : to fall out, to break up — **quebrarse** *vr*
queda *nf* : curfew
quedar *vi* **1** PERMANECER : to remain, to stay **2** : to be ⟨quedamos contentos con las mejoras : we were pleased with the improvements⟩ **3** : to be situated ⟨queda muy lejos : it's very far, it's too far away⟩ **4** : to be left ⟨quedan sólo dos alternativas : there are only two options left⟩ **5** : to fit, to suit ⟨estos zap-

atos no me quedan : these shoes don't fit⟩ **6 quedar bien (mal)** : to turn out well (badly) **7 ~ en** : to agree, to arrange ⟨¿en qué quedamos? : what's the arrangement, then?⟩ — **quedarse** *vr* **1** : to stay ⟨se quedó en casa : she stayed at home⟩ **2** : to keep on ⟨se quedó esperando : he kept on waiting⟩ **3 quedarse atrás** : to stay behind ⟨no quedarse atrás : to be no slouch⟩ **4 ~ con** : to remain ⟨me quedé con hambre después de comer : I was still hungry after I ate⟩

quedo[1] *adv* : softly, quietly

quedo[2], **-da** *adj* : quiet, still

quehacer *nm* **1** : work **2 quehaceres** *nmpl* : chores

queja *nf* : complaint

quejarse *vr* **1** : to complain **2** : to groan, to moan

quejido *nm* **1** : groan, moan **2** : whine, whimper

quejoso, -sa *adj* : complaining, whining

quejumbroso, -sa *adj* : querulous, whining

quema *nf* **1** FUEGO : fire **2** : burning

quemado, -da *adj* **1** : burned, burnt **2** : annoyed **3** : burned-out

quemador *nm* : burner

quemadura *nf* : burn

quemar *vt* : to burn, to set fire to — *vi* : to be burning hot — **quemarse** *vr*

quemarropa *nf* **a ~** : point-blank

quemazón *nf, pl* **-zones** **1** : burning **2** : intense heat **3** : itch **4** : cutting remark

quena *nf* : Peruvian reed flute

quepa, etc. → **caber**

querella *nf* **1** : complaint **2** : lawsuit

querellante *nmf* : plaintiff

querellarse *vr* **~ contra** : to bring suit against, to sue

querer[1] {64} *vt* **1** DESEAR : to want, to desire ⟨quiere ser profesor : he wants to be a teacher⟩ ⟨¿cuánto quieres por esta computadora? : how much do you want for this computer?⟩ **2** : to love, to like, to be fond of ⟨te quiero : I love you⟩ **3** (*indicating a request*) ⟨¿quieres pasarme la leche? : please pass the milk⟩ **4 querer decir** : to mean **5 sin ~** : unintentionally — *vi* : like, want ⟨si quieras : if you like⟩

querer[2] *nm* : love, affection

querido[1], **-da** *adj* : dear, beloved

querido[2], **-da** *n* : dear, sweetheart

queroseno *nm* : kerosene

querrá, etc. → **querer**

querúbico, -ca *adj* : cherubic

querubín *nm, pl* **-bines** : cherub

quesadilla *nf* : quesadilla

quesería *nf* : cheese shop

queso *nm* : cheese

quetzal *nm* **1** : quetzal (bird) **2** : monetary unit of Guatemala

quicio *nm* **1 estar fuera de quicio** : to be beside oneself **2 sacar de quicio** : to exasperate, to drive crazy

quid *nm* : crux, gist ⟨el quid de la cuestión : the crux of the matter⟩

quiebra[1], **etc.** → **quebrar**

quiebra[2] *nf* **1** : break, crack **2** BANCARROTA : failure, bankruptcy

quien *pron, pl* **quienes** **1** : who, whom ⟨no sé quien ganará : I don't know who will win⟩ ⟨las personas con quienes trabajo : the people with whom I work⟩ **2** : whoever, whomever ⟨quien quiere salir que salga : whoever wants to can leave⟩ **3** : anyone, some people ⟨hay quienes no están de acuerdo : some people don't agree⟩

quién *pron, pl* **quiénes** **1** : who, whom ⟨¿quién sabe? : who knows?⟩ ⟨¿con quién hablo? : with whom am I speaking?⟩ **2 de ~** : whose ⟨¿de quién es este libro? : whose book is this?⟩

quienquiera *pron, pl* **quienesquiera** : whoever, whomever

quiere, etc. → **querer**

quieto, -ta *adj* **1** : calm, quiet **2** INMÓVIL : still

quietud *nf* **1** : calm, tranquility **2** INMOVILIDAD : stillness

quijada *nf* : jaw, jawbone

quijotesco, -ca *adj* : quixotic

quilate *nm* : karat

quilla *nf* : keel

quimera *nf* : chimera, illusion

quimérico, -ca *adj* : chimeric, fanciful

química *nf* : chemistry

químico[1], **-ca** *adj* : chemical

químico[2], **-ca** *n* : chemist

quimioterapia *nf* : chemotherapy

quimono *nm* : kimono

quince *adj & nm* : fifteen

quinceañero, -ra *n* : fifteen-year-old, teenager

quinceavo[1], **-va** *adj* : fifteenth

quinceavo[2] *nm* : fifteenth (fraction)

quincena *nf* : two week period, fortnight

quincenal *adj* : bimonthly, twice a month

quincuagésimo[1], **-ma** *adj* : fiftieth, fifty-

quincuagésimo[2], **-ma** *n* : fiftieth, fifty- (in a series)

quingombó *nm* : okra

quiniela *nf* : sports lottery

quinientos[1], **-tas** *adj* : five hundred

quinientos[2] *nms & pl* : five hundred

quinina *nf* : quinine

quino *nm* : cinchona

quinqué *nm* : oil lamp

quinquenal *adj* : five-year ⟨un plan quinquenal : a five-year plan⟩

quinta *nf* : country house, villa

quintaesencia *nf* : quintessence — **quintaesencial** *adj*

quintal *nm* : hundredweight

quinteto *nm* : quintet

quintillizo, -za *n* : quintuplet

quinto, -ta *adj* : fifth — **quinto, -ta** *n*

quíntuplo, -la *adj* : quintuple, five-fold

quiosco *nm* **1** : kiosk **2** : newsstand **3 quiosco de música** : bandstand

quirófano *nm* : operating room

quiromancia *nf* : palmistry
quiropráctica *nf* : chiropractic
quiropráctico, -ca *n* : chiropractor
quirúrgico, -ca *adj* : surgical — **quirúrgicamente** *adv*
quiso, etc. → **querer**
quisquilloso[1], **-sa** *adj* : fastidious, fussy
quisquilloso[2], **-sa** *n* : fussy person, fussbudget
quiste *nm* : cyst
quitaesmalte *nm* : nail polish remover
quitamanchas *nms & pl* : stain remover
quitanieves *nms & pl* : snowplow
quitar *vt* **1** : to remove, to take away **2** : to take off (clothes) **3** : to get rid of, to relieve — **quitarse** *vr* **1** : to withdraw, to leave **2** : to take off (one's clothes) **3** ∼ **de** : to give up (a habit) **4 quitar de encima** : to get rid of
quitasol *nm* : parasol
quiteño[1], **-ña** *adj* : of or from Quito
quiteño[2], **-ña** *n* : person from Quito
quizá *or* **quizás** *adv* : maybe, perhaps
quórum *nm, pl* **quórums** : quorum

R

r *nf* : nineteenth letter of the Spanish alphabet
rábano *nm* **1** : radish **2 rábano picante** : horseradish
rabí *nmf, pl* **rabíes** : rabbi
rabia *nf* **1** HIDROFOBIA : rabies, hydrophobia **2** : rage, anger
rabiar *vi* **1** : to rage, to be furious **2** : to be in great pain **3 a** ∼ *fam* : like crazy, like mad
rabieta *nf* BERRINCHE : tantrum
rabino, -na *n* : rabbi
rabioso, -sa *adj* **1** : enraged, furious **2** : rabid
rabo *nm* **1** COLA : tail **2 el rabo del ojo** : the corner of one's eye
racha *nf* **1** : gust of wind **2** : run, series, string ⟨racha perdedora : losing streak⟩
racheado, -da *adj* : gusty, windy
racial *adj* : racial
racimo *nm* : bunch, cluster ⟨un racimo de uvas : a bunch of grapes⟩
raciocinio *nm* : reason, reasoning
ración *nf, pl* **raciones** **1** : share, ration **2** PORCIÓN : portion, helping
racional *adj* : rational, reasonable — **racionalmente** *adv*
racionalidad *nf* : rationality
racionalización *nf, pl* **-ciones** : rationalization
racionalizar {21} *vt* **1** : to rationalize **2** : to streamline
racionamiento *nm* : rationing
racionar *vt* : to ration
racismo *nm* : racism
racista *adj & nmf* : racist
radar *nm* : radar
radiación *nf, pl* **-ciones** : radiation, irradiation
radiactividad *nf* : radioactivity
radiactivo, -va *adj* : radioactive
radiador *nm* : radiator
radial *adj* **1** : radial **2** : radio, broadcasting ⟨emisora radial : radio transmitter⟩
radiante *adj* : radiant
radiar *vt* **1** : to radiate **2** : to irradiate **3** : to broadcast (on the radio)
radical[1] *adj* : radical, extreme — **radicalmente** *adv*
radical[2] *nmf* : radical
radicalismo *nm* : radicalism
radicar {72} *vi* **1** : to be found, to lie **2** ARRAIGAR : to take root — **radicarse** *vr* : to settle, to establish oneself
radio[1] *nm* **1** : radius **2** : radium
radio[2] *nmf* : radio
radioactividad *nf* : radioactivity
radioactivo, -va *adj* : radioactive
radioaficionado, -da *n* : ham radio operator
radiodifusión *nf, pl* **-siones** : radio broadcasting
radiodifusora *nf* : radio station
radioemisora *nf* : radio station
radiofaro *nm* : radio beacon
radiofónico, -ca *adj* : radio ⟨estación radiofónica pública : public radio station⟩
radiofrecuencia *nf* : radio frequency
radiografía *nf* : X ray (photograph)
radiografiar {85} *vt* : to x-ray
radiología *nf* : radiology
radiólogo, -ga *n* : radiologist
radón *nm* : radon
raer {65} *vt* RASPAR : to scrape, to scrape off
ráfaga *nf* **1** : gust (of wind) **2** : flash, burst ⟨una ráfaga de luz : a flash of light⟩
raid *nm CA, Mex fam* : lift, ride
raído, -da *adj* : worn, shabby
raiga, etc. → **raer**
raíz *nf, pl* **raíces** **1** : root **2** : origin, source **3 a raíz de** : following, as a result of **4 echar raíces** : to take root
raja *nf* **1** : crack, slit **2** : slice, wedge
rajá *nm* : raja
rajadura *nf* : crack, split
rajar *vt* HENDER : to crack, to split — *vi* **1** *fam* : to chatter **2** *fam* : to boast, to brag — **rajarse** *vr* **1** : to crack, to split open **2** *fam* : to back out
rajatabla *adv* **a** ∼ : strictly, to the letter
ralea *nf* : kind, sort, ilk ⟨son de la misma valea : they're two of a kind⟩
ralentí *nm* **dejar al ralentí** : to leave (a motor) idling
rallado, -da *adj* **1** : grated **2 pan rallado** : bread crumbs *pl*
rallador *nm* : grater

rallar *vt* : to grate
ralo, -la *adj* : sparse, thin
RAM *nf* : RAM, random-access memory
rama *nf* : branch
ramaje *nm* : branches *pl*
ramal *nm* **1** : branchline **2** : halter, strap
ramera *nf* : harlot, prostitute
ramificación *nf, pl* **-ciones** : ramification
ramificarse {72} *vr* : to branch out, to divide into branches
ramillete *nm* **1** RAMO : bouquet **2** : select group, cluster
ramo *nm* **1** : branch **2** RAMILLETE : bouquet **3** : division (of science or industry) **4 Domingo de Ramos** : Palm Sunday
rampa *nf* : ramp, incline
rana *nf* **1** : frog **2 rana toro** : bullfrog
ranchera *nf Mex* : traditional folk song
ranchería *nf* : settlement
ranchero, -ra *n* : rancher, farmer
rancho *nm* **1** : ranch, farm **2** : hut **3** : settlement, camp **4** : food, mess (for soldiers, etc.)
rancio, -cia *adj* **1** : aged, mellow (of wine) **2** : ancient, old **3** : rancid
rango *nm* **1** : rank, status **2** : high social standing **3** : pomp, splendor
ranúnculo *nm* : buttercup
ranura *nf* : groove, slot
rap *nm* : rap (music)
rapacidad *nf* : rapacity
rapar *vt* **1** : to crop **2** : to shave
rapaz[1] *adj, pl* **rapaces** : rapacious, predatory
rapaz[2], **-paza** *n, mpl* **rapaces** : youngster, child
rape *nm* : close haircut
rapé *nm* : snuff
rapero, -ra *n* : rapper, rap artist
rapidez *nf* : rapidity, speed
rápido[1] *adv* : quickly, fast ⟨¡manejas tan rápido! : you drive so fast!⟩
rápido[2], **-da** *adj* : rapid, quick — **rápidamente** *adv*
rápido[3] *nm* **1** : express train **2 rápidos** *nmpl* : rapids
rapiña *nf* **1** : plunder, pillage **2 ave de rapiña** : bird of prey
raposa *nf* : vixen (fox)
rapsodia *nf* : rhapsody
raptar *vt* SECUESTRAR : to abduct, to kidnap
rapto *nm* **1** SECUESTRO : kidnapping, abduction **2** ARREBATO : fit, outburst
raptor, -tora *n* SECUESTRADOR : kidnapper
raque *nm* : beachcombing
raquero, -ra *n* : beachcomber
raqueta *nf* **1** : racket (in sports) **2** : snowshoe
raquítico, -ca *adj* **1** : scrawny, weak **2** : measly, skimpy
raquitismo *nm* : rickets
raramente *adv* : seldom, rarely
rareza *nf* **1** : rarity **2** : peculiarity, oddity
raro, -ra *adj* **1** EXTRAÑO : odd, strange, peculiar **2** : unusual, rare **3** : exceptional **4 rara vez** : seldom, rarely
ras *nm* **a ras de** : level with
rasar *vt* **1** : to skim, to graze **2** : to level
rascacielos *nms & pl* : skyscraper
rascar {72} *vt* **1** : to scratch **2** : to scrape — **rascarse** *vr* : to scratch an itch
rasgadura *nf* : tear, rip
rasgar {52} *vt* : to rip, to tear — **rasgarse** *vr*
rasgo *nm* **1** : stroke (of a pen) ⟨a grandes rasgos : in broad outlines⟩ **2** CARACTERÍSTICA : trait, characteristic **3** : gesture, deed **4 rasgos** *nmpl* FACCIONES : features
rasgón *nm, pl* **rasgones** : rip, tear
rasgue, etc. → **rasgar**
rasguear *vt* : to strum
rasguñar *vt* **1** : to scratch **2** : to sketch, to outline
rasguño *nm* **1** : scratch **2** : sketch
raso[1], **-sa** *adj* **1** : level, flat **2 soldado raso** : private (in the army) ⟨los soldados rasos : the ranks⟩
raso[2] *nm* : satin
raspadura *nf* **1** : scratching, scraping **2 raspaduras** *nfpl* : scrapings
raspar *vt* **1** : to scrape **2** : to file down, to smooth — *vi* : to be rough
rasque, etc. → **rascar**
rastra *nf* **1** : harrow **2 a rastras** : by dragging, unwillingly
rastrear *vt* **1** : to track, to trace **2** : to comb, to search **3** : to trawl
rastrero, -ra *adj* **1** : creeping, crawling **2** : vile, despicable
rastrillar *vt* : to rake, to harrow
rastrillo *nm* **1** : rake **2** *Mex* : razor
rastro *nm* **1** PISTA : trail, track **2** VESTIGIO : trace, sign
rastrojo *nm* : stubble (of plants)
rasuradora *nf Mex, CA* : electric razor, shaver
rasurar *vt* AFEITAR : to shave — **rasurarse** *vr*
rata[1] *nm fam* : pickpocket, thief
rata[2] *nf* **1** : rat **2** *Col, Pan, Peru* : rate, percentage
ratear *vt* : to pilfer, to steal
ratero, -ra *n* : petty thief
ratificación *nf, pl* **-ciones** : ratification
ratificar {72} *vt* **1** : to ratify **2** : to confirm
rato *nm* **1** : while **2 pasar el rato** : to pass the time **3 a cada rato** : all the time, constantly ⟨les sacaba dinero a cada rato : he was always taking money from them⟩ **4 al poco rato** : later, shortly after
ratón[1], **-tona** *n, mpl* **ratones 1** : mouse **2 ratón de biblioteca** *fam* : bookworm
ratón[2] *nm, pl* **ratones 1** : (computer) mouse **2** *CoRi* : biceps
ratonera *nf* : mousetrap
raudal *nm* **1** : torrent **2 a raudales** : in abundance

raya[1], **etc.** → **raer**
raya[2] *nf* **1** : line **2** : stripe **3** : skate, ray **4** : part (in the hair) **5** : crease (in clothing)
rayar *vt* **1** ARAÑAR : to scratch **2** : to scrawl on, to mark up ⟨rayaron las paredes : they covered the walls with graffiti⟩ — *vi* **1** : to scratch **2** AMANECER : to dawn, to break ⟨al rayar el alba : at break of day⟩ **3 ~ con** : to be adjacent to, to be next to **4 ~ en** : to border on, to verge on ⟨su respuesta raya en lo ridículo : his answer borders on the ridiculous⟩ — **rayarse** *vr*
rayo *nm* **1** : ray, beam ⟨rayo láser : laser beam⟩ ⟨rayo de gamma : gamma ray⟩ ⟨rayo de sol : sunbeam⟩ **2** RELÁMPAGO : lightning bolt **3 rayo X** : X-ray
rayón *nm, pl* **rayones** : rayon
raza *nf* **1** : race ⟨raza humana : human race⟩ **2** : breed, strain **3 de ~** : thoroughbred, pedigreed
razón *nf, pl* **razones 1** MOTIVO : reason, motive ⟨en razón de : by reason of, because of⟩ **2** JUSTICIA : rightness, justice ⟨tener razón : to be right⟩ **3** : reasoning, sense ⟨perder la razón : to lose one's mind⟩ **4** : ratio, proportion
razonable *adj* : reasonable — **razonablemente** *adv*
razonado, -da *adj* : itemized, detailed
razonamiento *nm* : reasoning
razonar *v* : to reason, to think
reabastecimiento *nm* : replenishment
reabierto *pp* → **reabrir**
reabrir {2} *vt* : to reopen — **reabrirse** *vr*
reacción *nf, pl* **-ciones 1** : reaction **2 motor a reacción** : jet engine
reaccionar *vi* : to react, to respond
reaccionario, -ria *adj & n* : reactionary
reacio, -cia *adj* : resistant, opposed
reacondicionar *vt* : to recondition
reactivación *nf, pl* **-ciones** : reactivation, revival
reactivar *vt* : reactivate, revive
reactor *nm* **1** : reactor ⟨reactor nuclear : nuclear reactor⟩ **2** : jet engine **3** : jet airplane, jet
reafirmar *vt* : to reaffirm, to assert, to strengthen
reajustar *vt* : to readjust, to adjust
reajuste *nm* : readjustment ⟨reajuste de precios : price increase⟩
real *adj* **1** : real, true **2** : royal
realce *nm* **1** : embossing, relief **2 dar realce** : to highlight, to bring out
realeza *nf* : royalty
realidad *nf* **1** : reality **2 en ~** : in truth, actually
realinear *vt* : to realign
realismo *nm* **1** : realism **2** : royalism
realista[1] *adj* **1** : realistic **2** : realist **3** : royalist
realista[2] *nmf* **1** : realist **2** : royalist
realización *nf, pl* **-ciones** : execution, realization
realizar {21} *vt* **1** : to carry out, to execute **2** : to produce, to direct (a film or play) **3** : to fulfill, to achieve **4** : to realize (a profit) — **realizarse** *vr* **1** : to come true **2** : to fulfill oneself
realmente *adv* : really, in reality
realzar {21} *vt* **1** : to heighten, to raise **2** : to highlight, to enhance
reanimación *nf, pl* **-ciones** : revival, resuscitation
reanimar *vt* **1** : to revive, to restore **2** : to resuscitate — **reanimarse** *vr* : to come around, to recover
reanudación *nf, pl* **-ciones** : resumption, renewal
reanudar *vt* : to resume, to renew — **reanudarse** *vr* : to resume, to continue
reaparecer {53} *vi* **1** : to reappear **2** : to make a comeback
reaparición *nf, pl* **-ciones** : reappearance
reapertura *nf* : reopening
reata *nf* **1** : rope **2** *Mex* : lasso, lariat **3 de ~** : single file
reavivar *vt* : to revive, to reawaken
rebaja *nf* **1** : reduction **2** DESCUENTO : discount **3 rebajas** *nfpl* : sale
rebajar *vt* **1** : to reduce, to lower ⟨a precios rebajados : at reduced prices, on sale⟩ **2** : to lessen, to diminish **3** : to humiliate — **rebajarse** *vr* **1** : to humble oneself **2 rebajarse a** : to stoop to
rebanada *nf* : slice
rebañar *vt* : to mop up, to sop up
rebaño *nm* **1** : flock **2** : herd
rebasar *vt* **1** : to surpass, to exceed **2** *Mex* : to pass, to overtake
rebatiña *nf* : scramble, fight (over something)
rebatir *vt* REFUTAR : to refute
rebato *nm* **1** : surprise attack **2 tocar a rebato** : to sound the alarm
rebelarse *vr* : to rebel
rebelde[1] *adj* : rebellious, unruly
rebelde[2] *nmf* **1** : rebel **2** : defaulter
rebeldía *nf* **1** : rebelliousness **2 en ~** : in default
rebelión *nf, pl* **-liones** : rebellion
rebobinar *vt* : to rewind
reborde *nm* : border, flange, rim
rebosante *adj* : brimming, overflowing ⟨rebosante de salud : brimming with health⟩
rebosar *vi* **1** : to overflow **2 ~ de** : to abound in, to be bursting with — *vt* : to radiate
rebotar *vi* **1** : to bounce **2** : to ricochet, to rebound
rebote *nm* **1** : bounce **2** : rebound, ricochet
rebozar {21} *vt* : to coat in batter
rebozo *nm* **1** : shawl, wrap **2 sin ~** : frankly, openly
rebullir {38} *v* : to move, to stir — **rebullirse** *vr*
rebuscado, -da *adj* : affected, pretentious
rebuscar {72} *vi* : to search thoroughly

rebuznar *vi* : to bray
rebuzno *nm* : bray, braying
recabar *vt* **1** : to gather, to obtain, to collect **2 recabar fondos** : to raise money
recado *nm* **1** : message ⟨mandar recado : to send word⟩ **2** *Spain* : errand
recaer {13} *vi* **1** : to relapse **2 ~ en** *or* **~ sobre** : to fall on, to fall to
recaída *nf* : relapse
recaiga, etc. → **recaer**
recalar *vi* : to arrive
recalcar {72} *vt* : to emphasize, to stress
recalcitrante *adj* : recalcitrant
recalentar {55} *vt* **1** : to reheat, to warm up **2** : to overheat
recámara *nf* **1** *Col, Mex, Pan* : bedroom **2** : chamber (of a firearm)
recamarera *nf Mex* : chambermaid
recambio *nm* **1** : spare part **2** : refill (for a pen, etc.)
recapacitar *vi* **1** : to reconsider **2 ~ en** : to reflect on, to weigh
recapitular *v* : to recapitulate — **recapitulación** *nf*
recargable *adj* : rechargeable
recargado, -da *adj* : overly elaborate or ornate
recargar {52} *vt* **1** : to recharge **2** : to overload
recargo *nm* : surcharge
recatado, -da *adj* MODESTO : modest, demure
recato *nm* PUDOR : modesty
recaudación *nf, pl* **-ciones** **1** : collection **2** : earnings *pl*, takings *pl*
recaudador, -dora *n* **recaudador de impuestos** : tax collector
recaudar *vt* : to collect
recaudo *nm* : safe place ⟨a (buen) recaudo : in safe keeping⟩
recayó, etc. → **recaer**
rece, etc. → **rezar**
recelo *nm* : distrust, suspicion
receloso, -sa *adj* : distrustful, suspicious
recepción *nf, pl* **-ciones** : reception
recepcionista *nmf* : receptionist
receptáculo *nm* : receptacle
receptividad *nf* : receptivity, receptiveness
receptivo, -va *adj* : receptive
receptor[1], -tora *adj* : receiving
receptor[2], -tora *n* **1** : recipient **2** : catcher (in baseball), receiver (in football)
receptor[3] *nm* : receiver ⟨receptor de televisión : television set⟩
recesión *nf, pl* **-siones** : recession
recesivo, -va *adj* : recessive
receso *nm* : recess, adjournment
receta *nf* **1** : recipe **2** : prescription
recetar *vt* : to prescribe (medications)
rechazar {21} *vt* **1** : to reject **2** : to turn down, to refuse
rechazo *nm* : rejection, refusal
rechifla *nf* : booing, jeering
rechinar *vi* **1** : to squeak **2** : to grind, to gnash ⟨hacer rechinar los dientes : to grind one's teeth⟩
rechoncho, -cha *adj fam* : chubby, squat
recibidor *nm* : vestibule, entrance hall
recibimiento *nm* : reception, welcome
recibir *vt* **1** : to receive, to get **2** : to welcome — *vi* : to receive visitors — **recibirse** *vr* **~ de** : to qualify as
recibo *nm* : receipt
reciclable *adj* : recyclable
reciclado → **reciclaje**
reciclaje *nm* **1** : recycling **2** : retraining
reciclar *vt* **1** : to recycle **2** : to retrain
recién *adv* **1** : newly, recently ⟨recién nacido : newborn⟩ ⟨recién casados : newlyweds⟩ ⟨recién llegado : newcomer⟩ **2** : just, only just ⟨recién ahora me acordé : I just now remembered⟩
reciente *adj* : recent — **recientemente** *adv*
recinto *nm* **1** : enclosure **2** : site, premises *pl*
recio[1] *adv* **1** : strongly, hard **2** : loudly, loud
recio[2], -cia *adj* **1** : severe, harsh **2** : tough, strong
recipiente[1] *nm* : container, receptacle
recipiente[2] *nmf* : recipient
reciprocar {72} *vi* : to reciprocate
reciprocidad *nf* : reciprocity
recíproco, -ca *adj* : reciprocal, mutual
recitación *nf, pl* **-ciones** : recitation, recital
recital *nm* : recital
recitar *vt* : to recite
reclamación *nf, pl* **-ciones** **1** : claim, demand **2** QUEJA : complaint
reclamar *vt* **1** EXIGIR : to demand, to require **2** : to claim — *vi* : to complain
reclamo *nm* **1** : bird call, lure **2** : lure, decoy **3** : inducement, attraction **4** : advertisement **5** : complaint
reclinar *vt* : to rest, to lean — **reclinarse** *vr* : to recline, to lean back
recluir {41} *vt* : to confine, to lock up — **recluirse** *vr* : to shut oneself up, to withdraw
reclusión *nf, pl* **-siones** : imprisonment
recluso, -sa *n* **1** : inmate, prisoner **2** SOLITARIO : recluse
recluta *nmf* : recruit, draftee
reclutamiento *nm* : recruitment, recruiting
reclutar *vt* ENROLAR : to recruit, to enlist
recobrar *vt* : to recover, to regain — **recobrarse** *vr* : to recover, to recuperate
recocer {14} *vt* : to overcook, to cook again
recodo *nm* : bend
recogedor *nm* : dustpan
recoger {15} *vt* **1** : to collect, to gather **2** : to get, to retrieve, to pick up **3** : to clean up, to tidy (up)
recogido, -da *adj* : quiet, secluded
recogimiento *nm* **1** : collecting, gathering **2** : withdrawal **3** : absorption, concentration

recolección *nf, pl* **-ciones 1** : collection ⟨recolección de basura : trash pickup⟩ **2** : harvest
recolectar *vt* **1** : to gather, to collect **2** : to harvest, to pick
recomendable *adj* : advisable, recommended
recomendación *nf, pl* **-ciones** : recommendation
recomendar {55} *vt* **1** : to recommend **2** ACONSEJAR : to advise
recompensa *nf* : reward, recompense
recompensar *vt* **1** PREMIAR : to reward **2** : to compensate
reconciliación *nf, pl* **-ciones** : reconciliation
reconciliar *vt* : to reconcile — **reconciliarse** *vr*
recóndito, -ta *adj* **1** : remote, isolated **2** : hidden, recondite **3 en lo más recóndito de** : in the depths of
reconfortar *vt* : to comfort — **reconfortante** *adj*
reconocer {18} *vt* **1** : to recognize **2** : to admit **3** : to examine
reconocible *adj* : recognizable
reconocido, -da *adj* **1** : recognized, accepted **2** : grateful
reconocimiento *nm* **1** : acknowledgment, recognition, avowal **2** : (medical) examination **3** : reconnaissance
reconquista *nf* : reconquest
reconquistar *vt* **1** : to reconquer, to recapture **2** RECUPERAR : to regain, to recover
reconsiderar *vt* : to reconsider — **reconsideración** *nf*
reconstrucción *nf, pl* **-ciones** : reconstruction
reconstruir {41} *vt* : to rebuild, to reconstruct
reconversión *nf, pl* **-siones** : restructuring
reconvertir {76} *vt* **1** : to restructure **2** : to retrain
recopilación *nf, pl* **-ciones 1** : summary **2** : collection, compilation
recopilar *vt* : to compile, to collect
récord *or* **record** ['rɛkɔr] *nm, pl* **récords** *or* **records** [-kɔrs] : record ⟨record mundial : world record⟩ — **récord** *or* **record** *adj*
recordar {19} *vt* **1** : to recall, to remember **2** : to remind — *vi* **1** ACORDARSE : to remember **2** DESPERTAR : to wake up
recordatorio¹, -ria *adj* : commemorative
recordatorio² *nm* : reminder
recorrer *vt* **1** : to travel through, to tour **2** : to cover (a distance) **3** : to go over, to look over
recorrido *nm* **1** : journey, trip **2** : path, route, course **3** : round (in golf)
recortar *vt* **1** : to cut, to reduce **2** : to cut out **3** : to trim, to cut off **4** : to outline — **recortarse** *vr* : to stand out ⟨los árboles se recortaban en el horizonte : the trees were silhouetted against the horizon⟩
recorte *nm* **1** : cut, reduction **2** : clipping ⟨recortes de periódicos : newspaper clippings⟩
recostar {19} *vt* : to lean, to rest — **recostarse** *vr* : to lie down, recline
recoveco *nm* **1** VUELTA : bend, turn **2** : nook, corner **3 recovecos** *nmpl* : intricacies, ins and outs
recreación *nf, pl* **-ciones 1** : re-creation **2** DIVERSIÓN : recreation, entertainment
recrear *vt* **1** : to re-create **2** : to entertain, to amuse — **recrearse** *vr* : to enjoy oneself
recreativo, -va *adj* : recreational
recreo *nm* **1** DIVERSIÓN : entertainment, amusement **2** : recess, break
recriminación *nf, pl* **-ciones** : reproach, recrimination
recriminar *vt* : to reproach — *vi* : to recriminate — **recriminarse** *vr*
recrudecer {53} *v* : to intensify, to worsen — **recrudecerse** *vr*
rectal *adj* : rectal
rectangular *adj* : rectangular
rectángulo *nm* : rectangle
rectificación *nf, pl* **-ciones** : rectification, correction
rectificar {72} *vt* **1** : to rectify, to correct **2** : to straighten (out)
rectitud *nf* **1** : straightness **2** : honesty, rectitude
recto¹ *adv* : straight
recto², -ta *adj* **1** : straight **2** : upright, honorable **3** : sound
recto³ *nm* : rectum
rector¹, -tora *adj* : governing, managing
rector², -tora *n* : rector
rectoría *nf* : rectory
recubierto *pp* → **recubrir**
recubrir {2} *vt* : to cover, to coat
recuento *nm* : recount, count ⟨un recuento de los votos : a recount of the votes⟩
recuerdo *nm* **1** : memory **2** : souvenir, memento **3 recuerdos** *nmpl* : regards
recular *vi* **1** : to back up **2** REPLEGARSE : to retreat, to fall back **3** RETRACTARSE : to back down
recuperación *nf, pl* **-ciones 1** : recovery, recuperation **2 recuperación de datos** : data retrieval
recuperar *vt* **1** : to recover, to get back, to retrieve **2** : to recuperate **3** : to make up for ⟨recuperar el tiempo perdido : to make up for lost time⟩ — **recuperarse** *vr* **~ de** : to recover from, to get over
recurrente *adj* : recurrent, recurring
recurrir *vi* **1 ~ a** : to turn to, to appeal to **2 ~ a** : to resort to **3** : to appeal (in law)
recurso *nm* **1** : recourse ⟨el último recurso : the last resort⟩ **2** : appeal (in law) **3 recursos** *nmpl* : resources, means ⟨recursos naturales : natural resources⟩

red *nf* **1** : net, mesh **2** : network, system, chain **3** : trap, snare
redacción *nf, pl* **-ciones 1** : writing, composition **2** : editing
redactar *vt* **1** : to write, to draft **2** : to edit
redactor, -tora *n* : editor
redada *nf* **1** : raid **2** : catch, haul
redefinir *vt* : to redefine — **redefinición** *nf*
redención *nf, pl* **-ciones** : redemption
redentor[1], **-tora** *adj* : redeeming
redentor[2], **-tora** *n* : redeemer
redescubierto *pp* → **redescubrir**
redescubrir {2} *vt* : to rediscover
redicho, -cha *adj fam* : affected, pretentious
redil *nm* **1** : sheepfold **2 volver al redil** : to return to the fold
redimir *vt* : to redeem, to deliver (from sin)
rediseñar *vt* : to redesign
redistribuir {41} *vt* : to redistribute — **redistribución** *nf*
rédito *nm* : return, yield
redituar {3} *vt* : to produce, to yield
redoblar *vt* : to redouble, to strengthen — **redoblado, -da** *adj*
redoble *nm* : drum roll
redomado, -da *adj* **1** : sly, crafty **2** : utter, out-and-out
redonda *nf* **1** : region, surrounding area **2 a la redonda** ALREDEDOR : around ⟨de diez millas a la redonda : for ten miles around⟩
redondear *vt* : to round off, to round out
redondel *nm* **1** : ring, circle **2** : bullring, arena
redondez *nf* : roundness
redondo, -da *adj* **1** : round ⟨mesa redonda : round table⟩ **2** : great, perfect ⟨un negocio redondo : an excellent deal⟩ **3** : straightforward, flat ⟨un rechazo redondo : a flat refusal⟩ **4** *Mex* : round-trip **5 en ~** : around
reducción *nf, pl* **-ciones** : reduction, decrease
reducido, -da *adj* **1** : reduced, limited **2** : small
reducir {61} *vt* **1** DISMINUIR : to reduce, to decrease, to cut **2** : to subdue **3** : to boil down — **reducirse** *vr* **~ a** : to come down to, to be nothing more than
redundancia *nf* : redundancy
redundante *adj* : redundant
reedición *nf, pl* **-ciones** : reprint
reelegir {28} *vt* : to reelect — **reelección** *nf*
reembolsable *adj* : refundable
reembolsar *vt* **1** : to refund, to reimburse **2** : to repay
reembolso *nm* : refund, reimbursement
reemplazable *adj* : replaceable
reemplazar {21} *vt* : to replace, to substitute
reemplazo *nm* : replacement, substitution
reencarnación *nf, pl* **-ciones** : reincarnation
reencuentro *nm* : reunion
reestablecer {53} *vt* : to reestablish
reestructurar *vt* : to restructure
reexaminar *vt* : to reexamine
refaccionar *vt* : to repair, to renovate
refacciones *nfpl* : repairs, renovations
referencia *nf* **1** : reference **2 hacer referencia a** : to refer to
referendo → **referéndum**
referéndum *nm, pl* **-dums** : referendum
referente *adj* **~ a** : concerning
réferi *or* **referi** [ˈrɛfɛri] *nmf* : referee
referir {76} *vt* **1** : to relate, to tell **2** : to refer ⟨nos refirió al diccionario : she referred us to the dictionary⟩ — **referirse** *vr* **~ a 1** : to refer to **2 ~ a** : to be concerned, to be in reference to ⟨en lo que se refiere a la educación : as far as education is concerned⟩
refinado[1], **-da** *adj* : refined
refinado[2] *nm* : refining
refinamiento *nm* **1** : refining **2** FINURA : refinement
refinanciar *vt* : to refinance
refinar *vt* : to refine
refinería *nf* : refinery
reflectante *adj* : reflective, reflecting
reflector[1], **-tora** *adj* : reflecting
reflector[2] *nm* **1** : spotlight, searchlight **2** : reflector
reflejar *vt* : to reflect — **reflejarse** *vr* : to be reflected ⟨la decepción se refleja en su rostro : the disappointment shows on her face⟩
reflejo *nm* **1** : reflection **2** : reflex **3 reflejos** *nmpl* : highlights, streaks (in hair)
reflexión *nf, pl* **-xiones** : reflection, thought
reflexionar *vi* : to reflect, to think
reflexivo, -va *adj* **1** : reflective, thoughtful **2** : reflexive
reflujo *nm* : ebb, ebb tide
reforma *nf* **1** : reform **2** : alteration, renovation
reformador, -dora *n* : reformer
reformar *vt* **1** : to reform **2** : to change, to alter **3** : to renovate, to repair — **reformarse** *vr* : to mend one's ways
reformatorio *nm* : reformatory
reformular *vt* : to reformulate — **reformulación** *nf*
reforzar {36} *vt* **1** : to reinforce, to strengthen **2** : to encourage, to support
refracción *nf, pl* **-ciones** : refraction
refractar *vt* : to refract — **refractarse** *vr*
refractario, -ria *adj* : refractory, obstinate
refrán *nm, pl* **refranes** ADAGIO : proverb, saying
refregar {49} *vt* : to scrub
refrenar *vt* **1** : to rein in (a horse) **2** : to restrain, to check — **refrenarse** *vr* : to restrain oneself
refrendar *vt* **1** : to countersign, to endorse **2** : to stamp (a passport)
refrescante *adj* : refreshing

refrescar {72} *vt* **1** : to refresh, to cool **2** : to brush up (on) **3 refrescar la memoria** : to refresh one's memory — *vi* : to turn cooler
refresco *nm* : refreshment, soft drink
refriega *nf* : skirmish, scuffle
refrigeración *nf, pl* **-ciones 1** : refrigeration **2** : air-conditioning
refrigerador *nmf* NEVERA : refrigerator
refrigeradora *nf Col, Peru* : refrigerator
refrigerante *nm* : coolant
refrigerar *vt* **1** : to refrigerate **2** : to air-condition
refrigerio *nm* : snack, refreshments *pl*
refrito[1], **-ta** *adj* : refried
refrito[2] *nm* : rehash
refuerzo *nm* : reinforcement, support
refugiado, -da *n* : refugee
refugiar *vt* : to shelter — **refugiarse** *vr* ACOGERSE : to take refuge
refugio *nm* : refuge, shelter
refulgencia *nf* : brilliance, splendor
refulgir {35} *vi* : to shine brightly
refundir *vt* **1** : to recast (metals) **2** : to revise, to rewrite
refunfuñar *vi* : to grumble, to groan
refutar *vt* : to refute — **refutación** *nf*
regadera *nf* **1** : watering can **2** : shower head, shower **3** : sprinkler
regaderazo *nm Mex* : shower
regalar *vt* **1** OBSEQUIAR : to present (as a gift), to give away **2** : to regale, to entertain **3** : to flatter, to make a fuss over — **regalarse** *vr* : to pamper oneself
regalía *nf* : royalty, payment
regaliz *nm, pl* **-lices** : licorice
regalo *nm* **1** OBSEQUIO : gift, present **2** : pleasure, comfort **3** : treat
regañadientes *mpl* **a ~** : reluctantly, unwillingly
regañar *vt* : to scold, to give a talking to — *vi* **1** QUEJARSE : to grumble, to complain **2** REÑIR : to quarrel, to argue
regaño *nm fam* : scolding
regañon, -ñona *adj, mpl* **-ñones** *fam* : grumpy, irritable
regar {49} *vt* **1** : to irrigate **2** : to water **3** : to wash, to hose down **4** : to spill, to scatter
regata *nf* : regatta, yacht race
regate *nm* : dodge, feint
regatear *vt* **1** : to haggle over **2** ESCATIMAR : to skimp on, to be sparing with — *vi* : to bargain, to haggle
regateo *nm* : bargaining, haggling
regatón *nm, pl* **-tones** : ferrule, tip
regazo *nm* : lap (of a person)
regencia *nf* : regency
regenerar *vt* : to regenerate — **regenerarse** *vr* — **regeneración** *nf*
regentar *vt* : to run, to manage
regente *nmf* : regent
regidor, -dora *n* : town councillor
régimen *nm, pl* **regímenes 1** : regime **2** : diet **3** : regimen, rules *pl* ⟨régimen de vida : lifestyle⟩
regimiento *nm* : regiment
regio, -gia *adj* **1** : great, magnificent **2** : regal, royal
región *nf, pl* **regiones** : region, area
regional *adj* : regional — **regionalmente** *adv*
regir {28} *vt* **1** : to rule **2** : to manage, to run **3** : to control, to govern ⟨las costumbres que rigen la conducta : the customs which govern behavior⟩ — *vi* : to apply, to be in force ⟨las leyes rigen en los tres países : the laws apply in all three countries⟩ — **regirse** *vr* **~ por** : to go by, to be guided by
registrador[1], **-dora** *adj* **caja registradora** : cash register
registrador[2], **-dora** *n* : registrar, recorder
registrar *vt* **1** : to register, to record **2** GRABAR : to record, to tape **3** : to search, to examine — **registrarse** *vr* **1** INSCRIBIRSE : to register **2** OCURRIR : to happen, to occur
registro *nm* **1** : register **2** : registration **3** : registry, record office **4** : range (of a voice or musical instrument) **5** : search
regla *nf* **1** NORMA : rule, regulation **2** : ruler ⟨regla de cálculo : slide rule⟩ **3** MENSTRUACIÓN : period, menstruation
reglamentación *nf, pl* **-ciones 1** : regulation **2** : rules *pl*
reglamentar *vt* : to regulate, to set rules for
reglamentario, -ria *adj* : regulation, official ⟨equipo reglamentario : standard equipment⟩
reglamento *nm* : regulations *pl*, rules *pl* ⟨reglamento de tráfico : traffic regulations⟩
regocijar *vt* : to gladden, to delight — **regocijarse** *vr* : to rejoice
regocijo *nm* : delight, rejoicing
regordete, -ta *adj fam* LLENITO : chubby
regresar *vt* DEVOLVER : to give back — *vi* : to return, to come back, to go back
regresión *nf, pl* **-siones** : regression, return
regresivo, -va *adj* : regressive
regreso *nm* **1** : return **2 estar de regreso** : to be back, to be home
reguero *nm* **1** : irrigation ditch **2** : trail, trace **3 propagarse como reguero de pólvora** : to spread like wildfire
regulable *adj* : adjustable
regulación *nf, pl* **-ciones** : regulation, control
regulador[1], **-dora** *adj* : regulating, regulatory
regulador[2] *nm* **1** : regulator, governor **2 regulador de tiro** : damper (in a chimney)
regular[1] *vt* : to regulate, to control
regular[2] *adj* **1** : regular **2** : fair, OK, so-so **3** : medium, average **4 por lo regular** : in general, generally
regularidad *nf* : regularity

regularización *nf, pl* **-ciones** NORMALIZACIÓN : normalization
regularizar {21} *vt* NORMALIZAR : to normalize, to make regular
regularmente *adv* : regularly
regusto *nm* : aftertaste
rehabilitar *vt* **1** : to rehabilitate **2** : to reinstate **3** : renovate, to restore — **rehabilitación** *nf*
rehacer {40} *vt* **1** : to redo **2** : to remake, to repair, to renew — **rehacerse** *vr* **1** : to recover **2 ~ de** : to get over
rehecho *pp* → **rehacer**
rehén *nm, pl* **rehenes** : hostage
rehicieron, etc. → **rehacer**
rehizo → **rehacer**
rehuir {41} *vt* : to avoid, to shun
rehusar {8} *v* : to refuse
reimprimir *vt* : to reprint
reina *nf* : queen
reinado *nm* : reign
reinante *adj* **1** : reigning **2** : prevailing, current
reinar *vi* **1** : to reign **2** : to prevail
reincidencia *nf* : recidivism, relapse
reincidente *nmf* : backslider, recidivist
reincidir *vi* : to backslide, to retrogress
reincorporar *vt* : to reinstate — **reincorporarse** *vr* **~ a** : to return to, to rejoin
reiniciar *vt* **1** : to resume, to restart **2** : to reboot (a computer)
reino *nm* : kingdom, realm 〈reino animal : animal kingdom〉
reinstalar *vt* **1** : to reinstall **2** : to reinstate
reintegración *nf, pl* **-ciones** **1** : reinstatement, reintegration **2** : refund, reimbursement
reintegrar *vt* **1** : to reintegrate, reinstate **2** : to refund, to reimburse — **reintegrarse** *vr* **~ a** : to return to, to rejoin
reír {66} *vi* : to laugh — *vt* : to laugh at — **reírse** *vr*
reiteración *nf, pl* **-ciones** : reiteration, repetition
reiterado, -da *adj* : repeated 〈lo explicó en reiteradas ocasiones : he explained it repeatedly〉 — **reiteradamente** *adv*
reiterar *vt* : to reiterate, to repeat
reiterativo, -va *adj* : repetitive, repetitious
reivindicación *nf, pl* **-ciones** **1** : demand, claim **2** : vindication
reivindicar {72} *vt* **1** : to vindicate **2** : to demand, to claim **3** : to restore
reja *nf* **1** : grille, grating 〈entre rejas : behind bars〉 **2** : plowshare
rejilla *nf* : grille, grate, screen
rejuvenecer {53} *vt* : to rejuvenate — *vi* : to be rejuvenated — **rejuvenecerse** *vr*
rejuvenecimiento *nm* : rejuvenation
relación *nf, pl* **-ciones** **1** : relation, connection, relevance **2** : relationship **3** RELATO : account **4** LISTA : list **5 con relación a** *or* **en relación con** : in relation to, concerning **6 relaciones públicas** : public relations
relacionar *vt* : to relate, to connect — **relacionarse** *vr* **~ con** : to be connected to, to be linked with
relajación *nf, pl* **-ciones** : relaxation
relajado, -da *adj* **1** : relaxed, loose **2** : dissolute, depraved
relajante *adj* : relaxing
relajar *vt* : to relax, to slacken — *vi* : to be relaxing — **relajarse** *vr*
relajo *nm* **1** : commotion, ruckus **2** : joke, laugh 〈lo hizo de relajo : he did it for a laugh〉
relamerse *vr* : to smack one's lips, to lick one's chops
relámpago *nm* : flash of lightning
relampaguear *vi* : to flash
relanzar {21} *vt* : to relaunch
relatar *vt* : to relate, to tell
relatividad *nf* : relativity
relativo, -va *adj* **1** : relative **2 en lo relativo a** : with regard to, concerning — **relativamente** *adv*
relato *nm* **1** : story, tale **2** : account
releer {20} *vt* : to reread
relegar {52} *vt* **1** : to relegate **2 relegar al olvido** : to consign to oblivion
relevante *adj* : outstanding, important
relevar *vt* **1** : to relieve, to take over from **2 ~ de** : to exempt from — **relevarse** *vr* : to take turns
relevo *nm* **1** : relief, replacement **2** : relay 〈carrera de relevos : relay race〉
relicario *nm* **1** : reliquary **2** : locket
relieve *nm* **1** : relief, projection 〈mapa en relieve : relief map〉 〈letras en relieve : embossed letters〉 **2** : prominence, importance **3 poner en relieve** : to highlight, to emphasize
religión *nf, pl* **-giones** : religion
religiosamente *adv* : religiously, faithfully
religioso[1], -sa *adj* : religious
religioso[2], -sa *n* : monk *m*, nun *f*
relinchar *vi* : to neigh, to whinny
relincho *nm* : neigh, whinny
reliquia *nf* **1** : relic **2 reliquia de familia** : family heirloom
rellenar *vt* **1** : to refill **2** : to stuff, to fill **3** : to fill out
relleno[1], -na *adj* : stuffed, filled
relleno[2] *nm* : stuffing, filling
reloj *nm* **1** : clock **2** : watch **3 reloj de arena** : hourglass **4 reloj de pulsera** : wristwatch **5 como un reloj** : like clockwork
relojería *nf* **1** : watchmaker's shop **2** : watchmaking, clockmaking
reluciente *adj* : brilliant, shining
relucir {45} *vi* **1** : to glitter, to shine **2 salir a relucir** : to come to the surface **3 sacar a relucir** : to bring up, to mention
relumbrante *adj* : dazzling
relumbrar *vi* : to shine brightly
relumbrón *nm, pl* **-brones** **1** : flash, glare **2 de ~** : flashy, showy

remachar *vt* **1** : to rivet **2** : to clinch (a nail) **3** : to stress, to drive home — *vi* : to smash, to spike (a ball)
remache *nm* **1** : rivet **2** : smash, spike (in sports)
remanente *nm* **1** : remainder, balance **2** : surplus
remanso *nm* : pool
remar *vi* **1** : to row, to paddle **2** : to struggle, to toil
remarcar {72} *vt* : to emphasize, to stress
rematado, -da *adj* : utter, complete
rematador, -dora *n* : auctioneer
rematar *vt* **1** : to finish off **2** : to auction — *vi* **1** : to shoot **2** : to end
remate *nm* **1** : shot (in sports) **2** : auction **3** : end, conclusion **4 como ~** : to top it off **5 de ~** : completely, utterly
remecer {86} *vt* : to sway, to swing
remedar *vt* **1** IMITAR : to imitate, to copy **2** : to mimic, to ape
remediar *vt* **1** : to remedy, to repair **2** : to help out, to assist **3** EVITAR : to prevent, to avoid
remedio *nm* **1** : remedy, cure **2** : solution **3** : option ‹no me quedó más remedio : I had no other choice› ‹no hay remedio : it can't be helped› **4 poner remedio a** : to put a stop to **5 sin ~** : unavoidable, inevitable
remedo *nm* : imitation
rememorar *vi* : to recall ‹rememorar los viejos tiempos : to reminisce›
remendar {55} *vt* **1** : to mend, to patch, to darn **2** : to correct
remero, -ra *n* : rower
remesa *nf* **1** : remittance **2** : shipment
remezón *nm, pl* **-zones** : mild earthquake, tremor
remiendo *nm* **1** : patch **2** : correction
remilgado, -da *adj* **1** : prim, prudish **2** : affected
remilgo *nm* : primness, affectation
reminiscencia *nf* : reminiscence
remisión *nf, pl* **-siones 1** ENVÍO : sending, delivery **2** : remission **3** : reference, cross-reference
remiso, -sa *adj* **1** : lax, remiss **2** : reluctant
remitente[1] *nm* : return address
remitente[2] *nmf* : sender (of a letter, etc.)
remitir *vt* **1** : to send, to remit **2 ~ a** : to refer to, to direct to ‹nos remitió al diccionario : he referred us to the dictionary› — *vi* : to subside, to let up
remo *nm* **1** : paddle, oar **2** : rowing (sport)
remoción *nf, pl* **-ciones 1** : removal **2** : dismissal
remodelación *nf, pl* **-ciones 1** : remodeling **2** : reorganization, restructuring
remodelar *vt* **1** : to remodel **2** : to restructure
remojar *vt* **1** : to soak, to steep **2** : to dip, to dunk **3** : to celebrate with a drink
remojo *nm* **1** : soaking, steeping **2 poner en remojo** : to soak, to leave soaking
remolacha *nf* : beet
remolcador *nm* : tugboat
remolcar {72} *vt* : to tow, to haul
remolino *nm* **1** : whirlwind **2** : eddy, whirlpool **3** : crowd, throng **4** : cowlick
remolque *nm* **1** : towing, tow **2** : trailer **3 a ~** : in tow
remontar *vt* **1** : to overcome **2** SUBIR : to go up — **remontarse** *vr* **1** : to soar **2 ~ a** : to date from, to go back to
rémora *nf* : obstacle, hindrance
remorder {47} *vt* INQUIETAR : to trouble, to distress
remordimiento *nm* : remorse
remotamente *adv* : remotely, vaguely
remoto, -ta *adj* **1** : remote, unlikely ‹hay una posibilidad remota : there is a slim possibility› **2** : distant, far-off
remover {47} *vt* **1** : to stir **2** : to move around, to turn over **3** : to stir up **4** : to remove **5** : to dismiss
remozamiento *nm* : renovation
remozar {21} *vt* **1** : to renew, to brighten up **2** : to redo, to renovate
remuneración *nf, pl* **-ciones** : remuneration, pay
remunerar *vt* : to pay, to remunerate
remunerativo, -va *adj* : remunerative
renacer {48} *vi* : to be reborn, to revive
renacimiento *nm* **1** : rebirth, revival **2 el Renacimiento** : the Renaissance
renacuajo *nm* : tadpole, pollywog
renal *adj* : renal, kidney
rencilla *nf* : quarrel
renco, -ca *adj* : lame
rencor *nm* **1** : rancor, enmity, hostility **2 guardar rencor** : to hold a grudge
rencoroso, -sa *adj* : resentful, rancorous
rendición *nf, pl* **-ciones 1** : surrender, submission **2** : yield, return
rendido, -da *adj* **1** : submissive **2** : worn-out, exhausted **3** : devoted
rendija *nf* GRIETA : crack, split
rendimiento *nm* **1** : performance **2** : yield
rendir {54} *vt* **1** : to render, to give ‹rendir las gracias : to give thanks› ‹rendir homenaje a : to pay homage to› **2** : to yield **3** CANSAR : to exhaust — *vi* **1** CUNDIR : to progress, to make headway **2** : to last, to go a long way — **rendirse** *vr* : to surrender, to give up
renegado, -da *n* : renegade
renegar {49} *vi* **1 ~ de** : to renounce, to disown, to give up **2 ~ de** : to complain about — *vt* **1** : to deny vigorously **2** : to abhor, to hate
renegociar *vt* : to renegotiate — **renegociación** *nf*
renglón *nm, pl* **renglones 1** : line (of writing) **2** : merchandise, line (of products)

rengo, -ga *adj* : lame
renguear *vi* : to limp
reno *nm* : reindeer
renombrado, -da *adj* : renowned, famous
renombre *nm* NOMBRADÍA : renown, fame
renovable *adj* : renewable
renovación *nf, pl* **-ciones** **1** : renewal ⟨renovación de un contrato : renewal of a contract⟩ **2** : change, renovation
renovar {19} *vt* **1** : to renew, to restore **2** : to renovate
renquear *vi* : to limp, to hobble
renquera *nf* COJERA : limp, lameness
renta *nf* **1** : income **2** : rent **3 impuesto sobre la renta** : income tax
rentable *adj* : profitable
rentar *vt* **1** : to produce, to yield **2** ALQUILAR : to rent
renuencia *nf* : reluctance, unwillingness
renuente *adj* : reluctant, unwilling
renuncia *nf* **1** : resignation **2** : renunciation **3** : waiver
renunciar *vi* **1** : to resign **2 ~ a** : to renounce, to relinquish ⟨renunció al título : herelinquished the title⟩
reñido, -da *adj* **1** : tough, hard-fought **2** : at odds, on bad terms
reñir {67} *vi* **1** : to argue **2 ~ con** : to fall out with, to go up against — *vt* : to scold, to reprimand
reo, rea *n* **1** : accused, defendant **2** : offender, culprit
reojo *nm* **de ~** : out of the corner of one's eye ⟨una mirada de reojo : a sidelong glance⟩
reorganizar {21} *vt* : to reorganize — **reorganización** *nf*
repantigarse {52} *vr* : to slouch, to loll about
reparación *nf, pl* **-ciones** **1** : reparation, amends **2** : repair
reparar *vt* **1** : to repair, to fix, to mend **2** : to make amends for **3** : to correct **4** : to restore, to refresh — *vi* **1 ~ en** : to observe, to take notice of **2 ~ en** : to consider, to think about
reparo *nm* **1** : repair, restoration **2** : reservation, qualm ⟨no tuvieron reparos en decírmelo : they didn't hesitate to tell me⟩ **3 poner reparos a** : to find fault with, to object to
repartición *nf, pl* **-ciones** **1** : distribution **2** : department, division
repartidor[1], -dora *adj* : delivery ⟨camión repartidor : delivery truck⟩
repartidor[2], -dora *n* : delivery person, distributor
repartimiento *nm* → **repartición**
repartir *vt* **1** : to allocate **2** DISTRIBUIR : to distribute, to hand out **3** : to spread
reparto *nm* **1** : allocation **2** : distribution **3** : cast (of characters)
repasar *vt* **1** : to pass by again **2** : to review, to go over **3** : to mend
repaso *nm* **1** : review **2** : mending **3** : checkup, overhaul
repatriar {85} *vt* : to repatriate — **repatriación** *nf*
repavimentar *vt* : to resurface
repelente[1] *adj* : repellent, repulsive
repelente[2] *nm* : repellent ⟨repelente de insectos : insect repellent⟩
repeler *vt* **1** : to repel, to resist, to repulse **2** : to reject **3** : to disgust ⟨el sabor me repele : I find the taste repulsive⟩
repensar {55} *v* : to rethink, to reconsider
repente *nm* **1** : sudden movement, start ⟨de repente : suddenly⟩ **2** : fit, outburst ⟨un repente de ira : a fit of anger⟩
repentino, -na *adj* : sudden — **repentinamente** *adv*
repercusión *nf, pl* **-siones** : repercussion
repercutir *vi* **1** : to reverberate, to echo **2 ~ en** : to have effects on, to have repercussions on
repertorio *nm* : repertoire
repetición *nf, pl* **-ciones** **1** : repetition **2** : rerun, repeat
repetidamente *adv* : repeatedly
repetido, -da *adj* **1** : repeated, numerous **2 repetidas veces** : repeatedly, time and again
repetir {54} *vt* **1** : to repeat **2** : to have a second helping of — **repetirse** *vr* **1** : to repeat oneself **2** : to recur
repetitivo, -va *adj* : repetitive, repetitious
repicar {72} *vt* : to ring — *vi* : to ring out, to peal
repique *nm* : ringing, pealing
repisa *nf* : shelf, ledge ⟨repisa de chimenea : mantelpiece⟩ ⟨repisa de ventana : windowsill⟩
replantear *vt* : to redefine, to restate — **replantearse** *vr* : to reconsider
replegar {49} *vt* : to fold — **replegarse** *vr* RETIRARSE : to retreat, to withdraw
repleto, -ta *adj* **1** : replete, full **2 ~ de** : packed with, crammed with
réplica *nf* **1** : reply **2** : replica, reproduction **3** *Chile, Mex* : aftershock
replicación *nf, pl* **-ciones** : replication
replicar {72} *vi* **1** : to reply, to retort **2** : to argue, to answer back
repliegue *nm* **1** : fold **2** : retreat, withdrawal
repollo *nm* COL : cabbage
reponer {60} *vt* **1** : to replace, to put back **2** : to reinstate **3** : to reply — **reponerse** *vr* : to recover
reportaje *nm* : article, story, report
reportar *vt* **1** : to check, to restrain **2** : to bring, to carry, to yield ⟨me reportó numerosos beneficios : it brought me many benefits⟩ **3** : to report — **reportarse** *vr* **1** CONTENERSE : to control oneself **2** PRESENTARSE : to report, to show up
reporte *nm* : report
reportear *vt* : to report on, to cover

reportero, -ra *n* **1** : reporter **2 reportero gráfico** : photojournalist
reposado, -da *adj* : calm
reposar *vi* **1** : to rest, to repose **2** : to stand, to settle ⟨deje reposar la masa media hora : let the dough stand for half an hour⟩ **3** : to lie, to be buried — **reposarse** *vr* : to settle
reposición *nf, pl* **-ciones 1** : replacement **2** : reinstatement **3** : revival
repositorio *nm* : repository
reposo *nm* : repose, rest
repostar *vi* **1** : to stock up **2** : to refuel
repostería *nf* **1** : confectioner's shop **2** : pastry-making
repostero, -ra *n* : confectioner
repreguntar *vt* : to cross-examine
repreguntas *nfpl* : cross-examination
reprender *vt* : to reprimand, to scold
reprensible *adj* : reprehensible
represa *nf* : dam
represalia *nf* **1** : reprisal, retaliation **2 tomar represalias** : to retaliate
represar *vt* : to dam
representación *nf, pl* **-ciones 1** : representation **2** : performance **3 en representación de** : on behalf of
representante *nmf* **1** : representative **2** : performer
representar *vt* **1** : to represent, to act for **2** : to perform **3** : to look, to appear as **4** : to symbolize, to stand for **5** : to signify, to mean — **representarse** *vr* : to imagine, to picture
representativo, -va *adj* : representative
represión *nf, pl* **-siones** : repression
represivo, -va *adj* : repressive
reprimenda *nf* : reprimand
reprimir *vt* **1** : to repress **2** : to suppress, to stifle
reprobable *adj* : reprehensible, culpable
reprobación *nf* : disapproval
reprobar {19} *vt* **1** DESAPROBAR : to condemn, to disapprove of **2** : to fail (a course)
reprobatorio, -ria *adj* : disapproving, admonitory
reprochable *adj* : reprehensible, reproachable
reprochar *vt* : to reproach — **reprocharse** *vr*
reproche *nm* : reproach
reproducción *nf, pl* **-ciones** : reproduction
reproducir {61} *vt* : to reproduce — **reproducirse** *vr* **1** : to breed, to reproduce **2** : to recur
reproductor, -tora *adj* : reproductive
reptar *vi* : to crawl, to slither
reptil[1] *adj* : reptilian
reptil[2] *nm* : reptile
república *nf* : republic
republicanismo *nm* : republicanism
republicano, -na *adj & n* : republican
repudiar *vt* : to repudiate — **repudiación** *nf*
repudio *nm* : repudiation
repuesto[1] *pp* → **reponer**
repuesto[2] *nm* **1** : spare part **2 de ~** : spare ⟨rueda de repuesto : spare wheel⟩
repugnancia *nf* : repugnance
repugnante *adj* : repulsive, repugnant, revolting
repugnar *vt* : to cause repugnance, to disgust — **repugnarse** *vr*
repujar *vt* : to emboss
repulsivo, -va *adj* : repulsive
repuntar *vt Arg, Chile* : to round up (cattle) — *vi* : to begin to appear — **repuntarse** *vr* : to fall out, to quarrel
repuso, etc. → **reponer**
reputación *nf, pl* **-ciones** : reputation
reputar *vt* : to consider, to deem
requerir {76} *vt* **1** : to require, to call for **2** : to summon, to send for
requesón *nm, pl* **-sones** : curd cheese, cottage cheese
réquiem *nm* : requiem
requisa *nf* **1** : requisition **2** : seizure **3** : inspection
requisar *vt* **1** : to requisition **2** : to seize **3** INSPECCIONAR : to inspect
requisito *nm* **1** : requirement **2 requisito previo** : prerequisite
res *nf* **1** : beast, animal **2** *CA, Mex* : beef **3 reses** *nfpl* : cattle ⟨60 reses : 60 head of cattle⟩
resabio *nm* **1** VICIO : bad habit, vice **2** DEJO : aftertaste
resaca *nf* **1** : undertow **2** : hangover
resaltar *vi* **1** SOBRESALIR : to stand out **2 hacer resaltar** : to bring out, to highlight — *vt* : to stress, to emphasize
resarcimiento *nm* **1** : compensation **2** : reimbursement
resarcir {83} *vt* : to compensate, to indemnify — **resarcirse** *vr* **~ de** : to make up for
resbaladizo, -za *adj* **1** RESBALOSO : slippery **2** : tricky, ticklish, delicate
resbalar *vi* **1** : to slip, to slide **2** : to slip up, to make a mistake **3** : to skid — **resbalarse** *vr*
resbalón *nm, pl* **-lones** : slip
resbaloso, -sa *adj* : slippery
rescatar *vt* **1** : to rescue, to save **2** : to recover, to get back
rescate *nm* **1** : rescue **2** : recovery **3** : ransom
rescindir *vt* : to rescind, to annul, to cancel
rescisión *nf, pl* **-siones** : annulment, cancellation
rescoldo *nm* : embers *pl*
resecar {72} *vt* : to make dry, to dry up — **resecarse** *vr* : to dry up
reseco, -ca *adj* : dry, dried-up
resentido, -da *adj* : resentful
resentimiento *nm* : resentment
resentirse {76} *vr* **1** : to suffer, to be weakened **2** OFENDERSE : to be upset ⟨se resintió porque la insultaron : she got upset when they insulted her, she resented being insulted⟩ **3 ~ de** : to feel the effects of

reseña *nf* **1** : report, summary, review **2** : description

reseñar *vt* **1** : to review **2** DESCRIBIR : to describe

reserva *nf* **1** : reservation **2** : reserve **3** : confidence, privacy ⟨con la mayor reserva : in strictest confidence⟩ **4 de ~** : spare, in reserve **5 reservas** *nfpl* : reservations, doubts

reservación *nf, pl* **-ciones** : reservation

reservado, -da *adj* **1** : reserved, reticent **2** : confidential

reservar *vt* : to reserve — **reservarse** *vr* **1** : to save oneself **2** : to conceal, to keep to oneself

reservorio *nm* : reservoir, reserve

resfriado *nm* CATARRO : cold

resfriar {85} *vt* : to cool — **resfriarse** *vr* **1** : to cool off **2** : to catch a cold

resfrío *nm* : cold

resguardar *vt* : to safeguard, to protect — **resguardarse** *vr*

resguardo *nm* **1** : safeguard, protection **2** : receipt, voucher **3** : border guard, coast guard

residencia *nf* **1** : residence **2** : boarding house

residencial *adj* : residential

residente *adj & nmf* : resident

residir *vi* **1** VIVIR : to reside, to dwell **2 ~ en** : to lie in, to consist of

residual *adj* : residual

residuo *nm* **1** : residue **2** : remainder **3 residuos** *nmpl* : waste ⟨residuos nucleares : nuclear waste⟩

resignación *nf, pl* **-ciones** : resignation

resignar *vt* : to resign — **resignarse** *vr* **~ a** : to resign oneself to

resina *nf* **1** : resin **2 resina epoxídica** : epoxy

resistencia *nf* **1** : resistance **2** AGUANTE : endurance, strength, stamina

resistente *adj* **1** : resistant **2** : strong, tough

resistir *vt* **1** : to stand, to bear, to tolerate **2** : to withstand — *vi* : to resist ⟨resistió hasta el último minuto : he held out until the last minute⟩ — **resistirse** *vr* **~ a** : to be resistant to, to be reluctant

resollar {19} *vi* : to breathe heavily, to wheeze

resolución *nf, pl* **-ciones** **1** : resolution, settlement **2** : decision **3** : determination, resolve

resolver {89} *vt* **1** : to resolve, to settle **2** : to decide — **resolverse** *vr* : to make up one's mind

resonancia *nf* **1** : resonance **2** : impact, repercussions *pl*

resonante *adj* **1** : resonant **2** : tremendous, resounding ⟨un éxito resonante : a resounding success⟩

resonar {19} *vi* : to resound, to ring

resoplar *vi* **1** : to puff, to pant **2** : to snort

resoplo *nm* **1** : puffing, panting **2** : snort

resorte *nm* **1** MUELLE : spring **2** : elasticity **3** : influence, means *pl* ⟨tocar resortes : to pull strings⟩

resortera *nf Mex* : slingshot

respaldar *vt* : to back, to support, to endorse — **respaldarse** *vr* : to lean back

respaldo *nm* **1** : back (of an object) **2** : support, backing

respectar *vt* : to concern, to relate to ⟨por lo que a mí respecta : as far as I'm concerned⟩

respectivo, -va *adj* : respective — **respectivamente** *adv*

respecto *nm* **1 ~ a** : in regard to, concerning **2 al respecto** : on this matter, in this respect

respetable *adj* : respectable — **respetabilidad** *nf*

respetar *vt* : to respect

respeto *nm* **1** : respect, consideration **2 respetos** *nmpl* : respects ⟨presentar sus respetos : to pay one's respects⟩

respetuosidad *nf* : respectfulness

respetuoso, -sa *adj* : respectful — **respetuosamente** *adv*

respingo *nm* : start, jump

respiración *nf, pl* **-ciones** : respiration, breathing

respiradero *nm* : vent, ventilation shaft

respirador *nm* : respirator

respirar *v* : to breathe

respiratorio, -ria *adj* : respiratory

respiro *nm* **1** : breath **2** : respite, break

resplandecer {53} *vi* **1** : to shine **2** : to stand out

resplandeciente *adj* **1** : resplendent, shining **2** : radiant

resplandor *nm* **1** : brightness, brilliance, radiance **2** : flash

responder *vt* : to answer — *vi* **1** : to answer, to reply, to respond **2 ~ a** : to respond to ⟨responder al tratamiento : to respond to treatment⟩ **3 ~ de** : to answer for, to vouch for (something) **4 ~ por** : to vouch for (someone)

responsabilidad *nf* : responsibility

responsable *adj* : responsible — **responsablemente** *adv*

respuesta *nf* : answer, response

resquebrajar *vt* : to split, to crack — **resquebrajarse** *vr*

resquemor *nm* : resentment, bitterness

resquicio *nm* **1** : crack **2** : opportunity, chance **3** : trace ⟨sin un resquicio de remordimiento : without a trace of remorse⟩ **4 resquicio legal** : loophole

resta *nf* SUSTRACCIÓN : subtraction

restablecer {53} *vt* : to reestablish, to restore — **restablecerse** *vr* : to recover

restablecimiento *nm* **1** : reestablishment, restoration **2** : recovery

restallar *vi* : to crack, to crackle, to click

restallido *nm* : crack, crackle

restante *adj* **1** : remaining **2 lo restante, los restantes** : the rest

restañar *vt* : to stanch

restar *vt* **1** : to deduct, to subtract ⟨restar un punto : to deduct a point⟩

2 : to minimize, to play down — *vi* : to remain, to be left
restauración *nf, pl* **-ciones** **1** : restoration **2** : catering, food service
restaurante *nm* : restaurant
restaurar *vt* : to restore
restitución *nf, pl* **-ciones** : restitution, return
restituir {41} *vt* : to return, to restore, to reinstate
resto *nm* **1** : rest, remainder **2 restos** *nmpl* : remains ⟨restos de comida : leftovers⟩ ⟨restos arqueológicos : archeological ruins⟩ **3 restos mortales** : mortal remains
restorán *nm, pl* **-ranes** : restaurant
restregadura *nf* : scrub, scrubbing
restregar {49} *vt* **1** : to rub **2** : to scrub — **restregarse** *vr*
restricción *nf, pl* **-ciones** : restriction, limitation
restrictivo, -va *adj* : restrictive
restringido, -da *adj* LIMITADO : limited, restricted
restringir {35} *vt* LIMITAR : to restrict, to limit
restructuración *nf* : restructuring
restructurar *vt* : to restructure
resucitación *nf* : resuscitation ⟨resucitación cardiopulmonar : CPR, cardiopulmonary resuscitation⟩
resucitar *vt* **1** : to resuscitate, to revive, to resurrect **2** : to revitalize
resuello *nm* **1** : puffing, heavy breathing, wheezing **2** : break, breather
resuelto[1] *pp* → **resolver**
resuelto[2], **-ta** *adj* : determined, resolved, resolute
resulta *nf* **1** : consequence, result **2 a resultas de** *or* **de resultas de** : as a result of
resultado *nm* : result, outcome
resultante *adj & nf* : resultant
resultar *vi* **1** : to work, to work out ⟨mi idea no resultó : my idea didn't work out⟩ **2** : to prove, to turn out to be ⟨resultó bien simpático : he turned out to be very nice⟩ **3 ~ en** : to lead to, to result in **4 ~ de** : to be the result of
resumen *nm, pl* **-súmenes** **1** : summary, summation **2 en ~** : in summary, in short
resumidero *nm* : drain
resumir *v* : to summarize, to sum up
resurgimiento *nm* : resurgence
resurgir {35} *vi* : to reappear, to revive
resurrección *nf, pl* **-ciones** : resurrection
retablo *nm* **1** : tableau **2** : altarpiece
retador, -dora *n* : challenger (in sports)
retaguardia *nf* : rear guard
retahíla *nf* : string, series ⟨una retahíla de insultos : a volley of insults⟩
retaliación *nf, pl* **-ciones** : retaliation
retama *nf* : broom (plant)
retar *vt* DESAFIAR : to challenge, to defy
retardante *adj* : retardant
retardar *vt* **1** RETRASAR : to delay, to retard **2** : to postpone
retazo *nm* **1** : remnant, scrap **2** : fragment, piece ⟨retazos de su obra : bits and pieces from his writings⟩
retención *nf, pl* **-ciones** **1** : retention **2** : deduction, withholding
retener {80} *vt* **1** : to retain, to keep **2** : to withhold **3** : to detain
retentivo, -va *adj* : retentive
reticencia *nf* **1** : reluctance, reticence **2** : insinuation
reticente *adj* **1** : reluctant, reticent **2** : insinuating, misleading
retina *nf* : retina
retintín *nm, pl* **-tines** **1** : jingle, jangle **2 con ~** : sarcastically
retirada *nf* **1** : retreat ⟨batirse en retirada : to withdraw, to beat a retreat⟩ **2** : withdrawal (of funds) **3** : retirement **4** : refuge, haven
retirado, -da *adj* **1** : remote, distant, far off **2** : secluded, quiet
retirar *vt* **1** : to remove, to take away, to recall **2** : to withdraw, to take out — **retirarse** *vr* **1** REPLEGARSE : to retreat, to withdraw **2** JUBILARSE : to retire
retiro *nm* **1** JUBILACIÓN : retirement **2** : withdrawal, retreat **3** : seclusion
reto *nm* DESAFÍO : challenge, dare
retocar {72} *vt* : to touch up
retoñar *vi* : to sprout
retoño *nm* : sprout, shoot
retoque *nm* : retouching
retorcer {14} *vt* **1** : to twist **2** : to wring — **retorcerse** *vr* **1** : to get twisted, to get tangled up **2** : to squirm, to writhe, to wiggle about
retorcijón *nm, pl* **-jones** : cramp, sharp pain
retorcimiento *nm* **1** : twisting, wringing **2** : deviousness
retórica *nf* : rhetoric
retórico, -ca *adj* : rhetorical — **retóricamente** *adv*
retornar *v* : to return
retorno *nm* : return
retozar {21} *vi* : to frolic, to romp
retozo *nm* : frolicking
retozón, -zona *adj, mpl* **-zones** : playful
retracción *nf, pl* **-ciones** : retraction, withdrawal
retractable *adj* : retractable
retractación *nf, pl* **-ciones** : retraction (of a statement, etc.)
retractarse *vr* **1** : to withdraw, to back down **2 ~ de** : to take back, to retract
retraer {81} *vt* **1** : to bring back **2** : to dissuade — **retraerse** *vr* **1** RETIRARSE : to withdraw, to retire **2** REFUGIARSE : to take refuge
retraído, -da *adj* : withdrawn, retiring, shy
retraimiento *nm* **1** : shyness, timidity **2** : withdrawal
retrasado, -da *adj* **1** : retarded, mentally slow **2** : behind, in arrears **3**

: backward (of a country) **4** : slow (of a watch)
retrasar *vt* **1** DEMORAR, RETARDAR : to delay, to hold up **2** : to put off, to postpone — **retrasarse** *vr* **1** : to be late **2** : to fall behind
retraso *nm* **1** ATRASO : delay, lateness **2 retraso mental** : mental retardation
retratar *vt* **1** : to portray, to depict **2** : to photograph **3** : to paint a portrait of
retrato *nm* **1** : depiction, portrayal **2** : portrait, photograph
retrete *nm* : restroom, toilet
retribución *nf, pl* **-ciones** **1** : pay, payment **2** : reward
retribuir {41} *vt* **1** : to pay **2** : to reward
retroactivo, -va *adj* : retroactive — **retroactivamente** *adv*
retroalimentación *nf, pl* **-ciones** : feedback
retroceder *vi* **1** : to move back, to turn back **2** : to back off, to back down **3** : to recoil (of a firearm)
retroceso *nm* **1** : backward movement **2** : backing down **3** : setback, relapse **4** : recoil
retrógrado, -da *adj* **1** : reactionary **2** : retrograde
retropropulsión *nf* : jet propulsion
retrospectiva *nf* : retrospective, hindsight
retrospectivo, -va *adj* **1** : retrospective **2 mirada retrospectiva** : backward glance
retrovisor *nm* : rearview mirror
retruécano *nm* : pun, play on words
retumbar *vi* **1** : to boom, to thunder **2** : to resound, to reverberate
retumbo *nm* : booming, thundering, roll
retuvo, etc. → **retener**
reubicar {72} *vt* : to relocate — **reubicación** *nf*
reuma *or* **reúma** *nmf* → **reumatismo**
reumático, -ca *adj* : rheumatic
reumatismo *nm* : rheumatism
reunión *nf, pl* **-niones** **1** : meeting **2** : gathering, reunion
reunir {68} *vt* **1** : to unite, to join, to bring together **2** : to have, to possess <reunieron los requisitos necesarios : they fulfilled the necessary requirements> **3** : to gather, to collect, to raise (funds) — **reunirse** *vr* : to meet
reutilizable *adj* : reusable
reutilizar {21} *vt* : to recycle, to reuse
revalidar *vt* **1** : to confirm, to ratify **2** : to defend (a title)
revaluar {3} *vt* : to reevaluate — **revaluación** *n*
revancha *nf* **1** DESQUITE : revenge, requital **2** : rematch
revelación *nf, pl* **-ciones** : revelation
revelado *nm* : developing (of film)
revelador[1], **-dora** *adj* : revealing
revelador[2] *nm* : developer
revelar *vt* **1** : to reveal, to disclose **2** : to develop (film)
revendedor, -dora *n* **1** : scalper **2** DETALLISTA : retailer
revender *vt* **1** : to resell **2** : to scalp
reventa *nf* **1** : resale **2** : scalping
reventar {55} *vi* **1** ESTALLAR, EXPLOTAR : to burst, to blow up **2** ~ **de** : to be bursting with — *vt* **1** : to burst **2** *fam* : to annoy, to rile
reventón *nm, pl* **-tones** **1** : burst, bursting **2** : blowout, flat tire **3** *Mex fam* : bash, party
reverberar *vi* : to reverberate — **reverberación** *nf*
reverdecer {53} *vi* **1** : to grow green again **2** : to revive
reverencia *nf* **1** : reverence **2** : bow, curtsy
reverenciar *vt* : to revere, to venerate
reverendo[1], **-da** *adj* **1** : reverend **2** *fam* : total, absolute <es un reverendo imbécil : he is a complete idiot>
reverendo[2], **-da** *n* : reverend
reverente *adj* : reverent
reversa *nf Col, Mex* : reverse (gear)
reversible *adj* : reversible
reversión *nf, pl* **-siones** : reversion
reverso *nm* **1** : back, other side **2 el reverso de la medalla** : the complete opposite
revertir {76} *vi* **1** : to revert, to go back **2** ~ **en** : to result in, to end up as
revés *nm, pl* **reveses** **1** : back, wrong side **2** : setback, reversal **3** : backhand (in sports) **4 al revés** : the other way around, upside down, inside out **5 al revés de** : contrary to
revestimiento *nm* : covering, facing (of a building)
revestir {54} *vt* **1** : to coat, to cover, to surface **2** : to conceal, to disguise **3** : to take on, to assume <la reunión revistió gravedad : the meeting took on a serious note>
revisar *vt* **1** : to examine, to inspect, to check **2** : to check over, to overhaul (machinery) **3** : to revise
revisión *nf, pl* **-siones** **1** : revision **2** : inspection, check
revisor, -sora *n* **1** : inspector **2** : conductor (on a train)
revista *nf* **1** : magazine, journal **2** : revue **3 pasar revista** : to review, to inspect
revistar *vt* : to review, to inspect
revitalizar {21} *vt* : to revitalize — **revitalización** *nf*
revivir *vi* : to revive, to come alive again — *vt* : to relive
revocación *nf, pl* **-ciones** : revocation, repeal
revocar {72} *vt* **1** : to revoke, to repeal **2** : to plaster (a wall)
revolcar {82} *vt* : to knock over, to knock down — **revolcarse** *vr* : to roll around, to wallow
revolcón *nm, pl* **-cones** *fam* : tumble, fall
revolotear *vi* : to flutter around, to flit
revoloteo *nm* : fluttering, flitting

revoltijo *nm* **1** FÁRRAGO : mess, jumble **2** *Mex* : traditional seafood dish
revoltoso, -sa *adj* : unruly, rebellious
revolución *nf, pl* **-ciones** : revolution
revolucionar *vt* : to revolutionize
revolucionario, -ria *adj & n* : revolutionary
revolver {89} *vt* **1** : to move about, to mix, to shake, to stir **2** : to upset (one's stomach) **3** : to mess up, to rummage through ⟨revolver la casa : to turn the house upside down⟩ — **revolverse** *vr* **1** : to toss and turn **2** VOLVERSE : to turn around
revólver *nm* : revolver
revoque *nm* : plaster
revuelo *nm* **1** : fluttering **2** : commotion, stir
revuelta *nf* : uprising, revolt
revuelto[1] *pp* → **revolver**
revuelto[2]**, -ta** *adj* **1** : choppy, rough ⟨mar revuelto : rough sea⟩ **2** : untidy **3 huevos revueltos** : scrambled eggs
rey *nm* : king
reyerta *nf* : brawl, fight
rezagado, -da *n* : straggler, latecomer
rezagar {52} *vt* **1** : to leave behind **2** : to postpone — **rezagarse** *vr* : to fall behind, to lag
rezar {21} *vi* **1** : to pray **2** : to say ⟨como reza el refrán : as the saying goes⟩ **3 ~ con** : to concern, to have to do with — *vt* : to say, to recite ⟨rezar un Ave María : to say a Hail Mary⟩
rezo *nm* : prayer, praying
rezongar {52} *vi* : to gripe, to grumble
rezumar *v* : to ooze, to leak
ría[1]**, etc.** → **reír**
ría[2] *nf* : estuary
riachuelo *nm* ARROYO : brook, stream
riada *nf* : flood
ribera *nf* : bank, shore
ribete *nm* **1** : border, trim **2** : frill, adornment **3 ribetes** *nmpl* : hint, touch ⟨tiene sus ribetes de genio : there's a touch of genius in him⟩
ribetear *vt* : to border, to edge, to trim
ricamente *adv* : richly, splendidly
rice, etc. → **rizar**
rico[1]**, -ca** *adj* **1** : rich, wealthy **2** : fertile **3** : luxurious, valuable **4** : delicious **5** : adorable, lovely **6** : great, wonderful
rico[2]**, -ca** *n* : rich person
ridiculez *nf, pl* **-leces** : ridiculousness, absurdity
ridiculizar {21} *vt* : to ridicule
ridículo[1]**, -la** *adj* ABSURDO, DISPARATADO : ridiculous, ludicrous — **ridículamente** *adv*
ridículo[2]**, -la** *n* **1 hacer el ridículo** : to make a fool of oneself **2 poner en ridículo** : to ridicule
ríe, etc. → **reír**
riega, riegue etc. → **regar**
riego *nm* : irrigation
riel *nm* : rail, track
rienda *nf* **1** : rein **2 dar rienda suelta a** : to give free rein to **3 llevar las riendas** : to be in charge **4 tomar las riendas** : to take control
riesgo *nm* : risk
riesgoso, -sa *adj* : risky
rifa *nf* : raffle
rifar *vt* : to raffle — *vi* : to quarrel, to fight
rifle *nm* : rifle
rige, rija etc. → **regir**
rigidez *nf, pl* **-deces** **1** : rigidity, stiffness ⟨rigidez cadavérica : rigor mortis⟩ **2** : inflexibility
rígido, -da *adj* **1** : rigid, stiff **2** : strict — **rígidamente** *adv*
rigor *nm* **1** : rigor, harshness **2** : precision, meticulousness **3 de ~** : usual ⟨la respuesta de rigor : the standard reply⟩ **4 de ~** : essential, obligatory **5 en ~** : strictly speaking, in reality
riguroso, -sa *adj* : rigorous — **rigurosamente** *adv*
rima *nf* **1** : rhyme **2 rimas** *nfpl* : verse, poetry
rimar *vi* : to rhyme
rimbombante *adj* **1** : grandiose, showy **2** : bombastic, pompous
rímel *or* **rimel** *nm* : mascara
rin *nm Col, Mex* : wheel, rim (of a tire)
rincón *nm, pl* **rincones** : corner, nook
rinde, etc. → **rendir**
rinoceronte *nm* : rhinoceros
riña *nf* **1** : fight, brawl **2** : dispute, quarrel
riñe, etc. → **reñir**
riñón *nm, pl* **riñones** : kidney
río[1] → **reír**
río[2] *nm* **1** : river **2** : torrent, stream ⟨un río de lágrimas : a flood of tears⟩
ripio *nm* **1** : debris, rubble **2** : gravel
riqueza *nf* **1** : wealth, riches *pl* **2** : richness **3 riquezas naturales** : natural resources
risa *nf* **1** : laughter, laugh **2 dar risa** : to make laugh ⟨me dio mucha risa : I found it very funny⟩ **3** *fam* **morirse de la risa** : to die laughing, to crack up
risco *nm* : crag, cliff
risible *adj* IRRISORIO : ludicrous, laughable
risita *nf* : giggle, titter, snicker
risotada *nf* : guffaw
ristra *nf* : string, series *pl*
risueño, -ña *adj* **1** : cheerful, pleasant **2** : promising
rítmico, -ca *adj* : rhythmical, rhythmic — **rítmicamente** *adv*
ritmo *nm* **1** : rhythm **2** : pace, tempo ⟨trabajó a ritmo lento : she worked at a slow pace⟩
rito *nm* : rite, ritual
ritual *adj & nm* : ritual — **ritualmente** *adv*
rival *adj & nmf* COMPETIDOR : rival
rivalidad *nf* : rivalry, competition
rivalizar {21} *vi* **~ con** : to rival, to compete with

rizado, -da *adj* **1** : curly **2** : ridged **3** : ripply, undulating

rizar {21} *vt* **1** : to curl **2** : to ripple, to ruffle (a surface) **3** : to crumple, to fold — **rizarse** *vr* **1** : to frizz **2** : to ripple

rizo *nm* **1** : curl **2** : loop (in aviation)

robalo *or* **róbalo** *nm* : sea bass

robar *vt* **1** : to steal **2** : to rob, to burglarize **3** SECUESTRAR : to abduct, to kidnap **4** : to captivate — *vi* **~ en** : to break into

roble *nm* : oak

robo *nm* : robbery, theft

robot *nm, pl* **robots** : robot

robótica *nf* : robotics

robustecer {53} *vt* : to grow stronger, to strengthen

robustez *nf* : sturdiness, robustness

robusto, -ta *adj* : robust, sturdy

roca *nf* : rock, boulder

roce[1], **etc.** → **rozar**

roce[2] *nm* **1** : rubbing, chafing **2** : brush, graze, touch **3** : close contact, familiarity **4** : friction, disagreement

rociador *nm* : sprinkler

rociar {85} *vt* : to spray, to sprinkle

rocío *nm* **1** : dew **2** : shower, light rain

rock *or* **rock and roll** *nm* : rock, rock and roll

rocola *nf* : jukebox

rocoso, -sa *adj* : rocky

rodada *nf* : track (of a tire), rut

rodado, -da *adj* **1** : wheeled **2** : dappled (of a horse)

rodadura *nf* : rolling, taxiing

rodaja *nf* : round, slice

rodaje *nm* **1** : filming, shooting **2** : breaking in (of a vehicle)

rodamiento *nm* **1** : bearing ⟨rodamiento de bolas : ball bearings⟩ **2** : rolling

rodante *adj* : rolling

rodar {19} *vi* **1** : to roll, to roll down, to roll along ⟨rodé por la escalera : I tumbled down the stairs⟩ ⟨todo rodaba bien : everthing was going along well⟩ **2** GIRAR : to turn, to go around **3** : to move about, to travel ⟨andábamos rodando por todas partes : we drifted along from place to place⟩ — *vt* **1** : to film, to shoot **2** : to break in (a new vehicle)

rodear *vt* **1** : to surround **2** : to round up (cattle) — *vi* **1** : to go around **2** : to beat around the bush — **rodearse** *vr* **~ de** : to surround oneself with

rodeo *nm* **1** : rodeo, roundup **2** DESVÍO : detour **3** : evasion ⟨andar con rodeos : to beat around the bush⟩ ⟨sin rodeos : without reservations⟩

rodilla *nf* : knee

rodillo *nm* **1** : roller **2** : rolling pin

rododendro *nm* : rhododendron

roedor[1], **-dora** *adj* : gnawing

roedor[2] *nm* : rodent

roer {69} *vt* **1** : to gnaw **2** : to eat away at, to torment

rogar {16} *vt* : to beg, to request — *vi* **1** : to beg, to plead **2** : to pray

roiga, etc. → **roer**

rojez *nf* : redness

rojizo, -za *adj* : reddish

rojo[1], **-ja** *adj* **1** : red **2 ponerse rojo** : to blush

rojo[2] *nm* : red

rol *nm* **1** : role **2** : list, roll

rollo *nm* **1** : roll, coil ⟨un rollo de cinta : a roll of tape⟩ ⟨en rollo : rolled up⟩ **2** *fam* : roll of fat **3** *fam* : boring speech, lecture

romance *nm* **1** : Romance language **2** : ballad **3** : romance **4 en buen romance** : simply stated, simply put

romano, -na *adj & n* : Roman

romanticismo *nm* : romanticism

romántico, -ca *adj* : romantic — **románticamente** *adv*

rombo *nm* : rhombus

romería *nf* **1** : pilgrimage, procession **2** : crowd, gathering

romero[1], **-ra** *n* PEREGRINO : pilgrim

romero[2] *nm* : rosemary

romo, -ma *adj* : blunt, dull

rompecabezas *nms & pl* : puzzle, riddle

rompehielos *nms & pl* : icebreaker (ship)

rompehuelgas *nmfs & pl* ESQUIROL : strikebreaker, scab

rompenueces *nms & pl* : nutcracker

rompeolas *ns & pl* : breakwater, jetty

romper {70} *vt* **1** : to break, to smash **2** : to rip, to tear **3** : to break off (relations), to break (a contract) **4** : to break through, to break down **5** GASTAR : to wear out — *vi* **1** : to break ⟨al romper del día : at the break of day⟩ **2 ~ a** : to begin to, to burst out with ⟨romper a llorar : to burst into tears⟩ **3 ~ con** : to break off with

rompope *nm CA, Mex* : drink similar to eggnog

ron *nm* : rum

roncar {72} *vi* **1** : to snore **2** : to roar

ronco, -ca *adj* **1** : hoarse **2** : husky (of the voice) — **roncamente** *adv*

ronda *nf* **1** : beat, patrol **2** : round (of drinks, of negotiations, of a game)

rondar *vt* **1** : to patrol **2** : to hang around ⟨siempre está rondando la calle : he's always hanging around the street⟩ **3** : to be approximately ⟨debe rondar los cincuenta : he must be about 50⟩ — *vi* **1** : to be on patrol **2** : to prowl around, to roam about

ronque, etc. → **roncar**

ronquera *nf* : hoarseness

ronquido *nm* **1** : snore **2** : roar

ronronear *vi* : to purr

ronroneo *nm* : purr, purring

ronzal *nm* : halter (for an animal)

ronzar {21} *v* : to munch, to crunch

roña *nf* **1** : mange **2** : dirt, filth **3** *fam* : stinginess

roñoso, -sa *adj* **1** : mangy **2** : dirty **3** *fam* : stingy

ropa *nf* **1** : clothes *pl,* clothing **2 ropa interior** : underwear

ropaje *nm* : apparel, garments *pl,* regalia

ropero *nm* ARMARIO, CLÓSET : wardrobe, closet

rosa[1] *adj* : rose-colored, pink

rosa[2] *nm* : rose, pink (color)

rosa[3] *nf* : rose (flower)

rosáceo, -cea *adj* : pinkish

rosado[1], **-da** *adj* **1** : pink **2 vino rosado** : rosé

rosado[2] *nm* : pink (color)

rosal *nm* : rosebush

rosario *nm* **1** : rosary **2** : series ⟨un rosario de islas : a string of islands⟩

rosbif *nm* : roast beef

rosca *nf* **1** : thread (of a screw) ⟨una tapa a rosca : a screw top⟩ **2** : ring, coil

roseta *nf* : rosette

rosquilla *nf* : ring-shaped pastry, doughnut

rostro *nm* : face, countenance

rotación *nf, pl* **-ciones** : rotation

rotar *vt* : to rotate, to turn — *vi* : to turn, to spin

rotativo[1], **-va** *adj* : rotary

rotativo[2] *nm* : newspaper

rotatorio, -ria *adj* → **rotativo**[1]

roto[1] *pp* → **romper**

roto[2], **-ta** *adj* **1** : broken **2** : ripped, torn

rotonda *nf* **1** : traffic circle, rotary **2** : rotunda

rotor *nm* : rotor

rótula *nf* : kneecap

rotular *vt* **1** : to head, to entitle **2** : to label

rótulo *nm* **1** : heading, title **2** : label, sign

rotundo, -da *adj* **1** REDONDO : round **2** : categorical, absolute ⟨un éxito rotundo : a resounding success⟩ — **rotundamente** *adv*

rotura *nf* : break, tear, fracture

roya *nf* : plant rust

roya, etc. → **roer**

rozado, -da *adj* GASTADO : worn

rozadura *nf* **1** : scratch, abrasion **2** : rubbed spot, sore

rozar {21} *vt* **1** : to chafe, to rub against **2** : to border on, to touch on **3** : to graze, to touch lightly — **rozarse** *vr* **~ con** *fam* : to rub shoulders with

ruandés, -desa *adj & n* : Rwandan

ruano, -na *adj* : roan

rubí *nm, pl* **rubíes** : ruby

rubio, -bia *adj & n* : blond

rublo *nm* : ruble

rubor *nm* **1** : flush, blush **2** : rouge, blusher

ruborizarse {21} *vr* : to blush

rubrica *nf* : title, heading

rubricar {72} *vt* **1** : sign with a flourish ⟨firmado y rubricado : signed and sealed⟩ **2** : to endorse, to sanction

rubro *nm* **1** : heading, title **2** : line, area (in business)

rudeza *nf* ASPEREZA : roughness, coarseness

rudimentario, -ria *adj* : rudimentary — **rudimentariamente** *adv*

rudimento *nm* : rudiment, basics *pl*

rudo, -da *adj* **1** : rough, harsh **2** : coarse, unpolished — **rudamente** *adv*

rueda[1], **etc.** → **rodar**

rueda[2] *nf* **1** : wheel **2** RODAJA : round slice **3** : circle, ring **4 rueda de andar** : treadmill **5 rueda de prensa** : press conference **6 ir sobre ruedas** : to go smoothly

ruedita *nf* : caster (on furniture)

ruedo *nm* **1** : bullring, arena **2** : rotation, turn **3** : hem

ruega, ruegue etc. → **rogar**

ruego *nm* : request, appeal, plea

rugido *nm* : roar

rugir {35} *vi* : to roar

ruibarbo *nm* : rhubarb

ruido *nm* : noise, sound

ruidoso, -sa *adj* : loud, noisy — **ruidosamente** *adv*

ruin *adj* **1** : base, despicable **2** : mean, stingy

ruina *nf* **1** : ruin, destruction **2** : downfall, collapse **3 ruinas** *nfpl* : ruins, remains

ruinoso, -sa *adj* **1** : run-down, dilapidated **2** : ruinous, disastrous

ruiseñor *nm* : nightingale

ruja, etc. → **rugir**

ruleta *nf* : roulette

rulo *nm* : curler, roller

rumano, -na *n* : Romanian, Rumanian

rumbo *nm* **1** : direction, course ⟨con rumbo a : bound for, heading for⟩ ⟨perder el rumbo : to go off course, to lose one's bearings⟩ ⟨sin rumbo : aimless, aimlessly⟩ **2** : ostentation, pomp **3** : lavishness, generosity

rumiante *adj & nm* : ruminant

rumiar *vt* : to ponder, to mull over — *vi* **1** : to chew the cud **2** : to ruminate, to ponder

rumor *nm* **1** : rumor **2** : murmur

rumorearse *or* **rumorarse** *vr* : to be rumored ⟨se rumorea que se va : rumor has it that she's leaving⟩

rumoroso, -sa *adj* : murmuring, babbling ⟨un arroyo rumoroso : a babbling brook⟩

rupia *nf* : rupee

ruptura *nf* **1** : break **2** : breaking, breach (of a contract) **3** : breaking off, breakup

rural *adj* : rural

ruso[1], **-sa** *adj & n* : Russian

ruso[2] *nm* : Russian (language)

rústico[1], **-ca** *adj* : rural, rustic

rústico[2], **-ca** *n* : rustic, country dweller

ruta *nf* : route

rutina *nf* : routine, habit

rutinario, -ria *adj* : routine, ordinary ⟨visita rutinaria : routine visit⟩ — **rutinariamente** *adv*

S

s *nf* : twentieth letter of the Spanish alphabet

sábado *nm* **1** : Saturday **2** : Sabbath

sábalo *nm* : shad

sabana *nf* : savanna

sábana *nf* : sheet, bedsheet

sabandija *nf* BICHO : bug, small reptile, pesky creature

sabático, -ca *adj* : sabbatical

sabedor, -dora *adj* : aware, informed

sabelotodo *nmf fam* : know-it-all

saber[1] {71} *vt* **1** : to know **2** : to know how to, to be able to ⟨sabe tocar el violín : she can play the violin⟩ **3** : to learn, to find out **4 a ~** : to wit, namely — *vi* **1** : to know, to suppose **2** : to be informed ⟨supimos del desastre : we heard about the disaster⟩ **3** : to taste ⟨esto no sabe bien : this doesn't taste right⟩ **4 ~ a** : to taste like ⟨sabe a naranja : it tastes like orange⟩ — **saberse** *vr* : to know ⟨ese chiste no me lo sé : I don't know that joke⟩

saber[2] *nm* : knowledge, learning

sabiamente *adv* : wisely

sabido, -da *adj* : well-known

sabiduría *nf* **1** : wisdom **2** : learning, knowledge

sabiendas *adv* **1 a ~** : knowingly **2 a sabiendas de que** : knowing full well that

sabio[1], **-bia** *adj* **1** PRUDENTE : wise, sensible **2** DOCTO : learned

sabio[2], **-bia** *n* **1** : wise person **2** : savant, learned person

sable *nm* : saber, cutlass

sabor *nm* **1** : flavor, taste **2 sin ~** : flavorless

saborear *vt* **1** : to taste, to savor **2** : to enjoy, to relish

sabotaje *nm* : sabotage

saboteador, -dora *n* : saboteur

sabotear *vt* : to sabotage

sabrá, etc. → **saber**

sabroso, -sa *adj* **1** RICO : delicious, tasty **2** AGRADABLE : pleasant, nice, lovely

sabueso *nm* **1** : bloodhound **2** *fam* : detective, sleuth

sacacorchos *nms & pl* : corkscrew

sacapuntas *nms & pl* : pencil sharpener

sacar {72} *vt* **1** : to pull out, to take out ⟨saca el pollo del congelador : take the chicken out of the freezer⟩ **2** : to get, to obtain ⟨saqué un 100 en el examen : I got 100 on the exam⟩ **3** : to get out, to extract ⟨le saqué la información : I got the information from him⟩ **4** : to stick out ⟨sacar la lengua : to stick out one's tongue⟩ **5** : to bring out, to introduce ⟨sacar un libro : to publish a book⟩ ⟨sacaron una moda nueva : they introduced a new style⟩ **6** : to take (photos) **7** : to make (copies) — *vi* **1** : to kick off (in soccer or football) **2** : to serve (in sports)

sacarina *nf* : saccharin

sacarosa *nf* : sucrose

sacerdocio *nm* : priesthood

sacerdotal *adj* : priestly

sacerdote, -tisa *n* : priest *m*, priestess *f*

saciar *vt* **1** HARTAR : to sate, to satiate **2** SATISFACER : to satisfy

saciedad *nf* : satiety

saco *nm* **1** : bag, sack **2** : sac **3** : jacket, sport coat

sacramento *nm* : sacrament — **sacramental** *adj*

sacrificar {72} *vt* : to sacrifice — **sacrificarse** *vr* : to sacrifice oneself, to make sacrifices

sacrificio *nm* : sacrifice

sacrilegio *nm* : sacrilege

sacrílego, -ga *adj* : sacrilegious

sacristán *nm, pl* **-tanes** : sexton, sacristan

sacristía *nf* : sacristy, vestry

sacro, -cra *adj* SAGRADO : sacred ⟨arte sacro : sacred art⟩

sacrosanto, -ta *adj* : sacrosanct

sacudida *nf* **1** : shaking **2** : jerk, jolt, shock **3** : shake-up, upheaval

sacudir *vt* **1** : to shake, to beat **2** : to jerk, to jolt **3** : to dust off **4** CONMOVER : to shake up, to shock — **sacudirse** *vr* : to shake off

sacudón *nm, pl* **-dones** : intense jolt or shake-up

sádico[1], **-ca** *adj* : sadistic

sádico[2], **-ca** *n* : sadist

sadismo *nm* : sadism

safari *nm* : safari

saga *nf* : saga

sagacidad *nf* : sagacity, shrewdness

sagaz *adj, pl* **sagaces** PERSPICAZ : shrewd, discerning, sagacious

Sagitario *nmf* : Sagittarius, Sagittarian

sagrado, -da *adj* : sacred, holy

sainete *nm* : comedy sketch, one-act farce ⟨este proceso es un sainete : these proceedings are a farce⟩

sajar *vt* : to lance, to cut open

sal[1] → **salir**

sal[2] *nf* **1** : salt **2** *CA, Mex* : misfortune, bad luck

sala *nf* **1** : living room **2** : room, hall ⟨sala de conferencias : lecture hall⟩ ⟨sala de urgencias : emergency room⟩ ⟨sala de baile : ballroom⟩

salado, -da *adj* **1** : salty **2 agua salada** : salt water

salamandra *nf* : salamander

salami *nm* : salami

salar *vt* **1** : to salt **2** : to spoil, to ruin **3** *CoRi, Mex* : to jinx, to bring bad luck

salarial *adj* : salary, salary-related

salario *nm* **1** : salary **2 salario mínimo** : minimum wage

salaz *adj, pl* **salaces** : salacious, lecherous

salchicha *nf* **1** : sausage **2** : frankfurter, wiener
salchichón *nf, pl* **-chones** : a type of deli meat
salchichonería *nf Mex* **1** : delicatessen **2** : cold cuts *pl*
saldar *vt* : to settle, to pay off ⟨saldar una cuenta : to settle an account⟩
saldo *nm* **1** : settlement, payment **2** : balance ⟨saldo de cuenta : account balance⟩ **3** : remainder, leftover merchandise
saldrá, etc. → **salir**
salero *nm* **1** : saltshaker **2** : wit, charm
salga, etc. → **salir**
salida *nf* **1** : exit ⟨salida de emergencia : emergency exit⟩ **2** : leaving, departure **3** SOLUCIÓN : way out, solution **4** : start (of a race) **5** OCURRENCIA : wisecrack, joke **6 salida del sol** : sunrise
saliente¹ *adj* **1** : departing, outgoing **2** : projecting **3** DESTACADO : salient, prominent
saliente² *nm* **1** : projection, protrusion **2 ventana en saliente** : bay window
salinidad *nf* : salinity, saltiness
salino, -na *adj* : saline ⟨solución salina : saline solution⟩
salir {73} *vi* **1** : to go out, to come out, to get out ⟨salimos todas las noches : we go out every night⟩ ⟨su libro acaba de salir : her book just came out⟩ **2** PARTIR : to leave, to depart **3** APARECER : to appear ⟨salió en todos los diarios : it came out in all the papers⟩ **4** : to project, to stick out **5** : to cost, to come to **6** RESULTAR : to turn out, to prove **7** : to come up, to occur ⟨salga lo que salga : whatever happens⟩ ⟨salió una oportunidad : an opportunity came up⟩ **8 ~ a** : to take after, to look like, to resemble **9 ~ con** : to go out with, to date — **salirse** *vr* **1** : to escape, to get out, to leak out **2** : to come loose, to come off **3 salirse con la suya** : to get one's own way
saliva *nf* : saliva
salivar *vi* : to salivate
salmo *nm* : psalm
salmón¹ *adj* : salmon-colored
salmón² *nm, pl* **salmones** : salmon
salmuera *nf* : brine
salobre *adj* : brackish, briny
salón *nm, pl* **salones** **1** : hall, large room ⟨salón de clase : classroom⟩ ⟨salón de baile : ballroom⟩ **2** : salon ⟨salón de belleza : beauty salon⟩ **3** : parlor, sitting room
salpicadera *nf Mex* : fender
salpicadura *nf* : spatter, splash
salpicar {72} *vt* **1** : to spatter, to splash **2** : to sprinkle, to scatter about
salpimentar {55} *vt* **1** : to season (with salt and pepper) **2** : to spice up
salsa *nf* **1** : sauce ⟨salsa picante : hot sauce⟩ ⟨salsa inglesa : Worcestershire sauce⟩ ⟨salsa tártara : tartar sauce⟩ **2** : gravy **3** : salsa (music) **4 salsa mexicana** : salsa (sauce)
salsero, -ra *n* : salsa musician
saltador, -dora *n* : jumper
saltamontes *nms & pl* : grasshopper
saltar *vi* **1** BRINCAR : to jump, to leap **2** : to bounce **3** : to come off, to pop out **4** : to shatter, to break **5** : to explode, to blow up — *vt* **1** : to jump, to jump over **2** : to skip, to miss — **saltarse** *vr* OMITIR : to skip, to omit ⟨me salté ese capítulo : I skipped that chapter⟩
saltarín, -rina *adj, mpl* **-rines** : leaping, hopping ⟨frijol saltarín : jumping bean⟩
salteado, -da *adj* **1** : sautéed **2** : jumbled up ⟨los episodios se transmitieron salteados : the episodes were broadcast in random order⟩
salteador *nm* : highwayman
saltear *vt* **1** SOFREÍR : to sauté **2** : to skip around, to skip over
saltimbanqui *nmf* : acrobat
salto *nm* **1** BRINCO : jump, leap, skip **2** : jump, dive (in sports) **3** : gap, omission **4 dar saltos** : to jump up and down **5** *or* **salto de agua** CATARATA : waterfall
saltón, -tona *adj, mpl* **saltones** : bulging, protruding
salubre *adj* : healthful, salubrious
salubridad *nf* : healthfulness, health
salud *nf* **1** : health ⟨buena salud : good health⟩ **2 ¡salud!** : bless you! (when someone sneezes) **3 ¡salud!** : cheers!, to your health!
saludable *adj* **1** SALUBRE : healthful **2** SANO : healthy, well
saludar *vt* **1** : to greet, to say hello to **2** : to salute — **saludarse** *vr*
saludo *nm* **1** : greeting, regards *pl* **2** : salute
salutación *nf, pl* **-ciones** : salutation
salva *nf* **1** : salvo, volley **2 salva de aplausos** : round of applause
salvación *nf, pl* **-ciones** **1** : salvation **2** RESCATE : rescue
salvado *nm* : bran
salvador, -dora *n* **1** : savior, rescuer **2 el Salvador** : the Savior
salvadoreño, -ña *adj & n* : Salvadoran, El Salvadoran
salvaguardar *vt* : to safeguard
salvaguardia *or* **salvaguarda** *nf* : safeguard, defense
salvajada *nf* ATROCIDAD : atrocity, act of savagery
salvaje¹ *adj* **1** : wild ⟨animales salvajes : wild animals⟩ **2** : savage, cruel **3** : primitive, uncivilized
salvaje² *nmf* : savage
salvajismo *nm* : savagery
salvamento *nm* **1** : rescuing, lifesaving **2** : salvation **3** : refuge
salvar *vt* **1** : to save, to rescue **2** : to cover (a distance) **3** : to get around (an obstacle), to overcome (a difficulty) **4**

: to cross, to jump across **5 salvando** : except for, excluding — **salvarse** *vr* **1** : to survive, to escape **2** : to save one's soul
salvavidas[1] *nms & pl* **1** : life preserver **2 bote salvavidas** : lifeboat
salvavidas[2] *nmf* : lifeguard
salvedad *nf* **1** EXCEPCIÓN : exception **2** : proviso, stipulation
salvia *nf* : sage (plant)
salvo[1], **-va** *adj* **1** : unharmed, sound ⟨sano y salvo : safe and sound⟩ **2 a ~** : safe from danger
salvo[2] *prep* **1** EXCEPTO : except (for), save ⟨todos asistirán salvo Jaime : all will attend except for Jaime⟩ **2 salvo que** : unless ⟨salvo que llueva : unless it rains⟩
salvoconducto *nm* : safe-conduct
samba *nf* : samba
San *adj* → **santo**[1]
sanar *vt* : to heal, to cure — *vi* : to get well, to recover
sanatorio *nm* **1** : sanatorium **2** : clinic, private hospital
sanción *nf, pl* **sanciones** : sanction
sancionar *vt* **1** : to penalize, to impose a sanction on **2** : to sanction, to approve
sancochar *vt* : to parboil
sandalia *nf* : sandal
sándalo *nm* : sandalwood
sandez *nf, pl* **sandeces** ESTUPIDEZ : nonsense, silly thing to say
sandía *nf* : watermelon
sandwich [ˈsandwitʃ, ˈsaŋgwitʃ] *nm, pl* **sandwiches** [-dwitʃɛs, -gwi-] EMPAREDADO : sandwich
saneamiento *nm* **1** : cleaning up, sanitation **2** : reorganizing, streamlining
sanear *vt* **1** : to clean up, to sanitize **2** : to reorganize, to streamline
sangrante *adj* **1** : bleeding **2** : flagrant, blatant
sangrar *vi* : to bleed — *vt* : to indent (a paragraph, etc.)
sangre *nf* **1** : blood **2 a sangre fría** : in cold blood **3 a sangre y fuego** : by violent force **4 pura sangre** : thoroughbred
sangría *nf* **1** : bloodletting **2** : sangria (wine punch) **3** : drain, draining ⟨una sangría fiscal : a financial drain⟩ **4** : indentation, indenting
sangriento, -ta *adj* **1** : bloody **2** : cruel
sanguijuela *nf* **1** : leech, bloodsucker **2** : sponger, leech
sanguinario, -ria *adj* : bloodthirsty
sanguíneo, -nea *adj* **1** : blood ⟨vaso sanguíneo : blood vessel⟩ **2** : sanguine, ruddy
sanidad *nf* **1** : health **2** : public health, sanitation
sanitario[1], **-ria** *adj* **1** : sanitary **2** : health ⟨centro sanitario : health center⟩
sanitario[2], **-ria** *n* : sanitation worker
sanitario[3] *nm Col, Mex, Ven* : toilet ⟨los sanitarios : the toilets, the restroom⟩
sano, -na *adj* **1** SALUDABLE : healthy **2** : wholesome **3** : whole, intact
santiaguino, -na *adj* : of or from Santiago, Chile
santiamén *nm* **en un santiamén** : in no time at all
santidad *nf* : holiness, sanctity
santificar {72} *vt* : to sanctify, to consecrate, to hallow
santiguarse {10} *vr* PERSIGNARSE : to cross oneself
santo[1], **-ta** *adj* **1** : holy, saintly ⟨el Santo Padre : the Holy Father⟩ ⟨una vida santa : a saintly life⟩ **2 Santo, Santa** (**San** *before names of masculine saints except those beginning with D or T*) : Saint ⟨Santa Clara : Saint Claire⟩ ⟨Santo Tomás : Saint Thomas⟩ ⟨San Francisco : Saint Francis⟩
santo[2], **-ta** *n* : saint
santo[3] *nm* **1** : saint's day **2** CUMPLEAÑOS : birthday
santuario *nm* : sanctuary
santurrón, -rrona *adj, mpl* **-rrones** : overly pious, sanctimonious — **santurronamente** *adv*
saña *nf* **1** : fury, rage **2** : viciousness ⟨con saña : viciously⟩
sapo *nm* : toad
saque[1], **etc.** → **sacar**
saque[2] *nm* **1** : kickoff (in soccer or football) **2** : serve, service (in sports)
saqueador, -dora *n* DEPREDADOR : plunderer, looter
saquear *vt* : to sack, to plunder, to loot
saqueo *nm* DEPREDACIÓN : sacking, plunder, looting
sarampión *nm* : measles *pl*
sarape *nm CA, Mex* : serape, blanket
sarcasmo *nm* : sarcasm
sarcástico, -ca *adj* : sarcastic
sarcófago *nm* : sarcophagus
sardina *nf* : sardine
sardónico, -ca *adj* : sardonic
sarga *nf* : serge
sargento *nmf* : sergeant
sarna *nf* : mange
sarnoso, -sa *adj* : mangy
sarpullido *nm* ERUPCIÓN : rash
sarro *nm* **1** : deposit, coating **2** : tartar, plaque
sarta *nf* **1** : string, series (of insults, etc.) **2** : string (of pearls, etc.)
sartén *nmf, pl* **sartenes** **1** : frying pan **2 tener la sartén por el mango** : to call the shots, to be in control
sasafrás *nm* : sassafras
sastre, -tra *n* : tailor
sastrería *nf* **1** : tailoring **2** : tailor's shop
Satanás *or* **Satán** *nm* : Satan, the devil
satánico, -ca *adj* : satanic
satélite *nm* : satellite
satín *or* **satén** *nm, pl* **satines** *or* **satenes** : satin
satinado, -da *adj* : satiny, glossy
sátira *nf* : satire
satírico, -ca *adj* : satirical, satiric
satirizar {21} *vt* : to satirize

sátiro *nm* : satyr
satisfacción *nf, pl* **-ciones** : satisfaction
satisfacer {74} *vt* **1** : to satisfy **2** : to fulfill, to meet **3** : to pay, to settle — **satisfacerse** *vr* **1** : to be satisfied **2** : to take revenge
satisfactorio, -ria *adj* : satisfactory — **satisfactoriamente** *adv*
satisfecho, -cha *adj* : satisfied, content, pleased
saturación *nf, pl* **-ciones** : saturation
saturar *vt* **1** : to saturate, to fill up **2** : to satiate, to surfeit
saturnismo *nm* : lead poisoning
Saturno *nm* : Saturn
sauce *nm* : willow
saúco *nm* : elder (tree)
saudí *or* **saudita** *adj & nmf* : Saudi, Saudi Arabian
sauna *nmf* : sauna
savia *nf* : sap
saxofón *nm, pl* **-fones** : saxophone
sazón[1] *nf, pl* **sazones** **1** : flavor, seasoning **2** : ripeness, maturity ⟨en sazón : in season, ripe⟩ **3 a la sazón** : at that time, then
sazón[2] *nmf, pl* **sazones** *Mex* : flavor, seasoning
sazonar *vt* CONDIMENTAR : to season, to spice
scanner *nm* → **escáner**
sé → **saber, ser**
se *pron* **1** : to him, to her, to you, to them ⟨se los daré a ella : I'll give them to her⟩ **2** : each other, one another ⟨se abrazaron : they hugged each other⟩ **3** : himself, herself, itself, yourself, yourselves, themselves ⟨se afeitó antes de salir : he shaved before leaving⟩ **4** (*used in passive constructions*) ⟨se dice que es hermosa : they say she's beautiful⟩ ⟨se habla inglés : English spoken⟩
sea, etc. → **ser**
sebo *nm* **1** : grease, fat **2** : tallow **3** : suet
secado *nm* : drying
secador *nm* : hair dryer
secadora *nf* **1** : dryer, clothes dryer **2** *Mex* : hair dryer
secante *nm* : blotting paper, blotter
secar {72} *v* : to dry — **secarse** *vr* **1** : to get dry **2** : to dry up
sección *nf, pl* **secciones** **1** : section ⟨sección transversal : cross section⟩ **2** : department, division
seco, -ca *adj* **1** : dry **2** DISECADO : dried ⟨fruta seca : dried fruit⟩ **3** : thin, lean **4** : curt, brusque **5** : sharp ⟨un golpe seco : a sharp blow⟩ **6 a secas** : simply, just ⟨se llama Chico, a secas : he's just called Chico⟩ **7 en ~** : abruptly, suddenly ⟨frenar en seco : to make a sudden stop⟩
secoya *nf* : sequoia, redwood
secreción *nf, pl* **-ciones** : secretion
secretar *vt* : to secrete
secretaría *nf* **1** : secretariat, administrative department **2** *Mex* : ministry, cabinet office
secretariado *nm* **1** : secretariat **2** : secretarial profession
secretario, -ria *n* : secretary — **secretarial** *adj*
secreto[1], **-ta** *adj* **1** : secret **2** : secretive — **secretamente** *adv*
secreto[2] *nm* **1** : secret **2** : secrecy
secta *nf* : sect
sectario, -ria *adj & n* : sectarian
sector *nm* : sector
secuaz *nmf, pl* **secuaces** : follower, henchman, underling
secuela *nf* : consequence, sequel ⟨las secuelas de la guerra : the aftermath of the war⟩
secuencia *nf* : sequence
secuestrador, -dora *n* **1** : kidnapper, abductor **2** : hijacker
secuestrar *vt* **1** RAPTAR : to kidnap, to abduct **2** : to hijack, to commandeer **3** CONFISCAR : to confiscate, to seize
secuestro *nm* **1** RAPTO : kidnapping, abduction **2** : hijacking **3** : seizure, confiscation
secular *adj* : secular — **secularismo** *nm* — **secularización** *nf*
secundar *vt* : to support, to second
secundaria *nf* **1** : secondary education, high school **2** *Mex* : junior high school, middle school
secundario, -ria *adj* : secondary
secuoya *nf* : sequoia
sed *nf* **1** : thirst ⟨tener sed : to be thirsty⟩ **2 tener sed de** : to hunger for, to thirst for
seda *nf* : silk
sedación *nf, pl* **-ciones** : sedation
sedal *nm* : fishing line
sedán *nm, pl* **sedanes** : sedan
sedante *adj & nm* CALMANTE : sedative
sedar *vt* : to sedate
sede *nf* **1** : seat, headquarters **2** : venue, site **3 la Santa Sede** : the Holy See
sedentario, -ria *adj* : sedentary
sedición *nf, pl* **-ciones** : sedition — **sedicioso, -sa** *adj*
sediento, -ta *adj* : thirsty, thirsting
sedimentación *nf, pl* **-ciones** : sedimentation
sedimentario, -ria *adj* : sedimentary
sedimento *nm* : sediment
sedoso, -sa *adj* : silky, silken
seducción *nf, pl* **-ciones** : seduction
seducir {61} *vt* **1** : to seduce **2** : to captivate, to charm
seductivo, -va *adj* : seductive
seductor[1], **-tora** *adj* **1** SEDUCTIVO : seductive **2** ENCANTADOR : charming, alluring
seductor[2], **-tora** *n* : seducer
segador, -dora *n* : harvester
segar {49} *vt* **1** : to reap, to harvest, to cut **2** : to sever abruptly ⟨una vida segada por la enfermedad : a life cut short by illness⟩
seglar[1] *adj* LAICO : lay, secular
seglar[2] *nm* LAICO : layperson, layman *m*, laywoman *f*

segmentación *nf, pl* **-ciones** : segmentation
segmentado, -da *adj* : segmented
segmento *nm* : segment
segregar {52} *vt* **1** : to segregate **2** SECRETAR : to secrete
seguida *nf* **en ~** : right away, immediately ⟨vuelvo en seguida : I'll be right back⟩
seguidamente *adv* **1** : next, immediately after **2** : without a break, continuously
seguido[1] *adv* **1** RECTO : straight, straight ahead **2** : often, frequently
seguido[2], **-da** *adj* **1** CONSECUTIVO : consecutive, successive ⟨tres días seguidos : three days in a row⟩ **2** : straight, unbroken **3 ~ por** *or* **~ de** : followed by
seguidor, -dora *n* : follower, supporter
seguimiento *nm* **1** : following, pursuit **2** : continuation **3** : tracking, monitoring
seguir {75} *vt* **1** : to follow ⟨el sol sigue la lluvia : sunshine follows the rain⟩ ⟨seguiré tu consejo : I'll follow your advice⟩ ⟨me siguieron con la mirada : they followed me with their eyes⟩ **2** : to go along, to keep on ⟨seguimos toda la carretera panamericana : we continued along the PanAmerican Highway⟩ ⟨siguió hablando : he kept on talking⟩ ⟨seguir el curso : to stay on course⟩ **3** : to take (a course, a treatment) — *vi* **1** : to go on, to keep going ⟨sigue adelante : keep going, carry on⟩ **2** : to remain, to continue to be ⟨¿todavía sigues aquí? : you're still here?⟩ ⟨sigue con vida : she's still alive⟩ **3** : to follow, to come after ⟨la frase que sigue : the following sentence⟩
según[1] *adv* : it depends ⟨según y como : it all depends on⟩
según[2] *conj* **1** COMO, CONFORME : as, just as ⟨según lo dejé : just as I left it⟩ **2** : depending on how ⟨según se vea : depending on how one sees it⟩
según[3] *prep* **1** : according to ⟨según los rumores : according to the rumors⟩ **2** : depending on ⟨según los resultados : depending on the results⟩
segundo[1], **-da** *adj* : second ⟨el segundo lugar : second place⟩
segundo[2], **-da** *n* **1** : second (in a series) **2** : second (person), second-in-command
segundo[3] *nm* : second ⟨sesenta segundos : sixty seconds⟩
seguramente *adv* **1** : for sure, surely **2** : probably
seguridad *nf* **1** : safety, security **2** : (financial) security ⟨seguridad social : Social Security⟩ **3** CERTEZA : certainty, assurance ⟨con toda seguridad : with complete certainty⟩ **4** : confidence, self-confidence
seguro[1] *adv* : certainly, definitely ⟨va a llover, seguro : it's going to rain for sure⟩ ⟨¡seguro que sí! : of course!⟩
seguro[2], **-ra** *adj* **1** : safe, secure **2** : sure, certain ⟨estoy segura que es él : I'm sure that's him⟩ **3** : reliable, trustworthy **4** : self-assured
seguro[3] *nm* **1** : insurance ⟨seguro de vida : life insurance⟩ **2** : fastener, clasp **3** *Mex* : safety pin
seis *adj & nm* : six
seiscientos[1], **-tas** *adj* : six hundred
seiscientos[2] *nms & pl* : six hundred
selección *nf, pl* **-ciones** **1** ELECCIÓN : selection, choice **2 selección natural** : natural selection
seleccionar *vt* ELEGIR : to select, to choose
selectivo, -va *adj* : selective — **selectivamente** *adv*
selecto, -ta *adj* **1** : choice, select **2** EXCLUSIVO : exclusive
selenio *nm* : selenium
sellar *vt* **1** : to seal **2** : to stamp
sello *nm* **1** : seal **2** ESTAMPILLA, TIMBRE : postage stamp **3** : hallmark, characteristic
selva *nf* **1** BOSQUE : woods *pl,* forest ⟨selva húmeda : rain forest⟩ **2** JUNGLA : jungle
selvático, -ca *adj* **1** : forest, jungle ⟨sendero selvático : jungle path⟩ **2** : wild
semáforo *nm* **1** : traffic light **2** : stop signal
semana *nf* : week
semanal *adj* : weekly — **semanalmente** *adv*
semanario *nm* : weekly (publication)
semántica *nf* : semantics
semántico, -ca *adj* : semantic
semblante *nm* **1** : countenance, face **2** : appearance, look
semblanza *nf* : biographical sketch, profile
sembrado *nm* : cultivated field
sembrador, -dora *n* : planter, sower
sembradora *nf* : seeder (machine)
sembrar {55} *vt* **1** : to plant, to sow **2** : to scatter, to strew ⟨sembrar el pánico : to spread panic⟩
semejante[1] *adj* **1** PARECIDO : similar, alike **2** TAL : such ⟨nunca he visto cosa semejante : I have never seen such a thing⟩
semejante[2] *nm* PRÓJIMO : fellowman
semejanza *nf* PARECIDO : similarity, resemblance
semejar *vi* : to resemble, to look like — **semejarse** *vr* : to be similar, to look alike
semen *nm* : semen
semental *nm* : stud (animal) ⟨caballo semental : stallion⟩
semestre *nm* : semester
semicírculo *nm* : semicircle, half circle
semiconductor *nm* : semiconductor
semidiós *nm, pl* **-dioses** : demigod *m*
semifinal *nf* : semifinal
semifinalista[1] *adj* : semifinal
semifinalista[2] *nmf* : semifinalist

semiformal *adj* : semiformal
semilla *nf* : seed
semillero *nm* **1** : seedbed **2** : hotbed, breeding ground
seminario *nm* **1** : seminary **2** : seminar, graduate course
seminarista *nm* : seminarian
semiprecioso, **-sa** *adj* : semiprecious
semita[1] *adj* : Semitic
semita[2] *nmf* : Semite
sémola *nf* : semolina
sempiterno, **-na** *adj* ETERNO : eternal, everlasting
senado *nm* : senate
senador, **-dora** *n* : senator
sencillamente *adv* : simply, plainly
sencillez *nf* : simplicity
sencillo[1], **-lla** *adj* **1** : simple, easy **2** : plain, unaffected **3** : single
sencillo[2] *nm* **1** : single (recording) **2** : small change (coins) **3** : one-way ticket
senda *nf* CAMINO, SENDERO : path, way
sendero *nm* CAMINO, SENDA : path, way
sendos, **-das** *adj pl* : each, both ⟨llevaban sendos vestidos nuevos : they were each wearing a new dress⟩
senectud *nf* ANCIANIDAD : old age
senegalés, **-lesa** *adj & n, mpl* **-leses** : Senegalese
senil *adj* : senile — **senilidad** *nf*
seno *nm* **1** : breast, bosom ⟨los senos : the breasts⟩ ⟨el seno de la familia : the bosom of the family⟩ **2** : sinus **3 seno materno** : womb
sensación *nf, pl* **-ciones 1** IMPRESIÓN : feeling ⟨tener la sensación : to have a feeling⟩ **2** : sensation ⟨causar sensación : to cause a sensation⟩
sensacional *adj* : sensational
sensacionalista *adj* : sensationalistic, lurid
sensatez *nf* **1** : good sense **2 con ~** : sensibly
sensato, **-ta** *adj* : sensible, sound — **sensatamente** *adv*
sensibilidad *nf* **1** : sensitivity, sensibility **2** SENSACIÓN : feeling
sensibilizar {21} *vt* : to sensitize
sensible *adj* **1** : sensitive **2** APRECIABLE : considerable, significant
sensiblemente *adv* : considerably, significantly
sensiblería *nf* : sentimentality, mush
sensiblero, **-ra** *adj* : mawkish, sentimental, mushy
sensitivo, **-va** *adj* **1** : sense ⟨órganos sensitivos : sense organs⟩ **2** : sentient, capable of feeling
sensor *nm* : sensor
sensorial *adj* : sensory
sensual *adj* : sensual, sensuous — **sensualmente** *adv*
sensualidad *nf* : sensuality
sentado, **-da** *adj* **1** : sitting, seated **2** : established, settled ⟨dar por sentado : to take for granted⟩ ⟨dejar sentado : to make clear⟩ **3** : sensible, steady, judicious
sentar {55} *vt* **1** : to seat, to sit **2** : to establish, to set — *vi* **1** : to suit ⟨ese color te sienta : that color suits you⟩ **2** : to agree with (of food or drink) ⟨las cebollas no me sientan : onions don't agree with me⟩ **3** : to please ⟨le sentó mal el paseo : she didn't enjoy the trip⟩ — **sentarse** *vr* : to sit, to sit down ⟨siéntese, por favor : please have a seat⟩
sentencia *nf* **1** : sentence, judgment **2** : maxim, saying
sentenciar *vt* : to sentence
sentido[1], **-da** *adj* **1** : heartfelt, sincere ⟨mi más sentido pésame : my sincerest condolences⟩ **2** : touchy, sensitive **3** : offended, hurt
sentido[2] *nm* **1** : sense ⟨sentido común : common sense⟩ ⟨los cinco sentidos : the five senses⟩ ⟨sin sentido : senseless⟩ **2** CONOCIMIENTO : consciousness **3** SIGNIFICADO : meaning, sense ⟨doble sentido : double entendre⟩ **4** : direction ⟨calle de sentido único : one-way street⟩
sentimental[1] *adj* **1** : sentimental **2** : love, romantic ⟨vida sentimental : love life⟩
sentimental[2] *nmf* : sentimentalist
sentimentalismo *nm* : sentimentality, sentimentalism
sentimiento *nm* **1** : feeling, emotion **2** PESAR : regret, sorrow
sentir {76} *vt* **1** : to feel, to experience ⟨no siento nada de dolor : I don't feel any pain⟩ ⟨sentía sed : he was feeling thirsty⟩ ⟨sentir amor : to feel love⟩ **2** PERCIBIR : to perceive, to sense ⟨sentir un ruido : to hear a noise⟩ **3** LAMENTAR : to regret, to feel sorry for ⟨lo siento mucho : I'm very sorry⟩ — *vi* **1** : to have feeling, to feel **2 sin ~** : without noticing, inadvertently — **sentirse** *vr* **1** : to feel ⟨¿te sientes mejor? : are you feeling better?⟩ **2** *Chile, Mex* : to take offense
seña *nf* **1** : sign, signal **2 dar señas de** : to show signs of
señal *nf* **1** : signal **2** : sign ⟨señal de tráfico : traffic sign⟩ **3** INDICIO : indication ⟨en señal de : as a token of⟩ **4** VESTIGIO : trace, vestige **5** : scar, mark **6** : deposit, down payment
señalado, **-da** *adj* : distinguished, notable
señalador *nm* : marker ⟨señalador de libros : bookmark⟩
señalar *vt* **1** INDICAR : to indicate, to show **2** : to mark **3** : to point out, to stress **4** : to fix, to set — **señalarse** *vr* : to distinguish oneself
señor, **-ñora** *n* **1** : gentleman *m,* man *m,* lady *f,* woman *f,* wife *f* **2** : Sir *m,* Madam *f* ⟨estimados señores : Dear Sirs⟩ **3** : Mr. *m,* Mrs. *f* **4** : lord *m,* lady *f* ⟨el Señor : the Lord⟩
señoría *nf* **1** : lordship **2 Su Señoría** : Your Honor
señorial *adj* : stately, regal

señorío *nm* **1** : manor, estate **2** : dominion, power **3** : elegance, class

señorita *nf* **1** : young lady, young woman **2** : Miss

señuelo *nm* **1** : decoy **2** : bait

sépalo *nm* : sepal

sepa, etc. → **saber**

separación *nf, pl* **-ciones** **1** : separation, division **2** : gap, space

separadamente *adv* : separately, apart

separado, -da *adj* **1** : separated **2** : separate ⟨vidas separadas : separate lives⟩ **3 por ~** : separately

separar *vt* **1** : to separate, to divide **2** : to split up, to pull apart — **separarse** *vr*

sepelio *nm* : interment, burial

sepia[1] *adj & nm* : sepia

sepia[2] *nf* : cuttlefish

septentrional *adj* : northern

séptico, -ca *adj* : septic

septiembre *nm* : September

séptimo[1], **-ma** *adj* : seventh

séptimo[2] *nm* : seventh

septuagésimo[1], **-ma** *adj* : seventieth

septuagésimo[2] *nm* : seventieth

sepulcral *adj* **1** : sepulchral **2** : dismal, gloomy

sepulcro *nm* TUMBA : tomb, sepulchre

sepultar *vt* ENTERRAR : to bury

sepultura *nf* **1** : burial **2** TUMBA : grave, tomb

seque, etc. → **secar**

sequedad *nf* **1** : dryness **2** : brusqueness, curtness

sequía *nf* : drought

séquito *nm* : retinue, entourage

ser[1] {77} *vi* **1** : to be ⟨él es mi hermano : he is my brother⟩ ⟨Camila es linda : Camila is pretty⟩ **2** : to exist, to live ⟨ser, o no ser : to be or not to be⟩ **3** : to take place, to occur ⟨el concierto es el domingo : the concert is on Sunday⟩ **4** (*used with expressions of time, date, season*) ⟨son las diez : it's ten o'clock⟩ ⟨hoy es el 9 : today's the 9th⟩ **5** : to cost, to come to ⟨¿cuánto es? : how much is it?⟩ **6** (*with the future tense*) : to be able to be ⟨¿será posible? : can it be possible?⟩ **7 ~ de** : to come from ⟨somos de Managua : we're from Managua⟩ **8 ~ de** : to belong to ⟨ese lápiz es de Juan : that's Juan's pencil⟩ **9 es que** : the thing is that ⟨es que no lo conozco : it's just that I don't know him⟩ **10 ¡sea!** : agreed!, all right! **11 sea . . . sea** : either . . . or — *v aux* (*used in passive constructions*) : to be ⟨la cuenta ha sido pagada : the bill has been paid⟩ ⟨él fue asesinado : he was murdered⟩

ser[2] *nm* : being ⟨ser humano : human being⟩

seráfico, -ca *adj* : angelic, seraphic

serbio[1], **-bia** *adj & n* : Serb, Serbian

serbio[2] *nm* : Serbian (language)

serbocroata[1] *adj* : Serbo-Croatian

serbocroata[2] *nm* : Serbo-Croatian (language)

serenar *vt* : to calm, to soothe — **serenarse** *vr* CALMARSE : to calm down

serenata *nf* : serenade

serendipia *nf* : serendipity

serenidad *nf* : serenity, calmness

sereno[1], **-na** *adj* **1** SOSEGADO : serene, calm, composed **2** : fair, clear (of weather) **3** : calm, still (of the sea) — **serenamente** *adv*

sereno[2] *nm* : night watchman

seriado, -da *adj* : serial

serial *nm* : serial (on radio or television)

seriamente *adv* : seriously

serie *nf* **1** : series **2** SERIAL : serial **3 fabricación en serie** : mass production **4 fuera de serie** : extraordinary, amazing

seriedad *nf* **1** : seriousness, earnestness **2** : gravity, importance

serio, -ria *adj* **1** : serious, earnest **2** : reliable, responsible **3** : important **4 en ~** : seriously, in earnest — **seriamente** *adv*

sermón *nm, pl* **sermones** **1** : sermon **2** *fam* : harangue, lecture

sermonear *vt fam* : to harangue, to lecture

serpentear *vi* : to twist, to wind — **serpenteante** *adj*

serpentina *nf* : paper streamer

serpiente *nf* : serpent, snake

serrado, -da *adj* DENTADO : serrated

serranía *nf* : mountainous area

serrano, -na *adj* : from the mountains

serrar {55} *vt* : to saw

serrín *nm, pl* **serrines** : sawdust

serruchar *vt* : to saw up

serrucho *nm* : saw, handsaw

servicentro *nm Peru* : gas station

servicial *adj* : obliging, helpful

servicio *nm* **1** : service **2** SAQUE : serve (in sports) **3 servicios** *nmpl* : restroom

servidor, -dora *n* **1** : servant **2 su seguro servidor** : yours truly (in correspondence)

servidumbre *nf* **1** : servitude **2** : help, servants *pl*

servil *adj* **1** : servile, subservient **2** : menial

servilismo *nm* : servility, subservience

servilleta *nf* : napkin

servir {54} *vt* **1** : to serve, to be of use to **2** : to serve, to wait **3** SURTIR : to fill (an order) — *vi* **1** : to work ⟨mi radio no sirve : my radio isn't working⟩ **2** : to be of use, to be helpful ⟨esa computadora no sirve para nada : that computer's perfectly useless⟩ — **servirse** *vr* **1** : to help oneself to **2** : to be kind enough ⟨sírvase enviarnos un catálogo : please send us a catalog⟩

sésamo *nm* AJONJOLÍ : sesame, sesame seeds *pl*

sesenta *adj & nm* : sixty

sesentavo[1], **-va** *adj* : sixtieth

sesentavo[2] *n* : sixtieth (fraction)

sesgado, -da *adj* **1** : inclined, tilted **2** : slanted, biased

sesgar {52} *vt* **1** : to cut on the bias **2** : to tilt **3** : to bias, to slant
sesgo *nm* : bias
sesgue, etc. → **sesgar**
sesión *nf, pl* **sesiones 1** : session **2** : showing, performance
sesionar *vi* REUNIRSE : to meet, to be in session
seso *nm* **1** : brains, intelligence **2 sesos** *nmpl* : brains (as food)
sesudo, -da *adj* **1** : prudent, sensible **2** : brainy
set *nm, pl* **sets** : set (in tennis)
seta *nf* : mushroom
setecientos[1], **-tas** *adj* : seven hundred
setecientos[2] *nms & pl* : seven hundred
setenta *adj & nm* : seventy
setentavo[1], **-va** *adj* : seventieth
setentavo[2] *nm* : seventieth
setiembre → **septiembre**
seto *nm* **1** : fence, enclosure **2 seto vivo** : hedge
seudónimo *nm* : pseudonym
severidad *nf* **1** : harshness, severity **2** : strictness
severo, -ra *adj* **1** : harsh, severe **2** ESTRICTO : strict — **severamente** *adv*
sexagésimo[1], **-ma** *adj* : sixtieth, sixty-
sexagésimo[2], **-ma** *n* : sixtieth, sixty- (in a series)
sexismo *nm* : sexism — **sexista** *adj & nmf*
sexo *nm* : sex
sextante *nm* : sextant
sexteto *nm* : sextet
sexto, -ta *adj* : sixth — **sexto, -ta** *n*
sexual *adj* : sexual, sex ⟨educación sexual : sex education⟩ — **sexualmente** *adv*
sexualidad *nf* : sexuality
sexy *adj, pl* **sexy** *or* **sexys** : sexy
shock [ˈʃɔk, ˈtʃɔk] *nm* : shock ⟨estado de shock : state of shock⟩
short *nm, pl* **shorts** : shorts *pl*
show *nm, pl* **shows** : show
si *conj* **1** : if ⟨lo haré si me pagan : I'll do it if they pay me⟩ ⟨si lo supiera te lo diría : if I knew it I would tell you⟩ **2** : whether, if ⟨no importa si funciona o no : it doesn't matter whether it works (or not)⟩ **3** (*expressing desire, protest, or surprise*) ⟨si supiera la verdad : if only I knew the truth⟩ ⟨¡si no quiero! : but I don't want to!⟩ **4 si bien** : although ⟨si bien se ha progresado : although progress has been made⟩ **5 si no** : otherwise, or else ⟨si no, no voy : otherwise I won't go⟩
sí[1] *adv* **1** : yes ⟨sí, gracias : yes, please⟩ ⟨creo que sí : I think so⟩ **2 sí que** : indeed, absolutely ⟨esta vez sí que ganaré : this time I'm sure to win⟩ **3 porque sí** *fam* : because, just because ⟨lo hizo porque sí : she did it just because⟩
sí[2] *nm* : yes ⟨dar el sí : to say yes, to express consent⟩
sí[3] *pron* **1 de por sí** *or* **en sí** : by itself, in itself, per se **2 fuera de sí** : beside oneself **3 para sí (mismo)** : to himself, to herself, for himself, for herself **4 entre ~** : among themselves
siamés, -mesa *adj & n, mpl* **siameses** : Siamese
sibilante *adj & nf* : sibilant
siciliano, -na *adj & n* : Sicilian
sico- → **psico-**
sicomoro *or* **sicómoro** *nm* : sycamore
SIDA *or* **sida** *nm* (*s*índrome de *i*nmun*o*deficiencia *a*dquirida) : AIDS
siderurgia *nf* : iron and steel industry
siderúrgico, -ca *adj* : steel, iron ⟨la industria siderúrgica : the steel industry⟩
sidra *nf* : hard cider
siega[1], **siegue, etc.** → **segar**
siega[2] *nf* **1** : harvesting **2** : harvest time **3** : harvested crop
siembra[1], **etc.** → **sembrar**
siembra[2] *nf* **1** : sowing **2** : sowing season **3** SEMBRADO : cultivated field
siempre *adv* **1** : always ⟨siempre tienes hambre : you're always hungry⟩ **2** : still ⟨¿siempre te vas? : are you still going?⟩ **3** *Mex* : after all ⟨siempre no fui : I didn't go after all⟩ **4 siempre que** : whenever, every time ⟨siempre que pasa : every time he walks by⟩ **5 para ~** : forever, for good **6 siempre y cuando** : provided that
sien *nf* : temple (on the forehead)
sienta, etc. → **sentar**
siente, etc. → **sentir**
sierpe *nf* : serpent, snake
sierra[1], **etc.** → **serrar**
sierra[2] *nf* **1** : saw ⟨sierra de vaivén : jigsaw⟩ **2** CORDILLERA : mountain range **3** : mountains *pl* ⟨viven en la sierra : they live in the mountains⟩
siervo, -va *n* **1** : slave **2** : serf
siesta *nf* : nap, siesta
siete *adj & nm* : seven
sífilis *nf* : syphilis
sifón *nm, pl* **sifones** : siphon
siga, sigue etc. → **seguir**
sigilo *nm* : secrecy, stealth
sigiloso, -sa *adj* FURTIVO : furtive, stealthy — **sigilosamente** *adv*
sigla *nf* : acronym, abbreviation
siglo *nm* **1** : century **2** : age ⟨el Siglo de Oro : the Golden Age⟩ ⟨hace siglos que no te veo : I haven't seen you in ages⟩ **3** : world, secular life
signar *vt* : to sign (a treaty or agreement)
signatario, -ria *n* : signatory
significación *nf, pl* **-ciones 1** : significance, importance **2** : signification, meaning
significado *nm* **1** : sense, meaning **2** : significance
significante *adj* : significant
significar {72} *vt* **1** : to mean, to signify **2** : to express, to make known — **significarse** *vr* **1** : to draw attention, to become known **2** : to take a stance
significativo, -va *adj* **1** : significant, important **2** : meaningful — **significativamente** *adv*

signo *nm* **1** : sign ⟨signo de igual : equal sign⟩ ⟨un signo de alegría : a sign of happiness⟩ **2** : (punctuation) mark ⟨signo de interrogación : question mark⟩ ⟨signo de admiración : exclamation point⟩ ⟨signo de intercalación : caret⟩
siguiente *adj* : next, following
sílaba *nf* : syllable
silábico, -ca *adj* : syllabic
silbar *v* : to whistle
silbato *nm* PITO : whistle
silbido *nm* : whistle, whistling
silenciador *nm* **1** : muffler (of an automobile) **2** : silencer
silenciar *vt* **1** : to silence **2** : to muffle
silencio *nm* **1** : silence, quiet ⟨¡silencio! : be quiet!⟩ **2** : rest (in music)
silencioso, -sa *adj* : silent, quiet — **silenciosamente** *adv*
sílice *nf* : silica
silicio *nm* : silicon
silla *nf* **1** : chair **2 silla de ruedas** : wheelchair
sillón *nm, pl* **sillones** : armchair, easy chair
silo *nm* : silo
silueta *nf* **1** : silhouette **2** : figure, shape
silvestre *adj* : wild ⟨flor silvestre : wildflower⟩
silvicultor, -tora *n* : forester
silvicultura *nf* : forestry
sima *nf* ABISMO : chasm, abyss
simbólico, -ca *adj* : symbolic — **simbólicamente** *adj*
simbolismo *nm* : symbolism
simbolizar {21} *vt* : to symbolize
símbolo *nm* : symbol
simetría *nf* : symmetry
simétrico, -ca *adj* : symmetrical, symmetric
simiente *nf* : seed
símil *nm* **1** : simile **2** : analogy, comparison
similar *adj* SEMEJANTE : similar, alike
similitud *nf* : similarity, resemblance
simio *nm* : ape
simpatía *nf* **1** : liking, affection ⟨tomarle simpatía a : to take a liking to⟩ **2** : warmth, friendliness **3** : support, solidarity
simpático, -ca *adj* : nice, friendly, likeable
simpatizante *nf* : sympathizer, supporter
simpatizar {21} *vi* **1** : to get along, to hit it off ⟨simpaticé mucho con él : I really liked him⟩ **2 ~ con** : to sympathize with, to support
simple¹ *adj* **1** SENCILLO : plain, simple, easy **2** : pure, mere ⟨por simple vanidad : out of pure vanity⟩ **3** : simpleminded, foolish
simple² *n* : fool, simpleton
simplemente *adv* : simply, merely, just
simpleza *nf* **1** : foolishness, simpleness **2** NECEDAD : nonsense
simplicidad *nf* : simplicity
simplificar {72} *vt* : to simplify — **simplificación** *nf*
simplista *adj* : simplistic
simposio *or* **simposium** *nm* : symposium
simulación *nf, pl* **-ciones** : simulation
simulacro *nm* : imitation, sham ⟨simulacro de juicio : mock trial⟩
simular *vt* **1** : to simulate **2** : to feign, to pretend
simultáneo, -nea *adj* : simultaneous — **simultáneamente** *adv*
sin *prep* **1** : without ⟨sin querer : unintentionally⟩ ⟨sin refinar : unrefined⟩ **2 sin que** : without ⟨lo hicimos sin que él se diera cuenta : we did it without him noticing⟩
sinagoga *nf* : synagogue
sinceridad *nf* : sincerity
sincero, -ra *adj* : sincere, honest, true — **sinceramente** *adv*
síncopa *nf* : syncopation
sincopar *vt* : to syncopate
sincronizar {21} *vt* : to synchronize — **sincronización** *nf*
sindical *adj* GREMIAL : union, labor ⟨representante sindical : union representative⟩
sindicalización *nf, pl* **-ciones** : unionizing, unionization
sindicalizar {21} *vt* : to unionize — **sindicalizarse** *vr* **1** : to form a union **2** : to join a union
sindicar → **sindicalizar**
sindicato *nm* GREMIO : union, guild
síndrome *nm* : syndrome
sinecura *nf* : sinecure
sinfín *nm* : endless number ⟨un sinfín de problemas : no end of problems⟩
sinfonía *nf* : symphony
sinfónica *nf* : symphony orchestra
sinfónico, -ca *adj* : symphonic, symphony
singular¹ *adj* **1** : singular, unique **2** PARTICULAR : peculiar, odd **3** : singular (in grammar) — **singularmente** *adv*
singular² *nm* : singular
singularidad *nf* : uniqueness, singularity
singularizar {21} *vt* : to make unique or distinct — **singularizarse** *vr* : to stand out, to distinguish oneself
siniestrado, -da *adj* : damaged, wrecked ⟨zona siniestrada : disaster zone⟩
siniestro¹, -tra *adj* **1** IZQUIERDO : left, left-hand **2** MALVADO : sinister, evil
siniestro² *nm* : accident, disaster
sinnúmero → **sinfín**
sino *conj* **1** : but, rather ⟨no será hoy, sino mañana : it won't be today, but tomorrow⟩ **2** EXCEPTO : but, except ⟨no hace sino despertar suspicacias : it does nothing but arouse suspicion⟩
sinónimo¹, -ma *adj* : synonymous
sinónimo² *nm* : synonym
sinopsis *nfs & pl* RESUMEN : synopsis, summary
sinrazón *nf, pl* **-zones** : wrong, injustice

sinsabores *nmpl* : woes, troubles
sinsonte *nm* : mockingbird
sintáctico, -ca *adj* : syntactic, syntactical
sintaxis *nfs & pl* : syntax
síntesis *nfs & pl* **1** : synthesis, fusion **2** SINOPSIS : synopsis, summary
sintético, -ca *adj* : synthetic — **sintéticamente** *adv*
sintetizar {21} *vt* **1** : to synthesize **2** RESUMIR : to summarize
sintió, etc. → **sentir**
síntoma *nm* : symptom
sintomático, -ca *adj* : symptomatic
sintonía *nf* **1** : tuning in (of a radio) **2 en sintonía con** : in tune with, attuned to
sintonizador *nm* : tuner, knob for tuning (of a radio, etc.)
sintonizar {21} *vt* : to tune (in) to — *vi* **1** : to tune in **2 ~ con** : to be in tune with, to empathize with
sinuosidad *nf* : sinuosity
sinuoso, -sa *adj* **1** : winding, sinuous **2** : devious
sinvergüenza[1] *adj* **1** DESCARADO : shameless, brazen, impudent **2** TRAVIESO : naughty
sinvergüenza[2] *nmf* **1** : rogue, scoundrel **2** : brat, rascal
sionista *adj & nmf* : Zionist — **sionismo** *nm*
siqui- → **psiqui-**
siquiera *adv* **1** : at least ⟨dame siquiera un poquito : at least give me a little bit⟩ **2** (*in negative constructions*) : not even ⟨ni siquiera nos saludaron : they didn't even say hello to us⟩
sirena *nf* **1** : mermaid **2** : siren ⟨sirena de niebla : foghorn⟩
sirio, -ria *adj & n* : Syrian
sirope *nm* : syrup
sirve, etc. → **servir**
sirviente, -ta *n* : servant, maid *f*
sisal *nm* : sisal
sisear *vi* : to hiss
siseo *nm* : hiss
sísmico, -ca *adj* : seismic
sismo *nm* **1** TERREMOTO : earthquake **2** TEMBLOR : tremor
sismógrafo *nm* : seismograph
sistema *nm* : system
sistemático, -ca *adj* : systematic — **sistemáticamente** *adv*
sistematizar {21} *vt* : to systematize
sistémico, -ca *adj* : systemic
sitiar *vt* ASEDIAR : to besiege
sitio *nm* **1** LUGAR : place, site ⟨vámonos a otro sitio : let's go somewhere else⟩ **2** ESPACIO : room, space ⟨hacer sitio a : to make room for⟩ **3** : siege ⟨estado de sitio : state of siege⟩ **4** *Mex* : taxi stand
situación *nf, pl* **-ciones** : situation
situado, -da *adj* : situated, placed
situar {3} *vt* UBICAR : to situate, to place, to locate — **situarse** *vr* **1** : to be placed, to be located **2** : to make a place for oneself, to do well
sketch *nm* : sketch, skit
slip *nm* : briefs *pl*, underpants *pl*
smog *nm* : smog
smoking *nm* ESMOQUIN : tuxedo
snob → **esnob**
so *prep* : under ⟨so pena de : under penalty of⟩
sobaco *nm* : armpit
sobado, -da *adj* **1** : worn, shabby **2** : well-worn, hackneyed
sobar *vt* **1** : to finger, to handle **2** : to knead **3** : to rub, to massage **4** *fam* : to beat, to pummel
soberanía *nf* : sovereignty
soberano, -na *adj & n* : sovereign
soberbia *nf* **1** ORGULLO : pride, arrogance **2** MAGNIFICENCIA : magnificence
soberbio, -bia *adj* **1** : proud, arrogant **2** : grand, magnificent
sobornable *adv* : venal, bribable
sobornar *vt* : to bribe
soborno *nm* **1** : bribery **2** : bribe
sobra *nf* **1** : excess, surplus **2 de ~** : extra, to spare **3 sobras** *nfpl* : leftovers, scraps
sobrado, -da *adj* : abundant, excessive, more than enough
sobrante[1] *adj* : remaining, superfluous
sobrante[2] *nm* : remainder, surplus
sobrar *vi* : to be in excess, to be superfluous ⟨más vale que sobre a que falte : it's better to have too much than not enough⟩
sobre[1] *nm* **1** : envelope **2** : packet ⟨un sobre de sazón : a packet of seasoning⟩
sobre[2] *prep* **1** : on, on top of ⟨sobre la mesa : on the table⟩ **2** : over, above **3** : about ⟨¿tiene libros sobre Bolivia? : do you have books on Bolivia?⟩ **4 sobre todo** : especially, above all
sobrealimentar *vt* : to overfeed
sobrecalentar {55} *vt* : to overheat — **sobrecalentarse** *vr*
sobrecama *nmf* : bedspread
sobrecargar {52} *vt* : to overload, to overburden, to weigh down
sobrecoger {15} *vt* **1** : to surprise, to startle **2** : to scare — **sobrecogerse** *vr*
sobrecubierta *nf* : dust jacket
sobredosis *nfs & pl* : overdose
sobreentender {56} *vt* : to infer, to understand
sobreestimar *vt* : to overestimate, to overrate
sobreexcitado, -da *adj* : overexcited
sobreexponer {60} *vt* : to overexpose
sobregirar *vt* : to overdraw
sobregiro *nm* : overdraft
sobrehumano, -na *adj* : superhuman
sobrellevar *vt* : to endure, to bear
sobremanera *adv* : exceedingly
sobremesa *nf* : after-dinner conversation
sobrenatural *adj* : supernatural
sobrenombre *nm* APODO : nickname
sobrentender → **sobreentender**

sobrepasar *vt* : to exceed, to surpass — **sobrepasarse** *vr* PASARSE : to go too far

sobrepelliz *nf, pl* **-pellices** : surplice

sobrepeso *nm* **1** : excess weight **2** : overweight, obesity

sobrepoblación, sobrepoblado → **superpoblación, superpoblado**

sobreponer {60} *vt* **1** SUPERPONER : to superimpose **2** ANTEPONER : to put first, to give priority to — **sobreponerse** *vr* **1** : to pull oneself together **2** **~ a** : to overcome

sobreprecio *nm* : surcharge

sobreproducción *nf, pl* **-ciones** : overproduction

sobreproducir {61} *vt* : to overproduce

sobreprotector, -tora *adj* : overprotective

sobreproteger {15} *vt* : to overprotect

sobresaliente[1] *adj* **1** : protruding, projecting **2** : outstanding, noteworthy **3** : significant, salient

sobresaliente[2] *nmf* : understudy

sobresalir {73} *vi* **1** : to protrude, to jut out, to project **2** : to stand out, to excel

sobresaltar *vt* : to startle, to frighten — **sobresaltarse** *vr*

sobresalto *nm* : start, fright

sobresueldo *nm* : bonus, additional pay

sobretasa *nf* : surcharge ⟨sobretasa a la gasolina : gas tax⟩

sobretodo *nm* : overcoat

sobrevalorar *or* **sobrevaluar** {3} *vt* : to overvalue, to overrate

sobrevender *vt* : to oversell

sobrevenir {87} *vi* ACAECER : to take place, to come about ⟨podrían sobrevenir complicaciones : complications could occur⟩

sobrevivencia → **supervivencia**

sobreviviente → **superviviente**

sobrevivir *vi* : to survive — *vt* : to outlive, to outlast

sobrevolar {19} *vt* : to fly over, to overfly

sobriedad *nf* : sobriety, moderation

sobrino, -na *n* : nephew *m*, niece *f*

sobrio, -bria *adj* : sober — **sobriamente** *adv*

socarrón, -rrona *adj, mpl* **-rrones** **1** : sly, cunning **2** : sarcastic

socavar *vt* : to undermine

sociabilidad *nf* : sociability

sociable *adj* : sociable

social *adj* : social — **socialmente** *adv*

socialista *adj & nmf* : socialist — **socialismo** *nm*

sociedad *nf* **1** : society **2** : company, enterprise **3** **sociedad anónima** : incorporated company

socio, -cia *n* **1** : member **2** : partner

socioeconómico, -ca *adj* : socioeconomic

sociología *nf* : sociology

sociológico, -ca *adj* : sociological — **sociológicamente** *adv*

sociólogo, -ga *n* : sociologist

socorrer *vt* : to assist, to come to the aid of

socorrido, -da *adj* ÚTIL : handy, practical

socorrista *nmf* **1** : rescue worker **2** : lifeguard

socorro *nm* AUXILIO **1** : aid, help ⟨equipo de socorro : rescue team⟩ **2** **¡socorro!** : help!

soda *nf* : soda, soda water

sodio *nf* : sodium

soez *adj, pl* **soeces** GROSERO : rude, vulgar — **soezmente** *adv*

sofá *nm* : couch, sofa

sofistería *nf* : sophistry — **sofista** *nmf*

sofisticación *nf, pl* **-ciones** : sophistication

sofisticado, -da *adj* : sophisticated

sofocante *adj* : suffocating, stifling

sofocar {72} *vt* **1** AHOGAR : to suffocate, to smother **2** EXTINGUIR : to extinguish, to put out (a fire) **3** APLASTAR : to crush, to put down ⟨sofocar una rebelión : to crush a rebellion⟩ — **sofocarse** *vr* **1** : to suffocate **2** *fam* : to get upset, to get mad

sofreír {66} *vt* : to sauté

sofrito[1]**, -ta** *adj* : sautéed

sofrito[2] *nm* : seasoning sauce

softbol *nm* : softball

software *nm* : software

soga *nf* : rope

soja → **soya**

sojuzgar *vt* : to subdue, to conquer, to subjugate

sol *nm* **1** : sun **2** : Peruvian unit of currency

solamente *adv* SÓLO : only, just

solapa *nf* **1** : lapel (of a jacket) **2** : flap (of an envelope)

solapado, -da *adj* : secret, underhanded

solapar *vt* : to cover up, to keep secret — **solaparse** *vr* : to overlap

solar[1] {19} *vt* : to floor, to tile

solar[2] *adj* : solar, sun

solar[3] *nm* **1** TERRENO : lot, piece of land, site **2** *Cuba, Peru* : tenement building

solariego, -ga *adj* : ancestral

solaz *nm, pl* **solaces** **1** CONSUELO : solace, comfort **2** DESCANSO : relaxation, recreation

solazarse {21} *vr* : to relax, to enjoy oneself

soldado *nm* **1** : soldier **2** **soldado raso** : private, enlisted man

soldador[1]**, -dora** *n* : welder

soldador[2] *nm* : soldering iron

soldadura *nf* **1** : welding **2** : soldering, solder

soldar {19} *vt* **1** : to weld **2** : to solder

soleado, -da *adj* : sunny

soledad *nf* : loneliness, solitude

solemne *adj* : solemn — **solemnemente** *adv*

solemnidad *nf* : solemnity

soler {78} *vi* : to be in the habit of, to tend to ⟨solía tomar café por la tarde : she usually drank coffee in the afternoon⟩ ⟨eso suele ocurrir : that frequently happens⟩
solera *nf* **1** : prop, support **2** : tradition
solicitante *nmf* : applicant
solicitar *vt* **1** : to request, to solicit **2** : to apply for ⟨solicitar empleo : to apply for employment⟩
solícito, -ta *adj* : solicitous, attentive, obliging
solicitud *nf* **1** : solicitude, concern **2** : request **3** : application
solidaridad *nf* : solidarity
solidario, -ria *adj* : supportive, united in support ⟨se declararon solidarios con la nueva ley : they declared their support for the new law⟩ ⟨espíritu solidario : spirit of solidarity⟩
solidarizar {21} *vi* : to be in solidarity ⟨solidarizamos con la huelga : we support the strike⟩
solidez *nf* **1** : solidity, firmness **2** : soundness (of an argument, etc.)
solidificar {72} *vt* : to solidify, to make solid — **solidificarse** *vr* — **solidificación** *nf*
sólido[1], -da *adj* **1** : solid, firm **2** : sturdy, well-made **3** : sound, well-founded — **sólidamente** *adv*
sólido[2] *nm* : solid
soliloquio *nm* : soliloquy
solista *nmf* : soloist
solitaria *nf* TENIA : tapeworm
solitario[1], -ria *adj* **1** : lonely **2** : lone, solitary **3** DESIERTO : deserted, lonely ⟨una calle solitaria : a deserted street⟩
solitario[2], -ria *n* : recluse, loner
solitario[3] *nm* : solitaire
sollozar {21} *vi* : to sob
sollozo *nm* : sob
solo[1], -la *adj* **1** : alone, by oneself **2** : lonely **3** ÚNICO : only, sole, unique ⟨hay un solo problema : there's only one problem⟩ **4 a solas** : alone
solo[2] *nm* : solo
sólo *adv* SOLAMENTE : just, only ⟨sólo quieren comer : they just want to eat⟩
solomillo *nm* : sirloin, loin
solsticio *nm* : solstice
soltar {19} *vt* **1** : to let go of, to drop **2** : to release, to set free **3** AFLOJAR : to loosen, to slacken
soltería *nf* : bachelorhood, spinsterhood
soltero[1], -ra *adj* : single, unmarried
soltero[2], -ra *n* **1** : bachelor *m,* single man *m,* single woman *f* **2 apellido de soltera** : maiden name
soltura *nf* **1** : looseness, slackness **2** : fluency (of language) **3** : agility, ease of movement
soluble *adj* : soluble — **solubilidad** *nf*
solución *nf, pl* **-ciones 1** : solution (in a liquid) **2** : answer, solution
solucionar *vt* RESOLVER : to solve, to resolve — **solucionarse** *vr*
solvencia *nf* **1** : solvency **2** : settling, payment (of debts) **3** : reliability ⟨solvencia moral : trustworthiness⟩
solvente[1] *adj* **1** : solvent **2** : reliable, trustworthy
solvente[2] *nm* : solvent
somalí *adj & nmf* : Somalian
sombra *nf* **1** : shadow **2** : shade **3 sombras** *nfpl* : darkness, shadows *pl* **4 sin sombra de duda** : without a shadow of a doubt
sombreado, -da *adj* **1** : shady **2** : shaded, darkened
sombrear *vt* : to shade
sombrerero, -ra *n* : milliner, hatter
sombrero *nm* **1** : hat **2 sin ~** : bareheaded **3 sombrero hongo** : derby
sombrilla *nf* : parasol, umbrella
sombrío, -bría *adj* LÓBREGO : dark, somber, gloomy — **sombríamente** *adv*
someramente *adv* : cursorily, summarily
somero, -ra *adj* : superficial, cursory, shallow
someter *vt* **1** : to subjugate, to conquer **2** : to subordinate **3** : to subject (to treatment or testing) **4** : to submit, to present — **someterse** *vr* **1** : to submit, to yield **2** : to undergo
sometimiento *nm* **1** : submission, subjection **2** : presentation
somnífero[1], -ra *adj* : soporific
somnífero[2] *nm* : sleeping pill
somnolencia *nf* : drowsiness, sleepiness
somnoliento, -ta *adj* : drowsy, sleepy
somorgujo *or* **somormujo** *nm* : loon, grebe
somos → **ser[1]**
son[1] → **ser**
son[2] *nm* **1** : sound ⟨al son de la trompeta : at the sound of the trumpet⟩ **2** : news, rumor **3 en son de** : as, in the manner of, by way of ⟨en son de broma : as a joke⟩ ⟨en son de paz : in peace⟩
sonado, -da *adj* : celebrated, famous, much-discussed
sonaja *nf* : rattle
sonajero *nm* : rattle (toy)
sonámbulo, -la *n* : sleepwalker
sonar[1] {19} *vi* **1** : to sound ⟨suena bien : it sounds good⟩ **2** : to ring (bells) **3** : to look or sound familiar ⟨me suena ese nombre : that name rings a bell⟩ **4 ~ a** : to sound like — *vt* **1** : to ring **2** : to blow (a trumpet, a nose) — **sonarse** *vr* : to blow one's nose
sonar[2] *nm* : sonar
sonata *nf* : sonata
sonda *nf* **1** : sounding line **2** : probe **3** CATÉTER : catheter
sondar *vt* **1** : to sound, to probe (in medicine, drilling, etc.) **2** : to probe, to explore (outer space)
sondear *vt* **1** : to sound **2** : to probe **3** : to sound out, to test (opinions, markets)

sondeo *nm* **1** : sounding, probing **2** : drilling **3** ENCUESTA : survey, poll
soneto *nm* : sonnet
sónico, -ca *adj* : sonic
sonido *nm* : sound
sonoridad *nf* : sonority, resonance
sonoro, -ra *adj* **1** : resonant, sonorous, voiced (in linguistics) **2** : resounding, loud **3 banda sonora** : soundtrack
sonreír {66} *vi* : to smile
sonriente *adj* : smiling
sonrisa *nf* : smile
sonrojar *vt* : to cause to blush — **sonrojarse** *vr* : to blush
sonrojo *nm* RUBOR : blush
sonrosado, -da *adj* : rosy, pink
sonsacar {72} *vt* : to wheedle, to extract
sonsonete *nm* **1** : tapping **2** : drone **3** : mocking tone
soñador¹, -dora *adj* : dreamy
soñador², -dora *n* : dreamer
soñar {19} *v* **1** : to dream **2 ~ con** : to dream about **3 soñar despierto** : to daydream
soñoliento, -ta *adj* : sleepy, drowsy
sopa *nf* **1** : soup **2 estar hecho una sopa** : to be soaked to the bone
sopera *nf* : soup tureen
sopesar *vt* : to weigh, to evaluate
soplar *vi* : to blow — *vt* : to blow on, to blow out, to blow off
soplete *nm* : blowtorch
soplido *nm* : puff
soplo *nm* : puff, gust
soplón, -plona *n, mpl* **soplones** *fam* : tattletale, sneak
sopor *nm* SOMNOLENCIA : drowsiness, sleepiness
soporífero, -ra *adj* : soporific
soportable *adj* : bearable, tolerable
soportar *vt* **1** SOSTENER : to support, to hold up **2** RESISTIR : to withstand, to resist **3** AGUANTAR : to bear, to tolerate
soporte *nm* : base, stand, support
soprano *nmf* : soprano
sor *nf* : Sister (religious title)
sorber *vt* **1** : to sip, to suck in **2** : to absorb, to soak up
sorbete *nm* : sherbet
sorbo *nm* **1** : sip, gulp, swallow **2 beber a sorbos** : to sip
sordera *nf* : deafness
sordidez *nf, pl* **-deces** : sordidness, squalor
sórdido, -da *adj* : sordid, dirty, squalid
sordina *nf* : mute (for a musical instrument)
sordo, -da *adj* **1** : deaf **2** : muted, muffled
sordomudo, -da *n* : deaf-mute
sorgo *nm* : sorghum
soriasis *nfs & pl* : psoriasis
sorna *nf* : sarcasm, mocking tone
sorprendente *adj* : surprising — **sorprendentemente** *adv*
sorprender *vt* : to surprise — **sorprenderse** *vr*
sorpresa *nf* : surprise
sorpresivo, -va *adj* **1** : surprising, surprise **2** IMPREVISTO : sudden, unexpected
sortear *vt* **1** RIFAR : to raffle, to draw lots for **2** : to dodge, to avoid
sorteo *nm* : drawing, raffle
sortija *nf* **1** ANILLO : ring **2** : curl, ringlet
sortilegio *nm* **1** HECHIZO : spell, charm **2** HECHICERÍA : sorcery
SOS *nm* : SOS
sosegado, -da *adj* SERENO : calm, tranquil, serene
sosegar {49} *vt* : to calm, to pacify — **sosegarse** *vr*
sosiego *nm* : tranquillity, serenity, calm
soslayar *vt* ESQUIVAR : to dodge, to evade
soslayo *nm* **de ~** : obliquely, sideways ⟨mirar de soslayo : to look askance⟩
soso, -sa *adj* **1** INSÍPIDO : bland, flavorless **2** ABURRIDO : dull, boring
sospecha *nf* : suspicion
sospechar *vt* : to suspect — *vi* : to be suspicious
sospechosamente *adv* : suspiciously
sospechoso¹, -sa *adj* : suspicious, suspect
sospechoso², -sa *n* : suspect
sostén *nm, pl* **sostenes** **1** APOYO : support **2** : sustenance **3** : brassiere, bra
sostener {80} *vt* **1** : to support, to hold up **2** : to hold ⟨sostenme la puerta : hold the door for me⟩ ⟨sostener una conversación : to hold a conversation⟩ **3** : to sustain, to maintain — **sostenerse** *vr* **1** : to stand, to hold oneself up **2** : to continue, to remain
sostenible *adj* : sustainable, tenable
sostenido¹, -da *adj* **1** : sustained, prolonged **2** : sharp (in music)
sostenido² *nm* : sharp (in music)
sostuvo, etc. → **sostener**
sotana *nf* : cassock
sótano *nm* : basement
sotavento *nm* : lee ⟨a sotavento : leeward⟩
soterrar {55} *vt* **1** : to bury **2** : to conceal, to hide away
soto *nm* : grove, copse
souvenir *nm, pl* **-nirs** RECUERDO : souvenir, memento
soviético, -ca *adj* : Soviet
soy → **ser**
soya *nf* : soy, soybean
spaghetti → **espagueti**
sport [ɛ'spor] *adj* : sport, casual
sprint [ɛ'sprin, -'sprint] *nm* : sprint — **sprinter** *nmf*
squash [ɛ'skwaʃ, -'skwatʃ] *nm* : squash (sport)
Sr. *nm* : Mr.
Sra. *nf* : Mrs., Ms.
Srta. *or* **Srita.** *nf* : Miss, Ms.
standard → **estándar**
stress → **estrés**
su *adj* **1** : his, her, its, their, one's ⟨su libro : her book⟩ ⟨sus consecuencias

: its consequences⟩ 2 (*formal*) : your ⟨tómese su medicina, señor : take your medicine, sir⟩
suave *adj* 1 BLANDO : soft 2 LISO : smooth 3 : gentle, mild 4 *Mex fam* : great, fantastic
suavemente *adj* : smoothly, gently, softly
suavidad *nf* : softness, smoothness, mellowness
suavizante *nm* : softener, fabric softener
suavizar {21} *vt* 1 : to soften, to smooth out 2 : to tone down — **suavizarse** *vr*
subacuático, -ca *adj* : underwater
subalterno[1], **-na** *adj* 1 SUBORDINADO : subordinate 2 SECUNDARIO : secondary
subalterno[2], **-na** *n* SUBORDINADO : subordinate
subarrendar {55} *vt* : to sublet
subasta *nf* : auction
subastador, -dora *n* : auctioneer
subastar *vt* : to auction, to auction off
subcampeón, -peona *n, mpl* **-peones** : runner-up
subcomité *nm* : subcommittee
subconsciente *adj & nm* : subconscious — **subconscientemente** *adv*
subcontratar *vt* : to subcontract
subcontratista *nmf* : subcontractor
subcultura *nf* : subculture
subdesarrollado, -da *adj* : underdeveloped
subdirector, -tora *n* : assistant manager
súbdito, -ta *n* : subject (of a monarch)
subdividir *vt* : to subdivide
subdivisión *nf, pl* **-siones** : subdivision
subestimar *vt* : to underestimate, to undervalue
subexponer {60} *vt* : to underexpose
subexposición *nf, pl* **-ciones** : underexposure
subgrupo *nm* : subgroup
subibaja *nm* : seesaw
subida *nf* 1 : ascent, climb 2 : rise, increase 3 : slope, hill ⟨ir de subida : to go uphill⟩
subido, -da *adj* 1 : intense, strong ⟨amarillo subido : bright yellow⟩ 2 **subido de tono** : risqué
subir *vt* 1 : to bring up, to take up 2 : to climb, to go up 3 : to raise — *vi* 1 : to go up, to come up 2 : to rise, to increase 3 : to be promoted 4 **∼ a** : to get on, to mount ⟨subir a un tren : to get on a train⟩ — **subirse** *vr* 1 : to climb (up) 2 : to pull up (clothing) 3 **subirse a la cabeza** : to go to one's head
súbito, -ta *adj* 1 REPENTINO : sudden 2 **de ∼** : all of a sudden, suddenly — **súbitamente** *adv*
subjetivo, -va *adj* : subjective — **subjetivamente** *adv* — **subjetividad** *nf*
subjuntivo[1], **-va** *adj* : subjunctive
subjuntivo[2] *nm* : subjunctive
sublevación *nf, pl* **-ciones** ALZAMIENTO : uprising, rebellion
sublevar *vt* : to incite to rebellion — **sublevarse** *vr* : to rebel, to rise up
sublimar *vt* : to sublimate — **sublimación** *nf*
sublime *adj* : sublime
submarinismo *nm* : scuba diving
submarinista *nmf* : scuba diver
submarino[1], **-na** *adj* : submarine, undersea
submarino[2] *nm* : submarine
suboficial *nmf* : noncommissioned officer, petty officer
subordinado, -da *adj & n* : subordinate
subordinar *vt* : to subordinate — **subordinarse** *vr* — **subordinación** *nf*
subproducto *nm* : by-product
subrayar *vt* 1 : to underline, to underscore 2 ENFATIZAR : to highlight, to emphasize
subrepticio, -cia *adj* : surreptitious — **subrepticiamente** *adv*
subsahariano, -na *adj* : sub-Saharan
subsanar *vt* 1 RECTIFICAR : to rectify, to correct 2 : to overlook, to excuse 3 : to make up for
subscribir → **suscribir**
subsecretario, -ria *n* : undersecretary
subsecuente *adj* : subsequent — **subsecuentemente** *adv*
subsidiar *vt* : to subsidize
subsidiaria *nf* : subsidiary
subsidio *nm* : subsidy
subsiguiente *adj* : subsequent
subsistencia *nf* 1 : subsistence 2 : sustenance
subsistir *vi* 1 : to subsist, to live 2 : to endure, to survive
substancia → **sustancia**
subteniente *nmf* : second lieutenant
subterfugio *nm* : subterfuge
subterráneo[1], **-nea** *adj* : underground, subterranean
subterráneo[2] *nm* 1 : underground passage, tunnel 2 *Arg, Uru* : subway
subtítulo *nm* : subtitle, subheading
subtotal *nm* : subtotal
suburbano, -na *adj* : suburban
suburbio *nm* 1 : suburb 2 : slum (outside a city)
subvención *nf, pl* **-ciones** : subsidy, grant
subvencionar *vt* : to subsidize
subversivo, -va *adj & n* : subversive — **subversión** *nf*
subvertir {76} *vt* : to subvert
subyacente *adj* : underlying
subyugar {52} *vt* : to subjugate — **subyugación** *nf*
succión *nf, pl* **succiones** : suction
succionar *vt* : to suck up, to draw in
sucedáneo *nm* : substitute ⟨sucedáneo de azucar : sugar substitute⟩
suceder *vi* 1 OCURRIR : to happen, to occur ⟨¿qué sucede? : what's going on?⟩ ⟨suceda lo que suceda : come what may⟩ 2 **∼ a** : to follow, to succeed ⟨suceder al trono : to succeed to the throne⟩ ⟨a la primavera sucede el verano : summer follows spring⟩

sucesión *nf, pl* **-siones** **1** : succession **2** : sequence, series **3** : issue, heirs *pl*

sucesivamente *adv* : successively, consecutively ⟨y así sucesivamente : and so on⟩

sucesivo, -va *adj* : successive ⟨en los días sucesivos : in the days that followed⟩

suceso *nm* **1** : event, happening, occurrence **2** : incident, crime

sucesor, -sora *n* : successor

suciedad *nf* **1** : dirtiness, filthiness **2** MUGRE : dirt, filth

sucinto, -ta *adj* CONCISO : succinct, concise — **sucintamente** *adv*

sucio, -cia *adj* : dirty, filthy

sucre *nm* : Ecuadoran unit of currency

suculento, -ta *adj* : succulent

sucumbir *vi* : to succumb

sucursal *nf* : branch (of a business)

sudadera *nf* : sweatshirt

sudado, -da → **sudoroso**

sudafricano, -na *adj & n* : South African

sudamericano, -na *adj & n* : South American

sudanés, -nesa *adj & n, mpl* **-neses** : Sudanese

sudar *vi* TRANSPIRAR : to sweat, to perspire

sudario *nm* : shroud

sudeste → **sureste**

sudoeste → **suroeste**

sudor *nm* TRANSPIRACIÓN : sweat, perspiration

sudoroso, -sa *adj* : sweaty

sueco[1]**, -ca** *adj* : Swedish

sueco[2]**, -ca** *n* : Swede

sueco[3] *nm* : Swedish (language)

suegro, -gra *n* **1** : father-in-law *m*, mother-in-law *f* **2 suegros** *nmpl* : in-laws

suela *nf* : sole (of a shoe)

suelda, etc. → **soldar**

sueldo *nm* : salary, wage

suele, etc. → **soler**

suelo *nm* **1** : ground ⟨caerse al suelo : to fall down, to hit the ground⟩ **2** : floor, flooring **3** TIERRA : soil, land

suelta, etc. → **soltar**

suelto[1]**, -ta** *adj* : loose, free, unattached

suelto[2] *nm* : loose change

suena, etc. → **sonar**

sueña, etc. → **soñar**

sueño *nm* **1** : dream **2** : sleep ⟨perder el sueño : to lose sleep⟩ **3** : sleepiness ⟨tener sueño : to be sleepy⟩

suero *nm* **1** : serum **2** : whey

suerte *nf* **1** FORTUNA : luck, fortune ⟨tener suerte : to be lucky⟩ ⟨por suerte : luckily⟩ **2** DESTINO : fate, destiny, lot **3** CLASE, GÉNERO : sort, kind ⟨toda suerte de cosas : all kinds of things⟩

suertudo, -da *adj fam* : lucky

suéter *nm* : sweater

suficiencia *nf* **1** : adequacy, sufficiency **2** : competence, fitness **3** : smugness, self-satisfaction

suficiente *adj* **1** BASTANTE : enough, sufficient ⟨tener suficiente : to have enough⟩ **2** : suitable, fit **3** : smug, complacent

suficientemente *adv* : sufficiently, enough

sufijo *nm* : suffix

suflé *nm* : soufflé

sufragar {52} *vt* **1** AYUDAR : to help out, to support **2** : to defray (costs) — *vi* : to vote

sufragio *nm* : suffrage, vote

sufrido, -da *adj* **1** : long-suffering, patient **2** : sturdy, serviceable (of clothing)

sufrimiento *nm* : suffering

sufrir *vt* **1** : to suffer ⟨sufrir una pérdida : to suffer a loss⟩ **2** : to tolerate, to put up with ⟨ella no lo puede sufrir : she can't stand him⟩ — *vi* : to suffer

sugerencia *nf* : suggestion

sugerir {76} *vt* **1** PROPONER, RECOMENDAR : to suggest, to recommend, to propose **2** : to suggest, to bring to mind

sugestión *nf, pl* **-tiones** : suggestion, prompting ⟨poder de sugestión : power of suggestion⟩

sugestionable *adj* : suggestible, impressionable

sugestionar *vt* : to influence, to sway — **sugestionarse** *vr* **~ con** : to talk oneself into, to become convinced of

sugestivo, -va *adj* **1** : suggestive **2** : interesting, stimulating

suicida[1] *adj* : suicidal

suicida[2] *nmf* : suicide victim, suicide

suicidarse *vr* : to commit suicide

suicidio *nm* : suicide

suite *nf* : suite

suizo, -za *adj & n* : Swiss

sujeción *nf, pl* **-ciones** **1** : holding, fastening **2** : subjection

sujetador *nm* **1** : fastener **2** : holder ⟨sujetador de tazas : cup holder⟩

sujetalibros *nms & pl* : bookend

sujetapapeles *nms & pl* CLIP : paper clip

sujetar *vt* **1** : to hold on to, to steady, to hold down **2** FIJAR : to fasten, to attach **3** DOMINAR : to subdue, to conquer — **sujetarse** *vr* **1** : to hold on, to hang on **2 ~ a** : to abide by

sujeto[1]**, -ta** *adj* **1** : secure, fastened **2 ~ a** : subject to

sujeto[2] *nm* **1** INDIVIDUO : individual, character **2** : subject (in grammar)

sulfúrico, -ca *adj* : sulfuric

sulfuro *nm* : sulfur

sultán *nm, pl* **sultanes** : sultan

suma *nf* **1** CANTIDAD : sum, quantity **2** : addition

sumamente *adv* : extremely, exceedingly

sumar *vt* **1** : to add, to add up **2** : to add up to, to total — *vi* : to add up — **sumarse** *vr* **~ a** : to join

sumario[1]**, -ria** *adj* SUCINTO : succinct, summary — **sumariamente** *adv*

sumario[2] *nm* : summary

sumergir {35} *vt* : to submerge, to immerse, to plunge — **sumergirse** *vr*

sumersión *nf, pl* **-siones** : submersion, immersion

sumidero *nm* : drain, sewer

suministrar *vt* : to supply, to provide

suministro *nm* : supply, provision

sumir *vt* SUMERGIR : to plunge, to immerse, to sink — **sumirse** *vr*

sumisión *nf, pl* **-siones 1** : submission **2** : submissiveness

sumiso, -sa *adj* : submissive, acquiescent, docile

sumo, -ma *adj* **1** : extreme, great, high ⟨la suma autoridad : the highest authority⟩ **2 a lo sumo** : at the most — **sumamente** *adv*

suntuoso, -sa *adj* : sumptuous, lavish — **suntuosamente** *adv*

supeditar *vt* SUBORDINAR : to subordinate — **supeditación** *nf*

super[1] *or* **súper** *adj fam* : super, great

super[2] *nm* SUPERMERCADO : market, supermarket

superable *adj* : surmountable

superabundancia *nf* : overabundance, superabundance — **superabundante** *adj*

superar *vt* **1** : to surpass, to exceed **2** : to overcome, to surmount — **superarse** *vr* : to improve oneself

superávit *nm, pl* **-vit** *or* **-vits** : surplus

superchería *nf* : trickery, fraud

supercomputadora *nf* : supercomputer

superestructura *nf* : superstructure

superficial *adj* : superficial — **superficialmente** *adv*

superficialidad *nf* : superficiality

superficie *nf* **1** : surface **2** : area ⟨la superficie de un triángulo : the area of a triangle⟩

superfluidad *nf* : superfluity

superfluo, -flua *adj* : superfluous

superintendente *nmf* : supervisor, superintendent

superior[1] *adj* **1** : superior **2** : upper ⟨nivel superior : upper level⟩ **3** : higher ⟨educación superior : higher education⟩ **4 ~ a** : above, higher than, in excess of

superior[2] *nm* : superior

superioridad *nf* : superiority

superlativo[1], **-va** *adj* : superlative

superlativo[2] *nm* : superlative

supermercado *nm* : supermarket

superpoblación *nf, pl* **-ciones** : overpopulation

superpoblado, -da *adj* : overpopulated

superponer {60} *vt* : to superimpose

superpotencia *nf* : superpower

superproducción → **sobreproducción**

supersónico, -ca *adj* : supersonic

superstición *nf, pl* **-ciones** : superstition

supersticioso, -sa *adj* : superstitious

supervisar *vt* : to supervise, to oversee

supervisión *nf, pl* **-siones** : supervision

supervisor, -sora *n* : supervisor, overseer

supervivencia *nf* : survival

superviviente *nmf* : survivor

supino, -na *adj* : supine

suplantar *vt* : to supplant, to replace

suplemental → **suplementario**

suplementario, -ria *adj* : supplementary, additional, extra

suplemento *nm* : supplement

suplencia *nf* : substitution, replacement

suplente *adj & nmf* : substitute ⟨equipo suplente : replacement team⟩

supletorio, -ria *adj* : extra, additional ⟨teléfono supletorio : extension phone⟩ ⟨cama supletoria : spare bed⟩

súplica *nf* : plea, entreaty

suplicar {72} *vt* IMPLORAR, ROGAR : to entreat, to implore, to supplicate

suplicio *nm* TORMENTO : ordeal, torture

suplir *vt* **1** COMPENSAR : to make up for, to compensate for **2** REEMPLAZAR : to replace, to substitute

supo, etc. → **saber**

suponer {60} *vt* **1** PRESUMIR : to suppose, to assume ⟨supongo que sí : I guess so, I suppose so⟩ ⟨se supone que van a llegar mañana : they're supposed to arrive tomorrow⟩ **2** : to imply, to suggest **3** : to involve, to entail ⟨el éxito supone mucho trabajo : success involves a lot of work⟩

suposición *nf, pl* **-ciones** PRESUNCIÓN : supposition, assumption

supositorio *nm* : suppository

supremacía *nf* : supremacy

supremo, -ma *adj* : supreme

supresión *nf, pl* **-siones 1** : suppression, elimination **2** : deletion

suprimir *vt* **1** : to suppress, to eliminate **2** : to delete

supuestamente *adv* : supposedly, allegedly

supuesto, -ta *adj* **1** : supposed, alleged **2 por ~** : of course, absolutely

supurar *vi* : to ooze, to discharge

supuso, etc. → **suponer**

sur[1] *adj* : southern, southerly, south

sur[2] *nm* **1** : south, South **2** : south wind

surafricano, -na → **sudafricano**

suramericano, -na → **sudamericano**

surcar {72} *vt* **1** : to plow (through) **2** : to groove, to score, to furrow

surco *nm* : groove, furrow, rut

sureño[1], **-ña** *adj* : southern, Southern

sureño[2], **-ña** *n* : Southerner

sureste[1] *adj* **1** : southeast, southeastern **2** : southeasterly

sureste[2] *nm* : southeast, Southeast

surf *nm* : surfing

surfear *vi* : to surf

surfing → **surf**

surfista *nmf* : surfer

surgimiento *nm* : rise, emergence

surgir {35} *vi* : to rise, to arise, to emerge

suroeste[1] *adj* **1** : southwest, southwestern **2** : southwesterly

suroeste[2] *nm* : southwest, Southwest

surtido[1], **-da** *adj* **1** : assorted, varied **2** : stocked, provisioned

surtido[2] *nm* : assortment, selection
surtidor *nm* **1** : jet, spout **2** *Arg, Chile, Spain* : gas pump
surtir *vt* **1** : to supply, to provide ⟨surtir un pedido : to fill an order⟩ **2 surtir efecto** : to have an effect — *vi* : to spout, to spurt up — **surtirse** *vr* : to stock up
susceptible *adj* : susceptible, sensitive — **susceptibilidad** *nf*
suscitar *vt* : to provoke, to give rise to
suscribir {33} *vt* **1** : to sign (a formal document) **2** : to endorse, to sanction — **suscribirse** *vr* **~ a** : to subscribe to
suscripción *nf, pl* **-ciones** **1** : subscription **2** : endorsement, sanction **3** : signing
suscriptor, -tora *n* : subscriber
susodicho, -cha *adj* : aforementioned, aforesaid
suspender *vt* **1** COLGAR : to suspend, to hang **2** : to suspend, to discontinue **3** : to suspend, to dismiss
suspensión *nf, pl* **-siones** : suspension
suspenso *nm* : suspense
suspicacia *nf* : suspicion, mistrust
suspicaz *adj, pl* **-caces** DESCONFIADO : suspicious, wary
suspirar *vi* : to sigh
suspiro *nm* : sigh
surque, etc. → **surcar**
suscrito *pp* → **suscribir**
sustancia *nf* **1** : substance **2 sin ~** : shallow, lacking substance
sustancial *adj* **1** : substantial **2** ESENCIAL, FUNDAMENTAL : essential, fundamental — **sustancialmente** *adv*
sustancioso, -sa *adj* **1** NUTRITIVO : hearty, nutritious **2** : substantial, solid
sustantivo *nm* : noun
sustentación *nf, pl* **-ciones** SOSTÉN : support
sustentar *vt* **1** : to support, to hold up **2** : to sustain, to nourish **3** : to maintain, to hold (an opinion) — **sustentarse** *vr* : to support oneself
sustento *nm* **1** : means of support, livelihood **2** : sustenance, food
sustitución *nf, pl* **-ciones** : replacement, substitution
sustituir {41} *vt* **1** : to replace, to substitute for **2** : to stand in for
sustituto, -ta *n* : substitute, stand-in
susto *nm* : fright, scare
sustracción *nf, pl* **-ciones** **1** RESTA : subtraction **2** : theft
sustraer {81} *vt* **1** : to remove, to take away **2** RESTAR : to subtract **3** : to steal — **sustraerse** *vr* **~ a** : to avoid, to evade
susurrar *vi* **1** : to whisper **2** : to murmur **3** : to rustle (leaves, etc.) — *vt* : to whisper
susurro *nm* **1** : whisper **2** : murmur **3** : rustle, rustling
sutil *adj* **1** : delicate, thin, fine **2** : subtle
sutileza *nf* **1** : delicacy **2** : subtlety
sutura *nf* : suture
suturar *vt* : to suture
suyo[1], **-ya** *adj* **1** : his, her, its, theirs ⟨los libros suyos : his books⟩ ⟨un amigo suyo : a friend of hers⟩ ⟨esta casa es suya : this house is theirs⟩ **2** (*formal*) : yours ⟨¿este abrigo es suyo, señor? : is this your coat, sir?⟩
suyo[2], **-ya** *pron* **1** : his, hers, theirs ⟨mi guitarra y la suya : my guitar and hers⟩ ⟨ellos trajeron las suyas : they brought theirs, they brought their own⟩ **2** (*formal*) : yours ⟨usted olvidó la suya : you forgot yours⟩
switch *nm* : switch

T

t *nf* : twenty-first letter of the Spanish alphabet
taba *nf* : anklebone
tabacalero[1], **-ra** *adj* : tobacco ⟨industria tabacalera : tobacco industry⟩
tabacalero[2], **-ra** *n* : tobacco grower
tabaco *nm* : tobacco
tábano *nm* : horsefly
taberna *nf* : tavern, bar
tabernáculo *nm* : tabernacle
tabicar {72} *vt* : to wall up
tabique *nm* : thin wall, partition
tabla *nf* **1** : table, list ⟨tabla de multiplicar : multiplication table⟩ **2** : board, plank, slab ⟨tabla de planchar : ironing board⟩ **3** : plot, strip (of land) **4 tablas** *nfpl* : stage, boards *pl*
tablado *nm* **1** : floor **2** : platform, scaffold **3** : stage
tablero *nm* **1** : bulletin board **2** : board (in games) ⟨tablero de ajedrez : chessboard⟩ ⟨tablero de damas : checkerboard⟩ **3** PIZARRA : blackboard **4** : switchboard **5 tablero de instrumentos** : dashboard, instrument panel
tableta *nf* **1** COMPRIMIDO, PÍLDORA : tablet, pill **2** : bar (of chocolate)
tabletear *vi* : to rattle, to clack
tableteo *nm* : clack, rattling
tablilla *nf* **1** : small board or tablet **2** : bulletin board **3** : splint
tabloide *nm* : tabloid
tablón *nm, pl* **tablones** **1** : plank, beam **2 tablón de anuncios** : bulletin board
tabú[1] *adj* : taboo
tabú[2] *nm, pl* **tabúes** *or* **tabús** : taboo
tabulador *nm* : tabulator
tabular[1] *vt* : to tabulate
tabular[2] *adj* : tabular
taburete *nm* : footstool, stool
tacañería *nf* : miserliness, stinginess

tacaño[1], **-ña** *adj* MEZQUINO : stingy, miserly
tacaño[2], **-ña** *n* : miser, tightwad
tacha *nf* **1** : flaw, blemish, defect **2 poner tacha a** : to find fault with **3 sin ~** : flawless
tachadura *nf* : erasure, correction
tachar *vt* **1** : to cross out, to delete **2 ~ de** : to accuse of, to label as ⟨lo tacharon de mentiroso : they accused him of being a liar⟩
tachón *nm, pl* **tachones** : stud, hobnail
tachonar *vt* : to stud
tachuela *nf* : tack, hobnail, stud
tácito, -ta *adj* : tacit, implicit — **tácitamente** *adv*
taciturno, -na *adj* **1** : taciturn **2** : sullen, gloomy
tacle *nm* : tackle
taclear *vt* : to tackle (in football)
taco *nm* **1** : wad, stopper, plug **2** : pad (of paper) **3** : cleat **4** : heel (of a shoe) **5** : cue (in billiards) **6** : light snack, bite **7** : taco
tacón *nm, pl* **tacones** : heel (of a shoe) ⟨de tacón alto : high-heeled⟩
táctica *nf* : tactic, tactics *pl*
táctico[1], **-ca** *adj* : tactical
táctico[2], **-ca** *n* : tactician
táctil *adj* : tactile
tacto *nm* **1** : touch, touching, feel **2** DELICADEZA : tact
tafetán *nm, pl* **-tanes** : taffeta
tahúr *nm, pl* **tahúres** : gambler
tailandés[1], **-desa** *adj & n, pl* **-deses** : Thai
tailandés[2] *nm* : Thai (language)
taimado, -da *adj* **1** : crafty, sly **2** *Chile* : sullen, sulky
tajada *nf* **1** : slice **2 sacar tajada** *fam* : to get one's share
tajante *adj* **1** : cutting, sharp **2** : decisive, categorical
tajantemente *adj* : emphatically, categorically
tajar *vt* : to cut, to slice
tajo *nm* **1** : cut, slash, gash **2** ESCARPA : steep cliff
tal[1] *adv* **1** : so, in such a way **2 tal como** : just as ⟨tal como lo hice : just the way I did it⟩ **3 con tal que** : provided that, as long as **4 ¿qué tal?** : how are you?, how's it going?
tal[2] *adj* **1** : such, such a **2 tal vez** : maybe, perhaps
tal[3] *pron* **1** : such a one, someone **2** : such a thing, something **3 tal para cual** : two of a kind
tala *nf* : felling (of trees)
taladrar *vt* : to drill
taladro *nm* : drill, auger ⟨taladro eléctrico : power drill⟩
talante *nm* **1** HUMOR : mood, disposition **2** VOLUNTAD : will, willingness
talar *vt* **1** : to cut down, to fell **2** DEVASTAR : to devastate, to destroy
talco *nm* **1** : talc **2** : talcum powder
talego *nm* : sack
talento *nm* : talent, ability
talentoso, -sa *adj* : talented, gifted
talismán *nm, pl* **-manes** AMULETO : talisman, charm
talla *nf* **1** ESTATURA : height **2** : size (in clothing) **3** : stature, status **4** : sculpture, carving
tallar *vt* **1** : to sculpt, to carve **2** : to measure (someone's height) **3** : to deal (cards)
tallarín *nf, pl* **-rines** : noodle
talle *nm* **1** : size **2** : waist, waistline **3** : figure, shape
taller *nm* **1** : shop, workshop **2** : studio (of an artist)
tallo *nm* : stalk, stem ⟨tallo de maíz : cornstalk⟩
talón *nm, pl* **talones** **1** : heel (of the foot) **2** : stub (of a check) **3 talón de Aquiles** : Achilles' heel
talud *nm* : slope, incline
tamal *nm* : tamale
tamaño[1], **-ña** *adj* : such a big ⟨¿crees tamaña mentira? : do you believe such a lie?⟩
tamaño[2] *nm* **1** : size **2 de tamaño natural** : life-size
tamarindo *nm* : tamarind
tambalearse *vr* **1** : to teeter **2** : to totter, to stagger, to sway — **tambaleante** *adj*
tambaleo *nm* : staggering, lurching, swaying
también *adv* : too, as well, also
tambor *nm* : drum
tamborilear *vi* : to drum, to tap
tamborileo *nm* : tapping, drumming
tamiz *nm* : sieve
tamizar {21} *vt* : to sift
tampoco *adv* : neither, not either ⟨ni yo tampoco : me neither⟩
tampón *nm, pl* **tampones** **1** : ink pad **2** : tampon
tam–tam *nm* : tom-tom
tan *adv* **1** : so, so very ⟨no es tan difícil : it is not that difficult⟩ **2** : as ⟨tan pronto como : as soon as⟩ **3 tan siquiera** : at least, at the least **4 tan sólo** : only, merely
tanda *nf* **1** : turn, shift **2** : batch, lot, series
tándem *nm* **1** : tandem (bicycle) **2** : duo, pair
tangente *adj & nf* : tangent — **tangencial** *adj*
tangible *adj* : tangible
tango *nm* : tango
tanino *nm* : tannin
tanque *nm* **1** : tank, reservoir **2** : tanker, tank (vehicle)
tanteador *nm* MARCADOR : scoreboard
tantear *vt* **1** : to feel, to grope **2** : to size up, to weigh — *vi* **1** : to keep score **2** : to feel one's way
tanteo *nm* **1** : estimate, rough calculation **2** : testing, sizing up **3** : scoring
tanto[1] *adv* **1** : so much ⟨tanto mejor : so much the better⟩ **2** : so long ⟨¿por qué

te tardaste tanto? : why did you take so long?⟩
tanto[2], **-ta** *adj* **1** : so much, so many, such ⟨no hagas tantas preguntas : don't ask so many questions⟩ ⟨tiene tanto encanto : he has such charm, he's so charming⟩ **2** : as much, as many ⟨come tantos dulces como yo : she eats as many sweets as I do⟩ **3** : odd, however many ⟨cuarenta y tantos años : forty-odd years⟩
tanto[3] *nm* **1** : certain amount **2** : goal, point (in sports) **3 al tanto** : abreast, in the picture **4 un tanto** : somewhat, rather ⟨un tanto cansado : rather tired⟩
tanto[4], **-ta** *pron* **1** : so much, so many ⟨tiene tanto que hacer : she has so much to do⟩ ⟨¡no me des tantos! : don't give me so many!⟩ **2 entre ~** : meanwhile **3 por lo tanto** : therefore
tañer {79} *vt* **1** : to ring (a bell) **2** : to play (a musical instrument)
tañido *nm* **1** CAMPANADA : ring, peal, toll **2** : sound (of an instrument)
tapa *nf* **1** : cover, top, lid **2** *Spain* : bar snack
tapacubos *nms & pl* : hubcap
tapadera *nf* **1** : cover, lid **2** : front, cover (for an organization or person)
tapar *vt* **1** CUBRIR : to cover, to cover up **2** OBSTRUIR : to block, to obstruct — **taparse** *vr*
tapete *nm* **1** : small rug, mat **2** : table cover **3 poner sobre el tapete** : to bring up for discussion
tapia *nf* : (adobe) wall, garden wall
tapiar *vt* **1** : to wall in **2** : to enclose, to block off
tapicería *nf* **1** : upholstery **2** TAPIZ : tapestry
tapicero, **-ra** *n* : upholsterer
tapioca *nf* : tapioca
tapir *nm* : tapir
tapiz *nm, pl* **tapices** : tapestry
tapizar {21} *vt* **1** : to upholster **2** : to cover, to carpet
tapón *nm, pl* **tapones** **1** : cork **2** : bottle cap **3** : plug, stopper
tapujo *nm* **1** : deceit, pretension **2 sin tapujos** : openly, frankly
taquigrafía *nf* : stenography, shorthand
taquigráfico, **-ca** *adj* : stenographic
taquígrafo, **-fa** *n* : stenographer
taquilla *nf* **1** : box office, ticket office **2** : earnings *pl*, take
taquillero, **-ra** *adj* : box-office, popular ⟨un éxito taquillero : a box-office success⟩
tarántula *nf* : tarantula
tararear *vt* : to hum
tardanza *nf* : lateness, delay
tardar *vi* **1** : to delay, to take a long time **2** : to be late **3 a más tardar** : at the latest — *vt* DEMORAR : to take (time) ⟨tarda una hora : it takes an hour⟩
tarde[1] *adv* **1** : late **2 tarde o temprano** : sooner or later
tarde[2] *nf* **1** : afternoon, evening **2 ¡buenas tardes!** : good afternoon!, good evening! **3 en la tarde** *or* **por la tarde** : in the afternoon, in the evening
tardío, **-día** *adj* : late, tardy
tardo, **-da** *adj* : slow
tarea *nf* **1** : task, job **2** : homework
tarifa *nf* **1** : rate ⟨tarifas postales : postal rates⟩ **2** : fare (for transportation) **3** : price list **4** ARANCEL : duty
tarima *nf* PLATAFORMA : dais, platform, stage
tarjeta *nf* : card ⟨tarjeta de crédito : credit card⟩ ⟨tarjeta postal : postcard⟩
tarro *nm* **1** : jar, pot **2** *Arg, Chile* : can, tin
tarta *nf* **1** : tart **2** : cake
tartaleta *nf* : tart
tartamudear *vi* : to stammer, to stutter
tartamudeo *nm* : stutter, stammer
tartán *nm, pl* **tartanes** : tartan, plaid
tártaro *nm* : tartar
tasa *nf* **1** : rate ⟨tasa de desempleo : unemployment rate⟩ **2** : tax, fee **3** : appraisal, valuation
tasación *nf, pl* **-ciones** : appraisal, assessment
tasador, **-dora** *n* : assessor, appraiser
tasar *vt* **1** VALORAR : to appraise, to value **2** : to set the price of **3** : to ration, to limit
tasca *nf* : cheap bar, dive
tatuaje *nm* : tattoo, tattooing
tatuar {3} *vt* : to tattoo
taurino, **-na** *adj* : bull, bullfighting
Tauro *nmf* : Taurus
tauromaquia *nf* : (art of) bullfighting
taxi *nm, pl* **taxis** : taxi, taxicab
taxidermia *nf* : taxidermy
taxidermista *nmf* : taxidermist
taxímetro *nm* : taximeter
taxista *nmf* : taxi driver
taza *nf* **1** : cup **2** : cupful **3** : (toilet) bowl **4** : basin (of a fountain)
tazón *nm, pl* **tazones** **1** : bowl **2** : large cup, mug
te *pron* **1** : you ⟨te quiero : I love you⟩ **2** : for you, to you, from you ⟨me gustaría dártelo : I would like to give it to you⟩ **3** : yourself, for yourself, to yourself, from yourself ⟨¡cálmate! : calm yourself!⟩ ⟨¿te guardaste uno? : did you keep one for yourself?⟩ **4** : thee
té *nm* **1** : tea **2** : tea party
tea *nf* : torch
teatral *adj* : theatrical — **teatralmente** *adv*
teatro *nm* **1** : theater **2 hacer teatro** : to put on an act, to exaggerate
teca *nf* : teak
techado *nm* **1** : roof **2 bajo techado** : under cover, indoors
techar *vt* : to roof, to shingle
techo *nm* **1** TEJADO : roof **2** : ceiling **3** : upper limit, ceiling
techumbre *nf* : roofing
tecla *nf* **1** : key (of a musical instrument or a machine) **2 dar en la tecla** : to hit the nail on the head

teclado *nm* : keyboard
teclear *vt* : to type in, to enter
técnica *nf* **1** : technique, skill **2** : technology
técnico[1], -ca *adj* : technical — **técnicamente** *adv*
técnico[2], -ca *n* : technician, expert, engineer
tecnología *nf* : technology
tecnológico, -ca *adj* : technological — **tecnológicamente** *adv*
tecolote *nm Mex* : owl
tedio *nm* : tedium, boredom
tedioso, -sa *adj* : tedious, boring — **tediosamente** *adv*
teja *nf* : tile
tejado *nm* TECHO : roof
tejedor, -dora *n* : weaver
tejer *vt* **1** : to knit, to crochet **2** : to weave **3** FABRICAR : to concoct, to make up, to fabricate
tejido *nm* **1** TELA : fabric, cloth **2** : weave, texture **3** : tissue ⟨tejido muscular : muscle tissue⟩
tejo *nm* **1** : yew **2** : hopscotch (children's game)
tejón *nm, pl* **tejones** : badger
tela *nf* **1** : fabric, cloth, material **2 tela de araña** : spiderweb **3 poner en tela de juicio** : to call into question, to doubt
telar *nm* : loom
telaraña *nf* : spiderweb, cobweb
tele *nf fam* : TV, television
telecomunicación *nf, pl* **-ciones** : telecommunication
teleconferencia *nf* : teleconference
teledifusión *nf, pl* **-siones** : television broadcasting
teledirigido, -da *adj* : remote-controlled
telefonear *v* : to telephone, to call
telefónico, -ca *adj* : phone, telephone ⟨llamada telefónica : phone call⟩
telefonista *nmf* : telephone operator
teléfono *nm* **1** : telephone **2 llamar por teléfono** : to telephone, to make a phone call
telegrafiar {85} *v* : to telegraph
telegráfico, -ca *adj* : telegraphic
telégrafo *nm* : telegraph
telegrama *nm* : telegram
telenovela *nf* : soap opera
telepatía *nf* : telepathy
telepático, -ca *adj* : telepathic — **telepáticamente** *adv*
telescópico, -ca *adj* : telescopic
telescopio *nm* : telescope
telespectador, -dora *n* : television viewer
telesquí *nm, pl* **-squís** : ski lift
televidente *nmf* : television viewer
televisar *vt* : to televise
televisión *nf, pl* **-siones** : television, TV
televisivo, -va *adj* : television ⟨serie televisiva : television series⟩
televisor *nm* : television set
telón *nm, pl* **telones** **1** : curtain (in theater) **2 telón de fondo** : backdrop, background
tema *nm* **1** ASUNTO : theme, topic, subject **2** MOTIVO : motif, central theme
temario *nm* **1** : set of topics (for study) **2** : agenda
temática *nf* : subject matter
temático, -ca *adj* : thematic
temblar {55} *vi* **1** : to tremble, to shake, to shiver ⟨le temblaban las rodillas : his knees were shaking⟩ **2** : to shudder, to be afraid ⟨tiemblo con sólo pensarlo : I shudder to think of it⟩
temblor *nm* **1** : shaking, trembling **2** : tremor, earthquake
tembloroso, -sa *adj* : tremulous, trembling, shaking ⟨con la voz temblorosa : with a shaky voice⟩
temer *vt* : to fear, to dread — *vi* : to be afraid
temerario, -ria *adj* : reckless, rash — **temerariamente** *adv*
temeridad *nf* **1** : temerity, recklessness, rashness **2** : rash act
temeroso, -sa *adj* MIEDOSO : fearful, frightened
temible *adj* : fearsome, dreadful
temor *nm* MIEDO : fear, dread
témpano *nm* : ice floe
temperamento *nm* : temperament — **temperamental** *adj*
temperancia *nf* : temperance
temperar *vt* MODERAR : to temper, to moderate — *vi* : to have a change of air
temperatura *nf* : temperature
tempestad *nf* **1** : storm, tempest **2 tempestad de arena** : sandstorm
tempestuoso, -sa *adj* : tempestuous, stormy
templado, -da *adj* **1** : temperate, mild **2** : moderate, restrained **3** : warm, lukewarm **4** VALIENTE : courageous, bold
templanza *nf* **1** : temperance, moderation **2** : mildness (of weather)
templar *vt* **1** : to temper (steel) **2** : to restrain, to moderate **3** : to tune (a musical instrument) **4** : to warm up, to cool down — **templarse** *vr* **1** : to be moderate **2** : to warm up, to cool down
temple *nm* **1** : temper (of steel, etc.) **2** HUMOR : mood ⟨de buen temple : in a good mood⟩ **3** : tuning **4** VALOR : courage
templo *nm* **1** : temple **2** : church, chapel
tempo *nm* : tempo (in music)
temporada *nf* **1** : season, time ⟨temporada de béisbol : baseball season⟩ **2** : period, spell ⟨por temporadas : on and off⟩
temporal[1] *adj* **1** : temporal **2** : temporary
temporal[2] *nm* **1** : storm **2 capear el temporal** : to weather the storm
temporalmente *adv* : temporarily
temporario, -ria *adj* : temporary — **temporariamente** *adv*
temporero[1], -ra *adj* : temporary, seasonal

temporero[2], **-ra** *n* : temporary or seasonal worker
temporizador *nm* : timer
tempranero, -ra *adj* **1** : early **2** : early-rising
temprano[1] *adv* : early ⟨lo más temprano posible : as soon as possible⟩
temprano[2], **-na** *adj* : early ⟨la parte temprana del siglo : the early part of the century⟩
ten → **tener**
tenacidad *nf* : tenacity, perseverance
tenaz *adj, pl* **tenaces** **1** : tenacious, persistent **2** : strong, tough
tenaza *nf, or* **tenazas** *nfpl* **1** : pliers, pincers **2** : tongs **3** : claw (of a crustacean)
tenazmente *adv* : tenaciously
tendedero *nm* : clothesline
tendencia *nf* **1** PROPENSIÓN : tendency, inclination **2** : trend
tendencioso, -sa *adj* : tendentious, biased
tendente → **tendiente**
tender {56} *vt* **1** EXTENDER : to spread out, to lay out **2** : to hang out (clothes) **3** : to lay (cables, etc.) **4** : to set (a trap) — *vi* **~ a** : to tend to, to have a tendency towards — **tenderse** *vr* : to stretch out, to lie down
tendero, -ra *n* : shopkeeper, storekeeper
tendido *nm* **1** : laying (of cables, etc.) **2** : seats *pl,* section (at a bullfight)
tendiente *adj* **~ a** : aimed at, designed to
tendón *nm, pl* **tendones** : tendon
tenebrosidad *nf* : darkness, gloom
tendrá, etc. → **tener**
tenebroso, -sa *adj* **1** OSCURO : gloomy, dark **2** SINIESTRO : sinister
tenedor[1], **-dora** *n* **1** : holder **2 tenedor de libros, tenedora de libros** : bookkeeper
tenedor[2] *nm* : table fork
tenencia *nf* **1** : possession, holding **2** : tenancy **3** : tenure
tener {80} *vt* **1** : to have ⟨tiene ojos verdes : she has green eyes⟩ ⟨tengo mucho que hacer : I have a lot to do⟩ ⟨tiene veinte años : he's twenty years old⟩ ⟨tiene un metro de largo : it's one meter long⟩ **2** : to hold ⟨ten esto un momento : hold this for a moment⟩ **3** : to feel, to make ⟨tengo frío : I'm cold⟩ ⟨eso nos tiene contentos : that makes us happy⟩ **4 ~ por** : to think, to consider ⟨me tienes por loco : you think I'm crazy⟩ — *v aux* **1 tener que** : to have to ⟨tengo que salir : I have to leave⟩ ⟨tiene que estar aquí : it has to be here, it must be here⟩ **2** (*with past participle*) ⟨tenía pensado escribirte : I've been thinking of writing to you⟩ — **tenerse** *vr* **1** : to stand up **2 ~ por** : to consider oneself ⟨me tengo por afortunado : I consider myself lucky⟩
tenería *nf* CURTIDURÍA : tannery
tenga, etc. → **tener**
tenia *nf* SOLITARIA : tapeworm
teniente *nmf* **1** : lieutenant **2 teniente coronel** : lieutenant colonel
tenis *nms & pl* **1** : tennis **2 tenis** *nmpl* : sneakers *pl*
tenista *nmf* : tennis player
tenor *nm* **1** : tenor **2** : tone, sense
tensar *vt* **1** : to tense, to make taut **2** : to draw (a bow) — **tensarse** *vr* : to become tense
tensión *nf, pl* **tensiones** **1** : tension, tautness **2** : stress, strain **3 tensión arterial** : blood pressure
tenso, -sa *adj* : tense
tentación *nf, pl* **-ciones** : temptation
tentáculo *nm* : tentacle, feeler
tentador[1], **-dora** *adj* : tempting
tentador[2], **-dora** *n* : tempter, temptress *f*
tentar {55} *vt* **1** TOCAR : to feel, to touch **2** PROBAR : to test, to try **3** ATRAER : to tempt, to entice
tentativa *nf* : attempt, try
tentempié *nm fam* : snack, bite
tenue *adj* **1** : tenuous **2** : faint, weak, dim **3** : light, fine **4** : thin, slender
teñir {67} *vt* **1** : to dye **2** : to stain
teodolito *nm* : theodolite, transit (for surveying)
teología *nf* : theology
teológico, -ca *adj* : theological
teólogo, -ga *n* : theologian
teorema *nm* : theorem
teoría *nf* : theory
teórico[1], **-ca** *adj* : theoretical — **teóricamente** *adv*
teórico[2], **-ca** *n* : theorist
teorizar {21} *vi* : to theorize
tepe *nm* : sod, turf
teponaztle *nm Mex* : traditional drum
tequila *nm* : tequila
terapeuta *nmf* : therapist
terapéutica *nf* : therapeutics
terapéutico, -ca *adj* : therapeutic
terapia *nf* **1** : therapy **2 terapia intensiva** : intensive care
tercer → **tercero**
tercermundista *adj* : third-world
tercero[1], **-ra** *adj* (**tercer** *before masculine singular nouns*) **1** : third **2 el Tercer Mundo** : the Third World
tercero[2], **-ra** *n* : third (in a series)
terceto *nm* **1** : tercet, triplet (in literature) **2** : trio (in music)
terciar *vt* **1** : to place diagonally **2** : to divide into three parts — *vi* **1** : to mediate **2 ~ en** : to take part in
terciario, -ria *adj* : tertiary
tercio[1], **-cia** → **tercero**
tercio[2] *nm* : third ⟨dos tercios : two thirds⟩
terciopelo *nm* : velvet
terco, -ca *adj* OBSTINADO : obstinate, stubborn
tergiversación *nf, pl* **-ciones** : distortion
tergiversar *vt* : to distort, to twist
termal *adj* : thermal, hot
termas *nfpl* : hot springs
térmico, -ca *adj* : thermal, heat ⟨energía térmica : thermal energy⟩

terminación *nf, pl* **-ciones** : termination, conclusion
terminal[1] *adj* : terminal — **terminalmente** *adv*
terminal[2] *nm* (*in some regions f*) : (electric or electronic) terminal
terminal[3] *nf* (*in some regions m*) : terminal, station
terminante *adj* : final, definitive, categorical — **terminantemente** *adv*
terminar *vt* **1** CONCLUIR : to end, to conclude **2** ACABAR : to complete, to finish off — *vi* **1** : to finish **2** : to stop, to end — **terminarse** *vr* **1** : to run out **2** : to come to an end
término *nm* **1** CONCLUSIÓN : end, conclusion **2** : term, expression **3** : period, term of office **4 término medio** : happy medium **5 términos** *nmpl* : terms, specifications ⟨los términos del acuerdo : the terms of the agreement⟩
terminología *nf* : terminology
termita *nf* : termite
termo *nm* : thermos
termodinámica *nf* : thermodynamics
termómetro *nm* : thermometer
termostato *nm* : thermostat
ternera *nf* : veal
ternero, -ra *n* : calf
terno *nm* **1** : set of three **2** : three-piece suit
ternura *nf* : tenderness
terquedad *nf* OBSTINACIÓN : obstinacy, stubbornness
terracota *nf* : terra-cotta
terraplén *nm, pl* **-plenes** : terrace, embankment
terráqueo, -quea *adj* **1** : earth **2 globo terráqueo** : the earth, globe (of the earth)
terrateniente *nmf* : landowner
terraza *nf* **1** : terrace, veranda **2** : balcony (in a theater) **3** : terrace (in agriculture)
terremoto *nm* : earthquake
terrenal *adj* : worldly, earthly
terreno *nm* **1** : terrain **2** SUELO : earth, ground **3** : plot, tract of land **4 perder terreno** : to lose ground **5 preparar el terreno** : to pave the way
terrestre *adj* : terrestrial
terrible *adj* : terrible, horrible — **terriblemente** *adv*
terrier *nmf* : terrier
territorial *adj* : territorial
territorio *nm* : territory
terrón *nm, pl* **terrones 1** : clod (of earth) **2 terrón de azúcar** : lump of sugar
terror *nm* : terror
terrorífico, -ca *adj* : horrific, terrifying
terrorismo *nm* : terrorism
terrorista *adj & nmf* : terrorist
terroso, -sa *adj* : earthy ⟨colores terrosos : earthy colors⟩
terruño *nm* : native land, homeland
terso, -sa *adj* **1** : smooth **2** : glossy, shiny **3** : polished, flowing (of a style)
tersura *nf* **1** : smoothness **2** : shine
tertulia *nf* : gathering, group ⟨tertulia literaria : literary circle⟩
tesauro *nm* : thesaurus
tesis *nfs & pl* : thesis
tesón *nm* : persistence, tenacity
tesonero, -ra *adj* : persistent, tenacious
tesorería *nf* : treasurer's office
tesorero, -ra *n* : treasurer
tesoro *nm* **1** : treasure **2** : thesaurus
test *nm* : test
testaferro *nm* : figurehead
testamentario[1], **-ria** *adj* : testamentary
testamentario[2], **-ria** *n* ALBACEA : executor, executrix *f*
testamento *nm* : testament, will
testar *vi* : to draw up a will
testarudo, -da *adj* : stubborn, pigheaded
testículo *nm* : testicle
testificar {72} *v* : to testify
testigo *nmf* : witness
testimonial *adj* **1** : testimonial **2** : token
testimoniar *vi* : to testify
testimonio *nm* : testimony, statement
teta *nf* : teat
tétano *or* **tétanos** *nm* : tetanus, lockjaw
tetera *nf* **1** : teapot **2** : teakettle
tetilla *nf* **1** : teat **2** : nipple
tetina *nf* : nipple (on a bottle)
tétrico, -ca *adj* : somber, gloomy
textil *adj & nm* : textile
texto *nm* : text
textual *adj* : literal, exact — **textualmente** *adv*
textura *nf* : texture
tez *nf, pl* **teces** : complexion, coloring
ti *pron* **1** : you ⟨es para ti : it's for you⟩ **2 ti mismo, ti misma** : yourself **3** : thee
tía → **tío**
tiamina *nf* : thiamine
tianguis *nm Mex* : open-air market
tibetano[1], **-na** *adj & n* : Tibetan
tibetano[2] *nm* : Tibetan (language)
tibia *nf* : tibia
tibieza *nf* **1** : tepidness **2** : halfheartedness
tibio, -bia *adj* **1** : lukewarm, tepid **2** : cool, unenthusiastic
tiburón *nm, pl* **-rones 1** : shark **2** : raider (in finance)
tic *nm* **1** : click, tick **2 tic nervioso** : tic
tico, -ca *adj & n fam* : Costa Rican
tictac *nm* **1** : ticking, tick-tock **2 hacer tictac** : to tick
tiembla, etc. → **temblar**
tiempo *nm* **1** : time ⟨justo a tiempo : just in time⟩ ⟨perder tiempo : to waste time⟩ ⟨tiempo libre : spare time⟩ **2** : period, age ⟨en los tiempos que corren : nowadays⟩ **3** : season, moment ⟨antes de tiempo : prematurely⟩ **4** : weather ⟨hace buen tiempo : the weather is fine, it's nice outside⟩ **5** : tempo (in music) **6** : half (in sports) **7** : tense (in grammar)
tienda *nf* **1** : store, shop **2** *or* **tienda de campaña** : tent
tiende, etc. → **tender**

tiene, etc. → **tener**
tienta[1], etc. → **tentar**
tienta[2] *nf* **andar a tientas** : to feel one's way, to grope around
tiernamente *adv* : tenderly
tierno, **-na** *adj* **1** : affectionate, tender **2** : tender, young
tierra *nf* **1** : land **2** SUELO : ground, earth **3** : country, homeland, soil **4 tierra natal** : native land **5 tierras altas** : highlands **6 la Tierra** : the Earth
tieso, **-sa** *adj* **1** : stiff, rigid **2** : upright, erect
tiesto *nm* **1** : potsherd **2** MACETA : flowerpot
tiesura *nf* : stiffness, rigidity
tifoidea *nf* : typhoid
tifoideo, **-dea** *adj* : typhoid ⟨fiebre tifoidea : typhoid fever⟩
tifón *nm, pl* **tifones** : typhoon
tifus *nm* : typhus
tigre, **-gresa** *n* **1** : tiger, tigress *f* **2** : jaguar
tijera *nf* **1** *or* **tijeras** *nfpl* : scissors **2 de ~** : folding ⟨escalera de tijera : stepladder⟩
tijereta *nf* : earwig
tijeretada *nf or* **tijeretazo** *nm* : cut, snip
tildar *vt* **~ de** : to brand as, to call ⟨lo tildaron de traidor : they branded him as a traitor⟩
tilde *nf* **1** : accent mark **2** : tilde (accent over *ñ*)
tilo *nm* : linden (tree)
timador, **-dora** *n* : swindler
timar *vt* : to swindle, to cheat
timbal *nm* **1** : kettledrum **2 timbales** *nmpl* : timpani
timbre *nm* **1** : bell ⟨tocar el timbre : to ring the doorbell⟩ **2** : tone, timbre **3** SELLO : seal, stamp **4** *CA, Mex* : postage stamp
timidez *nf* : timidity, shyness
tímido, **-da** *adj* : timid, shy — **tímidamente** *adv*
timo *nm fam* : swindle, trick, hoax
timón *nm, pl* **timones** : rudder ⟨estar al timón : to beat the helm⟩
timonel *nm* : helmsman, coxswain
timorato, **-ta** *adj* **1** : timorous **2** : sanctimonious
tímpano *nm* **1** : eardrum **2 tímpanos** *nmpl* : timpani, kettledrums
tina *nf* **1** BAÑERA : tub, bathtub **2** : vat
tinaco *nm Mex* : water tank
tinieblas *nfpl* **1** OSCURIDAD : darkness **2** : ignorance
tino *nm* **1** : good judgment, sense **2** : tact, sensitivity, insight
tinta *nf* : ink
tinte *nm* **1** : dye, coloring **2** : overtone ⟨tintes raciales : racial overtones⟩
tintero *nm* **1** : inkwell **2 quedarse en el tintero** : to remain unsaid
tintinear *vt* : to jingle, to clink, to tinkle
tintineo *nm* : clink, jingle, tinkle
tinto, **-ta** *adj* **1** : dyed, stained ⟨tinto en sangre : bloodstained⟩ **2** : red (of wine)
tintorería *nf* : dry cleaner (service)
tintura *nf* **1** : dye, tint **2** : tincture ⟨tintura de yodo : tincture of iodine⟩
tiña *nf* : ringworm
tiñe, etc. → **teñir**
tío, **tía** *n* : uncle *m*, aunt *f*
tiovivo *nm* : merry-go-round
tipi *nm* : tepee
típico, **-ca** *adj* : typical — **típicamente** *adv*
tipificar {72} *vt* **1** : to classify, to categorize **2** : to typify
tiple *nm* : soprano
tipo[1] *nm* **1** CLASE : type, kind, sort **2** : figure, build, appearance **3** : rate ⟨tipo de interés : interest rate⟩ **4** : (printing) type, typeface **5** : style, model ⟨un vestido tipo 60's : a 60's-style dress⟩
tipo[2], **-pa** *n fam* : guy *m*, gal *f*, character
tipografía *nf* : typography, printing
tipográfico, **-ca** *adj* : typographic, typographical
tipográfo, **-fa** *n* : printer, typographer
tique *or* **tiquet** *nm* **1** : ticket **2** : receipt
tira *nf* **1** : strip, strap **2 tira cómica** : comic, comic strip
tirabuzón *nf, pl* **-zones** : corkscrew
tirada *nf* **1** : throw **2** : distance, stretch **3** IMPRESIÓN : printing, issue
tiradero *nm Mex* **1** : dump **2** : mess, clutter
tirador[1] *nm* : handle, knob
tirador[2], **-dora** *n* : marksman *m*, markswoman *f*
tiragomas *nms & pl* : slingshot
tiranía *nf* : tyranny
tiránico, **-ca** *adj* : tyrannical
tiranizar {21} *vt* : to tyrannize
tirano[1], **-na** *adj* : tyrannical, despotic
tirano[2], **-na** *n* : tyrant
tirante[1] *adj* **1** : tense, strained **2** : taut
tirante[2] *nm* **1** : shoulder strap **2 tirantes** *nmpl* : suspenders
tirantez *nf* **1** : tautness **2** : tension, friction, strain
tirar *vt* **1** : to throw, to hurl, to toss **2** BOTAR : to throw away, to throw out, to waste **3** DERRIBAR : to knock down **4** : to shoot, to fire, to launch **5** : to take (a photo) **6** : to print, to run off — *vi* **1** : to pull, to draw **2** : to shoot **3** : to attract **4** : to get by, to manage ⟨va tirando : he's getting along, he's managing⟩ **5 ~ a** : to tend towards, to be rather ⟨tira a picante : it's a bit spicy⟩ — **tirarse** *vr* **1** : to throw oneself **2** *fam* : to spend (time)
tiritar *vi* : to shiver, to tremble
tiro *nm* **1** BALAZO, DISPARO : shot, gunshot **2** : shot, kick (in sports) **3** : flue **4** : team (of horses, etc.) **5 a ~** : within range **6 al tiro** : right away **7 tiro de gracia** : coup de grace, death blow
tiroideo, **-dea** *adj* : thyroid
tiroides *nmf* : thyroid, thyroid gland — **tiroides** *adj*

tirolés, **-lesa** *adj* : Tyrolean
tirón *nm, pl* **tirones** **1** : pull, tug, yank **2 de un tirón** : all at once, in one go
tiroteo *nm* **1** : shooting **2** : gunfight, shoot-out
tirria *nf* **tener tirria a** *fam* : to have a grudge against
titánico, **-ca** *adj* : titanic, huge
titanio *nm* : titanium
títere *nm* : puppet
tití *nm* : marmoset
titilar *vi* : to twinkle, to flicker
titileo *nm* : twinkle, flickering
titiritero, **-ra** *n* **1** : puppeteer **2** : acrobat
titubear *vi* **1** : to hesitate **2** : to stutter, to stammer — **titubeante** *adj*
titubeo *nm* **1** : hesitation **2** : stammering
titulado, **-da** *adj* **1** : titled, entitled **2** : qualified
titular[1] *vt* : to title, to entitle — **titularse** *vr* **1** : to be called, to be entitled **2** : to receive a degree
titular[2] *adj* : titular, official
titular[3] *nm* : headline
titular[4] *nmf* **1** : owner, holder **2** : officeholder, incumbent
titularidad *nf* **1** : ownership, title **2** : position, office (with a title) **3** : starting position (in sports)
título *nm* **1** : title **2** : degree, qualification **3** : security, bond **4 a título de** : by way of, in the capacity of
tiza *nf* : chalk
tiznar *vt* : to blacken (with soot, etc.)
tizne *nm* HOLLÍN : soot
tiznón *nm, pl* **tiznones** : stain, smudge
tlapalería *nf Mex* : hardware store
TNT *nm* (*tri*nitro*to*lueno) : TNT
toalla *nf* : towel
toallita *nf* : washcloth
tobillo *nm* : ankle
tobogán *nm, pl* **-ganes** **1** : toboggan, sled **2** : slide, chute
tocadiscos *nms & pl* : record player, phonograph
tocado[1], **-da** *adj* **1** : bad, bruised (of fruit) **2** *fam* : touched, not all there
tocado[2] *nm* : headdress
tocador[1] *nm* **1** : dressing table, vanity table **2 artículos de tocador** : toiletries
tocador[2], **-dora** *n* : player (of music)
tocante *adj* **~ a** : with regard to, regarding
tocar {72} *vt* **1** : to touch, to feel, to handle **2** : to touch on, to refer to **3** : to concern, to affect **4** : to play (a musical instrument) — *vi* **1** : to knock, to ring ⟨tocar a la puerta : to rap on the door⟩ **2 ~ en** : to touch on, to border on ⟨eso toca en lo ridículo : that's almost ludicrous⟩ **3 tocarle a** : to fall to, to be up to, to be one's turn ⟨¿a quién le toca manejar? : whose turn is it to drive?⟩
tocayo, **-ya** *n* : namesake
tocineta *nf Col, Ven* : bacon
tocino *nm* **1** : bacon **2** : salt pork
tocología *nf* OBSTETRICIA : obstetrics
tocólogo, **-ga** *n* OBSTETRA : obstetrician
tocón *nm, pl* **tocones** CEPA : stump (of a tree)
todavía *adv* **1** AÚN : still, yet ⟨todavía puedes verlo : you can still see it⟩ **2** : even ⟨todavía más rápido : even faster⟩ **3 todavía no** : not yet
todo[1], **-da** *adj* **1** : all, whole, entire ⟨con toda sinceridad : with all sincerity⟩ ⟨toda la comunidad : the whole community⟩ **2** : every, each ⟨a todo nivel : at every level⟩ **3** : maximum ⟨a toda velocidad : at top speed⟩ **4 todo el mundo** : everyone, everybody
todo[2] *nm* : whole
todo[3], **-da** *pron* **1** : everything, all, every bit ⟨lo sabe todo : he knows it all⟩ ⟨es todo un soldado : he's every inch a soldier⟩ **2 todos, -das** *pl* : everybody, everyone, all
todopoderoso, **-sa** *adj* OMNIPOTENTE : almighty, all-powerful
toga *nf* **1** : toga **2** : gown, robe (for magistrates, etc.)
toldo *nm* : awning, canopy
tolerable *adj* : tolerable — **tolerablemente** *adv*
tolerancia *nf* : tolerance, toleration
tolerante *adj* : tolerant — **tolerantemente** *adv*
tolerar *vt* : to tolerate
tolete *nm* : oarlock
tolva *nf* : hopper (container)
toma *nf* **1** : taking, seizure, capture **2** DOSIS : dose **3** : take, shot **4 toma de corriente** : wall socket, outlet **5 toma y daca** : give-and-take
tomar *vt* **1** : to take ⟨tomé el libro : I took the book⟩ ⟨tomar un taxi : to take a taxi⟩ ⟨tomar una foto : to take a photo⟩ ⟨toma dos años : it takes two years⟩ ⟨tomaron medidas drásticas : they took drastic measures⟩ **2** BEBER : to drink **3** CAPTURAR : to capture, to seize **4 tomar el sol** : to sunbathe **5 tomar tierra** : to land — *vi* : to drink (alcohol) — **tomarse** *vr* **1** : to take ⟨tomarse la molestia de : to take the trouble to⟩ **2** : to drink, to eat, to have
tomate *nm* : tomato
tomillo *nm* : thyme
tomo *nm* : volume, tome
ton *nm* **sin ton ni son** : without rhyme or reason
tonada *nf* **1** : tune, song **2** : accent
tonalidad *nf* : tonality
tonel *nm* BARRICA : barrel, cask
tonelada *nf* : ton
tonelaje *nm* : tonnage
tónica *nf* **1** : tonic (water) **2** : tonic (in music) **3** : trend, tone ⟨dar la tónica : to set the tone⟩
tónico[1], **-ca** *adj* : tonic
tónico[2] *nm* : tonic ⟨tónico capilar : hair tonic⟩
tono *nm* **1** : tone ⟨tono muscular : muscle tone⟩ **2** : shade (of colors) **3** : key (in music)

tontamente *adv* : foolishly, stupidly

tontear *vi* **1** : to fool around, to play the fool **2** : to flirt

tontería *nf* **1** : foolishness **2** : stupid remark or action **3 decir tonterías** : to talk nonsense

tonto[1], **-ta** *adj* **1** : dumb, stupid **2** : silly **3 a tontas y a locas** : without thinking, haphazardly

tonto[2], **-ta** *n* : fool, idiot

topacio *nm* : topaz

toparse *vr* **~ con** : to bump into, to run into, to come across ⟨me topé con algunas dificultades : I ran into some problems⟩

tope *nm* **1** : limit, end ⟨hasta el tope : to the limit, to the brim⟩ **2** : stop, check, buffer ⟨tope de puerta : doorstop⟩ **3** : bump, collision **4** *Mex* : speed bump

tópico[1], **-ca** *adj* **1** : topical, external **2** : trite, commonplace

tópico[2] *nm* **1** : topic, subject **2** : cliché, trite expression

topo *nm* **1** : mole (animal) **2** *fam* : clumsy person, blunderer

topografía *nf* : topography

topográfico, -ca *adj* : topographic, topographical

topógrafo, -fa *n* : topographer

toque[1], **etc.** → **tocar**

toque[2] *nm* **1** : touch ⟨el último toque : the finishing touch⟩ ⟨un toque de color : a touch of color⟩ **2** : ringing, peal, chime **3** *Mex* : shock, jolt **4 toque de queda** : curfew **5 toque de diana** : reveille

toquetear *vt* : to touch, to handle, to finger

tórax *nm* : thorax

torbellino *nm* : whirlwind

torcedura *nf* **1** : twisting, buckling **2** : sprain

torcer {14} *vt* **1** : to bend, to twist **2** : to sprain **3** : to turn (a corner) **4** : to wring, to wring out **5** : to distort — *vi* : to turn — **torcerse** *vr*

torcido, -da *adj* **1** : twisted, crooked **2** : devious

tordo *nm* ZORZAL : thrush

torear *vt* **1** : to fight (bulls) **2** : to dodge, to sidestep

toreo *nm* : bullfighting

torero, -ra *n* MATADOR : bullfighter, matador

tormenta *nf* **1** : storm ⟨tormenta de nieve : snowstorm⟩ **2** : turmoil, frenzy

tormento *nm* **1** : torment, anguish **2** : torture

tormentoso, -sa *adj* : stormy, turbulent

tornado *nm* : tornado

tornamesa *nmf* : turntable

tornar *vt* **1** : to return, to give back **2** : to make, to render — *vi* : to go back — **tornarse** *vr* : to become, to turn into

tornasol *nm* **1** : reflected light **2** : sunflower **3** : litmus

tornear *vt* : to turn (in carpentry)

torneo *nm* : tournament

tornillo *nm* **1** : screw **2 tornillo de banco** : vise

torniquete *nm* **1** : tourniquet **2** : turnstile

torno *nm* **1** : lathe **2** : winch **3 torno de banco** : vise **4 en torno a** : around, about ⟨en torno a este asunto : about this issue⟩ ⟨en torno suyo : around him⟩

toro *nm* : bull

toronja *nf* : grapefruit

toronjil *nm* : balm, lemon balm

torpe *adj* **1** DESMAÑADO : clumsy, awkward **2** : stupid, dull — **torpemente** *adv*

torpedear *vt* : to torpedo

torpedo *nm* : torpedo

torpeza *nf* **1** : clumsiness, awkwardness **2** : stupidity **3** : blunder

torre *nf* **1** : tower ⟨torre de perforación : oil rig⟩ **2** : turret **3** : rook, castle (in chess)

torrencial *adj* : torrential — **torrencialmente** *adv*

torrente *nm* **1** : torrent **2 torrente sanguíneo** : bloodstream

torreón *nm, pl* **-rreones** : tower (of a castle)

torreta *nf* : turret (of a tank, ship, etc.)

tórrido, -da *adj* : torrid

torsión *nf, pl* **torsiones** : torsion — **torsional** *adj*

torso *nm* : torso, trunk

torta *nf* **1** : torte, cake **2** *Mex* : sandwich

tortazo *nm fam* : blow, wallop

tortilla *nf* **1** : tortilla **2** *or* **tortilla de huevo** : omelet

tórtola *nf* : turtledove

tortuga *nf* **1** : turtle, tortoise **2 tortuga de agua dulce** : terrapin **3 tortuga boba** : loggerhead

tortuoso, -sa *adj* : tortuous, winding

tortura *nf* : torture

torturador, -dora *n* : torturer

torturar *vt* : to torture, to torment

torvo, -va *adj* : grim, stern, baleful

torzamos, etc. → **torcer**

tos *nf* **1** : cough **2 tos ferina** : whooping cough

tosco, -ca *adj* : rough, coarse

toser *vi* : to cough

tosquedad *nf* : crudeness, coarseness, roughness

tostada *nf* **1** : piece of toast **2** : tostada

tostador *nm* **1** : toaster **2** : roaster (for coffee)

tostar {19} *vt* **1** : to toast **2** : to roast (coffee) **3** : to tan — **tostarse** *vr* : to get a tan

tostón *nm, pl* **tostones** *Car* : fried plantain chip

total[1] *adv* : in the end, so ⟨total, que no fui : in short, I didn't go⟩

total[2] *adj & nm* : total — **totalmente** *adv*

totalidad *nf* : totality, whole

totalitario, -ria *adj & n* : totalitarian

totalitarismo *nm* : totalitarianism

totalizar {21} *vt* : total, to add up to
tótem *nm, pl* **tótems** : totem
totopo *nm CA, Mex* : tortilla chip
totuma *nf* : calabash
tour ['tur] *nm, pl* **tours** : tour, excursion
toxicidad *nf* : toxicity
tóxico[1], **-ca** *adj* : toxic, poisonous
tóxico[2] *nm* : poison
toxicomanía *nf* : drug addiction
toxicómano, -na *n* : drug addict
toxina *nf* : toxin
tozudez *nf* : stubbornness, obstinacy
tozudo, -da *adj* : stubborn, obstinate — **tozudamente** *adv*
traba *nf* **1** : tie, bond **2** : obstacle, hindrance
trabajador[1], **-dora** *adj* : hardworking
trabajador[2], **-dora** *n* : worker
trabajar *vi* **1** : to work ⟨trabaja mucho : he works hard⟩ ⟨trabajo de secretaria : I work as a secretary⟩ **2** : to strive ⟨trabajan por mejores oportunidades : they're striving for better opportunities⟩ **3** : to act, to perform ⟨trabajar en una película : to be in a movie⟩ — *vt* **1** : to work (metal) **2** : to knead **3** : to till **4** : to work on ⟨tienes que trabajar el español : you need to work on your Spanish⟩
trabajo *nm* **1** : work, job **2** LABOR : labor, work ⟨tengo mucho trabajo : I have a lot of work to do⟩ **3** TAREA : task **4** ESFUERZA : effort **5 costar trabajo** : to be difficult **6 tomarse el trabajo** : to take the trouble **7 trabajo en equipo** : teamwork **8 trabajos** *nmpl* : hardships, difficulties
trabajoso, -sa *adj* LABORIOSO : laborious — **trabajosamente** *adv*
trabalenguas *nms & pl* : tongue twister
trabar *vt* **1** : to join, to connect **2** : to impede, to hold back **3** : to strike up (a conversation), to form (a friendship) **4** : to thicken (sauces) — **trabarse** *vr* **1** : to jam **2** : to become entangled **3** : to be tongue-tied, to stammer
trabucar {72} *vt* : to confuse, to mix up
trabuco *nm* : blunderbuss
tracalero, -ra *adj Mex* : dishonest, tricky
tracción *nf* : traction
trace, etc. → **trazar**
tracto *nm* : tract
tractor *nm* : tractor
tradición *nf, pl* **-ciones** : tradition
tradicional *adj* : traditional — **tradicionalmente** *adv*
traducción *nf, pl* **-ciones** : translation
traducible *adj* : translatable
traducir {61} *vt* **1** : to translate **2** : to convey, to express — **traducirse** *vr* **~ en** : to result in
traductor, -tora *n* : translator
traer {81} *vt* **1** : to bring ⟨trae una ensalada : bring a salad⟩ **2** CAUSAR : to cause, to bring about ⟨el problema puede traer graves consecuencias : the problem could have serious consequences⟩ **3** : to carry, to have ⟨todos los periódicos traían las mismas noticias : all of the newspapers carried the same news⟩ **4** LLEVAR : to wear — **traerse** *vr* **1** : to bring along **2 traérselas** : to be difficult
traficante *nmf* : dealer, trafficker
traficar {72} *vi* **1** : to trade, to deal **2 ~ con** : to traffic in
tráfico *nm* **1** : trade **2** : traffic
tragaluz *nf, pl* **-luces** : skylight, fanlight
tragar {52} *v* : to swallow — **tragarse** *vr*
tragedia *nf* : tragedy
trágico, -ca *adj* : tragic — **trágicamente** *adv*
trago *nm* **1** : swallow, swig **2** : drink, liquor **3 trago amargo** : hard time
trague, etc. → **tragar**
traición *nf, pl* **traiciones** **1** : treason **2** : betrayal, treachery
traicionar *vt* : to betray
traicionero, -ra → **traidor**
traidor[1], **-dora** *adj* : traitorous, treasonous
traidor[2], **-dora** *n* : traitor
traiga, etc. → **traer**
tráiler *or* **trailer** *nm* : trailer
traílla *nf* **1** : leash **2** : harrow
traje *nm* **1** : suit **2** : dress **3** : costume **4 traje de baño** : bathing suit
trajín *nm, pl* **trajines** **1** : transport **2** *fam* : hustle and bustle
trajinar *vt* : to transport, to carry — *vi* : to rush around
trajo, etc. → **traer**
trama *nf* **1** : plot **2** : weave, weft (fabric)
tramar *vt* **1** : to plot, to plan **2** : to weave
tramitar *vt* : to transact, to negotiate, to handle
trámite *nm* : procedure, step
tramo *nm* **1** : stretch, section **2** : flight (of stairs)
trampa *nf* **1** : trap **2 hacer trampas** : to cheat
trampear *vt* : to cheat
trampero, -ra *n* : trapper
trampilla *nf* : trapdoor
trampolín *nm, pl* **-lines** **1** : diving board **2** : trampoline **3** : springboard ⟨un trampolín al éxito : a springboard to success⟩
tramposo[1], **-sa** *adj* : crooked, cheating
tramposo[2], **-sa** *n* : cheat, swindler
tranca *nf* **1** : stick, club **2** : bar, crossbar
trancar {72} *vt* : to bar (a door or window)
trancazo *nm* GOLPE : blow, hit
trance *nm* **1** : critical juncture, tough time **2** : trance **3 en trance de** : in the process of ⟨en trance de extinción : on the verge of extinction⟩
tranco *nm* **1** : stride **2** UMBRAL : threshold
tranque, etc. → **trancar**
tranquilidad *nf* : tranquility, peace
tranquilizador, -dora *adj* **1** : soothing **2** : reassuring
tranquilizante[1] *adj* **1** : reassuring **2** : tranquilizing

tranquilizante[2] *nm* : tranquilizer

tranquilizar {21} *vt* CALMAR : to calm down, to soothe ⟨tranquilizar la conciencia : to ease the conscience⟩ — **tranquilizarse** *vr*

tranquilo, -la *adj* CALMO : calm, tranquil ⟨una vida tranquila : a quiet life⟩ — **tranquilamente** *adv*

transacción *nf, pl* **-ciones** : transaction

transar *vi* TRANSIGIR : to give way, to compromise — *vt* : to buy and sell

transatlántico[1], **-ca** *adj* : transatlantic

transatlántico[2] *nm* : ocean liner

transbordador *nm* **1** : ferry **2 transbordador espacial** : space shuttle

transbordar *v* : to transfer

transbordo *nm* : transfer

transcendencia → **trascendencia**

transcender → **trascender**

transcribir {33} *vt* : to transcribe

transcrito *pp* → **transcribir**

transcripción *nf, pl* **-ciones** : transcription

transcurrir *vi* : to elapse, to pass

transcurso *nm* : course, progression ⟨en el transcurso de cien años : over the course of a hundred years⟩

transeúnte *nmf* **1** : passerby **2** : transient

transferencia *nf* : transfer, transference

transferir {76} *vt* TRASLADAR : to transfer — **transferible** *adj*

transfigurar *vt* : to transfigure, to transform — **transfiguración** *nf*

transformación *nf, pl* **-ciones** : transformation, conversion

transformador *nm* : transformer

transformar *vt* **1** CONVERTIR : to convert **2** : to transform, to change, to alter — **transformarse** *vr*

transfusión *nf, pl* **-siones** : transfusion

transgredir {1} *vt* : to transgress — **transgresión** *nf*

transgresor, -sora *n* : transgressor

transición *nf, pl* **-ciones** : transition ⟨período de transición : transition period⟩

transido, -da *adj* : overcome, beset ⟨transido de dolor : racked with pain⟩

transigir {35} *vi* **1** : to give in, to compromise **2 ~ con** : to tolerate, to put up with

transistor *nm* : transistor

transitable *adj* : passable

transitar *vi* : to go, to pass, to travel ⟨transitar por la ciudad : to travel through the city⟩

transitivo, -va *adj* : transitive

tránsito *nm* **1** TRÁFICO : traffic ⟨hora de máximo tránsito : rush hour⟩ **2** : transit, passage, movement **3** : death, passing

transitorio, -ria *adj* **1** : transitory **2** : provisional, temporary — **transitoriamente** *adv*

translúcido, -da *adj* : translucent

translucir → **traslucir**

transmisible *adj* : transmissible

transmisión *nf, pl* **-siones** **1** : transmission, broadcast **2** : transfer **3** : transmission (of an automobile)

transmisor *nm* : transmitter

transmitir *vt* **1** : to transmit, to broadcast **2** : to pass on, to transfer — *vi* : to transmit, to broadcast

transparencia *nf* : transparency

transparentar *vt* : to reveal, to betray — **transparentarse** *vr* **1** : to be transparent **2** : to show through

transparente[1] *adj* : transparent — **transparentemente** *adv*

transparente[2] *nm* : shade, blind

transpiración *nf, pl* **-ciones** SUDOR : perspiration, sweat

transpirado, -da *adj* : sweaty

transpirar *vi* **1** SUDAR : to perspire, to sweat **2** : to transpire

transplantar, transplante → **trasplantar, trasplante**

transponer {60} *vt* **1** : to transpose, to move about **2** TRASPLANTAR : to transplant — **transponerse** *vr* **1** OCULTARSE : to hide **2** PONERSE : to set, to go down (of the sun or moon) **3** DORMITAR : to doze off

transportación *nf, pl* **-ciones** : transportation

transportador *nm* **1** : protractor **2** : conveyor

transportar *vt* **1** : to transport, to carry **2** : to transmit **3** : to transpose (music) — **transportarse** *vr* : to get carried away

transporte *nm* : transport, transportation

transportista *nmf* : hauler, carrier, trucker

transpuso, etc. → **transponer**

transversal *adj* : transverse, cross ⟨corte transversal : cross section⟩

transversalmente *adv* : obliquely

transverso, -sa *adj* : transverse

tranvía *nm* : streetcar, trolley

trapeador *nm* : mop

trapear *vt* : to mop

trapecio *nm* **1** : trapezoid **2** : trapeze

trapezoide *nm* : trapezoid

trapo *nm* **1** : cloth, rag ⟨trapo de polvo : dust cloth⟩ **2 soltar el trapo** : to burst into tears **3 trapos** *nmpl fam* : clothes

tráquea *nf* : trachea, windpipe

traquetear *vi* : to clatter, to jolt

traqueteo *nm* **1** : jolting **2** : clattering, clatter

tras *prep* **1** : after ⟨día tras día : day after day⟩ ⟨uno tras otro : one after another⟩ **2** : behind ⟨tras la puerta : behind the door⟩

trasbordar, trasbordo → **transbordar, transbordo**

trascendencia *nf* **1** : importance, significance **2** : transcendence

trascendental *adj* **1** : transcendental **2** : important, momentous

trascendente *adj* **1** : important, significant **2** : transcendent

trascender {56} *vi* **1** : to leak out, to become known **2** : to spread, to have a wide effect **3 ~ a** : to smell of ⟨la casa trascendía a flores : the house smelled of flowers⟩ **4 ~ de** : to transcend, to go beyond — *vt* : to transcend

trasero[1], **-ra** *adj* POSTERIOR : rear, back

trasero[2] *nm* : buttocks

trasfondo *nm* **1** : background, backdrop **2** : undertone, undercurrent

trasformación → **transformación**

trasgo *nm* : goblin, imp

trasgredir → **transgredir**

trasladar *vt* **1** TRANSFERIR : to transfer, to move **2** POSPONER : to postpone **3** TRADUCIR : to translate **4** COPIAR : to copy, to transcribe — **trasladarse** *vr* MUDARSE : to move, to relocate

traslado *nm* **1** : transfer, move **2** : copy

traslapar *vt* : to overlap — **traslaparse** *vr*

traslapo *nm* : overlap

traslúcido, -da → **translúcido**

traslucir {45} *vi* : to reveal, to show — **traslucirse** *vr* : to show through

trasmano *nm* **a ~** : out of the way, out of reach

trasmisión, trasmitir → **transmisión, transmitir**

trasnochar *vi* : to stay up all night

trasparencia *nf* **trasparente** → **transparencia, transparente**

traspasar *vt* **1** PERFORAR : to pierce, to go through **2** : to go beyond ⟨traspasar los límites : to overstep the limits⟩ **3** ATRAVESAR : to cross, to go across **4** : to sell, to transfer

traspaso *nm* : transfer, sale

traspié *nm* **1** : stumble **2** : blunder

traspiración → **transpiración**

trasplantar *vt* : to transplant

trasplante *nm* : transplant

trasponer → **transponer**

trasportar → **transportar**

trasquilar *vt* ESQUILAR : to shear

traste *nm* **1** : fret (on a guitar) **2** *CA, Mex, PRi* : kitchen utensil ⟨lavar los trastes : to do the dishes⟩ **3 dar al traste con** : to ruin, to destroy **4 irse al traste** : to fall through

trastornar *vt* : to disturb, to upset, to disrupt — **trastornarse** *vr*

trastorno *nm* **1** : disorder ⟨trastorno mental : mental disorder⟩ **2** : disturbance, upset

trastos *nmpl* **1** : implements, utensils **2** *fam* : pieces of junk, stuff

trasunto *nm* : image, likeness

tratable *adj* **1** : friendly, sociable **2** : treatable

tratado *nm* **1** : treatise **2** : treaty

tratamiento *nm* : treatment

tratante *nmf* : dealer, trader

tratar *vi* **1 ~ con** : to deal with, to have contact with ⟨no trato mucho con los clientes : I don't have much contact with customers⟩ **2 ~ de** : to try to ⟨estoy tratando de comer : I am trying to eat⟩ **3 ~ de** *or* **~ sobre** : to be about, to concern ⟨el libro trata de las plantas : the book is about plants⟩ **4 ~ en** : to deal in ⟨trata en herramientas : he deals in tools⟩ — *vt* **1** : to treat ⟨tratan bien a sus empleados : they treat their employees well⟩ **2** : to handle ⟨trató el tema con delicadeza : he handled the subject tactfully⟩ — **tratarse** *vr* **~ de** : to be about, to concern

trato *nm* **1** : deal, agreement **2** : relationship, dealings *pl* **3** : treatment ⟨malos tratos : ill-treatment⟩

trauma *nm* : trauma

traumático, -ca *adj* : traumatic — **traumáticamente** *adv*

traumatismo *nm* : injury ⟨traumatismo cervical : whiplash⟩

través *nm* **1 a través de** : across, through **2 al través** : crosswise, across **3 de través** : sideways

travesaño *nm* **1** : crossbar **2** : crossbeam, crosspiece, transom (of a window)

travesía *nf* : voyage, crossing (of the sea)

travesura *nf* **1** : prank, mischievous act **2 travesuras** *nfpl* : mischief

travieso, -sa *adj* : mischievous, naughty — **traviesamente** *adv*

trayecto *nm* **1** : journey **2** : route **3** : trajectory, path

trayectoria *nf* : course, path, trajectory

trayendo → **traer**

traza *nf* **1** DISEÑO : design, plan **2** : appearance

trazado *nm* **1** BOSQUEJO : outline, sketch **2** PLAN : plan, layout

trazar {21} *vt* **1** : to trace **2** : to draw up, to devise **3** : to outline, to sketch

trazo *nm* **1** : stroke, line **2** : sketch, outline

trébol *nm* **1** : clover, shamrock **2** : club (playing card)

trece *adj & nm* : thirteen

treceavo[1], **-va** *adj* : thirteenth

treceavo[2] *nm* : thirteenth (fraction)

trecho *nm* **1** : stretch, period ⟨de trecho en trecho : at intervals⟩ **2** : distance, space

tregua *nf* **1** : truce **2** : lull, respite **3 sin ~** : relentless, unrelenting

treinta *adj & nm* : thirty

treintavo[1], **-va** *adj* : thirtieth

treintavo[2] *nm* : thirtieth (fraction)

tremendo, -da *adj* **1** : tremendous, enormous **2** : terrible, dreadful **3** *fam* : great, super

trementina *nf* AGUARRÁS : turpentine

trémulo, -la *adj* **1** : trembling, shaky **2** : flickering

tren *nm* **1** : train **2** : set, assembly ⟨tren de aterrizaje : landing gear⟩ **3** : speed, pace ⟨a todo tren : at top speed⟩

trence, etc. → **trenzar**

trenza *nf* : braid, pigtail

trenzar {21} *vt* : to braid — **trenzarse** *vr* : to get involved

trepador, -dora *adj* : climbing ⟨rosal trepador : rambling rose⟩

trepadora *nf* **1** : climbing plant, climber **2** : nuthatch
trepar *vi* **1** : to climb ⟨trepar a un árbol : to climb up a tree⟩ **2** : to creep, to spread (of a plant)
trepidación *nf, pl* **-ciones** : vibration
trepidante *adj* **1** : vibrating **2** : fast, frantic
trepidar *vi* **1** : to shake, to vibrate **2** : to hesitate, to waver
tres *adj & nm* : three
trescientos[1], **-tas** *adj* : three hundred
trescientos[2] *nms & pl* : three hundred
treta *nf* : trick, ruse
tríada *nf* : triad
triángulo *nm* : triangle — **triangular** *adj*
tribal *adj* : tribal
tribu *nf* : tribe
tribulación *nf, pl* **-ciones** : tribulation
tribuna *nf* **1** : dais, platform **2** : stands *pl*, bleachers *pl*, grandstand
tribunal *nm* : court, tribunal
tributar *vt* : to pay, to render — *vi* : to pay taxes
tributario[1], **-ria** *adj* : tax ⟨evasión tributaria : tax evasion⟩
tributario[2] *nm* : tributary
tributo *nm* **1** : tax **2** : tribute
triciclo *nm* : tricycle
tricolor *adj* : tricolor, tricolored
tridente *nm* : trident
tridimensional *adj* : three-dimensional, 3-D
trienal *adj* : triennial
trifulca *nf fam* : row, ruckus
trigésimo[1], **-ma** *adj* : thirtieth, thirty-
trigésimo[2], **-ma** *n* : thirtieth, thirty- (in a series)
trigo *nm* **1** : wheat **2 trigo rubión** : buckwheat
trigonometría *nf* : trigonometry
trigueño, -ña *adj* **1** : light brown (of hair) **2** MORENO : dark, olive-skinned
trillado, -da *adj* : trite, hackneyed
trilladora *nf* : thresher, threshing machine
trillar *vt* : to thresh
trillizo, -za *n* : triplet
trilogía *nf* : trilogy
trimestral *adj* : quarterly — **trimestralmente** *adv*
trinar *vi* **1** : to thrill **2** : to warble
trinchar *vt* : to carve, to cut up
trinchera *nf* **1** : trench, ditch **2** : trench coat
trineo *nm* : sled, sleigh
trinidad *nf* **la Trinidad** : the Trinity
trino *nm* : trill, warble
trinquete *nm* : ratchet
trío *nm* : trio
tripa *nf* **1** INTESTINO : gut, intestine **2 tripas** *nfpl fam* : belly, tummy, insides *pl* ⟨dolerle a uno las tripas : to have a stomach ache⟩
tripartito, -ta *adj* : tripartite
triple *adj & nm* : triple
triplicado *nm* : triplicate
triplicar {72} *vt* : to triple, to treble
trípode *nm* : tripod
tripulación *nf, pl* **-ciones** : crew
tripulante *nmf* : crew member
tripular *vt* : to man
tris *nm* **estar en un tris de** : to be within an inch of, to be very close to
triste *adj* **1** : sad, gloomy ⟨ponerse triste : to become sad⟩ **2** : desolate, dismal ⟨una perspectiva triste : a dismal outlook⟩ **3** : sorry, sorry-looking ⟨la triste verdad : the sorry truth⟩
tristeza *nf* DOLOR : sadness, grief
tristón, -tona *adj, mpl* **-tones** : melancholy, downhearted
tritón *nm, pl* **tritones** : newt
triturar *vt* : to crush, to grind
triunfal *adj* : triumphal, triumphant — **triunfalmente** *adv*
triunfante *adj* : triumphant, victorious
triunfar *vi* : to triumph, to win
triunfo *nm* **1** : triumph, victory **2** ÉXITO : success **3** : trump (in card games)
triunvirato *nm* : triumvirate
trivial *adj* **1** : trivial **2** : trite, commonplace
trivialidad *nf* : triviality
triza *nf* **1** : shred, bit **2 hacer trizas** : to tear into shreds, to smash to pieces
trocar {82} *vt* **1** CAMBIAR : to exchange, to trade **2** CAMBIAR : to change, to alter, to transform **3** CONFUNDIR : to confuse, to mix up
trocha *nf* : path, trail
troce, etc. → **trozar**
trofeo *nm* : trophy
tromba *nf* **1** : whirlwind **2 tromba de agua** : downpour, cloudburst
trombón *nm, pl* **trombones** **1** : trombone **2** : trombonist — **trombonista** *nmf*
trombosis *nf* : thrombosis
trompa *nf* **1** : trunk (of an elephant), proboscis (of an insect) **2** : horn ⟨trompa de caza : hunting horn⟩ **3** : tube, duct (in the body)
trompada *nf fam* **1** : punch, blow **2** : bump, collision (of persons)
trompeta *nf* : trumpet
trompetista *nmf* : trumpet player, trumpeter
trompo *nm* : spinning top
tronada *nf* : thunderstorm
tronar {19} *vi* **1** : to thunder, to roar **2** : to be furious, to rage **3** *CA, Mex fam* : to shoot — *v impers* : to thunder ⟨está tronando : it's thundering⟩
tronchar *vt* **1** : to snap, to break off **2** : to cut off (relations)
tronco *nm* **1** : trunk (of a tree) **2** : log **3** : torso
trono *nm* **1** : throne **2** *fam* : toilet
tropa *nf* **1** : troop, soldiers *pl* **2** : crowd, mob **3** : herd (of livestock)
tropel *nm* : mob, swarm
tropezar {29} *vi* **1** : to trip, to stumble **2** : to slip up, to blunder **3 ~ con** : to run into, to bump into **4 ~ con** : to come up against (a problem)

tropezón *nm, pl* **-zones** **1** : stumble **2** : mistake, slip
tropical *adj* : tropical
trópico *nm* **1** : tropic ⟨trópico de Cáncer : tropic of Cancer⟩ **2 el trópico** : the tropics
tropiezo *nm* **1** CONTRATIEMPO : snag, setback **2** EQUIVOCACIÓN : mistake, slip
troqué, etc. → **trocar**
troquel *nm* : die (for stamping)
trotamundos *nmf* : globe-trotter
trotar *vi* **1** : to trot **2** : to jog **3** *fam* : to rush about
trote *nm* **1** : trot **2** *fam* : rush, bustle **3 de ~** : durable, for everyday use
trovador, -dora *n* : troubadour
trozar {21} *vt* : to cut up, to dice
trozo *nm* **1** PEDAZO : piece, bit, chunk **2** : passage, extract
trucha *nf* : trout
truco *nm* **1** : trick **2** : knack
truculento, -ta *adj* : horrifying, gruesome
trueca, trueque etc. → **trocar**
truena, etc. → **tronar**
trueno *nm* : thunder
trueque *nm* : barter, exchange
trufa *nf* : truffle
truncar {72} *vt* **1** : to truncate, to cut short **2** : to thwart, to frustrate ⟨truncó sus esperanzas : she shattered their hopes⟩
trunco, -ca *adj* **1** : truncated **2** : unfinished, incomplete
trunque, etc. → **truncar**
tu *adj* **1** : your ⟨tu vestido : your dress⟩ ⟨toma tus vitaminas : take your vitamins⟩ **2** : thy
tú *pron* **1** : you ⟨tú eres mi hijo : you are my son⟩ **2** : thou
tuba *nf* : tuba
tubérculo *nm* : tuber
tuberculosis *nf* : tuberculosis
tuberculoso, -sa *adj* : tuberculous, tubercular
tubería *nf* : pipes *pl*, tubing
tuberoso, -sa *adj* : tuberous
tubo *nm* **1** : tube ⟨tubo de ensayo : test tube⟩ **2** : pipe ⟨tubo de desagüe : drainpipe⟩ **3 tubo digestivo** : alimentary canal
tubular *adj* : tubular
tuerca *nf* : nut ⟨tuercas y tornillos : nuts and bolts⟩
tuerce, etc. → **torcer**
tuerto, -ta *adj* : one-eyed, blind in one eye
tuerza, etc. → **torcer**
tuesta, etc. → **tostar**
tuétano *nm* : marrow
tufo *nm* **1** : fume, vapor **2** *fam* : stench, stink
tugurio *nm* : hovel
tulipán *nm, pl* **-panes** : tulip
tumba *nf* **1** SEPULCRO : tomb **2** FOSA : grave **3** : felling of trees
tumbar *vt* **1** : to knock down **2** : to fell, to cut down — *vi* : to fall down — **tumbarse** *vr* ACOSTARSE : to lie down
tumbo *nm* **1** : tumble, fall **2 dar tumbos** : to jolt, to bump around
tumor *nm* : tumor
túmulo *nm* : burial mound
tumulto *nm* **1** ALBOROTO : commotion, tumult **2** MOTÍN : riot **3** MULTITUD : crowd
tumultuoso, -sa *adj* : tumultuous
tuna *nf* : prickly pear (fruit)
tundra *nf* : tundra
tunecino, -na *adj & n* : Tunisian
túnel *nm* : tunnel
tungsteno *nm* : tungsten
túnica *nf* : tunic
tupé *nm* PELUQUÍN : toupee
tupido, -da *adj* **1** DENSO : dense, thick **2** OBSTRUIDO : obstructed, blocked up
turba *nf* **1** : peat **2** : mob, throng
turbación *nf, pl* **-ciones** **1** : disturbance **2** : alarm, concern **3** : confusion
turbante *nm* : turban
turbar *vt* **1** : to disturb, to disrupt **2** : to worry, to upset **3** : to confuse
turbina *nf* : turbine
turbio, -bia *adj* **1** : cloudy, murky, turbid **2** : dim, blurred **3** : shady, crooked
turbopropulsor *nm* : turboprop
turborreactor *nm* : turbojet
turbulencia *nf* : turbulence
turbulento, -ta *adj* : turbulent
turco[1], **-ca** *adj* : Turkish
turco[2], **-ca** *n* : Turk
turco[3] *nm* : Turkish (language)
turgente *adj* : turgid, swollen
turismo *nm* : tourism, tourist industry
turista *nmf* : tourist, vacationer
turístico, -ca *adj* : tourist, travel
turnar *vi* : to take turns, to alternate
turno *nm* **1** : turn ⟨ya te tocará tu turno : you'll get your turn⟩ **2** : shift, duty ⟨turno de noche : night shift⟩ **3 por turno** : alternately
turón *nm, pl* **turones** : polecat
turquesa *nf* : turquoise
turrón *nm, pl* **turrones** : nougat
tusa *nf* : corn husk
tutear *vt* : to address as *tú*
tutela *nf* **1** : guardianship **2** : tutelage, protection
tuteo *nm* : addressing as *tú*
tutor, -tora *n* **1** : tutor **2** : guardian
tuvo, etc. → **tener**
tuyo[1], **-ya** *adj* : yours, of yours ⟨un amigo tuyo : a friend of yours⟩ ⟨¿es tuya esta casa? : is this house yours?⟩
tuyo[2], **-ya** *pron* **1** : yours ⟨ése es el tuyo : that one is yours⟩ ⟨trae la tuya : bring your own⟩ **2 los tuyos** : your relations, your friends ⟨¿vendrán los tuyos? : are your folks coming?⟩
tweed ['twið] *nm* : tweed

U

u[1] *nf* : twenty-second letter of the Spanish alphabet
u[2] *conj (used instead of* **o** *before words beginning with o- or ho-)* : or
ualabí *nm* : wallaby
uapití *nm* : American elk, wapiti
ubicación *nf, pl* **-ciones** : location, position
ubicar {72} *vt* **1** SITUAR : to place, to put, to position **2** LOCALIZAR : to locate, to find — **ubicarse** *vr* **1** LOCALIZARSE : to be placed, to be located **2** SITUARSE : to position oneself
ubicuidad *nf* OMNIPRESENCIA : ubiquity
ubicuo, -cua *adj* OMNIPRESENTE : ubiquitous
ubre *nf* : udder
ucraniano[1], **-na** *adj & n* : Ukranian
ucraniano[2] *nm* : Ukranian (language)
Ud., Uds. → **usted**
ufanarse *vr* **~ de** : to boast about, to pride oneself on
ufano, -na *adj* **1** ORGULLOSO : proud **2** : self-satisfied, smug
ugandés, -desa *adj & n, mpl* **-deses** : Ugandan
ukelele *nm* : ukulele
úlcera *nf* : ulcer — **ulceroso, -sa** *adj*
ulcerar *vt* : to ulcerate — **ulcerarse** *vr* — **ulceración** *nf*
ulceroso, -sa *adj* : ulcerous
ulterior *adj* : later, subsequent — **ulteriormente** *adv*
últimamente *adv* : lately, recently
ultimar *vt* **1** CONCLUIR : to complete, to finish, to finalize **2** MATAR : to kill
ultimátum *nm, pl* **-tums** : ultimatum
último, -ma *adj* **1** : last, final ⟨la última galleta : the last cookie⟩ ⟨en último caso : as a last resort⟩ **2** : last, latest, most recent ⟨su último viaje a España : her last trip to Spain⟩ ⟨en los últimos años : in recent years⟩ **3 por ~** : finally
ultrajar *vt* INSULTAR : to offend, to outrage, to insult
ultraje *nm* INSULTO : outrage, insult
ultramar *nm* **de ~** *or* **en ~** : overseas, abroad
ultranza *nf* **1 a ~** : to the extreme ⟨lo defendió a ultranza : she defended him fiercely⟩ **2 a ~** : extreme, out-and-out ⟨perfeccionismo a ultranza : rabid perfectionism⟩
ultrarrojo, -ja *adj* : infrared
ultravioleta *adj* : ultraviolet
ulular *vi* **1** : to hoot **2** : to howl, to wail
ululato *nm* : hoot (of an owl), wail (of a person)
umbilical *adj* : umbilical ⟨cordón umbilical : umbilical cord⟩
umbral *nm* : threshold, doorstep
un[1] *adj* → **uno**[1]
un[2], **una** *art, mpl* **unos** **1** : a, an **2 unos** *or* **unas** *pl* : some, a few ⟨hace unas semanas : a few weeks ago⟩ **3 unos** *or* **unas** *pl* : about, approximately ⟨unos veinte años antes : about twenty years before⟩
unánime *adj* : unanimous — **unánimemente** *adv*
unanimidad *nf* **1** : unanimity **2 por ~** : unanimously
unción *nf, pl* **-ciones** : unction
uncir {83} *vt* : to yoke
undécimo[1], **-ma** *adj* : eleventh
undécimo[2], **-ma** *n* : eleventh (in a series)
ungir {35} *vt* : to anoint
ungüento *nm* : ointment, salve
únicamente *adv* : only, solely
unicelular *adj* : unicellular
único[1], **-ca** *adj* **1** : only, sole **2** : unique, extraordinary
único[2], **-ca** *n* : only one ⟨los únicos que vinieron : the only ones who showed up⟩
unicornio *nm* : unicorn
unidad *nf* **1** : unity **2** : unit
unidireccional *adj* : unidirectional
unido, -da *adj* **1** : joined, united **2** : close ⟨unos amigos muy unidos : very close friends⟩
unificar {72} *vt* : to unify — **unificación** *nf*
uniformado, -da *adj* : uniformed
uniformar *vt* ESTANDARIZAR : to standardize, to make uniform
uniforme[1] *adj* : uniform — **uniformemente** *adv*
uniforme[2] *nm* : uniform
uniformidad *nf* : uniformity
unilateral *adj* : unilateral — **unilateralmente** *adv*
unión *nf, pl* **uniones** **1** : union **2** JUNTURA : joint, coupling
unir *vt* **1** JUNTAR : to unite, to join, to link **2** COMBINAR : to combine, to blend — **unirse** *vr* **1** : to join together **2** : to combine, to mix together **3 ~ a** : to join ⟨se unieron al grupo : they joined the group⟩
unísono *nm* : unison ⟨al unísono : in unison⟩
unitario, -ria *adj* : unitary, unit ⟨precio unitario : unit price⟩
universal *adj* : universal — **universalmente** *adv*
universidad *nf* : university
universitario[1], **-ria** *adj* : university, college
universitario[2], **-ria** *n* : university student, college student
universo *nm* : universe
unja, etc. → **ungir**
uno[1], **una** *adj* (**un** *before masculine singular nouns*) : one ⟨una silla : one chair⟩ ⟨tiene treinta y un años : he's thirty-one years old⟩ ⟨el tomo uno : volume one⟩
uno[2] *nm* : one, number one

uno[3], **una** *pron* **1** : one (number) ⟨uno por uno : one by one⟩ ⟨es la una : it's one o'clock⟩ **2** : one (person or thing) ⟨una es mejor que las otras : one (of them) is better than the others⟩ ⟨hacerlo uno mismo : to do it oneself⟩ **3 unos, unas** *pl* : some (ones), some people **4 uno y otro** : both **5 unos y otros** : all of them **6 el uno al otro** : one another, each other ⟨se enseñaron los unos a los otros : they taught each other⟩
untar *vt* **1** : to anoint **2** : to smear, to grease **3** : to bribe
unza, etc. → **uncir**
uña *nf* **1** : fingernail, toenail **2** : claw, hoof, stinger
uranio *nm* : uranium
Urano *nm* : Uranus
urbanidad *nf* : urbanity, courtesy
urbanización *nf, pl* **-ciones** : housing development, residential area
urbanizar {21} *vt* : to develop (an area)
urbano, -na *adj* **1** : urban **2** CORTÉS : urbane, polite
urbe *nf* : large city, metropolis
urdimbre *nf* : warp (in a loom)
urdu *nm* : Urdu
uretra *nf* : urethra
urgencia *nf* **1** : urgency **2** EMERGENCIA : emergency
urgente *adj* : urgent — **urgentemente** *adv*
urgir {35} *v impers* : to be urgent, to be pressing ⟨me urge localizarlo : I urgently need to find him⟩ ⟨el tiempo urge : time is running out⟩
urinario[1], **-ria** *adj* : urinary
urinario[2] *nm* : urinal (place)
urja, etc. → **urgir**
urna *nf* **1** : urn **2** : ballot box ⟨acudir a las urnas : to go to the polls⟩
urogallo *nm* : grouse (bird)
urraca *nf* **1** : magpie **2 urraca de América** : blue jay
urticaria *nf* : hives
uruguayo, -ya *adj & n* : Uruguayan
usado, -da *adj* **1** : used, secondhand **2** : worn, worn-out
usanza *nf* : custom, usage
usar *vt* **1** EMPLEAR, UTILIZAR : to use, to make use of **2** CONSUMIR : to consume, to use (up) **3** LLEVAR : to wear **4 de usar y tirar** : disposable — **usarse** *vr* **1** : to be used **2** : to be in fashion
uso *nm* **1** EMPLEO, UTILIZACIÓN : use ⟨de uso personal : for personal use⟩ ⟨hacer uso de : to make use of⟩ **2** : wear ⟨uso y desgaste : wear and tear⟩ **3** USANZA : custom, usage, habit ⟨al uso de : in the manner of, in the style of⟩
usted *pron* **1** (*formal form of address in most countries; often written as* **Ud.** *or* **Vd.**) : you **2 ustedes** *pl* (*often written as* **Uds.** *or* **Vds.**) : you, all of you
usual *adj* : usual, common, normal ⟨poco usual : not very common⟩ — **usualmente** *adv*
usuario, -ria *n* : user
usura *nf* : usury — **usurario, -ria** *adj*
usurero, -ra *n* : usurer
usurpador, -dora *n* : usurper
usurpar *vt* : to usurp — **usurpación** *nf*
utensilio *nm* : utensil, tool
uterino, -na *adj* : uterine
útero *nm* : uterus, womb
útil *adj* : useful, handy, helpful
útiles *nmpl* : implements, tools
utilidad *nf* **1** : utility, usefulness **2 utilidades** *nfpl* : profits
utilitario, -ria *adj* : utilitarian
utilizable *adj* : usable, fit for use
utilización *nf, pl* **-ciones** : utilization, use
utilizar {21} *vt* : to use, to utilize
útilmente *adv* : usefully
utopía *nf* : utopia
utópico, -ca *adj* : utopian
uva *nf* : grape
uvular *adj* : uvular

V

v *nf* : twenty-third letter of the Spanish alphabet
va → **ir**
vaca *nf* : cow
vacación *nf, pl* **-ciones 1** : vacation ⟨dos semanas de vacaciones : two weeks of vacation⟩ **2 estar de vacaciones** : to be on vacation **3 irse de vacaciones** : to go on vacation
vacacionar *vi Mex* : to vacation
vacacionista *nmf CA, Mex* : vacationer
vacante[1] *adj* : vacant, empty
vacante[2] *nf* : vacancy (for a job)
vaciado *nm* : cast, casting ⟨vaciado de yeso : plaster cast⟩
vaciar {85} *vt* **1** : to empty, to empty out, to drain **2** AHUECAR : to hollow out **3** : to cast (in a mold) — *vi* **~ en** : to flow into, to empty into
vacilación *nf, pl* **-ciones** : hesitation, vacillation
vacilante *adj* **1** : hesitant, unsure **2** : shaky, unsteady **3** : flickering
vacilar *vi* **1** : to hesitate, to vacillate, to waver **2** : to be unsteady, to wobble **3** : to flicker **4** *fam* : to joke, to fool around
vacío[1], **-cía** *adj* **1** : vacant **2** : empty **3** : meaningless
vacío[2] *nm* **1** : emptiness, void **2** : space, gap **3** : vacuum **4 hacerle el vacío a alguien** : to ostracize someone, to give someone the cold shoulder
vacuidad *nf* : vacuity, vacuousness

vacuna *nf* : vaccine
vacunación *nf, pl* **-ciones** INOCULACIÓN : vaccination, inoculation
vacunar *vt* INOCULAR : to vaccinate, to inoculate
vacuno[1], **-na** *adj* : bovine ⟨ganado vacuno : beef cattle⟩
vacuno[2] *nm* : bovine
vacuo, -cua *adj* : empty, shallow, inane
vadear *vt* : to ford, to wade across
vado *nm* : ford
vagabundear *vi* : to wander, to roam about
vagabundo[1], **-da** *adj* **1** ERRANTE : wandering **2** : stray
vagabundo[2], **-da** *n* : vagrant, bum, vagabond
vagamente *adv* : vaguely
vagancia *nf* **1** : vagrancy **2** PEREZA : laziness, idleness
vagar {52} *vi* ERRAR : to roam, to wander
vagina *nf* : vagina — **vaginal** *adj*
vago[1], **-ga** *adj* **1** : vague **2** PEREZOSO : lazy, idle
vago[2], **-ga** *n* **1** : idler, loafer **2** VAGABUNDO : vagrant, bum
vagón *nm, pl* **vagones** : car (of a train)
vague, etc. → **vagar**
vaguear *vi* **1** : to loaf, to lounge around **2** VAGAR : to wander
vaguedad *nf* : vagueness
vahído *nm* : dizzy spell
vaho *nm* **1** : breath **2** : vapor, steam (on glass, etc.)
vaina *nf* **1** : sheath, scabbard **2** : pod (of a pea or bean) **3** *fam* : nuisance, bother
vainilla *nf* : vanilla
vaivén *nm, pl* **vaivenes** **1** : swinging, swaying, rocking **2** : change, fluctuation ⟨los vaivenes de la vida : life's ups and downs⟩
vajilla *nf* : dishes *pl*, set of dishes
valdrá, etc. → **valer**
vale *nm* **1** : voucher **2** PAGARÉ : promissory note, IOU
valedero, -ra *adj* : valid
valentía *nf* : courage, valor
valer {84} *vt* **1** : to be worth ⟨valen una fortuna : they're worth a fortune⟩ ⟨no vale protestar : there's no point in protesting⟩ ⟨valer la pena : to be worth the trouble⟩ **2** : to cost ⟨¿cuánto vale? : how much does it cost?⟩ **3** : to earn, to gain ⟨le valió una reprimenda : it earned him a reprimand⟩ **4** : to protect, to aid ⟨¡válgame Dios! : God help me!⟩ **5** : to be equal to — *vi* **1** : to have value ⟨sus consejos no valen para nada : his advice is worthless⟩ **2** : to be valid, to count ⟨¡eso no vale! : that doesn't count!⟩ **3 hacerse valer** : to assert oneself **4 más vale** : it's better ⟨más vale que te vayas : you'd better go⟩ — **valerse** *vr* **1 ~ de** : to take advantage of **2 valerse solo** *or* **valerse por sí mismo** : to look after oneself **3** *Mex* : to be fair ⟨no se vale : it's not fair⟩
valeroso, -sa *adj* : brave, valiant
valet ['balɛt, -'le] *nm* : jack (in playing cards)
valga, etc. → **valer**
valía *nf* : value, worth
validar *vt* : to validate — **validación** *nf*
validez *nf* : validity
válido, -da *adj* : valid
valiente *adj* **1** : brave, valiant **2** (*used ironically*) : fine, great ⟨¡valiente amiga! : what a fine friend!⟩ — **valientemente** *adv*
valija *nf* : suitcase, valise
valioso, -sa *adj* PRECIOSO : valuable, precious
valla *nf* **1** : fence, barricade **2** : hurdle (in sports) **3** : obstacle, hindrance
vallar *vt* : to fence, to put a fence around
valle *nm* : valley, vale
valor *nm* **1** : value, worth, importance **2** CORAJE : courage, valor **3 valores** *nmpl* : values, principles **4 valores** *nmpl* : securities, bonds **5 sin ~** : worthless
valoración *nf, pl* **-ciones** **1** EVALUACIÓN : valuation, appraisal, assessment **2** APRECIACIÓN : appreciation
valorar *vt* **1** EVALUAR : to evaluate, to appraise, to assess **2** APRECIAR : to value, to appreciate
valorizarse {21} *vr* : to appreciate, to increase in value — **valorización** *nf*
vals *nm* : waltz
valsar *vi* : to waltz
valuación *nf, pl* **-ciones** : valuation, appraisal
valuar {3} *vt* : to value, to appraise, to assess
válvula *nf* **1** : valve **2 válvula reguladora** : throttle
vamos → **ir**
vampiro *nm* : vampire
van → **ir**
vanadio *nm* : vanadium
vanagloriarse *vr* : to boast, to brag
vanamente *adv* : vainly, in vain
vandalismo : vandalism
vándalo *nm* : vandal — **vandalismo** *nm*
vanguardia *nf* **1** : vanguard **2** : avant-garde **3 a la vanguardia** : at the forefront
vanidad *nf* : vanity
vanidoso, -sa *adj* PRESUMIDO : vain, conceited
vano, -na *adj* **1** INÚTIL : vain, useless **2** : vain, worthless ⟨vanas promesas : empty promises⟩ **3 en ~** : in vain, of no avail
vapor *nm* **1** : vapor, steam **2** : steamer, steamship **3 al vapor** : steamed
vaporizador *nm* : vaporizer
vaporizar {21} *vt* : to vaporize — **vaporizarse** *vr* — **vaporización** *nf*
vaporoso, -sa *adj* **1** : vaporous **2** : sheer, airy
vapulear *vt* : to beat, to thrash
vaquero[1], **-ra** *adj* : cowboy ⟨pantalón vaquero : jeans⟩

vaquero[2], **-ra** *n* : cowboy *m,* cowgirl *f*
vaqueros *nmpl* JEANS : jeans
vaquilla *nf* : heifer
vara *nf* **1** : pole, stick, rod **2** : staff (of office) **3** : lance, pike (in bullfighting) **4** : yardstick **5 vara de oro** : goldenrod
varado, -da *adj* **1** : beached, aground **2** : stranded
varar *vt* : to beach (a ship), to strand — *vi* : to run aground
variable *adj & nf* : variable — **variabilidad** *nf*
variación *nf, pl* **-ciones** : variation
variado, -da *adj* : varied, diverse
variante *adj & nf* : variant
varianza *nf* : variance
variar {85} *vt* **1** : to change, to alter **2** : to diversify — *vi* **1** : to vary, to change **2 variar de opinión** : to change one's mind
varicela *nf* : chicken pox
varices *or* **várices** *nfpl* : varicose veins
varicoso, -sa *adj* : varicose
variedad *nf* DIVERSIDAD : variety, diversity
varilla *nf* **1** : rod, bar **2** : spoke (of a wheel) **3** : rib (of an umbrella)
vario, -ria *adj* **1** : varied, diverse **2** : variegated, motley **3** : changeable **4 varios, varias** *pl* : various, several
variopinto, -ta *adj* : diverse, assorted, motley
varita *nf* : wand ⟨varita mágica : magic wand⟩
varón *nm, pl* **varones 1** HOMBRE : man, male **2** NIÑO : boy
varonil *adj* **1** : masculine, manly **2** : mannish
vas → **ir**
vasallo *nm* : vassal — **vasallaje** *nm*
vasco[1], **-ca** *adj & n* : Basque
vasco[2] *nm* : Basque (language)
vascular *adj* : vascular
vasija *nf* : container, vessel
vaso *nm* **1** : glass, tumbler **2** : glassful **3** : vessel ⟨vaso sanguíneo : blood vessel⟩
vástago *nm* **1** : offspring, descendant **2** : shoot (of a plant)
vastedad *nf* : vastness, immensity
vasto, -ta *adj* : vast, immense
vataje *nm* : wattage
vaticinar *vt* : to predict, to foretell
vaticinio *nm* : prediction, prophecy
vatio *nm* : watt
vaya, etc. → **ir**
Vd., Vds. → **usted**
ve, etc. → **ir, ver**
vea, etc. → **ver**
vecinal *adj* : local
vecindad *nf* **1** : neighborhood, vicinity **2 casa de vecindad** : tenement
vecindario *nm* **1** : neighborhood, area **2** : residents *pl*
vecino, -na *n* **1** : neighbor **2** : resident, inhabitant
veda *nf* **1** PROHIBICIÓN : prohibition **2** : closed season (for hunting or fishing)
vedar *vt* **1** : to prohibit, to ban **2** IMPEDIR : to impede, to prevent
vega *nf* : fertile lowland
vegetación *nf, pl* **-ciones 1** : vegetation **2 vegetaciones** *nfpl* : adenoids
vegetal *adj & nm* : vegetable, plant
vegetar *vi* : to vegetate
vegetarianismo *nm* : vegetarianism
vegetariano, -na *adj & n* : vegetarian
vegetativo, -va *adj* : vegetative
vehemente *adj* : vehement — **vehemencia** *nf*
vehículo *nm* : vehicle — **vehicular** *adj*
veía, etc. → **ver**
veinte *adj & nm* : twenty
veinteavo[1], **-va** *adj* : twentieth
veinteavo[2] *nm* : twentieth (fraction)
veintena *nf* : group of twenty, score ⟨una veintena de participantes : about twenty participants⟩
vejación *nf, pl* **-ciones** : ill-treatment, humiliation
vejar *vt* : to mistreat, to ridicule, to harass
vejete *nm* : old fellow, codger
vejez *nf* : old age
vejiga *nf* **1** : bladder **2** AMPOLLA : blister
vela *nf* **1** VIGILIA : wakefulness ⟨pasé la noche en vela : I stayed awake all night⟩ **2** : watch, vigil, wake **3** : candle **4** : sail
velada *nf* : evening party, soirée
velado, -da *adj* **1** : veiled, hidden **2** : blurred **3** : muffled
velador[1], **-dora** *n* : guard, night watchman
velador[2] *nm* **1** : candlestick **2** : night table
velar *vt* **1** : to hold a wake over **2** : to watch over, to sit up with **3** : to blur, to expose (a photo) **4** : to veil, to conceal — *vi* **1** : to stay awake **2 ~ por** : to watch over, to look after
velatorio *nm* VELORIO : wake (for the dead)
veleidad *nf* **1** : fickleness **2** : whim, caprice
veleidoso, -sa : fickle, capricious
velero *nm* **1** : sailing ship **2** : sailboat
veleta *nf* : weather vane
vello *nm* **1** : body hair **2** : down, fuzz
vellocino *nm* : fleece
vellón *nm, pl* **vellones 1** : fleece, sheepskin **2** *PRi* : nickel (coin)
vellosidad *nf* : downiness, hairiness
velloso, -sa *adj* : downy, fluffy, hairy
velo *nm* : veil
velocidad *nf* **1** : speed, velocity ⟨velocidad máxima : speed limit⟩ **2** MARCHA : gear (of an automobile)
velocímetro *nm* : speedometer
velocista *nmf* : sprinter
velorio *nm* VELATORIO : wake (for the dead)
velour *nm* : velour, velours
veloz *adj, pl* **veloces** : fast, quick, swift — **velozmente** *adv*
ven → **venir**

vena *nf* **1** : vein ⟨vena yugular : jugular vein⟩ **2** : vein, seam, lode **3** : grain (of wood) **4** : style ⟨en vena lírica : in a lyrical vein⟩ **5** : strain, touch ⟨una vena de humor : a touch of humor⟩ **6** : mood

venado *nm* **1** : deer **2** : venison

venal *adj* : venal — **venalidad** *nf*

vencedor, -dora *n* : winner, victor

vencejo *nm* : swift (bird)

vencer {86} *vt* **1** DERROTAR : to vanquish, to defeat **2** SUPERAR : to overcome, to surmount — *vi* **1** GANAR : to win, to triumph **2** CADUCAR : to expire ⟨el plazo vence el jueves : the deadline is Thursday⟩ **3** : to fall due, to mature — **vencerse** *vr* **1** DOMINARSE : to control oneself **2** : to break, to collapse

vencido, -da *adj* **1** : defeated **2** : expired **3** : due, payable **4 darse por vencido** : to give up

vencimiento *nm* **1** : defeat **2** : expiration **3** : maturity (of a loan)

venda *nf* : bandage

vendaje *nm* : bandage, dressing

vendar *vt* **1** : to bandage **2 vendar los ojos** : to blindfold

vendaval *nm* : gale, strong wind

vendedor, -dora *n* : salesperson, salesman *m*, saleswoman *f*

vender *vt* **1** : to sell **2** : to sell out, to betray — **venderse** *vr* **1** : to be sold ⟨se vende : for sale⟩ **2** : to sell out

vendetta *nf* : vendetta

vendible *adj* : salable, marketable

vendimia *nf* : grape harvest

vendrá, etc. → **venir**

veneno *nm* **1** : poison **2** : venom

venenoso, -sa *adj* : poisonous, venomous

venerable *adj* : venerable

veneración *nf, pl* **-ciones** : veneration, reverence

venerar *vt* : to venerate, to revere

venéreo, -rea *adj* : venereal

venero *nm* **1** VENA : seam, lode, vein **2** MANANTIAL : spring **3** FUENTE : origin, source

venezolano, -na *adj & n* : Venezuelan

venga, etc. → **venir**

vengador, -dora *n* : avenger

venganza *nf* : vengeance, revenge

vengar {52} *vt* : to avenge — **vengarse** *vr* : to get even, to revenge oneself

vengativo, -va *adj* : vindictive, vengeful

vengue, etc. → **vengar**

venia *nf* **1** PERMISO : permission, leave **2** PERDÓN : pardon **3** : bow (of the head)

venial *adj* : venial

venida *nf* **1** LLEGADA : arrival, coming **2** REGRESO : return **3 idas y venidas** : comings and goings

venidero, -ra *adj* : coming, future

venir {87} *vi* **1** : to come ⟨lo vi venir : I saw him coming⟩ ⟨¡venga! : come on!⟩ **2** : to arrive ⟨vinieron en coche : they came by car⟩ **3** : to come, to originate ⟨sus zapatos vienen de Italia : her shoes are from Italy⟩ **4** : to come, to be available ⟨viene envuelto en plástico : it comes wrapped in plastic⟩ **5** : to come back, to return **6** : to affect, to overcome ⟨me vino un vahído : a dizzy spell came over me⟩ **7** : to fit ⟨te viene un poco grande : it's a little big for you⟩ **8** (*with the present participle*) : to have been ⟨viene entrenando diariamente : he's been training daily⟩ **9 ~ a** (*with the infinitive*) : to end up, to turn out ⟨viene a ser lo mismo : it comes out the same⟩ **10 que viene** : coming, next ⟨el año que viene : next year⟩ **11 venir bien** : to be suitable, to be just right — **venirse** *vr* **1** : to come, to arrive **2** : to come back **3 venirse abajo** : to fall apart, to collapse

venta *nf* **1** : sale **2 venta al por menor** *or* **venta al detalle** : retail sales

ventaja *nf* **1** : advantage **2** : lead, head start **3 ventajas** *nfpl* : perks, extras

ventajoso, -sa *adj* **1** : advantageous **2** : profitable — **ventajosamente** *adv*

ventana *nf* **1** : window (of a building) **2 ventana de la nariz** : nostril

ventanal *nm* : large window

ventanilla *nf* **1** : window (of a vehicle or airplane) **2** : ticket window, box office

ventero, -ra *n* : innkeeper

ventilación *nf, pl* **-ciones** : ventilation

ventilador *nm* **1** : ventilator **2** : fan

ventilar *vt* **1** : to ventilate, to air out **2** : to air, to discuss **3** : to make public, to reveal — **ventilarse** *vr* : to get some air

ventisca *nf* : snowstorm, blizzard

ventisquero *nm* : snowdrift

ventosear *vi* : to break wind

ventosidad *nf* : wind, flatulence

ventoso, -sa *adj* : windy

ventrículo *nm* : ventricle

ventrílocuo, -cua *n* : ventriloquist

ventriloquia *nf* : ventriloquism

ventura *nf* **1** : fortune, luck, chance **2** : happiness **3 a la ventura** : at random, as it comes

venturoso, -sa *adj* **1** AFORTUNADO : fortunate, lucky **2** : successful

Venus *nm* : Venus

venza, etc. → **vencer**

ver[1] {88} *vt* **1** : to see ⟨vimos la película : we saw the movie⟩ **2** ENTENDER : to understand ⟨ya lo veo : now I get it⟩ **3** EXAMINAR : to examine, to look into ⟨lo veré : I'll take a look at it⟩ **4** JUZGAR : to see, to judge ⟨a mi manera de ver : to my way of thinking⟩ **5** VISITAR : to meet with, to visit **6** AVERIGUAR : to find out **7 a ver** *or* **vamos a ver** : let's see — *vi* **1** : to see **2** ENTERARSE : to learn, to find out **3** ENTENDER : to understand — **verse** *vr* **1** HALLARSE : to find oneself **2** PARECER : to look, to appear **3** ENCONTRARSE : to see each other, to meet

ver[2] *nm* **1** : looks *pl*, appearance **2** : opinion ⟨a mi ver : in my view⟩

vera *nf* : side ⟨a la vera del camino : alongside the road⟩

veracidad *nf* : truthfulness, veracity

veranda *nf* : veranda

veraneante *nmf* : summer vacationer

veranear *vi* : to spend the summer

veraniego, -ga *adj* **1** ESTIVAL : summer ⟨el sol veraniego : the summer sun⟩ **2** : summery

verano *nm* : summer

veras *nfpl* **de ~** : really, truly

veraz *adj, pl* **veraces** : truthful, veracious

verbal *adj* : verbal — **verbalmente** *adv*

verbalizar {21} *vt* : to verbalize, to express

verbena *nf* **1** FIESTA : festival, fair **2** : verbena, vervain

verbigracia *adv* : for example

verbo *nm* : verb

verborrea *nf* : verbiage

verbosidad *nf* : verbosity, wordiness

verboso, -sa *adj* : verbose, wordy

verdad *nf* **1** : truth **2 de ~** : really, truly **3 ¿verdad?** : right?, isn't that so?

verdaderamente *adv* : really, truly

verdadero, -dera *adj* **1** REAL, VERÍDICO : true, real **2** AUTÉNTICO : genuine

verde[1] *adj* **1** : green (in color) **2** : green, unripe **3** : inexperienced, green **4** : dirty, risqué

verde[2] *nm* : green

verdear *vi* : to turn green, to become verdant

verdín *nm, pl* **verdines** : slime, scum

verdor *nm* **1** : greenness **2** : verdure

verdoso, -sa *adj* : greenish

verdugo *nm* **1** : executioner, hangman **2** : tyrant

verdugón *nm, pl* **-gones** : welt, wheal

verdura *nf* : vegetable(s), green(s)

vereda *nf* **1** SENDA : path, trail **2** : sidewalk, pavement

veredicto *nm* : verdict

verga *nf* : spar, yard (of a ship)

vergonzoso, -sa *adj* **1** : disgraceful, shameful **2** : bashful, shy — **vergonzosamente** *adv*

vergüenza *nf* **1** : disgrace, shame **2** : embarrassment **3** : bashfulness, shyness

vericueto *nm* : rough terrain

verídico, -ca *adj* **1** REAL, VERDADERO : true, real **2** VERAZ : truthful

verificación *nf, pl* **-ciones** **1** : verification **2** : testing, checking

verificador, -dora *n* : inspector, tester

verificar {72} *vt* **1** : to verify, to confirm **2** : to test, to check **3** : to carry out, to conduct — **verificarse** *vr* **1** : to take place, to occur **2** : to come true

verja *nf* **1** : rails *pl* (of a fence) **2** : grating, grille **3** : gate

vermut *nm, pl* **vermuts** : vermouth

vernáculo, -la *adj* : vernacular

vernal *adj* : vernal, spring

verosímil *adj* **1** : probable, likely **2** : credible, realistic

verosimilitud *nf* **1** : probability, likeliness **2** : verisimilitude

verraco *nm* : boar

verruga *nf* : wart

versado, -da *adj* **~ en** : versed in, knowledgeable about

versar *vi* **~ sobre** : to deal with, to be about

versátil *adj* **1** : versatile **2** : fickle

versatilidad *nf* **1** : versatility **2** : fickleness

versículo *nm* : verse (in the Bible)

versión *nf, pl* **versiones** **1** : version **2** : translation

verso *nm* : verse

versus *prep* : versus, against

vértebra *nf* : vertebra — **vertebral** *adj*

vertebrado[1]**, -da** *adj* : vertebrate

vertebrado[2] *nm* : vertebrate

vertedero *nm* **1** : garbage dump **2** DESAGÜE : drain, outlet

verter {56} *vt* **1** : to pour **2** : to spill, to shed **3** : to empty out **4** : to express, to voice **5** : to translate, to render — *vi* : to flow

vertical *adj & nf* : vertical — **verticalmente** *adv*

vértice *nm* : vertex, apex

vertido *nm* : spilling, spill

vertiente *nf* **1** : slope **2** : aspect, side, element

vertiginoso, -sa *adj* : vertiginous — **vertiginosamente** *adv*

vértigo *nm* : vertigo, dizziness

vesícula *nf* **1** : vesicle **2 vesícula biliar** : gallbladder

vesicular *adj* : vesicular

vestíbulo *nm* : vestibule, hall, lobby, foyer

vestido *nm* **1** : dress, costume, clothes *pl* **2** : dress (garment)

vestidor *nm* : dressing room

vestiduras *nfpl* **1** : clothing, raiment, regalia **2** *or* **vestiduras sacerdotales** : vestments

vestigio *nm* : vestige, sign, trace

vestimenta *nf* ROPA : clothing, clothes *pl*

vestir {54} *vt* **1** : to dress, to clothe **2** LLEVAR : to wear **3** ADORNAR : to decorate, to dress up — *vi* **1** : to dress ⟨vestir bien : to dress well⟩ **2** : to look good, to suit the occasion — **vestirse** *vr* **1** : to get dressed **2 ~ de** : to dress up as ⟨se vistieron de soldados : they dressed up as soldiers⟩ **3 ~ de** : to wear, to dress in

vestuario *nm* **1** : wardrobe **2** : dressing room, locker room

veta *nf* **1** : grain (in wood) **2** : vein, seam, lode **3** : trace, streak ⟨una veta de terco : a stubborn streak⟩

vetar *vt* : to veto

veteado, -da *adj* : streaked, veined

veterano, -na *adj & n* : veteran

veterinaria *nf* : veterinary medicine

veterinario[1]**, -ria** *adj* : veterinary

veterinario[2]**, -ria** *n* : veterinarian

veto *nm* : veto
vetusto, -ta *adj* ANTIGUO : ancient, very old
vez *nf, pl* **veces** **1** : time, occasion ⟨a la vez : at the same time⟩ ⟨a veces : at times, occasionally⟩ ⟨de vez en cuando : from time to time⟩ **2** (*with numbers*) : time ⟨una vez : once⟩ ⟨de una vez : all at once⟩ ⟨de una vez para siempre : once and for all⟩ ⟨dos veces : twice⟩ **3** : turn ⟨a su vez : in turn⟩ ⟨en vez de : instead of⟩ ⟨hacer las veces de : to act as, to stand in for⟩
vía[1] *nf* **1** RUTA, CAMINO : road, route, way ⟨Vía Láctea : Milky Way⟩ **2** MEDIO : means, way ⟨por vía oficial : through official channels⟩ **3** : track, line (of a railroad) **4** : tract, passage ⟨por vía oral : orally⟩ **5 en vías de** : in the process of ⟨en vías de solución : on the road to a solution⟩ **6 por ~** : by (in transportation) ⟨por vía aérea : by air, airmail⟩
vía[2] *prep* : via
viable *adj* : viable, feasible — **viabilidad** *nf*
viaducto *nm* : viaduct
viajante *mf* : traveling salesman, traveling saleswoman
viajar *vi* : to travel, to journey
viaje *nm* : trip, journey ⟨viaje de negocios : business trip⟩
viajero[1], **-ra** *adj* : traveling
viajero[2], **-ra** *n* **1** : traveler **2** PASAJERO : passenger
vial *adj* : road, traffic
viático *nm* : travel allowance, travel expenses *pl*
víbora *nf* : viper
vibración *nf, pl* **-ciones** : vibration
vibrador *nm* : vibrator
vibrante *adj* **1** : vibrant **2** : vibrating
vibrar *vi* : to vibrate
vibratorio, -ria *adj* : vibratory
vicario, -ria *n* : vicar
vicealmirante *nmf* : vice admiral
vicepresidente, -ta *n* : vice president — **vicepresidencia** *nf*
viceversa *adv* : vice versa, conversely
viciado, -da *adj* : stuffy, close
viciar *vt* **1** : to corrupt **2** : to invalidate **3** FALSEAR : to distort **4** : to pollute, to adulterate
vicio *nm* **1** : vice, depravity **2** : bad habit **3** : defect, blemish
vicioso, -sa *adj* : depraved, corrupt
vicisitud *nf* : vicissitude
víctima *nf* : victim
victimario, -ria *n* ASESINO : killer, murderer
victimizar {21} *vt Arg, Mex* : to victimize
victoria *nf* : victory — **victorioso, -sa** *adj* — **victoriosamente** *adv*
victoriano, -na *adj* : Victorian
vid *nf* : vine, grapevine
vida *nf* **1** : life ⟨la vida cotidiana : everyday life⟩ **2** : life span, lifetime **3** BIOGRAFÍA : biography, life **4** : way of life, lifestyle **5** : livelihood ⟨ganarse la vida : to earn one's living⟩ **6** VIVEZA : liveliness **7 media vida** : half-life
vidente *nmf* **1** : psychic, clairvoyant **2** : sighted person
video *or* **vídeo** *nm* : video
videocasete *or* **videocassette** *nm* : videocassette
videocasetera *or* **videocassettera** *nf* : videocassette recorder, VCR
videocinta *nf* : videotape
videograbar *vt* : to videotape
vidriado *nm* : glaze
vidriar *vt* : to glaze (pottery, tile, etc.)
vidriera *nf* **1** : stained-glass window **2** : glass door or window **3** : store window
vidriero, -ra *n* : glazier
vidrio *nm* **1** : glass, piece of glass **2** : windowpane
vidrioso, -sa *adj* **1** : brittle, fragile **2** : slippery **3** : glassy, glazed (of eyes) **4** : touchy, delicate
vieira *nf* **1** : scallop **2** : scallop shell
viejo[1], **-ja** *adj* **1** ANCIANO : old, elderly **2** ANTIGUO : former, longstanding ⟨viejas tradiciones : old traditions⟩ ⟨viejos amigos : old friends⟩ **3** GASTADO : old, worn, worn-out
viejo[2], **-ja** *n* ANCIANO : old man *m*, old woman *f*
viene, etc. → **venir**
viento *nm* **1** : wind **2 hacer viento** : to be windy **3 contra viento y marea** : against all odds **4 viento alisio** : trade wind **5 viento en popa** : splendidly, successfully
vientre *nm* **1** : abdomen, belly **2** : womb **3** : bowels *pl*
viernes *nms & pl* : Friday
vierte, etc. → **verter**
vietnamita[1] *adj & nmf* : Vietnamese
vietnamita[2] *nm* : Vietnamese (language)
viga *nf* **1** : beam, rafter, girder **2 viga voladiza** : cantilever
vigencia *nf* **1** : validity **2** : force, effect ⟨entrar en vigencia : to go into effect⟩
vigente *adj* : valid, in force
vigésimo[1], **-ma** *adj* : twentieth, twenty- ⟨la vigésima segunda edición : the twenty-second edition⟩
vigésimo[2], **-ma** *n* : twentieth, twenty- (in a series)
vigía *nmf* : lookout
vigilancia *nf* : vigilance, watchfulness ⟨bajo vigilancia : under surveillance⟩
vigilante[1] *adj* : vigilant, watchful
vigilante[2] *nmf* : watchman, guard
vigilar *vt* **1** CUIDAR : to look after, to keep an eye on **2** GUARDAR : to watch over, to guard — *vi* **1** : to be watchful **2** : to keep watch
vigilia *nf* **1** VELA : wakefulness **2** : night work **3** : vigil (in religion)
vigor *nm* **1** : vigor, energy, strength **2** VIGENCIA : force, effect
vigorizante *adj* : invigorating

vigorizar {21} *vt* : to strengthen, to invigorate
vigoroso, -sa *adj* : vigorous — **vigorosamente** *adv*
VIH *nm* (*v*irus de *i*nmunodeficiencia *h*umana) : HIV
vikingo, -ga *adj & n* : Viking
vil *adj* : vile, despicable
vileza *nf* **1** : vileness **2** : despicable action, villainy
vilipendiar *vt* : to vilify, to revile
villa *nf* **1** : town, village **2** : villa
villancico *nm* : carol, Christmas carol
villano, -na *n* **1** : villain **2** : peasant
vilo *nm* **1 en ~** : in the air **2 en ~** : uncertain, in suspense
vinagre *nm* : vinegar
vinagrera *nf* : cruet (for vinegar)
vinatería *nf* : wine shop
vinculación *nf, pl* **-ciones 1** : linking **2** RELACIÓN : bond, link, connection
vincular *vt* CONECTAR, RELACIONAR : to tie, to link, to connect
vínculo *nm* LAZO : tie, link, bond
vindicación *nf, pl* **-ciones** : vindication
vindicar *vt* **1** : to vindicate **2** : to avenge
vinilo *nm* : vinyl
vino[1], **etc.** → **venir**
vino[2] *nm* : wine
viña *nf* : vineyard
viñedo *nm* : vineyard
vio, etc. → **ver**
viola *nf* : viola
violación *nf, pl* **-ciones 1** : violation, offense **2** : rape
violador[1], **-dora** *n* : violator, offender
violador[2] *nm* : rapist
violar *vt* **1** : to rape **2** : to violate (a law or right) **3** PROFANAR : to desecrate
violencia *nf* : violence
violentamente *adv* : by force, violently
violentar *vt* **1** FORZAR : to break open, to force **2** : to distort (words or ideas) — **violentarse** *vr* : to force oneself
violento, -ta *adj* **1** : violent **2** EMBARAZOSO, INCÓMODO : awkward, embarassing
violeta[1] *adj & nm* : violet (color)
violeta[2] *nf* : violet (flower)
violín *nm, pl* **-lines** : violin
violinista *nmf* : violinist
violonchelista *nmf* : cellist
violonchelo *nm* : cello, violoncello
VIP *nmf, pl* **VIPs** : VIP
vira *nf* : welt (of a shoe)
virago *nf* : virago, shrew
viraje *nm* **1** : turn, swerve **2** : change
viral *adj* : viral
virar *vi* : to tack, to turn, to veer
virgen[1] *adj* : virgin ⟨lana virgen : virgin wool⟩
virgen[2] *nmf, pl* **vírgenes** : virgin ⟨la Santísima Virgen : the Blessed Virgin⟩
virginal *adj* : virginal, chaste
virginidad *nf* : virginity
Virgo *nmf* : Virgo
vírico, -ca *adj* : viral
viril *adj* : virile — **virilidad** *nf*
virrey, -rreina *n* : viceroy *m*, vicereine *f*
virtual *adj* : virtual — **virtualmente** *adv*
virtud *nf* **1** : virtue **2 en virtud de** : by virtue of
virtuosismo *nm* : virtuosity
virtuoso[1], **-sa** *adj* : virtuous — **virtuosamente** *adv*
virtuoso[2], **-sa** *n* : virtuoso
viruela *nf* **1** : smallpox **2** : pockmark
virulencia *nf* : virulence
virulento, -ta *adj* : virulent
virus *nm* : virus
viruta *nf* : shaving
visa *nf* : visa
visado *nm Spain* : visa
visaje *nm* : face, grimace ⟨hacer visajes : to make faces⟩
visceral *adj* : visceral
vísceras *nfpl* : viscera, entrails
visconde, -desa *n* : viscount *m*, viscountess *f*
viscosidad *nf* : viscosity
viscoso, -sa *adj* : viscous
visera *nf* : visor
visibilidad *nf* : visibility
visible *adj* : visible — **visiblemente** *adv*
visión *nf, pl* **visiones 1** : vision, eyesight **2** : view, perspective **3** : vision, illusion ⟨ver visiones : to be seeing things⟩
visionario, -ria *adj & n* : visionary
visita *nf* **1** : visit, call **2** : visitor **3 ir de visita** : to go visiting
visitador, -dora *n* : visitor, frequent caller
visitante[1] *adj* : visiting
visitante[2] *nmf* : visitor
visitar *vt* : to visit
vislumbrar *vt* **1** : to discern, to make out **2** : to begin to see, to have an inkling of
vislumbre *nf* : glimmer, gleam
viso *nm* **1** APARIENCIA : appearance ⟨tener visos de : to seem, to show signs of⟩ **2** DESTELLO : glint, gleam **3** : sheen, iridescence
visón *nm, pl* **visones** : mink
víspera *nf* **1** : eve, day before **2 vísperas** *nfpl* : vespers
vista *nf* **1** VISIÓN : vision, eyesight **2** MIRADA : look, gaze, glance **3** PANORAMA : view, vista, panorama **4** : hearing (in court) **5 a primera vista** : at first sight **6 en vista de** : in view of **7 hacer la vista gorda** : to turn a blind eye **8 ¡hasta la vista!** : so long!, see you! **9 perder de vista** : to lose sight of **10 punto de vista** : point of view
vistazo *nm* : glance, look
viste, etc. → **ver**[1], **vestir**
visto[1] *pp* → **ver**
visto[2], **-ta** *adj* **1** : obvious, clear **2** : in view of, considering **3 estar bien visto** : to be approved of **4 estar mal visto** : to be frowned upon **5 por lo visto** : apparently **6 nunca visto** : unheard-of **7 visto que** : since, given that
visto[3] *nm* **visto bueno** : approval

vistoso, -sa *adj* : colorful, bright
visual *adj* : visual — **visualmente** *adv*
visualización *nf, pl* **-ciones** : visualization
visualizar {21} *vt* **1** : to visualize **2** : to display (on a screen)
vital *adj* **1** : vital **2** : lively, dynamic
vitalicio, -cia *adj* : life, lifetime
vitalidad *nf* : vitality
vitamina *nf* : vitamin
vitamínico, -ca *adj* : vitamin 〈complejos vitamínicos : vitamin compounds〉
vitorear *vt* : to cheer, to acclaim
vitral *nm* : stained-glass window
vítreo, -rea *adj* : vitreous, glassy
vitrina *nf* **1** : showcase, display case **2** : store window
vitriolo *nm* : vitriol
vituperar *vt* : to condemn, to vituperate against
vituperio *nm* : vituperation, censure
viudez *nf* : widowerhood, widowhood
viudo, -da *n* : widower *m,* widow *f*
vivacidad *nf* VIVEZA : vivacity, liveliness
vivamente *adv* **1** : in a lively manner **2** : vividly **3** : strongly, acutely 〈lo recomendamos vivamente : we strongly recommend it〉
vivaque *nm* : bivouac
vivaquear *vi* : to bivouac
vivar *vi* : to cheer
vivaz *adj, pl* **vivaces** **1** : lively, vivacious **2** : clever, sharp **3** : perennial
víveres *nmpl* : provisions, supplies, food
vivero *nm* **1** : nursery (for plants) **2** : hatchery, fish farm
viveza *nf* **1** VIVACIDAD : liveliness **2** BRILLO : vividness, brightness **3** ASTUCIA : cleverness, sharpness
vívido, -da *adj* : vivid, lively
vividor, -dora *n* : sponger, parasite
vivienda *nf* **1** : housing **2** MORADA : dwelling, home
viviente *adj* : living
vivificar {72} *vt* : to vivify, to give life to
vivir[1] *vi* **1** : to live, to be alive **2** SUBSISTIR : to subsist, to make a living **3** RESIDIR : to reside **4** : to spend one's life 〈vive para trabajar : she lives to work〉 **5** **~ de** : to live on — *vt* **1** : to live 〈vivir su vida : to live one's life〉 **2** EXPERIMENTAR : to go through, to experience
vivir[2] *nm* **1** : life, lifestyle **2** **de mal vivir** : disreputable
vivisección *nf, pl* **-ciones** : vivisection
vivo, -va *adj* **1** : alive **2** INTENSO : vivid, bright, intense **3** ANIMADO : lively, vivacious **4** ASTUTO : sharp, clever **5** **en ~** : live 〈transmisión en vivo : live broadcast〉 **6** **al rojo vivo** : red-hot
vizconde, -desa *n* : viscount *m,* viscountess *f*
vocablo *nm* PALABRA : word
vocabulario *nm* : vocabulary
vocación *nf, pl* **-ciones** : vocation
vocacional *adj* : vocational
vocal[1] *adj* : vocal
vocal[2] *nmf* : member (of a committee, board, etc.)
vocal[3] *nf* : vowel
vocalista *nmf* CANTANTE : singer, vocalist
vocalizar {21} *vi* : to vocalize
vocear *v* : to shout
vocerío *nm* : clamor, shouting
vocero, -ra *n* PORTAVOZ : spokesperson, spokesman *m,* spokeswoman *f*
vociferante *adj* : vociferous
vociferar *vi* GRITAR : to shout, to yell
vodevil *nm* : vaudeville
vodka *nm* : vodka
voladizo[1], **-za** *adj* : projecting
voladizo[2] *nm* : projection
volador, -dora *adj* : flying
volando *adv* : quickly, in a hurry
volante[1] *adj* : flying
volante[2] *nm* **1** : steering wheel **2** FOLLETO : flier, circular **3** : shuttlecock **4** : flywheel **5** : balance wheel (of a watch) **6** : ruffle, flounce
volar {19} *vi* **1** : to fly **2** CORRER : to hurry, to rush 〈el tiempo vuela : time flies〉 〈pasar volando : to fly past〉 **3** DIVULGARSE : to spread 〈unos rumores volaban : rumors were spreading around〉 **4** DESAPARECER : to disappear 〈el dinero ya voló : the money's already gone〉 — *vt* **1** : to blow up, to demolish **2** : to irritate
volátil *adj* : volatile — **volatilidad** *nf*
volatilizar {21} *vt* : to volatize — **volatilizarse** *vr*
volcán *nm, pl* **volcanes** : volcano
volcánico, -ca *adj* : volcanic
volcar {82} *vt* **1** : to upset, to knock over, to turn over **2** : to empty out **3** : to make dizzy **4** : to cause a change of mind in **5** : to irritate — *vi* **1** : to overturn, to tip over **2** : to capsize — **volcarse** *vr* **1** : to overturn **2** : to do one's utmost
volea *nf* : volley (in sports)
volear *vi* : to volley (in sports)
voleibol *nm* : volleyball
voleo *nm* **al voleo** : haphazardly, at random
volframio *nm* : wolfram, tungsten
volición *nf, pl* **-ciones** : volition
volqué, etc. → **volcar**
voltaje *nm* : voltage
voltear *vt* **1** : to turn over, to turn upside down **2** : to reverse, to turn inside out **3** : to turn 〈voltear la cara : to turn one's head〉 **4** : to knock down — *vi* **1** : to roll over, to do somersaults **2** : to turn 〈volteó a la izquierda : he turned left〉 — **voltearse** *vr* **1** : to turn around **2** : to change one's allegiance
voltereta *nf* : somersault, tumble
voltio *nm* : volt
volubilidad *nf* : fickleness, changeableness
voluble *adj* : fickle, changeable
volumen *nm, pl* **-lúmenes** **1** TOMO : volume, book **2** : capacity, size, bulk **3** CANTIDAD : amount 〈el volumen de

ventas : the volume of sales⟩ **4** : volume, loudness
voluminoso, -sa *adj* : voluminous, massive, bulky
voluntad *nf* **1** : will, volition **2** DESEO : desire, wish **3** INTENCIÓN : intention **4 a voluntad** : at will **5 buena voluntad** : good will **6 mala voluntad** : ill will **7 fuerza de voluntad** : willpower
voluntario[1], -ria *adj* : voluntary — **voluntariamente** *adv*
voluntario[2], -ria *n* : volunteer
voluntarioso, -sa *adj* **1** : stubborn **2** : willing, eager
voluptuosidad *nf* : voluptuousness
voluptuoso, -sa *adj* : voluptuous — **voluptuosamente** *adv*
voluta *nf* : spiral, column (of smoke)
volver {89} *vi* **1** : to return, to come or go back ⟨volver a casa : to return home⟩ **2** : to revert ⟨volver al tema : to get back to the subject⟩ **3 ~ a** : to do again ⟨volvieron a llamar : they called again⟩ **4 volver en sí** : to come to, to regain consciousness — *vt* **1** : to turn, to turn over, to turn inside out **2** : to return, to repay, to restore **3** : to cause, to make ⟨la volvía loca : it was driving her crazy⟩ — **volverse** *vr* **1** : to become ⟨se volvió deprimido : he became depressed⟩ **2** : to turn around
vomitar *vi* : to vomit — *vt* **1** : to vomit **2** : to spew out (lava, etc.)
vómito *nm* **1** : vomiting **2** : vomit
voracidad *nf* : voracity
vorágine *nf* : whirlpool, maelstrom
voraz *adj, pl* **voraces** : voracious — **vorazmente** *adv*
vórtice *nm* **1** : whirlpool, vortex **2** TORBELLINO : whirlwind
vos *pron* (*in some regions of Latin America*) : you
vosear *vt* : to address as *vos*
vosotros, -tras *pron pl Spain* **1** : you, yourselves **2** : ye
votación *nf, pl* **-ciones** : vote, voting
votante *nmf* : voter
votar *vi* : to vote — *vt* : to vote for
votivo, -va *adj* : votive
voto *nm* **1** : vote **2** : vow (in religion) **3 votos** *nmpl* : good wishes
voy → **ir**
voz *nf, pl* **voces** **1** : voice **2** : opinion, say **3** GRITO : shout, yell **4** : sound **5** VOCABLO : word, term **6** : rumor **7 a voz en cuello** : at the top of one's lungs **8 dar voces** : to shout **9 en voz alta** : aloud, in a loud voice **10 en voz baja** : softly, in a low voice
vudú *nm* : voodoo
vuelco *nm* : upset, overturning ⟨me dio un vuelco el corazón : my heart skipped a beat⟩
vuela, etc. → **volar**
vuelca, vuelque etc. → **volcar**
vuelo *nm* **1** : flight, flying ⟨alzar el vuelo : to take flight⟩ **2** : flight (of an aircraft) ⟨vuelo espacial : space flight⟩ **3** : flare, fullness (of clothing) **4 al vuelo** : on the wing
vuelta *nf* **1** GIRO : turn ⟨se dio la vuelta : he turned around⟩ **2** REVOLUCIÓN : circle, revolution ⟨dio la vuelta al mundo : she went around the world⟩ ⟨las ruedas daban vueltas : the wheels were spinning⟩ **3** : flip, turn ⟨le dio la vuelta : she flipped it over⟩ **4** : bend, curve ⟨a la vuelta de la esquina : around the corner⟩ **5** REGRESO : return ⟨de ida y vuelta : round trip⟩ ⟨a vuelta de correo : return mail⟩ **6** : round, lap (in sports or games) **7** PASEO : walk, drive, ride ⟨dio una vuelta : he went for a walk⟩ **8** DORSO, REVÉS : back, other side ⟨a la vuelta : on the back⟩ **9** : cuff (of pants) **10 darle vueltas** : to think over **11 estar de vuelta** : to be back
vuelto *pp* → **volver**
vuelve, etc. → **volver**
vuestro[1], -stra *adj Spain* : your, of yours ⟨vuestros coches : your cars⟩ ⟨una amiga vuestra : a friend of yours⟩
vuestro[2], -stra *pron Spain,* (*with definite article*) : yours ⟨la vuestra es más grande : yours is bigger⟩ ⟨esos son los vuestros : those are yours⟩
vulcanizar {21} *vt* : to vulcanize
vulgar *adj* **1** : common **2** : vulgar
vulgaridad *nf* : vulgarity
vulgarismo *nm* : vulgarism
vulgarizar {21} *vt* : to vulgarize, to popularize
vulgarmente *adv* : vulgarly, popularly
vulgo *nm* **el vulgo** : the masses, common people
vulnerable *adj* : vulnerable — **vulnerabilidad** *nf*
vulnerar *vt* **1** : to injure, to damage (one's reputation or honor) **2** : to violate, to break (a law or contract)

W

w *nf* : twenty-fourth letter of the Spanish alphabet
wafle *nm* : waffle
waflera *nf* : waffle iron
wapití *nm* : wapiti, elk
whisky *nm, pl* **whiskys** *or* **whiskies** : whiskey
wigwam *nm* : wigwam

X

x *nf* : twenty-fifth letter of the Spanish alphabet
xenofobia *nf* : xenophobia
xenófobo[1], **-ba** *adj* : xenophobic
xenófobo[2], **-ba** *n* : xenophobe
xenón *nm* : xenon
xerocopiar *vt* : to photocopy, to xerox
xilófono *nm* : xylophone

Y

y[1] *nf* : twenty-sixth letter of the Spanish alphabet
y[2] *conj* (**e** *before words beginning with i- or hi-*) **1** : and ⟨mi hermano y yo : my brother and I⟩ ⟨¿y los demás? : and (what about) the others?⟩ **2** (*used in numbers*) ⟨cincuenta y cinco : fifty-five⟩ **3** *fam* : well ⟨y por supuesto : well, of course⟩
ya[1] *adv* **1** : already ⟨ya terminó : she's finished already⟩ **2** : now, right now ⟨¡hazlo ya! : do it now!⟩ ⟨ya mismo : right away⟩ **3** : later, soon ⟨ya iremos : we'll go later on⟩ **4** : no longer, anymore ⟨ya no fuma : he no longer smokes⟩ **5** (*used for emphasis*) ⟨¡ya lo sé! : I know!⟩ ⟨ya lo creo : of course⟩ **6 no ya** : not only ⟨no ya lloran sino gritan : they're not only crying but screaming⟩ **7 ya que** : now that, since ⟨ya que sabe la verdad : now that she knows the truth⟩
ya[2] *conj* **ya . . . ya** : whether . . . or, first . . . then ⟨ya le gusta, ya no : first he likes it, then he doesn't⟩
yac *nm* : yak
yacer {90} *vi* : to lie ⟨en esta tumba yacen sus abuelos : his grandparents lie in this grave⟩
yacimiento *nm* : bed, deposit ⟨yacimiento petrolífero : oil field⟩
yaga, etc. → **yacer**
yanqui *adj & nmf* : Yankee
yarda *nf* : yard
yate *nm* : yacht
yaz, yazca, yazga etc. → **yacer**
yedra *nf* : ivy
yegua *nf* : mare
yelmo *nm* : helmet
yema *nf* **1** : bud, shoot **2** : yolk (of an egg) **3 yema del dedo** : fingertip
yemenita *adj & nmf* : Yemenite
yen *nm* : yen (currency)
yendo → **ir**
yerba *nf* **1** *or* **yerba mate** : maté **2** → **hierba**
yerga, yergue etc. → **erguir**
yermo[1], **-ma** *adj* : barren, deserted
yermo[2] *nm* : wasteland
yerno *nm* : son-in-law
yerra, etc. → **errar**
yerro *nm* : blunder, mistake
yerto, -ta *adj* : rigid, stiff
yesca *nf* : tinder
yeso *nm* **1** : plaster **2** : gypsum
yo[1] *nm* : ego, self
yo[2] *pron* **1** : I **2** : me ⟨todos menos yo : everyone except me⟩ ⟨tan bajo como yo : as short as me⟩ **3 soy yo** : it is I, it's me
yodado, -da *adj* : iodized
yodo *nm* : iodine
yoduro *nm* : iodide
yoga *nm* : yoga
yogui *nm* : yogi
yogurt *or* **yogur** *nm* : yogurt
yola *nf* : yawl
yoyo *or* **yoyó** *nm* : yo-yo
yuca *nf* **1** : yucca (plant) **2** : cassava, manioc
yucateco[1], **-ca** *adj* : of or from the Yucatán
yucateco[2], **-ca** *n* : person from the Yucatán
yudo → **judo**
yugo *nm* : yoke
yugoslavo, -va *adj & n* : Yugoslavian
yugular *adj* : jugular ⟨vena yugular : jugular vein⟩
yungas *nfpl Bol, Chile, Peru* : warm tropical valleys
yunque *nm* : anvil
yunta *nf* : yoke, team (of oxen)
yuppy *nmf, pl* **yuppies** : yuppie
yute *nm* : jute
yuxtaponer {60} *vt* : to juxtapose — **yuxtaposición** *nf*

Z

z *nf* : twenty-seventh letter of the Spanish alphabet
zacate *nm CA, Mex* **1** : grass, forage **2** : hay
zafacón *nm, pl* **-cones** *Car* : wastebasket
zafar *vt* : to loosen, to untie — **zafarse** *vr* **1** : to loosen up, to come undone **2** : to get free of
zafio, -fia *adj* : coarse, crude
zafiro *nm* : sapphire
zaga *nf* **1** : defense (in sports) **2 a la zaga** *or* **en ∼** : behind, in the rear
zagual *nm* : paddle (of a canoe)

zaguán *nm, pl* **zaguanes** : front hall, vestibule
zaherir {76} *vt* **1** : to criticize sharply **2** : to wound, to mortify
zahones *nmpl* : chaps
zaino, -na *adj* : chestnut (color)
zalamería *nf* : flattery, sweet talk
zalamero[1], **-ra** *adj* : flattering, fawning
zalamero[2], **-ra** *n* : flatterer
zambiano, -na *adj & nmf* : Zambian
zambullida *nf* : dive, plunge
zambullirse {38} *vr* : to dive, to plunge
zanahoria *nf* : carrot
zancada *nf* : stride, step
zancadilla *nf* **1** : trip, stumble **2** *fam* : trick, ruse
zancos *nmpl* : stilts
zancuda *nf* : wading bird
zancudo *nm* MOSQUITO : mosquito
zángano *nm* : drone, male bee
zanja *nf* : ditch, trench
zanjar *vt* ACLARAR : to settle, to clear up, to resolve
zapallo *nm Arg, Chile, Peru, Uru* : pumpkin
zapapico *nm* : pickax
zapata *nf* : brake shoe
zapatería *nf* **1** : shoemaker's, shoe factory **2** : shoe store
zapatero[1], **-ra** *adj* : dry, tough, poorly cooked
zapatero[2], **-ra** *n* : shoemaker, cobbler
zapatilla *nf* **1** PANTUFLA : slipper **2** *or* **zapatilla de deporte** : sneaker
zapato *nm* : shoe
zar, zarina *n* : czar *m,* czarina *f*
zarandear *vt* **1** : to sift, to sieve **2** : to shake, to jostle, to jiggle
zarapito *nm* : curlew
zarcillo *nm* **1** : earring **2** : tendril (of a plant)
zarigüeya *nf* : opossum
zarista *adj & nmf* : czarist
zarpa *nf* : paw
zarpar *vi* : to set sail, to raise anchor
zarza *nf* : bramble, blackberry bush
zarzamora *nf* **1** : blackberry **2** : bramble, blackberry bush
zarzaparrilla *nf* : sarsaparilla
zepelín *nm, pl* **-lines** : zeppelin
zigoto *nm* : zygote
zigzag *nm, pl* **zigzags** *or* **zigzagues** : zigzag
zigzaguear *vi* : to zigzag
zimbabuense *adj & nmf* : Zimbabwean
zinc *nm* : zinc
zinnia *nf* : zinnia
zíper *nm CA, Mex* : zipper
zircón *nm, pl* **zircones** : zircon
zócalo *nm Mex* : main square
zodíaco *or* **zodiaco** *nm* : zodiac — **zodíacal** *adj*
zombi *or* **zombie** *nmf* : zombie
zona *nf* : zone, district, area
zonzo[1], **-za** *adj* : stupid, silly
zonzo[2], **-za** *n* : idiot, nitwit
zoo *nm* : zoo
zoología *nf* : zoology
zoológico[1], **-ca** *adj* : zoological
zoológico[2] *nm* : zoo
zoólogo, -ga *n* : zoologist
zoom *nm* : zoom lens
zopilote *nm CA, Mex* : buzzard
zoquete *nmf fam* : oaf, blockhead
zorrillo *nm* MOFETA : skunk
zorro[1], **-rra** *adj* : sly, crafty
zorro[2], **-rra** *n* **1** : fox, vixen **2** : sly crafty person
zorzal *nm* : thrush
zozobra *nf* : anxiety, worry
zozobrar *vi* : to capsize
zueco *nm* : clog (shoe)
zulú[1] *adj & nmf* : Zulu
zulú[2] *nm* : Zulu (language)
zumaque *nm* : sumac
zumbar *vi* : to buzz, to hum — *vt fam* **1** : to hit, to thrash **2** : to make fun of
zumbido *nm* : buzzing, humming
zumo *nf* JUGO : juice
zurcir {83} *vt* : to darn, to mend
zurdo[1], **-da** *adj* : left-handed
zurdo[2], **-da** *n* : left-handed person
zurza, etc. → **zurcir**
zutano, -na → **fulano**

English–Spanish Dictionary

A

a[1] [ˈeɪ] *n, pl* **a's** *or* **as** [ˈeɪz] : primera letra del alfabeto inglés
a[2] [ə, ˈeɪ] *art* (**an** [ən, ˈæn] before vowel or silent h) **1** : un *m*, una *f* ⟨a house : una casa⟩ ⟨half an hour : media hora⟩ ⟨what a surprise! : ¡qué sorpresa!⟩ **2** PER : por, a la, al ⟨30 kilometers an hour : 30 kilómetros por hora⟩ ⟨twice a month : dos veces al mes⟩
aardvark [ˈɑrdˌvɑrk] *n* : oso *m* hormiguero
aback [əˈbæk] *adv* **1** : por sorpresa **2 to be taken aback** : quedarse desconcertado
abacus [ˈæbəkəs] *n, pl* **abaci** [ˈæbəˌsaɪ, -ˌkiː] *or* **abacuses** : ábaco *m*
abaft [əˈbæft] *adv* : a popa
abalone [ˌæbəˈloːni] *n* : abulón *m*, oreja *f* marina
abandon[1] [əˈbændən] *vt* **1** DESERT, FORSAKE : abandonar, desamparar (a alguien), desertar de (algo) **2** GIVE UP, SUSPEND : renunciar a, suspender ⟨he abandoned the search : suspendió la búsqueda⟩ **3** EVACUATE, LEAVE : abandonar, evacuar, dejar ⟨to abandon ship : abandonar el buque⟩ **4 to abandon oneself** : entregarse, abandonarse
abandon[2] *n* : desenfreno *m* ⟨with wild abandon : desenfrenadamente⟩
abandoned [əˈbændənd] *adj* **1** DESERTED : abandonado **2** UNRESTRAINED : desenfrenado, desinhibido
abandonment [əˈbændənmənt] *n* : abandono *m*, desamparo *m*
abase [əˈbeɪs] *vt* **abased; abasing** : degradar, humillar, rebajar
abash [əˈbæʃ] *vt* : avergonzar, abochornar
abashed [əˈbæʃt] *adj* : avergonzado
abate [əˈbeɪt] *vi* **abated; abating** : amainar, menguar, disminuir
abattoir [ˈæbəˌtwɑr] *n* : matadero *m*
abbess [ˈæbɪs, -ˌbɛs, -bəs] *n* : abadesa *f*
abbey [ˈæbi] *n, pl* **-beys** : abadía *f*
abbot [ˈæbət] *n* : abad *m*
abbreviate [əˈbriːviˌeɪt] *vt* **-ated; -ating** : abreviar
abbreviation [əˌbriːviˈeɪʃən] *n* : abreviación *f*, abreviatura *f*
ABC's [ˌeɪˌbiːˈsiːz] *npl* : abecé *m*
abdicate [ˈæbdɪˌkeɪt] *v* **-cated; -cating** : abdicar
abdication [ˌæbdɪˈkeɪʃən] *n* : abdicación *f*
abdomen [ˈæbdəmən, æbˈdoːmən] *n* : abdomen *m*, vientre *m*
abdominal [æbˈdɑmənəl] *adj* : abdominal — **abdominally** *adv*
abduct [æbˈdʌkt] *vt* : raptar, secuestrar
abduction [æbˈdʌkʃən] *n* : rapto *m*, secuestro *m*
abductor [æbˈdʌktər] *n* : raptor *m*, -tora *f*; secuestrador *m*, -dora *f*
abed [əˈbɛd] *adv & adj* : en cama
aberrant [æˈbɛrənt, ˈæbərənt] *adj* **1** ABNORMAL : anormal, aberrante **2** ATYPICAL : anómalo, atípico
aberration [ˌæbəˈreɪʃən] *n* **1** : aberración *f* **2** DERANGEMENT : perturbación *f* mental
abet [əˈbɛt] *vt* **abetted; abetting** ASSIST : ayudar ⟨to aid and abet : ser cómplice de⟩
abeyance [əˈbeɪənts] *n* : desuso *m*, suspensión *f*
abhor [əbˈhɔr, æb-] *vt* **-horred; -horring** : abominar, aborrecer
abhorrence [əbˈhɔrənts, æb-] *n* : aborrecimiento *m*, odio *m*
abhorrent [əbˈhɔrənt, æb-] *adj* : abominable, aborrecible, odioso
abide [əˈbaɪd] *v* **abode** [əˈboːd] *or* **abided; abiding** *vt* STAND : soportar, tolerar ⟨I can't abide them : no los puedo ver⟩ — *vi* **1** ENDURE : quedar, permanecer **2** DWELL : morar, residir **3 to abide by** : atenerse a
ability [əˈbɪləṭi] *n, pl* **-ties** **1** CAPABILITY : aptitud *f*, capacidad *f*, facultad *f* **2** COMPETENCE : competencia *f* **3** TALENT : talento *m*, don *m*, habilidad *f*
abject [ˈæbˌʤɛkt, æbˈ-] *adj* **1** WRETCHED : miserable, desdichado **2** HOPELESS : abatido, desesperado **3** SERVILE : servil ⟨abject flattery : halagos serviles⟩ — **abjectly** *adv*
abjure [æbˈʤʊr] *vt* **-jured; -juring** : abjurar de
ablaze [əˈbleɪz] *adj* **1** BURNING : ardiendo, en llamas **2** RADIANT : resplandeciente, radiante
able [ˈeɪbəl] *adj* **abler; ablest** **1** CAPABLE : capaz, hábil **2** COMPETENT : competente
ablution [əˈbluːʃən] *n* : ablución *f* ⟨to perform one's ablutions : lavarse⟩
ably [ˈeɪbəli] *adv* : hábilmente, eficientemente
abnormal [æbˈnɔrməl] *adj* : anormal — **abnormally** *adv*
abnormality [ˌæbnərˈmæləṭi, -nɔr-] *n, pl* **-ties** : anormalidad *f*
aboard[1] [əˈbord] *adv* : a bordo
aboard[2] *prep* : a bordo de
abode[1] → **abide**
abode[2] [əˈboːd] *n* : morada *f*, residencia *f*, vivienda *f*
abolish [əˈbɑlɪʃ] *vt* : abolir, suprimir
abolition [ˌæbəˈlɪʃən] *n* : abolición *f*, supresión *f*
abominable [əˈbɑmənəbəl] *adj* DETESTABLE : abominable, aborrecible, espantoso
abominate [əˈbɑməˌneɪt] *vt* **-nated; -nating** : abominar, aborrecer
abomination [əˌbɑməˈneɪʃən] *n* : abominación *f*
aboriginal [ˌæbəˈrɪʤənəl] *adj* : aborigen, indígena
aborigine [ˌæbəˈrɪʤəni] *n* NATIVE : aborigen *mf*, indígena *mf*

abort [əˈbɔrt] *vt* **1** : abortar (en medicina) **2** CALL OFF : suspender, abandonar — *vi* : abortar, hacerse un aborto
abortion [əˈbɔrʃən] *n* : aborto *m*
abortive [əˈbɔrt̬ɪv] *adj* UNSUCCESSFUL : fracasado, frustrado, malogrado
abound [əˈbaʊnd] *vi* **to abound in** : abundar en, estar lleno de
about[1] [əˈbaʊt] *adv* **1** APPROXIMATELY : aproximadamente, casi, más o menos **2** AROUND : por todas partes, alrededor ⟨the children are running about : los niños están corriendo por todas partes⟩ **3 to be about to** : estar a punto de **4 to be up and about** : estar levantado
about[2] *prep* **1** AROUND : alrededor de **2** CONCERNING : de, acerca de, sobre ⟨he always talks about politics : siempre habla de política⟩
above[1] [əˈbʌv] *adv* **1** OVERHEAD : por encima, arriba **2** : más arriba ⟨as stated above : como se indica más arriba⟩
above[2] *adj* : anterior, antedicho ⟨for the above reasons : por las razones antedichas⟩
above[3] *prep* **1** OVER : encima de, arriba de, sobre **2** : superior a, por encima de ⟨he's above those things : él está por encima de esas cosas⟩ **3** : más de, superior a ⟨he earns above $50,000 : gana más de $50,000⟩ ⟨a number above 10 : un número superior a 10⟩ **4 above all** : sobre todo
aboveboard[1] [əˈbʌvˈbord, -ˌbord] *adv* **open and aboveboard** : sin tapujos
aboveboard[2] *adj* : legítimo, sincero
abrade [əˈbreɪd] *vt* **abraded; abrading** **1** ERODE : erosionar, corroer **2** SCRAPE : escoriar, raspar
abrasion [əˈbreɪʒən] *n* **1** SCRAPE, SCRATCH : raspadura *f*, rasguño *m* **2** EROSION : erosión *f*
abrasive[1] [əˈbreɪsɪv] *adj* **1** ROUGH : abrasivo, áspero **2** BRUSQUE, IRRITATING : brusco, irritante
abrasive[2] *n* : abrasivo *m*
abreast [əˈbrɛst] *adv* **1** : en fondo, al lado ⟨to march three abreast : marchar de tres en fondo⟩ **2 to keep abreast** : mantenerse al día
abridge [əˈbrɪʤ] *vt* **abridged; abridging** : compendiar, resumir
abridgment *or* **abridgement** [əˈbrɪʤmənt] *n* : compendio *m*, resumen *m*
abroad [əˈbrɔd] *adv* **1** ABOUT, WIDELY : por todas partes, en todas direcciones ⟨the news spread abroad : la noticia corrió por todas partes⟩ **2** OVERSEAS : en el extranjero, en el exterior
abrogate [ˈæbrəˌgeɪt] *vt* **-gated; -gating** : abrogar
abrupt [əˈbrʌpt] *adj* **1** SUDDEN : abrupto, repentino, súbito **2** BRUSQUE, CURT : brusco, cortante — **abruptly** *adv*
abscess [ˈæbˌsɛs] *n* : absceso *m*
abscond [æbˈskɑnd] *vi* : huir, fugarse
absence [ˈæbsənts] *n* **1** : ausencia *f* (de una persona) **2** LACK : falta *f*, carencia *f*
absent[1] [æbˈsɛnt] *vt* **to absent oneself** : ausentarse
absent[2] [ˈæbsənt] *adj* : ausente
absentee [ˌæbsənˈtiː] *n* : ausente *mf*
absentminded [ˌæbsəntˈmaɪndəd] *adj* : distraído, despistado
absentmindedly [ˌæbsəntˈmaɪndədli] *adv* : distraídamente
absentmindedness [ˌæbsəntˈmaɪndədnəs] *n* : distracción *f*, despiste *m*
absolute [ˈæbsəˌluːt, ˌæbsəˈluːt] *adj* **1** COMPLETE, PERFECT : completo, pleno, perfecto **2** UNCONDITIONAL : absoluto, incondicional **3** DEFINITE : categórico, definitivo
absolutely [ˈæbsəˌluːtli, ˌæbsəˈluːtli] *adv* **1** COMPLETELY : completamente, absolutamente **2** CERTAINLY : desde luego ⟨do you agree? absolutely! : ¿estás de acuerdo? ¡desde luego!⟩
absolution [ˌæbsəˈluːʃən] *n* : absolución *f*
absolutism [ˈæbsəˌluːˌtɪzəm] *n* : absolutismo *m*
absolve [əbˈzɑlv, æb-, -ˈsɑlv] *vt* **-solved; -solving** : absolver, perdonar
absorb [əbˈzɔrb, æb-, -ˈsɔrb] *vt* **1** : absorber, embeber (un líquido), amortiguar (un golpe, la luz) **2** ENGROSS : absorber **3** ASSIMILATE : asimilar
absorbed [əbˈzɔrbd, æb-, -ˈsɔrbd] *adj* ENGROSSED : absorto, ensimismado
absorbency [əbˈzɔrbəntsi, æb-, -ˈsɔr-] *n* : absorbencia *f*
absorbent [əbˈzɔrbənt, æb-, -ˈsɔr-] *adj* : absorbente
absorbing [əbˈzɔrbɪŋ, æb-, -ˈsɔr-] *adj* : absorbente, fascinante
absorption [əbˈzɔrpʃən, æb-, -ˈsɔrp-] *n* **1** : absorción *f* **2** CONCENTRATION : concentración *f*
abstain [əbˈsteɪn, æb-] *vi* : abstenerse
abstainer [əbˈsteɪnər, æb-] *n* : abstemio *m*, -mia *f*
abstemious [æbˈstiːmiəs] *adj* : abstemio, sobrio — **abstemiously** *adv*
abstention [əbˈstɛntʃən, æb-] *n* : abstención *f*
abstinence [ˈæbstənənts] *n* : abstinencia *f*
abstract[1] [æbˈstrækt, ˈæbˌ-] *vt* **1** EXTRACT : abstraer, extraer **2** SUMMARIZE : compendiar, resumir
abstract[2] *adj* : abstracto — **abstractly** [æbˈstræktli, ˈæbˌ-] *adv*
abstract[3] [ˈæbˌstrækt] *n* : resumen *m*, compendio *m*, sumario *m*
abstraction [æbˈstrækʃən] *n* **1** : abstracción *f*, idea *f* abstracta **2** ABSENTMINDEDNESS : distracción *f*
abstruse [əbˈstruːs, æb-] *adj* : abstruso, recóndito — **abstrusely** *adv*
absurd [əbˈsərd, -ˈzərd] *adj* : absurdo, ridículo, disparatado — **absurdly** *adv*

absurdity [əb'sərdət̬i, -'zər-] *n, pl* **-ties** **1** : absurdo *m* **2** NONSENSE : disparate *m*, despropósito *m*
abundance [ə'bʌndənts] *n* : abundancia *f*
abundant [ə'bʌndənt] *adj* : abundante, cuantioso, copioso
abundantly [ə'bʌndəntli] *adv* : abundantemente, en abundancia
abuse¹ [ə'bju:z] *vt* **abused; abusing** **1** MISUSE : abusar de **2** MISTREAT : maltratar **3** REVILE : insultar, injuriar, denostar
abuse² [ə'bju:s] *n* **1** MISUSE : abuso *m* **2** MISTREATMENT : abuso *m*, maltrato *m* **3** INSULTS : insultos *mpl*, improperios *mpl* ⟨a string of abuse : una serie de improperios⟩
abuser [ə'bju:zər] *n* : abusador *m*, -dora *f*
abusive [ə'bju:sɪv] *adj* **1** ABUSING : abusivo **2** INSULTING : ofensivo, injurioso, insultante — **abusively** *adv*
abut [ə'bʌt] *v* **abutted; abutting** *vt* : bordear — *vi* **to abut on** : colindar con
abutment [ə'bʌtmənt] *n* **1** BUTTRESS : contrafuerte *m*, estribo *m* **2** CLOSENESS : contigüidad *f*
abysmal [ə'bɪzməl] *adj* **1** DEEP : abismal, insondable **2** TERRIBLE : atroz, desastroso
abysmally [ə'bɪzməli] *adv* : desastrosamente, terriblemente
abyss [ə'bɪs, 'æbɪs] *n* : abismo *m*, sima *f*
acacia [ə'keɪʃə] *n* : acacia *f*
academic¹ [ˌækə'dɛmɪk] *adj* **1** : académico **2** THEORETICAL : teórico — **academically** [-mɪkli] *adv*
academic² *n* : académico *m*, -ca *f*
academician [ˌækədə'mɪʃən] *n* → **academic**
academy [ə'kædəmi] *n, pl* **-mies** : academia *f*
acanthus [ə'kæntθəs] *n* : acanto *m*
accede [æk'si:d] *vi* **-ceded; -ceding** **1** AGREE : acceder, consentir **2** ASCEND : subir, acceder ⟨he acceded to the throne : subió al trono⟩
accelerate [ɪk'sɛləˌreɪt, æk-] *v* **-ated; -ating** *vt* : acelerar, apresurar — *vi* : acelerar (dícese de un carro)
acceleration [ɪkˌsɛlə'reɪʃən, æk-] *n* : aceleración *f*
accelerator [ɪk'sɛləˌreɪt̬ər, æk-] *n* : acelerador *m*
accent¹ ['ækˌsɛnt, æk'sɛnt] *vt* : acentuar
accent² ['ækˌsɛnt, -sənt] *n* **1** : acento *m* **2** EMPHASIS, STRESS : énfasis *m*, acento *m*
accentuate [ɪk'sɛntʃʊˌeɪt, æk-] *vt* **-ated; -ating** : acentuar, poner énfasis en
accept [ɪk'sɛpt, æk-] *vt* **1** : aceptar **2** ACKNOWLEDGE : admitir, reconocer
acceptability [ɪkˌsɛptə'bɪlət̬i, æk-] *n* : aceptabilidad *f*
acceptable [ɪk'sɛptəbəl, æk-] *adj* : aceptable, admisible — **acceptably** [-bli] *adv*
acceptance [ɪk'sɛptənts, æk-] *n* : aceptación *f*, aprobación *f*
access¹ ['ækˌsɛs] *vt* : obtener acceso a, entrar a
access² *n* : acceso *m*
accessibility [ɪkˌsɛsə'bɪlət̬i] *n, pl* **-ties** : accesibilidad *f*
accessible [ɪk'sɛsəbəl, æk-] *adj* : accesible, asequible
accession [ɪk'sɛʃən, æk-] *n* **1** : ascenso *f*, subida *f* (al trono, etc.) **2** ACQUISITION : adquisición *f*
accessory¹ [ɪk'sɛsəri, æk-] *adj* : auxiliar
accessory² *n, pl* **-ries** **1** : accesorio *m*, complemento *m* **2** ACCOMPLICE : cómplice *mf*
accident ['æksədənt] *n* **1** MISHAP : accidente *m* **2** CHANCE : casualidad *f*
accidental [ˌæksə'dɛntəl] *adj* : accidental, casual, imprevisto, fortuito
accidentally [ˌæksə'dɛntəli, -'dɛntli] *adv* **1** BY CHANCE : por casualidad **2** UNINTENTIONALLY : sin querer, involuntariamente
acclaim¹ [ə'kleɪm] *vt* : aclamar, elogiar
acclaim² *n* : aclamación *f*, elogio *m*
acclamation [ˌæklə'meɪʃən] *n* : aclamación *f*
acclimate ['ækləˌmeɪt, ə'klaɪmət] → **acclimatize**
acclimatize [ə'klaɪməˌtaɪz] *v* **-tized; -tizing** *vt* **1** : aclimatar **2 to acclimatize oneself** : aclimatarse
accolade ['ækəˌleɪd, -ˌlɑd] *n* **1** PRAISE : elogio *m* **2** AWARD : galardón *m*
accommodate [ə'kɑməˌdeɪt] *vt* **-dated; -dating** **1** ADAPT : acomodar, adaptar **2** SATISFY : tener en cuenta, satisfacer **3** HOLD : dar cabida a, tener cabida para
accommodation [əˌkɑmə'deɪʃən] *n* **1** : adaptación *f*, adecuación *f* **2 accommodations** *npl* LODGING : alojamiento *m*, hospedaje *m*
accompaniment [ə'kʌmpənəmənt, -'kɑm-] *n* : acompañamiento *m*
accompanist [ə'kʌmpənɪst, -'kɑm-] *n* : acompañante *mf*
accompany [ə'kʌmpəni, -'kɑm-] *vt* **-nied; -nying** : acompañar
accomplice [ə'kɑmpləs, -'kʌm-] *n* : cómplice *mf*
accomplish [ə'kɑmplɪʃ, -'kʌm-] *vt* : efectuar, realizar, lograr, llevar a cabo
accomplished [ə'kɑmplɪʃt, -'kʌm-] *adj* : consumado, logrado
accomplishment [ə'kɑmplɪʃmənt, -'kʌm-] *n* **1** ACHIEVEMENT : logro *m*, éxito *m* **2** SKILL : destreza *f*, habilidad *f*
accord¹ [ə'kɔrd] *vt* GRANT : conceder, otorgar — *vi* **to accord with** : concordar con, conformarse con
accord² *n* **1** AGREEMENT : acuerdo *m*, convenio *m* **2** VOLITION : voluntad *f*

⟨on one's own accord : voluntariamente, de motu proprio⟩
accordance [əˈkɔrdənts] *n* **1** ACCORD : acuerdo *m*, conformidad *f* **2 in accordance with** : conforme a, según, de acuerdo con
accordingly [əˈkɔrdɪŋli] *adv* **1** CORRESPONDINGLY : en consecuencia **2** CONSEQUENTLY : por consiguiente, por lo tanto
according to [əˈkɔrdɪŋ] *prep* : según, de acuerdo con, conforme a
accordion [əˈkɔrdiən] *n* : acordeón *m*
accordionist [əˈkɔrdiənɪst] *n* : acordeonista *mf*
accost [əˈkɔst] *vt* : abordar, dirigirse a
account[1] [əˈkaʊnt] *vt* : considerar, estimar ⟨he accounts himself lucky : se considera afortunado⟩ — *vi* **to account for** : dar cuenta de, explicar
account[2] *n* **1** : cuenta *f* ⟨savings account : cuenta de ahorros⟩ **2** EXPLANATION : versión *f*, explicación *f* **3** REPORT : relato *m*, informe *m* **4** IMPORTANCE : importancia *f* ⟨to be of no account : no tener importancia⟩ **5 on account of** BECAUSE OF : a causa de, debido a, por **6 on no account** : de ninguna manera
accountability [əˌkaʊntəˈbɪləṭi] *n* : responsabilidad *f*
accountable [əˈkaʊntəbəl] *adj* : responsable
accountant [əˈkaʊntənt] *n* : contador *m*, -dora *f*; contable *mf Spain*
accounting [əˈkaʊntɪŋ] *n* : contabilidad *f*
accoutrements *or* **accouterments** [əˈku:trəmənts, -ˈku:ṭər-] *npl* **1** EQUIPMENT : equipo *m*, avíos *mpl* **2** ACCESSORIES : accesorios *mpl* **3** TRAPPINGS : símbolos *mpl* ⟨the accoutrements of power : los símbolos del poder⟩
accredit [əˈkrɛdət] *vt* : acreditar, autorizar
accreditation [əˌkrɛdəˈteɪʃən] *n* : acreditación *f*, homologación *f*
accretion [əˈkri:ʃən] *n* **1** : acrecentamiento *m* (proceso) **2** : acreción *f*, acrecencia *f* (producto)
accrual [əˈkru:əl] *n* : incremento *m*, acumulación *f*
accrue [əˈkru:] *vi* **-crued; -cruing** : acumularse, aumentarse
accumulate [əˈkju:mjəˌleɪt] *v* **-lated; -lating** *vt* : acumular, amontonar — *vi* : acumularse, amontonarse
accumulation [əˌkju:mjəˈleɪʃən] *n* : acumulación *f*, amontonamiento *m*
accuracy [ˈækjərəsi] *n* : exactitud *f*, precisión *f*
accurate [ˈækjərət] *adj* : exacto, correcto, fiel, preciso — **accurately** *adv*
accusation [ˌækjəˈzeɪʃən] *n* : acusación *f*
accusatory [əˈkju:zəˌtori] *adj* : acusatorio
accuse [əˈkju:z] *vt* **-cused; -cusing** : acusar, delatar, denunciar
accused [əˈkju:zd] *ns & pl* DEFENDANT : acusado *m*, -da *f*
accuser [əˈkju:zər] *n* : acusador *m*, -dora *f*
accustom [əˈkʌstəm] *vt* : acostumbrar, habituar
ace [ˈeɪs] *n* : as *m*
acerbic [əˈsərbɪk, æ-] *adj* : acerbo, mordaz
acetate [ˈæsəˌteɪt] *n* : acetato *m*
acetic [əˈsi:ṭɪk] *adj* : acético
acetone [ˈæsəˌto:n] *n* : acetona *f*
acetylene [əˈsɛṭələn, -ṭəˌli:n] *n* : acetileno *m*
ache[1] [ˈeɪk] *vi* **ached; aching 1** : doler **2 to ache for** : anhelar, ansiar
ache[2] *n* : dolor *m*
achieve [əˈʧi:v] *vt* **achieved; achieving** : lograr, alcanzar, conseguir, realizar
achievement [əˈʧi:vmənt] *n* : logro *m*, éxito *m*, realización *f*
acid[1] [ˈæsəd] *adj* **1** SOUR : ácido, agrio **2** CAUSTIC, SHARP : acerbo, mordaz — **acidly** *adv*
acid[2] *n* : ácido *m*
acidic [əˈsɪdɪk, æ-] *adj* : ácido
acidity [əˈsɪdəṭi, æ-] *n, pl* **-ties** : acidez *f*
acknowledge [ɪkˈnɑlɪʤ, æk-] *vt* **-edged; -edging 1** ADMIT : reconocer, admitir **2** RECOGNIZE : reconocer **3 to acknowledge receipt of** : acusar recibo de
acknowledgment [ɪkˈnɑlɪʤmənt, æk-] *n* **1** RECOGNITION : reconocimiento *m* **2** THANKS : agradecimiento *m*
acme [ˈækmi] *n* : colmo *m*, apogeo *m*, cúspide *f*
acne [ˈækni] *n* : acné *m*
acolyte [ˈækəˌlaɪt] *n* : acólito *m*
acorn [ˈeɪˌkɔrn, -kərn] *n* : bellota *f*
acoustic [əˈku:stɪk] *or* **acoustical** [-stɪkəl] *adj* : acústico — **acoustically** *adv*
acoustics [əˈku:stɪks] *ns & pl* : acústica *f*
acquaint [əˈkweɪnt] *vt* **1** INFORM : enterar, informar **2** FAMILIARIZE : familiarizar **3 to be acquainted with** : conocer a (una persona), estar al tanto de (un hecho)
acquaintance [əˈkweɪntənts] *n* **1** KNOWLEDGE : conocimiento *m* **2** : conocido *m*, -da *f* ⟨friends and acquaintances : amigos y conocidos⟩
acquiesce [ˌækwiˈɛs] *vi* **-esced; -escing** : consentir, conformarse
acquiescence [ˌækwiˈɛsənts] *n* : consentimiento *m*, aquiescencia *f*
acquire [əˈkwaɪr] *vt* **-quired; -quiring** : adquirir, obtener
acquisition [ˌækwəˈzɪʃən] *n* : adquisición *f*
acquisitive [əˈkwɪzəṭɪv] *adj* : adquisitivo, codicioso
acquit [əˈkwɪt] *vt* **-quitted; -quitting 1** : absolver, exculpar **2 to acquit oneself** : comportarse, defenderse
acquittal [əˈkwɪṭəl] *n* : absolución *f*, exculpación *f*

acre [ˈeɪkər] *n* : acre *m*

acreage [ˈeɪkərɪʤ] *n* : superficie *f* en acres

acrid [ˈækrəd] *adj* **1** BITTER : acre **2** CAUSTIC : acre, mordaz — **acridly** *adv*

acrimonious [ˌækrəˈmo:niəs] *adj* : áspero, cáustico, sarcástico

acrimony [ˈækrəˌmo:ni] *n, pl* **-nies** : acrimonia *f*

acrobat [ˈækrəˌbæt] *n* : acróbata *mf*, saltimbanqui *mf*

acrobatic [ˌækrəˈbæt̬ɪk] *adj* : acrobático

acrobatics [ˌækrəˈbæt̬ɪks] *ns & pl* : acrobacia *f*

acronym [ˈækrəˌnɪm] *n* : acrónimo *m*

across[1] [əˈkrɔs] *adv* **1** CROSSWISE : al través **2** : a través, del otro lado ⟨he's already across : ya está del otro lado⟩ **3** : de ancho ⟨40 feet across : 40 pies de ancho⟩

across[2] *prep* **1** : al otro lado de ⟨across the street : al otro lado de la calle⟩ **2** : a través de ⟨a log across the road : un tronco a través del camino⟩

acrylic [əˈkrɪlɪk] *n* : acrílico *m*

act[1] [ˈækt] *vi* **1** PERFORM : actuar, interpretar **2** FEIGN, PRETEND : fingir, simular **3** BEHAVE : comportarse **4** FUNCTION : actuar, servir, funcionar **5** : tomar medidas ⟨he acted to save the business : tomó medidas para salvar el negocio⟩ **6 to act as** : servir de, hacer de

act[2] *n* **1** DEED : acto *m*, hecho *m*, acción *f* **2** DECREE : ley *f*, decreto *m* **3** : acto *m* (en una obra de teatro), número *m* (en un espectáculo) **4** PRETENSE : fingimiento *m*

action [ˈækʃən] *n* **1** DEED : acción *f*, acto *m*, hecho *m* **2** BEHAVIOR : actuación *f*, comportamiento *m* **3** LAWSUIT : demanda *f* **4** MOVEMENT : movimiento *m* **5** COMBAT : combate *m* **6** PLOT : acción *f*, trama *f* **7** MECHANISM : mecanismo *m*

activate [ˈæktəˌveɪt] *vt* **-vated; -vating** : activar

activation [ˌæktəˈveɪʃən] *n* : activación *f*

active [ˈæktɪv] *adj* **1** MOVING : activo, en movimiento **2** LIVELY : vigoroso, enérgico **3** : en actividad ⟨an active volcano : un volcán en actividad⟩ **4** OPERATIVE : vigente

actively [ˈæktɪvli] *adv* : activamente, enérgicamente

activist [ˈæktɪvɪst] *n* : activista *mf* — **activist** *adj*

activity [ækˈtɪvət̬i] *n, pl* **-ties** **1** MOVEMENT : actividad *f*, movimiento *m* **2** VIGOR : vigor *m*, energía *f* **3** OCCUPATION : actividad *f*, ocupación *f*

actor [ˈæktər] *n* : actor *m*, artista *mf*

actress [ˈæktrəs] *n* : actriz *f*

actual [ˈæktʃʊəl] *adj* : real, verdadero

actuality [ˌæktʃʊˈæləti] *n, pl* **-ties** : realidad *f*

actually [ˈæktʃʊəli, -ʃəli] *adv* : realmente, en realidad

actuary [ˈæktʃʊˌɛri] *n, pl* **-aries** : actuario *m*, -ria *f* de seguros

acumen [əˈkju:mən] *n* : perspicacia *f*

acupuncture [ˈækjʊˌpʌŋktʃər] *n* : acupuntura *f*

acute [əˈkju:t] *adj* **acuter; acutest** **1** SHARP : agudo **2** PERCEPTIVE : perspicaz, sagaz **3** KEEN : fino, muy desarrollado, agudo ⟨an acute sense of smell : un fino olfato⟩ **4** SEVERE : grave **5 acute angle** : ángulo *m* agudo

acutely [əˈkju:tli] *adv* : intensamente ⟨to be acutely aware : estar perfectamente consciente⟩

acuteness [əˈkju:tnəs] *n* : agudeza *f*

ad [ˈæd] → **advertisement**

adage [ˈædɪʤ] *n* : adagio *m*, refrán *m*, dicho *m*

adamant [ˈædəmənt, -ˌmænt] *adj* : firme, categórico, inflexible — **adamantly** *adv*

Adam's apple [ˈædəmz] *n* : nuez *f* de Adán

adapt [əˈdæpt] *vt* : adaptar, ajustar — *vi* : adaptarse

adaptability [əˌdæptəˈbɪlət̬i] *n* : adaptabilidad *f*, flexibilidad *f*

adaptable [əˈdæptəbəl] *adj* : adaptable, amoldable

adaptation [ˌæˌdæpˈteɪʃən, -dəp-] *n* **1** : adaptación *f*, modificación *f* **2** VERSION : versión *f*

adapter [əˈdæptər] *n* : adaptador *m*

add [ˈæd] *vt* **1** : añadir, agregar ⟨to add a comment : añadir una observación⟩ **2** : sumar ⟨add these numbers : suma estos números⟩ — *vi* : sumar (en total)

adder [ˈædər] *n* : víbora *f*

addict[1] [əˈdɪkt] *vt* : causar adicción en

addict[2] [ˈædɪkt] *n* **1** : adicto *m*, -ta *f* **2** **drug addict** : drogadicto *m*, -ta *f*; toxicómano *m*, -na *f*

addiction [əˈdɪkʃən] *n* **1** : adicción *f*, dependencia *f* **2** **drug addiction** : drogadicción *f*

addictive [əˈdɪktɪv] *adj* : adictivo

addition [əˈdɪʃən] *n* **1** : adición *f*, añadidura *f* **2 in ~** : además, también

additional [əˈdɪʃənəl] *adj* : extra, adicional, de más

additionally [əˈdɪʃənəli] *adv* : además, adicionalmente

additive [ˈædət̬ɪv] *n* : aditivo *m*

addle [ˈædəl] *vt* **-dled; -dling** : confundir, enturbiar

address[1] [əˈdrɛs] *vt* **1** : dirigirse a, pronunciar un discurso ante ⟨to address a jury : dirigirse a un jurado⟩ **2** : dirigir, ponerle la dirección a ⟨to address a letter : dirigir una carta⟩

address[2] [əˈdrɛs, ˈæˌdrɛs] *n* **1** SPEECH : discurso *m*, alocución *f* **2** : dirección *f* (de una residencia, etc.)

addressee [ˌæˌdrɛˈsi:, ə-] *n* : destinatario *m*, -ria *f*

adduce [ə-ˈduːs, ˈdjuːs] *vt* **-duced; -ducing** : aducir
adenoids [ˈædˌnɔɪd, -dənˌɔɪd] *npl* : adenoides *fpl*
adept [əˈdɛpt] *adj* : experto, hábil — **adeptly** *adv*
adequacy [ˈædɪkwəsi] *n, pl* **-cies** : cantidad *f* suficiente
adequate [ˈædɪkwət] *adj* **1** SUFFICIENT : adecuado, suficiente **2** ACCEPTABLE, PASSABLE : adecuado, aceptable
adequately [ˈædɪkwətli] *adv* : suficientemente, apropiadamente
adhere [ædˈhɪr, əd-] *vi* **-hered; -hering 1** STICK : pegarse, adherirse **2 to adhere to** : adherirse a (una política, etc.), cumplir con (una promesa)
adherence [ædˈhɪrənts, əd-] *n* : adhesión *f*, adherencia *f*, observancia *f* (de una ley, etc.)
adherent[1] [ædˈhɪrənt, əd-] *adj* : adherente, adhesivo, pegajoso
adherent[2] *n* : adepto *m*, -ta *f*; partidario *m*, -ria *f*
adhesion [ædˈhiːʒən, əd-] *n* : adhesión *f*
adhesive[1] [ædˈhiːsɪv, əd-, -zɪv] *adj* : adhesivo
adhesive[2] *n* : adhesivo *m*, pegamento *m*
adjacent [əˈdʒeɪsənt] *adj* : adyacente, colindante, contiguo
adjective [ˈædʒɪktɪv] *n* : adjetivo *m* — **adjectival** [ˌædʒɪkˈtaɪvəl] *adj*
adjoin [əˈdʒɔɪn] *vt* : lindar con, colindar con
adjoining [əˈdʒɔɪnɪŋ] *adj* : contiguo, colindante
adjourn [əˈdʒərn] *vt* : levantar, suspender ⟨the meeting is adjourned : se levanta la sesión⟩ — *vi* : aplazarse
adjournment [əˈdʒərnmənt] *n* : suspensión *f*, aplazamiento *m*
adjudicate [əˈdʒuːdɪˌkeɪt] *vt* **-cated; -cating** : juzgar, arbitrar
adjudication [əˌdʒuːdɪˈkeɪʃən] *n* **1** JUDGING : arbitrio *m* (judicial) **2** JUDGMENT : fallo *m*
adjunct [ˈæˌdʒʌŋkt] *n* : adjunto *m*, complemento *m*
adjust [əˈdʒʌst] *vt* : ajustar, arreglar, regular — *vi* **to adjust to** : adaptarse a
adjustable [əˈdʒʌstəbəl] *adj* : ajustable, regulable, graduable
adjustment [əˈdʒʌstmənt] *n* : ajuste *m*, modificación *f*
ad–lib[1] [ˈædˈlɪb] *v* **-libbed; -libbing** : improvisar
ad–lib[2] *adj* : improvisado
administer [ædˈmɪnəstər, əd-] *vt* : administrar
administration [ædˌmɪnəˈstreɪʃən, əd-] *n* **1** MANAGING : administración *f*, dirección *f* **2** GOVERNMENT, MANAGEMENT : administración *f*, gobierno *m*
administrative [ædˈmɪnəˌstreɪţɪv, əd-] *adj* : administrativo — **administratively** *adv*
administrator [ædˈmɪnəˌstreɪţər, əd-] *n* : administrador *m*, -dora *f*
admirable [ˈædmərəbəl] *adj* : admirable, loable — **admirably** *adv*
admiral [ˈædmərəl] *n* : almirante *mf*
admiration [ˌædməˈreɪʃən] *n* : admiración *f*
admire [ædˈmaɪr] *vt* **-mired; -miring** : admirar
admirer [ædˈmaɪrər] *n* : admirador *m*, -dora *f*
admiring [ædˈmaɪrɪŋ] *adj* : admirativo, de admiración
admiringly [ædˈmaɪrɪŋli] *adv* : con admiración
admissible [ædˈmɪsəbəl] *adj* : admisible, aceptable
admission [ædˈmɪʃən] *n* **1** ADMITTANCE : entrada *f*, admisión *f* **2** ACKNOWLEDGMENT : reconocimiento *m*, admisión *f*
admit [ædˈmɪt, əd-] *vt* **-mitted; -mitting 1** : admitir, dejar entrar ⟨the museum admits children : el museo deja entrar a los niños⟩ **2** ACKNOWLEDGE : reconocer, admitir
admittance [ædˈmɪtənts, əd-] *n* : admisión *f*, entrada *f*, acceso *m*
admittedly [ædˈmɪţədli, əd-] *adv* : la verdad es que, lo cierto es que ⟨admittedly we went too fast : la verdad es que fuimos demasiado de prisa⟩
admonish [ædˈmɑnɪʃ, əd-] *vt* : amonestar, reprender
admonition [ˌædməˈnɪʃən] *n* : admonición *f*
ado [əˈduː] *n* **1** FUSS : ruido *m*, alboroto *m* **2** TROUBLE : dificultad *f*, lío *m* **3 without further ado** : sin más preámbulos
adobe [əˈdoːbi] *n* : adobe *m*
adolescence [ˌædəlˈɛsənts] *n* : adolescencia *f*
adolescent[1] [ˌædəlˈɛsənt] *adj* : adolescente, de adolescencia
adolescent[2] *n* : adolescente *mf*
adopt [əˈdɑpt] *vt* : adoptar
adoption [əˈdɑpʃən] *n* : adopción *f*
adoptive [əˈdɑptɪv] *adj* : adoptivo
adorable [əˈdorəbəl] *adj* : adorable, encantador
adorably [əˈdorəbli] *adv* : de manera adorable
adoration [ˌædəˈreɪʃən] *n* : adoración *f*
adore [əˈdor] *vt* **adored; adoring 1** WORSHIP : adorar **2** LOVE : querer, adorar **3** LIKE : encantarle (algo a uno), gustarle mucho (algo a uno) ⟨I adore your new dress : me encanta tu vestido nuevo⟩
adorn [əˈdɔrn] *vt* : adornar, ornar, engalanar
adornment [əˈdɔrnmənt] *n* : adorno *m*, decoración *f*
adrenaline [əˈdrɛnələn] *n* : adrenalina *f*
adrift [əˈdrɪft] *adj & adv* : a la deriva
adroit [əˈdrɔɪt] *adj* : diestro, hábil — **adroitly** *adv*
adroitness [əˈdrɔɪtnəs] *n* : destreza *f*, habilidad *f*

adult[1] [ə'dʌlt, 'æˌdʌlt] *adj* : adulto

adult[2] *n* : adulto *m*, -ta *f*

adulterate [ə'dʌltəˌreɪt] *vt* **-ated; -ating** : adulterar

adulterous [ə'dʌltərəs] *adj* : adúltero

adultery [ə'dʌltəri] *n, pl* **-teries** : adulterio *m*

adulthood [ə'dʌltˌhʊd] *n* : adultez *f*, edad *f* adulta

advance[1] [æd'vænts, əd-] *v* **-vanced; -vancing** *vt* **1** : avanzar, adelantar ⟨to advance troops : avanzar las tropas⟩ **2** PROMOTE : ascender, promover **3** PROPOSE : proponer, presentar **4** : adelantar, anticipar ⟨they advanced me next month's salary : me adelantaron el sueldo del próximo mes⟩ — *vi* **1** PROCEED : avanzar, adelantarse **2** PROGRESS : progresar

advance[2] *adj* : anticipado ⟨advance notice : previo aviso⟩

advance[3] *n* **1** PROGRESSION : avance *m* **2** PROGRESS : adelanto *m*, mejora *f*, progreso *m* **3** RISE : aumento *m*, alza *f* **4** LOAN : anticipo *m*, préstamo *m* **5** **in ~** : por adelantado

advanced [æd'væntst, əd-] *adj* **1** DEVELOPED : avanzado, desarrollado **2** PRECOCIOUS : adelantado, precoz **3** HIGHER : superior

advancement [æd'væntsmənt, əd-] *n* **1** FURTHERANCE : fomento *m*, adelantamiento *m*, progreso *m* **2** PROMOTION : ascenso *m*

advantage [əd'væntɪʤ, æd-] *n* **1** SUPERIORITY : ventaja *f*, superioridad *f* **2** GAIN : provecho *m*, partido *m* **3** **to take advantage of** : aprovecharse de

advantageous [ˌædˌvæn'teɪʤəs, -vən-] *adj* : ventajoso, provechoso — **advantageously** *adv*

advent ['ædˌvɛnt] *n* **1** **Advent** : Adviento *m* **2** ARRIVAL : advenimiento *m*, venida *f*

adventure [æd'vɛnʧər, əd-] *n* : aventura *f*

adventurer [æd'vɛnʧərər, əd-] *n* : aventurero *m*, -ra *f*

adventurous [æd'vɛnʧərəs, əd-] *adj* **1** : intrépido, aventurero ⟨an adventurous traveler : un viajero intrépido⟩ **2** RISKY : arriesgado, aventurado

adverb ['ædˌvərb] *n* : adverbio *m* — **adverbial** [æd'vərbiəl] *adj*

adversary ['ædvərˌsɛri] *n, pl* **-saries** : adversario *m*, -ria *f*

adverse [æd'vərs, 'ædˌ] *adj* **1** OPPOSING : opuesto, contrario **2** UNFAVORABLE : adverso, desfavorable — **adversely** *adv*

adversity [æd'vərsət̬i, əd-] *n, pl* **-ties** : adversidad *f*

advertise ['ædvərˌtaɪz] *v* **-tised; -tising** *vt* : anunciar, hacerle publicidad a — *vi* : hacer publicidad, hacer propaganda

advertisement ['ædvərˌtaɪzmənt; æd'vərt̬əzmənt] *n* : anuncio *m*

advertiser ['ædvərˌtaɪzər] *n* : anunciante *mf*

advertising ['ædvərˌtaɪzɪŋ] *n* : publicidad *f*, propaganda *f*

advice [æd'vaɪs] *n* : consejo *m*, recomendación *f* ⟨take my advice : sigue mis consejos⟩

advisability [ædˌvaɪzə'bɪlət̬i, əd-] *n* : conveniencia *f*

advisable [æd'vaɪzəbəl, əd-] *adj* : aconsejable, recomendable, conveniente

advise [æd'vaɪz, əd-] *v* **-vised; -vising** *vt* **1** COUNSEL : aconsejar, asesorar **2** RECOMMEND : recomendar **3** INFORM : informar, notificar — *vi* : dar consejo

adviser *or* **advisor** [æd'vaɪzər, əd-] *n* : consejero *m*, -ra *f*; asesor *m*, -sora *f*

advisory [æd'vaɪzəri, əd-] *adj* **1** : consultivo **2** **in an advisory capacity** : como asesor

advocacy ['ædvəkəsi] *n* : promoción *f*, apoyo *m*

advocate[1] ['ædvəˌkeɪt] *vt* **-cated; -cating** : recomendar, abogar por, ser partidario de

advocate[2] ['ædvəkət] *n* : defensor *m*, -sora *f*; partidario *m*, -ria *f*

adze ['ædz] *n* : azuela *f*

aeon ['iːən, 'iːˌɑn] *n* : eón *m*, siglo *m*, eternidad *f*

aerate ['ærˌeɪt] *vt* **-ated; -ating** : gasear (un líquido), oxigenar (la sangre)

aerial[1] ['æriəl] *adj* : aéreo

aerial[2] *n* : antena *f*

aerie ['æri, 'ɪri, 'eɪəri] *n* : aguilera *f*

aerobic [ˌær'oːbɪk] *adj* : aerobio, aeróbico ⟨aerobic exercises : ejercicios aeróbicos⟩

aerobics [ˌær'oːbɪks] *ns & pl* : aeróbic *m*

aerodynamic [ˌæroːdaɪ'næmɪk] *adj* : aerodinámico — **aerodynamically** [-mikli] *adv*

aerodynamics [ˌæroːdaɪ'næmɪks] *n* : aerodinámica *f*

aeronautical [ˌærə'nɔt̬ɪkəl] *adj* : aeronáutico

aeronautics [ˌærə'nɔt̬ɪks] *n* : aeronáutica *f*

aerosol ['ærəˌsɔl] *n* : aerosol *m*

aerospace[1] ['æroˌspeɪs] *adj* : aeroespacial

aerospace[2] *n* : espacio *m*

aesthetic [ɛs'θɛt̬ɪk] *adj* : estético — **aesthetically** [-t̬ɪkli] *adv*

aesthetics [ɛs'θɛt̬ɪks] *n* : estética *f*

afar [ə'fɑr] *adv* : lejos, a lo lejos

affability [ˌæfə'bɪlət̬i] *n* : afabilidad *f*

affable ['æfəbəl] *adj* : afable — **affably** *adv*

affair [ə'fær] *n* **1** MATTER : asunto *m*, cuestión *f*, caso *m* **2** EVENT : ocasión *f*, acontecimiento *m* **3** LIAISON : amorío *m*, aventura *f* **4** **business affairs** : negocios *mpl* **5** **current affairs** : actualidades *fpl*

affect [ə'fɛkt, æ-] *vt* **1** INFLUENCE, TOUCH : afectar, tocar **2** FEIGN : fingir

affectation [ˌæˌfɛk'teɪʃən] *n* : afectación *f*

affected [ə'fɛktəd, æ-] *adj* **1** FEIGNED : afectado, fingido **2** MOVED : conmovido

affecting [ə'fɛktɪŋ, æ-] *adj* : conmovedor

affection [ə'fɛkʃən] *n* : afecto *m*, cariño *m*

affectionate [ə'fɛkʃənət] *adj* : afectuoso, cariñoso — **affectionately** *adv*

affidavit [ˌæfə'deɪvət, 'æfəˌ-] *n* : declaración *f* jurada, affidávit *m*

affiliate[1] [ə'fɪliˌeɪt] *v* **-ated; -ating** *vt* : afiliar, asociar ⟨to be affiliated with : estar afiliado a⟩

affiliate[2] [ə'fɪliət] *n* : afiliado *m*, -da *f* (persona), filial *f* (organización)

affiliation [əˌfɪli'eɪʃən] *n* : afiliación *f*, filiación *f*

affinity [ə'fɪnəṭi] *n, pl* **-ties** : afinidad *f*

affirm [ə'fərm] *vt* : afirmar, aseverar, declarar

affirmation [ˌæfər'meɪʃən] *n* : afirmación *f*, aserto *m*, declaración *f*

affirmative[1] [ə'fərməṭɪv] *adj* : afirmativo ⟨affirmative action : acción afirmativa⟩

affirmative[2] *n* **1** : afirmativa *f* **2 to answer in the affirmative** : responder afirmativamente, dar una respuesta afirmativa

affix [ə'fɪks] *vt* : fijar, poner, pegar

afflict [ə'flɪkt] *vt* **1** : afligir, aquejar **2 to be afflicted with** : padecer de, sufrir de

affliction [ə'flɪkʃən] *n* **1** TRIBULATION : aflicción *f*, tribulación *f* **2** AILMENT : enfermedad *f*, padecimiento *m*

affluence ['æˌflu:ənts; æ'flu:-, ə-] *n* : afluencia *f*, abundancia *f*, prosperidad *f*

affluent ['æˌflu:ənt; æ'flu:-, ə-] *adj* : próspero, adinerado

afford [ə'ford] *vt* **1** : tener los recursos para, permitirse el lujo de ⟨I can afford it : puedo permitírmelo, tengo con que comprarlo⟩ **2** PROVIDE : ofrecer, proporcionar, dar

affront[1] [ə'frʌnt] *vt* : afrentar, insultar, ofender

affront[2] *n* : afrenta *f*, insulto *m*, ofensa *f*

Afghan ['æfˌgæn, -gən] *n* : afgano *m*, -na *f* — **Afghan** *adj*

afire [ə'faɪr] *adj* : ardiendo, en llamas

aflame [ə'fleɪm] *adj* : llameante, en llamas

afloat [ə'flo:t] *adv & adj* : a flote

afoot [ə'fʊt] *adj* **1** WALKING : a pie, andando **2** UNDER WAY : en marcha ⟨something suspicious is afoot : algo sospechoso se está tramando⟩

aforementioned [ə'for'mentʃənd] *adj* : antedicho, susodicho

aforesaid [ə'forˌsɛd] *adj* : antes mencionado, antedicho

afraid [ə'freɪd] *adj* **1 to be afraid** : tener miedo **2 to be afraid that** : temerse que ⟨I'm afraid not : me temo que no⟩

afresh [ə'frɛʃ] *adv* **1** : de nuevo, otra vez **2 to start afresh** : volver a empezar

African ['æfrɪkən] *n* : africano *m*, -na *f* — **African** *adj*

Afro-American[1] [ˌæfroə'mɛrɪkən] *adj* : afroamericano *m*, -na *f*

Afro-American[2] *n* : afroamericano

aft ['æft] *adv* : a popa

after[1] ['æftər] *adv* **1** AFTERWARD : después **2** BEHIND : detrás, atrás

after[2] *adj* : posterior, siguiente ⟨in after years : en los años posteriores⟩

after[3] *conj* : después de, después de que ⟨after we ate : después de que comimos, después de comer⟩

after[4] *prep* **1** FOLLOWING : después de, tras ⟨after Saturday : después del sábado⟩ ⟨day after day : día tras día⟩ **2** BEHIND : tras de, después de ⟨I ran after the dog : corrí tras del perro⟩ **3** CONCERNING : por ⟨they asked after you : preguntaron por ti⟩ **4 after all** : después de todo

aftereffect ['æftərɪˌfɛkt] *n* : efecto *m* secundario

afterlife ['æftərˌlaɪf] *n* : vida *f* venidera, vida *f* después de la muerte

aftermath ['æftərˌmæθ] *n* : consecuencias *fpl*, resultados *mpl*

afternoon [ˌæftər'nu:n] *n* : tarde *f*

aftertaste ['æftərˌteɪst] *n* : resabio *m*, regusto *m*

afterthought ['æftərˌθɔt] *n* : ocurrencia *f* tardía, idea *f* tardía

afterward ['æftərwərd] *or* **afterwards** [-wərdz] *adv* : después, luego ⟨soon afterward : poco después⟩

again [ə'gɛn, -'gɪn] *adv* **1** ANEW, OVER : de nuevo, otra vez **2** BESIDES : además **3 then again** : por otra parte ⟨I may stay, then again I may not : puede ser que me quede, por otra parte, puede que no⟩

against [ə'gɛntst, -'gɪntst] *prep* **1** TOUCHING : contra ⟨against the wall : contra la pared⟩ **2** OPPOSING : contra, en contra de ⟨I will vote against the proposal : votaré en contra de la propuesta⟩ ⟨against the grain : a contrapelo⟩

agape [ə'geɪp] *adj* : boquiabierto

agate ['ægət] *n* : ágata *f*

age[1] ['eɪʤ] *vi* **aged; aging** : envejecer, madurar

age[2] *n* **1** : edad *f* ⟨ten years of age : diez años de edad⟩ ⟨to be of age : ser mayor de edad⟩ **2** PERIOD : era *f*, siglo *m*, época *f* **3 old age** : vejez *f* **4 ages** *npl* : siglos *mpl*, eternidad *f*

aged *adj* **1** ['eɪʤəd, 'eɪʤd] OLD : anciano, viejo, vetusto **2** ['eɪʤd] (*indicating a specified age*) ⟨a girl aged 10 : una niña de 10 años de edad⟩

ageless ['eɪʤləs] *adj* **1** YOUTHFUL : eternamente joven **2** TIMELESS : eterno, perenne

agency ['eɪʤəntsi] *n, pl* **-cies** **1** : agencia *f*, oficina *f* ⟨travel agency : agencia de viajes⟩ **2 through the agency of** : a través de, por medio de

agenda [əˈʤɛndə] *n* : agenda *f*, orden *m* del día

agent [ˈeɪʤənt] *n* **1** MEANS : agente *m*, medio *m*, instrumento *m* **2** REPRESENTATIVE : agente *mf*, representante *mf*

aggravate [ˈægrəˌveɪt] *vt* **-vated; -vating 1** WORSEN : agravar, empeorar **2** ANNOY : irritar, exasperar

aggravation [ˌægrəˈveɪʃən] *n* **1** WORSENING : empeoramiento *m* **2** ANNOYANCE : molestia *f*, irritación *f*, exasperación *f*

aggregate[1] [ˈægrɪˌgeɪt] *vt* **-gated; -gating** : juntar, sumar

aggregate[2] [ˈægrɪgət] *adj* : total, global, conjunto

aggregate[3] [ˈægrɪgət] *n* **1** CONGLOMERATE : agregado *m*, conglomerado *m* **2** WHOLE : total *m*, conjunto *m*

aggression [əˈgrɛʃən] *n* **1** ATTACK : agresión *f* **2** AGGRESSIVENESS : agresividad *f*

aggressive [əˈgrɛsɪv] *adj* : agresivo — **aggressively** *adv*

aggressiveness [əˈgrɛsɪvnəs] *n* : agresividad *f*

aggressor [əˈgrɛsər] *n* : agresor *m*, -sora *f*

aggrieved [əˈgri:vd] *adj* : ofendido, herido

aghast [əˈgæst] *adj* : espantado, aterrado, horrorizado

agile [ˈæʤəl] *adj* : ágil

agility [əˈʤɪləṭi] *n, pl* **-ties** : agilidad *f*

agitate [ˈæʤəˌteɪt] *v* **-tated; -tating** *vt* **1** SHAKE : agitar **2** UPSET : inquietar, perturbar — *vi* **to agitate against** : hacer campaña en contra de

agitation [ˌæʤəˈteɪʃən] *n* : agitación *f*, inquietud *f*

agitator [ˈæʤəˌteɪṭər] *n* : agitador *m*, -dora *f*

agnostic [ægˈnɑstɪk] *n* : agnóstico *m*, -ca *f*

ago [əˈgo:] *adv* : hace ⟨two years ago : hace dos años⟩ ⟨long ago : hace tiempo, hace mucho tiempo⟩

agog [əˈgɑg] *adj* : ansioso, curioso

agonize [ˈægəˌnaɪz] *vi* **-nized; -nizing** : tormentarse, angustiarse

agonizing [ˈægəˌnaɪzɪŋ] *adj* : angustioso, terrible — **agonizingly** [-zɪŋli] *adv*

agony [ˈægəni] *n, pl* **-nies 1** PAIN : dolor *m* **2** ANGUISH : angustia *f*

agrarian [əˈgrɛriən] *adj* : agrario

agree [əˈgri:] *v* **agreed; agreeing** *vt* ACKNOWLEDGE : estar de acuerdo ⟨he agreed that I was right : estuvo de acuerdo en que tenía razón⟩ — *vi* **1** CONCUR : estar de acuerdo **2** CONSENT : ponerse de acuerdo **3** TALLY : concordar **4 to agree with** : sentarle bien (a alguien) ⟨this climate agrees with me : este clima me sienta bien⟩

agreeable [əˈgri:əbəl] *adj* **1** PLEASING : agradable, simpático **2** WILLING : dispuesto **3** AGREEING : de acuerdo, conforme

agreeably [əˈgri:əbli] *adv* : agradablemente

agreement [əˈgri:mənt] *n* **1** : acuerdo *m*, conformidad *f* ⟨in agreement with : de acuerdo con⟩ **2** CONTRACT, PACT : acuerdo *m*, pacto *m*, convenio *m* **3** CONCORD, HARMONY : concordia *f*

agriculture [ˈægrɪˌkʌlʧər] *n* : agricultura *f* — **agricultural** [ˌægrɪˈkʌlʧərəl] *adj*

aground [əˈgraʊnd] *adj* : encallado, varado

ahead [əˈhɛd] *adv* **1** : al frente, delante, adelante ⟨he walked ahead : caminó delante⟩ **2** BEFOREHAND : por adelantado, con antelación **3** LEADING : a la delantera **4 to get ahead** : adelantar, progresar

ahead of *prep* **1** : al frente de, delante de, antes de **2 to get ahead of** : adelantarse a

ahoy [əˈhɔɪ] *interj* **ship ahoy!** : ¡barco a la vista!

aid[1] [ˈeɪd] *vt* : ayudar, auxiliar

aid[2] *n* **1** HELP : ayuda *f*, asistencia *f* **2** ASSISTANT : asistente *mf*

aide [ˈeɪd] *n* : ayudante *mf*

AIDS [ˈeɪdz] *n* : SIDA *m*, sida *m*

ail [ˈeɪl] *vt* : molestar, afligir — *vi* : sufrir, estar enfermo

aileron [ˈeɪləˌrɑn] *n* : alerón *m*

ailment [ˈeɪlmənt] *n* : enfermedad *f*, dolencia *f*, achaque *m*

aim[1] [ˈeɪm] *vt* **1** : apuntar (un arma), dirigir (una observación) **2** INTEND : proponerse, querer ⟨he aims to do it tonight : se propone hacerlo esta noche⟩ — *vi* **1** POINT : apuntar **2 to aim at** : aspirar a

aim[2] *n* **1** MARKSMANSHIP : puntería *f* **2** GOAL : propósito *m*, objetivo *m*, fin *m*

aimless [ˈeɪmləs] *adj* : sin rumbo, sin objeto

aimlessly [ˈeɪmləsli] *adv* : sin rumbo, sin objeto

air[1] [ˈær] *vt* **1** : airear, ventilar ⟨to air out a mattress : airear un colchón⟩ **2** EXPRESS : airear, manifestar, comunicar **3** BROADCAST : transmitir, emitir

air[2] *n* **1** : aire *m* **2** MELODY : aire *m* **3** APPEARANCE : aire *m*, aspecto *m* **4 airs** *npl* : aires *mpl*, afectación *f* **5 by ~** : por avión (dícese de una carta), en avión (dícese de una persona) **6 to be on the air** : estar en el aire, estar emitiendo

airborne [ˈærˌborn] *adj* **1** : aerotransportado ⟨airborne troops : tropas aerotransportadas⟩ **2** FLYING : volando, en el aire

air–condition [ˌærkənˈdɪʃən] *vt* : climatizar, condicionar con el aire

air conditioner [ˌærkənˈdɪʃənər] *n* : acondicionador *m* de aire

air-conditioning [ˌærkənˈdɪʃənɪŋ] *n* : aire *m* acondicionado
aircraft [ˈærˌkræft] *ns & pl* **1** : avión *m*, aeronave *f* **2 aircraft carrier** : portaaviones *m*
airfield [ˈærˌfiːld] *n* : aeródromo *m*, campo *m* de aviación
air force *n* : fuerza *f* aérea
airlift [ˈærˌlɪft] *n* : puente *m* aéreo, transporte *m* aéreo
airline [ˈærˌlaɪn] *n* : aerolínea *f*, línea *f* aérea
airliner [ˈærˌlaɪnər] *n* : avión *m* de pasajeros
airmail[1] [ˈærˌmeɪl] *vt* : enviar por vía aérea
airmail[2] *n* : correo *m* aéreo
airman [ˈærmən] *n, pl* **-men** [-mən, -ˌmɛn] **1** AVIATOR : aviador *m*, -dora *f* **2** : soldado *m* de la fuerza aérea
airplane [ˈærˌpleɪn] *n* : avión *m*
airport [ˈærˌport] *n* : aeropuerto *m*
airship [ˈærˌʃɪp] *n* : dirigible *m*, zepelín *m*
airstrip [ˈærˌstrɪp] *n* : pista *f* de aterrizaje
airtight [ˈærˈtaɪt] *adj* : hermético, herméticamente cerrado
airwaves [ˈærˌweɪvz] *npl* : radio *m*, televisión *f*
airy [ˈæri] *adj* **airier** [-iər]; **-est** **1** DELICATE, LIGHT : delicado, ligero **2** BREEZY : aireado, bien ventilado
aisle [ˈaɪl] *n* : pasillo *m*, nave *f* lateral (de una iglesia)
ajar [əˈʤɑr] *adj* : entreabierto, entornado
akimbo [əˈkɪmbo] *adj & adv* : en jarras
akin [əˈkɪn] *adj* **1** RELATED : emparentado **2** SIMILAR : semejante, parecido
alabaster [ˈæləˌbæstər] *n* : alabastro *m*
alacrity [əˈlækrəṭi] *n* : presteza *f*, prontitud *f*
alarm[1] [əˈlɑrm] *vt* **1** WARN : alarmar, alertar **2** FRIGHTEN : asustar
alarm[2] *n* **1** WARNING : alarma *f*, alerta *f* **2** APPREHENSION, FEAR : aprensión *f*, inquietud *f*, temor *m* **3 alarm clock** : despertador *m*
alarming [əˈlɑrmɪŋ] *adj* : alarmante
alas [əˈlæs] *interj* : ¡ay!
Albanian [ælˈbeɪniən] *n* : albanés *m*, -nesa *f* — **Albanian** *adj*
albatross [ˈælbəˌtrɔs] *n, pl* **-tross** *or* **-trosses** : albatros *m*
albeit [ɔlˈbiːət, æl-] *conj* : aunque
albino [ælˈbaɪno] *n, pl* **-nos** : albino *m*, -na *f*
album [ˈælbəm] *n* : álbum *m*
albumen [ælˈbjuːmən] *n* **1** : clara *f* de huevo **2** → **albumin**
albumin [ælˈbjuːmən] *n* : albúmina *f*
alchemist [ˈælkəmɪst] *n* : alquimista *mf*
alchemy [ˈælkəmi] *n, pl* **-mies** : alquimia *f*
alcohol [ˈælkəˌhɔl] *n* **1** ETHANOL : alcohol *m*, etanol *m* **2** LIQUOR : alcohol *m*, bebidas *fpl* alcohólicas
alcoholic[1] [ˌælkəˈhɔlɪk] *adj* : alcohólico
alcoholic[2] *n* : alcohólico *m*, -ca *f*
alcoholism [ˈælkəhɔˌlɪzəm] *n* : alcoholismo *m*
alcove [ˈælˌkoːv] *n* : nicho *m*, hueco *m*
alderman [ˈɔldərmən] *n, pl* **-men** [-mən, -ˌmɛn] : concejal *mf*
ale [ˈeɪl] *n* : cerveza *f*
alert[1] [əˈlərt] *vt* : alertar, poner sobre aviso
alert[2] *adj* **1** WATCHFUL : alerta, vigilante **2** QUICK : listo, vivo
alert[3] *n* : alerta *f*, alarma *f*
alertly [əˈlərtli] *adv* : con listeza
alertness [əˈlərtnəs] *n* **1** WATCHFULNESS : vigilancia *f* **2** ASTUTENESS : listeza *f*, viveza *f*
alfalfa [ælˈfælfə] *n* : alfalfa *f*
alga [ˈælgə] *n, pl* **-gae** [ˈælˌʤiː] : alga *f*
algebra [ˈælʤəbrə] *n* : álgebra *m*
algebraic [ˌælʤəˈbreɪɪk] *adj* : algebraico — **algebraically** [-ɪkli] *adv*
Algerian [ælˈʤɪriən] *n* : argelino *m*, -na *f* — **Algerian** *adj*
algorithm [ˈælgəˌrɪðəm] *n* : algoritmo *m*
alias[1] [ˈeɪliəs] *adv* : alias
alias[2] *n* : alias *m*
alibi[1] [ˈæləˌbaɪ] *vi* : ofrecer una coartada
alibi[2] *n* **1** : coartada *f* **2** EXCUSE : pretexto *m*, excusa *f*
alien[1] [ˈeɪliən] *adj* **1** STRANGE : ajeno, extraño **2** FOREIGN : extranjero, foráneo **3** EXTRATERRESTRIAL : extraterrestre
alien[2] *n* **1** FOREIGNER : extranjero *m*, -ra *f*; forastero *m*, -ra *f* **2** EXTRATERRESTRIAL : extraterrestre *mf*
alienate [ˈeɪliəˌneɪt] *vt* **-ated; -ating** **1** ESTRANGE : alienar, enajenar **2 to alienate oneself** : alejarse, distanciarse
alienation [ˌeɪliəˈneɪʃən] *n* : alienación *f*, enajenación *f*
alight [əˈlaɪt] *vi* **1** DISMOUNT : bajarse, apearse **2** LAND : posarse, aterrizar
align [əˈlaɪn] *vt* : alinear
alignment [əˈlaɪnmənt] *n* : alineación *f*, alineamiento *m*
alike[1] [əˈlaɪk] *adv* : igual, del mismo modo
alike[2] *adj* : igual, semejante, parecido
alimentary [ˌæləˈmɛntəri] *adj* **1** : alimenticio **2 alimentary canal** : tubo *m* digestivo
alimony [ˈæləˌmoːni] *n, pl* **-nies** : pensión *f* alimenticia
alive [əˈlaɪv] *adj* **1** LIVING : vivo, viviente **2** LIVELY : animado, activo **3** ACTIVE : vigente, en uso **4** AWARE : consciente ⟨alive to the danger : consciente del peligro⟩
alkali [ˈælkəˌlaɪ] *n, pl* **-lies** [-ˌlaɪz] *or* **-lis** [-ˌlaɪz] : álcali *m*
alkaline [ˈælkələn, -ˌlaɪn] *adj* : alcalino
all[1] [ˈɔl] *adv* **1** COMPLETELY : todo, completamente **2** : igual ⟨the score is 14 all : es 14 iguales, están empatados a 14⟩

3 all the better : tanto mejor **4 all the more** : aún más, todavía más
all[2] *adj* : todo ⟨all the children : todos los niños⟩ ⟨in all likelihood : con toda probabilidad, con la mayor probabilidad⟩
all[3] *pron* **1** : todo, -da ⟨they ate it all : lo comieron todo⟩ ⟨that's all : eso es todo⟩ ⟨enough for all : suficiente para todos⟩ **2 all in all** : en general **3 not at all** (*in negative constructions*) : en absoluto, para nada
Allah [ˈɑlɑ, ɑˈlɑ] *n* : Alá *m*
all–around [ˌɔləˈraʊnd] *adj* : completo, amplio
allay [əˈleɪ] *vt* **1** ALLEVIATE : aliviar, mitigar **2** CALM : aquietar, calmar
allegation [ˌælɪˈgeɪʃən] *n* : alegato *m*, acusación *f*
allege [əˈlɛʤ] *vt* **-leged; -leging 1** : alegar, afirmar **2 to be alleged** : decirse, pretenderse ⟨she is alleged to be wealthy : se dice que es adinerada⟩
alleged [əˈlɛʤd, əˈlɛʤəd] *adj* : presunto, supuesto
allegedly [əˈlɛʤədli] *adv* : supuestamente, según se alega
allegiance [əˈliːʤənts] *n* : lealtad *f*, fidelidad *f*
allegorical [ˌæləˈgɔrɪkəl] *adj* : alegórico
allegory [ˈæləˌgori] *n, pl* **-ries** : alegoría *f*
alleluia [ˌɑləˈluːjə, ˌæ-] → **hallelujah**
allergen [ˈælərʤən] *n* : alérgeno *m*
allergic [əˈlərʤɪk] *adj* : alérgico
allergy [ˈælərʤi] *n, pl* **-gies** : alergia *f*
alleviate [əˈliːviˌeɪt] *vt* **-ated; -ating** : aliviar, mitigar, paliar
alleviation [əˌliːviˈeɪʃən] *n* : alivio *m*
alley [ˈæli] *n, pl* **-leys 1** : callejón *m* **2 bowling alley** : bolera *f*
alliance [əˈlaɪənts] *n* : alianza *f*, coalición *f*
alligator [ˈæləˌgeɪṭər] *n* : caimán *m*
alliteration [əˌlɪṭəˈreɪʃən] *n* : aliteración *f*
allocate [ˈæləˌkeɪt] *vt* **-cated; -cating** : asignar, adjudicar
allocation [ˌæləˈkeɪʃən] *n* : asignación *f*, reparto *m*, distribución *f*
allot [əˈlɑt] *vt* **-lotted; -lotting** : repartir, distribuir, asignar
allotment [əˈlɑtmənt] *n* : reparto *m*, asignación *f*, distribución *f*
allow [əˈlaʊ] *vt* **1** PERMIT : permitir, dejar **2** ALLOT : conceder, dar **3** ADMIT, CONCEDE : admitir, conceder — *vi* **to allow for** : tener en cuenta
allowable [əˈlaʊəbəl] *adj* **1** PERMISSIBLE : permisible, lícito **2** : deducible ⟨allowable expenditure : gasto deducible⟩
allowance [əˈlaʊənts] *n* **1** : complemento *m* (para gastos, etc.), mesada *f* (para niños) **2 to make allowance(s)** : tener en cuenta, disculpar
alloy [ˈæˌlɔɪ] *n* : aleación *f*
all–purpose [ˈɔlˈpərpəs] *adj* : multiuso ⟨all-purpose flour : harina común⟩
all right[1] *adv* **1** YES : sí, por supuesto **2** WELL : bien ⟨I did all right : me fue bien⟩ **3** DEFINITELY : bien, ciertamente, sin duda ⟨he's sick all right : está bien enfermo⟩
all right[2] *adj* **1** OK : bien ⟨are you all right? : ¿estás bien?⟩ **2** SATISFACTORY : bien, bueno ⟨your work is all right : tu trabajo es bueno⟩
all–round [ˌɔlˈraʊnd] → **all–around**
allspice [ˈɔlspaɪs] *n* : pimienta *f* de Jamaica
allude [əˈluːd] *vi* **-luded; -luding** : aludir, referirse
allure[1] [əˈlʊr] *vt* **-lured; -luring** : cautivar, atraer
allure[2] *n* : atractivo *m*, encanto *m*
allusion [əˈluːʒən] *n* : alusión *f*
ally[1] [əˈlaɪ, ˈæˌlaɪ] *vi* **-lied; -lying** : aliarse
ally[2] [ˈæˌlaɪ, əˈlaɪ] *n* : aliado *m*, -da *f*
almanac [ˈɔlməˌnæk, ˈæl-] *n* : almanaque *m*
almighty [ɔlˈmaɪṭi] *adj* : omnipotente, todopoderoso
almond [ˈɑmənd, ˈɑl-, ˈæ-, ˈæl-] *n* : almendra *f*
almost [ˈɔlˌmoːst, ɔlˈmoːst] *adv* : casi, prácticamente
alms [ˈɑmz, ˈɑlmz, ˈælmz] *ns & pl* : limosna *f*, caridad *f*
aloe [ˈæloː] *n* : áloe *m*
aloft [əˈlɔft] *adv* : en alto, en el aire
alone[1] [əˈloːn] *adv* : sólo, solamente, únicamente
alone[2] *adj* : solo ⟨they're alone in the house : están solos en la casa⟩
along[1] [əˈlɔŋ] *adv* **1** FORWARD : adelante ⟨farther along : más adelante⟩ ⟨move along! : ¡circulen, por favor!⟩ **2 to bring along** : traer **3 ~ with** : con, junto con **4 all along** : desde el principio
along[2] *prep* **1** : por, a lo largo de ⟨along the coast : a lo largo de la costa⟩ **2** : en, en el curso de, por ⟨along the way : en el curso del viaje⟩
alongside[1] [əˌlɔŋˈsaɪd] *adv* : al costado, al lado
alongside[2] *or* **alongside of** *prep* : junto a, al lado de
aloof [əˈluːf] *adj* : distante, reservado
aloofness [əˈluːfnəs] *n* : reserva *f*, actitud *f* distante
aloud [əˈlaʊd] *adv* : en voz alta
alpaca [ælˈpækə] *n* : alpaca *f*
alphabet [ˈælfəˌbɛt] *n* : alfabeto *m*
alphabetical [ˌælfəˈbɛṭɪkəl] *or* **alphabetic** [-ˈbɛṭɪk] *adj* : alfabético — **alphabetically** [-ṭɪkli] *adv*
alphabetize [ˈælfəbəˌtaɪz] *vt* **-ized; -izing** : alfabetizar, poner en orden alfabético
alpine [ˈælˌpaɪn] *adj* : alpino
already [ɔlˈrɛdi] *adv* : ya
also [ˈɔlˌsoː] *adv* : también, además
altar [ˈɔltər] *n* : altar *m*
alter [ˈɔltər] *vt* : alterar, cambiar, modificar

alteration [ˌɔltəˈreɪʃən] *n* : alteración *f*, cambio *m*, modificación *f*
altercation [ˌɔltərˈkeɪʃən] *n* : altercado *m*, disputa *f*
alternate[1] [ˈɔltərˌneɪt] *v* **-nated; -nating** : alternar
alternate[2] [ˈɔltərnət] *adj* **1** : alterno ‹alternate cycles of inflation and depression : ciclos alternos de inflación y depresión› **2** : uno sí y otro no ‹he cooks on alternate days : cocina un día sí y otro no›
alternate[3] [ˈɔltərnət] *n* : suplente *mf*; sustituto *m*, -ta *f*
alternately [ˈɔltərnətli] *adv* : alternativamente, por turno
alternating current [ˈɔltərˌneɪṭɪŋ] *n* : corriente *f* alterna
alternation [ˌɔltərˈneɪʃən] *n* : alternancia *f*, rotación *f*
alternative[1] [ɔlˈtərnəṭɪv] *adj* : alternativo
alternative[2] *n* : alternativa *f*
alternator [ˈɔltərˌneɪṭər] *n* : alternador *m*
although [ɔlˈðoː] *conj* : aunque, a pesar de que
altitude [ˈæltəˌtuːd, -ˌtjuːd] *n* : altitud *f*, altura *f*
alto [ˈælˌtoː] *n, pl* **-tos** : alto *mf*, contralto *mf*
altogether [ˌɔltəˈgɛðər] *adv* **1** COMPLETELY : completamente, totalmente, del todo **2** ON THE WHOLE : en suma, en general
altruism [ˈæltrʊˌɪzəm] *n* : altruismo *m*
altruistic [ˌæltrʊˈɪstɪk] *adj* : altruista — **altruistically** [-tɪkli] *adv*
alum [ˈæləm] *n* : alumbre *m*
aluminum [əˈluːmənəm] *n* : aluminio *m*
alumna [əˈlʌmnə] *n, pl* **-nae** [-ˌniː] : exalumna *f*
alumnus [əˈlʌmnəs] *n, pl* **-ni** [-ˌnaɪ] : exalumno *m*
always [ˈɔlwiz, -ˌweɪz] *adv* **1** INVARIABLY : siempre, invariablemente **2** FOREVER : para siempre
am → **be**
amalgam [əˈmælgəm] *n* : amalgama *f*
amalgamate [əˈmælgəˌmeɪt] *vt* **-ated; -ating** : amalgamar, unir, fusionar
amalgamation [əˌmælgəˈmeɪʃən] *n* : fusión *f*, unión *f*
amaryllis [ˌæməˈrɪləs] *n* : amarilis *f*
amass [əˈmæs] *vt* : amasar, acumular
amateur [ˈæməʧər, -tər, -ˌtʊr, -ˌtjʊr] *n* **1** : amateur *mf* **2** BEGINNER : principiante *mf*; aficionado *m*, -da *f*
amateurish [ˈæməˌʧərɪʃ, -ˌtər-, -ˌtʊr-, -ˌtjʊr-] *adj* : amateur, inexperto
amaze [əˈmeɪz] *vt* **amazed; amazing** : asombrar, maravillar, pasmar
amazement [əˈmeɪzmənt] *n* : asombro *m*, sorpresa *f*
amazing [əˈmeɪzɪŋ] *adj* : asombroso, sorprendente — **amazingly** [-zɪŋli] *adv*
Amazon [ˈæməˌzɑn] *n* : amazona *f* (en mitología)
Amazonian [ˌæməˈzoːniən] *adj* : amazónico
ambassador [æmˈbæsədər] *n* : embajador *m*, -dora *f*
amber [ˈæmbər] *n* : ámbar *m*
ambergris [ˈæmbərˌgrɪs, -ˌgriːs] *n* : ámbar *m* gris
ambidextrous [ˌæmbɪˈdɛkstrəs] *adj* : ambidextro — **ambidextrously** *adv*
ambience *or* **ambiance** [ˈæmbiən*t*s, ˈɑmbiˌɑn*t*s] *n* : ambiente *m*, atmósfera *f*
ambiguity [ˌæmbəˈgjuːəṭi] *n, pl* **-ties** : ambigüedad *f*
ambiguous [æmˈbɪgjʊəs] *adj* : ambiguo
ambition [æmˈbɪʃən] *n* : ambición *f*
ambitious [æmˈbɪʃəs] *adj* : ambicioso — **ambitiously** *adv*
ambivalence [æmˈbɪvələn*t*s] *n* : ambivalencia *f*
ambivalent [æmˈbɪvələnt] *adj* : ambivalente
amble[1] [ˈæmbəl] *vi* **-bled; -bling** : ir tranquilamente, pasearse despreocupadamente
amble[2] *n* : paseo *m* tranquilo
ambulance [ˈæmbjələn*t*s] *n* : ambulancia *f*
ambush[1] [ˈæmˌbʊʃ] *vt* : emboscar
ambush[2] *n* : emboscada *f*, celada *f*
ameliorate [əˈmiːljəˌreɪt] *v* **-rated; -rating** IMPROVE : mejorar
amelioration [əˌmiːljəˈreɪʃən] *n* : mejora *f*
amen [ˈeɪˈmɛn, ˈɑ-] *interj* : amén
amenable [əˈmiːnəbəl, -ˈmɛ-] *adj* RESPONSIVE : susceptible, receptivo, sensible
amend [əˈmɛnd] *vt* **1** IMPROVE : mejorar, enmendar **2** CORRECT : enmendar, corregir
amendment [əˈmɛndmənt] *n* : enmienda *f*
amends [əˈmɛndz] *ns & pl* : compensación *f*, reparación *f*, desagravio *m*
amenity [əˈmɛnəṭi, -ˈmiː-] *n, pl* **-ties** **1** PLEASANTNESS : lo agradable, amenidad *f* **2 amenities** *npl* : servicios *mpl*, comodidades *fpl*
American [əˈmɛrɪkən] *n* : americano *m*, -na *f* — **American** *adj*
American Indian *n* : indio *m* (americano), india *f* (americana)
amethyst [ˈæməθəst] *n* : amatista *f*
amiability [ˌeɪmiːəˈbɪləṭi] *n* : amabilidad *f*, afabilidad *f*
amiable [ˈeɪmiːəbəl] *adj* : amable, afable — **amiably** [-bli] *adv*
amicable [ˈæmɪkəbəl] *adj* : amigable, amistoso, cordial — **amicably** [-bli] *adv*
amid [əˈmɪd] *or* **amidst** [əˈmɪdst] *prep* : en medio de, entre
amino acid [əˈmiːno] *n* : aminoácido *m*
amiss[1] [əˈmɪs] *adv* : mal, fuera de lugar ‹to take amiss : tomar a mal, llevar a mal›
amiss[2] *adj* **1** WRONG : malo, inoportuno **2 there's something amiss** : pasa algo, algo anda mal
ammeter [ˈæˌmiːṭər] *n* : amperímetro *m*

ammonia [əˈmo:njə] *n* : amoníaco *m*
ammunition [ˌæmjəˈnɪʃən] *n* **1** : municiones *fpl* **2** ARGUMENTS : argumentos *mpl*
amnesia [æmˈni:ʒə] *n* : amnesia *f*
amnesty [ˈæmnəsti] *n, pl* **-ties** : amnistía *f*
amoeba [əˈmi:bə] *n, pl* **-bas** *or* **-bae** [-ˌbi:] : ameba *f*
amoebic [əˈmi:bɪk] *adj* : amébico
amok [əˈmʌk, -ˈmɑk] *adv* **to run amok** : correr a ciegas, enloquecerse, desbocarse (dícese de la economía, etc.)
among [əˈmʌŋ] *prep* : entre
amoral [eɪˈmɔrəl] *adj* : amoral
amorous [ˈæmərəs] *adj* **1** PASSIONATE : enamoradizo, apasionado **2** ENAMORED : enamorado **3** LOVING : amoroso, cariñoso
amorously [ˈæmərəsli] *adv* : con cariño
amorphous [əˈmɔrfəs] *adj* : amorfo, informe
amortize [ˈæmərˌtaɪz, əˈmɔr-] *vt* **-tized; -tizing** : amortizar
amount[1] [əˈmaʊnt] *vi* **to amount to** **1** : equivaler a, significar ⟨that amounts to treason : eso equivale a la traición⟩ **2** : ascender (a) ⟨my debts amount to $2000 : mis deudas ascienden a $2000⟩
amount[2] *n* : cantidad *f*, suma *f*
ampere [ˈæmˌpɪr] *n* : amperio *m*
ampersand [ˈæmpərˌsænd] *n* : el signo &
amphetamine [æmˈfɛt̬əˌmi:n] *n* : anfetamina *f*
amphibian [æmˈfɪbiən] *n* : anfibio *m*
amphibious [æmˈfɪbiəs] *adj* : anfibio
amphitheater [ˈæmfəˌθi:ət̬ər] *n* : anfiteatro *m*
ample [ˈæmpəl] *adj* **-pler; -plest** **1** LARGE, SPACIOUS : amplio, extenso, grande **2** ABUNDANT : abundante, generoso
amplifier [ˈæmpləˌfaɪər] *n* : amplificador *m*
amplify [ˈæmpləˌfaɪ] *vt* **-fied; -fying** : amplificar
amply [ˈæmpli] *adv* : ampliamente, abundantemente, suficientemente
amputate [ˈæmpjəˌteɪt] *vt* **-tated; -tating** : amputar
amputation [ˌæmpjəˈteɪʃən] *n* : amputación *f*
amuck [əˈmʌk] → **amok**
amulet [ˈæmjələt] *n* : amuleto *m*, talismán *m*
amuse [əˈmju:z] *vt* **amused; amusing** **1** ENTERTAIN : entretener, distraer **2** : hacer reír, divertir ⟨the joke amused us : la broma nos hizo reír⟩
amusement [əˈmju:zmənt] *n* **1** ENTERTAINMENT : diversión *f*, entretenimiento *m*, pasatiempo *m* **2** LAUGHTER : risa *f*
an *art* → **a**[2]
anachronism [əˈnækrəˌnɪzəm] *n* : anacronismo *m*
anachronistic [əˌnækrəˈnɪstɪk] *adj* : anacrónico
anaconda [ˌænəˈkɑndə] *n* : anaconda *f*
anagram [ˈænəˌgræm] *n* : anagrama *m*
anal [ˈeɪnəl] *adj* : anal
analgesic [ˌænəlˈdʒi:zɪk, -sɪk] *n* : analgésico *m*
analog [ˈænəˌlɔg] *adj* : analógico
analogical [ˌænəˈlɑdʒɪkəl] *adj* : analógico — **analogically** [-kli] *adv*
analogous [əˈnæləgəs] *adj* : análogo
analogy [əˈnælədʒi] *n, pl* **-gies** : analogía *f*
analysis [əˈnæləsəs] *n, pl* **-yses** [-ˌsi:z] **1** : análisis *m* **2** PSYCHOANALYSIS : psicoanálisis *m*
analyst [ˈænəlɪst] *n* **1** : analista *mf* **2** PSYCHOANALYST : psicoanalista *mf*
analytic [ˌænəˈlɪt̬ɪk] *or* **analytical** [-t̬ɪkəl] *adj* : analítico — **analytically** [-t̬ɪkli] *adv*
analyze [ˈænəˌlaɪz] *vt* **-lyzed; -lyzing** : analizar
anarchic [æˈnɑrkɪk] *adj* : anárquico — **anarchically** [-kɪkli] *adv*
anarchism [ˈænərˌkɪzəm, -nɑr-] *n* : anarquismo *m*
anarchist [ˈænərkɪst, -nɑr-] *n* : anarquista *mf*
anarchy [ˈænərki, -nɑr-] *n* : anarquía *f*
anathema [əˈnæθəmə] *n* : anatema *m*
anatomic [ˌænəˈtɑmɪk] *or* **anatomical** [-mɪkəl] *adj* : anatómico — **anatomically** [-mɪkli] *adv*
anatomy [əˈnæt̬əmi] *n, pl* **-mies** : anatomía *f*
ancestor [ˈænˌsɛstər] *n* : antepasado *m*, -da *f*; antecesor *m*, -sora *f*
ancestral [ænˈsɛstrəl] *adj* : ancestral, de los antepasados
ancestry [ˈænˌsɛstri] *n* **1** DESCENT : ascendencia *f*, linaje *m*, abolengo *m* **2** ANCESTORS : antepasados *mpl*, -das *fpl*
anchor[1] [ˈæŋkər] *vt* **1** MOOR : anclar, fondear **2** FASTEN : sujetar, asegurar, fijar
anchor[2] *n* **1** : ancla *f* **2** : presentador *m*, -dora *f* (en televisión)
anchorage [ˈæŋkərɪdʒ] *n* : anclaje *m*
anchovy [ˈænˌtʃo:vi, ænˈtʃo:-] *n, pl* **-vies** *or* **-vy** : anchoa *f*
ancient [ˈeɪntʃənt] *adj* **1** : antiguo ⟨ancient history : historia antigua⟩ **2** OLD : viejo
ancients [ˈeɪntʃənts] *npl* : los antiguos *mpl*
and [ˈænd] *conj* **1** : y (**e** *before words beginning with i- or hi-*) **2** : con ⟨ham and eggs : huevos con jamón⟩ **3** : a ⟨go and see : ve a ver⟩ **4** : de ⟨try and finish it soon : trata de terminarlo pronto⟩
Andalusian [ˌændəˈlu:ʒən] *n* : andaluz *m*, -luza *f* — **Andalusian** *adj*
Andean [ˈændiən] *adj* : andino
andiron [ˈænˌdaɪərn] *n* : morillo *m*
Andorran [ænˈdɔrən] *n* : andorrano *m*, -na *f* — **Andorran** *adj*
androgynous [ænˈdrɑdʒənəs] *adj* : andrógino
anecdotal [ˌænɪkˈdo:t̬əl] *adj* : anecdótico

anecdote [ˈænɪkˌdoːt] *n* : anécdota *f*
anemia [əˈniːmiə] *n* : anemia *f*
anemic [əˈniːmɪk] *adj* : anémico
anemone [əˈnɛməni] *n* : anémona *f*
anesthesia [ˌænəsˈθiːʒə] *n* : anestesia *f*
anesthetic[1] [ˌænəsˈθɛt̬ɪk] *adj* : anestésico
anesthetic[2] *n* : anestésico *m*
anesthetist [əˈnɛsθətɪst] *n* : anestesista *mf*
anesthetize [əˈnɛsθəˌtaɪz] *vt* **-tize; -tized** : anestesiar
aneurysm [ˈænjəˌrɪzəm] *n* : aneurisma *mf*
anew [əˈnuː, -ˈnjuː] *adv* : de nuevo, otra vez, nuevamente
angel [ˈeɪndʒəl] *n* : ángel *m*
angelic [ænˈdʒɛlɪk] *or* **angelical** [-lɪkəl] *adj* : angélico, angelical — **angelically** [-lɪkli] *adv*
anger[1] [ˈæŋgər] *vt* : enojar, enfadar
anger[2] *n* : enojo *m*, enfado *m*, ira *f*, cólera *f*, rabia *f*
angina [ænˈdʒaɪnə] *n* : angina *f*
angle[1] [ˈæŋgəl] *v* **angled; angling** *vt* DIRECT, SLANT : orientar, dirigir — *vi* FISH : pescar (con caña)
angle[2] *n* **1** : ángulo *m* **2** POINT OF VIEW : perspectiva *f*, punto *m* de vista
angler [ˈæŋglər] *n* : pescador *m*, -dora *f*
Anglican [ˈæŋglɪkən] *n* : anglicano *m*, -na *f* — **Anglican** *adj*
Anglo–Saxon[1] [ˌæŋgloˈsæksən] *adj* : anglosajón
Anglo–Saxon[2] *n* : anglosajón *m*, -jona *f*
Angolan [æŋˈgoːlən, æn-] *n* : angoleño *m*, -ña *f* — **Angolan** *adj*
angora [æŋˈgorə, æn-] *n* : angora *f*
angrily [ˈæŋgrəli] *adv* : furiosamente, con ira
angry [ˈæŋgri] *adj* **-grier; -est** : enojado, enfadado, furioso
anguish [ˈæŋgwɪʃ] *n* : angustia *f*, congoja *f*
anguished [ˈæŋgwɪʃt] *adj* : angustiado, acongojado
angular [ˈæŋgjələr] *adj* : angular (dícese de las formas), anguloso (dícese de las caras)
animal [ˈænəməl] *n* **1** : animal *m* **2** BRUTE : bruto *m*, -ta *f*
animate[1] [ˈænəˌmeɪt] *vt* **-mated; -mating** : animar
animate[2] [ˈænəmət] *adj* : animado
animated [ˈænəˌmeɪt̬əd] *adj* **1** LIVELY : animado, vivo, vivaz **2 animated cartoon** : dibujos *mpl* animados
animation [ˌænəˈmeɪʃən] *n* : animación *f*
animosity [ˌænəˈmɑsət̬i] *n, pl* **-ties** : animosidad *f*, animadversión *f*
anise [ˈænəs] *n* : anís *m*
aniseed [ˈænəsˌsiːd] *n* : anís *m*, semilla *f* de anís
ankle [ˈæŋkəl] *n* : tobillo *m*
anklebone [ˈæŋkəlˌboːn] *n* : taba *f*
annals [ˈænəlz] *npl* : anales *mpl*, crónica *f*
anneal [əˈniːl] *vt* **1** TEMPER : templar **2** STRENGTHEN : fortalecer
annex[1] [əˈnɛks, ˈæˌnɛks] *vt* : anexar
annex[2] [ˈæˌnɛks, -nɪks] *n* : anexo *m*, anejo *m*
annexation [ˌæˌnɛkˈseɪʃən] *n* : anexión *f*
annihilate [əˈnaɪəˌleɪt] *vt* **-lated; -lating** : aniquilar
annihilation [əˌnaɪəˈleɪʃən] *n* : aniquilación *f*, aniquilamiento *m*
anniversary [ˌænəˈvərsəri] *n, pl* **-ries** : aniversario *m*
annotate [ˈænəˌteɪt] *vt* **-tated; -tating** : anotar
annotation [ˌænəˈteɪʃən] *n* : anotación *f*
announce [əˈnaʊnts] *vt* **-nounced; -nouncing** : anunciar
announcement [əˈnaʊntsmənt] *n* : anuncio *m*
announcer [əˈnaʊntsər] *n* : anunciador *m*, -dora *f*; comentarista *mf*; locutor *m*, -tora *f*
annoy [əˈnɔɪ] *vt* : molestar, fastidiar, irritar
annoyance [əˈnɔɪənts] *n* **1** IRRITATION : irritación *f*, fastidio *m* **2** NUISANCE : molestia *f*, fastidio *m*
annoying [əˈnɔɪɪŋ] *adj* : molesto, fastidioso, engorroso — **annoyingly** [-ɪŋli] *adv*
annual[1] [ˈænjʊəl] *adj* : anual — **annually** *adv*
annual[2] *n* **1** : planta *f* anual **2** YEARBOOK : anuario *m*
annuity [əˈnuːət̬i] *n, pl* **-ties** : anualidad *f*
annul [əˈnʌl] *vt* **anulled; anulling** : anular, invalidar
annulment [əˈnʌlmənt] *n* : anulación *f*
anode [ˈæˌnoːd] *n* : ánodo
anoint [əˈnɔɪnt] *vt* : ungir
anomalous [əˈnɑmələs] *adj* : anómalo
anomaly [əˈnɑməli] *n, pl* **-lies** : anomalía *f*
anonymity [ˌænəˈnɪmət̬i] *n* : anonimato *m*
anonymous [əˈnɑnəməs] *adj* : anónimo — **anonymously** *adv*
anorexia [ˌænəˈrɛksiə] *n* : anorexia *f*
anorexic [ˌænəˈrɛksɪk] *adj* : anoréxico
another[1] [əˈnʌðər] *adj* : otro
another[2] *pron* : otro, otra
answer[1] [ˈæntsər] *vt* **1** : contestar (a), responder (a) ⟨to answer the telephone : contestar el teléfono⟩ **2** FULFILL : satisfacer **3 to answer for** : ser responsable de, pagar por ⟨she'll answer for that mistake : pagará por ese error⟩ — *vi* : contestar, responder
answer[2] *n* **1** REPLY : respuesta *f*, contestación *f* **2** SOLUTION : solución *f*
answerable [ˈæntsərəbəl] *adj* : responsable
ant [ˈænt] *n* : hormiga *f*
antacid [æntˈæsəd, ˈænˌtæ-] *n* : antiácido *m*
antagonism [ænˈtægəˌnɪzəm] *n* : antagonismo *m*, hostilidad *f*
antagonist [ænˈtægənɪst] *n* : antagonista *mf*

antagonistic [æn,tægə'nɪstɪk] *adj* : antagonista, hostil
antagonize [æn'tægə,naɪz] *vt* **-nized; -nizing** : antagonizar
antarctic [ænt'ɑrktɪk, -'ɑrt̬ɪk] *adj* : antártico
antarctic circle *n* : círculo *m* antártico
anteater ['ænt,i:t̬ər] *n* : oso *m* hormiguero
antebellum [,æntɪ'bɛləm] *adj* : prebélico
antecedent[1] [,æntə'si:dənt] *adj* : antecedente, precedente
antecedent[2] *n* : antecedente *mf*; precursor *m*, -sora *f*
antelope ['æntəl,o:p] *n, pl* **-lope** *or* **-lopes** : antílope *m*
antenna [æn'tɛnə] *n, pl* **-nae** [-,ni:, -,naɪ] *or* **-nas** : antena *f*
anterior [æn'tɪriər] *adj* : anterior
anthem ['ænθəm] *n* : himno *m* ⟨national anthem : himno nacional⟩
anther ['ænθər] *n* : antera *f*
anthill ['ænt,hɪl] *n* : hormiguero *m*
anthology [æn'θɑləʤi] *n, pl* **-gies** : antología *f*
anthracite ['ænθrə,saɪt] *n* : antracita *f*
anthropoid[1] ['ænθrə,pɔɪd] *adj* : antropoide
anthropoid[2] *n* : antropoide *mf*
anthropological [,ænθrəpə'lɑʤɪkəl] *adj* : antropológico
anthropologist [,ænθrə'pɑləʤɪst] *n* : antropólogo *m*, -ga *f*
anthropology [,ænθrə'pɑləʤi] *n* : antropología *f*
antiabortion [,æntiə'bɔrʃən, ,æntaɪ-] *adj* : antiaborto
antiaircraft [,ænti'ær,kræft, ,æntaɪ-] *adj* : antiaéreo
anti–American [,æntiə'mɛrɪkən, ,æntaɪ-] *adj* : antiamericano
antibiotic[1] [,æntibaɪ'ɑt̬ɪk, ,æntaɪ-, -bi-] *adj* : antibiótico
antibiotic[2] *n* : antibiótico *m*
antibody ['ænti,bɑdi] *n, pl* **-bodies** : anticuerpo *m*
antic[1] ['æntɪk] *adj* : extravagante, juguetón
antic[2] *n* : payasada *f*, travesura *f*
anticipate [æn'tɪsə,peɪt] *vt* **-pated; -pating 1** FORESEE : anticipar, prever **2** EXPECT : esperar, contar con
anticipation [æn,tɪsə'peɪʃən] *n* **1** FORESIGHT : previsión *f* **2** EXPECTATION : anticipación *f*, expectación *f*, esperanza *f*
anticipatory [æn'tɪsəpə,tori] *adj* : en anticipación, en previsión
anticlimactic [,æntiklaɪ'mæktɪk] *adj* : anticlimático, decepcionante
anticlimax [,ænti'klaɪ,mæks] *n* : anticlímax *m*
anticommunism [,ænti'kɑmjə,nɪzəm, ,æntaɪ-] *n* : anticomunismo *m*
anticommunist[1] [,ænti'kɑmjənɪst, ,æntaɪ-] *adj* : anticomunista
anticommunist[2] *n* : anticomunista *mf*
antidemocratic [,ænti,dɛmə'kræt̬ɪk, ,æntaɪ-] *adj* : antidemocrático
antidepressant [,æntidi'prɛsənt] *n* : antidepresivo *m* — **antidepressant** *adj*
antidote ['æntɪ,do:t] *n* : antídoto *m*
antidrug [,ænti'drʌg, ,æntaɪ-; 'ænti ,drʌg, 'æntaɪ-] *adj* : antidrogas
antifascist [,ænti'fæʃɪst, ,æntaɪ-] *adj* : antifascista
antifeminist [,ænti'fɛmənɪst, ,æntaɪ-] *adj* : antifeminista
antifreeze ['ænti,fri:z] *n* : anticongelante *m*
antigen ['æntɪʤən, -,ʤɛn] *n* : antígeno *m*
antihistamine [,ænti'hɪstə,mi:n, -mən] *n* : antihistamínico *m*
anti–imperialism [,æntiɪm'pɪriə,lɪzəm, ,æntaɪ-] *n* : antiimperialismo *m*
anti–imperialist [,æntiɪm'pɪriəlɪst, ,æntaɪ-] *adj* : antiimperialista
anti–inflammatory [,ætiɪn'flæmətori] *adj* : antiinflamatorio
anti–inflationary [,æntiɪn'fleɪʃə,nɛri, ,æntaɪ-] *adj* : antiinflacionario
antimony ['æntə,mo:ni] *n* : antimonio *m*
antipathy [æn'tɪpəθi] *n, pl* **-thies** : antipatía *f*, aversión *f*
antiperspirant [,ænti'pərspərənt, ,æntaɪ-] *n* : antitranspirante *m*
antiquarian[1] [,æntə'kwɛriən] *adj* : antiguo, anticuario ⟨an antiquarian book : un libro antiguo⟩
antiquarian[2] *n* : anticuario *m*, -ria *f*
antiquary ['æntə,kwɛri] *n* → **antiquarian**[2]
antiquated ['æntə,kweɪt̬əd] *adj* : anticuado, pasado de moda
antique[1] [æn'ti:k] *adj* **1** OLD : antiguo, de época ⟨an antique mirror : un espejo antiguo⟩ **2** OLD-FASHIONED : anticuado, pasado de moda
antique[2] *n* : antigüedad *f*
antiquity [æn'tɪkwət̬i] *n, pl* **-ties** : antigüedad
antirevolutionary [,ænti,rɛvə'lu:ʃə,nɛri, ,æntaɪ-] *adj* : antirrevolucionario
anti–Semitic [,æntisə'mɪt̬ɪk, ,æntaɪ-] *adj* : antisemita
anti–Semitism [,ænti'sɛmə,tɪzəm, ,æntaɪ-] *n* : antisemitismo *m*
antiseptic[1] [,æntə'sɛptɪk] *adj* : antiséptico — **antiseptically** [-tɪkli] *adv*
antiseptic[2] *n* : antiséptico *m*
antismoking [,ænti'smo:kɪŋ, ,æntaɪ-] *adj* : antitabaco
antisocial [,ænti'so:ʃəl, ,æntaɪ-] *adj* **1** : antisocial **2** UNSOCIABLE : poco sociable
antitheft [,ænti'θɛft, ,æntaɪ-] *adj* : antirrobo
antithesis [æn'tɪθəsɪs] *n, pl* **-eses** [-,si:z] : antítesis *f*
antitoxin [,ænti'tɑksən, ,æntaɪ-] *n* : antitoxina *f*
antitrust [,ænti'trʌst, ,æntaɪ-] *adj* : antimonopolista
antler ['æntlər] *n* : asta *f*, cuerno *m*

antonym ['æntə,nɪm] *n* : antónimo *m*
anus ['eɪnəs] *n* : ano *m*
anvil ['ænvəl, -vɪl] *n* : yunque *m*
anxiety [æŋk'zaɪəṭi] *n, pl* **-eties** **1** UNEASINESS : inquietud *f*, preocupación *f*, ansiedad *f* **2** APPREHENSION : ansiedad *f*, angustia *f*
anxious ['æŋkʃəs] *adj* **1** WORRIED : inquieto, preocupado, ansioso **2** WORRISOME : preocupante, inquietante **3** EAGER : ansioso, deseoso
anxiously ['æŋkʃəsli] *adv* : con inquietud, con ansiedad
any[1] ['ɛni] *adv* **1** : algo ⟨is it any better? : ¿está (algo) mejor?⟩ **2** : para nada ⟨it is not any good : no sirve para nada⟩
any[2] *adj* **1** : alguno ⟨is there any doubt? : ¿hay alguna duda?⟩ ⟨call me if you have any questions : llámeme si tiene alguna pregunta⟩ **2** : cualquier ⟨I can answer any question : puedo responder a cualquier pregunta⟩ **3** : todo ⟨in any case : en todo caso⟩ **4** : ningún ⟨he would not accept it under any circumstances : no lo aceptaría bajo ninguna circunstancia⟩
any[3] *pron* **1** : alguno *m*, -na *f* ⟨are there any left? : ¿queda alguno?⟩ **2** : ninguno *m*, -na *f* ⟨I don't want any : no quiero ninguno⟩
anybody ['ɛni,bʌdi, -,bɑ-] → **anyone**
anyhow ['ɛni,haʊ] *adv* **1** HAPHAZARDLY : de cualquier manera **2** IN ANY CASE : de todos modos, en todo caso
anymore [,ɛni'mor] *adv* **1** : ya, ya más ⟨he doesn't dance anymore : ya no baila más⟩ **2** : todavía ⟨do they sing anymore? : ¿cantan todavía?⟩
anyone ['ɛni,wʌn] *pron* **1** : alguien ⟨is anyone here? : ¿hay alguien aquí?⟩ ⟨if anyone wants to come : si alguno quiere venir⟩ **2** : cualquiera ⟨anyone can play : cualquiera puede jugar⟩ **3** : nadie ⟨I don't want anyone here : no quiero a nadie aquí⟩
anyplace ['ɛni,pleɪs] → **anywhere**
anything ['ɛni,θɪŋ] *pron* **1** : algo, alguna cosa ⟨do you want anything? : ¿quieres algo?, ¿quieres alguna cosa?⟩ **2** : nada ⟨hardly anything : casi nada⟩ **3** : cualquier cosa ⟨I eat anything : como de todo⟩
anytime ['ɛni,taɪm] *adv* : en cualquier momento, a cualquier hora, cuando sea
anyway ['ɛni,weɪ] → **anyhow**
anywhere ['ɛni,*h*wɛr] *adv* **1** : en algún sitio, en alguna parte ⟨do you see it anywhere? : ¿lo ves en alguna parte?⟩ **2** : en ningún sitio, por ninguna parte ⟨I can't find it anywhere : no puedo encontrarlo por ninguna parte⟩ **3** : en cualquier parte, dondequiera, donde sea ⟨put it anywhere : ponlo dondequiera⟩
aorta [eɪ'ɔrṭə] *n, pl* **-tas** *or* **-tae** [-ṭi, -ṭaɪ] : aorta *f*
Apache [ə'pæʧi] *n, pl* **Apache** *or* **Apaches** : apache *mf*
apart [ə'pɑrt] *adv* **1** SEPARATELY : aparte, separadamente **2** ASIDE : aparte, a un lado **3 to fall apart** : deshacerse, hacerse pedazos **4 to take apart** : desmontar, desmantelar
apartheid [ə'pɑr,teɪt, -,taɪt] *n* : apartheid *m*
apartment [ə'pɑrtmənt] *n* : apartamento *m*, departamento *m*, piso *m Spain*
apathetic [,æpə'θɛṭɪk] *adj* : apático, indiferente — **apathetically** [-ṭɪkli] *adv*
apathy ['æpəθi] *n* : apatía *f*, indiferencia *f*
ape[1] ['eɪp] *vt* **aped; aping** : imitar, remedar
ape[2] *n* : simio *m*; mono *m*, -na *f*
aperitif [ə,pɛrə'ti:f] *n* : aperitivo *m*
aperture ['æpərʧər, -,ʧʊr] *n* : abertura *f*, rendija *f*, apertura *f* (en fotografía)
apex ['eɪ,pɛks] *n, pl* **apexes** *or* **apices** ['eɪpə,si:z, 'æ-] : ápice *m*, cúspide *f*, cima *f*
aphid ['eɪfɪd, 'æ-] *n* : áfido *m*
aphorism ['æfə,rɪzəm] *n* : aforismo *m*
aphrodisiac [,æfrə'di:zi,æk, -'dɪ-] *n* : afrodisíaco *m*
apiary ['eɪpi,ɛri] *n, pl* **-aries** : apiario *m*, colmenar *m*
apiece [ə'pi:s] *adv* : cada uno
aplenty [ə'plɛnti] *adj* : en abundancia
aplomb [ə'plɑm, -'plʌm] *n* : aplomo *m*
apocalypse [ə'pɑkə,lɪps] *n* : apocalipsis *m*
apocalyptic [ə,pɑkə'lɪptɪk] *adj* : apocalíptico
apocrypha [ə'pɑkrəfə] *n* : textos *mpl* apócrifos
apocryphal [ə'pɑkrəfəl] *adj* : apócrifo
apologetic [ə,pɑlə'ʤɛṭɪk] *adj* : lleno de disculpas
apologetically [ə,pɑlə'ʤɛṭɪkli] *adv* : disculpándose, con aire de disculpas
apologize [ə'pɑlə,ʤaɪz] *vi* **-gized; -gizing** : disculparse, pedir perdón
apology [ə'pɑləʤi] *n, pl* **-gies** : disculpa *f*, excusa *f*
apoplectic [,æpə'plɛktɪk] *adj* : apoplético
apoplexy ['æpə,plɛksi] *n* : apoplejía *f*
apostasy [ə'pɑstəsi] *n, pl* **-sies** : apostasía *f*
apostate [ə'pɑs,teɪt] *n* : apóstata *mf*
apostle [ə'pɑsəl] *n* : apóstol *m*
apostolic [,æpə'stɑlɪk] *adj* : apostólico
apostrophe [ə'pɑstrə,fi:] *n* : apóstrofo *m* (ortográfico)
apothecary [ə'pɑθə,kɛri] *n, pl* **-caries** : boticario *m*, -ria *f*
appall [ə'pɔl] *vt* : consternar, horrorizar
apparatus [,æpə'ræṭəs, -'reɪ-] *n, pl* **-tuses** *or* **-tus** : aparato *m*, equipo *m*
apparel [ə'pærəl] *n* : atavío *m*, ropa *f*
apparent [ə'pærənt] *adj* **1** VISIBLE : visible **2** OBVIOUS : claro, evidente, manifiesto **3** SEEMING : aparente, ostensible

apparently [ə'pærəntli] *adv* : aparentemente, al parecer

apparition [ˌæpə'rɪʃən] *n* : aparición *f*, visión *f*

appeal[1] [ə'pi:l] *vt* : apelar ⟨to appeal a decision : apelar contra una decisión⟩ — *vi* **1 to appeal for** : pedir, solicitar **2 to appeal to** : atraer a ⟨that doesn't appeal to me : eso no me atrae⟩

appeal[2] *n* **1** : apelación *f* (en derecho) **2** PLEA : ruego *m*, súplica *f* **3** ATTRACTION : atracción *f*, atractivo *m*, interés *m*

appear [ə'pɪr] *vi* **1** : aparecer, aparecerse, presentarse ⟨he suddenly appeared : apareció de repente⟩ **2** COME OUT : aparecer, salir, publicarse **3** : comparecer (ante el tribunal), actuar (en el teatro) **4** SEEM : parecer

appearance [ə'pɪrənts] *n* **1** APPEARING : aparición *f*, presentación *f*, comparecencia *f* (ante un tribunal), publicación *f* (de un libro) **2** LOOK : apariencia *f*, aspecto *m*

appease [ə'pi:z] *vt* **-peased; -peasing 1** CALM, PACIFY : aplacar, apaciguar, sosegar **2** SATISFY : satisfacer, mitigar

appeasement [ə'pi:zmənt] *n* : aplacamiento *m*, apaciguamiento *m*

append [ə'pɛnd] *vt* : agregar, añadir, adjuntar

appendage [ə'pɛndɪʤ] *n* **1** ADDITION : apéndice *m*, añadidura *f* **2** LIMB : miembro *m*, extremidad *f*

appendectomy [ˌæpən'dɛktəmi] *n, pl* **-mies** : apendicectomía *f*

appendicitis [əˌpɛndə'saɪt̬əs] *n* : apendicitis *f*

appendix [ə'pɛndɪks] *n, pl* **-dixes** *or* **-dices** [-dəˌsi:z] : apéndice *m*

appetite ['æpəˌtaɪt] *n* **1** CRAVING : apetito *m*, deseo *m*, ganas *fpl* **2** PREFERENCE : gusto *m*, preferencia *f* ⟨the cultural appetites of today : los gustos culturales de hoy⟩

appetizer ['æpəˌtaɪzər] *n* : aperitivo *m*, entremés *m*, botana *f Mex*, tapa *f Spain*

appetizing ['æpəˌtaɪzɪŋ] *adj* : apetecible, apetitoso — **appetizingly** [-zɪŋli] *adv*

applaud [ə'plɔd] *v* : aplaudir

applause [ə'plɔz] *n* : aplauso *m*

apple ['æpəl] *n* : manzana *f*

appliance [ə'plaɪənts] *n* **1** : aparato *m* **2 household appliance** : electrodoméstico *m*, aparato *m* electrodoméstico

applicability [ˌæplɪkə'bɪlət̬i, əˌplɪkə-] *n* : aplicabilidad *f*

applicable ['æplɪkəbəl, ə'plɪkə-] *adj* : aplicable, pertinente

applicant ['æplɪkənt] *n* : solicitante *mf*, aspirante *mf*, postulante *mf*; candidato *m*, -ta *f*

application [ˌæplə'keɪʃən] *n* **1** USE : aplicación *f*, empleo *m*, uso *m* **2** DILIGENCE : aplicación *f*, diligencia *f*, dedicación *f* **3** REQUEST : solicitud *f*, petición *f*, demanda *f*

applicator ['æpləˌkeɪt̬ər] *n* : aplicador *m*

appliqué[1] [ˌæplə'keɪ] *vt* : decorar con apliques

appliqué[2] *n* : aplique *m*

apply [ə'plaɪ] *v* **-plied; -plying** *vt* **1** : aplicar (una sustancia, los frenos, el conocimiento) **2 to apply oneself** : dedicarse, aplicarse — *vi* **1** : aplicarse, referirse ⟨the rules apply to everyone : las reglas se aplican a todos⟩ **2 to apply for** : solicitar, pedir

appoint [ə'pɔɪnt] *vt* **1** NAME : nombrar, designar **2** FIX, SET : fijar, señalar, designar ⟨to appoint a date : fijar una fecha⟩ **3** EQUIP : equipar ⟨a well-appointed office : una oficina bien equipada⟩

appointee [əˌpɔɪn'ti:, ˌæ-] *n* : persona *f* designada

appointment [ə'pɔɪntmənt] *n* **1** APPOINTING : nombramiento *m*, designación *f* **2** ENGAGEMENT : cita *f*, hora *f* **3** POST : puesto *m*

apportion [ə'porʃən] *vt* : distribuir, repartir

apportionment [ə'porʃənmənt] *n* : distribución *f*, repartición *f*, reparto *m*

apposite ['æpəzət] *adj* : apropiado, oportuno, pertinente — **appositely** *adv*

appraisal [ə'preɪzəl] *n* : evaluación *f*, valoración *f*, tasación *f*, apreciación *f*

appraise [ə'preɪz] *vt* **-praised; -praising** : evaluar, valorar, tasar, apreciar

appraiser [ə'preɪzər] *n* : tasador *m*, -dora *f*

appreciable [ə'pri:ʃəbəl, -'prɪʃiə-] *adj* : apreciable, sensible, considerable — **appreciably** [-bli] *adv*

appreciate [ə'pri:ʃiˌeɪt, -'prɪ-] *v* **-ated; -ating** *vt* **1** VALUE : apreciar, valorar **2** : agradecer ⟨we appreciate his frankness : agradecemos su franqueza⟩ **3** UNDERSTAND : darse cuenta de, entender — *vi* : apreciarse, valorizarse

appreciation [əˌpri:ʃi'eɪʃən, -ˌprɪ-] *n* **1** GRATITUDE : agradecimiento *m*, reconocimiento *m* **2** VALUING : apreciación *f*, valoración *f*, estimación *f* ⟨art appreciation : apreciación artística⟩ **3** UNDERSTANDING : comprensión *f*, entendimiento *m*

appreciative [ə'pri:ʃət̬ɪv, -'prɪ-; ə'pri:ʃiˌeɪ-] *adj* **1** : apreciativo ⟨an appreciative audience : un público apreciativo⟩ **2** GRATEFUL : agradecido **3** ADMIRING : de admiración

apprehend [ˌæprɪ'hɛnd] *vt* **1** ARREST : aprehender, detener, arrestar **2** DREAD : temer **3** COMPREHEND : comprender, entender

apprehension [ˌæprɪ'hɛnʧən] *n* **1** ARREST : arresto *m*, detención *f*, aprehensión *f* **2** ANXIETY : aprensión *f*, ansiedad *f*, temor *m* **3** UNDERSTANDING : comprensión *f*, percepción *f*

apprehensive [ˌæprɪ'hɛntsɪv] *adj* : aprensivo, inquieto — **apprehensively** *adv*

apprentice[1] [ə'prɛntɪs] *vt* **-ticed; -ticing** : colocar de aprendiz
apprentice[2] *n* : aprendiz *m*, -diza *f*
apprenticeship [ə'prɛntɪs,ʃɪp] *n* : aprendizaje *f*
apprise [ə'praɪz] *vt* **-prised; -prising** : informar, avisar
approach[1] [ə'pro:ʧ] *vt* **1** NEAR : acercarse a **2** APPROXIMATE : aproximarse a **3** : abordar, dirigirse a ⟨I approached my boss with the proposal : me dirigí a mi jefe con la propuesta⟩ **4** TACKLE : abordar, enfocar, considerar — *vi* : acercarse, aproximarse
approach[2] *n* **1** NEARING : acercamiento *m*, aproximación *f* **2** POSITION : enfoque *m*, planteamiento *m* **3** OFFER : propuesta *f*, oferta *f* **4** ACCESS : acceso *m*, vía *f* de acceso
approachable [ə'pro:ʧəbəl] *adj* : accesible, asequible
approbation [,æprə'beɪʃən] *n* : aprobación *f*
appropriate[1] [ə'pro:pri,eɪt] *vt* **-ated; -ating 1** SEIZE : apropiarse de **2** ALLOCATE : destinar, asignar
appropriate[2] [ə'pro:priət] *adj* : apropiado, adecuado, idóneo — **appropriately** *adv*
appropriateness [ə'pro:priətnəs] *n* : idoneidad *f*, propiedad *f*
appropriation [ə,pro:pri'eɪʃən] *n* **1** SEIZURE : apropiación *f* **2** ALLOCATION : asignación *f*
approval [ə'pru:vəl] *n* **1** : aprobación *f*, visto *m* bueno **2 on approval** : a prueba
approve [ə'pru:v] *vt* **-proved; -proving 1** : aprobar, sancionar, darle el visto bueno a **2 to approve of** : consentir en, aprobar ⟨he doesn't approve of smoking : está en contra del tabaco⟩
approximate[1] [ə'prɑksə,meɪt] *vt* **-mated; -mating** : aproximarse a, acercarse a
approximate[2] [ə'prɑksəmət] *adj* : aproximado
approximately [ə'prɑksəmətli] *adv* : aproximadamente, más o menos
approximation [ə,prɑksə'meɪʃən] *n* : aproximación *f*
appurtenance [ə'pərtənənts] *n* : accesorio *m*
apricot ['æprə,kɑt, 'eɪ-] *n* : albaricoque *m*, chabacano *m Mex*
April ['eɪprəl] *n* : abril *m*
apron ['eɪprən] *n* : delantal *m*, mandil *m*
apropos[1] [,æprə'po:, 'æprə,po:] *adv* : a propósito
apropos[2] *adj* : pertinente, oportuno, acertado
apropos of *prep* : a propósito de
apt ['æpt] *adj* **1** FITTING : apto, apropiado, acertado, oportuno **2** LIABLE : propenso, inclinado **3** CLEVER, QUICK : listo, despierto
aptitude ['æptə,tu:d, -,tju:d] *n* **1** : aptitud *f*, capacidad *f* ⟨aptitude test : prueba de aptitud⟩ **2** TALENT : talento *m*, facilidad *f*
aptly ['æptli] *adv* : acertadamente
aqua ['ækwə, 'ɑ-] *n* : color *m* aguamarina
aquarium [ə'kwæriəm] *n, pl* **-iums** *or* **-ia** [-iə] : acuario *m*
Aquarius [ə'kwæriəs] *n* : Acuario *mf*
aquatic [ə'kwɑt̬ɪk, -'kwæ-] *adj* : acuático
aqueduct ['ækwə,dʌkt] *n* : acueducto *m*
aqueous ['eɪkwiəs, 'æ-] *adj* : acuoso
aquiline ['ækwə,laɪn, -lən] *adj* : aguileño
Arab[1] ['ærəb] *adj* : árabe
Arab[2] *n* : árabe *mf*
arabesque [,ærə'bɛsk] *n* : arabesco *m*
Arabian[1] [ə'reɪbiən] *adj* : árabe
Arabian[2] *n* → **Arab**[2]
Arabic[1] ['ærəbɪk] *adj* : árabe
Arabic[2] *n* : árabe *m* (idioma)
arable ['ærəbəl] *adj* : arable, cultivable
arbiter ['ɑrbət̬ər] *n* : árbitro *m*, -tra *f*
arbitrary ['ɑrbə,trɛri] *adj* : arbitrario — **arbitrarily** [,ɑrbə'trɛrəli] *adv*
arbitrate ['ɑrbə,treɪt] *v* **-trated; -trating** : arbitrar
arbitration [,ɑrbə'treɪʃən] *n* : arbitraje *m*
arbitrator ['ɑrbə,treɪt̬ər] *n* : árbitro *m*, -tra *f*
arbor ['ɑrbər] *n* : cenador *m*, pérgola *f*
arboreal [ɑr'boriəl] *adj* : arbóreo
arc[1] ['ɑrk] *vi* **arced; arcing** : formar un arco
arc[2] *n* : arco *m*
arcade [ɑr'keɪd] *n* **1** ARCHES : arcada *f* **2** MALL : galería *f* comercial
arcane [ɑr'keɪn] *adj* : arcano, secreto, misterioso
arch[1] ['ɑrʧ] *vt* : arquear, enarcar — *vi* : formar un arco, arquearse
arch[2] *adj* **1** CHIEF : principal **2** MISCHIEVOUS : malicioso, pícaro
arch[3] *n* : arco *m*
archaeological [,ɑrkiə'lɑʤɪkəl] *adj* : arqueológico
archaeologist [,ɑrki'ɑləʤɪst] *n* : arqueólogo *m*, -ga *f*
archaeology *or* **archeology** [,ɑrki'ɑləʤi] *n* : arqueología *f*
archaic [ɑr'keɪɪk] *adj* : arcaico — **archaically** [-ɪkli] *adv*
archangel ['ɑrk,eɪnʤəl] *n* : arcángel *m*
archbishop [ɑrʧ'bɪʃəp] *n* : arzobispo *m*
archdiocese [ɑrʧ'daɪəsəs, -,si:z, -,si:s] *n* : archidiócesis *f*
archer ['ɑrʧər] *n* : arquero *m*, -ra *f*
archery ['ɑrʧəri] *n* : tiro *m* al arco
archetypal [,ɑrkɪ'taɪpəl] *adj* : arquetípico
archetype ['ɑrkɪ,taɪp] *n* : arquetipo *m*
archipelago [,ɑrkə'pɛlə,go:, ,ɑrʧə-] *n, pl* **-goes** *or* **-gos** [-go:z] : archipiélago *m*
architect ['ɑrkə,tɛkt] *n* : arquitecto *m*, -ta *f*
architectural [,ɑrkə'tɛkʧərəl] *adj* : arquitectónico — **architecturally** *adv*
architecture ['ɑrkə,tɛkʧər] *n* : arquitectura *f*
archive ['ɑr,kaɪv] *n or* **archives** ['ɑr,kaɪvz] *npl* : archivo *m*

archivist [ˈɑrkəvɪst, -ˌkaɪ-] *n* : archivero *m*, -ra *f*; archivista *mf*

archway [ˈɑrʧˌweɪ] *n* : arco *m*, pasadizo *m* abovedado

arctic [ˈɑrktɪk, ˈɑrt̬-] *adj* **1** : ártico ⟨arctic regions : zonas árticas⟩ **2** FRIGID : glacial

arctic circle *n* : círculo *m* ártico

ardent [ˈɑrdənt] *adj* **1** PASSIONATE : ardiente, fogoso, apasionado **2** FERVENT : ferviente, fervoroso — **ardently** *adv*

ardor [ˈɑrdər] *n* : ardor *m*, pasión *f*, fervor *m*

arduous [ˈɑrʤʊəs] *adj* : arduo, duro, riguroso — **arduously** *adv*

arduousness [ˈɑrʤʊəsnəs] *n* : dureza *f*, rigor *m*

are → **be**

area [ˈæriə] *n* **1** SURFACE : área *f*, superficie *f* **2** REGION : área *f*, región *f*, zona *f* **3** FIELD : área *f*, terreno *m*, campo *m* (de conocimiento)

area code *n* : código *m* de la zona, prefijo *m Spain*

arena [əˈriːnə] *n* **1** : arena *f*, estadio *m* ⟨sports arena : estadio deportivo⟩ **2** : arena *f*, ruedo *m* ⟨the political arena : el ruedo político⟩

Argentine [ˈɑrʤənˌtaɪn, -ˌtiːn] *or* **Argentinean** *or* **Argentinian** [ˌɑrʤənˈtɪniən] *n* : argentino *m*, -na *f* — **Argentine** *or* **Argentinean** *or* **Argentinian** *adj*

argon [ˈɑrˌgɑn] *n* : argón *m*

argot [ˈɑrgət, -ˌgoː] *n* : argot *m*

arguable [ˈɑrgjʊəbəl] *adj* : discutible

argue [ˈɑrˌgjuː] *v* **-gued; -guing** *vi* **1** REASON : argüir, argumentar, razonar **2** DISPUTE : discutir, pelear(se), alegar — *vt* **1** SUGGEST : sugerir **2** MAINTAIN : alegar, argüir, sostener **3** DISCUSS : discutir, debatir

argument [ˈɑrgjəmənt] *n* **1** REASONING : argumento *m*, razonamiento *m* **2** DISCUSSION : discusión *f*, debate *m* **3** QUARREL : pelea *f*, riña *f*, disputa *f*

argumentative [ˌɑrgjəˈmɛntət̬ɪv] *adj* : discutidor

argyle [ˈɑrˌgaɪl] *n* : diseño *m* de rombos

aria [ˈɑriə] *n* : aria *f*

arid [ˈærəd] *adj* : árido

aridity [əˈrɪdət̬i, æ-] *n* : aridez *f*

Aries [ˈɛriːz, -iˌiːz] *n* : Aries *mf*

arise [əˈraɪz] *vi* **arose** [əˈroːz]; **arisen** [əˈrɪzən]; **arising** **1** ASCEND : ascender, subir, elevarse **2** ORIGINATE : originarse, surgir, presentarse **3** GET UP : levantarse

aristocracy [ˌærəˈstɑkrəsi] *n, pl* **-cies** : aristocracia *f*

aristocrat [əˈrɪstəˌkræt] *n* : aristócrata *mf*

aristocratic [əˌrɪstəˈkræt̬ɪk] *adj* : aristocrático, noble

arithmetic[1] [ˌærɪθˈmɛt̬ɪk] *or* **arithmetical** [-t̬ɪkəl] *adj* : aritmético

arithmetic[2] [əˈrɪθməˌtɪk] *n* : aritmética

ark [ˈɑrk] *n* : arca *f*

arm[1] [ˈɑrm] *vt* : armar — *vi* : armarse

arm[2] *n* **1** : brazo *m* (del cuerpo o de un sillón), manga *f* (de una prenda) **2** BRANCH : rama *f*, sección *f* **3** WEAPON : arma *f* ⟨to take up arms : tomar las armas⟩ **4** → **coat of arms**

armada [ɑrˈmɑdə, -ˈmeɪ-] *n* : armada *f*, flota *f*

armadillo [ˌɑrməˈdɪlo] *n, pl* **-los** : armadillo *m*

armament [ˈɑrməmənt] *n* : armamento *m*

armchair [ˈɑrmˌʧɛr] *n* : butaca *f*, sillón *m*

armed [ˈɑrmd] *adj* **1** : armado ⟨armed robbery : robo a mano armada⟩ **2** **armed forces** : fuerzas *fpl* armadas

Armenian [ɑrˈmiːniən] *n* : armenio *m*, -nia *f* — **Armenian** *adj*

armistice [ˈɑrməstɪs] *n* : armisticio *m*

armor [ˈɑrmər] *n* : armadura *f*, coraza *f*

armored [ˈɑrmərd] *adj* : blindado, acorazado

armory [ˈɑrməri] *n, pl* **-mories** : arsenal *m* (almacén), armería *f* (museo), fábrica *f* de armas

armpit [ˈɑrmˌpɪt] *n* : axila *f*, sobaco *m*

army [ˈɑrmi] *n, pl* **-mies** **1** : ejército *m* (militar) **2** MULTITUDE : legión *f*, multitud *f*, ejército *m*

aroma [əˈroːmə] *n* : aroma *f*

aromatic [ˌærəˈmæt̬ɪk] *adj* : aromático

around[1] [əˈraʊnd] *adv* **1** : de circunferencia ⟨a tree three feet around : un árbol de tres pies de circunferencia⟩ **2** : alrededor, a la redonda ⟨for miles around : por millas a la redonda⟩ ⟨all around : por todos lados, todo alrededor⟩ **3** : por ahí ⟨they're somewhere around : deben estar por ahí⟩ **4** APPROXIMATELY : más o menos, aproximadamente ⟨around 5 o'clock : a eso de las 5⟩ **5** **to turn around** : darse la vuelta, voltearse

around[2] *prep* **1** SURROUNDING : alrededor de, en torno a **2** THROUGH : por, en ⟨he traveled around Mexico : viajó por México⟩ ⟨around the house : en casa⟩ **3** : a la vuelta de ⟨around the corner : a la vuelta de la esquina⟩ **4** NEAR : alrededor de, cerca de

arousal [əˈraʊzəl] *n* : excitación *f*

arouse [əˈraʊz] *vt* **aroused; arousing** **1** AWAKE : despertar **2** EXCITE : despertar, suscitar, excitar

arraign [əˈreɪn] *vt* : hacer comparecer (ante un tribunal)

arraignment [əˈreɪnmənt] *n* : orden *m* de comparecencia, acusación *f*

arrange [əˈreɪnʤ] *vt* **-ranged; -ranging** **1** ORDER : arreglar, poner en orden, disponer **2** SETTLE : arreglar, fijar, concertar **3** ADAPT : arreglar, adaptar

arrangement [əˈreɪnʤmənt] *n* **1** ORDER : arreglo *m*, orden *m* **2** ARRANGING : disposición *f* ⟨floral arrangement : arreglo floral⟩ **3** AGREEMENT : arreglo *m*, acuerdo *m*, convenio *m* **4** **arrange-**

ments *npl* : preparativos *mpl*, planes *mpl*

array[1] [əˈreɪ] *vt* **1** ORDER : poner en orden, presentar, formar **2** GARB : vestir, ataviar, engalanar

array[2] *n* **1** ORDER : orden *m*, formación *f* **2** ATTIRE : atavío *m*, galas *mpl* **3** RANGE, SELECTION : selección *f*, serie *f*, gama *f* ⟨an array of problems : una serie de problemas⟩

arrears [əˈrɪrz] *npl* : atrasos *mpl* ⟨to be in arrears : estar atrasado en los pagos⟩

arrest[1] [əˈrɛst] *vt* **1** APPREHEND : arrestar, detener **2** CHECK, STOP : detener, parar

arrest[2] *n* **1** APPREHENSION : arresto *m*, detención *f* ⟨under arrest : detenido⟩ **2** STOPPING : paro *m*

arrival [əˈraɪvəl] *n* : llegada *f*, venida *f*, arribo *m*

arrive [əˈraɪv] *vi* **-rived; -riving 1** COME : llegar, arribar **2** SUCCEED : triunfar, tener éxito

arrogance [ˈærəgən*t*s] *n* : arrogancia *f*, soberbia *f*, altanería *f*, altivez *f*

arrogant [ˈærəgənt] *adj* : arrogante, soberbio, altanero, altivo — **arrogantly** *adv*

arrogate [ˈærəˌgeɪt] *vt* **-gated; -gating to arrogate to oneself** : arrogarse

arrow [ˈæro] *n* : flecha *f*

arrowhead [ˈæroˌhɛd] *n* : punta *f* de flecha

arroyo [əˈrɔɪo] *n* : arroyo *m*

arsenal [ˈɑrsənəl] *n* : arsenal *m*

arsenic [ˈɑrsənɪk] *n* : arsénico *m*

arson [ˈɑrsən] *n* : incendio *m* premeditado

arsonist [ˈɑrsənɪst] *n* : incendiario *m*, -ria *f*; pirómano *m*, -na *f*

art [ˈɑrt] *n* **1** : arte *m* **2** SKILL : destreza *f*, habilidad *f*, maña *f* **3 arts** *npl* : letras *fpl* (en la educación) **4 fine arts** : bellas artes *fpl*

arterial [ɑrˈtɪriəl] *adj* : arterial

arteriosclerosis [ɑrˌtɪriosklәˈroːsɪs] *n* : arteriosclerosis *f*

artery [ˈɑrt̬əri] *n, pl* **-teries 1** : arteria *f* **2** THOROUGHFARE : carretera *f* principal, arteria *f*

artesian well [ɑrˈtiːʒən] *n* : pozo *m* artesiano

artful [ˈɑrtfəl] *adj* **1** INGENIOUS : ingenioso, diestro **2** CRAFTY : astuto, taimado, ladino, artero — **artfully** *adv*

arthritic [ɑrˈθrɪt̬ɪk] *adj* : artrítico

arthritis [ɑrˈθraɪt̬əs] *n, pl* **-tides** [ɑrˈθrɪt̬əˌdiːz] : artritis *f*

arthropod [ˈɑrθrəˌpɑd] *n* : artrópodo *m*

artichoke [ˈɑrt̬əˌʧoːk] *n* : alcachofa *f*

article [ˈɑrtɪkəl] *n* **1** ITEM : artículo *m*, objeto *m* **2** ESSAY : artículo *m* **3** CLAUSE : artículo *m*, cláusula *f* **4** : artículo *m* ⟨definite article : artículo determinado⟩

articulate[1] [ɑrˈtɪkjəˌleɪt] *vt* **-lated; -lating 1** UTTER : articular, enunciar, expresar **2** CONNECT : articular (en anatomía)

articulate[2] [ɑrˈtɪkjələt] *adj* **to be articulate** : poder articular palabras, expresarse bien

articulately [ɑrˈtɪkjələtli] *adv* : elocuentemente, con fluidez

articulateness [ɑrˈtɪkjələtnəs] *n* : elocuencia *f*, fluidez *f*

articulation [ɑrˌtɪkjəˈleɪʃən] *n* **1** JOINT : articulación *f* **2** UTTERANCE : articulación *f*, declaración *f* **3** ENUNCIATION : articulación *f*, pronunciación *f*

artifact [ˈɑrt̬əˌfækt] *n* : artefacto *m*

artifice [ˈɑrt̬əfəs] *n* : artificio *m*

artificial [ˌɑrt̬əˈfɪʃəl] *adj* **1** SYNTHETIC : artificial, sintético **2** FEIGNED : artificial, falso, afectado

artificially [ˌɑrt̬əˈfɪʃəli] *adv* : artificialmente, con afectación

artillery [ɑrˈtɪləri] *n, pl* **-leries** : artillería *f*

artisan [ˈɑrt̬əzən, -sən] *n* : artesano *m*, -na *f*

artist [ˈɑrt̬ɪst] *n* : artista *mf*

artistic [ɑrˈtɪstɪk] *adj* : artístico — **artistically** [-tɪkli] *adv*

artistry [ˈɑrt̬əstri] *n* : maestría *f*, arte *m*

artless [ˈɑrtləs] *adj* : sencillo, natural, ingenuo, cándido — **artlessly** *adv*

artlessness [ˈɑrtləsnəs] *n* : ingenuidad *f*, candidez *f*

arty [ˈɑrt̬i] *adj* **artier; -est** : pretenciosamente artístico

as[1] [ˈæz] *adv* **1** : tan, tanto ⟨this one's not as difficult : éste no es tan difícil⟩ **2** : como ⟨some trees, as oak and pine : algunos árboles, como el roble y el pino⟩

as[2] *conj* **1** LIKE : como, igual que **2** WHEN, WHILE : cuando, mientras, a la vez que **3** BECAUSE : porque **4** THOUGH : aunque, por más que ⟨strange as it may appear : por extraño que parezca⟩ **5 as is** : tal como está

as[3] *prep* **1** : de ⟨I met her as a child : la conocí de pequeña⟩ **2** LIKE : como ⟨behave as a man : compórtate como un hombre⟩

as[4] *pron* : que ⟨in the same building as my brother : en el mismo edificio que mi hermano⟩

asbestos [æzˈbɛstəs, æs-] *n* : asbesto *m*, amianto *m*

ascend [əˈsɛnd] *vi* : ascender, subir — *vt* : subir, subir a, escalar

ascendancy [əˈsɛndən*t*si] *n* : ascendiente *m*, predominio *m*

ascendant[1] [əˈsɛndənt] *adj* **1** RISING : ascendente **2** DOMINANT : superior, dominante

ascendant[2] *n* **to be in the ascendant** : estar en alza, ir ganando predominio

ascension [əˈsɛnʧən] *n* : ascensión *f*

ascent [əˈsɛnt] *n* **1** RISE : ascensión *f*, subida *f*, ascenso *m* **2** SLOPE : cuesta *f*, pendiente *f*

ascertain [ˌæsərˈteɪn] *vt* : determinar, establecer, averiguar

ascertainable [ˌæsərˈteɪnəbəl] *adj* : determinable, averiguable

ascetic[1] [ə'sɛt̬ɪk] *adj* : ascético
ascetic[2] *n* : asceta *mf*
asceticism [ə'sɛt̬əˌsɪzəm] *n* : ascetismo *m*
ascribable [ə'skraɪbəbəl] *adj* : atribuible, imputable
ascribe [ə'skraɪb] *vt* **-cribed; -cribing** : atribuir, imputar
aseptic [eɪ'sɛptɪk] *adj* : aséptico
asexual [ˌeɪ'sɛkʃʊəl] *adj* : asexual
as for *prep* CONCERNING : en cuanto a, respecto a, para
ash ['æʃ] *n* **1** : ceniza *f* ⟨to reduce to ashes : reducir a cenizas⟩ **2** : fresno *m* (árbol)
ashamed [ə'ʃeɪmd] *adj* : avergonzado, abochornado, apenado — **ashamedly** [ə'ʃeɪmədli] *adv*
ashen ['æʃən] *adj* : lívido, ceniciento, pálido
ashore [ə'ʃor] *adv* **1** : en tierra **2 to go ashore** : desembarcar
ashtray ['æʃˌtreɪ] *n* : cenicero *m*
Asian[1] ['eɪʒən, -ʃən] *adj* : asiático
Asian[2] *n* : asiático *m*, -ca *f*
aside [ə'saɪd] *adv* **1** : a un lado ⟨to step aside : hacerse a un lado⟩ **2** : de lado, aparte ⟨jesting aside : bromas aparte⟩ **3 to set aside** : guardar, apartar, reservar
aside from *prep* **1** BESIDES : además de **2** EXCEPT : aparte de, menos
as if *conj* : como si
asinine ['æsənˌaɪn] *adj* : necio, estúpido
ask ['æsk] *vt* **1** : preguntar ⟨ask him if he's coming : pregúntale si viene⟩ **2** REQUEST : pedir, solicitar ⟨to ask a favor : pedir un favor⟩ **3** INVITE : invitar — *vi* **1** INQUIRE : preguntar ⟨I asked about her children : pregunté por sus niños⟩ **2** REQUEST : pedir ⟨we asked for help : pedimos ayuda⟩
askance [ə'skænts] *adv* **1** SIDELONG : de reojo, de soslayo **2** SUSPICIOUSLY : con recelo, con desconfianza
askew [ə'skju:] *adj* : torcido, ladeado
asleep [ə'sli:p] *adj* **1** : dormido, durmiendo **2 to fall asleep** : quedarse dormido
as of *prep* : desde, a partir de
asparagus [ə'spærəgəs] *n* : espárrago *m*
aspect ['æˌspɛkt] *n* : aspecto *m*
aspen ['æspən] *n* : álamo *m* temblón
asperity [æ'spɛrət̬i, ə-] *n, pl* **-ties** : aspereza *f*
aspersion [ə'spərʒən] *n* : difamación *f*, calumnia *f*
asphalt ['æsˌfɔlt] *n* : asfalto *m*
asphyxia [æ'sfɪksiə, ə-] *n* : asfixia *f*
asphyxiate [æ'sfɪksiˌeɪt] *v* **-ated; -ating** *vt* : asfixiar — *vi* : asfixiarse
asphyxiation [æˌsfɪksi'eɪʃən] *n* : asfixia *f*
aspirant ['æspərənt, ə'spaɪrənt] *n* : aspirante *mf*, pretendiente *mf*
aspiration [ˌæspə'reɪʃən] *n* **1** DESIRE : aspiración *f*, anhelo *m*, ambición *f* **2** BREATHING : aspiración *f*
aspire [ə'spaɪr] *vi* **-pired; -piring** : aspirar
aspirin ['æsprən, 'æspə-] *n, pl* **aspirin** *or* **aspirins** : aspirina *f*
ass ['æs] *n* **1** : asno *m* **2** IDIOT : imbécil *mf*, idiota *mf*
assail [ə'seɪl] *vt* : atacar, asaltar
assailant [ə'seɪlənt] *n* : asaltante *mf*, atacante *mf*
assassin [ə'sæsən] *n* : asesino *m*, -na *f*
assassinate [ə'sæsənˌeɪt] *vt* **-nated; -nating** : asesinar
assassination [əˌsæsən'eɪʃən] *n* : asesinato *m*
assault[1] [ə'sɔlt] *vt* : atacar, asaltar, agredir
assault[2] *n* : ataque *m*, asalto *m*, agresión *f*
assay[1] [æ'seɪ, 'æˌseɪ] *vt* : ensayar
assay[2] ['æˌseɪ, æ'seɪ] *n* : ensayo *m*
assemble [ə'sɛmbəl] *v* **-bled; -bling** *vt* **1** GATHER : reunir, recoger, juntar **2** CONSTRUCT : ensamblar, montar, construir — *vi* : reunirse, congregarse
assembly [ə'sɛmbli] *n, pl* **-blies 1** MEETING : reunión *f* **2** CONSTRUCTING : ensamblaje *m*, montaje *m*
assemblyman [ə'sɛmblimən] *n, pl* **-men** [-mən, -ˌmɛn] : asambleísta *m*
assemblywoman [ə'sɛmbliˌwʊmən] *n, pl* **-women** [-ˌwɪmən] : asambleísta *f*
assent[1] [ə'sɛnt] *vi* : asentir, consentir
assent[2] *n* : asentimiento *m*, aprobación *f*
assert [ə'sərt] *vt* **1** AFFIRM : afirmar, aseverar, mantener **2 to assert oneself** : imponerse, hacerse valer
assertion [ə'sərʃən] *n* : afirmación *f*, aseveración *f*, aserto *m*
assertive [ə'sərt̬ɪv] *adj* : firme, enérgico
assertiveness [ə'sərt̬ɪvnəs] *n* : seguridad *f* en sí mismo
assess [ə'sɛs] *vt* **1** IMPOSE : gravar (un impuesto), imponer **2** EVALUATE : evaluar, valorar, aquilatar
assessment [ə'sɛsmənt] *n* : evaluación *f*, valoración *f*
assessor [ə'sɛsər] *n* : evaluador *m*, -dora *f*; tasador *m*, -dora *f*
asset ['æˌsɛt] *n* **1** : ventaja *f*, recurso *m* **2 assets** *npl* : bienes *mpl*, activo *m* ⟨assets and liabilities : activo y pasivo⟩
assiduous [ə'sɪʤʊəs] *adj* : diligente, aplicado, asiduo — **assiduously** *adv*
assign [ə'saɪn] *vt* **1** APPOINT : designar, nombrar **2** ALLOT : asignar, señalar **3** ATTRIBUTE : atribuir, dar, conceder
assignment [ə'saɪnmənt] *n* **1** TASK : función *f*, tarea *f*, misión *f* **2** HOMEWORK : tarea *f*, asignación *f PRi*, deberes *mpl Spain* **3** APPOINTMENT : nombramiento *m* **4** ALLOCATION : asignación *f*
assimilate [ə'sɪməˌleɪt] *v* **-lated; -lating** *vt* : asimilar — *vi* : adaptarse, integrarse
assimilation [əˌsɪmə'leɪʃən] *n* : asimilación *f*
assist[1] [ə'sɪst] *vt* : asistir, ayudar
assist[2] *n* : asistencia *f*, contribución *f*

assistance [ə'sɪstənts] *n* : asistencia *f*, ayuda *f*, auxilio *m*
assistant [ə'sɪstənt] *n* : ayudante *mf*, asistente *mf*
associate[1] [ə'soːʃi,eɪt, -si-] *v* **-ated; -ating** *vt* **1** CONNECT, RELATE : asociar, relacionar **2 to be associated with** : estar relacionado con, estar vinculado a — *vi* **to associate with** : relacionarse con, frecuentar
associate[2] [ə'soːʃiət, -siət] *n* : asociado *m*, -da *f*; colega *mf*; socio *m*, -cia *f*
association [ə,soːʃi'eɪʃən, -si-] *n* **1** ORGANIZATION : asociación *f*, sociedad *f* **2** RELATIONSHIP : asociación *f*, relación *f*
as soon as *conj* : en cuanto, tan pronto como
assorted [ə'sɔrṭəd] *adj* : surtido
assortment [ə'sɔrtmənt] *n* : surtido *m*, variedad *f*, colección *f*
assuage [ə'sweɪʤ] *vt* **-suaged; -suaging 1** EASE : aliviar, mitigar **2** CALM : calmar, aplacar **3** SATISFY : saciar, satisfacer
assume [ə'suːm] *vt* **-sumed; -suming 1** SUPPOSE : suponer, asumir **2** UNDERTAKE : asumir, encargarse de **3** TAKE ON : adquirir, adoptar, tomar ⟨to assume importance : tomar importancia⟩ **4** FEIGN : adoptar, afectar, simular
assumption [ə'sʌmpʃən] *n* : asunción *f*, presunción *f*
assurance [ə'ʃʊrənts] *n* **1** CERTAINTY : certidumbre *f*, certeza *f* **2** CONFIDENCE : confianza *f*, aplomo *m*, seguridad *f*
assure [ə'ʃʊr] *vt* **-sured; -suring** : asegurar, garantizar ⟨I assure you that I'll do it : te aseguro que lo haré⟩
assured [ə'ʃʊrd] *adj* **1** CERTAIN : seguro, asegurado **2** CONFIDENT : confiado, seguro de sí mismo
aster ['æstər] *n* : aster *m*
asterisk ['æstə,rɪsk] *n* : asterisco *m*
astern [ə'stərn] *adv* **1** BEHIND : detrás, a popa **2** BACKWARDS : hacia atrás
asteroid ['æstə,rɔɪd] *n* : asteroide *m*
asthma ['æzmə] *n* : asma *m*
asthmatic [æz'mæṭɪk] *adj* : asmático
as though → **as if**
astigmatism [ə'stɪgmə,tɪzəm] *n* : astigmatismo *m*
as to *prep* **1** ABOUT : sobre, acerca de **2** → **according to**
astonish [ə'stɑnɪʃ] *vt* : asombrar, sorprender, pasmar
astonishing [ə'stɑnɪʃɪŋ] *adj* : asombroso, sorprendente, increíble — **astonishingly** *adv*
astonishment [ə'stɑnɪʃmənt] *n* : asombro *m*, estupefacción *f*, sorpresa *f*
astound [ə'staʊnd] *vt* : asombrar, pasmar, dejar estupefacto
astounding [ə'staʊndɪŋ] *adj* : asombroso, pasmoso — **astoundingly** *adv*
astraddle [ə'strædəl] *adv* : a horcajadas
astral ['æstrəl] *adj* : astral
astray [ə'streɪ] *adv & adj* : perdido, extraviado, descarriado
astride [ə'straɪd] *adv* : a horcajadas
astringency [ə'strɪnʤəntsi] *n* : astringencia *f*
astringent[1] [ə'strɪnʤənt] *adj* : astringente
astringent[2] *n* : astringente *m*
astrologer [ə'strɑləʤər] *n* : astrólogo *m*, -ga *f*
astrological [,æstrə'lɑʤɪkəl] *adj* : astrológico
astrology [ə'strɑləʤi] *n* : astrología *f*
astronaut ['æstrə,nɔt] *n* : astronauta *mf*
astronautic [,æstrə'nɔṭɪk] *or* **astronautical** [-ṭɪkəl] *adj* : astronáutico
astronautics [,æstrə'nɔṭɪks] *ns & pl* : astronáutica *f*
astronomer [ə'strɑnəmər] *n* : astrónomo *m*, -ma *f*
astronomical [,æstrə'nɑmɪkəl] *adj* **1** : astronómico **2** ENORMOUS : astronómico, enorme, gigantesco
astronomy [ə'strɑnəmi] *n, pl* **-mies** : astronomía *f*
astute [ə'stuːt, -'stjuːt] *adj* : astuto, sagaz, perspicaz — **astutely** *adv*
astuteness [ə'stuːtnəs, -'stjuːt-] *n* : astucia *f*, sagacidad *f*, perspicacia *f*
asunder [ə'sʌndər] *adv* : en dos, en pedazos ⟨to tear asunder : hacer pedazos⟩
as well as[1] *conj* : tanto como
as well as[2] *prep* BESIDES : además de, aparte de
as yet *adv* : aún, todavía
asylum [ə'saɪləm] *n* **1** REFUGE : refugio *m*, santuario *m*, asilo *m* **2 insane asylum** : manicomio *m*
asymmetrical [,eɪsə'mɛtrɪkəl] *or* **asymmetric** [-'mɛtrɪk] *adj* : asimétrico
asymmetry [,eɪ'sɪmətri] *n* : asimetría *f*
at ['æt] *prep* **1** : en ⟨at the top : en lo alto⟩ ⟨at peace : en paz⟩ ⟨at Ann's house : en casa de Ana⟩ **2** : a ⟨at the rear : al fondo⟩ ⟨at 10 o'clock : a las diez⟩ **3** : por ⟨at last : por fin⟩ ⟨to be surprised at something : sorprenderse por algo⟩ **4** : de ⟨he's laughing at you : está riéndose de ti⟩ **5** : para ⟨you're good at this : eres bueno para esto⟩
at all *adv* : en absoluto, para nada
ate → **eat**
atheism ['eɪθi,ɪzəm] *n* : ateísmo *m*
atheist ['eɪθiɪst] *n* : ateo *m*, atea *f*
atheistic [,eɪθi'ɪstɪk] *adj* : ateo
athlete ['æθ,liːt] *n* : atleta *mf*
athletic [æθ'lɛṭɪk] *adj* : atlético
athletics [æθ'lɛṭɪks] *ns & pl* : atletismo *m*
Atlantic [ət'læntɪk, æt-] *adj* : atlántico
atlas ['ætləs] *n* : atlas *m*
ATM [,eɪ,tiː'ɛm] *n* : cajero *m* automático
atmosphere ['ætmə,sfɪr] *n* **1** AIR : atmósfera *f*, aire *m* **2** AMBIENCE : ambiente *m*, atmósfera *f*, clima *m*
atmospheric [,ætmə'sfɪrɪk, -'sfɛr-] *adj* : atmosférico — **atmospherically** [-ɪkli] *adv*

atoll [ˈæˌtɔl, ˈeɪ-, -ˌtɑl] *n* : atolón *m*
atom [ˈæṭəm] *n* **1** : átomo *m* **2** SPECK : ápice *m*, pizca *f*
atomic [əˈtɑmɪk] *adj* : atómico
atomic bomb *n* : bomba *f* atómica
atomizer [ˈæṭəˌmaɪzər] *n* : atomizador *m*, pulverizador *m*
atone [əˈto:n] *vt* **atoned; atoning to atone for** : expiar
atonement [əˈto:nmənt] *n* : expiación *f*, desagravio *m*
atop[1] [əˈtɑp] *adj* : encima
atop[2] *prep* : encima de, sobre
atrium [ˈeɪtriəm] *n, pl* **atria** [-triə] *or* **atriums** **1** : atrio *m* **2** : aurícula *f* (del corazón)
atrocious [əˈtro:ʃəs] *adj* : atroz — **atrociously** *adv*
atrocity [əˈtrɑsəṭi] *n, pl* **-ties** : atrocidad *f*
atrophy[1] [ˈætrəfi] *vt* **-phied; -phying** : atrofiar
atrophy[2] *n, pl* **-phies** : atrofia *f*
attach [əˈtæʧ] *vt* **1** FASTEN : sujetar, atar, amarrar, pegar **2** JOIN : juntar, adjuntar **3** ATTRIBUTE : dar, atribuir ⟨I attached little importance to it : le di poca importancia⟩ **4** SEIZE : embargar **5 to become attached to someone** : encariñarse con alguien
attaché [ˌæṭəˈʃeɪ, ˌæˌtæ-, əˌtæ-] *n* : agregado *m*, -da *f*
attachment [əˈtæʧmənt] *n* **1** ACCESSORY : accesorio *m* **2** CONNECTION : conexión *f*, acoplamiento *m* **3** FONDNESS : apego *m*, cariño *m*, afición *f*
attack[1] [əˈtæk] *vt* **1** ASSAULT : atacar, asaltar, agredir **2** TACKLE : acometer, combatir, enfrentarse con
attack[2] *n* **1** : ataque *m*, asalto *m*, acometida *f* ⟨to launch an attack : lanzar un ataque⟩ **2** : ataque *m*, crisis *f* ⟨heart attack : ataque cardíaco, infarto⟩ ⟨attack of nerves : crisis nerviosa⟩
attacker [əˈtækər] *n* : asaltante *mf*
attain [əˈteɪn] *vt* **1** ACHIEVE : lograr, conseguir, alcanzar, realizar **2** REACH : alcanzar, llegar a
attainable [əˈteɪnəbəl] *adj* : alcanzable, realizable, asequible
attainment [əˈteɪnmənt] *n* : logro *m*, consecución *f*, realización *f*
attempt[1] [əˈtɛmpt] *vt* : intentar, tratar de
attempt[2] *n* : intento *m*, tentativa *f*
attend [əˈtɛnd] *vt* **1** : asistir a ⟨to attend a meeting : asistir a una reunión⟩ **2** : atender, ocuparse de, cuidar ⟨to attend a patient : atender a un paciente⟩ **3** HEED : atender a, hacer caso de **4** ACCOMPANY : acompañar
attendance [əˈtɛndənts] *n* **1** ATTENDING : asistencia *f* **2** TURNOUT : concurrencia *f*
attendant[1] [əˈtɛndənt] *adj* : concomitante, inherente
attendant[2] *n* : asistente *mf*, acompañante *mf*, guarda *mf*
attention [əˈtɛnʧən] *n* **1** : atención *f* **2 to pay attention** : prestar atención, hacer caso **3 to stand at attention** : estar firme
attentive [əˈtɛntɪv] *adj* : atento — **attentively** *adv*
attentiveness [əˈtɛntɪvnəs] *n* **1** THOUGHTFULNESS : cortesía *f*, consideración *f* **2** CONCENTRATION : atención *f*, concentración *f*
attest [əˈtɛst] *vt* : atestiguar, dar fe de
attestation [ˌæˌtsˈteɪʃən] *n* : testimonio *m*
attic [ˈæṭɪk] *n* : ático *m*, desván *m*, buhardilla *f*
attire[1] [əˈtaɪr] *vt* **-tired; -tiring** : ataviar
attire[2] *n* : atuendo *m*, atavío *m*
attitude [ˈæṭəˌtu:d, -ˌtju:d] *n* **1** FEELING : actitud *f* **2** POSTURE : postura *f*
attorney [əˈtərni] *n, pl* **-neys** : abogado *m*, -da *f*
attract [əˈtrækt] *vt* **1** : atraer **2 to attract attention** : llamar la atención
attraction [əˈtrækʃən] *n* : atracción *f*, atractivo *m*
attractive [əˈtræktɪv] *adj* : atractivo, atrayente
attractively [əˈtræktɪvli] *adv* : de manera atractiva, de buen gusto, hermosamente
attractiveness [əˈtræktɪvnəs] *n* : atractivo *m*
attributable [əˈtrɪbjʊṭəbəl] *adj* : atribuible, imputable
attribute[1] [əˈtrɪˌbju:t] *vt* **-tributed; -tributing** : atribuir
attribute[2] [ˈætrəˌbju:t] *n* : atributo *m*, cualidad *f*
attribution [ˌætrəˈbju:ʃən] *n* : atribución *f*
attune [əˈtu:n, -ˈtju:n] *vt* **-tuned; -tuning** **1** ADAPT : adaptar, adecuar **2 to be attuned to** : estar en armonía con
atypical [ˌeɪˈtɪpɪkəl] *adj* : atípico
auburn [ˈɔbərn] *adj* : castaño rojizo
auction[1] [ˈɔkʃən] *vt* : subastar, rematar
auction[2] *n* : subasta *f*, remate *m*
auctioneer [ˌɔkʃəˈnɪr] *n* : subastador *m*, -dora *f*; rematador *m*, -dora *f*
audacious [ɔˈdeɪʃəs] *adj* : audaz, atrevido
audacity [ɔˈdæsəṭi] *n, pl* **-ties** : audacia *f*, atrevimiento *m*, descaro *m*
audible [ˈɔdəbəl] *adj* : audible — **audibly** [-bli] *adv*
audience [ˈɔdiənts] *n* **1** INTERVIEW : audiencia *f* **2** PUBLIC : audiencia *f*, público *m*, auditorio *m*, espectadores *mpl*
audio[1] [ˈɔdiˌo:] *adj* : de sonido, de audio
audio[2] *n* : audio *m*
audiovisual [ˌɔdioˈvɪʒʊəl] *adj* : audiovisual
audit[1] [ˈɔdət] *vt* **1** : auditar (finanzas) **2** : asistir como oyente a (una clase o un curso)
audit[2] *n* : auditoría *f*
audition[1] [ɔˈdɪʃən] *vi* : hacer una audición

audition[2] *n* : audición *f*
auditor [ˈɔdəṭər] *n* **1** : auditor *m*, -tora *f* (de finanzas) **2** STUDENT : oyente *mf*
auditorium [ˌɔdəˈtoriəm] *n, pl* **-riums** *or* **-ria** [-riə] : auditorio *m*, sala *f*
auditory [ˈɔdəˌtori] *adj* : auditivo
auger [ˈɔgər] *n* : taladro *m*, barrena *f*
augment [ɔgˈmɛnt] *vt* : aumentar, incrementar
augmentation [ˌɔgmənˈteɪʃən] *n* : aumento *m*, incremento *m*
augur[1] [ˈɔgər] *vt* : augurar, presagiar — *vi* **to augur well** : ser de buen agüero
augur[2] *n* : augur *m*
augury [ˈɔgjʊri, -gər-] *n, pl* **-ries** : augurio *m*, presagio *m*, agüero *m*
august [ɔˈgʌst] *adj* : augusto
August [ˈɔgəst] *n* : agosto *m*
auk [ˈɔk] *n* : alca *f*
aunt [ˈænt, ˈɑnt] *n* : tía *f*
aura [ˈɔrə] *n* : aura *f*
aural [ˈɔrəl] *adj* : auditivo
auricle [ˈɔrɪkəl] *n* : aurícula *f*
aurora borealis [əˈrorəˌboriˈæləs] *n* : aurora *f* boreal
auspices [ˈɔspəsəz, -ˌsiːz] *npl* : auspicios *mpl*
auspicious [ɔˈspɪʃəs] *adj* : prometedor, propicio, de buen augurio
austere [ɔˈstɪr] *adj* : austero, severo, adusto — **austerely** *adv*
austerity [ɔˈstɛrəṭi] *n, pl* **-ties** : austeridad *f*
Australian [ɔˈstreɪljən] *n* : australiano *m*, -na *f* — **Australian** *adj*
Austrian [ˈɔstriən] *n* : austriaco *m*, -ca *f* — **Austrian** *adj*
authentic [əˈθɛntɪk, ɔ-] *adj* : auténtico, genuino — **authentically** [-tɪkli] *adv*
authenticate [əˈθɛntɪˌkeɪt, ɔ-] *vt* **-cated; -cating** : autenticar, autentificar
authenticity [ɔˌθɛnˈtɪsəṭi] *n* : autenticidad *f*
author [ˈɔθər] *n* **1** WRITER : escritor *m*, -tora *f*; autor *m*, -tora *f* **2** CREATOR : autor *m*, -tora *f*; creador *m*, -dora *f*; artífice *mf*
authoritarian [ɔˌθɔrəˈtɛriən, ə-] *adj* : autoritario
authoritative [əˈθɔrəˌteɪṭɪv, ɔ-] *adj* **1** RELIABLE : fidedigno, autorizado **2** DICTATORIAL : autoritario, dictatorial, imperioso
authoritatively [əˈθɔrəˌteɪṭɪvli, ɔ-] *adv* **1** RELIABLY : con autoridad **2** DICTATORIALLY : de manera autoritaria
authority [əˈθɔrəṭi, ɔ-] *n, pl* **-ties** **1** EXPERT : autoridad *f*; experto *m*, -ta *f* **2** POWER : autoridad *f*, poder *m* **3** AUTHORIZATION : autorización *f*, licencia *f* **4 the authorities** : las autoridades **5 on good authority** : de buena fuente
authorization [ˌɔθərəˈzeɪʃən] *n* : autorización *f*
authorize [ˈɔθəˌraɪz] *vt* **-rized; -rizing** : autorizar, facultar
authorship [ˈɔθərˌʃɪp] *n* : autoría *f*
autism [ˈɔˌtɪzəm] *n* : autismo *m*
autistic [ɔˈtɪstɪk] *adj* : autista
auto [ˈɔṭo] → **automobile**
autobiographical [ˌɔṭoˌbaɪəˈgræfɪkəl] *adj* : autobiográfico
autobiography [ˌɔṭobaɪˈɑgrəfi] *n, pl* **-phies** : autobiografía *f*
autocracy [ɔˈtɑkrəsi] *n, pl* **-cies** : autocracia *f*
autocrat [ˈɔṭəˌkræt] *n* : autócrata *mf*
autocratic [ˌɔṭəˈkræṭɪk] *adj* : autocrático — **autocratically** [-ṭɪkli] *adv*
autograph[1] [ˈɔṭəˌgræf] *vt* : autografiar
autograph[2] *n* : autógrafo *m*
automaker [ˈɔṭoːmeɪkər] *n* : fabricante *mf* de autos, automotriz *f*
automate [ˈɔṭəˌmeɪt] *vt* **-mated; -mating** : automatizar
automatic [ˌɔṭəˈmæṭɪk] *adj* : automático — **automatically** [-ṭɪkli] *adv*
automation [ˌɔṭəˈmeɪʃə n] *n* : automatización *f*
automaton [ɔˈtɑməˌtɑn] *n, pl* **-atons** *or* **-ata** [-ṭə, -ˌtɑ] : autómata *m*
automobile [ˌɔṭəmoˈbiːl, -ˈmoːˌbiːl] *n* : automóvil *m*, auto *m*, carro *m*, coche *m*
automotive [ˌɔṭəˈmoːṭɪv] *adj* : automotor
autonomous [ɔˈtɑnəməs] *adj* : autónomo — **autonomously** *adv*
autonomy [ɔˈtɑnəmi] *n, pl* **-mies** : autonomía *f*
autopsy [ˈɔˌtɑpsi, -təp-] *n, pl* **-sies** : autopsia *f*
autumn [ˈɔṭəm] *n* : otoño *m*
autumnal [ɔˈtʌmnəl] *adj* : otoñal
auxiliary[1] [ɔgˈzɪljəri, -ˈzɪləri] *adj* : auxiliar
auxiliary[2] *n, pl* **-ries** : auxiliar *mf*, ayudante *mf*
avail[1] [əˈveɪl] *vt* **to avail oneself** : aprovecharse, valerse
avail[2] *n* **1** : provecho *m*, utilidad *f* **2 to no avail** : en vano **3 to be of no avail** : no servir de nada, ser inútil
availability [əˌveɪləˈbɪləṭi] *n, pl* **-ties** : disponibilidad *f*
available [əˈveɪləbəl] *adj* : disponible
avalanche [ˈævəˌlæntʃ] *n* : avalancha *f*, alud *m*
avarice [ˈævərəs] *n* : avaricia *f*, codicia *f*
avaricious [ˌævəˈrɪʃəs] *adj* : avaricioso, codicioso
avenge [əˈvɛndʒ] *vt* **avenged; avenging** : vengar
avenger [əˈvɛndʒər] *n* : vengador *m*, -dora *f*
avenue [ˈævəˌnuː, -ˌnjuː] *n* **1** : avenida *f* **2** MEANS : vía *f*, camino *m*
average[1] [ˈævrɪdʒ, ˈævə-] *vt* **-aged; -aging** **1** : hacer un promedio de ⟨he averages 8 hours a day : hace un promedio de 8 horas diarias⟩ **2** : calcular el promedio de, promediar (en matemáticas)
average[2] *adj* **1** MEAN : medio ⟨the average temperature : la temperatura media⟩ **2** ORDINARY : común, ordinario ⟨the average man : el hombre común⟩

average[3] *n* : promedio *m*
averse [ə'vərs] *adj* : reacio, opuesto
aversion [ə'vərʒən] *n* : aversión *f*
avert [ə'vərt] *vt* **1** : apartar, desviar ⟨he averted his eyes from the scene : apartó los ojos de la escena⟩ **2** AVOID, PREVENT : evitar, prevenir
aviary ['eɪvi,ɛri] *n, pl* **-aries** : pajarera *f*
aviation [,eɪvi'eɪʃən] *n* : aviación *f*
aviator ['eɪvi,eɪt̬ər] *n* : aviador *m*, -dora *f*
avid ['ævɪd] *adj* **1** GREEDY : ávido, codicioso **2** ENTHUSIASTIC : ávido, entusiasta, ferviente — **avidly** *adv*
avocado [,ævə'kɑdo, ,ɑvə-] *n, pl* **-dos** : aguacate *m*, palta *f*
avocation [,ævə'keɪʃən] *n* : pasatiempo *m*, afición *f*
avoid [ə'vɔɪd] *vt* **1** SHUN : evitar, eludir **2** FORGO : evitar, abstenerse de ⟨I always avoided gossip : siempre evitaba los chismes⟩ **3** EVADE : evitar ⟨if I can avoid it : si puedo evitarlo⟩
avoidable [ə'vɔɪdəbəl] *adj* : evitable
avoidance [ə'vɔɪdənts] *n* : el evitar
avoirdupois [,ævərdə'pɔɪz] *n* : sistema *m* inglés de pesos y medidas
avow [ə'vaʊ] *vt* : reconocer, confesar
avowal [ə'vaʊəl] *n* : reconocimiento *m*, confesión *f*
await [ə'weɪt] *vt* : esperar
awake[1] [ə'weɪk] *v* **awoke** [ə'wo:k]; **awoken** [ə'wo:kən] *or* **awaked**; **awaking** : despertar
awake[2] *adj* : despierto
awaken [ə'weɪkən] → **awake**[1]
award[1] [ə'wɔrd] *vt* : otorgar, conceder, conferir
award[2] *n* **1** PRIZE : premio *m*, galardón *m* **2** MEDAL : condecoración *f*
aware [ə'wær] *adj* : consciente ⟨to be aware of : darse cuenta de, estar consciente de⟩
awareness [ə'wærnəs] *n* : conciencia *f*, conocimiento *m*
awash [ə'wɔʃ] *adj* : inundado
away[1] [ə'weɪ] *adv* **1** : de aquí ⟨go away! : ¡fuera de aquí!, ¡vete!⟩ **2** : de distancia ⟨10 miles away : 10 millas de distancia, queda a 10 millas⟩ **3 far away** : lejos, a lo lejos **4 right away** : en seguida, ahora mismo **5 to be away** : estar ausente, estar de viaje **6 to give away** : regalar (una posesión), revelar (un secreto) **7 to go away** : irse, largarse **8 to put away** : guardar **9 to turn away** : volver la cara
away[2] *adj* **1** ABSENT : ausente ⟨away for the week : ausente por la semana⟩ **2 away game** : partido *m* que se juega fuera
awe[1] ['ɔ] *vt* **awed**; **awing** : abrumar, asombrar, impresionar
awe[2] *n* : asombro *m*
awesome ['ɔsəm] *adj* **1** IMPOSING : imponente, formidable **2** AMAZING : asombroso
awestruck ['ɔ,strʌk] *adj* : asombrado
awful ['ɔfəl] *adj* **1** AWESOME : asombroso **2** DREADFUL : horrible, terrible, atroz **3** ENORMOUS : enorme, tremendo ⟨an awful lot of people : muchísima gente, la mar de gente⟩
awfully ['ɔfəli] *adv* **1** EXTREMELY : terriblemente, extremadamente **2** BADLY : muy mal, espantosamente
awhile [ə'*h*waɪl] *adv* : un rato, algún tiempo
awkward ['ɔkwərd] *adj* **1** CLUMSY : torpe, desmañado **2** EMBARRASSING : embarazoso, delicado — **awkwardly** *adv*
awkwardness ['ɔkwərdnəs] *n* **1** CLUMSINESS : torpeza *f* **2** INCONVENIENCE : incomodidad *f*
awl ['ɔl] *n* : punzón *m*
awning ['ɔnɪŋ] *n* : toldo *m*
awry [ə'raɪ] *adj* **1** ASKEW : torcido **2 to go awry** : salir mal, fracasar
ax *or* **axe** ['æks] *n* : hacha *m*
axiom ['æksiəm] *n* : axioma *m*
axiomatic [,æksiə'mæt̬ɪk] *adj* : axiomático
axis ['æksɪs] *n, pl* **axes** [-,si:z] : eje *m*
axle ['æksəl] *n* : eje *m*
aye[1] ['aɪ] *adv* : sí
aye[2] *n* : sí *m*
azalea [ə'zeɪljə] *n* : azalea *f*
azimuth ['æzəməθ] *n* : azimut *m*, acimut *m*
Aztec ['æz,tɛk] *n* : azteca *mf*
azure[1] ['æʒər] *adj* : azur, celeste
azure[2] *n* : azur *m*

B

b ['bi:] *n, pl* **b's** *or* **bs** ['bi:z] : segunda letra del alfabeto inglés
babble[1] ['bæbəl] *vi* **-bled**; **-bling 1** PRATTLE : balbucear **2** CHATTER : charlatanear, parlotear *fam* **3** MURMUR : murmurar
babble[2] *n* : balbuceo *m* (de bebé), parloteo *m* (de adultos), murmullo *m* (de voces, de un arroyo)
babe ['beɪb] *n* → **baby**[3]
babel ['beɪbəl, 'bæ-] *n* : babel *f*, caos *m*
baboon [bæ'bu:n] *n* : babuino *m*
baby[1] ['beɪbi] *vt* **-bied**; **-bying** : mimar, consentir
baby[2] *adj* **1** : de niño ⟨a baby carriage : un cochecito⟩ ⟨baby talk : habla infantil⟩ **2** TINY : pequeño, minúsculo
baby[3] *n, pl* **-bies** : bebé *m*; niño *m*, -ña *f*
babyhood ['beɪbi,hʊd] *n* : niñez *f*, primera infancia *f*
babyish ['beɪbiɪʃ] *adj* : infantil, pueril

baby–sit [ˈbeɪbiˌsɪt] *vi* **-sat** [-ˌsæt]; **-sitting** : cuidar niños, hacer de canguro *Spain*

baby–sitter [ˈbeɪbiˌsɪtər] *n* : niñero *m*, -ra *f*; canguro *mf Spain*

baccalaureate [ˌbækəˈlɔriət] *n* : licenciatura *f*

bachelor [ˈbætʃələr] *n* **1** : soltero *m* **2** : licenciado *m*, -da *f* ⟨bachelor of arts degree : licenciatura en filosofía y letras⟩

bacillus [bəˈsɪləs] *n, pl* **-li** [-ˌlaɪ] : bacilo *m*

back[1] [ˈbæk] *vt* **1** *or* **to back up** SUPPORT : apoyar, respaldar **2** *or* **to back up** REVERSE : darle marcha atrás a (un vehículo) **3** : estar detrás de, formar el fondo de ⟨trees back the garden : unos árboles están detrás del jardín⟩ — *vi* **1** *or* **to back up** : retroceder **2 to back away** : echarse atrás **3 to back down** *or* **to back out** : volverse atrás, echarse para atrás

back[2] *adv* **1** : atrás, hacia atrás, detrás ⟨to move back : moverse atrás⟩ ⟨back and forth : de acá para allá⟩ **2** AGO : atrás, antes, ya ⟨some years back : unos años atrás, ya unos años⟩ ⟨10 months back : hace diez meses⟩ **3** : de vuelta, de regreso ⟨we're back : estamos de vuelta⟩ ⟨she ran back : volvió corriendo⟩ ⟨to call back : llamar de nuevo⟩

back[3] *adj* **1** REAR : de atrás, posterior, trasero **2** OVERDUE : atrasado **3 back pay** : atrasos *mpl*

back[4] *n* **1** : espalda *f* (de un ser humano), lomo *m* (de un animal) **2** : respaldo *m* (de una silla), espalda *f* (de ropa) **3** REVERSE : reverso *m*, dorso *m*, revés *m* **4** REAR : fondo *m*, parte *f* de atrás **5** : defensa *mf* (en deportes)

backache [ˈbækˌeɪk] *n* : dolor *m* de espalda

backbite [ˈbækˌbaɪt] *v* **-bit** [-ˌbɪt]; **-bitten** [-ˌbɪtən]; **-biting** *vt* : calumniar, hablar mal de — *vi* : murmurar

backbiter [ˈbækˌbaɪt̬ər] *n* : calumniador *m*, -dora *f*

backbone [ˈbækˌbo:n] *n* **1** : columna *f* vertebral **2** FIRMNESS : firmeza *f*, carácter *m*

backdrop [ˈbækˌdrɑp] *n* : telón *m* de fondo

backer [ˈbækər] *n* **1** SUPPORTER : partidario *m*, -ria *f* **2** SPONSOR : patrocinador *m*, -dora *f*

backfire[1] [ˈbækˌfaɪr] *vi* **-fired; -firing 1** : petardear (dícese de un automóvil) **2** FAIL : fallar, salir el tiro por la culata

backfire[2] *n* : petardeo *m*, explosión *f*

background [ˈbækˌgraʊnd] *n* **1** : fondo *m* (de un cuadro, etc.), antecedentes *mpl* (de una situación) **2** EXPERIENCE, TRAINING : experiencia *f* profesional, formación *f*

backhand[1] [ˈbækˌhænd] *adv* : de revés, con el revés

backhand[2] *n* : revés *m*

backhanded [ˈbækˌhændəd] *adj* **1** : dado con el revés, de revés **2** INDIRECT : indirecto, ambiguo

backing [ˈbækɪŋ] *n* **1** SUPPORT : apoyo *m*, respaldo *m* **2** REINFORCEMENT : refuerzo *m* **3** SUPPORTERS : partidarios *mpl*, -rias *fpl*

backlash [ˈbækˌlæʃ] *n* : reacción *f* violenta

backlog [ˈbækˌlɔg] *n* : atraso *m*, trabajo *m* acumulado

backpack[1] [ˈbækˌpæk] *vi* : viajar con mochila

backpack[2] *n* : mochila *f*

backrest [ˈbækˌrɛst] *n* : respaldo *m*

backside [ˈbækˌsaɪd] *n* : trasero *m*

backslide [ˈbækˌslaɪd] *vi* **-slid** [-ˌslɪd]; **-slid** *or* **-slidden** [-ˌslɪdən]; **-sliding** : recaer, reincidir

backstage [ˌbækˈsteɪʤ, ˈbækˌ-] *adv & adj* : entre bastidores

backtrack [ˈbækˌtræk] *vi* : dar marcha atrás, volverse atrás

backup [ˈbækˌʌp] *n* **1** SUPPORT : respaldo *m*, apoyo *m* **2** : copia *f* de seguridad (para computadoras)

backward[1] [ˈbækwərd] *or* **backwards** [-wərdz] *adv* **1** : hacia atrás **2** : de espaldas ⟨he fell backwards : se cayó de espaldas⟩ **3** : al revés ⟨you're doing it backwards : lo estás haciendo al revés⟩ **4 to bend over backwards** : hacer todo lo posible

backward[2] *adj* **1** : hacia atrás ⟨a backward glance : una mirada hacia atrás⟩ **2** RETARDED : retrasado **3** SHY : tímido **4** UNDERDEVELOPED : atrasado

backwardness [ˈbækwərdnəs] *n* : atraso *m* (dícese de una región), retraso *m* (dícese de una persona)

backwoods [ˌbækˈwʊdz] *npl* : monte *m*, región *f* alejada

bacon [ˈbeɪkən] *n* : tocino *m*, tocineta *f Col, Ven*, bacon *m Spain*

bacterial [bækˈtɪriəl] *adj* : bacteriano

bacteriologist [bækˌtɪriˈɑləʤɪst] *n* : bacteriólogo *m*, -ga *f*

bacteriology [bækˌtɪriˈɑləʤi] *n* : bacteriología *f*

bacterium [bækˈtɪriəm] *n, pl* **-ria** [-iə] : bacteria *f*

bad[1] [ˈbæd] *adv* → **badly**

bad[2] *adj* **1** : malo **2** ROTTEN : podrido **3** SERIOUS, SEVERE : grave **4** DEFECTIVE : defectuoso ⟨a bad check : un cheque sin fondos⟩ **5** HARMFUL : perjudicial **6** CORRUPT, EVIL : malo, corrompido **7** NAUGHTY : travieso **8 from bad to worse** : de mal en peor **9 too bad!** : ¡qué lástima!

bad[3] *n* : lo malo ⟨the good and the bad : lo bueno y lo malo⟩

bade → **bid**

badge [ˈbæʤ] *n* : insignia *f*, botón *m*, chapa *f*

badger[1] [ˈbæʤər] *vt* : fastidiar, acosar, importunar

badger[2] *n* : tejón *m*
badly ['bædli] *adv* **1** : mal **2** URGENTLY : mucho, con urgencia **3** SEVERELY : gravemente
badminton ['bæd,mɪntən, -,mɪt-] *n* : bádminton *m*
badness ['bædnəs] *n* : maldad *f*
baffle[1] ['bæfəl] *vi* **-fled; -fling 1** PERPLEX : desconcertar, confundir **2** FRUSTRATE : frustrar
baffle[2] *n* : deflector *m*, bafle *m* (acústico)
bafflement ['bæfəlmənt] *n* : desconcierto *m*, confusión *f*
bag[1] ['bæg] *v* **bagged; bagging** *vi* SAG : formar bolsas — *vt* **1** : ensacar, poner en una bolsa **2** : cobrar (en la caza), cazar
bag[2] *n* **1** : bolsa *f*, saco *m* **2** HANDBAG : cartera *f*, bolso *m*, bolsa *f Mex* **3** SUITCASE : maleta *f*, valija *f*
bagatelle [,bægə'tɛl] *n* : bagatela *f*
bagel ['beɪgəl] *n* : rosquilla *f* de pan
baggage ['bægɪʤ] *n* : equipaje *m*
baggy ['bægi] *adj* **-gier; -est** : holgado, ancho
bagpipe ['bæg,paɪp] *n or* **bagpipes** ['bæg,paɪps] *npl* : gaita *f*
bail[1] ['beɪl] *vt* **1** : achicar (agua de un bote) **2 to bail out** : poner en libertad (de una cárcel) bajo fianza **3 to bail out** EXTRICATE : sacar de apuros
bail[2] *n* : fianza *f*, caución *f*
bailiff ['beɪləf] *n* : alguacil *mf*
bailiwick ['beɪli,wɪk] *n* : dominio *m*
bailout ['beɪl,aʊt] *n* : rescate *m* (financiero)
bait[1] ['beɪt] *vt* **1** : cebar (un anzuelo o cepo) **2** HARASS : acosar
bait[2] *n* : cebo *m*, carnada *f*
bake[1] ['beɪk] *vt* **baked; baking** : hornear, hacer al horno
bake[2] *n* : fiesta con platos hechos al horno
baker ['beɪkər] *n* : panadero *m*, -ra *f*
baker's dozen *n* : docena *f* de fraile
bakery ['beɪkəri] *n, pl* **-ries** : panadería *f*
bakeshop ['beɪk,ʃɑp] *n* : pastelería *f*, panadería *f*
baking powder *n* : levadura *f* en polvo
baking soda → sodium bicarbonate
balance[1] ['bælənts] *v* **-anced; -ancing** *vt* **1** : hacer el balance de (una cuenta) ⟨to balance the books : cuadrar las cuentas⟩ **2** EQUALIZE : balancear, equilibrar **3** HARMONIZE : armonizar — *vi* : balancearse
balance[2] *n* **1** SCALES : balanza *f*, báscula *f* **2** COUNTERBALANCE : contrapeso *m* **3** EQUILIBRIUM : equilibrio *m* **4** REMAINDER : balance *m*, resto *m*
balanced ['bælən*t*st] *adj* : equilibrado, balanceado
balcony ['bælkəni] *n, pl* **-nies 1** : balcón *m*, terraza *f* (de un edificio) **2** : galería *f* (de un teatro)
bald ['bɔld] *adj* **1** : calvo, pelado, pelón **2** PLAIN : simple, puro ⟨the bald truth : la pura verdad⟩
balding ['bɔldɪŋ] *adj* : quedándose calvo
baldly ['bɔldli] *adv* : sin reparos, sin rodeos, francamente
baldness ['bɔldnəs] *n* : calvicie *f*
bale[1] ['beɪl] *vt* **baled; baling** : empacar, hacer balas de
bale[2] *n* : bala *f*, fardo *m*, paca *f*
baleful ['beɪlfəl] *adj* **1** DEADLY : mortífero **2** SINISTER : siniestro, funesto, torvo ⟨a baleful glance : una mirada torva⟩
balk[1] ['bɔk] *vt* : obstaculizar, impedir — *vi* **1** : plantarse *fam* (dícese de un caballo, etc.) **2 to balk at** : resistarse a, mostrarse reacio a
balk[2] *n* : obstáculo *m*
Balkan ['bɔlkən] *adj* : balcánico
balky ['bɔki] *adj* **balkier; -est** : reacio, obstinado, terco
ball[1] ['bɔl] *vt* : apelotonar, ovillar
ball[2] *n* **1** : pelota *f*, bola *f*, balón *m*, ovillo *m* (de lana) **2** : juego *m* con pelota o bola **3** DANCE : baile *m*, baile *m* de etiqueta
ballad ['bæləd] *n* : romance *m*, balada *f*
balladeer [,bælə'dɪr] *n* : cantante *mf* de baladas
ballast[1] ['bæləst] *vt* : lastrar
ballast[2] *n* : lastre *m*
ball bearing *n* : cojinete *m* de bola
ballerina [,bælə'ri:nə] *n* : bailarina *f*
ballet [bæ'leɪ, 'bæ,leɪ] *n* : ballet *m*
ballistic [bə'lɪstɪk] *adj* : balístico
ballistics [bə'lɪstɪks] *ns & pl* : balística *f*
balloon[1] [bə'lu:n] *vi* **1** : viajar en globo **2** SWELL : hincharse, inflarse
balloon[2] *n* : globo *m*
balloonist [bə'lu:nɪst] *n* : aeróstata *mf*
ballot[1] ['bælət] *vi* : votar
ballot[2] *n* **1** : papeleta *f* (de voto) **2** BALLOTING : votación *f* **3** VOTE : voto *m*
ballpoint pen ['bɔl,pɔɪnt] *n* : bolígrafo *m*
ballroom ['bɔl,ru:m, -,rʊm] *n* : sala *f* de baile
ballyhoo ['bæli,hu:] *n* : propaganda *f*, publicidad *f*, bombo *m fam*
balm ['bɑm, 'bɑlm] *n* : bálsamo *m*, ungüento *m*
balmy ['bɑmi, 'bɑl-] *adj* **balmier; -est 1** MILD : templado, agradable **2** SOOTHING : balsámico **3** CRAZY : chiflado *fam*, chalado *fam*
baloney [bə'lo:ni] *n* NONSENSE : tonterías *fpl*, estupideces *fpl*
balsa ['bɔlsə] *n* : balsa *f*
balsam ['bɔlsəm] *n* **1** : bálsamo *m* **2** *or* **balsam fir** : abeto *m* balsámico
Baltic ['bɔltɪk] *adj* : báltico
baluster ['bæləstər] *n* : balaustre *m*
balustrade ['bælə,streɪd] *n* : balaustrada *f*
bamboo [bæm'bu:] *n* : bambú *m*
bamboozle [bæm'bu:zəl] *vt* **-zled; -zling** : engañar, embaucar

ban[1] ['bæn] *vt* **banned; banning** : prohibir, proscribir
ban[2] *n* : prohibición *f*, proscripción *f*
banal [bə'nɑl, bə'næl, 'beɪnəl] *adj* : banal, trivial
banality [bə'næləṭi] *n, pl* **-ties** : banalidad *f*, trivialidad *f*
banana [bə'nænə] *n* : banano *m*, plátano *m*, banana *f*, cambur *m Ven*, guineo *m Car*
band[1] ['bænd] *vt* **1** BIND : fajar, atar **2 to band together** : unirse, juntarse
band[2] *n* **1** STRIP : banda *f*, cinta *f* (de un sombrero, etc.) **2** STRIPE : franja *f* **3** : banda *f* (de radiofrecuencia) **4** RING : anillo *m* **5** GROUP : banda *f*, grupo *m*, conjunto *m* ⟨jazz band : conjunto de jazz⟩
bandage[1] ['bændɪʤ] *vt* **-daged; -daging** : vendar
bandage[2] *n* : vendaje *m*, venda *f*
bandanna *or* **bandana** [bæn'dænə] *n* : pañuelo *m* (de colores)
bandit ['bændət] *n* : bandido *m*, -da *f*; bandolero *m*, -ra *f*
banditry ['bændətri] *n* : bandolerismo *m*, bandidaje *m*
bandstand ['bænd,stænd] *n* : quiosco *m* de música
bandwagon ['bænd,wægən] *n* **1** : carroza *f* de músicos **2 to jump on the bandwagon** : subirse al carro, seguir la moda
bandy[1] ['bændi] *vt* **-died; -dying 1** EXCHANGE : intercambiar **2 to bandy about** : circular, propagar
bandy[2] *adj* : arqueado, torcido ⟨bandy-legged : de piernas arqueadas⟩
bane ['beɪn] *n* **1** POISON : veneno *m* **2** RUIN : ruina *f*, pesadilla *f*
baneful ['beɪnfəl] *adj* : nefasto, funesto
bang[1] ['bæŋ] *vt* **1** STRIKE : golpear, darse ⟨he banged his elbow against the door : se dio con el codo en la puerta⟩ **2** SLAM : cerrar (la puerta) con un portazo — *vi* **1** SLAM : cerrarse de un golpe **2 to bang on** : aporrear, golpear ⟨she was banging on the table : aporreaba la mesa⟩
bang[2] *adv* : directamente, exactamente
bang[3] *n* **1** BLOW : golpe *m*, porrazo *m*, trancazo *m* **2** EXPLOSION : explosión *f*, estallido *m* **3** SLAM : portazo *m* **4 bangs** *npl* : flequillo *m*, fleco *m*
Bangladeshi [,bɑŋglə'dɛʃi, ,bæŋ-, ,bʌŋ-, -'deɪ-] *n* : bangladesí *mf* — **Bangladeshi** *adj*
bangle ['bæŋgəl] *n* : brazalete *m*, pulsera *f*
banish ['bænɪʃ] *vt* **1** EXILE : desterrar, exiliar **2** EXPEL : expulsar
banishment ['bænɪʃmənt] *n* **1** EXILE : destierro *m*, exilio *m* **2** EXPULSION : expulsión *f*
banister ['bænəstər] *n* **1** BALUSTER : balaustre *m* **2** HANDRAIL : pasamanos *m*, barandilla *f*, barandal *m*
banjo ['bæn,ʤo:] *n, pl* **-jos** : banjo *m*
bank[1] ['bæŋk] *vt* **1** TILT : peraltar (una carretera), ladear (un avión) **2** HEAP : amontonar **3** : cubrir (un fuego) **4** : depositar (dinero en un banco) — *vi* **1** : ladearse (dícese de un avión) **2** : tener una cuenta (en un banco) **3 to bank on** : contar con
bank[2] *n* **1** MASS : montón *m*, montículo *m*, masa *f* **2** : orilla *f*, ribera *f* (de un río) **3** : peralte *m* (de una carretera) **4** : banco *m* ⟨World Bank : Banco Mundial⟩ ⟨banco de sangre : blood bank⟩
bankbook ['bæŋk,bʊk] *n* : libreta *f* bancaria, libreta *f* de ahorros
banker ['bæŋkər] *n* : banquero *m*, -ra *f*
banking ['bæŋkɪŋ] *n* : banca *f*
bankrupt[1] ['bæŋ,krʌpt] *vt* : hacer quebrar, llevar a la quiebra, arruinar
bankrupt[2] *adj* **1** : en bancarrota, en quiebra **2 ~ of** LACKING : carente de, falto de
bankrupt[3] *n* : fallido *m*, -da *f*; quebrado *m*, -da *f*
bankruptcy ['bæŋ,krʌptsi] *n, pl* **-cies** : ruina *f*, quiebra *f*, bancarrota *f*
banner[1] ['bænər] *adj* : excelente
banner[2] *n* : estandarte *m*, bandera *f*
banns ['bænz] *npl* : amonestaciones *fpl*
banquet[1] ['bæŋkwət] *vi* : celebrar un banquete
banquet[2] *n* : banquete *m*
banter[1] ['bæntər] *vi* : bromear, hacer bromas
banter[2] *n* : bromas *fpl*
baptism ['bæp,tɪzəm] *n* : bautismo *m*
baptismal [bæp'tɪzməl] *adj* : bautismal
Baptist ['bæptɪst] *n* : bautista *mf* — **Baptist** *adj*
baptize [bæp'taɪz, 'bæp,taɪz] *vt* **-tized; -tizing** : bautizar
bar[1] ['bɑr] *vt* **barred; barring 1** OBSTRUCT : obstruir, bloquear **2** EXCLUDE : excluir **3** PROHIBIT : prohibir **4** SECURE : atrancar, asegurar ⟨bar the door! : ¡atranca la puerta!⟩
bar[2] *n* **1** : barra *f*, barrote *m* (de una ventana), tranca *f* (de una puerta) **2** BARRIER : barrera *f*, obstáculo *m* **3** LAW : abogacía *f* **4** STRIPE : franja *f* **5** COUNTER : mostrador *m*, barra *f* **6** TAVERN : bar *m*, taberna *f*
bar[3] *prep* **1** : excepto, con excepción de **2 bar none** : sin excepción
barb ['bɑrb] *n* **1** POINT : púa *f*, lengüeta *f* **2** GIBE : pulla *f*
barbarian[1] [bɑr'bæriən] *adj* **1** : bárbaro **2** CRUDE : tosco, bruto
barbarian[2] *n* : bárbaro *m*, -ra *f*
barbaric [bɑr'bærɪk] *adj* **1** PRIMITIVE : primitivo **2** CRUEL : brutal, cruel
barbarity [bɑr'bærəṭi] *n, pl* **-ties** : barbaridad *f*
barbarous ['bɑrbərəs] *adj* **1** UNCIVILIZED : bárbaro **2** MERCILESS : despiadado, cruel
barbarously ['bɑrbərəsli] *adv* : bárbaramente

barbecue[1] ['bɑrbɪˌkju:] *vt* **-cued; -cuing** : asar a la parrilla
barbecue[2] *n* : barbacoa *f*, parrillada *f*
barbed ['bɑrbd] *adj* **1** : con púas ⟨barbed wire : alambre de púas⟩ **2** BITING : mordaz
barber ['bɑrbər] *n* : barbero *m*, -ra *f*
barbiturate [bɑr'bɪʧərət] *n* : barbitúrico *m*
bard ['bɑrd] *n* : bardo *m*
bare[1] ['bær] *vt* **bared; baring** : desnudar
bare[2] *adj* **1** NAKED : desnudo **2** EXPOSED : descubierto, sin protección **3** EMPTY : desprovisto, vacío **4** MINIMUM : mero, mínimo ⟨the bare necessities : las necesidades mínimas⟩ **5** PLAIN : puro, sencillo
bareback ['bærˌbæk] *or* **barebacked** [-ˌbækt] *adv & adj* : a pelo
barefaced ['bærˌfeɪst] *adj* : descarado
barefoot ['bærˌfʊt] *or* **barefooted** [-ˌfʊt̬əd] *adv & adj* : descalzo
bareheaded ['bær'hɛdəd] *adv & adj* : sin sombrero, con la cabeza descubierta
barely ['bærli] *adv* : apenas, por poco
bareness ['bærnəs] *n* : desnudez *f*
bargain[1] ['bɑrgən] *vi* HAGGLE : regatear, negociar — *vt* BARTER : trocar, cambiar
bargain[2] *n* **1** AGREEMENT : acuerdo *m*, convenio *m* ⟨to strike a bargain : cerrar un trato⟩ **2** : ganga *f* ⟨bargain price : precio de ganga⟩
barge[1] ['bɑrʤ] *vi* **barged; barging 1** : mover con torpeza **2 to barge in** : entrometerse, interrumpir
barge[2] *n* : barcaza *f*, gabarra *f*
bar graph *n* : gráfico *m* de barras
baritone ['bærəˌto:n] *n* : barítono *m*
barium ['bæriəm] *n* : bario *m*
bark[1] ['bɑrk] *vi* : ladrar — *vt or* **to bark out** : gritar ⟨to bark out an order : dar una orden a gritos⟩
bark[2] *n* **1** : ladrido *m* (de un perro) **2** : corteza *f* (de un árbol) **3** *or* **barque** : tipo de embarcación con velas de proa y popa
barley ['bɑrli] *n* : cebada *f*
barn ['bɑrn] *n* : granero *m* (para cosechas), establo *m* (para ganado)
barnacle ['bɑrnɪkəl] *n* : percebe *m*
barnyard ['bɑrnˌjɑrd] *n* : corral *m*
barometer [bə'rɑmət̬ər] *n* : barómetro *m*
barometric [ˌbærə'mɛtrɪk] *adj* : barométrico
baron ['bærən] *n* **1** : barón *m* **2** TYCOON : magnate *mf*
baroness ['bærənɪs, -nəs, -ˌnɛs] *n* : baronesa *f*
baronet [ˌbærə'nɛt, 'bærənət] *n* : baronet *m*
baronial [bə'ro:niəl] *adj* **1** : de barón **2** STATELY : señorial, majestuoso
baroque [bə'ro:k, -'rɑk] *adj* : barroco
barracks ['bærəks] *ns & pl* : cuartel *m*
barracuda [ˌbærə'ku:də] *n, pl* **-da** *or* **-das** : barracuda *f*
barrage [bə'rɑʒ, -'rɑʤ] *n* **1** : descarga *f* (de artillería) **2** DELUGE : aluvión *m* ⟨a barrage of questions : un aluvión de preguntas⟩
barred ['bɑrd] *adj* : excluido, prohibido
barrel[1] ['bærəl] *v* **-reled** *or* **-relled; -reling** *or* **-relling** *vt* : embarrilar — *vi* : ir disparado
barrel[2] *n* **1** : barril *m*, tonel *m* **2** : cañón *m* (de un arma de fuego), cilindro *m* (de una cerradura)
barren ['bærən] *adj* **1** STERILE : estéril (dícese de las plantas o la mujer), árido (dícese del suelo) **2** DESERTED : yermo, desierto
barrette [bɑ'rɛt, bə-] *n* : pasador *m*, broche *m* para el cabello
barricade[1] ['bærəˌkeɪd, ˌbærə'-] *vt* **-caded; -cading** : cerrar con barricadas
barricade[2] *n* : barricada *f*
barrier ['bæriər] *n* **1** : barrera *f* **2** OBSTACLE : obstáculo *m*, impedimento *m*
barring ['bɑrɪŋ] *prep* : excepto, salvo, a excepción de
barrio ['bɑrio, 'bær-] *n* : barrio *m*
barroom ['bɑrˌru:m, -ˌrʊm] *n* : bar *m*
barrow ['bærˌo:] → **wheelbarrow**
bartender ['bɑrˌtɛndər] *n* : camarero *m*, -ra *f*; barman *m*
barter[1] ['bɑrt̬ər] *vt* : cambiar, trocar
barter[2] *n* : trueque *m*, permuta *f*
basalt [bə'sɔlt, 'beɪˌ-] *n* : basalto *m*
base[1] ['beɪs] *vt* **based; basing** : basar, fundamentar, establecer
base[2] *adj* **baser; basest 1** : de baja ley (dícese de un metal) **2** CONTEMPTIBLE : vil, despreciable
base[3] *n, pl* **bases** : base *f*
baseball ['beɪsˌbɔl] *n* : beisbol *m*, béisbol *m*
baseless ['beɪsləs] *adj* : infundado
basely ['beɪsli] *adv* : vilmente
basement ['beɪsmənt] *n* : sótano *m*
baseness ['beɪsnəs] *n* : vileza *f*, bajeza *f*
bash[1] ['bæʃ] *vt* : golpear violentamente
bash[2] *n* **1** BLOW : golpe *m*, porrazo *m*, madrazo *m Mex fam* **2** PARTY : fiesta *f*, juerga *f fam*
bashful ['bæʃfəl] *adj* : tímido, vergonzoso, penoso
bashfulness ['bæʃfəlnəs] *n* : timidez *f*
basic[1] ['beɪsɪk] *adj* **1** FUNDAMENTAL : básico, fundamental **2** RUDIMENTARY : básico, elemental **3** : básico (en química)
basic[2] *n* : fundamento *m*, rudimento *m*
basically ['beɪsɪkli] *adv* : fundamentalmente
basil ['beɪzəl, 'bæzəl] *n* : albahaca *f*
basilica [bə'sɪlɪkə] *n* : basílica *f*
basin ['beɪsən] *n* **1** WASHBOWL : palangana *f*, lavamanos *m*, lavabo *m* **2** : cuenca *f* (de un río)
basis ['beɪsəs] *n, pl* **bases** [-ˌsi:z] **1** BASE : base *f*, pilar *m* **2** FOUNDATION : fundamento *m*, base *f* **3 on a weekly basis** : semanalmente

bask ['bæsk] *vi* : disfrutar, deleitarse ⟨to bask in the sun : disfrutar del sol⟩

basket ['bæskət] *n* : cesta *f*, cesto *m*, canasta *f*

basketball ['bæskət,bɔl] *n* : baloncesto *m*, basquetbol *m*

bas–relief [,bɑrı'li:f] *n* : bajorrelieve *m*

bass[1] ['bæs] *n, pl* **bass** *or* **basses** : róbalo *m* (pesca)

bass[2] ['beɪs] *n* : bajo *m* (tono, voz, cantante)

bass drum *n* : bombo *m*

basset hound ['bæsət,haʊnd] *n* : basset *m*

bassinet [,bæsə'nɛt] *n* : moisés *m*, cuna *f*

bassist ['beɪsɪst] *n* : bajista *mf*

bassoon [bə'su:n, bæ-] *n* : fagot *m*

bass viol ['beɪs'vaɪəl, -,o:l] → **double bass**

bastard[1] ['bæstərd] *adj* : bastardo

bastard[2] *n* : bastardo *m*, -da *f*

bastardize ['bæstər,daɪz] *vt* **-ized; -izing** DEBASE : degradar, envilecer

baste ['beɪst] *vt* **basted; basting 1** STITCH : hilvanar **2** : bañar (con su jugo durante la cocción)

bastion ['bæstʃən] *n* : bastión *m*, baluarte *m*

bat[1] ['bæt] *vt* **batted; batting 1** HIT : batear **2 without batting an eye** : sin pestañear

bat[2] *n* **1** : murciélago *m* (animal) **2** : bate *m* ⟨baseball bat : bate de beisbol⟩

batch ['bætʃ] *n* : hornada *f*, tanda *f*, grupo *m*, cantidad *f*

bate ['beɪt] *vt* **bated; bating 1** : aminorar, reducir **2 with bated breath** : con ansiedad, aguantando la respiración

bath ['bæθ, 'baθ] *n, pl* **baths** ['bæðz, 'bæθs, 'baðz, 'baθs] **1** BATHING : baño *m* ⟨to take a bath : bañarse⟩ **2** : baño *m* (en fotografía, etc.) **3** BATHROOM : baño *m*, cuarto *m* de baño **4** SPA : balneario *m* **5** LOSS : pérdida *f*

bathe ['beɪð] *v* **bathed; bathing** *vt* **1** WASH : bañar, lavar **2** SOAK : poner en remojo **3** FLOOD : inundar ⟨to bathe with light : inundar de luz⟩ — *vi* : bañarse, ducharse

bather ['beɪðər] *n* : bañista *mf*

bathrobe ['bæθ,ro:b] *n* : bata *f* (de baño)

bathroom ['bæθ,ru:m, -,rʊm] *n* : baño *m*, cuarto *m* de baño

bathtub ['bæθ,tʌb] *n* : bañera *f*, tina *f* (de baño)

batiste [bə'ti:st] *n* : batista *f*

baton [bə'tɑn] *n* : batuta *f*, bastón *m*

battalion [bə'tæljən] *n* : batallón *m*

batten ['bætən] *vt* **to batten down the hatches** : cerrar las escotillas

batter[1] ['bæţər] *vt* **1** BEAT : aporrear, golpear **2** MISTREAT : maltratar

batter[2] *n* **1** : masa *f* para rebozar **2** HITTER : bateador *m*, -dora *f*

battering ram *n* : ariete *m*

battery ['bæţəri] *n, pl* **-teries 1** : lesiones *fpl* ⟨assault and battery : agresión con lesiones⟩ **2** ARTILLERY : batería *f* **3** : batería *f*, pila *f* (de electricidad) **4** SERIES : serie *f*

batting ['bæţɪŋ] *n* **1** *or* **cotton batting** : algodón *m* en láminas **2** : bateo *m* (en beisbol)

battle[1] ['bæţəl] *vi* **-tled; -tling** : luchar, pelear

battle[2] *n* : batalla *f*, lucha *f*, pelea *f*

battle–ax ['bæţəl,æks] *n* : hacha *f* de guerra

battlefield ['bæţəl,fɪ:ld] *n* : campo *m* de batalla

battlements ['bæţəlmənts] *npl* : almenas *fpl*

battleship ['bæţəl,ʃɪp] *n* : acorazado *m*

batty ['bæţi] *adj* **-tier; -est** : chiflado *fam*, chalado *fam*

bauble ['bɔbəl] *n* : chuchería *f*, baratija *f*

Bavarian [bə'vɛriən] *n* : bávaro *m*, -ra *f* — **Bavarian** *adj*

bawdiness ['bɔdinəs] *n* : picardía *f*

bawdy ['bɔdi] *adj* **bawdier; -est** : subido de tono, verde, colorado *Mex*

bawl[1] ['bɔl] *vi* : llorar a gritos

bawl[2] *n* : grito *m*, alarido *m*

bawl out *vt* SCOLD : regañar

bay[1] ['beɪ] *vi* HOWL : aullar

bay[2] *adj* : castaño, zaino (dícese de los caballos)

bay[3] *n* **1** : bahía *f* ⟨Bay of Campeche : Bahía de Campeche⟩ **2** *or* **bay horse** : caballo *m* castaño **3** LAUREL : laurel *m* **4** HOWL : aullido *m* **5** : saliente *m* ⟨bay window : ventana en saliente⟩ **6** COMPARTMENT : área *f*, compartimento *m* **7 at ~** : acorralado

bayberry ['beɪ,bɛri] *n, pl* **-ries** : arrayán *m* brabántico

bayonet[1] [,beɪə'nɛt, 'beɪə,nɛt] *vt* **-neted; -neting** : herir *o* matar) con bayoneta

bayonet[2] *n* : bayoneta *f*

bayou ['baɪ,u:, -,o:] *n* : pantano *m*

bazaar [bə'zɑr] *n* **1** : bazar *m* **2** SALE : venta *f* benéfica

bazooka [bə'zu:kə] *n* : bazuca *f*

BB ['bi:bi] *n* : balín *m*

be ['bi:] *v* **was** ['wəz, 'wɑz]; **were** ['wər]; **been** ['bɪn]; **being; am** ['æm]; **is** ['ɪz]; **are** ['ɑr] *vi* **1** (*expressing equality*) : ser ⟨José is a doctor : José es doctor⟩ ⟨I'm Ann's sister : soy la hermana de Ana⟩ **2** (*expressing quality*) : ser ⟨the tree is tall : el árbol es alto⟩ ⟨you're silly! : ¡eres tonto!⟩ **3** (*expressing origin or possession*) : ser ⟨she's from Managua : es de Managua⟩ ⟨it's mine : es mío⟩ **4** (*expressing location*) : estar ⟨my mother is at home : mi madre está en casa⟩ ⟨the cups are on the table : las tazas están en la mesa⟩ **5** (*expressing existence*) : ser, existir ⟨to be or not to be : ser, o no ser⟩ ⟨I think, therefore I am : pienso, luego existo⟩ **6** (*expressing a state of being*) : estar, tener ⟨how are you? : ¿cómo estás?⟩ ⟨I'm cold : tengo frío⟩ ⟨she's 10 years old : tiene 10 años⟩ ⟨they're both sick : están enfermos los dos⟩ — *v impers* **1** (*indicating time*) : ser ⟨it's eight o'clock : son las ocho⟩ ⟨it's Friday : hoy es viernes⟩ **2** (*indicating a condition*) : hacer, estar ⟨it's sunny : hace sol⟩ ⟨it's very dark outside : está bien oscuro afuera⟩ — *v aux* **1** (*expressing progression*) : estar ⟨what are you doing?—I'm working : ¿qué haces?—estoy trabajando⟩ **2** (*expressing occurrence*) : ser ⟨it was finished yesterday : fue acabado ayer, se acabó ayer⟩ ⟨it was cooked in the oven : se cocinó en el horno⟩ **3** (*expressing possibility*) : poderse ⟨can she be trusted? : ¿se puede confiar en ella?⟩ **4** (*expressing obligation*) : deber ⟨you are to stay here : debes quedarte aquí⟩ ⟨he was to come yesterday : se esperaba que viniese ayer⟩

beach[1] ['bi:ʧ] *vt* : hacer embarrancar, hacer varar, hacer encallar

beach[2] *n* : playa *f*

beachcomber ['bi:ʧ,ko:mər] *n* : raquero *m*, -ra *f*

beachhead ['bi:ʧ,hɛd] *n* : cabeza *f* de playa

beacon ['bi:kən] *n* : faro *m*

bead[1] ['bi:d] *vi* : formarse en gotas

bead[2] *n* **1** : cuenta *f* **2** DROP : gota *f* **3 beads** *npl* NECKLACE : collar *m*

beady ['bi:di] *adj* **beadier; -est 1** : de forma de cuenta **2 beady eyes** : ojos *mpl* pequeños y brillantes

beagle ['bi:gəl] *n* : beagle *m*

beak ['bi:k] *n* : pico *m*

beaker ['bi:kər] *n* **1** CUP : taza *f* alta **2** : vaso *m* de precipitados (en un laboratorio)

beam[1] ['bi:m] *vi* **1** SHINE : brillar **2** SMILE : sonreír radiantemente — *vt* BROADCAST : transmitir, emitir

beam[2] *n* **1** : viga *f*, barra *f* **2** RAY : rayo *m*, haz *m* de luz **3** : haz *m* de radiofaro (para guiar pilotos, etc.)

bean ['bi:n] *n* **1** : habichuela *f*, frijol *m* **2 broad bean** : haba *f* **3 string bean** : judía *f*

bear[1] ['bær] *v* **bore** ['bor]; **borne** ['bɔrn]; **bearing** *vt* **1** CARRY : llevar, portar **2** : dar a luz a (un niño) **3** PRODUCE : dar (frutas, cosechas) **4** ENDURE, SUPPORT : soportar, resistir, aguantar — *vi* **1** TURN : doblar, dar la vuelta ⟨bear right : doble a la derecha⟩ **2 to bear up** : resistir

bear[2] *n, pl* **bears** *or* **bear** : oso *m*, osa *f*

bearable ['bærəbəl] *adj* : soportable

beard ['bɪrd] *n* **1** : barba *f* **2** : arista *f* (de plantas)

bearded ['bɪrdəd] *adj* : barbudo, de barba

bearer ['bærər] *n* : portador *m*, -dora *f*

bearing ['bærɪŋ] *n* **1** CONDUCT, MANNERS : comportamiento *m*, modales *mpl* **2** SUPPORT : soporte *f* **3** SIGNIFICANCE : relación *f*, importancia *f* ⟨to have no bearing on : no tener nada que ver con⟩ **4** : cojinete *m*, rodamiento *m* (de una máquina) **5** COURSE, DIRECTION : dirección *f*, rumbo *m* ⟨to get one's bearings : orientarse⟩

beast ['bi:st] *n* **1** : bestia *f*, fiera *f* ⟨beast of burden : animal de carga⟩ **2** BRUTE : bruto *m*, -ta *f*; bestia *mf*

beastly ['bi:stli] *adj* : detestable, repugnante

beat[1] ['bi:t] *v* **beat; beaten** ['bi:tən] *or* **beat; beating** *vt* **1** STRIKE : golpear, pegar, darle una paliza (a alguien) **2** DEFEAT : vencer, derrotar **3** AVOID : anticiparse a, evitar ⟨to beat the crowd : evitar el gentío⟩ **4** MASH, WHIP : batir — *vi* THROB : palpitar, latir

beat[2] *adj* EXHAUSTED : derrengado, muy cansado ⟨I'm beat! : ¡estoy molido!⟩

beat[3] *n* **1** : golpe *m*, redoble *m* (de un tambor), latido *m* (del corazón) **2** RHYTHM : ritmo *m*, tiempo *m*

beater ['bi:t̬ər] *n* **1** : batidor *m*, -dora *f* **2** EGGBEATER : batidor *m*

beatific [,bi:ə'tɪfɪk] *adj* : beatífico

beatitude [bi'æt̬ə,tu:d] *n* **1** : beatitud *f* **2 the Beatitudes** : las bienaventuranzas

beau ['bo:] *n, pl* **beaux** *or* **beaus** : pretendiente *m*, galán *m*

beautification [,bju:t̬əfə'keɪʃən] *n* : embellecimiento *m*

beautiful ['bju:t̬ɪfəl] *adj* : hermoso, bello, lindo, precioso

beautifully ['bju:t̬ɪfəli] *adv* **1** ATTRACTIVELY : hermosamente **2** EXCELLENTLY : maravillosamente, excelentemente

beauty ['bju:t̬i] *n, pl* **-ties** : belleza *f*, hermosura *f*, beldad *f*

beauty shop *or* **beauty salon** *n* : salón *m* de belleza

beaver ['bi:vər] *n* : castor *m*

because [bɪ'kʌz, -'kɔz] *conj* : porque

because of *prep* : por, a causa de, debido a

beck ['bɛk] *n* **to be at the beck and call of** : estar a la entera disposición de, estar sometido a la voluntad de

beckon ['bɛkən] *vi* **to beckon to someone** : hacerle señas a alguien

become [bɪ'kʌm] *v* **-came** [-'keɪm]; **-come; -coming** *vi* : hacerse, volverse, ponerse ⟨he became famous : se hizo famoso⟩ ⟨to become sad : ponerse triste⟩ ⟨to become accustomed to : acostumbrarse a⟩ — *vt* **1** BEFIT : ser apropiado para **2** SUIT : favorecer, quedarle bien (a alguien) ⟨that dress becomes you : ese vestido te favorece⟩

becoming [bɪ'kʌmɪŋ] *adj* **1** SUITABLE : apropiado **2** FLATTERING : favorecedor

bed[1] ['bɛd] *v* **bedded; bedding** *vt* : acostar — *vi* : acostarse

bed[2] *n* **1** : cama *f*, lecho *m* **2** : cauce *m* (de un río), fondo *m* (del mar) **3** : arriate *m* (para plantas) **4** LAYER, STRATUM : estrato *m*, capa *f*

bedbug [ˈbɛdˌbʌg] *n* : chinche *f*
bedclothes [ˈbɛdˌkloːðz, -ˌkloːz] *npl* : ropa *f* de cama, sábanas *fpl*
bedding [ˈbɛdɪŋ] *n* **1** → **bedclothes 2** : cama *f* (para animales)
bedeck [bɪˈdɛk] *vt* : adornar, engalanar
bedevil [bɪˈdɛvəl] *vt* **-iled** *or* **-illed; -iling** *or* **-illing** : acosar, plagar
bedlam [ˈbɛdləm] *n* : locura *f*, caos *m*, alboroto *m*
bedraggled [bɪˈdrægəld] *adj* : desaliñado, despeinado
bedridden [ˈbɛdˌrɪdən] *adj* : postrado en cama
bedrock [ˈbɛdˌrɑk] *n* : lecho *m* de roca
bedroom [ˈbɛdˌruːm, -ˌrʊm] *n* : dormitorio *m*, habitación *f*, pieza *f*, recámara *f Col, Mex, Pan*
bedspread [ˈbɛdˌsprd] *n* : cubrecama *m*, colcha *f*, cobertor *m*
bee [ˈbiː] *n* **1** : abeja *f* (insecto) **2** GATHERING : círculo *m*, reunión *f*
beech [ˈbiːʧ] *n, pl* **beeches** *or* **beech** : haya *f*
beechnut [ˈbiːʧˌnʌt] *n* : hayuco *m*
beef[1] [ˈbiːf] *vt* **to beef up** : fortalecer, reforzar — *vi* COMPLAIN : quejarse
beef[2] *n, pl* **beefs** [ˈbiːfs] *or* **beeves** [ˈbiːvz] : carne *f* de vaca, carne *f* de res *CA, Mex*
beefsteak [ˈbiːfˌsteɪk] *n* : filete *m*, bistec *m*
beehive [ˈbiːˌhaɪv] *n* : colmena *f*
beekeeper [ˈbiːˌkiːpər] *n* : apicultor *m*, -tora *f*
beeline [ˈbiːˌlaɪn] *n* **to make a beeline for** : ir derecho a, ir directo hacia
been → **be**
beep[1] [ˈbiːp] *v* : pitar
beep[2] *n* : pitido *m*
beeper [ˈbiːpər] *n* : busca *m*, buscapersonas *m*
beer [ˈbɪr] *n* : cerveza *f*
beeswax [ˈbiːzˌwæks] *n* : cera *f* de abejas
beet [ˈbiːt] *n* : remolacha *f*, betabel *m Mex*
beetle [ˈbiːt̬əl] *n* : escarabajo *m*
befall [bɪˈfɔl] *v* **-fell** [-ˈfl]; **-fallen** [-ˈfɔlən] *vt* : sucederle a, acontecerle a — *vi* : acontecer
befit [bɪˈfɪt] *vt* **-fitted; -fitting** : convenir a, ser apropiado para
before[1] [bɪˈfor] *adv* **1** : antes ⟨before and after : antes y después⟩ **2** : anterior ⟨the month before : el mes anterior⟩
before[2] *conj* : antes que ⟨he would die before surrendering : moriría antes que rendirse⟩
before[3] *prep* **1** : antes de ⟨before eating : antes de comer⟩ **2** : delante de, ante ⟨I stood before the house : estaba parada delante de la casa⟩ ⟨before the judge : ante el juez⟩
beforehand [bɪˈforˌhænd] *adv* : antes, por adelantado, de antemano, con anticipación
befriend [bɪˈfrɛnd] *vt* : hacerse amigo de
befuddle [bɪˈfʌdəl] *vt* **-dled; -dling** : aturdir, ofuscar, confundir
beg [ˈbɛg] *v* **begged; begging** *vt* : pedir, mendigar, suplicar ⟨I begged him to go : le supliqué que fuera⟩ — *vi* : mendigar, pedir limosna
beget [bɪˈgɛt] *vt* **-got** [-ˈgɑt]; **-gotten** [-ˈgɑtən] *or* **-got; -getting** : engendrar
beggar [ˈbɛgər] *n* : mendigo *m*, -ga *f*; pordiosero *m*, -ra *f*
begin [bɪˈgɪn] *v* **-gan** [-ˈgæn]; **-gun** [-ˈgʌn]; **-ginning** *vt* : empezar, comenzar, iniciar — *vi* **1** START : empezar, comenzar, iniciarse **2** ORIGINATE : nacer, originarse **3 to begin with** : en primer lugar, para empezar
beginner [bɪˈgɪnər] *n* : principiante *mf*
beginning [bɪˈgɪnɪŋ] *n* : principio *m*, comienzo *m*
begone [biˈgɔn] *interj* : ¡fuera de aquí!
begonia [bɪˈgoːnjə] *n* : begonia *f*
begrudge [bɪˈgrʌʤ] *vt* **-grudged; -grudging 1** : dar de mala gana **2** ENVY : envidiar, resentir
beguile [bɪˈgaɪl] *vt* **-guiled; -guiling 1** DECEIVE : engañar **2** AMUSE : divertir, entretener
behalf [bɪˈhæf, -ˈhaf] *n* **1** : favor *m*, beneficio *m*, parte *f* **2 on behalf of** *or* **in behalf of** : de parte de, en nombre de
behave [bɪˈheɪv] *vi* **-haved; -having** : comportarse, portarse
behavior [bɪˈheɪvjər] *n* : comportamiento *m*, conducta *f*
behead [bɪˈhd] *vt* : decapitar
behest [bɪˈhɛst] *n* **1** : mandato *m*, orden *f* **2 at the behest of** : a instancia de
behind[1] [bɪˈhaɪnd] *adv* : atrás, detrás ⟨to fall behind : quedarse atrás⟩
behind[2] *prep* **1** : atrás de, detrás de, tras ⟨behind the house : detrás de la casa⟩ ⟨one behind another : uno tras otro⟩ **2** : atrasado con, después de ⟨behind schedule : atrasado con el trabajo⟩ ⟨I arrived behind the others : llegué después de los otros⟩ **3** SUPPORTING : en apoyo de, detrás
behind[3] [bɪˈhaɪnd, ˈbiːˌhaɪnd] *n* : trasero *m*
behold [bɪˈhoːld] *vt* **-held; -holding** : contemplar
beholder [bɪˈhoːldər] *n* : observador *m*, -dora *f*
behoove [bɪˈhuːv] *vt* **-hooved; -hooving** : convenirle a, corresponderle a ⟨it behooves us to help him : nos conviene ayudarlo⟩
beige[1] [ˈbeɪʒ] *adj* : beige
beige[2] *n* : beige *m*
being [ˈbiːɪŋ] *n* **1** EXISTENCE : ser *m*, existencia *f* **2** CREATURE : ser *m*, ente *m*
belabor [bɪˈleɪbər] *vt* **to belabor the point** : extenderse sobre el tema
belated [bɪˈleɪt̬əd] *adj* : tardío, retrasado
belch[1] [ˈbɛlʧ] *vi* **1** BURP : eructar **2** EXPEL : expulsar, arrojar
belch[2] *n* : eructo *m*

beleaguer [bɪˈli:gər] *vt* **1** BESIEGE : asediar, sitiar **2** HARASS : fastidiar, molestar
belfry [ˈbɛlfri] *n, pl* **-fries** : campanario *m*
Belgian [ˈbɛlʤən] *n* : belga *mf* — **Belgian** *adj*
belie [bɪˈlaɪ] *vt* **-lied; -lying** **1** MISREPRESENT : falsear, ocultar **2** CONTRADICT : contradecir, desmentir
belief [bəˈli:f] *n* **1** TRUST : confianza *f* **2** CONVICTION : creencia *f*, convicción *f* **3** FAITH : fe *f*
believable [bəˈli:vəbəl] *adj* : verosímil, creíble
believe [bəˈli:v] *v* **-lieved; -lieving** : creer
believer [bəˈli:vər] *n* **1** : creyente *mf* **2** : partidario *m*, -ria *f*; entusiasta *mf* ⟨she's a great believer in vitamins : ella es una gran partidaria de las vitaminas⟩
belittle [bɪˈlɪt̬əl] *vt* **-littled; -littling** **1** DISPARAGE : menospreciar, denigrar, rebajar **2** MINIMIZE : minimizar, quitar importancia a
Belizean [bəˈli:ziən] *n* : beliceño *m*, -ña *f* — **Belizean** *adj*
bell[1] [ˈbɛl] *vt* : ponerle un cascabel a
bell[2] *n* : campana *f*, cencerro *m* (para una vaca o cabra), cascabel *m* (para un gato), timbre *m* (de teléfono, de la puerta)
belle [ˈbɛl] *n* : belleza *f*, beldad *f*
bellhop [ˈbɛlˌhɑp] *n* : botones *m*
bellicose [ˈbɛlɪˌko:s] *adj* : belicoso *m* — **bellicosity** [ˌbɛlɪˈkɑsət̬i] *n*
belligerence [bəˈlɪʤərənts] *n* : agresividad *f*, beligerancia *f*
belligerent[1] [bəˈlɪʤərənt] *adj* : agresivo, beligerante
belligerent[2] *n* : beligerante *mf*
bellow[1] [ˈbɛˌlo:] *vi* : bramar, mugir — *vt* : gritar
bellow[2] *n* : bramido *m*, grito *m*
bellows [ˈbɛˌlo:z] *ns & pl* : fuelle *m*
bellwether [ˈbɛlˌwɛðər] *n* : líder *mf*
belly[1] [ˈbɛli] *vi* **-lied; -lying** SWELL : hincharse, inflarse
belly[2] *n, pl* **-lies** : abdomen *m*, vientre *m*, barriga *f*, panza *f*
belong [bɪˈlɔŋ] *vi* **1** : pertenecer (a), ser propiedad (de) ⟨it belongs to her : pertenece a ella, es suyo, es de ella⟩ **2** : ser parte (de), ser miembro (de) ⟨he belongs to the club : es miembro del club⟩ **3** : deber estar, ir ⟨your coat belongs in the closet : tu abrigo va en el ropero⟩
belongings [bɪˈlɔŋɪŋz] *npl* : pertenencias *fpl*, efectos *mpl* personales
beloved[1] [bɪˈlʌvəd, -ˈlʌvd] *adj* : querido, amado
beloved[2] *n* : amado *m*, -da *f*; enamorado *m*, -da *f*; amor *m*
below[1] [bɪˈlo:] *adv* : abajo
below[2] *prep* **1** : abajo de, debajo de ⟨below the window : debajo de la ventana⟩ **2** : por debajo de, bajo ⟨below average : por debajo del promedio⟩ ⟨5 degrees below zero : 5 grados bajo cero⟩
belt[1] [ˈbɛlt] *vt* **1** : ceñir con un cinturón, ponerle un cinturón a **2** THRASH : darle una paliza a, darle un trancazo a
belt[2] *n* **1** : cinturón *m*, cinto *m* (para el talle) **2** BAND, STRAP : cinta *f*, correa *f*, banda *f Mex* **3** AREA : frente *m*, zona *f*
beltway [ˈbɛltˌweɪ] *n* : carretera *f* de circunvalación; periférico *m CA, Mex*; libramiento *m Mex*
bemoan [bɪˈmo:n] *vt* : lamentarse de
bemuse [bɪˈmju:z] *vt* **-mused; -musing** **1** BEWILDER : confundir, desconcertar **2** ENGROSS : absorber
bench [ˈbɛntʃ] *n* **1** SEAT : banco *m*, escaño *m*, banca *f* **2** : estrado *m* (de un juez) **3** COURT : tribunal *m*
bend[1] [ˈbɛnd] *v* **bent** [ˈbnt;]; **bending** *vt* : torcer, doblar, curvar, flexionar — *vi* **1** : torcerse, agacharse ⟨to bend over : inclinarse⟩ **2** TURN : torcer, hacer una curva
bend[2] *n* **1** TURN : vuelta *f*, recodo *m* **2** CURVE : curva *f*, ángulo *m*, codo *m*
beneath[1] [bɪˈni:θ] *adv* : bajo, abajo, debajo
beneath[2] *prep* : bajo de, abajo de, por debajo de
benediction [ˌbɛnəˈdɪkʃən] *n* : bendición *f*
benefactor [ˈbɛnəˌfæktər] *n* : benefactor *m*, -tora *f*
beneficence [bəˈnɛfəsənts] *n* : beneficencia *f*
beneficent [bəˈnɛfəsənt] *adj* : benéfico, caritativo
beneficial [ˌbɛnəˈfɪʃəl] *adj* : beneficioso, provechoso — **beneficially** *adv*
beneficiary [ˌbɛnəˈfɪʃiˌɛri, -ˈfɪʃəri] *n, pl* **-ries** : beneficiario *m*, -ria *f*
benefit[1] [ˈbɛnəfɪt] *vt* : beneficiar — *vi* : beneficiarse
benefit[2] *n* **1** ADVANTAGE : beneficio *m*, ventaja *f*, provecho *m* **2** AID : asistencia *f*, beneficio *m* **3** : función *f* benéfica (para recaudar fondos)
benevolence [bəˈnɛvələnts] *n* : bondad *f*, benevolencia *f*
benevolent [bəˈnɛvələnt] *adj* : benévolo, bondadoso — **benevolently** *adv*
Bengali [bɛnˈgɔli, bɛŋ-] *n* **1** : bengalí *mf* **2** : bengalí *m* (idioma) — **Bengali** *adj*
benign [bɪˈnaɪn] *adj* **1** GENTLE, KIND : benévolo, amable **2** FAVORABLE : propicio, favorable **3** MILD : benigno ⟨a benign tumor : un tumor benigno⟩
Beninese [bəˌnɪˈni:z, -ˌni:-, -ˈni:s; ˌbɪnɪˈ-] *n* : beninés *m*, -nesa *f* — **Beninese** *adj*
bent [ˈbɛnt] *n* : aptitud *f*, inclinación *f*
benumb [bɪˈnʌm] *vt* : entumecer
benzene [ˈbɛnˌzi:n] *n* : benceno *m*
bequeath [bɪˈkwi:θ, -ˈkwi:ð] *vt* : legar, dejar en testamento
bequest [bɪˈkwɛst] *n* : legado *m*
berate [bɪˈreɪt] *vt* **-rated; -rating** : reprender, regañar
bereaved[1] [bɪˈri:vd] *adj* : que está de luto, afligido (por la muerte de alguien)

bereaved[2] *n* **the bereaved** : los deudos del difunto (o de la difunta)

bereavement [bɪˈri:vmənt] *n* **1** SORROW : dolor *m*, pesar *m* **2** LOSS : pérdida *f*

bereft [bɪˈrɛft] *adj* : privado, desprovisto

beret [bəˈreɪ] *n* : boina *f*

beriberi [ˌbɛriˈbɛri] *n* : beriberi *m*

berm [ˈbərm] *n* : arcén *m*

berry [ˈbɛri] *n, pl* **-ries** : baya *f*

berserk [bərˈsərk, -ˈzərk] *adj* **1** : enloquecido **2 to go beserk** : volverse loco

berth[1] [ˈbərθ] *vi* : atracar

berth[2] *n* **1** DOCK : atracadero *m* **2** ACCOMMODATION : litera *f*, camarote *m* **3** POSITION : trabajo *m*, puesto *m*

beryl [ˈbɛrəl] *n* : berilo *m*

beseech [bɪˈsi:ʧ] *vt* **-seeched** *or* **-sought** [-ˈsɔt]; **-seeching** : suplicar, implorar, rogar

beset [bɪˈsɛt] *vt* **-set; -setting 1** HARASS : acosar **2** SURROUND : rodear

beside [bɪˈsaɪd] *prep* : al lado de, junto a

besides[1] [bɪˈsaɪdz] *adv* **1** ALSO : además, también, aparte **2** MOREOVER : además, por otra parte

besides[2] *prep* **1** : además de, aparte de ⟨six others besides you : seis otros además de ti⟩ **2** EXCEPT : excepto, fuera de, aparte de

besiege [bɪˈsi:ʤ] *vt* **-sieged; -sieging** : asediar, sitiar, cercar

besmirch [bɪˈsmərʧ] *vt* : ensuciar, mancillar

best[1] [ˈbɛst] *vt* : superar, ganar a

best[2] *adv* (*superlative* of **well**) : mejor ⟨as best I can : lo mejor que puedo⟩

best[3] *adj* (*superlative* of **good**) : mejor ⟨my best friend : mi mejor amigo⟩

best[4] *n* **1 the best** : lo mejor, el mejor, la mejor, los mejores, las mejores **2 at ~** : a lo más **3 to do one's best** : hacer todo lo posible

bestial [ˈbɛsʧəl, ˈbi:s-] *adj* **1** : bestial **2** BRUTISH : brutal, salvaje

best man *n* : padrino *m*

bestow [bɪˈsto:] *vt* : conferir, otorgar, conceder

bestowal [bɪˈsto:əl] *n* : concesión *f*, otorgamiento *m*

bet[1] [ˈbɛt] *v* **bet; betting** *vt* : apostar — *vi* **to bet on** : apostarle a

bet[2] *n* : apuesta *f*

betoken [bɪˈto:kən] *vt* : denotar, ser indicio de

betray [bɪˈtreɪ] *vt* **1** : traicionar ⟨to betray one's country : traicionar uno a su patria⟩ **2** DIVULGE, REVEAL : delatar, revelar ⟨to betray a secret : revelar un secreto⟩

betrayal [bɪˈtreɪəl] *n* : traición *f*, delación *f*, revelación *f* ⟨betrayal of trust : abuso de confianza⟩

betrothal [bɪˈtro:ðəl, -ˈtrɔ-] *n* : esponsales *mpl*, compromiso *m*

betrothed [bɪˈtro:ðd, -ˈtrɔθt] *n* FIANCÉ : prometido *m*, -da *f*

better[1] [ˈbɛt̬ər] *vt* **1** IMPROVE : mejorar **2** SURPASS : superar

better[2] *adv* (*comparative* of **well**) **1** : mejor **2** MORE : más ⟨better than 50 miles : más de 50 millas⟩

better[3] *adj* (*comparative* of **good**) **1** : mejor ⟨the weather is better today : hace mejor tiempo hoy⟩ ⟨I was sick, but now I'm better : estuve enfermo, pero ahora estoy mejor⟩ **2** : mayor ⟨the better part of a month : la mayor parte de un mes⟩

better[4] *n* **1** : el mejor, la mejor ⟨the better of the two : el mejor de los dos⟩ **2 to get the better of** : vencer a, quedar por encima de, superar

betterment [ˈbɛt̬ərmənt] *n* : mejoramiento *m*, mejora *f*

bettor *or* **better** [ˈbɛt̬ər] *n* : apostador *m*, -dora *f*

between[1] [bɪˈtwi:n] *adv* **1** : en medio, por lo medio **2 in ~** : intermedio

between[2] *prep* : entre

bevel[1] [ˈbɛvəl] *v* **-eled** *or* **-elled; -eling** *or* **-elling** *vt* : biselar — *vi* INCLINE : inclinarse

bevel[2] *n* : bisel *m*

beverage [ˈbɛvrɪʤ, ˈbɛvə-] *n* : bebida *f*

bevy [ˈbɛvi] *n, pl* **bevies** : grupo *m* (de personas), bandada *f* (de pájaros)

bewail [bɪˈweɪl] *vt* : lamentarse de, llorar

beware [bɪˈwær] *vi* **to beware of** : tener cuidado con ⟨beware of the dog! : ¡cuidado con el perro!⟩ — *vt* : guardarse de, cuidarse de

bewilder [bɪˈwɪldər] *vt* : desconcertar, dejar perplejo

bewilderment [bɪˈwɪldərmənt] *n* : desconcierto *m*, perplejidad *f*

bewitch [bɪˈwɪʧ] *vt* **1** : hechizar, embrujar **2** CHARM : cautivar, encantar

bewitchment [bɪˈwɪʧmənt] *n* : hechizo *m*

beyond[1] [biˈjɑnd] *adv* **1** FARTHER, LATER : más allá, más lejos (en el espacio), más adelante (en el tiempo) **2** MORE : más ⟨$50 and beyond : $50 o más⟩

beyond[2] *n* **the beyond** : el más allá, lo desconocido

beyond[3] *prep* **1** : más allá de ⟨beyond the frontier : más allá de la frontera⟩ **2** : fuera de ⟨beyond one's reach : fuera de su alcance⟩ **3** BESIDES : además de

biannual [ˌbaɪˈænjuəl] *adj* : bianual — **biannually** *adv*

bias[1] [ˈbaɪəs] *vt* **-ased** *or* **-assed; -asing** *or* **-assing 1** : predisponer, sesgar, influir en, afectar **2 to be biased against** : tener prejuicio contra

bias[2] *n* **1** : sesgo *m*, bies *m* (en la costura) **2** PREJUDICE : prejuicio *m* **3** TENDENCY : inclinación *f*, tendencia *f*

biased [ˈbaɪəst] *adj* : tendencioso, parcial

bib [ˈbɪb] *n* **1** : peto *m* **2** : babero *m* (para niños)

Bible [ˈbaɪbəl] *n* : Biblia *f*

biblical [ˈbɪblɪkəl] *adj* : bíblico

bibliographer [ˌbɪbliˈɑgrəfər] *n* : bibliógrafo *m*, -fa *f*
bibliographic [ˌbɪbliəˈgræfɪk] *adj* : bibliográfico
bibliography [ˌbɪbliˈɑgrəfi] *n, pl* **-phies** : bibliografía *f*
bicameral [ˌbaɪˈkæmərəl] *adj* : bicameral
bicarbonate [ˌbaɪˈkɑrbənət, -ˌneɪt] *n* : bicarbonato *m*
bicentennial [ˌbaɪsɛnˈtɛniəl] *n* : bicentenario *m*
biceps [ˈbaɪˌsɛps] *ns & pl* : bíceps *m*
bicker¹ [ˈbɪkər] *vi* : pelear, discutir, reñir
bicker² *n* : pelea *f*, riña *f*, discusión *f*
bicuspid [baɪˈkʌspɪd] *n* : premolar *m*, diente *m* bicúspide
bicycle¹ [ˈbaɪsɪkəl, -ˌsɪ-] *vi* **-cled; -cling** : ir en bicicleta
bicycle² *n* : bicicleta *f*
bicycling [ˈbaɪsɪkəlɪŋ] *n* : ciclismo *m*
bicyclist [ˈbaɪsɪkəlɪst] *n* : ciclista *mf*
bid¹ [ˈbɪd] *vt* **bade** [ˈbæd, ˈbeɪd] *or* **bid; bidden** [ˈbɪdən] *or* **bid; bidding 1** ORDER : pedir, mandar **2** INVITE : invitar **3** SAY : dar, decir ⟨to bid good evening : dar las buenas noches⟩ ⟨to bid farewell to : decir adiós a⟩ **4** : ofrecer (en una subasta), declarar (en juegos de cartas)
bid² *n* **1** OFFER : oferta *f* (en una subasta), declaración *f* (en juegos de cartas) **2** INVITATION : invitación *f* **3** ATTEMPT : intento *m*, tentativa *f*
bidder [ˈbɪdər] *n* : postor *m*, -tora *f*
bide [ˈbaɪd] *v* **bode** [ˈbo:d] *or* **bided; bided; biding** *vt* : esperar, aguardar ⟨to bide one's time : esperar el momento oportuno⟩ — *vi* DWELL : morar, vivir
biennial [baɪˈɛniəl] *adj* : bienal — **biennially** *adv*
bier [ˈbɪr] *n* **1** STAND : andas *fpl* **2** COFFIN : ataúd *m*, féretro *m*
bifocals [ˈbaɪˌfo:kəlz] *npl* : lentes *mpl* bifocales, bifocales *mpl*
big [ˈbɪg] *adj* **bigger; biggest 1** LARGE : grande **2** PREGNANT : embarazada **3** IMPORTANT, MAJOR : importante, grande ⟨a big decision : una gran decisión⟩ **4** POPULAR : popular, famoso, conocido
bigamist [ˈbɪgəmɪst] *n* : bígamo *m*, -ma *f*
bigamous [ˈbɪgəməs] *adj* : bígamo
bigamy [ˈbɪgəmi] *n* : bigamia *f*
Big Dipper → **dipper**
bighorn [ˈbɪgˌhɔrn] *n, pl* **-horn** *or* **-horns** *or* **bighorn sheep** : oveja *f* salvaje de las montañas
bight [ˈbaɪt] *n* : bahía *f*, ensenada *f*, golfo *m*
bigot [ˈbɪgət] *n* : intolerante *mf*
bigoted [ˈbɪgəṭəd] *adj* : intolerante, prejuiciado, fanático
bigotry [ˈbɪgətri] *n, pl* **-tries** : intolerancia *f*
big shot *n* : pez *m* gordo *fam*, mandamás *mf*
bigwig [ˈbɪgˌwɪg] → **big shot**
bike [ˈbaɪk] *n* **1** : bicicleta *f*, bici *f fam* **2** : motocicleta *f*, moto *f*
bikini [bəˈki:ni] *n* : bikini *m*
bilateral [baɪˈlæṭərəl] *adj* : bilateral — **bilaterally** *adv*
bile [ˈbaɪl] *n* **1** : bilis *f* **2** IRRITABILITY : mal genio *m*
bilingual [baɪˈlɪŋgwəl] *adj* : bilingüe
bilious [ˈbɪliəs] *adj* **1** : bilioso **2** IRRITABLE : bilioso, colérico
bilk [ˈbɪlk] *vt* : burlar, estafar, defraudar
bill¹ [ˈbɪl] *vt* : pasarle la cuenta a — *vi* : acariciar ⟨to bill and coo : acariciarse⟩
bill² *n* **1** LAW : proyecto *m* de ley, ley *f* **2** INVOICE : cuenta *f*, factura *f* **3** POSTER : cartel *m* **4** PROGRAM : programa *m* (del teatro) **5** : billete *m* ⟨a five-dollar bill : un billete de cinco dólares⟩ **6** BEAK : pico *m*
billboard [ˈbɪlˌbɔrd] *n* : cartelera *f*
billet¹ [ˈbɪlət] *vt* : acuartelar, alojar
billet² *n* : alojamiento *m*
billfold [ˈbɪlˌfo:ld] *n* : billetera *f*, cartera *f*
billiards [ˈbɪljərdz] *n* : billar *m*
billion [ˈbɪljən] *n, pl* **billions** *or* **billion** : mil millones *mpl*
billow¹ [ˈbɪlo] *vi* : hincharse, inflarse
billow² *n* **1** WAVE : ola *f* **2** CLOUD : nube *f* ⟨a billow of smoke : un nube de humo⟩
billowy [ˈbɪlowi] *adj* : ondulante
billy goat [ˈbɪliˌgo:t] *n* : macho *m* cabrío
bin [ˈbɪn] *n* : cubo *m*, cajón *m*
binary [ˈbaɪnəri, -ˌnɛri] *adj* : binario *m*
bind [ˈbaɪnd] *vt* **bound** [ˈbaʊnd]; **binding 1** TIE : atar, amarrar **2** OBLIGATE : obligar **3** UNITE : aglutinar, ligar, unir **4** BANDAGE : vendar **5** : encuadernar (un libro)
binder [ˈbaɪndər] *n* **1** FOLDER : carpeta *f* **2** : encuadernador *m*, -dora *f* (de libros)
binding [ˈbaɪndɪŋ] *n* **1** : encuadernación *f* (de libros) **2** COVER : cubierta *f*, forro *m*
binge [ˈbɪndʒ] *n* : juerga *f*, parranda *f fam*
bingo [ˈbɪŋˌgo:] *n, pl* **-gos** : bingo *m*
binocular [baɪˈnɑkjələr, bə-] *adj* : binocular
binoculars [bəˈnɑkjələrz, baɪ-] *npl* : binoculares *mpl*
biochemical¹ [ˌbaɪoˈkɛmɪkəl] *adj* : bioquímico
biochemical² *n* : bioquímico *m*
biochemist [ˌbaɪoˈkɛmɪst] *n* : bioquímico *m*, -ca *f*
biochemistry [ˌbaɪoˈkɛməstri] *n* : bioquímica *f*
biodegradable [ˌbaɪodɪˈgreɪdəbəl] *adj* : biodegradable
biodegradation [ˌbaɪodɛgrəˈdeɪʃən] *n* : biodegradación *f*
biodegrade [ˌbaɪodɪˈgreɪd] *vi* **-graded; -grading** : biodegradarse

biodiversity [ˌbaɪodəˈvərsət̬i, -daɪ-] *n, pl* **-ties** : bioversidad *f*
biographer [baɪˈɑgrəfər] *n* : biógrafo *m*, -fa *f*
biographical [ˌbaɪəˈgræfɪkəl] *adj* : biográfico
biography [baɪˈɑgrəfi, biː-] *n, pl* **-phies** : biografía *f*
biologic [ˌbaɪəˈlɑʤɪk] *or* **biological** [-ʤɪkəl] *adj* : biológico
biologist [baɪˈɑləʤɪst] *n* : biólogo *m*, -ga *f*
biology [baɪˈɑləʤi] *n* : biología *f*
biophysical [ˌbaɪoˈfɪzɪkəl] *adj* : biofísico
biophysicist [ˌbaɪoˈfɪzəsɪst] *n* : biofísico *m*, -ca *f*
biophysics [ˌbaɪoˈfɪzɪks] *ns & pl* : biofísica *f*
biopsy [ˈbaɪˌɑpsi] *n, pl* **-sies** : biopsia *f*
biosphere [ˈbaɪəˌsfɪr] *n* : biosfera *f*, biósfera *f*
biotechnology [ˌbaɪotɛkˈnɑləʤi] *n* : biotecnología *f*
biotic [baɪˈɑtɪk] *adj* : biótico
bipartisan [baɪˈpɑrt̬əzən, -sən] *adj* : bipartidista, de dos partidas
biped [ˈbaɪˌpɛd] *n* : bípedo *m*
birch [ˈbərʧ] *n* : abedul *m*
bird [ˈbərd] *n* : pájaro *m* (pequeño), ave *f* (grande)
birdbath [ˈbərdˌbæθ, -ˌbaθ] *n* : pila *f* para pájaros
bird dog *n* : perro *m*, -rra *f* de caza
bird of prey *n* : ave *f* rapaz, ave *f* de presa
birdseed [ˈbərdˌsiːd] *n* : alpiste *m*
bird's–eye [ˈbərdzˌaɪ] *adj* **1** : visto desde arriba ⟨bird's-eye view : vista aérea⟩ **2** CURSORY : rápido, somero
birth [ˈbərθ] *n* **1** : nacimiento *m*, parto *m* **2** ORIGIN : origen *m*, nacimiento *m*
birthday [ˈbərθˌdeɪ] *n* : cumpleaños *m*, aniversario *m*
birthmark [ˈbərθˌmɑrk] *n* : mancha *f* de nacimiento
birthplace [ˈbərθˌpleɪs] *n* : lugar *m* de nacimiento
birthrate [ˈbərθˌreɪt] *n* : índice *m* de natalidad
birthright [ˈbərθˌraɪt] *n* : derecho *m* de nacimiento
biscuit [ˈbɪskət] *n* : bizcocho *m*
bisect [ˈbaɪˌsɛkt, ˌbaɪˈ-] *vt* : bisecar
bisexual [ˌbaɪˈsekʃʊəl] *adj* : bisexual
bishop [ˈbɪʃəp] *n* **1** : obispo *m* **2** : alfil *m* (en ajedrez)
bismuth [ˈbɪzməθ] *n* : bismuto *m*
bison [ˈbaɪzən, -sən] *ns & pl* : bisonte *m*
bistro [ˈbiːstro, ˈbɪs-] *n, pl* **-tros** : bar *m*, restaurante *m* pequeño
bit [ˈbɪt] *n* **1** FRAGMENT, PIECE : pedazo *m*, trozo *m* ⟨a bit of luck : un poco de suerte⟩ **2** : freno *m*, bocado *m* (de una brida) **3** : broca *f* (de un taladro) **4** : bit *m* (de información)
bitch¹ [ˈbɪʧ] *vi* COMPLAIN : quejarse, reclamar
bitch² *n* : perra *f*
bite¹ [ˈbaɪt] *v* **bit** [ˈbɪt]; **bitten** [ˈbɪtən]; **biting** *vt* **1** : morder **2** STING : picar **3** PUNCTURE : punzar, pinchar **4** GRIP : agarrar — *vi* **1** : morder ⟨that dog bites : ese perro muerde⟩ **2** STING : picar (dícese de un insecto), cortar (dícese del viento) **3** : picar ⟨the fish are biting now : ya están picando los peces⟩ **4** GRAB : agarrarse
bite² *n* **1** BITING : mordisco *m*, dentellada *f* **2** SNACK : bocado *m* ⟨a bite to eat : algo de comer⟩ **3** : picadura *f* (de un insecto), mordedura *f* (de un animal) **4** SHARPNESS : mordacidad *f*, penetración *f*
biting *adj* **1** PENETRATING : cortante, penetrante **2** CAUSTIC : mordaz, sarcástico
bitter [ˈbɪt̬ər] *adj* **1** ACRID : amargo, acre **2** PENETRATING : cortante, penetrante ⟨bitter cold : frío glacial⟩ **3** HARSH : duro, amargo ⟨to the bitter end : hasta el final⟩ **4** INTENSE, RELENTLESS : intenso, extremo, implacable ⟨bitter hatred : odio implacable⟩
bitterly [ˈbɪt̬ərli] *adv* : amargamente
bitterness [ˈbɪt̬ərnəs] *n* : amargura *f*
bittersweet [ˈbɪt̬ərˌswiːt] *adj* : agridulce
bivalve [ˈbaɪˌvælv] *n* : bivalvo *m* — **bivalve** *adj*
bivouac¹ [ˈbɪvəˌwæk, ˈbɪvˌwæk] *vi* **-ouacked; -ouacking** : acampar, vivaquear
bivouac² *n* : vivaque *m*
bizarre [bəˈzɑr] *adj* : extraño, singular, estrafalario, estrambótico — **bizarrely** *adv*
blab [ˈblæb] *vi* **blabbed; blabbing** : parlotear *fam*, cotorrear *fam*
black¹ [ˈblæk] *vt* : ennegrecer
black² *adj* **1** : negro (color, raza) **2** SOILED : sucio **3** DARK : oscuro, negro **4** WICKED : malvado, perverso, malo **5** GLOOMY : negro, sombrío, deprimente
black³ *n* **1** : negro *m* (color) **2** : negro *m*, -gra *f* (persona)
black–and–blue [ˌblækənˈbluː] *adj* : amoratado
blackball [ˈblækˌbɔl] *vt* **1** OSTRACIZE : hacerle el vacío a, aislar **2** BOYCOTT : boicotear
blackberry [ˈblækˌbɛri] *n, pl* **-ries** : mora *f*
blackbird [ˈblækˌbərd] *n* : mirlo *m*
blackboard [ˈblækˌbɔrd] *n* : pizarra *f*, pizarrón *m*
blacken [ˈblækən] *vt* **1** BLACK : ennegrecer **2** DEFAME : deshonrar, difamar, manchar
blackhead [ˈblækˌhɛd] *n* : espinilla *f*, punto *m* negro
black hole *n* : agujero *m* negro
blackjack [ˈblækˌʤæk] *n* **1** : cachiporra *f* (arma) **2** : veintiuna *f* (juego de cartas)
blacklist¹ [ˈblækˌlɪst] *vt* : poner en la lista negra

blacklist² *n* : lista *f* negra

blackmail¹ [ˈblæk,meɪl] *vt* : chantajear, hacer chantaje a

blackmail² *n* : chantaje *m*

blackmailer [ˈblæk,meɪlər] *n* : chantajista *mf*

blackout [ˈblæk,aʊt] *n* **1** : apagón *m* (de poder eléctrico) **2** FAINT : desmayo *m*, desvanecimiento *m*

black out *vt* : dejar sin luz — *vi* FAINT : perder el conocimiento, desmayarse

blacksmith [ˈblæk,smɪθ] *n* : herrero *m*

blacktop [ˈblæk,tɑp] *n* : asfalto *m*

bladder [ˈblædər] *n* : vejiga *f*

blade [ˈbleɪd] *n* : hoja *f* (de un cuchillo), cuchilla *f* (de un patín), pala *f* (de un remo o una hélice), brizna *f* (de hierba)

blamable [ˈbleɪməbəl] *adj* : culpable

blame¹ [ˈbleɪm] *vt* **blamed; blaming** : culpar, echar la culpa a

blame² *n* : culpa *f*

blameless [ˈbleɪmləs] *adj* : intachable, sin culpa, inocente — **blamelessly** *adv*

blameworthiness [ˈbleɪm,wərðinəs] *n* : culpa *f*, culpabilidad *f*

blameworthy [ˈbleɪm,wərði] *adj* : culpable, reprochable, censurable

blanch [ˈblæntʃ] *vt* WHITEN : blanquear — *vi* PALE : palidecer

bland [ˈblænd] *adj* : soso, insulso, desabrido ⟨a bland smile : una sonrisa insulsa⟩ ⟨a bland diet : una dieta fácil de digerir⟩

blandishments [ˈblændɪʃmənts] *npl* : lisonjas *fpl*, halagos *mpl*

blandly [ˈblændli] *adv* : de manera insulsa

blandness [ˈblændnəs] *n* : lo insulso, lo desabrido

blank¹ [ˈblæŋk] *vt* OBLITERATE : borrar

blank² *adj* **1** DAZED : perplejo, desconcertado **2** EXPRESSIONLESS : sin expresión, inexpresivo **3** : en blanco (dícese de un papel), liso (dícese de una pared) **4** EMPTY : vacío, en blanco ⟨a blank stare : una mirada vacía⟩ ⟨his mind went blank : se quedó en blanco⟩

blank³ *n* **1** SPACE : espacio *m* en blanco **2** FORM : formulario *m* **3** CARTRIDGE : cartucho *m* de fogueo **4** *or* **blank key** : llave *f* ciega

blanket¹ [blæŋkət] *vt* : cubrir

blanket² *adj* : global

blanket³ *n* : manta *f*, cobija *f*, frazada *f*

blankly [ˈblænkli] *adv* : sin comprender

blankness [ˈblænknəs] *n* **1** PERPLEXITY : desconcierto *m*, perplejidad *f* **2** EMPTINESS : vacío *m*, vacuidad *f*

blare¹ [ˈblær] *vi* **blared; blaring** : resonar

blare² *n* : estruendo *m*

blarney [ˈblɑrni] *n* : labia *f fam*

blasé [blɑˈzeɪ] *adj* : displicente, indiferente

blaspheme [blæsˈfiːm, ˈblæs,-] *vi* **-phemed; -pheming** : blasfemar

blasphemer [blæsˈfiːmər, ˈblæs,-] *n* : blasfemo *m*, -ma *f*

blasphemous [ˈblæsfəməs] *adj* : blasfemo

blasphemy [ˈblæsfəmi] *n, pl* **-mies** : blasfemia *f*

blast¹ [ˈblæst] *vt* **1** BLOW UP : volar, hacer volar **2** ATTACK : atacar, arremeter contra

blast² *n* **1** GUST : ráfaga *f* **2** EXPLOSION : explosión *f*

blast–off [ˈblæst,ɔf] *n* : despegue *m*

blast off *vi* : despegar

blatant [ˈbleɪtənt] *adj* : descarado — **blatantly** [ˈbleɪtəntli] *adv*

blaze¹ [ˈbleɪz] *v* **blazed; blazing** *vi* SHINE : arder, brillar, resplandecer — *vt* MARK : marcar, señalar ⟨to blaze a trail : abrir un camino⟩

blaze² *n* **1** FIRE : fuego *m* **2** BRIGHTNESS : resplandor *m*, brillantez *f* **3** OUTBURST : arranque *m* ⟨a blaze of anger : un arranque de cólera⟩ **4** DISPLAY : alarde *m*, llamarada *f* ⟨a blaze of color : un derroche de color⟩

blazer [ˈbleɪzər] *n* : chaqueta *f* deportiva, blazer *m*

bleach¹ [ˈbliːtʃ] *vt* : blanquear, decolorar

bleach² *n* : lejía *f*, blanqueador *m*

bleachers [ˈbliːtʃərz] *ns & pl* : gradas *fpl*, tribuna *f* descubierta

bleak [ˈbliːk] *adj* **1** DESOLATE : inhóspito, sombrío, desolado **2** DEPRESSING : deprimente, triste, sombrío

bleakly [ˈbliːkli] *adv* : sombríamente

bleakness [ˈbliːknəs] *n* : lo inhóspito, lo sombrío

blear [ˈblɪr] *adj* : empañado, nublado

bleary [ˈblɪri] *adj* **1** : adormilado, fatigado **2** **bleary–eyed** : con los ojos nublados

bleat¹ [ˈbliːt] *vi* : balar

bleat² *n* : balido *m*

bleed [ˈbliːd] *v* **bled** [ˈbɛld]; **bleeding** *vi* **1** : sangrar **2** GRIEVE : sufrir, afligirse **3** EXUDE : exudar (dícese de una planta), correrse (dícese de los colores) — *vt* **1** : sangrar (a una persona), purgar (frenos) **2** **to bleed someone dry** : sacarle todo el dinero a alguien

blemish¹ [ˈblɛmɪʃ] *vt* : manchar, marcar

blemish² *n* : imperfección *f*, mancha *f*, marca *f*

blend¹ [ˈblɛnd] *vt* **1** MIX : mezclar **2** COMBINE : combinar, aunar

blend² *n* : mezcla *f*, combinación *f*

blender [ˈblɛndər] *n* : licuadora *f*

bless [ˈblɛs] *vt* **blessed** [ˈblɛst]; **blessing** **1** CONSECRATE : bendecir, consagrar **2** : bendecir ⟨may God bless you! : ¡que Dios te bendiga!⟩ **3 to bless with** : dotar de **4 to bless oneself** : santiguarse

blessed [ˈblɛsəd] *or* **blest** [ˈblɛst] *adj* : bienaventurado, bendito, dichoso

blessedly [ˈblɛsədli] *adv* : felizmente, alegremente, afortunadamente

blessing [ˈblɛsɪŋ] *n* **1** : bendición *f* **2** APPROVAL : aprobación *f*, consentimiento *m*

blew → **blow**
blight[1] ['blaɪt] *vt* : arruinar, infestar
blight[2] *n* **1** : añublo *m* **2** PLAGUE : peste *f*, plaga *f* **3** DECAY : deterioro *m*, ruina *f*
blimp ['blɪmp] *n* : dirigible *m*
blind[1] ['blaɪnd] *vt* **1** : cegar, dejar ciego **2** DAZZLE : deslumbrar
blind[2] *adj* **1** SIGHTLESS : ciego **2** INSENSITIVE : ciego, insensible, sin razón **3** CLOSED : sin salida ⟨blind alley : callejón sin salida⟩
blind[3] *n* **1** : persiana *f* (para una ventana) **2** COVER : escondite *m*, escondrijo *m*
blinders ['blaɪndərz] *npl* : anteojeras *fpl*
blindfold[1] ['blaɪnd,fo:ld] *vt* : vendar los ojos
blindfold[2] *n* : venda *f* (para los ojos)
blinding ['blaɪndɪŋ] *adj* : enceguecedor, cegador ⟨with blinding speed : con una rapidez inusitada⟩
blindly ['blaɪndli] *adv* : a ciegas, ciegamente
blindness ['blaɪndnəs] *n* : ceguera *f*
blink[1] ['blɪŋk] *vi* **1** WINK : pestañear, parpadear **2** : brillar intermitentemente
blink[2] *n* : pestañeo *m*, parpadeo *m*
blinker ['blɪŋkər] *n* : intermitente *m*, direccional *f*
bliss ['blɪs] *n* **1** HAPPINESS : dicha *f*, felicidad *f* absoluta **2** PARADISE : paraíso *m*
blissful ['blɪsfəl] *adj* : dichoso, feliz — **blissfully** *adv*
blister[1] ['blɪstər] *vi* : ampollarse
blister[2] *n* : ampolla *f* (en la piel o una superficie), burbuja *f* (en una superficie)
blithe ['blaɪθ, 'blaɪð] *adj* **blither; blithest** **1** CAREFREE : despreocupado **2** CHEERFUL : alegre, risueño — **blithely** *adv*
blitz[1] ['blɪts] *vt* **1** BOMBARD : bombardear **2** : atacar con rapidez
blitz[2] *n* **1** : bombardeo *m* aéreo **2** CAMPAIGN : ataque *m*, acometida *f*
blizzard ['blɪzərd] *n* : tormenta *f* de nieve, ventisca *f*
bloat ['blo:t] *vi* : hincharse, inflarse
blob ['blɑb] *n* : gota *f*, mancha *f*, borrón *m*
bloc ['blɑk] *n* : bloque *m*
block[1] ['blɑk] *vt* **1** OBSTRUCT : obstruir, bloquear **2** CLOG : atascar, atorar
block[2] *n* **1** PIECE : bloque *m* ⟨building blocks : cubos de construcción⟩ ⟨auction block : plataforma de subastas⟩ ⟨starting block : taco de salida⟩ **2** OBSTRUCTION : obstrucción *f*, bloqueo *m* **3** : cuadra *f*, manzana *f* (de edificios) ⟨to go around the block : dar la vuelta a la cuadra⟩ **4** BUILDING : edificio *m* (de apartamentos, oficinas, etc.) **5** GROUP, SERIES : serie *f*, grupo *m* ⟨a block of tickets : una serie de entradas⟩ **6 block and tackle** : aparejo *m* de poleas
blockade[1] [blɑ'keɪd] *vt* **-aded; -ading** : bloquear
blockade[2] *n* : bloqueo *m*
blockage ['blɑkɪdʒ] *n* : bloqueo *m*, obstrucción *f*
blockhead ['blɑk,hɛd] *n* : bruto *m*, -ta *f*; estúpido *m*, -da *f*
blond[1] *or* **blonde** ['blɑnd] *adj* : rubio, güero *Mex*, claro (dícese de la madera)
blond[2] *or* **blonde** *n* : rubio *m*, -bia *f*; güero *m*, -ra *f Mex*
blood ['blʌd] *n* **1** : sangre *f* **2** LIFEBLOOD : vida *f*, alma *f* **3** LINEAGE : linaje *m*, sangre *f*
blood bank *n* : banco *m* de sangre
bloodcurdling ['blʌd,kərdəlɪŋ] *adj* : espeluznante, aterrador
blooded ['blʌdəd] *adj* : de sangre ⟨cold-blooded animal : animal de sangre fría⟩
bloodhound ['blʌd,haʊnd] *n* : sabueso *m*
bloodless ['blʌdləs] *adj* **1** : incruento, sin derramamiento de sangre **2** LIFELESS : desanimado, insípido, sin vida
bloodmobile ['blʌdmo,bi:l] *n* : unidad *f* móvil para donantes de sangre
blood pressure *n* : tensión *f*, presión *f* (arterial)
bloodshed ['blʌd,ʃɛd] *n* : derramamiento *m* de sangre
bloodshot ['blʌd,ʃɑt] *adj* : inyectado de sangre
bloodstain ['blʌd,steɪn] *n* : mancha *f* de sangre
bloodstained ['blʌd,steɪnd] *adj* : manchado de sangre
bloodstream ['blʌd,stri:m] *n* : torrente *m* sanguíneo, corriente *f* sanguínea
bloodsucker ['blʌd,sʌkər] *n* : sanguijuela *f*
bloodthirsty ['blʌd,θərsti] *adj* : sanguinario
blood vessel *n* : vaso *m* sanguíneo
bloody ['blʌdi] *adj* **bloodier; -est** : ensangrentado, sangriento
bloom[1] ['blu:m] *vi* **1** FLOWER : florecer **2** MATURE : madurar
bloom[2] *n* **1** FLOWER : flor *f* ⟨to be in bloom : estar en flor⟩ **2** FLOWERING : floración *f* ⟨in full bloom : en plena floración⟩ **3** : rubor *m* (de la tez) ⟨in the bloom of youth : en plena juventud, en la flor de la vida⟩
bloomers ['blu:mərz] *npl* : bombachos *mpl*
blooper ['blu:pər] *n* : metedura *f* de pata *fam*
blossom[1] ['blɑsəm] *vi* : florecer, dar flor
blossom[2] *n* : flor *f*
blot[1] ['blɑt] *vt* **blotted; blotting** **1** SPOT : emborronar, borronear **2** DRY : secar
blot[2] *n* **1** STAIN : mancha *f*, borrón *m* **2** BLEMISH : mancha *f*, tacha *f*
blotch[1] ['blɑtʃ] *vt* : emborronar, borronear
blotch[2] *n* : mancha *f*, borrón *m*
blotchy ['blɑtʃi] *adj* **blotchier; -est** : lleno de manchas

blotter ['blɑt̬ər] *n* : hoja *f* de papel secante, secante *m*
blouse ['blaʊs, 'blaʊz] *n* : blusa *f*
blow[1] ['blo:] *v* **blew** ['blu:]; **blown** ['blo:n]; **blowing** *vi* **1** : soplar, volar ⟨the wind is blowing hard : el viento está soplando con fuerza⟩ ⟨it blew out the door : voló por la puerta⟩ ⟨the window blew shut : se cerró la ventana⟩ **2** SOUND : sonar ⟨the whistle blew : sonó el silbato⟩ **3 to blow out** : fundirse (dícese de un fusible eléctrico), reventarse (dícese de una llanta) **4 to blow off** : dejar plantado (a alguien), flatar a (una cita, etc.) — *vt* **1** : soplar, echar ⟨to blow smoke : echar humo⟩ **2** SOUND : tocar, sonar **3** SHAPE : soplar, dar forma a ⟨to blow glass : soplar vidrio⟩ **4** BUNGLE : echar a perder
blow[2] *n* **1** PUFF : soplo *m*, soplido *m* **2** GALE : vendaval *f* **3** HIT, STROKE : golpe *m* **4** CALAMITY : golpe *m*, desastre *m* **5 to come to blows** : llegar a las manos
blower ['blo:ər] *n* FAN : ventilador *m*
blowout ['blo:ˌaʊt] *n* : reventón *m*
blowtorch ['blo:ˌtɔrʧ] *n* : soplete *m*
blow up *vi* EXPLODE : estallar, hacer explosión — *vt* BLAST : volar, hacer volar
blubber[1] ['blʌbər] *vi* : lloriquear
blubber[2] *n* : esperma *f* de ballena
bludgeon ['blʌʤən] *vt* : aporrear
blue[1] ['blu:] *adj* **bluer; bluest 1** : azul **2** MELANCHOLY : melancólico, triste
blue[2] *n* : azul *m*
blueberry ['blu:ˌbɛri] *n, pl* **-ries** : arándano *m*
bluebird ['blu:ˌbərd] *n* : azulejo *m*
blue cheese *n* : queso *m* azul
blueprint ['blu:ˌprɪnt] *n* **1** : plano *m*, proyecto *m*, cianotipo *m* **2** PLAN : anteproyecto *m*, programa *m*
blues ['blu:z] *npl* **1** DEPRESSION : depresión *f*, melancolía *f* **2** : blues *m* ⟨to sing the blues : cantar blues⟩
bluff[1] ['blʌf] *vi* : hacer un farol, blofear *Col, Mex*
bluff[2] *adj* **1** STEEP : escarpado **2** FRANK : campechano, franco, directo
bluff[3] *n* **1** : farol *m*, blof *m Col, Mex* **2** CLIFF : acantilado *m*, risco *m*
bluing *or* **blueing** ['blu:ɪŋ] *n* : añil *m*, azulete *m*
bluish ['blu:ɪʃ] *adj* : azulado
blunder[1] ['blʌndər] *vi* **1** STUMBLE : tropezar, dar traspiés **2** ERR : cometer un error, tropezar, meter la pata *fam*
blunder[2] *n* : error *m*, fallo *m* garrafal, metedura *f* de pata *fam*
blunderbuss ['blʌndərˌbʌs] *n* : trabuco *m*
blunt[1] ['blʌnt] *vt* : despuntar (aguja o lápiz), desafilar (cuchillo o tijeras), suavizar (crítica)
blunt[2] *adj* **1** DULL : desafilado, despuntado **2** DIRECT : directo, franco, categórico
bluntly ['blʌntli] *adv* : sin rodeos, francamente, bruscamente
bluntness ['blʌntnəs] *n* **1** DULLNESS : falta *f* de filo, embotadura *f* **2** FRANKNESS : franqueza *f*
blur[1] ['blər] *vt* **blurred; blurring** : desdibujar, hacer borroso
blur[2] *n* **1** SMEAR : mancha *f*, borrón *m* **2** : aspecto *m* borroso ⟨everything was just a blur : todo se volvió borroso⟩
blurb ['blərb] *n* : propaganda *f*, nota *f* publicitaria
blurry ['bləri] *adj* : borroso
blurt ['blərt] *vt* : espetar, decir impulsivamente
blush[1] ['blʌʃ] *vi* : ruborizarse, sonrojarse, hacerse colorado
blush[2] *n* : rubor *m*, sonrojo *m*
bluster[1] ['blʌstər] *vi* **1** BLOW : soplar con fuerza **2** BOAST : fanfarronear, echar bravatas
bluster[2] *n* : fanfarronada *f*, bravatas *fpl*
blustery ['blʌstəri] *adj* : borrascoso, tempestuoso
boa ['bo:ə] *n* : boa *f*
boar ['bor] *n* : cerdo *m* macho, verraco *m*
board[1] ['bord] *vt* **1** : embarcarse en, subir a bordo de (una nave o un avión), subir a (un tren o carro) **2** LODGE : hospedar, dar hospedaje con comidas a **3 to board up** : cerrar con tablas
board[2] *n* **1** PLANK : tabla *f*, tablón *m* **2** : tablero *m* ⟨chessboard : tablero de ajedrez⟩ **3** MEALS : comida *f* ⟨board and lodging : comida y alojamiento⟩ **4** COMMITTEE, COUNCIL : junta *f*, consejo *m*
boarder ['bordər] *n* LODGER : huésped *m*, -peda *f*
boardinghouse ['bordɪŋˌhaʊs] *n* : casa *f* de huéspedes
boarding school *n* : internado *m*
boardwalk ['bordˌwɔk] *n* : paseo *m* marítimo
boast[1] ['bo:st] *vi* : alardear, presumir, jactarse
boast[2] *n* : jactancia *f*, alarde *m*
boaster ['bo:stər] *n* : presumido *m*, -da *f*; fanfarrón *m*, -rrona *f fam*
boastful ['bo:stfəl] *adj* : jactancioso, fanfarrón *fam*
boastfully ['bo:stfəli] *adv* : de manera jactanciosa
boat[1] ['bo:t] *vt* : transportar en barco, poner a bordo
boat[2] *n* : barco *m*, embarcación *f*, bote *m*, barca *f*
boatman ['bo:tmən] *n, pl* **-men** [-mən, -ˌmɛn] : barquero *m*
boatswain ['bo:sən] *n* : contramaestre *m*
bob[1] ['bɑb] *v* **bobbed; bobbing** *vi* **1** : balancearse, mecerse ⟨to bob up and down : subir y bajar⟩ **2** *or* **to bob up** APPEAR : presentarse, surgir — *vt* **1** : inclinar (la cabeza o el cuerpo) **2** CUT : cortar, recortar ⟨she bobbed her hair : se cortó el pelo⟩

bob[2] *n* **1** : inclinación *f* (de la cabeza, del cuerpo), sacudida *f* **2** FLOAT : flotador *m*, corcho *m* (de pesca) **3** : pelo *m* corto
bobbin [ˈbɑbən] *n* : bobina *f*, carrete *m*
bobby pin [ˈbɑbi,pɪn] *n* : horquilla *f*
bobcat [ˈbɑb,kæt] *n* : lince *m* rojo
bobolink [ˈbɑbə,lɪŋk] *n* : tordo *m* arrocero
bobsled [ˈbɑb,slɛd] *n* : bobsleigh *m*
bobwhite [ˈbɑbˈhwaɪt] *n* : codorniz *m* (del Nuevo Mundo)
bode[1] [ˈbo:d] *v* **boded; boding** *vt* : presagiar, augurar — *vi* **to bode well** : ser de buen agüero
bode[2] → **bide**
bodice [ˈbɑdəs] *n* : corpiño *m*
bodied [ˈbɑdid] *adj* : de cuerpo ⟨lean-bodied : de cuerpo delgado⟩ ⟨able-bodied : no discapacitado⟩
bodiless [ˈbɑdiləs, ˈbɑdələs] *adj* : incorpóreo
bodily[1] [ˈbɑdəli] *adv* : en peso ⟨to lift someone bodily : levantar a alguien en peso⟩
bodily[2] *adj* : corporal, del cuerpo ⟨bodily harm : daños corporales⟩
body [ˈbɑdi] *n, pl* **bodies** **1** : cuerpo *m*, organismo *m* **2** CORPSE : cadáver *m* **3** PERSON : persona *f*, ser *m* humano **4** : nave *f* (de una iglesia), carrocería (de un automóvil), fuselaje *m* (de un avión), casco *m* (de una nave) **5** COLLECTION, MASS : conjunto *m*, grupo *m*, masa *f* ⟨in a body : todos juntos, en masa⟩ **6** ORGANIZATION : organismo *m*, organización *f*
bodyguard [ˈbɑdi,gɑrd] *n* : guardaespaldas *mf*
bog[1] [ˈbɑg, ˈbɔg] *vt* **bogged; bogging** : empantanar, inundar ⟨to get bogged down : empantanarse⟩
bog[2] *n* : lodazal *m*, ciénaga *f*, cenagal *m*
bogey [ˈbʊgi, ˈbo:-] *n, pl* **-geys** : terror *m*, coco *m fam*
boggle [ˈbɑgəl] *vi* **-gled; -gling** : quedarse atónito, quedarse pasmado ⟨the mind boggles! : ¡es increíble!⟩
boggy [ˈbɑgi, ˈbɔ-] *adj* **boggier; -est** : cenagoso
bogus [ˈbo:gəs] *adj* : falso, fingido, falaz
bohemian [bo:ˈhi:miən] *n* : bohemio *m*, -mia *f* — **bohemian** *adj*
boil[1] [ˈbɔɪl] *vi* **1** : hervir **2 to make one's blood boil** : hervirle la sangre a uno — *vt* **1** : hervir, hacer hervir ⟨to boil water : hervir agua⟩ **2** : cocer, hervir ⟨to boil potatoes : cocer papas⟩
boil[2] *n* **1** BOILING : hervor *m* **2** : furúnculo *m*, divieso *m* (en medicina)
boiler [ˈbɔɪlər] *n* : caldera *f*
boisterous [ˈbɔɪstərəs] *adj* : bullicioso, escandaloso — **boisterously** *adv*
bold [ˈbo:ld] *adj* **1** COURAGEOUS : valiente **2** INSOLENT : insolente, descarado **3** DARING : atrevido, audaz — **boldly** *adv*
boldface [ˈbo:ld,feɪs] *or* **boldface type** *n* : negrita *f*
boldness [ˈbo:ldnəs] *n* **1** COURAGE : valor *m*, coraje *m* **2** INSOLENCE : atrevimiento *m*, insolencia *f*, descaro *m* **3** DARING : audacia *f*
bolero [bəˈlɛro] *n, pl* **-ros** : bolero *m*
Bolivian [bəˈlɪviən] *n* : boliviano *m*, -na *f* — **Bolivian** *adj*
boll [ˈbo:l] *n* : cápsula *f* (del algodón)
boll weevil *n* : gorgojo *m* del algodón
bologna [bəˈlo:ni] *n* : salchicha *f* ahumada
bolster[1] [ˈbo:lstər] *vt* **-stered; -stering** : reforzar, reafirmar ⟨to bolster morale : levantar la moral⟩
bolster[2] *n* : cabezal *m*, almohadón *m*
bolt[1] [ˈbo:lt] *vt* **1** : atornillar, sujetar con pernos ⟨bolted to the floor : sujetado con pernos al suelo⟩ **2** : cerrar con pestillo, echar el cerrojo a ⟨to bolt the door : echar el cerrojo a la puerta⟩ **3 to bolt down** : engullir ⟨she bolted down her dinner : engulló su comida⟩ — *vi* : echar a correr, salir corriendo ⟨he bolted from the room : salió corriendo de la sala⟩
bolt[2] *n* **1** LATCH : pestillo *m*, cerrojo *m* **2** : tornillo *m*, perno *m* ⟨nuts and bolts : tuercas y tornillos⟩ **3** : rollo *m* ⟨a bolt of cloth : un rollo de tela⟩ **4 lightning bolt** : relámpago *m*, rayo *m*
bomb[1] [ˈbɑm] *vt* : bombardear
bomb[2] *n* : bomba *f*
bombard [bɑmˈbɑrd, bəm-] *vt* : bombardear
bombardier [,bɑmbəˈdɪr] *n* : bombardero *m*, -ra *f*
bombardment [bɑmˈbɑrdmənt] *n* : bombardeo *m*
bombast [ˈbɑm,bæst] *n* : grandilocuencia *f*, ampulosidad *f*
bombastic [bɑmˈbæstɪk] *adj* : grandilocuente, ampuloso, bombástico
bomber [ˈbɑmər] *n* : bombardero *m*
bombproof [ˈbɑm,pru:f] *adj* : a prueba de bombas
bombshell [ˈbɑm,ʃɛl] *n* : bomba *f* ⟨a political bombshell : una bomba política⟩
bona fide [ˈbo:nə,faɪd, ˈbɑ-; ,bo:nəˈfaɪdi] *adj* **1** : de buena fe ⟨a bona fide offer : una oferta de buena fe⟩ **2** GENUINE : genuino, auténtico
bonanza [bəˈnænzə] *n* : bonanza *f*
bonbon [ˈbɑn,bɑn] *n* : bombón *m*
bond[1] [ˈbɑnd] *vt* **1** INSURE : dar fianza a, asegurar **2** STICK : adherir, pegar — *vi* : adherirse, pegarse
bond[2] *n* **1** LINK, TIE : vínculo *m*, lazo *m* **2** BAIL : fianza *f*, caución *f* **3** : bono *m* ⟨stocks and bonds : acciones y bonos⟩ **4 bonds** *npl* FETTERS : cadenas *fpl*
bondage [ˈbɑndɪʤ] *n* : esclavitud *f*
bondholder [ˈbɑnd,ho:ldər] *n* : tenedor *m*, -dora *f* de bonos
bondsman [ˈbɑndzmən] *n, pl* **-men** [-mən, -,mɛn] **1** SLAVE : esclavo *m* **2** SURETY : fiador *m*, -dora *f*
bone[1] [ˈbo:n] *vt* **boned; boning** : deshuesar

bone[2] *n* : hueso *m*
boneless [ˈbo:nləs] *adj* : sin huesos, sin espinas
boner [ˈbo:nər] *n* : metedura *f* de pata, metida *f* de pata
bonfire [ˈbɑn,faɪr] *n* : hoguera *f*, fogata *f*, fogón *m*
bonito [bəˈni:t̬o] *n, pl* **-tos** *or* **-to** : bonito *m*
bonnet [ˈbɑnət] *n* : sombrero *m* (de mujer), gorra *f* (de niño)
bonus [ˈbo:nəs] *n* **1** : prima *f*, bonificación *f* (pagado al empleado) **2** ADVANTAGE, BENEFIT : beneficio *m*, provecho *m*
bony [ˈbo:ni] *adj* **bonier; -est** : huesudo
boo[1] [ˈbu:] *vt* : abuchear
boo[2] *n, pl* **boos** : abucheo *m*
booby [ˈbu:bi] *n, pl* **-bies** : bobo *m*, -ba *f*; tonto *m*, -ta *f*
book[1] [ˈbʊk] *vt* : reservar ⟨to book a flight : reservar un vuelo⟩
book[2] *n* **1** : libro *m* **2 the Book** : la Biblia **3 by the book** : según las reglas
bookcase [ˈbʊk,keɪs] *n* : estantería *f*, librero *m Mex*
bookend [ˈbʊk,ɛnd] *n* : sujetalibros *m*
bookie [ˈbʊki] → **bookmaker**
bookish [ˈbʊkɪʃ] *adj* : libresco
bookkeeper [ˈbʊk,ki:pər] *n* : tenedor *m*, -dora *f* de libros; contable *mf Spain*
bookkeeping [ˈbʊk,ki:pɪŋ] *n* : contabilidad *f*, teneduría *f* de libros
booklet [ˈbʊklət] *n* : folleto *m*
bookmaker [ˈbʊk,meɪkər] *n* : corredor *m*, -dora *f* de apuestas
bookmark [ˈbʊk,mɑrk] *n* : señalador *m* de libros, marcador *m* de libros
bookseller [ˈbʊk,slər] *n* : librero *m*, -ra *f*
bookshelf [ˈbʊk,ʃɛlf] *n, pl* **-shelves 1** : estante *m* **2 bookshelves** *npl* : estantería *f*
bookstore [ˈbʊk,stor] *n* : librería *f*
bookworm [ˈbʊk,wərm] *n* : ratón *m* de biblioteca *fam*
boom[1] [ˈbu:m] *vi* **1** THUNDER : tronar, resonar **2** FLOURISH, PROSPER : estar en auge, prosperar
boom[2] *n* **1** BOOMING : bramido *m*, estruendo *m* **2** FLOURISHING : auge *m* ⟨population boom : auge de población⟩
boomerang [ˈbu:mə,ræŋ] *n* : bumerán *m*
boon[1] [ˈbu:n] *adj* **boon companion** : amigo *m*, -ga *f* del alma
boon[2] *n* : ayuda *f*, beneficio *m*, adelanto *m*
boondocks [ˈbu:n,dɑks] *npl* : área *f* rural remota, región *f* alejada
boor [ˈbʊr] *n* : grosero *m*, -ra *f*
boorish [ˈbʊrɪʃ] *adj* : grosero
boost[1] [ˈbu:st] *vt* **1** LIFT : levantar, alzar **2** INCREASE : aumentar, incrementar **3** PROMOTE : promover, fomentar, hacer publicidad por
boost[2] *n* **1** THRUST : impulso *m*, empujón *m* **2** ENCOURAGEMENT : estímulo *m*, aliento *m* **3** INCREASE : aumento *m*, incremento *m*
booster [ˈbu:stər] *n* **1** SUPPORTER : partidario *m*, -ria *f* **2 booster rocket** : cohete *m* propulsor **3 booster shot** : vacuna *f* de refuerzo
boot[1] [ˈbu:t] *vt* KICK : dar una patada a, patear
boot[2] *n* **1** : bota *f*, botín *m* **2** KICK : puntapié *m*, patada *f*
bootee *or* **bootie** [ˈbu:t̬i] *n* : botita *f*, botín *m*
booth [ˈbu:θ] *n, pl* **booths** [ˈbu:ðz, ˈbu:θs] : cabina *f* (de teléfono, de votar), caseta *f* (de información), barraca *f* (a una feria)
bootlegger [ˈbu:t,lɛgər] *n* : contrabandista *mf* del alcohol
booty [ˈbu:t̬i] *n, pl* **-ties** : botín *m*
booze [ˈbu:z] *n fam* : alcohol *m*
borax [ˈbɔr,æks] *n* : bórax *m*
border[1] [ˈbɔrdər] *vt* **1** EDGE : ribetear, bordear **2** BOUND : limitar con, lindar con — *vi* VERGE : rayar, lindar ⟨that borders on absurdity : eso raya en el absurdo⟩
border[2] *n* **1** EDGE : borde *m*, orilla *f* **2** TRIM : ribete *m* **3** FRONTIER : frontera *f*
bore[1] [ˈbor] *vt* **bored; boring 1** PIERCE : taladrar, perforar ⟨to bore metals : taladrar metales⟩ **2** OPEN : hacer, abrir ⟨to bore a tunnel : abrir un túnel⟩ **3** WEARY : aburrir
bore[2] → **bear**[1]
bore[3] *n* **1** : pesado *m*, -da *f* (persona aburrida) **2** TEDIOUSNESS : pesadez *f*, lo aburrido **3** DIAMETER : calibre *m*
boredom [ˈbordəm] *n* : aburrimiento *m*
boring [ˈborɪŋ] *adj* : aburrido, pesado
born [ˈbɔrn] *adj* **1** : nacido **2** : nato ⟨she's a born singer : es una cantante nata⟩ ⟨he's a born leader : nació para mandar⟩
borne *pp* → **bear**[1]
boron [ˈbor,ɑn] *n* : boro *m*
borough [ˈbəro] *n* : distrito *m* municipal
borrow [ˈbɑro] *vt* **1** : pedir prestado, tomar prestado **2** APPROPRIATE : apropiarse de, adoptar
borrower [ˈbɑrəwər] *n* : prestatario *m*, -ria *f*
Bosnian [ˈbɑzniən, ˈbɔz-] *n* : bosnio *m*, -nia *f* — **Bosnian** *adj*
bosom[1] [ˈbʊzəm, ˈbu:-] *adj* : íntimo
bosom[2] *n* **1** CHEST : pecho *m* **2** BREAST : pecho *m*, seno *m* **3** CLOSENESS : seno *m* ⟨in the bosom of her family : en el seno de su familia⟩
bosomed [ˈbʊzəmd, ˈbu:-] *adj* : con busto ⟨big-bosomed : con mucho busto⟩
boss[1] [ˈbɔs] *vt* **1** SUPERVISE : dirigir, supervisar **2 to boss around** : mandonear *fam*, mangonear *fam*
boss[2] *n* : jefe *m*, -fa *f*; patrón *m*, -trona *f*
bossy [ˈbɔsi] *adj* **bossier; -est** : mandón *fam*, autoritario, dominante

botanist [ˈbɑtənɪst] *n* : botánico *m*, -ca *f*
botany [ˈbɑtəni] *n* : botánica *f* — **botanical** [bəˈtænɪkəl] *adj*
botch[1] [ˈbɑʧ] *vt* : hacer una chapuza de, estropear
botch[2] *n* : chapuza *f*
both[1] [ˈbo:θ] *adj* : ambos, los dos, las dos ⟨both books : ambos libros, los dos libros⟩
both[2] *conj* : tanto como ⟨both Ann and her mother are tall : tanto Ana como su madre son altas⟩
both[3] *pron* : ambos *m*, -bas *f*; los dos, las dos
bother[1] [ˈbɑðər] *vt* **1** IRK : preocupar ⟨nothing's bothering me : nada me preocupa⟩ ⟨what's bothering him? : ¿qué le pasa?⟩ **2** PESTER : molestar, fastidiar — *vi* **to bother to** : molestarse en, tomar la molestia de
bother[2] *n* **1** TROUBLE : molestia *f*, problemas *mpl* **2** ANNOYANCE : molestia *f*, fastidio *m*
bothersome [ˈbɑðərsəm] *adj* : molesto, fastidioso
bottle[1] [ˈbɑtəl] *vt* **bottled; bottling** : embotellar, envasar
bottle[2] *n* : botella *f*, frasco *m*
bottleneck [ˈbɑtəlˌnɛk] *n* **1** : cuello *m* de botella (en un camino) **2** : embotellamiento *m*, atasco *m* (de tráfico) **3** OBSTACLE : obstáculo *m*
bottom[1] [ˈbɑt̬əm] *adj* : más bajo, inferior, de abajo
bottom[2] *n* **1** : fondo *m* (de una caja, de una taza, del mar), pie *m* (de una escalera, una página, una montaña), asiento *m* (de una silla), parte *f* de abajo (de una pila) **2** CAUSE : origen *m*, causa *f* ⟨to get to the bottom of : llegar al fondo de⟩ **3** BUTTOCKS : trasero *m*, nalgas *fpl*
bottomless [ˈbɑt̬əmləs] *adj* : sin fondo, sin límites
botulism [ˈbɑʧəˌlɪzəm] *n* : botulismo *m*
boudoir [bəˈdwɑr, bʊ-; ˈbu:ˌ-, ˈbʊ-] *n* : tocador *m*
bough [ˈbaʊ] *n* : rama *f*
bought → **buy**[1]
bouillon [ˈbu:ˌjɑn; ˈbʊlˌjɑn, -jən] *n* : caldo *m*
boulder [ˈbo:ldər] *n* : canto *m* rodado, roca *f* grande
boulevard [ˈbʊləˌvɑrd, ˈbu:-] *n* : bulevar *m*, boulevard *m*
bounce[1] [ˈbaʊnts] *v* **bounced; bouncing** *vt* : hacer rebotar — *vi* : rebotar
bounce[2] *n* : rebote *m*
bouncy [ˈbaʊntsi] *adj* **bouncier; -est** **1** LIVELY : vivo, exuberante, animado **2** RESILIENT : elástico, flexible **3** : que rebota (dícese de una pelota)
bound[1] [ˈbaʊnd] *vt* : delimitar, rodear — *vi* LEAP : saltar, dar brincos
bound[2] *adj* **1** OBLIGED : obligado **2** : encuadernado, empastado ⟨a book bound in leather : un libro encuadernado en cuero⟩ **3** DETERMINED : decidido, empeñado **4 to be bound to** : ser seguro que, tener que, no caber duda que ⟨it was bound to happen : tenía que suceder⟩ **5 bound for** : con rumbo a ⟨bound for Chicago : con rumbo a Chicago⟩ ⟨to be homeward bound : ir camino a casa⟩
bound[3] *n* **1** LIMIT : límite *m* **2** LEAP : salto *m*, brinco *m*
boundary [ˈbaʊndri, -dəri] *n, pl* **-aries** : límite *m*, línea *f* divisoria, linde *mf*
boundless [ˈbaʊndləs] *adj* : sin límites, infinito
bounteous [ˈbaʊntiəs] *adj* **1** GENEROUS : generoso **2** ABUNDANT : copioso, abundante — **bounteously** *adv*
bountiful [ˈbaʊntɪfəl] *adj* **1** GENEROUS, LIBERAL : munificente, pródigo, generoso **2** ABUNDANT : copioso, abundante
bounty [ˈbaʊnti] *n, pl* **-ties** **1** GENEROSITY : generosidad *f*, munificencia *f* **2** REWARD : recompensa *f*
bouquet [bo:ˈkeɪ, bu:-] *n* **1** : ramo *m*, ramillete *m* **2** FRAGRANCE : bouquet *m*, aroma *m*
bourbon [ˈbərbən, ˈbʊr-] *n* : bourbon *m*, whisky *m* americano
bourgeois[1] [ˈbʊrʒˌwɑ, bʊrʒˈwɑ] *adj* : burgués
bourgeois[2] *n* : burgués *m*, -guesa *f*
bourgeoisie [ˌbʊrʒˌwɑˈzi] *n* : burguesía *f*
bout [ˈbaʊt] *n* **1** : encuentro *m*, combate *m* (en deportes) **2** ATTACK : ataque *m* (de una enfermedad) **3** PERIOD, SPELL : período *m* (de actividad)
boutique [bu:ˈti:k] *n* : boutique *f*
bovine[1] [ˈbo:ˌvaɪn, -ˌvi:n] *adj* : bovino, vacuno
bovine[2] *n* : bovino *m*
bow[1] [ˈbaʊ] *vi* **1** : hacer una reverencia, inclinarse **2** SUBMIT : ceder, resignarse, someterse — *vt* **1** LOWER : inclinar, bajar **2** BEND : doblar
bow[2] [ˈbaʊ:] *n* **1** BOWING : reverencia *f*, inclinación *f* **2** : proa *f* (de un barco)
bow[3] [ˈbo:] *vi* CURVE : arquearse, doblarse
bow[4] [ˈbo:] *n* **1** ARCH, CURVE : arco *m*, curva *f* **2** : arco *m* (arma o vara para tocar varios instrumentos de música) **3** : lazo *m*, moño *m* ⟨to tie a bow : hacer un moño⟩
bowels [ˈbaʊəls] *npl* **1** INTESTINES : intestinos *mpl* **2** : entrañas *fpl* ⟨in the bowels of the earth : en las entrañas de la tierra⟩
bower [ˈbaʊər] *n* : enramada *f*
bowl[1] [ˈbo:l] *vi* : jugar a los bolos
bowl[2] *n* : tazón *m*, cuenco *m*
bowler [ˈbo:lər] *n* : jugador *m*, -dora *f* de bolos
bowling [ˈbo:lɪŋ] *n* : bolos *mpl*
box[1] [ˈbɑks] *vt* **1** PACK : empaquetar, embalar, encajonar **2** SLAP : bofetear, cachetear — *vi* : boxear

box[2] *n* 1 CONTAINER : caja *f*, cajón *m* 2 COMPARTMENT : compartimento *m*, palco *m* (en el teatro) 3 SLAP : bofetada *f*, cachetada *f* 4 : boj *m* (planta)
boxcar [ˈbɑksˌkɑr] *n* : vagón *m* de carga, furgón *m*
boxer [ˈbɑksər] *n* : boxeador *m*, -dora *f*
boxing [ˈbɑksɪŋ] *n* : boxeo *m*
box office *n* : taquilla *f*, boletería *f*
boxwood [ˈbɑksˌwʊd] *n* : boj *m*
boy [ˈbɔɪ] *n* 1 : chico *m*, muchacho *m* 2 *or* **little boy** : niño *m*, chico *m* 3 SON : hijo *m*
boycott[1] [ˈbɔɪˌkɑt] *vt* : boicotear
boycott[2] *n* : boicot *m*
boyfriend [ˈbɔɪˌfrɛnd] *n* 1 FRIEND : amigo *m* 2 SWEETHEART : novio *m*
boyhood [ˈbɔɪˌhʊd] *n* : niñez *f*
boyish [ˈbɔɪɪʃ] *adj* : de niño, juvenil
bra [ˈbrɑ] → **brassiere**
brace[1] [ˈbreɪs] *v* **braced; bracing** *vt* 1 PROP UP, SUPPORT : apuntalar, apoyar, sostener 2 INVIGORATE : vigorizar 3 REINFORCE : reforzar — *vi* **to brace oneself** PREPARE : prepararse
brace[2] *n* 1 : berbiquí *m* ⟨brace and bit : berbiquí y barrena⟩ 2 CLAMP, REINFORCEMENT : abrazadera *f*, refuerzo *m* 3 : llave *f* (signo de puntuación) 4 **braces** *npl* : aparatos *mpl* (de ortodoncia), frenos *mpl Mex*
bracelet [ˈbreɪslət] *n* : brazalete *m*, pulsera *f*
bracken [ˈbrækən] *n* : helecho *m*
bracket[1] [ˈbrækət] *vt* 1 SUPPORT : asegurar, apuntalar 2 : poner entre corchetes 3 CATEGORIZE, GROUP : catalogar, agrupar
bracket[2] *n* 1 SUPPORT : soporte *m* 2 : corchete *m* (marca de puntuación) 3 CATEGORY, CLASS : clase *f*, categoría *f*
brackish [ˈbrækɪʃ] *adj* : salobre
brad [ˈbræd] *n* : clavo *m* con cabeza pequeña, clavito *m*
brag[1] [ˈbræg] *vi* **bragged; bragging** : alardear, fanfarronear, jactarse
brag[2] *n* : alarde *m*, jactancia *f*, fanfarronada *f*
braggart [ˈbrægərt] *n* : fanfarrón *m*, -rrona *f fam*; jactancioso *m*, -sa *f*
braid[1] [ˈbreɪd] *vt* : trenzar
braid[2] *n* : trenza *f*
braille [ˈbreɪl] *n* : braille *m*
brain[1] [ˈbreɪn] *vt* : romper la crisma a, aplastar el cráneo a
brain[2] *n* 1 : cerebro *m* 2 **brains** *npl* INTELLECT : inteligencia *f*, sesos *mpl*
brainless [ˈbreɪnləs] *adj* : estúpido, tonto
brainstorm [ˈbreɪnˌstɔrm] *n* : idea *f* brillante, idea *f* genial
brainy [ˈbreɪni] *adj* **brainier; -est** : inteligente, listo
braise [ˈbreɪz] *vt* **braised; braising** : cocer a fuego lento, estofar
brake[1] [ˈbreɪk] *v* **braked; braking** : frenar
brake[2] *n* : freno *m*
bramble [ˈbræmbəl] *n* : zarza *f*, zarzamora *f*
bran [ˈbræn] *n* : salvado *m*
branch[1] [ˈbræntʃ] *vi* 1 : echar ramas (dícese de una planta) 2 DIVERGE : ramificarse, separarse
branch[2] *n* 1 : rama *f* (de una planta) 2 EXTENSION : ramal *m* (de un camino, un ferrocarril, un río), rama *f* (de una familia o un campo de estudiar), sucursal *f* (de una empresa), agencia *f* (del gobierno)
brand[1] [ˈbrænd] *vt* 1 : marcar (ganado) 2 LABEL : tachar, tildar ⟨they branded him as a liar : lo tacharon de mentiroso⟩
brand[2] *n* 1 : marca *f* (de ganado) 2 STIGMA : estigma *m* 3 MAKE : marca *f* ⟨brand name : marca de fábrica⟩
brandish [ˈbrændɪʃ] *vt* : blandir
brand–new [ˈbrændˈnuː, -ˈnjuː] *adj* : nuevo, flamante
brandy [ˈbrændi] *n, pl* **-dies** : brandy *m*
brash [ˈbræʃ] *adj* 1 IMPULSIVE : impulsivo, impetuoso 2 BRAZEN : excesivamente desenvuelto, descarado
brass [ˈbræs] *n* 1 : latón *m* 2 GALL, NERVE : descaro *m*, cara *f fam* 3 OFFICERS : mandamases *mpl fam*
brassiere [brəˈzɪr, brɑ-] *n* : sostén *m*, brasier *m Col, Mex*
brassy [ˈbræsi] *adj* **brassier; -est** : dorado
brat [ˈbræt] *n* : mocoso *m*, -sa *f*; niño *m* mimado, niña *f* mimada
bravado [brəˈvɑdo] *n, pl* **-does** *or* **-dos** : bravuconadas *fpl*, bravatas *fpl*
brave[1] [ˈbreɪv] *vt* **braved; braving** : afrontar, hacer frente a
brave[2] *adj* **braver; bravest** : valiente, valeroso — **bravely** *adv*
brave[3] *n* : guerrero *m* indio
bravery [ˈbreɪvəri] *n* : valor *m*, valentía *f*
bravo [ˈbrɑˌvoː] *n, pl* **-vos** : bravo *m*
brawl[1] [ˈbrɔl] *vi* : pelearse, pegarse
brawl[2] *n* : pelea *f*, reyerta *f*
brawn [ˈbrɔn] *n* : fuerza *f* muscular
brawny [ˈbrɔni] *adj* **brawnier; -est** : musculoso
bray[1] [ˈbreɪ] *vi* : rebuznar
bray[2] *n* : rebuzno *m*
brazen [ˈbreɪzən] *adj* 1 : de latón 2 BOLD : descarado, directo
brazenly [ˈbreɪzənli] *adv* : descaradamente, insolentemente
brazenness [ˈbreɪzənnəs] *n* : descaro *m*, atrevimiento *m*
brazier [ˈbreɪʒər] *n* : brasero *m*
Brazilian [brəˈzɪljən] *n* : brasileño *m*, -ña *f* — **Brazilian** *adj*
Brazil nut [brəˈzɪlˌnʌt] *n* : nuez *f* de Brasil
breach[1] [ˈbriːtʃ] *vt* 1 PENETRATE : abrir una brecha en, penetrar 2 VIOLATE : infringir, violar
breach[2] *n* 1 VIOLATION : infracción *f*, violación *f* ⟨breach of trust : abuso de confianza⟩ 2 GAP, OPENING : brecha *f*

bread[1] [ˈbrɛd] *vt* : empanar
bread[2] *n* : pan *m*
breadth [ˈbrɛtθ] *n* : ancho *m*, anchura *f*
breadwinner [ˈbrɛdˌwɪnər] *n* : sostén *m* de la familia
break[1] [ˈbreɪk] *v* **broke** [ˈbroːk]; **broken** [ˈbroːkən]; **breaking** *vt* **1** SMASH : romper, quebrar **2** VIOLATE : infringir, violar, romper **3** SURPASS : batir, superar **4** CRUSH, RUIN : arruinar, deshacer, destrozar ⟨to break one's spirit : quebrantar su espíritu⟩ **5** : dar, comunicar ⟨to break the news : dar las noticias⟩ **6** INTERRUPT : cortar, interrumpir — *vi* **1** : romperse, quebrarse ⟨my calculator broke : se me rompió la calculadora⟩ **2** DISPERSE : dispersarse, despejarse **3** : estallar (dícese de una tormenta), romper (dícese del día) **4** CHANGE : cambiar (dícese del tiempo o de la voz) **5** DECREASE : bajar ⟨my fever broke : me bajó la fiebre⟩ **6** : divulgarse, revelarse ⟨the news broke : la noticia se divulgó⟩ **7 to break into** : forzar, abrir **8 to break out of** : escaparse de **9 to break through** : penetrar
break[2] *n* **1** : ruptura *f*, rotura *f*, fractura *f* (de un hueso), claro *m* (entre las nubes), cambio *m* (del tiempo) **2** CHANCE : oportunidad *f* ⟨a lucky break : un golpe de suerte⟩ **3** REST : descanso *m* ⟨to take a break : tomar(se) un descanso⟩
breakable [ˈbreɪkəbəl] *adj* : quebradizo, frágil
breakage [ˈbreɪkɪʤ] *n* **1** BREAKING : rotura *f* **2** DAMAGE : destrozos *mpl*, daños *mpl*
breakdown [ˈbreɪkˌdaʊn] *n* **1** : avería *f* (de máquinas), interrupción *f* (de comunicaciones), fracaso *m* (de negociaciones) **2** ANALYSIS : análisis *m*, desglose *m* **3** *or* **nervous breakdown** : crisis *f* nerviosa
break down *vi* **1** : estropearse, descomponerse ⟨the machine broke down : la máquina se descompuso⟩ **2** FAIL : fracasar **3** CRY : echarse a llorar — *vt* **1** DESTROY : derribar, echar abajo **2** OVERCOME : vencer (la resistencia), disipar (sospechas) **3** ANALYZE : analizar, descomponer
breaker [ˈbreɪkər] *n* **1** WAVE : ola *f* grande **2** : interruptor *m* automático (de electricidad)
breakfast[1] [ˈbrɛkfəst] *vi* : desayunar
breakfast[2] *n* : desayuno *m*
breakneck [ˈbreɪkˌnɛk] *adj* **at breakneck speed** : a una velocidad vertiginosa
break out *vi* **1** : salirse ⟨she broke out in spots : le salieron granos⟩ **2** ERUPT : estallar (dícese de una guerra, la violencia, etc.) **3** ESCAPE : fugarse, escaparse
breakup [ˈbreɪkˌəp] *n* **1** DIVISION : desintegración *f* **2** : ruptura *f*
break up *vt* **1** DIVIDE : dividir **2** : disolver (una muchedumbre, una pelea, etc.) — *vi* **1** BREAK : romperse **2** SEPARATE : deshacerse, separarse ⟨I broke up with him : terminé con él⟩
breast [ˈbrɛst] *n* **1** : pecho *m*, seno *m* (de una mujer) **2** CHEST : pecho *m*
breastbone [ˈbrɛstˌboːn] *n* : esternón *m*
breast–feed [ˈbrɛstˌfiːd] *vt* **-fed** [-ˌfɛd]; **-feeding** : amamantar, darle de mamar (a un niño)
breath [ˈbrɛθ] *n* **1** BREATHING : aliento *m* ⟨to hold one's breath : aguantar la respiración⟩ **2** BREEZE : soplo *m* ⟨a breath of fresh air : un soplo de aire freso⟩
breathe [ˈbriːð] *v* **breathed; breathing** *vi* **1** : respirar **2** LIVE : vivir, respirar — *vt* **1** : respirar, aspirar ⟨to breathe fresh air : respirar el aire fresco⟩ **2** UTTER : decir ⟨I won't breathe a word of this : no diré nada de esto⟩
breathless [ˈbrɛθləs] *adj* : sin aliento, jadeante
breathlessly [ˈbrɛθləsli] *adv* : entrecortadamente, jadeando
breathlessness [ˈbrɛθləsnəs] *n* : dificultad *f* al respirar
breathtaking [ˈbrɛθˌteɪkɪŋ] *adj* IMPRESSIVE : impresionante, imponente
breeches [ˈbrɪʧəz, ˈbriː-] *npl* : pantalones *mpl*, calzones *mpl*, bombachos *mpl*
breed[1] [ˈbriːd] *v* **bred** [ˈbrɛd]; **breeding** *vt* **1** : criar (animales) **2** ENGENDER : engendrar, producir ⟨familiarity breeds contempt : la confianza hace perder el respeto⟩ **3** RAISE, REAR : criar, educar — *vi* REPRODUCE : reproducirse
breed[2] *n* **1** : variedad *f* (de plantas), raza *f* (de animales) **2** CLASS : clase *f*, tipo *m*
breeder [ˈbriːdər] *n* : criador *m*, -dora *f* (de animales); cultivador *m*, -dora *f* (de plantas)
breeze[1] [ˈbriːz] *vi* **breezed; breezing** : pasar con ligereza ⟨to breeze in : entrar como si nada⟩
breeze[2] *n* : brisa *f*, soplo *m* (de aire)
breezy [ˈbriːzi] *adj* **breezier; -est 1** AIRY, WINDY : aireado, ventoso **2** LIVELY : animado, alegre **3** NONCHALANT : despreocupado
brethren → **brother**
brevity [ˈbrɛvəṭi] *n, pl* **-ties** : brevedad *f*, concisión *f*
brew[1] [ˈbruː] *vt* **1** : fabricar, elaborar (cerveza) **2** FOMENT : tramar, maquinar, fomentar — *vi* **1** : fabricar cerveza **2** : amenazar ⟨a storm is brewing : una tormenta amenaza⟩
brew[2] *n* **1** BEER : cerveza *f* **2** POTION : brebaje *m*
brewer [ˈbruːər] *n* : cervecero *m*, -ra *f*
brewery [ˈbruːəri, ˈbrʊri] *n, pl* **-eries** : cervecería *f*
briar [ˈbraɪər] → **brier**

bribe[1] ['braɪb] *vt* **bribed; bribing** : sobornar, cohechar, coimear *Arg, Chile, Peru*

bribe[2] *n* : soborno *m*, cohecho *m*, coima *f Arg, Chile, Peru*, mordida *f CA, Mex*

bribery ['braɪbəri] *n, pl* **-eries** : soborno *m*, cohecho *m*, coima *f*, mordida *f CA, Mex*

bric–a–brac ['brɪkəˌbræk] *npl* : baratijas *fpl*, chucherías *fpl*

brick[1] ['brɪk] *vt* **to brick up** : tabicar, tapiar

brick[2] *n* : ladrillo *m*

bricklayer ['brɪkˌleɪər] *n* : albañil *mf*

bricklaying ['brɪkˌleɪɪŋ] *n* : albañilería *f*

bridal ['braɪdəl] *adj* : nupcial, de novia

bride ['braɪd] *n* : novia *f*

bridegroom ['braɪdˌgruːm] *n* : novio *m*

bridesmaid ['braɪdzˌmeɪd] *n* : dama *f* de honor

bridge[1] ['brɪʤ] *vt* **bridged; bridging** 1 : tender un puente sobre 2 **to bridge the gap** : salvar las diferencias

bridge[2] *n* 1 : puente *m* 2 : caballete *m* (de la nariz) 3 : puente *m* de mando (de un barco) 4 DENTURE : puente *m* (dental) 5 : bridge *m* (juego de naipes)

bridle[1] ['braɪdəl] *v* **-dled; -dling** *vt* 1 : embridar (un caballo) 2 RESTRAIN : refrenar, dominar, contener — *vi* **to bridle at** : molestarse por, picarse por

bridle[2] *n* : brida *f*

brief[1] ['briːf] *vt* : dar órdenes a, instruir

brief[2] *adj* : breve, sucinto, conciso

brief[3] *n* 1 : resumen *m*, sumario *m* 2 **briefs** *npl* : calzoncillos *mpl*

briefcase ['briːfˌkeɪs] *n* : portafolio *m*, maletín *m*

briefly ['briːfli] *adv* : brevemente, por poco tiempo ⟨to speak briefly : discursar en pocas palabras⟩

brier ['braɪər] *n* 1 BRAMBLE : zarza *f*, rosal *m* silvestre 2 HEATH : brezo *m* veteado

brig ['brɪg] *n* 1 : bergantín *m* (barco) 2 : calabozo *m* (en un barco)

brigade [brɪ'geɪd] *n* : brigada *f*

brigadier general [ˌbrɪgə'dɪr] *n* : general *m* de brigada

brigand ['brɪgənd] *n* : bandolero *m*, -ra *f*; forajido *m*, -da *f*

bright ['braɪt] *adj* 1 : brillante (dícese del sol, de los ojos), vivo (dícese de un color), claro, fuerte 2 CHEERFUL : alegre, animado ⟨bright and early : muy temprano⟩ 3 INTELLIGENT : listo, inteligente ⟨a bright idea : una idea luminosa⟩

brighten ['braɪtən] *vt* 1 ILLUMINATE : iluminar 2 ENLIVEN : alegrar, animar — *vi* 1 : hacerse más brillante 2 **to brighten up** : animarse, alegrarse, mejorar

brightly ['braɪtli] *adv* : vivamente, intensamente, alegremente

brightness ['braɪtnəs] *n* 1 LUMINOSITY : luminosidad *f*, brillantez *f*, resplandor *m*, brillo *m* 2 CHEERFULNESS : alegría *f*, ánimo *m*

brilliance ['brɪljənts] *n* 1 BRIGHTNESS : resplandor *m*, fulgor *m*, brillo *m*, brillantez *f* 2 INTELLIGENCE : inteligencia *f*, brillantez *f*

brilliancy ['brɪljəntsi] → **brilliance**

brilliant ['brɪljənt] *adj* : brillante

brilliantly ['brɪljəntli] *adv* : brillantemente, con brillantez

brim[1] ['brɪm] *vi* **brimmed; brimming** 1 *or* **to brim over** : desbordarse, rebosar 2 **to brim with tears** : llenarse de lágrimas

brim[2] *n* 1 : ala *f* (de un sombrero) 2 : borde *m* (de una taza o un vaso)

brimful ['brɪm'fʊl] *adj* : lleno hasta el borde, repleto, rebosante

brimless ['brɪmləs] *adj* : sin ala

brimstone ['brɪmˌstoːn] *n* : azufre *m*

brindled ['brɪndəld] *adj* : manchado, pinto

brine ['braɪn] *n* 1 : salmuera *f*, escabeche *m* (para encurtir) 2 OCEAN : océano *m*, mar *m*

bring ['brɪŋ] *vt* **brought** ['brɔt]; **bringing** 1 CARRY : traer ⟨bring me some coffee : tráigame un café⟩ 2 PRODUCE : traer, producir, conseguir ⟨his efforts will bring him success : sus esfuerzos le conseguirán el éxito⟩ 3 PERSUADE : convencer, persuadir 4 YIELD : rendir, alcanzar, venderse por ⟨to bring a good price : alcanzar un precio alto⟩ 5 **to bring to an end** : terminar (con) 6 **to bring to light** : sacar a la luz

bring about *vt* : ocasionar, provocar, determinar

bring forth *vt* PRODUCE : producir

bring out *vt* : sacar, publicar (un libro, etc.)

bring to *vt* REVIVE : resucitar

bring up *vt* 1 REAR : criar 2 MENTION : sacar, mencionar

brininess ['braɪninəs] *n* : salinidad *f*

brink ['brɪŋk] *n* : borde *m*

briny ['braɪni] *adj* **brinier; -est** : salobre

briquette *or* **briquet** [brɪ'kɛt] *n* : briqueta *f*

brisk ['brɪsk] *adj* 1 LIVELY : rápido, enérgico, brioso 2 INVIGORATING : fresco, estimulante

brisket ['brɪskət] *n* : falda *f*

briskly ['brɪskli] *adv* : rápidamente, enérgicamente, con brío

briskness ['brɪsknəs] *n* : brío *m*, rapidez *f*

bristle[1] ['brɪsəl] *vi* **-tled; -tling** 1 : erizarse, ponerse de punta 2 : enfurecerse, enojarse ⟨she bristled at the suggestion : se enfureció ante tal sugerencia⟩ 3 : estar plagado, estar repleto ⟨a city bristling with tourists : una ciudad repleta de turistas⟩

bristle[2] *n* : cerda *f* (de un animal), pelo *m* (de una planta)

bristly ['brɪsəli] *adj* **bristlier; -est** : áspero y erizado

British[1] ['brɪtɪʃ] *adj* : británico

British[2] *n* **the British** *npl* : los británicos

brittle ['brɪtəl] *adj* **-tler; -tlest** : frágil, quebradizo
brittleness ['brɪtəlnəs] *n* : fragilidad *f*
broach ['bro:ʧ] *vt* BRING UP : mencionar, abordar, sacar
broad ['brɔd] *adj* **1** WIDE : ancho **2** SPACIOUS : amplio, extenso **3** FULL : pleno ⟨in broad daylight : en pleno día⟩ **4** OBVIOUS : claro, evidente **5** TOLERANT : tolerante, liberal **6** GENERAL : general **7** ESSENTIAL : principal, esencial ⟨the broad outline : los rasgos esenciales⟩
broadcast[1] ['brɔd,kæst] *vt* **-cast; -casting** **1** SCATTER : esparcir, diseminar **2** CIRCULATE, SPREAD : divulgar, difundir, propagar **3** TRANSMIT : transmitir, emitir
broadcast[2] *n* **1** TRANSMISSION : transmisión *f*, emisión *f* **2** PROGRAM : programa *m*, emisión *f*
broadcaster ['brɔd,kæstər] *n* : presentador *m*, -dora *f*; locutor *m*, -tora *f*
broadcloth ['brɔd,klɔθ] *n* : paño *m* fino
broaden ['brɔdən] *vt* : ampliar, ensanchar — *vi* : ampliarse, ensancharse
broadloom ['brɔd,lu:m] *adj* : tejido en telar ancho
broadly ['brɔdli] *adv* **1** GENERALLY : en general, aproximadamente **2** WIDELY : extensivamente
broad-minded ['brɔd'maɪndəd] *adj* : tolerante, de amplias miras
broad-mindedness [brɔd'maɪndədnəs] *n* : tolerancia *f*
broadside ['brɔd,saɪd] *n* **1** VOLLEY : andanada *f* **2** ATTACK : ataque *m*, invectiva *f*, andanada *f*
brocade [bro'keɪd] *n* : brocado *m*
broccoli ['brɑkəli] *n* : brócoli *m*, brécol *m*
brochure [bro'ʃʊr] *n* : folleto *m*
brogue ['bro:g] *n* : acento *m* irlandés
broil[1] ['brɔɪl] *vt* : asar a la parrilla
broil[2] *n* : asado *m*
broiler ['brɔɪlər] *n* **1** GRILL : parrilla *f* **2** : pollo *m* para asar
broke[1] ['bro:k] → **break**[1]
broke[2] *adj* : pelado, arruinado ⟨to go broke : arruinarse, quebrar⟩
broken ['bro:kən] *adj* **1** DAMAGED, SHATTERED : roto, quebrado, fracturado **2** IRREGULAR, UNEVEN : accidentado, irregular, recortado **3** VIOLATED : roto, quebrantado **4** INTERRUPTED : interrumpido, descontinuo **5** CRUSHED : abatido, quebrantado ⟨a broken man : un hombre destrozado⟩ **6** IMPERFECT : mal ⟨to speak broken English : hablar el inglés con dificultad⟩
brokenhearted [,bro:kən'hɑrt̬əd] *adj* : descorazonado, desconsolado
broker[1] ['bro:kər] *vt* : hacer corretaje de
broker[2] *n* **1** : agente *mf*; corredor *m*, -dora *f* **2** → **stockbroker**
brokerage ['bro:kərɪʤ] *n* : corretaje *m*, agencia *f* de corredores
bromine ['bro:,mi:n] *n* : bromo *m*
bronchitis [brɑn'kaɪt̬əs, brɑŋ-] *n* : bronquitis *f*
bronze[1] ['brɑnz] *vt* **bronzed; bronzing** : broncear
bronze[2] *n* : bronce *m*
brooch ['bro:ʧ, 'bru:ʧ] *n* : broche *m*, prendedor *m*
brood[1] ['bru:d] *vt* **1** INCUBATE : empollar, incubar **2** PONDER : sopesar, considerar — *vi* **1** INCUBATE : empollar **2** REFLECT : rumiar, reflexionar **3** WORRY : ponerse melancólico, inquietarse
brood[2] *adj* : de cría
brood[3] *n* : nidada *f* (de pájaros), camada *f* (de mamíferos)
brooder ['bru:dər] *n* **1** THINKER : pensador *m*, -dora *f* **2** INCUBATOR : incubadora *f*
brook[1] ['brʊk] *vt* TOLERATE : tolerar, admitir
brook[2] *n* : arroyo *m*
broom ['bru:m, 'brʊm] *n* **1** : retama *f*, hiniesta *f* **2** : escoba *f* (para barrer)
broomstick ['bru:m,stɪk, 'brʊm-] *n* : palo *m* de escoba
broth ['brɔθ] *n, pl* **broths** ['brɔθs, 'brɔðz] : caldo *m*
brothel ['brɑθəl, 'brɔ-] *n* : burdel *m*
brother ['brʌðər] *n, pl* **brothers** *also* **brethren** ['brðrən, -ðərn] **1** : hermano *m* **2** KINSMAN : pariente *m*, familiar *m*
brotherhood ['brʌðər,hʊd] *n* **1** FELLOWSHIP : fraternidad *f* **2** ASSOCIATION : hermandad *f*
brother-in-law ['brʌðərɪn,lɔ] *n, pl* **brothers-in-law** : cuñado *m*
brotherly ['brʌðərli] *adj* : fraternal
brought → **bring**
brow ['braʊ] *n* **1** EYEBROW : ceja *f* **2** FOREHEAD : frente *f* **3** : cima *f* ⟨the brow of a hill : la cima de una colina⟩
browbeat ['braʊ,bi:t] *vt* **-beat; -beaten** [-,bi:tən] *or* **-beat; -beating** : intimidar
brown[1] ['braʊn] *vt* **1** : dorar (en cocina) **2** TAN : broncear — *vi* **1** : dorarse (en cocina) **2** TAN : broncearse
brown[2] *adj* : marrón, café, castaño (dícese del pelo), moreno (dícese de la piel)
brown[3] *n* : marrón *m*, café *m*
brownish ['braʊnɪʃ] *adj* : pardo
browse ['braʊz] *vi* **browsed; browsing** **1** GRAZE : pacer **2** LOOK : mirar, echar un vistazo
bruin ['bru:ɪn] *n* BEAR : oso *m*
bruise[1] ['bru:z] *vt* **bruised; bruising** **1** : contusionar, machucar, magullar (a una persona) **2** DAMAGE : magullar, dañar (frutas) **3** CRUSH : majar **4** HURT : herir (los sentimientos)
bruise[2] *n* : moretón *m*, cardenal *m*, magulladura *f* (dícese de frutas)
brunch ['brʌnʧ] *n* : combinación *f* de desayuno y almuerzo
brunet[1] *or* **brunette** [bru:'nɛt] *adj* : moreno
brunet[2] *or* **brunette** *n* : moreno *m*, -na *f*

brunt [ˈbrʌnt] *n* **to bear the brunt of** : llevar el peso de, aguantar el mayor impacto de
brush[1] [ˈbrʌʃ] *vt* **1** : cepillar ⟨to brush one's teeth : cepillarse uno los dientes⟩ **2** SWEEP : barrer, quitar con un cepillo **3** GRAZE : rozar **4 to brush off** DISREGARD : hacer caso omiso de, ignorar — *vi* **to brush up on** : repasar, refrescar, dar un repaso a
brush[2] *n* **1** *or* **brushwood** [ˈbrʌʃˌwʊd] : broza *f* **2** SCRUB, UNDERBRUSH : maleza *f* **3** : cepillo *m*, pincel *m* (de artista), brocha *f* (de pintor) **4** TOUCH : roce *m* **5** SKIRMISH : escaramuza *f*
brush–off [ˈbrʌʃˌɔf] *n* **to give the brush–off to** : dar calabazas a
brusque [ˈbrʌsk] *adj* : brusco — **brusquely** *adv*
brussels sprout [ˈbrʌsəlzˌspraʊt] *n* : col *f* de Bruselas
brutal [ˈbruːt̬əl] *adj* : brutal, cruel, salvaje — **brutally** *adv*
brutality [bruːˈtælət̬i] *n, pl* **-ties** : brutalidad *f*
brutalize [ˈbruːt̬əlˌaɪz] *vt* **-ized; -izing** : brutalizar, maltratar
brute[1] [ˈbruːt] *adj* : bruto ⟨brute force : fuerza bruta⟩
brute[2] *n* **1** BEAST : bestia *f*, animal *m* **2** : bruto *m*, -ta *f*; bestia *mf* (persona)
brutish [ˈbruːt̬ɪʃ] *adj* **1** : de animal **2** CRUEL : brutal, salvaje **3** STUPID : bruto, estúpido
bubble[1] [ˈbʌbəl] *vi* **-bled; -bling** : burbujear ⟨to bubble over with joy : rebosar de alegría⟩
bubble[2] *n* : burbuja *f*
bubbly [ˈbʌbəli] *adj* **bubblier; -est** **1** BUBBLING : burbujeante **2** LIVELY : vivaz, lleno de vida
bubonic plague [buːˈbɑnɪk, ˈbjuː-] *n* : peste *f* bubónica
buccaneer [ˌbʌkəˈnɪr] *n* : bucanero *m*
buck[1] [ˈbʌk] *vi* **1** : corcovear (dícese de un caballo o un burro) **2** JOLT : dar sacudidas **3 to buck against** : resistirse a, rebelarse contra **4 to buck up** : animarse, levantar el ánimo — *vt* OPPOSE : oponerse a, ir en contra de
buck[2] *n, pl* **buck** *or* **bucks** **1** : animal *m* macho, ciervo *m* (macho) **2** DOLLAR : dólar *m* **3 to pass the buck** *fam* : pasar la pelota *fam*
bucket [ˈbʌkət] *n* : balde *m*, cubo *m*, cubeta *f Mex*
bucketful [ˈbʌkətˌfʊl] *n* : balde *m* lleno
buckle[1] [ˈbʌkəl] *v* **-led; -ling** *vt* **1** FASTEN : abrochar **2** BEND, TWIST : combar, torcer — *vi* **1** BEND, TWIST : combarse, torcerse, doblarse (dícese de las rodillas) **2 to buckle down** : ponerse a trabajar con esmero **3 to buckle up** : abrocharse
buckle[2] *n* **1** : hebilla *f* **2** TWISTING : torcedura *f*
buckshot [ˈbʌkˌʃɑt] *n* : perdigón *m*
buckskin [ˈbʌkˌskɪn] *n* : gamuza *f*
bucktooth [ˈbʌkˌtuːθ] *n* : diente *m* saliente, diente *m* salido
buckwheat [ˈbʌkˌhwiːt] *n* : trigo *m* rubión, alforfón *m*
bucolic [bjuːˈkɑlɪk] *adj* : bucólico
bud[1] [ˈbʌd] *v* **budded; budding** *vt* GRAFT : injertar — *vi* : brotar, hacer brotes
bud[2] *n* : brote *m*, yema *f*, capullo *m* (de una flor)
Buddhism [ˈbuːˌdɪzəm, ˈbʊ-] *n* : budismo *m*
Buddhist [ˈbuːdɪst, ˈbʊ-] *n* : budista *mf* — **Buddhist** *adj*
buddy [ˈbʌdi] *n, pl* **-dies** : amigo *m*, -ga *f*; compinche *mf fam*; cuate *m*, -ta *f Mex fam*
budge [ˈbʌʤ] *vi* **budged; budging** **1** MOVE : moverse, desplazarse **2** YIELD : ceder
budget[1] [ˈbʌʤət] *vt* : presupuestar (gastos), asignar (dinero) — *vi* : presupuestar, planear el presupuesto
budget[2] *n* : presupuesto
budgetary [ˈbʌʤəˌtɛri] *adj* : presupuestario
buff[1] [ˈbʌf] *vt* POLISH : pulir, sacar brillo a, lustrar
buff[2] *adj* : beige, amarillento
buff[3] *n* **1** : beige *m*, amarillento *m* **2** ENTHUSIAST : aficionado *m*, -da *f*; entusiasta *mf*
buffalo [ˈbʌfəˌloː] *n, pl* **-lo** *or* **-loes** **1** : búfalo *m* **2** BISON : bisonte *m*
buffer [ˈbʌfər] *n* **1** BARRIER : barrera *f* ⟨buffer state : estado tapón⟩ **2** SHOCK ABSORBER : amortiguador *m*
buffet[1] [ˈbʌfət] *vt* : golpear, zarandear, sacudir
buffet[2] *n* BLOW : golpe *m*
buffet[3] [ˌbʌˈfeɪ, ˌbuː-] *n* **1** : bufete *m*, bufé *m* (comida) **2** SIDEBOARD : aparador *m*
buffoon [ˌbʌˈfuːn] *n* : bufón *m*, -fona *f*; payaso *m*, -sa *f*
buffoonery [ˌbʌˈfuːnəri] *n, pl* **-eries** : bufonada *f*, payasada *f*
bug[1] [ˈbʌg] *vt* **bugged; bugging** **1** PESTER : fastidiar, molestar **2** : ocultar micrófonos en
bug[2] *n* **1** INSECT : bicho *m*, insecto *m* **2** DEFECT : defecto *m*, falla *f*, problema *m* **3** GERM : microbio *m*, virus *m* **4** MICROPHONE : micrófono *m*
bugaboo [ˈbʌgəˌbuː] → **bogey**
bugbear [ˈbʌgˌbær] *n* : pesadilla *f*, coco *m*
buggy [ˈbʌgi] *n, pl* **-gies** : calesa *f* (tirada por caballos), cochecito *m* (para niños)
bugle [ˈbjuːgəl] *n* : clarín *m*, corneta *f*
bugler [ˈbjuːgələr] *n* : corneta *mf*
build[1] [ˈbɪld] *v* **built** [ˈbɪlt]; **building** *vt* **1** CONSTRUCT : construir, edificar, ensamblar, levantar **2** DEVELOP : desarrollar, elaborar, forjar **3** INCREASE : incrementar, aumentar — *vi* **to build up** : aumentar, intensificar
build[2] *n* PHYSIQUE : físico *m*, complexión *f*

builder [ˈbɪldər] *n* : constructor *m*, -tora *f*; contratista *mf*
building [ˈbɪldɪŋ] *n* **1** EDIFICE : edificio *m* **2** CONSTRUCTION : construcción *f*
built–in [ˈbɪltˈɪn] *adj* **1** : empotrado ⟨built-in cabinets : armarios empotrados⟩ **2** INHERENT : incorporado, intrínseco
bulb [ˈbʌlb] *n* **1** : bulbo *m* (de una planta), cabeza *f* (de ajo), cubeta *f* (de un termómetro) **2** LIGHTBULB : bombilla *f*, foco *m*, bombillo *m CA, Col, Ven*
bulbous [ˈbʌlbəs] *adj* : bulboso
Bulgarian [bʌlˈgæriən, bʊl-] *n* **1** : búlgaro *m*, -ra *f* **2** : búlgaro *m* (idioma) — **Bulgarian** *adj*
bulge[1] [ˈbʌlʤ] *vi* **bulged; bulging** : abultar, sobresalir
bulge[2] *n* : bulto *m*, protuberancia *f*
bulk[1] [ˈbʌlk] *vt* : hinchar — *vi* EXPAND, SWELL : ampliarse, hincharse
bulk[2] *n* **1** SIZE, VOLUME : volumen *m*, tamaño *m* **2** FIBER : fibra *f* **3** MASS : mole *f* **4 the bulk of** : la mayor parte de **5 in ~** : en grandes cantidades
bulkhead [ˈbʌlkˌhɛd] *n* : mamparo *m*
bulky [ˈbʌlki] *adj* **bulkier; -est** : voluminoso, grande
bull[1] [ˈbʊl] *adj* : macho
bull[2] *n* **1** : toro *m*, macho *m* (de ciertas especies) **2** : bula *f* (papal) **3** DECREE : decreto *m*, edicto *m*
bulldog [ˈbʊlˌdɔg] *n* : bulldog *m*
bulldoze [ˈbʊlˌdoːz] *vt* **-dozed; -dozing** **1** LEVEL : nivelar (el terreno), derribar (un edificio) **2** FORCE : forzar ⟨he bulldozed his way through : se abrió paso a codazos⟩
bulldozer [ˈbʊlˌdoːzər] *n* : bulldozer *m*
bullet [ˈbʊlət] *n* : bala *f*
bulletin [ˈbʊlətən, -lətən] *n* **1** NOTICE : comunicado *m*, anuncio *m*, boletín *m* **2** NEWSLETTER : boletín *m* (informativo)
bulletin board *n* : tablón *m* de anuncios
bulletproof [ˈbʊlətˌpruːf] *adj* : antibalas, a prueba de balas
bullfight [ˈbʊlˌfaɪt] *n* : corrida *f* (de toros)
bullfighter [ˈbʊlˌfaɪtər] *n* : torero *m*, -ra *f*; matador *m*
bullfrog [ˈbʊlˌfrɔg] *n* : rana *f* toro
bullheaded [ˈbʊlˈhɛdəd] *adj* : testarudo
bullion [ˈbʊljən] *n* : oro *m* en lingotes, plata *f* en lingotes
bullock [ˈbʊlək] *n* **1** STEER : buey *m*, toro *m* castrado **2** : toro *m* joven, novillo *m*
bull's–eye [ˈbʊlzˌaɪ] *n, pl* **bull's–eyes** : diana *f*, blanco *m*
bully[1] [ˈbʊli] *vt* **-lied; -lying** : intimidar, amedrentar, mangonear
bully[2] *n, pl* **-lies** : matón *m*; bravucón *m*, -cona *f*
bulrush [ˈbʊlˌrʌʃ] *n* : especie *f* de junco
bulwark [ˈbʊlˌwərk, -ˌwɔrk; ˈbʌlˌwərk] *n* : baluarte *m*, bastión *f*
bum[1] [ˈbʌm] *v* **bummed; bumming** *vi* **to bum around** : vagabundear, vagar — *vt* : gorronear *fam*, sablear *fam*
bum[2] *adj* : inútil, malo ⟨a bum rap : una acusación falsa⟩
bum[3] *n* **1** LOAFER : vago *m*, -ga *f* **2** HOBO, TRAMP : vagabundo *m*, -da *f*
bumblebee [ˈbʌmbəlˌbiː] *n* : abejorro *m*
bump[1] [ˈbʌmp] *vt* : chocar contra, golpear contra, dar ⟨to bump one's head : darse (un golpe) en la cabeza⟩ — *vi* **to bump into** MEET : encontrarse con, tropezarse con
bump[2] *n* **1** BULGE : bulto *m*, protuberancia *f* **2** IMPACT : golpe *m*, choque *m* **3** JOLT : sacudida *f*
bumper[1] [ˈbʌmpər] *adj* : extraordinario, récord ⟨a bumper crop : una cosecha abundante⟩
bumper[2] *n* : parachoques *mpl*
bumpkin [ˈbʌmpkən] *n* : palurdo *m*, -da *f*
bumpy [ˈbʌmpi] *adj* **bumpier; -est** : desigual, lleno de baches (dícese de un camino), agitado (dícese de un vuelo en avión)
bun [ˈbʌn] *n* : bollo *m*
bunch[1] [ˈbʌntʃ] *vt* : agrupar, amontonar — *vi* **to bunch up** : amontonarse, agruparse, fruncirse (dícese de una tela)
bunch[2] *n* : grupo *m*, montón *m*, ramo *m* (de flores)
bundle[1] [ˈbʌndəl] *vt* **-dled; -dling** : liar, atar
bundle[2] *n* **1** : fardo *m*, atado *m*, bulto *m*, haz *m* (de palos) **2** PARCEL : paquete *m* **3** LOAD : montón *m* ⟨a bundle of money : un montón de dinero⟩
bungalow [ˈbʌŋgəˌloː] *n* : tipo de casa de un solo piso
bungle[1] [ˈbʌŋgəl] *vt* **-gled; -gling** : echar a perder, malograr
bungle[2] *n* : chapuza *f*, desatino *m*
bungler [ˈbʌŋgələr] *n* : chapucero *m*, -ra *f*; inepto *m*, -ta *f*
bunion [ˈbʌnjən] *n* : juanete *m*
bunk[1] [ˈbʌŋk] *vi* : dormir (en una litera)
bunk[2] *n* **1** *or* **bunk bed** : litera *f* **2** NONSENSE : tonterías *fpl*, bobadas *fpl*
bunker [ˈbʌŋkər] *n* **1** : carbonera *f* (en un barco) **2** SHELTER : búnker *m*
bunny [ˈbʌni] *n, pl* **-nies** : conejo *m*, -ja *f*
buoy[1] [ˈbuːi, ˈbɔɪ] *vt* **to buoy up** **1** : mantener a flote **2** CHEER, HEARTEN : animar, levantar el ánimo a
buoy[2] *n* : boya *f*
buoyancy [ˈbɔɪən*t*si, ˈbuːjən-] *n* **1** : flotabilidad *f* **2** OPTIMISM : confianza *f*, optimismo *m*
buoyant [ˈbɔɪənt, ˈbuːjənt] *adj* : boyante, flotante
bur *or* **burr** [ˈbər] *n* : abrojo *m* (de una planta)
burden[1] [ˈbərdən] *vt* : cargar, oprimir
burden[2] *n* : carga *f*, peso *m*
burdensome [ˈbərdənsəm] *adj* : oneroso
burdock [ˈbərˌdɑk] *n* : bardana *f*
bureau [ˈbjʊro] *n* **1** CHEST OF DRAWERS : cómoda *f* **2** DEPARTMENT : departamento *m* (del gobierno) **3** AGENCY

: agencia *f* ⟨travel bureau : agencia de viajes⟩

bureaucracy [bjʊˈrɑkrəsi] *n, pl* **-cies** : burocracia *f*

bureaucrat [ˈbjʊrəˌkræt] *n* : burócrata *mf*

bureaucratic [ˌbjʊrəˈkræt̬ɪk] *adj* : burocrático

burgeon [ˈbərʤən] *vi* : florecer, retoñar, crecer

burglar [ˈbərglər] *n* : ladrón *m*, -drona *f*

burglarize [ˈbərgləˌraɪz] *vt* **-ized; -izing** : robar

burglary [ˈbərgləri] *n, pl* **-glaries** : robo *m*

burgle [ˈbərgəl] *vt* **-gled; -gling** : robar

burgundy [ˈbərgəndi] *n, pl* **-dies** : borgoña *m*, vino *m* de Borgoña

burial [ˈbɛriəl] *n* : entierro *m*, sepelio *m*

burlap [ˈbərˌlæp] *n* : arpillera *f*

burlesque[1] [bərˈlɛsk] *vt* **-lesqued; -lesquing** : parodiar

burlesque[2] *n* **1** PARODY : parodia *f* **2** REVUE : revista *f* (musical)

burly [ˈbərli] *adj* **-lier; -liest** : fornido, corpulento, musculoso

Burmese [ˌbərˈmiːz, -ˈmiːs] *n* : birmano *m*, -na *f* — **Burmese** *adj*

burn[1] [ˈbərn] *v* **burned** [ˈbərnd, ˈbərnt] *or* **burnt** [ˈbərnt]; **burning** *vt* **1** : quemar, incendiar ⟨to burn a building : incendiar un edificio⟩ ⟨I burned my hand : me quemé la mano⟩ **2** CONSUME : usar, gastar, consumir — *vi* **1** : arder (dícese de un fuego o un edificio), quemarse (dícese de la comida, etc.) **2** : estar prendido, estar encendido ⟨we left the lights burning : dejamos las luces encendidas⟩ **3 to burn out** : consumirse, apagarse **4 to burn with** : arder de ⟨he was burning with jealousy : ardía de celos⟩

burn[2] *n* : quemadura *f*

burner [ˈbərnər] *n* : quemador *m*

burnish [ˈbərnɪʃ] *vt* : bruñir

burp[1] [ˈbərp] *vi* : eructar — *vt* : hacer eructar

burp[2] *n* : eructo *m*

burr → **bur**

burro [ˈbəro, ˈbʊr-] *n, pl* **-os** : burro *m*

burrow[1] [ˈbəro] *vi* **1** : cavar, hacer una madriguera **2 to burrow into** : hurgar en — *vt* : cavar, excavar

burrow[2] *n* : madriguera *f*, conejera *f* (de un conejo)

bursar [ˈbərsər] *n* : administrador *m*, -dora *f*

bursitis [bərˈsaɪt̬əs] *n* : bursitis *f*

burst[1] [ˈbərst] *v* **burst; bursting** *vi* **1** : reventarse (dícese de una llanta o un globo), estallar (dícese de obuses o fuegos artificiales), romperse (dícese de un dique) **2 to burst in** : irrumpir en **3 to burst into** : empezar a, echar a ⟨to burst into tears : echarse a llorar⟩ — *vt* : reventar

burst[2] *n* **1** EXPLOSION : estallido *m*, explosión *f*, reventón *m* (de una llanta) **2** OUTBURST : arranque *m* (de actividad, de velocidad), arrebato *m* (de ira), salva *f* (de aplausos)

Burundian [bʊˈruːndiən, -ˈrʊn-] *n* : burundés *m*, -desa *f* — **Burundian** *adj*

bury [ˈbɛri] *vt* **buried; burying 1** INTER : enterrar, sepultar **2** HIDE : esconder, ocultar **3 to bury oneself in** : enfrascarse en

bus[1] [ˈbʌs] *v* **bused** *or* **bussed** [ˈbʌst]; **busing** *or* **bussing** [ˈbʌsɪŋ] *vt* : transportar en autobús — *vi* : viajar en autobús

bus[2] *n* : autobús *m*, bus *m*, camión *m Mex*, colectivo *m Arg, Bol, Peru*

busboy [ˈbʌsˌbɔɪ] *n* : ayudante *mf* de camarero

bush [ˈbʊʃ] *n* **1** SHRUB : arbusto *m*, mata *f* **2** THICKET : maleza *f*, matorral *m*

bushel [ˈbʊʃəl] *n* : medida de áridos igual a 35.24 litros

bushing [ˈbʊʃɪŋ] *n* : cojinete *m*

bushy [ˈbʊʃi] *adj* **bushier; -est** : espeso, poblado ⟨bushy eyebrows : cejas pobladas⟩

busily [ˈbɪzəli] *adv* : afanosamente, diligentemente

business [ˈbɪznəs, -nəz] *n* **1** OCCUPATION : ocupación *f*, oficio *m* **2** DUTY, MISSION : misión *f*, deber *m*, responsabilidad *f* **3** ESTABLISHMENT, FIRM : empresa *f*, firma *f*, negocio *m*, comercio *m* **4** COMMERCE : negocios *mpl*, comercio *m* **5** AFFAIR, MATTER : asunto *m*, cuestión *f*, cosa *f* ⟨it's none of your business : no es asunto tuyo⟩

businessman [ˈbɪznəsˌmæn, -nəz-] *n, pl* **-men** [-mən, -ˌmɛn] : empresario *m*, hombre *m* de negocios

businesswoman [ˈbɪznəsˌwʊmən, -nəz-] *n, pl* **-women** [-ˌwɪmən] : empresaria *f*, mujer *f* de negocios

bust[1] [ˈbʌst] *vt* **1** BREAK, SMASH : romper, estropear, destrozar **2** TAME : domar, amansar (un caballo) — *vi* : romperse, estropearse

bust[2] *n* **1** : busto *m* (en la escultura) **2** BREASTS : pecho *m*, senos *mpl*, busto *m*

bustle[1] [ˈbʌsəl] *vi* **-tled; -tling to bustle about** : ir y venir, trajinar, ajetrearse

bustle[2] *n* **1** *or* **hustle and bustle** : bullicio *m*, ajetreo *m* **2** : polisón *m* (en la ropa feminina)

busy[1] [ˈbɪzi] *vt* **busied; busying to busy oneself with** : ocuparse con, ponerse a, entretenerse con

busy[2] *adj* **busier; -est 1** OCCUPIED : ocupado, atareado ⟨he's busy working : está ocupado en su trabajo⟩ ⟨the telephone was busy : el teléfono estaba ocupado⟩ **2** BUSTLING : concurrido, animado ⟨a busy street : una calle concurrida, una calle con mucho tránsito⟩

busybody [ˈbɪziˌbɑdi] *n, pl* **-bodies** : entrometido *m*, -da *f*; metiche *mf fam*; metomentodo *mf*

but[1] [ˈbʌt] *conj* **1** THAT : que ⟨there is no doubt but he is lazy : no cabe duda que sea perezoso⟩ **2** WITHOUT : sin que **3** NEVERTHELESS : pero, no obstante, sin embargo ⟨I called her but she didn't answer : la llamé pero no contestó⟩ **4** YET : pero ⟨he was poor but proud : era pobre pero orgulloso⟩

but[2] *prep* EXCEPT : excepto, menos ⟨everyone but Carlos : todos menos Carlos⟩ ⟨the last but one : el penúltimo⟩

butcher[1] ['bʊtʃər] *vt* **1** SLAUGHTER : matar (animales) **2** KILL : matar, asesinar, masacrar **3** BOTCH : estropear, hacer una chapuza

butcher[2] *n* **1** : carnicero *m*, -ra *f* **2** KILLER : asesino *m*, -na *f* **3** BUNGLER : chapucero *m*, -ra *f*

butler ['bʌtlər] *n* : mayordomo *m*

butt[1] ['bʌt] *vt* **1** : embestir (con los cuernos), darle un cabezazo a **2** ABUT : colindar con, bordear — *vi* **to butt in** **1** INTERRUPT : interrumpir **2** MEDDLE : entrometerse, meterse

butt[2] *n* **1** BUTTING : embestida *f* (de cuernos), cabezazo *m* **2** TARGET : blanco *m* ⟨the butt of their jokes : el blanco de sus bromas⟩ **3** BOTTOM, END : extremo *m*, culata *f* (de un rifle), colilla *f* (de un cigarrillo)

butte ['bju:t] *n* : colina *f* empinada y aislada

butter[1] ['bʌt̬ər] *vt* **1** : untar con mantequilla **2 to butter up** : halagar

butter[2] *n* : mantequilla *f*

buttercup ['bʌt̬ər,kʌp] *n* : ranúnculo *m*

butterfat ['bʌt̬ər,fæt] *n* : grasa *f* de la leche

butterfly ['bʌt̬ər,flaɪ] *n, pl* **-flies** : mariposa *f*

buttermilk ['bʌt̬ər,mɪlk] *n* : suero *m* de la leche

butternut ['bʌt̬ər,nʌt] *n* : nogal *m* ceniciento (árbol)

butterscotch ['bʌt̬ər,skɑtʃ] *n* : caramelo *m* duro hecho con mantequilla

buttery ['bʌt̬əri] *adj* : mantecoso

buttocks ['bʌt̬əks, -,tɑks] *npl* : nalgas *fpl*, trasero *m*

button[1] ['bʌtən] *vt* : abrochar, abotonar — *vi* : abrocharse, abotonarse

button[2] *n* : botón *m*

buttonhole[1] ['bʌtən,ho:l] *vt* **-holed; -holing** : acorralar

buttonhole[2] *n* : ojal *m*

buttress[1] ['bʌtrəs] *vt* : apoyar, reforzar

buttress[2] *n* **1** : contrafuerte *m* (en la arquitectura) **2** SUPPORT : apoyo *m*, sostén *m*

buxom ['bʌksəm] *adj* : con mucho busto, con mucho pecho

buy[1] ['baɪ] *vt* **bought** ['bɔt]; **buying** : comprar

buy[2] *n* BARGAIN : compra *f*, ganga *f*

buyer ['baɪər] *n* : comprador *m*, -dora *f*

buzz[1] ['bʌz] *vi* : zumbar (dícese de un insecto), sonar (dícese de un teléfono o un despertador)

buzz[2] *n* **1** : zumbido *m* (de insectos) **2** : murmullo *m*, rumor *m* (de voces)

buzzard ['bʌzərd] *n* VULTURE : buitre *m*, zopilote *m CA*, *Mex*

buzzer ['bʌzər] *n* : timbre *m*, chicharra *f*

buzzword ['bʌz,wərd] *n* : palabra *f* de moda

by[1] ['baɪ] *adv* **1** NEAR : cerca ⟨he lives close by : vive muy cerca⟩ **2 to stop by** : pasar por casa, hacer una visita **3 to go by** : pasar ⟨they rushed by : pasaron corriendo⟩ **4 to put by** : reservar, poner a un lado **5 by and by** : poco después, dentro de poco **6 by and large** : en general

by[2] *prep* **1** NEAR : cerca de, al lado de, junto a **2** VIA : por ⟨she left by the door : salió por la puerta⟩ **3** PAST : por, por delante de ⟨they walked by him : pasaron por delante de él⟩ **4** DURING : de, durante ⟨by night : de noche⟩ **5** (*in expressions of time*) : para ⟨we'll be there by ten : estaremos allí para las diez⟩ ⟨by then : para entonces⟩ **6** (*indicating cause or agent*) : por, de, a ⟨built by the Romans : construido por los romanos⟩ ⟨a book by Borges : un libro de Borges⟩ ⟨made by hand : hecho a mano⟩

by and by *adv* : dentro de poco

bygone[1] ['baɪ,gɔn] *adj* : pasado

bygone[2] *n* **let bygones be bygones** : lo pasado, pasado está

bylaw *or* **byelaw** ['baɪ,lɔ] *n* : norma *f*, reglamento *m*

by–line ['baɪ,laɪn] *n* : data *f*

bypass[1] ['baɪ,pæs] *vt* : evitar

bypass[2] *n* **1** BELTWAY : carretera *f* de circunvalación **2** DETOUR : desvío *m*

by–product ['baɪ,prɑdəkt] *n* : subproducto *m*, producto *m* derivado

bystander ['baɪ,stændər] *n* : espectador *m*, -dora *f*

byte ['baɪt] *n* : byte *m*

byway ['baɪ,weɪ] *n* : camino *m* (apartado), carretera *f* secundaria

byword ['baɪ,wərd] *n* **1** PROVERB : proverbio *m*, refrán *m* **2 to be a byword for** : estar sinónimo de

C

c ['si:] *n, pl* **c's** *or* **cs** : tercera letra del alfabeto inglés
cab ['kæb] *n* **1** TAXI : taxi *m* **2** : cabina *f* (de un camión o una locomotora) **3** CARRIAGE : coche *m* de caballos
cabal [kə'bɑl, -'bæl] *n* **1** INTRIGUE, PLOT : conspiración *f*, complot *m*, intriga *f* **2** : grupo *m* de conspiradores
cabaret [ˌkæbə'reɪ] *n* : cabaret *m*
cabbage ['kæbɪʤ] *n* : col *f*, repollo *m*
cabbie *or* **cabby** ['kæbi] *n* : taxista *mf*
cabin ['kæbən] *n* **1** HUT : cabaña *f*, choza *f*, barraca *f* **2** STATEROOM : camarote *m* **3** : cabina *f* (de un automóvil o avión)
cabinet ['kæbnət] *n* **1** CUPBOARD : armario *m* **2** : gabinete *m*, consejo *m* de ministros **3 medicine cabinet** : botiquín *m*
cabinetmaker ['kæbnətˌmeɪkər] *n* : ebanista *mf*
cabinetmaking ['kæbnətˌmeɪkɪŋ] *n* : ebanistería *f*
cable¹ ['keɪbəl] *vt* **-bled; -bling** : enviar un cable, telegrafiar
cable² *n* **1** : cable *m* (para colgar o sostener algo) **2** : cable *m* eléctrico **3** → **cablegram**
cablegram ['keɪbəlˌgræm] *n* : telegrama *m*, cable *m*
caboose [kə'bu:s] *n* : furgón *m* de cola, cabús *m Mex*
cabstand ['kæbˌstænd] *n* : parada *f* de taxis
cacao [kə'kaʊ, -'keɪo] *n, pl* **cacaos** : cacao *m*
cache¹ ['kæʃ] *vt* **cached; caching** : esconder, guardar en un escondrijo
cache² *n* **1** : escondite *m*, escondrijo *m* ⟨cache of weapons : escondite de armas⟩ **2** : cache *m* ⟨cache memory : memoria cache⟩
cachet [kæ'ʃeɪ] *n* : caché *m*, prestigio *m*
cackle¹ ['kækəl] *vi* **-led; -ling 1** CLUCK : cacarear **2** : reírse o carcajearse estridentemente ⟨he was cackling with delight : estaba carcajeándose de gusto⟩
cackle² *n* **1** : cacareo *m* (de una polla) **2** LAUGH : risa *f* estridente
cacophony [kæ'kɑfəni, -'kɔ-] *n, pl* **-nies** : cacofonía *f*
cactus ['kæktəs] *n, pl* **cacti** [-ˌtaɪ] *or* **-tuses** : cacto *m*, cactus *m*
cadaver [kə'dævər] *n* : cadáver *m*
cadaverous [kə'dævərəs] *adj* : cadavérico
caddie¹ *or* **caddy** ['kædi] *vi* **caddied; caddying** : trabajar de caddie, hacer de caddie
caddie² *or* **caddy** *n, pl* **-dies** : caddie *mf*
caddy ['kædi] *n, pl* **-dies** : cajita *f* para té
cadence ['keɪdənts] *n* : cadencia *f*, ritmo *m*
cadenced ['keɪdəntst] *adj* : cadencioso, rítmico
cadet [kə'dɛt] *n* : cadete *mf*
cadmium ['kædmiəm] *n* : cadmio *m*
cadre ['kæˌdreɪ, 'kɑ-, -ˌdri:] *n* : cuadro *m* (de expertos)
café [kæ'feɪ, kə-] *n* : café *m*, cafetería *f*
cafeteria [ˌkæfə'tɪriə] *n* : cafetería *f*, restaurante *m* de autoservicio
caffeine [kæ'fi:n] *n* : cafeína *f*
cage¹ ['keɪʤ] *vt* **caged; caging** : enjaular
cage² *n* : jaula *f*
cagey ['keɪʤi] *adj* **-gier; -est 1** CAUTIOUS : cauteloso, reservado **2** SHREWD : astuto, vivo — **cagily** [-ʤəli] *adv*
caisson ['keɪˌsɑn, -sən] *n* **1** : cajón *m* de municiones **2** : cajón *m* hidráulico
cajole [kə'ʤo:l] *vt* **-joled; -joling** : engatusar
cajolery [kə'ʤo:ləri] *n* : engatusamiento *m*
cake¹ ['keɪk] *v* **caked; caking** *vt* : cubrir ⟨caked with mud : cubierto de barro⟩ — *vi* : endurecerse
cake² *n* **1** : torta *f*, bizcocho *m*, pastel *m* **2** : pastilla *f* (de jabón) **3 to take the cake** : llevarse la palma, ser el colmo
calabash ['kæləˌbæʃ] *n* : calabaza *f*
calamari [ˌkɑlə'mɑri] *ns & pl* : calamares *mpl*
calamine ['kæləˌmaɪn] *n* : calamina *f* ⟨calamine lotion : loción de calamina⟩
calamitous [kə'læmət̬əs] *adj* : desastroso, catastrófico, calamitoso — **calamitously** *adv*
calamity [kə'læmət̬i] *n, pl* **-ties** : desastre *m*, desgracia *f*, calamidad *f*
calcium ['kælsiəm] *n* : calcio *m*
calcium carbonate ['kɑrbəˌneɪt, -nət] *n* : carbonato *m* de calcio
calculable ['kælkjələbəl] *adj* : calculable, computable
calculate ['kælkjəˌleɪt] *v* **-lated; -lating** *vt* **1** COMPUTE : calcular, computar **2** ESTIMATE : calcular, creer **3** INTEND : planear, tener la intención de ⟨I calculated on spending $100 : planeaba gastar $100⟩ — *vi* : calcular, hacer cálculos
calculated ['kælkjəˌleɪt̬əd] *adj* **1** ESTIMATED : calculado **2** DELIBERATE : intencional, premeditado, deliberado
calculating ['kælkjəˌleɪt̬ɪŋ] *adj* SHREWD : calculador, astuto
calculation [ˌkælkjə'leɪʃən] *n* : cálculo *m*
calculator ['kælkjəˌleɪt̬ər] *n* : calculadora *f*
calculus ['kælkjələs] *n, pl* **-li** [-ˌlaɪ] **1** : cálculo *m* ⟨differential calculus : cálculo diferencial⟩ **2** TARTAR : sarro *m* (dental)
caldron ['kɔldrən] → **cauldron**
calendar ['kæləndər] *n* **1** : calendario *m* **2** SCHEDULE : calendario *m*, programa *m*, agenda *f*

calf ['kæf, 'kaf] *n, pl* **calves** ['kævz, 'kavz] **1** : becerro *m*, -rra *f*; ternero *m*, -ra *f* (de vacunos) **2** : cría *f* (de otros mamíferos) **3** : pantorrilla *f* (de la pierna)
calfskin ['kæf,skın] *n* : piel *f* de becerro
caliber *or* **calibre** ['kæləbər] *n* **1** : calibre *m* ⟨a .38 caliber gun : una pistola de calibre .38⟩ **2** ABILITY : calibre *m*, valor *m*, capacidad *f*
calibrate ['kælə,breıt] *vt* **-brated; -brating** : calibrar (armas), graduar (termómetros)
calibration [,kælə'breıʃən] *n* : calibrado *m*, calibración *f*
calico ['kælı,ko:] *n, pl* **-coes** *or* **-cos 1** : calicó *m*, percal *m* **2** *or* **calico cat** : gato *m* manchado
calipers ['kæləpərz] *npl* : calibrador *m*
caliph *or* **calif** ['keıləf, 'kæ-] *n* : califa *m*
calisthenics [,kæləs'θɛnıks] *ns & pl* : calistenia *f*
calk ['kɔk] → **caulk**
call[1] ['kɔl] *vi* **1** CRY, SHOUT : gritar, vociferar **2** VISIT : hacer (una) visita, visitar **3 to call for** : exigir, requerir, necesitar ⟨it calls for patience : requiere mucha paciencia⟩ — *vt* **1** SUMMON : llamar, convocar **2** TELEPHONE : llamar por teléfono, telefonear **3** NAME : llamar, apodar
call[2] *n* **1** SHOUT : grito *m*, llamada *f* **2** : grito *m* (de un animal), reclamo *m* (de un pájaro) **3** SUMMONS : llamada *f* **4** DEMAND : llamado *m*, petición *f* **5** VISIT : visita *f* **6** DECISION : decisión *f* (en deportes) **7** *or* **telephone call** : llamada *f* (telefónica)
call down *vt* REPRIMAND : reprender, reñir
caller ['kɔlər] *n* **1** VISITOR : visita *f* **2** : persona *f* que llama (por teléfono)
calligraphy [kə'lıgrəfi] *n, pl* **-phies** : caligrafía *f*
calling ['kɔlıŋ] *n* : vocación *f*, profesión *f*
calliope [kə'laıə,pi:, 'kæli,o:p] *n* : órgano *m* de vapor
call off *vt* CANCEL : cancelar, suspender
callous[1] ['kæləs] *vt* : encallecer
callous[2] *adj* **1** CALLUSED : calloso, encallecido **2** UNFEELING : insensible, desalmado, cruel
callously ['kæləsli] *adv* : cruelmente, insensiblemente
callousness ['kæləsnəs] *n* : insensibilidad *f*, crueldad *f*
callow ['kælo] *adj* : inexperto, inmaduro
callus ['kæləs] *n* : callo *m*
callused ['kæləst] *adj* : encallecido, calloso
calm[1] ['kam, 'kalm] *vt* : tranquilizar, calmar, sosegar — *vi* : tranquilizarse, calmarse ⟨calm down! : ¡tranquilízate!⟩
calm[2] *adj* **1** TRANQUIL : calmo, tranquilo, sereno, ecuánime **2** STILL : en calma (dícese del mar), sin viento (dícese del aire)
calm[3] *n* : tranquilidad *f*, calma *f*
calmly ['kamli, 'kalm-] *adv* : con calma, tranquilamente
calmness ['kamnəs, 'kalm-] *n* : calma *f*, tranquilidad *f*
caloric [kə'lɔrık] *adj* : calórico (dícese de los alimentos), calorífico (dícese de la energía)
calorie ['kæləri] *n* : caloría *f*
calumniate [kə'lʌmni,eıt] *vt* **-ated; -ating** : calumniar, difamar
calumny ['kæləmni] *n, pl* **-nies** : calumnia *f*, difamación *f*
calve ['kæv, 'kav] *vi* **calved; calving** : parir (dícese de los mamíferos)
calves → **calf**
calypso [kə'lıp,so:] *n, pl* **-sos** : calipso *m*
calyx ['keılıks, 'kæ-] *n, pl* **-lyxes** *or* **-lyces** [-lə,si:z] : cáliz *m*
cam ['kæm] *n* : leva *f*
camaraderie [,kam'radəri, ,kæm-; ,kamə'ra-] *n* : compañerismo *m*, camaradería *f*
Cambodian [kæm'bo:diən] *n* : camboyano *m*, -na *f* — **Cambodian** *adj*
came → **come**
camel ['kæməl] *n* : camello *m*
camellia [kə'mi:ljə] *n* : camelia *f*
cameo ['kæmi,o:] *n, pl* **-eos 1** : camafeo *m* **2** *or* **cameo performance** : actuación *f* especial
camera ['kæmrə, 'kæmərə] *n* : cámara *f*, máquina *f* fotográfica
Cameroonian [,kæmə'ru:niən] *n* : camerunés *m*, -nesa *f*
camouflage[1] ['kæmə,flaʒ, -,fladʒ] *vt* **-flaged; -flaging** : camuflajear, camuflar
camouflage[2] *n* : camuflaje *m*
camp[1] ['kæmp] *vi* : acampar, ir de camping
camp[2] *n* **1** : campamento *m* **2** FACTION : campo *m*, bando *m* ⟨in the same camp : del mismo bando⟩ **3 to pitch camp** : acampar, poner el campamento **4 to break camp** : levantar el campamento
campaign[1] [kæm'peın] *vi* : hacer (una) campaña
campaign[2] *n* : campaña *f*
campanile [,kæmpə'ni:,li:, -'ni:l] *n, pl* **-niles** *or* **-nili** [-'ni:,li:] : campanario *m*
camper ['kæmpər] *n* **1** : campista *mf* (persona) **2** : cámper *m* (vehículo)
campground ['kæmp,graund] *n* : campamento *m*, camping *m*
camphor ['kæmpfər] *n* : alcanfor *m*
campsite ['kæmp,saıt] *n* : campamento *m*, camping *m*
campus ['kæmpəs] *n* : campus *m*, recinto *m* universitario
can[1] ['kæn] *v aux, past* **could** ['kud]; *present s & pl* **can 1** : poder ⟨could you help me? : ¿podría ayudarme?⟩ **2** : saber ⟨she can't drive yet : todavía no sabe manejar⟩ **3** MAY : poder, tener permiso para ⟨can I sit down? : ¿puedo sentarme?⟩ **4** : poder ⟨it can't be! : ¡no

puede ser!⟩ ⟨where can they be? : ¿dónde estarán?⟩

can[2] [ˈkæn] *vt* **canned; canning 1** : enlatar, envasar ⟨to can tomatoes : enlatar tomates⟩ **2** DISMISS, FIRE : despedir, echar

can[3] *n* : lata *f*, envase *m*, cubo *m* ⟨a can of beer : una lata de cerveza⟩ ⟨garbage can : cubo de basura⟩

Canadian [kəˈneɪdiən] *n* : canadiense *mf* — **Canadian** *adj*

canal [kəˈnæl] *n* **1** : canal *m*, tubo *m* ⟨alimentary canal : tubo digestivo⟩ **2** : canal *m* ⟨Panama Canal : Canal de Panamá⟩

canapé [ˈkænəpi, -ˌpeɪ] *n* : canapé *m*

canary [kəˈnɛri] *n, pl* **-naries** : canario *m*

cancel [ˈkæntsəl] *vt* **-celed** *or* **-celled; -celing** *or* **-celling** : cancelar

cancellation [ˌkæntsəˈleɪʃən] *n* : cancelación *f*

cancer [ˈkæntsər] *n* : cáncer *m*

Cancer *n* : Cáncer *mf*

cancerous [ˈkæntsərəs] *adj* : canceroso

candelabrum [ˌkændəˈlɑbrəm, -ˈlæ-] *or* **candelabra** [-brə] *n, pl* **-bra** *or* **-bras** : candelabro *m*

candid [ˈkændɪd] *adj* **1** FRANK : franco, sincero, abierto **2** : natural, espontáneo (en la fotografía)

candidacy [ˈkændədəsi] *n, pl* **-cies** : candidatura *f*

candidate [ˈkændəˌdeɪt, -dət] *n* : candidato *m*, -ta *f*

candidly [ˈkændɪdli] *adv* : con franqueza

candied [ˈkændid] *adj* : confitado

candle [ˈkændəl] *n* : vela *f*, candela *f*, cirio *m* (ceremonial)

candlestick [ˈkændəlˌstɪk] *n* : candelero *m*

candor [ˈkændər] *n* : franqueza *f*

candy [ˈkændi] *n, pl* **-dies** : dulce *m*, caramelo *m*

cane[1] [ˈkeɪn] *vt* **caned; caning 1** : tapizar (muebles) con mimbre **2** FLOG : azotar con una vara

cane[2] *n* **1** : bastón *m* (para andar), vara *f* (para castigar) **2** REED : caña *f*, mimbre *m* (para muebles)

canine[1] [ˈkeɪˌnaɪn] *adj* : canino

canine[2] *n* **1** DOG : canino *m*; perro *m*, -rra *f* **2** *or* **canine tooth** : colmillo *m*, diente *m* canino

canister [ˈkænəstər] *n* : lata *f*, bote *m*

canker [ˈkæŋkər] *n* : úlcera *f* bucal

cannery [ˈkænəri] *n, pl* **-ries** : fábrica *f* de conservas

cannibal [ˈkænəbəl] *n* : caníbal *mf*; antropófago *m*, -ga *f*

cannibalism [ˈkænəbəˌlɪzəm] *n* : canibalismo *m*, antropofagia *f*

cannibalize [ˈkænəbəˌlaɪz] *vt* **-ized; -izing** : canibalizar

cannily [ˈkænəli] *adv* : astutamente, sagazmente

cannon [ˈkænən] *n, pl* **-nons** *or* **-non** : cañón *m*

cannot **(can not)** [ˈkænˌɑt, kəˈnɑt] → **can**[1]

canny [ˈkæni] *adj* **-nier; -est** SHREWD : astuto, sagaz

canoe[1] [kəˈnuː] *vt* **-noed; -noeing** : ir en canoa

canoe[2] *n* : canoa *f*, piragua *f*

canon [ˈkænən] *n* **1** : canon *m* ⟨canon law : derecho canónico⟩ **2** WORKS : canon *m* ⟨the canon of American literature : el canon de la literatura americana⟩ **3** : canónigo *m* (de una catedral) **4** STANDARD : canon *m*, norma *f*

canonical [kəˈnɑnɪkəl] *adj* : canónico

canonize [ˈkænəˌnaɪz] *vt* **-ized; -izing** : canonizar

canopy [ˈkænəpi] *n, pl* **-pies** : dosel *m*, toldo *m*

cant[1] [ˈkænt] *vt* TILT : ladear, inclinar — *vi* **1** SLANT : ladearse, inclinarse, escorar (dícese de un barco) **2** : hablar insinceramente

cant[2] *n* **1** SLANT : plano *m* inclinado **2** JARGON : jerga *f* **3** : palabras *fpl* insinceras

can't [ˈkænt, ˈkant] (*contraction of* **can not**) → **can**[1]

cantaloupe [ˈkæntəlˌoːp] *n* : melón *m*, cantalupo *m*

cantankerous [kænˈtæŋkərəs] *adj* : irritable, irascible — **cantankerously** *adv*

cantankerousness [kænˈtæŋkərəsnəs] *n* : irritabilidad *f*, irascibilidad *f*

cantata [kənˈtɑt̬ə] *n* : cantata *f*

canteen [kænˈtiːn] *n* **1** FLASK : cantimplora *f* **2** CAFETERIA : cantina *f*, comedor *m* **3** : club *m* para actividades sociales y recreativas

canter[1] [ˈkæntər] *vi* : ir a medio galope

canter[2] *n* : medio galope *m*

cantilever [ˈkæntəˌliːvər, -ˌlɛvər] *n* **1** : viga *f* voladiza **2** **cantilever bridge** : puente *m* voladizo

canto [ˈkænˌtoː] *n, pl* **-tos** : canto *m*

canton [ˈkæntən, -ˌtɑn] *n* : cantón *m*

Cantonese [ˌkæntənˈiːz, -ˈiːs] *n* **1** : cantonés *m*, -nesa *f* **2** : cantonés *m* (idioma) — **Cantonese** *adj*

cantor [ˈkæntər] *n* : solista *mf*

canvas [ˈkænvəs] *n* **1** : lona *f* **2** SAILS : velas *fpl* (de un barco) **3** : lienzo *m*, tela *f* (de pintar) **4** PAINTING : pintura *f*, óleo *m*, cuadro *m*

canvass[1] [ˈkænvəs] *vt* **1** SOLICIT : solicitar votos o pedidos de, hacer campaña entre **2** SOUND OUT : sondear (opiniones, etc.)

canvass[2] *n* SURVEY : sondeo *m*, encuesta *f*

canyon [ˈkænjən] *n* : cañón *m*

cap[1] [ˈkæp] *vt* **capped; capping 1** COVER : tapar (un recipiente), enfundar (un diente), cubrir (una montaña) **2** CLIMAX : coronar, ser el punto culminante de ⟨to cap it all off : para colmo⟩ **3** LIMIT : limitar, poner un tope a

cap[2] *n* **1** : gorra *f*, gorro *m*, cachucha *f* *Mex* ⟨baseball cap : gorra de béisbol⟩

2 COVER, TOP : tapa *f*, tapón *m* (de botellas), corcholata *f Mex* 3 LIMIT : tope *m*, límite *m*
capability [ˌkeɪpəˈbɪləṭi] *n, pl* **-ties** : capacidad *f*, habilidad *f*, competencia *f*
capable [ˈkeɪpəbəl] *adj* : competente, capaz, hábil — **capably** [-bli] *adv*
capacious [kəˈpeɪʃəs] *adj* : amplio, espacioso, de gran capacidad
capacity[1] [kəˈpæsəṭi] *adj* : completo, total ⟨a capacity crowd : un lleno completo⟩
capacity[2] *n, pl* **-ties** 1 ROOM, SPACE : capacidad *f*, cabida *f*, espacio *m* 2 CAPABILITY : habilidad *f*, competencia *f* 3 FUNCTION, ROLE : calidad *f*, función *f* ⟨in his capacity as ambassador : en su calidad de embajador⟩
cape [ˈkeɪp] *n* 1 : capa *f* 2 : cabo *m* ⟨Cape Horn : el Cabo de Hornos⟩
caper[1] [ˈkeɪpər] *vi* : dar saltos, correr y brincar
caper[2] *n* 1 : alcaparra *f* ⟨olives and capers : aceitunas y alcaparras⟩ 2 ANTIC, PRANK : broma *f*, travesura *f* 3 LEAP : brinco *m*, salto *m*
Cape Verdean [ˈkeɪpˈvərdiən] *n* : caboverdiano *m*, -na *f* — **Cape Verdean** *adj*
capful [ˈkæpˌfʊl] *n* : tapa *f*, tapita *f*
capillary[1] [ˈkæpəˌlɛri] *adj* : capilar
capillary[2] *n, pl* **-ries** : capilar *m*
capital[1] [ˈkæpəṭəl] *adj* 1 : capital ⟨capital punishment : pena capital⟩ 2 : mayúsculo (dícese de las letras) 3 : de capital ⟨capital assets : activo fijo⟩ ⟨capital gain : ganancia de capital, plusvalía⟩ 4 EXCELLENT : excelente, estupendo
capital[2] *n* 1 *or* **capital city** : capital *f*, sede *f* del gobierno 2 WEALTH : capital *m* 3 *or* **capital letter** : mayúscula *f* 4 : capitel *m* (de una columna)
capitalism [ˈkæpəṭəlˌɪzəm] *n* : capitalismo *m*
capitalist[1] [ˈkæpəṭəlɪst] *or* **capitalistic** [ˌkæpəṭəlˈɪstɪk] *adj* : capitalista
capitalist[2] *n* : capitalista *mf*
capitalization [ˌkæpəṭələˈzeɪʃən] *n* : capitalización *f*
capitalize [ˈkæpəṭəlˌaɪz] *v* **-ized; -izing** *vt* 1 FINANCE : capitalizar, financiar 2 : escribir con mayúscula — *vi* **to capitalize on** : sacar partido de, aprovechar
capitol [ˈkæpəṭəl] *n* : capitolio *m*
capitulate [kəˈpɪʧəˌleɪt] *vi* **-lated; -lating** : capitular
capitulation [kəˌpɪʧəˈleɪʃən] *n* : capitulación *f*
capon [ˈkeɪˌpɑn, -pən] *n* : capón *m*
cappuccino [ˌkɑpəˈʧiːnoː] *n* : capuchino *m* (café)
caprice [kəˈpriːs] *n* : capricho *m*, antojo *m*
capricious [kəˈprɪʃəs, -ˈpriː-] *adj* : caprichoso — **capriciously** *adv*
Capricorn [ˈkæprɪˌkɔrn] *n* : Capricornio *mf*
capsize [ˈkæpˌsaɪz, kæpˈsaɪz] *v* **-sized; -sizing** *vi* : volcar, volcarse — *vt* : hacer volcar
capstan [ˈkæpstən, -ˌstæn] *n* : cabrestante *m*
capsule [ˈkæpsəl, -ˌsuːl] *n* 1 : cápsula *f* (en la farmacéutica y botánica) 2 **space capsule** : cápsula *f* espacial
captain[1] [ˈkæptən] *vt* : capitanear
captain[2] *n* 1 : capitán *m*, -tana *f* 2 HEADWAITER : jefe *m*, -fa *f* de comedor 3 **captain of industry** : magnate *mf*
caption[1] [ˈkæpʃən] *vt* : ponerle una leyenda a (una ilustración), titular (un artículo), subtitular (una película)
caption[2] *n* 1 HEADING : titular *m*, encabezamiento *m* 2 : leyenda *f* (al pie de una ilustración) 3 SUBTITLE : subtítulo *m*
captivate [ˈkæptəˌveɪt] *vt* **-vated; -vating** CHARM : cautivar, hechizar, encantar
captivating [ˈkæptəˌveɪṭɪŋ] *adj* : cautivador, hechicero, encantador
captive[1] [ˈkæptɪv] *adj* : cautivo
captive[2] *n* : cautivo *m*, -va *f*
captivity [kæpˈtɪvəṭi] *n* : cautiverio *m*
captor [ˈkæptər] *n* : captor *m*, -tora *f*
capture[1] [ˈkæpʃər] *vt* **-tured; -turing** 1 SEIZE : capturar, apresar 2 CATCH : captar ⟨to capture one's interest : captar el interés de uno⟩
capture[2] *n* : captura *f*, apresamiento *m*
car [ˈkɑr] *n* 1 AUTOMOBILE : automóvil *m*, coche *m*, carro *m* 2 : vagón *m*, coche *m* (de un tren) 3 : cabina *f* (de un ascensor)
carafe [kəˈræf, -ˈrɑf] *n* : garrafa *f*
caramel [ˈkɑrməl; ˈkærəməl, -ˌmɛl] *n* 1 : caramelo *m*, azúcar *f* quemada 2 *or* **caramel candy** : caramelo *m*, dulce *m* de leche
carat [ˈkærət] *n* : quilate *m*
caravan [ˈkærəˌvæn] *n* : caravana *f*
caraway [ˈkærəˌweɪ] *n* : alcaravea *f*
carbine [ˈkɑrˌbaɪn, -ˌbiːn] *n* : carabina *f*
carbohydrate [ˌkɑrboˈhaɪˌdreɪt, -drət] *n* : carbohidrato *m*, hidrato *m* de carbono
carbon [ˈkɑrbən] *n* 1 : carbono *m* 2 → **carbon paper** 3 → **carbon copy**
carbonated [ˈkɑrbəˌneɪṭəd] *adj* : carbonatado (dícese del agua), gaseoso (dícese de las bebidas)
carbon copy *n* 1 : copia *f* al carbón 2 DUPLICATE : duplicado *m*, copia *f* exacta
carbon paper *n* : papel *m* carbón
carbuncle [ˈkɑrˌbʌŋkəl] *n* : carbunco *m*
carburetor [ˈkɑrbəˌreɪṭər, -bjə-] *n* : carburador *m*
carcass [ˈkɑrkəs] *n* : cuerpo *m* (de un animal muerto)
carcinogen [kɑrˈsɪnəʤən, ˈkɑrsənəˌʤɛn] *n* : carcinógeno *m*, cancerígeno *m*
carcinogenic [ˌkɑrsənoˈʤɛnɪk] *adj* : carcinogénico
carcinoma [ˌkɑrsəˈnoːmə] *n* : carcinoma *m*

card[1] ['kɑrd] *vt* : cardar (fibras)
card[2] *n* **1** : carta *f*, naipe *m* ⟨to play cards : jugar a las cartas⟩ ⟨a deck of cards : una baraja⟩ **2** : tarjeta *f* ⟨birthday card : tarjeta de cumpleaños⟩ ⟨business card : tarjeta (de visita)⟩
cardboard ['kɑrd,bord] *n* : cartón *m*, cartulina *f*
cardiac ['kɑrdi,æk] *adj* : cardíaco, cardiaco
cardigan ['kɑrdɪgən] *n* : cárdigan *m*, chaqueta *f* de punto
cardinal[1] ['kɑrdənəl] *adj* FUNDAMENTAL : cardinal, fundamental
cardinal[2] *n* : cardenal *m*
cardinal number *n* : número *m* cardinal
cardinal point *n* : punto *m* cardinal
cardiologist [,kɑrdi'ɑləʤɪst] *n* : cardiólogo *m*, -ga *f*
cardiology [,kɑrdi'ɑləʤi] *n* : cardiología *f*
cardiovascular [,kɑrdio'væskjələr] *adj* : cardiovascular
care[1] ['kær] *v* **cared; caring** *vi* **1** : importarle a uno ⟨they don't care : no les importa⟩ **2** : preocuparse, inquietarse ⟨she cares about the poor : se preocupa por los pobres⟩ **3 to care for** TEND : cuidar (de), atender, encargarse de **4 to care for** CHERISH : querer, sentir cariño por **5 to care for** LIKE : gustarle (algo a uno) ⟨I don't care for your attitude : tu actitud no me agrada⟩ — *vt* WISH : desear, querer ⟨if you care to go : si deseas ir⟩
care[2] *n* **1** ANXIETY : inquietud *f*, preocupación *f* **2** CAREFULNESS : cuidado *m*, atención *f* ⟨handle with care : manejar con cuidado⟩ **3** CHARGE : cargo *m*, cuidado *m* **4 to take care of** : cuidar (de), atender, encargarse de
careen [kə'ri:n] *vi* **1** SWAY : oscilar, balancearse **2** CAREER : ir a toda velocidad
career[1] [kə'rɪr] *vi* : ir a toda velocidad
career[2] *n* VOCATION : vocación *f*, profesión *f*, carrera *f*
carefree ['kær,fri:, ,kær'-] *adj* : despreocupado
careful ['kærfəl] *adj* **1** CAUTIOUS : cuidadoso, cauteloso **2** PAINSTAKING : cuidadoso, esmerado, meticuloso
carefully ['kærfəli] *adv* : con cuidado, cuidadosamente
carefulness ['kærfəlnəs] *n* **1** CAUTION : cuidado *m*, cautela *f* **2** METICULOUSNESS : esmero *m*, meticulosidad *f*
caregiver ['kær,gɪvər] *n* : persona *f* que cuida a niños o enfermos
careless ['kærləs] *adj* : descuidado, negligente — **carelessly** *adv*
carelessness ['kærləsnəs] *n* : descuido *m*, negligencia *f*
caress[1] [kə'rɛs] *vt* : acariciar
caress[2] *n* : caricia *f*
caret ['kærət] *n* : signo *m* de intercalación
caretaker ['kɛr,teɪkər] *n* : conserje *mf*; velador *m*, -dora *f*
cargo ['kɑr,go:] *n, pl* **-goes** *or* **-gos** : cargamento *m*, carga *f*
Caribbean [kærə'bi:ən, kə'rɪbiən] *adj* : caribeño ⟨the Caribbean Sea : el mar Caribe⟩
caribou ['kærə,bu:] *n, pl* **-bou** *or* **-bous** : caribú *m*
caricature[1] ['kærɪkə,ʧʊr] *vt* **-tured; -turing** : caricaturizar
caricature[2] *n* : caricatura *f*
caricaturist ['kærɪkə,ʧʊrɪst] *n* : caricaturista *mf*
caries ['kær,i:z] *ns & pl* : caries *f*
carillon ['kærə,lɑn] *n* : carillón *m*
carmine ['kɑrmən, -,maɪn] *n* : carmín *m*
carnage ['kɑrnɪʤ] *n* : matanza *f*, carnicería *f*
carnal ['kɑrnəl] *adj* : carnal
carnation [kɑr'neɪʃən] *n* : clavel *m*
carnival ['kɑrnəvəl] *n* : carnaval *m*, feria *f*
carnivore ['kɑrnə,vor] *n* : carnívoro *m*
carnivorous [kɑr'nɪvərəs] *adj* : carnívoro
carol[1] ['kærəl] *vi* **-oled** *or* **-olled; -oling** *or* **-olling** : cantar villancicos
carol[2] *n* : villancico *m*
caroler *or* **caroller** ['kærələr] *n* : persona *f* que canta villancicos
carom[1] ['kærəm] *vi* **1** REBOUND : rebotar ⟨the bullet caromed off the wall : la bala rebotó contra el muro⟩ **2** : hacer carambola (en billar)
carom[2] *n* : carambola *f*
carouse [kə'raʊz] *vt* **-roused; -rousing** : irse de parranda, irse de juerga
carousel *or* **carrousel** [,kærə'sɛl, 'kærə,-] *n* : carrusel *m*, tiovivo *m*
carouser [kə'raʊzər] *n* : juerguista *mf*
carp[1] ['kɑrp] *vi* **1** COMPLAIN : quejarse **2 to carp at** : criticar
carp[2] *n, pl* **carp** *or* **carps** : carpa *f*
carpel ['kɑrpəl] *n* : carpelo *m*
carpenter ['kɑrpəntər] *n* : carpintero *m*, -ra *f*
carpentry ['kɑrpəntri] *n* : carpintería *f*
carpet[1] ['kɑrpət] *vt* : alfombrar
carpet[2] *n* : alfombra *f*
carpeting ['kɑrpəṭɪŋ] *n* : alfombrado *m*
carport ['kɑr,pɔrt] *n* : cochera *f*, garaje *m* abierto
carriage ['kærɪʤ] *n* **1** TRANSPORT : transporte *m* **2** POSTURE : porte *m*, postura *f* **3 horse–drawn carriage** : carruaje *m*, coche *m* **4 baby carriage** : cochecito *m*
carrier ['kæriər] *n* **1** : transportista *mf*, empresa *f* de transportes **2** : portador *m*, -dora *f* (de una enfermedad) **3 aircraft carrier** : portaaviones *m*
carrier pigeon : paloma *f* mensajera
carrion ['kæriən] *n* : carroña *f*
carrot ['kærət] *n* : zanahoria *f*
carry ['kæri] *v* **-ried; -rying** *vt* **1** TRANSPORT : llevar, cargar, transportar (cargamento), conducir (electricidad), portar (un virus) ⟨to carry a bag : cargar una bolsa⟩ ⟨to carry money : llevar dinero encima, traer dinero consi-

go⟩ **2** BEAR : soportar, aguantar, resistir (peso) **3** STOCK : vender, tener en abasto **4** ENTAIL : llevar, implicar, acarrear **5** WIN : ganar (una elección o competición), aprobar (una moción) **6 to carry oneself** : portarse, comportarse ⟨he carried himself honorably : se comportó dignamente⟩ — *vi* : oírse, proyectarse ⟨her voice carries well : su voz se puede oír desde lejos⟩

carryall [ˈkæriˌɔl] *n* : bolsa *f* de viaje

carry away *vt* **to get carried away** : exaltarse, entusiasmarse

carry on *vt* CONDUCT : realizar, ejercer, mantener ⟨to carry on research : realizar investigaciones⟩ ⟨to carry on a correspondence : mantener una correspondencia⟩ — *vi* **1** : portarse de manera escandalosa o inapropiada ⟨it's embarrassing how he carries on : su manera de comportarse da vergüenza⟩ **2** CONTINUE : seguir, continuar

carry out *vt* **1** PERFORM : llevar a cabo, realizar **2** FULFILL : cumplir

cart[1] [ˈkɑrt] *vt* : acarrear, llevar

cart[2] *n* : carreta *f*, carro *m*

cartel [kɑrˈtɛl] *n* : cártel *m*

cartilage [ˈkɑrt̬əlɪʤ] *n* : cartílago *m*

cartilaginous [ˌkɑrt̬əlˈæʤənəs] *adj* : cartilaginoso

cartographer [kɑrˈtɑgrəfər] *n* : cartógrafo *m*, -fa *f*

cartography [kɑrˈtɑgrəfi] *n* : cartografía *f*

carton [ˈkɑrtən] *n* : caja *f* de cartón

cartoon [kɑrˈtu:n] *n* **1** : chiste *m* (gráfico), caricatura *f* ⟨a political cartoon : un chiste político⟩ **2** COMIC STRIP : tira *f* cómica, historieta *f* **3** *or* **animated cartoon** : dibujo *m* animado

cartoonist [kɑrˈtu:nɪst] *n* : caricaturista *mf*, dibujante *mf* (de chistes)

cartridge [ˈkɑrtrɪʤ] *n* : cartucho *m*

carve [ˈkɑrv] *vt* **carved; carving** **1** : tallar (madera), esculpir (piedra), grabar ⟨he carved his name in the bark : grabó su nombre en la corteza⟩ **2** SLICE : cortar, trinchar (carne)

cascade[1] [kæsˈkeɪd] *vi* **-caded; -cading** : caer en cascada

cascade[2] *n* : cascada *f*, salto *m* de agua

case[1] [ˈkeɪs] *vt* **cased; casing** **1** BOX, PACK : embalar, encajonar **2** INSPECT : observar, inspeccionar (antes de cometer un delito)

case[2] *n* **1** : caso *m* ⟨an unusual case : un caso insólito⟩ ⟨ablative case : caso ablativo⟩ ⟨a case of the flu : un caso de gripe⟩ **2** BOX : caja *f* **3** CONTAINER : funda *f*, estuche *m* **4 in any case** : de todos modos, en cualquier caso **5 in case** : como precaución ⟨just in case : por si acaso⟩ **6 in case of** : en caso de

casement [ˈkeɪsmənt] *n* : ventana *f* con bisagras

cash[1] [ˈkæʃ] *vt* : convertir en efectivo, cobrar, cambiar (un cheque)

cash[2] *n* : efectivo *m*, dinero *m* en efectivo

cashew [ˈkæˌʃu:, kəˈʃu:] *n* : anacardo *m*

cashier[1] [kæˈʃɪr] *vt* : destituir, despedir

cashier[2] *n* : cajero *m*, -ra *f*

cashmere [ˈkæʒˌmɪr, ˈkæʃ-] *n* : cachemir *m*

casino [kəˈsi:ˌno:] *n, pl* **-nos** : casino *m*

cask [ˈkæsk] *n* : tonel *m*, barrica *f*, barril *m*

casket [ˈkæskət] *n* COFFIN : ataúd *m*, féretro *m*

cassava [kəˈsɑvə] *n* : mandioca *f*, yuca *f*

casserole [ˈkæsəˌro:l] *n* **1** : cazuela *f* **2** : guiso *m*, guisado *m* ⟨tuna casserole : guiso de atún⟩

cassette [kəˈsɛt, kæ-] *n* : cassette *mf*

cassock [ˈkæsək] *n* : sotana *f*

cast[1] [ˈkæst] *vt* **cast; casting** **1** THROW : tirar, echar, arrojar ⟨the die is cast : la suerte está echada⟩ **2** : depositar (un voto) **3** : asignar (papeles en una obra de teatro) **4** MOLD : moldear, fundir, vaciar **5 to cast off** ABANDON : desamparar, abandonar

cast[2] *n* **1** THROW : lance *m*, lanzamiento *m* **2** APPEARANCE : aspecto *m*, forma *f* **3** : elenco *m*, reparto *m* (de una obra de teatro) **4 plaster cast** : molde *m* de yeso, escayola *f*

castanets [ˌkæstəˈnɛts] *npl* : castañuelas *fpl*

castaway[1] [ˈkæstəˌweɪ] *adj* : náufrago

castaway[2] *n* : náufrago *m*, -ga *f*

caste [ˈkæst] *n* : casta *f*

caster [ˈkæstər] *n* : ruedita *f* (de un mueble)

castigate [ˈkæstəˌgeɪt] *vt* **-gated; -gating** : castigar severamente, censurar, reprobar

Castilian [kæˈstɪljən] *n* **1** : castellano *m*, -na *f* **2** : castellano *m* (idioma) — **Castilian** *adj*

cast iron *n* : hierro *m* fundido

castle [ˈkæsəl] *n* **1** : castillo *m* **2** : torre *f* (en ajedrez)

cast–off [ˈkæstˌɔf] *adj* : desechado

castoff [ˈkæstˌɔf] *n* : desecho *m*

castrate [ˈkæsˌtreɪt] *vt* **-trated; -trating** : castrar

castration [kæˈstreɪʃən] *n* : castración *f*

casual [ˈkæʒuəl] *adj* **1** FORTUITOUS : casual, fortuito **2** INDIFFERENT : indiferente, despreocupado **3** INFORMAL : informal — **casually** [ˈkæʒuəli, ˈkæʒəli] *adv*

casualness [ˈkæʒuəlnəs] *n* **1** FORTUITOUSNESS : casualidad *f* **2** INDIFFERENCE : indiferencia *f*, despreocupación *f* **3** INFORMALITY : informalidad *f*

casualty [ˈkæʒuəlti, ˈkæʒəl-] *n, pl* **-ties** **1** ACCIDENT : accidente *m* serio, desastre *m* **2** VICTIM : víctima *f*; baja *f*; herido *m*, -da *f*

cat [ˈkæt] *n* : gato *m*, -ta *f*

cataclysm [ˈkæt̬əˌklɪzəm] *n* : cataclismo *m*

cataclysmal [ˌkæt̬əˈklɪzməl] *or* **cataclysmic** [ˌkæt̬əˈklɪzmɪk] *adj* : catastrófico
catacombs [ˈkæt̬əˌkoːmz] *npl* : catacumbas *fpl*
Catalan [ˈkæt̬ələn, -ˌlæn] *n* **1** : catalán *m*, catalana *f* **2** : catalán *m* (idioma) — **Catalan** *adj*
catalog[1] *or* **catalogue** [ˈkæt̬əˌlɔg] *vt* **-loged** *or* **-logued**; **-loging** *or* **-loguing** : catalogar
catalog[2] *n* : catálogo *m*
catalyst [ˈkæt̬ələst] *n* : catalizador *m*
catalytic [ˌkæt̬əlˈɪtɪk] *adj* : catalítico
catamaran [ˌkæt̬əməˈræn, ˈkæt̬əməˌræn] *n* : catamarán *m*
catapult[1] [ˈkæt̬əˌpʌlt, -ˌpʊlt] *vt* : catapultar
catapult[2] *n* : catapulta *f*
cataract [ˈkæt̬əˌrækt] *n* : catarata *f*
catarrh [kəˈtɑr] *n* : catarro *m*
catastrophe [kəˈtæstrəˌfiː] *n* : catástrofe *f*
catastrophic [ˌkæt̬əˈstrɑfɪk] *adj* : catastrófico — **catastrophically** [-fɪkli] *adv*
catcall [ˈkætˌkɔl] *n* : rechifla *f*, abucheo *m*
catch[1] [ˈkætʃ, ˈkɛtʃ] *v* **caught** [ˈkɔt]; **catching** *vt* **1** CAPTURE, TRAP : capturar, agarrar, atrapar, coger **2** : agarrar, pillar *fam*, tomar de sorpresa ⟨they caught him red-handed : lo pillaron con las manos en la masa⟩ **3** GRASP : agarrar, captar **4** ENTANGLE : enganchar, enredar **5** : tomar (un tren, etc.) **6** : contagiarse de ⟨to catch a cold : contagiarse de un resfriado, resfriarse⟩ — *vi* **1** GRASP : agarrar **2** HOOK : engancharse **3** IGNITE : prender, agarrar
catch[2] *n* **1** CATCHING : captura *f*, atrapada *f*, parada *f* (de una pelota) **2** : redada *f* (de pescado), presa *f* (de caza) ⟨he's a good catch : es un buen partido⟩ **3** LATCH : pestillo *m*, pasador *m* **4** DIFFICULTY, TRICK : problema *m*, trampa *f*, truco *m*
catcher [ˈkætʃər, ˈkɛ-] *n* : catcher *mf*; receptor *m*, -tora *f* (en béisbol)
catching [ˈkætʃɪŋ, ˈkɛ-] *adj* : contagioso
catchup [ˈkætʃəp, ˈkɛ-] → **ketchup**
catchword [ˈkætʃˌwərd, ˈkɛtʃ-] *n* : eslogan *m*, lema *m*
catchy [ˈkætʃi, ˈkɛ-] *adj* **catchier**; **-est** : pegajoso ⟨a catchy song : una canción pegajosa⟩
catechism [ˈkæt̬əˌkɪzəm] *n* : catecismo *m*
categorical [ˌkæt̬əˈgɔrɪkəl] *adj* : categórico, absoluto, rotundo — **categorically** [-kli] *adv*
categorize [ˈkæt̬ɪgəˌraɪz] *vt* **-rized**; **-rizing** : clasificar, catalogar
category [ˈkæt̬əˌgori] *n, pl* **-ries** : categoría *f*, género *m*, clase *f*
cater [ˈkeɪt̬ər] *vi* **1** : proveer alimentos (para fiestas, bodas, etc.) **2 to cater to** : atender a ⟨to cater to all tastes : atender a todos los gustos⟩
catercorner[1] [ˈkæt̬iˌkɔrnər, ˈkæt̬ə-, ˈkɪt̬i-] *or* **cater–cornered** [-ˌkɔrnərd] *adv* : diagonalmente, en diagonal
catercorner[2] *or* **cater–cornered** *adj* : diagonal
caterer [ˈkeɪt̬ərər] *n* : proveedor *m*, -dora *f* de comida
caterpillar [ˈkæt̬ərˌpɪlər] *n* : oruga *f*
catfish [ˈkætˌfɪʃ] *n* : bagre *m*
catgut [ˈkætˌgʌt] *n* : cuerda *f* de tripa
catharsis [kəˈθɑrsɪs] *n, pl* **catharses** [-ˌsiːz] : catarsis *f*
cathartic[1] [kəˈθɑrt̬ɪk] *adj* : catártico
cathartic[2] *n* : purgante *m*
cathedral [kəˈθiːdrəl] *n* : catedral *f*
catheter [ˈkæθət̬ər] *n* : catéter *m*, sonda *f*
cathode [ˈkæˌθoːd] *n* : cátodo *m*
catholic [ˈkæθəlɪk] *adj* **1** BROAD, UNIVERSAL : liberal, universal **2 Catholic** : católico
Catholic *n* : católico *m*, -ca *f*
Catholicism [kəˈθɑləˌsɪzəm] *n* : catolicismo *m*
catlike [ˈkætˌlaɪk] *adj* : gatuno, felino
catnap[1] [ˈkætˌnæp] *vi* **-napped**; **-napping** : tomarse una siestecita
catnap[2] *n* : siesta *f* breve, siestecita *f*
catnip [ˈkætˌnɪp] *n* : nébeda *f*
catsup [ˈkɛtʃəp, ˈkætsəp] → **ketchup**
cattail [ˈkætˌteɪl] *n* : espadaña *f*, anea *f*
cattiness [ˈkæt̬inəs] *n* : malicia *f*
cattle [ˈkæt̬əl] *npl* : ganado *m*, reses *fpl*
cattleman [ˈkæt̬əlmən, -ˌmæn] *n, pl* **-men** [-mən, -ˌmɛn] : ganadero *m*
catty [ˈkæt̬i] *adj* **-tier**; **-est** : malicioso, malintencionado
catwalk [ˈkætˌwɔk] *n* : pasarela *f*
Caucasian[1] [kɔˈkeɪʒən] *adj* : caucásico
Caucasian[2] *n* : caucásico *m*, -ca *f*
caucus [ˈkɔkəs] *n* : junta *f* de políticos
caught → **catch**
cauldron [ˈkɔldrən] *n* : caldera *f*
cauliflower [ˈkɑlɪˌflaʊər, ˈkɔ-] *n* : coliflor *f*
caulk[1] [ˈkɔk] *vt* : calafatear (un barco), enmasillar (una grieta)
caulk[2] *n* : masilla *f*
causal [ˈkɔzəl] *adj* : causal
causality [kɔˈzæləti] *n* : causalidad *f*
cause[1] [ˈkɔz] *vt* **caused**; **causing** : causar, provocar, ocasionar
cause[2] *n* **1** ORIGIN : causa *f*, origen *m* **2** REASON : causa *f*, razón *f*, motivo *m* **3** LAWSUIT : litigio *m*, pleito *m* **4** MOVEMENT : causa *f*, movimiento *m*
causeless [ˈkɔzləs] *adj* : sin causa
causeway [ˈkɔzˌweɪ] *n* : camino *m* elevado
caustic [ˈkɔstɪk] *adj* **1** CORROSIVE : cáustico, corrosivo **2** BITING : mordaz, sarcástico
cauterize [ˈkɔt̬əˌraɪz] *vt* **-ized**; **-izing** : cauterizar
caution[1] [ˈkɔʃən] *vt* : advertir
caution[2] *n* **1** WARNING : advertencia *f*, aviso *m* **2** CARE, PRUDENCE : precaución *f*, cuidado *m*, cautela *f*

cautionary [ˈkɔʃəˌnɛri] *adv* : admonitorio ⟨cautionary tale : cuento moral⟩
cautious [ˈkɔʃəs] *adj* : cauteloso, cuidadoso, precavido
cautiously [ˈkɔʃəsli] *adv* : cautelosamente, con precaución
cautiousness [ˈkɔʃəsnəs] *n* : cautela *f*, precaución *f*
cavalcade [ˌkævəlˈkeɪd, ˈkævəlˌ-] *n* **1** : cabalgata *f* **2** SERIES : serie *f*
cavalier¹ [ˌkævəˈlɪr] *adj* : altivo, desdeñoso — **cavalierly** *adv*
cavalier² *n* : caballero *m*
cavalry [ˈkævəlri] *n, pl* **-ries** : caballería *f*
cave¹ [ˈkeɪv] *vi* **caved; caving** *or* **to cave in** : derrumbarse
cave² *n* : cueva *f*
cavern [ˈkævərn] *n* : caverna *f*
cavernous [ˈkævərnəs] *adj* : cavernoso — **cavernously** *adv*
caviar *or* **caviare** [ˈkæviˌɑr, ˈkɑ-] *n* : caviar *m*
cavity [ˈkævət̬i] *n, pl* **-ties** **1** HOLE : cavidad *f*, hueco *m* **2** CARIES : caries *f*
cavort [kəˈvɔrt] *vi* : brincar, hacer cabriolas
caw¹ [ˈkɔ] *vi* : graznar
caw² *n* : graznido *m*
cayenne pepper [ˌkaɪˈɛn, ˌkeɪ-] *n* : pimienta *f* cayena, pimentón *m*
CD [ˌsiːˈdiː] *n* : CD *m*, disco *m* compacto
CD-ROM [ˌsiːˌdiːˈrɑm] *n* : CD-ROM *m*
cease [ˈsiːs] *v* **ceased; ceasing** *vt* : dejar de ⟨they ceased bickering : dejaron de discutir⟩ — *vi* : cesar, pasarse
ceaseless [ˈsiːsləs] *adj* : incesante, continuo
cedar [ˈsiːdər] *n* : cedro *m*
cede [ˈsiːd] *vt* **ceded; ceding** : ceder, conceder
ceiling [ˈsiːlɪŋ] *n* **1** : techo *m*, cielo *m* raso **2** LIMIT : límite *m*, tope *m*
celebrant [ˈsɛləbrənt] *n* : celebrante *mf*, oficiante *mf*
celebrate [ˈsɛləˌbreɪt] *v* **-brated; -brating** *vt* **1** : celebrar, oficiar ⟨to celebrate Mass : celebrar la misa⟩ **2** : celebrar, festejar ⟨we're celebrating our anniversary : estamos celebrando nuestro aniversario⟩ **3** EXTOL : alabar, ensalzar, exaltar — *vi* : estar de fiesta, divertirse
celebrated [ˈsɛləˌbreɪt̬əd] *adj* : célebre, famoso, renombrado
celebration [ˌsɛləˈbreɪʃən] *n* : celebración *f*, festejos *mpl*
celebrity [səˈlɛbrət̬i] *n, pl* **-ties** **1** RENOWN : fama *f*, renombre *m*, celebridad *f* **2** PERSONALITY : celebridad *f*, personaje *m*
celery [ˈsɛləri] *n, pl* **-eries** : apio *m*
celestial [səˈlɛstʃəl, -ˈlɛstiəl] *adj* **1** : celeste **2** HEAVENLY : celestial, paradisiaco
celibacy [ˈsɛləbəsi] *n* : celibato *m*
celibate¹ [ˈsɛləbət] *adj* : célibe
celibate² *n* : célibe *mf*
cell [ˈsɛl] *n* **1** : célula *f* (de un organismo) **2** : celda *f* (en una cárcel, etc.) **3** : elemento *m* (de una pila)
cellar [ˈsɛlər] *n* **1** BASEMENT : sótano *m* **2** : bodega *f* (de vinos)
cellist [ˈtʃɛlɪst] *n* : violonchelista *mf*
cello [ˈtʃɛˌloː] *n, pl* **-los** : violonchelo *m*
cellophane [ˈsɛləˌfeɪn] *n* : celofán *m*
cell phone *n* : teléfono *m* celular
cellular [ˈsɛljələr] *adj* : celular
celluloid [ˈsɛljəˌlɔɪd] *n* : celuloide
cellulose [ˈsɛljəˌloːs] *n* : celulosa *f*
Celsius [ˈsɛlsiəs] *adj* : centígrado ⟨100 degrees Celsius : 100 grados centígrados⟩
Celt [ˈkɛlt, ˈsɛlt] *n* : celta *mf*
Celtic¹ [ˈkɛltɪk, ˈsɛl-] *adj* : celta
Celtic² *n* : celta *m*
cement¹ [sɪˈmɛnt] *vt* : unir o cubrir algo con cemento, cementar
cement² *n* **1** : cemento *m* **2** GLUE : pegamento *m*
cemetery [ˈsɛməˌtɛri] *n, pl* **-teries** : cementerio *m*, panteón *m*
censer [ˈsɛntsər] *n* : incensario *m*
censor¹ [ˈsɛntsər] *vt* : censurar
censor² *n* : censor *m*, -sora *f*
censorious [sɛnˈsoriəs] *adj* : de censura, crítico
censorship [ˈsɛntsərˌʃɪp] *n* : censura *f*
censure¹ [ˈsɛntʃər] *vt* **-sured; -suring** : censurar, criticar, reprobar — **censurable** [-tʃərəbəl] *adj*
censure² *n* : censura *f*, reproche *m* oficial
census [ˈsɛntsəs] *n* : censo *m*
cent [ˈsɛnt] *n* : centavo *m*
centaur [ˈsɛnˌtɔr] *n* : centauro *m*
centennial¹ [sɛnˈtɛniəl] *adj* : del centenario
centennial² *n* : centenario *m*
center¹ [ˈsɛntər] *vt* **1** : centrar **2** CONCENTRATE : concentrar, fijar, enfocar — *vi* : centrarse, enfocarse
center² *n* **1** : centro *m* ⟨center of gravity : centro de gravedad⟩ **2** : centro *mf* (en futbol americano), pívot *mf* (en basquetbol)
centerpiece [ˈsɛntərˌpiːs] *n* : centro *m* de mesa
centigrade [ˈsɛntəˌgreɪd, ˈsɑn-] *adj* : centígrado
centigram [ˈsɛntəˌgræm, ˈsɑn-] *n* : centigramo *m*
centimeter [ˈsɛntəˌmiːt̬ər, ˈsɑn-] *n* : centímetro *m*
centipede [ˈsɛntəˌpiːd] *n* : ciempiés *m*
central [ˈsɛntrəl] *adj* **1** : céntrico, central ⟨in a central location : en un lugar céntrico⟩ **2** MAIN, PRINCIPAL : central, fundamental, principal
Central American¹ *adj* : centroamericano
Central American² *n* : centroamericano *m*, -na *f*
centralization [ˌsɛntrələˈzeɪʃən] *n* : centralización *f*
centralize [ˈsɛntrəˌlaɪz] *vt* **-ized; -izing** : centralizar

centrally ['sɛntrəli] *adv* **1 centrally heated** : con calefacción central **2 centrally located** : céntrico, en un lugar céntrico

centre ['sɛntər] → **center**

centrifugal [sɛn'trɪfjəgəl, -'trɪfɪ-] *adj* : centrífugo

centrifugal force *n* : fuerza *f* centrífuga

century ['sɛntʃəri] *n, pl* **-ries** : siglo *m*

ceramic[1] [sə'ræmɪk] *adj* : de cerámica

ceramic[2] *n* **1** : objeto *m* de cerámica, cerámica *f* **2 ceramics** *npl* : cerámica *f*

cereal[1] ['sɪriəl] *adj* : cereal

cereal[2] *n* : cereal *m*

cerebellum [ˌsɛrə'bɛləm] *n, pl* **-bellums** *or* **-bella** [-'bɛlə] : cerebelo *m*

cerebral [sə'ri:brəl, 'sɛrə-] *adj* : cerebral

cerebral palsy *n* : parálisis *f* cerebral

cerebrum [sə'ri:brəm, 'sɛrə-] *n, pl* **-brums** *or* **-bra** [-brə] : cerebro *m*

ceremonial[1] [ˌsɛrə'mo:niəl] *adj* : ceremonial

ceremonial[2] *n* : ceremonial *m*

ceremonious [ˌsɛrə'mo:niəs] *adj* **1** FORMAL : ceremonioso, formal **2** CEREMONIAL : ceremonial

ceremony ['sɛrəˌmo:ni] *n, pl* **-nies** : ceremonia *f*

cerise [sə'ri:s] *n* : rojo *m* cereza

certain[1] ['sərtən] *adj* **1** DEFINITE : cierto, determinado ⟨a certain percentage : un porcentaje determinado⟩ **2** TRUE : cierto, con certeza ⟨I don't know for certain : no sé exactamente⟩ **3** : cierto, alguno ⟨it has a certain charm : tiene cierta gracia⟩ **4** INEVITABLE : seguro, inevitable **5** ASSURED : seguro, asegurado ⟨she's certain to do well : seguro que le irá bien⟩

certain[2] *pron* : ciertos *pl*, algunos *pl* ⟨certain of my friends : algunos de mis amigos⟩

certainly ['sərtənli] *adv* **1** DEFINITELY : ciertamente, seguramente **2** OF COURSE : por supuesto

certainty ['sərtənti] *n, pl* **-ties** : certeza *f*, certidumbre *f*, seguridad *f*

certifiable [ˌsərṭə'faɪəbəl] *adj* : certificable

certificate [sər'tɪfɪkət] *n* : certificado *m*, acta *f* ⟨birth certificate : acta de nacimiento⟩

certification [ˌsərṭəfə'keɪʃən] *n* : certificación *f*

certify ['sərṭəˌfaɪ] *vt* **-fied; -fying 1** VERIFY : certificar, verificar, confirmar **2** ENDORSE : endosar, aprobar oficialmente

certitude ['sərṭəˌtu:d, -ˌtju:d] *n* : certeza *f*, certidumbre *f*

cervical ['sərvɪkəl] *adj* **1** : cervical (dícese del cuello) **2** : del cuello del útero

cervix ['sərvɪks] *n, pl* **-vices** [-və-ˌsi:z] *or* **-vixes 1** NECK : cerviz *f* **2** *or* **uterine cervix** : cuello *m* del útero

cesarean[1] [sɪ'zæriən] *adj* : cesáreo

cesarean[2] *n* : cesárea *f*

cesium ['si:ziəm] *n* : cesio *m*

cessation [s'seɪʃən] *n* : cesación *f*, cese *m*

cesspool ['sɛsˌpu:l] *n* : pozo *m* séptico

Chadian ['tʃædiən] *n* : chadiano *m*, -na *f* — **Chadian** *adj*

chafe ['tʃeɪf] *v* **chafed; chafing** *vi* : enojarse, irritarse — *vt* : rozar

chaff ['tʃæf] *n* **1** : barcia *f*, granzas *fpl* **2 to separate the wheat from the chaff** : separar el grano de la paja

chafing dish ['tʃeɪfɪŋˌdɪʃ] *n* : escalfador *m*

chagrin[1] [ʃə'grɪn] *vt* : desilusionar, avergonzar

chagrin[2] *n* : desilusión *f*, disgusto *m*

chain[1] ['tʃeɪn] *vt* : encadenar

chain[2] *n* **1** : cadena *f* ⟨steel chain : cadena de acero⟩ ⟨restaurant chain : cadena de restaurantes⟩ **2** SERIES : serie *f* ⟨chain of events : serie de eventos⟩ **3 chains** *npl* FETTERS : grillos *mpl*

chair[1] ['tʃɛr] *vt* : presidir, moderar

chair[2] *n* **1** : silla *f* **2** CHAIRMANSHIP : presidencia *f* **3** → **chairman, chairwoman**

chairman ['tʃɛrmən] *n, pl* **-men** [-mən, -ˌmɛn] : presidente *m*

chairmanship ['tʃɛrmənˌʃɪp] *n* : presidencia *f*

chairwoman ['tʃɛrˌwʊmən] *n, pl* **-women** [-ˌwɪmən] : presidenta *f*

chaise longue ['ʃeɪz'lɔŋ] *n, pl* **chaise longues** [-lɔŋ, -'lɔŋz] : chaise longue *f*

chalet [ʃæ'leɪ] *n* : chalet *m*, chalé *m*

chalice ['tʃælɪs] *n* : cáliz *m*

chalk[1] ['tʃɔk] *vt* : escribir con tiza

chalk[2] *n* **1** LIMESTONE : creta *f*, caliza *f* **2** : tiza *f*, gis *m Mex* (para escribir)

chalkboard ['tʃɔkˌbord] → **blackboard**

chalk up *vt* **1** ASCRIBE : atribuir, adscribir **2** SCORE : apuntarse, anotarse (una victoria, etc.)

chalky ['tʃɔki] *adj* **chalkier; -est 1** : calcáreo **2** PALE : pálido **3** POWDERY : polvoriento

challenge[1] ['tʃælɪndʒ] *vt* **-lenged; -lenging 1** DISPUTE : disputar, cuestionar, poner en duda **2** DARE : desafiar, retar **3** STIMULATE : estimular, incentivar

challenge[2] *n* : reto *m*, desafío *m*

challenger ['tʃælɪndʒər] *n* : retador *m*, -dora *f*; contendiente *mf*

chamber ['tʃeɪmbər] *n* **1** ROOM : cámara *f*, sala *f* ⟨the senate chamber : la cámara del senado⟩ **2** : recámara *f* (de un arma de fuego), cámara *f* (de combustión) **3** : cámara *f* ⟨chamber of commerce : cámara de comercio⟩ **4 chambers** *npl or* **judge's chambers** : despacho *m* del juez

chambermaid ['tʃeɪmbərˌmeɪd] *n* : camarera *f*

chamber music *n* : música *f* de cámara

chameleon [kə'mi:ljən, -liən] *n* : camaleón *m*

chamois [ˈʃæmi] *n, pl* **chamois** [-mi, -miz] : gamuza *f*
champ[1] [ˈʧæmp, ˈʧɑmp] *vi* **1** : masticar ruidosamente **2 to champ at the bit** : impacientarse, comerle a uno la impaciencia
champ[2] [ˈʧæmp] *n* : campeón *m*, -peona *f*
champagne [ʃæmˈpeɪn] *n* : champaña *m*, champán *m*
champion[1] [ˈʧæmpiən] *vt* : defender, luchar por (una causa)
champion[2] *n* **1** ADVOCATE, DEFENDER : paladín *m*; campeón *m*, -peona *f*; defensor *m*, -sora *f* **2** WINNER : campeón *m*, -peona *f* ⟨world champion : campeón mundial⟩
championship [ˈʧæmpiənˌʃɪp] *n* : campeonato *m*
chance[1] [ˈʧænts] *v* **chanced; chancing** *vi* **1** HAPPEN : ocurrir por casualidad **2 to chance upon** : encontrar por casualidad — *vt* RISK : arriesgar
chance[2] *adj* : fortuito, casual ⟨a chance encounter : un encuentro casual⟩
chance[3] *n* **1** FATE, LUCK : azar *m*, suerte *f*, fortuna *f* **2** OPPORTUNITY : oportunidad *f*, ocasión *f* **3** PROBABILITY : probabilidad *f*, posibilidad *f* **4** RISK : riesgo *m* **5** : boleto *m* (de una rifa o lotería) **6 by chance** : por casualidad
chancellor [ˈʧæntsələr] *n* **1** : canciller *m* **2** : rector *m*, -tora *f* (de una universidad)
chancre [ˈʃæŋkər] *n* : chancro *m*
chancy [ˈʧæntsi] *adj* **chancier; -est** : riesgoso, arriesgado
chandelier [ˌʃændəˈlɪr] *n* : araña *f* de luces
change[1] [ˈʧeɪnʤ] *v* **changed; changing** *vt* **1** ALTER : cambiar, alterar, modificar **2** EXCHANGE : cambiar de, intercambiar ⟨to change places : cambiar de sitio⟩ — *vi* **1** VARY : cambiar, variar, transformarse ⟨you haven't changed : no has cambiado⟩ **2** *or* **to change clothes** : cambiarse (de ropa)
change[2] *n* **1** ALTERATION : cambio *m* **2** : cambio *m*, vuelto *m* ⟨two dollars change : dos dólares de vuelto⟩ **3** COINS : cambio *m*, monedas *fpl*
changeable [ˈʧeɪnʤəbəl] *adj* : cambiante, variable
changeless [ˈʧeɪnʤləs] *adj* : invariable, constante
changer [ˈʧeɪnʤər] *n* **1** : cambiador *m* ⟨record changer : cambiador de discos⟩ **2** *or* **money changer** : cambista *mf* (de dinero)
channel[1] [ˈʧænəl] *vt* **-neled** *or* **-nelled; -neling** *or* **-nelling** : encauzar, canalizar
channel[2] *n* **1** RIVERBED : cauce *m* **2** STRAIT : canal *m*, estrecho *m* ⟨English Channel : Canal de la Mancha⟩ **3** COURSE, MEANS : vía *f*, conducto *m* ⟨the usual channels : las vías normales⟩ **4** : canal *m* (de televisión)
chant[1] [ˈʧænt] *v* : salmodiar, cantar
chant[2] *n* **1** : salmodia *f* **2 Gregorian chant** : canto *m* gregoriano
Chanukah [ˈxɑnəkə, ˈhɑ-] → **Hanukkah**
chaos [ˈkeɪˌɑs] *n* : caos *m*
chaotic [keɪˈɑṭɪk] *adj* : caótico — **chaotically** [-ṭɪkli] *adv*
chap[1] [ˈʧæp] *vi* **chapped; chapping** : partirse, agrietarse
chap[2] *n* FELLOW : tipo *m*, hombre *m*
chapel [ˈʧæpəl] *n* : capilla *f*
chaperon[1] *or* **chaperone** [ˈʃæpəˌroːn] *vt* **-oned; -oning** : ir de chaperón, acompañar
chaperon[2] *or* **chaperone** *n* : chaperón *m*, -rona *f*; acompañante *mf*
chaplain [ˈʧæplɪn] *n* : capellán *m*
chapter [ˈʧæptər] *n* **1** : capítulo *m* (de un libro) **2** BRANCH : sección *f*, división *f* (de una organización)
char [ˈʧɑr] *vt* **charred; charring 1** BURN : carbonizar **2** SCORCH : chamuscar
character [ˈkærɪktər] *n* **1** LETTER, SYMBOL : carácter *m* ⟨Chinese characters : caracteres chinos⟩ **2** DISPOSITION : carácter *m*, personalidad *f* ⟨of good character : de buena reputación⟩ **3** : tipo *m*, personaje *m* peculiar ⟨he's quite a character! : ¡él es algo serio!⟩ **4** : personaje *m* (ficticio)
characteristic[1] [ˌkærɪktəˈrɪstɪk] *adj* : característico, típico — **characteristically** [-tɪkli] *adv*
characteristic[2] *n* : característica *f*
characterization [ˌkærɪktərəˈzeɪʃən] *n* : caracterización *f*
characterize [ˈkærɪktəˌraɪz] *vt* **-ized; -izing** : caracterizar
charades [ʃəˈreɪdz] *ns & pl* : charada *f*
charcoal [ˈʧɑrˌkoːl] *n* : carbón *m*
chard [ˈʧɑrd] → **Swiss chard**
charge[1] [ˈʧɑrʤ] *v* **charged; charging** *vt* **1** : cargar ⟨to charge the batteries : cargar las pilas⟩ **2** ENTRUST : encomendar, encargar **3** COMMAND : ordenar, mandar **4** ACCUSE : acusar ⟨charged with robbery : acusado de robo⟩ **5** : cargar a una cuenta, comprar a crédito — *vi* **1** : cargar (contra el enemigo) ⟨charge! : ¡a la carga!⟩ **2** : cobrar ⟨they charge too much : cobran demasiado⟩
charge[2] *n* **1** : carga *f* (eléctrica) **2** BURDEN : carga *f*, peso *m* **3** RESPONSIBILITY : cargo *m*, responsabilidad *f* ⟨to take charge of : hacerse cargo de⟩ **4** ACCUSATION : cargo *m*, acusación *f* **5** COST : costo *m*, cargo *m*, precio *m* **6** ATTACK : carga *f*, ataque *m*
charge card → **credit card**
chargeable [ˈʧɑrʤəbəl] *adj* **1** : acusable, perseguible (dícese de un delito) **2 ~ to** : a cargo de (una cuenta)
charger [ˈʧɑrʤər] *n* : corcel *m*, caballo *m* (de guerra)
chariot [ˈʧæriət] *n* : carro *m* (de guerra)
charisma [kəˈrɪzmə] *n* : carisma *m*
charismatic [ˌkærəzˈmætɪk] *adj* : carismático

charitable ['ʧærəṭəbəl] *adj* **1** GENEROUS : caritativo ⟨a charitable organization : una organización benéfica⟩ **2** KIND, UNDERSTANDING : generoso, benévolo, comprensivo — **charitably** [-bli] *adv*

charitableness ['ʧærəṭəbəlnəs] *n* : caridad *f*

charity ['ʧærəṭi] *n, pl* **-ties 1** GENEROSITY : caridad *f* **2** ALMS : caridad *f*, limosna *f* **3** : organización *f* benéfica, obra *f* de beneficencia

charlatan ['ʃɑrlətən] *n* : charlatán *m*, -tana *f*; farsante *mf*

charley horse ['ʧɑrli,hɔrs] *n* : calambre *m*

charm[1] ['ʧɑrm] *vt* : encantar, cautivar, fascinar

charm[2] *n* **1** AMULET : amuleto *m*, talismán *m* **2** ATTRACTION : encanto *m*, atractivo *m* ⟨it has a certain charm : tiene cierto atractivo⟩ **3** : dije *m*, colgante *m* ⟨charm bracelet : pulsera de dijes⟩

charmer ['ʧɑrmər] *n* : persona *f* encantadora

charming ['ʧɑrmɪŋ] *adj* : encantador, fascinante

chart[1] ['ʧɑrt] *vt* **1** : trazar un mapa de, hacer un gráfico de **2** PLAN : trazar, planear ⟨to chart a course : trazar un derrotero⟩

chart[2] *n* **1** MAP : carta *f*, mapa *m* **2** DIAGRAM : gráfico *m*, cuadro *m*, tabla *f*

charter[1] ['ʧɑrṭər] *vt* **1** : establecer los estatutos de (una organización) **2** RENT : alquilar, fletar

charter[2] *n* **1** STATUTES : estatutos *mpl* **2** CONSTITUTION : carta *f*, constitución *f*

chartreuse [ʃɑr'tru:z, -'tru:s] *n* : color *m* verde-amarillo intenso

chary ['ʧæri] *adj* **charier; -est 1** WARY : cauteloso, precavido **2** SPARING : parco

chase[1] ['ʧeɪs] *vt* **chased; chasing 1** PURSUE : perseguir, ir a la caza de **2** DRIVE : ahuyentar, echar ⟨he chased the dog from the garden : ahuyentó al perro del jardín⟩ **3** : grabar (metales)

chase[2] *n* **1** PURSUIT : persecución *f*, caza *f* **2 the chase** HUNTING : caza *f*

chaser ['ʧeɪsər] *n* **1** PURSUER : perseguidor *m*, -dora *f* **2** : bebida *f* que se toma después de un trago de licor

chasm ['kæzəm] *n* : abismo *m*, sima *f*

chassis ['ʧæsi, 'ʃæsi] *n, pl* **chassis** [-siz] : chasis *m*, armazón *m*

chaste ['ʧeɪst] *adj* **chaster; -est 1** : casto **2** MODEST : modesto, puro **3** AUSTERE : austero, sobrio

chastely ['ʧeɪstli] *adv* : castamente

chasten ['ʧeɪsən] *vt* : castigar, sancionar

chasteness ['ʧeɪstnəs] *n* **1** MODESTY : modestia *f*, castidad *f* **2** AUSTERITY : sobriedad *f*, austeridad *f*

chastise ['ʧæs,taɪz, ʧæs'-] *vt* **-tised; -tising 1** REPRIMAND : reprender, corregir, reprobar **2** PUNISH : castigar

chastisement ['ʧæs,taɪzmənt, ʧæs'taɪz-, 'ʧæstəz-] *n* : castigo *m*, corrección *f*

chastity ['ʧæstəṭi] *n* : castidad *f*, decencia *f*, modestia *f*

chat[1] ['ʧæt] *vi* **chatted; chatting** : charlar, platicar

chat[2] *n* : charla *f*, plática *f*

château [ʃæ'to:] *n, pl* **-teaus** [-'to:z] *or* **-teaux** [-'to:, -'to:z] : mansión *f* campestre

chattel ['ʧæṭəl] *n* : bienes *fpl* muebles, enseres *mpl*

chatter[1] ['ʧæṭər] *vi* **1** : castañetear (dícese de los dientes) **2** GAB : parlotear *fam*, cotorrear *fam*

chatter[2] *n* **1** CHATTERING : castañeteo *m* (de dientes) **2** GABBING : parloteo *m fam*, cotorreo *m fam*, cháchara *f fam*

chatterbox ['ʧæṭər,bɑks] *n* : parlanchín *m*, -china *f*; charlatán *m*, -tana *f*; hablador *m*, -dora *f*

chatty ['ʧæṭi] *adj* **chattier; chattiest 1** TALKATIVE : parlanchín, charlatán **2** CONVERSATIONAL : familiar, conversador ⟨a chatty letter : una carta llena de noticias⟩

chauffeur[1] ['ʃo:fər, ʃo'fər] *vi* : trabajar de chofer privado — *vt* : hacer de chofer para

chauffeur[2] *n* : chofer *m* privado

chauvinism ['ʃo:və,nɪzəm] *n* : chauvinismo *m*, patriotería *f*

chauvinist ['ʃo:vənɪst] *n* : chauvinista *mf*; patriotero *m*, -ra *f*

chauvinistic [,ʃo:və'nɪstɪk] *adj* : chauvinista, patriotero

cheap[1] ['ʧi:p] *adv* : barato ⟨to sell cheap : vender barato⟩

cheap[2] *adj* **1** INEXPENSIVE : barato, económico **2** SHODDY : barato, mal hecho **3** STINGY : tacaño, agarrado *fam*, codo *Mex*

cheapen ['ʧi:pən] *vt* : degradar, rebajar

cheaply ['ʧi:pli] *adv* : barato, a precio bajo

cheapness ['ʧi:pnəs] *n* **1** : baratura *f*, precio *m* bajo **2** STINGINESS : tacañería *f*

cheapskate ['ʧi:p,skeɪt] *n* : tacaño *m*, -ña *f*; codo *m*, -da *f Mex*

cheat[1] ['ʧi:t] *vt* : defraudar, estafar, engañar — *vi* : hacer trampa

cheat[2] *n* **1** CHEATING : engaño *m*, fraude *m*, trampa *f* **2** → **cheater**

cheater ['ʧi:ṭər] *n* : estafador *m*, -dora *f*; tramposo *m*, -sa *f*

check[1] ['ʧɛk] *vt* **1** HALT : frenar, parar, detener **2** RESTRAIN : refrenar, contener, reprimir **3** VERIFY : verificar, comprobar **4** INSPECT : revisar, chequear, inspeccionar **5** MARK : marcar, señalar **6** : chequear, facturar (maletas, equipaje) **7** CHECKER : marcar con cuadros **8 to check in** : registrarse en un hotel **9 to check out** : irse de un hotel

check² *n* **1** HALT : detención *f* súbita, parada *f* **2** RESTRAINT : control *m*, freno *m* **3** INSPECTION : inspección *f*, verificación *f*, chequeo *m* **4** : cheque *m* <to pay by check : pagar con cheque> **5** VOUCHER : resguardo *m*, comprobante *m* **6** BILL : cuenta *f* (en un restaurante) **7** SQUARE : cuadro *m* **8** MARK : marca *f* **9** : jaque *m* (en ajedrez)
checkbook [ˈʧɛkˌbʊk] *n* : chequera *f*
checker¹ [ˈʧɛkər] *vt* : marcar con cuadros
checker² *n* **1** : pieza *f* (en el juego de damas) **2** : verificador *m*, -dora *f* **3** CASHIER : cajero *m*, -ra *f*
checkerboard [ˈʧɛkərˌbord] *n* : tablero *m* de damas
checkers [ˈʧɛkərz] *n* : damas *fpl*
checkmate¹ [ˈʧɛkˌmeɪt] *vt* **-mated; -mating 1** : dar jaque mate a (en ajedrez) **2** THWART : frustrar, arruinar
checkmate² *n* : jaque mate *m*
checkout [ˈʧɛkˌaʊt] *n or* **checkout counter** : caja *f*
checkpoint [ˈʧɛkˌpɔɪnt] *n* : puesto *m* de control
checkup [ˈʧɛkˌʌp] *n* : examen *m* médico, chequeo *m*
cheddar [ˈʧɛdər] *n* : queso *m* Cheddar
cheek [ˈʧi:k] *n* **1** : mejilla *f*, cachete *m* **2** IMPUDENCE : insolencia *f*, descaro *m*
cheekbone [ˈʧi:kˌbo:n] *n* : pómulo *m*
cheeky [ˈʧi:ki] *adj* **cheekier; -est** : descarado, insolente, atrevido
cheep¹ [ˈʧi:p] *vi* : piar
cheep² *n* : pío *m*
cheer¹ [ˈʧɪr] *vt* **1** ENCOURAGE : alentar, animar **2** GLADDEN : alegrar, levantar el ánimo a **3** ACCLAIM : aclamar, vitorear, echar porras a
cheer² *n* **1** CHEERFULNESS : alegría *f*, buen humor *m*, jovialidad *f* **2** APPLAUSE : aclamación *f*, ovación *f*, aplausos *mpl* <three cheers for the chief! : ¡viva el jefe!> **3 cheers!** : ¡salud!
cheerful [ˈʧɪrfəl] *adj* : alegre, de buen humor
cheerfully [ˈʧɪrfəli] *adv* : alegremente, jovialmente
cheerfulness [ˈʧɪrfəlnəs] *n* : buen humor *m*, alegría *f*
cheerily [ˈʧɪrəli] *adv* : alegremente
cheeriness [ˈʧɪrinəs] *n* : buen humor *m*, alegría *f*
cheerleader [ˈʧɪrˌli:dər] *n* : porrista *mf*
cheerless [ˈʧɪrləs] *adj* BLEAK : triste, sombrío
cheerlessly [ˈʧɪrləsli] *adv* : desanimadamente
cheery [ˈʧɪri] *adj* **cheerier; -est** : alegre, de buen humor
cheese [ˈʧi:z] *n* : queso *m*
cheesecloth [ˈʧi:zˌklɔθ] *n* : estopilla *f*
cheesy [ˈʧi:zi] *adj* **cheesier; -est 1** : a queso **2** : que contiene queso **3** CHEAP : barato, de mala calidad
cheetah [ˈʧi:t̬ə] *n* : guepardo *m*
chef [ˈʃɛf] *n* : chef *m*
chemical¹ [ˈkɛmɪkəl] *adj* : químico — **chemically** [-mɪkli] *adv*
chemical² *n* : sustancia *f* química
chemise [ʃəˈmi:z] *n* **1** : camiseta *f*, prenda *f* interior de una pieza **2** : vestido *m* holgado
chemist [ˈkɛmɪst] *n* : químico *m*, -ca *f*
chemistry [ˈkɛmɪstri] *n, pl* **-tries** : química *f*
chemotherapy [ˌki:moˈθɛrəpi, ˌkɛmo-] *n, pl* **-pies** : quimioterapia *f*
chenille [ʃəˈni:l] *n* : felpilla *f*
cherish [ˈʧɛrɪʃ] *vt* **1** VALUE : apreciar, valorar **2** HARBOR : abrigar, albergar
cherry [ˈʧɛri] *n, pl* **-ries 1** : cereza *f* (fruta) **2** : cerezo *m* (árbol)
cherub [ˈʧɛrəb] *n* **1** *pl* **-ubim** [ˈʧɛrəˌbɪm, ˈʧɛrjə-] ANGEL : ángel *m*, querubín *m* **2** *pl* **-ubs** : niño *m* regordete, niña *f* regordeta
cherubic [ʧəˈru:bɪk] *adj* : querúbico, angelical
chess [ˈʧɛs] *n* : ajedrez *m*
chessboard [ˈʧɛsˌbord] *n* : tablero *m* de ajedrez
chessman [ˈʧɛsmən, -ˌmæn] *n, pl* **-men** [-mən, -ˌmɛn] : pieza *f* de ajedrez
chest [ˈʧɛst] *n* **1** : cofre *m*, baúl *m* **2** : pecho *m* <chest pains : dolores de pecho>
chestnut [ˈʧɛs*t*ˌnʌt] *n* **1** : castaña *f* (fruto) **2** : castaño *m* (árbol)
chest of drawers *n* : cómoda *f*
chevron [ˈʃɛvrən] *n* : galón *m* (de un oficial militar)
chew¹ [ˈʧu:] *vt* : masticar, mascar
chew² *n* : algo que se masca (como tabaco)
chewable [ˈʧu:əbəl] *adj* : masticable
chewing gum *n* : goma *f* de mascar, chicle *m*
chewy [ˈʧu:i] *adj* **chewier; -est 1** : fibroso (dícese de las carnes o los vegetales) **2** : pegajoso, chicloso (dícese de los dulces)
chic¹ [ˈʃi:k] *adj* : chic, elegante, de moda
chic² *n* : chic *m*, elegancia *f*
Chicano [ʧɪˈkɑno] *n* : chicano *m*, -na *f* — **Chicano** *adj*
chick [ˈʧɪk] *n* : pollito *m*, -ta *f*; polluelo *m*, -la *f*
chicken [ˈʧɪkən] *n* **1** FOWL : pollo *m* **2** COWARD : cobarde *mf*
chickenhearted [ˈʧɪkənˌhɑrt̬əd] *n* : miedoso, cobarde
chicken pox *n* : varicela *f*
chickpea [ˈʧɪkˌpi:] *n* : garbanzo *m*
chicle [ˈʧɪkəl] *n* : chicle *m* (resina)
chicory [ˈʧɪkəri] *n, pl* **-ries 1** : endibia *f* (para ensaladas) **2** : achicoria *f* (aditivo de café)
chide [ˈʧaɪd] *vt* **chid** [ˈʧɪd] *or* **chided; chid** *or* **chidden** [ˈʧɪdən] *or* **chided; chiding** [ˈʧaɪdɪŋ] : regañar, reprender
chief¹ [ˈʧi:f] *adj* : principal, capital <chief negotiator : negociador en jefe> — **chiefly** *adv*
chief² *n* : jefe *m*, -fa *f*

chieftain ['ʧi:ftən] *n* : jefe *m*, -fa *f* (de una tribu)
chiffon [ʃɪ'fɑn, 'ʃɪ,-] *n* : chifón *m*
chigger ['ʧɪgər] *n* : nigua *f*
chignon ['ʃi:n,jɑn, -,jɔn] *n* : moño *m*, chongo *m Mex*
chilblain ['ʧɪl,bleɪn] *n* : sabañón *m*
child ['ʧaɪld] *n, pl* **children** ['ʧɪldrən] **1** BABY, YOUNGSTER : niño *m*, -ña *f*; criatura *f* **2** OFFSPRING : hijo *m*, -ja *f*; progenie *f*
childbearing[1] ['ʧaɪlbɛrɪŋ] *adj* : relativo al parto ⟨of childbearing age : en edad fértil⟩
childbearing[2] → **childbirth**
childbirth ['ʧaɪld,bərθ] *n* : parto *m*
childhood ['ʧaɪld,hʊd] *n* : infancia *f*, niñez *f*
childish ['ʧaɪldɪʃ] *adj* : infantil, inmaduro — **childishly** *adv*
childishness ['ʧaɪldɪʃnəs] *n* : infantilismo *m*, inmadurez *f*
childless ['ʧaɪldləs] *adj* : sin hijos
childlike ['ʧaɪld,laɪk] *adj* : infantil, inocente ⟨a childlike imagination : una imaginación infantil⟩
childproof ['ʧaɪld,pru:f] *adj* : a prueba de niños
Chilean ['ʧɪliən, ʧɪ'leɪən] *n* : chileno *m*, -na *f* — **Chilean** *adj*
chili *or* **chile** *or* **chilli** ['ʧɪli] *n, pl* **chilies** *or* **chiles** *or* **chillies** **1** *or* **chili pepper** : chile *m*, ají *m* **2** : chile *m* con carne
chill[1] ['ʧɪl] *v* : enfriar
chill[2] *adj* : frío, gélido ⟨a chill wind : un viento frío⟩
chill[3] *n* **1** CHILLINESS : fresco *m*, frío *m* **2** SHIVER : escalofrío *m* **3** DAMPER : enfriamiento *m*, frío *m* ⟨to cast a chill over : enfriar⟩
chilliness ['ʧɪlinəs] *n* : frío *m*, fresco *m*
chilly ['ʧɪli] *adj* **chillier; -est** : frío ⟨it's chilly tonight : hace frío esta noche⟩
chime[1] ['ʧaɪm] *v* **chimed; chiming** *vt* : hacer sonar (una campana) — *vi* : sonar una campana, dar campanadas
chime[2] *n* **1** BELLS : juego *m* de campanitas sintonizadas, carillón *m* **2** PEAL : tañido *m*, campanada *f*
chime in *vi* : meterse en una conversación
chimera *or* **chimaera** [kaɪ'mɪrə, kə-] *n* : quimera *f*
chimney ['ʧɪmni] *n, pl* **-neys** : chimenea *f*
chimney sweep *n* : deshollinador *m*, -dora *f*
chimp ['ʧɪmp, 'ʃɪmp] → **chimpanzee**
chimpanzee [,ʧɪm,pæn'zi:, ,ʃɪm-; ʧɪm 'pænzi, ʃɪm-] *n* : chimpancé *m*
chin ['ʧɪn] *n* : barbilla *f*, mentón *m*, barba *f*
china ['ʧaɪnə] *n* **1** PORCELAIN : porcelana *f*, loza *f* **2** CROCKERY, TABLEWARE : loza *f*, vajilla *f*
chinchilla [ʧɪn'ʧɪlə] *n* : chinchilla *f*
Chinese ['ʧaɪ'ni:z, -'ni:s] *n* **1** : chino *m*, -na *f* **2** : chino *m* (idioma) — **Chinese** *adj*
chink ['ʧɪŋk] *n* : grieta *f*, abertura *f*
chintz ['ʧɪnts] *n* : chintz *m*, chinz *m*
chip[1] ['ʧɪp] *v* **chipped; chipping** *vt* : desportillar, desconchar, astillar (madera) — *vi* : desportillarse, desconcharse, descascararse (dícese de la pintura, etc.)
chip[2] *n* **1** : astilla *f* (de madera o vidrio), lasca *f* (de piedra) ⟨he's a chip off the old block : de tal palo, tal astilla⟩ **2** : bocado *m* pequeño (en rodajas o rebanadas) ⟨tortilla chips : totopos, tortillitas tostadas⟩ **3** : ficha *f* (de póker, etc.) **4** NICK : desportilladura *f*, mella *f* **5** : chip *m* ⟨memory chip : chip de memoria⟩
chip in *v* CONTRIBUTE : contribuir
chipmunk ['ʧɪp,mʌŋk] *n* : ardilla *f* listada
chipper ['ʧɪpər] *adj* : alegre y vivaz
chiropodist [kə'rɑpədɪst, ʃə-] *n* : podólogo *m*, -ga *f*
chiropody [kə'rɑpədi, ʃə-] *n* : podología *f*
chiropractic ['kaɪrə,præktɪk] *n* : quiropráctica *f*
chiropractor ['kaɪrə,præktər] *n* : quiropráctico *m*, -ca *f*
chirp[1] ['ʧərp] *vi* : gorjear (dícese de los pájaros), chirriar (dícese de los grillos)
chirp[2] *n* : gorjeo *m* (de un pájaro), chirrido *m* (de un grillo)
chisel[1] ['ʧɪzəl] *vt* **-eled** *or* **-elled; -eling** *or* **-elling** **1** : cincelar, tallar, labrar **2** CHEAT : estafar, defraudar
chisel[2] *n* : cincel *m* (para piedras y metales), escoplo *m* (para madera), formón *m*
chiseler ['ʧɪzələr] *n* SWINDLER : estafador *m*, -dora *f*; fraude *mf*
chit ['ʧɪt] *n* : resguardo *m*, recibo *m*
chitchat ['ʧɪt,ʧæt] *n* : cotorreo *m*, charla *f*
chivalric [ʃə'vælrɪk] → **chivalrous**
chivalrous ['ʃɪvəlrəs] *adj* **1** KNIGHTLY : caballeresco, relativo a la caballería **2** GENTLEMANLY : caballeroso, honesto, cortés
chivalrousness ['ʃɪvəlrəsnəs] *n* : caballerosidad *f*, cortesía *f*
chivalry ['ʃɪvəlri] *n, pl* **-ries** **1** KNIGHTHOOD : caballería *f* **2** CHIVALROUSNESS : caballerosidad *f*, nobleza *f*, cortesía *f*
chive ['ʧaɪv] *n* : cebollino *m*
chloride ['klor,aɪd] *n* : cloruro *m*
chlorinate ['klorə,neɪt] *vt* **-nated; -nating** : clorar
chlorination [,klorə'neɪʃən] *n* : cloración *f*
chlorine ['klor,i:n] *n* : cloro *m*
chloroform ['klorə,fɔrm] *n* : cloroformo *m*
chlorophyll ['klorə,fɪl] *n* : clorofila *f*
chock–full ['ʧɑk'fʊl, 'ʧʌk-] *adj* : colmado, repleto
chocolate ['ʧɑkələt, 'ʧɔk-] *n* **1** : chocolate *m* **2** BONBON : bombón *m* **3** : color *m* chocolate, marrón *m*

choice[1] [ˈʧɔɪs] *adj* **choicer; -est** : selecto, escogido, de primera calidad
choice[2] *n* **1** CHOOSING : elección *f,* selección *f* **2** OPTION : elección *f,* opción *f* ⟨I have no choice : no tengo alternativa⟩ **3** PREFERENCE : preferencia *f,* elección *f* **4** VARIETY : surtido *m,* selección *f* ⟨a wide choice : un gran surtido⟩
choir [ˈkwaɪr] *n* : coro *m*
choirboy [ˈkwaɪrˌbɔɪ] *n* : niño *m* de coro
choke[1] [ˈʧoːk] *v* **choked; choking** *vt* **1** ASPHYXIATE, STRANGLE : sofocar, asfixiar, ahogar, estrangular **2** BLOCK : tapar, obstruir — *vi* **1** SUFFOCATE : asfixiarse, sofocarse, ahogarse, atragantarse (con comida) **2** CLOG : taparse, obstruirse
choke[2] *n* **1** CHOKING : estrangulación *f* **2** : choke *m* (de un motor)
choker [ˈʧoːkər] *n* : gargantilla *f*
cholera [ˈkɑlərə] *n* : cólera *m*
cholesterol [kəˈlɛstəˌrɔl] *n* : colesterol *m*
choose [ˈʧuːz] *v* **chose** [ˈʧoːz]; **chosen** [ˈʧoːzən]; **choosing** *vt* **1** SELECT : escoger, elegir ⟨choose only one : escoja sólo uno⟩ **2** DECIDE : decidir ⟨he chose to leave : decidió irse⟩ **3** PREFER : preferir ⟨which one do you choose? : ¿cuál prefiere?⟩ — *vi* : escoger ⟨much to choose from : mucho de donde escoger⟩
choosy *or* **choosey** [ˈʧuːzi] *adj* **choosier; -est** : exigente, remilgado
chop[1] [ˈʧɑp] *vt* **chopped; chopping 1** MINCE : picar, cortar, moler (carne) **2 to chop down** : cortar, talar (un árbol)
chop[2] *n* **1** CUT : hachazo *m* (con una hacha), tajo *m* (con una cuchilla) **2** BLOW : golpe *m* (penetrante) ⟨karate chop : golpe de karate⟩ **3** : chuleta *f* ⟨pork chops : chuletas de cerdo⟩
chopper [ˈʧɑpər] → **helicopter**
choppy [ˈʧɑpi] *adj* **choppier; -est 1** : agitado, picado (dícese del mar) **2** DISCONNECTED : incoherente, inconexo
chops [ˈʧɑps] *npl* **1** : quijada *f,* mandíbula *f,* boca *f* (de una persona) **2 to lick one's chops** : relamerse
chopsticks [ˈʧɑpˌstɪks] *npl* : palillos *mpl*
choral [ˈkorəl] *adj* : coral
chorale [kəˈræl, -ˈrɑl] *n* **1** : coral *f* (composición musical vocal) **2** CHOIR, CHORUS : coral *f,* coro *m*
chord [ˈkɔrd] *n* **1** : acorde *m* (en música) **2** : cuerda *f* (en anatomía o geometría)
chore [ˈʧor] *n* **1** TASK : tarea *f* rutinaria **2** BOTHER, NUISANCE : lata *f fam,* fastidio *m* **3 chores** *npl* WORK : quehaceres *mpl,* faenas *fpl*
choreograph [ˈkoriəˌgræf] *vt* : coreografiar
choreographer [ˌkoriˈɑgrəfər] *n* : coreógrafo *m,* -fa *f*
choreographic [ˌkoriəˈgræfɪk] *adj* : coreográfico
choreography [ˌkoriˈɑgrəfi] *n, pl* **-phies** : coreografía *f*
chorister [ˈkorəstər] *n* : corista *mf*
chortle[1] [ˈʧɔrtəl] *vi* **-tled; -tling** : reírse (con satisfacción o júbilo)
chortle[2] *n* : risa *f* (de satisfacción o júbilo)
chorus[1] [ˈkorəs] *vt* : corear
chorus[2] *n* **1** : coro *m* (grupo o composición musical) **2** REFRAIN : coro *m,* estribillo *m*
chose → **choose**
chosen [ˈʧoːzən] *adj* : elegido, selecto
chow [ˈʧaʊ] *n* **1** FOOD : comida *f* **2** : chow-chow *m* (perro)
chowder [ˈʧaʊdər] *n* : sopa *f* de pescado
Christ [ˈkraɪst] *n* **1** : Cristo *m* **2 for Christ's sake** : ¡por Dios!
christen [ˈkrɪsən] *vt* **1** BAPTIZE : bautizar **2** NAME : bautizar con el nombre de
Christendom [ˈkrɪsəndəm] *n* : cristiandad *f*
christening [ˈkrɪsənɪŋ] *n* : bautismo *m,* bautizo *m*
Christian[1] [ˈkrɪsʧən] *adj* : cristiano
Christian[2] *n* : cristiano *m,* -na *f*
Christianity [ˌkrɪsʧiˈænəti, ˌkrɪsˈʧæ-] *n* : cristianismo *m*
Christian name *n* : nombre *m* de pila
Christmas [ˈkrɪsməs] *n* : Navidad *f* ⟨Christmas season : las Navidades⟩
chromatic [kroːˈmætɪk] *adj* : cromático ⟨chromatic scale : escala cromática⟩
chrome [ˈkroːm] *n* : cromo *m* (metal)
chromium [ˈkroːmiəm] *n* : cromo *m* (elemento)
chromosome [ˈkroːməˌsoːm, -ˌzoːm] *n* : cromosoma *m*
chronic [ˈkrɑnɪk] *adj* : crónico — **chronically** [-nɪkli] *adv*
chronicle[1] [ˈkrɑnɪkəl] *vt* **-cled; -cling** : escribir (una crónica o historia)
chronicle[2] *n* : crónica *f,* historia *f*
chronicler [ˈkrɑnɪklər] *n* : historiador *m,* -dora *f;* cronista *mf*
chronological [ˌkrɑnəlˈɑʤɪkəl] *adj* : cronológico — **chronologically** [-kli] *adv*
chronology [krəˈnɑləʤi] *n, pl* **-gies** : cronología *f*
chronometer [krəˈnɑmətər] *n* : cronómetro *m*
chrysalis [ˈkrɪsələs] *n, pl* **chrysalides** [krɪˈsæləˌdiːz] *or* **chrysalises** : crisálida *f*
chrysanthemum [krɪˈsænʧθəməm] *n* : crisantemo *m*
chubbiness [ˈʧʌbinəs] *n* : gordura *f*
chubby [ˈʧʌbi] *adj* **-bier; -est** : gordito, regordete, rechoncho
chuck[1] [ˈʧʌk] *vt* **1** TOSS : tirar, lanzar, aventar *Col, Mex* **2 to chuck under the chin** : hacer la mamola
chuck[2] *n* **1** PAT : mamola *f,* palmada *f* **2** TOSS : lanzamiento *m* **3** *or* **chuck steak** : corte *m* de carne de res
chuckle[1] [ˈʧʌkəl] *vi* **-led; -ling** : reírse entre dientes
chuckle[2] *n* : risita *f,* risa *f* ahogada

chug[1] [ˈʧʌg] *vi* **chugged; chugging** : resoplar, traquetear
chug[2] *n* : resoplido *m*, traqueteo *m*
chum[1] [ˈʧʌm] *vi* **chummed; chumming** : ser camaradas, ser cuates *Mex fam*
chum[2] *n* : amigo *m*, -ga *f*; camarada *mf*; compinche *mf fam*
chummy [ˈʧʌmi] *adj* **-mier; -est** : amistoso ⟨they're very chummy : son muy amigos⟩
chump [ˈʧʌmp] *n* : tonto *m*, -ta *f*; idiota *mf*
chunk [ˈʧʌnk] *n* **1** PIECE : cacho *m*, pedazo *m*, trozo *m* **2** : cantidad *f* grande ⟨a chunk of money : mucho dinero⟩
chunky [ˈʧʌnki] *adj* **chunkier; -est 1** STOCKY : fornido, robusto **2** : que contiene pedazos
church [ˈʧərʧ] *n* **1** : iglesia *f* ⟨to go to church : ir a la iglesia⟩ **2** CHRISTIANS : iglesia *f*, conjunto *m* de fieles cristianos **3** DENOMINATION : confesión *f*, secta *f* **4** CONGREGATION : feligreses *mpl*, fieles *mpl*
churchgoer [ˈʧərʧˌgoːər] *n* : practicante *mf*
churchyard [ˈʧərʧˌjɑrd] *n* : cementerio *m* (junto a una iglesia)
churn[1] [ˈʧərn] *vt* **1** : batir (crema), hacer (mantequilla) **2** : agitar con fuerza, revolver — *vi* : agitarse, arremolinarse
churn[2] *n* : mantequera *f*
chute [ˈʃuːt] *n* : conducto *m* inclinado, vertedero *m* (para basuras)
chutney [ˈʧʌtni] *n, pl* **-neys** : chutney *m*
chutzpah [ˈhʊtspə, ˈxʊt-, -ˌspɑ] *n* : descaro *m*, frescura *f*, cara *f fam*
cicada [səˈkeɪdə, -ˈkɑ-] *n* : cigarra *f*, chicharra *f*
cider [ˈsaɪdər] *n* **1** : jugo *m* (de manzana, etc.) **2 hard cider** : sidra *f*
cigar [sɪˈgɑr] *n* : puro *m*, cigarro *m*
cigarette [ˌsɪgəˈrɛt, ˈsɪgəˌrɛt] *n* : cigarrillo *m*, cigarro *m*
cilantro [sɪˈlɑntroː, -ˈlæn-] *n* : cilantro *m*
cinch[1] [ˈsɪnʧ] *vt* **1** : cinchar (un caballo) **2** ASSURE : asegurar
cinch[2] *n* **1** : cincha *f* (para caballos) **2** : algo fácil o seguro ⟨it's a cinch : es bien fácil, es pan comido⟩
cinchona [sɪŋˈkoːnə] *n* : quino *m*
cinder [ˈsɪndər] *n* **1** EMBER : brasa *f*, ascua *f* **2 cinders** *npl* ASHES : cenizas *fpl*
cinema [ˈsɪnəmə] *n* : cine *m*
cinematic [ˌsɪnəˈmæt̬ɪk] *adj* : cinematográfico
cinnamon [ˈsɪnəmən] *n* : canela *f*
cipher [ˈsaɪfər] *n* **1** ZERO : cero *m* **2** CODE : cifra *f*, clave *f*
circa [ˈsərkə] *prep* : alrededor de, hacia ⟨circa 1800 : hacia el año 1800⟩
circle[1] [ˈsərkəl] *v* **-cled; -cling** *vt* **1** : encerrar en un círculo, poner un círculo alrededor de **2** : girar alrededor de, dar vueltas a ⟨we circled the building twice : le dimos vueltas al edificio dos veces⟩ — *vi* : dar vueltas
circle[2] *n* **1** : círculo *m* **2** CYCLE : ciclo *m* ⟨to come full circle : volver al punto de partida⟩ **3** GROUP : círculo *m*, grupo *m* (social)
circuit [ˈsərkət] *n* **1** BOUNDARY : circuito *m*, perímetro *m* (de una zona o un territorio) **2** TOUR : circuito *m*, recorrido *m*, tour *m* **3** : circuito *m* (eléctrico) ⟨a short circuit : un cortocircuito⟩
circuitous [ˌsərˈkjuːət̬əs] *adj* : sinuoso, tortuoso
circuitry [ˈsərkətri] *n, pl* **-ries** : sistema *m* de circuitos
circular[1] [ˈsərkjələr] *adj* ROUND : circular, redondo
circular[2] *n* : circular *f*
circulate [ˈsərkjəˌleɪt] *v* **-lated; -lating** *vi* : circular — *vt* **1** : circular (noticias, etc.) **2** DISSEMINATE : hacer circular, divulgar
circulation [ˌsərkjəˈleɪʃən] *n* : circulación *f*
circulatory [ˈsərkjələˌtori] *adj* : circulatorio
circumcise [ˈsərkəmˌsaɪz] *vt* **-cised; -cising** : circuncidar
circumcision [ˌsərkəmˈsɪʒən, ˈsərkəmˌ-] *n* : circuncisión *f*
circumference [sərˈkʌmpfrənts] *n* : circunferencia *f*
circumflex [ˈsərkəmˌflɛks] *n* : acento *m* circunflejo
circumlocution [ˌsərkəmloˈkjuːʃən] *n* : circunlocución *f*
circumnavigate [ˌsərkəmˈnævəˌgeɪt] *vt* **-gated; -gating** : circunnavegar
circumscribe [ˈsərkəmˌskraɪb] *vt* **-scribed; -scribing 1** : circunscribir, trazar una figura alrededor de **2** LIMIT : circunscribir, limitar
circumspect [ˈsərkəmˌspɛkt] *adj* : circunspecto, prudente, cauto
circumspection [ˌsərkəmˈspɛkʃən] *n* : circunspección *f*, cautela *f*
circumstance [ˈsərkəmˌstænts] *n* **1** EVENT : circunstancia *f*, acontecimiento *m* **2 circumstances** *npl* SITUATION : circunstancias *fpl*, situación *f* ⟨under the circumstances : dadas las circunstancias⟩ ⟨under no circumstances : de ninguna manera, bajo ningún concepto⟩ **3 circumstances** *npl* : situación *f* económica
circumstantial [ˌsərkəmˈstænʧəl] *adj* : circunstancial
circumvent [ˌsərkəmˈvɛnt] *vt* : evadir, burlar (una ley o regla), sortear (una responsabilidad o dificultad)
circumvention [ˌsərkəmˈvɛnʧən] *n* : evasión *f*
circus [ˈsərkəs] *n* : circo *m*
cirrhosis [səˈroːsɪs] *n, pl* **-rhoses** [-ˈroːˌsiːz] : cirrosis *f*
cirrus [ˈsɪrəs] *n, pl* **-ri** [ˈsɪrˌaɪ] : cirro *m*
cistern [ˈsɪstərn] *n* : cisterna *f*, aljibe *m*
citadel [ˈsɪt̬ədəl, -ˌdɛl] *n* FORTRESS : ciudadela *f*, fortaleza *f*

citation [saɪˈteɪʃən] *n* **1** SUMMONS : emplazamiento *m*, citación *f*, convocatoria *f* (judicial) **2** QUOTATION : cita *f* **3** COMMENDATION : elogio *m*, mención *f* (de honor)

cite [ˈsaɪt] *vt* **cited; citing** **1** ARRAIGN, SUBPOENA : emplazar, citar, hacer comparecer (ante un tribunal) **2** QUOTE : citar **3** COMMEND : elogiar, honrar (oficialmente)

citizen [ˈsɪţəzən] *n* : ciudadano *m*, -na *f*

citizenry [ˈsɪţəzənri] *n, pl* **-ries** : ciudadanía *f*, conjunto *m* de ciudadanos

citizenship [ˈsɪţəzənˌʃɪp] *n* : ciudadanía *f* ⟨Nicaraguan citizenship : ciudadanía nicaragüense⟩

citron [ˈsɪtrən] *n* : cidra *f*

citrus [ˈsɪtrəs] *n, pl* **-rus** *or* **-ruses** : cítrico *m*

city [ˈsɪţi] *n, pl* **cities** : ciudad *f*

civic [ˈsɪvɪk] *adj* : cívico

civics [ˈsɪvɪks] *ns & pl* : civismo *m*

civil [ˈsɪvəl] *adj* **1** : civil ⟨civil law : derecho civil⟩ **2** POLITE : civil, cortés

civilian [səˈvɪljən] *n* : civil *mf* ⟨soldiers and civilians : soldados y civiles⟩

civility [səˈvɪləţi] *n, pl* **-ties** : cortesía *f*, educación *f*

civilization [ˌsɪvələˈzeɪʃən] *n* : civilización *f*

civilize [ˈsɪvəˌlaɪz] *vt* **-lized; -lizing** : civilizar — **civilized** *adj*

civil liberties *npl* : derechos *mpl* civiles

civilly [ˈsɪvəli] *adv* : cortésmente

civil rights *npl* : derechos *mpl* civiles

civil service *n* : administración *f* pública

civil war *n* : guerra *f* civil

clack[1] [ˈklæk] *vi* : tabletear

clack[2] *n* : tableteo *m*

clad [ˈklæd] *adj* **1** CLOTHED : vestido **2** COVERED : cubierto

claim[1] [ˈkleɪm] *vt* **1** DEMAND : reclamar, reivindicar ⟨she claimed her rights : reclamó sus derechos⟩ **2** MAINTAIN : afirmar, sostener ⟨they claim it's theirs : sostienen que es suyo⟩

claim[2] *n* **1** DEMAND : demanda *f*, reclamación *f* **2** DECLARATION : declaración *f*, afirmación *f* **3 to stake a claim** : reclamar, reivindicar

claimant [ˈkleɪmənt] *n* : demandante *mf* (ante un juez), pretendiente *mf* (al trono, etc.)

clairvoyance [klærˈvɔɪənts] *n* : clarividencia *f*

clairvoyant[1] [klærˈvɔɪənt] *adj* : clarividente

clairvoyant[2] *n* : clarividente *mf*

clam [ˈklæm] *n* : almeja *f*

clamber [ˈklæmbər] *vi* : treparse o subirse torpemente

clammy [ˈklæmi] *adj* **-mier; -est** : húmedo y algo frío

clamor[1] [ˈklæmər] *vi* : gritar, clamar

clamor[2] *n* : clamor *m*

clamorous [ˈklæmərəs] *adj* : clamoroso, ruidoso, estrepitoso

clamp[1] [ˈklæmp] *vt* : sujetar con abrazaderas

clamp[2] *n* : abrazadera *f*

clan [ˈklæn] *n* : clan *m*

clandestine [klænˈdɛstɪn] *adj* : clandestino, secreto

clang[1] [ˈklæŋ] *vi* : hacer resonar (dícese de un objeto metálico)

clang[2] *n* : ruido *m* metálico fuerte

clangor [ˈklæŋər, -gər] *n* : estruendo *m* metálico

clank[1] [ˈklæŋk] *vi* : producir un ruido metálico seco

clank[2] *n* : ruido *m* metálico seco

clannish [ˈklænɪʃ] *adj* : exclusivista

clap[1] [ˈklæp] *v* **clapped; clapping** *vt* **1** SLAP, STRIKE : golpear ruidosamente, dar una palmada ⟨to clap one's hands : batir palmas, dar palmadas⟩ **2** APPLAUD : aplaudir — *vi* APPLAUD : aplaudir

clap[2] *n* **1** SLAP : palmada *f*, golpecito *m* **2** NOISE : ruido *m* seco ⟨a clap of thunder : un trueno⟩

clapboard [ˈklæbərd, ˈklæpˌbord] *n* : tabla *f* de madera (para revestir muros)

clapper [ˈklæpər] *n* : badajo *m* (de una campana)

clarification [ˌklærəfəˈkeɪʃən] *n* : clarificación *f*

clarify [ˈklærəˌfaɪ] *vt* **-fied; -fying** **1** EXPLAIN : aclarar **2** : clarificar (un líquido)

clarinet [ˌklærəˈnɛt] *n* : clarinete *m*

clarion [ˈklæriən] *adj* : claro y sonoro

clarity [ˈklærəţi] *n* : claridad *f*, nitidez *f*

clash[1] [ˈklæʃ] *vi* **1** : sonar, chocarse ⟨the cymbals clashed : los platillos sonaron⟩ **2** : chocar, enfrentarse ⟨the students clashed with the police : los estudiantes se enfrentaron con la policía⟩ **3** CONFLICT : estar en conflicto, oponerse **4** : desentonar (dícese de los colores), coincidir (dícese de los datos)

clash[2] *n* **1** : ruido *m* (producido por un choque) **2** CONFLICT, CONFRONTATION : enfrentamiento *m*, conflicto *m*, choque *m* **3** : desentono *m* (de colores), coincidencia *f* (de datos)

clasp[1] [ˈklæsp] *vt* **1** FASTEN : sujetar, abrochar **2** EMBRACE, GRASP : agarrar, sujetar, abrazar

clasp[2] *n* **1** FASTENING : broche *m*, cierre *m* **2** EMBRACE, SQUEEZE : apretón *m*, abrazo *m*

class[1] [ˈklæs] *vt* : clasificar, catalogar

class[2] *n* **1** KIND, TYPE : clase *f*, tipo *m*, especie *f* **2** : clase *f*, rango *m* social ⟨the working class : la clase obrera⟩ **3** LESSON : clase *f*, curso *m* ⟨English class : clase de inglés⟩ **4** : conjunto *m* de estudiantes, clase *f* ⟨the class of '97 : la promoción del 97⟩

classic[1] [ˈklæsɪk] *adj* : clásico

classic[2] *n* : clásico *m*, obra *f* clásica

classical [ˈklæsɪkəl] *adj* : clásico — **classically** [-kli] *adv*

classicism [ˈklæsəˌsɪzəm] *n* : clasicismo *m*
classification [ˌklæsəfəˈkeɪʃən] *n* : clasificación *f*
classified [ˈklæsəˌfaɪd] *adj* **1** : clasificado ⟨classified ads : avisos clasificados⟩ **2** RESTRICTED : confidencial, secreto ⟨classified documents : documentos secretos⟩
classify [ˈklæsəˌfaɪ] *vt* **-fied; -fying** : clasificar, catalogar
classless [ˈklæsləs] *adj* : sin clases
classmate [ˈklæsˌmeɪt] *n* : compañero *m*, -ra *f* de clase
classroom [ˈklæsˌruːm] *n* : aula *f*, salón *m* de clase
clatter[1] [ˈklæt̬ər] *vi* : traquetear, hacer ruido
clatter[2] *n* : traqueteo *m*, ruido *m*, estrépito *m*
clause [ˈklɔz] *n* : cláusula *f*
claustrophobia [ˌklɔstrəˈfoːbiə] *n* : claustrofobia *f*
claustrophobic [ˌklɔstrəˈfoːbɪk] *adj* : claustrofóbico
clavicle [ˈklævɪkəl] *n* : clavícula *f*
claw[1] [ˈklɔ] *v* : arañar
claw[2] *n* : garra *f*, uña *f* (de un gato), pinza *f* (de un crustáceo)
clay [ˈkleɪ] *n* : arcilla *f*, barro *m*
clayey [ˈkleɪi] *adj* : arcilloso
clean[1] [ˈkliːn] *vt* : limpiar, lavar, asear
clean[2] *adv* : limpio, limpiamente ⟨to play clean : jugar limpio⟩
clean[3] *adj* **1** : limpio **2** UNADULTERATED : puro **3** IRREPROACHABLE : intachable, sin mancha ⟨to have a clean record : no tener antecedentes penales⟩ **4** DECENT : decente **5** COMPLETE : completo, absoluto ⟨a clean break with the past : un corte radical con el pasado⟩
cleaner [ˈkliːnər] *n* **1** : limpiador *m*, -dora *f* **2** : producto *m* de limpieza **3** DRY CLEANER : tintorería *f* (servicio)
cleanliness [ˈklɛnlinəs] *n* : limpieza *f*, aseo *m*
cleanly[1] [ˈkliːnli] *adv* : limpiamente, con limpieza
cleanly[2] [ˈklɛnli] *adj* **-lier; -est** : limpio, pulcro
cleanness [ˈkliːnnəs] *n* : limpieza *f*
cleanse [ˈklɛnz] *vt* **cleansed; cleansing** : limpiar, purificar
cleanser [ˈklɛnzər] *n* : limpiador *m*, purificador *m*
clear[1] [ˈklɪr] *vt* **1** CLARIFY : aclarar, clarificar (un líquido) **2** : despejar (una superficie), desatascar (un tubo), desmontar (una selva) ⟨to clear the table : levantar la mesa⟩ ⟨to clear one's throat : carraspear, aclararse la voz⟩ **3** EXONERATE : absolver, limpiar el nombre de **4** EARN : ganar, sacar (una ganancia de) **5** : pasar sin tocar ⟨he cleared the hurdle : saltó por encima de la valla⟩ **6 to clear up** RESOLVE : aclarar, resolver, esclarecer — *vi* **1** DISPERSE : irse, despejarse, disiparse **2** : ser compensado (dícese de un cheque) **3 to clear up** : despejar (dícese del tiempo), mejorarse (dícese de una enfermedad)
clear[2] *adv* : claro, claramente
clear[3] *adj* **1** BRIGHT : claro, lúcido **2** FAIR : claro, despejado **3** TRANSPARENT : transparente, translúcido **4** EVIDENT, UNMISTAKABLE : evidente, claro, obvio **5** CERTAIN : seguro **6** UNOBSTRUCTED : despejado, libre
clear[4] *n* **1 in the clear** : inocente, libre de toda sospecha **2 in the clear** SAFE : fuera de peligro
clearance [ˈklɪrənts] *n* **1** CLEARING : despeje *m* **2** SPACE : espacio *m* (libre), margen *m* **3** AUTHORIZATION : autorización *f*, despacho *m* (de la aduana)
clearing [ˈklɪrɪŋ] *n* : claro *m* (de un bosque)
clearly [ˈklɪrli] *adv* **1** DISTINCTLY : claramente, directamente **2** OBVIOUSLY : obviamente, evidentemente
cleat [ˈkliːt] *n* **1** : taco *m* **2 cleats** *npl* : zapatos *mpl* deportivos (con tacos)
cleavage [ˈkliːvɪʤ] *n* **1** CLEFT : hendidura *f*, raja *f* **2** : escote *m* (del busto)
cleave[1] [ˈkliːv] *vi* **cleaved** [ˈkliːvd] *or* **clove** [ˈkloːv]; **cleaving** ADHERE : adherirse, unirse
cleave[2] *vt* **cleaved; cleaving** SPLIT : hender, dividir, partir
cleaver [ˈkliːvər] *n* : cuchilla *f* de carnicero
clef [ˈklɛf] *n* : clave *f*
cleft [ˈklɛft] *n* : hendidura *f*, raja *f*, grieta *f*
clemency [ˈklɛməntsi] *n* : clemencia *f*
clement [ˈklɛmənt] *adj* **1** MERCIFUL : clemente, piadoso **2** MILD : clemente, apacible
clench [ˈklɛntʃ] *vt* **1** CLUTCH : agarrar **2** TIGHTEN : apretar (el puño, los dientes)
clergy [ˈklərʤi] *n, pl* **-gies** : clero *m*
clergyman [ˈklərʤimən] *n, pl* **-men** [-mən, -ˌmɛn] : clérigo *m*
cleric [ˈklɛrɪk] *n* : clérigo *m*, -ga *f*
clerical [ˈklɛrɪkəl] *adj* **1** : clerical ⟨a clerical collar : un alzacuello⟩ **2** : de oficina ⟨clerical staff : personal de oficina⟩
clerk[1] [ˈklərk, *Brit* ˈklɑrk] *vi* : trabajar de oficinista, trabajar de dependiente
clerk[2] *n* **1** : funcionario *m*, -ria *f* (de una oficina gubernamental) **2** : oficinista *mf*, empleado *m*, -da *f* de oficina **3** SALESPERSON : dependiente *m*, -ta *f*
clever [ˈklɛvər] *adj* **1** SKILLFUL : ingenioso, hábil **2** SMART : listo, inteligente, astuto
cleverly [ˈklɛvərli] *adv* **1** SKILLFULLY : ingeniosamente, hábilmente **2** INTELLIGENTLY : inteligentemente
cleverness [ˈklɛvərnəs] *n* **1** SKILL : ingenio *m*, habilidad *f* **2** INTELLIGENCE : inteligencia *f*

clew ['klu:] → **clue**
cliché [kli'ʃeɪ] *n* : cliché *m*, tópico *m*
click[1] ['klɪk] *vt* **1** : chasquear (los dedos, etc.) ⟨to click one's heels : dar un taconazo⟩ **2** : hacer clic en (un botón, etc.) — *vi* **1** : hacer clic **2** SNAP : chasquear **3** SUCCEED : tener éxito **4** GET ALONG : congeniar, llevarse bien
click[2] *n* : chasquido *m* (de los dedos, etc.), clic *m* (de un botón, etc.)
client ['klaɪənt] *n* : cliente *m*, -ta *f*
clientele [ˌklaɪən'tɛl, ˌkli:-] *n* : clientela *f*
cliff ['klɪf] *n* : acantilado *m*, precipicio *m*, risco *m*
climate ['klaɪmət] *n* : clima *m*
climatic [klaɪ'mæṭɪk, klə-] *adj* : climático
climax[1] ['klaɪˌmæks] *vi* : llegar al punto culminante, culminar — *vt* : ser el punto culminante de
climax[2] *n* : clímax *m*, punto *m* culminante
climb[1] ['klaɪm] *vt* : escalar, trepar a, subir a ⟨to climb a mountain : escalar una montaña⟩ — *vi* **1** RISE : subir, ascender ⟨prices are climbing : los precios están subiendo⟩ **2** : subirse, treparse ⟨to climb up a tree : treparse a un árbol⟩
climb[2] *n* : ascenso *m*, subida *f*
climber ['klaɪmər] *n* **1** : escalador *m*, -dora *f* ⟨a mountain climber : un alpinista⟩ **2** : trepadora *f* (planta)
clinch[1] ['klɪntʃ] *vt* **1** FASTEN, SECURE : remachar (un clavo), afianzar, abrochar **2** SETTLE : decidir, cerrar ⟨to clinch the title : ganar el título⟩
clinch[2] *n* : abrazo *m*, clinch *m* (en el boxeo)
clincher ['klɪntʃər] *n* : argumento *m* decisivo
cling ['klɪŋ] *vi* **clung** ['klʌŋ]; **clinging 1** STICK : adherirse, pegarse **2** : aferrarse, agarrarse ⟨he clung to the railing : se aferró a la barandilla⟩
clinic ['klɪnɪk] *n* : clínica *f*
clinical ['klɪnɪkəl] *adj* : clínico — **clinically** [-kli] *adv*
clink[1] ['klɪŋk] *vi* : tintinear
clink[2] *n* : tintineo *m*
clip[1] ['klɪp] *vt* **clipped; clipping 1** CUT : cortar, recortar **2** HIT : golpear, dar un puñetazo a **3** FASTEN : sujetar (con un clip)
clip[2] *n* **1** → **clippers 2** BLOW : golpe *m*, puñetazo *m* **3** PACE : paso *m* rápido **4** FASTENER : clip *m* ⟨a paper clip : un sujetapapeles⟩
clipper ['klɪpər] *n* **1** : clíper *m* (buque de vela) **2 clippers** *npl* : tijeras *fpl* ⟨nail clippers : cortauñas⟩
clique ['kli:k, 'klɪk] *n* : grupo *m* exclusivo, camarilla *f* (de políticos)
clitoris ['klɪṭərəs, klɪ'tɔrəs] *n, pl* **clitorides** [-'tɔrəˌdi:z] : clítoris *m*
cloak[1] ['klo:k] *vt* : encubrir, envolver (en un manto de)
cloak[2] *n* : capa *f*, capote *m*, manto *m* ⟨under the cloak of darkness : al amparo de la oscuridad⟩
clobber ['klɑbər] *vt* : dar una paliza a
clock[1] ['klɑk] *vt* : cronometrar
clock[2] *n* **1** : reloj *m* (de pared), cronómetro *m* (en deportes o competencias) **2 around the clock** : las veinticuatro horas
clockwise ['klɑkˌwaɪz] *adv & adj* : en la dirección de las manecillas del reloj
clockwork ['klɑkˌwərk] *n* : mecanismo *m* de relojería
clod ['klɑd] *n* **1** : terrón *m* **2** OAF : zoquete *mf*
clog[1] ['klɑg] *v* **clogged; clogging** *vt* **1** HINDER : estorbar, impedir **2** BLOCK : atascar, tapar — *vi* : atascarse, taparse
clog[2] *n* **1** OBSTACLE : traba *f*, impedimento *m*, estorbo *m* **2** : zueco *m* (zapato)
cloister[1] ['klɔɪstər] *vt* : enclaustrar
cloister[2] *n* : claustro *m*
clone ['klo:n] *n* **1** : clon *m* (de un organismo) **2** COPY : copia *f*, reproducción *f*
close[1] ['klo:z] *v* **closed; closing** *vt* : cerrar — *vi* **1** : cerrarse, cerrar **2** TERMINATE : concluirse, terminar **3 to close in** APPROACH : acercarse, aproximarse
close[2] ['klo:s] *adv* : cerca, de cerca
close[3] *adj* **closer; closest 1** CONFINING : restrictivo, estrecho **2** SECRETIVE : reservado **3** STRICT : estricto, detallado **4** STUFFY : cargado, bochornoso (dícese del tiempo) **5** TIGHT : apretado, entallado, ceñido ⟨it's a close fit : es muy apretado⟩ **6** NEAR : cercano, próximo **7** INTIMATE : íntimo ⟨close friends : amigos íntimos⟩ **8** ACCURATE : fiel, exacto **9** : reñido ⟨a close election : una elección muy reñida⟩
close[4] ['klo:z] *n* : fin *m*, final *m*, conclusión *f*
closely ['klo:sli] *adv* : cerca, de cerca
closeness ['klo:snəs] *n* **1** NEARNESS : cercanía *f*, proximidad *f* **2** INTIMACY : intimidad *f*
closet[1] ['klɑzət] *vt* **to be closeted with** : estar encerrado con
closet[2] *n* : armario *m*, guardarropa *f*, clóset *m*
closure ['klo:ʒər] *n* **1** CLOSING, END : cierre *m*, clausura *f*, fin *m* **2** FASTENER : cierre *m*
clot[1] ['klɑt] *v* **clotted; clotting** *vt* : coagular, cuajar — *vi* : cuajarse, coagularse
clot[2] *n* : coágulo *m*
cloth ['klɔθ] *n, pl* **cloths** ['klɔðz, 'klɔθs] **1** FABRIC : tela *f* **2** RAG : trapo *m* **3** TABLECLOTH : mantel *m*
clothe ['klo:ð] *vt* **clothed** *or* **clad** ['klæd]; **clothing** DRESS : vestir, arropar, ataviar
clothes ['klo:z, 'klo:ðz] *npl* **1** CLOTHING : ropa *f* **2** BEDCLOTHES : ropa *f* de cama
clothespin ['klo:zˌpɪn] *n* : pinza *f* (para la ropa)

clothing ['klo:ðɪŋ] *n* : ropa *f*, indumentaria *f*

cloud[1] ['klaʊd] *vt* : nublar, oscurecer — *vi* **to cloud over** : nublarse

cloud[2] *n* : nube *f*

cloudburst ['klaʊdˌbərst] *n* : chaparrón *m*, aguacero *m*

cloudless ['klaʊdləs] *adj* : despejado, claro

cloudy ['klaʊdi] *adj* **cloudier; -est** : nublado, nuboso

clout[1] ['klaʊt] *vt* : bofetear, dar un tortazo a

clout[2] *n* **1** BLOW : golpe *m*, tortazo *m fam* **2** INFLUENCE : influencia *f*, palanca *f fam*

clove[1] ['klo:v] *n* **1** : diente *m* (de ajo) **2** : clavo *m* (especia)

clove[2] → **cleave**

cloven hoof ['klo:vən] *n* : pezuña *f* hendida

clover ['klo:vər] *n* : trébol *m*

cloverleaf ['klo:vərˌli:f] *n, pl* **-leafs** *or* **-leaves** [-ˌli:vz] : intersección *f* en trébol

clown[1] ['klaʊn] *vi* : payasear, bromear ⟨stop clowning around : déjate de payasadas⟩

clown[2] *n* : payaso *m*, -sa *f*

clownish ['klaʊnɪʃ] *adj* **1** : de payaso **2** BOORISH : grosero — **clownishly** *adv*

cloying ['klɔɪɪŋ] *adj* : empalagoso, meloso

club[1] ['klʌb] *vt* **clubbed; clubbing** : aporrear, dar garrotazos a

club[2] *n* **1** CUDGEL : garrote *m*, porra *f* **2** : palo *m* ⟨golf club : palo de golf⟩ **3** : trébol *m* (naipe) **4** ASSOCIATION : club *m*

clubfoot ['klʌbˌfʊt] *n, pl* **-feet** : pie *m* deforme

clubhouse ['klʌbˌhaʊs] *n* : sede *f* de un club

cluck[1] ['klʌk] *vi* : cloquear, cacarear

cluck[2] *n* : cloqueo *m*, cacareo *m*

clue[1] ['klu:] *vt* **clued; clueing** *or* **cluing** *or* **to clue in** : dar una pista a, informar

clue[2] *n* : pista *f*, indicio *m*

clump[1] ['klʌmp] *vi* **1** : caminar con pisadas fuertes **2** LUMP : agruparse, aglutinarse — *vt* : amontonar

clump[2] *n* **1** : grupo *m* (de arbustos o árboles), terrón *m* (de tierra) **2** : pisada *f* fuerte

clumsily ['klʌmzəli] *adv* : torpemente, sin gracia

clumsiness ['klʌmzinəs] *n* : torpeza *f*

clumsy ['klʌmzi] *adj* **-sier; -est 1** AWKWARD : torpe, desmañado **2** TACTLESS : carente de tacto, poco delicado

clung → **cling**

clunky ['klʌŋki] *adj* : torpe, poco elegante

cluster[1] ['klʌstər] *vt* : agrupar, juntar — *vi* : agruparse, apiñarse, arracimarse

cluster[2] *n* : grupo *m*, conjunto *m*, racimo *m* (de uvas)

clutch[1] ['klʌʧ] *vt* : agarrar, asir — *vi* **to clutch at** : tratar de agarrar

clutch[2] *n* **1** GRASP, GRIP : agarre *m*, apretón *m* **2** : embrague *m*, clutch *m* (de una máquina) **3 clutches** *npl* : garras *fpl* ⟨he fell into their clutches : cayó en sus garras⟩

clutter[1] ['klʌt̬ər] *vt* : atiborrar o atestar de cosas, llenar desordenadamente

clutter[2] *n* : desorden *m*, revoltijo *m*

coach[1] ['ko:ʧ] *vt* : entrenar (atletas, artistas), preparar (alumnos)

coach[2] *n* **1** CARRIAGE : coche *m*, carruaje *m*, carroza *f* **2** : vagón *m* de pasajeros (de un tren) **3** BUS : autobús *m*, ómnibus *m* **4** : pasaje *m* aéreo de segunda clase **5** TRAINER : entrenador *m*, -dora *f*

coagulate [ko'ægjəˌleɪt] *v* **-lated; -lating** *vt* : coagular, cuajar — *vi* : coagularse, cuajarse

coal ['ko:l] *n* **1** EMBER : ascua *f*, brasa *f* **2** : carbón *m* ⟨a coal mine : una mina de carbón⟩

coalesce [ˌko:ə'lɛs] *vi* **-alesced; -alescing** : unirse

coalition [ˌko:ə'lɪʃən] *n* : coalición *f*

coarse ['kors] *adj* **coarser; -est 1** : grueso (dícese de la arena o la sal), basto (dícese de las telas), áspero (dícese de la piel) **2** CRUDE, ROUGH : basto, tosco, ordinario **3** VULGAR : grosero — **coarsely** *adv*

coarsen ['korsən] *vt* : hacer áspero o basto — *vi* : volverse áspero o basto

coarseness ['korsnəs] *n* : aspereza *f*, tosquedad *f*

coast[1] ['ko:st] *vi* : deslizarse, rodar sin impulso

coast[2] *n* : costa *f*, litoral *m*

coastal ['ko:stəl] *adj* : costero

coaster ['ko:stər] *n* : posavasos *m*

coast guard *n* : guardia *f* costera, guardacostas *mpl*

coastline ['ko:stˌlaɪn] *n* : costa *f*

coat[1] ['ko:t] *vt* : cubrir, revestir, bañar (en un líquido)

coat[2] *n* **1** : abrigo *m* ⟨a sport coat : una chaqueta, un saco⟩ **2** : pelaje *m* (de animales) **3** LAYER : capa *f*, mano *f* (de pintura)

coating ['ko:t̬ɪŋ] *n* : capa *f*

coat of arms *n* : escudo *m* de armas

coax ['ko:ks] *vt* : engatusar, persuadir

cob ['kɑb] → **corncob**

cobalt ['ko:ˌbɔlt] *n* : cobalto *m*

cobble ['kɑbəl] *vt* **cobbled; cobbling 1** : fabricar o remendar (zapatos) **2 to cobble together** : improvisar, hacer apresuradamente

cobbler ['kɑblər] *n* **1** SHOEMAKER : zapatero *m*, -ra *f* **2 fruit cobbler** : tarta *f* de fruta

cobblestone ['kɑbəlˌsto:n] *n* : adoquín *m*

cobra ['ko:brə] *n* : cobra *f*

cobweb ['kɑbˌwɛb] *n* : telaraña *f*

coca ['ko:kə] *n* : coca *f*

cocaine [ko:ˈkeɪn, ˈko:ˌkeɪn] *n* : cocaína *f*

cock[1] [ˈkɑk] *vt* **1** : ladear ⟨to cock one's head : ladear la cabeza⟩ **2** : montar, amartillar (un arma de fuego)

cock[2] *n* **1** ROOSTER : gallo *m* **2** FAUCET : grifo *m*, llave *f* **3** : martillo *m* (de un arma de fuego)

cockatoo [ˈkɑkəˌtu:] *n, pl* **-toos** : cacatúa *f*

cockeyed [ˈkɑkˌaɪd] *adj* **1** ASKEW : ladeado, torcido, chueco **2** ABSURD : disparatado, absurdo

cockfight [ˈkɑkˌfaɪt] *n* : pelea *f* de gallos

cockiness [ˈkɑkinəs] *n* : arrogancia *f*

cockle [ˈkɑkəl] *n* : berberecho *m*

cockpit [ˈkɑkˌpɪt] *n* : cabina *f*

cockroach [ˈkɑkˌro:ʧ] *n* : cucaracha *f*

cocktail [ˈkɑkˌteɪl] *n* **1** : coctel *m*, cóctel *m* **2** APPETIZER : aperitivo *m*

cocky [ˈkɑki] *adj* **cockier; -est** : creído, engreído

cocoa [ˈko:ˌko:] *n* **1** CACAO : cacao *m* **2** : cocoa *f*, chocolate *m* (bebida)

coconut [ˈko:kəˌnʌt] *n* : coco *m*

cocoon [kəˈku:n] *n* : capullo *m*

cod [ˈkɑd] *n, pl* **cod** : bacalao *m*

coddle [ˈkɑdəl] *vt* **-dled; -dling** : mimar, consentir

code [ˈko:d] *n* **1** : código *m* ⟨civil code : código civil⟩ **2** : código *m*, clave *f* ⟨secret code : clave secreta⟩

codeine [ˈko:ˌdi:n] *n* : codeína *f*

codex [ˈko:ˌdɛks] *n, pl* **-dexes** [-ˌdɛksəz] *or* **-dices** [-dəˌsi:z] : códice *m*

codger [ˈkɑʤər] *n* : viejo *m*, vejete *m*

codify [ˈkɑdəˌfaɪ, ˈko:-] *vt* **-fied; -fying** : codificar

coeducation [ˌko:ˌɛʤəˈkeɪʃən] *n* : coeducación *f*, enseñanza *f* mixta

coeducational [ˌko:ˌɛʤəˈkeɪʃənəl] *adj* : mixto

coefficient [ˌko:əˈfɪʃənt] *n* : coeficiente *m*

coerce [koˈərs] *vt* **-erced; -ercing** : coaccionar, forzar, obligar

coercion [koˈərʒən, -ʃən] *n* : coacción *f*

coercive [koˈərsɪv] *adj* : coactivo

coexist [ˌko:ɪgˈzɪst] *vi* : coexistir

coexistence [ˌko:ɪgˈzɪstənts] *n* : coexistencia *f*

coffee [ˈkɔfi] *n* : café *m*

coffeepot [ˈkɔfiˌpɑt] *n* : cafetera *f*

coffee table *n* : mesa *f* de centro

coffer [ˈkɔfər] *n* : cofre *m*

coffin [ˈkɔfən] *n* : ataúd *m*, féretro *m*

cog [ˈkɑg] *n* : diente *m* (de una rueda dentada)

cogent [ˈko:ʤənt] *adj* : convincente, persuasivo

cogitate [ˈkɑʤəˌteɪt] *vi* **-tated; -tating** : reflexionar, meditar, discurrir

cogitation [ˌkɑʤəˈteɪʃən] *n* : reflexión *f*, meditación *f*

cognac [ˈko:nˌjæk] *n* : coñac *m*

cognate [ˈkɑgˌneɪt] *adj* : relacionado, afín

cognition [kɑgˈnɪʃən] *n* : cognición *f*

cognitive [ˈkɑgnət̮ɪv] *adj* : cognitivo

cogwheel [ˈkɑgˌhwi:l] *n* : rueda *f* dentada

cohabit [ˌko:ˈhæbət] *vi* : cohabitar

cohere [koˈhɪr] *vi* **-hered; -hering** **1** ADHERE : adherirse, pegarse **2** : ser coherente o congruente

coherence [koˈhɪrənts] *n* : coherencia *f*, congruencia *f*

coherent [koˈhɪrənt] *adj* : coherente, congruente — **coherently** *adv*

cohesion [koˈhi:ʒən] *n* : cohesión *f*

cohesive [ko:ˈhi:sɪv, -zɪv] *adj* : cohesivo

cohort [ˈko:ˌhɔrt] *n* **1** : cohorte *f* (de soldados) **2** COMPANION : compañero *m*, -ra *f*; colega *mf*

coiffure [kwɑˈfjʊr] *n* : peinado *m*

coil[1] [ˈkɔɪl] *vt* : enrollar — *vi* : enrollarse, enroscarse

coil[2] *n* : rollo *m* (de cuerda, etc.), espiral *f* (de humo)

coin[1] [ˈkɔɪn] *vt* **1** MINT : acuñar (moneda) **2** INVENT : acuñar, crear, inventar ⟨to coin a phrase : como se suele decir⟩

coin[2] *n* : moneda *f*

coincide [ˌko:ɪnˈsaɪd, ˈko:ɪnˌsaɪd] *vi* **-cided; -ciding** : coincidir

coincidence [koˈɪntsədənts] *n* : coincidencia *f*, casualidad *f* ⟨what a coincidence! : ¡qué casualidad!⟩

coincident [koˈɪntsədənt] *adj* : coincidente, concurrente

coincidental [koˌɪntsəˈdɛntəl] *adj* : casual, accidental, fortuito

coitus [ˈko:ət̮əs] *n* : coito *m*

coke [ˈko:k] *n* : coque *m*

colander [ˈkɑləndər, ˈkʌ-] *n* : colador *m*

cold[1] [ˈko:ld] *adj* : frío ⟨it's cold out : hace frío⟩ ⟨a cold reception : una fría recepción⟩ ⟨in cold blood : a sangre fría⟩

cold[2] *n* **1** : frío *m* ⟨to feel the cold : sentir frío⟩ **2** : resfriado *m*, catarro *m* ⟨to catch a cold : resfriarse⟩

cold–blooded [ˈko:ldˈblʌdəd] *adj* **1** CRUEL : cruel, despiadado **2** : de sangre fría (dícese de los reptiles, etc.)

coldly [ˈko:ldli] *adv* : fríamente, con frialdad

coldness [ˈko:ldnəs] *n* : frialdad *f* (de una persona o una actitud), frío *m* (de la temperatura)

coleslaw [ˈko:lˌslɔ] *n* : ensalada *f* de col

colic [ˈkɑlɪk] *n* : cólico *m*

coliseum [ˌkɑləˈsi:əm] *n* : coliseo *m*, arena *f*

collaborate [kəˈlæbəˌreɪt] *vi* **-rated; -rating** : colaborar

collaboration [kəˌlæbəˈreɪʃə n] *n* : colaboración *f*

collaborator [kəˈlæbəˌreɪt̮ər] *n* **1** COLLEAGUE : colaborador *m*, -dora *f* **2** TRAITOR : colaboracionista *mf*

collage [kəˈlɑʒ] *n* : collage *m*

collapse[1] [kəˈlæps] *vi* **-lapsed; -lapsing** **1** : derrumbarse, desplomarse, hundirse ⟨the building collapsed : el edificio se derrumbó⟩ **2** FALL : desplomarse, caerse ⟨he collapsed on the bed : se desplomó en la cama⟩ ⟨to collapse with laughter : morirse de risa⟩ **3** FAIL : fracasar, quebrar, arruinarse **4** FOLD : plegarse

collapse[2] *n* **1** FALL : derrumbe *m*, desplome *m* **2** BREAKDOWN, FAILURE : fracaso *m*, colapso *m* (físico), quiebra *f* (económica)

collapsible [kəˈlæpsəbəl] *adj* : plegable

collar[1] [ˈkɑlər] *vt* : agarrar, atrapar

collar[2] *n* : cuello *m*

collarbone [ˈkɑlərˌbo:n] *n* : clavícula *f*

collate [kəˈleɪt; ˈkɑˌleɪt, ˈko:-] *vt* **-lated; -lating** **1** COMPARE : cotejar, comparar **2** : ordenar, recopilar (páginas)

collateral[1] [kəˈlæt̬ərəl] *adj* : colateral

collateral[2] *n* : garantía *f*, fianza *f*, prenda *f*

colleague [ˈkɑˌli:g] *n* : colega *mf*; compañero *m*, -ra *f*

collect[1] [kəˈlɛkt] *vt* **1** GATHER : recopilar, reunir, recoger ⟨she collected her thoughts : puso en orden sus ideas⟩ **2** : coleccionar, juntar ⟨to collect stamps : coleccionar timbres⟩ **3** : cobrar (una deuda), recaudar (un impuesto) **4** DRAW : cobrar, percibir (un sueldo, etc.) — *vi* **1** ACCUMULATE : acumularse, juntarse **2** CONGREGATE : congregarse, reunirse

collect[2] *adv & adj* : por cobrar, a cobro revertido

collectible *or* **collectable** [kəˈlɛktəbəl] *adj* : coleccionable

collection [kəˈlɛkʃən] *n* **1** COLLECTING : colecta *f* (de contribuciones), cobro *m* (de deudas), recaudación *f* (de impuestos) **2** GROUP : colección *f* (de objetos), grupo *m* (de personas)

collective[1] [kəˈlɛktɪv] *adj* : colectivo — **collectively** *adv*

collective[2] *n* : colectivo *m*

collector [kəˈlɛktər] *n* **1** : coleccionista *mf* (de objetos) **2** : cobrador *m*, -dora *f* (de deudas)

college [ˈkɑlɪʤ] *n* **1** : universidad *f* **2** : colegio *m* (de electores o profesionales)

collegiate [kəˈli:ʤət] *adj* : universitario

collide [kəˈlaɪd] *vi* **-lided; -liding** : chocar, colisionar, estrellarse

collie [ˈkɑli] *n* : collie *mf*

collision [kəˈlɪʒən] *n* : choque *m*, colisión *f*

colloquial [kəˈlo:kwiəl] *adj* : coloquial

colloquialism [kəˈlo:kwiəˌlɪzəm] *n* : expresión *f* coloquial

collusion [kəˈlu:ʒən] *n* : colusión *f*

cologne [kəˈlo:n] *n* : colonia *f*

Colombian [kəˈlʌmbiən] *n* : colombiano *m*, -na *f* — **Colombian** *adj*

colon[1] [ˈko:lən] *n, pl* **colons** *or* **cola** [-lə] : colon *m* (de los intestinos)

colon[2] *n, pl* **colons** : dos puntos *mpl* (signo ortográfico)

colonel [ˈkərnəl] *n* : coronel *m*

colonial[1] [kəˈlo:niəl] *adj* : colonial

colonial[2] *n* : colono *m*, -na *f*

colonist [ˈkɑlənɪst] *n* : colono *m*, -na *f*; colonizador *m*, -dora *f*

colonization [ˌkɑlənəˈzeɪʃən] *n* : colonización *f*

colonize [ˈkɑləˌnaɪz] *vt* **-nized; -nizing** **1** : establecer una colonia en **2** SETTLE : colonizar

colonnade [ˌkɑləˈneɪd] *n* : columnata *f*

colony [ˈkɑləni] *n, pl* **-nies** : colonia *f*

color[1] [ˈkʌlər] *vt* **1** : colorear, pintar **2** INFLUENCE : influir en, influenciar — *vi* BLUSH : sonrojarse, ruborizarse

color[2] *n* **1** : color *m* ⟨primary colors : colores primarios⟩ **2** INTEREST, VIVIDNESS : color *m*, colorido *m* ⟨local color : color local⟩

coloration [kʌləˈreɪʃən] *n* : coloración *f*

color–blind [ˈkʌlərˌblaɪnd] *adj* : daltónico

color blindness *n* : daltonismo *m*

colored [ˈkʌlərd] *adj* **1** : de color (dícese de los objetos) **2** : de color, negro (dícese de las personas)

colorfast [ˈkʌlərˌfæst] *adj* : que no se destiñe

colorful [ˈkʌlərfəl] *adj* **1** : lleno de colorido, de colores vivos **2** PICTURESQUE, STRIKING : pintoresco, llamativo

coloring [ˈkələrɪŋ] *n* **1** : color *m*, colorido *m* **2 food coloring** : colorante *m*

colorless [ˈkʌlərləs] *adj* **1** : incoloro, sin color **2** DULL : soso, aburrido

colossal [kəˈlɑsəl] *adj* : colosal

colossus [kəˈlɑsəs] *n, pl* **-si** [-ˌsaɪ] : coloso *m*

colt [ˈko:lt] *n* : potro *m*, potranco *m*

column [ˈkɑləm] *n* : columna *f*

columnist [ˈkɑləmnɪst, -ləmɪst] *n* : columnista *mf*

coma [ˈko:mə] *n* : coma *m*, estado *m* de coma

Comanche [kəˈmænʧi] *n* : comanche *mf* — **Comanche** *adj*

comatose [ˈko:məˌto:s, ˈkɑ-] *adj* : comatoso, en estado de coma

comb[1] [ˈko:m] *vt* **1** : peinar (el pelo) **2** SEARCH : peinar, rastrear, registrar a fondo

comb[2] *n* **1** : peine *m* **2** : cresta *f* (de un gallo)

combat[1] [kəmˈbæt, ˈkɑmˌbæt] *vt* **-bated** *or* **-batted; -bating** *or* **-batting** : combatir, luchar contra

combat[2] [ˈkɑmˌbæt] *n* : combate *m*, lucha *f*

combatant [kəmˈbætənt] *n* : combatiente *mf*

combative [kəmˈbæt̬ɪv] *adj* : combativo

combination [ˌkɑmbəˈneɪʃən] *n* : combinación *f*

combine[1] [kəmˈbaɪn] *v* **-bined; -bining** *vt* : combinar, aunar — *vi* : combinarse, mezclarse

combine[2] [ˈkɑmˌbaɪn] *n* **1** ALLIANCE : alianza *f* comercial o política **2** HARVESTER : cosechadora *f*

combustible [kəm'bʌstəbəl] *adj* : inflamable, combustible

combustion [kəm'bʌstʃən] *n* : combustión *f*

come ['kʌm] *vi* **came** ['keɪm]; **come; coming 1** APPROACH : venir, aproximarse ⟨here they come : acá vienen⟩ **2** ARRIVE : venir, llegar, alcanzar ⟨they came yesterday : vinieron ayer⟩ **3** ORIGINATE : venir, provenir ⟨this wine comes from France : este vino viene de Francia⟩ **4** AMOUNT : llegar, ascender ⟨the investment came to two million : la inversión llegó a dos millones⟩ **5 to come clean** : confesar, desahogar la conciencia **6 to come into** ACQUIRE : adquirir ⟨to come into a fortune : heredar una fortuna⟩ **7 to come off** SUCCEED : tener éxito, ser un éxito **8 to come out** : salir, aparecer, publicarse **9 to come to** REVIVE : recobrar el conocimiento, volver en sí **10 to come to pass** HAPPEN : acontecer **11 to come to terms** : llegar a un acuerdo

comeback ['kʌm,bæk] *n* **1** RETORT : réplica *f*, respuesta *f* **2** RETURN : retorno *m*, regreso *m* ⟨the champion announced his comeback : el campeón anunció su regreso⟩

come back *vi* **1** RETORT : replicar, contestar **2** RETURN : volver ⟨come back here! : ¡vuelve acá!⟩ ⟨that style's coming back : ese estilo está volviendo⟩

comedian [kə'mi:diən] *n* : cómico *m*, -ca *f*; humorista *mf*

comedienne [kə,mi:di'ɛn] *n* : cómica *f*, humorista *f*

comedy ['kɑmədi] *n, pl* **-dies** : comedia *f*

comely ['kʌmli] *adj* **-lier; -est** : bello, bonito

comet ['kɑmət] *n* : cometa *m*

comfort[1] ['kʌmpfərt] *vt* **1** CHEER : confortar, alentar **2** CONSOLE : consolar

comfort[2] *n* **1** CONSOLATION : consuelo *m* **2** WELL-BEING : confort *m*, bienestar *m* **3** CONVENIENCE : comodidad *f* ⟨the comforts of home : las comodidades del hogar⟩

comfortable ['kʌmpfərṭəbəl, 'kʌmpftə-] *adj* : cómodo, confortable — **comfortably** ['kʌmpfərṭəbli, 'kʌmpftə-] *adv*

comforter ['kʌmpfərṭər] *n* QUILT : edredón *m*, cobertor *m*

comic[1] ['kɑmɪk] *adj* : cómico, humorístico

comic[2] *n* **1** COMEDIAN : cómico *m*, -ca *f*; humorista *mf* **2** *or* **comic book** : historieta *f*, cómic *m*

comical ['kɑmɪkəl] *adj* : cómico, gracioso, chistoso

comic strip *n* : tira *f* cómica, historieta *f*

coming ['kʌmɪŋ] *adj* : siguiente, próximo, que viene

comma ['kɑmə] *n* : coma *f*

command[1] [kə'mænd] *vt* **1** ORDER : ordenar, mandar **2** CONTROL, DIRECT : comandar, tener el mando de — *vi* **1** : dar órdenes **2** GOVERN : estar al mando *m*, gobernar

command[2] *n* **1** CONTROL, LEADERSHIP : mando *m*, control *m*, dirección *f* **2** ORDER : orden *f*, mandato *m* **3** MASTERY : maestría *f*, destreza *f*, dominio *m* **4** : tropa *f* asignada a un comandante

commandant ['kɑmən,dɑnt, -,dænt] *n* : comandante *mf*

commandeer [,kɑmən'dɪr] *vt* : piratear, secuestrar (un vehículo, etc.)

commander [kə'mændər] *n* : comandante *mf*

commandment [kə'mændmənt] *n* : mandamiento *m*, orden *f* ⟨the Ten Commandments : los diez mandamientos⟩

commando [kə'mændo:] *n* : comando *m*

commemorate [kə'mɛmə,reɪt] *vt* **-rated; -rating** : conmemorar

commemoration [kə,mɛmə'reɪʃən] *n* : conmemoración *f*

commemorative [kə'mɛmrəṭɪv, -'mɛmə,reɪṭɪv] *adj* : conmemorativo

commence [kə'mɛnts] *v* **-menced; -mencing** *vt* : iniciar, comenzar — *vi* : iniciarse, comenzar

commencement [kə'mɛntsmənt] *n* **1** BEGINNING : inicio *m*, comienzo *m* **2** : ceremonia *f* de graduación

commend [kə'mɛnd] *vt* **1** ENTRUST : encomendar **2** RECOMMEND : recomendar **3** PRAISE : elogiar, alabar

commendable [kə'mɛndəbəl] *adj* : loable, meritorio, encomiable

commendation [,kɑmən'deɪʃən, -,mɛn-] *n* : elogio *m*, encomio *m*

commensurate [kə'mɛntsərət, -'mɛntʃʊrət] *adj* : proporcionado ⟨commensurate with : en proporción a⟩

comment[1] ['kɑ,mɛnt] *vi* **1** : hacer comentarios **2 to comment on** : comentar, hacer observaciones sobre

comment[2] *n* : comentario *m*, observación *f*

commentary ['kɑmən,tɛri] *n, pl* **-taries** : comentario *m*, crónica *f* (deportiva)

commentator ['kɑmən,teɪṭər] *n* : comentarista *mf*, cronista *mf* (de deportes)

commerce ['kɑmərs] *n* : comercio *m*

commercial[1] [kə'mərʃəl] *adj* : comercial — **commercially** *adv*

commercial[2] *n* : comercial *m*

commercialize [kə'mərʃə,laɪz] *vt* **-ized; -izing** : comercializar

commiserate [kə'mɪzə,reɪt] *vi* **-ated; -ating** : compadecerse, consolarse

commiseration [kə,mɪzə'reɪʃən] *n* : conmiseración *f*

commission[1] [kə'mɪʃən] *vt* **1** : nombrar (un oficial) **2** : comisionar, encargar ⟨to commission a painting : encargar una pintura⟩

commission[2] *n* **1** : nombramiento *m* (al grado de oficial) **2** COMMITTEE : comisión *f*, comité *m* **3** COMMITTING : comisión *f*, realización *f* (de un acto) **4** PERCENTAGE : comisión *f* ⟨sales commissions : comisiones de venta⟩

commissioned officer *n* : oficial *mf*

commissioner [kəˈmɪʃənər] *n* **1** : comisionado *m*, -da *f*; miembro *m* de una comisión **2** : comisario *m*, -ria *f* (de policía, etc.)

commit [kəˈmɪt] *vt* **-mitted; -mitting 1** ENTRUST : encomendar, confiar **2** CONFINE : internar (en un hospital), encarcelar (en una prisión) **3** PERPETRATE : cometer ⟨to commit a crime : cometer un crimen⟩ **4 to commit oneself** : comprometerse

commitment [kəˈmɪtmənt] *n* **1** RESPONSIBILITY : compromiso *m*, responsabilidad *f* **2** DEDICATION : dedicación *f*, devoción *f* ⟨commitment to the cause : devoción a la causa⟩

committee [kəˈmɪt̬i] *n* : comité *m*

commodious [kəˈmoːdiəs] *adj* SPACIOUS : amplio, espacioso

commodity [kəˈmɑdət̬i] *n, pl* **-ties** : artículo *m* de comercio, mercancía *f*, mercadería *f*

commodore [ˈkɑməˌdor] *n* : comodoro *m*

common[1] [ˈkɑmən] *adj* **1** PUBLIC : común, público ⟨the common good : el bien común⟩ **2** SHARED : común ⟨a common interest : un interés común⟩ **3** GENERAL : común, general ⟨it's common knowledge : todo el mundo lo sabe⟩ **4** ORDINARY : ordinario, común y corriente ⟨the common man : el hombre medio, el hombre de la calle⟩

common[2] *n* **1** : tierra *f* comunal **2 in ~** : en común

common cold *n* : resfriado *m* común

common denominator *n* : denominador *m* común

commoner [ˈkɑmənər] *n* : plebeyo *m*, -ya *f*

commonly [ˈkɑmənli] *adv* **1** FREQUENTLY : comúnmente, frecuentemente **2** USUALLY : normalmente

common noun *n* : nombre *m* común

commonplace[1] [ˈkɑmənˌpleɪs] *adj* : común, ordinario

commonplace[2] *n* : cliché *m*, tópico *m*

common sense *n* : sentido *m* común

commonwealth [ˈkɑmənˌwɛlθ] *n* : entidad *f* política ⟨the British Commonwealth : la Mancomunidad Británica⟩

commotion [kəˈmoːʃən] *n* **1** RUCKUS : alboroto *m*, jaleo *m*, escándalo *m* **2** STIR, UPSET : revuelo *m*, conmoción *f*

communal [kəˈmjuːnəl] *adj* : comunal

commune[1] [kəˈmjuːn] *vi* **-muned; -muning** : estar en comunión

commune[2] [ˈkɑˌmjuːn, kəˈmjuːn] *n* : comuna *f*

communicable [kəˈmjuːnɪkəbəl] *adj* CONTAGIOUS : transmisible, contagioso

communicate [kəˈmjuːnəˌkeɪt] *v* **-cated; -cating** *vt* **1** CONVEY : comunicar, expresar, hacer saber **2** TRANSMIT : transmitir (una enfermedad), contagiar — *vi* : comunicarse, expresarse

communication [kəˌmjuːnəˈkeɪʃən] *n* : comunicación *f*

communicative [kəˈmjuːnɪˌkeɪt̬ɪv, -kət̬ɪv] *adj* : comunicativo

communion [kəˈmjuːnjən] *n* **1** SHARING : comunión *f* **2 Communion** : comunión *f*, eucaristía *f*

communiqué [kəˈmjuːnəˌkeɪ, -ˌmjuːnəˈkeɪ] *n* : comunicado *m*

communism *or* **Communism** [ˈkɑmjəˌnɪzəm] *n* : comunismo *m*

communist[1] *or* **Communist** [ˈkɑmjəˌnɪst] *adj* : comunista ⟨the Communist Party : el Partido Comunista⟩

communist[2] *or* **Communist** *n* : comunista *mf*

communistic *or* **Communistic** [ˌkɑmjəˈnɪstɪk] *adj* : comunista

community [kəˈmjuːnət̬i] *n, pl* **-ties** : comunidad *f*

commute [kəˈmjuːt] *v* **-muted; -muting** *vt* REDUCE : conmutar, reducir (una sentencia) — *vi* : viajar de la residencia al trabajo

commuter [kəˈmjuːt̬ər] *n* : persona *f* que viaja diariamente al trabajo

compact[1] [kəmˈpækt, ˈkɑmˌpækt] *vt* : compactar, consolidar, comprimir

compact[2] [kəmˈpækt, ˈkɑmˌpækt] *adj* **1** DENSE, SOLID : compacto, macizo, denso **2** CONCISE : breve, conciso

compact[3] [ˈkɑmˌpækt] *n* **1** AGREEMENT : acuerdo *m*, pacto *m* **2** : polvera *f*, estuche *m* de maquillaje **3** *or* **compact car** : auto *m* compacto

compact disc [ˈkɑmˌpæktˈdɪsk] *n* : disco *m* compacto, compact disc *m*

compactly [kəmˈpæktli, ˈkɑmˌpækt-] *adv* **1** DENSELY : densamente, macizamente **2** CONCISELY : concisamente, brevemente

companion [kəmˈpænjən] *n* **1** COMRADE : compañero *m*, -ra *f*; acompañante *mf* **2** MATE : pareja *f* (de un zapato, etc.)

companionable [kəmˈpænjənəbəl] *adj* : sociable, amigable

companionship [kəmˈpænjənˌʃɪp] *n* : compañerismo *m*, camaradería *f*

company [ˈkʌmpəni] *n, pl* **-nies 1** FIRM : compañía *f*, empresa *f* **2** GROUP : compañía *f* (de actores o soldados) **3** GUESTS : visita *f* ⟨we have company : tenemos visita⟩

comparable [ˈkɑmpərəbəl] *adj* : comparable, parecido

comparative[1] [kəmˈpærət̬ɪv] *adj* RELATIVE : comparativo, relativo — **comparatively** *adv*

comparative[2] *n* : comparativo *m*

compare[1] [kəm'pær] *v* **-pared; -paring** *vt* : comparar — *vi* **to compare with** : poder comparar con, tener comparación con
compare[2] *n* : comparación *f* ⟨beyond compare : sin igual, sin par⟩
comparison [kəm'pærəsən] *n* : comparación *f*
compartment [kəm'pɑrtmənt] *n* : compartimento *m*, compartimiento *m*
compass ['kʌmpəs, 'kɑm-] *n* **1** RANGE, SCOPE : alcance *m*, extensión *f*, límites *mpl* **2** : compás *m* (para trazar circunferencias) **3** : compás *m*, brújula *f* ⟨the points of the compass : los puntos cardinales⟩
compassion [kəm'pæʃən] *n* : compasión *f*, piedad *f*, misericordia *f*
compassionate [kəm'pæʃənət] *adj* : compasivo
compatibility [kəm,pæt̬ə'bɪlət̬i] *n* : compatibilidad *f*
compatible [kəm'pæt̬əbəl] *adj* : compatible, afín
compatriot [kəm'peɪtriət, -'pæ-] *n* : compatriota *mf*; paisano *m*, -na *f*
compel [kəm'pɛl] *vt* **-pelled; -pelling** : obligar, compeler
compelling [kəm'pɛlɪŋ] *adj* **1** FORCEFUL : fuerte **2** ENGAGING : absorbente **3** PERSUASIVE : persuasivo, convincente
compendium [kəm'pɛndiəm] *n, pl* **-diums** *or* **-dia** [-diə] : compendio *m*
compensate ['kɑmpən,seɪt] *v* **-sated; -sating** *vi* **to compensate for** : compensar — *vt* : indemnizar, compensar
compensation [,kɑmpən'seɪʃən] *n* : compensación *f*, indemnización *f*
compensatory [kəm'pɛntsə,tori] *adj* : compensatorio
compete [kəm'pi:t] *vi* **-peted; -peting** : competir, contender, rivalizar
competence ['kɑmpətənts] *n* : competencia *f*, aptitud *f*
competency ['kɑmpətəntsi] → **competence**
competent ['kɑmpətənt] *adj* : competente, capaz
competition [,kɑmpə'tɪʃən] *n* : competencia *f*, concurso *m*
competitive [kəm'pɛt̬ət̬ɪv] *adj* : competitivo
competitor [kəm'pɛt̬ət̬ər] *n* : competidor *m*, -dora *f*
compilation [,kɑmpə'leɪʃən] *n* : recopilación *f*, compilación *f*
compile [kəm'paɪl] *vt* **-piled; -piling** : compilar, recopilar
complacency [kəm'pleɪsəntsi] *n* : satisfacción *f* consigo mismo, suficiencia *f*
complacent [kəm'pleɪsənt] *adj* : satisfecho de sí mismo, suficiente
complain [kəm'pleɪn] *vi* **1** GRIPE : quejarse, regañar, rezongar **2** PROTEST : reclamar, protestar
complaint [kəm'pleɪnt] *n* **1** GRIPE : queja *f* **2** AILMENT : afección *f*, dolencia *f* **3** ACCUSATION : reclamo *m*, acusación *f*
complement[1] ['kɑmplə,mɛnt] *vt* : complementar
complement[2] ['kɑmpləmənt] *n* : complemento *m*
complementary [,kɑmplə'mɛntəri] *adj* : complementario
complete[1] [kəm'pli:t] *vt* **-pleted; -pleting** **1** : completar, hacer entero ⟨this piece completes the collection : esta pieza completa la colección⟩ **2** FINISH : completar, acabar, terminar ⟨she completed her studies : completó sus estudios⟩
complete[2] *adj* **-pleter; -est** **1** WHOLE : completo, entero, íntegro **2** FINISHED : terminado, acabado **3** TOTAL : completo, total, absoluto
completely [kəm'pli:tli] *adv* : completamente, totalmente
completion [kəm'pli:ʃən] *n* : finalización *f*, cumplimiento *m*
complex[1] [kɑm'plɛks, kəm-; 'kɑm,plɛks] *adj* : complejo, complicado
complex[2] ['kɑm,plɛks] *n* : complejo *m*
complexion [kəm'plɛkʃən] *n* : cutis *m*, tez *f* ⟨of dark complexion : de tez morena⟩
complexity [kəm'plɛksət̬i, kɑm-] *n, pl* **-ties** : complejidad *f*
compliance [kəm'plaɪənts] *n* : conformidad *f* ⟨in compliance with the law : conforme a la ley⟩
compliant [kəm'plaɪənt] *adj* : dócil, sumiso
complicate ['kɑmplə,keɪt] *vt* **-cated; -cating** : complicar
complicated ['kɑmplə,keɪt̬əd] *adj* : complicado
complication [,kɑmplə'keɪʃən] *n* : complicación *f*
complicity [kəm'plɪsət̬i] *n, pl* **-ties** : complicidad *f*
compliment[1] ['kɑmplə,mɛnt] *vt* : halagar, florear *Mex*
compliment[2] ['kɑmpləmənt] *n* **1** : halago *m*, cumplido *m* **2 compliments** *npl* : saludos *mpl* ⟨give them my compliments : déles saludos de mi parte⟩
complimentary [,kɑmplə'mɛntəri] *adj* **1** FLATTERING : halagador, halagüeño **2** FREE : de cortesía, gratis
comply [kəm'plaɪ] *vi* **-plied; -plying** : cumplir, acceder, obedecer
component[1] [kəm'po:nənt, 'kɑm-,po:-] *adj* : componente
component[2] *n* : componente *m*, elemento *m*, pieza *f*
compose [kəm'po:z] *vt* **-posed; -posing** **1** : componer, crear ⟨to compose a melody : componer una melodía⟩ **2** CALM : calmar, serenar ⟨to compose oneself : serenarse⟩ **3** CONSTITUTE : constar, componer ⟨to be composed of : constar de⟩ **4** : componer (un texto a imprimirse)
composer [kəm'po:zər] *n* : compositor *m*, -tora *f*

composite[1] [kɑm'pɑzət, kəm-; 'kɑmpəzət] *adj* : compuesto (de varias partes)
composite[2] *n* : compuesto *m*, mezcla *f*
composition [ˌkɑmpə'zɪʃən] *n* **1** MAKE-UP : composición *f* **2** ESSAY : ensayo *m*, trabajo *m*
compost ['kɑmˌpo:st] *n* : abono *m* vegetal
composure [kəm'po:ʒər] *n* : compostura *f*, serenidad *f*
compound[1] [kɑm'paʊnd, kəm-; 'kɑmˌpaʊnd] *vt* **1** COMBINE, COMPOSE : combinar, componer **2** AUGMENT : agravar, aumentar ⟨to compound a problem : agravar un problema⟩
compound[2] ['kɑmˌpaʊnd; kɑm'paʊnd, kəm-] *adj* : compuesto ⟨compound interest : interés compuesto⟩
compound[3] ['kɑmˌpaʊnd] *n* **1** MIXTURE : compuesto *m*, mezcla *f* **2** ENCLOSURE : recinto *m* (de residencias, etc.)
compound fracture *n* : fractura *f* complicada
comprehend [ˌkɑmprɪ'hɛnd] *vt* **1** UNDERSTAND : comprender, entender **2** INCLUDE : comprender, incluir, abarcar
comprehensible [ˌkɑmprɪ'hɛntsəbəl] *adj* : comprensible
comprehension [ˌkɑmprɪ'hɛntʃən] *n* : comprensión *f*
comprehensive [ˌkɑmprɪ'hɛntsɪv] *adj* **1** INCLUSIVE : inclusivo, exhaustivo **2** BROAD : extenso, amplio
compress[1] [kəm'prɛs] *vt* : comprimir
compress[2] ['kɑmˌprɛs] *n* : compresa *f*
compression [kəm'prɛʃən] *n* : compresión *f*
compressor [kəm'prɛsər] *n* : compresor *m*
comprise [kəm'praɪz] *vt* **-prised; -prising** **1** INCLUDE : comprender, incluir **2** : componerse de, constar de ⟨the installation comprises several buildings : la instalación está compuesta de varios edificios⟩
compromise[1] ['kɑmprəˌmaɪz] *v* **-mised; -mising** *vi* : transigir, avenirse — *vt* JEOPARDIZE : comprometer, poner en peligro
compromise[2] *n* : acuerdo *m* mutuo, compromiso *m*
comptroller [kən'tro:lər, 'kɑmp-ˌtro:-] *n* : contralor *m*, -lora *f*; interventor *m*, -tora *f*
compulsion [kəm'pʌlʃən] *n* **1** COERCION : coacción *f* **2** URGE : compulsión *f*, impulso *m*
compulsive [kəm'pʌlsɪv] *adj* : compulsivo
compulsory [kəm'pʌlsəri] *adj* : obligatorio
compunction [kəm'pʌŋkʃən] *n* **1** QUALM : reparo *m*, escrúpulo *m* **2** REMORSE : remordimiento *m*
computation [ˌkɑmpjʊ'teɪʃən] *n* : cálculo *m*, cómputo *m*
compute [kəm'pju:t] *vt* **-puted; -puting** : computar, calcular
computer [kəm'pju:ţər] *n* : computadora *f*, computador *m*, ordenador *m Spain*
computerize [kəm'pju:ţəˌraɪz] *vt* **-ized; -izing** : computarizar, informatizar
comrade ['kɑmˌræd] *n* : camarada *mf*; compañero *m*, -ra *f*
con[1] ['kɑn] *vt* **conned; conning** SWINDLE : estafar, timar
con[2] *adv* : contra
con[3] *n* : contra *m* ⟨the pros and cons : los pros y los contras⟩
concave [kɑn'keɪv, 'kɑnˌkeɪv] *adj* : cóncavo
conceal [kən'si:l] *vt* : esconder, ocultar, disimular
concealment [kən'si:lmənt] *n* : escondimiento *m*, ocultación *f*
concede [kən'si:d] *vt* **-ceded; -ceding** **1** ALLOW, GRANT : conceder **2** ADMIT : conceder, reconocer ⟨to concede defeat : reconocer la derrota⟩
conceit [kən'si:t] *n* : engreimiento *m*, presunción *f*
conceited [kən'si:ţəd] *adj* : presumido, engreído, presuntuoso
conceivable [kən'si:vəbəl] *adj* : concebible, imaginable
conceivably [kən'si:vəbli] *adv* : posiblemente, de manera concebible
conceive [kən'si:v] *v* **-ceived; -ceiving** *vi* : concebir, embarazarse — *vt* IMAGINE : concebir, imaginar
concentrate[1] ['kɑntsənˌtreɪt] *v* **-trated; -trating** *vt* : concentrar — *vi* : concentrarse
concentrate[2] *n* : concentrado *m*
concentration [ˌkɑntsən'treɪʃən] *n* : concentración *f*
concentric [kən'sɛntrɪk] *adj* : concéntrico
concept ['kɑnˌspt] *n* : concepto *m*, idea *f*
conception [kən'sɛpʃən] *n* **1** : concepción *f* (de un bebé) **2** IDEA : concepto *m*, idea *f*
concern[1] [kən'sərn] *vt* **1** : tratarse de, tener que ver con ⟨the novel concerns a sailor : la novela se trata de un marinero⟩ **2** INVOLVE : concernir, incumbir a, afectar ⟨that does not concern me : eso no me incumbe⟩
concern[2] *n* **1** AFFAIR : asunto *m* **2** WORRY : inquietud *f*, preocupación *f* **3** BUSINESS : negocio *m*
concerned [kən'sərnd] *adj* **1** ANXIOUS : preocupado, ansioso **2** INTERESTED, INVOLVED : interesado, afectado
concerning [kən'sərnɪŋ] *prep* REGARDING : con respecto a, acerca de, sobre
concert ['kɑnˌsərt] *n* **1** AGREEMENT : concierto *m*, acuerdo *m* **2** : concierto *m* (musical)
concerted [kən'sərţəd] *adj* : concertado, coordinado ⟨to make a concerted effort : coordinar los esfuerzos⟩
concertina [ˌkɑntsər'ti:nə] *n* : concertina *f*

concerto [kən'ʧɛrˌto:] *n, pl* **-ti** [-ˌti, -ˌti:] *or* **-tos** : concierto *m* ⟨violin concerto : concierto para violín⟩
concession [kən'sɛʃən] *n* : concesión *f*
conch ['kaŋk, 'kanʧ] *n, pl* **conchs** ['kaŋks] *or* **conches** ['kanʧəz] : caracol *m* (animal), caracola *f* (concha)
conciliatory [kən'sɪliəˌtori] *adj* : conciliador, conciliatorio
concise [kən'saɪs] *adj* : conciso, breve — **concisely** *adv*
conclave ['kanˌkleɪv] *n* : cónclave *m*
conclude [kən'klu:d] *v* **-cluded; -cluding** *vt* **1** END : concluir, finalizar ⟨to conclude a meeting : concluir una reunión⟩ **2** DECIDE : concluir, llegar a la conclusión de — *vi* END : concluir, terminar
conclusion [kən'klu:ʒən] *n* **1** INFERENCE : conclusión *f* **2** END : fin *m*, final *m*
conclusive [kən'klu:sɪv] *adj* : concluyente, decisivo — **conclusively** *adv*
concoct [kən'kakt, kan-] *vt* **1** PREPARE : preparar, confeccionar **2** DEVISE : inventar, tramar
concoction [kən'kakʃən] *n* : invención *f*, mejunje *m*, brebaje *m*
concomitant [kən'kaməṭənt] *adj* : concomitante
concord ['kanˌkɔrd, 'kaŋ-] *n* **1** HARMONY : concordia *f*, armonía *f* **2** AGREEMENT : acuerdo *m*
concordance [kən'kɔrdənts] *n* : concordancia *f*
concourse ['kanˌkors] *n* : explanada *f*, salón *m* (para pasajeros)
concrete[1] [kan'kri:t, 'kanˌkri:t] *adj* **1** REAL : concreto ⟨concrete objects : objetos concretos⟩ **2** SPECIFIC : determinado, específico **3** : de concreto, de hormigón ⟨concrete walls : paredes de concreto⟩
concrete[2] ['kanˌkri:t, kan'kri:t] *n* : concreto *m*, hormigón *m*
concur [kən'kər] *vi* **concurred; concurring** **1** COINCIDE : concurrir, coincidir **2** AGREE : concurrir, estar de acuerdo
concurrent [kən'kərənt] *adj* : concurrente, simultáneo
concussion [kən'kʌʃən] *n* : conmoción *f* cerebral
condemn [kən'dɛm] *vt* **1** CENSURE : condenar, reprobar, censurar **2** : declarar insalubre (alimentos), declarar ruinoso (un edificio) **3** SENTENCE : condenar ⟨condemned to death : condenado a muerte⟩
condemnation [ˌkanˌdɛm'neɪʃən] *n* : condena *f*, reprobación *f*
condensation [ˌkanˌdɛn'seɪʃən, -dən-] *n* : condensación *f*
condense [kən'dɛnts] *v* **-densed; -densing** *vt* **1** ABRIDGE : condensar, resumir **2** : condensar (vapor, etc.) — *vi* : condensarse
condescend [ˌkandɪ'sɛnd] *vi* **1** DEIGN : condescender, dignarse **2 to condescend to someone** : tratar a alguien con condescendencia
condescension [ˌkandɪ'sɛnʧən] *n* : condescendencia *f*
condiment ['kandəmənt] *n* : condimento *m*
condition[1] [kən'dɪʃən] *vt* **1** DETERMINE : condicionar, determinar **2** : acondicionar (el pelo o el aire), poner en forma (el cuerpo)
condition[2] *n* **1** STIPULATION : condición *f*, estipulación *f* ⟨on the condition that : a condición de que⟩ **2** STATE : condición *f*, estado *m* ⟨in poor condition : en malas condiciones⟩ **3 conditions** *npl* : condiciones *fpl*, situación *f* ⟨working conditions : condiciones del trabajo⟩
conditional [kən'dɪʃənəl] *adj* : condicional — **conditionally** *adv*
conditioner [kən'dɪʃənər] *n* : acondicionador *m*
condo ['kando:] → **condominium**
condolence [kən'do:lənts] *n* **1** SYMPATHY : condolencia *f* **2 condolences** *npl* : pésame *m*
condom ['kandəm] *n* : condón *m*
condominium [ˌkandə'mɪniəm] *n, pl* **-ums** : condominio *m*
condone [kən'do:n] *vt* **-doned; -doning** : aprobar, perdonar, tolerar
condor ['kandər, -ˌdɔr] *n* : cóndor *m*
conducive [kən'du:sɪv, -'dju:-] *adj* : propicio, favorable
conduct[1] [kən'dʌkt] *vt* **1** GUIDE : guiar, conducir ⟨to conduct a tour : guiar una visita⟩ **2** DIRECT : conducir, dirigir ⟨to conduct an orchestra : dirigir una orquesta⟩ **3** CARRY OUT : realizar, llevar a cabo ⟨to conduct an investigation : llevar a cabo una investigación⟩ **4** TRANSMIT : conducir, transmitir (calor, electricidad, etc.) **5 to conduct oneself** BEHAVE : conducirse, comportarse
conduct[2] ['kanˌdʌkt] *n* **1** MANAGEMENT : conducción *f*, dirección *f*, manejo *m* ⟨the conduct of foreign affairs : la conducción de asuntos exteriores⟩ **2** BEHAVIOR : conducta *f*, comportamiento *m*
conduction [kən'dʌkʃən] *n* : conducción *f*
conductivity [ˌkanˌdʌk'tɪvəṭi] *n, pl* **-ties** : conductividad *f*
conductor [kən'dʌktər] *n* **1** : conductor *m*, -tora *f*; revisor *m*, -sora *f* (en un tren); cobrador *m*, -dora *f* (en un bus); director *m*, -tora *f* (de una orquesta) **2** : conductor *m* (de electricidad, etc.)
conduit ['kanˌdu:ət, -ˌdju:-] *n* : conducto *m*, canal *m*, vía *f*
cone ['ko:n] *n* **1** : piña *f* (fruto de las coníferas) **2** : cono *m* (en geometría) **3 ice–cream cone** : cono *m*, barquillo *m*, cucurucho *m*
confection [kən'fɛkʃən] *n* : dulce *m*

confectioner [kənˈfɛkʃənər] *n* : confitero *m*, -ra *f*

confederacy [kənˈfɛdərəsi] *n, pl* **-cies** : confederación *f*

confederate[1] [kənˈfɛdəˌreɪt] *v* **-ated; -ating** *vt* : unir, confederar — *vi* : confederarse, aliarse

confederate[2] [kənˈfɛdərət] *adj* : confederado

confederate[3] *n* : cómplice *mf*; aliado *m*, -da *f*

confederation [kənˌfɛdəˈreɪʃən] *n* : confederación *f*, alianza *f*

confer [kənˈfər] *v* **-ferred; -ferring** *vt* : conferir, otorgar — *vi* **to confer with** : consultar

conference [ˈkɑnfrənts, -fərənts] *n* : conferencia *f* ⟨press conference : conferencia de prensa⟩

confess [kənˈfɛs] *vt* : confesar — *vi* **1** : confesar ⟨the prisoner confessed : el detenido confesó⟩ **2** : confesarse (en religión)

confession [kənˈfɛʃən] *n* : confesión *f*

confessional [kənˈfɛʃənəl] *n* : confesionario *m*

confessor [kənˈfɛsər] *n* : confesor *m*

confetti [kənˈfɛt̬i] *n* : confeti *m*

confidant [ˈkɑnfəˌdɑnt, -ˌdænt] *n* : confidente *mf*

confide [kənˈfaɪd] *v* **-fided; -fiding** : confiar

confidence [ˈkɑnfədənts] *n* **1** TRUST : confianza *f* **2** SELF-ASSURANCE : confianza *f* en sí mismo, seguridad *f* en sí mismo **3** SECRET : confidencia *f*, secreto *m*

confident [ˈkɑnfədənt] *adj* **1** SURE : seguro **2** SELF-ASSURED : confiado, seguro de sí mismo

confidential [ˌkɑnfəˈdɛntʃəl] *adj* : confidencial — **confidentially** [ˌkɑnfəˈdɛntʃəli] *adv*

confidently [ˈkɑnfədəntli] *adv* : con seguridad, con confianza

configuration [kənˌfɪgjəˈreɪʃən] *n* : configuración *f*

confine [kənˈfaɪn] *vt* **-fined; -fining** **1** LIMIT : confinar, restringir, limitar **2** IMPRISON : recluir, encarcelar, encerrar

confinement [kənˈfaɪnmənt] *n* : confinamiento *m*, reclusión *f*, encierro *m*

confines [ˈkɑnˌfaɪnz] *npl* : límites *mpl*, confines *mpl*

confirm [kənˈfərm] *vt* **1** RATIFY : ratificar **2** VERIFY : confirmar, verificar **3** : confirmar (en religión)

confirmation [ˌkɑnfərˈmeɪʃən] *n* : confirmación *f*

confiscate [ˈkɑnfəˌskeɪt] *vt* **-cated; -cating** : confiscar, incautar, decomisar

confiscation [ˌkɑnfəˈskeɪʃən] *n* : confiscación *f*, incautación *f*, decomiso *m*

conflagration [ˌkɑnfləˈgreɪʃən] *n* : conflagración *f*

conflict[1] [kənˈflɪkt] *vi* : estar en conflicto, oponerse

conflict[2] [ˈkɑnˌflɪkt] *n* : conflicto *m* ⟨to be in conflict : estar en desacuerdo⟩

confluence [ˈkɑnˌfluːənts, kənˈfluːənts] *n* : confluencia *f*

conform [kənˈfɔrm] *vi* **1** ACCORD, COMPLY : ajustarse, adaptarse, conformarse ⟨it conforms with our standards : se ajusta a nuestras normas⟩ **2** CORRESPOND : corresponder, encajar ⟨to conform to the truth : corresponder a la verdad⟩

conformity [kənˈfɔrmət̬i] *n, pl* **-ties** : conformidad *f*

confound [kənˈfaʊnd, kɑn-] *vt* : confundir, desconcertar

confront [kənˈfrʌnt] *vt* : afrontar, enfrentarse a, encarar

confrontation [ˌkɑnfrənˈteɪʃən] *n* : enfrentamiento *m*, confrontación *f*

confuse [kənˈfjuːz] *vt* **-fused; -fusing** **1** PUZZLE : confundir, enturbiar **2** COMPLICATE : confundir, enredar, complicar ⟨to confuse the issue : complicar las cosas⟩

confusing [kənˈfjuːzɪŋ] *adj* : complicado, que confunde

confusion [kənˈfjuːʒən] *n* **1** PERPLEXITY : confusión *f* **2** MESS, TURMOIL : confusión *f*, embrollo *m*, lío *m fam*

congeal [kənˈdʒiːl] *vi* **1** FREEZE : congelarse **2** COAGULATE, CURDLE : coagularse, cuajarse

congenial [kənˈdʒiːniəl] *adj* : agradable, simpático

congenital [kənˈdʒɛnət̬əl] *adj* : congénito

congest [kənˈdʒɛst] *vt* **1** : congestionar (en la medicina) **2** OVERCROWD : abarrotar, atestar, congestionar (el tráfico) — *vi* : congestionarse

congestion [kənˈdʒɛstʃən] *n* : congestión *f*

conglomerate[1] [kənˈglɑmərət] *adj* : conglomerado

conglomerate[2] [kənˈglɑmərət] *n* : conglomerado *m*

conglomeration [kənˌglɑməˈreɪʃən] *n* : conglomerado *m*, acumulación *f*

Congolese [ˌkɑŋgəˈliːz, -ˈliːs] *n* : congoleño *m*, -ña *f* — **Congolese** *adj*

congratulate [kənˈgrædʒəˌleɪt, -ˈgrætʃə-] *vt* **-lated; -lating** : felicitar

congratulation [kənˌgrædʒəˈleɪʃən, -ˌgrætʃə-] *n* : felicitación *f* ⟨congratulations! : ¡felicidades!, ¡enhorabuena!⟩

congregate [ˈkɑŋgrɪˌgeɪt] *v* **-gated; -gating** *vt* : congregar, reunir — *vi* : congregarse, reunirse

congregation [ˌkɑŋgrɪˈgeɪʃən] *n* **1** GATHERING : congregación *f*, fieles *mpl* (a un servicio religioso) **2** PARISHIONERS : feligreses *mpl*

congress [ˈkɑŋgrəs] *n* : congreso *m*

congressional [kənˈgrɛʃənəl, kɑn-] *adj* : del congreso

congressman [ˈkɑŋgrəsmən] *n, pl* **-men** [-mən, -ˌmɛn] : congresista *m*, diputado *m*

congresswoman [ˈkɑŋgrəsˌwʊmən] *n, pl* **-women** [-ˌwɪmən] : congresista *f*, diputada *f*
congruence [kənˈgruːənts, ˈkɑŋgrʊənts] *n* : congruencia *f*
congruent [kənˈgruːənt, ˈkɑŋgrʊənt] *adj* : congruente
conic [ˈkɑnɪk] → **conical**
conical [ˈkɑnɪkəl] *adj* : cónico
conifer [ˈkɑnəfər, ˈkoː-] *n* : conífera *f*
coniferous [koːˈnɪfərəs, kə-] *adj* : conífero
conjecture¹ [kənˈʤɛkʧər] *v* **-tured; -turing** : conjeturar
conjecture² *n* : conjetura *f*, presunción *f*
conjugal [ˈkɑnʤɪgəl, kənˈʤuː-] *adj* : conyugal
conjugate [ˈkɑnʤəˌgeɪt] *vt* **-gated; -gating** : conjugar
conjugation [ˌkɑnʤəˈgeɪʃən] *n* : conjugación *f*
conjunction [kənˈʤʌŋkʃən] *n* : conjunción *f* ⟨in conjunction with : en combinación con⟩
conjure [ˈkɑnʤər, ˈkʌn-] *v* **-jured; -juring** *vt* **1** ENTREAT : rogar, suplicar **2 to conjure up** : hacer aparecer (apariciones), evocar (memorias, etc.) — *vi* : practicar la magia
conjurer *or* **conjuror** [ˈkɑnʤərər, ˈkʌn-] *n* : mago *m*, -ga *f*; prestidigitador *m*, -dora *f*
connect [kəˈnɛkt] *vi* : conectar, enlazar, empalmar, comunicarse — *vt* **1** JOIN, LINK : conectar, unir, juntar, vincular **2** RELATE : relacionar, asociar (ideas)
connection [kənˈnɛkʃən] *n* : conexión *f*, enlace *m* ⟨professional connections : relaciones profesionales⟩
connective [kəˈnɛktɪv] *adj* : conectivo, conjuntivo ⟨connective tissue : tejido conjuntivo⟩
connector [kəˈnɛktər] *n* : conector *m*
connivance [kəˈnaɪvənts] *n* : connivencia *f*, complicidad *f*
connive [kəˈnaɪv] *vi* **-nived; -niving** CONSPIRE, PLOT : actuar en connivencia, confabularse, conspirar
connoisseur [ˌkɑnəˈsər, -ˈsʊr] *n* : conocedor *m*, -dora *f*; entendido *m*, -da *f*
connotation [ˌkɑnəˈteɪʃən] *n* : connotación *f*
connote [kəˈnoːt] *vt* **-noted; -noting** : connotar
conquer [ˈkɑŋkər] *vt* : conquistar, vencer
conqueror [ˈkɑŋkərər] *n* : conquistador *m*, -dora *f*
conquest [ˈkɑnˌkwɛst, ˈkɑŋ-] *n* : conquista *f*
conscience [ˈkɑnʧənts] *n* : conciencia *f*, consciencia *f* ⟨to have a clear conscience : tener la conciencia limpia⟩
conscientious [ˌkɑnʧiˈɛnʧəs] *adj* : concienzudo — **conscientiously** *adv*
conscious [ˈkɑnʧəs] *adj* **1** AWARE : consciente ⟨to become conscious of : darse cuenta de⟩ **2** ALERT, AWAKE : consciente **3** INTENTIONAL : intencional, deliberado
consciously [ˈkɑnʧəsli] *adv* INTENTIONALLY : intencionalmente, deliberadamente, a propósito
consciousness [ˈkɑnʧəsnəs] *n* **1** AWARENESS : conciencia *f*, consciencia *f* **2** : conocimiento *m* ⟨to lose consciousness : perder el conocimiento⟩
conscript¹ [kənˈskrɪpt] *vt* : reclutar, alistar, enrolar
conscript² [ˈkɑnˌskrɪpt] *n* : conscripto *m*, -ta *f*; recluta *mf*
consecrate [ˈkɑntsəˌkreɪt] *vt* **-crated; -crating** : consagrar
consecration [ˌkɑntsəˈkreɪʃən] *n* : consagración *f*, dedicación *f*
consecutive [kənˈsɛkjət̬ɪv] *adj* : consecutivo, seguido ⟨on five consecutive days : cinco días seguidos⟩
consecutively [kənˈsɛkjət̬ivli] *adv* : consecutivamente
consensus [kənˈsɛntsəs] *n* : consenso *m*
consent¹ [kənˈsɛnt] *vi* **1** AGREE : acceder, ponerse de acuerdo **2 to consent to do something** : consentir en hacer algo
consent² *n* : consentimiento *m*, permiso *m* ⟨by common consent : de común acuerdo⟩
consequence [ˈkɑntsəˌkwɛnts, -kwənts] *n* **1** RESULT : consecuencia *f*, secuela *f* **2** IMPORTANCE : importancia *f*, trascendencia *f*
consequent [ˈkɑntsəkwənt, -ˌkwɛnt] *adj* : consiguiente
consequential [ˌkɑntsəˈkwɛnʧəl] *adj* **1** CONSEQUENT : consiguiente **2** IMPORTANT : importante, trascendente, trascendental
consequently [ˈkɑntsəkwəntli, -ˌkwɛnt-] *adv* : por consiguiente, por ende, por lo tanto
conservation [ˌkɑntsərˈveɪʃən] *n* : conservación *f*, protección *f*
conservationist [ˌkɑntsərˈveɪʃənɪst] *n* : conservacionista *mf*
conservatism [kənˈsərvəˌtɪzəm] *n* : conservadurismo *m*
conservative¹ [kənˈsərvət̬ɪv] *adj* **1** : conservador **2** CAUTIOUS : moderado, cauteloso ⟨a conservative estimate : un cálculo moderado⟩
conservative² *n* : conservador *m*, -dora *f*
conservatory [kənˈsərvəˌtori] *n, pl* **-ries** : conservatorio *m*
conserve¹ [kənˈsərv] *vt* **-served; -serving** : conservar, preservar
conserve² [ˈkɑnˌsərv] *n* PRESERVES : confitura *f*
consider [kənˈsɪdər] *vt* **1** CONTEMPLATE : considerar, pensar en ⟨we'd considered attending : habíamos pensado en asistir⟩ **2** : considerar, tener en cuenta ⟨consider the consequences : considera las consecuencias⟩ **3** JUDGE, REGARD : considerar, estimar

considerable [kən'sɪdərəbəl] *adj* : considerable — **considerably** [-bli] *adv*
considerate [kən'sɪdərət] *adj* : considerado, atento
consideration [kən,sɪdə'reɪʃən] *n* : consideración *f* ⟨to take into consideration : tener en cuenta⟩
considering [kən'sɪdərɪŋ] *prep* : teniendo en cuenta, visto
consign [kən'saɪn] *vt* **1** COMMIT, ENTRUST : confiar, encomendar **2** TRANSFER : consignar, transferir **3** SEND : consignar, enviar (mercancía)
consignment [kən'saɪnmənt] *n* **1** : envío *m*, remesa *f* **2 on ~** : en consignación
consist [kən'sɪst] *vi* **1** LIE : consistir ⟨success consists in hard work : el éxito consiste en trabajar duro⟩ **2** : constar, componerse ⟨the set consists of 5 pieces : el juego se compone de 5 piezas⟩
consistency [kən'sɪstəntsi] *n, pl* **-cies 1** : consistencia *f* (de una mezcla o sustancia) **2** COHERENCE : coherencia *f* **3** UNIFORMITY : regularidad *f*, uniformidad *f*
consistent [kən'sɪstənt] *adj* **1** COMPATIBLE : compatible, coincidente ⟨consistent with policy : coincidente con la política⟩ **2** UNIFORM : uniforme, constante, regular — **consistently** [kən'sɪstəntli] *adv*
consolation [,kantsə'leɪʃə n] *n* **1** : consuelo *m* **2 consolation prize** : premio *m* de consolación
console[1] [kən'so:l] *vt* **-soled; -soling** : consolar
console[2] ['kan,so:l] *n* : consola *f*
consolidate [kən'salə,deɪt] *vt* **-dated; -dating** : consolidar, unir
consolidation [kən,salə'deɪʃən] *n* : consolidación *f*
consommé [,kantsə'meɪ] *n* : consomé *m*
consonant ['kantsənənt] *n* : consonante *m*
consort[1] [kən'sɔrt] *vi* : asociarse, relacionarse, tener trato ⟨to consort with criminals : tener trato con criminales⟩
consort[2] ['kan,sɔrt] *n* : consorte *mf*
consortium [kən'sɔrʃəm] *n, pl* **-tia** [-ʃə] *or* **-tiums** [-ʃəmz] : consorcio *m*
conspicuous [kən'spɪkjʊəs] *adj* **1** OBVIOUS : visible, evidente **2** STRIKING : llamativo
conspicuously [kən'spɪkjʊəsli] *adv* : de manera llamativa
conspiracy [kən'spɪrəsi] *n, pl* **-cies** : conspiración *f*, complot *m*, confabulación *f*
conspirator [kən'spɪrət̬ər] *n* : conspirador *m*, -dora *f*
conspire [kən'spaɪr] *vi* **-spired; -spiring** : conspirar, confabularse
constable ['kantstəbəl, 'kʌntstə-] *n* : agente *mf* de policía (en un pueblo)
constancy ['kantstəntsi] *n, pl* **-cies** : constancia *f*
constant[1] ['kantstənt] *adj* **1** FAITHFUL : leal, fiel **2** INVARIABLE : constante, invariable **3** CONTINUAL : constante, continuo
constant[2] *n* : constante *f*
constantly ['kantstəntli] *adv* : constantemente, continuamente
constellation [,kantstə'leɪʃən] *n* : constelación *f*
consternation [,kantstər'neɪʃən] *n* : consternación *f*
constipate ['kantstə,peɪt] *vt* **-pated; -pating** : estreñir
constipation ['kantstə'peɪʃən] *n* : estreñimiento *m*, constipación *f* (de vientre)
constituency [kən'stɪtʃʊəntsi] *n, pl* **-cies 1** : distrito *m* electoral **2** : residentes *mpl* de un distrito electoral
constituent[1] [kən'stɪtʃʊənt] *adj* **1** COMPONENT : constituyente, componente **2** : constituyente, constitutivo ⟨a constituent assembly : una asamblea constituyente⟩
constituent[2] *n* **1** COMPONENT : componente *m* **2** ELECTOR, VOTER : elector *m*, -tora *f*; votante *mf*
constitute ['kantstə,tu:t, -,tju:t] *vt* **-tuted; -tuting 1** ESTABLISH : constituir, establecer **2** COMPOSE, FORM : constituir, componer
constitution [,kantstə'tu:ʃən, -'tju:-] *n* : constitución *f*
constitutional [,kantstə'tu:ʃənəl, -'tju:-] *adj* : constitucional
constitutionality [,kantstə,tu:ʃə'næləṭi, -,tju:-] *n* : constitucionalidad *f*
constrain [kən'streɪn] *vt* **1** COMPEL : constreñir, obligar **2** CONFINE : constreñir, limitar, restringir **3** RESTRAIN : contener, refrenar
constraint [kən'streɪnt] *n* : restricción *f*, limitación *f*
constrict [kən'strɪkt] *vt* : estrechar, apretar, comprimir
constriction [kən'strɪkʃən] *n* : estrechamiento *m*, compresión *f*
construct [kən'strʌkt] *vt* : construir
construction [kən'strʌkʃən] *n* : construcción *f*
constructive [kən'strʌktɪv] *adj* : constructivo
construe [kən'stru:] *vt* **-strued; -struing** : interpretar
consul ['kantsəl] *n* : cónsul *mf*
consular ['kantsələr] *adj* : consular
consulate ['kantsələt] *n* : consulado *m*
consult [kən'sʌlt] *vt* : consultar — *vi* **to consult with** : consultar con, solicitar la opinión de
consultant [kən'sʌltənt] *n* : consultor *m*, -tora *f*; asesor *m*, -sora *f*
consultation [,kantsəl'teɪʃən] *n* : consulta *f*
consumable [kən'su:məbəl] *adj* : consumible
consume [kən'su:m] *vt* **-sumed; -suming** : consumir, usar, gastar

consumer [kən'su:mər] *n* : consumidor *m*, -dora *f*

consummate[1] ['kɑntsə,meɪt] *vt* **-mated; -mating** : consumar

consummate[2] [kən'sʌmət, 'kɑntsə-mət] *adj* : consumado, perfecto

consummation [,kɑntsə'meɪʃən] *n* : consumación *f*

consumption [kən'sʌmpʃən] *n* **1** USE : consumo *m*, uso *m* ⟨consumption of electricity : consumo de electricidad⟩ **2** TUBERCULOSIS : tisis *f*, consunción *f*

contact[1] ['kɑn,tækt, kən'-] *vt* : ponerse en contacto con, contactar (con)

contact[2] ['kɑn,tækt] *n* **1** TOUCHING : contacto *m* ⟨to come into contact with : entrar en contacto con⟩ **2** TOUCH : contacto *m*, comunicación *f* ⟨to lose contact with : perder contacto con⟩ **3** CONNECTION : contacto *m* (en negocios) **4** → **contact lens**

contact lens ['kɑn,tækt'lɛnz] *n* : lente *mf* de contacto, pupilente *m Mex*

contagion [kən'teɪdʒən] *n* : contagio *m*

contagious [kən'teɪdʒəs] *adj* : contagioso

contain [kən'teɪn] *vt* **1** : contener **2 to contain oneself** : contenerse

container [kən'teɪnər] *n* : recipiente *m*, envase *m*

containment [kən'teɪnmənt] *n* : contención *f*

contaminant [kən'tæmənənt] *n* : contaminante *m*

contaminate [kən'tæmə,neɪt] *vt* **-nated; -nating** : contaminar

contamination [kən,tæmə'neɪʃən] *n* : contaminación *f*

contemplate ['kɑntəm,pleɪt] *v* **-plated; -plating** *vt* **1** VIEW : contemplar **2** PONDER : contemplar, considerar **3** CONSIDER, PROPOSE : proponerse, proyectar, pensar en ⟨to contemplate a trip : pensar en viajar⟩ — *vi* MEDITATE : meditar

contemplation [,kɑntəm'pleɪʃən] *n* : contemplación *f*

contemplative [kən'tɛmplət̬ɪv, 'kɑntəm,pleɪt̬ɪv] *adj* : contemplativo

contemporaneous [kən,tɛmpə'reɪniəs] *adj* → **contemporary**[1]

contemporary[1] [kən'tɛmpə,rɛri] *adj* : contemporáneo

contemporary[2] *n, pl* **-raries** : contemporáneo *m*, -nea *f*

contempt [kən'tɛmpt] *n* **1** DISDAIN : desprecio *m*, desdén *m* ⟨to hold in contempt : despreciar⟩ **2** : desacato *m* (ante un tribunal)

contemptible [kən'tɛmptəbəl] *adj* : despreciable, vil

contemptuous [kən'tɛmptʃʊəs] *adj* : despectivo, despreciativo, desdeñoso

contemptuously [kən'tɛmptʃʊəsli] *adv* : despectivamente, con desprecio

contend [kən'tɛnd] *vi* **1** STRUGGLE : luchar, lidiar, contender ⟨to contend with a problem : lidiar con un problema⟩ **2** COMPETE : competir ⟨to contend for a position : competir por un puesto⟩ — *vt* **1** ARGUE, MAINTAIN : argüir, sostener, afirmar ⟨he contended that he was right : afirmó que tenía razón⟩ **2** CONTEST : protestar contra (una decisión, etc.), disputar

contender [kən'tɛndər] *n* : contendiente *mf*; aspirante *mf*; competidor *m*, -dora *f*

content[1] [kən'tɛnt] *vt* SATISFY : contentar, satisfacer

content[2] *adj* : conforme, contento, satisfecho

content[3] *n* CONTENTMENT : contento *m*, satisfacción *f* ⟨to one's heart's content : hasta quedar satisfecho, a más no poder⟩

content[4] ['kɑn,tɛnt] *n* **1** MEANING : contenido *m*, significado *m* **2** PROPORTION : contenido *m*, proporción *f* ⟨fat content : contenido de grasa⟩ **3 contents** *npl* : contenido *m*, sumario *m* (de un libro) ⟨table of contents : índice de materias⟩

contented [kən'tɛntəd] *adj* : conforme, satisfecho ⟨a contented smile : una sonrisa de satisfacción⟩

contentedly [kən'tɛntədli] *adv* : con satisfacción

contention [kən'tɛntʃən] *n* **1** DISPUTE : disputa *f*, discusión *f* **2** COMPETITION : competencia *f*, contienda *f* **3** OPINION : argumento *m*, opinión *f*

contentious [kən'tɛntʃəs] *adj* : disputador, pugnaz, combativo

contentment [kən'tɛntmənt] *n* : satisfacción *f*, contento *m*

contest[1] [kən'tɛst] *vt* : disputar, cuestionar, impugnar ⟨to contest a will : impugnar un testamento⟩

contest[2] ['kɑn,tɛst] *n* **1** STRUGGLE : lucha *f*, contienda *f* **2** GAME : concurso *m*, competencia *f*

contestable [kən'tɛstəbəl] *adj* : discutible, cuestionable

contestant [kən'tɛstənt] *n* : concursante *mf*; competidor *m*, -dora *f*

context ['kɑn,tɛkst] *n* : contexto *m*

contiguous [kən'tɪgjʊəs] *adj* : contiguo

continence ['kɑntənənts] *n* : continencia *f*

continent[1] ['kɑntənənt] *adj* : continente

continent[2] *n* : continente *m* — **continental** [,kɑntən'ɛntəl] *adj*

contingency [kən'tɪndʒəntsi] *n, pl* **-cies** : contingencia *f*, eventualidad *f*

contingent[1] [kən'tɪndʒənt] *adj* **1** POSSIBLE : contingente, eventual **2** ACCIDENTAL : fortuito, accidental **3 to be contingent on** : depender de, estar sujeto a

contingent[2] *n* : contingente *m*

continual [kən'tɪnjʊəl] *adj* : continuo, constante — **continually** [kən-'tɪnjʊəli, -'tɪnjəli] *adv*

continuance [kən'tɪnjʊənts] *n* **1** CONTINUATION : continuación *f* **2** DURA-

TION : duración *f* **3** : aplazamiento *m* (de un proceso)

continuation [kən,tɪnjʊ'eɪʃən] *n* : continuación *f*, prolongación *f*

continue [kən'tɪnju:] *v* **-tinued; -tinuing** *vi* **1** CARRY ON : continuar, seguir, proseguir ⟨please continue : continúe, por favor⟩ **2** ENDURE, LAST : continuar, prolongarse, durar **3** RESUME : continuar, reanudarse — *vt* **1** : continuar, seguir ⟨she continued writing : continuó escribiendo⟩ **2** RESUME : continuar, reanudar **3** EXTEND, PROLONG : continuar, prolongar

continuity [,kantə-'nu:əṭi, -'nju:-] *n, pl* **-ties** : continuidad *f*

continuous [kən'tɪnjʊəs] *adj* : continuo — **continuously** *adv*

contort [kən'tɔrt] *vt* : torcer, retorcer, contraer (el rostro) — *vi* : contraerse, demudarse

contortion [kən'tɔrʃən] *n* : contorsión *f*

contour ['kan,tʊr] *n* **1** OUTLINE : contorno *m* **2 contours** *npl* SHAPE : forma *f*, curvas *fpl* **3 contour map** : mapa *m* topográfico

contraband ['kantrə,bænd] *n* : contrabando *m*

contraception [,kantrə'sɛpʃən] *n* : anticoncepción *f*, contracepción *f*

contraceptive[1] [,kantrə'sɛptɪv] *adj* : anticonceptivo, contraceptivo

contraceptive[2] *n* : anticonceptivo *m*, contraceptivo *m*

contract[1] [kən'trækt, 1 *usu* 'kan-,trækt] *vt* **1** : contratar (servicios profesionales) **2** : contraer (una enfermedad, una deuda) **3** TIGHTEN : contraer (un músculo) **4** SHORTEN : contraer (una palabra) — *vi* : contraerse, reducirse

contract[2] ['kan,trækt] *n* : contrato *m*

contraction [kən'trækʃən] *n* : contracción *f*

contractor ['kan,træktər, kən'træk-] *n* : contratista *mf*

contractual [kən'træktʃʊəl] *adj* : contractual — **contractually** *adv*

contradict [,kantrə'dɪkt] *vt* : contradecir, desmentir

contradiction [,kantrə'dɪkʃən] *n* : contradicción *f*

contradictory [,kantrə'dɪktəri] *adj* : contradictorio

contralto [kən'træl,to:] *n, pl* **-tos** : contralto *m* (voz), contralto *mf* (vocalista)

contraption [kən'træpʃən] *n* DEVICE : aparato *m*, artefacto *m*

contrary[1] ['kan,trɛri, *2 often* kən-'trɛri] *adj* **1** OPPOSITE : contrario, opuesto **2** BALKY, STUBBORN : terco, testarudo **3 contrary to** : al contrario de, en contra de ⟨contrary to the facts : en contra de los hechos⟩

contrary[2] ['kan,trɛri] *n, pl* **-traries** **1** OPPOSITE : lo contrario, lo opuesto **2 on the contrary** : al contrario, todo lo contrario

contrast[1] [kən'træst] *vi* DIFFER : contrastar, diferir — *vt* COMPARE : contrastar, comparar

contrast[2] ['kan,træst] *n* : contraste *m*

contravene [,kantrə'vi:n] *vt* **-vened; -vening** : contravenir, infringir

contribute [kən'trɪbjət] *v* **-uted; -uting** *vt* : contribuir, aportar (dinero, bienes, etc.) — *vi* : contribuir

contribution [,kantrə'bju:ʃən] *n* : contribución *f*

contributor [kən'trɪbjəṭər] *n* : contribuidor *m*, -dora *f*; colaborador *m*, -dora *f* (en periodismo)

contrite ['kan,traɪt, kən'traɪt] *adj* REPENTANT : contrito, arrepentido

contrition [kən'trɪʃən] *n* : contrición *f*, arrepentimiento *m*

contrivance [kən'traɪvənts] *n* **1** DEVICE : aparato *m*, artefacto *m* **2** SCHEME : artimaña *f*, treta *f*, ardid *m*

contrive [kən'traɪv] *vt* **-trived; -triving** **1** DEVISE : idear, ingeniar, maquinar **2** MANAGE : lograr, ingeniárselas para ⟨she contrived a way out of the mess : se las ingenió para salir del enredo⟩

control[1] [kən'tro:l] *vt* **-trolled; -trolling** : controlar, dominar

control[2] *n* **1** : control *m*, dominio *m*, mando *m* ⟨to be under control : estar bajo control⟩ **2** RESTRAINT : control *m*, limitación *f* ⟨birth control : control natal⟩ **3** : control *m*, dispositivo *m* de mando ⟨remote control : control remoto⟩

controllable [kən'tro:ləbəl] *adj* : controlable

controller [kən'tro:lər, 'kan,-] *n* **1** → **comptroller** **2** : controlador *m*, -dora *f* ⟨air traffic controller : controlador aéreo⟩

controversial [,kantrə'vərʃəl, -siəl] *adj* : controvertido ⟨a controversial decision : una decisión controvertida⟩

controversy ['kantrə,vərsi] *n, pl* **-sies** : controversia *f*

controvert ['kantrə,vərt, ,kantrə'-] *vt* : controvertir, contradecir

contusion [kən'tu:ʒən, -tju:-] *n* BRUISE : contusión *f*, moretón *m*

conundrum [kə'nʌndrəm] *n* RIDDLE : acertijo *m*, adivinanza *f*

convalesce [,kanvə'lɛs] *vi* **-lesced; -lescing** : convalecer

convalescence [,kanvə'lɛsənts] *n* : convalecencia *f*

convalescent[1] [,kanvə'lɛsənt] *adj* : convaleciente

convalescent[2] *n* : convaleciente *mf*

convection [kən'vɛkʃən] *n* : convección *f*

convene [kən'vi:n] *v* **-vened; -vening** *vt* : convocar — *vi* : reunirse

convenience [kən'vi:njənts] *n* **1** : conveniencia *f* ⟨at your convenience : cuando le resulte conveniente⟩ **2** AMENITY : comodidad *f* ⟨modern conveniences : comodidades modernas⟩

convenience store *n* : tienda *f* de conveniencia

convenient [kən'vi:njənt] *adj* : conveniente, cómodo — **conveniently** *adv*

convent ['kɑnvənt, -ˌvɛnt] *n* : convento *m*

convention [kən'vɛnʧən] *n* **1** PACT : convención *f*, convenio *m*, pacto *m* ⟨the Geneva Convention : la Convención de Ginebra⟩ **2** MEETING : convención *f*, congreso *m* **3** CUSTOM : convención *f*, convencionalismo *m*

conventional [kən'vɛnʧənəl] *adj* : convencional — **conventionally** *adv*

converge [kən'vərʤ] *vi* **-verged; -verging** : converger, convergir

convergence [kən'vərʤənts] *n* : convergencia *f*

convergent [kən'vərʤənt] *adj* : convergente

conversant [kən'vərsənt] *adj* **conversant with** : versado con, experto en

conversation [ˌkɑnvər'seɪʃən] *n* : conversación *f*

conversational [ˌkɑnvər'seɪʃənəl] *adj* : familiar ⟨a conversational style : un estilo familiar⟩

converse[1] [kən'vərs] *vi* **-versed; -versing** : conversar

converse[2] [kən'vərs, 'kɑnˌvərs] *adj* : contrario, opuesto, inverso

conversely [kən'vərsli, 'kɑnˌvərs-] *adv* : a la inversa

conversion [kən'vərʒən] *n* **1** CHANGE : conversión *f*, transformación *f*, cambio *m* **2** : conversión *f* (a una religión)

convert[1] [kən'vərt] *vt* **1** : convertir (a una religión o un partido) **2** CHANGE : convertir, cambiar — *vi* : convertirse

convert[2] ['kɑnˌvərt] *n* : converso *m*, -sa *f*

converter *or* **convertor** [kən'vərt̬ər] *n* : convertidor *m*

convertible[1] [kən'vərt̬əbəl] *adj* : convertible

convertible[2] *n* : convertible *m*, descapotable *m*

convex [kɑn'vɛks, 'kɑnˌ-, kən'-] *adj* : convexo

convey [kən'veɪ] *vt* **1** TRANSPORT : transportar, conducir **2** TRANSMIT : transmitir, comunicar, expresar (noticias, ideas, etc.)

conveyance [kən'veɪənts] *n* **1** TRANSPORT : transporte *m*, transportación *f* **2** COMMUNICATION : transmisión *f*, comunicación *f* **3** TRANSFER : transferencia *f*, traspaso *m* (de una propiedad)

conveyor [kən'veɪər] *n* : transportador *m*, -dora *f* ⟨conveyor belt : cinta transportadora⟩

convict[1] [kən'vɪkt] *vt* : declarar culpable

convict[2] ['kɑnˌvɪkt] *n* : preso *m*, -sa *f*; presidiario *m*, -ria *f*; recluso *m*, -sa *f*

conviction [kən'vɪkʃən] *n* **1** : condena *f* (de un acusado) **2** BELIEF : convicción *f*, creencia *f*

convince [kən'vɪnts] *vt* **-vinced; -vincing** : convencer

convincing [kən'vɪntsɪŋ] *adj* : convincente, persuasivo

convincingly [kən'vɪntsɪŋli] *adv* : de forma convincente

convivial [kən'vɪvjəl, -'vɪviəl] *adj* : jovial, festivo, alegre

conviviality [kənˌvɪvi'æləṯi] *n, pl* **-ties** : jovialidad *f*

convoke [kən'vo:k] *vt* **-voked; -voking** : convocar

convoluted ['kɑnvəˌlu:t̬əd] *adj* : intrincado, complicado

convoy ['kɑnˌvɔɪ] *n* : convoy *m*

convulse [kən'vʌls] *v* **-vulsed; -vulsing** *vt* : convulsionar ⟨convulsed with laughter : muerto de risa⟩ — *vi* : sufrir convulsiones

convulsion [kən'vʌlʃən] *n* : convulsión *f*

convulsive [kən'vʌlsɪv] *adj* : convulsivo — **convulsively** *adv*

coo[1] ['ku:] *vi* : arrullar

coo[2] *n* : arrullo *m* (de una paloma)

cook[1] ['kʊk] *vi* : cocinar — *vt* **1** : preparar (comida) **2 to cook up** CONCOCT : inventar, tramar

cook[2] *n* : cocinero *m*, -ra *f*

cookbook ['kʊkˌbʊk] *n* : libro *m* de cocina

cookery ['kʊkəri] *n, pl* **-eries** : cocina *f*

cookie *or* **cooky** ['kʊki] *n, pl* **-ies** : galleta *f* (dulce)

cooking ['kʊkɪŋ] *n* **1** COOKERY : cocina *f* **2** : cocción *f*, cocimiento *m* ⟨cooking time : tiempo de cocción⟩

cookout ['kʊkˌaʊt] *n* : comida *f* al aire libre

cool[1] ['ku:l] *vt* : refrescar, enfriar — *vi* **1** : refrescarse, enfriarse ⟨the pie is cooling : el pastel se está enfriando⟩ **2** : calmarse, tranquilizarse ⟨his anger cooled : su ira se calmó⟩

cool[2] *adj* **1** : fresco, frío ⟨cool weather : tiempo fresco⟩ **2** CALM : tranquilo, sereno **3** ALOOF : frío, distante

cool[3] *n* **1** : fresco *m* ⟨the cool of the evening : el fresco de la tarde⟩ **2** COMPOSURE : calma *f*, serenidad *f*

coolant ['ku:lənt] *n* : refrigerante *m*

cooler ['ku:lər] *n* : nevera *f* portátil

coolie ['ku:li] *n* : culi *m*

coolly ['ku:lli] *adv* **1** CALMLY : con calma, tranquilamente **2** COLDLY : fríamente, con frialdad

coolness ['ku:lnəs] *n* **1** : frescura *f*, frescor *m* ⟨the coolness of the evening : el frescor de la noche⟩ **2** CALMNESS : tranquilidad *f*, serenidad *f* **3** COLDNESS, INDIFFERENCE : frialdad *f*, indiferencia

coop[1] ['ku:p, 'kʊp] *vt or* **to coop up** : encerrar ⟨cooped up in the house : encerrado en la casa⟩

coop[2] *n* : gallinero *m*

co–op ['ko:ˌɑp] *n* → **cooperative[2]**

cooperate [ko'ɑpəˌreɪt] *vi* **-ated; -ating** : cooperar, colaborar

cooperation [ko,ɑpə'reɪʃən] *n* : cooperación *f*, colaboración *f*
cooperative[1] [ko'ɑpərəṯɪv, -'ɑpə,reɪṯɪv] *adj* : cooperativo
cooperative[2] [ko'ɑpərəṯɪv] *n* : cooperativa *f*
co–opt [ko'ɑpt] *vt* **1** : nombrar como miembro, cooptar **2** APPROPRIATE : apropiarse de
coordinate[1] [ko'ɔrdən,eɪt] *v* **-nated; -nating** *vt* : coordinar — *vi* : coordinarse, combinar, acordar
coordinate[2] [ko'ɔrdənət] *adj* **1** COORDINATED : coordinado **2** EQUAL : igual, semejante
coordinate[3] [ko'ɔrdənət] *n* : coordenada *f*
coordination [ko,ɔrdən'eɪʃən] *n* : coordinación *f*
coordinator [ko'ɔrdən,eɪṯər] *n* : coordinador *m*, -dora *f*
cop ['kɑp] → **police officer**
cope ['ko:p] *vi* **coped; coping 1** : arreglárselas **2 to cope with** : hacer frente a, poder con ⟨I can't cope with all this! : ¡no puedo con todo esto!⟩
copier ['kɑpiər] *n* : copiadora *f*, fotocopiadora *f*
copilot ['ko:,paɪlət] *n* : copiloto *m*
copious ['ko:piəs] *adj* : copioso, abundante — **copiously** *adv*
copiousness ['ko:piəsnəs] *n* : abundancia *f*
copper ['kɑpər] *n* : cobre *m*
coppery ['kɑpəri] *adj* : cobrizo
copra ['ko:prə, 'kɑ-] *n* : copra *f*
copse ['kɑps] *n* THICKET : soto *m*, matorral *m*
copulate ['kɑpjə,leɪt] *vi* **-lated; -lating** : copular
copulation [,kɑpjə'leɪʃən] *n* : cópula *f*, relaciones *fpl* sexuales
copy[1] ['kɑpi] *vt* **copied; copying 1** DUPLICATE : hacer una copia de, duplicar, reproducir **2** IMITATE : copiar, imitar
copy[2] *n, pl* **copies 1** : copia *f*, duplicado *m* (de un documento), reproducción *f* (de una obra de arte) **2** : ejemplar *m* (de un libro), número *m* (de una revista) **3** TEXT : manuscrito *m*, texto *m*
copyright[1] ['kɑpi,raɪt] *vt* : registrar los derechos de
copyright[2] *n* : derechos *mpl* de autor
coral[1] ['kɔrəl] *adj* : de coral ⟨a coral reef : un arrecife de coral⟩
coral[2] *n* : coral *m*
coral snake *n* : serpiente *f* de coral
cord ['kɔrd] *n* **1** ROPE, STRING : cuerda *f*, cordón *m*, cordel *m* **2** : cuerda *f*, cordón *m*, médula *f* (en la anatomía) ⟨vocal cords : cuerdas vocales⟩ **3** : cuerda *f* ⟨a cord of firewood : una cuerda de leña⟩ **4** *or* **electric cord** : cable *m* eléctrico
cordial[1] ['kɔrdʒəl] *adj* : cordial — **cordially** *adv*
cordial[2] *n* : cordial *m*
cordiality [,kɔrdʒi'æləṯi] *n* : cordialidad *f*
cordless ['kɔrdləs] *adj* : inalámbrico
cordon[1] ['kɔrdən] *vt* **to cordon off** : acordonar
cordon[2] *n* : cordón *m*
corduroy ['kɔrdə,rɔɪ] *n* **1** : pana *f* **2 corduroys** *npl* : pantalones *mpl* de pana
core[1] ['kor] *vt* **cored; coring** : quitar el corazón a (una fruta)
core[2] *n* **1** : corazón *m*, centro *m* (de algunas frutas) **2** CENTER : núcleo *m*, centro *m* **3** ESSENCE : núcleo *m*, meollo *m* ⟨to the core : hasta la médula⟩
coriander ['kori,ændər] *n* : cilantro *m*
cork[1] ['kɔrk] *vt* : ponerle un corcho a
cork[2] *n* : corcho *m*
corkscrew ['kɔrk,skru:] *n* : tirabuzón *m*, sacacorchos *m*
cormorant ['kɔrmərənt, -,rænt] *n* : cormorán *m*
corn[1] ['kɔrn] *vt* : conservar en salmuera ⟨corned beef : carne en conserva⟩
corn[2] *n* **1** GRAIN : grano *m* **2** : maíz *m*, elote *m Mex* ⟨corn tortillas : tortillas de maíz⟩ **3** : callo *m* ⟨corn plaster : emplasto para callos⟩
corncob ['kɔrn,kɑb] *n* : mazorca *f* (de maíz), choclo *m*, elote *m CA, Mex*
cornea ['kɔrniə] *n* : córnea *f*
corner[1] ['kɔrnər] *vt* **1** TRAP : acorralar, arrinconar **2** MONOPOLIZE : monopolizar, acaparar (un mercado) — *vi* : tomar una curva, doblar una esquina (en un automóvil)
corner[2] *n* **1** ANGLE : rincón *m*, esquina *f*, ángulo *m* ⟨the corner of a room : el rincón de una sala⟩ ⟨all corners of the world : todos los rincones del mundo⟩ ⟨to cut corners : atajar, economizar esfuerzos⟩ **2** INTERSECTION : esquina *f* **3** IMPASSE, PREDICAMENT : aprieto *m*, impasse *m* ⟨to be backed into a corner : estar acorralado⟩
cornerstone ['kɔrnər,sto:n] *n* : piedra *f* angular
cornet [kɔr'nɛt] *n* : corneta *f*
cornfield ['kɔrn,fi:ld] *n* : maizal *m*; milpa *f CA, Mex*
cornice ['kɔrnɪs] *n* : cornisa *f*
cornmeal ['kɔrn,mi:l] *n* : harina *f* de maíz
cornstalk ['kɔrn,stɔk] *n* : tallo *m* del maíz
cornstarch ['kɔrn,stɑrtʃ] *n* : maicena *f*, almidón *m* de maíz
cornucopia [,kɔrnə'ko:piə, -njə-] *n* : cornucopia *f*
corolla [kə'rɑlə] *n* : corola *f*
corollary ['kɔrə,lɛri] *n, pl* **-laries** : corolario *m*
corona [kə'ro:nə] *n* : corona *f* (del sol)
coronary[1] ['kɔrə,nɛri] *adj* : coronario
coronary[2] *n, pl* **-naries 1** : trombosis *f* coronaria **2** HEART ATTACK : infarto *m*, ataque *m* al corazón
coronation [,kɔrə'neɪʃən] *n* : coronación *f*

coroner [ˈkɔrənər] *n* : médico *m* forense

corporal[1] [ˈkɔrpərəl] *adj* : corporal ⟨corporal punishment : castigos corporales⟩

corporal[2] *n* : cabo *m*

corporate [ˈkɔrpərət] *adj* : corporativo, empresarial

corporation [ˌkɔrpəˈreɪʃən] *n* : sociedad *f* anónima, corporación *f*, empresa *f*

corporeal [kɔrˈporiəl] *adj* **1** PHYSICAL : corpóreo **2** MATERIAL : material, tangible — **corporeally** *adv*

corps [ˈkor] *n, pl* **corps** [ˈkorz] : cuerpo *m* ⟨medical corps : cuerpo médico⟩ ⟨diplomatic corps : cuerpo diplomático⟩

corpse [ˈkɔrps] *n* : cadáver *m*

corpulence [ˈkɔrpjələnts] *n* : obesidad *f*, gordura *f*

corpulent [ˈkɔrpjələnt] *adj* : obeso, gordo

corpuscle [ˈkɔrˌpʌsəl] *n* : corpúsculo *m*, glóbulo *m* (sanguíneo)

corral[1] [kəˈræl] *vt* **-ralled; -ralling** : acorralar, encorralar (ganado)

corral[2] *n* : corral *m*

correct[1] [kəˈrɛkt] *vt* **1** RECTIFY : corregir, rectificar **2** REPRIMAND : corregir, reprender

correct[2] *adj* **1** ACCURATE, RIGHT : correcto, exacto ⟨to be correct : estar en lo cierto⟩ **2** PROPER : correcto, apropiado

correction [kəˈrɛkʃən] *n* : corrección *f*

corrective [kəˈrɛktɪv] *adj* : correctivo

correctly [kəˈrɛktli] *adv* : correctamente

correctness [kəˈrɛk(t)nəs] *n* **1** ACCURACY : exactitud *f* **2** PROPRIETY : corrección *f*

correlate [ˈkɔrəˌleɪt] *vt* **-lated; -lating** : relacionar, poner en correlación

correlation [ˌkɔrəˈleɪʃən] *n* : correlación *f*

correspond [ˌkɔrəˈspand] *vi* **1** MATCH : corresponder, concordar, coincidir **2** WRITE : corresponderse, escribirse

correspondence [ˌkɔrəˈspandənts] *n* : correspondencia *f*

correspondent [ˌkɔrəˈspandənt] *n* : corresponsal *mf*

corresponding [kɔrəˈspandɪŋ, kar-] *adj* : correspondiente

correspondingly [ˌkɔrəˈspandɪŋli] *adv* : en consecuencia, de la misma manera

corridor [ˈkɔrədər, -ˌdɔr] *n* : corredor *m*, pasillo *m*

corroborate [kəˈrabəˌreɪt] *vt* **-rated; -rating** : corroborar

corroboration [kəˌrabəˈreɪʃən] *n* : corroboración *f*

corrode [kəˈro:d] *v* **-roded; -roding** *vt* : corroer — *vi* : corroerse

corrosion [kəˈro:ʒən] *n* : corrosión *f*

corrosive [kəˈro:sɪv] *adj* : corrosivo

corrugate [ˈkɔrəˌgeɪt] *vt* **-gated; -gating** : ondular, acanalar, corrugar

corrugated [ˈkɔrəˌgeɪţəd] *adj* : ondulado, acanalado ⟨corrugated cardboard : cartón ondulado⟩

corrupt[1] [kəˈrʌpt] *vt* **1** PERVERT : corromper, pervertir, degradar (información) **2** BRIBE : sobornar

corrupt[2] *adj* : corrupto, corrompido

corruptible [kəˈrʌptəbəl] *adj* : corruptible

corruption [kəˈrʌpʃən] *n* : corrupción *f*

corsage [kɔrˈsaʒ, -ˈsaʤ] *n* : ramillete *m* que se lleva como adorno

corset [ˈkɔrsət] *n* : corsé *m*

cortex [ˈkɔrˌtɛks] *n, pl* **-tices** [ˈkɔrţəˌsi:z] *or* **-texes** : corteza *f* ⟨cerebral cortex : corteza cerebral⟩

cortisone [ˈkɔrţəˌso:n, -zo:n] *n* : cortisona *f*

cosmetic[1] [kazˈmɛţɪk] *adj* : cosmético

cosmetic[2] *n* : cosmético *m*

cosmic [ˈkazmɪk] *adj* **1** : cósmico ⟨cosmic ray : rayo cósmico⟩ **2** VAST : grandioso, inmenso, vasto

cosmonaut [ˈkazməˌnɔt] *n* : cosmonauta *mf*

cosmopolitan[1] [ˌkazməˈpalətən] *adj* : cosmopolita

cosmopolitan[2] *n* : cosmopolita *mf*

cosmos [ˈkazməs, -ˌmo:s, -ˌmas] *n* : cosmos *m*, universo *m*

cost[1] [ˈkɔst] *v* **cost; costing** *vt* : costar ⟨how much does it cost? : ¿cuánto cuesta?, ¿cuánto vale?⟩ — *vi* : costar ⟨these cost more : éstos cuestan más⟩

cost[2] *n* : costo *m*, precio *m*, coste *m* ⟨cost of living : costo de vida⟩ ⟨victory at all costs : victoria a toda costa⟩

Costa Rican[1] [ˌkɔstəˈri:kən] *adj* : costarricense

Costa Rican[2] *n* : costarricense *mf*

costly [ˈkɔstli] *adj* : costoso, caro

costume [ˈkasˌtu:m, -ˌtju:m] *n* **1** : traje *m* ⟨national costume : traje típico⟩ **2** : disfraz *m* ⟨costume party : fiesta de disfraces⟩ **3** OUTFIT : vestimenta *f*, traje *m*, conjunto *m*

cosy [ˈko:zi] → **cozy**

cot [ˈkat] *n* : catre *m*

coterie [ˈko:ţəˌri, ˌko:ţəˈ-] *n* : tertulia *f*, círculo *m* (social)

cottage [ˈkaţɪʤ] *n* : casita *f* (de campo)

cottage cheese *n* : requesón *m*

cotton [ˈkatən] *n* : algodón *m*

cottonmouth [ˈkatənˌmaʊθ] → **moccasin**

cottonseed [ˈkatənˌsi:d] *n* : semilla *f* de algodón

cotton swab → **swab**

cottontail [ˈkatənˌteɪl] *n* : conejo *m* de cola blanca

couch[1] [ˈkaʊʧ] *vt* : expresar, formular ⟨couched in strong language : expresado en lenguaje enérgico⟩

couch[2] *n* SOFA : sofá *m*

couch potato *n* : haragán *m*, -gana *f*; vago *m*, -ga *f*

cougar [ˈku:gər] *n* : puma *m*

cough[1] [ˈkɔf] *vi* : toser

cough[2] *n* : tos *f*
could [ˈkʊd] → **can**
council [ˈkaʊntsəl] *n* **1** : concejo *m* ⟨city council : concejo municipal, ayuntamiento⟩ **2** MEETING : concejo *m*, junta *f* **3** BOARD : consejo *m* **4** : concilio *m* (eclesiástico)
councillor *or* **councilor** [ˈkaʊntsələr] *n* : concejal *m*, -jala *f*
councilman [ˈkaʊntsəlmən] *n, pl* **-men** [-mən, -ˌmɛn] : concejal *m*
councilwoman [ˈkaʊntsəlˌwʊmən] *n, pl* **-women** [-ˌwɪmən] : concejala *f*
counsel[1] [ˈkaʊntsəl] *v* **-seled** *or* **-selled; -seling** *or* **-selling** *vt* ADVISE : aconsejar, asesorar, recomendar — *vi* CONSULT : consultar
counsel[2] *n* **1** ADVICE : consejo *m*, recomendación *f* **2** CONSULTATION : consulta *f* **3 counsel** *ns & pl* LAWYER : abogado *m*, -da *f*
counselor *or* **counsellor** [ˈkaʊntsələr] *n* : consejero *m*, -ra *f*; consultor *m*, -tora *f*; asesor *m*, -sora *f*
count[1] [ˈkaʊnt] *vt* : contar, enumerar — *vi* **1** : contar ⟨to count out loud : contar en voz alta⟩ **2** MATTER : contar, valer, importar ⟨that's what counts : eso es lo que cuenta⟩ **3 to count on** : contar con
count[2] *n* **1** COMPUTATION : cómputo *m*, recuento *m*, cuenta *f* ⟨to lose count : perder la cuenta⟩ **2** CHARGE : cargo *m* ⟨two counts of robbery : dos cargos de robo⟩ **3** : conde *m* (noble)
countable [ˈkaʊntəbəl] *adj* : numerable
countdown [ˈkaʊntˌdaʊn] *n* : cuenta *f* atrás
countenance[1] [ˈkaʊntənənts] *vt* **-nanced; -nancing** : permitir, tolerar
countenance[2] *n* FACE : semblante *m*, rostro *m*
counter[1] [ˈkaʊntər] *vt* **1** → **counteract** **2** OPPOSE : oponerse a, resistir — *vi* RETALIATE : responder, contraatacar
counter[2] *adv* **counter to** : contrario a, en contra de
counter[3] *adj* : contrario, opuesto
counter[4] *n* **1** PIECE : ficha *f* (de un juego) **2** : mostrador *m* (de un negocio), ventanilla *f* (en un banco) **3** : contador *m* (aparato) **4** COUNTERBALANCE : fuerza *f* opuesta, contrapeso *m*
counteract [ˌkaʊntərˈækt] *vt* : contrarrestar
counterattack [ˈkaʊntərəˌtæk] *n* : contraataque *m*
counterbalance[1] [ˌkaʊntərˈbæləntś] *vt* **-anced; -ancing** : contrapesar
counterbalance[2] [ˈkaʊntərˌbæləntś] *n* : contrapeso *m*
counterclockwise [ˌkaʊntərˈklɑkˌwaɪz] *adv & adj* : en el sentido opuesto al de las manecillas del reloj
counterfeit[1] [ˈkaʊntərˌfɪt] *vt* **1** : falsificar (dinero) **2** PRETEND : fingir, aparentar
counterfeit[2] *adj* : falso, inauténtico
counterfeit[3] *n* : falsificación *f*
counterfeiter [ˈkaʊntərˌfɪţər] *n* : falsificador *m*, -dora *f*
countermand [ˈkaʊntərˌmænd, ˌkaʊntərˈ-] *vt* : contramandar
countermeasure [ˈkaʊntərˌmɛʒər] *n* : contramedida *f*
counterpart [ˈkaʊntərˌpɑrt] *n* : homólogo *m*, contraparte *f Mex*
counterpoint [ˈkaʊntərˌpɔɪnt] *n* : contrapunto *m*
counterproductive [ˌkaʊntərprəˈdʌktɪv] *adj* : contraproducente
counterrevolution [ˌkaʊntərˌrɛvəˈluːʃən] *n* : contrarrevolución *f*
counterrevolutionary[1] [ˌkaʊntərˌrɛvəˈluːʃənˌɛri] *adj* : contrarrevolucionario
counterrevolutionary[2] *n, pl* **-ries** : contrarrevolucionario *m*, -ria *f*
countersign [ˈkaʊntərˌsaɪn] *n* : contraseña *f*
countess [ˈkaʊntɪs] *n* : condesa *f*
countless [ˈkaʊntləs] *adj* : incontable, innumerable
country[1] [ˈkʌntri] *adj* : campestre, rural
country[2] *n, pl* **-tries** **1** NATION : país *m*, nación *f*, patria *f* ⟨country of origin : país de origen⟩ ⟨love of one's country : amor a la patria⟩ **2** : campo *m* ⟨they left the city for the country : se fueron de la ciudad al campo⟩
countryman [ˈkʌntrimən] *n, pl* **-men** [-mən, -ˌmɛn] : compatriota *mf*; paisano *m*, -na *f*
countryside [ˈkʌntriˌsaɪd] *n* : campo *m*, campiña *f*
county [ˈkaʊnti] *n, pl* **-ties** : condado *m*
coup [ˈkuː] *n, pl* **coups** [ˈkuːz] **1** : golpe *m* maestro **2** *or* **coup d'etat** : golpe *m* (de estado), cuartelazo *m*
coupe [ˈkuːp] *n* : cupé *m*
couple[1] [ˈkʌpəl] *vt* **-pled; -pling** : acoplar, enganchar, conectar
couple[2] *n* **1** PAIR : par *m* ⟨a couple of hours : un par de horas, unas dos horas⟩ **2** : pareja *f* ⟨a young couple : una pareja joven⟩
coupling [ˈkʌplɪŋ] *n* : acoplamiento *m*
coupon [ˈkuːˌpɑn, ˈkjuː-] *n* : cupón *m*
courage [ˈkərɪʤ] *n* : valor *m*, valentía *f*, coraje *m*
courageous [kəˈreɪʤəs] *adj* : valiente, valeroso
courier [ˈkʊriər, ˈkəriər] *n* : mensajero *m*, -ra *f*
course[1] [ˈkors] *vi* **coursed; coursing** : correr (a toda velocidad)
course[2] *n* **1** PROGRESS : curso *m*, transcurso *m* ⟨to run its course : seguir su curso⟩ **2** DIRECTION : rumbo *m* (de un avión), derrota *f*, derrotero *m* (de un barco) **3** PATH, WAY : camino *m*, vía *f* ⟨course of action : línea de conducta⟩ **4** : plato *m* (de una cena) ⟨the main course : el plato principal⟩ **5** : curso *m* (académico) **6 of course** : desde luego, por supuesto ⟨yes, of course! : ¡claro que sí!⟩

court[1] ['kort] *vt* WOO : cortejar, galantear

court[2] *n* **1** PALACE : palacio *m* **2** RETINUE : corte *f*, séquito *m* **3** COURTYARD : patio *m* **4** : cancha *f* (de tenis, baloncesto, etc.) **5** TRIBUNAL : corte *f*, tribunal *m* ⟨the Supreme Court : la Corte Suprema⟩

courteous ['kərt̬iəs] *adj* : cortés, atento, educado — **courteously** *adv*

courtesan ['kort̬əzən, 'kər-] *n* : cortesana *f*

courtesy ['kərt̬əsi] *n, pl* **-sies** : cortesía *f*

courthouse ['kort,haʊs] *n* : palacio *m* de justicia, juzgado *m*

courtier ['kort̬iər, 'kortjər] *n* : cortesano *m*, -na *f*

courtly ['kortli] *adj* **-lier; -est** : distinguido, elegante, cortés

court–martial[1] ['kort,mɑrʃəl] *vt* : someter a consejo de guerra

court–martial[2] *n, pl* **courts–martial** ['korts,mɑrʃəl] : consejo *m* de guerra

court order *n* : mandamiento *m* judicial

courtroom ['kort,ru:m] *n* : tribunal *m*, corte *f*

courtship ['kort,ʃɪp] *n* : cortejo *m*, noviazgo *m*

courtyard ['kort,jɑrd] *n* : patio *m*

cousin ['kʌzən] *n* : primo *m*, -ma *f*

couture [ku:'tʊr] *n* : industria *f* de la moda ⟨haute couture : alta costura⟩

cove ['ko:v] *n* : ensenada *f*, cala *f*

covenant ['kʌvənənt] *n* : pacto *m*, contrato *m*

cover[1] ['kʌvər] *vt* **1** : cubrir, tapar ⟨cover your head : tápate la cabeza⟩ ⟨covered with mud : cubierto de lodo⟩ **2** HIDE, PROTECT : encubrir, proteger **3** TREAT : tratar **4** INSURE : asegurar, cubrir

cover[2] *n* **1** SHELTER : cubierta *f*, abrigo *m*, refugio *m* ⟨to take cover : ponerse a cubierto⟩ ⟨under cover of darkness : al amparo de la oscuridad⟩ **2** LID, TOP : cubierta *f*, tapa *f* **3** : cubierta *f* (de un libro), portada *f* (de una revista) **4 covers** *npl* BEDCLOTHES : ropa *f* de cama, cobijas *fpl*, mantas *fpl*

coverage ['kʌvərɪʤ] *n* : cobertura *f*

coverlet ['kʌvərlət] *n* : cobertor *m*

covert[1] ['ko:,vərt, 'kʌvərt] *adj* : encubierto, secreto ⟨covert operations : operaciones encubiertas⟩

covert[2] ['kʌvərt, 'ko:-] *n* THICKET : espesura *f*, maleza *f*

cover–up ['kʌvər,ʌp] *n* : encubrimiento *m* (de algo ilícito)

covet ['kʌvət] *vt* : codiciar

covetous ['kʌvət̬əs] *adj* : codicioso

covey ['kʌvi] *n, pl* **-eys 1** : bandada *f* pequeña (de codornices, etc.) **2** GROUP : grupo *m*

cow[1] ['kaʊ] *vt* : intimidar, acobardar

cow[2] *n* : vaca *f*, hembra *f* (de ciertas especies)

coward ['kaʊərd] *n* : cobarde *mf*

cowardice ['kaʊərdɪs] *n* : cobardía *f*

cowardly ['kaʊərdli] *adj* : cobarde

cowboy ['kaʊ,bɔɪ] *n* : vaquero *m*, cowboy *m*

cower ['kaʊər] *vi* : encogerse (de miedo), acobardarse

cowgirl ['kaʊ,gərl] *n* : vaquera *f*

cowherd ['kaʊ,hərd] *n* : vaquero *m*, -ra *f*

cowhide ['kaʊ,haɪd] *n* : cuero *m*, piel *f* de vaca

cowl ['kaʊl] *n* : capucha *f* (de un monje)

cowlick ['kaʊ,lɪk] *n* : remolino *m*

cowpuncher ['kaʊ,pʌnʧər] → **cowboy**

cowslip ['kaʊ,slɪp] *n* : prímula *f*, primavera *f*

coxswain ['kɑksən, -,sweɪn] *n* : timonel *m*

coy ['kɔɪ] *adj* **1** SHY : tímido, cohibido **2** COQUETTISH : coqueto

coyote [kaɪ'o:t̬i, 'kaɪ,o:t] *n, pl* **coyotes** *or* **coyote** : coyote *m*

cozy ['ko:zi] *adj* **-zier; -est** : acogedor, cómodo

CPU [,si:,pi:'ju:] *n* (*c*entral *p*rocessing *u*nit) : CPU *f*

crab ['kræb] *n* : cangrejo *m*, jaiba *f*

crabby ['kræbi] *adj* **-bier; -est** : gruñón, malhumorado

crabgrass ['kræb,græs] *n* : garranchuelo *m*

crack[1] ['kræk] *vi* **1** : chasquear, restallar ⟨the whip cracked : el látigo restalló⟩ **2** SPLIT : rajarse, resquebrajarse, agrietarse **3** : quebrarse (dícese de la voz) — *vt* **1** : restallar, chasquear (un látigo, etc.) **2** SPLIT : rajar, agrietar, resquebrajar **3** BREAK : romper (un huevo), cascar (nueces), forzar (una caja fuerte) **4** SOLVE : resolver, descifrar (un código)

crack[2] *adj* FIRST-RATE : buenísimo, de primera

crack[3] *n* **1** : chasquido *m*, restallido *m*, estallido *m* (de un arma de fuego), crujido *m* (de huesos) ⟨a crack of thunder : un trueno⟩ **2** WISECRACK : chiste *m*, ocurrencia *f*, salida *f* **3** CREVICE : raja *f*, grieta *f*, fisura *f* **4** BLOW : golpe *m* **5** ATTEMPT : intento *m*

crackdown ['kræk,daʊn] *n* : medidas *fpl* enérgicas

crack down *vt* : tomar medidas enérgicas

cracker ['krækər] *n* : galleta *f* (de soda, etc.)

crackle[1] ['krækəl] *vi* **-led; -ling** : crepitar, chisporrotear

crackle[2] *n* : crujido *m*, chisporroteo *m*

crackpot ['kræk,pɑt] *n* : excéntrico *m*, -ca *f*; chiflado *m*, -da *f*

crack–up ['kræk,ʌp] *n* **1** CRASH : choque *m*, estrellamiento *m* **2** BREAKDOWN : crisis *f* nerviosa

crack up *vt* **1** : estrellar (un vehículo) **2** : hacer reír **3** : elogiar ⟨it isn't all that it's cracked up to be : no es tan bueno como se dice⟩ — *vi* **1** : estrellarse **2** LAUGH : echarse a reír

cradle[1] [ˈkreɪdəl] *vt* **-dled; -dling** : acunar, mecer (a un niño)

cradle[2] *n* : cuna *f*

craft [ˈkræft] *n* **1** TRADE : oficio *m* <the craft of carpentry : el oficio de carpintero> **2** CRAFTSMANSHIP, SKILL : arte *m*, artesanía *f*, destreza *f* **3** CRAFTINESS : astucia *f*, maña *f* **4** *pl usually* **craft** BOAT : barco *m*, embarcación *f* **5** *pl usually* **craft** AIRCRAFT : avión *m*, aeronave *f*

craftiness [ˈkræftinəs] *n* : astucia *f*, maña *f*

craftsman [ˈkræftsmən] *n, pl* **-men** [-mən, -ˌmɛn] : artesano *m*, -na *f*

craftsmanship [ˈkræftsmənˌʃɪp] *n* : artesanía *f*, destreza *f*

crafty [ˈkræfti] *adj* **craftier; -est** : astuto, taimado

crag [ˈkræg] *n* : peñasco *m*

craggy [ˈkrægi] *adj* **-gier; -est** : peñascoso

cram [ˈkræm] *v* **crammed; cramming** *vt* **1** JAM : embutir, meter **2** STUFF : atiborrar, abarrotar <crammed with people : atiborrado de gente> — *vi* : estudiar a última hora, memorizar (para un examen)

cramp[1] [ˈkræmp] *vt* **1** : dar calambre en **2** RESTRICT : limitar, restringir, entorpecer <to cramp someone's style : cortarle el vuelo a alguien> — *vi or* **to cramp up** : acalambrarse

cramp[2] *n* **1** SPASM : calambre *m*, espasmo *m* (de los músculos) **2 cramps** *npl* : retorcijones *mpl* <stomach cramps : retorcijones de estómago>

cranberry [ˈkrænˌbɛri] *n, pl* **-berries** : arándano *m* (rojo y agrio)

crane[1] [ˈkreɪn] *vt* **craned; craning** : estirar <to crane one's neck : estirar el cuello>

crane[2] *n* **1** : grulla *f* (ave) **2** : grúa *f* (máquina)

cranial [ˈkreɪniəl] *adj* : craneal, craneano

cranium [ˈkreɪniəm] *n, pl* **-niums** *or* **-nia** [-niə] : cráneo *m*

crank[1] [ˈkræŋk] *vt or* **to crank up** : arrancar (con una manivela)

crank[2] *n* **1** : manivela *f*, manubrio *m* **2** ECCENTRIC : excéntrico *m*, -ca *f*

cranky [ˈkræŋki] *adj* **crankier; -est** : irritable, malhumorado, enojadizo

cranny [ˈkræni] *n, pl* **-nies** : grieta *f* <every nook and cranny : todos los rincones>

crash[1] [ˈkræʃ] *vi* **1** SMASH : caerse con estrépito, estrellarse **2** COLLIDE : estrellarse, chocar **3** BOOM, RESOUND : retumbar, resonar — *vt* **1** SMASH : estrellar **2 to crash a party** : colarse en una fiesta **3 to crash one's car** : tener un accidente

crash[2] *n* **1** DIN : estrépito *m* **2** COLLISION : choque *m*, colisión *f* <car crash : accidente automovilístico> **3** FAILURE : quiebra *f* (de un negocio), crac *m* (de la bolsa)

crass [ˈkræs] *adj* : grosero, de mal gusto

crate[1] [ˈkreɪt] *vt* **crated; crating** : empacar en un cajón

crate[2] *n* : cajón *m* (de madera)

crater [ˈkreɪt̬ər] *n* : cráter *m*

cravat [krəˈvæt] *n* : corbata *f*

crave [ˈkreɪv] *vt* **craved; craving** : ansiar, apetecer, tener muchas ganas de

craven [ˈkreɪvən] *adj* : cobarde, pusilánime

craving [ˈkreɪvɪŋ] *n* : ansia *f*, antojo *m*, deseo *m*

crawfish [ˈkrɔˌfɪʃ] → **crayfish**

crawl[1] [ˈkrɔl] *vi* **1** CREEP : arrastrarse, gatear (dícese de un bebé) **2** TEEM : estar plagado

crawl[2] *n* : paso *m* lento

crayfish [ˈkreɪˌfɪʃ] *n* **1** : ástaco *m* (de agua dulce) **2** : langostino *m* (de mar)

crayon [ˈkreɪˌɑn, -ən] *n* : crayón *m*

craze [ˈkreɪz] *n* : moda *f* pasajera, manía *f*

crazed [ˈkreɪzd] *adj* : enloquecido

crazily [ˈkreɪzəli] *adv* : locamente, erráticamente, insensatamente

craziness [ˈkreɪzinəs] *n* : locura *f*, demencia *f*

crazy [ˈkreɪzi] *adj* **-zier; -est 1** INSANE : loco, demente <to go crazy : volverse loco> **2** ABSURD, FOOLISH : loco, insensato, absurdo **3 like crazy** : como loco **4 to be crazy about** : estar loco por

creak[1] [ˈkriːk] *vi* : chirriar, rechinar, crujir

creak[2] *n* : chirrido *m*, crujido *m*

creaky [ˈkriːki] *adj* **creakier; -est** : chirriante, que cruje

cream[1] [ˈkriːm] *vt* **1** BEAT, MIX : batir, mezclar (azúcar y mantequilla, etc.) **2** : preparar (alimentos) con crema

cream[2] *n* **1** : crema *f* (de leche) **2** LOTION : crema *f*, loción *f* **3** ELITE : crema *f*, elite *f* <the cream of the crop : la crema y nata, lo mejor>

creamery [ˈkriːməri] *n, pl* **-eries** : fábrica *f* de productos lácteos

creamy [ˈkriːmi] *adj* **creamier; -est** : cremoso

crease[1] [ˈkriːs] *vt* **creased; creasing 1** : plegar, poner una raya en (pantalones) **2** WRINKLE : arrugar

crease[2] *n* : pliegue *m*, doblez *m*, raya *f* (de pantalones)

create [kriˈeɪt] *vt* **-ated; -ating** : crear, hacer

creation [kriˈeɪʃən] *n* : creación *f*

creative [kriˈeɪt̬ɪv] *adj* : creativo, original <creative people : personas creativas> <a creative work : un obra original>

creatively [kriˈeɪt̬ɪvli] *adv* : creativamente, con originalidad

creativity [ˌkriːeɪˈtɪvət̬i] *n* : creatividad *f*

creator [kriˈeɪt̬ər] *n* : creador *m*, -dora *f*

creature [ˈkriːtʃər] *n* : ser *m* viviente, criatura *f*, animal *m*

credence [ˈkri:dənts] *n* : crédito *m*
credentials [krɪˈdɛnʧəlz] *npl* : referencias *fpl* oficiales, cartas *fpl* credenciales
credibility [ˌkrɛdəˈbɪləṭi] *n* : credibilidad *f*
credible [ˈkrɛdəbəl] *adj* : creíble
credit[1] [ˈkrɛdɪt] *vt* **1** BELIEVE : creer, dar crédito a **2** : ingresar, abonar ⟨to credit $100 to an account : ingresar $100 en (una) cuenta⟩ **3** ATTRIBUTE : atribuir ⟨they credit the invention to him : a él se le atribuye el invento⟩
credit[2] *n* **1** : saldo *m* positivo, saldo *m* a favor (de una cuenta) **2** : crédito *m* ⟨to buy on credit : comprar a crédito⟩ ⟨credit card : tarjeta de crédito⟩ **3** CREDENCE : crédito *m* ⟨I gave credit to everything he said : di crédito a todo lo que dijo⟩ **4** RECOGNITION : reconocimiento *m* **5** : orgullo *m*, honor *m* ⟨she's a credit to the school : ella es el orgullo de la escuela⟩
creditable [ˈkrɛdɪṭəbəl] *adj* : encomiable, loable — **creditably** [-bli] *adv*
credit card *n* : tarjeta de crédito
creditor [ˈkrɛdɪṭər] *n* : acreedor *m*, -dora *f*
credo [ˈkri:do:, ˈkreɪ-] *n* : credo *m*
credulity [krɪˈdu:ləṭi, -ˈdju:-] *n* : credulidad *f*
credulous [ˈkrɛʤələs] *adj* : crédulo
creed [ˈkri:d] *n* : credo *m*
creek [ˈkri:k, ˈkrɪk] *n* : arroyo *m*, riachuelo *m*
creel [ˈkri:l] *n* : nasa *f*, cesta *f* (de pescador)
creep[1] [ˈkri:p] *vi* **crept** [ˈkrɛpt]; **creeping** **1** CRAWL : arrastrarse, gatear **2** : moverse lentamente o sigilosamente ⟨he crept out of the house : salió sigilosamente de la casa⟩ **3** SPREAD : trepar (dícese de una planta)
creep[2] *n* **1** CRAWL : paso *m* lento **2** : asqueroso *m*, -sa *f* **3 creeps** *npl* : escalofríos *mpl* ⟨that gives me the creeps : eso me da escalofríos⟩
creeper [ˈkri:pər] *n* : planta *f* trepadora, trepadora *f*
creepy [ˈkri:pi] *adj* **1** SPOOKY : espeluznante **2** UNPLEASANT : asqueroso
cremate [ˈkri:ˌmeɪt] *vt* **-mated; -mating** : cremar
cremation [krɪˈmeɪʃən] *n* : cremación *f*
Creole [ˈkri:ˌo:l] *n* **1** : criollo *m*, criolla *f* **2** : criollo *m* (idioma) — **Creole** *adj*
creosote [ˈkri:əˌso:t] *n* : creosota *f*
crepe *or* **crêpe** [ˈkreɪp] *n* **1** : crespón *m* (tela) **2** PANCAKE : crepe *mf*, crepa *f* *Mex*
crescendo [krɪˈʃɛnˌdo:] *n, pl* **-dos** *or* **-does** : crescendo *m*
crescent [ˈkrɛsənt] *n* : creciente *m*
crest [ˈkrɛst] *n* **1** : cresta *f*, penacho *m* (de un ave) **2** PEAK, TOP : cresta *f* (de una ola), cima *f* (de una colina) **3** : emblema *m* (sobre un escudo de armas)
crestfallen [ˈkrɛstˌfɔlən] *adj* : alicaído, abatido
cretin [ˈkri:tən] *n* : cretino *m*, -na *f*
crevasse [krɪˈvæs] *n* : grieta *f*, fisura *f*
crevice [ˈkrɛvɪs] *n* : grieta *f*, hendidura *f*
crew [ˈkru:] *n* **1** : tripulación *f* (de una nave) **2** TEAM : equipo *m* (de trabajadores o atletas)
crib [ˈkrɪb] *n* **1** MANGER : pesebre *m* **2** GRANARY : granero *m* **3** : cuna *f* (de un bebé)
crick [ˈkrɪk] *n* : calambre *m*, espasmo *m* muscular
cricket [ˈkrɪkət] *n* **1** : grillo *m* (insecto) **2** : críquet *m* (juego)
crime [ˈkraɪm] *n* **1** : crimen *m*, delito *m* ⟨to commit a crime : cometer un delito⟩ **2** : crimen *m*, delincuencia *f* ⟨organized crime : crimen organizado⟩
criminal[1] [ˈkrɪmənəl] *adj* : criminal
criminal[2] *n* : criminal *mf*, delincuente *mf*
crimp [ˈkrɪmp] *vt* : ondular, rizar (el pelo), arrugar (una tela, etc.)
crimson [ˈkrɪmzən] *n* : carmesí *m*
cringe [ˈkrɪnʤ] *vi* **cringed; cringing** : encogerse
crinkle[1] [ˈkrɪŋkəl] *v* **-kled; -kling** *vt* : arrugar — *vi* : arrugarse
crinkle[2] *n* : arruga *f*
crinkly [ˈkrɪŋkəli] *adj* : arrugado
cripple[1] [ˈkrɪpəl] *vt* **-pled; -pling** **1** DISABLE : lisiar, dejar inválido **2** INCAPACITATE : inutilizar, incapacitar
cripple[2] *n* : lisiado *m*, -da *f*
crisis [ˈkraɪsɪs] *n, pl* **crises** [-ˌsi:z] : crisis *f*
crisp[1] [ˈkrɪsp] *vt* : tostar, hacer crujiente
crisp[2] *adj* **1** CRUNCHY : crujiente, crocante **2** FIRM, FRESH : firme, fresco ⟨crisp lettuce : lechuga fresca⟩ **3** LIVELY : vivaz, alegre ⟨a crisp tempo : un ritmo alegre⟩ **4** INVIGORATING : fresco, vigorizante ⟨the crisp autumn air : el fresco aire otoñal⟩ — **crisply** *adv*
crisp[3] *n* : postre *m* de fruta (con pedacitos de masa dulce por encima)
crispy [ˈkrɪspi] *adj* **crispier; -est** : crujiente ⟨crispy potato chips : papitas crujientes⟩
crisscross [ˈkrɪsˌkrɔs] *vt* : entrecruzar
criterion [kraɪˈtɪriən] *n, pl* **-ria** [-iə] : criterio *m*
critic [ˈkrɪṭɪk] *n* **1** : crítico *m*, -ca *f* (de las artes) **2** FAULTFINDER : detractor *m*, -tora *f*; criticón *m*, -cona *f*
critical [ˈkrɪṭɪkəl] *adj* : crítico
critically [ˈkrɪṭɪkli] *adv* : críticamente ⟨critically ill : gravemente enfermo⟩
criticism [ˈkrɪṭəˌsɪzəm] *n* : crítica *f*
criticize [ˈkrɪṭəˌsaɪz] *vt* **-cized; -cizing** **1** EVALUATE, JUDGE : criticar, analizar, evaluar **2** CENSURE : criticar, reprobar
critique [krɪˈti:k] *n* : crítica *f*, evaluación *f*
croak[1] [ˈkro:k] *vi* : croar
croak[2] *n* : croar *m*, canto *m* (de la rana)
Croatian [kroˈeɪʃən] *n* : croata *mf* — **Croatian** *adj*

crochet[1] [kro:ˈʃeɪ] *v* : tejer al croché
crochet[2] *n* : croché *m*, crochet *m*
crock [ˈkrɑk] *n* : vasija *f* de barro
crockery [ˈkrɑkəri] *n* : vajilla *f* (de barro)
crocodile [ˈkrɑkəˌdaɪl] *n* : cocodrilo *m*
crocus [ˈkro:kəs] *n, pl* **-cuses** : azafrán *m*
croissant [krəˈsɑnt] *n* : croissant *m*
crone [ˈkro:n] *n* : vieja *f* arpía, vieja *f* bruja
crony [ˈkro:ni] *n, pl* **-nies** : amigote *m fam*; compinche *mf fam*
crook[1] [ˈkrʊk] *vt* : doblar (el brazo o el dedo)
crook[2] *n* **1** STAFF : cayado *m* (de pastor), báculo *m* (de obispo) **2** THIEF : ratero *m*, -ra *f*; ladrón *m*, -drona *f*
crooked [ˈkrʊkəd] *adj* **1** BENT : chueco, torcido **2** DISHONEST : deshonesto
crookedness [ˈkrʊkədnəs] *n* **1** : lo torcido, lo chueco **2** DISHONESTY : falta *f* de honradez
croon [ˈkru:n] *v* : cantar suavemente
crop[1] [ˈkrɑp] *v* **cropped; cropping** *vt* TRIM : recortar, cortar — *vi* **to crop up** : aparecer, surgir ⟨these problems keep cropping up : estos problemas no cesan de surgir⟩
crop[2] *n* **1** : buche *m* (de un ave o insecto) **2** WHIP : fusta *f* (de jinete) **3** HARVEST : cosecha *f*, cultivo *m*
croquet [ˌkro:ˈkeɪ] *n* : croquet *m*
croquette [ˌkro:ˈkɛt] *n* : croqueta *f*
cross[1] [ˈkrɔs] *vt* **1** : cruzar, atravesar ⟨to cross the street : cruzar la calle⟩ ⟨several canals cross the city : varios canales atraviesan la ciudad⟩ **2** CANCEL : tachar, cancelar ⟨he crossed his name off the list : tachó su nombre de la planilla⟩ **3** INTERBREED : cruzar (en genética)
cross[2] *adj* **1** : que atraviesa ⟨cross ventilation : ventilación que atraviesa un cuarto⟩ **2** CONTRARY : contrario, opuesto ⟨cross purposes : objetivos opuestos⟩ **3** ANGRY : enojado, de mal humor
cross[3] *n* **1** : cruz *f* ⟨the sign of the cross : la señal de la cruz⟩ **2** : cruza *f* (en biología)
crossbones [ˈkrɔsˌbo:nz] *npl* **1** : huesos *mpl* cruzados **2** → **skull**
crossbow [ˈkrɔsˌbo:] *n* : ballesta *f*
crossbreed [ˈkrɔsˌbri:d] *vt* **-bred** [-ˌbrɛd]; **-breeding** : cruzar
crosscurrent [ˈkrɔsˌkərənt] *n* : contracorriente *f*
cross–examination [ˌkrɔsɪgˌzæməˈneɪʃən] *n* : repreguntas *fpl*, interrogatorio *m*
cross–examine [ˌkrɔsɪgˈzæmən] *vt* **-ined; -ining** : repreguntar
cross–eyed [ˈkrɔsˌaɪd] *adj* : bizco
crossing [ˈkrɔsɪŋ] *n* **1** INTERSECTION : cruce *m*, paso *m* ⟨pedestrian crossing : paso de peatones⟩ **2** VOYAGE : travesía *f* (del mar)
crossly [ˈkrɔsli] *adv* : con enojo, con enfado
cross–reference [ˌkrɔsˈrɛfrənts, -ˈrɛfərənts] *n* : referencia *f*, remisión *f*
crossroads [ˈkrɔsˌro:dz] *n* : cruce *m*, encrucijada *f*, crucero *m Mex*
cross section *n* **1** SECTION : corte *m* transversal **2** SAMPLE : muestra *f* representativa ⟨a cross section of the population : una muestra representativa de la población⟩
crosswalk [ˈkrɔsˌwɔk] *n* : cruce *m* peatonal, paso *m* de peatones
crossways [ˈkrɔsˌweɪz] → **crosswise**
crosswise[1] [ˈkrɔsˌwaɪz] *adv* : transversalmente, diagonalmente
crosswise[2] *adj* : transversal, diagonal
crossword puzzle [ˈkrɔsˌwərd] *n* : crucigrama *m*
crotch [ˈkrɑʧ] *n* : entrepierna *f*
crotchety [ˈkrɑʧət̬i] *adj* CRANKY : malhumorado, irritable, enojadizo
crouch [ˈkraʊʧ] *vi* : agacharse, ponerse de cuclillas
croup [ˈkru:p] *n* : crup *m*
crouton [ˈkru:ˌtɑn] *n* : crutón *m*
crow[1] [ˈkro:] *vi* **1** : cacarear, cantar (como un cuervo) **2** BRAG : alardear, presumir
crow[2] *n* **1** : cuervo *m* (ave) **2** : cantar *m* (del gallo)
crowbar [ˈkro:ˌbɑr] *n* : palanca *f*
crowd[1] [ˈkraʊd] *vi* : aglomerarse, amontonarse — *vt* : atestar, atiborrar, llenar
crowd[2] *n* : multitud *f*, muchedumbre *f*, gentío *m*
crown[1] [ˈkraʊn] *vt* : coronar
crown[2] *n* : corona *f*
crow's nest *n* : cofa *f*
crucial [ˈkru:ʃəl] *adj* : crucial, decisivo
crucible [ˈkru:səbəl] *n* : crisol *m*
crucifix [ˈkru:səˌfɪks] *n* : crucifijo *m*
crucifixion [ˌkru:səˈfɪkʃən] *n* : crucifixión *f*
crucify [ˈkru:səˌfaɪ] *vt* **-fied; -fying** : crucificar
crude [ˈkru:d] *adj* **cruder; -est** **1** RAW, UNREFINED : crudo, sin refinar ⟨crude oil : petróleo crudo⟩ **2** VULGAR : grosero, de mal gusto **3** ROUGH : tosco, burdo, rudo
crudely [ˈkru:dli] *adv* **1** VULGARLY : groseramente **2** ROUGHLY : burdamente, de manera rudimentaria
crudity [ˈkru:dət̬i] *n, pl* **-ties** **1** VULGARITY : grosería *f* **2** COARSENESS, ROUGHNESS : tosquedad *f*, rudeza *f*
cruel [ˈkru:əl] *adj* **-eler** *or* **-eller; -elest** *or* **-ellest** : cruel
cruelly [ˈkru:əli] *adv* : cruelmente
cruelty [ˈkru:əlti] *n, pl* **-ties** : crueldad *f*
cruet [ˈkru:ɪt] *n* : vinagrera *f*, aceitera *f*
cruise[1] [ˈkru:z] *vi* **cruised; cruising** **1** : hacer un crucero **2** : navegar o conducir a una velocidad constante ⟨cruising speed : velocidad de crucero⟩
cruise[2] *n* : crucero *m*

cruiser [ˈkru:zər] *n* **1** WARSHIP : crucero *m*, buque *m* de guerra **2** : patrulla *f* (de policía)

crumb [ˈkrʌm] *n* : miga *f*, migaja *f*

crumble [ˈkrʌmbəl] *v* **-bled; -bling** *vt* : desmigajar, desmenuzar — *vi* : desmigajarse, desmoronarse, desmenuzarse

crumbly [ˈkrʌmbli] *adj* : que se desmenuza fácilmente, friable

crumple [ˈkrʌmpəl] *v* **-pled; -pling** *vt* RUMPLE : arrugar — *vi* **1** WRINKLE : arrugarse **2** COLLAPSE : desplomarse

crunch[1] [ˈkrʌntʃ] *vt* **1** : ronzar (con los dientes) **2** : hacer crujir (con los pies, etc.) — *vi* : crujir

crunch[2] *n* : crujido *m*

crunchy [ˈkrʌntʃi] *adj* **crunchier; -est** : crujiente

crusade[1] [kru:ˈseɪd] *vi* **-saded; -sading** : hacer una campaña (a favor de o contra algo)

crusade[2] *n* **1** : campaña *f* (de reforma, etc.) **2 Crusade** : cruzada *f*

crusader [kru:ˈseɪdər] *n* **1** : cruzado *m* (en la Edad Media) **2** : campeón *m*, -peona *f* (de una causa)

crush[1] [ˈkrʌʃ] *vt* **1** SQUASH : aplastar, apachurrar **2** GRIND, PULVERIZE : triturar, machacar **3** SUPPRESS : aplastar, suprimir

crush[2] *n* **1** CROWD, MOB : gentío *m*, multitud *f*, aglomeración *f* **2** INFATUATION : enamoramiento *m*

crushing [ˈkrʌʃɪŋ] *adj* : aplastante, abrumador

crust [ˈkrʌst] *n* **1** : corteza *f*, costra *f* (de pan) **2** : tapa *f* de masa, pasta *f* (de un pastel) **3** LAYER : capa *f*, corteza *f* ⟨the earth's crust : la corteza terrestre⟩

crustacean [ˌkrʌsˈteɪʃən] *n* : crustáceo *m*

crusty [ˈkrʌsti] *adj* **crustier; -est** **1** : de corteza dura **2** CROSS, GRUMPY : enojado, malhumorado

crutch [ˈkrʌtʃ] *n* : muleta *f*

crux [ˈkrʌks, ˈkrʊks] *n, pl* **cruxes** : quid *m*, esencia *f*, meollo *m* ⟨the crux of the problem : el quid del problema⟩

cry[1] [ˈkraɪ] *vi* **cried; crying** **1** SHOUT : gritar ⟨they cried for more : a gritos pidieron más⟩ **2** WEEP : llorar

cry[2] *n, pl* **cries** **1** SHOUT : grito *m* **2** WEEPING : llanto *m* **3** : chillido *m* (de un animal)

crybaby [ˈkraɪˌbeɪbi] *n, pl* **-bies** : llorón *m*, -rona *f*

crypt [ˈkrɪpt] *n* : cripta *f*

cryptic [ˈkrɪptɪk] *adj* : enigmático, críptico

crystal [ˈkrɪstəl] *n* : cristal *m*

crystalline [ˈkrɪstəlɪn] *adj* : cristalino

crystallize [ˈkrɪstəˌlaɪz] *v* **-lized; -lizing** *vt* : cristalizar, materializar ⟨to crystallize one's thoughts : cristalizar uno sus pensamientos⟩ — *vi* : cristalizarse

cub [ˈkʌb] *n* : cachorro *m*

Cuban [ˈkju:bən] *n* : cubano *m*, -na *f* — **Cuban** *adj*

cubbyhole [ˈkʌbiˌho:l] *n* : chiribitil *m*

cube[1] [ˈkju:b] *vt* **cubed; cubing** **1** : elevar (un número) al cubo **2** : cortar en cubos

cube[2] *n* **1** : cubo *m* **2 ice cube** : cubito *m* de hielo **3 sugar cube** : terrón *m* de azúcar

cubic [ˈkju:bɪk] *adj* : cúbico

cubicle [ˈkju:bɪkəl] *n* : cubículo *m*

cuckoo[1] [ˈku:ˌku:, ˈkʊ-] *adj* : loco, chiflado

cuckoo[2] *n, pl* **-oos** : cuco *m*, cuclillo *m*

cucumber [ˈkju:ˌkʌmbər] *n* : pepino *m*

cud [ˈkʌd] *n* **to chew the cud** : rumiar

cuddle [ˈkʌdəl] *v* **-dled; -dling** *vi* : abrazarse tiernamente, acurrucarse — *vt* : abrazar

cudgel[1] [ˈkʌdʒəl] *vt* **-geled** *or* **-gelled; -geling** *or* **-gelling** : apalear, aporrear

cudgel[2] *n* : garrote *m*, porra *f*

cue[1] [ˈkju:] *vt* **cued; cuing** *or* **cueing** : darle el pie a, darle la señal a

cue[2] *n* **1** SIGNAL : señal *f*, pie *m* (en teatro), entrada *f* (en música) **2** : taco *m* (de billar)

cuff[1] [ˈkʌf] *vt* : bofetear, cachetear

cuff[2] *n* **1** : puño *m* (de una camisa), vuelta *f* (de pantalones) **2** SLAP : bofetada *f*, cachetada *f* **3 cuffs** *npl* HANDCUFFS : esposas *fpl*

cuisine [kwɪˈzi:n] *n* : cocina *f* ⟨Mexican cuisine : la cocina mexicana⟩

culinary [ˈkʌləˌnɛri, ˈkju:lə-] *adj* : culinario

cull [ˈkʌl] *vt* : seleccionar, entresacar

culminate [ˈkʌlməˌneɪt] *vi* **-nated; -nating** : culminar

culmination [ˌkʌlməˈneɪʃən] *n* : culminación *f*, punto *m* culminante

culpable [ˈkʌlpəbəl] *adj* : culpable

culprit [ˈkʌlprɪt] *n* : culpable *mf*

cult [ˈkʌlt] *n* : culto *m*

cultivate [ˈkʌltəˌveɪt] *vt* **-vated; -vating** **1** TILL : cultivar, labrar **2** FOSTER : cultivar, fomentar **3** REFINE : cultivar, refinar ⟨to cultivate the mind : cultivar la mente⟩

cultivation [ˌkʌltəˈveɪʃən] *n* **1** : cultivo *m* ⟨under cultivation : en cultivo⟩ **2** CULTURE, REFINEMENT : cultura *f*, refinamiento *m*

cultural [ˈkʌltʃərəl] *adj* : cultural — **culturally** *adv*

culture [ˈkʌltʃər] *n* **1** CULTIVATION : cultivo *m* **2** REFINEMENT : cultura *f*, educación *f*, refinamiento *m* **3** CIVILIZATION : cultura *f*, civilización *f* ⟨the Incan culture : la cultura inca⟩

cultured [ˈkʌltʃərd] *adj* **1** EDUCATED, REFINED : culto, educado, refinado **2** : de cultivo, cultivado ⟨cultured pearls : perlas de cultivo⟩

culvert [ˈkʌlvərt] *n* : alcantarilla *f*

cumbersome [ˈkʌmbərsəm] *adj* : torpe y pesado, difícil de manejar

cumin [ˈkʌmən] *n* : comino *m*

cumulative [ˈkju:mjələt̬ɪv, -ˌleɪt̬ɪv] *adj* : acumulativo

cumulus ['kju:mjələs] *n, pl* **-li** [-ˌlaɪ, -ˌli:] : cúmulo *m*
cunning¹ ['kʌnɪŋ] *adj* **1** CRAFTY : astuto, taimado **2** CLEVER : ingenioso, hábil **3** CUTE : mono, gracioso, lindo
cunning² *n* **1** SKILL : habilidad *f* **2** CRAFTINESS : astucia *f*, maña *f*
cup¹ ['kʌp] *vt* **cupped; cupping** : ahuecar (las manos)
cup² *n* **1** : taza *f* ⟨a cup of coffee : una taza de café⟩ **2** CUPFUL : taza *f* **3** : media pinta *f* (unidad de medida) **4** GOBLET : copa *f* **5** TROPHY : copa *f*, trofeo *m*
cupboard ['kʌbərd] *n* : alacena *f*, armario *m*
cupcake ['kʌpˌkeɪk] *n* : pastelito *m*
cupful ['kʌpˌfʊl] *n* : taza *f*
cupola ['kju:pələ, -ˌlo:] *n* : cúpula *f*
cur ['kər] *n* : perro *m* callejero, perro *m* corriente *Mex*
curate ['kjʊrət] *n* : cura *m*, párroco *m*
curator ['kjʊrˌeɪṭər, kjʊ'reɪṭər] *n* : conservador *m*, -dora *f* (de un museo); director *m*, -tora *f* (de un zoológico)
curb¹ ['kərb] *vt* : refrenar, restringir, controlar
curb² *n* **1** RESTRAINT : freno *m*, control *m* **2** : borde *m* de la acera
curd ['kərd] *n* : cuajada *f*
curdle ['kərdəl] *v* **-dled; -dling** *vi* : cuajarse — *vt* : cuajar ⟨to curdle one's blood : helarle la sangre a uno⟩
cure¹ ['kjʊr] *vt* **cured; curing 1** HEAL : curar, sanar **2** REMEDY : remediar **3** PROCESS : curar (alimentos, etc.)
cure² *n* **1** RECOVERY : curación *f*, recuperación *f* **2** REMEDY : cura *f*, remedio *m*
curfew ['kərˌfju:] *n* : toque *m* de queda
curio ['kjʊriˌo:] *n, pl* **-rios** : curiosidad *f*, objeto *m* curioso
curiosity [ˌkjʊri'ɑsəṭi] *n, pl* **-ties** : curiosidad *f*
curious ['kjʊriəs] *adj* **1** INQUISITIVE : curioso **2** STRANGE : curioso, raro
curl¹ ['kərl] *vt* **1** : rizar, ondular (el pelo) **2** COIL : enrollar **3** TWIST : torcer ⟨to curl one's lip : hacer una mueca⟩ — *vi* **1** : rizarse, ondularse **2 to curl up** : acurrucarse (con un libro, etc.)
curl² *n* **1** RINGLET : rizo *m* **2** COIL : espiral *f*, rosca *f*
curler ['kərlər] *n* : rulo *m*
curlew ['kərˌlu:, 'kərlˌju:] *n, pl* **-lews** *or* **-lew** : zarapito *m*
curly ['kərli] *adj* **curlier; -est** : rizado, crespo
currant ['kərənt] *n* **1** : grosella *f* (fruta) **2** RAISIN : pasa *f* de Corinto
currency ['kərən*t*si] *n, pl* **-cies 1** PREVALENCE, USE : uso *m*, aceptación *f*, difusión *f* ⟨to be in currency : estar en uso⟩ **2** MONEY : moneda *f*, dinero *m*
current¹ ['kərənt] *adj* **1** PRESENT : actual ⟨current events : actualidades⟩ **2** PREVALENT : corriente, común — **currently** *adv*
current² *n* : corriente *f*
curriculum [kə'rɪkjələm] *n, pl* **-la** [-lə] : currículum *m*, currículo *m*, programa *m* de estudio
curriculum vitae ['vi:ˌtaɪ, 'vaɪṭi] *n, pl* **curricula vitae** : currículum *m*, currículo *m*
curry¹ ['kəri] *vt* **-ried; -rying 1** GROOM : almohazar (un caballo) **2** : condimentar con curry **3 to curry favor** : congraciarse (con alguien)
curry² *n, pl* **-ries** : curry *m*
curse¹ ['kərs] *v* **cursed; cursing** *vt* **1** DAMN : maldecir **2** INSULT : injuriar, insultar, decir malas palabras a **3** AFFLICT : afligir — *vi* : maldecir, decir malas palabras
curse² *n* **1** : maldición *f* ⟨to put a curse on someone : echarle una maldición a alguien⟩ **2** AFFLICTION : maldición *f*, aflicción *f*, cruz *f*
cursor ['kərsər] *n* : cursor *m*
cursory ['kərsəri] *adj* : rápido, superficial, somero
curt ['kərt] *adj* : cortante, brusco, seco — **curtly** *adv*
curtail [kər'teɪl] *vt* : acortar, limitar, restringir
curtailment [kər'teɪlmənt] *n* : restricción *f*, limitación *f*
curtain ['kərtən] *n* : cortina *f* (de una ventana), telón *m* (en un teatro)
curtness ['kərtnəs] *n* : brusquedad *f*, sequedad *f*
curtsy¹ *or* **curtsey** ['kərtsi] *vt* **-sied** *or* **-seyed; -sying** *or* **-seying** : hacer una reverencia
curtsy² *or* **curtsey** *n, pl* **-sies** *or* **-seys** : reverencia *f*
curvature ['kərvəˌtʃʊr] *n* : curvatura *f*
curve¹ ['kərv] *v* **curved; curving** *vi* : torcerse, describir una curva — *vt* : encorvar
curve² *n* : curva *f*
cushion¹ ['kʊʃən] *vt* **1** : poner cojines o almohadones a **2** SOFTEN : amortiguar, mitigar, suavizar ⟨to cushion a blow : amortiguar un golpe⟩
cushion² *n* **1** : cojín *m*, almohadón *m* **2** PROTECTION : colchón *m*, protección *f*
cusp ['kʌsp] *n* : cúspide *f* (de un diente), cuerno *m* (de la luna)
cuspid ['kʌspɪd] *n* : diente *m* canino, colmillo *m*
custard ['kʌstərd] *n* : natillas *fpl*
custodian [ˌkʌ'sto:diən] *n* : custodio *m*, -dia *f*; guardián, -diana *f*
custody ['kʌstədi] *n, pl* **-dies** : custodia *f*, cuidado *m* ⟨to be in custody : estar detenido⟩
custom¹ ['kʌstəm] *adj* : a la medida, a la orden
custom² *n* **1** : costumbre *f*, tradición *f* **2 customs** *npl* : aduana *f*
customarily [ˌkʌstə'mɛrəli] *adv* : habitualmente, normalmente, de costumbre

customary [ˈkʌstəˌmɛri] *adj* **1** TRADITIONAL : tradicional **2** USUAL : habitual, de costumbre
customer [ˈkʌstəmər] *n* : cliente *m*, -ta *f*
custom–made [ˈkʌstəmˈmeɪd] *adj* : hecho a la medida
cut[1] [ˈkʌt] *v* **cut; cutting** *vt* **1** : cortar ⟨to cut paper : cortar papel⟩ **2** : cortarse ⟨to cut one's finger : cortarse uno el dedo⟩ **3** TRIM : cortar, recortar ⟨to have one's hair cut : cortarse el pelo⟩ **4** INTERSECT : cruzar, atravesar **5** SHORTEN : acortar, abreviar **6** REDUCE : reducir, rebajar ⟨to cut prices : rebajar los precios⟩ **7 to cut one's teeth** : salirle los dientes a uno — *vi* **1** : cortar, cortarse **2 to cut in** : entrometerse
cut[2] *n* **1** : corte *m* ⟨a cut of meat : un corte de carne⟩ **2** SLASH : tajo *m*, corte *m*, cortadura *f* **3** REDUCTION : rebaja *f*, reducción *f* ⟨a cut in the rates : una rebaja en las tarifas⟩
cute [ˈkjuːt] *adj* **cuter; -est** : mono *fam*, lindo
cuticle [ˈkjuːtɪkəl] *n* : cutícula *f*
cutlass [ˈkʌtləs] *n* : alfanje *m*
cutlery [ˈkʌtləri] *n* : cubiertos *mpl*
cutlet [ˈkʌtlət] *n* : chuleta *f*
cutter [ˈkʌt̬ər] *n* **1** : cortadora *f* (implemento) **2** : cortador *m*, -dora *f* (persona) **3** : cúter *m* (embarcación)
cutthroat [ˈkʌtˌθroːt] *adj* : despiadado, desalmado ⟨cutthroat competition : competencia feroz⟩
cutting[1] [ˈkʌt̬ɪŋ] *adj* **1** : cortante ⟨a cutting wind : un viento cortante⟩ **2** CAUSTIC : mordaz
cutting[2] *n* : esqueje *m* (de una planta)
cuttlefish [ˈkʌt̬əlˌfɪʃ] *n, pl* **-fish** *or* **-fishes** : jibia *f*, sepia *f*
cyanide [ˈsaɪəˌnaɪd, -nɪd] *n* : cianuro *m*
cycle[1] [ˈsaɪkəl] *vi* **-cled; -cling** : andar en bicicleta, ir en bicicleta
cycle[2] *n* **1** : ciclo *m* ⟨life cycle : ciclo de vida, ciclo vital⟩ **2** BICYCLE : bicicleta *f* **3** MOTORCYCLE : motocicleta *f*
cyclic [ˈsaɪklɪk, ˈsɪ-] *or* **cyclical** [-klɪkəl] *adj* : cíclico
cyclist [ˈsaɪklɪst] *n* : ciclista *mf*
cyclone [ˈsaɪˌkloːn] *n* **1** : ciclón *m* **2** TORNADO : tornado *m*
cyclopedia *or* **cyclopaedia** [ˌsaɪkləˈpiːdiə] → **encyclopedia**
cylinder [ˈsɪləndər] *n* : cilindro *m*
cylindrical [səˈlɪndrɪkəl] *adj* : cilíndrico
cymbal [ˈsɪmbəl] *n* : platillo *m*, címbalo *m*
cynic [ˈsɪnɪk] *n* : cínico *m*, -ca *f*
cynical [ˈsɪnɪkəl] *adj* : cínico
cynicism [ˈsɪnəˌsɪzəm] *n* : cinismo *m*
cypress [ˈsaɪprəs] *n* : ciprés *m*
Cypriot [ˈsɪpriət, -ˌɑt] *n* : chipriota *mf* — **Cypriot** *adj*
cyst [ˈsɪst] *n* : quiste *m*
cytoplasm [ˈsaɪt̬oˌplæzəm] *n* : citoplasma *m*
czar [ˈzɑr, ˈsɑr] *n* : zar *m*
czarina [zɑˈriːnə, sɑ-] *n* : zarina *f*
Czech [ˈʧɛk] *n* **1** : checo *m*, -ca *f* **2** : checo *m* (idioma) — **Czech** *adj*
Czechoslovak [ˌʧɛkoˈsloːˌvɑk, -ˌvæk] *or* **Czechoslovakian** [-sloˈvɑkiən, -ˈvæ-] *n* : checoslovaco *m*, -ca *f* — **Czechoslovak** *or* **Czechoslovakian** *adj*

D

d [ˈdiː] *n, pl* **d's** *or* **ds** [ˈdiːz] : cuarta letra del alfabeto inglés
dab[1] [ˈdæb] *vt* **dabbed; dabbing** : darle toques ligeros a, aplicar suavemente
dab[2] *n* **1** BIT : toque *m*, pizca *f*, poco *m* ⟨a dab of ointment : un toque de ungüento⟩ **2** PAT : toque *m* ligero, golpecito *m*
dabble [ˈdæbəl] *v* **-bled; -bling** *vt* SPATTER : salpicar — *vi* **1** SPLASH : chapotear **2** TRIFLE : jugar, interesarse superficialmente
dabbler [ˈdæbələr] *n* : diletante *mf*
dachshund [ˈdɑksˌhʊnt, -ˌhʊnd; ˈdɑksənt, -sənd] *n* : perro *m* salchicha
dad [ˈdæd] *n* : papá *m fam*
daddy [ˈdædi] *n, pl* **-dies** : papi *m fam*
daffodil [ˈdæfəˌdɪl] *n* : narciso *m*
daft [ˈdæft] *adj* : tonto, bobo
dagger [ˈdægər] *n* : daga *f*, puñal *m*
dahlia [ˈdæljə, ˈdɑl-, ˈdeɪl-] *n* : dalia *f*
daily[1] [ˈdeɪli] *adv* : a diario, diariamente
daily[2] *adj* : diario, cotidiano
daily[3] *n, pl* **-lies** : diario *m*, periódico *m*
daintily [ˈdeɪntəli] *adv* : delicadamente, con delicadeza
daintiness [ˈdeɪntinəs] *n* : delicadeza *f*, finura *f*
dainty[1] [ˈdeɪnti] *adj* **-tier; -est** **1** DELICATE : delicado **2** FASTIDIOUS : remilgado, melindroso **3** DELICIOUS : exquisito, sabroso
dainty[2] *n, pl* **-ties** DELICACY : exquisitez *f*, manjar *m*
dairy [ˈdæri] *n, pl* **-ies** **1** *or* **dairy store** : lechería *f* **2** *or* **dairy farm** : granja *f* lechera
dairymaid [ˈdæriˌmeɪd] *n* : lechera *f*
dairyman [ˈdærimən, -ˌmæn] *n, pl* **-men** [-mən, -ˌmɛn] : lechero *m*
dais [ˈdeɪəs] *n* : tarima *f*, estrado *m*
daisy [ˈdeɪzi] *n, pl* **-sies** : margarita *f*
dale [ˈdeɪl] *n* : valle *m*
dally [ˈdæli] *vi* **-lied; -lying** **1** TRIFLE : juguetear **2** DAWDLE : entretenerse, perder tiempo
dalmatian [dælˈmeɪʃən, dɔl-] *n* : dálmata *m*
dam[1] [ˈdæm] *vt* **dammed; damming** : represar, embalsar
dam[2] *n* **1** : represa *f*, dique *m* **2** : madre *f* (de animales domésticos)

damage[1] [ˈdæmɪʤ] *vt* **-aged; -aging** : dañar (un objeto o una máquina), perjudicar (la salud o una reputación)
damage[2] *n* **1** : daño *m*, perjuicio *m* **2 damages** *npl* : daños y perjuicios *mpl*
damaging [ˈdæməʤɪŋ] *adj* : perjudicial
damask [ˈdæməsk] *n* : damasco *m*
dame [ˈdeɪm] *n* LADY : dama *f*, señora *f*
damn[1] [ˈdæm] *vt* **1** CONDEMN : condenar **2** CURSE : maldecir
damn[2] *or* **damned** [ˈdæmd] *adj* : condenado *fam*, maldito *fam*
damn[3] *n* : pito *m*, bledo *m*, comino *m* ⟨it's not worth a damn : no vale un pito⟩ ⟨I don't give a damn : me importa un comino⟩
damnable [ˈdæmnəbəl] *adj* : condenable, detestable
damnation [dæmˈneɪʃən] *n* : condenación *f*
damned[1] [ˈdæmd] *adv* VERY : muy
damned[2] *adj* **1** → **damnable** **2** REMARKABLE : extraordinario
damp[1] [ˈdæmp] *vt* → **dampen**
damp[2] *adj* : húmedo
damp[3] *n* MOISTURE : humedad *f*
dampen [ˈdæmpən] *vt* **1** MOISTEN : humedecer **2** DISCOURAGE : desalentar, desanimar
damper [ˈdæmpər] *n* **1** : regulador *m* de tiro (de una chimenea) **2** : sordina *f* (de un piano) **3 to put a damper on** : desanimar, apagar (el entusiasmo), enfriar
dampness [ˈdæmpnəs] *n* : humedad *f*
damsel [ˈdæmzəl] *n* : damisela *f*
dance[1] [ˈdænts] *v* **danced; dancing** : bailar
dance[2] *n* : baile *m*
dancer [ˈdæntsər] *n* : bailarín *m*, -rina *f*
dandelion [ˈdændəlˌaɪən] *n* : diente *m* de león
dandruff [ˈdændrəf] *n* : caspa *f*
dandy[1] [ˈdændi] *adj* **-dier; -est** : excelente, magnífico, macanudo *fam*
dandy[2] *n, pl* **-dies** **1** FOP : dandi *m* **2** : algo *m* excelente ⟨this new program is a dandy : este programa nuevo es algo excelente⟩
Dane [ˈdeɪn] *n* : danés *m*, -nesa *f*
danger [ˈdeɪnʤər] *n* : peligro *m*
dangerous [ˈdeɪnʤərəs] *adj* : peligroso
dangle [ˈdæŋgəl] *v* **-gled; -gling** *vi* HANG : colgar, pender — *vt* **1** SWING : hacer oscilar **2** PROFFER : ofrecer (como incentivo) **3 to keep someone dangling** : dejar a alguien en suspenso
Danish[1] [ˈdeɪnɪʃ] *adj* : danés
Danish[2] *n* : danés *m* (idioma)
dank [ˈdæŋk] *adj* : frío y húmedo
dapper [ˈdæpər] *adj* : pulcro, atildado
dappled [ˈdæpəld] *adj* : moteado ⟨a dappled horse : un caballo rodado⟩
dare[1] [ˈdær] *v* **dared; daring** *vi* : osar, atreverse ⟨how dare you! : ¡cómo te atreves!⟩ — *vt* **1** CHALLENGE : desafiar, retar **2 to dare to do something** : atreverse a hacer algo, osar hacer algo
dare[2] *n* : desafío *m*, reto *m*
daredevil [ˈdærˌdɛvəl] *n* : persona *f* temeraria
daring[1] [ˈdærɪŋ] *adj* : osado, atrevido, audaz
daring[2] *n* : arrojo *m*, coraje *m*, audacia *f*
dark [ˈdɑrk] *adj* **1** : oscuro (dícese del ambiente o de los colores), moreno (dícese del pelo o de la piel) **2** SOMBER : sombrío, triste
darken [ˈdɑrkən] *vt* **1** DIM : oscurecer **2** SADDEN : entristecer — *vi* : ensombrecerse, nublarse
darkly [ˈdɑrkli] *adv* **1** DIMLY : oscuramente **2** GLOOMILY : tristemente **3** MYSTERIOUSLY : misteriosamente, enigmáticamente
darkness [ˈdɑrknəs] *n* : oscuridad *f*, tinieblas *f*
darling[1] [ˈdɑrlɪŋ] *adj* **1** BELOVED : querido, amado **2** CHARMING : encantador, mono *fam*
darling[2] *n* **1** BELOVED : querido *m*, -da *f*; amado *m*, -da *f*; cariño *m*, -ña *f* **2** FAVORITE : preferido *m*, -da *f*; favorito *m*, -ta *f*
darn[1] [ˈdɑrn] *vt* : zurcir
darn[2] *n* **1** : zurcido *m* **2** → **damn**[3]
dart[1] [ˈdɑrt] *vt* THROW : lanzar, tirar — *vi* DASH : lanzarse, precipitarse
dart[2] *n* **1** : dardo *m* **2 darts** *npl* : juego *m* de dardos
dash[1] [ˈdæʃ] *vt* **1** SMASH : romper, estrellar **2** HURL : arrojar, lanzar **3** SPLASH : salpicar **4** FRUSTRATE : frustrar **5 to dash off** : hacer (algo) rápidamente — *vi* **1** SMASH : romperse, estrellarse **2** DART : lanzarse, irse apresuradamente
dash[2] *n* **1** BURST, SPLASH : arranque *m*, salpicadura *f* (de aguas) **2** : guión *m* largo (signo de puntuación) **3** DROP : gota *f*, pizca *f* **4** VERVE : brío *m* **5** RACE : carrera *f* ⟨a 100-meter dash : una carrera de 100 metros⟩ **6 to make a dash for it** : precipitarse (hacia), echarse a correr **7** → **dashboard**
dashboard [ˈdæʃˌbord] *n* : tablero *m* de instrumentos
dashing [ˈdæʃɪŋ] *adj* : gallardo, apuesto
data [ˈdeɪt̬ə, ˈdæ-, ˈdɑ-] *ns & pl* : datos *mpl*, información *f*
database [ˈdeɪt̬əˌbeɪs, ˈdæ-, ˈdɑ-] *n* : base *f* de datos
date[1] [ˈdeɪt] *v* **dated; dating** *vt* **1** : fechar (una carta, etc.), datar (un objeto) ⟨it was dated June 9 : estaba fechada el 9 de junio⟩ **2** : salir con ⟨she's dating my brother : sale con mi hermano⟩ — *vi* : datar
date[2] *n* **1** : fecha *f* ⟨to date : hasta la fecha⟩ **2** EPOCH, PERIOD : época *f*, período *m* **3** APPOINTMENT : cita *f* **4** COMPANION : acompañante *mf* **5** : dátil *m* (fruta)
dated [ˈdeɪt̬əd] *adj* OUT-OF-DATE : anticuado, pasado de moda

datum ['deɪṭəm, 'dæ-, 'dɑ-] *n, pl* **-ta** [-ṭə] *or* **-tums** : dato *m*
daub[1] ['dɔb] *vt* : embadurnar
daub[2] *n* : mancha *f*
daughter ['dɔṭər] *n* : hija *f*
daughter–in–law ['dɔṭərɪn,lɔ] *n, pl* **daughters–in–law** : nuera *f*, hija *f* política
daunt ['dɔnt] *vt* : amilanar, acobardar, intimidar
dauntless ['dɔntləs] *adj* : intrépido, impávido
davenport ['dævən,port] *n* : sofá *m*
dawdle ['dɔdəl] *vi* **-dled; -dling 1** DALLY : demorarse, entretenerse, perder tiempo **2** LOITER : vagar, holgazanear, haraganear
dawn[1] ['dɔn] *vi* **1** : amanecer, alborear, despuntar ⟨Saturday dawned clear and bright : el sábado amaneció claro y luminoso⟩ **2 to dawn on** : hacerse obvio ⟨it dawned on me that she was right : me di cuenta de que tenía razón⟩
dawn[2] *n* **1** DAYBREAK : amanecer *m*, alba *f* **2** BEGINNING : albor *m*, comienzo *m* ⟨the dawn of history : los albores de la historia⟩ **3 from dawn to dusk** : de sol a sol
day ['deɪ] *n* **1** : día *m* **2** DATE : fecha *f* **3** TIME : día *m*, tiempo *m* ⟨in olden days : intaño⟩ **4** WORKDAY : jornada *f* laboral
daybreak ['deɪ,breɪk] *n* : alba *f*, amanecer *m*
day care *n* : servicio *m* de guardería infantil
daydream[1] ['deɪ,dri:m] *vi* : soñar despierto, fantasear
daydream[2] *n* : ensueño *m*, ensoñación *f*, fantasía *f*
daylight ['deɪ,laɪt] *n* **1** : luz *f* del día ⟨in broad daylight : a plena luz del día⟩ **2** → **daybreak 3** → **daytime**
daylight saving time *n* : hora *f* de verano
daytime ['deɪ,taɪm] *n* : horas *fpl* diurnas, día *m*
daze[1] ['deɪz] *vt* **dazed; dazing 1** STUN : aturdir **2** DAZZLE : deslumbrar, ofuscar
daze[2] *n* **1** : aturdimiento *m* **2 in a daze** : aturdido, atontado
dazzle[1] ['dæzəl] *vt* **-zled; -zling** : deslumbrar, ofuscar
dazzle[2] *n* : resplandor *m*, brillo *m*
DDT [,di:,di:'ti:] *n* : DDT *m*
deacon ['di:kən] *n* : diácono *m*
dead[1] ['dɛd] *adv* **1** ABRUPTLY : repentinamente, súbitamente ⟨to stop dead : parar en seco⟩ **2** ABSOLUTELY : absolutamente ⟨I'm dead certain : estoy absolutamente seguro⟩ **3** DIRECTLY : justo ⟨dead ahead : justo adelante⟩
dead[2] *adj* **1** LIFELESS : muerto **2** NUMB : entumecido **3** INDIFFERENT : indiferente, frío **4** INACTIVE : inactivo ⟨a dead volcano : un volcán inactivo⟩ **5** : desconectado (dícese del teléfono), descargado (dícese de una batería) **6** EXHAUSTED : agotado, derrengado, muerto **7** OBSOLETE : obsoleto, muerto ⟨a dead language : una lengua muerta⟩ **8** EXACT : exacto ⟨in the dead center : justo en el blanco⟩
dead[3] *n* **1 the dead** : los muertos **2 in the dead of night** : a las altas horas de la noche **3 in the dead of winter** : en pleno invierno
deadbeat ['dɛd,bi:t] *n* **1** LOAFER : vago *m*, -ga *f*; holgazán *m*, -zana *f* **2** FREELOADER : gorrón *m*, -rrona *f fam*; gorrero *m*, -ra *f fam*
deaden ['dɛdən] *vt* **1** : atenuar (un dolor), entorpecer (sensaciones) **2** DULL : deslustrar **3** DISPIRIT : desanimar **4** MUFFLE : amortiguar, reducir (sonidos)
dead–end ['dɛd'ɛnd] *adj* **1** : sin salida ⟨dead-end street : calle sin salida⟩ **2** : sin futuro ⟨a dead-end job : un trabajo sin porvenir⟩
dead end *n* : callejón *m* sin salida
dead heat *n* : empate *m*
deadline ['dɛd,laɪn] *n* : fecha *f* límite, fecha *f* tope, plazo *m* (determinado)
deadlock[1] ['dɛd,lɑk] *vt* : estancar — *vi* : estancarse, llegar a punto muerto
deadlock[2] *n* : punto *m* muerto, impasse *m*
deadly[1] ['dɛdli] *adv* : extremadamente, sumamente ⟨deadly serious : muy en serio⟩
deadly[2] *adj* **-lier; -est 1** LETHAL : mortal, letal, mortífero **2** ACCURATE : certero, preciso ⟨a deadly aim : una puntería infalible⟩ **3** CAPITAL : capital ⟨the seven deadly sins : los siete pecados capitales⟩ **4** DULL : funesto, aburrido **5** EXTREME : extremo, absoluto ⟨a deadly calm : una calma absoluta⟩
deadpan[1] ['dɛd,pæn] *adv* : de manera inexpresiva, sin expresión
deadpan[2] *adj* : inexpresivo, impasible
deaf ['dɛf] *adj* : sordo
deafen ['dɛfən] *vt* **-ened; -ening** : ensordecer
deafening ['dɛfənɪŋ] *adj* : ensordecedor
deaf–mute ['dɛf'mju:t] *n* : sordomudo *m*, -da *f*
deafness ['dɛfnəs] *n* : sordera *f*
deal[1] ['di:l] *v* **dealt; dealing** *vt* **1** APPORTION : repartir ⟨to deal justice : repartir la justicia⟩ **2** DISTRIBUTE : repartir, dar (naipes) **3** DELIVER : asestar, propinar ⟨to deal a blow : asestar un golpe⟩ — *vi* **1** : dar, repartir (en juegos de naipes) **2 to deal in** : comerciar en, traficar con (drogas) **3 to deal with** CONCERN : tratar de, tener que ver con ⟨the book deals with poverty : el libro trata de la pobreza⟩ **4 to deal with** HANDLE : tratar (con), encargarse de **5 to deal with** TREAT : tratar ⟨the judge dealt with him severely : el juez lo trató con severidad⟩ **6 to deal with** ACCEPT : aceptar (una situación o desgracia)

deal[2] *n* **1** : reparto *m* (de naipes) **2** AGREEMENT, TRANSACTION : trato *m*, acuerdo *m*, transacción *f* **3** TREATMENT : trato *m* ⟨he got a raw deal : le hicieron una injusticia⟩ **4** BARGAIN : ganga *f*, oferta *f* **5 a good deal** *or* **a great deal** : mucho, una gran cantidad
dealer [ˈdiːlər] *n* : comerciante *mf*, traficante *mf*
dealership [ˈdiːlərˌʃɪp] *n* : concesión *f*
dealings [ˈdiːlɪŋz] *npl* **1** : relaciones *fpl* (personales) **2** TRANSACTIONS : negocios *mpl*, transacciones *fpl*
dean [ˈdiːn] *n* **1** : deán *m* (del clero) **2** : decano *m*, -na *f* (de una facultad o profesión)
dear[1] [ˈdɪr] *adj* **1** ESTEEMED, LOVED : querido, estimado ⟨a dear friend : un amigo querido⟩ ⟨Dear Sir : Estimado Señor⟩ **2** COSTLY : caro, costoso
dear[2] *n* : querido *m*, -da *f*; amado *m*, -da *f*
dearly [ˈdɪrli] *adv* **1** : mucho ⟨I love them dearly : los quiero mucho⟩ **2** : caro ⟨to pay dearly : pagar caro⟩
dearth [ˈdərθ] *n* : escasez *f*, carestía *f*
death [ˈdɛθ] *n* **1** : muerte *f*, fallecimiento *m* ⟨to be the death of : matar⟩ **2** FATALITY : víctima *f* (mortal); muerto *m*, -ta *f* **3** END : fin *m* ⟨the death of civilization : el fin de la civilización⟩
deathbed [ˈdɛθˌbɛd] *n* : lecho *m* de muerte
deathblow [ˈdɛθˌbloː] *n* : golpe *m* mortal
deathless [ˈdɛθləs] *adj* : eterno, inmortal
deathly [ˈdɛθli] *adj* : de muerte, sepulcral (dícese del silencio), cadavérico (dícese de la palidez)
debacle [dɪˈbɑkəl, -ˈbæ-] *n* : desastre *m*, debacle *m*, fiasco *m*
debar [diˈbɑr] *vt* **-barred; -barring** : excluir, prohibir
debase [diˈbeɪs] *vt* **-based; -basing** : degradar, envilecer
debasement [diˈbeɪsmənt] *n* : degradación *f*, envilecimiento *m*
debatable [diˈbeɪt̬əbəl] *adj* : discutible
debate[1] [diˈbeɪt] *vt* **-bated; -bating** : debatir, discutir
debate[2] *n* : debate *m*, discusión *f*
debauch [diˈbɔtʃ] *vt* : pervertir, corromper
debauchery [diˈbɔtʃəri] *n, pl* **-eries** : libertinaje *m*, disipación *f*, intemperancia *f*
debilitate [diˈbɪləˌteɪt] *vt* **-tated; -tating** : debilitar
debility [diˈbɪlət̬i] *n, pl* **-ties** : debilidad *f*
debit[1] [ˈdɛbɪt] *vt* : adeudar, cargar, debitar
debit[2] *n* : débito *m*, cargo *m*, debe *m*
debonair [ˌdɛbəˈnær] *adj* : elegante y desenvuelto, apuesto
debris [dəˈbriː, deɪ-; ˈdeɪˌbriː] *n, pl* **-bris** [-ˈbriːz, -ˌbriːz] **1** RUBBLE, RUINS : escombros *mpl*, ruinas *fpl*, restos *mpl* **2** RUBBISH : basura *f*, deshechos *mpl*
debt [ˈdɛt] *n* **1** : deuda *f* ⟨to pay a debt : saldar una deuda⟩ **2** INDEBTEDNESS : endeudamiento *m*
debtor [ˈdɛt̬ər] *n* : deudor *m*, -dora *f*
debunk [diˈbʌŋk] *vt* DISCREDIT : desacreditar, desprestigiar
debut[1] [deɪˈbjuː, ˈdeɪˌbjuː] *vi* : debutar
debut[2] *n* **1** : debut *m* (de un actor), estreno *m* (de una obra) **2** : debut *m*, presentación *f* (en sociedad)
debutante [ˈdɛbjʊˌtɑnt] *n* : debutante *f*
decade [ˈdɛˌkeɪd, dɛˈkeɪd] *n* : década *f*
decadence [ˈdɛkədənts] *n* : decadencia *f*
decadent [ˈdɛkədənt] *adj* : decadente
decaf[1] [ˈdiːˌkæf] → **decaffeinated**
decaf[2] *n* : café *m* descafeinado
decaffeinated [diˈkæfəˌneɪt̬əd] *adj* : descafeinado
decal [ˈdiːˌkæl, diˈkæl] *n* : calcomanía *f*
decamp [diˈkæmp] *vi* : irse, largarse *fam*
decant [diˈkænt] *vt* : decantar
decanter [diˈkæntər] *n* : licorera *f*, garrafa *f*
decapitate [diˈkæpəˌteɪt] *vt* **-tated; -tating** : decapitar
decay[1] [diˈkeɪ] *vi* **1** DECOMPOSE : descomponerse, pudrirse **2** DETERIORATE : deteriorarse **3** : cariarse (dícese de los dientes)
decay[2] *n* **1** DECOMPOSITION : descomposición *f* **2** DECLINE, DETERIORATION : decadencia *f*, deterioro *m* **3** : caries *f* (de los dientes)
decease[1] [diˈsiːs] *vi* **-ceased; -ceasing** : morir, fallecer
decease[2] *n* : fallecimiento *m*, defunción *f*, deceso *m*
deceit [diˈsiːt] *n* **1** DECEPTION : engaño *m* **2** DISHONESTY : deshonestidad *f*
deceitful [diˈsiːtfəl] *adj* : falso, embustero, engañoso, mentiroso
deceitfully [diˈsiːtfəli] *adv* : con engaño, con falsedad
deceitfulness [diˈsiːtfəlnəs] *n* : falsedad *f*, engaño *m*
deceive [diˈsiːv] *vt* **-ceived; -ceiving** : engañar, burlar
deceiver [diˈsiːvər] *n* : impostor *m*, -tora *f*
decelerate [diˈsɛləˌreɪt] *vi* **-ated; -ating** : reducir la velocidad, desacelerar
December [diˈsɛmbər] *n* : diciembre *m*
decency [ˈdisəntsi] *n, pl* **-cies** : decencia *f*, decoro *m*
decent [ˈdiːsənt] *adj* **1** CORRECT, PROPER : decente, decoroso, correcto **2** CLOTHED : vestido, presentable **3** MODEST : púdico, modesto **4** ADEQUATE : decente, adecuado ⟨decent wages : paga adecuada⟩
decently [ˈdiːsəntli] *adv* : decentemente
decentralize [diˈsɛntrəˌlaɪz] *v* **-lized** [-ˌlaɪzd]; **-lizing** [-ˌlaɪzɪŋ] *vt* : descentralizar — *vi* : descentralizarse
deception [diˈsɛpʃən] *n* : engaño *m*

deceptive [di'sɛptɪv] *adj* : engañoso, falaz — **deceptively** *adv*
decibel ['dɛsəbəl, -ˌbɛl] *n* : decibelio *m*
decide [di'saɪd] *v* **-cided; -ciding** *vt* **1** CONCLUDE : decidir, llegar a la conclusión de ⟨he decided what to do : decidió qué iba a hacer⟩ **2** DETERMINE : decidir, determinar ⟨one blow decided the fight : un solo golpe determinó la pelea⟩ **3** CONVINCE : decidir ⟨her pleas decided me to help : sus súplicas me decidieron a ayudarla⟩ **4** RESOLVE : resolver — *vi* : decidirse
decided [di'saɪdəd] *adj* **1** UNQUESTIONABLE : indudable **2** RESOLUTE : decidido, resuelto — **decidedly** *adv*
deciduous [di'sɪʤuəs] *adj* : caduco, de hoja caduca
decimal¹ ['dɛsəməl] *adj* : decimal
decimal² *n* : número *m* decimal
decipher [di'saɪfər] *vt* : descifrar — **decipherable** [-əbəl] *adj*
decision [dɪ'sɪʒən] *n* : decisión *f*, determinación *f* ⟨to make a decision : tomar una decisión⟩
decisive [dɪ'saɪsɪv] *adj* **1** DECIDING : decisivo ⟨the decisive vote : el voto decisivo⟩ **2** CONCLUSIVE : decisivo, concluyente, contundente ⟨a decisive victory : una victoria contundente⟩ **3** RESOLUTE : decidido, resuelto, firme
decisively [dɪ'saɪsɪvli] *adv* : con decisión, de manera decisiva
decisiveness [dɪ'saɪsɪvnəs] *n* **1** FORCEFULNESS : contundencia *f* **2** RESOLUTION : firmeza *f*, decisión *f*, determinación *f*
deck¹ ['dɛk] *vt* **1** FLOOR : tumbar, derribar ⟨she decked him with one blow : lo tumbó de un solo golpe⟩ **2 to deck out** : adornar, engalanar
deck² *n* **1** : cubierta *f* (de un barco) **2** *or* **deck of cards** : baraja *f* (de naipes)
declaim [di'kleɪm] *v* : declamar
declaration [ˌdɛklə'reɪʃən] *n* : declaración *f*, pronunciamiento *m* (oficial)
declare [di'klær] *vt* **-clared; -claring** : declarar, manifestar ⟨to declare war : declarar la guerra⟩ ⟨they declared their support : manifestaron su apoyo⟩
decline¹ [di'klaɪn] *v* **-clined; -clining** *vi* **1** DESCEND : descender **2** DETERIORATE : deteriorarse, decaer ⟨her health is declining : su salud se está deteriorando⟩ **3** DECREASE : disminuir, decrecer, decaer **4** REFUSE : rehusar — *vt* **1** INFLECT : declinar **2** REFUSE, TURN DOWN : declinar, rehusar
decline² *n* **1** DETERIORATION : decadencia *f*, deterioro *m* **2** DECREASE : disminución *f*, descenso *m* **3** SLOPE : declive *m*, pendiente *f*
decode [di'ko:d] *vt* **-coded; -coding** : descifrar (un mensaje), descodificar (una señal)
decoder [di'ko:dər] *n* : descodificador *m*
decompose [ˌdi:kəm'po:z] *v* **-posed; -posing** *vt* **1** BREAK DOWN : descomponer **2** ROT : descomponer, pudrir — *vi* : descomponerse, pudrirse
decomposition [ˌdi:ˌkɑmpə'zɪʃən] *n* : descomposición *f*
decongestant [ˌdi:kən'ʤɛstənt] *n* : descongestionante *m*
decor *or* **décor** [deɪ'kɔr, 'deɪˌkɔr] *n* : decoración *f*
decorate ['dɛkəˌreɪt] *vt* **-rated; -rating** **1** ADORN : decorar, adornar **2** : condecorar ⟨he was decorated for bravery : lo condecoraron por valor⟩
decoration [ˌdɛkə'reɪʃən] *n* **1** ADORNMENT : decoración *f*, adorno *m* **2** : condecoración *f* (de honor)
decorative ['dɛkərət̬ɪv, -ˌreɪ-] *adj* : decorativo, ornamental, de adorno
decorator ['dɛkəˌreɪt̬ər] *n* : decorador *m*, -dora *f*
decorum [di'korəm] *n* : decoro *m*
decoy¹ ['di:ˌkɔɪ, di'-] *vt* : atraer (con señuelo)
decoy² *n* : señuelo *m*, reclamo *m*, cimbel *m*
decrease¹ [di'kri:s] *v* **-creased; -creasing** *vi* : decrecer, disminuir, bajar — *vt* : reducir, disminuir
decrease² ['di:ˌkri:s] *n* : disminución *f*, descenso *m*, bajada *f*
decree¹ [di'kri:] *vt* **-creed; -creeing** : decretar
decree² *n* : decreto *m*
decrepit [di'krɛpɪt] *adj* **1** FEEBLE : decrépito, débil **2** DILAPIDATED : deteriorado, ruinoso
decry [di'kraɪ] *vt* **-cried; -crying** : censurar, criticar
dedicate ['dɛdɪˌkeɪt] *vt* **-cated; -cating** **1** : dedicar ⟨she dedicated the book to Carlos : le dedicó el libro a Carlos⟩ **2** : consagrar, dedicar ⟨to dedicate one's life : consagrar uno su vida⟩
dedication [ˌdɛdɪ'keɪʃən] *n* **1** DEVOTION : dedicación *f*, devoción *f* **2** : dedicatoria *f* (de un libro, una canción, etc.) **3** CONSECRATION : dedicación *f*
deduce [di'du:s, -'dju:s] *vt* **-duced; -ducing** : deducir, inferir
deduct [di'dʌkt] *vt* : deducir, descontar, restar
deductible [di'dʌktəbəl] *adj* : deducible
deduction [di'dʌkʃən] *n* : deducción *f*
deed¹ ['di:d] *vt* : ceder, transferir
deed² *n* **1** ACT : acto *m*, acción *f*, hecho *m* ⟨a good deed : una buena acción⟩ **2** FEAT : hazaña *f*, proeza *f* **3** TITLE : escritura *f*, título *m*
deem ['di:m] *vt* : considerar, juzgar
deep¹ ['di:p] *adv* : hondo, profundamente ⟨to dig deep : cavar hondo⟩
deep² *adj* **1** : hondo, profundo ⟨the deep end : la parte honda⟩ ⟨a deep wound : una herida profunda⟩ **2** WIDE : ancho **3** INTENSE : profundo, intenso **4** DARK : intenso, subido ⟨deep red : rojo subido⟩ **5** LOW : profundo ⟨a deep tone

: un tono profundo> **6** ABSORBED : absorto <deep in thought : absorto en la meditación>
deep³ *n* **1 the deep** : lo profundo, el piélago **2 the deep of night** : lo más profundo de la noche
deepen [ˈdi:pən] *vt* **1** : ahondar, profundizar **2** INTENSIFY : intensificar — *vi* **1** : hacerse más profundo **2** INTENSIFY : intensificarse
deeply [ˈdi:pli] *adv* : hondo, profundamente <I'm deeply sorry : lo siento sinceramente>
deep–seated [ˈdi:pˈsi:t̬əd] *adj* : profundamente arraigado, enraizado
deer [ˈdɪr] *ns & pl* : ciervo *m*, venado *m*
deerskin [ˈdɪrˌskɪn] *n* : piel *f* de venado
deface [diˈfeɪs] *vt* **-faced; -facing** MAR : desfigurar
defacement [diˈfeɪsmənt] *n* : desfiguración *f*
defamation [ˌdɛfəˈmeɪʃən] *n* : difamación *f*
defamatory [diˈfæməˌtori] *adj* : difamatorio
defame [diˈfeɪm] *vt* **-famed; -faming** : difamar, calumniar
default¹ [diˈfɔlt, ˈdi:ˌfɔlt] *vi* **1** : no cumplir (con una obligación), no pagar **2** : no presentarse (en un tribunal)
default² *n* **1** NEGLECT : omisión *f*, negligencia *f* **2** NONPAYMENT : impago *m*, falta *f* de pago **3 to win by default** : ganar por abandono
defaulter [diˈfɔltər] *n* : moroso *m*, -sa *f*; rebelde *mf* (en un tribunal)
defeat¹ [diˈfi:t] *vt* **1** FRUSTRATE : frustrar **2** BEAT : vencer, derrotar
defeat² *n* : derrota *f*, rechazo *m* (de legislación), fracaso *m* (de planes, etc.)
defecate [ˈdɛfɪˌkeɪt] *vi* **-cated; -cating** : defecar
defect¹ [diˈfɛkt] *vi* : desertar
defect² [ˈdi:ˌfɛkt, diˈfɛkt] *n* : defecto *m*
defection [diˈfɛkʃən] *n* : deserción *f*, defección *f*
defective [diˈfɛktɪv] *adj* **1** FAULTY : defectuoso **2** DEFICIENT : deficiente
defector [diˈfɛktər] *n* : desertor *m*, -tora *f*
defend [diˈfɛnd] *vt* : defender
defendant [diˈfɛndənt] *n* : acusado *m*, -da *f*; demandado *m*, -da *f*
defender [diˈfɛndər] *n* **1** ADVOCATE : defensor *m*, -sora *f* **2** : defensa *mf* (en deportes)
defense [diˈfɛnts, ˈdi:ˌfɛnts] *n* : defensa *f*
defenseless [diˈfɛntsləs] *adj* : indefenso
defensive¹ [diˈfɛntsɪv] *adj* : defensivo
defensive² *n* **on the defensive** : a la defensiva
defer [diˈfər] *v* **-ferred; -ferring** *vt* POSTPONE : diferir, aplazar, posponer — *vi* **to defer to** : deferir a
deference [ˈdɛfərənts] *n* : deferencia *f*
deferential [ˌdɛfəˈrɛntʃəl] *adj* : respetuoso
deferment [diˈfərmənt] *n* : aplazamiento *m*
defiance [diˈfaɪənts] *n* : desafío *m*
defiant [diˈfaɪənt] *adj* : desafiante, insolente
deficiency [diˈfɪʃəntsi] *n, pl* **-cies** : deficiencia *f*, carencia *f*
deficient [diˈfɪʃənt] *adj* : deficiente, carente
deficit [ˈdɛfəsɪt] *n* : déficit *m*
defile [diˈfaɪl] *vt* **-filed; -filing 1** DIRTY : ensuciar, manchar **2** CORRUPT : corromper **3** DESECRATE, PROFANE : profanar **4** DISHONOR : deshonrar
defilement [diˈfaɪlmənt] *n* **1** DESECRATION : profanación *f* **2** CORRUPTION : corrupción *f* **3** CONTAMINATION : contaminación *f*
define [diˈfaɪn] *vt* **-fined; -fining 1** BOUND : delimitar, demarcar **2** CLARIFY : aclarar, definir **3** : definir <to define a word : definir una palabra>
definite [ˈdɛfənɪt] *adj* **1** CERTAIN : definido, determinado **2** CLEAR : claro, explícito **3** UNQUESTIONABLE : seguro, incuestionable
definite article *n* : artículo *m* definido
definitely [ˈdɛfənɪtli] *adv* **1** DOUBTLESSLY : indudablemente, sin duda **2** DEFINITIVELY : definitivamente, seguramente
definition [ˌdɛfəˈnɪʃən] *n* : definición *f*
definitive [diˈfɪnət̬ɪv] *adj* **1** CONCLUSIVE : definitivo, decisivo **2** AUTHORITATIVE : de autoridad, autorizado
deflate [diˈfleɪt] *v* **-flated; -flating** *vt* **1** : desinflar (una llanta, etc.) **2** REDUCE : rebajar <to deflate one's ego : bajarle los humos a uno> — *vi* : desinflarse
deflation [diˈfleɪʃən] *n* **1** : desinflación *f* (de una llanta, etc.) **2** : deflación *f* (económica)
deflect [diˈflɛkt] *vt* : desviar — *vi* : desviarse
defoliant [diˈfo:liənt] *n* : defoliante *m*
deforestation [diˌfɔrəˈsteɪʃən] *n* : deforestación *f*, desforestación *f*
deform [diˈfɔrm] *vt* : deformar
deformation [ˌdi:ˌfɔrˈmeɪʃən] *n* : deformación *f*
deformed [diˈfɔrmd] *adj* : deforme
deformity [diˈfɔrmət̬i] *n, pl* **-ties** : deformidad *f*
defraud [diˈfrɔd] *vt* : estafar, defraudar
defray [diˈfreɪ] *vt* : sufragar, costear
defrost [diˈfrɔst] *vt* : descongelar, deshelar — *vi* : descongelarse, deshelarse
deft [ˈdɛft] *adj* : hábil, diestro — **deftly** *adv*
defunct [diˈfʌŋkt] *adj* **1** DECEASED : difunto, fallecido **2** EXTINCT : extinto, fenecido
defuse [diˈfju:z] *vt* : desactivar <to defuse the situation : reducir las tensiones>
defy [diˈfaɪ] *vt* **-fied; -fying 1** CHALLENGE : desafiar, retar **2** DISOBEY : desobedecer **3** RESIST : resistir, hacer imposible, hacer inútil

degenerate[1] [di'ʤɛnə,reɪt] *vi* **-ated; -ating** : degenerar
degenerate[2] [di'ʤɛnərət] *adj* : degenerado
degeneration [di,ʤɛnə'reɪʃən] *n* : degeneración *f*
degenerative [di'ʤɛnərətɪv] *adj* : degenerative
degradation [,dɛgrə'deɪʃən] *n* : degradación *f*
degrade [di'greɪd] *vt* **-graded; -grading 1** : degradar, envilecer **2 to degrade oneself** : rebajarse
degrading [di'greɪdɪŋ] *adj* : degradante
degree [di'gri:] *n* **1** EXTENT : grado *m* ⟨a third degree burn : una quemadura de tercer grado⟩ **2** : título *m* (de enseñanza superior) **3** : grado *m* (de un círculo, de la temperatura) **4 by degrees** : gradualmente, poco a poco
dehydrate [di'haɪ,dreɪt] *v* **-drated; -drating** *vt* : deshidratar — *vi* : deshidratarse
dehydration [,di:haɪ'dreɪʃən] *n* : deshidratación *f*
deice [,di:'aɪs] *vt* **-iced; -icing** : deshelar, descongelar
deify ['di:ə,faɪ, 'deɪ-] *vt* **-fied; -fying** : deificar
deign ['deɪn] *vi* : dignarse, condescender
deity ['di:əṯi, 'deɪ-] *n, pl* **-ties 1 the Deity** : Dios *m* **2** GOD, GODDESS : deidad *f*; dios *m*, diosa *f*
dejected [di'ʤɛktəd] *adj* : abatido, desalentado, desanimado
dejection [di'ʤɛkʃən] *n* : abatimiento *m*, desaliento *m*, desánimo *m*
delay[1] [di'leɪ] *vt* **1** POSTPONE : posponer, postergar **2** HOLD UP : retrasar, demorar — *vi* : tardar, demorar
delay[2] *n* **1** LATENESS : tardanza *f* **2** HOLDUP : demora *f*, retraso *m*
delectable [di'lɛktəbəl] *adj* **1** DELICIOUS : delicioso, exquisito **2** DELIGHTFUL : encantador
delegate[1] ['dɛlɪ,geɪt] *v* **-gated; -gating** : delegar
delegate[2] ['dɛlɪgət, -,geɪt] *n* : delegado *m*, -da *f*
delegation [,dɛlɪ'geɪʃən] *n* : delegación *f*
delete [di'li:t] *vt* **-leted; -leting** : suprimir, tachar, eliminar
deletion [di'li:ʃən] *n* : supresión *f*, tachadura *f*, eliminación *f*
deli ['dɛli] → **delicatessen**
deliberate[1] [dɪ'lɪbə,reɪt] *v* **-ated; -ating** *vt* : deliberar sobre, reflexionar sobre, considerar — *vi* : deliberar
deliberate[2] [dɪ'lɪbərət] *adj* **1** CONSIDERED : reflexionado, premeditado **2** INTENTIONAL : deliberado, intencional **3** SLOW : lento, pausado
deliberately [dɪ'lɪbərətli] *adv* **1** INTENTIONALLY : adrede, a propósito **2** SLOWLY : pausadamente, lentamente
deliberation [dɪ,lɪbə'reɪʃən] *n* **1** CONSIDERATION : deliberación *f*, consideración *f* **2** SLOWNESS : lentitud *f*
delicacy ['dɛlɪkəsi] *n, pl* **-cies 1** : manjar *m*, exquisitez *f* ⟨caviar is a real delicacy : el caviar es un verdadero manjar⟩ **2** FINENESS : delicadeza *f* **3** FRAGILITY : fragilidad *f*
delicate ['dɛlɪkət] *adj* **1** SUBTLE : delicado ⟨a delicate fragrance : una fragancia delicada⟩ **2** DAINTY : delicado, primoroso, fino **3** FRAGILE : frágil **4** SENSITIVE : delicado ⟨a delicate matter : un asunto delicado⟩
delicately ['dɛlɪkətli] *adv* : delicadamente, con delicadeza
delicatessen [,dɛlɪkə'tɛsən] *n* : charcutería *f*, fiambrería *f*, salchichonería *f* *Mex*
delicious [di'lɪʃəs] *adj* : delicioso, exquisito, rico — **deliciously** *adv*
delight[1] [dɪ'laɪt] *vt* : deleitar, encantar — *vi* **to delight in** : deleitarse con, complacerse en
delight[2] *n* **1** JOY : placer *m*, deleite *m*, gozo *m* **2** : encanto *m* ⟨your garden is a delight : su jardín es un encanto⟩
delightful [dɪ'laɪtfəl] *adj* : delicioso, encantador
delightfully [dɪ'laɪtfəli] *adv* : de manera encantadora, de maravilla
delineate [di'lɪni,eɪt] *vt* **-eated; -eating** : delinear, trazar, bosquejar
delinquency [di'lɪŋkwəntsi] *n, pl* **-cies** : delincuencia *f*
delinquent[1] [di'lɪŋkwənt] *adj* **1** : delincuente **2** OVERDUE : vencido y sin pagar, moroso
delinquent[2] *n* : delincuente *mf* ⟨juvenile delinquent : delincuente juvenil⟩
delirious [di'lɪriəs] *adj* : delirante ⟨delirious with joy : loco de alegría⟩
delirium [di'lɪriəm] *n* : delirio *m*, desvarío *m*
deliver [di'lɪvər] *vt* **1** FREE : liberar, librar **2** DISTRIBUTE, HAND : entregar, repartir **3** : asistir en el parto de (un niño) **4** : pronunciar ⟨to deliver a speech : pronunciar un discurso⟩ **5** PROJECT : despachar, lanzar ⟨he delivered a fast ball : lanzó un pelota rápida⟩ **6** DEAL : propinar, asestar ⟨to deliver a blow : asestar un golpe⟩
deliverance [di'lɪvərənts] *n* : liberación *f*, rescate *m*, salvación *f*
deliverer [di'lɪvərər] *n* RESCUER : libertador *m*, -dora *f*; salvador *m*, -dora *f*
delivery [di'lɪvəri] *n, pl* **-eries 1** LIBERATION : liberación *f* **2** : entrega *f*, reparto *m* ⟨cash on delivery : entrega contra reembolso⟩ ⟨home delivery : servicio a domicilio⟩ **3** CHILDBIRTH : parto *m*, alumbramiento *m* **4** SPEECH : expresión *f* oral, modo *m* de hablar **5** THROW : lanzamiento *m*
dell ['dɛl] *n* : hondonada *f*, valle *m* pequeño
delta ['dɛltə] *n* : delta *m*
delude [di'lu:d] *vt* **-luded; -luding 1** : engañar **2 to delude oneself** : engañarse

deluge[1] [ˈdɛlˌjuːʤ, -ˌjuːʒ] *vt* **-uged; -uging** **1** FLOOD : inundar **2** OVERWHELM : abrumar ⟨deluged with requests : abrumado de pedidos⟩
deluge[2] *n* **1** FLOOD : inundación *f* **2** DOWNPOUR : aguacero *m* **3** BARRAGE : aluvión *m*
delusion [diˈluːʒən] *n* **1** : ilusión *f* (falsa) **2 delusions of grandeur** : delirios *mpl* de grandeza
deluxe [diˈlʌks, -ˈlʊks] *adj* : de lujo
delve [ˈdɛlv] *vi* **delved; delving** **1** DIG : escarbar **2 to delve into** PROBE : cavar en, ahondar en
demagogue [ˈdɛməˌgɑg] *n* : demagogo *m*, demagoga *f*
demand[1] [diˈmænd] *vt* : demandar, exigir, reclamar
demand[2] *n* **1** REQUEST : petición *f*, pedido *m*, demanda *f* ⟨by popular demand : a petición del público⟩ **2** CLAIM : reclamación *f*, exigencia *f* **3** MARKET : demanda *f* ⟨supply and demand : la oferta y la demanda⟩
demanding [diˈmændɪŋ] *adj* : exigente
demarcation [ˌdiːˌmɑrˈkeɪʃən] *n* : demarcación *f*, deslinde *m*
demean [diˈmiːn] *vt* : degradar, rebajar
demeanor [diˈmiːnər] *n* : comportamiento *m*, conducta *f*
demented [diˈmɛntəd] *adj* : demente, loco
dementia [diˈmɛntʃə] *n* : demencia *f*
demerit [diˈmɛrət] *n* : demérito *m*
demigod [ˈdɛmiˌgɑd, -ˌgɔd] *n* : semidiós *m*
demise [dɪˈmaɪz] *n* **1** DEATH : fallecimiento *m*, deceso *m* **2** END : hundimiento *m*, desaparición *f* (de una institución, etc.)
demitasse [ˈdɛmiˌtæs, -ˌtɑs] *n* : taza *f* pequeña (de café)
demobilization [diˌmoːbələˈzeɪʃən] *n* : desmovilización *f*
demobilize [diˈmoːbəˌlaɪz] *vt* **-lized; -lizing** : desmovilizar
democracy [diˈmɑkrəsi] *n, pl* **-cies** : democracia *f*
democrat [ˈdɛməˌkræt] *n* : demócrata *mf*
democratic [ˌdɛməˈkræṭɪk] *adj* : democrático — **democratically** [-ṭɪkli] *adv*
demographic [dɛməˈgræfɪk] *adj* : demográfico
demolish [diˈmɑlɪʃ] *vt* **1** RAZE : demoler, derribar, arrasar **2** DESTROY : destruir, destrozar
demolition [ˌdɛməˈlɪʃən, ˌdiː-] *n* : demolición *f*, derribo *m*
demon [ˈdiːmən] *n* : demonio *m*, diablo *m*
demonstrably [diˈmɑntstrəbli] *adv* : manifiestamente, claramente
demonstrate [ˈdɛmənˌstreɪt] *vt* **-strated; -strating** **1** SHOW : demostrar **2** PROVE : probar, demostrar **3** EXPLAIN : explicar, ilustrar
demonstration [ˌdɛmənˈstreɪʃən] *n* **1** SHOW : muestra *f*, demostración *f* **2** RALLY : manifestación *f*
demonstrative [diˈmɑntstrəṭɪv] *adj* **1** EFFUSIVE : efusivo, expresivo, demostrativo **2** : demostrativo (en lingüística) ⟨demonstrative pronoun : pronombre demostrativo⟩
demonstrator [ˈdɛmənˌstreɪṭər] *n* **1** : demostrador *m*, -dora *f* (de productos) **2** PROTESTER : manifestante *mf*
demoralize [diˈmɔrəˌlaɪz] *vt* **-ized; -izing** : desmoralizar
demote [diˈmoːt] *vt* **-moted; -moting** : degradar, bajar de categoría
demotion [diˈmoːʃən] *n* : degradación *f*, descenso *m* de categoría
demur [diˈmər] *vi* **-murred; -murring** **1** OBJECT : oponerse **2 to demur at** : ponerle objeciones a (algo)
demure [diˈmjʊr] *adj* : recatado, modesto — **demurely** *adv*
den [ˈdɛn] *n* **1** LAIR : cubil *m*, madriguera *f* **2** HIDEOUT : guarida *f* **3** STUDY : estudio *m*, gabinete *m*
denature [diˈneɪʧər] *vt* **-tured; -turing** : desnaturalizar
denial [diˈnaɪəl] *n* **1** REFUSAL : rechazo *m*, denegación *f*, negativa *f* **2** REPUDIATION : negación *f* (de una creencia, etc.), rechazo *m*
denigrate [ˈdɛnɪˌgreɪt] *vt* **-grated; -grating** : denigrar
denim [ˈdɛnəm] *n* **1** : tela *f* vaquera, mezclilla *f Chile, Mex* **2 denims** *npl* → **jeans**
denizen [ˈdɛnəzən] *n* : habitante *mf*; morador *m*, -dora *f*
denomination [dɪˌnɑməˈneɪʃən] *n* **1** FAITH : confesión *f*, fe *f* **2** VALUE : denominación *f*, valor *m* (de una moneda)
denominator [dɪˈnɑməˌneɪṭər] *n* : denominador *m*
denote [diˈnoːt] *vt* **-noted; -noting** **1** INDICATE, MARK : indicar, denotar, señalar **2** MEAN : significar
denouement [ˌdeɪˌnuːˈmɑ] *n* : desenlace *m*
denounce [diˈnaʊnts] *vt* **-nounced; -nouncing** **1** CENSURE : denunciar, censurar **2** ACCUSE : denunciar, acusar, delatar
dense [ˈdɛnts] *adj* **denser; -est** **1** THICK : espeso, denso ⟨dense vegetation : vegetación densa⟩ ⟨a dense fog : una niebla espesa⟩ **2** STUPID : estúpido, burro *fam*
densely [ˈdɛntsli] *adv* **1** THICKLY : densamente **2** STUPIDLY : torpemente
denseness [ˈdɛntsnəs] *n* **1** → **density** **2** STUPIDITY : estupidez *f*
density [ˈdɛntsəṭi] *n, pl* **-ties** : densidad *f*
dent[1] [ˈdɛnt] *vt* : abollar, mellar
dent[2] *n* : abolladura *f*, mella *f*
dental [ˈdɛntəl] *adj* : dental
dental floss *n* : hilo *m* dental

dentifrice [ˈdɛntəfrɪs] *n* : dentífrico *m*, pasta *f* de dientes
dentist [ˈdɛntɪst] *n* : dentista *mf*
dentistry [ˈdɛntɪstri] *n* : odontología *f*
dentures [ˈdɛntʃərz] *npl* : dentadura *f* postiza
denude [diˈnu:d, -ˈnju:d] *vt* **-nuded; -nuding** STRIP : desnudar, despojar
denunciation [di̩nʌntsiˈeɪʃən] *n* : denuncia *f*, acusación *f*
deny [diˈnaɪ] *vt* **-nied; -nying 1** REFUTE : desmentir, negar **2** DISOWN, REPUDIATE : negar, renegar de **3** REFUSE : denegar **4 to deny oneself** : privarse, sacrificarse
deodorant [diˈo:dərənt] *n* : desodorante *m*
deodorize [diˈo:də̩raɪz] *vt* **-ized; -izing** : desodorizar
depart [diˈpɑrt] *vt* : salirse de — *vi* **1** LEAVE : salir, partir, irse **2** DIE : morir
department [diˈpɑrtmənt] *n* **1** DIVISION : sección *f* (de una tienda, una organización, etc.), departamento *m* (de una empresa, una universidad, etc.), ministerio *m* (del gobierno) **2** PROVINCE, SPHERE : esfera *f*, campo *m*, competencia *f*
departmental [di̩pɑrtˈmɛntəl, ̩di:-] *adj* : departamental
department store *n* : grandes almacenes *mpl*
departure [diˈpɑrtʃər] *n* **1** LEAVING : salida *f*, partida *f* **2** DEVIATION : desviación *f*
depend [diˈpɛnd] *vi* **1** RELY : contar (con), confiar (en) <depend on me! : ¡cuenta conmigo!> **2 to depend on** : depender de <success depends on hard work : el éxito depende de trabajar duro> **3 that depends** : según, eso depende
dependable [diˈpɛndəbəl] *adj* : responsable, digno de confianza, fiable
dependence [diˈpɛndənts] *n* : dependencia *f*
dependency [diˈpɛndəntsi] *n, pl* **-cies 1** → **dependence 2** : posesión *f* (de una unidad política)
dependent[1] [diˈpɛndənt] *adj* : dependiente
dependent[2] *n* : persona *f* a cargo de alguien
depict [diˈpɪkt] *vt* **1** PORTRAY : representar **2** DESCRIBE : describir
depiction [diˈpɪkʃən] *n* : representación *f*, descripción *f*
deplete [diˈpli:t] *vt* **-pleted; -pleting 1** EXHAUST : agotar **2** REDUCE : reducir
depletion [diˈpli:ʃən] *n* **1** EXHAUSTION : agotamiento *m* **2** REDUCTION : reducción *f*, disminución *f*
deplorable [diˈplorəbəl] *adj* **1** CONTEMPTIBLE : deplorable, despreciable **2** LAMENTABLE : lamentable
deplore [diˈplor] *vt* **-plored; -ploring 1** REGRET : deplorar, lamentar **2** CONDEMN : condenar, deplorar
deploy [diˈplɔɪ] *vt* : desplegar
deployment [diˈplɔɪmənt] *n* : despliegue *m*
deport [diˈport] *vt* **1** EXPEL : deportar, expulsar (de un país) **2 to deport oneself** BEHAVE : comportarse
deportation [̩di:̩porˈteɪʃən] *n* : deportación *f*
depose [diˈpo:z] *vt* **-posed; -posing** : deponer
deposit[1] [diˈpɑzət] *vt* **-ited; -iting** : depositar
deposit[2] *n* **1** : depósito *m* (en el banco) **2** DOWN PAYMENT : entrega *f* inicial **3** : depósito *m*, yacimiento *m* (en geología)
deposition [̩dɛpəˈzɪʃən] *n* TESTIMONY : deposición *f*
depositor [diˈpɑzət̬ər] *n* : depositante *mf*
depository [diˈpɑzə̩tori] *n, pl* **-ries** : almacén *m*, depósito *m*
depot [*in sense 1 usu* ˈdɛ̩po:, *2 usu* ˈdi:-] *n* **1** STOREHOUSE : almacén *m*, depósito *m* **2** STATION, TERMINAL : terminal *mf*, estación *f* (de autobuses, ferrocarriles, etc.)
deprave [diˈpreɪv] *vt* **-praved; -praving** : depravar, pervertir
depraved [diˈpreɪvd] *adj* : depravado, degenerado
depravity [diˈprævət̬i] *n, pl* **-ties** : depravación *f*
depreciate [diˈpri:ʃi̩eɪt] *v* **-ated; -ating** *vt* **1** DEVALUE : depreciar, devaluar **2** DISPARAGE : menospreciar, despreciar — *vi* : depreciarse, devaluarse
depreciation [di̩pri:ʃiˈeɪʃən] *n* : depreciación *f*, devaluación *f*
depress [diˈprɛs] *vt* **1** PRESS, PUSH : apretar, presionar, pulsar **2** REDUCE : reducir, hacer bajar (precios, ventas, etc.) **3** SADDEN : deprimir, abatir, entristecer **4** DEVALUE : depreciar
depressant[1] [diˈprɛsənt] *adj* : depresivo
depressant[2] *n* : depresivo *m*
depressed [diˈprɛst] *adj* **1** DEJECTED : deprimido, abatido **2** : deprimido, en crisis (dícese de la economía)
depressing [diˈprɛsɪŋ] *adj* : deprimente, triste
depression [diˈprɛʃən] *n* **1** DESPONDENCY : depresión *f*, abatimiento *m* **2** : depresión (en una superficie) **3** RECESSION : depresión *f* económica, crisis *f*
deprivation [̩dɛprəˈveɪʃən] *n* : privación *f*
deprive [diˈpraɪv] *vt* **-prived; -priving** : privar
depth [ˈdɛpθ] *n, pl* **depths** [ˈdɛpθs, ˈdɛps] : profundidad *f*, fondo *m* <to study in depth : estudiar a fondo> <in the depths of winter : en pleno invierno>
deputize [ˈdɛpjʊ̩taɪz] *vt* **-tized; -tizing** : nombrar como segundo
deputy [ˈdɛpjʊt̬i] *n, pl* **-ties** : suplente *mf*; sustituto *m*, -ta *f*
derail [diˈreɪl] *v* : descarrilar

derailment [di'reɪlmənt] *n* : descarrilamiento *m*
derange [di'reɪndʒ] *vt* **-ranged; -ranging** 1 DISARRANGE : desarreglar, desordenar 2 DISTURB, UPSET : trastornar, perturbar 3 MADDEN : enloquecer, volver loco
derangement [di'reɪndʒmənt] *n* 1 DISTURBANCE, UPSET : trastorno *m* 2 INSANITY : locura *f*, perturbación *f* mental
derby ['dərbi] *n, pl* **-bies** 1 : derby *m* ⟨the Kentucky Derby : el Derby de Kentucky⟩ 2 : sombrero *m* hongo
deregulate [di'rɛgjʊˌleɪt] *vt* **-lated; -lating** : desregular
deregulation [diˌrɛgjʊ'leɪʃən] *n* : desregulación *f*
derelict[1] ['dɛrəˌlɪkt] *adj* 1 ABANDONED : abandonado, en ruinas 2 REMISS : negligente, remiso
derelict[2] *n* 1 : propiedad *f* abandonada 2 VAGRANT : vagabundo *m*, -da *f*
deride [di'raɪd] *vt* **-rided; -riding** : ridiculizar, burlarse de
derision [di'rɪʒən] *n* : escarnio *m*, irrisión *f*, mofa *f*
derisive [di'raɪsɪv] *adj* : burlón
derivation [ˌdɛrə'veɪʃən] *n* : derivación *f*
derivative[1] [di'rɪvət̬ɪv] *adj* 1 DERIVED : derivado 2 BANAL : carente de originalidad, banal
derivative[2] *n* : derivado *m*
derive [di'raɪv] *v* **-rived; -riving** *vt* 1 OBTAIN : obtener, sacar 2 DEDUCE : deducir, inferir — *vi* : provenir, derivar, proceder
dermatologist [ˌdərmə'tɑlədʒɪst] *n* : dermatólogo *m*, -ga *f*
dermatology [ˌdərmə'tɑlədʒi] *n* : dermatología *f*
derogatory [di'rɑgəˌtori] *adj* : despectivo, despreciativo
derrick ['dɛrɪk] *n* 1 CRANE : grúa *f* 2 : torre *f* de perforación (sobre un pozo de petróleo)
descend [di'sɛnd] *vt* : descender, bajar — *vi* 1 : descender, bajar ⟨he descended from the platform : descendió del estrado⟩ 2 DERIVE : descender, provenir 3 STOOP : rebajarse ⟨I descended to his level : me rebajé a su nivel⟩ 4 **to descend upon** : caer sobre, invadir
descendant[1] [di'sɛndənt] *adj* : descendente
descendant[2] *n* : descendiente *mf*
descent [di'sɛnt] *n* 1 : bajada *f*, descenso *m* ⟨the descent from the mountain : el descenso de la montaña⟩ 2 ANCESTRY : ascendencia *f*, linaje *f* 3 SLOPE : pendiente *f*, cuesta *f* 4 FALL : caída *f* 5 ATTACK : incursión *f*, ataque *m*
describe [di'skraɪb] *vt* **-scribed; -scribing** : describir
description [di'skrɪpʃən] *n* : descripción *f*
descriptive [di'skrɪptɪv] *adj* : descriptivo ⟨descriptive adjective : adjetivo calificativo⟩
desecrate ['dɛsɪˌkreɪt] *vt* **-crated; -crating** : profanar
desecration [ˌdɛsɪ'kreɪʃən] *n* : profanación *f*
desegregate [di'sɛgrəˌgeɪt] *vt* **-gated; -gating** : eliminar la segregación racial de
desegregation [diˌsɛgrə'geɪʃən] *n* : eliminación *f* de la segregación racial
desert[1] [di'zərt] *vt* : abandonar (una persona o un lugar), desertar de (una causa, etc.) — *vi* : desertar
desert[2] ['dɛzərt] *adj* : desierto ⟨a desert island : una isla desierta⟩
desert[3] *n* 1 ['dɛzərt] : desierto *m* (en geografía) 2 [di'zərt] → **deserts**
deserter [di'zərt̬ər] *n* : desertor *m*, -tora *f*
desertion [di'zərʃən] *n* : abandono *m*, deserción *f* (militar)
deserts [di'zərts] *npl* : merecido *m* ⟨to get one's just deserts : llevarse uno su merecido⟩
deserve [di'zərv] *vt* **-served; -serving** : merecer, ser digno de
deserving [di'zərvɪŋ] *adj* : meritorio ⟨deserving of : digno de⟩
desiccate ['dɛsɪˌkeɪt] *vt* **-cated; -cating** : desecar, deshidratar
design[1] [di'zaɪn] *vt* 1 DEVISE : diseñar, concebir, idear 2 PLAN : proyectar 3 SKETCH : trazar, bosquejar
design[2] *n* 1 PLAN, SCHEME : plan *m*, proyecto *m* ⟨by design : a propósito, intencionalmente⟩ 2 SKETCH : diseño *m*, bosquejo *m* 3 PATTERN, STYLE : diseño *m*, estilo *m* 4 **designs** *npl* INTENTIONS : propósitos *mpl*, designios *mpl*
designate ['dɛzɪgˌneɪt] *vt* **-nated; -nating** 1 INDICATE, SPECIFY : indicar, especificar 2 APPOINT : nombrar, designar
designation [ˌdɛzɪg'neɪʃən] *n* 1 NAMING : designación *f* 2 NAME : denominación *f*, nombre *m* 3 APPOINTMENT : designación *f*, nombramiento *m*
designer [di'zaɪnər] *n* : diseñador *m*, -dora *f*
desirability [diˌzaɪrə'bɪlət̬i] *n, pl* **-ties** 1 ADVISABILITY : conveniencia *f* 2 ATTRACTIVENESS : atractivo *m*
desirable [di'zaɪrəbəl] *adj* 1 ADVISABLE : conveniente, aconsejable 2 ATTRACTIVE : deseable, atractivo
desire[1] [di'zaɪr] *vt* **-sired; -siring** 1 WANT : desear 2 REQUEST : rogar, solicitar
desire[2] *n* : deseo *m*, anhelo *m*, ansia *m*
desist [di'sɪst, -'zɪst] *vi* **to desist from** : desistir de, abstenerse de
desk ['dɛsk] *n* : escritorio *m*, pupitre *m* (en la escuela)
desktop ['dɛskˌtɑp] *adj* : de escritorio
desolate[1] ['dɛsəˌleɪt, -zə-] *vt* **-lated; -lating** : devastar, desolar

desolate[2] ['dɛsələt, -zə-] *adj* **1** BARREN : desolado, desierto, yermo **2** DISCONSOLATE : desconsolado, desolado
desolation [ˌdɛsə'leɪʃən, -zə-] *n* : desolación *f*
despair[1] [di'spær] *vi* : desesperar, perder las esperanzas
despair[2] *n* : desesperación *f*, desesperanza *f*
desperate ['dɛspərət] *adj* **1** HOPELESS : desesperado, sin esperanzas **2** RASH : desesperado, precipitado **3** SERIOUS, URGENT : grave, urgente, apremiante ⟨a desperate need : una necesidad apremiante⟩
desperately ['dɛspərətli] *adv* : desesperadamente, urgentemente
desperation [ˌdɛspə'reɪʃən] *n* : desesperación *f*
despicable [di'spɪkəbəl, 'dɛspɪ-] *adj* : vil, despreciable, infame
despise [di'spaɪz] *vt* **-spised; -spising** : despreciar
despite [də'spaɪt] *prep* : a pesar de, aún con
despoil [di'spɔɪl] *vt* : saquear
despondency [di'spɑndəntsi] *n* : desaliento *m*, desánimo *m*, depresión *f*
despondent [di'spɑndənt] *adj* : desalentado, desanimado
despot ['dɛspət, -ˌpɑt] *n* : déspota *mf*; tirano *m*, -na *f*
despotic [dɛs'pɑṭɪk] *adj* : despótico
despotism ['dɛspəˌtɪzəm] *n* : despotismo *m*
dessert [di'zərt] *n* : postre *m*
destination [ˌdɛstə'neɪʃən] *n* : destino *m*, destinación *f*
destined ['dɛstənd] *adj* **1** FATED : predestinado **2** BOUND : destinado, con destino (a), con rumbo (a)
destiny ['dɛstəni] *n, pl* **-nies** : destino *m*
destitute ['dɛstəˌtu:t, -ˌtju:t] *adj* **1** LACKING : carente, desprovisto **2** POOR : indigente, en miseria
destitution [ˌdɛstə'tu:ʃən, -'tju:-] *n* : indigencia *f*, miseria *f*
destroy [di'strɔɪ] *vt* **1** KILL : matar **2** DEMOLISH : destruir, destrozar
destroyer [di'strɔɪər] *n* : destructor *m* (buque)
destructible [di'strʌktəbəl] *adj* : destructible
destruction [di'strʌkʃən] *n* : destrucción *f*, ruina *f*
destructive [di'strʌktɪv] *adj* : destructor, destructivo
desultory ['dɛsəlˌtori] *adj* **1** AIMLESS : sin rumbo, sin objeto **2** DISCONNECTED : inconexo
detach [di'tætʃ] *vt* : separar, quitar, desprender
detached [di'tætʃt] *adj* **1** SEPARATE : separado, suelto **2** ALOOF : distante, indiferente **3** IMPARTIAL : imparcial, objetivo
detachment [di'tætʃmənt] *n* **1** SEPARATION : separación *f* **2** DETAIL : destacamento *m* (de tropas) **3** ALOOFNESS : reserva *f*, indiferencia *f* **4** IMPARTIALITY : imparcialidad *f*
detail[1] [di'teɪl, 'di:ˌteɪl] *vt* : detallar, exponer en detalle
detail[2] *n* **1** : detalle *m*, pormenor *m* **2** : destacamento *m* (de tropas)
detailed [di'teɪld, 'di:ˌteɪld] *adj* : detallado, minucioso
detain [di'teɪn] *vt* **1** HOLD : detener **2** DELAY : entretener, demorar, retrasar
detect [di'tɛkt] *vt* : detectar, descubrir
detection [di'tɛkʃən] *n* : descubrimiento *m*
detective [di'tɛktɪv] *n* : detective *mf* ⟨private detective : detective privado⟩
detector [di'tɛktər] *n* : detector *m*
detention [di'tɛntʃən] *n* : detención *m*
deter [di'tər] *vt* **-terred; -terring** : disuadir, impedir
detergent [di'tərdʒənt] *n* : detergente *m*
deteriorate [di'tɪriəˌreɪt] *vi* **-rated; -rating** : deteriorarse, empeorar
deterioration [diˌtɪriə'reɪʃən] *n* : deterioro *m*, empeoramiento *m*
determinant[1] [di'tərmənənt] *adj* : determinante
determinant[2] *n* **1** : factor *m* determinante **2** : determinante *m* (en matemáticas)
determination [dɪˌtərmə'neɪʃən] *n* **1** DECISION : determinación *f*, decisión *f* **2** RESOLUTION : resolución *f*, determinación *f* ⟨with grim determination : con una firme resolución⟩
determine [di'tərmən] *vt* **-mined; -mining** **1** ESTABLISH : determinar, establecer **2** SETTLE : decidir **3** FIND OUT : averiguar **4** BRING ABOUT : determinar
determined [di'tərmənd] *adj* RESOLUTE : decidido, resuelto
deterrent [di'tərənt] *n* : medida *f* disuasiva
detest [di'tɛst] *vt* : detestar, odiar, aborrecer
detestable [di'tɛstəbəl] *adj* : detestable, odioso, aborrecible
dethrone [di'θro:n] *vt* **-throned; -throning** : destronar
detonate ['dɛtənˌeɪt] *v* **-nated; -nating** *vt* : hacer detonar — *vi* : detonar, estallar
detonation [ˌdɛṭə'neɪʃən] *n* : detonación *f*
detour[1] ['di:ˌtʊr, di'tʊr] *vi* : desviarse
detour[2] *n* : desvío *m*, rodeo *m*
detract [di'trækt] *vi* **to detract from** : restarle valor a, quitarle méritos a
detractor [di'træktər] *n* : detractor *m*, -tora *f*
detriment ['dɛtrəmənt] *n* : detrimento *m*, perjuicio *m*
detrimental [ˌdɛtrə'mɛntəl] *adj* : perjudicial — **detrimentally** *adv*
devaluation [diˌvæljʊ'eɪʃən] *n* : devaluación *f*
devalue [di'vælˌju:] *vt* **-ued; -uing** : devaluar, depreciar

devastate ['dɛvə,steɪt] *vt* **-tated; -tating** : devastar, arrasar, asolar
devastation [,dɛvə'steɪʃən] *n* : devastación *f*, estragos *mpl*
develop [di'vɛləp] *vt* **1** FORM, MAKE : desarrollar, elaborar, formar **2** : revelar (en fotografía) **3** FOSTER : desarrollar, fomentar **4** EXPLOIT : explotar (recursos), urbanizar (un área) **5** ACQUIRE : adquirir ⟨to develop an interest : adquirir un interés⟩ **6** CONTRACT : contraer (una enfermedad) — *vi* **1** GROW : desarrollarse **2** ARISE : aparecer, surgir
developed [di'vɛləpt] *adj* : avanzado, desarrollado
developer [di'vɛləpər] *n* **1** : inmobiliaria *f*, urbanizadora *f* **2** : revelador *m* (en fotografía)
development [di'vɛləpmənt] *n* **1** : desarrollo *m* ⟨physical development : desarrollo físico⟩ **2** : urbanización *f* (de un área), explotación *f* (de recursos), creación *f* (de inventos) **3** EVENT : acontecimiento *m*, suceso *m* ⟨to await developments : esperar acontecimientos⟩
deviant ['di:viənt] *adj* : desviado, anormal
deviate ['di:vi,eɪt] *v* **-ated; -ating** *vi* : desviarse, apartarse — *vt* : desviar
deviation [,di:vi'eɪʃən] *n* : desviación *f*
device [di'vaɪs] *n* **1** MECHANISM : dispositivo *m*, aparato *m*, mecanismo *m* **2** EMBLEM : emblema *m*
devil¹ ['dɛvəl] *vt* **-iled** *or* **-illed; -iling** *or* **-illing** **1** : sazonar con picante y especias **2** PESTER : molestar
devil² *n* **1** SATAN : el diablo, Satanás *m* **2** DEMON : diablo *m*, demonio *m* **3** FIEND : persona *f* diabólica; malvado *m*, -da *f*
devilish ['dɛvəlɪʃ] *adj* : diabólico
devilry ['dɛvəlri] *n, pl* **-ries** : diabluras *fpl*, travesuras *fpl*
devious ['di:viəs] *adj* **1** CRAFTY : taimado, artero **2** WINDING : tortuoso, sinuoso
devise [di'vaɪz] *vt* **-vised; -vising** **1** INVENT : idear, concebir, inventar **2** PLOT : tramar
devoid [di'vɔɪd] *adj* ~ **of** : carente de, desprovisto de
devote [di'vo:t] *vt* **-voted; -voting** **1** DEDICATE : consagrar, dedicar ⟨to devote one's life : dedicar uno su vida⟩ **2** **to devote oneself** : dedicarse
devoted [di'vo:t̬əd] *adj* **1** FAITHFUL : leal, fiel **2** **to be devoted to someone** : tenerle mucho cariño a alguien
devotee [,dɛvə'ti:, -'teɪ] *n* : devoto *m*, -ta *f*
devotion [di'vo:ʃən] *n* **1** DEDICATION : dedicación *f*, devoción *f* **2** **devotions** PRAYERS : oraciones *fpl*, devociones *fpl*
devour [di'vaʊər] *vt* : devorar
devout [di'vaʊt] *adj* **1** PIOUS : devoto, piadoso **2** EARNEST, SINCERE : sincero, ferviente — **devoutly** *adv*
devoutness [di'vaʊtnəs] *n* : devoción *f*, piedad *f*
dew ['du:, 'dju:] *n* : rocío *m*
dewlap ['du,læp, 'dju-] *n* : papada *f*
dew point *n* : punto *m* de condensación
dewy ['du:i, 'dju:i] *adj* **dewier; -est** : cubierto de rocío
dexterity [dɛk'stɛrət̬i] *n, pl* **-ties** : destreza *f*, habilidad *f*
dexterous ['dɛkstrəs] *adj* : diestro, hábil
dexterously ['dɛkstrəsli] *adv* : con destreza, con habilidad, hábilmente
dextrose ['dɛk,stro:s] *n* : dextrosa *f*
diabetes [,daɪə'bi:t̬iz] *n* : diabetes *f*
diabetic¹ [,daɪə'bɛt̬ɪk] *adj* : diabético
diabetic² *n* : diabético *m*, -ca *f*
diabolic [,daɪə'bɑlɪk] *or* **diabolical** [-lɪkəl] *adj* : diabólico, satánico
diacritical mark [,daɪə'krɪt̬ɪkəl] *n* : signo *m* diacrítico
diadem ['daɪə,dɛm, -dəm] *n* : diadema *f*
diagnose ['daɪɪg,no:s, ,daɪɪg'no:s] *vt* **-nosed; -nosing** : diagnosticar
diagnosis [,daɪɪg'no:sɪs] *n, pl* **-noses** [-'no:,si:z] : diagnóstico *m*
diagnostic [,daɪɪg'nɑstɪk] *adj* : diagnóstico
diagonal¹ [daɪ'ægənəl] *adj* : diagonal, en diagonal
diagonal² *n* : diagonal *f*
diagonally [daɪ'ægənəli] *adv* : diagonalmente, en diagonal
diagram¹ ['daɪə,græm] *vt* **-gramed** *or* **-grammed; -graming** *or* **-gramming** : hacer un diagrama de
diagram² *n* : diagrama *m*, gráfico *m*, esquema *m*
dial¹ ['daɪl] *v* **dialed** *or* **dialled; dialing** *or* **dialling** : marcar, discar
dial² *n* : esfera *f* (de un reloj), dial *m* (de un radio), disco *m* (de un teléfono)
dialect ['daɪə,lɛkt] *n* : dialecto *m*
dialogue ['daɪə,lɔg] *n* : diálogo *m*
diameter [daɪ'æmət̬ər] *n* : diámetro *m*
diamond ['daɪmənd, 'daɪə-] *n* **1** : diamante *m*, brillante *m* ⟨a diamond necklace : un collar de brillantes⟩ **2** : rombo *m*, forma *f* de rombo **3** : diamante *m* (en naipes) **4** INFIELD : cuadro *m*, diamante *m* (en béisbol)
diaper ['daɪpər, 'daɪə-] *n* : pañal *m*
diaphragm ['daɪə,fræm] *n* : diafragma *m*
diarrhea [,daɪə'ri:ə] *n* : diarrea *f*
diary ['daɪəri] *n, pl* **-ries** : diario *m*
diatribe ['daɪə,traɪb] *n* : diatriba *f*
dice¹ ['daɪs] *vt* **diced; dicing** : cortar en cubos
dice² *ns & pl* **1** → **die²** **2** : dados *mpl* (juego)
dicker ['dɪkər] *vt* : regatear
dictate¹ ['dɪk,teɪt, dɪk'teɪt] *v* **-tated; -tating** *vt* **1** : dictar ⟨to dictate a letter : dictar una carta⟩ **2** ORDER : mandar, ordenar — *vi* : dar órdenes

dictate[2] [ˈdɪkˌteɪt] *n* **1** : mandato *m*, orden *f* **2 dictates** *npl* : dictados *mpl* ⟨the dictates of conscience : los dictados de la conciencia⟩
dictation [dɪkˈteɪʃən] *n* : dictado *m*
dictator [ˈdɪkˌteɪt̬ər] *n* : dictador *m*, -dora *f*
dictatorial [ˌdɪktəˈtoriəl] *adj* : dictatorial — **dictatorially** *adv*
dictatorship [dɪkˈteɪt̬ərˌʃɪp, ˈdɪkˌ-] *n* : dictadura *f*
diction [ˈdɪkʃən] *n* **1** : lenguaje *m*, estilo *m* **2** ENUNCIATION : dicción *f*, articulación *f*
dictionary [ˈdɪkʃəˌnɛri] *n, pl* **-naries** : diccionario *m*
did → **do**
didactic [daɪˈdæktɪk] *adj* : didáctico
die[1] [ˈdaɪ] *vi* **died** [ˈdaɪd]; **dying** [ˈdaɪɪŋ] **1** : morir **2** CEASE : morir, morirse ⟨a dying civilization : una civilización moribunda⟩ **3** STOP : apagarse, dejar de funcionar ⟨the motor died : el motor se apagó⟩ **4 to die down** SUBSIDE : amainar, disminuir **5 to die out** : extinguirse **6 to be dying for** *or* **to be dying to** : morirse por ⟨I'm dying to leave : me muero por irme⟩
die[2] [ˈdaɪ] *n, pl* **dice** [ˈdaɪs] : dado *m*
die[3] *n, pl* **dies** [ˈdaɪz] **1** STAMP : troquel *m*, cuño *m* **2** MOLD : matriz *f*, molde *m*
diesel [ˈdi:zəl, -səl] *n* : diesel *m*
diet[1] [ˈdaɪət] *vi* : ponerse a régimen, hacer dieta
diet[2] *n* : régimen *m*, dieta *f*
dietary [ˈdaɪəˌtɛri] *adj* : alimenticio, dietético
dietitian *or* **dietician** [ˌdaɪəˈtɪʃən] *n* : dietista *mf*
differ [ˈdɪfər] *vi* **-ferred; -ferring 1** : diferir, diferenciarse **2** VARY : variar **3** DISAGREE : discrepar, diferir, no estar de acuerdo
difference [ˈdɪfrənts, ˈdɪfərənts] *n* : diferencia *f*
different [ˈdɪfrənt, ˈdɪfərənt] *adj* : distinto, diferente
differentiate [ˌdɪfəˈrɛntʃiˌeɪt] *v* **-ated; -ating** *vt* **1** : hacer diferente **2** DISTINGUISH : distinguir, diferenciar — *vi* : distinguir
differentiation [ˌdɪfəˌrɛntʃiˈeɪʃən] *n* : diferenciación *f*
differently [ˈdɪfrəntli, ˈdɪfərənt-] *adv* : de otra manera, de otro modo, distintamente
difficult [ˈdɪfɪˌkʌlt] *adj* : difícil
difficulty [ˈdɪfɪˌkʌlti] *n, pl* **-ties 1** : dificultad *f* **2** PROBLEM : problema *f*, dificultad *f*
diffidence [ˈdɪfədənts] *n* **1** SHYNESS : retraimiento *m*, timidez *f*, apocamiento *m* **2** RETICENCE : reticencia *f*
diffident [ˈdɪfədənt] *adj* **1** SHY : tímido, apocado, inseguro **2** RESERVED : reservado
diffuse[1] [dɪˈfju:z] *v* **-fused; -fusing** *vt* : difundir, esparcir — *vi* : difundirse, esparcirse
diffuse[2] [dɪˈfju:s] *adj* **1** WORDY : prolijo, verboso **2** WIDESPREAD : difuso
diffusion [dɪˈfju:ʒən] *n* : difusión *f*
dig[1] [ˈdɪg] *v* **dug** [ˈdʌg]; **digging** *vt* **1** : cavar, excavar ⟨to dig a hole : cavar un hoyo⟩ **2** EXTRACT : sacar ⟨to dig up potatoes : sacar papas del suelo⟩ **3** POKE, THRUST : clavar, hincar ⟨he dug me in the ribs : me dio un codazo en las costillas⟩ **4 to dig up** DISCOVER : descubrir, sacar a luz — *vi* : cavar, excavar
dig[2] *n* **1** POKE : codazo *m* **2** GIBE : pulla *f* **3** EXCAVATION : excavación *f*
digest[1] [daɪˈdʒɛst, dɪ-] *vt* **1** ASSIMILATE : digerir, asimilar **2** : digerir (comida) **3** SUMMARIZE : compendiar, resumir
digest[2] [ˈdaɪˌdʒɛst] *n* : compendio *m*, resumen *m*
digestible [daɪˈdʒɛstəbəl, dɪ-] *adj* : digerible
digestion [daɪˈdʒɛstʃən, dɪ-] *n* : digestión *f*
digestive [daɪˈdʒɛstɪv, dɪ-] *adj* : digestivo ⟨the digestive system : el sistema digestivo⟩
digit [ˈdɪdʒət] *n* **1** NUMERAL : dígito *m*, número *m* **2** FINGER, TOE : dedo *m*
digital [ˈdɪdʒət̬əl] *adj* : digital — **digitally** *adv*
dignified [ˈdɪgnəˌfaɪd] *adj* : digno, decoroso
dignify [ˈdɪgnəˌfaɪ] *vt* **-fied; -fying** : dignificar, honrar
dignitary [ˈdɪgnəˌtɛri] *n, pl* **-taries** : dignatario *m*, -ria *f*
dignity [ˈdɪgnət̬i] *n, pl* **-ties** : dignidad *f*
digress [daɪˈgrɛs, də-] *vi* : desviarse del tema, divagar
digression [daɪˈgrɛʃən, də-] *n* : digresión *f*
dike *or* **dyke** [ˈdaɪk] *n* : dique *m*
dilapidated [dəˈlæpəˌdeɪt̬əd] *adj* : ruinoso, desvencijado, destartalado
dilapidation [dəˌlæpəˈdeɪʃən] *n* : deterioro *m*, estado *m* ruinoso
dilate [daɪˈleɪt, ˈdaɪˌleɪt] *v* **-lated; -lating** *vt* : dilatar — *vi* : dilatarse
dilemma [dɪˈlɛmə] *n* : dilema *m*
dilettante [ˈdɪləˌtɑnt, -ˌtænt] *n, pl* **-tantes** [-ˌtɑnts, -ˌtænts] *or* **-tanti** [ˌdɪləˈtɑnti, -ˈtæn-] : diletante *mf*
diligence [ˈdɪlədʒənts] *n* : diligencia *f*, aplicación *f*
diligent [ˈdɪlədʒənt] *adj* : diligente ⟨a diligent search : una búsqueda minuciosa⟩ — **diligently** *adv*
dill [ˈdɪl] *n* : eneldo *m*
dillydally [ˈdɪliˌdæli] *vi* **-lied; lying** : demorarse, perder tiempo
dilute [daɪˈlu:t, də-] *vt* **-luted; -luting** : diluir, aguar
dilution [daɪˈlu:ʃən, də-] *n* : dilución *f*
dim[1] [ˈdɪm] *v* **dimmed; dimming** *vt* : atenuar (la luz), nublar (la vista), bo-

rrar (la memoria), opacar (una superficie) — *vi* : oscurecerse, apagarse

dim[2] *adj* **dimmer; dimmest** **1** FAINT : oscuro, tenue (dícese de la luz), nublado (dícese de la vista), borrado (dícese de la memoria) **2** DULL : deslustrado **3** STUPID : tonto, torpe

dime [ˈdaɪm] *n* : moneda *f* de diez centavos

dimension [dəˈmɛntʃən, daɪ-] *n* **1** : dimensión *f* **2 dimensions** *npl* EXTENT, SCOPE : dimensiones *fpl*, extensión *f*, medida *f*

diminish [dəˈmɪnɪʃ] *vt* LESSEN : disminuir, reducir, amainar — *vi* DWINDLE, WANE : menguar, reducirse

diminutive [dəˈmɪnjʊt̬ɪv] *adj* : diminutivo, minúsculo

dimly [ˈdɪmli] *adv* : indistintamente, débilmente

dimmer [ˈdɪmər] *n* : potenciómetro *m*, conmutador *m* de luces (en automóviles)

dimness [ˈdɪmnəs] *n* : oscuridad *f*, debilidad *f* (de la vista), imprecisión *f* (de la memoria)

dimple [ˈdɪmpəl] *n* : hoyuelo *m*

din [ˈdɪn] *n* : estrépito *m*, estruendo *m*

dine [ˈdaɪn] *vi* **dined; dining** : cenar

diner [ˈdaɪnər] *n* **1** : comensal *mf* (persona) **2** : vagón *m* restaurante (en un tren) **3** : cafetería *f*, restaurante *m* barato

dinghy [ˈdɪŋi, ˈdɪŋgi, ˈdɪŋki] *n, pl* **-ghies** : bote *m*

dinginess [ˈdɪndʒinəs] *n* **1** DIRTINESS : suciedad *f* **2** SHABBINESS : lo gastado, lo deslucido

dingy [ˈdɪndʒi] *adj* **-gier; -est** **1** DIRTY : sucio **2** SHABBY : gastado, deslucido

dinner [ˈdɪnər] *n* : cena *f*, comida *f*

dinosaur [ˈdaɪnəˌsɔr] *n* : dinosaurio *m*

dint [ˈdɪnt] *n* **by dint of** : a fuerza de

diocese [ˈdaɪəsəs, -ˌsiːz, -ˌsiːs] *n, pl* **-ceses** [ˈdaɪəsəsəz] : diócesis *f*

dip[1] [ˈdɪp] *v* **dipped; dipping** *vt* **1** DUNK, PLUNGE : sumergir, mojar, meter **2** LADLE : servir con cucharón **3** LOWER : bajar, arriar (una bandera) — *vi* **1** DESCEND, DROP : bajar en picada, descender **2** SLOPE : bajar, inclinarse

dip[2] *n* **1** SWIM : chapuzón *m* **2** DROP : descenso *m*, caída *f* **3** SLOPE : cuesta *f*, declive *m* **4** SAUCE : salsa *f*

diphtheria [dɪfˈθɪriə] *n* : difteria *f*

diphthong [ˈdɪfˌθɔŋ] *n* : diptongo *m*

diploma [dəˈploːmə] *n, pl* **-mas** : diploma *m*

diplomacy [dəˈploːməsi] *n* **1** : diplomacia *f* **2** TACT : tacto *m*, discreción *f*

diplomat [ˈdɪpləˌmæt] *n* **1** : diplomático *m*, -ca *f* (en relaciones internacionales) **2** : persona *f* diplomática

diplomatic [ˌdɪpləˈmæt̬ɪk] *adj* : diplomático ⟨diplomatic immunity : inmunidad diplomática⟩

dipper [ˈdɪpər] *n* **1** LADLE : cucharón *m*, cazo *m* **2 Big Dipper** : Osa *f* Mayor **3 Little Dipper** : Osa *f* Menor

dire [ˈdaɪr] *adj* **direr; direst** **1** HORRIBLE : espantoso, terrible, horrendo **2** EXTREME : extremo ⟨dire poverty : pobreza extrema⟩

direct[1] [dəˈrɛkt, daɪ-] *vt* **1** ADDRESS : dirigir, mandar **2** AIM, POINT : dirigir **3** GUIDE : indicarle el camino (a alguien), orientar **4** MANAGE : dirigir ⟨to direct a film : dirigir una película⟩ **5** COMMAND : ordenar, mandar

direct[2] *adv* : directamente

direct[3] *adj* **1** STRAIGHT : directo **2** FRANK : franco

direct current *n* : corriente *f* continua

direction [dəˈrɛkʃən, daɪ-] *n* **1** SUPERVISION : dirección *f* **2** INSTRUCTION, ORDER : instrucción *f*, orden *f* **3** COURSE : dirección *f*, rumbo *m* ⟨to change direction : cambiar de dirección⟩ **4 to ask directions** : pedir indicaciones

directional [dəˈrɛkʃənəl, daɪ-] *adj* : direccional

directive [dəˈrɛktɪv, daɪ-] *n* : directiva *f*

directly [dəˈrɛktli, daɪ-] *adv* **1** STRAIGHT : directamente ⟨directly north : directamente al norte⟩ **2** FRANKLY : francamente **3** EXACTLY : exactamente, justo ⟨directly opposite : justo enfrente⟩ **4** IMMEDIATELY : en seguida, inmediatamente

directness [dəˈrɛktnəs, daɪ-] *n* : franqueza *f*

director [dəˈrɛktər, daɪ-] *n* **1** : director *m*, -tora *f* **2 board of directors** : junta *f* directiva, directorio *m*

directory [dəˈrɛktəri, daɪ-] *n, pl* **-ries** : guía *f*, directorio *m* ⟨telephone directory : directorio telefónico⟩

dirge [ˈdərdʒ] *n* : canto *m* fúnebre

dirigible [ˈdɪrədʒəbəl, dəˈrɪdʒə-] *n* : dirigible *m*, zepelín *m*

dirt [ˈdərt] *n* **1** FILTH : suciedad *f*, mugre *f*, porquería *f* **2** SOIL : tierra *f*

dirtiness [ˈdərt̬inəs] *n* : suciedad *f*

dirty[1] [ˈdərt̬i] *vt* **dirtied; dirtying** : ensuciar, manchar

dirty[2] *adj* **dirtier; -est** **1** SOILED, STAINED : sucio, manchado **2** DISHONEST : sucio, deshonesto ⟨a dirty player : un jugador tramposo⟩ ⟨a dirty trick : una mala pasada⟩ **3** INDECENT : indecente, cochino ⟨a dirty joke : un chiste verde⟩

disability [ˌdɪsəˈbɪlət̬i] *n, pl* **-ties** : minusvalía *f*, discapacidad *f*, invalidez *f*

disable [dɪsˈeɪbəl] *vt* **-abled; -abling** : dejar inválido, inutilizar, incapacitar

disabled [dɪsˈeɪbəld] *adj* : minusválido, discapacitado

disabuse [ˌdɪsəˈbjuːz] *vt* **-bused; -busing** : desengañar, sacar del error

disadvantage [ˌdɪsədˈvæntɪdʒ] *n* : desventaja *f*

disadvantageous [ˌdɪsˌædˌvænˈteɪ-dʒəs] *adj* : desventajoso, desfavorable

disagree [ˌdɪsəˈgriː] *vi* **1** DIFFER : discrepar, no coincidir **2** DISSENT : disentir, discrepar, no estar de acuerdo
disagreeable [ˌdɪsəˈgriːəbəl] *adj* : desagradable
disagreement [ˌdɪsəˈgriːmənt] *n* **1** : desacuerdo *m* **2** DISCREPANCY : discrepancia *f* **3** ARGUMENT : discusión *f*, altercado *m*, disputa *f*
disappear [ˌdɪsəˈpɪr] *vi* : desaparecer, desvanecerse ⟨to disappear from view : perderse de vista⟩
disappearance [ˌdɪsəˈpɪrənts] *n* : desaparición *f*
disappoint [ˌdɪsəˈpɔɪnt] *vt* : decepcionar, defraudar, fallar
disappointing [ˌdɪsəˈpɔɪntɪŋ] *adj* : decepcionante
disappointment [ˌdɪsəˈpɔɪntmənt] *n* : decepción *f*, desilusión *f*, chasco *m*
disapproval [ˌdɪsəˈpruːvəl] *n* : desaprobación *f*
disapprove [ˌdɪsəˈpruːv] *vi* **-proved; -proving** : desaprobar, estar en contra
disapprovingly [ˌdɪsəˈpruːvɪŋli] *adv* : con desaprobación
disarm [dɪsˈɑrm] *vt* : desarmar
disarmament [dɪsˈɑrməmənt] *n* : desarme *m* ⟨nuclear disarmament : desarme nuclear⟩
disarrange [ˌdɪsəˈreɪnʤ] *vt* **-ranged; -ranging** : desarreglar, desordenar
disarray [ˌdɪsəˈreɪ] *n* : desorden *m*, confusión *f*, desorganización *f*
disaster [dɪˈzæstər] *n* : desastre *m*, catástrofe *f*
disastrous [dɪˈzæstrəs] *adj* : desastroso
disband [dɪsˈbænd] *vt* : disolver — *vi* : disolverse, dispersarse
disbar [dɪsˈbɑr] *vt* **-barred; -barring** : prohibir de ejercer la abogacía
disbelief [ˌdɪsbɪˈliːf] *n* : incredulidad *f*
disbelieve [ˌdɪsbɪˈliːv] *v* **-lieved; -lieving** : no creer, dudar
disburse [dɪsˈbərs] *vt* **-bursed; -bursing** : desembolsar
disbursement [dɪsˈbərsmənt] *n* : desembolso *m*
disc → **disk**
discard [dɪsˈkɑrd, ˈdɪsˌkɑrd] *vt* : desechar, deshacerse de, botar — *vi* : descartarse (en juegos de naipes)
discern [dɪˈsərn, -ˈzərn] *vt* : discernir, distinguir, percibir
discernible [dɪˈsərnəbəl, -ˈzər-] *adj* : perceptible, visible
discernment [dɪˈsərnmənt, -ˈzərn-] *n* : discernimiento *m*, criterio *m*
discharge¹ [dɪsˈʧɑrʤ, ˈdɪsˌ-] *v* **-charged; -charging** **1** UNLOAD : descargar (carga), desembarcar (pasajeros) **2** SHOOT : descargar, disparar **3** FREE : liberar, poner en libertad **4** DISMISS : despedir **5** EMIT : despedir (humo, etc.), descargar (electricidad) **6** : cumplir con (una obligación), saldar (una deuda) — *vi* **1** : descargarse (dícese de una batería) **2** OOZE : supurar
discharge² [ˈdɪsˌʧɑrʤ, dɪsˈ-] *n* **1** EMISSION : descarga *f* (de electricidad), emisión *f* (de gases) **2** DISMISSAL : despido *m* (del empleo), baja *f* (del ejército) **3** SECRETION : secreción *f*
disciple [dɪˈsaɪpəl] *n* : discípulo *m*, -la *f*
discipline¹ [ˈdɪsəplən] *vt* **-plined; -plining** **1** PUNISH : castigar, sancionar (a los empleados) **2** CONTROL : disciplinar **3 to discipline oneself** : disciplinarse
discipline² *n* **1** FIELD : disciplina *f*, campo *m* **2** TRAINING : disciplina *f* **3** PUNISHMENT : castigo *m* **4** SELF-CONTROL : dominio *m* de sí mismo
disc jockey *n* : disc jockey *mf*
disclaim [dɪsˈkleɪm] *vt* DENY : negar
disclose [dɪsˈkloːz] *vt* **-closed; -closing** : revelar, poner en evidencia
disclosure [dɪsˈkloːʒər] *n* : revelación *f*
disco [ˈdɪskoː] *n* **1** → **discotheque** **2** *or* **disco music** : disco *f*, música *f* disco
discolor [dɪsˈkʌlər] *vt* **1** BLEACH : decolorar **2** FADE : desteñir **3** STAIN : manchar — *vi* : decolorarse, desteñirse
discoloration [dɪsˌkʌləˈreɪʃən] *n* **1** FADING : decoloración *f* **2** STAIN : mancha *f*
discomfort [dɪsˈkʌmfərt] *n* **1** PAIN : molestia *f*, malestar *m* **2** UNEASINESS : inquietud *f*
disconcert [ˌdɪskənˈsərt] *vt* : desconcertar
disconcerting [ˌdɪskənˈsərt̬ɪŋ] *adj* : desconcertante
disconnect [ˌdɪskəˈnɛkt] *vt* : desconectar
disconnected [ˌdɪskəˈnɛktəd] *adj* : inconexo
disconsolate [dɪsˈkɑntsələt] *adj* : desconsolado
discontent [ˌdɪskənˈtɛnt] *n* : descontento *m*
discontented [ˌdɪskənˈtɛntəd] *adj* : descontento
discontinue [ˌdɪskənˈtɪnˌjuː] *vt* **-ued; -uing** : suspender, descontinuar
discontinuity [dɪsˌkɑntəˈnuːət̬i, -ˈnjuː-] *n, pl* **-ties** : discontinuidad *f*
discontinuous [ˌdɪskənˈtɪnjəwəs] *adj* : discontinuo
discord [ˈdɪsˌkɔrd] *n* **1** STRIFE : discordia *f*, discordancia *f* **2** : disonancia *f* (en música)
discordant [dɪsˈkɔrdənt] *adj* : discordante, discorde — **discordantly** *adv*
discotheque [ˈdɪskəˌtɛk, ˌdɪskəˈtɛk] *n* : discoteca *f*
discount¹ [ˈdɪsˌkaʊnt, dɪsˈ-] *vt* **1** REDUCE : descontar, rebajar (precios) **2** DISREGARD : descartar, ignorar
discount² [ˈdɪsˌkaʊnt] *n* : descuento *m*, rebaja *f*
discourage [dɪsˈkərɪʤ] *vt* **-aged; -aging** **1** DISHEARTEN : desalentar, desanimar **2** DISSUADE : disuadir
discouragement [dɪsˈkərɪʤmənt] *n* : desánimo *m*, desaliento *m*

discouraging [dɪsˈkərəʤɪŋ] *adj* : desalentador

discourse[1] [dɪsˈkors] *vi* **-coursed; -coursing** : disertar, conversar

discourse[2] [ˈdɪsˌkors] *n* **1** TALK : conversación *f* **2** SPEECH, TREATISE : discurso *m*, tratado *m*

discourteous [dɪsˈkərt̬iəs] *adj* : descortés — **discourteously** *adv*

discourtesy [dɪsˈkərt̬əsi] *n, pl* **-sies** : descortesía *f*

discover [dɪsˈkʌvər] *vt* : descubrir

discoverer [dɪsˈkʌvərər] *n* : descubridor *m*, -dora *f*

discovery [dɪsˈkʌvəri] *n, pl* **-ries** : descubrimiento *m*

discredit[1] [dɪsˈkrɛdət] *vt* **1** DISBELIEVE : no creer, dudar **2** : desacreditar, desprestigiar, poner en duda ⟨they discredited his research : desacreditaron sus investigaciones⟩

discredit[2] *n* **1** DISREPUTE : descrédito *m*, desprestigio *m* **2** DOUBT : duda *f*

discreet [dɪsˈkri:t] *adj* : discreto — **discreetly** *adv*

discrepancy [dɪsˈkrɛpən*t*si] *n, pl* **-cies** : discrepancia *f*

discretion [dɪsˈkrɛʃən] *n* **1** CIRCUMSPECTION : discreción *f*, circunspección *f* **2** JUDGMENT : discernimiento *m*, criterio *m*

discretionary [dɪsˈkrɛʃəˌnɛri] *adj* : discrecional

discriminate [dɪsˈkrɪməˌneɪt] *v* **-nated; -nating** *vt* DISTINGUISH : distinguir, discriminar, diferenciar — *vi* : discriminar ⟨to discriminate against women : discriminar a las mujeres⟩

discrimination [dɪsˌkrɪməˈneɪʃən] *n* **1** PREJUDICE : discriminación *f* **2** DISCERNMENT : discernimiento *m*

discriminatory [dɪsˈkrɪmənəˌtori] *adj* : discriminatorio

discus [ˈdɪskəs] *n, pl* **-cuses** [-kəsəz] : disco *m*

discuss [dɪsˈkʌs] *vt* : hablar de, discutir, tratar (de)

discussion [dɪsˈkʌʃən] *n* : discusión *f*, debate *m*, conversación *f*

disdain[1] [dɪsˈdeɪn] *vt* : desdeñar, despreciar ⟨they disdained to reply : no se dignaron a responder⟩

disdain[2] *n* : desdén *m*

disdainful [dɪsˈdeɪnfəl] *adj* : desdeñoso — **disdainfully** *adv*

disease [dɪˈzi:z] *n* : enfermedad *f*, mal *m*, dolencia *f*

diseased [dɪˈzi:zd] *adj* : enfermo

disembark [ˌdɪsɪmˈbɑrk] *v* : desembarcar

disembarkation [dɪsˌɛmˌbɑrˈkeɪʃən] *n* : desembarco *m*, desembarque *m*

disembodied [ˌdɪsɪmˈbɑdid] *adj* : incorpóreo

disenchant [ˌdɪsɪnˈʧænt] *vt* : desilusionar, desencantar, desengañar

disenchantment [ˌdɪsɪnˈʧæntmənt] *n* : desencanto *m*, desilusión *f*

disengage [ˌdɪsɪnˈgeɪʤ] *vt* **-gaged; -gaging 1** : soltar, desconectar (un mecanismo) **2 to disengage the clutch** : desembragar

disentangle [ˌdɪsɪnˈtæŋgəl] *vt* **-gled; -gling** UNTANGLE : desenredar, desenmarañar

disfavor [dɪsˈfeɪvər] *n* : desaprobación *f*

disfigure [dɪsˈfɪgjər] *vt* **-ured; -uring** : desfigurar (a una persona), afear (un edificio, un área)

disfigurement [dɪsˈfɪgjərmənt] *n* : desfiguración *f*, afeamiento *m*

disfranchise [dɪsˈfrænˌʧaɪz] *vt* **-chised; -chising** : privar del derecho a votar

disgrace[1] [dɪˈskreɪs] *vt* **-graced; -gracing** : deshonrar

disgrace[2] *n* **1** DISHONOR : desgracia *f*, deshonra *f* **2** SHAME : vergüenza *f* ⟨he's a disgrace to his family : es una vergüenza para su familia⟩

disgraceful [dɪˈskreɪsfəl] *adj* : vergonzoso, deshonroso, ignominioso

disgracefully [dɪˈskreɪsfəli] *adv* : vergonzosamente

disgruntle [dɪsˈgrʌntəl] *vt* **-tled; -tling** : enfadar, contrariar

disguise[1] [dɪˈskaɪz] *vt* **-guised; -guising 1** : disfrazar, enmascarar (el aspecto) **2** CONCEAL : encubrir, disimular

disguise[2] *n* : disfraz *m*

disgust[1] [dɪˈskʌst] *vt* : darle asco (a alguien), asquear, repugnar ⟨that disgusts me : eso me da asco⟩

disgust[2] *n* : asco *m*, repugnancia *f*

disgusting [dɪˈskʌstɪŋ] *adj* : asqueroso, repugnante — **disgustingly** *adv*

dish[1] [ˈdɪʃ] *vt* SERVE : servir

dish[2] *n* **1** : plato *m* ⟨the national dish : el plato nacional⟩ **2** PLATE : plato *m* ⟨to wash the dishes : lavar los platos⟩ **3 serving dish** : fuente *f*

dishcloth [ˈdɪʃˌklɔth] *n* : paño *m* de cocina (para secar), trapo *m* de fregar (para lavar)

dishearten [dɪsˈhɑrtən] *vt* : desanimar, desalentar

dishevel [dɪˈʃɛvəl] *vt* **-eled** *or* **-elled; -eling** *or* **-elling** : desarreglar, despeinar (el pelo)

disheveled *or* **dishevelled** [dɪˈʃɛvəld] *adj* : despeinado (dícese del pelo), desarreglado, desaliñado

dishonest [dɪˈsɑnəst] *adj* : deshonesto, fraudulento — **dishonestly** *adv*

dishonesty [dɪˈsɑnəsti] *n, pl* **-ties** : deshonestidad *f*, falta *f* de honradez

dishonor[1] [dɪˈsɑnər] *vt* : deshonrar

dishonor[2] *n* : deshonra *f*

dishonorable [dɪˈsɑnərəbəl] *adj* : deshonroso — **dishonorably** [-bli] *adv*

dishrag [ˈdɪʃˌræg] → **dishcloth**

dishwasher [ˈdɪʃˌwɔʃər] *n* : lavaplatos *m*, lavavajillas *m*

disillusion [ˌdɪsəˈlu:ʒən] *vt* : desilusionar, desencantar, desengañar

disillusionment [ˌdɪsəˈlu:ʒənmənt] *n* : desilusión *f*, desencanto *m*

disinclination [dɪs,ɪnklə'neɪʃən, -,ɪŋ-] *n* : aversión *f*
disinclined [,dɪsɪn'klaɪnd] *adv* : poco dispuesto
disinfect [,dɪsɪn'fɛkt] *vt* : desinfectar
disinfectant¹ [,dɪsɪn'fɛktənt] *adj* : desinfectante
disinfectant² *n* : desinfectante *m*
disinherit [,dɪsɪn'hɛrət] *vt* : desheredar
disintegrate [dɪs'ɪntə,greɪt] *v* **-grated; -grating** *vt* : desintegrar, deshacer — *vi* : desintegrarse, deshacerse
disintegration [dɪs,ɪntə'greɪʃən] *n* : desintegración *f*
disinterested [dɪs'ɪntərəstəd, -,rɛs-] *adj* **1** INDIFFERENT : indiferente **2** IMPARTIAL : imparcial, desinteresado
disinterestedness [dɪs'ɪntərəstədnəs, -,rɛs-] *n* : desinterés *m*
disjointed [dɪs'ʤɔɪntəd] *adj* : inconexo, incoherente
disk *or* **disc** ['dɪsk] *n* : disco *m*
disk drive *n* : unidad *f* de disco
diskette [,dɪs'kɛt] *n* : diskette *m*, disquete *m*
dislike¹ [dɪs'laɪk] *vt* **-liked; -liking** : tenerle aversión a (algo), tenerle antipatía (a alguien), no gustarle (algo a uno)
dislike² *n* : aversión *f*, antipatía *f*
dislocate ['dɪslo,keɪt, dɪs'lo:-] *vt* **-cated; -cating** : dislocar
dislocation [,dɪslo'keɪʃən] *n* : dislocación *f*
dislodge [dɪs'lɑʤ] *vt* **-lodged; -lodging** : sacar, desalojar, desplazar
disloyal [dɪs'lɔɪəl] *adj* : desleal
disloyalty [dɪs'lɔɪəlti] *n, pl* **-ties** : deslealtad *f*
dismal ['dɪzməl] *adj* **1** GLOOMY : sombrío, lúgubre, tétrico **2** DEPRESSING : deprimente, triste
dismantle [dɪs'mæntəl] *vt* **-tled; -tling** : desmantelar, desmontar, desarmar
dismay¹ [dɪs'meɪ] *vt* : consternar
dismay² *n* : consternación *f*
dismember [dɪs'mɛmbər] *vt* : desmembrar
dismiss [dɪs'mɪs] *vt* **1** : dejar salir, darle permiso (a alguien) para retirarse **2** DISCHARGE : despedir, destituir **3** REJECT : descartar, desechar, rechazar
dismissal [dɪs'mɪsəl] *n* **1** : permiso *m* para retirarse **2** DISCHARGE : despido *m* (de un empleado), destitución *f* (de un funcionario) **3** REJECTION : rechazo *m*
dismount [dɪs'maʊnt] *vi* : desmontar, bajarse, apearse
disobedience [,dɪsə'bi:diənts] *n* : desobediencia *f* — **disobedient** [-ənt] *adj*
disobey [,dɪsə'beɪ] *v* : desobedecer
disorder¹ [dɪs'ɔrdər] *vt* : desordenar, desarreglar
disorder² *n* **1** DISARRAY : desorden *m* **2** UNREST : disturbios *mpl*, desórdenes *mpl* **3** AILMENT : afección *f*, indisposición *f*, dolencia *f*
disorderly [dɪs'ɔrdərli] *adj* **1** UNTIDY : desordenado, desarreglado **2** UNRULY : indisciplinado, alborotado **3 disorderly conduct** : conducta *f* escandalosa
disorganization [dɪs,ɔrgənə'zeɪʃən] *n* : desorganización *f*
disorganize [dɪs'ɔrgə,naɪz] *vt* **-nized; -nizing** : desorganizar
disorient [dɪs'ori,ɛnt] *vt* : desorientar
disown [dɪs'o:n] *vt* : renegar de, repudiar
disparage [dɪs'pærɪʤ] *vt* **-aged; -aging** : menospreciar, denigrar
disparagement [dɪs'pærɪʤmənt] *n* : menosprecio *m*
disparate ['dɪspərət, dɪs'pærət] *adj* : dispar, diferente
disparity [dɪs'pærəṭi] *n, pl* **-ties** : disparidad *f*
dispassionate [dɪs'pæʃənət] *adj* : desapasionado, imparcial — **dispassionately** *adv*
dispatch¹ [dɪs'pæʧ] *vt* **1** SEND : despachar, enviar **2** KILL : despachar, matar **3** HANDLE : despachar
dispatch² *n* **1** SENDING : envío *m*, despacho *m* **2** MESSAGE : despacho *m*, reportaje *m* (de un periodista), parte *m* (en el ejército) **3** PROMPTNESS : prontitud *f*, rapidez *f*
dispel [dɪs'pɛl] *vt* **-pelled; -pelling** : disipar, desvanecer
dispensable [dɪ'spɛntsəbəl] *adj* : prescindible
dispensation [,dɪspɛn'seɪʃən] *n* EXEMPTION : exención *m*, dispensa *f*
dispense [dɪs'pɛnts] *v* **-pensed; -pensing** *vt* **1** DISTRIBUTE : repartir, distribuir, dar **2** ADMINISTER, BESTOW : administrar (justicia), conceder (favores, etc.) **3** : preparar y despachar (medicamentos) — *vi* **to dispense with** : prescindir de
dispenser [dɪs'pɛntsər] *n* : dispensador *m*, distribuidor *m* automático
dispersal [dɪs'pərsəl] *n* : dispersión *f*
disperse [dɪs'pərs] *v* **-persed; -persing** *vt* : dispersar, diseminar — *vi* : dispersarse
dispersion [dɪ'spərʒən] *n* : dispersión *f*
dispirit [dɪ'spɪrət] *vt* : desalentar, desanimar
displace [dɪs'pleɪs] *vt* **-placed; -placing** **1** : desplazar (un líquido, etc.) **2** REPLACE : reemplazar
displacement [dɪs'pleɪsmənt] *n* **1** : desplazamiento *m* (de personas) **2** REPLACEMENT : sustitución *f*, reemplazo *m*
display¹ [dɪs'pleɪ] *vt* : exponer, exhibir, mostrar
display² *n* **1** : muestra *f*, exposición *f*, alarde *m* **2** : visualizador *m* (de una computadora)
displease [dɪs'pli:z] *vt* **-pleased; -pleasing** : desagradar a, disgustar, contrariar

displeasure [dɪsˈplɛʒər] *n* : desagrado *m*
disposable [dɪsˈpoːzəbəl] *adj* **1** : desechable ⟨disposable diapers : pañales desechables⟩ **2** AVAILABLE : disponible
disposal [dɪsˈpoːzəl] *n* **1** PLACEMENT : disposición *f*, colocación *f* **2** REMOVAL : eliminación *f* **3 to have at one's disposal** : disponer de, tener a su disposición
dispose [dɪsˈpoːz] *v* **-posed; -posing** *vt* **1** ARRANGE : disponer, colocar **2** INCLINE : predisponer — *vi* **1 to dispose of** DISCARD : desechar, deshacerse de **2 to dispose of** HANDLE : despachar
disposition [ˌdɪspəˈzɪʃən] *n* **1** ARRANGEMENT : disposición *f* **2** TENDENCY : predisposición *f*, inclinación *f* **3** TEMPERAMENT : temperamento *m*, carácter *m*
dispossess [ˌdɪspəˈzɛs] *vt* : deposeer
disproportion [ˌdɪsprəˈporʃən] *n* : desproporción *f*
disproportionate [ˌdɪsprəˈporʃənət] *adj* : desproporcionado — **disproportionately** *adv*
disprove [dɪsˈpruːv] *vt* **-proved; -proving** : rebatir, refutar
disputable [dɪsˈpjuːt̬əbəl, ˈdɪspjʊt̬əbəl] *adj* : disputable, discutible
dispute[1] [dɪsˈpjuːt] *v* **-puted; -puting** *vt* **1** QUESTION : discutir, cuestionar **2** OPPOSE : combatir, resistir — *vi* ARGUE, DEBATE : discutir
dispute[2] *n* **1** DEBATE : debate *m*, discusión *f* **2** QUARREL : disputa *f*, discusión *f*
disqualification [dɪsˌkwɑləfəˈkeɪʃən] *n* : descalificación *f*
disqualify [dɪsˈkwɑləˌfaɪ] *vt* **-fied; -fying** : descalificar, inhabilitar
disquiet[1] [dɪsˈkwaɪət̬] *vt* : inquietar
disquiet[2] *n* : ansiedad *f*, inquietud *f*
disregard[1] [ˌdɪsrɪˈgɑrd] *vt* : ignorar, no prestar atención a
disregard[2] *n* : indiferencia *f*
disrepair [ˌdɪsrɪˈpær] *n* : mal estado *m*
disreputable [dɪsˈrɛpjʊt̬əbəl] *adj* : de mala fama (dícese de una persona o un lugar), vergonzoso (dícese de la conducta)
disreputably [dɪsˈrɛpjʊt̬əbli] *adv* : vergonzosamente
disrepute [ˌdɪsrɪˈpjuːt] *n* : descrédito *m*, mala fama *f*, deshonra *f*
disrespect [ˌdɪsrɪˈspɛkt] *n* : falta *f* de respeto
disrespectful [ˌdɪsrɪˈspɛktfəl] *adj* : irrespetuoso — **disrespectfully** *adv*
disrobe [dɪsˈroːb] *v* **-robed; -robing** *vt* : desvestir, desnudar — *vi* : desvestirse, desnudarse
disrupt [dɪsˈrʌpt] *vt* : trastornar, perturbar
disruption [dɪsˈrʌpʃən] *n* : trastorno *m*
disruptive [dɪsˈrʌptɪv] *adj* : perjudicial, perturbador — **disruptively** *adv*
dissatisfaction [dɪsˌsæt̬əsˈfækʃən] *n* : descontento *m*, insatisfacción *f*
dissatisfied [dɪsˈsæt̬əsˌfaɪd] *adj* : descontento, insatisfecho
dissatisfy [dɪsˈsæt̬əsˌfaɪ] *vt* **-fied; -fying** : no contentar, no satisfacer
dissect [dɪˈsɛkt] *vt* : disecar
dissection [dɪˈsɛkʃən] *n* : disección *f*
dissemble [dɪˈsɛmbəl] *v* **-bled; -bling** *vt* HIDE : ocultar, disimular — *vi* PRETEND : fingir, disimular
disseminate [dɪˈsɛməˌneɪt] *vt* **-nated; -nating** : diseminar, difundir, divulgar
dissemination [dɪˌsɛməˈneɪʃən] *n* : diseminación *f*, difusión *f*
dissension [dɪˈsɛntʃən] *n* : disensión *f*, desacuerdo *m*
dissent[1] [dɪˈsɛnt] *vi* : disentir
dissent[2] *n* : disentimiento *m*, disensión *f*
dissertation [ˌdɪsərˈteɪʃən] *n* **1** DISCOURSE : disertación *f*, discurso *m* **2** THESIS : tesis *f*
disservice [dɪsˈsərvɪs] *n* : perjuicio *m*
dissident[1] [ˈdɪsədənt] *adj* : disidente
dissident[2] *n* : disidente *mf*
dissimilar [dɪˈsɪmələr] *adj* : distinto, diferente, disímil
dissipate [ˈdɪsəˌpeɪt] *vt* **-pated; -pating** **1** DISPERSE : disipar, dispersar **2** SQUANDER : malgastar, desperdiciar, derrochar, disipar
dissipation [ˌdɪsəˈpeɪʃən] *n* : disipación *f*, libertinaje *m*
dissociate [dɪˈsoːʃiˌeɪt, -si-] *v* **-ated** [-ˌeɪt̬əd]; **-ating** [-ˌeɪt̬ɪŋ] *vt* : disociar ⟨to disassociate oneself : disociarse⟩ — *vi* : disociarse
dissociation [dɪˌsoːʃiˈeɪʃən, -si-] *n* : disociación *f*
dissolute [ˈdɪsəˌluːt] *adj* : disoluto
dissolution [ˌdɪsəˈluːʃən] *n* : disolución *f*
dissolve [dɪˈzɑlv] *v* **-solved; -solving** *vt* : disolver — *vi* : disolverse
dissonance [ˈdɪsənənts] *n* : disonancia *f*
dissuade [dɪˈsweɪd] *vt* **-suaded; -suading** : disuadir
distance[1] [ˈdɪstənts] *vt* **-tanced** [-təntst]; **-tancing** [-təntsɪŋ] **to distance oneself** : distanciarse
distance[2] *n* **1** : distancia *f* ⟨the distance between two points : la distancia entre dos puntos⟩ ⟨in the distance : a lo lejos⟩ **2** RESERVE : actitud *f* distante, reserva *f* ⟨to keep one's distance : guardar las distancias⟩
distant [ˈdɪstənt] *adj* **1** FAR : distante, lejano **2** REMOTE : distante, lejano, remoto **3** ALOOF : distante, frío
distantly [ˈdɪstəntli] *adv* **1** LOOSELY : aproximadamente, vagamente **2** COLDLY : fríamente, con frialdad
distaste [dɪsˈteɪst] *n* : desagrado *m*, aversión *f*
distasteful [dɪsˈteɪstfəl] *adj* : desagradable, de mal gusto
distemper [dɪsˈtɛmpər] *n* : moquillo *m*
distend [dɪsˈtɛnd] *vt* : dilatar, hinchar — *vi* : dilatarse, hincharse

distill [dɪˈstɪl] *vt* : destilar
distillation [ˌdɪstəˈleɪʃən] *n* : destilación *f*
distiller [dɪˈstɪlər] *n* : destilador *m*, -dora *f*
distillery [dɪˈstɪləri] *n, pl* **-ries** [-riz] : destilería *f*
distinct [dɪˈstɪŋkt] *adj* **1** DIFFERENT : distinto, diferente **2** CLEAR, UNMISTAKABLE : marcado, claro, evidente ⟨a distinct possibility : una clara posibilidad⟩
distinction [dɪˈstɪŋkʃən] *n* **1** DIFFERENTIATION : distinción *f* **2** DIFFERENCE : diferencia *f* **3** EXCELLENCE : distinción *f*, excelencia *f* ⟨a writer of distinction : un escritor destacado⟩
distinctive [dɪˈstɪŋktɪv] *adj* : distintivo, característico — **distinctively** *adv*
distinctiveness [dɪˈstɪŋktɪvnəs] *n* : peculiaridad *f*
distinctly [dɪˈstɪŋktli] *adv* : claramente, con claridad
distinguish [dɪsˈtɪŋgwɪʃ] *vt* **1** DIFFERENTIATE : distinguir, diferenciar **2** DISCERN : distinguir ⟨he distinguished the sound of the piano : distinguió el sonido del piano⟩ **3 to distinguish oneself** : señalarse, distinguirse — *vi* DISCRIMINATE : distinguir
distinguishable [dɪsˈtɪŋgwɪʃəbəl] *adj* : distinguible
distinguished [dɪsˈtɪŋgwɪʃt] *adj* : distinguido
distort [dɪˈstɔrt] *vt* **1** MISREPRESENT : distorsionar, tergiversar **2** DEFORM : distorsionar, deformar
distortion [dɪˈstɔrʃən] *n* : distorsión *f*, deformación *f*, tergiversación *f*
distract [dɪˈstrækt] *vt* : distraer, entretener
distracted [dɪˈstræktəd] *adj* : distraído
distraction [dɪˈstrækʃən] *n* **1** INTERRUPTION : distracción *f*, interrupción *f* **2** CONFUSION : confusión *f* **3** AMUSEMENT : diversión *f*, entretenimiento *m*, distracción *f*
distraught [dɪˈstrɔt] *adj* : afligido, turbado
distress[1] [dɪˈstɛs] *vt* : afligir, darle pena (a alguien), hacer sufrir
distress[2] *n* **1** SORROW : dolor *m*, angustia *f*, aflicción *f* **2** PAIN : dolor *m* **3 in ~** : en peligro
distressful [dɪˈstrɛsfəl] *adj* : doloroso, penoso
distribute [dɪˈstrɪˌbjuːt, -bjʊt] *vt* **-uted; -uting** : distribuir, repartir
distribution [ˌdɪstrəˈbjuːʃən] *n* : distribución *f*, reparto *m*
distributive [dɪˈstrɪbjʊt̬ɪv] *adj* : distributivo
distributor [dɪˈstrɪbjʊt̬ər] *n* : distribuidor *m*, -dora *f*
district [ˈdɪsˌtrɪkt] *n* **1** REGION : región *f*, zona *f*, barrio *m* (de una ciudad) **2** : distrito *m* (zona política)
distrust[1] [dɪsˈtrʌst] *vt* : desconfiar de
distrust[2] *n* : desconfianza *f*, recelo *m*
distrustful [dɪsˈtrʌstfəl] *adj* : desconfiado, receloso, suspicaz
disturb [dɪˈstərb] *vt* **1** BOTHER : molestar, perturbar ⟨sorry to disturb you : perdone la molestia⟩ **2** DISARRANGE : desordenar **3** WORRY : inquietar, preocupar **4 to disturb the peace** : alterar el orden público
disturbance [dɪˈstərbənts] *n* **1** COMMOTION : alboroto *m*, disturbio *m* **2** INTERRUPTION : interrupción *f*
disuse [dɪsˈjuːs] *n* : desuso *m*
ditch[1] [ˈdɪʧ] *vt* **1** : cavar zanjas en **2** DISCARD : deshacerse de, botar
ditch[2] *n* : zanja *f*, fosa *f*, cuneta *f* (en una carretera)
dither [ˈdɪðər] *n* **to be in a dither** : estar nervioso, ponerse como loco
ditto [ˈdɪt̬oː] *n, pl* **-tos 1** : lo mismo, ídem *m* **2 ditto marks** : comillas *fpl*
ditty [ˈdɪt̬i] *n, pl* **-ties** : canción *f* corta y simple
diurnal [daɪˈərnəl] *adj* **1** DAILY : diario, cotidiano **2** : diurno ⟨a diurnal animal : un animal diurno⟩
divan [ˈdaɪˌvæn, dɪˈ-] *n* : diván *m*
dive[1] [ˈdaɪv] *vi* **dived** *or* **dove** [ˈdoːv]; **dived; diving 1** PLUNGE : tirarse al agua, zambullirse, dar un clavado **2** SUBMERGE : sumergirse **3** DROP : bajar en picada (dícese de un avión), caer en picada
dive[2] *n* **1** PLUNGE : zambullida *f*, clavado *m* (en el agua) **2** DESCENT : descenso *m* en picada **3** BAR, JOINT : antro *m*
diver [ˈdaɪvər] *n* : saltador *m*, -dora *f*; clavadista *mf*
diverge [dəˈvərʤ, daɪ-] *vi* **-verged; -verging 1** SEPARATE : divergir, separarse **2** DIFFER : divergir, discrepar
divergence [dəˈvərʤənts, daɪ-] *n* : divergencia *f* — **divergent** [-ənt] *adj*
diverse [daɪˈvərs, də-, ˈdaɪˌvərs] *adj* : diverso, variado
diversification [daɪˌvərsəfəˈkeɪʃən, də-] *n* : diversificación *f*
diversify [daɪˈvərsəˌfaɪ, də-] *vt* **-fied; -fying** : diversificar, variar
diversion [daɪˈvərʒən, də-] *n* **1** DEVIATION : desviación *f* **2** AMUSEMENT, DISTRACTION : diversión *f*, distracción *f*, entretenimiento *m*
diversity [daɪˈvərsət̬i, də-] *n, pl* **-ties** : diversidad *f*
divert [dəˈvərt, daɪ-] *vt* **1** DEFLECT : desviar **2** DISTRACT : distraer **3** AMUSE : divertir, entretener
divest [daɪˈvɛst, də-] *vt* **1** UNDRESS : desnudar, desvestir **2 to divest of** : despojar de
divide [dəˈvaɪd] *v* **-vided; -viding** *vt* **1** HALVE : dividir, partir por la mitad **2** SHARE : repartir, dividir **3** : dividir (números) — *vi* : dividirse, dividir (en matemáticas)

dividend ['dɪvə,dɛnd, -dənd] *n* **1** : dividendo *m* (en finanzas) **2** BONUS : benefício *m*, provecho *m* **3** : dividendo *m* (en matemáticas)

divider [dɪ'vaɪdər] *n* **1** : separador *m* (para ficheros, etc.) **2** *or* **room divider** : mampara *f*, biombo *m*

divination [,dɪvə'neɪʃən] *n* : adivinación *f*

divine[1] [də'vaɪn] *adj* **-viner; -est 1** : divino **2** SUPERB : divino, espléndido — **divinely** *adv*

divine[2] *n* : clérigo *m*, eclesiástico *m*

divinity [də'vɪnəṯi] *n, pl* **-ties** : divinidad *f*

divisible [dɪ'vɪzəbəl] *adj* : divisible

division [dɪ'vɪʒən] *n* **1** DISTRIBUTION : división *f*, reparto *m* ⟨division of labor : distribución del trabajo⟩ **2** PART : división *f*, sección *f* **3** : división *f* (en matemáticas)

divisive [də'vaɪsɪv] *adj* : divisivo

divisor [dɪ'vaɪzər] *n* : divisor *m*

divorce[1] [də'vors] *v* **-vorced; -vorcing** *vt* : divorciar — *vi* : divorciarse

divorce[2] *n* : divorcio *m*

divorcé [dɪ,vor'seɪ, -'si:; -'vor,-] *n* : divorciado *m*

divorcée [dɪ,vor'seɪ, -'si:; -'vor,-] *n* : divorciada *f*

divulge [də'vʌlʤ, daɪ-] *vt* **-vulged; -vulging** : revelar, divulgar

dizzily ['dɪzəli] *adv* : vertiginosamente

dizziness ['dɪzinəs] *n* : mareo *m*, vahído *m*, vértigo *m*

dizzy ['dɪzi] *adj* **dizzier; -est 1** : mareado ⟨I feel dizzy : estoy mareado⟩ **2** : vertiginoso ⟨a dizzy speed : una velocidad vertiginosa⟩

DNA [,di:,ɛn'eɪ] *n* : ADN *m*

do ['du:] *v* **did** ['dɪd]; **done** ['dʌn]; **doing; does** ['dʌz] *vt* **1** CARRY OUT, PERFORM : hacer, realizar, llevar a cabo ⟨she did her best : hizo todo lo posible⟩ **2** PREPARE : preparar, hacer ⟨do your homework : haz tu tarea⟩ **3** ARRANGE : arreglar, peinar (el pelo) **4 to do in** RUIN : estropear, arruinar **5 to do in** KILL : matar, liquidar *fam* — *vi* **1** : hacer ⟨you did well : hiciste bien⟩ **2** FARE : estar, ir, andar ⟨how are you doing? : ¿cómo estás?, ¿cómo te va?⟩ **3** FINISH : terminar ⟨now I'm done : ya terminé⟩ **4** SERVE : servir, ser suficiente, alcanzar ⟨this will do for now : esto servirá por el momento⟩ **5 to do away with** ABOLISH : abolir, suprimir **6 to do away with** KILL : eliminar, matar **7 to do by** TREAT : tratar ⟨he does well by her : él la trata bien⟩ — *v aux* **1** (*used in interrogative sentences and negative statements*) ⟨do you know her? : ¿la conoces?⟩ ⟨I don't like that : a mí no me gusta eso⟩ **2** (*used for emphasis*) ⟨I do hope you'll come : espero que vengas⟩ **3** (*used as a substitute verb to avoid repetition*) ⟨do you speak English? yes, I do : ¿habla inglés? sí⟩

docile ['dɑsəl] *adj* : dócil, sumiso

dock[1] ['dɑk] *vt* **1** CUT : cortar **2** : descontar dinero de (un sueldo) — *vi* ANCHOR, LAND : fondear, atracar

dock[2] *n* **1** PIER : atracadero *m* **2** WHARF : muelle *m* **3** : banquillo *m* de los acusados (en un tribunal)

doctor[1] ['dɑktər] *vt* **1** TREAT : tratar, curar **2** ALTER : adulterar, alterar, falsificar (un documento)

doctor[2] *n* **1** : doctor *m*, -tora *f* ⟨Doctor of Philosophy : doctor en filosofía⟩ **2** PHYSICIAN : médico *m*, -ca *f*; doctor *m*, -tora *f*

doctorate ['dɑktərət] *n* : doctorado *m*

doctrine ['dɑktrɪn] *n* : doctrina *f*

document[1] ['dɑkjʊ,mɛnt] *vt* : documentar

document[2] ['dɑkjʊmənt] *n* : documento *m*

documentary[1] [,dɑkjʊ'mɛntəri] *adj* : documental

documentary[2] *n, pl* **-ries** : documental *m*

documentation [,dɑkjʊmən'teɪʃən] *n* : documentación *f*

dodge[1] ['dɑʤ] *v* **dodged; dodging** *vt* : esquivar, eludir, evadir (impuestos) — *vi* : echarse a un lado

dodge[2] *n* **1** RUSE : truco *m*, treta *f*, artimaña *f* **2** EVASION : regate *m*, evasión *f*

dodo ['do:,do:] *n, pl* **-does** *or* **-dos** : dodo *m*

doe ['do:] *n, pl* **does** *or* **doe** : gama *f*, cierva *f*

doer ['du:ər] *n* : hacedor *m*, -dora *f*

does → **do**

doff ['dɑf, 'dɔf] *vt* : quitarse ⟨to doff one's hat : quitarse el sombrero⟩

dog[1] ['dɔg, 'dɑg] *vt* **dogged; dogging** : seguir de cerca, perseguir, acosar ⟨to dog someone's footsteps : seguir los pasos de alguien⟩ ⟨dogged by bad luck : perseguido por la mala suerte⟩

dog[2] *n* : perro *m*, -rra *f*

dogcatcher ['dɔg,kæʧər] *n* : perrero *m*, -ra *f*

dog–eared ['dɔg,ɪrd] *adj* : con las esquinas dobladas

dogged ['dɔgəd] *adj* : tenaz, terco, obstinado

doggy ['dɔgi] *n, pl* **doggies** : perrito *m*, -ta *f*

doghouse ['dɔg,haʊs] *n* : casita *f* de perro

dogma ['dɔgmə] *n* : dogma *m*

dogmatic [dɔg'mæṯɪk] *adj* : dogmático

dogmatism ['dɔgmə,tɪzəm] *n* : dogmatismo *m*

dogwood ['dɔg,wʊd] *n* : cornejo *m*

doily ['dɔɪli] *n, pl* **-lies** : pañito *m*

doings ['du:ɪŋz] *npl* : eventos *mpl*, actividades *fpl*

doldrums ['do:ldrəmz, 'dɑl-] *npl* **1** : zona *f* de las calmas ecuatoriales **2 to be in the doldrums** : estar abatido (dícese de una persona), estar estancado (dícese de una empresa)

dole [ˈdo:l] *n* **1** ALMS : distribución *f* a los necesitados, limosna *f* **2** : subsidios *mpl* de desempleo
doleful [ˈdo:lfəl] *adj* : triste, lúgubre
dolefully [ˈdo:lfəli] *adv* : con pesar, de manera triste
dole out *vt* **doled out; doling out** : repartir
doll [ˈdɑl, ˈdɔl] *n* : muñeco *m*, -ca *f*
dollar [ˈdɑlər] *n* : dólar *m*
dolly [ˈdɑli] *n, pl* **-lies** **1** → **doll** **2** : plataforma *f* rodante
dolphin [ˈdɑlfən, ˈdɔl-] *n* : delfín *m*
dolt [ˈdo:lt] *n* : imbécil *mf*; tonto *m*, -ta *f*
domain [doˈmeɪn, də-] *n* **1** TERRITORY : dominio *m*, territorio *m* **2** FIELD : campo *m*, esfera *f*, ámbito *m* ⟨the domain of art : el ámbito de las artes⟩
dome [ˈdo:m] *n* : cúpula *f*, bóveda *f*
domestic[1] [dəˈmɛstɪk] *adj* **1** HOUSEHOLD : doméstico, casero **2** : nacional, interno ⟨domestic policy : política interna⟩ **3** TAME : domesticado
domestic[2] *n* : empleado *m* doméstico, empleada *f* doméstica
domestically [dəˈmɛstɪkli] *adv* : domésticamente
domesticate [dəˈmɛstɪˌkeɪt] *vt* **-cated; -cating** : domesticar
domicile [ˈdɑməˌsaɪl, ˈdo:-; ˈdɑməsɪl] *n* : domicilio *m*
dominance [ˈdɑmənənts] *n* : dominio *m*, dominación *f*
dominant [ˈdɑmənənt] *adj* : dominante
dominate [ˈdɑməˌneɪt] *v* **-nated; -nating** : dominar
domination [ˌdɑməˈneɪʃən] *n* : dominación *f*
domineer [ˌdɑməˈnɪr] *vt* : dominar sobre, avasallar, tiranizar
Dominican [dəˈmɪnɪkən] *n* : dominicano *m*, -na *f* — **Dominican** *adj*
dominion [dəˈmɪnjən] *n* **1** POWER : dominio *m* **2** DOMAIN, TERRITORY : dominio *m*, territorio *m*
domino [ˈdɑməˌno:] *n, pl* **-noes** *or* **-nos** **1** : dominó *m* **2** **dominoes** *npl* : dominó *m* (juego)
don [ˈdɑn] *vt* **donned; donning** : ponerse
donate [ˈdo:ˌneɪt, do:ˈ-] *vt* **-nated; -nating** : donar, hacer un donativo de
donation [do:ˈneɪʃən] *n* : donación *f*, donativo *m*
done[1] [ˈdʌn] → **do**
done[2] *adj* **1** FINISHED : terminado, acabado, concluido **2** COOKED : cocinado
donkey [ˈdɑŋki, ˈdʌŋ-] *n, pl* **-keys** : burro *m*, asno *m*
donor [ˈdo:nər] *n* : donante *mf*; donador *m*, -dora *f*
don't [ˈdo:nt] (*contraction* of **do not**) → **do**
doodle[1] [ˈdu:dəl] *v* **-dled; -dling** : garabatear
doodle[2] *n* : garabato *m*
doom[1] [ˈdu:m] *vt* : condenar
doom[2] *n* **1** JUDGMENT : sentencia *f*, condena *f* **2** DEATH : muerte *f* **3** FATE : destino *m* **4** RUIN : perdición *f*, ruina *f*
door [ˈdor] *n* : puerta *f*
doorbell [ˈdorˌbɛl] *n* : timbre *m*
doorknob [ˈdorˌnɑb] *n* : pomo *m*, perilla *f*
doorman [ˈdormən] *n, pl* **-men** [-mən, -ˌmɛn] : portero *m*
doormat [ˈdorˌmæt] : felpudo *m*
doorstep [ˈdorˌstɛp] *n* : umbral *m*
doorway [ˈdorˌweɪ] *n* : entrada *f*, portal *m*
dope[1] [ˈdo:p] *vt* **doped; doping** : drogar, narcotizar
dope[2] *n* **1** DRUG : droga *f*, estupefaciente *m*, narcótico *m* **2** IDIOT : idiota *mf*; tonto *m*, -ta *f* **3** INFORMATION : información *f*
dormant [ˈdɔrmənt] *adj* : inactivo, latente
dormer [ˈdɔrmər] *n* : buhardilla *f*
dormitory [ˈdɔrməˌtori] *n, pl* **-ries** : dormitorio *m*, residencia *f* de estudiantes
dormouse [ˈdɔrˌmaʊs] *n* : lirón *m*
dorsal [ˈdɔrsəl] *adj* : dorsal — **dorsally** *adv*
dory [ˈdori] *n, pl* **-ries** : bote *m* de fondo plano
dosage [ˈdo:sɪʤ] *n* : dosis *f*
dose[1] [ˈdo:s] *vt* **dosed; dosing** : medicinar
dose[2] *n* : dosis *f*
dossier [ˈdɔsˌjeɪ, ˈdɑs-] *n* : dossier *m*
dot[1] [ˈdɑt] *vt* **dotted; dotting** **1** : poner el punto sobre (una letra) **2** SCATTER : esparcir, salpicar
dot[2] *n* : punto *m* ⟨at six on the dot : a las seis en punto⟩ ⟨dots and dashes : puntos y rayas⟩
dote [ˈdo:t] *vi* **doted; doting** : chochear
double[1] [ˈdʌbəl] *v* **-bled; -bling** *vt* **1** : doblar, duplicar (una cantidad), redoblar (esfuerzos) **2** FOLD : doblar, plegar **3** **to double one's fist** : apretar el puño — *vi* **1** : doblarse, duplicarse **2** **to double over** : retorcerse
double[2] *adj* : doble — **doubly** *adv*
double[3] *n* : doble *mf*
double bass *n* : contrabajo *m*
double–cross [ˌdʌbəlˈkrɔs] *vt* : traicionar
double–crosser [ˌdʌbəlˈkrɔsər] *n* : traidor *m*, -dora *f*
double–jointed [ˌdʌbəlˈʤɔintəd] *adj* : con articulaciones dobles
double–talk [ˈdʌbəlˌtɔk] *n* : ambigüedades *fpl*, lenguaje *m* con doble sentido
doubt[1] [ˈdaʊt] *vt* **1** QUESTION : dudar de, cuestionar **2** DISTRUST : desconfiar de **3** : dudar, creer poco probable ⟨I doubt it very much : lo dudo mucho⟩
doubt[2] *n* **1** UNCERTAINTY : duda *f*, incertidumbre *f* **2** DISTRUST : desconfianza *f* **3** SKEPTICISM : duda *f*, escepticismo *m*

doubtful ['daʊtfəl] *adj* **1** QUESTIONABLE : dudoso **2** UNCERTAIN : dudoso, incierto

doubtfully ['daʊtfəli] *adv* : dudosamente, sin estar convencido

doubtless ['daʊtləs] *or* **doubtlessly** *adv* : sin duda

douche1 ['du:ʃ] *vt* **douched; douching** : irrigar

douche2 *n* : ducha *f*, irrigación *f*

dough ['do:] *n* : masa *f*

doughnut *or* **donut** ['do:ˌnʌt] *n* : rosquilla *f*, dona *f Mex*

doughty ['daʊt̬i] *adj* **-tier; -est** : fuerte, valiente

dour ['daʊər, 'dʊr] *adj* **1** STERN : severo, adusto **2** SULLEN : hosco, taciturno — **dourly** *adv*

douse ['daʊs, 'daʊz] *vt* **doused; dousing 1** DRENCH : empapar, mojar **2** EXTINGUISH : extinguir, apagar

dove1 ['do:v] → **dive**

dove2 ['dʌv] *n* : paloma *f*

dovetail ['dʌvˌteɪl] *vi* : encajar, enlazar

dowdy ['daʊdi] *adj* **dowdier; -est** : sin gracia, poco elegante

dowel ['daʊəl] *n* : clavija *f*

down1 ['daʊn] *vt* **1** FELL : tumbar, derribar, abatir **2** DEFEAT : derrotar

down2 *adv* **1** DOWNWARD : hacia abajo **2 to lie down** : acostarse, echarse **3 to put down (money)** : pagar un depósito (de dinero) **4 to sit down** : sentarse **5 to take down, to write down** : apuntar, anotar

down3 *adj* **1** DESCENDING : de bajada ⟨the down elevator : el ascensor de bajada⟩ **2** REDUCED : reducido, rebajado ⟨attendance is down : la concurrencia ha disminuido⟩ **3** DOWNCAST : abatido, deprimido

down4 *n* **1** : plumón *m* **2** : down *m* (en deportes) **3 ups and downs** : altibajos *mpl*

down5 *prep* **1** : (hacia) abajo ⟨down the mountain : montaña abajo⟩ ⟨I walked down the stairs : bajé por la escalera⟩ **2** ALONG : por, a lo largo de ⟨we ran down the beach : corrimos por la playa⟩ **3** : a través de ⟨down the years : a través de los años⟩

downcast ['daʊnˌkæst] *adj* **1** SAD : triste, abatido **2 with downcast eyes** : con los ojos bajos, con los ojos mirando al suelo

downfall ['daʊnˌfɔl] *n* : ruina *f*, perdición *f*

downgrade1 ['daʊnˌgreɪd] *vt* **-graded; -grading** : bajar de categoría

downgrade2 *n* : bajada *f*

downhearted ['daʊnˌhɑrt̬əd] *adj* : desanimado, descorazonado

downhill ['daʊn'hɪl] *adv & adj* : cuesta abajo

download1 ['daʊnˌlo:d] *vt* : descargar (un archivo)

download2 *n* : descarga *f* (de archivos, etc.)

down payment *n* : entrega *f* inicial

downplay ['daʊnˌpleɪ] *vt* : minimizar

downpour ['daʊnˌpor] *n* : aguacero *m*, chaparrón *m*

downright1 ['daʊnˌraɪt] *adv* THOROUGHLY : absolutamente, completamente

downright2 *adj* : patente, manifiesto, absoluto ⟨a downright refusal : un rechazo categórico⟩

downside ['daʊnˌsaɪd] *n* : desventaja *f*

downstairs1 ['daʊn'stærz] *adv* : abajo

downstairs2 ['daʊnˌstærz] *adj* : del piso de abajo

downstairs3 ['daʊn'stærz, -ˌstærz] *n* : planta *f* baja

downstream ['daʊn'stri:m] *adv* : río abajo

down–to–earth [ˌdaʊntu'ərth] *adj* : práctico, realista

downtown1 [ˌdaʊn'taʊn] *adv* : hacia el centro, al centro, en el centro (de la ciudad)

downtown2 *adj* : del centro (de la ciudad) ⟨downtown Chicago : el centro de Chicago⟩

downtown3 [ˌdaʊn'taʊn, 'daʊnˌtaʊn] *n* : centro *m* (de la ciudad)

downtrodden ['daʊnˌtrɑdən] *adj* : oprimido

downward ['daʊnwərd] *or* **downwards** [-wərdz] *adv & adj* : hacia abajo

downwind ['daʊn'wɪnd] *adv & adj* : en la dirección del viento

downy ['daʊni] *adj* **downier; -est 1** : cubierto de plumón, plumoso **2** VELVETY : aterciopelado, velloso

dowry ['daʊri] *n, pl* **-ries** : dote *f*

doze1 ['do:z] *vi* **dozed; dozing** : dormitar

doze2 *n* : sueño *m* ligero, cabezada *f*

dozen ['dʌzən] *n, pl* **dozens** *or* **dozen** : docena *f*

drab ['dræb] *adj* **drabber; drabbest 1** BROWNISH : pardo **2** DULL, LACKLUSTER : monótono, gris, deslustrado

draft1 ['dræft, 'draft] *vt* **1** CONSCRIPT : reclutar **2** COMPOSE, SKETCH : hacer el borrador de, redactar

draft2 *adj* **1** : de barril ⟨draft beer : cerveza de barril⟩ **2** : de tiro ⟨draft horses : caballos de tiro⟩

draft3 *n* **1** HAULAGE : tiro *m* **2** DRINK, GULP : trago *m* **3** OUTLINE, SKETCH : bosquejo *m*, borrador *m*, versión *f* **4** : corriente *f* de aire, chiflón *m*, tiro *m* (de una chimenea) **5** CONSCRIPTION : conscripción *f* **6 bank draft** : giro *m* bancario, letra *f* de cambio

draftee [dræf'ti:] *n* : recluta *mf*

draftsman ['dræftsmən] *n, pl* **-men** [-mən, -ˌmɛn] : dibujante *mf*

drafty ['dræfti] *adj* **draftier; -est** : con corrientes de aire

drag1 ['dræg] *v* **dragged; dragging** *vt* **1** HAUL : arrastrar, jalar **2** DREDGE : dragar — *vi* **1** TRAIL : arrastrarse **2** LAG : rezagarse **3** : hacerse pesado, hacerse largo ⟨the day dragged on : el día se hizo largo⟩

drag[2] *n* **1** RESISTANCE : resistencia *f* (aerodinámica) **2** HINDRANCE : traba *f*, estorbo *m* **3** BORE : pesadez *f*, plomo *m fam*

dragnet [ˈdræg,nɛt] *n* **1** : red *f* barredera (en pesca) **2** : operativo *m* policial de captura

dragon [ˈdrægən] *n* : dragón *m*

dragonfly [ˈdrægən,flaɪ] *n, pl* **-flies** : libélula *f*

drain[1] [ˈdreɪn] *vt* **1** EMPTY : vaciar, drenar **2** EXHAUST : agotar, consumir — *vi* **1** : escurrir, escurrirse ⟨the dishes are draining : los platos están escurriéndose⟩ **2** EMPTY : desaguar **3 to drain away** : irse agotando

drain[2] *n* **1** : desagüe *m* **2** SEWER : alcantarilla *f* **3** GRATING : sumidero *m*, resumidero *m*, rejilla *f* **4** EXHAUSTION : agotamiento *m*, disminución *f* (de energía, etc.) ⟨to be a drain on : agotar, consumir⟩ **5 to throw down the drain** : tirar por la ventana

drainage [ˈdreɪnɪʤ] *n* : desagüe *m*, drenaje *m*

drainpipe [ˈdreɪn,paɪp] *n* : tubo *m* de desagüe, caño *m*

drake [ˈdreɪk] *n* : pato *m* (macho)

drama [ˈdrɑmə, ˈdræ-] *n* **1** THEATER : drama *m*, teatro *m* **2** PLAY : obra *f* de teatro, drama *m*

dramatic [drəˈmæṭɪk] *adj* : dramático — **dramatically** [-ṭɪkli] *adv*

dramatist [ˈdræməṭɪst, ˈdrɑ-] *n* : dramaturgo *m*, -ga *f*

dramatization [,dræməṭəˈzeɪʃən, ,drɑ-] *n* : dramatización *f*

dramatize [ˈdræmə,taɪz, ˈdrɑ-] *vt* **-tized; -tizing** : dramatizar

drank → **drink**

drape[1] [ˈdreɪp] *vt* **draped; draping 1** COVER : cubrir (con tela) **2** HANG : drapear, disponer los pliegues de

drape[2] *n* **1** HANG : caída *f* **2 drapes** *npl* : cortinas *fpl*

drapery [ˈdreɪpəri] *n, pl* **-eries 1** CLOTH : pañería *f*, tela *f* para cortinas **2 draperies** *npl* : cortinas *fpl*

drastic [ˈdræstɪk] *adj* **1** HARSH, SEVERE : drástico, severo **2** EXTREME : radical, excepcional — **drastically** [-tɪkli] *adv*

draught [ˈdræft, ˈdraft] *n* → **draft**[3]

draughty [ˈdrafti] → **drafty**

draw[1] [ˈdrɔ] *v* **drew** [ˈdru:]; **drawn** [ˈdrɔn]; **drawing** *vt* **1** PULL : tirar de, jalar, correr (cortinas) **2** ATTRACT : atraer **3** PROVOKE : provocar, suscitar **4** INHALE : aspirar ⟨to draw breath : respirar⟩ **5** EXTRACT : sacar, extraer **6** TAKE : sacar ⟨to draw a number : sacar un número⟩ **7** COLLECT : cobrar, percibir (un sueldo, etc.) **8** BEND : tensar (un arco) **9** TIE : empatar (en deportes) **10** SKETCH : dibujar, trazar **11** FORMULATE : sacar, formular, llegar a ⟨to draw a conclusion : llegar a una conclusión⟩ **12 to draw out** : hacer hablar (sobre algo), hacer salir de sí mismo **13 to draw up** DRAFT : redactar — *vi* **1** SKETCH : dibujar **2** TUG : tirar, jalar **3 to draw near** : acercarse **4 to draw to a close** : terminar, finalizar **5 to draw up** STOP : parar

draw[2] *n* **1** DRAWING, RAFFLE : sorteo *m* **2** TIE : empate *m* **3** ATTRACTION : atracción *f* **4** PUFF : chupada *f* (de un cigarrillo, etc.)

drawback [ˈdrɔ,bæk] *n* : desventaja *f*, inconveniente *m*

drawbridge [ˈdrɔ,brɪʤ] *n* : puente *m* levadizo

drawer [ˈdrɔr, ˈdrɔər] *n* **1** ILLUSTRATOR : dibujante *mf* **2** : gaveta *f*, cajón *m* (en un mueble) **3 drawers** *npl* UNDERPANTS : calzones *mpl*

drawing [ˈdrɔɪŋ] *n* **1** LOTTERY : sorteo *m*, lotería *f* **2** SKETCH : dibujo *m*, bosquejo *m*

drawl[1] [ˈdrɔl] *vi* : hablar arrastrando las palabras

drawl[2] *n* : habla *f* lenta y con vocales prolongadas

dread[1] [ˈdrɛd] *vt* : tenerle pavor a, temer

dread[2] *adj* : pavoroso, aterrado

dread[3] *n* : pavor *m*, temor *m*

dreadful [ˈdrɛdfəl] *adj* **1** DREAD : pavoroso **2** TERRIBLE : espantoso, atroz, terrible — **dreadfully** *adv*

dream[1] [ˈdri:m] *v* **dreamed** [ˈdrɛmpt, ˈdri:md] *or* **dreamt** [ˈdrɛmpt]; **dreaming** *vi* **1** : soñar ⟨to dream about : soñar con⟩ **2** FANTASIZE : fantasear — *vt* **1** : soñar **2** IMAGINE : imaginarse **3 to dream up** : inventar, idear

dream[2] *n* **1** : sueño *m*, ensueño *m* **2 bad dream** NIGHTMARE : pesadilla *f*

dreamer [ˈdri:mər] *n* : soñador *m*, -dora *f*

dreamlike [ˈdri:m,laɪk] *adj* : de ensueño

dreamy [ˈdri:mi] *adj* **dreamier; -est 1** DISTRACTED : soñador, distraído **2** DREAMLIKE : de ensueño **3** MARVELOUS : maravilloso

drearily [ˈdrɪrəli] *adv* : sombríamente

dreary [ˈdrɪri] *adj* **-rier; -est** : deprimente, lóbrego, sombrío

dredge[1] [ˈdrɛʤ] *vt* **dredged; dredging 1** DIG : dragar **2** COAT : espolvorear, enharinar

dredge[2] *n* : draga *f*

dredger [ˈdrɛʤər] *n* : draga *f*

dregs [ˈdrɛgz] *npl* **1** LEES : posos *mpl*, heces *fpl* (de un líquido) **2** : heces *fpl*, escoria *f* ⟨the dregs of society : la escoria de la sociedad⟩

drench [ˈdrɛnʧ] *vt* : empapar, mojar, calar

dress[1] [ˈdrɛs] *vt* **1** CLOTHE : vestir **2** DECORATE : decorar, adornar **3** : preparar (pollo o pescado), aliñar (ensalada) **4** : curar, vendar (una herida) **5** FERTILIZE : abonar (la tierra) — *vi* **1** : vestirse **2 to dress up** : ataviarse, engalanarse, ponerse de etiqueta

dress[2] *n* **1** APPAREL : indumentaria *f*, ropa *f* **2** : vestido *m*, traje *m* (de mujer)

dresser ['drɛsər] *n* : cómoda *f* con espejo

dressing ['drɛsɪŋ] *n* **1** : vestirse *m* **2** : aderezo *m*, aliño *m* (de ensalada), relleno *m* (de pollo) **3** BANDAGE : vendaje *m*, gasa *f*

dressmaker ['drɛs,meɪkər] *n* : modista *mf*

dressmaking ['drɛs,meɪkɪŋ] *n* : costura *f*

dressy ['drɛsi] *adj* **dressier; -est** : de mucho vestir, elegante

drew → **draw**

dribble[1] ['drɪbəl] *vi* **-bled; -bling** **1** DRIP : gotear **2** DROOL : babear **3** : driblar (en basquetbol)

dribble[2] *n* **1** TRICKLE : goteo *m*, hilo *m* **2** DROOL : baba *f* **3** : drible *m* (en basquetbol)

drier → **dry**[2], **dryer**

driest *adj* → **dry**[2]

drift[1] ['drɪft] *vi* **1** : dejarse llevar por la corriente, ir a la deriva (dícese de un bote), ir sin rumbo (dícese de una persona) **2** ACCUMULATE : amontonarse, acumularse, apilarse

drift[2] *n* **1** DRIFTING : deriva *f* **2** HEAP, MASS : montón *m* (de arena, etc.), ventisquero *m* (de nieve) **3** MEANING : sentido *m*

drifter ['drɪftər] *n* : vagabundo *m*, -da *f*

driftwood ['drɪft,wʊd] *n* : madera *f* flotante

drill[1] ['drɪl] *vt* **1** BORE : perforar, taladrar **2** INSTRUCT : instruir por repetición — *vi* **1** TRAIN : entrenarse **2 to drill for oil** : perforar en busca de petróleo

drill[2] *n* **1** : taladro *m*, barrena *f* **2** EXERCISE, PRACTICE : ejercicio *m*, instrucción *f*

drily → **dryly**

drink[1] ['drɪŋk] *v* **drank** ['dræŋk]; **drunk** ['drʌŋk] *or* **drank; drinking** *vt* **1** IMBIBE : beber, tomar **2 to drink up** ABSORB : absorber — *vi* **1** : beber **2** : beber alcohol, tomar

drink[2] *n* **1** : bebida *f* **2** : bebida *f* alcohólica

drinkable ['drɪŋkəbəl] *adj* : potable

drinker ['drɪŋkər] *n* : bebedor *m*, -dora *f*

drip[1] ['drɪp] *vi* **dripped; dripping** : gotear, chorrear

drip[2] *n* **1** DROP : gota *f* **2** DRIPPING : goteo *m*

drive[1] ['draɪv] *v* **drove** ['dro:v]; **driven** ['drɪvən]; **driving** *vt* **1** IMPEL : impeler, impulsar **2** OPERATE : guiar, conducir, manejar (un vehículo) **3** COMPEL : obligar, forzar **4** : clavar, hincar ⟨to drive a stake : clavar una estaca⟩ **5** *or* **to drive away** : ahuyentar, echar **6 to drive crazy** : volver loco — *vi* : manejar, conducir ⟨do you know how to drive? : ¿sabes manejar?⟩

drive[2] *n* **1** RIDE : paseo *m* en coche **2** CAMPAIGN : campaña *f* ⟨fund-raising drive : campaña para recaudar fondos⟩ **3** DRIVEWAY : camino *m* de entrada, entrada *f* **4** TRANSMISSION : transmisión *f* ⟨front-wheel drive : tracción delantera⟩ **5** ENERGY : dinamismo *m*, energía *f* **6** INSTINCT, NEED : instinto *m*, necesidad *f* básica **7** → **disk drive**

drivel ['drɪvəl] *n* : tontería *f*, estupidez *f*

driver ['draɪvər] *n* : conductor *m*, -tora *f*; chofer *m*

driveway ['draɪv,weɪ] *n* : camino *m* de entrada, entrada *f* (para coches)

drizzle[1] ['drɪzəl] *vi* **-zled; -zling** : lloviznar, garuar

drizzle[2] *n* : llovizna *f*, garúa *f*

droll ['dro:l] *adj* : cómico, gracioso, chistoso — **drolly** *adv*

dromedary ['drɑmə,dɛri] *n, pl* **-daries** : dromedario *m*

drone[1] ['dro:n] *vi* **droned; droning** **1** BUZZ : zumbar **2** MURMUR : hablar con monotonía, murmurar

drone[2] *n* **1** : zángano *m* (abeja) **2** FREELOADER : gorrón *m*, -rrona *f fam*; parásito *m*, -ta *f* **3** BUZZ, HUM : zumbido *m*, murmullo *m*

drool[1] ['dru:l] *vi* : babear

drool[2] *n* : baba *f*

droop[1] ['dru:p] *vi* **1** HANG : inclinarse (dícese de la cabeza), encorvarse (dícese de los escombros), marchitarse (dícese de las flores) **2** FLAG : decaer, flaquear ⟨his spirits drooped : se desanimó⟩

droop[2] *n* : inclinación *f*, caída *f*

drop[1] ['drɑp] *v* **dropped; dropping** *vt* **1** : dejar caer, soltar ⟨she dropped the glass : se le cayó el vaso⟩ ⟨to drop a hint : dejar caer una indirecta⟩ **2** SEND : mandar ⟨drop me a line : mándame unas líneas⟩ **3** ABANDON : abandonar, dejar ⟨to drop the subject : cambiar de tema⟩ **4** LOWER : bajar ⟨he dropped his voice : bajó la voz⟩ **5** OMIT : omitir **6 to drop off** : dejar — *vi* **1** DRIP : gotear **2** FALL : caer(se) **3** DECREASE, DESCEND : bajar, descender ⟨the wind dropped : amainó el viento⟩ **4 to drop back** *or* **to drop behind** : rezagarse, quedarse atrás **5 to drop by** *or* **to drop in** : pasar

drop[2] *n* **1** : gota *f* (de líquido) **2** DECLINE : caída *f*, bajada *f*, descenso *m* **3** INCLINE : caída *f*, pendiente *f* ⟨a 20-foot drop : una caída de 20 pies⟩ **4** SWEET : pastilla *f*, dulce *m* **5 drops** *npl* : gotas *fpl* (de medicina)

droplet ['drɑplət] *n* : gotita *f*

dropper ['drɑpər] *n* : gotero *m*, cuentagotas *m*

dross ['drɑs, 'drɔs] *n* : escoria *f*

drought ['draʊt] *n* : sequía *f*

drove[1] → **drive**

drove[2] ['dro:v] *n* : multitud *f*, gentío *m*, manada *f* (de ganado) ⟨in droves : en manada⟩

drown ['draʊn] *vt* **1** : ahogar **2** INUNDATE : anegar, inundar **3 to drown out** : ahogar — *vi* : ahogarse

drowse¹ ['draʊz] *vi* **drowsed; drowsing** DOZE : dormitar

drowse² *n* : sueño *m* ligero, cabezada *f*

drowsiness ['draʊzinəs] *n* : somnolencia *f*, adormecimiento *m*

drowsy ['draʊzi] *adj* **drowsier; -est** : somnoliento, soñoliento

drub ['drʌb] *vt* **drubbed; drubbing 1** BEAT, THRASH : golpear, apalear **2** DEFEAT : derrotar por completo

drudge¹ ['drʌʤ] *vi* **drudged; drudging** : trabajar como esclavo, trabajar duro

drudge² *n* : esclavo *m*, -va *f* del trabajo

drudgery ['drʌʤəri] *n, pl* **-eries** : trabajo *m* pesado

drug¹ ['drʌg] *vt* **drugged; drugging** : drogar, narcotizar

drug² *n* **1** MEDICATION : droga *f*, medicina *f*, medicamento *m* **2** NARCOTIC : narcótico *m*, estupefaciente *m*, droga *f*

druggist ['drʌgɪst] *n* : farmacéutico *m*, -ca *f*

drugstore ['drʌg,stor] *n* : farmacia *f*, botica *f*, droguería *f*

drum¹ ['drʌm] *v* **drummed; drumming** *vt* : meter a fuerza ⟨he drummed it into my head : me lo metió en la cabeza a fuerza⟩ — *vi* : tocar el tambor

drum² *n* **1** : tambor *m* **2** : bidón *m* ⟨oil drum : bidón de petróleo⟩

drummer ['drʌmər] *n* : baterista *mf*

drumstick ['drʌm,stɪk] *n* **1** : palillo *m* (de tambor), baqueta *f* **2** : muslo *m* de pollo

drunk¹ *pp* → **drink¹**

drunk² ['drʌŋk] *adj* : borracho, embriagado, ebrio

drunk³ *n* : borracho *m*, -cha *f*

drunkard ['drʌŋkərd] *n* : borracho *m*, -cha *f*

drunken ['drʌŋkən] *adj* : borracho, ebrio ⟨drunken driver : conductor ebrio⟩ ⟨drunken brawl : pleito de borrachos⟩

drunkenly ['drʌŋkənli] *adv* : como un borracho

drunkenness ['drʌŋkənnəs] *n* : borrachera *f*, embriaguez *f*, ebriedad *f*

dry¹ ['draɪ] *v* **dried; drying** *vt* : secar — *vi* : secarse

dry² *adj* **drier; driest 1** : seco **2** THIRSTY : sediento **3** : donde la venta de bebidas alcohólicas está prohibida ⟨a dry county : un condado seco⟩ **4** DULL : aburrido, árido **5** : seco (dícese del vino), brut (dícese de la champaña)

dry–clean ['draɪ,kli:n] *v* : limpiar en seco

dry cleaner *n* : tintorería *f* (servicio)

dry cleaning *n* : limpieza *f* en seco

dryer ['draɪər] *n* **1 hair dryer** : secador *m* **2 clothes dryer** : secadora *f*

dry goods *npl* : artículos *mpl* de confección

dry ice *n* : hielo *m* seco

dryly ['draɪli] *adv* : secamente

dryness ['draɪnəs] *n* : sequedad *f*, aridez *f*

dual ['du:əl, 'dju:-] *adj* : doble

dualism ['du:ə,lɪzəm] *n* : dualismo *m*

dub ['dʌb] *vt* **dubbed; dubbing 1** CALL : apodar **2** : doblar (una película), mezclar (una grabación)

dubious ['du:biəs, 'dju:-] *adj* **1** UNCERTAIN : dudoso, indeciso **2** QUESTIONABLE : sospechoso, dudoso, discutible

dubiously ['du:biəsli, 'dju:-] *adv* **1** UNCERTAINLY : dudosamente, con desconfianza **2** SUSPICIOUSLY : de modo sospechoso, con recelo

duchess ['dʌʧəs] *n* : duquesa *f*

duck¹ ['dʌk] *vt* **1** LOWER : agachar, bajar (la cabeza) **2** PLUNGE : zambullir **3** EVADE : eludir, evadir — *vi* **to duck down** : agacharse

duck² *n, pl* **duck** *or* **ducks** : pato *m*, -ta *f*

duckling ['dʌklɪŋ] *n* : patito *m*, -ta *f*

duct ['dʌkt] *n* : conducto *m*

ductile ['dʌktəl] *adj* : dúctil

dude ['du:d, 'dju:d] *n* **1** DANDY : dandi *m*, dandy *m* **2** GUY : tipo *m*

due¹ ['du:, 'dju:] *adv* : justo a, derecho hacia ⟨due north : derecho hacia el norte⟩

due² *adj* **1** PAYABLE : pagadero, sin pagar **2** APPROPRIATE : debido, apropiado ⟨after due consideration : con las debidas consideraciones⟩ **3** EXPECTED : esperado ⟨the train is due soon : esperamos el tren muy pronto, el tren debe llegar pronto⟩ **4 due to** : debido a, por

due³ *n* **1 to give someone his (her) due** : darle a alguien su merecido **2 dues** *npl* : cuota *f*

duel¹ ['du:əl, 'dju:-] *vi* : batirse en duelo

duel² *n* : duelo *m*

duet [du'ɛt, dju-] *n* : dúo *m*

due to *prep* : debido a

dug → **dig**

dugout ['dʌg,aʊt] *n* **1** CANOE : piragua *f* **2** SHELTER : refugio *m* subterráneo

duke ['du:k, 'dju:k] *n* : duque *m*

dull¹ ['dʌl] *vt* **1** DIM : opacar, quitar el brillo a, deslustrar **2** BLUNT : embotar (un filo), entorpecer (los sentidos), aliviar (el dolor), amortiguar (sonidos)

dull² *adj* **1** STUPID : torpe, lerdo, lento **2** BLUNT : desafilado, despuntado **3** LACKLUSTER : sin brillo, deslustrado **4** BORING : aburrido, soso, pesado — **dully** *adv*

dullness ['dʌlnəs] *n* **1** STUPIDITY : estupidez *f* **2** : embotamiento *m* (de los sentidos) **3** MONOTONY : monotonía *f*, insipidez *f* **4** : falta *f* de brillo **5** BLUNTNESS : falta *f* de filo, embotadura *f*

duly ['du:li, 'dju:-] *adv* PROPERLY : debidamente, a su debido tiempo

dumb ['dʌm] *adj* **1** MUTE : mudo **2** STUPID : estúpido, tonto, bobo — **dumbly** *adv*

dumbbell ['dʌm,bɛl] *n* **1** WEIGHT : pesa *f* **2** : estúpido *m*, -da *f*
dumbfound *or* **dumfound** [,dʌm-'faʊnd] *vt* : dejar atónito, dejar sin habla
dummy ['dʌmi] *n, pl* **-mies** **1** SHAM : imitación *f*, sustituto *m* **2** PUPPET : muñeco *m* **3** MANNEQUIN : maniquí *m* **4** IDIOT : tonto *m*, -ta *f*; idiota *mf*
dump[1] ['dʌmp] *vt* : descargar, verter
dump[2] *n* **1** : vertedero *m*, tiradero *m Mex* **2 down in the dumps** : triste, deprimido
dumpling ['dʌmplɪŋ] *n* : bola *f* de masa hervida
dumpy ['dʌmpi] *adj* **dumpier; -est** : rechoncho, regordete
dun[1] ['dʌn] *vt* **dunned; dunning** : apremiar (a un deudor)
dun[2] *adj* : pardo (color)
dunce ['dʌnts] *n* : estúpido *m*, -da *f*; burro *m*, -rra *f fam*
dune ['du:n, 'dju:n] *n* : duna *f*
dung ['dʌŋ] *n* **1** FECES : excrementos *mpl* **2** MANURE : estiércol *m*
dungaree [,dʌŋgə'ri:] *n* **1** DENIM : tela *f* vaquera, mezclilla *f Chile, Mex* **2 dungarees** *npl* : pantalones *mpl* de trabajo hechos de tela vaquera
dungeon ['dʌndʒən] *n* : mazmorra *f*, calabozo *m*
dunk ['dʌŋk] *vt* : mojar, ensopar
duo ['du:o:, 'dju:-] *n, pl* **duos** : dúo *m*, par *m*
dupe[1] ['du:p, dju:p] *vt* **duped; duping** : engañar, embaucar
dupe[2] *n* : inocentón *m*, -tona *f*; simple *mf*
duplex[1] ['du:,plɛks, 'dju:-] *adj* : doble
duplex[2] *n* : casa *f* de dos viviendas, dúplex *m*
duplicate[1] ['du:plɪ,keɪt, 'dju:-] *vt* **-cated; -cating** **1** COPY : duplicar, hacer copias de **2** REPEAT : repetir, reproducir
duplicate[2] ['du:plɪkət, 'dju:-] *adj* : duplicado <a duplicate invoice : una factura por duplicado>
duplicate[3] ['du:plɪkət, 'dju:-] *n* : duplicado *m*, copia *f*
duplication [,du:plɪ'keɪʃən, ,dju:-] *n* **1** DUPLICATING : duplicación *f*, repetición *f* (de esfuerzos) **2** DUPLICATE : copia *f*, duplicado *m*
duplicity [dʊ'plɪsət̬i, ,dju:-] *n, pl* **-ties** : duplicidad *f*
durability [,dʊrə'bɪlət̬i, ,djʊr-] *n* : durabilidad *f* (de un producto) permanencia *f*
durable ['dʊrəbəl, 'djʊr-] *adj* : duradero
duration [dʊ'reɪʃən, djʊ-] *n* : duración *f*
duress [dʊ'rɛs, djʊ-] *n* : coacción *f*
during ['dʊrɪŋ, 'djʊr-] *prep* : durante
dusk ['dʌsk] *n* : anochecer *m*, crepúsculo *m*
dusky ['dʌski] *adj* **duskier; -est** : oscuro (dícese de los colores)
dust[1] ['dʌst] *vt* **1** : quitar el polvo de **2** SPRINKLE : espolvorear
dust[2] *n* : polvo *m*
duster ['dʌstər] *n* **1** *or* **dust cloth** : trapo *m* de polvo **2** HOUSECOAT : guardapolvo *m* **3 feather duster** : plumero *m*
dustpan ['dʌst,pæn] *n* : recogedor *m*
dusty ['dʌsti] *adj* **dustier; -est** : cubierto de polvo, polvoriento
Dutch[1] ['dʌtʃ] *adj* : holandés
Dutch[2] *n* **1** : holandés *m* (idioma) **2 the Dutch** *npl* : los holandeses
Dutch treat *n* : invitación o pago a escote
dutiful ['du:t̬ɪfəl, 'dju:-] *adj* : motivado por sus deberes, responsable
duty ['du:t̬i, 'dju:-] *n, pl* **-ties** **1** OBLIGATION : deber *m*, obligación *f*, responsabilidad *f* **2** TAX : impuesto *m*, arancel *m*
DVD [,di:,vi:'di:] *n* : DVD *m*
dwarf[1] ['dwɔrf] *vt* **1** STUNT : arrestar el crecimiento de **2** : hacer parecer pequeño
dwarf[2] *n, pl* **dwarfs** ['dwɔrfs] *or* **dwarves** ['dwɔrvz] : enano *m*, -na *f*
dwell ['dwɛl] *vi* **dwelled** *or* **dwelt** ['dwɛlt]; **dwelling** **1** RESIDE : residir, morar, vivir **2 to dwell on** : pensar demasiado en, insistir en
dweller ['dwɛlər] *n* : habitante *mf*
dwelling ['dwɛlɪŋ] *n* : morada *f*, vivienda *f*, residencia *f*
dwindle ['dwɪndəl] *vi* **-dled; -dling** : menguar, reducirse, disminuir
dye[1] ['daɪ] *vt* **dyed; dyeing** : teñir
dye[2] *n* : tintura *f*, tinte *m*
dying → **die**
dyke → **dike**
dynamic [daɪ'næmɪk] *adj* : dinámico
dynamics [daɪ'næmɪks] *npl* : dinámica *f*
dynamite[1] ['daɪnə,maɪt] *vt* **-mited; -miting** : dinamitar
dynamite[2] *n* : dinamita *f*
dynamo ['daɪnə,mo:] *n, pl* **-mos** : dínamo *m*, generador *m* de electricidad
dynasty ['daɪnəsti, -,næs-] *n, pl* **-ties** : dinastía *f*
dysentery ['dɪsən,tɛri] *n, pl* **-teries** : disentería *f*
dysfunction [dɪs'fʌŋkʃən] *n* : disfunción *f*
dystrophy ['dɪstrəfi] *n, pl* **-phies** **1** : distrofia *f* **2** → **muscular dystrophy**

E

e [ˈiː] *n, pl* **e's** *or* **es** [ˈiːz] : quinta letra del alfabeto inglés

each[1] [ˈiːʧ] *adv* : cada uno, por persona ⟨they cost $10 each : costaron $10 cada uno⟩

each[2] *adj* : cada ⟨each student : cada estudiante⟩ ⟨each and every one : todos sin excepción⟩

each[3] *pron* **1** : cada uno *m*, cada una *f* ⟨each of us : cada uno de nosotros⟩ **2 each other** : el uno al otro, mutuamente ⟨we are helping each other : nos ayudamos el uno al otro⟩ ⟨they love each other : se aman⟩

eager [ˈiːgər] *adj* **1** ENTHUSIASTIC : entusiasta, ávido, deseoso **2** ANXIOUS : ansioso, impaciente

eagerly [ˈiːgərli] *adv* : con entusiasmo, ansiosamente

eagerness [ˈiːgərnəs] *n* : entusiasmo *m*, deseo *m*, impaciencia *f*

eagle [ˈiːgəl] *n* : águila *f*

ear [ˈɪr] *n* **1** : oído *m*, oreja *f* ⟨inner ear : oído interno⟩ ⟨big ears : orejas grandes⟩ **2 ear of corn** : mazorca *f*, choclo *m*

earache [ˈɪrˌeɪk] *n* : dolor *m* de oído

eardrum [ˈɪrˌdrʌm] *n* : tímpano *m*

earl [ˈərl] *n* : conde *m*

earlobe [ˈɪrˌloːb] *n* : lóbulo *m* de la oreja, perilla *f* de la oreja

early[1] [ˈərli] *adv* **earlier; -est** : temprano, pronto ⟨he arrived early : llegó temprano⟩ ⟨as early as possible : lo más pronto posible, cuanto antes⟩ ⟨ten minutes early : diez minutos de adelanto⟩

early[2] *adj* **earlier; -est 1** (*referring to a beginning*) : primero ⟨the early stages : las primeras etapas⟩ ⟨in early May : a principios de mayo⟩ **2** (*referring to antiquity*) : primitivo, antiguo ⟨early man : el hombre primitivo⟩ ⟨early painting : la pintura antigua⟩ **3** (*referring to a designated time*) : temprano, antes de la hora, prematuro ⟨he was early : llegó temprano⟩ ⟨early fruit : frutas tempraneras⟩ ⟨an early death : una muerte prematura⟩

earmark [ˈirˌmɑrk] *vt* : destinar ⟨earmarked funds : fondos destinados⟩

earn [ˈərn] *vt* **1** : ganar ⟨to earn money : ganar dinero⟩ **2** DESERVE : ganarse, merecer

earnest[1] [ˈərnəst] *adj* : serio, sincero

earnest[2] *n* **in ~** : en serio, de verdad ⟨we began in earnest : empezamos de verdad⟩

earnestly [ˈərnəstli] *adv* **1** SERIOUSLY : con seriedad, en serio **2** FERVENTLY : de todo corazón

earnestness [ˈərnəstnəs] *n* : seriedad *f*, sinceridad *f*

earnings [ˈərnɪŋz] *npl* : ingresos *mpl*, ganancias *fpl*, utilidades *fpl*

earphone [ˈɪrˌfoːn] *n* : audífono *m*

earring [ˈɪrˌrɪŋ] *n* : zarcillo *m*, arete *m*, aro *m Arg, Chile, Uru*, pendiente *m Spain*

earshot [ˈɪrˌʃɑt] *n* : alcance *m* del oído

earth [ˈərθ] *n* **1** LAND, SOIL : tierra *f*, suelo *m* **2 the Earth** : la Tierra

earthen [ˈərθən, -ðən] *adj* : de tierra, de barro

earthenware [ˈərθənˌwær, -ðən-] *n* : loza *f*, vajillas *fpl* de barro

earthly [ˈərθli] *adj* : terrenal, mundano

earthquake [ˈərθˌkweɪk] *n* : terremoto *m*, temblor *m*

earthworm [ˈərθˌwərm] *n* : lombriz *f* (de tierra)

earthy [ˈərθi] *adj* **earthier; -est 1** : terroso ⟨earthy colors : colores terrosos⟩ **2** DOWN-TO-EARTH : realista, práctico, llano **3** COARSE, CRUDE : basto, grosero, tosco ⟨earthy jokes : chistes groseros⟩

earwax [ˈɪrˌwæks] *n* → **wax**[2]

earwig [ˈɪrˌwɪg] *n* : tijereta *f*

ease[1] [ˈiːz] *v* **eased; easing** *vt* **1** ALLEVIATE : aliviar, calmar, hacer disminuir **2** LOOSEN, RELAX : aflojar (una cuerda), relajar (restricciones), descargar (tensiones) **3** FACILITATE : facilitar — *vi* : calmarse, relajarse

ease[2] *n* **1** CALM, RELIEF : tranquilidad *f*, comodidad *f*, desahogo *m* **2** FACILITY : facilidad *f* **3 at ~** : relajado, cómodo ⟨to put someone at ease : tranquilizar a alguien⟩

easel [ˈiːzəl] *n* : caballete *m*

easily [ˈiːzəli] *adv* **1** : fácilmente, con facilidad **2** UNQUESTIONABLY : con mucho, de lejos

easiness [ˈiːzinəs] *n* : facilidad *f*, soltura *f*

east[1] [ˈiːst] *adv* : al este

east[2] *adj* : este, del este, oriental ⟨east winds : vientos del este⟩

east[3] *n* **1** : este *m* **2 the East** : el Oriente

Easter [ˈiːstər] *n* : Pascua *f* (de Resurrección)

easterly [ˈiːstərli] *adv & adj* : del este

eastern [ˈiːstərn] *adj* **1** : Oriental, del Este ⟨Eastern Europe : Europa del Este⟩ **2** : oriental, este

Easterner [ˈiːstərnər] *n* : habitante *mf* del este

eastward [ˈiːstwərd] *adv & adj* : hacia el este

easy [ˈiːzi] *adj* **easier; -est 1** : fácil **2** LENIENT : indulgente

easygoing [ˌiːziˈgoːɪŋ] *adj* : acomodaticio, tolerante, poco exigente

eat [ˈiːt] *v* **ate** [ˈeɪt]; **eaten** [ˈiːtən]; **eating** *vt* **1** : comer **2** CONSUME : consumir, gastar, devorar ⟨expenses ate up profits : los gastos devoraron las ganancias⟩ **3** CORRODE : corroer — *vi* **1** : comer **2 to eat away at** *or* **to eat into** : comerse **3 to eat out** : comer fuera

eatable1 ['iːt̬əbəl] *adj* : comestible, comible *fam*
eatable2 *n* **1** : algo para comer **2 eatables** *npl* : comestibles *mpl*, alimentos *mpl*
eater ['iːt̬ər] *n* : comedor *m*, -dora *f*
eaves ['iːvz] *npl* : alero *m*
eavesdrop ['iːvz,drɑp] *vi* **-dropped; -dropping** : escuchar a escondidas
eavesdropper ['iːvz,drɑpər] *n* : persona *f* que escucha a escondidas
ebb1 ['ɛb] *vi* **1** : bajar, menguar (dícese de la marea) **2** DECLINE : decaer, disminuir
ebb2 *n* **1** : reflujo *m* (de una marea) **2** DECLINE : decadencia *f*, declive *m*, disminución *f*
ebony1 ['ɛbəni] *adj* **1** : de ébano **2** BLACK : de color ébano, negro
ebony2 *n, pl* **-nies** : ébano *m*
ebullience [ɪ'bʊljənts, -'bʌl-] *n* : efervescencia *f*, vivacidad *f*
ebullient [ɪ'bʊljənt, -'bʌl-] *adj* : efervescente, vivaz
eccentric1 [ɪk'sɛntrɪk] *adj* **1** : excéntrico ⟨an eccentric wheel : una rueda excéntrica⟩ **2** ODD, SINGULAR : excéntrico, extraño, raro — **eccentrically** [-trɪkli] *adv*
eccentric2 *n* : excéntrico *m*, -ca *f*
eccentricity [,ɛk,sɛn'trɪsət̬i] *n, pl* **-ties** : excentricidad *f*
ecclesiastic [ɪ,kliːzi'æstɪk] *n* : eclesiástico *m*, clérigo *m*
ecclesiastical [ɪ,kliːzi'æstɪkəl] *or* **ecclesiastic** *adj* : eclesiástico — **ecclesiastically** *adv*
echelon ['ɛʃə,lɑn] *n* **1** : escalón *m* (de tropas o aviones) **2** LEVEL : nivel *m*, esfera *f*, estrato *m*
echo1 ['ɛ,koː] *v* **echoed; echoing** *vi* : hacer eco, resonar — *vt* : repetir
echo2 *n, pl* **echoes** : eco *m*
éclair [eɪ'klær, i-] *n* : pastel *m* relleno de crema
eclectic [ɛ'klɛktɪk, ɪ-] *adj* : ecléctico
eclipse1 [ɪ'klɪps] *vt* **eclipsed; eclipsing** : eclipsar
eclipse2 *n* : eclipse *m*
ecological [,iːkə'lɑʤɪkəl, ,ɛkə-] *adj* : ecológico — **ecologically** *adv*
ecologist [i'kɑləʤɪst, ɛ-] *n* : ecólogo *m*, -ga *f*
ecology [i'kɑləʤi, ɛ-] *n, pl* **-gies** : ecología *f*
economic [,iːkə'nɑmɪk, ,ɛkə-] *adj* : económico
economical [,iːkə'nɑmɪkəl, ,ɛkə-] *adj* : económico — **economically** *adv*
economics [,iːkə'nɑmɪks, ,ɛkə-] *n* : economía *f*
economist [i'kɑnəmɪst] *n* : economista *mf*
economize [i'kɑnə,maɪz] *v* **-mized; -mizing** : economizar, ahorrar
economy [i'kɑnəmi] *n, pl* **-mies** **1** : economía *f*, sistema *m* económico **2** THRIFT : economía *f*, ahorro *m*
ecosystem ['iːko,sɪstəm] *n* : ecosistema *m*
ecru ['ɛ,kruː, 'eɪ-] *n* : color *m* crudo
ecstasy ['ɛkstəsi] *n, pl* **-sies** : éxtasis *m*
ecstatic [ɛk'stæt̬ɪk, ɪk-] *adj* : extático
ecstatically [ɛk'stæt̬ɪkli, ɪk-] *adv* : con éxtasis, con gran entusiasmo
Ecuadoran [,ɛkwə'dorən] *or* **Ecuadorean** *or* **Ecuadorian** [-'doriən] *n* : ecuatoriano *m*, -na *f* — **Ecuadorean** *or* **Ecuadorian** *adj*
ecumenical [,ɛkjʊ'mnɪkəl] *adj* : ecuménico
eczema [ɪg'ziːmə, 'ɛgzəmə, 'ɛksə-] *n* : eczema *m*
eddy1 ['ɛdi] *vi* **eddied; eddying** : arremolinarse, hacer remolinos
eddy2 *n, pl* **-dies** : remolino *m*
edema [ɪ'diːmə] *n* : edema *m*
Eden ['iːdən] *n* : Edén *m*
edge1 ['ɛʤ] *v* **edged; edging** *vt* **1** BORDER : bordear, ribetear, orlar **2** SHARPEN : afilar, aguzar **3** *or* **to edge one's way** : avanzar poco a poco **4 to edge out** : derrotar por muy poco — *vi* ADVANCE : ir avanzando (poco a poco)
edge2 *n* **1** : filo *m* (de un cuchillo) **2** BORDER : borde *m*, orilla *f*, margen *m* **3** ADVANTAGE : ventaja *f*
edger ['ɛʤər] *n* : cortabordes *m*
edgewise ['ɛʤ,waɪz] *adv* SIDEWAYS : de lado, de canto
edginess ['ɛʤinəs] *n* : tensión *f*, nerviosismo *m*
edgy ['ɛʤi] *adj* **edgier; -est** : tenso, nervioso
edible ['ɛdəbəl] *adj* : comestible
edict ['iː,dɪkt] *n* : edicto *m*, mandato *m*, orden *f*
edification [,ɛdəfə'keɪʃən] *n* : edificación *f*, instrucción *f*
edifice ['ɛdəfɪs] *n* : edificio *m*
edify ['ɛdə,faɪ] *vt* **-fied; -fying** : edificar
edit ['ɛdɪt] *vt* **1** : editar, redactar, corregir **2** *or* **to edit out** DELETE : recortar, cortar
edition [ɪ'dɪʃən] *n* : edición *f*
editor ['ɛdɪt̬ər] *n* : editor *m*, -tora *f*; redactor *m*, -tora *f*
editorial1 [,ɛdɪ'toriəl] *adj* **1** : de redacción **2** : editorial ⟨an editorial comment : un comentario editorial⟩
editorial2 *n* : editorial *m*
editorship ['ɛdət̬ər,ʃɪp] *n* : dirección *f*
educable ['ɛʤəkəbəl] *adj* : educable
educate ['ɛʤə,keɪt] *vt* **-cated; -cating** **1** TEACH : educar, enseñar **2** INSTRUCT : formar, educar, instruir **3** INFORM : informar, concientizar
education [,ɛʤə'keɪʃən] *n* : educación *f*
educational [,ɛʤə'keɪʃənəl] *adj* **1** : docente, de enseñanza ⟨an educational institution : una institución docente⟩ **2** PEDAGOGICAL : pedagógico **3** INSTRUCTIONAL : educativo, instructivo
educator ['ɛʤə,keɪt̬ər] *n* : educador *m*, -dora *f*
eel ['iːl] *n* : anguila *f*

eerie [ˈɪri] *adj* **-rier; -est 1** SPOOKY : que da miedo, espeluznante **2** GHOSTLY : fantasmagórico
eerily [ˈɪrəli] *adv* : de manera extraña y misteriosa
efface [ɪˈfeɪs, -] *vt* **-faced; -facing** : borrar
effect[1] [ɪˈfɛkt] *vt* **1** CARRY OUT : efectuar, llevar a cabo **2** ACHIEVE : lograr, realizar
effect[2] *n* **1** RESULT : efecto *m*, resultado *m*, consecuencia *f* ⟨to no effect : sin resultado⟩ **2** MEANING : sentido *m* ⟨something to that effect : algo por el estilo⟩ **3** INFLUENCE : efecto *m*, influencia *f* **4 effects** *npl* BELONGINGS : efectos *mpl*, pertenencias *fpl* **5 to go into effect** : entrar en vigor **6 in ~** REALLY : en realidad, efectivamente
effective [ɪˈfɛktɪv] *adj* **1** EFFECTUAL : efectivo, eficaz **2** OPERATIVE : vigente — **effectively** *adv*
effectiveness [ɪˈfɛktɪvnəs] *n* : eficacia *f*, efectividad *f*
effectual [ɪˈfɛkʧuəl] *adj* : eficaz, efectivo — **effectually** *adv*
effeminate [əˈfɛmənət] *adj* : afeminado
effervesce [ˌɛfərˈvɛs] *vi* **-vesced; -vescing 1** : estar en efervescencia, burbujear (dícese de líquidos) **2** : estar eufórico, estar muy animado (dícese de las personas)
effervescence [ˌɛfərˈvɛsənts] *n* **1** : efervescencia *f* **2** LIVELINESS : vivacidad *f*
effervescent [ˌɛfərˈvɛsənt] *adj* **1** : efervescente **2** LIVELY, VIVACIOUS : vivaz, animado
effete [ˈɛfiːt, ɪ-] *adj* **1** WORN-OUT : desgastado, agotado **2** DECADENT : decadente **3** EFFEMINATE : afeminado
efficacious [ˌɛfəˈkeɪʃəs] *adj* : eficaz, efectivo
efficacy [ˈɛfɪkəsi] *n, pl* **-cies** : eficacia *f*
efficiency [ɪˈfɪʃəntsi] *n, pl* **-cies** : eficiencia *f*
efficient [ɪˈfɪʃənt] *adj* : eficiente — **efficiently** *adv*
effigy [ˈɛfəʤi] *n, pl* **-gies** : efigie *f*
effluent [ˈɛˌfluːənt, ɛˈfluː-] *n* : efluente *m* — **effluent** *adj*
effort [ˈɛfərt] *n* **1** EXERTION : esfuerzo *m* **2** ATTEMPT : tentativa *f*, intento *m* ⟨it's not worth the effort : no vale la pena⟩
effortless [ˈɛfərtləs] *adj* : fácil, sin esfuerzo
effortlessly [ˈɛfərtləsli] *adv* : sin esfuerzo, fácilmente
effrontery [ɪˈfrʌntəri] *n, pl* **-teries** : insolencia *f*, desfachatez *f*, descaro *m*
effusion [ɪˈfjuːʒən, ɛ-] *n* : efusión *f*
effusive [ɪˈfjuːsɪv, ɛ-] *adj* : efusivo — **effusively** *adv*
egg[1] [ˈɛg] *vt* **to egg on** : incitar, azuzar, provocar
egg[2] *n* **1** : huevo *m* **2** OVUM : óvulo *m*
eggbeater [ˈɛgˌbiːt̬ər] *n* : batidor *m* (de huevos)
eggnog [ˈɛgˌnɑg] *n* : ponche *m* de huevo, rompope *m CA, Mex*
eggplant [ˈɛgˌplænt] *n* : berenjena *f*
eggshell [ˈɛgˌʃl] *n* : cascarón *m*
ego [ˈiːˌgoː] *n, pl* **egos 1** SELF-ESTEEM : amor *m* propio **2** SELF : ego *m*, yo *m*
egocentric [ˌiːgoˈsɛntrɪk] *adj* : egocéntrico
egoism [ˈiːgoˌwɪzəm] *n* : egoísmo *m*
egoist [ˈiːgowɪst] *n* : egoísta *mf*
egoistic [ˌiːˌgoˈwɪstɪk] *adj* : egoísta
egotism [ˈiːgəˌtɪzəm] *n* : egotismo *m*
egotist [ˈiːgətɪst] *n* : egotista *mf*
egotistic [ˌiːgəˈtɪstɪk] *or* **egotistical** [-ˈtɪstɪkəl] *adj* : egotista — **egotistically** *adv*
egregious [ɪˈgriːʤəs] *adj* : atroz, flagrante, mayúsculo — **egregiously** *adv*
egress [ˈiːˌgrɛs] *n* : salida *f*
egret [ˈiːgrət, -ˌgrɛt] *n* : garceta *f*
Egyptian [ɪˈʤɪpʃən] *n* **1** : egipcio *m*, -cia *f* **2** : egipcio *m* (idioma) — **Egyptian** *adj*
eiderdown [ˈaɪdərˌdaʊn] *n* **1** : plumón *m* **2** COMFORTER : edredón *m*
eight[1] [ˈeɪt] *adj* : ocho
eight[2] *n* : ocho *m*
eight hundred[1] *adj* : ochocientos
eight hundred[2] *n* : ochocientos *m*
eighteen[1] [eɪtˈtiːn] *adj* : dieciocho
eighteen[2] *n* : dieciocho *m*
eighteenth[1] [eɪtˈtiːnθ] *adj* : decimoctavo
eighteenth[2] *n* **1** : decimoctavo *m*, -va *f* (en una serie) **2** : dieciochoavo *m*, dieciochoava parte *f*
eighth[1] [ˈeɪtθ] *adj* : octavo
eighth[2] *n* **1** : octavo *m*, -va *f* (en una serie) **2** : octavo *m*, octava parte *f*
eightieth[1] [ˈeɪt̬iəθ] *adj* : octogésimo
eightieth[2] *n* **1** : octogésimo *m*, -ma *f* (en una serie) **2** : ochentavo *m*, ochentava parte *f*
eighty[1] [ˈeɪt̬i] *adj* : ochenta
eighty[2] *n, pl* **eighties 1** : ochenta *m* **2 the eighties** : los ochenta *mpl*
either[1] [ˈiːðər, ˈaɪ-] *adj* **1** : cualquiera (de los dos) ⟨we can watch either movie : podemos ver cualquiera de las dos películas⟩ **2** : ninguno de los dos ⟨she wasn't in either room : no estaba en ninguna de las dos salas⟩ **3** EACH : cada ⟨on either side of the street : a cada lado de la calle⟩
either[2] *pron* **1** : cualquiera *mf* (de los dos) ⟨either is fine : cualquiera de los dos está bien⟩ **2** : ninguno *m*, -na *f* (de los dos) ⟨I don't like either : no me gusta ninguno⟩ **3** : algún *m*, alguna *f* ⟨is either of you interested? : ¿está alguno de ustedes (dos) interesado?⟩
either[3] *conj* **1** : o, u ⟨either David or Daniel could go : puede ir (o) David o Daniel⟩ **2** : ni ⟨we won't watch either this movie or the other : no veremos ni esta película ni la otra⟩
ejaculate [iˈʤækjəˌleɪt] *v* **-lated; -lating** *vt* **1** : eyacular **2** EXCLAIM : exclamar — *vi* : eyacular

ejaculation [iˌʤækjəˈleɪʃən] *n* **1** : eyaculación *f* (en fisiología) **2** EXCLAMATION : exclamación *f*
eject [iˈʤɛkt] *vt* : expulsar, expeler
ejection [iˈʤɛkʃən] *n* : expulsión *f*
eke [ˈiːk] *vt* **eked; eking** *or* **to eke out** : ganar a duras penas
elaborate[1] [iˈlæbəˌreɪt] *v* **-rated; -rating** *vt* : elaborar, idear, desarrollar — *vi* **to elaborate on** : ampliar, entrar en detalles
elaborate[2] [iˈlæbərət] *adj* **1** DETAILED : detallado, minucioso, elaborado **2** COMPLICATED : complicado, intrincado, elaborado — **elaborately** *adv*
elaboration [iˌlæbəˈreɪʃən] *n* : elaboración *f*
elapse [iˈlæps] *vi* **elapsed; elapsing** : transcurrir, pasar
elastic[1] [iˈlæstɪk] *adj* : elástico
elastic[2] *n* **1** : elástico *m* **2** RUBBER BAND : goma *f*, gomita *f*, elástico *m*, liga *f*
elasticity [iˌlæsˈtɪsət̬i, ˌiːˌlæs-] *n, pl* **-ties** : elasticidad *f*
elate [iˈleɪt] *vt* **elated; elating** : alborozar, regocijar
elation [iˈleɪʃən] *n* : euforia *f*, júbilo *m*, alborozo *m*
elbow[1] [ˈɛlˌboː] *vt* : darle un codazo a
elbow[2] *n* : codo *m*
elder[1] [ˈɛldər] *adj* : mayor
elder[2] *n* **1 to be someone's elder** : ser mayor que alguien **2** : anciano *m*, -na *f* (de un pueblo o una tribu) **3** : miembro *m* del consejo (en varias religiones)
elderberry [ˈɛldərˌbɛri] *n, pl* **-berries** : baya *f* de saúco (fruta), saúco *m* (árbol)
elderly [ˈɛldərli] *adj* : mayor, de edad, anciano
eldest [ˈɛldəst] *adj* : mayor, de más edad
elect[1] [iˈlɛkt] *vt* : elegir
elect[2] *adj* : electo ⟨the president-elect : el presidente electo⟩
elect[3] *npl* **the elect** : los elegidos *mpl*
election [iˈlɛkʃən] *n* : elección *f*
elective[1] [iˈlɛktɪv] *adj* **1** : electivo **2** OPTIONAL : facultativo, optativo
elective[2] *n* : asignatura *f* electiva
elector [iˈlɛktər] *n* : elector *m*, -tora *f*
electoral [iˈlɛktərəl] *adj* : electoral
electorate [iˈlɛktərət] *n* : electorado *m*
electric [iˈlɛktrɪk] *adj* **1** *or* **electrical** [-trɪkəl] : eléctrico **2** THRILLING : electrizante, emocionante
electrician [iˌlɛkˈtrɪʃən] *n* : electricista *mf*
electricity [iˌlɛkˈtrɪsət̬i] *n, pl* **-ties 1** : electricidad *f* **2** CURRENT : corriente *m* eléctrica
electrification [iˌlɛktrəfəˈkeɪʃən] *n* : electrificación *f*
electrify [iˈlɛktrəˌfaɪ] *vt* **-fied; -fying 1** : electrificar **2** THRILL : electrizar, emocionar
electrocardiogram [iˌlɛktroˈkɑrdiəˌgræm] *n* : electrocardiograma *m*
electrocardiograph [iˌlɛktroˈkɑrdiəˌgræf] *n* : electrocardiógrafo *m*
electrocute [iˈlɛktrəˌkjuːt] *vt* **-cuted; -cuting** : electrocutar
electrocution [iˌlɛktrəˈkjuːʃən] *n* : electrocución *f*
electrode [iˈlɛkˌtroːd] *n* : electrodo *m*
electrolysis [iˌlɛkˈtrɑləsɪs] *n* : electrólisis *f*
electrolyte [iˈlɛktrəˌlaɪt] *n* : electrolito *m*
electromagnet [iˌlɛktroˈmægnət] *n* : electroimán *m*
electromagnetic [iˌlɛktromægˈnɛt̬ɪk] *adj* : electromagnético — **electromagnetically** [-t̬ɪkli] *adv*
electromagnetism [iˌlɛktroˈmægnəˌtɪzəm] *n* : electromagnetismo *m*
electron [iˈlɛkˌtrɑn] *n* : electrón *m*
electronic [iˌlɛkˈtrɑnɪk] *adj* : electrónico — **electronically** [-nɪkli] *adv*
electronic mail *n* : correo *m* electrónico
electronics [iˌlɛkˈtrɑnɪks] *n* : electrónica *f*
electroplate [iˈlɛktrəˌpleɪt] *vt* **-plated; plating** : galvanizar mediante electrólisis
elegance [ˈɛlɪgənts] *n* : elegancia *f*
elegant [ˈɛlɪgənt] *adj* : elegante — **elegantly** *adv*
elegy [ˈɛləʤi] *n, pl* **-gies** : elegía *f*
element [ˈɛləmənt] *n* **1** COMPONENT : elemento *m*, factor *m* **2** : elemento *m* (en la química) **3** MILIEU : elemento *m*, medio *m* ⟨to be in one's element : estar en su elemento⟩ **4 elements** *npl* RUDIMENTS : elementos *mpl*, rudimentos *mpl*, bases *fpl* **5 the elements** WEATHER : los elementos *mpl*
elemental [ˌɛləˈmɛntəl] *adj* **1** BASIC : elemental, primario **2** : elemental (dícese de los elementos químicos)
elementary [ˌɛləˈmɛntri] *adj* **1** SIMPLE : elemental, simple, fundamental **2** : de enseñanza primaria
elementary school *n* : escuela *f* primaria
elephant [ˈɛləfənt] *n* : elefante *m*, -ta *f*
elevate [ˈɛləˌveɪt] *vt* **-vated; -vating 1** RAISE : elevar, levantar, alzar **2** EXALT, PROMOTE : elevar, exaltar, ascender **3** ELATE : alborozar, regocijar
elevation [ˌɛləˈveɪʃən] *n* **1** : elevación *f* **2** ALTITUDE : altura *f*, altitud *f* **3** PROMOTION : ascenso *m*
elevator [ˈɛləˌveɪt̬ər] *n* : ascensor *m*, elevador *m*
eleven[1] [ɪˈlɛvən] *adj* : once
eleven[2] *n* : once *m*
eleventh[1] [ɪlɛvəntθ] *adj* : undécimo
eleventh[2] *n* **1** : undécimo *m*, -ma *f* (en una serie) **2** : onceavo *m*, onceava parte *f*
elf [ˈɛlf] *n, pl* **elves** [ˈɛlvz] : elfo *m*, geniecillo *m*, duende *m*
elfin [ˈɛlfən] *adj* **1** : de elfo, menudo **2** ENCHANTING, MAGIC : mágico, encantador
elfish [ˈɛlfɪʃ] *adj* **1** : de elfo **2** MISCHIEVOUS : travieso
elicit [ɪˈlɪsət] *vt* : provocar

eligibility [ˌɛləʤəˈbɪləṭi] *n, pl* **-ties** : elegibilidad *f*
eligible [ˈɛləʤəbəl] *adj* **1** QUALIFIED : elegible **2** SUITABLE : idóneo
eliminate [ɪˈlɪməˌneɪt] *vt* **-nated; -nating** : eliminar
elimination [ɪˌlɪməˈneɪʃən] *n* : eliminación *f*
elite [eɪˈli:t, i-] *n* : elite *f*
elixir [iˈlɪksər] *n* : elixir *m*
elk [ˈɛlk] *n* : alce *m* (de Europa), uapití *m* (de América)
ellipse [ɪˈlɪps, -] *n* : elipse *f*
ellipsis [ɪˈlɪpsəs, -] *n, pl* **-lipses** [-ˌsi:z] **1** : elipsis *f* **2** : puntos *mpl* suspensivos (en la puntuación)
elliptical [ɪˈlɪptɪkəl, -] *or* **elliptic** [-tɪk] *adj* : elíptico
elm [ˈɛlm] *n* : olmo *m*
elocution [ˌɛləˈkju:ʃən] *n* : elocución *f*
elongate [iˈlɔŋˌgeɪt] *vt* **-gated; -gating** : alargar
elongation [ˌi:ˌlɔŋˈgeɪʃən] *n* : alargamiento *m*
elope [iˈlo:p] *vi* **eloped; eloping** : fugarse
elopement [iˈlo:pmənt] *n* : fuga *f*
eloquence [ˈɛləkwənts] *n* : elocuencia *f*
eloquent [ˈɛləkwənt] *adj* : elocuente — **eloquently** *adv*
El Salvadoran [ˌɛlˌsælvəˈdorən] *n* : salvadoreño *m*, -ña *f* — **El Salvadoran** *adj*
else[1] [ˈɛls] *adv* **1** DIFFERENTLY : de otro modo, de otra manera ⟨how else? : ¿de qué otro modo?⟩ **2** ELSEWHERE : de otro sitio, de otro lugar ⟨where else? : ¿en qué otro sitio?⟩ **3 or else** OTHERWISE : si no, de lo contrario
else[2] *adj* **1** OTHER : otro ⟨anyone else : cualquier otro⟩ ⟨everyone else : todos los demás⟩ ⟨nobody else : ningún otro, nadie más⟩ ⟨somebody else : otra persona⟩ **2** MORE : más ⟨nothing else : nada más⟩ ⟨what else? : ¿qué más?⟩
elsewhere [ˈɛlsˌhwɛr] *adv* : en otra parte, en otro sitio, en otro lugar
elucidate [iˈlu:səˌdeɪt] *vt* **-dated; -dating** : dilucidar, elucidar, esclarecer
elucidation [iˌlu:səˈdeɪʃən] *n* : elucidación *f*, esclarecimiento *m*
elude [iˈlu:d] *vt* **eluded; eluding** : eludir, evadir
elusive [iˈlu:sɪv] *adj* **1** EVASIVE : evasivo, esquivo **2** SLIPPERY : huidizo, escurridizo **3** FLEETING, INTANGIBLE : impalpable, fugaz
elusively [iˈlu:sɪvli] *adv* : de manera esquiva
elves → **elf**
emaciate [iˈmeɪʃiˌeɪt] *vt* **-ated; -ating** : enflaquecer
emaciation [iˌmeɪsiˈeɪʃən, -ʃi-] *n* : enflaquecimiento *m*, escualidez *f*, delgadez *f* extrema
e–mail [ˈi:ˌmeɪl] *n* : e-mail *m*
emanate [ˈɛməˌneɪt] *v* **-nated; -nating** *vi* : emanar, provenir, proceder — *vt* : emanar
emanation [ˌɛməˈneɪʃən] *n* : emanación *f*
emancipate [iˈmæntsəˌpeɪt] *vt* **-pated; -pating** : emancipar
emancipation [iˌmæntsəˈpeɪʃən] *n* : emancipación *f*
emasculate [iˈmæskjəˌleɪt] *vt* **-lated; -lating** **1** CASTRATE : castrar, emascular **2** WEAKEN : debilitar
embalm [ɪmˈbɑm, ɛm-, -ˈbɑlm] *vt* : embalsamar
embankment [ɪmˈbæŋkmənt, ɛm-] *n* : terraplén *m*, muro *m* de contención
embargo[1] [ɪmˈbɑrgo, ɛm-] *vt* **-goed; -going** : imponer un embargo sobre
embargo[2] *n, pl* **-goes** : embargo *m*
embark [ɪmˈbɑrk, ɛm-] *vt* : embarcar — *vi* **1** : embarcarse **2 to embark on** START : emprender, embarcarse en
embarkation [ˌɛmˌbɑrˈkeɪʃən] *n* : embarque *m*, embarco *m*
embarrass [ɪmˈbærəs, ɛm-] *vt* : avergonzar, abochornar
embarrassing [ɪmˈbærəsɪŋ, ɛm-] *adj* : embarazoso, violento
embarrassment [ɪmˈbærəsmənt, ɛm-] *n* : vergüenza *f*, pena *f*
embassy [ˈɛmbəsi] *n, pl* **-sies** : embajada *f*
embed [ɪmˈbɛd, ɛm-] *vt* **-bedded; -bedding** : incrustar, empotrar, grabar (en la memoria)
embellish [ɪmˈbɛlɪʃ, ɛm-] *vt* : adornar, embellecer
embellishment [ɪmˈbɛlɪʃmənt, ɛm-] *n* : adorno *m*
ember [ˈɛmbər] *n* : ascua *f*, brasa *f*
embezzle [ɪmˈbɛzəl, ɛm-] *vt* **-zled; -zling** : desfalcar, malversar
embezzlement [ɪmˈbɛzəlmənt, ɛm-] *n* : desfalco *m*, malversación *f*
embezzler [ɪmˈbɛzələr, ɛm-] *n* : desfalcador *m*, -dora *f*; malversador *m*, -dora *f*
embitter [ɪmˈbɪṭər, ɛm-] *vt* : amargar
emblem [ˈɛmbləm] *n* : emblema *m*, símbolo *m*
emblematic [ˌɛmbləˈmæṭɪk] *adj* : emblemático, simbólico
embodiment [ɪmˈbɑdɪmənt, ɛm-] *n* : encarnación *f*, personificación *f*
embody [ɪmˈbɑdi, ɛm-] *vt* **-bodied; -bodying** : encarnar, personificar
emboss [ɪmˈbɑs, ɛm-, -ˈbɔs] *vt* : repujar, grabar en relieve
embrace[1] [ɪmˈbreɪs, ɛm-] *vt* **-braced; -bracing** **1** HUG : abrazar **2** ADOPT, TAKE ON : adoptar, aceptar **3** INCLUDE : abarcar, incluir
embrace[2] *n* : abrazo *m*
embroider [ɪmˈbrɔɪdər, ɛm-] *vt* : bordar (una tela), adornar (una historia)
embroidery [ɪmˈbrɔɪdəri, ɛm-] *n, pl* **-deries** : bordado *m*
embroil [ɪmˈbrɔɪl, ɛm-] *vt* : embrollar, enredar
embryo [ˈɛmbriˌo:] *n, pl* **embryos** : embrión *m*

embryonic [ˌɛmbriˈɑnɪk] *adj* : embrionario
emend [iˈmɛnd] *vt* : enmendar, corregir
emendation [ˌiːˌmɛnˈdeɪʃən] *n* : enmienda *f*
emerald¹ [ˈɛmrəld, ˈɛmə-] *adj* : verde esmeralda
emerald² *n* : esmeralda *f*
emerge [iˈmərʤ] *vi* **emerged; emerging** : emerger, salir, aparecer, surgir
emergence [iˈmərʤənts] *n* : aparición *f*, surgimiento *m*
emergency [iˈmərʤəntsi] *n, pl* **-cies** : emergencia *f*
emergent [iˈmərʤənt] *adj* : emergente
emery [ˈɛməri] *n, pl* **-eries** : esmeril *m*
emetic¹ [iˈmɛt̬ɪk] *adj* : vomitivo, emético
emetic² *n* : vomitivo *m*, emético *m*
emigrant [ˈɛmɪgrənt] *n* : emigrante *mf*
emigrate [ˈɛməˌgreɪt] *vi* **-grated; -grating** : emigrar
emigration [ˌɛməˈgreɪʃən] *n* : emigración *f*
eminence [ˈɛmənənts] *n* **1** PROMINENCE : eminencia *f*, prestigio *m*, renombre *m* **2** DIGNITARY : eminencia *f*; dignatario *m*, -ria *f* ⟨Your Eminence : Su Eminencia⟩
eminent [ˈɛmənənt] *adj* : eminente, ilustre
eminently [ˈɛmənəntli] *adv* : sumamente
emissary [ˈɛməˌsɛri] *n, pl* **-saries** : emisario *m*, -ria *f*
emission [iˈmɪʃən] *n* : emisión *f*
emit [iˈmɪt] *vt* **emitted; emitting** : emitir, despedir, producir
emote [iˈmoːt] *vi* **emoted; emoting** : exteriorizar las emociones
emotion [iˈmoːʃən] *n* : emoción *f*, sentimiento *m*
emotional [iˈmoːʃənəl] *adj* **1** : emocional, afectivo ⟨an emotional reaction : una reacción emocional⟩ **2** MOVING : emocionante, emotivo, conmovedor
emotionally [iˈmoːʃənəli] *adv* : emocionalmente
empathy [ˈɛmpəθi] *n* : empatía *f*
emperor [ˈɛmpərər] *n* : emperador *m*
emphasis [ˈɛmfəsɪs] *n, pl* **-phases** [-ˌsiːz] : énfasis *m*, hincapié *m*
emphasize [ˈɛmfəˌsaɪz] *vt* **-sized; -sizing** : enfatizar, destacar, subrayar, hacer hincapié en
emphatic [ɪmˈfæt̬ɪk, ɛm-] *adj* : enfático, enérgico, categórico — **emphatically** [-ɪkli] *adv*
empire [ˈɛmˌpaɪr] *n* : imperio *m*
empirical [ɪmˈpɪrɪkəl, ɛm-] *adj* : empírico — **empirically** [-ɪkli] *adv*
employ¹ [ɪmˈplɔɪ, ɛm-] *vt* **1** USE : usar, utilizar **2** HIRE : contratar, emplear **3** OCCUPY : ocupar, dedicar, emplear
employ² [ɪmˈplɔɪ, ɛm-; ˈɪmˌ-, ˈɛmˌ-] *n* **1** : puesto *m*, cargo *m*, ocupación *f* **2 to be in the employ of** : estar al servicio de, trabajar para
employee [ɪmˌplɔɪˈiː, ɛm-, -ˈplɔɪˌiː] *n* : empleado *m*, -da *f*
employer [ɪmˈplɔɪər, ɛm-] *n* : patrón *m*, -trona *f*; empleador *m*, -dora *f*
employment [ɪmˈplɔɪmənt, ɛm-] *n* : trabajo *m*, empleo *m*
empower [ɪmˈpaʊər, ɛm-] *vt* : facultar, autorizar, conferirle poder a
empowerment [ɪmˈpaʊərmənt, ɛm-] *n* : autorización *f*
empress [ˈɛmprəs] *n* : emperatriz *f*
emptiness [ˈɛmptinəs] *n* : vacío *m*, vacuidad *f*
empty¹ [ˈɛmpti] *v* **-tied; -tying** *vt* : vaciar — *vi* : desaguar (dícese de un río)
empty² *adj* **emptier; -est 1** : vacío **2** VACANT : desocupado, libre **3** MEANINGLESS : vacío, hueco, vano
empty–handed [ˌɛmptiˈhændəd] *adj* : con las manos vacías
empty–headed [ˌɛmptiˈhɛdəd] *adj* : cabeza hueca, tonto
emu [ˈiːˌmjuː] *n* : emú *m*
emulate [ˈɛmjəˌleɪt] *vt* **-lated; -lating** : emular
emulation [ˌɛmjəˈleɪʃən] *n* : emulación *f*
emulsifier [ɪˈmʌlsəˌfaɪər] *n* : emulsionante *m*
emulsify [ɪˈmʌlsəˌfaɪ] *vt* **-fied; -fying** : emulsionar
emulsion [ɪˈmʌlʃən] *n* : emulsión *f*
enable [ɪˈneɪbəl, ɛ-] *vt* **-abled; -abling 1** EMPOWER : habilitar, autorizar, facultar **2** PERMIT : hacer posible, posibilitar, permitir
enact [ɪˈnækt, ɛ-] *vt* **1** : promulgar (un ley o decreto) **2** : representar (un papel en el teatro)
enactment [ɪˈnæktmənt, ɛ-] *n* : promulgación *f*
enamel¹ [ɪˈnæməl] *vt* **-eled** *or* **-elled; -eling** *or* **-elling** : esmaltar
enamel² *n* : esmalte *m*
enamor [ɪˈnæmər] *vt* **1** : enamorar **2 to be enamored of** : estar enamorado de (una persona), estar entusiasmado con (algo)
encamp [ɪnˈkæmp, ɛn-] *vi* : acampar
encampment [ɪnˈkæmpmənt, ɛn-] *n* : campamento *m*
encase [ɪnˈkeɪs, ɛn-] *vt* **-cased; -casing** : encerrar, revestir
encephalitis [ɪnˌsɛfəˈlaɪt̬əs, ɛn-] *n, pl* **-litides** [ˈlɪt̬əˌdiːz] : encefalitis *f*
enchant [ɪnˈʧænt, ɛn-] *vt* **1** BEWITCH : hechizar, encantar, embrujar **2** CHARM, FASCINATE : cautivar, fascinar, encantar
enchanting [ɪnˈʧæntɪŋ, ɛn-] *adj* : encantador
enchanter [ɪnˈʧæntər, ɛn-] *n* SORCERER : mago *m*, encantador *m*
enchantment [ɪnˈʧæntmənt, ɛn-] *n* **1** SPELL : encanto *m*, hechizo *m* **2** CHARM : encanto *m*
enchantress [ɪnˈʧæntrəs, ɛn-] *n* **1** SORCERESS : maga *f*, hechicera *f* **2** CHARMER : mujer *f* cautivadora
encircle [ɪnˈsərkəl, ɛn-] *vt* **-cled; -cling** : rodear, ceñir, cercar

enclose [ɪn'klo:z, ɛn-] *vt* **-closed; -closing** 1 SURROUND : encerrar, cercar, rodear 2 INCLUDE : incluir, adjuntar, acompañar ⟨please find enclosed : le enviamos adjunto⟩
enclosure [ɪn'klo:ʒər, ɛn-] *n* 1 ENCLOSING : encierro *m* 2 : cercado *m* (de terreno), recinto *m* ⟨an enclosure for the press : un recinto para la prensa⟩ 3 ADJUNCT : anexo *m* (con una carta), documento *m* adjunto
encode [ɪn'ko:d, ɛn-] *vt* : cifrar (mensajes, etc.), codificar (en informática)
encompass [ɪn'kʌmpəs, ɛn-, -'kɑm-] *vt* 1 SURROUND : circundar, rodear 2 INCLUDE : abarcar, comprender
encore ['ɑn,kor] *n* : bis *m*, repetición *f*
encounter[1] [ɪn'kaʊntər, ɛn-] *vt* 1 MEET : encontrar, encontrarse con, toparse con, tropezar con 2 FIGHT : combatir, luchar contra
encounter[2] *n* : encuentro *m*
encourage [ɪn'kərɪʤ, ɛn-] *vt* **-aged; -aging** 1 HEARTEN, INSPIRE : animar, alentar 2 FOSTER : fomentar, promover
encouragement [ɪn'kərɪʤmənt, ɛn-] *n* : ánimo *m*, aliento *m*
encouraging [ɪn'kərəʤɪŋ, ɛn-] *adj* : alentador, esperanzador
encroach [ɪn'kro:ʧ, ɛn-] *vi* **to encroach on** : invadir, abusar (derechos), quitar (tiempo)
encroachment [ɪn'kro:ʧmənt, ɛn-] *n* : invasión *f*, usurpación *f*
encrust [ɪn'krʌst, ɛn-] *vt* 1 : recubrir con una costra 2 INLAY : incrustar ⟨encrusted with gems : incrustado de gemas⟩
encumber [ɪn'kʌmbər, ɛn-] *vt* 1 BLOCK : obstruir, estorbar 2 BURDEN : cargar, gravar
encumbrance [ɪn'kʌmbrən*t*s, ɛn-] *n* : estorbo *m*, carga *f*, gravamen *m*
encyclopedia [ɪn,saɪklə'pi:diə, ɛn-] *n* : enciclopedia *f*
encyclopedic [ɪn,saɪklə'pi:dɪk, ɛn-] *adj* : enciclopédico
end[1] ['ɛnd] *vt* 1 STOP : terminar, poner fin a 2 CONCLUDE : concluir, terminar — *vi* : terminar(se), acabar, concluir(se)
end[2] *n* 1 EXTREMITY : extremo *m*, final *m*, punta *f* 2 CONCLUSION : fin *m*, final *m* 3 AIM : fin *m*
endanger [ɪn'deɪnʤər, ɛn-] *vt* : poner en peligro
endear [ɪn'dɪr, ɛn-] *vt* **to endear oneself to** : ganarse la simpatía de, granjearse el cariño de
endearment [ɪn'dɪrmənt, ɛn-] *n* : expresión *f* de cariño
endeavor[1] [ɪn'dɛvər, ɛn-] *vt* : intentar, esforzarse por ⟨he endeavored to improve his work : intentó por mejorar su trabajo⟩
endeavor[2] *n* : intento *m*, esfuerzo *m*
endemic [ɛn'dɛmɪk, ɪn-] *adj* : endémico
ending ['ɛndɪŋ] *n* 1 CONCLUSION : final *m*, desenlace *m* 2 SUFFIX : sufijo *m*, terminación *f*
endive ['ɛn,daɪv, ,ɑn'di:v] *n* : endibia *f*, endivia *f*
endless ['ɛndləs] *adj* 1 INTERMINABLE : interminable, inacabable, sin fin 2 INNUMERABLE : innumerable, incontable
endlessly ['ɛndləsli] *adv* : interminablemente, eternamente, sin parar
endocrine ['ɛndəkrən, -,kraɪn, -,kri:n] *adj* : endocrino
endorse [ɪn'dɔrs, ɛn-] *vt* **-dorsed; -dorsing** 1 SIGN : endosar, firmar 2 APPROVE : aprobar, sancionar
endorsement [ɪn'dɔrsmənt, ɛn-] *n* 1 SIGNATURE : endoso *m*, firma *f* 2 APPROVAL : aprobación *f*, aval *m*
endow [ɪn'daʊ, ɛn-] *vt* : dotar
endowment [ɪn'daʊmənt, ɛn-] *n* 1 FUNDING : dotación *f* 2 DONATION : donación *f*, legado *m* 3 ATTRIBUTE, GIFT : atributo *m*, dotes *fpl*
endurable [ɪn'dʊrəbəl, ɛn-, -'djʊr-] *adj* : tolerable, soportable
endurance [ɪn'dʊrən*t*s, ɛn-, -'djʊr-] *n* : resistencia *f*, aguante *m*
endure [ɪn'dʊr, ɛn-, -'djʊr] *v* **-dured; -during** *vt* 1 BEAR : resistir, soportar, aguantar 2 TOLERATE : tolerar, soportar — *vi* LAST : durar, perdurar
enema ['ɛnəmə] *n* : enema *m*, lavativa *f*
enemy ['ɛnəmi] *n, pl* **-mies** : enemigo *m*, -ga *f*
energetic [,ɛnər'ʤɛṭɪk] *adj* : enérgico, vigoroso — **energetically** [-ṭɪkli] *adv*
energize ['ɛnər,ʤaɪz] *vt* **-gized; -gizing** 1 ACTIVATE : activar 2 INVIGORATE : vigorizar
energy ['ɛnərʤi] *n, pl* **-gies** 1 VITALITY : energía *f*, vitalidad *f* 2 EFFORT : esfuerzo *m*, energías *fpl* 3 POWER : energía *f* ⟨atomic energy : energía atómica⟩
enervate ['ɛnər,veɪt] *vt* **-vated; -vating** : enervar, debilitar
enfold [ɪn'fo:ld, ɛn-] *vt* : envolver
enforce [ɪn'fors, ɛn-] *vt* **-forced; -forcing** 1 : hacer respetar, hacer cumplir (una ley, etc.) 2 IMPOSE : imponer ⟨to enforce obedience : imponer la obediencia⟩
enforcement [ɪn'forsmənt, ɛn-] *n* : imposición *f*
enfranchise [ɪn'fræn,ʧaɪz, ɛn-] *vt* **-chised; -chising** : conceder el voto a
enfranchisement [ɪn'fræn,ʧaɪzmənt, ɛn-] *n* : concesión *f* del voto
engage [ɪn'geɪʤ, ɛn-] *v* **-gaged; -gaging** *vt* 1 ATTRACT : captar, atraer, llamar ⟨to engage one's attention : captar la atención⟩ 2 MESH : engranar ⟨to engage the clutch : embragar⟩ 3 COMMIT : comprometer ⟨to get engaged : comprometerse⟩ 4 HIRE : contratar 5 : entablar combate con (un enemigo)

— *vi* **1** PARTICIPATE : participar **2 to engage in combat** : entrar en combate

engagement [ɪnˈgeɪʤmənt, ɛn-] *n* **1** APPOINTMENT : cita *f*, hora *f* **2** BETROTHAL : compromiso *m*

engaging [ɪnˈgeɪʤɪŋ, ɛn-] *adj* : atractivo, encantador, interesante

engender [ɪnˈʤndər, ɛn-] *vt* **-dered; -dering** : engendrar

engine [ˈɛnʤən] *n* **1** MOTOR : motor *m* **2** LOCOMOTIVE : locomotora *f*, máquina *f*

engineer[1] [ˌɛnʤəˈnɪr] *vt* **1** : diseñar, construir (un sistema, un mecanismo, etc.) **2** CONTRIVE : maquinar, tramar, fraguar

engineer[2] *n* **1** : ingeniero *m*, -ra *f* **2** : maquinista *mf* (de locomotoras)

engineering [ˌɛnʤəˈnɪrɪŋ] *n* : ingeniería *f*

English[1] [ˈɪŋglɪʃ, ˈŋlɪʃ] *adj* : inglés

English[2] *n* **1** : inglés *m* (idioma) **2 the English** : los ingleses

Englishman [ˈɪŋglɪʃmən, ˈɪŋlɪʃ-] *n, pl* **-men** [-mən, -ˌmɛn] : inglés *m*

Englishwoman [ˈɪŋglɪʃˌwʊmən, ˈɪŋlɪʃ-] *n, pl* **-women** [-ˌwɪmən] : inglesa *f*

engrave [ɪnˈgreɪv, ɛn-] *vt* **-graved; -graving** : grabar

engraver [ɪnˈgreɪvər, ɛn-] *n* : grabador *m*, -dora *f*

engraving [ɪnˈgreɪvɪŋ, ɛn-] *n* : grabado *m*

engross [ɪnˈgroːs, ɛn-] *vt* : absorber

engrossed [ɪnˈgroːst, ɛn-] *adj* : absorto

engrossing [ɪnˈgroːsɪŋ, ɛn-] *adj* : fascinante, absorbente

engulf [ɪnˈgʌlf, ɛn-] *vt* : envolver, sepultar

enhance [ɪnˈhænts, ɛn-] *vt* **-hanced; -hancing** : realzar, aumentar, mejorar

enhancement [ɪnˈhæntsmənt, ɛn-] *n* : mejora *f*, realce *m*, aumento *m*

enigma [ɪˈnɪgmə] *n* : enigma *m*

enigmatic [ˌɛnɪgˈmæṭɪk, ˌiːnɪg-] *adj* : enigmático — **enigmatically** [-ṭɪkli] *adv*

enjoin [ɪnˈʤɔɪn, ɛn-] *vt* **1** COMMAND : ordenar, imponer **2** FORBID : prohibir, vedar

enjoy [ɪnˈʤɔɪ, ɛn-] *vt* **1** : disfrutar, gozar de ⟨did you enjoy the book? : ¿te gustó el libro?⟩ ⟨to enjoy good health : gozar de buena salud⟩ **2 to enjoy oneself** : divertirse, pasarlo bien

enjoyable [ɪnˈʤɔɪəbəl, ɛn-] *adj* : agradable, placentero, divertido

enjoyment [ɪnˈʤɔɪmənt, ɛn-] *n* : placer *m*, goce *m*, disfrute *m*, deleite *m*

enlarge [ɪnˈlɑrʤ, ɛn-] *v* **-larged; -larging** *vt* : extender, agrandar, ampliar — *vi* **1** : ampliarse **2 to enlarge upon** : extenderse sobre, entrar en detalles sobre

enlargement [ɪnˈlɑrʤmənt, ɛn-] *n* : expansión *f*, ampliación *f* (dícese de fotografías)

enlarger [ɪnˈlɑrʤər, ɛn-] *n* : ampliadora *f*

enlighten [ɪnˈlaɪtən, ɛn-] *vt* : iluminar, aclarar

enlightenment [ɪnˈlaɪtənmənt, ɛn-] *n* **1** : ilustración *f* ⟨the Enlightenment : la Ilustración⟩ **2** CLARIFICATION : aclaración *f*

enlist [ɪnˈlɪst, ɛn-] *vt* **1** ENROLL : alistar, reclutar **2** SECURE : conseguir ⟨to enlist the support of : conseguir el apoyo de⟩ — *vi* : alistarse

enlisted man [ɪnˈlɪstəd, ɛn-] *n* : soldado *m* raso

enlistment [ɪnˈlɪstmənt, ɛn-] *n* : alistamiento *m*, reclutamiento *m*

enliven [ɪnˈlaɪvən, ɛn-] *vt* : animar, alegrar, darle vida a

enmity [ˈɛnməṭi] *n, pl* **-ties** : enemistad *f*, animadversión *f*

ennoble [ɪˈnoːbəl, ɛ-] *vt* **-bled; -bling** : ennoblecer

ennui [ˌɑnˈwiː] *n* : hastío *m*, tedio *m*, fastidio *m*, aburrimiento *m*

enormity [ɪˈnɔrməṭi] *n, pl* **-ties** **1** ATROCITY : atrocidad *f*, barbaridad *f* **2** IMMENSITY : enormidad *f*, inmensidad *f*

enormous [ɪˈnɔrməs] *adj* : enorme, inmenso, tremendo — **enormously** *adv*

enough[1] [ɪˈnʌf] *adv* **1** : bastante, suficientemente **2 fair enough!** : ¡está bien!, ¡de acuerdo! **3 strangely enough** : por extraño que parezca **4 sure enough** : en efecto, sin duda alguna **5 well enough** : muy bien, bastante bien

enough[2] *adj* : bastante, suficiente ⟨do we have enough chairs? : ¿tenemos suficientes sillas?⟩

enough[3] *pron* : (lo) suficiente, (lo) bastante ⟨enough to eat : lo suficiente para comer⟩ ⟨it's not enough : no basta⟩ ⟨I've had enough! : ¡estoy harto!, ¡está bueno ya!⟩

enquire [ɪnˈkwaɪr, ɛn-] **enquiry** [ˈɪnˌkwaɪri, ˈɛn-, -kwəri; ɪnˈkwaɪri, ɛnˈ-] → **inquire, inquiry**

enrage [ɪnˈreɪʤ, ɛn-] *vt* **-raged; -raging** : enfurecer, encolerizar

enraged [ɪnˈreɪʤd, ɛn-] *adj* : enfurecido, furioso

enrich [ɪnˈrɪʧ, ɛn-] *vt* : enriquecer

enrichment [ɪnˈrɪʧmənt, ɛn-] *n* : enriquecimiento *m*

enroll *or* **enrol** [ɪnˈroːl, ɛn-] *v* **-rolled; -rolling** *vt* : matricular, inscribir — *vi* : matricularse, inscribirse

enrollment [ɪnˈroːlmənt, ɛn-] *n* : matrícula *f*, inscripción *f*

en route [ɑˈruːt, ɛnˈraʊt] *adv* : de camino, por el camino

ensconce [ɪnˈskɑnts, ɛn-] *vt* **-sconced; -sconcing** : acomodar, instalar, establecer cómodamente

ensemble [ɑnˈsɑmbəl] *n* : conjunto *m*

enshrine [ɪnˈʃraɪn, ɛn-] *vt* **-shrined; -shrining** : conservar religiosamente, preservar

ensign [ˈntsən, ˈɛnˌsaɪn] *n* **1** FLAG : enseña *f*, pabellón *m* **2** : alférez *mf* (de fragata)

enslave [ɪn'sleɪv, ɛn-] *vt* **-slaved; -slaving** : esclavizar
enslavement [ɪn'sleɪvmənt, ɛn-] *n* : esclavización *f*
ensnare [ɪn'snær, ɛn-] *vt* **-snared; -snaring** : atrapar
ensue [ɪn'su:, ɛn-] *vi* **-sued; -suing** : seguir, resultar
ensure [ɪn'ʃʊr, ɛn-] *vt* **-sured; -suring** : asegurar, garantizar
entail [ɪn'teɪl, ɛn-] *vt* : implicar, suponer, conllevar
entangle [ɪn'tæŋgəl, ɛn-] *vt* **-gled; -gling** : enredar
entanglement [ɪn'tæŋgəlmənt, ɛn-] *n* : enredo *m*
enter ['ɛntər] *vt* **1** : entrar en, entrar a **2** BEGIN : entrar en, comenzar, iniciar **3** RECORD : anotar, inscribir, dar entrada a ⟨to enter data : introducir datos⟩ **4** JOIN : entrar en, alistarse en, hacerse socio de — *vi* **1** : entrar **2 to enter into** : entrar en, firmar (un acuerdo), entablar (negociaciones, etc.)
enterprise ['ɛntər,praɪz] *n* **1** UNDERTAKING : empresa *f* **2** BUSINESS : empresa *f*, firma *f* **3** INITIATIVE : iniciativa *f*, empuje *m*
enterprising ['ɛntər,praɪzɪŋ] *adj* : emprendedor
entertain [,ɛntər'teɪn] *vt* **1** : recibir, agasajar ⟨to entertain guests : tener invitados⟩ **2** CONSIDER : considerar, contemplar **3** AMUSE : entretener, divertir
entertainer [,ɛntər'teɪnər] *n* : artista *mf*
entertaining [,ɛntər'teɪnɪŋ] *adj* : entretenido, divertido
entertainment [,ɛntər'teɪnmənt] *n* : entretenimiento *m*, diversión *f*
enthrall *or* **enthral** [ɪn'θrɔl, ɛn-] *vt* **-thralled; -thralling** : cautivar, embelesar
enthuse [ɪn'θuiz, ɛn-] *v* **-thused; -thusing** *vt* **1** EXCITE : entusiasmar **2** : decir con entusiasmo — *vi* **to enthuse over** : hablar con entusiasmo sobre
enthusiasm [ɪn'θu:zi,æzəm, ɛn-, -'θju:-] *n* : entusiasmo *m*
enthusiast [ɪn'θu:zi,æst, ɛn-, -'θju:-, -əst] *n* : entusiasta *mf*; aficionado *m*, -da *f*
enthusiastic [ɪn,θu:zi'æstɪk, ɛn-, -,θju:-] *adj* : entusiasta, aficionado
enthusiastically [ɪn,θu:zi'æstɪkli, ɛn-, -,θju:-] *adv* : con entusiasmo
entice [ɪn'taɪs, ɛn-] *vt* **-ticed; -ticing** : atraer, tentar
enticement [ɪn'taɪsmənt, ɛn-] *n* : tentación *f*, atracción *f*, señuelo *m*
entire [ɪn'taɪr, ɛn-] *adj* : entero, completo
entirely [ɪn'taɪrli, ɛn-] *adv* : completamente, totalmente
entirety [ɪn'taɪrṭi, ɛn-, -'taɪrəṭi] *n, pl* **-ties** : totalidad *f*
entitle [ɪn'taɪṭəl, ɛn-] *vt* **-tled; -tling 1** NAME : titular, intitular **2** : dar derecho a ⟨it entitles you to enter free : le da derecho a entrar gratis⟩ **3 to be entitled to** : tener derecho a
entitlement [ɪn'taɪṭəlmənt, ɛn-] *n* RIGHT : derecho *m*
entity ['ɛntəṭi] *n, pl* **-ties** : entidad *f*, ente *m*
entomologist [,ɛntə'mɑləʤɪst] *n* : entomólogo *m*, -ga *f*
entomology [,ɛntə'mɑləʤi] *n* : entomología *f*
entourage [,ɑntʊ'rɑʒ] *n* : séquito *m*
entrails ['ɛn,treɪlz, -trəlz] *npl* : entrañas *fpl*, vísceras *fpl*
entrance[1] [ɪn'træn*t*s, ɛn-] *vt* **-tranced; -trancing** : encantar, embelesar, fascinar
entrance[2] ['ɛntrən*t*s] *n* **1** ENTERING : entrada *f* ⟨to make an entrance : entrar en escena⟩ **2** ENTRY : entrada *f*, puerta *f* **3** ADMISSION : entrada *f*, ingreso *m* ⟨entrance examination : examen de ingreso⟩
entrant ['ɛntrənt] *n* : candidato *m*, -ta *f* (en un examen); participante *mf* (en un concurso)
entrap [ɪn'træp, ɛn-] *vt* **-trapped; -trapping** : atrapar, entrampar, hacer caer en una trampa
entrapment [ɪn'træpmənt, ɛn-] *n* : captura *f*
entreat [ɪn'tri:t, ɛn-] *vt* : suplicar, rogar
entreaty [ɪn'tri:ṭi, ɛn-] *n, pl* **-treaties** : ruego *m*, súplica *f*
entrée *or* **entree** ['ɑn,treɪ, ,ɑn'-] *n* : plato *m* principal
entrench [ɪn'trɛnʧ, ɛn-] *vt* **1** FORTIFY : atrincherar (una posición militar) **2** : consolidar, afianzar ⟨firmly entrenched in his job : afianzado en su puesto⟩
entrepreneur [,ɑntrəprə'nər, -'njʊr] *n* : empresario *m*, -ria *f*
entrust [ɪn'trʌst, ɛn-] *vt* : confiar, encomendar
entry ['ɛntri] *n, pl* **-tries 1** ENTRANCE : entrada *f* **2** NOTATION : entrada *f*, anotación *f*
entwine [ɪn'twaɪn, ɛn-] *vt* **-twined; -twining** : entrelazar, entretejer, entrecruzar
enumerate [ɪ'nu:mə,reɪt, ɛ-, -'nju:-] *vt* **-ated; -ating 1** LIST : enumerar **2** COUNT : contar, enumerar
enumeration [ɪ,nu:mə'reɪʃən, ɛ-, -,nju:-] *n* : enumeración *f*, lista *f*
enunciate [i'nʌn*t*si,eɪt, ɛ-] *vt* **-ated; -ating 1** STATE : enunciar, decir **2** PRONOUNCE : articular, pronunciar
enunciation [i,nʌn*t*si'eɪʃən, ɛ-] *n* **1** STATEMENT : enunciación *f*, declaración *f* **2** ARTICULATION : articulación *f*, pronunciación *f*, dicción *f*
envelop [ɪn'vləp, ɛn-] *vt* : envolver, cubrir
envelope ['ɛnvə,lo:p, 'ɑn-] *n* : sobre *m*
enviable ['ɛnviəbəl] *adj* : envidiable
envious ['ɛnviəs] *adj* : envidioso — **enviously** *adv*

environment [ɪnˈvaɪrənmənt, ɛn-, -ˈvaɪərn-] *n* : medio *m* (ambiente), ambiente *m*, entorno *m*
environmental [ɪnˌvaɪrənˈmɛntəl, ɛn-, -ˌvaɪərn-] *adj* : ambiental
environmentalist [ɪnˌvaɪrənˈmɛntəlɪst, ɛn-, -ˌvaɪərn-] *n* : ecologista *mf*
environs [ɪnˈvaɪrənz, ɛn-, -ˈvaɪərnz] *npl* : alrededores *mpl*, entorno *m*, inmediaciones *fpl*
envisage [ɪnˈvɪzɪʤ, ɛn-] *vt* **-aged; -aging** 1 IMAGINE : imaginarse, concebir 2 FORESEE : prever
envision [ɪnˈvɪʒən, ɛn-] *vt* : imaginar
envoy [ˈɛnˌvɔɪ, ˈɑn-] *n* : enviado *m*, -da *f*
envy¹ [ˈɛnvi] *vt* **-vied; -vying** : envidiar
envy² *n, pl* **envies** : envidia *f*
enzyme [ˈɛnˌzaɪm] *n* : enzima *f*
eon [ˈi:ən, i:ˌɑn] → **aeon**
epaulet [ˌpəˈlɛt] *n* : charretera *f*
ephemeral [ɪˈfɛmərəl, -ˈfi:-] *adj* : efímero, fugaz
epic¹ [ˈɛpɪk] *adj* : épico
epic² *n* : poema *m* épico, epopeya *f*
epicure [ˈɛpɪˌkjʊr] *n* : epicúreo *m*, -rea *f*; gastrónomo *m*, -ma *f*
epicurean [ˌɛpɪkjʊˈri:ən, -ˈkjʊriən] *adj* : epicúreo
epidemic¹ [ˌɛpəˈdɛmɪk] *adj* : epidémico
epidemic² *n* : epidemia *f*
epidermis [ˌɛpəˈdərməs] *n* : epidermis *f*
epigram [ˈɛpəˌgræm] *n* : epigrama *m*
epilepsy [ˈɛpəˌlɛpsi] *n, pl* **-sies** : epilepsia *f*
epileptic¹ [ˌɛpəˈlɛptɪk] *adj* : epiléptico
epileptic² *n* : epiléptico *m*, -ca *f*
epilogue [ˈɛpəˌlɔg, -ˌlɑg] *n* : epílogo *m*
epiphany [ɪˈpɪfəni] *n, pl* **-nies** 1 **Epiphany** : Epifanía *f* 2 **to have an epiphany** : tener una revelación
episcopal [ɪˈpɪskəpəl] *adj* : episcopal
Episcopalian [ɪˌpɪskəˈpeɪljən] *n* : episcopalista *mf*; episcopaliano *m*, -na *f*
episode [ˈɛpəˌso:d] *n* : episodio *m*
episodic [ˌɛpəˈsɑdɪk] *adj* : episódico
epistle [ɪˈpɪsəl] *n* : epístola *f*, carta *f*
epitaph [ˈɛpəˌtæf] *n* : epitafio *m*
epithet [ˈɛpəˌθɛt, -θət] *n* : epíteto *m*
epitome [ɪˈpɪṭəmi] *n* 1 SUMMARY : epítome *m*, resumen *m* 2 EMBODIMENT : personificación *f*
epitomize [ɪˈpɪṭəˌmaɪz] *vt* **-mized; -mizing** 1 SUMMARIZE : resumir 2 EMBODY : ser la personificación de, personificar
epoch [ˈɛpək, ˈɛˌpɑk, ˈi:ˌpɑk] *n* : época *f*, era *f*
epoxy [ɪˈpɑksi] *n, pl* **epoxies** : resina *f* epoxídica
equable [ˈɛkwəbəl, ˈi:-] *adj* 1 CALM, STEADY : ecuánime 2 UNIFORM : estable (dícese de la temperatura), constante (dícese del clima), uniforme
equably [ˈɛkwəbli, ˈi:-] *adv* : con ecuanimidad
equal¹ [ˈi:kwəl] *vt* **equaled** *or* **equalled; equaling** *or* **equalling** 1 : ser igual a ‹two plus three equals five : dos más tres es igual a cinco› 2 MATCH : igualar
equal² *adj* 1 SAME : igual 2 ADEQUATE : adecuado, capaz
equal³ *n* : igual *mf*
equality [ɪˈkwɑləṭi] *n, pl* **-ties** : igualdad *f*
equalize [ˈi:kwəˌlaɪz] *vt* **-ized; -izing** : igualar, equiparar
equally [ˈi:kwəli] *adv* : igualmente, por igual
equanimity [ˌi:kwəˈnɪməṭi, ˌɛ-] *n, pl* **-ties** : ecuanimidad *f*
equate [ɪˈkweɪt] *vt* **equated; equating** : equiparar, identificar
equation [ɪˈkweɪʒən] *n* : ecuación *f*
equator [ɪˈkweɪṭər] *n* : ecuador *m*
equatorial [ˌi:kwəˈtoriəl, ˌɛ-] *adj* : ecuatorial
equestrian¹ [ɪˈkwɛstriən, ɛ-] *adj* : ecuestre
equestrian² *n* : jinete *mf*, caballista *mf*
equilateral [ˌi:kwəˈlæṭərəl, ˌɛ-] *adj* : equilátero
equilibrium [ˌi:kwəˈlɪbriəm, ˌɛ-] *n, pl* **-riums** *or* **-ria** [-briə] : equilibrio *m*
equine [ˈi:ˌkwaɪn, ˈɛ-] *adj* : equino, hípico
equinox [ˈi:kwəˌnɑks, ˈɛ-] *n* : equinoccio *m*
equip [ɪˈkwɪp] *vt* **equipped; equipping** 1 FURNISH : equipar 2 PREPARE : preparar
equipment [ɪˈkwɪpmənt] *n* : equipo *m*
equitable [ˈɛkwəṭəbəl] *adj* : equitativo, justo, imparcial
equity [ˈɛkwəṭi] *n, pl* **-ties** 1 FAIRNESS : equidad *f*, imparcialidad *f* 2 VALUE : valor *m* líquido
equivalence [ɪˈkwɪvələn*t*s] *n* : equivalencia *f*
equivalent¹ [ɪˈkwɪvələnt] *adj* : equivalente
equivalent² *n* : equivalente *m*
equivocal [ɪˈkwɪvəkəl] *adj* 1 AMBIGUOUS : equívoco, ambiguo 2 QUESTIONABLE : incierto, dudoso, sospechoso
equivocate [ɪˈkwɪvəˌkeɪt] *vi* **-cated; -cating** : usar lenguaje equívoco, andarse con evasivas
equivocation [ɪˌkwɪvəˈkeɪʃən] *n* : evasiva *f*, subterfugio *m*
era [ˈɪrə, ˈɛrə, ˈi:rə] *n* : era *f*, época *f*
eradicate [ɪˈrædəˌkeɪt] *vt* **-cated; -cating** : erradicar
erase [ɪˈreɪs] *vt* **erased; erasing** : borrar
eraser [ɪˈreɪsər] *n* : goma *f* de borrar, borrador *m*
erasure [ɪˈreɪʃər] *n* : tachadura *f*
ere¹ [ˈɛr] *conj* : antes de que
ere² *prep* 1 : antes de 2 **ere long** : dentro de poco
erect¹ [ɪˈrɛkt] *vt* 1 CONSTRUCT : erigir, construir 2 RAISE : levantar 3 ESTABLISH : establecer
erect² *adj* : erguido, derecho, erecto

erection [ɪ'rɛkʃən] *n* **1** : erección *f* (en fisiología) **2** BUILDING : construcción *f*

ergonomics [ˌərgə'nɑmɪks] *npl* : ergonomía *f*

ermine ['ərmən] *n* : armiño *m*

erode [ɪ'ro:d] *vt* **eroded; eroding** : erosionar (el suelo), corroer (metales)

erosion [ɪ'ro:ʒən] *n* : erosión *f*, corrosión *f*

erotic [ɪ'rɑt̬ɪk] *adj* : erótico — **erotically** [-t̬ɪkli] *adv*

eroticism [ɪ'rɑt̬əˌsɪzəm] *n* : erotismo *m*

err ['ɛr, 'ər] *vi* : cometer un error, equivocarse, errar

errand ['ɛrənd] *n* : mandado *m*, encargo *m*, recado *m Spain* ⟨an errand of mercy : una misión de caridad⟩

errant ['ɛrənt] *adj* **1** WANDERING : errante **2** ASTRAY : descarriado

erratic [ɪ'ræt̬ɪk] *adj* **1** INCONSISTENT : errático, irregular, inconsistente **2** ECCENTRIC : excéntrico, raro

erratically [ɪ'ræt̬ɪkli] *adv* : erráticamente, de manera irregular

erroneous [ɪ'ro:niəs, ɛ-] *adj* : erróneo — **erroneously** *adv*

error ['ɛrər] *n* : error *m*, equivocación *f* ⟨to be in error : estar equivocado⟩

ersatz ['ɛrˌsɑts, 'ərˌsæts] *adj* : artificial, sustituto

erstwhile ['ərstˌ*h*waɪl] *adj* : antiguo

erudite ['ɛrəˌdaɪt, 'ɛrjʊ-] *adj* : erudito, letrado

erudition [ˌɛrə'dɪʃən, ˌɛrjʊ-] *n* : erudición *f*

erupt [ɪ'rʌpt] *vi* **1** : hacer erupción (dícese de un volcán o un sarpullido) **2** : estallar (dícese de la cólera o la violencia)

eruption [ɪ'rʌpʃən] *n* : erupción *f*, estallido *m*

eruptive [ɪ'rʌptɪv] *adj* : eruptivo

escalate ['ɛskəˌleɪt] *v* **-lated; -lating** *vt* : intensificar (un conflicto), aumentar (precios) — *vi* : intensificarse, aumentarse

escalation [ˌɛskə'leɪʃən] *n* : intensificación *f*, escalada *f*, aumento *m*, subida *f*

escalator ['ɛskəˌleɪt̬ər] *n* : escalera *f* mecánica

escapade ['ɛskəˌpeɪd] *n* : aventura *f*

escape[1] [ɪ'skeɪp, ɛ-] *v* **-caped; -caping** *vt* : escaparse de, librarse de, evitar — *vi* : escaparse, fugarse, huir

escape[2] *n* **1** FLIGHT : fuga *f*, huida *f*, escapada *f* **2** LEAKAGE : escape *m*, fuga *f* **3** : escapatoria *f*, evasión *f* ⟨to have no escape : no tener escapatoria⟩ ⟨escape from reality : evasión de la realidad⟩

escapee [ɪˌskeɪ'pi:, ˌɛ-] *n* : fugitivo *m*, -va *f*

escarole ['ɛskəˌro:l] *n* : escarola *f*

escarpment [ɪs'kɑrpmənt, ɛs-] *n* : escarpa *f*, escarpadura *f*

eschew [ɛ'ʃu:, ɪs'ʧu:] *vt* : evitar, rehuir, abstenerse de

escort[1] [ɪ'skɔrt, ɛ-] *vt* **1** : escoltar ⟨to escort a ship : escoltar un barco⟩ **2** ACCOMPANY : acompañar

escort[2] ['ɛsˌkɔrt] *n* **1** : escolta *f* ⟨armed escort : escolta armada⟩ **2** COMPANION : acompañante *mf*; compañero *m*, -ra *f*

escrow ['ɛsˌkro:] *n* **in escrow** : en depósito, en custodia de un tercero

Eskimo ['ɛskəˌmo:] *n* **1** : esquimal *mf* **2** : esquimal *m* (idioma) — **Eskimo** *adj*

esophagus [ɪ'sɑfəgəs, i:-] *n, pl* **-gi** [-ˌgaɪ, -ˌʤaɪ] : esófago *m*

esoteric [ˌɛsə'tɛrɪk] *adj* : esotérico, hermético

especially [ɪ'spɛʃəli] *adv* : especialmente, particularmente

espionage ['ɛspiəˌnɑʒ, -ˌnɑʤ] *n* : espionaje *m*

espouse [ɪ'spaʊz, ɛ-] *vt* **espoused; espousing** **1** MARRY : casarse con **2** ADOPT, ADVOCATE : apoyar, adherirse a, adoptar

espresso ['ɛsprɛˌso:] *n, pl* **-sos** : café *m* exprés

essay[1] ['ɛseɪ, 'ɛˌseɪ] *vt* : intentar, tratar

essay[2] ['ɛˌseɪ] *n* **1** COMPOSITION : ensayo *m*, trabajo *m* **2** ATTEMPT : intento *m*

essayist ['ɛˌseɪɪst] *n* : ensayista *mf*

essence ['ɛsən*t*s] *n* **1** CORE : esencia *f*, núcleo *m*, meollo *m* ⟨in essence : esencialmente⟩ **2** EXTRACT : esencia *f*, extracto *m* **3** PERFUME : esencia *f*, perfume *m*

essential[1] [ɪ'sɛnʧəl] *adj* : esencial, imprescindible, fundamental — **essentially** *adv*

essential[2] *n* : elemento *m* esencial, lo imprescindible

establish [ɪ'stæblɪʃ, ɛ-] *vt* **1** FOUND : establecer, fundar **2** SET UP : establecer, instaurar, instituir **3** PROVE : demostrar, probar

establishment [ɪ'stæblɪʃmənt, ɛ-] *n* **1** ESTABLISHING : establecimiento *m*, fundación *f*, instauración *f* **2** BUSINESS : negocio *m*, establecimiento *m* **3 the Establishment** : la clase dirigente

estate [ɪ'steɪt, ɛ-] *n* **1** POSSESSIONS : bienes *mpl*, propiedad *f*, patrimonio *m* **2** PROPERTY : hacienda *f*, finca *f*, propiedad *f*

esteem[1] [ɪ'sti:m, ɛ-] *vt* : estimar, apreciar

esteem[2] *n* : estima *f*, aprecio *m*

ester ['ɛstər] *n* : éster *m*

esthetic [ɛs'θɛt̬ɪk] → **aesthetic**

estimable ['ɛstəməbəl] *adj* : estimable

estimate[1] ['ɛstəˌmeɪt] *vt* **-mated; -mating** : calcular, estimar

estimate[2] ['ɛstəmət] *n* **1** : cálculo *m* aproximado ⟨to make an estimate : hacer un cálculo⟩ **2** ASSESSMENT : valoración *f*, estimación *f*

estimation [ˌɛstə'meɪʃən] *n* **1** JUDGMENT : juicio *m*, opinión *f* ⟨in my estimation : en mi opinión, según mis cálculos⟩ **2** ESTEEM : estima *f*, aprecio *m*

estimator [ˈɛstəˌmeɪt̬ər] *n* : tasador *m*, -dora *f*

Estonian [ɛˈsto:niən] *n* : estonio *m*, -nia *f* — **Estonian** *adj*

estrange [ɪˈstreɪnʤ, ɛ-] *vt* **-tranged; -tranging** : enajenar, apartar, alejar

estrangement [ɪˈstreɪnʤmənt, ɛ-] *n* : alejamiento *m*, distanciamiento *m*

estrogen [ˈɛstrəʤən] *n* : estrógeno *m*

estrus [ˈɛstrəs] *n* : celo *m*

estuary [ˈɛsʧʊˌwɛri] *n, pl* **-aries** : estuario *m*, -ría *f*

et cetera [ɛtˈsɛt̬ərə, -ˈsɛtrə] : etcétera

etch [ˈɛʧ] *v* : grabar al aguafuerte

etching [ˈɛʧɪŋ] *n* : aguafuerte *m*, grabado *m* al aguafuerte

eternal [ɪˈtərnəl, i:-] *adj* **1** EVERLASTING : eterno **2** INTERMINABLE : constante, incesante

eternally [ɪˈtərnəli, i:-] *adv* : eternamente, para siempre

eternity [ɪˈtərnət̬i, i:-] *n, pl* **-ties** : eternidad *f*

ethane [ˈɛˌθeɪn] *n* : etano *m*

ethanol [ˈɛθəˌnɔl, -ˌno:l] *n* : etanol *m*

ether [ˈi:θər] *n* : éter *m*

ethereal [ɪˈθɪriəl, i:-] *adj* **1** CELESTIAL : etéreo, celeste **2** DELICATE : delicado

ethical [ˈɛθɪkəl] *adj* : ético — **ethically** *adv*

ethics [ˈɛθɪks] *ns & pl* **1** : ética *f* **2** MORALITY : ética *f*, moral *f*, moralidad *f*

Ethiopian [ˌi:θiˈo:piən] *n* : etíope *mf* — **Ethiopian** *adj*

ethnic [ˈɛθnɪk] *adj* : étnico

ethnologist [ɛθˈnɑləʤɪst] *n* : etnólogo *m*, -ga *f*

ethnology [ɛθˈnɑləʤi] *n* : etnología *f*

etiquette [ˈɛt̬ɪkət, -ˌkɛt] *n* : etiqueta *f*, protocolo *m*

etymological [ˌɛt̬əməˈlɑʤɪkəl] *adj* : etimológico

etymology [ˌɛt̬əˈmɑləʤi] *n, pl* **-gies** : etimología *f*

eucalyptus [ˌju:kəˈlɪptəs] *n, pl* **-ti** [-ˌtaɪ] *or* **-tuses** [-təsəz] : eucalipto *m*

Eucharist [ˈju:kərɪst] *n* : Eucaristía *f*

eulogize [ˈju:ləˌʤaɪz] *vt* **-gized; -gizing** : elogiar, encomiar

eulogy [ˈju:ləʤi] *n, pl* **-gies** : elogio *m*, encomio *m*, panegírico *m*

eunuch [ˈju:nək] *n* : eunuco *m*

euphemism [ˈju:fəˌmɪzəm] *n* : eufemismo *m*

euphemistic [ˌju:fəˈmɪstɪk] *adj* : eufemístico

euphony [ˈju:fəni] *n, pl* **-nies** : eufonía *f*

euphoria [jʊˈforiə] *n* : euforia *f*

euphoric [jʊˈforɪk] *adj* : eufórico

European [ˌjʊrəˈpi:ən] *n* : europeo *m*, europea *f* — **European** *adj*

euthanasia [ˌju:θəˈneɪʒə, -ʒiə] *n* : eutanasia *f*

evacuate [ɪˈvækjʊˌeɪt] *v* **-ated; -ating** *vt* VACATE : evacuar, desalojar — *vi* WITHDRAW : retirarse

evacuation [ɪˌvækjʊˈeɪʃən] *n* : evacuación *f*, desalojo *m*

evade [ɪˈveɪd] *vt* **evaded; evading** : evadir, eludir, esquivar

evaluate [ɪˈvæljʊˌeɪt] *vt* **-ated; -ating** : evaluar, valorar, tasar

evaluation [ɪˌvæljʊˈeɪʃən] *n* : evaluación *f*, valoración *f*, tasación *f*

evangelical [ˌi:ˌvænˈʤɛlɪkəl, ˌɛvən-] *adj* : evangélico

evangelist [ɪˈvænʤəlɪst] *n* **1** : evangelista *m* **2** PREACHER : predicador *m*, -dora *f*

evaporate [ɪˈvæpəˌreɪt] *vi* **-rated; -rating** **1** VAPORIZE : evaporarse **2** VANISH : evaporarse, desvanecerse, esfumarse

evaporation [ɪˌvæpəˈreɪʃən] *n* : evaporación *f*

evasion [ɪˈveɪʒən] *n* : evasión *f*

evasive [ɪˈveɪsɪv] *adj* : evasivo

evasiveness [ɪˈveɪsɪvnəs] *n* : carácter *m* evasivo

eve [ˈi:v] *n* **1** : víspera *f* ⟨on the eve of the festivities : en vísperas de las festividades⟩ **2** → **evening**

even¹ [ˈi:vən] *vt* **1** LEVEL : allanar, nivelar, emparejar **2** EQUALIZE : igualar, equilibrar — *vi* **to even out** : nivelarse, emparejarse

even² *adv* **1** : hasta, incluso ⟨even a child can do it : hasta un niño puede hacerlo⟩ ⟨he looked content, even happy : se le veía satisfecho, incluso feliz⟩ **2** (*in negative constructions*) : ni siquiera ⟨he didn't even try : ni siquiera lo intentó⟩ **3** (*in comparisons*) : aún, todavía ⟨even better : aún mejor, todavía mejor⟩ **4** **even if** : aunque **5** **even so** : aun así **6** **even though** : aun cuando, a pesar de que

even³ *adj* **1** SMOOTH : uniforme, liso, parejo **2** FLAT : plano, llano **3** EQUAL : igual, igualado ⟨an even score : un marcador igualado⟩ **4** REGULAR : regular, constante ⟨an even pace : un ritmo constante⟩ **5** EXACT : exacto, justo **6** : par ⟨even number : número par⟩ **7** **to be even** : estar en paz, estar a mano **8** **to get even** : desquitarse, vengarse

evening [ˈi:vnɪŋ] *n* : tarde *f*, noche *f* ⟨in the evening : por la noche⟩

evenly [ˈi:vənli] *adv* **1** UNIFORMLY : de modo uniforme, de manera constante **2** FAIRLY : igualmente, equitativamente

evenness [ˈi:vənnəs] *n* : uniformidad *f*, igualdad *f*, regularidad *f*

event [ɪˈvɛnt] *n* **1** : acontecimiento *m*, suceso *m*, prueba *f* (en deportes) **2** **in the event that** : en caso de que

eventful [ɪˈvɛntfəl] *adj* : lleno de incidentes, memorable

eventual [ɪˈvɛnʧʊəl] *adj* : final, consiguiente

eventuality [ɪˌvɛnʧʊˈælət̬i] *n, pl* **-ties** : eventualidad *f*

eventually [ɪˈvɛnʧʊəli] *adv* : al fin, con el tiempo, algún día

ever [ˈɛvər] *adv* **1** ALWAYS : siempre ⟨as ever : como siempre⟩ ⟨ever since : desde entonces⟩ **2** (*in questions*) : alguna vez, algún día ⟨have you ever been to Mexico? : ¿has estado en México alguna vez?⟩ **3** (*in negative constructions*) : nunca ⟨doesn't he ever work? : ¿es que nunca trabaja?⟩ ⟨nobody ever helps me : nadie nunca me ayuda⟩ **4** (*in comparisons*) : nunca ⟨better than ever : mejor que nunca⟩ **5** (*as intensifier*) ⟨I'm ever so happy! : ¡estoy tan y tan feliz!⟩ ⟨he looks ever so angry : parece estar muy enojado⟩
evergreen[1] [ˈɛvərˌgriːn] *adj* : de hoja perenne
evergreen[2] *n* : planta *f* de hoja perenne
everlasting [ˌɛvərˈlæstɪŋ] *adj* : eterno, perpetuo, imperecedero
evermore [ˌɛvərˈmor] *adv* : eternamente
every [ˈɛvri] *adj* **1** EACH : cada ⟨every time : cada vez⟩ ⟨every other house : cada dos casas⟩ **2** ALL : todo ⟨every month : todos los meses⟩ ⟨every woman : toda mujer, todas las mujeres⟩ **3** COMPLETE : pleno, entero ⟨to have every confidence : tener plena confianza⟩
everybody [ˈɛvriˌbʌdi, -ˌbɑ-] *pron* : todos *mpl*, -das *fpl*; todo el mundo
everyday [ˌɛvriˈdeɪ, ˈɛvriˌ-] *adj* : cotidiano, diario, corriente ⟨everyday clothes : ropa de todos los días⟩
everyone [ˈɛvriˌwʌn] → **everybody**
everything [ˈɛvriˌθɪŋ] *pron* : todo
everywhere [ˈɛvriˌ*h*wɛr] *adv* : en todas partes, por todas partes, dondequiera ⟨I looked everywhere : busqué en todas partes⟩ ⟨everywhere we go : dondequiera que vayamos⟩
evict [ɪˈvɪkt] *vt* : desalojar, desahuciar
eviction [ɪˈvɪkʃən] *n* : desalojo *m*, desahucio *m*
evidence [ˈɛvədən*t*s] *n* **1** INDICATION : indicio *m*, señal *m* ⟨to be in evidence : estar a la vista⟩ **2** PROOF : evidencia *f*, prueba *f* **3** TESTIMONY : testimonio *m*, declaración *f* ⟨to give evidence : declarar como testigo, prestar declaración⟩
evident [ˈɛvidənt] *adj* : evidente, patente, manifiesto
evidently [ˈɛvidəntli, ˌɛviˈdɛntli] *adv* **1** CLEARLY : claramente, obviamente **2** APPARENTLY : aparentemente, evidentemente, al parecer
evil[1] [ˈiːvəl, -vɪl] *adj* **eviler** *or* **eviller; evilest** *or* **evillest 1** WICKED : malvado, malo, maligno **2** HARMFUL : nocivo, dañino, pernicioso **3** UNPLEASANT : desagradable ⟨an evil odor : un olor horrible⟩
evil[2] *n* **1** WICKEDNESS : mal *m*, maldad *f* **2** MISFORTUNE : desgracia *f*, mal *m*
evildoer [ˌiːvəlˈduːər, ˌiːvɪl-] *n* : malvado *m*, -da *f*
evince [ɪˈvɪn*t*s] *vt* **evinced; evincing** : mostrar, manifestar, revelar
eviscerate [ɪˈvɪsəˌreɪt] *vt* **-ated; -ating** : eviscerar, destripar (un pollo, etc.)
evocation [ˌiːvoˈkeɪʃən, ˌɛ-] *n* : evocación *f*
evocative [iˈvɑkət̬ɪv] *adj* : evocador
evoke [iˈvoːk] *vt* **evoked; evoking** : evocar, provocar
evolution [ˌɛvəˈluːʃən, ˌiː-] *n* : evolución *f*, desarrollo *m*
evolutionary [ˌɛvəˈluːʃəˌnɛri, ˌiː-] *adj* : evolutivo
evolve [iˈvɑlv] *vi* **evolved; evolving** : evolucionar, desarrollarse
ewe [ˈjuː] *n* : oveja *f*
exacerbate [ɪgˈzæsərˌbeɪt] *vt* **-bated; -bating** : exacerbar
exact[1] [ɪgˈzækt, ɛ-] *vt* : exigir, imponer, arrancar
exact[2] *adj* : exacto, preciso — **exactly** *adv*
exacting [ɪˈzæktɪŋ, ɛg-] *adj* : exigente, riguroso
exactitude [ɪgˈzæktəˌtuːd, ɛg-, -ˌtjuːd] *n* : exactitud *f*, precisión *f*
exaggerate [ɪgˈzæʤəˌreɪt, ɛg-] *v* **-ated; -ating** : exagerar
exaggerated [ɪgˈzæʤəˌreɪt̬əd, ɛg-] *adj* : exagerado — **exaggeratedly** *adv*
exaggeration [ɪgˌzæʤəˈreɪʃən, ɛg-] *n* : exageración *f*
exalt [ɪgˈzɔlt, ɛg-] *vt* : exaltar, ensalzar, glorificar
exaltation [ˌɛgˌzɔlˈteɪʃən, ˌɛkˌsɔl-] *n* : exaltación *f*
exam [ɪgˈzæm, ɛg-] → **examination**
examination [ɪgˌzæməˈneɪʃən, ɛg-] *n* **1** TEST : examen *m* **2** INSPECTION : inspección *f*, revisión *f* **3** INVESTIGATION : examen *m*, estudio *m*
examine [ɪgˈzæmən, ɛg-] *vt* **-ined; -ining 1** TEST : examinar **2** INSPECT : inspeccionar, revisar **3** STUDY : examinar
example [ɪgˈzæmpəl, ɛg-] *n* : ejemplo *m* ⟨for example : por ejemplo⟩ ⟨to set an example : dar ejemplo⟩
exasperate [ɪgˈzæspəˌreɪt, ɛg-] *vt* **-ated; -ating** : exasperar, sacar de quicio
exasperation [ɪgˌzæspəˈreɪʃən, ɛg-] *n* : exasperación *f*
excavate [ˈɛkskəˌveɪt] *vt* **-vated; -vating** : excavar
excavation [ˌɛkskəˈveɪʃən] *n* : excavación *f*
exceed [ɪkˈsiːd, ɛk-] *vt* **1** SURPASS : exceder, rebasar, sobrepasar **2** : exceder de, sobrepasar ⟨not exceeding two months : que no exceda de dos meses⟩
exceedingly [ɪkˈsiːdɪŋli, ɛk-] *adv* : extremadamente, sumamente
excel [ɪkˈsɛl, ɛk-] *v* **-celled; -celling** *vi* : sobresalir, descollar, lucirse — *vt* : superar
excellence [ˈɛksələn*t*s] *n* : excelencia *f*
excellency [ˈɛksələn*t*si] *n, pl* **-cies** : excelencia *f* ⟨His Excellency : Su Excelencia⟩
excellent [ˈɛksələnt] *adj* : excelente, sobresaliente — **excellently** *adv*

except[1] [ɪk'sɛpt] *vt* : exceptuar, excluir
except[2] *conj* : pero, si no fuera por
except[3] *prep* : excepto, menos, salvo ⟨everyone except Carlos : todos menos Carlos⟩
exception [ɪk'sɛpʃən] *n* **1** : excepción *f* **2 to take exception to** : ofenderse por, objetar a
exceptional [ɪk'sɛpʃənəl] *adj* : excepcional, extraordinario — **exceptionally** *adv*
excerpt[1] [ɛk'sərpt, ɛg'zərpt, 'ɛk,-, 'g,-] *vt* : escoger, seleccionar
excerpt[2] ['ɛk,sərpt, 'ɛg,zərpt] *n* : pasaje *m*, selección *f*
excess[1] ['ɛk,sɛs, ɪk'sɛs] *adj* **1** : excesivo, de sobra **2 excess baggage** : exceso *m* de equipaje
excess[2] [ɪk'sɛs, 'ɛk,sɛs] *n* **1** SUPERFLUITY : exceso *m*, superfluidad *f* ⟨an excess of energy : un exceso de energía⟩ **2** SURPLUS : excedente *m*, sobrante *m* ⟨in excess of : superior a⟩
excessive [ɪk'sɛsɪv, ɛk-] *adj* : excesivo, exagerado, desmesurado — **excessively** *adv*
exchange[1] [ɪks'ʧeɪnʤ, ɛks-; 'ɛks,ʧeɪnʤ] *vt* **-changed; -changing** : cambiar, intercambiar, canjear
exchange[2] *n* **1** : cambio *m*, intercambio *m*, canje *m* **2 stock exchange** : bolsa *f* (de valores)
exchangeable [ɪks'ʧeɪnʤəbəl, ɛks-] *adj* : canjeable
excise[1] [ɪk'saɪz, ɛk-] *vt* **-cised; -cising** : extirpar
excise[2] ['ɛk,saɪz] *n* **excise tax** : impuesto *m* interno, impuesto *m* sobre el consumo
excision [ɪk'sɪʒən, ɛk-] *n* : extirpación *f*, excisión *f*
excitability [ɪk,saɪtə'bɪləṭi, ɛk-] *n* : excitabilidad *f*
excitable [ɪk'saɪṭəbəl, ɛk-] *adj* : excitable
excitation [,ɛk,saɪ'teɪʃən] *n* : excitación *f*
excite [ɪk'saɪt, ɛk-] *vt* **-cited; -citing** **1** AROUSE, STIMULATE : excitar, mover, estimular **2** ANIMATE : entusiasmar, animar **3** EVOKE, PROVOKE : provocar, despertar, suscitar ⟨to excite curiosity : despertar la curiosidad⟩
excited [ɪk'saɪṭəd, ɛk-] *adj* **1** STIMULATED : excitado, estimulado **2** ENTHUSIASTIC : entusiasmado, emocionado
excitedly [ɪk'saɪṭədli, ɛk-] *adv* : con excitación, con entusiasmo
excitement [ɪk'saɪtmənt, ɛk-] *n* **1** ENTHUSIASM : entusiasmo *m*, emoción *f* **2** AGITATION : agitación *f*, alboroto *m*, conmoción *f* **3** AROUSAL : excitación *f*
exciting [ɪk'saɪṭɪŋ, ɛk-] *adj* **1** : emocionante **2** AROUSING : excitante
exclaim [ɪks'kleɪm, ɛk-] *v* : exclamar
exclamation [,ɛksklə'meɪʃən] *n* : exclamación *f*
exclamation point *n* : signo *m* de admiración
exclamatory [ɪks'klæmə,tori, ɛks-] *adj* : exclamativo
exclude [ɪks'klu:d, ɛks-] *vt* **-cluded; -cluding** **1** BAR : excluir, descartar, no admitir **2** EXPEL : expeler, expulsar
exclusion [ɪks'klu:ʒən, ɛks-] *n* : exclusión *f*
exclusive[1] [ɪks'klu:sɪv, ɛks-] *adj* **1** SOLE : exclusivo, único **2** SELECT : exclusivo, selecto
exclusive[2] *n* : exclusiva *f*
exclusively [ɪks'klu:sɪvli, ɛks-] *adv* : exclusivamente, únicamente
exclusiveness [ɪks'klu:sɪvnəs, ɛks-] *n* : exclusividad *f*
excommunicate [,ɛkskə'mju:nə,keɪt] *vt* **-cated; -cating** : excomulgar
excommunication [,ɛkskə,mju:nə'keɪʃən] *n* : excomunión *f*
excrement ['ɛkskrəmənt] *n* : excremento *m*
excrete [ɪk'skri:t, ɛk-] *vt* **-creted; -creting** : excretar
excretion [ɪk'skri:ʃən, ɛk-] *n* : excreción *f*
excruciating [ɪk'skru:ʃi,eɪṭɪŋ, ɛk-] *adj* : insoportable, atroz, terrible — **excruciatingly** *adv*
exculpate ['ɛkskəl,peɪt] *vt* **-pated; -pating** : exculpar
excursion [ɪk'skərʒən, ɛk-] *n* **1** OUTING : excursión *f*, paseo *m* **2** DIGRESSION : digresión *f*
excuse[1] [ɪk'skju:z, ɛk-] *vt* **-cused; -cusing** **1** PARDON : disculpar, perdonar ⟨excuse me : con permiso, perdóneme, perdón⟩ **2** EXEMPT : eximir, disculpar **3** JUSTIFY : excusar, justificar
excuse[2] [ɪk'skju:s, ɛk-] *n* **1** JUSTIFICATION : excusa *f*, justificación *f* **2** PRETEXT : pretexto *m* **3 to make one's excuses to someone** : pedirle disculpas a alguien
execute ['ɛksɪ,kju:t] *vt* **-cuted; -cuting** **1** CARRY OUT : ejecutar, llevar a cabo, desempeñar **2** ENFORCE : ejecutar, cumplir (un testamento, etc.) **3** KILL : ejecutar, ajusticiar
execution [,ɛksɪ'kju:ʃən] *n* **1** PERFORMANCE : ejecución *f*, desempeño *m* **2** IMPLEMENTATION : cumplimiento *m* **3** : ejecución *f* (por un delito)
executioner [,ɛksɪ'kju:ʃənər] *n* : verdugo *m*
executive[1] [ɪg'zɛkjəṭɪv, ɛg-] *adj* : ejecutivo
executive[2] *n* : ejecutivo *m*, -va *f*
executor [ɪg'zɛkjəṭər, ɛg-] *n* : albacea *m*, testamentario *m*
executrix [ɪg'zɛkjə,trɪks, ɛg-] *n, pl* **executrices** [-,zɛkjə'traɪ,si:z] *or* **executrixes** [-'zɛkjə,trɪksəz] : albacea *f*, testamentaria *f*
exemplary [ɪg'zɛmpləri, ɛg-] *adj* : ejemplar
exemplify [ɪg'zɛmplə,faɪ, ɛg-] *vt* **-fied; -fying** : ejemplificar, ilustrar, demostrar

exempt[1] [ɪg'zɛmpt, ɛg-] *vt* : eximir, dispensar, exonerar
exempt[2] *adj* : exento, eximido
exemption [ɪg'zɛmpʃən, ɛg-] *n* : exención *f*
exercise[1] ['ɛksər,saɪz] *v* **-cised; -cising** *vt* **1** : ejercitar (el cuerpo) **2** USE : ejercer, hacer uso de — *vi* : hacer ejercicio
exercise[2] *n* **1** : ejercicio *m* **2 exercises** *npl* WORKOUT : ejercicios *mpl* físicos **3 exercises** *npl* CEREMONY : ceremonia *f*
exert [ɪg'zərt, ɛg-] *vt* **1** : ejercer, emplear **2 to exert oneself** : esforzarse
exertion [ɪg'zərʃən, ɛg-] *n* **1** USE : ejercicio *m* (de autoridad, etc.), uso *m* (de fuerza, etc.) **2** EFFORT : esfuerzo *m*, empeño *m*
exhalation [,ɛksə'leɪʃən, ,ɛkshə-] *n* : exhalación *f*, espiración *f*
exhale [ɛks'heɪl] *v* **-haled; -haling** *vt* **1** : exhalar, espirar **2** EMIT : exhalar, despedir, emitir — *vi* : espirar
exhaust[1] [ɪg'zɔst, ɛg-] *vt* **1** DEPLETE : agotar **2** TIRE : cansar, fatigar, agotar **3** EMPTY : vaciar
exhaust[2] *n* **1 exhaust fumes** : gases *mpl* de escape **2 exhaust pipe** : tubo *m* de escape **3 exhaust system** : sistema *m* de escape
exhausted [ɪg'zɔstəd, ɛg-] *adj* : agotado, derrengado
exhausting [ɪg'zɔstɪŋ, ɛg-] *adj* : extenuante, agotador
exhaustion [ɪg'zɔstʃən, ɛg-] *n* : agotamiento *m*
exhaustive [ɪg'zɔstɪv, ɛg-] *adj* : exhaustivo
exhibit[1] [ɪg'zɪbət, ɛg-] *vt* **1** DISPLAY : exhibir, exponer **2** PRODUCE, SHOW : mostrar, presentar
exhibit[2] *n* **1** OBJECT : objeto *m* expuesto **2** EXHIBITION : exposición *f*, exhibición *f* **3** EVIDENCE : prueba *f* instrumental
exhibition [,ɛksə'bɪʃən] *n* **1** : exposición *f*, exhibición *f* **2 to make an exhibition of oneself** : dar el espectáculo, hacer el ridículo
exhibitor [ɪg'zɪbət̬ər] *n* : expositor *m*, -tora *f*
exhilarate [ɪg'zɪlə,reɪt, ɛg-] *vt* **-rated; -rating** : alegrar, levantar el ánimo de
exhilaration [ɪg,zɪlə'reɪʃən, ɛg-] *n* : alegría *f*, regocijo *m*, júbilo *m*
exhort [ɪg'zɔrt, ɛg-] *vt* : exhortar
exhortation [,ɛk,sɔr'teɪʃən, -sər-; ,ɛg-,zɔr-] *n* : exhortación *f*
exhumation [,ɛksju'meɪʃən, -hju-; ,ɛgzu-, -zju-] *n* : exhumación *f*
exhume [ɪg'zu:m, -'zju:m; ɪks'ju:m, -'hju:m] *vt* **-humed; -huming** : exhumar, desenterrar
exigencies ['ɛksɪdʒəntsiz, ɪg'zɪdʒən,si:z] *npl* : exigencias *fpl*
exile[1] ['ɛg,zaɪl, 'ɛk,saɪl] *vt* **exiled; exiling** : exiliar, desterrar
exile[2] *n* **1** BANISHMENT : exilio *m*, destierro *m* **2** OUTCAST : exiliado *m*, -da *f*; desterrado *m*, -da *f*
exist [ɪg'zɪst, ɛg-] *vi* **1** BE : existir **2** LIVE : subsistir, vivir
existence [ɪg'zɪstənts, ɛg-] *n* : existencia *f*
existent [ɪg'zɪstənt, ɛg-] *adj* : existente
existing [ɪg'zɪstɪŋ] *adj* : existente
exit[1] ['ɛgzət, 'ɛksət] *vi* : salir, hacer mutis (en el teatro) — *vt* : salir de
exit[2] *n* **1** DEPARTURE : salida *f*, partida *f* **2** EGRESS : salida *f* <emergency exit : salida de emergencia>
exodus ['ɛksədəs] *n* : éxodo *m*
exonerate [ɪg'zɑnə,reɪt, ɛg-] *vt* **-ated; -ating** : exonerar, disculpar, absolver
exoneration [ɪg,zɑnə'reɪʃən, ɛg-] *n* : exoneración *f*
exorbitant [ɪg'zɔrbətənt, ɛg-] *adj* : exorbitante, excesivo
exorcise ['ɛk,sɔr,saɪz, -sər-] *vt* **-cised; -cising** : exorcizar
exorcism ['ɛksər,sɪzəm] *n* : exorcismo *m*
exotic[1] [ɪg'zɑtɪk, ɛg-] *adj* : exótico — **exotically** [-ɪkli] *adv*
exotic[2] *n* : planta *f* exótica
expand [ɪk'spænd, ɛk-] *vt* **1** ENLARGE : expandir, dilatar, aumentar, ampliar **2** EXTEND : extender — *vi* **1** ENLARGE : ampliarse, extenderse **2** : expandirse, dilatarse (dícese de los metales, gases, etc.)
expanse [ɪk'spænts, ɛk-] *n* : extensión *f*
expansion [ɪk'spæntʃən, ɛk-] *n* **1** ENLARGEMENT : expansión *f*, ampliación *f* **2** EXPANSE : extensión *f*
expansive [ɪk'spæntsɪv, ɛk-] *adj* **1** : expansivo **2** OUTGOING : expansivo, comunicativo **3** AMPLE : ancho, amplio — **expansively** *adv*
expansiveness [ɪk'spæntsɪvnəs, ɛk-] *n* : expansibilidad *f*
expatriate[1] [ɛks'peɪtri,eɪt] *vt* **-ated; -ating** : expatriar
expatriate[2] [ɛks'peɪtriət, -,eɪt] *adj* : expatriado
expatriate[3] [ɛks'peɪtriət, -,eɪt] *n* : expatriado *m*, -da *f*
expect [ɪk'spkt, ɛk-] *vt* **1** SUPPOSE : suponer, imaginarse **2** ANTICIPATE : esperar **3** COUNT ON, REQUIRE : contar con, esperar — *vi* **to be expecting** : estar embarazada
expectancy [ɪk'spɛktəntsi, ɛk-] *n, pl* **-cies** : expectativa *f*, esperanza *f*
expectant [ɪk'spɛktənt, ɛk-] *adj* **1** ANTICIPATING : expectante **2** EXPECTING : futuro <expectant mother : futura madre>
expectantly [ɪk'spɛktəntli, ɛk-] *adv* : con expectación
expectation [,ɛk,spɛk'teɪʃən] *n* **1** ANTICIPATION : expectación *f* **2** EXPECTANCY : expectativa *f*
expedient[1] [ɪk'spi:diənt, ɛk-] *adj* : conveniente, oportuno
expedient[2] *n* : expediente *m*, recurso *m*

expedite ['ɛkspəˌdaɪt] *vt* **-dited; -diting 1** FACILITATE : facilitar, dar curso a **2** HASTEN : acelerar
expedition [ˌɛkspə'dɪʃən] *n* : expedición *f*
expeditious [ˌɛkspə'dɪʃəs] *adj* : pronto, rápido
expel [ɪk'spɛl, ɛk-] *vt* **-pelled; -pelling** : expulsar, expeler
expend [ɪk'spɛnd, ɛk-] *vt* **1** DISBURSE : gastar, desembolsar **2** CONSUME : consumir, agotar
expendable [ɪk'spɛndəbəl, ɛk-] *adj* : prescindible
expenditure [ɪk'spɛndɪʧər, ɛk-, -ˌʧur] *n* : gasto *m*
expense [ɪk'spɛnts, ɛk-] *n* **1** COST : gasto *m* **2 expenses** *npl* : gastos *mpl*, expensas *fpl* **3 at the expense of** : a expensas de
expensive [ɪk'spɛntsɪv, ɛk-] *adj* : costoso, caro — **expensively** *adv*
experience[1] [ɪk'spɪriənts, ɛk-] *vt* **-enced; -encing** : experimentar (sentimientos), tener (dificultades), sufrir (una pérdida)
experience[2] *n* : experiencia *f*
experienced [ɪk'spɪriəntst, ɛk-] *adj* : con experiencia, experimentado
experiment[1] [ɪk'spɛrəmənt, ɛk-, -'spɪr-] *vi* : experimentar, hacer experimentos
experiment[2] *n* : experimento *m*
experimental [ɪkˌspɛrə'mntəl, ɛk-, -ˌspɪr-] *adj* : experimental — **experimentally** *adv*
experimentation [ɪkˌspɛrəmən'teɪʃən, ɛk-, -ˌspɪr-] *n* : experimentación *f*
expert[1] ['ɛkˌspərt, ɪk'spərt] *adj* : experto, de experto, pericial (dícese de un testigo) — **expertly** *adv*
expert[2] ['ɛkˌspərt] *n* : experto *m*, -ta *f*; perito *m*, -ta *f*; especialista *mf*
expertise [ˌɛkspər'ti:z] *n* : pericia *f*, competencia *f*
expiate ['ɛkspiˌeɪt] *vt* **-ated; -ating** : expiar
expiation [ˌɛkspi'eɪʃən] *n* : expiación *f*
expiration [ˌɛkspə'reɪʃən] *n* **1** EXHALATION : exhalación *f*, espiración *f* **2** DEATH : muerte *f* **3** TERMINATION : vencimiento *m*, caducidad *f*
expire [ɪk'spaɪr, ɛk-] *vi* **-pired; -piring 1** EXHALE : espirar **2** DIE : expirar, morir **3** TERMINATE : caducar, vencer
explain [ɪk'spleɪn, ɛk-] *vt* : explicar
explanation [ˌɛksplə'neɪʃən] *n* : explicación *f*
explanatory [ɪk'splænəˌtori, ɛk-] *adj* : explicativo, aclaratorio
expletive ['ɛkspləṭɪv] *n* : improperio *m*, palabrota *f fam*, grosería *f*
explicable [ɛk'splɪkəbəl, 'ɛksplɪ-] *adj* : explicable
explicit [ɪk'splɪsət, ɛk-] *adj* : explícito, claro, categórico, rotundo — **explicitly** *adv*
explicitness [ɪk'splɪsətnəs, ɛk-] *n* : claridad *f*, carácter *m* explícito
explode [ɪk'splo:d, ɛk-] *v* **-ploded; -ploding** *vt* **1** BURST : hacer explosionar, hacer explotar **2** REFUTE : rebatir, refutar, desmentir — *vi* **1** BURST : explotar, estallar, reventar **2** SKYROCKET : dispararse
exploit[1] [ɪk'splɔɪt, ɛk-] *vt* : explotar, aprovecharse de
exploit[2] ['ɛkˌsplɔɪt] *n* : hazaña *f*, proeza *f*
exploitation [ˌɛkˌsplɔɪ'teɪʃən] *n* : explotación *f*
exploration [ˌɛksplə'reɪʃən] *n* : exploración *f*
exploratory [ɪk'splorəˌtori, ɛk-] *adj* : exploratorio
explore [ɪk'splor, ɛk-] *vt* **-plored; -ploring** : explorar, investigar, examinar
explorer [ɪk'splorər, ɛk-] *n* : explorador *m*, -dora *f*
explosion [ɪk'splo:ʒən, ɛk-] *n* : explosión *f*, estallido *m*
explosive[1] [ɪk'splo:sɪv, ɛk-] *adj* : explosivo, fulminante — **explosively** *adv*
explosive[2] *n* : explosivo *m*
exponent [ɪk'spo:nənt, 'ɛkˌspo:-] *n* **1** : exponente *m* **2** ADVOCATE : defensor *m*, -sora *f*; partidario *m*, -ria *f*
exponential [ˌɛkspə'nɛnʧəl] *adj* : exponencial — **exponentially** *adv*
export[1] [ɛk'sport, 'ɛkˌsport] *vt* : exportar
export[2] ['ɛkˌsport] *n* **1** : artículo *m* de exportación **2** → **exportation**
exportation [ˌɛkˌspor'teɪʃən] *n* : exportación *f*
exporter [ɛk'sporṭər, 'ɛkˌspor-] *n* : exportador *m*, -dora *f*
expose [ɪk'spo:z, ɛk-] *vt* **-posed; -posing 1** : exponer (al peligro, a los elementos, a una enfermedad) **2** : exponer (una película a la luz) **3** DISCLOSE : descubrir, revelar, poner en evidencia **4** UNMASK : desenmascarar
exposé *or* **expose** [ˌɛkspo'zeɪ] *n* : exposición *f* (de hechos), revelación *f* (de un escándalo)
exposed [ɪk'spo:zd, ɛk-] *adj* : descubierto, sin protección
exposition [ˌɛkspə'zɪʃən] *n* : exposición *f*
exposure [ɪk'spo:ʒər, ɛk-] *n* **1** : exposición *f* **2** CONTACT : exposición *f*, experiencia *f*, contacto *m* **3** UNMASKING : desenmascaramiento *m* **4** ORIENTATION : orientación *f* ⟨a room with a northern exposure : una sala orientada al norte⟩
expound [ɪk'spaʊnd, ɛk-] *vt* : exponer, explicar — *vi* : hacer comentarios detallados
express[1] [ɪk'sprɛs, ɛk-] *vt* **1** SAY : expresar, comunicar **2** SHOW : expresar, manifestar, externar *Mex* **3** SQUEEZE : exprimir ⟨to express the juice from a lemon : exprimir el jugo de un limón⟩
express[2] *adv* : por correo exprés, por correo urgente

express[3] *adj* **1** EXPLICIT : expreso, manifiesto **2** SPECIFIC : específico ⟨for that express purpose : con ese fin específico⟩ **3** RAPID : expreso, rápido
express[4] *n* **1** : correo *m* exprés, correo *m* urgente **2** : expreso *m* (tren)
expression [ɪkˈsprɛʃən, ɛk-] *n* **1** UTTERANCE : expresión *f* ⟨freedom of expression : libertad de expresión⟩ **2** : expresión *f* (en la matemática) **3** PHRASE : frase *f*, expresión *f* **4** LOOK : expresión *f*, cara *f*, gesto *m* ⟨with a sad expression : con un gesto de tristeza⟩
expressionless [ɪkˈsprɛʃənləs, ɛk-] *adj* : inexpresivo
expressive [ɪkˈsprɛsɪv, ɛk-] *adj* : expresivo
expressway [ɪkˈsprɛsˌweɪ, ɛk-] *n* : autopista *f*
expulsion [ɪkˈspʌlʃən, ɛk-] *n* : expulsión *f*
expurgate [ˈɛkspərˌgeɪt] *vt* **-gated; -gating** : expurgar
exquisite [ɛkˈskwɪzət, ˈɛkˌskwɪ-] *adj* **1** FINE : exquisito, delicado, primoroso **2** INTENSE : intenso, extremo
extant [ˈɛkstənt, ɛkˈstænt] *adj* : existente
extemporaneous [ɛkˌstɛmpəˈreɪniəs] *adj* : improvisado — **extemporaneously** *adv*
extend [ɪkˈstɛnd, ɛk-] *vt* **1** STRETCH : extender, tender **2** PROLONG : prolongar, prorrogar **3** ENLARGE : agrandar, ampliar, aumentar **4** PROFFER : extender, dar, ofrecer — *vi* : extenderse
extended [ɪkˈstɛndəd, ɛk-] *adj* LENGTHY : prolongado, largo
extension [ɪkˈstɛntʃən, ɛk-] *n* **1** EXTENDING : extensión *f*, ampliación *f*, prórroga *f*, prolongación *f* **2** ANNEX : ampliación *f*, anexo *m* **3** : extensión *f* (de teléfono)
extensive [ɪkˈstɛntsɪv, ɛk-] *adj* : extenso, vasto, amplio — **extensively** *adv*
extent [ɪkˈstɛnt, ɛk-] *n* **1** SIZE : extensión *f*, magnitud *f* **2** DEGREE, SCOPE : alcance *m*, grado *m* ⟨to a certain extent : hasta cierto punto⟩
extenuate [ɪkˈstɛnjəˌweɪt, ɛk-] *vt* **-ated; -ating** : atenuar, aminorar, mitigar ⟨extenuating circumstances : circunstancias atenuantes⟩
extenuation [ɪkˌstɛnjəˈweɪʃən, ɛk-] *n* : atenuación *f*, aminoración *f*
exterior[1] [ɛkˈstɪriər] *adj* : exterior
exterior[2] *n* : exterior *m*
exterminate [ɪkˈstərməˌneɪt, ɛk-] *vt* **-nated; -nating** : exterminar
extermination [ɪkˌstərməˈneɪʃən, ɛk-] *n* : exterminación *f*, exterminio *m*
exterminator [ɪkˈstərməˌneɪt̬ər, ɛk-] *n* : exterminador *m*, -dora *f*
external [ɪkˈstərnəl, ɛk-] *adj* : externo, exterior — **externally** *adv*
extinct [ɪkˈstɪŋkt, ɛk-] *adj* : extinto
extinction [ɪkˈstɪŋkʃən, ɛk-] *n* : extinción *f*
extinguish [ɪkˈstɪŋgwɪʃ, ɛk-] *vt* : extinguir, apagar
extinguisher [ɪkˈstɪŋgwɪʃər, ɛk-] *n* : extinguidor *m*, extintor *m*
extirpate [ˈɛkstərˌpeɪt] *vt* **-pated; -pating** : extirpar, exterminar
extol [ɪkˈsto:l, ɛk-] *vt* **-tolled; -tolling** : exaltar, ensalzar, alabar
extort [ɪkˈstɔrt, ɛk-] *vt* : extorsionar
extortion [ɪkˈstɔrʃən, ɛk-] *n* : extorsión *f*
extra[1] [ˈɛkstrə] *adv* : extra, más, extremadamente, super ⟨extra special : super especial⟩
extra[2] *adj* **1** ADDITIONAL : adicional, suplementario, de más **2** SUPERIOR : superior
extra[3] *n* : extra *m*
extract[1] [ɪkˈstrækt, ɛk-] *vt* : extraer, sacar
extract[2] [ˈɛkˌstrækt] *n* **1** EXCERPT : pasaje *m*, selección *f*, trozo *m* **2** : extracto *m* ⟨vanilla extract : extracto de vainilla⟩
extraction [ɪkˈstrækʃən, ɛk-] *n* : extracción *f*
extractor [ɪkˈstræktər, ɛk-] *n* : extractor *m*
extracurricular [ˌɛkstrəkəˈrɪkjələr] *adj* : extracurricular
extradite [ˈɛkstrəˌdaɪt] *vt* **-dited; -diting** : extraditar
extradition [ˌɛkstrəˈdɪʃən] *n* : extradición *f*
extramarital [ˌɛkstrəˈmærət̬əl] *adj* : extramatrimonial
extraneous [ɛkˈstreɪniəs] *adj* **1** OUTSIDE : extrínseco, externo **2** SUPERFLUOUS : superfluo, ajeno — **extraneously** *adv*
extraordinary [ɪkˈstrɔrdənˌɛri, ˌɛkstrəˈɔrd-] *adj* : extraordinario, excepcional — **extraordinarily** [ɪkˌstrɔrdənˈɛrəli, ˌkstrəˌɔrd-] *adv*
extrasensory [ˌɛkstrəˈsɛntsəri] *adj* : extrasensorial
extraterrestrial[1] [ˌɛkstrətəˈrɛstriəl] *adj* : extraterrestre
extraterrestrial[2] *n* : extraterrestre *mf*
extravagance [ɪkˈstrævɪgənts, ɛk-] *n* **1** EXCESS : exceso *m*, extravagancia *f* **2** WASTEFULNESS : derroche *m*, despilfarro *m* **3** LUXURY : lujo *m*
extravagant [ɪkˈstrævɪgənt, ɛk-] *adj* **1** EXCESSIVE : excesivo, extravagante **2** WASTEFUL : despilfarrador, derrochador, gastador **3** EXORBITANT : costoso, exorbitante
extravagantly [ɪkˈstrævɪgəntli, ɛk-] *adv* **1** LAVISHLY : a lo grande **2** EXCESSIVELY : exageradamente, desmesuradamente
extravaganza [ɪkˌstrævəˈgænzə, ɛk-] *n* : gran espectáculo *m*
extreme[1] [ɪkˈstri:m, ɛk-] *adj* **1** UTMOST : extremo, sumo ⟨of extreme importance : de suma importancia⟩ **2** INTENSE : intenso, extremado ⟨extreme cold : frío extremado⟩ **3** EXCESSIVE : excesivo, extremo ⟨extreme views : opiniones extremas⟩ ⟨extreme measures : medidas excepcionales, medi-

das drásticas⟩ **4** OUTERMOST : extremo ⟨the extreme north : el norte extremo⟩
extreme² *n* **1** : extremo *m* **2 in the extreme** : en extremo, en sumo grado
extremely [ɪkˈstri:mli, ɛk-] *adv* : sumamente, extremadamente, terriblemente
extremist [ɪkˈstri:mɪst, ɛk-] *n* : extremista *mf* — **extremist** *adj*
extremity [ɪkˈstrɛmət̬i, ɛk-] *n, pl* **-ties 1** EXTREME : extremo *m* **2 extremities** *npl* LIMBS : extremidades *fpl*
extricate [ˈɛkstrəˌkeɪt] *vt* **-cated; -cating** : librar, sacar
extrinsic [ɪkˈstrɪnzɪk, -ˈstrɪntsɪk] *adj* : extrínseco
extrovert [ˈɛkstrəˌvərt] *n* : extrovertido *m*, -da *f*
extroverted [ˈɛkstrəˌvərt̬əd] *adj* : extrovertido
extrude [ɪkˈstru:d, ɛk-] *vt* **-truded; -truding** : extrudir, expulsar
exuberance [ɪgˈzu:bərənts, ɛg-] *n* **1** JOYOUSNESS : euforia *f*, exaltación *f* **2** VIGOR : exuberancia *f*, vigor *m*
exuberant [ɪgˈzu:bərənt, ɛg-] *adj* **1** JOYOUS : eufórico **2** LUSH : exuberante — **exuberantly** *adv*
exude [ɪgˈzu:d, ɛg-] *vt* **-uded; -uding 1** OOZE : rezumar, exudar **2** EMANATE : emanar, irradiar
exult [ɪgˈzʌlt, ɛg-] *vi* : exultar, regocijarse
exultant [ɪgˈzʌltənt, ɛg-] *adj* : exultante, jubiloso — **exultantly** *adv*
exultation [ˌɛksəlˈteɪʃən, ˌɛgzəl-] *n* : exultación *f*, júbilo *m*, alborozo *m*
eye¹ [ˈaɪ] *vt* **eyed; eyeing** *or* **eying** : mirar, observar
eye² *n* **1** : ojo *m* **2** VISION : visión *f*, vista *f*, ojo *m* ⟨a good eye for bargains : un buen ojo para las gangas⟩ **3** GLANCE : mirada *f*, ojeada *f* **4** ATTENTION : atención *f* ⟨to catch one's eye : llamar la atención⟩ **5** POINT OF VIEW : punto *m* de vista ⟨in the eyes of the law : según la ley⟩ **6** : ojo *m* (de una aguja, una papa, una tormenta)
eyeball [ˈaɪˌbɔl] *n* : globo *m* ocular
eyebrow [ˈaɪˌbraʊ] *n* : ceja *f*
eyedropper [ˈaɪˌdrɑpər] *n* : cuentagotas *f*
eyeglasses [ˈaɪˌglæsəz] *npl* : anteojos *mpl*, lentes *mpl*, espejuelos *mpl*, gafas *fpl*
eyelash [ˈaɪˌlæʃ] *n* : pestaña *f*
eyelet [ˈaɪlət] *n* : ojete *m*
eyelid [ˈaɪˌlɪd] *n* : párpado *m*
eye–opener [ˈaɪˌo:pənər] *n* : revelación *f*, sorpresa *f*
eye–opening [ˈaɪˌo:pənɪŋ] *adj* : revelador
eyepiece [ˈaɪˌpi:s] *n* : ocular *m*
eyesight [ˈaɪˌsaɪt] *n* : vista *f*, visión *f*
eyesore [ˈaɪˌsor] *n* : monstruosidad *f*, adefesio *m*
eyestrain [ˈaɪˌstreɪn] *n* : fatiga *f* visual, vista *f* cansada
eyetooth [ˈaɪˌtu:θ] *n* : colmillo *m*
eyewitness [ˈaɪˈwɪtnəs] *n* : testigo *mf* ocular, testigo *mf* presencial
eyrie [ˈaɪri] → **aerie**

F

f [ˈɛf] *n, pl* **f's** *or* **fs** [ˈɛfs] : sexta letra del alfabeto inglés
fable [ˈfeɪbəl] *n* : fábula *f*
fabled [ˈfeɪbəld] *adj* : legendario, fabuloso
fabric [ˈfæbrɪk] *n* **1** MATERIAL : tela *f*, tejido *m* **2** STRUCTURE : estructura *f* ⟨the fabric of society : la estructura de la sociedad⟩
fabricate [ˈfæbrɪˌkeɪt] *vt* **-cated; -cating 1** CONSTRUCT, MANUFACTURE : construir, fabricar **2** INVENT : inventar (excusas o mentiras)
fabrication [ˌfæbrɪˈkeɪʃən] *n* **1** LIE : mentira *f*, invención *f* **2** MANUFACTURE : fabricación *f*
fabulous [ˈfæbjələs] *adj* **1** LEGENDARY : fabuloso, legendario **2** INCREDIBLE : increíble, fabuloso ⟨fabulous wealth : riqueza fabulosa⟩ **3** WONDERFUL : magnífico, estupendo, fabuloso — **fabulously** *adv*
facade [fəˈsɑd] *n* : fachada *f*
face¹ [ˈfeɪs] *v* **faced; facing** *vt* **1** LINE : recubrir (una superficie), forrar (ropa) **2** CONFRONT : enfrentarse a, afrontar, hacer frente a ⟨to face the music : afrontar las consecuencias⟩ ⟨to face the facts : aceptar la realidad⟩ **3** : estar de cara a, estar enfrente de ⟨she's facing her brother : está de cara a su hermano⟩ **4** OVERLOOK : dar a — *vi* : mirar (hacia), estar orientado (a)
face² *n* **1** : cara *f*, rostro *m* ⟨he told me to my face : me lo dijo a la cara⟩ **2** EXPRESSION : cara *f*, expresión *f* ⟨to pull a long face : poner mala cara⟩ **3** GRIMACE : mueca *f* ⟨to make faces : hacer muecas⟩ **4** APPEARANCE : fisonomía *f*, aspecto *m* ⟨the face of society : la fisonomía de la sociedad⟩ **5** EFFRONTERY : desfachatez *f* **6** PRESTIGE : prestigio *m* ⟨to lose face : desprestigiarse⟩ **7** FRONT, SIDE : cara *f* (de una moneda), esfera *f* (de un reloj), fachada *f* (de un edificio), pared *f* (de una montaña) **8** SURFACE : superficie *f*, faz *f* (de la tierra), cara *f* (de la luna) **9 in the face of** DESPITE : en medio de, en visto de, ante
facedown [ˈfeɪsˌdaʊn] *adv* : boca abajo
faceless [ˈfeɪsləs] *adj* ANONYMOUS : anónimo
face–lift [ˈfeɪsˌlɪft] *n* **1** : estiramiento *m*

facial 2 RENOVATION : renovación *f*, remozamiento *m*

facet [ˈfæsət] *n* **1** : faceta *f* (de una piedra) **2** ASPECT : faceta *f*, aspecto *m*

facetious [fəˈsiːʃəs] *adj* : gracioso, burlón, bromista

facetiously [fəˈsiːʃəsli] *adv* : en tono de burla

facetiousness [fəˈsiːʃəsnəs] *n* : jocosidad *f*

face–to–face *adv & adj* : cara a cara

faceup [ˈfeɪsˈʌp] *adv* : boca arriba

face value *n* : valor *m* nominal

facial[1] [ˈfeɪʃəl] *adj* : de la cara, facial

facial[2] *n* : tratamiento *m* facial, limpieza *f* de cutis

facile [ˈfæsəl] *adj* SUPERFICIAL : superficial, simplista

facilitate [fəˈsɪləˌteɪt] *vt* **-tated; -tating** : facilitar

facility [fəˈsɪləṭi] *n, pl* **-ties** **1** EASE : facilidad *f* **2** CENTER, COMPLEX : centro *m*, complejo *m* **3 facilities** *npl* AMENITIES : comodidades *fpl*, servicios *mpl*

facing [ˈfeɪsɪŋ] *n* **1** LINING : entretela *f* (de una prenda) **2** : revestimiento *m* (de un edificio)

facsimile [fækˈsɪməli] *n* : facsímile *m*, facsímil *m*

fact [ˈfækt] *n* **1** : hecho *m* ⟨as a matter of fact : de hecho⟩ **2** INFORMATION : información *f*, datos *mpl* ⟨facts and figures : datos y cifras⟩ **3** REALITY : realidad *f* ⟨in fact : en realidad⟩

faction [ˈfækʃən] *n* : facción *m*, bando *m*

factional [ˈfækʃənəl] *adj* : entre facciones

factious [ˈfækʃəs] *adj* : faccioso, contencioso

factitious [fækˈtɪʃəs] *adj* : artificial, facticio

factor [ˈfæktər] *n* : factor *m*

factory [ˈfæktəri] *n, pl* **-ries** : fábrica *f*

factual [ˈfæktʃʊəl] *adj* : basado en hechos, objetivo

factually [ˈfæktʃʊəli] *adv* : en cuanto a los hechos

faculty [ˈfækəlti] *n, pl* **-ties** **1** : facultad *f* ⟨the faculty of sight : las facultades visuales, el sentido de la vista⟩ **2** APTITUDE : aptitud *f*, facilidad *f* **3** TEACHERS : cuerpo *m* docente

fad [ˈfæd] *n* : moda *f* pasajera, manía *f*

fade [ˈfeɪd] *v* **faded; fading** *vi* **1** WITHER : debilitarse (dícese de las personas), marchitarse (dícese de las flores y las plantas) **2** DISCOLOR : desteñirse, decolorarse **3** DIM : apagarse (dícese de la luz), perderse (dícese de los sonidos), fundirse (dícese de las imágenes) **4** VANISH : desvanecerse, decaer — *vt* DISCOLOR : desteñir

fag [ˈfæg] *vt* **fagged; fagging** EXHAUST : cansar, fatigar

fagot *or* **faggot** [ˈfægət] *n* : haz *m* de leña

Fahrenheit [ˈfærənˌhaɪt] *adj* : Fahrenheit

fail[1] [ˈfeɪl] *vi* **1** WEAKEN : fallar, deteriorarse **2** STOP : fallar, detenerse ⟨his heart failed : le falló el corazón⟩ **3** : fracasar, fallar ⟨her plan failed : su plan fracasó⟩ ⟨the crops failed : se perdió la cosecha⟩ **4** : quebrar ⟨a business about to fail : una empresa a punto de quebrar⟩ **5 to fail in** : faltar a, no cumplir con ⟨to fail in one's duties : faltar a sus deberes⟩ — *vt* **1** FLUNK : reprobar (un examen) **2** : fallar ⟨words fail me : las palabras me fallan, no encuentro palabras⟩ **3** DISAPPOINT : fallar, decepcionar ⟨don't fail me! : ¡no me falles!⟩

fail[2] *n* : fracaso *m*

failing [ˈfeɪlɪŋ] *n* : defecto *m*

failure [ˈfeɪljər] *n* **1** : fracaso *m*, malogro *m* ⟨crop failure : pérdida de la cosecha⟩ ⟨heart failure : insuficiencia cardíaca⟩ ⟨engine failure : falla mecánica⟩ **2** BANKRUPTCY : bancarrota *f*, quiebra *f* **3** : fracaso *m* (persona) ⟨he was a failure as a manager : como gerente, fue un fracaso⟩

faint[1] [ˈfeɪnt] *vi* : desmayarse

faint[2] *adj* **1** COWARDLY, TIMID : cobarde, tímido **2** DIZZY : mareado ⟨faint with hunger : desfallecido de hambre⟩ **3** SLIGHT : leve, ligero, vago ⟨I haven't the faintest idea : no tengo la más mínima idea⟩ **4** INDISTINCT : tenue, indistinto, apenas perceptible

faint[3] *n* : desmayo *m*

fainthearted [ˈfeɪntˈhɑrṭəd] *adj* : cobarde, pusilánime

faintly [ˈfeɪntli] *adv* : débilmente, ligeramente, levemente

faintness [ˈfeɪntnəs] *n* **1** INDISTINCTNESS : lo débil, falta *f* de claridad **2** FAINTING : desmayo *m*, desfallecimiento *m*

fair[1] [ˈfær] *adj* **1** ATTRACTIVE, BEAUTIFUL : bello, hermoso, atractivo **2** (*relating to weather*) : bueno, despejado ⟨fair weather : tiempo despejado⟩ **3** JUST : justo, imparcial **4** ALLOWABLE : permisible **5** BLOND, LIGHT : rubio (dícese del pelo), blanco (dícese de la tez) **6** ADEQUATE : bastante, adecuado ⟨fair to middling : mediano, regular⟩ **7 fair game** : presa *f* fácil **8 to play fair** : jugar limpio

fair[2] *n* : feria *f*

fairground [ˈfærˌgraʊnd] *n* : parque *m* de diversiones

fairly [ˈfærli] *adv* **1** IMPARTIALLY : imparcialmente, limpiamente, equitativamente **2** QUITE : bastante **3** MODERATELY : medianamente

fairness [ˈfærnəs] *n* **1** IMPARTIALITY : imparcialidad *f*, justicia *f* **2** LIGHTNESS : blancura *f* (de la piel), lo rubio (del pelo)

fairy [ˈfæri] *n, pl* **fairies** **1** : hada *f* **2 fairy tale** : cuento *m* de hadas

fairyland [ˈfæriˌlænd] *n* **1** : país *m* de las hadas **2** : lugar *m* encantador

faith [ˈfeɪθ] *n, pl* **faiths** [ˈfeɪθs, ˈfeɪðz] **1** BELIEF : fe *f* **2** ALLEGIANCE : lealtad *f* **3** CONFIDENCE, TRUST : confianza *f*, fe *f* **4** RELIGION : religión *f*

faithful [ˈfeɪθfəl] *adj* : fiel — **faithfully** *adv*

faithfulness [ˈfeɪθfəlnəs] *n* : fidelidad *f*

faithless [ˈfeɪθləs] *adj* **1** DISLOYAL : desleal **2** : infiel (en la religión) — **faithlessly** *adv*

faithlessness [ˈfeɪθləsnəs] *n* : deslealtad *f*

fake[1] [ˈfeɪk] *v* **faked; faking** *vt* **1** FALSIFY : falsificar, falsear **2** FEIGN : fingir — *vi* **1** PRETEND : fingir **2** : hacer un engaño, hacer una finta (en deportes)

fake[2] *adj* : falso, fingido, postizo

fake[3] *n* **1** IMITATION : imitación *f*, falsificación *f* **2** IMPOSTOR : impostor *m*, -tora *f*; charlatán *m*, -tana *f*; farsante *mf* **3** FEINT : engaño *m*, finta *f* (en deportes)

faker [ˈfeɪkər] *n* : impostor *m*, -tora *f*; charlatán *m*, -tana *f*; farsante *mf*

fakir [fəˈkɪr, ˈfeɪkər] *n* : faquir *m*

falcon [ˈfælkən, ˈfɔl-] *n* : halcón *m*

falconry [ˈfælkənri, ˈfɔl-] *n* : cetrería *f*

fall[1] [ˈfɔl] *vi* **fell** [ˈfɛl]; **fallen** [fɔlən]; **falling** **1** : caer, caerse ⟨to fall out of bed : caer de la cama⟩ ⟨to fall down : caerse⟩ **2** HANG : caer **3** DESCEND : caer (dícese de la lluvia o de la noche), bajar (dícese de los precios), descender (dícese de la temperatura) **4** : caer (a un enemigo), rendirse ⟨the city fell : la ciudad se rindió⟩ **5** OCCUR : caer ⟨Christmas falls on a Friday : la Navidad cae en viernes⟩ **6 to fall asleep** : dormirse, quedarse dormido **7 to fall from grace** SIN : perder la gracia **8 to fall sick** : caer enfermo, enfermarse **9 to fall through** : fracasar, caer en la nada **10 to fall to** : tocar a, corresponder a ⟨the task fell to him : le tocó hacerlo⟩

fall[2] *n* **1** TUMBLE : caída *f* ⟨to break one's fall : frenar uno su caída⟩ ⟨a fall of three feet : una caída de tres pies⟩ **2** FALLING : derrumbe *m* (de rocas), aguacero *m* (de lluvia), nevada *f* (de nieve), bajada *f* (de precios), disminución *f* (de cantidades) **3** AUTUMN : otoño *m* **4** DOWNFALL : caída *f*, ruina *f* **5 falls** *npl* WATERFALL : cascada *f*, catarata *f*

fallacious [fəˈleɪʃəs] *adj* : erróneo, engañoso, falaz

fallacy [ˈfæləsi] *n, pl* **-cies** : falacia *f*

fall back *vi* **1** RETREAT : retirarse, replegarse **2 to fall back on** : recurrir a

fall guy *n* SCAPEGOAT : chivo *m* expiatorio

fallible [ˈfæləbəl] *adj* : falible

fallout [ˈfɔl,aʊt] *n* **1** : lluvia *f* radioactiva **2** CONSEQUENCES : secuelas *fpl*, consecuencias *fpl*

fallow[1] [ˈfælo] *vt* : barbechar

fallow[2] *adj* **to lie fallow** : estar en barbecho

fallow[3] *n* : barbecho *m*

false [ˈfɔls] *adj* **falser; falsest** **1** UNTRUE : falso **2** ERRONEOUS : erróneo, equivocado **3** FAKE : falso, postizo **4** UNFAITHFUL : infiel **5** FRAUDULENT : fraudulento ⟨under false pretenses : por fraude⟩

falsehood [ˈfɔls,hʊd] *n* : mentira *f*, falsedad *f*

falsely [ˈfɔlsli] *adv* : falsamente, con falsedad

falseness [ˈfɔlsnəs] *n* : falsedad *f*

falsetto [fɔlˈsɛt̬o:] *n, pl* **-tos** : falsete *m*

falsification [ˌfɔlsəfəˈkeɪʃən] *n* : falsificación *f*, falseamiento *m*

falsify [ˈfɔlsə,faɪ] *vt* **-fied; fying** : falsificar, falsear

falsity [ˈfɔlsət̬i] *n, pl* **-ties** : falsedad *f*

falter [ˈfɔltər] *vi* **-tered; -tering** **1** TOTTER : tambalearse **2** STAMMER : titubear, tartamudear **3** WAVER : vacilar

faltering [ˈfɔltərɪŋ] *adj* : titubeante, vacilante

fame [ˈfeɪm] *n* : fama *f*

famed [ˈfeɪmd] *adj* : famoso, célebre, afamado

familial [fəˈmɪljəl, -liəl] *adj* : familiar

familiar[1] [fəˈmɪljər] *adj* **1** KNOWN : familiar, conocido ⟨to be familiar with : estar familiarizado con⟩ **2** INFORMAL : familiar, informal **3** INTIMATE : íntimo, de confianza **4** FORWARD : confianzudo, atrevido — **familiarly** *adv*

familiar[2] *n* : espíritu *m* guardián

familiarity [fə,mɪliˈærət̬i, -ˌmɪlˈjær-] *n, pl* **-ties** **1** KNOWLEDGE : conocimiento *m*, familiaridad *f* **2** INFORMALITY, INTIMACY : confianza *f*, familiaridad *f* **3** FORWARDNESS : exceso *m* de confianza, descaro *m*

familiarize [fəˈmɪljə,raɪz] *vt* **-ized; -izing** **1** : familiarizar **2 to familiarize oneself** : familiarizarse

family [ˈfæmli, ˈfæmə-] *n, pl* **-lies** : familia *f*

family room *n* : living *m*, sala *f* (informal)

family tree *n* : árbol *m* genealógico

famine [ˈfæmən] *n* : hambre *f*, hambruna *f*

famish [ˈfæmɪʃ] *vi* **to be famished** : estar famélico, estar hambriento, morir de hambre *fam*

famous [ˈfeɪməs] *adj* : famoso

famously [ˈfeɪməsli] *adv* **to get on famously** : llevarse de maravilla

fan[1] [ˈfæn] *vt* **fanned; fanning** **1** : abanicar (a una persona), avivar (un fuego) **2** STIMULATE : avivar, estimular

fan[2] *n* **1** : ventilador *m*, abanico *m* **2** ADMIRER, ENTHUSIAST : aficionado *m*, -da *f*; entusiasta *mf*; admirador *m*, -dora *f*

fanatic[1] [fəˈnæt̬ɪk] *or* **fanatical** [-t̬ɪ-kəl] *adj* : fanático

fanatic[2] *n* : fanático *m*, -ca *f*

fanaticism [fəˈnæṭəˌsɪzəm] *n* : fanatismo *m*
fanciful [ˈfæn*t*sɪfəl] *adj* **1** CAPRICIOUS : caprichoso, fantástico, extravagante **2** IMAGINATIVE : imaginativo — **fancifully** *adv*
fancy¹ [ˈfæn*t*si] *vt* **-cied; -cying 1** IMAGINE : imaginarse, figurarse ⟨fancy that! : ¡figúrate!, ¡imagínate!⟩ **2** CRAVE : apetecer, tener ganas de
fancy² *adj* **-cier; -est 1** ELABORATE : elaborado **2** LUXURIOUS : lujoso, elegante — **fancily** [ˈfæn*t*səli] *adv*
fancy³ *n, pl* **-cies 1** LIKING : gusto *m*, afición *f* **2** WHIM : antojo *m*, capricho *m* **3** IMAGINATION : fantasía *f*, imaginación *f*
fandango [fænˈdæŋgo] *n, pl* **-gos** : fandango *m*
fanfare [ˈfænˌfær] *n* : fanfarria *f*
fang [ˈfæŋ] *n* : colmillo *m* (de un animal), diente *m* (de una serpiente)
fanlight [ˈfænˌlaɪt] *n* : tragaluz *m*
fantasia [fænˈteɪʒə, -ziə; ˌfæntəˈziːə] *n* : fantasía *f*
fantasize [ˈfæntəˌsaɪz] *vi* **-sized; -sizing** : fantasear
fantastic [fænˈtæstɪk] *adj* **1** UNBELIEVABLE : fantástico, increíble, extraño **2** ENORMOUS : fabuloso, inmenso ⟨fantastic sums : sumas fabulosas⟩ **3** WONDERFUL : estupendo, fantástico, bárbaro *fam*, macanudo *fam* — **fantastically** [-tɪkli] *adv*
fantasy [ˈfæntəsi] *n, pl* **-sies** : fantasía *f*
far¹ [ˈfɑr] *adv* **farther** [ˈfɑrðər] *or* **further** [ˈfər-]; **farthest** *or* **furthest** [-ðəst] **1** : lejos ⟨far from here : lejos de aquí⟩ ⟨to go far : llegar lejos⟩ ⟨as far as Chicago : hasta Chicago⟩ ⟨far away : a lo lejos⟩ **2** MUCH : muy, mucho ⟨far bigger : mucho más grande⟩ ⟨far superior : muy superior⟩ ⟨it's by far the best : es con mucho el mejor⟩ **3** (*expressing degree or extent*) ⟨the results are far off : salieron muy inexactos los resultados⟩ ⟨to go so far as : decir tanto como⟩ ⟨to go far enough : tener el alcance necesario⟩ **4** (*expressing progress*) ⟨the work is far advanced : el trabajo está muy avanzado⟩ ⟨to take (something) too far : llevar (algo) demasiado lejos⟩ **5 far and wide** : por todas partes **6 far from it!** : ¡todo lo contrario! **7 so far** : hasta ahora, todavía
far² *adj* **farther** *or* **further; farthest** *or* **furthest 1** REMOTE : lejano, remoto ⟨the Far East : el Lejano Oriente, el Extremo Oriente⟩ ⟨a far country : un país lejano⟩ **2** LONG : largo ⟨a far journey : un viaje largo⟩ **3** EXTREME : extremo ⟨the far right : la extrema derecha⟩ ⟨at the far end of the room : en el otro extremo de la sala⟩
faraway [ˈfɑrəˌweɪ] *adj* : remoto, lejano
farce [ˈfɑrs] *n* : farsa *f*
farcical [ˈfɑrsɪkəl] *adj* : absurdo, ridículo
fare¹ [ˈfær] *vi* **fared; faring** : ir, salir ⟨how did you fare? : ¿cómo te fue?⟩
fare² *n* **1** : pasaje *m*, billete *m*, boleto *m* ⟨half fare : medio pasaje⟩ **2** FOOD : comida *f*
farewell¹ [færˈwɛl] *adj* : de despedida
farewell² *n* : despedida *f*
far–fetched [ˈfɑrˈfɛtʃt] *adj* : improbable, exagerado
farina [fəˈriːnə] *n* : harina *f*
farm¹ [ˈfɑrm] *vt* **1** : cultivar, labrar **2** : criar (animales) — *vi* : ser agricultor
farm² *n* : granja *f*, hacienda *f*, finca *f*, estancia *f*
farmer [ˈfɑrmər] *n* : agricultor *m*, granjero *m*
farmhand [ˈfɑrmˌhænd] *n* : peón *m*
farmhouse [ˈfɑrmˌhaʊs] *n* : granja *f*, vivienda *f* del granjero, casa *f* de hacienda
farming [ˈfɑrmɪŋ] *n* : labranza *f*, cultivo *m*, crianza *f* (de animales)
farmland [ˈfɑrmˌlænd] *n* : tierras *fpl* de labranza
farmyard [ˈfɑrmˌjɑrd] *n* : corral *m*
far–off [ˈfɑrˌɔf, -ˈɔf] *adj* : remoto, distante, lejano
far–reaching [ˈfɑrˈriːtʃɪŋ] *adj* : de gran alcance
farsighted [ˈfɑrˌsaɪṭəd] *adj* **1** : hipermétrope **2** JUDICIOUS : con visión de futuro, previsor, precavido
farsightedness [ˈfɑrˌsaɪṭədnəs] *n* **1** : hipermetropía *f* **2** PRUDENCE : previsión *f*
farther¹ [ˈfɑrðər] *adv* **1** AHEAD : más lejos (en el espacio), más adelante (en el tiempo) **2** MORE : más
farther² *adj* : más lejano, más remoto
farthermost [ˈfɑrðərˌmoːst] *adj* : (el) más lejano
farthest¹ [ˈfɑrðəst] *adv* **1** : lo más lejos ⟨I jumped farthest : salté lo más lejos⟩ **2** : lo más avanzado ⟨he progressed farthest : progresó al punto más avanzado⟩ **3** : más ⟨the farthest developed plan : el plan más desarrollado⟩
farthest² *adj* : más lejano
fascicle [ˈfæsɪkəl] *n* : fascículo *m*
fascinate [ˈfæsənˌeɪt] *vt* **-nated; -nating** : fascinar, cautivar
fascinating [ˈfæsənˌeɪṭɪŋ] *adj* : fascinante
fascination [ˌfæsənˈeɪʃən] *n* : fascinación *f*
fascism [ˈfæʃˌɪzəm] *n* : fascismo *m*
fascist¹ [ˈfæʃɪst] *adj* : fascista
fascist² *n* : fascista *mf*
fashion¹ [ˈfæʃən] *vt* : formar, moldear
fashion² *n* **1** MANNER : manera *f*, modo *m* **2** CUSTOM : costumbre *f* **3** STYLE : moda *f*
fashionable [ˈfæʃənəbəl] *adj* : de moda, chic
fashionably [ˈfæʃənəbli] *adv* : a la moda
fast¹ [ˈfæst] *vi* : ayunar
fast² *adv* **1** SECURELY : firmemente, seguramente ⟨to hold fast : agarrarse

bien⟩ **2** RAPIDLY : rápidamente, rápido, de prisa **3 to run fast** : ir adelantado (dícese de un reloj) **4** SOUNDLY : profundamente ⟨fast asleep : profundamente dormido⟩
fast[3] *adj* **1** SECURE : firme, seguro ⟨to make fast : amarrar (un barco)⟩ **2** FAITHFUL : leal ⟨fast friends : amigos leales⟩ **3** RAPID : rápido, veloz **4** : adelantado ⟨my watch is fast : tengo el reloj adelantado⟩ **5** DEEP : profundo ⟨a fast sleep : un sueño profundo⟩ **6** COLORFAST : inalterable, que no destiñe **7** DISSOLUTE : extravagante, disipado, disoluto
fast[4] *n* : ayuno *m*
fasten [ˈfæsən] *vt* **1** ATTACH : sujetar, atar **2** FIX : fijar ⟨to fasten one's eyes on : fijar los ojos en⟩ **3** SECURE : abrochar (ropa o cinturones), atar (cordones), cerrar (una maleta) — *vi* : abrocharse, cerrar
fastener [ˈfæsənər] *n* : cierre *m*, sujetador *m*
fastening [ˈfæsənɪŋ] *n* : cierre *m*, sujetador *m*
fast food *n* : comida *f* rápida
fastidious [fæsˈtɪdiəs] *adj* : quisquilloso, exigente — **fastidiously** *adv*
fat[1] [ˈfæt] *adj* **fatter; fattest** **1** OBESE : gordo, obeso **2** THICK : grueso
fat[2] *n* : grasa *f*
fatal [ˈfeɪt̬əl] *adj* **1** DEADLY : mortal **2** ILL-FATED : malhadado, fatal **3** MOMENTOUS : fatídico
fatalism [ˈfeɪt̬əlˌɪzəm] *n* : fatalismo *m*
fatalist [ˈfeɪt̬əlɪst] *n* : fatalista *mf*
fatalistic [ˌfeɪt̬əlˈɪstɪk] *adj* : fatalista
fatality [feɪˈtæləṭi, fə-] *n, pl* **-ties** : víctima *f* mortal
fatally [ˈfeɪt̬əli] *adv* : mortalmente
fate [ˈfeɪt] *n* **1** DESTINY : destino *m* **2** END, LOT : final *m*, suerte *f*
fated [ˈfeɪt̬əd] *adj* : predestinado
fateful [ˈfeɪtfəl] *adj* **1** MOMENTOUS : fatídico, aciago **2** PROPHETIC : profético — **fatefully** *adv*
father[1] [ˈfɑðər] *vt* : engendrar
father[2] *n* **1** : padre *m* ⟨my father and my mother : mi padre y mi madre⟩ ⟨Father Smith : el padre Smith⟩ **2 the Father** GOD : el Padre, Dios *m*
fatherhood [ˈfɑðərˌhʊd] *n* : paternidad *f*
father-in-law [ˈfɑðərɪnˌlɔ] *n, pl* **fathers-in-law** : suegro *m*
fatherland [ˈfɑðərˌlænd] *n* : patria *f*
fatherless [ˈfɑðərləs] *adj* : huérfano de padre, sin padre
fatherly [ˈfɑðərli] *adj* : paternal
fathom[1] [ˈfæðəm] *vt* UNDERSTAND : entender, comprender
fathom[2] *n* : braza *f*
fatigue[1] [fəˈtiːg] *vt* **-tigued; -tiguing** : fatigar, cansar
fatigue[2] *n* : fatiga *f*
fatness [ˈfætnəs] *n* : gordura *f* (de una persona o un animal), grosor *m* (de un objeto)
fatten [ˈfætən] *vt* : engordar, cebar
fatty [ˈfæṭi] *adj* **fattier; -est** : graso, grasoso, adiposo (dícese de los tejidos)
fatuous [ˈfætʃʊəs] *adj* : necio, fatuo — **fatuously** *adv*
faucet [ˈfɔsət] *n* : llave *f*, canilla *f Arg, Uru*, grifo *m*
fault[1] [ˈfɔlt] *vt* : encontrar defectos a
fault[2] *n* **1** SHORTCOMING : defecto *m*, falta *f* **2** DEFECT : falta *f*, defecto *m*, falla *f* **3** BLAME : culpa *f* **4** FRACTURE : falla *f* (geológica)
faultfinder [ˈfɔltˌfaɪndər] *n* : criticón *m*, -cona *f*
faultfinding [ˈfɔltˌfaɪndɪŋ] *n* : crítica *f*
faultless [ˈfɔltləs] *adj* : sin culpa, sin imperfecciones, impecable
faultlessly [ˈfɔltləsli] *adv* : impecablemente, perfectamente
faulty [ˈfɔlti] *adj* **faultier; -est** : defectuoso, imperfecto — **faultily** [ˈfɔltəli] *adv*
fauna [ˈfɔnə] *n* : fauna *f*
faux [ˈfoː] *adj* : de imitación
faux pas [ˌfoːˈpɑ] *n, pl* **faux pas** [*same or* -ˈpɑz] : metedura *f* de pata *fam*
favor[1] [ˈfeɪvər] *vt* **1** SUPPORT : estar a favor de, ser partidario de, apoyar **2** OBLIGE : hacerle un favor a **3** PREFER : preferir **4** RESEMBLE : parecerse a, salir a
favor[2] *n* : favor *m* ⟨in favor of : a favor de⟩ ⟨an error in his favor : un error a su favor⟩
favorable [ˈfeɪvərəbəl] *adj* : favorable, propicio
favorably [ˈfeɪvərəbli] *adv* : favorablemente, bien
favorite[1] [ˈfeɪvərət] *adj* : favorito, preferido
favorite[2] *n* : favorito *m*, -ta *f*; preferido *m*, -da *f*
favoritism [ˈfeɪvərəˌtɪzəm] *n* : favoritismo *m*
fawn[1] [ˈfɔn] *vi* : adular, lisonjear
fawn[2] *n* : cervato *m*
fax [ˈfæks] *n* : facsímil *m*, facsímile *m*
faze [ˈfeɪz] *vt* **fazed; fazing** : desconcertar, perturbar
fear[1] [ˈfɪr] *vt* : temer, tener miedo de — *vi* : temer
fear[2] *n* : miedo *m*, temor *m* ⟨for fear of : por temor a⟩
fearful [ˈfɪrfəl] *adj* **1** FRIGHTENING : espantoso, aterrador, horrible **2** FRIGHTENED : temeroso, miedoso
fearfully [ˈfɪrfəli] *adv* **1** EXTREMELY : extremadamente, terriblemente **2** TIMIDLY : con temor
fearless [ˈfɪrləs] *adj* : intrépido, impávido
fearlessly [ˈfɪrləsli] *adv* : sin temor
fearlessness [ˈfɪrləsnəs] *n* : intrepidez *f*, impavidez *f*
fearsome [ˈfɪrsəm] *adj* : aterrador
feasibility [ˌfiːzəˈbɪləṭi] *n* : viabilidad *f*, factibilidad *f*
feasible [ˈfiːzəbəl] *adj* : viable, factible, realizable

feast[1] [ˈfiːst] *vi* : banquetear — *vt* **1** : agasajar, festejar **2 to feast one's eyes on** : regalarse la vista con

feast[2] *n* **1** BANQUET : banquete *m*, festín *m* **2** FESTIVAL : fiesta *f*

feat [ˈfiːt] *n* : proeza *f*, hazaña *f*

feather[1] [ˈfɛðər] *vt* **1** : emplumar **2 to feather one's nest** : hacer su agosto

feather[2] *n* **1** : pluma *f* **2 a feather in one's cap** : un triunfo personal

feathered [ˈfɛðərd] *adj* : con plumas

feathery [ˈfɛðəri] *adj* **1** DOWNY : plumoso **2** LIGHT : liviano

feature[1] [ˈfiːʧər] *v* **-tured; -turing** *vt* **1** IMAGINE : imaginarse **2** PRESENT : presentar — *vi* : figurar

feature[2] *n* **1** CHARACTERISTIC : característica *f*, rasgo *m* **2** : largometraje *m* (en el cine), artículo *m* (en un periódico), documental *m* (en la televisión) **3 features** *npl* : rasgos *mpl*, facciones *fpl* ⟨delicate features : facciones delicadas⟩

February [ˈfɛbjʊˌri, ˈfɛbʊ-, ˈfbrʊ-] *n* : febrero *m*

fecal [ˈfiːkəl] *adj* : fecal

feces [ˈfiːˌsiːz] *npl* : heces *fpl*, excrementos *mpl*

feckless [ˈfɛkləs] *adj* : irresponsable

fecund [ˈfɛkənd, ˈfiː-] *adj* : fecundo

fecundity [fɪˈkʌndəṯi, fɛ-] *n* : fecundidad *f*

federal [ˈfɛdrəl, -dərəl] *adj* : federal

federalism [ˈfɛdrəˌlɪzəm, -dərə-] *n* : federalismo *m*

federalist[1] [ˈfɛdrəlɪst, -dərə-] *adj* : federalista

federalist[2] *n* : federalista *mf*

federate [ˈfɛdəˌreɪt] *vt* **-ated; -ating** : federar

federation [ˌfɛdəˈreɪʃən] *n* : federación *f*

fedora [fɪˈdorə] *n* : sombrero *m* flexible de fieltro

fed up *adj* : harto

fee [ˈfiː] *n* **1** : honorarios *mpl* (a un médico, un abogado, etc.) **2 entrance fee** : entrada *f*

feeble [ˈfiːbəl] *adj* **-bler; -blest 1** WEAK : débil, endeble **2** INEFFECTIVE : flojo, pobre, poco convincente

feebleminded [ˌfiːbəlˈmaɪndəd] *adj* **1** : débil mental **2** FOOLISH, STUPID : imbécil, tonto

feebleness [ˈfiːbəlnəs] *n* : debilidad *f*

feebly [ˈfiːbli] *adv* : débilmente

feed[1] [ˈfiːd] *v* **fed** [ˈfɛd]; **feeding** *vt* **1** : dar de comer a, nutrir, alimentar (a una persona) **2** : alimentar (un fuego o una máquina), proveer (información), introducir (datos) — *vi* : comer, alimentarse

feed[2] *n* **1** NOURISHMENT : alimento *m* **2** FODDER : pienso *m*

feedback [ˈfiːdˌbæk] *n* **1** : realimentación *f* (electrónica) **2** RESPONSE : reacción *f*

feeder [ˈfiːdər] *n* : comedero *m* (para animales)

feel[1] [ˈfiːl] *v* **felt** [ˈflt]; **feeling** *vi* **1** : sentirse, encontrarse ⟨I feel tired : me siento cansada⟩ ⟨he feels hungry : tiene hambre⟩ ⟨she feels like a fool : se siente como una idiota⟩ ⟨to feel like doing something : tener ganas de hacer algo⟩ **2** SEEM : parecer ⟨it feels like spring : parece primavera⟩ **3** THINK : parecerse, opinar, pensar ⟨how does he feel about that? : ¿qué opina él de eso?⟩ — *vt* **1** TOUCH : tocar, palpar **2** SENSE : sentir ⟨to feel the cold : sentir el frío⟩ **3** CONSIDER : sentir, creer, considerar ⟨to feel (it) necessary : creer necesario⟩

feel[2] *n* **1** SENSATION, TOUCH : sensación *f*, tacto *m* **2** ATMOSPHERE : ambiente *m*, atmósfera *f* **3 to have a feel for** : tener un talento especial para

feeler [ˈfiːlər] *n* : antena *f*, tentáculo *m*

feeling [ˈfiːlɪŋ] *n* **1** SENSATION : sensación *f*, sensibilidad *f* **2** EMOTION : sentimiento *m* **3** OPINION : opinión *f* **4 feelings** *npl* SENSIBILITIES : sentimientos *mpl* ⟨to hurt someone's feelings : herir los sentimientos de alguien⟩

feet → **foot**

feign [ˈfeɪn] *vt* : simular, aparentar, fingir

feint[1] [ˈfeɪnt] *vi* : fintar, fintear

feint[2] *n* : finta *f*

feldspar [ˈfɛl*d*ˌspɑr] *n* : feldespato *m*

felicitate [fɪˈlɪsəˌteɪt] *vt* **-tated; -tating** : felicitar, congratular

felicitation [fɪˌlɪsəˈteɪʃən] *n* : felicitación *f*

felicitous [fɪˈlɪsəṯəs] *adj* : acertado, oportuno

feline[1] [ˈfiːˌlaɪn] *adj* : felino

feline[2] *n* : felino *m*, -na *f*

fell[1] [ˈfɛl] *vt* : talar (un árbol), derribar (a una persona)

fell[2] → **fall**

fellow [ˈfɛˌloː] *n* **1** COMPANION : compañero *m*, -ra *f*; camarada *mf* **2** ASSOCIATE : socio *m*, -cia *f* **3** MAN : tipo *m*, hombre *m*

fellowman [ˌfɛloˈmæn] *n, pl* **-men** : prójimo *m*, semejante *m*

fellowship [ˈfɛloˌʃɪp] *n* **1** COMPANIONSHIP : camaradería *f*, compañerismo *m* **2** ASSOCIATION : fraternidad *f* **3** GRANT : beca *f* (de investigación)

felon [ˈfɛlən] *n* : malhechor *m*, -chora *f*; criminal *mf*

felonious [fəˈloːniəs] *adj* : criminal

felony [ˈfɛləni] *n, pl* **-nies** : delito *m* grave

felt[1] [ˈfɛlt] *n* : fieltro *m*

felt[2] → **feel**

female[1] [ˈfiːˌmeɪl] *adj* : femenino

female[2] *n* **1** : hembra *f* (de animal) **2** WOMAN : mujer *f*

feminine [ˈfɛmənən] *adj* : femenino

femininity [ˌfɛməˈnɪnəṯi] *n* : feminidad *f*, femineidad *f*

feminism [ˈfɛməˌnɪzəm] *n* : feminismo *m*

feminist[1] [ˈfɛmənɪst] *adj* : feminista

feminist[2] *n* : feminista *mf*

femoral [ˈfɛmərəl] *adj* : femoral
femur [ˈfi:mər] *n, pl* **femurs** *or* **femora** [ˈfɛmərə] : fémur *m*
fence[1] [ˈfɛnts] *v* **fenced; fencing** *vt* : vallar, cercar — *vi* : hacer esgrima
fence[2] *n* : cerca *f*, valla *f*, cerco *m*
fencer [ˈfɛntsər] *n* : esgrimista *mf*; esgrimidor *m*, -dora *f*
fencing [ˈfɛntsɪŋ] *n* **1** : esgrima *m* (deporte) **2** : materiales *mpl* para cercas **3** ENCLOSURE : cercado *m*
fend [ˈfɛnd] *vt* **to fend off** : rechazar (un enemigo), parar (un golpe), eludir (una pregunta) — *vi* **to fend for oneself** : arreglárselas sólo, valerse por sí mismo
fender [ˈfɛndər] *n* : guardabarros *mpl*, salpicadera *f Mex*
fennel [ˈfɛnəl] *n* : hinojo *m*
ferment[1] [fərˈmɛnt] *v* : fermentar
ferment[2] [ˈfərˌmɛnt] *n* **1** : fermento *m* (en la química) **2** TURMOIL : agitación *f*, conmoción *f*
fermentation [ˌfərmənˈteɪʃən, -ˌmɛn-] *n* : fermentación *f*
fern [ˈfərn] *n* : helecho *m*
ferocious [fəˈro:ʃəs] *adj* : feroz — **ferociously** *adv*
ferociousness [fəˈro:ʃəsnəs] *n* : ferocidad *f*
ferocity [fəˈrɑsət̬i] *n* : ferocidad *f*
ferret[1] [ˈfɛrət] *vi* SNOOP : hurgar, husmear — *vt* **to ferret out** : descubrir
ferret[2] *n* : hurón *m*
ferric [ˈfɛrɪk] *or* **ferrous** [ˈfɛrəs] *adj* : férrico
Ferris wheel [ˈfɛrɪs] *n* : noria *f*
ferry[1] [ˈfɛri] *vt* **-ried; -rying** : llevar, transportar
ferry[2] *n, pl* **-ries** : transbordador *m*, ferry *m*
ferryboat [ˈfɛriˌbo:t] *n* : transbordador *m*, ferry *m*
fertile [ˈfərt̬əl] *adj* : fértil, fecundo
fertility [fərˈtɪlət̬i] *n* : fertilidad *f*
fertilization [ˌfərt̬ələˈzeɪʃən] *n* : fertilización *f* (del suelo), fecundación (de un huevo)
fertilize [ˈfərt̬əlˌaɪz] *vt* **-ized; -izing 1** : fecundar (un huevo) **2** : fertilizar, abonar (el suelo)
fertilizer [ˈfərt̬əlˌaɪzər] *n* : fertilizante *m*, abono *m*
fervent [ˈfərvənt] *adj* : ferviente, fervoroso, ardiente — **fervently** *adv*
fervid [ˈfərvɪd] *adj* : ardiente, apasionado — **fervidly** *adv*
fervor [ˈfərvər] *n* : fervor *m*, ardor *m*
fester [ˈfɛstər] *vi* : enconarse, supurar
festival [ˈfɛstəvəl] *n* : fiesta *f*, festividad *f*, festival *m*
festive [ˈfɛstɪv] *adj* : festivo — **festively** *adv*
festivity [fɛsˈtɪvət̬i] *n, pl* **-ties** : festividad *f*, celebración *f*
festoon[1] [fɛsˈtu:n] *vt* : adornar, engalanar
festoon[2] *n* GARLAND : guirnalda *f*
fetal [ˈfi:t̬əl] *adj* : fetal
fetch [ˈfɛtʃ] *vt* **1** BRING : traer, recoger, ir a buscar **2** REALIZE : realizar, venderse por ⟨the jewelry fetched $10,000 : las joyas se vendieron por $10,000⟩
fetching [ˈfɛtʃɪŋ] *adj* : atractivo, encantador
fête[1] [ˈfeɪt, ˈfɛt] *vt* **fêted; fêting** : festejar, agasajar
fête[2] *n* : fiesta *f*
fetid [ˈfɛt̬əd] *adj* : fétido
fetish [ˈfɛt̬ɪʃ] *n* : fetiche *m*
fetlock [ˈfɛtˌlɑk] *n* : espolón *m*
fetter [ˈfɛt̬ər] *vt* : encadenar, poner grillos a
fetters [ˈfɛt̬ərz] *npl* : grillos *mpl*, grilletes *mpl*, cadenas *fpl*
fettle [ˈfɛt̬əl] *n* **in fine fettle** : en buena forma, en plena forma
fetus [ˈfi:t̬əs] *n* : feto *m*
feud[1] [ˈfju:d] *vi* : pelear, contender
feud[2] *n* : contienda *f*, enemistad *f* (heredada)
feudal [ˈfju:dəl] *adj* : feudal
feudalism [ˈfju:dəlˌɪzəm] *n* : feudalismo *m*
fever [ˈfi:vər] *n* : fiebre *f*, calentura *f*
feverish [ˈfi:vərɪʃ] *adj* **1** : afiebrado, con fiebre, febril **2** FRANTIC : febril, frenético
few[1] [ˈfju:] *adj* : pocos ⟨with few exceptions : con pocas excepciones⟩ ⟨a few times : varias veces⟩
few[2] *pron* **1** : pocos ⟨few (of them) were ready : pocos estaban listos⟩ **2 a few** : algunos, unos cuantos **3 few and far between** : contados
fewer [ˈfju:ər] *pron* : menos ⟨the fewer the better : cuantos menos mejor⟩
fez [ˈfɛz] *n, pl* **fezzes** : fez *m*
fiancé [ˌfi:ˌɑnˈseɪ, ˌfi:ˈɑnˌseɪ] *n* : prometido *m*, novio *m*
fiancée [ˌfi:ˌɑnˈseɪ, ˌfi:ˈɑnˌseɪ] *n* : prometida *f*, novia *f*
fiasco [fiˈæsˌko:] *n, pl* **-coes** : fiasco *m*, fracaso *m*
fiat [ˈfi:ˌɑt, -ˌæt, -ət; ˈfaɪət, -ˌæt] *n* : decreto *m*, orden *m*
fib[1] [ˈfɪb] *vi* **fibbed; fibbing** : decir mentirillas
fib[2] *n* : mentirilla *f*, bola *f fam*
fibber [ˈfɪbər] *n* : mentirosillo *m*, -lla *f*; cuentista *mf fam*
fiber *or* **fibre** [ˈfaɪbər] *n* : fibra *f*
fiberboard [ˈfaɪbərˌbord] *n* : cartón *m* madera
fiberglass [ˈfaɪbərˌglæs] *n* : fibra *f* de vidrio
fibrillate [ˈfɪbrəˌleɪt, ˈfaɪ-] *vi* **-lated; -lating** : fibrilar
fibrillation [ˌfɪbrəˈleɪʃən, ˌfaɪ-] *n* : fibrilación *f*
fibrous [ˈfaɪbrəs] *adj* : fibroso
fibula [ˈfɪbjələ] *n, pl* **-lae** [-ˌli:, -ˌlaɪ] *or* **-las** : peroné *m*
fickle [ˈfɪkəl] *adj* : inconstante, voluble, veleidoso
fickleness [ˈfɪkəlnəs] *n* : volubilidad *f*, inconstancia *f*, veleidad *f*

fiction ['fɪkʃən] *n* : ficción *f*
fictional ['fɪkʃənəl] *adj* : ficticio
fictitious [fɪk'tɪʃəs] *adj* **1** IMAGINARY : ficticio, imaginario **2** FALSE : falso, ficticio
fiddle[1] ['fɪdəl] *vi* **-dled; -dling 1** : tocar el violín **2 to fiddle with** : juguetear con, toquetear
fiddle[2] *n* : violín *m*
fiddler ['fɪdlər, 'fɪdələr] *n* : violinista *mf*
fiddlesticks ['fɪdəl,stɪks] *interj* : ¡tonterías!
fidelity [fə'dɛləṭi, faɪ-] *n, pl* **-ties** : fidelidad *f*
fidget[1] ['fɪʤət] *vi* **1** : moverse, estarse inquieto **2 to fidget with** : juguetear con
fidget[2] *n* **1** : persona *f* inquieta **2 fidgets** *npl* RESTLESSNESS : inquietud *f*
fidgety ['fɪʤəṭi] *adj* : inquieto
fiduciary[1] [fə'du:ʃi,ɛri, -'dju:-, -ʃəri] *adj* : fiduciario
fiduciary[2] *n, pl* **-ries** : fiduciario *m*, -ria *f*
field[1] ['fi:ld] *vt* : interceptar y devolver (una pelota), presentar (un candidato), sortear (una pregunta)
field[2] *adj* : de campaña, de campo ⟨field hospital : hospital de campaña⟩ ⟨field goal : gol de campo⟩ ⟨field trip : viaje de estudio⟩
field[3] *n* **1** : campo *m* (de cosechas, de batalla, de magnetismo) **2** : campo *m*, cancha *f* (en deportes) **3** : campo *m* (de trabajo), esfera *f* (de actividades)
fielder ['fi:ldər] *n* : jugador *m*, -dora *f* de campo; fildeador *m*, -dora *f*
field glasses *n* : binoculares *mpl*, gemelos *mpl*
fiend ['fi:nd] *n* **1** DEMON : demonio *m* **2** EVILDOER : persona *f* maligna; malvado *m*, -da *f* **3** FANATIC : fanático *m*, -ca *f*
fiendish ['fi:ndɪʃ] *adj* : diabólico — **fiendishly** *adv*
fierce ['fɪrs] *adj* **fiercer; -est 1** FEROCIOUS : fiero, feroz **2** HEATED : acalorado **3** INTENSE : intenso, violento, fuerte — **fiercely** *adv*
fierceness ['fɪrsnəs] *n* **1** FEROCITY : ferocidad *f*, fiereza *f* **2** INTENSITY : intensidad *f*, violencia *f*
fieriness ['faɪərinəs] *n* : pasión *f*, ardor *m*
fiery ['faɪəri] *adj* **fierier; -est 1** BURNING : ardiente, llameante **2** GLOWING : encendido **3** PASSIONATE : acalorado, ardiente, fogoso
fiesta [fi'ɛstə] *n* : fiesta *f*
fife ['faɪf] *n* : pífano *m*
fifteen[1] [fɪf'ti:n] *adj* : quince
fifteen[2] *n* : quince *m*
fifteenth[1] [fɪf'ti:nθ] *adj* : decimoquinto
fifteenth[2] *n* **1** : decimoquinto *m*, -ta *f* (en una serie) **2** : quinceavo *m*, quinceava parte *f*
fifth[1] ['fɪfθ] *adj* : quinto
fifth[2] *n* **1** : quinto *m*, -ta *f* (en una serie) **2** : quinto *m*, quinta parte *f* **3** : quinta *f* (en la música)
fiftieth[1] ['fɪftiəθ] *adj* : quincuagésimo
fiftieth[2] *n* **1** : quincuagésimo *m*, -ma *f* (en una serie) **2** : cincuentavo *m*, cincuentava parte *f*
fifty[1] ['fɪfti] *adj* : cincuenta
fifty[2] *n, pl* **-ties** : cincuenta *m*
fifty–fifty[1] [,fɪfti'fɪfti] *adv* : a medias, mitad y mitad
fifty–fifty[2] *adj* **to have a fifty–fifty chance** : tener un cincuenta por ciento de posibilidades
fig ['fɪg] *n* : higo *m*
fight[1] ['faɪt] *v* **fought** ['fɔt]; **fighting** *vi* : luchar, combatir, pelear — *vt* : luchar contra, combatir contra
fight[2] *n* **1** COMBAT : lucha *f*, pelea *f*, combate *m* **2** MATCH : pelea *f*, combate *m* (en boxeo) **3** QUARREL : disputa *f*, pelea *f*, pleito *m*
fighter ['faɪṭər] *n* **1** COMBATANT : luchador *m*, -dora *f*; combatiente *mf* **2** BOXER : boxeador *m*, -dora *f*
figment ['fɪgmənt] *n* **figment of the imagination** : producto *m* de la imaginación
figurative ['fɪgjərəṭɪv, -gə-] *adj* : figurado, metafórico
figuratively ['fɪgjərəṭɪvli, -gə-] *adv* : en sentido figurado, de manera metafórica
figure[1] ['fɪgjər, -gər] *v* **-ured; -uring** *vt* **1** CALCULATE : calcular **2** ESTIMATE : figurarse, calcular ⟨he figured it was possible : se figuró que era posible⟩ — *vi* **1** FEATURE, STAND OUT : figurar, destacar **2 that figures!** : ¡obvio!, ¡no me extraña nada!
figure[2] *n* **1** DIGIT : número *m*, cifra *f* **2** PRICE : precio *m*, cifra *f* **3** PERSONAGE : figura *f*, personaje *m* **4** : figura *f*, tipo *m*, físico *m* ⟨to have a good figure : tener buen tipo, tener un buen físico⟩ **5** DESIGN, OUTLINE : figura *f* **6 figures** *npl* : aritmética *f*
figurehead ['fɪgjər,hɛd, -gər-] *n* : testaferro *m*, líder *mf* sin poder
figure of speech *n* : figura *f* retórica, figura *f* de hablar
figure out *vt* **1** UNDERSTAND : entender **2** RESOLVE : resolver (un problema, etc.)
figurine [,fɪgjə'ri:n] *n* : estatuilla *f*
Fijian ['fi:ʤiən, fɪ'ji:ən] *n* : fijiano *m*, -na *f* — **Fijian** *adj*
filament ['fɪləmənt] *n* : filamento *m*
filbert ['fɪlbərt] *n* : avellana *f*
filch ['fɪlʧ] *vt* : hurtar, birlar *fam*
file[1] ['faɪl] *v* **filed; filing** *vt* **1** CLASSIFY : clasificar **2** : archivar (documentos) **3** SUBMIT : presentar ⟨to file charges : presentar cargos⟩ **4** SMOOTH : limar — *vi* : desfilar, entrar (o salir) en fila
file[2] *n* **1** : lima *f* ⟨nail file : lima de uñas⟩ **2** DOCUMENTS : archivo *m* **3** LINE : fila *f*

filial ['fɪliəl, 'fɪljəl] *adj* : filial

filibuster[1] ['fɪlə,bʌstər] *vi* : practicar el obstruccionismo

filibuster[2] *n* : obstruccionismo *m*

filibusterer ['fɪlə,bʌstərər] *n* : obstruccionista *mf*

filigree ['fɪlə,gri:] *n* : filigrana *f*

Filipino [,fɪlə'pi:no:] *n* : filipino *m*, -na *f* — **Filipino** *adj*

fill[1] ['fɪl] *vt* **1** : llenar, ocupar ⟨to fill a cup : llenar una taza⟩ ⟨to fill a room : ocupar una sala⟩ **2** STUFF : rellenar **3** PLUG : tapar, rellenar, empastar (un diente) **4** SATISFY : cumplir con, satisfacer **5** *or* **to fill out** : llenar, re- llenar ⟨to fill out a form : rellenar un formulario⟩

fill[2] *n* **1** FILLING, STUFFING : relleno *m* **2 to eat one's fill** : comer lo suficiente **3 to have one's fill of** : estar harto de

filler ['fɪlər] *n* : relleno *m*

fillet[1] ['fɪlət, fɪ'leɪ, 'fɪ,leɪ] *vt* : cortar en filetes

fillet[2] *n* : filete *m*

fill in *vt* INFORM : informar, poner al corriente — *vi* **to fill in for** : reemplazar a

filling ['fɪlɪŋ] *n* **1** : relleno *m* **2** : empaste *m* (de un diente)

filling station → **gas station**

filly ['fɪli] *n, pl* **-lies** : potra *f*, potranca *f*

film[1] ['fɪlm] *vt* : filmar — *vi* : rodar

film[2] *n* **1** COATING : capa *f*, película *f* **2** : película *f* (fotográfica) **3** MOVIE : película *f*, filme *m*

filmmaker ['fɪlm,meɪkər] *n* : cineasta *mf*

filmy ['fɪlmi] *adj* **filmier; -est 1** GAUZY : diáfano, vaporoso **2** : cubierto de una película

filter[1] ['fɪltər] *vt* : filtrar

filter[2] *n* : filtro *m*

filth ['fɪlθ] *n* : mugre *f*, porquería *f*, roña *f*

filthiness ['fɪlθinəs] *n* : suciedad *f*

filthy ['fɪlθi] *adj* **filthier; -est 1** DIRTY : mugriento, sucio **2** OBSCENE : obsceno, indecente

filtration [fɪl'treɪʃən] *n* : filtración *f*

fin ['fɪn] *n* **1** : aleta *f* **2** : alerón *m* (de un automóvil o un avión)

finagle [fə'neɪgəl] *vt* **-gled; -gling** : arreglárselas para conseguir

final[1] ['faɪnəl] *adj* **1** DEFINITIVE : definitivo, final, inapelable **2** ULTIMATE : final **3** LAST : último, final

final[2] *n* **1** : final *f* (en deportes) **2 finals** *npl* : exámenes *mpl* finales

finale [fɪ'næli, -'nɑ-] *n* : final *m* ⟨grand finale : final triunfal⟩

finalist ['faɪnəlɪst] *n* : finalista *mf*

finality [faɪ'næləṭi, fə-] *n, pl* **-ties** : finalidad *f*

finalize ['faɪnəl,aɪz] *vt* **-ized; -izing** : finalizar

finally ['faɪnəli] *adv* **1** LASTLY : por último, finalmente **2** EVENTUALLY : por fin, al final **3** DEFINITIVELY : definitivamente

finance[1] [fə'nænts, 'faɪ,nænts] *vt* **-nanced; -nancing** : financiar

finance[2] *n* **1** : finanzas *fpl* **2 finances** *npl* RESOURCES : recursos *mpl* financieros

financial [fə'næntʃəl, faɪ-] *adj* : financiero, económico

financially [fə'næntʃəli, faɪ-] *adv* : económicamente

financier [,fɪnən'sɪr, ,faɪ,næn-] *n* : financiero *m*, -ra *f*; financista *mf*

financing [fə'næntsɪŋ, 'fæɪ,næntsɪŋ] *n* : financiación *f*, financiamiento *m*

finch ['fɪntʃ] *n* : pinzón *m*

find[1] ['faɪnd] *vt* **found** ['faʊnd]; **finding 1** LOCATE : encontrar, hallar ⟨I can't find it : no lo encuentro⟩ ⟨to find one's way : encontrar el camino, orientarse⟩ **2** DISCOVER, REALIZE : descubrir, darse cuenta de ⟨he found it difficult : descubrió que era difícil⟩ **3** DECLARE : declarar, hallar ⟨they found him guilty : lo declararon culpable⟩

find[2] *n* : hallazgo *m*

finder ['faɪndər] *n* : descubridor *m*, -dora *f*

finding ['faɪndɪŋ] *n* **1** FIND : hallazgo *m* **2 findings** *npl* : conclusiones *fpl*

find out *vt* DISCOVER : descubrir, averiguar — *vi* LEARN : enterarse

fine[1] ['faɪn] *vt* **fined; fining** : multar

fine[2] *adj* **finer; -est 1** PURE : puro (dícese del oro y de la plata) **2** THIN : fino, delgado **3** : fino ⟨fine sand : arena fina⟩ **4** SMALL : pequeño, minúsculo ⟨fine print : letras minúsculas⟩ **5** SUBTLE : sutil, delicado **6** EXCELLENT : excelente, magnífico, selecto **7** FAIR : bueno ⟨it's a fine day : hace buen tiempo⟩ **8** EXQUISITE : exquisito, delicado, fino **9 fine arts** : bellas artes *fpl*

fine[3] *n* : multa *f*

finely ['faɪnli] *adv* **1** EXCELLENTLY : con arte **2** ELEGANTLY : elegantemente **3** PRECISELY : con precisión **4 to chop finely** : picar muy fino, picar en trozos pequeños

fineness ['faɪnnəs] *n* **1** EXCELLENCE : excelencia *f* **2** ELEGANCE : elegancia *f*, refinamiento *m* **3** DELICACY : delicadeza *f*, lo fino **4** PRECISION : precisión *f* **5** SUBTLETY : sutileza *f* **6** PURITY : ley *f* (de oro y plata)

finery ['faɪnəri] *n* : galas *fpl*, adornos *mpl*

finesse[1] [fə'nɛs] *vt* **-nessed; -nessing** : ingeniar

finesse[2] *n* **1** REFINEMENT : refinamiento *m*, finura *f* **2** TACT : delicadeza *f*, tacto *m*, diplomacia *f* **3** CRAFTINESS : astucia *f*

finger[1] ['fɪŋgər] *vt* **1** HANDLE : tocar, toquetear **2** ACCUSE : acusar, delatar

finger[2] *n* : dedo *m*

fingerling ['fɪŋgərlɪŋ] *n* : pez *m* pequeño y joven

fingernail ['fɪŋgər,neɪl] *n* : uña *f*

fingerprint[1] ['fɪŋgər,prɪnt] *vt* : tomar las huellas digitales a

fingerprint² *n* : huella *f* digital
fingertip [ˈfɪŋgərˌtɪp] *n* : punta *f* del dedo, yema *f* del dedo
finicky [ˈfɪnɪki] *adj* : maniático, melindroso, mañoso
finish¹ [ˈfɪnɪʃ] *vt* **1** COMPLETE : acabar, terminar **2** : aplicar un acabado a (muebles, etc.)
finish² *n* **1** END : fin *m*, final *m* **2** REFINEMENT : refinamiento *m* **3** : acabado *m* ⟨a glossy finish : un acabado brillante⟩
finite [ˈfaɪˌnaɪt] *adj* : finito
fink [ˈfɪŋk] *n* : mequetrefe *mf fam*
Finn [ˈfɪn] *n* : finlandés *m*, -desa *f*
Finnish¹ [ˈfɪnɪʃ] *adj* : finlandés
Finnish² *n* : finlandés *m* (idioma)
fiord [fiˈɔrd] → **fjord**
fir [ˈfər] *n* : abeto *m*
fire¹ [ˈfaɪr] *vt* **fired; firing 1** IGNITE, KINDLE : encender **2** ENLIVEN : animar, avivar **3** DISMISS : despedir **4** SHOOT : disparar **5** BAKE : cocer (cerámica)
fire² *n* **1** : fuego *m* **2** BURNING : incendio *m* ⟨fire alarm : alarma contra incendios⟩ ⟨to be on fire : estar en llamas⟩ **3** ENTHUSIASM : ardor *m*, entusiasmo *m* **4** SHOOTING : disparos *mpl*, fuego *m*
firearm [ˈfaɪrˌɑrm] *n* : arma *f* de fuego
fireball [ˈfaɪrˌbɔl] *n* **1** : bola *f* de fuego **2** METEOR : bólido *m*
firebreak [ˈfaɪrˌbreɪk] *n* : cortafuegos *m*
firebug [ˈfaɪrˌbʌg] *n* : pirómano *m*, -na *f*; incendiario *m*, -ria *f*
firecracker [ˈfaɪrˌkrækər] *n* : petardo *m*
fire escape *n* : escalera *f* de incendios
firefighter [ˈfaɪrˌfaɪṭər] *n* : bombero *m*, -ra *f*
firefly [ˈfaɪrˌflaɪ] *n, pl* **-flies** : luciérnaga *f*
fireman [ˈfaɪrmən] *n, pl* **-men** [-mən, -ˌmɛn] **1** FIREFIGHTER : bombero *m*, -ra *f* **2** STOKER : fogonero *m*, -ra *f*
fireplace [ˈfaɪrˌpleɪs] *n* : hogar *m*, chimenea *f*
fireproof¹ [ˈfaɪrˌpruːf] *vt* : hacer incombustible
fireproof² *adj* : incombustible, ignífugo
fireside¹ [ˈfaɪrˌsaɪd] *adj* : informal ⟨fireside chat : charla informal⟩
fireside² *n* **1** HEARTH : chimenea *f*, hogar *m* **2** HOME : hogar *m*, casa *f*
firewall [ˈfaɪrˌwɔl] *n* : cortafuegos *m*
firewood [ˈfaɪrˌwʊd] *n* : leña *f*
fireworks [ˈfaɪrˌwərks] *npl* : fuegos *mpl* artificiales, pirotecnia *f*
firm¹ [ˈfərm] *vt or* **to firm up** : endurecer
firm² *adj* **1** VIGOROUS : fuerte, vigoroso **2** SOLID, UNYIELDING : firme, duro, sólido **3** UNCHANGING : firme, inalterable **4** RESOLUTE : firme, resuelto
firm³ *n* : empresa *f*, firma *f*, compañía *f*
firmament [ˈfərməmənt] *n* : firmamento *m*
firmly [ˈfərmli] *adv* : firmemente
firmness [ˈfərmnəs] *n* : firmeza *f*
first¹ [ˈfərst] *adv* **1** : primero ⟨finish your homework first : primero termina tu tarea⟩ ⟨first and foremost : ante todo⟩ ⟨first of all : en primer lugar⟩ **2** : por primera vez ⟨I saw it first in Boston : lo vi por primera vez en Boston⟩
first² *adj* **1** : primero ⟨the first time : la primera vez⟩ ⟨at first sight : a primera vista⟩ ⟨in the first place : en primer lugar⟩ ⟨the first ten applicants : los diez primeros candidatos⟩ **2** FOREMOST : principal, primero ⟨first tenor : tenor principal⟩
first³ *n* **1** : primero *m*, -ra *f* **2** *or* **first gear** : primera *f* **3 at ~** : al principio
first aid *n* : primeros auxilios *mpl*
first–class¹ [ˈfərstˈklæs] *adv* : en primera ⟨to travel first-class : viajar en primera⟩
first–class² *adj* : de primera
first class *n* : primera clase *f*
firsthand¹ [ˈfərstˈhænd] *adv* : directamente
firsthand² *adj* : de primera mano
first lieutenant *n* : teniente *mf*; teniente primero *m*, teniente primera *f*
firstly [ˈfərstli] *adv* : primeramente, principalmente, en primer lugar
first–rate¹ [ˈfərstˈreɪt] *adv* : muy bien
first–rate² *adj* : de primera, de primera clase
first sergeant *n* : sargento *mf*
firth [ˈfərθ] *n* : estuario *m*
fiscal [ˈfɪskəl] *adj* : fiscal — **fiscally** *adv*
fish¹ [ˈfɪʃ] *vi* **1** : pescar **2 to fish for** SEEK : buscar, rebuscar ⟨to fish for compliments : andar a la caza de cumplidos⟩ — *vt* : pescar
fish² *n, pl* **fish** *or* **fishes** : pez *m* (vivo), pescado *m* (para comer)
fisherman [ˈfɪʃərmən] *n, pl* **-men** [-mən, -ˌmɛn] : pescador *m*, -dora *f*
fishery [ˈfɪʃəri] *n, pl* **-eries 1** → **fishing 2** : zona *f* pesquera, pesquería *f*
fishhook [ˈfɪʃˌhʊk] *n* : anzuelo *m*
fishing [ˈfɪʃɪŋ] *n* : pesca *f*, industria *f* pesquera
fishing pole *n* : caña *f* de pescar
fish market *n* : pescadería *f*
fishy [ˈfɪʃi] *adj* **fishier; -est 1** : a pescado ⟨a fishy taste : un sabor a pescado⟩ **2** QUESTIONABLE : dudoso, sospechoso ⟨there's something fishy going on : aquí hay gato encerrado⟩
fission [ˈfɪʃən, -ʒən] *n* : fisión *f*
fissure [ˈfɪʃər] *n* : fisura *f*, hendidura *f*
fist [ˈfɪst] *n* : puño *m*
fistful [ˈfɪstˌfʊl] *n* : puñado *m*
fisticuffs [ˈfɪstɪˌkʌfs] *npl* : lucha *f* a puñetazos
fit¹ [ˈfɪt] *v* **fitted; fitting** *vt* **1** MATCH : corresponder a, coincidir con ⟨the punishment fits the crime : el castigo corresponde al crimen⟩ **2** : quedar ⟨the dress doesn't fit me : el vestido no me queda⟩ **3** GO : caber, encajar en ⟨her key fits the lock : su llave encaja en la cerradura⟩ **4** INSERT, INSTALL : poner, colocar **5** ADAPT : adecuar, ajustar, adaptar **6** *or* **to fit out** EQUIP : equipar

— *vi* **1** : quedar, entallar ⟨these pants don't fit : estos pantalones no me quedan⟩ **2** CONFORM : encajar, cuadrar **3 to fit in** : encajar, estar integrado

fit[2] *adj* **fitter; fittest** **1** SUITABLE : adecuado, apropiado, conveniente **2** QUALIFIED : calificado, competente **3** HEALTHY : sano, en forma

fit[3] *n* **1** ATTACK : ataque *m*, acceso *m*, arranque *m* **2 to be a good fit** : quedar bien **3 to be a tight fit** : ser muy entallado (de ropa), estar apretado (de espacios)

fitful ['fɪtfəl] *adj* : irregular, intermitente — **fitfully** *adv*

fitness ['fɪtnəs] *n* **1** HEALTH : salud *f*, buena forma *f* (física) **2** SUITABILITY : idoneidad *f*

fitting[1] ['fɪtɪŋ] *adj* : adecuado, apropiado

fitting[2] *n* : accesorio *m*

five[1] ['faɪv] *adj* : cinco

five[2] *n* : cinco *m*

five hundred[1] *adj* : quinientos

five hundred[2] *n* : quinientos *m*

fix[1] ['fɪks] *vt* **1** ATTACH, SECURE : sujetar, asegurar, fijar **2** ESTABLISH : fijar, concretar, establecer **3** REPAIR : arreglar, reparar **4** PREPARE : preparar ⟨to fix dinner : preparar la cena⟩ **5** : arreglar, amañar ⟨to fix a race : arreglar una carrera⟩ **6** RIVET : fijar (los ojos, la mirada, etc.)

fix[2] *n* **1** PREDICAMENT : aprieto *m*, apuro *m* **2** : posición *f* ⟨to get a fix on : establecer la posición de⟩

fixate ['fɪk,seɪt] *vi* **-ated; -ating** : obsesionarse

fixation [fɪk'seɪʃən] *n* : fijación *f*, obsesión *f*

fixed ['fɪkst] *adj* **1** STATIONARY : estacionario, inmóvil **2** UNCHANGING : fijo, inalterable **3** INTENT : fijo ⟨a fixed stare : una mirada fija⟩ **4 to be comfortably fixed** : estar en posición acomodada

fixedly ['fɪksədli] *adv* : fijamente

fixedness ['fɪksədnəs, 'fikst-] *n* : rigidez *f*

fixture ['fɪkstʃər] *n* **1** : parte *f* integrante, elemento *m* fijo **2 fixtures** *npl* : instalaciones *fpl* (de una casa)

fizz[1] ['fɪz] *vi* : burbujear

fizz[2] *n* : efervescencia *f*, burbujeo *m*

fizzle[1] ['fɪzəl] *vi* **-zled; -zling** **1** FIZZ : burbujear **2** FAIL : fracasar

fizzle[2] *n* : fracaso *m*, fiasco *m*

fjord [fi'ɔrd] *n* : fiordo *m*

flab ['flæb] *n* : gordura *f*

flabbergast ['flæbər,gæst] *vt* : asombrar, pasmar, dejar atónito

flabby ['flæbi] *adj* **-bier; -est** : blando, fofo, aguado *CA*, *Col*, *Mex*

flaccid ['flæksəd, 'flæsəd] *adj* : fláccido

flag[1] ['flæg] *vi* **flagged; flagging** **1** : hacer señales con banderas **2** WEAKEN : flaquear, desfallecer

flag[2] *n* : bandera *f*, pabellón *m*, estandarte *m*

flagon ['flægən] *n* : jarra *f* grande

flagpole ['flæg,po:l] *n* : asta *f*, mástil *m*

flagrant ['fleɪgrənt] *adj* : flagrante — **flagrantly** *adv*

flagship ['flæg,ʃɪp] *n* : buque *m* insignia

flagstaff ['flæg,stæf] → **flagpole**

flagstone ['flæg,sto:n] *n* : losa *f*, piedra *f*

flail[1] ['fleɪl] *vt* **1** : trillar (grano) **2** : sacudir, agitar (los brazos)

flail[2] *n* : mayal *m*

flair ['flær] *n* : don *m*, facilidad *f*

flak ['flæk] *ns & pl* **1** : fuego *m* antiaéreo **2** CRITICISM : críticas *fpl*

flake[1] ['fleɪk] *vi* **flaked; flaking** : desmenuzarse, pelarse (dícese de la piel)

flake[2] *n* : copo *m* (de nieve), escama *f* (de la piel), astilla *f* (de madera)

flamboyance [flæm'bɔɪən*t*s] *n* : extravagancia *f*, rimbombancia *f*

flamboyant [flæm'bɔɪənt] *adj* : exuberante, extravagante, rimbombante

flame[1] ['fleɪm] *vi* **flamed; flaming** **1** BLAZE : arder, llamear **2** GLOW : brillar, encenderse

flame[2] *n* BLAZE : llama *f* ⟨to burst into flames : estallar en llamas⟩ ⟨to go up in flame : incendiarse⟩

flamethrower ['fleɪm,θro:ər] *n* : lanzallamas *m*

flamingo [flə'mɪŋgo] *n, pl* **-gos** : flamenco *m*

flammable ['flæməbəl] *adj* : inflamable, flamable

flange ['flændʒ] *n* : reborde *m*, pestaña *f*

flank[1] ['flæŋk] *vt* **1** : flanquear (para defender o atacar) **2** BORDER, LINE : bordear

flank[2] *n* : ijada *f* (de un animal), costado *m* (de una persona), falda *f* (de una colina), flanco *m* (de un cuerpo de soldados)

flannel ['flænəl] *n* : franela *f*

flap[1] ['flæp] *v* **flapped; flapping** *vi* **1** : aletear ⟨the bird was flapping (its wings) : el pájaro aleteaba⟩ **2** FLUTTER : ondear, agitarse — *vt* : batir, agitar

flap[2] *n* **1** FLAPPING : aleteo *m*, aletazo *m* (de alas) **2** : soplada *f* (de un sobre), hoja *f* (de una mesa), faldón *m* (de una chaqueta)

flapjack ['flæp,dʒæk] → **pancake**

flare[1] ['flær] *vi* **flared; flaring** **1** FLAME, SHINE : llamear, brillar **2 to flare up** : estallar, explotar (de cólera)

flare[2] *n* **1** FLASH : destello *m* **2** SIGNAL : (luz *f* de) bengala *f* **3 solar flare** : erupción *f* solar

flash[1] ['flæʃ] *vi* **1** SHINE, SPARKLE : destellar, brillar, relampaguear **2** : pasar como un relámpago ⟨an idea flashed through my mind : una idea me cruzó la mente como un relámpago⟩ — *vt* : despedir, lanzar (una luz), transmitir (un mensaje)

flash² *adj* SUDDEN : repentino
flash³ *n* **1** : destello *m* (de luz), fogonazo *m* (de una explosión) **2 flash of lightning** : relámpago *m* **3 in a flash** : de repente, de un abrir y cerrar los ojos
flashback ['flæʃˌbæk] *n* : flashback *m*
flashiness ['flæʃinəs] *n* : ostentación *f*
flashlight ['flæʃˌlaɪt] *n* : linterna *f*
flashy ['flæʃi] *adj* **flashier; -est** : llamativo, ostentoso
flask ['flæsk] *n* : frasco *m*
flat¹ ['flæt] *vt* **flatted; flatting 1** FLATTEN : aplanar, achatar **2** : bajar de tono (en música)
flat² *adv* **1** EXACTLY : exactamente ⟨in ten minutes flat : en diez minutos exactos⟩ **2** : desafinado, demasiado bajo (en la música)
flat³ *adj* **flatter; flattest 1** EVEN, LEVEL : plano, llano **2** SMOOTH : liso **3** DEFINITE : categórico, rotundo, explícito ⟨a flat refusal : una negativa categórica⟩ **4** DULL : aburrido, soso, monótono (dícese la voz) **5** DEFLATED : desinflado, pinchado, ponchado *Mex* **6** : bemol (en música) ⟨to sing flat : cantar desafinado⟩
flat⁴ *n* **1** PLAIN : llano *m*, terreno *m* llano **2** : bemol *m* (en la música) **3** APARTMENT : apartamento *m*, departamento *m* **4** *or* **flat tire** : pinchazo *m*, ponchadura *f Mex*
flatbed ['flætˌbɛd] *n* : camión *m* de plataforma
flatcar ['flætˌkɑr] *n* : vagón *m* abierto
flatfish ['flætˌfɪʃ] *n* : platija *f*
flat-footed ['flætˌfʊṭəd, ˌflæt'-] *adj* : de pies planos
flatly ['flætli] *adv* DEFINITELY : categóricamente, rotundamente
flatness ['flætnəs] *n* **1** EVENNESS : lo llano, lisura *f*, uniformidad *f* **2** DULLNESS : monotonía *f*
flat-out ['flæt'aʊt] *adj* **1** : frenético, a toda máquina ⟨a flat-out effort : un esfuerzo frenético⟩ **2** CATEGORICAL : descarado, rotundo, categórico
flatten ['flætən] *vt* : aplanar, achatar
flatter ['flæṭər] *vt* **1** OVERPRAISE : adular **2** COMPLIMENT : halagar **3** : favorecer ⟨the photo flatters you : la foto te favorece⟩
flatterer ['flæṭərər] *n* : adulador *m*, -dora *f*
flattering ['flæṭərɪŋ] *adj* **1** COMPLIMENTARY : halagador **2** BECOMING : favorecedor
flattery ['flæṭəri] *n, pl* **-ries** : halagos *mpl*
flatulence ['flætʃələnts] *n* : flatulencia *f*, ventosidad *f*
flatulent ['flætʃələnt] *adj* : flatulento
flatware ['flætˌwær] *n* : cubertería *f*, cubiertos *mpl*
flaunt¹ ['flɔnt] *vt* : alardear, hacer alarde de
flaunt² *n* : alarde *m*, ostentación *f*
flavor¹ ['fleɪvər] *vt* : dar sabor a, sazonar
flavor² *n* **1** : gusto *m*, sabor *m* **2** FLAVORING : sazón *f*, condimento *m*
flavorful ['fleɪvərfəl] *adj* : sabroso
flavoring ['fleɪvərɪŋ] *n* : condimento *m*, sazón *f*
flavorless ['fleɪvərləs] *adj* : sin sabor
flaw ['flɔ] *n* : falla *f*, defecto *m*, imperfección *f*
flawed ['flɔd] *adj* : imperfecto, con defectos
flawless ['flɔləs] *adj* : impecable, perfecto — **flawlessly** *adv*
flax ['flæks] *n* : lino *m*
flaxen ['flæksən] *adj* : rubio, blondo (dícese del pelo)
flay ['fleɪ] *vt* **1** SKIN : desollar, despellejar **2** VILIFY : criticar con dureza, vilipendiar
flea ['fli:] *n* : pulga *f*
fleck¹ ['flɛk] *vt* : salpicar
fleck² *n* : mota *f*, pinta *f*
fledgling ['flɛʤlɪŋ] *n* : polluelo *m*, pollito *m*
flee ['fli:] *v* **fled** ['flɛd]; **fleeing** *vi* : huir, escapar(se) — *vt* : huir de
fleece¹ ['fli:s] *vt* **fleeced; fleecing 1** SHEAR : esquilar, trasquilar **2** SWINDLE : estafar, defraudar
fleece² *n* : lana *f*, vellón *m*
fleet¹ ['fli:t] *vi* : moverse con rapidez
fleet² *adj* SWIFT : rápido, veloz
fleet³ *n* : flota *f*
fleet admiral *n* : almirante *mf*
fleeting ['fli:ṭɪŋ] *adj* : fugaz, breve
flesh ['flɛʃ] *n* **1** : carne *f* (de seres humanos y animales) **2** : pulpa *f* (de frutas)
flesh out *vt* : desarrollar, darle cuerpo a
fleshy ['flɛʃi] *adj* **fleshier; -est** : gordo (dícese de las personas), carnoso (dícese de la fruta)
flew → **fly**
flex ['flɛks] *vt* : doblar, flexionar
flexibility [ˌflɛksə'bɪləṭi] *n, pl* **-ties** : flexibilidad *f*, elasticidad *f*
flexible ['flɛksəbəl] *adj* : flexible — **flexibly** [-bli] *adv*
flick¹ ['flɪk] *vt* : dar un capirotazo a (con el dedo) ⟨to flick a switch : darle al interruptor⟩ — *vi* **1** FLIT : revolotear **2 to flick through** : hojear (un libro)
flick² *n* : coletazo *m* (de una cola), capirotazo *m* (de un dedo)
flicker¹ ['flɪkər] *vi* **1** FLUTTER : revolotear, aletear **2** BLINK, TWINKLE : parpadear, titilar
flicker² *n* **1** : parpadeo *m*, titileo *m* **2** HINT, TRACE : indicio *m*, rastro *m* ⟨a flicker of hope : un rayo de esperanza⟩
flier ['flaɪər] *n* **1** AVIATOR : aviador *m*, -dora *f* **2** CIRCULAR : folleto *m* publicitario, circular *f*
flight ['flaɪt] *n* **1** : vuelo *m* (de aves o aviones), trayectoria *f* (de proyectiles) **2** TRIP : vuelo *m* **3** FLOCK, SQUADRON : bandada *f* (de pájaros), escuadrilla *f* (de aviones) **4** ESCAPE : huida *f*, fuga

f **5 flight of fancy** : ilusiones *fpl*, fantasía *f* **6 flight of stairs** : tramo *m*
flight attendant *n* : auxiliar *mf* de vuelo
flightless [ˈflaɪtləs] *adj* : no volador
flighty [ˈflaɪt̬i] *adj* **flightier; -est** : caprichoso, frívolo
flimsy [flɪmzi] *adj* **flimsier; -est 1** LIGHT, THIN : ligero, fino **2** WEAK : endeble, poco sólido **3** IMPLAUSIBLE : pobre, flojo, poco convincente ⟨a flimsy excuse : una excusa floja⟩
flinch [ˈflɪntʃ] *vi* **1** WINCE : estremecerse **2** RECOIL : recular, retroceder
fling[1] [ˈflɪŋ] *vt* **flung** [ˈflʌŋ]; **flinging 1** THROW : lanzar, tirar, arrojar **2 to fling oneself** : lanzarse, tirarse, precipitarse
fling[2] *n* **1** THROW : lanzamiento *m* **2** ATTEMPT : intento *m* **3** AFFAIR : aventura *f* **4** BINGE : juerga *f*
flint [ˈflɪnt] *n* : pedernal *m*
flinty [ˈflɪnti] *adj* **flintier; -est 1** : de pedernal **2** STERN, UNYIELDING : severo, inflexible
flip[1] [ˈflɪp] *v* **flipped; flipping** *vt* **1** TOSS : tirar ⟨to flip a coin : echar a cara o cruz⟩ **2** OVERTURN : dar la vuelta a, voltear — *vi* **1** : moverse bruscamente **2 to flip through** : hojear (un libro)
flip[2] *adj* : insolente, descarado
flip[3] *n* **1** FLICK : capirotazo *m*, golpe *m* ligero **2** SOMERSAULT : voltereta *f*
flip–flop [ˈflɪpˌflɑp] *n* **1** REVERSAL : giro *m* radical **2** THONG : chancla *f*, chancleta *f*
flippancy [ˈflɪpəntsi] *n, pl* **-cies** : ligereza *f*, falta *f* de seriedad
flippant [ˈflɪpənt] *adj* : ligero, frívolo, poco serio
flipper [ˈflɪpər] *n* : aleta *f*
flirt[1] [ˈflərt] *vi* **1** : coquetear, flirtear **2** TRIFLE : jugar ⟨to flirt with death : jugar con la muerte⟩
flirt[2] *n* : coqueto *m*, -ta *f*
flirtation [ˌflərˈteɪʃən] *n* : devaneo *m*, coqueteo *m*
flirtatious [ˌflərˈteɪʃəs] *adj* : insinuante, coqueto
flit [ˈflɪt] *vi* **flitted; flitting 1** : revolotear **2 to flit about** : ir y venir rápidamente
float[1] [ˈfloːt] *vi* **1** : flotar **2** WANDER : vagar, errar — *vt* **1** : poner a flote, hacer flotar (un barco) **2** LAUNCH : hacer flotar (una empresa) **3** ISSUE : emitir (acciones en la bolsa)
float[2] *n* **1** : flotador *m*, corcho *m* (para pescar) **2** BUOY : boya *f* **3** : carroza *f* (en un desfile)
floating [ˈfloːt̬ɪŋ] *adj* : flotante
flock[1] [ˈflɑk] *vi* **1** : moverse en rebaño **2** CONGREGATE : congregarse, reunirse
flock[2] *n* : rebaño *m* (de ovejas), bandada *f* (de pájaros)
floe [ˈfloː] *n* : témpano *m* de hielo
flog [ˈflɑg] *vt* **flogged; flogging** : azotar, fustigar
flood[1] [ˈflʌd] *vt* : inundar, anegar
flood[2] *n* **1** INUNDATION : inundación *f* **2** TORRENT : avalancha *f*, diluvio *m*, torrente *m* ⟨a flood of tears : un mar de lágrimas⟩
floodlight [ˈflʌdˌlaɪt] *n* : foco *m*
floodwater [ˈflʌdˌwɔt̬ər] *n* : crecida *f*, creciente *f*
floor[1] [ˈflor] *vt* **1** : solar, poner suelo a (una casa o una sala) **2** KNOCK DOWN : derribar, echar al suelo **3** NONPLUS : desconcertar, confundir, dejar perplejo
floor[2] *n* **1** : suelo *m*, piso *m* ⟨dance floor : pista de baile⟩ **2** STORY : piso *m*, planta *f* ⟨ground floor : planta baja⟩ ⟨second floor : primer piso⟩ **3** : mínimo *m* (de sueldos, precios, etc.)
floorboard [ˈflorˌbord] *n* : tabla *f* del suelo, suelo *m*, piso *m*
flooring [ˈflorɪŋ] *n* : entarimado *m*
flop[1] [ˈflɑp] *vi* **flopped; flopping 1** FLAP : golpearse, agitarse **2** COLLAPSE : dejarse caer, desplomarse **3** FAIL : fracasar
flop[2] *n* **1** FAILURE : fracaso *m* **2 to take a flop** : caerse
floppy [ˈflɑpi] *adj* **-pier; -est 1** : blando, flexible **2 floppy disk** : diskette *m*, disquete *m*
flora [ˈflorə] *n* : flora *f*
floral [ˈflorəl] *adj* : floral, floreado
florid [ˈflorɪd] *adj* **1** FLOWERY : florido **2** REDDISH : rojizo
florist [ˈflorɪst] *n* : florista *mf*
floss[1] [ˈflɔs] *vi* : limpiarse los dientes con hilo dental
floss[2] *n* **1** : hilo *m* de seda (de bordar) **2 → dental floss**
flotation [floˈteɪʃən] *n* : flotación *f*
flotilla [floˈtɪlə] *n* : flotilla *f*
flotsam [ˈflɑtsəm] *n* **1** : restos *mpl* flotantes (en el mar) **2 flotsam and jetsam** : desechos *mpl*, restos *mpl*
flounce[1] [ˈflaʊnts] *vi* **flounced; flouncing** : moverse haciendo aspavientos ⟨she flounced into the room : entró en la sala haciendo aspavientos⟩
flounce[2] *n* **1** RUFFLE : volante *m* **2** FLOURISH : aspaviento *m*
flounder[1] [ˈflaʊndər] *vi* **1** STRUGGLE : forcejear **2** STUMBLE : no saber qué hacer o decir, perder el hilo (en un discurso)
flounder[2] *n, pl* **flounder** *or* **flounders** : platija *f*
flour[1] [ˈflaʊər] *vt* : enharinar
flour[2] *n* : harina *f*
flourish[1] [ˈflərɪʃ] *vi* THRIVE : florecer, prosperar, crecer (dícese de las plantas) — *vt* BRANDISH : blandir
flourish[2] *n* : floritura *f*, floreo *m*
flourishing [ˈflərɪʃɪŋ] *adj* : floreciente, próspero
flout [ˈflaʊt] *vt* : desacatar, burlarse de
flow[1] [ˈfloː] *vi* **1** COURSE : fluir, manar, correr **2** CIRCULATE : circular, correr ⟨traffic is flowing smoothly : el tránsito está circulando con fluidez⟩

flow² *n* **1** FLOWING : flujo *m*, circulación *f* **2** STREAM : corriente *f*, chorro *m*
flower¹ ['flaʊər] *vi* : florecer, florear
flower² *n* : flor *f*
flowered ['flaʊərd] *adj* : florido, floreado
floweriness ['flaʊərinəs] *n* : floritura *f*
flowering¹ ['flaʊərɪŋ] *adj* : floreciente
flowering² *n* : floración *f*, florecimiento *m*
flowerpot ['flaʊərˌpɑt] *n* : maceta *f*, tiesto *m*, macetero *m*
flowery ['flaʊəri] *adj* **1** : florido **2** FLOWERED : floreado, de flores
flowing ['flo:ɪŋ] *adj* : fluido, corriente
flown → **fly**
flu ['flu:] *n* : gripe *f*, gripa *f Col, Mex*
fluctuate ['flʌktʃʊˌeɪt] *vi* **-ated; -ating** : fluctuar
fluctuation [ˌflʌktʃʊ'eɪʃən] *n* : fluctuación *f*
flue ['flu:] *n* : tiro *m*, salida *f* de humos
fluency ['flu:əntsi] *n* : fluidez *f*, soltura *f*
fluent ['flu:ənt] *adj* : fluido
fluently ['flu:əntli] *adv* : con soltura, con fluidez
fluff¹ ['flʌf] *vt* **1** : mullir ⟨to fluff up the pillows : mullir las almohadas⟩ **2** BUNGLE : echar a perder, equivocarse
fluff² *n* **1** FUZZ : pelusa *f* **2** DOWN : plumón *m*
fluffy ['flʌfi] *adj* **fluffier; -est** **1** DOWNY : lleno de pelusa, velloso **2** SPONGY : esponjoso
fluid¹ ['flu:ɪd] *adj* : fluido
fluid² *n* : fluido *m*, líquido *m*
fluidity [flu'ɪdət̬i] *n* : fluidez *f*
fluid ounce *n* : onza *f* líquida (29.57 mililitros)
fluke ['flu:k] *n* : golpe *m* de suerte, chiripa *f*, casualidad *f*
flung → **fling**
flunk ['flʌŋk] *vt* FAIL : reprobar — *vi* : salir reprobando
fluorescence [ˌflʊr'ɛsənts, ˌflɔr-] *n* : fluorescencia *f*
fluorescent [ˌflʊr'ɛsənt, ˌflɔr-] *adj* : fluorescente
fluoridate ['flɔrəˌdeɪt, 'flʊr-] *vt* **-dated; -dating** : fluorizar
fluoridation [ˌflɔrə'deɪʃən, ˌflʊr-] *n* : fluorización *f*, fluoración *f*
fluoride ['flɔrˌaɪd, 'flʊr-] *n* : fluoruro *m*
fluorine ['flʊrˌi:n] *n* : flúor *m*
fluorocarbon [ˌflɔro'kɑrbən, ˌflʊr-] *n* : fluorocarbono *m*
flurry ['fləri] *n, pl* **-ries** **1** GUST : ráfaga *f* **2** SNOWFALL : nevisca *f* **3** BUSTLE : frenesí *m*, bullicio *m* **4** BARRAGE : aluvión *m*, oleada *f* ⟨a flurry of questions : un aluvión de preguntas⟩
flush¹ ['flʌʃ] *vt* **1** : limpiar con agua ⟨to flush the toilet : jalar la cadena⟩ **2** RAISE : hacer salir, levantar (en la caza) — *vi* BLUSH : ruborizarse, sonrojarse
flush² *adv* : al mismo nivel, a ras
flush³ *adj* **1** *or* **flushed** ['flʌʃt] : colorado, rojo, encendido (dícese de la cara) **2** FILLED : lleno a rebosar **3** ABUNDANT : copioso, abundante **4** AFFLUENT : adinerado **5** ALIGNED, SMOOTH : alineado, liso **6** **flush against** : pegado a, contra
flush⁴ *n* **1** FLOW, JET : chorro *m*, flujo *m* rápido **2** SURGE : arrebato *m*, arranque *m* ⟨a flush of anger : un arrebato de cólera⟩ **3** BLUSH : rubor *m*, sonrojo *m* **4** GLOW : resplandor *m*, flor *f* ⟨the flush of youth : la flor de la juventud⟩ ⟨in the flush of victory : en la euforia del triunfo⟩
fluster¹ ['flʌstər] *vt* : poner nervioso, aturdir
fluster² *n* : agitación *f*, confusión *f*
flute ['flu:t] *n* : flauta *f*
fluted ['flu:t̬əd] *adj* **1** GROOVED : estriado, acanalado **2** WAVY : ondulado
fluting ['flu:t̬ɪŋ] *n* : estrías *fpl*
flutist ['flu:t̬ɪst] *n* : flautista *mf*
flutter¹ ['flʌt̬ər] *vi* **1** : revolotear (dícese de un pájaro), ondear (dícese de una bandera), palpitar con fuerza (dícese del corazón) **2** **to flutter about** : ir y venir, revolotear — *vt* : sacudir, batir
flutter² *n* **1** FLUTTERING : revoloteo *m*, aleteo *m* **2** COMMOTION, STIR : revuelo *m*, agitación *f*
flux ['flʌks] *n* **1** : flujo *m* (en física y medicina) **2** CHANGE : cambio *m* ⟨to be in a state of flux : estar cambiando continuamente⟩
fly¹ ['flaɪ] *v* **flew** ['flu:]; **flown** ['flo:n]; **flying** *vi* **1** : volar (dícese de los pájaros, etc.) **2** TRAVEL : volar (dícese de los aviones), ir en avión (dícese de los pasajeros) **3** FLOAT : flotar, ondear **4** FLEE : huir, escapar **5** RUSH : correr, irse volando **6** PASS : pasar (volando) ⟨how time flies! : ¡cómo pasa el tiempo!⟩ **7** **to fly open** : abrir de golpe — *vt* : pilotar (un avión), hacer volar (una cometa)
fly² *n, pl* **flies** **1** : mosca *f* ⟨to drop like flies : caer como moscas⟩ **2** : bragueta *f* (de pantalones, etc.)
flyer → **flier**
flying saucer *n* : platillo *m* volador
flypaper ['flaɪˌpeɪpər] *n* : papel *m* matamoscas
flyspeck ['flaɪˌspɛk] *n* **1** : excremento *m* de mosca **2** SPECK : motita *f*, puntito *m*
flyswatter ['flaɪˌswɑt̬ər] *n* : matamoscas *m*
flywheel ['flaɪˌhwi:l] *n* : volante *m*
foal¹ ['fo:l] *vi* : parir
foal² *n* : potro *m*, -tra *f*
foam¹ ['fo:m] *vi* : hacer espuma
foam² *n* : espuma *f*
foamy ['fo:mi] *adj* **foamier; -est** : espumoso
focal ['fo:kəl] *adj* **1** : focal, central **2** **focal point** : foco *m*, punto *m* de referencia
fo'c'sle ['fo:ksəl] → **forecastle**

focus[1] [ˈfoːkəs] *v* **-cused** *or* **-cussed; -cusing** *or* **-cussing** *vt* **1** : enfocar (un instrumento) **2** CONCENTRATE : concentrar, centrar — *vi* : enfocar, fijar la vista

focus[2] *n, pl* **-ci** [ˈfoːˌsaɪ, -ˌkaɪ] **1** : foco *m* ⟨to be in focus : estar enfocado⟩ **2** FOCUSING : enfoque *m* **3** CENTER : centro *m*, foco *m*

fodder [ˈfɑdər] *n* : pienso *m*, forraje *m*

foe [ˈfoː] *n* : enemigo *m*, -ga *f*

fog[1] [ˈfɔg, ˈfɑg] *v* **fogged; fogging** *vt* : empañar — *vi* **to fog up** : empañarse

fog[2] *n* : niebla *f*, neblina *f*

foggy [ˈfɔgi, ˈfɑ-] *adj* **foggier; -est** : nebuloso, brumoso

foghorn [ˈfɔgˌhɔrn, ˈfɑg-] *n* : sirena *f* de niebla

fogy [ˈfoːgi] *n, pl* **-gies** : carca *mf fam*, persona *f* chapada a la antigua

foible [ˈfɔɪbəl] *n* : flaqueza *f*, debilidad *f*

foil[1] [ˈfɔɪl] *vt* : frustrar, hacer fracasar

foil[2] *n* **1** : lámina *f* de metal, papel *m* de aluminio **2** CONTRAST : contraste *m*, complemento *m* **3** SWORD : florete *m* (en esgrima)

foist [ˈfɔɪst] *vt* : encajar, endilgar *fam*, colocar

fold[1] [ˈfoːld] *vt* **1** BEND : doblar, plegar **2** CLASP : cruzar (brazos), enlazar (manos), plegar (alas) **3** EMBRACE : estrechar, abrazar **4 to fold in** : incorporar ⟨fold in the cream : incorpore la crema⟩ — *vi* **1** FAIL : fracasar **2 to fold up** : doblarse, plegarse

fold[2] *n* **1** SHEEPFOLD : redil *m* (para ovejas) **2** FLOCK : rebaño *m* ⟨to return to the fold : volver al redil⟩ **3** CREASE : pliegue *m*, doblez *m*

folder [ˈfoːldər] *n* **1** CIRCULAR : circular *f*, folleto *m* **2** BINDER : carpeta *f*

foliage [ˈfoːliɪʤ, -lɪʤ] *n* : follaje *m*

folio [ˈfoːliˌoː] *n, pl* **-lios** : folio *m*

folk[1] [ˈfoːk] *adj* : popular, folklórico ⟨folk customs : costumbres populares⟩ ⟨folk dance : danza folklórica⟩

folk[2] *n, pl* **folk** *or* **folks 1** PEOPLE : gente *f* **2 folks** *npl* : familia *f*, padres *mpl*

folklore [ˈfoːkˌlor] *n* : folklore *m*

folklorist [ˈfoːkˌlorɪst] *n* : folklorista *mf*

folksy [ˈfoːksi] *adj* **folksier; -est** : campechano

follicle [ˈfɑlɪkəl] *n* : folículo *m*

follow [ˈfɑlo] *vt* **1** : seguir ⟨follow the guide : siga al guía⟩ ⟨she followed the road : siguió el camino, continuó por el camino⟩ **2** PURSUE : perseguir, seguir **3** OBEY : seguir, cumplir, observar **4** UNDERSTAND : entender — *vi* **1** : seguir **2** UNDERSTAND : entender **3 it follows that . . .** : se deduce que . . .

follower [ˈfɑloər] *n* : seguidor *m*, -dora *f*

following[1] [ˈfɑloɪŋ] *adj* NEXT : siguiente

following[2] *n* FOLLOWERS : seguidores *mpl*

following[3] *prep* AFTER : después de

follow through *vi* **to follow through with** : continuar con, realizar

follow up *vt* : seguir (una sugerencia, etc.), investigar (una huella)

folly [ˈfɑli] *n, pl* **-lies** : locura *f*, desatino *m*

foment [foˈmɛnt] *vt* : fomentar

fond [ˈfɑnd] *adj* **1** LOVING : cariñoso, tierno **2** PARTIAL : aficionado **3** FERVENT : ferviente, fervoroso

fondle [ˈfɑndəl] *vt* **-dled; -dling** : acariciar

fondly [ˈfɑndli] *adv* : cariñosamente, afectuosamente

fondness [ˈfɑndnəs] *n* **1** LOVE : cariño *m* **2** LIKING : afición *f*

fondue [fɑnˈduː, -ˈdjuː] *n* : fondue *f*

font [ˈfɑnt] *n* **1** *or* **baptismal font** : pila *f* bautismal **2** FOUNTAIN : fuente *f*

food [ˈfuːd] *n* : comida *f*, alimento *m*

food chain *n* : cadena *f* alimenticia

foodstuffs [ˈfuːdˌstʌfs] *npl* : comestibles *mpl*

fool[1] [ˈfuːl] *vi* **1** JOKE : bromear, hacer el tonto **2** TOY : jugar, juguetear ⟨don't fool with the computer : no juegues con la computadora⟩ **3 to fool around** : perder el tiempo ⟨he fools around instead of working : pierde el tiempo en vez de trabajar⟩ — *vt* DECEIVE : engañar, burlar

fool[2] *n* **1** IDIOT : idiota *mf*; tonto *m*, -ta *f*; bobo *m*, -ba *f* **2** JESTER : bufón *m*, -fona *f*

foolhardiness [ˈfuːlˌhɑrdinəs] *n* : imprudencia *f*

foolhardy [ˈfuːlˌhɑrdi] *adj* RASH : imprudente, temerario, precipitado

foolish [ˈfuːlɪʃ] *adj* **1** STUPID : insensato, estúpido **2** SILLY : idiota, tonto

foolishly [ˈfuːlɪʃli] *adv* : tontamente

foolishness [ˈfuːlɪʃnəs] *n* : insensatez *f*, estupidez *f*, tontería *f*

foolproof [ˈfuːlˌpruːf] *adj* : infalible

foot [ˈfʊt] *n, pl* **feet** [ˈfiːt] : pie *m*

footage [ˈfʊt̬ɪʤ] *n* : medida *f* en pies, metraje *m* (en el cine)

football [ˈfʊtˌbɔl] *n* : futbol *m* americano, fútbol *m* americano

footbridge [ˈfʊtˌbrɪʤ] *n* : pasarela *f*, puente *m* peatonal

foothills [ˈfʊtˌhɪlz] *npl* : estribaciones *fpl*

foothold [ˈfʊtˌhoːld] *n* **1** : punto *m* de apoyo **2 to gain a foothold** : afianzarse en una posición

footing [ˈfʊt̬ɪŋ] *n* **1** BALANCE : equilibrio *m* **2** FOOTHOLD : punto *m* de apoyo **3** BASIS : base *f* ⟨on an equal footing : en igualdad⟩

footlights [ˈfʊtˌlaɪts] *npl* : candilejas *fpl*

footlocker [ˈfʊtˌlɑkər] *n* : baúl *m* pequeño, cofre *m*

footloose [ˈfʊtˌluːs] *adj* : libre y sin compromiso

footman [ˈfʊtmən] *n, pl* **-men** [-mən, -ˌmɛn] : lacayo *m*

footnote [ˈfʊtˌnoːt] *n* : nota *f* al pie de la página

footpath [ˈfʊtˌpæθ] *n* : sendero *m*, senda *f*, vereda *f*

footprint [ˈfʊtˌprɪnt] *n* : huella *f*

footrace [ˈfʊtˌreɪs] *n* : carrera *f* pedestre

footrest [ˈfʊtˌrɛst] *n* : apoyapiés *m*, reposapiés *m*

footstep [ˈfʊtˌstɛp] *n* **1** STEP : paso *m* **2** FOOTPRINT : huella *f*

footstool [ˈfʊtˌstuːl] *n* : taburete *m*, escabel *m*

footwear [ˈfʊtˌwær] *n* : calzado *m*

footwork [ˈfʊtˌwərk] *n* : juego *m* de piernas, juego *m* de pies

fop [ˈfɑp] *n* : petimetre *m*, dandi *m*

for[1] [ˈfɔr] *conj* : puesto que, porque

for[2] *prep* **1** (*indicating purpose*) : para, de ⟨clothes for children : ropa para niños⟩ ⟨it's time for dinner : es la hora de comer⟩ **2** BECAUSE OF : por ⟨for fear of : por miedo de⟩ **3** (*indicating a recipient*) : para, por ⟨a gift for you : un regalo para ti⟩ **4** (*indicating support*) : por ⟨he fought for his country : luchó por su patria⟩ **5** (*indicating a goal*) : por, para ⟨a cure for cancer : una cura para el cáncer⟩ ⟨for your own good : por tu propio bien⟩ **6** (*indicating correspondence or exchange*) : por, para ⟨I bought it for $5 : lo compré por $5⟩ ⟨a lot of trouble for nothing : mucha molestia para nada⟩ **7** AS FOR : para, con respecto a **8** (*indicating duration*) : durante, por ⟨he's going for two years : se va por dos años⟩ ⟨I spoke for ten minutes : hablé (durante) diez minutos⟩ ⟨she has known it for three months : lo sabe desde hace tres meses⟩

forage[1] [ˈfɔrɪʤ] *v* **-aged; -aging** *vi* : hurgar (en busca de alimento) — *vt* : buscar (provisiones)

forage[2] *n* : forraje *m*

foray [ˈfɔrˌeɪ] *n* : incursión *f*

forbear[1] [fɔrˈbær] *vi* **-bore** [-ˈbor]; **-borne** [-ˈborn]; **-bearing 1** ABSTAIN : abstenerse **2** : tener paciencia

forbear[2] → **forbear**

forbearance [fɔrˈbærənts] *n* **1** ABSTAINING : abstención *f* **2** PATIENCE : paciencia *f*

forbid [fərˈbɪd] *vt* **-bade** [-ˈbæd, -ˈbeɪd]; **-bidden** [-ˈbɪdən]; **-bidding 1** PROHIBIT : prohibir **2** PREVENT : impedir

forbidding [fərˈbɪdɪŋ] *adj* **1** IMPOSING : imponente **2** DISAGREEABLE : desagradable, ingrato **3** GRIM : severo

force[1] [ˈfors] *vt* **forced; forcing 1** COMPEL : obligar, forzar **2** : forzar ⟨to force open the window : forzar la ventana⟩ ⟨to force a lock : forzar una cerradura⟩ **3** IMPOSE : imponer, obligar

force[2] *n* **1** : fuerza *f* **2 by force** : por la fuerza **3 in force** : en vigor, en vigencia

forced [ˈforst] *adj* : forzado, forzoso

forceful [ˈforsfəl] *adj* : fuerte, energético, contundente

forcefully [ˈforsfəli] *adv* : con energía, con fuerza

forcefulness [ˈforsfəlnəs] *n* : contundencia *f*, fuerza *f*

forceps [ˈfɔrsəps, -ˌsɛps] *ns & pl* : fórceps *m*

forcible [ˈforsəbəl] *adj* **1** FORCED : forzoso **2** CONVINCING : contundente, convincente — **forcibly** [-bli] *adv*

ford[1] [ˈford] *vt* : vadear

ford[2] *n* : vado *m*

fore[1] [ˈfor] *adv* **1** FORWARD : hacia adelante **2 fore and aft** : de popa a proa

fore[2] *adj* **1** FORWARD : delantero, de adelante **2** FORMER : anterior

fore[3] *n* **1** : frente *m*, delantera *f* **2 to come to the fore** : empezar a destacar, saltar a primera plana

fore–and–aft [ˈforənˈæft, -ənd-] *adj* : longitudinal

forearm [ˈforˌɑrm] *n* : antebrazo *m*

forebear [ˈforˌbær] *n* : antepasado *m*, -da *f*

foreboding [forˈboːdɪŋ] *n* : premonición *f*, presentimiento *m*

forecast[1] [ˈforˌkæst] *vt* **-cast; -casting** : pronosticar, predecir

forecast[2] *n* : predicción *f*, pronóstico *m*

forecastle [ˈfoːksəl] *n* : castillo *m* de proa

foreclose [forˈkloːz] *vt* **-closed; -closing** : ejecutar (una hipoteca)

forefather [ˈforˌfɑðər] *n* : antepasado *m*, ancestro *m*

forefinger [ˈforˌfɪŋgər] *n* : índice *m*, dedo *m* índice

forefoot [ˈforˌfʊt] *n* : pata *f* delantera

forefront [ˈforˌfrʌnt] *n* : frente *m*, vanguardia *f* ⟨in the forefront : a la vanguardia⟩

forego [forˈgoː] *vt* **-went; -gone; -going 1** PRECEDE : preceder **2** → **forgo**

foregoing [forˈgoːɪŋ] *adj* : precedente, anterior

foregone [forˈgɔn] *adj* : previsto ⟨a foregone conclusion : un resultado inevitable⟩

foreground [ˈforˌgraʊnd] *n* : primer plano *m*

forehand[1] [ˈforˌhænd] *adj* : directo, derecho

forehand[2] *n* : golpe *m* del derecho

forehead [ˈfɔrəd, ˈforˌhɛd] *n* : frente *f*

foreign [ˈfɔrən] *adj* **1** : extranjero, exterior ⟨foreign countries : países extranjeros⟩ ⟨foreign trade : comercio exterior⟩ **2** ALIEN : ajeno, extraño ⟨foreign to their nature : ajeno a su carácter⟩ ⟨a foreign body : un cuerpo extraño⟩

foreigner [ˈfɔrənər] *n* : extranjero *m*, -ra *f*

foreknowledge [forˈnɑlɪʤ] *n* : conocimiento *m* previo

foreleg [ˈforˌlɛg] *n* : pata *f* delantera

foreman [ˈformən] *n, pl* **-men** [-mən, -ˌmɛn] : capataz *mf* ⟨foreman of the jury : presidente del jurado⟩

foremost[1] [ˈforˌmoːst] *adv* : en primer lugar

foremost[2] *adj* : más importante, principal, grande

forenoon [ˈforˌnuːn] *n* : mañana *m*

forensic [fəˈrɛntsɪk] *adj* **1** RHETORICAL : retórico, de argumentación **2** : forense ⟨forensic medicine : medicina forense⟩
foreordain [ˌforɔrˈdeɪn] *vt* : predestinar, predeterminar
forequarter [ˈforˌkwɔrt̬ər] *n* : cuarto *m* delantero
forerunner [ˈforˌrʌnər] *n* : precursor *m*, -sora *f*
foresee [forˈsiː] *vt* **-saw; -seen; -seeing** : prever
foreseeable [forˈsiːəbəl] *adj* : previsible ⟨in the foreseeable future : en el futuro inmediato⟩
foreshadow [forˈʃædoː] *vt* : anunciar, prefigurar
foresight [ˈforˌsaɪt] *n* : previsión *f*
foresighted [ˈforˌsaɪt̬əd] *adj* : previsto
forest [ˈfɔrəst] *n* : bosque *m* (en zonas templadas), selva *f* (en zonas tropicales)
forestall [forˈstɔl] *vt* **1** PREVENT : prevenir, impedir **2** PREEMPT : adelantarse a
forested [ˈfɔrəstəd] *adj* : arbolado
forester [ˈfɔrəstər] *n* : silvicultor *m*, -tora *f*
forestland [ˈfɔrəstˌlænd] *n* : zona *f* boscosa
forest ranger → **ranger**
forestry [ˈfɔrəstri] *n* : silvicultura *f*, ingeniería *f* forestal
foreswear → **forswear**
foretaste[1] [ˈforˌteɪst] *vt* **-tasted; -tasting** : anticipar
foretaste[2] *n* : anticipo *m*
foretell [forˈtɛl] *vt* **-told; -telling** : predecir, pronosticar, profetizar
forethought [ˈforˌθɔt] *n* : previsión *f*, reflexión *f* previa
forever [fɔrˈɛvər] *adv* **1** PERPETUALLY : para siempre, eternamente **2** CONTINUALLY : siempre, constantemente
forevermore [fɔrˌɛvərˈmor] *adv* : por siempre jamás
forewarn [forˈwɔrn] *vt* : prevenir, advertir
foreword [ˈforwərd] *n* : prólogo *m*
forfeit[1] [ˈfɔrfət] *vt* : perder el derecho a
forfeit[2] *n* **1** FINE, PENALTY : multa *f* **2** : prenda *f* (en un juego)
forge[1] [ˈforʤ] *v* **forged; forging** *vt* **1** : forjar (metal o un plan) **2** COUNTERFEIT : falsificar — *vi* **to forge ahead** : avanzar, seguir adelante
forge[2] *n* : forja *f*
forger [ˈforʤər] *n* : falsificador *m*, -dora *f*
forgery [ˈforʤəri] *n, pl* **-eries** : falsificación *f*
forget [fərˈgɛt] *v* **-got** [-ˈgɑt]; **-gotten** [-ˈgɑtən] *or* **-got; -getting** *vt* : olvidar — *vi* **to forget about** : olvidarse de, no acordarse de
forgetful [fərˈgɛtfəl] *adj* : olvidadizo
forget–me–not [fərˈgɛtmiˌnɑt] *n* : nomeolvides *mf*
forgettable [fərˈgɛt̬əbəl] *adj* : poco memorable
forgivable [fərˈgɪvəbəl] *adj* : perdonable
forgive [fərˈgɪv] *vt* **-gave** [-ˈgeɪv]; **-given** [-ˈgɪvən]; **-giving** : perdonar
forgiveness [fərˈgɪvnəs] *n* : perdón *m*
forgiving [fərˈgɪvɪŋ] *adj* : indulgente, comprensivo, clemente
forgo *or* **forego** [forˈgoː] *vt* **-went; -gone; -going** : privarse de, renunciar a
fork[1] [ˈfɔrk] *vi* : ramificarse, bifurcarse — *vt* **1** : levantar (con un tenedor, una horca, etc.) **2 to fork over** : desembolsar
fork[2] *n* **1** : tenedor *m* (utensilio de cocina) **2** PITCHFORK : horca *f*, horquilla *f* **3** : bifurcación *f* (de un río o camino), horqueta *f* (de un árbol)
forked [ˈfɔrkt, ˈfɔrkəd] *adj* : bífido, ahorquillado
forklift [ˈfɔrkˌlɪft] *n* : carretilla *f* elevadora
forlorn [fɔrˈlɔrn] *adj* **1** DESOLATE : abandonado, desolado, desamparado **2** SAD : triste **3** DESPERATE : desesperado
forlornly [fɔrˈlɔrnli] *adv* **1** SADLY : con tristeza **2** HALFHEARTEDLY : sin ánimo
form[1] [ˈfɔrm] *vt* **1** FASHION, MAKE : formar **2** DEVELOP : moldear, desarrollar **3** CONSTITUTE : constituir, formar **4** ACQUIRE : adquirir (un hábito), formar (una idea) — *vi* : tomar forma, formarse
form[2] *n* **1** SHAPE : forma *f*, figura *f* **2** MANNER : manera *f*, forma *f* **3** DOCUMENT : formulario *m* **4** : forma *f* ⟨in good form : en buena forma⟩ ⟨true to form : en forma consecuente⟩ **5** MOLD : molde *m* **6** KIND, VARIETY : clase *f*, tipo *m* **7** : forma *f* (en gramática) ⟨plural forms : formas plurales⟩
formal[1] [ˈfɔrməl] *adj* **1** CEREMONIOUS : formal, de etiqueta, ceremonioso **2** OFFICIAL : formal, oficial, de forma
formal[2] *n* **1** BALL : baile *m* formal, baile *m* de etiqueta **2** *or* **formal dress** : traje *m* de etiqueta
formaldehyde [fɔrˈmældəˌhaɪd] *n* : formaldehído *m*
formality [fɔrˈmæləṭi] *n, pl* **-ties** : formalidad *f*
formalize [ˈfɔrməˌlaɪz] *vt* **-ized; -izing** : formalizar
formally [ˈfɔrməli] *adv* : formalmente
format[1] [ˈfɔrˌmæt] *vt* **-matted; -matting** : formatear
format[2] *n* : formato *m*
formation [fɔrˈmeɪʃən] *n* **1** FORMING : formación *f* **2** SHAPE : forma *f* **3 in formation** : en formación
formative [ˈfɔrmət̬ɪv] *adj* : formativo
former [ˈfɔrmər] *adj* **1** PREVIOUS : antiguo, anterior ⟨the former president : el antiguo presidente⟩ **2** : primero (de dos)
formerly [ˈfɔrmərli] *adv* : anteriormente, antes

formidable [ˈfɔrmədəbəl, fɔrˈmɪdə-] *adj* : formidable — **formidably** *adv*

formless [ˈfɔrmləs] *adj* : informe, amorfo

formula [ˈfɔrmjələ] *n, pl* **-las** *or* **-lae** [-ˌliː, -ˌlaɪ] **1** : fórmula *f* **2 baby formula** : preparado *m* para biberón

formulate [ˈfɔrmjəˌleɪt] *vt* **-lated; -lating** : formular, hacer

formulation [ˌfɔrmjəˈleɪʃən] *n* : formulación *f*

fornicate [ˈfɔrnəˌkeɪt] *vi* **-cated; -cating** : fornicar

fornication [ˌfɔrnəˈkeɪʃən] *n* : fornicación *f*

forsake [fərˈseɪk] *vt* **-sook** [-ˈsʊk]; **-saken** [-ˈseɪkən]; **-saking 1** ABANDON : abandonar, desamparar **2** RELINQUISH : renunciar a

forswear [fɔrˈswær] *v* **-swore; -sworn; -swearing** *vt* RENOUNCE : renunciar a — *vi* : perjurar

forsythia [fərˈsɪθiə] *n* : forsitia *f*

fort [ˈfort] *n* **1** STRONGHOLD : fuerte *m*, fortaleza *f*, fortín *m* **2** BASE : base *f* militar

forte [ˈfort, ˈforˌteɪ] *n* : fuerte *m*

forth [ˈforθ] *adv* **1** : adelante ⟨from this day forth : de hoy en adelante⟩ **2 and so forth** : etcétera

forthcoming [forθˈkʌmɪŋ, ˈforθˌ-] *adj* **1** COMING : próximo **2** DIRECT, OPEN : directo, franco, comunicativo

forthright [ˈforθˌraɪt] *adj* : directo, franco — **forthrightly** *adv*

forthrightness [ˈforθˌraɪtnəs] *n* : franqueza *f*

forthwith [forθˈwɪθ, -ˈwɪð] *adv* : inmediatamente, en el acto, enseguida

fortieth[1] [ˈfɔrt̬iəθ] *adj* : cuadragésimo

fortieth[2] *n* **1** : cuadragésimo *m*, -ma *f* (en una serie) **2** : cuarentavo *m*, cuarentava parte *f*

fortification [ˌfɔrt̬əfəˈkeɪʃən] *n* : fortificación *f*

fortify [ˈfɔrt̬əˌfaɪ] *vt* **-fied; -fying** : fortificar

fortitude [ˈfɔrt̬əˌtuːd, -ˌtjuːd] *n* : fortaleza *f*, valor *m*

fortnight [ˈfortˌnaɪt] *n* : quince días *mpl*, dos semanas *fpl*

fortnightly[1] [ˈfortˌnaɪtli] *adv* : cada quince días

fortnightly[2] *adj* : quincenal

fortress [ˈfɔrtrəs] *n* : fortaleza *f*

fortuitous [fɔrˈtuːət̬əs, -ˈtjuː-] *adj* : fortuito, accidental

fortunate [ˈfɔrtʃənət] *adj* : afortunado

fortunately [ˈfɔrtʃənətli] *adv* : afortunadamente, con suerte

fortune [ˈfɔrtʃən] *n* **1** : fortuna *f* ⟨to seek one's fortune : buscar uno su fortuna⟩ **2** LUCK : suerte *f*, fortuna *f* **3** DESTINY, FUTURE : destino *m*, buenaventura *f* **4** : dineral *m*, platal *m* ⟨she spent a fortune : se gastó un dineral⟩

fortune–teller [ˈfɔrtʃənˌtɛlər] *n* : adivino *m*, -na *f*

fortune–telling [ˈfɔrtʃənˌtɛlɪŋ] *n* : adivinación *f*

forty[1] [ˈfɔrt̬i] *adj* : cuarenta

forty[2] *n, pl* **forties** : cuarenta *m*

forum [ˈforəm] *n, pl* **-rums** : foro *m*

forward[1] [ˈfɔrwərd] *vt* **1** PROMOTE : promover, adelantar, fomentar **2** SEND : remitir, enviar

forward[2] *adv* **1** : adelante, hacia adelante ⟨to go forward : irse adelante⟩ **2 from this day forward** : de aquí en adelante

forward[3] *adj* **1** : hacia adelante, delantero **2** BRASH : atrevido, descarado

forward[4] *n* : delantero *m*, -ra *f* (en deportes)

forwarder [ˈfɔrwərdər] *n* : agencia *f* de transportes, agente *mf* expedidor

forwardness [ˈfɔrwərdnəs] *n* : atrevimiento *m*, descaro *m*

forwards [ˈfɔrwərdz] *adv* → **forward**[2]

fossil[1] [ˈfɑsəl] *adj* : fósil

fossil[2] *n* : fósil *m*

fossilize [ˈfɑsəˌlaɪz] *vt* **-ized; -izing** : fosilizar — *vi* : fosilizarse

foster[1] [ˈfɔstər] *vt* : promover, fomentar

foster[2] *adj* : adoptivo ⟨foster child : niño adoptivo⟩

fought → **fight**

foul[1] [ˈfaʊl] *vi* : cometer faltas (en deportes) — *vt* **1** DIRTY, POLLUTE : contaminar, ensuciar **2** TANGLE : enredar

foul[2] *adv* **1** → **foully 2** : contra las reglas

foul[3] *adj* **1** REPULSIVE : asqueroso, repugnante **2** CLOGGED : atascado, obstruido **3** TANGLED : enredado **4** OBSCENE : obsceno **5** BAD : malo ⟨foul weather : mal tiempo⟩ **6** : antirreglamentario (en deportes)

foul[4] *n* : falta *f*, faul *m*

foully [ˈfaʊli] *adv* : asquerosamente

foulmouthed [ˈfaʊlˌmæuːðd, -ˌmaʊθt] *adj* : malhablado

foulness [ˈfaʊlnəs] *n* **1** DIRTINESS : suciedad *f* **2** INCLEMENCY : inclemencia *f* **3** OBSCENITY : obscenidad *f*, grosería *f*

foul play *n* : actos *mpl* criminales

foul–up [ˈfaʊlˌʌp] *n* : lío *m*, confusión *f*, desastre *m*

foul up *vt* SPOIL : estropear, arruinar — *vi* BUNGLE : echar todo a perder

found[1] → **find**

found[2] [ˈfaʊnd] *vt* : fundar, establecer

foundation [faʊnˈdeɪʃən] *n* **1** FOUNDING : fundación *f* **2** BASIS : fundamento *m*, base *f* **3** INSTITUTION : fundación *f* **4** : cimientos *mpl* (de un edificio)

founder[1] [ˈfaʊndər] *vi* SINK : hundirse, irse a pique

founder[2] *n* : fundador *m*, -dora *f*

founding [ˈfaʊndɪŋ] *adj* : fundador ⟨the founding fathers : los fundadores⟩

foundling [ˈfaʊndlɪŋ] *n* : expósito *m*, -ta *f*

foundry [ˈfaʊndri] *n, pl* **-dries** : fundición *f*

fount ['faʊnt] *n* SOURCE : fuente *f*, origen *m*
fountain ['faʊntən] *n* **1** SPRING : fuente *f*, manantial *m* **2** SOURCE : fuente *f*, origen *m* **3** JET : chorro *m* (de agua), surtidor *m*
fountain pen *n* : pluma *f* fuente
four¹ ['for] *adj* : cuatro
four² *n* **1** : cuatro *m* **2 on all fours** : a gatas
fourfold ['for,fo:ld, -'fo:ld] *adj* : cuadruple
four hundred¹ *adj* : cuatrocientos
four hundred² *n* : cuatrocientos *m*
fourscore ['for'skor] *adj* EIGHTY : ochenta *m*
fourteen¹ [for'ti:n] *adj* : catorce
fourteen² *n* : catorce *m*
fourteenth¹ [for'ti:nθ] *adj* : decimocuarto
fourteenth² *n* **1** : decimocuarto *m*, -ta *f* (en una serie) **2** : catorceavo *m*, catorceava parte *f*
fourth¹ ['forθ] *adj* : cuarto
fourth² *n* **1** : cuarto *m*, -ta *f* (en una serie) **2** : cuarto *m*, cuarta parte *f*
fowl ['faʊl] *n, pl* **fowl** *or* **fowls** **1** BIRD : ave *f* **2** CHICKEN : pollo *m*
fox¹ ['fɑks] *vt* **1** TRICK : engañar **2** BAFFLE : confundir
fox² *n, pl* **foxes** : zorro *m*, -ra *f*
foxglove ['fɑks,glʌv] *n* : dedalera *f*, digital *f*
foxhole ['fɑks,ho:l] *n* : hoyo *m* para atrincherarse, trinchera *f* individual
foxy ['fɑksi] *adj* **foxier; -est** SHREWD : astuto
foyer ['fɔɪər, 'fɔɪ,jeɪ] *n* : vestíbulo *m*
fracas ['freɪkəs, 'fræ-] *n, pl* **-cases** [-kəsəz] : altercado *m*, pelea *f*, reyerta *f*
fraction ['frækʃən] *n* **1** : fracción *f*, quebrado *m* **2** PORTION : porción *f*, parte *f*
fractional ['frækʃənəl] *adj* **1** : fraccionario **2** TINY : minúsculo, mínimo, insignificante
fractious ['frækʃəs] *adj* **1** UNRULY : rebelde **2** IRRITABLE : malhumorado, irritable
fracture¹ ['fræktʃər] *vt* **-tured; -turing** : fracturar
fracture² *n* **1** : fractura *f* (de un hueso) **2** CRACK : fisura *f*, grieta *f*, falla *f* (geológica)
fragile ['frædʒəl, -,dʒaɪl] *adj* : frágil
fragility [frə'dʒɪləṭi] *n, pl* **-ties** : fragilidad *f*
fragment¹ ['fræg,mɛnt] *vt* : fragmentar — *vi* : fragmentarse, hacerse añicos
fragment² ['frægmənt] *n* : fragmento *m*, trozo *m*, pedazo *m*
fragmentary ['frægmən,tɛri] *adj* : fragmentario, incompleto
fragmentation [,frægmən'teɪʃən, -,mn-] *n* : fragmentación *f*
fragrance ['freɪgrənts] *n* : fragancia *f*, aroma *m*
fragrant ['freɪgrənt] *adj* : fragante, aromático — **fragrantly** *adv*
frail ['freɪl] *adj* : débil, delicado
frailty ['freɪlti] *n, pl* **-ties** : debilidad *f*, flaqueza *f*
frame¹ ['freɪm] *vt* **framed; framing** **1** FORMULATE : formular, elaborar **2** BORDER : enmarcar, encuadrar **3** INCRIMINATE : incriminar
frame² *n* **1** BODY : cuerpo *m* **2** : armazón *f* (de un edificio, un barco, o un avión), bastidor *m* (de un automóvil), cuadro *m* (de una bicicleta), marco *m* (de un cuadro, una ventana, una puerta, etc.) **3 frames** *npl* : armazón *mf*, montura *f* (para anteojos) **4 frame of mind** : estado *m* de ánimo
framework ['freɪm,wərk] *n* **1** SKELETON, STRUCTURE : armazón *f*, estructura *f* **2** BASIS : marco *m*
franc ['fræŋk] *n* : franco *m*
franchise ['fræn,tʃaɪz] *n* **1** LICENSE : licencia *f* exclusiva, concesión *f* (en comercio) **2** SUFFRAGE : sufragio *m*
franchisee [,fræn,tʃaɪ'zi:, -tʃə-] *n* : concesionario *m*, -ria *f*
Franciscan [fræn'sɪskən] *n* : franciscano *m*, -na *f* — **Franciscan** *adj*
frank¹ ['fræŋk] *vt* : franquear
frank² *adj* : franco, sincero, cándido — **frankly** *adv*
frank³ *n* : franqueo *m* (de correo)
frankfurter ['fræŋkfərṭər, -,fər-] *or* **frankfurt** [-fərt] *n* : salchicha *f* (de Frankfurt, de Viena), perro *m* caliente
frankincense ['fræŋkən,sɛnts] *n* : incienso *m*
frankness ['fræŋknəs] *n* : franqueza *f*, sinceridad *f*, candidez *f*
frantic ['fræntɪk] *adj* : frenético, desesperado — **frantically** *adv*
fraternal [frə'tərnəl] *adj* : fraterno, fraternal
fraternity [frə'tərnəṭi] *n, pl* **-ties** : fraternidad *f*
fraternization [,fræṭərnə'zeɪʃən] *n* : fraternización *f*, confraternización *f*
fraternize ['fræṭər,naɪz] *vi* **-nized; -nizing** : fraternizar, confraternizar
fratricidal [,frætrə'saɪdəl] *adj* : fratricida
fratricide ['frætrə,saɪd] *n* : fratricidio *m*
fraud ['frɔd] *n* **1** DECEPTION, SWINDLE : fraude *m*, estafa *f*, engaño *m* **2** IMPOSTOR : impostor *m*, -tora *f*; farsante *mf*
fraudulent ['frɔdʒələnt] *adj* : fraudulento — **fraudulently** *adv*
fraught ['frɔt] *adj* **fraught with** : lleno de, cargado de
fray¹ ['freɪ] *vt* **1** WEAR : desgastar, deshilachar **2** IRRITATE : crispar, irritar (los nervios) — *vi* : desgastarse, deshilacharse
fray² *n* : pelea *f* ⟨to join the fray : salir a la palestra⟩ ⟨to return to the fray : volver a la carga⟩

frazzle[1] ['fræzəl] *vt* **-zled; -zling 1** FRAY : desgastar, deshilachar **2** EXHAUST : agotar, fatigar
frazzle[2] *n* EXHAUSTION : agotamiento *m*
freak ['fri:k] *n* **1** ODDITY : ejemplar *m* anormal, fenómeno *m*, rareza *f* **2** ENTHUSIAST : entusiasta *mf*
freakish ['fri:kɪʃ] *adj* : extraño, estrafalario, raro
freak out *vi* : ponerse como loco — *vt* : darle un ataque (a alguien)
freckle[1] ['frɛkəl] *vi* **-led; -ling** : cubrirse de pecas
freckle[2] *n* : peca *f*
free[1] ['fri:] *vt* **freed; freeing 1** LIBERATE : libertar, liberar, poner en libertad **2** RELIEVE, RID : librar, eximir **3** RELEASE, UNTIE : desatar, soltar **4** UNCLOG : desatascar, destapar
free[2] *adv* **1** FREELY : libremente **2** GRATIS : gratuitamente, gratis
free[3] *adj* **freer; freest 1** : libre ⟨free as a bird : libre como un pájaro⟩ **2** EXEMPT : libre ⟨tax-free : libre de impuestos⟩ **3** GRATIS : gratuito, gratis **4** VOLUNTARY : espontáneo, voluntario, libre **5** UNOCCUPIED : desocupado, libre **6** LOOSE : suelto
freebooter ['fri:ˌbu:t̬ər] *n* : pirata *mf*
freeborn ['fri:'bɔrn] *adj* : nacido libre
freedom ['fri:dəm] *n* : libertad *f*
free–for–all ['fri:fərˌɔl] *n* : pelea *f*, batalla *f* campal
freelance[1] ['fri:ˌlænts] *vi* **-lanced; -lancing** : trabajar por cuenta propia
freelance[2] *adj* : por cuenta propia, independiente
freeload ['fri:ˌlo:d] *vi* : gorronear *fam*, gorrear *fam*
freeloader ['fri:ˌlo:dər] *n* : gorrón *m*, -rrona *f*; gorrero *m*, -ra *f*; vividor *m*, -dora *f*
freely ['fri:li] *adv* **1** FREE : libremente **2** GRATIS : gratis, gratuitamente
freestanding ['fri:'stændɪŋ] *adj* : de pie, no empotrado, independiente
freeway ['fri:ˌweɪ] *n* : autopista *f*
freewill ['fri:ˌwɪl] *adj* : de propia voluntad
free will *n* : libre albedrío *m*, propia voluntad *f*
freeze[1] ['fri:z] *v* **froze** ['fro:z]; **frozen** ['fro:zən]; **freezing** *vi* **1** : congelarse, helarse ⟨the water froze in the lake : el agua se congeló en el lago⟩ ⟨my blood froze : se me heló la sangre⟩ ⟨I'm freezing : me estoy helando⟩ **2** STOP : quedarse inmóvil — *vt* : helar, congelar (líquidos), congelar (alimentos, precios, activos)
freeze[2] *n* **1** FROST : helada *f* **2** FREEZING : congelación *f*, congelamiento *m*
freeze–dried ['fri:z'draɪd] *adj* : liofilizado
freeze–dry ['fri:z'draɪ] *vt* **-dried; -drying** : liofilizar
freezer ['fri:zər] *n* : congelador *m*
freezing ['fri:zɪŋ] *adj* : helando ⟨it's freezing! : ¡hace un frío espantoso!⟩
freezing point *n* : punto *m* de congelación
freight[1] ['freɪt] *vt* : enviar como carga
freight[2] *n* **1** SHIPPING, TRANSPORT : transporte *m*, porte *m*, flete *m* **2** GOODS : mercancías *fpl*, carga *f*
freighter ['freɪt̬ər] *n* : carguero *m*, buque *m* de carga
French[1] ['frɛntʃ] *adj* : francés
French[2] *n* **1** : francés *m* (idioma) **2 the French** *npl* : los franceses
french fries ['frɛntʃˌfraɪz] *npl* : papas *fpl* fritas
Frenchman ['frɛntʃmən] *n, pl* **-men** [-mən, -ˌmɛn] : francés *m*
Frenchwoman ['frɛntʃˌwʊmən] *n, pl* **-women** [-ˌwɪmən] : francesa *f*
frenetic [frɪ'nɛt̬ɪk] *adj* : frenético — **frenetically** [-t̬ɪkli] *adv*
frenzied ['frɛnzid] *adj* : frenético
frenzy ['frɛnzi] *n, pl* **-zies** : frenesí *m*
frequency ['fri:kwəntsi] *n, pl* **-cies** : frecuencia *f*
frequent[1] [fri'kwɛnt, 'fri:kwənt] *vt* : frecuentar
frequent[2] ['fri:kwənt] *adj* : frecuente — **frequently** *adv*
fresco ['frɛsˌko:] *n, pl* **-coes** : fresco *m*
fresh ['frɛʃ] *adj* **1** : dulce ⟨freshwater : agua dulce⟩ **2** PURE : puro **3** : fresco ⟨fresh fruits : frutas frescas⟩ **4** CLEAN, NEW : limpio, nuevo ⟨fresh clothes : ropa limpia⟩ ⟨fresh evidence : evidencia nueva⟩ **5** REFRESHED : fresco, descansado **6** IMPERTINENT : descarado, impertinente
freshen ['frɛʃən] *vt* : refrescar, arreglar — *vi* **to freshen up** : arreglarse, lavarse
freshet ['frɛʃət] *n* : arroyo *m* desbordado
freshly ['frɛʃli] *adv* : recientemente, recién
freshman ['frɛʃmən] *n, pl* **-men** [-mən, -ˌmɛn] : estudiante *mf* de primer año universitario
freshness ['frɛʃnəs] *n* : frescura *f*
freshwater ['frɛʃˌwɔt̬ər] *n* : agua *f* dulce
fret[1] ['frɛt] *vi* **fretted; fretting** : preocuparse, inquietarse
fret[2] *n* **1** VEXATION : irritación *f*, molestia *f* **2** WORRY : preocupación *f* **3** : traste *m* (de un instrumento musical)
fretful ['frɛtfəl] *adj* : fastidioso, quejoso, neurótico
fretfully ['frɛtfəli] *adv* : ansiosamente, fastidiosamente, inquieto
fretfulness ['frɛtfəlnəs] *n* : inquietud *f*, irritabilidad *f*
friable ['fraɪəbəl] *adj* : friable, pulverizable
friar ['fraɪər] *n* : fraile *m*
fricassee[1] ['frɪkəˌsi:, ˌfrɪkə'si:] *vt* **-seed; -seeing** : cocinar al fricasé
fricassee[2] *n* : fricasé *m*
friction ['frɪkʃən] *n* **1** RUBBING : fricción *f* **2** CONFLICT : fricción *f*, roce *m*
Friday ['fraɪˌdeɪ, -di] *n* : viernes *m*
fridge ['frɪʤ] → **refrigerator**

friend ['frɛnd] *n* : amigo *m*, -ga *f*

friendless ['frɛndləs] *adj* : sin amigos

friendliness ['frɛndlinəs] *n* : simpatía *f*, amabilidad *f*

friendly ['frɛndli] *adj* **-lier; -est 1** : simpático, amable, de amigo ⟨a friendly child : un niño simpático⟩ ⟨friendly advice : consejo de amigo⟩ **2** : agradable, acogedor ⟨a friendly atmosphere : un ambiente agradable⟩ **3** GOOD-NATURED : amigable, amistoso ⟨friendly competition : competencia amistosa⟩

friendship [frɛnd,ʃɪp] *n* : amistad *f*

frieze ['fri:z] *n* : friso *m*

frigate ['frɪgət] *n* : fragata *f*

fright ['fraɪt] *n* : miedo *m*, susto *m*

frighten ['fraitən] *vt* : asustar, espantar

frightened ['fraitənd] *adj* : asustado, temeroso

frightening ['fraitənɪŋ] *adj* : espantoso, aterrador

frightful ['fraɪtfəl] *adj* **1** → **frightening 2** TREMENDOUS : espantoso, tremendo

frightfully ['fraɪtfəli] *adv* : terriblemente, tremendamente

frigid ['frɪʤɪd] *adj* : glacial, extremadamente frío

frigidity [frɪ'ʤɪdət̬i] *n* **1** COLDNESS : frialdad *f* **2** : frigidez *f* (sexual)

frill ['frɪl] *n* **1** RUFFLE : volante *m* **2** EMBELLISHMENT : floritura *f*, adorno *m*

frilly ['frɪli] *adj* **frillier; -est 1** RUFFLY : con volantes **2** OVERDONE : recargado

fringe[1] ['frɪnʤ] *vt* **fringed; fringing** : orlar, bordear

fringe[2] *n* **1** BORDER : fleco *m*, orla *f* **2** EDGE : periferia *f*, margen *m* **3 fringe benefits** : incentivos *mpl*, extras *mpl*

frisk ['frɪsk] *vi* FROLIC : retozar, juguetear — *vt* SEARCH : cachear, registrar

friskiness ['frɪskinəs] *n* : vivacidad *f*

frisky ['frɪski] *adj* **friskier; -est** : retozón, juguetón

fritter[1] ['frɪt̬ər] *vt* : desperdiciar, malgastar ⟨I frittered away the money : malgasté el dinero⟩

fritter[2] *n* : buñuelo *m*

frivolity [frɪ'vɑlət̬i] *n, pl* **-ties** : frivolidad *f*

frivolous ['frɪvələs] *adj* : frívolo, de poca importancia

frivolously ['frɪvələsli] *adv* : frívolamente, a la ligera

frizz[1] ['frɪz] *vi* : rizarse, encresparse, ponerse chino *Mex*

frizz[2] *n* : rizos *mpl* muy apretados

frizzy ['frɪzi] *adj* **frizzier; -est** : rizado, crespo, chino *Mex*

fro ['fro:] *adv* **to and fro** : de aquí para allá, de un lado para otro

frock ['frɑk] *n* DRESS : vestido *m*

frog ['frɔg, 'frɑg] *n* **1** : rana *f* **2** FASTENER : alamar *m* **3 to have a frog in one's throat** : tener carraspera

frogman ['frɔg,mæn, 'frɑg-, -mən] *n, pl* **-men** [-mən, -,mɛn] : hombre *m* rana, submarinista *mf*

frolic[1] ['frɑlɪk] *vi* **-icked; -icking** : retozar, juguetear

frolic[2] *n* FUN : diversión *f*

frolicsome ['frɑlɪksəm] *adj* : juguetón

from ['frʌm, 'frɑm] *prep* **1** (*indicating a starting point*) : desde, de, a partir de ⟨from Cali to Bogota : de Cali a Bogotá⟩ ⟨where are you from? : ¿de dónde eres?⟩ ⟨from that time onward : desde entonces⟩ ⟨from tomorrow : a partir de mañana⟩ **2** (*indicating a source or sender*) : de ⟨a letter from my friend : una carta de mi amiga⟩ ⟨a quote from Shakespeare : una cita de Shakespeare⟩ **3** (*indicating distance*) : de ⟨10 feet from the entrance : a 10 pies de la entrada⟩ **4** (*indicating a cause*) : de ⟨red from crying : rojos de llorar⟩ ⟨he died from the cold : murió del frío⟩ **5** OFF, OUT OF : de ⟨she took it from the drawer : lo sacó del cajón⟩ **6** (*with adverbs or adverbial phrases*) : de, desde ⟨from above : desde arriba⟩ ⟨from among : de entre⟩

frond ['frɑnd] *n* : fronda *f*, hoja *f*

front[1] ['frʌnt] *vi* **1** FACE : dar, estar orientado ⟨the house fronts north : la casa da al norte⟩ **2** : servir de pantalla ⟨he fronts for his boss : sirve de pantalla para su jefe⟩

front[2] *adj* : delantero, de adelante, primero ⟨the front row : la primera fila⟩

front[3] *n* **1** : frente *m*, parte *f* de adelante, delantera *f* ⟨the front of the class : el frente de la clase⟩ ⟨at the front of the train : en la parte delantera del tren⟩ **2** AREA, ZONE : frente *m*, zona *f* ⟨the Eastern front : el frente oriental⟩ ⟨on the educational front : en el frente de la enseñanza⟩ **3** FACADE : fachada *f* (de un edificio o una persona) **4** : frente *m* (en meteorología)

frontage ['frʌntɪʤ] *n* : fachada *f*, frente *m*

frontal ['frʌntəl] *adj* : frontal, de frente

frontier [,frʌn'tɪr] *n* : frontera *f*

frontiersman [,frʌn'tɪrzmən] *n, pl* **-men** [-mən, -,mɛn] : hombre *m* de la frontera

frontispiece ['frʌntəs,pi:s] *n* : frontispicio *m*

frost[1] ['frɔst] *vt* **1** FREEZE : helar **2** ICE : escarchar (pasteles)

frost[2] *n* **1** : helada *f* (en meteorología) **2** : escarcha *f* ⟨frost on the window : escarcha en la ventana⟩

frostbite ['frɔst,baɪt] *n* : congelación *f*

frostbitten ['frɔst,bɪtən] *adj* : congelado (dícese de una persona), quemado (dícese de una planta)

frosting ['frɔstɪŋ] *n* ICING : glaseado *m*, betún *m Mex*

frosty ['frɔsti] *adj* **frostier; -est 1** CHILLY : helado, frío **2** COOL, UNFRIENDLY : frío, glacial

froth ['frɔθ] *n, pl* **froths** ['frɔθs, 'frɔðz] : espuma *f*

frothy ['frɔθi] *adj* **frothier; -est** : espumoso

frown[1] ['fraʊn] *vi* **1** : fruncir el ceño, fruncir el entrecejo **2 to frown at** : mirar (algo) con ceño, mirar (a alguien) con ceño

frown[2] *n* : ceño *m* (fruncido)

frowsy *or* **frowzy** ['fraʊzi] *adj* **frowsier** *or* **frowzier; -est** : desaliñado, desaseado

froze → **freeze**

frozen → **freeze**

frugal ['fru:gəl] *adj* : frugal, ahorrativo, parco — **frugally** *adv*

frugality [fru'gæləṭi] *n* : frugalidad *f*

fruit[1] ['fru:t] *vi* : dar fruto

fruit[2] *n* **1** : fruta *f* (término genérico), fruto *m* (término particular) **2 fruits** *npl* REWARDS : frutos *mpl* ⟨the fruits of his labor : los frutos de su trabajo⟩

fruitcake ['fru:t,keɪk] *n* : pastel *m* de frutas

fruitful ['fru:tfəl] *adj* : fructífero, provechoso

fruition [fru'ɪʃən] *n* **1** : cumplimiento *m*, realización *f* **2 to bring to fruition** : realizar

fruitless ['fru:tləs] *adj* : infructuoso, inútil — **fruitlessly** *adv*

fruity ['fru:ṭi] *adj* **fruitier; -est** : (con sabor) a fruta

frumpy ['frʌmpi] *adj* **frumpier; -est** : anticuado y sin atractivo

frustrate ['frʌs,treɪt] *vt* **-trated; -trating** : frustrar

frustrating ['frʌs,treɪṭɪŋ] *adj* : frustrante — **frustratingly** *adv*

frustration [,frʌs'treɪʃən] *n* : frustración *f*

fry[1] ['fraɪ] *vt* **fried; frying** : freír

fry[2] *n, pl* **fries** **1** : fritura *f*, plato *m* frito **2** : fiesta *f* en que se sirven frituras **3** *pl* **fry** : alevín *m* (pez)

frying pan *n* : sartén *mf*

fuchsia ['fju:ʃə] *n* **1** : fucsia *f* (planta) **2** : fucsia *m* (color)

fuddle ['fʌdəl] *vt* **-dled; -dling** : confundir, atontar

fuddy–duddy ['fʌdi,dʌdi] *n, pl* **-dies** : persona *f* chapada a la antigua, carca *mf*

fudge[1] ['fʌʤ] *vt* **fudged; fudging** **1** FALSIFY : amañar, falsificar **2** DODGE : esquivar

fudge[2] *n* : dulce *m* blando de chocolate y leche

fuel[1] ['fju:əl] *vt* **-eled** *or* **-elled; -eling** *or* **-elling** **1** : abastecer de combustible **2** STIMULATE : estimular

fuel[2] *n* : combustible *m*, carburante *m* (para motores)

fugitive[1] ['fju:ʤəṭɪv] *adj* **1** RUNAWAY : fugitivo **2** FLEETING : efímero, pasajero, fugaz

fugitive[2] *n* : fugitivo *m*, -va *f*

fugue ['fju:g] *n* : fuga *f*

fulcrum ['fʊlkrəm, 'fʌl-] *n, pl* **-crums** *or* **-cra** [-krə] : fulcro *m*

fulfill *or* **fulfil** [fʊl'fɪl] *vt* **-filled; -filling** **1** PERFORM : cumplir con, realizar, llevar a cabo **2** SATISFY : satisfacer

fulfillment [fʊl'fɪlmənt] *n* **1** PERFORMANCE : cumplimiento *m*, ejecución *f* **2** SATISFACTION : satisfacción *f*, realización *f*

full[1] ['fʊl, 'fʌl] *adv* **1** VERY : muy ⟨full well : muy bien, perfectamente⟩ **2** ENTIRELY : completamente ⟨she swung full around : giró completamente⟩ **3** DIRECTLY : de lleno, directamente ⟨he looked me full in the face : me miró directamente a la cara⟩

full[2] *adj* **1** FILLED : lleno **2** COMPLETE : completo, detallado **3** MAXIMUM : todo, pleno ⟨at full speed : a toda velocidad⟩ ⟨in full bloom : en plena flor⟩ **4** PLUMP : redondo, llenito *fam*, regordete *fam* ⟨a full face : una cara redonda⟩ ⟨a full figure : un cuerpo llenito⟩ **5** AMPLE : amplio ⟨a full skirt : una falda amplia⟩

full[3] *n* **1 to pay in full** : pagar en su totalidad **2 to the full** : al máximo

full–fledged ['fʊl'flɛʤd] *adj* : hecho y derecho

fullness ['fʊlnəs] *n* **1** ABUNDANCE : plenitud *f*, abundancia *f* **2** : amplitud *f* (de una falda)

fully ['fʊli] *adv* **1** COMPLETELY : completamente, totalmente **2** : al menos, por lo menos ⟨fully half of them : al menos la mitad de ellos⟩

fulsome ['fʊlsəm] *adj* : excesivo, exagerado, efusivo

fumble[1] ['fʌmbəl] *v* **-bled; -bling** *vt* **1** : dejar caer, fumblear **2 to fumble one's way** : ir a tientas — *vi* **1** GROPE : hurgar, tantear **2 to fumble with** : manejar con torpeza

fumble[2] *n* : fumble *m* (en futbol americano)

fume[1] ['fju:m] *vi* **fumed; fuming** **1** SMOKE : echar humo, humear **2** : estar furioso

fume[2] *n* : gas *m*, humo *m*, vapor *m*

fumigate ['fju:mə,geɪt] *vt* **-gated; -gating** : fumigar

fumigation [,fju:mə'geɪʃən] *n* : fumigación *m*

fun[1] ['fʌn] *adj* : divertido, entretenido

fun[2] *n* **1** AMUSEMENT : diversión *f*, entretenimiento *m* **2** ENJOYMENT : disfrute *m* **3 to have fun** : divertirse **4 to make fun of** : reírse de, burlarse de

function[1] ['fʌŋkʃən] *vi* : funcionar, desempeñarse, servir

function[2] *n* **1** PURPOSE : función *f* **2** GATHERING : reunión *f* social, recepción *f* **3** CEREMONY : ceremonia *f*, acto *m*

functional ['fʌŋkʃənəl] *adj* : funcional — **functionally** *adv*

functionary ['fʌŋkʃə,nɛri] *n, pl* **-aries** : funcionario *m*, -ria *f*

fund[1] ['fʌnd] *vt* : financiar

fund[2] *n* **1** SUPPLY : reserva *f*, cúmulo *m* **2** : fondo *m* ⟨investment fund : fondo de inversiones⟩ **3 funds** *npl* RESOURCES : fondos *mpl*
fundamental[1] [ˌfʌndəˈmɛntəl] *adj* **1** BASIC : fundamental, básico **2** PRINCIPAL : esencial, principal **3** INNATE : innato, intrínseco
fundamental[2] *n* : fundamento *m*
fundamentalism [ˌfʌndəˈmɛntəlˌɪzəm] *n* : integrismo *m*, fundamentalismo *m*
fundamentalist [ˌfʌndəˈmɛntəlɪst] *n* : integrista *mf*, fundamentalista *mf* — **fundamentalist** *adj*
fundamentally [ˌfʌndəˈmɛntəli] *adv* : fundamentalmente, básicamente
funding [ˈfʌndɪŋ] *n* : financiación *f*
fund–raiser [ˈfʌndˌreɪzər] *n* : función *f* para recaudar fondos
funeral[1] [ˈfjuːnərəl] *adj* **1** : funeral, funerario, fúnebre ⟨funeral procession : cortejo fúnebre⟩ **2 funeral home** : funeraria *f*
funeral[2] *n* : funeral *m*, funerales *mpl*
funereal [fjuːˈnɪriəl] *adj* : fúnebre
fungal [ˈfʌŋgəl] *adj* : de hongos, micótico
fungicidal [ˌfʌnʤəˈsaɪdəl, ˌfʌngə-] *adj* : fungicida
fungicide [ˈfʌnʤəˌsaɪd, ˈfʌŋgə-] *n* : fungicida *m*
fungous [ˈfʌŋgəs] *adj* : fungoso
fungus [ˈfʌŋgəs] *n, pl* **fungi** [ˈfʌnˌʤaɪ, ˈfʌŋˌgaɪ] : hongo *m*
funk [ˈfʌŋk] *n* **1** FEAR : miedo *m* **2** DEPRESSION : depresión *f*
funky [ˈfʌŋki] *adj* **funkier; -est** ODD, QUAINT : raro, extraño, original
funnel[1] [ˈfʌnəl] *vt* **-neled; -neling** CHANNEL : canalizar, encauzar
funnel[2] *n* **1** : embudo *m* **2** SMOKESTACK : chimenea *f* (de un barco o vapor)
funnies [ˈfʌniz] *npl* : tiras *fpl* cómicas
funny [ˈfʌni] *adj* **funnier; -est 1** AMUSING : divertido, cómico **2** STRANGE : extraño, raro
fur[1] [ˈfər] *adj* : de piel
fur[2] *n* **1** : pelaje *m*, piel *f* **2** : prenda *f* de piel
furbish [ˈfərbɪʃ] *vt* : pulir, limpiar
furious [ˈfjʊriəs] *adj* **1** ANGRY : furioso **2** FRANTIC : violento, frenético, vertiginoso (dícese de la velocidad)
furiously [ˈfjʊriəsli] *adv* **1** ANGRILY : furiosamente **2** FRANTICALLY : frenéticamente
furlong [ˈfərˌlɔŋ] *n* : estadio *m* (201.2 m)
furlough[1] [ˈfərˌloː] *vt* : dar permiso a, dar licencia a
furlough[2] *n* LEAVE : permiso *m*, licencia *f*
furnace [ˈfərnəs] *n* : horno *m*
furnish [ˈfərnɪʃ] *vt* **1** SUPPLY : proveer, suministrar **2** : amueblar ⟨furnished apartment : departamento amueblado⟩
furnishings [ˈfərnɪʃɪŋz] *npl* **1** ACCESSORIES : accesorios *mpl* **2** FURNITURE : muebles *mpl*, mobiliario *m*
furniture [ˈfərnɪʧər] *n* : muebles *mpl*, mobiliario *m*
furor [ˈfjʊrˌɔr, -ər] *n* **1** RAGE : furia *f*, rabia *f* **2** UPROAR : escándalo *m*, jaleo *m*, alboroto *m*
furrier [ˈfəriər] *n* : peletero *m*, -ra *f*
furrow[1] [ˈfəroː] *vt* **1** : surcar **2 to furrow one's brow** : fruncir el ceño
furrow[2] *n* **1** GROOVE : surco *m* **2** WRINKLE : arruga *f*, surco *m*
furry [ˈfəri] *adj* **furrier; -est** : peludo (dícese de un animal), peluche (dícese de un objeto)
further[1] [ˈfərðər] *vt* : promover, fomentar
further[2] *adv* **1** FARTHER : más lejos, más adelante **2** MOREOVER : además **3** MORE : más ⟨I'll consider it further in the morning : lo consideraré más en la mañana⟩
further[3] *adj* **1** FARTHER : más lejano **2** ADDITIONAL : adicional, más
furtherance [ˈfərðərən*t*s] *n* : promoción *f*, fomento *m*, adelantamiento *m*
furthermore [ˈfərðərˌmor] *adv* : además
furthermost [ˈfərðərˌmoːst] *adj* : más lejano, más distante
furthest [ˈfərðəst] → **farthest**[1], **farthest**[2]
furtive [ˈfərṭɪv] *adj* : furtivo, sigiloso — **furtively** *adv*
furtiveness [ˈfərṭɪvnəs] *n* STEALTH : sigilo *m*
fury [ˈfjʊri] *n, pl* **-ries 1** RAGE : furia *f*, ira *f* **2** VIOLENCE : furia *f*, furor *m*
fuse[1] [ˈfjuːz] *or* **fuze** *vt* **fused** *or* **fuzed; fusing** *or* **fuzing** : equipar con un fusible
fuse[2] *v* **fused; fusing** *vt* **1** SMELT : fundir **2** MERGE : fusionar, fundir — *vi* : fundirse, fusionarse
fuse[3] *n* : fusible *m*
fuselage [ˈfjuːsəˌlɑʒ, -zə-] *n* : fuselaje *m*
fusillade [ˈfjuːsəˌlɑd, -ˌleɪd, ˌfjuːsəˈ-, -zə-] *n* : descarga *f* de fusilería
fusion [ˈfjuːʒən] *n* : fusión *f*
fuss[1] [ˈfʌs] *vi* **1** WORRY : preocuparse **2 to fuss with** : juguetear con, toquetear **3 to fuss over** : mimar
fuss[2] *n* **1** COMMOTION : alboroto *m*, escándalo *m* **2** ATTENTION : atenciones *fpl* **3** COMPLAINT : quejas *fpl*
fussbudget [ˈfʌsˌbʌʤət] *n* : quisquilloso *m*, -sa *f*; melindroso *m*, -sa *f*
fussiness [ˈfʌsinəs] *n* **1** IRRITABILITY : irritabilidad *f* **2** ORNATENESS : lo recargado **3** METICULOUSNESS : meticulosidad *f*
fussy [ˈfʌsi] *adj* **fussier; -est 1** IRRITABLE : irritable, nervioso **2** OVERELABORATE : recargado **3** METICULOUS : meticuloso **4** FASTIDIOUS : quisquilloso, exigente
futile [ˈfjuːṭəl, ˈfjuːˌtaɪl] *adj* : inútil, vano
futility [fjuˈtɪləṭi] *n, pl* **-ties** : inutilidad *f*
future[1] [ˈfjuːʧər] *adj* : futuro
future[2] *n* : futuro *m*
futuristic [ˌfjuːʧəˈrɪstɪk] *adj* : futurista
fuze → **fuse**[1]

fuzz [ˈfʌz] *n* : pelusa *f*
fuzziness [ˈfʌzinəs] *n* **1** DOWNINESS : vellosidad *f* **2** INDISTINCTNESS : falta *f* de claridad
fuzzy [ˈfʌzi] *adj* **fuzzier; -est** **1** FLUFFY, FURRY : con pelusa, peludo **2** INDISTINCT : indistinto ⟨a fuzzy image : una imagen borrosa⟩

G

g [ˈʤiː] *n, pl* **g's** *or* **gs** [ˈʤiːz] : séptima letra del alfabeto inglés
gab[1] [ˈgæb] *vi* **gabbed; gabbing** : charlar, cotorrear *fam*, parlotear *fam*
gab[2] *n* CHATTER : cotorreo *m fam*, parloteo *m fam*
gabardine [ˈgæbərˌdiːn] *n* : gabardina *f*
gabby [ˈgæbi] *adj* **gabbier; -est** : hablador, parlanchín
gable [ˈgeɪbəl] *n* : hastial *m*, aguilón *m*
Gabonese [ˌgæbəˈniːz, -ˈniːs] *n* : gabonés *m*, -nesa *f* — **Gabonese** *adj*
gad [ˈgæd] *vi* **gadded; gadding** WANDER : deambular, vagar, callejear
gadfly [ˈgædˌflaɪ] *n, pl* **-flies** **1** : tábano *m* (insecto) **2** FAULTFINDER : criticón *m*, -cona *f fam*
gadget [ˈgæʤət] *n* : artilugio *m*, aparato *m*
gadgetry [ˈgæʤətri] *n* : artilugios *mpl*, aparatos *mpl*
Gaelic [ˈgeɪlɪk, ˈgæ] *n* : gaélico *m* (idioma) — **Gaelic** *adj*
gaff [ˈgæf] *n* **1** : garfio *m* **2** → **gaffe**
gaffe [ˈgæf] *n* : metedura *f* de pata *fam*
gag[1] [ˈgæg] *v* **gagged; gagging** *vt* : amordazar ⟨to tie up and gag : atar y amordazar⟩ — *vi* **1** CHOKE : atragantarse **2** RETCH : hacer arcadas
gag[2] *n* **1** : mordaza *f* (para la boca) **2** JOKE : chiste *m*
gage → **gauge**
gaggle [ˈgægəl] *n* : bandada *f*, manada *f* (de gansos)
gaiety [ˈgeɪəṭi] *n, pl* **-eties** **1** MERRYMAKING : juerga *f* **2** MERRIMENT : alegría *f*, regocijo *m*
gaily [ˈgeɪli] *adv* : alegremente
gain[1] [ˈgeɪn] *vt* **1** ACQUIRE, OBTAIN : ganar, obtener, adquirir, conseguir ⟨to gain knowledge : adquirir conocimientos⟩ ⟨to gain a victory : obtener una victoria⟩ **2** REACH : alcanzar, llegar a **3** INCREASE : ganar, aumentar ⟨to gain weight : aumentar de peso⟩ **4** : adelantarse, ganar ⟨the watch gains two minutes a day : el reloj se adelanta dos minutos por día⟩ — *vi* **1** PROFIT : beneficiarse **2** INCREASE : aumentar
gain[2] *n* **1** PROFIT : beneficio *m*, ganancia *f*, lucro *m*, provecho *m* **2** INCREASE : aumento *m*
gainful [ˈgeɪnfəl] *adj* : lucrativo, beneficioso, provechoso ⟨gainful employment : trabajo remunerado⟩
gait [ˈgeɪt] *n* : paso *m*, andar *m*, manera *f* de caminar
gal [ˈgæl] *n* : muchacha *f*
gala[1] [ˈgeɪlə, ˈgæ-, ˈgɑ-] *adj* : de gala
gala[2] *n* : gala *f*, fiesta *f*
galactic [gəˈlæktɪk] *adj* : galáctico
galaxy [ˈgæləksi] *n, pl* **-axies** : galaxia *f*
gale [ˈgeɪl] *n* **1** WIND : vendaval *f*, viento *m* fuerte **2 gales of laughter** : carcajadas *fpl*
gall[1] [ˈgɔl] *vt* **1** CHAFE : rozar **2** IRRITATE, VEX : irritar, molestar
gall[2] *n* **1** BILE : bilis *f*, hiel *f* **2** INSOLENCE : audacia *f*, insolencia *f*, descaro *m* **3** SORE : rozadura *f* (de un caballo) **4** : agalla *f* (de una planta)
gallant [ˈgælənt] *adj* **1** BRAVE : valiente, gallardo **2** CHIVALROUS, POLITE : galante, cortés
gallantry [ˈgæləntri] *n, pl* **-ries** : galantería *f*, caballerosidad *f*
gallbladder [ˈgɔlˌblædər] *n* : vesícula *f* biliar
galleon [ˈgæljən] *n* : galeón *m*
gallery [ˈgæləri] *n, pl* **-leries** **1** BALCONY : galería *f* (para espectadores) **2** CORRIDOR : pasillo *m*, galería *f*, corredor *m* **3** : galería *f* (para exposiciones)
galley [ˈgæli] *n, pl* **-leys** : galera *f*
gallium [ˈgæliəm] *n* : galio *m*
gallivant [ˈgæləˌvænt] *vi* : callejear
gallon [ˈgælən] *n* : galón *m*
gallop[1] [ˈgæləp] *vi* : galopar
gallop[2] *n* : galope *m*
gallows [ˈgæˌloːz] *n, pl* **-lows** *or* **-lowses** [-ˌloːzəz] : horca *f*
gallstone [ˈgɔlˌstoːn] *n* : cálculo *m* biliar
galore [gəˈlor] *adj* : en abundancia ⟨bargains galore : muchísimas gangas⟩
galoshes [gəˈlɑʃəz] *npl* : galochas *fpl*, chanclos *mpl*
galvanize [ˈgælvənˌaɪz] *vt* **-nized; -nizing** **1** STIMULATE : estimular, excitar, impulsar **2** : galvanizar (metales)
Gambian [ˈgæmbiən] *n* : gambiano *m*, -na *f* — **Gambian** *adj*
gambit [ˈgæmbɪt] *n* **1** : gambito *m* (en ajedrez) **2** STRATAGEM : estratagema *f*, táctica *f*
gamble[1] [ˈgæmbəl] *v* **-bled; -bling** *vi* : jugar, arriesgarse — *vt* **1** BET, WAGER : apostar, jugarse **2** RISK : arriesgar
gamble[2] *n* **1** BET : apuesta *f* **2** RISK : riesgo *m*
gambler [ˈgæmbələr] *n* : jugador *m*, -dora *f*
gambling [ˈgæmbəlɪŋ] *n* : juego *m*
gambol [ˈgæmbəl] *vi* **-boled** *or* **-bolled; -boling** *or* **-bolling** FROLIC : retozar, juguetear
game[1] [ˈgeɪm] *adj* **1** READY : listo, dispuesto ⟨we're game for anything : es-

tamos listos para lo que sea⟩ **2** LAME : cojo

game[2] *n* **1** AMUSEMENT : juego *m*, diversión *f* **2** CONTEST : juego *m*, partido *m*, concurso *m* **3** : caza *f* ⟨big game : caza mayor⟩

gamecock [ˈgeɪm,kɑk] *n* : gallo *m* de pelea

gamekeeper [ˈgeɪm,kiːpər] *n* : guardabosque *mf*

gamely [ˈgeɪmli] *adv* : animosamente

gamma ray [ˈgæmə] *n* : rayo *m* gamma

gamut [ˈgæmət] *n* : gama *f*, espectro *m* ⟨to run the gamut : pasar por toda la gama⟩

gamy *or* **gamey** [ˈgeɪmi] *adj* **gamier; -est** : con sabor de animal de caza, fuerte

gander [ˈgændər] *n* **1** : ganso *m* (animal) **2** GLANCE : mirada *f*, vistazo *m*, ojeada *f*

gang[1] [ˈgæŋ] *vi* **to gang up** : agruparse, unirse

gang[2] *n* : banda *f*, pandilla *f*

gangling [ˈgæŋglɪŋ] *adj* LANKY : larguirucho *fam*

ganglion [ˈgæŋgliən] *n, pl* **-glia** [-gliə] : ganglio *m*

gangplank [ˈgæŋ,plæŋk] *n* : pasarela *f*

gangrene [ˈgæŋ,griːn, ˈgæn-; gæŋˈ-, gænˈ-] *n* : gangrena *f*

gangrenous [ˈgæŋgrənəs] *adj* : gangrenoso

gangster [ˈgæŋstər] *n* : gángster *mf*

gangway [ˈgæŋ,weɪ] *n* **1** : pasarela *f* **2 gangway!** : ¡abran paso!

gap [ˈgæp] *n* **1** BREACH, OPENING : espacio *m*, brecha *f*, abertura *f* **2** GORGE : desfiladero *m*, barranco *m* **3** : laguna *f* ⟨a gap in my education : una laguna en mi educación⟩ **4** INTERVAL : pausa *f*, intervalo *m* **5** DISPARITY : brecha *f*, disparidad *f*

gape[1] [ˈgeɪp] *vi* **gaped; gaping 1** OPEN : abrirse, estar abierto **2** STARE : mirar fijamente con la boca abierta, mirar boquiabierto

gape[2] *n* **1** OPENING : abertura *f*, brecha *f* **2** STARE : mirada *f* boquiabierta

garage[1] [gəˈrɑʒ, -ˈrɑʤ] *vt* **-raged; -raging** : dejar en un garaje

garage[2] *n* : garaje *m*, cochera *f*

garb[1] [ˈgɑrb] *vt* : vestir, ataviar

garb[2] *n* : vestimenta *f*, atuendo *f*

garbage [ˈgɑrbɪʤ] *n* : basura *f*, desechos *mpl*

garbageman [ˈgɑrbɪʤmən] *n, pl* **-men** [-mən, -,mɛn] : basurero *m*

garble [ˈgɑrbəl] *vt* **-bled; -bling** : tergiversar, distorsionar

garbled [ˈgɑrbəld] *adj* : incoherente, incomprensible

garden[1] [ˈgɑrdən] *vi* : trabajar en el jardín

garden[2] *n* : jardín *m*

gardener [ˈgɑrdənər] *n* : jardinero *m*, -ra *f*

gardenia [gɑrˈdiːnjə] *n* : gardenia *f*

gardening [ˈgɑrdənɪŋ] *n* : jardinería *f*

gargantuan [gɑrˈgænʧuən] *adj* : gigantesco, colosal

gargle[1] [ˈgɑrgəl] *vi* **-gled; -gling** : hacer gárgaras, gargarizar

gargle[2] *n* : gárgara *f*

gargoyle [ˈgɑr,gɔɪl] *n* : gárgola *f*

garish [ˈgærɪʃ] *adj* GAUDY : llamativo, chillón, charro — **garishly** *adv*

garland[1] [ˈgɑrlənd] *vt* : adornar con guirnaldas

garland[2] *n* : guirnalda *f*

garlic [ˈgɑrlɪk] *n* : ajo *m*

garment [ˈgɑrmənt] *n* : prenda *f*

garner [ˈgɑrnər] *vt* : recoger, cosechar

garnet [ˈgɑrnət] *n* : granate *m*

garnish[1] [ˈgɑrnɪʃ] *vt* : aderezar, guarnecer

garnish[2] *n* : aderezo *m*, guarnición *f*

garret [ˈgærət] *n* : buhardilla *f*, desván *m*

garrison[1] [ˈgærəsən] *vt* **1** QUARTER : acuartelar (tropas) **2** OCCUPY : guarnecer, ocupar (con tropas)

garrison[2] *n* **1** : guarnición *f* (ciudad) **2** FORT : fortaleza *f*, poste *m* militar

garrulous [ˈgærələs] *adj* : charlatán, parlanchín, garlero *Col fam*

garter [ˈgɑrt̬ər] *n* : liga *f*

gas[1] [ˈgæs] *v* **gassed; gassing** *vt* : gasear — *vi* **to gas up** : llenar el tanque con gasolina

gas[2] *n, pl* **gases** [ˈgæsəz] **1** : gas *m* ⟨tear gas : gas lacrimógeno⟩ **2** GASOLINE : gasolina *f*

gaseous [ˈgæʃəs, ˈgæsiəs] *adj* : gaseoso

gash[1] [ˈgæʃ] *vt* : hacer un tajo en, cortar

gash[2] *n* : cuchillada *f*, tajo *m*

gasket [ˈgæskət] *n* : junta *f*

gas mask *n* : máscara *f* antigás

gasoline [ˈgæsə,liːn, ,gæsəˈ-] *n* : gasolina *f*, nafta *f*

gasp[1] [ˈgæsp] *vi* **1** : boquear ⟨to gasp with surprise : gritar de asombro⟩ **2** PANT : jadear, respirar con dificultad

gasp[2] *n* **1** : boqueada *f* ⟨a gasp of surprise : un grito sofocado⟩ **2** PANTING : jadeo *m*

gas station *n* : estación *f* de servicio, gasolinera *f*

gastric [ˈgæstrɪk] *adj* : gástrico ⟨gastric juice : jugo gástrico⟩

gastronomic [,gæstrəˈnɑmɪk] *adj* : gastronómico

gastronomy [gæsˈtrɑnəmi] *n* : gastronomía *f*

gate [ˈgeɪt] *n* : portón *m*, verja *f*, puerta *f*

gatekeeper [ˈgeɪt,kiːpər] *n* : guarda *mf*; guardián *m*, -diana *f*

gateway [ˈgeɪt,weɪ] *n* : puerta *f* (de acceso), entrada *f*

gather [ˈgæðər] *vt* **1** ASSEMBLE : juntar, recoger, reunir **2** HARVEST : recoger, cosechar **3** : fruncir (una tela) **4** INFER : deducir, suponer

gathering [ˈgæðərɪŋ] *n* : reunión *f*

gauche [ˈgoːʃ] *adj* : torpe, falto de tacto

gaudy ['gɔdi] *adj* **gaudier; -est** : chillón, llamativo

gauge¹ ['geɪʤ] *vt* **gauged; gauging 1** MEASURE : medir **2** ESTIMATE, JUDGE : estimar, evaluar, juzgar

gauge² *n* **1** : indicador *m* ⟨pressure gauge : indicador de presión⟩ **2** CALIBER : calibre *m* **3** INDICATION : indicio *m*, muestra *f*

gaunt ['gɔnt] *adj* : demacrado, enjuto, descarnado

gauntlet ['gɔntlət] *n* : guante *m* ⟨to run the gauntlet of : exponerse a⟩

gauze ['gɔz] *n* : gasa *f*

gauzy ['gɔzi] *adj* **gauzier; -est** : diáfano, vaporoso

gave → **give**

gavel ['gævəl] *n* : martillo *m* (de un juez, un subastador, etc.)

gawk ['gɔk] *vi* GAPE : mirar boquiabierto

gawky ['gɔki] *adj* **gawkier; -est** : desmañado, torpe, desgarbado

gay ['geɪ] *adj* **1** MERRY : alegre **2** BRIGHT, COLORFUL : vistoso, vivo **3** HOMOSEXUAL : homosexual

gaze¹ ['geɪz] *vi* **gazed; gazing** : mirar (fijamente)

gaze² *n* : mirada *f* (fija)

gazelle [gə'zɛl] *n* : gacela *f*

gazette [gə'zɛt] *n* : gaceta *f*

gazetteer [ˌgæzə'tɪr] *n* : diccionario *m* geográfico

gear¹ ['gɪr] *vt* ADAPT, ORIENT : adaptar, ajustar, orientar ⟨a book geared to children : un libro adaptado a los niños⟩ — *vi* **to gear up** : prepararse

gear² *n* **1** CLOTHING : ropa *f* **2** BELONGINGS : efectos *mpl* personales **3** EQUIPMENT, TOOLS : equipo *m*, aparejo *m*, herramientas *fpl* ⟨fishing gear : aparejo de pescar⟩ ⟨landing gear : tren de aterrizaje⟩ **4** COGWHEEL : rueda *f* dentada **5** : marcha *f*, velocidad *f* (de un vehículo) ⟨to put in gear : poner en marcha⟩ ⟨to change gear(s) : cambiar de velocidad⟩

gearshift ['gɪrˌʃɪft] *n* : palanca *f* de cambio, palanca *f* de velocidad

geek ['gi:k] *n fam* : intelectual *mf*

geese → **goose**

Geiger counter ['gaɪgərˌkaʊntər] *n* : contador *m* Geiger

gel ['ʤɛl] *n* : gel *m*

gelatin ['ʤɛlətən] *n* : gelatina *f*

gem ['ʤɛm] *n* : joya *f*, gema *f*, alhaja *f*

Gemini ['ʤɛməˌnaɪ] *n* : Géminis *mf*

gemstone ['ʤɛmˌsto:n] *n* : piedra *f* (semipreciosa o preciosa), gema *f*

gender ['ʤɛndər] *n* **1** SEX : sexo *m* **2** : género *m* (en la gramática)

gene ['ʤi:n] *n* : gen *m*, gene *m*

genealogical [ˌʤi:niə'lɑʤɪkəl] *adj* : genealógico

genealogy [ˌʤi:ni'ɑləʤi, ˌʤɛ-, -'æ-] *n, pl* **-gies** : genealogía *f*

genera → **genus**

general¹ ['ʤɛnrəl, 'ʤɛnə-] *adj* : general ⟨in general : en general, por lo general⟩

general² *n* : general *mf*

generality [ˌʤɛnə'ræləṯi] *n, pl* **-ties** : generalidad *f*

generalization [ˌʤɛnrələ'zeɪʃən, ˌʤɛnərə-] *n* : generalización *f*

generalize ['ʤɛnrəˌlaɪz, 'ʤɛnərə-] *v* **-ized; -izing** : generalizar

generally ['ʤɛnrəli, 'ʤɛnərə-] *adv* : generalmente, por lo general, en general

generate ['ʤɛnəˌreɪt] *vt* **-ated; -ating** : generar, producir

generation [ˌʤɛnə'reɪʃən] *n* : generación *f*

generator ['ʤɛnəˌreɪṯər] *n* : generador *m*

generic [ʤə'nɛrɪk] *adj* : genérico

generosity [ˌʤɛnə'rɑsəṯi] *n, pl* **-ties** : generosidad *f*

generous ['ʤɛnərəs] *adj* **1** OPENHANDED : generoso, dadivoso, desprendido **2** ABUNDANT, AMPLE : abundante, amplio, generoso — **generously** *adv*

genetic [ʤə'nɛṯɪk] *adj* : genético — **genetically** [-ṯɪkli] *adv*

geneticist [ʤə'nɛṯəsɪst] *n* : genetista *mf*

genetics [ʤə'nɛṯɪks] *n* : genética *f*

genial ['ʤi:niəl] *adj* GRACIOUS : simpático, cordial, afable — **genially** *adv*

geniality [ˌʤi:ni'æləṯi] *n* : simpatía *f*, afabilidad *f*

genie ['ʤi:ni] *n* : genio *m*

genital ['ʤɛnəṯəl] *adj* : genital

genitals ['ʤɛnəṯəlz] *npl* : genitales *mpl*

genius ['ʤi:njəs] *n* : genio *m*

genocide ['ʤɛnəˌsaɪd] *n* : genocidio *m*

genre ['ʒɑnrə, 'ʒɑr] *n* : género *m*

genteel [ʤɛn'ti:l] *adj* : cortés, fino, refinado

gentile¹ ['ʤɛnˌtaɪl] *adj* : gentil

gentile² *n* : gentil *mf*

gentility [ʤɛn'tɪləṯi] *n, pl* **-ties 1** : nobleza *f* (de nacimiento) **2** POLITENESS, REFINEMENT : cortesía *f*, refinamiento *m*

gentle ['ʤɛntəl] *adj* **-tler; -tlest 1** NOBLE : bien nacido, noble **2** DOCILE : dócil, manso **3** KINDLY : bondadoso, amable **4** MILD : suave, apacible ⟨a gentle breeze : una brisa suave⟩ **5** SOFT : suave (dícese de un sonido), ligero (dícese del tacto) **6** MODERATE : moderado, gradual ⟨a gentle slope : una cuesta gradual⟩

gentleman ['ʤɛntəlmən] *n, pl* **-men** [-mən, -ˌmɛn] : caballero *m*, señor *m*

gentlemanly ['ʤɛntəlmənli] *adj* : caballeroso

gentleness ['ʤɛntəlnəs] *n* : delicadeza *f*, suavidad *f*, ternura *f*

gentlewoman ['ʤɛntəlˌwʊmən] *n, pl* **-women** [-ˌwɪmən] : dama *f*, señora *f*

gently ['ʤɛntli] *adv* **1** CAREFULLY, SOFTLY : con cuidado, suavemente, ligeramente **2** KINDLY : amablemente, con delicadeza

gentry [ˈʤɛntri] *n, pl* **-tries** : aristocracia *f*
genuflect [ˈʤɛnjʊˌflɛkt] *vi* : doblar la rodilla, hacer una genuflexión
genuflection [ˌʤɛnjʊˈflɛkʃən] *n* : genuflexión *f*
genuine [ˈʤɛnjʊwən] *adj* **1** AUTHENTIC, REAL : genuino, verdadero, auténtico **2** SINCERE : sincero — **genuinely** *adv*
genus [ˈʤiːnəs] *n, pl* **genera** [ˈʤ-nərə] : género *m*
geographer [ʤiˈɑgrəfər] *n* : geógrafo *m*, -fa *f*
geographical [ˌʤiːəˈgræfɪkəl] *or* **geographic** [-fɪk] *adj* : geográfico — **geographically** [-fɪkli] *adv*
geography [ʤiˈɑgrəfi] *n, pl* **-phies** : geografía *f*
geologic [ˌʤiːəˈlɑʤɪk] *or* **geological** [-ʤɪkəl] *adj* : geológico — **geologically** [-ʤɪkli] *adv*
geologist [ʤiˈɑləʤɪst] *n* : geólogo *m*, -ga *f*
geology [ʤiˈɑləʤi] *n* : geología *f*
geometric [ˌʤiːəˈmɛtrɪk] *or* **geometrical** [-trɪkəl] *adj* : geométrico
geometry [ʤiˈɑmətri] *n, pl* **-tries** : geometría *f*
geopolitical [ˌʤiːopəˈlɪt̬ɪkəl] *adj* : geopolítico
Georgian [ˈʤɔrʤən] *n* **1** : georgiano *m* (idioma) **2** : georgiano *m*, -na *f* — **Georgian** *adj*
geranium [ʤəˈreɪniəm] *n* : geranio *m*
gerbil [ˈʤərbəl] *n* : jerbo *m*, gerbo *m*
geriatric [ˌʤɛriˈætrɪk] *adj* : geriátrico
geriatrics [ˌʤɛriˈætrɪks] *n* : geriatría *f*
germ [ˈʤərm] *n* **1** MICROORGANISM : microbio *m*, germen *m* **2** BEGINNING : germen *m*, principio *m* ⟨the germ of a plan : el germen de un plan⟩
German [ˈʤərmən] *n* **1** : alemán *m*, -mana *f* **2** : alemán *m* (idioma) — **German** *adj*
germane [ʤərˈmeɪn] *adj* : relevante, pertinente
Germanic[1] [ʤərˈmænɪk] *adj* : germánico, germano
Germanic[2] *n* : germánico *m* (idioma)
germanium [ʤərˈmeɪniəm] *n* : germanio *m*
germ cell *n* : célula *f* germen
germicide [ˈʤərməˌsaɪd] *n* : germicida *m*
germinate [ˈʤərməˌneɪt] *v* **-nated; -nating** *vi* : germinar — *vt* : hacer germinar
germination [ˌʤərməˈneɪʃən] *n* : germinación *f*
gerund [ˈʤɛrənd] *n* : gerundio *m*
gestation [ʤɛˈsteɪʃən] *n* : gestación *f*
gesture[1] [ˈʤɛsʧər] *vi* **-tured; -turing** : gesticular, hacer gestos
gesture[2] *n* **1** : gesto *m*, ademán *m* **2** SIGN, TOKEN : gesto *m*, señal *f* ⟨a gesture of friendship : una señal de amistad⟩
get [ˈgɛt] *v* **got** [ˈgɑt]; **got** *or* **gotten** [ˈgɑtən]; **getting** *vt* **1** OBTAIN : conseguir, obtener, adquirir **2** RECEIVE : recibir ⟨to get a letter : recibir una carta⟩ **3** EARN : ganar ⟨he gets $10 an hour : gana $10 por hora⟩ **4** FETCH : traer ⟨get me my book : tráigame el libro⟩ **5** CATCH : tomar (un tren, etc.), agarrar (una pelota, una persona, etc.) **6** CONTRACT : contagiarse de, contraer ⟨she got the measles : le dio el sarampión⟩ **7** PREPARE : preparar (una comida) **8** PERSUADE : persuadir, mandar a hacer ⟨I got him to agree : logré convencerlo⟩ **9** (*to cause to be*) ⟨to get one's hair cut : cortarse el pelo⟩ **10** UNDERSTAND : entender ⟨now I get it! : ¡ya entiendo!⟩ **11 to have got** : tener ⟨I've got a headache : tengo un dolor de cabeza⟩ **12 to have got to** : tener que ⟨you've got to come : tienes que venir⟩ — *vi* **1** BECOME : ponerse, volverse, hacerse ⟨to get angry : ponerse furioso, enojarse⟩ **2** GO, MOVE : ir, avanzar ⟨he didn't get far : no avanzó mucho⟩ **3** ARRIVE : llegar ⟨to get home : llegar a casa⟩ **4 to get to be** : llegar a ser ⟨she got to be the director : llegó a ser directora⟩ **5 to get ahead** : adelantarse, progresar **6 to get along** : llevarse bien (con alguien), congeniar **7 to get by** MANAGE : arreglárselas **8 to get over** OVERCOME : superar, consolarse de **9 to get together** MEET : reunirse **10 to get up** : levantarse
getaway [ˈgɛt̬əˌweɪ] *n* ESCAPE : fuga *f*, huida *f*, escapada *f*
geyser [ˈgaɪzər] *n* : géiser *m*
Ghanaian [ˈgɑniən, ˈgæ-] *n* : ghanés *m*, -nesa *f* — **Ghanaian** *adj*
ghastly [ˈgæstli] *adj* **-lier; -est** **1** HORRIBLE : horrible, espantoso **2** PALE : pálido, cadavérico
gherkin [ˈgərkən] *n* : pepinillo *m*
ghetto [ˈgɛt̬oː] *n, pl* **-tos** *or* **-toes** : gueto *m*
ghost [ˈgoːst] *n* **1** : fantasma *f*, espectro *m* **2 the Holy Ghost** : el Espíritu Santo
ghostly [ˈgoːstli] *adv* : fantasmal
ghoul [ˈguːl] *n* **1** : demonio *m* necrófago **2** : persona *f* de gustos macabros
GI [ˌʤiːˈaɪ] *n, pl* **GI's** *or* **GIs** : soldado *m* estadounidense
giant[1] [ˈʤaɪənt] *adj* : gigante, gigantesco, enorme
giant[2] *n* : gigante *m*, -ta *f*
gibberish [ˈʤɪbərɪʃ] *n* : galimatías *m*, jerigonza *f*
gibbon [ˈgɪbən] *n* : gibón *m*
gibe[1] [ˈʤaɪb] *vi* **gibed; gibing** : mofarse, burlarse
gibe[2] *n* : pulla *f*, burla *f*, mofa *f*
giblets [ˈʤɪbləts] *npl* : menudos *mpl*, menudencias *fpl*
giddiness [ˈgɪdinəs] *n* **1** DIZZINESS : vértigo *m*, mareo *m* **2** SILLINESS : frivolidad *f*, estupidez *f*

giddy [ˈgɪdi] *adj* **-dier; -est 1** DIZZY : mareado, vertiginoso **2** FRIVOLOUS, SILLY : frívolo, tonto

gift [ˈgɪft] *n* **1** TALENT : don *m*, talento *m*, dotes *fpl* **2** PRESENT : regalo *m*, obsequio *m*

gifted [ˈgɪftəd] *adj* TALENTED : talentoso

gig [ˈgɪg] *vi* : trabajo *m* (de duración limitada) ⟨to play a gig : tocar en un concierto⟩

gigabyte [ˈʤɪgəˌbaɪt, ˈgɪ-] *n* : gigabyte *m*

gigantic [ʤaɪˈgæntɪk] *adj* : gigantesco, enorme, colosal

giggle[1] [ˈgɪgəl] *vi* **-gled; -gling** : reírse tontamente

giggle[2] *n* : risita *f*, risa *f* tonta

gild [ˈgɪld] *vt* **gilded** *or* **gilt** [ˈgɪlt]; **gilding** : dorar

gill [ˈgɪl] *n* : agalla *f*, branquia *f*

gilt[1] [ˈgɪlt] *adj* : dorado

gilt[2] *n* : dorado *m*

gimlet [ˈgɪmlət] *n* **1** : barrena *f* (herramienta) **2** : bebida *f* de vodka o ginebra y limón

gimmick [ˈgɪmɪk] *n* **1** GADGET : artilugio *m* **2** CATCH : engaño *m*, trampa *f* **3** SCHEME, TRICK : ardid *m*, truco *m*

gin [ˈʤɪn] *n* **1** : desmotadora *f* (de algodón) **2** : ginebra *f* (bebida alcohólica)

ginger [ˈʤɪnʤər] *n* : jengibre *m*

ginger ale *n* : ginger ale *m*, gaseosa *f* de jengibre

gingerbread [ˈʤɪnʤərˌbrɛd] *n* : pan *m* de jengibre

gingerly [ˈʤɪnʤərli] *adv* : con cuidado, cautelosamente

gingham [ˈgɪŋəm] *n* : guinga *f*

ginseng [ˈʤɪnˌsɪŋ, -ˌsɛŋ] *n* : ginseng *m*

giraffe [ʤəˈræf] *n* : jirafa *f*

gird [ˈgərd] *vt* **girded** *or* **girt** [ˈgərt]; **girding 1** BIND : ceñir, atar **2** ENCIRCLE : rodear **3 to gird oneself** : prepararse

girder [ˈgərdər] *n* : viga *f*

girdle[1] [ˈgərdəl] *vt* **-dled; -dling 1** GIRD : ceñir, atar **2** SURROUND : rodear, circundar

girdle[2] *n* : faja *f*

girl [ˈgərl] *n* **1** : chica *f*, muchacha *f* **2** *or* **little girl** : niña *f*, chica *f* **3** SWEETHEART : novia *f* **4** DAUGHTER : hija *f*

girlfriend [ˈgərlˌfrɛnd] *n* : novia *f*, amiga *f*

girlhood [ˈgərlˌhʊd] *n* : niñez *f*, juventud *f* (de una muchacha)

girlish [ˈgərlɪʃ] *adj* : de niña

girth [ˈgərθ] *n* **1** : circunferencia *f* (de un árbol, etc.), cintura *f* (de una persona) **2** CINCH : cincha *f* (para caballos, etc.)

gist [ˈʤɪst] *n* : quid *m*, meollo *m*

give[1] [ˈgɪv] *v* **gave** [ˈgeɪv]; **given** [ˈgɪvən]; **giving** *vt* **1** HAND, PRESENT : dar, regalar, obsequiar ⟨give it to me : dámelo⟩ ⟨they gave him a gold watch : le regalaron un reloj de oro⟩ **2** PAY : dar, pagar ⟨I'll give you $10 for this one : te daré $10 por éste⟩ **3** UTTER : dar, pronunciar ⟨to give a shout : dar un grito⟩ ⟨to give a speech : pronunciar un discurso⟩ ⟨to give a verdict : dictar sentencia⟩ **4** PROVIDE : dar ⟨to give one's word : dar uno su palabra⟩ ⟨to give a party : dar una fiesta⟩ **5** CAUSE : dar, causar, ocasionar ⟨to give trouble : causar problemas⟩ ⟨to give someone to understand : darle a entender a alguien⟩ **6** GRANT : dar, otorgar ⟨to give permission : dar permiso⟩ — *vi* **1** : hacer regalos **2** YIELD : ceder, romperse ⟨it gave under the weight of the crowd : cedió bajo el peso de la muchedumbre⟩ **3 to give in** *or* **to give up** SURRENDER : rendirse, entregarse **4 to give out** : agotarse, acabarse ⟨the supplies gave out : las provisiones se agotaron⟩

give[2] *n* FLEXIBILITY : flexibilidad *f*, elasticidad *f*

giveaway [ˈgɪvəˌweɪ] *n* **1** : revelación *f* involuntaria **2** GIFT : regalo *m*, obsequio *m*

given [ˈgɪvən] *adj* **1** INCLINED : dado, inclinado ⟨he's given to quarreling : es muy dado a discutir⟩ **2** SPECIFIC : dado, determinado ⟨at a given time : en un momento dado⟩

given name *n* : nombre *m* de pila

give up *vt* : dejar, renunciar a, abandonar ⟨to give up smoking : dejar de fumar⟩

gizzard [ˈgɪzərd] *n* : molleja *f*

glacial [ˈgleɪʃəl] *adj* : glacial — **glacially** *adv*

glacier [ˈgleɪʃər] *n* : glaciar *m*

glad [ˈglæd] *adj* **gladder; gladdest 1** PLEASED : alegre, contento ⟨she was glad I came : se alegró de que haya venido⟩ ⟨glad to meet you! : ¡mucho gusto!⟩ **2** HAPPY, PLEASING : feliz, agradable ⟨glad tidings : buenas nuevas⟩ **3** WILLING : dispuesto, gustoso ⟨I'll be glad to do it : lo haré con mucho gusto⟩

gladden [ˈglædən] *vt* : alegrar

glade [ˈgleɪd] *n* : claro *m*

gladiator [ˈglædiˌeɪt̬ər] *n* : gladiador *m*

gladiolus [ˌglædiˈo:ləs] *n, pl* **-li** [-li, -ˌlaɪ] : gladiolo *m*, gladíolo *m*

gladly [ˈglædli] *adv* : con mucho gusto

gladness [ˈglædnəs] *n* : alegría *f*, gozo *m*

glamor *or* **glamour** [ˈglæmər] *n* : atractivo *m*, hechizo *m*, encanto *m*

glamorous [ˈglæmərəs] *adj* : atractivo, encantador

glance[1] [ˈglænts] *vi* **glanced; glancing 1** RICOCHET : rebotar ⟨it glanced off the wall : rebotó en la pared⟩ **2 to glance at** : mirar, echar un vistazo a **3 to glance away** : apartar los ojos

glance[2] *n* : mirada *f*, vistazo *m*, ojeada *f*

gland [ˈglænd] *n* : glándula *f*

glandular [ˈglænʤʊlər] *adj* : glandular

glare[1] [ˈglær] *vi* **glared; glaring 1** SHINE : brillar, relumbrar **2** STARE : mirar con ira, lanzar una mirada feroz

glare[2] *n* **1** BRIGHTNESS : resplandor *m*, luz *f* deslumbrante **2** : mirada *f* feroz

glaring [ˈglærɪŋ] *adj* **1** BRIGHT : deslumbrante, brillante **2** FLAGRANT, OBVIOUS : flagrante, manifiesto ⟨a glaring error : un error que salta a la vista⟩

glass [ˈglæs] *n* **1** : vidrio *m*, cristal *m* ⟨stained glass : vidrio de color⟩ **2** : vaso *m* ⟨a glass of milk : un vaso de leche⟩ **3 glasses** *npl* SPECTACLES : gafas *fpl*, anteojos *mpl*, lentes *mpl*, espejuelos *mpl*

glassblowing [ˈglæsˌbloːɪŋ] *n* : soplado *m* del vidrio

glassful [ˈglæsˌfʊl] *n* : vaso *m*, copa *f*

glassware [ˈglæsˌwær] *n* : cristalería *f*

glassy [ˈglæsi] *adj* **glassier; -est 1** VITREOUS : vítreo **2** : vidrioso ⟨glassy eyes : ojos vidriosos⟩

glaucoma [glaʊˈkoːmə, glɔ-] *n* : glaucoma *m*

glaze[1] [ˈgleɪz] *vt* **glazed; glazing 1** : ponerle vidrios a (una ventana, etc.) **2** : vidriar (cerámica) **3** : glasear (papel, verduras, etc.)

glaze[2] *n* : vidriado *m*, glaseado *m*, barniz *m*

glazier [ˈgleɪʒər] *n* : vidriero *m*, -ra *f*

gleam[1] [ˈgliːm] *vi* : brillar, destellar, relucir

gleam[2] *n* **1** LIGHT : luz *f* (oscura) **2** GLINT : destello *m* **3** GLIMMER : rayo *m*, vislumbre *f* ⟨a gleam of hope : un rayo de esperanza⟩

glean [ˈgliːn] *vt* : recoger, espigar

glee [ˈgliː] *n* : alegría *f*, júbilo *m*, regocijo *m*

gleeful [ˈgliːfəl] *adj* : lleno de alegría

glen [ˈglɛn] *n* : cañada *f*

glib [ˈglɪb] *adj* **glibber; glibbest 1** : simplista ⟨a glib reply : una respuesta simplista⟩ **2** : con mucha labia (dícese de una persona)

glibly [ˈglɪbli] *adv* : con mucha labia

glide[1] [ˈglaɪd] *vi* **glided; gliding** : deslizarse (en una superficie), planear (en el aire)

glide[2] *n* : planeo *m*

glider [ˈglaɪdər] *n* **1** : planeador *m* (aeronave) **2** : mecedor *m* (tipo de columpio)

glimmer[1] [ˈglɪmər] *vi* : brillar con luz trémula

glimmer[2] *n* **1** : luz *f* trémula, luz *f* tenue **2** GLEAM : rayo *m*, vislumbre *f* ⟨a glimmer of understanding : un rayo de entendimiento⟩

glimpse[1] [ˈglɪmps] *vt* **glimpsed; glimpsing** : vislumbrar, entrever

glimpse[2] *n* : mirada *f* breve ⟨to catch a glimpse of : alcanzar a ver, vislumbrar⟩

glint[1] [ˈglɪnt] *vi* GLEAM, SPARKLE : destellar, fulgurar

glint[2] *n* **1** SPARKLE : destello *m*, centelleo *m* **2 to have a glint in one's eye** : chispearle los ojos a uno

glisten[1] [ˈglɪsən] *vi* : brillar, centellear

glisten[2] *n* : brillo *m*, centelleo *m*

glitch [ˈglɪʧ] *n* **1** MALFUNCTION : mal funcionamiento *m* **2** SNAG : problema *m*, complicación *f*

glitter[1] [ˈglɪt̬ər] *vi* **1** SPARKLE : destellar, relucir, brillar **2** FLASH : relampaguear ⟨his eyes glittered in anger : le relampagueaban los ojos de ira⟩

glitter[2] *n* **1** BRIGHTNESS : brillo *m* **2** : purpurina *f* (para decoración)

glitz [ˈglɪts] *n* : oropel *m*

gloat [ˈgloːt] *vi* **to gloat over** : regodearse en

glob [ˈglɑb] *n* : plasta *f*, masa *f*, grumo *m*

global [ˈgloːbəl] *adj* **1** SPHERICAL : esférico **2** WORLDWIDE : global, mundial — **globally** *adv*

globe [ˈgloːb] *n* **1** SPHERE : esfera *f*, globo *m* **2** EARTH : globo *m*, Tierra *f* **3** : globo *m* terráqueo (modelo de la Tierra)

globe–trotter [ˈgloːbˌtrɑt̬ər] *n* : trotamundos *mf*

globular [ˈglɑbjʊlər] *adj* : globular

globule [ˈglɑˌbjuːl] *n* : glóbulo *m*

gloom [ˈgluːm] *n* **1** DARKNESS : penumbra *f*, oscuridad *f* **2** MELANCHOLY : melancolía *f*, tristeza *f*

gloomily [ˈgluːməli] *adv* : tristemente

gloomy [ˈgluːmi] *adj* **gloomier; -est 1** DARK : oscuro, tenebroso ⟨gloomy weather : tiempo gris⟩ **2** MELANCHOLY : melancólico **3** PESSIMISTIC : pesimista **4** DEPRESSING : deprimente, lúgubre

glorification [ˌglorəfəˈkeɪʃən] *n* : glorificación *f*

glorify [ˈglorəˌfaɪ] *vt* **-fied; -fying** : glorificar

glorious [ˈgloriəs] *adj* **1** ILLUSTRIOUS : glorioso, ilustre **2** MAGNIFICENT : magnífico, espléndido, maravilloso — **gloriously** *adv*

glory[1] [ˈglori] *vi* **-ried; -rying** EXULT : exultar, regocijarse

glory[2] *n, pl* **-ries 1** RENOWN : gloria *f*, fama *f*, honor *m* **2** PRAISE : gloria *f* ⟨glory to God : gloria a Dios⟩ **3** MAGNIFICENCE : magnificencia *f*, esplendor *m*, gloria *f* **4 to be in one's glory** : estar uno en su gloria

gloss[1] [ˈglɔs, ˈglɑs] *vt* **1** EXPLAIN : glosar, explicar **2** POLISH : lustrar, pulir **3 to gloss over** : quitarle importancia a, minimizar

gloss[2] *n* **1** SHINE : lustre *m*, brillo *m* **2** EXPLANATION : glosa *f*, explicación *f* breve **3** → **glossary**

glossary [ˈglɔsəri, ˈglɑ-] *n, pl* **-ries** : glosario *m*

glossy [ˈglɔsi, ˈglɑ-] *adj* **glossier; -est** : brillante, lustroso, satinado (dícese del papel)

glove [ˈglʌv] *n* : guante *m*

glow[1] [ˈgloː] *vi* **1** SHINE : brillar, resplandecer **2** BRIM : rebosar ⟨to glow with health : rebosar de salud⟩

glow[2] *n* **1** BRIGHTNESS : resplandor *m*, brillo *m*, luminosidad *f* **2** FEELING : sensación *f* (de bienestar), oleada *f* (de sentimiento) **3** INCANDESCENCE : incandescencia *f*

glower [ˈglaʊər] *vi* : fruncir el ceño

glowworm [ˈgloːˌwərm] *n* : luciérnaga *f*

glucose [ˈgluːˌkoːs] *n* : glucosa *f*

glue[1] [ˈgluː] *vt* **glued; gluing** *or* **glueing** : pegar, encolar

glue[2] *n* : pegamento *m*, cola *f*

gluey [ˈgluːi] *adj* **gluier; -est** : pegajoso

glum [ˈglʌm] *adj* **glummer; glummest** **1** SULLEN : hosco, sombrío **2** DREARY, GLOOMY : sombrío, triste, melancólico

glut[1] [ˈglʌt] *vt* **glutted; glutting** **1** SATIATE : saciar, hartar **2** : inundar (el mercado)

glut[2] *n* : exceso *m*, superabundancia *f*

glutinous [ˈgluːtənəs] *adj* STICKY : pegajoso, glutinoso

glutton [ˈglʌtən] *n* : glotón *m*, -tona *f*

gluttonous [ˈglʌtənəs] *adj* : glotón

gluttony [ˈglʌtəni] *n, pl* **-tonies** : glotonería *f*, gula *f*

gnarled [ˈnɑrld] *adj* **1** KNOTTY : nudoso **2** TWISTED : retorcido

gnash [ˈnæʃ] *vt* : hacer rechinar (los dientes)

gnat [ˈnæt] *n* : jején *m*

gnaw [ˈnɔ] *vt* : roer

gnome [ˈnoːm] *n* : gnomo *m*

gnu [ˈnuː, ˈnjuː] *n, pl* **gnu** *or* **gnus** : ñu *m*

go[1] [ˈgoː] *v* **went** [ˈwɛnt]; **gone** [ˈgɔn, ˈgɑn]; **going; goes** [ˈgoːz] *vi* **1** PROCEED : ir ⟨to go slow : ir despacio⟩ ⟨to go shopping : ir de compras⟩ **2** LEAVE : irse, marcharse, salir ⟨let's go! : ¡vámonos!⟩ ⟨the train went on time : el tren salió a tiempo⟩ **3** DISAPPEAR : desaparecer, pasarse, irse ⟨her fear is gone : se le ha pasado el miedo⟩ ⟨my pen is gone! : ¡mi pluma desapareció!⟩ **4** EXTEND : ir, extenderse, llegar ⟨this road goes to the river : este camino se extiende hasta el río⟩ ⟨to go from top to bottom : ir de arriba abajo⟩ **5** FUNCTION : funcionar, marchar ⟨the car won't go : el coche no funciona⟩ ⟨to get something going : poner algo en marcha⟩ **6** SELL : venderse ⟨it goes for $15 : se vende por $15⟩ **7** PROGRESS : ir, andar, seguir ⟨my exam went well : me fue bien en el examen⟩ ⟨how did the meeting go? : ¿qué tal la reunión?⟩ **8** BECOME : volverse, quedarse ⟨he's going crazy : está volviéndose loco⟩ ⟨the tire went flat : la llanta se desinfló⟩ **9** FIT : caber ⟨it will go through the door : cabe por la puerta⟩ **10 anything goes!** : ¡todo vale! **11 to go** : faltar ⟨only 10 days to go : faltan sólo 10 días⟩ **12 to go back on** : faltar uno a (su promesa) **13 to go bad** SPOIL : estropearse, echarse a perder **14 to go for** : interesarse uno en, gustarle a uno (algo, alguien) ⟨I don't go for that : eso no me interesa⟩ **15 to go off** EXPLODE : estallar **16 to go with** MATCH : armonizar con, hacer juego con — *v aux* **to be going to** : ir a ⟨I'm going to write a letter : voy a escribir una carta⟩ ⟨it's not going to last : no va a durar⟩

go[2] *n, pl* **goes** **1** ATTEMPT : intento *m* ⟨to have a go at : intentar, probar⟩ **2** SUCCESS : éxito *m* **3** ENERGY : energía *f*, empuje *m* ⟨to be on the go : no parar, no descansar⟩

goad[1] [ˈgoːd] *vt* : aguijonear (un animal), incitar (a una persona)

goad[2] *n* : aguijón *m*

goal [ˈgoːl] *n* **1** : gol *m* (en deportes) ⟨to score a goal : anotar un gol⟩ **2** *or* **goalposts** : portería *f* **3** AIM, OBJECTIVE : meta *m*, objetivo *m*

goalie [ˈgoːli] → **goalkeeper**

goalkeeper [ˈgoːlˌkiːpər] *n* : portero *m*, -ra *f*; guardameta *mf*; arquero *m*, -ra *f*

goaltender [ˈgoːlˌtɛndər] → **goalkeeper**

goat [ˈgoːt] *n* **1** : cabra *f* (hembra) **2 billy goat** : macho *m* cabrío, chivo *m*

goatee [goːˈtiː] *n* : barbita *f* de chivo, piocha *f Mex*

goatskin [ˈgoːtˌskɪn] *n* : piel *f* de cabra

gob [ˈgɑb] *n* : masa *f*, grumo *m*

gobble [ˈgɑbəl] *v* **-bled; -bling** *vt* **to gobble up** : tragar, engullir — *vi* : hacer ruidos de pavo

gobbledygook [ˈgɑbəldiˌgʊk, -ˌguːk] *n* GIBBERISH : jerigonza *f*

go–between [ˈgoːbɪˌtwiːn] *n* : intermediario *m*, -ria *f*; mediador *m*, -dora *f*

goblet [ˈgɑblət] *n* : copa *f*

goblin [ˈgɑblən] *n* : duende *m*, trasgo *m*

god [ˈgɑd, ˈgɔd] *n* **1** : dios *m* **2 God** : Dios *m*

godchild [ˈgɑdˌtʃaɪld, ˈgɔd-] *n, pl* **-children** : ahijado *m*, -da *f*

goddess [ˈgɑdəs, ˈgɔ-] *n* : diosa *f*

godfather [ˈgɑdˌfɑðər, ˈgɔd-] *n* : padrino *m*

godless [ˈgɑdləs, ˈgɔd-] *adj* : ateo

godlike [ˈgɑdˌlaɪk, ˈgɔd-] *adj* : divino

godly [ˈgɑdli, ˈgɔd-] *adj* **-lier; -est** **1** DIVINE : divino **2** DEVOUT, PIOUS : piadoso, devoto, beato

godmother [ˈgɑdˌmʌðər, ˈgɔd-] *n* : madrina *f*

godparents [ˈgɑdˌpærənts, ˈgɔd-] *npl* : padrinos *mpl*

godsend [ˈgɑdˌsɛnd, ˈgɔd-] *n* : bendición *f*, regalo *m* divino

goes → **go**

go–getter [ˈgoːˌgɛt̬ər] *n* : persona *f* ambiciosa, buscavidas *mf fam*

goggle [ˈgɑgəl] *vi* **-gled; -gling** : mirar con ojos desorbitados

goggles [ˈgɑgəlz] *npl* : gafas *fpl* (protectoras), anteojos *mpl*

goings–on [ˌgoːɪŋzˈɑn, -ˈɔn] *npl* : sucesos *mpl*, ocurrencias *fpl*

goiter [ˈgɔɪt̬ər] *n* : bocio *m*

gold [ˈgoːld] *n* : oro *m*

golden [ˈgoːldən] *adj* **1** : (hecho) de oro **2** : dorado, de color oro ⟨golden hair

: pelo rubio〉 **3** FLOURISHING, PROSPEROUS : dorado, próspero 〈golden years : años dorados〉 **4** FAVORABLE : favorable, excelente 〈a golden opportunity : una excelente oportunidad〉

goldenrod ['go:ldən,rɑd] *n* : vara *f* de oro

golden rule *n* : regla *f* de oro

goldfinch ['go:ld,fɪntʃ] *n* : jilguero *m*

goldfish ['go:ld,fɪʃ] *n* : pez *m* de colores

goldsmith ['go:ld,smɪθ] *n* : orífice *mf*, orfebre *mf*

golf[1] ['gɑlf, 'gɔlf] *vi* : jugar (al) golf

golf[2] *n* : golf *m*

golfer ['gɑlfər, 'gɔl-] *n* : golfista *mf*

gondola ['gɑndələ, gɑn'do:lə] *n* : góndola *f*

gone ['gɔn] *adj* **1** DEAD : muerto **2** PAST : pasado, ido **3** LOST : perdido, desaparecido **4 to be far gone** : estar muy avanzado **5 to be gone on** : estar loco por

goner ['gɔnər] *n* **to be a goner** : estar en las últimas

gong ['gɔŋ, 'gɑŋ] *n* : gong *m*

gonorrhea [,gɑnə'ri:ə] *n* : gonorrea *f*

good[1] ['gʊd] *adv* **1** (*used as an intensifier*) : bien 〈a good strong rope : una cuerda bien fuerte〉 **2** WELL : bien

good[2] *adj* **better** ['bɛt̬ər]; **best** ['bɛst] **1** PLEASANT : bueno, agradable 〈good news : buenas noticias〉 〈to have a good time : divertirse〉 **2** BENEFICIAL : bueno, beneficioso 〈good for a cold : beneficioso para los resfriados〉 〈it's good for you : es bueno para uno〉 **3** FULL : completo, entero 〈a good hour : una hora entera〉 **4** CONSIDERABLE : bueno, bastante 〈a good many people : muchísima gente, un buen número de gente〉 **5** ATTRACTIVE, DESIRABLE : bueno, bien 〈a good salary : un buen sueldo〉 〈to look good : quedar bien〉 **6** KIND, VIRTUOUS : bueno, amable 〈she's a good person : es buena gente〉 〈that's good of you! : ¡qué amable!〉 〈good deeds : buenas obras〉 **7** SKILLED : bueno, hábil 〈to be good at : tener facilidad para〉 **8** SOUND : bueno, sensato 〈good advice : buenos consejos〉 **9** (*in greetings*) : bueno 〈good morning : buenos días〉 〈good afternoon (evening) : buenas tardes〉 〈good night : buenas noches〉

good[3] *n* **1** RIGHT : bien *m* 〈to do good : hacer el bien〉 **2** GOODNESS : bondad *f* **3** BENEFIT : bien *m*, provecho *m* 〈it's for your own good : es por tu propio bien〉 **4 goods** *npl* PROPERTY : efectos *mpl* personales, posesiones *fpl* **5 goods** *npl* WARES : mercancía *f*, mercadería *f*, artículos *mpl* **6 for ~** : para siempre

good–bye *or* **good–by** [gʊd'baɪ] *n* : adiós *m*

good–for–nothing ['gʊdfər,nʌθɪŋ] *n* : inútil *mf*; haragán *m*, -gana *f*; holgazán *m*, -zana *f*

Good Friday *n* : Viernes *m* Santo

good–hearted ['gʊd'hɑrt̬əd] *adj* : bondadoso, benévolo, de buen corazón

good–looking ['gʊd'lʊkɪŋ] *adj* : bello, bonito, guapo

goodly ['gʊdli] *adj* **-lier; -est** : considerable, importante 〈a goodly number : un número considerable〉

good–natured ['gʊd'neɪtʃərd] *adj* : amigable, amistoso, bonachón *fam*

goodness ['gʊdnəs] *n* **1** : bondad *f* **2 thank goodness!** : ¡gracias a Dios!, ¡menos mal!

good–tempered ['gʊd'tɛmpərd] *adj* : de buen genio

goodwill [,gʊd'wɪl] *n* **1** BENEVOLENCE : benevolencia *f*, buena voluntad *f* **2** : buen nombre *m* (de comercios), renombre *m* comercial

goody ['gʊdi] *n, pl* **goodies** : cosa *f* rica para comer, golosina *f*

gooey ['gu:i] *adj* **gooier; gooiest** : pegajoso

goof[1] ['gu:f] *vi* **1 to goof off** : holgazanear **2 to goof around** : hacer tonterías **3 to goof up** BLUNDER : cometer un error

goof[2] *n* **1** : bobo *m*, -ba *f*; tonto *m*, -ta *f* **2** BLUNDER : error *m*, planchazo *m fam*

goofy ['gu:fi] *adj* **goofier; -est** SILLY : tonto, bobo

goose ['gu:s] *n, pl* **geese** ['gi:s] : ganso *m*, -sa *f*; ánsar *m*; oca *f*

gooseberry ['gu:s,bɛri:, 'gu:z-] *n, pl* **-berries** : grosella *f* espinosa

goose bumps *npl* : carne *f* de gallina

gooseflesh ['gu:s,flɛʃ] → **goose bumps**

goose pimples → **goose bumps**

gopher ['go:fər] *n* : taltuza *f*

gore[1] ['gor] *vt* **gored; goring** : cornear

gore[2] *n* BLOOD : sangre *f*

gorge[1] ['gɔrdʒ] *vt* **gorged; gorging 1** SATIATE : saciar, hartar **2 to gorge oneself** : hartarse, atiborrarse, atracarse *fam*

gorge[2] *n* RAVINE : desfiladero *m*

gorgeous ['gɔrdʒəs] *adj* : hermoso, espléndido, magnífico

gorilla [gə'rɪlə] *n* : gorila *m*

gory ['gori] *adj* **gorier; -est** BLOODY : sangriento

gosling ['gɑzlɪŋ, 'gɔz-] *n* : ansarino *m*

gospel ['gɑspəl] *n* **1** *or* **Gospel** : evangelio *m* 〈the four Gospels : los cuatro evangelios〉 **2 the gospel truth** : el evangelio, la pura verdad

gossamer ['gɑsəmər, 'gɑzə-] *adj* : tenue, sutil 〈gossamer wings : alas tenues〉

gossip[1] ['gɑsɪp] *vi* : chismear, contar chismes

gossip[2] *n* **1** : chismoso *m*, -sa *f* (persona) **2** RUMOR : chisme *m*, rumor *m*

gossipy ['gɑsɪpi] *adj* : chismoso

got → **get**

Gothic ['gɑθɪk] *adj* : gótico

gotten → **get**

gouge[1] ['gaʊdʒ] *vt* **gouged; gouging 1** : excavar, escoplear (con una gubia) **2** SWINDLE : estafar, extorsionar

gouge[2] *n* **1** CHISEL : gubia *f*, formón *m* **2** GROOVE : ranura *f*, hoyo *m* (hecho por un formón)
goulash ['gu:ˌlɑʃ, -ˌlæʃ] *n* : estofado *m*, guiso *m* al estilo húngaro
gourd ['gord, 'gʊrd] *n* : calabaza *f*
gourmand ['gʊrˌmɑnd] *n* **1** GLUTTON : glotón *m*, -tona *f* **2** → **gourmet**
gourmet ['gʊrˌmeɪ, gʊr'meɪ] *n* : gourmet *mf*; gastrónomo *m*, -ma *f*
gout ['gaʊt] *n* : gota *f*
govern ['gʌvərn] *vt* **1** RULE : gobernar **2** CONTROL, DETERMINE : determinar, controlar, guiar **3** RESTRAIN : dominar (las emociones, etc.) — *vi* : gobernar
governess ['gʌvərnəs] *n* : institutriz *f*
government ['gʌvərmənt] *n* : gobierno *m*
governmental [ˌgʌvər'mɛntəl] *adj* : gubernamental, gubernativo
governor ['gʌvənər, 'gʌvərnər] *n* **1** : gobernador *m*, - dora *f* (de un estado, etc.) **2** : regulador *m* (de una máquina)
governorship ['gʌvənərˌʃɪp, 'gʌvərnər-] *n* : cargo *m* de gobernador
gown ['gaʊn] *n* **1** : vestido *m* ⟨evening gown : traje de fiesta⟩ **2** : toga *f* (de magistrados, clérigos, etc.)
grab[1] ['græb] *v* **grabbed; grabbing** *vt* SNATCH : agarrar, arrebatar — *vi* : agarrarse
grab[2] *n* **1 to make a grab for** : tratar de agarrar **2 up for grabs** : disponible, libre
grace[1] ['greɪs] *vt* **graced; gracing 1** HONOR : honrar **2** ADORN : adornar, embellecer
grace[2] *n* **1** : gracia *f* ⟨by the grace of God : por la gracia de Dios⟩ **2** BLESSING : bendición *f* (de la mesa) **3** RESPITE : plazo *m*, gracia *f* ⟨a five days' grace (period) : un plazo de cinco días⟩ **4** GRACIOUSNESS : gentileza *f*, cortesía *f* **5** ELEGANCE : elegancia *f*, gracia *f* **6 to be in the good graces of** : estar en buenas relaciones con **7 with good grace** : de buena gana
graceful ['greɪsfəl] *adj* : lleno de gracia, garboso, grácil
gracefully ['greɪsfəli] *adv* : con gracia, con garbo
gracefulness ['greɪsfəlnəs] *n* : gracilidad *f*, apostura *f*, gallardía *f*
graceless ['greɪsləs] *adj* **1** DISCOURTEOUS : descortés **2** CLUMSY, INELEGANT : torpe, desgarbado, poco elegante
gracious ['greɪʃəs] *adj* : cortés, gentil, cordial
graciously ['greɪʃəsli] *adv* : gentilmente
graciousness ['greɪʃəsnəs] *n* : gentileza *f*
gradation [greɪ'deɪʃən, grə-] *n* : gradación *f*
grade[1] ['greɪd] *vt* **graded; grading 1** SORT : clasificar **2** LEVEL : nivelar **3** : calificar (exámenes, alumnos)
grade[2] *n* **1** QUALITY : categoría *f*, calidad *f* **2** RANK : grado *m*, rango *m* (militar) **3** YEAR : grado *m*, curso *m*, año *m* ⟨sixth grade : el sexto grado⟩ **4** MARK : nota *f*, calificación *f* (en educación) **5** SLOPE : cuesta *f*, pendiente *f*, gradiente *f*
grade school → **elementary school**
gradient ['greɪdiənt] *n* : gradiente *f*
gradual ['grædʒʊəl] *adj* : gradual, paulatino
gradually ['grædʒʊəli, 'grædʒəli] *adv* : gradualmente, poco a poco
graduate[1] ['grædʒʊˌeɪt] *v* **-ated; -ating** *vi* : graduarse, licenciarse — *vt* : graduar ⟨a graduated thermometer : un termómetro graduado⟩
graduate[2] ['grædʒʊət] *adj* : de postgrado ⟨graduate course : curso de postgrado⟩
graduate[3] *n* **1** : licenciado *m*, -da *f*; graduado *m*, -da *f* (de la universidad) **2** : bachiller *mf* (de la escuela secundaria)
graduate student *n* : postgraduado *m*, -da *f*
graduation [ˌgrædʒʊ'eɪʃən] *n* : graduación *f*
graffiti [grə'fi:t̬i, græ-] *npl* : pintadas *fpl*, graffiti *mpl*
graft[1] ['græft] *vt* : injertar
graft[2] *n* **1** : injerto *m* ⟨skin graft : injerto cutáneo⟩ **2** CORRUPTION : soborno *m* (político), ganancia *f* ilegal
grain ['greɪn] *n* **1** : grano *m* ⟨a grain of corn : un grano de maíz⟩ ⟨like a grain of sand : como grano de arena⟩ **2** CEREALS : cereales *mpl* **3** : veta *f*, vena *f*, grano *m* (de madera) **4** SPECK, TRACE : pizca *f*, ápice *m* ⟨a grain of truth : una pizca de verdad⟩ **5** grano *m* (unidad de peso)
gram ['græm] *n* : gramo *m*
grammar ['græmər] *n* : gramática *f*
grammar school → **elementary school**
grammatical [grə'mæt̬ɪkəl] *adj* : gramatical — **grammatically** [-kli] *adv*
granary ['greɪnəri, 'græ-] *n, pl* **-ries** : granero *m*
grand ['grænd] *adj* **1** FOREMOST : grande **2** IMPRESSIVE : impresionante, magnífico ⟨a grand view : una vista magnífica⟩ **3** LAVISH : grandioso, suntuoso, lujoso ⟨to live in a grand manner : vivir a lo grande⟩ **4** FABULOUS : fabuloso, magnífico ⟨to have a grand time : pasarlo estupendamente, pasarlo en grande⟩ **5 grand total** : total *m*, suma *f* total
grandchild ['grændˌtʃaɪld] *n, pl* **-children** : nieto *m*, -ta *f*
granddaughter ['grændˌdɔt̬ər] *n* : nieta *f*
grandeur ['grændʒər] *n* : grandiosidad *f*, esplendor *m*
grandfather ['grændˌfɑðər] *n* : abuelo *m*
grandiose ['grændiˌo:s, ˌgrændi'-] *adj* **1** IMPOSING : imponente, grandioso **2** POMPOUS : pomposo, presuntuoso
grandma ['græn̩ˌmɑ, -ˌmɔ] *n* : abuelita *f*, nana *f*

grandmother [ˈgrændˌmʌðər] *n* : abuela *f*
grandpa [ˈgræmˌpɑ, -ˌpɔ] *n* : abuelito *m*
grandparents [ˈgrændˌpærənts] *npl* : abuelos *mpl*
grandson [ˈgrændˌsʌn] *n* : nieto *m*
grandstand [ˈgrændˌstænd] *n* : tribuna *f*
granite [ˈgrænɪt] *n* : granito *m*
grant[1] [ˈgrænt] *vt* **1** ALLOW : conceder ⟨to grant a request : conceder una petición⟩ **2** BESTOW : conceder, dar, otorgar ⟨to grant a favor : otorgar un favor⟩ **3** ADMIT : reconocer, admitir ⟨I'll grant that he's clever : reconozco que es listo⟩ **4 to take for granted** : dar (algo) por sentado
grant[2] *n* **1** GRANTING : concesión *f*, otorgamiento *m* **2** SCHOLARSHIP : beca *f* **3** SUBSIDY : subvención *f*
granular [ˈgrænjʊlər] *adj* : granular
granulated [ˈgrænjʊˌleɪt̬əd] *adj* : granulado
grape [ˈgreɪp] *n* : uva *f*
grapefruit [ˈgreɪpˌfruːt] *n* : toronja *f*, pomelo *m*
grapevine [ˈgreɪpˌvaɪn] *n* **1** : vid *f*, parra *f* **2 through the grapevine** : por vías secretas ⟨I heard it through the grapevine : me lo contaron⟩
graph [ˈgræf] *n* : gráfica *f*, gráfico *m*
graphic [ˈgræfɪk] *adj* **1** VIVID : vívido, gráfico **2 graphic arts** : artes gráficas
graphically [ˈgræfɪkli] *adv* : gráficamente
graphite [ˈgræˌfaɪt] *n* : grafito *m*
grapnel [ˈgræpnəl] *n* : rezón *m*
grapple [ˈgræpəl] *v* **-pled; -pling** *vt* GRIP : agarrar (con un garfio) — *vi* STRUGGLE : forcejear, luchar (con un problema, etc.)
grasp[1] [ˈgræsp] *vt* **1** GRIP, SEIZE : agarrar, asir **2** COMPREHEND : entender, comprender — *vi* **to grasp at** : aprovechar
grasp[2] *n* **1** GRIP : agarre *m* **2** CONTROL : control *m*, garras *fpl* **3** REACH : alcance *m* ⟨within your grasp : a su alcance⟩ **4** UNDERSTANDING : comprensión *f*, entendimiento *m*
grass [ˈgræs] *n* **1** : hierba *f* (planta) **2** PASTURE : pasto *m*, zacate *m CA, Mex* **3** LAWN : césped *m*, pasto *m*
grasshopper [ˈgræsˌhɑpər] *n* : saltamontes *m*
grassland [ˈgræsˌlænd] *n* : pradera *f*
grassy [ˈgræsi] *adj* **grassier; -est** : cubierto de hierba
grate[1] [ˈgreɪt] *v* **grated; -ing** *vt* **1** : rallar (en cocina) **2** SCRAPE : rascar **3 to grate one's teeth** : hacer rechinar los dientes — *vi* **1** RASP, SQUEAK : chirriar **2** IRRITATE : irritar ⟨to grate on one's nerves : crisparle los nervios a uno⟩
grate[2] *n* **1** : parrilla *f* (para cocinar) **2** GRATING : reja *f*, rejilla *f*, verja *f* (en una ventana)
grateful [ˈgreɪtfəl] *adj* : agradecido
gratefully [ˈgreɪtfəli] *adv* : con agradecimiento
gratefulness [ˈgreɪtfəlnəs] *n* : gratitud *f*, agradecimiento *m*
grater [ˈgreɪt̬ər] *n* : rallador *m*
gratification [ˌgræt̬əfəˈkeɪʃən] *n* : gratificación *f*
gratify [ˈgræt̬əˌfaɪ] *vt* **-fied; -fying** **1** PLEASE : complacer **2** SATISFY : satisfacer, gratificar
grating [ˈgreɪt̬ɪŋ] *n* : reja *f*, rejilla *f*
gratis[1] [ˈgræt̬əs, ˈgreɪ-] *adv* : gratis, gratuitamente
gratis[2] *adj* : gratis, gratuito
gratitude [ˈgræt̬əˌtuːd, -ˌtjuːd] *n* : gratitud *f*, agradecimiento *m*
gratuitous [grəˈtuːət̬əs] *adj* : gratuito
gratuity [grəˈtuːət̬i] *n, pl* **-ities** TIP : propina *f*
grave[1] [ˈgreɪv] *adj* **graver; -est** **1** IMPORTANT : grave, de mucha gravedad **2** SERIOUS, SOLEMN : grave, serio
grave[2] *n* : tumba *f*, sepultura *f*
gravel [ˈgrævəl] *n* : grava *f*, gravilla *f*
gravelly [ˈgrævəli] *adj* **1** : de grava **2** HARSH : áspero (dícese de la voz)
gravely [ˈgreɪvli] *adv* : gravemente
gravestone [ˈgreɪvˌstoːn] *n* : lápida *f*
graveyard [ˈgreɪvˌjɑrd] *n* CEMETERY : cementerio *m*, panteón *m*, camposanto *m*
gravitate [ˈgrævəˌteɪt] *vi* **-tated; -tating** : gravitar
gravitation [ˌgrævəˈteɪʃən] *n* : gravitación *f*
gravitational [ˌgrævəˈteɪʃənəl] *adj* : gravitacional
gravity [ˈgrævət̬i] *n, pl* **-ties** **1** SERIOUSNESS : gravedad *f*, seriedad *f* **2** : gravedad *f* ⟨the law of gravity : la ley de la gravedad⟩
gravy [ˈgreɪvi] *n, pl* **-vies** : salsa *f* (preparada con el jugo de la carne asada)
gray[1] [ˈgreɪ] *vt* : hacer gris — *vi* : encanecer, ponerse gris
gray[2] *adj* **1** : gris (dícese del color) **2** : cano, canoso ⟨gray hair : pelo canoso⟩ ⟨to go gray : volverse cano⟩ **3** DISMAL, GLOOMY : gris, triste
gray[3] *n* : gris *m*
grayish [ˈgreɪɪʃ] *adj* : grisáceo
graze [ˈgreɪz] *v* **grazed; grazing** *vi* : pastar, pacer — *vt* **1** : pastorear (ganado) **2** BRUSH : rozar **3** SCRATCH : raspar
grease[1] [ˈgriːs, ˈgriːz] *vt* **greased; greasing** : engrasar, lubricar
grease[2] [ˈgriːs] *n* : grasa *f*
greasy [ˈgriːsi, -zi] *adj* **greasier; -est** **1** : grasiento **2** OILY : graso, grasoso
great [ˈgreɪt] *adj* **1** LARGE : grande ⟨a great mountain : una montaña grande⟩ ⟨a great crowd : una gran muchedumbre⟩ **2** INTENSE : intenso, fuerte, grande ⟨great pain : gran dolor⟩ **3** EMINENT : grande, eminente, distinguido ⟨a great poet : un gran poeta⟩ **4** EXCELLENT, TERRIFIC : excelente, estu-

pendo, fabuloso ⟨to have a great time : pasarlo en grande⟩ **5 a great while** : mucho tiempo

great–aunt [ˌgreɪtˈænt, -ˈant] *n* : tía *f* abuela

greater [ˈgreɪt̬ər] (*comparative* of **great**) : mayor

greatest [ˈgreɪt̬əst] (*superlative* of **great**) : el mayor, la mayor

great–grandchild [ˌgreɪtˈgrænd-ˌʧaɪld] *n, pl* **-children** [-ˌʧɪldrən] : bisnieto *m*, -ta *f*

great–grandfather [ˌgreɪtˈgrænd-ˌfɑðər] *n* : bisabuelo *m*

great–grandmother [ˌgreɪtˈgrænd-ˌmʌðər] *n* : bisabuela *f*

greatly [ˈgreɪtli] *adv* **1** MUCH : mucho, sumamente ⟨to be greatly improved : haber mejorado mucho⟩ **2** VERY : muy ⟨greatly superior : muy superior⟩

greatness [ˈgreɪtnəs] *n* : grandeza *f*

great–uncle [ˌgreɪtˈʌŋkəl] *n* : tío *m* abuelo

grebe [ˈgri:b] *n* : somorgujo *m*

greed [ˈgri:d] *n* **1** AVARICE : avaricia *f*, codicia *f* **2** GLUTTONY : glotonería *f*, gula *f*

greedily [ˈgri:dəli] *adv* : con avaricia, con gula

greediness [ˈgri:dinəs] → **greed**

greedy [ˈgri:di] *adj* **greedier; -est** **1** AVARICIOUS : codicioso, avaricioso **2** GLUTTONOUS : glotón

Greek [ˈgri:k] *n* **1** : griego *m*, -ga *f* **2** : griego *m* (idioma) — **Greek** *adj*

green¹ [ˈgri:n] *adj* **1** : verde (dícese del color) **2** UNRIPE : verde, inmaduro **3** INEXPERIENCED : verde, novato

green² *n* **1** : verde *m* **2** **greens** *npl* VEGETABLES : verduras *fpl*

greenery [ˈgri:nəri] *n, pl* **-eries** : plantas *fpl* verdes, vegetación *f*

greenhorn [ˈgri:nˌhɔrn] *n* : novato *m*, -ta *f*

greenhouse [ˈgri:nˌhaʊs] *n* : invernadero *m*

greenhouse effect : efecto *m* invernadero

greenish [ˈgri:nɪʃ] *adj* : verdoso

Greenlander [ˈgri:nləndər, -ˌlæn-] *n* : groenlandés *m*, -desa *f*

greenness [ˈgri:nnəs] *n* **1** : verdor *m* **2** INEXPERIENCE : inexperiencia *f*

green thumb *n* **to have a green thumb** : tener buena mano para las plantas

greet [ˈgri:t] *vt* **1** : saludar ⟨to greet a friend : saludar a un amigo⟩ **2** : acoger, recibir ⟨they greeted him with boos : lo recibieron con abucheos⟩

greeting [ˈgri:t̬ɪŋ] *n* **1** : saludo *m* **2** **greetings** *npl* REGARDS : saludos *mpl*, recuerdos *mpl*

gregarious [grɪˈgæriəs] *adj* : gregario (dícese de los animales), sociable (dícese de las personas) — **gregariously** *adv*

gregariousness [grɪˈgæriəsnəs] *n* : sociabilidad *f*

gremlin [ˈgrɛmlən] *n* : duende *m*

grenade [grəˈneɪd] *n* : granada *f*

Grenadian [grəˈneɪdiən] *n* : granadino *m*, -na *f* — **Grenadian** *adj*

grew → **grow**

grey → **gray**

greyhound [ˈgreɪˌhaʊnd] *n* : galgo *m*

grid [ˈgrɪd] *n* **1** GRATING : rejilla *f* **2** NETWORK : red *f* (de electricidad, etc.) **3** : cuadriculado *m* (de un mapa)

griddle [ˈgrɪdəl] *n* : plancha *f*

griddle cake → **pancake**

gridiron [ˈgrɪdˌaɪərn] *n* **1** GRILL : parrilla *f* **2** : campo *m* de futbol americano

gridlock [ˈgrɪdˌlɑk] *n* : atasco *m* completo (de una red de calles)

grief [ˈgri:f] *n* **1** SORROW : dolor *m*, pena *f* **2** ANNOYANCE, TROUBLE : problemas *mpl*, molestia *f*

grievance [ˈgri:vənts] *n* COMPLAINT : queja *f*

grieve [ˈgri:v] *v* **grieved; grieving** *vt* DISTRESS : afligir, entristecer, apenar — *vi* **1** : sufrir, afligirse **2 to grieve for** *or* **to grieve over** : llorar, lamentar

grievous [ˈgri:vəs] *adj* **1** OPPRESSIVE : gravoso, opresivo, severo **2** GRAVE, SERIOUS : grave, severo, doloroso

grievously [ˈgri:vəsli] *adv* : gravemente, de gravedad

grill¹ [ˈgrɪl] *vt* **1** : asar (a la parrilla) **2** INTERROGATE : interrogar

grill² *n* **1** : parrilla *f* (para cocinar) **2** : parrillada *f* (comida) **3** RESTAURANT : grill *m*

grille *or* **grill** [ˈgrɪl] *n* : reja *f*, enrejado *m*

grim [ˈgrɪm] *adj* **grimmer; grimmest** **1** CRUEL : cruel, feroz **2** STERN : adusto, severo ⟨a grim expression : un gesto severo⟩ **3** GLOOMY : sombrío, deprimente **4** SINISTER : macabro, siniestro **5** UNYIELDING : inflexible, persistente ⟨with grim determination : con una voluntad de hierro⟩

grimace¹ [ˈgrɪməs, grɪˈmeɪs] *vi* **-maced; -macing** : hacer muecas

grimace² *n* : mueca *f*

grime [ˈgraɪm] *n* : mugre *f*, suciedad *f*

grimly [ˈgrɪmli] *adv* **1** STERNLY : severamente **2** RESOLUTELY : inexorablemente

grimy [ˈgraɪmi] *adj* **grimier; -est** : mugriento, sucio

grin¹ [ˈgrɪn] *vi* **grinned; grinning** : sonreír abiertamente

grin² *n* : sonrisa *f* abierta

grind¹ [ˈgraɪnd] *v* **ground** [ˈgraʊnd]; **grinding** *vt* **1** CRUSH : moler, machacar, triturar **2** SHARPEN : afilar **3** POLISH : pulir, esmerilar (lentes, espejos) **4 to grind one's teeth** : rechinarle los dientes a uno **5 to grind down** OPPRESS : oprimir, agobiar — *vi* **1** : funcionar con dificultad, rechinar ⟨to grind to a halt : pararse poco a poco, llegar a un punto muerto⟩ **2** STUDY : estudiar mucho

grind[2] *n* : trabajo *m* pesado ⟨the daily grind : la rutina diaria⟩
grinder [ˈgraɪndər] *n* : molinillo *m* ⟨coffee grinder : molinillo de café⟩
grindstone [ˈgraɪndˌsto:n] *n* : piedra *m* de afilar
grip[1] [ˈgrɪp] *vt* **gripped; gripping** **1** GRASP : agarrar, asir **2** HOLD, INTEREST : captar el interés de
grip[2] *n* **1** GRASP : agarre *m*, asidero *m* ⟨to have a firm grip on something : agarrarse bien de algo⟩ **2** CONTROL, HOLD : control *m*, dominio *m* ⟨to lose one's grip on : perder el control de⟩ ⟨inflation tightened its grip on the economy : la inflación se afianzó en su dominio de la economía⟩ **3** UNDERSTANDING : comprensión *f*, entendimiento *m* ⟨to come to grips with : llegar a entender⟩ **4** HANDLE : asidero *m*, empuñadura *f* (de un arma)
gripe[1] [ˈgraɪp] *v* **griped; griping** *vt* IRRITATE, VEX : irritar, fastidiar, molestar — *vi* COMPLAIN : quejarse, rezongar
gripe[2] *n* : queja *f*
grippe [ˈgrɪp] *n* : influenza *f*, gripe *f*, gripa *f Col, Mex*
grisly [ˈgrɪzli] *adj* **-lier; -est** : horripilante, horroroso, truculento
grist [ˈgrɪst] *n* : molienda *f* ⟨it's all grist for the mill : todo ayuda, todo es provechoso⟩
gristle [ˈgrɪsəl] *n* : cartílago *m*
gristly [ˈgrɪsli] *adj* **-tlier; -est** : cartilaginoso
grit[1] [ˈgrɪt] *vt* **gritted; gritting** : hacer rechinar (los dientes, etc.)
grit[2] *n* **1** SAND : arena *f* **2** GRAVEL : grava *f* **3** COURAGE : valor *m*, coraje *m* **4** **grits** *npl* : sémola *f* de maíz
gritty [ˈgrɪt̬i] *adj* **-tier; -est** **1** : arenoso ⟨a gritty surface : una superficie arenosa⟩ **2** PLUCKY : valiente
grizzled [ˈgrɪzəld] *adj* : entrecano
grizzly bear [ˈgrɪzli] *n* : oso *m* pardo
groan[1] [ˈgro:n] *vi* **1** MOAN : gemir, quejarse **2** CREAK : crujir
groan[2] *n* **1** MOAN : gemido *m*, quejido *m* **2** CREAK : crujido *m*
grocer [ˈgro:sər] *n* : tendero *m*, -ra *f*
grocery [ˈgro:səri, -ʃəri] *n, pl* **-ceries** **1** *or* **grocery store** : tienda *f* de comestibles, tienda *f* de abarrotes **2** **groceries** *npl* : comestibles *mpl*, abarrotes *mpl*
groggy [ˈgrɑgi] *adj* **-gier; -est** : atontado, grogui, tambaleante
groin [ˈgrɔɪn] *n* : ingle *f*
grommet [ˈgrɑmət, ˈgrʌ-] *n* : arandela *f*
groom[1] [ˈgru:m, ˈgrʊm] *vt* **1** : cepillar, almohazar (un animal) **2** : arreglar, cuidar ⟨well-groomed : bien arreglado⟩ **3** PREPARE : preparar
groom[2] *n* **1** : mozo *m*, -za *f* de cuadra **2** BRIDEGROOM : novio *m*
groove[1] [ˈgru:v] *vt* **grooved; grooving** : acanalar, hacer ranuras en, surcar
groove[2] *n* **1** FURROW, SLOT : ranura *f*, surco *m* **2** RUT : rutina *f*
grope [ˈgro:p] *v* **groped; groping** *vi* : andar a tientas, tantear ⟨he groped for the switch : buscó el interruptor a tientas⟩ — *vt* **to grope one's way** : avanzar a tientas
gross[1] [ˈgro:s] *vt* : tener entrada bruta de, recaudar en bruto
gross[2] *adj* **1** FLAGRANT : flagrante, grave ⟨a gross error : un error flagrante⟩ ⟨a gross injustice : una injusticia grave⟩ **2** FAT : muy gordo, obeso **3** : bruto ⟨gross national product : producto nacional bruto⟩ **4** COARSE, VULGAR : grosero, basto
gross[3] *n* **1** *pl* **gross** : gruesa *f* (12 docenas) **2** *or* **gross income** : ingresos *mpl* brutos
grossly [ˈgro:sli] *adv* **1** EXTREMELY : extremadamente ⟨grossly unfair : totalmente injusto⟩ **2** CRUDELY : groseramente
grotesque [gro:ˈtɛsk] *adj* : grotesco
grotesquely [gro:ˈtɛskli] *adv* : de forma grotesca
grotto [ˈgrɑt̬o:] *n, pl* **-toes** : gruta *f*
grouch[1] [ˈgraʊʧ] *vi* : refunfuñar, rezongar
grouch[2] *n* **1** COMPLAINT : queja *f* **2** GRUMBLER : gruñón *m*, -ñona *f*; cascarrabias *mf fam*
grouchy [ˈgraʊʧi] *adj* **grouchier; -est** : malhumorado, gruñón
ground[1] [ˈgraʊnd] *vt* **1** BASE : fundar, basar **2** INSTRUCT : enseñar los conocimientos básicos a ⟨to be well grounded in : ser muy entendido en⟩ **3** : conectar a tierra (un aparato eléctrico) **4** : varar, hacer encallar (un barco) **5** : restringir (un avión o un piloto) a la tierra
ground[2] *n* **1** EARTH, SOIL : suelo *m*, tierra *f* ⟨to dig (in) the ground : cavar la tierra⟩ ⟨to fall to the ground : caerse al suelo⟩ **2** LAND, TERRAIN : terreno *m* ⟨hilly ground : terreno alto⟩ ⟨to lose ground : perder terreno⟩ **3** BASIS, REASON : razón *f*, motivo *m* ⟨grounds for complaint : motivos de queja⟩ **4** BACKGROUND : fondo *m* **5** FIELD : campo *m*, plaza *f* ⟨parade ground : plaza de armas⟩ **6** : tierra *f* (para electricidad) **7** **grounds** *npl* PREMISES : recinto *m*, terreno *m* **8** **grounds** *npl* DREGS : posos *mpl* (de café)
ground[3] → **grind**
groundhog [ˈgraʊndˌhɔg] *n* : marmota *f* (de América)
groundless [ˈgraʊndləs] *adj* : infundado
groundwork [ˈgraʊndˌwərk] *n* **1** FOUNDATION : fundamento *m*, base *f* **2** PREPARATION : trabajo *m* preparatorio
group[1] [ˈgru:p] *vt* : agrupar
group[2] *n* : grupo *m*, agrupación *f*, conjunto *m*, compañía *f*
grouper [ˈgru:pər] *n* : mero *m*

grouse[1] [ˈgraʊs] *vi* **groused; grousing** : quejarse, rezongar, refunfuñar

grouse[2] *n, pl* **grouse** *or* **grouses** : urogallo *m* (ave)

grout [ˈgraʊt] *n* : lechada *f*

grove [ˈgro:v] *n* : bosquecillo *m*, arboleda *f*, soto *m*

grovel [ˈgrɑvəl, ˈgrʌ-] *vi* **-eled** *or* **-elled; -eling** *or* **-elling 1** CRAWL : arrastrarse **2** : humillarse, postrarse ⟨to grovel before someone : postrarse ante alguien⟩

grow [ˈgro:] *v* **grew** [ˈgru:]; **grown** [ˈgro:n]; **growing** *vi* **1** : crecer ⟨palm trees grow on the islands : las palmas crecen en las islas⟩ ⟨my hair grows very fast : mi pelo crece muy rápido⟩ **2** DEVELOP, MATURE : desarrollarse, madurar **3** INCREASE : crecer, aumentar **4** BECOME : hacerse, volverse, ponerse ⟨she was growing angry : se estaba poniendo furiosa⟩ ⟨to grow dark : oscurecerse⟩ **5 to grow up** : hacerse mayor ⟨grow up! : ¡no seas niño!⟩ — *vt* **1** CULTIVATE, RAISE : cultivar **2** : dejar crecer ⟨to grow one's hair : dejarse crecer el pelo⟩

grower [ˈgro:ər] *n* : cultivador *m*, -dora *f*

growl[1] [ˈgraʊl] *vi* : gruñir (dícese de un animal), refunfuñar (dícese de una persona)

growl[2] *n* : gruñido *m*

grown–up[1] [ˈgro:nˌəp] *adj* : adulto, mayor

grown–up[2] *n* : adulto *m*, -ta *f*; persona *f* mayor

growth [ˈgro:θ] *n* **1** : crecimiento *m* ⟨to stunt one's growth : detener el crecimiento⟩ **2** INCREASE : aumento *m*, crecimiento *m*, expansión *f* **3** DEVELOPMENT : desarrollo *m* ⟨economic growth : desarrollo económico⟩ ⟨a five days' growth of beard : una barba de cinco días⟩ **4** LUMP, TUMOR : bulto *m*, tumor *m*

grub[1] [ˈgrʌb] *vi* **grubbed; grubbing 1** DIG : escarbar **2** RUMMAGE : hurgar, buscar **3** DRUDGE : trabajar duro

grub[2] *n* **1** : larva *f* ⟨beetle grub : larva del escarabajo⟩ **2** DRUDGE : esclavo *m*, -va *f* del trabajo **3** FOOD : comida *f*

grubby [ˈgrʌbi] *adj* **grubbier; -est** : mugriento, sucio

grudge[1] [ˈgrʌʤ] *vt* **grudged; grudging** : resentir, envidiar

grudge[2] *n* : rencor *m*, resentimiento *m* ⟨to hold a grudge : guardar rencor⟩

grueling *or* **gruelling** [ˈgru:lɪŋ, ˈgru:ə-] *adj* : extenuante, agotador, duro

gruesome [ˈgru:səm] *adj* : horripilante, truculento, horroroso

gruff [ˈgrʌf] *adj* **1** BRUSQUE : brusco ⟨a gruff reply : una respuesta brusca⟩ **2** HOARSE : ronco — **gruffly** *adv*

grumble[1] [ˈgrʌmbəl] *vi* **-bled; -bling 1** COMPLAIN : refunfuñar, rezongar, quejarse **2** RUMBLE : hacer un ruido sordo, retumbar (dícese del trueno)

grumble[2] *n* **1** COMPLAINT : queja *f* **2** RUMBLE : ruido *m* sordo, estruendo *m*

grumbler [ˈgrʌmbələr] *n* : gruñón *m*, -ñona *f*

grumpy [ˈgrʌmpi] *adj* **grumpier; -est** : malhumorado, gruñón

grungy [ˈgrʌnʤi] *adj* : sucio

grunt[1] [ˈgrʌnt] *vi* : gruñir

grunt[2] *n* : gruñido *m*

guacamole [ˌgwɑkəˈmo:li] *n* : guacamole *m*, guacamol *m*

guarantee[1] [ˌgærənˈti:] *vt* **-teed; -teeing 1** PROMISE : asegurar, prometer **2** : poner bajo garantía, garantizar (un producto o servicio)

guarantee[2] *n* **1** PROMISE : garantía *f*, promesa *f* ⟨lifetime guarantee : garantía de por vida⟩ **2** → **guarantor**

guarantor [ˌgærənˈtɔr] *n* : garante *mf*; fiador *m*, -dora *f*

guaranty [ˌgærənˈti:] → **guarantee**

guard[1] [ˈgɑrd] *vt* **1** DEFEND, PROTECT : defender, proteger **2** : guardar, vigilar, custodiar ⟨to guard the frontier : vigilar la frontera⟩ ⟨she guarded my secret well : guardó bien mi secreto⟩ — *vi* **to guard against** : protegerse contra, evitar

guard[2] *n* **1** WATCHMAN : guarda *mf* ⟨security guard : guarda de seguridad⟩ **2** VIGILANCE : guardia *f*, vigilancia *f* ⟨to be on guard : estar en guardia⟩ ⟨to let one's guard down : bajar la guardia⟩ **3** SAFEGUARD : salvaguardia *f*, dispositivo *m* de seguridad (en una máquina) **4** PRECAUTION : precaución *f*, protección *f*

guardhouse [ˈgɑrdˌhaʊs] *n* : cuartel *m* de la guardia

guardian [ˈgɑrdiən] *n* **1** PROTECTOR : guardián *m*, -diana *f*; custodio *m*, -dia *f* **2** : tutor *m*, -tora *f* (de un niño)

guardianship [ˈgɑrdiənˌʃɪp] *n* : custodia *f*, tutela *f*

Guatemalan [ˌgwɑt̬əˈmɑlən] *n* : guatemalteco *m*, -ca *f* — **Guatemalan** *adj*

guava [ˈgwɑvə] *n* : guayaba *f*

gubernatorial [ˌgu:bənəˈtori:əl, ˌgju:-] *adj* : del gobernador

guerrilla *or* **guerilla** [gəˈrɪlə] *n* : guerrillero *m*, -ra *f*

guess[1] [ˈgɛs] *vt* **1** CONJECTURE : adivinar, conjeturar ⟨guess what happened! : ¡adivina lo que pasó!⟩ **2** SUPPOSE : pensar, creer, suponer ⟨I guess so : supongo que sí⟩ **3** : adivinar correctamente, acertar ⟨to guess the answer : acertar la respuesta⟩ — *vi* : adivinar

guess[2] *n* : conjetura *f*, suposición *f*

guesswork [ˈgɛsˌwərk] *n* : suposiciones *fpl*, conjeturas *fpl*

guest [ˈgɛst] *n* : huésped *mf*; invitado *m*, -da *f*

guffaw[1] [gəˈfɔ] *vi* : reírse a carcajadas, carcajearse *fam*

guffaw[2] [gəˈfɔ, ˈgʌˌfɔ] *n* : carcajada *f*, risotada *f*

guidance [ˈgaɪdənts] *n* : orientación *f*, consejos *mpl*
guide¹ [ˈgaɪd] *vt* **guided; guiding 1** DIRECT, LEAD : guiar, dirigir, conducir **2** ADVISE, COUNSEL : aconsejar, orientar
guide² *n* : guía *f*
guidebook [ˈgaɪd,bʊk] *n* : guía *f* (para viajeros)
guideline [ˈgaɪd,laɪn] *n* : pauta *f*, directriz *f*
guild [ˈgɪld] *n* : gremio *m*, sindicato *m*, asociación *f*
guile [ˈgaɪl] *n* : astucia *f*, engaño *m*
guileless [ˈgaɪlləs] *adj* : inocente, cándido, sin malicia
guillotine¹ [ˈgɪlə,ti:n, ˈgi:jə,-] *vt* **-tined; -tining** : guillotinar
guillotine² *n* : guillotina *f*
guilt [ˈgɪlt] *n* : culpa *f*, culpabilidad *f*
guilty [ˈgɪlti] *adj* **guiltier; -est** : culpable
guinea fowl [ˈgɪni] *n* : gallina *f* de Guinea
guinea pig *n* : conejillo *m* de Indias, cobaya *f*
guise [ˈgaɪz] *n* : apariencia *f*, aspecto *m*, forma *f*
guitar [gəˈtɑr, gɪ-] *n* : guitarra *f*
guitarist [gəˈtɑrɪst, gɪ-] *n* : guitarrista *mf*
gulch [ˈgʌltʃ] *n* : barranco *m*, quebrada *f*
gulf [ˈgʌlf] *n* **1** : golfo *m* ⟨the Gulf of Mexico : el Golfo de México⟩ **2** GAP : brecha *f* ⟨the gulf between generations : la brecha entre las generaciones⟩ **3** CHASM : abismo *m*
gull [ˈgʌl] *n* : gaviota *f*
gullet [ˈgʌlət] *n* : garganta *f*
gullible [ˈgʌlɪbəl] *adj* : crédulo
gully [ˈgʌli] *n, pl* **-lies** : barranco *m*, hondonada *f*
gulp¹ [ˈgʌlp] *vt* **1** : engullir, tragar ⟨he gulped down the whiskey : engulló el whisky⟩ **2** SUPPRESS : suprimir, reprimir, tragar ⟨to gulp down a sob : reprimir un sollozo⟩ — *vi* : tragar saliva, tener un nudo en la garganta
gulp² *n* : trago *m*
gum [ˈgʌm] *n* **1** CHEWING GUM : goma *f* de mascar, chicle *m* **2 gums** *npl* : encías *fpl*
gumbo [ˈgʌm,bo:] *n* : sopa *f* de quingombó
gumdrop [ˈgʌm,drɑp] *n* : pastilla *f* de goma
gummy [ˈgʌmi] *adj* **gummier; -est** : gomoso
gumption [ˈgʌmpʃən] *n* : iniciativa *f*, agallas *fpl fam*
gun¹ [ˈgʌn] *vt* **gunned; gunning 1** *or* **to gun down** : matar a tiros, asesinar **2** : acelerar (rápidamente) ⟨to gun the engine : acelerar el motor⟩
gun² *n* **1** CANNON : cañón *m* **2** FIREARM : arma *f* de fuego **3** SPRAY GUN : pistola *f* **4 to jump the gun** : adelantarse, salir antes de tiempo
gunboat [ˈgʌn,bo:t] *n* : cañonero *m*
gunfight [ˈgʌn,faɪt] *n* : tiroteo *m*, balacera *f*
gunfire [ˈgʌn,faɪr] *n* : disparos *mpl*
gunman [ˈgʌnmən] *n, pl* **-men** [-mən, -,mɛn] : pistolero *m*, gatillero *m Mex*
gunner [ˈgʌnər] *n* : artillero *m*, -ra *f*
gunnysack [ˈgʌni,sæk] *n* : saco *m* de yute
gunpowder [ˈgʌn,paʊdər] *n* : pólvora *f*
gunshot [ˈgʌn,ʃɑt] *n* : disparo *m*, tiro *m*, balazo *m*
gunwale [ˈgʌnəl] *n* : borda *f*
guppy [ˈgʌpi] *n, pl* **-pies** : lebistes *m*
gurgle¹ [ˈgərgəl] *vi* **-gled; -gling 1** : borbotar, gorgotear (dícese de un líquido) **2** : gorjear (dícese de un niño)
gurgle² *n* **1** : borboteo *m*, gorgoteo *m* (de un líquido) **2** : gorjeo *m* (de un niño)
gush [ˈgʌʃ] *vi* **1** SPOUT : surgir, salir a chorros, chorrear **2** : hablar con entusiasmo efusivo ⟨she gushed with praise : se deshizo en elogios⟩
gust [ˈgʌst] *n* : ráfaga *f*, racha *f*
gusto [ˈgʌs,to:] *n, pl* **gustoes** : entusiasmo *m* ⟨with gusto : con deleite, con ganas⟩
gusty [ˈgʌsti] *adj* **gustier; -est** : racheado
gut¹ [ˈgʌt] *vt* **gutted; gutting 1** EVISCERATE : destripar (un pollo, etc.), limpiar (un pescado) **2** : destruir el interior de (un edificio)
gut² *n* **1** INTESTINE : intestino *m* **2 guts** *npl* INNARDS : tripas *fpl fam*, entrañas *fpl* **3 guts** *npl* COURAGE : valentía *f*, agallas *fpl*
gutter [ˈgʌt̬ər] *n* **1** : canal *mf*, canaleta *f* (de un techo) **2** : cuneta *f*, arroyo *m* (de una calle)
guttural [ˈgʌt̬ərəl] *adj* : gutural
guy [ˈgaɪ] *n* **1** *or* **guyline** : cuerda *f* tensora, cable *m* **2** FELLOW : tipo *m*, hombre *m*
guzzle [ˈgʌzəl] *vt* **-zled; -zling** : chupar, tragarse
gym [ˈdʒɪm] → **gymnasium**
gymnasium [dʒɪmˈneɪziəm, -ʒəm] *n, pl* **-siums** *or* **-sia** [-zi:ə, -ʒə] : gimnasio *m*
gymnast [ˈdʒɪmnəst, -,næst] *n* : gimnasta *mf*
gymnastic [dʒɪmˈnæstɪk] *adj* : gimnástico
gymnastics [dʒɪmˈnæstɪks] *ns & pl* : gimnasia *f*
gynecologist [,gaɪnəˈkɑlədʒɪst, ,dʒɪnə-] *n* : ginecólogo *m*, -ga *f*
gynecology [,gaɪnəˈkɑlədʒi, ,dʒɪnə-] *n* : ginecología *f*
gyp¹ [ˈdʒɪp] *vt* **gypped; gypping** : estafar, timar
gyp² *n* **1** SWINDLER : estafador *m*, -dora *f* **2** FRAUD, SWINDLE : estafa *f*, timo *m fam*
gypsum [ˈdʒɪpsəm] *n* : yeso *m*
Gypsy [ˈdʒɪpsi] *n, pl* **-sies** : gitano *m*, -na *f*
gyrate [ˈdʒaɪ,reɪt] *vi* **-rated; -rating** : girar, rotar
gyration [dʒaɪˈreɪʃən] *n* : giro *m*, rotación *f*
gyroscope [ˈdʒaɪrə,sko:p] *n* : giroscopio *m*, giróscopo *m*

H

h [ˈeɪtʃ] *n, pl* **h's** *or* **hs** [ˈeɪtʃəz] : octava letra del alfabeto inglés
ha [ˈhɑ] *interj* : ¡ja!
haberdashery [ˈhæbərˌdæʃəri] *n, pl* **-eries** : tienda *f* de ropa para caballeros
habit [ˈhæbɪt] *n* **1** CUSTOM : hábito *m*, costumbre *f* **2** : hábito *m* (de un monje o una religiosa) **3** ADDICTION : dependencia *f*, adicción *f*
habitable [ˈhæbɪt̬əbəl] *adj* : habitable
habitat [ˈhæbɪˌtæt] *n* : hábitat *m*
habitation [ˌhæbɪˈteɪʃən] *n* **1** OCCUPANCY : habitación *f* **2** RESIDENCE : residencia *f*, morada *f*
habit–forming [ˈhæbɪtˌfɔrmɪŋ] *adj* : que crea dependencia
habitual [həˈbɪtʃʊəl] *adj* **1** CUSTOMARY : habitual, acostumbrado **2** INVETERATE : incorregible, empedernido — **habitually** *adv*
habituate [həˈbɪtʃʊˌeɪt] *vt* **-ated; -ating** : habituar, acostumbrar
hack[1] [ˈhæk] *vt* : cortar, tajear (a hachazos, etc.) ⟨to hack one's way : abrirse paso⟩ — *vi* **1** : hacer tajos **2** COUGH : toser
hack[2] *n* **1** CHOP : hachazo *m*, tajo *m* **2** HORSE : caballo *m* de alquiler **3** WRITER : escritor *m*, -tora *f* a sueldo; escritorzuelo *m*, -la *f* **4** COUGH : tos *f* seca
hackles [ˈhækəlz] *npl* **1** : pluma *f* erizada (de un ave), pelo *m* erizado (de un perro, etc.) **2 to get one's hackles up** : ponerse furioso
hackney [ˈhækni] *n, pl* **-neys** : caballo *m* de silla, caballo *m* de tiro
hackneyed [ˈhæknid] *adj* TRITE : trillado, gastado
hacksaw [ˈhækˌsɔ] *n* : sierra *f* para metales
had → **have**
haddock [ˈhædək] *ns & pl* : eglefino *m*
hadn't [ˈhædənt] (*contraction* of **had not**) → **have**
haft [ˈhæft] *n* : mango *m*, empuñadura *f*
hag [ˈhæg] *n* **1** WITCH : bruja *f*, hechicera *f* **2** CRONE : vieja *f* fea
haggard [ˈhægərd] *adj* : demacrado, macilento — **haggardly** *adv*
haggle [ˈhægəl] *vi* **-gled; -gling** : regatear
ha–ha [ˌhɑˈhɑ, ˈhɑˈhɑ] *interj* : ¡ja, ja!
hail[1] [ˈheɪl] *vt* **1** GREET : saludar **2** SUMMON : llamar ⟨to hail a taxi : llamar un taxi⟩ — *vi* : granizar (en meteorología)
hail[2] *n* **1** : granizo *m* **2** BARRAGE : aluvión *m*, lluvia *f*
hail[3] *interj* : ¡salve!
hailstone [ˈheɪlˌstoːn] *n* : granizo *m*, piedra *f* de granizo
hailstorm [ˈheɪlˌstɔrm] *n* : granizada *f*
hair [ˈhær] *n* **1** : pelo *m*, cabello *m* ⟨to get one's hair cut : cortarse el pelo⟩ **2** : vello *m* (en las piernas, etc.)
hairbreadth [ˈhærˌbrɛdθ] *or* **hairsbreadth** [ˈhærz-] *n* **by a hairbreadth** : por un pelo
hairbrush [ˈhærˌbrʌʃ] *n* : cepillo *m* (para el pelo)
haircut [ˈhærˌkʌt] *n* : corte *m* de pelo
hairdo [ˈhærˌduː] *n, pl* **-dos** : peinado *m*
hairdresser [ˈhærˌdrɛsər] *n* : peluquero *m*, -ra *f*
hairiness [ˈhærinəs] *n* : vellosidad *f*
hairless [ˈhærləs] *adj* : sin pelo, calvo, pelón
hairline [ˈhærˌlaɪn] *n* **1** : línea *f* delgada **2** : nacimiento *m* del pelo ⟨to have a receding hairline : tener entradas⟩
hairpin [ˈhærˌpɪn] *n* : horquilla *f*
hair–raising [ˈhærˌreɪzɪŋ] *adj* : espeluznante
hair spray *n* : laca *f*, fijador *m* (para el pelo)
hairstyle [ˈhærˌstaɪl] *n* : peinado *m*
hairy [ˈhæri] *adj* **hairier; -est** : peludo, velludo
Haitian [ˈheɪʃən, ˈheɪt̬iən] *n* : haitiano *m*, -na *f* — **Haitian** *adj*
hake [ˈheɪk] *n* : merluza *f*
hale[1] [ˈheɪl] *vt* **haled; haling** : arrastrar, halar ⟨to hale to court : arrastrar al tribunal⟩
hale[2] *adj* : saludable, robusto
half[1] [ˈhæf, ˈhaf] *adv* : medio, a medias ⟨half cooked : medio cocido⟩
half[2] *adj* : medio, a medias ⟨a half hour : una media hora⟩ ⟨a half truth : una verdad a medias⟩
half[3] *n, pl* **halves** [ˈhævz, ˈhavz] **1** : mitad *f* ⟨half of my friends : la mitad de mis amigos⟩ ⟨in half : por la mitad⟩ **2** : tiempo *m* (en deportes)
half brother *n* : medio hermano *m*, hermanastro *m*
halfhearted [ˈhæfˈhɑrt̬əd] *adj* : sin ánimo, poco entusiasta
halfheartedly [ˈhæfˈhɑrt̬ədli] *adv* : con poco entusiasmo, sin ánimo
half–life [ˈhæfˌlaɪf] *n, pl* **half–lives** : media vida *f*
half sister *n* : media hermana *f*, hermanastra *f*
halfway[1] [ˈhæfˈweɪ] *adv* : a medio camino, a mitad de camino
halfway[2] *adj* : medio, intermedio ⟨a halfway point : un punto intermedio⟩
half–wit [ˈhæfˌwɪt] *n* : tonto *m*, -ta *f*; imbécil *mf*
half–witted [ˈhæfˌwɪt̬əd] *adj* : estúpido
halibut [ˈhælɪbət] *ns & pl* : halibut *m*
hall [ˈhɔl] *n* **1** BUILDING : residencia *f* estudiantil, facultad *f* (de una universidad) **2** VESTIBULE : entrada *f*, vestíbulo *m*, zaguán *m* **3** CORRIDOR : corredor *m*, pasillo *m* **4** AUDITORIUM : sala *f*, salón *m* ⟨concert hall : sala de conciertos⟩ **5 city hall** : ayuntamiento *m*
hallelujah [ˌhæləˈluːjə, ˌhɑ-] *interj* : ¡aleluya!

hallmark [ˈhɔl͵mɑrk] *n* : sello *m* (distintivo)
hallow [ˈhæ͵lo:] *vt* : santificar, consagrar
hallowed [ˈhæ͵lo:d, ˈhæ͵lo:əd, ˈhɑ͵lo:d] *adj* : sagrado
Halloween [͵hæləˈwi:n, ͵hɑ-] *n* : víspera *f* de Todos los Santos
hallucinate [hæˈlu:sən͵eɪt] *vi* **-nated; -nating** : alucinar
hallucination [hə͵lu:sənˈeɪʃən] *n* : alucinación *f*
hallucinatory [həˈlu:sənə͵tori] *adj* : alucinante
hallucinogen [həˈlu:sənəʤən] *n* : alucinógeno *m*
hallucinogenic [hə͵lu:sənəˈʤɛnɪk] *adj* : alucinógeno
hallway [ˈhɔl͵weɪ] *n* **1** ENTRANCE : entrada *f* **2** CORRIDOR : corredor *m*, pasillo *m*
halo [ˈheɪ͵lo:] *n, pl* **-los** *or* **-loes** : aureola *f*, halo *m*
halt[1] [ˈhɔlt] *vi* : detenerse, pararse — *vt* **1** STOP : detener, parar (a una persona) **2** INTERRUPT : interrumpir (una actividad)
halt[2] *n* **1** : alto *m*, parada *f* **2 to come to a halt** : pararse, detenerse
halter [ˈhɔltər] *n* **1** : cabestro *m*, ronzal *m* (para un animal) **2** : blusa *f* sin espalda
halting [ˈhɔltɪŋ] *adj* HESITANT : vacilante, titubeante — **haltingly** *adv*
halve [ˈhæv, ˈhav] *vt* **halved; halving 1** DIVIDE : partir por la mitad **2** REDUCE : reducir a la mitad
halves → **half**
ham [ˈhæm] *n* **1** : jamón *m* **2** *or* **ham actor** : comicastro *m*, -tra *f* **3** *or* **ham radio operator** : radioaficionado *m*, -da *f* **4 hams** *npl* HAUNCHES : ancas *fpl*
hamburger [ˈhæm͵bərgər] *or* **hamburg** [-͵bərg] *n* **1** : carne *f* molida **2** : hamburguesa *f* (emparedado)
hamlet [ˈhæmlət] *n* VILLAGE : aldea *f*, poblado *m*
hammer[1] [ˈhæmər] *vt* **1** STRIKE : clavar, golpear **2** NAIL : clavar, martillar **3 to hammer out** NEGOTIATE : elaborar, negociar, llegar a — *vi* : martillar, golpear
hammer[2] *n* **1** : martillo *m* **2** : percusor *m*, percutor *m* (de un arma de fuego)
hammock [ˈhæmək] *n* : hamaca *f*
hamper[1] [ˈhæmpər] *vt* : obstaculizar, dificultar
hamper[2] *n* : cesto *m*, canasta *f*
hamster [ˈhæm*p*stər] *n* : hámster *m*
hamstring [ˈhæm͵strɪŋ] *vt* **-strung** [-͵strʌŋ]; **-stringing 1** : cortarle el tendón del corvejón a (un animal) **2** INCAPACITATE : incapacitar, inutilizar
hand[1] [ˈhænd] *vt* : pasar, dar, entregar
hand[2] *n* **1** : mano *f* ⟨made by hand : hecho a mano⟩ **2** POINTER : manecilla *f*, aguja *f* (de un reloj o instrumento) **3** SIDE : lado *m* ⟨on the other hand : por otro lado⟩ **4** HANDWRITING : letra *f*, escritura *f* **5** APPLAUSE : aplauso *m* **6** : mano *f*, cartas *fpl* (en juegos de naipes) **7** WORKER : obrero *m*, -ra *f*; trabajador *m*, -dora *f* **8 to ask for someone's hand (in marriage)** : pedir la mano de alguien **9 to lend a hand** : echar una mano
handbag [ˈhænd͵bæg] *n* : cartera *f*, bolso *m*, bolsa *f Mex*
handball [ˈhænd͵bɔl] *n* : frontón *m*, pelota *f*
handbill [ˈhænd͵bɪl] *n* : folleto *m*, volante *m*
handbook [ˈhænd͵bʊk] *n* : manual *m*
handcuff [ˈhænd͵kʌf] *vt* : esposar, ponerle esposas (a alguien)
handcuffs [ˈhænd͵kʌfs] *npl* : esposas *fpl*
handful [ˈhænd͵fʊl] *n* : puñado *m*
handgun [ˈhænd͵gʌn] *n* : pistola *f*, revólver *m*
handheld [ˈhænd͵hɛld] *adj* : de mano
handicap[1] [ˈhændi͵kæp] *vt* **-capped; -capping 1** : asignar un handicap a (en deportes) **2** HAMPER : obstaculizar, poner en desventaja
handicap[2] *n* **1** DISABILITY : minusvalía *f*, discapacidad *f* **2** DISADVANTAGE : desventaja *f*, handicap *m* (en deportes)
handicapped [ˈhændi͵kæpt] *adj* DISABLED : minusválido, discapacitado
handicraft [ˈhændi͵kræft] *n* : artesanía *f*
handily [ˈhændəli] *adv* EASILY : fácilmente, con facilidad
handiwork [ˈhændi͵wərk] *n* **1** WORK : trabajo *m* **2** CRAFTS : artesanías *fpl*
handkerchief [ˈhæŋkərʧəf, -͵ʧi:f] *n, pl* **-chiefs** : pañuelo *m*
handle[1] [ˈhændəl] *v* **-dled; -dling** *vt* **1** TOUCH : tocar **2** MANAGE : tratar, manejar, despachar **3** SELL : comerciar con, vender — *vi* : responder, conducirse (dícese de un vehículo)
handle[2] *n* : asa *m*, asidero *m*, mango *m* (de un cuchillo, etc.), pomo *m* (de una puerta), tirador *m* (de un cajón)
handlebars [ˈhændəl͵bɑrz] *npl* : manubrio *m*, manillar *m*
handler [ˈhændələr] *n* : cuidador *m*, -dora *f*
handling [ˈhændəlɪŋ] *n* **1** MANAGEMENT : manejo *m* **2** TOUCHING : manoseo *m* **3 shipping and handling** : porte *m*, transporte *m*
handmade [ˈhænd͵meɪd] *adj* : hecho a mano
hand-me-downs [ˈhænd*d*mi͵daʊnz] *npl* : ropa *f* usada
handout [ˈhænd͵aʊt] *n* **1** AID : dádiva *f*, limosna *f* **2** LEAFLET : folleto *m*
handpick [ˈhændˈpɪk] *vt* : seleccionar con cuidado
handrail [ˈhænd͵reɪl] *n* : pasamanos *m*, barandilla *f*, barandal *m*
handsaw [ˈhænd͵sɔ] *n* : serrucho *m*
hands down *adv* **1** EASILY : con facilidad **2** UNQUESTIONABLY : con mucho, de lejos
handshake [ˈhænd͵ʃeɪk] *n* : apretón *m* de manos

handsome ['hæntsəm] *adj* **-somer; -est** **1** ATTRACTIVE : apuesto, guapo, atractivo **2** GENEROUS : generoso **3** SIZABLE : considerable

handsomely ['hæntsəmli] *adv* **1** ELEGANTLY : elegantemente **2** GENEROUSLY : con generosidad

handspring ['hænd,sprɪŋ] *n* : voltereta *f*

handstand ['hænd,stænd] *n* **to do a handstand** : pararse de manos

hand–to–hand ['hændtə'hænd] *adj* : cuerpo a cuerpo

handwriting ['hænd,raɪṭɪŋ] *n* : letra *f*, escritura *f*

handwritten ['hænd,rɪtən] *adj* : escrito a mano

handy ['hændi] *adj* **handier; -est** **1** NEARBY : a mano, cercano **2** USEFUL : útil, práctico **3** DEXTEROUS : hábil

hang[1] ['hæŋ] *v* **hung** ['hʌŋ]; **hanging** *vt* **1** SUSPEND : colgar, tender, suspender **2** *past tense often* **hanged** EXECUTE : colgar, ahorcar **3 to hang one's head** : bajar la cabeza — *vi* **1** FALL : caer (dícese de las telas y la ropa) **2** DANGLE : colgar **3** HOVER : flotar, sostenerse en el aire **4** : ser ahorcado **5** DROOP : inclinarse **6 to hang up** : colgar ⟨he hung up on me : me colgó⟩

hang[2] *n* **1** DRAPE : caída *f* **2 to get the hang of something** : agarrarle la onda a algo

hangar ['hæŋər, 'hæŋgər] *n* : hangar *m*

hanger ['hæŋər] *n* : percha *f*, gancho *m* (para ropa)

hangman ['hæŋmən] *n, pl* **-men** [-mən, -,mɛn] : verdugo *m*

hangnail ['hæŋ,neɪl] *n* : padrastro *m*

hangout ['hæŋ,aʊt] *n* : lugar *m* popular, sitio *m* muy frecuentado

hangover ['hæŋ,o:vər] *n* : resaca *f*

hank ['hæŋk] *n* : madeja *f*

hanker ['hæŋkər] *vi* **to hanker for** : tener ansias de, tener ganas de

hankering ['hæŋkərɪŋ] *n* : ansia *f*, anhelo *m*

hansom ['hæntsəm] *n* : coche *m* de caballos

Hanukkah ['xɑnəkə, 'hɑ-] *n* : Janucá, Hanukkah

haphazard [hæp'hæzərd] *adj* : casual, fortuito, al azar — **haphazardly** *adv*

hapless ['hæpləs] *adj* UNFORTUNATE : desafortunado, desventurado — **haplessly** *adv*

happen ['hæpən] *vi* **1** OCCUR : pasar, ocurrir, suceder, tener lugar **2** BEFALL : pasar, acontecer ⟨what happened to her? : ¿qué le ha pasado?⟩ **3** CHANCE : resultar, ocurrir por casualidad ⟨it happened that I wasn't home : resulta que estaba fuera de casa⟩ ⟨he happens to be right : da la casualidad de que tiene razón⟩

happening ['hæpənɪŋ] *n* : suceso *m*, acontecimiento *m*

happiness ['hæpinəs] *n* : felicidad *f*, dicha *f*

happy ['hæpi] *adj* **-pier; -est** **1** JOYFUL : feliz, contento, alegre **2** FORTUNATE : afortunado, feliz — **happily** [-pəli] *adv*

happy–go–lucky ['hæpigo:'lʌki] *adj* : despreocupado

harangue[1] [hə'ræŋ] *vt* **-rangued; -ranguing** : arengar

harangue[2] *n* : arenga *f*

harass [hə'ræs, 'hærəs] *vt* **1** BESIEGE, HOUND : acosar, asediar, hostigar **2** ANNOY : molestar

harassment [hə'ræsmənt, 'hærəsmənt] *n* : acoso *m*, hostigamiento *m* ⟨sexual harrassment : acoso sexual⟩

harbinger ['hɑrbɪnʤər] *n* **1** HERALD : heraldo *m*, precursor *m* **2** OMEN : presagio *m*

harbor[1] ['hɑrbər] *vt* **1** SHELTER : dar refugio a, albergar **2** CHERISH, KEEP : abrigar, guardar, albergar ⟨to harbor doubts : guardar dudas⟩

harbor[2] *n* **1** REFUGE : refugio *m* **2** PORT : puerto *m*

hard[1] ['hɑrd] *adv* **1** FORCEFULLY : fuerte, con fuerza ⟨the wind blew hard : el viento sopló fuerte⟩ **2** STRENUOUSLY : duro, mucho ⟨to work hard : trabajar duro⟩ **3 to take something hard** : tomarse algo muy mal, estar muy afectado por algo

hard[2] *adj* **1** FIRM, SOLID : duro, firme, sólido **2** DIFFICULT : difícil, arduo **3** SEVERE : severo, duro ⟨a hard winter : un invierno severo⟩ **4** UNFEELING : insensible, duro **5** DILIGENT : diligente ⟨to be a hard worker : ser muy trabajador⟩ **6 hard liquor** : bebidas *fpl* fuertes **7 hard water** : agua *f* dura

hardcover ['hɑrd,kʌvər] *adj* : de pasta dura, de tapa dura

hard disk *n* : disco *m* duro

hard drive → **hard disk**

harden ['hɑrdən] *vt* : endurecer

hardheaded [,hɑrd'hɛdəd] *adj* **1** STUBBORN : testarudo, terco **2** REALISTIC : realista, práctico — **hardheadedly** *adv*

hard–hearted [,hɑrd'hɑrṭəd] *adj* : despiadado, insensible — **hard–heartedly** *adv*

hard–heartedness [,hɑrd'hɑrṭədnəs] *n* : dureza *f* de corazón

hardly ['hɑrdli] *adv* **1** SCARCELY : apenas, casi ⟨I hardly knew her : apenas la conocía⟩ ⟨hardly ever : casi nunca⟩ **2** NOT : difícilmente, poco, no ⟨they can hardly blame me! : ¡difícilmente pueden echarme la culpa!⟩ ⟨it's hardly likely : es poco probable⟩

hardness ['hɑrdnəs] *n* **1** FIRMNESS : dureza *f* **2** DIFFICULTY : dificultad *f* **3** SEVERITY : severidad *f*

hardship ['hɑrd,ʃɪp] *n* : dificultad *f*, privación *f*

hardware ['hɑrd,wær] *n* **1** TOOLS : ferretería *f* **2** : hardware *m* (de una computadora)

hardwood ['hɑrd,wʊd] *n* : madera *f* dura, madera *f* noble

hardworking ['hɑrd'wərkɪŋ] *adj* : trabajador
hardy ['hɑrdi] *adj* **-dier; -est** : fuerte, robusto, resistente (dícese de las plantas) — **hardily** [-dəli] *adv*
hare ['hær] *n, pl* **hare** *or* **hares** : liebre *f*
harebrained ['hær,breɪnd] *adj* : estúpido, absurdo, disparatado
harelip ['hær,lɪp] *n* : labio *m* leporino
harem ['hærəm] *n* : harén *m*
hark ['hɑrk] *vi* **1** (*used only in the imperative*) LISTEN : escuchar **2 hark back** RETURN : volver **3 hark back** RECALL : recordar
harlequin ['hɑrlɪkən, -kwən] *n* : arlequín *m*
harm¹ ['hɑrm] *vt* : hacerle daño a, perjudicar
harm² *n* : daño *m*, perjuicio *m*
harmful ['hɑrmfəl] *adj* : dañino, perjudicial — **harmfully** *adv*
harmless ['hɑrmləs] *adj* : inofensivo, inocuo — **harmlessly** *adv*
harmlessness ['hɑrmləsnəs] *n* : inocuidad *f*
harmonic [hɑr'mɑnɪk] *adj* : armónico — **harmonically** [-nɪkli] *adv*
harmonica [hɑr'mɑnɪkə] *n* : armónica *f*
harmonious [hɑr'mo:niəs] *adj* : armonioso — **harmoniously** *adv*
harmonize ['hɑrmə,naɪz] *v* **-nized; -nizing** : armonizar
harmony ['hɑrməni] *n, pl* **-nies** : armonía *f*
harness¹ ['hɑrnəs] *vt* **1** : enjaezar (un animal) **2** UTILIZE : utilizar, aprovechar
harness² *n* : arreos *mpl*, guarniciones *fpl*, arnés *m*
harp¹ ['hɑrp] *vi* **to harp on** : insistir sobre, machacar sobre
harp² *n* : arpa *m*
harpist ['hɑrpɪst] *n* : arpista *mf*
harpoon¹ [hɑr'pu:n] *vt* : arponear
harpoon² *n* : arpón *m*
harpsichord ['hɑrpsɪ,kɔrd] *n* : clavicémbalo *m*
harrow¹ ['hær,o:] *vt* **1** CULTIVATE : gradar, labrar (la tierra) **2** TORMENT : atormentar
harrow² *n* : grada *f*, rastra *f*
harry ['hæri] *vt* **-ried; -rying** HARASS : acosar, hostigar
harsh ['hɑrʃ] *adj* **1** ROUGH : áspero **2** SEVERE : duro, severo **3** : discordante (dícese de los sonidos) — **harshly** *adv*
harshness ['hɑrʃnəs] *n* **1** ROUGHNESS : aspereza *f* **2** SEVERITY : dureza *f*, severidad *f*
harvest¹ ['hɑrvəst] *v* : cosechar
harvest² *n* **1** HARVESTING : siega *f*, recolección *f* **2** CROP : cosecha *f*
harvester ['hɑrvəstər] *n* : segador *m*, -dora *f*; cosechadora *f* (máquina)
has → **have**
hash¹ ['hæʃ] *vt* **1** MINCE : picar **2 to hash over** DISCUSS : discutir, repasar
hash² *n* **1** : picadillo *m* (comida) **2** JUMBLE : revoltijo *m*, fárrago *m*
hasn't ['hæzənt] (*contraction* of **has not**) → **has**
hasp ['hæsp] *n* : picaporte *m*, pestillo *m*
hassle¹ ['hæsəl] *vt* **-sled; -sling** : fastidiar, molestar
hassle² *n* **1** ARGUMENT : discusión *f*, disputa *f*, bronca *f* **2** FIGHT : pelea *f*, riña *f* **3** BOTHER, TROUBLE : problemas *mpl*, lío *m*
hassock ['hæsək] *n* **1** CUSHION : almohadón *m*, cojín *m* **2** FOOTSTOOL : escabel *m*
haste ['heɪst] *n* **1** : prisa *f*, apuro *m* **2 to make haste** : darse prisa, apurarse
hasten ['heɪsən] *vt* : acelerar, precipitar — *vi* : apresurarse, apurarse
hasty ['heɪsti] *adj* **hastier; -est 1** HURRIED, QUICK : rápido, apresurado, apurado **2** RASH : precipitado — **hastily** [-təli] *adv*
hat ['hæt] *n* : sombrero *m*
hatch¹ ['hætʃ] *vt* **1** : incubar, empollar (huevos) **2** DEVISE : idear, tramar — *vi* : salir del cascarón
hatch² *n* : escotilla *f*
hatchery ['hætʃəri] *n, pl* **-ries** : criadero *m*
hatchet ['hætʃət] *n* : hacha *f*
hatchway ['hætʃ,weɪ] *n* : escotilla *f*
hate¹ ['heɪt] *vt* **hated; hating** : odiar, aborrecer, detestar
hate² *n* : odio *m*
hateful ['heɪtfəl] *adj* : odioso, aborrecible, detestable — **hatefully** *adv*
hatred ['heɪtrəd] *n* : odio *m*
hatter ['hæt̬ər] *n* : sombrerero *m*, -ra *f*
haughtiness ['hɔt̬inəs] *n* : altanería *f*, altivez *f*
haughty ['hɔt̬i] *adj* **-tier; -est** : altanero, altivo — **haughtily** [-t̬əli] *adv*
haul¹ ['hɔl] *vt* **1** DRAG, PULL : arrastrar, jalar **2** TRANSPORT : transportar
haul² *n* **1** PULL : tirón *m*, jalón *m* **2** CATCH : redada *f* **3** JOURNEY : viaje *m*, trayecto *m* ⟨it's a long haul : es un trayecto largo⟩
haulage ['hɔlɪdʒ] *n* : transporte *m*, tiro *m*
hauler ['hɔlər] *n* : transportista *mf*
haunch ['hɔntʃ] *n* **1** HIP : cadera *f* **2 haunches** *npl* HINDQUARTERS : ancas *fpl*, cuartos *mpl* traseros
haunt¹ ['hɔnt] *vt* **1** : aparecer en (dícese de un fantasma) **2** FREQUENT : frecuentar, rondar **3** PREOCCUPY : perseguir, obsesionar
haunt² *n* : guarida *f* (de animales o ladrones), lugar *m* predilecto
haunting ['hɔntɪŋ] *adj* : obsesionante, evocador — **hauntingly** *adv*
haute ['o:t] *adj* **1** : de moda, de categoría **2 haute couture** [,o:tku'tʊr] : alta costura *f* **3 haute cuisine** [,o:tkwɪ'zi:n] : alta cocina *f*
have ['hæv, *in sense 3 as an auxiliary verb usu* 'hæf] *v* **had** ['hæd]; **having; has** ['hæz, *in sense 3 as an auxiliary verb usu* 'hæs] *vt* **1** POSSESS : tener ⟨do you have

change? : ¿tienes cambio?⟩ **2** EXPERIENCE, UNDERGO : tener, experimentar, sufrir ⟨I have a toothache : tengo un dolor de muelas⟩ **3** INCLUDE : tener, incluir ⟨April has 30 days : abril tiene 30 días⟩ **4** CONSUME : comer, tomar **5** RECEIVE : tener, recibir ⟨he had my permission : tenía mi permiso⟩ **6** ALLOW : permitir, dejar ⟨I won't have it! : ¡no lo permitiré!⟩ **7** HOLD : hacer ⟨to have a party : dar una fiesta⟩ ⟨to have a meeting : convocar una reunión⟩ **8** HOLD : tener ⟨he had me in his power : me tenía en su poder⟩ **9** BEAR : tener (niños) **10** (*indicating causation*) ⟨she had a dress made : mandó hacer un vestido⟩ ⟨to have one's hair cut : cortarse el pelo⟩ — *v aux* **1** : haber ⟨she has been very busy : ha estado muy ocupada⟩ ⟨I've lived here three years : hace tres años que vivo aquí⟩ **2** (*used in tags*) ⟨you've finished, haven't you? : ha terminado, ¿no?⟩ **3 to have to** : deber, tener que ⟨we have to leave : tenemos que salir⟩

haven [ˈheɪvən] *n* : refugio *m*

havoc [ˈhævək] *n* **1** DESTRUCTION : estragos *mpl*, destrucción *f* **2** CHAOS, DISORDER : desorden *m*, caos *m*

Hawaiian[1] [həˈwaɪən] *adj* : hawaiano

Hawaiian[2] *n* : hawaiano *m*, -na *f*

hawk[1] [ˈhɔk] *vt* : pregonar, vender (mercancías) en la calle

hawk[2] *n* : halcón *m*

hawker [ˈhɔkər] *n* : vendedor *m*, -dora *f* ambulante

hawthorn [ˈhɔˌθɔrn] *n* : espino *m*

hay [ˈheɪ] *n* : heno *m*

hay fever *n* : fiebre *f* del heno

hayloft [ˈheɪˌlɔft] *n* : pajar *m*

hayseed [ˈheɪˌsiːd] *n* : palurdo *m*, -da *f*

haystack [ˈheɪˌstæk] *n* : almiar *m*

haywire [ˈheɪˌwaɪr] *adj* : descompuesto, desbaratado ⟨to go haywire : estropearse⟩

hazard[1] [ˈhæzərd] *vt* : arriesgar, aventurar

hazard[2] *n* **1** DANGER : peligro *m*, riesgo *m* **2** CHANCE : azar *m*

hazardous [ˈhæzərdəs] *adj* : arriesgado, peligroso

haze[1] [ˈheɪz] *vt* **hazed; hazing** : abrumar, acosar

haze[2] *n* : bruma *f*, neblina *f*

hazel [ˈheɪzəl] *n* **1** : avellano *m* (árbol) **2** : color *m* avellana

hazelnut [ˈheɪzəlˌnʌt] *n* : avellana *f*

haziness [ˈheɪzinəs] *n* **1** MISTINESS : nebulosidad *f* **2** VAGUENESS : vaguedad *f*

hazy [ˈheɪzi] *adj* **hazier; -est 1** MISTY : brumoso, neblinoso, nebuloso **2** VAGUE : vago, confuso

he [ˈhiː] *pron* : él

head[1] [ˈhɛd] *vt* **1** LEAD : encabezar **2** DIRECT : dirigir — *vi* : dirigirse

head[2] *adj* MAIN : principal ⟨the head office : la oficina central, la sede⟩

head[3] *n* **1** : cabeza *f* ⟨from head to foot : de pies a cabeza⟩ **2** MIND : mente *f*, cabeza *f* **3** TIP, TOP : cabeza *f* (de un clavo, un martillo, etc.), cabecera *f* (de una mesa o un río), punta *f* (de una flecha), flor *m* (de un repollo, etc.), encabezamiento *m* (de una carta, etc.), espuma *f* (de cerveza) **4** DIRECTOR, LEADER : director *m*, -tora *f*; jefe *m*, -fa *f*; cabeza *f* (de una familia) **5** : cara *f* (de una moneda) ⟨heads or tails : cara o cruz⟩ **6** : cabeza *f* ⟨500 head of cattle : 500 cabezas de ganado⟩ ⟨$10 a head : $10 por cabeza⟩ **7 to come to a head** : llegar a un punto crítico

headache [ˈhɛdˌeɪk] *n* : dolor *m* de cabeza, jaqueca *f*

headband [ˈhɛdˌbænd] *n* : cinta *f* del pelo

headdress [ˈhɛdˌdrɛs] *n* : tocado *m*

headfirst [ˈhɛdˈfərst] *adv* : de cabeza

headgear [ˈhɛdˌgɪr] *n* : gorro *m*, casco *m*, sombrero *m*

heading [ˈhɛdɪŋ] *n* **1** DIRECTION : dirección *f* **2** TITLE : encabezamiento *m*, título *m* **3** : membrete *m* (de una carta)

headland [ˈhɛdlənd, -ˌlænd] *n* : cabo *m*

headlight [ˈhɛdˌlaɪt] *n* : faro *m*, foco *m*, farol *m Mex*

headline [ˈhɛdˌlaɪn] *n* : titular *m*

headlong[1] [ˈhɛdˈlɔŋ] *adv* **1** HEADFIRST : de cabeza **2** HASTILY : precipitadamente

headlong[2] [ˈhɛdˌlɔŋ] *adj* : precipitado

headmaster [ˈhɛdˌmæstər] *n* : director *m*

headmistress [ˈhɛdˌmɪstrəs, -ˈmɪs-] *n* : directora *f*

head–on [ˈhɛdˈɑn, -ˈɔn] *adv & adj* : de frente

headphones [ˈhɛdˌfoːnz] *npl* : audífonos *mpl*, cascos *mpl*

headquarters [ˈhɛdˌkwɔrt̬ərz] *ns & pl* **1** SEAT : oficina *f* central, sede *f* **2** : cuartel *m* general (de los militares)

headrest [ˈhɛdˌrɛst] *n* : apoyacabezas *m*

headship [ˈhɛdˌʃɪp] *n* : dirección *f*

head start *n* : ventaja *f*

headstone [ˈhɛdˌstoːn] *n* : lápida *f*

headstrong [ˈhɛdˈstrɔŋ] *adj* : testarudo, obstinado, empecinado

headwaiter [ˈhɛdˈweɪt̬ər] *n* : jefe *m*, -fa *f* de comedor

headwaters [ˈhɛdˌwɔt̬ərz, -ˌwɑ-] *npl* : cabecera *f*

headway [ˈhɛdˌweɪ] *n* : progreso *m* ⟨to make headway against : avanzar contra⟩

heady [ˈhɛdi] *adj* **headier; -est 1** INTOXICATING : embriagador, excitante **2** SHREWD : astuto, sagaz

heal [ˈhiːl] *vt* : curar, sanar — *vi* **1** : sanar, curarse **2 to heal up** : cicatrizarse

healer [ˈhiːlər] *n* **1** : curandero *m*, -dera *f* **2** : curador *m*, -dora *f* (cosa)

health [ˈhɛlθ] *n* : salud *f*

healthful ['hɛlθfəl] *adj* : saludable, salubre — **healthfully** *adv*
healthy ['hɛlθi] *adj* **healthier; -est** : sano, bien — **healthily** [-θəli] *adv*
heap[1] ['hi:p] *vt* **1** PILE : amontonar, apilar **2** SHOWER : colmar
heap[2] *n* : montón *m*, pila *f*
hear ['hɪr] *v* **heard** ['hərd]; **hearing** *vt* **1** : oír ⟨do you hear me? : ¿me oyes?⟩ **2** HEED : oír, prestar atención a **3** LEARN : oír, enterarse de — *vi* **1** : oír ⟨to hear about : oír hablar de⟩ **2 to hear from** : tener noticias de
hearing ['hɪrɪŋ] *n* **1** : oído *m* ⟨hard of hearing : duro de oído⟩ **2** : vista *f* (en un tribunal) **3** ATTENTION : consideración *f*, oportunidad *f* de expresarse **4** EARSHOT : alcance *m* del oído
hearing aid *n* : audífono *m*
hearken ['hɑrkən] *vt* : escuchar
hearsay ['hɪr,seɪ] *n* : rumores *mpl*
hearse ['hərs] *n* : coche *m* fúnebre
heart ['hɑrt] *n* **1** : corazón *m* **2** CENTER, CORE : corazón *m*, centro *m* ⟨the heart of the matter : el meollo del asunto⟩ **3** FEELINGS : corazón *m*, sentimientos *mpl* ⟨a broken heart : un corazón destrozado⟩ ⟨to have a good heart : tener buen corazón⟩ ⟨to take something to heart : tomarse algo a pecho⟩ **4** COURAGE : valor *m*, corazón *m* ⟨to take heart : animarse, cobrar ánimos⟩ **5 hearts** *npl* : corazones *mpl* (en juegos de naipes) **6 by heart** : de memoria
heartache ['hɑrṭ,eɪk] *n* : pena *f*, angustia *f*
heart attack *n* : infarto *m*, ataque *m* al corazón
heartbeat ['hɑrt,bi:t] *n* : latido *m* (del corazón)
heartbreak ['hɑrt,breɪk] *n* : congoja *f*, angustia *f*
heartbreaking ['hɑrt,breɪkɪŋ] *adj* : desgarrador, que parte el corazón
heartbroken ['hɑrt,bro:kən] *adj* : desconsolado, destrozado
heartburn ['hɑrt,bərn] *n* : acidez *f* estomacal
hearten ['hɑrtən] *vt* : alentar, animar
heartfelt ['hɑrt,fɛlt] *adj* : sentido
hearth ['hɑrθ] *n* : hogar *m*, chimenea *f*
heartily ['hɑrṭəli] *adv* **1** ENTHUSIASTICALLY : de buena gana, con entusiasmo **2** TOTALLY : totalmente, completamente
heartless ['hɑrtləs] *adj* : desalmado, despiadado, cruel
heartsick ['hɑrt,sɪk] *adj* : abatido, desconsolado
heartstrings ['hɑrt,strɪŋz] *npl* : fibras *fpl* del corazón
heartwarming ['hɑrt,wɔrmɪŋ] *adj* : conmovedor, emocionante
hearty ['hɑrṭi] *adj* **heartier; -est 1** CORDIAL, WARM : cordial, caluroso **2** STRONG : fuerte ⟨to have a hearty appetite : ser de buen comer⟩ **3** SUBSTANTIAL : abundante, sustancioso ⟨a hearty breakfast : un desayuno abundante⟩
heat[1] ['hi:t] *vt* : calentar
heat[2] *n* **1** WARMTH : calor *m* **2** HEATING : calefacción *f* **3** EXCITEMENT : calor *m*, entusiasmo *m* ⟨in the heat of the moment : en el calor del momento⟩ **4** ESTRUS : celo *m*
heated ['hi:ṭəd] *adj* **1** WARMED : calentado **2** IMPASSIONED : acalorado, apasionado
heater ['hi:ṭər] *n* : calentador *m*, estufa *f*, calefactor *m*
heath ['hi:θ] *n* **1** MOOR : brezal *m*, páramo *m* **2** HEATHER : brezo *m*
heathen[1] ['hi:ðən] *adj* : pagano
heathen[2] *n, pl* **-thens** *or* **-then** : pagano *m*, -na *f*; infiel *mf*
heather ['hɛðər] *n* : brezo *m*
heave[1] ['hi:v] *v* **heaved** *or* **hove** ['ho:v]; **heaving** *vt* **1** LIFT, RAISE : levantar con esfuerzo **2** HURL : lanzar, tirar **3 to heave a sigh** : echar un suspiro, suspirar — *vi* **1** : subir y bajar, palpitar (dícese del pecho) **2 to heave up** RISE : levantarse
heave[2] *n* **1** EFFORT : gran esfuerzo *m* (para levantar algo) **2** THROW : lanzamiento *m*
heaven ['hɛvən] *n* **1** : cielo *m* ⟨for heaven's sake : por Dios⟩ **2 heavens** *npl* SKY : cielo *m* ⟨the heavens opened up : empezó a llover a cántaros⟩
heavenly ['hɛvənli] *adj* **1** : celestial, celeste **2** DELIGHTFUL : divino, encantador
heavily ['hɛvəli] *adv* **1** : pesadamente, con mucho peso **2** LABORIOUSLY : trabajosamente, penosamente **3** : mucho
heaviness ['hɛvinəs] *n* : peso *m*, pesadez *f*
heavy ['hɛvi] *adj* **heavier; -est 1** WEIGHTY : pesado **2** DENSE, THICK : denso, espeso, grueso **3** BURDENSOME : oneroso, gravoso **4** PROFOUND : profundo **5** SLUGGISH : lento, tardo **6** STOUT : corpulento **7** SEVERE : severo, duro, fuerte
heavy–duty ['hɛvi'du:ṭi, -'dju:-] *adj* : muy resistente, fuerte
heavyweight ['hɛvi,weɪt] *n* : peso *m* pesado (en deportes)
Hebrew[1] ['hi:,bru:] *adj* : hebreo
Hebrew[2] *n* **1** : hebreo *m*, -brea *f* **2** : hebreo *m* (idioma)
heck ['hɛk] *n* : ¡caramba!, ¡caray! ⟨a heck of a lot : un montón⟩ ⟨what the heck is . . . ? : ¿que diablos es . . . ?⟩
heckle ['hɛkəl] *vt* **-led; -ling** : interrumpir (a un orador)
hectare ['hɛk,tær] *n* : hectárea *f*
hectic ['hɛktɪk] *adj* : agitado, ajetreado — **hectically** [-tɪkli] *adv*
he'd ['hi:d] (*contraction* of **he had** *or* **he would**) → **have, would**
hedge[1] ['hɛʤ] *v* **hedged; hedging** *vt* **1** : cercar con un seto **2 to hedge one's bet** : cubrirse — *vi* **1** : dar rodeos, con-

testar con evasivas **2 to hedge against** : cubrirse contra, protegerse contra
hedge[2] *n* **1** : seto *m* vivo **2** SAFEGUARD : salvaguardia *f*, protección *f*
hedgehog ['hɛʤ,hɔg, -hɑg] *n* : erizo *m*
heed[1] ['hi:d] *vt* : prestar atención a, hacer caso de
heed[2] *n* : atención *f*
heedless ['hi:dləs] *adj* : descuidado, despreocupado, inconsciente ⟨to be heedless of : hacer caso omiso de⟩ — **heedlessly** *adv*
heel[1] ['hi:l] *vi* : inclinarse
heel[2] *n* : talón *m* (del pie), tacón *m* (de calzado)
heft ['hɛft] *vt* : sopesar
hefty ['hɛfti] *adj* **heftier; -est** : robusto, fornido, pesado
hegemony [hɪ'ʤɛməni] *n, pl* **-nies** : hegemonía *f*
heifer ['hɛfər] *n* : novilla *f*
height ['haɪt] *n* **1** PEAK : cumbre *f*, cima *f*, punto *m* alto ⟨at the height of her career : en la cumbre de su carrera⟩ ⟨the height of stupidity : el colmo de la estupidez⟩ **2** TALLNESS : estatura *f* (de una persona), altura *f* (de un objeto) **3** ALTITUDE : altura *f*
heighten ['haɪtən] *vt* **1** : hacer más alto **2** INTENSIFY : aumentar, intensificar — *vi* : aumentarse, intensificarse
heinous ['heɪnəs] *adj* : atroz, abominable, nefando
heir ['ær] *n* : heredero *m*, -ra *f*
heiress ['ærəs] *n* : heredera *f*
heirloom ['ær,lu:m] *n* : reliquia *f* de familia
held → **hold**
helicopter ['hɛlə,kɑptər] *n* : helicóptero *m*
helium ['hi:liəm] *n* : helio *m*
helix ['hi:lɪks] *n, pl* **helices** ['hɛlə,si:z, 'hi:-] *or* **helixes** ['hi:lɪksəz] : hélice *f*
hell ['hɛl] *n* : infierno *m*
he'll ['hi:l, 'hɪl] (*contraction of* **he shall** *or* **he will**) → **shall, will**
hellish ['hɛlɪʃ] *adj* : horroroso, infernal
hello [hə'lo:, hɛ-] *interj* : ¡hola!
helm ['hɛlm] *n* **1** : timón *m* **2 to take the helm** : tomar el mando
helmet ['hɛlmət] *n* : casco *m*
help[1] ['hɛlp] *vt* **1** AID, ASSIST : ayudar, auxiliar, socorrer, asistir **2** ALLEVIATE : aliviar **3** SERVE : servir ⟨help yourself! : ¡sírvete!⟩ **4** AVOID : evitar ⟨it can't be helped : no lo podemos evitar, no hay más remedio⟩ ⟨I couldn't help smiling : no pude menos que sonreír⟩
help[2] *n* **1** ASSISTANCE : ayuda *f* ⟨help! : ¡socorro!, ¡auxilio!⟩ **2** STAFF : personal *m* (en una oficina), servicio *m* doméstico
helper ['hɛlpər] *n* : ayudante *mf*
helpful ['hɛlpfəl] *adj* **1** OBLIGING : servicial, amable, atento **2** USEFUL : útil, práctico — **helpfully** *adv*
helpfulness ['hɛlpfəlnəs] *n* **1** KINDNESS : bondad *f*, amabilidad *f* **2** USEFULNESS : utilidad *f*
helping ['hɛlpɪŋ] *n* : porción *f*
helpless ['hɛlpləs] *adj* **1** POWERLESS : incapaz, impotente **2** DEFENSELESS : indefenso
helplessly ['hɛlpləsli] *adv* : en vano, inútilmente
helplessness ['hɛlpləsnəs] *n* POWERLESSNESS : incapacidad *f*, impotencia *f*
helter–skelter [,hɛltər'skɛltər] *adv* : atropelladamente, precipitadamente
hem[1] ['hɛm] *vt* **hemmed; hemming 1** : dobladillar **2 to hem in** : encerrar
hem[2] *n* : dobladillo *m*, bastilla *f*
hemisphere ['hɛmə,sfɪr] *n* : hemisferio *m*
hemispheric [,hɛmə'sfɪrɪk, -'sfɛr-] *or* **hemispherical** [-ɪkəl] *adj* : hemisférico
hemlock ['hɛm,lɑk] *n* : cicuta *f*
hemoglobin ['hi:mə,glo:bən] *n* : hemoglobina *f*
hemophilia [,hi:mə'fɪliə] *n* : hemofilia *f*
hemorrhage[1] ['hɛmərɪʤ] *vi* **-rhaged; -rhaging** : sufrir una hemorragia
hemorrhage[2] *n* : hemorragia *f*
hemorrhoids ['hɛmə,rɔɪdz, 'hɛm-,rɔɪdz] *npl* : hemorroides *fpl*, almorranas *fpl*
hemp ['hɛmp] *n* : cáñamo *m*
hen ['hɛn] *n* : gallina *f*
hence ['hɛnts] *adv* **1** : de aquí, de ahí ⟨10 years hence : de aquí a 10 años⟩ ⟨a dog bit me, hence my dislike of animals : un perro me mordió, de ahí mi aversión a los animales⟩ **2** THEREFORE : por lo tanto, por consiguiente
henceforth ['hɛnts,forθ, ,hɛnts'-] *adv* : de ahora en adelante
henchman ['hɛntʃmən] *n, pl* **-men** [-mən, -,mɛn] : secuaz *mf*, esbirro *m*
henpeck ['hɛn,pɛk] *vt* : dominar (al marido)
hepatitis [,hɛpə'taɪṭəs] *n, pl* **-titides** [-'tɪṭə,di:z] : hepatitis *f*
her[1] ['hər] *adj* : su, sus, de ella ⟨her house : su casa, la casa de ella⟩
her[2] ['hər, ər] *pron* **1** (*used as direct object*) : la ⟨I saw her yesterday : la vi ayer⟩ **2** (*used as indirect object*) : le, se ⟨he gave her the book : le dio el libro⟩ ⟨he sent it to her : se lo mandó⟩ **3** (*used as object of a preposition*) : ella ⟨we did it for her : lo hicimos por ella⟩ ⟨taller than her : más alto que ella⟩
herald[1] ['hɛrəld] *vt* ANNOUNCE : anunciar, proclamar
herald[2] *n* **1** MESSENGER : heraldo *m* **2** HARBINGER : precursor *m*
heraldic [hɛ'rældɪk, hə-] *adj* : heráldico
heraldry ['hɛrəldri] *n, pl* **-ries** : heráldica *f*
herb ['ərb, 'hərb] *n* : hierba *f*
herbal ['ərbəl, 'hər-] *adj* : herbario
herbicide ['ərbə,saɪd, 'hər-] *n* : herbicida *m*
herbivore ['ərbə,vor, 'hər-] *n* : herbívoro *m*
herbivorous [,ər'bɪvərəs, ,hər-] *adj* : herbívoro
herculean [,hərkjə'li:ən, ,hər'kju:-liən] *adj* : hercúleo, sobrehumano

herd[1] ['hərd] *vt* : reunir en manada, conducir en manada — *vi* : ir en manada (dícese de los animales), apiñarse (dícese de la gente)
herd[2] *n* : manada *f*
herder ['hərdər] → **herdsman**
herdsman ['hərdzmən] *n, pl* **-men** [-mən, -ˌmɛn] : vaquero *m* (de ganado), pastor *m* (de ovejas)
here ['hɪr] *adv* **1** : aquí, acá ⟨come here! : ¡ven acá!⟩ ⟨right here : aquí mismo⟩ **2** NOW : en este momento, ahora, ya ⟨here he comes : ya viene⟩ ⟨here it's three o'clock (already) : ahora son las tres⟩ **3** : en este punto ⟨here we agree : estamos de acuerdo en este punto⟩ **4** **here you are!** : ¡toma!
hereabouts ['hɪrəˌbaʊts] *or* **hereabout** [-ˌbaʊt] *adv* : por aquí (cerca)
hereafter[1] [hɪr'æftər] *adv* **1** : de aquí en adelante, a continuación **2** : en el futuro
hereafter[2] *n* **the hereafter** : el más allá
hereby [hɪr'baɪ] *adv* : por este medio
hereditary [hə'rɛdəˌtɛri] *adj* : hereditario
heredity [hə'rɛdəţi] *n* : herencia *f*
herein [hɪr'ɪn] *adv* : aquí
hereof [hɪr'ʌv] *adv* : de aquí
hereon [hɪr'ɑn, -'ɔn] *adv* : sobre esto
heresy ['hɛrəsi] *n, pl* **-sies** : herejía *f*
heretic ['hɛrəˌtɪk] *n* : hereje *mf*
heretical [hə'rɛţɪkəl] *adj* : herético
hereto [hɪr'tu:] *adv* : a esto
heretofore ['hɪrţəˌfor] *adv* HITHERTO : hasta ahora
hereunder [hɪr'ʌndər] *adv* : a continuación, abajo
hereupon [hɪrə'pɑn, -'pɔn] *adv* : con esto, en ese momento
herewith [hɪr'wɪθ] *adv* : adjunto
heritage ['hɛrəţɪʤ] *n* : patrimonio *m* (nacional)
hermaphrodite [hər'mæfrəˌdaɪt] *n* : hermafrodita *mf*
hermetic [hər'mɛţɪk] *adj* : hermético — **hermetically** [-ţɪkli] *adv*
hermit ['hərmət] *n* : ermitaño *m*, -ña *f*; eremita *mf*
hernia ['hərniə] *n, pl* **-nias** *or* **-niae** [-niˌi:, -niˌaɪ] : hernia *f*
hero ['hi:ˌro:, 'hɪrˌo:] *n, pl* **-roes** **1** : héroe *m* **2** PROTAGONIST : protagonista *mf*
heroic [hɪ'ro:ɪk] *adj* : heroico — **heroically** [-ɪkli] *adv*
heroics [hɪ'ro:ɪks] *npl* : actos *mpl* heroicos
heroin ['hɛroən] *n* : heroína *f*
heroine ['hɛroən] *n* **1** : heroína *f* **2** PROTAGONIST : protagonista *f*
heroism ['hɛroˌɪzəm] *n* : heroísmo *m*
heron ['hɛrən] *n* : garza *f*
herpes ['hərˌpi:z] *n* : herpes *m*
herring ['hɛrɪŋ] *n, pl* **-ring** *or* **-rings** : arenque *m*
hers ['hərz] *pron* : suyo, -ya; suyos, -yas; de ella ⟨these shoes are hers : estos zapatos son suyos⟩ ⟨hers are bigger : los de ella son más grandes⟩
herself [hər'sɛlf] *pron* **1** (*used reflexively*) : se ⟨she dressed herself : se vistió⟩ **2** (*used emphatically*) : ella misma ⟨she fixed it herself : lo arregló ella misma, lo arregló por sí sola⟩
hertz ['hərts, 'hrts] *ns & pl* : hercio *m*
he's ['hi:z] (*contraction of* **he is** *or* **he has**) → **be, have**
hesitancy ['hɛzəţən*t*si] *n, pl* **-cies** : vacilación *f*, titubeo *m*, indecisión *f*
hesitant ['hɛzəţənt] *adj* : titubeante, vacilante — **hesitantly** *adv*
hesitate ['hɛzəˌteɪt] *vi* **-tated; -tating** : vacilar, titubear
hesitation [ˌhɛzə'teɪʃən] *n* : vacilación *f*, indecisión *f*, titubeo *m*
heterogeneous [ˌhɛţərə'ʤi:niəs, -njəs] *adj* : heterogéneo
heterosexual[1] [ˌhɛţəro'sɛkʃʊəl] *adj* : heterosexual
heterosexual[2] *n* : heterosexual *mf*
heterosexuality [ˌhɛţəroˌsɛkʃʊ'æləţi] *n* : heterosexualidad *f*
hew ['hju:] *v* **hewed; hewed** *or* **hewn** ['hju:n]; **hewing** *vt* **1** CUT : cortar, talar (árboles) **2** SHAPE : labrar, tallar — *vi* CONFORM : conformarse, ceñirse
hex[1] ['hɛks] *vt* : hacerle un maleficio (a alguien)
hex[2] *n* : maleficio *m*
hexagon ['hɛksəˌgɑn] *n* : hexágono *m*
hexagonal [hɛk'sægənəl] *adj* : hexagonal
hey ['heɪ] *interj* : ¡eh!, ¡oye!
heyday ['heɪˌdeɪ] *n* : auge *m*, apogeo *m*
hi ['haɪ] *interj* : ¡hola!
hiatus [haɪ'eɪţəs] *n* **1** : hiato *m* **2** PAUSE : pausa *f*
hibernate ['haɪbərˌneɪt] *vi* **-nated; -nating** : hibernar, invernar
hibernation [ˌhaɪbər'neɪʃən] *n* : hibernación *f*
hiccup[1] ['hɪkəp] *vi* **-cuped; -cuping** : hipar, tener hipo
hiccup[2] *n* : hipo *m* ⟨to have the hiccups : tener hipo⟩
hick ['hɪk] *n* BUMPKIN : palurdo *m*, -da *f*
hickory ['hɪkəri] *n, pl* **-ries** : nogal *m* americano
hidden ['hɪdən] *adj* : oculto
hide[1] ['haɪd] *v* **hid** ['hɪd]; **hidden** ['hɪdən] *or* **hid; hiding** *vt* **1** CONCEAL : esconder **2** : ocultar ⟨to hide one's motives : ocultar uno sus motivos⟩ **3** SCREEN : tapar, no dejar ver — *vi* : esconderse
hide[2] *n* : piel *f*, cuero *m* ⟨to save one's hide : salvar el pellejo⟩
hide–and–seek ['haɪdənd'si:k] *n* **to play hide–and–seek** : jugar a las escondidas
hidebound ['haɪdˌbaʊnd] *adj* : rígido, conservador
hideous ['hɪdiəs] *adj* : horrible, horroroso, espantoso — **hideously** *adv*
hideout ['haɪdˌaʊt] *n* : guarida *f*, escondrijo *m*
hierarchical [ˌhaɪə'rɑrkɪkəl] *adj* : jerárquico

hierarchy [ˈhaɪəˌrɑrki] *n, pl* **-chies** : jerarquía *f*

hieroglyphic [ˌhaɪərəˈglɪfɪk] *n* : jeroglífico *m*

hi–fi [ˈhaɪˈfaɪ] *n* **1** → **high fidelity** **2** : equipo *m* de alta fidelidad

high[1] [ˈhaɪ] *adv* : alto

high[2] *adj* **1** TALL : alto ⟨a high wall : una pared alta⟩ **2** ELEVATED : alto, elevado ⟨high prices : precios elevados⟩ ⟨high blood pressure : presión alta⟩ **3** GREAT, IMPORTANT : grande, importante, alto ⟨a high number : un número grande⟩ ⟨high society : alta sociedad⟩ ⟨high hopes : grandes esperanzas⟩ **4** : alto (en música) **5** INTOXICATED : borracho, drogado

high[3] *n* **1** : récord *m*, punto *m* máximo ⟨to reach an all-time high : batir el récord⟩ **2** : zona *f* de alta presión (en meteorología) **3** *or* **high gear** : directa *f* **4 on high** : en las alturas

highbrow [ˈhaɪˌbraʊ] *n* : intelectual *mf*

higher [ˈhaɪər] *adj* : superior

high fidelity *n* : alta fidelidad *f*

high–flown [ˈhaɪˈfloːn] *adj* : altisonante

high–handed [ˈhaɪˈhændəd] *adj* : arbitrario

highlands [ˈhaɪləndz] *npl* : tierras *fpl* altas, altiplano *m*

highlight[1] [ˈhaɪˌlaɪt] *vt* **1** EMPHASIZE : destacar, poner en relieve, subrayar **2** : ser el punto culminante de

highlight[2] *n* : punto *m* culminante

highly [ˈhaɪli] *adv* **1** VERY : muy, sumamente **2** FAVORABLY : muy bien ⟨to speak highly of : hablar muy bien de⟩ ⟨to think highly of : tener en mucho a⟩

highness [ˈhaɪnəs] *n* **1** HEIGHT : altura *f* **2 Highness** : Alteza *f* ⟨Your Royal Highness : Su Alteza Real⟩

high–pitched [ˈhaɪˈpɪtʃt] *adj* : agudo

high–rise [ˈhaɪˌraɪz] *adj* : alto, de muchas plantas

high school *n* : escuela *f* superior, escuela *f* secundaria

high seas *npl* : alta mar *f*

high–spirited [ˈhaɪˈspɪrət̬əd] *adj* : vivaz, muy animado, brioso

high–strung [ˌhaɪˈstrʌŋ] *adj* : nervioso, excitable

highway [ˈhaɪˌweɪ] *n* : carretera *f*

highwayman [ˈhaɪˌweɪmən] *n, pl* **-men** [-mən, -ˌmɛn] : salteador *m* (de caminos), bandido *m*

hijack[1] [ˈhaɪˌdʒæk] *vt* : secuestrar

hijack[2] *n* : secuestro *m*

hijacker [ˈhaɪˌdʒækər] *n* : secuestrador *m*, -dora *f*

hike[1] [ˈhaɪk] *v* **hiked; hiking** *vi* : hacer una caminata — *vt* RAISE : subir

hike[2] *n* **1** : caminata *f*, excursión *f* **2** INCREASE : subida *f* (de precios)

hiker [ˈhaɪkər] *n* : excursionista *mf*

hilarious [hɪˈlæriəs, haɪˈ-] *adj* : muy divertido, hilarante

hilarity [hɪˈlærət̬i, haɪ-] *n* : hilaridad *f*

hill [ˈhɪl] *n* **1** : colina *f*, cerro *m* **2** SLOPE : cuesta *f*, pendiente *f*

hillbilly [ˈhɪlˌbɪli] *n, pl* **-lies** : palurdo *m*, -da *f* (de las montañas)

hillock [ˈhɪlək] *n* : loma *f*, altozano *m*, otero *m*

hillside [ˈhɪlˌsaɪd] *n* : ladera *f*, cuesta *f*

hilltop [ˈhɪlˌtɑp] *n* : cima *f*, cumbre *f*

hilly [ˈhɪli] *adj* **hillier; -est** : montañoso, accidentado

hilt [ˈhɪlt] *n* : puño *m*, empuñadura *f*

him [ˈhɪm, əm] *pron* **1** (*used as direct object*) : lo ⟨I found him : lo encontré⟩ **2** (*used as indirect object*) : le, se ⟨we gave him a present : le dimos un regalo⟩ ⟨I sent it to him : se lo mandé⟩ **3** (*used as object of a preposition*) : él ⟨she was thinking of him : pensaba en él⟩ ⟨younger than him : más joven que él⟩

himself [hɪmˈsɛlf] *pron* **1** (*used reflexively*) : se ⟨he washed himself : se lavó⟩ **2** (*used emphatically*) : él mismo ⟨he did it himself : lo hizo él mismo, lo hizo por sí solo⟩

hind[1] [ˈhaɪnd] *adj* : trasero, posterior ⟨hind legs : patas traseras⟩

hind[2] *n* : cierva *f*

hinder [ˈhɪndər] *vt* : dificultar, impedir, estorbar

Hindi [ˈhɪndiː] *n* : hindi *m*

hindquarters [ˈhaɪndˌkwɔrt̬ərz] *npl* : cuartos *mpl* traseros

hindrance [ˈhɪndrənts] *n* : estorbo *m*, obstáculo *m*, impedimento *m*

hindsight [ˈhaɪndˌsaɪt] *n* : retrospectiva *f* ⟨with the benefit of hindsight : en retrospectiva, con la perspectiva que da la experiencia⟩

Hindu[1] [ˈhɪnˌduː] *adj* : hindú

Hindu[2] *n* : hindú *mf*

Hinduism [ˈhɪnduːˌɪzəm] *n* : hinduismo *m*

hinge[1] [ˈhɪndʒ] *v* **hinged; hinging** *vt* : unir con bisagras — *vi* **to hinge on** : depender de

hinge[2] *n* : bisagra *f*, gozne *m*

hint[1] [ˈhɪnt] *vt* : insinuar, dar a entender — *vi* : soltar indirectas

hint[2] *n* **1** INSINUATION : insinuación *f*, indirecta *f* **2** TIP : consejo *m*, sugerencia *f* **3** TRACE : pizca *f*, indicio *m*

hinterland [ˈhɪntərˌlænd, -lənd] *n* : interior *m* (de un país)

hip [ˈhɪp] *n* : cadera *f*

hip–hop [ˈhɪpˌhɑp] *n* : hip-hop *m*

hippie [ˈhɪpi] *n* : hippie *mf*, hippy *mf*

hippopotamus [ˌhɪpəˈpɑt̬əməs] *n, pl* **-muses** *or* **-mi** [-ˌmaɪ] : hipopótamo *m*

hippo [ˈhɪpoː] *n, pl* **hippos** → **hippopotamus**

hire[1] [ˈhaɪr] *vt* **hired; hiring** **1** EMPLOY : contratar, emplear **2** RENT : alquilar, arrendar

hire[2] *n* **1** RENT : alquiler *m* ⟨for hire : se alquila⟩ **2** WAGES : paga *f*, sueldo *m* **3** EMPLOYEE : empleado *m*, -da *f*

his[1] [ˈhɪz, ɪz] *adj* : su, sus, de él ⟨his hat : su sombrero, el sombrero de él⟩

his[2] *pron* : suyo, -ya; suyos, suyas; de él ⟨the decision is his : la decisión es suya⟩ ⟨it's his, not hers : es de él, no de ella⟩

Hispanic[1] [hɪˈspænɪk] *adj* : hispano, hispánico
Hispanic[2] *n* : hispano *m*, -na *f*; hispánico *m*, -ca *f*
hiss[1] [ˈhɪs] *vi* : sisear, silbar — *vt* : decir entre dientes
hiss[2] *n* : siseo *m*, silbido *m*
historian [hɪˈstɔriən] *n* : historiador *m*, -dora *f*
historic [hɪˈstɔrɪk] *or* **historical** [-ɪkəl] *adj* : histórico — **historically** [-ɪkli] *adv*
history [ˈhɪstəri] *n, pl* **-ries** **1** : historia *f* **2** RECORD : historial *m*
histrionics [ˌhɪstriˈɑnɪks] *ns & pl* : histrionismo *m*
hit[1] [ˈhɪt] *v* **hit; hitting** *vt* **1** STRIKE : golpear, pegar, batear (una pelota) ⟨he hit the dog : le pegó al perro⟩ **2** : chocar contra, dar con, dar en (el blanco) ⟨the car hit a tree : el coche chocó contra un árbol⟩ **3** AFFECT : afectar ⟨the news hit us hard : la noticia nos afectó mucho⟩ **4** ENCOUNTER : tropezar con, toparse con ⟨to hit a snag : tropezar con un obstáculo⟩ **5** REACH : llegar a, alcanzar ⟨the price hit $10 a pound : el precio alcanzó los $10 dólares por libra⟩ ⟨to hit town : llegar a la ciudad⟩ ⟨to hit the headlines : ser noticia⟩ **6** **to hit on** *or* **to hit upon** : dar con — *vi* : golpear
hit[2] *n* **1** BLOW : golpe *m* **2** : impacto *m* (de un arma) **3** SUCCESS : éxito *m*
hitch[1] [ˈhɪʧ] *vt* **1** : mover con sacudidas **2** ATTACH : enganchar, atar, amarrar **3** → **hitchhike** **4** **to hitch up** : subirse (los pantalones, etc.)
hitch[2] *n* **1** JERK : tirón *m*, jalón *m* **2** OBSTACLE : obstáculo *m*, impedimento *m*, tropiezo *m*
hitchhike [ˈhɪʧˌhaɪk] *vi* **-hiked; -hiking** : hacer autostop, ir de aventón *Col, Mex fam*
hitchhiker [ˈhɪʧˌhaɪkər] *n* : autostopista *mf*
hither [ˈhɪðər] *adv* : acá, por aquí
hitherto [ˈhɪðərˌtuː, ˌhɪðərˈ-] *adv* : hasta ahora
hitter [ˈhɪtər] *n* BATTER : bateador *m*, -dora *f*
HIV [ˌeɪʧˌaɪˈviː] *n* (*h*uman *i*mmunodeficiency *v*irus) : VIH *m*, virus *m* del sida
hive [ˈhaɪv] *n* **1** : colmena *f* **2** SWARM : enjambre *m* **3** : lugar *m* muy activo ⟨a hive of activity : un hervidero de actividad⟩
hives [ˈhaɪvz] *ns & pl* : urticaria *f*
hoard[1] [ˈhord] *vt* : acumular, atesorar
hoard[2] *n* : tesoro *m*, reserva *f*, provisión *f*
hoarfrost [ˈhorˌfrɔst] *n* : escarcha *f*
hoarse [ˈhors] *adj* **hoarser; -est** : ronco — **hoarsely** *adv*
hoarseness [ˈhorsnəs] *n* : ronquera *f*
hoary [ˈhori] *adj* **hoarier; -est** **1** : cano, canoso **2** OLD : vetusto, antiguo
hoax[1] [ˈhoːks] *vt* : engañar, embaucar, bromear
hoax[2] *n* : engaño *m*, broma *f*
hobble[1] [ˈhɑbəl] *v* **-bled; -bling** *vi* LIMP : cojear, renguear — *vt* : manear (un animal)
hobble[2] *n* **1** LIMP : cojera *f*, rengo *m* **2** : maniota *f* (para un animal)
hobby [ˈhɑbi] *n, pl* **-bies** : pasatiempo *m*, afición *f*
hobgoblin [ˈhɑbˌgɑblən] *n* : duende *m*
hobnail [ˈhɑbˌneɪl] *n* : tachuela *f*
hobnob [ˈhɑbˌnɑb] *vi* **-nobbed; -nobbing** : codearse
hobo [ˈhoːˌboː] *n, pl* **-boes** : vagabundo *m*, -da *f*
hock[1] [ˈhɑk] *vt* PAWN : empeñar
hock[2] *n* **in hock** : empeñado
hockey [ˈhɑki] *n* : hockey *m*
hodgepodge [ˈhɑʤˌpɑʤ] *n* : mezcolanza *f*
hoe[1] [ˈhoː] *vt* **hoed; hoeing** : azadonar
hoe[2] *n* : azada *f*, azadón *m*
hog[1] [ˈhɔg, ˈhɑg] *vt* **hogged; hogging** : acaparar, monopolizar
hog[2] *n* **1** PIG : cerdo *m*, -da *f* **2** GLUTTON : glotón *m*, -tona *f*
hogshead [ˈhɔgzˌhɛd, ˈhɑgz-] *n* : tonel *m*
hoist[1] [ˈhɔɪst] *vt* : levantar, alzar, izar (una bandera, una vela)
hoist[2] *n* : grúa *f*
hold[1] [ˈhoːld] *v* **held** [ˈhɛld]; **holding** *vt* **1** POSSESS : tener ⟨to hold office : ocupar un puesto⟩ **2** RESTRAIN : detener, controlar ⟨to hold one's temper : controlar su mal genio⟩ **3** CLASP, GRASP : agarrar, coger ⟨to hold hands : agarrarse de la mano⟩ **4** : sujetar, mantener fijo ⟨hold this nail for me : sujétame este clavo⟩ **5** CONTAIN : contener, dar cabida a **6** SUPPORT : aguantar, sostener **7** REGARD : considerar, tener ⟨he held me responsible : me consideró responsable⟩ **8** CONDUCT : celebrar (una reunión), realizar (un evento), mantener (una conversación) — *vi* **1** : aguantar, resistir ⟨the rope will hold : la cuerda resistirá⟩ **2** : ser válido, valer ⟨my offer still holds : mi oferta todavía es válida⟩ **3** **to hold forth** : perorar, arengar **4** **to hold to** : mantenerse firme en **5** **to hold with** : estar de acuerdo con
hold[2] *n* **1** GRIP : agarre *m*, llave *f* (en deportes) **2** CONTROL : control *m*, dominio *m* ⟨to get hold of oneself : controlarse⟩ **3** DELAY : demora *f* ⟨to put on hold : suspender temporalmente⟩ **4** : bodega *f* (en un barco o un avión) **5** **to get hold of** : conseguir, localizar
holder [ˈhoːldər] *n* : poseedor *m*, -dora *f*; titular *mf*
holdings [ˈhoːldɪŋz] *npl* : propiedades *fpl*
hold out *vi* **1** LAST : aguantar, durar **2** RESIST : resistir
holdup [ˈhoːldˌʌp] *n* **1** ROBBERY : atraco *m* **2** DELAY : retraso *m*, demora *f*
hold up *vt* **1** ROB : robarle (a alguien), atracar, asaltar **2** DELAY : retrasar
hole [ˈhoːl] *n* : agujero *m*, hoyo *m*

holiday [ˈhɑləˌdeɪ] *n* **1** : día *m* feriado, fiesta *f* **2** VACATION : vacaciones *fpl*
holiness [ˈhoːlinəs] *n* **1** : santidad *f* **2** **His Holiness** : Su Santidad
holistic [hoːˈlɪstɪk] *adj* : holístico
holler[1] [ˈhɑlər] *vi* : gritar, chillar
holler[2] *n* : grito *m*, chillido *m*
hollow[1] [ˈhɑˌloː] *vt or* **to hollow out** : ahuecar
hollow[2] *adj* **-lower; -est** **1** : hueco, hundido (dícese de las mejillas, etc.), cavernoso (dícese de un sonido) **2** EMPTY, FALSE : vacío, falso
hollow[3] *n* **1** CAVITY : hueco *m*, depresión *f*, cavidad *f* **2** VALLEY : hondonada *f*, valle *m*
hollowness [ˈhɑˌloːnəs] *n* **1** HOLLOW : hueco *m*, cavidad *f* **2** FALSENESS : falsedad *f* **3** EMPTINESS : vacuidad *f*
holly [ˈhɑli] *n, pl* **-lies** : acebo *m*
hollyhock [ˈhɑliˌhɑk] *n* : malvarrosa *f*
holocaust [ˈhɑləˌkɔst, ˈhoː-, ˈhɔ-] *n* : holocausto *m*
hologram [ˈhoːləˌɡræm, ˈhɑ-] *n* : holograma *m*
holster [ˈhoːlstər] *n* : pistolera *f*
holy [ˈhoːli] *adj* **-lier; -est** : santo, sagrado
Holy Ghost → Holy Spirit
Holy Spirit *n* **the Holy Spirit** : el Espíritu Santo
homage [ˈɑmɪʤ, ˈhɑ-] *n* : homenaje *m*
home [ˈhoːm] *n* **1** : casa *f*, hogar *m*, domicilio *m* ⟨to feel at home : sentirse en casa⟩ **2** INSTITUTION : residencia *f*, asilo *m*
homecoming [ˈhoːmˌkʌmɪŋ] *n* : regreso *m* (a casa)
homegrown [ˈhoːmˈɡroːn] *adj* **1** : de cosecha propia **2** LOCAL : local
homeland [ˈhoːmˌlænd] *n* : patria *f*, tierra *f* natal, terruño *m*
homeless [ˈhoːmləs] *adj* : sin hogar, sin techo
homely [ˈhoːmli] *adj* **-lier; -est** **1** DOMESTIC : casero, hogareño **2** UGLY : feo, poco atractivo
homemade [ˈhoːmˈmeɪd] *adj* : casero, hecho en casa
homemaker [ˈhoːmˌmeɪkər] *n* : ama *f* de casa, persona *f* que se ocupa de la casa
home plate *n* : base *f* del bateador
home run *n* : jonrón *m*
homesick [ˈhoːmˌsɪk] *adj* : nostálgico ⟨to be homesick : echar de menos a la familia⟩
homesickness [ˈhoːmˌsɪknəs] *n* : nostalgia *f*, morriña *f*
homespun [ˈhoːmˌspʌn] *adj* : simple, sencillo
homestead [ˈhoːmˌstɛd] *n* : estancia *f*, hacienda *f*
homeward[1] [ˈhoːmwərd] *or* **homewards** [-wərdz] *adv* : de vuelta a casa, hacia casa
homeward[2] *adj* : de vuelta, de regreso
homework [ˈhoːmˌwərk] *n* : tarea *f*, deberes *mpl Spain*, asignación *f PRi*
homey [ˈhoːmi] *adj* **homier; -est** : hogareño
homicidal [ˌhɑməˈsaɪdəl, ˌhoː-] *adj* : homicida
homicide [ˈhɑməˌsaɪd, ˈhoː-] *n* : homicidio *m*
hominy [ˈhɑməni] *n* : maíz *m* descascarillado
homogeneity [ˌhoːməʤəˈniːəṭi, -ˈneɪ-] *n, pl* **-ties** : homogeneidad *f*
homogeneous [ˌhoːməˈʤiːniəs, -njəs] *adj* : homogéneo — **homogeneously** *adv*
homogenize [hoːˈmɑʤəˌnaɪz, hə-] *vt* **-nized; -nizing** : homogeneizar
homograph [ˈhɑməˌɡræf, ˈhoː-] *n* : homógrafo *m*
homologous [hoːˈmɑləɡəs, hə-] *adj* : homólogo
homonym [ˈhɑməˌnɪm, ˈhoː-] *n* : homónimo *m*
homophone [ˈhɑməˌfoːn, ˈhoː-] *n* : homófono *m*
homosexual[1] [ˌhoːməˈsɛkʃuəl] *adj* : homosexual
homosexual[2] *n* : homosexual *mf*
homosexuality [ˌhoːməˌsɛkʃʊˈæləṭi] *n* : homosexualidad *f*
honcho [ˈhɑnˌʧoː] *n* : pez *m* gordo ⟨the head honcho : el jefe⟩
Honduran [hɑnˈdʊrən, -ˈdjʊr-] *n* : hondureño *m*, -ña *f* — **Honduran** *adj*
hone [ˈhoːn] *vt* **honed; honing** : afilar
honest [ˈɑnəst] *adj* : honesto, honrado — **honestly** *adv*
honesty [ˈɑnəsti] *n, pl* **-ties** : honestidad *f*, honradez *f*
honey [ˈhʌni] *n, pl* **-eys** : miel *f*
honeybee [ˈhʌniˌbiː] *n* : abeja *f*
honeycomb [ˈhʌniˌkoːm] *n* : panal *m*
honeymoon[1] [ˈhʌniˌmuːn] *vi* : pasar la luna de miel
honeymoon[2] *n* : luna *f* de miel
honeysuckle [ˈhʌniˌsʌkəl] *n* : madreselva *f*
honk[1] [ˈhɑŋk, ˈhɔŋk] *vi* **1** : graznar (dícese del ganso) **2** : tocar la bocina (dícese de un vehículo), pitar
honk[2] *n* : graznido *m* (del ganso), bocinazo *m* (de un vehículo)
honor[1] [ˈɑnər] *vt* **1** RESPECT : honrar **2** : cumplir con ⟨to honor one's word : cumplir con su palabra⟩ **3** : aceptar (un cheque, etc.)
honor[2] *n* **1** : honor *m* ⟨in honor of : en honor de⟩ **2** **honors** *npl* AWARDS : honores *mpl*, condecoraciones *fpl* **3** **Your Honor** : Su Señoría
honorable [ˈɑnərəbəl] *adj* : honorable, honroso — **honorably** [-bli] *adv*
honorary [ˈɑnəˌrɛri] *adj* : honorario
hood [ˈhʊd] *n* **1** : capucha *f* **2** : capó *m*, bonete *m Car* (de un automóvil)
hooded [ˈhʊdəd] *adj* : encapuchado
hoodlum [ˈhʊdləm, ˈhuːd-] *n* THUG : maleante *mf*, matón *m*
hoodwink [ˈhʊdˌwɪŋk] *vt* : engañar

hoof [ˈhʊf, ˈhu:f] *n, pl* **hooves** [ˈhʊvz, ˈhu:vz] *or* **hoofs** : pezuña *f*, casco *m*

hoofed [ˈhʊft, ˈhu:ft] *adj* : ungulado

hook[1] [ˈhʊk] *vt* : enganchar — *vi* : abrocharse, engancharse

hook[2] *n* : gancho *m*, percha *f*

hooked [ˈhʊkt] *adj* **1** : en forma de gancho **2 to be hooked on** : estar enganchado a

hooker [ˈhʊkər] *n* : prostituta *f*, fulana *f fam*

hookworm [ˈhʊkˌwərm] *n* : anquilostoma *m*

hooligan [ˈhu:lɪgən] *n* : gamberro *m*, -rra *f*

hoop [ˈhu:p] *n* : aro *m*

hooray [hʊˈreɪ] → **hurrah**

hoot[1] [ˈhu:t] *vi* **1** SHOUT : gritar ⟨to hoot with laughter : morirse de risa, reírse a carcajadas⟩ **2** : ulular (dícese de un búho), tocar la bocina (dícese de un vehículo), silbar (dícese de un tren o un barco)

hoot[2] *n* **1** : ululato *m* (de un búho), silbido *m* (de un tren), bocinazo *m* (de un vehículo) **2** GUFFAW : carcajada *f*, risotada *f* **3 I don't give a hoot** : me vale un comino, me importa un pito

hop[1] [ˈhɑp] *vi* **hopped; hopping** : brincar, saltar

hop[2] *n* **1** LEAP : salto *m*, brinco *m* **2** FLIGHT : vuelo *m* corto **3** : lúpulo *m* (planta)

hope[1] [ˈho:p] *v* **hoped; hoping** *vi* : esperar — *vt* : esperar que ⟨we hope she comes : esperamos que venga⟩ ⟨I hope not : espero que no⟩

hope[2] *n* : esperanza *f*

hopeful [ˈho:pfəl] *adj* : esperanzado — **hopefully** *adv*

hopeless [ˈho:pləs] *adj* **1** DESPAIRING : desesperado **2** IMPOSSIBLE : imposible ⟨a hopeless case : un caso perdido⟩

hopelessly [ˈho:pləsli] *adv* **1** : sin esperanzas, desesperadamente **2** COMPLETELY : totalmente, completamente **3** IMPOSSIBLY : imposiblemente

hopelessness [ˈho:pləsnəs] *n* : desesperanza *f*

hopper [ˈhɑpər] *n* : tolva *f*

hopscotch [ˈhɑpˌskɑʧ] *n* : tejo *m*

horde [ˈhord] *n* : horda *f*, multitud *f*

horizon [həˈraɪzən] *n* : horizonte *m*

horizontal [ˌhorəˈzɑntəl] *adj* : horizontal — **horizontally** *adv*

hormone [ˈhɔrˌmo:n] *n* : hormona *f* — **hormonal** [hɔrˈmo:nəl] *adj*

horn [ˈhɔrn] *n* **1** : cuerno *m* (de un toro, una vaca, etc.) **2** : cuerno *m*, trompa *f* (instrumento musical) **3** : bocina *f*, claxon *m* (de un vehículo)

horned [ˈhɔrnd, ˈhɔrnəd] *adj* : cornudo, astado, con cuernos

hornet [ˈhɔrnət] *n* : avispón *m*

horny [ˈhɔrni] *adj* **hornier; -est 1** CALLOUS : calloso **2** LUSTFUL *fam* : caliente *fam*

horoscope [ˈhɔrəˌsko:p] *n* : horóscopo *m*

horrendous [hɔˈrɛndəs] *adj* : horrendo, horroroso, atroz

horrible [ˈhɔrəbəl] *adj* : horrible, espantoso, horroroso — **horribly** [-bli] *adv*

horrid [ˈhɔrɪd] *adj* : horroroso, horrible — **horridly** *adv*

horrific [hɔˈrɪfɪk] *adj* : terrorífico, horroroso

horrify [ˈhɔrəˌfaɪ] *vt* **-fied; -fying** : horrorizar

horrifying [ˈhɔrəˌfaɪɪŋ] *adj* : horripilante, horroroso

horror [ˈhɔrər] *n* : horror *m*

hors d'oeuvre [ɔrˈdərv] *n, pl* **hors d'oeuvres** [-ˈdərvz] : entremés *m*

horse [ˈhɔrs] *n* : caballo *m*

horseback [ˈhɔrsˌbæk] *n* **on ~** : a caballo

horse chestnut *n* : castaña *f* de Indias

horsefly [ˈhɔrsˌflaɪ] *n, pl* **-flies** : tábano *m*

horsehair [ˈhɔrsˌhær] *n* : crin *f*

horseman [ˈhɔrsmən] *n, pl* **-men** [-mən, -ˌmɛn] : jinete *m*, caballista *m*

horsemanship [ˈhɔrsmənˌʃɪp] *n* : equitación *f*

horseplay [ˈhɔrsˌpleɪ] *n* : payasadas *fpl*

horsepower [ˈhɔrsˌpaʊər] *n* : caballo *m* de fuerza

horseradish [ˈhɔrsˌrædɪʃ] *n* : rábano *m* picante

horseshoe [ˈhɔrsˌʃu:] *n* : herradura *f*

horsewhip [ˈhɔrsˌ*h*wɪp] *vt* **-whipped; -whipping** : azotar, darle fuetazos (a alguien)

horsewoman [ˈhɔrsˌwʊmən] *n, pl* **-women** [-ˌwɪmən] : amazona *f*, jinete *f*, caballista *f*

horsey *or* **horsy** [ˈhɔrsi] *adj* **horsier; -est** : relacionado a los caballos, caballar

horticultural [ˌhɔrt̬əˈkʌlʧərəl] *adj* : hortícola

horticulture [ˈhɔrt̬əˌkʌlʧər] *n* : horticultura *f*

hose[1] [ˈho:z] *vt* **hosed; hosing** : regar o lavar con manguera

hose[2] *n* **1** *pl* **hose** SOCKS : calcetines *mpl*, medias *fpl* **2** *pl* **hose** STOCKINGS : medias *fpl* **3** *pl* **hoses** : manguera *f*, manga *f*

hosiery [ˈho:ʒəri, ˈho:zə-] *n* : calcetería *f*, medias *fpl*

hospice [ˈhɑspəs] *n* : hospicio *m*

hospitable [hɑˈspɪt̬əbəl, ˈhɑsˌpɪ-] *adj* : hospitalario — **hospitably** [-bli] *adv*

hospital [ˈhɑsˌpɪt̬əl] *n* : hospital *m*

hospitality [ˌhɑspəˈtæləti] *n, pl* **-ties** : hospitalidad *f*

hospitalization [ˌhɑsˌpɪt̬ələˈzeɪʃən] *n* : hospitalización *f*

hospitalize [ˈhɑsˌpɪt̬əlˌaɪz] *vt* **-ized; -izing** : hospitalizar

host[1] [ˈho:st] *vt* : presentar (un programa de televisión, etc.)

host[2] *n* **1** : anfitrión *m*, -triona *f* (en la casa, a un evento); presentador *m*, -dora *f* (de un programa de televisión, etc.) **2** *or* **host organism** : huésped *m*

3 TROOPS : huestes *fpl* 4 MULTITUDE : multitud *f* ⟨for a host of reasons : por muchas razones⟩ 5 EUCHARIST : hostia *f*, Eucaristía *f*

hostage [ˈhɑstɪʤ] *n* : rehén *m*

hostel [ˈhɑstəl] *n* : albergue *m* juvenil

hostess [ˈho:stɪs] *n* : anfitriona *f* (en la casa), presentadora *f* (de un programa)

hostile [ˈhɑstəl, -ˌtaɪl] *adj* : hostil — **hostilely** *adv*

hostility [hɑsˈtɪləti] *n, pl* **-ties** : hostilidad *f*

hot [ˈhɑt] *adj* **hotter; hottest** 1 : caliente, cálido, caluroso ⟨hot water : agua caliente⟩ ⟨a hot climate : un clima cálido⟩ ⟨a hot day : un día caluroso⟩ 2 ARDENT, FIERY : ardiente, acalorado ⟨to have a hot temper : tener mal genio⟩ 3 SPICY : picante 4 FRESH : reciente, nuevo ⟨hot news : noticias de última hora⟩ 5 EAGER : ávido 6 STOLEN : robado

hot air *n* : palabrería *f*

hotbed [ˈhɑtˌbɛd] *n* 1 : semillero *m* (de plantas) 2 : hervidero *m*, semillero *m* (de crimen, etc.)

hot dog *n* : perro *m* caliente

hotel [ho:ˈtɛl] *n* : hotel *m*

hothead [ˈhɑtˌhɛd] *n* : exaltado *m*, -da *f*

hotheaded [ˈhɑtˈhɛdəd] *adj* : exaltado

hothouse [ˈhɑtˌhaʊs] *n* : invernadero *m*

hot plate *n* : placa *f* (de cocina)

hot rod *n* : coche *m* con motor modificado

hot water *n* **to get into hot water** : meterse en un lío

hound[1] [ˈhaʊnd] *vt* : acosar, perseguir

hound[2] *n* : perro *m* (de caza)

hour [ˈaʊər] *n* : hora *f*

hourglass [ˈaʊərˌglæs] *n* : reloj *m* de arena

hourly [ˈaʊərli] *adv & adj* : cada hora, por hora

house[1] [ˈhaʊz] *vt* **housed; housing** : albergar, alojar, hospedar

house[2] [ˈhaʊs] *n, pl* **houses** [ˈhaʊzəz, -səz] 1 HOME : casa *f* 2 : cámara *f* (del gobierno) 3 BUSINESS : casa *f*, empresa *f*

houseboat [ˈhaʊsˌbo:t] *n* : casa *f* flotante

housebroken [ˈhaʊsˌbro:kən] *adj* : enseñado

housefly [ˈhaʊsˌflaɪ] *n, pl* **-flies** : mosca *f* común

household[1] [ˈhaʊsˌho:ld] *adj* 1 DOMESTIC : doméstico, de la casa 2 FAMILIAR : conocido por todos

household[2] *n* : casa *f*, familia *f*

householder [ˈhaʊsˌho:ldər] *n* : dueño *m*, -ña *f* de casa

housekeeper [ˈhaʊsˌki:pər] *n* : ama *f* de llaves

housekeeping [ˈhaʊsˌki:pɪŋ] *n* : gobierno *m* de la casa, quehaceres *mpl* domésticos

housemaid [ˈhaʊsˌmeɪd] *n* : criada *f*, mucama *f*, muchacha *f*, sirvienta *f*

housewarming [ˈhaʊsˌwɔrmɪŋ] *n* : fiesta *f* de estreno de una casa

housewife [ˈhaʊsˌwaɪf] *n, pl* **-wives** : ama *f* de casa

housework [ˈhaʊsˌwərk] *n* : faenas *fpl* domésticas, quehaceres *mpl* domésticos

housing [ˈhaʊzɪŋ] *n* 1 HOUSES : vivienda *f* 2 COVERING : caja *f* protectora

hove → **heave**

hovel [ˈhʌvəl, ˈhɑ-] *n* : casucha *f*, tugurio *m*

hover [ˈhʌvər, ˈhɑ-] *vi* 1 : cernerse, sostenerse en el aire 2 **to hover about** : rondar

how [ˈhaʊ] *adv* 1 : cómo ⟨how are you? : ¿cómo estás?⟩ ⟨I don't know how to fix it : no se cómo arreglarlo⟩ 2 : qué ⟨how beautiful! : ¡qué bonito!⟩ 3 : cuánto ⟨how old are you? : ¿cuántos años tienes?⟩ 4 **how about . . . ?** : ¿qué te parece . . . ?

however[1] [haʊˈɛvər] *adv* 1 : por mucho que, por más que ⟨however hot it is : por mucho calor que haga⟩ 2 NEVERTHELESS : sin embargo, no obstante

however[2] *conj* : comoquiera que, de cualquier manera que

howl[1] [ˈhaʊl] *vi* : aullar

howl[2] *n* : aullido *m*, alarido *m*

hub [ˈhʌb] *n* 1 CENTER : centro *m* 2 : cubo *m* (de una rueda)

hubbub [ˈhʌˌbʌb] *n* : algarabía *f*, alboroto *m*, jaleo *m*

hubcap [ˈhʌbˌkæp] *n* : tapacubos *m*

huckster [ˈhʌkstər] *n* : buhonero *m*, -ra *f*; vendedor *m*, -dora *f* ambulante

huddle[1] [ˈhʌdəl] *vi* **-dled; -dling** 1 : apiñarse, amontonarse 2 **to huddle together** : acurrucarse

huddle[2] *n* : grupo *m* (cerrado) ⟨to go into a huddle : conferenciar en secreto⟩

hue [ˈhju:] *n* : color *m*, tono *m*

huff [ˈhʌf] *n* : enojo *m*, enfado *m* ⟨to be in a huff : estar enojado⟩

huffy [ˈhʌfi] *adj* **huffier; -est** : enojado, enfadado

hug[1] [ˈhʌg] *vt* **hugged; hugging** 1 EMBRACE : abrazar 2 : ir pegado a ⟨the road hugs the river : el camino está pegado al río⟩

hug[2] *n* : abrazo *m*

huge [ˈhju:ʤ] *adj* **huger; hugest** : inmenso, enorme — **hugely** *adv*

hulk [ˈhʌlk] *n* 1 : persona *f* fornida 2 : casco *m* (barco), armatoste *m* (edificio, etc.)

hulking [ˈhʌlkɪŋ] *adj* : grandote *fam*, pesado

hull[1] [ˈhʌl] *vt* : pelar

hull[2] *n* 1 HUSK : cáscara *f* 2 : casco *m* (de un barco, un avión, etc.)

hullabaloo [ˈhʌləbəˌlu:] *n, pl* **-loos** : alboroto *m*, jaleo *m*

hum[1] [ˈhʌm] *v* **hummed; humming** *vi* 1 BUZZ : zumbar 2 : estar muy activo, moverse ⟨to hum with activity : bullir de actividad⟩ — *vt* : tararear (una melodía)

hum² *n* : zumbido *m*, murmullo *m*
human¹ ['hju:mən, 'ju:-] *adj* : humano — **humanly** *adv*
human² *n* : ser *m* humano
humane [hju:'meɪn, ju:-] *adj* : humano, humanitario — **humanely** *adv*
humanism ['hju:məˌnɪzəm, 'ju:-] *n* : humanismo *m*
humanist¹ ['hju:mənɪst, 'ju:-] *n* : humanista *mf*
humanist² *or* **humanistic** [ˌhju:mə'nɪstɪk, ˌju:-] *adj* : humanístico
humanitarian¹ [hju:ˌmænə'triən, ju:-] *adj* : humanitario
humanitarian² *n* : humanitario *m*, -ria *f*
humanity [hju:'mænəṭi, ju:-] *n, pl* **-ties** : humanidad *f*
humankind ['hju:mən'kaɪnd, 'ju:-] *n* : género *m* humano
humble¹ ['hʌmbəl] *vt* **-bled; -bling 1** : humillar **2 to humble oneself** : humillarse
humble² *adj* **-bler; -blest** : humilde, modesto — **humbly** ['hʌmbli] *adv*
humbug ['hʌmˌbʌg] *n* **1** FRAUD : charlatán *m*, -tana *f*; farsante *mf* **2** NONSENSE : patrañas *fpl*, tonterías *fpl*
humdrum ['hʌmˌdrʌm] *adj* : monótono, rutinario
humid ['hju:məd, 'ju:-] *adj* : húmedo
humidifier [hju:'mɪdəˌfaɪər, ju:-] *n* : humidificador *m*
humidify [hju:'mɪdəˌfaɪ, ju:-] *vt* **-fied; -fying** : humidificar
humidity [hju:'mɪdəṭi, ju:-] *n, pl* **-ties** : humedad *f*
humiliate [hju:'mɪliˌeɪt, ju:-] *vt* **-ated; -ating** : humillar
humiliating [hju:'mɪliˌeɪṭɪŋ, ju:-] *adj* : humillante
humiliation [hju:ˌmɪli'eɪʃən, ju:-] *n* : humillación *f*
humility [hju:'mɪləṭi, ju:-] *n* : humildad *f*
hummingbird ['hʌmɪŋˌbərd] *n* : colibrí *m*, picaflor *m*
hummock ['hʌmək] *n* : montículo *m*
humor¹ ['hju:mər, 'ju:-] *vt* : seguir el humor a, complacer
humor² *n* : humor *m*
humorist ['hju:mərɪst, 'ju:-] *n* : humorista *mf*
humorless ['hju:mərləs, 'ju:-] *adj* : sin sentido del humor 〈a humorless smile : una sonrisa forzada〉
humorous ['hju:mərəs, 'ju:-] *adj* : humorístico, cómico — **humorously** *adv*
hump ['hʌmp] *n* : joroba *f*, giba *f*
humpback ['hʌmpˌbæk] *n* **1** HUMP : joroba *f*, giba *f* **2** HUNCHBACK : jorobado *m*, -da *f*; giboso *m*, -sa *f*
humpbacked ['hʌmpˌbækt] *adj* : jorobado, giboso
humus ['hju:məs, 'ju:-] *n* : humus *m*
hunch¹ ['hʌntʃ] *vt* : encorvar — *vi or* **to hunch up** : encorvarse
hunch² *n* PREMONITION : presentimiento *m*
hunchback ['hʌntʃˌbæk] *n* **1** HUMP : joroba *f*, giba *f* **2** HUMPBACK : jorobado *m*, -da *f*; giboso *m*, -sa *f*
hunchbacked ['hʌntʃˌbækt] *adj* : jorobado, giboso
hundred¹ ['hʌndrəd] *adj* : cien, ciento
hundred² *n, pl* **-dreds** *or* **-dred** : ciento *m*
hundredth¹ ['hʌndrədθ] *adj* : centésimo
hundredth² *n* **1** : centésimo *m*, -ma *f* (en una serie) **2** : centésimo *m*, centésima parte *f*
hung → **hang**
Hungarian [hʌŋ'gæriən] *n* **1** : húngaro *m*, -ra *f* **2** : húngaro *m* (idioma) — **Hungarian** *adj*
hunger¹ ['hʌŋgər] *vi* **1** : tener hambre **2 to hunger for** : ansiar, anhelar
hunger² *n* : hambre *m*
hungrily ['hʌŋgrəli] *adv* : ávidamente
hungry ['hʌŋgri] *adj* **-grier; -est 1** : hambriento **2 to be hungry** : tener hambre
hunk ['hʌŋk] *n* : trozo *m*, pedazo *m*
hunt¹ ['hʌnt] *vt* **1** PURSUE : cazar **2 to hunt for** : buscar
hunt² *n* **1** PURSUIT : caza *f*, cacería *f* **2** SEARCH : búsqueda *f*, busca *f*
hunter ['hʌntər] *n* : cazador *m*, -dora *f*
hunting ['hʌntɪŋ] *n* : caza *f* 〈to go hunting : ir de caza〉
hurdle¹ ['hərdəl] *vt* **-dled; -dling** : saltar, salvar (un obstáculo)
hurdle² *n* : valla *f* (en deportes), obstáculo *m*
hurl ['hərl] *vt* : arrojar, tirar, lanzar
hurrah [hʊ'rɑ, -'rɔ] *interj* : ¡hurra!
hurricane ['hərəˌkeɪn] *n* : huracán *m*
hurried ['hərid] *adj* : apresurado, precipitado
hurriedly ['hərədli] *adv* : apresuradamente, de prisa
hurry¹ ['həri] *v* **-ried; -rying** *vi* : apurarse, darse prisa, apresurarse — *vt* : apurar, darle prisa (a alguien)
hurry² *n* : prisa *f*, apuro *f*
hurt¹ ['hərt] *v* **hurt; hurting** *vt* **1** INJURE : hacer daño a, herir, lastimar 〈to hurt oneself : hacerse daño〉 **2** DISTRESS, OFFEND : hacer sufrir, ofender, herir — *vi* : doler 〈my foot hurts : me duele el pie〉
hurt² *n* **1** INJURY : herida *f* **2** DISTRESS, PAIN : dolor *m*, pena *f*
hurtful ['hərtfəl] *adj* : hiriente, doloroso
hurtle ['hərṭəl] *vi* **-tled; -tling** : lanzarse, precipitarse
husband¹ ['hʌzbənd] *vt* : economizar, bien administrar
husband² *n* : esposo *m*, marido *m*
husbandry ['hʌzbəndri] *n* **1** MANAGEMENT, THRIFT : economía *f*, buena administración *f* **2** AGRICULTURE : agricultura *f* 〈animal husbandry : cría de animales〉
hush¹ ['hʌʃ] *vt* **1** SILENCE : hacer callar, acallar **2** CALM : calmar, apaciguar
hush² *n* : silencio *m*

hush–hush [ˈhʌʃˌhʌʃ, ˌhʌʃˈhʌʃ] *adj* : muy secreto, confidencial
husk[1] [ˈhʌsk] *vt* : descascarar
husk[2] *n* : cáscara *f*
huskily [ˈhʌskəli] *adv* : con voz ronca
husky[1] [ˈhʌski] *adj* **-kier; -est 1** HOARSE : ronco **2** BURLY : fornido
husky[2] *n, pl* **-kies** : perro *m*, -rra *f* esquimal
hustle[1] [ˈhəsəl] *v* **-tled; -tling** *vt* : darle prisa (a alguien), apurar ⟨they hustled me in : me hicieron entrar a empujones⟩ — *vi* : apurarse, ajetrearse
hustle[2] *n* BUSTLE : ajetreo *m*
hut [ˈhʌt] *n* : cabaña *f*, choza *f*, barraca *f*
hutch [ˈhʌʧ] *n* **1** CUPBOARD : alacena *f* **2 rabbit hutch** : conejera *f*
hyacinth [ˈhaɪəˌsɪnθ] *n* : jacinto *m*
hybrid[1] [ˈhaɪbrɪd] *adj* : híbrido
hybrid[2] *n* : híbrido *m*
hydrant [ˈhaɪdrənt] *n* : boca *f* de riego, hidrante *m CA, Col* ⟨fire hydrant : boca de incendios⟩
hydraulic [haɪˈdrɔlɪk] *adj* : hidráulico — **hydraulically** *adv*
hydrocarbon [ˌhaɪdroˈkɑrbən] *n* : hidrocarburo *m*
hydrochloric acid [ˌhaɪdroˈklorɪk] *n* : ácido *m* clorhídrico
hydroelectric [ˌhaɪdroɪˈlɛktrɪk] *adj* : hidroeléctrico
hydrogen [ˈhaɪdrəʤən] *n* : hidrógeno *m*
hydrogen bomb *n* : bomba *f* de hidrógeno
hydrogen peroxide *n* : agua *f* oxigenada, peróxido *m* de hidrógeno
hydrophobia [ˌhaɪdrəˈfo:biə] *n* : hidrofobia *f*, rabia *f*
hydroplane [ˈhaɪdrəˌpleɪn] *n* : hidroplano *m*
hyena [haɪˈi:nə] *n* : hiena *f*
hygiene [ˈhaɪˌʤi:n] *n* : higiene *f*
hygienic [haɪˈʤɛnɪk, -ˈʤi:-; ˌhaɪ-ʤiˈnɪk] *adj* : higiénico — **hygienically** [-nɪkli] *adv*
hygienist [haɪˈʤi:nɪst, -ˈʤɛ-; ˈhaɪ-ˌʤi:-] *n* : higienista *mf*
hygrometer [haɪˈgrɑmət̬ər] *n* : higrómetro *m*
hymn [ˈhɪm] *n* : himno *m*
hymnal [ˈhɪmnəl] *n* : himnario *m*
hype [ˈhaɪp] *n* : bombo *m* publicitario
hyperactive [ˌhaɪpərˈæktɪv] *adj* : hiperactivo
hyperactivity [ˌhaɪpərˌækˈtɪvət̬i] *n, pl* **-ties** : hiperactividad *f*
hyperbole [haɪˈpərbəli] *n* : hipérbole *f*
hyperbolic [ˌhaɪpərˈbɑlɪk] *adj* : hiperbólico
hypercritical [ˌhaɪpərˈkrɪt̬ɪkəl] *adj* : hipercrítico
hypersensitivity [ˌhaɪpərˌsɛntsəˈtɪ-vət̬i] *n* : hipersensibilidad *f*
hypertension [ˈhaɪpərˌtɛnʧən] *n* : hipertensión *f*
hyphen [ˈhaɪfən] *n* : guión *m*
hyphenate [ˈhaɪfənˌeɪt] *vt* **-ated; -ating** : escribir con guión
hypnosis [hɪpˈno:sɪs] *n, pl* **-noses** [-ˌsi:z] : hipnosis *f*
hypnotic [hɪpˈnɑt̬ɪk] *adj* : hipnótico, hipnotizador
hypnotism [ˈhɪpnəˌtɪzəm] *n* : hipnotismo *m*
hypnotize [ˈhɪpnəˌtaɪz] *vt* **-tized; -tizing** : hipnotizar
hypochondria [ˌhaɪpəˈkɑndriə] *n* : hipocondría *f*
hypochondriac [ˌhaɪpəˈkɑndriˌæk] *n* : hipocondríaco *m*, -ca *f*
hypocrisy [hɪpˈɑkrəsi] *n, pl* **-sies** : hipocresía *f*
hypocrite [ˈhɪpəˌkrɪt] *n* : hipócrita *mf*
hypocritical [ˌhɪpəˈkrɪt̬ɪkəl] *adj* : hipócrita
hypodermic[1] [ˌhaɪpəˈdərmɪk] *adj* : hipodérmico
hypodermic[2] *n* : aguja *f* hipodérmica
hypotenuse [haɪˈpɑtənˌu:s, -ˌu:z, -ˌju:s, -ˌju:z] *n* : hipotenusa *f*
hypothesis [haɪˈpɑθəsɪs] *n, pl* **-eses** [-ˌsi:z] : hipótesis *f*
hypothetical [ˌhaɪpəˈθɛt̬ɪkəl] *adj* : hipotético — **hypothetically** [-t̬ɪkli] *adv*
hysteria [hɪsˈtɛriə, -tɪr-] *n* : histeria *f*, histerismo *m*
hysterical [hɪsˈtɛrɪkəl] *adj* : histérico — **hysterically** [-ɪkli] *adv*
hysterics [hɪsˈtɛrɪks] *n* : histeria *f*, histerismo *m*

I

i [ˈaɪ] *n, pl* **i's** *or* **is** [ˈaɪz] : novena letra del alfabeto inglés
I [ˈaɪ] *pron* : yo
Iberian [aɪˈbɪriən] *adj* : ibérico
ibis [ˈaɪbəs] *n, pl* **ibis** *or* **ibises** : ibis *f*
ice[1] [ˈaɪs] *v* **iced; icing** *vt* **1** FREEZE : congelar, helar **2** CHILL : enfriar **3 to ice a cake** : escarchar un pastel — *vi* : helarse, congelarse
ice[2] *n* **1** : hielo *m* **2** SHERBET : sorbete *m*, nieve *f Cuba, Mex, PRi*
iceberg [ˈaɪsˌbərg] *n* : iceberg *m*
icebox [ˈaɪsˌbɑks] → **refrigerator**
icebreaker [ˈaɪsˌbreɪkər] *n* : rompehielos *m*
ice cap *n* : casquete *m* glaciar
ice–cold [ˈaɪsˈko:ld] *adj* : helado
ice cream *n* : helado *m*, mantecado *m PRi*
Icelander [ˈaɪsˌlændər, -lən-] *n* : islandés *m*, -desa *f*
Icelandic[1] [aɪsˈlændɪk] *adj* : islandés

Icelandic[2] *n* : islandés *m* (idioma)
ice–skate [ˈaɪsˌskeɪt] *vi* **-skated; -skating** : patinar
ice skater *n* : patinador *m*, -dora *f*
ichthyology [ˌɪkthiˈɑləʤi] *n* : ictiología *f*
icicle [ˈaɪˌsɪkəl] *n* : carámbano *m*
icily [ˈaɪsəli] *adv* : fríamente, con frialdad ⟨he stared at me icily : me fijó la mirada con mucha frialdad⟩
icing [ˈaɪsɪŋ] *n* : glaseado *m*, betún *m Mex*
icon [ˈaɪˌkɑn, -kən] *n* : icono *m*
iconoclasm [aɪˈkɑnəˌklæzəm] *n* : iconoclasia *f*
iconoclast [aɪˈkɑnəˌklæst] *n* : iconoclasta *mf*
icy [ˈaɪsi] *adj* **icier; -est** **1** : cubierto de hielo ⟨an icy road : una carretera cubierta de hielo⟩ **2** FREEZING : helado, gélido, glacial **3** ALOOF : frío, distante
id [ˈɪd] *n* : id *m*
I'd [ˈaɪd] (*contraction of* **I should** *or* **I would**) → **should, would**
idea [aɪˈdiːə] *n* : idea *f*
ideal[1] [aɪˈdiːəl] *adj* : ideal
ideal[2] *n* : ideal *m*
idealism [aɪˈdiːəˌlɪzəm] *n* : idealismo *m*
idealist [aɪˈdiːəlɪst] *n* : idealista *mf*
idealistic [aɪˌdiːəˈlɪstɪk] *adj* : idealista
idealistically [aɪˌdiːəˈlɪstɪkli] *adv* : con idealismo
idealization [aɪˌdiːələˈzeɪʃən] *n* : idealización *f*
idealize [aɪˈdiːəˌlaɪz] *vt* **-ized; -izing** : idealizar
ideally [aɪˈdiːəli] *adv* : perfectamente
identical [aɪˈdɛntɪkəl] *adj* : idéntico — **identically** [-tɪkli] *adv*
identifiable [aɪˌdɛntəˈfaɪəbəl] *adj* : identificable
identification [aɪˌdɛntəfəˈkeɪʃən] *n* **1** : identificación *f* **2 identification card** : carnet *m*, cédula *f* de identidad, identificación *f*
identify [aɪˈdɛntəˌfaɪ] *v* **-fied; -fying** *vt* : identificar — *vi* **to identify with** : identificarse con
identity [aɪˈdɛntət̬i] *n, pl* **-ties** : identidad *f*
ideological [ˌaɪdiəˈlɑʤɪkəl, ˌɪ-] *adj* : ideológico — **ideologically** [-ʤɪkli] *adv*
ideology [ˌaɪdiˈɑləʤi, ˌɪ-] *n, pl* **-gies** : ideología *f*
idiocy [ˈɪdiəsi] *n, pl* **-cies** **1** : idiotez *f* **2** NONSENSE : estupidez *f*, tontería *f*
idiom [ˈɪdiəm] *n* **1** LANGUAGE : lenguaje *m* **2** EXPRESSION : modismo *m*, expresión *f* idiomática
idiomatic [ˌɪdiəˈmæt̬ɪk] *adj* : idiomático
idiosyncrasy [ˌɪdioˈsɪŋkrəsi] *n, pl* **-sies** : idiosincrasia *f*
idiosyncratic [ˌɪdiosɪnˈkræt̬ɪk] *adj* : idiosincrásico — **idiosyncratically** [-t̬ɪkli] *adv*
idiot [ˈɪdiət] *n* **1** : idiota *mf* (en medicina) **2** FOOL : idiota *mf*; tonto *m*, -ta *f*; imbécil *mf fam*
idiotic [ˌɪdiˈɑt̬ɪk] *adj* : estúpido, idiota
idiotically [ˌɪdiˈɑt̬ɪkli] *adv* : estúpidamente
idle[1] [ˈaɪdəl] *v* **idled; idling** *vi* **1** LOAF : holgazanear, flojear, haraganear **2** : andar al ralentí (dícese de un automóvil), marchar en vacío (dícese de una máquina) — *vt* : dejar sin trabajo
idle[2] *adj* **idler; idlest** **1** VAIN : frívolo, vano, infundado ⟨idle curiosity : pura curiosidad⟩ **2** INACTIVE : inactivo, parado, desocupado **3** LAZY : holgazán, haragán, perezoso
idleness [ˈaɪdəlnəs] *n* **1** INACTIVITY : inactividad *f*, ociosidad *f* **2** LAZINESS : holgazanería *f*, flojera *f*, pereza *f*
idler [ˈaɪdələr] *n* : haragán *m*, -gana *f*; holgazán *m*, -zana *f*
idly [ˈaɪdəli] *adv* : ociosamente
idol [ˈaɪdəl] *n* : ídolo *m*
idolater *or* **idolator** [aɪˈdɑlət̬ər] *n* : idólatra *mf*
idolatrous [aɪˈdɑlətrəs] *adj* : idólatra
idolatry [aɪˈdɑlətri] *n, pl* **-tries** : idolatría *f*
idolize [ˈaɪdəlaɪz] *vt* **-ized; -izing** : idolatrar
idyll [ˈaɪdəl] *n* : idilio *m*
idyllic [aɪˈdɪlɪk] *adj* : idílico
if [ˈɪf] *conj* **1** : si ⟨I would do it if I could : lo haría si pudiera⟩ ⟨if so : si es así⟩ ⟨as if : como si⟩ ⟨if I were you : yo que tú⟩ **2** WHETHER : si ⟨I don't know if they're ready : no sé si están listos⟩ **3** THOUGH : aunque, si bien ⟨it's pretty, if somewhat old-fashioned : es lindo aunque algo anticuado⟩
igloo [ˈɪˌgluː] *n, pl* **-loos** : iglú *m*
ignite [ɪgˈnaɪt] *v* **-nited; -niting** *vt* : prenderle fuego a, encender — *vi* : prender, encenderse
ignition [ɪgˈnɪʃən] *n* **1** IGNITING : ignición *f*, encendido *m* **2** *or* **ignition switch** : encendido *m*, arranque *m* ⟨to turn on the ignition : arrancar el motor⟩
ignoble [ɪgˈnoːbəl] *adj* : innoble — **ignobly** *adv*
ignominious [ˌɪgnəˈmɪniəs] *adj* : ignominioso, deshonroso — **ignominiously** *adv*
ignominy [ˈɪgnəˌmɪni] *n, pl* **-nies** : ignominia *f*
ignoramus [ˌɪgnəˈreɪməs] *n* : ignorante *mf*; bestia *mf*; bruto *m*, -ta *f*
ignorance [ˈɪgnərən*t*s] *n* : ignorancia *f*
ignorant [ˈɪgnərənt] *adj* **1** : ignorante **2 to be ignorant of** : no ser consciente de, desconocer, ignorar
ignorantly [ˈɪgnərəntli] *adv* : ignorantemente, con ignorancia
ignore [ɪgˈnor] *vt* **-nored; -noring** : ignorar, hacer caso omiso de, no hacer caso de
iguana [ɪˈgwɑnə] *n* : iguana *f*, garrobo *f CA*
ilk [ˈɪlk] *n* : tipo *m*, clase *f*, índole *f*
ill[1] [ˈɪl] *adv* **worse** [ˈwərs]; **worst** [ˈwərst] : mal ⟨to speak ill of : hablar mal de⟩

⟨he can ill afford to fail : mal puede permitirse el lujo de fracasar⟩

ill[2] *adj* **worse; worst 1** SICK : enfermo **2** BAD : malo ⟨ill luck : mala suerte⟩

ill[3] *n* **1** EVIL : mal *m* **2** MISFORTUNE : mal *m*, desgracia *f* **3** AILMENT : enfermedad *f*

I'll ['aɪl] (*contraction of* **I shall** *or* **I will**) → **shall, will**

illegal [ɪl'li:gəl] *adj* : ilegal — **illegally** *adv*

illegality [ɪli'gæləti] *n* : ilegalidad *f*

illegibility [ɪl,lɛʤə'bɪləti] *n, pl* **-ties** : ilegibilidad *f*

illegible [ɪl'lɛʤəbəl] *adj* : ilegible — **illegibly** [-bli] *adv*

illegitimacy [,ɪlɪ'ʤɪtəməsi] *n* : ilegitimidad *f*

illegitimate [,ɪlɪ'ʤɪtəmət] *adj* **1** BASTARD : ilegítimo, bastardo **2** UNLAWFUL : ilegítimo, ilegal — **illegitimately** *adv*

ill–fated ['ɪl'feɪtəd] *adj* : malhadado, infortunado, desventurado

illicit [ɪl'lɪsət] *adj* : ilícito — **illicitly** *adv*

illiteracy [ɪl'lɪtərəsi] *n, pl* **-cies** : analfabetismo *m*

illiterate[1] [ɪl'lɪtərət] *adj* : analfabeto

illiterate[2] *n* : analfabeto *m*, -ta *f*

ill–mannered [,ɪl'manərd] *adj* : descortés, maleducado

ill–natured [,ɪl'neɪʧərd] *adj* : desagradable, de mal genio

ill–naturedly [,ɪl'neɪʧərdli] *adv* : desagradablemente

illness ['ɪlnəs] *n* : enfermedad *f*

illogical [ɪl'lɑʤɪkəl] *adj* : ilógico — **illogically** [-kli] *adv*

ill–tempered [,ɪl'tempərd] → **ill–natured**

ill–treat [,ɪl'tri:t] *vt* : maltratar

ill–treatment [,ɪl'tri:tmənt] *n* : maltrato *m*

illuminate [ɪ'lu:mə,neɪt] *vt* **-nated; -nating 1** : iluminar, alumbrar **2** ELUCIDATE : esclarecer, elucidar

illumination [ɪ,lu:mə'neɪʃən] *n* **1** LIGHTING : iluminación *f*, luz *f* **2** ELUCIDATION : esclarecimiento *m*, elucidación *f*

ill–use ['ɪl'ju:z] → **ill–treat**

illusion [ɪ'lu:ʒən] *n* : ilusión *f*

illusory [ɪ'lu:səri, -zəri] *adj* : engañoso, ilusorio

illustrate ['ɪləs,treɪt] *v* **-trated; -trating** : ilustrar

illustration [,ɪlə'streɪʃən] *n* **1** PICTURE : ilustración *f* **2** EXAMPLE : ejemplo *m*, ilustración *f*

illustrative [ɪ'lʌstrətɪv, 'ɪlə,streɪtɪv] *adj* : ilustrativo — **illustratively** *adv*

illustrator ['ɪlə,streɪtər] *n* : ilustrador *m*, -dora *f*; dibujante *mf*

illustrious [ɪ'lʌstriəs] *adj* : ilustre, eminente, glorioso

illustriousness [ɪ'lʌstriəsnəs] *n* : eminencia *f*, prestigio *m*

ill will *n* : animosidad *f*, malquerencia *f*, mala voluntad *f*

I'm ['aɪm] (*contraction of* **I am**) → **be**

image[1] ['ɪmɪʤ] *vt* **-aged; -aging** : imaginar, crear una imagen de

image[2] *n* : imagen *f*

imagery ['ɪmɪʤri] *n, pl* **-eries 1** IMAGES : imágenes *fpl* **2** : imaginería *f* (en el arte)

imaginable [ɪ'mæʤənəbəl] *adj* : imaginable — **imaginably** [-bli] *adv*

imaginary [ɪ'mæʤə,nɛri] *adj* : imaginario

imagination [ɪ,mæʤə'neɪʃən] *n* : imaginación *f*

imaginative [ɪ'mæʤənətɪv, -ə,neɪtɪv] *adj* : imaginativo — **imaginatively** *adv*

imagine [ɪ'mæʤən] *vt* **-ined; -ining** : imaginar(se)

imbalance [ɪm'bæləns] *n* : desajuste *m*, desbalance *m*, desequilibrio *m*

imbecile[1] ['ɪmbəsəl, -,sɪl] *or* **imbecilic** [,ɪmbə'sɪlɪk] *adj* : imbécil, estúpido

imbecile[2] *n* **1** : imbécil *mf* (en medicina) **2** FOOL : idiota *mf*; imbécil *mf fam*; estúpido *m*, -da *f*

imbecility [,ɪmbə'sɪləti] *n, pl* **-ties** : imbecilidad *f*

imbibe [ɪm'baɪb] *v* **-bibed; -bibing** *vt* **1** DRINK : beber **2** ABSORB : absorber, embeber — *vi* : beber

imbue [ɪm'bju:] *vt* **-bued; -buing** : imbuir

imitate ['ɪmə,teɪt] *vt* **-tated; -tating** : imitar, remedar

imitation[1] [,ɪmə'teɪʃən] *adj* : de imitación, artificial

imitation[2] *n* : imitación *f*

imitative ['ɪmə,teɪtɪv] *adj* : imitativo, imitador, poco original

imitator ['ɪmə,teɪtər] *n* : imitador *m*, -dora *f*

immaculate [ɪ'mækjələt] *adj* **1** PURE : inmaculado, puro **2** FLAWLESS : impecable, intachable — **immaculately** *adv*

immaterial [,ɪmə'tɪriəl] *adj* **1** INCORPOREAL : incorpóreo **2** UNIMPORTANT : irrelevante, sin importancia

immature [,ɪmə'ʧʊr, -'tjʊr, -'tʊr] *adj* : inmaduro, verde (dícese de la fruta)

immaturity [,ɪmə'ʧʊrəti, -'tjʊr-, -'tʊr-] *n, pl* **-ties** : inmadurez *f*, falta *f* de madurez

immeasurable [ɪ'mɛʒərəbəl] *adj* : inconmensurable, incalculable — **immeasurably** [-bli] *adv*

immediacy [ɪ'mi:diəsi] *n* : inmediatez *f*

immediate [ɪ'mi:diət] *adj* **1** INSTANT : inmediato, instantáneo ⟨immediate relief : alivio instantáneo⟩ **2** DIRECT : inmediato, directo ⟨the immediate cause of death : la causa directa de la muerte⟩ **3** URGENT : urgente, apremiante **4** CLOSE : cercano, próximo, inmediato ⟨her immediate family : sus familiares más cercanos⟩ ⟨in the immediate vicinity : en los alrededores, en las inmediaciones⟩

immediately [ɪ'mi:diətli] *adv* : inmediatamente, enseguida

immemorial [ˌɪmə'moriəl] *adj* : inmemorial
immense [ɪ'mɛnts] *adj* : inmenso, enorme — **immensely** *adv*
immensity [ɪ'mɛntsət̬i] *n, pl* **-ties** : inmensidad *f*
immerse [ɪ'mərs] *vt* **-mersed; -mersing** **1** SUBMERGE : sumergir **2 to immerse oneself in** : enfrascarse en
immersion [ɪ'mərʒən] *n* **1** : inmersión *f* (en un líquido) **2** : enfrascamiento *m* (en una actividad)
immigrant ['ɪmɪgrənt] *n* : inmigrante *mf*
immigrate ['ɪməˌgreɪt] *vi* **-grated; -grating** : inmigrar
immigration [ˌɪmə'greɪʃən] *n* : inmigración *f*
imminence ['ɪmənənts] *n* : inminencia *f*
imminent ['ɪmənənt] *adj* : inminente — **imminently** *adv*
immobile [ɪm'oːbəl] *adj* **1** FIXED, IMMOVABLE : inmovible, fijo **2** MOTIONLESS : inmóvil
immobility [ˌɪmo'bɪlət̬i] *n, pl* **-ties** : inmovilidad *f*
immobilize [ɪ'moːbəˌlaɪz] *vt* **-lized; -lizing** : inmovilizar, paralizar
immoderate [ɪ'mɑdərət] *adj* : inmoderado, desmesurado, desmedido, excesivo — **immoderately** *adv*
immodest [ɪ'mɑdəst] *adj* **1** INDECENT : inmodesto, indecente, impúdico **2** CONCEITED : inmodesto, presuntuoso, engreído — **immodestly** *adv*
immodesty [ɪ'mɑdəsti] *n* : inmodestia *f*
immoral [ɪ'mɔrəl] *adj* : inmoral
immorality [ˌɪmɔ'rælət̬i, ˌɪmə-] *n, pl* **-ties** : inmoralidad *f*
immorally [ɪ'mɔrəli] *adv* : de manera inmoral
immortal[1] [ɪ'mɔrtəl] *adj* : inmortal
immortal[2] *n* : inmortal *mf*
immortality [ˌɪˌmɔr'tælət̬i] *n* : inmortalidad *f*
immortalize [ɪ'mɔrtəlˌaɪz] *vt* **-ized; -izing** : inmortalizar
immovable [ɪ'muːvəbəl] *adj* **1** FIXED : fijo, inmovible **2** UNYIELDING : inflexible
immune [ɪ'mjuːn] *adj* **1** : inmune ⟨immune to smallpox : inmune a la viruela⟩ **2** EXEMPT : exento, inmune
immune system *n* : sistema *m* inmunológico
immunity [ɪ'mjuːnət̬i] *n, pl* **-ties** **1** : inmunidad *f* **2** EXEMPTION : exención *f*
immunization [ˌɪmjʊnə'zeɪʃən] *n* : inmunización *f*
immunize ['ɪmjʊˌnaɪz] *vt* **-nized; -nizing** : inmunizar
immunology [ˌɪmjʊ'nɑləʤi] *n* : inmunología *f*
immutable [ɪ'mjuːt̬əbəl] *adj* : inmutable
imp ['ɪmp] *n* RASCAL : diablillo *m*; pillo *m*, -lla *f*
impact[1] [ɪm'pækt] *vt* **1** STRIKE : chocar con, impactar **2** AFFECT : afectar, impactar, impresionar — *vi* **1** STRIKE : hacer impacto, golpear **2 to impact on** : tener un impacto sobre
impact[2] ['ɪmˌpækt] *n* **1** COLLISION : impacto *m*, choque *m*, colisión *f* **2** EFFECT : efecto *m*, impacto *m*, consecuencias *fpl*
impacted [ɪm'pæktəd] *adj* : impactado, incrustado (dícese de los dientes)
impair [ɪm'pær] *vt* : perjudicar, dañar, afectar
impairment [ɪm'pærmənt] *n* : perjuicio *m*, daño *m*
impala [ɪm'pɑlə, -'pæ-] *n, pl* **impalas** *or* **impala** : impala *m*
impale [ɪm'peɪl] *vt* **-paled; -paling** : empalar
impanel [ɪm'pænəl] *vt* **-eled** *or* **-elled; -eling** *or* **-elling** : elegir (un jurado)
impart [ɪm'pɑrt] *vt* **1** CONVEY : impartir, dar, conferir **2** DISCLOSE : revelar, divulgar
impartial [ɪm'pɑrʃəl] *adj* : imparcial — **impartially** *adv*
impartiality [ɪmˌpɑrʃi'ælət̬i] *n, pl* **-ties** : imparcialidad *f*
impassable [ɪm'pæsəbəl] *adj* : infranqueable, intransitable — **impassably** [-bli] *adv*
impasse ['ɪmˌpæs] *n* **1** DEADLOCK : impasse *m*, punto *m* muerto **2** DEAD END : callejón *m* sin salida
impassioned [ɪm'pæʃənd] *adj* : apasionado, vehemente
impassive [ɪm'pæsɪv] *adj* : impasible, indiferente
impassively [ɪm'pæsɪvli] *adv* : impasiblemente, sin emoción
impatience [ɪm'peɪʃənts] *n* : impaciencia *f*
impatient [ɪm'peɪʃənt] *adj* : impaciente — **impatiently** *adv*
impeach [ɪm'piːʧ] *vt* : destituir (a un funcionario) de su cargo
impeachment [ɪm'piːʧmənt] *n* **1** ACCUSATION : acusación *f* **2** DISMISSAL : destitución *f*
impeccable [ɪm'pɛkəbəl] *adj* : impecable — **impeccably** [-bli] *adv*
impecunious [ˌɪmpɪ'kjuːniəs] *adj* : falto de dinero
impede [ɪm'piːd] *vt* **-peded; -peding** : impedir, dificultar, obstaculizar
impediment [ɪm'pɛdəmənt] *n* **1** HINDRANCE : impedimento *m*, obstáculo *m* **2 speech impediment** : defecto *m* del habla
impel [ɪm'pɛl] *vt* **-pelled; -pelling** : impeler
impend [ɪm'pɛnd] *vi* : ser inminente
impenetrable [ɪm'pɛnətrəbəl] *adj* **1** : impenetrable ⟨an impenetrable forest : una selva impenetrable⟩ **2** INSCRUTABLE : incomprensible, inescrutable, impenetrable — **impenetrably** [-bli] *adv*
impenitent [ɪm'pɛnətənt] *adj* : impenitente

imperative[1] [ɪm'pɛrət̬ɪv] *adj* **1** AUTHORITATIVE : imperativo, imperioso **2** NECESSARY : imprescindible — **imperatively** *adv*
imperative[2] *n* : imperativo *m*
imperceptible [ˌɪmpər'sɛptəbəl] *adj* : imperceptible — **imperceptibly** [-bli] *adv*
imperfect [ɪm'pərfɪkt] *adj* : imperfecto, defectuoso — **imperfectly** *adv*
imperfection [ɪmˌpər'fkʃən] *n* : imperfección *f*, defecto *m*
imperial [ɪm'pɪriəl] *adj* **1** : imperial **2** SOVEREIGN : soberano **3** IMPERIOUS : imperioso, señorial
imperialism [ɪm'pɪriəˌlɪzəm] *n* : imperialismo *m*
imperialist[1] [ɪm'pɪriəlɪst] *adj* : imperialista
imperialist[2] *n* : imperialista *mf*
imperialistic [ɪmˌpɪri:ə'lɪstɪk] *adj* : imperialista
imperil [ɪm'pɛrəl] *vt* **-iled** *or* **-illed; -iling** *or* **-illing** : poner en peligro
imperious [ɪm'pɪriəs] *adj* : imperioso — **imperiously** *adv*
imperishable [ɪm'pɛrɪʃəbəl] *adj* : imperecedero
impermanent [ɪm'pərmənənt] *adj* : pasajero, inestable, efímero — **impermanently** *adv*
impermeable [ɪm'pərmiəbəl] *adj* : impermeable
impersonal [ɪm'pərsənəl] *adj* : impersonal — **impersonally** *adv*
impersonate [ɪm'pərsənˌeɪt] *vt* **-ated; -ating** : hacerse pasar por, imitar
impersonation [ɪmˌpərsən'eɪʃən] *n* : imitación *f*
impersonator [ɪm'pərsənˌeɪt̬ər] *n* : imitador *m*, -dora *f*
impertinence [ɪm'pərtənənts] *n* : impertinencia *f*
impertinent [ɪm'pərtənənt] *adj* **1** IRRELEVANT : impertinente, irrelevante **2** INSOLENT : impertinente, insolente
impertinently [ɪm'pərtənəntli] *adv* : con impertinencia, impertinentemente
imperturbable [ˌɪmpər'tərbəbəl] *adj* : imperturbable
impervious [ɪm'pərviəs] *adj* **1** IMPENETRABLE : impermeable **2** INSENSITIVE : insensible ⟨impervious to criticism : insensible a la crítica⟩
impetuosity [ɪmˌpɛʧʊ'ɑsət̬i] *n, pl* **-ties** : impetuosidad *f*
impetuous [ɪm'pɛʧʊəs] *adj* : impetuoso, impulsivo
impetuously [ɪm'pɛʧʊəsli] *adv* : de manera impulsiva, impetuosamente
impetus ['ɪmpət̬əs] *n* : ímpetu *m*, impulso *m*
impiety [ɪm'paɪət̬i] *n, pl* **-ties** : impiedad *f*
impinge [ɪm'pɪnʤ] *vi* **-pinged; -pinging** **1 to impinge on** AFFECT : afectar a, incidir en **2 to impinge on** VIOLATE : violar, vulnerar
impious ['ɪmpiəs, ɪm'paɪəs] *adj* : impío, irreverente
impish ['ɪmpɪʃ] *adj* MISCHIEVOUS : pícaro, travieso
impishly ['ɪmpɪʃli] *adv* : con picardía
implacable [ɪm'plækəbəl] *adj* : implacable — **implacably** [-bli] *adv*
implant[1] [ɪm'plænt] *vt* **1** INCULCATE, INSTILL : inculcar, implantar **2** INSERT : implantar, insertar
implant[2] ['ɪmˌplænt] *n* : implante *m* (de pelo), injerto *m* (de piel)
implantation [ˌɪmˌplæn'teɪʃən] *n* : implantación *f*
implausibility [ɪmˌplɔzə'bɪlət̬i] *n, pl* **-ties** : inverosimilitud *f*
implausible [ɪm'plɔzəbəl] *adj* : inverosímil, poco convincente
implement[1] ['ɪmpləˌmnt] *vt* : poner en práctica, implementar
implement[2] ['ɪmpləmənt] *n* : utensilio *m*, instrumento *m*, implemento *m*
implementation [ˌɪmpləmən'teɪʃən] *n* : implementación *f*, ejecución *f*, cumplimiento *m*
implicate ['ɪmpləˌkeɪt] *vt* **-cated; -cating** : implicar, involucrar
implication [ˌɪmplə'keɪʃən] *n* **1** CONSEQUENCE : implicación *f*, consecuencia *f* **2** INFERENCE : insinuación *f*, inferencia *f*
implicit [ɪm'plɪsət] *adj* **1** IMPLIED : implícito, tácito **2** ABSOLUTE : absoluto, completo ⟨implicit faith : fe ciega⟩ — **implicitly** *adv*
implied [ɪm'plaɪd] *adj* : implícito, tácito
implode [ɪm'plo:d] *vi* **-ploded; -ploding** : implosionar
implore [ɪm'plor] *vt* **-plored; -ploring** : implorar, suplicar
implosion [ɪm'plo:ʒən] *n* : implosión *f*
imply [ɪm'plaɪ] *vt* **-plied; -plying** **1** SUGGEST : insinuar, dar a entender **2** INVOLVE : implicar, suponer ⟨rights imply obligations : los derechos implican unas obligaciones⟩
impolite [ˌɪmpə'laɪt] *adj* : descortés, maleducado
impoliteness [ˌɪmpə'laɪtnəs] *n* : descortesía *f*, falta *f* de educación
impolitic [ɪm'pɑləˌtɪk] *adj* : imprudente, poco político
imponderable[1] [ɪm'pɑndərəbəl] *adj* : imponderable
imponderable[2] *n* : imponderable *m*
import[1] [ɪm'port] *vt* **1** SIGNIFY : significar **2** : importar ⟨to import foreign cars : importar autos extranjeros⟩
import[2] ['ɪmˌport] *n* **1** SIGNIFICANCE : importancia *f*, significación *f* **2** → **importation**
importance [ɪm'portənts] *n* : importancia *f*
important [ɪm'pɔrtənt] *adj* : importante
importantly [ɪm'pɔrtəntli] *adv* **1** : con importancia **2 more importantly** : lo que es más importante
importation [ˌɪmˌpɔr'teɪʃən] *n* : importación *f*
importer [ɪm'port̬ər] *n* : importador *m*, -dora *f*

importunate [ɪm'pɔrʧənət] *adj* : importuno, insistente
importune [ˌɪmpər'tu:n, -'tju:n; ɪm'pɔrʧən] *vt* **-tuned; -tuning** : importunar, implorar
impose [ɪm'po:z] *v* **-posed; -posing** *vt* : imponer ⟨to impose a tax : imponer un impuesto⟩ — *vi* **to impose on** : abusar de, molestar ⟨to impose on her kindness : abusar de su bondad⟩
imposing [ɪm'po:zɪŋ] *adj* : imponente, impresionante
imposition [ˌɪmpə'zɪʃən] *n* : imposición *f*
impossibility [ɪmˌpɑsə'bɪləṱi] *n, pl* **-ties** : imposibilidad *f*
impossible [ɪm'pɑsəbəl] *adj* **1** : imposible ⟨an impossible task : una tarea imposible⟩ ⟨to make life impossible for : hacerle la vida imposible a⟩ **2** UNACCEPTABLE : inaceptable
impossibly [ɪm'pɑsəbli] *adv* : imposiblemente, increíblemente
impostor *or* **imposter** [ɪm'pɑstər] *n* : impostor *m*, -tora *f*
impotence ['ɪmpətənts] *n* : impotencia *f*
impotency ['ɪmpətəntsi] → **impotence**
impotent ['ɪmpətənt] *adj* : impotente
impound [ɪm'paʊnd] *vt* : incautar, embargar, confiscar
impoverish [ɪm'pɑvərɪʃ] *vt* : empobrecer
impoverishment [ɪm'pɑvərɪʃmənt] *n* : empobrecimiento *m*
impracticable [ɪm'præktɪkəbəl] *adj* : impracticable
impractical [ɪm'præktɪkəl] *adj* : poco práctico
imprecise [ˌɪmprɪ'saɪs] *adj* : impreciso
imprecisely [ˌɪmprɪ'saɪsli] *adv* : con imprecisión
impreciseness [ˌɪmprɪ'saɪsnəs] → **imprecision**
imprecision [ˌɪmprɪ'sɪʒən] *n* : imprecisión *f*, falta de precisión *f*
impregnable [ɪm'prɛgnəbəl] *adj* : inexpugnable, impenetrable, inconquistable
impregnate [ɪm'prɛgˌneɪt] *vt* **-nated; -nating 1** FERTILIZE : fecundar **2** PERMEATE, SATURATE : impregnar, empapar, saturar
impresario [ˌɪmprə'sɑriˌo, -'sær-] *n, pl* **-rios** : empresario *m*, -ria *f*
impress [ɪm'prɛs] *vt* **1** IMPRINT : imprimir, estampar **2** : impresionar, causar impresión a ⟨I was not impressed : no me hizo buena impresión⟩ **3 to impress (something) on someone** : recalcarle (algo) a alguien — *vi* : impresionar, hacer una impresión
impression [ɪm'prɛʃən] *n* **1** IMPRINT : marca *f*, huella *f*, molde *m* (de los dientes) **2** EFFECT : impresión *f*, efecto *m*, impacto *m* **3** PRINTING : impresión *f* **4** NOTION : impresión *f*, noción *f*
impressionable [ɪm'prɛʃənəbəl] *adj* : impresionable
impressionism [ɪm'prɛʃəˌnɪzəm] *n* : impresionismo *m*
impressionist [ɪm'prɛʃənɪst] *n* : impresionista *mf* — **impressionist** *adj*
impressive [ɪm'prɛsɪv] *adj* : impresionante — **impressively** *adv*
impressiveness [ɪm'prɛsɪvnəs] *n* : calidad de ser impresionante
imprint[1] [ɪm'prɪnt, 'ɪmˌ-] *vt* : imprimir, estampar
imprint[2] ['ɪmˌprɪnt] *n* : marca *f*, huella *f*
imprison [ɪm'prɪzən] *vt* **1** JAIL : encarcelar, aprisionar **2** CONFINE : recluir, encerrar
imprisonment [ɪm'prɪzənmənt] *n* : encarcelamiento *m*
improbability [ɪmˌprɑbə'bɪləṱi] *n, pl* **-ties** : improbabilidad *f*, inverosimilitud *f*
improbable [ɪm'prɑbəbəl] *adj* : improbable, inverosímil
impromptu[1] [ɪm'prɑmpˌtu:, -ˌtju:] *adv* : sin preparación, espontáneamente
impromptu[2] *adj* : espontáneo, improvisado
impromptu[3] *n* : improvisación *f*
improper [ɪm'prɑpər] *adj* **1** INCORRECT : incorrecto, impropio **2** INDECOROUS : indecoroso
improperly [ɪm'prɑpərli] *adv* : incorrectamente, indebidamente
impropriety [ˌɪmprə'praɪəṱi] *n, pl* **-eties 1** INDECOROUSNESS : indecoro *m*, falta *f* de decoro **2** ERROR : impropiedad *f*, incorrección *f*
improve [ɪm'pru:v] *v* **-proved; -proving** : mejorar
improvement [ɪm'pru:vmənt] *n* : mejoramiento *m*, mejora *f*
improvidence [ɪm'prɑvədənts] *n* : imprevisión *f*
improvisation [ɪmˌprɑvə'zeɪʃən, ˌɪmprəvə-] *n* : improvisación *f*
improvise ['ɪmprəˌvaɪz] *v* **-vised; -vising** : improvisar
imprudence [ɪm'pru:dənts] *n* : imprudencia *f*, indiscreción *f*
imprudent [ɪm'pru:dənt] *adj* : imprudente, indiscreto
impudence ['ɪmpjədənts] *n* : insolencia *f*, descaro *m*
impudent ['ɪmpjədənt] *adj* : insolente, descarado — **impudently** *adv*
impugn [ɪm'pju:n] *vt* : impugnar
impulse ['ɪmˌpʌls] *n* **1** : impulso *m* **2 on impulse** : sin reflexionar
impulsive [ɪm'pʌlsɪv] *adj* : impulsivo — **impulsively** *adv*
impulsiveness [ɪm'pʌlsɪvnəs] *n* : impulsividad *f*
impunity [ɪm'pju:nəṱi] *n* **1** : impunidad *f* **2 with impunity** : impunemente
impure [ɪm'pjʊr] *adj* **1** : impuro ⟨impure thoughts : pensamientos impuros⟩ **2** CONTAMINATED : con impurezas, impuro
impurity [ɪm'pjʊrəṱi] *n, pl* **-ties** : impureza *f*

impute [ɪm'pju:t] *vt* **-puted; -puting** ATTRIBUTE : imputar, atribuir

in[1] ['ɪn] *adv* **1** INSIDE : dentro, adentro ⟨let's go in : vamos adentro⟩ **2** HARVESTED : recogido ⟨the crops are in : las cosechas ya están recogidas⟩ **3 to be in** : estar ⟨is Linda in? : ¿está Linda?⟩ **4 to be in** : estar en poder ⟨the Democrats are in : los demócratas están en el poder⟩ **5 to be in for** : ser objeto de, estar a punto de ⟨they're in for a treat : los van a agasajar⟩ ⟨he's in for a surprise : se va a llevar una sorpresa⟩ **6 to be in on** : participar en, tomar parte en

in[2] *adj* **1** INSIDE : interior ⟨the in part : la parte interior⟩ **2** FASHIONABLE : de moda

in[3] *prep* **1** (*indicating location or position*) ⟨in the lake : en el lago⟩ ⟨a pain in the leg : un dolor en la pierna⟩ ⟨in the sun : al sol⟩ ⟨in the rain : bajo la lluvia⟩ ⟨the best restaurant in Buenos Aires : el mejor restaurante de Buenos Aires⟩ **2** INTO : en, a ⟨he broke it in pieces : lo rompió en pedazos⟩ ⟨she went in the house : se metió a la casa⟩ **3** DURING : por, durante ⟨in the afternoon : por la tarde⟩ **4** WITHIN : dentro de ⟨I'll be back in a week : vuelvo dentro de una semana⟩ **5** (*indicating manner*) : en, con, de ⟨in Spanish : en español⟩ ⟨written in pencil : escrito con lápiz⟩ ⟨in this way : de esta manera⟩ **6** (*indicating states or circumstances*) ⟨to be in luck : tener suerte⟩ ⟨to be in love : estar enamorado⟩ ⟨to be in a hurry : tener prisa⟩ **7** (*indicating purpose*) : en ⟨in reply : en respuesta, como réplica⟩

in[4] *n* **ins and outs** : pormenores *mpl*

inability [ˌɪnə'bɪləṭi] *n, pl* **-ties** : incapacidad *f*

inaccessibility [ˌɪnɪkˌsɛsə'bɪləṭi] *n, pl* **-ties** : inaccesibilidad *f*

inaccessible [ˌɪnɪk'sɛsəbəl] *adj* : inaccesible

inaccuracy [ɪn'ækjərəsi] *n, pl* **-cies 1** : inexactitud *f* **2** MISTAKE : error *m*

inaccurate [ɪn'ækjərət] *n* : inexacto, erróneo, incorrecto

inaccurately [ɪn'ækjərətli] *adv* : incorrectamente, con inexactitud

inaction [ɪn'ækʃən] *n* : inactividad *f*, inacción *f*

inactive [ɪn'æktɪv] *adj* : inactivo

inactivity [ˌɪnˌæk'tɪvəṭi] *n, pl* **-ties** : inactividad *f*, ociosidad *f*

inadequacy [ɪn'ædɪkwəsi] *n, pl* **-cies 1** INSUFFICIENCY : insuficiencia *f* **2** INCOMPETENCE : ineptitud *f*, incompetencia *f*

inadequate [ɪn'ædɪkwət] *adj* **1** INSUFFICIENT : insuficiente, inadecuado **2** INCOMPETENT : inepto, incompetente

inadmissible [ˌɪnæd'mɪsəbəl] *adj* : inadmisible

inadvertent [ˌɪnəd'vərtənt] *adj* : inadvertido, involuntario — **inadvertently** *adv*

inadvisable [ˌɪnæd'vaɪzəbəl] *adj* : desaconsejable

inalienable [ɪn'eɪljənəbəl, -'eɪliənə-] *adj* : inalienable

inane [ɪ'neɪn] *adj* **inaner; -est** : estúpido, idiota, necio

inanimate [ɪn'ænəmət] *adj* : inanimado, exánime

inanity [ɪ'nænəṭi] *n, pl* **-ties 1** STUPIDITY : estupidez *f* **2** NONSENSE : idiotez *f*, disparate *m*

inapplicable [ɪn'æplɪkəbəl, ˌɪnə-'plɪkəbəl] *adj* IRRELEVANT : inaplicable, irrelevante

inappreciable [ˌɪnə'pri:ʃəbəl] *adj* : inapreciable, imperceptible

inappropriate [ˌɪnə'pro:priət] *adj* : inapropiado, inadecuado, impropio

inappropriateness [ˌɪnə'pro:priətnəs] *n* : lo inapropiado, impropiedad *f*

inapt [ɪn'æpt] *adj* **1** UNSUITABLE : inadecuado, inapropiado **2** INEPT : inepto

inarticulate [ˌɪnɑr'tɪkjələt] *adj* : inarticulado, incapaz de expresarse

inarticulately [ˌɪnɑr'tɪkjələtli] *adv* : inarticuladamente

inasmuch as [ˌɪnæz'mʌʧæz] *conj* : ya que, dado que, puesto que

inattention [ˌɪnə'tɛnʧən] *n* : falta *f* de atención, distracción *f*

inattentive [ˌɪnə'tɛntɪv] *adj* : distraído, despistado

inattentively [ˌɪnə'tɛntɪvli] *adv* : distraídamente, sin prestar atención

inaudible [ɪn'ɔdəbəl] *adj* : inaudible

inaudibly [ɪn'ɔdəbli] *adv* : de forma inaudible

inaugural[1] [ɪ'nɔgjərəl, -gərəl] *adj* : inaugural, de investidura

inaugural[2] *n* **1** *or* **inaugural address** : discurso *m* de investidura **2** INAUGURATION : investidura *f* (de una persona)

inaugurate [ɪ'nɔgjəˌreɪt, -gə-] *vt* **-rated; -rating 1** BEGIN : inaugurar **2** INDUCT : investir ⟨to inaugurate the president : investir al presidente⟩

inauguration [ɪˌnɔgjə'reɪʃən, -gə-] *n* **1** : inauguración *f* (de un edificio, un sistema, etc.) **2** : investidura *f* (de una persona)

inauspicious [ˌɪnɔ'spɪʃəs] *adj* : desfavorable, poco propicio

inborn ['ɪnˌbɔrn] *adj* **1** CONGENITAL, INNATE : innato, congénito **2** HEREDITARY : hereditario

inbred ['ɪnˌbrɛd] *adj* **1** : engendrado por endogamia **2** INNATE : innato

inbreed ['ɪnˌbri:d] *vt* **-bred; -breeding** : engendrar por endogamia

inbreeding ['ɪnˌbri:dɪŋ] *n* : endogamia *f*

Inca ['ɪŋkə] *n* : inca *mf*

incalculable [ɪn'kælkjələbəl] *adj* : incalculable — **incalculably** [-bli] *adv*

incandescence [ˌɪnkənˈdɛsənts] *n* : incandescencia *f*
incandescent [ˌɪnkənˈdɛsənt] *adj* **1** : incandescente **2** BRILLIANT : brillante
incantation [ˌɪnˌkænˈteɪʃən] *n* : conjuro *m*, ensalmo *m*
incapable [ɪnˈkeɪpəbəl] *adj* : incapaz
incapacitate [ˌɪnkəˈpæsəˌteɪt] *vt* **-tated; -tating** : incapacitar
incapacity [ˌɪnkəˈpæsəṭi] *n, pl* **-ties** : incapacidad *f*
incarcerate [ɪnˈkɑrsəˌreɪt] *vt* **-ated; -ating** : encarcelar
incarceration [ɪnˌkɑrsəˈreɪʃən] *n* : encarcelamiento *m*, encarcelación *f*
incarnate[1] [ɪnˈkɑrˌneɪt] *vt* **-nated; -nating** : encarnar
incarnate[2] [ɪnˈkɑrnət, -ˌneɪt] *adj* : encarnado
incarnation [ˌɪnˌkɑrˈneɪʃən] *n* : encarnación *f*
incendiary[1] [ɪnˈsɛndiˌri] *adj* : incendiario
incendiary[2] *n, pl* **-aries** : incendiario *m*, -ria *f*; pirómano *m*, -na *f*
incense[1] [ɪnˈsɛnts] *vt* **-censed; -censing** : indignar, enfadar, enfurecer
incense[2] [ˈɪnˌsɛnts] *n* : incienso *m*
incentive [ɪnˈsɛntɪv] *n* : incentivo *m*, aliciente *m*, motivación *f*, acicate *m*
inception [ɪnˈsɛpʃən] *n* : comienzo *m*, principio *m*
incessant [ɪnˈsɛsənt] *adj* : incesante, continuo — **incessantly** *adv*
incest [ˈɪnˌsɛst] *n* : incesto *m*
incestuous [ɪnˈsɛstʃʊəs] *adj* : incestuoso
inch[1] [ˈɪntʃ] *v* : avanzar poco a poco
inch[2] *n* **1** : pulgada *f* **2 every inch** : absoluto, seguro ⟨every inch a winner : un seguro ganador⟩ **3 within an inch of** : a punto de
incidence [ˈɪntsədənts] *n* **1** FREQUENCY : frecuencia *f*, índice *m* ⟨a high incidence of crime : un alto índice de crímenes⟩ **2 angle of incidence** : ángulo *m* de incidencia
incident[1] [ˈɪntsədənt] *adj* : incidente
incident[2] *n* : incidente *m*, incidencia *f*, episodio *m* (en una obra de ficción)
incidental[1] [ˌɪntsəˈdɛntəl] *adj* **1** SECONDARY : incidental, secundario **2** ACCIDENTAL : casual, fortuito
incidental[2] *n* **1** : algo incidental **2 incidentals** *npl* : imprevistos *mpl*
incidentally [ˌɪntsəˈdɛntəli, -ˈdɛntli] *adv* **1** BY CHANCE : incidentalmente, casualmente **2** BY THE WAY : a propósito, por cierto
incinerate [ɪnˈsɪnəˌreɪt] *vt* **-ated; -ating** : incinerar
incinerator [ɪnˈsɪnəˌreɪṭər] *n* : incinerador *m*
incipient [ɪnˈsɪpiənt] *adj* : incipiente, naciente
incise [ɪnˈsaɪz] *vt* **-cised; -cising 1** ENGRAVE : grabar, cincelar, inscribir **2** : hacer una incisión en
incision [ɪnˈsɪʒən] *n* : incisión *f*
incisive [ɪnˈsaɪsɪv] *adj* : incisivo, penetrante
incisively [ɪnˈsaɪsɪvli] *adv* : con agudeza
incisor [ɪnˈsaɪzər] *n* : incisivo *m*
incite [ɪnˈsaɪt] *vt* **-cited; -citing** : incitar, instigar
incitement [ɪnˈsaɪtmənt] *n* : incitación *f*
inclemency [ɪnˈklɛməntsi] *n, pl* **-cies** : inclemencia *f*
inclement [ɪnˈklɛmənt] *adj* : inclemente, tormentoso
inclination [ˌɪnkləˈneɪʃən] *n* **1** PROPENSITY : inclinación *f*, tendencia *f* **2** DESIRE : deseo *m*, ganas *fpl* **3** BOW : inclinación *f*
incline[1] [ɪnˈklaɪn] *v* **-clined; -clining** *vi* **1** SLOPE : inclinarse **2** TEND : inclinarse, tender ⟨he is inclined to be late : tiende a llegar tarde⟩ — *vt* **1** LOWER : inclinar, bajar ⟨to incline one's head : bajar la cabeza⟩ **2** SLANT : inclinar **3** PREDISPOSE : predisponer
incline[2] [ˈɪnˌklaɪn] *n* : inclinación *f*, pendiente *f*
inclined [ɪnˈklaɪnd] *adj* **1** SLOPING : inclinado **2** PRONE : prono, dispuesto, dado
inclose, inclosure → **enclose, enclosure**
include [ɪnˈkluːd] *vt* **-cluded; -cluding** : incluir, comprender
inclusion [ɪnˈkluːʒən] *n* : inclusión *f*
inclusive [ɪnˈkluːsɪv] *adj* : inclusivo
incognito [ˌɪnˌkɑgˈniːṭo, ɪnˈkɑgnəˌtoː] *adv & adj* : de incógnito
incoherence [ˌɪnkoˈhɪrənts, -ˈhɛr-] *n* : incoherencia *f*
incoherent [ˌɪnkoˈhɪrənt, -ˈhɛr-] *adj* : incoherente — **incoherently** *adv*
incombustible [ˌɪnkəmˈbʌstəbəl] *adj* : incombustible
income [ˈɪnˌkʌm] *n* : ingresos *mpl*, entradas *fpl*
income tax *n* : impuesto *m* sobre la renta
incoming [ˈɪnˌkʌmɪŋ] *adj* **1** ARRIVING : que se recibe (dícese del correo), que llega (dícese de las personas), ascendente (dícese de la marea) **2** NEW : nuevo, entrante ⟨the incoming president : el nuevo presidente⟩ ⟨the incoming year : el año entrante⟩
incommunicado [ˌɪnkəˌmjuːnəˈkɑdo] *adj* : incomunicado
incomparable [ɪnˈkɑmpərəbəl] *adj* : incomparable, sin igual
incompatible [ˌɪnkəmˈpæṭəbəl] *adj* : incompatible
incompetence [ɪnˈkɑmpəṭənts] *n* : incompetencia *f*, impericia *f*, ineptitud *f*
incompetent [ɪnˈkɑmpəṭənt] *adj* : incompetente, inepto, incapaz
incomplete [ˌɪnkəmˈpliːt] *adj* : incompleto — **incompletely** *adv*
incomprehensible [ˌɪnˌkɑmpriˈhɛntsəbəl] *adj* : incomprensible
inconceivable [ˌɪnkənˈsiːvəbəl] *adj* **1** INCOMPREHENSIBLE : incomprensible **2** UNBELIEVABLE : inconcebible, increíble

inconceivably [ˌɪnkən'siːvəbli] *adv* : inconcebiblemente, increíblemente
inconclusive [ˌɪnkən'kluːsɪv] *adj* : inconcluyente, no decisivo
incongruity [ˌɪnkən'gruːəṯi, -ˌkɑn-] *n, pl* **-ties** : incongruencia *f*
incongruous [ɪn'kɑŋgrʊəs] *adj* : incongruente, inapropiado, fuera de lugar
incongruously [ɪn'kɑŋgrʊəsli] *adv* : de manera incongruente, inapropiadamente
inconsequential [ˌɪnˌkɑnsə'kwɛnʧəl] *adj* : intrascendente, de poco importancia
inconsiderable [ˌɪnkən'sɪdərəbəl] *adj* : insignificante
inconsiderate [ˌɪnkən'sɪdərət] *adj* : desconsiderado, sin consideración — **inconsiderately** *adv*
inconsistency [ˌɪnkən'sɪstəntsi] *n, pl* **-cies** : inconsecuencia *f*, inconsistencia *f*
inconsistent [ˌɪnkən'sɪstənt] *adj* : inconsecuente, inconsistente
inconsolable [ˌɪnkən'soːləbəl] *adj* : inconsolable — **inconsolably** [-bli] *adv*
inconspicuous [ˌɪnkən'spɪkjʊəs] *adj* : discreto, no conspicuo, que no llama la atención
inconspicuously [ˌɪnkən'spɪkjʊəsli] *adv* : discretamente, sin llamar la atención
incontestable [ˌɪnkən'tɛstəbəl] *adj* : incontestable, indiscutible — **incontestably** [-bli] *adv*
incontinence [ɪn'kɑntənənts] *n* : incontinencia *f*
incontinent [ɪn'kɑntənənt] *adj* : incontinente
inconvenience[1] [ˌɪnkən'viːnjənts] *vt* **-nienced; -niencing** : importunar, incomodar, molestar
inconvenience[2] *n* : incomodidad *f*, molestia *f*
inconvenient [ˌɪnkən'viːnjənt] *adj* : inconveniente, importuno, incómodo — **inconveniently** *adv*
incorporate [ɪn'kɔrpəˌreɪt] *vt* **-rated; -rating** 1 INCLUDE : incorporar, incluir 2 : incorporar, constituir en sociedad (dícese de un negocio)
incorporation [ɪnˌkɔrpə'reɪʃən] *n* : incorporación *f*
incorporeal [ˌɪnˌkɔr'poriəl] *adj* : incorpóreo
incorrect [ˌɪnkə'rɛkt] *adj* 1 INACCURATE : incorrecto 2 WRONG : equivocado, erróneo 3 IMPROPER : impropio — **incorrectly** *adv*
incorrigible [ɪn'kɔrəʤəbəl] *adj* : incorregible
incorruptible [ˌɪnkə'rʌptəbəl] *adj* : incorruptible
increase[1] [ɪn'kriːs, 'ɪnˌkriːs] *v* **-creased; -creasing** *vi* GROW : aumentar, crecer, subir (dícese de los precios) — *vt* AUGMENT : aumentar, acrecentar
increase[2] ['ɪnˌkriːs, ɪn'kriːs] *n* : aumento *m*, incremento *m*, subida *f* (de precios)
increasing [ɪn'kriːsɪŋ, 'ɪnˌkriːsɪŋ] *adj* : creciente
increasingly [ɪn'kriːsɪŋli] *adv* : cada vez más
incredible [ɪn'krɛdəbəl] *adj* : increíble — **incredibly** [-bli] *adv*
incredulity [ˌɪnkrɪ'duːləṯi, -'djuː-] *n* : incredulidad *f*
incredulous [ɪn'krɛʤələs] *adj* : incrédulo, escéptico
incredulously [ɪn'krɛʤələsli] *adv* : con incredulidad
increment ['ɪŋkrəmənt, 'ɪn-] *n* : incremento *m*, aumento *m*
incremental [ˌɪŋkrə'mɛntəl, ˌɪn-] *adj* : de incremento
incriminate [ɪn'krɪməˌneɪt] *vt* **-nated; -nating** : incriminar
incrimination [ɪnˌkrɪmə'neɪʃən] *n* : incriminación *f*
incriminatory [ɪn'krɪmənəˌtori] *adj* : incriminatorio
incubate ['ɪŋkjʊˌbeɪt, 'ɪn-] *v* **-bated; -bating** *vt* : incubar, empollar — *vi* : incubar(se), empollar
incubation [ˌɪŋkjʊ'beɪʃən, ˌɪn-] *n* : incubación *f*
incubator ['ɪŋkjʊˌbeɪṯər, 'ɪn-] *n* : incubadora *f*
inculcate [ɪn'kʌlˌkeɪt, 'ɪnˌkʌl-] *vt* **-cated; -cating** : inculcar
incumbency [ɪn'kʌmbəntsi] *n, pl* **-cies** 1 OBLIGATION : incumbencia *f* 2 : mandato *m* (en la política)
incumbent[1] [ɪn'kʌmbənt] *adj* : obligatorio
incumbent[2] *n* : titular *mf*
incur [ɪn'kər] *vt* **incurred; incurring** : provocar (al enojo), incurrir en (gastos, obligaciones)
incurable [ɪn'kjʊrəbəl] *adj* : incurable, sin remedio
incursion [ɪn'kərʒən] *n* : incursión *f*
indebted [ɪn'dɛṯəd] *adj* 1 : endeudado 2 **to be indebted to** : estar en deuda con, estarle agradecido a
indebtedness [ɪn'dɛṯədnəs] *n* : endeudamiento *m*
indecency [ɪn'diːsəntsi] *n, pl* **-cies** : indecencia *f*
indecent [ɪn'diːsənt] *adj* : indecente — **indecently** *adv*
indecipherable [ˌɪndɪ'saɪfərəbəl] *adj* : indescifrable
indecision [ˌɪndɪ'sɪʒən] *n* : indecisión *f*, irresolución *f*
indecisive [ˌɪndɪ'saɪsɪv] *adj* 1 INCONCLUSIVE : indeciso, que no es decisivo 2 IRRESOLUTE : indeciso, irresoluto, vacilante 3 INDEFINITE : indefinido — **indecisively** *adv*
indecorous [ɪn'dɛkərəs, ˌɪndɪ'korəs] *adj* : indecoroso — **indecorously** *adv*
indecorousness [ɪn'dkərəsnəs, ˌɪndɪ'korəs-] *n* : indecoro *m*
indeed [ɪn'diːd] *adv* 1 TRULY : verdaderamente, de veras 2 (*used as intensifier*) ‹thank you very much indeed

: muchísimas gracias⟩ **3** OF COURSE : claro, por supuesto
indefatigable [ˌɪndɪˈfæt̬ɪgəbəl] *adj* : incansable, infatigable — **indefatigably** [-bli] *adv*
indefensible [ˌɪndɪˈfɛntsəbəl] *adj* **1** VULNERABLE : indefendible, vulnerable **2** INEXCUSABLE : inexcusable
indefinable [ˌɪndɪˈfaɪnəbəl] *adj* : indefinible
indefinite [ɪnˈdɛfənət] *adj* **1** : indefinido, indeterminado ⟨indefinite pronouns : pronombres indefinidos⟩ **2** VAGUE : vago, impreciso
indefinitely [ɪnˈdɛfənətli] *adv* : indefinidamente, por un tiempo indefinido
indelible [ɪnˈdɛləbəl] *adj* : indeleble, imborrable — **indelibly** [-bli] *adv*
indelicacy [ɪnˈdɛləkəsi] *n* : falta *f* de delicadeza
indelicate [ɪnˈdɛlɪkət] *adj* **1** IMPROPER : indelicado, indecoroso **2** TACTLESS : indiscreto, falto de tacto
indemnify [ɪnˈdɛmnəˌfaɪ] *vt* **-fied; -fying** **1** INSURE : asegurar **2** COMPENSATE : indemnizar, compensar
indemnity [ɪnˈdɛmnət̬i] *n, pl* **-ties** **1** INSURANCE : indemnidad *f* **2** COMPENSATION : indemnización *f*
indent [ɪnˈdɛnt] *vt* : sangrar (un párrafo)
indentation [ˌɪnˌdɛnˈteɪʃən] *n* **1** NOTCH : muesca *f*, mella *f* **2** INDENTING : sangría *f* (de un párrafo)
indenture¹ [ɪnˈdɛntʃər] *vt* **-tured; -turing** : ligar por contrato
indenture² *n* : contrato de aprendizaje
independence [ˌɪndəˈpɛndənts] *n* : independencia *f*
Independence Day *n* : día *m* de la Independencia (4 de julio en los EE.UU.)
independent¹ [ˌɪndəˈpɛndənt] *adj* : independiente — **independently** *adv*
independent² *n* : independiente *mf*
indescribable [ˌɪndɪˈskraɪbəbəl] *adj* : indescriptible, incalificable — **indescribably** [-bli] *adv*
indestructibility [ˌɪndɪˌstrʌktəˈbɪlət̬i] *n* : indestructibilidad *f*
indestructible [ˌɪndɪˈstrʌktəbəl] *adj* : indestructible
indeterminate [ˌɪndɪˈtərmənət] *adj* **1** VAGUE : vago, impreciso, indeterminado **2** INDEFINITE : indeterminado, indefinido
index¹ [ˈɪnˌdɛks] *vt* **1** : ponerle un índice a (un libro o una revista) **2** : incluir en un índice ⟨all proper names are indexed : todos los nombres propios están incluidos en el índice⟩ **3** INDICATE : indicar, señalar **4** REGULATE : indexar, indiciar ⟨to index prices : indiciar los precios⟩
index² *n, pl* **-dexes** *or* **-dices** [ˈɪndəˌsiːz] **1** : índice *m* (de un libro, de precios) **2** INDICATION : indicio *m*, índice *m*, señal *f* ⟨an index of her character : una señal de su carácter⟩
index finger *n* FOREFINGER : dedo *m* índice
Indian [ˈɪndiən] *n* **1** : indio *m*, -dia *f* **2** → **American Indian** — **Indian** *adj*
indicate [ˈɪndəˌkeɪt] *vt* **-cated; -cating** **1** POINT OUT : indicar, señalar **2** SHOW, SUGGEST : ser indicio de, ser señal de **3** EXPRESS : expresar, señalar **4** REGISTER : marcar, poner (una medida, etc.)
indication [ˌɪndəˈkeɪʃən] *n* : indicio *m*, señal *f*
indicative [ɪnˈdɪkət̬ɪv] *adj* : indicativo
indicator [ˈɪndəˌkeɪt̬ər] *n* : indicador *m*
indict [ɪnˈdaɪt] *vt* : acusar, procesar (por un crimen)
indictment [ɪnˈdaɪtmənt] *n* : acusación *f*
indifference [ɪnˈdɪfrənts, -ˈdɪfə-] *n* : indiferencia *f*
indifferent [ɪnˈdɪfrənt, -ˈdɪfə-] *adj* **1** UNCONCERNED : indiferente **2** MEDIOCRE : mediocre
indifferently [ɪnˈdɪfrəntli, -ˈdɪfə-] *adv* **1** : con indiferencia, indiferentemente **2** SO-SO : de modo regular, más o menos
indigence [ˈɪndɪʤənts] *n* : indigencia *f*
indigenous [ɪnˈdɪʤənəs] *adj* : indígena, nativo
indigent [ˈɪndɪʤənt] *adj* : indigente, pobre
indigestible [ˌɪndaɪˈʤɛstəbəl, -dɪ-] *adj* : difícil de digerir
indigestion [ˌɪndaɪˈʤɛstʃən, -dɪ-] *n* : indigestión *f*, empacho *m*
indignant [ɪnˈdɪgnənt] *adj* : indignado
indignantly [ɪnˈdɪgnəntli] *adv* : con indignación
indignation [ˌɪndɪgˈneɪʃən] *n* : indignación *f*
indignity [ɪnˈdɪgnət̬i] *n, pl* **-ties** : indignidad *f*
indigo [ˈɪndɪˌgoː] *n, pl* **-gos** *or* **-goes** : añil *m*, índigo *m*
indirect [ˌɪndəˈrɛkt, -daɪ-] *adj* : indirecto — **indirectly** *adv*
indiscernible [ˌɪndɪˈsərnəbəl, -ˈzər-] *adj* : imperceptible
indiscreet [ˌɪndɪˈskriːt] *adj* : indiscreto, imprudente — **indiscreetly** *adv*
indiscretion [ˌɪndɪˈskrɛʃən] *n* : indiscreción *f*, imprudencia *f*
indiscriminate [ˌɪndɪˈskrɪmənət] *adj* : indiscriminado
indiscriminately [ˌɪndɪˈskrɪmənətli] *adv* : sin discriminación, sin discernimiento
indispensable [ˌɪndɪˈspɛntsəbəl] *adj* : indispensable, necesario, imprescindible — **indispensably** [-bli] *adv*
indisposed [ˌɪndɪˈspoːzd] *adj* **1** ILL : indispuesto, enfermo **2** AVERSE, DISINCLINED : opuesto, reacio ⟨to be indisposed toward working : no tener ganas de trabajar⟩
indisputable [ˌɪndɪˈspjuːt̬əbəl, ɪnˈdɪspjʊt̬ə-] *adj* : indiscutible, incuestionable, incontestable — **indisputably** [-bli] *adv*

indistinct [ˌɪndɪˈstɪŋkt] *adj* : indistinto — **indistinctly** *adv*
indistinctness [ˌɪndɪˈstɪŋktnəs] *n* : falta *f* de claridad
indistinguishable [ˌɪndɪˈstɪŋgwɪʃəbəl] *adj* : indistinguible
individual[1] [ˌɪndəˈvɪʤʊəl] *adj* **1** PERSONAL : individual, personal ⟨individual traits : características personales⟩ **2** SEPARATE : individual, separado **3** PARTICULAR : particular, propio
individual[2] *n* : individuo *m*
individualism [ˌɪndəˈvɪʤəwəˌlɪzəm] *n* : individualismo *m*
individualist [ˌɪndəˈvɪʤʊəlɪst] *n* : individualista *mf*
individuality [ˌɪndəˌvɪʤʊˈæləṭi] *n, pl* **-ties** : individualidad *f*
individually [ˌɪndəˈvɪʤʊəli, -ʤəli] *adv* : individualmente
indivisible [ˌɪndɪˈvɪzəbəl] *adj* : indivisible
indoctrinate [ɪnˈdɑktrəˌneɪt] *vt* **-nated; -nating** **1** TEACH : enseñar, instruir **2** PROPAGANDIZE : adoctrinar
indoctrination [ɪnˌdɑktrəˈneɪʃən] *n* : adoctrinamiento *m*
indolence [ˈɪndələnts] *n* : indolencia *f*
indolent [ˈɪndələnt] *adj* : indolente
indomitable [ɪnˈdɑməṭəbəl] *adj* : invencible, indomable, indómito — **indomitably** [-bli] *adv*
Indonesian [ˌɪndoˈni:ʒən, -ʃən] *n* : indonesio *m*, -sia *f* — **Indonesian** *adj*
indoor [ˈɪnˈdor] *adj* : interior (dícese de las plantas), para estar en casa (dícese de la ropa), cubierto (dícese de las piscinas, etc.), bajo techo (dícese de los deportes)
indoors [ˈɪnˈdorz] *adv* : adentro, dentro
indubitable [ɪnˈdu:bəṭəbəl, -ˈdju:-] *adj* : indudable, incuestionable, indiscutible
indubitably [ɪnˈdu:bəṭəbli, -ˈdju:-] *adv* : indudablemente
induce [ɪnˈdu:s, -ˈdju:s] *vt* **-duced; -ducing** **1** PERSUADE : persuadir, inducir **2** CAUSE : inducir, provocar ⟨to induce labor : provocar un parto⟩
inducement [ɪnˈdu:smənt, -ˈdju:s-] *n* **1** INCENTIVE : incentivo *m*, aliciente *m* **2** : inducción *f*, provocación *f* (de un parto)
induct [ɪnˈdʌkt] *vt* **1** INSTALL : instalar, investir **2** ADMIT : admitir (como miembro) **3** CONSCRIPT : reclutar (al servicio militar)
inductee [ˌɪnˌdʌkˈti:] *n* : recluta *mf*, conscripto *m*, -ta *f*
induction [ɪnˈdʌkʃən] *n* **1** INTRODUCTION : iniciación *f*, introducción *f* **2** : inducción *f* (en la lógica o la electricidad)
inductive [ɪnˈdʌktɪv] *adj* : inductivo
indulge [ɪnˈdʌlʤ] *v* **-dulged; -dulging** *vt* **1** GRATIFY : gratificar, satisfacer **2** SPOIL : consentir, mimar — *vi* **to indulge in** : permitirse
indulgence [ɪnˈdʌlʤənts] *n* **1** SATISFYING : satisfacción *f*, gratificación *f* **2** HUMORING : complacencia *f*, indulgencia *f* **3** SPOILING : consentimiento *m* **4** : indulgencia *f* (en la religión)
indulgent [ɪŋˈdʌlʤənt] *adj* : indulgente, consentido — **indulgently** *adv*
industrial [ɪnˈdʌstriəl] *adj* : industrial — **industrially** *adv*
industrialist [ɪnˈdʌstriəlɪst] *n* : industrial *mf*
industrialization [ɪnˌdʌstriələˈzeɪ-ʃən] *n* : industrialización *f*
industrialize [ɪnˈdʌstriəˌlaɪz] *vt* **-ized; -izing** : industrializar
industrious [ɪnˈdʌstriəs] *adj* : diligente, industrioso, trabajador
industriously [ɪnˈdʌstriəsli] *adv* : con diligencia, con aplicación
industriousness [ɪnˈdʌstriəsnəs] *n* : diligencia *f*, aplicación *f*
industry [ˈɪndəstri] *n, pl* **-tries** **1** DILIGENCE : diligencia *f*, aplicación *f* **2** : industria *f* ⟨the steel industry : la industria siderúrgica⟩
inebriated [ɪˈni:briˌeɪṭəd] *adj* : ebrio, embriagado
inebriation [ɪˌni:briˈeɪʃən] *n* : ebriedad *f*, embriaguez *f*
ineffable [ɪnˈɛfəbəl] *adj* : inefable — **ineffably** [-bli] *adv*
ineffective [ˌɪnɪˈfɛktɪv] *adj* **1** INEFFECTUAL : ineficaz, inútil **2** INCAPABLE : incompetente, ineficiente, incapaz
ineffectively [ˌɪnɪˈfɛktɪvli] *adv* : ineficazmente, infructuosamente
ineffectual [ˌɪnɪˈfɛktʃʊəl] *adj* : inútil, ineficaz — **ineffectually** *adv*
inefficiency [ˌɪnɪˈfɪʃəntsi] *n, pl* **-cies** : ineficiencia *f*, ineficacia *f*
inefficient [ˌɪnɪˈfɪʃənt] *adj* **1** : ineficiente, ineficaz **2** INCAPABLE, INCOMPETENT : incompetente, incapaz — **inefficiently** *adv*
inelegance [ɪnˈɛləgənts] *n* : inelegancia *f*
inelegant [ɪnˈɛləgənt] *adj* : inelegante, poco elegante
ineligibility [ɪnˌɛləʤəˈbɪləṭi] *n* : inelegibilidad *f*
ineligible [ɪnˈɛləʤəbəl] *adj* : inelegible
inept [ɪˈɛnpt] *adj* : inepto ⟨inept at : incapaz para⟩
ineptitude [ɪˈɛnptəˌtu:d, -ˌtju:d] *n* : ineptitud *f*, incompetencia *f*, incapacidad *f*
inequality [ˌɪnɪˈkwɑləṭi] *n, pl* **-ties** : desigualdad *f*
inert [ɪˈnərt] *adj* **1** INACTIVE : inerte, inactivo **2** SLUGGISH : lento
inertia [ɪˈnərʃə] *n* : inercia *f*
inescapable [ˌɪnɪˈskeɪpəbəl] *adj* : inevitable, ineludible — **inescapably** [-bli] *adv*
inessential [ˌɪnɪˈsɛntʃəl] *adj* : que no es esencial, innecesario
inestimable [ɪnˈɛstəməbəl] *adj* : inestimable, inapreciable

inevitability [ɪn͵ɛvət̬əˈbɪlət̬i] *n, pl* **-ties** : inevitabilidad *f*
inevitable [ɪnˈɛvət̬əbəl] *adj* : inevitable — **inevitably** [-bli] *adv*
inexact [͵ɪnɪgˈzækt] *adj* : inexacto
inexactly [͵ɪnɪgˈzæktli] *adv* : sin exactitud
inexcusable [͵ɪnɪkˈskjuːzəbəl] *adj* : inexcusable, imperdonable — **inexcusably** [-bli] *adv*
inexhaustible [͵ɪnɪgˈzɔstəbəl] *adj* **1** INDEFATIGABLE : infatigable, incansable **2** ENDLESS : inagotable — **inexhaustibly** [-bli] *adv*
inexorable [ɪnˈɛksərəbəl] *adj* : inexorable — **inexorably** [-bli] *adv*
inexpensive [͵ɪnɪkˈspɛntsɪv] *adj* : barato, económico
inexperience [͵ɪnɪkˈspɪriənts] *n* : inexperiencia *f*
inexperienced [͵ɪnɪkˈspɪriəntst] *adj* : inexperto, novato
inexplicable [͵ɪnɪkˈsplɪkəbəl] *adj* : inexplicable — **inexplicably** [-bli] *adv*
inexpressible [͵ɪnɪkˈsprɛsəbəl] *adj* : inexpresable, inefable
inextricable [͵ɪnɪkˈstrɪkəbəl, ɪˈnɛk-͵strɪ-] *adj* : inextricable — **inextricably** [-bli] *adv*
infallibility [ɪn͵fæləˈbɪlət̬i] *n* : infalibilidad *f*
infallible [ɪnˈfæləbəl] *adj* : infalible — **infallibly** [-bli] *adv*
infamous [ˈɪnfəməs] *adj* : infame — **infamously** *adv*
infamy [ˈɪnfəmi] *n, pl* **-mies** : infamia *f*
infancy [ˈɪnfəntsi] *n, pl* **-cies** : infancia *f*
infant [ˈɪnfənt] *n* : bebé *m*; niño *m*, -ña *f*
infantile [ˈɪnfən͵taɪl, -təl, -͵tiːl] *adj* : infantil, pueril
infantile paralysis → **poliomyelitis**
infantry [ˈɪnfəntri] *n, pl* **-tries** : infantería *f*
infatuated [ɪnˈfætʃʊ͵eɪt̬əd] *adj* **to be infatuated with** : estar encaprichado con
infatuation [ɪn͵fætʃʊˈeɪʃən] *n* : encaprichamiento *m*, enamoramiento *m*
infect [ɪnˈfɛkt] *vt* : infectar, contagiar
infection [ɪnˈfɛkʃən] *n* : infección *f*, contagio *m*
infectious [ɪnˈfɛkʃəs] *adj* : infeccioso, contagioso
infer [ɪnˈfər] *vt* **inferred; inferring** **1** DEDUCE : deducir, inferir **2** SURMISE : concluir, suponer, tener entendido **3** IMPLY : sugerir, insinuar
inference [ˈɪnfərənts] *n* : deducción *f*, inferencia *f*, conclusión *f*
inferior[1] [ɪnˈfɪriər] *adj* : inferior, malo
inferior[2] *n* : inferior *mf*
inferiority [ɪn͵fɪriˈɔrət̬i] *n, pl* **-ties** : inferioridad *f* ⟨inferiority complex : complejo de inferioridad⟩
infernal [ɪnˈfərnəl] *adj* **1** : infernal ⟨infernal fires : fuegos infernales⟩ **2** DIABOLICAL : infernal, diabólico **3** DAMNABLE : maldito, condenado
inferno [ɪnˈfər͵noː] *n, pl* **-nos** : infierno *m*
infertile [ɪnˈfərt̬əl, -͵taɪl] *adj* : estéril, infecundo
infertility [͵ɪnfərˈtɪlət̬i] *n* : esterilidad *f*, infecundidad *f*
infest [ɪnˈfɛst] *vt* : infestar, plagar
infestation [͵ɪn͵fɛsˈteɪʃən] *n* : infestación *f*, plaga *f*
infidel [ˈɪnfədəl, -͵dɛl] *n* : infiel *mf*
infidelity [͵ɪnfəˈdɛlət̬i, -faɪ-] *n, pl* **-ties** **1** UNFAITHFULNESS : infidelidad *f* **2** DISLOYALTY : deslealtad *f*
infield [ˈɪn͵fiːld] *n* : cuadro *m*, diamante *m*
infiltrate [ɪnˈfɪl͵treɪt, ˈɪnfɪl-] *v* **-trated; -trating** *vt* : infiltrar — *vi* : infiltrarse
infiltration [͵ɪnfɪlˈtreɪʃən] *n* : infiltración *f*
infinite [ˈɪnfənət] *adj* **1** LIMITLESS : infinito, sin límites **2** VAST : infinito, vasto, extenso
infinitely [ˈɪnfənətli] *adv* : infinitamente
infinitesimal [͵ɪn͵fɪnəˈtɛsəməl] *adj* : infinitésimo, infinitesimal — **infinitesimally** *adv*
infinitive [ɪnˈfɪnət̬ɪv] *n* : infinitivo *m*
infinity [ɪnˈfɪnət̬i] *n, pl* **-ties** **1** : infinito *m* (en matemáticas, etc.) **2** : infinidad *f* ⟨an infinity of stars : una infinidad de estrellas⟩
infirm [ɪnˈfərm] *adj* **1** FEEBLE : enfermizo, endeble **2** INSECURE : inseguro
infirmary [ɪnˈfərməri] *n, pl* **-ries** : enfermería *f*, hospital *m*
infirmity [ɪnˈfərmət̬i] *n, pl* **-ties** **1** FRAILTY : debilidad *f*, endeblez *f* **2** AILMENT : enfermedad *f*, dolencia *f* ⟨the infirmities of age : los achaques de la vejez⟩
inflame [ɪnˈfleɪm] *v* **-flamed; -flaming** *vt* **1** KINDLE : inflamar, encender **2** : inflamar (una herida) **3** STIR UP : encender, provocar, inflamar — *vi* : inflamarse
inflammable [ɪnˈflæməbəl] *adj* **1** FLAMMABLE : inflamable **2** IRASCIBLE : irascible, explosivo
inflammation [͵ɪnfləˈmeɪʃən] *n* : inflamación *f*
inflammatory [ɪnˈflæmə͵tori] *adj* : inflamatorio, incendiario
inflatable [ɪnˈfleɪt̬əbəl] *adj* : inflable
inflate [ɪnˈfleɪt] *vt* **-flated; -flating** : inflar, hinchar
inflation [ɪnˈfleɪʃən] *n* : inflación *f*
inflationary [ɪnˈfleɪʃə͵nɛri] *adj* : inflacionario, inflacionista
inflect [ɪnˈflɛkt] *vt* **1** CONJUGATE, DECLINE : conjugar, declinar **2** MODULATE : modular (la voz)
inflection [ɪnˈflɛkʃən] *n* : inflexión *f*
inflexibility [ɪn͵flɛksəˈbɪlət̬i] *n, pl* **-ties** : inflexibilidad *f*
inflexible [ɪnˈflɛksɪbəl] *adj* : inflexible
inflict [ɪnˈflɪkt] *vt* **1** : infligir, causar, imponer **2 to inflict oneself on** : imponer uno su presencia (a alguien)
infliction [ɪnˈflɪkʃən] *n* : imposición *f*

influence[1] [ˈɪnˌflu:ənts, ɪnˈflu:ənts] *vt* **-enced; -encing** : influenciar, influir en
influence[2] *n* **1** : influencia *f*, influjo *m* <to exert influence over : ejercer influencia sobre> <the influence of gravity : el influjo de la gravidad> **2 under the influence** : bajo la influencia del alcohol, embriagado
influential [ˌɪnfluˈɛntʃəl] *adj* : influyente
influenza [ˌɪnfluˈɛnzə] *n* : gripe *f*, influenza *f*, gripa *f Col, Mex*
influx [ˈɪnˌflʌks] *n* : afluencia *f* (de gente), entrada *f* (de mercancías), llegada *f* (de ideas)
inform [ɪnˈfɔrm] *vt* : informar, notificar, avisar — *vi* **to inform on** : delatar, denunciar
informal [ɪnˈfɔrməl] *adj* **1** UNCEREMONIOUS : sin ceremonia, sin etiqueta **2** CASUAL : informal, familiar (dícese del lenguaje) **3** UNOFFICIAL : extraoficial
informality [ˌɪnfɔrˈmæləṭi, -fər-] *n, pl* **-ties** : informalidad *f*, familiaridad *f*, falta *f* de ceremonia
informally [ɪnˈfɔrməli] *adv* : sin ceremonias, de manera informal, informalmente
informant [ɪnˈfɔrmənt] *n* : informante *mf*; informador *m*, -dora *f*
information [ˌɪnfərˈmeɪʃən] *n* : información *f*
informative [ɪnˈfɔrməṭɪv] *adj* : informativo, instructivo
informer [ɪnˈfɔrmər] *n* : informante *mf*; informador *m*, -dora *f*
infraction [ɪnˈfrækʃən] *n* : infracción *f*, violación *f*, transgresión *f*
infrared [ˌɪnfrəˈrɛd] *adj* : infrarrojo
infrastructure [ˈɪnfrəˌstrʌktʃər] *n* : infraestructura *f*
infrequent [ɪnˈfri:kwənt] *adj* : infrecuente, raro
infrequently [ɪnˈfri:kwəntli] *adv* : raramente, con poca frecuencia
infringe [ɪnˈfrɪnʤ] *v* **-fringed; -fringing** *vt* : infringir, violar — *vi* **to infringe on** : abusar de, violar
infringement [ɪnˈfrɪnʤmənt] *n* **1** VIOLATION : violación *f* (de la ley), incumplimiento *m* (de un contrato) **2** ENCROACHMENT : usurpación *f* (de derechos, etc.)
infuriate [ɪnˈfjʊriˌeɪt] *vt* **-ated; -ating** : enfurecer, poner furioso
infuriating [ɪnˈfjʊriˌeɪṭɪŋ] *adj* : indignante, exasperante
infuse [ɪnˈfju:z] *vt* **-fused; -fusing 1** INSTILL : infundir **2** STEEP : hacer una infusión de
infusion [ɪnˈfju:ʒən] *n* : infusión *f*
ingenious [ɪnˈʤi:njəs] *adj* : ingenioso — **ingeniously** *adv*
ingenue *or* **ingénue** [ˈɑnʤəˌnu:, ˈæn-; ˈæʒə-, ˈɑ-] *n* : ingenua *f*
ingenuity [ˌɪnʤəˈnu:əṭi, -ˈnju:-] *n, pl* **-ities** : ingenio
ingenuous [ɪnˈʤɛnjʊəs] *adj* **1** FRANK : cándido, franco **2** NAIVE : ingenuo — **ingenuously** *adv*
ingenuousness [ɪnˈʤɛnjʊəsnəs] *n* **1** FRANKNESS : candidez *f*, candor *m* **2** NAÏVETÉ : ingenuidad *f*
ingest [ɪnˈʤɛst] *vt* : ingerir
ingestion [ɪnˈʤɛstʃən] *n* : ingestión *f*
inglorious [ɪnˈgloriəs] *adj* : deshonroso, ignominioso
ingot [ˈɪŋgət] *n* : lingote *m*
ingrained [ɪnˈgreɪnd] *adj* : arraigado
ingrate [ˈɪnˌgreɪt] *n* : ingrato *m*, -ta *f*
ingratiate [ɪnˈgreɪʃiˌeɪt] *vt* **-ated; -ating** : conseguir la benevolencia de <to ingratiate oneself with someone : congraciarse con alguien>
ingratiating [ɪnˈgreɪʃiˌeɪṭɪŋ] *adj* : halagador, zalamero, obsequioso
ingratitude [ɪnˈgræṭəˌtu:d, -ˌtju:d] *n* : ingratitud *f*
ingredient [ɪnˈgri:diənt] *n* : ingrediente *m*, componente *m*
ingrown [ˈɪnˌgro:n] *adj* **1** : crecido hacia adentro **2 ingrown toenail** : uña *f* encarnada
inhabit [ɪnˈhæbət] *vt* : vivir en, habitar, ocupar
inhabitable [ɪnˈhæbəṭəbəl] *adj* : habitable
inhabitant [ɪnˈhæbəṭənt] *n* : habitante *mf*
inhalant [ɪnˈheɪlənt] *n* : inhalante *m*
inhalation [ˌɪnhəˈleɪʃən, ˌɪnə-] *n* : inhalación *f*
inhale [ɪnˈheɪl] *v* **-haled; -haling** *vt* : inhalar, aspirar — *vi* : inspirar
inhaler [ɪnˈheɪlər] *n* : inhalador *m*
inhere [ɪnˈhɪr] *vi* **-hered; -hering** : ser inherente
inherent [ɪnˈhɪrənt, -ˈhɛr-] *adj* : inherente, intrínseco — **inherently** *adv*
inherit [ɪnˈhɛrət] *vt* : heredar
inheritance [ɪnˈhɛrəṭənts] *n* : herencia *f*
inheritor [ɪnˈhɛrəṭər] *n* : heredero *m*, -da *f*
inhibit [ɪnˈhɪbət] *vt* IMPEDE : inhibir, impedir
inhibition [ˌɪnhəˈbɪʃən, ˌɪnə-] *n* : inhibición *f*, cohibición *f*
inhuman [ɪnˈhju:mən, -ˈju:-] *adj* : inhumano, cruel — **inhumanly** *adv*
inhumane [ˌɪnhjuˈmeɪn, -ju-] *adj* INHUMAN : inhumano, cruel
inhumanity [ˌɪnhjuˈmænəṭi, -ju-] *n, pl* **-ties** : inhumanidad *f*, crueldad *f*
inimical [ɪˈnɪmɪkəl] *adj* **1** UNFAVORABLE : adverso, desfavorable **2** HOSTILE : hostil — **inimically** *adv*
inimitable [ɪˈnɪməṭəbəl] *adj* : inimitable
iniquitous [ɪˈnɪkwəṭəs] *adj* : inicuo, malvado
iniquity [ɪˈnɪkwəṭi] *n, pl* **-ties** : iniquidad *f*
initial[1] [ɪˈnɪʃəl] *vt* **-tialed** *or* **-tialled; -tialing** *or* **-tialling** : poner las iniciales a, firmar con las iniciales
initial[2] *adj* : inicial, primero — **initially** *adv*

initial³ *n* : inicial *f*
initiate¹ [ɪˈnɪʃi,eɪt] *vt* **-ated; -ating 1** BEGIN : comenzar, iniciar **2** INDUCT : instruir **3** INTRODUCE : introducir, instruir
initiate² [ɪˈnɪʃiət] *n* : iniciado *m*, -da *f*
initiation [ɪ,nɪʃiˈeɪʃən] *n* : iniciación *f*
initiative [ɪˈnɪʃət̬ɪv] *n* : iniciativa *f*
initiatory [ɪˈnɪʃiə,tori] *adj* **1** INTRODUCTORY : introductorio **2** : de iniciación ⟨initiatory rites : ritos de iniciación⟩
inject [ɪnˈʤɛkt] *vt* : inyectar
injection [ɪnˈʤɛkʃən] *n* : inyección *f*
injudicious [,ɪnʤʊˈdɪʃəs] *adj* : imprudente, indiscreto, poco juicioso
injunction [ɪnˈʤʌŋkʃən] *n* **1** ORDER : orden *f*, mandato *m* **2** COURT ORDER : mandamiento *m* judicial
injure [ˈɪnʤər] *vt* **-jured; -juring 1** WOUND : herir, lesionar **2** HURT : lastimar, dañar, herir **3 to injure oneself** : hacerse daño
injurious [ɪnˈʤʊriəs] *adj* : perjudicial ⟨injurious to one's health : perjudicial a la salud⟩
injury [ˈɪnʤəri] *n, pl* **-ries 1** WRONG : mal *m*, injusticia *f* **2** DAMAGE, HARM : herida *f*, daño *m*, perjuicio *m*
injustice [ɪnˈʤʌstəs] *n* : injusticia *f*
ink¹ [ˈɪŋk] *vt* : entintar
ink² *n* : tinta *f*
inkling [ˈɪŋklɪŋ] *n* : presentimiento *m*, indicio *m*, sospecha *f*
inkwell [ˈɪŋk,wɛl] *n* : tintero *m*
inky [ˈɪŋki] *adj* **1** : manchado de tinta **2** BLACK : negro, impenetrable ⟨inky darkness : negra oscuridad⟩
inland¹ [ˈɪn,lænd, -lənd] *adv* : hacia el interior, tierra adentro
inland² *adj* : interior
inland³ *n* : interior *m*
in–law [ˈɪn,lɔ] *n* **1** : pariente *m* político **2 in–laws** *npl* : suegros *mpl*
inlay¹ [ɪnˈleɪ, ˈɪn,leɪ] *vt* **-laid** [-ˈleɪd, -,leɪd]; **-laying** : incrustar, taracear
inlay² [ˈɪn,leɪ] *n* **1** : incrustación *f* **2** : empaste *m* (de un diente)
inlet [ˈɪn,lɛt, -lət] *n* : cala *f*, ensenada *f*
inmate [ˈɪn,meɪt] *n* : paciente *mf* (en un hospital); preso *m*, -sa *f* (en una prisión); interno *m*, -na *f* (en un asilo)
in memoriam [,ɪnməˈmoriəm] *prep* : en memoria de
inmost [ˈɪn,mo:st] → **innermost**
inn [ˈɪn] *n* **1** : posada *f*, hostería *f*, fonda *f* **2** TAVERN : taberna *f*
innards [ˈɪnərdz] *npl* : entrañas *fpl*, tripas *fpl fam*
innate [ɪˈneɪt] *adj* **1** INBORN : innato **2** INHERENT : inherente
inner [ˈɪnər] *adj* : interior, interno
innermost [ˈɪnər,mo:st] *adj* : más íntimo, más profundo
innersole [ˈɪnərˈso:l] → **insole**
inning [ˈɪnɪŋ] *n* : entrada *f*
innkeeper [ˈɪn,ki:pər] *n* : posadero *m*, -ra *f*
innocence [ˈɪnəsənts] *n* : inocencia *f*
innocent¹ [ˈɪnəsənt] *adj* : inocente — **innocently** *adv*
innocent² *n* : inocente *mf*
innocuous [ɪˈnɑkjəwəs] *adj* **1** HARMLESS : inocuo **2** INOFFENSIVE : inofensivo
innovate [ˈɪnə,veɪt] *vi* **-vated; -vating** : innovar
innovation [,ɪnəˈveɪʃən] *n* : innovación *f*, novedad *f*
innovative [ˈɪnə,veɪt̬ɪv] *adj* : innovador
innovator [ˈɪnə,veɪt̬ər] *n* : innovador *m*, -dora *f*
innuendo [,ɪnjʊˈɛndo] *n, pl* **-dos** *or* **-does** : insinuación *f*, indirecta *f*
innumerable [ɪˈnu:mərəbəl, -ˈnju:-] *adj* : innumerable
inoculate [ɪˈnɑkjə,leɪt] *vt* **-lated; -lating** : inocular
inoculation [ɪ,nɑkjəˈleɪʃən] *n* : inoculación *f*
inoffensive [,ɪnəˈfɛntsɪv] *adj* : inofensivo
inoperable [ɪnˈɑpərəbəl] *adj* : inoperable
inoperative [ɪnˈɑpərət̬ɪv, -,reɪ-] *adj* : inoperante
inopportune [ɪn,ɑpərˈtu:n, -ˈtju:n] *adj* : inoportuno — **inopportunely** *adv*
inordinate [ɪnˈɔrdənət] *adj* : excesivo, inmoderado, desmesurado — **inordinately** *adv*
inorganic [,ɪn,ɔrˈgænɪk] *adj* : inorgánico
inpatient [ˈɪn,peɪʃənt] *n* : paciente *mf* hospitalizado
input¹ [ˈɪn,pʊt] *vt* **inputted** *or* **input; inputting** : entrar (datos, información)
input² *n* **1** CONTRIBUTION : aportación *f*, contribución *f* **2** ENTRY : entrada *f* (de datos) **3** ADVICE, OPINION : consejos *mpl*, opinión *f*
inquest [ˈɪn,kwɛst] *n* INQUIRY, INVESTIGATION : investigación *f*, averiguación *f*, pesquisa *f* (judicial)
inquire [ɪnˈkwaɪr] *v* **-quired; -quiring** *vt* : preguntar, informarse de, inquirir ⟨he inquired how to get in : preguntó como entrar⟩ — *vi* **1** ASK : preguntar, informarse ⟨to inquire about : informarse sobre⟩ ⟨to inquire after (someone) : preguntar por (alguien)⟩ **2 to inquire into** INVESTIGATE : investigar, inquirir sobre
inquiringly [ɪnˈkwaɪrɪŋli] *adv* : inquisitivamente
inquiry [ˈɪn,kwaɪri, ɪnˈkwaɪri; ˈɪnkwəri, ˈɪŋ-] *n, pl* **-ries 1** QUESTION : pregunta *f* ⟨to make inquiries about : pedir información sobre⟩ **2** INVESTIGATION : investigación *f*, inquisición *f*, pesquisa *f*
inquisition [,ɪnkwəˈzɪʃən, ,ɪŋ-] *n* **1** : inquisición *f*, interrogatorio *m*, investigación *f* **2 the Inquisition** : la Inquisición *f*
inquisitive [ɪnˈkwɪzət̬ɪv] *adj* : inquisidor, inquisitivo, curioso — **inquisitively** *adv*

inquisitiveness [ɪn'kwɪzət̬ɪvnəs] *n* : curiosidad *f*
inquisitor [ɪn'kwɪzət̬ər] *n* : inquisidor *m*, -dora *f*; interrogador *m*, -dora *f*
inroad ['ɪn,ro:d] *n* **1** ENCROACHMENT, INVASION : invasión *f*, incursión *f* **2 to make inroads into** : ocupar parte de (un tiempo), agotar parte de (ahorros, recursos), invadir (un territorio)
insane [ɪn'seɪn] *adj* **1** MAD : loco, demente ⟨to go insane : volverse loco⟩ **2** ABSURD : absurdo, insensato ⟨an insane scheme : un proyecto insensato⟩
insanely [ɪn'seɪnli] *adv* : como un loco ⟨insanely suspicious : loco de recelo⟩
insanity [ɪn'sænət̬i] *n, pl* **-ties 1** MADNESS : locura *f* **2** FOLLY : locura *f*, insensatez *f*
insatiable [ɪn'seɪʃəbəl] *adj* : insaciable — **insatiably** [-bli] *adv*
inscribe [ɪn'skraɪb] *vt* **-scribed; -scribing 1** ENGRAVE : inscribir, grabar **2** ENROLL : inscribir **3** DEDICATE : dedicar (un libro)
inscription [ɪn'skrɪpʃən] *n* : inscripción *f* (en un monumento), dedicación *f* (en un libro), leyenda *f* (de una ilustración, etc.)
inscrutable [ɪn'skru:t̬əbəl] *adj* : inescrutable, misterioso — **inscrutably** [-bli] *adv*
inseam ['ɪn,si:m] *n* : entrepierna *f*
insect ['ɪn,sɛkt] *n* : insecto *m*
insecticidal [ɪn,sɛktə'saɪdəl] *adj* : insecticida
insecticide [ɪn'sɛktə,saɪd] *n* : insecticida *m*
insecure [,ɪnsɪ'kjʊr] *adj* : inseguro, poco seguro — **insecurely** *adv*
insecurely [,ɪnsɪ'kjʊrli] *adv* : inseguramente
insecurity [,ɪnsɪ'kjʊrət̬i] *n, pl* **-ties** : inseguridad *f*
inseminate [ɪn'sɛmə,neɪt] *vt* **-nated; -nating** : inseminar
insemination [ɪn,sɛmə'neɪʃən] *n* : inseminación *f*
insensibility [ɪn,sɛntsə'bɪlət̬i] *n, pl* **-ties** : insensibilidad *f*
insensible [ɪn'sɛntsəbəl] *adj* **1** UNCONSCIOUS : inconsciente, sin conocimiento **2** NUMB : insensible, entumecido **3** UNAWARE : inconsciente
insensitive [ɪn'sɛntsət̬ɪv] *adj* : insensible
insensitivity [ɪn,sɛntsə'tɪvət̬i] *n, pl* **-ties** : insensibilidad *f*
inseparable [ɪn'sɛpərəbəl] *adj* : inseparable
insert[1] [ɪn'sərt] *vt* **1** : insertar, introducir, poner, meter ⟨insert your key in the lock : mete tu llave en la cerradura⟩ **2** INTERPOLATE : interpolar, intercalar
insert[2] ['ɪn,sərt] *n* : inserción *f*, hoja *f* insertada (en una revista, etc.)
insertion [ɪn'sərʃən] *n* : inserción *f*
inset ['ɪn,sɛt] *n* : página *f* intercalada (en un libro), entredós *m* (de encaje en la ropa)
inshore[1] ['ɪn'ʃor] *adv* : hacia la costa
inshore[2] *adj* : cercano a la costa, costero ⟨inshore fishing : pesca costera⟩
inside[1] [ɪn'saɪd, 'ɪn,saɪd] *adv* : adentro, dentro ⟨to run inside : correr para adentro⟩ ⟨inside and out : por dentro y por fuera⟩
inside[2] *adj* **1** : interior, de adentro, de dentro ⟨the inside lane : el carril interior⟩ **2** : confidencial ⟨inside information : información confidencial⟩
inside[3] *n* **1** : interior *m*, parte *f* de adentro **2 insides** *npl* BELLY, GUTS : tripas *fpl fam* **3 inside out** : al revés
inside[4] *prep* **1** INTO : al interior de **2** WITHIN : dentro de **3** (*referring to time*) : en menos de ⟨inside an hour : en menos de una hora⟩
inside of *prep* INSIDE : dentro de
insider [ɪn'saɪdər] *n* : persona *f* enterada
insidious [ɪn'sɪdiəs] *adj* : insidioso — **insidiously** *adv*
insidiousness [ɪn'sɪdiəsnəs] *n* : insidia *f*
insight ['ɪn,saɪt] *n* : perspicacia *f*, penetración *f*
insightful [ɪn'saɪtfəl] *adj* : perspicaz
insignia [ɪn'sɪgniə] *or* **insigne** [-,ni:] *n, pl* **-nia** *or* **-nias** : insignia *f*, enseña *f*
insignificance [,ɪnsɪg'nɪfɪkənts] *n* : insignificancia *f*
insignificant [,ɪnsɪg'nɪfɪkənt] *adj* : insignificante
insincere [,ɪnsɪn'sɪr] *adj* : insincero, poco sincero
insincerely [,ɪnsɪn'sɪrli] *adv* : con poca sinceridad
insincerity [,ɪnsɪn'sɛrət̬i, -'sɪr-] *n, pl* **-ties** : insinceridad *f*
insinuate [ɪn'sɪnjʊ,eɪt] *vt* **-ated; -ating** : insinuar
insinuation [ɪn,sɪnjʊ'eɪʃən] *n* : insinuación *f*
insipid [ɪn'sɪpəd] *adj* : insípido
insist [ɪn'sɪst] *v* : insistir
insistence [ɪn'sɪstənts] *n* : insistencia *f*
insistent [ɪn'sɪstənt] *adj* : insistente — **insistently** *adv*
insofar as [,ɪnso'fɑræz] *conj* : en la medida en que, en tanto que, en cuanto a
insole ['ɪn,so:l] *n* : plantilla *f*
insolence ['ɪntsələnts] *n* : insolencia *f*
insolent ['ɪntsələnt] *adj* : insolente
insolubility [ɪn,sɑljʊ'bɪlət̬i] *n* : insolubilidad *f*
insoluble [ɪn'sɑljʊbəl] *adj* : insoluble
insolvency [ɪn'sɑlvəntsi] *n, pl* **-cies** : insolvencia *f*
insolvent [ɪn'sɑlvənt] *adj* : insolvente
insomnia [ɪn'sɑmniə] *n* : insomnio *m*
insomuch as [,ɪnso'mʌʧæz] → **inasmuch as**
insomuch that *conj* SO : así que, de manera que
inspect [ɪn'spɛkt] *vt* : inspeccionar, examinar, revisar
inspection [ɪn'spɛkʃən] *n* : inspección *f*, examen *m*, revisión *f*, revista *f* (de tropas)

inspector [ɪnˈspɛktər] *n* : inspector *m*, -tora *f*
inspiration [ˌɪntspəˈreɪʃən] *n* : inspiración *f*
inspirational [ˌɪntspəˈreɪʃənəl] *adj* : inspirador
inspire [ɪnˈspaɪr] *v* **-spired; -spiring** *vt* **1** INHALE : inhalar, aspirar **2** STIMULATE : estimular, animar, inspirar **3** INSTILL : inspirar, infundir — *vi* : inspirar
instability [ˌɪntstəˈbɪləṭi] *n, pl* **-ties** : inestabilidad *f*
install [ɪnˈstɔl] *vt* **-stalled; -stalling 1** : instalar ⟨to install the new president : instalar el presidente nuevo⟩ ⟨to install a fan : montar un abanico⟩ **2 to install oneself** : instalarse
installation [ˌɪntstəˈleɪʃən] *n* : instalación *f*
installment [ɪnˈstɔlmənt] *n* **1** : plazo *m*, cuota *f* ⟨to pay in four installments : pagar a cuatro plazos⟩ **2** : entrega *f* (de una publicación o telenovela) **3** INSTALLATION : instalación *f*
instance [ˈɪntstənts] *n* **1** INSTIGATION : instancia *f* **2** EXAMPLE : ejemplo *m* ⟨for instance : por ejemplo⟩ **3** OCCASION : instancia *f*, caso *m*, ocasión *f* ⟨he prefers, in this instance, to remain anonymous : en este caso prefiere quedarse anónimo⟩
instant[1] [ˈɪntstənt] *adj* **1** IMMEDIATE : inmediato, instantáneo ⟨an instant reply : una respuesta inmediata⟩ **2** : instantáneo ⟨instant coffee : café instantáneo⟩
instant[2] *n* : momento *m*, instante *m*
instantaneous [ˌɪntstənˈteɪniəs] *adj* : instantáneo
instantaneously [ˌɪntstənˈteɪniəsli] *adv* : instantáneamente, al instante
instantly [ˈɪntstəntli] *adv* : al instante, instantáneamente
instead [ɪnˈstɛd] *adv* **1** : en cambio, en lugar de eso, en su lugar ⟨Dad was going, but Mom went instead : papá iba a ir, pero mamá fue en su lugar⟩ **2** RATHER : al contrario
instead of *prep* : en vez de, en lugar de
instep [ˈɪnˌstɛp] *n* : empeine *m*
instigate [ˈɪntstəˌgeɪt] *vt* **-gated; -gating** INCITE, PROVOKE : instigar, incitar, provocar, fomentar
instigation [ˌɪntstəˈgeɪʃən] *n* : instancia *f*, incitación *f*
instigator [ˈɪntstəˌgeɪṭər] *n* : instigador *m*, -dora *f*; incitador *m*, -dora *f*
instill [ɪnˈstɪl] *vt* **-stilled; -stilling** : inculcar, infundir
instinct [ˈɪnˌstɪŋkt] *n* **1** TALENT : instinto *m*, don *m* ⟨an instinct for the right word : un don para escoger la palabra apropiada⟩ **2** : instinto *m* ⟨maternal instincts : instintos maternales⟩
instinctive [ɪnˈstɪŋktɪv] *adj* : instintivo
instinctively [ɪnˈstɪŋktɪvli] *adv* : instintivamente, por instinto
instinctual [ɪnˈstɪŋktʃʊəl] *adj* : instintivo
institute[1] [ˈɪntstəˌtuːt, -ˌtjuːt] *vt* **-tuted; -tuting 1** ESTABLISH : establecer, instituir, fundar **2** INITIATE : iniciar, empezar, entablar
institute[2] *n* : instituto *m*
institution [ˌɪntstəˈtuːʃən, -ˈtjuː-] *n* **1** ESTABLISHING : institución *f*, establecimiento *m* **2** CUSTOM : institución *f*, tradición *f* ⟨the institution of marriage : la institución del matrimonio⟩ **3** ORGANIZATION : institución *f*, organismo *m* **4** ASYLUM : asilo *m*
institutional [ˌɪntstəˈtuːʃənəl, -ˈtjuː-] *adj* : institucional
institutionalize [ˌɪntstəˈtuːʃənəˌlaɪz, -ˈtjuː-] *vt* **-ized; -izing 1** : institucionalizar ⟨institutionalized values : valores institucionalizados⟩ **2** : internar ⟨institutionalized orphans : huérfanos internados⟩
instruct [ɪnˈstrʌkt] *vt* **1** TEACH, TRAIN : instruir, adiestrar, enseñar **2** COMMAND : mandar, ordenar, dar instrucciones a
instruction [ɪnˈstrʌkʃən] *n* **1** TEACHING : instrucción *f*, enseñanza *f* **2** COMMAND : orden *f*, instrucción *f* **3 instructions** *npl* DIRECTIONS : instrucciones *fpl*, modo *m* de empleo
instructional [ɪnˈstrʌkʃənəl] *adj* : instructivo, educativo
instructive [ɪnˈstrʌktɪv] *adj* : instructivo
instructor [ɪnˈstrʌktər] *n* : instructor *m*, -tora *f*
instrument [ˈɪntstrəmənt] *n* : instrumento *m*
instrumental [ˌɪntstrəˈmɛntəl] *adj* : instrumental
instrumentalist [ˌɪntstrəˈmɛntəlɪst] *n* : instrumentista *mf*
insubordinate [ˌɪnsəˈbɔrdənət] *adj* : insubordinado
insubordination [ˌɪnsəˌbɔrdənˈeɪʃən] *n* : insubordinación *f*
insubstantial [ˌɪnsəbˈstæntʃəl] *adj* : insustancial, poco nutritivo (dícese de una comida), poco sólido (dícese de una estructura o un argumento)
insufferable [ɪnˈsʌfərəbəl] *adj* UNBEARABLE : insufrible, intolerable, inaguantable, insoportable — **insufferably** [-bli] *adv*
insufficiency [ˌɪnsəˈfɪʃəntsi] *n, pl* **-cies** : insuficiencia *f*
insufficient [ˌɪnsəˈfɪʃənt] *adj* : insuficiente — **insufficiently** *adv*
insular [ˈɪntsʊlər, -sjʊ-] *adj* **1** : isleño (dícese de la gente), insular (dícese del clima) ⟨insular residents : residentes de la isla⟩ **2** NARROW-MINDED : de miras estrechas
insularity [ˌɪntsʊˈlærəṭi, -sjʊ-] *n* : insularidad *f*
insulate [ˈɪntsəˌleɪt] *vt* **-lated; -lating** : aislar
insulation [ˌɪntsəˈleɪʃən] *n* : aislamiento *m*
insulator [ˈɪntsəˌleɪṭər] *n* : aislador *m* (pieza), aislante *m* (material)

insulin ['ɪntsələn] *n* : insulina *f*
insult[1] [ɪn'sʌlt] *vt* : insultar, ofender, injuriar
insult[2] ['ɪn,sʌlt] *n* : insulto *m*, injuria *f*, agravio *m*
insulting [ɪn'sʌltɪŋ] *adj* : ofensivo, injurioso, insultante
insultingly [ɪn'sʌltɪŋli] *adv* : ofensivamente, de manera insultante
insuperable [ɪn'su:pərəbəl] *adj* : insuperable — **insuperably** [-bli] *adv*
insurable [ɪn'ʃʊrəbəl] *adj* : asegurable
insurance [ɪn'ʃʊrənts, 'ɪn,ʃʊr-] *n* : seguro *m* ⟨life insurance : seguro de vida⟩ ⟨insurance company : compañía de seguros⟩
insure [ɪn'ʃʊr] *vt* **-sured; -suring 1** UNDERWRITE : asegurar **2** ENSURE : asegurar, garantizar
insured [ɪn'ʃʊrd] *n* : asegurado *m*, -da *f*
insurer [ɪn'ʃʊrər] *n* : asegurador *m*, -dora *f*
insurgent[1] [ɪn'sərdʒənt] *adj* : insurgente
insurgent[2] *n* : insurgente *mf*
insurmountable [,ɪnsər'maʊntəbəl] *adj* : insuperable, insalvable — **insurmountably** [-bli] *adv*
insurrection [,ɪnsə'rɛkʃən] *n* : insurrección *f*, levantamiento *m*, alzamiento *m*
intact [ɪn'tækt] *adj* : intacto
intake ['ɪn,teɪk] *n* **1** OPENING : entrada *f*, toma *f* ⟨fuel intake : toma de combustible⟩ **2** : entrada *f* (de agua o aire), consumo *m* (de sustancias nutritivas) **3 intake of breath** : inhalación *f*
intangible [ɪn'tændʒəbəl] *adj* : intangible, impalpable — **intangibly** [-bli] *adv*
integer ['ɪntɪdʒər] *n* : entero *m*
integral ['ɪntɪgrəl] *adj* : integral, esencial
integrate ['ɪntə,greɪt] *v* **-grated; -grating** *vt* **1** UNITE : integrar, unir **2** DESEGREGATE : eliminar la segregación de — *vi* : integrarse
integration [,ɪntə'greɪʃən] *n* : integración *f*
integrity [ɪn'tɛgrət̬i] *n* : integridad *f*
intellect ['ɪntəl,ɛkt] *n* : intelecto *m*, inteligencia *f*, capacidad *f* intelectual
intellectual[1] [,ɪntə'lɛktʃʊəl] *adj* : intelectual — **intellectually** *adv*
intellectual[2] *n* : intelectual *mf*
intellectualism [,ɪntə'lɛktʃʊə,lɪzəm] *n* : intelectualismo *m*
intelligence [ɪn'tɛlədʒənts] *n* **1** : inteligencia *f* **2** INFORMATION, NEWS : inteligencia *f*, información *f*, noticias *fpl*
intelligent [ɪn'tɛlədʒənt] *adj* : inteligente — **intelligently** *adv*
intelligentsia [ɪn,tɛlə'dʒɛntsiə, -'gɛn-] *ns & pl* : intelectualidad *f*
intelligibility [ɪn,tɛlədʒə'bɪlət̬i] *n* : inteligibilidad *f*
intelligible [ɪn'tɛlədʒəbəl] *adj* : inteligible, comprensible — **intelligibly** [-bli] *adv*
intemperance [ɪn'tɛmpərənts] *n* : inmoderación *f*, intemperancia *f*
intemperate [ɪn'tɛmpərət] *adj* : excesivo, inmoderado, desmedido
intend [ɪn'tɛnd] *vt* **1** MEAN : querer decir ⟨that's not what I intended : eso no es lo que quería decir⟩ **2** PLAN : tener planeado, proyectar, proponerse ⟨I intend to finish by Thursday : me propongo acabar para el jueves⟩
intended [ɪn'tɛndəd] *adj* **1** PLANNED : previsto, proyectado **2** INTENTIONAL : intencional, deliberado
intense [ɪn'tɛnts] *adj* **1** EXTREME : intenso, extremo ⟨intense pain : dolor intenso⟩ **2** : profundo, intenso ⟨to my intense relief : para mi alivio profundo⟩ ⟨intense enthusiasm : entusiasmo ardiente⟩
intensely [ɪn'tɛntsli] *adv* : sumamente, profundamente, intensamente
intensification [ɪn,tɛntsəfə'keɪʃən] *n* : intensificación *f*
intensify [ɪn'tɛntsə,faɪ] *v* **-fied; -fying** *vt* **1** STRENGTHEN : intensificar, redoblar ⟨to intensify one's efforts : redoblar uno sus esfuerzos⟩ **2** SHARPEN : intensificar, agudizar (dolor, ansiedad) — *vi* : intensificarse, hacerse más intenso
intensity [ɪn'tɛntsət̬i] *n, pl* **-ties** : intensidad *f*
intensive [ɪn'tɛntsɪv] *adj* : intensivo — **intensively** *adv*
intent[1] [ɪn'tɛnt] *adj* **1** FIXED : concentrado, fijo ⟨an intent stare : una mirada fija⟩ **2 intent on** *or* **intent upon** : resuelto a, atento a
intent[2] *n* **1** PURPOSE : intención *f*, propósito *m* **2 for all intents and purposes** : a todos los efectos, prácticamente
intention [ɪn'tɛntʃən] *n* : intención *f*, propósito *m*
intentional [ɪn'tɛntʃənəl] *adj* : intencional, deliberado
intentionally [ɪn'tɛntʃənəli] *adv* : a propósito, adrede
intently [ɪn'tɛntli] *adv* : atentamente, fijamente
inter [ɪn'tər] *vt* **-terred; -terring** : enterrar, inhumar
interact [,ɪntər'ækt] *vi* : interactuar, actuar recíprocamente, relacionarse
interaction [,ɪntər'ækʃən] *n* : interacción *f*, interrelación *f*
interactive [,ɪntər'æktɪv] *adj* : interactivo
interbreed [,ɪntər'bri:d] *v* **-bred** [-'brɛd]; **-breeding** *vt* : cruzar — *vi* : cruzarse
intercalate [ɪn'tərkə,leɪt] *vt* **-lated; -lating** : intercalar
intercede [,ɪntər'si:d] *vi* **-ceded; -ceding** : interceder
intercept [,ɪntər'sɛpt] *vt* : interceptar
interception [,ɪntər'sɛpʃən] *n* : intercepción *f*
intercession [,ɪntər'sɛʃən] *n* : intercesión *f*

interchange[1] [ˌɪntərˈʧeɪnʤ] *vt* **-changed; -changing** : intercambiar
interchange[2] [ˈɪntərˌʧeɪnʤ] *n* **1** EXCHANGE : intercambio *m*, cambio *m* **2** JUNCTION : empalme *m*, enlace *m* de carreteras
interchangeable [ˌɪntərˈʧeɪnʤəbəl] *adj* : intercambiable
intercity [ˈɪntərˈsɪṭi] *adj* : interurbano
intercollegiate [ˌɪntərkəˈliːʤət, -ʤiət] *adj* : interuniversitario
interconnect [ˌɪntərkəˈnɛkt] *vt* **1** : conectar, interconectar (en tecnología) **2** RELATE : interrelacionar — *vi* **1** : conectar **2** : interrelacionarse
intercontinental [ˌɪntərˌkɑntənˈnɛtəl] *adj* : intercontinental
intercourse [ˈɪntərˌkors] *n* **1** RELATIONS : relaciones *fpl*, trato *m* **2** COPULATION : acto *m* sexual, relaciones *fpl* sexuales, coito *m*
interdenominational [ˌɪntərdɪˌnɑməˈneɪʃənəl] *adj* : interconfesional
interdepartmental [ˌɪntərdɪˌpɑrtˈmɛntəl, -ˌdiː-] *adj* : interdepartamental
interdependence [ˌɪntərdɪˈpɛndənts] *n* : interdependencia *f*
interdependent [ˌɪntərdɪˈpɛndənt] *adj* : interdependiente
interdict [ˌɪntərˈdɪkt] *vt* **1** PROHIBIT : prohibir **2** : cortar (las líneas de comunicación o provisión del enemigo)
interest[1] [ˈɪntrəst, -təˌrɛst] *vt* : interesar
interest[2] *n* **1** SHARE, STAKE : interés *m*, participación *f* **2** BENEFIT : provecho *m*, beneficio *m*, interés *m* ⟨in the public interest : en el interés público⟩ **3** CHARGE : interés *m*, cargo *m* ⟨compound interest : interés compuesto⟩ **4** CURIOSITY : interés *m*, curiosidad *f* **5** COLOR : color *m*, interés *m* ⟨places of local interest : lugares de color local⟩ **6** HOBBY : afición *f*
interesting [ˈɪntrəstɪŋ, -təˌrɛstɪŋ] *adj* : interesante — **interestingly** *adv*
interface [ˈɪntərˌfeɪs] *n* **1** : punto *m* de contacto ⟨oil-water interface : punto de contacto entre el agua y el aceite⟩ **2** : interfaz *f* (de una computadora), interfase *f*
interfere [ˌɪntərˈfɪr] *vi* **-fered; -fering 1** INTERPOSE : interponerse, hacer interferencia ⟨to interfere with a play : obstruir una jugada⟩ **2** MEDDLE : entrometerse, interferir, intervenir **3 to interfere with** DISRUPT : afectar (una actividad), interferir (la radiotransmisión) **4 to interfere with** TOUCH : tocar ⟨someone interfered with my papers : alguien tocó mis papeles⟩
interference [ˌɪntərˈfɪrənts] *n* : interferencia *f*, intromisión *f*
intergalactic [ˌɪntərgəˈlæktɪk] *adj* : intergaláctico
intergovernmental [ˌɪntərˌgʌvər-ˈmɛntəl, -vərn-] *adj* : intergubernamental
interim[1] [ˈɪntərəm] *adj* : interino, provisional
interim[2] *n* **1** : interín *m*, intervalo *m* **2 in the interim** : en el interín, mientras tanto
interior[1] [ɪnˈtɪriər] *adj* : interior
interior[2] *n* : interior *m*
interject [ˌɪntərˈʤɛkt] *vt* : interponer, agregar
interjection [ˌɪntərˈʤɛkʃən] *n* **1** : interjección *f* (en lingüística) **2** EXCLAMATION : exclamación *f* **3** INTERPOSITION, INTERRUPTION : interposición *f*, interrupción *f*
interlace [ˌɪntərˈleɪs] *vt* **-laced; -lacing 1** INTERWEAVE : entrelazar **2** INTERSPERSE : intercalar
interlock [ˌɪntərˈlɑk] *vt* **1** UNITE : trabar, unir **2** ENGAGE, MESH : engranar — *vi* : entrelazarse, trabarse
interloper [ˌɪntərˈloːpər] *n* **1** INTRUDER : intruso *m*, -sa *f* **2** MEDDLER : entrometido *m*, -da *f*
interlude [ˈɪntərˌluːd] *n* **1** INTERVAL : intervalo *m*, intermedio *m* (en el teatro) **2** : interludio *m* (en música)
intermarriage [ˌɪntərˈmærɪʤ] *n* **1** : matrimonio *m* mixto (entre miembros de distintas razas o religiones) **2** : matrimonio *m* entre miembros del mismo grupo
intermarry [ˌɪntərˈmæri] *vi* **-married; -marrying 1** : casarse (con miembros de otros grupos) **2** : casarse entre sí (con miembros del mismo grupo)
intermediary[1] [ˌɪntərˈmiːdiˌɛri] *adj* : intermediario
intermediary[2] *n, pl* **-aries** : intermediario *m*, -ria *f*
intermediate[1] [ˌɪntərˈmiːdiət] *adj* : intermedio
intermediate[2] *n* GO-BETWEEN : intermediario *m*, -ria *f*; mediador *m*, -dora *f*
interment [ɪnˈtərmənt] *n* : entierro *m*
interminable [ɪnˈtərmənəbəl] *adj* : interminable, constante — **interminably** [-bli] *adv*
intermingle [ˌɪntərˈmɪŋgəl] *vt* **-mingled; -mingling** : entremezclar, mezclar — *vi* : entremezclarse
intermission [ˌɪntərˈmɪʃən] *n* : intermisión *f*, intervalo *m*, intermedio *m*
intermittent [ˌɪntərˈmɪtənt] *adj* : intermitente — **intermittently** *adv*
intermix [ˌɪntərˈmɪks] *vt* : entremezclar
intern[1] [ˈɪnˌtərn, ɪnˈtərn] *vt* : confinar (durante la guerra) — *vi* : servir de interno, hacer las prácticas
intern[2] [ˈɪnˌtərn] *n* : interno *m*, -na *f*
internal [ɪnˈtərnəl] *adj* : interno, interior ⟨internal bleeding : hemorragia interna⟩ ⟨internal affairs : asuntos interiores, asuntos domésticos⟩ — **internally** *adv*
international [ˌɪntərˈnæʃənəl] *adj* : internacional — **internationally** *adv*
internationalize [ˌɪntərˈnæʃənəˌlaɪz] *vt* **-ized; -izing** : internacionalizar
internee [ˌɪnˌtərˈniː] *n* : interno *m*, -na *f*
Internet [ˈɪntərˌnɛt] *n* : Internet *mf*

internist [ˈɪn,tərnɪst] *n* : internista *mf*
interpersonal [,ɪntərˈpərsənəl] *adj* : interpersonal
interplay [ˈɪntər,pleɪ] *n* : interacción *f*, juego *m*
interpolate [ɪnˈtərpə,leɪt] *vt* **-lated; -lating** : interpolar
interpose [,ɪntərˈpo:z] *v* **-posed; -posing** *vt* : interponer, interrumpir con — *vi* : interponerse
interposition [,ɪntərpəˈzɪʃən] *n* : interposición *f*
interpret [ɪnˈtərprət] *vt* : interpretar
interpretation [ɪn,tərprəˈteɪʃən] *n* : interpretación *f*
interpretative [ɪnˈtərprə,teɪt̬ɪv] *adj* : interpretativo
interpreter [ɪnˈtərprət̬ər] *n* : intérprete *mf*
interpretive [ɪnˈtərprət̬ɪv] *adj* : interpretativo
interracial [,ɪntərˈreɪʃəl] *adj* : interracial
interrelate [,ɪntərɪˈleɪt] *v* **-related; -relating** : interrelacionar
interrelationship [,ɪntərɪˈleɪʃən,ʃɪp] *n* : interrelación *f*
interrogate [ɪnˈtɛrə,geɪt] *vt* **-gated; -gating** : interrogar, someter a un interrogatorio
interrogation [ɪn,tɛrəˈgeɪʃən] *n* : interrogación *f*
interrogative¹ [,ɪntəˈrɑgət̬ɪv] *adj* : interrogativo
interrogative² *n* : interrogativo *m*
interrogator [ɪnˈtɛrə,geɪt̬ər] *n* : interrogador *m*, -dora *f*
interrogatory [,ɪntəˈrɑgə,tɔri] *adj* → **interrogative**¹
interrupt [,ɪntəˈrʌpt] *v* : interrumpir
interruption [,ɪntəˈrʌpʃən] *n* : interrupción *f*
intersect [,ɪntərˈsɛkt] *vt* : cruzar, cortar — *vi* : cruzarse (dícese de los caminos), intersectarse (dícese de las líneas o figuras), cortarse
intersection [,ɪntərˈsɛkʃən] *n* : intersección *f*, cruce *m*
intersperse [,ɪntərˈspərs] *vt* **-spersed; -spersing** : intercalar, entremezclar
interstate [,ɪntərˈsteɪt] *adj* : interestatal
interstellar [,ɪntərˈstɛlər] *adj* : interestelar
interstice [ɪnˈtərstəs] *n, pl* **-stices** [-stə,si:z, -stəsəz] : intersticio *m*
intertwine [,ɪntərˈtwaɪn] *vi* **-twined; -twining** : entrelazarse
interval [ˈɪntərvəl] *n* : intervalo *m*
intervene [,ɪntərˈvi:n] *vi* **-vened; -vening 1** ELAPSE : transcurrir, pasar ⟨the intervening years : los años intermediarios⟩ **2** INTERCEDE : intervenir, interceder, mediar
intervention [,ɪntərˈvɛntʃən] *n* : intervención *f*
interview¹ [ˈɪntər,vju:] *vt* : entrevistar — *vi* : hacer entrevistas
interview² *n* : entrevista *f*
interviewer [ˈɪntər,vju:ər] *n* : entrevistador *m*, -dora *f*
interweave [,ɪntərˈwi:v] *v* **-wove** [-ˈwo:v]; **-woven** [-ˈwo:vən]; **-weaving** *vt* : entretejer, entrelazar — *vi* INTERTWINE : entrelazarse, entretejerse
interwoven [,ɪntərˈwo:vən] *adj* : entretejido
intestate [ɪnˈtɛs,teɪt, -tət] *adj* : intestado
intestinal [ɪnˈtɛstənəl] *adj* : intestinal
intestine [ɪnˈtɛstən] *n* **1** : intestino *m* **2 small intestine** : intestino *m* delgado **3 large intestine** : intestino *m* grueso
intimacy [ˈɪntəməsi] *n, pl* **-cies 1** CLOSENESS : intimidad *f* **2** FAMILIARITY : familiaridad *f*
intimate¹ [ˈɪntə,meɪt] *vt* **-mated; -mating** : insinuar, dar a entender
intimate² [ˈɪntəmət] *adj* **1** CLOSE : íntimo, de confianza ⟨intimate friends : amigos íntimos⟩ **2** PRIVATE : íntimo, privado ⟨intimate clubs : clubes íntimos⟩ **3** INNERMOST, SECRET : íntimo, secreto ⟨intimate fantasies : fantasías secretas⟩
intimate³ *n* : amigo *m* íntimo, amiga *f* íntima
intimidate [ɪnˈtɪmə,deɪt] *vt* **-dated; -dating** : intimidar
intimidation [ɪn,tɪməˈdeɪʃən] *n* : intimidación *f*
into [ˈɪn,tu:] *prep* **1** (*indicating motion*) : en, a, contra, dentro de ⟨she got into bed : se metió en la cama⟩ ⟨to get into a plane : subir a un avión⟩ ⟨he crashed into the wall : chocó contra la pared⟩ ⟨looking into the sun : mirando al sol⟩ **2** (*indicating state or condition*) : a, en ⟨to burst into tears : echarse a llorar⟩ ⟨the water turned into ice : el agua se convirtió en hielo⟩ ⟨to translate into English : traducir al inglés⟩ **3** (*indicating time*) ⟨far into the night : hasta bien entrada la noche⟩ ⟨he's well into his eighties : tiene los ochenta bien cumplidos⟩ **4** (*in mathematics*) ⟨3 into 12 is 4 : 12 dividido por 3 es 4⟩
intolerable [ɪnˈtɑlərəbəl] *adj* : intolerable — **intolerably** [-bli] *adv*
intolerance [ɪnˈtɑlərənts] *n* : intolerancia *f*
intolerant [ɪnˈtɑlərənt] *adj* : intolerante
intonation [,ɪntoˈneɪʃən] *n* : entonación *f*
intone [ɪnˈto:n] *vt* **-toned; -toning** : entonar
intoxicant [ɪnˈtɑksɪkənt] *n* : bebida *f* alcohólica
intoxicate [ɪnˈtɑksə,keɪt] *vt* **-cated; -cating** : emborrachar, embriagar
intoxicated [ɪnˈtɑksə,keɪt̬əd] *adj* : borracho, embriagado
intoxicating [ɪnˈtɑksə,keɪt̬ɪŋ] *adj* : embriagador
intoxication [ɪn,tɑksəˈkeɪʃən] *n* : embriaguez *f*
intractable [ɪnˈtræktəbəl] *adj* : obstinado, intratable
intramural [,ɪntrəˈmjʊrəl] *adj* : interno, dentro de la universidad

intransigence [ɪn'træntsədʒənts, -'trænzə-] *n* : intransigencia *f*
intransigent [ɪn'træntsədʒənt, -'trænzə-] *adj* : intransigente
intransitive [ɪn'træntsət̬ɪv, -'trænzə-] *adj* : intransitivo
intravenous [ˌɪntrə'vi:nəs] *adj* : intravenoso — **intravenously** *adv*
intrepid [ɪn'trɛpəd] *adj* : intrépido
intricacy ['ɪntrɪkəsi] *n, pl* **-cies** : complejidad *f*, lo intrincado
intricate ['ɪntrɪkət] *adj* : intrincado, complicado — **intricately** *adv*
intrigue[1] [ɪn'tri:g] *v* **-trigued; -triguing** : intrigar
intrigue[2] ['ɪnˌtri:g, ɪn'tri:g] *n* : intriga *f*
intriguing [ɪn'tri:gɪŋ] *adj* : intrigante, fascinante
intrinsic [ɪn'trɪnzɪk, -'trɪntsɪk] *adj* : intrínseco, esencial — **intrinsically** [-zɪkli, -sɪ-] *adv*
introduce [ˌɪntrə'du:s, -'dju:s] *vt* **-duced; -ducing 1** : presentar ⟨let me introduce my father : permítame presentar a mi padre⟩ **2** : introducir (algo nuevo), lanzar (un producto), presentar (una ley), proponer (una idea o un tema)
introduction [ˌɪntrə'dʌkʃən] *n* : introducción *f*, presentación *f*
introductory [ˌɪntrə'dʌktəri] *adj* : introductorio, preliminar, de introducción
introspection [ˌɪntrə'spɛkʃən] *n* : introspección *f*
introspective [ˌɪntrə'spɛktɪv] *adj* : introspectivo — **introspectively** *adv*
introvert ['ɪntrəˌvərt] *n* : introvertido *m*, -da *f*
introverted ['ɪntrəˌvərt̬əd] *adj* : introvertido
intrude [ɪn'tru:d] *v* **-truded; -truding** *vi* **1** INTERFERE : inmiscuirse, entrometerse **2** DISTURB, INTERRUPT : molestar, estorbar, interrumpir — *vt* : introducir por fuerza
intruder [ɪn'tru:dər] *n* : intruso *m*, -sa *f*
intrusion [ɪn'tru:ʒən] *n* : intrusión *f*
intrusive [ɪn'tru:sɪv] *adj* : intruso
intuit [ɪn'tu:ɪt, -'tju:-] *vt* : intuir
intuition [ˌɪntʊ'ɪʃən, -tjʊ-] *n* : intuición *f*
intuitive [ɪn'tu:ət̬ɪv, -'tju:-] *adj* : intuitivo — **intuitively** *adv*
inundate ['ɪnənˌdeɪt] *vt* **-dated; -dating** : inundar
inundation [ˌɪnən'deɪʃən] *n* : inundación *f*
inure [ɪ'nʊr, -'njʊr] *vt* **-ured; -uring** : acostumbrar, habituar
invade [ɪn'veɪd] *vt* **-vaded; -vading** : invadir
invader [ɪn'veɪdər] *n* : invasor *m*, -sora *f*
invalid[1] [ɪn'væləd] *adj* : inválido, nulo
invalid[2] ['ɪnvələd] *adj* : inválido, discapacitado
invalid[3] ['ɪnvələd] *n* : inválido *m*, -da *f*
invalidate [ɪn'væləˌdeɪt] *vt* **-dated; -dating** : invalidar
invalidity [ˌɪnvə'lɪdət̬i] *n, pl* **-ties** : invalidez *f*, falta de validez *f*
invaluable [ɪn'væljəbəl, -'væljʊə-] *adj* : invalorable, inestimable, inapreciable
invariable [ɪn'væriəbəl] *adj* : invariable, constante — **invariably** [-bli] *adv*
invasion [ɪn'veɪʒən] *n* : invasión *f*
invasive [ɪn'veɪsɪv] *adj* : invasivo
invective [ɪn'vɛktɪv] *n* : invectiva *f*, improperio *m*, vituperio *m*
inveigh [ɪn'veɪ] *vi* **to inveigh against** : arremeter contra, lanzar invectivas contra
inveigle [ɪn'veɪgəl, -'vi:-] *vt* **-gled; -gling** : engatusar, embaucar, persuadir con engaños
invent [ɪn'vɛnt] *vt* : inventar
invention [ɪn'vɛntʃən] *n* : invención *f*, invento *m*
inventive [ɪn'vɛntɪv] *adj* : inventivo
inventiveness [ɪn'vɛntɪvnəs] *n* : ingenio *m*, inventiva *f*
inventor [ɪn'vɛntər] *n* : inventor *m*, -tora *f*
inventory[1] ['ɪnvənˌtɔri] *vt* **-ried; -rying** : inventariar
inventory[2] *n, pl* **-ries 1** LIST : inventario *m* **2** STOCK : existencias *fpl*
inverse[1] [ɪn'vərs, 'ɪnˌvərs] *adj* : inverso — **inversely** *adv*
inverse[2] *n* : inverso *m*
inversion [ɪn'vɛrʒən] *n* : inversión *f*
invert [ɪn'vərt] *vt* : invertir
invertebrate[1] [ɪn'vərt̬əbrət, -ˌbreɪt] *adj* : invertebrado
invertebrate[2] *n* : invertebrado *m*
invest [ɪn'vɛst] *vt* **1** AUTHORIZE : investir, autorizar **2** CONFER : conferir **3** : invertir, dedicar ⟨he invested his savings in stocks : invirtió sus ahorros en acciones⟩ ⟨to invest one's time : dedicar uno su tiempo⟩
investigate [ɪn'vɛstəˌgeɪt] *v* **-gated; -gating** : investigar
investigation [ɪnˌvɛstə'geɪʃən] *n* : investigación *f*, estudio *m*
investigative [ɪn'vɛstəˌgeɪt̬ɪv] *adj* : investigador
investigator [ɪn'vɛstəˌgeɪt̬ər] *n* : investigador *m*, -dora *f*
investiture [ɪn'vɛstəˌtʃʊr, -tʃər] *n* : investidura *f*
investment [ɪn'vɛstmənt] *n* : inversión *f*
investor [ɪn'vɛstər] *n* : inversor *m*, -sora *f*; inversionista *mf*
inveterate [ɪn'vɛt̬ərət] *adj* **1** DEEP-SEATED : inveterado, enraizado **2** HABITUAL : empedernido, incorregible
invidious [ɪn'vɪdiəs] *adj* **1** OBNOXIOUS : repugnante, odioso **2** UNJUST : injusto — **invidiously** *adv*
invigorate [ɪn'vɪgəˌreɪt] *vt* **-rated; -rating** : vigorizar, animar
invigorating [ɪn'vɪgəˌreɪt̬ɪŋ] *adj* : vigorizante, estimulante
invigoration [ɪnˌvɪgə'reɪʃən] *n* : animación *f*
invincibility [ɪnˌvɪntsə'bɪlət̬i] *n* : invencibilidad *f*

invincible [ɪnˈvɪntsəbəl] *adj* : invencible — **invincibly** [-bli] *adv*
inviolable [ɪnˈvaɪələbəl] *adj* : inviolable
inviolate [ɪnˈvaɪələt] *adj* : inviolado, puro
invisibility [ɪnˌvɪzəˈbɪləṭi] *n* : invisibilidad *f*
invisible [ɪnˈvɪzəbəl] *adj* : invisible — **invisibly** [-bli] *adv*
invitation [ˌɪnvəˈteɪʃən] *n* : invitación *f*
invite [ɪnˈvaɪt] *vt* **-vited; -viting** **1** ATTRACT : atraer, tentar ⟨a book that invites interest : un libro que atrae el interés⟩ **2** PROVOKE : provocar, buscar ⟨to invite trouble : buscarse problemas⟩ **3** ASK : invitar ⟨we invited them for dinner : los invitamos acenar⟩ **4** SOLICIT : solicitar, buscar (preguntas, comentarios, etc.)
inviting [ɪnˈvaɪṭɪŋ] *adj* : atractivo, atrayente
invocation [ˌɪnvəˈkeɪʃən] *n* : invocación *f*
invoice[1] [ˈɪnˌvɔɪs] *vt* **-voiced; -voicing** : facturar
invoice[2] *n* : factura *f*
invoke [ɪnˈvoːk] *vt* **-voked; -voking** **1** : invocar, apelar a ⟨she invoked our aid : apeló a nuestra ayuda⟩ **2** CITE : invocar, citar ⟨to invoke a precedent : invocar un precedente⟩ **3** CONJURE UP : hacer aparecer, invocar
involuntary [ɪnˈvɑlənˌtɛri] *adj* : involuntario — **involuntarily** [ɪn-ˌvɑlənˈtrəli] *adv*
involve [ɪnˈvɑlv] *vt* **-volved; -volving** **1** ENGAGE : ocupar (con una tarea, etc.) **2** IMPLICATE : involucrar, enredar, implicar ⟨to be involved in a crime : estar involucrado en un crimen⟩ **3** CONCERN : concernir, afectar **4** CONNECT : conectar, relacionar **5** ENTAIL, INCLUDE : suponer, incluir, consistir en ⟨what does the job involve? : ¿en qué consiste el trabajo?⟩ **6 to be involved with someone** : tener una relación (amorosa) con alguien
involved [ɪnˈvɑlvd] *adj* **1** COMPLEX, INTRICATE : complicado, complejo **2** CONCERNED : interesado, afectado
involvement [ɪnˈvɑlvmənt] *n* **1** PARTICIPATION : participación *f*, complicidad *f* **2** RELATIONSHIP : relación *f*
invulnerable [ɪnˈvʌlnərəbəl] *adj* : invulnerable
inward[1] [ˈɪnwərd] *or* **inwards** [-wərdz] *adv* : hacia adentro, hacia el interior
inward[2] *adj* INSIDE : interior, interno
inwardly [ˈɪnwərdli] *adv* **1** MENTALLY, SPIRITUALLY : por dentro **2** INTERNALLY : internamente, interiormente **3** PRIVATELY : para sus adentros, para sí
iodide [ˈaɪəˌdaɪd] *n* : yoduro *m*
iodine [ˈaɪəˌdaɪn, -dən] *n* : yodo *m*, tintura *f* de yodo
iodize [ˈaɪəˌdaɪz] *vt* **-dized; -dizing** : yodar
ion [ˈaɪən, ˈaɪˌɑn] *n* : ion *m*
ionic [aɪˈɑnɪk] *adj* : iónico
ionize [ˈaɪəˌnaɪz] *v* **ionized; ionizing** : ionizar
ionosphere [aɪˈɑnəˌsfɪr] *n* : ionosfera *f*
iota [aɪˈoːṭə] *n* : pizca *f*, ápice *m*
IOU [ˌaɪˌoˈjuː] *n* : pagaré *m*, vale *m*
IPA [ˌaɪˌpiːˈeɪ] *n* *I*nternational *P*honetic *A*lphabet : AFI *m*
IQ [ˌaɪˈkjuː] *n* (*i*ntelligence *q*uotient) : CI *m*, coeficiente *m* intelectual
Iranian [ɪˈreɪniən, -ˈræ-, -ˈrɑ-; aɪˈ-] *n* : iraní *mf* — **Iranian** *adj*
Iraqi [ɪˈrɑkiː] *n* : iraquí *mf* — **Iraqi** *adj*
irascibility [ɪˌræsəˈbɪləṭi] *n* : irascibilidad *f*
irascible [ɪˈræsəbəl] *adj* : irascible
irate [aɪˈreɪt] *adj* : furioso, airado, iracundo — **irately** *adv*
ire [ˈaɪr] *n* : ira *f*, cólera *f*
iridescence [ˌɪrəˈdɛsənts] *n* : iridiscencia *f*
iridescent [ˌɪrəˈdɛsənt] *adj* : iridiscente
iridium [ɪˈrɪdiəm] *n* : iridio *m*
iris [ˈaɪrəs] *n, pl* **irises** *or* **irides** [ˈaɪrəˌdiːz, ˈɪr-] **1** : iris *m* (del ojo) **2** : lirio *m* (planta)
Irish[1] [ˈaɪrɪʃ] *adj* : irlandés
Irish[2] **1** : irlandés *m* (idioma) **2 the Irish** *npl* : los irlandeses
Irishman [ˈaɪrɪʃmən] *n, pl* **-men** : irlandés *m*
Irishwoman [ˈaɪrɪʃˌwʊmən] *n, pl* **-women** : irlandesa *f*
irk [ˈərk] *vt* : fastidiar, irritar, preocupar
irksome [ˈərksəm] *adj* : irritante, fastidioso — **irksomely** *adv*
iron[1] [ˈaɪərn] *v* : planchar
iron[2] *n* **1** : hierro *m*, fierro *m* ⟨a will of iron : una voluntad de hierro, una voluntad férrea⟩ **2** : plancha *f* (para planchar la ropa)
ironclad [ˈaɪərnˈklæd] *adj* **1** : acorazado, blindado **2** STRICT : riguroso, estricto
ironic [aɪˈrɑnɪk] *or* **ironical** [-nɪkəl] *adj* : irónico — **ironically** [-kli] *adv*
ironing [ˈaɪərnɪŋ] *n* **1** PRESSING : planchada *f* **2** : ropa *f* para planchar
ironing board *n* : tabla *f* (de planchar)
ironwork [ˈaɪərnˌwərk] *n* **1** : obra *f* de hierro **2 ironworks** *npl* : fundición *f*
ironworker [ˈaɪərnˌwərkər] *n* : fundidor *m*, -dora *f*
irony [ˈaɪrəni] *n, pl* **-nies** : ironía *f*
irradiate [ɪˈreɪdiˌeɪt] *vt* **-ated; -ating** : irradiar, radiar
irradiation [ɪˌreɪdiˈeɪʃən] *n* : irradiación *f*, radiación *f*
irrational [ɪˈræʃənəl] *adj* : irracional — **irrationally** *adv*
irrationality [ɪˌræʃəˈnæləṭi] *n, pl* **-ties** : irracionalidad *f*
irreconcilable [ɪˌrɛkənˈsaɪləbəl] *adj* : irreconciliable
irrecoverable [ˌɪrɪˈkʌvərəbəl] *adj* : irrecuperable — **irrecoverably** [-bli] *adv*

irredeemable [ˌɪrɪˈdiːməbəl] *adj* **1** : irredimible (dícese de un bono) **2** HOPELESS : irremediable, irreparable
irreducible [ˌɪrɪˈduːsəbəl, -ˈdjuː-] *adj* : irreducible — **irreducibly** [-bli] *adv*
irrefutable [ˌɪrɪˈfjuːt̬əbəl, ɪrˈrɛfjə-] *adj* : irrefutable
irregular[1] [ɪˈrɛgjələr] *adj* : irregular — **irregularly** *adv*
irregular[2] *n* **1** : soldado *m* irregular **2** **irregulars** *npl* : artículos *mpl* defectuosos
irregularity [ɪˌrɛgjəˈlærət̬i] *n, pl* **-ties** : irregularidad *f*
irrelevance [ɪˈrɛləvən*t*s] *n* : irrelevancia *f*
irrelevant [ɪˈrɛləvənt] *adj* : irrelevante
irreligious [ˌɪrɪˈlɪʤəs] *adj* : irreligioso
irreparable [ɪˈrɛpərəbəl] *adj* : irreparable
irreplaceable [ˌɪrɪˈpleɪsəbəl] *adj* : irreemplazable, insustituible
irrepressible [ˌɪrɪˈprɛsəbəl] *adj* : incontenible, incontrolable
irreproachable [ɪrɪˈproːʧəbəl] *adj* : irreprochable, intachable
irresistible [ˌɪrɪˈzɪst̬əbəl] *adj* : irresistible — **irresistibly** [-bli] *adv*
irresolute [ɪˈrɛzəˌluːt] *adj* : irresoluto, indeciso
irresolutely [ɪˈrɛzəˌluːtli, -ˌrzəˈluːt-] *adv* : de manera indecisa
irresolution [ɪˌrɛzəˈluːʃən] *n* : irresolución *f*
irrespective of [ˌɪrɪˈspɛktɪvəv] *prep* : sin tomar en consideración, sin tener en cuenta
irresponsibility [ˌɪrɪˌspɑn*t*səˈbɪlət̬i] *n, pl* **-ties** : irresponsabilidad *f*, falta *f* de responsabilidad
irresponsible [ˌɪrɪˈspɑn*t*səbəl] *adj* : irresponsable — **irresponsibly** [-bli] *adv*
irretrievable [ˌɪrɪˈtriːvəbəl] *adj* IRRECOVERABLE : irrecuperable
irreverence [ɪˈrɛvərən*t*s] *n* : irreverencia *f*, falta *f* de respeto
irreverent [ɪˈrɛvərənt] *adj* : irreverente, irrespetuoso
irreversible [ˌɪrɪˈvərsəbəl] *adj* : irreversible
irrevocable [ɪˈrɛvəkəbəl] *adj* : irrevocable — **irrevocably** [-bli] *adv*
irrigate [ˈɪrəˌgeɪt] *vt* **-gated; -gating** : irrigar, regar
irrigation [ˌɪrəˈgeɪʃən] *n* : irrigación *f*, riego *m*
irritability [ˌɪrət̬əˈbɪlət̬i] *n, pl* **-ties** : irritabilidad *f*
irritable [ˈɪrət̬əbəl] *adj* : irritable, colérico
irritably [ˈɪrət̬əbli] *adv* : con irritación
irritant[1] [ˈɪrətənt] *adj* : irritante
irritant[2] *n* : agente *m* irritante
irritate [ˈɪrəˌteɪt] *vt* **-tated; -tating** **1** ANNOY : irritar, molestar **2** : irritar (en medicina)
irritating [ˈɪrəˌteɪt̬ɪŋ] *adj* : irritante
irritatingly [ˈɪrəˌteɪt̬ɪŋli] *adv* : de modo irritante, fastidiosamente
irritation [ˌɪrəˈteɪʃən] *n* : irritación *f*
is → **be**
Islam [ɪsˈlɑm, ɪz-, -ˈlæm; ˈɪsˌlɑm, ˈɪz-, -ˌlæm] *n* : el Islam
Islamic [ɪsˈlɑmɪk, ɪz-, -ˈlæ-] *adj* : islámico
island [ˈaɪlənd] *n* : isla *f*
islander [ˈaɪləndər] *n* : isleño *m*, -ña *f*
isle [ˈaɪl] *n* : isla *f*, islote *m*
islet [ˈaɪlət] *n* : islote *m*
isolate [ˈaɪsəˌleɪt] *vt* **-lated; -lating** : aislar
isolated [ˈaɪsəˌleɪt̬əd] *adj* : aislado, solo
isolation [ˌaɪsəˈleɪʃən] *n* : aislamiento *m*
isometric [ˌaɪsəˈmɛtrɪk] *adj* : isométrico
isometrics [ˌaɪsəˈmɛtrɪks] *ns & pl* : isometría *f*
isosceles [aɪˈsɑsəˌliːz] *adj* : isósceles
isotope [ˈaɪsəˌtoːp] *n* : isótopo *m*
Israeli [ɪzˈreɪli] *n* : israelí *mf* — **Israeli** *adj*
issue[1] [ˈɪˌʃuː] *v* **-sued; -suing** *vi* **1** EMERGE : emerger, salir, fluir **2** DESCEND : descender (dícese de los padres o antepasados específicos) **3** EMANATE, RESULT : emanar, surgir, resultar — *vt* **1** EMIT : emitir **2** DISTRIBUTE : emitir, distribuir ⟨to issue a new stamp : emitir un sello nuevo⟩ **3** PUBLISH : publicar
issue[2] *n* **1** EMERGENCE, FLOW : emergencia *f*, flujo *m* **2** PROGENY : descendencia *f*, progenie *f* **3** OUTCOME, RESULT : desenlace *m*, resultado *m*, consecuencia *f* **4** MATTER, QUESTION : asunto *m*, cuestión *f* **5** PUBLICATION : publicación *f*, distribución *f*, emisión *f* **6** : número *m* (de un periódico o una revista)
isthmus [ˈɪsməs] *n* : istmo *m*
it [ˈɪt] *pron* **1** (*as subject; generally omitted*) : él, ella, ello ⟨it's a big building : es un edificio grande⟩ ⟨who was it? : ¿quién era?⟩ **2** (*as indirect object*) : le ⟨I'll give it some water : voy a darle agua⟩ **3** (*as direct object*) : lo, la ⟨give it to me : dámelo⟩ **4** (*as object of a preposition; generally omitted*) : él, ella, ello ⟨behind it : detrás, detrás de él⟩ **5** (*in impersonal constructions*) ⟨it's raining : está lloviendo⟩ ⟨it's 8 o'clock : son las ocho⟩ **6** (*as the implied subject or object of a verb*) ⟨it is necessary to study : es necesario estudiar⟩ ⟨to give it all one's got : dar lo mejor de sí⟩
Italian [ɪˈtæliən, aɪ-] *n* **1** : italiano *m*, -na *f* **2** : italiano *m* (idioma) — **Italian** *adj*
italic[1] [ɪˈtælɪk, aɪ-] *adj* : en cursiva, en bastardilla
italic[2] *n* : cursiva *f*, bastardilla *f*
italicize [ɪˈtæləˌsaɪz, aɪ-] *vt* **-cized; -cizing** : poner en cursiva
itch[1] [ˈɪʧ] *vi* **1** : picar ⟨her arm itched : le pica el brazo⟩ **2** : morirse ⟨they were itching to go outside : se morían por salir⟩ — *vt* : dar picazón, hacer picar

itch[2] *n* **1** ITCHING : picazón *f*, picor *m*, comezón *f* **2** RASH : sarpullido *m*, erupción *f* **3** DESIRE : ansia *f*, deseo *m*
itchy [ˈɪʧi] *adj* **itchier; -est** : que pica, que da comezón
it'd [ˈɪṭəd] (*contraction of* **it had** *or* **it would**) → **have, would**
item [ˈaɪṭəm] *n* **1** OBJECT : artículo *m*, pieza *f* ⟨item of clothing : prenda de vestir⟩ **2** : punto *m* (en una agenda), número *m* (en el teatro), ítem *m* (en un documento) **3 news item** : noticia *f*
itemize [ˈaɪṭəˌmaɪz] *vt* **-ized; -izing** : detallar, enumerar, listar
itinerant [aɪˈtɪnərənt] *adj* : itinerante, ambulante
itinerary [aɪˈtɪnəˌrɛri] *n, pl* **-aries** : itinerario *m*
it'll [ˈɪṭəl] (*contraction of* **it shall** *or* **it will**) → **shall, will**
its [ˈɪts] *adj* : su, sus ⟨its kennel : su perrera⟩ ⟨a city and its inhabitants : una ciudad y sus habitantes⟩
it's [ˈɪts] (*contraction of* **it is** *or* **it has**) → **be, have**
itself [ɪtˈsɛlf] *pron* **1** (*used reflexively*) : se ⟨the cat gave itself a bath : el gato se bañó⟩ **2** (*used for emphasis*) : (él) mismo, (ella) misma, sí (mismo), solo ⟨he is courtesy itself : es la misma cortesía⟩ ⟨in and of itself : por sí mismo⟩ ⟨it opened by itself : se abrió solo⟩
IUD [ˌaɪˌjuːˈdiː] *n* *i*ntra*u*terine *d*evice : DIU *m*, dispositivo *m* intrauterino
I've [ˈaɪv] (*contraction of* **I have**) → **have**
ivory [ˈaɪvəri] *n, pl* **-ries** **1** : marfil *m* **2** : color *m* de marfil
ivy [ˈaɪvi] *n, pl* **ivies** **1** : hiedra *f*, yedra *f* **2** → **poison ivy**

J

j [ˈʤeɪ] *n, pl* **j's** *or* **js** [ˈʤeɪz] : décima letra del alfabeto inglés
jab[1] [ˈʤæb] *v* **jabbed; jabbing** *vt* **1** PUNCTURE : clavar, pinchar **2** POKE : dar, golpear (con la punta de algo) ⟨he jabbed me in the ribs : me dio un codazo en las costillas⟩ — *vi* **to jab at** : dar, golpear
jab[2] *n* **1** PRICK : pinchazo *m* **2** POKE : golpe *m* abrupto
jabber[1] [ˈʤæbər] *v* : farfullar
jabber[2] *n* : galimatías *m*, farfulla *f*
jack[1] [ˈʤæk] *vt* **to jack up** **1** : levantar (con un gato) **2** INCREASE : subir, aumentar
jack[2] *n* **1** : gato *m*, cric *m* ⟨hydraulic jack : gato hidráulico⟩ **2** FLAG : pabellón *m* **3** SOCKET : enchufe *m* hembra **4** : jota *f*, valet *m* ⟨jack of hearts : jota de corazones⟩ **5 jacks** *npl* : cantillos *mpl*
jackal [ˈʤækəl] *n* : chacal *m*
jackass [ˈʤækˌæs] *n* : asno *m*, burro *m*
jacket [ˈʤækət] *n* **1** : chaqueta *f* **2** COVER : sobrecubierta *f* (de un libro), carátula *f* (de un disco)
jackhammer [ˈʤækˌhæmər] *n* : martillo *m* neumático
jack–in–the–box [ˈʤækɪnðəˌbɑks] *n* : caja *f* de sorpresa
jackknife[1] [ˈʤækˌnaɪf] *vi* **-knifed; -knifing** : doblarse como una navaja, plegarse
jackknife[2] *n* : navaja *f*
jack–of–all–trades *n* : persona *f* que sabe un poco de todo, persona *f* de muchos oficios
jack–o'–lantern [ˈʤækəˌlæntərn] *n* : linterna *f* hecha de una calabaza
jackpot [ˈʤækˌpɑt] *n* **1** : primer premio *m*, gordo *m* **2 to hit the jackpot** : sacarse la lotería, sacarse el gordo
jackrabbit [ˈʤækˌræbət] *n* : liebre *f* grande de Norteamérica
jade [ˈʤeɪd] *n* : jade *m*
jaded [ˈʤeɪdəd] *adj* **1** TIRED : agotado **2** BORED : hastiado
jagged [ˈʤægəd] *adj* : dentado, mellado
jaguar [ˈʤægˌwɑr, ˈʤægjʊˌwɑr] *n* : jaguar *m*
jai alai [ˈhaɪˌlaɪ] *n* : jai alai *m*, pelota *f* vasca
jail[1] [ˈʤeɪl] *vt* : encarcelar
jail[2] *n* : cárcel *f*
jailbreak [ˈʤeɪlˌbreɪk] *n* : fuga *f*, huida *f* (de la cárcel)
jailer *or* **jailor** [ˈʤeɪlər] *n* : carcelero *m*, -ra *f*
jalapeño [ˌhɑləˈpeɪnjo, ˌhæ-, -ˈpiːno] *n* : jalapeño *m*
jalopy [ʤəˈlɑpi] *n, pl* **-lopies** : cacharro *m fam*, carro *m* destartalado
jalousie [ˈʤæləsi] *n* : celosía *f*
jam[1] [ˈʤæm] *v* **jammed; jamming** *vt* **1** CRAM : apiñar, embutir **2** BLOCK : atascar, atorar **3 to jam on the brakes** : frenar en seco — *vi* STICK : atascarse, atrancarse
jam[2] *n* **1** *or* **traffic jam** : atasco *m*, embotellamiento *m* (de tráfico) **2** PREDICAMENT : lío *m*, aprieto *m*, apuro *m* **3** : mermelada *f* ⟨strawberry jam : mermelada de fresa⟩
Jamaican [ʤəˈmeɪkən] *n* : jamaiquino *m*, -na *f*; jamaicano *m*, -na *f* — **Jamaican** *adj*
jamb [ˈʤæm] *n* : jamba *f*
jamboree [ˌʤæmbəˈriː] *n* : fiesta *f* grande
jangle[1] [ˈʤæŋgəl] *v* **-gled; -gling** *vi* : hacer un ruido metálico — *vt* **1** : hacer sonar **2 to jangle one's nerves** : irritar, crispar
jangle[2] *n* : ruido *m* metálico
janitor [ˈʤænəṭər] *n* : portero *m*, -ra *f*; conserje *mf*
January [ˈʤænjʊˌɛri] *n* : enero *m*
Japanese [ˌʤæpəˈniːz, -ˈniːs] *n* **1**

: japonés *m*, -nesa *f* **2** : japonés *m* (idioma) — **Japanese** *adj*

jar[1] [ˈʤɑr] *v* **jarred; jarring** *vi* **1** GRATE : chirriar **2** CLASH : desentonar **3** SHAKE : sacudirse **4 to jar on** : crispar, enervar — *vt* JOLT : sacudir

jar[2] *n* **1** GRATING : chirrido *m* **2** JOLT : vibración *f*, sacudida *f* **3** : tarro *m*, bote *m*, pote *m* ⟨a jar of honey : un tarro de miel⟩

jargon [ˈʤɑrgən] *n* : jerga *f*

jasmine [ˈʤæzmən] *n* : jazmín *m*

jasper [ˈʤæspər] *n* : jaspe *m*

jaundice [ˈʤɔndɪs] *n* : ictericia *f*

jaundiced [ˈʤɔndɪst] *adj* **1** : ictérico **2** EMBITTERED, RESENTFUL : amargado, resentido, negativo ⟨with a jaundiced eye : con una actitud de cinismo⟩

jaunt [ˈʤɔnt] *n* : excursión *f*, paseo *m*

jauntily [ˈʤɔntəli] *adv* : animadamente

jauntiness [ˈʤɔntinəs] *n* : animación *f*, vivacidad *f*

jaunty [ˈʤɔnti] *adj* **-tier; -est 1** SPRIGHTLY : animado, alegre **2** RAKISH : desenvuelto, desenfadado

Javanese [ˌʤævəˈniːz, ˌʤɑ-, -ˈniːs] *n* **1** : javanés *m* (idioma) **2** : javanés *m*, -nesa *f* — **Javanese** *adj*

javelin [ˈʤævələn] *n* : jabalina *f*

jaw[1] [ˈʤɔ] *vi* GAB : cotorrear *fam*, parlotear *fam*

jaw[2] *n* **1** : mandíbula *f*, quijada *f* **2** : mordaza *f* (de una herramienta) **3 the jaws of death** : las garras *f* de la muerte

jawbone [ˈʤɔˌboːn] *n* : mandíbula *f*

jay [ˈʤeɪ] *n* : arrendajo *m*, chara *f Mex*, azulejo *m Mex*

jaybird [ˈʤeɪˌbərd] → **jay**

jaywalk [ˈʤeɪˌwɔk] *vi* : cruzar la calle sin prudencia

jaywalker [ˈʤeɪˌwɔkər] *n* : peatón *m* imprudente

jazz[1] [ˈʤæz] *vt* **to jazz up** : animar, alegrar

jazz[2] *n* : jazz *m*

jazzy [ˈʤæzi] *adj* **jazzier; -est 1** : con ritmo de jazz **2** FLASHY, SHOWY : llamativo, ostentoso

jealous [ˈʤɛləs] *adj* : celoso, envidioso — **jealously** *adv*

jealousy [ˈʤɛləsi] *n* : celos *mpl*, envidia *f*

jeans [ˈʤiːnz] *npl* : jeans *mpl*, vaqueros *mpl*

jeep [ˈʤiːp] *n* : jeep *m*

jeer[1] [ˈʤɪr] *vi* **1** BOO : abuchear **2** SCOFF : mofarse, burlarse — *vt* RIDICULE : mofarse de, burlarse de

jeer[2] *n* **1** : abucheo *m* **2** TAUNT : mofa *f*, burla *f*

Jehovah [ʤɪˈhoːvə] *n* : Jehová *m*

jell [ˈʤɛl] *vi* **1** SET : gelificarse, cuajar **2** FORM : cuajar, formarse (una idea, etc.)

jelly[1] [ˈʤɛli] *v* **jellied; jellying** *vi* **1** JELL : gelificarse, cuajar **2** : hacer jalea — *vt* : gelificar

jelly[2] *n, pl* **-lies 1** : jalea *f* **2** GELATIN : gelatina *f*

jellyfish [ˈʤɛliˌfɪʃ] *n* : medusa *f*

jeopardize [ˈʤɛpərˌdaɪz] *vt* **-dized; -dizing** : arriesgar, poner en peligro

jeopardy [ˈʤɛpərdi] *n* : peligro *m*, riesgo *m*

jerk[1] [ˈʤərk] *vt* **1** JOLT : sacudir **2** TUG, YANK : darle un tirón a — *vi* JOLT : dar sacudidas ⟨the train jerked along : el tren iba moviéndose a sacudidas⟩

jerk[2] *n* **1** TUG : tirón *m*, jalón *m* **2** JOLT : sacudida *f* brusca **3** FOOL : estúpido *m*, -da *f*; idiota *mf*

jerkin [ˈʤərkən] *n* : chaqueta *f* sin mangas, chaleco *m*

jerky [ˈʤərki] *adj* **jerkier; -est 1** : espasmódico (dícese de los movimientos) **2** CHOPPY : inconexo (dícese de la prosa) — **jerkily** [-kəli] *adv*

jerry–built [ˈʤɛriˌbɪlt] *adj* : mal construido, chapucero

jersey [ˈʤərzi] *n, pl* **-seys** : jersey *m*

jest[1] [ˈʤɛst] *vi* : bromear

jest[2] *n* : broma *f*, chiste *m*

jester [ˈʤɛstər] *n* : bufón *m*, -fona *f*

Jesuit [ˈʤɛzuət] *n* : jesuita *m* — **Jesuit** *adj*

Jesus [ˈʤiːzəs, -zəz] *n* **1** : Jesús *m* **2 Jesus Christ** : Jesucristo *m* **3 Jesus (Christ)!** *fam* : ¡por Dios!

jet[1] [ˈʤɛt] *v* **jetted; jetting** *vt* SPOUT : arrojar a chorros — *vi* **1** GUSH : salir a chorros, chorrear **2** FLY : viajar en avión, volar

jet[2] *n* **1** STREAM : chorro *m* **2** *or* **jet airplane** : avión *m* a reacción, reactor *m* **3** : azabache *m* (mineral) **4 jet engine** : reactor *m*, motor *m* a reacción **5 jet lag** : desajuste *m* de horario (debido a un vuelo largo)

jet–propelled *adj* : a reacción

jetsam [ˈʤɛtsəm] *n* **flotsam and jetsam** : restos *mpl*, desechos *mpl*

jettison [ˈʤɛṭəsən] *vt* **1** : echar al mar **2** DISCARD : desechar, deshacerse de

jetty [ˈʤɛṭi] *n, pl* **-ties 1** PIER, WHARF : desembarcadero *m*, muelle *m* **2** BREAKWATER : malecón *m*, rompeolas *m*

Jew [ˈʤuː] *n* : judío *m*, -día *f*

jewel [ˈʤuːəl] *n* **1** : joya *f*, alhaja *f* **2** GEM : piedra *f* preciosa, gema *f* **3** : rubí *m* (de un reloj) **4** TREASURE : joya *f*, tesoro *m*

jeweler *or* **jeweller** [ˈʤuːələr] *n* : joyero *m*, -ra *f*

jewelry [ˈʤuːəlri] *n* : joyas *fpl*, alhajas *fpl*

Jewish [ˈʤuːɪʃ] *adj* : judío

jib [ˈʤɪb] *n* : foque *m* (de un barco)

jibe [ˈʤaɪb] *vi* **jibed; jibing** AGREE : concordar

jiffy [ˈʤɪfi] *n, pl* **-fies** : santiamén *m*, segundo *m*, momento *m*

jig[1] [ˈʤɪg] *vi* **jigged; jigging** : bailar la giga

jig[2] *n* **1** : giga *f* **2 the jig is up** : se acabó la fiesta

jigger [ˈʤɪgər] *n* : medida de 1 a 2 onzas (para licores)

jiggle[1] ['ʤɪgəl] *v* **-gled; -gling** *vt* : agitar o sacudir ligeramente — *vi* : agitarse, vibrar
jiggle[2] *n* : sacudida *f*, vibración *f*
jigsaw ['ʤɪg,sɔ] *n* **1** : sierra *f* de vaivén **2 jigsaw puzzle** : rompecabezas *m*
jilt ['ʤɪlt] *vt* : dejar plantado, dar calabazas a
jimmy[1] ['ʤɪmi] *vt* **-mied; -mying** : forzar con una palanqueta
jimmy[2] *n, pl* **-mies** : palanqueta *f*
jingle[1] ['ʤɪŋgəl] *v* **-gled; -gling** *vi* : tintinear — *vt* : hacer sonar
jingle[2] *n* **1** TINKLE : tintineo *m*, retintín *m* **2** : canción *f* rimada
jingoism ['ʤɪŋgo,ɪzəm] *n* : jingoísmo *m*, patriotería *f*
jingoistic [,ʤɪŋgo'ɪstɪk] *or* **jingoist** ['ʤɪŋgoɪst] *adj* : jingoísta, patriotero
jinx[1] ['ʤɪŋks] *vt* : traer mala suerte a, salar *CoRi, Mex*
jinx[2] *n* **1** : cenizo *m*, -za *f* **2 to put a jinx on** : echarle el mal de ojo a
jitters ['ʤɪt̬ərz] *npl* : nervios *mpl* ⟨he got the jitters : se puso nervioso⟩
jittery ['ʤɪt̬əri] *adj* : nervioso
job ['ʤɑb] *n* **1** : trabajo *m* ⟨he did odd jobs for her : le hizo algunos trabajos⟩ **2** CHORE, TASK : tarea *f*, quehacer *m* **3** EMPLOYMENT : trabajo *m*, empleo *m*, puesto *m*
jobber ['ʤɑbər] *n* MIDDLEMAN : intermediario *m*, -ria *f*
jock ['ʤɑk] *n* : deportista *mf*, atleta *mf*
jockey[1] ['ʤɑki] *v* **-eyed; -eying** *vt* **1** MANIPULATE : manipular **2** MANEUVER : maniobrar — *vi* **to jockey for position** : maniobrar para conseguir algo
jockey[2] *n, pl* **-eys** : jockey *mf*
jocose [ʤo'ko:s] *adj* : jocoso
jocular ['ʤɑkjʊlər] *adj* : jocoso — **jocularly** *adv*
jocularity [,ʤɑkjʊ'lærət̬i] *n* : jocosidad *f*
jodhpurs ['ʤɑdpərz] *npl* : pantalones *mpl* de montar
jog[1] ['ʤɑg] *v* **jogged; jogging** *vt* **1** NUDGE : dar, empujar, codear **2 to jog one's memory** : refrescar la memoria — *vi* **1** RUN : correr despacio, trotar, hacer footing (como ejercicio) **2** TRUDGE : andar a trote corto
jog[2] *n* **1** PUSH, SHAKE : empujoncito *m*, sacudida *f* leve **2** TROT : trote *m* corto, footing *m* (en deportes) **3** TWIST : recodo *m*, vuelta *f*, curva *f*
jogger ['ʤɑgər] *n* : persona *f* que hace footing
join ['ʤɔɪn] *vt* **1** CONNECT, LINK : unir, juntar ⟨to join in marriage : unir en matrimonio⟩ **2** ADJOIN : lindar con, colindar con **3** MEET : reunirse con, encontrarse con ⟨we joined them for lunch : nos reunimos con ellos para almorzar⟩ **4** : hacerse socio de (una organización), afiliarse a (un partido), entrar en (una empresa) — *vi* **1** UNITE : unirse **2** MERGE : empalmar (dícese de las carreteras), confluir (dícese de los ríos) **3 to join up** : hacerse socio, enrolarse
joiner ['ʤɔɪnər] *n* **1** CARPENTER : carpintero *m*, -ra *f* **2** : persona *f* que se une a varios grupos
joint[1] ['ʤɔɪnt] *adj* : conjunto, colectivo, mutuo ⟨a joint effort : un esfuerzo conjunto⟩ — **jointly** *adv*
joint[2] *n* **1** : articulación *f*, coyuntura *f* ⟨out of joint : dislocado⟩ **2** ROAST : asado *m* **3** JUNCTURE : juntura *f*, unión *f* **4** DIVE : antro *m*, tasca *f*
joist ['ʤɔɪst] *n* : viga *f*
joke[1] ['ʤo:k] *vi* **joked; joking** : bromear
joke[2] *n* **1** STORY : chiste *m* **2** PRANK : broma *f*
joker ['ʤo:kər] *n* **1** PRANKSTER : bromista *mf* **2** : comodín *m* (en los naipes)
jokingly ['ʤo:kɪŋli] *adv* : en broma
jollity ['ʤɑlət̬i] *n, pl* **-ties** MERRIMENT : alegría *f*, regocijo *m*
jolly ['ʤɑli] *adj* **-lier; -est** : alegre, jovial
jolt[1] ['ʤo:lt] *vi* JERK : dar tumbos, dar sacudidas — *vt* : sacudir
jolt[2] *n* **1** JERK : sacudida *f* brusca **2** SHOCK : golpe *m* (emocional)
jonquil ['ʤɑnkwɪl] *n* : junquillo *m*
Jordanian [ʤɔr'deɪniən] *n* : jordano *m*, -na *f* — **Jordanian** *adj*
josh ['ʤɑʃ] *vt* TEASE : tomarle el pelo (a alguien) — *vi* JOKE : bromear
jostle ['ʤɑsəl] *v* **-tled; -tling** *vi* **1** SHOVE : empujar, dar empellones **2** CONTEND : competir — *vt* **1** SHOVE : empujar **2 to jostle one's way** : abrirse paso a empellones
jot[1] ['ʤɑt] *vt* **jotted; jotting** : anotar, apuntar ⟨jot it down : apúntalo⟩
jot[2] *n* BIT : ápice *m*, jota *f*, pizca *f*
jounce[1] ['ʤæʊnts] *v* **jounced; jouncing** *vt* JOLT : sacudir — *vi* : dar tumbos, dar sacudidas
jounce[2] *n* JOLT : sacudida *f*, tumbo *m*
journal ['ʤərnəl] *n* **1** DIARY : diario *m* **2** PERIODICAL : revista *f*, publicación *f* periódica **3** NEWSPAPER : periódico *m*, diario *m*
journalism ['ʤərnəl,ɪzəm] *n* : periodismo *m*
journalist ['ʤərnəlɪst] *n* : periodista *mf*
journalistic [,ʤərnəl'ɪstɪk] *adj* : periodístico
journey[1] ['ʤərni] *vi* **-neyed; -neying** : viajar
journey[2] *n, pl* **-neys** : viaje *m*
journeyman ['ʤərnimən] *n, pl* **-men** [-mən, -,mn] : oficial *m*
joust[1] ['ʤæʊst] *vi* : justar
joust[2] *n* : justa *f*
jovial ['ʤo:viəl] *adj* : jovial — **jovially** *adv*
joviality [,ʤo:vi'ælət̬i] *n* : jovialidad *f*
jowl ['ʤæʊl] *n* **1** JAW : mandíbula *f* **2** CHEEK : mejilla *f*, cachete *m*
joy ['ʤɔɪ] *n* **1** HAPPINESS : gozo *m*, alegría *f*, felicidad *f* **2** DELIGHT : placer *m*, deleite *m* ⟨the child is a real joy : el niño es un verdadero placer⟩

joyful [ˈʤɔɪfəl] *adj* : gozoso, alegre, feliz — **joyfully** *adv*

joyless [ˈʤɔɪləs] *adj* : sin alegría, triste

joyous [ˈʤɔɪəs] *adj* : alegre, feliz, eufórico — **joyously** *adv*

joyousness [ˈʤɔɪəsnəs] *n* : alegría *f*, felicidad *f*, euforia *f*

joyride [ˈʤɔɪˌraɪd] *n* : paseo *m* temerario e irresponsable (en coche)

joystick [ˈʤɔɪˌstɪk] *n* : joystick *m*

jubilant [ˈʤuːbələnt] *adj* : jubiloso, alborozado — **jubilantly** *adv*

jubilation [ˌʤuːbəˈleɪʃən] *n* : júbilo *m*

jubilee [ˈʤuːbəˌliː] *n* **1** : quincuagésimo aniversario *m* **2** CELEBRATION : celebración *f*, festejos *mpl*

Judaic [ʤʊˈdeɪɪk] *adj* : judaico

Judaism [ˈʤuːdəˌɪzəm, ˈʤuːdi-, ˈʤuː-ˌdeɪ-] *n* : judaísmo *m*

judge[1] [ˈʤʌʤ] *vt* **judged; judging 1** ASSESS : evaluar, juzgar **2** DEEM : juzgar, considerar **3** TRY : juzgar (ante el tribunal) **4 judging by** : a juzgar por

judge[2] *n* **1** : juez *mf*, jueza *f* **2 to be a good judge of** : saber juzgar a, entender mucho de

judgment *or* **judgement** [ˈʤʌʤ-mənt] *n* **1** RULING : fallo *m*, sentencia *f* **2** OPINION : opinión *f* **3** DISCERNMENT : juicio *m*, discernimiento *m*

judgmental [ˌʤʌʤˈmntəl] *adj* : crítico — **judgmentally** *adv*

judicature [ˈʤuːdɪkəˌʧʊr] *n* : judicatura *f*

judicial [ʤʊˈdɪʃəl] *adj* : judicial — **judicially** *adv*

judiciary[1] [ʤʊˈdɪʃiˌri, -ˈdɪʃəri] *adj* : judicial

judiciary[2] *n* **1** JUDICATURE : judicatura *f* **2** : poder *m* judicial

judicious [ʤʊˈdɪʃəs] *adj* SOUND, WISE : juicioso, sensato — **judiciously** *adv*

judo [ˈʤuːˌdoː] *n* : judo *m*

jug [ˈʤʌg] *n* **1** : jarra *f*, jarro *m*, cántaro *m* **2** JAIL : cárcel *f*, chirona *f fam*

juggernaut [ˈʤʌgərˌnɔt] *n* : gigante *m*, fuerza *f* irresistible ⟨a political juggernaut : un gigante político⟩

juggle [ˈʤʌgəl] *v* **-gled; -gling** *vt* **1** : hacer juegos malabares con **2** MANIPULATE : manipular, jugar con — *vi* : hacer juegos malabares

juggler [ˈʤʌgələr] *n* : malabarista *mf*

jugular [ˈʤʌgjʊlər] *adj* : yugular ⟨jugular vein : vena yugular⟩

juice [ˈʤuːs] *n* **1** : jugo *m* (de carne, de frutas) *m*, zumo *m* (de frutas) **2** ELECTRICITY : electricidad *f*, luz *f*

juicer [ˈʤuːsər] *n* : exprimidor *m*

juiciness [ˈʤuːsinəs] *n* : jugosidad *f*

juicy [ˈʤuːsi] *adj* **juicier; -est 1** SUCCULENT : jugoso, suculento **2** PROFITABLE : jugoso, lucrativo **3** RACY : picante

jukebox [ˈʤuːkˌbɑks] *n* : rocola *f*, máquina *f* de discos

julep [ˈʤuːləp] *n* : bebida *f* hecha con whisky americano y menta

July [ʤʊˈlaɪ] *n* : julio *m*

jumble[1] [ˈʤʌmbəl] *vt* **-bled; -bling** : mezclar, revolver

jumble[2] *n* : revoltijo *m*, fárrago *m*, embrollo *m*

jumbo[1] [ˈʤʌmˌboː] *adj* : gigante, enorme, de tamaño extra grande

jumbo[2] *n, pl* **-bos** : coloso *m*, cosa *f* de tamaño extra grande

jump[1] [ˈʤʌmp] *vi* **1** LEAP : saltar, brincar **2** START : levantarse de un salto, sobresaltarse **3** MOVE, SHIFT : moverse, pasar ⟨to jump from job to job : pasar de un empleo a otro⟩ **4** INCREASE, RISE : dar un salto, aumentarse de golpe, subir bruscamente **5** BUSTLE : animarse, ajetrearse **6 to jump to conclusions** : sacar conclusiones precipitadas — *vt* **1** : saltar ⟨to jump a fence : saltar una valla⟩ **2** SKIP : saltarse **3** ATTACK : atacar, asaltar **4 to jump the gun** : precipitarse

jump[2] *n* **1** LEAP : salto *m* **2** START : sobresalto *m*, respingo *m* **3** INCREASE : subida *f* brusca, aumento *m* **4** ADVANTAGE : ventaja *f* ⟨we got the jump on them : les llevamos la ventaja⟩

jumper [ˈʤʌmpər] *n* **1** : saltador *m*, -dora *f* (en deportes) **2** : jumper *m*, vestido *m* sin mangas

jumpy [ˈʤʌmpi] *adj* **jumpier; -est** : asustadizo, nervioso

junction [ˈʤʌŋkʃən] *n* **1** JOINING : unión *f* **2** : cruce *m* (de calles), empalme *m* (de un ferrocarril), confluencia *f* (de ríos)

juncture [ˈʤʌŋkʧər] *n* **1** UNION : juntura *f*, unión *f* **2** MOMENT, POINT : coyuntura *f* ⟨at this juncture : en esta coyuntura, en este momento⟩

June [ˈʤuːn] *n* : junio *m*

jungle [ˈʤʌŋgəl] *n* : jungla *f*, selva *f*

junior[1] [ˈʤuːnjər] *adj* **1** YOUNGER : más joven ⟨John Smith, Junior : John Smith, hijo⟩ **2** SUBORDINATE : subordinado, subalterno

junior[2] *n* **1** : persona *f* de menor edad ⟨she's my junior : es menor que yo⟩ **2** SUBORDINATE : subalterno *m*, -na *f*; subordinado *m*, -da *f* **3** : estudiante *mf* de penúltimo año

juniper [ˈʤuːnəpər] *n* : enebro *m*

junk[1] [ˈʤʌŋk] *vt* : echar a la basura

junk[2] *n* **1** RUBBISH : desechos *mpl*, desperdicios *mpl* **2** STUFF : trastos *mpl fam*, cachivaches *mpl fam* **3 piece of junk** : cacharro *m*, porquería *f*

junket [ˈʤʌŋkət] *n* : viaje *m* (pagado con dinero público)

junta [ˈhʊntə, ˈʤʌn-, ˈhʌn-] *n* : junta *f* militar

Jupiter [ˈʤuːpəţər] *n* : Júpiter *m*

jurisdiction [ˌʤʊrəsˈdɪkʃən] *n* : jurisdicción *f*

jurisprudence [ˌʤʊrəsˈpruːdən*t*s] *n* : jurisprudencia *f*

jurist [ˈʤʊrɪst] *n* : jurista *mf*; magistrado *m*, -da *f*

juror [ˈʤʊrər] *n* : jurado *m*, -da *f*
jury [ˈʤʊri] *n, pl* **-ries** : jurado *m*
just[1] [ˈʤʌst] *adv* **1** EXACTLY : justo, precisamente, exactamente **2** POSSIBLY : posiblemente ⟨it just might work : tal vez resulte⟩ **3** BARELY : justo, apenas ⟨just in time : justo a tiempo⟩ **4** ONLY : sólo, solamente, nada más ⟨just us : sólo nosotros⟩ **5** QUITE : muy, simplemente ⟨it's just horrible! : ¡qué horrible!⟩ **6 to have just (done something)** : acabar de (hacer algo) ⟨he just called : acaba de llamar⟩
just[2] *adj* : justo — **justly** *adv*
justice [ˈʤʌstɪs] *n* **1** : justicia *f* **2** JUDGE : juez *mf*, jueza *f*
justification [ˌʤʌstəfəˈkeɪʃən] *n* : justificación *f*
justify [ˈʤʌstəˌfaɪ] *vt* **-fied; -fying** : justificar — **justifiable** [ˌʤʌstə-ˈfaɪəbəl] *adj*
jut [ˈʤʌt] *vi* **jutted; jutting** : sobresalir
jute [ˈʤu:t] *n* : yute *m*
juvenile[1] [ˈʤu:vəˌnaɪl, -vənəl] *adj* **1** : juvenil ⟨juvenile delinquent : delincuente juvenil⟩ ⟨juvenile court : tribunal de menores⟩ **2** CHILDISH : infantil
juvenile[2] *n* : menor *mf*
juxtapose [ˈʤʌkstəˌpo:z] *vt* **-posed; -posing** : yuxtaponer
juxtaposition [ˌʤʌkstəpəˈzɪʃən] *n* : yuxtaposición *f*

K

k [ˈkeɪ] *n, pl* **k's** *or* **ks** [ˈkeɪz] : undécima letra del alfabeto inglés
kaiser [ˈkaɪzər] *n* : káiser *m*
kale [ˈkeɪl] *n* : col *f* rizada
kaleidoscope [kəˈlaɪdəˌsko:p] *n* : calidoscopio *m*
kamikaze [ˌkɑmɪˈkɑzi] *n* : kamikaze *m* — **kamikaze** *adj*
kangaroo [ˌkæŋgəˈru:] *n, pl* **-roos** : canguro *m*
kaolin [ˈkeɪələn] *n* : caolín *m*
karaoke [ˌkæriˈo:ki] *n* : karaoke *m*
karat [ˈkærət] *n* : quilate *m*
karate [kəˈrɑṭi] *n* : karate *m*
katydid [ˈkeɪṭiˌdɪd] *n* : saltamontes *m*
kayak [ˈkaɪˌæk] *n* : kayac *m*, kayak *m*
keel[1] [ˈki:l] *vi* **to keel over** : volcar (dícese de un barco), desplomarse (dícese de una persona)
keel[2] *n* : quilla *f*
keen [ˈki:n] *adj* **1** SHARP : afilado, filoso ⟨a keen blade : una hoja afilada⟩ **2** PENETRATING : cortante, penetrante ⟨a keen wind : un viento cortante⟩ **3** ENTHUSIASTIC : entusiasta **4** ACUTE : agudo, fino ⟨keen hearing : oído fino⟩ ⟨keen intelligence : inteligencia aguda⟩
keenly [ˈki:nli] *adv* **1** ENTHUSIASTICALLY : con entusiasmo **2** INTENSELY : vivamente, profundamente ⟨keenly aware of : muy consciente de⟩
keenness [ˈki:nnəs] *n* **1** SHARPNESS : lo afilado, lo filoso **2** ENTHUSIASM : entusiasmo *m* **3** ACUTENESS : agudeza *f*
keep[1] [ˈki:p] *v* **kept** [ˈkpt]; **keeping** *vt* **1** : cumplir (la palabra a uno), acudir a (una cita) **2** OBSERVE : observar (una fiesta) **3** GUARD : guardar, cuidar **4** CONTINUE : mantener ⟨to keep silence : mantener silencio⟩ **5** SUPPORT : mantener (una familia) **6** RAISE : criar (animales) **7** : llevar, escribir (un diario, etc.) **8** RETAIN : guardar, conservar, quedarse con **9** STORE : guardar **10** DETAIN : hacer quedar, detener **11** PRESERVE : guardar ⟨to keep a secret : guardar un secreto⟩ — *vi* **1** : conservarse (dícese de los alimentos) **2** CONTINUE : seguir, no dejar ⟨he keeps on pestering us : no deja de molestarnos⟩ **3 to keep from** : abstenerse de ⟨I couldn't keep from laughing : no podía contener la risa⟩
keep[2] *n* **1** TOWER : torreón *m* (de un castillo), torre *f* del homenaje **2** SUSTENANCE : manutención *f*, sustento *m* **3 for keeps** : para siempre
keeper [ˈki:pər] *n* **1** : guarda *mf* (en un zoológico); conservador *m*, -dora *f* (en un museo) **2** GAMEKEEPER : guardabosque *mf*
keeping [ˈki:pɪŋ] *n* **1** CONFORMITY : conformidad *f*, acuerdo *m* ⟨in keeping with : de acuerdo con⟩ **2** CARE : cuidado *m* ⟨in the keeping of : al cuidado de⟩
keepsake [ˈki:pˌseɪk] *n* : recuerdo *m*
keep up *vt* CONTINUE, MAINTAIN : mantener, seguir con — *vi* **1** : mantenerse al corriente ⟨he kept up with the news : se mantenía al tanto de las noticias⟩ **2** CONTINUE : continuar **3 to keep up with someone** : mantener contacto con alguien
keg [ˈkɛg] *n* : barril *m*
kelp [ˈkɛlp] *n* : alga *f* marina
ken [ˈkɛn] *n* **1** SIGHT : vista *f*, alcance *m* de la vista **2** UNDERSTANDING : comprensión *f*, alcance *m* del conocimiento ⟨it's beyond his ken : no lo puede entender⟩
kennel [ˈkɛnəl] *n* : caseta *f* para perros, perrera *f*
Kenyan [ˈkɛnjən, ˈki:n-] *n* : keniano *m*, -na *f* — **Kenyan** *adj*
kept → **keep**
kerchief [ˈkərʧəf, -ˌʧi:f] *n* : pañuelo *m*
kernel [ˈkərnəl] *n* **1** : almendra *f* (de semillas y nueces) **2** : grano *m* (de cereales) **3** CORE : meollo *m* ⟨a kernel of truth : un fondo de verdad⟩
kerosene *or* **kerosine** [ˈkɛrəˌsi:n, ˌkɛrəˈ-] *n* : queroseno *m*, kerosén *m*, kerosene *m*

ketchup [ˈkɛtʃəp, ˈkæ-] *n* : salsa *f* catsup
kettle [ˈkɛtəl] *n* **1** : hervidor *m*, pava *f* *Arg, Bol, Chile* **2** → **teakettle**
kettledrum [ˈkɛtəlˌdrʌm] *n* : timbal *m*
key[1] [ˈkiː] *vt* **1** ATTUNE : adaptar, adecuar **2 to key up** : poner nervioso, inquietar
key[2] *adj* : clave, fundamental
key[3] *n* **1** : llave *f* **2** SOLUTION : clave *f*, soluciones *fpl* **3** : tecla *f* (de un piano o una máquina) **4** : tono *m*, tonalidad *f* (en la música) **5** ISLET, REEF : cayo *m*, islote *m*
keyboard [ˈkiːˌbord] *n* : teclado *m*
keyhole [ˈkiːˌhoːl] *n* : bocallave *f*, ojo *m* (de una cerradura)
keynote[1] [ˈkiːˌnoːt] *vt* **-noted; -noting** **1** : establecer la tónica de (en música) **2** : pronunciar el discurso principal de
keynote[2] *n* **1** : tónica *f* (en música) **2** : idea *f* fundamental
keystone [ˈkiːˌstoːn] *n* : clave *f*, dovela *f*
keystroke [ˈkiːˌstroːk] *n* : pulsación *f* (de tecla)
khaki [ˈkæki, ˈkɑ-] *n* : caqui *m*
khan [ˈkɑn, ˈkæn] *n* : kan *m*
kibbutz [kəˈbʊts, -ˈbuːts] *n, pl* **-butzim** [-ˌbʊtˈsiːm, -ˌbuːt-] : kibutz *m*
kibitz [ˈkɪbɪts] *vi* : dar consejos molestos
kibitzer [ˈkɪbɪtsər, kɪˈbɪt-] *n* : persona *f* que da consejos molestos
kick[1] [ˈkɪk] *vi* **1** : dar patadas (dícese de una persona), cocear (dícese de un animal) **2** PROTEST : patalear, protestar **3** RECOIL : dar un culatazo (dícese de un arma de fuego) — *vt* : patear, darle una patada (a alguien)
kick[2] *n* **1** : patada *f*, puntapié *m*, coz *f* (de un animal) **2** RECOIL : culatazo *m* (de un arma de fuego) **3** : fuerza *f* ⟨a drink with a kick : una bebida fuerte⟩
kicker [ˈkɪkər] *n* : pateador *m*, -dora *f* (en deportes)
kickoff [ˈkɪkˌɔf] *n* : saque *m* (inicial)
kick off *vi* **1** : hacer el saque inicial (en deportes) **2** BEGIN : empezar — *vt* : empezar
kid[1] [ˈkɪd] *v* **kidded; kidding** *vt* **1** FOOL : engañar **2** TEASE : tomarle el pelo (a alguien) — *vi* JOKE : bromear ⟨I'm only kidding : lo digo en broma⟩
kid[2] *n* **1** : chivo *m*, -va *f*; cabrito *m*, -ta *f* **2** CHILD : chico *m*, -ca *f*; niño *m*, -ña *f*
kidder [ˈkɪdər] *n* : bromista *mf*
kiddingly [ˈkɪdɪŋli] *adv* : en broma
kidnap [ˈkɪdˌnæp] *vt* **-napped** *or* **-naped** [-ˌnæpt]; **-napping** *or* **-naping** [-ˌnæpɪŋ] : secuestrar, raptar
kidnapper *or* **kidnaper** [ˈkɪdˌnæpər] *n* : secuestrador *m*, -dora *f*; raptor *m*, -tora *f*
kidnapping [ˈkɪdˌnæpɪŋ] *n* : secuestro *m*
kidney [ˈkɪdni] *n, pl* **-neys** : riñón *m*
kidney bean *n* : frijol *m*
kill[1] [ˈkɪl] *vt* **1** : matar **2** END : acabar con, poner fin a **3 to kill time** : matar el tiempo
kill[2] *n* **1** KILLING : matanza *f* **2** PREY : presa *f*
killer [ˈkɪlər] *n* : asesino *m*, -na *f*
killjoy [ˈkɪlˌdʒɔɪ] *n* : aguafiestas *mf*
kiln [ˈkɪl, ˈkɪln] *n* : horno *m*
kilo [ˈkiːˌloː] *n, pl* **-los** : kilo *m*
kilobyte [ˈkɪləˌbaɪt] *n* : kilobyte *m*
kilocycle [ˈkɪləˌsaɪkəl] *n* : kilociclo *m*
kilogram [ˈkɪləˌgræm, ˈkiː-] *n* : kilogramo *m*
kilohertz [ˈkɪləˌhərts] *n* : kilohertzio *m*
kilometer [kɪˈlɑmət̬ər, ˈkɪləˌmiː-] *n* : kilómetro *m*
kilowatt [ˈkɪləˌwɑt] *n* : kilovatio *m*
kilt [ˈkɪlt] *n* : falda *f* escocesa
kilter [ˈkɪltər] *n* **1** ORDER : buen estado *m* **2 out of kilter** : descompuesto, estropeado
kimono [kəˈmoːno, -nə] *n, pl* **-nos** : kimono *m*, quimono *m*
kin [ˈkɪn] *n* : familiares *mpl*, parientes *mpl*
kind[1] [ˈkaɪnd] *adj* : amable, bondadoso, benévolo
kind[2] *n* **1** ESSENCE : esencia *f* ⟨a difference in degree, not in kind : una diferencia cuantitativa y no cualitativa⟩ **2** CATEGORY : especie *f*, género *m* **3** TYPE : clase *f*, tipo *m*, índole *f*
kindergarten [ˈkɪndərˌgɑrtən, -dən] *n* : kinder *m*, kindergarten *m*, jardín *m* de infantes, jardín *m* de niños *Mex*
kindhearted [ˌkaɪndˈhɑrt̬əd] *adj* : bondadoso, de buen corazón
kindle [ˈkɪndəl] *v* **-dled; -dling** *vt* **1** IGNITE : encender **2** AROUSE : despertar, suscitar — *vi* : encenderse
kindliness [ˈkaɪndlinəs] *n* : bondad *f*
kindling [ˈkɪndlɪŋ, ˈkɪndlən] *n* : astillas *fpl*, leña *f*
kindly[1] [ˈkaɪndli] *adv* **1** AMIABLY : amablemente, bondadosamente **2** COURTEOUSLY : cortésmente, con cortesía ⟨we kindly ask you not smoke : les rogamos que no fumen⟩ **3** PLEASE : por favor **4 to take kindly to** : aceptar de buena gana
kindly[2] *adj* **-lier; -est** : bondadoso, amable
kindness [ˈkaɪndnəs] *n* : bondad *f*
kind of *adv* SOMEWHAT : un tanto, algo
kindred[1] [ˈkɪndrəd] *adj* SIMILAR : similar, afín ⟨kindred spirits : almas gemelas⟩
kindred[2] *n* **1** FAMILY : familia *f*, parentela *f* **2** → **kin**
kinfolk [ˈkɪnˌfoːk] *or* **kinfolks** [-ˌfoːks] *npl* → **kin**
king [ˈkɪŋ] *n* : rey *m*
kingdom [ˈkɪŋdəm] *n* : reino *m*
kingfisher [ˈkɪŋˌfɪʃər] *n* : martín *m* pescador
kingly [ˈkɪŋli] *adj* **-lier; -est** : regio, real
king–size [ˈkɪŋˌsaɪz] *or* **king–sized** [-ˌsaɪzd] *adj* : de tamaño muy grande, extra largo (dícese de cigarrillos)
kink [ˈkɪŋk] *n* **1** : rizo *m* (en el pelo), vuelta *f* (en una cuerda) **2** CRAMP

: calambre *m* ⟨to have a kink in the neck : tener tortícolis⟩

kinky [ˈkɪŋki] *adj* **-kier; -est** : rizado (dícese del pelo), enroscado (dícese de una cuerda)

kinship [ˈkɪnˌʃɪp] *n* : parentesco *m*

kinsman [ˈkɪnzmən] *n, pl* **-men** [-mən, -ˌmɛn] : familiar *m*, pariente *m*

kinswoman [ˈkɪnzˌwʊmən] *n, pl* **-women** [-ˌwɪmən] : familiar *f*, pariente *f*

kiosk [ˈkiːˌɑsk] *n* : quiosco *m*

kipper [ˈkɪpər] *n* : arenque *m* ahumado

kiss1 [ˈkɪs] *vt* : besar — *vi* : besarse

kiss2 *n* : beso *m*

kit [ˈkɪt] *n* **1** SET : juego *m*, kit *m* **2** CASE : estuche *m*, caja *f* **3 first–aid kit** : botiquín *m* **4 tool kit** : caja *f* de herramientas **5 travel kit** : neceser *m*

kitchen [ˈkɪʧən] *n* : cocina *f*

kite [ˈkaɪt] *n* **1** : milano *m* (ave) **2** : cometa *f*, papalote *m Mex* ⟨to fly a kite : hacer volar una cometa⟩

kith [ˈkɪθ] *n* : amigos *mpl* ⟨kith and kin : amigos y parientes⟩

kitten [ˈkɪtən] *n* : gatito *m*, -ta *f*

kitty [ˈkɪṭi] *n, pl* **-ties** **1** FUND, POOL : bote *m*, fondo *m* común **2** CAT : gato *m*, gatito *m*

kitty–corner [ˈkɪṭiˌkɔrnər] *or* **kitty–cornered** [-nərd] → **catercorner**

kiwi [ˈkiːˌwiː] *n* : kiwi *m*

kleptomania [ˌklɛptəˈmeɪniə] *n* : cleptomanía *f*

kleptomaniac [ˌklɛptəˈmeɪniˌæk] *n* : cleptómano *m*, -na *f*

knack [ˈnæk] *n* : maña *f*, facilidad *f*

knapsack [ˈnæpˌsæk] *n* : mochila *f*, morral *m*

knave [ˈneɪv] *n* : bellaco *m*, pícaro *m*

knead [ˈniːd] *vt* **1** : amasar, sobar **2** MASSAGE : masajear

knee [ˈniː] *n* : rodilla *f*

kneecap [ˈniːˌkæp] *n* : rótula *f*

kneel [ˈniːl] *vi* **knelt** [ˈnɛlt] *or* **kneeled** [ˈniːld]; **kneeling** : arrodillarse, ponerse de rodillas

knell [ˈnɛl] *n* : doble *m*, toque *m* ⟨death knell : toque de difuntos⟩

knew → **know**

knickers [ˈnɪkərz] *npl* : pantalones *mpl* bombachos de media pierna

knickknack [ˈnɪkˌnæk] *n* : chuchería *f*, baratija *f*

knife1 [ˈnaɪf] *vt* **knifed** [ˈnaɪft]; **knifing** : acuchillar, apuñalar

knife2 *n, pl* **knives** [ˈnaɪvz] : cuchillo *m*

knight1 [ˈnaɪt] *vt* : conceder el título de *Sir* a

knight2 *n* **1** : caballero *m* ⟨knight errant : caballero andante⟩ **2** : caballo *m* (en ajedrez) **3** : uno que tiene el título de *Sir*

knighthood [ˈnaɪtˌhʊd] *n* **1** : caballería *f* **2** : título *m* de *Sir*

knightly [ˈnaɪtli] *adj* : caballeresco

knit1 [ˈnɪt] *v* **knit** *or* **knitted** [ˈnɪṭəd]; **knitting** *vt* **1** UNITE : unir, enlazar **2** : tejer ⟨to knit a sweater : tejer un suéter⟩ **3 to knit one's brows** : fruncir el ceño — *vi* **1** : tejer **2** : soldarse (dícese de los huesos)

knit2 *n* : prenda *f* tejida

knitter [ˈnɪṭər] *n* : tejedor *m*, -dora *f*

knob [ˈnɑb] *n* **1** LUMP : bulto *m*, protuberancia *f* **2** HANDLE : perilla *f*, tirador *m*, botón *m*

knobbed [ˈnɑbd] *adj* **1** KNOTTY : nudoso **2** : que tiene perilla o botón

knobby [ˈnɑbi] *adj* **knobbier; -est** **1** KNOTTY : nudoso **2 knobby knees** : rodillas *fpl* huesudas

knock1 [ˈnɑk] *vt* **1** HIT, RAP : golpear, golpetear **2** : hacer chocar ⟨they knocked heads : se dieron en la cabeza⟩ **3** CRITICIZE : criticar — *vi* **1** RAP : dar un golpe, llamar (a la puerta) **2** COLLIDE : darse, chocar

knock2 *n* : golpe *m*, llamada *f* (a la puerta), golpeteo *m* (de un motor)

knock down *vt* : derribar, echar al suelo

knocker [ˈnɑkər] *n* : aldaba *f*, llamador *m*

knock–kneed [ˈnɑkˈniːd] *adj* : patizambo

knockout [ˈnɑkˌaʊt] *n* : nocaut *m*, knockout *m* (en deportes)

knock out *vt* : dejar sin sentido, poner fuera de combate (en el boxeo)

knoll [ˈnoːl] *n* : loma *f*, otero *m*, montículo *m*

knot1 [ˈnɑt] *v* **knotted; knotting** *vt* : anudar — *vi* : anudarse

knot2 *n* **1** : nudo *m* (en cordel o madera), nódulo *m* (en los músculos) **2** CLUSTER : grupo *m* **3** : nudo *m* (unidad de velocidad)

knotty [ˈnɑṭi] *adj* **-tier; -est** **1** GNARLED : nudoso **2** COMPLEX : espinoso, enredado, complejo

know [ˈnoː] *v* **knew** [ˈnuː, ˈnjuː]; **known** [ˈnoːn]; **knowing** *vt* **1** : saber ⟨he knows the answer : sabe la respuesta⟩ **2** : conocer (a una persona, un lugar) ⟨do you know Julia? : ¿conoces a Julia?⟩ **3** RECOGNIZE : reconocer **4** DISCERN, DISTINGUISH : distinguir, discernir **5 to know how to** : saber ⟨I don't know how to dance : no sé bailar⟩ — *vi* : saber

knowable [ˈnoːəbəl] *adj* : conocible

knowing [ˈnoːɪŋ] *adj* **1** KNOWLEDGEABLE : informado ⟨a knowing look : una mirada de complicidad⟩ **2** ASTUTE : astuto **3** DELIBERATE : deliberado, intencional

knowingly [ˈnoːɪŋli] *adv* **1** : con complicidad ⟨she smiled knowingly : sonrió con una mirada de complicidad⟩ **2** DELIBERATELY : a sabiendas, adrede, a propósito

know–it–all [ˈnoːɪṭˌɔl] *n* : sabelotodo *mf fam*

knowledge [ˈnɑlɪʤ] *n* **1** AWARENESS : conocimiento *m* **2** LEARNING : conocimientos *mpl*, saber *m*

knowledgeable [ˈnɑlɪʤəbəl] *adj* : informado, entendido, enterado

known [ˈnoːn] *adj* : conocido, familiar
knuckle [ˈnʌkəl] *n* : nudillo *m*
koala [koˈwɑlə] *n* : koala *m*
kohlrabi [ˌkoːlˈrɑbi, -ˈræ-] *n, pl* **-bies** : colinabo *m*
Koran [kəˈrɑn, -ˈræn] *n* **the Koran** : el Corán
Korean [kəˈriːən] *n* **1** : coreano *m*, -na *f* **2** : coreano *m* (idioma) — **Korean** *adj*
kosher [ˈkoːʃər] *adj* : aprobado por la ley judía
kowtow [ˌkaʊˈtaʊ, ˈkaʊˌtaʊ] *vi* **to kowtow to** : humillarse ante, doblegarse ante
krypton [ˈkrɪpˌtɑn] *n* : criptón *m*
kudos [ˈkjuːˌdɑs, ˈkuː-, -ˌdoːz] *n* : fama *f*, renombre *m*
kumquat [ˈkʌmˌkwɑt] *n* : naranjita *f* china
Kurd [ˈkʊrd, ˈkərd] *n* : kurdo *m*, -da *f*
Kurdish [ˈkʊrdɪʃ, ˈkər-] *adj* : kurdo
Kuwaiti [kʊˈweɪt̬i] *n* : kuwaití *mf* — **Kuwaiti** *adj*

L

l [ˈɛl] *n, pl* **l's** *or* **ls** [ˈlz] : duodécima letra del alfabeto inglés
lab [ˈlæb] → **laboratory**
label[1] [ˈleɪbəl] *vt* **-beled** *or* **-belled; -beling** *or* **-belling** **1** : etiquetar, poner etiqueta a **2** BRAND, CATEGORIZE : calificar, tildar, tachar ⟨they labeled him as a fraud : lo calificaron de farsante⟩
label[2] *n* **1** : etiqueta *f*, rótulo *m* **2** DESCRIPTION : calificación *f*, descripción *f* **3** BRAND : marca *f*
labial [ˈleɪbiəl] *adj* : labial
labor[1] [ˈleɪbər] *vi* **1** WORK : trabajar **2** STRUGGLE : avanzar penosamente (dícese de una persona), funcionar con dificultad (dícese de un motor) **3 to labor under a delusion** : hacerse ilusiones, tener una falsa impresión — *vt* BELABOR : insistir en, extenderse sobre
labor[2] *n* **1** EFFORT, WORK : trabajo *m*, esfuerzos *mpl* **2** : parto *m* ⟨to be in labor : estar de parto⟩ **3** TASK : tarea *f*, labor *m* **4** WORKERS : mano *f* de obra
laboratory [ˈlæbrəˌtori, ləˈbɔrə-] *n, pl* **-ries** : laboratorio *m*
Labor Day *n* : Día *m* del Trabajo
laborer [ˈleɪbərər] *n* : peón *m*; trabajador *m*, -dora *f*
laborious [ləˈboriəs] *adj* : laborioso, difícil
laboriously [ləˈboriəsli] *adv* : laboriosamente, trabajosamente
labor union → **union**
labyrinth [ˈlæbəˌrɪnθ] *n* : laberinto *m*
lace[1] [ˈleɪs] *vt* **laced; lacing** **1** TIE : acordonar, atar los cordones de **2** : adornar de encaje ⟨I laced the dress in white : adorné el vestido de encaje blanco⟩ **3** SPIKE : echar licor a
lace[2] *n* **1** : encaje *m* **2** SHOELACE : cordón *m* (de zapatos), agujeta *f Mex*
lacerate [ˈlæsəˌreɪt] *vt* **-ated; -ating** : lacerar
laceration [ˌlæsəˈreɪʃən] *n* : laceración *f*
lack[1] [ˈlæk] *vt* : carecer de, no tener ⟨she lacks patience : carece de paciencia⟩ — *vi* : faltar ⟨they lack for nothing : no les falta nada⟩
lack[2] *n* : falta *f*, carencia *f*
lackadaisical [ˌlækəˈdeɪzɪkəl] *adj* : apático, indiferente, lánguido — **lackadaisically** [-kli] *adv*
lackey [ˈlæki] *n, pl* **-eys** **1** FOOTMAN : lacayo *m* **2** TOADY : adulador *m*, -dora *f*
lackluster [ˈlækˌlʌstər] *adj* **1** DULL : sin brillo, apagado, deslustrado **2** MEDIOCRE : deslucido, mediocre
laconic [ləˈkɑnɪk] *adj* : lacónico — **laconically** [-nɪkli] *adv*
lacquer[1] [ˈlækər] *vt* : laquear, pintar con laca
lacquer[2] *n* : laca *f*
lacrosse [ləˈkrɔs] *n* : lacrosse *f*
lactic acid [ˈlæktɪk] *n* : ácido *m* láctico
lacuna [ləˈkuːnə, -ˈkjuː-] *n, pl* **-nae** [-ˌniː, -ˌnaɪ] *or* **-nas** : laguna *f*
lacy [ˈleɪsi] *adj* **lacier; -est** : de encaje, como de encaje
lad [ˈlæd] *n* : muchacho *m*, niño *m*
ladder [ˈlædər] *n* : escalera *f*
laden [ˈleɪdən] *adj* : cargado
ladle[1] [ˈleɪdəl] *vt* **-dled; -dling** : servir con cucharón
ladle[2] *n* : cucharón *m*, cazo *m*
lady [ˈleɪdi] *n, pl* **-dies** **1** : señora *f*, dama *f* **2** WOMAN : mujer *f*
ladybird [ˈleɪdiˌbərd] → **ladybug**
ladybug [ˈleɪdiˌbʌg] *n* : mariquita *f*
lag[1] [ˈlæg] *vi* **lagged; lagging** : quedarse atrás, retrasarse, rezagarse
lag[2] *n* **1** DELAY : retraso *m*, demora *f* **2** INTERVAL : lapso *m*, intervalo *m*
lager [ˈlɑgər] *n* : cerveza *f* rubia
laggard[1] [ˈlægərd] *adj* : retardado, retrasado
laggard[2] *n* : rezagado *m*, -da *f*
lagoon [ləˈguːn] *n* : laguna *f*
laid → **lay**[1]
laid–back [ˈleɪdˈbæk] *adj* : tranquilo, relajado
lain *pp* → **lie**[1]
lair [ˈlær] *n* : guarida *f*, madriguera *f*
laissez–faire [ˌlɛˌseɪˈfær, ˌleɪˌzeɪ-] *n* : liberalismo *m* económico
laity [ˈleɪət̬i] *n* **the laity** : los laicos, el laicado
lake [ˈleɪk] *n* : lago *m*
lama [ˈlɑmə] *n* : lama *m*
lamb [ˈlæm] *n* **1** : cordero *m*, borrego *m* (animal) **2** : carne *f* de cordero

lambaste [læm'beɪst] *or* **lambast** [-'bæst] *vt* **-basted; -basting 1** BEAT, THRASH : golpear, azotar, darle una paliza (a alguien) **2** CENSURE : arremeter contra, censurar
lame[1] ['leɪm] *vt* **lamed; laming** : lisiar, hacer cojo
lame[2] *adj* **lamer; lamest 1** : cojo, renco, rengo **2** WEAK : pobre, débil, poco convincente ⟨a lame excuse : una excusa débil⟩
lamé [lɑ'meɪ, læ-] *n* : lamé *m*
lame duck *n* : persona *f* sin poder ⟨a lame-duck President : un presidente saliente⟩
lamely ['leɪmli] *adv* : sin convicción
lameness ['leɪmnəs] *n* **1** : cojera *f*, renquera *f* **2** : falta *f* de convicción, debilidad *f*, pobreza *f* ⟨the lameness of her response : la pobreza de su respuesta⟩
lament[1] [lə'mɛnt] *vt* **1** MOURN : llorar, llorar por **2** DEPLORE : lamentar, deplorar — *vi* : llorar
lament[2] *n* : lamento *m*
lamentable ['læməntəbəl, lə'mɛntə-] *adj* : lamentable, deplorable — **lamentably** [-bli] *adv*
lamentation [ˌlæmən'teɪʃən] *n* : lamentación *f*, lamento *m*
laminate[1] ['læməˌneɪt] *vt* **-nated; -nating** : laminar
laminate[2] ['læmənət] *n* : laminado *m*
laminated ['læməˌneɪţəd] *adj* : laminado
lamp ['læmp] *n* : lámpara *f*
lampoon[1] [læm'puːn] *vt* : satirizar
lampoon[2] *n* : sátira *f*
lamprey ['læmpri] *n, pl* **-preys** : lamprea *f*
lance[1] ['lænts] *vt* **lanced; lancing** : abrir con lanceta, sajar
lance[2] *n* : lanza *f*
lance corporal *n* : cabo *m* interino, soldado *m* de primera clase
lancet ['læntsət] *n* : lanceta *f*
land[1] ['lænd] *vt* **1** : desembarcar (pasajeros de un barco), hacer aterrizar (un avión) **2** CATCH : pescar, sacar (un pez) del agua **3** GAIN, SECURE : conseguir, ganar ⟨to land a job : conseguir empleo⟩ **4** DELIVER : dar, asestar ⟨he landed a punch : asestó un puñetazo⟩ — *vi* **1** : aterrizar, tomar tierra, atracar ⟨the plane just landed : el avión acaba de aterrizar⟩ ⟨the ship landed an hour ago : el barco atracó hace una hora⟩ **2** ALIGHT : posarse, aterrizar ⟨to land on one's feet : caer de pie⟩
land[2] *n* **1** GROUND : tierra *f* ⟨dry land : tierra firme⟩ **2** TERRAIN : terreno *m* **3** NATION : país *m*, nación *f* **4** DOMAIN : mundo *m*, dominio *m* ⟨the land of dreams : el mundo de los sueños⟩
landfill ['lændˌfɪl] *n* : vertedero *m* (de basuras)
landing ['lændɪŋ] *n* **1** : aterrizaje *m* (de aviones), desembarco *m* (de barcos) **2** : descansillo *m* (de una escalera)
landing field *n* : campo *m* de aterrizaje
landing strip → **airstrip**
landlady ['lændˌleɪdi] *n, pl* **-dies** : casera *f*, dueña *f*, arrendadora *f*
landless ['lændləs] *adj* : sin tierra
landlocked ['lændˌlɑkt] *adj* : sin salida al mar
landlord ['lændˌlɔrd] *n* : dueño *m*, casero *m*, arrendador *m*
landlubber ['lændˌlʌbər] *n* : marinero *m* de agua dulce
landmark ['lændˌmɑrk] *n* **1** : señal *f* (geográfica), punto *m* de referencia **2** MILESTONE : hito *m* ⟨a landmark in our history : un hito en nuestra historia⟩ **3** MONUMENT : monumento *m* histórico
landowner ['lændˌoːnər] *n* : hacendado *m*, -da *f*; terrateniente *mf*
landscape[1] ['lændˌskeɪp] *vt* **-scaped; -scaping** : ajardinar
landscape[2] *n* : paisaje *m*
landslide ['lændˌslaɪd] *n* **1** : desprendimiento *m* de tierras, derrumbe *m* **2** **landslide victory** : victoria *f* arrolladora
landward ['lændwərd] *adv* : en dirección de la tierra, hacia tierra
lane ['leɪn] *n* **1** PATH, WAY : camino *m*, sendero *m* **2** : carril *m* (de una carretera)
language ['læŋgwɪʤ] *n* **1** : idioma *m*, lengua *f* ⟨the English language : el idioma inglés⟩ **2** : lenguaje *m* ⟨body language : lenguaje corporal⟩
languid ['læŋgwɪd] *adj* : lánguido — **languidly** *adv*
languish ['læŋgwɪʃ] *vi* **1** WEAKEN : languidecer, debilitarse **2** PINE : consumirse, suspirar (por) ⟨to languish for love : suspirar por el amor⟩ ⟨he languished in prison : estuvo pudriéndose en la cárcel⟩
languor ['læŋgər] *n* : languidez *f*
languorous ['læŋgərəs] *adj* : lánguido — **languorously** *adv*
lank ['læŋk] *adj* **1** THIN : delgado, larguirucho *fam* **2** LIMP : lacio
lanky ['læŋki] *adj* **lankier; -est** : delgado, larguirucho *fam*
lanolin ['lænəlɪn] *n* : lanolina *f*
lantern ['læntərn] *n* : linterna *f*, farol *m*
Laotian [leɪ'oːʃən, 'laʊʃən] *n* : laosiano *m*, -na *f* — **Laotian** *adj*
lap[1] ['læp] *v* **lapped; lapping** *vt* **1** FOLD : plegar, doblar **2** WRAP : envolver **3** : lamer, besar ⟨waves were lapping the shore : las olas lamían la orilla⟩ **4 to lap up** : beber a lengüetadas (como un gato) — *vi* OVERLAP : traslaparse
lap[2] *n* **1** : falda *f*, regazo *m* (del cuerpo) **2** OVERLAP : traslapo *m* **3** : vuelta *f* (en deportes) **4** STAGE : etapa *f* (de un viaje)
lapdog ['læpˌdɔg] *n* : perro *m* faldero
lapel [lə'pɛl] *n* : solapa *f*
Lapp ['læp] *n* : lapón *m*, -pona *f* — **Lapp** *adj*
lapse[1] ['læps] *vi* **lapsed; lapsing 1** FALL, SLIP : caer ⟨to lapse into bad habits : caer en malos hábitos⟩ ⟨to lapse into

unconsciousness : perder el conocimiento⟩ ⟨to lapse into silence : quedarse callado⟩ **2** FADE : decaer, desvanecerse ⟨her dedication lapsed : su dedicación se desvaneció⟩ **3** CEASE : cancelarse, perderse **4** ELAPSE : transcurrir, pasar **5** EXPIRE : caducar

lapse[2] *n* **1** SLIP : lapsus *m*, desliz *m*, falla *f* ⟨a lapse of memory : una falla de memoria⟩ **2** INTERVAL : lapso *m*, intervalo *m*, período *m* **3** EXPIRATION : caducidad *f*

laptop[1] [ˈlæpˌtɑp] *adj* : portátil, laptop

laptop[2] *n* : laptop *m*

larboard [ˈlɑrbərd] *n* : babor *m*

larcenous [ˈlɑrsənəs] *adj* : de robo

larceny [ˈlɑrsəni] *n, pl* **-nies** : robo *m*, hurto *m*

larch [ˈlɑrʧ] *n* : alerce *f*

lard [ˈlɑrd] *n* : manteca *f* de cerdo

larder [ˈlɑrdər] *n* : despensa *f*, alacena *f*

large [ˈlɑrʤ] *adj* **larger; largest** **1** BIG : grande **2** COMPREHENSIVE : amplio, extenso **3 by and large** : por lo general

largely [ˈlɑrʤli] *adv* : en gran parte, en su mayoría

largeness [ˈlɑrʤnəs] *n* : lo grande

largesse *or* **largess** [lɑrˈʒɛs, -ˈʤɛs] *n* : generosidad *f*, largueza *f*

lariat [ˈlæriət] *n* : lazo *m*

lark [ˈlɑrk] *n* **1** FUN : diversión *f* ⟨what a lark! : ¡qué divertido!⟩ **2** : alondra *f* (pájaro)

larva [ˈlɑrvə] *n, pl* **-vae** [-ˌvi:, -ˌvaɪ] : larva *f* — **larval** [-vəl] *adj*

laryngitis [ˌlærənˈʤaɪţəs] *n* : laringitis *f*

larynx [ˈlærɪŋks] *n, pl* **-rynges** [ləˈrɪnˌʤi:z] *or* **-ynxes** [ˈlærɪŋksəz] : laringe *f*

lasagna [ləˈzɑnjə] *n* : lasaña *f*

lascivious [ləˈsɪviəs] *adj* : lascivo

lasciviousness [ləˈsɪviəsnəs] *n* : lascivia *f*, lujuria *f*

laser [ˈleɪzər] *n* : láser *m*

laser disc *n* : disco *m* láser

lash[1] [ˈlæʃ] *vt* **1** WHIP : azotar **2** BIND : atar, amarrar

lash[2] *n* **1** WHIP : látigo *m* **2** STROKE : latigazo *m* **3** EYELASH : pestaña *f*

lass [ˈlæs] *or* **lassie** [ˈlæsi] *n* : muchacha *f*, chica *f*

lassitude [ˈlæsəˌtu:d, -ˌtju:d] *n* : lasitud *f*

lasso[1] [ˈlæˌso:, læˈsu:] *vt* : lazar

lasso[2] *n, pl* **-sos** *or* **-soes** : lazo *m*, reata *f Mex*

last[1] [ˈlæst] *vi* **1** CONTINUE : durar ⟨how long will it last? : ¿cuánto durará?⟩ **2** ENDURE : aguantar, durar **3** SURVIVE : durar, sobrevivir **4** SUFFICE : durar, bastar — *vt* **1** : durar ⟨it will last a lifetime : durará toda la vida⟩ **2 to last out** : aguantar

last[2] *adv* **1** : en último lugar, al último ⟨we came in last : llegamos en último lugar⟩ **2** : por última vez, la última vez ⟨I saw him last in Bogota : lo vi por última vez en Bogotá⟩ **3** FINALLY : por último, en conclusión

last[3] *adj* **1** FINAL : último, final **2** PREVIOUS : pasado ⟨last year : el año pasado⟩

last[4] *n* **1** : el último, la última, lo último ⟨at last : por fin, al fin, finalmente⟩ **2** : horma *f* (de zapatero)

lasting [ˈlæstɪŋ] *adj* : perdurable, duradero, estable

lastly [ˈlæstli] *adv* : por último, finalmente

latch[1] [ˈlæʧ] *vt* : cerrar con picaporte

latch[2] *n* : picaporte *m*, pestillo *m*, pasador *m*

late[1] [ˈleɪt] *adv* **later; latest** **1** : tarde ⟨to arrive late : llegar tarde⟩ ⟨to sleep late : dormir hasta tarde⟩ **2** : a última hora, a finales ⟨late in the month : a finales del mes⟩ **3** RECENTLY : recién, últimamente ⟨as late as last year : todavía en el año pasado⟩

late[2] *adj* **later; latest** **1** TARDY : tardío, de retraso ⟨to be late : llegar tarde⟩ **2** : avanzado ⟨because of the late hour : a causa de la hora avanzada⟩ **3** DECEASED : difunto, fallecido **4** RECENT : reciente, último ⟨our late quarrel : nuestra última pelea⟩

latecomer [ˈleɪtˌkʌmər] *n* : rezagado *m*, -da *f*

lately [ˈleɪtli] *adv* : recientemente, últimamente

lateness [ˈleɪtnəs] *n* **1** DELAY : retraso *m*, atraso *m*, tardanza *f* **2** : lo avanzado (de la hora)

latent [ˈleɪtənt] *adj* : latente — **latently** *adv*

lateral [ˈlæţərəl] *adj* : lateral — **laterally** *adv*

latex [ˈleɪˌtɛks] *n, pl* **-tices** [ˈleɪţəˌsi:z, ˈlæţə-] *or* **-texes** : látex *m*

lath [ˈlæθ, ˈlæð] *n, pl* **laths** *or* **lath** : listón *m*

lathe [ˈleɪð] *n* : torno *m*

lather[1] [ˈlæðər] *vt* : enjabonar — *vi* : espumar, hacer espuma

lather[2] *n* **1** : espuma *f* (de jabón) **2** : sudor *m* (de caballo) **3 to get into a lather** : ponerse histérico

Latin[1] *adj* : latino

Latin[2] *n* **1** : latín *m* (idioma) **2** → **Latin American**

Latin–American [ˈlætənəˈmrikən] *adj* : latinoamericano

Latin American *n* : latinoamericano *m*, -na *f*

latitude [ˈlæţəˌtu:d, -ˌtju:d] *n* : latitud *f*

latrine [ləˈtri:n] *n* : letrina *f*

latte [ˈlɑˌteɪ] *n* : café *m* con leche

latter[1] [ˈlæţər] *adj* **1** SECOND : segundo **2** LAST : último

latter[2] *pron* **the latter** : éste, ésta, éstos *pl*, éstas *pl*

lattice [ˈlæţəs] *n* : enrejado *m*, celosía *f*

Latvian [ˈlætviən] *n* : letón *m*, -tona *f* — **Latvian** *adj*

laud[1] [ˈlɔd] *vt* : alabar, loar

laud[2] *n* : alabanza *f*, loa *f*

laudable [ˈlɔdəbəl] *adj* : loable — **laudably** [-bli] *adv*
laugh[1] [ˈlæf] *vi* : reír, reírse
laugh[2] *n* **1** LAUGHTER : risa *f* **2** JOKE : chiste *m*, broma *f* ⟨he did it for a laugh : lo hizo en broma, lo hizo para divertirse⟩
laughable [ˈlæfəbəl] *adj* : risible, de risa
laughingstock [ˈlæfɪŋˌstɑk] *n* : hazmerreír *m*
laughter [ˈlæftər] *n* : risa *f*, risas *fpl*
launch[1] [ˈlɔntʃ] *vt* **1** HURL : lanzar **2** : botar (un barco) **3** START : iniciar, empezar
launch[2] *n* **1** : lancha *f* (bote) **2** LAUNCHING : lanzamiento *m*
launder [ˈlɔndər] *vt* **1** : lavar y planchar (ropa) **2** : blanquear, lavar (dinero)
launderer [ˈlɔndərər] *n* : lavandero *m*, -ra *f*
laundress [ˈlɔndrəs] *n* : lavandera *f*
laundry [ˈlɔndri] *n, pl* **laundries** **1** : ropa *f* sucia, ropa *f* para lavar ⟨to do the laundry : lavar la ropa⟩ **2** : lavandería *f* (servicio de lavar)
laureate [ˈlɔriət] *n* : laureado *m*, -da *f* ⟨poet laureate : poeta laureado⟩
laurel [ˈlɔrəl] *n* **1** : laurel *m* (planta) **2** **laurels** *npl* : laureles *mpl* ⟨to rest on one's laurels : dormirse uno en sus laureles⟩
lava [ˈlɑvə, ˈlæ-] *n* : lava *f*
lavatory [ˈlævəˌtori] *n, pl* **-ries** : baño *m*, cuarto *m* de baño
lavender [ˈlævəndər] *n* : lavanda *f*, espliego *m*
lavish[1] [ˈlævɪʃ] *vt* : prodigar (a), colmar (de)
lavish[2] *adj* **1** EXTRAVAGANT : pródigo, generoso, derrochador **2** ABUNDANT : abundante **3** LUXURIOUS : lujoso, espléndido
lavishly [ˈlævɪʃli] *adv* : con generosidad, espléndidamente ⟨to live lavishly : vivir a lo grande⟩
lavishness [ˈlævɪʃnəs] *n* : generosidad *f*, esplendidez *f*
law [ˈlɔ] *n* **1** : ley *f* ⟨to break the law : violar la ley⟩ **2** : derecho *m* ⟨criminal law : derecho criminal⟩ **3** : abogacía *f* ⟨to practice law : ejercer la abogacía⟩
law–abiding [ˈlɔəˌbaɪdɪŋ] *adj* : observante de la ley
lawbreaker [ˈlɔˌbreɪkər] *n* : infractor *m*, -tora *f* de la ley
lawful [ˈlɔfəl] *adj* : legal, legítimo, lícito — **lawfully** *adv*
lawgiver [ˈlɔˌgɪvər] *n* : legislador *m*, -dora *f*
lawless [ˈlɔləs] *adj* : anárquico, ingobernable — **lawlessly** *adv*
lawlessness [ˈlɔləsnəs] *n* : anarquía *f*, desorden *m*
lawmaker [ˈlɔˌmeɪkər] *n* : legislador *m*, -dora *f*
lawman [ˈlɔmən] *n, pl* **-men** [-mən, -ˌmɛn] : agente *m* del orden
lawn [ˈlɔn] *n* : césped *m*, pasto *m*
lawn mower *n* : cortadora *f* de césped
lawsuit [ˈlɔˌsuːt] *n* : pleito *m*, litigio *m*, demanda *f*
lawyer [ˈlɔɪər, ˈlɔjər] *n* : abogado *m*, -da *f*
lax [ˈlæks] *adj* : laxo, relajado — **laxly** *adv*
laxative [ˈlæksət̬ɪv] *n* : laxante *m*
laxity [ˈlæksət̬i] *n* : relajación *f*, descuido *m*, falta *f* de rigor
lay[1] [ˈleɪ] *vt* **laid** [ˈleɪd]; **laying** **1** PLACE, PUT : poner, colocar ⟨she laid it on the table : lo puso en la mesa⟩ ⟨to lay eggs : poner huevos⟩ **2** : hacer ⟨to lay a bet : hacer una apuesta⟩ **3** IMPOSE : imponer ⟨to lay a tax : imponer un impuesto⟩ ⟨to lay the blame on : echarle la culpa a⟩ **4** **to lay out** PRESENT : presentar, exponer ⟨he laid out his plan : presentó su proyecto⟩ **5** **to lay out** DESIGN : diseñar (el trazado de)
lay[2] → **lie**[1]
lay[3] *adj* SECULAR : laico, lego
lay[4] *n* **1** : disposición *f*, configuración *f* ⟨the lay of the land : la configuración del terreno⟩ **2** BALLAD : romance *m*, balada *f*
layer [ˈleɪər] *n* **1** : capa *f* (de pintura, etc.), estrato *m* (de roca) **2** : gallina *f* ponedora
layman [ˈleɪmən] *n, pl* **-men** [-mən, -ˌmɛn] : laico *m*, lego *m*
layoff [ˈleɪˌɔf] *n* : despido *m*
lay off *vt* : despedir
layout [ˈleɪˌaʊt] *n* : disposición *f*, distribución *f* (de una casa, etc.), trazado *m* (de una ciudad)
lay up *vt* **1** STORE : guardar, almacenar **2** **to be laid up** : estar enfermo, tener que guardar cama
laywoman [ˈleɪˌwʊmən] *n, pl* **-women** [-ˌwɪmən] : laica *f*, lega *f*
laziness [ˈleɪzinəs] *n* : pereza *f*, flojera *f*
lazy [ˈleɪzi] *adj* **-zier**; **-est** : perezoso, holgazán — **lazily** [ˈleɪzəli] *adv*
leach [ˈliːtʃ] *vt* : filtrar
lead[1] [ˈliːd] *vt* **led** [ˈlɛd]; **leading** **1** GUIDE : conducir, llevar, guiar **2** DIRECT : dirigir **3** HEAD : encabezar, ir al frente de **4** **to lead to** : resultar en, llevar a ⟨it only leads to trouble : sólo resulta en problemas⟩
lead[2] *n* : delantera *f*, primer lugar *m* ⟨to take the lead : tomar la delantera⟩
lead[3] [ˈlɛd] *n* **1** : plomo *m* (metal) **2** : mina *f* (de lápiz) **3** **lead poisoning** : saturnismo *m*
leaden [ˈlɛdən] *adj* **1** : plomizo ⟨a leaden sky : un ciel plomizo⟩ **2** HEAVY : pesado
leader [ˈliːdər] *n* : jefe *m*, -fa *f*; líder *mf*; dirigente *mf*; gobernante *mf*
leadership [ˈliːdərˌʃɪp] *n* : mando *m*, dirección *f*
leaf[1] [ˈliːf] *vi* **1** : echar hojas (dícese de un árbol) **2** **to leaf through** : hojear (un libro)

leaf[2] *n, pl* **leaves** [ˈliːvz] **1** : hoja *f* (de plantas o libros) **2 to turn over a new leaf** : hacer borrón y cuenta nueva
leafless [ˈliːfləs] *adj* : sin hojas, pelado
leaflet [ˈliːflət] *n* : folleto *m*
leafy [ˈliːfi] *adj* **leafier; -est** : frondoso
league[1] [ˈliːg] *v* **leagued; leaguing** *vt* : aliar, unir — *vi* : aliarse, unirse
league[2] *n* **1** : legua *f* (medida de distancia) **2** ASSOCIATION : alianza *f*, sociedad *f*, liga *f*
leak[1] [ˈliːk] *vt* **1** : perder, dejar escapar (un líquido o un gas) **2** : filtrar (información) — *vi* **1** : gotear, escaparse, fugarse (dícese de un líquido o un gas) **2** : hacer agua (dícese de un bote) **3** : filtrarse, divulgarse (dícese de información)
leak[2] *n* **1** HOLE : agujero *m* (en recipientes), gotera *f* (en un tejado) **2** ESCAPE : fuga *f*, escape *m* **3** : filtración *f* (de información)
leakage [ˈliːkɪʤ] *n* : escape *m*, fuga *f*
leaky [ˈliːki] *adj* **leakier; -est** : agujereado (dícese de un recipiente), que hace agua (dícese de un bote), con goteras (dícese de un tejado)
lean[1] [ˈliːn] *vi* **1** BEND : inclinarse, ladearse **2** RECLINE : reclinarse **3** RELY : apoyarse (en), depender (de) **4** INCLINE, TEND : inclinarse, tender — *vt* : apoyar
lean[2] *adj* **1** THIN : delgado, flaco **2** : sin grasa, magro (dícese de la carne)
leanness [ˈliːnnəs] *n* : delgadez *f*
lean–to [ˈliːnˌtuː] *n* : cobertizo *m*
leap[1] [ˈliːp] *vi* **leaped** [ˈliːpt, ˈlɛpt] *or* **leapt; leaping** : saltar, brincar
leap[2] *n* : salto *m*, brinco *m*
leap year *n* : año *m* bisiesto
learn [ˈlərn] *vt* **1** : aprender ⟨to learn to sing : aprender a cantar⟩ **2** MEMORIZE : aprender de memoria **3** DISCOVER : saber, enterarse de — *vi* **1** : aprender ⟨to learn from experience : aprender por experiencia⟩ **2** FIND OUT : enterarse, saber
learned [ˈlərnəd] *adj* : erudito
learner [ˈlərnər] *n* : principiante *mf*, estudiante *mf*
learning [ˈlərnɪŋ] *n* : erudición *f*, saber *m*
lease[1] [ˈliːs] *vt* **leased; leasing** : arrendar
lease[2] *n* : contrato *m* de arrendamiento
leash[1] [ˈliːʃ] *vt* : atraillar (un animal)
leash[2] *n* : traílla *f*
least[1] [ˈliːst] *adv* : menos ⟨when least expected : cuando menos se espera⟩
least[2] *adj* (*superlative of* **little**) : menor, más mínimo
least[3] *n* **1** : lo menos ⟨at least : por lo menos⟩ **2 to say the least** : por no decir más
leather [ˈlɛðər] *n* : cuero *m*
leathery [ˈlɛðəri] *adj* : curtido (dícese de la piel), correoso (dícese de la carne)
leave[1] [ˈliːv] *v* **left** [ˈlɛft]; **leaving** *vt* **1** BEQUEATH : dejar, legar **2** DEPART : dejar, salir(se) de **3** ABANDON : abandonar, dejar **4** FORGET : dejar, olvidarse de ⟨I left the books at the library : dejé los libros en la biblioteca⟩ **5 to be left** : quedar ⟨it's all I have left : es todo lo que me queda⟩ **6 to be left over** : sobrar **7 to leave out** : omitir, excluir — *vi* : irse, salir, partir, marcharse ⟨she left yesterday morning : se fue ayer por la mañana⟩
leave[2] *n* **1** PERMISSION : permiso *m* ⟨by your leave : con su permiso⟩ **2** *or* **leave of absence** : permiso *m*, licencia *f* ⟨maternity leave : licencia por maternidad⟩ **3 to take one's leave** : despedirse
leaven [ˈlɛvən] *n* : levadura *f*
leaves → **leaf**[2]
leaving [ˈliːvɪŋ] *n* **1** : salida *f*, partida *f* **2 leavings** *npl* : restos *mpl*, sobras *fpl*
Lebanese [ˌlɛbəˈniːz, -ˈniːs] *n* : libanés *m*, -nesa *f* — **Lebanese** *adj*
lecherous [ˈlɛʧərəs] *adj* : lascivo, libidinoso — **lecherously** *adv*
lechery [ˈlɛʧəri] *n* : lascivia *f*, lujuria *f*
lecture[1] [ˈlɛkʧər] *v* **-tured; -turing** *vi* : dar clase, dictar clase, dar una conferencia — *vt* SCOLD : sermonear, echar una reprimenda a, regañar
lecture[2] *n* **1** : conferencia *f* **2** REPRIMAND : reprimenda *f*
lecturer [ˈlɛkʧərər] *n* **1** SPEAKER : conferenciante *mf* **2** TEACHER : profesor *m*, -sora *f*
led → **lead**[1]
ledge [ˈlɛʤ] *n* : repisa *f* (de una pared), antepecho *m* (de una ventana), saliente *m* (de una montaña)
ledger [ˈlɛʤər] *n* : libro *m* mayor, libro *m* de contabilidad
lee[1] [ˈliː] *adj* : de sotavento
lee[2] *n* : sotavento *m*
leech [ˈliːʧ] *n* : sanguijuela *f*
leek [ˈliːk] *n* : puerro *m*
leer[1] [ˈlɪr] *vi* : mirar con lascivia
leer[2] *n* : mirada *f* lasciva
leery [ˈlɪri] *adj* : receloso
lees [ˈliːz] *npl* : posos *mpl*, heces *fpl*
leeward[1] [ˈliːwərd, ˈluːərd] *adj* : de sotavento
leeward[2] *n* : sotavento *m*
leeway [ˈliːˌweɪ] *n* : libertad *f*, margen *m*
left[1] [ˈlɛft] *adv* : hacia la izquierda
left[2] → **leave**[1]
left[3] *adj* : izquierdo
left[4] *n* : izquierda *f* ⟨on the left : a la izquierda⟩
left–hand [ˈlɛftˈhænd] *adj* **1** : de la izquierda **2** → **left–handed**
left–handed [ˈlɛftˈhændəd] *adj* **1** : zurdo (dícese de una persona) **2** : con doble sentido ⟨a left-handed compliment : un cumplido a medias⟩
leftist [ˈlɛftɪst] *n* : izquierdista *mf* — **leftist** *adj*
leftover [ˈlɛftˌoːvər] *adj* : sobrante, que sobra

leftovers [ˈlɛftˌoːvərz] *npl* : restos *mpl*, sobras *fpl*
left wing *n* **the left wing** : la izquierda
left–winger [ˈlɛftˈwɪŋər] *n* : izquierdista *mf*
leg [ˈlɛg] *n* **1** : pierna *f* (de una persona, de carne, de ropa), pata *f* (de un animal, de muebles) **2** STAGE : etapa *f* (de un viaje), vuelta *f* (de una carrera)
legacy [ˈlɛgəsi] *n, pl* **-cies** : legado *m*, herencia *f*
legal [ˈliːgəl] *adj* **1** : legal, jurídico ⟨legal advisor : asesor jurídico⟩ ⟨the legal profession : la abogacía⟩ **2** LAWFUL : legítimo, legal
legalistic [ˌliːgəˈlɪstɪk] *adj* : legalista
legality [liˈgæləṭi] *n, pl* **-ties** : legalidad *f*
legalize [ˈliːgəˌlaɪz] *vt* **-ized; -izing** : legalizar
legally [ˈliːgəli] *adv* : legalmente
legate [ˈlɛgət] *n* : legado *m*
legation [lɪˈgeɪʃən] *n* : legación *f*
legend [ˈlɛʤənd] *n* **1** STORY : leyenda *f* **2** INSCRIPTION : leyenda *f*, inscripción *f* **3** : signos *mpl* convencionales (en un mapa)
legendary [ˈlɛʤənˌdɛri] *adj* : legendario
legerdemain [ˌlɛʤərdəˈmeɪn] → **sleight of hand**
leggings [ˈlɛgɪŋz, ˈlɛgənz] *npl* : mallas *fpl*
legibility [ˌlɛʤəˈbɪləṭi] *n* : legibilidad *f*
legible [ˈlɛʤəbəl] *adj* : legible
legibly [ˈlɛʤəbli] *adv* : de manera legible
legion [ˈliːʤən] *n* : legión *f*
legionnaire [ˌliːʤəˈnær] *n* : legionario *m*, -ria *f*
legislate [ˈlɛʤəsˌleɪt] *vi* **-lated; -lating** : legislar
legislation [ˌlɛʤəsˈleɪʃən] *n* : legislación *f*
legislative [ˈlɛʤəsˌleɪṭɪv] *adj* : legislativo, legislador
legislator [ˈlɛʤəsˌleɪṭər] *n* : legislador *m*, -dora *f*
legislature [ˈlɛʤəsˌleɪʧər] *n* : asamblea *f* legislativa
legitimacy [lɪˈʤɪṭəməsi] *n* : legitimidad *f*
legitimate [lɪˈʤɪṭəmət] *adj* **1** VALID : legítimo, válido, justificado **2** LAWFUL : legítimo, legal
legitimately [lɪˈʤɪṭəmətli] *adv* : legítimamente
legitimize [lɪˈʤɪṭəˌmaɪz] *vt* **-mized; -mizing** : legitimar, hacer legítimo
legume [ˈlɛˌgjuːm, lɪˈgjuːm] *n* : legumbre *f*
leisure [ˈliːʒər, ˈlɛ-] *n* **1** : ocio *m*, tiempo *m* libre ⟨a life of leisure : una vida de ocio⟩ **2 to take one's leisure** : reposar **3 at your leisure** : cuando te venga bien, cuando tengas tiempo
leisurely [ˈliːʒərli, ˈlɛ-] *adj & adv* : lento, sin prisas
lemming [ˈlɛmɪŋ] *n* : lemming *m*
lemon [ˈlɛmən] *n* : limón *m*
lemonade [ˌlɛməˈneɪd] *n* : limonada *f*
lemony [ˈlɛməni] *adj* : a limón
lend [ˈlɛnd] *vt* **lent** [ˈlɛnt]; **lending 1** : prestar ⟨to lend money : prestar dinero⟩ **2** GIVE : dar ⟨it lends force to his criticism : da fuerza a su crítica⟩ **3 to lend oneself to** : prestarse a
length [ˈlɛŋkθ] *n* **1** : longitud *f*, largo *m* ⟨10 feet in length : 10 pies de largo⟩ **2** DURATION : duración *f* **3** : trozo *m* (de madera), corte *m* (de tela) **4 to go to any lengths** : hacer todo lo posible **5 at ~** : extensamente ⟨to speak at length : hablar largo y tendido⟩
lengthen [ˈlɛŋkθən] *vt* **1** : alargar ⟨can they lengthen the dress? : ¿se puede alargar el vestido?⟩ **2** EXTEND, PROLONG : prolongar, extender — *vi* : alargarse, crecer ⟨the days are lengthening : los días están creciendo⟩
lengthways [ˈlɛŋkθˌweɪz] → **lengthwise**
lengthwise [ˈlɛŋkθˌwaɪz] *adv* : a lo largo, longitudinalmente
lengthy [ˈlɛŋkθi] *adj* **lengthier; -est 1** OVERLONG : largo y pesado **2** EXTENDED : prolongado, largo
leniency [ˈliːniəntsi] *n, pl* **-cies** : lenidad *f*, indulgencia *f*
lenient [ˈliːniənt] *adj* : indulgente, poco severo
leniently [ˈliːniəntli] *adv* : con lenidad, con indulgencia
lens [ˈlɛnz] *n* **1** : cristalino *m* (del ojo) **2** : lente *mf* (de un instrumento o una cámara) **3** → **contact lens**
lent → **lend**
Lent [ˈlɛnt] *n* : Cuaresma *f*
lentil [ˈlɛntəl] *n* : lenteja *f*
Leo [ˈliːoː] *n* : Leo *mf*
leopard [ˈlɛpərd] *n* : leopardo *m*
leotard [ˈliːəˌtɑrd] *n* : leotardo *m*, malla *f*
leper [ˈlɛpər] *n* : leproso *m*, -sa *f*
leprechaun [ˈlɛprəˌkɑn] *n* : duende *m* (irlandés)
leprosy [ˈlɛprəsi] *n* : lepra *f* — **leprous** [ˈlɛprəs] *adj*
lesbian[1] [ˈlɛzbiən] *adj* : lesbiano
lesbian[2] *n* : lesbiana *f*
lesbianism [ˈlɛzbiəˌnɪzəm] *n* : lesbianismo *m*
lesion [ˈliːʒən] *n* : lesión *f*
less[1] [ˈlɛs] *adv* (*comparative of* **little**[1]) : menos ⟨the less you know, the better : cuanto menos sepas, mejor⟩ ⟨less and less : cada vez menos⟩
less[2] *adj* (*comparative of* **little**[2]) : menos ⟨less than three : menos de tres⟩ ⟨less money : menos dinero⟩ ⟨nothing less than perfection : nada menos que la perfección⟩
less[3] *pron* : menos ⟨I'm earning less : estoy ganando menos⟩
less[4] *prep* : menos ⟨one month less two days : un mes menos dos días⟩
lessee [lɛˈsiː] *n* : arrendatario *m*, -ria *f*
lessen [ˈlɛsən] *vt* : disminuir, reducir — *vi* : disminuir, reducirse

lesser ['lɛsər] *adj* : menor ⟨to a lesser degree : en menor grado⟩

lesson ['lɛsən] *n* **1** CLASS : clase *f*, curso *m* **2** : lección *f* ⟨the lessons of history : las lecciones de la historia⟩

lessor ['lɛˌsɔr, lˈsɔr] *n* : arrendador *m*, -dora *f*

lest ['lɛst] *conj* : para (que) no ⟨lest we forget : para que no olvidemos⟩

let ['lɛt] *vt* **let; letting** **1** ALLOW : dejar, permitir ⟨let me see it : déjame verlo⟩ **2** MAKE : hacer ⟨let me know : házmelo saber, avísame⟩ ⟨let them wait : que esperen, haz que esperen⟩ **3** RENT : alquilar **4** (*used in the first person plural imperative*) ⟨let's go! : ¡vamos!, ¡vámonos!⟩ ⟨let us pray : oremos⟩ **5 to let down** DISAPPOINT : fallar **6 to let off** FORGIVE : perdonar **7 to let out** REVEAL : revelar **8 to let up** ABATE : amainar, disminuir ⟨the pace never lets up : el ritmo nunca disminuye⟩

letdown *n* : chasco *m*, decepción *f*

lethal ['li:θəl] *adj* : letal — **lethally** *adv*

lethargic [lɪ'θɑrʤɪk] *adj* : letárgico

lethargy ['lɛθərʤi] *n* : letargo *m*

let on *vi* **1** ADMIT : reconocer ⟨don't let on! : ¡no digas nada!⟩ **2** PRETEND : fingir

let's ['lɛts] (*contraction of* **let us**) → **let**

letter[1] ['lɛt̬ər] *vt* : marcar con letras, inscribir letras en

letter[2] *n* **1** : letra *f* (del alfabeto) **2** : carta *f* ⟨a letter to my mother : una carta a mi madre⟩ **3 letters** *npl* ARTS : letras *fpl* **4 to the letter** : al pie de la letra

lettering ['lɛt̬ərɪŋ] *n* : letra *f*

lettuce ['lɛt̬əs] *n* : lechuga *f*

leukemia [lu:'ki:miə] *n* : leucemia *f*

levee ['lɛvi] *n* : dique *m*

level[1] ['lɛvəl] *vt* **-eled** *or* **-elled; -eling** *or* **-elling** **1** FLATTEN : nivelar, aplanar **2** AIM : apuntar (una pistola), dirigir (una acusación) **3** RAZE : rasar, arrasar

level[2] *adj* **1** EVEN : llano, plano, parejo **2** CALM : tranquilo ⟨to keep a level head : no perder la cabeza⟩

level[3] *n* : nivel *m*

leveler ['lɛvələr] *n* : nivelador *m*, -dora *f*

levelheaded ['lɛvəl'hɛdəd] *adj* : sensato, equilibrado

levelly ['lɛvəli] *adv* CALMLY : con ecuanimidad *f*, con calma

levelness ['lɛvəlnəs] *n* : uniformidad *f*

lever ['lɛvər, 'li:-] *n* : palanca *f*

leverage ['lɛvərɪʤ, 'li:-] *n* **1** : apalancamiento *m* (en física) **2** INFLUENCE : influencia *f*, palanca *f fam*

leviathan [lɪ'vaɪəθən] *n* : leviatán *m*, gigante *m*

levity ['lɛvət̬i] *n* : ligereza *f*, frivolidad *f*

levy[1] ['lɛvi] *vt* **levied; levying** **1** IMPOSE : imponer, exigir, gravar (un impuesto) **2** COLLECT : recaudar (un impuesto)

levy[2] *n, pl* **levies** : impuesto *m*, gravamen *m*

lewd ['lu:d] *adj* : lascivo — **lewdly** *adv*

lewdness ['lu:dnəs] *n* : lascivia *f*

lexical ['lɛksikəl] *adj* : léxico

lexicographer [ˌlɛksə'kɑgrəfər] *n* : lexicógrafo *m*, -fa *f*

lexicographical [ˌlɛksəko'græfɪkəl] *or* **lexicographic** [-'græfɪk] *adj* : lexicográfico

lexicography [ˌlɛksə'kɑgrəfi] *n* : lexicografía *f*

lexicon ['lɛksɪˌkɑn] *n, pl* **-ica** [-kə] *or* **-icons** : léxico *m*, lexicón *m*

liability [ˌlaɪə'bɪlət̬i] *n, pl* **-ties** **1** RESPONSIBILITY : responsabilidad *f* **2** SUSCEPTIBILITY : propensión *f* **3** DRAWBACK : desventaja *f* **4 liabilities** *npl* DEBTS : deudas *fpl*, pasivo *m*

liable ['laɪəbəl] *adj* **1** RESPONSIBLE : responsable **2** SUSCEPTIBLE : propenso **3** PROBABLE : probable ⟨it's liable to happen : es probable que suceda⟩

liaison ['li:əˌzɑn, li'eɪ-] *n* **1** CONNECTION : enlace *m*, relación *f* **2** AFFAIR : amorío *m*, aventura *f*

liar ['laɪər] *n* : mentiroso *m*, -sa *f*; embustero *m*, -ra *f*

libel[1] ['laɪbəl] *vt* **-beled** *or* **-belled; -beling** *or* **-belling** : difamar, calumniar

libel[2] *n* : difamación *f*, calumnia *f*

libeler ['laɪbələr] *n* : difamador *m*, -dora *f*; calumniador *m*, -dora *f*; libelista *mf*

libelous *or* **libellous** ['laɪbələs] *adj* : difamatorio, calumnioso, injurioso

liberal[1] ['lɪbrəl, 'lɪbərəl] *adj* **1** TOLERANT : liberal, tolerante **2** GENEROUS : generoso **3** ABUNDANT : abundante **4 liberal arts** : humanidades *fpl*, artes *fpl* liberales

liberal[2] *n* : liberal *mf*

liberalism ['lɪbrəˌlɪzəm, 'lɪbərə-] *n* : liberalismo *m*

liberality [ˌlɪbə'rælət̬i] *n, pl* **-ties** : liberalidad *f*, generosidad *f*

liberalize ['lɪbrəˌlaɪz, 'lɪbərə-] *vt* **-ized; -izing** : liberalizar

liberally ['lɪbrəli, 'lɪbərə-] *adv* **1** GENEROUSLY : generosamente **2** ABUNDANTLY : abundantemente **3** FREELY : libremente

liberate ['lɪbəˌreɪt] *vt* **-ated; -ating** : liberar, libertar

liberation [ˌlɪbə'reɪʃən] *n* : liberación *f*

liberator ['lɪbəˌreɪt̬ər] *n* : libertador *m*, -dora *f*

Liberian [laɪ'bɪriən] *n* : liberiano *m*, -na *f* — **Liberian** *adj*

libertine ['lɪbərˌti:n] *n* : libertino *m*, -na *f*

liberty ['lɪbərt̬i] *n, pl* **-ties** **1** : libertad *f* **2 to take the liberty of** : tomarse la libertad de **3 to take liberties with** : tomarse confianzas con, tomarse libertades con

libido [lə'bi:do:, -'baɪ-] *n, pl* **-dos** : libido *f* — **libidinous** [lə'bɪdənəs] *adj*

Libra ['li:brə] *n* : Libra *mf*

librarian [laɪ'brɛriən] *n* : bibliotecario *m*, -ria *f*

library ['laɪˌbrɛri] *n, pl* **-braries** : biblioteca *f*

librettist [lɪˈbrɛt̬ɪst] *n* : libretista *mf*
libretto [lɪˈbrɛt̬o] *n, pl* **-tos** *or* **-ti** [-t̬i:] : libreto *m*
Libyan [ˈlɪbiən] *n* : libio *m*, -bia *f* — **Libyan** *adj*
lice → **louse**
license[1] [ˈlaɪsənts] *vt* **licensed; licensing** : licenciar, autorizar, dar permiso a
license[2] *or* **licence** *n* **1** PERMISSION : licencia *f*, permiso *m* **2** PERMIT : licencia *f*, carnet *m Spain* ⟨driver's license : licencia de conducir⟩ **3** FREEDOM : libertad *f* **4** LICENTIOUSNESS : libertinaje *m*
licentious [laɪˈsɛntʃəs] *adj* : licencioso, disoluto — **licentiously** *adv*
licentiousness [laɪˈsɛntʃəsnəs] *n* : libertinaje *m*
lichen [ˈlaɪkən] *n* : liquen *m*
licit [ˈlɪsət] *adj* : lícito
lick[1] [ˈlɪk] *vt* **1** : lamer **2** BEAT : darle una paliza (a alguien)
lick[2] *n* **1** : lamida *f*, lengüetada *f* ⟨a lick of paint : una mano de pintura⟩ **2** BIT : pizca *f*, ápice *m* **3 a lick and a promise** : una lavada a la carrera
licorice [ˈlɪkərɪʃ, -rəs] *n* : regaliz *m*, dulce *m* de regaliz
lid [ˈlɪd] *n* **1** COVER : tapa *f* **2** EYELID : párpado *m*
lie[1] [ˈlaɪ] *vi* **lay** [ˈleɪ]; **lain** [ˈleɪn]; **lying** [ˈlaɪɪŋ] **1** : acostarse, echarse ⟨I lay down : me acosté⟩ **2** : estar, estar situado, encontrarse ⟨the book lay on the table : el libro estaba en la mesa⟩ ⟨the city lies to the south : la ciudad se encuentra al sur⟩ **3** CONSIST : consistir **4 to lie in** : residir en ⟨the power lies in the people : el poder reside en el pueblo⟩
lie[2] *vi* **lied; lying** [ˈlaɪɪŋ] : mentir
lie[3] *n* **1** UNTRUTH : mentira *f* ⟨to tell lies : decir mentiras⟩ **2** POSITION : posición *f*
liege [ˈli:ʤ] *n* : señor *m* feudal
lien [ˈli:n, ˈli:ən] *n* : derecho *m* de retención
lieutenant [lu:ˈtɛnənt] *n* : teniente *mf*
lieutenant colonel *n* : teniente *mf* coronel
lieutenant commander *n* : capitán *m*, -tana *f* de corbeta
lieutenant general *n* : teniente *mf* general
life [ˈlaɪf] *n, pl* **lives** [ˈlaɪvz] **1** : vida *f* ⟨plant life : la vida vegetal⟩ **2** EXISTENCE : vida *f*, existencia *f* **3** BIOGRAPHY : biografía *f*, vida *f* **4** DURATION : duración *f*, vida *f* **5** LIVELINESS : vivacidad *f*, animación *f*
lifeblood [ˈlaɪfˌblʌd] *n* : parte *f* vital, sustento *m*
lifeboat [ˈlaɪfˌbo:t] *n* : bote *m* salvavidas
lifeguard [ˈlaɪfˌgɑrd] *n* : socorrista *mf*, salvavidas *mf*
lifeless [ˈlaɪfləs] *adj* : sin vida, muerto
lifelike [ˈlaɪfˌlaɪk] *adj* : que parece vivo, natural, verosímil
lifelong [ˈlaɪfˈlɔŋ] *adj* : de toda la vida ⟨a lifelong friend : un amigo de toda la vida⟩
life preserver *n* : salvavidas *m*
lifesaver [ˈlaɪfˌseɪvər] *n* **1** : salvación *f* **2** → **lifeguard**
lifesaving [ˈlaɪfˌseɪvɪŋ] *n* : socorrismo *m*
lifestyle [ˈlaɪfˌstaɪl] *n* : estilo *m* de vida
lifetime [ˈlaɪfˌtaɪm] *n* : vida *f*, curso *m* de la vida
lift[1] [ˈlɪft] *vt* **1** RAISE : levantar, alzar, subir **2** END : levantar ⟨to lift a ban : levantar una prohibición⟩ — *vi* **1** RISE : levantarse, alzarse **2** CLEAR UP : despejar ⟨the fog lifted : se disipó la niebla⟩
lift[2] *n* **1** LIFTING : levantamiento *m*, alzamiento *m* **2** BOOST : impulso *m*, estímulo *m* **3 to give someone a lift** : llevar en coche a alguien
liftoff [ˈlɪftˌɔf] *n* : despegue *m*
ligament [ˈlɪgəmənt] *n* : ligamento *m*
ligature [ˈlɪgəˌtʃʊr, -tʃər] *n* : ligadura *f*
light[1] [ˈlaɪt] *v* **lit** [ˈlɪt] *or* **lighted; lighting** *vt* **1** ILLUMINATE : iluminar, alumbrar **2** IGNITE : encender, prenderle fuego a — *vi* : encenderse, prender
light[2] *vi* **lighted** *or* **lit** [ˈlɪt]; **lighting** **1** LAND, SETTLE : posarse **2** DISMOUNT : bajarse, apearse
light[3] [ˈlaɪt] *adv* **1** LIGHTLY : suavemente, ligeramente **2 to travel light** : viajar con poco equipaje
light[4] *adj* **1** LIGHTWEIGHT : ligero, liviano, poco pesado **2** EASY : fácil, ligero, liviano ⟨light reading : lectura fácil⟩ ⟨light work : trabajo liviano⟩ **3** GENTLE, MILD : fino, suave, leve ⟨a light breeze : una brisa suave⟩ ⟨a light rain : una lluvia fina⟩ **4** FRIVOLOUS : de poca importancia, superficial **5** BRIGHT : bien iluminado, claro **6** PALE : claro (dícese de los colores), rubio (dícese del pelo)
light[5] *n* **1** ILLUMINATION : luz *f* **2** DAYLIGHT : luz *f* del día **3** DAWN : amanecer *m*, madrugada *f* **4** LAMP : lámpara *f* ⟨to turn on off the light : apagar la luz⟩ **5** ASPECT : aspecto *m* ⟨in a new light : con otros ojos⟩ ⟨in the light of : en vista de, a la luz de⟩ **6** MATCH : fósforo *m*, cerillo *m* **7 to bring to light** : sacar a (la) luz
lightbulb [ˈlaɪtˌbʌlb] *n* : bombilla *f*, foco *m*, bombillo *m CA, Col, Ven*
lighten [ˈlaɪtən] *vt* **1** ILLUMINATE : iluminar, dar más luz a **2** : aclararse (el pelo) **3** : aligerar (una carga, etc.) **4** RELIEVE : aliviar **5** GLADDEN : alegrar ⟨it lightened his heart : alegró su corazón⟩
lighter [ˈlaɪt̬ər] *n* : encendedor *m*
lighthearted [ˈlaɪtˈhɑrt̬əd] *adj* : alegre, despreocupado, desenfadado — **lightheartedly** *adv*
lightheartedness [ˈlaɪtˈhɑrt̬ədnəs] *n* : desenfado *m*, alegría *f*
lighthouse [ˈlaɪtˌhaʊs] *n* : faro *m*

lighting [ˈlaɪt̬ɪŋ] *n* : iluminación *f*

lightly [ˈlaɪtli] *adv* **1** GENTLY : suavemente **2** SLIGHTLY : ligeramente **3** FRIVOLOUSLY : a la ligera **4 to let off lightly** : tratar con indulgencia

lightness [ˈlaɪtnəs] *n* **1** BRIGHTNESS : luminosidad *f*, claridad *f* **2** GENTLENESS : ligereza *f*, suavidad *f*, delicadeza *f* **3** : ligereza *f*, liviandad *f* (de peso)

lightning [ˈlaɪtnɪŋ] *n* : relámpago *m*, rayo *m*

lightning bug → firefly

lightproof [ˈlaɪtˌpruːf] *adj* : impenetrable por la luz, opaco

lightweight [ˈlaɪtˈweɪt] *adj* : ligero, liviano, de poco peso

light–year [ˈlaɪtˌjɪr] *n* : año *m* luz

lignite [ˈlɪgˌnaɪt] *n* : lignito *m*

likable *or* **likeable** [ˈlaɪkəbəl] *adj* : simpático, agradable

like[1] [ˈlaɪk] *v* **liked; liking** *vt* **1** : agradar, gustarle (algo a uno) ⟨he likes rice : le gusta el arroz⟩ ⟨she doesn't like flowers : a ella no le gustan las flores⟩ ⟨I like you : me caes bien⟩ **2** WANT : querer, desear ⟨I'd like a hamburger : quiero una hamburguesa⟩ ⟨he would like more help : le gustaría tener más ayuda⟩ — *vi* : querer ⟨do as you like : haz lo que quieras⟩

like[2] *adj* : parecido, semejante, similar

like[3] *n* **1** PREFERENCE : preferencia *f*, gusto *m* **2 the like** : cosa *f* parecida, cosas *fpl* por el estilo ⟨I've never seen the like : nunca he visto cosa parecida⟩

like[4] *conj* **1** AS IF : como si ⟨they looked at me like I was crazy : se me quedaron mirando como si estuviera loca⟩ **2** AS : como, igual que ⟨she doesn't love you like I do : ella no te quiere como yo⟩

like[5] *prep* **1** : como, parecido a ⟨she acts like my mother : se comporta como mi madre⟩ ⟨he looks like me : se parece a mí⟩ **2** : propio de, típico de ⟨that's just like her : eso es muy típico de ella⟩ **3** : como ⟨animals like cows : animales como vacas⟩ **4 like this, like that** : así ⟨do it like that : hazlo así⟩

likelihood [ˈlaɪkliˌhʊd] *n* : probabilidad *f* ⟨in all likelihood : con toda probabilidad⟩

likely[1] [ˈlaɪkli] *adv* : probablemente ⟨most likely he's sick : lo más probable es que esté enfermo⟩ ⟨they're likely to come : es probable que vengan⟩

likely[2] *adj* **-lier; -est 1** PROBABLE : probable ⟨to be likely to : ser muy probable que⟩ **2** SUITABLE : apropiado, adecuado **3** BELIEVABLE : verosímil, creíble **4** PROMISING : prometedor

liken [ˈlaɪkən] *vt* : comparar

likeness [ˈlaɪknəs] *n* **1** SIMILARITY : semejanza *f*, parecido *m* **2** PORTRAIT : retrato *m*

likewise [ˈlaɪkˌwaɪz] *adv* **1** SIMILARLY : de la misma manera, asimismo **2** ALSO : también, además, asimismo

liking [ˈlaɪkɪŋ] *n* **1** FONDNESS : afición *f* (por una cosa), simpatía *f* (por una persona) **2** TASTE : gusto *m* ⟨is it to your liking? : ¿te gusta?⟩

lilac [ˈlaɪlək, -ˌlæk, -ˌlɑk] *n* : lila *f*

lilt [ˈlɪlt] *n* : cadencia *f*, ritmo *m* alegre

lily [ˈlɪli] *n, pl* **lilies 1** : lirio *m*, azucena *f* **2 lily of the valley** : lirio *m* de los valles, muguete *m*

lima bean [ˈlaɪmə] *n* : frijol *m* de media luna

limb [ˈlɪm] *n* **1** APPENDAGE : miembro *m*, extremidad *f* **2** BRANCH : rama *f*

limber[1] [ˈlɪmbər] *vi or* **to limber up** : calentarse, prepararse

limber[2] *adj* : ágil (dícese de las personas), flexible (dícese de los objetos)

limbo [ˈlɪmˌboː] *n, pl* **-bos 1** : limbo *m* (en la religión) **2** OBLIVION : olvido *m* ⟨the project is in limbo : el proyecto ha caído en el olvido⟩

lime [ˈlaɪm] *n* **1** : cal *f* (óxido) **2** : lima *f* (fruta), limón *m* verde *Mex*

limelight [ˈlaɪmˌlaɪt] *n* **to be in the limelight** : ser el centro de atención, estar en el candelero

limerick [ˈlɪmərɪk] *n* : poema *m* jocoso de cinco versos

limestone [ˈlaɪmˌstoːn] *n* : piedra *f* caliza, caliza *f*

limit[1] [ˈlɪmət] *vt* : limitar, restringir

limit[2] *n* **1** MAXIMUM : límite *m*, máximo *m* ⟨speed limit : límite de velocidad⟩ **2 limits** *npl* : límites *mpl*, confines *mpl* ⟨city limits : límites de la ciudad⟩ **3 that's the limit!** : ¡eso es el colmo!

limitation [ˌlɪməˈteɪʃən] *n* : limitación *f*, restricción *f*

limited [ˈlɪmət̬əd] *adj* : limitado, restringido

limitless [ˈlɪmətləs] *adj* : ilimitado, sin límites

limousine [ˈlɪməˌziːn, ˌlɪməˈ-] *n* : limusina *f*

limp[1] [ˈlɪmp] *vi* : cojear

limp[2] *adj* **1** FLACCID : fláccido **2** LANK : lacio (dícese del pelo) **3** WEAK : débil ⟨to feel limp : sentirse desfallecer, sentirse sin fuerzas⟩

limp[3] *n* : cojera *f*

limpid [ˈlɪmpəd] *adj* : límpido, claro

limply [ˈlɪmpli] *adv* : sin fuerzas

limpness [ˈlɪmpnəs] *n* : flaccidez *f*, debilidad *f*

linden [ˈlɪndən] *n* : tilo *m*

line[1] [ˈlaɪn] *v* **lined; lining** *vt* **1** : forrar, cubrir ⟨to line a dress : forrar un vestido⟩ ⟨to line the walls : cubrir las paredes⟩ **2** MARK : rayar, trazar líneas en **3** BORDER : bordear **4** ALIGN : alinear — *vi* **to line up** : ponerse in fila, hacer cola

line[2] *n* **1** CORD, ROPE : cuerda *f* **2** WIRE : cable *m* ⟨power line : cable eléctrico⟩ **3** : línea *f* (de teléfono) **4** ROW : fila *f*, hilera *f* **5** NOTE : nota *f*, líneas *fpl* ⟨drop me a line : mándame unas líneas⟩ **6** COURSE : línea *f* ⟨line of inquiry : línea de investigación⟩ **7** AGREEMENT : conformidad *f* ⟨to be in line with : ser conforme a⟩ ⟨to fall into line : estar de acuerdo⟩ **8** OCCUPATION : ocupación *f*, rama *f*, especialidad *f* **9** LIMIT : línea *f*, límite *m* ⟨dividing line : línea divisoria⟩ ⟨to draw the line : fijar límites⟩ **10** SERVICE : línea *f* ⟨bus line : línea de autobuses⟩ **11** MARK : línea *f*, arruga *f* (de la cara)

lineage [ˈlɪniɪʤ] *n* : linaje *m*, abolengo *m*

lineal [ˈlɪniəl] *adj* : en línea directa

lineaments [ˈlɪniəmənts] *npl* : facciones *fpl* (de la cara), rasgos *mpl*

linear [ˈlɪniər] *adj* : lineal

linen [ˈlɪnən] *n* : lino *m*

liner [ˈlaɪnər] *n* **1** LINING : forro *m* **2** SHIP : buque *m*, transatlántico *m*

lineup [ˈlaɪnˌəp] *n* **1** : fila *f* de sospechosos **2** : formación *f* (en deportes) **3** ALIGNMENT : alineación *f*

linger [ˈlɪŋgər] *vi* **1** TARRY : quedarse, entretenerse, rezagarse **2** PERSIST : persistir, sobrevivir

lingerie [ˌlɑnʤəˈreɪ, ˌlænʒəˈriː] *n* : ropa *f* íntima femenina, lencería *f*

lingo [ˈlɪŋgo] *n, pl* **-goes 1** LANGUAGE : idioma *m* **2** JARGON : jerga *f*

linguist [ˈlɪŋgwɪst] *n* : lingüista *mf*

linguistic [lɪŋˈgwɪstɪk] *adj* : lingüístico

linguistics [lɪŋˈgwɪstɪks] *n* : lingüística *f*

liniment [ˈlɪnəmənt] *n* : linimento *m*

lining [ˈlaɪnɪŋ] *n* : forro *m*

link¹ [ˈlɪŋk] *vt* : unir, enlazar, conectar — *vi* **to link up** : unirse, conectar

link² *n* **1** : eslabón *m* (de una cadena) **2** BOND : conexión *f*, lazo *m*, vínculo *m*

linkage [ˈlɪŋkɪʤ] *n* : conexión *f*, unión *f*, enlace *m*

linoleum [ləˈnoːliəm] *n* : linóleo *m*

linseed oil [ˈlɪnˌsiːd] *n* : aceite *m* de linaza

lint [ˈlɪnt] *n* : pelusa *f*

lintel [ˈlɪntəl] *n* : dintel *m*

lion [ˈlaɪən] *n* : león *m*

lioness [ˈlaɪənɪs] *n* : leona *f*

lionize [ˈlaɪəˌnaɪz] *vt* **-ized; -izing** : tratar a una persona como muy importante

lip [ˈlɪp] *n* **1** : labio *m* **2** EDGE, RIM : pico *m* (de una jarra), borde *m* (de una taza)

lipreading [ˈlɪpˌriːdɪŋ] *n* : lectura *f* de los labios

lipstick [ˈlɪpˌstɪk] *n* : lápiz *m* de labios, barra *f* de labios

liquefy [ˈlɪkwəˌfaɪ] *v* **-fied; -fying** *vt* : licuar — *vi* : licuarse

liqueur [lɪˈkʊr, -ˈkər, -ˈkjʊr] *n* : licor *m*

liquid¹ [ˈlɪkwəd] *adj* : líquido

liquid² *n* : líquido *m*

liquidate [ˈlɪkwəˌdeɪt] *vt* **-dated; -dating** : liquidar

liquidation [ˌlɪkwəˈdeɪʃən] *n* : liquidación *f*

liquidity [lɪkˈwɪdəṭi] *n* : liquidez *f*

liquor [ˈlɪkər] *n* : alcohol *m*, bebidas *fpl* alcohólicas, licor *m*

lisp¹ [ˈlɪsp] *vi* : cecear

lisp² *n* : ceceo *m*

lissome [ˈlɪsəm] *adj* **1** FLEXIBLE : flexible **2** LITHE : ágil y grácil

list¹ [ˈlɪst] *vt* **1** ENUMERATE : hacer una lista de, enumerar **2** INCLUDE : poner en una lista, incluir — *vi* : escorar (dícese de un barco)

list² *n* **1** ENUMERATION : lista *f* **2** SLANT : escora *f*, inclinación *f*

listen [ˈlɪsən] *vi* **1** : escuchar, oír **2 to listen to** HEED : prestar atención a, hacer caso de, escuchar **3 to listen to reason** : atender a razones

listener [ˈlɪsənər] *n* : oyente *mf*, persona *f* que sabe escuchar

listless [ˈlɪstləs] *adj* : lánguido, apático — **listlessly** *adv*

listlessness [ˈlɪstləsnəs] *n* : apatía *f*, languidez *f*, desgana *f*

lit [ˈlɪt] → **light**

litany [ˈlɪtəni] *n, pl* **-nies** : letanía *f*

liter [ˈliːṭər] *n* : litro *m*

literacy [ˈlɪṭərəsi] *n* : alfabetismo *m*

literal [ˈlɪṭərəl] *adj* : literal — **literally** *adv*

literary [ˈlɪṭəˌrri] *adj* : literario

literate [ˈlɪṭərət] *adj* : alfabetizado

literature [ˈlɪṭərəˌʧʊr, -ʧər] *n* : literatura *f*

lithe [ˈlaɪð, ˈlaɪθ] *adj* : ágil y grácil

lithesome [ˈlaɪðsəm, ˈlaɪθ-] → **lissome**

lithium [ˈlɪθiəm] *n* : litio *m*

lithograph [ˈlɪθəˌgræf] *n* : litografía *f*

lithographer [lɪˈθɑgrəfər, ˈlɪθəˌgræfər] *n* : litógrafo *m*, -fa *f*

lithography [lɪˈθɑgrəfi] *n* : litografía *f*

lithosphere [ˈlɪθəˌsfɪr] *n* : litosfera *f*

Lithuanian [ˌlɪθəˈweɪniən] *n* **1** : lituano *m* (idioma) **2** : lituano *m*, -na *f* — **Lithuanian** *adj*

litigant [ˈlɪṭɪgənt] *n* : litigante *mf*

litigate [ˈlɪṭəˌgeɪt] *vi* **-gated; -gating** : litigar

litigation [ˌlɪṭəˈgeɪʃən] *n* : litigio *m*

litmus paper [ˈlɪtməs] *n* : papel *m* de tornasol

litter¹ [ˈlɪṭər] *vt* : tirar basura en, ensuciar — *vi* : tirar basura

litter² *n* **1** : camada *f*, cría *f* ⟨a litter of kittens : una cría de gatitos⟩ **2** STRETCHER : camilla *f* **3** RUBBISH : basura *f* **4** : arena *f* higiénica (para gatos)

little¹ [ˈlɪṭəl] *adv* **less** [ˈlɛs]; **least** [ˈliːst] **1** : poco ⟨she sings very little : canta muy poco⟩ **2 little did I know that . . .** : no tenía la menor idea de que . . . **3 as little as possible** : lo menos posible

little² *adj* **littler** *or* **less** [ˈlɛs] *or* **lesser** [ˈlɛsər]; **littlest** *or* **least** [ˈliːst] **1** SMALL : pequeño **2** : poco ⟨they speak little Spanish : hablan poco español⟩ ⟨little by little : poco a poco⟩ **3** TRIVIAL : sin importancia, trivial

little³ *n* **1** : poco *m* ⟨little has changed : poco ha cambiado⟩ **2 a little** : un poco, algo ⟨it's a little surprising : es algo sorprendente⟩

Little Dipper → **dipper**

liturgical [ləˈtərʤɪkəl] *adj* : litúrgico — **liturgically** [-kli] *adv*

liturgy ['lɪt̬ərʤi] *n, pl* **-gies** : liturgia *f*
livable ['lɪvəbəl] *adj* : habitable
live[1] ['lɪv] *vi* **lived; living** **1** EXIST : vivir ⟨as long as I live : mientras viva⟩ ⟨to live from day to day : vivir al día⟩ **2** : llevar una vida, vivir ⟨he lived simply : llevó una vida sencilla⟩ **3** SUBSIST : mantenerse, vivir **4** RESIDE : vivir, residir
live[2] ['laɪv] *adj* **1** LIVING : vivo **2** BURNING : encendido ⟨a live coal : una brasa⟩ **3** : con corriente ⟨live wires : cables con corriente⟩ **4** : cargado, sin estallar ⟨a live bomb : una bomba sin estallar⟩ **5** CURRENT : de actualidad ⟨a live issue : un asunto de actualidad⟩ **6** : en vivo, en directo ⟨a live interview : una entrevista en vivo⟩
livelihood ['laɪvli,hʊd] *n* : sustento *m*, vida *f*, medio *m* de vida
liveliness ['laɪvlinəs] *n* : animación *f*, vivacidad *f*
livelong ['lɪv'lɔŋ] *adj* : entero, completo
lively ['laɪvli] *adj* **-lier; -est** : animado, vivaz, vivo, enérgico
liven ['laɪvən] *vt* : animar — *vi* : animarse
liver ['lɪvər] *n* : hígado *m*
livery ['lɪvəri] *n, pl* **-eries** : librea *f*
lives → **life**
livestock ['laɪv,stɑk] *n* : ganado *m*
live wire *n* : persona *f* vivaz y muy activa
livid ['lɪvəd] *adj* **1** BLACK-AND-BLUE : amoratado **2** PALE : lívido **3** ENRAGED : furioso
living[1] ['lɪvɪŋ] *adj* : vivo
living[2] *n* **to make a living** : ganarse la vida
living room *n* : living *m*, sala *f* de estar
lizard ['lɪzərd] *n* : lagarto *m*
llama ['lɑmə, 'jɑ-] *n* : llama *f*
load[1] ['lo:d] *vt* : cargar, embarcar
load[2] *n* **1** CARGO : carga *f* **2** WEIGHT : peso *m* **3** BURDEN : carga *f*, peso *m* **4 loads** *npl* : montón *m*, pila *f*, cantidad *f* ⟨loads of work : un montón de trabajo⟩
loaf[1] ['lo:f] *vi* : holgazanear, flojear, haraganear
loaf[2] *n, pl* **loaves** ['lo:vz] **1** : pan *m*, pan *m* de molde, barra *f* de pan **2 meat loaf** : pan *m* de carne
loafer ['lo:fər] *n* : holgazán *m*, -zana *f*; haragán *m*, -gana *f*; vago *m*, -ga *f*
loam ['lo:m] *n* : marga *f*, suelo *m*
loan[1] ['lo:n] *vt* : prestar
loan[2] *n* : préstamo *m*, empréstito *m* (del banco)
loath ['lo:θ, 'lo:ð] *adj* : poco dispuesto ⟨I am loath to say it : me resisto a decirlo⟩
loathe ['lo:ð] *vt* **loathed; loathing** : odiar, aborrecer
loathing ['lo:ðɪŋ] *n* : aversión *f*, odio *m*, aborrecimiento *m*
loathsome ['lo:θsəm, 'lo:ð-] *adj* : odioso, repugnante
lob[1] ['lɑb] *vt* **lobbed; lobbing** : hacerle un globo (a otro jugador)
lob[2] *n* : globo *m* (en deportes)
lobby[1] ['lɑbi] *v* **-bied; -bying** *vt* : presionar, ejercer presión sobre — *vi* **to lobby for** : presionar para (lograr algo)
lobby[2] *n, pl* **-bies** **1** FOYER : vestíbulo *m* **2** LOBBYISTS : grupo *m* de presión, lobby *m*
lobbyist ['lɑbiɪst] *n* : miembro *m* de un lobby
lobe ['lo:b] *n* : lóbulo *m*
lobed ['lo:bd] *adj* : lobulado
lobotomy [lə'bɑt̬əmi, lo-] *n, pl* **-mies** : lobotomía *f*
lobster ['lɑbstər] *n* : langosta *f*
local[1] ['lo:kəl] *adj* : local
local[2] *n* **1** : anestesia *f* local **2 the locals** : los vecinos del lugar, los habitantes
locale [lo'kæl] *n* : lugar *m*, escenario *m*
locality [lo'kæləţi] *n, pl* **-ties** : localidad *f*
localize ['lo:kə,laɪz] *vt* **-ized; -izing** : localizar
locally ['lo:kəli] *adv* : en la localidad, en la zona
locate ['lo:,keɪt, lo'keɪt] *v* **-cated; -cating** *vt* **1** POSITION : situar, ubicar **2** FIND : localizar, ubicar — *vi* SETTLE : establecerse
location [lo'keɪʃən] *n* **1** POSITION : posición *f*, emplazamiento *m*, ubicación *f* **2** PLACE : lugar *m*, sitio *m*
lock[1] ['lɑk] *vt* **1** FASTEN : cerrar **2** CONFINE : encerrar ⟨they locked me in the room : me encerraron en la sala⟩ **3** IMMOBILIZE : bloquear (una rueda) — *vi* **1** : cerrarse (dícese de una puerta) **2** : trabarse, bloquearse (dícese de una rueda)
lock[2] *n* **1** : mechón *m* (de pelo) **2** FASTENER : cerradura *f*, cerrojo *m*, chapa *f* **3** : esclusa *f* (de un canal)
locker ['lɑkər] *n* : armario *m*, cajón *m* con llave, lócker *m*
locket ['lɑkət] *n* : medallón *m*, guardapelo *m*, relicario *m*
lockjaw ['lɑk,jɔ] *n* : tétano *m*
lockout ['lɑk,aʊt] *n* : cierre *m* patronal, lockout *m*
locksmith ['lɑk,smɪθ] *n* : cerrajero *m*, -ra *f*
lockup ['lɑk,ʌp] *n* JAIL : cárcel *f*
locomotion [,lo:kə'mo:ʃən] *n* : locomoción *f*
locomotive[1] [,lo:kə'mo:ţɪv] *adj* : locomotor
locomotive[2] *n* : locomotora *f*
locust ['lo:kəst] *n* **1** : langosta *f*, chapulín *m CA, Mex* **2** CICADA : cigarra *f*, chicharra *f* **3** : acacia *f* blanca (árbol)
locution [lo'kju:ʃən] *n* : locución *f*
lode ['lo:d] *n* : veta *f*, vena *f*, filón *m*
lodestar ['lo:d,stɑr] *n* : estrella *f* polar
lodestone ['lo:d,sto:n] *n* : piedra *f* imán
lodge[1] ['lɑʤ] *v* **lodged; lodging** *vt* **1** HOUSE : hospedar, alojar **2** FILE : presentar ⟨to lodge a complaint : presentar una demanda⟩ — *vi* **1** : posarse, meterse ⟨the bullet lodged in the door

: la bala se incrustó en la puerta⟩ **2** STAY : hospedarse, alojarse
lodge[2] *n* **1** : pabellón *m*, casa *f* de campo ⟨hunting lodge : refugio de caza⟩ **2** : madriguera *f* (de un castor) **3** : logia *f* ⟨Masonic lodge : logia masónica⟩
lodger [ˈlɑʤər] *n* : inquilino *m*, -na *f*; huésped *m*, -peda *f*
lodging [ˈlɑʤɪŋ] *n* **1** : alojamiento *m* **2 lodgings** *npl* ROOMS : habitaciones *fpl*
loft [ˈlɔft] *n* **1** ATTIC : desván *m*, ático *m*, buhardilla *f* **2** : loft *m* (en un depósito comercial) **3** HAYLOFT : pajar *m* **4** : galería *f* ⟨choir loft : galería del coro⟩
loftily [ˈlɔftəli] *adv* : altaneramente, con altivez
loftiness [ˈlɔftinəs] *n* **1** NOBILITY : nobleza *f* **2** ARROGANCE : altanería *f*, arrogancia *f* **3** HEIGHT : altura *f*, elevación *f*
lofty [ˈlɔfti] *adj* **loftier; -est 1** NOBLE : noble, elevado **2** HAUGHTY : altivo, arrogante, altanero **3** HIGH : majestuoso, elevado
log[1] [ˈlɔg, ˈlɑg] *vi* **logged; logging 1** : talar (árboles) **2** RECORD : registrar, anotar **3 to log on** : entrar (al sistema) **4 to log off** : salir (del sistema)
log[2] *n* **1** : tronco *m*, leño *m* **2** RECORD : diario *m*
logarithm [ˈlɔgəˌrɪðəm, ˈlɑ-] *n* : logaritmo *m*
logger [ˈlɔgər, ˈlɑ-] *n* : leñador *m*, -dora *f*
loggerhead [ˈlɔgərˌhd, ˈlɑ-] *n* **1** : tortuga *f* boba **2 to be at loggerheads** : estar en pugna, estar en desacuerdo
logic [ˈlɑʤɪk] *n* : lógica *f* — **logical** [ˈlɑʤɪkəl] *adj* — **logically** [-kli] *adv*
logistic [ləˈʤɪstɪk, lo-] *adj* : logístico
logistics [ləˈʤɪstɪks, lo-] *ns & pl* : logística *f*
logo [ˈloːˌgoː] *n, pl* **logos** [-ˌgoːz] : logotipo *m*
loin [ˈlɔɪn] *n* **1** : lomo *m* ⟨pork loin : lomo de cerdo⟩ **2 loins** *npl* : lomos *mpl* ⟨to gird one's loins : prepararse para la lucha⟩
loiter [ˈlɔɪt̬ər] *vi* : vagar, perder el tiempo
loll [ˈlɑl] *vi* **1** SLOUCH : repantigarse **2** IDLE : holgazanear, hacer el vago
lollipop *or* **lollypop** [ˈlɑliˌpɑp] *n* : dulce *m* en palito, chupete *m Chile, Peru*, paleta *f CA, Mex*
lone [ˈloːn] *adj* **1** SOLITARY : solitario **2** ONLY : único
loneliness [ˈloːnlinəs] *n* : soledad *f*
lonely [ˈloːnli] *adj* **-lier; -est 1** SOLITARY : solitario, aislado **2** LONESOME : solo ⟨to feel lonely : sentirse muy solo⟩
loner [ˈloːnər] *n* : solitario *m*, -ria *f*; recluso *m*, -sa *f*
lonesome [ˈloːnsəm] *adj* : solo, solitario
long[1] [ˈlɔŋ] *vi* **1 to long for** : añorar, desear, anhelar **2 to long to** : anhelar, estar deseando ⟨they longed to see her : estaban deseando verla, tenían muchas ganas de verla⟩
long[2] *adv* **1** : mucho, mucho tiempo ⟨it didn't take long : no llevó mucho tiempo⟩ ⟨will it last long? : ¿va a durar mucho?⟩ **2 all day long** : todo el día **3 as long as** *or* **so long as** : mientras, con tal que **4 long before** : mucho antes **5 so long!** : ¡hasta luego!, ¡adiós!
long[3] *adj* **longer** [ˈlɔŋgər]; **longest** [ˈlɔŋgəst] **1** (*indicating length*)) : largo ⟨the dress is too long : el vestido es demasiado largo⟩ ⟨a long way from : bastante lejos de⟩ ⟨in the long run : a la larga⟩ **2** (*indicating time*)) : largo, prolongado ⟨a long illness : una enfermedad prolongada⟩ ⟨a long walk : un paseo largo⟩ ⟨at long last : por fin⟩ **3 to be long on** : estar cargado de
long[4] *n* **1 before long** : dentro de poco **2 the long and the short** : lo esencial, lo fundamental
longevity [lɑnˈʤɛvət̬i] *n* : longevidad *f*
longhand [ˈlɔŋˌhænd] *n* : escritura *f* a mano, escritura *f* cursiva
longhorn [ˈlɔŋˌhɔrn] *n* : longhorn *mf*
longing [lɔŋɪŋ] *n* : vivo deseo *m*, ansia *f*, anhelo *m*
longingly [lɔŋɪŋlli] *adv* : ansiosamente, con ansia
longitude [ˈlɑnʤəˌtuːd, -ˌtjuːd] *n* : longitud *f*
longitudinal [ˌlɑnʤəˈtuːdənəl, -ˈtjuː-] *adj* : longitudinal — **longitudinally** *adv*
long–lived [ˈlɔŋˈlɪvd, -ˈlaɪvd] *adj* : longevo
longshoreman [ˈlɔŋˈʃormən] *n, pl* **-men** [-mən, -ˌmɛn] : estibador *m*, -dora *f*
long–standing [ˈlɔŋˈstændɪŋ] *adj* : de larga data
long–suffering [ˈlɔŋˈsʌfərɪŋ] *adj* : paciente, sufrido
look[1] [ˈlʊk] *vi* **1** GLANCE : mirar ⟨to look out the window : mirar por la ventana⟩ **2** INVESTIGATE : buscar, mirar ⟨look in the closet : busca en el closet⟩ ⟨look before you leap : mira lo que haces⟩ **3** SEEM : parecer ⟨he looks happy : parece estar contento⟩ ⟨I look like my mother : me parezco a mi madre⟩ **4 to look after** : cuidar, cuidar de **5 to look for** EXPECT : esperar **6 to look for** SEEK : buscar — *vt* : mirar
look[2] *n* **1** GLANCE : mirada *f* **2** EXPRESSION : cara *f* ⟨a look of disapproval : una cara de desaprobación⟩ **3** ASPECT : aspecto *m*, apariencia *f*, aire *m* **4 looks** *npl* : belleza *f*
lookout [ˈlʊkˌaʊt] *n* **1** : centinela *mf*, vigía *mf* **2 to be on the lookout for** : estar al acecho de, andar a la caza de
loom[1] [ˈluːm] *vi* **1** : aparecer, surgir ⟨the city loomed up in the distance : la ciudad surgió en la distancia⟩ **2** IMPEND : amenazar, ser inminente **3 to loom large** : cobrar mucha importancia
loom[2] *n* : telar *m*
loon [ˈluːn] *n* : somorgujo *m*, somormujo *m*
loony *or* **looney** [ˈluːni] *adj* **-nier; -est** : loco, chiflado *fam*

loop[1] ['lu:p] *vt* **1** : hacer lazadas con **2 to loop around** : pasar alrededor de — *vi* **1** : rizar el rizo (dícese de un avión) **2** : serpentear (dícese de una carretera)

loop[2] *n* **1** : lazada *f* (en hilo o cuerda) **2** BEND : curva *f* **3** CIRCUIT : circuito *m* cerrado **4** : rizo *m* (en la aviación) ⟨to loop the loop : rizar el rizo⟩

loophole ['lu:p,ho:l] *n* : escapatoria *f*, pretexto *m*

loose[1] ['lu:s] *vt* **loosed; loosing 1** RELEASE : poner en libertad, soltar **2** UNTIE : deshacer, desatar **3** DISCHARGE, UNLEASH : descargar, desatar

loose[2] → **loosely**

loose[3] *adj* **looser; -est 1** INSECURE : flojo, suelto, poco seguro ⟨a loose tooth : un diente flojo⟩ **2** ROOMY : suelto, holgado ⟨loose clothing : ropa holgada⟩ **3** OPEN : suelto, abierto ⟨loose soil : suelo suelto⟩ ⟨a loose weave : una tejida abierta⟩ **4** FREE : suelto ⟨to break loose : soltarse⟩ **5** SLACK : flojo, flexible **6** APPROXIMATE : libre, aproximado ⟨a loose translation : una traducción aproximada⟩

loosely ['lu:sli] *adv* **1** : sin apretar **2** ROUGHLY : aproximadamente, más o menos

loosen ['lu:sən] *vt* : aflojar

loose–leaf ['lu:s'li:f] *adj* : de hojas sueltas

looseness ['lu:snəs] *n* **1** : aflojamiento *m*, holgura *f* (de ropa) **2** IMPRECISION : imprecisión *f*

loot[1] ['lu:t] *vt* : saquear, robar

loot[2] *n* : botín *m*

looter ['lu:ṭər] *n* : saqueador *m*, -dora *f*

lop ['lɑp] *vt* **lopped; lopping** : cortar, podar

lope[1] ['lo:p] *vi* **loped; loping** : correr a paso largo

lope[2] *n* : paso *m* largo

lopsided ['lɑp,saɪdəd] *adj* **1** CROOKED : torcido, chueco, ladeado **2** ASYMETRICAL : asimétrico

loquacious [lo'kweɪʃəs] *adj* : locuaz

lord ['lɔrd] *n* **1** : señor *m*, noble *m* **2** : lord *m* (en la Gran Bretaña) **3 the Lord** : el Señor **4 good Lord!** : ¡Dios mío!

lordly ['lɔrdli] *adj* **-lier; -est** HAUGHTY : arrogante, altanero

lordship ['lɔrd,ʃɪp] *n* : señoría *f*

Lord's Supper *n* : Eucaristía *f*

lore ['lor] *n* : saber *m* popular, tradición *f*

lose ['lu:z] *v* **lost** ['lɔst]; **losing** ['lu:-zɪŋ] *vt* **1** : perder ⟨I lost my umbrella : perdí mi paraguas⟩ ⟨to lose blood : perder sangre⟩ ⟨to lose one's voice : quedarse fónico⟩ ⟨to have nothing to lose : no tener nada que perder⟩ ⟨to lose no time : no perder tiempo⟩ ⟨to lose weight : perder peso, adelgazar⟩ ⟨to lose one's temper : perder los estribos, enojarse, enfadarse⟩ ⟨to lose sight of : perder de vista⟩ **2** : costar, hacer perder ⟨the errors lost him his job : los errores le costaron su empleo⟩ **3** : atrasar ⟨my watch loses 5 minutes a day : mi reloj atrasa 5 minutos por día⟩ **4 to lose oneself** : perderse, ensimismarse — *vi* **1** : perder ⟨we lost to the other team : perdimos contra el otro equipo⟩ **2** : atrasarse ⟨the clock loses time : el reloj se atrasa⟩

loser ['lu:zər] *n* : perdedor *m*, -dora *f*

loss ['lɔs] *n* **1** LOSING : pérdida *f* ⟨loss of memory : pérdida de memoria⟩ ⟨to sell at a loss : vender con pérdida⟩ ⟨to be at a loss to : no saber como⟩ **2** DEFEAT : derrota *f*, juego *m* perdido **3 losses** *npl* DEATHS : muertos *mpl*

lost ['lɔst] *adj* **1** : perdido ⟨a lost cause : una causa perdida⟩ ⟨lost in thought : absorto⟩ **2 to get lost** : perderse **3 to make up for lost time** : recuperar el tiempo perdido

lot ['lɑt] *n* **1** DRAWING : sorteo *m* ⟨by lot : por sorteo⟩ **2** SHARE : parte *f*, porción *f* **3** FATE : suerte *f* **4** LAND, PLOT : terreno *m*, solar *m*, lote *m*, parcela *f* ⟨parking lot : estacionamiento⟩ **5 a lot of** *or* **lots of** : mucho, un montón de, bastante ⟨lots of books : un montón de libros, muchos libros⟩ ⟨a lot of people : mucha gente⟩

loth ['lo:θ, 'lo:ð] → **loath**

lotion ['lo:ʃən] *n* : loción *f*

lottery ['lɑṭəri] *n, pl* **-teries** : lotería *f*

lotus ['lo:ṭəs] *n* : loto *m*

loud[1] ['laʊd] *adv* : alto, fuerte ⟨out loud : en voz alta⟩

loud[2] *adj* **1** : alto, fuerte ⟨a loud voice : una voz alta⟩ **2** NOISY : ruidoso ⟨a loud party : una fiesta ruidosa⟩ **3** FLASHY : llamativo, chillón

loudly ['laʊdli] *adv* : alto, fuerte, en voz alta

loudness ['laʊdnəs] *n* : volumen *m*, fuerza *f* (del ruido)

loudspeaker ['laʊd,spi:kər] *n* : altavoz *m*, altoparlante *m*

lounge[1] ['laʊndʒ] *vi* **lounged; lounging** : holgazanear, gandulear

lounge[2] *n* : salón *m*, sala *f* de estar

louse ['laʊs] *n, pl* **lice** ['laɪs] : piojo *m*

lousy ['laʊzi] *adj* **lousier; -est 1** : piojoso, lleno de piojos **2** BAD : pésimo, muy malo

lout ['laʊt] *n* : bruto *m*, patán *m*

louver *or* **louvre** ['lu:vər] *n* : persiana *f*, listón *m* de persiana

lovable ['lʌvəbəl] *adj* : adorable, amoroso, encantador

love[1] ['lʌv] *v* **loved; loving** *vt* **1** : querer, amar ⟨I love you : te quiero⟩ **2** ENJOY : encantarle a alguien, ser (muy) aficionado a, gustarle mucho a uno (algo) ⟨she loves flowers : le encantan las flores⟩ ⟨he loves golf : es muy aficionado al golf⟩ ⟨I'd love to go with you : me gustaría mucho acompañarte⟩ — *vi* : querer, amar

love[2] *n* **1** : amor *m*, cariño *m* ⟨to be in love with : estar enamorado de⟩ ⟨to fall in love with : enamorarse de⟩ **2** ENTHUSIASM, INTEREST : amor *m*, afición *m*, gusto *m* ⟨love of music : afición a la música⟩ **3** BELOVED : amor *m*; amado *m*, -da *f*; enamorado *m*, -da *f*

loveless [ˈlʌvləs] *adj* : sin amor

loveliness [ˈlʌvlinəs] *n* : belleza *f*, hermosura *f*

lovelorn [ˈlʌvˌlɔrn] *adj* : herido de amor, perdidamente enamorado

lovely [ˈlʌvli] *adj* **-lier; -est** : hermoso, bello, lindo, precioso

lover [ˈlʌvər] *n* : amante *mf* (de personas); aficionado *m*, -da *f* (a alguna actividad)

loving [ˈlʌvɪŋ] *adj* : amoroso, cariñoso

lovingly [ˈlʌvɪŋli] *adv* : cariñosamente

low1 [ˈloː] *vi* : mugir

low2 *adv* : bajo, profundo ⟨to aim low : apuntar bajo⟩ ⟨to lie low : mantenerse escondido⟩ ⟨to turn the lights down low : bajar las luces⟩

low3 *adj* **lower** [ˈloːər]; **-est** **1** : bajo ⟨a low building : un edificio bajo⟩ ⟨a low bow : una profunda reverencia⟩ **2** SOFT : bajo, suave ⟨in a low voice : en voz baja⟩ **3** SHALLOW : bajo, poco profundo **4** HUMBLE : humilde, modesto **5** DEPRESSED : deprimido, bajo de moral **6** INFERIOR : bajo, inferior **7** UNFAVORABLE : mal ⟨to have a low opinion of him : tener un mal concepto de él⟩ **8 to be low on** : tener poco de, estar escaso de

low4 *n* **1** : punto *m* bajo ⟨to reach an all-time low : estar más bajo que nunca⟩ **2** *or* **low gear** : primera velocidad *f* **3** : mugido *m* (de una vaca)

lowbrow [ˈloːˌbraʊ] *n* : persona *f* inculta

lower1 [ˈloːər] *vt* **1** DROP : bajar ⟨to lower one's voice : bajar la voz⟩ **2** : arriar, bajar ⟨to lower the flag : arriar la bandera⟩ **3** REDUCE : reducir, bajar **4 to lower oneself** : rebajarse

lower2 [ˈloːər] *adj* : inferior, más bajo, de abajo

lowland [ˈloːlənd, -ˌlænd] *n* : tierras *fpl* bajas

lowly [ˈloːli] *adj* **-lier; -est** : humilde, modesto

loyal [ˈlɔɪəl] *adj* : leal, fiel — **loyally** *adv*

loyalist [ˈlɔɪəlɪst] *n* : partidario *m*, -ria *f* del régimen

loyalty [ˈlɔɪəlti] *n, pl* **-ties** : lealtad *f*, fidelidad *f*

lozenge [ˈlɑzənʤ] *n* : pastilla *f*

LSD [ˌɛlˌɛsˈdiː] *n* : LSD *m*

lubricant [ˈluːbrɪkənt] *n* : lubricante *m*

lubricate [ˈluːbrɪˌkeɪt] *vt* **-cated; -cating** : lubricar — **lubrication** [ˌluːbrɪˈkeɪʃən] *n*

lucid [ˈluːsəd] *adj* : lúcido, claro — **lucidly** *adv*

lucidity [luːˈsɪdət̬i] *n* : lucidez *f*

luck [ˈlʌk] *n* **1** : suerte *f* **2 to have bad luck** : tener mala suerte **3 good luck!** : ¡(buena) suerte!

luckily [ˈlʌkəli] *adv* : afortunadamente, por suerte

luckless [ˈlʌkləs] *adj* : desafortunado

lucky [ˈlʌki] *adj* **luckier; -est** **1** : afortunado, que tiene suerte ⟨a lucky woman : una mujer afortunada⟩ **2** FORTUITOUS : fortuito, de suerte **3** OPPORTUNE : oportuno **4** : de (la) suerte ⟨lucky number : número de la suerte⟩

lucrative [ˈluːkrət̬ɪv] *adj* : lucrativo, provechoso — **lucratively** *adv*

ludicrous [ˈluːdəkrəs] *adj* : ridículo, absurdo — **ludicrously** *adv*

ludicrousness [ˈluːdəkrəsnəs] *n* : ridiculez *f*, absurdo *m*

lug [ˈlʌg] *vt* **lugged; lugging** : arrastrar, transportar con dificultad

luggage [ˈlʌgɪʤ] *n* : equipaje *m*

lugubrious [lʊˈguːbriəs] *adj* : lúgubre — **lugubriously** *adv*

lukewarm [ˈluːkˈwɔrm] *adj* **1** TEPID : tibio **2** HALFHEARTED : poco entusiasta

lull1 [ˈlʌl] *vt* **1** CALM, SOOTHE : calmar, sosegar **2 to lull to sleep** : arrullar, adormecer

lull2 *n* : calma *f*, pausa *f*

lullaby [ˈlʌləˌbaɪ] *n, pl* **-bies** : canción *f* de cuna, arrullo *m*, nana *f*

lumber1 [ˈlʌmbər] *vt* : aserrar (madera) — *vi* : moverse pesadamente

lumber2 *n* : madera *f*

lumberjack [ˈlʌmbərˌʤæk] *n* : leñador *m*, -dora *f*

lumberyard [ˈlʌmbərˌjɑrd] *n* : almacén *m* de maderas

luminary [ˈluːməˌnɛri] *n, pl* **-naries** : lumbrera *f*, luminaria *f*

luminescence [ˌluːməˈnɛsənts] *n* : luminiscencia *f* — **luminescent** [-ˈnɛsənt] *adj*

luminosity [ˌluːməˈnɑsət̬i] *n, pl* **-ties** : luminosidad *f*

luminous [ˈluːmənəs] *adj* : luminoso — **luminously** *adv*

lump1 [ˈlʌmp] *vt or* **to lump together** : juntar, agrupar, amontonar — *vi* CLUMP : agruparse, aglutinarse

lump2 *n* **1** GLOB : grumo *m* **2** PIECE : pedazo *m*, trozo *m*, terrón *m* ⟨a lump of coal : un trozo de carbón⟩ ⟨a lump of sugar : un terrón de azúcar⟩ **3** SWELLING : bulto *m*, hinchazón *f*, protuberancia *f* **4 to have a lump in one's throat** : tener un nudo en la garganta

lumpy [ˈlʌmpi] *adj* **lumpier; -est** **1** : lleno de grumos (dícese de una salsa) **2** UNEVEN : desigual, disparejo

lunacy [ˈluːnəsi] *n, pl* **-cies** : locura *f*

lunar [ˈluːnər] *adj* : lunar

lunatic1 [ˈluːnəˌtɪk] *adj* : lunático, loco

lunatic2 *n* : loco *m*, -ca *f*

lunch1 [ˈlʌnʧ] *vi* : almorzar, comer

lunch2 *n* : almuerzo *m*, comida *f*, lonche *m*

luncheon [ˈlʌnʧən] *n* **1** : comida *f*, almuerzo *m* **2 luncheon meat** : fiambres *fpl*

lung [ˈlʌŋ] *n* : pulmón *m*
lunge¹ [ˈlʌndʒ] *vi* **lunged; lunging** 1 THRUST : atacar (en la esgrima) 2 **to lunge forward** : arremeter, lanzarse
lunge² *n* 1 : arremetida *f*, embestida *f* 2 : estocada *f* (en la esgrima)
lurch¹ [ˈlərtʃ] *vi* 1 PITCH : cabecear, dar bandazos, dar sacudidas 2 STAGGER : tambalearse
lurch² *n* 1 : sacudida *f*, bandazo *m* (de un vehículo) 2 : tambaleo *m* (de una persona)
lure¹ [ˈlʊr] *vt* **lured; luring** : atraer
lure² *n* 1 ATTRACTION : atractivo *m* 2 ENTICEMENT : señuelo *m*, aliciente *m* 3 BAIT : cebo *m* artificial (en la pesca)
lurid [ˈlʊrəd] *adj* 1 GRUESOME : espeluznante, horripilante 2 SENSATIONAL : sensacionalista, chocante 3 GAUDY : chillón
lurk [ˈlərk] *vi* : estar al acecho
luscious [ˈlʌʃəs] *adj* 1 DELICIOUS : delicioso, exquisito 2 SEDUCTIVE : seductor, cautivador
lush [ˈlʌʃ] *adj* 1 LUXURIANT : exuberante, lozano 2 LUXURIOUS : suntuoso, lujoso
lust¹ [ˈlʌst] *vi* **to lust after** : desear (a una persona), codiciar (riquezas, etc.)
lust² *n* 1 LASCIVIOUSNESS : lujuria *f*, lascivia *f* 2 CRAVING : deseo *m*, ansia *f*, anhelo *m*
luster *or* **lustre** [ˈlʌstər] *n* 1 GLOSS, SHEEN : lustre *m*, brillo *m* 2 SPLENDOR : lustre *m*, esplendor *m*
lusterless [ˈlʌstərləs] *adj* : deslustrado, sin brillo
lustful [ˈlʌstfəl] *adj* : lujurioso, lascivo, lleno de deseo
lustrous [ˈlʌstrəs] *adj* : brillante, brilloso, lustroso
lusty [ˈlʌsti] *adj* **lustier; -est** : fuerte, robusto, vigoroso — **lustily** [ˈlʌstəli] *adv*
lute [ˈluːt] *n* : laúd *m*
luxuriant [ˌlʌgˈʒʊriənt, ˌlʌkˈʃʊr-] *adj* 1 : exuberante, lozano (dícese de las plantas) 2 : abundante y hermoso (dícese del pelo) — **luxuriantly** *adv*
luxuriate [ˌlʌgˈʒʊriˌeɪt, ˌlʌkˈʃʊr-] *vi* **-ated; -ating** 1 : disfrutar 2 **to luxuriate in** : deleitarse con
luxurious [ˌlʌgˈʒʊriəs, ˌlʌkˈʃʊr-] *adj* : lujoso, suntuoso — **luxuriously** *adv*
luxury [ˈlʌkʃəri, ˈlʌgʒə-] *n, pl* **-ries** : lujo *m*
lye [ˈlaɪ] *n* : lejía *f*
lying → **lie¹**, **lie²**
lymph [ˈlɪmpf] *n* : linfa *f*
lymphatic [lɪmˈfæt̬ɪk] *adj* : linfático
lynch [ˈlɪntʃ] *vt* : linchar
lynx [ˈlɪŋks] *n, pl* **lynx** *or* **lynxes** : lince *m*
lyre [ˈlaɪr] *n* : lira *f*
lyric¹ [ˈlɪrɪk] *adj* : lírico
lyric² *n* 1 : poema *m* lírico 2 **lyrics** *npl* : letra *f* (de una canción)
lyrical [ˈlɪrɪkəl] *adj* : lírico, elocuente

M

m [ˈɛm] *n, pl* **m's** *or* **ms** [ˈɛmz] : decimotercera letra del alfabeto inglés
ma'am [ˈmæm] → **madam**
macabre [məˈkɑb, -ˈkɑbər, -ˈkɑbrə] *adj* : macabro
macadam [məˈkædəm] *n* : macadán *m*
macaroni [ˌmækəˈroːni] *n* : macarrones *mpl*
macaroon [ˌmækəˈruːn] *n* : macarrón *m*, mostachón *m*
macaw [məˈkɔ] *n* : guacamayo *m*
mace [ˈmeɪs] *n* 1 : maza *f* (arma o símbolo) 2 : macis *f* (especia)
machete [məˈʃɛt̬i] *n* : machete *m*
machination [ˌmækəˈneɪʃən, ˌmæʃə-] *n* : maquinación *f*, intriga *f*
machine¹ [məˈʃiːn] *vt* **-chined; -chining** : trabajar a máquina
machine² *n* 1 : máquina *f* ⟨machine shop : taller de máquinas⟩ ⟨machine language : lenguaje de la máquina⟩ 2 : aparato *m*, maquinaria *f* (en política)
machine gun *n* : ametralladora *f*
machinery [məˈʃiːnəri] *n, pl* **-eries** 1 : maquinaria *f* 2 WORKS : mecanismo *m*
machinist [məˈʃiːnɪst] *n* : maquinista *mf*
machismo [mɑˈtʃiːzmoː] *n* : machismo *m*, masculinidad *f*
macho [ˈmɑtʃoː] *adj* : machote, macho
mackerel [ˈmækərəl] *n, pl* **-el** *or* **-els** : caballa *f*
mackinaw [ˈmækəˌnɔ] *n* : chaqueta *f* escocesa de lana
mad [ˈmæd] *adj* **madder; maddest** 1 INSANE : loco, demente 2 RABID : rabioso 3 FOOLISH : tonto, insensato 4 ANGRY : enojado, furioso 5 CRAZY : loco ⟨I'm mad about you : estoy loco por ti⟩
Madagascan [ˌmædəˈgæskən] *n* : malgache *mf* — **Madagascan** *adj*
madam [ˈmædəm] *n, pl* **mesdames** [meɪˈdɑm, -ˈdæm] : señora *f*
madcap¹ [ˈmædˌkæp] *adj* ZANY : alocado, disparatado
madcap² *n* : alocado *m*, -da *f*
madden [ˈmædən] *vt* : enloquecer, enfurecer
maddening [ˈmædənɪŋ] *adj* : enloquecedor, exasperante ⟨I find it maddening : me saca de quicio⟩
made → **make¹**
madhouse [ˈmædˌhaʊs] *n* : manicomio *m* ⟨the office was a madhouse : la oficina parecía una casa de locos⟩
madly [ˈmædli] *adv* : como un loco, locamente

madman ['mæd,mæn, -mən] *n, pl* **-men** [-mən, -,mɛn] : loco *m*, demente *m*

madness ['mædnəs] *n* : locura *f*, demencia *f*

madwoman ['mæd,wʊmən] *n, pl* **-women** [-,wɪmən] : loca *f*, demente *f*

maelstrom ['meɪlstrəm] *n* : remolino *m*, vorágine *f*

maestro ['maɪ,stro:] *n, pl* **-stros** *or* **-stri** [-,stri:] : maestro *m*

Mafia ['mɑfiə] *n* : Mafia *f*

magazine ['mægə,zi:n] *n* **1** STOREHOUSE : almacén *m*, polvorín *m* (de explosivos) **2** PERIODICAL : revista *f* **3** : cargador *m* (de un arma de fuego)

magenta [mə'ʤɛntə] *n* : magenta *f*, color *m* magenta

maggot ['mægət] *n* : gusano *m*

magic¹ ['mæʤɪk] *or* **magical** ['mæʤɪkəl] *adj* : mágico

magic² *n* : magia *f*

magically ['mæʤɪkli] *adv* : mágicamente ⟨they magically appeared : aparecieron como por arte de magia⟩

magician [mə'ʤɪʃən] *n* **1** SORCERER : mago *m*, -ga *f* **2** CONJURER : prestidigitador *m*, -dora *f*; mago *m*, -ga *f*

magistrate ['mæʤə,streɪt] *n* : magistrado *m*, -da *f*

magma ['mægmə] *n* : magma *m*

magnanimity [,mægnə'nɪməṭi] *n, pl* **-ties** : magnanimidad *f*

magnanimous [mæg'nænəməs] *adj* : magnánimo, generoso — **magnanimously** *adv*

magnate ['mæg,neɪt, -nət] *n* : magnate *mf*

magnesium [mæg'ni:ziəm, -ʒəm] *n* : magnesio *m*

magnet ['mægnət] *n* : imán *m*

magnetic [mæg'nɛṭɪk] *adj* : magnético — **magnetically** [-ṭɪkli] *adv*

magnetic field *n* : campo *m* magnético

magnetism ['mægnə,tɪzəm] *n* : magnetismo *m*

magnetize ['mægnə,taɪz] *vt* **-tized; -tizing 1** : magnetizar, imantar **2** ATTRACT : magnetizar, atraer

magnification [,mægnəfə'keɪʃən] *n* : aumento *m*, ampliación *f*

magnificence [mæg'nɪfəsənts] *n* : magnificencia *f*

magnificent [mæg'nɪfəsənt] *adj* : magnífico — **magnificently** *adv*

magnify ['mægnə,faɪ] *vt* **-fied; -fying 1** ENLARGE : ampliar **2** EXAGGERATE : magnificar, exagerar

magnifying glass *n* : lupa *f*

magnitude ['mægnə,tu:d, -,tju:d] *n* **1** GREATNESS : magnitud *f*, grandeza *f* **2** QUANTITY : cantidad *f* **3** IMPORTANCE : magnitud *f*, envergadura *f*

magnolia [mæg'no:ljə] *n* : magnolia *f* (flor), magnolio *m* (árbol)

magpie ['mæg,paɪ] *n* : urraca *f*

mahogany [mə'hɑgəni] *n, pl* **-nies** : caoba *f*

maid ['meɪd] *n* **1** MAIDEN : doncella *f* **2** *or* **maidservant** ['meɪd,sərvənt] : sirvienta *f*, muchacha *f*, mucama *f*, criada *f*

maiden¹ ['meɪdən] *adj* **1** UNMARRIED : soltera **2** FIRST : primero ⟨maiden voyage : primera travesía⟩

maiden² *n* : doncella *f*

maidenhood ['meɪdən,hʊd] *n* : doncellez *f*

maiden name *n* : nombre *m* de soltera

mail¹ ['meɪl] *vt* : enviar por correo, echar al correo

mail² *n* **1** : correo *m* ⟨airmail : correo aéreo⟩ **2** : malla *f* ⟨coat of mail : cota de malla⟩

mailbox ['meɪl,bɑks] *n* : buzón *m*

mailman ['meɪl,mæn, -mən] *n, pl* **-men** [-mən, -,mn] : cartero *m*

maim ['meɪm] *vt* : mutilar, desfigurar, lisiar

main¹ ['meɪn] *adj* : principal, central ⟨the main office : la oficina central⟩

main² *n* **1** HIGH SEAS : alta mar *f* **2** : tubería *f* principal (de agua o gas), cable *m* principal (de un circuito) **3 with might and main** : con todas sus fuerzas

mainframe ['meɪn,freɪm] *n* : mainframe *m*, computadora *f* central

mainland ['meɪn,lænd, -lənd] *n* : continente *m*

mainly ['meɪnli] *adv* **1** PRINCIPALLY : principalmente, en primer lugar **2** MOSTLY : principalmente, en la mayor parte

mainstay ['meɪn,steɪ] *n* : pilar *m*, sostén *m* principal

mainstream¹ ['meɪn,stri:m] *adj* : dominante, corriente, convencional

mainstream² *n* : corriente *f* principal

maintain [meɪn'teɪn] *vt* **1** SERVICE : dar mantenimiento a (una máquina) **2** PRESERVE : mantener, conservar ⟨to maintain silence : guardar silencio⟩ **3** SUPPORT : mantener, sostener **4** ASSERT : mantener, sostener, afirmar

maintenance ['meɪntənənts] *n* : mantenimiento *m*

maize ['meɪz] *n* : maíz *m*

majestic [mə'ʤɛstɪk] *adj* : majestuoso — **majestically** [-tɪkli] *adv*

majesty ['mæʤəsti] *n, pl* **-ties 1** : majestad *f* ⟨Your Majesty : su Majestad⟩ **2** SPLENDOR : majestuosidad *f*, esplendor *m*

major¹ ['meɪʤər] *vi* **-jored; -joring** : especializarse

major² *adj* **1** GREATER : mayor **2** NOTEWORTHY : mayor, notable **3** SERIOUS : grave **4** : mayor (en la música)

major³ *n* **1** : mayor *mf*, comandante *mf* (en las fuerzas armadas) **2** : especialidad *f* (universitaria)

Majorcan [mɑ'ʤɔrkən, mə-, -'jɔr-] *n* : mallorquín *m*, -quina *f* — **Majorcan** *adj*

major general *n* : general *mf* de división

majority [mə'ʤɔrət̬i] *n, pl* **-ties** **1** ADULTHOOD : mayoría *f* de edad **2** : mayoría *f*, mayor parte *f* ⟨the vast majority : la inmensa mayoría⟩

make[1] ['meɪk] *v* **made** ['meɪd;]; **making** *vt* **1** CREATE : hacer ⟨to make noise : hacer ruido⟩ **2** FASHION, MANUFACTURE : hacer, fabricar ⟨she made a dress : hizo un vestido⟩ **3** DEVISE, FORM : desarrollar, elaborar, formar **4** CONSTITUTE : hacer, constituir ⟨made of stone : hecho de piedra⟩ **5** PREPARE : hacer, preparar **6** RENDER : hacer, poner ⟨it makes him nervous : lo pone nervioso⟩ ⟨to make someone happy : hacer feliz a alguien⟩ ⟨it made me sad : me dio pena⟩ **7** PERFORM : hacer ⟨to make a gesture : hacer un gesto⟩ **8** COMPEL : hacer, forzar, obligar **9** EARN : ganar ⟨to make a living : ganarse la vida⟩ — *vi* **1** HEAD : ir, dirigirse ⟨we made for home : nos fuimos a casa⟩ **2 to make do** : arreglárselas **3 to make good** REPAY : pagar **4 to make good** SUCCEED : tener éxito

make[2] *n* BRAND : marca *f*

make–believe[1] [ˌmeɪkbə'li:v] *adj* : imaginario

make–believe[2] *n* : fantasía *f*, invención *f* ⟨a world of make-believe : un mundo de ensueño⟩

make out *vt* **1** WRITE : hacer (un cheque) **2** DISCERN : distinguir, divisar **3** UNDERSTAND : comprender, entender — *vi* : arreglárselas ⟨how did you make out? : ¿qué tal te fue?⟩

maker ['meɪkər] *n* : fabricante *mf*

makeshift ['meɪkˌʃɪft] *adj* : provisional, improvisado

makeup ['meɪkˌʌp] *n* **1** COMPOSITION : composición *f* **2** CHARACTER : carácter *m*, temperamento *m* **3** COSMETICS : maquillaje *m*

make up *vt* **1** INVENT : inventar **2** : recuperar ⟨she made up the time : recuperó las horas perdidas⟩ — *vi* RECONCILE : hacer las paces, reconciliarse

making ['meɪkɪŋ] *n* **1** : creación *f*, producción *f* ⟨in the making : en ciernes⟩ **2 to have the makings of** : tener madera de (dícese de personas), tener los ingredientes para

maladjusted [ˌmælə'ʤʌstəd] *adj* : inadaptado

malady ['mælədi] *n, pl* **-dies** : dolencia *f*, enfermedad *f*, mal *m*

malaise [mə'leɪz, mæ-] *n* : malestar *m*

malapropism ['mæləˌprɑˌpɪzəm] *n* : uso *m* incorrecto y cómico de una palabra

malaria [mə'lɛriə] *n* : malaria *f*, paludismo *m*

malarkey [mə'lɑrki] *n* : tonterías *fpl*, estupideces *fpl*

Malawian [mə'lɑwiən] *n* : malauiano *m*, -na *f* — **Malawian** *adj*

Malay [mə'leɪ, 'meɪˌleɪ] *n* **1** *or* **Malayan** [mə'leɪən, meɪ-; 'meɪˌleɪən] : malayo *m*, -ya *f* **2** : malayo *m* (idioma) — **Malay** *or* **Malayan** *adj*

Malaysian [mə'leɪʒən, -ʃən] *n* : malasio *m*, -sia *f*; malaisio *m*, -sia *f* — **Malaysian** *adj*

male[1] ['meɪl] *adj* **1** : macho **2** MASCULINE : masculino

male[2] *n* : macho *m* (de animales o plantas), varón *m* (de personas)

malefactor ['mæləˌfæktər] *n* : malhechor *m*, -chora *f*

maleness ['meɪlnəs] *n* : masculinidad *f*

malevolence [mə'lɛvələnts] *n* : malevolencia *f*

malevolent [mə'lɛvələnt] *adj* : malévolo

malformation [ˌmælfɔr'meɪʃən] *n* : malformación *f*

malformed [mæl'fɔrmd] *adj* : mal formado, deforme

malfunction[1] [mæl'fʌŋkʃən] *vi* : funcionar mal

malfunction[2] *n* : mal funcionamiento *m*

malice ['mælɪs] *n* **1** : malicia *f*, malevolencia *f* **2 with malice aforethought** : con premeditación

malicious [mə'lɪʃəs] *adj* : malicioso, malévolo — **maliciously** *adv*

malign[1] [mə'laɪn] *vt* : calumniar, difamar

malign[2] *adj* : maligno

malignancy [mə'lɪgnəntsi] *n, pl* **-cies** : malignidad *f*

malignant [mə'lɪgnənt] *adj* : maligno

malinger [mə'lɪŋgər] *vi* : fingirse enfermo

malingerer [mə'lɪŋgərər] *n* : uno que se finge enfermo

mall ['mɔl] *n* **1** PROMENADE : alameda *f*, paseo *m* (arbolado) **2** : centro *m* comercial ⟨shopping mall : galería comercial⟩

mallard ['mælərd] *n, pl* **-lard** *or* **-lards** : pato *m* real, ánade *mf* real

malleable ['mæliəbəl] *adj* : maleable

mallet ['mælət] *n* : mazo *m*

malnourished [mæl'nərɪʃt] *adj* : desnutrido, malnutrido

malnutrition [ˌmælnʊ'trɪʃən, -njʊ-] *n* : desnutrición *f*, malnutrición *f*

malodorous [mæl'o:dərəs] *adj* : maloliente

malpractice [ˌmæl'præktəs] *n* : mala práctica *f*, negligencia *f*

malt ['mɔlt] *n* : malta *f*

maltreat [mæl'tri:t] *vt* : maltratar

mama *or* **mamma** ['mɑmə] *n* : mamá *f*

mammal ['mæməl] *n* : mamífero *m*

mammalian [mə'meɪliən, mæ-] *adj* : mamífero

mammary ['mæməri] *adj* **1** : mamario **2 mammary gland** : glándula mamaria

mammogram ['mæməˌgræm] *n* : mamografía *f*

mammoth[1] ['mæməθ] *adj* : colosal, gigantesco

mammoth[2] *n* : mamut *m*

man[1] ['mæn] *vt* **manned; manning** : tripular (un barco o avión), encargarse de (un servicio)

man[2] *n, pl* **men** [ˈmɛn] **1** PERSON : hombre *m*, persona *f* **2** MALE : hombre *m* **3** MANKIND : humanidad *f*
manacles [ˈmænɪkəlz] *npl* HANDCUFFS : esposas *fpl*
manage [ˈmænɪʤ] *v* **-aged; -aging** *vt* **1** HANDLE : controlar, manejar **2** DIRECT : administrar, dirigir **3** CONTRIVE : lograr, ingeniárselas para — *vi* COPE : arreglárselas
manageable [ˈmænɪʤəbəl] *adj* : manejable
management [ˈmænɪʤmənt] *n* **1** DIRECTION : administración *f*, gestión *f*, dirección *f* **2** HANDLING : manejo *m* **3** MANAGERS : dirección *f*, gerencia *f*
manager [ˈmænɪʤər] *n* : director *m*, -tora *f*; gerente *mf*; administrador *m*, -dora *f*
managerial [ˌmænəˈʤɪriəl] *adj* : directivo, gerencial
mandarin [ˈmændərən] *n* **1** : mandarín *m* **2** *or* **mandarin orange** : mandarina *f*
mandate [ˈmænˌdeɪt] *n* : mandato *m*
mandatory [ˈmændəˌtori] *adj* : obligatorio
mandible [ˈmændəbəl] *n* : mandíbula *f*
mandolin [ˌmændəˈlɪn, ˈmændələn] *n* : mandolina *f*
mane [ˈmeɪn] *n* : crin *f* (de un caballo), melena *f* (de un león o una persona)
maneuver[1] [məˈnuːvər, -ˈnjuː-] *vt* **1** PLACE, POSITION : maniobrar, posicionar, colocar **2** MANIPULATE : manipular, maniobrar — *vi* : maniobrar
maneuver[2] *n* : maniobra *f*
manfully [ˈmænfəli] *adv* : valientemente
manganese [ˈmæŋgəˌniːz, -ˌniːs] *n* : manganeso *m*
mange [ˈmeɪnʤ] *n* : sarna *f*
manger [ˈmeɪnʤər] *n* : pesebre *m*
mangle [ˈmæŋgəl] *vt* **-gled; -gling** **1** CRUSH, DESTROY : aplastar, despedazar, destrozar **2** MUTILATE : mutilar ⟨to mangle a text : mutilar un texto⟩
mango [ˈmæŋˌgoː] *n, pl* **-goes** : mango *m*
mangrove [ˈmænˌgroːv, ˈmæŋ-] *n* : mangle *m*
mangy [ˈmeɪnʤi] *adj* **mangier; -est** **1** : sarnoso **2** SHABBY : gastado
manhandle [ˈmænˌhændəl] *vt* **-dled; -dling** : maltratar, tratar con poco cuidado
manhole [ˈmænˌhoːl] *n* : boca *f* de alcantarilla
manhood [ˈmænˌhʊd] *n* **1** : madurez *f* (de un hombre) **2** COURAGE, MANLINESS : hombría *f*, valor *m* **3** MEN : hombres *mpl*
manhunt [ˈmænˌhʌnt] *n* : búsqueda *f* (de un criminal)
mania [ˈmeɪniə, -njə] *n* : manía *f*
maniac [ˈmeɪniˌæk] *n* : maníaco *m*, -ca *f*; maniático *m*, -ca *f*
maniacal [məˈnaɪəkəl] *adj* : maníaco, maniaco
manicure[1] [ˈmænəˌkjʊr] *vt* **-cured; -curing** **1** : hacer la manicura a **2** TRIM : recortar
manicure[2] *n* : manicura *f*
manicurist [ˈmænəˌkjʊrɪst] *n* : manicuro *m*, -ra *f*
manifest[1] [ˈmænəˌfɛst] *vt* : manifestar
manifest[2] *adj* : manifiesto, patente — **manifestly** *adv*
manifestation [ˌmænəfəˈsteɪʃən] *n* : manifestación *f*
manifesto [ˌmænəˈfɛsˌtoː] *n, pl* **-tos** *or* **-toes** : manifiesto *m*
manifold[1] [ˈmænəˌfoːld] *adj* : diverso, variado
manifold[2] *n* : colector *m* (de escape)
manipulate [məˈnɪpjəˌleɪt] *vt* **-lated; -lating** : manipular
manipulation [məˌnɪpjəˈleɪʃən] *n* : manipulación *f*
manipulative [məˈnɪpjəˌleɪṭɪv, -ləṭɪv] *adj* : manipulador
mankind [ˈmænˈkaɪnd, ˌkaɪnd] *n* : género *m* humano, humanidad *f*
manliness [ˈmænlinəs] *n* : hombría *f*, masculinidad *f*
manly [ˈmænli] *adj* **-lier; -est** : varonil, viril
man–made [ˈmænˈmeɪd] *adj* : artificial ⟨man-made fabrics : telas sintéticas⟩
manna [ˈmænə] *n* : maná *m*
mannequin [ˈmænɪkən] *n* **1** DUMMY : maniquí *m* **2** MODEL : modelo *mf*
manner [ˈmænər] *n* **1** KIND, SORT : tipo *m*, clase *f* **2** WAY : manera *f*, modo *m* **3** STYLE : estilo *m* (artístico) **4 manners** *npl* CUSTOMS : costumbres *fpl* ⟨Victorian manners : costumbres victorianas⟩ **5 manners** *npl* ETIQUETTE : modales *mpl*, educación *f*, etiqueta *f* ⟨good manners : buenos modales⟩
mannered [ˈmænərd] *adj* **1** AFFECTED, ARTIFICIAL : amanerado, afectado **2 well–mannered** : educado, cortés **3** → **ill–mannered**
mannerism [ˈmænəˌrɪzəm] *n* : peculiaridad *f*, gesto *m* particular
mannerly [ˈmænərli] *adj* : cortés, bien educado
mannish [ˈmænɪʃ] *adj* : masculino, hombruno
man–of–war [ˌmænəˈwɔr, -əvˈwɔr] *n, pl* **men–of–war** [ˌmɛn-] WARSHIP : buque *m* de guerra
manor [ˈmænər] *n* **1** : casa *f* solariega, casa *f* señorial **2** ESTATE : señorío *m*
manpower [ˈmænˌpaʊər] *n* : personal *m*, mano *f* de obra
mansion [ˈmænʧən] *n* : mansión *f*
manslaughter [ˈmænˌslɔṭər] *n* : homicidio *m* sin premeditación
mantel [ˈmæntəl] *n* : repisa *f* de chimenea
mantelpiece [ˈmæntəlˌpiːs] → **mantel**
mantis [ˈmæntəs] *n, pl* **-tises** *or* **-tes** [ˈmænˌtiːz] : mantis *f* religiosa
mantle [ˈmæntəl] *n* : manto *m*

manual[1] ['mænjʊəl] *adj* : manual — **manually** *adv*

manual[2] *n* : manual *m*

manufacture[1] [ˌmænjə'fæktʃər] *vt* **-tured; -turing** : fabricar, manufacturar, confeccionar (ropa), elaborar (comestibles)

manufacture[2] *n* : manufactura *f*, fabricación *f*, confección *f* (de ropa), elaboración *f* (de comestibles)

manufacturer [ˌmænjə'fæktʃərər] *n* : fabricante *m*; manufacturero *m*, -ra *f*

manure [mə'nʊr, -'njʊr] *n* : estiércol *m*

manuscript ['mænjəˌskrɪpt] *n* : manuscrito *m*

many[1] ['mɛni] *adj* **more** ['mor]; **most** ['mo:st] : muchos

many[2] *pron* : muchos *pl*, -chas *pl*

map[1] ['mæp] *vt* **mapped; mapping** 1 : trazar el mapa de 2 PLAN : planear, proyectar ⟨to map out a program : planear un programa⟩

map[2] *n* : mapa *m*

maple ['meɪpəl] *n* : arce *m*

mar ['mɑr] *vt* **marred; marring** 1 SPOIL : estropear, echar a perder 2 DEFACE : desfigurar

maraschino [ˌmærə'ski:no:, -'ʃi:-] *n, pl* **-nos** : cereza *f* al marrasquino

marathon ['mærəˌθɑn] *n* 1 RACE : maratón *m* 2 CONTEST : competencia *f* de resistencia

maraud [mə'rɔd] *vi* : merodear

marauder [mə'rɔdər] *n* : merodeador *m*, -dora *f*

marble ['mɑrbəl] *n* 1 : mármol *m* 2 : canica *f* ⟨to play marbles : jugar a las canicas⟩

march[1] ['mɑrtʃ] *vi* 1 : marchar, desfilar ⟨they marched past the grandstand : desfilaron ante la tribuna⟩ 2 : caminar con resolución ⟨she marched right up to him : se le acercó sin vacilación⟩

march[2] *n* 1 MARCHING : marcha *f* 2 PASSAGE : paso *m* (del tiempo) 3 PROGRESS : avance *m*, progreso *m* 4 : marcha *f* (en música)

March ['mɑrtʃ] *n* : marzo *m*

marchioness ['mɑrʃənɪs] *n* : marquesa *f*

Mardi Gras ['mɑrdiˌgrɑ] *n* : martes *m* de Carnaval

mare ['mær] *n* : yegua *f*

margarine ['mɑrdʒərən] *n* : margarina *f*

margin ['mɑrdʒən] *n* : margen *m*

marginal ['mɑrdʒənəl] *adj* 1 : marginal 2 MINIMAL : mínimo — **marginally** *adv*

marigold ['mærəˌgo:ld] *n* : maravilla *f*, caléndula *f*

marijuana [ˌmærə'*h*wɑnə] *n* : marihuana *f*

marina [mə'ri:nə] *n* : puerto *m* deportivo

marinade [ˌmærə'nɑd] *n* : adobo *m*, marinada *f*

marinate ['mærəˌneɪt] *vt* **-nated; -nating** : marinar

marine[1] [mə'ri:n] *adj* 1 : marino ⟨marine life : vida marina⟩ 2 NAUTICAL : náutico, marítimo 3 : de la infantería de marina

marine[2] *n* : soldado *m* de marina

mariner ['mærɪnər] *n* : marinero *m*, marino *m*

marionette [ˌmæriə'nɛt] *n* : marioneta *f*, títere *m*

marital ['mærəṭəl] *adj* 1 : matrimonial 2 **marital status** : estado *m* civil

maritime ['mærəˌtaɪm] *adj* : marítimo

marjoram ['mɑrdʒərəm] *n* : mejorana *f*

mark[1] ['mɑrk] *vt* 1 : marcar 2 CHARACTERIZE : caracterizar 3 SIGNAL : señalar 4 NOTICE : prestar atención a, hacer caso de 5 **to mark off** : demarcar, delimitar

mark[2] *n* 1 TARGET : blanco *m* 2 : marca *f*, señal *f* ⟨put a mark where you left off : pon una señal donde terminaste⟩ 3 INDICATION : señal *f*, indicio *m* 4 GRADE : nota *f* 5 IMPRINT : huella *f*, marca *f* 6 BLEMISH : marca *f*, imperfección *f*

marked ['mɑrkt] *adj* : marcado, notable — **markedly** ['mɑrkədli] *adv*

marker ['mɑrkər] *n* : marcador *m*

market[1] ['mɑrkət] *vt* : poner en venta, comercializar

market[2] *n* 1 MARKETPLACE : mercado *m* ⟨the open market : el mercado libre⟩ 2 DEMAND : demanda *f*, mercado *m* 3 STORE : tienda *f* 4 → **stock market**

marketable ['mɑrkəṭəbəl] *adj* : vendible

marketing ['mɑrkəṭɪŋ] *n* : mercadotecnia *f*, mercadeo *m*

marketplace ['mɑrkətˌpleɪs] *n* : mercado *m*

marksman ['mɑrksmən] *n, pl* **-men** [-mən, -ˌmn] : tirador *m*

marksmanship ['mɑrksmənˌʃɪp] *n* : puntería *f*

marlin ['mɑrlɪn] *n* : marlín *m*

marmalade ['mɑrməˌleɪd] *n* : mermelada *f*

marmoset ['mɑrməˌsɛt] *n* : tití *m*

marmot ['mɑrmət] *n* : marmota *f*

maroon[1] [mə'ru:n] *vt* : abandonar, aislar

maroon[2] *n* : rojo *m* oscuro, granate *m*

marquee [mɑr'ki:] *n* : marquesina *f*

marquess ['mɑrkwɪs] *or* **marquis** ['mɑrkwɪs, mɑr'ki:] *n, pl* **-quesses** *or* **-quises** [-'ki:z, -'ki:zəz] *or* **-quis** [-'ki:, -'ki:z] : marqués *m*

marquise [mɑr'ki:z] → **marchioness**

marriage ['mærɪdʒ] *n* 1 : matrimonio *m* 2 WEDDING : casamiento *m*, boda *f*

marriageable ['mærɪdʒəbəl] *adj* **of marriageable age** : de edad de casarse

married ['mærid] *adj* 1 : casado 2 **to get married** : casarse

marrow ['mæro:] *n* : médula *f*, tuétano *m*

marry ['mæri] *vt* **-ried; -rying** 1 : casar ⟨the priest married them : el cura los casó⟩ 2 : casarse con ⟨she married John : se casó con John⟩

Mars ['mɑrz] *n* : Marte *m*
marsh ['mɑrʃ] *n* **1** : pantano *m* **2 salt marsh** : marisma *f*
marshal¹ ['mɑrʃəl] *vt* **-shaled** *or* **-shalled; -shaling** *or* **-shalling 1** : poner en orden, reunir **2** USHER : conducir
marshal² *n* **1** : maestro *m* de ceremonias **2** : mariscal *m* (en el ejército); jefe *m*, -fa *f* (de la policía, de los bomberos, etc.)
marshmallow ['mɑrʃˌmɛlo:, -ˌmælo:] *n* : malvavisco *m*
marshy ['mɑrʃi] *adj* **marshier; -est** : pantanoso
marsupial [mɑr'su:piəl] *n* : marsupial *m*
mart ['mɑrt] *n* MARKET : mercado *m*
marten ['mɑrtən] *n, pl* **-ten** *or* **-tens** : marta *f*
martial ['mɑrʃəl] *adj* : marcial
martin ['mɑrtən] *n* **1** SWALLOW : golondrina *f* **2** SWIFT : vencejo *m*
martyr¹ ['mɑrt̬ər] *vt* : martirizar
martyr² *n* : mártir *mf*
martyrdom ['mɑrt̬ərdəm] *n* : martirio *m*
marvel¹ ['mɑrvəl] *vi* **-veled** *or* **-velled; -veling** *or* **-velling** : maravillarse
marvel² *n* : maravilla *f*
marvelous ['mɑrvələs] *or* **marvellous** *adj* : maravilloso — **marvelously** *adv*
Marxism ['mɑrkˌsɪzəm] *n* : marxismo *m*
Marxist¹ ['mɑrksɪst] *adj* : marxista
Marxist² *n* : marxista *mf*
mascara [mæs'kærə] *n* : rímel *m*, rimel *m*
mascot ['mæsˌkɑt, -kət] *n* : mascota *f*
masculine ['mæskjələn] *adj* : masculino
masculinity [ˌmæskjə'lɪnət̬i] *n* : masculinidad *f*
mash¹ ['mæʃ] *vt* **1** : hacer puré de (papas, etc.) **2** CRUSH : aplastar, majar
mash² *n* **1** FEED : afrecho *m* **2** : malta *f* (para hacer bebidas alcohólicas) **3** PASTE, PULP : papilla *f*, pasta *f*
mask¹ ['mæsk] *vt* **1** CONCEAL, DISGUISE : enmascarar, ocultar **2** COVER : cubrir, tapar
mask² *n* : máscara *f*, careta *f*, mascarilla *f* (de un cirujano o dentista)
masochism ['mæsəˌkɪzəm, 'mæzə-] *n* : masoquismo *m*
masochist ['mæsəˌkɪst, 'mæzə-] *n* : masoquista *mf*
masochistic [ˌmæsə'kɪstɪk, ˌmæzə-] *adj* : masoquista
mason ['meɪsən] *n* **1** BRICKLAYER : albañil *mf* **2** *or* **stonemason** ['sto:nˌ-] : mampostero *m*, cantero *m*
masonry ['meɪsənri] *n, pl* **-ries 1** BRICKLAYING : albañería *f* **2** *or* **stonemasonry** ['sto:nˌ-] : mampostería *f*
masquerade¹ [ˌmæskə'reɪd] *vi* **-aded; -ading 1** : disfrazarse (de), hacerse pasar (por) **2** : asistir a una mascarada
masquerade² *n* **1** : mascarada *f*, baile *m* de disfraces **2** FACADE : farsa *f*, fachada *f*
mass¹ ['mæs] *vi* : concentrarse, juntarse en masa — *vt* : concentrar
mass² *n* **1** : masa *f* ⟨atomic mass : masa atómica⟩ **2** BULK : mole *f*, volumen *m* **3** MULTITUDE : cantidad *f*, montón *m* (de cosas), multitud *f* (de gente) **4 the masses** : las masas, el pueblo, el populacho
Mass ['mæs] *n* : misa *f*
massacre¹ ['mæsɪkər] *vt* **-cred; -cring** : masacrar
massacre² *n* : masacre *f*
massage¹ [mə'sɑʒ, -'sɑʤ] *vt* **-saged; -saging** : masajear
massage² *n* : masaje *m*
masseur [mæ'sər] *n* : masajista *m*
masseuse [mæ'søz, -'su:z] *n* : masajista *f*
massive ['mæsɪv] *adj* **1** BULKY : voluminoso, macizo **2** HUGE : masivo, enorme — **massively** *adv*
mast ['mæst] *n* : mástil *m*, palo *m*
master¹ ['mæstər] *vt* **1** SUBDUE : dominar **2** : llegar a dominar ⟨she mastered French : llegó a dominar el francés⟩
master² *n* **1** TEACHER : maestro *m*, profesor *m* **2** EXPERT : experto *m*, -ta *f*; maestro *m*, -tra *f* **3** : amo *m* (de animales o esclavos), señor *m* (de la casa) **4 master's degree** : maestría *f*
masterful ['mæstərfəl] *adj* **1** IMPERIOUS : autoritario, imperioso, dominante **2** SKILLFUL : magistral — **masterfully** *adv*
masterly ['mæstərli] *adj* : magistral
mastermind ['mæstərˌmaɪnd] *n* : cerebro *m*, artífice *mf*
masterpiece ['mæstərˌpi:s] *n* : obra *f* maestra
masterwork ['mæstərˌwərk] → **masterpiece**
mastery ['mæstəri] *n* **1** DOMINION : dominio *m*, autoridad *f* **2** SUPERIORITY : superioridad *f* **3** EXPERTISE : maestría *f*
masticate ['mæstəˌkeɪt] *v* **-cated; -cating** : masticar
mastiff ['mæstɪf] *n* : mastín *m*
mastodon ['mæstəˌdɑn] *n* : mastodonte *m*
masturbate ['mæstərˌbeɪt] *v* **-bated; bating** *vi* : masturbarse — *vt* : masturbar
masturbation [ˌmæstər'beɪʃən] *n* : masturbación *f*
mat¹ ['mæt] *v* **matted; matting** *vt* TANGLE : enmarañar — *vi* : enmarañarse
mat² *n* **1** : estera *f* **2** TANGLE : maraña *f* **3** PAD : colchoneta *f* (de gimnasia) **4** *or* **matt** *or* **matte** ['mæt] FRAME : marco *m* (de cartón)
mat³ → **matte**
matador ['mæt̬əˌdɔr] *n* : matador *m*
match¹ ['mæʧ] *vt* **1** PIT : enfrentar, oponer **2** EQUAL, FIT : igualar, corresponder a, coincidir con **3** : combinar con, hacer juego con ⟨her shoes match her dress : sus zapatos hacen juego con su vestido⟩ — *vi* **1** CORRESPOND : concordar, coincidir **2** : hacer juego ⟨with a tie to match : con una corbata que hace juego⟩

match[2] *n* **1** EQUAL : igual *mf* ⟨he's no match for her : no puede competir con ella⟩ **2** FIGHT, GAME : partido *m*, combate *m* (en boxeo) **3** MARRIAGE : matrimonio *m*, casamiento *m* **4** : fósforo *m*, cerilla *f*, cerillo *m in various countries*) ⟨he lit a match : encendió un fósforo⟩ **5 to be a good match** : hacer buena pareja (dícese de las personas), hacer juego (dícese de la ropa)

matchless [ˈmætʃləs] *adj* : sin igual, sin par

matchmaker [ˈmætʃˌmeɪkər] *n* : casamentero *m*, -ra *f*

mate[1] [ˈmeɪt] *v* **mated; mating** *vi* **1** FIT : encajar **2** PAIR : emparejarse **3** (*relating to animals*) : aparearse, copular — *vt* : aparear, acoplar (animales)

mate[2] *n* **1** COMPANION : compañero *m*, -ra *f*; camarada *mf* **2** : macho *m*, hembra *f* (de animales) **3** : oficial *mf* (de un barco) ⟨first mate : primer oficial⟩ **4** : compañero *m*, -ra *f*; pareja *f* (de un zapato, etc.)

material[1] [məˈtɪriəl] *adj* **1** PHYSICAL : material, físico ⟨the material world : el mundo material⟩ ⟨material needs : necesidades materiales⟩ **2** IMPORTANT : importante, esencial **3 material evidence** : prueba *f* sustancial

material[2] *n* **1** : material *m* **2** CLOTH : tejido *m*, tela *f*

materialism [məˈtɪriəˌlɪzəm] *n* : materialismo *m*

materialist [məˈtɪriəlɪst] *n* : materialista *mf*

materialistic [məˌtɪriəˈlɪstɪk] *adj* : materialista

materialize [məˈtɪriəˌlaɪz] *v* **-ized; -izing** *vt* : materializar, hacer aparecer — *vi* : materializarse, aparecer

maternal [məˈtərnəl] *adj* MOTHERLY : maternal — **maternally** *adv*

maternity[1] [məˈtərnəṭi] *adj* : de maternidad ⟨maternity clothes : ropa de futura mamá⟩ ⟨maternity leave : licencia por maternidad⟩

maternity[2] *n, pl* **-ties** : maternidad *f*

math [ˈmæθ] → **mathematics**

mathematical [ˌmæθəˈmæṭɪkəl] *adj* : matemático — **mathematically** *adv*

mathematician [ˌmæθəməˈtɪʃən] *n* : matemático *m*, -ca *f*

mathematics [ˌmæθəˈmæṭɪks] *ns & pl* : matemáticas *fpl*, matemática *f*

matinee *or* **matinée** [ˌmætənˈeɪ] *n* : matiné *f*

matriarch [ˈmeɪtriˌɑrk] *n* : matriarca *f*

matriarchy [ˈmeɪtriˌɑrki] *n, pl* **-chies** : matriarcado *m*

matriculate [məˈtrɪkjəˌleɪt] *v* **-lated; -lating** *vt* : matricular — *vi* : matricularse

matriculation [məˌtrɪkjəˈleɪʃən] *n* : matrícula *f*, matriculación *f*

matrimony [ˈmætrəˌmoːni] *n* : matrimonio *m* — **matrimonial** [ˌmætrəˈmoːniəl] *adj*

matrix [ˈmeɪtrɪks] *n, pl* **-trices** [ˈmeɪtrəˌsiːz, ˈmæ-] *or* **-trixes** [ˈmeɪtrɪksəz] : matriz *f*

matron [ˈmeɪtrən] *n* : matrona *f*

matronly [ˈmeɪtrənli] *adj* : de matrona, matronal

matte [ˈmæt] *adj* : mate, de acabado mate

matter[1] [ˈmæṭər] *vi* : importar ⟨it doesn't matter : no importa⟩

matter[2] *n* **1** QUESTION : asunto *m*, cuestión *f* ⟨a matter of taste : una cuestión de gusto⟩ **2** SUBSTANCE : materia *f*, sustancia *f* **3 matters** *npl* CIRCUMSTANCES : situación *f*, cosas *fpl* ⟨to make matters worse : para colmo de males⟩ **4 to be the matter** : pasar ⟨what's the matter? : ¿qué pasa?⟩ **5 as a matter of fact** : en efecto, en realidad **6 for that matter** : de hecho **7 no matter how much** : por mucho que

matter–of–fact [ˈmæṭərəvˈfækt] *adj* : práctico, realista

mattress [ˈmætrəs] *n* : colchón *m*

mature[1] [məˈtʊr, -ˈtjʊr, -ˈtʃʊr] *vi* **-tured; -turing 1** : madurar **2** : vencer ⟨when does the loan mature? : ¿cuándo vence el préstamo?⟩

mature[2] *adj* **-turer; -est 1** : maduro **2** DUE : vencido

maturity [məˈtʊrəṭi, -ˈtjʊr-, -ˈtʃʊr-] *n* : madurez *f*

maudlin [ˈmɔdlɪn] *adj* : sensiblero

maul[1] [ˈmɔl] *vt* **1** BEAT : golpear, pegar **2** MANGLE : mutilar **3** MANHANDLE : maltratar

maul[2] *n* MALLET : mazo *m*

Mauritanian [ˌmɔrəˈteɪniən] *n* : mauritano *m*, -na *f* — **Mauritanian** *adj*

mausoleum [ˌmɔsəˈliːəm, ˌmɔzə-] *n, pl* **-leums** *or* **-lea** [-ˈliːə] : mausoleo *m*

mauve [ˈmoːv, ˈmɔv] *n* : malva *m*

maven *or* **mavin** [ˈmeɪvən] *n* EXPERT : experto *m*, -ta *f*

maverick [ˈmævrɪk, ˈmævə-] *n* **1** : ternero *m* sin marcar **2** NONCONFORMIST : inconformista *mf*, disidente *mf*

mawkish [ˈmɔkɪʃ] *adj* : sensiblero

maxim [ˈmæksəm] *n* : máxima *f*

maximize [ˈmæksəˌmaɪz] *vt* **-mized; -mizing** : maximizar, llevar al máximo

maximum[1] [ˈmæksəməm] *adj* : máximo

maximum[2] *n, pl* **-ma** [ˈmæksəmə] *or* **-mums** : máximo *m*

may [ˈmeɪ] *v aux, past* **might** [ˈmaɪt] *present s & pl* **may 1** (*expressing permission*) : poder ⟨you may go : puedes ir⟩ **2** (*expressing possibility or probability*) : poder ⟨you may be right : puede que tengas razón⟩ ⟨it may happen occasionally : puede pasar de vez en cuando⟩ **3** (*expressing desires, intentions, or contingencies*) ⟨may the best man win : que gane el mejor⟩ ⟨I laugh that I may not weep : me río para no llorar⟩ ⟨come what may : pase lo que pase⟩

May [ˈmeɪ] *n* : mayo *m*

Maya [ˈmaɪə] *or* **Mayan** [ˈmaɪən] *n* : maya *mf* — **Maya** *or* **Mayan** *adj*
maybe [ˈmeɪbi] *adv* PERHAPS : quizás, tal vez
mayfly [ˈmeɪˌflaɪ] *n, pl* **-flies** : efímera *f*
mayhem [ˈmeɪˌhɛm, ˈmeɪəm] *n* **1** MUTILATION : mutilación *f* **2** DEVASTATION : estragos *mpl*
mayonnaise [ˈmeɪəˌneɪz] *n* : mayonesa *f*
mayor [ˈmeɪər, ˈmɛr] *n* : alcalde *m*, -desa *f*
mayoral [ˈmeɪərəl, ˈmɛrəl] *adj* : de alcalde
maze [ˈmeɪz] *n* : laberinto *m*
me [ˈmiː] *pron* **1** : me ⟨she called me : me llamó⟩ ⟨give it to me : dámelo⟩ **2** (*after a preposition*) : mí ⟨for me : para mí⟩ ⟨with me : conmigo⟩ **3** (*after conjunctions and verbs*) : yo ⟨it's me : soy yo⟩ ⟨as big as me : tan grande como yo⟩ **4** (*emphatic use*) : yo ⟨me, too! : ¡yo también!⟩ ⟨who, me? : ¿quién, yo?⟩
meadow [ˈmɛdoː] *n* : prado *m*, pradera *f*
meadowland [ˈmɛdoˌlænd] *n* : pradera *f*
meadowlark [ˈmɛdoˌlɑrk] *n* : pájaro *m* cantor con el pecho amarillo
meager *or* **meagre** [ˈmiːgər] *adj* **1** THIN : magro, flaco **2** POOR, SCANTY : exiguo, escaso, pobre
meagerly [ˈmiːgərli] *adv* : pobremente
meagerness [ˈmiːgərnəs] *n* : escasez *f*, pobreza *f*
meal [ˈmiːl] *n* **1** : comida *f* ⟨a hearty meal : una comida sustanciosa⟩ **2** : harina *f* (de maíz, etc.)
mealtime [ˈmiːlˌtaɪm] *n* : hora *f* de comer
mean[1] [ˈmiːn] *vt* **meant** [ˈmɛnt]; **meaning** **1** INTEND : querer, pensar, tener la intención de ⟨I didn't mean to do it : lo hice sin querer⟩ ⟨what do you mean to do? : ¿qué piensas hacer?⟩ **2** SIGNIFY : querer decir, significar ⟨what does that mean? : ¿qué quiere decir eso?⟩ **3** : importar ⟨health means everything : lo que más importa es la salud⟩
mean[2] *adj* **1** HUMBLE : humilde **2** NEGLIGIBLE : despreciable ⟨it's no mean feat : no es poca cosa⟩ **3** STINGY : mezquino, tacaño **4** CRUEL : malo, cruel ⟨to be mean to someone : tratar mal a alguien⟩ **5** AVERAGE, MEDIAN : medio
mean[3] *n* **1** MIDPOINT : término *m* medio **2** AVERAGE : promedio *m*, media *f* aritmética **3 means** *npl* WAY : medio *m*, manera *f*, vía *f* **4 means** *npl* RESOURCES : medios *mpl*, recursos *mpl* **5 by all means** : por supuesto, cómo no **6 by means of** : por medio de **7 by no means** : de ninguna manera, de ningún modo
meander [miˈændər] *vi* **-dered; -dering** **1** WIND : serpentear **2** WANDER : vagar, andar sin rumbo fijo
meaning [ˈmiːnɪŋ] *n* **1** : significado *m*, sentido *m* ⟨double meaning : doble sentido⟩ **2** INTENT : intención *f*, propósito *m*
meaningful [ˈmiːnɪŋfəl] *adj* : significativo — **meaningfully** *adv*
meaningless [ˈmiːnɪŋləs] *adj* : sin sentido
meanness [ˈmiːnnəs] *n* **1** CRUELTY : crueldad *f*, mezquindad *f* **2** STINGINESS : tacañería *f*
meantime[1] [ˈmiːnˌtaɪm] *adv* → **meanwhile**[1]
meantime[2] *n* **1** : interín *m* **2 in the meantime** : entretanto, mientras tanto
meanwhile[1] [ˈmiːnˌ*h*waɪl] *adv* : entretanto, mientras tanto
meanwhile[2] *n* → **meantime**[2]
measles [ˈmiːzəlz] *ns & pl* : sarampión *m*
measly [ˈmiːzli] *adj* **-slier; -est** : miserable, mezquino
measurable [ˈmɛʒərəbəl, ˈmeɪ-] *adj* : mensurable — **measurably** [-bli] *adv*
measure[1] [ˈmɛʒər, ˈmeɪ-] *v* **-sured; -suring** : medir ⟨he measured the table : midió la mesa⟩ ⟨it measures 15 feet tall : mide 15 pies de altura⟩
measure[2] *n* **1** AMOUNT : medida *f*, cantidad *f* ⟨in large measure : en gran medida⟩ ⟨a full measure : una cantidad exacta⟩ ⟨a measure of proficiency : una cierta competencia⟩ ⟨for good measure : de ñapa, por añadidura⟩ **2** DIMENSIONS, SIZE : medida *f*, tamaño *m* **3** RULER : regla *f* ⟨tape measure : cinta métrica⟩ **4** MEASUREMENT : medida *f* ⟨cubic measure : medida de capacidad⟩ **5** MEASURING : medición *f* **6 measures** *npl* : medidas *fpl* ⟨security measures : medidas de seguridad⟩
measureless [ˈmɛʒərləs, ˈmeɪ-] *adj* : inmensurable
measurement [ˈmɛʒərmənt, ˈmeɪ-] *n* **1** MEASURING : medición *f* **2** DIMENSION : medida *f*
measure up *vi* **to measure up to** : estar a la altura de
meat [ˈmiːt] *n* **1** FOOD : comida *f* **2** : carne *f* ⟨meat and fish : carne y pescado⟩ **3** SUBSTANCE : sustancia *f*, esencia *f* ⟨the meat of the story : la sustancia del cuento⟩
meatball [ˈmiːtˌbɔl] *n* : albóndiga *f*
meaty [ˈmiːṭi] *adj* **meatier; -est** : con mucha carne, carnoso
mechanic [mɪˈkænɪk] *n* : mecánico *m*, -ca *f*
mechanical [mɪˈkænɪkəl] *adj* : mecánico — **mechanically** *adv*
mechanics [mɪˈkænɪks] *ns & pl* **1** : mecánica *f* ⟨fluid mechanics : la mecánica de fluidos⟩ **2** MECHANISMS : mecanismos *mpl*, aspectos *mpl* prácticos
mechanism [ˈmɛkəˌnɪzəm] *n* : mecanismo *m*
mechanization [ˌmɛkənəˈzeɪʃən] *n* : mecanización *f*

mechanize ['mɛkə,naɪz] *vt* **-nized; -nizing** : mecanizar
medal ['mɛdəl] *n* : medalla *f*, condecoración *f*
medalist ['mɛdəlɪst] *or* **medallist** *n* : medallista *mf*
medallion [mə'dæljən] *n* : medallón *m*
meddle ['mɛdəl] *vi* **-dled; -dling** : meterse, entrometerse
meddler ['mɛdələr] *n* : entrometido *m*, -da *f*
meddlesome ['mɛdəlsəm] *adj* : entrometido
media ['mi:diə] *npl* : medios *mpl* de comunicación
median¹ ['mi:diən] *adj* : medio
median² *n* : valor *m* medio
mediate ['mi:di,eɪt] *vi* **-ated; -ating** : mediar
mediation [,mi:di'eɪʃən] *n* : mediación *f*
mediator ['mi:di,eɪt̬ər] *n* : mediador *m*, -dora *f*
medical ['mɛdɪkəl] *adj* : médico
medicate ['mɛdə,keɪt] *vt* **-cated; -cating** : medicar ⟨medicated powder : polvos medicinales⟩
medication [,mɛdə'keɪʃən] *n* **1** TREATMENT : tratamiento *m*, medicación *f* **2** MEDICINE : medicamento *m* ⟨to be on medication : estar medicado⟩
medicinal [mə'dɪsənəl] *adj* : medicinal
medicine ['mɛdəsən] *n* **1** MEDICATION : medicina *f*, medicamento *m* **2** : medicina *f* ⟨he's studying medicine : estudia medicina⟩
medicine man *n* : hechicero *m*
medieval *or* **mediaeval** [mɪ'di:vəl, ,mi:-, ,mɛ-, -di'i:vəl] *adj* : medieval
mediocre [,mi:di'o:kər] *adj* : mediocre
mediocrity [,mi:di'ɑkrət̬i] *n, pl* **-ties** : mediocridad *f*
meditate ['mɛdə,teɪt] *vi* **-tated; -tating** : meditar
meditation [,mɛdə'teɪʃən] *n* : meditación *f*
meditative ['mɛdə,teɪt̬ɪv] *adj* : meditabundo
medium¹ ['mi:diəm] *adj* : mediano ⟨of medium height : de estatura mediana, de estatura regular⟩
medium² *n, pl* **-diums** *or* **-dia** ['mi:-diə] **1** MEAN : punto *m* medio, término *m* medio ⟨happy medium : justo medio⟩ **2** MEANS : medio *m* **3** SUBSTANCE : medio *m*, sustancia *f* ⟨a viscous medium : un medio viscoso⟩ **4** : medio *m* de comunicación **5** : medio *m* (artístico)
medley ['mɛdli] *n, pl* **-leys** : popurrí *m* (de canciones)
meek ['mi:k] *adj* **1** LONG-SUFFERING : paciente, sufrido **2** SUBMISSIVE : sumiso, dócil, manso
meekly ['mi:kli] *adv* : dócilmente
meekness ['mi:knəs] *n* : mansedumbre *f*, docilidad *f*
meet¹ ['mi:t] *v* **met** ['mɛt]; **meeting** *vt* **1** ENCOUNTER : encontrarse con **2** JOIN : unirse con **3** CONFRONT : enfrentarse a **4** SATISFY : satisfacer, cumplir con ⟨to meet costs : pagar los gastos⟩ **5** : conocer ⟨I met his sister : conocí a su hermana⟩ — *vi* ASSEMBLE : reunirse, congregarse
meet² *n* : encuentro *m*
meeting ['mi:t̬ɪŋ] *n* **1** : reunión *f* ⟨to open the meeting : abrir la sesión⟩ **2** ENCOUNTER : encuentro *m* **3** : entrevista *f* (formal)
meetinghouse ['mi:t̬ɪŋ,haʊs] *n* : iglesia *f* (de ciertas confesiones protestantes)
megabyte ['mɛgə,baɪt] *n* : megabyte *m*
megahertz ['mɛgə,hərts, -,hrts] *n* : megahercio *m*
megaphone ['mɛgə,fo:n] *n* : megáfono *m*
melancholy¹ ['mɛlən,kɑli] *adj* : melancólico, triste, sombrío
melancholy² *n, pl* **-cholies** : melancolía *f*
melanoma [,mɛlə'no:mə] *n, pl* **-mas** : melanoma *m*
meld ['mɛld] *vt* : fusionar, unir — *vi* : fusionarse, unirse
melee ['meɪ,leɪ, meɪ'leɪ] *n* BRAWL : reyerta *f*, riña *f*, pelea *f*
meliorate ['mi:ljə,reɪt, 'mi:liə-] → **ameliorate**
mellow¹ ['mɛlo:] *vt* : suavizar, endulzar — *vi* : suavizarse, endulzarse
mellow² *adj* **1** RIPE : maduro **2** MILD : apacible ⟨a mellow character : un carácter apacible⟩ ⟨mellow wines : vinos añejos⟩ **3** : suave, dulce ⟨mellow colors : colores suaves⟩ ⟨mellow tones : tonos dulces⟩
mellowness ['mɛlonəs] *n* : suavidad *f*, dulzura *f*
melodic [mə'lɑdɪk] *adj* : melódico — **melodically** [-dɪkli] *adv*
melodious [mə'lo:diəs] *adj* : melodioso — **melodiously** *adv*
melodiousness [mə'lo:diəsnəs] *n* : calidad *f* de melódico
melodrama ['mɛlə,drɑmə, -,dræ-] *n* : melodrama *m*
melodramatic [,mɛlədrə'mæt̬ɪk] *adj* : melodramático — **melodramatically** [-t̬ɪkli] *adv*
melody ['mɛlədi] *n, pl* **-dies** : melodía *f*, tonada *f*
melon ['mɛlən] *n* : melón *m*
melt ['mɛlt] *vt* **1** : derretir, disolver **2** SOFTEN : ablandar ⟨it melted his heart : ablandó su corazón⟩ — *vi* **1** : derretirse, disolverse **2** SOFTEN : ablandarse **3** DISAPPEAR : desvanecerse, esfumarse ⟨the clouds melted away : las nubes se desvanecieron⟩
melting point *n* : punto *m* de fusión
member ['mɛmbər] *n* **1** LIMB : miembro *m* **2** : miembro *m* (de un grupo); socio *m*, -cia *f* (de un club) **3** PART : miembro *m*, parte *f*
membership ['mɛmbər,ʃɪp] *n* **1** : membresía *f* ⟨application for membership

: solicitud de entrada⟩ **2** MEMBERS : membresía *f*, miembros *mpl*, socios *mpl*
membrane [ˈmɛmˌbreɪn] *n* : membrana *f* — **membranous** [ˈmɛmbrə-nəs] *adj*
memento [mɪˈmɛnˌtoː] *n, pl* **-tos** *or* **-toes** : recuerdo *m*
memo [ˈmɛmoː] *n, pl* **memos** : memorándum *m*
memoirs [ˈmɛmˌwɑrz] *npl* : memorias *fpl*, autobiografía *f*
memorabilia [ˌmɛmərəˈbiliə, -ˈbɪljə] *npl* **1** : objetos *mpl* de interés histórico **2** MEMENTOS : recuerdos *mpl*
memorable [ˈmɛmərəbəl] *adj* : memorable, notable — **memorably** [-bli] *adv*
memorandum [ˌmɛməˈrændəm] *n, pl* **-dums** *or* **-da** [-də] : memorándum *m*
memorial¹ [məˈmoriəl] *adj* : conmemorativo
memorial² *n* : monumento *m* conmemorativo
Memorial Day *n* : el último lunes de mayo (observado en Estados Unidos como día feriado para conmemorar a los caídos en guerra)
memorialize [məˈmoriəˌlaɪz] *vt* **-ized; -izing** COMMEMORATE : conmemorar
memorization [ˌmɛmərəˈzeɪʃən] *n* : memorización *f*
memorize [ˈmɛməˌraɪz] *vt* **-rized; -rizing** : memorizar, aprender de memoria
memory [ˈmɛmri, ˈmɛmə-] *n, pl* **-ries** **1** : memoria *f* ⟨he has a good memory : tiene buena memoria⟩ **2** RECOLLECTION : recuerdo *m* **3** COMMEMORATION : memoria *f*, conmemoración *f*
men → **man²**
menace¹ [ˈmɛnəs] *vt* **-aced; -acing** **1** THREATEN : amenazar **2** ENDANGER : poner en peligro
menace² *n* : amenaza *f*
menacing [ˈmɛnəsɪŋ] *adj* : amenazador, amenazante
menagerie [məˈnæʤəri, -ˈnæʒəri] *n* : colección *f* de animales salvajes
mend¹ [ˈmɛnd] *vt* **1** CORRECT : enmendar, corregir ⟨to mend one's ways : enmendarse⟩ **2** REPAIR : remendar, arreglar, reparar — *vi* HEAL : curarse
mend² *n* : remiendo *m*
mendicant [ˈmɛndɪkənt] *n* BEGGAR : mendigo *m*, -ga *f*
menhaden [mɛnˈheɪdən, mən-] *ns & pl* : pez *m* de la misma familia que los arenques
menial¹ [ˈmiːniəl] *adj* : servil, bajo
menial² *n* : sirviente *m*, -ta *f*
meningitis [ˌmɛnənˈʤaɪt̬əs] *n, pl* **-gitides** [-ˈʤɪt̬əˌdiːz] : meningitis *f*
menopause [ˈmɛnəˌpɔz] *n* : menopausia *f*
menorah [məˈnorə] *n* : candelabro *m* (usado en los oficios religiosos judíos)
menstrual [ˈmɛn*t*struəl] *adj* : menstrual
menstruate [ˈmɛn*t*struˌeɪt] *vi* **-ated; -ating** : menstruar
menstruation [ˌmɛn*t*struˈeɪʃən] *n* : menstruación *f*
mental [ˈmɛntəl] *adj* : mental ⟨mental hospital : hospital psiquiátrico⟩ — **mentally** *adv*
mentality [mɛnˈtæləṯi] *n, pl* **-ties** : mentalidad *f*
menthol [ˈmɛnˌθɔl, -ˌθoːl] *n* : mentol *m*
mentholated [ˌmɛn*t*θəˌleɪt̬əd] *adj* : mentolado
mention¹ [ˈmɛnʧən] *vt* : mencionar, mentar, referirse a ⟨don't mention it! : ¡de nada!, ¡no hay de qué!⟩
mention² *n* : mención *f*
mentor [ˈmɛnˌtɔr, ˈmɛntər] *n* : mentor *m*
menu [ˈmɛnˌjuː] *n* **1** : menú *m*, carta *f* (en un restaurante) **2** : menú *m* (de computadoras)
meow¹ [miːˈaʊ] *vi* : maullar
meow² *n* : maullido *m*, miau *m*
mercantile [ˈmərkənˌtiːl, -ˌtaɪl] *adj* : mercantil
mercenary¹ [ˈmərsənɛˌri] *adj* : mercenario
mercenary² *n, pl* **-naries** : mercenario *m*, -ria *f*
merchandise [ˈmərʧənˌdaɪz, -ˌdaɪs] *n* : mercancía *f*, mercadería *f*
merchandiser [ˈmərʧənˌdaɪzər] *n* : comerciante *mf*; vendedor *m*, -dora *f*
merchant [ˈmərʧənt] *n* : comerciante *mf*
merchant marine *n* : marina *f* mercante
merciful [ˈmərsɪfəl] *adj* : misericordioso, clemente
mercifully [ˈmərsɪfli] *adv* **1** : con misericordia, con compasión **2** FORTUNATELY : afortunadamente
merciless [ˈmərsɪləs] *adj* : despiadado — **mercilessly** *adv*
mercurial [ˌmərˈkjʊriəl] *adj* TEMPERAMENTAL : temperamental, volátil
mercury [ˈmərkjəri] *n, pl* **-ries** : mercurio *m*
Mercury *n* : Mercurio *m*
mercy [ˈmərsi] *n, pl* **-cies** **1** CLEMENCY : misericordia *f*, clemencia *f* **2** BLESSING : bendición *f*
mere [ˈmɪr] *adj, superlative* **merest** : mero, simple
merely [ˈmɪrli] *adv* : solamente, simplemente
merge [ˈmərʤ] *v* **merged; merging** *vi* : unirse, fusionarse (dícese de las compañías), confluir (dícese de los ríos, las calles, etc.) — *vt* : unir, fusionar, combinar
merger [ˈmərʤər] *n* : unión *f*, fusión *f*
meridian [məˈrɪdiən] *n* : meridiano *m*
meringue [məˈræŋ] *n* : merengue *m*
merino [məˈriːno] *n, pl* **-nos** **1** : merino *m*, -na *f* **2** *or* **merino wool** : lana *f* merino
merit¹ [ˈmɛrət] *vt* : merecer, ser digno de
merit² *n* : mérito *m*, valor *m*
meritorious [ˌmɛrəˈtoriəs] *adj* : meritorio
mermaid [ˈmərˌmeɪd] *n* : sirena *f*
merriment [ˈmɛrɪmənt] *n* : alegría *f*, júbilo *m*, regocijo *m*

merry ['mɛri] *adj* **-rier; -est** : alegre — **merrily** ['mɛrəli] *adv*
merry–go–round ['mɛrigo,raʊnd] *n* : carrusel *m*, tiovivo *m*
merrymaker ['mɛri,meɪkər] *n* : juerguista *mf*
merrymaking ['mɛri,meɪkɪŋ] *n* : juerga *f*
mesa ['meɪsə] *n* : mesa *f*
mesdames → **madam, Mrs.**
mesh[1] ['mɛʃ] *vi* **1** ENGAGE : engranar (dícese de las piezas mecánicas) **2** TANGLE : enredarse **3** COORDINATE : coordinarse, combinar
mesh[2] *n* **1** : malla *f* ⟨wire mesh : malla metálica⟩ **2** NETWORK : red *f* **3** MESHING : engranaje *m* ⟨in mesh : engranado⟩
mesmerize ['mɛzmə,raɪz] *vt* **-ized; -izing 1** HYPNOTIZE : hipnotizar **2** FASCINATE : cautivar, embelesar, fascinar
mess[1] ['mɛs] *vt* **1** SOIL : ensuciar **2 to mess up** DISARRANGE : desordenar, desarreglar **3 to mess up** BUNGLE : echar a perder — *vi* **1** PUTTER : entretenerse **2** INTERFERE : meterse, entrometerse ⟨don't mess with me : no te metas conmigo⟩
mess[2] *n* **1** : rancho *m* (para soldados, etc.) **2** DISORDER : desorden *m* ⟨your room is a mess : tienes el cuarto hecho un desastre⟩ **3** CONFUSION, TURMOIL : confusión *f*, embrollo *m*, lío *m fam*
message ['mɛsɪʤ] *n* : mensaje *m*, recado *m*
messenger ['mɛsənʤər] *n* : mensajero *m*, -ra *f*
Messiah [mə'saɪə] *n* : Mesías *m*
Messrs. → **Mr.**
messy ['mɛsi] *adj* **messier; -est** UNTIDY : desordenado, sucio
met → **meet**
metabolic [,mɛt̬ə'bɑlɪk] *adj* : metabólico
metabolism [mə'tæbə,lɪzəm] *n* : metabolismo *m*
metabolize [mə'tæbə,laɪz] *vt* **-lized; -lizing** : metabolizar
metal ['mɛt̬əl] *n* : metal *m*
metallic [mə'tælɪk] *adj* : metálico
metallurgical [,mɛt̬əl'ərʤɪkəl] *adj* : metalúrgico
metallurgy ['mɛt̬əl,ərʤi] *n* : metalurgia *f*
metalwork ['mɛt̬əl,wərk] *n* : objeto *m* de metal
metalworking ['mɛt̬əl,wərkɪŋ] *n* : metalistería *f*
metamorphosis [,mɛt̬ə'mɔrfəsɪs] *n, pl* **-phoses** [-,si:z] : metamorfosis *f*
metaphor ['mɛt̬ə,fɔr, -fər] *n* : metáfora *f*
metaphoric [,mɛt̬ə'fɔrɪk] *or* **metaphorical** [-ɪkəl] *adj* : metafórico
metaphysical [,mɛt̬ə'fɪzəkəl] *adj* : metafísico
metaphysics [,mɛt̬ə'fɪzɪks] *n* : metafísica *f*
mete ['mi:t] *vt* **meted; meting** ALLOT : repartir, distribuir ⟨to mete out punishment : imponer castigos⟩
meteor ['mi:t̬iər, -t̬i:,ɔr] *n* : meteoro *m*
meteoric [,mi:t̬i'ɔrɪk] *adj* : meteórico
meteorite ['mi:t̬iə,raɪt] *n* : meteorito *m*
meteorologic [,mi:t̬i,ɔrə'lɑʤɪk] *or* **meteorological** [-'lɑʤɪkəl] *adj* : meteorológico
meteorologist [,mi:t̬iə'rɑləʤɪst] *n* : meteorólogo *m*, -ga *f*
meteorology [,mi:t̬iə'rɑləʤi] *n* : meteorología *f*
meter ['mi:t̬ər] *n* **1** : metro *m* ⟨it measures 2 meters : mide 2 metros⟩ **2** : contador *m*, medidor *m* (de electricidad, etc.) ⟨parking meter : parquímetro⟩ **3** : metro *m* (en literatura o música)
methane ['mɛ,θeɪn] *n* : metano *m*
method ['mɛθəd] *n* : método *m*
methodical [mə'θɑdɪkəl] *adj* : metódico — **methodically** *adv*
Methodist ['mɛθədɪst] *n* : metodista *mf* — **Methodist** *adj*
methodology [,mɛθə'dɑləʤi] *n, pl* **-gies** : metodología *f*
meticulous [mə'tɪkjələs] *adj* : meticuloso — **meticulously** *adv*
meticulousness [mə'tɪkjələsnəs] *n* : meticulosidad *f*
metric ['mɛtrɪk] *or* **metrical** [-trɪkəl] *adj* : métrico
metric system *n* : sistema *m* métrico
metronome ['mɛtrə,no:m] *n* : metrónomo *m*
metropolis [mə'trɑpələs] *n* : metrópoli *f*, metrópolis *f*
metropolitan [,mɛtrə'pɑlətən] *adj* : metropolitano
mettle ['mɛt̬əl] *n* : temple *m*, valor *m* ⟨on one's mettle : dispuesto a mostrar su valía⟩
Mexican ['mɛksɪkən] *n* : mexicano *m*, -na *f* — **Mexican** *adj*
mezzanine ['mɛzə,ni:n, ,mɛzə'ni:n] *n* **1** : entrepiso *m*, entresuelo *m* **2** : primer piso *m* (de un teatro)
miasma [maɪ'æzmə] *n* : miasma *m*
mica ['maɪkə] *n* : mica *f*
mice → **mouse**
micro ['maɪkro] *adj* : muy pequeño, microscópico
microbe ['maɪ,kro:b] *n* : microbio *m*
microbiology [,maɪkrobaɪ'ɑləʤi] *n* : microbiología *f*
microchip ['maɪkro,ʧɪp] *n* : microchip *m*
microcomputer ['maɪkrokəm,pju:t̬ər] *n* : microcomputadora *f*
microcosm ['maɪkro,kɑzəm] *n* : microcosmo *m*
microfilm ['maɪkro,fɪlm] *n* : microfilm *m*
micrometer [maɪ'krɑmət̬ər] *n* : micrómetro *m*
micron ['maɪ,krɑn] *n* : micrón *m*
microorganism [,maɪkro'ɔrgə,nɪzəm] *n* : microorganismo *m*, microbio *m*

microphone [ˈmaɪkrəˌfo:n] *n* : micrófono *m*
microprocessor [ˈmaɪkroˌprɑˌsɛsər] *n* : microprocesador *m*
microscope [ˈmaɪkrəˌsko:p] *n* : microscopio *m*
microscopic [ˌmaɪkrəˈskɑpɪk] *adj* : microscópico
microscopy [maɪˈkrɑskəpi] *n* : microscopía *f*
microwave [ˈmaɪkrəˌweɪv] *n* **1** : microonda *f* **2** *or* **microwave oven** : microondas *m*
mid [ˈmɪd] *adj* : medio ⟨mid morning : a media mañana⟩ ⟨in mid-August : a mediados de agosto⟩ ⟨in mid ocean : en alta mar⟩
midair [ˈmɪdˈær] *n* **in ~** : en el aire ⟨to catch in midair : agarrar al vuelo⟩
midday [ˈmɪdˈdeɪ] *n* NOON : mediodía *m*
middle[1] [ˈmɪdəl] *adj* **1** CENTRAL : medio, del medio, de en medio **2** INTERMEDIATE : intermedio, mediano ⟨middle age : la mediana edad⟩
middle[2] *n* **1** CENTER : medio *m*, centro *m* ⟨fold it down the middle : dóblalo por la mitad⟩ **2 in the middle of** : en medio de (un espacio), a mitad de (una actividad) ⟨in the middle of the month : a mediados del mes⟩
Middle Ages *npl* : Edad *f* Media
middle class *n* : clase *f* media
middleman [ˈmɪdəlˌmæn] *n, pl* **-men** [-mən, -ˌmɛn] : intermediario *m*, -ria *f*
middling [ˈmɪdlɪŋ, -lən] *adj* **1** MEDIUM, MIDDLE : mediano **2** MEDIOCRE : mediocre, regular
midfielder [ˈmɪdˌfi:ldər] *n* : mediocampista *mf*
midge [ˈmɪdʒ] *n* : mosca *f* pequeña
midget [ˈmɪdʒət] *n* **1** : enano *m*, -na *f* (persona) **2** : cosa *f* diminuta
midland [ˈmɪdlənd, -ˌlænd] *n* : región *f* central (de un país)
midnight [ˈmɪdˌnaɪt] *n* : medianoche *f*
midpoint [ˈmɪdˌpɔɪnt] *n* : punto *m* medio, término *m* medio
midriff [ˈmɪdˌrɪf] *n* : diafragma *m*
midshipman [ˈmɪdˌʃɪpmən, ˌmɪdˈʃɪp-] *n, pl* **-men** [-mən, -ˌmɛn] : guardiamarina *m*
midst[1] [ˈmɪdst] *n* : medio *m* ⟨in our midst : entre nosotros⟩ ⟨in the midst of : en medio de⟩
midst[2] *prep* : entre
midstream [ˈmɪdˈstri:m, -ˌstri:m] *n* : medio *m* de la corriente ⟨in the midstream of his career : en medio de su carrera⟩
midsummer [ˈmɪdˈsʌmər, -ˌsʌ-] *n* : pleno verano *m*
midtown [ˈmɪdˌtaʊn] *n* : centro *m* (de una ciudad)
midway [ˈmɪdˌweɪ] *adv* HALFWAY : a mitad de camino
midweek [ˈmɪdˌwi:k] *n* : medio *m* de la semana ⟨in midweek : a media semana⟩
midwife [ˈmɪdˌwaɪf] *n, pl* **-wives** [-ˌwaɪvz] : partera *f*, comadrona *f*
midwinter [ˈmɪdˈwɪntər, -ˌwin-] *n* : pleno invierno *m*
midyear [ˈmɪdˌjɪr] *n* : medio *m* del año ⟨at midyear : a mediados del año⟩
mien [ˈmi:n] *n* : aspecto *m*, porte *m*, semblante *m*
miff [ˈmɪf] *vt* : ofender
might[1] [ˈmaɪt] (*used to express permission or possibility or as a polite alternative to* **may**) → **may** ⟨it might be true : podría ser verdad⟩ ⟨might I speak with Sarah? : ¿se puede hablar con Sarah?⟩
might[2] *n* : fuerza *f*, poder *m*
mightily [ˈmaɪtəli] *adv* : con mucha fuerza, poderosamente
mighty[1] [ˈmaɪti] *adv* VERY : muy ⟨mighty good : muy bueno, buenísimo⟩
mighty[2] *adj* **mightier; -est 1** POWERFUL : poderoso, potente **2** GREAT : grande, imponente
migraine [ˈmaɪˌgreɪn] *n* : jaqueca *f*, migraña *f*
migrant [ˈmaɪgrənt] *n* : trabajador *m*, -dora *f* ambulante
migrate [ˈmaɪˌgreɪt] *vi* **-grated; -grating** : emigrar
migration [maɪˈgreɪʃən] *n* : migración *f*
migratory [ˈmaɪgrəˌtori] *adj* : migratorio
mild [ˈmaɪld] *adj* **1** GENTLE : apacible, suave ⟨a mild disposition : un temperamento suave⟩ **2** LIGHT : leve, ligero ⟨a mild punishment : un castigo leve, un castigo poco severo⟩ **3** TEMPERATE : templado (dícese del clima) — **mildly** *adv*
mildew[1] [ˈmɪlˌdu:, -ˌdju:] *vi* : enmohecerse
mildew[2] *n* : moho *m*
mildness [ˈmaɪldnəs] *n* : apacibilidad *f*, suavidad *f*
mile [ˈmaɪl] *n* : milla *f*
mileage [ˈmaɪlɪdʒ] *n* **1** ALLOWANCE : viáticos *mpl* (pagados por milla recorrida) **2** : distancia *f* recorrida (en millas), kilometraje *m*
milestone [ˈmaɪlˌsto:n] *n* LANDMARK : hito *m*, jalón *m* ⟨a milestone in his life : un hito en su vida⟩
milieu [mi:lˈju:, -ˈjø] *n, pl* **-lieus** *or* **-lieux** [-ˈju:z, -ˈjø] SURROUNDINGS : entorno *m*, medio *m*, ambiente *m*
militant[1] [ˈmɪlətənt] *adj* : militante, combativo
militant[2] *n* : militante *mf*
militarism [ˈmɪlətəˌrɪzəm] *n* : militarismo *m*
militaristic [ˌmɪlətəˈrɪstɪk] *adj* : militarista
military[1] [ˈmɪləˌtɛri] *adj* : militar
military[2] *n* **the military** : las fuerzas armadas
militia [məˈlɪʃə] *n* : milicia *f*
milk[1] [ˈmɪlk] *vt* **1** : ordeñar (una vaca, etc.) **2** EXPLOIT : explotar

milk² *n* : leche *f*
milkman [ˈmɪlk,mæn, -mən] *n, pl* **-men** [-mən, -,mɛn] : lechero *m*
milk shake *n* : batido *m*, licuado *m*
milkweed [ˈmɪlk,wi:d] *n* : algodoncillo *m*
milky [ˈmɪlki] *adj* **milkier; -est** : lechoso
Milky Way *n* : Vía *f* Láctea
mill¹ [ˈmɪl] *vt* : moler (granos), fresar (metales), acordonar (monedas) — *vi* **to mill about** : arremolinarse
mill² *n* **1** : molino *m* (para moler granos) **2** FACTORY : fábrica *f* ⟨textile mill : fábrica textil⟩ **3** GRINDER : molinillo *m*
millennium [məˈlɛniəm] *n, pl* **-nia** [-niə] *or* **-niums** : milenio *m*
miller [ˈmɪlər] *n* : molinero *m*, -ra *f*
millet [ˈmɪlət] *n* : mijo *m*
milligram [ˈmɪlə,græm] *n* : miligramo *m*
milliliter [ˈmɪlə,li:ţər] *n* : mililitro *m*
millimeter [ˈmɪlə,mi:ţər] *n* : milímetro *m*
milliner [ˈmɪlənər] *n* : sombrerero *m*, -ra *f* (de señoras)
millinery [ˈmɪlə,nɛri] *n* : sombreros *mpl* de señora
million¹ [ˈmɪljən] *adj* **a million** : un millón de
million² *n, pl* **millions** *or* **million** : millón *m*
millionaire [,mɪljəˈnær, ˈmɪljə,nær] *n* : millonario *m*, -ria *f*
millionth¹ [ˈmɪljənθ] *adj* : millonésimo
millionth² *n* : millonésimo *m*
millipede [ˈmɪlə,pi:d] *n* : milpiés *m*
millstone [ˈmɪl,sto:n] *n* : rueda *f* de molino, muela *f*
mime¹ [ˈmaɪm] *v* **mimed; miming** *vt* MIMIC : imitar, remedar — *vi* PANTOMIME : hacer la mímica
mime² *n* **1** : mimo *mf* **2** PANTOMIME : pantomima *f*
mimeograph [ˈmɪmiə,græf] *n* : mimeógrafo *m*
mimic¹ [ˈmɪmɪk] *vt* **-icked; -icking** : imitar, remedar
mimic² *n* : imitador *m*, -dora *f*
mimicry [ˈmɪmɪkri] *n, pl* **-ries** : mímica *f*, imitación *f*
minaret [,mɪnəˈrɛt] *n* : alminar *m*, minarete *m*
mince [ˈmɪnts] *v* **minced; mincing** *vt* **1** CHOP : picar, moler (carne) **2 not to mince one's words** : no tener uno pelos en la lengua — *vi* : caminar de manera afectada
mincemeat [ˈmɪnts,mi:t] *n* : mezcla *f* de fruta picada, sebo, y especias
mind¹ [ˈmaɪnd] *vt* **1** TEND : cuidar, atender ⟨mind the children : cuida a los niños⟩ **2** OBEY : obedecer **3** : preocuparse por, sentirse molestado por ⟨I don't mind his jokes : sus bromas no me molestan⟩ **4** : tener cuidado con ⟨mind the ladder! : ¡cuidado con la escalera!⟩ — *vi* **1** OBEY : obedecer **2** CARE : importarle a uno ⟨I don't mind : no me importa, me es igual⟩
mind² *n* **1** MEMORY : memoria *f*, recuerdo *m* ⟨keep it in mind : téngalo en cuenta⟩ **2** : mente *f* ⟨the mind and the body : la mente y el cuerpo⟩ **3** INTENTION : intención *f*, propósito *m* ⟨to have a mind to do something : tener intención de hacer algo⟩ **4** : razón *f* ⟨he's out of his mind : está loco⟩ **5** OPINION : opinión *f* ⟨to change one's mind : cambiar de opinión⟩ **6** INTELLECT : capacidad *f* intelectual
minded [ˈmaɪndəd] *adj* **1** (*used in combination*) ⟨narrow-minded : de mentalidad cerrada⟩ ⟨health-minded : preocupado por la salud⟩ **2** INCLINED : inclinado
mindful [ˈmaɪndfəl] *adj* AWARE : consciente — **mindfully** *adv*
mindless [ˈmaɪndləs] *adj* **1** SENSELESS : estúpido, sin sentido ⟨mindless violence : violencia sin sentido⟩ **2** HEEDLESS : inconsciente
mindlessly [ˈmaɪndləsli] *adv* **1** SENSELESSLY : sin sentido **2** HEEDLESSLY : inconscientemente
mine¹ [ˈmaɪn] *vt* **mined; mining 1** : extraer (oro, etc.) **2** : minar (con artefactos explosivos)
mine² *n* : mina *f* ⟨gold mine : mina de oro⟩
mine³ *pron* : mío, mía ⟨that one's mine : ése es el mío⟩ ⟨some friends of mine : unos amigos míos⟩
minefield [ˈmaɪn:fi:ld] *n* : campo *m* de minas
miner [ˈmaɪnər] *n* : minero *m*, -ra *f*
mineral [ˈmɪnərəl] *n* : mineral *m* — **mineral** *adj*
mineralogy [,mɪnəˈrɑləʤi, -ˈræ-] *n* : mineralogía *f*
mingle [ˈmɪŋgəl] *v* **-gled; -gling** *vt* MIX : mezclar — *vi* **1** MIX : mezclarse **2** CIRCULATE : circular
miniature¹ [ˈmɪniə,ʧʊr, ˈmɪnɪ,ʧʊr, -ʧər] *adj* : en miniatura, diminuto
miniature² *n* : miniatura *f*
minibus [ˈmɪni,bʌs] *n* : microbús *m*, pesera *f* *Mex*
minicomputer [ˈmɪnikəm,pju:ţər] *n* : minicomputadora *f*
minimal [ˈmɪnəməl] *adj* : mínimo
minimally [ˈmɪnəməli] *adv* : en grado mínimo
minimize [ˈmɪnə,maɪz] *vt* **-mized; -mizing** : minimizar
minimum¹ [ˈmɪnəməm] *adj* : mínimo
minimum² *n, pl* **-ma** [ˈmɪnəmə] *or* **-mums** : mínimo *m*
miniseries [ˈmɪni,sɪri:z] *n* : miniserie *f*
miniskirt [ˈmɪni,skərt] *n* : minifalda *f*
minister¹ [ˈmɪnəstər] *vi* **to minister to** : cuidar (de), atender a
minister² *n* **1** : pastor *m*, -tora *f* (de una iglesia) **2** : ministro *m*, -tra *f* (en política)
ministerial [,mɪnəˈstɪriəl] *adj* : ministerial
ministry [ˈmɪnəstri] *n, pl* **-tries 1** : ministerio *m* (en política) **2** : sacerdocio *m* (en el catolicismo), clerecía *f* (en el protestantismo)

minivan ['mɪni,væn] *n* : minivan *f*
mink ['mɪŋk] *n, pl* **mink** *or* **minks** : visón *m*
minnow ['mɪno:] *n, pl* **-nows** : pececillo *m* de agua dulce
minor[1] ['maɪnər] *adj* : menor
minor[2] *n* **1** : menor *mf* (de edad) **2** : asignatura *f* secundaria (de estudios)
minority [mə'nɔrəṭi, maɪ-] *n, pl* **-ties** : minoría *f*
minstrel ['mɪn*t*strəl] *n* : juglar *m*, trovador *m* (en el medioevo)
mint[1] ['mɪnt] *vt* : acuñar
mint[2] *adj* : sin usar ⟨in mint condition : como nuevo⟩
mint[3] *n* **1** : menta *f* ⟨mint tea : té de menta⟩ **2** : pastilla *f* de menta **3** : casa *f* de la moneda ⟨the U.S. Mint : la casa de la moneda de los EE.UU.⟩ **4** FORTUNE : dineral *m*, fortuna *f*
minuet [,mɪnjʊ'ɛt] *n* : minué *m*
minus[1] ['maɪnəs] *n* **1** : cantidad *f* negativa **2 minus sign** : signo *m* de menos
minus[2] *prep* **1** : menos ⟨four minus two : cuatro menos dos⟩ **2** WITHOUT : sin ⟨minus his hat : sin su sombrero⟩
minuscule *or* **miniscule** ['mɪnəs,kju:l, mɪ'nʌs-] *adj* : minúsculo
minute[1] [maɪ'nu:t, mɪ-, -'nju:t] *adj* **-nuter; -est 1** TINY : diminuto, minúsculo **2** DETAILED : minucioso
minute[2] ['mɪnət] *n* **1** : minuto *m* ⟨ten minutes late : diez minutos de retraso⟩ **2** MOMENT : momento *m* **3 minutes** *npl* : actas *fpl* (de una reunión)
minutely [maɪ'nu:tli, mɪ-, -'nju:t-] *adv* : minuciosamente
miracle ['mɪrɪkəl] *n* : milagro *m*
miraculous [mə'rækjələs] *adj* : milagroso — **miraculously** *adv*
mirage [mɪ'rɑʒ, *chiefly Brit* 'mɪr,ɑʒ] *n* : espejismo *m*
mire[1] ['maɪr] *vi* **mired; miring** : atascarse
mire[2] *n* **1** MUD : barro *m*, lodo *m* **2** : atolladero *m* ⟨stuck in a mire of debt : agobiado por la deuda⟩
mirror[1] ['mɪrər] *vt* : reflejar
mirror[2] *n* : espejo *m*
mirth ['mərθ] *n* : alegría *f*, regocijo *m*
mirthful ['mərθfəl] *adj* : alegre, regocijado
misadventure [,mɪsəd'vɛnʧər] *n* : malaventura *f*, desventura *f*
misanthrope ['mɪsən,θro:p] *n* : misántropo *m*, -pa *f*
misanthropic [,mɪsən'θrɑpɪk] *adj* : misantrópico
misanthropy [mɪ'sænθrəpi] *n* : misantropía *f*
misapprehend [,mɪs,æprə'hɛnd] *vt* : entender mal
misapprehension [,mɪs,æprə'hɛnʧən] *n* : malentendido *m*
misappropriate [,mɪsə'pro:pri,eɪt] *vt* **-ated; -ating** : malversar
misbegotten [,mɪsbi'gɑtən] *adj* **1** ILLEGITIMATE : ilegítimo **2** : mal concebido ⟨misbegotten laws : leyes mal concebidas⟩
misbehave [,mɪsbi'heɪv] *vi* **-haved; -having** : portarse mal
misbehavior [,mɪsbi'heɪvjər] *n* : mala conducta *f*
miscalculate [mɪs'kælkjə,leɪt] *v* **-lated; -lating** : calcular mal
miscalculation [mɪs,kælkjə'leɪʃən] *n* : error *m* de cálculo, mal cálculo *m*
miscarriage [,mɪs'kærɪʤ, 'mɪs,kærɪʤ] *n* **1** : aborto *m* **2** FAILURE : fracaso *m*, malogro *m* ⟨a miscarriage of justice : una injusticia, un error judicial⟩
miscarry [,mɪs'kæri, 'mɪs,kæri] *vi* **-ried; -rying 1** ABORT : abortar **2** FAIL : malograrse, fracasar
miscellaneous [,mɪsə'leɪniəs] *adj* : misceláneo
miscellany ['mɪsə,leɪni] *n, pl* **-nies** : miscelánea *f*
mischance [mɪs'ʧæn*t*s] *n* : desgracia *f*, infortunio *m*, mala suerte *f*
mischief ['mɪsʧəf] *n* : diabluras *fpl*, travesuras *fpl*
mischievous ['mɪsʧəvəs] *adj* : travieso, pícaro
mischievously ['mɪsʧəvəsli] *adv* : de manera traviesa
misconception [,mɪskən'sɛpʃən] *n* : concepto *m* erróneo, idea *f* falsa
misconduct [mɪs'kɑndəkt] *n* : mala conducta *f*
misconstrue [,mɪskən'stru:] *vt* **-strued; -struing** : malinterpretar
misdeed [mɪs'di:d] *n* : fechoría *f*
misdemeanor [,mɪsdɪ'mi:nər] *n* : delito *m* menor
miser ['maɪzər] *n* : avaro *m*, -ra *f*; tacaño *m*, -ña *f*
miserable ['mɪzərəbəl] *adj* **1** UNHAPPY : triste, desdichado **2** WRETCHED : miserable, desgraciado ⟨a miserable hut : una choza miserable⟩ **3** UNPLEASANT : desagradable, malo ⟨miserable weather : tiempo malísimo⟩ **4** CONTEMPTIBLE : despreciable, mísero ⟨for a miserable $10 : por unos míseros diez dólares⟩
miserably ['mɪzərəbli] *adv* **1** SADLY : tristemente **2** WRETCHEDLY : miserablemente, lamentablemente **3** UNFORTUNATELY : desgraciadamente
miserly ['maɪzərli] *adj* : avaro, tacaño
misery ['mɪzəri] *n, pl* **-eries** : miseria *f*, sufrimiento *m*
misfire [mɪs'faɪr] *vi* **-fired; -firing** : fallar
misfit ['mɪs,fɪt] *n* : inadaptado *m*, -da *f*
misfortune [mɪs'fɔrʧən] *n* : desgracia *f*, desventura *f*, infortunio *m*
misgiving [mɪs'gɪvɪŋ] *n* : duda *f*, recelo *m*
misguided [mɪs'gaɪdəd] *adj* : desacertado, equivocado, mal informado
mishap ['mɪs,hæp] *n* : contratiempo *m*, percance *m*, accidente *m*
misinform [,mɪsɪn'fɔrm] *vt* : informar mal
misinterpret [,mɪsɪn'tərprət] *vt* : malinterpretar

misinterpretation [ˌmɪsɪnˌtərprəˈteɪ-ʃən] *n* : mala interpretación *f*, malentendido *m*
misjudge [mɪsˈʤʌʤ] *vt* **-judged; -judging** : juzgar mal
mislay [mɪsˈleɪ] *vt* **-laid** [-leɪd]; **-laying** : extraviar, perder
mislead [mɪsˈliːd] *vt* **-led** [-ˈlɛd]; **-leading** : engañar
misleading [mɪsˈliːdɪŋ] *adj* : engañoso
mismanage [mɪsˈmænɪʤ] *vt* **-aged; -aging** : administrar mal
mismanagement [mɪsˈmænɪʤmənt] *n* : mala administración *f*
misnomer [mɪsˈnoːmər] *n* : nombre *m* inapropiado
misogynist [mɪˈsɑʤənɪst] *n* : misógino *m*
misogyny [məˈsɑʤəni] *n* : misoginia *f*
misplace [mɪsˈpleɪs] *vt* **-placed; -placing** : extraviar, perder
misprint [ˈmɪsˌprɪnt, mɪsˈ-] *n* : errata *f*, error *m* de imprenta
mispronounce [ˌmɪsprəˈnaʊnts] *vt* **-nounced; -nouncing** : pronunciar mal
mispronunciation [ˌmɪsprəˌnʌntsiˈeɪʃən] *n* : pronunciación *f* incorrecta
misquote [mɪsˈkwoːt] *vt* **-quoted; -quoting** : citar incorrectamente
misread [mɪsˈriːd] *vt* **-read; -reading** **1** : leer mal ⟨she misread the sentence : leyó mal la frase⟩ **2** MISUNDERSTAND : malinterpretar ⟨they misread his intention : malinterpretaron su intención⟩
misrepresent [ˌmɪsˌrɛprɪˈzɛnt] *vt* : distorsionar, falsear, tergiversar
misrule[1] [mɪsˈruːl] *vt* **-ruled; -ruling** : gobernar mal
misrule[2] *n* : mal gobierno *m*
miss[1] [ˈmɪs] *vt* **1** : errar, faltar ⟨to miss the target : no dar en el blanco⟩ **2** : no encontrar, perder ⟨they missed each other : no se encontraron⟩ ⟨I missed the plane : perdí el avión⟩ **3** : echar de menos, extrañar ⟨we miss him a lot : lo echamos mucho de menos⟩ **4** OVERLOOK : pasar por alto, perder (una oportunidad, etc.) **5** AVOID : evitar ⟨they just missed hitting the tree : por muy poco chocan contra el árbol⟩ **6** OMIT : saltarse ⟨he missed breakfast : se saltó el desayuno⟩
miss[2] *n* **1** : fallo *m* (de un tiro, etc.) **2** FAILURE : fracaso *m* **3** : señorita *f* ⟨Miss Jones called us : nos llamó la señorita Jones⟩ ⟨excuse me, miss : perdone, señorita⟩
missal [ˈmɪsəl] *n* : misal *m*
misshapen [mɪˈʃeɪpən] *adj* : deforme
missile [ˈmɪsəl] *n* **1** : misil *m* ⟨guided missile : misil guiado⟩ **2** PROJECTILE : proyectil *m*
missing [ˈmɪsɪŋ] *adj* **1** ABSENT : ausente ⟨who's missing? : ¿quién falta?⟩ **2** LOST : perdido, desaparecido ⟨missing persons : los desaparecidos⟩
mission [ˈmɪʃən] *n* **1** : misión *f* (mandada por una iglesia) **2** DELEGATION : misión *f*, delegación *f*, embajada *f* **3** TASK : misión *f*
missionary[1] [ˈmɪʃəˌnɛri] *adj* : misionero
missionary[2] *n, pl* **-aries** : misionero *m*, -ra *f*
missive [ˈmɪsɪv] *n* : misiva *f*
misspell [mɪsˈspɛl] *vt* : escribir mal
misspelling [mɪsˈspɛlɪŋ] *n* : falta *f* de ortografía
misstep [ˈmɪsˌstɛp] *n* : traspié *m*, tropezón *m*
mist [ˈmɪst] *n* **1** HAZE : neblina *f*, niebla *f* **2** SPRAY : rocío *m*
mistake[1] [mɪˈsteɪk] *vt* **-took** [-ˈstʊk]; **-taken** [-ˈsteɪkən]; **-taking** **1** MISINTERPRET : malinterpretar **2** CONFUSE : confundir ⟨he mistook her for Clara : la confundió con Clara⟩
mistake[2] *n* **1** MISUNDERSTANDING : malentendido *m*, confusión *f* **2** ERROR : error *m* ⟨I made a mistake : me equivoqué, cometí un error⟩
mistaken [mɪˈsteɪkən] *adj* WRONG : equivocado — **mistakenly** *adv*
mister [ˈmɪstər] *n* : señor *m* ⟨watch out, mister : cuidado, señor⟩
mistiness [ˈmɪstinəs] *n* : nebulosidad *f*
mistletoe [ˈmɪsəlˌtoː] *n* : muérdago *m*
mistreat [mɪsˈtriːt] *vt* : maltratar
mistreatment [mɪsˈtriːtmənt] *n* : maltrato *m*, abuso *m*
mistress [ˈmɪstrəs] *n* **1** : dueña *f*, señora *f* (de una casa) **2** LOVER : amante *f*
mistrust[1] [mɪsˈtrʌst] *vt* : desconfiar de
mistrust[2] *n* : desconfianza *f*
mistrustful [mɪsˈtrʌstfəl] *adj* : desconfiado
misty [ˈmɪsti] *adj* **mistier; -est** **1** : neblinoso, nebuloso **2** TEARFUL : lloroso
misunderstand [ˌmɪsˌʌndərˈstænd] *vt* **-stood** [-ˈstʊd]; **-standing** **1** : entender mal **2** MISINTERPRET : malinterpretar ⟨don't misunderstand me : no me malinterpretes⟩
misunderstanding [ˌmɪsˌʌndərˈstændɪŋ] *n* **1** MISINTERPRETATION : malentendido *m* **2** DISAGREEMENT, QUARREL : disputa *f*, discusión *f*
misuse[1] [mɪsˈjuːz] *vt* **-used; -using** **1** : emplear mal **2** ABUSE, MISTREAT : abusar de, maltratar
misuse[2] [mɪsˈjuːs] *n* **1** : mal empleo *m*, mal uso *m* **2** WASTE : derroche *m*, despilfarro *m* **3** ABUSE : abuso *m*
mite [ˈmaɪt] *n* **1** : ácaro *m* **2** BIT : poco *m* ⟨a mite tired : un poquito cansado⟩
miter *or* **mitre** [ˈmaɪt̬ər] *n* **1** : mitra *f* (de un obispo) **2** *or* **miter joint** : inglete *m*
mitigate [ˈmɪt̬əˌgeɪt] *vt* **-gated; -gating** : mitigar, aliviar
mitigation [ˌmɪt̬əˈgeɪʃən] *n* : mitigación *f*, alivio *m*
mitosis [maɪˈtoːsɪs] *n, pl* **-toses** [-ˌsiːz] : mitosis *f*
mitt [ˈmɪt] *n* : manopla *f*, guante *m* (de béisbol)

mitten [ˈmɪtən] *n* : manopla *f*, mitón *m*
mix[1] [ˈmɪks] *vt* **1** COMBINE : mezclar **2** STIR : remover, revolver **3 to mix up** CONFUSE : confundir — *vi* : mezclarse
mix[2] *n* : mezcla *f*
mixer [ˈmɪksər] *n* **1** : batidora *f* (de la cocina) **2 cement mixer** : hormigonera *f*
mixture [ˈmɪkstʃər] *n* : mezcla *f*
mix–up [ˈmɪksˌʌp] *n* CONFUSION : confusión *f*, lío *m fam*
mnemonic [nɪˈmɑnɪk] *adj* : mnemónico
moan[1] [ˈmoːn] *vi* : gemir
moan[2] *n* : gemido *m*
moat [ˈmoːt] *n* : foso *m*
mob[1] [ˈmɑb] *vt* **mobbed; mobbing 1** ATTACK : atacar en masa **2** HOUND : acosar, rodear
mob[2] *n* **1** THRONG : multitud *f*, turba *f*, muchedumbre *f* **2** GANG : pandilla *f*
mobile[1] [ˈmoːbəl, -ˌbiːl, -ˌbaɪl] *adj* : móvil ⟨mobile home : caravana, casa rodante⟩
mobile[2] [ˈmoˌbiːl] *n* : móvil *m*
mobility [moˈbɪləṭi] *n* : movilidad *f*
mobilize [ˈmoːbəˌlaɪz] *vt* **-lized; -lizing** : movilizar
moccasin [ˈmɑkəsən] *n* **1** : mocasín *m* **2** *or* **water moccasin** : serpiente *f* venenosa de Norteamérica
mocha [ˈmoːkə] *n* **1** : mezcla *f* de café y chocolate **2** : color *m* chocolate
mock[1] [ˈmɑk, ˈmɔk] *vt* **1** RIDICULE : burlarse de, mofarse de **2** MIMIC : imitar, remedar (de manera burlona)
mock[2] *adj* **1** SIMULATED : simulado **2** PHONY : falso
mockery [ˈmɑkəri, ˈmɔ-] *n, pl* **-eries 1** JEER, TAUNT : burla *f*, mofa *f* ⟨to make a mockery of : burlarse de⟩ **2** FAKE : imitación *f* (burlona)
mockingbird [ˈmɑkɪŋˌbərd, ˈmɔ-] *n* : sinsonte *m*
mode [ˈmoːd] *n* **1** FORM : modo *m*, forma *f* **2** MANNER : modo *m*, manera *f*, estilo *m* **3** FASHION : moda *f*
model[1] [ˈmɑdəl] *v* **-eled** *or* **-elled; -eling** *or* **-elling** *vt* SHAPE : modelar — *vi* : trabajar de modelo
model[2] *adj* **1** EXEMPLARY : modelo, ejemplar ⟨a model student : un estudiante modelo⟩ **2** MINIATURE : en miniatura
model[3] *n* **1** PATTERN : modelo *m* **2** MINIATURE : modelo *m*, miniatura *f* **3** EXAMPLE : modelo *m*, ejemplo *m* **4** MANNEQUIN : modelo *mf* **5** DESIGN : modelo *m* ⟨the '97 model : el modelo '97⟩
modem [ˈmoːdəm, -ˌdɛm] *n* : módem *m*
moderate[1] [ˈmɑdəˌreɪt] *v* **-ated; -ating** *vt* : moderar, temperar — *vi* **1** CALM : moderarse, calmarse **2** : fungir como moderador (en un debate, etc.)
moderate[2] [ˈmɑdərət] *adj* : moderado
moderate[3] [ˈmɑdərət] *n* : moderado *m*, -da *f*
moderately [ˈmɑdərətli] *adv* **1** : con moderación **2** FAIRLY : medianamente
moderation [ˌmɑdəˈreɪʃən] *n* : moderación *f*
moderator [ˈmɑdəˌreɪṭər] *n* : moderador *m*, -dora *f*
modern [ˈmɑdərn] *adj* : moderno
modernism [ˈmɑdərˌnɪzəm] *n* : modernismo *m*
modernist [ˈmɑdərnɪst] *n* : modernista *mf* — **modernist** *adj*
modernity [məˈdərnəṭi] *n* : modernidad *f*
modernization [ˌmɑdərnəˈzeɪʃən] *n* : modernización *f*
modernize [ˈmɑdərˌnaɪz] *v* **-ized; -izing** *vt* : modernizar — *vi* : modernizarse
modest [ˈmɑdəst] *adj* **1** HUMBLE : modesto **2** DEMURE : recatado, pudoroso **3** MODERATE : modesto, moderado — **modestly** *adv*
modesty [ˈmɑdəsti] *n* : modestia *f*
modicum [ˈmɑdɪkəm] *n* : mínimo *m*, pizca *f*
modification [ˌmɑdəfəˈkeɪʃən] *n* : modificación *f*
modifier [ˈmɑdəˌfaɪər] *n* : modificante *m*, modificador *m*
modify [ˈmɑdəˌfaɪ] *vt* **-fied; -fying** : modificar, calificar (en gramática)
modish [ˈmoːdɪʃ] *adj* STYLISH : a la moda, de moda
modular [ˈmɑdʒələr] *adj* : modular
modulate [ˈmɑdʒəˌleɪt] *vt* **-lated; -lating** : modular
modulation [ˌmɑdʒəˈleɪʃən] *n* : modulación *f*
module [ˈmɑˌdʒuːl] *n* : módulo *m*
mogul [ˈmoːgəl] *n* : magnate *mf*; potentado *m*, -da *f*
mohair [ˈmoːˌhær] *n* : mohair *m*
moist [ˈmɔɪst] *adj* : húmedo
moisten [ˈmɔɪsən] *vt* : humedecer
moistness [ˈmɔɪstnəs] *n* : humedad *f*
moisture [ˈmɔɪstʃər] *n* : humedad *f*
moisturize [ˈmɔɪstʃəˌraɪz] *vt* **-ized; -izing** : humedecer (el aire), humectar (la piel)
moisturizer [ˈmɔɪtʃəˌraɪzər] *n* : crema *f* hidratante, crema *f* humectante
molar [ˈmoːlər] *n* : muela *f*, molar *m*
molasses [məˈlæsəz] *n* : melaza *f*
mold[1] [ˈmoːld] *vt* : moldear, formar (carácter, etc.) — *vi* : enmohecerse ⟨the bread will mold : el pan se enmohecerá⟩
mold[2] *n* **1** *or* **leaf mold** : mantillo *m* **2** FORM : molde *m* ⟨to break the mold : romper el molde⟩ **3** FUNGUS : moho *m*
molder [ˈmoːldər] *vi* CRUMBLE : desmoronarse
molding [ˈmoːldɪŋ] *n* : moldura *f* (en arquitectura)
moldy [ˈmoːldi] *adj* **moldier; -est** : mohoso
mole [ˈmoːl] *n* **1** : lunar *m* (en la piel) **2** : topo *m* (animal)

molecule ['mɑlɪˌkjuːl] *n* : molécula *f* — **molecular** [mə'lɛkjələr] *adj*
molehill ['moːlˌhɪl] *n* : topera *f*
molest [mə'lɛst] *vt* **1** ANNOY, DISTURB : molestar **2** : abusar (sexualmente)
mollify ['mɑləˌfaɪ] *vt* **-fied; -fying** : apaciguar, aplacar
mollusk *or* **mollusc** ['mɑləsk] *n* : molusco *m*
mollycoddle ['mɑliˌkɑdəl] *vt* **-dled; -dling** PAMPER : consentir, mimar
molt ['moːlt] *vi* : mudar, hacer la muda
molten ['moːltən] *adj* : fundido
mom ['mɑm, 'mʌm] *n* : mamá *f*
moment ['moːmənt] *n* **1** INSTANT : momento *m* ⟨one moment, please : un momento, por favor⟩ **2** TIME : momento *m* ⟨at the moment : de momento, actualmente⟩ ⟨from that moment : desde entonces⟩ **3** IMPORTANCE : importancia *f* ⟨of great moment : de gran importancia⟩
momentarily [ˌmoːmən'tɛrəli] *adv* **1** : momentáneamente **2** SOON : dentro de poco, pronto
momentary ['moːmənˌtɛri] *adj* : momentáneo
momentous [mo'mɛntəs] *adj* : de suma importancia, fatídico
momentum [mo'mɛntəm] *n, pl* **-ta** [-tə] *or* **-tums 1** : momento *m* (en física) **2** IMPETUS : ímpetu *m*, impulso *m*
mommy ['mɑmi, 'mʌ-] *n* : mami *f*
monarch ['mɑˌnɑrk, -nərk] *n* : monarca *mf*
monarchism ['mɑˌnɑrˌkɪzəm, -nər-] *n* : monarquismo *m*
monarchist ['mɑˌnɑrkɪst, -nər-] *n* : monárquico *m*, -ca *f*
monarchy ['mɑˌnɑrki, -nər-] *n, pl* **-chies** : monarquía *f*
monastery ['mɑnəˌstɛri] *n, pl* **-teries** : monasterio *m*
monastic [mə'næstɪk] *adj* : monástico — **monastically** [-tɪkli] *adv*
Monday ['mʌnˌdeɪ, -di] *n* : lunes *m*
monetary ['mɑnəˌtɛri, 'mʌnə-] *adj* : monetario
money ['mʌni] *n, pl* **-eys** *or* **-ies** ['mʌniz] : dinero *m*, plata *f*
moneyed ['mʌnid] *adj* : adinerado
moneylender ['mʌniˌlɛndər] *n* : prestamista *mf*
money order *n* : giro *m* postal
Mongol ['mɑŋgəl, -ˌgoːl] → **Mongolian**
Mongolian [mɑn'goːliən, mɑŋ-] *n* : mongol *m*, -gola *f* — **Mongolian** *adj*
mongoose ['mɑnˌguːs, 'mɑŋ-] *n, pl* **-gooses** : mangosta *f*
mongrel ['mɑŋgrəl, 'mʌŋ-] *n* **1** : perro *m* mestizo, perro *m* corriente *Mex* **2** HYBRID : híbrido *m*
monitor[1] ['mɑnəṭər] *vt* : controlar, monitorear
monitor[2] *n* **1** : ayudante *mf* (en una escuela) **2** : monitor *m* (de una computadora, etc.)
monk ['mʌŋk] *n* : monje *m*
monkey[1] ['mʌŋki] *vi* **-keyed; -keying 1 to monkey around** : hacer payasadas, payasear **2 to monkey with** : juguetear con
monkey[2] *n, pl* **-keys** : mono *m*, -na *f*
monkeyshines ['mʌŋkiˌʃaɪnz] *npl* PRANKS : picardías *fpl*, travesuras *fpl*
monkey wrench *n* : llave *f* inglesa
monocle ['mɑnɪkəl] *n* : monóculo *m*
monogamous [mə'nɑgəməs] *adj* : monógamo
monogamy [mə'nɑgəmi] *n* : monogamia *f*
monogram[1] ['mɑnəˌgræm] *vt* **-grammed; -gramming** : marcar con monograma ⟨monogrammed towels : toallas con monograma⟩
monogram[2] *n* : monograma *m*
monograph ['mɑnəˌgræf] *n* : monografía *f*
monolingual [ˌmɑnə'lɪŋgwəl] *adj* : monolingüe
monolith ['mɑnəˌlɪθ] *n* : monolito *m*
monolithic [ˌmɑnə'lɪθɪk] *adj* : monolítico
monologue ['mɑnəˌlɔg] *n* : monólogo *m*
monoplane ['mɑnəˌpleɪn] *n* : monoplano *m*
monopolize [mə'nɑpəˌlaɪz] *vt* **-lized; -lizing** : monopolizar
monopoly [mə'nɑpəli] *n, pl* **-lies** : monopolio *m*
monosyllabic [ˌmɑnosə'læbɪk] *adj* : monosilábico
monosyllable ['mɑnoˌsɪləbəl] *n* : monosílabo *m*
monotheism ['mɑnoθiːˌɪzəm] *n* : monoteísmo *m*
monotheistic [ˌmɑnoθiː'ɪstɪk] *adj* : monoteísta
monotone ['mɑnəˌtoːn] *n* : voz *f* monótona
monotonous [mə'nɑtənəs] *adj* : monótono — **monotonously** *adv*
monotony [mə'nɑtəni] *n* : monotonía *f*, uniformidad *f*
monoxide [mə'nɑkˌsaɪd] *n* : monóxido *m*
monsoon [mɑn'suːn] *n* : monzón *m*
monster ['mɑntstər] *n* : monstruo *m*
monstrosity [mɑn'strɑsəṭi] *n, pl* **-ties** : monstruosidad *f*
monstrous ['mɑntstrəs] *adj* : monstruoso — **monstrously** *adv*
montage [mɑn'tɑʒ] *n* : montaje *m*
month ['mʌnθ] *n* : mes *m*
monthly[1] ['mʌnθli] *adv* : mensualmente
monthly[2] *adj* : mensual
monthly[3] *n, pl* **-lies** : publicación *f* mensual
monument ['mɑnjəmənt] *n* : monumento *m*
monumental [ˌmɑnjə'mɛntəl] *adj* : monumental — **monumentally** *adv*
moo[1] ['muː] *vi* : mugir
moo[2] *n* : mugido *m*
mood ['muːd] *n* : humor *m* ⟨to be in a good mood : estar de buen humor⟩ ⟨to

be in the mood for : tener ganas de⟩ ⟨to be in no mood for : no estar para⟩
moodiness [ˈmuːdinəs] *n* **1** SADNESS : melancolía *f*, tristeza *f* **2** : cambios *mpl* de humor, carácter *m* temperamental
moody [ˈmuːdi] *adj* **moodier; -est 1** GLOOMY : melancólico, deprimido **2** TEMPERAMENTAL : temperamental, de humor variable
moon [ˈmuːn] *n* : luna *f*
moonbeam [ˈmuːnˌbiːm] *n* : rayo *m* de luna
moonlight¹ [ˈmuːnˌlaɪt] *vi* : estar pluriempleado
moonlight² *n* : claro *m* de luna, luz *f* de la luna
moonlit [ˈmuːnˌlɪt] *adj* : iluminado por la luna ⟨a moonlit night : una noche de luna⟩
moonshine [ˈmuːnˌʃaɪn] *n* **1** MOONLIGHT : luz *f* de la luna **2** NONSENSE : disparates *mpl*, tonterías *fpl* **3** : whisky *m* destilado ilegalmente
moor¹ [ˈmʊr, ˈmɔr] *vt* : amarrar
moor² *n* : brezal *m*, páramo *m*
Moor [ˈmʊr] *n* : moro *m*, -ra *f*
mooring [ˈmʊrɪŋ, ˈmɔr-] *n* DOCK : atracadero *m*
Moorish [ˈmʊrɪʃ] *adj* : moro
moose [ˈmuːs] *ns & pl* : alce *m* (norteamericano)
moot [ˈmuːt] *adj* DEBATABLE : discutible
mop¹ [ˈmɑp] *vt* **mopped; mopping** : trapear
mop² *n* : trapeador *m*
mope [ˈmoːp] *vi* **moped; moping** : andar deprimido, quedar abatido
moped [ˈmoːˌpɛd] *n* : ciclomotor *m*
moraine [məˈreɪn] *n* : morena *f*
moral¹ [ˈmɔrəl] *adj* : moral ⟨moral judgment : juicio moral⟩ ⟨moral support : apoyo moral⟩ — **morally** *adv*
moral² *n* **1** : moraleja *f* (de un cuento, etc.) **2 morals** *npl* : moral *f*, moralidad *f*
morale [məˈræl] *n* : moral *f*
moralist [ˈmɔrəlɪst] *n* : moralista *mf*
moralistic [ˌmɔrəˈlɪstɪk] *adj* : moralista
morality [məˈræləṭi] *n, pl* **-ties** : moralidad *f*
morass [məˈræs] *n* **1** SWAMP : ciénaga *f*, pantano *m* **2** CONFUSION, MESS : lío *m fam*, embrollo *m*
moratorium [ˌmɔrəˈtoriəm] *n, pl* **-riums** *or* **-ria** [-iə] : moratoria *f*
moray [ˈmɔrˌeɪ, məˈreɪ] *n* : morena *f*
morbid [ˈmɔrbɪd] *adj* **1** : mórbido, morboso (en medicina) **2** GRUESOME : morboso, horripilante
morbidity [mɔrˈbɪdəṭi] *n, pl* **-ties** : morbosidad *f*
more¹ [ˈmor] *adv* : más ⟨what more can I say? : ¿qué más puedo decir?⟩ ⟨more important : más importante⟩ ⟨once more : una vez más⟩
more² *adj* : más ⟨nothing more than that : nada más que eso⟩ ⟨more work : más trabajo⟩
more³ *n* : más *m* ⟨the more you eat, the more you want : cuanto más comes, tanto más quieres⟩
more⁴ *pron* : más ⟨more were found : se encontraron más⟩
moreover [morˈoːvər] *adv* : además
mores [ˈmɔrˌeɪz, -iːz] *npl* CUSTOMS : costumbres *fpl*, tradiciones *fpl*
morgue [ˈmɔrg] *n* : morgue *f*
moribund [ˈmɔrəˌbʌnd] *adj* : moribundo
Mormon [ˈmɔrmən] *n* : mormón *m*, -mona *f* — **Mormon** *adj*
morn [ˈmɔrn] → **morning**
morning [ˈmɔrnɪŋ] *n* : mañana *f* ⟨good morning! : ¡buenos días!⟩
Moroccan [məˈrɑkən] *n* : marroquí *mf* — **Moroccan** *adj*
moron [ˈmorˌɑn] *n* **1** : retrasado *m*, -da *f* mental **2** DUNCE : estúpido *m*, -da *f*; tonto *m*, -ta *f*
morose [məˈroːs] *adj* : hosco, sombrío — **morosely** *adv*
moroseness [məˈroːsnəs] *n* : malhumor *m*
morphine [ˈmɔrˌfiːn] *n* : morfina *f*
morphology [mɔrˈfɑləʤi] *n, pl* **-gies** : morfología *f*
morrow [ˈmɑroː] *n* : día *m* siguiente
Morse code [ˈmɔrs] *n* : código *m* morse
morsel [ˈmɔrsəl] *n* **1** BITE : bocado *m* **2** FRAGMENT : pedazo *m*
mortal¹ [ˈmɔrṭəl] *adj* : mortal ⟨mortal blow : golpe mortal⟩ ⟨mortal fear : miedo mortal⟩ — **mortally** *adv*
mortal² *n* : mortal *mf*
mortality [mɔrˈtæləṭi] *n* : mortalidad *f*
mortar [ˈmɔrṭər] *n* **1** : mortero *m*, molcajete *m Mex* ⟨mortar and pestle : mortero y maja⟩ **2** : mortero *m* ⟨mortar shell : granada de mortero⟩ **3** CEMENT : mortero *m*, argamasa *f*
mortgage¹ [ˈmɔrgɪʤ] *vt* **-gaged; -gaging** : hipotecar
mortgage² *n* : hipoteca *f*
mortification [ˌmɔrṭəfəˈkeɪʃən] *n* **1** : mortificación *f* **2** HUMILIATION : humillación *f*, vergüenza *f*
mortify [ˈmɔrṭəˌfaɪ] *vt* **-fied; -fying 1** : mortificar (en religión) **2** HUMILIATE : humillar, avergonzar
mortuary [ˈmɔrʧəˌwɛri] *n, pl* **-aries** FUNERAL HOME : funeraria *f*
mosaic [moˈzeɪɪk] *n* : mosaico *m*
Moslem [ˈmɑzləm] → **Muslim**
mosque [ˈmɑsk] *n* : mezquita *f*
mosquito [məˈskiːṭo] *n, pl* **-toes** : mosquito *m*, zancudo *m*
moss [ˈmɔs] *n* : musgo *m*
mossy [ˈmɔsi] *adj* **-ier; -est** : musgoso
most¹ [ˈmoːst] *adv* : más ⟨the most interesting book : el libro más interesante⟩
most² *adj* **1** : la mayoría de, la mayor parte de ⟨most people : la mayoría de la gente⟩ **2** GREATEST : más (dícese de los números), mayor (dícese de las cantidades) ⟨the most ability : la mayor capacidad⟩

most[3] *n* : más *m*, máximo *m* ⟨the most I can do : lo más que puedo hacer⟩ ⟨three weeks at the most : tres semanas como máximo⟩
most[4] *pron* : la mayoría, la mayor parte ⟨most will go : la mayoría irá⟩
mostly [ˈmoːstli] *adv* MAINLY : en su mayor parte, principalmente
mote [ˈmoːt] *n* SPECK : mota *f*
motel [moˈtɛl] *n* : motel *m*
moth [ˈmɔθ] *n* : palomilla *f*, polilla *f*
mother[1] [ˈmʌðər] *vt* **1** BEAR : dar a luz a **2** PROTECT : cuidar de, proteger
mother[2] *n* : madre *f*
motherhood [ˈmʌðərˌhʊd] *n* : maternidad *f*
mother–in–law [ˈmʌðərɪnˌlɔ] *n, pl* **mothers–in–law** : suegra *f*
motherland [ˈmʌðərˌlænd] *n* : patria *f*
motherly [ˈmʌðərli] *adj* : maternal
mother–of–pearl [ˌmʌðərəvˈpərl] *n* : nácar *m*, madreperla *f*
motif [moˈtiːf] *n* : motivo *m*
motion[1] [ˈmoːʃən] *vt* : hacerle señas (a alguien) ⟨she motioned us to come in : nos hizo señas para que entráramos⟩
motion[2] *n* **1** MOVEMENT : movimiento *m* ⟨to set in motion : poner en marcha⟩ **2** PROPOSAL : moción *f* ⟨to second a motion : apoyar una moción⟩
motionless [ˈmoːʃənləs] *adj* : inmóvil, quieto
motion picture *n* MOVIE : película *f*
motivate [ˈmoːţəˌveɪt] *vt* **-vated; -vating** : motivar, mover, inducir
motivation [ˌmoːţəˈveɪʃən] *n* : motivación *f*
motive[1] [ˈmoːţɪv] *adj* : motor ⟨motive power : fuerza motriz⟩
motive[2] *n* : motivo *m*, móvil *m*
motley [ˈmɑtli] *adj* : abigarrado, variopinto
motor[1] [ˈmoːţər] *vi* : viajar en coche
motor[2] *n* : motor *m*
motorbike [ˈmoːţərˌbaɪk] *n* : motocicleta *f* (pequeña), moto *f*
motorboat [ˈmoːţərˌboːt] *n* : bote *m* a motor, lancha *f* motora
motorcar [ˈmoːţərˌkɑr] *n* : automóvil *m*
motorcycle [ˈmoːţərˌsaɪkəl] *n* : motocicleta *f*
motorcyclist [ˈmoːţərˌsaɪkəlɪst] *n* : motociclista *mf*
motorist [ˈmoːţərɪst] *n* : automovilista *mf*, motorista *mf*
mottle [ˈmɑţəl] *vt* **-tled; -tling** : manchar, motear ⟨mottled skin : piel manchada⟩ ⟨a mottled surface : una superficie moteada⟩
motto [ˈmɑţoː] *n, pl* **-toes** : lema *m*
mould [ˈmoːld] → **mold**
mound [ˈmaʊnd] *n* **1** PILE : montón *m* **2** KNOLL : montículo *m* **3 burial mound** : túmulo *m*
mount[1] [ˈmaʊnt] *vt* **1** : montar a (un caballo), montar en (una bicicleta), subir a **2** : montar (artillería, etc.) — *vi* INCREASE : aumentar
mount[2] *n* **1** SUPPORT : soporte *m* **2** HORSE : caballería *f*, montura *f* **3** MOUNTAIN : monte *m*, montaña *f*
mountain [ˈmaʊntən] *n* : montaña *f*
mountaineer [ˌmaʊntənˈɪr] *n* : alpinista *mf*; montañero *m*, -ra *f*
mountaineering [ˌmaʊntənˈɪrɪŋ] *n* : alpinismo *m*
mountainous [ˈmaʊntənəs] *adj* : montañoso
mountaintop [ˈmaʊntənˌtɑp] *n* : cima *f*, cumbre *f*
mourn [ˈmorn] *vt* : llorar (por), lamentar ⟨to mourn the death of : llorar la muerte de⟩ — *vi* : llorar, estar de luto
mourner [ˈmornər] *n* : doliente *mf*
mournful [ˈmornfəl] *adj* **1** SORROWFUL : lloroso, plañidero, triste **2** GLOOMY : deprimente, entristecedor — **mournfully** *adv*
mourning [ˈmornɪŋ] *n* : duelo *m*, luto *m*
mouse [ˈmaʊs] *n, pl* **mice** [ˈmaɪs] **1** : ratón *m*, -tona *f* **2** : ratón *m* (de una computadora)
mousetrap [ˈmaʊsˌtræp] *n* : ratonera *f*
mousse [ˈmuːs] *n* : mousse *mf*
moustache [ˈmʌˌstæʃ, məˈstæʃ] → **mustache**
mouth[1] [ˈmaʊð] *vt* **1** : decir con poca sinceridad, repetir sin comprensión **2** : articular en silencio ⟨she mouthed the words : formó las palabras con los labios⟩
mouth[2] [ˈmaʊθ] *n* : boca *f* (de una persona o un animal), entrada *f* (de un túnel), desembocadura *f* (de un río)
mouthful [ˈmaʊθˌfʊl] *n* : bocado *m* (de comida), bocanada *f* (de líquido o humo)
mouthpiece [ˈmaʊθˌpiːs] *n* : boquilla *f* (de un instrumento musical)
mouthwash [ˈmaʊθˌwɔʃ, -ˌwɑʃ] *n* : enjuague *m* bucal
movable [ˈmuːvəbəl] *or* **moveable** *adj* : movible, móvil
move[1] [ˈmuːv] *v* **moved; moving** *vi* **1** GO : ir **2** RELOCATE : mudarse, trasladarse **3** STIR : moverse ⟨don't move! : ¡no te muevas!⟩ **4** ACT : actuar — *vt* **1** : mover ⟨move it over there : ponlo allí⟩ ⟨he kept moving his feet : no dejaba de mover los pies⟩ **2** INDUCE, PERSUADE : inducir, persuadir, mover **3** TOUCH : conmover ⟨it moved him to tears : lo hizo llorar⟩ **4** PROPOSE : proponer
move[2] *n* **1** MOVEMENT : movimiento *m* **2** RELOCATION : mudanza *f* (de casa), traslado *m* **3** STEP : paso *m* ⟨a good move : un paso acertado⟩
movement [ˈmuːvmənt] *n* : movimiento *m*
mover [ˈmuːvər] *n* : persona *f* que hace mudanzas
movie [ˈmuːvi] *n* **1** : película *f* **2 movies** *npl* : cine *m*
moving [ˈmuːvɪŋ] *adj* **1** : en movimiento ⟨a moving target : un blanco móvil⟩

2 TOUCHING : conmovedor, emocionante
mow[1] [ˈmoː] *vt* **mowed; mowed** *or* **mown** [ˈmoːn]; **mowing** : cortar (la hierba)
mow[2] [ˈmaʊ] *n* : pajar *m*
mower [ˈmoːər] → **lawn mower**
Mr. [ˈmɪstər] *n, pl* **Messrs.** [ˈmɛsərz] : señor *m*
Mrs. [ˈmɪsəz, -səs, *esp South* ˈmɪzəz, -zəs] *n, pl* **Mesdames** [meɪˈdɑm, -ˈdæm] : señora *f*
Ms. [ˈmɪz] *n* : señora *f*, señorita *f*
much[1] [ˈmʌʧ] *adv* **more** [ˈmor]; **most** [ˈmoːst] : mucho ‹I'm much happier : estoy mucho más contenta› ‹she talks as much as I do : habla tanto como yo›
much[2] *adj* **more; most** : mucho ‹it has much validity : tiene mucha validez› ‹too much time : demasiado tiempo›
much[3] *pron* : mucho, -cha ‹I don't need much : no necesito mucho›
mucilage [ˈmjuːsəlɪʤ] *n* : mucílago *m*
muck [ˈmʌk] *n* **1** MANURE : estiércol *m* **2** DIRT, FILTH : mugre *f*, suciedad *f* **3** MIRE, MUD : barro *m*, fango *m*, lodo *m*
mucous [ˈmjuːkəs] *adj* : mucoso ‹mucous membrane : membrana mucosa›
mucus [ˈmjuːkəs] *n* : mucosidad *f*
mud [ˈmʌd] *n* : barro *m*, fango *m*, lodo *m*
muddle[1] [ˈmʌdəl] *v* **-dled; -dling** *vt* **1** CONFUSE : confundir **2** BUNGLE : echar a perder, malograr — *vi* : andar confundido ‹to muddle through : arreglárselas›
muddle[2] *n* : confusión *f*, embrollo *m*, lío *m*
muddleheaded [ˌmʌdəlˈhɛdəd, ˈmʌdəlˌ-] *adj* CONFUSED : confuso, despistado
muddy[1] [ˈmʌdi] *vt* **-died; -dying** : llenar de barro
muddy[2] *adj* **-dier; -est** : barroso, fangoso, lodoso, enlodado ‹you're all muddy : estás cubierto de barro›
muff[1] [ˈmʌf] *vt* BUNGLE : echar a perder, fallar (un tiro, etc.)
muff[2] *n* : manguito *m*
muffin [ˈmʌfən] *n* : magdalena *f*, mantecada *f Mex*
muffle [ˈmʌfəl] *vt* **-fled; -fling 1** ENVELOP : cubrir, tapar **2** DEADEN : amortiguar (un sonido)
muffler [ˈmʌflər] *n* **1** SCARF : bufanda *f* **2** : silenciador *m*, mofle *m CA, Mex* (de un automóvil)
mug[1] [ˈmʌg] *v* **mugged; mugging** *vi* : posar (con afectación), hacer muecas ‹mugging for the camera : haciendo muecas para la cámara› — *vt* ASSAULT : asaltar, atracar
mug[2] *n* CUP : tazón *m*
mugger [ˈmʌgər] *n* : atracador *m*, -dora *f*
mugginess [ˈmʌginəs] *n* : bochorno *m*
muggy [ˈmʌgi] *adj* **-gier; -est** : bochornoso
mulatto [mʊˈlɑṭo, -ˈlæ-] *n, pl* **-toes** *or* **-tos** : mulato *m*, -ta *f*
mulberry [ˈmʌlˌbɛri] *n, pl* **-ries** : morera *f* (árbol), mora *f* (fruta)
mulch[1] [ˈmʌlʧ] *vt* : cubrir con pajote
mulch[2] *n* : pajote *m*
mule [ˈmjuːl] *n* **1** : mula *f* **2** : obstinado *m*, -da *f*; terco *m*, -ca *f*
mulish [ˈmjuːlɪʃ] *adj* : obstinado, terco
mull [ˈmʌl] *vt* **to mull over** : reflexionar sobre
mullet [ˈmʌlət] *n, pl* **-let** *or* **-lets** : mújol *m*, múgil *m*
multicolored [ˌmʌltiˈkʌlərd, ˌmʌltaɪ-] *adj* : multicolor, abigarrado
multicultural [ˌmʌltiˈkʌlʧərəl] *adj* : multicultural
multifaceted [ˌmʌltiˈfæsəṭəd, ˌmʌltaɪ-] *adj* : multifacético
multifamily [ˌmʌltiˈfæmli, ˌmʌltaɪ-] *adj* : multifamiliar
multifarious [ˌmʌltəˈfæriəs] *adj* DIVERSE : diverso, variado
multilateral [ˌmʌltiˈlæṭərəl, ˌmʌltaɪ-] *adj* : multilateral
multimedia [ˌmʌltiˈmiːdiə, ˌmʌltaɪ-] *adj* : multimedia
multimillionaire [ˌmʌltiˌmɪljəˈnær, ˌmʌltaɪ-, -ˈmɪljəˌnær] *adj* : multimillonario
multinational [ˌmʌltiˈnæʃənəl, ˌmʌltaɪ-] *adj* : multinacional
multiple[1] [ˈmʌltəpəl] *adj* : múltiple
multiple[2] *n* : múltiplo *m*
multiple sclerosis [skləˈroːsɪs] *n* : esclerosis *f* múltiple
multiplication [ˌmʌltəpləˈkeɪʃən] *n* : multiplicación *f*
multiplicity [ˌmʌltəˈplɪsəṭi] *n, pl* **-ties** : multiplicidad *f*
multiplier [ˈmʌltəˌplaɪər] *n* : multiplicador *m* (en matemáticas)
multiply [ˈmʌltəˌplaɪ] *v* **-plied; -plying** *vt* : multiplicar — *vi* : multiplicarse
multipurpose [ˌmʌltiˈpərpəs, ˌmʌltaɪ-] *adj* : multiuso
multitude [ˈmʌltəˌtuːd, -ˌtjuːd] *n* **1** CROWD : multitud *f*, muchedumbre *f* **2** HOST : multitud *f*, gran cantidad *f* ‹a multitude of ideas : numerosas ideas›
multivitamin [ˌmʌltiˈvaɪṭəmən, ˌmʌltaɪ-] *adj* : multivitamínico
mum[1] [ˈmʌm] *adj* SILENT : callado
mum[2] *n* → **chrysanthemum**
mumble[1] [ˈmʌmbəl] *v* **-bled; -bling** *vt* : mascullar, musitar — *vi* : mascullar, hablar entre dientes, murmurar
mumble[2] *n* **to speak in a mumble** : hablar entre dientes
mummy [ˈmʌmi] *n, pl* **-mies** : momia *f*
mumps [ˈmʌmps] *ns & pl* : paperas *fpl*
munch [ˈmʌnʧ] *v* : mascar, masticar
mundane [ˌmʌnˈdeɪn, ˈmʌnˌ-] *adj* **1** EARTHLY, WORLDLY : mundano, terrenal **2** COMMONPLACE : rutinario, ordinario
municipal [mjʊˈnɪsəpəl] *adj* : municipal
municipality [mjʊˌnɪsəˈpæləṭi] *n, pl* **-ties** : municipio *m*
munitions [mjʊˈnɪʃənz] *npl* : municiones *fpl*

mural[1] ['mjʊrəl] *adj* : mural
mural[2] ['mjʊrəlɪst] *n* : mural *m*
murder[1] ['mərdər] *vt* : asesinar, matar — *vi* : matar
murder[2] *n* : asesinato *m*, homicidio *m*
murderer ['mərdərər] *n* : asesino *m*, -na *f*; homicida *mf*
murderess ['mərdərɪs, -dəˌrɛs, -dərəs] *n* : asesina *f*, homicida *f*
murderous ['mərdərəs] *adj* : asesino, homicida
murk ['mərk] *n* DARKNESS : oscuridad *f*, tinieblas *fpl*
murkiness ['mərkinəs] *n* : oscuridad *f*, tenebrosidad *f*
murky ['mərki] *adj* **-kier; -est** : oscuro, tenebroso
murmur[1] ['mərmər] *vi* **1** DRONE : murmurar **2** GRUMBLE : refunfuñar, regañar, rezongar — *vt* MUMBLE : murmurar
murmur[2] *n* **1** COMPLAINT : queja *f* **2** DRONE : murmullo *m*, rumor *m*
muscle[1] ['mʌsəl] *vi* **-cled; -cling** : meterse ⟨to muscle in on : meterse por la fuerza en, entrometerse en⟩
muscle[2] *n* **1** : músculo *m* **2** STRENGTH : fuerza *f*
muscular ['mʌskjələr] *adj* **1** : muscular ⟨muscular tissue : tejido muscular⟩ **2** BRAWNY : musculoso
muscular dystrophy *n* : distrofia *f* muscular
musculature ['mʌskjələˌʧʊr, -ʧər] *n* : musculatura *f*
muse[1] ['mju:z] *vi* **mused; musing** PONDER, REFLECT : cavilar, meditar, reflexionar
muse[2] *n* : musa *f*
museum [mjʊ'zi:əm] *n* : museo *m*
mush ['mʌʃ] *n* **1** : gachas *fpl* (de maíz) **2** SENTIMENTALITY : sensiblería *f*
mushroom[1] ['mʌʃˌru:m, -ˌrʊm] *vi* GROW, MULTIPLY : crecer rápidamente, multiplicarse
mushroom[2] *n* : hongo *m*, champiñón *m*, seta *f*
mushy ['mʌʃi] *adj* **mushier; -est 1** SOFT : blando **2** MAWKISH : sensiblero
music ['mju:zɪk] *n* : música *f*
musical[1] ['mju:zɪkəl] *adj* : musical, de música — **musically** *adv*
musical[2] *n* : comedia *f* musical
music box *n* : cajita *f* de música
musician [mjʊ'zɪʃən] *n* : músico *m*, -ca *f*
musk ['mʌsk] *n* : almizcle *m*
musket ['mʌskət] *n* : mosquete *m*
musketeer [ˌmʌskə'tɪr] *n* : mosquetero *m*
muskrat ['mʌskˌræt] *n, pl* **-rat** *or* **-rats** : rata *f* almizclera
Muslim[1] ['mʌzləm, 'mʊs-, 'mʊz-] *adj* : musulmán
Muslim[2] *n* : musulmán *m*, -mana *f*
muslin ['mʌzlən] *n* : muselina *f*
muss[1] ['mʌs] *vt* : desordenar, despeinar (el pelo)
muss[2] *n* : desorden *m*
mussel ['mʌsəl] *n* : mejillón *m*
must[1] ['mʌst] *v aux* **1** (*expressing obligation or necessity*) : deber, tener que ⟨you must stop : debes parar⟩ ⟨we must obey : tenemos que obedecer⟩ **2** (*expressing probability*) : deber (de), haber de ⟨you must be tired : debes de estar cansado⟩ ⟨it must be late : ha de ser tarde⟩
must[2] *n* : necesidad *f* ⟨exercise is a must : el ejercicio es imprescindible⟩
mustache ['mʌˌstæʃ, mʌ'stæʃ] *n* : bigote *m*, bigotes *mpl*
mustang ['mʌˌstæŋ] *n* : mustang *m*
mustard ['mʌstərd] *n* : mostaza *f*
muster[1] ['mʌstər] *vt* **1** ASSEMBLE : reunir **2 to muster up** : armarse de, cobrar (valor, fuerzas, etc.)
muster[2] *n* **1** INSPECTION : revista *f* (de tropas) ⟨it didn't pass muster : no resistió un examen minucioso⟩ **2** COLLECTION : colección *f*
mustiness ['mʌstinəs] *n* : lo mohoso
musty ['mʌsti] *adj* **mustier; -est** : mohoso, que huele a moho, que huele a encerrado
mutant[1] ['mju:tənt] *adj* : mutante
mutant[2] *n* : mutante *m*
mutate ['mju:ˌteɪt] *vi* **-tated; -tating 1** : mutar (genéticamente) **2** CHANGE : transformarse
mutation [mju:'teɪʃən] *n* : mutación *f* (genética)
mute[1] ['mju:t] *vt* **muted; muting** MUFFLE : amortiguar, ponerle sordina a (un instrumento musical)
mute[2] *adj* **muter; mutest** : mudo — **mutely** *adv*
mute[3] *n* **1** : mudo *m*, -da *f* (persona) **2** : sordina *f* (para un instrumento musical)
mutilate ['mju:ţəˌleɪt] *vt* **-lated; -lating** : mutilar
mutilation [ˌmju:ţə'leɪʃən] *n* : mutilación *f*
mutineer [ˌmju:tən'ɪr] *n* : amotinado *m*, -da *f*
mutinous ['mju:tənəs] *adj* : amotinado
mutiny[1] ['mju:təni] *vi* **-nied; -nying** : amotinarse
mutiny[2] *n, pl* **-nies** : amotinamiento *m*, motín *m*
mutt ['mʌt] *n* MONGREL : perro *m* mestizo, perro *m* corriente *Mex*
mutter ['mʌţər] *vi* **1** MUMBLE : mascullar, hablar entre dientes, murmurar **2** GRUMBLE : refunfuñar, regañar, rezongar
mutton ['mʌtən] *n* : carne *f* de carnero
mutual ['mju:ʧʊəl] *adj* **1** : mutuo ⟨mutual respect : respeto mutuo⟩ **2** COMMON : común ⟨a mutual friend : un amigo común⟩
mutually ['mju:ʧʊəli, -ʧəli] *adv* **1** : mutuamente ⟨mutually beneficial : mutuamente beneficioso⟩ **2** JOINTLY : conjuntamente

muzzle[1] ['mʌzəl] *vt* **-zled; -zling** : ponerle un bozal a (un animal), amordazar
muzzle[2] *n* **1** SNOUT : hocico *m* **2** : bozal *m* (para un perro, etc.) **3** : boca *f* (de un arma de fuego)
my[1] ['maɪ] *adj* : mi ⟨my parents : mis padres⟩
my[2] *interj* : ¡caramba!, ¡Dios mío!
myopia [maɪ'o:piə] *n* : miopía *f*
myopic [maɪ'o:pɪk, -'ɑ-] *adj* : miope
myriad[1] ['mɪriəd] *adj* INNUMERABLE : innumerable
myriad[2] *n* : miríada *f*
myrrh ['mər] *n* : mirra *f*
myrtle ['mərṭəl] *n* : mirto *m*, arrayán *m*
myself [maɪ'sɛlf] *pron* **1** (*used reflexively*) : me ⟨I washed myself : me lavé⟩ **2** (*used for emphasis*) : yo mismo, yo misma ⟨I did it myself : lo hice yo mismo⟩
mysterious [mɪ'stɪriəs] *adj* : misterioso — **mysteriously** *adv*
mysteriousness [mɪ'stɪriəsnəs] *n* : lo misterioso
mystery ['mɪstəri] *n, pl* **-teries** : misterio *m*
mystic[1] ['mɪstɪk] *adj* : místico
mystic[2] *n* : místico *m*, -ca *f*
mystical ['mɪstɪkəl] *adj* : místico — **mystically** *adv*
mysticism ['mɪstə,sɪzəm] *n* : misticismo *m*
mystify ['mɪstə,faɪ] *vt* **-fied; -fying** : dejar perplejo, confundir
mystique [mɪ'sti:k] *n* : aura *f* de misterio
myth ['mɪθ] *n* : mito *m*
mythic ['mɪθɪk] *adj* : mítico
mythical ['mɪθɪkəl] *adj* : mítico
mythological [,mɪθə'lɑʤɪkəl] *adj* : mitológico
mythology [mɪ'θɑləʤi] *n, pl* **-gies** : mitología *f*

N

n ['ɛn] *n, pl* **n's** *or* **ns** ['ɛnz] : decimocuarta letra del alfabeto inglés
nab ['næb] *vt* **nabbed; nabbing** : prender, pillar *fam*, pescar *fam*
nadir ['neɪdər, 'neɪ,dɪr] *n* : nadir *m*, punto *m* más bajo
nag[1] ['næg] *v* **nagged; nagging** *vi* **1** COMPLAIN : quejarse, rezongar **2 to nag at** HASSLE : molestar, darle (la) lata (a alguien) — *vt* **1** PESTER : molestar, fastidiar **2** SCOLD : regañar, estarle encima a *fam*
nag[2] *n* **1** GRUMBLER : gruñón *m*, -ñona *f* **2** HORSE : jamelgo *m*
naiad ['neɪəd, 'naɪ-, -,æd] *n, pl* **-iads** *or* **-iades** [-ə,di:z] : náyade *f*
nail[1] ['neɪl] *vt* : clavar, sujetar con clavos
nail[2] *n* **1** FINGERNAIL : uña *f* ⟨nail file : lima (de uñas)⟩ ⟨nail polish : laca de uñas⟩ **2** : clavo *m* ⟨to hit the nail on the head : dar en el clavo⟩
naive *or* **naïve** [nɑ'i:v] *adj* **-iver; -est 1** INGENUOUS : ingenuo, cándido **2** GULLIBLE : crédulo
naively [nɑ'i:vli] *adv* : ingenuamente
naïveté [,nɑ,i:və'teɪ, nɑ'i:və,-] *n* : ingenuidad *f*
naked ['neɪkəd] *adj* **1** UNCLOTHED : desnudo **2** UNCOVERED : desenvainado (dícese de una espada), pelado (dícese de los árboles), expuesto al aire (dícese de una llama) **3** OBVIOUS, PLAIN : manifiesto, puro, desnudo ⟨the naked truth : la pura verdad⟩ **4 to the naked eye** : a simple vista
nakedly ['neɪkədli] *adv* : manifiestamente
nakedness ['neɪkədnəs] *n* : desnudez *f*
name[1] ['neɪm] *vt* **named; naming 1** CALL : llamar, bautizar, ponerle nombre a **2** MENTION : mentar, mencionar, dar el nombre de ⟨they have named a suspect : han dado el nombre de un sospechoso⟩ **3** APPOINT : nombrar **4 to name a price** : fijar un precio
name[2] *adj* **1** KNOWN : de nombre ⟨name brand : marca conocida⟩ **2** PROMINENT : de renombre, de prestigio
name[3] *n* **1** : nombre *m* ⟨what is your name? : ¿cómo se llama?⟩ **2** SURNAME : apellido *m* **3** EPITHET : epíteto *m* ⟨to call somebody names : llamar a alguien de todo⟩ **4** REPUTATION : fama *f*, reputación *f* ⟨to make a name for oneself : darse a conocer, hacerse famoso⟩
nameless ['neɪmləs] *adj* **1** ANONYMOUS : anónimo **2** INDESCRIBABLE : indecible, indescriptible
namelessly ['neɪmləsli] *adv* : anónimamente
namely ['neɪmli] *adv* : a saber
namesake ['neɪm,seɪk] *n* : tocayo *m*, -ya *f*; homónimo *m*, -ma *f*
Namibian [nə'mɪbiən] *n* : namibio *m*, -bia *f* — **Namibian** *adj*
nanny ['næni] *n, pl* **nannies** : niñera *f*; nana *f CA, Col, Mex, Ven*
nap[1] ['næp] *vi* **napped; napping 1** : dormir, dormir la siesta **2 to be caught napping** : estar desprevenido
nap[2] *n* **1** SLEEP : siesta *f* ⟨to take a nap : echarse una siesta⟩ **2** FUZZ, PILE : pelo *m*, pelusa *f* (de telas)
nape ['neɪp, 'næp] *n* : nuca *f*, cerviz *f*, cogote *m*
naphtha ['næfθə] *n* : nafta *f*
napkin ['næpkən] *n* : servilleta *f*
narcissism ['nɑrsə,sɪzəm] *n* : narcisismo *m*
narcissist ['nɑrsəsɪst] *n* : narcisista *mf*
narcissistic [,nɑrsə'sɪstɪk] *adj* : narcisista
narcissus [nɑr'sɪsəs] *n, pl* **-cissus** *or**

-cissuses *or* -cissi [-ˈsɪˌsaɪ, -ˌsiː] : narciso *m*
narcotic[1] [nɑrˈkɑt̬ɪk] *adj* : narcótico
narcotic[2] *n* : narcótico *m*, estupefaciente *m*
narrate [ˈnærˌeɪt] *vt* **-rated; -rating** : narrar, relatar
narration [næˈreɪʃən] *n* : narración *f*
narrative[1] [ˈnærət̬ɪv] *adj* : narrativo
narrative[2] *n* : narración *f*, narrativa *f*, relato *m*
narrator [ˈnærˌeɪt̬ər] *n* : narrador *m*, -dora *f*
narrow[1] [ˈnærˌoː] *vi* : estrecharse, angostarse ⟨the river narrowed : el río se estrechó⟩ — *vt* **1** : estrechar, angostar **2** LIMIT : restringir, limitar ⟨to narrow the search : limitar la búsqueda⟩
narrow[2] *adj* **1** : estrecho, angosto **2** LIMITED : estricto, limitado ⟨in the narrowest sense of the word : en el sentido más estricto de la palabra⟩ **3 to have a narrow escape** : escapar por un pelo
narrowly [ˈnæroli] *adv* **1** BARELY : por poco **2** CLOSELY : de cerca
narrow–minded [ˌnæroˈmaɪndəd] *adj* : de miras estrechas
narrowness [ˈnæronəs] *n* : estrechez *f*
narrows [ˈnæroːz] *npl* STRAIT : estrecho *m*
narwhal [ˈnɑrˌ*h*wɑl, ˈnɑrwəl] *n* : narval *m*
nasal [ˈneɪzəl] *adj* : nasal, gangoso ⟨a nasal voice : una voz gangosa⟩
nasally [ˈneɪzəli] *adv* **1** : por la nariz **2** : con voz gangosa
nastily [ˈnæstəli] *adv* : con maldad, cruelmente
nastiness [ˈnæstinəs] *n* : porquería *f*
nasturtium [nəˈstərʃəm, næ-] *n* : capuchina *f*
nasty [ˈnæsti] *adj* **-tier; -est** **1** FILTHY : sucio, mugriento **2** OBSCENE : obsceno **3** MEAN, SPITEFUL : malo, malicioso **4** UNPLEASANT : desagradable, feo **5** REPUGNANT : asqueroso, repugnante ⟨a nasty smell : un olor asqueroso⟩
natal [ˈneɪt̬əl] *adj* : natal
nation [ˈneɪʃən] *n* : nación *f*
national[1] [ˈnæʃənəl] *adj* : nacional
national[2] *n* : ciudadano *m*, -na *f*; nacional *mf*
nationalism [ˈnæʃənəˌlɪzəm] *n* : nacionalismo *m*
nationalist[1] [ˈnæʃənəlɪst] *adj* : nacionalista
nationalist[2] *n* : nacionalista *mf*
nationalistic [ˌnæʃənəˈlɪstɪk] *adj* : nacionalista
nationality [ˌnæʃəˈnælət̬i] *n, pl* **-ties** : nacionalidad *f*
nationalization [ˌnæʃənələˈzeɪʃən] *n* : nacionalización *f*
nationalize [ˈnæʃənəˌlaɪz] *vt* **-ized; -izing** : nacionalizar
nationally [ˈnæʃənəli] *adv* : a escala nacional, a nivel nacional
nationwide [ˈneɪʃənˈwaɪd] *adj* : en toda la nación, por todo el país
native[1] [ˈneɪt̬ɪv] *adj* **1** INNATE : innato **2** : natal ⟨her native city : su ciudad natal⟩ **3** INDIGENOUS : indígena, autóctono
native[2] *n* **1** ABORIGINE : nativo *m*, -va *f*; indígena *mf* **2** : natural *m* ⟨he's a native of Mexico : es natural de México⟩
Native American → **American Indian**
nativity [nəˈtɪvət̬i, neɪ-] *n, pl* **-ties** **1** BIRTH : navidad *f* **2 the Nativity** : la Natividad, la Navidad
natty [ˈnæt̬i] *adj* **-tier; -est** : elegante, garboso
natural[1] [ˈnætʃərəl] *adj* **1** : natural, de la naturaleza ⟨natural woodlands : bosques naturales⟩ ⟨natural childbirth : parto natural⟩ **2** INNATE : innato, natural **3** UNAFFECTED : natural, sin afectación **4** LIFELIKE : natural, vivo
natural[2] *n* **to be a natural** : tener un talento innato (para algo)
natural gas *n* : gas *m* natural
natural history *n* : historia *f* natural
naturalism [ˈnætʃərəˌlɪzəm] *n* : naturalismo *m*
naturalist [ˈnætʃərəlɪst] *n* : naturalista *mf* — **naturalist** *adj*
naturalistic [ˌnætʃərəˈlɪstɪk] *adj* : naturalista
naturalization [ˌnætʃərələˈzeɪʃən] *n* : naturalización *f*
naturalize [ˈnætʃərəˌlaɪz] *vt* **-ized; -izing** : naturalizar
naturally [ˈnætʃərəli] *adv* **1** INHERENTLY : naturalmente, intrínsecamente **2** UNAFFECTEDLY : de manera natural **3** OF COURSE : por supuesto, naturalmente
naturalness [ˈnætʃərəlnəs] *n* : naturalidad *f*
natural science *n* : ciencias *fpl* naturales
nature [ˈneɪtʃər] *n* **1** : naturaleza *f* ⟨the laws of nature : las leyes de la naturaleza⟩ **2** KIND, SORT : índole *f*, clase *f* ⟨things of this nature : cosas de esta índole⟩ **3** DISPOSITION : carácter *m*, natural *m*, naturaleza *f* ⟨it is his nature to be friendly : es de natural simpático⟩ ⟨human nature : la naturaleza humana⟩
naught [ˈnɔt] *n* **1** : nada *f* ⟨to come to naught : reducirse a nada, fracasar⟩ **2** ZERO : cero *m*
naughtily [ˈnɔt̬əli] *adv* : traviesamente, con malicia
naughtiness [ˈnɔt̬inəs] *n* : mala conducta *f*, travesuras *fpl*, malicia *f*
naughty [ˈnɔt̬i] *adj* **-tier; -est** **1** MISCHIEVOUS : travieso, pícaro **2** RISQUÉ : picante, subido de tono
nausea [ˈnɔziə, ˈnɔʃə] *n* **1** SICKNESS : náuseas *fpl* **2** DISGUST : asco *m*
nauseate [ˈnɔziˌeɪt, -ʒi-, -si-, -ʃi-] *vt* **-ated; -ating** **1** SICKEN : darle náuseas (a alguien) **2** DISGUST : asquear, darle asco (a alguien)

nauseating *adj* : nauseabundo, repugnante
nauseatingly [ˈnɔziˌeɪt̬ɪŋli, -ʒi-, -si-, -ʃi-] *adv* : hasta el punto de dar asco ⟨nauseatingly sweet : tan dulce que da asco⟩
nauseous [ˈnɔʃəs, -ziəs] *adj* **1** SICK : mareado, con náuseas **2** SICKENING : nauseabundo
nautical [ˈnɔt̬ɪkəl] *adj* : náutico
nautilus [ˈnɔt̬ələs] *n, pl* **-luses** *or* **-li** [-ˌlaɪ, -ˌliː] : nautilo *m*
Navajo [ˈnævəˌhoː, ˈnɑ-] *n* : navajo *m*, -ja *f* — **Navajo** *adj*
naval [ˈneɪvəl] *adj* : naval
nave [ˈneɪv] *n* : nave *f*
navel [ˈneɪvəl] *n* : ombligo *m*
navigability [ˌnævɪgəˈbɪlət̬i] *n* : navegabilidad *f*
navigable [ˈnævɪgəbəl] *adj* : navegable
navigate [ˈnævəˌgeɪt] *v* **-gated; -gating** *vi* : navegar — *vt* **1** STEER : gobernar (un barco), pilotar (un avión) **2** : navegar por (un río, etc.)
navigation [ˌnævəˈgeɪʃən] *n* : navegación *f*
navigator [ˈnævəˌgeɪt̬ər] *n* : navegante *mf*
navy [ˈneɪvi] *n, pl* **-vies** **1** FLEET : flota *f* **2** : marina *f* de guerra, armada *f* ⟨the United States Navy : la armada de los Estados Unidos⟩ **3** *or* **navy blue** : azul *m* marino
nay[1] [ˈneɪ] *adv* : no
nay[2] *n* : no *m*, voto *m* en contra
Nazi [ˈnɑtsi, ˈnæt-] *n* : nazi *mf*
Nazism [ˈnɑtˌsɪzəm, ˈnæt-] *or* **Naziism** [ˈnɑtsiˌɪzəm, ˈnæt-] *n* : nazismo *m*
Neanderthal man [niˈændərˌθɔl, -ˌtɔl] *n* : hombre *m* de Neanderthal
near[1] [ˈnɪr] *vt* **1** : acercarse a ⟨the ship is nearing port : el barco se está acercando al puerto⟩ **2** : estar a punto de ⟨she is nearing graduation : está a punto de graduarse⟩
near[2] *adv* **1** CLOSE : cerca ⟨my family lives quite near : mi familia vive muy cerca⟩ **2** NEARLY : casi ⟨I came near to finishing : casi terminé⟩
near[3] *adj* **1** CLOSE : cercano, próximo **2** SIMILAR : parecido, semejante
near[4] *prep* : cerca de
nearby[1] [nɪrˈbaɪ, ˈnɪrˌbaɪ] *adv* : cerca
nearby[2] *adj* : cercano
nearly [ˈnɪrli] *adv* **1** ALMOST : casi ⟨nearly asleep : casi dormido⟩ **2 not nearly** : ni con mucho, ni mucho menos ⟨it was not nearly so bad as I had expected : no fue ni con mucho tan malo como esperaba⟩
nearness [ˈnɪrnəs] *n* : proximidad *f*
nearsighted [ˈnɪrˌsaɪt̬əd] *adj* : miope, corto de vista
nearsightedly [ˈnɪrˌsaɪt̬ədli] *adv* : con miopía
nearsightedness [ˈnɪrˌsaɪt̬ədnəs] *n* : miopía *f*
neat [ˈniːt] *adj* **1** CLEAN, ORDERLY : ordenado, pulcro, limpio **2** UNDILUTED : solo, sin diluir **3** SIMPLE, TASTEFUL : sencillo y de buen gusto **4** CLEVER : hábil, ingenioso ⟨a neat trick : un truco ingenioso⟩
neatly [ˈniːtli] *adv* **1** TIDILY : ordenadamente **2** CLEVERLY : ingeniosamente
neatness [ˈniːtnəs] *n* : pulcritud *f*, limpieza *f*, orden *m*
nebula [ˈnɛbjʊlə] *n, pl* **-lae** [-ˌliː, -ˌlaɪ] : nebulosa *f*
nebulous [ˈnɛbjʊləs] *adj* : nebuloso, vago
necessarily [ˌnɛsəˈsɛrəli] *adv* : necesariamente, forzosamente
necessary[1] [ˈnɛsəˌsɛri] *adj* **1** INEVITABLE : inevitable **2** COMPULSORY : necesario, obligatorio **3** ESSENTIAL : imprescindible, preciso, necesario
necessary[2] *n, pl* **-saries** : lo esencial, lo necesario
necessitate [nɪˈsɛsəˌteɪt] *vt* **-tated; -tating** : necesitar, requerir
necessity [nɪˈsɛsət̬i] *n, pl* **-ties** **1** NEED : necesidad *f* **2** REQUIREMENT : requisito *m* indispensable **3** POVERTY : indigencia *f*, necesidad *f* **4** INEVITABILITY : inevitabilidad *f*
neck[1] [ˈnɛk] *vi* : besuquearse
neck[2] *n* **1** : cuello *m* (de una persona), pescuezo *m* (de un animal) **2** COLLAR : cuello *m* **3** : cuello *m* (de una botella), mástil *m* (de una guitarra)
neckerchief [ˈnɛkərʧəf, -ˌʧiːf] *n, pl* **-chiefs** [-ʧəfs, -ˌʧiːfs] : pañuelo *m* (para el cuello), mascada *f Mex*
necklace [ˈnɛkləs] *n* : collar *m*
neckline [ˈnɛkˌlaɪn] *n* : escote *m*
necktie [ˈnɛkˌtaɪ] *n* : corbata *f*
nectar [ˈnɛktər] *n* : néctar *m*
nectarine [ˌnɛktəˈriːn] *n* : nectarina *f*
née *or* **nee** [ˈneɪ] *adj* : de soltera ⟨Mrs. Smith, née Whitman : la señora Smith, de soltera Whitman⟩
need[1] [ˈniːd] *vt* **1** : necesitar ⟨I need your help : necesito su ayuda⟩ ⟨I need money : me falta dinero⟩ **2** REQUIRE : requerir, exigir ⟨that job needs patience : ese trabajo exige paciencia⟩ **3 to need to** : tener que ⟨he needs to study : tiene que estudiar⟩ ⟨they need to be scolded : hay que reprenderlos⟩ — *v aux* **1** MUST : tener que, deber ⟨need you shout? : ¿tienes que gritar?⟩ **2 to be needed** : hacer falta ⟨you needn't worry : no hace falta que te preocupes, no hay por qué preocuparse⟩
need[2] *n* **1** NECESSITY : necesidad *f* ⟨in case of need : en caso de necesidad⟩ **2** LACK : falta *f* ⟨the need for better training : la falta de mejor capacitación⟩ ⟨to be in need : necesitar⟩ **3** POVERTY : necesidad *f*, indigencia *f* **4 needs** *npl* : requisitos *mpl*, carencias *fpl*
needful [ˈniːdfəl] *adj* : necesario
needle[1] [ˈniːdəl] *vt* **-dled; -dling** : pinchar
needle[2] *n* **1** : aguja *f* ⟨to thread a needle : enhebrar una aguja⟩ ⟨knitting

needle : aguja de tejer⟩ **2** POINTER : aguja *f*, indicador *m*

needlepoint [ˈni:dəlˌpɔint] *n* **1** LACE : encaje *m* de mano **2** EMBROIDERY : bordado *m* en cañamazo

needless [ˈni:dləs] *adj* : innecesario

needlessly [ˈni:dləsli] *adv* : sin ninguna necesidad, innecesariamente

needlework [ˈni:dəlˌwərk] *n* : bordado *m*

needn't [ˈni:dənt] (*contraction of* **need not**) → **need**

needy[1] [ˈni:di] *adj* **needier; -est** : necesitado

needy[2] *n* **the needy** : los necesitados *mpl*

nefarious [nɪˈfæriəs] *adj* : nefario, nefando, infame

negate [nɪˈgeɪt] *vt* **-gated; -gating** **1** DENY : negar **2** NULLIFY : invalidar, anular

negation [nɪˈgeɪʃən] *n* : negación *f*

negative[1] [ˈnɛgət̬ɪv] *adj* : negativo

negative[2] *n* **1** : negación *f* (en lingüística) **2** : negativa *f* ⟨to answer in the negative : contestar con una negativa⟩ **3** : término *m* negativo (en matemáticas) **4** : negativo *m*, imagen *f* en negativo (en fotografía)

negatively [ˈnɛgət̬ɪvli] *adv* : negativamente

neglect[1] [nɪˈglɛkt] *vt* **1** : desatender, descuidar ⟨to neglect one's health : descuidar la salud⟩ **2** : no cumplir con, faltar a ⟨to neglect one's obligations : faltar uno a sus obligaciones⟩ ⟨he neglected to tell me : omitió decírmelo⟩

neglect[2] *n* **1** : negligencia *f*, descuido *m*, incumplimiento *m* ⟨through neglect : por negligencia⟩ ⟨neglect of duty : incumplimiento del deber⟩ **2 in a state of neglect** : abandonado, descuidado

neglectful [nɪˈglɛktfəl] *adj* : descuidado *m*

negligee [ˌnɛgləˈʒeɪ] *n* : negligé *m*

negligence [ˈnɛglɪʤənts] *n* : descuido *m*, negligencia *f*

negligent [ˈnɛglɪʤənt] *adj* : negligente, descuidado — **negligently** *adv*

negligible [ˈnɛglɪʤəbəl] *adj* : insignificante, despreciable

negotiable [nɪˈgo:ʃəbəl, -ʃiə-] *adj* : negociable

negotiate [nɪˈgo:ʃiˌeɪt] *v* **-ated; -ating** *vi* : negociar — *vt* **1** : negociar, gestionar ⟨to negotiate a treaty : negociar un trato⟩ **2** : salvar, franquear ⟨they negotiated the obstacles : salvaron los obstáculos⟩ ⟨to negotiate a turn : tomar una curva⟩

negotiation [nɪˌgo:ʃiˈeɪʃən, -siˈeɪ-] *n* : negociación *f*

negotiator [nɪˈgo:ʃiˌeɪt̬ər, -siˌeɪ-] *n* : negociador *m*, -dora *f*

Negro [ˈni:ˌgro:] *n, pl* **-groes** : negro *m*, -gra *f*

neigh[1] [ˈneɪ] *vi* : relinchar

neigh[2] *n* : relincho *m*

neighbor[1] [ˈneɪbər] *vt* : ser vecino de, estar junto a ⟨her house neighbors mine : su casa está junto a la mía⟩ — *vi* : estar cercano, lindar, colindar ⟨her land neighbors on mine : sus tierras lindan con las mías⟩

neighbor[2] *n* **1** : vecino *m*, -na *f* **2 love thy neighbor** : ama a tu prójimo

neighborhood [ˈneɪbərˌhʊd] *n* **1** : barrio *m*, vecindad *f*, vecindario *m* **2 in the neighborhood of** : alrededor de, cerca de

neighborly [ˈneɪbərli] *adv* : amable, de buena vecindad

neither[1] [ˈni:ðər, ˈnaɪ-] *adj* : ninguno (de los dos)

neither[2] *conj* **1** : ni ⟨neither asleep nor awake : ni dormido ni despierto⟩ **2** NOR : ni (tampoco) ⟨I'm not asleep—neither am I : no estoy dormido—ni yo tampoco⟩

neither[3] *pron* : ninguno

nemesis [ˈnɛməsɪs] *n, pl* **-eses** [-ˌsi:z] **1** RIVAL : rival *mf* **2** RETRIBUTION : justo castigo *m*

Neoclassical [ˌni:oˈklæsɪkəl] *adj* : neoclásico

neologism [niˈɑləˌʤɪzəm] *n* : neologismo *m*

neon[1] [ˈni:ˌɑn] *adj* : de neón ⟨neon sign : letrero de neón⟩

neon[2] *n* : neón *m*

neophyte [ˈni:əˌfaɪt] *n* : neófito *m*, -ta *f*

Nepali [nəˈpɔli, -ˈpɑ-, -ˈpæ-] *n* : nepalés *m*, -lesa *f* — **Nepali** *adj*

nephew [ˈnɛˌfju:, *chiefly British* ˈnɛˌvju:] *n* : sobrino *m*

nepotism [ˈnɛpəˌtɪzəm] *n* : nepotismo *m*

Neptune [ˈnɛpˌtu:n, -ˌtju:n] *n* : Neptuno *m*

nerd [ˈnərd] *n* : ganso *m*, -sa *f*

nerve [ˈnərv] *n* **1** : nervio *m* **2** COURAGE : coraje *m*, valor *m*, fuerza *f* de la voluntad ⟨to lose one's nerve : perder el valor⟩ **3** AUDACITY, GALL : atrevimiento *m*, descaro *m* ⟨of all the nerve! : ¡qué descaro!⟩ **4 nerves** *npl* : nervios *mpl* ⟨a fit of nerves : un ataque de nervios⟩

nervous [ˈnərvəs] *adj* **1** : nervioso ⟨the nervous system : el sistema nervioso⟩ **2** EXCITABLE : nervioso, excitable ⟨to get nervous : excitarse, ponerse nervioso⟩ **3** FEARFUL : miedoso, temeroso

nervously [ˈnərvəsli] *adv* : nerviosamente

nervousness [ˈnərvəsnəs] *n* : nerviosismo *m*, nerviosidad *f*, ansiedad *f*

nervy [ˈnərvi] *adj* **nervier; -est** **1** COURAGEOUS : valiente **2** IMPUDENT : atrevido, descarado, fresco *fam* **3** NERVOUS : nervioso

nest[1] [ˈnɛst] *vi* : anidar

nest[2] *n* **1** : nido *m* (de un ave), avispero *m* (de una avispa), madriguera *f* (de un animal) **2** REFUGE : nido *m*, refugio *m* **3** SET : juego *m* ⟨a nest of tables : un juego de mesitas⟩

nestle [ˈnɛsəl] *vi* **-tled; -tling** : acurrucarse, arrimarse cómodamente

net[1] ['nɛt] *vt* **netted; netting 1** CATCH : pescar, atrapar con una red **2** CLEAR : ganar neto ⟨they netted $5000 : ganaron $5000 netos⟩ **3** YIELD : producir neto
net[2] *adj* : neto ⟨net weight : peso neto⟩ ⟨net gain : ganancia neta⟩
net[3] *n* : red *f*, malla *f*
nether ['nɛðər] *adj* **1** : inferior, más bajo **2 the nether regions** : el infierno
nettle[1] ['nɛtəl] *vt* **-tled; -tling** : irritar, provocar, molestar
nettle[2] *n* : ortiga *f*
network ['nɛt,wərk] *n* **1** SYSTEM : red *f* **2** CHAIN : cadena *f* ⟨a network of supermarkets : una cadena de supermercados⟩
neural ['nʊrəl, 'njʊr-] *adj* : neural
neuralgia [nʊ'rælʤə, njʊ-] *n* : neuralgia *f*
neuritis [nʊ'raɪtəs, njʊ-] *n, pl* **-ritides** [-'rɪtə,di:z] *or* **-ritises** : neuritis *f*
neurological [,nʊrə'lɑʤɪkəl, ,njʊr-] *or* **neurologic** [,nʊrə'lɑʤɪk, ,njʊr-] *adj* : neurológico
neurologist [nʊ'rɑləʤɪst, njʊ-] *n* : neurólogo *m*, -ga *f*
neurology [nʊ'rɑləʤi, njʊ-] *n* : neurología *f*
neurosis [nʊ'ro:sɪs, njʊ-] *n, pl* **-roses** [-,si:z] : neurosis *f*
neurotic[1] [nʊ'rɑtɪk, njʊ-] *adj* : neurótico
neurotic[2] *n* : neurótico *m*, -ca *f*
neuter[1] ['nu:tər, 'nju:-] *vt* : castrar
neuter[2] *adj* : neutro
neutral[1] ['nu:trəl, 'nju:-] *adj* **1** IMPARTIAL : neutral, imparcial ⟨to remain neutral : permanecer neutral⟩ **2** : neutro ⟨a neutral color : un color neutro⟩ **3** : neutro (en la química o la electricidad)
neutral[2] *n* : punto *m* muerto (de un automóvil)
neutrality [nu:'træləti:, nju:-] *n* : neutralidad *f*
neutralization [,nu:trələ'zeɪʃən, ,nju:-] *n* : neutralización *f*
neutralize ['nu:trə,laɪz, 'nju:-] *vt* **-ized; -izing** : neutralizar
neutron ['nu:,trɑn, 'nju:-] *n* : neutrón *m*
never ['nɛvər] *adv* **1** : nunca, jamás ⟨he never studies : nunca estudia⟩ **2 never again** : nunca más, nunca jamás **3 never mind** : no importa
nevermore [,nɛvər'mor] *adv* : nunca más
nevertheless [,nɛvərðə'lɛs] *adv* : sin embargo, no obstante
new ['nu:, 'nju:] *adj* **1** : nuevo ⟨a new dress : un vestido nuevo⟩ **2** RECENT : nuevo, reciente ⟨what's new? : ¿qué hay de nuevo?⟩ ⟨a new arrival : un recién llegado⟩ **3** DIFFERENT : nuevo, distinto ⟨this problem is new : este problema es distinto⟩ ⟨new ideas : ideas nuevas⟩ **4 like new** : como nuevo
newborn ['nu:,bɔrn, 'nju:-] *adj* : recién nacido
newcomer ['nu:,kʌmər, 'nju:-] *n* : recién llegado *m*, recién llegada *f*
newfangled ['nu:'fæŋgəld, 'nju:-] *adj* : novedoso
newfound ['nu:'faʊnd, 'nju:-] *adj* : recién descubierto
newly ['nu:li, 'nju:-] *adv* : recién, recientemente
newlywed ['nu:li,wɛd, 'nju:-] *n* : recién casado *m*, -da *f*
new moon *n* : luna *f* nueva
newness ['nu:nəs, 'nju:-] *n* : novedad *f*
news ['nu:z, 'nju:z] *n* : noticias *fpl*
newscast ['nu:z,kæst, 'nju:z-] *n* : noticiero *m*, informativo *m*
newscaster ['nu:z,kæstər, 'nju:z-] *n* : presentador *m*, -dora *f*; locutor *m*, -tora *f*
newsletter ['nu:z,lɛtər, 'nju:z-] *n* : boletín *m* informativo
newsman ['nu:zmən, 'nju:z-, -,mæn] *n, pl* **-men** [-mən, -,mɛn] : periodista *m*, reportero *m*
newspaper ['nu:z,peɪpər, 'nju:z-] *n* : periódico *m*, diario *m*
newspaperman ['nu:z,peɪpər,mæn, 'nju:z-] *n, pl* **-men** [-mən, -,mɛn] **1** REPORTER : periodista *m*, reportero *m* **2** : dueño *m* de un periódico
newsprint ['nu:z,prɪnt, 'nju:z-] *n* : papel *m* de prensa
newsstand ['nu:z,stænd, 'nju:z-] *n* : quiosco *m*, puesto *m* de periódicos
newswoman ['nu:z,wʊmən, 'nju:z-] *n, pl* **-women** [-,wɪmən] : periodista *f*, reportera *f*
newsworthy ['nu:z,wərði, 'nju:z-] *adj* : de interés periodístico
newsy ['nu:zi:, 'nju:-] *adj* **newsier; -est** : lleno de noticias
newt ['nu:t, 'nju:t] *n* : tritón *m*
New Testament *n* : Nuevo Testamento *m*
New Year *n* : Año *m* Nuevo
New Year's Day *n* : día *m* del Año Nuevo
New Yorker [nu:'jɔrkər, nju:-] *n* : neoyorquino *m*, -na *f*
New Zealander [nu:'zi:ləndər, nju:-] *n* : neozelandés *m*, -desa *f*
next[1] ['nɛkst] *adv* **1** AFTERWARD : después, luego ⟨what will you do next? : ¿qué harás después?⟩ **2** NOW : después, ahora, entonces ⟨next I will sing a song : ahora voy a cantar una canción⟩ **3** : la próxima vez ⟨when next we meet : la próxima vez que nos encontremos⟩
next[2] *adj* **1** ADJACENT : contiguo, de al lado **2** COMING : que viene, próximo ⟨next Friday : el viernes que viene⟩ **3** FOLLOWING : siguiente ⟨the next year : el año siguiente⟩
next–door ['nɛkst'dor] *adj* : de al lado
next to[1] *adv* ALMOST : casi, prácticamente ⟨next to impossible : casi imposible⟩

next to[2] *prep* : junto a, al lado de
nexus [ˈnɛksəs] *n* : nexo *m*
nib [ˈnɪb] *n* : plumilla *f*
nibble[1] [ˈnɪbəl] *v* **-bled; -bling** *vt* : pellizcar, mordisquear, picar — *vi* : picar
nibble[2] *n* : mordisco *m*
Nicaraguan [ˌnɪkəˈrɑgwən] *n* : nicaragüense *mf* — **Nicaraguan** *adj*
nice [ˈnaɪs] *adj* **nicer; nicest 1** REFINED : pulido, refinado **2** SUBTLE : fino, sutil **3** PLEASING : agradable, bueno, lindo ⟨nice weather : buen tiempo⟩ **4** RESPECTABLE : bueno, decente **5 nice and** : bien, muy ⟨nice and hot : bien caliente⟩ ⟨nice and slow : despacito⟩
nicely [ˈnaɪsli] *adv* **1** KINDLY : amablemente **2** POLITELY : con buenos modales **3** ATTRACTIVELY : de buen gusto
niceness [ˈnaɪsnəs] *n* : simpatía *f*, amabilidad *f*
nicety [ˈnaɪsət̬i] *n, pl* **-ties 1** DETAIL, SUBTLETY : sutileza *f*, detalle *m* **2 niceties** *npl* : lujos *mpl*, detalles *mpl*
niche [ˈnɪʧ] *n* **1** RECESS : nicho *m*, hornacina *f* **2** : nicho *m*, hueco *m* ⟨to make a niche for oneself : hacerse un hueco, encontrarse una buena posición⟩
nick[1] [ˈnɪk] *vt* : cortar, hacer una muesca en
nick[2] *n* **1** CUT : corte *m*, muesca *f* **2 in the nick of time** : en el momento crítico, justo a tiempo
nickel [ˈnɪkəl] *n* **1** : níquel *m* **2** : moneda *f* de cinco centavos
nickname[1] [ˈnɪkˌneɪm] *vt* **-named; -naming** : apodar
nickname[2] *n* : apodo *m*, mote *m*, sobrenombre *m*
nicotine [ˈnɪkəˌtiːn] *n* : nicotina *f*
niece [ˈniːs] *n* : sobrina *f*
Nigerian [naɪˈʤɪriən] *n* : nigeriano *m*, -na *f* — **Nigerian** *adj*
niggardly [ˈnɪgərdli] *adj* : mezquino, tacaño
niggling [ˈnɪgəlɪŋ] *adj* **1** PETTY : insignificante **2** PERSISTENT : constante, persistente ⟨a niggling doubt : una duda constante⟩
nigh[1] [ˈnaɪ] *adv* **1** NEARLY : casi **2 to draw nigh** : acercarse, avecinarse
nigh[2] *adj* : cercano, próximo
night[1] [ˈnaɪt] *adj* : nocturno, de la noche ⟨the night sky : el cielo nocturno⟩ ⟨night shift : turno de la noche⟩
night[2] *n* **1** EVENING : noche *f* ⟨at night : de noche⟩ ⟨last night : anoche⟩ ⟨tomorrow night : mañana por la noche⟩ **2** DARKNESS : noche *f*, oscuridad *f* ⟨night fell : cayó la noche⟩
nightclothes [ˈnaɪtˌkloːðz, -ˌkloːz] *npl* : ropa *f* de dormir
nightclub [ˈnaɪtˌklʌb] *n* : cabaret *m*, club *m* nocturno
night crawler [ˈnaɪtˌkrɔlər] *n* EARTHWORM : lombriz *f* (de tierra)
nightfall [ˈnaɪtˌfɔl] *n* : anochecer *m*
nightgown [ˈnaɪtˌgaʊn] *n* : camisón *m* (de noche)
nightingale [ˈnaɪtənˌgeɪl, ˈnaɪt̬ɪŋ-] *n* : ruiseñor *m*
nightly[1] [ˈnaɪtli] *adv* : cada noche, todas las noches
nightly[2] *adj* : de todas las noches
nightmare [ˈnaɪtˌmær] *n* : pesadilla *f*
nightmarish [ˈnaɪtˌmærɪʃ] *adj* : de pesadilla
night owl *n* : noctámbulo *m*, -la *f*
nightshade [ˈnaɪtˌʃeɪd] *n* : hierba *f* mora
nightshirt [ˈnaɪtˌʃərt] *n* : camisa *f* de dormir
nightstick [ˈnaɪtˌstɪk] *n* : porra *f*
nighttime [ˈnaɪtˌtaɪm] *n* : noche *f*
nihilism [ˈnaɪəˌlɪzəm] *n* : nihilismo *m*
nil [ˈnɪl] *n* : nada *f*, cero *m*
nimble [ˈnɪmbəl] *adj* **-bler; -blest 1** AGILE : ágil **2** CLEVER : hábil, ingenioso
nimbleness [ˈnɪmbəlnəs] *n* : agilidad *f*
nimbly [ˈnɪmbli] *adv* : con agilidad, ágilmente
nincompoop [ˈnɪnkəmˌpuːp, ˈnɪŋ-] *n* FOOL : tonto *m*, -ta *f*; bobo *m*, -ba *f*
nine[1] [ˈnaɪn] *adj* **1** : nueve **2 nine times out of ten** : casi siempre
nine[2] *n* : nueve *m*
nine hundred[1] *adj* : novecientos
nine hundred[2] *n* : novecientos *m*
ninepins [ˈnaɪnˌpɪnz] *n* : bolos *mpl*
nineteen[1] [naɪnˈtiːn] *adj* : diecinueve
nineteen[2] *n* : diecinueve *m*
nineteenth[1] [naɪnˈtiːnθ] *adj* : decimonoveno, decimonono ⟨the nineteenth century : el siglo diecinueve⟩
nineteenth[2] *n* **1** : decimonoveno *m*, -na *f*; decimonono *m*, -na *f* (en una serie) **2** : diecinueveavo *m*, diecinueveava parte *f*
ninetieth[1] [ˈnaɪnt̬iəθ] *adj* : nonagésimo
ninetieth[2] *n* **1** : nonagésimo *m*, -ma *f* (en una serie) **2** : noventavo *m*, noventava parte *f*
ninety[1] [ˈnaɪnt̬i] *adj* : noventa
ninety[2] *n, pl* **-ties** : noventa *m*
ninth[1] [ˈnaɪnθ] *adj* : noveno
ninth[2] *n* **1** : noveno *m*, -na *f* (en una serie) **2** : noveno *m*, novena parte *f*
ninny [ˈnɪni] *n, pl* **ninnies** FOOL : tonto *m*, -ta *f*; bobo *m*, -ba *f*
nip[1] [ˈnɪp] *vt* **nipped; nipping 1** PINCH : pellizcar **2** BITE : morder, mordisquear **3 to nip in the bud** : cortar de raíz
nip[2] *n* **1** TANG : sabor *m* fuerte **2** PINCH : pellizco *m* **3** NIBBLE : mordisco *m* **4** SWALLOW : trago *m*, traguito *m* **5 there's a nip in the air** : hace fresco
nipple [ˈnɪpəl] *n* : pezón *m* (de una mujer), tetilla *f* (de un hombre)
nippy [ˈnɪpi] *adj* **-pier; -est 1** SHARP : fuerte, picante **2** CHILLY : frío ⟨it's nippy today : hoy hace frío⟩
nit [ˈnɪt] *n* : liendre *f*
nitrate [ˈnaɪˌtreɪt] *n* : nitrato *m*
nitric acid [ˈnaɪtrɪk] *n* : ácido *m* nítrico
nitrite [ˈnaɪˌtraɪt] *n* : nitrito *m*
nitrogen [ˈnaɪtrəʤən] *n* : nitrógeno *m*
nitroglycerin *or* **nitroglycerine** [ˌnaɪtroˈglɪsərən] *n* : nitroglicerina *f*

nitwit ['nɪt,wɪt] *n* : zonzo *m*, -za *f*; bobo *m*, -ba *f*
no¹ ['no:] *adv* : no ⟨are you leaving?—no : ¿te vas?—no⟩ ⟨no less than : no menos de⟩ ⟨to say no : decir que no⟩ ⟨like it or no : quieras o no quieras⟩
no² *adj* **1** : ninguno ⟨it's no trouble : no es ningún problema⟩ ⟨she has no money : no tiene dinero⟩ **2** (*indicating a small amount*) ⟨we'll be there in no time : llegamos dentro de poco, no tardamos nada⟩ **3** (*expressing a negation*) ⟨he's no liar : no es mentiroso⟩
no³ *n, pl* **noes** *or* **nos** ['no:z] **1** DENIAL : no *m* ⟨I won't take no for an answer : no aceptaré un no por respuesta⟩ **2** : voto *f* en contra ⟨the noes have it : se ha rechazado la moción⟩
nobility [no'bɪləṭi] *n* : nobleza *f*
noble¹ ['no:bəl] *adj* **-bler; -blest 1** ILLUSTRIOUS : noble, glorioso **2** ARISTOCRATIC : noble **3** STATELY : majestuoso, magnífico **4** LOFTY : noble, elevado ⟨noble sentiments : sentimientos elevados⟩
noble² *n* : noble *mf*, aristócrata *mf*
nobleman ['no:bəlmən] *n, pl* **-men** [-mən, -,mɛn] : noble *m*, aristócrata *m*
nobleness ['no:bəlnəs] *n* : nobleza *f*
noblewoman ['no:bəl,wumən] *n, pl* **-women** [-,wɪmən] : noble *f*, aristócrata *f*
nobly ['no:bli] *adv* : noblemente
nobody¹ ['no:bədi, -,badi] *n, pl* **-bodies** : don nadie *m* ⟨he's a mere nobody : es un don nadie⟩
nobody² *pron* : nadie
nocturnal [nak'tərnəl] *adj* : nocturno
nocturne ['nak,tərn] *n* : nocturno *m*
nod¹ ['nad] *v* **nodded; nodding** *vi* **1** : saludar con la cabeza, asentir con la cabeza **2 to nod off** : dormirse, quedarse dormido — *vt* : inclinar (la cabeza) ⟨to nod one's head in agreement : asentir con la cabeza⟩
nod² *n* : saludo *m* con la cabeza, señal *m* con la cabeza, señal *m* de asentimiento
node ['no:d] *n* : nudo *m* (de una planta)
nodule ['na,ʤu:l] *n* : nódulo *m*
noel [no'ɛl] *n* **1** CAROL : villancico *m* de Navidad **2 Noel** CHRISTMAS : Navidad *f*
noes → **no³**
noise¹ ['nɔɪz] *vt* **noised; noising** : rumorear, publicar
noise² *n* : ruido *m*
noiseless ['nɔɪzləs] *adj* : silencioso, sin ruido
noiselessly ['nɔɪzləsli] *adv* : silenciosamente
noisemaker ['nɔɪz,meɪkər] *n* : matraca *f*
noisiness ['nɔɪzinəs] *n* : ruido *m*
noisome ['nɔɪsəm] *adj* : maloliente, fétido
noisy ['nɔɪzi] *adj* **noisier; -est** : ruidoso — **noisily** ['nɔɪzəli] *adv*
nomad¹ ['no:,mæd] → **nomadic**
nomad² *n* : nómada *mf*
nomadic [no'mædɪk] *adj* : nómada
nomenclature ['no:mən,kleɪʧər] *n* : nomenclatura *f*
nominal ['namənəl] *adj* **1** : nominal ⟨the nominal head of his party : el jefe nominal de su partido⟩ **2** TRIFLING : insignificante
nominally ['namənəli] *adv* : sólo de nombre, nominalmente
nominate ['namə,neɪt] *vt* **-nated; -nating 1** PROPOSE : proponer (como candidato), nominar **2** APPOINT : nombrar
nomination [,namə'neɪʃən] *n* **1** PROPOSAL : propuesta *f*, postulación *f* **2** APPOINTMENT : nombramiento *m*
nominative¹ ['namənəṭɪv] *adj* : nominativo
nominative² *n or* **nominative case** : nominativo *m*
nominee [,namə'ni:] *n* : candidato *m*, -ta *f*
nonaddictive [,nanə'dɪktɪv] *adj* : que no crea dependencia
nonalcoholic [,nan,ælkə'hɔlɪk] *adj* : sin alcohol, no alcohólico
nonaligned [,nanə'laɪnd] *adj* : no alineado
nonbeliever [,nanbə'li:vər] *n* : no creyente *mf*
nonbreakable [,nan'breɪkəbəl] *adj* : irrompible
nonce ['nan*t*s] *n* **for the nonce** : por el momento
nonchalance [,nanʃə'lan*t*s] *n* : indiferencia *f*, despreocupación *f*
nonchalant [,nanʃə'lant] *adj* : indiferente, despreocupado, impasible
nonchalantly [,nanʃə'lantli] *adv* : con aire despreocupado, con indiferencia
noncombatant [,nankəm'bætənt, -'kambə-] *n* : no combatiente *mf*
noncommissioned officer [,nankə'mɪʃənd] *n* : suboficial *mf*
noncommittal [,nankə'mɪṭəl] *adj* : evasivo, que no se compromete
nonconductor [,nankən'dʌktər] *n* : aislante *m*
nonconformist [,nankən'fɔrmɪst] *n* : inconformista *mf*, inconforme *mf*
nonconformity [,nankən'fɔrməṭi] *n* : inconformidad *f*, no conformidad *f*
noncontagious [,nankən'teɪʤəs] *adj* : no contagioso
nondenominational [,nandɪ,namə'neɪʃənəl] *adj* : no sectario
nondescript [,nandɪ'skrɪpt] *adj* : anodino, soso
nondiscriminatory [,nandɪ'skrɪmənə,tori] *adj* : no discriminatorio
nondrinker [,nan'drɪŋkər] *n* : abstemio *m*, -mia *f*
none¹ ['nʌn] *adv* : de ninguna manera, de ningún modo, nada ⟨he was none too happy : no se sintió nada contento⟩ ⟨I'm none the worse for it : no estoy peor por ello⟩ ⟨none too soon : a buena hora⟩

none[2] *pron* : ninguno, ninguna
nonentity [ˌnɑnˈɛntət̬i] *n, pl* **-ties** : persona *f* insignificante, nulidad *f*
nonessential [ˌnɑnɪˈsɛntʃəl] *adj* : secundario, no esencial
nonessentials [ˌnɑnɪˈsɛntʃəlz] *npl* : cosas *fpl* secundarias, cosas *fpl* accesorias
nonetheless [ˌnʌnðəˈlɛs] *adv* : sin embargo, no obstante
nonexistence [ˌnɑnɪgˈzɪstənts] *n* : inexistencia *f*
nonexistent [ˌnɑnɪgˈzɪstənt] *adj* : inexistente
nonfat [ˌnɑnˈfæt] *adj* : sin grasa
nonfattening [ˌnɑnˈfætənɪŋ] *adj* : que no engorda
nonfiction [ˌnɑnˈfɪkʃən] *n* : no ficción *f*
nonflammable [ˌnɑnˈflæməbəl] *adj* : no inflamable
nonintervention [ˌnɑnˌɪntərˈvɛntʃən] *n* : no intervención *f*
nonmalignant [ˌnɑnməˈlɪgnənt] *adj* : no maligno, benigno
nonnegotiable [ˌnɑnnɪˈgoːʃəbəl, -ʃiə-] *adj* : no negociable
nonpareil[1] [ˌnɑnpəˈrɛl] *adj* : sin parangón, sin par
nonpareil[2] *n* : persona *f* sin igual, cosa *f* sin par
nonpartisan [ˌnɑnˈpɑrt̬əzən, -sən] *adj* : imparcial
nonpaying [ˌnɑnˈpeɪɪŋ] *adj* : que no paga
nonpayment [ˌnɑnˈpeɪmənt] *n* : impago *m*, falta *f* de pago
nonperson [ˌnɑnˈpərsən] *n* : persona *f* sin derechos
nonplus [ˌnɑnˈplʌs] *vt* **-plussed; -plussing** : confundir, desconcertar, dejar perplejo
nonprescription [ˌnɑnprɪˈskrɪpʃən] *adj* : disponible sin receta del médico
nonproductive [ˌnɑnprəˈdʌktɪv] *adj* : improductivo
nonprofit [ˌnɑnˈprɑfət] *adj* : sin fines lucrativos
nonproliferation [ˌnɑnprəˌlɪfəˈreɪʃən] *adj* : no proliferación
nonresident [ˌnɑnˈrɛzədənt, -ˌdɛnt] *n* : no residente *mf*
nonscheduled [ˌnɑnˈskɛˌdʒuːld] *adj* : no programado, no regular
nonsectarian [ˌnɑnˌsɛkˈtæriən] *adj* : no sectario
nonsense [ˈnɑnˌsɛnts, ˈnɑntsənts] *n* : tonterías *fpl*, disparates *mpl*
nonsensical [nɑnˈsɛntsɪkəl] *adj* ABSURD : absurdo, disparatado — **nonsensically** [-kli] *adv*
nonsmoker [ˌnɑnˈsmoːkər] *n* : no fumador *m*, -dora *f*; persona *f* que no fuma
nonstandard [ˌnɑnˈstændərd] *adj* : no regular, no estándar
nonstick [ˌnɑnˈstɪk] *adj* : antiadherente
nonstop[1] [ˌnɑnˈstɑp] *adv* : sin parar ⟨he talked nonstop : habló sin parar⟩
nonstop[2] *adj* : directo, sin escalas ⟨nonstop flight : vuelo directo⟩
nonsupport [ˌnɑnsəˈpɔrt] *n* : falta *f* de manutención
nontaxable [ˌnɑnˈtæksəbəl] *adj* : exento de impuestos
nontoxic [ˌnɑnˈtɑksɪk] *adj* : no tóxico
nonviolence [ˌnɑnˈvaɪlənts, -ˈvaɪə-] *n* : no violencia *f*
nonviolent [ˌnɑnˈvaɪlənt, -ˈvaɪə-] *adj* : pacífico, no violento
noodle [ˈnuːdəl] *n* : fideo *m*, tallarín *m*
nook [ˈnʊk] *n* : rincón *m*, recoveco *m*, escondrijo *m* ⟨in every nook and cranny : en todos los rincones⟩
noon [ˈnuːn] *n* : mediodía *m*
noonday [ˈnuːnˌdeɪ] *n* : mediodía *m* ⟨the noonday sun : el sol de mediodía⟩
no one *pron* NOBODY : nadie
noontime [ˈnuːnˌtaɪm] *n* : mediodía *m*
noose [ˈnuːs] *n* **1** LASSO : lazo *m* **2 hangman's noose** : dogal *m*, soga *f*
nor [ˈnɔr] *conj* : ni ⟨neither good nor bad : ni bueno ni malo⟩ ⟨nor I! : ¡ni yo tampoco!⟩
Nordic [ˈnɔrdɪk] *adj* : nórdico
norm [ˈnɔrm] *n* **1** STANDARD : norma *f*, modelo *m* **2** CUSTOM, RULE : regla *f* general, lo normal
normal [ˈnɔrməl] *adj* : normal — **normally** *adv*
normalcy [ˈnɔrməlsi] *n* : normalidad *f*
normality [nɔrˈmælət̬i] *n* : normalidad *f*
normalize [ˈnɔrməˌlaɪz] *vt* : normalizar
Norse [ˈnɔrs] *adj* : nórdico
north[1] [ˈnɔrθ] *adv* : al norte
north[2] *adj* : norte, del norte ⟨the north coast : la costa del norte⟩
north[3] *n* **1** : norte *m* **2 the North** : el Norte *m*
North American *n* : norteamericano *m*, -na *f* — **North American** *adj*
northbound [ˈnɔrθˌbaʊnd] *adv* : con rumbo al norte
northeast[1] [nɔrθˈiːst] *adv* : hacia el nordeste
northeast[2] *adj* : nordeste, del nordeste
northeast[3] *n* : nordeste *m*, noreste *m*
northeasterly[1] [nɔrθˈiːstərli] *adv* : hacia el nordeste
northeasterly[2] *adj* : nordeste, del nordeste
northeastern [nɔrθˈiːstərn] *adj* : nordeste, del nordeste
northerly[1] [ˈnɔrðərli] *adv* : hacia el norte
northerly[2] *adj* : del norte ⟨a northerly wind : un viento del norte⟩
northern [ˈnɔrðərn] *adj* : norte, norteño, septentrional
Northerner [ˈnɔrðərnər] *n* : norteño *m*, -ña *f*
northern lights → aurora borealis
North Pole : Polo *m* Norte
North Star *n* : estrella *f* polar
northward [ˈnɔrθwərd] *adv & adj* : hacia el norte
northwest[1] [nɔrθˈwɛst] *adv* : hacia el noroeste
northwest[2] *adj* : del noroeste
northwest[3] *n* : noroeste *m*

northwesterly[1] [nɔrθ'wɛstərli] *adv* : hacia el noroeste

northwesterly[2] *adj* : del noroeste

northwestern [nɔrθ'wɛstərn] *adj* : noroeste, del noroeste

Norwegian [nɔr'wi:ʤən] *n* **1** : noruego *m*, -ga*f* **2** : noruego *m* (idioma) — **Norwegian** *adj*

nose[1] ['no:z] *v* **nosed; nosing** *vt* **1** SMELL : olfatear **2** : empujar con el hocico ⟨the dog nosed open the bag : el perro abrió el saco con el hocico⟩ **3** EDGE, MOVE : mover poco a poco — *vi* **1** PRY : entrometerse, meter las narices **2** EDGE : avanzar poco a poco

nose[2] *n* **1** : nariz *f* (de una persona), hocico *m* (de un animal) ⟨to blow one's nose : sonarse las narices⟩ **2** SMELL : olfato *m*, sentido *m* del olfato **3** FRONT : parte *f* delantera, nariz *f* (de un avión), proa *f* (de un barco) **4 to follow one's nose** : dejarse guiar por el instinto

nosebleed ['no:z,bli:d] *n* : hemorragia *f* nasal

nosedive ['no:z,daɪv] *n* **1** : descenso *m* en picada (de un avión) **2** : caída *f* súbita (de precios, etc.)

nose–dive ['no:z,daɪv] *vi* : descender en picada, caer en picada

nostalgia [nɑ'stælʤə, nə-] *n* : nostalgia *f*

nostalgic [nɑ'stælʤɪk, nə-] *adj* : nostálgico

nostril ['nɑstrəl] *n* : ventana *f* de la nariz

nostrum ['nɑstrəm] *n* : panacea *f*

nosy *or* **nosey** ['no:zi] *adj* **nosier; -est** : entrometido

not ['nɑt] *adv* **1** (*used to form a negative*) : no ⟨she is not tired : no está cansada⟩ ⟨not to say something would be wrong : no decir nada sería injusto⟩ **2** (*used to replace a negative clause*) : no ⟨are we going or not? : ¿vamos a ir o no?⟩ ⟨of course not! : ¡claro que no!⟩

notable[1] ['no:t̬əbəl] *adj* **1** NOTEWORTHY : notable, de notar **2** DISTINGUISHED, PROMINENT : distinguido, destacado

notable[2] *n* : persona *f* importante, personaje *m*

notably ['no:t̬əbli] *adv* : notablemente, particularmente

notarize ['no:t̬ə,raɪz] *vt* **-rized; -rizing** : autenticar, autorizar

notary public ['no:t̬əri] *n, pl* **-ries public** *or* **-ry publics** : notario *m*, -ria *f*; escribano *m*, -na *f*

notation [no'teɪʃən] *n* **1** NOTE : anotación *f*, nota *f* **2** : notación *f* ⟨musical notation : notación musical⟩

notch[1] ['nɑʧ] *vt* : hacer una muesca en, cortar

notch[2] *n* : muesca *f*, corte *m*

note[1] ['no:t] *vt* **noted; noting 1** NOTICE : notar, observar, tomar nota de **2** RECORD : anotar, apuntar

note[2] *n* **1** : nota *f* (musical) **2** COMMENT : nota *f*, comentario *m* **3** LETTER : nota *f*, cartita *f* **4** PROMINENCE : prestigio *m* ⟨a musician of note : un músico destacado⟩ **5** ATTENTION : atención *f* ⟨to take note of : prestar atención a⟩

notebook ['no:t,bʊk] *n* **1** : libreta *f*, cuaderno *m* **2** : notebook *m* (computadora)

noted ['no:t̬əd] *adj* EMINENT : renombrado, eminente, celebrado

noteworthy ['no:t,wərði] *adj* : notable, de notar, de interés

nothing[1] ['nʌθɪŋ] *adv* **1** : de ninguna manera ⟨nothing daunted, we carried on : sin amilanarnos, seguimos adelante⟩ **2 nothing like** : no . . . en nada ⟨he's nothing like his brother : no se parece en nada a su hermano⟩

nothing[2] *n* **1** NOTHINGNESS : nada *f* **2** ZERO : cero *m* **3** : persona *f* de poca importancia, cero *m* **4** TRIFLE : nimiedad *f*

nothing[3] *pron* : nada ⟨there's nothing better : no hay nada mejor⟩ ⟨nothing else : nada más⟩ ⟨nothing but : solamente⟩ ⟨they mean nothing to me : ellos me son indiferentes⟩

nothingness ['nʌθɪŋnəs] *n* **1** VOID : vacío *m*, nada *f* **2** NONEXISTENCE : inexistencia *f* **3** TRIFLE : nimiedad *f*

notice[1] ['no:t̬ɪs] *vt* **-ticed; -ticing** : notar, observar, advertir, darse cuenta de

notice[2] *n* **1** NOTIFICATION : aviso *m*, notificación *f* **2** ATTENTION : atención *f* ⟨to take notice of : prestar atención a⟩

noticeable ['no:t̬ɪsəbəl] *adj* : evidente, perceptible — **noticeably** [-bli] *adv*

notification [,no:t̬əfə'keɪʃən] *n* : notificación *f*, aviso *m*

notify ['no:t̬ə,faɪ] *vt* **-fied; -fying** : notificar, avisar

notion ['no:ʃən] *n* **1** IDEA : idea *f*, noción *f* **2** WHIM : capricho *m*, antojo *m* **3 notions** *npl* : artículos *mpl* de mercería

notoriety [,no:t̬ə'raɪət̬i] *n* : mala fama *f*, notoriedad *f*

notorious [no'to:riəs] *adj* : de mala fama, célebre, bien conocido

notwithstanding[1] [,nɑtwɪθ'stændɪŋ, -wɪð-] *adv* NEVERTHELESS : no obstante, sin embargo

notwithstanding[2] *conj* : a pesar de que

notwithstanding[3] *prep* : a pesar de, no obstante

nougat ['nu:gət] *n* : turrón *m*

nought ['nɔt, 'nɑt] → **naught**

noun ['naʊn] *n* : nombre *m*, sustantivo *m*

nourish ['nərɪʃ] *vt* **1** FEED : alimentar, nutrir, sustentar **2** FOSTER : fomentar, alentar

nourishing ['nərɪʃɪŋ] *adj* : alimenticio, nutritivo

nourishment ['nərɪʃmənt] *n* : nutrición *f*, alimento *m*, sustento *m*

novel[1] ['nɑvəl] *adj* : original, novedoso

novel[2] *n* : novela *f*
novelist [ˈnɑvəlɪst] *n* : novelista *mf*
novelty [ˈnɑvəlti] *n, pl* **-ties 1** : novedad *f* **2 novelties** *npl* TRINKETS : baratijas *fpl*, chucherías *fpl*
November [noˈvɛmbər] *n* : noviembre *m*
novice [ˈnɑvɪs] *n* : novato *m*, -ta *f*; principiante *mf*; novicio *m*, -cia *f*
now[1] [ˈnaʊ] *adv* **1** PRESENTLY : ahora, ya, actualmente ⟨from now on : de ahora en adelante⟩ ⟨long before now : ya hace tiempo⟩ ⟨now and then : de vez en cuando⟩ **2** IMMEDIATELY : ahora (mismo), inmediatamente ⟨do it right now! : ¡hazlo ahora mismo!⟩ **3** THEN : ya, entonces ⟨now they were ready : ya estaban listos⟩ **4** (*used to introduce a statement, a question, a command, or a transition*) ⟨now hear this! : ¡presten atención!⟩ ⟨now what do you think of that? : ¿qué piensas de eso?⟩
now[2] *n* (*indicating the present time*) ⟨until now : hasta ahora⟩ ⟨by now : ya⟩ ⟨ten years from now : dentro de 10 años⟩
now[3] *conj* **now that** : ahora que, ya que
nowadays [ˈnaʊəˌdeɪz] *adv* : hoy en día, actualmente, en la actualidad
nowhere[1] [ˈnoːˌ*h*wɛr] *adv* **1** : en ninguna parte, a ningún lado ⟨nowhere to be found : en ninguna parte, por ningún lado⟩ ⟨you're going nowhere : no estás yendo a ningún lado, no estás yendo a ninguna parte⟩ **2 nowhere near** : ni con mucho, nada cerca ⟨it's nowhere near here : no está nada cerca de aquí⟩
nowhere[2] *n* **1** : ninguna parte *f* **2 out of nowhere** : de la nada
noxious [ˈnɑkʃəs] *adj* : nocivo, dañino, tóxico
nozzle [ˈnɑzəl] *n* : boca *f*
nuance [ˈnuːˌɑn*t*s, ˈnjuː-] *n* : matiz *m*
nub [ˈnʌb] *n* **1** KNOB, LUMP : protuberancia *f*, nudo *m* **2** GIST : quid *m*, meollo *m*
nuclear [ˈnuːkliər, ˈnjuː-] *adj* : nuclear
nucleus [ˈnuːkliəs, ˈnjuː-] *n, pl* **-clei** [-kliˌaɪ] : núcleo *m*
nude[1] [ˈnuːd, ˈnjuːd] *adj* **nuder; nudest** : desnudo
nude[2] *n* : desnudo *m*
nudge[1] [ˈnʌʤ] *vt* **nudged; nudging** : darle con el codo (a alguien)
nudge[2] *n* : toque *m* que se da con el codo
nudism [ˈnuːˌdɪzəm, ˈnjuː-] *n* : nudismo *m*
nudist [ˈnuːdɪst, ˈnjuː-] *n* : nudista *mf*
nudity [ˈnuːdəti, ˈnjuː-] *n* : desnudez *f*
nugget [ˈnʌgət] *n* : pepita *f*
nuisance [ˈnuːsən*t*s, ˈnjuː-] *n* **1** BOTHER : fastidio *m*, molestia *f*, lata *f* **2** PEST : pesado *m*, -da *f fam*
null [ˈnʌl] *adj* : nulo ⟨null and void : nulo y sin efecto⟩
nullify [ˈnʌləˌfaɪ] *vt* **-fied; -fying** : invalidar, anular
nullity [ˈnʌləti] *n, pl* **-ties** : nulidad *f*
numb[1] [ˈnʌm] *vt* : entumecer, adormecer
numb[2] *adj* : entumecido, dormido ⟨numb with fear : paralizado de miedo⟩
number[1] [ˈnʌmbər] *vt* **1** COUNT, INCLUDE : contar, incluir **2** : numerar ⟨number the pages : numera las páginas⟩ **3** TOTAL : ascender a, sumar
number[2] *n* **1** : número *m* ⟨in round numbers : en números redondos⟩ ⟨telephone number : número de teléfono⟩ **2 a number of** : varios, unos pocos, unos cuantos
numberless [ˈnʌmbərləs] *adj* : innumerable, sin número
numbness [ˈnʌmnəs] *n* : entumecimiento *m*
numeral [ˈnuːmərəl, ˈnjuː-] *n* : número *m* ⟨Roman numeral : número romano⟩
numerator [ˈnuːməˌreɪtər, ˈnjuː-] *n* : numerador *m*
numeric [nʊˈmɛrɪk, njʊ-] *adj* : numérico
numerical [nʊˈmɛrɪkəl, njʊ-] *adj* : numérico — **numerically** [-kli] *adv*
numerous [ˈnuːmərəs, ˈnjuː-] *adj* : numeroso
numismatics [ˌnuːməzˈmætɪks, ˌnjuː-] *n* : numismática *f*
numskull [ˈnʌmˌskʌl] *n* : tonto *m*, -ta *f*; mentecato *m*, -ta *f*; zoquete *m fam*
nun [ˈnʌn] *n* : monja *f*
nuptial [ˈnʌpʃəl] *adj* : nupcial
nuptials [ˈnʌpʃəlz] *npl* WEDDING : nupcias *fpl*, boda *f*
nurse[1] [ˈnərs] *vt* **nursed; nursing 1** SUCKLE : amamantar **2** : cuidar (de), atender ⟨to nurse the sick : cuidar a los enfermos⟩ ⟨to nurse a cold : curarse de un resfriado⟩
nurse[2] *n* **1** : enfermero *m*, -ra *f* **2** → **nursemaid**
nursemaid [ˈnərsˌmeɪd] *n* : niñera *f*
nursery [ˈnərsəri] *n, pl* **-eries 1** *or* **day nursery** : guardería *f* **2** : vivero *m* (de plantas)
nursing home *n* : hogar *m* de ancianos, clínica *f* de reposo
nurture[1] [ˈnərʧər] *vt* **-tured; -turing 1** FEED, NOURISH : nutrir, alimentar **2** EDUCATE : criar, educar **3** FOSTER : alimentar, fomentar
nurture[2] *n* **1** UPBRINGING : crianza *f*, educación *f* **2** FOOD : alimento *m*
nut [ˈnʌt] *n* **1** : nuez *f* **2** : tuerca *f* ⟨nuts and bolts : tuercas y tornillos⟩ **3** LUNATIC : loco *m*, -ca *f*; chiflado *m*, -da *f fam* **4** ENTHUSIAST : fanático *m*, -ca *f*; entusiasta *mf*
nutcracker [ˈnʌtˌkrækər] *n* : cascanueces *m*
nuthatch [ˈnʌtˌhæʧ] *n* : trepador *m*
nutmeg [ˈnʌtˌmɛg] *n* : nuez *f* moscada
nutrient [ˈnuːtriənt, ˈnjuː-] *n* : nutriente *m*, alimento *m* nutritivo
nutriment [ˈnuːtrəmənt, ˈnjuː-] *n* : nutrimento *m*
nutrition [nʊˈtrɪʃən, njʊ-] *n* : nutrición *f*
nutritional [nʊˈtrɪʃənəl, njʊ-] *adj* : alimenticio
nutritious [nʊˈtrɪʃəs, njʊ-] *adj* : nutritivo, alimenticio

nuts ['nʌts] *adj* **1** FANATICAL : fanático **2** CRAZY : loco, chiflado *fam*
nutshell ['nʌt,ʃɛl] *n* **1** : cáscara *f* de nuez **2 in a nutshell** : en pocas palabras
nutty ['nʌt̬i] *adj* **-tier; -tiest** : loco, chiflado *fam*
nuzzle ['nʌzəl] *v* **-zled; -zling** *vi* NESTLE : acurrucarse, arrimarse — *vt* : acariciar con el hocico
nylon ['naɪ,lɑn] *n* **1** : nilón *m* **2 nylons** *npl* : medias *fpl* de nilón
nymph ['nɪmpf] *n* : ninfa *f*

O

o ['o:] *n, pl* **o's** *or* **os** ['o:z] **1** : decimoquinta letra del alfabeto inglés **2** ZERO : cero *m*
O ['o:] → **oh**
oaf ['o:f] *n* : zoquete *m*; bruto *m*, -ta *f*
oafish ['o:fɪʃ] *adj* : torpe, lerdo
oak ['o:k] *n, pl* **oaks** *or* **oak** : roble *m*
oaken ['o:kən] *adj* : de roble
oar ['or] *n* : remo *m*
oarlock ['or,lɑk] *n* : tolete *m*, escálamo *m*
oasis [o'eɪsɪs] *n, pl* **oases** [-,si:z] : oasis *m*
oat ['o:t] *n* : avena *f*
oath ['o:θ] *n, pl* **oaths** ['o:ðz, 'o:θs] **1** : juramento *m* ⟨to take an oath : prestar juramento⟩ **2** SWEARWORD : mala palabra *f*, palabrota *f*
oatmeal ['o:t,mi:l] *n* : avena *f* ⟨instant oatmeal : avena instantánea⟩
obdurate ['ɑbdʊrət, -djʊ-] *adj* : inflexible, firme, obstinado
obedience [o'bi:diənts] *n* : obediencia *f*
obedient [o'bi:diənt] *adj* : obediente — **obediently** *adv*
obelisk ['ɑbə,lɪsk] *n* : obelisco *m*
obese [o'bi:s] *adj* : obeso
obesity [o'bi:sət̬i] *n* : obesidad *f*
obey [o'beɪ] *v* **obeyed; obeying** : obedecer ⟨to obey the law : cumplir la ley⟩
obfuscate ['ɑbfə,skeɪt] *vt* **-cated; -cating** : ofuscar, confundir
obituary [ə'bɪtʃʊ,ɛri] *n, pl* **-aries** : obituario *m*, necrología *f*
object¹ [əb'dʒɛkt] *vt* : objetar — *vi* : oponerse, poner reparos, hacer objeciones
object² ['ɑbdʒɪkt] *n* **1** : objeto *m* **2** OBJECTIVE, PURPOSE : objetivo *m*, propósito *m* **3** : complemento *m* (en gramática)
objection [əb'dʒɛkʃən] *n* : objeción *f*
objectionable [əb'dʒɛkʃənəbəl] *adj* : ofensivo, indeseable — **objectionably** [-bli] *adv*
objective¹ [əb'dʒɛktɪv] *adj* **1** IMPARTIAL : objetivo, imparcial **2** : de complemento, directo (en gramática)
objective² *n* **1** : objetivo *m* **2** *or* **objective case** : acusativo *m*
objectively [əb'dʒɛktɪvli] *adv* : objetivamente
objectivity [,ɑb,dʒɛk'tɪvət̬i] *n, pl* **-ties** : objetividad *f*
obligate ['ɑblə,geɪt] *vt* **-gated; -gating** : obligar
obligation [,ɑblə'geɪʃən] *n* : obligación *f*
obligatory [ə'blɪgə,tori] *adj* : obligatorio
oblige [ə'blaɪdʒ] *vt* **obliged; obliging 1** COMPEL : obligar **2** : hacerle un favor (a alguien), complacer ⟨to oblige a friend : hacerle un favor a un amigo⟩ **3 to be much obliged** : estar muy agradecido
obliging [ə'blaɪdʒɪŋ] *adj* : servicial, complaciente — **obligingly** *adv*
oblique [o'bli:k] *adj* **1** SLANTING : oblicuo **2** INDIRECT : indirecto — **obliquely** *adv*
obliterate [ə'blɪt̬ə,reɪt] *vt* **-ated; -ating 1** ERASE : obliterar, borrar **2** DESTROY : destruir, eliminar
obliteration [ə,blɪt̬ə'reɪʃən] *n* : obliteración *f*
oblivion [ə'blɪviən] *n* : olvido *m*
oblivious [ə'blɪviəs] *adj* : inconsciente — **obliviously** *adv*
oblong¹ ['ɑ,blɔŋ] *adj* : oblongo
oblong² *n* : figura *f* oblonga, rectángulo *m*
obnoxious [ɑb'nɑkʃəs, əb-] *adj* : repugnante, odioso — **obnoxiously** *adv*
oboe ['o:,bo:] *n* : oboe *m*
oboist ['o,boɪst] *n* : oboe *mf*
obscene [ɑb'si:n, əb-] *adj* : obsceno, indecente — **obscenely** *adv*
obscenity [ɑb'sɛnət̬i, əb-] *n, pl* **-ties** : obscenidad *f*
obscure¹ [ɑb'skjʊr, əb-] *vt* **-scured; -scuring 1** CLOUD, DIM : oscurecer, nublar **2** HIDE : ocultar
obscure² *adj* **1** DIM : oscuro **2** REMOTE, SECLUDED : recóndito **3** VAGUE : oscuro, confuso, vago **4** UNKNOWN : desconocido ⟨an obscure poet : un poeta desconocido⟩ — **obscurely** *adv*
obscurity [ɑb'skjʊrət̬i, əb-] *n, pl* **-ties** : oscuridad *f*
obsequious [əb'si:kwiəs] *adj* : servil, excesivamente atento
observable [əb'zərvəbəl] *adj* : observable, perceptible
observance [əb'zərvənts] *n* **1** FULFILLMENT : observancia *f*, cumplimiento *m* **2** PRACTICE : práctica *f*
observant [əb'zərvənt] *adj* : observador
observation [,ɑbsər'veɪʃən, -zər-] *n* : observación *f*
observatory [əb'zərvə,tori] *n, pl* **-ries** : observatorio *m*
observe [əb'zərv] *v* **-served; -serving** *vt* **1** OBEY : observar, obedecer **2** CELEBRATE : celebrar, guardar (una práctica religiosa) **3** WATCH : observar, mi-

rar 4 REMARK : observar, comentar — *vi* LOOK : mirar
observer [ɑb'zərvər] *n* : observador *m*, -dora *f*
obsess [əb'sɛs] *vt* : obsesionar
obsession [ɑb'sɛʃən, əb-] *n* : obsesión *f*
obsessive [ɑb'sɛsɪv, əb-] *adj* : obsesivo — **obsessively** *adv*
obsolescence [ˌɑbsə'lɛsənts] *n* : obsolescencia *f*
obsolescent [ˌɑbsə'lɛsənt] *adj* : obsolescente ⟨to become obsolescent : caer en desuso⟩
obsolete [ˌɑbsə'li:t, 'ɑbsəˌ-] *adj* : obsoleto, anticuado
obstacle ['ɑbstɪkəl] *n* : obstáculo *m*, impedimento *m*
obstetric [əb'stɛtrɪk] *or* **obstetrical** [-trɪkəl] *adj* : obstétrico
obstetrician [ˌɑbstə'trɪʃən] *n* : obstetra *mf*; tocólogo *m*, -ga *f*
obstetrics [əb'stɛtrɪks] *ns & pl* : obstetricia *f*, tocología *f*
obstinacy ['ɑbstənəsi] *n, pl* **-cies** : obstinación *f*, terquedad *f*
obstinate ['ɑbstənət] *adj* : obstinado, terco — **obstinately** *adv*
obstreperous [əb'strɛpərəs] *adj* **1** CLAMOROUS : ruidoso, clamoroso **2** UNRULY : rebelde, indisciplinado
obstruct [əb'strʌkt] *vt* : obstruir, bloquear
obstruction [əb'strʌkʃən] *n* : obstrucción *f*, bloqueo *m*
obstructive [əb'strəktɪv] *adj* : obstructor
obtain [əb'teɪn] *vt* : obtener, conseguir — *vi* PREVAIL : imperar, prevalecer
obtainable [əb'teɪnəbəl] *adj* : obtenible, asequible
obtrude [əb'tru:d] *v* **-truded; -truding** *vt* **1** EXTRUDE : expulsar **2** IMPOSE : imponer — *vi* INTRUDE : inmiscuirse, entrometerse
obtrusive [əb'tru:sɪv] *adj* **1** IMPERTINENT, MEDDLESOME : impertinente, entrometido **2** PROTRUDING : prominente
obtuse [ɑb'tu:s, əb-, -'tju:s] *adj* : obtuso, torpe
obtuse angle *n* : ángulo obtuso
obviate ['ɑbviˌeɪt] *vt* **-ated; -ating** : obviar, evitar
obvious ['ɑbviəs] *adj* : obvio, evidente, manifiesto
obviously ['ɑbviəsli] *adv* **1** CLEARLY : obviamente, evidentemente **2** OF COURSE : claro, por supuesto
occasion[1] [ə'keɪʒən] *vt* : ocasionar, causar
occasion[2] *n* **1** OPPORTUNITY : oportunidad *f*, ocasión *f* **2** CAUSE : motivo *m*, razón *f* **3** INSTANCE : ocasión *f* **4** EVENT : ocasión *f*, acontecimiento *m* **5 on ~** : de vez en cuando, ocasionalmente
occasional [ə'keɪʒənəl] *adj* : ocasional
occasionally [ə'keɪʒənəli] *adv* : de vez en cuando, ocasionalmente
occidental [ˌɑksə'dɛntəl] *adj* : oeste, del oeste, occidental
occult[1] [ə'kʌlt, 'ɑˌkʌlt] *adj* **1** HIDDEN, SECRET : oculto, secreto **2** ARCANE : arcano, esotérico
occult[2] *n* **the occult** : las ciencias ocultas
occupancy ['ɑkjəpəntsi] *n, pl* **-cies** : ocupación *f*, habitación *f*
occupant ['ɑkjəpənt] *n* : ocupante *mf*
occupation [ˌɑkjə'peɪʃən] *n* : ocupación *f*, profesión *f*, oficio *m*
occupational [ˌɑkjə'peɪʃənəl] *adj* : ocupacional
occupy ['ɑkjəˌpaɪ] *vt* **-pied; -pying** : ocupar
occur [ə'kər] *vi* **occurred; occurring 1** EXIST : encontrarse, existir **2** HAPPEN : ocurrir, acontecer, suceder, tener lugar **3** : ocurrirse ⟨it occurred to him that . . . : se le ocurrió que . . . ⟩
occurrence [ə'kərənts] *n* : acontecimiento *m*, suceso *m*, ocurrencia *f*
ocean ['o:ʃən] *n* : océano *m*
oceanic [ˌo:ʃi'ænɪk] *adj* : oceánico
oceanography [ˌo:ʃə'nɑgrəfi] *n* : oceanografía *f*
ocelot ['ɑsəˌlɑt, 'o:-] *n* : ocelote *m*
ocher *or* **ochre** ['o:kər] *n* : ocre *m*
o'clock [ə'klɑk] *adv* (*used in telling time*) ⟨it's ten o'clock : son las diez⟩ ⟨at six o'clock : a las seis⟩
octagon ['ɑktəˌgɑn] *n* : octágono *m*
octagonal [ɑk'tægənəl] *adj* : octagonal
octave ['ɑktɪv] *n* : octava *f*
October [ɑk'to:bər] *n* : octubre *m*
octopus ['ɑktəˌpʊs, -pəs] *n, pl* **-puses** *or* **-pi** [-ˌpaɪ] : pulpo *m*
ocular ['ɑkjələr] *adj* : ocular
oculist ['ɑkjəlɪst] *n* **1** OPHTHALMOLOGIST : oftalmólogo *m*, -ga *f*; oculista *mf* **2** OPTOMETRIST : optometrista *mf*
odd ['ɑd] *adj* **1** : sin pareja, suelto ⟨an odd sock : un calcetín sin pareja⟩ **2** UNEVEN : impar ⟨odd numbers : números impares⟩ **3** : y pico, y tantos ⟨forty odd years ago : hace cuarenta y pico años⟩ **4** : alguno, uno que otro ⟨odd jobs : algunos trabajos⟩ **5** STRANGE : extraño, raro
oddball ['ɑdˌbɔl] *n* : excéntrico *m*, -ca *f*; persona *f* rara
oddity ['ɑdəṭi] *n, pl* **-ties** : rareza *f*, cosa *f* rara
oddly ['ɑdli] *adv* : de manera extraña
oddness ['ɑdnəs] *n* : rareza *f*, excentricidad *f*
odds ['ɑdz] *npl* **1** CHANCES : probabilidades *fpl* **2** : puntos *mpl* de ventaja (de una apuesta) **3 to be at odds** : estar en desacuerdo
odds and ends *npl* : costillas *fpl*, cosas *fpl* sueltas, cachivaches *mpl*
ode ['o:d] *n* : oda *f*
odious ['o:diəs] *adj* : odioso — **odiously** *adv*
odor ['o:dər] *n* : olor *m*
odorless ['o:dərləs] *adj* : inodoro, sin olor

odorous ['oːdərəs] *adj* : oloroso
odyssey ['ɑdəsi] *n, pl* **-seys** : odisea *f*
o'er ['or] → **over**
of ['ʌv, 'ɑv] *prep* **1** FROM : de ⟨a man of the city : un hombre de la ciudad⟩ **2** (*indicating character or background*) : de ⟨a woman of great ability : una mujer de gran capacidad⟩ **3** (*indicating cause*) : de ⟨he died of the flu : murió de la gripe⟩ **4** BY : de ⟨the works of Shakespeare : las obras de Shakespeare⟩ **5** (*indicating contents, material, or quantity*) : de ⟨a house of wood : una casa de madera⟩ ⟨a glass of water : un vaso de agua⟩ **6** (*indicating belonging or connection*) : de ⟨the front of the house : el frente de la casa⟩ **7** ABOUT : sobre, de ⟨tales of the West : los cuentos del Oeste⟩ **8** (*indicating a particular example*) : de ⟨the city of Caracas : la ciudad de Caracas⟩ **9** FOR : por, a ⟨love of country : amor por la patria⟩ **10** (*indicating time or date*) ⟨five minutes of ten : las diez menos cinco⟩ ⟨the eighth of April : el ocho de abril⟩
off¹ ['ɔf] *adv* **1** (*indicating change of position or state*) ⟨to march off : marcharse⟩ ⟨he dozed off : se puso a dormir⟩ **2** (*indicating distance in space or time*) ⟨some miles off : a varias millas⟩ ⟨the holiday is three weeks off : faltan tres semanas para la fiesta⟩ **3** (*indicating removal*) ⟨the knob came off : se le cayó el pomo⟩ **4** (*indicating termination*) ⟨shut the television off : apaga la televisión⟩ **5** (*indicating suspension of work*) ⟨to take a day off : tomarse un día de descanso⟩ **6 off and on** : de vez en cuando
off² *adj* **1** FARTHER : más remoto, distante ⟨the off side of the building : el lado distante del edificio⟩ **2** STARTED : empezado ⟨to be off on a spree : irse de juerga⟩ **3** OUT : apagado ⟨the light is off : la luz está apagada⟩ **4** CANCELED : cancelado, suspendido **5** INCORRECT : erróneo, incorrecto **6** REMOTE : remoto, lejano ⟨an off chance : una posibilidad remota⟩ **7** FREE : libre ⟨I'm off today : hoy estoy libre⟩ **8 to be well off** : vivir con desahogo, tener bastante dinero
off³ *prep* **1** (*indicating physical separation*) : de ⟨she took it off the table : lo tomó de la mesa⟩ ⟨a shop off the main street : una tienda al lado de la calle principal⟩ **2** : a la costa de, a expensas de ⟨he lives off his sister : vive a expensas de su hermana⟩ **3** (*indicating the suspension of an activity*) ⟨to be off duty : estar libre⟩ ⟨he's off liquor : ha dejado el alcohol⟩ **4** BELOW : por debajo de ⟨he's off his game : está por debajo de su juego normal⟩
offal ['ɔfəl] *n* **1** RUBBISH, WASTE : desechos *mpl*, desperdicios *mpl* **2** VISCERA : vísceras *fpl*, asaduras *fpl*
offend [ə'fɛnd] *vt* **1** VIOLATE : violar, atentar contra **2** HURT : ofender ⟨to be easily offended : ser muy susceptible⟩
offender [ə'fɛndər] *n* : delincuente *mf*; infractor *m*, -tora *f*
offense *or* **offence** [ə'fɛnts, 'ɔˌfɛnts] *n* **1** INSULT : ofensa *f*, injuria *f*, agravio *m* ⟨to take offense : ofenderse⟩ **2** ASSAULT : ataque *m* **3** : ofensiva *f* (en deportes) **4** CRIME, INFRACTION : infracción *f*, delito *m*
offensive¹ [ə'fɛntsɪv, 'ɔˌfɛnt-] *adj* : ofensivo — **offensively** *adv*
offensive² *n* : ofensiva *f*
offer¹ ['ɔfər] *vt* **1** : ofrecer ⟨they offered him the job : le ofrecieron el puesto⟩ **2** PROPOSE : proponer, sugerir **3** SHOW : ofrecer, mostrar ⟨to offer resistance : ofrecer resistencia⟩
offer² *n* : oferta *f*, ofrecimiento *m*, propuesta *f*
offering ['ɔfərɪŋ] *n* : ofrenda *f*
offhand¹ ['ɔf'hænd] *adv* : sin preparación, sin pensarlo
offhand² *adj* **1** IMPROMPTU : improvisado **2** ABRUPT : brusco
office ['ɔfəs] *n* **1** : cargo *m* ⟨to run for office : presentarse como candidato⟩ **2** : oficina *f*, despacho *m*, gabinete *m* (en la casa) ⟨office hours : horas de oficina⟩
officeholder ['ɔfəsˌhoːldər] *n* : titular *mf*
officer ['ɔfəsər] *n* **1** *or* **police officer** : policía *mf*, agente *mf* de policía **2** OFFICIAL : oficial *mf*; funcionario *m*, -ria *f*; director *m*, -tora *f* (en una empresa) **3** COMMISSIONED OFFICER : oficial *mf*
official¹ [ə'fɪʃəl] *adj* : oficial — **officially** *adv*
official² *n* : funcionario *m*, -ria *f*; oficial *mf*
officiate [ə'fɪʃiˌeɪt] *v* **-ated; -ating** *vi* **1** : arbitrar (en deportes) **2 to officiate at** : oficiar, celebrar — *vt* : arbitrar
officious [ə'fɪʃəs] *adj* : oficioso
offing ['ɔfɪŋ] *n* **in the offing** : en perspectiva
offset ['ɔfˌsɛt] *vt* **-set; -setting** : compensar
offshoot ['ɔfˌʃuːt] *n* **1** OUTGROWTH : producto *m*, resultado *m* **2** BRANCH, SHOOT : retoño *m*, rama *f*, vástago *m* (de una planta)
offshore¹ ['ɔf'ʃor] *adv* : a una distancia de la costa
offshore² *adj* **1** : de (la) tierra ⟨an offshore wind : un viento que sopla de tierra⟩ **2** : (de) costa afuera, cercano a la costa ⟨an offshore island : una isla costera⟩
offspring ['ɔfˌsprɪŋ] *ns & pl* **1** YOUNG : crías *fpl* (de los animales) **2** PROGENY : prole *f*, progenie *f*
off–white ['ɔf'hwaɪt] *adj* : blancuzco
often ['ɔfən, 'ɔftən] *adv* : muchas veces, a menudo, seguido

oftentimes [ˈɔfən,taɪmz, ˈɔftən-] *or* **ofttimes** [ˈɔft,taɪms] → **often**

ogle [ˈoːgəl] *vt* **ogled; ogling** : comerse con los ojos, quedarse mirando a

ogre [ˈoːgər] *n* : ogro *m*

oh [ˈoː] *interj* : ¡oh!, ¡ah!, ¡ay! ⟨oh, of course : ah, por supuesto⟩ ⟨oh no! : ¡ay no!⟩ ⟨oh really? : ¿de veras?⟩

ohm [ˈoːm] *n* : ohm *m*, ohmio *m*

oil[1] [ˈɔɪl] *vt* : lubricar, engrasar, aceitar

oil[2] *n* **1** : aceite *m* **2** PETROLEUM : petróleo *m* **3** *or* **oil painting** : óleo *m*, pintura *f* al óleo **4** *or* **oil paint(s)** : óleo *m*

oilcloth [ˈɔɪl,klɔθ] *n* : hule *m*

oiliness [ˈɔɪlinəs] *n* : lo aceitoso

oilskin [ˈɔɪl,skɪn] *n* **1** : hule *m* **2** **oilskins** *npl* : impermeable *m*

oily [ˈɔɪli] *adj* **oilier; -est** : aceitoso, grasiento, grasoso ⟨oily fingers : dedos grasientos⟩

ointment [ˈɔɪntmənt] *n* : ungüento *m*, pomada *f*

OK[1] [,oːˈkeɪ] *vt* **OK'd** *or* **okayed** [,oːˈkeɪd]; **OK'ing** *or* **okaying** APPROVE, AUTHORIZE : dar el visto bueno a, autorizar, aprobar

OK[2] *or* **okay** [,oːˈkeɪ] *adv* **1** WELL : bien **2** YES : sí, por supuesto

OK[3] *adj* : bien ⟨he's OK : está bien⟩ ⟨it's OK with me : estoy de acuerdo⟩

OK[4] *n* : autorización *f*, visto *m* bueno

okra [ˈoːkrə, *South also* -kri] *n* : quingombó *m*

old[1] [ˈoːld] *adj* **1** ANCIENT : antiguo ⟨old civilizations : civilizaciones antiguas⟩ **2** FAMILIAR : viejo ⟨old friends : viejos amigos⟩ ⟨the same old story : el mismo cuento⟩ **3** (*indicating a certain age*) ⟨he's ten years old : tiene diez años (de edad)⟩ **4** AGED : viejo, anciano ⟨an old woman : una anciana⟩ **5** FORMER : antiguo ⟨her old neighborhood : su antiguo barrio⟩ **6** WORN-OUT : viejo, gastado

old[2] *n* **1 the old** : los viejos, los ancianos **2 in the days of old** : antaño, en los tiempos antiguos

olden [ˈoːldən] *adj* : de antaño, de antigüedad

old–fashioned [ˈoːldˈfæʃənd] *adj* : anticuado, pasado de moda

old maid *n* **1** SPINSTER : soltera *f* **2** FUSSBUDGET : maniático *m*, -ca *f*; melindroso *m*, -sa *f*

Old Testament *n* : Antiguo Testamento *m*

old–time [ˈoːldˈtaɪm] *adj* : antiguo

old–timer [ˈoːldˈtaɪmər] *n* **1** VETERAN : veterano *m*, -na *f* **2** *or* **oldster** : anciano *m*, -na *f*

old–world [ˈoːldˈwərld] *adj* : pintoresco (de antaño)

oleander [ˈoːli,ændər] *n* : adelfa *f*

oleomargarine [,oːlioˈmɑrdʒərən] → **margarine**

olfactory [ɑlˈfæktəri, ol-] *adj* : olfativo

oligarchy [ˈɑlə,gɑrki, ˈoːlə-] *n, pl* **-chies** : oligarquía *f*

olive [ˈɑlɪv, -ləv] *n* **1** : aceituna *f*, oliva *f* (fruta) **2** : olivo *m* (árbol) **3** *or* **olive green** : color *m* aceituna, verde *m* oliva

Olmec [ˈɑl,mɛk, ˈoːl-] *n* : olmeca *mf* — **Olmec** *adj*

Olympic [əˈlɪmpɪk, o-] *adj* : olímpico

Olympic Games *npl* : Juegos *mpl* Olímpicos

Olympics [əˈlɪmpɪks, o-] *npl* : olimpiadas *fpl*

Omani [oˈmɑni, -ˈmæ-] *n* : omaní *mf* — **Omani** *adj*

ombudsman [ˈɑm,bʊdzmən, ɑmˈbʊdz-] *n, pl* **-men** [-mən, -,mɛn] : ombudsman *m*

omelet *or* **omelette** [ˈɑmlət, ˈɑmə-] *n* : omelette *mf*, tortilla *f* (de huevo)

omen [ˈoːmən] *n* : presagio *m*, augurio *m*, agüero *m*

ominous [ˈɑmənəs] *adj* : ominoso, agorero, de mal agüero

ominously [ˈɑmənəsli] *adv* : de manera amenazadora

omission [oˈmɪʃən] *n* : omisión *f*

omit [oˈmɪt] *vt* **omitted; omitting** **1** LEAVE OUT : omitir, excluir **2** NEGLECT : omitir ⟨they omitted to tell us : omitieron decírnoslo⟩

omnipotence [ɑmˈnɪpətənts] *n* : omnipotencia *f* — **omnipotent** [ɑmˈnɪpətənt] *adj*

omnipresent [,ɑmnɪˈprɛzənt] *adj* : omnipresente

omniscient [ɑmˈnɪʃənt] *adj* : omnisciente

omnivorous [ɑmˈnɪvərəs] *adj* **1** : omnívoro **2** AVID : ávido, voraz

on[1] [ˈɑn, ˈɔn] *adv* **1** (*indicating contact with a surface*) ⟨put the top on : pon la tapa⟩ ⟨he has a hat on : lleva un sombrero puesto⟩ **2** (*indicating forward movement*) ⟨from that moment on : a partir de ese momento⟩ ⟨farther on : más adelante⟩ **3** (*indicating operation or an operating position*) ⟨turn the light on : prende la luz⟩

on[2] *adj* **1** (*being in operation*) ⟨the radio is on : el radio está prendido⟩ **2** (*taking place*) ⟨the game is on : el juego ha comenzado⟩ **3 to be on to** : estar enterado de

on[3] *prep* **1** (*indicating position*) : en, sobre, encima de ⟨on the table : en (sobre, encima de) la mesa⟩ ⟨shadows on the wall : sombras en la pared⟩ ⟨on horseback : a caballo⟩ **2** AT, TO : a ⟨on the right : a la derecha⟩ **3** ABOARD, IN : en, a ⟨on the plane : en el avión⟩ ⟨he got on the train : subió al tren⟩ **4** (*indicating time*) ⟨she worked on Saturdays : trabajaba los sábados⟩ ⟨every hour on the hour : a la hora en punto⟩ **5** (*indicating means or agency*) : por ⟨he cut himself on a tin can : se cortó con una lata⟩ ⟨to talk on the telephone : hablar por teléfono⟩ **6** (*indicating a state or process*) : en ⟨on fire : en llamas⟩ ⟨on the increase : en aumento⟩ **7** (*indicating connection or membership*) : en ⟨on a committee : en una comisión⟩ **8** (*indicating an activity*) ⟨on vacation : de vacaciones⟩ ⟨on a diet : a dieta⟩ **9** ABOUT, CONCERNING : sobre ⟨a book on insects : un libro sobre insectos⟩ ⟨reflect on that : reflexiona sobre eso⟩

once[1] [ˈwʌnts] *adv* **1** : una vez ⟨once a month : una vez al mes⟩ ⟨once and for all : de una vez por todas⟩ **2** EVER : alguna vez **3** FORMERLY : antes, anteriormente

once[2] *adj* FORMER : antiguo

once[3] *n* **1** : una vez **2 at ~** SIMULTANEOUSLY : al mismo tiempo, simultáneamente **3 at ~** IMMEDIATELY : inmediatamente, en seguida

once[4] *conj* : una vez que, tan pronto como

once–over [ˌwʌntsˈoːvər, ˈwʌntsˌ-] *n* **to give someone the once–over** : echarle un vistazo a alguien

oncoming [ˈɑnˌkʌmɪŋ, ˈɔn-] *adj* : que viene

one[1] [ˈwʌn] *adj* **1** (*being a single unit*) : un, una ⟨he only wants one apple : sólo quiere una manzana⟩ **2** (*being a particular one*) : un, una ⟨he arrived early one morning : llegó temprano una mañana⟩ **3** (*being the same*) : mismo, misma ⟨they're all members of one team : todos son miembros del mismo equipo⟩ ⟨one and the same thing : la misma cosa⟩ **4** SOME : alguno, alguna; un, una ⟨I'll see you again one day : algún día te veré otra vez⟩ ⟨at one time or another : en una u otra ocasión⟩

one[2] *n* **1** : uno *m* (número) **2** (*indicating the first of a set or series*) ⟨from day one : desde el primer momento⟩ **3** (*indicating a single person or thing*) ⟨the one (girl) on the right : la de la derecha⟩ ⟨he has the one but needs the other : tiene uno pero necesita el otro⟩

one[3] *pron* **1** : uno, una ⟨one of his friends : una de sus amigas⟩ ⟨one never knows : uno nunca sabe, nunca se sabe⟩ ⟨to cut one's finger : cortarse el dedo⟩ **2 one and all** : todos, todo el mundo **3 one another** : el uno al otro, se ⟨they loved one another : se amaban⟩ **4 that one** : aquél, aquella **5 which one?** : ¿cuál?

one–on–one [wʌnɔnˈwʌn, -ɑn-] *adj* : uno a uno — **one–on–one** *adv*

onerous [ˈɑnərəs, ˈoːnə-] *adj* : oneroso, gravoso

oneself [ˌwʌnˈsɛlf] *pron* **1** (*used reflexively or for emphasis*) : se, sí mismo, uno mismo ⟨to control oneself : controlarse⟩ ⟨to talk to oneself : hablarse a sí mismo⟩ ⟨to do it oneself : hacérselo uno mismo⟩ **2 by ~** : solo

one–sided [ˈwʌnˈsaɪdəd] *adj* **1** : de un solo lado **2** LOPSIDED : asimétrico **3** BIASED : parcial, tendencioso **4** UNILATERAL : unilateral

onetime [ˈwʌnˈtaɪm] *adj* FORMER : antiguo

one–way [ˈwʌnˈweɪ] *adj* **1** : de sentido único, de una sola dirección ⟨a one-way street : una calle de sentido único⟩ **2** : de ida, sencillo ⟨a one-way ticket : un boleto de ida⟩

ongoing [ˈɑnˌgoːɪŋ] *adj* **1** CONTINUING : en curso, corriente **2** DEVELOPING : en desarrollo

onion [ˈʌnjən] *n* : cebolla *f*

online [ˈɔnˈlaɪn, ˈɑn-] *adj* : en línea

onlooker [ˈɔnˌlʊkər, ˈɑn-] *n* : espectador *m*, -dora *f*, circunstante *mf*

only[1] [ˈoːnli] *adv* **1** MERELY : sólo, solamente, nomás ⟨for only two dollars : por tan sólo dos dólares⟩ ⟨only once : sólo una vez, no más de una vez⟩ ⟨I only did it to help : lo hice por ayudar nomás⟩ **2** SOLELY : únicamente, sólo, solamente ⟨only he knows it : solamente él lo sabe⟩ **3** (*indicating a result*) ⟨it will only cause him problems : no hará más que crearle problemas⟩ **4 if only** : ojalá, por lo menos ⟨if only it were true! : ¡ojalá sea cierto!⟩ ⟨if he could only dance : si por lo menos pudiera bailar⟩

only[2] *adj* : único ⟨an only child : un hijo único⟩ ⟨the only chance : la única oportunidad⟩

only[3] *conj* BUT : pero ⟨I would go, only I'm sick : iría, pero estoy enfermo⟩

onset [ˈɑnˌsɛt] *n* : comienzo *m*, llegada *f*

onslaught [ˈɑnˌslɔt, ˈɔn-] *n* : arremetida *f*, embestida *f*, embate *m*

onto [ˈɑnˌtuː, ˈɔn-] *prep* : sobre

onus [ˈoːnəs] *n* : responsabilidad *f*, carga *f*

onward[1] [ˈɑnwərd, ˈɔn-] *or* **onwards** *adv* FORWARD : adelante, hacia adelante

onward[2] *adj* : hacia adelante

onyx [ˈɑnɪks] *n* : ónix *m*

ooze[1] [ˈuːz] *v* **oozed; oozing** *vi* : rezumar — *vt* **1** : rezumar **2** EXUDE : irradiar, rebosar ⟨to ooze confidence : irradiar confianza⟩

ooze[2] *n* SLIME : cieno *m*, limo *m*

opacity [oˈpæsəṭi] *n, pl* **-ties** : opacidad *f*

opal [ˈoːpəl] *n* : ópalo *m*

opaque [oˈpeɪk] *adj* **1** : opaco **2** UNCLEAR : poco claro

open[1] [ˈoːpən] *vt* **1** : abrir ⟨open the door : abre la puerta⟩ **2** UNCOVER : destapar **3** UNFOLD : desplegar, abrir **4** CLEAR : abrir (un camino, etc.) **5** INAUGURATE : abrir (una tienda), inaugurar (una exposición, etc.) **6** INITIATE : iniciar, entablar, abrir ⟨to open the meeting : abrir la sesión⟩ ⟨to open a discussion : entablar un debate⟩ — *vi* **1** : abrirse **2** BEGIN : empezar, comenzar

open[2] *adj* **1** : abierto ⟨an open window : una ventana abierta⟩ **2** FRANK : abierto, franco, directo **3** UNCOV-

ERED : descubierto, abierto **4** EXTENDED : extendido, abierto ⟨with open arms : con los brazos abiertos⟩ **5** UNRESTRICTED : libre, abierto **6** UNDECIDED : pendiente, por decidir, sin resolver ⟨an open question : una cuestión pendiente⟩ **7** AVAILABLE : vacante, libre ⟨the job is open : el puesto está vacante⟩

open[3] *n* **in the open 1** OUTDOORS : al aire libre **2** KNOWN : conocido, sacado a la luz

open–air [ˈoːpənˈær] *adj* OUTDOOR : al aire libre

open–and–shut [ˈoːpənəndˈʃʌt] *adj* : claro, evidente ⟨an open-and-shut case : un caso muy claro⟩

opener [ˈoːpənər] *n* : destapador *m*, abrelatas *m*, abridor *m*

openhanded [ˌoːpənˈhændəd] *adj* : generoso, liberal

openhearted [ˌoːpənˈhɑrt̬əd] *adj* **1** FRANK : franco, sincero **2** : generoso, de gran corazón

opening [ˈoːpənɪŋ] *n* **1** BEGINNING : comienzo *m*, principio *m*, apertura *f* **2** APERTURE : abertura *f*, brecha *f*, claro *m* (en el bosque) **3** OPPORTUNITY : oportunidad *f*

openly [ˈoːpənli] *adv* **1** FRANKLY : abiertamente, francamente **2** PUBLICLY : públicamente, declaradamente

openness [ˈoːpənnəs] *n* : franqueza *f*

opera [ˈɑprə, ˈɑpərə] *n* **1** : ópera *f* **2** → **opus**

opera glasses *npl* : gemelos *mpl* de teatro

operate [ˈɑpəˌreɪt] *v* **-ated; -ating** *vi* **1** ACT, FUNCTION : operar, funcionar, actuar **2 to operate on (someone)** : operar a (alguien) — *vt* **1** WORK : operar, manejar, hacer funcionar (una máquina) **2** MANAGE : manejar, administrar (un negocio)

operatic [ˌɑpəˈræt̬ɪk] *adj* : operístico

operation [ˌɑpəˈreɪʃən] *n* **1** FUNCTIONING : funcionamiento *m* **2** USE : uso *m*, manejo *m* (de máquinas) **3** SURGERY : operación *f*, intervención *f* quirúrgica

operational [ˌɑpəˈreɪʃənəl] *adj* : operacional, de operación

operative [ˈɑpərət̬ɪv, -ˌreɪ-] *adj* **1** OPERATING : vigente, en vigor **2** WORKING : operativo **3** SURGICAL : quirúrgico

operator [ˈɑpəˌreɪt̬ər] *n* : operador *m*, -dora *f*

operetta [ˌɑpəˈrɛt̬ə] *n* : opereta *f*

ophthalmologist [ˌɑfˌθælˈmɑləʤɪst, -θəˈmɑ-] *n* : oftalmólogo *m*, -ga *f*

ophthalmology [ˌɑfˌθælˈmɑləʤi, -θəˈmɑ-] *n* : oftalmología *f*

opiate [ˈoːpiət, -piˌeɪt] *n* : opiato *m*

opinion [əˈpɪnjən] *n* : opinión *f*

opinionated [əˈpɪnjəˌneɪt̬əd] *adj* : testarudo, dogmático

opium [ˈoːpiəm] *n* : opio *m*

opossum [əˈpɑsəm] *n* : zarigüeya *f*, oposum *m*

opponent [əˈpoːnənt] *n* : oponente *mf*; opositor *m*, -tora *f*; contrincante *mf* (en deportes)

opportune [ˌɑpərˈtuːn, -ˈtjuːn] *adj* : oportuno — **opportunely** *adv*

opportunist [ˌɑpərˈtuːnɪst, -ˈtjuː-] *n* : oportunista *mf*

opportunistic [ˌɑpərtuˈnɪstɪk, -tju-] *adj* : oportunista *mf*

opportunity [ˌɑpərˈtuːnət̬i, -ˈtjuː-] *n, pl* **-ties** : oportunidad *f*, ocasión *f*, chance *m*, posibilidades *fpl*

oppose [əˈpoːz] *vt* **-posed; -posing 1** : ir en contra de, oponerse a ⟨good opposes evil : el bien se opone al mal⟩ **2** COMBAT : luchar contra, combatir, resistir

opposite[1] [ˈɑpəzət] *adv* : enfrente

opposite[2] *adj* **1** FACING : de enfrente ⟨the opposite side : el lado de enfrente⟩ **2** CONTRARY : opuesto, contrario ⟨in opposite directions : en direcciones contrarias⟩ ⟨the opposite sex : el sexo opuesto, el otro sexo⟩

opposite[3] *n* : lo contrario, lo opuesto

opposite[4] *prep* : enfrente de, frente a

opposition [ˌɑpəˈzɪʃən] *n* **1** : oposición *f*, resistencia *f* **2 in opposition to** AGAINST : en contra de

oppress [əˈprɛs] *vt* **1** PERSECUTE : oprimir, perseguir **2** BURDEN : oprimir, agobiar

oppression [əˈprɛʃən] *n* : opresión *f*

oppressive [əˈprɛsɪv] *adj* **1** HARSH : opresivo, severo **2** STIFLING : agobiante, sofocante ⟨oppressive heat : calor sofocante⟩

oppressor [əˈprɛsər] *n* : opresor *m*, -sora *f*

opprobrium [əˈproːbriəm] *n* : oprobio *m*

opt [ˈɑpt] *vi* : optar

optic [ˈɑptɪk] *or* **optical** [-tɪkəl] *adj* : óptico

optical disk *n* : disco *m* óptico

optician [ɑpˈtɪʃən] *n* : óptico *m*, -ca *f*

optics [ˈɑptɪks] *npl* : óptica *f*

optimal [ˈɑptəməl] *adj* : óptimo

optimism [ˈɑptəˌmɪzəm] *n* : optimismo *m*

optimist [ˈɑptəmɪst] *n* : optimista *mf*

optimistic [ˌɑptəˈmɪstɪk] *adj* : optimista

optimistically [ˌɑptəˈmɪstɪkli] *adv* : con optimismo, positivamente

optimum[1] [ˈɑptəməm] *adj* → **optimal**

optimum[2] *n, pl* **-ma** [ˈɑptəmə] : lo óptimo, lo ideal

option [ˈɑpʃən] *n* : opción *f* ⟨she has no option : no tiene más remedio⟩

optional [ˈɑpʃənəl] *adj* : facultativo, optativo

optometrist [ɑpˈtɑmətrɪst] *n* : optometrista *mf*

optometry [ɑpˈtɑmətri] *n* : optometría *f*

opulence [ˈɑpjələnts] *n* : opulencia *f*

opulent [ˈɑpjələnt] *adj* : opulento

opus [ˈoːpəs] *n, pl* **opera** [ˈoːpərə, ˈɑpə-] : opus *m*, obra *f* (de música)

or [ˈɔr] *conj* **1** (*indicating an alternative*) : o (u *before words beginning with o or ho*) ⟨coffee or tea : café o té⟩ ⟨one day

or another : un día u otro⟩ **2** (*following a negative*) : ni ⟨he didn't have his keys or his wallet : no llevaba ni sus llaves ni su billetera⟩
oracle [ˈɔrəkəl] *n* : oráculo *m*
oral [ˈorəl] *adj* : oral — **orally** *adv*
orange [ˈɔrɪnʤ] *n* **1** : naranja *f*, china *f PRi* (fruto) **2** : naranja *m* (color), color *m* de china *PRi*
orangeade [ˌɔrɪnʤˈeɪd] *n* : naranjada *f*
orangutan [əˈræŋəˌtæŋ, -ˈræŋgə-, -ˌtæn] *n* : orangután *m*
oration [əˈreɪʃən] *n* : oración *f*, discurso *m*
orator [ˈɔrəṭər] *n* : orador *m*, -dora *f*
oratorio [ˌɔrəˈtoriˌo:] *n, pl* **-rios** : oratorio *m*
oratory [ˈɔrəˌtori] *n, pl* **-ries** : oratoria *f*
orb [ˈɔrb] *n* : orbe *m*
orbit[1] [ˈɔrbət] *vt* **1** CIRCLE : girar alrededor de, orbitar **2** : poner en órbita (un satélite, etc.) — *vi* : orbitar
orbit[2] *n* : órbita *f*
orbital [ˈɔrbəṭəl] *adj* : orbital
orchard [ˈɔrʧərd] *n* : huerto *m*
orchestra [ˈɔrkəstrə] *n* : orquesta *f*
orchestral [ɔrˈkɛstrəl] *adj* : orquestal
orchestrate [ˈɔrkəˌstreɪt] *vt* **-trated; -trating** **1** : orquestar, instrumentar (en música) **2** ORGANIZE : arreglar, organizar
orchestration [ˌɔrkəˈstreɪʃən] *n* : orquestación *f*
orchid [ˈɔrkɪd] *n* : orquídea *f*
ordain [ɔrˈdeɪn] *vt* **1** : ordenar (en religión) **2** DECREE : decretar, ordenar
ordeal [ɔrˈdi:l, ˈɔrˌdi:l] *n* : prueba *f* dura, experiencia *f* terrible
order[1] [ˈɔrdər] *vt* **1** ORGANIZE : arreglar, ordenar, poner en orden **2** COMMAND : ordenar, mandar **3** REQUEST : pedir, encargar ⟨to order a meal : pedir algo de comer⟩ — *vi* : hacer un pedido
order[2] *n* **1** : orden *f* ⟨a religious order : una orden religiosa⟩ **2** COMMAND : orden *f*, mandato *m* ⟨to give an order : dar una orden⟩ **3** REQUEST : orden *f*, pedido *m* ⟨purchase order : orden de compra⟩ **4** ARRANGEMENT : orden *m* ⟨in chronological order : por orden cronológico⟩ **5** DISCIPLINE : orden *m* ⟨law and order : el orden público⟩ **6** **in order to** : para **7** **out of order** : descompuesto, averiado **8** **orders** *npl or* **holy orders** : órdenes *fpl* sagradas
orderliness [ˈɔrdərlinəs] *n* : orden *m*
orderly[1] [ˈɔrdərli] *adj* **1** METHODICAL : ordenado, metódico **2** PEACEFUL : pacífico, disciplinado
orderly[2] *n, pl* **-lies** **1** : ordenanza *m* (en el ejército) **2** : camillero *m* (en un hospital)
ordinal [ˈɔrdənəl] *n or* **ordinal number** : ordinal *m*, número *m* ordinal
ordinance [ˈɔrdənənts] *n* : ordenanza *f*, reglamento *m*
ordinarily [ˌɔrdənˈɛrəli] *adv* : ordinariamente, por lo general
ordinary [ˈɔrdənˌɛri] *adj* **1** NORMAL, USUAL : normal, usual **2** AVERAGE : común y corriente, normal **3** MEDIOCRE : mediocre, ordinario
ordination [ˌɔrdənˈeɪʃən] *n* : ordenación *f*
ordnance [ˈɔrdnənts] *n* : artillería *f*
ore [ˈor] *n* : mineral *m* (metalífero), mena *f*
oregano [əˈrɛgəˌno:] *n* : orégano *m*
organ [ˈɔrgən] *n* **1** : órgano *m* (instrumento) **2** : órgano *m* (del cuerpo) **3** PERIODICAL : publicación *f* periódica, órgano *m*
organic [ɔrˈgænɪk] *adj* : orgánico — **organically** *adv*
organism [ˈɔrgəˌnɪzəm] *n* : organismo *m*
organist [ˈɔrgənɪst] *n* : organista *mf*
organization [ˌɔrgənəˈzeɪʃən] *n* **1** ORGANIZING : organización *f* **2** BODY : organización *f*, organismo *m*
organizational [ˌɔrgənəˈzeɪʃənəl] *adj* : organizativo
organize [ˈɔrgəˌnaɪz] *vt* **-nized; -nizing** : organizar, arreglar, poner en orden
organizer [ˈɔrgəˌnaɪzər] *n* : organizador *m*, -dora *f*
orgasm [ˈɔrˌgæzəm] *n* : orgasmo *m*
orgy [ˈɔrʤi] *n, pl* **-gies** : orgía *f*
orient [ˈoriˌɛnt] *vt* : orientar
Orient *n* **the Orient** : el Oriente
oriental [ˌoriˈɛntəl] *adj* : del Oriente, oriental
Oriental *n* : oriental *mf*
orientation [ˌoriənˈteɪʃən] *n* : orientación *f*
orifice [ˈɔrəfəs] *n* : orificio *m*
origin [ˈɔrəʤən] *n* **1** ANCESTRY : origen *m*, ascendencia *f* **2** SOURCE : origen *m*, raíz *f*, fuente *f*
original[1] [əˈrɪʤənəl] *adj* : original
original[2] *n* : original *m*
originality [əˌrɪʤəˈnæləṭi] *n* : originalidad *f*
originally [əˈrɪʤənəli] *adv* **1** AT FIRST : al principio, originariamente **2** CREATIVELY : originalmente, con originalidad
originate [əˈrɪʤəˌneɪt] *v* **-nated; -nating** *vt* : originar, iniciar, crear — *vi* **1** BEGIN : originarse, empezar **2** COME : provenir, proceder, derivarse
originator [əˈrɪʤəˌneɪṭər] *n* : creador *m*, -dora *f*; inventor *m*, -tora *f*
oriole [ˈoriˌo:l, -iəl] *n* : oropéndola *f*
ornament[1] [ˈɔrnəmənt] *vt* : adornar, decorar, ornamentar
ornament[2] *n* : ornamento *m*, adorno *m*, decoración *f*
ornamental [ˌɔrnəˈmɛntəl] *adj* : ornamental, de adorno, decorativo
ornamentation [ˌɔrnəmənˈteɪʃən, -mɛn-] *n* : ornamentación *f*
ornate [ɔrˈneɪt] *adj* : elaborado, recargado
ornery [ˈɔrnəri, ˈɑrnəri] *adj* **ornerier; -est** : de mal genio, malhumorado
ornithologist [ˌɔrnəˈθɑləʤɪst] *n* : ornitólogo *m*, -ga *f*

ornithology [ˌɔrnəˈθɑləʤi] *n, pl* **-gies** : ornitología *f*
orphan[1] [ˈɔrfən] *vt* : dejar huérfano
orphan[2] *n* : huérfano *m*, -na *f*
orphanage [ˈɔrfənɪʤ] *n* : orfelinato *m*, orfanato *m*
orthodontics [ˌɔrθəˈdɑntɪks] *n* : ortodoncia *f*
orthodontist [ˌɔrθəˈdɑntɪst] *n* : ortodoncista *mf*
orthodox [ˈɔrθəˌdɑks] *adj* : ortodoxo
orthodoxy [ˈɔrθəˌdɑksi] *n, pl* **-doxies** : ortodoxia *f*
orthographic [ˌɔrθəˈgræfɪk] *adj* : ortográfico
orthography [ɔrˈθɑgrəfi] *n, pl* **-phies** SPELLING : ortografía *f*
orthopedic [ˌɔrθəˈpiːdɪk] *adj* : ortopédico
orthopedics [ˌɔrθəˈpiːdɪks] *ns & pl* : ortopedia *f*
orthopedist [ˌɔrθəˈpiːdɪst] *n* : ortopedista *mf*
oscillate [ˈɑsəˌleɪt] *vi* **-lated; -lating** : oscilar
oscillation [ˌɑsəˈleɪʃən] *n* : oscilación *f*
osmosis [ɑzˈmoːsɪs, ɑs-] *n* : ósmosis *f*, osmosis *f*
osprey [ˈɑspri, -ˌpreɪ] *n* : pigargo *m*
ostensible [ɑˈstɛn*t*səbəl] *adj* APPARENT : aparente, ostensible — **ostensibly** [-bli] *adv*
ostentation [ˌɑstənˈteɪʃən] *n* : ostentación *f*, boato *m*
ostentatious [ˌɑstənˈteɪʃəs] *adj* : ostentoso — **ostentatiously** *adv*
osteopath [ˈɑstiəˌpæθ] *n* : osteópata *f*
osteopathy [ˌɑstiˈɑpəθi] *n* : osteopatía *f*
osteoporosis [ˌɑstiopəˈroːsɪs] *n, pl* **-roses** [-ˌsiːz] : osteoporosis *f*
ostracism [ˈɑstrəˌsɪzəm] *n* : ostracismo *m*
ostracize [ˈɑstrəˌsaɪz] *vt* **-cized; -cizing** : condenar al ostracismo, marginar, aislar
ostrich [ˈɑstrɪʧ, ˈɔs-] *n* : avestruz *m*
other[1] [ˈʌðər] *adv* **other than** : aparte de, fuera de
other[2] *adj* : otro ⟨the other boys : los otros muchachos⟩ ⟨smarter than other people : más inteligente que los demás⟩ ⟨on the other hand : por otra parte, por otro lado⟩ ⟨every other day : cada dos días⟩
other[3] *pron* : otro, otra ⟨one in front of the other : uno tras otro⟩ ⟨myself and three others : yo y tres otros, yo y tres más⟩ ⟨somewhere or other : en alguna parte⟩
otherwise[1] [ˈʌðərˌwaɪz] *adv* **1** DIFFERENTLY : de otro modo, de manera distinta ⟨he could not act otherwise : no pudo actuar de manera distinta⟩ **2** : eso aparte, por lo demás ⟨I'm dizzy, but otherwise I'm fine : estoy mareado pero, por lo demás, estoy bien⟩ **3** OR ELSE : de lo contrario, si no ⟨do what I tell you, otherwise you'll be sorry : haz lo que te digo, de lo contrario, te arrepentirás⟩
otherwise[2] *adj* : diferente, distinto ⟨the facts are otherwise : la realidad es diferente⟩
otter [ˈɑt̬ər] *n* : nutria *f*
Ottoman [ˈɑt̬əmən] *n* **1** : otomano *m*, -na *f* **2** : otomana *f* (mueble) — **Ottoman** *adj*
ouch [ˈaʊʧ] *interj* : ¡ay!, ¡huy!
ought [ˈɔt] *v aux* : deber ⟨you ought to take care of yourself : deberías cuidarte⟩
oughtn't [ˈɔtənt] (*contraction of* **ought not**) → **ought**
ounce [ˈaʊn*t*s] *n* : onza *f*
our [ˈɑr, ˈaʊr] *adj* : nuestro
ours [ˈaʊrz, ˈɑrz] *pron* : nuestro, nuestra ⟨a cousin of ours : un primo nuestro⟩
ourselves [ɑrˈsɛlvz, aʊr-] *pron* **1** (*used reflexively*) : nos, nosotros ⟨we amused ourselves : nos divertimos⟩ ⟨we were always thinking of ourselves : siempre pensábamos en nosotros⟩ **2** (*used for emphasis*) : nosotros mismos, nosotras mismas ⟨we did it ourselves : lo hicimos nosotros mismos⟩
oust [ˈaʊst] *vt* : desbancar, expulsar
ouster [ˈaʊstər] *n* : expulsión *f* (de un país, etc.), destitución *f* (de un puesto)
out[1] [ˈaʊt] *vi* : revelarse, hacerse conocido
out[2] *adv* **1** (*indicating direction or movement*) : para afuera ⟨she opened the door and looked out : abrió la puerta y miró para afuera⟩ **2** (*indicating a location away from home or work*) : fuera, afuera ⟨to eat out : comer afuera⟩ **3** (*indicating loss of control or possession*) ⟨they let the secret out : sacaron el secreto a la luz⟩ **4** (*indicating completion or discontinuance*) ⟨his money ran out : se le acabó el dinero⟩ ⟨to turn out the light : apagar la luz⟩ **5** OUTSIDE : fuera, afuera ⟨out in the garden : afuera en el jardín⟩ **6** ALOUD : en voz alta, en alto ⟨to cry out : gritar⟩
out[3] *adj* **1** EXTERNAL : externo, exterior **2** OUTLYING : alejado, distante ⟨the out islands : las islas distantes⟩ **3** ABSENT : ausente **4** UNFASHIONABLE : fuera de moda **5** EXTINGUISHED : apagado
out[4] *prep* **1** (*used to indicate an outward movement*) : por ⟨I looked out the window : miré por la ventana⟩ ⟨she ran out the door : corrió por la puerta⟩ **2** → **out of**
out–and–out [ˈaʊtənˈaʊt] *adj* UTTER : redomado, absoluto
outboard motor [ˈaʊtˌbord] *n* : motor *m* fuera de borde
outbound [ˈaʊtˌbaʊnd] *adj* : que sale, de salida
outbreak [ˈaʊtˌbreɪk] *n* : brote *m* (de una enfermedad), comienzo *m* (de guerra), ola *f* (de violencia), erupción *f* (de granos)

outbuilding ['aʊt,bɪldɪŋ] *n* : edificio *m* anexo
outburst ['aʊt,bərst] *n* : arranque *m*, arrebato *m*
outcast ['aʊt,kæst] *n* : marginado *m*, -da *f*; paria *mf*
outcome ['aʊt,kʌm] *n* : resultado *m*, desenlace *m*, consecuencia *f*
outcrop ['aʊt,krɑp] *n* : afloramiento *m*
outcry ['aʊt,kraɪ] *n, pl* **-cries** : clamor *m*, protesta *f*
outdated [,aʊt'deɪṭəd] *adj* : anticuado, fuera de moda
outdistance [,aʊt'dɪstənts] *vt* **-tanced; -tancing** : aventajar, dejar atrás
outdo [,aʊt'du:] *vt* **-did** [-'dɪd]; **-done** [-'dʌn]; **-doing; -does** [-'dʌz] : superar
outdoor ['aʊt'dor] *adj* : al aire libre ⟨outdoor sports : deportes al aire libre⟩ ⟨outdoor clothing : ropa de calle⟩
outdoors[1] ['aʊt'dorz] *adv* : afuera, al aire libre
outdoors[2] *n* : aire *m* libre
outer ['aʊṭər] *adj* **1** : exterior, externo **2 outer space** : espacio *m* exterior
outermost ['aʊṭər,mo:st] *adj* : más remoto, más exterior, extremo
outfield ['aʊt,fi:ld] *n* **the outfield** : los jardines
outfielder ['aʊt,fi:ldər] *n* : jardinero *m*, -ra *f*
outfit[1] ['aʊt,fɪt] *vt* **-fitted; -fitting** EQUIP : equipar
outfit[2] *n* **1** EQUIPMENT : equipo *m* **2** COSTUME, ENSEMBLE : traje *m*, conjunto *m* **3** GROUP : conjunto *m*
outgo ['aʊt,go:] *n, pl* **outgoes** : gasto *m*
outgoing ['aʊt,go:ɪŋ] *adj* **1** OUTBOUND : que sale **2** DEPARTING : saliente ⟨an outgoing president : un presidente saliente⟩ **3** EXTROVERTED : extrovertido, expansivo
outgrow [,aʊt'gro:] *vt* **-grew** [-'gru:]; **-grown** [-'gro:n]; **-growing** **1** : crecer más que ⟨that tree outgrew all the others : ese árbol creció más que todos los otros⟩ **2 to outgrow one's clothes** : quedarle pequeña la ropa a uno
outgrowth ['aʊt,gro:θ] *n* **1** OFFSHOOT : brote *m*, vástago *m* (de una planta) **2** CONSEQUENCE : consecuencia *f*, producto *m*, resultado *m*
outing ['aʊṭɪŋ] *n* : excursión *f*
outlandish [aʊt'lændɪʃ] *adj* : descabellado, muy extraño
outlast [,aʊt'læst] *vt* : durar más que
outlaw[1] ['aʊt,lɔ] *vt* : hacerse ilegal, declarar fuera de la ley, prohibir
outlaw[2] *n* : bandido *m*, -da *f*; bandolero *m*, -ra *f*; forajido *m*, -da *f*
outlay ['aʊt,leɪ] *n* : gasto *m*, desembolso *m*
outlet ['aʊt,lɛt, -lət] *n* **1** EXIT : salida *f*, escape *m* ⟨electrical outlet : toma de corriente⟩ **2** RELIEF : desahogo *m* **3** MARKET : mercado *m*, salida *f*
outline[1] ['aʊt,laɪn] *vt* **-lined; -lining** **1** SKETCH : diseñar, esbozar, bosquejar **2** DEFINE, EXPLAIN : perfilar, delinear, explicar ⟨she outlined our responsibilities : delineó nuestras responsabilidades⟩
outline[2] *n* **1** PROFILE : perfil *m*, silueta *f*, contorno *m* **2** SKETCH : bosquejo *m*, boceto *m* **3** SUMMARY : esquema *m*, resumen *m*, sinopsis *m* ⟨an outline of world history : un esquema de la historia mundial⟩
outlive [,aʊt'lɪv] *vt* **-lived; -living** : sobrevivir a
outlook ['aʊt,lʊk] *n* **1** VIEW : vista *f*, panorama *f* **2** POINT OF VIEW : punto *m* de vista **3** PROSPECTS : perspectivas *fpl*
outlying ['aʊt,laɪɪŋ] *adj* : alejado, distante, remoto ⟨the outlying areas : las afueras⟩
outmoded [,aʊt'mo:dəd] *adj* : pasado de moda, anticuado
outnumber [,aʊt'nʌmbər] *vt* : superar en número a, ser más numeroso de
out of *prep* **1** (*indicating direction or movement from within*) : de, por ⟨we ran out of the house : salimos corriendo de la casa⟩ ⟨to look out of the window : mirar por la ventana⟩ **2** (*being beyond the limits of*) ⟨out of control : fuera de control⟩ ⟨to be out of sight : desaparecer de vista⟩ **3** OF : de ⟨one out of four : uno de cada cuatro⟩ **4** (*indicating absence or loss*) : sin ⟨out of money : sin dinero⟩ ⟨we're out of matches : nos hemos quedado sin fósforos⟩ **5** BECAUSE OF : por ⟨out of curiosity : por curiosidad⟩ **6** FROM : de ⟨made out of plastic : hecho de plástico⟩
out–of–date [,aʊṭəv'deɪt] *adj* : anticuado, obsoleto, pasado de moda
out–of–door [,aʊṭəv'dor] *or* **out–of–doors** [-'dorz] → **outdoor**
out–of–doors *n* → **outdoors**[2]
outpatient ['aʊt,peɪʃənt] *n* : paciente *m* externo, paciente *f* externa
outpost ['aʊt,po:st] *n* : puesto *m* avanzado
output[1] ['aʊt,pʊt] *vt* **-putted** *or* **-put; -putting** : producir
output[2] *n* : producción *f* (de una fábrica), rendimiento *m* (de una máquina), productividad *f* (de una persona)
outrage[1] ['aʊt,reɪʤ] *vt* **-raged; -raging** **1** INSULT : ultrajar, injuriar **2** INFURIATE : indignar, enfurecer
outrage[2] *n* **1** ATROCITY : atropello *m*, atrocidad *f*, atentado *m* **2** SCANDAL : escándalo *m* **3** ANGER : ira *f*, furia *f*
outrageous [,aʊt'reɪʤəs] *adj* **1** SCANDALOUS : escandaloso, ofensivo, atroz **2** UNCONVENTIONAL : poco convencional, extravagante **3** EXORBITANT : exorbitante, excesivo (dícese de los precios, etc.)
outright[1] [,aʊt'raɪt] *adv* **1** COMPLETELY : por completo, totalmente ⟨to sell outright : vender por completo⟩ ⟨he refused it outright : lo rechazó rotunda-

mente⟩ **2** DIRECTLY : directamente, sin reserva **3** INSTANTLY : al instante, en el acto

outright[2] [ˈaʊtˌraɪt] *adj* **1** COMPLETE : completo, absoluto, categórico ⟨an outright lie : una mentira absoluta⟩ **2** : sin reservas ⟨an outright gift : un regalo sin reservas⟩

outset [ˈaʊtˌsɛt] *n* : comienzo *m*, principio *m*

outshine [ˌaʊtˈʃaɪn] *vt* **-shone** [-ˈʃoːn, -ˈʃɑn] *or* **-shined; -shining** : eclipsar

outside[1] [ˌaʊtˈsaɪd, ˈaʊtˌ-] *adv* : fuera, afuera

outside[2] *adj* **1** : exterior, externo ⟨the outside edge : el borde exterior⟩ ⟨outside influences : influencias externas⟩ **2** REMOTE : remoto ⟨an outside chance : una posibilidad remota⟩

outside[3] *n* **1** EXTERIOR : parte *f* de afuera, exterior *m* **2** MOST : máximo *m* ⟨three weeks at the outside : tres semanas como máximo⟩ **3 from the outside** : desde afuera, desde fuera

outside[4] *prep* : fuera de, afuera de ⟨outside my window : fuera de mi ventana⟩ ⟨outside regular hours : fuera del horario normal⟩ ⟨outside the law : afuera de la ley⟩

outside of *prep* **1** → **outside**[4] **2** → **besides**[2]

outsider [ˌaʊtˈsaɪdər] *n* : forastero *m*, -ra *f*

outskirts [ˈaʊtˌskərts] *npl* : afueras *fpl*, alrededores *mpl*

outsmart [ˌaʊtˈsmɑrt] → **outwit**

outspoken [ˌaʊtˈspoːkən] *adj* : franco, directo

outstanding [ˌaʊtˈstændɪŋ] *adj* **1** UNPAID : pendiente **2** NOTABLE : destacado, notable, excepcional, sobresaliente

outstandingly [ˌaʊtˈstændɪŋli] *adv* : excepcionalmente

outstretched [ˌaʊtˈstrɛtʃt] *adj* : extendido

outstrip [ˌaʊtˈstrɪp] *vt* **-stripped** *or* **-stript** [-ˈstrɪpt]; **-stripping** **1** : aventajar, dejar atrás ⟨he outstripped the other runners : aventajó a los otros corredores⟩ **2** SURPASS : aventajar, sobrepasar

outward[1] [ˈaʊtwərd] *or* **outwards** [-wərdz] *adv* : hacia afuera, hacia el exterior

outward[2] *adj* **1** : hacia afuera ⟨an outward flow : un flujo hacia afuera⟩ **2** : externo ⟨outward beauty : belleza externa⟩

outwardly [ˈaʊtwərdli] *adv* **1** EXTERNALLY : exteriormente **2** APPARENTLY : aparentemente ⟨outwardly friendly : aparentemente simpático⟩

outwit [ˌaʊtˈwɪt] *vt* **-witted; -witting** : ser más listo que

ova → **ovum**

oval[1] [ˈoːvəl] *adj* : ovalado, oval

oval[2] *n* : óvalo *m*

ovarian [oˈværiən] *adj* : ovárico

ovary [ˈoːvəri] *n, pl* **-ries** : ovario *m*

ovation [oˈveɪʃən] *n* : ovación *f*

oven [ˈʌvən] *n* : horno *m*

over[1] [ˈoːvər] *adv* **1** (*indicating movement across*) ⟨he flew over to London : voló a Londres⟩ ⟨come on over! : ¡ven acá!⟩ **2** (*indicating an additional amount*) ⟨the show ran 10 minutes over : el espectáculo terminó 10 minutos de tarde⟩ **3** ABOVE, OVERHEAD : por encima **4** AGAIN : otra vez, de nuevo ⟨over and over : una y otra vez⟩ ⟨to start over : volver a empezar⟩ **5 all over** EVERYWHERE : por todas partes **6 to fall over** : caerse **7 to turn over** : poner boca abajo, voltear

over[2] *adj* **1** HIGHER, UPPER : superior **2** REMAINING : sobrante, que sobra **3** ENDED : terminado, acabado ⟨the work is over : el trabajo está terminado⟩

over[3] *prep* **1** ABOVE : encima de, arriba de, sobre ⟨over the fireplace : encima de la chimenea⟩ ⟨the hawk flew over the hills : el halcón voló sobre los cerros⟩ **2** : más de ⟨over $50 : más de $50⟩ **3** ALONG : por, sobre ⟨to glide over the ice : deslizarse sobre el hielo⟩ **4** (*indicating motion through a place or thing*) ⟨they showed me over the house : me mostraron la casa⟩ **5** ACROSS : por encima de, sobre ⟨he jumped over the ditch : saltó por encima de la zanja⟩ **6** UPON : sobre ⟨a cape over my shoulders : una capa sobre los hombros⟩ **7** ON : por ⟨to speak over the telephone : hablar por teléfono⟩ **8** DURING : en, durante ⟨over the past 25 years : durante los últimos 25 años⟩ **9** BECAUSE OF : por ⟨they fought over the money : se pelearon por el dinero⟩

overabundance [ˌoːvərəˈbʌndən*t*s] *n* : superabundancia *f*

overabundant [ˌoːvərəˈbʌndənt] *adj* : superabundante

overactive [ˌoːvərˈæktɪv] *adj* : hiperactivo

overall [ˌoːvərˈɔl] *adj* : total, global, de conjunto

overalls [ˈoːvərˌɔlz] *npl* : overol *m*

overawe [ˌoːvərˈɔ] *vt* **-awed; -awing** : intimidar, impresionar

overbearing [ˌoːvərˈbærɪŋ] *adj* : dominante, imperioso, prepotente

overblown [ˌoːvərˈbloːn] *adj* **1** INFLATED : inflado, exagerado **2** BOMBASTIC : grandilocuente, rimbombante

overboard [ˈoːvərˌbord] *adv* : por la borda, al agua

overburden [ˌoːvərˈbərdən] *vt* : sobrecargar, agobiar

overcast [ˈoːvərˌkæst] *adj* CLOUDY : nublado

overcharge [ˌoːvərˈtʃɑrdʒ] *vt* **-charged; -charging** : cobrarle de más (a alguien)

overcoat [ˈoːvərˌkoːt] *n* : abrigo *m*

overcome [ˌoːvərˈkʌm] *v* **-came** [-ˈkeɪm]; **-come; -coming** *vt* **1** CON-

QUER : vencer, derrotar, superar 2 OVERWHELM : abrumar, agobiar — *vi* : vencer

overconfidence [ˌo:vərˈkɑnfədənts] *n* : exceso *m* de confianza

overconfident [ˌo:vərˈkɑnfədənt] *adj* : demasiado confiado

overcook [ˌo:vərˈkʊk] *vt* : recocer, cocer demasiado

overcrowded [ˌo:vərˈkraʊdəd] *adj* 1 PACKED : abarrotado, atestado de gente 2 OVERPOPULATED : superpoblado

overdo [ˌo:vərˈdu:] *vt* **-did** [-ˈdɪd]; **-done** [-ˈdʌn]; **-doing; -does** [-ˈdʌz] 1 : hacer demasiado 2 EXAGGERATE : exagerar 3 OVERCOOK : recocer

overdose [ˈo:vərˌdo:s] *n* : sobredosis *f*

overdraft [ˈo:vərˌdræft] *n* : sobregiro *m*, descubierto *m*

overdraw [ˌo:vərˈdrɔ] *vt* **-drew** [-ˈdru:]; **-drawn** [-ˈdrɔn]; **-drawing** 1 : sobregirar ⟨my account is overdrawn : tengo la cuenta en descubierto⟩ 2 EXAGGERATE : exagerar

overdue [ˌo:vərˈdu:] *adj* 1 UNPAID : vencido y sin pagar 2 TARDY : de retraso, tardío

overeat [ˌo:vərˈi:t] *vi* **-ate** [-ˈeɪt]; **-eaten** [-ˈi:tən]; **-eating** : comer demasiado

overelaborate [ˌo:vərɪˈlæbərət] *adj* : recargado

overestimate [ˌo:vərˈɛstəˌmeɪt] *vt* **-mated; -mating** : sobreestimar

overexcited [ˌo:vərɪkˈsaɪt̬əd] *adj* : sobreexcitado

overexpose [ˌo:vərɪkˈspo:z] *vt* **-posed; -posing** : sobreexponer

overfeed [ˌo:vərˈfi:d] *vt* **-fed** [-ˈfɛd]; **-feeding** : sobrealimentar

overflow¹ [ˌo:vərˈflo:] *vt* 1 : desbordar 2 INUNDATE : inundar — *vi* : desbordarse, rebosar

overflow² [ˈo:vərˌflo:] *n* 1 : derrame *m*, desbordamiento *m* (de un río) 2 SURPLUS : exceso *m*, excedente *m*

overfly [ˌo:vərˈflaɪ] *vt* **-flew** [-ˈflu:]; **-flown** [-ˈflo:n]; **-flying** : sobrevolar

overgrown [ˌo:vərˈgro:n] *adj* 1 : cubierto ⟨overgrown with weeds : cubierto de malas hierbas⟩ 2 : demasiado grande

overhand¹ [ˈo:vərˌhænd] *adv* : por encima de la cabeza

overhand² *adj* : por lo alto (tirada)

overhang¹ [ˌo:vərˈhæŋ] *v* **-hung** [-ˈhʌŋ]; **-hanging** *vt* 1 : sobresalir por encima de 2 THREATEN : amenazar — *vi* : sobresalir

overhang² [ˈo:vərˌhæŋ] *n* : saliente *mf*

overhaul [ˌo:vərˈhɔl] *vt* 1 : revisar ⟨to overhaul an engine : revisar un motor⟩ 2 OVERTAKE : adelantar

overhead¹ [ˌo:vərˈhɛd] *adv* : por encima, arriba, por lo alto

overhead² [ˈo:vərˌhɛd] *adj* : de arriba

overhead³ [ˈo:vərˌhɛd] *n* : gastos *mpl* generales

overhear [ˌo:vərˈhɪr] *vt* **-heard; -hearing** : oír por casualidad

overheat [ˌo:vərˈhi:t] *vt* : recalentar, sobrecalentar, calentar demasiado

overjoyed [ˌo:vərˈʤɔɪd] *adj* : rebosante de alegría

overkill [ˈo:vərˌkɪl] *n* : exceso *m*, excedente *m*

overland¹ [ˈo:vərˌlænd, -lənd] *adv* : por tierra

overland² *adj* : terrestre, por tierra

overlap¹ [ˌo:vərˈlæp] *v* **-lapped; -lapping** *vt* : traslapar — *vi* : traslaparse, solaparse

overlap² [ˈo:vərˌlæp] *n* : traslapo *m*

overlay¹ [ˌo:vərˈleɪ] *vt* **-laid** [-ˈleɪd]; **-laying** : recubrir, revestir

overlay² [ˈo:vərˌleɪ] *n* : revestimiento *m*

overload [ˌo:vərˈlo:d] *vt* : sobrecargar

overlong [ˌo:vərˈlɔŋ] *adj* : excesivamente largo, largo y pesado

overlook [ˌo:vərˈlʊk] *vt* 1 INSPECT : inspeccionar, revisar 2 : tener vista a, dar a ⟨a house overlooking the valley : una casa que tiene vista al valle⟩ 3 MISS : pasar por alto 4 EXCUSE : dejar pasar, disculpar

overly [ˈo:vərli] *adv* : demasiado

overnight¹ [ˌo:vərˈnaɪt] *adv* 1 : por la noche, durante la noche 2 : de la noche a la mañana ⟨we can't do it overnight : no podemos hacerlo de la noche a la mañana⟩

overnight² [ˈo:vərˈnaɪt] *adj* 1 : de noche ⟨an overnight stay : una estancia de una noche⟩ ⟨an overnight bag : una bolsa de viaje⟩ 2 SUDDEN : repentino

overpass [ˈo:vərˌpæs] *n* : paso *m* elevado, paso *m* a desnivel *Mex*

overpopulated [ˌo:vərˈpɑpjəˌleɪt̬əd] *adj* : sobrepoblado

overpower [ˌo:vərˈpaʊər] *vt* 1 CONQUER, SUBDUE : vencer, superar 2 OVERWHELM : abrumar, agobiar ⟨overpowered by the heat : sofocado por el calor⟩

overpraise [ˌo:vərˈpreɪz] *vt* **-praised; -praising** : adular

overrate [ˌo:vərˈreɪt] *vt* **-rated; -rating** : sobrevalorar, sobrevaluar

override [ˌo:vərˈraɪd] *vt* **-rode** [-ˈro:d]; **-ridden** [-ˈrɪdən]; **-riding** 1 : predominar sobre, contar más que ⟨hunger overrode our manners : el hambre predominó sobre los modales⟩ 2 ANNUL : anular, invalidar ⟨to override a veto : anular un veto⟩

overrule [ˌo:vərˈru:l] *vt* **-ruled; -ruling** : anular (una decisión), desautorizar (una persona), denegar (un pedido)

overrun [ˌo:vərˈrʌn] *v* **-ran** [-ˈræn]; **-running** *vt* 1 INVADE : invadir 2 INFEST : infestar, plagar 3 EXCEED : exceder, rebasar — *vi* : rebasar el tiempo previsto

overseas¹ [ˌo:vərˈsi:z] *adv* : en el extranjero ⟨to travel overseas : viajar al extranjero⟩

overseas[2] [ˈoːvər͵siːz] *adj* : extranjero, exterior

oversee [͵oːvərˈsiː] *vt* **-saw** [-ˈsɔ]; **-seen** [-ˈsiːn]; **-seeing** SUPERVISE : supervisar

overseer [ˈoːvər͵siːər] *n* : supervisor *m*, -sora *f*; capataz *mf*

overshadow [͵oːvərˈʃæ͵doː] *vt* **1** DARKEN : oscurecer, ensombrecer **2** ECLIPSE, OUTSHINE : eclipsar

overshoe [ˈoːvər͵ʃuː] *n* : chanclo *m*

overshoot [͵oːvərˈʃuːt] *vt* **-shot** [-ˈʃɑt]; **-shooting** : pasarse de ⟨to overshoot the mark : pasarse de la raya⟩

oversight [ˈoːvər͵saɪt] *n* : descuido *m*, inadvertencia *f*

oversleep [͵oːvərˈsliːp] *vi* **-slept** [-ˈslɛpt]; **-sleeping** : no despertarse a tiempo, quedarse dormido

overspread [͵oːvərˈsprɛd] *vt* **-spread**; **-spreading** : extenderse sobre

overstaffed [͵oːvərˈstæft] *adj* : con exceso de personal

overstate [͵oːvərˈsteɪt] *vt* **-stated**; **-stating** EXAGGERATE : exagerar

overstatement [͵oːvərˈsteɪtmənt] *n* : exageración *f*

overstep [͵oːvərˈstɛp] *vt* **-stepped**; **-stepping** EXCEED : sobrepasar, traspasar, exceder

overt [oˈvərt, ˈoː͵vərt] *adj* : evidente, manifiesto, patente

overtake [͵oːvərˈteɪk] *vt* **-took** [-ˈtʊk]; **-taken** [-ˈteɪkən]; **-taking** : pasar, adelantar, rebasar *Mex*

overthrow[1] [͵oːvərˈθroː] *vt* **-threw** [-ˈθruː]; **-thrown** [-ˈθroːn]; **-throwing** **1** OVERTURN : dar la vuelta a, volcar **2** DEFEAT, TOPPLE : derrocar, derribar, deponer

overthrow[2] [ˈoːvər͵θroː] *n* : derrocamiento *m*, caída *f*

overtime [ˈoːvər͵taɪm] *n* **1** : horas *fpl* extras (de trabajo) **2** : prórroga *f* (en deportes)

overtly [oˈvərtli, ˈoː͵vərt-] *adv* OPENLY : abiertamente

overtone [ˈoːvər͵toːn] *n* **1** : armónico *m* (en música) **2** HINT, SUGGESTION : tinte *m*, insinuación *f*

overture [ˈoːvər͵ʧʊr, -ʧər] *n* **1** PROPOSAL : propuesta *f* **2** : obertura *f* (en música)

overturn [͵oːvərˈtərn] *vt* **1** UPSET : dar la vuelta a, volcar **2** NULLIFY : anular, invalidar — *vi* TURN OVER : volcar, dar un vuelco

overuse [͵oːvərˈjuːz] *vt* **-used**; **-using** : abusar de

overview [ˈoːvər͵vjuː] *n* : resumen *m*, visión *f* general

overweening [͵oːvərˈwiːnɪŋ] *adj* **1** ARROGANT : arrogante, soberbio **2** IMMODERATE : desmesurado

overweight [͵oːvərˈweɪt] *adj* : demasiado gordo, demasiado pesado

overwhelm [͵oːvərˈhwɛlm] *vt* **1** CRUSH, DEFEAT : aplastar, arrollar **2** SUBMERGE : inundar, sumergir **3** OVERPOWER : abrumar, agobiar ⟨overwhelmed by remorse : abrumado de remordimiento⟩

overwhelming [͵oːvərˈhwɛlmɪŋ] *adj* **1** CRUSHING : abrumador, apabullante **2** SWEEPING : arrollador, aplastante ⟨an overwhelming majority : una mayoría aplastante⟩

overwork [͵oːvərˈwərk] *vt* **1** : hacer trabajar demasiado **2** OVERUSE : abusar de — *vi* : trabajar demasiado

overwrought [͵oːvərˈrɔt] *adj* : alterado, sobreexcitado

ovoid [ˈoː͵vɔɪd] *or* **ovoidal** [oˈvɔɪdəl] *adj* : ovoide

ovulate [ˈɑvjə͵leɪt, ˈoː-] *vi* **-lated**; **-lating** : ovular

ovulation [͵ɑvjəˈleɪʃən, ͵oː-] *n* : ovulación *f*

ovum [ˈoːvəm] *n, pl* **ova** [-və] : óvulo *m*

owe [ˈoː] *vt* **owed**; **owing** : deber ⟨you owe me $10 : me debes $10⟩ ⟨he owes his wealth to his father : le debe su riqueza a su padre⟩

owing to *prep* : debido a

owl [ˈaʊl] *n* : búho *m*, lechuza *f*, tecolote *m Mex*

own[1] [ˈoːn] *vt* **1** POSSESS : poseer, tener, ser dueño de **2** ADMIT : reconocer, admitir — *vi* **to own up** : reconocer (algo), admitir (algo)

own[2] *adj* : propio, personal, particular ⟨his own car : su propio coche⟩

own[3] *pron* **my; (your, his/her, our, their); own** : el mío, la mía; el tuyo, la tuya; el suyo, la suya; el nuestro, la nuestra ⟨to each his own : cada uno a lo suyo⟩ ⟨money of my own : mi propio dinero⟩ ⟨to be on one's own : estar solo⟩

owner [ˈoːnər] *n* : dueño *m*, -ña *f*; propietario *m*, -ria *f*

ownership [ˈoːnər͵ʃɪp] *n* : propiedad *f*

ox [ˈɑks] *n, pl* **oxen** [ˈɑksən] : buey *m*

oxidation [͵ɑksəˈdeɪʃən] *n* : oxidación *f*

oxide [ˈɑk͵saɪd] *n* : óxido *m*

oxidize [ˈɑksə͵daɪz] *vt* **-dized**; **-dizing** : oxidar

oxygen [ˈɑksɪʤən] *n* : oxígeno *m*

oyster [ˈɔɪstər] *n* : ostra *f*, ostión *m Mex*

ozone [ˈoː͵zoːn] *n* : ozono *m*

P

p [ˈpiː] *n, pl* **p's** *or* **ps** [ˈpiːz] : decimosexta letra del alfabeto inglés

pace[1] [ˈpeɪs] *v* **paced; pacing** *vi* : caminar, ir y venir — *vt* **1** : caminar por ⟨she paced the floor : caminaba de un lado a otro del cuarto⟩ **2 to pace a runner** : marcarle el ritmo a un corredor

pace[2] *n* **1** STEP : paso *m* **2** RATE : paso *m*, ritmo *m* ⟨to set the pace : marcar el paso, marcar la pauta⟩

pacemaker [ˈpeɪsˌmeɪkər] *n* : marcapasos *m*

pacific [pəˈsɪfɪk] *adj* : pacífico

pacifier [ˈpæsəˌfaɪər] *n* : chupete *m*, chupón *m*, mamila *f Mex*

pacifism [ˈpæsəˌfɪzəm] *n* : pacifismo *m*

pacifist [ˈpæsəfɪst] *n* : pacifista *mf*

pacify [ˈpæsəˌfaɪ] *vt* **-fied; -fying** **1** SOOTHE : apaciguar, pacificar **2** : pacificar (un país, una región, etc.)

pack[1] [ˈpæk] *vt* **1** PACKAGE : empaquetar, embalar, envasar **2** : empacar, meter (en una maleta) ⟨to pack one's bag : hacer la maleta⟩ **3** FILL : llenar, abarrotar ⟨a packed theater : un teatro abarrotado⟩ **4 to pack off** SEND : mandar — *vi* : empacar, hacer las maletas

pack[2] *n* **1** BUNDLE : bulto *m*, fardo *m* **2** BACKPACK : mochila *f* **3** PACKAGE : paquete *m*, cajetilla *f* (de cigarrillos, etc.) **4** : manada *f* (de lobos, etc.), jauría *f* (de perros) ⟨a pack of thieves : una pandilla de ladrones⟩

package[1] [ˈpækɪʤ] *vt* **-aged; -aging** : empaquetar, embalar

package[2] *n* : paquete *m*, bulto *m*

packaging [ˈpækɪʤɪŋ] *n* **1** : embalaje *m* **2** WRAPPING : envoltorio *m*

packer [ˈpækər] *n* : empacador *m*, -dora *f*

packet [ˈpækət] *n* : paquete *m*

packing [ˈpækɪŋ] *n* : embalaje *m*

pact [ˈpækt] *n* : pacto *m*, acuerdo *m*

pad[1] [ˈpæd] *vt* **padded; padding** **1** FILL, STUFF : rellenar, acolchar (una silla, una pared) **2** : meter paja en, rellenar ⟨to pad a speech : rellenar un discurso⟩

pad[2] *n* **1** CUSHION : almohadilla *f* ⟨a shoulder pad : una hombrera⟩ **2** TABLET : bloc *m* (de papel) **3** *or* **lily pad** : hoja *f* grande (de un nenúfar) **4 ink pad** : tampón *m* **5 launching pad** : plataforma *f* (de lanzamiento)

padding [ˈpædɪŋ] *n* **1** FILLING : relleno *m* **2** : paja *f* (en un discurso, etc.)

paddle[1] [ˈpædəl] *v* **-dled; -dling** *vt* **1** : hacer avanzar (una canoa) con canalete **2** HIT : azotar, darle nalgadas a (con una pala o paleta) — *vi* **1** : remar (en una canoa) **2** SPLASH : chapotear, mojarse los pies

paddle[2] *n* **1** : canalete *m*, zagual *m* (de una canoa, etc.) **2** : pala *f*, paleta *f* (en deportes)

paddock [ˈpædək] *n* **1** PASTURE : potrero *m* **2** : paddock *m*, cercado *m* (en un hipódromo)

paddy [ˈpædi] *n, pl* **-dies** : arrozal *m*

padlock[1] [ˈpædˌlɑk] *vt* : cerrar con candado

padlock[2] *n* : candado *m*

pagan[1] [ˈpeɪgən] *adj* : pagano

pagan[2] *n* : pagano *m*, -na *f*

paganism [ˈpeɪgənˌɪzəm] *n* : paganismo *m*

page[1] [ˈpeɪʤ] *vt* **paged; paging** : llamar por altavoz

page[2] *n* **1** BELLHOP : botones *m* **2** : página *f* (de un libro, etc.)

pageant [ˈpæʤənt] *n* **1** SPECTACLE : espectáculo *m* **2** PROCESSION : desfile *m*

pageantry [ˈpæʤəntri] *n* : pompa *f*, fausto *m*

pager [ˈpeɪʤər] *n* BEEPER : buscapersonas *m*

pagoda [pəˈgoːdə] *n* : pagoda *f*

paid → **pay**

pail [ˈpeɪl] *n* : balde *m*, cubo *m*, cubeta *f Mex*

pailful [ˈpeɪlˌfʊl] *n* : balde *m*, cubo *m*, cubeta *f Mex*

pain[1] [ˈpeɪn] *vt* : doler

pain[2] *n* **1** PENALTY : pena *f* ⟨under pain of death : so pena de muerte⟩ **2** SUFFERING : dolor *m*, malestar *m*, pena *f* (mental) **3 pains** *npl* EFFORT : esmero *m*, esfuerzo *m* ⟨to take pains : esmerarse⟩

painful [ˈpeɪnfəl] *adj* : doloroso — **painfully** *adv*

painkiller [ˈpeɪnˌkɪlər] *n* : analgésico *m*

painless [ˈpeɪnləs] *adj* : indoloro, sin dolor

painlessly [ˈpeɪnləsli] *adv* : sin dolor

painstaking [ˈpeɪnˌsteɪkɪŋ] *adj* : esmerado, cuidadoso, meticuloso — **painstakingly** *adv*

paint[1] [ˈpeɪnt] *v* : pintar

paint[2] *n* : pintura *f*

paintbrush [ˈpeɪntˌbrʌʃ] *n* : pincel *m* (de un artista), brocha *f* (para pintar casas, etc.)

painter [ˈpeɪntər] *n* : pintor *m*, -tora *f*

painting [ˈpeɪntɪŋ] *n* : pintura *f*

pair[1] [ˈpær] *vt* : emparejar, poner en parejas — *vi* : emparejarse

pair[2] *n* : par *m* (de objetos), pareja *f* (de personas o animales) ⟨a pair of scissors : unas tijeras⟩

pajamas [pəˈʤɑməz, -ˈʤæ-] *npl* : pijama *m*, piyama *mf*

Pakistani [ˌpækɪˈstæni, ˌpɑkɪˈstɑni] *n* : paquistaní *mf* — **Pakistani** *adj*

pal [ˈpæl] *n* : amigo *m*, -ga *f*; compinche *mf fam*; chamo *m*, -ma *f Ven fam*; cuate *m*, -ta *f Mex*

palace [ˈpæləs] *n* : palacio *m*

palatable [ˈpælət̬əbəl] *adj* : sabroso

palate [ˈpælət] *n* **1** : paladar *m* (de la boca) **2** TASTE : paladar *m*, gusto *m*

palatial [pə'leɪʃəl] *adj* : suntuoso, espléndido
palaver [pə'lævər, -'lɑ-] *n* : palabrería *f*
pale[1] ['peɪl] *v* **paled; paling** *vi* : palidecer — *vt* : hacer pálido
pale[2] *adj* **paler; palest** **1** : pálido ⟨to turn pale : palidecer, ponerse pálido⟩ **2** : claro (dícese de los colores)
paleness ['peɪlnəs] *n* : palidez *f*
paleontologist [ˌpeɪliˌɑn'tɑləʤɪst] *n* : paleontólogo *m*, -ga *f*
paleontology [ˌpeɪliˌɑn'tɑləʤi] *n* : paleontología *f*
Palestinian [ˌpælə'stɪniən] *n* : palestino *m*, -na *f* — **Palestinian** *adj*
palette ['pælət] *n* : paleta *f* (para mezclar pigmentos)
palisade [ˌpælə'seɪd] *n* **1** FENCE : empalizada *f*, estacada *f* **2** CLIFFS : acantilado *m*
pall[1] ['pɔl] *vi* : perder su sabor, dejar de gustar
pall[2] *n* **1** : paño *m* mortuorio (sobre un ataúd) **2** COVER : cortina *f* (de humo, etc.) **3 to cast a pall over** : ensombrecer
pallbearer ['pɔlˌbɛrər] *n* : portador *m*, -dora *f* del féretro
pallet ['pælət] *n* **1** BED : camastro *m* **2** PLATFORM : plataforma *f* de carga
palliative ['pæliˌeɪt̬ɪv, 'pæljət̬ɪv] *adj* : paliativo
pallid ['pæləd] *adj* : pálido
pallor ['pælər] *n* : palidez *f*
palm[1] ['pɑm, 'pɑlm] *vt* **1** CONCEAL : escamotear (un naipe, etc.) **2 to palm off** : encajar, endilgar *fam* ⟨he palmed it off on me : me lo endilgó⟩
palm[2] *n* **1** *or* **palm tree** : palmera *f* **2** : palma *f* (de la mano)
Palm Sunday *n* : Domingo *m* de Ramos
palomino [ˌpælə'miːˌnoː] *n, pl* **-nos** : caballo *m* de color dorado
palpable ['pælpəbəl] *adj* : palpable — **palpably** [-bli] *adv*
palpitate ['pælpəˌteɪt] *vi* **-tated; -tating** : palpitar
palpitation [ˌpælpə'teɪʃən] *n* : palpitación *f*
palsy ['pɔlzi] *n, pl* **-sies** **1** : parálisis *f* **2** → **cerebral palsy**
paltry ['pɔltri] *adj* **-trier; -est** : mísero, mezquino, insignificante ⟨a paltry excuse : una mala excusa⟩
pampas ['pæmpəz, 'pɑmpəs] *npl* : pampa *f*
pamper ['pæmpər] *vt* : mimar, consentir, chiquear *Mex*
pamphlet ['pæmpflət] *n* : panfleto *m*, folleto *m*
pan[1] ['pæn] *vt* **panned; panning** CRITICIZE : poner por los suelos — *vi* **to pan for gold** : cribar el oro con batea, lavar oro
pan[2] *n* **1** : cacerola *f*, cazuela *f* **2 frying pan** : sartén *mf*, freidera *f Mex*
panacea [ˌpænə'siːə] *n* : panacea *f*
Panamanian [ˌpænə'meɪniən] *n* : panameño *m*, -ña *f* — **Panamanian** *adj*
pancake ['pænˌkeɪk] *n* : panqueque *m*
pancreas ['pæŋkriəs, 'pæn-] *n* : páncreas *m*
panda ['pændə] *n* : panda *mf*
pandemonium [ˌpændə'moːniəm] *n* : pandemonio *m*, pandemónium *m*
pander ['pændər] *vi* **to pander to** : satisfacer, complacer (a alguien) ⟨to pander to popular taste : satisfacer el gusto popular⟩
pane ['peɪn] *n* : cristal *m*, vidrio *m*
panel[1] ['pænəl] *vt* **-eled** *or* **-elled; -eling** *or* **-elling** : adornar con paneles
panel[2] *n* **1** : lista *f* de nombres (de un jurado, etc.) **2** GROUP : panel *m*, grupo *m* ⟨discussion panel : panel de discusión⟩ **3** : panel *m* (de una pared, etc.) **4 instrument panel** : tablero *m* de instrumentos
paneling ['pænəlɪŋ] *n* : paneles *mpl*
pang ['pæŋ] *n* : puntada *f*, punzada *f*
panic[1] ['pænɪk] *v* **-icked; -icking** *vt* : llenar de pánico — *vi* : ser presa de pánico
panic[2] *n* : pánico *m*
panicky ['pænɪki] *adj* : presa de pánico
panorama [ˌpænə'ræmə, -'rɑ-] *n* : panorama *m*
panoramic [ˌpænə'ræmɪk, -'rɑ-] *adj* : panorámico
pansy ['pænzi] *n, pl* **-sies** : pensamiento *m*
pant[1] ['pænt] *vi* : jadear, resoplar
pant[2] *n* : jadeo *m*, resoplo *m*
pantaloons [ˌpæntə'luːnz] → **pants**
pantheon ['pænɪθiˌɑn, -ən] *n* : panteón *m*
panther ['pænθər] *n* : pantera *f*
panties ['pæntiz] *npl* : calzones *mpl*; pantaletas *fpl Mex, Ven*; bragas *fpl Spain*
pantomime[1] ['pæntəˌmaɪm] *v* **-mimed; -miming** *vt* : representar mediante la pantomima — *vi* : hacer la mímica
pantomime[2] *n* : pantomima *f*
pantry ['pæntri] *n, pl* **-tries** : despensa *f*
pants ['pænts] *npl* **1** TROUSERS : pantalón *m*, pantalones *mpl* **2** → **panties**
panty hose ['pænti] *ns & pl* : medias *fpl*, panties *mfpl*, pantimedias *fpl Mex*
pap ['pæp] *n* : papilla *f* (para bebés, etc.)
papa ['pɑpə] *n* : papá *m*
papal ['peɪpəl] *adj* : papal
papaya [pə'paɪə] *n* : papaya *f* (fruta)
paper[1] ['peɪpər] *vt* WALLPAPER : empapelar
paper[2] *adj* : de papel
paper[3] *n* **1** : papel *m* ⟨a piece of paper : un papel⟩ **2** DOCUMENT : papel *m*, documento *m* **3** NEWSPAPER : periódico *m*, diario *m*
paperback ['peɪpərˌbæk] *n* : libro *m* en rústica
paper clip *n* : clip *m*, sujetapapeles *m*
paperweight ['peɪpərˌweɪt] *n* : pisapapeles *m*

paperwork [ˈpeɪpərˌwərk] *n* : papeleo *m*

papery [ˈpeɪpəri] *adj* : parecido al papel

papier–mâché [ˌpeɪpərməˈʃeɪ, ˌpæˌpjeɪmæˈʃeɪ] *n* : papel *m* maché

papoose [pæˈpuːs, pə-] *n* : niño *m*, -ña *f* de los indios norteamericanos

paprika [pəˈpriːkə, pæ-] *n* : pimentón *m*, paprika *f*

papyrus [pəˈpaɪrəs] *n, pl* **-ruses** *or* **-ri** [-ri, -ˌraɪ] : papiro *m*

par [ˈpɑr] *n* **1** VALUE : valor *m* (nominal), par *f* ⟨below par : debajo de la par⟩ **2** EQUALITY : igualdad *f* ⟨to be on a par with : estar al mismo nivel que⟩ **3** : par *m* (en golf)

parable [ˈpærəbəl] *n* : parábola *f*

parabola [pəˈræbələ] *n* : parábola *f* (en matemáticas)

parachute[1] [ˈpærəˌʃuːt] *vi* **-chuted; -chuting** : lanzarse en paracaídas

parachute[2] *n* : paracaídas *m*

parachutist [ˈpærəˌʃuːt̬ɪst] *n* : paracaidista *mf*

parade[1] [pəˈreɪd] *vi* **-raded; -rading** **1** MARCH : desfilar **2** SHOW OFF : pavonearse, lucirse

parade[2] *n* **1** PROCESSION : desfile *m* **2** DISPLAY : alarde *m*

paradigm [ˈpærəˌdaɪm] *n* : paradigma *m*

paradise [ˈpærəˌdaɪs, -ˌdaɪz] *n* : paraíso *m*

paradox [ˈpærəˌdɑks] *n* : paradoja *f*

paradoxical [ˌpærəˈdɑksɪkəl] *adj* : paradójico — **paradoxically** *adv*

paraffin [ˈpærəfən] *n* : parafina *f*

paragon [ˈpærəˌgɑn, -gən] *n* : dechado *m*

paragraph[1] [ˈpærəˌgræf] *vt* : dividir en párrafos

paragraph[2] *n* : párrafo *m*, acápite *m*

Paraguayan [ˌpærəˈgwaɪən, -ˈgweɪ-] *n* : paraguayo *m*, -ya *f* — **Paraguayan** *adj*

parakeet [ˈpærəˌkiːt] *n* : periquito *m*

paralegal [ˌpærəˈliːgəl] *n* : asistente *mf* de abogado

parallel[1] [ˈpærəˌlɛl, -ləl] *vt* **1** MATCH, RESEMBLE : ser paralelo a, ser análogo a, corresponder con **2** : extenderse en línea paralela con ⟨the road parallels the river : el camino se extiende a lo largo del río⟩

parallel[2] *adj* : paralelo

parallel[3] *n* **1** : línea *f* paralela, superficie *f* paralela **2** : paralelo *m* (en geografía) **3** SIMILARITY : paralelismo *m*, semejanza *f*

parallelogram [ˌpærəˈlɛləˌgræm] *n* : paralelogramo *m*

paralysis [pəˈræləsɪs] *n, pl* **-yses** [-ˌsiːz] : parálisis *f*

paralyze [ˈpærəˌlaɪz] *vt* **-lyzed; -lyzing** : paralizar

parameter [pəˈræmət̬ər] *n* : parámetro *m*

paramount [ˈpærəˌmaʊnt] *adj* : supremo ⟨of paramount importance : de suma importancia⟩

paranoia [ˌpærəˈnɔɪə] *n* : paranoia *f*

paranoid [ˈpærəˌnɔɪd] *adj* : paranoico

parapet [ˈpærəpət, -ˌpɛt] *n* : parapeto *m*

paraphernalia [ˌpærəfəˈneɪljə, -fər-] *ns & pl* : parafernalia *f*

paraphrase[1] [ˈpærəˌfreɪz] *vt* **-phrased; -phrasing** : parafrasear

paraphrase[2] *n* : paráfrasis *f*

paraplegic[1] [ˌpærəˈpliːdʒɪk] *adj* : parapléjico

paraplegic[2] *n* : parapléjico *m*, -ca *f*

parasite [ˈpærəˌsaɪt] *n* : parásito *m*

parasitic [ˌpærəˈsɪt̬ɪk] *adj* : parasitario

parasol [ˈpærəˌsɔl] *n* : sombrilla *f*, quitasol *m*, parasol *m*

paratrooper [ˈpærəˌtruːpər] *n* : paracaidista *mf* (militar)

parboil [ˈpɑrˌbɔɪl] *vt* : sancochar, cocer a medias

parcel[1] [ˈpɑrsəl] *vt* **-celed** *or* **-celled; -celing** *or* **-celling** *or* **to parcel out** : repartir, parcelar (tierras)

parcel[2] *n* **1** LOT : parcela *f*, lote *m* **2** PACKAGE : paquete *m*, bulto *m*

parch [ˈpɑrtʃ] *vt* : resecar

parchment [ˈpɑrtʃmənt] *n* : pergamino *m*

pardon[1] [ˈpɑrdən] *vt* **1** FORGIVE : perdonar, disculpar ⟨pardon me! : ¡perdone!, ¡disculpe la molestia!⟩ **2** REPRIEVE : indultar (a un delincuente)

pardon[2] *n* **1** FORGIVENESS : perdón *m* **2** REPRIEVE : indulto *m*

pardonable [ˈpɑrdənəbəl] *adj* : perdonable, disculpable

pare [ˈpær] *vt* **pared; paring** **1** PEEL : pelar **2** TRIM : recortar **3** REDUCE : reducir ⟨he pared it (down) to 50 pages : lo redujo a 50 páginas⟩

parent [ˈpærənt] *n* **1** : madre *f*, padre *m* **2 parents** *npl* : padres *mpl*

parentage [ˈpærəntɪdʒ] *n* : linaje *m*, abolengo *m*, origen *m*

parental [pəˈrɛntəl] *adj* : de los padres

parenthesis [pəˈrɛnθəsɪs] *n, pl* **-theses** [-ˌsiːz] : paréntesis *m*

parenthetic [ˌpærənˈθɛt̬ɪk] *or* **parenthetical** [-t̬ɪkəl] *adj* : parentético — **parenthetically** [-t̬ɪkli] *adv*

parenthood [ˈpærəntˌhʊd] *n* : paternidad *f*

parfait [pɑrˈfeɪ] *n* : postre *m* elaborado con frutas y helado

pariah [pəˈraɪə] *n* : paria *mf*

parish [ˈpærɪʃ] *n* : parroquia *f*

parishioner [pəˈrɪʃənər] *n* : feligrés *m*, -gresa *f*

parity [ˈpærət̬i] *n, pl* **-ties** : paridad *f*

park[1] [ˈpɑrk] *vt* : estacionar, parquear, aparcar *Spain* — *vi* : estacionarse, parquearse, aparcar *Spain*

park[2] *n* : parque *m*

parka [ˈpɑrkə] *n* : parka *f*

parking [ˈpɑrkɪŋ] *n* : estacionamiento *m*, aparcamiento *m Spain*

parkway [ˈpɑrkˌweɪ] *n* : carretera *f* ajardinada, bulevar *m*

parley[1] [ˈpɑrli] *vi* : parlamentar, negociar

parley² *n, pl* **-leys** : negociación *f*, parlamento *m*
parliament [ˈpɑrləmənt, ˈpɑrljə-] *n* : parlamento *m*
parliamentary [ˌpɑrləˈmɛntəri, ˌpɑrljə-] *adj* : parlamentario
parlor [ˈpɑrlər] *n* **1** : sala *f*, salón *m* (en una casa) **2** : salón *m* ⟨beauty parlor : salón de belleza⟩ **3 funeral parlor** : funeraria *f*
parochial [pəˈroːkiəl] *adj* **1** : parroquial **2** PROVINCIAL : pueblerino, de miras estrechas
parody¹ [ˈpærədi] *vt* **-died; -dying** : parodiar
parody² *n, pl* **-dies** : parodia *f*
parole [pəˈroːl] *n* : libertad *f* condicional
paroxysm [ˈpærəkˌsɪzəm, pəˈrɑk-] *n* : paroxismo *m*
parquet [ˈpɑrˌkeɪ, pɑrˈkeɪ] *n* : parquet *m*, parqué *m*
parrakeet → **parakeet**
parrot [ˈpærət] *n* : loro *m*, papagayo *m*
parry¹ [ˈpæri] *v* **-ried; -rying** *vi* : parar un golpe — *vt* EVADE : esquivar (una pregunta, etc.)
parry² *n, pl* **-ries** : parada *f*
parsimonious [ˌpɑrsəˈmoːniəs] *adj* : tacaño, mezquino
parsley [ˈpɑrsli] *n* : perejil *m*
parsnip [ˈpɑrsnɪp] *n* : chirivía *f*
parson [ˈpɑrsən] *n* : pastor *m*, -tora *f*; clérigo *m*
parsonage [ˈpɑrsənɪʤ] *n* : rectoría *f*, casa *f* del párroco
part¹ [ˈpɑrt] *vi* **1** SEPARATE : separarse, despedirse ⟨we should part as friends : debemos separarnos amistosamente⟩ **2** OPEN : abrirse ⟨the curtains parted : las cortinas se abrieron⟩ **3 to part with** : deshacerse de — *vt* **1** SEPARATE : separar **2 to part one's hair** : hacerse la raya, peinarse con raya
part² *n* **1** SECTION, SEGMENT : parte *f*, sección *f* **2** PIECE : pieza *f* (de una máquina, etc.) **3** ROLE : papel *m* **4** : raya *f* (del pelo)
partake [pɑrˈteɪk, pər-] *vi* **-took** [-ˈtʊk]; **-taken** [-ˈteɪkən;]; **-taking 1 to partake of** CONSUME : comer, beber, tomar **2 to partake in** : participar en (una actividad, etc.)
partial [ˈpɑrʃəl] *adj* **1** BIASED : parcial, tendencioso **2** INCOMPLETE : parcial, incompleto **3 to be partial to** : ser aficionado a
partiality [ˌpɑrʃiˈæləṭi] *n, pl* **-ties** : parcialidad *f*
partially [ˈpɑrʃəli] *adv* : parcialmente
participant [pərˈtɪsəpənt, pɑr-] *n* : participante *mf*
participate [pərˈtɪsəˌpeɪt, pɑr-] *vi* **-pated; -pating** : participar
participation [pərˌtɪsəˈpeɪʃən, pɑr-] *n* : participación *f*
participle [ˈpɑrṭəˌsɪpəl] *n* : participio *m*
particle [ˈpɑrṭɪkəl] *n* : partícula *f*
particular¹ [pɑrˈtɪkjələr] *adj* **1** SPECIFIC : particular, en particular ⟨this particular person : esta persona en particular⟩ **2** SPECIAL : particular, especial ⟨with particular emphasis : con un énfasis especial⟩ **3** FUSSY : exigente, maniático ⟨to be very particular : ser muy especial⟩ ⟨I'm not particular : me da igual⟩
particular² *n* **1** DETAIL : detalle *m*, sentido *m* **2 in particular** : en particular, en especial
particularly [pɑrˈtɪkjələrli] *adv* **1** ESPECIALLY : particularmente, especialmente **2** SPECIFICALLY : específicamente, en especial
partisan [ˈpɑrṭəzən, -sən] *n* **1** ADHERENT : partidario *m*, -ria *f* **2** GUERRILLA : partisano *m*, -na *f*; guerrillero *m*, -ra *f*
partition¹ [pərˈtɪʃən, pɑr-] *vt* : dividir ⟨to partition off (a room) : dividir (una habitación) con un tabique⟩
partition² *n* **1** DISTRIBUTION : partición *f*, división *f*, reparto *m* **2** DIVIDER : tabique *m*, mampara *f*, biombo *m*
partly [ˈpɑrtli] *adv* : en parte, parcialmente
partner [ˈpɑrtnər] *n* **1** COMPANION : compañero *m*, -ra *f* **2** : pareja *f* (en un juego, etc.) ⟨dancing partner : pareja de baile⟩ **3** SPOUSE : cónyuge *mf* **4** *or* **business partner** : socio *m*, -cia *f*; asociado *m*, -da *f*
partnership [ˈpɑrtnərˌʃɪp] *n* **1** ASSOCIATION : asociación *f*, compañerismo *m* **2** : sociedad *f* (de negociantes) ⟨to form a partnership : asociarse⟩
part of speech : categoría *f* gramatical
partridge [ˈpɑrtrɪʤ] *n, pl* **-tridge** *or* **-tridges** : perdiz *f*
party [ˈpɑrṭi] *n, pl* **-ties 1** : partido *m* (político) **2** PARTICIPANT : parte *f*, participante *mf* **3** GROUP : grupo *m* (de personas) **4** GATHERING : fiesta *f* ⟨to throw a party : dar una fiesta⟩
parvenu [ˈpɑrvəˌnuː, -ˌnjuː] *n* : advenedizo *m*, -za *f*
pass¹ [ˈpæs] *vi* **1** : pasar, cruzarse ⟨a car passed by : pasó un coche⟩ ⟨we passed in the hallway : nos cruzamos en el pasillo⟩ **2** CEASE : pasarse ⟨the pain passed : se pasó el dolor⟩ **3** ELAPSE : pasar, transcurrir **4** PROCEED : pasar ⟨let me pass : déjame pasar⟩ **5** HAPPEN : pasar, ocurrir **6** : pasar, aprobar (en un examen) **7** RULE : fallar ⟨the jury passed on the case : el jurado falló en el caso⟩ **8** *or* **to pass down** : pasar ⟨the throne passed to his son : el trono pasó a su hijo⟩ **9 to let pass** OVERLOOK : pasar por alto **10 to pass as** : pasar por **11 to pass away** *or* **to pass on** DIE : fallecer, morir — *vt* **1** : pasar por ⟨they passed the house : pasaron por la casa⟩ **2** OVERTAKE : pasar, adelantar **3** SPEND : pasar (tiempo) **4** HAND : pasar ⟨pass me the salt : pásame la sal⟩ **5** : aprobar (un examen, una ley)

pass² *n* 1 CROSSING, GAP : paso *m*, desfiladero *m*, puerto *m* ⟨mountain pass : puerto de montaña⟩ 2 PERMIT : pase *m*, permiso *m* 3 : pase *m* (en deportes) 4 SITUATION : situación *f* (díficil) ⟨things have come to a pretty pass! : ¡hasta dónde hemos llegado!⟩
passable [ˈpæsəbəl] *adj* 1 ADEQUATE : adecuado, pasable 2 : transitable (dícese de un camino, etc.)
passably [ˈpæsəbli] *adv* : pasablemente
passage [ˈpæsɪʤ] *n* 1 PASSING : paso *m* ⟨the passage of time : el paso del tiempo⟩ 2 PASSAGEWAY : pasillo *m* (dentro de un edificio), pasaje *m* (entre edificios) 3 VOYAGE : travesía *f* (por el mar), viaje *m* ⟨to grant safe passage : dar un salvoconducto⟩ 4 SECTION : pasaje *m* (en música o literatura)
passageway [ˈpæsɪʤˌweɪ] *n* : pasillo *m*, pasadizo *m*, corredor *m*
passbook [ˈpæsˌbʊk] *n* BANKBOOK : libreta *f* de ahorros
passé [pæˈseɪ] *adj* : pasado de moda
passenger [ˈpæsənʤər] *n* : pasajero *m*, -ra *f*
passerby [ˌpæsərˈbaɪ, ˈpæsərˌ-] *n, pl* **passersby** : transeúnte *mf*
passing [ˈpæsɪŋ] *n* DEATH : fallecimiento *m*
passion [ˈpæʃən] *n* : pasión *f*, ardor *m*
passionate [ˈpæʃənət] *adj* 1 IRASCIBLE : irascible, iracundo 2 ARDENT : apasionado, ardiente, ferviente, fogoso
passionately [ˈpæʃənətli] *adv* : apasionadamente, fervientemente, con pasión
passive¹ [ˈpæsɪv] *adj* : pasivo — **passively** *adv*
passive² *n* : voz *f* pasiva (en gramática)
passivity [pæˈsɪvət̬i] *n* : pasividad *f*
Passover [ˈpæsˌoːvər] *n* : Pascua *f* (en el judaísmo)
passport [ˈpæsˌport] *n* : pasaporte *m*
password [ˈpæsˌwərd] *n* : contraseña *f*
past¹ [ˈpæst] *adv* : por delante ⟨he drove past : pasamos en coche⟩
past² *adj* 1 AGO : hace ⟨10 years past : hace 10 años⟩ 2 LAST : último ⟨the past few months : los últimos meses⟩ 3 BYGONE : pasado ⟨in past times : en tiempos pasados⟩ 4 : pasado (en gramática)
past³ *n* : pasado *m*
past⁴ *prep* 1 BY : por, por delante de ⟨he ran past the house : pasó por la casa corriendo⟩ 2 BEYOND : más allá de ⟨just past the corner : un poco más allá de la esquina⟩ ⟨we went past the exit : pasamos la salida⟩ 3 AFTER : después de ⟨past noon : después del mediodía⟩ ⟨half past two : las dos y media⟩
pasta [ˈpɑstə, ˈpæs-] *n* : pasta *f*
paste¹ [ˈpeɪst] *vt* **pasted; pasting** : pegar (con engrudo)
paste² *n* 1 : pasta *f* ⟨tomato paste : pasta de tomate⟩ 2 : engrudo *m* (para pegar)
pasteboard [ˈpeɪstˌbord] *n* : cartón *m*, cartulina *f*
pastel [pæˈstɛl] *n* : pastel *m* — **pastel** *adj*
pasteurization [ˌpæsʧərəˈzeɪʃən, ˌpæstjə-] *n* : pasteurización *f*
pasteurize [ˈpæsʧəˌraɪz, ˈpæstjə-] *vt* **-ized; -izing** : pasteurizar
pastime [ˈpæsˌtaɪm] *n* : pasatiempo *m*
pastor [ˈpæstər] *n* : pastor *m*, -tora *f*
pastoral [ˈpæstərəl] *adj* : pastoral
past participle *n* : participio *m* pasado
pastry [ˈpeɪstri] *n, pl* **-ries** 1 DOUGH : pasta *f*, masa *f* 2 **pastries** *npl* : pasteles *mpl*
pasture¹ [ˈpæsʧər] *v* **-tured; -turing** *vi* GRAZE : pacer, pastar — *vt* : apacentar, pastar
pasture² *n* : pastizal *m*, potrero *m*, pasto *m*
pasty [ˈpeɪsti] *adj* **pastier; -est** 1 : pastoso (en consistencia) 2 PALLID : pálido
pat¹ [ˈpæt] *vt* **patted; patting** : dar palmaditas a, tocar
pat² *adv* : de memoria ⟨to have down pat : saberse de memoria⟩
pat³ *adj* 1 APT : apto, apropiado 2 GLIB : fácil 3 UNYIELDING : firme ⟨to stand pat : mantenerse firme⟩
pat⁴ *n* 1 TAP : golpecito *m*, palmadita *f* ⟨a pat on the back : una palmadita en la espalda⟩ 2 CARESS : caricia *f* 3 : porción *f* ⟨a pat of butter : una porción de mantequilla⟩
patch¹ [ˈpæʧ] *vt* 1 MEND, REPAIR : remendar, parchar, ponerle un parche a 2 **to patch together** IMPROVISE : confeccionar, improvisar 3 **to patch up** : arreglar ⟨they patched things up : hicieron las paces⟩
patch² *n* 1 : parche *m*, remiendo *m* (para la ropa) ⟨eye patch : parche para el ojo⟩ 2 PIECE : mancha *f*, trozo *m* ⟨a patch of sky : un trozo de cielo⟩ 3 PLOT : parcela *f*, terreno *m* ⟨cabbage patch : parcela de repollos⟩
patchwork [ˈpæʧˌwərk] *n* : labor *f* de retazos
patchy [ˈpæʧi] *adj* **patchier; -est** 1 IRREGULAR : irregular, desigual 2 INCOMPLETE : parcial, incompleto
patent¹ [ˈpætənt] *vt* : patentar
patent² [ˈpætənt, ˈpeɪt-] *adj* 1 OBVIOUS : patente, evidente 2 [ˈpæt-] PATENTED : patentado
patent³ [ˈpætənt] *n* : patente *f*
patently [ˈpætəntli] *adv* : patentemente, evidentemente
paternal [pəˈtərnəl] *adj* 1 FATHERLY : paternal 2 : paterno ⟨paternal grandfather : abuelo paterno⟩
paternity [pəˈtərnət̬i] *n* : paternidad *f*
path [ˈpæθ, ˈpaθ] *n* 1 TRACK, TRAIL : camino *m*, sendero *m*, senda *f* 2 COURSE, ROUTE : recorrido *m*, trayecto *m*, trayectoria *f*
pathetic [pəˈθɛt̬ɪk] *adj* : patético — **pathetically** [-t̬ɪkli] *adv*
pathological [ˌpæθəˈlɑʤɪkəl] *adj* : patológico

pathologist [pə'θɑləʤɪst] *n* : patólogo *m*, -ga *f*
pathology [pə'θɑləʤi] *n, pl* **-gies** : patología *f*
pathos ['peɪˌθɑs, 'pæ-, -ˌθɔs] *n* : patetismo *m*
pathway ['pæθˌweɪ] *n* : camino *m*, sendero *m*, senda *f*, vereda *f*
patience ['peɪʃənts] *n* : paciencia *f*
patient[1] ['peɪʃənt] *adj* : paciente — **patiently** *adv*
patient[2] *n* : paciente *mf*
patio ['pæṭiˌo:] *n, pl* **-tios** : patio *m*
patriarch ['peɪtriˌɑrk] *n* : patriarca *m*
patriarchy ['peɪtriˌɑrki] *n, pl* **-chies** : patriarcado *m*
patrimony ['pætrəˌmo:ni] *n, pl* **-nies** : patrimonio *m*
patriot ['peɪtriət] *n* : patriota *mf*
patriotic [ˌpeɪtri'ɑṭɪk] *adj* : patriótico — **patriotically** *adv*
patriotism ['peɪtriəˌtɪzəm] *n* : patriotismo *m*
patrol[1] [pə'tro:l] *v* **-trolled; -trolling** : patrullar
patrol[2] *n* : patrulla *f*
patrolman [pə'tro:lmən] *n, pl* **-men** [-mən, -ˌmɛn] : policía *mf*, guardia *mf*
patron ['peɪtrən] *n* **1** SPONSOR : patrocinador *m*, -dora *f* **2** CUSTOMER : cliente *m*, -ta *f* **3** *or* **patron saint** : patrono *m*, -na *f*
patronage ['peɪtrənɪʤ, 'pæ-] *n* **1** SPONSORSHIP : patrocinio *m* **2** CLIENTELE : clientela *f* **3** : influencia *f* (política)
patronize ['peɪtrəˌnaɪz, 'pæ-] *vt* **-ized; -izing** **1** SPONSOR : patrocinar **2** : ser cliente de (un negocio) **3** : tratar con condescendencia
patter[1] ['pæṭər] *vi* **1** TAP : golpetear, tamborilear (dícese de la lluvia) **2 to patter about** : corretear (con pasos ligeros)
patter[2] *n* **1** TAPPING : golpeteo *m*, tamborileo *m* (de la lluvia), correteo *m* (de pies) **2** CHATTER : palabrería *f*, parloteo *m fam*
pattern[1] ['pæṭərn] *vt* **1** BASE : basar (en un modelo) **2 to pattern after** : hacer imitación de
pattern[2] *n* **1** MODEL : modelo *m*, patrón *m* (de costura) **2** DESIGN : diseño *m*, dibujo *m*, estampado *m* (de tela) **3** NORM, STANDARD : pauta *f*, norma *f*, patrón *m*
patty ['pæṭi] *n, pl* **-ties** : porción *f* de carne picada (u otro alimento) en forma de ruedita <a hamburger patty : una hamburguesa>
paucity ['pɔsəṭi] *n* : escasez *f*
paunch ['pɔntʃ] *n* : panza *f*, barriga *f*
pauper ['pɔpər] *n* : pobre *mf*, indigente *mf*
pause[1] ['pɔz] *vi* **paused; pausing** : hacer una pausa, pararse (brevemente)
pause[2] *n* : pausa *f*
pave ['peɪv] *vt* **paved; paving** : pavimentar <to pave with stones : empedrar>
pavement ['peɪvmənt] *n* : pavimento *m*, empedrado *m*
pavilion [pə'vɪljən] *n* : pabellón *m*
paving ['peɪvɪŋ] → **pavement**
paw[1] ['pɔ] *vt* : tocar, manosear, sobar
paw[2] *n* : pata *f*, garra *f*, zarpa *f*
pawn[1] ['pɔn] *vt* : empeñar, prendar
pawn[2] *n* **1** PLEDGE, SECURITY : prenda *f* **2** PAWNING : empeño *m* **3** : peón *m* (en ajedrez)
pawnbroker ['pɔnˌbro:kər] *n* : prestamista *mf*
pawnshop ['pɔnˌʃɑp] *n* : casa *f* de empeños, monte *m* de piedad
pay[1] ['peɪ] *v* **paid** ['peɪd]; **paying** *vt* **1** : pagar (una cuenta, a un empleado, etc.) **2 to pay attention** : poner atención, prestar atención, hacer caso **3 to pay back** : pagar, devolver <she paid them back : les devolvió el dinero> <I'll pay you back for what you did! : ¡me las pagarás!> **4 to pay off** SETTLE : saldar, cancelar (una deuda, etc.) **5 to pay one's respects** : presentar uno sus respetos **6 to pay a visit** : hacer una visita — *vi* : valer la pena <crime doesn't pay : no hay crimen sin castigo>
pay[2] *n* : paga *f*
payable ['peɪəbəl] *adj* DUE : pagadero
paycheck ['peɪˌtʃɛk] *n* : sueldo *m*, cheque *m* del sueldo
payee [peɪ'i:] *n* : beneficiario *m*, -ria *f* (de un cheque, etc.)
payment ['peɪmənt] *n* **1** : pago *m* **2** INSTALLMENT : plazo *m*, cuota *f* **3** REWARD : recompensa *f*
payoff ['peɪˌɔf] *n* **1** REWARD : recompensa *f* **2** PROFIT : ganancia *f* **3** BRIBE : soborno *m*
payroll ['peɪˌro:l] *n* : nómina *f*
PC [ˌpi:'si:] *n, pl* **PCs** *or* **PC's** : PC *mf*, computadora *f* personal
pea ['pi:] *n* : chícharo *m*, guisante *m*, arveja *f*
peace ['pi:s] *n* **1** : paz *f* <peace treaty : tratado de paz> <peace and tranquillity : paz y tranquilidad> **2** ORDER : orden *m* (público)
peaceable ['pi:səbəl] *adj* : pacífico — **peaceably** [-bli] *adv*
peaceful ['pi:sfəl] *adj* **1** PEACEABLE : pacífico **2** CALM, QUIET : tranquilo, sosegado — **peacefully** *adv*
peacemaker ['pi:sˌmeɪkər] *n* : conciliador *m*, -dora *f*; mediador *m*, -dora *f*
peach ['pi:tʃ] *n* : durazno *m*, melocotón *m*
peacock ['pi:ˌkɑk] *n* : pavo *m* real
peak[1] ['pi:k] *vi* : alcanzar su nivel máximo
peak[2] *adj* : máximo
peak[3] *n* **1** POINT : punta *f* **2** CREST, SUMMIT : cima *f*, cumbre *f* **3** APEX : cúspide *f*, apogeo *m*, nivel *m* máximo
peaked ['pi:kəd] *adj* SICKLY : pálido
peal[1] ['pi:l] *vi* : repicar
peal[2] *n* : repique *m*, tañido *m* (de campanada) <peals of laughter : carcajadas>

peanut ['pi:ˌnʌt] *n* : maní *m*, cacahuate *m Mex*, cacahuete *m Spain*
pear ['pær] *n* : pera *f*
pearl ['pərl] *n* : perla *f*
pearly ['pərli] *adj* **pearlier; -est** : nacarado
peasant ['pɛzənt] *n* : campesino *m*, -na *f*
peat ['pi:t] *n* : turba *f*
pebble ['pɛbəl] *n* : guijarro *m*, piedrecita *f*, piedrita *f*
pecan [pɪ'kɑn, -'kæn, 'pi:ˌkæn] *n* : pacana *f*, nuez *f Mex*
peccadillo [ˌpɛkə'dɪlo] *n, pl* **-loes** *or* **-los** : pecadillo *m*
peccary ['pɛkəri] *n, pl* **-ries** : pécari *m*, pecarí *m*
peck¹ ['pɛk] *vt* : picar, picotear
peck² *n* **1** : medida *f* de áridos equivalente a 8.810 litros **2** : picotazo *m* (de un pájaro) ⟨a peck on the cheek : un besito en la mejilla⟩
pectoral ['pɛktərəl] *adj* : pectoral
peculiar [pɪ'kju:ljər] *adj* **1** DISTINCTIVE : propio, peculiar, característico ⟨peculiar to this area : propio de esta zona⟩ **2** STRANGE : extraño, raro — **peculiarly** *adv*
peculiarity [pɪˌkju:l'jærəṭi, -ˌkju:li'ær-] *n, pl* **-ties** **1** DISTINCTIVENESS : peculiaridad *f* **2** ODDITY, QUIRK : rareza *f*, idiosincrasia *f*, excentricidad *f*
pecuniary [pɪ'kju:niˌɛri] *adj* : pecuniario
pedagogical [ˌpɛdə'gɑʤɪkəl, -'go:-] *adj* : pedagógico
pedagogy ['pɛdəˌgo:ʤi, -ˌgɑ-] *n* : pedagogía *f*
pedal¹ ['pɛdəl] *v* **-aled** *or* **-alled; -aling** *or* **-alling** *vi* : pedalear — *vt* : darle a los pedales de
pedal² *n* : pedal *m*
pedant ['pɛdənt] *n* : pedante *mf*
pedantic [pɪ'dæntɪk] *adj* : pedante
pedantry ['pɛdəntri] *n, pl* **-ries** : pedantería *f*
peddle ['pɛdəl] *vt* **-dled; -dling** : vender (en las calles)
peddler ['pɛdlər] *n* : vendedor *m*, -dora *f* ambulante; mercachifle *m*
pedestal ['pɛdəstəl] *n* : pedestal *m*
pedestrian¹ [pə'dɛstriən] *adj* **1** COMMONPLACE : pedestre, ordinario **2** : de peatón, peatonal ⟨pedestrian crossing : paso de peatones⟩
pedestrian² *n* : peatón *m*, -tona *f*
pediatric [ˌpi:di'ætrɪk] *adj* : pediátrico
pediatrician [ˌpi:diə'trɪʃən] *n* : pediatra *mf*
pediatrics [ˌpi:di'ætrɪks] *ns & pl* : pediatría *f*
pedigree ['pɛdəˌgri:] *n* **1** FAMILY TREE : árbol *m* genealógico **2** LINEAGE : pedigrí *m* (de un animal), linaje *m* (de una persona)
peek¹ ['pi:k] *vi* **1** PEEP : espiar, mirar furtivamente **2** GLANCE : echar un vistazo
peek² *n* **1** : miradita *f* (furtiva) **2** GLANCE : vistazo *m*, ojeada *f*
peel¹ ['pi:l] *vt* **1** : pelar (fruta, etc.) **2** *or* **to peel away** : quitar — *vi* : pelarse (dícese de la piel), desconcharse (dícese de la pintura)
peel² *n* : cáscara *f*
peep¹ ['pi:p] *vi* **1** PEEK : espiar, mirar furtivamente **2** CHEEP : piar **3 to peep out** SHOW : asomarse
peep² *n* **1** CHEEP : pío *m* (de un pajarito) **2** GLANCE : vistazo *m*, ojeada *f*
peer¹ ['pɪr] *vi* : mirar detenidamente, mirar con atención
peer² *n* **1** EQUAL : par *m*, igual *mf* **2** NOBLE : noble *mf*
peerage ['pɪrɪʤ] *n* : nobleza *f*
peerless ['pɪrləs] *adj* : sin par, incomparable
peeve¹ ['pi:v] *vt* **peeved; peeving** : fastidiar, irritar, molestar
peeve² *n* : queja *f*
peevish ['pi:vɪʃ] *adj* : quejoso, fastidioso — **peevishly** *adv*
peevishness ['pi:vɪʃnəs] *n* : irritabilidad *f*
peg¹ ['pɛg] *vt* **pegged; pegging** **1** PLUG : tapar (con una clavija) **2** FASTEN, FIX : sujetar (con estaquillas) **3 to peg out** MARK : marcar (con estaquillas)
peg² *n* : estaquilla *f* (para clavar), clavija *f* (para tapar)
pejorative [pɪ'ʤɔrəṭɪv] *adj* : peyorativo — **pejoratively** *adv*
pelican ['pɛlɪkən] *n* : pelícano *m*
pellagra [pə'lægrə, -'leɪ-] *n* : pelagra *f*
pellet ['pɛlət] *n* **1** BALL : bolita *f* ⟨food pellet : bolita de comida⟩ **2** SHOT : perdigón *m*
pell–mell ['pɛl'mɛl] *adv* : desordenadamente, atropelladamente
pelt¹ ['pɛlt] *vt* **1** THROW : lanzar, tirar (algo a alguien) **2 to pelt with stones** : apedrear — *vi* BEAT : golpear con fuerza ⟨the rain was pelting down : llovía a cántaros⟩
pelt² *n* : piel *f*, pellejo *m*
pelvic ['pɛlvɪk] *adj* : pélvico
pelvis ['pɛlvɪs] *n, pl* **-vises** *or* **-ves** ['pɛlˌvi:z] : pelvis *f*
pen¹ ['pɛn] *vt* **penned; penning** **1** *or* **pen in** : encerrar (animales) **2** WRITE : escribir
pen² *n* **1** CORRAL : corral *m*, redil *m* (para ovejas) **2** : pluma *f* ⟨fountain pen : pluma fuente⟩ ⟨ballpoint pen : bolígrafo⟩
penal ['pi:nəl] *adj* : penal
penalize ['pi:nəlˌaɪz, 'pɛn-] *vt* **-ized; -izing** : penalizar, sancionar, penar
penalty ['pɛnəlti] *n, pl* **-ties** **1** PUNISHMENT : pena *f*, castigo *m* **2** DISADVANTAGE : desventaja *f*, castigo *m*, penalty *m* (en deportes) **3** FINE : multa *f*
penance ['pɛnənts] *n* : penitencia *f*
pence → **penny**
penchant ['pɛntʃənt] *n* : inclinación *f*, afición *f*

pencil[1] [ˈpɛntsəl] *vt* **-ciled** *or* **-cilled; -ciling** *or* **-cilling** : escribir con lápiz, dibujar con lápiz

pencil[2] *n* : lápiz *m*

pendant [ˈpɛndənt] *n* : colgante *m*

pending[1] [ˈpɛndɪŋ] *adj* : pendiente

pending[2] *prep* **1** DURING : durante **2** AWAITING : en espera de

pendulum [ˈpɛndʒələm, -djʊləm] *n* : péndulo *m*

penetrate [ˈpɛnəˌtreɪt] *vt* **-trated; -trating** : penetrar

penetrating [ˈpɛnəˌtreɪt̬ɪŋ] *adj* : penetrante, cortante

penetration [ˌpɛnəˈtreɪʃən] *n* : penetración *f*

penguin [ˈpɛŋgwɪn, ˈpɛn-] *n* : pingüino *m*

penicillin [ˌpɛnəˈsɪlən] *n* : penicilina *f*

peninsula [pəˈnɪntsələ, -ˈnɪntʃʊlə] *n* : península *f*

penis [ˈpiːnəs] *n, pl* **-nes** [-ˌniːz] *or* **-nises** : pene *m*

penitence [ˈpɛnət̬ənts] *n* : arrepentimiento *m*, penitencia *f*

penitent[1] [ˈpɛnət̬ənt] *adj* : arrepentido, penitente

penitent[2] *n* : penitente *mf*

penitentiary [ˌpɛnəˈtɛntʃəri] *n, pl* **-ries** : penitenciaría *f*, prisión *m*, presidio *m*

penmanship [ˈpɛnmənˌʃɪp] *n* : escritura *f*, caligrafía *f*

pen name *n* : seudónimo *m*

pennant [ˈpɛnənt] *n* : gallardete *m* (de un barco), banderín *m*

penniless [ˈpɛniləs] *adj* : sin un centavo

penny [ˈpɛni] *n, pl* **-nies** *or* **pence** [ˈpɛnts] **1** : penique *m* (del Reino Unido) **2** *pl* **-nies** CENT : centavo *m* (de los Estados Unidos)

pension[1] [ˈpɛntʃən] *vt or* **to pension off** : jubilar

pension[2] *n* : pensión *m*, jubilación *f*

pensive [ˈpɛntsɪv] *adj* : pensativo, meditabundo — **pensively** *adv*

pent [ˈpɛnt] *adj* : encerrado ⟨pent-up feelings : emociones reprimidas⟩

pentagon [ˈpɛntəˌgɑn] *n* : pentágono *m*

pentagonal [pɛnˈtægənəl] *adj* : pentagonal

penthouse [ˈpɛntˌhaʊs] *n* : ático *m*, penthouse *m*

penultimate [pɪˈnʌltəmət] *adj* : penúltimo

penury [ˈpɛnjəri] *n* : penuria *f*, miseria *f*

peon [ˈpiːˌɑn, -ən] *n, pl* **-ons** *or* **-ones** [peɪˈoːniːz] : peón *m*

peony [ˈpiːəni] *n, pl* **-nies** : peonía *f*

people[1] [ˈpiːpəl] *vt* **-pled; -pling** : poblar

people[2] *ns & pl* **1 people** *npl* : gente *f*, personas *fpl* ⟨people like him : él le cae bien a la gente⟩ ⟨many people : mucha gente, muchas personas⟩ **2** *pl* **peoples** : pueblo *m* ⟨the Cuban people : el pueblo cubano⟩

pep[1] [ˈpɛp] *vt* **pepped; pepping** *or* **to pep up** : animar

pep[2] *n* : energía *f*, vigor *m*

pepper[1] [ˈpɛpər] *vt* **1** : añadir pimienta a **2** RIDDLE : acribillar (a balazos) **3** SPRINKLE : salpicar ⟨peppered with quotations : salpicado de citas⟩

pepper[2] *n* **1** : pimienta *f* (condimento) **2** : pimiento *m*, pimentón *m* (fruta) **3** → **chili**

peppermint [ˈpɛpərˌmɪnt] *n* : menta *f*

peppery [ˈpɛpəri] *adj* : picante

peppy [ˈpɛpi] *adj* **peppier; -est** : lleno de energía, vivaz

peptic [ˈpɛptɪk] *adj* **peptic ulcer** : úlcera *f* estomacal

per [ˈpər] *prep* **1** : por ⟨miles per hour : millas por hora⟩ **2** ACCORDING TO : según ⟨per his specifications : según sus especificaciones⟩

per annum [pərˈænəm] *adv* : al año, por año

percale [ˌpərˈkeɪl, ˈpər-ˌ; ˌpərˈkæl] *n* : percal *m*

per capita [pərˈkæpɪt̬ə] *adv & adj* : per cápita

perceive [pərˈsiːv] *vt* **-ceived; -ceiving** **1** REALIZE : percatarse de, concientizarse de, darse cuenta de **2** NOTE : percibir, notar

percent[1] [pərˈsɛnt] *adv* : por ciento

percent[2] *n, pl* **-cent** *or* **-cents** **1** : por ciento ⟨10 percent of the population : el 10 por ciento de la población⟩ **2** → **percentage**

percentage [pərˈsɛntɪdʒ] *n* : porcentaje *m*

perceptible [pərˈsɛptəbəl] *adj* : perceptible — **perceptibly** [-bli] *adv*

perception [pərˈsɛpʃən] *n* **1** : percepción *f* ⟨color perception : la percepción de los colores⟩ **2** INSIGHT : perspicacia *f* **3** IDEA : idea *f*, imagen *f*

perceptive [pərˈsɛptɪv] *adj* : perspicaz

perceptively [pərˈsɛptɪvli] *adv* : con perspicacia

perch[1] [ˈpərtʃ] *vi* **1** ROOST : posarse **2** SIT : sentarse (en un sitio elevado) — *vt* PLACE : posar, colocar

perch[2] *n* **1** ROOST : percha *f* (para los pájaros) **2** *pl* **perch** *or* **perches** : perca *f* (pez)

percolate [ˈpərkəˌleɪt] *vi* **-lated; -lating** : colarse, filtrarse ⟨percolated coffee : café filtrado⟩

percolator [ˈpərkəˌleɪt̬ər] *n* : cafetera *f* de filtro

percussion [pərˈkʌʃən] *n* **1** STRIKING : percusión *f* **2** *or* **percussion instruments** : instrumentos *mpl* de percusión

peremptory [pəˈrɛmptəri] *adj* : perentorio

perennial[1] [pəˈrɛniəl] *adj* **1** : perenne, vivaz ⟨perennial flowers : flores perennes⟩ **2** RECURRENT : perenne, continuo ⟨a perennial problem : un problema eterno⟩

perennial[2] *n* : planta *f* perenne, planta *f* vivaz

perfect[1] [pərˈfɛkt] *vt* : perfeccionar

perfect[2] [ˈpərfɪkt] *adj* : perfecto — **perfectly** *adv*
perfection [pərˈfɛkʃən] *n* : perfección *f*
perfectionist [pərˈfɛkʃənɪst] *n* : perfeccionista *mf*
perfidious [pərˈfɪdiəs] *adj* : pérfido
perforate [ˈpərfəˌreɪt] *vt* **-rated; -rating** : perforar
perforation [ˌpərfəˈreɪʃən] *n* : perforación *f*
perform [pərˈfɔrm] *vt* **1** CARRY OUT : realizar, hacer, desempeñar **2** PRESENT : representar, dar (una obra teatral, etc.) — *vi* : actuar (en una obra teatral), cantar (en una ópera, etc.), tocar (en un concierto, etc.), bailar (en un ballet, etc.)
performance [pərˈfɔrmənts] *n* **1** EXECUTION : ejecución *f*, realización *f*, desempeño *m*, rendimiento *m* **2** INTERPRETATION : interpretación *f* ⟨his performance of Hamlet : su interpretación de Hamlet⟩ **3** PRESENTATION : representación *f* (de una obra teatral), función *f*
performer [pərˈfɔrmər] *n* : artista *mf*; actor *m*, -triz *f*; intérprete *mf* (de música)
perfume[1] [pərˈfju:m, ˈpərˌ-] *vt* **-fumed; -fuming** : perfumar
perfume[2] [ˈpərˌfju:m, pərˈ-] *n* : perfume *m*
perfunctory [pərˈfʌŋktəri] *adj* : mecánico, superficial, somero
perhaps [pərˈhæps] *adv* : tal vez, quizá, quizás
peril [ˈpɛrəl] *n* : peligro *m*
perilous [ˈpɛrələs] *adj* : peligroso — **perilously** *adv*
perimeter [pəˈrɪmət̬ər] *n* : perímetro *m*
period [ˈpɪriəd] *n* **1** : punto *m* (en puntuación) **2** : período *m* ⟨a two-hour period : un período de dos horas⟩ **3** STAGE : época *f* (histórica), fase *f*, etapa *f*
periodic [ˌpɪriˈɑdɪk] *or* **periodical** [-dɪkəl] *adj* : periódico — **periodically** [-dɪkli] *adv*
periodical [ˌpɪriˈɑdɪkəl] *n* : publicación *f* periódica, revista *f*
peripheral [pəˈrɪfərəl] *adj* : periférico
periphery [pəˈrɪfəri] *n, pl* **-eries** : periferia *f*
periscope [ˈpɛrəˌsko:p] *n* : periscopio *m*
perish [ˈpɛrɪʃ] *vi* DIE : perecer, morirse
perishable[1] [ˈpɛrɪʃəbəl] *adj* : perecedero
perishable[2] *n* : producto *m* perecedero
perjure [ˈpərʤər] *vt* **-jured; -juring** (*used in law*) **to perjure oneself** : perjurar, perjurarse
perjury [ˈpərʤəri] *n* : perjurio *m*
perk[1] [ˈpərk] *vt* **1** : levantar (las orejas, etc.) **2** *or* **to perk up** FRESHEN : arreglar — *vi* **to perk up** : animarse, reanimarse
perk[2] *n* : extra *m*
perky [ˈpərki] *adj* **perkier; -est** : animado, alegre, lleno de vida
permanence [ˈpərmənənts] *n* : permanencia *f*
permanent[1] [ˈpərmənənt] *adj* : permanente — **permanently** *adv*
permanent[2] *n* : permanente *f*
permeability [ˌpərmiəˈbɪlət̬i] *n* : permeabilidad *f*
permeable [ˈpərmiəbəl] *adj* : permeable
permeate [ˈpərmiˌeɪt] *v* **-ated; -ating** *vt* **1** PENETRATE : penetrar, impregnar **2** PERVADE : penetrar, difundirse por — *vi* : penetrar
permissible [pərˈmɪsəbəl] *adj* : permisible, lícito
permission [pərˈmɪʃən] *n* : permiso *m*
permissive [pərˈmɪsɪv] *adj* : permisivo
permit[1] [pərˈmɪt] *vt* **-mitted; -mitting** : permitir, dejar ⟨weather permitting : si el tiempo lo permite⟩
permit[2] [ˈpərˌmɪt, pərˈ-] *n* : permiso *m*, licencia *f*
pernicious [pərˈnɪʃəs] *adj* : pernicioso
peroxide [pəˈrɑkˌsaɪd] *n* **1** : peróxido *m* **2** → **hydrogen peroxide**
perpendicular[1] [ˌpərpənˈdɪkjələr] *adj* **1** VERTICAL : vertical **2** : perpendicular ⟨perpendicular lines : líneas perpendiculares⟩ — **perpendicularly** *adv*
perpendicular[2] *n* : perpendicular *f*
perpetrate [ˈpərpəˌtreɪt] *vt* **-trated; -trating** : perpetrar, cometer (un delito)
perpetrator [ˈpərpəˌtreɪt̬ər] *n* : autor *m*, -tora *f* (de un delito)
perpetual [pərˈpɛʧʊəl] *adj* **1** EVERLASTING : perpetuo, eterno **2** CONTINUAL : perpetuo, continuo, constante
perpetually [pərˈpɛʧʊəli, -ʧəli] *adv* : para siempre, eternamente
perpetuate [pərˈpɛʧʊˌeɪt] *vt* **-ated; -ating** : perpetuar
perpetuity [ˌpərpəˈtu:ət̬i, -ˈtju:-] *n, pl* **-ties** : perpetuidad *f*
perplex [pərˈplɛks] *vt* : dejar perplejo, confundir
perplexed [pərˈplɛkst] *adj* : perplejo
perplexity [pərˈplɛksət̬i] *n, pl* **-ties** : perplejidad *f*, confusión *f*
persecute [ˈpərsɪˌkju:t] *vt* **-cuted; -cuting** : perseguir
persecution [ˌpərsɪˈkju:ʃən] *n* : persecución *f*
perseverance [ˌpərsəˈvɪrənts] *n* : perseverancia *f*
persevere [ˌpərsəˈvɪr] *vi* **-vered; -vering** : perseverar
Persian [ˈpərʒən] *n* **1** : persa *mf* **2** : persa *m* (idioma) — **Persian** *adj*
persist [pərˈsɪst] *vi* : persistir
persistence [pərˈsɪstənts] *n* **1** CONTINUATION : persistencia *f* **2** TENACITY : perseverancia *f*, tenacidad *f*
persistent [pərˈsɪstənt] *adj* : persistente — **persistently** *adv*
person [ˈpərsən] *n* **1** HUMAN, INDIVIDUAL : persona *f*, individuo *m*, ser *m* humano **2** : persona *f* (en gramática) **3** **in person** : en persona
personable [ˈpərsənəbəl] *adj* : agradable

personage [ˈpərsənɪʤ] *n* : personaje *m*

personal [ˈpərsənəl] *adj* **1** OWN, PRIVATE : personal, particular, privado ⟨for personal reasons : por razones personales⟩ **2** : en persona ⟨to make a personal appearance : presentarse en persona, hacerse acto de presencia⟩ **3** : íntimo, personal ⟨personal hygiene : higiene personal⟩ **4** INDISCREET, PRYING : indiscreto, personal

personal computer *n* : computadora *f* personal, ordenador *m* personal *Spain*

personal digital assistant *n* : asistente *m* personal digital

personality [ˌpərsənˈæləṭi] *n, pl* **-ties** **1** DISPOSITION : personalidad *f*, temperamento *m* **2** CELEBRITY : personalidad *f*, personaje *m*, celebridad *f*

personalize [ˈpərsənəˌlaɪz] *vt* **-ized; -izing** : personalizar

personally [ˈpərsənəli] *adv* **1** : personalmente, en persona ⟨I'll do it personally : lo haré personalmente⟩ **2** : como persona ⟨personally she's very amiable : como persona es muy amable⟩ **3** : personalmente ⟨personally, I don't believe it : yo, personalmente, no me lo creo⟩

personification [pərˌsɑnəfəˈkeɪʃən] *n* : personificación *f*

personify [pərˈsɑnəˌfaɪ] *vt* **-fied; -fying** : personificar

personnel [ˌpərsənˈɛl] *n* : personal *m*

perspective [pərˈspɛktɪv] *n* : perspectiva *f*

perspicacious [ˌpərspəˈkeɪʃəs] *adj* : perspicaz

perspiration [ˌpərspəˈreɪʃən] *n* : transpiración *f*, sudor *m*

perspire [pərˈspaɪr] *vi* **-spired; -spiring** : transpirar, sudar

persuade [pərˈsweɪd] *vt* **-suaded; -suading** : persuadir, convencer

persuasion [pərˈsweɪʒən] *n* : persuasión *f*

persuasive [pərˈsweɪsɪv, -zɪv] *adj* : persuasivo — **persuasively** *adv*

persuasiveness [pərˈsweɪsɪvnəs, -zɪv-] *n* : persuasión *f*

pert [ˈpərt] *adj* **1** SAUCY : descarado, impertinente **2** JAUNTY : alegre, animado ⟨a pert little hat : un sombrero coqueto⟩

pertain [pərˈteɪn] *vi* **1** BELONG : pertenecer (a) **2** RELATE : estar relacionado (con)

pertinence [ˈpərtənənts] *n* : pertinencia *f*

pertinent [ˈpərtənənt] *adj* : pertinente

perturb [pərˈtərb] *vt* : perturbar

perusal [pəˈruːzəl] *n* : lectura *f* cuidadosa

peruse [pəˈruːz] *vt* **-rused; -rusing** **1** READ : leer con cuidado **2** SCAN : recorrer con la vista ⟨he perused the newspaper : echó un vistazo al periódico⟩

Peruvian [pəˈruːviən] *n* : peruano *m*, -na *f* — **Peruvian** *adj*

pervade [pərˈveɪd] *vt* **-vaded; -vading** : penetrar, difundirse por

pervasive [pərˈveɪsɪv, -zɪv] *adj* : penetrante

perverse [pərˈvərs] *adj* **1** CORRUPT : perverso, corrompido **2** STUBBORN : obstinado, porfiado, terco (sin razón) — **perversely** *adv*

perversion [pərˈvərʒən] *n* : perversión *f*

perversity [pərˈvərsəṭi] *n, pl* **-ties** **1** CORRUPTION : corrupción *f* **2** STUBBORNNESS : obstinación *f*, terquedad *f*

pervert¹ [pərˈvərt] *vt* **1** DISTORT : pervertir, distorsionar **2** CORRUPT : pervertir, corromper

pervert² [ˈpərˌvərt] *n* : pervertido *m*, -da *f*

pesky [ˈpɛski] *adj* : molestoso, molesto

peso [ˈpeɪˌsoː] *n, pl* **-sos** : peso *m*

pessimism [ˈpɛsəˌmɪzəm] *n* : pesimismo *m*

pessimist [ˈpɛsəmɪst] *n* : pesimista *mf*

pessimistic [ˌpɛsəˈmɪstɪk] *adj* : pesimista

pest [ˈpɛst] *n* **1** NUISANCE : peste *f*; latoso *m*, -sa *f fam* ⟨to be a pest : dar (la) lata⟩ **2** : insecto *m* nocivo, animal *m* nocivo ⟨the squirrels were pests : las ardillas eran una plaga⟩

pester [ˈpɛstər] *vt* **-tered; -tering** : molestar, fastidiar

pesticide [ˈpɛstəˌsaɪd] *n* : pesticida *m*

pestilence [ˈpɛstələnts] *n* : pestilencia *f*, peste *f*

pestle [ˈpɛsəl, ˈpɛstəl] *n* : mano *f* de mortero, mazo *m*, maja *f*

pet¹ [ˈpɛt] *vt* **petted; petting** : acariciar

pet² *n* **1** : animal *m* doméstico **2** FAVORITE : favorito *m*, -ta *f*

petal [ˈpɛṭəl] *n* : pétalo *m*

petite [pəˈtiːt] *adj* : pequeña, menuda, chiquita

petition¹ [pəˈtɪʃən] *vt* : peticionar

petition² *n* : petición *f*

petitioner [pəˈtɪʃənər] *n* : peticionario *m*, -ria *f*

petrify [ˈpɛtrəˌfaɪ] *vt* **-fied; -fying** : petrificar

petroleum [pəˈtroːliəm] *n* : petróleo *m*

petticoat [ˈpɛṭiˌkoːt] *n* : enagua *f*, fondo *m Mex*

pettiness [ˈpɛṭinəs] *n* **1** INSIGNIFICANCE : insignificancia *f* **2** MEANNESS : mezquindad *f*

petty [ˈpɛṭi] *adj* **-tier; -est** **1** MINOR : menor ⟨petty cash : dinero para gastos menores⟩ **2** INSIGNIFICANT : insignificante, trivial, nimio **3** MEAN : mezquino

petty officer *n* : suboficial *mf*

petulance [ˈpɛʧələnts] *n* : irritabilidad *f*, mal genio *m*

petulant [ˈpɛʧələnt] *adj* : irritable, de mal genio

petunia [pɪˈtuːnjə, -ˈtjuː-] *n* : petunia *f*

pew [ˈpjuː] *n* : banco *m* (de iglesia)

pewter ['pju:ṭər] *n* : peltre *m*
pH [,pi:'eɪtʃ] *n* : pH *m*
phallic ['fælɪk] *adj* : fálico
phallus ['fæləs] *n, pl* **-li** ['fæ,laɪ] *or* **-luses** : falo *m*
phantasy ['fæntəsi] → **fantasy**
phantom ['fæntəm] *n* : fantasma *m*
pharaoh ['fɛr,o:, 'feɪ,ro:] *n* : faraón *m*
pharmaceutical [,fɑrmə'su:ṭɪkəl] *adj* : farmacéutico
pharmacist ['fɑrməsɪst] *n* : farmacéutico *m*, -ca *f*
pharmacology [,fɑrmə'kɑləʤi] *n* : farmacología *f*
pharmacy ['fɑrməsi] *n, pl* **-cies** : farmacia *f*
pharynx ['færɪŋks] *n, pl* **pharynges** [fə'rɪn,ʤi:z] : faringe *f*
phase[1] ['feɪz] *vt* **phased; phasing 1** SYNCHRONIZE : sincronizar, poner en fase **2** STAGGER : escalonar **3 to phase in** : introducir progresivamente **4 to phase out** : retirar progresivamente, dejar de producir
phase[2] *n* **1** : fase *f* (de la luna, etc.) **2** STAGE : fase *f*, etapa *f*
pheasant ['fɛzənt] *n, pl* **-ant** *or* **-ants** : faisán *m*
phenomenal [fɪ'nɑmənəl] *adj* : extraordinario, excepcional
phenomenon [fɪ'nɑmə,nɑn, -nən] *n, pl* **-na** [-nə] *or* **-nons 1** : fenómeno *m* **2** *pl* **-nons** PRODIGY : fenómeno *m*, prodigio *m*
philanthropic [,fɪlən'θrɑpɪk] *adj* : filantrópico
philanthropist [fə'lænʈθrəpɪst] *n* : filántropo *m*, -pa *f*
philanthropy [fə'lænʈθrəpi] *n, pl* **-pies** : filantropía *f*
philately [fə'lætəli] *n* : filatelia *f*
philodendron [,fɪlə'dɛndrən] *n, pl* **-drons** *or* **-dra** [-drə] : arácea *f*
philosopher [fə'lɑsəfər] *n* : filósofo *m*, -fa *f*
philosophic [,fɪlə'sɑfɪk] *or* **philosophical** [-fɪkəl] *adj* : filosófico — **philosophically** [-kli] *adv*
philosophize [fə'lɑsə,faɪz] *vi* **-phized; -phizing** : filosofar
philosophy [fə'lɑsəfi] *n, pl* **-phies** : filosofía *f*
phlebitis [flɪ'baɪṭəs] *n* : flebitis *f*
phlegm ['flɛm] *n* : flema *f*
phlox ['flɑks] *n, pl* **phlox** *or* **phloxes** : polemonio *m*
phobia ['fo:biə] *n* : fobia *f*
phoenix ['fi:nɪks] *n* : fénix *m*
phone[1] ['fo:n] *v* → **telephone**[1]
phone[2] *n* → **telephone**[2]
phoneme ['fo:,ni:m] *n* : fonema *m*
phonetic [fə'nɛṭɪk] *adj* : fonético
phonetics [fə'nɛṭɪks] *n* : fonética *f*
phonics ['fɑnɪks] *n* : método *m* fonético de aprender a leer
phonograph ['fo:nə,græf] *n* : fonógrafo *m*, tocadiscos *m*
phony[1] *or* **phoney** ['fo:ni] *adj* **-nier; -est** : falso
phony[2] *or* **phoney** *n, pl* **-nies** : farsante *mf*; charlatán *m*, -tana *f*
phosphate ['fɑs,feɪt] *n* : fosfato *m*
phosphorescence [,fɑsfə'rɛsənʈs] *n* : fosforescencia *f*
phosphorescent [,fɑsfə'rɛsənt] *adj* : fosforescente — **phosphorescently** *adv*
phosphorus ['fɑsfərəs] *n* : fósforo *m*
photo ['fo:ṭo:] *n, pl* **-tos** : foto *f*
photocopier ['fo:ṭo,kɑpiər] *n* : fotocopiadora *f*
photocopy[1] ['fo:ṭo,kɑpi] *vt* **-copied; -copying** : fotocopiar
photocopy[2] *n, pl* **-copies** : fotocopia *f*
photoelectric [,fo:ṭoɪ'lɛktrɪk] *adj* : fotoeléctrico
photogenic [,fo:ṭə'ʤɛnɪk] *adj* : fotogénico
photograph[1] ['fo:ṭə,græf] *vt* : fotografiar
photograph[2] *n* : fotografía *f*, foto *f* ⟨to take a photograph of : tomarle una fotografía a, tomar una fotografía de⟩
photographer [fə'tɑgrəfər] *n* : fotógrafo *m*, -fa *f*
photographic [,fo:ṭə'græfɪk] *adj* : fotográfico — **photographically** [-fɪkli] *adv*
photography [fə'tɑgrəfi] *n* : fotografía *f*
photosynthesis [,fo:ṭo'sɪnʈθəsɪs] *n* : fotosíntesis *f*
photosynthetic [,fo:ṭosɪn'θɛṭɪk] *adj* : fotosintético, de fotosíntesis
phrase[1] ['freɪz] *vt* **phrased; phrasing** : expresar
phrase[2] *n* : frase *f*, locución *f* ⟨to coin a phrase : para decirlo así⟩
phylum ['faɪləm] *n, pl* **-la** [-lə] : phylum *m*
physical[1] ['fɪzɪkəl] *adj* **1** : físico ⟨physical laws : leyes físicas⟩ **2** MATERIAL : material, físico **3** BODILY : físico, corpóreo — **physically** [-kli] *adv*
physical[2] *n* CHECKUP : chequeo *m*, reconocimiento *m* médico
physician [fə'zɪʃən] *n* : médico *m*, -ca *f*
physicist ['fɪzəsɪst] *n* : físico *m*, -ca *f*
physics ['fɪzɪks] *ns & pl* : física *f*
physiognomy [,fɪzi'ɑgnəmi] *n, pl* **-mies** : fisonomía *f*
physiological ['fɪziə'lɑʤɪkəl] *or* **physiologic** [-ʤɪk] *adj* : fisiológico
physiologist [,fɪzi'ɑləʤɪst] *n* : fisiólogo *m*, -ga *f*
physiology [,fɪzi'ɑləʤi] *n* : fisiología *f*
physique [fə'zi:k] *n* : físico *m*
pi ['paɪ] *n, pl* **pis** ['paɪz] : pi *f*
pianist [pi'ænɪst, 'pi:ənɪst] *n* : pianista *mf*
piano [pi'æno:] *n, pl* **-anos** : piano *m*
piazza [pi'æzə, -'ɑtsə] *n, pl* **-zas** *or* **-ze** [-'ɑt,seɪ] : plaza *f*
picaresque [,pɪkə'rɛsk, ,pi:-] *adj* : picaresco
picayune [,pɪki'ju:n] *adj* : trivial, nimio, insignificante
piccolo ['pɪkə,lo:] *n, pl* **-los** : flautín *m*
pick[1] ['pɪk] *vt* **1** : picar, labrar (con un pico) ⟨he picked the hard soil : picó la

tierra dura> **2** : quitar, sacar (poco a poco) <to pick meat off the bones : quitar pedazos de carne de los huesos> **3** : recoger, arrancar (frutas, flores, etc.) **4** SELECT : escoger, elegir **5** PROVOKE : provocar <to pick a quarrel : buscar pleito, buscar pelea> **6 to pick a lock** : forzar una cerradura **7 to pick someone's pocket** : robarle algo del bolsillo de alguien <someone picked my pocket! : ¡me robaron la cartera del bolsillo!> — *vi* **1** NIBBLE : picar, picotear **2 to pick and choose** : ser exigente **3 to pick at** : tocar, rascarse (una herida, etc.) **4 to pick on** TEASE : mofarse de, atormentar

pick[2] *n* **1** CHOICE : selección *f* **2** BEST : lo mejor <the pick of the crop : la crema y nata> **3** → **pickax**

pickax [ˈpɪkˌæks] *n* : pico *m*, zapapico *m*, piqueta *f*

pickerel [ˈpɪkərəl] *n, pl* **-el** *or* **-els** : lucio *m* pequeño

picket[1] [ˈpɪkət] *v* : piquetear

picket[2] *n* **1** STAKE : estaca *f* **2** STRIKER : huelguista *mf*, integrante *mf* de un piquete

pickle[1] [ˈpɪkəl] *vt* **-led; -ling** : encurtir, escabechar

pickle[2] *n* **1** BRINE : escabeche *m* **2** GHERKIN : pepinillo *m* (encurtido) **3** JAM, TROUBLE : lío *m*, apuro *m*

pickpocket [ˈpɪkˌpɑkət] *n* : carterista *mf*

pickup [ˈpɪkˌəp] *n* **1** IMPROVEMENT : mejora *f* **2** *or* **pickup truck** : camioneta *f*

pick up *vt* **1** LIFT : levantar **2** TIDY : arreglar, ordenar — *vi* IMPROVE : mejorar

picnic[1] [ˈpɪkˌnɪk] *vi* **-nicked; -nicking** : ir de picnic

picnic[2] *n* : picnic *m*

pictorial [pɪkˈtoriəl] *adj* : pictórico

picture[1] [ˈpɪktʃər] *vt* **-tured; -turing 1** DEPICT : representar **2** IMAGINE : imaginarse <can you picture it? : ¿te lo puedes imaginar?>

picture[2] *n* **1** : cuadro *m* (pintado o dibujado), ilustración *f*, fotografía *f* **2** DESCRIPTION : descripción *f* **3** IMAGE : imagen *f* <he's the picture of his father : es la viva imagen de su padre> **4** MOVIE : película *f*

picturesque [ˌpɪktʃəˈrɛsk] *adj* : pintoresco

pie [ˈpaɪ] *n* : pastel *m* (con fruta o carne), empanada *f* (con carne)

piebald [ˈpaɪˌbɔld] *adj* : picazo, pío

piece[1] [ˈpiːs] *vt* **pieced; piecing 1** PATCH : parchar, arreglar **2 to piece together** : construir pieza por pieza

piece[2] *n* **1** FRAGMENT : trozo *m*, pedazo *m* **2** COMPONENT : pieza *f* <a three-piece suit : un traje de tres piezas> **3** UNIT : pieza *f* <a piece of fruit : una (pieza de) fruta> **4** WORK : obra *f*, pieza *f* (de música, etc.) **5** (*in board games*) : ficha *f*, pieza *f*, figura *f* (en ajedrez)

piecemeal[1] [ˈpiːsˌmiːl] *adv* : poco a poco, por partes

piecemeal[2] *adj* : hecho poco a poco, poco sistemático

pied [ˈpaɪd] *adj* : pío

pier [ˈpɪr] *n* **1** : pila *f* (de un puente) **2** WHARF : muelle *m*, atracadero *m*, embarcadero *m* **3** PILLAR : pilar *m*

pierce [ˈpɪrs] *vt* **pierced; piercing 1** PENETRATE : atravesar, traspasar, penetrar (en) <the bullet pierced his leg : la bala le atravesó la pierna> <to pierce one's heart : traspasarle el corazón a uno> **2** PERFORATE : perforar, agujerear (las orejas, etc.) **3 to pierce the silence** : desgarrar el silencio

piety [ˈpaɪət̬i] *n, pl* **-eties** : piedad *f*

pig [ˈpɪg] *n* **1** HOG, SWINE : cerdo *m*, -da *f*; puerco *m*, -ca *f* **2** SLOB : persona *f* desaliñada; cerdo *m*, -da *f* **3** GLUTTON : glotón *m*, -tona *f* **4** *or* **pig iron** : lingote *m* de hierro

pigeon [ˈpɪdʒən] *n* : paloma *f*

pigeonhole [ˈpɪdʒənˌhoːl] *n* : casilla *f*

pigeon–toed [ˈpɪdʒənˌtoːd] *adj* : patituerto

piggish [ˈpɪgɪʃ] *adj* **1** GREEDY : glotón **2** DIRTY : cochino, sucio

piggyback [ˈpɪgiˌbæk] *adv & adj* : a cuestas

pigheaded [ˈpɪgˌhɛdəd] *adj* : terco, obstinado

piglet [ˈpɪglət] *n* : cochinillo *m*; lechón *m*, -chona *f*

pigment [ˈpɪgmənt] *n* : pigmento *m*

pigmentation [ˌpɪgmənˈteɪʃən] *n* : pigmentación *f*

pigmy → **pygmy**

pigpen [ˈpɪgˌpɛn] *n* : chiquero *m*, pocilga *f*

pigsty [ˈpɪgˌstaɪ] → **pigpen**

pigtail [ˈpɪgˌteɪl] *n* : coleta *f*, trenza *f*

pike [ˈpaɪk] *n, pl* **pike** *or* **pikes 1** : lucio *m* (pez) **2** LANCE : pica *f* **3** → **turnpike**

pile[1] [ˈpaɪl] *v* **piled; piling** *vt* : amontonar, apilar — *vi* **to pile up** : amontonarse, acumularse

pile[2] *n* **1** STAKE : pilote *m* **2** HEAP : montón *m*, pila *f* **3** NAP : pelo *m* (de telas)

piles [ˈpaɪlz] *npl* HEMORRHOIDS : hemorroides *fpl*, almorranas *fpl*

pilfer [ˈpɪlfər] *vt* : robar (cosas pequeñas), ratear

pilgrim [ˈpɪlgrəm] *n* : peregrino *m*, -na *f*

pilgrimage [ˈpɪlgrəmɪdʒ] *n* : peregrinación *f*

pill [ˈpɪl] *n* : pastilla *f*, píldora *f*

pillage[1] [ˈpɪlɪdʒ] *vt* **-laged; -laging** : saquear

pillage[2] *n* : saqueo *m*

pillar [ˈpɪlər] *n* : pilar *m*, columna *f*

pillory [ˈpɪləri] *n, pl* **-ries** : picota *f*

pillow [ˈpɪˌloː] *n* : almohada *f*

pillowcase [ˈpɪˌloːˌkeɪs] *n* : funda *f*

pilot[1] [ˈpaɪlət] *vt* : pilotar, pilotear

pilot[2] *n* : piloto *mf*

pilot light *n* : piloto *m*

pimento [pəˈmɛnˌtoː] → **pimiento**

pimiento [pəˈmɛnˌtoː, -ˈmjɛn-] *n, pl* **-tos** : pimiento *m* morrón
pimp [ˈpɪmp] *n* : proxeneta *m*
pimple [ˈpɪmpəl] *n* : grano *m*
pimply [ˈpɪmpəli] *adj* **-plier; -est** : cubierto de granos
pin¹ [ˈpɪn] *vt* **pinned; pinning 1** FASTEN : prender, sujetar (con alfileres) **2** HOLD, IMMOBILIZE : inmovilizar, sujetar **3 to pin one's hopes on** : poner sus esperanzas en
pin² *n* **1** : alfiler *m* ⟨safety pin : alfiler de gancho⟩ ⟨a bobby pin : una horquilla⟩ **2** BROOCH : alfiler *m*, broche *m*, prendedor *m* **3** *or* **bowling pin** : bolo *m*
pinafore [ˈpɪnəˌfor] *n* : delantal *m*
pincer [ˈpɪntsər] *n* **1** CLAW : pinza *f* (de una langosta, etc.) **2 pincers** *npl* : pinzas *fpl*, tenazas *fpl*, tenaza *f*
pinch¹ [ˈpɪntʃ] *vt* **1** : pellizcar ⟨she pinched my cheek : me pellizcó el cachete⟩ **2** STEAL : robar — *vi* : apretar ⟨my shoes pinch : me aprietan los zapatos⟩
pinch² *n* **1** EMERGENCY : emergencia *f* ⟨in a pinch : en caso necesario⟩ **2** PAIN : dolor *m*, tormento *m* **3** SQUEEZE : pellizco *m* (con los dedos) **4** BIT : pizca *f*, pellizco *m* ⟨a pinch of cinnamon : una pizca de canela⟩
pinch hitter *n* **1** SUBSTITUTE : sustituto *m*, -ta *f* **2** : bateador *m* emergente (en beisbol)
pincushion [ˈpɪnˌkuʃən] *n* : acerico *m*, alfiletero *m*
pine¹ [ˈpaɪn] *vi* **pined; pining 1 to pine away** : languidecer, consumirse **2 to pine for** : añorar, suspirar por
pine² *n* **1** : pino *m* (árbol) **2** : madera *f* de pino
pineapple [ˈpaɪnˌæpəl] *n* : piña *f*, ananá *m*, ananás *m*
ping-pong [ˈpɪŋˌpɑŋ, -ˌpɔŋ] *n* : ping-pong *m*
pinion¹ [ˈpɪnjən] *vt* : sujetar los brazos de, inmovilizar
pinion² *n* : piñón *m*
pink¹ [ˈpɪŋk] *adj* : rosa, rosado
pink² *n* **1** : clavelito *m* (flor) **2** : rosa *m*, rosado *m* (color) **3 to be in the pink** : estar en plena forma, rebosar de salud
pinkeye [ˈpɪŋkˌaɪ] *n* : conjuntivitis *f* aguda
pinkish [ˈpɪŋkɪʃ] *adj* : rosáceo
pinnacle [ˈpɪnɪkəl] *n* **1** : pináculo *m* (de un edificio) **2** PEAK : cima *f*, cumbre *f* (de una montaña) **3** ACME : pináculo *m*, cúspide *f*, apogeo *m*
pinpoint [ˈpɪnˌpɔɪnt] *vt* : precisar, localizar con precisión
pint [ˈpaɪnt] *n* : pinta *f*
pinto [ˈpɪnˌtoː] *n, pl* **pintos** : caballo *m* pinto
pinworm [ˈpɪnˌwərm] *n* : oxiuro *m*
pioneer¹ [ˌpaɪəˈnɪr] *vt* : promover, iniciar, introducir
pioneer² *n* : pionero *m*, -ra *f*
pious [ˈpaɪəs] *adj* **1** DEVOUT : piadoso, devoto **2** SANCTIMONIOUS : beato
piously [ˈpaɪəsli] *adv* **1** DEVOUTLY : piadosamente **2** SANCTIMONIOUSLY : santurronamente
pipe¹ [ˈpaɪp] *v* **piped; piping** *vi* : hablar en voz chillona — *vt* **1** PLAY : tocar (el caramillo o la flauta) **2** : conducir por tuberías ⟨to pipe water : transportar el agua por tubería⟩
pipe² *n* **1** : caramillo *m* (instrumento musical) **2** BAGPIPE : gaita *f* **3** : tubo *m*, caño *m* ⟨gas pipes : tubería de gas⟩ **4** : pipa *f* (para fumar)
pipeline [ˈpaɪpˌlaɪn] *n* **1** : conducto *m*, oleoducto *m* (para petróleo), gasoducto *m* (para gas) **2** CONDUIT : vía *f* (de información, etc.)
piper [ˈpaɪpər] *n* : músico *m*, -ca *f* que toca el caramillo o la gaita
piping [ˈpaɪpɪŋ] *n* **1** : música *f* del caramillo o de la gaita **2** TRIM : cordoncillo *m*, ribete *m* con cordón
piquant [ˈpiːkənt, ˈpɪkwənt] *adj* **1** SPICY : picante **2** INTRIGUING : intrigante, estimulante
pique¹ [ˈpiːk] *vt* **piqued; piquing 1** IRRITATE : picar, irritar **2** AROUSE : despertar (la curiosidad, etc.)
pique² *n* : pique *m*, resentimiento *m*
piracy [ˈpaɪrəsi] *n, pl* **-cies** : piratería *f*
piranha [pəˈrɑnə, -ˈrɑnjə, -ˈrænjə] *n* : piraña *f*
pirate¹ [ˈpaɪrət] *n* : pirata *mf*
pirate² *vt* **-rated; -rating** : piratear (software, etc.)
pirouette [ˌpɪrəˈwɛt] *n* : pirueta *f*
pis → **pi**
Pisces [ˈpaɪˌsiːz, ˈpɪ-; ˈpɪsˌkeɪs] *n* : Piscis *mf*
pistachio [pəˈstæʃiˌoː, -ˈstɑ-] *n, pl* **-chios** : pistacho *m*
pistil [ˈpɪstəl] *n* : pistilo *m*
pistol [ˈpɪstəl] *n* : pistola *f*
piston [ˈpɪstən] *n* : pistón *m*, émbolo *m*
pit¹ [ˈpɪt] *v* **pitted; pitting** *vt* **1** : marcar de hoyos, picar (una superficie) **2** : deshuesar (una fruta) **3 to pit against** : enfrentar a, oponer a — *vi* : quedar marcado
pit² *n* **1** HOLE : fosa *f*, hoyo *m* ⟨a bottomless pit : un pozo sin fondo⟩ **2** MINE : mina *f* **3** : foso *m* ⟨orchestra pit : foso orquestal⟩ **4** POCKMARK : marca *f* (en la cara), cicatriz *f* de viruela **5** STONE : hueso *m*, pepa *f* (de una fruta) **6 pit of the stomach** : boca *f* del estómago
pitch¹ [ˈpɪtʃ] *vt* **1** SET UP : montar, armar (una tienda) **2** THROW : lanzar, arrojar **3** ADJUST, SET : dar el tono de (un discurso, un instrumento musical) — *vi* **1** *or* **pitch forward** FALL : caerse **2** LURCH : cabecear (dícese de un barco o un avión), dar bandazos
pitch² *n* **1** LURCHING : cabezada *f*, cabeceo *m* (de un barco o un avión) **2** SLOPE : (grado de) inclinación *f*, pendiente *f* **3** : tono *m* (en música) ⟨per-

fect pitch : oído absoluto⟩ **4** THROW : lanzamiento *m* **5** DEGREE : grado *m*, nivel *m*, punto *m* ⟨the excitement reached a high pitch : la excitación llegó a un punto culminante⟩ **6** *or* **sales pitch** : presentación *f* (de un vendedor) **7** TAR : pez *f*, brea *f*

pitcher [ˈpɪʧər] *n* **1** JUG : jarra *f*, jarro *m*, cántaro *m*, pichel *m* **2** : lanzador *m*, -dora *f* (en béisbol, etc.)

pitchfork [ˈpɪʧˌfɔrk] *n* : horquilla *f*, horca *f*

piteous [ˈpɪṭiəs] *adj* : lastimoso, lastimero — **piteously** *adv*

pitfall [ˈpɪtˌfɔl] *n* : peligro *m* (poco obvio), dificultad *f*

pith [ˈpɪθ] *n* **1** : médula *f* (de una planta) **2** CORE : meollo *m*, entraña *f*

pithy [ˈpɪθi] *adj* **pithier; -est** : conciso y sustancioso ⟨pithy comments : comentarios sucintos⟩

pitiable [ˈpɪṭiəbəl] → **pitiful**

pitiful [ˈpɪṭɪfəl] *adj* **1** LAMENTABLE : lastimero, lastimoso, lamentable **2** CONTEMPTIBLE : despreciable, lamentable — **pitifully** [-fli] *adv*

pitiless [ˈpɪṭɪləs] *adj* : despiadado — **pitilessly** *adv*

pittance [ˈpɪtənts] *n* : miseria *f*

pituitary [pəˈtu:əˌtɛri, -ˈtju:-] *adj* : pituitario

pity¹ [ˈpɪṭi] *vt* **pitied; pitying** : compadecer, compadecerse de

pity² *n, pl* **pities** **1** COMPASSION : compasión *f*, piedad *f* **2** SHAME : lástima *f*, pena *f* ⟨what a pity! : ¡qué lástima!⟩

pivot¹ [ˈpɪvət] *vi* **1** : girar sobre un eje **2** **to pivot on** : girar sobre, depender de

pivot² *n* : pivote *m*

pivotal [ˈpɪvəṭəl] *adj* : fundamental, central

pixie *or* **pixy** [ˈpɪksi] *n, pl* **pixies** : elfo *m*, hada *f*

pizza [ˈpi:tsə] *n* : pizza *f*

pizzazz *or* **pizazz** [pəˈzæz] *n* **1** GLAMOR : encanto *m* **2** VITALITY : animación *f*, vitalidad *f*

placard [ˈplækərd, -ˌkɑrd] *n* POSTER : cartel *m*, póster *m*, afiche *m*

placate [ˈpleɪˌkeɪt, ˈplæ-] *vt* **-cated; -cating** : aplacar, apaciguar

place¹ [ˈpleɪs] *vt* **placed; placing** **1** PUT, SET : poner, colocar **2** SITUATE : situar, ubicar, emplazar ⟨to be well placed : estar bien situado⟩ ⟨to place in a job : colocar en un trabajo⟩ **3** IDENTIFY, RECALL : identificar, ubicar, recordar ⟨I can't place him : no lo ubico⟩ **4** **to place an order** : hacer un pedido

place² *n* **1** SPACE : sitio *m*, lugar *m* ⟨there's no place to sit : no hay sitio para sentarse⟩ **2** LOCATION, SPOT : lugar *m*, sitio *m*, parte *f* ⟨place of work : lugar de trabajo⟩ ⟨our summer place : nuestra casa de verano⟩ ⟨all over the place : por todas partes⟩ **3** RANK : lugar *m*, puesto *m* ⟨he took first place : ganó el primer lugar⟩ **4** POSITION : lugar *m* ⟨everything in its place : todo en su debido lugar⟩ ⟨to feel out of place : sentirse fuera de lugar⟩ **5** SEAT : asiento *m*, cubierto *m* (a la mesa) **6** JOB : puesto *m* **7** ROLE : papel *m*, lugar *m* ⟨to change places : cambiarse los papeles⟩ **8** **to take place** : tener lugar **9** **to take the place of** : sustituir a

placebo [pləˈsi:ˌbo:] *n, pl* **-bos** : placebo *m*

placement [ˈpleɪsmənt] *n* : colocación *f*

placenta [pləˈsɛntə] *n, pl* **-tas** *or* **-tae** [-ti, -ˌtaɪ] : placenta *f*

placid [ˈplæsəd] *adj* : plácido, tranquilo — **placidly** *adv*

plagiarism [ˈpleɪʤəˌrɪzəm] *n* : plagio *m*

plagiarist [ˈpleɪʤərɪst] *n* : plagiario *m*, -ria *f*

plagiarize [ˈpleɪʤəˌraɪz] *vt* **-rized; -rizing** : plagiar

plague¹ [ˈpleɪg] *vt* **plagued; plaguing** **1** AFFLICT : plagar, afligir **2** HARASS : acosar, atormentar

plague² *n* **1** : plaga *f* (de insectos, etc.) **2** : peste *f* (en medicina)

plaid¹ [ˈplæd] *adj* : escocés, de cuadros ⟨a plaid skirt : una falda escocesa⟩

plaid² *n* TARTAN : tela *f* escocesa, tartán *m*

plain¹ [ˈpleɪn] *adj* **1** SIMPLE, UNADORNED : liso, sencillo, sin adornos **2** CLEAR : claro ⟨in plain language : en palabras claras⟩ **3** FRANK : franco, puro ⟨the plain truth : la pura verdad⟩ **4** HOMELY : ordinario, poco atractivo **5** **in plain sight** : a la vista de todos

plain² *n* : llanura *f*, llano *m*, planicie *f*

plainly [ˈpleɪnli] *adv* **1** CLEARLY : claramente **2** FRANKLY : francamente, con franqueza **3** SIMPLY : sencillamente

plaintiff [ˈpleɪntɪf] *n* : demandante *mf*

plaintive [ˈpleɪntɪv] *adj* MOURNFUL : lastimero, plañidero

plait¹ [ˈpleɪt, ˈplæt] *vt* **1** PLEAT : plisar **2** BRAID : trenzar

plait² *n* **1** PLEAT : pliegue *m* **2** BRAID : trenza *f*

plan¹ [ˈplæn] *v* **planned; planning** *vt* **1** : planear, proyectar, planificar ⟨to plan a trip : planear un viaje⟩ ⟨to plan a city : planificar una ciudad⟩ **2** INTEND : tener planeado, proyectar — *vi* : hacer planes

plan² *n* **1** DIAGRAM : plano *m*, esquema *m* **2** SCHEME : plan *m*, proyecto *m*, programa *m* ⟨to draw up a plan : elaborar un proyecto⟩

plane¹ [ˈpleɪn] *vt* **planed; planing** : cepillar (madera)

plane² *adj* : plano

plane³ *n* **1** : plano *m* (en matemáticas, etc.) **2** LEVEL : nivel *m* **3** : cepillo *m* (de carpintero) **4** → **airplane**

planet [ˈplænət] *n* : planeta *f*

planetarium [ˌplænəˈtɛriəm] *n, pl* **-iums** *or* **-ia** [-iə] : planetario *m*

planetary [ˈplænəˌtɛri] *adj* : planetario

plank [ˈplæŋk] *n* **1** BOARD : tablón *m*, tabla *f* **2** : artículo *m*, punto *m* (de una plataforma política)

plankton ['plæŋktən] *n* : plancton *m*
plant[1] ['plænt] *vt* **1** : plantar, sembrar (semillas) <planted with flowers : plantado de flores> **2** PLACE : plantar, colocar <to plant an idea : inculcar una idea>
plant[2] *n* **1** : planta *f* <leafy plants : plantas frondosas> **2** FACTORY : planta *f*, fábrica *f* <hydroelectric plant : planta hidroeléctrica> **3** MACHINERY : maquinaria *f*, equipo *m*
plantain ['plæntən] *n* **1** : llantén *m* (mala hierba) **2** : plátano *m*, plátano *m* macho *Mex* (fruta)
plantation [plæn'teɪʃən] *n* : plantación *f*, hacienda *f* <a coffee plantation : un cafetal>
planter ['plæntər] *n* **1** : hacendado *m*, -da *f* (de una hacienda) **2** FLOWERPOT : tiesto *m*, maceta *f*
plaque ['plæk] *n* **1** TABLET : placa *f* **2** : placa *f* (dental)
plasma ['plæzmə] *n* : plasma *m*
plaster[1] ['plæstər] *vt* **1** : enyesar, revocar (con yeso) **2** COVER : cubrir, llenar <a wall plastered with notices : una pared cubierta de avisos>
plaster[2] *n* **1** : yeso *m*, revoque *m* (para paredes, etc.) **2** : escayola *f*, yeso *m* (en medicina) **3 plaster of Paris** ['pærɪs] : yeso *m* mate
plaster cast *n* : vaciado *m* de yeso
plasterer ['plæstərər] *n* : revocador *m*, -dora *f*
plastic[1] ['plæstɪk] *adj* **1** : de plástico **2** PLIABLE : plástico, flexible **3 plastic surgery** : cirugía *f* plástica
plastic[2] *n* : plástico *m*
plasticity [plæ'stɪsəṭi] *n, pl* **-ties** : plasticidad *f*
plate[1] ['pleɪt] *vt* **plated; plating** : chapar (en metal)
plate[2] *n* **1** PLAQUE, SHEET : placa *f* <a steel plate : una placa de acero> **2** UTENSILS : vajilla *f* (de metal) <silver plate : vajilla de plata> **3** DISH : plato *m* **4** DENTURES : dentadura *f* postiza **5** ILLUSTRATION : lámina *f* (en un libro) **6 license plate** : matrícula *f*, placa *f* de matrícula
plateau [plæ'to:] *n, pl* **-teaus** *or* **-teaux** [-'to:z] : meseta *f*
platform ['plæt,fɔrm] *n* **1** STAGE : plataforma *f*, estrado *m*, tribuna *f* **2** : andén *m* (de una estación de ferrocarril) **3 political platform** : plataforma *f* política, programa *m* electoral
plating ['pleɪṭɪŋ] *n* **1** : enchapado *m* **2 silver plating** : plateado *m*
platinum ['plætənəm] *n* : platino *m*
platitude ['plæṭə,tu:d, -,tju:d] *n* : lugar *m* común, perogrullada *f*
platonic [plə'tɑnɪk] *adj* : platónico
platoon [plə'tu:n] *n* : sección *f* (en el ejército)
platter ['plæṭər] *n* : fuente *f*
platypus ['plæṭɪpəs, -,pʊs] *n, pl* **platypuses** *or* **platypi** [-,paɪ, -,pi:] : ornitorrinco *m*
plausibility [,plɔzə'bɪləṭi] *n, pl* **-ties** : credibilidad *f*, verosimilitud *f*
plausible ['plɔzəbəl] *adj* : creíble, convincente, verosímil — **plausibly** [-bli] *adv*
play[1] ['pleɪ] *vi* **1** : jugar <to play with a doll : jugar con una muñeca> <to play with an idea : darle vueltas a una idea> **2** FIDDLE, TOY : jugar, juguetear <don't play with your food : no juegues con la comida> **3** : tocar <to play in a band : tocar en un grupo> **4** : actuar (en una obra de teatro) — *vt* **1** : jugar (un deporte, etc.), jugar a (un juego), jugar contra (un contrincante) **2** : tocar (música o un instrumento) **3** PERFORM : interpretar, hacer el papel de (un carácter), representar (una obra de teatro) <she plays the lead : hace el papel principal> **4 to play back** : poner (una grabación) **5 to play down** : minimizar **6 to play up** : resaltar
play[2] *n* **1** GAME, RECREATION : juego *m* <children at play : niños jugando> <a play on words : un juego de palabras> **2** ACTION : juego *m* <the ball is in play : la pelota está en juego> <to bring into play : poner en juego> **3** DRAMA : obra *f* de teatro, pieza *f* (de teatro) **4** MOVEMENT : juego *m* (de la luz, una brisa, etc.) **5** SLACK : juego *m* <there's not enough play in the wheel : la rueda no da lo suficiente>
playacting ['pleɪ,æktɪŋ] *n* : actuación *f*, teatro *m*
player ['pleɪər] *n* **1** : jugador *m*, -dora *f* (en un juego) **2** ACTOR : actor *m*, actriz *f* **3** MUSICIAN : músico *m*, -ca *f*
playful ['pleɪfəl] *adj* **1** FROLICSOME : juguetón **2** JOCULAR : jocoso — **playfully** *adv*
playfulness ['pleɪfəlnəs] *n* : lo juguetón, jocosidad *f*, alegría *f*
playground ['pleɪ,graʊnd] *n* : patio *m* de recreo, jardín *m* para jugar
playhouse ['pleɪ,haʊs] *n* **1** THEATER : teatro *m* **2** : casita *f* de juguete
playing card *n* : naipe *m*, carta *f*
playmate ['pleɪ,meɪt] *n* : compañero *m*, -ra *f* de juego
play–off ['pleɪ,ɔf] *n* : desempate *m*
playpen ['pleɪ,pɛn] *n* : corral *m* (para niños)
plaything ['pleɪ,θɪŋ] *n* : juguete *m*
playwright ['pleɪ,raɪt] *n* : dramaturgo *m*, -ga *f*
plaza ['plæzə, 'plɑ-] *n* **1** SQUARE : plaza *f* **2 shopping plaza** MALL : centro *m* comercial
plea ['pli:] *n* **1** : acto *m* de declararse <he entered a plea of guilty : se declaró culpable> **2** APPEAL : ruego *m*, súplica *f*
plead ['pli:d] *v* **pleaded** *or* **pled** ['plɛd]; **pleading** *vi* **1** : declararse (culpable o inocente) **2 to plead for** : suplicar, implorar — *vt* **1** : alegar, pretextar <he pleaded illness : pretextó la enfermedad> **2 to plead a case** : defender un caso

pleasant [ˈplɛzənt] *adj* : agradable, grato, bueno — **pleasantly** *adv*
pleasantness [ˈplɛzəntnəs] *n* : lo agradable, amenidad *f*
pleasantries [ˈplɛzəntriz] *npl* : cumplidos *mpl*, cortesías *fpl* ⟨to exchange pleasantries : intercambiar cumplidos⟩
please[1] [ˈpli:z] *v* **pleased; pleasing** *vt* **1** GRATIFY : complacer ⟨please yourself! : ¡cómo quieras!⟩ **2** SATISFY : contentar, satisfacer — *vi* **1** SATISFY : complacer, agradar ⟨anxious to please : deseoso de complacer⟩ **2** LIKE : querer ⟨do as you please : haz lo que quieras, haz lo que te parezca⟩
please[2] *adv* : por favor
pleased [ˈpli:zd] *adj* : contento, satisfecho, alegre
pleasing [ˈpli:zɪŋ] *adj* : agradable — **pleasingly** *adv*
pleasurable [ˈplɛʒərəbəl] *adj* PLEASANT : agradable
pleasure [ˈplɛʒər] *n* **1** WISH : deseo *m*, voluntad *f* ⟨at your pleasure : cuando guste⟩ **2** ENJOYMENT : placer *m*, disfrute *m*, goce *m* ⟨with pleasure : con mucho gusto⟩ **3** : placer *m*, gusto *m* ⟨it's a pleasure to be here : me da gusto estar aquí⟩ ⟨the pleasures of reading : los placeres de leer⟩
pleat[1] [ˈpli:t] *vt* : plisar
pleat[2] *n* : pliegue *m*
plebeian [plɪˈbiən] *adj* : ordinario, plebeyo
pledge[1] [ˈplɛʤ] *vt* **pledged; pledging 1** PAWN : empeñar, prendar **2** PROMISE : prometer, jurar
pledge[2] *n* **1** SECURITY : garantía *f*, prenda *f* **2** PROMISE : promesa *f*
plenteous [ˈplɛntiəs] *adj* : copioso, abundante
plentiful [ˈplɛntɪfəl] *adj* : abundante — **plentifully** [-fli] *adv*
plenty [ˈplɛnti] *n* : abundancia *f* ⟨plenty of time : tiempo de sobra⟩ ⟨plenty of visitors : muchos visitantes⟩
plethora [ˈplɛθərə] *n* : plétora *f*
pleurisy [ˈplʊrəsi] *n* : pleuresía *f*
pliable [ˈplaɪəbəl] *adj* : flexible, maleable
pliant [ˈplaɪənt] → **pliable**
pliers [ˈplaɪərz] *npl* : alicates *mpl*, pinzas *fpl*
plight [ˈplaɪt] *n* : situación *f* difícil, apuro *m*
plod [ˈplɑd] *vi* **plodded; plodding 1** TRUDGE : caminar pesadamente y lentamente **2** DRUDGE : trabajar laboriosamente
plot[1] [ˈplɑt] *v* **plotted; plotting** *vt* **1** DEVISE : tramar **2 to plot out** : trazar, determinar (una posición, etc.) — *vi* CONSPIRE : conspirar
plot[2] *n* **1** LOT : terreno *m*, parcela *f*, lote *m* **2** STORY : argumento *m* (en el teatro), trama *f* (en un libro, etc.) **3** CONSPIRACY, INTRIGUE : complot *m*, intriga *f*
plotter [ˈplɑt̬ər] *n* : conspirador *m*, -dora *f*; intrigante *mf*
plow[1] *or* **plough** [ˈplaʊ] *vt* **1** : arar (la tierra) **2 to plow the seas** : surcar los mares
plow[2] *or* **plough** *n* **1** : arado *m* **2** → **snowplow**
plowshare [ˈplaʊˌʃɛr] *n* : reja *f* del arado
ploy [ˈplɔɪ] *n* : estratagema *f*, maniobra *f*
pluck[1] [ˈplʌk] *vt* **1** PICK : arrancar **2** : desplumar (un pollo, etc.) — *vi* **to pluck at** : tirar de
pluck[2] *n* **1** TUG : tirón *m* **2** COURAGE, SPIRIT : valor *m*, ánimo *m*
plucky [ˈplʌki] *adj* **pluckier; -est** : valiente, animoso
plug[1] [ˈplʌg] *vt* **plugged; plugging 1** BLOCK : tapar **2** PROMOTE : hacerle publicidad a, promocionar **3 to plug in** : enchufar
plug[2] *n* **1** STOPPER : tapón *m* **2** : enchufe *m* (eléctrico) **3** ADVERTISEMENT : publicidad *f*, propaganda *f*
plum [ˈplʌm] *n* **1** : ciruela *f* (fruta) **2** : color *m* ciruela **3** PRIZE : premio *m*, algo muy atractivo
plumage [ˈplu:mɪʤ] *n* : plumaje *m*
plumb[1] [ˈplʌm] *vt* **1** : aplomar ⟨to plumb a wall : aplomar una pared⟩ **2** SOUND : sondear, sondar
plumb[2] *adv* **1** VERTICALLY : a plomo, verticalmente **2** EXACTLY : justo, exactamente **3** COMPLETELY : completamente, absolutamente ⟨plumb crazy : loco de remate⟩
plumb[3] *adj* : a plomo
plumb[4] *n or* **plumb line** : plomada *f*
plumber [ˈplʌmər] *n* : plomero *m*, -ra *f*; fontanero *m*, -ra *f*
plumbing [ˈplʌmɪŋ] *n* **1** : plomería *f*, fontanería *f* (trabajo del plomero) **2** PIPES : cañería *f*, tubería *f*
plume [ˈplu:m] *n* **1** FEATHER : pluma *f* **2** TUFT : penacho *m* (en un sombrero, etc.)
plumed [ˈplu:md] *adj* : con plumas ⟨white-plumed birds : aves de plumaje blanco⟩
plummet [ˈplʌmət] *vi* : caer en picada, desplomarse
plump[1] [ˈplʌmp] *vi or* **to plump down** : dejarse caer (pesadamente)
plump[2] *adv* **1** STRAIGHT : a plomo **2** DIRECTLY : directamente, sin rodeos ⟨he ran plump into the door : dio de cara con la puerta⟩
plump[3] *adj* : llenito *fam*, regordete *fam*, rechoncho *fam*
plumpness [ˈplʌmpnəs] *n* : gordura *f*
plunder[1] [ˈplʌndər] *vi* : saquear, robar
plunder[2] *n* : botín *m*
plunderer [ˈplʌndərər] *n* : saqueador *m*, -dora *f*
plunge[1] [ˈplʌnʤ] *v* **plunged; plunging** *vt* **1** IMMERSE : sumergir **2** THRUST : hundir, clavar — *vi* **1** DIVE : zambullirse (en el agua) **2** : meterse precipitadamente o violentamente ⟨they plunged into war : se enfrascaron en

una guerra⟩ ⟨he plunged into depression : cayó en la depresión⟩ **3** DESCEND : descender en picada ⟨the road plunges dizzily : la calle desciende vertiginosamente⟩

plunge[2] *n* **1** DIVE : zambullida *f* **2** DROP : descenso *m* abrupto ⟨the plunge in prices : el desplome de los precios⟩

plural[1] [ˈplʊrəl] *adj* : plural

plural[2] *n* : plural *m*

plurality [plʊˈrælət̬i] *n, pl* **-ties** : pluralidad *f*

pluralize [ˈplʊrəˌlaɪz] *vt* **-ized; -izing** : pluralizar

plus[1] [ˈplʌs] *adj* **1** POSITIVE : positivo ⟨a plus factor : un factor positivo⟩ **2** (*indicating a quantity in addition*) ⟨a grade of C plus : una calificación entre C y B⟩ ⟨a salary of $30,000 plus : un sueldo de más de $30,000⟩

plus[2] *n* **1** *or* **plus sign** : más *m*, signo *m* de más **2** ADVANTAGE : ventaja *f*

plus[3] *prep* : más (en matemáticas)

plus[4] *conj* AND : y

plush[1] [ˈplʌʃ] *adj* **1** : afelpado **2** LUXURIOUS : lujoso

plush[2] *n* : felpa *f*, peluche *m*

plushy [ˈplʌʃi] *adj* **plushier; -est** : lujoso

Pluto [ˈpluːt̬oː] *n* : Plutón *m*

plutocracy [pluːˈtɑkrəsi] *n, pl* **-cies** : plutocracia *f*

plutonium [pluːˈtoːniəm] *n* : plutonio *m*

ply[1] [ˈplaɪ] *v* **plied; plying** *vt* **1** USE, WIELD : manejar ⟨to ply an ax : manejar un hacha⟩ **2** PRACTICE : ejercer ⟨to ply a trade : ejercer un oficio⟩ **3 to ply with questions** : acosar con preguntas

ply[2] *n, pl* **plies** **1** LAYER : chapa *f* (de madera), capa *f* (de papel) **2** STRAND : cabo *m* (de hilo, etc.)

plywood [ˈplaɪˌwʊd] *n* : contrachapado *m*

pneumatic [nʊˈmæt̬ɪk, njʊ-] *adj* : neumático

pneumonia [nʊˈmoːnjə, njʊ-] *n* : pulmonía *f*, neumonía *f*

poach [ˈpoːʧ] *vt* **1** : cocer a fuego lento ⟨to poach an egg : escalfar un huevo⟩ **2 to poach game** : cazar ilegalmente — *vi* : cazar ilegalmente

poacher [ˈpoːʧər] *n* : cazador *m* furtivo, cazadora *f* furtiva

pock [ˈpɑk] *n* **1** PUSTULE : pústula *f* **2** → **pockmark**

pocket[1] [ˈpɑkət] *vt* **1** : meterse en el bolsillo ⟨he pocketed the pen : se metió la pluma en el bolsillo⟩ **2** STEAL : embolsarse

pocket[2] *n* **1** : bolsillo *m*, bolsa *f Mex* ⟨a coat pocket : el bolsillo de un abrigo⟩ ⟨air pockets : bolsas de aire⟩ **2** CENTER : foco *m*, centro *m* ⟨a pocket of resistance : un foco de resistencia⟩

pocketbook [ˈpɑkətˌbʊk] *n* **1** PURSE : cartera *f*, bolso *m*, bolsa *f Mex* **2** MEANS : recursos *mpl*

pocketknife [ˈpɑkətˌnaɪf] *n, pl* **-knives** : navaja *f*

pocket–size [ˈpɑkətˈsaɪz] *adj* : de bolsillo

pockmark [ˈpɑkˌmɑrk] *n* : cicatriz *f* de viruela, viruela *f*

pod [ˈpɑd] *n* : vaina *f* ⟨pea pod : vaina de guisantes⟩

podiatrist [pəˈdaɪətrɪst, po-] *n* : podólogo *m*, -ga *f*

podiatry [pəˈdaɪətri, po-] *n* : podología *f*, podiatría *f*

podium [ˈpoːdiəm] *n, pl* **-diums** *or* **-dia** [-diə] : podio *m*, estrado *m*, tarima *f*

poem [ˈpoːəm] *n* : poema *m*, poesía *f*

poet [ˈpoːət] *n* : poeta *mf*

poetic [poˈɛt̬ɪk] *or* **poetical** [-t̬ɪkəl] *adj* : poético

poetry [ˈpoːətri] *n* : poesía *f*

pogrom [ˈpoːgrəm, pəˈgrɑm, ˈpɑgrəm] *n* : pogrom *m*

poignancy [ˈpɔɪnjən*t*si] *n, pl* **-cies** : lo conmovedor

poignant [ˈpɔɪnjənt] *adj* **1** PAINFUL : penoso, doloroso ⟨poignant grief : profundo dolor⟩ **2** TOUCHING : conmovedor, emocionante

poinsettia [pɔɪnˈsɛt̬iə, -ˈsɛt̬ə] *n* : flor *f* de Nochebuena

point[1] [ˈpɔɪnt] *vt* **1** SHARPEN : afilar (la punta de) **2** INDICATE : señalar, indicar ⟨to point the way : señalar el camino⟩ **3** AIM : apuntar **4 to point out** : señalar, indicar — *vi* **1 to point at** : señalar (con el dedo) **2 to point to** INDICATE : señalar, indicar

point[2] *n* **1** ITEM : punto *m* ⟨the main points : los puntos principales⟩ **2** QUALITY : cualidad *f* ⟨her good points : sus buenas cualidades⟩ ⟨it's not his strong point : no es su (punto) fuerte⟩ **3** (*indicating a chief idea or meaning*) ⟨it's beside the point : no viene al caso⟩ ⟨to get to the point : ir al grano⟩ ⟨to stick to the point : no salirse del tema⟩ **4** PURPOSE : fin *m*, propósito *m* ⟨there's no point to it : no vale la pena, no sirve para nada⟩ **5** PLACE : punto *m*, lugar *m* ⟨points of interest : puntos interesantes⟩ **6** : punto *m* (en una escala) ⟨boiling point : punto de ebullición⟩ **7** MOMENT : momento *m*, coyuntura *f* ⟨at this point : en este momento⟩ **8** TIP : punta *f* **9** HEADLAND : punta *f*, cabo *m* **10** PERIOD : punto *m* (marca de puntuación) **11** UNIT : punto *m* ⟨he scored 15 points : ganó 15 puntos⟩ ⟨shares fell 10 points : las acciones bajaron 10 enteros⟩ **12 compass points** : puntos *mpl* cardinales **13 decimal point** : punto *m* decimal, coma *f*

point–blank[1] [ˈpɔɪntˈblæŋk] *adv* **1** : a quemarropa ⟨to shoot point-blank : disparar a quemarropa⟩ **2** BLUNTLY, DIRECTLY : a bocajarro, sin rodeos, francamente

point–blank[2] *adj* **1** : a quemarropa ⟨point-blank shots : disparos a quemarropa⟩ **2** BLUNT, DIRECT : directo, franco

pointed ['pɔɪntəd] *adj* **1** POINTY : puntiagudo **2** PERTINENT : atinado **3** CONSPICUOUS : marcado, manifiesto

pointedly ['pɔɪntədli] *adv* : intencionadamente, directamente

pointer ['pɔɪntər] *n* **1** STICK : puntero *m* (para maestros, etc.) **2** INDICATOR, NEEDLE : indicador *m*, aguja *f* **3** : perro *m* de muestra **4** HINT, TIP : consejo *m*

pointless ['pɔɪntləs] *adj* : inútil, ocioso, vano ⟨it's pointless to continue : no tiene sentido continuar⟩

point of view *n* : perspectiva *f*, punto *m* de vista

pointy ['pɔɪnti] *adj* : puntiagudo

poise¹ ['pɔɪz] *vt* **poised; poising** BALANCE : equilibrar, balancear

poise² *n* : aplomo *m*, compostura *f*

poison¹ ['pɔɪzən] *vt* **1** : envenenar, intoxicar **2** CORRUPT : corromper

poison² *n* : veneno *m*

poison ivy *n* : hiedra *f* venenosa

poisonous ['pɔɪzənəs] *adj* : venenoso, tóxico, ponzoñoso

poke¹ ['po:k] *v* **poked; poking** *vt* **1** JAB : golpear (con la punta de algo), dar ⟨he poked me with his finger : me dio con el dedo⟩ **2** THRUST : introducir, asomar ⟨I poked my head out the window : asomé la cabeza por la ventana⟩ — *vi* **1 to poke around** RUMMAGE : hurgar **2 to poke along** DAWDLE : demorarse, entretenerse

poke² *n* : golpe *m* abrupto (con la punta de algo)

poker ['po:kər] *n* **1** : atizador *m* (para el fuego) **2** : póker *m*, poker *m* (juego de naipes)

polar ['po:lər] *adj* : polar

polar bear *n* : oso *m* blanco

Polaris [po'lærɪs, -'lɑr-] → **North Star**

polarize ['po:lə,raɪz] *vt* **-ized; -izing** : polarizar

pole ['po:l] *n* **1** : palo *m*, poste *m*, vara *f* ⟨telephone pole : poste de teléfonos⟩ **2** : polo *m* ⟨the South Pole : el Polo Sur⟩ **3** : polo *m* (eléctrico o magnético)

Pole ['po:l] *n* : polaco *m*, -ca *f*

polecat ['po:l,kæt] *n, pl* **polecats** *or* **polecat 1** : turón *m* (de Europa) **2** SKUNK : mofeta *f*, zorrillo *m*

polemical [pə'lɛmɪkəl] *adj* : polémico

polemics [pə'lɛmɪks] *ns & pl* : polémica *f*

polestar ['po:l,stɑr] → **North Star**

police¹ [pə'li:s] *vt* **-liced; -licing** : mantener el orden en ⟨to police the streets : patrullar las calles⟩

police² *ns & pl* **1** : policía *f* (organización) **2** POLICE OFFICERS : policías *mfpl*

policeman [pə'li:smən] *n, pl* **-men** [-mən, -,mɛn] : policía *m*

police officer *n* : policía *mf*, agente *mf* de policía

policewoman [pə'li:s,wʊmən] *n, pl* **-women** [-,wɪmən] : policía *f*, mujer *f* policía

policy ['pɑləsi] *n, pl* **-cies 1** : política *f* ⟨foreign policy : política exterior⟩ **2** *or* **insurance policy** : póliza *f* de seguros, seguro *m*

polio¹ ['po:li,o:] *adj* : de polio ⟨polio vaccine : vacuna contra la polio⟩

polio² *n* → **poliomyelitis**

poliomyelitis [,po:li,o:,maɪə'laɪṱəs] *n* : poliomielitis *f*, polio *f*

polish¹ ['pɑlɪʃ] *vt* **1** : pulir, lustrar, sacar brillo a ⟨to polish one's nails : pintarse las uñas⟩ **2** REFINE : pulir, perfeccionar

polish² *n* **1** LUSTER : brillo *m*, lustre *m* **2** REFINEMENT : refinamiento *m* **3** : betún *m* (para zapatos), cera *f* (para suelos y muebles), esmalte *m* (para las uñas)

Polish¹ ['po:lɪʃ] *adj* : polaco

Polish² *n* : polaco *m* (idioma)

polite [pə'laɪt] *adj* **-liter; -est** : cortés, correcto, educado

politely [pə'laɪtli] *adv* : cortésmente, correctamente, con buenos modales

politeness [pə'laɪtnəs] *n* : cortesía *f*

politic ['pɑlə,tɪk] *adj* : diplomático, prudente

political [pə'lɪṱɪkəl] *adj* : político — **politically** [-ṱɪkli] *adv*

politician [,pɑlə'tɪʃən] *n* : político *m*, -ca *f*

politics ['pɑlə,tɪks] *ns & pl* : política *f*

polka ['po:lkə, 'po:kə] *n* : polka *f*

polka dot ['po:kə,dɑt] *n* : lunar *m* (en un diseño)

poll¹ ['po:l] *vt* **1** : obtener (votos) ⟨she polled over 1000 votes : obtuvo más de 1000 votos⟩ **2** CANVASS : encuestar, sondear — *vi* : obtener votos

poll² *n* **1** SURVEY : encuesta *f*, sondeo *m* **2 polls** *npl* : urnas *fpl* ⟨to go to the polls : acudir a las urnas, ir a votar⟩

pollen ['pɑlən] *n* : polen *m*

pollinate ['pɑlə,neɪt] *vt* **-nated; -nating** : polinizar

pollination [,pɑlə'neɪʃən] *n* : polinización *f*

pollster ['po:lstər] *n* : encuestador *m*, -dora *f*

pollutant [pə'lu:tənt] *n* : contaminante *m*

pollute [pə'lu:t] *vt* **-luted; -luting** : contaminar

pollution [pə'lu:ʃən] *n* : contaminación *f*

pollywog *or* **polliwog** ['pɑli,wɔg] *n* TADPOLE : renacuajo *m*

polo ['po:,lo:] *n* : polo *m*

poltergeist ['po:lṱər,gaɪst] *n* : poltergeist *m*, fantasma *m* travieso

polyester ['pɑli,ɛstər, ,pɑli'-] *n* : poliéster *m*

polygamous [pə'lɪgəməs] *adj* : polígamo

polygamy [pə'lɪgəmi] *n* : poligamia *f*

polygon ['pɑli,gɑn] *n* : polígono *m*

polymer [ˈpɑləmər] *n* : polímero *m*

Polynesian [ˌpɑləˈniːʒən, -ʃən] *n* : polinesio *m*, -sia *f* — **Polynesian** *adj*

polyunsaturated [ˌpɑliˌʌnˈsætʃə-ˌreɪt̬əd] *adj* : poliinsaturado

pomegranate [ˈpɑməˌgrænət, ˈpɑmˌgrænət] *n* : granada *f* (fruta)

pommel1 [ˈpʌməl] *vt* → **pummel**

pommel2 [ˈpʌməl, ˈpɑ-] *n* **1** : pomo *m* (de una espada) **2** : perilla *f* (de una silla de montar)

pomp [ˈpɑmp] *n* **1** SPLENDOR : pompa *f*, esplendor *m* **2** OSTENTATION : boato *m*, ostentación *f*

pom–pom [ˈpɑmˌpɑm] *n* : borla *f*, pompón *m*

pomposity [pɑmˈpɑsət̬i] *n, pl* **-ties** : pomposidad *f*

pompous [ˈpɑmpəs] *adj* : pomposo — **pompously** *adv*

poncho [ˈpɑnˌtʃoː] *n, pl* **-chos** : poncho *m*

pond [ˈpɑnd] *n* : charca *f* (natural), estanque *m* (artificial)

ponder [ˈpɑndər] *vt* : reflexionar, considerar — *vi* **to ponder over** : reflexionar sobre, sopesar

ponderous [ˈpɑndərəs] *adj* : pesado

pontiff [ˈpɑntɪf] *n* POPE : pontífice *m*

pontificate [pɑnˈtɪfəˌkeɪt] *vi* **-cated; -cating** : pontificar

pontoon [pɑnˈtuːn] *n* : pontón *m*

pony [ˈpoːni] *n, pl* **-nies** : poni *m*, poney *m*, jaca *f*

ponytail [ˈpoːniˌteɪl] *n* : cola *f* de caballo, coleta *f*

poodle [ˈpuːdəl] *n* : caniche *m*

pool1 [ˈpuːl] *vt* : mancomunar, hacer un fondo común de

pool2 *n* **1** : charca *f* ⟨a swimming pool : una piscina⟩ **2** PUDDLE : charco *m* **3** RESERVE, SUPPLY : fondo *m* común (de recursos), reserva *f* **4** : billar *m* (juego)

poor [ˈpʊr, ˈpor] *adj* **1** : pobre ⟨poor people : los pobres⟩ **2** SCANTY : pobre, escaso ⟨poor attendance : baja asistencia⟩ **3** UNFORTUNATE : pobre ⟨poor thing! : ¡pobrecito!⟩ **4** BAD : malo ⟨to be in poor health : estar mal de salud⟩

poorly [ˈpʊrli, ˈpor-] *adv* : mal

pop1 [ˈpɑp] *v* **popped; popping** *vi* **1** BURST : reventarse, estallar **2** : ir, venir, o aparecer abruptamente ⟨he popped into the house : se metió en la casa⟩ ⟨a menu pops up : aparece un menú⟩ **3 to pop out** PROTRUDE : salirse, saltarse ⟨my eyes popped out of my head : se me saltaban los ojos⟩ — *vt* **1** BURST : reventar **2** : hacer o meter abruptamente ⟨he popped it into his mouth : se lo metió en la boca⟩

pop2 *adj* : popular ⟨pop music : música popular⟩

pop3 *n* **1** : estallido *m* pequeño (de un globo, etc.) **2** SODA : refresco *m*, gaseosa *f*

popcorn [ˈpɑpˌkɔrn] *n* : palomitas *fpl* (de maíz)

pope [ˈpoːp] *n* : papa *m* ⟨Pope John : el Papa Juan⟩

poplar [ˈpɑplər] *n* : álamo *m*

poplin [ˈpɑplɪn] *n* : popelín *m*, popelina *f*

poppy [ˈpɑpi] *n, pl* **-pies** : amapola *f*

populace [ˈpɑpjələs] *n* **1** MASSES : pueblo *m* **2** POPULATION : población *f*

popular [ˈpɑpjələr] *adj* **1** : popular ⟨the popular vote : el voto popular⟩ **2** COMMON : generalizado, común ⟨popular beliefs : creencias generalizadas⟩ **3** : popular, de gran popularidad ⟨a popular singer : un cantante popular⟩

popularity [ˌpɑpjəˈlærət̬i] *n* : popularidad *f*

popularize [ˈpɑpjələˌraɪz] *vt* **-ized; -izing** : popularizar

popularly [ˈpɑpjələrli] *adv* : popularmente, vulgarmente

populate [ˈpɑpjəˌleɪt] *vt* **-lated; -lating** : poblar

population [ˌpɑpjəˈleɪʃən] *n* : población *f*

populist [ˈpɑpjəlɪst] *n* : populista *mf* — **populist** *adj*

populous [ˈpɑpjələs] *adj* : populoso

porcelain [ˈporsələn] *n* : porcelana *f*

porch [ˈportʃ] *n* : porche *m*

porcupine [ˈpɔrkjəˌpaɪn] *n* : puerco *m* espín

pore1 [ˈpor] *vi* **pored; poring 1** GAZE : mirar (con atención) **2 to pore over** : leer detenidamente, estudiar

pore2 *n* : poro *m*

pork [ˈpork] *n* : carne *f* de cerdo, carne *f* de puerco

pornographic [ˌpɔrnəˈgræfɪk] *adj* : pornográfico

pornography [pɔrˈnɑgrəfi] *n* : pornografía *f*

porous [ˈporəs] *adj* : poroso

porpoise [ˈpɔrpəs] *n* **1** : marsopa *f* **2** DOLPHIN : delfín *m*

porridge [ˈpɔrɪdʒ] *n* : sopa *f* espesa de harina, gachas *fpl*

port1 [ˈport] *adj* : de babor ⟨on the port side : a babor⟩

port2 *n* **1** HARBOR : puerto *m* **2** ORIFICE : orificio *m* (de una válvula, etc.) **3** : puerto *m* (de una computadora) **4** PORTHOLE : portilla *f* **5** *or* **port side** : babor *m* (de un barco) **6** : oporto *m* (vino)

portable [ˈport̬əbəl] *adj* : portátil

portal [ˈport̬əl] *n* : portal *m*

portend [pɔrˈtɛnd] *vt* : presagiar, augurar

portent [ˈpɔrˌtɛnt] *n* : presagio *m*, augurio *m*

portentous [pɔrˈtɛntəs] *adj* : profético, que presagia

porter [ˈport̬ər] *n* : maletero *m*, mozo *m* (de estación)

portfolio [portˈfoːliˌo] *n, pl* **-lios 1** FOLDER : cartera *f* (para llevar papeles), carpeta *f* **2** : cartera *f* (diplomática) **3 investment portfolio** : cartera de inversiones

porthole [ˈport,ho:l] *n* : portilla *f* (de un barco), ventanilla *f* (de un avión)

portico [ˈporṭɪ,ko] *n, pl* **-coes** *or* **-cos** : pórtico *m*

portion[1] [ˈporʃən] *vt* DISTRIBUTE : repartir

portion[2] *n* PART, SHARE : porción *f*, parte *f*

portly [ˈportli] *adj* **-lier; -est** : corpulento

portrait [ˈportrət, -,treɪt] *n* : retrato *m*

portray [porˈtreɪ] *vt* **1** DEPICT : representar, retratar **2** DESCRIBE : describir **3** PLAY : interpretar (un personaje)

portrayal [porˈtreɪəl] *n* **1** REPRESENTATION : representación *f* **2** PORTRAIT : retrato *m*

Portuguese [,portʃəˈgi:z, -ˈgi:s] *n* **1** : portugués *m*, -guesa *f* (persona) **2** : portugués *m* (idioma) — **Portuguese** *adj*

pose[1] [ˈpo:z] *v* **posed; posing** *vt* PRESENT : plantear (una pregunta, etc.), representar (una amenaza) — *vi* **1** : posar (para una foto, etc.) **2 to pose as** : hacerse pasar por

pose[2] *n* **1** : pose *f* ⟨to strike a pose : asumir una pose⟩ **2** PRETENSE : pose *f*, afectación *f*

posh [ˈpɑʃ] *adj* : elegante, de lujo

position[1] [pəˈzɪʃən] *vt* : colocar, situar, ubicar

position[2] *n* **1** APPROACH, STANCE : posición *f*, postura *f*, planteamiento *m* **2** LOCATION : posición *f*, ubicación *f* **3** STATUS : posición *f* (en una jerarquía) **4** JOB : puesto *m*

positive [ˈpɑzəṭɪv] *adj* **1** DEFINITE : incuestionable, inequívoco ⟨positive evidence : pruebas irrefutables⟩ **2** CONFIDENT : seguro **3** : positivo (en gramática, matemáticas, y física) **4** AFFIRMATIVE : positivo, afirmativo ⟨a positive response : una respuesta positiva⟩

positively [ˈpɑzəṭɪvli] *adv* **1** FAVORABLY : favorablemente **2** OPTIMISTICALLY : positivamente **3** DEFINITELY : definitivamente, en forma concluyente **4** (*used for emphasis*) : realmente, verdaderamente ⟨it's positively awful! : ¡es verdaderamente malo!⟩

possess [pəˈzɛs] *vt* **1** HAVE, OWN : poseer, tener **2** SEIZE : apoderarse de ⟨he was possessed by fear : el miedo se apoderó de él⟩

possession [pəˈzɛʃən] *n* **1** POSSESSING : posesión *f* **2** : posesión *f* (por un demonio, etc.) **3 possessions** *npl* PROPERTY : bienes *mpl*, propiedad *f*

possessive[1] [pəˈzɛsɪv] *adj* **1** : posesivo (en gramática) **2** JEALOUS : posesivo, celoso

possessive[2] *n or* **possessive case** : posesivo *m*

possessor [pəˈzɛsər] *n* : poseedor *m*, -dora *f*

possibility [,pɑsəˈbɪləṭi] *n, pl* **-ties** : posibilidad *f*

possible [ˈpɑsəbəl] *adj* : posible

possibly [ˈpɑsəbli] *adv* **1** CONCEIVABLY : posiblemente ⟨it can't possibly be true! : ¡no puede ser!⟩ **2** PERHAPS : quizás, posiblemente

possum [ˈpɑsəm] → **opossum**

post[1] [ˈpo:st] *vt* **1** MAIL : echar al correo, mandar por correo **2** ANNOUNCE : anunciar ⟨they've posted the grades : han anunciado las notas⟩ **3** AFFIX : fijar, poner (noticias, etc.) **4** STATION : apostar **5 to keep (someone) posted** : tener al corriente (a alguien)

post[2] *n* **1** POLE : poste *m*, palo *m* **2** STATION : puesto *m* **3** CAMP : puesto *m* (militar) **4** JOB, POSITION : puesto *m*, empleo *m*, cargo *m*

postage [ˈpo:stɪʤ] *n* : franqueo *m*

postal [ˈpo:stəl] *adj* : postal

postcard [ˈpo:st,kɑrd] *n* : postal *f*, tarjeta *f* postal

poster [ˈpo:stər] *n* : póster *m*, cartel *m*, afiche *m*

posterior[1] [pɑˈstɪriər, po-] *adj* : posterior

posterior[2] *n* BUTTOCKS : trasero *m*, nalgas *fpl*, asentaderas *fpl*

posterity [pɑˈstɛrəṭi] *n* : posteridad *f*

postgraduate[1] [,po:stˈgræʤʊət] *adj* : de postgrado

postgraduate[2] *n* : postgraduado *m*, -da *f*

posthaste [ˈpo:stˈheɪst] *adv* : a toda prisa

posthumous [ˈpɑstʃəməs] *adj* : póstumo — **posthumously** *adv*

postman [ˈpo:stmən, -,mæn] → **mailman**

postmark[1] [ˈpo:st,mɑrk] *vt* : matasellar

postmark[2] *n* : matasellos *m*

postmaster [ˈpo:st,mæstər] *n* : administrador *m*, -dora *f* de correos

postmodern [,po:stˈmɑdərn] *adj* : posmoderno

postmortem [,po:stˈmɔrṭəm] *n* : autopsia *f*

postnatal [,po:stˈneɪṭəl] *adj* : postnatal ⟨postnatal depression : depresión posparto⟩

post office *n* : correo *m*, oficina *f* de correos

postoperative [,po:stˈɑpərəṭɪv, -,reɪ-] *adj* : posoperatorio

postpaid [,po:stˈpeɪd] *adv* : con franqueo pagado

postpone [,po:stˈpo:n] *vt* **-poned; -poning** : postergar, aplazar, posponer

postponement [,po:stˈpo:nmənt] *n* : postergación *f*, aplazamiento *m*

postscript [ˈpo:st,skrɪpt] *n* : postdata *f*, posdata *f*

postulate [ˈpɑstʃə,leɪt] *vt* **-lated; -lating** : postular

posture[1] [ˈpɑstʃər] *vi* **-tured; -turing** : posar, asumir una pose

posture[2] *n* : postura *f*

postwar [,po:stˈwɔr] *adj* : de (la) posguerra

posy ['po:zi] *n, pl* **-sies** **1** FLOWER : flor *f* **2** BOUQUET : ramo *m*, ramillete *m*

pot[1] ['pɑt] *vt* **potted; potting** : plantar (en una maceta)

pot[2] *n* **1** : olla *f* (de cocina) **2 pots and pans** : cacharros *mpl*

potable ['po:t̬əbəl] *adj* : potable

potash ['pɑt,æʃ] *n* : potasa *f*

potassium [pə'tæsiəm] *n* : potasio *m*

potato [pə'teɪt̬o] *n, pl* **-toes** : papa *f*, patata *f Spain*

potato chips *npl* : papas *fpl* fritas (de bolsa)

potbellied ['pɑt,bɛlid] *adj* : panzón, barrigón *fam*

potbelly ['pɑt,bɛli] *n* : panza *f*, barriga *f*

potency ['po:təntsi] *n, pl* **-cies** **1** POWER : fuerza *f*, potencia *f* **2** EFFECTIVENESS : eficacia *f*

potent ['po:tənt] *adj* **1** POWERFUL : potente, poderoso **2** EFFECTIVE : eficaz ⟨a potent medicine : una medicina bien fuerte⟩

potential[1] [pə'tɛntʃəl] *adj* : potencial, posible

potential[2] *n* **1** : potencial *m* ⟨growth potential : potencial de crecimiento⟩ ⟨a child with potential : un niño que promete⟩ **2** : potencial *m* (eléctrico) — **potentially** *adv*

potful ['pɑt,fʊl] *n* : contenido *m* de una olla ⟨a potful of water : una olla de agua⟩

pothole ['pɑt,ho:l] *n* : bache *m*

potion ['po:ʃən] *n* : brebaje *m*, poción *f*

potluck ['pɑt,lʌk] *n* **to take potluck** : tomar lo que haya

potpourri [,po:pʊ'ri:] *n* : popurrí *m*

potshot ['pɑt,ʃɑt] *n* **1** : tiro *m* al azar ⟨to take potshots at : disparar al azar a⟩ **2** CRITICISM : crítica *f* (hecha al azar)

potter ['pɑt̬ər] *n* : alfarero *m*, -ra *f*

pottery ['pɑt̬əri] *n, pl* **-teries** : cerámica *f*

pouch ['paʊtʃ] *n* **1** BAG : bolsa *f* pequeña **2** : bolsa *f* (de un animal)

poultice ['po:lt̬əs] *n* : emplasto *m*, cataplasma *f*

poultry ['po:ltri] *n* : aves *fpl* de corral

pounce ['paʊnts] *vi* **pounced; pouncing** : abalanzarse

pound[1] ['paʊnd] *vt* **1** CRUSH : machacar, machucar, majar **2** BEAT : golpear, machacar ⟨she pounded the lessons into them : les machacaba las lecciones⟩ ⟨he pounded home his point : les hizo entender su razonamiento⟩ — *vi* **1** BEAT : palpitar (dícese del corazón) **2** RESOUND : retumbar, resonar **3** : andar con paso pesado ⟨we pounded through the mud : caminamos pesadamente por el barro⟩

pound[2] *n* **1** : libra *f* (unidad de peso) **2** : libra *f* (unidad monetaria) **3 dog pound** : perrera *f*

pour ['por] *vt* **1** : echar, verter, servir (bebidas) ⟨pour it into a pot : viértalo en una olla⟩ **2** : proveer con abundancia ⟨they poured money into it : le invirtieron mucho dinero⟩ **3 to pour out** : dar salida a ⟨he poured out his feelings to her : se desahogó con ella⟩ — *vi* **1** FLOW : manar, fluir, salir ⟨blood was pouring from the wound : la sangre le salía de la herida⟩ **2 it's pouring (outside)** : está lloviendo a cántaros

pout[1] ['paʊt] *vi* : hacer pucheros

pout[2] *n* : puchero *m*

poverty ['pɑvərt̬i] *n* : pobreza *f*, indigencia *f*

powder[1] ['paʊdər] *vt* **1** : empolvar ⟨to powder one's face : empolvarse la cara⟩ **2** PULVERIZE : pulverizar

powder[2] *n* : polvo *m*, polvos *mpl*

powdery ['paʊdəri] *adj* : polvoriento, como polvo

power[1] ['paʊər] *vt* : impulsar, propulsar

power[2] *n* **1** AUTHORITY : poder *m*, autoridad *f* ⟨executive powers : poderes ejecutivos⟩ **2** ABILITY : capacidad *f*, poder *m* **3** : potencia *f* (política) ⟨foreign powers : potencias extranjeras⟩ **4** STRENGTH : fuerza *f* **5** : potencia *f* (en física y matemáticas)

powerful ['paʊərfəl] *adj* : poderoso, potente — **powerfully** *adv*

powerhouse ['paʊər,haʊs] *n* : persona *f* dinámica

powerless ['paʊərləs] *adj* : impotente

power plant *n* : central *f* eléctrica

powwow ['paʊ,waʊ] *n* : conferencia *f*

pox ['pɑks] *n, pl* **pox** *or* **poxes** **1** CHICKEN POX : varicela *f* **2** SYPHILIS : sífilis *f*

practicable ['præktɪkəbəl] *adj* : practicable, viable, factible

practical ['præktɪkəl] *adj* : práctico

practicality [,præktɪ'kæləṭi] *n, pl* **-ties** : factibilidad *f*, viabilidad *f*

practical joke *n* : broma *f* (pesada)

practically ['præktɪkli] *adv* **1** : de manera práctica **2** ALMOST : casi, prácticamente

practice[1] *or* **practise** ['præktəs] *vt* **-ticed** *or* **-tised; -ticing** *or* **-tising** **1** : practicar ⟨he practiced his German on us : practicó el alemán con nosotros⟩ ⟨to practice politeness : practicar la cortesía⟩ **2** : ejercer ⟨to practice medicine : ejercer la medicina⟩

practice[2] *n* **1** USE : práctica *f* ⟨to put into practice : poner en práctica⟩ **2** CUSTOM : costumbre *f* ⟨it's a common practice here : por aquí se acostumbra hacerlo⟩ **3** TRAINING : práctica *f* **4** : ejercicio *m* (de una profesión)

practitioner [præk'tɪʃənər] *n* **1** : profesional *mf* **2 general practitioner** : médico *m*, -ca *f*

pragmatic [præg'mæt̬ɪk] *adj* : pragmático — **pragmatically** *adv*

pragmatism ['prægmə,tɪzəm] *n* : pragmatismo

prairie ['prɛri] *n* : pradera *f*, llanura *f*

praise[1] ['preɪz] *vt* **praised; praising** : elogiar, alabar ⟨to praise God : alabar a Dios⟩
praise[2] *n* : elogio *m*, alabanza *f*
praiseworthy ['preɪz,wərði] *adj* : digno de alabanza, loable
prance[1] ['prænts] *vi* **pranced; prancing** **1** : hacer cabriolas, cabriolar ⟨a prancing horse : un caballo haciendo cabriolas⟩ **2** SWAGGER : pavonearse
prance[2] *n* : cabriola *f*
prank ['præŋk] *n* : broma *f*, travesura *f*
prankster ['præŋkstər] *n* : bromista *mf*
prattle[1] ['prætəl] *vt* **-tled; -tling** : parlotear *fam*, cotorrear *fam*, balbucear (como un niño)
prattle[2] *n* : parloteo *m fam*, cotorreo *m fam*, cháchara *f fam*
prawn ['prɔn] *n* : langostino *m*, camarón *m*, gamba *f*
pray ['preɪ] *vt* ENTREAT : rogar, suplicar — *vi* : rezar
prayer ['prɛr] *n* **1** : plegaria *f*, oración *f* ⟨to say one's prayers : orar, rezar⟩ ⟨the Lord's Prayer : el Padrenuestro⟩ **2** PRAYING : rezo *m*, oración *f* ⟨to kneel in prayer : arrodillarse para rezar⟩
praying mantis → **mantis**
preach ['pri:ʧ] *vi* : predicar — *vt* ADVOCATE : abogar por ⟨to preach cooperation : promover la cooperación⟩
preacher ['pri:ʧər] *n* **1** : predicador *m*, -dora *f* **2** MINISTER : pastor *m*, -tora *f*
preamble ['pri:,æmbəl] *n* : preámbulo *m*
prearrange [,pri:ə'reɪnʤ] *vt* **-ranged; -ranging** : arreglar de antemano
precarious [pri'kæriəs] *adj* : precario — **precariously** *adv*
precariousness [pri'kæriəsnəs] *n* : precariedad *f*
precaution [pri'kɔʃən] *n* : precaución *f*
precautionary [pri'kɔʃə,nɛri] *adj* : preventivo, cautelar, precautorio
precede [pri'si:d] *v* **-ceded; -ceding** : preceder a
precedence ['prɛsədənts, prɪ'si:dənts] *n* : precedencia *f*
precedent ['prɛsədənt] *n* : precedente *m*
precept ['pri:,sɛpt] *n* : precepto *m*
precinct ['pri:,sɪŋkt] *n* **1** DISTRICT : distrito *m* (policial, electoral, etc.) **2** **precincts** *npl* PREMISES : recinto *m*, predio *m*, límites *mpl* (de una ciudad)
precious ['prɛʃəs] *adj* **1** : precioso ⟨precious gems : piedras preciosas⟩ **2** DEAR : querido **3** AFFECTED : afectado
precipice ['prɛsəpəs] *n* : precipicio *m*
precipitate [pri'sɪpə,teɪt] *v* **-tated; -tating** *vt* **1** HASTEN, PROVOKE : precipitar, provocar **2** HURL : arrojar **3** : precipitar (en química) — *vi* : precipitarse (en química), condensarse (en meteorología)
precipitation [pri,sɪpə'teɪʃən] *n* **1** HASTE : precipitación *f*, prisa *f* **2** : precipitaciones *fpl* (en meteorología)
precipitous [pri'sɪpət̬əs] *adj* **1** HASTY, RASH : precipitado **2** STEEP : escarpado, empinado ⟨a precipitous drop : una caída vertiginosa⟩
précis [preɪ'si:] *n, pl* **précis** [-'si:z] : resumen *m*
precise [pri'saɪs] *adj* **1** DEFINITE : preciso, explícito **2** EXACT : exacto, preciso ⟨precise calculations : cálculos precisos⟩ — **precisely** *adv*
preciseness [pri'saɪsnəs] *n* : precisión *f*, exactitud *f*
precision [pri'sɪʒən] *n* : precisión *f*
preclude [pri'klu:d] *vt* **-cluded; -cluding** : evitar, impedir, excluir (una posibilidad, etc.)
precocious [pri'ko:ʃəs] *adj* : precoz — **precociously** *adv*
precocity [pri'kɑsət̬i] *n* : precocidad *f*
preconceive [,pri:kən'si:v] *vt* **-ceived; -ceiving** : preconcebir
preconception [,pri:kən'spʃən] *n* : idea *f* preconcebida
precondition [,pri:kən'dɪʃən] *n* : precondición *f*, condición *f* previa
precook [,pri:'kʊk] *vt* : precocinar
precursor [pri'kərsər] *n* : precursor *m*, -sora *f*
predator ['prɛdət̬ər] *n* : depredador *m*, -dora *f*
predatory ['prɛdə,tori] *adj* : depredador
predecessor ['prɛdə,sɛsər, 'pri:-] *n* : antecesor *m*, -sora *f*; predecesor *m*, -sora *f*
predestination [pri,dɛstə'neɪʃən] *n* : predestinación *f*
predestine [pri'dɛstən] *vt* **-tined; -tining** : predestinar
predetermine [,pri:dɪ'tərmən] *vt* **-mined; -mining** : predeterminar
predicament [pri'dɪkəmənt] *n* : apuro *m*, aprieto *m*
predicate[1] ['prɛdə,keɪt] *vt* **-cated; -cating** **1** AFFIRM : afirmar, aseverar **2 to be predicated on** : estar basado en
predicate[2] ['prɛdɪkət] *n* : predicado *m*
predict [pri'dɪkt] *vt* : pronosticar, predecir
predictable [pri'dɪktəbəl] *adj* : previsible — **predictably** [-bli] *adv*
prediction [pri'dɪkʃən] *n* : pronóstico *m*, predicción *f*
predilection [,prɛdəl'ɛkʃən, ,pri:-] *n* : predilección *f*
predispose [,pri:dɪ'spo:z] *vt* **-posed; -posing** : predisponer
predisposition [,pri:,dɪspə'zɪʃən] *n* : predisposición *f*
predominance [pri'dɑmənənts] *n* : predominio *m*
predominant [pri'dɑmənənt] *adj* : predominante — **predominantly** *adv*
predominate [pri'dɑmə,neɪt] *vi* **-nated; -nating** **1** : predominar (en cantidad) **2** PREVAIL : prevalecer
preeminence [pri'ɛmənənts] *n* : preeminencia *f*
preeminent [pri'ɛmənənt] *adj* : preeminente
preeminently [pri'ɛmənəntli] *adv* : especialmente

preempt [pri'ɛmpt] *vt* **1** APPROPRIATE : apoderarse de, apropiarse de **2** : reemplazar (un programa de televisión, etc.) **3** FORESTALL : adelantarse a (un ataque, etc.)
preen ['pri:n] *vt* : arreglarse (el pelo, las plumas, etc.)
prefabricated [ˌpri:'fæbrəˌkeɪṭəd] *adj* : prefabricado
preface ['prɛfəs] *n* : prefacio *m*, prólogo *m*
prefatory ['prɛfəˌtori] *adj* : preliminar
prefer [pri'fər] *vt* **-ferred; -ferring 1** : preferir ⟨I prefer coffee : prefiero café⟩ **2 to prefer charges against** : presentar cargos contra
preferable ['prɛfərəbəl] *adj* : preferible
preferably ['prɛfərəbli] *adv* : preferentemente, de preferencia
preference ['prɛfrənts, 'prɛfər-] *n* : preferencia *f*, gusto *m*
preferential [ˌprɛfə'rɛntʃəl] *adj* : preferencial, preferente
prefigure [pri'fɪgjər] *vt* **-ured; -uring** FORESHADOW : prefigurar, anunciar
prefix ['pri:ˌfɪks] *n* : prefijo *m*
pregnancy ['prɛgnəntsi] *n, pl* **-cies** : embarazo *m*, preñez *f*
pregnant ['prɛgnənt] *adj* **1** : embarazada (dícese de una mujer), preñada (dícese de un animal) **2** MEANINGFUL : significativo
preheat [ˌpri:'hi:t] *vt* : precalentar
prehensile [pri'hɛntsəl, -'hɛnˌsaɪl] *adj* : prensil
prehistoric [ˌpri:hɪs'tɔrɪk] *or* **prehistorical** [-ɪkəl] *adj* : prehistórico
prejudge [ˌpri:'ʤʌʤ] *vt* **-judged; -judging** : prejuzgar
prejudice¹ ['prɛʤədəs] *vt* **-diced; -dicing 1** DAMAGE : perjudicar **2** BIAS : predisponer, influir en
prejudice² *n* **1** DAMAGE : perjuicio *m* (en derecho) **2** BIAS : prejuicio *m*
prelate ['prɛlət] *n* : prelado *m*
preliminary¹ [pri'lɪməˌnɛri] *adj* : preliminar
preliminary² *n, pl* **-naries 1** : preámbulo *m*, preludio *m* **2 preliminaries** *npl* : preliminares *mpl*
prelude ['prɛˌlu:d, 'prɛlˌju:d; 'preɪˌlu:d, 'pri:-] *n* : preludio *m*
premarital [ˌpri:'mærəṭəl] *adj* : prematrimonial
premature [ˌpri:mə'tʊr, -'tjʊr, -'ʧʊr] *adj* : prematuro — **prematurely** *adv*
premeditate [pri'mɛdəˌteɪt] *vt* **-tated; -tating** : premeditar
premeditation [priˌmɛdə'teɪʃən] *n* : premeditación *f*
premenstrual [pri'mɛntstruəl] *adj* : premenstrual
premier¹ [pri'mɪr, -'mjɪr; 'pri:miər] *adj* : principal
premier² *n* PRIME MINISTER : primer ministro *m*, primera ministra *f*
premiere¹ [prɪ'mjɛr, -'mɪr] *vt* **-miered; -miering** : estrenar
premiere² *n* : estreno *m*
premise ['prɛmɪs] *n* **1** : premisa *f* ⟨the premise of his arguments : la premisa de sus argumentos⟩ **2 premises** *npl* : recinto *m*, local *m*
premium ['pri:miəm] *n* **1** BONUS : prima *f* **2** SURCHARGE : recargo *m* ⟨to sell at a premium : vender (algo) muy caro⟩ **3 insurance premium** : prima *f* (de seguros) **4 to set a premium on** : darle un gran valor (a algo)
premonition [ˌpri:mə'nɪʃən, ˌprɛmə-] *n* : presentimiento *m*, premonición *f*
prenatal [ˌpri:'neɪṭəl] *adj* : prenatal
preoccupation [priˌɑkjə'peɪʃən] *n* : preocupación *f*
preoccupied [pri'ɑkjəˌpaɪd] *adj* : abstraído, ensimismado, preocupado
preoccupy [pri'ɑkjəˌpaɪ] *vt* **-pied; -pying** : preocupar
preparation [ˌprɛpə'reɪʃən] *n* **1** PREPARING : preparación *f* **2** MIXTURE : preparado *m* ⟨a preparation for burns : un preparado para quemaduras⟩ **3 preparations** *npl* ARRANGEMENTS : preparativos *mpl*
preparatory [pri'pærəˌtori] *adj* : preparatorio
prepare [pri'pær] *v* **-pared; -paring** *vt* : preparar — *vi* : prepararse
prepay [ˌpri:'peɪ] *vt* **-paid; -paying** : pagar por adelantado
preponderance [pri'pɑndərənts] *n* : preponderancia *f*
preponderant [pri'pɑndərənt] *adj* : preponderante — **preponderantly** *adv*
preposition [ˌprɛpə'zɪʃən] *n* : preposición *f*
prepositional [ˌprɛpə'zɪʃənəl] *adj* : preposicional
prepossessing [ˌpri:pə'zɛsɪŋ] *adj* : atractivo, agradable
preposterous [pri'pɑstərəs] *adj* : absurdo, ridículo
prerequisite¹ [pri'rɛkwəzət] *adj* : necesario, esencial
prerequisite² *n* : condición *f* necesario, requisito *m* previo
prerogative [pri'rɑgəṭɪv] *n* : prerrogativa *f*
presage ['prɛsɪʤ, pri'seɪʤ] *vt* **-saged; -saging** : presagiar
preschool ['pri:ˌsku:l] *adj* : preescolar ⟨preschool students : estudiantes de preescolar⟩
prescribe [pri'skraɪb] *vt* **-scribed; -scribing 1** ORDAIN : prescribir, ordenar **2** : recetar (medicinas, etc.)
prescription [pri'skrɪpʃən] *n* : receta *f*
presence ['prɛzənts] *n* : presencia *f*
present¹ [pri'zɛnt] *vt* **1** INTRODUCE : presentar ⟨to present oneself : presentarse⟩ **2** : presentar (una obra de teatro, etc.) **3** GIVE : entregar (un regalo, etc.), regalar, obsequiar **4** SHOW : presentar, ofrecer ⟨it presents a lovely view : ofrece una vista muy linda⟩
present² ['prɛzənt] *adj* **1** : actual ⟨present conditions : condiciones actuales⟩

2 : presente ⟨all the students were present : todos los estudiantes estaban presentes⟩

present[3] ['prɛzənt] *n* **1** GIFT : regalo *m*, obsequio *m* **2** : presente *m* ⟨at present : en este momento⟩ **3** *or* **present tense** : presente *m*

presentable [pri'zɛntəbəl] *adj* : presentable

presentation [ˌpri:ˌzɛn'teɪʃən, ˌprɛzən-] *n* : presentación *f* ⟨presentation ceremony : ceremonia de entrega⟩

presentiment [pri'zɛntəmənt] *n* : presentimiento *m*, premonición *f*

presently ['prɛzəntli] *adv* **1** SOON : pronto, dentro de poco **2** NOW : actualmente, ahora

present participle *n* : participio *m* presente, participio *m* activo

preservation [ˌprɛzər'veɪʃən] *n* : conservación *f*, preservación *f*

preservative [pri'zərvət̬ɪv] *n* : conservante *m*

preserve[1] [pri'zərv] *vt* **-served; -serving** **1** PROTECT : proteger, preservar **2** : conservar (los alimentos, etc.) **3** MAINTAIN : conservar, mantener

preserve[2] *n* **1** *or* **preserves** *npl* : conserva *f* ⟨peach preserves : duraznos en conserva⟩ **2** : coto *m* ⟨game preserve : coto de caza⟩

preside [pri'zaɪd] *vi* **-sided; -siding** **1 to preside over** : presidir ⟨he presided over the meeting : presidió la reunión⟩ **2 to preside over** : supervisar ⟨she presides over the department : dirige el departamento⟩

presidency ['prɛzədəntsi] *n, pl* **-cies** : presidencia *f*

president ['prɛzədənt] *n* : presidente *m*, -ta *f*

presidential [ˌprɛzə'dɛntʃəl] *adj* : presidencial

press[1] ['prɛs] *vt* **1** PUSH : apretar **2** SQUEEZE : apretar, prensar (frutas, flores, etc.) **3** IRON : planchar (ropa) **4** URGE : instar, apremiar ⟨he pressed me to come : insistió en que viniera⟩ — *vi* **1** PUSH : apretar ⟨press hard : aprieta con fuerza⟩ **2** CROWD : apiñarse **3** : abrirse paso ⟨I pressed through the crowd : me abrí paso entre el gentío⟩ **4** URGE : presionar

press[2] *n* **1** CROWD : multitud *f* **2** : imprenta *f*, prensa *f* ⟨to go to press : entrar en prensa⟩ **3** URGENCY : urgencia *f*, prisa *f* **4** PRINTER, PUBLISHER : imprenta *f*, editorial *f* **5 the press** : la prensa ⟨freedom of the press : libertad de prensa⟩

pressing ['prɛsɪŋ] *adj* URGENT : urgente

pressure[1] ['prɛʃər] *vt* **-sured; -suring** : presionar, apremiar

pressure[2] *n* **1** : presión *f* ⟨to be under pressure : estar bajo presión⟩ **2** → **blood pressure**

pressurize ['prɛʃəˌraɪz] *vt* **-ized; -izing** : presurizar

prestige [prɛ'sti:ʒ, -'sti:dʒ] *n* : prestigio *m*

prestigious [prɛ'stɪdʒəs] *adj* : prestigioso

presto ['prɛsˌto:] *adv* : de pronto

presumably [pri'zu:məbli] *adv* : es de suponer, supuestamente ⟨presumably, he's guilty : supone que es culpable⟩

presume [pri'zu:m] *vt* **-sumed; -suming** **1** ASSUME, SUPPOSE : suponer, asumir, presumir **2 to presume to** : atreverse a, osar

presumption [pri'zʌmpʃən] *n* **1** AUDACITY : atrevimiento *m*, osadía *f* **2** ASSUMPTION : presunción *f*, suposición *f*

presumptuous [pri'zʌmptʃʊəs] *adj* : descarado, atrevido

presuppose [ˌpri:sə'po:z] *vt* **-posed; -posing** : presuponer

pretend [pri'tɛnd] *vt* **1** CLAIM : pretender **2** FEIGN : fingir, simular — *vi* : fingir

pretender [pri'tɛndər] *n* : pretendiente *mf* (al trono, etc.)

pretense *or* **pretence** ['pri:ˌtɛnts, pri'tɛnts] *n* **1** CLAIM : afirmación *f* (falsa), pretensión *f* **2** FEIGNING : fingimiento *m*, simulación *f* ⟨to make a pretense of doing something : fingir hacer algo⟩ ⟨a pretense of order : una apariencia de orden⟩ **3** PRETEXT : pretexto *m* ⟨under false pretenses : con pretextos falsos, de manera fraudulenta⟩

pretension [pri'tɛntʃən] *n* **1** CLAIM : pretensión *f*, afirmación *f* **2** ASPIRATION : aspiración *f*, ambición *f* **3** PRETENTIOUSNESS : pretensiones *fpl*, presunción *f*

pretentious [pri'tɛntʃəs] *adj* : pretencioso

pretentiousness [pri'tɛntʃəsnəs] *n* : presunción *f*, pretensiones *fpl*

pretext ['pri:ˌtɛkst] *n* : pretexto *m*, excusa *f*

prettily ['prɪtəli] *adv* : atractivamente

prettiness ['prɪt̬inəs] *n* : lindeza *f*

pretty[1] ['prɪt̬i] *adv* : bastante, bien ⟨it's pretty obvious : está bien claro⟩ ⟨it's pretty much the same : es más o menos igual⟩

pretty[2] *adj* **-tier; -est** : bonito, lindo, guapo ⟨a pretty girl : una muchacha guapa⟩ ⟨what a pretty dress! : ¡qué vestido más lindo!⟩

pretzel ['prɛtsəl] *n* : galleta *f* salada (en forma de nudo)

prevail [pri'veɪl] *vi* **1** TRIUMPH : prevalecer **2** PREDOMINATE : predominar **3 to prevail upon** : persuadir, convencer ⟨I prevailed upon her to sing : la convencí para que cantara⟩

prevailing [pri'veɪlɪŋ] *adj* : imperante, prevaleciente

prevalence ['prɛvələnts] *n* : preponderancia *f*, predominio *m*

prevalent ['prɛvələnt] *adj* **1** COMMON : común y corriente, general **2** WIDESPREAD : extendido

prevaricate [pri'værə,keɪt] *vi* **-cated; -cating** LIE : mentir
prevarication [pri,værə'keɪʃən] *n* : mentira *f*
prevent [pri'vɛnt] *vt* **1** AVOID : prevenir, evitar ⟨steps to prevent war : medidas para evitar la guerra⟩ **2** HINDER : impedir
preventable [pri'vɛntəbəl] *adj* : evitable
preventative [pri'vɛntət̬ɪv] → **preventive**
prevention [pri'vɛntʃən] *n* : prevención *f*
preventive [pri'vɛntɪv] *adj* : preventivo
preview ['pri:,vju] *n* : preestreno *m*
previous ['pri:viəs] *adj* : previo, anterior ⟨previous knowledge : conocimientos previos⟩ ⟨the previous day : el día anterior⟩ ⟨in the previous year : en el año pasado⟩
previously ['pri:viəsli] *adv* : antes
prewar [,pri:'wɔr] *adj* : de antes de la guerra
prey ['preɪ] *n, pl* **preys** : presa *f*
prey on *vt* **1** : cazar, alimentarse de ⟨it preys on fish : se alimenta de peces⟩ **2 to prey on one's mind** : hacer presa en alguien, atormentar a alguien
price[1] ['praɪs] *vt* **priced; pricing** : poner un precio a
price[2] *n* : precio *m* ⟨peace at any price : la paz a toda costa⟩
priceless ['praɪsləs] *adj* : inestimable, inapreciable
pricey ['praɪsi] *adj* : caro
prick[1] ['prɪk] *vt* **1** : pinchar **2 to prick up one's ears** : levantar las orejas — *vi* : pinchar
prick[2] *n* **1** STAB : pinchazo *m* ⟨a prick of conscience : un remordimiento⟩ **2** → **pricker**
pricker ['prɪkər] *n* THORN : espina *f*
prickle[1] ['prɪkəl] *vi* **-led; -ling** : sentir un cosquilleo, tener un hormigueo
prickle[2] *n* **1** : espina *f* (de una planta) **2** TINGLE : cosquilleo *m*, hormigueo *m*
prickly ['prɪkəli] *adj* **1** THORNY : espinoso **2** : que pica ⟨a prickly sensation : un hormigueo⟩
prickly pear *n* : tuna *f*
pride[1] ['praɪd] *vt* **prided; priding** : estar orgulloso de ⟨to pride oneself on : preciarse de, enorgullecerse de⟩
pride[2] *n* : orgullo *m*
priest ['pri:st] *n* : sacerdote *m*, cura *m*
priestess ['pri:stɪs] *n* : sacerdotisa *f*
priesthood ['pri:st,hʊd] *n* : sacerdocio *m*
priestly ['pri:stli] *adj* : sacerdotal
prig ['prɪg] *n* : mojigato *m*, -ta *f*; gazmoño *m*, -ña *f*
prim ['prɪm] *adj* **primmer; primmest 1** PRISSY : remilgado **2** PRUDISH : mojigato, gazmoño
primarily [praɪ'mɛrəli] *adv* : principalmente, fundamentalmente
primary[1] ['praɪ,mɛri, 'praɪməri] *adj* **1** FIRST : primario **2** PRINCIPAL : principal **3** BASIC : fundamental
primary[2] *n, pl* **-ries** : elección *f* primaria
primary color *n* : color *m* primario
primary school → **elementary school**
primate *n* **1** ['praɪ,meɪt, -mət] : primado *m* (obispo) **2** [-,meɪt] : primate *m* (animal)
prime[1] ['praɪm] *vt* **primed; priming 1** : cebar ⟨to prime a pump : cebar una bomba⟩ **2** PREPARE : preparar (una superficie para pintar) **3** COACH : preparar (a un testigo, etc.)
prime[2] *adj* **1** CHIEF, MAIN : principal, primero **2** EXCELLENT : de primera (categoría), excelente
prime[3] *n* **the prime of one's life** : la flor de la vida
prime minister *n* : primer ministro *m*, primera ministra *f*
primer[1] ['prɪmər] *n* **1** READER : cartilla *f* **2** MANUAL : manual *m*
primer[2] ['praɪmər] *n* **1** : cebo *m* (para explosivos) **2** : base *f* (de pintura)
prime time *n* : horas *fpl* de mayor audiencia
primeval [praɪ'mi:vəl] *adj* : primitivo, primigenio
primitive ['prɪmət̬ɪv] *adj* : primitivo
primly ['prɪmli] *adv* : mojigatamente
primness ['prɪmnəs] *n* : mojigatería *f*, gazmoñería *f*
primordial [praɪ'mɔrdiəl] *adj* : primordial, fundamental
primp ['prɪmp] *vi* : arreglarse, acicalarse
primrose ['prɪm,ro:z] *n* : primavera *f*, prímula *f*
prince ['prɪnts] *n* : príncipe *m*
princely ['prɪntsli] *adj* : principesco
princess ['prɪntsəs, 'prɪn,sɛs] *n* : princesa *f*
principal[1] ['prɪntsəpəl] *adj* : principal — **principally** *adv*
principal[2] *n* **1** PROTAGONIST : protagonista *mf* **2** : director *m*, -tora *f* (de una escuela) **3** CAPITAL : principal *m*, capital *m* (en finanzas)
principality [,prɪntsə'pælət̬i] *n, pl* **-ties** : principado *m*
principle ['prɪntsəpəl] *n* : principio *m*
print[1] ['prɪnt] *vt* : imprimir (libros, etc.) — *vi* : escribir con letra de molde
print[2] *n* **1** IMPRESSION : marca *f*, huella *f*, impresión *f* **2** : texto *m* impreso ⟨to be out of print : estar agotado⟩ **3** LETTERING : letra *f* **4** ENGRAVING : grabado *m* **5** : copia *f* (en fotografía) **6** : estampado *m* (de tela)
printer ['prɪntər] *n* **1** : impresor *m*, -sora *f* (persona) **2** : impresora *f* (máquina)
printing ['prɪntɪŋ] *n* **1** : impresión *f* (acto) ⟨the third printing : la tercera tirada⟩ **2** : imprenta *f* (profesión) **3** LETTERING : letras *fpl* de molde
printing press *n* : prensa *f*
print out *vt* : imprimir (de una computadora)
printout ['prɪnt,aʊt] *n* : copia *f* impresa (de una computadora)
prior ['praɪər] *adj* **1** : previo **2 prior to** : antes de

priority [praɪ'ɔrət̬i] *n, pl* **-ties** : prioridad *f*
priory ['praɪəri] *n, pl* **-ries** : priorato *m*
prism ['prɪzəm] *n* : prisma *m*
prison ['prɪzən] *n* : prisión *f*, cárcel *f*
prisoner ['prɪzənər] *n* : preso *m*, -sa *f*; recluso *m*, -sa *f* ⟨prisoner of war : prisionero de guerra⟩
prissy ['prɪsi] *adj* **-sier; -est** : remilgado, melindroso
pristine ['prɪs,ti:n, prɪs'-] *adj* : puro, prístino
privacy ['praɪvəsi] *n, pl* **-cies** : privacidad *f*
private[1] ['praɪvət] *adj* **1** PERSONAL : privado, particular ⟨private property : propiedad privada⟩ **2** INDEPENDENT : privado, independiente ⟨private studies : estudios privados⟩ **3** SECRET : secreto **4** SECLUDED : aislado, privado — **privately** *adv*
private[2] *n* : soldado *m* raso
privateer [,praɪvə'tɪr] *n* : corsario *m*
privation [praɪ'veɪʃən] *n* : privación *f*
privilege ['prɪvlɪʤ, 'prɪvə-] *n* : privilegio *m*
privileged ['prɪvlɪʤd, 'prɪvə-] *adj* : privilegiado
privy[1] ['prɪvi] *adj* **to be privy to** : estar enterado de
privy[2] *n, pl* **privies** : excusado *m*, retrete *m* (exterior)
prize[1] ['praɪz] *vt* **prized; prizing** : valorar, apreciar
prize[2] *adj* **1** : premiado ⟨a prize stallion : un semental premiado⟩ **2** OUTSTANDING : de primera, excepcional
prize[3] *n* **1** AWARD : premio *m* ⟨third prize : el tercer premio⟩ **2** : joya *f*, tesoro *m* ⟨he's a real prize : es un tesoro⟩
prizefighter ['praɪz,faɪt̬ər] *n* : boxeador *m*, -dora *f* profesional
prizewinning ['praɪz,wɪnɪŋ] *adj* : premiado
pro[1] ['pro:] *adv* : a favor
pro[2] *adj* → **professional**[1]
pro[3] *n* **1** : pro *m* ⟨the pros and cons : los pros y los contras⟩ **2** → **professional**[2]
probability [,prɑbə'bɪlət̬i] *n, pl* **-ties** : probabilidad *f*
probable ['prɑbəbəl] *adj* : probable — **probably** [-bli] *adv*
probate[1] ['pro:,beɪt] *vt* **-bated; -bating** : autenticar (un testamento)
probate[2] *n* : autenticación *f* (de un testamento)
probation [pro'beɪʃən] *n* **1** : período *m* de prueba (para un empleado, etc.) **2** : libertad *f* condicional (para un preso)
probationary [pro'beɪʃə,nɛri] *adj* : de prueba
probe[1] ['pro:b] *vt* **probed; probing 1** : sondar (en medicina y tecnología) **2** INVESTIGATE : investigar, sondear
probe[2] *n* **1** : sonda *f* (en medicina, etc.) ⟨space probe : sonda espacial⟩ **2** INVESTIGATION : investigación *f*, sondeo *m*
probity ['pro:bət̬i] *n* : probidad *f*
problem[1] ['prɑbləm] *adj* : difícil
problem[2] *n* : problema *m*
problematic [,prɑblə'mæt̬ɪk] *or* **problematical** [-t̬ɪkəl] *adj* : problemático
proboscis [prə'bɑsɪs] *n, pl* **-cises** *also* **-cides** [-sə,di:z] : probóscide *f*
procedural [prə'si:ʤərəl] *adj* : de procedimiento
procedure [prə'si:ʤər] *n* : procedimiento *m* ⟨administrative procedures : trámites administrativos⟩
proceed [pro'si:d] *vi* **1** : proceder ⟨to proceed to do something : proceder a hacer algo⟩ **2** CONTINUE : continuar, proseguir, seguir ⟨he proceeded to the next phase : pasó a la segunda fase⟩ **3** ADVANCE : avanzar ⟨as the conference proceeded : mientras seguía avanzando la conferencia⟩ ⟨the road proceeds south : la calle sigue hacia el sur⟩
proceeding [pro'si:dɪŋ] *n* **1** PROCEDURE : procedimiento *m* **2 proceedings** *npl* EVENTS : acontecimientos *mpl* **3 proceedings** *npl* MINUTES : actas *fpl* (de una reunión, etc.)
proceeds ['pro:,si:dz] *npl* : ganancias *fpl*
process[1] ['prɑ,sɛs, 'pro:-] *vt* : procesar, tratar
process[2] *n, pl* **-cesses** ['prɑ,sɛsəz, 'pro:-, -səsəz, -sə,si:z] **1** : proceso *m* ⟨the process of elimination : el proceso de eliminación⟩ **2** METHOD : proceso *m*, método *m* ⟨manufacturing processes : procesos industriales⟩ **3** : acción *f* judicial ⟨due process of law : el debido proceso (de la ley)⟩ **4** SUMMONS : citación *f* **5** PROJECTION : protuberancia *f* (anatómica) **6 in the process of** : en vías de ⟨in the process of repair : en reparaciones⟩
procession [prə'sɛʃən] *n* : procesión *f*, desfile *m* ⟨a funeral procession : un cortejo fúnebre⟩
processional [prə'sɛʃənəl] *n* : himno *m* para una procesión
processor ['prɑ,sɛsər, 'pro:-, -səsər] *n* **1** : procesador *m* (de una computadora) **2 food processor** : procesador *m* de alimentos
proclaim [pro'kleɪm] *vt* : proclamar
proclamation [,prɑklə'meɪʃən] *n* : proclamación *f*
proclivity [pro'klɪvət̬i] *n, pl* **-ties** : proclividad *f*
procrastinate [prə'kræstə,neɪt] *vi* **-nated; -nating** : demorar, aplazar las responsabilidades
procrastination [prə,kræstə'neɪʃən] *n* : aplazamiento *m*, demora *f*, dilación *f*
procreate ['pro:kri,eɪt] *vi* **-ated; -ating** : procrear
procreation [,pro:kri'eɪʃən] *n* : procreación *f*
proctor[1] ['prɑktər] *vt* : supervisar (un examen)
proctor[2] *n* : supervisor *m*, -sora *f* (de un examen)

procure [prə'kjʊr] *vt* **-cured; -curing 1** OBTAIN : procurar, obtener **2** BRING ABOUT : provocar, lograr, conseguir
procurement [prə'kjʊrmənt] *n* : obtención *f*
prod[1] ['prɑd] *vt* **prodded; prodding 1** JAB, POKE : pinchar, golpear (con la punta de algo) **2** GOAD : incitar, estimular
prod[2] *n* **1** JAB, POKE : golpe *m* (con la punta de algo), pinchazo *m* **2** STIMULUS : estímulo *m* **3 cattle prod** : picana *f*, aguijón *m*
prodigal[1] ['prɑdɪgəl] *adj* SPENDTHRIFT : pródigo, despilfarrador, derrochador
prodigal[2] *n* : pródigo *m*, -ga *f*; derrochador *m*, -dora *f*
prodigious [prə'dɪʤəs] *adj* **1** MARVELOUS : prodigioso, maravilloso **2** HUGE : enorme, vasto ⟨prodigious sums : muchísimo dinero⟩ — **prodigiously** *adv*
prodigy ['prɑdəʤi] *n, pl* **-gies** : prodigio *m* ⟨child prodigy : niño prodigio⟩
produce[1] [prə'du:s, -'dju:s] *vt* **-duced; -ducing 1** EXHIBIT : presentar, mostrar **2** YIELD : producir **3** CAUSE : producir, causar **4** CREATE : producir ⟨to produce a poem : escribir un poema⟩ **5** : poner en escena (una obra de teatro), producir (una película)
produce[2] ['prɑˌdu:s, 'pro:-, -ˌdju:s] *n* : productos *mpl* agrícolas
producer [prə'du:sər, -'dju:-] *n* : productor *m*, -tora *f*
product ['prɑˌdʌkt] *n* : producto *m*
production [prə'dʌkʃən] *n* : producción *f*
productive [prə'dʌktɪv] *adj* : productivo
productivity [ˌpro:ˌdʌk'tɪvəṭi, ˌprɑ-] *n* : productividad *f*
profane[1] [pro'feɪn] *vt* **-faned; -faning** : profanar
profane[2] *adj* **1** SECULAR : profano **2** IRREVERENT : irreverente, impío
profanity [pro'fænəṭi] *n, pl* **-ties 1** IRREVERENCE : irreverencia *f*, impiedad *f* **2** : blasfemias *fpl*, obscenidades *fpl* ⟨don't use profanity : no digas blasfemias⟩
profess [prə'fɛs] *vt* **1** DECLARE : declarar, manifestar **2** CLAIM : pretender **3** : profesar (una religión, etc.)
professedly [prə'fɛsədli] *adv* **1** OPENLY : declaradamente **2** ALLEGEDLY : supuestamente
profession [prə'fɛʃən] *n* : profesión *f*
professional[1] [prə'fɛʃənəl] *adj* : profesional — **professionally** *adv*
professional[2] *n* : profesional *mf*
professionalism [prə'fɛʃənəˌlɪzəm] *n* : profesionalismo *m*
professor [prə'fɛsər] *n* : profesor *m* (universitario), profesora *f* (universitaria); catedrático *m*, -ca *f*
proffer ['prɑfər] *vt* **-fered; -fering** : ofrecer, dar
proficiency [prə'fɪʃəntsi] *n* : competencia *f*, capacidad *f*
proficient [prə'fɪʃənt] *adj* : competente, experto — **proficiently** *adv*
profile ['pro:ˌfaɪl] *n* : perfil *m* ⟨a portrait in profile : un retrato de perfil⟩ ⟨to keep a low profile : no llamar la atención, hacerse pasar desapercibido⟩
profit[1] ['prɑfət] *vi* : sacar provecho (de), beneficiarse (de)
profit[2] *n* **1** ADVANTAGE : provecho *m*, partido *m*, beneficio *m* **2** GAIN : beneficio *m*, utilidad *f*, ganancia *f* ⟨to make a profit : sacar beneficios⟩
profitable ['prɑfəṭəbəl] *adj* : rentable, lucrativo — **profitably** [-bli] *adv*
profitless ['prɑfətləs] *adj* : infructuoso, inútil
profligate ['prɑflɪgət, -ˌgeɪt] *adj* **1** DISSOLUTE : disoluto, licencioso **2** SPENDTHRIFT : despilfarrador, derrochador, pródigo
profound [prə'faʊnd] *adj* : profundo
profoundly [prə'faʊndli] *adv* : profundamente, en profundidad
profundity [prə'fʌndəṭi] *n, pl* **-ties** : profundidad *f*
profuse [prə'fju:s] *adj* **1** COPIOUS : profuso, copioso **2** LAVISH : pródigo — **profusely** *adv*
profusion [prə'fju:ʒən] *n* : abundancia *f*, profusión *f*
progenitor [pro'ʤɛnəṭər] *n* : progenitor *m*, -tora *f*
progeny ['prɑʤəni] *n, pl* **-nies** : progenie *f*
progesterone [pro'ʤɛstəˌro:n] *n* : progesterona *f*
prognosis [prɑg'no:sɪs] *n, pl* **-noses** [-ˌsi:z] : pronóstico *m* (médico)
program[1] ['pro:ˌgræm, -grəm] *vt* **-grammed** *or* **-gramed; -gramming** *or* **-graming** : programar
program[2] *n* : programa *m*
programmable ['pro:ˌgræməbəl] *adj* : programable
programmer ['pro:ˌgræmər] *n* : programador *m*, -dora *f*
programming ['pro:ˌgræmɪŋ] *n* : programación *f*
progress[1] [prə'grɛs] *vi* **1** PROCEED : progresar, adelantar **2** IMPROVE : mejorar
progress[2] ['prɑgrəs, -ˌgrɛs] *n* **1** ADVANCE : progreso *m*, adelanto *m*, avance *m* ⟨to make progress : hacer progresos⟩ **2** BETTERMENT : mejora *f*, mejoramiento *m*
progression [prə'grɛʃən] *n* **1** ADVANCE : avance *m* **2** SEQUENCE : desarrollo *m* (de eventos)
progressive [prə'grɛsɪv] *adj* **1** : progresista ⟨a progressive society : una sociedad progresista⟩ **2** : progresivo ⟨a progressive disease : una enfermedad progresiva⟩ **3** *or* **Progressive** : progresista (en política) **4** : progresivo (en gramática)

progressively [prəˈgrɛsɪvli] *adv* : progresivamente, poco a poco
prohibit [proˈhɪbət] *vt* : prohibir
prohibition [ˌpro:əˈbɪʃən, ˌpro:hə-] *n* : prohibición *f*
prohibitive [proˈhɪbət̬ɪv] *adj* : prohibitivo
project¹ [prəˈʤɛkt] *vt* **1** PLAN : proyectar, planear **2** : proyectar (imágenes, misiles, etc.) — *vi* PROTRUDE : sobresalir, salir
project² [ˈprɑˌʤɛkt, -ʤɪkt] *n* : proyecto *m*, trabajo *m* (de un estudiante) ⟨research project : proyecto de investigación⟩
projectile [prəˈʤɛktəl, -ˌtaɪl] *n* : proyectil *m*
projection [prəˈʤɛkʃən] *n* **1** PLAN : plan *m*, proyección *f* **2** : proyección *f* (de imágenes, misiles, etc.) **3** PROTRUSION : saliente *m*
projector [prəˈʤɛktər] *n* : proyector *m*
proletarian¹ [ˌpro:ləˈtɛriən] *adj* : proletario
proletarian² *n* : proletario *m*, -ria *f*
proletariat [ˌpro:ləˈtɛriət] *n* : proletariado *m*
proliferate [prəˈlɪfəˌreɪt] *vi* **-ated; -ating** : proliferar
proliferation [prəˌlɪfəˈreɪʃən] *n* : proliferación *f*
prolific [prəˈlɪfɪk] *adj* : prolífico
prologue [ˈpro:ˌlɔg] *n* : prólogo *m*
prolong [prəˈlɔŋ] *vt* : prolongar
prolongation [ˌpro:ˌlɔŋˈgeɪʃən] *n* : prolongación *f*
prom [ˈprɑm] *n* : baile *m* formal (de un colegio)
promenade¹ [ˌprɑməˈneɪd, -ˈnɑd] *vi* **-naded; -nading** : pasear, pasearse, dar un paseo
promenade² *n* : paseo *m*
prominence [ˈprɑmənənts] *n* **1** PROJECTION : prominencia *f* **2** EMINENCE : eminencia *f*, prestigio *m*
prominent [ˈprɑmənənt] *adj* **1** OUTSTANDING : prominente, destacado **2** PROJECTING : prominente, saliente
prominently [ˈprɑmənəntli] *adv* : destacadamente, prominentemente
promiscuity [ˌprɑmɪsˈkju:ət̬i] *n, pl* **-ties** : promiscuidad *f*
promiscuous [prəˈmɪskjuəs] *adj* : promiscuo — **promiscuously** *adv*
promise¹ [ˈprɑməs] *v* **-ised; -ising** : prometer
promise² *n* **1** : promesa *f* ⟨he kept his promise : cumplió su promesa⟩ **2 to show promise** : prometer
promising [ˈprɑməsɪŋ] *adj* : prometedor
promissory [ˈprɑməˌsori] *adj* : que promete ⟨a promissory note : un pagaré⟩
promontory [ˈprɑmənˌtori] *n, pl* **-ries** : promontorio *m*
promote [prəˈmo:t] *vt* **-moted; -moting** **1** : ascender (a un alumno o un empleado) **2** ADVERTISE : promocionar, hacerle publicidad a **3** FURTHER : promover, fomentar
promoter [prəˈmo:t̬ər] *n* : promotor *m*, -tora *f*; empresario *m*, -ria *f* (en deportes)
promotion [prəˈmo:ʃən] *n* **1** : ascenso *m* (de un alumno o un empleado) **2** FURTHERING : promoción *f*, fomento *m* **3** ADVERTISING : publicidad *f*, propaganda *f*
promotional [prəˈmo:ʃənəl] *adj* : promocional
prompt¹ [ˈprɑmpt] *vt* **1** INDUCE : provocar (una cosa), inducir (a una persona) ⟨curiosity prompted me to ask you : la curiosidad me indujo a preguntarle⟩ **2** : apuntar (a un actor, etc.)
prompt² *adj* : pronto, rápido ⟨prompt payment : pago puntual⟩
prompter [ˈprɑmptər] *n* : apuntador *m*, -dora *f* (en teatro)
promptly [ˈprɑmptli] *adv* : inmediatamente, rápidamente
promptness [ˈprɑmptnəs] *n* : prontitud *f*, rapidez *f*
promulgate [ˈprɑməlˌgeɪt] *vt* **-gated; -gating** : promulgar
prone [ˈpro:n] *adj* **1** LIABLE : propenso, proclive ⟨accident-prone : propenso a los accidentes⟩ **2** : boca abajo, decúbito prono ⟨in a prone position : en decúbito prono⟩
prong [ˈprɔŋ] *n* : punta *f*, diente *m*
pronoun [ˈpro:ˌnaʊn] *n* : pronombre *m*
pronounce [prəˈnaʊnts] *vt* **-nounced; -nouncing** **1** : pronunciar ⟨how do you pronounce your name? : ¿cómo se pronuncia su nombre?⟩ **2** DECLARE : declarar **3 to pronounce sentence** : dictar sentencia, pronunciar un fallo
pronounced [prəˈnaʊntst] *adj* MARKED : pronunciado, marcado
pronouncement [prəˈnaʊntsmənt] *n* : declaración *f*
pronunciation [prəˌnʌntsiˈeɪʃən] *n* : pronunciación *f*
proof¹ [ˈpru:f] *adj* : a prueba ⟨proof against tampering : a prueba de manipulación⟩
proof² *n* : prueba *f*
proofread [ˈpru:fˌri:d] *v* **-read; -reading** *vt* : corregir — *vi* : corregir pruebas
proofreader [ˈpru:fˌri:dər] *n* : corrector *m*, -tora *f* (de pruebas)
prop¹ [ˈprɑp] *vt* **propped; propping** **1 to prop against** : apoyar contra **2 to prop up** SUPPORT : apoyar, apuntalar, sostener **3 to prop up** SUSTAIN : alentar (a alguien), darle ánimo (a alguien)
prop² *n* **1** SUPPORT : puntal *m*, apoyo *m*, soporte *m* **2** : accesorio *m* (en teatro)
propaganda [ˌprɑpəˈgændə, ˌpro:-] *n* : propaganda *f*
propagandize [ˌprɑpəˈgænˌdaɪz, ˌpro:-] *v* **-dized; -dizing** *vt* : someter a propaganda — *vi* : hacer propaganda

propagate [ˈprɑpəˌgeɪt] *v* **-gated; -gating** *vi* : propagarse — *vt* : propagar
propagation [ˌprɑpəˈgeɪʃən] *n* : propagación *f*
propane [ˈproːˌpeɪn] *n* : propano *m*
propel [prəˈpɛl] *vt* **-pelled; -pelling** : impulsar, propulsar, impeler
propellant *or* **propellent** [prəˈpɛlənt] *n* : propulsor *m*
propeller [prəˈpɛlər] *n* : hélice *f*
propensity [prəˈpɛntsəṭi] *n, pl* **-ties** : propensión *f*, tendencia *f*, inclinación *f*
proper [ˈprɑpər] *adj* **1** RIGHT, SUITABLE : apropiado, adecuado **2** : propio, mismo ⟨the city proper : la propia ciudad⟩ **3** CORRECT : correcto **4** GENTEEL : fino, refinado, cortés **5** OWN, SPECIAL : propio ⟨proper name : nombre propio⟩ — **properly** *adv*
property [ˈprɑpərṭi] *n, pl* **-ties** **1** CHARACTERISTIC : característica *f*, propiedad *f* **2** POSSESSIONS : propiedad *f* **3** BUILDING : inmueble *m* **4** LAND, LOT : terreno *m*, lote *m*, parcela *f* **5** PROP : accesorio *m* (en teatro)
prophecy [ˈprɑfəsi] *n, pl* **-cies** : profecía *f*, vaticinio *m*
prophesy [ˈprɑfəˌsaɪ] *v* **-sied; -sying** *vt* **1** FORETELL : profetizar (como profeta) **2** PREDICT : profetizar, predecir, vaticinar — *vi* : hacer profecías
prophet [ˈprɑfət] *n* : profeta *m*, profetisa *f*
prophetic [prəˈfɛṭɪk] *or* **prophetical** [-ṭɪkəl] *adj* : profético — **prophetically** [-ṭɪkli] *adv*
propitiate [proˈpɪʃiˌeɪt] *vt* **-ated; -ating** : propiciar
propitious [prəˈpɪʃəs] *adj* : propicio
proponent [prəˈpoːnənt] *n* : defensor *m*, -sora *f*; partidario *m*, -ria *f*
proportion[1] [prəˈporʃən] *vt* : proporcionar ⟨well-proportioned : de buenas proporciones⟩
proportion[2] *n* **1** RATIO : proporción *f* **2** SYMMETRY : proporción *f*, simetría *f* ⟨out of proportion : desproporcionado⟩ **3** SHARE : parte *f* **4 proportions** *npl* SIZE : dimensiones *fpl*
proportional [prəˈporʃənəl] *adj* : proporcional — **proportionally** *adv*
proportionate [prəˈporʃənət] *adj* : proporcional — **proportionately** *adv*
proposal [prəˈpoːzəl] *n* **1** PROPOSITION : propuesta *f*, proposición *f* ⟨marriage proposal : propuesta de matrimonio⟩ **2** PLAN : proyecto *m*, propuesta *f*
propose [prəˈpoːz] *v* **-posed; -posing** *vi* : proponer matrimonio — *vt* **1** INTEND : pensar, proponerse **2** SUGGEST : proponer
proposition [ˌprɑpəˈzɪʃən] *n* **1** PROPOSAL : proposición *f*, propuesta *f* **2** STATEMENT : proposición *f*
propound [prəˈpaʊnd] *vt* : proponer, exponer
proprietary [prəˈpraɪəˌtɛri] *adj* : propietario, patentado
proprietor [prəˈpraɪəṭər] *n* : propietario *m*, -ria *f*
propriety [prəˈpraɪəṭi] *n, pl* **-eties** **1** DECORUM : decencia *f*, decoro *m* **2 proprieties** *npl* CONVENTIONS : convenciones *fpl*, cánones *mpl* sociales
propulsion [prəˈpʌlʃən] *n* : propulsión *f*
prosaic [proˈzeɪɪk] *adj* : prosaico
proscribe [proˈskraɪb] *vt* **-scribed; -scribing** : proscribir
prose [ˈproːz] *n* : prosa *f*
prosecute [ˈprɑsɪˌkjuːt] *vt* **-cuted; -cuting** **1** CARRY OUT : llevar a cabo **2** : procesar, enjuiciar ⟨prosecuted for fraud : procesado por fraude⟩
prosecution [ˌprɑsɪˈkjuːʃən] *n* **1** : procesamiento *m* ⟨the prosecution of forgers : el procesamiento de falsificadores⟩ **2** PROSECUTORS : acusación *f* ⟨witness for the prosecution : testigo de cargo⟩
prosecutor [ˈprɑsɪˌkjuːṭər] *n* : acusador *m*, -dora *f*; fiscal *mf*
prospect[1] [ˈprɑˌspɛkt] *vi* : prospectar (el terreno) ⟨to prospect for gold : buscar oro⟩
prospect[2] *n* **1** VISTA : vista *f*, panorama *m* **2** POSSIBILITY : posibilidad *f* **3** OUTLOOK : perspectiva *f* **4** : posible cliente *m*, -ta *f* ⟨a salesman looking for prospects : un vendedor buscando nuevos clientes⟩
prospective [prəˈspɛktɪv, ˈprɑˌspɛk-] *adj* **1** EXPECTANT : futuro ⟨prospective mother : futura madre⟩ **2** POTENTIAL : potencial, posible ⟨prospective employee : posible empleado⟩
prospector [ˈprɑˌspɛktər, prɑˈspɛk-] *n* : prospector *m*, -tora *f*; explorador *m*, -dora *f*
prospectus [prəˈspɛktəs] *n* : prospecto *m*
prosper [ˈprɑspər] *vi* : prosperar
prosperity [prɑˈspɛrəṭi] *n* : prosperidad *f*
prosperous [ˈprɑspərəs] *adj* : próspero
prostate [ˈprɑˌsteɪt] *n* : próstata *f*
prosthesis [prɑsˈθiːsɪs, ˈprɑsθə-] *n, pl* **-theses** [-ˌsiːz] : prótesis *f*
prostitute[1] [ˈprɑstəˌtuːt, -ˌtjuːt] *vt* **-tuted; -tuting** **1** : prostituir **2 to prostitute oneself** : prostituirse
prostitute[2] *n* : prostituto *m*, -ta *f*
prostitution [ˌprɑstəˈtuːʃən, -ˈtjuː-] *n* : prostitución *f*
prostrate[1] [ˈprɑˌstreɪt] *vt* **-trated; -trating** **1** : postrar **2 to prostrate oneself** : postrarse
prostrate[2] *adj* : postrado
prostration [prɑˈstreɪʃən] *n* : postración *f*
protagonist [proˈtægənɪst] *n* : protagonista *mf*
protect [prəˈtɛkt] *vt* : proteger
protection [prəˈtɛkʃən] *n* : protección *f*
protective [prəˈtɛktɪv] *adj* : protector
protector [prəˈtɛktər] *n* **1** : protector *m*, -tora *f* (persona) **2** GUARD : protector *m* (aparato)

protectorate [prə'tɛktərət] *n* : protectorado *m*
protégé ['pro:t̬ə,ʒeɪ] *n* : protegido *m*, -da *f*
protein ['pro:,ti:n] *n* : proteína *f*
protest[1] [pro'tɛst] *vt* **1** ASSERT : afirmar, declarar **2** : protestar ⟨they protested the decision : protestaron (por) la decisión⟩ — *vi* **to protest against** : protestar contra
protest[2] ['pro:,tɛst] *n* **1** DEMONSTRATION : manifestación *f* (de protesta) ⟨a public protest : una manifestación pública⟩ **2** COMPLAINT : queja *f*, protesta *f*
Protestant ['prɑt̬əstənt] *n* : protestante *mf*
Protestantism ['prɑt̬əstən,tɪzəm] *n* : protestantismo *m*
protocol ['pro:t̬ə,kɔl] *n* : protocolo *m*
proton ['pro,tɑn] *n* : protón *m*
protoplasm ['pro:t̬ə,plæzəm] *n* : protoplasma *m*
prototype ['pro:t̬ə,taɪp] *n* : prototipo *m*
protozoan [,pro:t̬ə'zo:ən] *n* : protozoario *m*, protozoo *m*
protract [pro'trækt] *vt* : prolongar
protractor [pro'træktər] *n* : transportador *m* (instrumento)
protrude [pro'tru:d] *vi* **-truded; -truding** : salir, sobresalir
protrusion [pro'tru:ʒən] *n* : protuberancia *f*, saliente *m*
protuberance [pro'tu:bərənts, -'tju:-] *n* : protuberancia *f*
proud ['praʊd] *adj* **1** HAUGHTY : altanero, orgulloso, arrogante **2** : orgulloso ⟨she was proud of her work : estaba orgullosa de su trabajo⟩ ⟨too proud to beg : demasiado orgulloso para rogar⟩ **3** GLORIOUS : glorioso — **proudly** *adv*
prove ['pru:v] *v* **proved; proved** *or* **proven** ['pru:vən]; **proving** *vt* **1** TEST : probar **2** DEMONSTRATE : probar, demostrar — *vi* : resultar ⟨it proved effective : resultó efectivo⟩
Provençal [,pro:vɑn'sɑl, ,prɑvən-] *n* **1** : provenzal *mf* **2** : provenzal *m* (idioma) — **Provençal** *adj*
proverb ['prɑ,vərb] *n* : proverbio *m*, refrán *m*
proverbial [prə'vərbiəl] *adj* : proverbial
provide [prə'vaɪd] *v* **-vided; -viding** *vt* **1** STIPULATE : estipular **2 to provide with** : proveer de, proporcionar — *vi* **1** : proveer ⟨the Lord will provide : el Señor proveerá⟩ **2 to provide for** SUPPORT : mantener **3 to provide for** ANTICIPATE : hacer previsiones para, prever
provided [prə'vaɪdəd] *or* **provided that** *conj* : con tal (de) que, siempre que
providence ['prɑvədənts] *n* **1** PRUDENCE : previsión *f*, prudencia *f* **2** *or* **Providence** : providencia *f* ⟨divine providence : la Divina Providencia⟩ **3 Providence** GOD : Providencia *f*
provident ['prɑvədənt] *adj* **1** PRUDENT : previsor, prudente **2** FRUGAL : frugal, ahorrativo
providential [,prɑvə'dɛntʃəl] *adj* : providencial
provider [prə'vaɪdər] *n* **1** PURVEYOR : proveedor *m*, -dora *f* **2** BREADWINNER : sostén *m* (económico)
providing that → **provided**
province ['prɑvɪnts] *n* **1** : provincia *f* (de un país) ⟨to live in the provinces : vivir en las provincias⟩ **2** FIELD, SPHERE : campo *m*, competencia *f* ⟨it's not in my province : no es de mi competencia⟩
provincial [prə'vɪntʃəl] *adj* **1** : provincial ⟨provincial government : gobierno provincial⟩ **2** : provinciano, pueblerino ⟨a provincial mentality : una mentalidad provinciana⟩
provision[1] [prə'vɪʒən] *vt* : aprovisionar, abastecer
provision[2] *n* **1** PROVIDING : provisión *f*, suministro *m* **2** STIPULATION : condición *f*, salvedad *f*, estipulación *f* **3 provisions** *npl* : despensa *f*, víveres *mpl*, provisiones *fpl*
provisional [prə'vɪʒənəl] *adj* : provisional, provisorio — **provisionally** *adv*
proviso [prə'vaɪ,zo:] *n, pl* **-sos** *or* **-soes** : condición *f*, salvedad *f*, estipulación *f*
provocation [,prɑvə'keɪʃən] *n* : provocación *f*
provocative [prə'vɑkət̬ɪv] *adj* : provocador, provocativo ⟨a provocative article : un artículo que hace pensar⟩
provoke [prə'vo:k] *vt* **-voked; -voking** : provocar
prow ['praʊ] *n* : proa *f*
prowess ['praʊəs] *n* **1** VALOR : valor *m*, valentía *f* **2** SKILL : habilidad *f*, destreza *f*
prowl ['praʊl] *vi* : merodear, rondar — *vt* : rondar por
prowler ['praʊlər] *n* : merodeador *m*, -dora *f*
proximity [prɑk'sɪmət̬i] *n* : proximidad *f*
proxy ['prɑksi] *n, pl* **proxies** **1** : poder *m* (de actuar en nombre de alguien) ⟨by proxy : por poder⟩ **2** AGENT : apoderado *m*, -da *f*; representante *mf*
prude ['pru:d] *n* : mojigato *m*, -ta *f*; gazmoño *m*, -ña *f*
prudence ['pru:dənts] *n* **1** SHREWDNESS : prudencia *f*, sagacidad *f* **2** CAUTION : prudencia *f*, cautela *f* **3** THRIFTINESS : frugalidad *f*
prudent ['pru:dənt] *adj* **1** SHREWD : prudente, sagaz **2** CAUTIOUS, FARSIGHTED : prudente, previsor, precavido **3** THRIFTY : frugal, ahorrativo — **prudently** *adv*
prudery ['pru:dəri] *n, pl* **-eries** : mojigatería *f*, gazmoñería *f*
prudish ['pru:dɪʃ] *adj* : mojigato, gazmoño

prune[1] ['pru:n] *vt* **pruned; pruning** : podar (arbustos, etc.), acortar (un texto), recortar (gastos, etc.)

prune[2] *n* : ciruela *f* pasa

prurient ['prʊriənt] *adj* : lascivo

pry ['praɪ] *v* **pried; prying** *vi* : curiosear, huronear ⟨to pry into other people's business : meterse uno en lo que no le importa⟩ — *vt or* **to pry open** : abrir (con una palanca), apalancar

psalm ['sɑm, 'sɑlm] *n* : salmo *m*

pseudonym ['su:də,nɪm] *n* : seudónimo *m*

psoriasis [sə'raɪəsɪs] *n* : soriasis *f*, psoriasis *f*

psyche ['saɪki] *n* : psique *f*, psiquis *f*

psychedelic[1] [,saɪkə'dɛlɪk] *adj* : psicodélico

psychedelic[2] *n* : droga *f* psicodélica

psychiatric [,saɪki'ætrɪk] *adj* : psiquiátrico, siquiátrico

psychiatrist [sə'kaɪətrɪst, saɪ-] *n* : psiquiatra *mf*, siquiatra *mf*

psychiatry [sə'kaɪətri, saɪ-] *n* : psiquiatría *f*, siquiatría *f*

psychic[1] ['saɪkɪk] *adj* **1** : psíquico, síquico (en psicología) **2** CLAIRVOYANT : clarividente

psychic[2] *n* : vidente *mf*, clarividente *mf*

psychoanalysis [,saɪkoə'næləsɪs] *n, pl* **-yses** : psicoanálisis *m*, sicoanálisis *m*

psychoanalyst [,saɪko'ænəlɪst] *n* : psicoanalista *mf*, sicoanalista *mf*

psychoanalytic [,saɪko,ænəl'ɪṭɪk] *adj* : psicoanalítico, sicoanalítico

psychoanalyze [,saɪko'ænəl,aɪz] *vt* **-lyzed; -lyzing** : psicoanalizar, sicoanalizar

psychological [,saɪkə'lɑʤɪkəl] *adj* : psicológico, sicológico — **psychologically** *adv*

psychologist [saɪ'kɑləʤɪst] *n* : psicólogo *m*, -ga *f*; sicólogo *m*, -ga *f*

psychology [saɪ'kɑləʤi] *n, pl* **-gies** : psicología *f*, sicología *f*

psychopath ['saɪkə,pæθ] *n* : psicópata *mf*, sicópata *mf*

psychopathic [,saɪkə'pæθɪk] *adj* : psicopático, sicopático

psychosis [saɪ'ko:sɪs] *n, pl* **-choses** [-'ko:,si:z] : psicosis *f*, sicosis *f*

psychosomatic [,saɪkəsə'mæṭɪk] *adj* : psicosomático, sicosomático

psychotherapist [,saɪko'θɛrəpɪst] *n* : psicoterapeuta *mf*, sicoterapeuta *mf*

psychotherapy [,saɪko'θɛrəpi] *n, pl* **-pies** : psicoterapia *f*, sicoterapia *f*

psychotic[1] [saɪ'kɑṭɪk] *adj* : psicótico, sicótico

psychotic[2] *n* : psicótico *m*, -ca *f*; sicótico *m*, -ca *f*

puberty ['pju:bərṭi] *n* : pubertad *f*

pubic ['pju:bɪk] *adj* : pubiano, púbico

public[1] ['pʌblɪk] *adj* : público — **publicly** *adv*

public[2] *n* : público *m*

publication [,pʌblə'keɪʃən] *n* : publicación *f*

publicist ['pʌbləsɪst] *n* : publicista *mf*

publicity [pə'blɪsəṭi] *n* : publicidad *f*

publicize ['pʌblə,saɪz] *vt* **-cized; -cizing** : publicitar

public school *n* : escuela *f* pública

publish ['pʌblɪʃ] *vt* : publicar

publisher ['pʌblɪʃər] *n* : casa *f* editorial (compañía); editor *m*, -tora *f* (persona)

publishing ['pʌblɪʃɪŋ] *n* : industria *f* editorial

pucker[1] ['pʌkər] *vt* : fruncir, arrugar — *vi* : arrugarse

pucker[2] *n* : arruga *f*, frunce *m*, fruncido *m*

pudding ['pʊdɪŋ] *n* : budín *m*, pudín *m*

puddle ['pʌdəl] *n* : charco *m*

pudgy ['pʌʤi] *adj* **pudgier; -est** : regordete *fam*, rechoncho *fam*, gordinflón *fam*

puerile ['pjʊrəl] *adj* : pueril

Puerto Rican[1] [,pwɛrṭə'ri:kən, ,porṭə-] *adj* : puertorriqueño

Puerto Rican[2] *n* : puertorriqueño *m*, -ña *f*

puff[1] ['pʌf] *vi* **1** BLOW : soplar **2** PANT : resoplar, jadear **3 to puff up** SWELL : hincharse — *vt* **1** BLOW : soplar ⟨to puff smoke : echar humo⟩ **2** INFLATE : inflar, hinchar ⟨to puff out one's cheeks : inflar las mejillas⟩

puff[2] *n* **1** GUST : soplo *m*, ráfaga *f*, bocanada *f* (de humo) **2** DRAW : chupada *f* (a un cigarrillo) **3** SWELLING : hinchazón *f* **4 cream puff** : pastelito *m* de crema **5 powder puff** : borla *f*

puffy ['pʌfi] *adj* **puffier; -est 1** SWOLLEN : hinchado, inflado **2** SPONGY : esponjoso, suave

pug ['pʌg] *n* **1** : doguillo *m* (perro) **2** *or* **pug nose** : nariz *f* achatada

pugnacious [,pʌg'neɪʃəs] *adj* : pugnaz, agresivo

puke ['pju:k] *vi* **puked; puking** : vomitar, devolver

pull[1] ['pʊl, 'pʌl] *vt* **1** DRAW, TUG : tirar de, jalar **2** EXTRACT : sacar, extraer ⟨to pull teeth : sacar muelas⟩ ⟨to pull a gun on : amenazar a (alguien) con pistola⟩ **3** TEAR : desgarrarse (un músculo, etc.) **4 to pull down** : bajar, echar abajo, derribar (un edificio) **5 to pull in** ATTRACT : atraer (una muchedumbre, etc.) ⟨to pull in votes : conseguir votos⟩ **6 to pull off** REMOVE : sacar, quitar **7 to pull oneself together** : calmarse, tranquilizarse **8 to pull up** RAISE : levantar, subir — *vi* **1** DRAW, TUG : tirar, jalar **2** (*indicating movement in a specific direction*) ⟨they pulled in front of us : se nos metieron delante⟩ ⟨to pull to a stop : pararse⟩ **3 to pull through** RECOVER : recobrarse, reponerse **4 to pull together** COOPERATE : trabajar juntos, cooperar

pull[2] *n* **1** TUG : tirón *m*, jalón *m* ⟨he gave it a pull : le dio un tirón⟩ **2** ATTRACTION : atracción *f*, fuerza *f* ⟨the pull of gravity : la fuerza de la gravedad⟩ **3**

INFLUENCE : influencia *f* **4** HANDLE : tirador *m* (de un cajón, etc.) **5 bell pull** : cuerda *f*
pullet ['pʊlət] *n* : polla *f*, gallina *f* (joven)
pulley ['pʊli] *n, pl* **-leys** : polea *f*
pullover ['pʊl,o:vər] *n* : suéter *m*
pulmonary ['pʊlmə,nɛri, 'pʌl-] *adj* : pulmonar
pulp ['pʌlp] *n* **1** : pulpa *f* (de una fruta, etc.) **2** MASH : papilla *f*, pasta *f* ⟨wood pulp : pasta de papel, pulpa de papel⟩ ⟨to beat to a pulp : hacer papilla (a alguien)⟩ **3** : pulpa *f* (de los dientes)
pulpit ['pʊl,pɪt] *n* : púlpito *m*
pulsate ['pʌl,seɪt] *vi* **-sated; -sating 1** BEAT : latir, palpitar **2** VIBRATE : vibrar
pulsation [,pʌl'seɪʃən] *n* : pulsación *f*
pulse ['pʌls] *n* : pulso *m*
pulverize ['pʌlvə,raɪz] *vt* **-ized; -izing** : pulverizar
puma ['pu:mə, 'pju:-] *n* : puma *m*; león *m*, leona *f* (in various countries)
pumice ['pʌməs] *n* : piedra *f* pómez
pummel ['pʌməl] *vt* **-meled; -meling** : aporrear, apalear
pump1 ['pʌmp] *vt* **1** : bombear ⟨to pump water : bombear agua⟩ ⟨to pump (up) a tire : inflar una llanta⟩ **2** : mover (una manivela, un pedal, etc.) de arriba abajo ⟨to pump someone's hand : darle un fuerte apretón de manos (a alguien)⟩ **3 to pump out** : sacar, vaciar (con una bomba)
pump2 *n* **1** : bomba *f* ⟨water pump : bomba de agua⟩ **2** SHOE : zapato *m* de tacón
pumpernickel ['pʌmpər,nɪkəl] *n* : pan *m* negro de centeno
pumpkin ['pʌmpkɪn, 'pʌŋkən] *n* : calabaza *f*, zapallo *m Arg, Chile, Peru, Uru*
pun1 ['pʌn] *vi* **punned; punning** : hacer juegos de palabras
pun2 *n* : juego *m* de palabras, albur *m Mex*
punch1 ['pʌntʃ] *vt* **1** HIT : darle un puñetazo (a alguien), golpear ⟨she punched him in the nose : le dio un puñetazo en la nariz⟩ **2** PERFORATE : perforar (papel, etc.), picar (un boleto)
punch2 *n* **1** : perforadora *f* ⟨paper punch : perforadora de papel⟩ **2** BLOW : golpe *m*, puñetazo *m* **3** : ponche *m* ⟨fruit punch : ponche de frutas⟩
punctilious [pəŋk'tɪliəs] *adj* : puntilloso
punctual ['pʌŋktʃʊəl] *adj* : puntual
punctuality [,pʌŋktʃʊ'æləṭi] *n* : puntualidad *f*
punctually ['pʌŋktʃʊəli] *adv* : puntualmente, a tiempo
punctuate ['pʌŋktʃʊ,eɪt] *vt* **-ated; -ating** : puntuar
punctuation [,pʌŋktʃʊ'eɪʃən] *n* : puntuación *f*
puncture1 ['pʌŋktʃər] *vt* **-tured; -turing** : pinchar, punzar, perforar, ponchar *Mex*
puncture2 *n* : pinchazo *m*, ponchadura *f Mex*
pundit ['pʌndɪt] *n* : experto *m*, -ta *f*
pungency ['pʌndʒəntsi] *n* : acritud *f*, acrimonia *f*
pungent ['pʌndʒənt] *adj* : acre
punish ['pʌnɪʃ] *vt* : castigar
punishable ['pʌnɪʃəbəl] *adj* : punible
punishment ['pʌnɪʃmənt] *n* : castigo *m*
punitive ['pju:nəṭɪv] *adj* : punitivo
punt1 ['pʌnt] *vt* : impulsar (un barco) con una pértiga — *vi* : despejar (en deportes)
punt2 *n* **1** : batea *f* (barco) **2** : patada *f* de despeje (en deportes)
puny ['pju:ni] *adj* **-nier; -est** : enclenque, endeble
pup ['pʌp] *n* : cachorro *m*, -rra *f* (de un perro); cría *f* (de otros animales)
pupa ['pju:pə] *n, pl* **-pae** [-pi, -,paɪ] *or* **-pas** : crisálida *f*, pupa *f*
pupil ['pju:pəl] *n* **1** : alumno *m*, -na *f* (de colegio) **2** : pupila *f* (del ojo)
puppet ['pʌpət] *n* : títere *m*, marioneta *f*
puppy ['pʌpi] *n, pl* **-pies** : cachorro *m*, -rra *f*
purchase1 ['pərtʃəs] *vt* **-chased; -chasing** : comprar
purchase2 *n* **1** PURCHASING : compra *f*, adquisición *f* **2** : compra *f* ⟨last-minute purchases : compras de última hora⟩ **3** GRIP : agarre *m*, asidero *m* ⟨she got a firm purchase on the wheel : se agarró bien del volante⟩
purchase order *n* : orden *f* de compra
pure ['pjʊr] *adj* **purer; purest** : puro
puree1 [pjʊ'reɪ, -'ri:] *vt* **-reed; -reeing** : hacer un puré con
puree2 *n* : puré *m*
purely ['pjʊrli] *adv* **1** WHOLLY : puramente, completamente ⟨purely by chance : por pura casualidad⟩ **2** SIMPLY : sencillamente, meramente
purgative ['pərgəṭɪv] *n* : purgante *m*
purgatory ['pərgə,tori] *n, pl* **-ries** : purgatorio *m*
purge1 ['pərdʒ] *vt* **purged; purging** : purgar
purge2 *n* : purga *f*
purification [,pjʊrəfə'keɪʃən] *n* : purificación *f*
purify ['pjʊrə,faɪ] *vt* **-fied; -fying** : purificar
puritan ['pjʊrətən] *n* : puritano *m*, -na *f* — **puritan** *adj*
puritanical [,pju:rə'tænɪkəl] *adj* : puritano
purity ['pjʊrəṭi] *n* : pureza *f*
purl1 ['pərl] *v* : tejer al revés, tejer del revés
purl2 *n* : punto *m* del revés
purloin [pər'lɔɪn, 'pər,lɔɪn] *vt* : hurtar, robar
purple ['pərpəl] *n* : morado *m*, color *m* púrpura
purport [pər'port] *vt* : pretender ⟨to purport to be : pretender ser⟩
purpose ['pərpəs] *n* **1** INTENTION : propósito *m*, intención *f* ⟨on purpose

: a propósito, adrede⟩ **2** FUNCTION : función *f* **3** RESOLUTION : resolución *f*, determinación *f*

purposeful [ˈpərpəsfəl] *adj* : determinado, decidido, resuelto

purposefully [ˈpərpəsfəli] *adv* : decididamente, resueltamente

purposely [ˈpərpəsli] *adv* : intencionadamente, a propósito, adrede

purr[1] [ˈpər] *vi* : ronronear

purr[2] *n* : ronroneo *m*

purse[1] [ˈpərs] *vt* **pursed; pursing** : fruncir ⟨to purse one's lips : fruncir la boca⟩

purse[2] *n* **1** HANDBAG : cartera *f*, bolso *m*, bolsa *f Mex* ⟨a change purse : un monedero⟩ **2** FUNDS : fondos *mpl* **3** PRIZE : premio *m*

pursue [pərˈsuː] *vt* **-sued; -suing 1** CHASE : perseguir **2** SEEK : buscar, tratar de encontrar ⟨to pursue pleasure : buscar el placer⟩ **3** FOLLOW : seguir ⟨the road pursues a northerly course : el camino sigue hacia el norte⟩ **4** : dedicarse a ⟨to pursue a hobby : dedicarse a un pasatiempo⟩

pursuer [pərˈsuːər] *n* : perseguidor *m*, -dora *f*

pursuit [pərˈsuːt] *n* **1** CHASE : persecución *f* **2** SEARCH : búsqueda *f*, busca *f* **3** ACTIVITY : actividad *f*, pasatiempo *m*

purveyor [pərˈveɪər] *n* : proveedor *m*, -dora *f*

pus [ˈpʌs] *n* : pus *m*

push[1] [ˈpʊʃ] *vt* **1** SHOVE : empujar **2** PRESS : apretar, pulsar ⟨push that button : aprieta ese botón⟩ **3** PRESSURE, URGE : presionar **4 to push around** BULLY : intimidar, mangonear — *vi* **1** SHOVE : empujar **2** INSIST : insistir, presionar **3 to push off** LEAVE : marcharse, irse, largarse *fam* **4 to push on** PROCEED : seguir

push[2] *n* **1** SHOVE : empujón *m* **2** DRIVE : empuje *m*, energía *f*, dinamismo *m* **3** EFFORT : esfuerzo *m*

push–button [ˈpʊʃˈbʌtən] *adj* : de botones

pushcart [ˈpʊʃˌkɑrt] *n* : carretilla *f* de mano

pushy [ˈpʊʃi] *adj* **pushier; -est** : mandón, prepotente

pussy [ˈpʊsi] *n, pl* **pussies** : gatito *m*, -ta *f*; minino *m*, -na *f*

pussy willow *n* : sauce *m* blanco

pustule [ˈpʌsˌʧuːl] *n* : pústula *f*

put [ˈpʊt] *v* **put; putting** *vt* **1** PLACE : poner, colocar ⟨put it on the table : ponlo en la mesa⟩ **2** INSERT : meter **3** (*indicating causation of a state or feeling*) : poner ⟨it put her in a good mood : la puso de buen humor⟩ ⟨to put into effect : poner en práctica⟩ **4** IMPOSE : imponer ⟨they put a tax on it : lo gravaron con un impuesto⟩ **5** SUBJECT : someter, poner ⟨to put to the test : poner a prueba⟩ ⟨to put to death : ejecutar⟩ **6** EXPRESS : expresar, decir ⟨he put it simply : lo dijo sencillamente⟩ **7** APPLY : aplicar ⟨to put one's mind to something : proponerse hacer algo⟩ **8** SET : poner ⟨I put him to work : lo puse a trabajar⟩ **9** ATTACH : dar ⟨to put a high value on : dar gran valor a⟩ **10** PRESENT : presentar, exponer ⟨to put a question to someone : hacer una pregunta a alguien⟩ — *vi* **1 to put to sea** : hacerse a la mar **2 to put up with** : aguantar, soportar

put away *vt* **1** KEEP : guardar **2** *or* **to put aside** : dejar a un lado

put by *vt* SAVE : ahorrar

put down *vt* **1** SUPPRESS : aplastar, suprimir **2** ATTRIBUTE : atribuir ⟨she put it down to luck : lo atribuyó a la suerte⟩

put in *vi* : presentarse ⟨I've put in for the position : me presenté para el puesto⟩ — *vt* DEVOTE : dedicar (unas horas, etc.)

put off *vt* DEFER : aplazar, posponer

put on *vt* **1** ASSUME : afectar, adoptar **2** PRODUCE : presentar (una obra de teatro, etc.) **3** WEAR : ponerse

put out *vt* INCONVENIENCE : importunar, incomodar

putrefy [ˈpjuːtrəˌfaɪ] *v* **-fied; -fying** *vt* : pudrir — *vi* : pudrirse

putrid [ˈpjuːtrɪd] *adj* : putrefacto, pútrido

putter [ˈpʌt̬ər] *vi or* **to putter around** : entretenerse

putty[1] [ˈpʌt̬i] *vt* **-tied; -tying** : poner masilla en

putty[2] *n, pl* **-ties** : masilla *f*

put up *vt* **1** LODGE : alojar **2** CONTRIBUTE : contribuir, pagar

puzzle[1] [ˈpʌzəl] *vt* **-zled; -zling 1** CONFUSE : confundir, dejar perplejo **2 to puzzle out** : dar vueltas a, tratar de resolver

puzzle[2] *n* **1** : rompecabezas *m* ⟨a crossword puzzle : un crucigrama⟩ **2** MYSTERY : misterio *m*, enigma *m*

puzzlement [ˈpʌzəlmənt] *n* : desconcierto *m*, perplejidad *f*

pygmy[1] [ˈpɪgmi] *adj* : enano, pigmeo

pygmy[2] *n, pl* **-mies 1** DWARF : enano *m*, -na *f* **2 Pygmy** : pigmeo *m*, -mea *f*

pylon [ˈpaɪˌlɑn, -lən] *n* **1** : torre *f* de conducta eléctrica **2** : pilón *m* (de un puente)

pyramid [ˈpɪrəˌmɪd] *n* : pirámide *f*

pyre [ˈpaɪr] *n* : pira *f*

pyromania [ˌpaɪroˈmeɪniə] *n* : piromanía *f*

pyromaniac [ˌpaɪroˈmeɪniˌæk] *n* : pirómano *m*, -na *f*

pyrotechnics [ˌpaɪrəˈtɛknɪks] *npl* **1** FIREWORKS : fuegos *mpl* artificiales **2** DISPLAY, SHOW : espectáculo *m*, muestra *f* de virtuosismo ⟨computer pyrotechnics : efectos especiales hechos por computadora⟩

python [ˈpaɪˌθɑn, -θən] *n* : pitón *f*, serpiente *f* pitón

Q

q [ˈkjuː] *n, pl* **q's** *or* **qs** [ˈkjuːz] : decimoséptima letra del alfabeto inglés
quack[1] [ˈkwæk] *vi* : graznar
quack[2] *n* **1** : graznido *m* (de pato) **2** CHARLATAN : curandero *m*, -ra *f*; matasanos *m fam*
quadrangle [ˈkwɑˌdræŋgəl] *n* **1** COURTYARD : patio *m* interior **2** → **quadrilateral**
quadrant [ˈkwɑdrənt] *n* : cuadrante *m*
quadrilateral [ˌkwɑdrəˈlæt̬ərəl] *n* : cuadrilátero *m*
quadruped [ˈkwɑdrəˌpɛd] *n* : cuadrúpedo *m*
quadruple [kwɑˈdruːpəl, -ˈdrʌ-; ˈkwɑdrə-] *v* **-pled; -pling** *vt* : cuadruplicar — *vi* : cuadruplicarse
quadruplet [kwɑˈdruːplət, -ˈdrʌ-; ˈkwɑdrə-] *n* : cuatrillizo *m*, -za *f*
quagmire [ˈkwægˌmaɪr, ˈkwɑg-] *n* **1** : lodazal *m*, barrizal *m* **2** PREDICAMENT : atolladero *m*
quail[1] [ˈkweɪl] *vi* : encogerse, acobardarse
quail[2] *n, pl* **quail** *or* **quails** : codorniz *f*
quaint [ˈkweɪnt] *adj* **1** ODD : extraño, curioso **2** PICTURESQUE : pintoresco — **quaintly** *adv*
quaintness [ˈkweɪntnəs] *n* : rareza *f*, lo curioso
quake[1] [ˈkweɪk] *vi* **quaked; quaking** : temblar
quake[2] *n* : temblor *m*, terremoto *m*
qualification [ˌkwɑləfəˈkeɪʃən] *n* **1** LIMITATION, RESERVATION : reserva *f*, limitación *f* ⟨without qualification : sin reservas⟩ **2** REQUIREMENT : requisito *m* **3 qualifications** *npl* ABILITY : aptitud *f*, capacidad *f*
qualified [ˈkwɑləˌfaɪd] *adj* : competente, capacitado
qualifier [ˈkwɑləˌfaɪər] *n* **1** : clasificado *m*, -da *f* (en deportes) **2** : calificativo *m* (en gramática)
qualify [ˈkwɑləˌfaɪ] *v* **-fied; -fying** *vt* **1** : matizar ⟨to qualify a statement : matizar una declaración⟩ **2** MODIFY : calificar (en gramática) **3** : habilitar ⟨the certificate qualified her to teach : el certificado la habilitó para enseñar⟩ — *vi* **1** : obtener el título, recibirse ⟨to qualify as an engineer : recibirse de ingeniero⟩ **2** : clasificarse (en deportes)
quality [ˈkwɑlət̬i] *n, pl* **-ties** **1** NATURE : carácter *m* **2** ATTRIBUTE : cualidad *f* **3** GRADE : calidad *f* ⟨of good quality : de buena calidad⟩
qualm [ˈkwɑm, ˈkwɑlm, ˈkwɔm] *n* **1** MISGIVING : duda *f*, aprensión *f* **2** RESERVATION, SCRUPLE : escrúpulo *m*, reparo *m*
quandary [ˈkwɑndri] *n, pl* **-ries** : dilema *m*
quantitative [ˈkwɑntəˌteɪt̬ɪv] *adj* : cuantitativo
quantity [ˈkwɑntət̬i] *n, pl* **-ties** : cantidad *f*
quantum[1] [ˈkwɑntəm] *n* : cuanto *m* (en física)
quantum[2] *adj* : cuántico
quantum theory [ˈkwɑntəm] *n* : teoría *f* cuántica
quarantine[1] [ˈkwɔrənˌtiːn] *vt* **-tined; -tining** : poner en cuarentena
quarantine[2] *n* : cuarentena *f*
quarrel[1] [ˈkwɔrəl] *vi* **-reled** *or* **-relled; -reling** *or* **-relling** : pelearse, reñir, discutir
quarrel[2] *n* : pelea *f*, riña *f*, disputa *f*
quarrelsome [ˈkwɔrəlsəm] *adj* : pendenciero, discutidor
quarry[1] [ˈkwɔri] *vt* **quarried; quarrying** **1** EXTRACT : extraer, sacar ⟨to quarry marble : extraer mármol⟩ **2** EXCAVATE : excavar ⟨to quarry a hill : excavar un cerro⟩
quarry[2] *n, pl* **quarries** **1** PREY : presa *f* **2** *or* **stone quarry** : cantera *f*
quart [ˈkwɔrt] *n* : cuarto *m* de galón
quarter[1] [ˈkwɔrt̬ər] *vt* **1** : dividir en cuatro partes **2** LODGE : alojar, acuartelar (tropas)
quarter[2] *n* **1** : cuarto *m*, cuarta parte *f* ⟨a foot and a quarter : un pie y cuarto⟩ ⟨a quarter after three : las tres y cuarto⟩ **2** : moneda *f* de 25 centavos, cuarto *m* de dólar **3** DISTRICT : barrio *m* ⟨business quarter : barrio comercial⟩ **4** PLACE : parte *f* ⟨from all quarters : de todas partes⟩ ⟨at close quarters : de muy cerca⟩ **5** MERCY : clemencia *f*, cuartel *m* ⟨to give no quarter : no dar cuartel⟩ **6 quarters** *npl* LODGING : alojamiento *m*, cuartel *m* (militar)
quarterback [ˈkwɔrt̬ərˌbæk] *n* : mariscal *m* de campo
quarterly[1] [ˈkwɔrt̬ərli] *adv* : cada tres meses, trimestralmente
quarterly[2] *adj* : trimestral
quarterly[3] *n, pl* **-lies** : publicación *f* trimestral
quartermaster [ˈkwɔrt̬ərˌmæstər] *n* : intendente *mf*
quartet [kwɔrˈtɛt] *n* : cuarteto *m*
quartz [ˈkwɔrts] *n* : cuarzo *m*
quash [ˈkwɑʃ, ˈkwɔʃ] *vt* **1** ANNUL : anular **2** QUELL : sofocar, aplastar
quaver[1] [ˈkweɪvər] *vi* **1** SHAKE : temblar ⟨her voice was quavering : le temblaba la voz⟩ **2** TRILL : trinar
quaver[2] *n* : temblor *m* (de la voz)
quay [ˈkiː, ˈkeɪ, ˈkweɪ] *n* : muelle *m*
queasiness [ˈkwiːzinəs] *n* : mareo *m*, náusea *f*
queasy [ˈkwiːzi] *adj* **-sier; -est** : mareado
queen [ˈkwiːn] *n* : reina *f*
queenly [ˈkwiːnli] *adj* **-lier; -est** : de reina, regio
queer [ˈkwɪr] *adj* : extraño, raro, curioso — **queerly** *adv*
quell [ˈkwl] *vt* : aplastar, sofocar

quench [ˈkwɛntʃ] *vt* **1** EXTINGUISH : apagar, sofocar **2** SATISFY : saciar, satisfacer (la sed)

querulous [ˈkwɛrələs, ˈkwɛrjələs, ˈkwɪr-] *adj* : quejumbroso, quejoso — **querulously** *adv*

query[1] [ˈkwɪri, ˈkwɛr-] *vt* **-ried; -rying 1** ASK : preguntar, interrogar ⟨we queried the professor : preguntamos al profesor⟩ **2** QUESTION : cuestionar, poner en duda ⟨to query a matter : cuestionar un asunto⟩

query[2] *n, pl* **-ries 1** QUESTION : pregunta *f* **2** DOUBT : duda *f*

quest[1] [ˈkwɛst] *v* : buscar

quest[2] *n* : búsqueda *f*

question[1] [ˈkwɛstʃən] *vt* **1** ASK : preguntar **2** DOUBT : poner en duda, cuestionar **3** INTERROGATE : interrogar — *vi* INQUIRE : inquirir, preguntar

question[2] *n* **1** QUERY : pregunta *f* **2** ISSUE : asunto *m*, problema *f*, cuestión *f* **3** POSSIBILITY : posibilidad *f* ⟨it's out of the question : es indiscutible⟩ **4** DOUBT : duda *f* ⟨to call into question : poner en duda⟩

questionable [ˈkwɛstʃənəbəl] *adj* : dudoso, discutible, cuestionable ⟨questionable results : resultados discutibles⟩ ⟨questionable motives : motivos sospechosos⟩

questioner [ˈkwɛstʃənər] *n* : interrogador *m*, -dora *f*

question mark *n* : signo *m* de interrogación

questionnaire [ˌkwɛstʃəˈnær] *n* : cuestionario *m*

queue[1] [ˈkju:] *vi* **queued; queuing** *or* **queueing** : hacer cola

queue[2] *n* **1** PIGTAIL : coleta *f*, trenza *f* **2** LINE : cola *f*, fila *f*

quibble[1] [ˈkwɪbəl] *vi* **-bled; -bling** : quejarse por nimiedades, andar con sutilezas

quibble[2] *n* : objeción *f* de poca monta, queja *f* insignificante

quick[1] [ˈkwɪk] *adv* : rápidamente

quick[2] *adj* **1** RAPID : rápido **2** ALERT, CLEVER : listo, vivo, agudo **3 a quick temper** : un genio vivo

quick[3] *n* **1** FLESH : carne *f* viva **2 to cut someone to the quick** : herir a alguien en lo más vivo

quicken [ˈkwɪkən] *vt* **1** REVIVE : resucitar **2** AROUSE : estimular, despertar **3** HASTEN : acelerar ⟨she quickened her pace : aceleró el paso⟩

quickly [ˈkwɪkli] *adv* : rápidamente, rápido, de prisa

quickness [ˈkwɪknəs] *n* : rapidez *f*

quicksand [ˈkwɪkˌsænd] *n* : arena *f* movediza

quicksilver [ˈkwɪkˌsɪlvər] *n* : mercurio *m*, azogue *m*

quick–tempered [ˈkwɪkˈtɛmpərd] *adj* : irascible, de genio vivo

quick–witted [ˈkwɪkˈwɪt̬əd] *adj* : agudo

quiet[1] [ˈkwaɪət] *vt* **1** SILENCE : hacer callar, acallar **2** CALM : calmar, tranquilizar — *vi* **to quiet down** : calmarse, tranquilizarse

quiet[2] *adv* : silenciosamente ⟨a quiet-running engine : un motor silencioso⟩

quiet[3] *adj* **1** CALM : tranquilo, calmoso **2** MILD : sosegado, suave ⟨a quiet disposition : un temperamento sosegado⟩ **3** SILENT : silencioso **4** UNOBTRUSIVE : discreto **5** SECLUDED : aislado ⟨a quiet nook : un rincón aislado⟩ — **quietly** *adv*

quiet[4] *n* **1** CALM : calma *f*, tranquilidad *f* **2** SILENCE : silencio *m*

quietness [ˈkwaɪətnəs] *n* : suavidad *f*, tranquilidad *f*, quietud *f*

quietude [ˈkwaɪəˌtu:d, -ˌtju:d] *n* : quietud *f*, reposo *m*

quill [ˈkwɪl] *n* **1** SPINE : púa *f* (de un puerco espín) **2** : pluma *f* (para escribir)

quilt[1] [ˈkwɪlt] *vt* : acolchar

quilt[2] *n* : colcha *f*, edredón *m*

quince [ˈkwɪnts] *n* : membrillo *m*

quinine [ˈkwaɪˌnaɪn] *n* : quinina *f*

quintessence [kwɪnˈtɛsənts] *n* : quintaesencia *f*

quintet [kwɪnˈtɛt] *n* : quinteto *m*

quintuple [kwɪnˈtu:pəl, -ˈtju:-, -ˈtʌ-; ˈkwɪntə-] *adj* : quíntuplo

quintuplet [kwɪnˈtʌplət, -ˈtu:-, -ˈtju:-; ˈkwɪntə-] *n* : quintillizo *m*, -za *f*

quip[1] [ˈkwɪp] *vi* **quipped; quipping** : bromear

quip[2] *n* : ocurrencia *f*, salida *f*

quirk [ˈkwərk] *n* : peculiaridad *f*, rareza *f* ⟨a quirk of fate : un capricho del destino⟩

quirky [ˈkwərki] *adj* **-kier; -est** : peculiar, raro

quit [ˈkwɪt] *v* **quit; quitting** *vt* : dejar, abandonar ⟨to quit smoking : dejar de fumar⟩ — *vi* **1** STOP : parar **2** RESIGN : dimitir, renunciar

quite [ˈkwaɪt] *adv* **1** COMPLETELY : completamente, totalmente **2** RATHER : bastante ⟨quite near : bastante cerca⟩

quits [ˈkwɪts] *adj* **to call it quits** : quedar en paz

quitter [ˈkwɪt̬ər] *n* : derrotista *mf*

quiver[1] [ˈkwɪvər] *vi* : temblar, estremecerse, vibrar

quiver[2] *n* **1** : carcaj *m*, aljaba *f* (para flechas) **2** TREMBLING : temblor *m*, estremecimiento *m*

quixotic [kwɪkˈsɑt̬ɪk] *adj* : quijotesco

quiz[1] [ˈkwɪz] *vt* **quizzed; quizzing** : interrogar, hacer una prueba a (en el colegio)

quiz[2] *n, pl* **quizzes** : examen *m* corto, prueba *f*

quizzical [ˈkwɪzɪkəl] *adj* **1** TEASING : burlón **2** CURIOUS : curioso, interrogativo

quorum [ˈkworəm] *n* : quórum *m*

quota [ˈkwoːt̬ə] *n* : cuota *f*, cupo *m*
quotable [ˈkwoːt̬əbəl] *adj* : citable
quotation [kwoˈteɪʃən] *n* **1** CITATION : cita *f* **2** ESTIMATE : presupuesto *m*, estimación *f* **3** PRICE : cotización *f*
quotation marks *npl* : comillas *fpl*
quote[1] [ˈkwoːt] *vt* **quoted; quoting 1** CITE : citar **2** VALUE : cotizar (en finanzas)
quote[2] *n* **1** → **quotation 2 quotes** *npl* → **quotation marks**
quotient [ˈkwoːʃənt] *n* : cociente *m*

R

r [ˈɑr] *n, pl* **r's** *or* **rs** [ˈɑrz] : decimoctava letra del alfabeto inglés
rabbi [ˈræˌbaɪ] *n* : rabino *m*, -na *f*
rabbit [ˈræbət] *n, pl* **-bit** *or* **-bits** : conejo *m*, -ja *f*
rabble [ˈræbəl] *n* **1** MASSES : populacho *m* **2** RIFFRAFF : chusma *f*, gentuza *f*
rabid [ˈræbɪd] *adj* **1** : rabioso, afectado con la rabia **2** FURIOUS : furioso **3** FANATIC : fanático
rabies [ˈreɪbiːz] *ns & pl* : rabia *f*
raccoon [ræˈkuːn] *n, pl* **-coon** *or* **-coons** : mapache *m*
race[1] [ˈreɪs] *vi* **raced; racing 1** : correr, competir (en una carrera) **2** RUSH : ir a toda prisa, ir corriendo
race[2] *n* **1** CURRENT : corriente *f* (de agua) **2** : carrera *f* ‹dog race : carrera de perros› ‹the presidential race : la carrera presidential› **3** : raza *f* ‹the black race : la raza negra› ‹the human race : el género humano›
racecourse [ˈreɪsˌkors] *n* : pista *f* (de carreras)
racehorse [ˈreɪsˌhors] *n* : caballo *m* de carreras
racer [ˈreɪsər] *n* : corredor *m*, -dora *f*
racetrack [ˈreɪsˌtræk] *n* : pista *f* (de carreras)
racial [ˈreɪʃəl] *adj* : racial — **racially** *adv*
racism [ˈreɪˌsɪzəm] *n* : racismo *m*
racist [ˈreɪsɪst] *n* : racista *mf*
rack[1] [ˈræk] *vt* **1** : atormentar ‹racked with pain : atormentado por el dolor› **2 to rack one's brains** : devanarse los sesos
rack[2] *n* **1** SHELF, STAND : estante *m* ‹a luggage rack : un portaequipajes› ‹a coatrack : un perchero, una percha› **2** : potro *m* (instrumento de la tortura)
racket [ˈrækət] *n* **1** : raqueta *f* (en deportes) **2** DIN : estruendo *m*, bulla *f*, jaleo *m fam* **3** SWINDLE : estafa *f*, timo *m fam*
racketeer [ˌrækəˈtɪr] *n* : estafador *m*, -dora *f*
raconteur [ˌræˌkɑnˈtər] *n* : anecdotista *mf*
racy [ˈreɪsi] *adj* **racier; -est** : subido de tono, picante
radar [ˈreɪˌdɑr] *n* : radar *m*
radial [ˈreɪdiəl] *adj* : radial
radiance [ˈreɪdiənts] *n* : resplandor *m*
radiant [ˈreɪdiənt] *adj* : radiante — **radiantly** *adv*
radiate [ˈreɪdiˌeɪt] *v* **-ated; -ating** *vt* : irradiar, emitir ‹to radiate heat : irradiar el calor› ‹to radiate happiness : rebosar de alegría› — *vi* **1** : irradiar **2** SPREAD : salir, extenderse ‹to radiate (out) from the center : salir del centro›
radiation [ˌreɪdiˈeɪʃən] *n* : radiación *f*
radiator [ˈreɪdiˌeɪt̬ər] *n* : radiador *m*
radical[1] [ˈrædɪkəl] *adj* : radical — **radically** [-kli] *adv*
radical[2] *n* : radical *mf*
radicalism [ˈrædɪkəˌlɪzəm] *n* : radicalismo *m*
radii → **radius**
radio[1] [ˈreɪdiˌoː] *v* : llamar por radio, transmitir por radio
radio[2] *n, pl* **-dios** : radio *m* (aparato), radio *f* (emisora, radiodifusión)
radioactive [ˈreɪdioˈæktɪv] *adj* : radiactivo, radioactivo
radioactivity [ˌreɪdioˌækˈtɪvət̬i] *n, pl* **-ties** : radiactividad *f*, radioactividad *f*
radiologist [ˌreɪdiˈɑləʤɪst] *n* : radiólogo *m*, -ga *f*
radiology [ˌreɪdiˈɑləʤi] *n* : radiología *f*
radish [ˈrædɪʃ] *n* : rábano *m*
radium [ˈreɪdiəm] *n* : radio *m*
radius [ˈreɪdiəs] *n, pl* **radii** [-diˌaɪ] : radio *m*
radon [ˈreɪˌdɑn] *n* : radón *m*
raffle[1] [ˈræfəl] *vt* **-fled; -fling** : rifar, sortear
raffle[2] *n* : rifa *f*, sorteo *m*
raft [ˈræft] *n* **1** : balsa *f* ‹rubber rafts : balsas de goma› **2** LOT, SLEW : montón *m* ‹a raft of documents : un montón de documentos›
rafter [ˈræftər] *n* : par *m*, viga *f*
rag [ˈræg] *n* **1** CLOTH : trapo *m* **2 rags** *npl* TATTERS : harapos *mpl*, andrajos *mpl*
ragamuffin [ˈrægəˌmʌfən] *n* : pilluelo *m*, -la *f*
rage[1] [ˈreɪʤ] *vi* **raged; raging 1** : estar furioso, rabiar ‹to fly into a rage : enfurecerse› **2** : bramar, hacer estragos ‹the wind was raging : el viento bramaba› ‹flu raged through the school : la gripe hizo estragos por el colegio›
rage[2] *n* **1** ANGER : furia *f*, ira *f*, cólera *f* **2** FAD : moda *f*, furor *m*
ragged [ˈrægəd] *adj* **1** UNEVEN : irregular, desigual **2** TORN : hecho jirones **3** TATTERED : andrajoso, harapiento
ragout [ræˈguː] *n* : ragú *m*, estofado *m*
ragtime [ˈrægˌtaɪm] *n* : ragtime *m*
ragweed [ˈrægˌwiːd] *n* : ambrosía *f*
raid[1] [ˈreɪd] *vt* **1** : invadir, hacer una incursión en ‹raided by enemy troops

: invadido por tropas enemigas〉 **2** : asaltar, atracar 〈the gang raided the warehouse : la pandilla asaltó el almacén〉 **3** : allanar, hacer una redada en 〈police raided the house : la policía allanó la vivienda〉
raid² *n* **1** : invasión *f* (militar) **2** : asalto *m* (por delincuentes) **3** : redada *f*, allanamiento *m* (por la policía)
raider [ˈreɪdər] *n* **1** ATTACKER : asaltante *mf*; invasor *m*, -sora *f* **2 corporate raider** : tiburón *m*
rail¹ [ˈreɪl] *vi* **1 to rail against** REVILE : denostar contra **2 to rail at** SCOLD : regañar, reprender
rail² *n* **1** BAR : barra *f*, barrera *f* **2** HANDRAIL : pasamanos *m*, barandilla *f* **3** TRACK : riel *m* (para ferrocarriles) **4** RAILROAD : ferrocarril *m*
railing [ˈreɪlɪŋ] *n* **1** : baranda *f* (de un balcón, etc.) **2** RAILS : verja *f*
raillery [ˈreɪləri] *n, pl* **-leries** : bromas *fpl*
railroad [ˈreɪl,roːd] *n* : ferrocarril *m*
railway [ˈreɪl,weɪ] → **railroad**
raiment [ˈreɪmənt] *n* : vestiduras *fpl*
rain¹ [ˈreɪn] *vi* **1** : llover 〈it's raining : está lloviendo〉 **2 to rain down** SHOWER : llover 〈insults rained down on him : le llovieron los insultos〉
rain² *n* : lluvia *f*
rainbow [ˈreɪn,boː] *n* : arco *m* iris
raincoat [ˈreɪn,koːt] *n* : impermeable *m*
raindrop [ˈreɪn,drɑp] *n* : gota *f* de lluvia
rainfall [ˈreɪn,fɔl] *n* : lluvia *f*, precipitación *f*
rainstorm [ˈreɪn,stɔrm] *n* : temporal *m* (de lluvia)
rainwater [ˈreɪn,wɔt̬ər] *n* : agua *f* de lluvia
rainy [ˈreɪni] *adj* **rainier; -est** : lluvioso
raise¹ [ˈreɪz] *vt* **raised; raising 1** LIFT : levantar, subir, alzar 〈to raise one's spirits : levantarle el ánimo a alguien〉 **2** ERECT : levantar, erigir **3** COLLECT : recaudar 〈to raise money : recaudar dinero〉 **4** REAR : criar 〈to raise one's children : criar uno a sus niños〉 **5** GROW : cultivar **6** INCREASE : aumentar, subir **7** PROMOTE : ascender **8** PROVOKE : provocar 〈it raised a laugh : provocó una risa〉 **9** BRING UP : sacar (temas, objeciones, etc.)
raise² *n* : aumento *m*
raisin [ˈreɪzən] *n* : pasa *f*
raja *or* **rajah** [ˈrɑʤə, -ˌʤɑ, -ˌʒɑ] *n* : rajá *m*
rake¹ [ˈreɪk] *v* **raked; raking** *vt* **1** : rastrillar 〈to rake leaves : rastrillar las hojas〉 **2** SWEEP : barrer 〈raked with gunfire : barrido con metralla〉 — *vi* **to rake through** : revolver, hurgar en
rake² *n* **1** : rastrillo *m* **2** LIBERTINE : libertino *m*, -na *f*; calavera *m*
rakish [ˈreɪkɪʃ] *adj* **1** JAUNTY : desenvuelto, desenfadado **2** DISSOLUTE : libertino, disoluto
rally¹ [ˈræli] *v* **-lied; -lying** *vi* **1** MEET, UNITE : reunirse, congregarse **2** RECOVER : recuperarse — *vt* **1** ASSEMBLE : reunir (tropas, etc.) **2** RECOVER : recobrar (la fuerza, el ánimo, etc.)
rally² *n, pl* **-lies** : reunión *f*, mitin *m*, manifestación *f*
ram¹ [ˈræm] *v* **rammed; ramming** *vt* **1** DRIVE : hincar, clavar 〈he rammed it into the ground : lo hincó en la tierra〉 **2** SMASH : estrellar, embestir — *vi* COLLIDE : chocar (contra), estrellarse
ram² *n* **1** : carnero *m* (animal) **2 battering ram** : ariete *m*
RAM [ˈræm] *n* : RAM *f*
ramble¹ [ˈræmbəl] *vi* **-bled; -bling 1** WANDER : pasear, deambular **2 to ramble on** : divagar, perder el hilo **3** SPREAD : trepar (dícese de una planta)
ramble² *n* : paseo *m*, excursión *f*
rambler [ˈræmblər] *n* **1** WALKER : excursionista *mf* **2** ROSE : rosa *f* trepadora
rambunctious [ræmˈbʌŋkʃəs] *adj* UNRULY : alborotado
ramification [ˌræməfəˈkeɪʃən] *n* : ramificación *f*
ramify [ˈræmə,faɪ] *vi* **-fied; -fying** : ramificarse
ramp [ˈræmp] *n* : rampa *f*
rampage¹ [ˈræm,peɪʤ, ræmˈpeɪʤ] *vi* **-paged; -paging** : andar arrasando todo, correr destrozando
rampage² [ˈræm,peɪʤ] *n* : alboroto *m*, frenesí *m* (de violencia)
rampant [ˈræmpənt] *adj* : desenfrenado
rampart [ˈræm,pɑrt] *n* : terraplén *m*, muralla *f*
ramrod [ˈræm,rɑd] *n* : baqueta *f*
ramshackle [ˈræm,ʃækəl] *adj* : destartalado
ran → **run**
ranch [ˈræntʃ] *n* **1** : hacienda *f*, rancho *m*, finca *f* ganadera **2** FARM : granja *f* 〈fruit ranch : granja de frutas〉
rancher [ˈræntʃər] *n* : estanciero *m*, -ra *f*; ranchero *m*, -ra *f*
rancid [ˈræntsɪd] *adj* : rancio
rancor [ˈræŋkər] *n* : rencor *m*
random [ˈrændəm] *adj* **1** : fortuito, aleatorio **2 at ~** : al azar — **randomly** *adv*
rang → **ring**
range¹ [ˈreɪnʤ] *v* **ranged; ranging** *vt* ARRANGE : alinear, ordenar, arreglar — *vi* **1** ROAM : deambular 〈to range through the town : deambular por el pueblo〉 **2** EXTEND : extenderse 〈the results range widely : los resultados se extienden mucho〉 **3** VARY : variar 〈discounts range from 20% to 40% : los descuentos varían entre 20% y 40%〉
range² *n* **1** ROW : fila *f*, hilera *f* 〈a mountain range : una cordillera〉 **2** GRASSLAND : pradera *f*, pampa *f* **3** STOVE : cocina *f* **4** VARIETY : variedad *f*, gama *f* **5** SPHERE : ámbito *m*, esfera *f*, campo *m* **6** REACH : registro *m* (de la voz), alcance *m* (de un arma de fuego) **7 shooting range** : campo *m* de tiro

ranger [ˈreɪndʒər] *n or* **forest ranger** : guardabosque *mf*
rangy [ˈreɪndʒi] *adj* **rangier; -est** : alto y delgado
rank[1] [ˈræŋk] *vt* **1** RANGE : alinear, ordenar, poner en fila **2** CLASSIFY : clasificar — *vi* **1 to rank above** : ser superior a **2 to rank among** : encontrarse entre, figurar entre
rank[2] *adj* **1** LUXURIANT : lozano, exuberante (dícese de una planta) **2** SMELLY : fétido, maloliente **3** OUTRIGHT : completo, absoluto ⟨a rank injustice : una injusticia manifiesta⟩
rank[3] *n* **1** LINE, ROW : fila *f* ⟨to close ranks : cerrar filas⟩ **2** GRADE, POSITION : grado *m*, rango *m* (militar) ⟨to pull rank : abusar de su autoridad⟩ **3** CLASS : categoría *f*, clase *f* **4 ranks** *npl* : soldados *mpl* rasos
rank and file *n* **1** RANKS : soldados *mpl* rasos **2** : bases *fpl* (de un partido, etc.)
rankle [ˈræŋkəl] *v* **-kled; -kling** *vi* : doler — *vt* : irritar, herir
ransack [ˈrænˌsæk] *vt* : revolver, desvalijar, registrar de arriba abajo
ransom[1] [ˈræn*t*səm] *vt* : rescatar, pagar un rescate por
ransom[2] *n* : rescate *m*
rant [ˈrænt] *vi or* **to rant and rave** : despotricar, desvariar
rap[1] [ˈræp] *v* **rapped; rapping** *vt* **1** KNOCK : golpetear, dar un golpe en **2** CRITICIZE : criticar — *vi* **1** CHAT : charlar, cotorrear *fam* **2** KNOCK : dar un golpe
rap[2] *n* **1** BLOW, KNOCK : golpe *m*, golpecito *m* **2** CHAT : charla *f* **3** *or* **rap music** : rap *m* **4 to take the rap** : pagar el pato *fam*
rapacious [rəˈpeɪʃəs] *adj* **1** GREEDY : avaricioso, codicioso **2** PREDATORY : rapaz, de rapiña **3** RAVENOUS : voraz
rape[1] [ˈreɪp] *vt* **raped; raping** : violar
rape[2] *n* **1** : colza *f* (planta) **2** : violación *f* (de una persona)
rapid [ˈræpɪd] *adj* : rápido — **rapidly** *adv*
rapidity [rəˈpɪdət̬i] *n* : rapidez *f*
rapids [ˈræpɪdz] *npl* : rápidos *mpl*
rapier [ˈreɪpiər] *n* : estoque *m*
rapist [ˈreɪpɪst] *n* : violador *m*, -dora *f*
rapper [ˈræpər] *n* : cantante *mf* de rap; rapero *m*, -ra *f*
rapport [ræˈpor] *n* : relación *f* armoniosa, entendimiento *m*
rapt [ˈræpt] *adj* : absorto, embelesado
rapture [ˈræptʃər] *n* : éxtasis *m*
rapturous [ˈræptʃərəs] *adj* : extasiado, embelesado
rare [ˈrær] *adj* **rarer; rarest 1** RAREFIED : enrarecido **2** FINE : excelente, excepcional ⟨a rare talent : un talento excepcional⟩ **3** UNCOMMON : raro, poco común **4** : poco cocido (dícese de la carne)
rarefy [ˈrærəˌfaɪ] *vt* **-fied; -fying** : rarificar, enrarecer
rarely [ˈrærli] *adv* SELDOM : pocas veces, rara vez
raring [ˈrærən, -ɪŋ] *adj* : lleno de entusiasmo, con muchas ganas
rarity [ˈrærət̬i] *n, pl* **-ties** : rareza *f*
rascal [ˈræskəl] *n* : pillo *m*, -lla *f*; pícaro *m*, -ra *f*
rash[1] [ˈræʃ] *adj* : imprudente, precipitado — **rashly** *adv*
rash[2] *n* : sarpullido *m*, erupción *f*
rashness [ˈræʃnəs] *n* : precipitación *f*, impetuosidad *f*
rasp[1] [ˈræsp] *vt* **1** SCRAPE : raspar, escofinar **2 to rasp out** : decir en voz áspera
rasp[2] *n* : escofina *f*
raspberry [ˈræzˌbɛri] *n, pl* **-ries** : frambuesa *f*
rat [ˈræt] *n* : rata *f*
ratchet [ˈrætʃət] *n* : trinquete *m*
rate[1] [ˈreɪt] *vt* **rated; rating 1** CONSIDER, REGARD : considerar, estimar **2** DESERVE : merecer
rate[2] *n* **1** PACE, SPEED : velocidad *f*, ritmo *m* ⟨at this rate : a este paso⟩ **2** : índice *m*, tasa *f* ⟨birth rate : índice de natalidad⟩ ⟨interest rate : tasa de interés⟩ **3** CHARGE, PRICE : precio *m*, tarifa *f*
rather [ˈræðər, ˈrʌ-, ˈrɑ-] *adv* **1** (*indicating preference*) ⟨she would rather stay in the house : preferiría quedarse en casa⟩ ⟨I'd rather not : mejor que no⟩ **2** (*indicating preciseness*) ⟨my father, or rather my stepfather : mi padre, o mejor dicho mi padrastro⟩ **3** INSTEAD : sino que, más que, al contrario ⟨I'm not pleased; rather I'm disappointed : no estoy satisfecho, sino desilusionado⟩ **4** SOMEWHAT : algo, un tanto ⟨rather strange : un poco extraño⟩ **5** QUITE : bastante ⟨rather difficult : bastante difícil⟩
ratification [ˌræt̬əfəˈkeɪʃən] *n* : ratificación *f*
ratify [ˈræt̬əˌfaɪ] *vt* **-fied; -fying** : ratificar
rating [ˈreɪt̬ɪŋ] *n* **1** STANDING : clasificación *f*, posición *f* **2 ratings** *npl* : índice *m* de audiencia
ratio [ˈreɪʃio] *n, pl* **-tios** : proporción *f*, relación *f*
ration[1] [ˈræʃən, ˈreɪʃən] *vt* : racionar
ration[2] *n* **1** : ración *f* **2 rations** *npl* PROVISIONS : víveres *mpl*
rational [ˈræʃənəl] *adj* : racional, razonable, lógico — **rationally** *adv*
rationale [ˌræʃəˈnæl] *n* **1** EXPLANATION : explicación *f* **2** BASIS : base *f*, razones *fpl*
rationality [ˌræʃəˈnælət̬i] *n, pl* **-ties** : racionalidad *f*
rationalization [ˌræʃənələˈzeɪʃən] *n* : racionalización *f*
rationalize [ˈræʃənəˌlaɪz] *vt* **-ized; -izing** : racionalizar
rattle[1] [ˈræt̬əl] *v* **-tled; -tling** *vi* **1** CLATTER : traquetear, hacer ruido **2 to rattle on** CHATTER : parlotear *fam* — *vt*

1 : hacer sonar, agitar ⟨the wind rattled the door : el viento sacudió la puerta⟩ **2** DISCONCERT, WORRY : desconcertar, poner nervioso **3 to rattle off** : despachar, recitar, decir de corrido

rattle[2] *n* **1** CLATTER : traqueteo *m*, ruido *m* **2** *or* **baby's rattle** : sonajero *m* **3** : cascabel *m* (de una culebra)

rattler [ˈrætələr] → **rattlesnake**

rattlesnake [ˈrætəlˌsneɪk] *n* : serpiente *f* de cascabel

ratty [ˈræti] *adj* **rattier; -est** : raído, andrajoso

raucous [ˈrɔkəs] *adj* **1** HOARSE : ronco **2** BOISTEROUS : escandaloso, bullicioso — **raucously** *adv*

ravage[1] [ˈrævɪʤ] *vt* **-aged; -aging** : devastar, arrasar, hacer estragos

ravage[2] *n* : destrozo *m*, destrucción *f* ⟨the ravages of war : los estragos de la guerra⟩

rave [ˈreɪv] *vi* **raved; raving 1** : delirar, desvariar ⟨to rave like a maniac : desvariar como un loco⟩ **2 to rave about** : hablar con entusiasmo sobre, entusiasmarse por

ravel [ˈrævəl] *v* **-eled** *or* **-elled; -eling** *or* **-elling** *vt* UNRAVEL : desenredar, desenmarañar — *vi* FRAY : deshilacharse

raven [ˈreɪvən] *n* : cuervo *m*

ravenous [ˈrævənəs] *adj* : hambriento, voraz — **ravenously** *adv*

ravine [rəˈviːn] *n* : barranco *m*, quebrada *f*

ravish [ˈrævɪʃ] *vt* **1** PLUNDER : saquear **2** ENCHANT : embelesar, cautivar, encantar

raw [ˈrɔ] *adj* **rawer; rawest 1** UNCOOKED : crudo **2** UNTREATED : sin tratar, sin refinar, puro ⟨raw data : datos en bruto⟩ ⟨raw materials : materias primas⟩ **3** INEXPERIENCED : novato, inexperto **4** OPEN : abierto, en carne viva ⟨a raw sore : una llaga abierta⟩ **5** : frío y húmedo ⟨a raw day : un día crudo⟩ **6** UNFAIR : injusto ⟨a raw deal : un trato injusto, una injusticia⟩

rawhide [ˈrɔˌhaɪd] *n* : cuero *m* sin curtir

ray [ˈreɪ] *n* **1** : rayo *m* (de la luz, etc.) ⟨a ray of hope : un resquicio de esperanza⟩ **2** : raya *f* (pez)

rayon [ˈreɪˌɑn] *n* : rayón *m*

raze [ˈreɪz] *vt* **razed; razing** : arrasar, demoler

razor [ˈreɪzər] *n* **1** *or* **straight razor** : navaja *f* (de afeitar) **2** *or* **safety razor** : maquinilla *f* de afeitar, rastrillo *m Mex* **3** SHAVER : afeitadora *f*, rasuradora *f*

reach[1] [ˈriːʧ] *vt* **1** EXTEND : extender, alargar ⟨to reach out one's hand : extender la mano⟩ **2** : alcanzar ⟨I couldn't reach the apple : no pude alcanzar la manzana⟩ **3** : llegar a, llegar hasta ⟨the shadow reached the wall : la sombra llegó hasta la pared⟩ **4** CONTACT : contactar, ponerse en contacto con — *vi* **1** *or* **to reach out** : extender la mano **2** STRETCH : extenderse **3 to reach for** : tratar de agarrar

reach[2] *n* : alcance *m*, extensión *f*

react [riˈækt] *vi* : reaccionar

reaction [riˈækʃən] *n* : reacción *f*

reactionary[1] [riˈækʃəˌnɛri] *adj* : reaccionario

reactionary[2] *n, pl* **-ries** : reaccionario *m*, -ria *f*

reactor [riˈæktər] *n* : reactor *m* ⟨nuclear reactor : reactor nuclear⟩

read[1] [ˈriːd] *v* **read** [ˈrɛd]; **reading** *vt* **1** : leer ⟨to read a story : leer un cuento⟩ **2** INTERPRET : interpretar ⟨it can be read two ways : se puede interpretar de dos maneras⟩ **3** : decir, poner ⟨the sign read "No smoking" : el letrero decía "No Fumar"⟩ **4** : marcar ⟨the thermometer reads 70° : el termómetro marca 70°⟩ — *vi* **1** : leer ⟨he can read : sabe leer⟩ **2** SAY : decir ⟨the list reads as follows : la lista dice lo siguiente⟩

read[2] *n* **to be a good read** : ser una lectura amena

readable [ˈriːdəbəl] *adj* : legible — **readably** [-bli] *adv*

reader [ˈriːdər] *n* : lector *m*, -tora *f*

readily [ˈrɛdəli] *adv* **1** WILLINGLY : de buena gana, con gusto **2** EASILY : fácilmente, con facilidad

readiness [ˈrɛdinəs] *n* **1** WILLINGNESS : buena disposición *f* **2 to be in readiness** : estar preparado

reading [ˈriːdɪŋ] *n* : lectura *f*

readjust [ˌriːəˈʤʌst] *vt* : reajustar — *vi* : volverse a adaptar

readjustment [ˌriːəˈʤʌstmənt] *n* : reajuste *m*

ready[1] [ˈrɛdi] *vt* **readied; readying** : preparar

ready[2] *adj* **readier; -est 1** PREPARED : listo, preparado **2** WILLING : dispuesto **3** : a punto de ⟨ready to cry : a punto de llorar⟩ **4** AVAILABLE : disponible ⟨ready cash : efectivo⟩ **5** QUICK : vivo, agudo ⟨a ready wit : un ingenio agudo⟩

ready–made [ˈrɛdiˈmeɪd] *adj* : preparado, confeccionado

reaffirm [ˌriːəˈfərm] *vt* : reafirmar

real[1] [ˈriːl] *adv* VERY : muy ⟨we had a real good time : lo pasamos muy bien⟩

real[2] *adj* **1** : inmobiliario ⟨real property : bien inmueble, bien raíz⟩ **2** GENUINE : auténtico, genuino **3** ACTUAL, TRUE : real, verdadero ⟨a real friend : un verdadero amigo⟩ **4 for real** SERIOUSLY : de veras, de verdad

real estate *n* : propiedad *f* inmobiliaria, bienes *mpl* raíces

realign [ˌriːəˈlaɪn] *vt* : realinear

realignment [ˌriːəˈlaɪnmənt] *n* : realineamiento *m*

realism [ˈriːəˌlɪzəm] *n* : realismo *m*

realist [ˈriːəlɪst] *n* : realista *mf*

realistic [ˌriːəˈlɪstɪk] *adj* : realista

realistically [ˌriːəˈlɪstɪkli] *adv* : de manera realista

reality [ri'æləṭi] *n, pl* **-ties** : realidad *f*
realizable [ˌriːə'laɪzəbəl] *adj* : realizable, alcanzable
realization [ˌriːələ'zeɪʃən] *n* : realización *f*
realize ['riːəˌlaɪz] *vt* **-ized; -izing 1** ACCOMPLISH : realizar, llevar a cabo **2** GAIN : obtener, realizar, sacar ⟨to realize a profit : realizar beneficios⟩ **3** UNDERSTAND : darse cuenta de, saber
really ['rɪli, 'riː-] *adv* **1** ACTUALLY : de verdad, en realidad **2** TRULY : verdaderamente, realmente **3** FRANKLY : francamente, en serio
realm ['rɛlm] *n* **1** KINGDOM : reino *m* **2** SPHERE : esfera *f*, campo *m*
ream[1] ['riːm] *vt* : escariar
ream[2] *n* **1** : resma *f* (de papel) **2 reams** *npl* LOADS : montones *mpl*
reap ['riːp] *v* : cosechar
reaper ['riːpər] *n* **1** : cosechador *m*, -dora *f* (persona) **2** : cosechadora *f* (máquina)
reappear [ˌriːə'pɪr] *vi* : reaparecer
reappearance [ˌriːə'pɪrənts] *n* : reaparición *f*
rear[1] ['rɪr] *vt* **1** LIFT, RAISE : levantar **2** BREED, BRING UP : criar — *vi or* **to rear up** : encabritarse
rear[2] *adj* : trasero, posterior, de atrás
rear[3] *n* **1** BACK : parte *f* de atrás ⟨to bring up the rear : cerrar la marcha⟩ **2** *or* **rear end** : trasero *m*
rear admiral *n* : contraalmirante *mf*
rearrange [ˌriːə'reɪndʒ] *vt* **-ranged; -ranging** : colocar de otra manera, volver a arreglar, reorganizar
rearview mirror ['rɪrˌvjuː-] *n* : retrovisor *m*
reason[1] ['riːzən] *vt* THINK : pensar — *vi* : razonar ⟨I can't reason with her : no puedo razonar con ella⟩
reason[2] *n* **1** CAUSE, GROUND : razón *f*, motivo *m* ⟨the reason for his trip : el motivo de su viaje⟩ ⟨for this reason : por esta razón, por lo cual⟩ ⟨the reason why : la razón por la cual, el porqué⟩ **2** SENSE : razón *f* ⟨to lose one's reason : perder los sesos⟩ ⟨to listen to reason : avenirse a razones⟩
reasonable ['riːzənəbəl] *adj* **1** SENSIBLE : razonable **2** INEXPENSIVE : barato, económico
reasonably ['riːzənəbli] *adv* **1** SENSIBLY : razonablemente **2** FAIRLY : bastante
reasoning ['riːzənɪŋ] *n* : razonamiento *m*, raciocinio *m*, argumentos *mpl*
reassess [ˌriːə'sɛs] *vt* : revaluar, reconsiderar
reassurance [ˌriːə'ʃʊrənts] *n* : consuelo *m*, palabras *fpl* alentadoras
reassure [ˌriːə'ʃʊr] *vt* **-sured; -suring** : tranquilizar
reassuring [ˌriːə'ʃʊrɪŋ] *adj* : tranquilizador
reawaken [ˌriːə'weɪkən] *vt* : volver a despertar, reavivar
rebate ['riːˌbeɪt] *n* : reembolso *m*, devolución *f*
rebel[1] [rɪ'bɛl] *vi* **-belled; -belling** : rebelarse, sublevarse
rebel[2] ['rɛbəl] *adj* : rebelde
rebel[3] ['rɛbəl] *n* : rebelde *mf*
rebellion [rɪ'bɛljən] *n* : rebelión *f*
rebellious [rɪ'bɛljəs] *adj* : rebelde
rebelliousness [rɪ'bɛljəsnəs] *n* : rebeldía *f*
rebirth [ˌriː'bərθ] *n* : renacimiento *m*
reboot [ri'buːt] *vt* : reiniciar (una computadora)
reborn [riː'bɔrn] *adj* **to be reborn** : renacer
rebound[1] ['riːˌbaʊnd, ˌriː'baʊnd] *vi* : rebotar
rebound[2] ['riːˌbaʊnd] *n* : rebote *m*
rebuff[1] [ri'bʌf] *vt* : desairar, rechazar
rebuff[2] *n* : desaire *m*, rechazo *m*
rebuild [ˌriː'bɪld] *vt* **-built** [-'bɪlt]; **-building** : reconstruir
rebuke[1] [ri'bjuːk] *vt* **-buked; -buking** : reprender, regañar
rebuke[2] *n* : reprimenda *f*, reproche *m*
rebut [ri'bʌt] *vt* **-butted; -butting** : rebatir, refutar
rebuttal [ri'bʌṭəl] *n* : refutación *f*
recalcitrant [ri'kælsətrənt] *adj* : recalcitrante
recall[1] [ri'kɔl] *vt* **1** : llamar, retirar ⟨recalled to active duty : llamado al servicio activo⟩ **2** REMEMBER : recordar, acordarse de **3** REVOKE : revocar
recall[2] [ri'kɔl, 'riːˌkɔl] *n* **1** : retirada *f* (de personas o mercancías) **2** MEMORY : memoria *f* ⟨to have total recall : poder recordar todo⟩
recant [ri'kænt] *vt* : retractarse de — *vi* : retractarse, renegar
recapitulate [ˌriːkə'pɪtʃəˌleɪt] *v* **-lated; -lating** : resumir, recapitular
recapture [ˌriː'kæptʃər] *vt* **-tured; -turing 1** REGAIN : volver a tomar, reconquistar **2** RELIVE : revivir (la juventud, etc.)
recast [riː'kæst] *vt* **-cast; -casting 1** : refundir (metales) **2** REWRITE : refundir, modificar
recede [ri'siːd] *vi* **-ceded; -ceding 1** WITHDRAW : retirarse, retroceder **2** FADE : desvanecerse, alejarse **3** SLANT : inclinarse **4 to have a receding hairline** : tener entradas
receipt [ri'siːt] *n* **1** : recibo *m* **2 receipts** *npl* : ingresos *mpl*, entradas *fpl*
receivable [ri'siːvəbəl] *adj* **accounts receivable** : cuentas por cobrar
receive [ri'siːv] *vt* **-ceived; -ceiving 1** GET : recibir ⟨to receive a letter : recibir una carta⟩ ⟨to receive a blow : recibir un golpe⟩ **2** WELCOME : acoger, recibir ⟨to receive guests : tener invitados⟩ **3** : recibir, captar (señales de radio)
receiver [ri'siːvər] *n* **1** : receptor *m*, -tora *f* (en futbol americano) **2** : receptor *m* (de radio o televisión) **3 telephone receiver** : auricular *m*
recent ['riːsənt] *adj* : reciente — **recently** *adv*

receptacle [ri'sɛptɪkəl] *n* : receptáculo *m*, recipiente *m*
reception [ri'sɛpʃən] *n* : recepción *f*
receptionist [ri'sɛpʃənɪst] *n* : recepcionista *mf*
receptive [ri'sɛptɪv] *adj* : receptivo
receptivity [ˌriːˌsɛp'tɪvəṭi] *n* : receptividad *f*
recess[1] ['riːˌsɛs, rɪ'sɛs] *vt* **1** : poner en un hueco ⟨recessed lighting : iluminación empotrada⟩ **2** ADJOURN : suspender, levantar
recess[2] *n* **1** ALCOVE : hueco *m*, nicho *m* **2** BREAK : receso *m*, descanso *m*, recreo *m* (en el colegio)
recession [ri'sɛʃən] *n* : recesión *f*, depresión *f* económica
recessive [ri'sɛsɪv] *adj* : recesivo
recharge [ˌriː'ʧɑrʤ] *vt* **-charged; -charging** : recargar
rechargeable [ˌriː'ʧɑrʤəbəl] *adj* : recargable
recipe ['rɛsəˌpiː] *n* : receta *f*
recipient [ri'sɪpiənt] *n* : recipiente *mf*
reciprocal [ri'sɪprəkəl] *adj* : recíproco
reciprocate [ri'sɪprəˌkeɪt] *vi* **-cated; -cating** : reciprocar
reciprocity [ˌrɛsə'prɑsəṭi] *n, pl* **-ties** : reciprocidad *f*
recital [ri'saɪṭəl] *n* **1** PERFORMANCE : recital *m* **2** ENUMERATION : relato *m*, enumeración *f*
recitation [ˌrsə'teɪʃən] *n* : recitación *f*
recite [ri'saɪt] *vt* **-cited; -citing 1** : recitar (un poema, etc.) **2** RECOUNT : narrar, relatar, enumerar
reckless ['rɛkləs] *adj* : imprudente, temerario — **recklessly** *adv*
recklessness ['rɛkləsnəs] *n* : imprudencia *f*, temeridad *f*
reckon ['rɛkən] *vt* **1** CALCULATE : calcular, contar **2** CONSIDER : considerar
reckoning ['rɛkənɪŋ] *n* **1** CALCULATION : cálculo *m* **2** SETTLEMENT : ajuste *m* de cuentas ⟨day of reckoning : día del juicio final⟩
reclaim [ri'kleɪm] *vt* **1** : ganar, sanear ⟨to reclaim marshy land : sanear las tierras pantanosas⟩ **2** RECOVER : recobrar, reciclar ⟨to reclaim old tires : reciclar llantas desechadas⟩ **3** REGAIN : reclamar, recuperar ⟨to reclaim one's rights : reclamar uno sus derechos⟩
recline [ri'klaɪn] *vi* **-clined; -clining 1** LEAN : reclinarse **2** REPOSE : recostarse
recluse ['rɛˌkluːs, ri'kluːs] *n* : solitario *m*, -ria *f*
recognition [ˌrɛkɪg'nɪʃən] *n* : reconocimiento *m*
recognizable ['rɛkəgˌnaɪzəbəl] *adj* : reconocible
recognize ['rɛkɪgˌnaɪz] *vt* **-nized; -nizing** : reconocer
recoil[1] [ri'kɔɪl] *vi* : retroceder, dar un culatazo
recoil[2] ['riːˌkɔɪl, ri'-] *n* : retroceso *m*, culatazo *m*
recollect [ˌrɛkə'lɛkt] *v* : recordar
recollection [ˌrɛkə'lɛkʃən] *n* : recuerdo *m*
recommend [ˌrɛkə'mɛnd] *vt* **1** : recomendar ⟨she recommended the medicine : recomendó la medicina⟩ **2** ADVISE, COUNSEL : aconsejar, recomendar
recommendation [ˌrɛkəmən'deɪʃən] *n* : recomendación *f*
recompense[1] ['rɛkəmˌpɛnts] *vt* **-pensed; -pensing** : indemnizar, recompensar
recompense[2] *n* : indemnización *f*, compensación *f*
reconcile ['rɛkənˌsaɪl] *v* **-ciled; -ciling** *vt* **1** : reconciliar (personas), conciliar (ideas, etc.) **2 to reconcile oneself to** : resignarse a — *vi* MAKE UP : reconciliarse, hacer las paces
reconciliation [ˌrɛkənˌsɪli'eɪʃən] *n* : reconciliación *f* (con personas), conciliación *f* (con ideas, etc.)
recondite ['rɛkənˌdaɪt, ri'kɑn-] *adj* : recóndito, abstruso
recondition [ˌriːkən'dɪʃən] *vt* : reacondicionar
reconnaissance [ri'kɑnəzənts, -sənts] *n* : reconocimiento *m*
reconnoiter *or* **reconnoitre** [ˌriːkə'nɔɪṭər, ˌrɛkə-] *v* **-tered** *or* **-tred; -tering** *or* **-tring** *vt* : reconocer — *vi* : hacer un reconocimiento
reconsider [ˌriːkən'sɪdər] *vt* : reconsiderar, repensar
reconsideration [ˌriːkənˌsɪdə'reɪʃən] *n* : reconsideración *f*
reconstruct [ˌriːkən'strʌkt] *vt* : reconstruir
reconstruction [ˌriːkən'strʌkʃən] *n* : reconstrucción *f*
record[1] [ri'kɔrd] *vt* **1** WRITE DOWN : anotar, apuntar **2** REGISTER : registrar, hacer constar **3** INDICATE : marcar (una temperatura, etc.) **4** TAPE : grabar
record[2] ['rɛkərd] *n* **1** DOCUMENT : registro *m*, documento *m* oficial **2** HISTORY : historial *m* ⟨a good academic record : un buen historial académico⟩ ⟨criminal record : antecedentes penales⟩ **3** : récord *m* ⟨the world record : el récord mundial⟩ **4** : disco *m* (de música, etc.) ⟨to make a record : grabar un disco⟩
recorder [ri'kɔrdər] *n* **1** : flauta *f* dulce (instrumento de viento) **2 tape recorder** : grabadora *f*
recording [ri'kɔrdɪŋ] *n* : grabación *f*
recount[1] [ri'kaʊnt] *vt* **1** NARRATE : narrar, relatar **2** : volver a contar (votos, etc.)
recount[2] ['riːˌkaʊnt, ˌri'-] *n* : recuento *m*
recoup [ri'kuːp] *vt* : recuperar, recobrar
recourse ['riːˌkors, ri'-] *n* : recurso *m* ⟨to have recourse to : recurrir a⟩
recover [ri'kʌvər] *vt* REGAIN : recobrar — *vi* RECUPERATE : recuperarse

recovery [riˈkʌvəri] *n, pl* **-eries** : recuperación *f*
re–create [ˌriːkriˈeɪt] *vt* **-ated; -ating** : recrear
recreation [ˌrɛkriˈeɪʃən] *n* : recreo *m*, esparcimiento *m*, diversión *f*
recreational [ˌrɛkriˈeɪʃənəl] *adj* : recreativo, de recreo
recrimination [riˌkrɪməˈneɪʃən] *n* : recriminación *f*
recruit[1] [riˈkruːt] *vt* : reclutar
recruit[2] *n* : recluta *mf*
recruitment [riˈkruːtmənt] *n* : reclutamiento *m*, alistamiento *m*
rectal [ˈrɛktəl] *adj* : rectal
rectangle [ˈrɛkˌtæŋgəl] *n* : rectángulo *m*
rectangular [rɛkˈtæŋgjələr] *adj* : rectangular
rectify [ˈrɛktəˌfaɪ] *vt* **-fied; -fying** : rectificar
rectitude [ˈrktəˌtuːd, -ˌtjuːd] *n* : rectitud *f*
rector [ˈrɛktər] *n* : rector *m*, -tora *f*
rectory [ˈrɛktəri] *n, pl* **-ries** : rectoría *f*
rectum [ˈrɛktəm] *n, pl* **-tums** *or* **-ta** [-tə] : recto *m*
recuperate [riˈkuːpəˌreɪt, -ˈkjuː-] *v* **-ated; -ating** *vt* : recuperar — *vi* : recuperarse, restablecerse
recuperation [riˌkuːpəˈreɪʃən, -ˌkjuː-] *n* : recuperación *f*
recur [riˈkər] *vi* **-curred; -curring** : volver a ocurrir, volver a producirse, repetirse
recurrence [riˈkərən*t*s] *n* : repetición *f*, reaparición *f*
recurrent [riˈkərənt] *adj* : recurrente, que se repite
recyclable [riˈsaɪkələbəl] *adj* : reciclable
recycle [riˈsaɪkəl] *vt* **-cled; -cling** : reciclar
recycling [riˈsaɪkəlɪŋ] *n* : reciclaje *m*
red[1] [ˈrɛd] *adj* **1** : rojo, colorado ⟨to be red in the face : ponerse colorado⟩ ⟨to have red hair : ser pelirrojo⟩ **2** COMMUNIST : rojo, comunista
red[2] *n* **1** : rojo *m*, colorado *m* **2 Red** COMMUNIST : comunista *mf*
red blood cell *n* : glóbulo *m* rojo
red–blooded [ˈrɛdˈblʌdəd] *adj* : vigoroso
redcap [ˈrɛdˌkæp] → **porter**
redden [ˈrɛdən] *vt* : enrojecer — *vi* BLUSH : enrojecerse, ruborizarse
reddish [ˈrɛdɪʃ] *adj* : rojizo
redecorate [ˌriːˈdɛkəˌreɪt] *vt* **-rated; -rating** : renovar, pintar de nuevo
redeem [riˈdiːm] *vt* **1** RESCUE, SAVE : rescatar, salvar **2** : desempeñar ⟨she redeemed it from the pawnshop : lo desempeñó de la casa de empeños⟩ **3** : redimir (en religión) **4** : canjear, vender ⟨to redeem coupons : canjear cupones⟩
redeemer [riˈdiːmər] *n* : redentor *m*, -tora *f*
redefine [ˌriːdɪˈfaɪn] *vt* : redefinir
redemption [riˈdɛmpʃən] *n* : redención *f*
redesign [ˌriːdiˈzaɪn] *vt* : rediseñar
red–handed [ˈrɛdˈhændəd] *adj* : con las manos en la masa
redhead [ˈrɛdˌhɛd] *n* : pelirrojo *m*, -ja *f*
red–hot [ˈrɛdˈhɑt] *adj* **1** : al rojo vivo, candente **2** CURRENT : de candente actualidad **3** POPULAR : de gran popularidad
rediscover [ˌriːdiˈskʌvər] *vt* : redescubrir
redistribute [ˌriːdiˈstrɪˌbjuːt] *vt* **-uted; -uting** : redistribuir
red–letter [ˈrɛdˈlɛt̬ər] *adj* **red–letter day** : día *m* memorable
redness [ˈrɛdnəs] *n* : rojez *f*
redo [ˌriːˈduː] *vt* **-did** [-dɪd]; **-done** [-ˈdʌn]; **-doing 1** : hacer de nuevo **2** → **redecorate**
redolence [ˈrɛdələn*t*s] *n* : fragancia *f*
redolent [ˈrɛdələnt] *adj* **1** FRAGRANT : fragante, oloroso **2** SUGGESTIVE : evocador
redouble [riˈdʌbəl] *vt* **-bled; -bling** : redoblar, intensificar (esfuerzos, etc.)
redoubtable [rˈdaʊt̬əbəl] *adj* : temible
redress [riˈdrɛs] *vt* : reparar, remediar, enmendar
red snapper *n* : pargo *m*, huachinango *m Mex*
red tape *n* : papeleo *m*
reduce [riˈduːs, -ˈdjuːs] *v* **-duced; -ducing** *vt* **1** LESSEN : reducir, disminuir, rebajar (precios) **2** DEMOTE : bajar de categoría, degradar **3 to be reduced to** : verse rebajado a, verse forzado a **4 to reduce someone to tears** : hacer llorar a alguien — *vi* SLIM : adelgazar
reduction [riˈdʌkʃən] *n* : reducción *f*, rebaja *f*
redundancy [riˈdʌndən*t*si] *n, pl* **-cies 1** : superfluidad *f* **2** REPETITION : redundancia *f*
redundant [riˈdʌndənt] *adj* : superfluo, redundante
redwood [ˈrɛdˌwʊd] *n* : secoya *f*
reed [ˈriːd] *n* **1** : caña *f*, carrizo *m*, junco *m* **2** : lengüeta *f* (para instrumentos de viento)
reef [ˈriːf] *n* : arrecife *m*, escollo *m*
reek[1] [ˈriːk] *vi* : apestar
reek[2] *n* : hedor *m*
reel[1] [ˈriːl] *vt* **1 to reel in** : enrollar, sacar (un pez) del agua **2 to reel off** : recitar de un tirón — *vi* **1** SPIN, WHIRL : girar, dar vueltas **2** STAGGER : tambalearse
reel[2] *n* **1** : carrete *m* (de pescar etc.), rollo *m* (de fotos) **2** : baile *m* escocés **3** STAGGER : tambaleo *m*
reelect [ˌriːɪˈlɛkt] *vt* : reelegir
reenact [ˌriːɪˈnækt] *vt* : representar de nuevo, reconstruir
reenter [ˌriːˈɛntər] *vt* : volver a entrar
reestablish [ˌriːɪˈstæblɪʃ] *vt* : restablecer
reevaluate [ˌriːɪˈvæljʊˌeɪt] *vt* **-ated; -ating** : revaluar
reevaluation [ˌriːɪˌvæljʊˈeɪʃən] *n* : revaluación *f*

reexamine [ˌriːɪgˈzæmən, -g-] *vt* **-ined; -ining** : volver a examinar, reexaminar

refer [riˈfər] *v* **-ferred; -ferring** *vt* DIRECT, SEND : remitir, enviar ⟨to refer a patient to a specialist : enviar a un paciente a un especialista⟩ — *vi* **to refer to** MENTION : referirse a, aludir a

referee[1] [ˌrɛfəˈriː] *v* **-eed; -eeing** : arbitrar

referee[2] *n* : árbitro *m*, -tra *f*; réferi *mf*

reference [ˈrɛfrən*t*s, ˈrɛfə-] *n* **1** ALLUSION : referencia *f*, alusión *f* ⟨to make reference to : hacer referencia a⟩ **2** CONSULTATION : consulta *f* ⟨for future reference : para futuras consultas⟩ **3** *or* **reference book** : libro *m* de consulta **4** TESTIMONIAL : informe *m*, referencia *f*, recomendación *f*

referendum [ˌrɛfəˈrɛndəm] *n, pl* **-da** [-də] *or* **-dums** : referéndum *m*

refill[1] [ˌriːˈfɪl] *vt* : rellenar

refill[2] [ˈriːˌfɪl] *n* : recambio *m*

refinance [ˌriːˈfaɪˌnæn*t*s] *vt* **-nanced; -nancing** : refinanciar

refine [riˈfaɪn] *vt* **-fined; -fining** **1** : refinar (azúcar, petróleo, etc.) **2** PERFECT : perfeccionar, pulir

refined [riˈfaɪnd] *adj* **1** : refinado (dícese del azúcar, etc.) **2** CULTURED : culto, educado, refinado

refinement [riˈfaɪnmənt] *n* : refinamiento *m*, fineza *f*, finura *f*

refinery [riˈfaɪnəri] *n, pl* **-eries** : refinería *f*

reflect [riˈflɛkt] *vt* **1** : reflejar ⟨to reflect light : reflejar la luz⟩ ⟨happiness is reflected in her face : la felicidad se refleja en su cara⟩ **2 to reflect that** : pensar que, considerar que — *vi* **1 to reflect on** : reflexionar sobre **2 to reflect badly on** : desacreditar, perjudicar

reflection [riˈflɛkʃən] *n* **1** : reflexión *f*, reflejo *m* (de la luz, de imágenes, etc.) **2** THOUGHT : reflexión *f*, meditación *f*

reflective [riˈflɛktɪv] *adj* **1** THOUGHTFUL : reflexivo, pensativo **2** : reflectante (en física)

reflector [riˈflɛktər] *n* : reflector *m*

reflex [ˈriːˌflɛks] *n* : reflejo *m*

reflexive [riˈflɛksɪv] *adj* : reflexivo ⟨a reflexive verb : un verbo reflexivo⟩

reform[1] [riˈfɔrm] *vt* : reformar — *vi* : reformarse

reform[2] *n* : reforma *f*

reformation [ˌrɛfərˈmeɪʃən] *n* : reforma *f* ⟨the Reformation : la Reforma⟩

reformatory [riˈfɔrməˌtori] *n, pl* **-ries** : reformatorio *m*

reformer [riˈfɔrmər] *n* : reformador *m*, -dora *f*

refract [riˈfrækt] *vt* : refractar — *vi* : refractarse

refraction [riˈfrækʃən] *n* : refracción *f*

refractory [riˈfræktəri] *adj* OBSTINATE : refractario, obstinado

refrain[1] [riˈfreɪn] *vi* **to refrain from** : abstenerse de

refrain[2] *n* : estribillo *m* (en música)

refresh [riˈfrɛʃ] *vt* : refrescar ⟨to refresh one's memory : refrescarle la memoria a uno⟩

refreshing [riˈfrɛʃɪŋ] *adj* : refrescante ⟨a refreshing sleep : un sueño reparador⟩

refreshment [riˈfrɛʃmənt] *n* **1** : refresco *m* **2 refreshments** *npl* : refrigerio *m*

refrigerate [riˈfrɪʤəˌreɪt] *vt* **-ated; -ating** : refrigerar

refrigeration [riˌfrɪʤəˈreɪʃən] *n* : refrigeración *f*

refrigerator [riˈfrɪʤəˌreɪt̬ər] *n* : refrigerador *m*, -dora *f*, nevera *f*

refuel [riːˈfjuːəl] *v* **-eled** *or* **-elled; -eling** *or* **-elling** *vi* : repostar — *vt* : llenar de combustible

refuge [ˈrɛˌfjuːʤ] *n* : refugio *m*

refugee [ˌrɛfjʊˈʤiː] *n* : refugiado *m*, -da *f*

refund[1] [riˈfʌnd, ˈriːˌfʌnd] *vt* : reembolsar, devolver

refund[2] [ˈriːˌfʌnd] *n* : reembolso *m*, devolución *f*

refundable [riˈfʌndəbəl] *adj* : reembolsable

refurbish [riˈfərbɪʃ] *vt* : renovar, restaurar

refusal [riˈfjuːzəl] *n* : negativa *f*, rechazo *m*, denegación *f* (de una petición)

refuse[1] [riˈfjuːz] *vt* **-fused; -fusing** **1** REJECT : rechazar, rehusar **2** DENY : negar, rehusar, denegar ⟨to refuse permission : negar el permiso⟩ **3 to refuse to** : negarse a

refuse[2] [ˈrɛˌfjuːs, -ˌfjuːz] *n* : basura *f*, desechos *mpl*, desperdicios *mpl*

refutation [ˌrɛfjʊˈteɪʃən] *n* : refutación *f*

refute [riˈfjuːt] *vt* **-futed; -futing** **1** DENY : desmentir, negar **2** DISPROVE : refutar, rebatir

regain [riːˈgeɪn] *vt* **1** RECOVER : recuperar, recobrar **2** REACH : alcanzar ⟨to regain the shore : llegar a la tierra⟩

regal [ˈriːgəl] *adj* : real, regio

regale [riˈgeɪl] *vt* **-galed; -galing** **1** ENTERTAIN : agasajar, entretener **2** AMUSE, DELIGHT : deleitar, divertir

regalia [riˈgeɪljə] *npl* : ropaje *m*, vestiduras *fpl*, adornos *mpl*

regard[1] [riˈgɑrd] *vt* **1** OBSERVE : observar, mirar **2** HEED : tener en cuenta, hacer caso de **3** CONSIDER : considerar **4** RESPECT : respetar ⟨highly regarded : muy estimado⟩ **5 as regards** : en cuanto a, en lo que se refiere a

regard[2] *n* **1** CONSIDERATION : consideración *f* **2** ESTEEM : respeto *m*, estima *f* **3** PARTICULAR : aspecto *m*, sentido *m* ⟨in this regard : en este sentido⟩ **4 regards** *npl* : saludos *mpl*, recuerdos *mpl* **5 with regard to** : con relación a, con respecto a

regarding [riˈgɑrdɪŋ] *prep* : con respecto a, en cuanto a

regardless [riˈgɑrdləs] *adv* : a pesar de todo

regardless of *prep* : a pesar de, sin tener en cuenta ⟨regardless of our mistakes : a pesar de nuestros errores⟩ ⟨regardless of age : sin tener en cuenta la edad⟩
regenerate [riˈʤɛnəˌreɪt] *v* **-ated; -ating** *vt* : regenerar — *vi* : regenerarse
regeneration [riˌʤɛnəˈreɪʃən] *n* : regeneración *f*
regent [ˈriːʤənt] *n* **1** RULER : regente *mf* **2** : miembro *m* de la junta directiva (de una universidad, etc.)
regime [reɪˈʒiːm, rɪ-] *n* : régimen *m*
regimen [ˈrɛʤəmən] *n* : régimen *m*
regiment[1] [ˈrɛʤəˌmɛnt] *vt* : reglamentar
regiment[2] [ˈrɛʤəmənt] *n* : regimiento *m*
region [ˈriːʤən] *n* **1** : región *f* **2 in the region of** : alrededor de
regional [ˈriːʤənəl] *adj* : regional — **regionally** *adv*
register[1] [ˈrɛʤəstər] *vt* **1** RECORD : registrar, inscribir **2** INDICATE : marcar (temperatura, medidas, etc.) **3** REVEAL : manifestar, acusar ⟨to register surprise : acusar sorpresa⟩ **4** : certificar (correo) — *vi* ENROLL : inscribirse, matricularse
register[2] *n* : registro *m*
registrar [ˈrɛʤəˌstrɑr] *n* : registrador *m*, -dora *f* oficial
registration [ˌrɛʤəˈstreɪʃən] *n* **1** REGISTERING : inscripción *f*, matriculación *f*, registro *m* **2** *or* **registration number** : matrícula *f*, número *m* de matrícula
registry [ˈrɛʤəstri] *n, pl* **-tries** : registro *m*
regress [riˈgrɛs] *vi* : retroceder
regression [riˈgrɛʃən] *n* : retroceso *m*, regresión *f*
regressive [riˈgrɛsɪv] *adj* : regresivo
regret[1] [riˈgrɛt] *vt* **-gretted; -gretting** : arrepentirse de, lamentar ⟨he regrets nothing : no se arrepiente de nada⟩ ⟨I regret to tell you : lamento decirle⟩
regret[2] *n* **1** REMORSE : arrepentimiento *m*, remordimientos *mpl* **2** SADNESS : pesar *m*, dolor *m* **3 regrets** *npl* : excusas *fpl* ⟨to send one's regrets : excusarse⟩
regretful [riˈgrɛtfəl] *adj* : arrepentido, pesaroso
regretfully [riˈgrɛtfəli] *adv* : con pesar
regrettable [riˈgrɛt̬əbəl] *adj* : lamentable — **regrettably** [-bli] *adv*
regular[1] [ˈrɛgjələr] *adj* **1** NORMAL : regular, normal, usual **2** STEADY : uniforme, regular ⟨a regular pace : un paso regular⟩ **3** CUSTOMARY, HABITUAL : habitual, de costumbre
regular[2] *n* : cliente *mf* habitual
regularity [ˌrɛgjəˈlærət̬i] *n, pl* **-ties** : regularidad *f*
regularly [ˈrɛgjələrli] *adv* : regularmente, con regularidad
regulate [ˈrɛgjəˌleɪt] *vt* **-lated; -lating** : regular
regulation [ˌrɛgjəˈleɪʃən] *n* **1** REGULATING : regulación *f* **2** RULE : regla *f*, reglamento *m*, norma *f* ⟨safety regulations : reglas de seguridad⟩
regulator [ˈrɛgjəˌleɪt̬ər] *n* **1** : regulador *m* (mecanismo) **2** : persona *f* que regula
regulatory [ˈrɛgjələˌtori] *adj* : regulador
regurgitate [riˈgərʤəˌteɪt] *v* **-tated; -tating** : regurgitar, vomitar
rehabilitate [ˌriːhəˈbɪləˌteɪt, ˌriːə-] *vt* **-tated; -tating** : rehabilitar
rehabilitation [ˌriːhəˌbɪləˈteɪʃən, ˌriːə-] *n* : rehabilitación *f*
rehearsal [riˈhərsəl] *n* : ensayo *m*
rehearse [riˈhərs] *v* **-hearsed; -hearsing** : ensayar
reheat [ˌriːˈhiːt] *vt* : recalentar
reign[1] [ˈreɪn] *vi* **1** RULE : reinar **2** PREVAIL : reinar, predominar ⟨the reigning champion : el actual campeón⟩
reign[2] *n* : reinado *m*
reimburse [ˌriːəmˈbərs] *vt* **-bursed; -bursing** : reembolsar
reimbursement [ˌriːəmˈbərsmənt] *n* : reembolso *m*
rein[1] [ˈreɪn] *vt* : refrenar (un caballo)
rein[2] *n* **1** : rienda *f* ⟨to give free rein to : dar rienda suelta a⟩ **2** CHECK : control *m* ⟨to keep a tight rein on : llevar un estricto control de⟩
reincarnation [ˌriːɪnˌkɑrˈneɪʃən] *n* : reencarnación *f*
reindeer [ˈreɪnˌdɪr] *n* : reno *m*
reinforce [ˌriːənˈfors] *vt* **-forced; -forcing** : reforzar
reinforcement [ˌriːənˈforsmənt] *n* : refuerzo *m*
reinstate [ˌriːənˈsteɪt] *vt* **-stated; -stating** **1** : reintegrar, restituir (una persona) **2** RESTORE : restablecer (un servicio, etc.)
reinstatement [ˌriːənˈsteɪtmənt] *n* : reintegración *f*, restitución *f*, restablecimiento *m*
reiterate [riˈɪt̬əˌreɪt] *vt* **-ated; -ating** : reiterar, repetir
reiteration [riˌɪt̬əˈreɪʃən] *n* : reiteración *f*, repetición *f*
reject[1] [riˈʤɛkt] *vt* : rechazar
reject[2] [ˈriːˌʤɛkt] *n* : desecho *m* (cosa), persona *f* rechazada
rejection [riˈʤɛkʃən] *n* : rechazo *m*
rejoice [riˈʤɔɪs] *vi* **-joiced; -joicing** : alegrarse, regocijarse
rejoin [ˌriːˈʤɔɪn] *vt* **1** : reincorporarse a, reintegrarse a ⟨he rejoined the firm : se reincorporó a la firma⟩ **2** [riˈ-] REPLY, RETORT : replicar
rejoinder [riˈʤɔɪndər] *n* : réplica *f*
rejuvenate [riˈʤuːvəˌneɪt] *vt* **-nated; -nating** : rejuvenecer
rejuvenation [riˌʤuːvəˈneɪʃən] *n* : rejuvenecimiento *m*
rekindle [ˌriːˈkɪndəl] *vt* **-dled; -dling** : reavivar
relapse[1] [riˈlæps] *vi* **-lapsed; -lapsing** : recaer, volver a caer
relapse[2] [ˈriːˌlæps, riˈlæps] *n* : recaída *f*

relate [ri'leɪt] *v* **-lated; -lating** *vt* **1** TELL : relatar, contar **2** ASSOCIATE : relacionar, asociar ⟨to relate crime to poverty : relacionar la delincuencia a la pobreza⟩ — *vi* **1** CONNECT : conectar, estar relacionado (con) **2** INTERACT : relacionarse (con), llevarse bien (con) **3 to relate to** UNDERSTAND : identificarse con, simpatizar con

related [ri'leɪt̬əd] *adj* : emparentado ⟨to be related to : ser pariente de⟩

relation [ri'leɪʃən] *n* **1** NARRATION : relato *m*, narración *f* **2** RELATIVE : pariente *mf*, familiar *mf* **3** RELATIONSHIP : relación *f* ⟨in relation to : en relación con, con relación a⟩ **4 relations** *npl* : relaciones *fpl* ⟨public relations : relaciones públicas⟩

relationship [ri'leɪʃən,ʃɪp] *n* **1** CONNECTION : relación *f* **2** KINSHIP : parentesco *m*

relative[1] ['rɛlət̬ɪv] *adj* : relativo — **relatively** *adv*

relative[2] *n* : pariente *mf*, familiar *mf*

relativism ['rɛlətɪ,vɪzəm] *n* : relativismo *m*

relativity [,rɛlə'tɪvət̬i] *n, pl* **-ties** : relatividad *f*

relax [ri'læks] *vt* : relajar, aflojar — *vi* : relajarse

relaxation [,ri:,læk'seɪʃən] *n* **1** RELAXING : relajación *f*, aflojamiento *m* **2** DIVERSION : esparcimiento *m*, distracción *f*

relaxing [ri'læksɪŋ] *adj* : relajante

relay[1] ['ri:,leɪ, ri'leɪ] *vt* **-layed; -laying** : transmitir

relay[2] ['ri:,leɪ] *n* **1** : relevo *m* **2** *or* **relay race** : carrera de relevos

release[1] [ri'li:s] *vt* **-leased; -leasing 1** FREE : liberar, poner en libertad **2** LOOSEN : soltar, aflojar ⟨to release the brake : soltar el freno⟩ **3** RELINQUISH : renunciar a, ceder **4** ISSUE : publicar (un libro), estrenar (una película), sacar (un disco)

release[2] *n* **1** LIBERATION : liberación *f*, puesta *f* en libertad **2** RELINQUISHMENT : cesión *f* (de propiedad, etc.) **3** ISSUE : estreno *m* (de una película), puesta *f* en venta (de un disco), publicación *f* (de un libro) **4** ESCAPE : escape *m*, fuga *f* (de un gas)

relegate ['rɛlə,geɪt] *vt* **-gated; -gating** : relegar

relent [ri'lɛnt] *vi* : ablandarse, ceder

relentless [ri'lɛntləs] *adj* : implacable, sin tregua

relentlessly [ri'lɛntləsli] *adv* : implacablemente

relevance ['rɛləvən*t*s] *n* : pertinencia *f*, relación *f*

relevant ['rɛləvənt] *adj* : pertinente — **relevantly** *adv*

reliability [ri,laɪə'bɪlət̬i] *n, pl* **-ties 1** : fiabilidad *f*, seguridad *f* (de una cosa) **2** : formalidad *f*, seriedad *f* (de una persona)

reliable [ri'laɪəbəl] *adj* : confiable, fiable, fidedigno, seguro

reliably [ri'laɪəbli] *adv* : sin fallar ⟨to be reliably informed : saber (algo) de fuentes fidedignas⟩

reliance [ri'laɪən*t*s] *n* **1** DEPENDENCE : dependencia *f* **2** CONFIDENCE : confianza *f*

reliant [ri'laɪənt] *adj* : dependiente

relic ['rɛlɪk] *n* **1** : reliquia *f* **2** VESTIGE : vestigio *m*

relief [ri'li:f] *n* **1** : alivio *m*, desahogo *m* ⟨relief from pain : alivio del dolor⟩ **2** AID, WELFARE : ayuda *f* (benéfica), asistencia *f* social **3** : relieve *m* (en la escultura) ⟨relief map : mapa en relieve⟩ **4** REPLACEMENT : relevo *m*

relieve [ri'li:v] *vt* **-lieved; -lieving 1** ALLEVIATE : aliviar, mitigar ⟨to feel relieved : sentirse aliviado⟩ **2** FREE : liberar, eximir ⟨to relieve someone of responsibility for : eximir a alguien de la responsabilidad de⟩ **3** REPLACE : relevar (a un centinela, etc.) **4** BREAK : romper ⟨to relieve the monotony : romper la monotonía⟩

religion [ri'lɪʤən] *n* : religión *f*

religious [ri'lɪʤəs] *adj* : religioso — **religiously** *adv*

relinquish [ri'lɪŋkwɪʃ, -'lɪn-] *vt* **1** GIVE UP : renunciar a, abandonar **2** RELEASE : soltar

relish[1] ['rɛlɪʃ] *vt* : saborear (comida), disfrutar con (una idea, una perspectiva, etc.)

relish[2] *n* **1** ENJOYMENT : gusto *m*, deleite *m* **2** : salsa *f* (condimento)

relive [,ri:'lɪv] *vt* **-lived; -living** : revivir

relocate [,ri:'lo:,keɪt, ,ri:lo'keɪt] *v* **-cated; -cating** *vt* : reubicar, trasladar — *vi* : trasladarse

relocation [,ri:lo'keɪʃən] *n* : reubicación *f*, traslado *m*

reluctance [ri'lʌktən*t*s] *n* : renuencia *f*, reticencia *f*, desgana *f*

reluctant [ri'lʌktənt] *adj* : renuente, reacio, reticente

reluctantly [ri'lʌktəntli] *adv* : a regañadientes

rely [ri'laɪ] *vi* **-lied; -lying 1** DEPEND : depender (de), contar (con) **2** TRUST : confiar (en)

remain [ri'meɪn] *vi* **1** : quedar ⟨very little remains : queda muy poco⟩ ⟨the remaining 10 minutes : los 10 minutos que quedan⟩ **2** STAY : quedarse, permanecer **3** CONTINUE : continuar, seguir ⟨to remain the same : continuar siendo igual⟩ **4 to remain to** : quedar por ⟨to remain to be done : quedar por hacer⟩ ⟨it remains to be seen : está por ver⟩

remainder [ri'meɪndər] *n* : resto *m*, remanente *m*

remains [ri'meɪnz] *npl* : restos *mpl* ⟨mortal remains : restos mortales⟩

remake[1] [ri:'meɪk] *vt* **-made; -making 1** TRANSFORM : rehacer **2** : hacer una nueva versión de (una película, etc.)

remake[2] [ˈriː,meɪk] *n* : nueva versión *f*

remark[1] [riˈmɑrk] *vt* **1** NOTICE : observar **2** SAY : comentar, observar — *vi* **to remark on** : hacer observaciones sobre

remark[2] *n* : comentario *m*, observación *f*

remarkable [riˈmɑrkəbəl] *adj* : extraordinario, notable — **remarkably** [-bli] *adv*

rematch [ˈriː,mætʃ] *n* : revancha *f*

remedial [riˈmiːdiəl] *adj* : correctivo ⟨remedial classes : clases para alumnos atrasados⟩

remedy[1] [ˈrɛmədi] *vt* **-died; -dying** : remediar

remedy[2] *n, pl* **-dies** : remedio *m*, medicamento *m*

remember [riˈmɛmbər] *vt* **1** RECOLLECT : acordarse de, recordar **2** : no olvidar ⟨remember my words : no olvides mis palabras⟩ ⟨to remember to : acordarse de⟩ **3** : dar saludos, dar recuerdos ⟨remember me to her : dale saludos de mi parte⟩ **4** COMMEMORATE : recordar, conmemorar

remembrance [riˈmɛmbrənts] *n* **1** RECOLLECTION : recuerdo *m* ⟨in remembrance of : en conmemoración de⟩ **2** MEMENTO : recuerdo *m*

remind [riˈmaɪnd] *vt* : recordar ⟨remind me to do it : recuérdame que lo haga⟩ ⟨she reminds me of Clara : me recuerda de Clara⟩

reminder [riˈmaɪndər] *n* : recuerdo *m*

reminisce [,rɛməˈnɪs] *vi* **-nisced; -niscing** : rememorar los viejos tiempos

reminiscence [,rɛməˈnɪsənts] *n* : recuerdo *m*, reminiscencia *f*

reminiscent [,rɛməˈnɪsənt] *adj* **1** NOSTALGIC : reminiscente, nostálgico **2** SUGGESTIVE : evocador, que recuerda — **reminiscently** *adv*

remiss [riˈmɪs] *adj* : negligente, descuidado, remiso

remission [riˈmɪʃən] *n* : remisión *f*

remit [riˈmɪt] *vt* **-mitted; -mitting 1** PARDON : perdonar **2** SEND : remitir, enviar (dinero)

remittance [riˈmɪtənts] *n* : remesa *f*

remnant [ˈrɛmnənt] *n* : restos *mpl*, vestigio *m*

remodel [riˈmɑdəl] *vt* **-eled** *or* **-elled; -eling** *or* **-elling** : remodelar, reformar

remonstrate [riˈmɑn,streɪt] *vi* **-strated; -strating** : protestar ⟨to remonstrate with someone : quejarse a alguien⟩

remorse [riˈmɔrs] *n* : remordimiento *m*

remorseful [riˈmɔrsfəl] *adj* : arrepentido, lleno de remordimiento

remorseless [riˈmɔrsləs] *adj* **1** PITILESS : despiadado **2** RELENTLESS : implacable

remote [riˈmoːt] *adj* **-moter; -est 1** FAR-OFF : lejano, remoto ⟨remote countries : países remotos⟩ ⟨in the remote past : en el pasado lejano⟩ **2** SECLUDED : recóndito **3** : a distancia, remoto ⟨remote control : control remoto⟩ **4** SLIGHT : remoto **5** ALOOF : distante

remotely [riˈmoːtli] *adv* **1** SLIGHTLY : remotamente **2** DISTANTLY : en un lugar remoto, muy lejos

remoteness [riˈmoːtnəs] *n* : lejanía *f*

removable [riˈmuːvəbəl] *adj* : removible

removal [riˈmuːvəl] *n* : separación *f*, extracción *f*, supresión *f* (en algo escrito), eliminación *f* (de problemas, etc.)

remove [riˈmuːv] *vt* **-moved; -moving 1** : quitar, quitarse ⟨remove the lid : quite la tapa⟩ ⟨to remove one's hat : quitarse el sombrero⟩ **2** EXTRACT : sacar, extraer ⟨to remove the contents of : sacar el contenido de⟩ **3** ELIMINATE : eliminar, disipar

remunerate [riˈmjuːnə,reɪt] *vt* **-ated; -ating** : remunerar

remuneration [ri,mjuːnəˈreɪʃən] *n* : remuneración *f*

remunerative [riˈmjuːnərəṭɪv, -,reɪ-] *adj* : remunerativo

renaissance [,rɛnəˈsɑnts, -ˈzɑnts; ˈrɛnə-,-] *n* : renacimiento *m* ⟨the Renaissance : el Renacimiento⟩

renal [ˈriːnəl] *adj* : renal

rename [,riːˈneɪm] *vt* **-named; -naming** : ponerle un nombre nuevo a

rend [ˈrɛnd] *vt* **rent** [ˈrɛnt]; **rending** : desgarrar

render [ˈrɛndər] *vt* **1** : derretir ⟨to render lard : derretir la manteca⟩ **2** GIVE : prestar, dar ⟨to render aid : prestar ayuda⟩ **3** MAKE : hacer, volver, dejar ⟨it rendered him helpless : lo dejó incapacitado⟩ **4** TRANSLATE : traducir, verter ⟨to render into English : traducir al inglés⟩

rendezvous [ˈrɑndɪ,vuː, -deɪ-] *ns & pl* : encuentro *m*, cita *f*

rendition [rɛnˈdɪʃən] *n* : interpretación *f*

renegade [ˈrɛnɪ,geɪd] *n* : renegado *m*, -da *f*

renege [riˈnɪg, -ˈnɛg] *vi* **-neged; -neging** : no cumplir con (una promesa, etc.)

renew [riˈnuː, -ˈnjuː] *vt* **1** REVIVE : renovar, reavivar ⟨to renew the sentiments of youth : renovar los sentimientos de la juventud⟩ **2** RESUME : reanudar **3** EXTEND : renovar ⟨to renew a subscription : renovar una suscripción⟩

renewable [riˈnuːəbəl, -ˈnjuː-] *adj* : renovable

renewal [riˈnuːəl, -ˈnjuː-] *n* : renovación *f*

renounce [riˈnaʊnts] *vt* **-nounced; -nouncing** : renunciar a

renovate [ˈrɛnə,veɪt] *vt* **-vated; -vating** : restaurar, renovar

renovation [,rɛnəˈveɪʃən] *n* : restauración *f*, renovación *f*

renown [riˈnaʊn] *n* : renombre *m*, fama *f*, celebridad *f*

renowned [riˈnaʊnd] *adj* : renombrado, célebre, famoso

rent[1] [ˈrɛnt] *vt* : rentar, alquilar

rent[2] *n* **1** : renta *f*, alquiler *m* ⟨for rent : se alquila⟩ **2** RIP : rasgadura *f*
rental[1] [ˈrɛntəl] *adj* RENT : de alquiler
rental[2] *n* : alquiler *m*
renter [ˈrɛntər] *n* : arrendatario *m*, -ria *f*
renunciation [riˌnʌntsiˈeɪʃən] *n* : renuncia *f*
reopen [ˌriːˈoːpən] *vt* : volver a abrir
reorganization [ˌriːˌɔrgənəˈzeɪʃən] *n* : reorganización *f*
reorganize [ˌriːˈɔrgənˌaɪz] *vt* **-nized; -nizing** : reorganizar
repair[1] [riˈpær] *vt* : reparar, arreglar, refaccionar
repair[2] *n* **1** : reparación *f*, arreglo *m* **2** CONDITION : estado *m* ⟨in bad repair : en mal estado⟩
reparation [ˌrɛpəˈreɪʃən] *n* **1** AMENDS : reparación *f* **2 reparations** *npl* COMPENSATION : indemnización *f*
repartee [ˌrɛpərˈtiː, -ˌpɑr-, -ˈteɪ] *n* : intercambio *m* de réplicas ingeniosas
repast [riˈpæst, ˈriːˌpæst] *n* : comida *f*
repatriate [riˈpeɪtriˌeɪt] *vt* **-ated; -ating** : repatriar
repay [riˈpeɪ] *vt* **-paid; -paying** : pagar, devolver, reembolsar
repeal[1] [riˈpiːl] *vt* : abrogar, revocar
repeal[2] *n* : abrogación *f*, revocación *f*
repeat[1] [riˈpiːt] *vt* : repetir
repeat[2] *n* : repetición *f*
repeatedly [riˈpiːt̬ədli] *adv* : repetidamente, repetidas veces
repel [riˈpɛl] *vt* **-pelled; -pelling 1** REPULSE : repeler (un enemigo, etc.) **2** RESIST : repeler **3** REJECT : rechazar, repeler **4** DISGUST : repugnar, darle asco (a alguien)
repellent *or* **repellant** [riˈpɛlənt] *n* : repelente *m*
repent [riˈpɛnt] *vi* : arrepentirse
repentance [riˈpɛntənts] *n* : arrepentimiento *m*
repentant [riˈpɛntənt] *adj* : arrepentido
repercussion [ˌriːpərˈkʌʃən, ˌrɛpər-] *n* : repercusión *f*
repertoire [ˈrɛpərˌtwɑr] *n* : repertorio *m*
repertory [ˈrɛpərˌtori] *n, pl* **-ries** : repertorio *m*
repetition [ˌrɛpəˈtɪʃən] *n* : repetición *f*
repetitious [ˌrɛpəˈtɪʃəs] *adj* : repetitivo, reiterativo — **repetitiously** *adv*
repetitive [riˈpt̬ət̬ɪv] *adj* : repetitivo, reiterativo
replace [riˈpleɪs] *vt* **-placed; -placing 1** : volver a poner ⟨replace it in the drawer : vuelve a ponerlo en el cajón⟩ **2** SUBSTITUTE : reemplazar, sustituir **3** : reponer ⟨to replace the worn carpet : reponer la alfombra raída⟩
replaceable [riˈpleɪsəbəl] *adj* : reemplazable
replacement [riˈpleɪsmənt] *n* **1** SUBSTITUTION : reemplazo *m*, sustitución *f* **2** SUBSTITUTE : sustituto *m*, -ta *f*; suplente *mf* (persona) **3 replacement part** : repuesto *m*, pieza *f* de recambio
replenish [riˈplɛnɪʃ] *vt* : rellenar, llenar de nuevo
replenishment [riˈplɛnɪʃmənt] *n* : reabastecimiento *m*
replete [riˈpliːt] *adj* : repleto, lleno
replica [ˈrɛplɪkə] *n* : réplica *f*, reproducción *f*
replicate [ˈrɛpləˌkeɪt] *v* **-cated; -cating** *vt* : duplicar, repetir — *vi* : duplicarse
replication [ˌrɛpləˈkeɪʃən] *n* **1** REPRODUCTION : reproducción *f* **2** REPETITION : repetición *f* **3** : replicación *f* (celular)
reply[1] [riˈplaɪ] *vi* **-plied; -plying** : contestar, responder
reply[2] *n, pl* **-plies** : respuesta *f*, contestación *f*
report[1] [riˈport] *vt* **1** ANNOUNCE : relatar, anunciar **2** : dar parte de, informar de, reportar ⟨he reported an accident : dio parte de un accidente⟩ ⟨to report a crime : denunciar un delito⟩ **3** : informar acerca de (en un periódico, la televisión, etc.) — *vi* **1** : hacer un informe, informar **2 to report for duty** : presentarse, reportarse
report[2] *n* **1** RUMOR : rumor *m* **2** REPUTATION : reputación *f* ⟨people of evil report : personas de mala fama⟩ **3** ACCOUNT : informe *m*, reportaje *m* (en un periódico, etc.) **4** BANG : estallido *m* (de un arma de fuego)
report card *n* : boletín *m* de calificaciones, boletín *m* de notas
reportedly [riˈport̬ədli] *adv* : según se dice, según se informa
reporter [riˈport̬ər] *n* : periodista *mf*; reportero *m*, -ra *f*
repose[1] [riˈpoːz] *vi* **-posed; -posing** : reposar, descansar
repose[2] *n* **1** : reposo *m*, descanso *m* **2** CALM : calma *f*, tranquilidad *f*
repository [riˈpɑzəˌtori] *n, pl* **-ries** : depósito *m*
repossess [ˌriːpəˈzɛs] *vt* : recuperar, recobrar la posesión de
reprehensible [ˌrɛpriˈhɛntsəbəl] *adj* : reprensible — **reprehensibly** *adv*
represent [ˌrɛprɪˈzɛnt] *vt* **1** SYMBOLIZE : representar ⟨the flag represents our country : la bandera representa a nuestro país⟩ **2** : representar, ser un representante de ⟨an attorney who represents his client : un abogado que representa su cliente⟩ **3** PORTRAY : presentar ⟨he represents himself as a friend : se presenta como amigo⟩
representation [ˌrɛprɪˌzɛnˈteɪʃən, -zən-] *n* : representación *f*
representative[1] [ˌrɛprɪˈzɛntət̬ɪv] *adj* : representativo
representative[2] *n* **1** : representante *mf* **2** : diputado *m*, -da *f* (en la política)
repress [riˈprɛs] *vt* : reprimir
repression [riˈprɛʃən] *n* : represión *f*
repressive [riˈprɛsɪv] *adj* : represivo
reprieve[1] [riˈpriːv] *vt* **-prieved; -prieving** : indultar
reprieve[2] *n* : indulto *m*
reprimand[1] [ˈrɛprəˌmænd] *vt* : reprender

reprimand[2] *n* : reprimenda *f*

reprint[1] [ri'prɪnt] *vt* : reimprimir

reprint[2] ['ri:ˌprɪnt, ri'prɪnt] *n* : reedición *f*

reprisal [ri'praɪzəl] *n* : represalia *f*

reproach[1] [ri'pro:ʧ] *vt* : reprochar

reproach[2] *n* **1** DISGRACE : deshonra *f* **2** REBUKE : reproche *m*, recriminación *f*

reproachful [ri'pro:ʧfəl] *adj* : de reproche

reproduce [ˌri:prə'du:s, -'dju:s] *v* **-duced; -ducing** *vt* : reproducir — *vi* BREED : reproducirse

reproduction [ˌri:prə'dʌkʃən] *n* : reproducción *f*

reproductive [ˌri:prə'dʌktɪv] *adj* : reproductor

reproof [ri'pru:f] *n* : reprobación *f*, reprimenda *f*, reproche *m*

reprove [ri'pru:v] *vt* **-proved; -proving** : reprender, censurar

reptile ['rɛpˌtaɪl] *n* : reptil *m*

republic [ri'pʌblɪk] *n* : república *f*

republican[1] [ri'pʌblɪkən] *adj* : republicano

republican[2] *n* : republicano *m*, -na *f*

repudiate [ri'pju:diˌeɪt] *vt* **-ated; -ating** **1** REJECT : rechazar **2** DISOWN : repudiar, renegar de

repudiation [riˌpju:di'eɪʃən] *n* : rechazo *m*, repudio *m*

repugnance [ri'pʌgnənts] *n* : repugnancia *f*

repugnant [ri'pʌgnənt] *adj* : repugnante, asqueroso

repulse[1] [ri'pʌls] *vt* **-pulsed; -pulsing** **1** REPEL : repeler **2** REBUFF : desairar, rechazar

repulse[2] *n* : rechazo *m*

repulsive [ri'pʌlsɪv] *adj* : repulsivo, repugnante, asqueroso — **repulsively** *adv*

reputable ['rɛpjəṭəbəl] *adj* : acreditado, de buena reputación

reputation [ˌrɛpjə'teɪʃən] *n* : reputación *f*, fama *f*

repute [ri'pju:t] *n* : reputación *f*, fama *f*

reputed [ri'pju:ṭəd] *adj* : reputado, supuesto ⟨she's reputed to be the best : tiene fama de ser la mejor⟩

reputedly [ri'pju:ṭədli] *adv* : supuestamente, según se dice

request[1] [ri'kwɛst] *vt* : pedir, solicitar, rogar ⟨to request assistance : solicitar asistencia, pedir ayuda⟩ ⟨I requested him to do it : le pedí que lo hiciera⟩

request[2] *n* : petición *f*, solicitud *f*, pedido *m*

requiem ['rɛkwiəm, 'reɪ-] *n* : réquiem *m*

require [ri'kwaɪr] *vt* **-quired; -quiring** **1** CALL FOR, DEMAND : requerir, exigir ⟨if required : si se requiere⟩ ⟨to require that something be done : exigir que algo se haga⟩ **2** NEED : necesitar, requerir

requirement [ri'kwaɪrmənt] *n* **1** NECESSITY : necesidad *f* **2** DEMAND : requisito *m*, demanda *f*

requisite[1] ['rɛkwəzɪt] *adj* : esencial, necesario

requisite[2] *n* : requisito *m*, necesidad *f*

requisition[1] [ˌrɛkwə'zɪʃən] *vt* : requisar

requisition[2] *n* : requisición *f*, requisa *f*

reread [ˌri:'ri:d] *vt* **-read; -reading** : releer

reroute [ˌri:'ru:t, -'raʊt] *vt* **-routed; -routing** : desviar

rerun[1] [ri:'rʌn] *vt* **-ran; -run; -running** : reponer (un programa televisivo)

rerun[2] ['ri:ˌrʌn] *n* **1** : reposición *f* (de un programa televisivo) **2** REPEAT : repetición *f*

resale ['ri:ˌseɪl, ˌri:'seɪl] *n* : reventa *f* ⟨resale price : precio de venta⟩

rescind [ri'sɪnd] *vt* **1** CANCEL : rescindir, cancelar **2** REPEAL : abrogar, revocar

rescue[1] ['rɛsˌkju:] *vt* **-cued; -cuing** : rescatar, salvar

rescue[2] *n* : rescate *m*

rescuer ['rɛskjuər] *n* : salvador *m*, -dora *f*

research[1] [ri'sərʧ, 'ri:ˌsərʧ] *v* : investigar

research[2] *n* : investigación *f*

researcher [ri'sərʧər, 'ri:ˌ-] *n* : investigador *m*, -dora *f*

resemblance [ri'zɛmblənts] *n* : semejanza *f*, parecido *m*

resemble [ri'zɛmbəl] *vt* **-sembled; -sembling** : parecerse a, asemejarse a

resent [ri'zɛnt] *vt* : resentirse de, ofenderse por

resentful [ri'zɛntfəl] *adj* : resentido, rencoroso — **resentfully** *adv*

resentment [ri'zɛntmənt] *n* : resentimiento *m*

reservation [ˌrɛzər'veɪʃən] *n* **1** : reservación *f*, reserva *f* ⟨to make a reservation : hacer una reservación⟩ **2** DOUBT, MISGIVING : reserva *f*, duda *f* ⟨without reservations : sin reservas⟩ **3** : reserva *f* (de indios americanos)

reserve[1] [ri'zərv] *vt* **-served; -serving** : reservar

reserve[2] *n* **1** STOCK : reserva *f* ⟨to keep in reserve : guardar en reserva⟩ **2** RESTRAINT : reserva *f*, moderación *f* **3 reserves** *npl* : reservas *fpl* (militares)

reserved [ri'zərvd] *adj* : reservado

reservoir ['rɛzərˌvwɑr, -ˌvwɔr, -ˌvɔr] *n* : embalse *m*

reset [ˌri:'sɛt] *vt* **-set; -setting** : reajustar, poner en hora (un reloj), reiniciar (una computadora)

reside [ri'zaɪd] *vi* **-sided; -siding** **1** DWELL : residir **2** LIE : radicar, residir ⟨the power resides in the presidency : el poder radica en la presidencia⟩

residence ['rɛzədənts] *n* : residencia *f*

resident[1] ['rɛzədənt] *adj* : residente

resident[2] *n* : residente *mf*

residential [ˌrɛzə'dɛnʧəl] *adj* : residencial

residual [ri'zɪʤʊəl] *adj* : residual

residue ['rɛzəˌdu:, -ˌdju:] *n* : residuo *m*, resto *m*

resign [ri'zaɪn] *vt* **1** QUIT : dimitir, renunciar **2 to resign oneself** : aguantarse, resignarse
resignation [ˌrɛzɪg'neɪʃən] *n* : resignación *f*
resignedly [ri'zaɪnədli] *adv* : con resignación
resilience [ri'zɪljənts] *n* **1** : capacidad *f* de recuperación, adaptabilidad *f* **2** ELASTICITY : elasticidad *f*
resiliency [ri'zɪljəntsi] → **resilience**
resilient [ri'zɪljənt] *adj* **1** STRONG : resistente, fuerte **2** ELASTIC : elástico
resin ['rɛzən] *n* : resina *f*
resist [ri'zɪst] *vt* **1** WITHSTAND : resistir ⟨to resist heat : resistir el calor⟩ **2** OPPOSE : oponerse a
resistance [ri'zɪstənts] *n* : resistencia *f*
resistant [ri'zɪstənt] *adj* : resistente
resolute ['rɛzəˌlu:t] *adj* : firme, resuelto, decidido
resolutely ['rɛzəˌlu:tli, ˌrzə'-] *adv* : resueltamente, firmemente
resolution [ˌrɛzə'lu:ʃən] *n* **1** SOLUTION : solución *f* **2** RESOLVE : resolución *f*, determinación *f* **3** DECISION : propósito *m*, decisión *f* ⟨New Year's resolutions : propósitos para el Año Nuevo⟩ **4** MOTION, PROPOSAL : moción *f*, resolución *f* (legislativa)
resolve¹ [ri'zɑlv] *vt* **-solved; -solving 1** SOLVE : resolver, solucionar **2** DECIDE : resolver ⟨she resolved to get more sleep : resolvió dormir más⟩
resolve² *n* : resolución *f*, determinación *f*
resonance ['rɛzənənts] *n* : resonancia *f*
resonant ['rɛzənənt] *adj* : resonante, retumbante
resort¹ [ri'zɔrt] *vi* **to resort to** : recurrir ⟨to resort to force : recurrir a la fuerza⟩
resort² *n* **1** RECOURSE : recurso *m* ⟨as a last resort : como último recurso⟩ **2** HANGOUT : lugar *m* popular, lugar *m* muy frecuentado **3** : lugar *m* de vacaciones ⟨tourist resort : centro turístico⟩
resound [ri'zaʊnd] *vi* : retumbar, resonar
resounding [ri'zaʊndɪŋ] *adj* **1** RESONANT : retumbante, resonante **2** ABSOLUTE, CATEGORICAL : rotundo, tremendo ⟨a resounding success : un éxito rotundo⟩
resource ['ri:ˌsors, ri'sors] *n* **1** RESOURCEFULNESS : ingenio *m*, recursos *mpl* **2 resources** *npl* : recursos *mpl* ⟨natural resources : recursos naturales⟩ **3 resources** *npl* MEANS : recursos *mpl*, medios *mpl*, fondos *mpl*
resourceful [ri'sorsfəl, -'zors-] *adj* : ingenioso
resourcefulness [ri'sorsfəlnəs, -'zors-] *n* : ingenio *m*, recursos *mpl*, inventiva *f*
respect¹ [ri'spɛkt] *vt* : respetar, estimar
respect² *n* **1** REFERENCE : relación *f*, respeto *m* ⟨with respect to : en lo que respecta a⟩ **2** ESTEEM : respeto *m*, estima *f* **3** DETAIL, PARTICULAR : detalle *m*, sentido *m*, respeto *m* ⟨in some respects : en algunos sentidos⟩ **4 respects** *npl* : respetos *mpl* ⟨to pay one's respects : presentar uno susrespetos⟩
respectability [riˌspɛktə'bɪləṯi] *n* : respetabilidad *f*
respectable [ri'spɛktəbəl] *adj* **1** PROPER : respetable, decente **2** CONSIDERABLE : considerable, respetable ⟨a respectable amount : una cantidad respetable⟩ — **respectably** [-bli] *adv*
respectful [ri'spɛktfəl] *adj* : respetuoso — **respectfully** *adv*
respectfulness [ri'spɛktfəlnəs] *n* : respetuosidad *f*
respective [ri'spɛktɪv] *adj* : respectivo ⟨their respective homes : sus casas respectivas⟩ — **respectively** *adv*
respiration [ˌrɛspə'reɪʃən] *n* : respiración *f*
respirator ['rɛspəˌreɪṯər] *n* : respirador *m*
respiratory ['rɛspərəˌtori, rɪ'spaɪrə-] *adj* : respiratorio
respite ['rɛspɪt, rɪ'spaɪt] *n* : respiro *m*, tregua *f*
resplendent [ri'splɛndənt] *adj* : resplandeciente — **resplendently** *adv*
respond [ri'spɑnd] *vi* **1** ANSWER : contestar, responder **2** REACT : responder, reaccionar ⟨to respond to treatment : responder al tratamiento⟩
response [ri'spɑnts] *n* : respuesta *f*
responsibility [riˌspɑntsə'bɪləṯi] *n, pl* **-ties** : responsabilidad *f*
responsible [ri'spɑntsəbəl] *adj* : responsable — **responsibly** [-bli] *adv*
responsive [ri'spɑntsɪv] *adj* **1** ANSWERING : que responde **2** SENSITIVE : sensible, receptivo
responsiveness [ri'spɑntsɪvnəs] *n* : receptividad *f*, sensibilidad *f*
rest¹ ['rɛst] *vi* **1** REPOSE : reposar, descansar **2** RELAX : quedarse tranquilo **3** STOP : pararse, detenerse **4** DEPEND : basarse (en), descansar (sobre), depender (de) ⟨the decision rests with her : la decisión pesa sobre ella⟩ **5 to rest on** : apoyarse en, descansar sobre ⟨to rest on one's arm : apoyarse en el brazo⟩ — *vt* **1** RELAX : descansar **2** SUPPORT : apoyar **3 to rest one's eyes on** : fijar la mirada en
rest² *n* **1** RELAXATION, REPOSE : reposo *m*, descanso *m* **2** SUPPORT : soporte *m*, apoyo *m* **3** : silencio *m* (en música) **4** REMAINDER : resto *m* **5 to come to rest** : pararse
restart [ri'stɑrt] *vt* **1** : volver a empezar **2** RESUME : reanudar **3** : volver a arrancar (un motor), reiniciar (una computadora) — *vi* **1** : reanudarse **2** : volver a arrancar
restatement [ˌri:'steɪtmənt] *n* : repetición *f*
restaurant ['rɛstəˌrɑnt, -rənt] *n* : restaurante *m*

restful [ˈrɛstfəl] *adj* **1** RELAXING : relajante **2** PEACEFUL : tranquilo, sosegado
restitution [ˌrɛstəˈtuːʃən, -ˈtjuː-] *n* : restitución *f*
restive [ˈrɛstɪv] *adj* : inquieto, nervioso
restless [ˈrɛstləs] *adj* **1** FIDGETY : inquieto, agitado **2** IMPATIENT : impaciente **3** SLEEPLESS : desvelado ⟨a restless night : una noche en blanco⟩
restlessly [ˈrɛstləsli] *adv* : nerviosamente
restlessness [ˈrɛstləsnəs] *n* : inquietud *f*, agitación *f*
restoration [ˌrɛstəˈreɪʃən] *n* : restauración *f*, restablecimiento *m*
restore [riˈstor] *vt* **-stored; -storing** **1** RETURN : volver **2** REESTABLISH : restablecer **3** REPAIR : restaurar
restrain [riˈstreɪn] *vt* **1** : refrenar, contener **2 to restrain oneself** : contenerse
restrained [riˈstreɪnd] *adj* : comedido, templado, contenido
restraint [riˈstreɪnt] *n* **1** RESTRICTION : restricción *f*, limitación *f*, control *m* **2** CONFINEMENT : encierro *m* **3** RESERVE : reserva *f*, control *m* de sí mismo
restrict [riˈstrɪkt] *vt* : restringir, limitar, constreñir
restricted [riˈstrɪktəd] *adj* **1** LIMITED : limitado, restringido **2** CLASSIFIED : secreto, confidencial
restriction [riˈstrɪkʃən] *n* : restricción *f*
restrictive [riˈstrɪktɪv] *adj* : restrictivo — **restrictively** *adv*
rest room *n* : servicios *mpl*, baño *m*
restructure [riˈstrʌktʃər] *vt* **-tured; -turing** : reestructurar
result[1] [riˈzʌlt] *vi* : resultar ⟨to result in : resultar en, tener por resultado⟩
result[2] *n* : resultado *m*, consecuencia *f* ⟨as a result of : como consecuencia de⟩
resultant [riˈzʌltənt] *adj* : resultante
resume [riˈzuːm] *v* **-sumed; -suming** *vt* : reanudar — *vi* : reanudarse
résumé *or* **resume** *or* **resumé** [ˈrɛzəˌmeɪ, ˌrɛzəˈ-] *n* **1** SUMMARY : resumen *m* **2** CURRICULUM VITAE : currículum *m*, currículo *m*
resumption [riˈzʌmpʃən] *n* : reanudación *f*
resurface [ˌriːˈsərfəs] *v* **-faced; -facing** *vt* : pavimentar (una carretera) de nuevo — *vi* : volver a salir en la superficie
resurgence [riˈsərdʒənts] *n* : resurgimiento *m*
resurrect [ˌrɛzəˈrɛkt] *vt* : resucitar, desempolvar
resurrection [ˌrɛzəˈrɛkʃən] *n* : resurrección *f*
resuscitate [riˈsʌsəˌteɪt] *vt* **-tated; -tating** : resucitar, revivir
resuscitation [riˌsʌsəˈteɪʃən] *n* : reanimación *f*, resucitación *f*
retail[1] [ˈriːˌteɪl] *vt* : vender al por menor, vender al detalle
retail[2] *adv* : al por menor, al detalle
retail[3] *adj* : detallista, minorista
retail[4] *n* : venta *f* al detalle, venta *f* al por menor
retailer [ˈriːˌteɪlər] *n* : detallista *mf*, minorista *mf*
retain [riˈteɪn] *vt* : retener, conservar, guardar
retainer [riˈteɪnər] *n* **1** SERVANT : criado *m*, -da *f* **2** ADVANCE : anticipo *m*
retaliate [riˈtæliˌeɪt] *vi* **-ated; -ating** : responder, contraatacar, tomar represalias
retaliation [riˌtæliˈeɪʃən] *n* : represalia *f*, retaliación *f*
retard [riˈtɑrd] *vt* : retardar, retrasar
retardation [ˌriːˌtɑrˈdeɪʃən] *n* **1** : retardación *f* **2** *or* **mental retardation** : retraso *m* mental
retarded [riˈtɑrdəd] *adj* : retrasado
retch [ˈrɛtʃ] *vi* : hacer arcadas
retention [riˈtɛntʃən] *n* : retención *f*
retentive [riˈtɛntɪv] *adj* : retentivo
rethink [riːˈθɪŋk] *vt* **-thought; -thinking** : reconsiderar, repensar
reticence [ˈrɛt̬əsənts] *n* : reticencia *f*
reticent [ˈrɛt̬əsənt] *adj* : reticente
retina [ˈrɛtənə] *n, pl* **-nas** *or* **-nae** [-əni, -ənˌaɪ] : retina *f*
retinue [ˈrɛtənˌuː, -ˌjuː] *n* : séquito *m*, comitiva *f*, cortejo *m*
retire [riˈtaɪr] *vi* **-tired; -tiring** **1** RETREAT, WITHDRAW : retirarse, retraerse **2** : retirarse, jubilarse (de su trabajo) **3** : acostarse, irse a dormir
retiree [riˌtaɪˈriː] *n* : jubilado *m*, -da *f*
retirement [riˈtaɪrmənt] *n* : jubilación *f*
retiring [riˈtaɪrɪŋ] *adj* SHY : retraído
retort[1] [riˈtɔrt] *vt* : replicar
retort[2] *n* : réplica *f*
retrace [ˌriːˈtreɪs] *vt* **-traced; -tracing** : volver sobre, desandar ⟨to retrace one's steps : volver uno sobre sus pasos⟩
retract [riˈtrækt] *vt* **1** TAKE BACK, WITHDRAW : retirar, retractarse de **2** : retraer (las garras) — *vi* : retractarse
retractable [riˈtræktəbəl] *adj* : retractable
retrain [ˌriːˈtreɪn] *vt* : reciclar, reconvertir
retreat[1] [riˈtriːt] *vi* : retirarse
retreat[2] *n* **1** WITHDRAWAL : retirada *f*, repliegue *m*, retiro *m* ⟨to beat a retreat : batirse en retirada⟩ **2** REFUGE : retiro *m*, refugio *m*
retrench [riˈtrɛntʃ] *vt* : reducir (gastos) — *vi* : economizar
retribution [ˌrɛtrəˈbjuːʃən] *n* PUNISHMENT : castigo *m*, pena *f* merecida
retrieval [riˈtriːvəl] *n* : recuperación *f* ⟨beyond retrieval : irrecuperable⟩ ⟨data retrieval : recuperación de datos⟩
retrieve [riˈtriːv] *vt* **-trieved; -trieving** **1** : cobrar ⟨to retrieve game : cobrar la caza⟩ **2** RECOVER : recuperar
retriever [riˈtriːvər] *n* : perro *m* cobrador

retroactive [ˌrɛtroˈæktɪv] *adj* : retroactivo — **retroactively** *adv*
retrograde [ˈrɛtrəˌgreɪd] *adj* : retrógrado
retrospect [ˈrɛtrəˌspɛkt] *n* **in retrospect** : mirando hacia atrás, retrospectivamente
retrospective [ˌrɛtrəˈspɛktɪv] *adj* : retrospectivo
return[1] [riˈtərn] *vi* **1** : volver, regresar ⟨to return home : regresar a casa⟩ **2** REAPPEAR : reaparecer, resurgir **3** ANSWER : responder — *vt* **1** REPLACE, RESTORE : devolver, volver (a poner), restituir ⟨to return something to its place : volver a poner algo en su lugar⟩ **2** YIELD : producir, redituar, rendir **3** REPAY : pagar, devolver ⟨to return a compliment : devolver un cumplido⟩
return[2] *adj* : de vuelta
return[3] *n* **1** RETURNING : regreso *m*, vuelta *f*, retorno *m* **2** *or* **tax return** : declaración *f* de impuestos **3** YIELD : rédito *m*, rendimiento *m*, ganancia *f* **4 returns** *npl* DATA, RESULTS : resultados *mpl*, datos *mpl*
reunion [riˈju:njən] *n* : reunión *f*, reencuentro *m*
reunite [ˌri:jʊˈnaɪt] *v* **-nited; -niting** *vt* : (volver a) reunir — *vi* : (volver a) reunirse
reusable [riˈju:zəbəl] *adj* : reutilizable
reuse [riˈju:z] *vt* **-used; -using** : reutilizar, usar de nuevo
revamp [ˌriˈvæmp] *vt* : renovar
reveal [riˈvi:l] *vt* **1** DIVULGE : revelar, divulgar ⟨to reveal a secret : revelar un secreto⟩ **2** SHOW : manifestar, mostrar, dejar ver
revealing [riˈvi:lɪŋ] *adj* : revelador
reveille [ˈrɛvəli] *n* : toque *m* de diana
revel[1] [ˈrɛvəl] *vi* **-eled** *or* **-elled; -eling** *or* **-elling 1** CAROUSE : ir de juerga **2 to revel in** : deleitarse en
revel[2] *n* : juerga *f*, parranda *f fam*
revelation [ˌrɛvəˈleɪʃən] *n* : revelación *f*
reveler *or* **reveller** [ˈrɛvələr] *n* : juerguista *mf*
revelry [ˈrɛvəlri] *n, pl* **–ries** : juerga *f*, parranda *f fam*, jarana *f fam*
revenge[1] [riˈvɛnʤ] *vt* **-venged; -venging** : vengar ⟨to revenge oneself on : vengarse de⟩
revenge[2] *n* : venganza *f*
revenue [ˈrɛvəˌnu:, -ˌnju:] *n* : ingresos *mpl*, rentas *fpl*
reverberate [riˈvərbəˌreɪt] *vi* **-ated; -ating** : reverberar
reverberation [riˌvərbəˈreɪʃən] *n* : reverberación *f*
revere [riˈvɪr] *vt* **-vered; -vering** : reverenciar, venerar
reverence [ˈrɛvərənts] *n* : reverencia *f*, veneración *f*
reverend [ˈrɛvərənd] *adj* : reverendo ⟨the Reverend John Chapin : el reverendo John Chapin⟩
reverent [ˈrɛvərənt] *adj* : reverente — **reverently** *adv*
reverie [ˈrɛvəri] *n, pl* **-eries** : ensueño *m*
reversal [ˈrɛvərsəl] *n* **1** INVERSION : inversión *f* (del orden normal) **2** CHANGE : cambio *m* total **3** SETBACK : revés *m*, contratiempo *m*
reverse[1] [riˈvərs] *v* **-versed; -versing** *vt* **1** INVERT : invertir **2** CHANGE : cambiar totalmente **3** ANNUL : anular, revocar — *vi* : dar marcha atrás
reverse[2] *adj* **1** : inverso ⟨in reverse order : en orden inverso⟩ ⟨the reverse side : el reverso⟩ **2** OPPOSITE : contrario, opuesto
reverse[3] *n* **1** OPPOSITE : lo contrario, lo opuesto **2** SETBACK : revés *m*, contratiempo *m* **3** BACK : reverso *m*, dorso *m*, revés *m* **4** *or* **reverse gear** : marcha *f* atrás, reversa *f Col, Mex*
reversible [riˈvərsəbəl] *adj* : reversible
reversion [riˈvərʒən] *n* : reversión *f*, vuelta *f*
revert [riˈvərt] *vi* : revertir
review[1] [riˈvju:] *vt* **1** REEXAMINE : volver a examinar, repasar (una lección) **2** CRITICIZE : reseñar, hacer una crítica de **3** EXAMINE : examinar, analizar ⟨to review one's life : examinar su vida⟩ **4 to review the troops** : pasar revista a las tropas
review[2] *n* **1** INSPECTION : revista *f* (de tropas) **2** ANALYSIS, OVERVIEW : resumen *m*, análisis *m* ⟨a review of current affairs : un análisis de las actualidades⟩ **3** CRITICISM : reseña *f*, crítica *f* (de un libro, etc.) **4** : repaso *m* (para un examen) **5** REVUE : revista *f* (musical)
reviewer [riˈvju:ər] *n* : crítico *m*, -ca *f*
revile [riˈvaɪl] *vt* **-viled; -viling** : injuriar, denostar
revise [riˈvaɪz] *vt* **-vised; -vising** : revisar, corregir, refundir ⟨to revise a dictionary : corregir un diccionario⟩
revision [riˈvɪʒən] *n* : revisión *f*
revival [riˈvaɪvəl] *n* **1** : renacimiento *m* (de ideas, etc.), restablecimiento *m* (de costumbres, etc.), reactivación *f* (de la economía) **2** : reanimación *f*, resucitación *f* (en medicina) **3** *or* **revival meeting** : asamblea *f* evangelista
revive [riˈvaɪv] *v* **-vived; -viving** *vt* **1** REAWAKEN : reavivar, reanimar, reactivar (la economía), resucitar (a un paciente) **2** REESTABLISH : restablecer — *vi* **1** : renacer, reanimarse, reactivarse **2** COME TO : recobrar el sentido, volver en sí
revoke [riˈvo:k] *vt* **-voked; -voking** : revocar
revolt[1] [riˈvo:lt] *vi* **1** REBEL : rebelarse, sublevarse **2 to revolt at** : sentir repugnancia por — *vt* DISGUST : darle asco (a alguien), repugnar
revolt[2] *n* REBELLION : rebelión *f*, revuelta *f*, sublevación *f*
revolting [riˈvo:ltɪŋ] *adj* : asqueroso, repugnante

revolution [ˌrɛvəˈluːʃən] *n* : revolución *f*
revolutionary[1] [ˌrɛvəˈluːʃənˌɛri] *adj* : revolucionario
revolutionary[2] *n, pl* **-aries** : revolucionario *m*, -ria *f*
revolutionize [ˌrɛvəˈluːʃənˌaɪz] *vt* **-ized; -izing** : cambiar radicalmente, revolucionar
revolve [riˈvɑlv] *v* **-volved; -volving** *vt* ROTATE : hacer girar — *vi* **1** ROTATE : girar ⟨to revolve around : girar alrededor de⟩ **2 to revolve in one's mind** : darle vueltas en la cabeza a alguien
revolver [riˈvɑlvər] *n* : revólver *m*
revue [riˈvjuː] *n* : revista *f* (musical)
revulsion [riˈvʌlʃən] *n* : repugnancia *f*
reward[1] [riˈwɔrd] *vt* : recompensar, premiar
reward[2] *n* : recompensa *f*
rewrite [ˌriːˈraɪt] *vt* **-wrote; -written; -writing** : escribir de nuevo, volver a escribir
rhapsody [ˈræpsədi] *n, pl* **-dies 1** : elogio *m* excesivo ⟨to go into rhapsodies over : extasiarse por⟩ **2** : rapsodia *f* (en música)
rhetoric [ˈrɛt̬ərɪk] *n* : retórica *f*
rhetorical [rɪˈtɔrɪkəl] *adj* : retórico
rheumatic [rʊˈmæt̬ɪk] *adj* : reumático
rheumatism [ˈruːməˌtɪzəm, ˈrʊ-] *n* : reumatismo *m*
rhinestone [ˈraɪnˌstoːn] *n* : diamante *m* de imitación
rhino [ˈraɪˌnoː] *n, pl* **rhino** *or* **rhinos** → **rhinoceros**
rhinoceros [raɪˈnɑsərəs] *n, pl* **-eroses** *or* **-eros** *or* **-eri** [-ˌraɪ] : rinoceronte *m*
rhododendron [ˌroːdəˈdɛndrən] *n* : rododendro *m*
rhombus [ˈrɑmbəs] *n, pl* **-buses** *or* **-bi** [-ˌbaɪ, -bi] : rombo *m*
rhubarb [ˈruːˌbɑrb] *n* : ruibarbo *m*
rhyme[1] [ˈraɪm] *vi* **rhymed; rhyming** : rimar
rhyme[2] *n* **1** : rima *f* **2** VERSE : verso *m* (en rima)
rhythm [ˈrɪðəm] *n* : ritmo *m*
rhythmic [ˈrɪðmɪk] *or* **rhythmical** [-mɪkəl] *adj* : rítmico — **rhythmically** [-mɪkli] *adv*
rib[1] [ˈrɪb] *vt* **ribbed; ribbing 1** : hacer en canalé ⟨a ribbed sweater : un suéter en canalé⟩ **2** TEASE : tomarle el pelo (a alguien)
rib[2] *n* **1** : costilla *f* (de una persona o un animal) **2** : nervio *m* (de una bóveda o una hoja), varilla *f* (de un paraguas), canalé *m* (de una prenda tejida)
ribald [ˈrɪbəld] *adj* : escabroso, procaz
ribbon [ˈrɪbən] *n* **1** : cinta *f* **2 to tear to ribbons** : hacer jirones
rice [ˈraɪs] *n* : arroz *m*
rich [ˈrɪʧ] *adj* **1** WEALTHY : rico **2** SUMPTUOUS : suntuoso, lujoso **3** : pesado ⟨rich foods : comida pesada⟩ **4** ABUNDANT : abundante **5** : vivo, intenso ⟨rich colors : colores vivos⟩ **6** FERTILE : fértil, rico
riches [ˈrɪʧəz] *npl* : riquezas *fpl*
richly [ˈrɪʧli] *adv* **1** SUMPTUOUSLY : suntuosamente, ricamente **2** ABUNDANTLY : abundantemente **3 richly deserved** : bien merecido
richness [ˈrɪʧnəs] *n* : riqueza *f*
rickets [ˈrɪkəts] *n* : raquitismo *m*
rickety [ˈrɪkət̬i] *adj* : desvencijado, destartalado
ricksha *or* **rickshaw** [ˈrɪkˌʃɔ] *n* : cochecillo *m* tirado por un hombre
ricochet[1] [ˈrɪkəˌʃeɪ] *vi* **-cheted** [-ˌʃeɪd] *or* **-chetted** [-ˌʃɛt̬əd]; **-cheting** [-ˌʃeɪɪŋ] *or* **-chetting** [-ˌʃɛt̬ɪŋ] : rebotar
ricochet[2] *n* : rebote *m*
rid [ˈrɪd] *vt* **rid; ridding 1** FREE : librar ⟨to rid the city of thieves : librar la ciudad de ladrones⟩ **2 to rid oneself of** : desembarazarse de
riddance [ˈrɪdənts] *n* : libramiento *m* ⟨good riddance! : ¡adiós y buen viaje!, ¡vete con viento fresco!⟩
riddle[1] [ˈrɪdəl] *vt* **-dled; -dling** : acribillar ⟨riddled with bullets : acribillado a balazos⟩ ⟨riddled with errors : lleno de errores⟩
riddle[2] *n* : acertijo *m*, adivinanza *f*
ride[1] [ˈraɪd] *v* **rode** [ˈroːd]; **ridden** [ˈrɪdən]; **riding** *vt* **1** : montar, ir, andar ⟨to ride a horse : montar a caballo⟩ ⟨to ride a bicycle : montar en bicicleta, andar en bicicleta⟩ ⟨to ride the bus : ir en autobús⟩ **2** TRAVERSE : recorrer ⟨he rode 5 miles : recorrió 5 millas⟩ **3** TEASE : burlarse de, ridiculizar **4** CARRY : llevar **5** WEATHER : capear ⟨they rode out the storm : capearon el temporal⟩ **6 to ride the waves** : surcar los mares — *vi* **1** : montar a caballo, cabalgar **2** TRAVEL : ir, viajar (en coche, en bicicleta, etc.) **3** RUN : andar, marchar ⟨the car rides well : el coche anda bien⟩ **4 to ride at anchor** : estar fondeado **5 to let things ride** : dejar pasar las cosas
ride[2] *n* **1** : paseo *m*, vuelta *f* (en coche, en bicicleta, a caballo) ⟨to go for a ride : dar una vuelta⟩ ⟨to give someone a ride : llevar en coche a alguien⟩ **2** : aparato *m* (en un parque de diversiones)
rider [ˈraɪdər] *n* **1** : jinete *mf* ⟨the rider fell off his horse : el jinete se cayó de su caballo⟩ **2** CYCLIST : ciclista *mf* **3** MOTORCYCLIST : motociclista *mf* **4** CLAUSE : cláusula *f* añadida
ridge [ˈrɪʤ] *n* **1** CHAIN : cadena *f* (de montañas o cerros) **2** : caballete *m* (de un techo), cresta *f* (de una ola o una montaña), cordoncillo *m* (de telas)
ridicule[1] [ˈrɪdəˌkjuːl] *vt* **-culed; -culing** : burlarse de, mofarse de, ridiculizar
ridicule[2] *n* : burlas *fpl*
ridiculous [rəˈdɪkjələs] *adj* : ridículo, absurdo
ridiculously [rəˈdɪkjələsli] *adv* : de forma ridícula
rife [ˈraɪf] *adj* : abundante, común ⟨to be rife with : estar plagado de⟩

riffraff ['rɪf,ræf] *n* : chusma *f*, gentuza *f*
rifle¹ ['raɪfəl] *v* **-fled; -fling** *vt* RANSACK : desvalijar, saquear — *vi* **to rifle through** : revolver
rifle² *n* : rifle *m*, fusil *m*
rift ['rɪft] *n* **1** FISSURE : grieta *f*, fisura *f* **2** BREAK : ruptura *f* (entre personas), división *f* (dentro de un grupo)
rig¹ ['rɪg] *vt* **rigged; rigging 1** : aparejar (un barco) **2** EQUIP : equipar **3** FIX : amañar (una elección, etc.) **4 to rig up** CONSTRUCT : construir, erigir **5 to rig oneself out as** : vestirse de
rig² *n* **1** : aparejo *m* (de un barco) **2** *or* **oil rig** : torre *f* de perforación, plataforma *f* petrolífera
rigging ['rɪgɪŋ, -gən] *n* : jarcia *f*, aparejo *m*
right¹ ['raɪt] *vt* **1** FIX, RESTORE : reparar ⟨to right the economy : reparar la economía⟩ **2** STRAIGHTEN : enderezar
right² *adv* **1** : bien ⟨to live right : vivir bien⟩ **2** PRECISELY : precisamente, justo ⟨right in the middle : justo en medio⟩ **3** DIRECTLY, STRAIGHT : derecho, directamente ⟨he went right home : fue derecho a casa⟩ **4** IMMEDIATELY : inmediatamente ⟨right after lunch : inmediatamente después del almuerzo⟩ **5** COMPLETELY : completamente ⟨he felt right at home : se sintió completamente cómodo⟩ **6** : a la derecha ⟨to look left and right : mirar a la izquierda y a la derecha⟩
right³ *adj* **1** UPRIGHT : bueno, honrado ⟨right conduct : conducta honrada⟩ **2** CORRECT : correcto ⟨the right answer : la respuesta correcta⟩ **3** APPROPRIATE : apropiado, adecuado, debido ⟨the right man for the job : el hombre perfecto para el trabajo⟩ **4** STRAIGHT : recto ⟨a right line : una línea recta⟩ **5** : derecho ⟨the right hand : la mano derecha⟩ **6** SOUND : bien ⟨he's not in his right mind : no está bien de la cabeza⟩
right⁴ *n* **1** GOOD : bien *m* ⟨to do right : hacer el bien⟩ **2** : derecha *f* ⟨on the right : a la derecha⟩ **3** *or* **right hand** : mano *f* derecha **4** ENTITLEMENT : derecho *m* ⟨the right to vote : el derecho a votar⟩ ⟨women's rights : los derechos de la mujer⟩ **5 the Right** : la derecha (en la política)
right angle *n* : ángulo *m* recto
right–angled ['raɪt'æŋgəld] *or* **right–angle** [-gəl] *adj* **1** : en ángulo recto **2 right–angled triangle** : triángulo *m* rectángulo
righteous ['raɪtʃəs] *adj* : recto, honrado — **righteously** *adv*
righteousness ['raɪtʃəsnəs] *n* : rectitud *f*, honradez *f*
rightful ['raɪtfəl] *adj* **1** JUST : justo **2** LAWFUL : legítimo — **rightfully** *adv*
right–hand ['raɪt'hænd] *adj* **1** : situado a la derecha **2** RIGHT-HANDED : para la mano derecha, con la mano derecha **3 right–hand man** : brazo *m* derecho
right–handed ['raɪt'hændəd] *adj* **1** : diestro ⟨a right-handed pitcher : un lanzador diestro⟩ **2** : para la mano derecha, con la mano derecha **3** CLOCKWISE : en la dirección de las manecillas del reloj
rightly ['raɪtli] *adv* **1** JUSTLY : justamente, con razón **2** PROPERLY : debidamente, apropiadamente **3** CORRECTLY : correctamente
right–of–way ['raɪtə'weɪ, -əv-] *n, pl* **rights–of–way 1** : preferencia (del tráfico) **2** ACCESS : derecho *m* de paso
rightward ['raɪtwərd] *adj* : a la derecha, hacia la derecha
right–wing ['raɪt'wɪŋ] *adj* : derechista
right wing *n* **the right wing** : la derecha
right–winger ['raɪt'wɪŋər] *n* : derechista *mf*
rigid ['rɪʤɪd] *adj* : rígido — **rigidly** *adv*
rigidity [rɪ'ʤɪdəti] *n, pl* **-ties** : rigidez *f*
rigmarole ['rɪgmə,ro:l, 'rɪgə-] *n* **1** NONSENSE : galimatías *m*, disparates *mpl* **2** PROCEDURES : trámites *mpl*
rigor ['rɪgər] *n* : rigor *m*
rigor mortis [,rɪgər'mɔrtəs] *n* : rigidez *f* cadavérica
rigorous ['rɪgərəs] *adj* : riguroso — **rigorously** *adv*
rile ['raɪl] *vt* **riled; riling** : irritar
rill ['rɪl] *n* : riachuelo *m*
rim ['rɪm] *n* **1** EDGE : borde *m* **2** : llanta *f*, rin *m* *Col, Mex* (de una rueda) **3** FRAME : montura *f* (de anteojos)
rime ['raɪm] *n* : escarcha *f*
rind ['raɪnd] *n* : corteza *f*
ring¹ ['rɪŋ] *v* **rang** ['ræŋ]; **rung** ['rʌŋ]; **ringing** *vi* **1** : sonar ⟨the doorbell rang : el timbre sonó⟩ ⟨to ring for : llamar⟩ **2** RESOUND : resonar **3** SEEM : parecer ⟨to ring true : parecer cierto⟩ — *vt* **1** : tocar, hacer sonar (un timbre, una alarma, etc.) **2** SURROUND : cercar, rodear
ring² *n* **1** : anillo *m*, sortija *f* ⟨wedding ring : anillo de matrimonio⟩ **2** BAND : aro *m*, anillo *m* ⟨piston ring : aro de émbolo⟩ **3** CIRCLE : círculo *m* **4** ARENA : arena *f*, ruedo *m* ⟨a boxing ring : un cuadrilátero, un ring⟩ **5** GANG : banda *f* (de ladrones, etc.) **6** SOUND : timbre *m*, sonido *m* **7** CALL : llamada *f* (por teléfono)
ringer ['rɪŋər] *n* **to be a dead ringer for** : ser un vivo retrato de
ringleader ['rɪŋ,li:dər] *n* : cabecilla *mf*
ringlet ['rɪŋlət] *n* : sortija *f*, rizo *m*
ringworm ['rɪŋ,wərm] *n* : tiña *f*
rink ['rɪŋk] *n* : pista *f* ⟨skating rink : pista de patinaje⟩
rinse¹ ['rɪnts] *vt* **rinsed; rinsing** : enjuagar ⟨to rinse out one's mouth : enjuagarse la boca⟩
rinse² *n* : enjuague *m*
riot¹ ['raɪət] *vi* : amotinarse
riot² *n* : motín *m*, tumulto *m*, alboroto *m*

rioter ['raɪəṭər] *n* : alborotador *m*, -dora *f*
riotous ['raɪəṭəs] *adj* **1** UNRULY, WILD : desenfrenado, alborotado **2** ABUNDANT : abundante
rip[1] ['rɪp] *v* **ripped; ripping** *vt* : rasgar, arrancar, desgarrar — *vi* : rasgarse, desgarrarse
rip[2] *n* : rasgón *m*, desgarrón *m*
ripe ['raɪp] *adj* **riper; ripest** **1** MATURE : maduro ⟨ripe fruit : fruta madura⟩ **2** READY : listo, preparado
ripen ['raɪpən] *v* : madurar
ripeness ['raɪpnəs] *n* : madurez *f*
rip–off ['rɪp,ɔf] *n* **1** THEFT : robo *m* **2** SWINDLE : estafa *f*, timo *m fam*
rip off *vt* **1** : rasgar, arrancar, desgarrar **2** SWINDLE *fam* : estafar, tifar
ripple[1] ['rɪpəl] *v* **-pled; -pling** *vi* : rizarse, ondear, ondular — *vt* : rizar
ripple[2] *n* : onda *f*, ondulación *f*
rise[1] ['raɪz] *vi* **rose** ['ro:z]; **risen** ['rɪz-ən]; **rising** **1** GET UP : levantarse ⟨to rise to one's feet : ponerse de pie⟩ **2** : elevarse, alzarse ⟨the mountains rose to the west : las montañas se elevaron al oeste⟩ **3** : salir (dícese del sol y de la luna) **4** : subir (dícese de las aguas, del humo, etc.) ⟨the river rose : las aguas subieron de nivel⟩ **5** INCREASE : aumentar, subir **6** ORIGINATE : nacer, proceder **7 to rise in rank** : ascender **8 to rise up** REBEL : sublevarse, rebelarse
rise[2] *n* **1** ASCENT : ascensión *f*, subida *f* **2** ORIGIN : origen *m* **3** ELEVATION : elevación *f* **4** INCREASE : subida *f*, aumento *m*, alzamiento *m* **5** SLOPE : pendiente *f*, cuesta *f*
riser ['raɪzər] *n* **1** : contrahuella *f* (de una escalera) **2 early riser** : madrugador *m*, -dora *f* **3 late riser** : dormilón *m*, -lona *f*
risk[1] ['rɪsk] *vt* : arriesgar
risk[2] *n* : riesgo *m*, peligro *m* ⟨at risk : en peligro⟩ ⟨at your own risk : por su cuenta y riesgo⟩
risky ['rɪski] *adj* **riskier; -est** : arriesgado, peligroso, riesgoso
risqué [rɪ'skeɪ] *adj* : escabroso, picante, subido de tono
rite ['raɪt] *n* : rito *m*
ritual[1] ['rɪʧʊəl] *adj* : ritual — **ritually** *adv*
ritual[2] *n* : ritual *m*
rival[1] ['raɪvəl] *vt* **-valed** *or* **-valled; -valing** *or* **-valling** : rivalizar con, competir con
rival[2] *adj* : competidor, rival
rival[3] *n* : rival *mf*; competidor *m*, -dora *f*
rivalry ['raɪvəlri] *n, pl* **-ries** : rivalidad *f*, competencia *f*
river ['rɪvər] *n* : río *m*
riverbank ['rɪvər,bæŋk] *n* : ribera *f*, orilla *f*
riverbed ['rɪvər,bɛd] *n* : cauce *m*, lecho *m*
riverside ['rɪvər,saɪd] *n* : ribera *f*, orilla *f*
rivet[1] ['rɪvət] *vt* **1** : remachar **2** FIX : fijar (los ojos, etc.) **3** FASCINATE : fascinar, cautivar
rivet[2] *n* : remache *m*
rivulet ['rɪvjələt] *n* : arroyo *m*, riachuelo *m* ⟨rivulets of sweat : gotas de sudor⟩
roach ['ro:ʧ] → **cockroach**
road ['ro:d] *n* **1** : carretera *f*, calle *f*, camino *m* **2** PATH : camino *m*, sendero *m*, vía *f* ⟨on the road to a solution : en vías de una solución⟩
roadblock ['ro:d,blɑk] *n* : control *m*
roadrunner ['ro:d,rʌnər] *n* : correcaminos *m*
roadside ['ro:d,saɪd] *n* : borde *m* de la carretera
roadway ['ro:d,weɪ] *n* : carretera *f*, calzada *f*
roam ['ro:m] *vi* : vagar, deambular, errar — *vt* : vagar por
roan[1] ['ro:n] *adj* : ruano
roan[2] *n* : caballo *m* ruano
roar[1] ['ror] *vi* : rugir, bramar ⟨to roar with laughter : reírse a carcajadas⟩ — *vt* : decir a gritos
roar[2] *n* **1** : rugido *m*, bramido *m* (de un animal) **2** DIN : clamor *m* (de gente), fragor *m* (del trueno), estruendo *m* (del tráfico, etc.)
roast[1] ['ro:st] *vt* : asar (carne, papas), tostar (café, nueces) — *vi* : asarse
roast[2] *adj* **1** : asado ⟨roast chicken : pollo asado⟩ **2 roast beef** : rosbif *m*
roast[3] *n* : asado *m*
rob ['rɑb] *v* **robbed; robbing** *vt* **1** STEAL : robar **2** DEPRIVE : privar, quitar — *vi* : robar
robber ['rɑbər] *n* : ladrón *m*, -drona *f*
robbery ['rɑbəri] *n, pl* **-beries** : robo *m*
robe[1] ['ro:b] *vt* **robed; robing** : vestirse
robe[2] *n* **1** : toga *f* (de magistrados, etc.), sotana *f* (de eclesiásticos) ⟨robe of office : traje de ceremonias⟩ **2** BATHROBE : bata *f*
robin ['rɑbən] *n* : petirrojo *m*
robot ['ro:,bɑt, -bət] *n* : robot *m*
robotic [ro'bɑṭɪk] *adj* : robótico, robotizado
robotics [ro'bɑṭɪks] *ns & pl* : robótica *f*
robust [ro'bʌst, 'ro:,bʌst] *adj* : robusto, fuerte — **robustly** *adv*
rock[1] ['rɑk] *vt* **1** : acunar (a un niño), mecer (una cuna) **2** SHAKE : sacudir — *vi* SWAY : mecerse, balancearse
rock[2] *adj* : de rock
rock[3] *n* **1** ROCKING : balanceo *m* **2** *or* **rock music** : rock *m*, música *f* rock **3** : roca *f* (substancia) **4** STONE : piedra *f*
rock and roll *n* : rock and roll *m*
rocker ['rɑkər] *n* **1** : balancín *m* **2** *or* **rocking chair** : mecedora *f*, balancín *m* **3 to be off one's rocker** : estar chiflado, estar loco
rocket[1] ['rɑkət] *vi* : dispararse, subir rápidamente
rocket[2] *n* : cohete *m*

rocking horse *n* : caballito *m* (de balancín)
rock salt *n* : sal *f* gema
rocky [ˈrɑki] *adj* **rockier; -est 1** : rocoso, pedregoso **2** UNSTEADY : inestable
rod [ˈrɑd] *n* **1** BAR : barra *f*, varilla *f*, vara *f* (de madera) ⟨a fishing rod : una caña (de pescar)⟩ **2** : medida *f* de longitud equivalente a 5.03 metros (5 yardas)
rode → **ride**[1]
rodent [ˈroːdənt] *n* : roedor *m*
rodeo [ˈroːdiˌoː, roˈdeɪˌoː] *n, pl* **-deos** : rodeo *m*
roe [ˈroː] *n* : hueva *f*
rogue [ˈroːg] *n* SCOUNDREL : pícaro *m*, -ra *f*; pillo *m*, -lla *f*
roguish [ˈroːgɪʃ] *adj* : pícaro, travieso
role [ˈroːl] *n* : papel *m*, función *f*, rol *m*
roll[1] [ˈroːl] *vt* **1** : hacer rodar ⟨to roll the ball : hacer rodar la pelota⟩ ⟨to roll one's eyes : poner los ojos en blanco⟩ **2** : liar (un cigarrillo) **3** *or* **to roll up** : enrollar ⟨to roll (oneself) up into a ball : hacerse una bola⟩ **4** FLATTEN : estirar (masa), laminar (metales), pasar el rodillo por (el césped) **5 to roll up one's sleeves** : arremangarse — *vi* **1** : rodar ⟨the ball kept on rolling : la pelota siguió rodando⟩ **2** SWAY : balancearse ⟨the ship rolled in the waves : el barco se balanceó en las olas⟩ **3** REVERBERATE, SOUND : tronar (dícese del trueno), redoblar (dícese de un tambor) **4 to roll along** PROCEED : ponerse en marcha **5 to roll around** : revolcarse **6 to roll by** : pasar **7 to roll over** : dar una vuelta
roll[2] *n* **1** LIST : lista *f* ⟨to call the roll : pasar lista⟩ ⟨to have on the roll : tener inscrito⟩ **2** *or* **bread roll** : panecito *m*, bolillo *m Mex* **3** : rollo *m* (de papel, de tela, etc.) ⟨a roll of film : un carrete⟩ ⟨a roll of bills : un fajo⟩ **4** : redoble *m* (de tambores), retumbo *m* (del trueno, etc.) **5** ROLLING, SWAYING : balanceo *m*
roller [ˈroːlər] *n* **1** : rodillo *m* **2** CURLER : rulo *m*
roller coaster [ˈroːlərˌkoːstər] *n* : montaña *f* rusa
roller–skate [ˈroːlərˌskeɪt] *vi* **-skated; -skating** : patinar (sobre ruedas)
roller skate *n* : patín *m* (de ruedas)
rollicking [ˈrɑlɪkɪŋ] *adj* : animado, alegre
rolling pin *n* : rodillo *m*
Roman[1] [ˈroːmən] *adj* : romano
Roman[2] *n* : romano *m*, -na *f*
Roman Catholic *n* : católico *m*, -ca *f* — **Roman Catholic** *adj*
Roman Catholicism *n* : catolicismo *m*
romance[1] [roˈmænts, ˈroːˌmænts] *vi* **-manced; -mancing** FANTASIZE : fantasear
romance[2] *n* **1** : romance *m*, novela *f* de caballerías **2** : novela *f* de amor, novela *f* romántica **3** AFFAIR : romance *m*, amorío *m*
Romanian [rʊˈmeɪniən, ro-] *n* **1** : rumano *m*, -na *f* **2** : rumano *m* (idioma) — **Romanian** *adj*
Roman numeral *n* : número *m* romano
romantic [roˈmæntɪk] *adj* : romántico — **romantically** [-tɪkli] *adv*
romp[1] [ˈrɑmp] *vi* FROLIC : retozar, juguetear
romp[2] *n* : retozo *m*
roof[1] [ˈruːf, ˈrʊf] *vt* : techar
roof[2] *n, pl* **roofs** [ˈruːfs, ˈrʊfs; ˈruːvz, ˈrʊvz] **1** : techo *m*, tejado *m*, techado *m* **2 roof of the mouth** : paladar *m*
roofing [ˈruːfɪŋ, ˈrʊfɪŋ] *n* : techumbre *f*
rooftop [ˈruːfˌtɑp, ˈrʊf-] *n* ROOF : tejado *m*
rook[1] [ˈrʊk] *vt* CHEAT : defraudar, estafar, timar
rook[2] *n* **1** : grajo *m* (ave) **2** : torre *f* (en ajedrez)
rookie [ˈrʊki] *n* : novato *m*, -ta *f*
room[1] [ˈruːm, ˈrʊm] *vi* LODGE : alojarse, hospedarse
room[2] *n* **1** SPACE : espacio *m*, sitio *m*, lugar *m* ⟨to make room for : hacer lugar para⟩ **2** : cuarto *m*, habitación *f* (en una casa), sala *f* (para reuniones, etc.) **3** BEDROOM : dormitorio *m*, habitación *f*, pieza *f* **4** (*indicating possibility or opportunity*) ⟨room for improvement : posibilidad de mejorar⟩ ⟨there's no room for error : no hay lugar para errores⟩
roomer [ˈruːmər, ˈrʊmər] *n* : inquilino *m*, -na *f*
rooming house *n* : pensión *f*
roommate [ˈruːmˌmeɪt, ˈrʊm-] *n* : compañero *m*, -ra *f* de cuarto
roomy [ˈruːmi, ˈrʊmi] *adj* **roomier; -est 1** SPACIOUS : espacioso, amplio **2** LOOSE : suelto, holgado ⟨a roomy blouse : una blusa holgada⟩
roost[1] [ˈruːst] *vi* : posarse, dormir (en una percha)
roost[2] *n* : percha *f*
rooster [ˈruːstər, ˈrʊs-] *n* : gallo *m*
root[1] [ˈruːt, ˈrʊt] *vi* **1** : arraigar ⟨the plant rooted easily : la planta arraigó con facilidad⟩ ⟨deeply rooted traditions : tradiciones profundamente arraigadas⟩ **2** : hozar (dícese de los cerdos) ⟨to root around in : hurgar en⟩ **3 to root for** : apoyar a, alentar — *vt* **to root out** *or* **to root up** : desarraigar (plantas), extirpar (problemas, etc.)
root[2] *n* **1** : raíz *f* (de una planta) **2** ORIGIN : origen *m*, raíz *f* **3** CORE : centro *m*, núcleo *m* ⟨to get to the root of the matter : ir al centro del asunto⟩
rootless [ˈruːtləs, ˈrʊt-] *adj* : desarraigado
rope[1] [ˈroːp] *vt* **roped; roping 1** TIE : amarrar, atar **2** LASSO : lazar **3 to rope off** : acordonar
rope[2] *n* : soga *f*, cuerda *f*
rosary [ˈroːzəri] *n, pl* **-ries** : rosario *m*
rose[1] → **rise**[1]
rose[2] [ˈroːz] *adj* : rosa, color de rosa

rose[3] *n* **1** : rosal *m* (planta), rosa *f* (flor) **2** : rosa *m* (color)
rosebush [ˈroːzˌbʊʃ] *n* : rosal *m*
rosemary [ˈroːzˌmɛri] *n, pl* **-maries** : romero *m*
rosette [roˈzɛt] *n* : escarapela *f* (hecho de cintas), roseta *f* (en arquitectura)
Rosh Hashanah [ˌrɑʃhɑˈʃɑnə, ˌroːʃ-] *n* : el Año Nuevo judío
rosin [ˈrɑzən] *n* : colofonia *f*
roster [ˈrɑstər] *n* : lista *f*
rostrum [ˈrɑstrəm] *n, pl* **-trums** *or* **-tra** [-trə] : tribuna *f*, estrado *m*
rosy [ˈroːzi] *adj* **rosier; -est** **1** : sonrosado, de color rosa **2** PROMISING : prometedor, halagüeño
rot[1] [ˈrɑt] *v* **rotted; rotting** *vi* : pudrirse, descomponerse — *vt* : pudrir, descomponer
rot[2] *n* : putrefacción *f*, descomposición *f*, podredumbre *f*
rotary[1] [ˈroːt̬əri] *adj* : rotativo, rotatorio
rotary[2] *n, pl* **-ries** **1** : máquina *f* rotativa **2** TRAFFIC CIRCLE : rotonda *f*, glorieta *f*
rotate [ˈroːˌteɪt] *v* **-tated; -tating** *vi* REVOLVE : girar, rotar — *vt* **1** TURN : hacer girar, darle vueltas a **2** ALTERNATE : alternar
rotation [roˈteɪʃən] *n* : rotación *f*
rote [ˈroːt] *n* **to learn by rote** : aprender de memoria
rotor [ˈroːt̬ər] *n* : rotor *m*
rotten [ˈrɑtən] *adj* **1** PUTRID : podrido, putrefacto **2** CORRUPT : corrompido **3** BAD : malo ⟨a rotten day : un día malísimo⟩
rottenness [ˈrɑtənnəs] *n* : podredumbre *f*
rotund [roˈtʌnd] *adj* **1** ROUNDED : redondeado **2** PLUMP : regordete *fam*, llenito *fam*
rouge [ˈruːʒ, ˈruːʤ] *n* : colorete *m*
rough[1] [ˈrʌf] *vt* **1** ROUGHEN : poner áspero **2 to rough out** SKETCH : esbozar, bosquejar **3 to rough up** BEAT : darle una paliza (a alguien) **4 to rough it** : vivir sin comodidades
rough[2] *adj* **1** COARSE : áspero, basto **2** UNEVEN : desigual, escabroso, accidentado (dícese del terreno) **3** : agitado (dícese del mar), tempestuoso (dícese del tiempo), violento (dícese del viento) **4** VIOLENT : violento, brutal ⟨a rough neighborhood : un barrio peligroso⟩ **5** DIFFICULT : duro, difícil **6** CRUDE : rudo, tosco, burdo ⟨a rough cottage : una casita tosca⟩ ⟨a rough draft : un borrador⟩ ⟨a rough sketch : un bosquejo⟩ **7** APPROXIMATE : aproximado ⟨a rough idea : una idea aproximada⟩
rough[3] *n* **1 the rough** : el rough (en golf) **2 in the rough** : en borrador
roughage [ˈrʌfɪʤ] *n* : fibra *f*
roughen [ˈrʌfən] *vt* : poner áspero — *vi* : ponerse áspero
roughly [ˈrʌfli] *adv* **1** : bruscamente ⟨to treat roughly : maltratar⟩ **2** CRUDELY : burdamente **3** APPROXIMATELY : aproximadamente, más o menos
roughneck [ˈrʌfˌnɛk] *n* : matón *m*
roughness [ˈrʌfnəs] *n* : rudeza *f*, aspereza *f*
roulette [ruːˈlɛt] *n* : ruleta *f*
round[1] [ˈraʊnd] *vt* **1** : redondear ⟨she rounded the edges : redondeó los bordes⟩ **2** TURN : doblar ⟨to round the corner : dar la vuelta a la esquina⟩ **3 to round off** : redondear (un número) **4 to round off** *or* **to round out** COMPLETE : rematar, terminar **5 to round up** GATHER : reunir
round[2] *adv* → **around**[1]
round[3] *adj* **1** : redondo ⟨a round table : una mesa redonda⟩ ⟨in round numbers : en números redondos⟩ ⟨round shoulders : espaldas cargadas⟩ **2 round trip** : viaje *m* de ida y vuelta
round[4] *n* **1** CIRCLE : círculo *m* **2** SERIES : serie *f*, sucesión *f* ⟨a round of talks : una ronda de negociaciones⟩ ⟨the daily round : la rutina cotidiana⟩ **3** : asalto *m* (en boxeo), recorrido *m* (en golf), vuelta *f* (en varios juegos) **4** : salva *f* (de aplausos) **5 round of drinks** : ronda *f* **6 round of ammunition** : disparo *m*, cartucho *m* **7 rounds** *npl* : recorridos *mpl* (de un cartero), rondas *fpl* (de un vigilante), visitas *fpl* (de un médico) ⟨to make the rounds : hacer visitas⟩
round[5] *prep* → **around**[2]
roundabout [ˈraʊndəˌbaʊt] *adj* : indirecto ⟨to speak in a roundabout way : hablar con rodeos⟩
roundly [ˈraʊndli] *adv* **1** THOROUGHLY : completamente **2** BLUNTLY : francamente, rotundamente **3** VIGOROUSLY : con vigor
roundness [ˈraʊndnəs] *n* : redondez *f*
roundup [ˈraʊndˌʌp] *n* **1** : rodeo *m* (de animales), redada *f* (de delincuentes, etc.) **2** SUMMARY : resumen *m*
round up *vt* **1** : rodear (ganado), reunir (personas) **2** SUMMARIZE : hacer un resumen de
roundworm [ˈraʊndˌwərm] *n* : lombriz *f* intestinal
rouse [ˈraʊz] *vt* **roused; rousing** **1** AWAKE : despertar **2** EXCITE : excitar ⟨it roused him to fury : lo enfureció⟩
rout[1] [ˈraʊt] *vt* **1** DEFEAT : derrotar, aplastar **2 to rout out** : hacer salir
rout[2] *n* **1** DISPERSAL : desbandada *f*, dispersión *f* **2** DEFEAT : derrota *f* aplastante
route[1] [ˈruːt, ˈraʊt] *vt* **routed; routing** : dirigir, enviar, encaminar
route[2] *n* : camino *m*, ruta *f*, recorrido *m*
routine[1] [ruːˈtiːn] *adj* : rutinario — **routinely** *adv*
routine[2] *n* : rutina *f*
rove [ˈroːv] *v* **roved; roving** *vi* : vagar, errar — *vt* : errar por
rover [ˈroːvər] *n* : vagabundo *m*, -da *f*

row[1] ['ro:] *vt* **1** : avanzar a remo ⟨to row a boat : remar⟩ **2** : llevar a remo ⟨he rowed me to shore : me llevó hasta la orilla⟩ — *vi* : remar

row[2] ['raʊ] *n* **1** : paseo *m* en barca ⟨to go for a row : salir a remar⟩ **2** LINE, RANK : fila *f*, hilera *f* **3** SERIES : serie *f* ⟨three days in a row : tres días seguidos⟩ **4** RACKET : estruendo *m*, bulla *f* **5** QUARREL : pelea *f*, riña *f*

rowboat ['ro:ˌbo:t] *n* : bote *m* de remos

rowdiness ['raʊdinəs] *n* : bulla *f*

rowdy[1] ['raʊdi] *adj* **-dier; -est** : escandaloso, alborotador

rowdy[2] *n, pl* **-dies** : alborotador *m*, -dora *f*

rower ['ro:ər] *n* : remero *m*, -ra *f*

royal[1] ['rɔɪəl] *adj* : real — **royally** *adv*

royal[2] *n* : persona de linaje real, miembro de la familia real

royalty ['rɔɪəlti] *n, pl* **-ties** **1** : realeza *f* (posición) **2** : miembros *mpl* de la familia real **3 royalties** *npl* : derechos *mpl* de autor

rub[1] ['rʌb] *v* **rubbed; rubbing** *vt* **1** : frotar, restregar ⟨to rub one's hands together : frotarse las manos⟩ **2** MASSAGE : friccionar, masajear **3** CHAFE : rozar **4** POLISH : frotar, pulir **5** SCRUB : fregar **6 to rub elbows with** : codearse con **7 to rub someone the wrong way** : sacar de quicio a alguien, caerle mal a alguien — *vi* **to rub against** : rozar

rub[2] *n* **1** RUBBING : frotamiento *m*, fricción *f* **2** DIFFICULTY : problema *m*

rubber ['rʌbər] *n* **1** : goma *f*, caucho *m*, hule *m Mex* **2 rubbers** *npl* OVERSHOES : chanclos *mpl*

rubber band *n* : goma *f* (elástica), gomita *f*

rubber–stamp ['rʌbər'stæmp] *vt* **1** APPROVE : aprobar, autorizar **2** STAMP : sellar

rubber stamp *n* : sello *m* (de goma)

rubbery ['rʌbəri] *adj* : gomoso

rubbish ['rʌbɪʃ] *n* : basura *f*, desechos *mpl*, desperdicios *mpl*

rubble ['rʌbəl] *n* : escombros *mpl*, ripio *m*

ruble ['ru:bəl] *n* : rublo *m*

ruby ['ru:bi] *n, pl* **-bies** **1** : rubí *m* (gema) **2** : color *m* de rubí

rudder ['rʌdər] *n* : timón *m*

ruddy ['rʌdi] *adj* **-dier; -est** : rubicundo (dícese de la cara, etc.), rojizo (dícese del cielo)

rude ['ru:d] *adj* **ruder; rudest** **1** CRUDE : tosco, rústico **2** IMPOLITE : grosero, descortés, maleducado **3** ABRUPT : brusco ⟨a rude awakening : una sorpresa desagradable⟩

rudely ['ru:dli] *adv* : groseramente

rudeness ['ru:dnəs] *n* **1** IMPOLITENESS : grosería *f*, descortesía *f*, falta *f* de educación **2** ROUGHNESS : tosquedad *f* **3** SUDDENNESS : brusquedad *f*

rudiment ['ru:dəmənt] *n* : rudimento *m*, noción *f* básica ⟨the rudiments of Spanish : los rudimentos del español⟩

rudimentary [ˌru:də'mɛntəri] *adj* : rudimentario, básico

rue ['ru:] *vt* **rued; ruing** : lamentar, arrepentirse de

rueful ['ru:fəl] *adj* **1** PITIFUL : lastimoso **2** REGRETFUL : arrepentido, pesaroso

ruffian ['rʌfiən] *n* : matón *m*

ruffle[1] ['rʌfəl] *vt* **-fled; -fling** **1** AGITATE : agitar, rizar (agua) **2** RUMPLE : arrugar (ropa), despeinar (pelo) **3** ERECT : erizar (plumas) **4** VEX : alterar, irritar, perturbar **5** : fruncir volantes en (tela)

ruffle[2] *n* FLOUNCE : volante *m*

ruffly ['rʌfəli] *adj* : con volantes

rug ['rʌg] *n* : alfombra *f*, tapete *m*

rugged ['rʌgəd] *adj* **1** ROUGH, UNEVEN : accidentado, escabroso ⟨rugged mountains : montañas accidentadas⟩ **2** HARSH : duro, severo **3** ROBUST, STURDY : robusto, fuerte

ruin[1] ['ru:ən] *vt* **1** DESTROY : destruir, arruinar **2** BANKRUPT : arruinar, hacer quebrar

ruin[2] *n* **1** : ruina *f* ⟨to fall into ruin : caer en ruinas⟩ **2** : ruina *f*, perdición *f* ⟨to be the ruin of : ser la perdición de⟩ **3 ruins** *npl* : ruinas *fpl*, restos *mpl* ⟨the ruins of the ancient temple : las ruinas del templo antiguo⟩

ruinous ['ru:ənəs] *adj* : ruinoso

rule[1] ['ru:l] *v* **ruled; ruling** *vt* **1** CONTROL, GOVERN : gobernar (un país), controlar (las emociones) **2** DECIDE : decidir, fallar ⟨the judge ruled that . . . : el juez falló que . . . ⟩ **3** DRAW : trazar con una regla — *vi* **1** GOVERN : gobernar, reinar **2** PREVAIL : prevalecer, imperar **3 to rule against** : fallar en contra de

rule[2] *n* **1** REGULATION : regla *f*, norma *f* **2** CUSTOM, HABIT : regla *f* general ⟨as a rule : por lo general⟩ **3** GOVERNMENT : gobierno *m*, dominio *m* **4** RULER : regla *f* (para medir)

ruler ['ru:lər] *n* **1** LEADER, SOVEREIGN : gobernante *mf*; soberano *m*, -na *f* **2** : regla *f* (para medir)

ruling ['ru:lɪŋ] *n* : resolución *f*, fallo *m*

rum ['rʌm] *n* : ron *m*

Rumanian [rʊ'meɪniən] → **Romanian**

rumble[1] ['rʌmbəl] *vi* **-bled; -bling** : retumbar, hacer ruidos (dícese del estómago)

rumble[2] *n* : estruendo *m*, ruido *m* sordo, retumbo *m*

ruminant[1] ['ru:mənənt] *adj* : rumiante

ruminant[2] *n* : rumiante *m*

ruminate ['ru:məˌneɪt] *vi* **-nated; -nating** **1** : rumiar (en zoología) **2** REFLECT : reflexionar, rumiar

rummage ['rʌmɪʤ] *v* **-maged; -maging** *vi* : hurgar — *vt* RANSACK : revolver ⟨they rummaged the attic : revolvieron el ático⟩

rummy [ˈrʌmi] *n* : rummy *m* (juego de naipes)
rumor[1] [ˈruːmər] *vt* : rumorear ⟨it is rumored that . . . : se rumorea que . . ., se dice que . . . ⟩
rumor[2] *n* : rumor *m*
rump [ˈrʌmp] *n* **1** : ancas *fpl*, grupa *f* (de un animal) **2** : cadera *f* ⟨rump steak : filete de cadera⟩
rumple [ˈrʌmpəl] *vt* **-pled; -pling** : arrugar (ropa, etc.), despeinar (pelo)
rumpus [ˈrʌmpəs] *n* : lío *m*, jaleo *m fam*
run[1] [ˈrʌn] *v* **ran** [ˈræn]; **run; running** *vi* **1** : correr ⟨she ran to catch the bus : corrió para alcanzar el autobús⟩ ⟨run and fetch the doctor : corre a buscar al médico⟩ **2** : circular, correr ⟨the train runs between Detroit and Chicago : el tren circula entre Detroit y Chicago⟩ ⟨to run on time : ser puntual⟩ **3** FUNCTION : funcionar, ir ⟨the engine runs on gasoline : el motor funciona con gasolina⟩ ⟨to run smoothly : ir bien⟩ **4** FLOW : correr, ir **5** LAST : durar ⟨the movie runs for two hours : la película dura dos horas⟩ ⟨the contract runs for three years : el contrato es válido por tres años⟩ **6** : desteñir, despintar (dícese de los colores) **7** EXTEND : correr, extenderse **8 to run for office** : postularse, presentarse — *vt* **1** : correr ⟨to run 10 miles : correr 10 millas⟩ ⟨to run errands : hacer los mandados⟩ ⟨to run out of town : hacer salir del pueblo⟩ **2** PASS : pasar **3** DRIVE : llevar en coche **4** OPERATE : hacer funcionar (un motor, etc.) **5** : echar ⟨to run water : echar agua⟩ **6** MANAGE : dirigir, llevar (un negocio, etc.) **7** EXTEND : tender (un cable, etc.) **8 to run a risk** : correr un riesgo
run[2] *n* **1** : carrera *f* ⟨at a run : a la carrera, corriendo⟩ ⟨to go for a run : ir a correr⟩ **2** TRIP : vuelta *f*, paseo *m* (en coche), viaje *m* (en avión) **3** SERIES : serie *f* ⟨a run of disappointments : una serie de desilusiones⟩ ⟨in the long run : a la larga⟩ ⟨in the short run : a corto plazo⟩ **4** DEMAND : gran demanda *f* ⟨a run on the banks : una corrida bancaria⟩ **5** (*used for theatrical productions and films*) ⟨to have a long run : mantenerse mucho tiempo en la cartelera⟩ **6** TYPE : tipo *m* ⟨the average run of students : el tipo más común de estudiante⟩ **7** : carrera *f* (en béisbol) **8** : carrera *f* (en una media) **9 to have the run of** : tener libre acceso de (una casa, etc.) **10 ski run** : pista *f* (de esquí)
runaway[1] [ˈrʌnəˌweɪ] *adj* **1** FUGITIVE : fugitivo **2** UNCONTROLLABLE : incontrolable, fuera de control ⟨runaway inflation : inflación desenfrenada⟩ ⟨a runaway success : un éxito aplastante⟩
runaway[2] *n* : fugitivo *m*, -va *f*
rundown [ˈrʌnˌdaʊn] *n* SUMMARY : resumen *m*
run–down [ˈrʌnˈdaʊn] *adj* **1** DILAPIDATED : ruinoso, destartalado **2** SICKLY, TIRED : cansado, débil
rung[1] *pp* → **ring**[1]
rung[2] [ˈrʌŋ] *n* : peldaño *m*, escalón *m*
run–in [ˈrʌnˌɪn] *n* : disputa *f*, altercado *m*
runner [ˈrʌnər] *n* **1** RACER : corredor *m*, -dora *f* **2** MESSENGER : mensajero *m*, -ra *f* **3** TRACK : riel *m* (de un cajón, etc.) **4** : patín *m* (de un trineo), cuchilla *f* (de un patín) **5** : estolón *m* (planta)
runner–up [ˌrʌnərˈʌp] *n, pl* **runners–up** : subcampeón *m*, -peona *f*
running [ˈrʌnɪŋ] *adj* **1** FLOWING : corriente ⟨running water : agua corriente⟩ **2** CONTINUOUS : continuo ⟨a running battle : una lucha continua⟩ **3** CONSECUTIVE : seguido ⟨six days running : por seis días seguidos⟩
runny [ˈrʌni] *adj* **-nier; -est 1** WATERY : caldoso **2 to have a runny nose** : moquear
run over *vt* : atropellar — *vi* OVERFLOW : rebosar
runt [ˈrʌnt] *n* : animal *m* pequeño ⟨the runt of the litter : el más pequeño de la camada⟩
runway [ˈrʌnˌweɪ] *n* : pista *f* de aterrizaje
rupee [ruːˈpiː, ˈruːˌ-] *n* : rupia *f*
rupture[1] [ˈrʌptʃər] *v* **-tured; -turing** *vt* **1** BREAK, BURST : romper, reventar **2** : causar una hernia en — *vi* : reventarse
rupture[2] *n* **1** BREAK : ruptura *f* **2** HERNIA : hernia *f*
rural [ˈrʊrəl] *adj* : rural, campestre
ruse [ˈruːs, ˈruːz] *n* : treta *f*, ardid *m*, estratagema *f*
rush[1] [ˈrʌʃ] *vi* : correr, ir de prisa ⟨to rush around : correr de un lado a otro⟩ ⟨to rush off : irse corriendo⟩ — *vt* **1** HURRY : apresurar, apurar **2** ATTACK : abalanzarse sobre, asaltar
rush[2] *adj* : urgente
rush[3] *n* **1** HASTE : prisa *f*, apuro *m* **2** SURGE : ráfaga *f* (de aire), torrente *m* (de aguas), avalancha *f* (de gente) **3** DEMAND : demanda *f* ⟨a rush on sugar : una gran demanda para el azúcar⟩ **4** : carga *f* (en futbol americano) **5** : junco *m* (planta)
russet [ˈrʌsət] *n* : color *m* rojizo
Russian [ˈrʌʃən] *n* **1** : ruso *m*, -sa *f* **2** : ruso *m* (idioma) — **Russian** *adj*
rust[1] [ˈrʌst] *vi* : oxidarse — *vt* : oxidar
rust[2] *n* **1** : herrumbre *f*, orín *m*, óxido *m* (en los metales) **2** : roya *f* (en las plantas)
rustic[1] [ˈrʌstɪk] *adj* : rústico, campestre — **rustically** [-tɪkli] *adv*
rustic[2] *n* : rústico *m*, -ca *f*; campesino *m*, -na *f*
rustle[1] [ˈrʌsəl] *v* **-tled; -tling** *vt* **1** : hacer susurrar, hacer crujir ⟨to rustle a newspaper : hacer crujir un periódico⟩ **2** STEAL : robar (ganado) — *vi* : susurrar, crujir

rustle[2] *n* : murmullo *m*, susurro *m*, crujido *m*
rustler [ˈrʌsələr] *n* : ladrón *m*, -drona *f* de ganado
rusty [ˈrʌsti] *adj* **rustier; -est** : oxidado, herrumbroso
rut [ˈrʌt] *n* **1** GROOVE, TRACK : rodada *f*, surco *m* **2 to be in a rut** : ser esclavo de la rutina
ruthless [ˈru:θləs] *adj* : despiadado, cruel — **ruthlessly** *adv*
ruthlessness [ˈru:θləsnəs] *n* : crueldad *f*, falta *f* de piedad
Rwandan [rʊˈandən] *n* : ruandés *m*, -desa *f* — **Rwandan** *adj*
rye [ˈraɪ] *n* **1** : centeno *m* **2** *or* **rye whiskey** : whisky *m* de centeno

S

s [ˈɛs] *n, pl* **s's** *or* **ss** [ˈɛsəz] : decimonovena letra del alfabeto inglés
Sabbath [ˈsæbəθ] *n* **1** : sábado *m* (en el judaísmo) **2** : domingo *m* (en el cristianismo)
saber [ˈseɪbər] *n* : sable *m*
sable [ˈseɪbəl] *n* **1** BLACK : negro *m* **2** : marta *f* cebellina (animal)
sabotage[1] [ˈsæbəˌtaʒ] *vt* **-taged; -taging** : sabotear
sabotage[2] *n* : sabotaje *m*
sac [ˈsæk] *n* : saco *m* (anatómico)
saccharin [ˈsækərən] *n* : sacarina *f*
saccharine [ˈsækərən, -ˌri:n, -ˌraɪn] *adj* : meloso, empalagoso
sachet [sæˈʃeɪ] *n* : bolsita *f* (perfumada)
sack[1] [ˈsæk] *vt* **1** FIRE : echar (del trabajo), despedir **2** PLUNDER : saquear
sack[2] *n* BAG : saco *m*
sacrament [ˈsækrəmənt] *n* : sacramento *m*
sacramental [ˌsækrəˈmɛntəl] *adj* : sacramental
sacred [ˈseɪkrəd] *adj* **1** RELIGIOUS : sagrado, sacro ⟨sacred texts : textos sagrados⟩ **2** HOLY : sagrado **3 sacred to** : consagrado a
sacrifice[1] [ˈsækrəˌfaɪs] *vt* **-ficed; -ficing 1** : sacrificar **2 to sacrifice oneself** : sacrificarse
sacrifice[2] *n* : sacrificio *m*
sacrilege [ˈsækrəlɪʤ] *n* : sacrilegio *m*
sacrilegious [ˌsækrəˈlɪʤəs, -ˈli:-] *adj* : sacrílego
sacrosanct [ˈsækroˌsæŋkt] *adj* : sacrosanto
sad [ˈsæd] *adj* **sadder; saddest** : triste — **sadly** *adv*
sadden [ˈsædən] *vt* : entristecer
saddle[1] [ˈsædəl] *vt* **-dled; -dling** : ensillar
saddle[2] *n* : silla *f* (de montar)
sadism [ˈseɪˌdɪzəm, ˈsæ-] *n* : sadismo *m*
sadist [ˈseɪdɪst, ˈsæ-] *n* : sádico *m*, -ca *f*
sadistic [səˈdɪstɪk] *adj* : sádico — **sadistically** [-tɪkli] *adv*
sadness [ˈsædnəs] *n* : tristeza *f*
safari [səˈfari, -ˈfær-] *n* : safari *m*
safe[1] [ˈseɪf] *adj* **safer; safest 1** UNHARMED : ileso ⟨safe and sound : sano y salvo⟩ **2** SECURE : seguro **3 to be on the safe side** : para mayor seguridad **4 to play it safe** : ir a la segura
safe[2] *n* : caja *f* fuerte
safeguard[1] [ˈseɪfˌgard] *vt* : salvaguardar, proteger
safeguard[2] *n* : salvaguarda *f*, protección *f*
safekeeping [ˈseɪfˈki:pɪŋ] *n* : custodia *f*, protección *f* ⟨to put into safekeeping : poner en buen recaudo⟩
safely [ˈseɪfli] *adv* **1** UNHARMED : sin incidentes, sin novedades ⟨they landed safely : aterrizaron sin novedades⟩ **2** SECURELY : con toda seguridad, sin peligro
safety [ˈseɪfti] *n, pl* **-ties** : seguridad *f*
safety belt *n* : cinturón *m* de seguridad
safety pin *n* : alfiler *m* de gancho, alfiler *m* de seguridad, imperdible *m Spain*
saffron [ˈsæfrən] *n* : azafrán *m*
sag[1] [ˈsæg] *vi* **sagged; sagging 1** DROOP, SINK : combarse, hundirse, inclinarse **2** : colgar, caer ⟨his jowls sagged : le colgaban las mejillas⟩ **3** FLAG : flaquear, decaer ⟨his spirits sagged : se le flaqueó el ánimo⟩
sag[2] *n* : combadura *f*
saga [ˈsagə, ˈsæ-] *n* : saga *f*
sagacious [səˈgeɪʃəs] *adj* : sagaz
sage[1] [ˈseɪʤ] *adj* **sager; -est** : sabio — **sagely** *adv*
sage[2] *n* **1** : sabio *m*, -bia *f* **2** : salvia *f* (planta)
sagebrush [ˈseɪʤˌbrʌʃ] *n* : artemisa *f*
Sagittarius [ˌsæʤəˈtɛriəs] *n* : Sagitario *mf*
said → **say**
sail[1] [ˈseɪl] *vi* **1** : navegar (en un barco) **2** : ir fácilmente ⟨we sailed right in : entramos sin ningún problema⟩ — *vt* **1** : gobernar (un barco) **2 to sail the seas** : cruzar los mares
sail[2] *n* **1** : vela *f* (de un barco) **2** : viaje *m* en velero ⟨to go for a sail : salir a navegar⟩
sailboat [ˈseɪlˌbo:t] *n* : velero *m*, barco *m* de vela
sailfish [ˈseɪlˌfɪʃ] *n* : pez *m* vela
sailor [ˈseɪlər] *n* : marinero *m*
saint [ˈseɪnt, *before a name* ˌseɪnt *or* sənt] *n* : santo *m*, -ta *f* ⟨Saint Francis : San Francisco⟩ ⟨Saint Rose : Santa Rosa⟩
saintliness [ˈseɪntlinəs] *n* : santidad *f*
saintly [ˈseɪntli] *adj* **saintlier; -est** : santo
sake [ˈseɪk] *n* **1** BENEFIT : bien *m* ⟨for the children's sake : por el bien de los

niños⟩ **2** (*indicating an end or a purpose*) ⟨art for art's sake : el arte por el arte⟩ ⟨let's say, for argument's sake, that he's wrong : pongamos que está equivocado⟩ **3 for goodness' sake!** : ¡por (el amor de) Dios!

salable *or* **saleable** ['seɪləbəl] *adj* : vendible

salacious [sə'leɪʃəs] *adj* : salaz — **salaciously** *adv*

salad ['sæləd] *n* : ensalada *f*

salamander ['sælə,mændər] *n* : salamandra *f*

salami [sə'lɑmi] *n* : salami *m*

salary ['sæləri] *n, pl* **-ries** : sueldo *m*

sale ['seɪl] *n* **1** SELLING : venta *f* **2** : liquidación *f*, rebajas *fpl* ⟨on sale : de rebaja⟩ **3 sales** *npl* : ventas *fpl* ⟨to work in sales : trabajar en ventas⟩

salesman ['seɪlzmən] *n, pl* **-men** [-mən, -,mɛn] **1** : vendedor *m*, dependiente *m* (en una tienda) **2 traveling salesman** : viajante *m*, representante *m*

salesperson ['seɪlz,pərsən] *n* : vendedor *m*, -dora *f*; dependiente *m*, -ta *f* (en una tienda)

saleswoman ['seɪlz,wʊmən] *n, pl* **-women** [-,wɪmən] **1** : vendedora *f*, dependienta *f* (en una tienda) **2 traveling saleswoman** : viajante *f*, representante *f*

salient ['seɪljənt] *adj* : saliente, sobresaliente

saline ['seɪ,li:n, -,laɪn] *adj* : salino

saliva [sə'laɪvə] *n* : saliva *f*

salivary ['sælə,vɛri] *adj* : salival ⟨salivary gland : glándula salival⟩

salivate ['sælə,veɪt] *vi* **-vated; -vating** : salivar

sallow ['sælo:] *adj* : amarillento, cetrino

sally[1] ['sæli] *vi* **-lied; -lying** SET OUT : salir, hacer una salida

sally[2] *n, pl* **-lies** **1** : salida *f* (militar), misión *f* **2** QUIP : salida *f*, ocurrencia *f*

salmon ['sæmən] *ns & pl* **1** : salmón *m* (pez) **2** : color *m* salmón

salon [sə'lɑn, 'sæ,lɑn, sæ'lɔ̃] *n* : salón *m* ⟨beauty salon : salón de belleza⟩

saloon [sə'lu:n] *n* **1** HALL : salón *m* (en un barco) **2** BARROOM : bar *m*

salsa ['sɔlsə, 'sɑl-] *n* : salsa *f* mexicana, salsa *f* picante

salt[1] ['sɔlt] *vt* : salar, echarle sal a

salt[2] *adj* : salado

salt[3] *n* : sal *f*

saltwater ['sɔlt,wɔt̬ər, -,wɑ-] *adj* : de agua salada

salty ['sɔlt̬i] *adj* **saltier; -est** : salado

salubrious [sə'lu:briəs] *adj* : salubre

salutary ['sæljə,tɛri] *adj* : saludable, salubre

salutation [,sæljə'teɪʃən] *n* : saludo *m*, salutación *f*

salute[1] [sə'lu:t] *v* **-luted; -luting** *vt* **1** : saludar (con gestos o ceremonias) **2** ACCLAIM : reconocer, aclamar — *vi* : hacer un saludo

salute[2] *n* **1** : saludo *m* (gesto), salva *f* (de cañonazos) **2** TRIBUTE : reconocimiento *m*, homenaje *m*

Salvadoran [,sælvə'dorən] → **El Salvadoran**

salvage[1] ['sælvɪʤ] *vt* **-vaged; -vaging** : salvar, rescatar

salvage[2] *n* **1** SALVAGING : salvamento *m*, rescate *m* **2** : objetos *mpl* salvados

salvation [sæl'veɪʃən] *n* : salvación *f*

salve[1] ['sæv, 'sav] *vt* **salved; salving** : calmar, apaciguar ⟨to salve one's conscience : aliviarse la conciencia⟩

salve[2] *n* : ungüento *m*

salvo ['sæl,vo:] *n, pl* **-vos** *or* **-voes** : salva *f*

same[1] ['seɪm] *adj* : mismo, igual ⟨the results are the same : los resultados son iguales⟩ ⟨he said the same thing as you : dijo lo mismo que tú⟩

same[2] *pron* : mismo ⟨it's all the same to me : me da lo mismo⟩ ⟨the same to you! : ¡igualmente!⟩

sameness ['seɪmnəs] *n* **1** SIMILARITY : identidad *f*, semejanza *f* **2** MONOTONY : monotonía *f*

sample[1] ['sæmpəl] *vt* **-pled; -pling** : probar

sample[2] *n* : muestra *f*, prueba *f*

sampler ['sæmplər] *n* **1** : dechado *m* (de bordado) **2** COLLECTION : colección *f* **3** ASSORTMENT : surtido *m*

sanatorium [,sænə'toriəm] *n, pl* **-riums** *or* **-ria** [-iə] : sanatorio *m*

sanctify ['sæŋktə,faɪ] *vt* **-fied; -fying** : santificar

sanctimonious [,sæŋktə'mo:niəs] *adj* : beato, santurrón

sanction[1] ['sæŋkʃən] *vt* : sancionar, aprobar

sanction[2] *n* **1** AUTHORIZATION : sanción *f*, autorización *f* **2 sanctions** *npl* : sanciones *fpl* ⟨to impose sanctions on : imponer sanciones a⟩

sanctity ['sæŋktət̬i] *n, pl* **-ties** : santidad *f*

sanctuary ['sæŋkʧʊ,ɛri] *n, pl* **-aries** **1** : presbiterio *m* (en una iglesia) **2** REFUGE : refugio *m*, asilo *m*

sand[1] ['sænd] *vt* : lijar (madera)

sand[2] *n* : arena *f*

sandal ['sændəl] *n* : sandalia *f*

sandbank ['sænd,bæŋk] *n* : banco *m* de arena

sandpaper *n* : papel *m* de lija

sandpiper ['sænd,paɪpər] *n* : andarríos *m*

sandstone ['sænd,sto:n] *n* : arenisca *f*

sandstorm ['sænd,stɔrm] *n* : tormenta *f* de arena

sandwich[1] ['sænd,wɪʧ] *vt* : intercalar, encajonar, meter (entre dos cosas)

sandwich[2] *n* : sandwich *m*, emparedado *m*, bocadillo *m Spain*

sandy ['sændi] *adj* **sandier; -est** : arenoso

sane ['seɪn] *adj* **saner; sanest** **1** : cuerdo **2** SENSIBLE : sensato, razonable

sang → **sing**

sanguine ['sæŋgwən] *adj* **1** RUDDY : sanguíneo, rubicundo **2** HOPEFUL : optimista

sanitarium [ˌsænə'tɛriəm] *n, pl* **-iums** *or* **-ia** [-iə] → **sanatorium**

sanitary ['sænətɛri] *adj* **1** : sanitario ⟨sanitary measures : medidas sanitarias⟩ **2** HYGIENIC : higiénico **3 sanitary napkin** : compresa *f*, paño *m* higiénico

sanitation [ˌsænə'teɪʃən] *n* : sanidad *f*

sanitize ['sænəˌtaɪz] *vt* **-tized; -tizing 1** : desinfectar **2** EXPURGATE : expurgar

sanity ['sænəṭi] *n* : cordura *f*, razón *f* ⟨to lose one's sanity : perder el juicio⟩

sank → **sink**

Santa Claus ['sæntəˌklɔz] *n* : Papá Noel, San Nicolás

sap[1] ['sæp] *vt* **sapped; sapping 1** UNDERMINE : socavar **2** WEAKEN : minar, debilitar

sap[2] *n* **1** : savia *f* (de una planta) **2** SUCKER : inocentón *m*, -tona *f*

sapling ['sæplɪŋ] *n* : árbol *m* joven

sapphire ['sæˌfaɪr] *n* : zafiro *m*

sarcasm ['sɑrˌkæzəm] *n* : sarcasmo *m*

sarcastic [sɑr'kæstɪk] *adj* : sarcástico — **sarcastically** [-ṭɪkli] *adv*

sarcophagus [sɑr'kɑfəgəs] *n, pl* **-gi** [-ˌgaɪ, -ˌʤaɪ] : sarcófago *m*

sardine [sɑr'di:n] *n* : sardina *f*

sardonic [sɑr'dɑnɪk] *adj* : sardónico — **sardonically** [-nɪkli] *adv*

sarsaparilla [ˌsæspə'rɪlə, ˌsɑrs-] *n* : zarzaparrilla *f*

sash ['sæʃ] *n* **1** : faja *f* (de un vestido), fajín *m* (de un uniforme) **2** *pl* **sash** : marco *m* (de una ventana)

sassafras ['sæsəˌfræs] *n* : sasafrás *m*

sassy ['sæsi] *adj* **sassier; -est** → **saucy**

sat → **sit**

Satan ['seɪtən] *n* : Satanás *m*, Satán *m*

satanic [sə'tænɪk, seɪ-] *adj* : satánico — **satanically** [-nɪkli] *adv*

satchel ['sæʧəl] *n* : cartera *f*, saco *m*

sate ['seɪt] *vt* **sated; sating** : saciar

satellite ['sæṭəˌlaɪt] *n* : satélite *m* ⟨spy satellite : satélite espía⟩

satiate ['seɪʃiˌeɪt] *vt* **-ated; -ating** : saciar, hartar

satin ['sætən] *n* : raso *m*, satín *m*, satén *m*

satire ['sæˌtaɪr] *n* : sátira *f*

satiric [sə'tɪrɪk] *or* **satirical** [-ɪkəl] *adj* : satírico

satirize ['sæṭəˌraɪz] *vt* **-rized; -rizing** : satirizar

satisfaction [ˌsæṭəs'fækʃən] *n* : satisfacción *f*

satisfactory [ˌsæṭəs'fæktəri] *adj* : satisfactorio, bueno — **satisfactorily** [-rəli] *adv*

satisfy ['sæṭəsˌfaɪ] *v* **-fied; -fying** *vt* **1** PLEASE : satisfacer, contentar **2** CONVINCE : convencer **3** FULFILL : satisfacer, cumplir con, llenar **4** SETTLE : pagar, saldar (una cuenta) — *vi* SUFFICE : bastar

saturate ['sæʧəˌreɪt] *vt* **-rated; -rating 1** SOAK : empapar **2** FILL : saturar

saturation [ˌsæʧə'reɪʃən] *n* : saturación *f*

Saturday ['sæṭərˌdeɪ, -di] *n* : sábado *m*

Saturn ['sæṭərn] *n* : Saturno *m*

satyr ['seɪṭər, 'sæ-] *n* : sátiro *m*

sauce ['sɔs] *n* : salsa *f*

saucepan ['sɔsˌpæn] *n* : cacerola *f*, cazo *m*, cazuela *f*

saucer ['sɔsər] *n* : platillo *m*

sauciness ['sɔsinəs] *n* : descaro *m*, frescura *f*

saucy ['sɔsi] *adj* **saucier; -est** IMPUDENT : descarado, fresco *fam* — **saucily** *adv*

Saudi ['saʊdi, 'sɔ-] → **Saudi Arabian**

Saudi Arabian *n* : saudita *mf*, saudí *mf* — **Saudi Arabian** *adj*

sauna ['sɔnə, 'saʊnə] *n* : sauna *mf*

saunter ['sɔntər, 'sɑn-] *vi* : pasear, parsearse

sausage ['sɔsɪʤ] *n* : salchicha *f*, embutido *m*

sauté [sɔ'teɪ, so:-] *vt* **-téed** *or* **-téd; -téing** : saltear, sofreír

savage[1] ['sævɪʤ] *adj* : salvaje, feroz — **savagely** *adv*

savage[2] *n* : salvaje *mf*

savagery ['sævɪʤri, -ʤəri] *n, pl* **-ries 1** FEROCITY : ferocidad *f* **2** WILDNESS : salvajismo *m*

savanna [sə'vænə] *n* : sabana *f*

save[1] ['seɪv] *vt* **saved; saving 1** RESCUE : salvar, rescatar **2** PRESERVE : preservar, conservar **3** KEEP : guardar, ahorrar (dinero), almacenar (alimentos) **4** : guardar (en informática)

save[2] *prep* EXCEPT : salvo, excepto, menos

savior ['seɪvjər] *n* **1** : salvador *m*, -dora *f* **2 the Savior** : el Salvador *m*

savor[1] ['seɪvər] *vt* : saborear

savor[2] *n* : sabor *m*

savory ['seɪvəri] *adj* : sabroso

saw[1] → **see**

saw[2] ['sɔ] *vt* **sawed; sawed** *or* **sawn** ['sɔn]; **sawing** : serrar, cortar (con sierra)

saw[3] *n* : sierra *f*

sawdust ['sɔˌdʌst] *n* : aserrín *m*, serrín *m*

sawhorse ['sɔˌhɔrs] *n* : caballete *m*, burro *m* (en carpintería)

sawmill ['sɔˌmɪl] *n* : aserradero *m*

saxophone ['sæksəˌfo:n] *n* : saxofón *m*

say[1] ['seɪ] *v* **said** ['sɛd]; **saying; says** ['sɛz] *vt* **1** EXPRESS, UTTER : decir, expresar ⟨to say no : decir que no⟩ ⟨that goes without saying : ni que decir tiene⟩ ⟨no sooner said than done : dicho y hecho⟩ ⟨to say again : repetir⟩ ⟨to say one's prayers : rezar⟩ **2** INDICATE : marcar, poner ⟨my watch says three o'clock : mi reloj marca las tres⟩ ⟨what does the sign say? : ¿qué pone el letrero?⟩ **3** ALLEGE : decir ⟨it's said that she's pretty : se dice que es bonita⟩ — *vi* : decir

say[2] *n, pl* **says** [ˈseɪz] : voz *f*, opinión *f* ⟨to have no say : no tener ni voz ni voto⟩ ⟨to have one's say : dar uno su opinión⟩
saying [ˈseɪɪŋ] *n* : dicho *m*, refrán *m*
scab [ˈskæb] *n* **1** : costra *f*, postilla *f* (en una herida) **2** STRIKEBREAKER : rompehuelgas *mf*, esquirol *mf*
scabbard [ˈskæbərd] *n* : vaina *f* (de una espada), funda *f* (de un puñal, etc.)
scabby [ˈskæbi] *adj* **scabbier; -est** : lleno de costras
scaffold [ˈskæfəld, -ˌfoːld] *n* **1** *or* **scaffolding** : andamio *m* (para obreros, etc.) **2** : patíbulo *m*, cadalso *m* (para ejecuciones)
scald [ˈskɔld] *vt* **1** BURN : escaldar **2** HEAT : calentar (hasta el punto de ebullición)
scale[1] [ˈskeɪl] *v* **scaled; scaling** *vt* **1** : escamar (un pescado) **2** CLIMB : escalar (un muro, etc.) **3 to scale down** : reducir — *vi* WEIGH : pesar ⟨he scaled in at 200 pounds : pesó 200 libras⟩
scale[2] *n* **1** *or* **scales** : balanza *f*, báscula *f* (para pesar) **2** : escama *f* (de un pez, etc.) **3** EXTENT : escala *f*, proporción *f* ⟨wage scale : escala salarial⟩ **4** : escala *f* (en música, en cartografía, etc.) ⟨to draw to scale : dibujar a escala⟩
scallion [ˈskæljən] *n* : cebollino *m*, cebolleta *f*
scallop [ˈskɑləp, ˈskæ-] *n* **1** : vieira *f* (molusco) **2** : festón *m* (decoración)
scalp[1] [ˈskælp] *vt* : arrancar la cabellera a
scalp[2] *n* : cuero *m* cabelludo
scalpel [ˈskælpəl] *n* : bisturí *m*, escalpelo *m*
scaly [ˈskeɪli] *adj* **scalier; -est** : escamoso
scam [ˈskæm] *n* : estafa *f*, timo *m fam*, chanchullo *m fam*
scamp [ˈskæmp] *n* : bribón *m*, -bona *f*; granuja *mf*; travieso *m*, -sa *f*
scamper [ˈskæmpər] *vi* : corretear
scan[1] [ˈskæn] *vt* **scanned; scanning 1** : escandir (versos) **2** SCRUTINIZE : escudriñar, escrutar ⟨to scan the horizon : escudriñar el horizonte⟩ **3** PERUSE : echarle un vistazo a (un periódico, etc.) **4** EXPLORE : explorar (con radar), hacer un escáner de (en ecografía) **5** : escanear (una imagen)
scan[2] *n* **1** : ecografía *f*, examen *m* ultrasónico (en medicina) **2** : imagen *f* escaneada (en una computadora)
scandal [ˈskændəl] *n* **1** DISGRACE, OUTRAGE : escándalo *m* **2** GOSSIP : habladurías *fpl*, chismes *mpl*
scandalize [ˈskændəlˌaɪz] *vt* **-ized; -izing** : escandalizar
scandalous [ˈskændələs] *adj* : de escándalo
Scandinavian[1] [ˌskændəˈneɪviən] *adj* : escandinavo
Scandinavian[2] *n* : escandinavo *m*, -va *f*
scanner [ˈskænər] *n* : escáner *m*, scanner *m*
scant [ˈskænt] *adj* : escaso
scanty [ˈskænti] *adj* **scantier; -est** : exiguo, escaso ⟨a scanty meal : una comida insuficiente⟩ — **scantily** [-təli] *adv*
scapegoat [ˈskeɪpˌgoːt] *n* : chivo *m* expiatorio, cabeza *f* de turco
scapula [ˈskæpjələ] *n, pl* **-lae** [-ˌliː, -ˌlaɪ] *or* **-las** → **shoulder blade**
scar[1] [ˈskɑr] *v* **scarred; scarring** *vt* : dejar una cicatriz en — *vi* : cicatrizar
scar[2] *n* : cicatriz *f*, marca *f*
scarab [ˈskærəb] *n* : escarabajo *m*
scarce [ˈskɛrs] *adj* **scarcer; -est** : escaso
scarcely [ˈskɛrsli] *adv* **1** BARELY : apenas **2** : ni mucho menos, ni nada que se le parezca ⟨he's scarcely an expert : ciertamente no es experto⟩
scarcity [ˈskɛrsət̬i] *n, pl* **-ties** : escasez *f*
scare[1] [ˈskɛr] *vt* **scared; scaring** : asustar, espantar
scare[2] *n* **1** FRIGHT : susto *m*, sobresalto *m* **2** ALARM : pánico *m*
scarecrow [ˈskɛrˌkroː] *n* : espantapájaros *m*, espantajo *m*
scarf [ˈskɑrf] *n, pl* **scarves** [ˈskɑrvz] *or* **scarfs 1** MUFFLER : bufanda *f* **2** KERCHIEF : pañuelo *m*
scarlet [ˈskɑrlət] *n* : escarlata *f* — **scarlet** *adj*
scarlet fever *n* : escarlatina *f*
scary [ˈskɛri] *adj* **scarier; -est** : espantoso, pavoroso
scathing [ˈskeɪðɪŋ] *adj* : mordaz, cáustico
scatter [ˈskæt̬ər] *vt* : esparcir, desparramar — *vi* DISPERSE : dispersarse
scavenge [ˈskævəndʒ] *v* **-venged; -venging** *vt* : rescatar (de la basura), pepenar *CA, Mex* — *vi* : rebuscar, hurgar en la basura ⟨to scavenge for food : andar buscando comida⟩
scavenger [ˈskævəndʒər] *n* **1** : persona *f* que rebusca en las basuras; pepenador *m*, -dora *f CA, Mex* **2** : carroñero *m*, -ra *f* (animal)
scenario [səˈnæriˌoː, -ˈnɑr-] *n, pl* **-ios 1** PLOT : argumento *m* (en teatro), guión *m* (en cine) **2** SITUATION : situación *f* hipotética ⟨in the worst-case scenario : en el peor de los casos⟩
scene [ˈsiːn] *n* **1** : escena *f* (en una obra de teatro) **2** SCENERY : decorado *m* (en el teatro) **3** VIEW : escena *f* **4** LOCALE : escenario *m* **5** COMMOTION, FUSS : escándalo *m*, escena *f* ⟨to make a scene : armar un escándalo⟩
scenery [ˈsiːnəri] *n, pl* **-eries 1** : decorado *m* (en el teatro) **2** LANDSCAPE : paisaje *m*
scenic [ˈsiːnɪk] *adj* : pintoresco
scent[1] [ˈsɛnt] *vt* **1** SMELL : oler, olfatear **2** PERFUME : perfumar **3** SENSE : sentir, percibir
scent[2] *n* **1** ODOR : olor *m*, aroma *m* **2** : olfato *m* ⟨a dog with a keen scent : un

perro con un buen olfato⟩ 3 PERFUME : perfume *m*
scented [ˈsɛntəd] *adj* : perfumado
scepter [ˈsɛptər] *n* : cetro *m*
sceptic [ˈskɛptɪk] → **skeptic**
schedule[1] [ˈskɛˌʤu:l, -ʤəl, *esp Brit* ˈʃɛdˌju:l] *vt* **-uled; -uling** : planear, programar
schedule[2] *n* **1** PLAN : programa *m*, plan *m* ⟨on schedule : según lo previsto⟩ ⟨behind schedule : atrasado, con retraso⟩ **2** TIMETABLE : horario *m*
scheme[1] [ˈski:m] *vi* **schemed; scheming** : intrigar, conspirar
scheme[2] *n* **1** PLAN : plan *m*, proyecto *m* **2** PLOT, TRICK : intriga *f*, ardid *m* **3** FRAMEWORK : esquema *f* ⟨a color scheme : una combinación de colores⟩
schemer [ˈski:mər] *n* : intrigante *mf*
schism [ˈsɪzəm, ˈskɪ-] *n* : cisma *m*
schizophrenia [ˌskɪtsəˈfri:niə, ˌskɪzə-, -ˈfrɛ-] *n* : esquizofrenia *f*
schizophrenic [ˌskɪtsəˈfrɛnɪk, ˌskɪzə-] *n* : esquizofrénico *m*, -ca *f* — **schizophrenic** *adj*
scholar [ˈskɑlər] *n* **1** STUDENT : escolar *mf*; alumno *m*, -na *f* **2** EXPERT : especialista *mf*
scholarly [ˈskɑlərli] *adj* : erudito
scholarship [ˈskɑlərˌʃɪp] *n* **1** LEARNING : erudición *f* **2** GRANT : beca *f*
scholastic [skəˈlæstɪk] *adj* : académico
school[1] [ˈsku:l] *vt* : instruir, enseñar
school[2] *n* **1** : escuela *f*, colegio *m* (institución) **2** : estudiantes *mfpl* y profesores *mpl* (de una escuela) **3** : escuela *f* (en pintura, etc.) ⟨the Flemish school : la escuela flamenca⟩ **4 school of fish** : banco *m*, cardumen *m*
schoolboy [ˈsku:lˌbɔɪ] *n* : escolar *m*, colegial *m*
schoolgirl [ˈsku:lˌgərl] *n* : escolar *f*, colegiala *f*
schoolhouse [ˈsku:lˌhaʊs] *n* : escuela *f*
schoolmate [ˈsku:lˌmeɪt] *n* : compañero *m*, -ra *f* de escuela
schoolroom [ˈsku:lˌru:m, -ˌrʊm] → **classroom**
schoolteacher [ˈsku:lˌti:ʧər] *n* : maestro *m*, -tra *f*; profesor *m*, -sora *f*
schoolwork [ˈsku:lˌwərk] *n* : trabajo *m* escolar
schooner [ˈsku:nər] *n* : goleta *f*
science [ˈsaɪən*t*s] *n* : ciencia *f*
science fiction *n* : ciencia ficción *f*
scientific [ˌsaɪənˈtɪfɪk] *adj* : científico — **scientifically** [-fɪkli] *adv*
scientist [ˈsaɪəntɪst] *n* : científico *m*, -ca *f*
scintillating [ˈsɪntəˌleɪṭɪŋ] *adj* : chispeante, brillante
scissors [ˈsɪzərz] *npl* : tijeras *fpl*
sclerosis [skləˈro:səs] *n, pl* **-roses** : esclerosis *f*
scoff [ˈskɑf] *vi* **to scoff at** : burlarse de, mofarse de
scold [ˈsko:ld] *vt* : regañar, reprender, reñir
scoop[1] [ˈsku:p] *vt* **1** : sacar (con pala o cucharón) **2 to scoop out** HOLLOW : vaciar, ahuecar
scoop[2] *n* : pala *f* (para harina, etc.), cucharón *m* (para helado, etc.)
scoot [ˈsku:t] *vi* : ir rápidamente ⟨she scooted around the corner : volvió la esquina a toda prisa⟩
scooter [ˈsku:ṭər] *n* : patineta *f*, monopatín *m*, patinete *m*
scope [ˈsko:p] *n* **1** RANGE : alcance *m*, ámbito *m*, extensión *f* **2** OPPORTUNITY : posibilidades *fpl*, libertad *f*
scorch [ˈskɔrʧ] *vt* : chamuscar, quemar
score[1] [ˈskor] *v* **scored; scoring** *vt* **1** RECORD : anotar **2** MARK, SCRATCH : marcar, rayar **3** : marcar, meter (en deportes) **4** GAIN : ganar, apuntarse **5** GRADE : calificar (exámenes, etc.) **6** : instrumentar, orquestar (música) — *vi* **1** : marcar (en deportes) **2** : obtener una puntuación (en un examen)
score[2] *n, pl* **scores 1** *or pl* **score** TWENTY : veintena *f* **2** LINE, SCRATCH : línea *f*, marca *f* **3** : resultado *m* (en deportes) ⟨what's the score? : ¿cómo va el marcador?⟩ **4** GRADE, POINTS : calificación *f* (en un examen), puntuación *f* (en un concurso) **5** ACCOUNT : cuenta *f* ⟨to settle a score : ajustar una cuenta⟩ ⟨on that score : a ese respecto⟩ **6** : partitura *f* (musical)
scorn[1] [ˈskɔrn] *vt* : despreciar, menospreciar, desdeñar
scorn[2] *n* : desprecio *m*, menosprecio *m*, desdén *m*
scornful [ˈskɔrnfəl] *adj* : desdeñoso, despreciativo — **scornfully** *adv*
Scorpio [ˈskɔrpiˌo:] *n* : Escorpio *mf*, Escorpión *mf*
scorpion [ˈskɔrpiən] *n* : alacrán *m*, escorpión *m*
Scot [ˈskɑt] *n* : escocés *m*, -cesa *f*
Scotch[1] [ˈskɑʧ] *adj* → **Scottish**[1]
Scotch[2] *npl* **the Scotch** : los escoceses
scot–free [ˈskɑtˈfri:] *adj* **to get off scot–free** : salir impune, quedar sin castigo
Scots [ˈskɑts] *n* : escocés *m* (idioma)
Scottish[1] [ˈskɑṭɪʃ] *adj* : escocés
Scottish[2] *n* → **Scots**
scoundrel [ˈskaʊndrəl] *n* : sinvergüenza *mf*; bellaco *m*, -ca *f*
scour [ˈskaʊər] *vt* **1** EXAMINE, SEARCH : registrar (un área), revisar (documentos, etc.) **2** SCRUB : fregar, restregar
scourge[1] [ˈskərʤ] *vt* **scourged; scourging** : azotar
scourge[2] *n* : azote *m*
scout[1] [ˈskaʊt] *vi* **1** RECONNOITER : reconocer **2 to scout around for** : explorar en busca de
scout[2] *n* **1** : explorador *m*, -dora *f* **2** *or* **talent scout** : cazatalentos *mf*
scow [ˈskaʊ] *n* : barcaza *f*, gabarra *f*
scowl[1] [ˈskaʊl] *vi* : fruncir el ceño
scowl[2] *n* : ceño *m* fruncido

scram ['skræm] *vi* **scrammed; scramming** : largarse

scramble[1] ['skræmbəl] *v* **-bled; -bling** *vi* **1** : trepar, gatear (con torpeza) ⟨he scrambled over the fence : se trepó a la cerca con dificultad⟩ **2** STRUGGLE : pelearse (por) ⟨they scrambled for seats : se pelearon por los asientos⟩ — *vt* **1** JUMBLE : mezclar **2 to scramble eggs** : hacer huevos revueltos

scramble[2] *n* : rebatiña *f*, pelea *f*

scrap[1] ['skræp] *v* **scrapped; scrapping** *vt* DISCARD : desechar — *vi* FIGHT : pelearse

scrap[2] *n* **1** FRAGMENT : pedazo *m*, trozo *m* **2** FIGHT : pelea *f* **3** *or* **scrap metal** : chatarra *f* **4 scraps** *npl* LEFTOVERS : restos *mpl*, sobras *fpl*

scrapbook ['skræp,bʊk] *n* : álbum *m* de recortes

scrape[1] ['skreɪp] *v* **scraped; scraping** *vt* **1** GRAZE, SCRATCH : rozar, rascar ⟨to scrape one's knee : rasparse la rodilla⟩ **2** CLEAN : raspar ⟨to scrape carrots : raspar zanahorias⟩ **3 to scrape off** : raspar (pintura, etc.) **4 to scrape up** *or* **to scrape together** : juntar, reunir poco a poco — *vi* **1** RUB : rozar **2 to scrape by** : arreglárselas, ir tirando

scrape[2] *n* **1** SCRAPING : raspadura *f* **2** SCRATCH : rasguño *m* **3** PREDICAMENT : apuro *m*, aprieto *m*

scratch[1] ['skrætʃ] *vt* **1** : arañar, rasguñar ⟨to scratch an itch : rascarse⟩ **2** MARK : rayar, marcar **3 to scratch out** : tachar

scratch[2] *n* **1** : rasguño *m*, arañazo *m* (en la piel), rayón *m* (en un mueble, etc.) **2** : sonido *m* rasposo ⟨I heard a scratch at the door : oí como que raspaban a la puerta⟩

scratchy ['skrætʃi] *adj* **scratchier; -est** : áspero, que pica ⟨a scratchy sweater : un suéter que pica⟩

scrawl[1] ['skrɔl] *v* : garabatear

scrawl[2] *n* : garabato *m*

scrawny ['skrɔni] *adj* **scrawnier; -est** : flaco, escuálido

scream[1] ['skri:m] *vi* : chillar, gritar

scream[2] *n* : chillido *m*, grito *m*

screech[1] ['skri:tʃ] *vi* : chillar (dícese de las personas o de los animales), chirriar (dícese de los frenos, etc.)

screech[2] *n* **1** : chillido *m*, grito *m* (de una persona o un animal) **2** : chirrido *m* (de frenos, etc.)

screen[1] ['skri:n] *vt* **1** SHIELD : proteger **2** CONCEAL : tapar, ocultar **3** EXAMINE : someter a una revisión, hacerle un chequeo (a un paciente) **4** SIEVE : cribar

screen[2] *n* **1** PARTITION : biombo *m*, pantalla *f* **2** SIEVE : criba *f* **3** : pantalla *f* (de un televisor, una computadora, etc.) **4** MOVIES : cine *m* **5** *or* **window screen** : ventana *f* de tela metálica

screenplay ['skri:n,pleɪ] *n* SCRIPT : guión *m*

screw[1] ['skru:] *vt* : atornillar — *vi* **1 to screw in** : atornillarse **2 to screw up** *fam* : meter la pata

screw[2] *n* **1** : tornillo *m* (para fijar algo) **2** TWIST : vuelta *f* **3** PROPELLER : hélice *f*

screwdriver ['skru:,draɪvər] *n* : destornillador *m*, desarmador *m Mex*

scribble[1] ['skrɪbəl] *v* **-bled; -bling** : garabatear

scribble[2] *n* : garabato *m*

scribe ['skraɪb] *n* : escriba *m*

scrimmage ['skrɪmɪdʒ] *n* : escaramuza *f*

scrimp ['skrɪmp] *vi* **1 to scrimp on** : escatimar **2 to scrimp and save** : hacer economías

script ['skrɪpt] *n* **1** HANDWRITING : letra *f*, escritura *f* **2** : guión *m* (de una película, etc.)

scriptural ['skrɪptʃərəl] *adj* : bíblico

scripture ['skrɪptʃər] *n* **1** : escritos *mpl* sagrados (de una religión) **2 the Scriptures** *npl* : las Sagradas Escrituras

scriptwriter ['skrɪpt,raɪt̬ər] *n* : guionista *mf*, libretista *mf*

scroll ['skro:l] *n* **1** : rollo *m* (de pergamino, etc.) **2** : voluta *f* (adorno en arquitectura)

scrotum ['skro:t̬əm] *n, pl* **scrota** [-t̬ə] *or* **scrotums** : escroto *m*

scrounge ['skraʊndʒ] *v* **scrounged; scrounging** *vt* **1** BUM : gorrear *fam*, sablear *fam* (dinero) **2 to scrounge around for** : buscar, andar a la busca de — *vi* **to scrounge off someone** : vivir a costa de alguien

scrub[1] ['skrʌb] *vt* **scrubbed; scrubbing** : restregar, fregar

scrub[2] *n* **1** THICKET, UNDERBRUSH : maleza *f*, matorral *m*, matorrales *mpl* **2** SCRUBBING : fregado *m*, restregadura *f*

scrubby ['skrʌbi] *adj* **-bier; -est 1** STUNTED : achaparrado **2** : cubierto de maleza

scruff ['skrʌf] *n* **by the scruff of the neck** : por el cogote, por el pescuezo

scrumptious ['skrʌmpʃəs] *adj* : delicioso, muy rico

scruple ['skru:pəl] *n* : escrúpulo *m*

scrupulous ['skru:pjələs] *adj* : escrupuloso — **scrupulously** *adv*

scrutinize ['skru:tən,aɪz] *vt* **-nized; -nizing** : escrutar, escudriñar

scrutiny ['skru:təni] *n, pl* **-nies** : escrutinio *m*, inspección *f*

scuba ['sku:bə] *n* **1** *or* **scuba gear** : equipo *m* de submarinismo **2 scuba diver** : submarinista *mf* **3 scuba diving** : submarinismo *m*

scuff ['skʌf] *vt* : rayar, raspar ⟨to scuff one's feet : arrastrar los pies⟩

scuffle[1] ['skʌfəl] *vi* **-fled; -fling 1** TUSSLE : pelearse **2** SHUFFLE : caminar arrastrando los pies

scuffle[2] *n* **1** TUSSLE : refriega *f*, pelea *f* **2** SHUFFLE : arrastre *m* de los pies

scull[1] ['skʌl] *vi* : remar (con espadilla)

scull2 *n* OAR : espadilla *f*
sculpt [ˈskʌlpt] *v* : esculpir
sculptor [ˈskʌlptər] *n* : escultor *m*, -tora *f*
scuptural [ˈskʌlptʃərəl] *adj* : escultórico
sculpture1 [ˈskʌlptʃər] *vt* **-tured; -turing** : esculpir
sculpture2 *n* : escultura *f*
scum [ˈskʌm] *n* **1** FROTH : espuma *f*, nata *f* **2** : verdín *m* (encima de un líquido)
scurrilous [ˈskərələs] *adj* : difamatorio, calumnioso, injurioso
scurry [ˈskəri] *vi* **-ried; -rying** : corretear
scurvy [ˈskərvi] *n* : escorbuto *m*
scuttle1 [ˈskʌṭəl] *v* **-tled; -tling** *vt* : hundir (un barco) — *vi* SCAMPER : corretear
scuttle2 *n* : cubo *m* (para carbón)
scythe [ˈsaɪð] *n* : guadaña *f*
sea1 [ˈsiː] *adj* : del mar
sea2 *n* **1** : mar *mf* ⟨the Black Sea : el Mar Negro⟩ ⟨on the high seas : en alta mar⟩ ⟨heavy seas : mar gruesa, mar agitada⟩ **2** MASS : mar *m*, multitud *f* ⟨a sea of faces : un mar de rostros⟩
seabird [ˈsiːˌbərd] *n* : ave *f* marina
seaboard [ˈsiːˌbord] *n* : litoral *m*
seacoast [ˈsiːˌkoːst] *n* : costa *f*, litoral *m*
seafarer [ˈsiːˌfærər] *n* : marinero *m*
seafaring1 [ˈsiːˌfærɪŋ] *adj* : marinero
seafaring2 *n* : navegación *f*
seafood [ˈsiːˌfuːd] *n* : mariscos *mpl*
seagull [ˈsiːˌgʌl] *n* : gaviota *f*
sea horse [ˈsiːˌhɔrs] *n* : hipocampo *m*, caballito *m* de mar
seal1 [ˈsiːl] *vt* **1** CLOSE : sellar, cerrar ⟨to seal a letter : cerrar una carta⟩ ⟨to seal an agreement : sellar un acuerdo⟩ **2 to seal up** : tapar, rellenar (una grieta, etc.)
seal2 *n* **1** : foca *f* (animal) **2** : sello *m* ⟨seal of approval : sello de aprobación⟩ **3** CLOSURE : cierre *m*, precinto *m*
sea level *n* : nivel *m* del mar
sea lion *n* : león *m* marino
sealskin [ˈsiːlˌskɪn] *n* : piel *f* de foca
seam1 [ˈsiːm] *vt* **1** STITCH : unir con costuras **2** MARK : marcar
seam2 *n* **1** STITCHING : costura *f* **2** LODE, VEIN : veta *f*, filón *m*
seaman [ˈsiːmən] *n, pl* **-men** [-mən, -ˌmɛn] **1** SAILOR : marinero *m* **2** : marino *m* (en la armada)
seamless [ˈsiːmləs] *adj* **1** : sin costuras, de una pieza **2** : perfecto ⟨a seamless transition : una transición fluida⟩
seamstress [ˈsiːmpstrəs] *n* : costurera *f*
seamy [ˈsiːmi] *adj* **seamier; -est** : sórdido
séance [ˈseɪˌɑnts] *n* : sesión *f* de espiritismo
seaplane [ˈsiːˌpleɪn] *n* : hidroavión *m*
seaport [ˈsiːˌport] *n* : puerto *m* marítimo
sear [ˈsɪr] *vt* **1** PARCH, WITHER : secar, resecar **2** SCORCH : chamuscar, quemar
search1 [ˈsərtʃ] *vt* : registrar (un edificio, un área), cachear (a una persona), buscar en — *vi* **to search for** : buscar
search2 *n* : búsqueda *f*, registro *m* (de un edificio, etc.), cacheo *m* (de una persona)
searchlight [ˈsərtʃˌlaɪt] *n* : reflector *m*
seashell [ˈsiːˌʃɛl] *n* : concha *f* (marina)
seashore [ˈsiːˌʃor] *n* : orilla *f* del mar
seasick [ˈsiːˌsɪk] *adj* : mareado ⟨to get seasick : marearse⟩
seasickness [ˈsiːˌsɪknəs] *n* : mareo *m*
seaside → **seacoast**
season1 [ˈsiːzən] *vt* **1** FLAVOR, SPICE : sazonar, condimentar **2** CURE : curar, secar ⟨seasoned wood : madera seca⟩ ⟨a seasoned veteran : un veterano avezado⟩
season2 *n* **1** : estación *f* (del año) **2** : temporada *f* (en deportes, etc.) ⟨baseball season : temporada de beisbol⟩
seasonable [ˈsiːzənəbəl] *adj* **1** : propio de la estación (dícese del tiempo, de las temperaturas, etc.) **2** TIMELY : oportuno
seasonal [ˈsiːzənəl] *adj* : estacional — **seasonally** *adv*
seasoning [ˈsiːzənɪŋ] *n* : condimento *m*, sazón *f*
seat1 [ˈsiːt] *vt* **1** SIT : sentar ⟨please be seated : siéntense, por favor⟩ **2** HOLD : tener cabida para ⟨the stadium seats 40,000 : el estadio tiene 40,000 asientos⟩
seat2 *n* **1** : asiento *m*, plaza *f* (en un vehículo) ⟨take a seat : tome asiento⟩ **2** BOTTOM : fondillos *mpl* (de la ropa), trasero *m* (del cuerpo) **3** : sede *f* (de un gobierno, etc.)
seat belt *n* : cinturón *m* de seguridad
sea urchin *n* : erizo *m* de mar
seawall [ˈsiːˌwɑl] *n* : rompeolas *m*, dique *m* marítimo
seawater [ˈsiːˌwɔṭər, -ˌwɑ-] *n* : agua *f* de mar
seaweed [ˈsiːˌwiːd] *n* : alga *f* marina
seaworthy [ˈsiːˌwərði] *adj* : en condiciones de navegar
secede [sɪˈsiːd] *vi* **-ceded; -ceding** : separarse (de una nación, etc.)
seclude [sɪˈkluːd] *vt* **-cluded; -cluding** : aislar
seclusion [sɪˈkluːʒən] *n* : aislamiento *m*
second1 [ˈsɛkənd] *vt* : secundar, apoyar (una moción)
second2 *or* **secondly** [ˈsɛkəndli] *adv* : en segundo lugar
second3 *adj* : segundo
second4 *n* **1** : segundo *m*, -da *f* (en una serie) **2** : segundo *m*, ayudante *m* (en deportes) **3** MOMENT : segundo *m*, momento *m*
secondary [ˈsɛkənˌdri] *adj* : secundario
secondhand [ˈsɛkəndˈhænd] *adj* : de segunda mano
second lieutenant *n* : alférez *mf*, subteniente *mf*
second–rate [ˈsɛkəndˈreɪt] *adj* : mediocre, de segunda categoría

secrecy ['si:krəsi] *n, pl* **-cies** : secreto *m*
secret[1] ['si:krət] *adj* : secreto — **secretly** *adv*
secret[2] *n* : secreto *m*
secretarial [ˌsɛkrə'triəl] *adj* : de secretario, de oficina
secretariat [ˌsɛkrə'triət] *n* : secretaría *f*, secretariado *m*
secretary ['sɛkrəˌtri] *n, pl* **-taries** **1** : secretario *m*, -ria *f* (en una oficina, etc.) **2** : ministro *m*, -tra *f*; secretario *m*, -ria *f* ⟨Secretary of State : Secretario de Estado⟩
secrete [sɪ'kri:t] *vt* **-creted; -creting** **1** : secretar, segregar (en fisiología) **2** HIDE : ocultar
secretion [sɪ'kri:ʃən] *n* : secreción *f*
secretive ['si:krət̬ɪv, sɪ'kri:t̬ɪv] *adj* : reservado, callado, secreto
sect ['sɛkt] *n* : secta *f*
sectarian [sɛk'triən] *adj* : sectario
section ['sɛkʃən] *n* : sección *f*, parte *f* (de un mueble, etc.), sector *m* (de la población), barrio *m* (de una ciudad)
sectional ['sɛkʃənəl] *adj* **1** : en sección, en corte ⟨a sectional diagram : un gráfico en corte⟩ **2** FACTIONAL : de grupo, entre facciones **3** : modular ⟨sectional furniture : muebles modulares⟩
sector ['sɛktər] *n* : sector *m*
secular ['sɛkjələr] *adj* **1** : secular, laico ⟨secular life : la vida secular⟩ **2** : seglar (dícese de los sacerdotes, etc.)
secure[1] [sɪ'kjʊr] *vt* **-cured; -curing** **1** FASTEN : asegurar (una puerta, etc.), sujetar **2** GET : conseguir
secure[2] *adj* **-curer; -est** : seguro — **securely** *adv*
security [sɪ'kjʊrət̬i] *n, pl* **-ties** **1** SAFETY : seguridad *f* **2** GUARANTEE : garantía *f* **3 securities** *npl* : valores *mpl*
sedan [sɪ'dæn] *n* **1** *or* **sedan chair** : silla *f* de manos **2** : sedán *m* (automóvil)
sedate[1] [sɪ'deɪt] *vt* **-dated; -dating** : sedar
sedate[2] *adj* : sosegado — **sedately** *adv*
sedation [sɪ'deɪʃən] *n* : sedación *f*
sedative[1] ['sɛdət̬ɪv] *adj* : sedante
sedative[2] *n* : sedante *m*, calmante *m*
sedentary ['sɛdənˌtɛri] *adj* : sedentario
sedge ['sɛʤ] *n* : juncia *f*
sediment ['sɛdəmənt] *n* : sedimento *m* (geológico), poso *m* (en un líquido)
sedimentary [ˌsɛdə'mɛntəri] *adj* : sedimentario
sedition [sɪ'dɪʃən] *n* : sedición *f*
seditious [sɪ'dɪʃəs] *adj* : sedicioso
seduce [sɪ'du:s, -'dju:s] *vt* **-duced; -ducing** : seducir
seduction [sɪ'dʌkʃən] *n* : seducción *f*
seductive [sɪ'dʌktɪv] *adj* : seductor, seductivo
see[1] ['si:] *v* **saw** ['sɔ]; **seen** ['si:n]; **seeing** *vt* **1** : ver ⟨I saw a dog : vi un perro⟩ ⟨see you later! : ¡hasta luego!⟩ **2** EXPERIENCE : ver, conocer **3** UNDERSTAND : ver, entender **4** ENSURE : asegurarse ⟨see that it's correct : asegúrese de que sea correcto⟩ **5** ACCOMPANY : acompañar **6 to see off** : despedir, despedirse de — *vi* **1** : ver ⟨seeing is believing : ver para creer⟩ **2** UNDERSTAND : entender, ver ⟨now I see! : ¡ya entiendo!⟩ **3** CONSIDER : ver ⟨let's see : vamos a ver⟩ **4 to see to** : ocuparse de
see[2] *n* : sede *f* ⟨the Holy See : la Santa Sede⟩
seed[1] ['si:d] *vt* **1** SOW : sembrar **2** : despepitar, quitarle las semillas a
seed[2] *n, pl* **seed** *or* **seeds** **1** : semilla *f*, pepita *f* (de una fruta) **2** SOURCE : germen *m*, semilla *f*
seedless ['si:dləs] *adj* : sin semillas
seedling ['si:dlɪŋ] *n* : plantón *m*
seedpod ['si:dˌpɑd] → **pod**
seedy ['si:di] *adj* **seedier; -est** **1** : lleno de semillas **2** SHABBY : raído (dícese de la ropa) **3** RUN-DOWN : ruinoso (dícese de los edificios, etc.), sórdido
seek ['si:k] *v* **sought** ['sɔt]; **seeking** *vt* **1** : buscar ⟨to seek an answer : buscar una solución⟩ **2** REQUEST : solicitar, pedir **3 to seek to** : tratar de, intentar de — *vi* SEARCH : buscar
seem ['si:m] *vi* : parecer
seeming ['si:mɪŋ] *adj* : aparente, ostensible
seemingly ['si:mɪŋli] *adv* : aparentemente, según parece
seemly ['si:mli] *adj* **seemlier; -est** : apropiado, decoroso
seep ['si:p] *vi* : filtrarse
seer ['si:ər] *n* : vidente *mf*, clarividente *mf*
seesaw[1] ['si:ˌsɔ] *vi* **1** : jugar en un subibaja **2** VACILLATE : vacilar, oscilar
seesaw[2] *n* : balancín *m*, subibaja *m*
seethe ['si:ð] *vi* **seethed; seething** **1** : bullir, hervir **2 to seethe with anger** : rabiar, estar furioso
segment ['sɛgmənt] *n* : segmento *m*
segmented ['sɛgˌmɛntəd, sɛg'mɛn-] *adj* : segmentado
segregate ['sɛgrɪˌgeɪt] *vt* **-gated; -gating** : segregar
segregation [ˌsɛgrɪ'geɪʃən] *n* : segregación *f*
seismic ['saɪzmɪk, 'saɪs-] *adj* : sísmico
seize ['si:z] *v* **seized; seizing** *vt* **1** CAPTURE : capturar, tomar, apoderarse de **2** ARREST : detener **3** CLUTCH, GRAB : agarrar, coger, aprovechar (una oportunidad) **4 to be seized with** : estar sobrecogido por — *vi or* **to seize up** : agarrotarse
seizure ['si:ʒər] *n* **1** CAPTURE : toma *f*, captura *f* **2** ARREST : detención *f* **3** : ataque *m* ⟨an epileptic seizure : un ataque epiléptico⟩
seldom ['sɛldəm] *adv* : pocas veces, rara vez, casi nunca
select[1] [sə'lɛkt] *vt* : escoger, elegir, seleccionar (a un candidato, etc.)
select[2] *adj* : selecto
selection [sə'lɛkʃən] *n* : selección *f*, elección *f*

selective [sə'lɛktɪv] *adj* : selectivo
selenium [sə'li:niəm] *n* : selenio *m*
self ['sɛlf] *n, pl* **selves** ['sɛlvz] **1** : ser *m*, persona *f* ⟨the self : el yo⟩ ⟨with his whole self : con todo su ser⟩ ⟨her own self : su propia persona⟩ **2** SIDE : lado (de la personalidad) ⟨his better self : su lado bueno⟩
self–addressed [ˌsɛlfə'drst] *adj* : con la dirección del remitente ⟨include a self-addressed envelope : incluya un sobre con su nombre y dirección⟩
self–appointed [ˌsɛlfə'pɔɪntəd] *adj* : autoproclamado, autonombrado
self–assurance [ˌsɛlfə'ʃʊrənts] *n* : seguridad *f* en sí mismo
self–assured [ˌsɛlfə'ʃʊrd] *adj* : seguro de sí mismo
self–centered [ˌsɛlf'sɛntərd] *adj* : egocéntrico
self–confidence [ˌsɛlf'kɑnfədənts] *n* : confianza *f* en sí mismo
self–confident [ˌsɛlf'kɑnfədənt] *adj* : seguro de sí mismo
self–conscious [ˌsɛlf'kɑntʃəs] *adj* : cohibido, tímido
self–consciously [ˌsɛlf'kɑntʃəsli] *adv* : de manera cohibida
self–consciousness [ˌsɛlf'kɑntʃəsnəs] *n* : vergüenza *f*, timidez *f*
self–contained [ˌsɛlfkən'teɪnd] *adj* **1** INDEPENDENT : independiente **2** RESERVED : reservado
self–control [ˌsɛlfkən'tro:l] *n* : autocontrol *m*, control *m* de sí mismo
self–defense [ˌsɛlfdɪ'fɛnts] *n* : defensa *f* propia, defensa *f* personal ⟨to act in self-defense : actuar en defensa propia⟩ ⟨self-defense class : clase de defensa personal⟩
self–denial [ˌsɛlfdɪ'naɪəl] *n* : abnegación *f*
self–destructive [ˌsɛlfdɪ'strʌktɪv] *adj* : autodestructivo
self–determination [ˌsɛlfdɪˌtərmə'neɪʃən] *n* : autodeterminación *f*
self–discipline [ˌsɛlf'dɪsəplən] *n* : autodisciplina *f*
self–employed [ˌsɛlfɪm'plɔɪd] *adj* : que trabaja por cuenta propia, autónomo
self–esteem [ˌsɛlfɪ'sti:m] *n* : autoestima *f*, amor *m* propio
self–evident [ˌsɛlf'ɛvədənt] *adj* : evidente, manifiesto
self–explanatory [ˌsɛlfɪk'splænəˌtori] *adj* : fácil de entender, evidente
self–expression [ˌsɛlfɪk'sprɛʃən] *n* : expresión *f* personal
self–government [ˌsɛlf'gʌvərmənt, -vərn-] *n* : autogobierno *m*
self–help [ˌsɛlf'hɛlp] *n* : autoayuda *f*
self–important [ˌsɛlfɪm'pɔrtənt] *adj* **1** VAIN : vanidoso, presumido **2** ARROGANT : arrogante
self–indulgent [ˌsɛlfɪn'dʌldʒənt] *adj* : que se permite excesos
self–inflicted [ˌsɛlfɪn'flɪktəd] *adj* : autoinfligido
self–interest [ˌsɛlf'ɪntrəst, -təˌrst] *n* : interés *m* personal
selfish ['sɛlfɪʃ] *adj* : egoísta
selfishly ['sɛlfɪʃli] *adv* : de manera egoísta
selfishness ['sɛlfɪʃnəs] *n* : egoísmo *m*
selfless ['sɛlfləs] *adj* UNSELFISH : desinteresado
self–made [ˌsɛlf'meɪd] *adj* : próspero gracias a sus propios esfuerzos
self–pity [ˌsɛlf'pɪt̬i] *n, pl* **-ties** : autocompasión *f*
self–portrait [ˌsɛlf'pɔrtrət] *n* : autorretrato *m*
self–propelled [ˌsɛlfpro'pɛld] *adj* : autopropulsado
self–reliance [ˌsɛlfri'laɪənts] *n* : independencia *f*, autosuficiencia *f*
self–respect [ˌsɛlfri'spɛkt] *n* : autoestima *f*, amor *m* propio
self–restraint [ˌsɛlfri'streɪnt] *n* : autocontrol *m*, moderación *f*
self–righteous [ˌsɛlf'raɪtʃəs] *adj* : santurrón, moralista
self–sacrifice [ˌsɛlf'sækrəˌfaɪs] *n* : abnegación *f*
selfsame ['sɛlfˌseɪm] *adj* : mismo
self–service [ˌsɛlf'sərvɪs] *adj* **1** : de autoservicio **2 self-service restaurant** : autoservicio *m*
self–sufficiency [ˌsɛlfsə'fɪʃəntsi] *n* : autosuficiencia *f*
self–sufficient [ˌsɛlfsə'fɪʃənt] *adj* : autosuficiente
self–taught [ˌsɛlf'tɔt] *adj* : autodidacta
sell ['sɛl] *v* **sold** ['so:ld]; **selling** *vt* : vender — *vi* : venderse
seller ['sɛlər] *n* : vendedor *m*, -dora *f*
selves → **self**
semantic [sɪ'mæntɪk] *adj* : semántico
semantics [sɪ'mæntɪks] *ns & pl* : semántica *f*
semaphore ['sɛməˌfor] *n* : semáforo *m*
semblance ['sɛmbləntss] *n* : apariencia *f*
semen ['si:mən] *n* : semen *m*
semester [sə'mɛstər] *n* : semestre *m*
semicolon ['sɛmiˌko:lən, 'sɛˌmaɪ-] *n* : punto y coma *m*
semiconductor ['sɛmikənˌdʌktər, 'sɛˌmaɪ-] *n* : semiconductor *m*
semifinal ['sɛmiˌfaɪnəl, 'sɛˌmaɪ-] *n* : semifinal *f*
seminar ['sɛməˌnɑr] *n* : seminario *m*
seminary ['sɛməˌnɛri] *n, pl* **-naries** : seminario *m*
Semitic [sə'mɪt̬ɪk] *adj* : semita
senate ['sɛnət] *n* : senado *m*
senator ['sɛnət̬ər] *n* : senador *m*, -dora *f*
send ['sɛnd] *vt* **sent** ['sɛnt]; **sending** **1** : mandar, enviar ⟨to send a letter : mandar una carta⟩ ⟨to send word : avisar, mandar decir⟩ **2** PROPEL : mandar, lanzar ⟨he sent it into left field : lo mandó al jardín izquierdo⟩ ⟨to send up dust : alzar polvo⟩ **3 to send into a rage** : poner furioso
sender ['sɛndər] *n* : remitente *mf* (de una carta, etc.)

Senegalese [ˌsɛnəgəˈliːz, -ˈliːs] *n* : senegalés *m*, -lesa *f* — **Senegalese** *adj*
senile [ˈsiːˌnaɪl] *adj* : senil
senility [sɪˈnɪləṭi] *n* : senilidad *f*
senior[1] [ˈsiːnjər] *adj* **1** ELDER : mayor ⟨John Doe, Senior : John Doe, padre⟩ **2** : superior (en rango), más antiguo (en años de servicio) ⟨a senior official : un alto oficial⟩
senior[2] *n* **1** : superior *m* (en rango) **2 to be someone's senior** : ser mayor que alguien ⟨she's two years my senior : me lleva dos años⟩
senior citizen *n* : persona *f* de la tercera edad
seniority [ˌsiːˈnjɔrəṭi] *n* : antigüedad *f* (en años de servicio)
sensation [sɛnˈseɪʃən] *n* : sensación *f*
sensational [sɛnˈseɪʃənəl] *adj* : que causa sensación ⟨sensational stories : historias sensacionalistas⟩
sense[1] [ˈsɛnts] *vt* **sensed; sensing** : sentir ⟨he sensed danger : se dio cuenta del peligro⟩
sense[2] *n* **1** MEANING : sentido *m*, significado *m* **2** : sentido *m* ⟨the sense of smell : el sentido del olfato⟩ **3 to make sense** : tener sentido
senseless [ˈsɛntsləs] *adj* **1** MEANINGLESS : sin sentido, sin razón **2** UNCONSCIOUS : inconsciente
senselessly [ˈsɛntsləsli] *adv* : sin sentido
sensibility [ˌsɛntsəˈbɪləṭi] *n, pl* **-ties** : sensibilidad *f*
sensible [ˈsɛntsəbəl] *adj* **1** PERCEPTIBLE : sensible, perceptible **2** AWARE : consciente **3** REASONABLE : sensato ⟨a sensible man : un hombre sensato⟩ ⟨sensible shoes : zapatos prácticos⟩ — **sensibly** [-bli] *adv*
sensibleness [ˈsɛntsəbəlnəs] *n* : sensatez *f*, solidez *f*
sensitive [ˈsɛntsəṭɪv] *adj* **1** : sensible, delicado ⟨sensitive skin : piel sensible⟩ **2** IMPRESSIONABLE : sensible, impresionable **3** TOUCHY : susceptible
sensitiveness [ˈsɛntsəṭɪvnəs] → **sensitivity**
sensitivity [ˌsɛntsəˈtɪvəṭi] *n, pl* **-ties** : sensibilidad *f*
sensitize [ˈsɛntsəˌtaɪz] *vt* **-tized; -tizing** : sensibilizar
sensor [ˈsɛnˌsɔr, ˈsɛntsər] *n* : sensor *m*
sensory [ˈsɛntsəri] *adj* : sensorial
sensual [ˈsɛntʃʊəl] *adj* : sensual — **sensually** *adv*
sensuality [ˌsɛntʃəˈwæləṭi] *n, pl* **-ties** : sensualidad *f*
sensuous [ˈsɛntʃʊəs] *adj* : sensual
sent → **send**
sentence[1] [ˈsɛntənts, -ənz] *vt* **-tenced; -tencing** : sentenciar
sentence[2] *n* **1** JUDGMENT : sentencia *f* **2** : oración *f*, frase *f* (en gramática)
sentiment [ˈsɛntəmənt] *n* **1** BELIEF : opinión *f* **2** FEELING : sentimiento *m* **3** → **sentimentality**
sentimental [ˌsɛntəˈmɛntəl] *adj* : sentimental
sentimentality [ˌsɛntəˌmɛnˈtæləṭi] *n, pl* **-ties** : sentimentalismo *m*, sensiblería *f*
sentinel [ˈsɛntənəl] *n* : centinela *mf*, guardia *mf*
sentry [ˈsɛntri] *n, pl* **-tries** : centinela *mf*
sepal [ˈsiːpəl, ˈsɛ-] *n* : sépalo *m*
separable [ˈsɛpərəbəl] *adj* : separable
separate[1] [ˈsɛpəˌreɪt] *v* **-rated; -rating** *vt* **1** DETACH, SEVER : separar **2** DISTINGUISH : diferenciar, distinguir — *vi* PART : separarse
separate[2] [ˈsɛprət, ˈsɛpə-] *adj* **1** INDIVIDUAL : separado, aparte ⟨a separate state : un estado separado⟩ ⟨in a separate envelope : en un sobre aparte⟩ **2** DISTINCT : distinto
separately [ˈsɛprətli, ˈsɛpə-] *adv* : por separado, separadamente, aparte
separation [ˌsɛpəˈreɪʃən] *n* : separación *f*
sepia [ˈsiːpiə] *n* : color *m* sepia
September [sɛpˈtɛmbər] *n* : septiembre *m*, setiembre *m*
septic [ˈsɛptɪk] *adj* : séptico ⟨septic tank : fosa séptica⟩
sepulchre [ˈsɛpəlkər] *n* : sepulcro *m*
sequel [ˈsiːkwəl] *n* **1** CONSEQUENCE : secuela *f*, consecuencia *f* **2** : continuación *f* (de una película, etc.)
sequence [ˈsiːkwənts] *n* **1** SERIES : serie *f*, sucesión *f*, secuencia *f* (matemática o musical) **2** ORDER : orden *m*
sequester [sɪˈkwɛstər] *vt* : aislar
sequin [ˈsiːkwən] *n* : lentejuela *f*
sequoia [sɪˈkwɔɪə] *n* : secoya *f*, secuoya *f*
sera → **serum**
Serb [ˈsərb] *or* **Serbian** [ˈsərbiən] *n* **1** : serbio *m*, -bia *f* **2** : serbio *m* (idioma) — **Serb** *or* **Serbian** *adj*
Serbo–Croatian [ˌsərbokroˈeɪʃən] *n* : serbocroata *m* (idioma) — **Serbo–Croatian** *adj*
serenade[1] [ˌsɛrəˈneɪd] *vt* **-naded; -nading** : darle una serenata (a alguien)
serenade[2] *n* : serenata *f*
serene [səˈriːn] *adj* : sereno — **serenely** *adv*
serenity [səˈrɛnəṭi] *n* : serenidad *f*
serf [ˈsərf] *n* : siervo *m*, -va *f*
serge [ˈsərdʒ] *n* : sarga *f*
sergeant [ˈsɑrdʒənt] *n* : sargento *mf*
serial[1] [ˈsɪriəl] *adj* : seriado
serial[2] *n* : serie *f*, serial *m* (de radio o televisión), publicación *f* por entregas
serially [ˈsɪriəli] *adv* : en serie
series [ˈsɪrˌiːz] *n, pl* **series** : serie *f*, sucesión *f*
serious [ˈsɪriəs] *adj* **1** SOBER : serio **2** DEDICATED, EARNEST : serio, dedicado ⟨to be serious about something : tomar algo en serio⟩ **3** GRAVE : serio, grave ⟨serious problems : problemas graves⟩
seriously [ˈsɪriəsli] *adv* **1** EARNESTLY : seriamente, con seriedad, en serio **2** SEVERELY : gravemente

seriousness [ˈsɪriəsnəs] *n* : seriedad *f*, gravedad *f*

sermon [ˈsərmən] *n* : sermón *m*

serpent [ˈsərpənt] *n* : serpiente *f*

serrated [səˈreɪṭəd, ˈsɛrˌeɪṭəd] *adj* : dentado, serrado

serum [ˈsɪrəm] *n, pl* **serums** *or* **sera** [ˈsɪrə] : suero *m*

servant [ˈsərvənt] *n* : criado *m*, -da *f*; sirviente *m*, -ta *f*

serve [ˈsərv] *v* **served; serving** *vi* **1** : servir ⟨to serve in the navy : servir en la armada⟩ ⟨to serve on a jury : ser miembro de un jurado⟩ **2** DO, FUNCTION : servir ⟨to serve as : servir de, servir como⟩ **3** : sacar (en deportes) — *vt* **1** : servir ⟨to serve God : servir a Dios⟩ **2** HELP : servir ⟨it serves no purpose : no sirve para nada⟩ **3** : servir (comida o bebida) ⟨dinner is served : la cena está servida⟩ **4** SUPPLY : abastecer **5** CARRY OUT : cumplir, hacer ⟨to serve time : servir una pena⟩ **6 to serve a summons** : entregar una citación

server [ˈsərvər] *n* **1** : camarero *m*, -ra *f*; mesero *m*, -ra *f* (en un restaurante) **2** *or* **serving dish** : fuente *f* (para servir comida) **3** : servidor *m* (en informática)

service¹ [ˈsərvəs] *vt* **-viced; -vicing 1** MAINTAIN : darle mantenimiento a (una máquina), revisar **2** REPAIR : arreglar, reparar

service² *n* **1** HELP, USE : servicio *m* ⟨to do someone a service : hacerle un servicio a alguien⟩ ⟨at your service : a sus órdenes⟩ ⟨to be out of service : no funcionar⟩ **2** CEREMONY : oficio *m* (religioso) **3** DEPARTMENT, SYSTEM : servicio *m* ⟨social services : servicios sociales⟩ ⟨train service : servicio de trenes⟩ **4** SET : juego *m*, servicio *m* ⟨tea service : juego de té⟩ **5** MAINTENANCE : mantenimiento *m*, revisión *f*, servicio *m* **6** : saque *m* (en deportes) **7 armed services** : fuerzas *fpl* armadas

serviceable [ˈsərvəsəbəl] *adj* **1** USEFUL : útil **2** DURABLE : duradero

serviceman [ˈsərvəsˌmæn, -mən] *n, pl* **-men** [-mən, -ˌmɛn] : militar *m*

service station → **gas station**

servicewoman [ˈsərvəsˌwʊmən] *n, pl* **-women** [-ˌwɪmən] : militar *f*

servile [ˈsərvəl, -ˌvaɪl] *adj* : servil

serving [ˈsərvɪŋ] *n* HELPING : porción *f*, ración *f*

servitude [ˈsərvəˌtuːd, -ˌtjuːd] *n* : servidumbre *f*

sesame [ˈsɛsəmi] *n* : ajonjolí *m*, sésamo *m*

session [ˈsɛʃən] *n* : sesión *f*

set¹ [ˈsɛt] *v* **set; setting** *vt* **1** SEAT : sentar **2** *or* **set down** PLACE : poner, colocar **3** ARRANGE : fijar, establecer ⟨to set the date : poner la fecha⟩ ⟨he set the agenda : estableció la agenda⟩ **4** ADJUST : poner (un reloj, etc.) **5** (*indicating the causing of a certain condition*) ⟨to set fire to : prenderle fuego a⟩ ⟨she set it free : lo soltó⟩ **6** MAKE, START : poner, hacer ⟨I set them working : los puse a trabajar⟩ — *vi* **1** SOLIDIFY : fraguar (dícese del cemento, etc.), cuajar (dícese de la gelatina, etc.) **2** : ponerse (dícese del sol o de la luna)

set² *adj* **1** ESTABLISHED, FIXED : fijo, establecido **2** RIGID : inflexible ⟨to be set in one's ways : tener costumbres muy arraigadas⟩ **3** READY : listo, preparado

set³ *n* **1** COLLECTION : juego *m* ⟨a set of dishes : un juego de platos, una vajilla⟩ ⟨a tool set : una caja de herramientas⟩ **2** *or* **stage set** : decorado *m* (en el teatro), plató *m* (en el cine) **3** APPARATUS : aparato *m* ⟨a television set : un televisor⟩ **4** : conjunto *m* (en matemáticas)

setback [ˈsɛtˌbæk] *n* : revés *m*, contratiempo *m*

set in *vi* BEGIN : comenzar, empezar

set off *vt* **1** PROVOKE : provocar **2** EXPLODE : hacer estallar (una bomba, etc.) — *vi or* **to set forth** : salir

set out *vi* : salir (de viaje) — *vt* INTEND : proponerse

settee [sɛˈtiː] *n* : sofá *m*

setter [ˈsɛṭər] *n* : setter *mf* ⟨Irish setter : setter irlandés⟩

setting [ˈsɛṭɪŋ] *n* **1** : posición *f*, ajuste *m* (de un control) **2** : engaste *m*, montura *f* (de una gema) **3** SCENE : escenario *m* (de una novela, etc.) **4** SURROUNDINGS : ambiente *m*, entorno *m*, marco *m*

settle [ˈsɛṭəl] *v* **settled; settling** *vi* **1** ALIGHT, LAND : posarse (dícese de las aves), depositarse (dícese del polvo) **2** SINK : asentarse (dícese de los edificios) ⟨he settled into the chair : se arrellanó en la silla⟩ **3** : instalarse (en una casa), establecerse (en una ciudad o región) **4 to settle down** : calmarse, tranquilizarse ⟨settle down! : ¡tranquilízate!, ¡cálmate!⟩ **5 to settle down** : sentar cabeza, hacerse sensato ⟨to marry and settle down : casarse y sentar cabeza⟩ — *vt* **1** ARRANGE, DECIDE : fijar, decidir, acordar (planes, etc.) **2** RESOLVE : resolver, solucionar ⟨to settle an argument : resolver una discusión⟩ **3** PAY : pagar ⟨to settle an account : saldar una cuenta⟩ **4** CALM : calmar (los nervios), asentar (el estómago) **5** COLONIZE : colonizar **6 to settle oneself** : acomodarse, hacerse cómodo

settlement [ˈsɛṭəlmənt] *n* **1** PAYMENT : pago *m*, liquidación *f* **2** COLONY : asentamiento *m* **3** RESOLUTION : acuerdo *m*

settler [ˈsɛṭələr] *n* : poblador *m*, -dora *f*; colono *m*, -na *f*

setup [ˈsɛtˌʌp] *n* **1** ASSEMBLY : montaje *m*, ensamblaje *m* **2** ARRANGEMENT : disposición *f* **3** PREPARATION : preparación *f* **4** TRAP, TRICK : encerrona *f*

set up *vt* **1** ASSEMBLE : montar, armar **2** ERECT : levantar, erigir **3** ESTABLISH : establecer, fundar, montar (un negocio) **4** CAUSE : armar ⟨they set up a clamor : armaron un alboroto⟩
seven[1] [ˈsɛvən] *adj* : siete
seven[2] *n* : siete *m*
seven hundred[1] *adj* : setecientos
seven hundred[2] *n* : setecientos *m*
seventeen[1] [ˌsɛvənˈtiːn] *adj* : diecisiete
seventeen[2] *n* : diecisiete *m*
seventeenth[1] [ˌsɛvənˈtiːnθ] *adj* : decimoséptimo
seventeenth[2] *n* **1** : decimoséptimo *m*, -ma *f* (en una serie) **2** : diecisieteavo *m*, diecisieteava parte *f*
seventh[1] [ˈsɛvənθ] *adj* : séptimo
seventh[2] *n* **1** : séptimo *m*, -ma *f* (en una serie) **2** : séptimo *m*, séptima parte *f*
seventieth[1] [ˈsɛvəntiəθ] *adj* : septuagésimo
seventieth[2] *n* **1** : septuagésimo *m*, -ma *f* (en una serie) **2** : setentavo *m*, setentava parte *f*, septuagésima parte *f*
seventy[1] [ˈsɛvənt̬i] *adj* : setenta
seventy[2] *n, pl* **-ties** : setenta *m*
sever [ˈsɛvər] *vt* **-ered; -ering** : cortar, romper
several[1] [ˈsɛvrəl, ˈsɛvə-] *adj* **1** DISTINCT : distinto **2** SOME : varios ⟨several weeks : varias semanas⟩
several[2] *pron* : varios, varias
severance [ˈsɛvrənts, sɛvə-] *n* **1** : ruptura *f* (de relaciones, etc.) **2 severance pay** : indemnización *f* (por despido)
severe [səˈvɪr] *adj* **severer; -est 1** STRICT : severo **2** AUSTERE : sobrio, austero **3** SERIOUS : grave ⟨a severe wound : una herida grave⟩ ⟨severe aches : dolores fuertes⟩ **4** DIFFICULT : duro, difícil — **severely** *adv*
severity [səˈvrət̬i] *n* **1** HARSHNESS : severidad *f* **2** AUSTERITY : sobriedad *f*, austeridad *f* **3** SERIOUSNESS : gravedad *f* (de una herida, etc.)
sew [ˈsoː] *v* **sewed; sewn** [ˈsoːn] *or* **sewed; sewing** : coser
sewage [ˈsuːɪʤ] *n* : aguas *fpl* negras, aguas *fpl* residuales
sewer[1] [ˈsoːər] *n* : uno que cose
sewer[2] [ˈsuːər] *n* : alcantarilla *f*, cloaca *f*
sewing [ˈsoːɪŋ] *n* : costura *f*
sex [ˈsɛks] *n* **1** : sexo *m* ⟨the opposite sex : el sexo opuesto⟩ **2** COPULATION : relaciones *fpl* sexuales
sexism [ˈsɛkˌsɪzəm] *n* : sexismo *m*
sexist[1] [ˈsɛksɪst] *adj* : sexista
sexist[2] *n* : sexista *mf*
sextant [ˈsɛkstənt] *n* : sextante *m*
sextet [sɛkˈstɛt] *n* : sexteto *m*
sexton [ˈsɛkstən] *n* : sacristán *m*
sexual [ˈsɛkʃʊəl] *adj* : sexual — **sexually** *adv*
sexuality [ˌsɛkʃʊˈælət̬i] *n* : sexualidad *f*
sexy [ˈsɛksi] *adj* **sexier; -est** : sexy
shabbily [ˈʃæbəli] *adv* **1** : pobremente ⟨shabbily dressed : pobremente vestido⟩ **2** UNFAIRLY : mal, injustamente
shabbiness [ˈʃæbinəs] *n* **1** : lo gastado (de ropa, etc.) **2** : lo mal vestido (de personas) **3** UNFAIRNESS : injusticia *f*
shabby [ˈʃæbi] *adj* **shabbier; -est 1** : gastado (dícese de la ropa, etc.) **2** : mal vestido (dícese de las personas) **3** UNFAIR : malo, injusto ⟨shabby treatment : mal trato⟩
shack [ˈʃæk] *n* : choza *f*, rancho *m*
shackle[1] [ˈʃækəl] *vt* **-led; -ling** : ponerle grilletes (a alguien)
shackle[2] *n* : grillete *m*
shad [ˈʃæd] *n* : sábalo *m*
shade[1] [ˈʃeɪd] *v* **shaded; shading** *vt* **1** SHELTER : proteger (del sol o de la luz) **2** *or* **to shade in** : matizar los colores de — *vi* : convertirse gradualmente ⟨his irritation shaded into rage : su irritación iba convirtiéndose en furia⟩
shade[2] *n* **1** : sombra *f* ⟨to give shade : dar sombra⟩ **2** : tono *m* (de un color) **3** NUANCE : matiz *m* **4** : pantalla *f* (de una lámpara), persiana *f* (de una ventana)
shadow[1] [ˈʃædoː] *vt* **1** DARKEN : ensombrecer **2** TRAIL : seguir de cerca, seguirle la pista (a alguien)
shadow[2] *n* **1** : sombra *f* **2** DARKNESS : oscuridad *f* **3** TRACE : sombra *f*, atisbo *m*, indicio *m* ⟨without a shadow of a doubt : sin sombra de duda, sin lugar a dudas⟩ **4 to cast a shadow over** : ensombrecer
shadowy [ˈʃædowi] *adj* **1** INDISTINCT : vago, indistinto **2** DARK : oscuro
shady [ˈʃeɪdi] *adj* **shadier; -est 1** : sombreado (dícese de un lugar), que da sombra (dícese de un árbol) **2** DISREPUTABLE : sospechoso (dícese de una persona), turbio (dícese de un negocio, etc.)
shaft [ˈʃæft] *n* **1** : asta *f* (de una lanza), astil *m* (de una flecha), mango *m* (de una herramienta) **2** *or* **mine shaft** : pozo *m*
shaggy [ˈʃægi] *adj* **shaggier; -est 1** HAIRY : peludo ⟨a shaggy dog : un perro peludo⟩ **2** UNKEMPT : enmarañado, despeinado (dícese del pelo, de las barbas, etc.)
shake[1] [ˈʃeɪk] *v* **shook** [ˈʃʊk]; **shaken** [ˈʃeɪkən]; **shaking** *vt* **1** : sacudir, agitar, hacer temblar ⟨he shook his head : negó con la cabeza⟩ **2** WEAKEN : debilitar, hacer flaquear ⟨it shook her faith : debilitó su confianza⟩ **3** UPSET : afectar, alterar **4 to shake hands with someone** : darle la mano a alguien, estrecharle la mano a alguien — *vi* : temblar, sacudirse
shake[2] *n* : sacudida *f*, apretón *m* (de manos)
shaker [ˈʃeɪkər] *n* **1 salt shaker** : salero *m* **2 pepper shaker** : pimentero *m* **3 cocktail shaker** : coctelera *f*
shake–up [ˈʃeɪkˌʌp] *n* : reorganización *f*
shakily [ˈʃeɪkəli] *adv* : temblorosamente

shaky [ˈʃeɪki] *adj* **shakier; -est 1** SHAKING : tembloroso **2** UNSTABLE : poco firme, inestable **3** PRECARIOUS : precario, incierto **4** QUESTIONABLE : dudoso, cuestionable ⟨shaky arguments : argumentos discutibles⟩

shale [ˈʃeɪl] *n* : esquisto *m*

shall [ˈʃæl] *v aux, past* **should** [ˈʃʊd] *present s & pl* **shall 1** (*used to express a command*) ⟨you shall do as I say : harás lo que te digo⟩ **2** (*used to express futurity*) ⟨we shall see : ya veremos⟩ ⟨when shall we expect you? : ¿cuándo te podemos esperar?⟩ **3** (*used to express determination*) ⟨you shall have the money : tendrás el dinero⟩ **4** (*used to express a condition*) ⟨if he should die : si muriera⟩ ⟨if they should call, tell me : si llaman, dímelo⟩ **5** (*used to express obligation*) ⟨he should have said it : debería haberlo dicho⟩ **6** (*used to express probability*) ⟨they should arrive soon : deben (de) llegar pronto⟩ ⟨why should he lie? : ¿porqué ha de mentir?⟩

shallow [ˈʃælo:] *adj* **1** : poco profundo (dícese del agua, etc.) **2** SUPERFICIAL : superficial

shallows [ˈʃælo:z] *npl* : bajío *m*, bajos *mpl*

sham¹ [ˈʃæm] *v* **shammed; shamming** : fingir

sham² *adj* : falso, fingido

sham³ *n* **1** FAKE, PRETENSE : farsa *f*, simulación *f*, imitación *f* **2** FAKER : impostor *m*, -tora *f*; farsante *mf*

shamble [ˈʃæmbəl] *vi* **-bled; -bling** : caminar arrastrando los pies

shambles [ˈʃæmbəlz] *ns & pl* : caos *m*, desorden *m*, confusión *f*

shame¹ [ˈʃeɪm] *vt* **shamed; shaming 1** : avergonzar ⟨he was shamed by their words : sus palabras le dieron vergüenza⟩ **2** DISGRACE : deshonrar

shame² *n* **1** : vergüenza *f* ⟨to have no shame : no tener vergüenza⟩ **2** DISGRACE : vergüenza *f*, deshonra *f* **3** PITY : lástima *f*, pena *f* ⟨what a shame! : ¡qué pena!⟩

shamefaced [ˈʃeɪm,feɪst] *adj* : avergonzado

shameful [ˈʃeɪmfəl] *adj* : vergonzoso — **shamefully** *adv*

shameless [ˈʃeɪmləs] *adj* : descarado, desvergonzado — **shamelessly** *adv*

shampoo¹ [ʃæmˈpu:] *vt* : lavar (el pelo)

shampoo² *n, pl* **-poos** : champú *m*

shamrock [ˈʃæm,rɑk] *n* : trébol *m*

shank [ˈʃæŋk] *n* : parte *f* baja de la pierna

shan't [ˈʃænt] (*contraction of* **shall not**) → **shall**

shanty [ˈʃænti] *n, pl* **-ties** : choza *f*, rancho *m*

shape¹ [ˈʃeɪp] *v* **shaped; shaping** *vt* **1** : dar forma a, modelar (arcilla, etc.), tallar (madera, piedra), formar (carácter) ⟨to be shaped like : tener forma de⟩ **2** DETERMINE : decidir, determinar — *vi or* **to shape up** : tomar forma

shape² *n* **1** : forma *f*, figura *f* ⟨in the shape of a circle : en forma de círculo⟩ **2** CONDITION : estado *m*, condiciones *fpl*, forma *f* (física) ⟨to get in shape : ponerse en forma⟩

shapeless [ˈʃeɪpləs] *adj* : informe

shapely [ˈʃeɪpli] *adj* **shapelier; -est** : curvilíneo, bien proporcionado

shard [ˈʃɑrd] *n* : fragmento *m*, casco *m* (de cerámica, etc.)

share¹ [ˈʃɛr] *v* **shared; sharing** *vt* **1** APPORTION : dividir, repartir **2** : compartir ⟨they share a room : comparten una habitación⟩ — *vi* : compartir

share² *n* **1** PORTION : parte *f*, porción *f* ⟨one's fair share : lo que le corresponde a uno⟩ **2** : acción *f* (en una compañía) ⟨to hold shares : tener acciones⟩

sharecropper [ˈʃɛr,krɑpər] *n* : aparcero *m*, -ra *f*

shareholder [ˈʃɛr,ho:ldər] *n* : accionista *mf*

shark [ˈʃɑrk] *n* : tiburón *m*

sharp¹ [ˈʃɑrp] *adv* : en punto ⟨at two o'clock sharp : a las dos en punto⟩

sharp² *adj* **1** : afilado, filoso ⟨a sharp knife : un cuchillo afilado⟩ **2** PENETRATING : cortante, fuerte **3** CLEVER : agudo, listo, perspicaz **4** ACUTE : agudo ⟨sharp eyesight : vista aguda⟩ **5** HARSH, SEVERE : duro, severo, agudo ⟨a sharp rebuke : una reprimenda mordaz⟩ **6** STRONG : fuerte ⟨sharp cheese : queso fuerte⟩ **7** ABRUPT : brusco, repentino **8** DISTINCT : nítido, definido ⟨a sharp image : una imagen bien definida⟩ **9** ANGULAR : anguloso (dícese de la cara) **10** : sostenido (en música)

sharp³ *n* : sostenido *m* (en música)

sharpen [ˈʃɑrpən] *vt* : afilar, aguzar ⟨to sharpen a pencil : sacarle punta a un lápiz⟩ ⟨to sharpen one's wits : aguzar el ingenio⟩

sharpener [ˈʃɑrpənər] *n* : afilador *m* (para cuchillos, etc.), sacapuntas *m* (para lápices)

sharply [ˈʃɑrpli] *adv* **1** ABRUPTLY : bruscamente **2** DISTINCTLY : claramente, marcadamente

sharpness [ˈʃɑrpnəs] *n* **1** : lo afilado (de un cuchillo, etc.) **2** ACUTENESS : agudeza *f* (de los sentidos o de la mente) **3** INTENSITY : intensidad *f*, agudeza *f* (de dolores, etc.) **4** HARSHNESS : dureza *f*, severidad *f* **5** ABRUPTNESS : brusquedad *f* **6** CLARITY : nitidez *f*

sharpshooter [ˈʃɑrp,ʃu:t̬ər] *n* : tirador *m*, -dora *f* de primera

shatter [ˈʃæt̬ər] *vt* **1** : hacer añicos ⟨to shatter the silence : romper el silencio⟩ **2 to be shattered by** : quedar destrozado por — *vi* : hacerse añicos, romperse en pedazos

shave[1] [ˈʃeɪv] *v* **shaved; shaved** *or* **shaven** [ˈʃeɪvən]; **shaving** *vt* **1** : afeitar, rasurar ⟨she shaved her legs : se rasuró las piernas⟩ ⟨they shaved (off) his beard : le afeitaron la barba⟩ **2** SLICE : cortar (en pedazos finos) — *vi* : afeitarse, rasurarse
shave[2] *n* : afeitada *f*, rasurada *f*
shaver [ˈʃeɪvər] *n* : afeitadora *f*, máquina *f* de afeitar, rasuradora *f*
shawl [ˈʃɔl] *n* : chal *m*, mantón *m*, rebozo *m*
she [ˈʃiː] *pron* : ella
sheaf [ˈʃiːf] *n, pl* **sheaves** [ˈʃiːvz] : gavilla *f* (de cereales), haz *m* (de flechas), fajo *m* (de papeles)
shear [ˈʃɪr] *vt* **sheared; sheared** *or* **shorn** [ˈʃorn]; **shearing 1** : esquilar, trasquilar ⟨to shear sheep : trasquilar ovejas⟩ **2** CUT : cortar (el pelo, etc.)
shears [ˈʃɪrz] *npl* : tijeras *fpl* (grandes)
sheath [ˈʃiːθ] *n, pl* **sheaths** [ˈʃiːðz, ˈʃiːθs] : funda *f*, vaina *f*
sheathe [ˈʃiːð] *vt* **sheathed; sheathing** : envainar, enfundar
shed[1] [ˈʃd] *vt* **shed; shedding 1** : derramar (sangre o lágrimas) **2** EMIT : emitir (luz) ⟨to shed light on : aclarar⟩ **3** DISCARD : mudar (la piel, etc.) ⟨to shed one's clothes : quitarse uno la ropa⟩
shed[2] *n* : cobertizo *m*
she'd [ˈʃiːd] (*contraction of* **she had** *or* **she would**) → **have, would**
sheen [ˈʃiːn] *n* : brillo *m*, lustre *m*
sheep [ˈʃiːp] *ns & pl* : oveja *f*
sheepfold [ˈʃiːpˌfoːld] *n* : redil *m*
sheepish [ˈʃiːpɪʃ] *adj* : avergonzado
sheepskin [ˈʃiːpˌskɪn] *n* : piel *f* de oveja, piel *f* de borrego
sheer[1] [ˈʃɪr] *adv* **1** COMPLETELY : completamente, totalmente **2** VERTICALLY : verticalmente
sheer[2] *adj* **1** TRANSPARENT : vaporoso, transparente **2** ABSOLUTE, UTTER : puro ⟨by sheer luck : por pura suerte⟩ **3** STEEP : escarpado, vertical
sheet [ˈʃiːt] *n* **1** *or* **bedsheet** [ˈbɛd-ˌʃiːt] : sábana *f* **2** : hoja *f* (de papel) **3** : capa *f* (de hielo, etc.) **4** : lámina *f*, placa *f* (de vidrio, metal, etc.), plancha *f* (de metal, madera, etc.) ⟨baking sheet : placa de horno⟩
sheikh *or* **sheik** [ˈʃiːk, ˈʃeɪk] *n* : jeque *m*
shelf [ˈʃɛlf] *n, pl* **shelves** [ˈʃɛlvz] **1** : estante *m*, anaquel *m* (en una pared) **2** : banco *m*, arrecife *m* (en geología) ⟨continental shelf : plataforma continental⟩
shell[1] [ˈʃɛl] *vt* **1** : desvainar (chícharos), pelar (nueces, etc.) **2** BOMBARD : bombardear
shell[2] *n* **1** SEASHELL : concha *f* **2** : cáscara *f* (de huevos, nueces, etc.), vaina *f* (de chícharos, etc.), caparazón *m* (de crustáceos, tortugas, etc.) **3** : cartucho *m*, casquillo *m* ⟨a .45 caliber shell : un cartucho calibre .45⟩ **4** *or* **racing shell** : bote *m* (para hacer regatas de remos)
she'll [ˈʃiːl, ˈʃɪl] (*contraction of* **she shall** *or* **she will**) → **shall, will**
shellac[1] [ʃəˈlæk] *vt* **-lacked; -lacking 1** : laquear (madera, etc.) **2** DEFEAT : darle una paliza (a alguien), derrotar
shellac[2] *n* : laca *f*
shellfish [ˈʃɛlˌfɪʃ] *n* : marisco *m*
shelter[1] [ˈʃɛltər] *vt* **1** PROTECT : proteger, abrigar **2** HARBOR : dar refugio a, albergar
shelter[2] *n* : refugio *m*, abrigo *m* ⟨to take shelter : refugiarse⟩
shelve [ˈʃɛlv] *vt* **shelved; shelving 1** : poner en estantes **2** DEFER : dar carpetazo a
shenanigans [ʃəˈnænɪgənz] *npl* **1** TRICKERY : artimañas *fpl* **2** MISCHIEF : travesuras *fpl*
shepherd[1] [ˈʃɛpərd] *vt* **1** : cuidar (ovejas, etc.) **2** GUIDE : conducir, guiar
shepherd[2] *n* : pastor *m*
shepherdess [ˈʃɛpərdəs] *n* : pastora *f*
sherbet [ˈʃərbət] *or* **sherbert** [-bərt] *n* : sorbete *m*, nieve *f Cuba, Mex, PRi*
sheriff [ˈʃɛrɪf] *n* : sheriff *mf*
sherry [ˈʃɛri] *n, pl* **-ries** : jerez *m*
she's [ˈʃiːz] (*contraction of* **she is** *or* **she has**) → **be, have**
shield[1] [ˈʃiːld] *vt* **1** PROTECT : proteger **2** CONCEAL : ocultar ⟨to shield one's eyes : taparse los ojos⟩
shield[2] *n* **1** : escudo *m* (armadura) **2** PROTECTION : protección *f*, blindaje *m* (de un cable)
shier, shiest → **shy**
shift[1] [ˈʃɪft] *vt* **1** CHANGE : cambiar ⟨to shift gears : cambiar de velocidad⟩ **2** MOVE : mover **3** TRANSFER : transferir ⟨to shift the blame : echarle la culpa (a otro)⟩ — *vi* **1** CHANGE : cambiar **2** MOVE : moverse **3 to shift for oneself** : arreglárselas solo
shift[2] *n* **1** CHANGE, TRANSFER : cambio *m* ⟨a shift in priorities : un cambio de prioridades⟩ **2** : turno *m* ⟨night shift : turno de noche⟩ **3** DRESS : vestido *m* (suelto) **4** → **gearshift**
shiftless [ˈʃɪftləs] *adj* : perezoso, vago, holgazán
shifty [ˈʃɪfti] *adj* **shiftier; -est** : taimado, artero ⟨a shifty look : una mirada huidiza⟩
shilling [ˈʃɪlɪŋ] *n* : chelín *m*
shimmer [ˈʃɪmər] *vi* GLIMMER : brillar con luz trémula
shin[1] [ˈʃɪn] *vi* **shinned; shinning** : trepar, subir ⟨she shinned up the pole : subió al poste⟩
shin[2] *n* : espinilla *f*, canilla *f*
shine[1] [ˈʃaɪn] *v* **shone** [ˈʃoːn] *or* **shined; shining** *vi* **1** : brillar, relucir ⟨the stars were shining : las estrellas brillaban⟩ **2** EXCEL : brillar, lucirse — *vt* **1** : alumbrar ⟨he shined the flashlight at it : lo alumbró con la linterna⟩ **2** POLISH : sacarle brillo a, lustrar
shine[2] *n* : brillo *m*, lustre *m*
shingle[1] [ˈʃɪŋgəl] *vt* **-gled; -gling** : techar

shingle[2] *n* : tablilla *f* (para techar)
shingles ['ʃɪŋgəlz] *npl* : herpes *m*
shinny ['ʃɪni] *vi* **-nied; -nying** → **shin**[1]
shiny ['ʃaɪni] *adj* **shinier; -est** : brillante
ship[1] ['ʃɪp] *vt* **shipped; shipping 1** LOAD : embarcar (en un barco) **2** SEND : transportar (en barco), enviar ⟨to ship by air : enviar por avión⟩
ship[2] *n* **1** : barco *m*, buque *m* **2** → **spaceship**
shipboard ['ʃɪp,bord] *n* **on ∼** : a bordo
shipbuilder ['ʃɪp,bɪldər] *n* : constructor *m*, -tora *f* naval
shipment ['ʃɪpmənt] *n* **1** SHIPPING : transporte *m*, embarque *m* **2** : envío *m*, remesa *f* ⟨a shipment of medicine : un envío de medicina⟩
shipping ['ʃɪpɪŋ] *n* **1** SHIPS : barcos *mpl*, embarcaciones *fpl* **2** TRANSPORTATION : transporte *m* (de mercancías)
shipshape ['ʃɪp'ʃeɪp] *adj* : ordenado
shipwreck[1] ['ʃɪp,rɛk] *vt* **to be shipwrecked** : naufragar
shipwreck[2] *n* : naufragio *m*
shipyard ['ʃɪp,jard] *n* : astillero *m*
shirk ['ʃərk] *vt* : eludir, rehuir ⟨to shirk one's responsibilities : esquivar uno sus responsabilidades⟩
shirt ['ʃərt] *n* : camisa *f*
shiver[1] ['ʃɪvər] *vi* **1** : tiritar (de frío) **2** TREMBLE : estremecerse, temblar
shiver[2] *n* : escalofrío *m*, estremecimiento *m*
shoal ['ʃo:l] *n* : banco *m*, bajío *m*
shock[1] ['ʃak] *vt* **1** UPSET : conmover, conmocionar **2** STARTLE : asustar, sobresaltar **3** SCANDALIZE : escandalizar **4** : darle una descarga eléctrica a
shock[2] *n* **1** COLLISION, JOLT : choque *m*, sacudida *f* **2** UPSET : conmoción *f*, golpe *m* emocional **3** : shock *m* (en medicina) **4** *or* **electric shock** : descarga *f* eléctrica **5** SHEAVES : gavillas *fpl* **6 shock of hair** : mata *f* de pelo
shock absorber *n* : amortiguador *m*
shocking ['ʃakɪŋ] *adj* **1** : chocante **2 shocking pink** : rosa *m* estridente
shoddy ['ʃadi] *adj* **shoddier; -est** : de mala calidad ⟨a shoddy piece of work : un trabajo chapucero⟩
shoe[1] ['ʃu:] *vt* **shod** ['ʃad]; **shoeing** : herrar (un caballo)
shoe[2] *n* **1** : zapato *m* ⟨the shoe industry : la industria del calzado⟩ **2** HORSESHOE : herradura *f* **3 brake shoe** : zapata *f*
shoelace ['ʃu:,leɪs] *n* : cordón *m* (de zapatos)
shoemaker ['ʃu:,meɪkər] *n* : zapatero *m*, -ra *f*
shone → **shine**
shook → **shake**
shoot[1] ['ʃu:t] *v* **shot** ['ʃat]; **shooting** *vt* **1** : disparar, tirar ⟨to shoot a bullet : tirar una bala⟩ **2** : pegarle un tiro a, darle un balazo a ⟨he shot her : le pegó un tiro⟩ ⟨they shot and killed him : lo mataron a balazos⟩ **3** THROW : lanzar (una pelota, etc.), echar (una mirada) **4** PHOTOGRAPH : fotografiar **5** FILM : filmar — *vi* **1** : disparar (con un arma de fuego) **2** DART : ir rápidamente ⟨it shot past : pasó como una bala⟩
shoot[2] *n* : brote *m*, retoño *m*, vástago *m*
shooting star *n* : estrella *f* fugaz
shop[1] ['ʃap] *vi* **shopped; shopping** : hacer compras ⟨to go shopping : ir de compras⟩
shop[2] *n* **1** WORKSHOP : taller *m* **2** STORE : tienda *f*
shopkeeper ['ʃap,ki:pər] *n* : tendero *m*, -ra *f*
shoplift ['ʃap,lɪft] *vi* : hurtar mercancía (de una tienda) — *vt* : hurtar (de una tienda)
shoplifter ['ʃap,lɪftər] *n* : ladrón *m*, -drona *f* (que roba en una tienda)
shopper ['ʃapər] *n* : comprador *m*, -dora *f*
shore[1] ['ʃor] *vt* **shored; shoring** : apuntalar ⟨they shored up the wall : apuntalaron la pared⟩
shore[2] *n* **1** : orilla *f* (del mar, etc.) **2** PROP : puntal *m*
shoreline ['ʃor,laɪn] *n* : orilla *f*
shorn → **shear**
short[1] ['ʃɔrt] *adv* **1** ABRUPTLY : repentinamente, súbitamente ⟨the car stopped short : el carro se paró en seco⟩ **2 to fall short** : no alcanzar, quedarse corto
short[2] *adj* **1** : corto (de medida), bajo (de estatura) **2** BRIEF : corto ⟨short and sweet : corto y bueno⟩ ⟨a short time ago : hace poco⟩ **3** CURT : brusco, cortante, seco **4** : corto (de tiempo, de dinero) ⟨I'm one dollar short : me falta un dólar⟩
short[3] *n* **1 shorts** *npl* : shorts *mpl*, pantalones *mpl* cortos **2** → **short circuit**
shortage ['ʃɔrtɪʤ] *n* : falta *f*, escasez *f*, carencia *f*
shortcake ['ʃɔrt,keɪk] *n* : tarta *f* de fruta
shortchange ['ʃɔrt'ʧeɪnʤ] *vt* **-changed; -changing** : darle mal el cambio (a alguien)
short circuit *n* : cortocircuito *m*, corto *m* (eléctrico)
shortcoming ['ʃɔrt,kʌmɪŋ] *n* : defecto *m*
shortcut ['ʃɔrt,kʌt] *n* **1** : atajo *m* ⟨to take a shortcut : cortar camino⟩ **2** : alternativa *f* fácil, método *m* rápido
shorten ['ʃɔrtən] *vt* : acortar — *vi* : acortarse
shorthand ['ʃɔrt,hænd] *n* : taquigrafía *f*
short–lived ['ʃɔrt'lɪvd, -'laɪvd] *adj* : efímero
shortly ['ʃɔrtli] *adv* **1** BRIEFLY : brevemente ⟨to put it shortly : para decirlo en pocas palabras⟩ **2** SOON : dentro de poco
shortness ['ʃɔrtnəs] *n* **1** : lo corto ⟨shortness of stature : estatura baja⟩ **2** BREVITY : brevedad *f* **3** CURTNESS : brusquedad *f* **4** SHORTAGE : falta *f*, escasez *f*, carencia *f*

shortsighted [ˈʃɔrtˌsaɪt̬əd] → **nearsighted**
shot [ˈʃɑt] *n* **1** : disparo *m*, tiro *m* ⟨to fire a shot : disparar⟩ **2** PELLETS : perdigones *mpl* **3** : tiro *m* (en deportes) **4** ATTEMPT : intento *m*, tentativa *f* ⟨to have a shot at : hacer un intento por⟩ **5** RANGE : alcance *m* ⟨a long shot : una posibilidad remota⟩ **6** PHOTOGRAPH : foto *f* **7** INJECTION : inyección *f* **8** : trago *m* (de licor)
shotgun [ˈʃɑtˌgʌn] *n* : escopeta *f*
should → **shall**
shoulder[1] [ˈʃoːldər] *vt* **1** JOSTLE : empujar (con el hombro) **2** : ponerse al hombro (una mochila, etc.) **3** : cargar con (la responsabilidad, etc.)
shoulder[2] *n* **1** : hombro *m* ⟨to shrug one's shoulders : encogerse los hombros⟩ **2** : arcén *m* (de una carretera)
shoulder blade *n* : omóplato *m*, omoplato *m*, escápula *f*
shouldn't [ˈʃʊdənt] (*contraction of* **should not**) → **shall**
shout[1] [ˈʃaʊt] *v* : gritar, vocear
shout[2] *n* : grito *m*
shove[1] [ˈʃʌv] *v* **shoved; shoving** : empujar bruscamente
shove[2] *n* : empujón *m*, empellón *m*
shovel[1] [ˈʃʌvəl] *vt* **-veled** *or* **-velled; -veling** *or* **-velling** **1** : mover con (una) pala ⟨they shoveled the dirt out : sacaron la tierra con palas⟩ **2** DIG : cavar (con una pala)
shovel[2] *n* : pala *f*
show[1] [ˈʃoː] *v* **showed; shown** [ˈʃoːn] *or* **showed; showing** *vt* **1** DISPLAY : mostrar, enseñar **2** REVEAL : demostrar, manifestar, revelar ⟨he showed himself to be a coward : se reveló como cobarde⟩ **3** TEACH : enseñar **4** PROVE : demostrar, probar **5** CONDUCT, DIRECT : llevar, acompañar ⟨to show someone the way : indicarle el camino a alguien⟩ **6** : proyectar (una película), dar (un programa de televisión) — *vi* **1** : notarse, verse ⟨the stain doesn't show : la mancha no se ve⟩ **2** APPEAR : aparecer, dejarse ver
show[2] *n* **1** : demostración *f* ⟨a show of force : una demostración de fuerza⟩ **2** EXHIBITION : exposición *f*, exhibición *f* ⟨flower show : exposición de flores⟩ ⟨to be on show : estar expuesto⟩ **3** : espectáculo *m* (teatral), programa *m* (de televisión, etc.) ⟨to go to a show : ir al teatro⟩
showcase [ˈʃoːˌkeɪs] *n* : vitrina *f*
showdown [ˈʃoːˌdaʊn] *n* : confrontación *f* (decisiva)
shower[1] [ˈʃaʊər] *vt* **1** SPRAY : regar, mojar **2** HEAP : colmar ⟨they showered him with gifts : lo colmaron de regalos, le llovieron los regalos⟩ — *vi* **1** BATHE : ducharse, darse una ducha **2** RAIN : llover
shower[2] *n* **1** : chaparrón *m*, chubasco *m* ⟨a chance of showers : una posibilidad de chaparrones⟩ **2** : ducha *f* ⟨to take a shower : ducharse⟩ **3** PARTY : fiesta *f* ⟨a bridal shower : una despedida de soltera⟩
show off *vt* : hacer alarde de, ostentar — *vi* : lucirse
show up *vi* APPEAR : aparecer — *vt* EXPOSE : revelar
showy [ˈʃoːi] *adj* **showier; -est** : llamativo, ostentoso — **showily** *adv*
shrank → **shrink**
shrapnel [ˈʃræpnəl] *ns & pl* : metralla *f*
shred[1] [ˈʃrɛd] *vt* **shredded; shredding** : hacer trizas, desmenuzar (con las manos), triturar (con una máquina) ⟨to shred vegetables : cortar verduras en tiras⟩
shred[2] *n* **1** STRIP : tira *f*, jirón *m* (de tela) **2** BIT : pizca *f* ⟨not a shred of evidence : ni la mínima prueba⟩
shrew [ˈʃruː] *n* **1** : musaraña *f* (animal) **2** : mujer *f* regañona, arpía *f*
shrewd [ˈʃruːd] *adj* : astuto, inteligente, sagaz — **shrewdly** *adv*
shrewdness [ˈʃruːdnəs] *n* : astucia *f*
shriek[1] [ˈʃriːk] *vi* : chillar, gritar
shriek[2] *n* : chillido *m*, alarido *m*, grito *m*
shrill [ˈʃrɪl] *adj* : agudo, estridente
shrilly [ˈʃrɪli] *adv* : agudamente
shrimp [ˈʃrɪmp] *n* : camarón *m*, langostino *m*
shrine [ˈʃraɪn] *n* **1** TOMB : sepulcro *m* (de un santo) **2** SANCTUARY : lugar *m* sagrado, santuario *m*
shrink [ˈʃrɪŋk] *vi* **shrank** [ˈʃræŋk] *or* **shrunk** [ˈʃrʌŋk]; **shrunk** *or* **shrunken** [ˈʃrʌŋkən]; **shrinking** **1** RECOIL : retroceder ⟨he shrank back : se echó para atrás⟩ **2** : encogerse (dícese de la ropa)
shrinkage [ˈʃrɪŋkɪʤ] *n* : encogimiento *m* (de ropa, etc.), contracción *f*, reducción *f*
shrivel [ˈʃrɪvəl] *vi* **-veled** *or* **-velled; -veling** *or* **-velling** : arrugarse, marchitarse
shroud[1] [ˈʃraʊd] *vt* : envolver
shroud[2] *n* **1** : sudario *m*, mortaja *f* **2** VEIL : velo *m* ⟨wrapped in a shroud of mystery : envuelto en un aura de misterio⟩
shrub [ˈʃrʌb] *n* : arbusto *m*, mata *f*
shrubbery [ˈʃrʌbəri] *n, pl* **-beries** : arbustos *mpl*, matas *fpl*
shrug [ˈʃrʌg] *vi* **shrugged; shrugging** : encogerse de hombros
shrunk → **shrink**
shuck[1] [ˈʃʌk] *vt* : pelar (mazorcas, etc.), abrir (almejas, etc.)
shuck[2] *n* **1** HUSK : cascarilla *f*, cáscara *f* (de una nuez, etc.), hojas *fpl* (de una mazorca) **2** SHELL : concha *f* (de una almeja, etc.)
shudder[1] [ˈʃʌdər] *vi* : estremecerse
shudder[2] *n* : estremecimiento *m*, escalofrío *m*
shuffle[1] [ˈʃʌfəl] *v* **-fled; -fling** *vt* MIX : mezclar, revolver, barajar (naipes) — *vi* : caminar arrastrando los pies

shuffle[2] *n* **1** : acto *m* de revolver ⟨each player gets a shuffle : a cada jugador le toca barajar⟩ **2** JUMBLE : revoltijo *m* **3** : arrastramiento *m* de los pies
shun [ˈʃʌn] *vi* **shunned; shunning** : evitar, esquivar, eludir
shunt [ˈʃʌnt] *vt* : desviar, cambiar de vía (un tren)
shut [ˈʃʌt] *v* **shut; shutting** *vt* **1** CLOSE : cerrar ⟨shut the lid : tápalo⟩ **2 to shut out** EXCLUDE : excluir, dejar fuera a (personas), no dejar que entre (luz, ruido, etc.) **3 to shut up** CONFINE : encerrar — *vi* : cerrarse ⟨the factory shut down : la fábrica cerró suspuertas⟩
shut–in [ˈʃʌtˌɪn] *n* : inválido *m*, -da *f* (que no puede salir de casa)
shutter [ˈʃʌt̬ər] *n* **1** : contraventana *f*, postigo *m* (de una ventana o puerta) **2** : obturador *m* (de una cámara)
shuttle[1] [ˈʃʌt̬əl] *v* **-tled; -tling** *vt* : transportar ⟨she shuttled him back and forth : lo llevaba de acá para allá⟩ — *vi* : ir y venir
shuttle[2] *n* **1** : lanzadera *f* (para tejer) **2** : vehículo *m* que hace recorridos cortos **3** → **space shuttle**
shuttlecock [ˈʃʌt̬əlˌkɑk] *n* : volante *m*
shut up *vi* : callarse ⟨shut up! : ¡cállate (la boca)!⟩
shy[1] [ˈʃaɪ] *vi* **shied; shying** : retroceder, asustarse
shy[2] *adj* **shier** *or* **shyer** [ˈʃaɪər]; **shiest** *or* **shyest** [ˈʃaɪəst] **1** TIMID : tímido **2** WARY : cauteloso ⟨he's not shy about asking : no vacila en preguntar⟩ **3** SHORT : corto (de dinero, etc.) ⟨I'm two dollars shy : me faltan dos dólares⟩
shyly [ˈʃaɪli] *adv* : tímidamente
shyness [ˈʃaɪnəs] *n* : timidez *f*
Siamese[1] [ˌsaɪəˈmiːz, -ˈmiːs-] *adj* : siamés ⟨Siamese twins : hermanos siameses⟩
Siamese[2] *n* **1** : siamés *m*, -mesa *f* **2** : siamés *m* (idioma) **3** *or* **Siamese cat** : gato *m* siamés
sibling [ˈsɪblɪŋ] *n* : hermano *m*, hermana *f*
Sicilian [səˈsɪljən] *n* : siciliano *m*, -na *f* — **Sicilian** *adj*
sick [ˈsɪk] *adj* **1** : enfermo **2** NAUSEOUS : mareado, con náuseas ⟨to get sick : vomitar⟩ **3** : para uso de enfermos ⟨sick day : día de permiso (por enfermedad)⟩
sickbed [ˈsɪkˌbɛd] *n* : lecho *m* de enfermo
sicken [ˈsɪkən] *vt* **1** : poner enfermo **2** REVOLT : darle asco (a alguien) — *vi* : enfermar(se), caer enfermo
sickening [ˈsɪkənɪŋ] *adj* : asqueroso, repugnante, nauseabundo
sickle [ˈsɪkəl] *n* : hoz *f*
sickly [ˈsɪkli] *adj* **sicklier; -est** **1** : enfermizo **2** → **sickening**
sickness [ˈsɪknəs] *n* **1** : enfermedad *f* **2** NAUSEA : náuseas *fpl*
side [ˈsaɪd] *n* **1** : lado *m*, costado *m* (de una persona), ijada *f* (de un animal) **2** : lado *m*, cara *f* (de una moneda, etc.) **3** : lado *m*, parte *f* ⟨he's on my side : está de mi parte⟩ ⟨to take sides : tomar partido⟩
sideboard [ˈsaɪdˌbord] *n* : aparador *m*
sideburns [ˈsaɪdˌbərnz] *npl* : patillas *fpl*
sided [ˈsaɪdəd] *adj* : que tiene lados ⟨one-sided : de un lado⟩
side effect *n* : efecto *m* secundario
sideline [ˈsaɪdˌlaɪn] *n* **1** : línea *f* de banda (en deportes) **2** : actividad *f* suplementaria (en negocios) **3 to be on the sidelines** : estar al margen
sidelong [ˈsaɪdˌlɔŋ] *adj* : de reojo, de soslayo
sideshow [ˈsaɪdˌʃoː] *n* : espectáculo *m* secundario, atracción *f* secundaria
sidestep [ˈsaɪdˌstɛp] *v* **-stepped; -stepping** *vi* : dar un paso hacia un lado — *vt* AVOID : esquivar, eludir
sidetrack [ˈsaɪdˌtræk] *vt* : desviar (una conversación, etc.), distraer (a una persona)
sidewalk [ˈsaɪdˌwɔk] *n* : acera *f*, vereda *f*, andén *m CA*, *Col*, banqueta *f Mex*
sideways[1] [ˈsaɪdˌweɪz] *adv* **1** : hacia un lado ⟨it leaned sideways : se inclinaba hacia un lado⟩ **2** : de lado, de costado ⟨lie sideways : acuéstese de costado⟩
sideways[2] *adj* : hacia un lado ⟨a sideways glance : una mirada de reojo⟩
siding [ˈsaɪdɪŋ] *n* **1** : apartadero *m* (para trenes) **2** : revestimiento *m* exterior (de un edificio)
sidle [ˈsaɪdəl] *vi* **-dled; -dling** : moverse furtivamente
siege [ˈsiːʤ, ˈsiːʒ] *n* : sitio *m* ⟨to be under siege : estar sitiado⟩
siesta [siːˈɛstə] *n* : siesta *f*
sieve [ˈsɪv] *n* : tamiz *m*, cedazo *m*, criba *f* (en mineralogía)
sift [ˈsɪft] *vt* **1** : tamizar, cerner ⟨sift the flour : tamice la harina⟩ **2** *or* **to sift through** : examinar cuidadosamente, pasar por el tamiz
sifter [ˈsɪftər] *n* : tamiz *m*, cedazo *m*
sigh[1] [ˈsaɪ] *vi* : suspirar
sigh[2] *n* : suspiro *m*
sight[1] [ˈsaɪt] *vt* : ver (a una persona), divisar (la tierra, un barco)
sight[2] *n* **1** : vista *f* (facultad) ⟨out of sight : fuera de vista⟩ **2** : algo visto ⟨it's a familiar sight : se ve con frecuencia⟩ ⟨she's a sight for sore eyes : da gusto verla⟩ **3** : lugar *m* de interés (para turistas, etc.) **4** : mira *f* (de un rifle, etc.) **5** GLIMPSE : mirada *f* breve ⟨I caught sight of her : la divisé, alcancé a verla⟩
sighting [ˈsaɪt̬ɪŋ] *n* : avistamiento *m*
sightless [ˈsaɪtləs] *adj* : invidente, ciego
sightseer [ˈsaɪtˌsiːər] *n* : turista *mf*
sign[1] [ˈsaɪn] *vt* **1** : firmar ⟨to sign a check : firmar un cheque⟩ **2** *or* **to sign on** HIRE : contratar (a un empleado), fichar (a un jugador) — *vi* **1** : hacer una seña ⟨she signed for him to stop : le hizo una seña para que se parara⟩ **2** : comunicarse por señas

sign[2] *n* **1** SYMBOL : símbolo *m*, signo *m* ⟨minus sign : signo de menos⟩ **2** GESTURE : seña *f*, señal *f*, gesto *m* **3** : letrero *m*, cartel *m* ⟨neon sign : letrero de neón⟩ **4** TRACE : señal *f*, indicio *m*
signal[1] ['sɪgnəl] *vt* **-naled** *or* **-nalled; -naling** *or* **-nalling 1** : hacerle señas (a alguien) ⟨she signaled me to leave : me hizo señas para que saliera⟩ **2** INDICATE : señalar, indicar — *vi* : hacer señas, comunicar por señas
signal[2] *adj* NOTABLE : señalado, notable
signal[3] *n* : señal *f*
signature ['sɪgnəˌʧʊr] *n* : firma *f*
signet ['sɪgnət] *n* : sello *m*
significance [sɪg'nɪfɪkənts] *n* **1** MEANING : significado *m* **2** IMPORTANCE : importancia *f*
significant [sɪg'nɪfɪkənt] *adj* **1** IMPORTANT : importante **2** MEANINGFUL : significativo — **significantly** *adv*
signify ['sɪgnəˌfaɪ] *vt* **-fied; -fying 1** : indicar ⟨he signified his desire for more : haciendo señas indicó que quería más⟩ **2** MEAN : significar
sign language *n* : lenguaje *m* por señas
signpost ['saɪnˌpo:st] *n* : poste *m* indicador
silence[1] ['saɪlənts] *vt* **-lenced; -lencing** : silenciar, acallar
silence[2] *n* : silencio *m*
silent ['saɪlənt] *adj* **1** : callado ⟨to remain silent : quedarse callado, guardar silencio⟩ **2** QUIET, STILL : silencioso **3** MUTE : mudo ⟨a silent letter : una letra muda⟩
silently ['saɪləntli] *adv* : silenciosamente, calladamente
silhouette[1] [ˌsɪlə'wɛt] *vt* **-etted; -etting** : destacar la silueta de ⟨it was silhouetted against the sky : se perfilaba contra el cielo⟩
silhouette[2] *n* : silueta *f*
silica ['sɪlɪkə] *n* : sílice *f*
silicon ['sɪlɪkən, -ˌkɑn] *n* : silicio *m*
silk ['sɪlk] *n* : seda *f*
silken ['sɪlkən] *adj* **1** : de seda ⟨a silken veil : un velo de seda⟩ **2** SILKY : sedoso ⟨silken hair : cabellos sedosos⟩
silkworm ['sɪlkˌwərm] *n* : gusano *m* de seda
silky ['sɪlki] *adj* **silkier; -est** : sedoso
sill ['sɪl] *n* : alféizar *m* (de una ventana), umbral *m* (de una puerta)
silliness ['sɪlinəs] *n* : tontería *f*, estupidez *f*
silly ['sɪli] *adj* **sillier; -est** : tonto, estúpido, ridículo
silo ['saɪˌlo:] *n, pl* **silos** : silo *m*
silt ['sɪlt] *n* : cieno *m*
silver[1] ['sɪlvər] *adj* **1** : de plata ⟨a silver spoon : una cuchara de plata⟩ **2** → **silvery**
silver[2] *n* **1** : plata *f* **2** COINS : monedas *fpl* **3** → **silverware 4** : color *m* plata
silverware ['sɪlvərˌwær] *n* **1** : artículos *mpl* de plata, platería *f* **2** FLATWARE : cubertería *f*
silvery ['sɪlvəri] *adj* : plateado
similar ['sɪmələr] *adj* : similar, parecido, semejante
similarity [ˌsɪmə'lærət̬i] *n, pl* **-ties** : semejanza *f*, parecido *m*
similarly ['sɪmələrli] *adv* : de manera similar
simile ['sɪməˌli:] *n* : símil *m*
simmer ['sɪmər] *v* : hervir a fuego lento
simper[1] ['sɪmpər] *vi* : sonreír como un tonto
simper[2] *n* : sonrisa *f* tonta
simple ['sɪmpəl] *adj* **simpler; -plest 1** INNOCENT : inocente **2** PLAIN : sencillo, simple **3** EASY : simple, sencillo, fácil **4** STRAIGHTFORWARD : puro, simple ⟨the simple truth : la pura verdad⟩ **5** NAIVE : ingenuo, simple
simpleton ['sɪmpəltən] *n* : bobo *m*, -ba *f*; tonto *m*, -ta *f*
simplicity [sɪm'plɪsət̬i] *n* : simplicidad *f*, sencillez *f*
simplification [ˌsɪmpləfə'keɪʃən] *n* : simplificación *f*
simplify ['sɪmpləˌfaɪ] *vt* **-fied; -fying** : simplificar
simply ['sɪmpli] *adv* **1** PLAINLY : sencillamente **2** SOLELY : simplemente, sólo **3** REALLY : absolutamente
simulate ['sɪmjəˌleɪt] *vt* **-lated; -lating** : simular
simulation [ˌsɪmjə'leɪʃən] *n* : simulación *f*
simultaneous [ˌsaɪməl'teɪniəs] *adj* : simultáneo — **simultaneously** *adv*
sin[1] ['sɪn] *vi* **sinned; sinning** : pecar
sin[2] *n* : pecado *m*
since[1] ['sɪnts] *adv* **1** : desde entonces ⟨they've been friends ever since : desde entonces han sido amigos⟩ ⟨she's since become mayor : más tarde se hizo alcalde⟩ **2** AGO : hace ⟨he's long since dead : murió hace mucho⟩
since[2] *conj* **1** : desde que ⟨since he was born : desde que nació⟩ **2** INASMUCH AS : ya que, puesto que, dado que
since[3] *prep* : desde
sincere [sɪn'sɪr] *adj* **-cerer; -est** : sincero — **sincerely** *adv*
sincerity [sɪn'sɛrət̬i] *n* : sinceridad *f*
sinew ['sɪnˌju:, 'sɪˌnu:] *n* **1** TENDON : tendón *m*, nervio *m* (en la carne) **2** POWER : fuerza *f*
sinewy ['sɪnjʊi, 'sɪnʊi] *adj* **1** STRINGY : fibroso **2** STRONG, WIRY : fuerte, nervudo
sinful ['sɪnfəl] *adj* : pecador (dícese de las personas), pecaminoso
sing ['sɪŋ] *v* **sang** ['sæŋ] *or* **sung** ['sʌŋ]; **sung; singing** : cantar
singe ['sɪnʤ] *vt* **singed; singeing** : chamuscar, quemar
singer ['sɪŋər] *n* : cantante *mf*
single[1] ['sɪŋgəl] *vt* **-gled; -gling** *or* **to single out 1** SELECT : escoger **2** DISTINGUISH : señalar
single[2] *adj* **1** UNMARRIED : soltero **2** SOLE : solo ⟨a single survivor : un solo

sobreviviente⟩ ⟨every single one : cada uno, todos⟩

single[3] *n* **1** : soltero *m*, -ra *f* ⟨for married couples and singles : para los matrimonios y los solteros⟩ **2** *or* **single room** : habitación *f* individual **3** DOLLAR : billete *m* de un dólar

single–handed [ˈsɪŋgəlˈhændəd] *adj* : sin ayuda, solo

singly [ˈsɪŋgli] *adv* : individualmente, uno por uno

singular[1] [ˈsɪŋgjələr] *adj* **1** : singular (en gramática) **2** OUTSTANDING : singular, sobresaliente **3** STRANGE : singular, extraño

singular[2] *n* : singular *m*

singularity [ˌsɪŋgjəˈlærət̬i] *n, pl* **-ties** : singularidad *f*

singularly [ˈsɪŋgjələrli] *adv* : singularmente

sinister [ˈsɪnəstər] *adj* : siniestro

sink[1] [ˈsɪŋk] *v* **sank** [ˈsæŋk] *or* **sunk** [ˈsʌŋk]; **sunk; sinking** *vi* **1** : hundirse (dícese de un barco) **2** DROP, FALL : descender, caer ⟨to sink into a chair : dejarse caer en una silla⟩ ⟨her heart sank : se le cayó el alma a los pies⟩ **3** DECREASE : bajar — *vt* **1** : hundir (un barco, etc.) **2** EXCAVATE : excavar (un pozo para minar), perforar (un pozo de agua) **3** PLUNGE, STICK : clavar, hincar **4** INVEST : invertir (fondos)

sink[2] *n* **1 kitchen sink** : fregadero *m*, lavaplatos *m Chile, Col, Mex* **2 bathroom sink** : lavabo *m*, lavamanos *m*

sinner [ˈsɪnər] *n* : pecador *m*, -dora *f*

sinuous [ˈsɪnjʊəs] *adj* : sinuoso — **sinuously** *adv*

sinus [ˈsaɪnəs] *n* : seno *m*

sip[1] [ˈsɪp] *v* **sipped; sipping** *vt* : sorber — *vi* : beber a sorbos

sip[2] *n* : sorbo *m*

siphon[1] [ˈsaɪfən] *vt* : sacar con sifón

siphon[2] *n* : sifón *m*

sir [ˈsər] *n* **1** (*in titles*) : sir *m* **2** (*as a form of address*) : señor *m* ⟨Dear Sir : Muy señor mío⟩ ⟨yes sir! : ¡sí, señor!⟩

sire[1] [ˈsaɪr] *vt* **sired; siring** : engendrar, ser el padre de

sire[2] *n* : padre *m*

siren [ˈsaɪrən] *n* : sirena *f*

sirloin [ˈsərˌlɔɪn] *n* : solomillo *m*

sirup → **syrup**

sisal [ˈsaɪsəl, -zəl] *n* : sisal *m*

sissy [ˈsɪsi] *n, pl* **-sies** : mariquita *f fam*

sister [ˈsɪstər] *n* **1** : hermana *f* **2 Sister** : hermana *f*, Sor *f* ⟨Sister Mary : Sor María⟩

sisterhood [ˈsɪstərˌhʊd] *n* **1** : condición *f* de ser hermana **2** : sociedad *f* de mujeres

sister–in–law [ˈsɪstərɪnˌlɔ] *n, pl* **sisters–in–law** : cuñada *f*

sisterly [ˈsɪstərli] *adj* : de hermana

sit [ˈsɪt] *v* **sat** [ˈsæt]; **sitting** *vi* **1** : sentarse, estar sentado ⟨he sat down : se sentó⟩ **2** ROOST : posarse **3** : sesionar ⟨the legislature is sitting : la legislatura está en sesión⟩ **4** POSE : posar (para un retrato) **5** LIE, REST : estar (ubicado) ⟨the house sits on a hill : la casa está en una colina⟩ — *vt* SEAT : sentar, colocar ⟨I sat him on the sofa : lo senté en el sofá⟩

sitcom [ˈsɪtˌkɑm] → **situation comedy**

site [ˈsaɪt] *n* **1** PLACE : sitio *m*, lugar *m* **2** LOCATION : emplazamiento *m*, ubicación *f*

sitter [ˈsɪt̬ər] → **baby–sitter**

sitting room → **living room**

situated [ˈsɪʧʊˌeɪt̬əd] *adj* LOCATED : ubicado, situado

situation [ˌsɪʧʊˈeɪʃən] *n* **1** LOCATION : situación *f*, ubicación *f*, emplazamiento *m* **2** CIRCUMSTANCES : situación *f* **3** JOB : empleo *m*

situation comedy *n* : comedia *f* de situación

six[1] [ˈsɪks] *adj* : seis

six[2] *n* : seis *m*

six–gun [ˈsɪksˌgʌn] *n* : revólver *m* (con seis cámaras)

six hundred[1] *adj* : seiscientos

six hundred[2] *n* : seiscientos *m*

six–shooter [ˈsɪksˌʃuːt̬ər] → **six–gun**

sixteen[1] [sɪksˈtiːn] *adj* : dieciséis

sixteen[2] *n* : dieciséis *m*

sixteenth[1] [sɪksˈtiːnθ] *adj* : decimosexto

sixteenth[2] *n* **1** : decimosexto *m*, -ta *f* (en una serie) **2** : dieciseisavo *m*, dieciseisava parte *f*

sixth[1] [ˈsɪksθ, ˈsɪkst] *adj* : sexto

sixth[2] *n* **1** : sexto *m*, -ta *f* (en una serie) **2** : sexto *m*, sexta parte *f*

sixtieth[1] [ˈsɪkst̬iəθ] *adj* : sexagésimo

sixtieth[2] *n* **1** : sexagésimo *m*, -ma *f* (en una serie) **2** : sesentavo *m*, sesentava parte *f*

sixty[1] [ˈsɪkst̬i] *adj* : sesenta

sixty[2] *n, pl* **-ties** : sesenta *m*

sizable *or* **sizeable** [ˈsaɪzəbəl] *adj* : considerable

size[1] [ˈsaɪz] *vt* **sized; sizing 1** : clasificar según el tamaño **2 to size up** : evaluar, apreciar

size[2] *n* **1** DIMENSIONS : tamaño *m*, talla *f* (de ropa), número *m* (de zapatos) **2** MAGNITUDE : magnitud *f*

sizzle [ˈsɪzəl] *vi* **-zled; -zling** : chisporrotear

skate[1] [ˈskeɪt] *vi* **skated; skating** : patinar

skate[2] *n* **1** : patín *m* ⟨roller skate : patín de ruedas⟩ **2** : raya *f* (pez)

skateboard [ˈskeɪtˌbord] *n* : monopatín *m*

skater [ˈskeɪt̬ər] *n* : patinador *m*, -dora *f*

skein [ˈskeɪn] *n* : madeja *f*

skeletal [ˈskələt̬əl] *adj* **1** : óseo (en anatomía) **2** EMACIATED : esquelético

skeleton [ˈskɛlətən] *n* **1** : esqueleto *m* (anatómico) **2** FRAMEWORK : armazón *mf*

skeptic [ˈskɛptɪk] *n* : escéptico *m*, -ca *f*

skeptical [ˈskɛptɪkəl] *adj* : escéptico

skepticism [ˈskɛptəˌsɪzəm] *n* : escepticismo *m*

sketch[1] [ˈskɛʧ] *vt* : bosquejar — *vi* : hacer bosquejos
sketch[2] *n* **1** DRAWING, OUTLINE : esbozo *m*, bosquejo *m* **2** ESSAY : ensayo *m*
sketchy [ˈskɛʧi] *adj* **sketchier; -est** : incompleto, poco detallado
skewer[1] [ˈskju:ər] *vt* : ensartar (carne, etc.)
skewer[2] *n* : brocheta *f*, broqueta *f*
ski[1] [ˈski:] *vi* **skied; skiing** : esquiar
ski[2] *n, pl* **skis** : esquí *m*
skid[1] [ˈskɪd] *vi* **skidded; skidding** : derrapar, patinar
skid[2] *n* : derrape *m*, patinazo *m*
skier [ˈski:ər] *n* : esquiador *m*, -dora *f*
skiff [ˈskɪf] *n* : esquife *m*
skill [ˈskɪl] *n* **1** DEXTERITY : habilidad *f*, destreza *f* **2** CAPABILITY : capacidad *f*, arte *m*, técnica *f* ⟨organizational skills : la capacidad para organizar⟩
skilled [ˈskɪld] *adj* : hábil, experto
skillet [ˈskɪlət] *n* : sartén *mf*
skillful [ˈskɪlfəl] *adj* : hábil, diestro
skillfully [ˈskɪlfəli] *adv* : con habilidad, con destreza
skim[1] [ˈskɪm] *vt* **skimmed; skimming 1** *or* **to skim off** : espumar, descremar (leche) **2** : echarle un vistazo a (un libro, etc.), pasar rozando (una superficie)
skim[2] *adj* : descremado ⟨skim milk : leche descremada⟩
skimp [ˈskɪmp] *vi* **to skimp on** : escatimar
skimpy [ˈskɪmpi] *adj* **skimpier; -est** : exiguo, escaso, raquítico
skin[1] [ˈskɪn] *vt* **skinned; skinning** : despellejar, desollar
skin[2] *n* **1** : piel *f*, cutis *m* (de la cara) ⟨dark skin : piel morena⟩ **2** RIND : piel *f*
skin diving *n* : buceo *m*, submarinismo *m*
skinflint [ˈskɪnˌflɪnt] *n* : tacaño *m*, -ña *f*
skinned [ˈskɪnd] *adj* : de piel ⟨tough-skinned : de piel dura⟩
skinny [ˈskɪni] *adj* **skinnier; -est** : flaco
skip[1] [ˈskɪp] *v* **skipped; skipping** *vi* : ir dando brincos — *vt* : saltarse
skip[2] *n* : brinco *m*, salto *m*
skipper [ˈskɪpər] *n* : capitán *m*, -tana *f*
skirmish[1] [ˈskərmɪʃ] *vi* : escaramuzar
skirmish[2] *n* : escaramuza *f*, refriega *f*
skirt[1] [ˈskərt] *vt* **1** BORDER : bordear **2** EVADE : evadir, esquivar
skirt[2] *n* : falda *f*, pollera *f*
skit [ˈskɪt] *n* : sketch *m* (teatral)
skittish [ˈskɪt̬ɪʃ] *adj* : asustadizo, nervioso
skulk [ˈskʌlk] *vi* : merodear
skull [ˈskʌl] *n* **1** : cráneo *m*, calavera *f* **2 skull and crossbones** : calavera *f* (bandera pirata)
skunk [ˈskʌŋk] *n* : zorrillo *m*, mofeta *f*
sky [ˈskaɪ] *n, pl* **skies** : cielo *m*
skylark [ˈskaɪˌlɑrk] *n* : alondra *f*
skylight [ˈskaɪˌlaɪt] *n* : claraboya *f*, tragaluz *m*
skyline [ˈskaɪˌlaɪn] *n* : horizonte *m*
skyrocket [ˈskaɪˌrɑkət] *vi* : dispararse
skyscraper [ˈskaɪˌskreɪpər] *n* : rascacielos *m*
slab [ˈslæb] *n* : losa *f* (de piedra), tabla *f* (de madera), pedazo *m* grueso (de pan, etc.)
slack[1] [ˈslæk] *adj* **1** CARELESS : descuidado, negligente **2** LOOSE : flojo **3** SLOW : de poco movimiento
slack[2] *n* **1** : parte *f* floja ⟨to take up the slack : tensar (una cuerda, etc.)⟩ **2 slacks** *npl* : pantalones *mpl*
slacken [ˈslækən] *vt* : aflojar — *vi* : aflojarse
slacker [ˈslækər] *n* : vago *m*, -ga *f*; holgazán *m*, -zana *f*
slag [ˈslæg] *n* : escoria *f*
slain → **slay**
slake [ˈsleɪk] *vt* **slaked; slaking** : saciar (la sed), satisfacer (la curiosidad)
slam[1] [ˈslæm] *v* **slammed; slamming** *vt* **1** : cerrar de golpe ⟨he slammed the door : dio un portazo⟩ **2** : tirar o dejar caer de golpe ⟨he slammed down the book : dejó caer el libro de un golpe⟩ — *vi* **1** : cerrarse de golpe **2 to slam into** : chocar contra
slam[2] *n* : golpe *m*, portazo *m* (de una puerta)
slander[1] [ˈslændər] *vt* : calumniar, difamar
slander[2] *n* : calumnia *f*, difamación *f*
slanderous [ˈslændərəs] *adj* : difamatorio, calumnioso
slang [ˈslæŋ] *n* : argot *m*, jerga *f*
slant[1] [ˈslænt] *vi* : inclinarse, ladearse — *vt* **1** SLOPE : inclinar **2** ANGLE : sesgar, orientar, dirigir ⟨a story slanted towards youth : un artículo dirigido a los jóvenes⟩
slant[2] *n* **1** INCLINE : inclinación *f* **2** PERSPECTIVE : perspectiva *f*, enfoque *m*
slap[1] [ˈslæp] *vt* **slapped; slapping** : bofetear, cachetear, dar una palmada (en la espalda, etc.)
slap[2] *n* : bofetada *f*, cachetada *f*, palmada *f*
slash[1] [ˈslæʃ] *vt* **1** GASH : cortar, hacer un tajo en **2** REDUCE : reducir, rebajar (precios)
slash[2] *n* : tajo *m*, corte *m*
slat [ˈslæt] *n* : tablilla *f*, listón *m*
slate [ˈsleɪt] *n* **1** : pizarra *f* ⟨a slate roof : un techo de pizarra⟩ **2** : lista *f* de candidatos (políticos)
slaughter[1] [ˈslɔt̬ər] *vt* **1** BUTCHER : matar (animales) **2** MASSACRE : masacrar (personas)
slaughter[2] *n* **1** : matanza *f* (de animales) **2** MASSACRE : masacre *f*, carnicería *f*
slaughterhouse [ˈslɔt̬ərˌhaʊs] *n* : matadero *m*
Slav [ˈslɑv, ˈslæv] *n* : eslavo *m*, -va *f*
slave[1] [ˈsleɪv] *vi* **slaved; slaving** : trabajar como un burro
slave[2] *n* : esclavo *m*, -va *f*
slaver [ˈslævər, ˈsleɪ-] *vi* : babear

slavery ['sleɪvəri] *n* : esclavitud *f*
Slavic ['slɑvɪk, 'slæ-] *adj* : eslavo
slavish ['sleɪvɪʃ] *adj* **1** SERVILE : servil **2** IMITATIVE : poco original
slay ['sleɪ] *vt* **slew** ['slu:]; **slain** ['sleɪn]; **slaying** : asesinar, matar
slayer ['sleɪər] *n* : asesino *m*, -na *f*
sleazy ['sli:zi] *adj* **sleazier; -est 1** SHODDY : chapucero, de mala calidad **2** DILAPIDATED : ruinoso **3** DISREPUTABLE : de mala fama
sled[1] ['slɛd] *v* **sledded; sledding** *vi* : ir en trineo — *vt* : transportar en trineo
sled[2] *n* : trineo *m*
sledge ['slɛʤ] *n* **1** : trineo *m* (grande) **2** → **sledgehammer**
sledgehammer ['slɛʤˌhæmər] *n* : almádena *f*, combo *m Chile, Peru*
sleek[1] ['sli:k] *vt* SLICK : alisar
sleek[2] *adj* : liso y brillante
sleep[1] ['sli:p] *vi* **slept** ['slɛpt]; **sleeping** : dormir
sleep[2] *n* **1** : sueño *m* **2 to go to sleep** : dormirse
sleeper ['sli:pər] *n* **1** : durmiente *mf* ⟨to be a light sleeper : tener el sueño ligero⟩ **2** *or* **sleeping car** : coche *m* cama, coche *m* dormitorio
sleepily ['sli:pəli] *adv* : de manera somnolienta
sleepiness ['sli:pinəs] *n* : somnolencia *f*
sleepless ['sli:pləs] *adj* : sin dormir, desvelado ⟨to have a sleepless night : pasar la noche en blanco⟩
sleepwalker ['sli:pˌwɔkər] *n* : sonámbulo *m*, -la *f*
sleepy ['sli:pi] *adj* **sleepier; -est 1** DROWSY : somnoliento, soñoliento ⟨to be sleepy : tener sueño⟩ **2** LETHARGIC : aletargado, letárgico
sleet[1] ['sli:t] *vi* **to be sleeting** : caer aguanieve
sleet[2] *n* : aguanieve *f*
sleeve ['sli:v] *n* : manga *f* (de una camisa, etc.)
sleeveless ['sli:vləs] *adj* : sin mangas
sleigh[1] ['sleɪ] *vi* : ir en trineo
sleigh[2] *n* : trineo *m* (tirado por caballos)
sleight of hand [ˌslaɪt̬əv'hænd] : prestidigitación *f*, juegos *mpl* de manos
slender ['slɛndər] *adj* **1** SLIM : esbelto, delgado **2** SCANTY : exiguo, escaso ⟨a slender hope : una esperanza lejana⟩
sleuth ['slu:θ] *n* : detective *mf*; sabueso *m*, -sa *f*
slew → **slay**
slice[1] ['slaɪs] *vt* **sliced; slicing** : cortar
slice[2] *n* : rebanada *f*, tajada *f*, lonja *f* (de carne, etc.), rodaja *f* (de una verdura, fruta, etc.), trozo *m* (de pastel, etc.)
slick[1] ['slɪk] *vt* : alisar
slick[2] *adj* **1** SLIPPERY : resbaladizo, resbaloso **2** CRAFTY : astuto, taimado
slicker ['slɪkər] *n* : impermeable *m*
slide[1] ['slaɪd] *v* **slid** ['slɪd]; **sliding** ['slaɪdɪŋ] *vi* **1** SLIP : resbalar **2** GLIDE : deslizarse **3** DECLINE : bajar ⟨to let things slide : dejar pasar las cosas⟩ — *vt* : correr, deslizar
slide[2] *n* **1** SLIDING : deslizamiento *m* **2** SLIP : resbalón *m* **3** : tobogán *m* (para niños) **4** TRANSPARENCY : diapositiva *f* (fotográfica) **5** DECLINE : descenso *m*
slier, sliest → **sly**
slight[1] ['slaɪt] *vt* : desairar, despreciar
slight[2] *adj* **1** SLENDER : esbelto, delgado **2** FLIMSY : endeble **3** TRIFLING : leve, insignificante ⟨a slight pain : un leve dolor⟩ **4** SMALL : pequeño, ligero ⟨not in the slightest : en absoluto⟩
slight[3] *n* SNUB : desaire *m*
slightly ['slaɪtli] *adv* : ligeramente, un poco
slim[1] ['slɪm] *v* **slimmed; slimming** : adelgazar
slim[2] *adj* **slimmer; slimmest 1** SLENDER : esbelto, delgado **2** SCANTY : exiguo, escaso
slime ['slaɪm] *n* **1** : baba *f* (secretada por un animal) **2** MUD, SILT : fango *m*, cieno *m*
slimy ['slaɪmi] *adj* **slimier; -est** : viscoso
sling[1] ['slɪŋ] *vt* **slung** ['slʌŋ]; **slinging 1** THROW : lanzar, tirar **2** HANG : colgar
sling[2] *n* **1** : honda *f* (arma) **2** : cabestrillo *m* ⟨my arm is in a sling : llevo el brazo en cabestrillo⟩
slingshot ['slɪŋˌʃɑt] *n* : tiragomas *m*, resortera *f Mex*
slink ['slɪŋk] *vi* **slunk** ['slʌŋk]; **slinking** : caminar furtivamente
slip[1] ['slɪp] *v* **slipped; slipping** *vi* **1** STEAL : ir sigilosamente ⟨to slip away : escabullirse⟩ ⟨to slip out the door : escaparse por la puerta⟩ **2** SLIDE : resbalarse, deslizarse **3** LAPSE : caer ⟨to slip into error : equivocarse⟩ **4 to let slip** : dejar escapar **5 to slip into** PUT ON : ponerse — *vt* **1** PUT : meter, poner **2** PASS : pasar ⟨she slipped me a note : me pasó una nota⟩ **3 to slip one's mind** : olvidársele a uno
slip[2] *n* **1** PIER : atracadero *m* **2** MISHAP : percance *m*, contratiempo *m* **3** MISTAKE : error *m*, desliz *m* ⟨a slip of the tongue : un lapsus⟩ **4** PETTICOAT : enagua *f* **5** : injerto *m*, esqueje *m* (de una planta) **6 slip of paper** : papelito *m*
slipper ['slɪpər] *n* : zapatilla *f*, pantufla *f*
slipperiness ['slɪpərinəs] *n* **1** : lo resbaloso, lo resbaladizo **2** TRICKINESS : astucia *f*
slippery ['slɪpəri] *adj* **slipperier; -est 1** : resbaloso, resbaladizo ⟨a slippery road : un camino resbaloso⟩ **2** TRICKY : artero, astuto, taimado **3** ELUSIVE : huidizo, escurridizo
slipshod ['slɪpˌʃɑd] *adj* : descuidado, chapucero
slip up *vi* : equivocarse
slit[1] ['slɪt] *vt* **slit; slitting** : cortar, abrir por lo largo

slit[2] *n* **1** OPENING : abertura *f*, rendija *f* **2** CUT : corte *m*, raja *f*, tajo *m*

slither [ˈslɪðər] *vi* : deslizarse

sliver [ˈslɪvər] *n* : astilla *f*

slob [ˈslɑb] *n* : persona *f* desaliñada ⟨what a slob! : ¡qué cerdo!⟩

slobber[1] [ˈslɑbər] *vi* : babear

slobber[2] *n* : baba *f*

slogan [ˈslo:gən] *n* : lema *m*, eslogan *m*

sloop [ˈslu:p] *n* : balandra *f*

slop[1] [ˈslɑp] *v* **slopped; slopping** *vt* : derramar — *vi* : derramarse

slop[2] *n* : bazofia *f*

slope[1] [ˈslo:p] *vi* **sloped; sloping** : inclinarse ⟨the road slopes upward : el camino sube (en pendiente)⟩

slope[2] *n* : inclinación *f*, pendiente *f*, declive *m*

sloppy [ˈslɑpi] *adj* **sloppier; -est** **1** MUDDY, SLUSHY : lodoso, fangoso **2** UNTIDY : descuidado (en el trabajo, etc.), desaliñado (de aspecto)

slot [ˈslɑt] *n* : ranura *f*

sloth [ˈslɔθ, ˈslo:θ] *n* **1** LAZINESS : pereza *f* **2** : perezoso *m* (animal)

slouch[1] [ˈslaʊʧ] *vi* : andar con los hombros caídos, repantigarse (en un sillón)

slouch[2] *n* **1** SLUMPING : mala postura *f* **2** BUNGLER, IDLER : haragán *m*, -gana *f*; inepto *m*, -ta *f* ⟨to be no slouch : no quedarse atrás⟩

slough[1] [ˈslʌf] *vt* : mudar de (piel)

slough[2] [ˈslu:, ˈslaʊ] *n* SWAMP : ciénaga *f*

Slovak [ˈslo:ˌvɑk, -ˌvæk] *or* **Slovakian** [slo:ˈvɑkiən, -ˈvæ-] *n* : eslovaco *m*, -ca *f* — **Slovak** *or* **Slovakian** *adj*

Slovene [ˈslo:ˌvi:n] *or* **Slovenian** [slo:ˈvi:niən] *n* : esloveno *m*, -na *f* — **Slovene** *or* **Slovenian** *adj*

slovenly [ˈslʌvənli, ˈslɑv-] *adj* : descuidado (en el trabajo, etc.), desaliñado (de aspecto)

slow[1] [slo:] *vt* : retrasar, reducir la marcha de — *vi* : ir más despacio

slow[2] *adv* : despacio, lentamente

slow[3] *adj* **1** : lento ⟨a slow process : un proceso lento⟩ **2** : atrasado ⟨my watch is slow : mi reloj está atrasado, mi reloj se atrasa⟩ **3** SLUGGISH : lento, poco activo **4** STUPID : lento, torpe, corto de alcances

slowly [slo:li] *adv* : lentamente, despacio

slowness [slo:nəs] *n* : lentitud *f*, torpeza *f*

sludge [ˈslʌʤ] *n* : aguas *fpl* negras, aguas *fpl* residuales

slug[1] [ˈslʌg] *vt* **slugged; slugging** : pegarle un porrazo (a alguien)

slug[2] *n* **1** : babosa *f* (molusco) **2** BULLET : bala *f* **3** TOKEN : ficha *f* **4** BLOW : porrazo *m*, puñetazo *m*

sluggish [ˈslʌgɪʃ] *adj* : aletargado, lento

sluice[1] [ˈslu:s] *vt* **sluiced; sluicing** : lavar en agua corriente

sluice[2] *n* : canal *m*

slum [ˈslʌm] *n* : barriada *f*, barrio *m* bajo

slumber[1] [ˈslʌmbər] *vi* : dormir

slumber[2] *n* : sueño *m*

slump[1] [ˈslʌmp] *vi* **1** DECLINE, DROP : disminuir, bajar **2** SLOUCH : encorvarse, dejarse caer (en una silla, etc.)

slump[2] *n* : bajón *m*, declive *m* (económico)

slung → **sling**

slunk → **slink**

slur[1] [ˈslər] *vt* **slurred; slurring** : ligar (notas musicales), tragarse (las palabras)

slur[2] *n* **1** : ligado *m* (en música), mala pronunciación *f* (de las palabras) **2** ASPERSION : calumnia *f*, difamación *f*

slurp[1] [ˈslərp] *vi* : beber o comer haciendo ruido — *vt* : sorber ruidosamente

slurp[2] *n* : sorbo *m* (ruidoso)

slush [ˈslʌʃ] *n* : nieve *f* medio derretida

slut [ˈslʌt] *n* PROSTITUTE : ramera *f*, fulana *f*

sly [ˈslaɪ] *adj* **slier** [ˈslaɪər]; **sliest** [ˈslaɪəst] **1** CUNNING : astuto, taimado **2** UNDERHANDED : soplado — **slyly** *adv*

slyness [ˈslaɪnəs] *n* : astucia *f*

smack[1] [ˈsmæk] *vi* **to smack of** : oler a, saber a — *vt* **1** KISS : besar, plantarle un beso (a alguien) **2** SLAP : pegarle una bofetada (a alguien) **3 to smack one's lips** : relamerse

smack[2] *adv* : justo, exactamente ⟨smack in the face : en plena cara⟩

smack[3] *n* **1** TASTE, TRACE : sabor *m*, indicio *m* **2** : chasquido *m* (de los labios) **3** SLAP : bofetada *f* **4** KISS : beso *m*

small [ˈsmɔl] *adj* **1** : pequeño, chico ⟨a small house : una casa pequeña⟩ ⟨small change : monedas de poco valor⟩ **2** TRIVIAL : pequeño, insignificante

smallness [ˈsmɔlnəs] *n* : pequeñez *f*

smallpox [ˈsmɔlˌpɑks] *n* : viruela *f*

smart[1] [ˈsmɑrt] *vi* **1** STING : escocer, picar, arder **2** HURT : dolerse, resentirse ⟨to smart under a rejection : dolerse ante un rechazo⟩

smart[2] *adj* **1** BRIGHT : listo, vivo, inteligente **2** STYLISH : elegante — **smartly** *adv*

smart[3] *n* **1** PAIN : escozor *m*, dolor *m* **2 smarts** *npl* : inteligencia *f*

smartness [ˈsmɑrtnəs] *n* **1** INTELLIGENCE : inteligencia *f* **2** ELEGANCE : elegancia *f*

smash[1] [ˈsmæʃ] *vt* **1** BREAK : romper, quebrar, hacer pedazos **2** WRECK : destrozar, arruinar **3** CRASH : estrellar, chocar — *vi* **1** SHATTER : hacerse pedazos, hacerse añicos **2** COLLIDE, CRASH : estrellarse, chocar

smash[2] *n* **1** BLOW : golpe *m* **2** COLLISION : choque *m* **3** BANG, CRASH : estrépito *m*

smattering [ˈsmæţərɪŋ] *n* **1** : nociones *fpl* ⟨she has a smattering of programming : tiene nociones de programación⟩ **2** : un poco, unos cuantos ⟨a

smattering of spectators : unos cuantos espectadores⟩
smear[1] ['smɪr] *vt* **1** DAUB : embadurnar, untar (mantequilla, etc.) **2** SMUDGE : emborronar **3** SLANDER : calumniar, difamar
smear[2] *n* **1** SMUDGE : mancha *f* **2** SLANDER : calumnia *f*
smell[1] ['smɛl] *v* **smelled** *or* **smelt** ['smɛlt]; **smelling** *vt* : oler, olfatear ⟨to smell danger : olfatear el peligro⟩ — *vi* : oler ⟨to smell good : oler bien⟩
smell[2] *n* **1** : olfato *m*, sentido *m* del olfato **2** ODOR : olor *m*
smelly ['smɛli] *adj* **smellier; -est** : maloliente
smelt[1] ['smɛlt] *vt* : fundir
smelt[2] *n, pl* **smelts** *or* **smelt** : eperlano *m* (pez)
smile[1] ['smaɪl] *vi* **smiled; smiling** : sonreír
smile[2] *n* : sonrisa *f*
smirk[1] ['smərk] *vi* : sonreír con suficiencia
smirk[2] *n* : sonrisa *f* satisfecha
smite ['smaɪt] *vt* **smote** ['smo:t]; **smitten** ['smɪtən] *or* **smote; smiting** **1** STRIKE : golpear **2** AFFLICT : afligir
smith ['smɪθ] *n* : herrero *m*, -ra *f*
smithy ['smɪθi] *n, pl* **smithies** : herrería *f*
smock ['smɑk] *n* : bata *f*, blusón *m*
smog ['smɑg, 'smɔg] *n* : smog *m*
smoke[1] ['smo:k] *v* **smoked; smoking** *vi* **1** : echar humo, humear ⟨a smoking chimney : una chimenea que echa humo⟩ **2** : fumar ⟨I don't smoke : no fumo⟩ — *vt* : ahumar (carne, etc.)
smoke[2] *n* : humo *m*
smoke detector [dɪ'tɛktər] *n* : detector *m* de humo
smoker ['smo:kər] *n* : fumador *m*, -dora *f*
smokestack ['smo:kˌstæk] *n* : chimenea *f*
smoky ['smo:ki] *adj* **smokier; -est** **1** SMOKING : humeante **2** : a humo ⟨a smoky flavor : un sabor a humo⟩ **3** : lleno de humo ⟨a smoky room : un cuarto lleno de humo⟩
smolder ['smo:ldər] *vi* **1** : arder sin llama **2** : arder (en el corazón) ⟨his anger smoldered : su rabia ardía⟩
smooth[1] ['smu:ð] *vt* : alisar
smooth[2] *adj* **1** : liso (dícese de una superficie) ⟨smooth skin : piel lisa⟩ **2** : suave (dícese de un movimiento) ⟨a smooth landing : un aterrizaje suave⟩ **3** : sin grumos ⟨a smooth sauce : una salsa sin grumos⟩ **4** : fluido ⟨smooth writing : escritura fluida⟩
smoothly ['smu:ðli] *adv* **1** GENTLY, SOFTLY : suavemente **2** EASILY : con facilidad, sin problemas
smoothness ['smu:ðnəs] *n* : suavidad *f*
smother ['smʌðər] *vt* **1** SUFFOCATE : ahogar, sofocar **2** COVER : cubrir **3** SUPPRESS : contener — *vi* : asfixiarse
smudge[1] ['smʌʤ] *v* **smudged; smudging** *vt* : emborronar — *vi* : correrse
smudge[2] *n* : mancha *f*, borrón *m*
smug ['smʌg] *adj* **smugger; smuggest** : suficiente, pagado de sí mismo
smuggle ['smʌgəl] *vt* **-gled; -gling** : contrabandear, pasar de contrabando
smuggler ['smʌgələr] *n* : contrabandista *mf*
smugly ['smʌgli] *adv* : con suficiencia
smut ['smʌt] *n* **1** SOOT : tizne *m*, hollín *m* **2** FUNGUS : tizón *m* **3** OBSCENITY : obscenidad *f*, inmundicia *f*
smutty ['smʌṯi] *adj* **smuttier; -est** **1** SOOTY : tiznado **2** OBSCENE : obsceno, indecente
snack ['snæk] *n* : refrigerio *m*, bocado *m*, tentempié *m fam* ⟨an afternoon snack : una merienda⟩
snag[1] ['snæg] *v* **snagged; snagging** *vt* : enganchar — *vi* : engancharse
snag[2] *n* : problema *m*, inconveniente *m*
snail ['sneɪl] *n* : caracol *m*
snake ['sneɪk] *n* : culebra *f*, serpiente *f*
snakebite ['sneɪkˌbaɪt] *n* : mordedura *f* de serpiente
snap[1] ['snæp] *v* **snapped; snapping** *vi* **1** : intentar morder (dícese de un perro, etc.), picar (dícese de un pez) **2** : hablar con severidad ⟨he snapped at me! : ¡me gritó!⟩ **3** BREAK : romperse, quebrarse (haciendo un chasquido) — *vt* **1** BREAK : partir (en dos), quebrar **2** : hacer (algo) de un golpe ⟨to snap open : abrir de golpe⟩ **3** RETORT : decir bruscamente **4** CLICK : chasquear ⟨to snap one's fingers : chasquear los dedos⟩
snap[2] *n* **1** CLICK, CRACK : chasquido *m* **2** FASTENER : broche *m* **3** CINCH : cosa *f* fácil ⟨it's a snap : es facilísimo⟩
snapdragon ['snæpˌdrægən] *n* : dragón *m* (flor)
snapper ['snæpər] → **red snapper**
snappy ['snæpi] *adj* **snappier; -est** **1** FAST : rápido ⟨make it snappy! : ¡date prisa!⟩ **2** LIVELY : vivaz **3** CHILLY : frío **4** STYLISH : elegante
snapshot ['snæpˌʃɑt] *n* : instantánea *f*
snare[1] ['snær] *vt* **snared; snaring** : atrapar
snare[2] *n* : trampa *f*, red *f*
snare drum *n* : tambor *m* con bordón
snarl[1] ['snɑrl] *vi* **1** TANGLE : enmarañar, enredar **2** GROWL : gruñir
snarl[2] *n* **1** TANGLE : enredo *m*, maraña *f* **2** GROWL : gruñido *m*
snatch[1] ['snæʧ] *vt* : arrebatar
snatch[2] *n* : fragmento *m*
sneak[1] ['sni:k] *vi* : ir a hurtadillas — *vt* : hacer furtivamente ⟨to sneak a look : mirar con disimulo⟩ ⟨he sneaked a smoke : fumó un cigarrillo a escondidas⟩
sneak[2] *n* : soplón *m*, -plona *f*
sneakers ['sni:kərz] *npl* : tenis *mpl*, zapatillas *fpl*
sneaky ['sni:ki] *adj* **sneakier; -est** : solapado

sneer[1] ['snɪr] *vi* : sonreír con desprecio
sneer[2] *n* : sonrisa *f* de desprecio
sneeze[1] ['sni:z] *vi* **sneezed; sneezing** : estornudar
sneeze[2] *n* : estornudo *m*
snicker[1] ['snɪkər] *vi* : reírse disimuladamente
snicker[2] *n* : risita *f*
snide ['snaɪd] *adj* : sarcástico
sniff[1] ['snɪf] *vi* **1** SMELL : oler, husmear (dícese de los animales) **2 to sniff at** : despreciar, desdeñar — *vt* **1** SMELL : oler **2 to sniff out** : olerse, husmear
sniff[2] *n* **1** SNIFFING : aspiración *f* por la nariz **2** SMELL : olor *m*
sniffle ['snɪfəl] *vi* **-fled; -fling** : respirar con la nariz congestionada
sniffles ['snɪfəlz] *npl* : resfriado *m*
snip[1] ['snɪp] *vt* **snipped; snipping** : cortar (con tijeras)
snip[2] *n* : tijeretada *f*, recorte *m*
snipe[1] ['snaɪp] *vi* **sniped; sniping** : disparar
snipe[2] *n, pl* **snipes** *or* **snipe** : agachadiza *f*
sniper ['snaɪpər] *n* : francotirador *m*, -dora *f*
snippet ['snɪpət] *n* : fragmento *m* (de un texto, etc.)
snivel ['snɪvəl] *vi* **-veled** *or* **-velled; -veling** *or* **-velling 1** → **snuffle 2** WHINE : lloriquear
snob ['snɑb] *n* : esnob *mf*, snob *mf*
snobbery ['snɑbəri] *n, pl* **-beries** : esnobismo *m*
snobbish ['snɑbɪʃ] *adj* : esnob, snob
snobbishness ['snɑbɪʃnəs] *n* : esnobismo *m*
snoop[1] ['snu:p] *vi* : husmear, curiosear
snoop[2] *n* : fisgón *m*, -gona *f*
snooze[1] ['snu:z] *vi* **snoozed; snoozing** : dormitar
snooze[2] *n* : siestecita *f*, siestita *f*
snore[1] ['snor] *vi* **snored; snoring** : roncar
snore[2] *n* : ronquido *m*
snort[1] ['snɔrt] *vi* : bufar, resoplar
snort[2] *n* : bufido *m*, resoplo *m*
snout ['snaʊt] *n* : hocico *m*, morro *m*
snow[1] ['sno:] *vi* **1** : nevar ⟨I'm snowed in : estoy aislado por la nieve⟩ **2 to be snowed under** : estar inundado
snow[2] *n* : nieve *f*
snowball ['sno:ˌbɔl] *n* : bola *f* de nieve
snowdrift ['sno:ˌdrɪft] *n* : ventisquero *m*
snowfall ['sno:ˌfɔl] *n* : nevada *f*
snowplow ['sno:ˌplaʊ] *n* : quitanieves *m*
snowshoe ['sno:ˌʃu:] *n* : raqueta *f* (para nieve)
snowstorm ['sno:ˌstorm] *n* : tormenta *f* de nieve, ventisca *f*
snowy ['sno:i] *adj* **snowier; -est** : nevoso ⟨a snowy road : un camino nevado⟩
snub[1] ['snʌb] *vt* **snubbed; snubbing** : desairar
snub[2] *n* : desaire *m*
snub–nosed ['snʌbˌno:zd] *adj* : de nariz respingada
snuff[1] ['snʌf] *vt* **1** : apagar (una vela) **2** : sorber (algo) por la nariz
snuff[2] *n* : rapé *m*
snuffle ['snʌfəl] *vi* **-fled; -fling** : respirar con la nariz congestionada
snug ['snʌg] *adj* **snugger; snuggest 1** COMFORTABLE : cómodo **2** TIGHT : ajustado, ceñido ⟨snug pants : pantalones ajustados⟩
snuggle ['snʌgəl] *vi* **-gled; -gling** : acurrucarse ⟨to snuggle up to someone : arrimársele a alguien⟩
snugly ['snʌgli] *adv* **1** COMFORTABLY : cómodamente **2** : de manera ajustada ⟨the shirt fits snugly : la camisa queda ajustada⟩
so[1] ['so:] *adv* **1** (*referring to something indicated or suggested*) ⟨do you think so? : ¿tú crees?⟩ ⟨so it would seem : eso parece⟩ ⟨I told her so : se lo dije⟩ ⟨he's ready, or so he says : según dice, está listo⟩ ⟨it so happened that . . . : resultó que . . . ⟩ ⟨do it like so : hazlo así⟩ ⟨so be it : así sea⟩ **2** ALSO : también ⟨so do I : yo también⟩ **3** THUS : así, de esta manera **4** : tan ⟨he'd never been so happy : nunca había estado tan contento⟩ **5** CONSEQUENTLY : por lo tanto
so[2] *conj* **1** THEREFORE : así que **2** *or* **so that** : para que, así que, de manera que **3 so what?** : ¿y qué?
soak[1] ['so:k] *vi* : estar en remojo — *vt* **1** : poner en remojo **2 to soak up** ABSORB : absorber
soak[2] *n* : remojo *m*
soap[1] ['so:p] *vt* : enjabonar
soap[2] *n* : jabón *m*
soapsuds ['so:pˌsʌdz] → **suds**
soapy ['so:pi] *adj* **soapier; -est** : jabonoso ⟨a soapy taste : un gusto a jabón⟩ ⟨a soapy texture : una textura de jabón⟩
soar ['sor] *vi* **1** FLY : volar **2** RISE : remontar el vuelo (dícese de las aves) ⟨her hopes soared : su esperanza renació⟩ ⟨prices are soaring : los precios están subiendo vertiginosamente⟩
sob[1] ['sɑb] *vi* **sobbed; sobbing** : sollozar
sob[2] *n* : sollozo *m*
sober ['so:bər] *adj* **1** : sobrio ⟨he's not sober enough to drive : está demasiado borracho para manejar⟩ **2** SERIOUS : serio
soberly ['so:bərli] *adv* **1** : sobriamente **2** SERIOUSLY : seriamente
sobriety [sə'braɪəṭi, so-] *n* **1** : sobriedad *f* ⟨sobriety test : prueba de alcoholemia⟩ **2** SERIOUSNESS : seriedad *f*
so–called ['so:'kɔld] *adj* : supuesto, presunto ⟨the so-called experts : los expertos, así llamados⟩
soccer ['sɑkər] *n* : futbol *m*, fútbol *m*
sociable ['so:ʃəbəl] *adj* : sociable
social[1] ['so:ʃəl] *adj* : social — **socially** *adv*
social[2] *n* : reunión *f* social

socialism [ˈsoːʃəˌlɪzəm] *n* : socialismo *m*
socialist[1] [ˈsoːʃəlɪst] *adj* : socialista
socialist[2] *n* : socialista *mf*
socialize [ˈsoːʃəˌlaɪz] *v* **-ized; -izing** *vt* **1** NATIONALIZE : nacionalizar **2** : socializar (en psicología) — *vi* : alternar, circular ⟨to socialize with friends : alternar con amigos⟩
social work *n* : asistencia *f* social
society [səˈsaɪət̬i] *n, pl* **-eties** **1** COMPANIONSHIP : compañía *f* **2** : sociedad *f* ⟨a democratic society : una sociedad democrática⟩ ⟨high society : alta sociedad⟩ **3** ASSOCIATION : sociedad *f*, asociación *f*
socioeconomic [ˌsoːsioˌiːkəˈnɑmɪk, -ˌɛkə-] *adj* : socioeconómico
sociology [ˌsoːsiˈɑləʤi] *n* : sociología *f*
sociological [ˌsoːsiəˈlɑʤɪkəl] *adj* : sociológico
sociologist [ˌsoːsiˈɑləʤɪst] *n* : sociólogo *m*, -ga *f*
sock[1] [ˈsɑk] *vt* : pegar, golpear, darle un puñetazo a
sock[2] *n* **1** *pl* **socks** *or* **sox** [ˈsɑks] : calcetín *m*, media *f* ⟨shoes and socks : zapatos y calcetines⟩ **2** *pl* **socks** [ˈsɑks] PUNCH : puñetazo *m*
socket [ˈsɑkət] *n* **1** *or* **electric socket** : enchufe *m*, toma *f* de corriente **2** : glena *f* (de una articulación) ⟨shoulder socket : glena del hombro⟩ **3** **eye socket** : órbita *f*, cuenca *f*
sod[1] [ˈsɑd] *vt* **sodded; sodding** : cubrir de césped
sod[2] *n* TURF : césped *m*, tepe *m*
soda [ˈsoːdə] *n* **1** *or* **soda water** : soda *f* **2** *or* **soda pop** : gaseosa *f*, refresco *m* **3** *or* **ice–cream soda** : refresco *m* con helado
sodden [ˈsɑdən] *adj* SOGGY : empapado
sodium [ˈsoːdiəm] *n* : sodio *m*
sodium bicarbonate *n* : bicarbonato *m* de soda
sodium chloride → **salt**
sofa [ˈsoːfə] *n* : sofá *m*
soft [ˈsɔft] *adj* **1** : blando ⟨a soft pillow : una almohada blanda⟩ **2** SMOOTH : suave (dícese de las texturas, de los sonidos, etc.) **3** NONALCOHOLIC : no alcohólico ⟨a soft drink : un refresco⟩
softball [ˈsɔftˌbɔl] *n* : softbol *m*
soften [ˈsɔfən] *vt* : ablandar (algo sólido), suavizar (la piel, un golpe, etc.), amortiguar (un impacto) — *vi* : ablandarse, suavizarse
softly [ˈsɔftli] *adv* : suavemente ⟨she spoke softly : habló en voz baja⟩
softness [ˈsɔftnəs] *n* **1** : blandura *f*, lo blando (de una almohada, de la mantequilla, etc.) **2** SMOOTHNESS : suavidad *f*
software [ˈsɔftˌwær] *n* : software *m*
soggy [ˈsɑgi] *adj* **soggier; -est** : empapado
soil[1] [ˈsɔɪl] *vt* : ensuciar — *vi* : ensuciarse
soil[2] *n* **1** DIRTINESS : suciedad *f* **2** DIRT, EARTH : suelo *m*, tierra *f* **3** COUNTRY : patria *f* ⟨her native soil : su tierra natal⟩
sojourn[1] [ˈsoːˌʤərn, soːˈʤərn] *vi* : pasar una temporada
sojourn[2] *n* : estadía *f*, estancia *f*, permanencia *f*
solace [ˈsɑləs] *n* : consuelo *m*
solar [ˈsoːlər] *adj* : solar ⟨the solar system : el sistema solar⟩
sold → **sell**
solder[1] [ˈsɑdər, ˈsɔ-] *vt* : soldar
solder[2] *n* : soldadura *f*
soldier[1] [ˈsoːlʤər] *vi* : servir como soldado
soldier[2] *n* : soldado *mf*
sole[1] [ˈsoːl] *adj* : único
sole[2] *n* **1** : suela *f* (de un zapato) **2** : lenguado *m* (pez)
solely [ˈsoːli] *adv* : únicamente, sólo
solemn [ˈsɑləm] *adj* : solemne, serio — **solemnly** *adv*
solemnity [səˈlɛmnət̬i] *n, pl* **-ties** : solemnidad *f*
solicit [səˈlɪsət] *vt* : solicitar
solicitous [səˈlɪsət̬əs] *adj* : solícito
solicitude [səˈlɪsəˌtuːd, -ˌtjuːd] *n* : solicitud *f*
solid[1] [ˈsɑləd] *adj* **1** : macizo ⟨a solid rubber ball : una bola maciza de caucho⟩ **2** CUBIC : tridimensional **3** COMPACT : compacto, denso **4** STURDY : sólido **5** CONTINUOUS : seguido, continuo ⟨two solid hours : dos horas seguidas⟩ ⟨a solid line : una línea continua⟩ **6** UNANIMOUS : unánime **7** DEPENDABLE : serio, fiable **8** PURE : macizo, puro ⟨solid gold : oro macizo⟩
solid[2] *n* : sólido *m*
solidarity [ˌsɑləˈdærət̬i] *n* : solidaridad *f*
solidify [səˈlɪdəˌfaɪ] *v* **-fied; -fying** *vt* : solidificar — *vi* : solidificarse
solidity [səˈlɪdət̬i] *n, pl* **-ties** : solidez *f*
solidly [ˈsɑlədli] *adv* **1** : sólidamente **2** UNANIMOUSLY : unánimemente
soliloquy [səˈlɪləkwi] *n, pl* **-quies** : soliloquio *m*
solitaire [ˈsɑləˌtɛr] *n* : solitario *m*
solitary [ˈsɑləˌtɛri] *adj* **1** ALONE : solitario **2** SECLUDED : apartado, retirado **3** SINGLE : solo
solitude [ˈsɑləˌtuːd, -ˌtjuːd] *n* : soledad *f*
solo[1] [ˈsoːˌloː] *vi* : volar en solitario (dícese de un piloto)
solo[2] *adv & adj* : en solitario, a solas
solo[3] *n, pl* **solos** : solo *m*
soloist [ˈsoːloɪst] *n* : solista *mf*
solstice [ˈsɑlstɪs] *n* : solsticio *m*
soluble [ˈsɑljəbəl] *adj* : soluble
solution [səˈluːʃən] *n* : solución *f*
solve [ˈsɑlv] *vt* **solved; solving** : resolver, solucionar
solvency [ˈsɑlvəntsi] *n* : solvencia *f*
solvent [ˈsɑlvənt] *n* : solvente *m*
Somali [soˈmɑli, sə-] *n* : somalí *mf* — **Somali** *adj*
somber [ˈsɑmbər] *adj* **1** DARK : sombrío, oscuro ⟨somber colors : colores

oscuros⟩ **2** GRAVE : sombrío, serio **3** MELANCHOLY : sombrío, lúgubre

sombrero [səmˈbrɛrˌo:] *n, pl* **-ros** : sombrero *m* (mexicano)

some[1] [ˈsʌm] *adj* **1** : un, algún ⟨some lady stopped me : una mujer me detuvo⟩ ⟨some distant galaxy : alguna galaxia lejana⟩ **2** : algo de, un poco de ⟨he drank some water : tomó (un poco de) agua⟩ **3** : unos ⟨do you want some apples? : ¿quieres unas manzanas?⟩ ⟨some years ago : hace varios años⟩

some[2] *pron* **1** : algunos ⟨some went, others stayed : algunos se fueron, otros se quedaron⟩ **2** : un poco, algo ⟨there's some left : queda un poco⟩ ⟨I have gum; do you want some? : tengo chicle, ¿quieres?⟩

somebody [ˈsʌmbədi, -ˌbɑdi] *pron* : alguien

someday [ˈsʌmˌdeɪ] *adv* : algún día

somehow [ˈsʌmˌhaʊ] *adv* **1** : de alguna manera, de algún modo ⟨I'll do it somehow : lo haré de alguna manera⟩ **2** : por alguna razón ⟨somehow I don't trust her : por alguna razón no me fío de ella⟩

someone [ˈsʌmˌwʌn] *pron* : alguien

someplace [ˈsʌmˌpleɪs] → **somewhere**

somersault[1] [ˈsʌmərˌsɔlt] *vi* : dar volteretas, dar un salto mortal

somersault[2] *n* : voltereta *f*, salto *m* mortal

something [ˈsʌmθɪŋ] *pron* : algo ⟨I want something else : quiero otra cosa⟩ ⟨she's writing a novel or something : está escribiendo una novela o no sé qué⟩

sometime [ˈsʌmˌtaɪm] *adv* : algún día, en algún momento ⟨sometime next month : durante el mes que viene⟩

sometimes [ˈsʌmˌtaɪmz] *adv* : a veces, algunas veces, de vez en cuando

somewhat [ˈsʌmˌhwʌt, -ˌhwɑt] *adv* : algo, un tanto

somewhere [ˈsʌmˌ*h*wɛr] *adv* **1** (*indicating location*) : en algún lugar ⟨it must be somewhere else : estará en otra parte⟩ **2** (*indicating destination*) : a algún lugar

son [ˈsʌn] *n* : hijo *m*

sonar [ˈso:ˌnɑr] *n* : sonar *m*

sonata [səˈnɑt̬ə] *n* : sonata *f*

song [ˈsɔŋ] *n* : canción *f*, canto *m* (de un pájaro)

songbird [ˈsɔŋˌbərd] *n* : pájaro *m* cantor

songwriter [ˈsɔŋˌraɪt̬ər] *n* : compositor *m*, -tora *f*

sonic [ˈsɑnɪk] *adj* **1** : sónico **2 sonic boom** : estampido *m* sónico

son–in–law [ˈsʌnɪnˌlɔ] *n, pl* **sons–in–law** : yerno *m*, hijo *m* político

sonnet [ˈsɑnət] *n* : soneto *m*

sonorous [ˈsɑnərəs, səˈnorəs] *adj* : sonoro

soon [ˈsu:n] *adv* **1** : pronto, dentro de poco ⟨he'll arrive soon : llegará pronto⟩ **2** QUICKLY : pronto ⟨as soon as possible : lo más pronto posible⟩ ⟨the sooner the better : cuanto antes mejor⟩ **3** : de buena gana ⟨I'd sooner walk : prefiero caminar⟩

soot [ˈsʊt, ˈsu:t, ˈsʌt] *n* : hollín *m*, tizne *m*

soothe [ˈsu:ð] *vt* **soothed; soothing 1** CALM : calmar, tranquilizar **2** RELIEVE : aliviar

soothsayer [ˈsu:θˌseɪər] *n* : adivino *m*, -na *f*

sooty [ˈsʊt̬i, ˈsu:-, ˈsʌ-] *adj* **sootier; -est** : cubierto de hollín, tiznado

sop[1] [ˈsɑp] *vt* **sopped; sopping 1** DIP : mojar **2** SOAK : empapar **3 to sop up** : rebañar, absorber

sop[2] *n* **1** CONCESSION : concesión *f* **2** BRIBE : soborno *m*

sophisticated [səˈfɪstəˌkeɪt̬əd] *adj* **1** COMPLEX : complejo **2** WORLDLY-WISE : sofisticado

sophistication [səˌfɪstəˈkeɪʃən] *n* **1** COMPLEXITY : complejidad *f* **2** URBANITY : sofisticación *f*

sophomore [ˈsɑfˌmor, ˈsɑfəˌmor] *n* : estudiante *mf* de segundo año

soporific [ˌsɑpəˈrɪfɪk, ˌso:-] *adj* : soporífero

soprano [səˈpræˌno:] *n, pl* **-nos** : soprano *mf*

sorcerer [ˈsɔrsərər] *n* : hechicero *m*, brujo *m*, mago *m*

sorceress [ˈsɔrsərəs] *n* : hechicera *f*, bruja *f*, maga *f*

sorcery [ˈsɔrsəri] *n* : hechicería *f*, brujería *f*

sordid [ˈsɔrdɪd] *adj* : sórdido

sore[1] [ˈsor] *adj* **sorer; sorest 1** PAINFUL : dolorido, doloroso ⟨I have a sore throat : me duele la garganta⟩ **2** ACUTE, SEVERE : extremo, grande ⟨in sore straits : en grandes apuros⟩ **3** ANGRY : enojado, enfadado

sore[2] *n* : llaga *f*

sorely [ˈsorli] *adv* : muchísimo ⟨it was sorely needed : se necesitaba urgentemente⟩ ⟨she was sorely missed : la echaban mucho de menos⟩

soreness [ˈsornəs] *n* : dolor *m*

sorghum [ˈsɔrgəm] *n* : sorgo *m*

sorority [səˈrɔrət̬i] *n, pl* **-ties** : hermandad *f* (de estudiantes femeninas)

sorrel [ˈsɔrəl] *n* **1** : alazán *m* (color o animal) **2** : acedera *f* (hierba)

sorrow [ˈsɑrˌo:] *n* : pesar *m*, dolor *m*, pena *f*

sorrowful [ˈsɑrofəl] *adj* : triste, afligido, apenado

sorrowfully [ˈsɑrofəli] *adv* : con tristeza

sorry [ˈsɑri] *adj* **sorrier; -est 1** PITIFUL : lastimero, lastimoso **2 to be sorry** : sentir, lamentar ⟨I'm sorry : lo siento⟩ **3 to feel sorry for** : compadecer ⟨I feel sorry for him : me da pena⟩

sort[1] [ˈsɔrt] *vt* **1** : dividir en grupos **2** CLASSIFY : clasificar **3 to sort out** ORGANIZE : poner en orden **4 to sort out** RESOLVE : resolver

sort² *n* **1** KIND : tipo *m*, clase *f* ⟨a sort of writer : una especie de escritor⟩ **2** NATURE : índole *f* **3 out of sorts** : de mal humor
sortie [ˈsɔrṭi, sɔrˈtiː] *n* : salida *f*
SOS [ˌɛsˌoːˈɛs] *n* : SOS *m*
so–so [ˈsoːˈsoː] *adj & adv* : así así, de modo regular
soufflé [suːˈfleɪ] *n* : suflé *m*
sought → **seek**
soul [ˈsoːl] *n* **1** SPIRIT : alma *f* **2** ESSENCE : esencia *f* **3** PERSON : persona *f*, alma *f*
soulful [ˈsoːlfəl] *adj* : conmovedor, lleno de emoción
sound¹ [ˈsaʊnd] *vt* **1** : sondar (en navegación) **2** *or* **to sound out** PROBE : sondear **3** : hacer sonar, tocar (una trompeta, etc.) — *vi* **1** : sonar ⟨the alarm sounded : la alarma sonó⟩ **2** SEEM : parecer
sound² *adj* **1** HEALTHY : sano ⟨safe and sound : sano y salvo⟩ ⟨of sound mind and body : en pleno uso de sus facultades⟩ **2** FIRM, SOLID : sólido **3** SENSIBLE : lógico, sensato **4** DEEP : profundo ⟨a sound sleep : un sueño profundo⟩
sound³ *n* **1** : sonido *m* ⟨the speed of sound : la velocidad del sonido⟩ **2** NOISE : sonido *m*, ruido *m* ⟨I heard a sound : oí un sonido⟩ **3** CHANNEL : brazo *m* de mar, canal *m* (ancho)
soundless [ˈsaʊndləs] *adj* : sordo
soundlessly [ˈsaʊndləsli] *adv* : silenciosamente
soundly [ˈsaʊndli] *adv* **1** SOLIDLY : sólidamente **2** SENSIBLY : lógicamente, sensatamente **3** DEEPLY : profundamente ⟨sleeping soundly : durmiendo profundamente⟩
soundness [ˈsaʊndnəs] *n* **1** SOLIDITY : solidez *f* **2** SENSIBLENESS : sensatez *f*, solidez *f*
soundproof [ˈsaʊndˌpruːf] *adj* : insonorizado
soundtrack [ˈsaʊndˌtræk] *n* : banda *f* sonora
sound wave *n* : onda *f* sonora
soup [ˈsuːp] *n* : sopa *f*
sour¹ [ˈsaʊər] *vi* : agriarse, cortarse (dícese de la leche) — *vt* : agriar, cortar (leche)
sour² *adj* **1** ACID : agrio, ácido (dícese de la fruta, etc.), cortado (dícese de la leche) **2** DISAGREEABLE : desagradable, agrio
source [ˈsors] *n* : fuente *f*, origen *m*, nacimiento *m* (de un río)
sourness [ˈsaʊərnəs] *n* : acidez *f*
south¹ [ˈsaʊθ] *adv* : al sur, hacia el sur ⟨the window looks south : la ventana mira al sur⟩ ⟨she continued south : continuó hacia el sur⟩
south² *adj* : sur, del sur ⟨the south entrance : la entrada sur⟩ ⟨South America : Sudamérica, América del Sur⟩
south³ *n* : sur *m*
South African *n* : sudafricano *m*, -na *f* — **South African** *adj*
South American¹ *adj* : sudamericano, suramericano
South American² *n* : sudamericano *m*, -na *f*; suramericano *m*, -na *f*
southbound [ˈsaʊθˌbaʊnd] *adj* : con rumbo al sur
southeast¹ [saʊˈθiːst] *adj* : sureste, sudeste, del sureste
southeast² *n* : sureste *m*, sudeste *m*
southeasterly [saʊˈθiːstərli] *adv & adj* **1** : del sureste (dícese del viento) **2** : hacia el sureste
southeastern [saʊˈθiːstərn] *adj* → **southeast**¹
southerly [ˈsʌðərli] *adv & adj* : del sur
southern [ˈsʌðərn] *adj* : sur, sureño, meridional, austral ⟨a southern city : una ciudad del sur del país, una ciudad meridional⟩ ⟨the southern side : el lado sur⟩
Southerner [ˈsʌðərnər] *n* : sureño *m*, -ña *f*
South Pole : Polo *m* Sur
southward [ˈsaʊθwərd] *or* **southwards** [-wərdz] *adv & adj* : hacia el sur
southwest¹ [saʊθˈwɛst, *as a nautical term often* saʊˈwɛst] *adj* : suroeste, sudoeste, del suroeste
southwest² *n* : suroeste *m*, sudoeste *m*
southwesterly [saʊθˈwɛstərli] *adv & adj* **1** : del suroeste (dícese del viento) **2** : hacia el suroeste
southwestern [saʊθˈwɛstərn] *adj* → **southwest**¹
souvenir [ˌsuːvəˈnɪr, ˈsuːvəˌ-] *n* : recuerdo *m*, souvenir *m*
sovereign¹ [ˈsɑvərən] *adj* : soberano
sovereign² *n* **1** : soberano *m*, -na *f* (monarca) **2** : soberano *m* (moneda)
sovereignty [ˈsɑvərənti] *n, pl* **-ties** : soberanía *f*
Soviet [ˈsoːviˌɛt, ˈsɑ-, -viət] *adj* : soviético
sow¹ [ˈsoː] *vt* **sowed; sown** [ˈsoːn] *or* **sowed; sowing 1** PLANT : sembrar **2** SCATTER : esparcir
sow² [ˈsaʊ] *n* : cerda *f*
sox → **sock**
soy [ˈsɔɪ] *n* : soya *f*, soja *f*
soybean [ˈsɔɪˌbiːn] *n* : soya *f*, soja *f*
spa [ˈspɑ] *n* : balneario *m*
space¹ [ˈspeɪs] *vt* **spaced; spacing** : espaciar
space² *n* **1** PERIOD : espacio *m*, lapso *m*, período *m* **2** ROOM : espacio *m*, sitio *m*, lugar *m* ⟨is there space for me? : ¿hay sitio para mí?⟩ **3** : espacio *m* ⟨blank space : espacio en blanco⟩ **4** : espacio *m* (en física) **5** PLACE : plaza *f*, sitio *m* ⟨to reserve space : reservar plazas⟩ ⟨parking space : sitio para estacionarse⟩
spacecraft [ˈspeɪsˌkræft] *n* : nave *f* espacial
spaceflight [ˈspeɪsˌflaɪt] *n* : vuelo *m* espacial

spaceman [ˈspeɪsmən, -ˌmæn] *n, pl* **-men** [-mən, -ˌmɛn] : astronauta *m*, cosmonauta *m*

spaceship [ˈspeɪsˌʃɪp] *n* : nave *f* espacial

space shuttle *n* : transbordador *m* espacial

space suit *n* : traje *m* espacial

spacious [ˈspeɪʃəs] *adj* : espacioso, amplio

spade[1] [ˈspeɪd] *v* **spaded; spading** *vt* : palear — *vi* : usar una pala

spade[2] *n* **1** SHOVEL : pala *f* **2** : pica *f* (naipe)

spaghetti [spəˈgɛţi] *n* : espagueti *m*, espaguetis *mpl*, spaghetti *mpl*

spam [ˈspæm] *n* : spam *m*, correo *m* electrónico no solicitado

span[1] [ˈspæn] *vt* **spanned; spanning** : abarcar (un período de tiempo), extenderse sobre (un espacio)

span[2] *n* **1** : lapso *m*, espacio *m* (de tiempo) ⟨life span : duración de la vida⟩ **2** : luz *f* (entre dos soportes)

spangle [ˈspæŋgəl] *n* : lentejuela *f*

Spaniard [ˈspænjərd] *n* : español *m*, -ñola *f*

spaniel [ˈspænjəl] *n* : spaniel *m*

Spanish[1] [ˈspænɪʃ] *adj* : español

Spanish[2] *n* **1** : español *m* (idioma) **2 the Spanish** *npl* : los españoles

spank [ˈspæŋk] *vt* : darle nalgadas (a alguien)

spar[1] [ˈspɑr] *vi* **sparred; sparring** : entrenarse (en boxeo)

spar[2] *n* : palo *m*, verga *f* (de un barco)

spare[1] [ˈspær] *vt* **spared; sparing 1** : perdonar ⟨to spare someone's life : perdonarle la vida a alguien⟩ **2** SAVE : ahorrar, evitar ⟨I'll spare you the trouble : le evitaré la molestia⟩ **3** : prescindir de ⟨I can't spare her : no puedo prescindir de ella⟩ ⟨can you spare a dollar? : ¿me das un dólar?⟩ **4** STINT : escatimar ⟨they spared no expense : no repararon en gastos⟩ **5 to spare** : de sobra

spare[2] *adj* **1** : de repuesto, de recambio ⟨spare tire : llanta de repuesto⟩ **2** EXCESS : de más, de sobra ⟨spare time : tiempo libre⟩ **3** LEAN : delgado

spare[3] *n or* **spare part** : repuesto *m*, recambio *m*

sparing [ˈspærɪŋ] *adj* : parco, económico — **sparingly** *adv*

spark[1] [ˈspɑrk] *vi* : chispear, echar chispas — *vt* PROVOKE : despertar, provocar ⟨to spark interest : despertar interés⟩

spark[2] *n* **1** : chispa *f* ⟨to throw off sparks : echar chispas⟩ **2** GLIMMER, TRACE : destello *m*, pizca *f*

sparkle[1] [ˈspɑrkəl] *vi* **-kled; -kling 1** FLASH, SHINE : destellar, centellear, brillar **2** : estar muy animado (dícese de una conversación, etc.)

sparkle[2] *n* : destello *m*, centelleo *m*

sparkler [ˈspɑrklər] *n* : luz *f* de bengala

spark plug *n* : bujía *f*

sparrow [ˈspæroː] *n* : gorrión *m*

sparse [ˈspɑrs] *adj* **sparser; -est** : escaso — **sparsely** *adv*

spasm [ˈspæzəm] *n* **1** : espasmo *m* (muscular) **2** BURST, FIT : arrebato *m*

spasmodic [spæzˈmɑdɪk] *adj* **1** : espasmódico **2** SPORADIC : irregular, esporádico — **spasmodically** [-dɪkli] *adv*

spastic [ˈspæstɪk] *adj* : espástico

spat[1] → **spit**[1]

spat[2] [ˈspæt] *n* : discusión *f*, disputa *f*, pelea *f*

spatial [ˈspeɪʃəl] *adj* : espacial

spatter[1] [ˈspæţər] *v* : salpicar

spatter[2] *n* : salpicadura *f*

spatula [ˈspætʃələ] *n* : espátula *f*, paleta *f* (para servir)

spawn[1] [ˈspɔn] *vi* : desovar, frezar — *vt* GENERATE : generar, producir

spawn[2] *n* : hueva *f*, freza *f*

spay [ˈspeɪ] *vt* : esterilizar (una perra, etc.)

speak [ˈspiːk] *v* **spoke** [ˈspoːk]; **spoken** [ˈspoːkən]; **speaking** *vi* **1** TALK : hablar ⟨to speak to someone : hablar con alguien⟩ ⟨who's speaking? : ¿de parte de quien?⟩ ⟨so to speak : por así decirlo⟩ **2 to speak out** : hablar claramente **3 to speak out against** : denunciar **4 to speak up** : hablar en voz alta **5 to speak up for** : defender — *vt* **1** SAY : decir ⟨she spoke her mind : habló con franqueza⟩ **2** : hablar (un idioma)

speaker [ˈspiːkər] *n* **1** : hablante *mf* ⟨a native speaker : un hablante nativo⟩ **2** : orador *m*, -dora *f* ⟨the keynote speaker : el orador principal⟩ **3** LOUDSPEAKER : altavoz *m*, altoparlante *m*

spear[1] [ˈspɪr] *vt* : atravesar con una lanza

spear[2] *n* : lanza *f*

spearhead[1] [ˈspɪrˌhɛd] *vt* : encabezar

spearhead[2] *n* : punta *f* de lanza

spearmint [ˈspɪrmɪnt] *n* : menta *f* verde

special [ˈspɛʃəl] *adj* : especial ⟨nothing special : nada en especial, nada en particular⟩ — **specially** *adv*

specialist [ˈspɛʃəlɪst] *n* : especialista *mf*

specialization [ˌspɛʃələˈzeɪʃən] *n* : especialización *f*

specialize [ˈspɛʃəˌlaɪz] *vi* **-ized; -izing** : especializarse

specialty [ˈspɛʃəlţi] *n, pl* **-ties** : especialidad *f*

species [ˈspiːˌʃiːz, -ˌsiːz] *ns & pl* : especie *f*

specific [spɪˈsɪfɪk] *adj* : específico, determinado — **specifically** [-fɪkli] *adv*

specification [ˌspɛsəfəˈkeɪʃən] *n* : especificación *f*

specify [ˈspɛsəˌfaɪ] *vt* **-fied; -fying** : especificar

specimen [ˈspɛsəmən] *n* **1** SAMPLE : espécimen *m*, muestra *f* **2** EXAMPLE : espécimen *m*, ejemplar *m*

speck [ˈspɛk] *n* **1** SPOT : manchita *f* **2** BIT, TRACE : mota *f*, pizca *f*, ápice *m*

speckled [ˈspɛkəld] *adj* : moteado

spectacle [ˈspɛktɪkəl] *n* **1** : espectáculo *m* **2 spectacles** *npl* GLASSES : lentes *fpl*, gafas *fpl*, anteojos *mpl*, espejuelos *mpl*
spectacular [spɛkˈtækjələr] *adj* : espectacular
spectator [ˈspɛkˌteɪt̬ər] *n* : espectador *m*, -dora *f*
specter *or* **spectre** [ˈspɛktər] *n* : espectro *m*, fantasma *m*
spectrum [ˈspɛktrəm] *n, pl* **spectra** [-trə] *or* **spectrums** **1** : espectro *m* (de colores, etc.) **2** RANGE : gama *f*, abanico *m*
speculate [ˈspɛkjəˌleɪt] *vi* **-lated; -lating** **1** : especular (en finanzas) **2** WONDER : preguntarse, hacer conjeturas
speculation [ˌspɛkjəˈleɪʃən] *n* : especulación *f*
speculative [ˈspɛkjəˌleɪt̬ɪv] *adj* : especulativo
speculator [ˈspɛkjəˌleɪt̬ər] *n* : especulador *m*, -dora *f*
speech [ˈspiːtʃ] *n* **1** : habla *f*, modo *m* de hablar, expresión *f* **2** ADDRESS : discurso *m*
speechless [ˈspiːtʃləs] *adj* : enmudecido, estupefacto
speed[1] [ˈspiːd] *v* **sped** [ˈspɛd] *or* **speeded; speeding** *vi* **1** : ir a toda velocidad, correr a toda prisa ⟨he sped off : se fue a toda velocidad⟩ **2** : conducir a exceso de velocidad ⟨a ticket for speeding : una multa por exceso de velocidad⟩ — *vt* **to speed up** : acelerar
speed[2] *n* **1** SWIFTNESS : rapidez *f* **2** VELOCITY : velocidad *f*
speedboat [ˈspiːdˌboːt] *n* : lancha *f* motora
speed bump *n* : badén *m*
speed limit *n* : velocidad *f* máxima, límite *m* de velocidad
speedometer [spɪˈdɑmət̬ər] *n* : velocímetro *m*
speedup [ˈspiːdˌʌp] *n* : aceleración *f*
speedy [ˈspiːdi] *adj* **speedier; -est** : rápido — **speedily** [-dəli] *adv*
spell[1] [ˈspɛl] *vt* **1** : escribir, deletrear (verbalmente) ⟨how do you spell it? : ¿cómo se escribe?, ¿cómo se deletrea?⟩ **2** MEAN : significar ⟨that could spell trouble : eso puede significar problemas⟩ **3** RELIEVE : relevar
spell[2] *n* **1** TURN : turno *m* **2** PERIOD, TIME : período *m* (de tiempo) **3** ENCHANTMENT : encanto *m*, hechizo *m*, maleficio *m*
spellbound [ˈspɛlˌbaʊnd] *adj* : embelesado
speller [ˈspɛlər] *n* : persona *f* que escribe ⟨she's a good speller : tiene buena ortografía⟩
spelling [ˈspɛlɪŋ] *n* : ortografía *f*
spend [ˈspɛnd] *vt* **spent** [ˈspɛnt]; **spending** **1** : gastar (dinero, etc.) **2** PASS : pasar (el tiempo) ⟨to spend time on : dedicar tiempo a⟩
spendthrift [ˈspɛndˌθrɪft] *n* : derrochador *m*, -dora *f*; despilfarrador *m*, -dora *f*
sperm [ˈspərm] *n, pl* **sperm** *or* **sperms** : esperma *mf*
spew [ˈspjuː] *vi* : salir a chorros — *vt* : vomitar, arrojar (lava, etc.)
sphere [ˈsfɪr] *n* : esfera *f*
spherical [ˈsfɪrɪkəl, ˈsfɛr-] *adj* : esférico
spice[1] [ˈspaɪs] *vt* **spiced; spicing** **1** SEASON : condimentar, sazonar **2** *or* **to spice up** : salpimentar, hacer más interesante
spice[2] *n* **1** : especia *f* **2** FLAVOR, INTEREST : sabor *m* ⟨the spice of life : la sal de la vida⟩
spick–and–span [ˈspɪkənd̬ˈspæn] *adj* : limpio y ordenado
spicy [ˈspaɪsi] *adj* **spicier; -est** **1** SPICED : condimentado, sazonado **2** HOT : picante **3** RACY : picante
spider [ˈspaɪdər] *n* : araña *f*
spigot [ˈspɪgət, -kət] *n* : llave *f*, grifo *m*, canilla *Arg, Uru*
spike[1] [ˈspaɪk] *vt* **spiked; spiking** **1** FASTEN : clavar (con clavos grandes) **2** PIERCE : atravesar **3** : añadir alcohol a ⟨he spiked her drink with rum : le puso ron a la bebida⟩
spike[2] *n* **1** : clavo *m* grande **2** CLEAT : clavo *m* **3** : remache *m* (en voleibol) **4** PEAK : pico *m*
spill[1] [ˈspɪl] *vt* **1** SHED : derramar, verter ⟨to spill blood : derrame sangre⟩ **2** DIVULGE : revelar, divulgar — *vi* : derramarse
spill[2] *n* **1** SPILLING : derrame *m*, vertido *m* ⟨oil spill : derrame de petróleo⟩ **2** FALL : caída *f*
spin[1] [ˈspɪn] *v* **spun** [ˈspʌn]; **spinning** *vi* **1** : hilar **2** TURN : girar **3** REEL : dar vueltas ⟨my head is spinning : la cabeza me está dando vueltas⟩ — *vt* **1** : hilar (hilo, etc.) **2** : tejer ⟨to spin a web : tejer una telaraña⟩ **3** TWIRL : hacer girar
spin[2] *n* : vuelta *f*, giro *m* ⟨to go for a spin : dar una vuelta (en coche)⟩
spinach [ˈspɪnɪtʃ] *n* : espinacas *fpl*, espinaca *f*
spinal column [ˈspaɪnəl] *n* BACKBONE : columna *f* vertebral
spinal cord *n* : médula *f* espinal
spindle [ˈspɪndəl] *n* **1** : huso *m* (para hilar) **2** : eje *m* (de un mecanismo)
spindly [ˈspɪndli] *adj* : larguirucho *fam*, largo y débil (dícese de una planta)
spine [ˈspaɪn] *n* **1** BACKBONE : columna *f* vertebral, espina *f* dorsal **2** QUILL : púa *f* (de un animal) **3** THORN : espina *f* **4** : lomo *m* (de un libro)
spineless [ˈspaɪnləs] *adj* **1** : sin púas, sin espinas **2** INVERTEBRATE : invertebrado **3** WEAK : débil (de carácter)
spinet [ˈspɪnət] *n* : espineta *f*
spinster [ˈspɪntstər] *n* : soltera *f*
spiny [ˈspaɪni] *adj* **spinier; -est** : con púas (dícese de los animales), espinoso (dícese de las plantas)

spiral[1] ['spaɪrəl] *vi* **-raled** *or* **-ralled; -raling** *or* **-ralling** : ir en espiral
spiral[2] *adj* : espiral, en espiral ⟨a spiral staircase : una escalera de caracol⟩
spiral[3] *n* : espiral *f*
spire ['spaɪr] *n* : aguja *f*
spirit[1] ['spɪrət] *vt* **to spirit away** : hacer desaparecer
spirit[2] *n* **1** : espíritu *m* ⟨body and spirit : cuerpo y espíritu⟩ **2** GHOST : espíritu *m*, fantasma *m* **3** MOOD : espíritu *m*, humor *m* ⟨in the spirit of friendship : en el espíritu de amistad⟩ ⟨to be in good spirits : estar de buen humor⟩ **4** ENTHUSIASM, VIVACITY : espíritu *m*, ánimo *m*, brío *m* **5 spirits** *npl* : licores *mpl*
spirited ['spɪrət̬əd] *adj* : animado, energético
spiritless ['spɪrətləs] *adj* : desanimado
spiritual[1] ['spɪrɪʧʊəl, -ʧəl] *adj* : espiritual — **spiritually** *adv*
spiritual[2] *n* : espiritual *m* (canción)
spiritualism ['spɪrɪʧʊəˌlɪzəm, -ʧə-] *n* : espiritismo *m*
spirituality [ˌspɪrɪʧʊ'æləṭi] *n, pl* **-ties** : espiritualidad *f*
spit[1] ['spɪt] *v* **spit** *or* **spat** ['spæt]; **spitting** : escupir
spit[2] *n* **1** SALIVA : saliva *f* **2** ROTISSERIE : asador *m* **3** POINT : lengua *f* (de tierra)
spite[1] ['spaɪt] *vt* **spited; spiting** : fastidiar, molestar
spite[2] *n* **1** : despecho *m*, rencor *m* **2 in spite of** : a pesar de (que), pese a (que)
spiteful ['spaɪtfəl] *adj* : malicioso, rencoroso
spitting image *n* **to be the spitting image of** : ser el vivo retrato de
spittle ['spɪṭəl] *n* : saliva *f*
splash[1] ['splæʃ] *vt* : salpicar — *vi* **1** : salpicar **2 to splash around** : chapotear
splash[2] *n* **1** SPLASHING : salpicadura *f* **2** SQUIRT : chorrito *m* **3** SPOT : mancha *f*
splatter ['splæṭər] → **spatter**
splay ['spleɪ] *vt* : extender (hacia afuera) ⟨to splay one's fingers : abrir los dedos⟩ — *vi* : extenderse (hacia afuera)
spleen ['spli:n] *n* **1** : bazo *m* (órgano) **2** ANGER, SPITE : ira *f*, rencor *m*
splendid ['splɛndəd] *adj* : espléndido — **splendidly** *adv*
splendor ['splɛndər] *n* : esplendor *m*
splice[1] ['splaɪs] *vt* **spliced; splicing** : empalmar, unir
splice[2] *n* : empalme *m*, unión *f*
splint ['splɪnt] *n* : tablilla *f*
splinter[1] ['splɪntər] *vt* : astillar — *vi* : astillarse
splinter[2] *n* : astilla *f*
split[1] ['splɪt] *v* **split; splitting** *vt* **1** CLEAVE : partir, hender ⟨to split wood : partir madera⟩ **2** BURST : romper, rajar ⟨to split open : abrir⟩ **3** DIVIDE, SHARE : dividir, repartir — *vi* **1** : partirse (dícese de la madera, etc.) **2** BURST, CRACK : romperse, rajarse **3** *or* **to split up** : dividirse
split[2] *n* **1** CRACK : rajadura *f* **2** TEAR : rotura *f* **3** DIVISION : división *f*, escisión *f*
splurge[1] ['splərʤ] *v* **splurged; splurging** *vt* : derrochar — *vi* : derrochar dinero
splurge[2] *n* : derroche *m*
spoil[1] ['spɔɪl] *vt* **1** PILLAGE : saquear **2** RUIN : estropear, arruinar **3** PAMPER : consentir, mimar — *vi* : estropearse, echarse a perder
spoil[2] *n* PLUNDER : botín *m*
spoke[1] → **speak**
spoke[2] ['spo:k] *n* : rayo *m* (de una rueda)
spoken → **speak**
spokesman ['spo:ksmən] *n, pl* **-men** [-mən, -ˌmɛn] : portavoz *mf*; vocero *m*, -ra *f*
spokeswoman ['spo:ksˌwʊmən] *n, pl* **-women** [-ˌwɪmən] : portavoz *f*, vocera *f*
sponge[1] ['spʌnʤ] *vt* **sponged; sponging** : limpiar con una esponja
sponge[2] *n* : esponja *f*
spongy ['spʌnʤi] *adj* **spongier; -est** : esponjoso
sponsor[1] ['spɑntsər] *vt* : patrocinar, auspiciar, apadrinar (a una persona)
sponsor[2] *n* : patrocinador *m*, -dora *f*; padrino *m*, madrina *f*
sponsorship ['spɑntsərˌʃɪp] *n* : patrocinio *m*, apadrinamiento *m*
spontaneity [ˌspɑntə'ni:əṭi, -'neɪ-] *n* : espontaneidad *f*
spontaneous [spɑn'teɪniəs] *adj* : espontáneo — **spontaneously** *adv*
spoof ['spu:f] *n* : burla *f*, parodia *f*
spook[1] ['spu:k] *vt* : asustar
spook[2] *n* : fantasma *m*, espíritu *m*, espectro *m*
spooky ['spu:ki] *adj* **spookier; -est** : que da miedo, espeluzante
spool ['spu:l] *n* : carrete *m*
spoon[1] ['spu:n] *vt* : comer, servir, o echar con cuchara
spoon[2] *n* : cuchara *f*
spoonful ['spu:nˌfʊl] *n* : cucharada *f* ⟨by the spoonful : a cucharadas⟩
spoor ['spʊr, 'spor] *n* : rastro *m*, pista *f*
sporadic [spə'rædɪk] *adj* : esporádico — **sporadically** [-dɪkli] *adv*
spore ['spor] *n* : espora *f*
sport[1] ['sport] *vi* FROLIC : retozar, juguetear — *vt* SHOW OFF : lucir, ostentar
sport[2] *n* **1** : deporte *m* ⟨outdoor sports : deportes al aire libre⟩ **2** JEST : broma *f* **3 to be a good sport** : tener espíritu deportivo
sporting ['sporṭɪŋ] *adj* : deportivo ⟨a sporting chance : buenas posibilidades⟩
sportsman ['sportsmən] *n, pl* **-men** [-mən, -ˌmɛn] : deportista *m*

sportsmanship ['sportsmən,ʃɪp] *n* : espíritu *m* deportivo, deportividad *f Spain*

sportswoman ['sports,wʊmən] *n, pl* **-women** [-,wɪmən] : deportista *f*

sporty ['sporṭi] *adj* **sportier; -est** : deportivo

spot[1] ['spɑt] *v* **spotted; spotting** *vt* **1** STAIN : manchar **2** RECOGNIZE, SEE : ver, reconocer ⟨to spot an error : descubrir un error⟩ — *vi* : mancharse

spot[2] *adj* : hecho al azar ⟨a spot check : un vistazo, un control aleatorio⟩

spot[3] *n* **1** STAIN : mancha *f* **2** DOT : punto *m* **3** PIMPLE : grano *m* ⟨to break out in spots : salirle granos a alguien⟩ **4** PREDICAMENT : apuro *m*, aprieto *m*, lío *m* ⟨in a tight spot : en apuros⟩ **5** PLACE : lugar *m*, sitio *m* ⟨to be on the spot : estar en el lugar⟩

spotless ['spɑtləs] *adj* : impecable, inmaculado — **spotlessly** *adv*

spotlight[1] ['spɑt,laɪt] *vt* **-lighted** *or* **-lit** [-,lɪt]; **-lighting 1** LIGHT : iluminar (con un reflector) **2** HIGHLIGHT : destacar, poner en relieve

spotlight[2] *n* **1** : reflector *m*, foco *m* **2 to be in the spotlight** : ser el centro de atención

spotty ['spɑṭi] *adj* **spottier; -est** : irregular, desigual

spouse ['spaʊs] *n* : cónyuge *mf*

spout[1] ['spaʊt] *vt* **1** : lanzar chorros de **2** DECLAIM : declamar — *vi* : salir a chorros

spout[2] *n* **1** : pico *m* (de una jarra, etc.) **2** STREAM : chorro *m*

sprain[1] ['spreɪn] *vt* : sufrir un esguince en

sprain[2] *n* : esguince *m*, torcedura *f*

sprawl[1] ['sprɔl] *vi* **1** LIE : tumbarse, echarse, despatarrarse **2** EXTEND : extenderse

sprawl[2] *n* **1** : postura *f* despatarrada **2** SPREAD : extensión *f*, expansión *f*

spray[1] ['spreɪ] *vt* : rociar (una superficie), pulverizar (un líquido)

spray[2] *n* **1** BOUQUET : ramillete *m* **2** MIST : rocío *m* **3** ATOMIZER : atomizador *m*, pulverizador *m*

spray gun *n* : pistola *f*

spread[1] ['sprɛd] *v* **spread; spreading** *vt* **1** *or* **to spread out** : desplegar, extender **2** SCATTER, STREW : esparcir **3** SMEAR : untar (mantequilla, etc.) **4** DISSEMINATE : difundir, sembrar, propagar — *vi* **1** : difundirse, correr, propagarse **2** EXTEND : extenderse

spread[2] *n* **1** EXTENSION : extensión *f*, difusión *f* (de noticias, etc.), propagación *f* (de enfermedades, etc.) **2** : colcha *f* (para una cama), mantel *m* (para una mesa) **3** PASTE : pasta *f* ⟨cheese spread : pasta de queso⟩

spreadsheet ['sprɛd,ʃi:t] *n* : hoja *f* de cálculo

spree ['spri] *n* **1** : acción *f* desenfrenada ⟨to go on a shopping spree : comprar como loco⟩ **2** BINGE : parranda *f*, juerga *f* ⟨on a spree : de parranda, de juerga⟩

sprig ['sprɪg] *n* : ramita *f*, ramito *m*

sprightly ['spraɪtli] *adj* **sprightlier; -est** : vivo, animado ⟨with a sprightly step : con paso ligero⟩

spring[1] ['sprɪŋ] *v* **sprang** ['spræŋ] *or* **sprung** ['sprʌŋ]; **sprung; springing** *vi* **1** LEAP : saltar **2** : mover rápidamente ⟨the lid sprang shut : la tapa se cerró de un golpe⟩ ⟨he sprang to his feet : se paró de un salto⟩ **3 to spring up** : brotar (dícese de las plantas), surgir **4 to spring from** : surgir de — *vt* **1** RELEASE : soltar (de repente) ⟨to spring the news on someone : sorprender a alguien con las noticias⟩ ⟨to spring a trap : hacer saltar una trampa⟩ **2** ACTIVATE : accionar (un mecanismo) **3 to spring a leak** : hacer agua

spring[2] *n* **1** SOURCE : fuente *f*, origen *m* **2** : manantial *m*, fuente *f* ⟨hot spring : fuente termal⟩ **3** : primavera *f* ⟨spring and summer : la primavera y el verano⟩ **4** : resorte *m*, muelle *m* (de metal, etc.) **5** LEAP : salto *m*, brinco *m* **6** RESILIENCE : elasticidad *f*

springboard ['sprɪŋ,bord] *n* : trampolín *m*

springtime ['sprɪŋ,taɪm] *n* : primavera *f*

springy ['sprɪŋi] *adj* **springier; -est 1** RESILIENT : elástico **2** LIVELY : enérgico

sprinkle[1] ['sprɪŋkəl] *vt* **-kled; -kling** : rociar (con agua), espolvorear (con azúcar, etc.), salpicar

sprinkle[2] *n* : llovizna *f*

sprinkler ['sprɪŋkələr] *n* : rociador *m*, aspersor *m*

sprint[1] ['sprɪnt] *vi* : echar la carrera, esprintar (en deportes)

sprint[2] *n* : esprint *m* (en deportes)

sprinter ['sprɪntər] *n* : esprínter *mf*

sprite ['spraɪt] *n* : hada *f*, elfo *m*

sprocket ['sprɑkət] *n* : diente *m* (de una rueda dentada)

sprout[1] ['spraʊt] *vi* : brotar

sprout[2] *n* : brote *m*, retoño *m*, vástago *m*

spruce[1] ['spru:s] *v* **spruced; sprucing** *vt* : arreglar — *vi or* **to spruce up** : arreglarse, acicalarse

spruce[2] *adj* **sprucer; sprucest** : pulcro, arreglado

spruce[3] *n* : picea *f* (árbol)

spry ['spraɪ] *adj* **sprier** *or* **spryer** ['spraɪər]; **spriest** *or* **spryest** ['spraɪəst] : ágil, activo

spun → **spin**

spunk ['spʌŋk] *n* : valor *m*, coraje *m*, agallas *fpl fam*

spunky ['spʌŋki] *adj* **spunkier; -est** : animoso, corajudo

spur[1] ['spər] *vt* **spurred; spurring** *or* **to spur on** : espolear (un caballo), motivar (a una persona, etc.)

spur[2] *n* **1** : espuela *f*, acicate *m* **2** STIMULUS : acicate *m* **3** : espolón *m* (de aves gallináceas)
spurious [ˈspjʊriəs] *adj* : espurio
spurn [ˈspərn] *vt* : desdeñar, rechazar
spurt[1] [ˈspərt] *vt* SQUIRT : lanzar un chorro de — *vi* SPOUT : salir a chorros
spurt[2] *n* **1** : actividad *f* repentina ⟨a spurt of energy : una explosión de energía⟩ ⟨to do in spurts : hacer por rachas⟩ **2** JET : chorro *m* (de agua, etc.)
sputter[1] [ˈspʌt̬ər] *vi* **1** JABBER : farfullar **2** : chisporrotear (dícese de la grasa, etc.), petardear (dícese de un motor)
sputter[2] *n* **1** JABBER : farfulla *f* **2** : chisporroteo *m* (de grasa, etc.), petardeo *m* (de un motor)
spy[1] [ˈspaɪ] *v* **spied; spying** *vt* SEE : ver, divisar — *vi* : espiar ⟨to spy on someone : espiar a alguien⟩
spy[2] *n* : espía *mf*
squab [ˈskwɑb] *n, pl* **squabs** *or* **squab** : pichón *m*
squabble[1] [ˈskwɑbəl] *vi* **-bled; -bling** : reñir, pelearse, discutir
squabble[2] *n* : riña *f*, pelea *f*, discusión *f*
squad [ˈskwɑd] *n* : pelotón *m* (militar), brigada *f* (de policías), cuadrilla *f* (de obreros, etc.)
squadron [ˈskwɑdrən] *n* : escuadrón *m* (de militares), escuadrilla *f* (de aviones), escuadra *f* (de naves)
squalid [ˈskwɑlɪd] *adj* : miserable
squall [ˈskwɔl] *n* **1** : aguacero *m* tormentoso, chubasco *m* tormentoso **2** **snow squall** : tormenta *f* de nieve
squalor [ˈskwɑlər] *n* : miseria *f*
squander [ˈskwɑndər] *vt* : derrochar (dinero, etc.), desaprovechar (una oportunidad, etc.), desperdiciar (talentos, energías, etc.)
square[1] [ˈskwær] *vt* **squared; squaring** **1** : cuadrar **2** : elevar al cuadrado (en matemáticas) **3** CONFORM : conciliar (con), ajustar (con) **4** SETTLE : saldar (una cuenta) ⟨I squared it with him : lo arreglé con él⟩
square[2] *adj* **squarer; -est** **1** : cuadrado ⟨a square house : una casa cuadrada⟩ **2** RIGHT-ANGLED : a escuadra, en ángulo recto **3** : cuadrado (en matemáticas) ⟨a square mile : una milla cuadrada⟩ **4** HONEST : justo ⟨a square deal : un buen acuerdo⟩ ⟨fair and square : en buena lid⟩
square[3] *n* **1** : escuadra *f* (instrumento) **2** : cuadrado *m*, cuadro *m* ⟨to fold into squares : plegar en cuadrados⟩ **3** : plaza *f* (de una ciudad) **4** : cuadrado *m* (en matemáticas)
squarely [ˈskwærli] *adv* **1** EXACTLY : exactamente, directamente, justo **2** HONESTLY : honradamente, justamente
square root *n* : raíz *f* cuadrada
squash[1] [ˈskwɑʃ, ˈskwɔʃ] *vt* **1** CRUSH : aplastar **2** SUPPRESS : acallar (protestas), sofocar (una rebelión)
squash[2] *n* **1** *pl* **squashes** *or* **squash** : calabaza *f* (vegetal) **2** *or* **squash racquets** : squash *m* (deporte)
squat[1] [ˈskwɑt] *vi* **squatted; squatting** **1** CROUCH : agacharse, ponerse en cuclillas **2** : ocupar un lugar sin derecho
squat[2] *adj* **squatter; squattest** : bajo y ancho, rechoncho *fam* (dícese de una persona)
squat[3] *n* **1** : posición *f* en cuclillas **2** : ocupación *f* ilegal (de un lugar)
squaw [ˈskwɔ] *n* : india *f* (norteamericana)
squawk[1] [ˈskwɔk] *vi* : graznar (dícese de las aves), chillar
squawk[2] *n* : graznido *m* (de un ave), chillido *m*
squeak[1] [ˈskwi:k] *vi* : chillar (dícese de un animal), chirriar (dícese de un objeto)
squeak[2] *n* : chillido *m*, chirrido *m*
squeaky [ˈskwi:ki] *adj* **squeakier; -est** : chirriante ⟨a squeaky voice : una voz chillona⟩
squeal[1] [ˈskwi:l] *vi* **1** : chillar (dícese de las personas o los animales), chirriar (dícese de los frenos, etc.) **2** PROTEST : quejarse
squeal[2] *n* **1** : chillido *m* (de una persona o un animal) **2** SCREECH : chirrido *m* (de frenos, etc.)
squeamish [ˈskwi:mɪʃ] *adj* : impresionable, sensible ⟨he's squeamish about cockroaches : las cucarachas le dan asco⟩
squeeze[1] [ˈskwi:z] *vt* **squeezed; squeezing** **1** PRESS : apretar, exprimir (naranjas, etc.) **2** EXTRACT : extraer (jugo, etc.)
squeeze[2] *n* : apretón *m*
squelch [ˈskwɛltʃ] *vt* : aplastar (una rebelión, etc.)
squid [ˈskwɪd] *n, pl* **squid** *or* **squids** : calamar *m*
squint[1] [ˈskwɪnt] *vi* : mirar con los ojos entornados
squint[2] *adj or* **squint–eyed** [ˈskwɪntˌaɪd] : bizco
squint[3] *n* : ojos *mpl* bizcos, bizquera *f*
squire [ˈskwaɪr] *n* : hacendado *m*, -da *f*; terrateniente *mf*
squirm [ˈskwərm] *vi* : retorcerse
squirrel [ˈskwərəl] *n* : ardilla *f*
squirt[1] [ˈskwərt] *vt* : lanzar un chorro de — *vi* SPURT : salir a chorros
squirt[2] *n* : chorrito *m*
stab[1] [stæb] *vt* **stabbed; stabbing** **1** KNIFE : acuchillar, apuñalar **2** STICK : clavar (con una aguja, etc.), golpear (con el dedo, etc.)
stab[2] *n* **1** : puñalada *f*, cuchillada *f* **2** JAB : pinchazo *m* (con una aguja, etc.), golpe *m* (con un dedo, etc.) **3** **to take a stab at** : intentar
stability [stəˈbɪlət̬i] *n, pl* **-ties** : estabilidad *f*
stabilize [ˈsteɪbəˌlaɪz] *v* **-lized; -lizing** *vt* : estabilizar — *vi* : estabilizarse

stable[1] [ˈsteɪbəl] *vt* **-bled; -bling** : poner (ganado) en un establo, poner (caballos) en una caballeriza
stable[2] *adj* **-bler; -blest** **1** FIXED, STEADY : fijo, sólido, estable **2** LASTING : estable, perdurable ⟨a stable government : un gobierno estable⟩ **3** : estacionario (en medicina), equilibrado (en psicología)
stable[3] *n* : establo *m* (para ganado), caballeriza *f* o cuadra *f* (para caballos)
staccato [stəˈkɑt̬o:] *adj* : staccato
stack[1] [ˈstæk] *vt* **1** PILE : amontonar, apilar **2** COVER : cubrir, llenar ⟨he stacked the table with books : cubrió la mesa de libros⟩
stack[2] *n* **1** PILE : montón *m*, pila *f* **2** SMOKESTACK : chimenea *f*
stadium [ˈsteɪdiəm] *n, pl* **-dia** [-diə] *or* **-diums** : estadio *m*
staff[1] [ˈstæf] *vt* : proveer de personal
staff[2] *n, pl* **staffs** [ˈstæfs, stævz] *or* **staves** [ˈstævz, ˈsteɪvz] **1** : bastón *m* (de mando), báculo *m* (de obispo) **2** *pl* **staffs** PERSONNEL : personal *m* **3** *or* **stave** : pentagrama *m* (en música)
stag[1] [ˈstæg] *adv* : solo, sin pareja ⟨to go stag : ir solo⟩
stag[2] *adj* : sólo para hombres
stag[3] *n, pl* **stags** *or* **stag** : ciervo *m*, venado *m*
stage[1] [ˈsteɪʤ] *vt* **staged; staging** : poner en escena (una obra de teatro)
stage[2] *n* **1** PLATFORM : estrado *m*, tablado *m*, escenario *m* (de un teatro) **2** PHASE, STEP : fase *f*, etapa *f* ⟨stage of development : fase de desarrollo⟩ ⟨in stages : por etapas⟩ **3 the stage** : el teatro *m*
stagecoach [ˈsteɪʤˌko:ʧ] *n* : diligencia *f*
stagger[1] [ˈstægər] *vi* TOTTER : tambalearse — *vt* **1** ALTERNATE : alternar, escalonar (turnos de trabajo) **2** : hacer tambalear ⟨to be staggered by : quedarse estupefacto por⟩
stagger[2] *n* : tambaleo *m*
staggering [ˈstægərɪŋ] *adj* : asombroso
stagnant [ˈstægnənt] *adj* : estancado
stagnate [ˈstægˌneɪt] *vi* **-nated; -nating** : estancarse
staid [ˈsteɪd] *adj* : serio, sobrio
stain[1] [ˈsteɪn] *vt* **1** DISCOLOR : manchar **2** DYE : teñir (madera, etc.) **3** SULLY : manchar, empañar
stain[2] *n* **1** SPOT : mancha *f* **2** DYE : tinte *m*, tintura *f* **3** BLEMISH : mancha *f*, mácula *f*
stainless [ˈsteɪnləs] *adj* : sin mancha ⟨stainless steel : acero inoxidable⟩
stair [ˈstær] *n* **1** STEP : escalón *m*, peldaño *m* **2 stairs** *npl* : escalera *f*, escaleras *fpl*
staircase [ˈstærˌkeɪs] *n* : escalera *f*, escaleras *fpl*
stairway [ˈstærˌweɪ] *n* : escalera *f*, escaleras *fpl*
stake[1] [ˈsteɪk] *vt* **staked; staking** **1** : estacar, marcar con estacas (una propiedad) **2** BET : jugarse, apostar **3 to stake a claim to** : reclamar, reivindicar
stake[2] *n* **1** POST : estaca *f* **2** BET : apuesta *f* ⟨to be at stake : estar en juego⟩ **3** INTEREST, SHARE : interés *m*, participación *f*
stalactite [stəˈlækˌtaɪt] *n* : estalactita *f*
stalagmite [stəˈlægˌmaɪt] *n* : estalagmita *f*
stale [ˈsteɪl] *adj* **staler; stalest** : viejo ⟨stale bread : pan duro⟩ ⟨stale news : viejas noticias⟩
stalemate [ˈsteɪlˌmeɪt] *n* : punto *m* muerto, impasse *m*
stalk[1] [ˈstɔk] *vt* : acechar — *vi* : caminar rígidamente (por orgullo, ira, etc.)
stalk[2] *n* : tallo *m* (de una planta)
stall[1] [ˈstɔl] *vt* **1** : parar (un motor) **2** DELAY : entretener (a una persona), demorar — *vi* **1** : pararse (dícese de un motor) **2** DELAY : demorar, andar con rodeos
stall[2] *n* **1** : compartimiento *m* (de un establo) **2** : puesto *m* (en un mercado, etc.)
stallion [ˈstæljən] *n* : caballo *m* semental
stalwart [ˈstɔlwərt] *adj* **1** STRONG : fuerte ⟨a stalwart supporter : un firme partidario⟩ **2** BRAVE : valiente, valeroso
stamen [ˈsteɪmən] *n* : estambre *m*
stamina [ˈstæmənə] *n* : resistencia *f*
stammer[1] [ˈstæmər] *vi* : tartamudear, titubear
stammer[2] *n* : tartamudeo *m*, titubeo *m*
stamp[1] [ˈstæmp] *vt* **1** : pisotear (con los pies) ⟨to stamp one's feet : patear, dar una patada⟩ **2** IMPRESS, IMPRINT : sellar (una factura, etc.), acuñar (monedas) **3** : franquear, ponerle estampillas a (correo)
stamp[2] *n* **1** : sello *m* (para documentos, etc.) **2** DIE : cuño *m* (para monedas) **3** *or* **postage stamp** : sello *m*, estampilla *f*, timbre *m* *CA, Mex*
stampede[1] [stæmˈpi:d] *vi* **-peded; -peding** : salir en estampida
stampede[2] *n* : estampida *f*
stance [ˈstænts] *n* : postura *f*
stanch [ˈstɔnʧ, ˈstɑnʧ] *vt* : detener, estancar (un líquido)
stand[1] [ˈstænd] *v* **stood** [ˈstʊd]; **standing** *vi* **1** : estar de pie, estar parado ⟨I was standing on the corner : estaba parada en la esquina⟩ **2** *or* **to stand up** : levantarse, pararse, ponerse de pie **3** (*indicating a specified position or location*) ⟨they stand third in the country : ocupan el tercer lugar en el país⟩ ⟨the machines are standing idle : las máquinas están paradas⟩ **4** (*referring to an opinion*) ⟨how does he stand on the matter? : ¿cuál es su postura respecto al asunto?⟩ **5** BE : estar ⟨the house stands on a hill : la casa está en una colina⟩ **6** CONTINUE : seguir ⟨the order still stands : el mandato sigue vi-

gente⟩ — *vt* **1** PLACE, SET : poner, colocar ⟨he stood them in a row : los colocó en hilera⟩ **2** TOLERATE : aguantar, soportar ⟨he can't stand her : no la puede tragar⟩ **3 to stand firm** : mantenerse firme **4 to stand guard** : hacer la guardia

stand[2] *n* **1** RESISTANCE : resistencia *f* ⟨to make a stand against : resistir a⟩ **2** BOOTH, STALL : stand *m*, puesto *m*, kiosko *m* (para vender periódicos, etc) **3** BASE : pie *m*, base *f* **4** : grupo *m* (de árboles, etc.) **5** POSITION : posición *f*, postura *f* **6 stands** *npl* GRANDSTAND : tribuna *f*

standard[1] [ˈstændərd] *adj* **1** ESTABLISHED : estándar, oficial ⟨standard measures : medidas oficiales⟩ ⟨standard English : el inglés estándar⟩ **2** NORMAL : normal, estándar, común **3** CLASSIC : estándar, clásico ⟨a standard work : una obra clásica⟩

standard[2] *n* **1** BANNER : estandarte *m* **2** CRITERION : criterio *m* **3** RULE : estándar *m*, norma *f*, regla *f* **4** LEVEL : nivel *m* ⟨standard of living : nivel de vida⟩ **5** SUPPORT : poste *m*, soporte *m*

standardization [ˌstændərdəˈzeɪʃən] *n* : estandarización *f*

standardize [ˈstændərˌdaɪz] *vt* **-ized; -izing** : estandarizar

standard time *n* : hora *f* oficial

stand by *vt* : atenerse a, cumplir con (una promesa, etc.) — *vi* **1** : mantenerse aparte ⟨to stand by and do nothing : mirar sin hacer nada⟩ **2** : estar preparado, estar listo (para un anuncio, un ataque, etc.)

stand for *vt* **1** REPRESENT : significar **2** PERMIT, TOLERATE : permitir, tolerar

standing [ˈstændɪŋ] *n* **1** POSITION, RANK : posición *f* **2** DURATION : duración *f*

stand out *vi* **1** : destacar(se) ⟨she stands out from the rest : se destaca entre los otros⟩ **2 to stand out against** RESIST : oponerse a

standpoint [ˈstændˌpɔint] *n* : punto *m* de vista

standstill [ˈstændˌstɪl] *n* **1** STOP : detención *f*, paro *m* ⟨to come to a standstill : pararse⟩ **2** DEADLOCK : punto *m* muerto, impasse *m*

stand up *vt* : dejar plantado ⟨he stood me up again : otra vez me dejó plantado⟩ — *vi* **1** ENDURE : durar, resistir **2 to stand up for** : defender **3 to stand up to** : hacerle frente (a alguien)

stank → **stink**

stanza [ˈstænzə] *n* : estrofa *f*

staple[1] [ˈsteɪpəl] *vt* **-pled; -pling** : engrapar, grapar

staple[2] *adj* : principal, básico ⟨a staple food : un alimento básico⟩

staple[3] *n* **1** : producto *m* principal **2** : grapa *f* (para engrapar papeles)

stapler [ˈsteɪplər] *n* : engrapadora *f*, grapadora *f*

star[1] [ˈstɑr] *v* **starred; starring** *vt* **1** : marcar con una estrella o un asterisco **2** FEATURE : estar protagonizado por — *vi* : tener el papel principal ⟨to star in : protagonizar⟩

star[2] *n* : estrella *f*

starboard [ˈstɑrbərd] *n* : estribor *m*

starch[1] [ˈstɑrtʃ] *vt* : almidonar

starch[2] *n* : almidón *m*, fécula *f* (comida)

starchy [ˈstɑrtʃi] *adj* **starchier; -est** : lleno de almidón ⟨a starchy diet : una dieta feculenta⟩

stardom [ˈstɑrdəm] *n* : estrellato *m*

stare[1] [ˈstær] *vi* **stared; staring** : mirar fijamente

stare[2] *n* : mirada *f* fija

starfish [ˈstɑrˌfɪʃ] *n* : estrella *f* de mar

stark[1] [ˈstɑrk] *adv* : completamente ⟨stark raving mad : loco de remate⟩ ⟨stark naked : completamente desnudo⟩

stark[2] *adj* **1** ABSOLUTE : absoluto **2** BARREN, DESOLATE : desolado, desierto **3** BARE : desnudo **4** HARSH : severo, duro

starlight [ˈstɑrˌlaɪt] *n* : luz *f* de las estrellas

starling [ˈstɑrlɪŋ] *n* : estornino *m*

starry [ˈstɑri] *adj* **starrier; -est** : estrellado

start[1] [ˈstɑrt] *vi* **1** JUMP : levantarse de un salto, sobresaltarse, dar un respingo **2** BEGIN : empezar, comenzar **3** SET OUT : salir (de viaje, etc.) **4** : arrancar (dícese de un motor) — *vt* **1** BEGIN : empezar, comenzar, iniciar **2** CAUSE : provocar, causar **3** ESTABLISH : fundar, montar, establecer ⟨to start a business : montar un negocio⟩ **4** : arrancar, poner en marcha, encender ⟨to start the car : arrancar el motor⟩

start[2] *n* **1** JUMP : sobresalto *m*, respingo *m* **2** BEGINNING : principio *m*, comienzo *m* ⟨to get an early start : salir temprano⟩

starter [ˈstɑrt̬ər] *n* **1** : participante *mf* (en una carrera, etc.); jugador *m* titular, jugadora *f* titular (en beisbol, etc.) **2** APPETIZER : entremés *m*, aperitivo *m* **3** *or* **starter motor** : motor *m* de arranque

startle [ˈstɑrt̬əl] *vt* **-tled; -tling** : asustar, sobresaltar

start–up [ˈstɑrtˈʌp] *adj* : de puesta en marcha

starvation [stɑrˈveɪʃən] *n* : inanición *f*, hambre *f*

starve [ˈstɑrv] *v* **starved; starving** *vi* : morirse de hambre — *vt* : privar de comida

stash [ˈstæʃ] *vt* : esconder, guardar (en un lugar secreto)

stat [ˈstæt] → **statistic**

state[1] [ˈsteɪt] *vt* **stated; stating** **1** REPORT : puntualizar, exponer (los hechos, etc.) ⟨state your name : diga su nombre⟩ **2** ESTABLISH, FIX : establecer, fijar

state[2] *n* **1** CONDITION : estado *m*, condición *f* ⟨a liquid state : un estado líquido⟩ ⟨state of mind : estado de ánimo⟩

⟨in a bad state : en malas condiciones⟩ **2** NATION : estado *m*, nación *f* **3** : estado *m* (dentro de un país) ⟨the States : los Estados Unidos⟩

stateliness ['steɪtlinəs] *n* : majestuosidad *f*

stately ['steɪtli] *adj* **statelier; -est** : majestuoso

statement ['steɪtmənt] *n* **1** DECLARATION : declaración *f*, afirmación *f* **2** *or* **bank statement** : estado *m* de cuenta

stateroom ['steɪtˌru:m, -ˌrʊm] *n* : camarote *m*

statesman ['steɪtsmən] *n, pl* **-men** [-mən, -ˌmɛn] : estadista *mf*

static[1] ['stæt̬ɪk] *adj* : estático

static[2] *n* : estática *f*, interferencia *f*

station[1] ['steɪʃən] *vt* : apostar, estacionar

station[2] *n* **1** : estación *f* (de trenes, etc.) **2** RANK, STANDING : condición *f* (social) **3** : canal *m* (de televisión), estación *f* o emisora *f* (de radio) **4 police station** : comisaría *f* **5 fire station** : estación *f* de bomberos, cuartel *m* de bomberos

stationary ['steɪʃəˌnɛri] *adj* **1** IMMOBILE : estacionario, inmovible **2** UNCHANGING : inmutable, inalterable

stationery ['steɪʃəˌnɛri] *n* : papel *m* y sobres *mpl* (para correspondencia)

station wagon *n* : camioneta *f* ranchera, camioneta *f* guayín *Mex*

statistic [stə'tɪstɪk] *n* : estadística *f* ⟨according to statistics : según las estadísticas⟩

statistical [stə'tɪstɪkəl] *adj* : estadístico

statistician [ˌstætə'stɪʃən] *n* : estadístico *m*, -ca *f*

statue ['stæˌʧu:] *n* : estatua *f*

statuesque [ˌstæʧʊ'ɛsk] *adj* : escultural

statuette [ˌstæʧʊ'ɛt] *n* : estatuilla *f*

stature ['stæʧər] *n* **1** HEIGHT : estatura *f*, talla *f* **2** PRESTIGE : talla *f*, prestigio *m*

status ['steɪt̬əs, 'stæ-] *n* : condición *f*, situación *f*, estatus *m* (social) ⟨marital status : estado civil⟩

statute ['stæˌʧu:t] *n* : ley *f*, estatuto *m*

staunch ['stɔnʧ] *adj* : acérrimo, incondicional, leal ⟨a staunch supporter : un partidario incondicional⟩ — **staunchly** *adv*

stave[1] ['steɪv] *vt* **staved** *or* **stove** ['sto:v]; **staving 1 to stave in** : romper **2 to stave off** : evitar (un ataque), prevenir (un problema)

stave[2] *n* : duela *f* (de un barril)

staves → **staff**

stay[1] ['steɪ] *vi* **1** REMAIN : quedarse, permanecer ⟨to stay in : quedarse en casa⟩ ⟨he stayed in the city : permaneció en la ciudad⟩ **2** CONTINUE : seguir, quedarse ⟨it stayed cloudy : siguió nublado⟩ ⟨to stay awake : mantenerse despierto⟩ **3** LODGE : hospedarse, alojarse (en un hotel, etc.) — *vt* **1** HALT : detener, suspender (una ejecución, etc.) **2 to stay the course** : aguantar hasta el final

stay[2] *n* **1** SOJOURN : estadía *f*, estancia *f*, permanencia *f* **2** SUSPENSION : suspensión *f* (de una sentencia) **3** SUPPORT : soporte *m*

stead ['stɛd] *n* **1** : lugar *m* ⟨she went in his stead : fue en su lugar⟩ **2 to stand (someone) in good stead** : ser muy útil a, servir de mucho a

steadfast ['stɛdˌfæst] *adj* : firme, resuelto ⟨a steadfast friend : un fiel amigo⟩ ⟨a steadfast refusal : una negativa categórica⟩

steadily ['stɛdəli] *adv* **1** CONSTANTLY : continuamente, sin parar **2** FIRMLY : con firmeza **3** FIXEDLY : fijamente

steady[1] ['stɛdi] *v* **steadied; steadying** *vt* : sujetar ⟨she steadied herself : recobró el equilibrio⟩ — *vi* : estabilizarse

steady[2] *adj* **steadier; -est 1** FIRM, SURE : seguro, firme ⟨to have a steady hand : tener buen pulso⟩ **2** FIXED, REGULAR : fijo ⟨a steady income : ingresos fijos⟩ **3** CALM : tranquilo, ecuánime ⟨she has steady nerves : es imperturbable⟩ **4** DEPENDABLE : responsable, fiable **5** CONSTANT : constante

steak ['steɪk] *n* : bistec *m*, filete *m*, churrasco *m*, bife *m Arg, Chile, Uru*

steal ['sti:l] *v* **stole** ['sto:l]; **stolen** ['sto:lən]; **stealing** *vt* : robar, hurtar — *vi* **1** : robar, hurtar **2** : ir sigilosamente ⟨to steal away : escabullirse⟩

stealth ['stɛlθ] *n* : sigilo *m*

stealthily ['stɛlθəli] *adv* : furtivamente

stealthy ['stɛlθi] *adj* **stealthier; -est** : furtivo, sigiloso

steam[1] ['sti:m] *vi* : echar vapor ⟨to steam away : moverse echando vapor⟩ — *vt* **1** : cocer al vapor (en cocina) **2 to steam open** : abrir con vapor

steam[2] *n* **1** : vapor *m* **2 to let off steam** : desahogarse

steamboat ['sti:mˌbo:t] → **steamship**

steam engine *n* : motor *m* de vapor

steamroller ['sti:mˌro:lər] *n* : apisonadora *f*

steamship ['sti:mˌʃɪp] *n* : vapor *m*, barco *m* de vapor

steamy ['sti:mi] *adj* **steamier; -est 1** : lleno de vapor **2** EROTIC : erótico ⟨a steamy romance : un tórrido romance⟩

steed ['sti:d] *n* : corcel *m*

steel[1] ['sti:l] *vt* **to steel oneself** : armarse de valor

steel[2] *adj* : de acero

steel[3] *n* : acero *m*

steely ['sti:li] *adj* **steelier; -est** : como acero ⟨a steely gaze : una mirada fría⟩ ⟨steely determination : determinación férrea⟩

steep[1] ['sti:p] *vt* : remojar, dejar (té, etc.) en infusión

steep[2] *adj* **1** : empinado, escarpado ⟨a steep cliff : un precipicio escarpado⟩ **2** CONSIDERABLE : considerable, marcado **3** EXCESSIVE : excesivo ⟨steep prices : precios muy altos⟩

steeple ['sti:pəl] *n* : aguja *f*, campanario *m*

steeplechase [ˈstiːpəlˌʧeɪs] *n* : carrera *f* de obstáculos
steeply [ˈstiːpli] *adv* : abruptamente
steer[1] [ˈstɪr] *vt* **1** : conducir (un coche), gobernar (un barco) **2** GUIDE : dirigir, guiar
steer[2] *n* : buey *m*
steering wheel *n* : volante *m*
stein [ˈstaɪn] *n* : jarra *f* (para cerveza)
stellar [ˈstɛlər] *adj* : estelar
stem[1] [ˈstɛm] *v* **stemmed; stemming** *vt* : detener, contener, parar ⟨to stem the tide : detener el curso⟩ — *vi* **to stem from** : provenir de, ser el resultado de
stem[2] *n* : tallo *m* (de una planta)
stench [ˈstɛnʧ] *n* : hedor *m*, mal olor *m*
stencil[1] [ˈstɛntsəl] *vt* **-ciled** *or* **-cilled; -ciling** *or* **-cilling** : marcar utilizando una plantilla
stencil[2] *n* : plantilla *f* (para marcar)
stenographer [stəˈnɑgrəfər] *n* : taquígrafo *m*, -fa *f*
stenographic [ˌstɛnəˈgræfɪk] *adj* : taquigráfico
stenography [stəˈnɑgrəfi] *n* : taquigrafía *f*
step[1] [ˈstɛp] *vi* **stepped; stepping** **1** : dar un paso ⟨step this way, please : pase por aquí, por favor⟩ ⟨he stepped outside : salió⟩ **2 to step on** : pisar
step[2] *n* **1** : paso *m* ⟨step by step : paso por paso⟩ **2** STAIR : escalón *m*, peldaño *m* **3** RUNG : escalón *m*, travesaño *m* **4** MEASURE, MOVE : medida *f*, paso *m* ⟨to take steps : tomar medidas⟩ **5** STRIDE : paso *m* ⟨with a quick step : con paso rápido⟩
stepbrother [ˈstɛpˌbrʌðər] *n* : hermanastro *m*
stepdaughter [ˈstɛpˌdɔt̬ər] *n* : hijastra *f*
stepfather [ˈstɛpˌfɑðər, -ˌfa-] *n* : padrastro *m*
stepladder [ˈstɛpˌlædər] *n* : escalera *f* de tijera
stepmother [ˈstɛpˌmʌðər] *n* : madrastra *f*
steppe [ˈstɛp] *n* : estepa *f*
stepping–stone [ˈstɛpɪŋˌstoːn] *n* : pasadera *f* (en un río, etc.), trampolín *m* (al éxito)
stepsister [ˈstɛpˌsɪstər] *n* : hermanastra *f*
stepson [ˈstɛpˌsʌn] *n* : hijastro *m*
step up *vt* INCREASE : aumentar
stereo[1] [ˈstɛriˌoː, ˈstɪr-] *adj* : estéreo
stereo[2] *n, pl* **stereos** : estéreo *m*
stereophonic [ˌstɛrioˈfɑnɪk, ˌstɪr-] *adj* : estereofónico
stereotype[1] [ˈstɛrioˌtaɪp, ˈstɪr-] *vt* **-typed; -typing** : estereotipar
stereotype[2] *n* : estereotipo *m*
sterile [ˈstɛrəl] *adj* : estéril
sterility [stəˈrɪlət̬i] *n* : esterilidad *f*
sterilization [ˌstɛrələˈzeɪʃən] *n* : esterilización *f*
sterilize [ˈstɛrəˌlaɪz] *vt* **-ized; -izing** : esterilizar
sterling [ˈstərlɪŋ] *adj* **1** : de ley ⟨sterling silver : plata de ley⟩ **2** EXCELLENT : excelente
stern[1] [ˈstərn] *adj* : severo, adusto — **sternly** *adv*
stern[2] *n* : popa *f*
sternness [ˈstərnnəs] *n* : severidad *f*
sternum [ˈstərnəm] *n, pl* **sternums** *or* **sterna** [-nə] : esternón *m*
stethoscope [ˈstɛθəˌskoːp] *n* : estetoscopio *m*
stevedore [ˈstiːvəˌdor] *n* : estibador *m*, -dora *f*
stew[1] [ˈstuː, ˈstjuː] *vt* : estofar, guisar — *vi* **1** : cocer (dícese de la carne, etc.) **2** FRET : preocuparse
stew[2] *n* **1** : estofado *m*, guiso *m* **2 to be in a stew** : estar agitado
steward [ˈstuːərd, ˈstjuː-] *n* **1** MANAGER : administrador *m* **2** : auxiliar *m* de vuelo (en un avión), camarero *m* (en un barco)
stewardess [ˈstuːərdəs, ˈstjuː-] *n* **1** MANAGER : administradora *f* **2** : camarera *f* (en un barco) **3** : auxiliar *f* de vuelo, azafata *f*, aeromoza *f* (en un avión)
stick[1] [ˈstɪk] *v* **stuck** [ˈstʌk]; **sticking** *vt* **1** STAB : clavar **2** ATTACH : pegar **3** PUT : poner **4 to stick out** : sacar (la lengua, etc.), extender (la mano) — *vi* **1** ADHERE : pegarse, adherirse **2** JAM : atascarse **3 to stick around** : quedarse **4 to stick out** PROJECT : sobresalir (de una superficie), asomar (por detrás o debajo de algo) **5 to stick to** : no abandonar ⟨stick to your guns : manténgase firme⟩ **6 to stick up** : estar parado (dícese del pelo, etc.), sobresalir (de una superficie) **7 to stick with** : serle fiel a (una persona), seguir con (una cosa) ⟨I'll stick with what I know : prefiero lo conocido⟩
stick[2] *n* **1** BRANCH, TWIG : ramita *f* **2** : palo *m*, vara *f* ⟨a walking stick : un bastón⟩
sticker [ˈstɪkər] *n* : etiqueta *f* adhesiva
stickler [ˈstɪklər] *n* : persona *f* exigente ⟨to be a stickler for : insistir mucho en⟩
sticky [ˈstɪki] *adj* **stickier; -est** **1** ADHESIVE : pegajoso, adhesivo **2** MUGGY : bochornoso **3** DIFFICULT : difícil
stiff [ˈstɪf] *adj* **1** RIGID : rígido, tieso ⟨a stiff dough : una masa firme⟩ **2** : agarrotado, entumecido ⟨stiff muscles : músculos entumecidos⟩ **3** STILTED : acartonado, poco natural **4** STRONG : fuerte (dícese del viento, etc.) **5** DIFFICULT, SEVERE : severo, difícil, duro
stiffen [ˈstɪfən] *vt* **1** STRENGTHEN : fortalecer, reforzar (tela, etc.) **2** : hacer más duro (un castigo, etc.) — *vi* **1** HARDEN : endurecerse **2** : entumecerse (dícese de los músculos)
stiffly [ˈstɪfli] *adv* **1** RIGIDLY : rígidamente **2** COLDLY : con frialdad
stiffness [ˈstɪfnəs] *n* **1** RIGIDITY : rigidez *f* **2** COLDNESS : frialdad *f* **3** SEVERITY : severidad *f*

stifle [ˈstaɪfəl] *vt* **-fled; -fling** SMOTHER, SUPPRESS : sofocar, reprimir, contener ⟨to stifle a yawn : reprimir un bostezo⟩
stigma [ˈstɪgmə] *n, pl* **stigmata** [stɪgˈmɑt̬ə, ˈstɪgmət̬ə] *or* **stigmas** : estigma *m*
stigmatize [ˈstɪgməˌtaɪz] *vt* **-tized; -tizing** : estigmatizar
stile [ˈstaɪl] *n* : escalones *mpl* para cruzar un cerco
stiletto [stəˈlɛˌt̬oː] *n, pl* **-tos** *or* **-toes** : estilete *m*
still[1] [ˈstɪl] *vt* CALM : pacificar, apaciguar — *vi* : pacificarse, apaciguarse
still[2] *adv* **1** QUIETLY : quieto ⟨sit still! : ¡quédate quieto!⟩ **2** : de todos modos, aún, todavía ⟨she still lives there : aún vive allí⟩ ⟨it's still the same : sigue siendo lo mismo⟩ **3** IN ANY CASE : de todos modos, aún así ⟨he still has doubts : aún así le quedan dudas⟩ ⟨I still prefer that you stay : de todos modos prefiero que te quedes⟩
still[3] *adj* **1** MOTIONLESS : quieto, inmóvil **2** SILENT : callado
still[4] *n* **1** SILENCE : quietud *f*, calma *f* **2** : alambique *m* (para destilar alcohol)
stillborn [ˈstɪlˌbɔrn] *adj* : nacido muerto
stillness [ˈstɪlnəs] *n* : calma *f*, silencio *m*
stilt [ˈstɪlt] *n* : zanco *m*
stilted [ˈstɪltəd] *adj* : afectado, poco natural
stimulant [ˈstɪmjələnt] *n* : estimulante *m* — **stimulant** *adj*
stimulate [ˈstɪmjəˌleɪt] *vt* **-lated; -lating** : estimular
stimulation [ˌstɪmjəˈleɪʃən] *n* **1** STIMULATING : estimulación *f* **2** STIMULUS : estímulo *m*
stimulus [ˈstɪmjələs] *n, pl* **-li** [-ˌlaɪ] **1** : estímulo *m* **2** INCENTIVE : acicate *m*
sting[1] [ˈstɪŋ] *v* **stung** [ˈstʌŋ]; **stinging** *vt* **1** : picar ⟨a bee stung him : le picó una abeja⟩ **2** HURT : hacer escocer (físicamente), herir (emocionalmente) — *vi* **1** : picar (dícese de las abejas, etc.) **2** SMART : escocer, arder
sting[2] *n* : picadura *f* (herida), escozor *m* (sensación)
stinger [ˈstɪŋər] *n* : aguijón *m* (de una abeja, etc.)
stinginess [ˈstɪnʤinəs] *n* : tacañería *f*
stingy [ˈstɪnʤi] *adj* **stingier; -est** **1** MISERLY : tacaño, avaro **2** PALTRY : mezquino, mísero
stink[1] [ˈstɪŋk] *vi* **stank** [ˈstæŋk] *or* **stunk** [ˈstʌŋk]; **stunk; stinking** : apestar, oler mal
stink[2] *n* : hedor *m*, mal olor *m*, peste *f*
stint[1] [ˈstɪnt] *vt* : escatimar ⟨to stint oneself of : privarse de⟩ — *vi* **to stint on** : escatimar
stint[2] *n* : período *m*
stipend [ˈstaɪˌpɛnd, -pənd] *n* : estipendio *m*
stipulate [ˈstɪpjəˌleɪt] *vt* **-lated; -lating** : estipular
stipulation [ˌstɪpjəˈleɪʃən] *n* : estipulación *f*
stir[1] [ˈstər] *v* **stirred; stirring** *vt* **1** AGITATE : mover, agitar **2** MIX : revolver, remover **3** INCITE : incitar, impulsar, motivar **4** *or* **to stir up** AROUSE : despertar (memorias, etc.), provocar (ira, etc.) — *vi* : moverse, agitarse
stir[2] *n* **1** MOTION : movimiento *m* **2** COMMOTION : revuelo *m*
stirrup [ˈstərəp, ˈstɪr-] *n* : estribo *m*
stitch[1] [ˈstɪʧ] *vt* : coser, bordar (para decorar) — *vi* : coser
stitch[2] *n* **1** : puntada *f* **2** TWINGE : punzada *f*, puntada *f*
stock[1] [ˈstɑk] *vt* : surtir, abastecer, vender — *vi* **to stock up** : abastecerse
stock[2] *n* **1** SUPPLY : reserva *f*, existencias *fpl* (en comercio) ⟨to be out of stock : estar agotadas las existencias⟩ **2** SECURITIES : acciones *fpl*, valores *mpl* **3** LIVESTOCK : ganado *m* **4** ANCESTRY : linaje *m*, estirpe *f* **5** BROTH : caldo *m* **6 to take stock** : evaluar
stockade [stɑˈkeɪd] *n* : estacada *f*
stockbroker [ˈstɑkˌbroːkər] *n* : corredor *m*, -dora *f* de bolsa
stockholder [ˈstɑkˌhoːldər] *n* : accionista *mf*
stocking [ˈstɑkɪŋ] *n* : media *f* ⟨a pair of stockings : unas medias⟩
stock market *n* : bolsa *f*
stockpile[1] [ˈstɑkˌpaɪl] *vt* **-piled; -piling** : acumular, almacenar
stockpile[2] *n* : reservas *fpl*
stocky [ˈstɑki] *adj* **stockier; -est** : robusto, fornido
stockyard [ˈstɑkˌjɑrd] *n* : corral *m*
stodgy [ˈstɑʤi] *adj* **stodgier; -est** **1** DULL : aburrido, pesado **2** OLD-FASHIONED : anticuado
stoic[1] [ˈstoːɪk] *or* **stoical** [-ɪkəl] *adj* : estoico — **stoically** [-ɪkli] *adv*
stoic[2] *n* : estoico *m*, -ca *f*
stoicism [ˈstoːəˌsɪzəm] *n* : estoicismo *m*
stoke [ˈstoːk] *vt* **stoked; stoking** : atizar (un fuego), echarle carbón a (un horno)
stole[1] → **steal**
stole[2] [ˈstoːl] *n* : estola *f*
stolen → **steal**
stolid [ˈstɑlɪd] *adj* : impasible, imperturbable — **stolidly** *adv*
stomach[1] [ˈstʌmɪk] *vt* : aguantar, soportar
stomach[2] *n* **1** : estómago *m* **2** BELLY : vientre *m*, barriga *f*, panza *f* **3** DESIRE : ganas *fpl* ⟨he had no stomach for a fight : no quería pelea⟩
stomachache [ˈstʌmɪkˌeɪk] *n* : dolor *m* de estómago
stomp [ˈstɑmp, ˈstɔmp] *vt* : pisotear — *vi* : pisar fuerte
stone[1] [ˈstoːn] *vt* **stoned; stoning** : apedrear, lapidar
stone[2] *n* **1** : piedra *f* **2** PIT : hueso *m*, pepa *f* (de una fruta)
Stone Age *n* : Edad *f* de Piedra

stony [ˈstoːni] *adj* **stonier; -est** **1** ROCKY : pedregoso **2** UNFEELING : insensible, frío ⟨a stony stare : una mirada glacial⟩
stood → **stand**
stool [ˈstuːl] *n* **1** SEAT : taburete *m*, banco *m* **2** FOOTSTOOL : escabel *m* **3** FECES : deposición *f* de heces
stoop¹ [ˈstuːp] *vi* **1** CROUCH : agacharse **2 to stoop to** : rebajarse a
stoop² *n* **1** : espaldas *fpl* encorvadas ⟨to have a stoop : ser encorvado⟩ **2** : entrada *f* (de una casa)
stop¹ [ˈstɑp] *v* **stopped; stopping** *vt* **1** PLUG : tapar **2** PREVENT : impedir, evitar ⟨she stopped me from leaving : me impidió que saliera⟩ **3** HALT : parar, detener **4** CEASE : dejar de ⟨he stopped talking : dejó de hablar⟩ — *vi* **1** HALT : detenerse, parar **2** CEASE : cesar, terminar ⟨the rain won't stop : no deja de llover⟩ **3** STAY : quedarse ⟨she stopped with friends : se quedó en casa de unos amigos⟩ **4 to stop by** : visitar
stop² *n* **1** STOPPER : tapón *m* **2** HALT : parada *f*, alto *m* ⟨to come to a stop : pararse, detenerse⟩ ⟨to put a stop to : poner fin a⟩ **3** : parada *f* ⟨bus stop : parada de autobús⟩
stopgap [ˈstɑpˌgæp] *n* : arreglo *m* provisorio
stoplight [ˈstɑpˌlaɪt] *n* : semáforo *m*
stoppage [ˈstɑpɪʤ] *n* : acto *m* de parar ⟨a work stoppage : un paro⟩
stopper [ˈstɑpər] *n* : tapón *m*
storage [ˈstorɪʤ] *n* : almacenamiento *m*, almacenaje *m*
storage battery *n* : acumulador *m*
store¹ [ˈstor] *vt* **stored; storing** : guardar, almacenar
store² *n* **1** RESERVE, SUPPLY : reserva *f* **2** SHOP : tienda *f* ⟨grocery store : tienda de comestibles⟩
storehouse [ˈstorˌhaʊs] *n* : almacén *m*, depósito *m*
storekeeper [ˈstorˌkiːpər] *n* : tendero *m*, -ra *f*
storeroom [ˈstorˌruːm, -ˌrʊm] *n* : almacén *m*, depósito *m*
stork [ˈstɔrk] *n* : cigüeña *f*
storm¹ [ˈstɔrm] *vi* **1** : llover o nevar tormentosamente **2** RAGE : ponerse furioso, vociferar **3 to storm out** : salir echando pestes — *vt* ATTACK : asaltar
storm² *n* **1** : tormenta *f*, tempestad *f* **2** UPROAR : alboroto *m*, revuelo *m*, escándalo *m* ⟨a storm of abuse : un torrente de abusos⟩
stormy [ˈstɔrmi] *adj* **stormier; -est** : tormentoso
story [ˈstori] *n, pl* **stories** **1** NARRATIVE : cuento *m*, relato *m* **2** ACCOUNT : historia *f*, relato *m* **3** : piso *m*, planta *f* (de un edificio) ⟨first story : planta baja⟩
stout [ˈstaʊt] *adj* **1** FIRM, RESOLUTE : firme, resuelto **2** STURDY : fuerte, robusto, sólido **3** FAT : corpulento, gordo
stove¹ [ˈstoːv] *n* : cocina *f* (para cocinar), estufa *f* (para calentar)
stove² → **stave¹**
stow [ˈstoː] *vt* **1** STORE : poner, meter, guardar **2** LOAD : cargar — *vi* **to stow away** : viajar de polizón
stowaway [ˈstoːəˌweɪ] *n* : polizón *m*
straddle [ˈstrædəl] *vt* **-dled; -dling** : sentarse a horcajadas sobre
straggle [ˈstrægəl] *vi* **-gled; -gling** : rezagarse, quedarse atrás
straggler [ˈstrægələr] *n* : rezagado *m*, -da *f*
straight¹ [ˈstreɪt] *adv* **1** : derecho, directamente ⟨go straight, then turn right : sigue derecho, luego gira a la derecha⟩ **2** HONESTLY : honestamente ⟨to go straight : enmendarse⟩ **3** CLEARLY : con claridad **4** FRANKLY : francamente, con franqueza
straight² *adj* **1** : recto (dícese de las líneas, etc.), derecho (dícese de algo vertical), lacio (dícese del pelo) **2** HONEST, JUST : honesto, justo **3** NEAT, ORDERLY : arreglado, ordenado
straighten [ˈstreɪtən] *vt* **1** : enderezar, poner derecho **2 to straighten up** : arreglar, ordenar ⟨he straightened up the house : arregló la casa⟩
straightforward [streɪtˈfɔrwərd] *adj* **1** FRANK : franco, sincero **2** CLEAR, PRECISE : puro, simple, claro
straightway [ˈstreɪtˈweɪ, -ˌweɪ] *adv* : inmediatamente
strain¹ [ˈstreɪn] *vt* **1** EXERT : forzar (la vista, la voz) ⟨to strain oneself : hacer un gran esfuerzo⟩ **2** FILTER : colar, filtrar **3** INJURE : lastimarse, hacerse daño en ⟨to strain a muscle : sufrir un esguince⟩
strain² *n* **1** LINEAGE : linaje *m*, abolengo *m* **2** STREAK, TRACE : veta *f* **3** VARIETY : tipo *m*, variedad *f* **4** STRESS : tensión *f*, presión *f* **5** SPRAIN : esguince *m*, torcedura *f* (del tobillo, etc.) **6 strains** *npl* TUNE : melodía *f*, acordes *mpl*, compases *fpl*
strainer [ˈstreɪnər] *n* : colador *m*
strait [ˈstreɪt] *n* **1** : estrecho *m* **2 straits** *npl* DISTRESS : aprietos *mpl*, apuros *mpl* ⟨in dire straits : en serios aprietos⟩
straitened [ˈstreɪtənd] *adj* **in straitened circumstances** : en apuros económicos
strand¹ [ˈstrænd] *vt* **1** : varar **2 to be left stranded** : quedar(se) varado, quedar colgado ⟨they left me stranded : me dejaron abandonado⟩
strand² *n* **1** : hebra *f* (de hilo, etc.) ⟨a strand of hair : un pelo⟩ **2** BEACH : playa *f*
strange [ˈstreɪnʤ] *adj* **stranger; -est** **1** QUEER, UNUSUAL : extraño, raro **2** UNFAMILIAR : desconocido, nuevo
strangely [ˈstreɪnʤli] *adv* ODDLY : de manera extraña ⟨to behave strangely : portarse de una manera rara⟩ ⟨strangely, he didn't call : curiosamente, no llamó⟩

strangeness [ˈstreɪndʒnəs] *n* **1** ODDNESS : rareza *f* **2** UNFAMILIARITY : lo desconocido
stranger [ˈstreɪndʒər] *n* : desconocido *m*, -da *f*; extraño *m*, -ña *f*
strangle [ˈstræŋgəl] *vt* **-gled; -gling** : estrangular
strangler [ˈstræŋglər] *n* : estrangulador *m*, -dora *f*
strap¹ [ˈstræp] *vt* **strapped; strapping 1** FASTEN : sujetar con una correa **2** FLOG : azotar (con una correa)
strap² *n* **1** : correa *f* **2 shoulder strap** : tirante *m*
strapless [ˈstræpləs] *n* : sin tirantes
strapping [ˈstræpɪŋ] *adj* : robusto, fornido
stratagem [ˈstræṭədʒəm, -ˌdʒɛm] *n* : estratagema *f*, artimaña *f*
strategic [strəˈtiːdʒɪk] *adj* : estratégico
strategist [ˈstræṭədʒɪst] *n* : estratega *mf*
strategy [ˈstræṭədʒi] *n, pl* **-gies** : estrategia *f*
stratified [ˈstræṭəˌfaɪd] *adj* : estratificado
stratosphere [ˈstræṭəˌsfɪr] *n* : estratosfera *f*
stratospheric [ˌstræṭəˈsfɪrɪk, -ˈsfɛr-] *adj* : estratosférico
stratum [ˈstreɪṭəm, ˈstræ-] *n, pl* **strata** [-ṭə] : estrato *m*, capa *f*
straw *n* **1** : paja *f* ⟨the last straw : el colmo⟩ **2** *or* **drinking straw** : pajita *f*, popote *m Mex*
strawberry [ˈstrɔˌbɛri] *n, pl* **-ries** : fresa *f*
stray¹ [ˈstreɪ] *vi* **1** WANDER : alejarse, extraviarse ⟨the cattle strayed away : el ganado se descarrió⟩ **2** DIGRESS : desviarse, divagar
stray² *adj* : perdido, callejero (dícese de un perro o un gato), descarriado (dícese del ganado)
stray³ *n* : animal *m* perdido, animal *m* callejero
streak¹ [ˈstriːk] *vt* : hacer rayas en ⟨blue streaked with grey : azul veteado con gris⟩ — *vi* : ir como una flecha
streak² *n* **1** : raya *f*, veta *f* (en mármol, queso, etc.), mechón *m* (en el pelo) **2** : rayo *m* (de luz) **3** TRACE : veta *f* **4** : racha *f* ⟨a streak of luck : una racha de suerte⟩
stream¹ [ˈstriːm] *vi* : correr, salir a chorros ⟨tears streamed from his eyes : las lágrimas brotaban de sus ojos⟩ — *vt* : derramar, dejar correr ⟨to stream blood : derramar sangre⟩
stream² *n* **1** BROOK : arroyo *m*, riachuelo *m* **2** RIVER : río *m* **3** FLOW : corriente *f*, chorro *m*
streamer [ˈstriːmər] *n* **1** PENNANT : banderín *m* **2** RIBBON : serpentina *f* (de papel), cinta *f* (de tela)
streamlined [ˈstriːmˌlaɪnd] *adj* **1** : aerodinámico (dícese de los automóviles, etc.) **2** EFFICIENT : eficiente, racionalizado
street [ˈstriːt] *n* : calle *f*
streetcar [ˈstriːtˌkɑr] *n* : tranvía *m*
strength [ˈstrɛŋkθ] *n* **1** POWER : fuerza *f* **2** SOLIDITY, TOUGHNESS : solidez *f*, resistencia *f*, dureza *f* **3** INTENSITY : intensidad *f* (de emociones, etc.), lo fuerte (de un sabor, etc.) **4** : punto *m* fuerte ⟨strengths and weaknesses : virtudes y defectos⟩ **5** NUMBER : número *m*, complemento *m* ⟨in full strength : en gran número⟩
strengthen [ˈstrɛŋkθən] *vt* **1** : fortalecer (los músculos, el espíritu, etc.) **2** REINFORCE : reforzar **3** INTENSIFY : intensificar, redoblar (esfuerzos, etc.) — *vi* **1** : fortalecerse, hacerse más fuerte **2** INTENSIFY : intensificarse
strenuous [ˈstrɛnjuəs] *adj* **1** VIGOROUS : vigoroso, enérgico **2** ARDUOUS : duro, riguroso
strenuously [ˈstrɛnjuəsli] *adv* : vigorosamente, duro
stress¹ [ˈstrɛs] *vt* **1** : someter a tensión (física) **2** EMPHASIZE : enfatizar, recalcar **3 to stress out** : estresar
stress² *n* **1** : tensión *f* (en un material) **2** EMPHASIS : énfasis *m*, acento *m* (en lingüística) **3** TENSION : tensión *f* (nerviosa), estrés *m*
stressful [ˈstrɛsfəl] *adj* : estresante
stretch¹ [ˈstrɛtʃ] *vt* **1** EXTEND : estirar, extender, desplegar (alas) **2 to stretch the truth** : forzar la verdad, exagerar — *vi* : estirarse
stretch² *n* **1** STRETCHING : extensión *f*, estiramiento *m* (de músculos) **2** ELASTICITY : elasticidad *f* **3** EXPANSE : tramo *m*, trecho *m* ⟨the home stretch : la recta final⟩ **4** PERIOD : período *m* (de tiempo)
stretcher [ˈstrɛtʃər] *n* : camilla *f*
strew [ˈstruː] *vt* **strewed; strewed** *or* **strewn** [ˈstruːn]; **strewing 1** SCATTER : esparcir (semillas, etc.), desparramar (papeles, etc.) **2 to strew with** : cubrir de
stricken [ˈstrɪkən] *adj* **stricken with** : aquejado de (una enfermedad), afligido por (tristeza, etc.)
strict [ˈstrɪkt] *adj* : estricto — **strictly** *adv*
strictness [ˈstrɪktnəs] *n* : severidad *f*, lo estricto
stricture [ˈstrɪktʃər] *n* : crítica *f*, censura *f*
stride¹ [ˈstraɪd] *vi* **strode** [ˈstroːd]; **stridden** [ˈstrɪdən]; **striding** : ir dando trancos, ir dando zancadas
stride² *n* : tranco *m*, zancada *f*
strident [ˈstraɪdənt] *adj* : estridente
strife [ˈstraɪf] *n* : conflictos *mpl*, disensión *f*
strike¹ [ˈstraɪk] *v* **struck** [ˈstrʌk]; **striking** *vt* **1** HIT : golpear (a una persona) ⟨to strike a blow : pegar un golpe⟩ **2** DELETE : suprimir, tachar **3** COIN, MINT : acuñar (monedas) **4** : dar (la hora) **5** AFFLICT : sobrevenir ⟨he was stricken with a fever : le sobrevino una

fiebre> **6** IMPRESS : impresionar, parecer <her voice struck me : su voz me impresionó> <it struck him as funny : le pareció chistoso> **7** : encender (un fósforo) **8** FIND : descubrir (oro, petróleo) **9** ADOPT : adoptar (una pose, etc.) — *vi* **1** HIT : golpear <to strike against : chocar contra> **2** ATTACK : atacar **3** : declararse en huelga

strike² *n* **1** BLOW : golpe *m* **2** : huelga *f*, paro *m* <to be on strike : estar en huelga> **3** ATTACK : ataque *m*

strikebreaker ['straɪk,breɪkər] *n* : rompehuelgas *mf*, esquirol *mf*

strike out *vi* **1** HEAD : salir (para) **2** : ser ponchado (en béisbol) <the batter struck out : poncharon al bateador>

striker ['straɪkər] *n* : huelguista *mf*

strike up *vt* START : entablar, empezar

striking ['straɪkɪŋ] *adj* : notable, sorprendente, llamativo <a striking beauty : una belleza imponente> — **strikingly** *adv*

string¹ ['strɪŋ] *vt* **strung** ['strʌŋ]; **stringing** **1** THREAD : ensartar <to string beads : ensartar cuentas> **2** HANG : colgar (con un cordel)

string² *n* **1** : cordel *m*, cuerda *f* **2** SERIES : serie *f*, sarta *f* (de insultos, etc.) **3 strings** *npl* : cuerdas *fpl* (en música)

string bean *n* : judía *f*, ejote *m Mex*

stringent ['strɪndʒənt] *adj* : estricto, severo

stringy ['strɪŋi] *adj* **stringier; -est** : fibroso

strip¹ ['strɪp] *v* **stripped; stripping** *vt* : quitar (ropa, pintura, etc.), desnudar, despojar — *vi* UNDRESS : desnudarse

strip² *n* : tira *f* <a strip of land : una faja>

stripe¹ ['straɪp] *vt* **striped** ['straɪpt]; **striping** : marcar con rayas o listas

stripe² *n* **1** : raya *f*, lista *f* **2** BAND : franja *f*

striped ['straɪpt, 'straɪpəd] *adj* : a rayas, de rayas, rayado, listado

strive ['straɪv] *vi* **strove** ['stro:v]; **striven** ['strɪvən] *or* **strived; striving** **1 to strive for** : luchar por lograr **2 to strive to** : esforzarse por

strobe ['stro:b] *or* **strobe light** *n* : luz *f* estroboscópica

strode → **stride**

stroke¹ ['stro:k] *vt* **stroked; stroking** : acariciar

stroke² *n* : golpe *m* <a stroke of luck : un golpe de suerte>

stroll¹ ['stro:l] *vi* : pasear, pasearse, dar un paseo

stroll² *n* : paseo *m*

stroller ['stro:lər] *n* : cochecito *m* (para niños)

strong ['strɔŋ] *adj* **1** : fuerte **2** HEALTHY : sano **3** ZEALOUS : ferviente

stronghold ['strɔŋ,ho:ld] *n* : fortaleza *f*, fuerte *m*, bastión *m* <a cultural stronghold : un baluarte de la cultura>

strongly ['strɔŋli] *adv* **1** POWERFULLY : fuerte, con fuerza **2** STURDILY : fuertemente, sólidamente **3** INTENSELY : intensamente, profundamente **4** WHOLEHEARTEDLY : totalmente

struck → **strike¹**

structural ['strʌktʃərəl] *adj* : estructural

structure¹ ['strʌktʃər] *vt* **-tured; -turing** : estructurar

structure² *n* **1** BUILDING : construcción *f* **2** ARRANGEMENT, FRAMEWORK : estructura *f*

struggle¹ ['strʌgəl] *vi* **-gled; -gling** **1** CONTEND : forcejear (físicamente), luchar, contender **2** : hacer con dificultad <she struggled forward : avanzó con dificultad>

struggle² *n* : lucha *f*, pelea *f* (física)

strum ['strʌm] *vt* **strummed; strumming** : rasguear

strung → **string¹**

strut¹ ['strʌt] *vi* **strutted; strutting** : pavonearse

strut² *n* **1** : pavoneo *m* <he walked with a strut : se pavoneaba> **2** : puntal *m* (en construcción, etc.)

strychnine ['strɪk,naɪn, -nən, -,ni:n] *n* : estricnina *f*

stub¹ ['stʌb] *vt* **stubbed; stubbing** **1 to stub one's toe** : darse en el dedo (del pie) **2 to stub out** : apagarse

stub² *n* : colilla *f* (de un cigarrillo), cabo *m* (de un lápiz, etc.), talón *m* (de un cheque)

stubble ['stʌbəl] *n* **1** : rastrojo *m* (de plantas) **2** BEARD : barba *f*

stubborn ['stʌbərn] *adj* **1** OBSTINATE : terco, obstinado, empecinado **2** PERSISTENT : pertinaz, persistente — **stubbornly** *adv*

stubbornness ['stʌbərnnəs] *n* **1** OBSTINACY : terquedad *f*, obstinación *f* **2** PERSISTENCE : persistencia *f*

stubby ['stʌbi] *adj* **stubbier; -est** : corto y grueso <stubby fingers : dedos regordetes>

stucco ['stʌko:] *n, pl* **stuccos** *or* **stuccoes** : estuco *m*

stuck → **stick¹**

stuck–up ['stʌk'ʌp] *adj* : engreído, creído *fam*

stud¹ ['stʌd] *vt* **studded; studding** : tachonar, salpicar

stud² *n* **1** *or* **stud horse** : semental *m* **2** : montante *m* (en construcción) **3** HOBNAIL : tachuela *f*, tachón *m*

student ['stu:dənt, 'stju:-] *n* : estudiante *mf*; alumno *m*, -na *f* (de un colegio)

studied ['stʌdid] *adj* : intencionado, premeditado

studio ['stu:di,o:, 'stju:-] *n, pl* **studios** : estudio *m*

studious ['stu:diəs, 'stju:-] *adj* : estudioso — **studiously** *adv*

study¹ ['stʌdi] *v* **studied; studying** **1** : estudiar **2** EXAMINE : examinar, estudiar

study² *n, pl* **studies** **1** STUDYING : estudio *m* **2** OFFICE : estudio *m*, gabi-

nete *m* (en una casa) **3** RESEARCH : investigación *f*, estudio *m*
stuff[1] ['stʌf] *vt* : rellenar, llenar, atiborrar ⟨a stuffed toy : un juguete de peluche⟩
stuff[2] *n* **1** POSSESSIONS : cosas *fpl* **2** ESSENCE : esencia *f* **3** SUBSTANCE : cosa *f*, cosas *fpl* ⟨some sticky stuff : una cosa pegajosa⟩ ⟨she knows her stuff : es experta⟩
stuffing ['stʌfɪŋ] *n* : relleno *m*
stuffy ['stʌfi] *adj* **stuffier; -est 1** CLOSE : viciado, cargado ⟨a stuffy room : una sala mal ventilada⟩ ⟨stuffy weather : tiempo bochornoso⟩ **2** : tapado (dícese de la nariz) **3** STODGY : pesado, aburrido
stumble[1] ['stʌmbəl] *vi* **-bled; -bling 1** TRIP : tropezar, dar un traspié **2** FLOUNDER : quedarse sin saber qué hacer o decir **3 to stumble across** *or* **to stumble upon** : dar con, tropezar con
stumble[2] *n* : tropezón *m*, traspié *m*
stump[1] ['stʌmp] *vt* : dejar perplejo ⟨to be stumped : no tener respuesta⟩
stump[2] *n* **1** : muñón *m* (de un brazo o una pierna) **2** *or* **tree stump** : cepa *f*, tocón *m* **3** STUB : cabo *m*
stun ['stʌn] *vt* **stunned; stunning 1** : aturdir (con un golpe) **2** ASTONISH, SHOCK : dejar estupefacto, dejar atónito, aturdir
stung → **sting**[1]
stunk → **stink**[1]
stunning ['stʌnɪŋ] *adj* **1** ASTONISHING : asombroso, pasmoso, increíble **2** STRIKING : imponente, impresionante (dícese de la belleza)
stunt[1] ['stʌnt] *vt* : atrofiar
stunt[2] *n* : proeza *f* (acrobática)
stupefy ['stu:pəˌfaɪ, 'stju:-] *vt* **-fied; -fying 1** : aturdir, atontar (con drogas, etc.) **2** AMAZE : dejar estupefacto, dejar atónito
stupendous [stʊ'pɛndəs, stjʊ-] *adj* **1** MARVELOUS : estupendo, maravilloso **2** TREMENDOUS : tremendo — **stupendously** *adv*
stupid ['stu:pəd, 'stju:-] *adj* **1** IDIOTIC, SILLY : tonto, bobo, estúpido **2** DULL, OBTUSE : lento, torpe, lerdo
stupidity [stʊ'pɪdət̬i, stjʊ-] *n* : tontería *f*, estupidez *f*
stupidly ['stu:pədli, 'stju:-] *adv* **1** IDIOTICALLY : estúpidamente, tontamente **2** DENSELY : torpemente
stupor ['stu:pər, 'stju:-] *n* : estupor *m*
sturdily ['stərdəli] *adv* : sólidamente
sturdiness ['stərdinəs] *n* : solidez *f* (de muebles, etc.), robustez *f* (de una persona)
sturdy ['stərdi] *adj* **sturdier; -est** : fuerte, robusto, sólido
sturgeon ['stərdʒən] *n* : esturión *m*
stutter[1] ['stʌt̬ər] *vi* : tartamudear
stutter[2] *n* STAMMER : tartamudeo *m*
sty ['staɪ] *n* **1** *pl* **sties** PIGPEN : chiquero *m*, pocilga *f* **2** *pl* **sties** *or* **styes** : orzuelo *m* (en el ojo)
style[1] ['staɪl] *vt* **styled; styling 1** NAME : llamar **2** : peinar (pelo), diseñar (vestidos, etc.) ⟨carefully styled prose : prosa escrita con gran esmero⟩
style[2] *n* **1** : estilo *m* ⟨that's just his style : él es así⟩ ⟨to live in style : vivir a lo grande⟩ **2** FASHION : moda *f*
stylish ['staɪlɪʃ] *adj* : de moda, elegante, chic
stylishly ['staɪlɪʃli] *adv* : con estilo
stylishness ['staɪlɪʃnəs] *n* : estilo *m*
stylist ['staɪlɪst] *n* : estilista *mf*
stylize ['staɪˌlaɪz, 'staɪə-] *vt* : estilizar
stylus ['staɪləs] *n, pl* **styli** ['staɪˌlaɪ] **1** PEN : estilo *m* **2** NEEDLE : aguja *f* (de un tocadiscos)
stymie ['staɪmi] *vt* **-mied; -mieing** : obstaculizar
suave ['swɑv] *adj* : fino, urbano
sub[1] ['sʌb] *vi* **subbed; subbing** → **substitute**[1]
sub[2] *n* **1** → **substitute**[2] **2** → **submarine**
subcommittee ['sʌbkəˌmɪt̬i] *n* : subcomité *m*
subconscious[1] [səb'kɑntʃəs] *adj* : subconsciente — **subconsciously** *adv*
subconscious[2] *n* : subconsciente *m*
subcontract [ˌsʌb'kɑnˌtrækt] *vt* : subcontratar
subculture ['sʌbˌkʌltʃər] *n* : subcultura *f*
subdivide [ˌsʌbdə'vaɪd, 'sʌbdəˌvaɪd] *vt* **-vided; -viding** : subdividir
subdivision ['sʌbdəˌvɪʒən] *n* : subdivisión *f*
subdue [səb'du:, -'dju:] *vt* **-dued; -duing 1** OVERCOME : sojuzgar (a un enemigo), vencer, superar **2** CONTROL : dominar **3** SOFTEN : suavizar, atenuar (luz, etc.), moderar (lenguaje)
subgroup ['sʌbˌgru:p] *n* : subgrupo *m*
subhead ['sʌbˌhɛd] *or* **subheading** [-ˌhɛdɪŋ] *n* : subtítulo *m*
subject[1] [səb'dʒɛkt] *vt* **1** CONTROL, DOMINATE : controlar, dominar **2** : someter ⟨they subjected him to pressure : lo sometieron a presiones⟩
subject[2] ['sʌbdʒɪkt] *adj* **1** : subyugado, sometido ⟨a subject nation : una nación subyugada⟩ **2** PRONE : sujeto, propenso ⟨subject to colds : sujeto a resfriarse⟩ **3 subject to** : sujeto a ⟨subject to congressional approval : sujeto a la aprobación del congreso⟩
subject[3] ['sʌbdʒɪkt] *n* **1** : súbdito *m*, -ta *f* (de un gobierno) **2** TOPIC : tema *m* **3** : sujeto *m* (en gramática)
subjection [səb'dʒɛkʃən] *n* : sometimiento *m*
subjective [səb'dʒɛktɪv] *adj* : subjetivo — **subjectively** *adv*
subjectivity [ˌsʌbˌdʒɛk'tɪvət̬i] *n* : subjetividad *f*
subjugate ['sʌbdʒɪˌgeɪt] *vt* **-gated; -gating** : subyugar, someter, sojuzgar

subjunctive [səbˈʤʌŋktɪv] *n* : subjuntivo *m* — **subjunctive** *adj*
sublet [ˈsʌbˌlɛt] *vt* **-let; -letting** : subarrendar
sublime [səˈblaɪm] *adj* : sublime
sublimely [səˈblaɪmli] *adv* **1** : de manera sublime **2** UTTERLY : absolutamente, completamente
submarine¹ [ˈsʌbməˌri:n, ˌsʌbməˈ-] *adj* : submarino
submarine² *n* : submarino *m*
submerge [səbˈmərʤ] *v* **-merged; -merging** *vt* : sumergir — *vi* : sumergirse
submission [səbˈmɪʃən] *n* **1** YIELDING : sumisión *f* **2** PRESENTATION : presentación *f*
submissive [səbˈmɪsɪv] *adj* : sumiso, dócil
submit [səbˈmɪt] *v* **-mitted; -mitting** *vi* YIELD : rendirse ⟨to submit to : someterse a⟩ — *vt* PRESENT : presentar
subnormal [ˌsʌbˈnɔrməl] *adj* : por debajo de lo normal
subordinate¹ [səˈbɔrdənˌeɪt] *vt* **-nated; -nating** : subordinar
subordinate² [səˈbɔrdənət] *adj* : subordinado ⟨a subordinate clause : una oración subordinada⟩
subordinate³ *n* : subordinado *m*, -da *f*; subalterno *m*, -na *f*
subordination [səˌbɔrdənˈeɪʃən] *n* : subordinación *f*
subpoena¹ [səˈpi:nə] *vt* **-naed; -naing** : citar
subpoena² *n* : citación *f*, citatorio *m*
subscribe [səbˈskraɪb] *vi* **-scribed; -scribing 1** : suscribirse (a una revista, etc.) **2 to subscribe to** : suscribir (una opinión, etc.), estar de acuerdo con
subscriber [səbˈskraɪbər] *n* : suscriptor *m*, -tora *f* (de una revista, etc.); abonado *m*, -da *f* (de un servicio)
subscription [səbˈskrɪpʃən] *n* : suscripción *f*
subsequent [ˈsʌbsɪkwənt, -səˌkwɛnt] *adj* : subsiguiente ⟨subsequent to : posterior a⟩
subsequently [ˈsʌbˌsɪkwɛntli, -kwənt-] *adv* : posteriormente
subservient [səbˈsərviənt] *adj* : servil
subside [səbˈsaɪd] *vi* **-sided; -siding 1** SINK : hundirse, descender **2** ABATE : calmarse (dícese de las emociones), amainar (dícese del viento, etc.)
subsidiary¹ [səbˈsɪdiˌɛri] *adj* : secundario
subsidiary² *n, pl* **-ries** : filial *f*, subsidiaria *f*
subsidize [ˈsʌbsəˌdaɪz] *vt* **-dized; -dizing** : subvencionar, subsidiar
subsidy [ˈsʌbsədi] *n, pl* **-dies** : subvención *f*, subsidio *m*
subsist [səbˈsɪst] *vi* : subsistir, mantenerse, vivir
subsistence [səbˈsɪstənts] *n* : subsistencia *f*
substance [ˈsʌbstənts] *n* **1** ESSENCE : sustancia *f*, esencia *f* **2** : sustancia *f* ⟨a toxic substance : una sustancia tóxica⟩ **3** WEALTH : riqueza *f* ⟨a woman of substance : una mujer acaudalada⟩
substandard [ˌsʌbˈstændərd] *adj* : inferior, deficiente
substantial [səbˈstænʧəl] *adj* **1** ABUNDANT : sustancioso ⟨a substantial meal : una comida sustanciosa⟩ **2** CONSIDERABLE : considerable, apreciable **3** SOLID, STURDY : sólido
substantially [səbˈstænʧəli] *adv* : considerablemente
substantiate [səbˈstænʧiˌeɪt] *vt* **-ated; -ating** : confirmar, probar, justificar
substitute¹ [ˈsʌbstəˌtu:t, -ˌtju:t] *v* **-tuted; -tuting** *vt* : sustituir — *vi* **to substitute for** : sustituir
substitute² *n* **1** : sustituto *m*, -ta *f*; suplente *mf* (persona) **2** : sucedáneo *m* ⟨sugar substitute : sucedáneo de azúcar⟩
substitute teacher *n* : profesor *m*, -sora *f* suplente
substitution [ˌsʌbstəˈtu:ʃən, -ˈtju:-] *n* : sustitución *f*
subterfuge [ˈsʌbtərˌfju:ʤ] *n* : subterfugio *m*
subterranean [ˌsʌbtəˈreɪniən] *adj* : subterráneo
subtitle [ˈsʌbˌtaɪt̬əl] *n* : subtítulo *m*
subtle [ˈsʌt̬əl] *adj* **-tler; -tlest 1** DELICATE, ELUSIVE : sutil, delicado **2** CLEVER : sutil, ingenioso
subtlety [ˈsʌt̬əlti] *n, pl* **-ties** : sutileza *f*
subtly [ˈsʌt̬əli] *adv* : sutilmente
subtotal [ˈsʌbˌto:t̬əl] *n* : subtotal *m*
subtract [səbˈtrækt] *vt* : restar, sustraer
subtraction [səbˈtrækʃən] *n* : resta *f*, sustracción *f*
suburb [ˈsʌˌbərb] *n* : municipio *m* periférico, suburbio *m*
suburban [səˈbərbən] *adj* : de las afueras (de una ciudad), suburbano
subversion [səbˈvərʒən] *n* : subversión *f*
subversive [səbˈvərsɪv] *adj* : subversivo
subway [ˈsʌbˌweɪ] *n* : metro *m*, subterráneo *m Arg, Uru*
succeed [səkˈsi:d] *vt* FOLLOW : suceder a — *vi* : tener éxito (dícese de las personas), dar resultado (dícese de los planes, etc.) ⟨she succeeded in finishing : logró terminar⟩
success [səkˈsɛs] *n* : éxito *m*
successful [səkˈsɛsfəl] *adj* : exitoso, logrado — **successfully** *adv*
succession [səkˈsɛʃən] *n* : sucesión *f* ⟨in succesion : sucesivamente⟩
successive [səkˈsɛsɪv] *adj* : sucesivo, consecutivo — **successively** *adv*
successor [səkˈsɛsər] *n* : sucesor *m*, -sora *f*
succinct [səkˈsɪŋkt, səˈsɪŋkt] *adj* : sucinto — **succinctly** *adv*
succor¹ [ˈsʌkər] *vt* : socorrer
succor² *n* : socorro *m*

succotash [ˈsʌkəˌtæʃ] *n* : guiso *m* de maíz y frijoles
succulent¹ [ˈsʌkjələnt] *adj* : suculento, jugoso
succulent² *n* : suculenta *f* (planta)
succumb [səˈkʌm] *vi* : sucumbir
such¹ [ˈsʌʧ] *adv* **1** SO : tan ‹such tall buildings : edificios tan grandes› **2** VERY : muy ‹he's not in such good shape : anda un poco mal› **3 such that** : de tal manera que
such² *adj* : tal ‹there's no such thing : no existe tal cosa› ‹in such cases : en tales casos› ‹animals such as cows and sheep : animales como vacas y ovejas›
such³ *pron* **1** : tal ‹such was the result : tal fue el resultado› ‹he's a child, and acts as such : es un niño, y se porta como tal› **2** : algo o alguien semejante ‹books, papers and such : libros, papeles y cosas por el estilo›
suck [ˈsʌk] *vi* **1** : chupar (por la boca), aspirar (dícese de las máquinas) **2** SUCKLE : mamar — *vt* : sorber (bebidas), chupar (dulces, etc.)
sucker [ˈsʌkər] *n* **1** : ventosa *f* (de un insecto, etc.) **2** : chupón *m* (de una planta) **3** → **lollipop 4** FOOL : tonto *m*, -ta *f*; idiota *mf*
suckle [ˈsʌkəl] *v* **-led; -ling** *vt* : amamantar — *vi* : mamar
suckling [ˈsʌklɪŋ] *n* : lactante *mf*
sucrose [ˈsuːˌkroːs, -ˌkroːz] *n* : sacarosa *f*
suction [ˈsʌkʃən] *n* : succión *f*
Sudanese [ˌsuːdənˈiːz, -ˈiːs] *n* : sudanés *m*, -nesa *f* — **Sudanese** *adj*
sudden [ˈsʌdən] *adj* **1** : repentino, súbito ‹all of a sudden : de pronto, de repente› **2** UNEXPECTED : inesperado, improviso **3** ABRUPT, HASTY : precipitado, brusco
suddenly [ˈsʌdənli] *adv* **1** : de repente, de pronto **2** ABRUPTLY : bruscamente
suddenness [ˈsʌdənnəs] *n* **1** : lo repentino **2** ABRUPTNESS : brusquedad *f* **3** HASTINESS : lo precipitado
suds [ˈsʌdz] *npl* : espuma *f* (de jabón)
sue [ˈsuː] *v* **sued; suing** *vt* : demandar — *vi* **to sue for** : demandar por (daños, etc.)
suede [ˈsweɪd] *n* : ante *m*, gamuza *f*
suet [ˈsuːət] *n* : sebo *m*
suffer [ˈsʌfər] *vi* : sufrir — *vt* **1** : sufrir, padecer (dolores, etc.) **2** PERMIT : permitir, dejar
sufferer [ˈsʌfərər] *n* : persona que padece (una enfermedad, etc.)
suffering [ˈsʌfərɪŋ] *n* : sufrimiento *m*
suffice [səˈfaɪs] *vi* **-ficed; -ficing** : ser suficiente, bastar
sufficient [səˈfɪʃənt] *adj* : suficiente
sufficiently [səˈfɪʃəntli] *adv* : (lo) suficientemente, bastante
suffix [ˈsʌˌfɪks] *n* : sufijo *m*
suffocate [ˈsʌfəˌkeɪt] *v* **-cated; -cating** *vt* : asfixiar, ahogar — *vi* : asfixiarse, ahogarse
suffocation [ˌsʌfəˈkeɪʃən] *n* : asfixia *f*, ahogo *m*
suffrage [ˈsʌfrɪʤ] *n* : sufragio *m*, derecho *m* al voto
suffuse [səˈfjuːz] *vt* **-fused; -fusing** : impregnar (de olores, etc.), bañar (de luz), teñir (de colores), llenar (de emociones)
sugar¹ [ˈʃʊgər] *vt* : azucarar
sugar² *n* : azúcar *mf*
sugarcane [ˈʃʊgərˌkeɪn] *n* : caña *f* de azúcar
sugary [ˈʃʊgəri] *adj* **1** : azucarado ‹sugary desserts : postres azucarados› **2** SACCHARINE : empalagoso
suggest [səgˈʤɛst, sə-] *vt* **1** PROPOSE : sugerir **2** IMPLY : indicar, dar a entender
suggestible [səgˈʤɛstəbəl, sə-] *adj* : influenciable
suggestion [səgˈʤɛsʧən, sə-] *n* **1** PROPOSAL : sugerencia *f* **2** INDICATION : indicio *m* **3** INSINUATION : insinuación *f*
suggestive [səgˈʤɛstɪv, sə-] *adj* : insinuante — **suggestively** *adv*
suicidal [ˌsuːəˈsaɪdəl] *adj* : suicida
suicide [ˈsuːəˌsaɪd] *n* **1** : suicidio *m* (acto) **2** : suicida *mf* (persona)
suit¹ [ˈsuːt] *vt* **1** ADAPT : adaptar **2** BEFIT : convenir a, ser apropiado a **3** BECOME : favorecer, quedarle bien (a alguien) ‹the dress suits you : el vestido te queda bien› **4** PLEASE : agradecer, satisfacer, convenirle bien (a alguien) ‹does Friday suit you? : ¿le conviene el viernes?› ‹suit yourself! : ¡como quieras!›
suit² *n* **1** LAWSUIT : pleito *m*, litigio *m* **2** : traje *m* (ropa) **3** : palo *m* (de naipes)
suitability [ˌsuːt̬əˈbɪləṯi] *n* : idoneidad *f*, lo apropiado
suitable [ˈsuːt̬əbəl] *adj* : apropiado, idóneo — **suitably** [-bli] *adv*
suitcase [ˈsuːtˌkeɪs] *n* : maleta *f*, valija *f*, petaca *f Mex*
suite [ˈswiːt, *for 2 also* ˈsuːt] *n* **1** : suite *f* (de habitaciones) **2** SET : juego *m* (de muebles)
suitor [ˈsuːt̬ər] *n* : pretendiente *m*
sulfur [ˈsʌlfər] *n* : azufre *m*
sulfuric acid [ˌsʌlˈfjʊrɪk] *adj* : ácido *m* sulfúrico
sulfurous [ˌsʌlˈfjʊrəs, ˈsʌlfərəs, ˈsʌlfjə-] *adj* : sulfuroso
sulk¹ [ˈsʌlk] *vi* : estar de mal humor, enfurruñarse *fam*
sulk² *n* : mal humor *m*
sulky [ˈsʌlki] *adj* **sulkier; -est** : malhumorado, taimado *Chile*
sullen [ˈsʌlən] *adj* **1** MOROSE : hosco, taciturno **2** DREARY : sombrío, deprimente
sullenly [ˈsʌlənli] *adv* **1** MOROSELY : hoscamente **2** GLOOMILY : sombríamente
sully [ˈsʌli] *vt* **sullied; sullying** : manchar, empañar

sultan [ˈsʌltən] *n* : sultán *m*
sultry [ˈsʌltri] *adj* **sultrier; -est 1** : bochornoso ⟨sultry weather : tiempo sofocante, tiempo bochornoso⟩ **2** SENSUAL : sensual, seductor
sum[1] [ˈsʌm] *vt* **summed; summing 1** : sumar (números) **2** → **sum up**
sum[2] *n* **1** AMOUNT : suma *f*, cantidad *f* **2** TOTAL : suma *f*, total *f* **3** : suma *f*, adición *f* (en matemáticas)
sumac [ˈʃuːˌmæk, ˈsuː-] *n* : zumaque *m*
summarize [ˈsʌməˌraɪz] *v* **-rized; -rizing** : resumir, compendiar
summary[1] [ˈsʌməri] *adj* **1** CONCISE : breve, conciso **2** IMMEDIATE : inmediato ⟨a summary dismissal : un despido inmediato⟩
summary[2] *n, pl* **-ries** : resumen *m*, compendio *m*
summer [ˈsʌmər] *n* : verano *m*
summery [ˈsʌməri] *adj* : veraniego
summit [ˈsʌmət] *n* **1** : cumbre *f*, cima *f* (de una montaña) **2** *or* **summit conference** : cumbre *f*
summon [ˈsʌmən] *vt* **1** CALL : convocar (una reunión, etc.), llamar (a una persona) **2** : citar (en derecho) **3 to summon up** : armarse de (valor, etc.) ⟨to summon up one's strength : reunir fuerzas⟩
summons [ˈsʌmənz] *n, pl* **summonses 1** SUBPOENA : citación *f*, citatorio *m Mex* **2** CALL : llamada *f*, llamamiento *m*
sumptuous [ˈsʌmptʃʊəs] *adj* : suntuoso
sum up *vt* **1** SUMMARIZE : resumir **2** EVALUATE : evaluar — *vi* : recapitular
sun[1] [ˈsʌn] *vt* **sunned; sunning 1** : poner al sol **2 to sun oneself** : asolearse, tomar el sol
sun[2] *n* **1** : sol *m* **2** SUNSHINE : luz *f* del sol
sunbeam [ˈsʌnˌbiːm] *n* : rayo *m* de sol
sunblock [ˈsʌnˌblɑk] *n* : filtro *m* solar
sunburn[1] [ˈsʌnˌbərn] *vi* **-burned** [-ˌbərnd] *or* **-burnt** [-ˌbərnt]; **-burning** : quemarse por el sol
sunburn[2] [ˈsʌnˌbərn] *n* : quemadura *f* de sol
sundae [ˈsʌndi] *n* : sundae *m*
Sunday [ˈsʌnˌdeɪ, -di] *n* : domingo *m*
sundial [ˈsʌnˌdaɪl] *n* : reloj *m* de sol
sundown [ˈsʌnˌdaʊn] → **sunset**
sundries [ˈsʌndriz] *npl* : artículos *mpl* diversos
sundry [ˈsʌndri] *adj* : varios, diversos
sunflower [ˈsʌnˌflaʊər] *n* : girasol *m*, mirasol *m*
sung → **sing**
sunglasses [ˈsʌnˌglæsəz] *npl* : gafas *fpl* de sol, lentes *mpl* de sol
sunk → **sink**[1]
sunken [ˈsʌŋkən] *adj* : hundido
sunlight [ˈsʌnˌlaɪt] *n* : sol *m*, luz *f* del sol
sunny [ˈsʌni] *adj* **sunnier; -est** : soleado
sunrise [ˈsʌnˌraɪz] *n* : salida *f* del sol
sunscreen [ˈsʌnˌskriːn] *n* : filtro *m* solar
sunset [ˈsʌnˌsɛt] *n* : puesta *f* del sol
sunshine [ˈsʌnˌʃaɪn] *n* : sol *m*, luz *f* del sol
sunspot [ˈsʌnˌspɑt] *n* : mancha *f* solar
sunstroke [ˈsʌnˌstroːk] *n* : insolación *f*
suntan [ˈsʌnˌtæn] *n* : bronceado *m*
sup [ˈsʌp] *vi* **supped; supping** : cenar
super [ˈsuːpər] *adj* : súper ⟨super! : ¡fantástico!⟩
superabundance [ˌsuːpərəˈbʌndən*t*s] *n* : superabundancia *f*
superb [sʊˈpərb] *adj* : magnífico, espléndido — **superbly** *adv*
supercilious [ˌsuːpərˈsɪliəs] *adj* : altivo, altanero, desdeñoso
supercomputer [ˈsuːpərkəmˌpjuːt̬ər] *n* : supercomputadora *f*
superficial [ˌsuːpərˈfɪʃəl] *adj* : superficial — **superficially** *adv*
superfluous [sʊˈpərflʊəs] *adj* : superfluo
superhighway [ˈsuːpərˌhaɪˌweɪ, ˌsuːpərˈ-] *n* : autopista *f*
superhuman [ˌsuːpərˈ*h*juːmən] *adj* **1** SUPERNATURAL : sobrenatural **2** HERCULEAN : sobrehumano
superimpose [ˌsuːpərɪmˈpoːz] *vt* **-posed; -posing** : superponer, sobreponer
superintend [ˌsuːpərɪnˈtɛnd] *vt* : supervisar
superintendent [ˌsuːpərɪnˈtɛndənt] *n* : portero *m*, -ra *f* (de un edificio); director *m*, -tora *f* (de una escuela, etc.); superintendente *mf* (de policía)
superior[1] [sʊˈpɪriər] *adj* **1** BETTER : superior **2** HAUGHTY : altivo, altanero
superior[2] *n* : superior *m*
superiority [sʊˌpɪriˈɔrət̬i] *n, pl* **-ties** : superioridad *f*
superlative[1] [sʊˈpərlət̬ɪv] *adj* **1** : superlativo (en gramática) **2** SUPREME : supremo **3** EXCELLENT : excelente, excepcional
superlative[2] *n* : superlativo *m*
supermarket [ˈsuːpərˌmɑrkət] *n* : supermercado *m*
supernatural [ˌsuːpərˈnætʃərəl] *adj* : sobrenatural
supernaturally [ˌsuːpərˈnætʃərəli] *adv* : de manera sobrenatural
superpower [ˈsuːpərˌpaʊər] *n* : superpotencia *f*
supersede [ˌsuːpərˈsiːd] *vt* **-seded; -seding** : suplantar, reemplazar, sustituir
supersonic [ˌsuːpərˈsɑnɪk] *adj* : supersónico
superstar [ˈsuːpərˌstɑr] *n* : superestrella *f*
superstition [ˌsuːpərˈstɪʃən] *n* : superstición *f*
superstitious [ˌsuːpərˈstɪʃəs] *adj* : supersticioso
superstructure [ˈsuːpərˌstrʌktʃər] *n* : superestructura *f*
supervise [ˈsuːpərˌvaɪz] *vt* **-vised; -vising** : supervisar, dirigir
supervision [ˌsuːpərˈvɪʒən] *n* : supervisión *f*, dirección *f*

supervisor [ˈsuːpərˌvaɪzər] *n* : supervisor *m*, -sora *f*
supervisory [ˌsuːpərˈvaɪzəri] *adj* : de supervisor
supine [sʊˈpaɪn] *adj* **1** : en decúbito supino, en decúbito dorsal **2** ABJECT, INDIFFERENT : indiferente, apático
supper [ˈsʌpər] *n* : cena *f*, comida *f*
supplant [səˈplænt] *vt* : suplantar
supple [ˈsʌpəl] *adj* **-pler; -plest** : flexible
supplement[1] [ˈsʌpləˌmɛnt] *vt* : complementar, completar
supplement[2] [ˈsʌpləmənt] *n* **1** : complemento *m* ⟨dietary supplement : complemento alimenticio⟩ **2** : suplemento *m* (de un libro o periódico)
supplementary [ˌsʌpləˈmɛntəri] *adj* : suplementario
supplicate [ˈsʌpləˌkeɪt] *v* **-cated; -cating** *vi* : rezar — *vt* : suplicar
supplier [səˈplaɪər] *n* : proveedor *m*, -dora *f*; abastecedor *m*, -dora *f*
supply[1] [səˈplaɪ] *vt* **-plied; -plying** : suministrar, proveer de, proporcionar
supply[2] *n, pl* **-plies** **1** PROVISION : provisión *f*, suministro *m* ⟨supply and demand : la oferta y la demanda⟩ **2** STOCK : reserva *f*, existencias *fpl* (de un negocio) **3 supplies** *npl* PROVISIONS : provisiones *fpl*, víveres *mpl*, despensa *f*
support[1] [səˈport] *vt* **1** BACK : apoyar, respaldar **2** MAINTAIN : mantener, sostener, sustentar **3** PROP UP : sostener, apoyar, apuntalar, soportar
support[2] *n* **1** : apoyo *m* (moral), ayuda *f* (económica) **2** PROP : soporte *m*, apoyo *m*
supporter [səˈporṭər] *n* : partidario *m*, -ria *f*
supportive [səˈporṭɪv] *adj* : que apoya ⟨his family is very supportive : su familia lo apoya mucho⟩
suppose [səˈpoːz] *vt* **-posed; -posing** **1** ASSUME : suponer, imaginarse **2** BELIEVE : suponer, creer **3 to be supposed to** : tener que, deber
supposed [səˈpoːzd, -ˈpoːzəd] *adj* : supuesto — **supposedly** [səˈpoːzədli] *adv*
supposition [ˌsʌpəˈzɪʃən] *n* : suposición *f*
suppository [səˈpɑzəˌtori] *n, pl* **-ries** : supositorio *m*
suppress [səˈprɛs] *vt* **1** SUBDUE : sofocar, suprimir, reprimir (una rebelión, etc.) **2** : suprimir, ocultar (información) **3** REPRESS : reprimir, contener ⟨to suppress a yawn : reprimir un bostezo⟩
suppression [səˈprɛʃən] *n* **1** SUBDUING : represión *f* **2** : supresión *f* (de información) **3** REPRESSION : represión *f*, inhibición *f*
supremacy [sʊˈprɛməsi] *n, pl* **-cies** : supremacía *f*
supreme [sʊˈpriːm] *adj* : supremo
Supreme Being *n* : Ser *m* Supremo
supremely [sʊˈpriːmli] *adv* : totalmente, sumamente
surcharge [ˈsərˌʧɑrʤ] *n* : recargo *m*
sure[1] [ˈʃʊr] *adv* **1** ALL RIGHT : por supuesto, claro **2** (*used as an intensifier*) ⟨it sure is hot! : ¡hace tanto calor!⟩ ⟨she sure is pretty! : ¡qué linda es!⟩
sure[2] *adj* **surer; -est** : seguro ⟨to be sure about something : estar seguro de algo⟩ ⟨a sure sign : una clara señal⟩ ⟨for sure : seguro, con seguridad⟩
surely [ˈʃʊrli] *adv* **1** CERTAINLY : seguramente **2** (*used as an intensifier*) ⟨you surely don't mean that! : ¡no me digas que estás hablando en serio!⟩
sureness [ˈʃʊrnəs] *n* : certeza *f*, seguridad *f*
surety [ˈʃʊrəṭi] *n, pl* **-ties** : fianza *f*, garantía *f*
surf [ˈsərf] *n* **1** WAVES : oleaje *m* **2** FOAM : espuma *f*
surface[1] [ˈsərfəs] *v* **-faced; -facing** *vi* : salir a la superficie — *vt* : revestir (una carretera)
surface[2] *n* **1** : superficie *f* **2 on the surface** : en apariencia
surfboard [ˈsərfˌbord] *n* : tabla *f* de surf, tabla *f* de surfing
surfeit [ˈsərfət] *n* : exceso *m*
surfer [ˈsərfər] *n* : surfista *mf*
surfing [ˈsərfɪŋ] *n* : surf *m*, surfing *m*
surge[1] [ˈsərʤ] *vi* **surged; surging** **1** : hincharse (dícese del mar), levantarse (dícese de las olas) **2** SWARM : salir en tropel (dícese de la gente, etc.)
surge[2] *n* **1** : oleaje *m* (del mar), oleada *f* (de gente) **2** FLUSH : arranque *m*, arrebato *m* (de ira, etc.) **3** INCREASE : aumento *m* (súbito)
surgeon [ˈsərʤən] *n* : cirujano *m*, -na *f*
surgery [ˈsərʤəri] *n, pl* **-geries** : cirugía *f*
surgical [ˈsərʤɪkəl] *adj* : quirúrgico — **surgically** [-kli] *adv*
surly [ˈsərli] *adj* **surlier; -est** : hosco, arisco
surmise[1] [sərˈmaɪz] *vt* **-mised; -mising** : conjeturar, suponer, concluir
surmise[2] *n* : conjetura *f*
surmount [sərˈmaʊnt] *vt* **1** OVERCOME : superar, vencer, salvar **2** CLIMB : escalar **3** CAP, TOP : coronar
surname [ˈsərˌneɪm] *n* : apellido *m*
surpass [sərˈpæs] *vt* : superar, exceder, rebasar, sobrepasar
surplus [ˈsərˌplʌs] *n* : excedente *m*, sobrante *m*, superávit *m* (de dinero)
surprise[1] [səˈpraɪz, sər-] *vt* **-prised; -prising** : sorprender
surprise[2] *n* : sorpresa *f* ⟨to take by surprise : sorprender⟩
surprising [səˈpraɪzɪŋ, sər-] *adj* : sorprendente — **surprisingly** *adv*
surrender[1] [səˈrɛndər] *vt* **1** : entregar, rendir **2 to surrender oneself** : entregarse — *vi* : rendirse
surrender[2] *n* : rendición *m* (de una ciudad, etc.), entrega *f* (de posesiones)

surreptitious [ˌsərəpˈtɪʃəs] *adj* : subrepticio — **surreptitiously** *adv*
surrogate [ˈsərəgət, -ˌgeɪt] *n* : sustituto *m*
surround [səˈraʊnd] *vt* : rodear
surroundings [səˈraʊndɪŋz] *npl* : ambiente *m*, entorno *m*
surveillance [sərˈveɪlənts, -ˈveɪljənts, -ˈveɪənts] *n* : vigilancia *f*
survey[1] [sərˈveɪ] *vt* **-veyed; -veying 1** : medir (un terreno) **2** EXAMINE : inspeccionar, examinar, revisar **3** POLL : hacer una encuesta de, sondear
survey[2] [ˈsərˌveɪ] *n, pl* **-veys 1** INSPECTION : inspección *f*, revisión *f* **2** : medición *f* (de un terreno) **3** POLL : encuesta *f*, sondeo *m*
surveyor [sərˈveɪər] *n* : agrimensor *m*, -sora *f*
survival [sərˈvaɪvəl] *n* : supervivencia *f*, sobrevivencia *f*
survive [sərˈvaɪv] *v* **-vived; -viving** *vi* : sobrevivir — *vt* OUTLIVE : sobrevivir a
survivor [sərˈvaɪvər] *n* : superviviente *mf*, sobreviviente *mf*
susceptibility [səˌsɛptəˈbɪləti] *n, pl* **-ties** : vulnerabilidad *f*, propensión *f* (a enfermedades, etc.)
susceptible [səˈsɛptəbəl] *adj* **1** VULNERABLE : vulnerable, sensible ⟨susceptible to flattery : sensible a halagos⟩ **2** PRONE : propenso ⟨susceptible to colds : propenso a resfriarse⟩
suspect[1] [səˈspɛkt] *vt* **1** DISTRUST : dudar de **2** : sospechar (algo), sospechar de (una persona) **3** IMAGINE, THINK : imaginarse, creer
suspect[2] [ˈsʌsˌpɛkt, səˈspɛkt] *adj* : sospechoso, dudoso, cuestionable
suspect[3] [ˈsʌsˌpɛkt] *n* : sospechoso *m*, -sa *f*
suspend [səˈspɛnd] *vt* : suspender
suspenders [səˈspɛndərz] *npl* : tirantes *mpl*
suspense [səˈspɛnts] *n* : incertidumbre *f*, suspenso *m* (en una película, etc.)
suspenseful [səˈspɛntsfəl] *adj* : de suspenso
suspension [səˈspɛntʃən] *n* : suspensión *f*
suspicion [səˈspɪʃən] *n* **1** : sospecha *f* **2** TRACE : pizca *f*, atisbo *m*
suspicious [səˈspɪʃəs] *adj* **1** QUESTIONABLE : sospechoso, dudoso **2** DISTRUSTFUL : suspicaz, desconfiado
suspiciously [səˈspɪʃəsli] *adv* : de modo sospechoso, con recelo
sustain [səˈsteɪn] *vt* **1** NOURISH : sustentar **2** PROLONG : sostener **3** SUFFER : sufrir **4** SUPPORT, UPHOLD : apoyar, respaldar, sostener
sustainable [səˈsteɪnəbəl] *adj* : sostenible
sustenance [ˈsʌstənənts] *n* **1** NOURISHMENT : sustento *m* **2** SUPPORT : sostén *m*
svelte [ˈsfɛlt] *adj* : esbelto
swab[1] [ˈswɑb] *vt* **swabbed; swabbing 1** CLEAN : lavar, limpiar **2** : aplicar a (con hisopo)
swab[2] *n or* **cotton swab** : hisopo *m* (para aplicar medicinas, etc.)
swaddle [ˈswɑdəl] *vt* **-dled; -dling** [ˈswɑdəlɪŋ] : envolver (en pañales)
swagger[1] [ˈswægər] *vi* : pavonearse
swagger[2] *n* : pavoneo *m*
swallow[1] [ˈswɑlo:] *vt* **1** : tragar (comida, etc.) **2** ENGULF : tragarse, envolver **3** REPRESS : tragarse (insultos, etc.) — *vi* : tragar
swallow[2] *n* **1** : golondrina *f* (pájaro) **2** GULP : trago *m*
swam → **swim**[1]
swamp[1] [ˈswɑmp] *vt* : inundar
swamp[2] *n* : pantano *m*, ciénaga *f*
swampy [ˈswɑmpi] *adj* **swampier; -est** : pantanoso, cenagoso
swan [ˈswɑn] *n* : cisne *f*
swap[1] [ˈswɑp] *vt* **swapped; swapping** : cambiar, intercambiar ⟨to swap places : cambiarse de sitio⟩
swap[2] *n* : cambio *m*, intercambio *m*
swarm[1] [ˈswɔrm] *vi* : enjambrar
swarm[2] *n* : enjambre *m*
swarthy [ˈswɔrði, -θi] *adj* **swarthier; -est** : moreno
swashbuckling [ˈswɑʃˌbʌklɪŋ] *adj* : de aventurero
swat[1] [ˈswɑt] *vt* **swatted; swatting** : aplastar (un insecto), darle una palmada (a alguien)
swat[2] *n* : palmada *f* (con la mano), golpe *m* (con un objeto)
swatch [ˈswɑtʃ] *n* : muestra *f*
swath [ˈswɑθ, ˈswɔθ] *or* **swathe** [ˈswɑð, ˈswɔð, ˈsweɪð] *n* : franja *f* (de grano segado)
swathe [ˈswɑð, ˈswɔð, ˈsweɪð] *vt* **swathed; swathing** : envolver
swatter [ˈswɑtər] → **flyswatter**
sway[1] [ˈsweɪ] *vi* : balancearse, mecerse — *vt* INFLUENCE : influir en, convencer
sway[2] *n* **1** SWINGING : balanceo *m* **2** INFLUENCE : influjo *m*
swear [ˈswær] *v* **swore** [ˈswor]; **sworn** [ˈsworn]; **swearing** *vi* **1** VOW : jurar **2** CURSE : decir palabrotas — *vt* : jurar
swearword [ˈswærˌwərd] *n* : mala palabra *f*, palabrota *f*
sweat[1] [ˈswɛt] *vi* **sweat** *or* **sweated; sweating 1** PERSPIRE : sudar, transpirar **2** OOZE : rezumar **3 to sweat over** : sudar la gota gorda por
sweat[2] *n* : sudor *m*, transpiración *f*
sweater [ˈswɛtər] *n* : suéter *m*
sweatshirt [ˈswɛtˌʃərt] *n* : sudadera *f*
sweaty [ˈswɛti] *adj* **sweatier; -est** : sudoroso, sudado, transpirado
Swede [ˈswi:d] *n* : sueco *m*, -ca *f*
Swedish[1] [ˈswi:dɪʃ] *adj* : sueco
Swedish[2] *n* **1** : sueco *m* (idioma) **2 the Swedish** *npl* : los suecos
sweep[1] [ˈswi:p] *v* **swept** [ˈswɛpt]; **sweeping** *vt* **1** : barrer (el suelo, etc.), limpiar (suciedad, etc.) ⟨he swept the books

aside : apartó los libros de un manotazo⟩ **2** *or* **to sweep through** : extenderse por (dícese del fuego, etc.), azotar (dícese de una tormenta) — *vi* **1** : barrer, limpiar **2** : extenderse (en una curva), describir una curva ⟨the sun swept across the sky : el sol describía una curva en el cielo⟩
sweep[2] *n* **1** : barrido *m*, barrida *f* (con una escoba) **2** : movimiento *m* circular **3** SCOPE : alcance *m*
sweeper [ˈswiːpər] *n* : barrendero *m*, -ra *f*
sweeping [ˈswiːpɪŋ] *adj* **1** WIDE : amplio (dícese de un movimiento) **2** EXTENSIVE : extenso, radical **3** INDISCRIMINATE : indiscriminado, demasiado general **4** OVERWHELMING : arrollador, aplastante
sweepstakes [ˈswiːpˌsteɪks] *ns & pl* **1** : carrera *f* (en que el ganador se lleva el premio entero) **2** LOTTERY : lotería *f*
sweet[1] [ˈswiːt] *adj* **1** : dulce ⟨sweet desserts : postres dulces⟩ **2** FRESH : fresco **3** : sin sal (dícese de la mantequilla, etc.) **4** PLEASANT : dulce, agradable **5** DEAR : querido
sweet[2] *n* : dulce *m*
sweeten [ˈswiːtən] *vt* : endulzar
sweetener [ˈswiːtənər] *n* : endulzante *m*
sweetheart [ˈswiːtˌhɑrt] *n* : novio *m*, -via *f* ⟨thanks, sweetheart : gracias, cariño⟩
sweetly [ˈswiːtli] *adv* : dulcemente
sweetness [ˈswiːtnəs] *n* : dulzura *f*
sweet potato *n* : batata *f*, boniato *m*
swell[1] [ˈswɛl] *vi* **swelled; swelled** *or* **swollen** [ˈswoːlən, ˈswʌl-]; **swelling 1** *or* **to swell up** : hincharse ⟨her ankle swelled : se le hinchó el tobillo⟩ **2** *or* **to swell out** : inflarse, hincharse (dícese de las velas, etc.) **3** INCREASE : aumentar, crecer
swell[2] *n* **1** : oleaje *m* (del mar) **2** → **swelling**
swelling [ˈswɛlɪŋ] *n* : hinchazón *f*
swelter [ˈswɛltər] *vi* : sofocarse de calor
swept → **sweep[1]**
swerve[1] [ˈswərv] *vi* **swerved; swerving** : virar bruscamente
swerve[2] *n* : viraje *m* brusco
swift[1] [ˈswɪft] *adj* **1** FAST : rápido, veloz **2** SUDDEN : repentino, súbito — **swiftly** *adv*
swift[2] *n* : vencejo *m* (pájaro)
swiftness [ˈswɪftnəs] *n* : rapidez *f*, velocidad *f*
swig[1] [ˈswɪg] *vi* **swigged; swigging** : tomar a tragos, beber a tragos
swig[2] *n* : trago *m*
swill[1] [ˈswɪl] *vt* : chupar, beber a tragos grandes
swill[2] *n* **1** SLOP : bazofia *f* **2** GARBAGE : basura *f*
swim[1] [ˈswɪm] *vi* **swam** [ˈswæm]; **swum** [ˈswʌm]; **swimming 1** : nadar **2** FLOAT : flotar **3** REEL : dar vueltas ⟨his head was swimming : la cabeza le daba vueltas⟩
swim[2] *n* : baño *m*, chapuzón *m* ⟨to go for a swim : ir a nadar⟩
swimmer [ˈswɪmər] *n* : nadador *m*, -dora *f*
swindle[1] [ˈswɪndəl] *vt* **-dled; -dling** : estafar, timar
swindle[2] *n* : estafa *f*, timo *m fam*
swindler [ˈswɪndələr] *n* : estafador *m*, -dora *f*; timador *m*, -dora *f*
swine [ˈswaɪn] *ns & pl* : cerdo *m*, -da *f*
swing[1] [ˈswɪŋ] *v* **swung** [ˈswʌŋ]; **swinging** *vt* **1** : describir una curva con ⟨he swung the ax at the tree : le dio al árbol con el hacha⟩ **2** : balancear (los brazos, etc.), hacer oscilar **3** SUSPEND : colgar — *vi* **1** SWAY : balancearse (dícese de los brazos, etc.), oscilar (dícese de un objeto), columpiarse, mecerse (en un columpio) **2** SWIVEL : girar (en un pivote) ⟨the door swung shut : la puerta se cerró⟩ **3** CHANGE : virar, cambiar (dícese de las opiniones, etc.)
swing[2] *n* **1** SWINGING : vaivén *m*, balanceo *m* **2** CHANGE, SHIFT : viraje *m*, movimiento *m* **3** : columpio *m* (para niños) **4 to take a swing at someone** : intentar pegarle a alguien
swipe[1] [ˈswaɪp] *vt* **swiped; swiping 1** STRIKE : dar, pegar (con un movimiento amplio) **2** WIPE : limpiar **3** STEAL : birlar *fam*, robar
swipe[2] *n* BLOW : golpe *m*
swirl[1] [ˈswərl] *vi* : arremolinarse
swirl[2] *n* **1** EDDY : remolino *m* **2** SPIRAL : espiral *f*
swish[1] [ˈswɪʃ] *vt* : mover (produciendo un sonido) ⟨she swished her skirt : movía la falda⟩ — *vi* : moverse (produciendo un sonido) ⟨the cars swished by : se oían pasar los coches⟩
swish[2] *n* : silbido *m* (de un látigo, etc.), susurro *m* (de agua), crujido *m* (de ropa, etc.)
Swiss [ˈswɪs] *n* : suizo *m*, -za *f* — **Swiss** *adj*
swiss chard *n* : acelga *f*
switch[1] [ˈswɪʧ] *vt* **1** LASH, WHIP : azotar **2** CHANGE : cambiar de **3** EXCHANGE : intercambiar **4 to switch on** : encender, prender **5 to switch off** : apagar — *vi* **1** : moverse de un lado al otro **2** CHANGE : cambiar **3** SWAP : intercambiarse
switch[2] *n* **1** WHIP : vara *f* **2** CHANGE, SHIFT : cambio *m* **3** : interruptor *m*, llave *f* (de la luz, etc.)
switchboard [ˈswɪʧˌbord] *n* : conmutador *m*, centralita *f*
swivel[1] [ˈswɪvəl] *vi* **-veled** *or* **-velled; -veling** *or* **-velling** : girar (sobre un pivote)
swivel[2] *n* : base *f* giratoria
swollen *pp* → **swell[1]**
swoon[1] [ˈswuːn] *vi* : desvanecerse, desmayarse
swoon[2] *n* : desvanecimiento *m*, desmayo *m*

swoop[1] ['swu:p] *vi* : abatirse (dícese de las aves), descender en picada (dícese de un avión)
swoop[2] *n* : descenso *m* en picada
sword ['sɔrd] *n* : espada *f*
swordfish ['sɔrd,fɪʃ] *n* : pez *m* espada
swore, sworn → **swear**
swum *pp* → **swim**[1]
swung → **swing**[1]
sycamore ['sɪkə,mor] *n* : sicomoro *m*
sycophant ['sɪkəfənt, -,fænt] *n* : adulador *m*, -dora *f*
syllabic [sə'læbɪk] *adj* : silábico
syllable ['sɪləbəl] *n* : sílaba *f*
syllabus ['sɪləbəs] *n, pl* **-bi** [-,baɪ] *or* **-buses** : programa *m* (de estudios)
symbol ['sɪmbəl] *n* : símbolo *m*
symbolic [sɪm'bɑlɪk] *adj* : simbólico — **symbolically** [-kli] *adv*
symbolism ['sɪmbə,lɪzəm] *n* : simbolismo *m*
symbolize ['sɪmbə,laɪz] *vt* **-ized; -izing** : simbolizar
symmetrical [sə'mɛtrɪkəl] *or* **symmetric** [-trɪk] *adj* : simétrico — **symmetrically** [-trɪkli] *adv*
symmetry ['sɪmətri] *n, pl* **-tries** : simetría *f*
sympathetic [,sɪmpə'θɛt̬ɪk] *adj* **1** PLEASING : agradable **2** RECEPTIVE : receptivo, favorable **3** COMPASSIONATE, UNDERSTANDING : comprensivo, compasivo
sympathetically [,sɪmpə'θɛt̬ɪkli] *adv* : con compasión, con comprensión
sympathize ['sɪmpə,θaɪz] *vi* **-thized; -thizing** : compadecer ⟨I sympathize with you : te compadezco⟩
sympathy ['sɪmpəθi] *n, pl* **-thies** **1** COMPASSION : compasión *f* **2** UNDERSTANDING : comprensión *f* **3** AGREEMENT : solidaridad *f* ⟨in sympathy with : de acuerdo con⟩ **4** CONDOLENCES : pésame *m*, condolencias *fpl*
symphonic [sɪm'fɑnɪk] *adj* : sinfónico
symphony ['sɪmpfəni] *n, pl* **-nies** : sinfonía *f*
symposium [sɪm'po:ziəm] *n, pl* **-sia** [-ziə] *or* **-siums** : simposio *m*
symptom ['sɪmptəm] *n* : síntoma *m*
symptomatic [,sɪmptə'mæt̬ɪk] *adj* : sintomático
synagogue ['sɪnə,gɑg, -,gɔg] *n* : sinagoga *f*
sync ['sɪŋk] *n* : sincronización *f* ⟨in sync : sincronizado⟩
synchronize ['sɪŋkrə,naɪz, 'sɪn-] *v* **-nized; -nizing** *vi* : estar sincronizado — *vt* : sincronizar
syncopate ['sɪŋkə,peɪt, 'sɪn-] *vt* **-pated; -pating** : sincopar
syncopation [,sɪŋkə'peɪʃən, ,sɪn-] *n* : síncopa *f*
syndicate[1] ['sɪndə,keɪt] *vi* **-cated; -cating** : formar una asociación
syndicate[2] ['sɪndɪkət] *n* : asociación *f*, agrupación *f*
syndrome ['sɪn,dro:m] *n* : síndrome *m*
synonym ['sɪnə,nɪm] *n* : sinónimo *m*
synonymous [sə'nɑnəməs] *adj* : sinónimo
synopsis [sə'nɑpsɪs] *n, pl* **-opses** [-,si:z] : sinopsis *f*
syntactic [sɪn'tæktɪk] *adj* : sintáctico
syntax ['sɪn,tæks] *n* : sintaxis *f*
synthesis ['sɪnθəsɪs] *n, pl* **-theses** [-,si:z] : síntesis *f*
synthesize ['sɪnθə,saɪz] *vt* **-sized; -sizing** : sintetizar
synthetic[1] [sɪn'θɛt̬ɪk] *adj* : sintético, artificial — **synthetically** [-t̬ɪkli] *adv*
synthetic[2] *n* : producto *m* sintético
syphilis ['sɪfələs] *n* : sífilis *f*
Syrian ['sɪriən] *n* : sirio *m*, -ria *f* — **Syrian** *adj*
syringe [sə'rɪnʤ, 'sɪrɪnʤ] *n* : jeringa *f*, jeringuilla *f*
syrup ['sərəp, 'sɪrəp] *n* : jarabe *m*, almíbar *m* (de azúcar y agua)
system ['sɪstəm] *n* **1** METHOD : sistema *m*, método *m* **2** APPARATUS : sistema *m*, instalación *f*, aparato *m* ⟨electrical system : instalación eléctrica⟩ ⟨digestive system : aparato digestivo⟩ **3** BODY : organismo *m*, cuerpo *m* ⟨diseases that affect the whole system : enfermedades que afectan el organismo entero⟩ **4** NETWORK : red *f*
systematic [,sɪstə'mæt̬ɪk] *adj* : sistemático — **systematically** [-t̬ɪkli] *adv*
systematize ['sɪstəmə,taɪz] *vt* **-tized; -tizing** : sistematizar
systemic [sɪs'tɛmɪk] *adj* : sistémico

T

t ['ti:] *n, pl* **t's** *or* **ts** ['ti:z] : vigésima letra del alfabeto inglés
tab ['tæb] *n* **1** FLAP, TAG : lengüeta *f* (de un sobre, una caja, etc.), etiqueta *f* (de ropa) **2** → **tabulator** **3** BILL, CHECK : cuenta *f* **4 to keep tabs on** : tener bajo vigilancia
tabby ['tæbi] *n, pl* **-bies** **1** *or* **tabby cat** : gato *m* atigrado **2** : gata *f*
tabernacle ['tæbər,nækəl] *n* : tabernáculo *m*
table ['teɪbəl] *n* **1** : mesa *f* ⟨a table for two : una mesa para dos⟩ **2** LIST : tabla *f* ⟨multiplication table : tabla de multiplicar⟩ **3 table of contents** : índice *m* de materias
tableau [tæ'blo:, 'tæ,-] *n, pl* **-leaux** [-'blo:z, -,blo:z] : retablo *m*, cuadro *m* vivo (en teatro)
tablecloth ['teɪbəl,klɔθ] *n* : mantel *m*
tablespoon ['teɪbəl,spu:n] *n* **1** : cuchara *f* (de mesa) **2** → **tablespoonful**

tablespoonful [ˈteɪbəlˌspu:nˌfʊl] *n* : cucharada *f*
tablet [ˈtæblət] *n* **1** PLAQUE : placa *f* **2** PAD : bloc *m* (de papel) **3** PILL : tableta *f*, pastilla *f*, píldora *f* ⟨an aspirin tablet : una tableta de aspirina⟩
table tennis *n* : tenis *m* de mesa
tableware [ˈteɪbəlˌwær] *n* : vajillas *fpl*, cubiertos *mpl* (de mesa)
tabloid [ˈtæˌblɔɪd] *n* : tabloide *m*
taboo[1] [təˈbu:, tæ-] *adj* : tabú
taboo[2] *n* : tabú *m*
tabular [ˈtæbjələr] *adj* : tabular
tabulate [ˈtæbjəˌleɪt] *vt* **-lated; -lating** : tabular
tabulator [ˈtæbjəˌleɪt̬ər] *n* : tabulador *m*
tacit [ˈtæsɪt] *adj* : tácito, implícito — **tacitly** *adv*
taciturn [ˈtæsɪˌtərn] *adj* : taciturno
tack[1] [ˈtæk] *vt* **1** : sujetar con tachuelas **2 to tack on** ADD : añadir, agregar
tack[2] *n* **1** : tachuela *f* **2** COURSE : rumbo *m* ⟨to change tack : cambiar de rumbo⟩
tackle[1] [ˈtækəl] *vt* **-led; -ling** **1** : taclear (en futbol americano) **2** CONFRONT : abordar, enfrentar, emprender (un problema, un trabajo, etc.)
tackle[2] *n* **1** EQUIPMENT, GEAR : equipo *m*, aparejo *m* **2** : aparejo *m* (de un buque) **3** : tacleada *f* (en futbol americano)
tacky [ˈtæki] *adj* **tackier; -est** **1** STICKY : pegajoso **2** CHEAP, GAUDY : de mal gusto, naco *Mex*
tact [ˈtækt] *n* : tacto *m*, delicadeza *f*, discreción *f*
tactful [ˈtæktfəl] *adj* : discreto, diplomático, de mucho tacto
tactfully [ˈtæktfəli] *adv* : discretamente, con mucho tacto
tactic [ˈtæktɪk] *n* : táctica *f*
tactical [ˈtæktɪkəl] *adj* : táctico, estratégico
tactics [ˈtæktɪks] *ns & pl* : táctica *f*, estrategia *f*
tactile [ˈtæktəl, -ˌtaɪl] *adj* : táctil
tactless [ˈtæktləs] *adj* : indiscreto, poco delicado
tactlessly [ˈtæktləsli] *adv* : rudamente, sin tacto
tadpole [ˈtædˌpo:l] *n* : renacuajo *m*
taffeta [ˈtæfət̬ə] *n* : tafetán *m*, tafeta *f* *Arg, Mex, Uru*
taffy [ˈtæfi] *n, pl* **-fies** : caramelo *m* de melaza, chicloso *m Mex*
tag[1] [ˈtæg] *v* **tagged; tagging** *vt* **1** LABEL : etiquetar **2** TAIL : seguir de cerca **3** TOUCH : tocar (en varios juegos) — *vi* **to tag along** : pegarse, acompañar
tag[2] *n* **1** LABEL : etiqueta *f* **2** SAYING : dicho *m*, refrán *m*
tail[1] [ˈteɪl] *vt* FOLLOW : seguir de cerca, pegarse
tail[2] *n* **1** : cola *f*, rabo *m* (de un animal) **2** : cola *f*, parte *f* posterior ⟨a comet's tail : la cola de un cometa⟩ **3 tails** *npl* : cruz *f* (de una moneda) ⟨heads or tails : cara o cruz⟩
tailed [ˈteɪld] *adj* : que tiene cola
tailgate[1] [ˈteɪlˌgeɪt] *vi* **-gated; -gating** : seguir a un vehículo demasiado de cerca
tailgate[2] *n* : puerta *f* trasera (de un vehículo)
taillight [ˈteɪlˌlaɪt] *n* : luz *f* trasera (de un vehículo), calavera *f Mex*
tailor[1] [ˈteɪlər] *vt* **1** : confeccionar o alterar (ropa) **2** ADAPT : adaptar, ajustar
tailor[2] *n* : sastre *m*, -tra *f*
tailpipe [ˈteɪlˌpaɪp] *n* : tubo *m* de escape
tailspin [ˈteɪlˌspɪn] *n* : barrena *f*
taint[1] [ˈteɪnt] *vt* : contaminar, corromper
taint[2] *n* : corrupción *f*, impureza *f*
take[1] [ˈteɪk] *v* **took** [ˈtʊk]; **taken** [ˈteɪkən]; **taking** *vt* **1** CAPTURE : capturar, apresar **2** GRASP : tomar, agarrar ⟨to take the bull by the horns : tomar al toro por los cuernos⟩ **3** CATCH : tomar, agarrar ⟨taken by surprise : tomado por sorpresa⟩ **4** CAPTIVATE : encantar, fascinar **5** INGEST : tomar, ingerir ⟨take two pills : tome dos píldoras⟩ **6** REMOVE : sacar, extraer ⟨take an orange : saca una naranja⟩ **7** : tomar, coger (un tren, un autobús, etc.) **8** NEED, REQUIRE : tomar, requerir ⟨these things take time : estas cosas toman tiempo⟩ **9** BRING, CARRY : llevar, sacar, cargar ⟨take them with you : llévalos contigo⟩ ⟨take the trash out : saca la basura⟩ **10** BEAR, ENDURE : soportar, aguantar (dolores, etc.) **11** ACCEPT : aceptar (un cheque, etc.), seguir (consejos), asumir (la responsabilidad) **12** SUPPOSE : suponer ⟨I take it that . . . : supongo que . . . ⟩ **13** (*indicating an action or an undertaking*) ⟨to take a walk : dar un paseo⟩ ⟨to take a class : tomar una clase⟩ **14 to take place** HAPPEN : tener lugar, suceder, ocurrir — *vi* : agarrar (dícese de un tinte), prender (dícese de una vacuna)
take[2] *n* **1** PROCEEDS : recaudación *f*, ingresos *mpl*, ganancias *fpl* **2** : toma *f* (de un rodaje o una grabación)
take back *vt* : retirar (palabras, etc.)
take in *vt* **1** : tomarle a, achicar (un vestido, etc.) **2** INCLUDE : incluir, abarcar **3** ATTEND : ir a ⟨to take in a movie : ir al cine⟩ **4** GRASP, UNDERSTAND : captar, entender **5** DECEIVE : engañar
takeoff [ˈteɪkˌɔf] *n* **1** PARODY : parodia *f* **2** : despegue *m* (de un avión o cohete)
take off *vt* REMOVE : quitar ⟨take off your hat : quítate el sombrero⟩ — *vi* **1** : despegar (dícese de un avión o un cohete) **2** LEAVE : irse, partir
take on *vt* **1** TACKLE : abordar, emprender (problemas, etc.) **2** ACCEPT : aceptar, encargarse de, asumir (una responsabilidad) **3** CONTRACT : contratar (trabajadores) **4** ASSUME : adoptar, asumir, adquirir ⟨the neighborhood took on a dingy look : el barrio asumió una apariencia deprimente⟩

takeover ['teɪk,oːvər] *n* : toma *f* (de poder o de control), adquisición *f* (de una empresa por otra)
take over *vt* : tomar el poder de, tomar las riendas de — *vi* : asumir el mando
taker ['teɪkər] *n* : persona *f* interesada ⟨available to all takers : disponible a cuantos estén interesados⟩
take up *vt* **1** LIFT : levantar **2** SHORTEN : acortar (una falda, etc.) **3** BEGIN : empezar, dedicarse a (un pasatiempo, etc.) **4** OCCUPY : ocupar, llevar (tiempo, espacio) **5** PURSUE : volver a (una cuestión, un asunto) **6** CONTINUE : seguir con
talc ['tælk] *n* : talco *m*
talcum powder ['tælkəm] *n* : talco *m*, polvos *mpl* de talco
tale ['teɪl] *n* **1** ANECDOTE, STORY : cuento *m*, relato *m*, anécdota *f* **2** FALSEHOOD : cuento *m*, mentira *f*
talent ['tælənt] *n* : talento *m*, don *m*
talented ['tæləntəd] *adj* : talentoso
talisman ['tælɪsmən, -lɪz-] *n, pl* **-mans** : talismán *m*
talk[1] ['tɔk] *vi* **1** : hablar ⟨he talks for hours : se pasa horas hablando⟩ **2** CHAT : charlar, platicar — *vt* **1** SPEAK : hablar ⟨to talk French : hablar francés⟩ ⟨to talk business : hablar de negocios⟩ **2** PERSUADE : influenciar, convencer ⟨she talked me out of it : me convenció que no lo hiciera⟩ **3 to talk over** DISCUSS : hablar de, discutir
talk[2] *n* **1** CONVERSATION : charla *f*, plática *f*, conversación *f* **2** GOSSIP, RUMOR : chisme *m*, rumores *mpl*
talkative ['tɔkət̬ɪv] *adj* : locuaz, parlanchín, charlatán
talker ['tɔkər] *n* : conversador *m*, -dora *f*; hablador *m*, -dora *f*
talk show *n* : programa *m* de entrevistas
tall ['tɔl] *adj* : alto ⟨how tall is he? : ¿cuánto mide?⟩
tallness ['tɔlnəs] *n* HEIGHT : estatura *f* (de una persona), altura *f* (de un objeto)
tallow ['tæloː] *n* : sebo *m*
tally[1] ['tæli] *v* **-lied; -lying** *vt* RECKON : contar, hacer una cuenta de — *vi* MATCH : concordar, corresponder, cuadrar
tally[2] *n, pl* **-lies** : cuenta *f* ⟨to keep a tally : llevar la cuenta⟩
talon ['tælən] *n* : garra *f* (de un ave de rapiña)
tambourine [,tæmbə'riːn] *n* : pandero *m*, pandereta *f*
tame[1] ['teɪm] *vt* **tamed; taming** : domar, amansar, domesticar
tame[2] *adj* **tamer; -est 1** DOMESTICATED : domesticado, manso **2** DOCILE : manso, dócil **3** DULL : aburrido, soso
tamely ['teɪmli] *adv* : mansamente, dócilmente
tamer ['teɪmər] *n* : domador *m*, -dora *f*
tamp ['tæmp] *vt* : apisonar
tamper ['tæmpər] *vi* **to tamper with** : adulterar (una sustancia), forzar (un sello, una cerradura), falsear (documentos), manipular (una máquina)
tampon ['tæm,pɑn] *n* : tampón *m*
tan[1] ['tæn] *v* **tanned; tanning** *vt* **1** : curtir (pieles) **2** : broncear — *vi* : broncearse
tan[2] *n* **1** SUNTAN : bronceado *m* ⟨to get a tan : broncearse⟩ **2** : color *m* canela, color *m* café con leche
tandem[1] ['tændəm] *adv or* **in tandem** : en tándem
tandem[2] *n* : tándem *m* (bicicleta)
tang ['tæŋ] *n* : sabor *m* fuerte
tangent ['tænʤənt] *n* : tangente *f* ⟨to go off on a tangent : irse por la tangente⟩
tangerine ['tænʤə,riːn, ,tænʤə'-] *n* : mandarina *f*
tangible ['tænʤəbəl] *adj* : tangible, palpable — **tangibly** [-bli] *adv*
tangle[1] ['tæŋgəl] *v* **-gled; -gling** *vt* : enredar, enmarañar — *vi* : enredarse
tangle[2] *n* : enredo *m*, maraña *f*
tango[1] ['tæŋ,goː] *vi* : bailar el tango
tango[2] *n, pl* **-gos** : tango *m*
tangy ['tæŋi] *adj* **tangier; -est** : que tiene un sabor fuerte
tank ['tæŋk] *n* : tanque *m*, depósito *m* ⟨fuel tank : depósito de combustibles⟩
tankard ['tæŋkərd] *n* : jarra *f*
tanker ['tæŋkər] *n* : buque *m* cisterna, camión *m* cisterna, avión *m* cisterna ⟨an oil tanker : un petrolero⟩
tanner ['tænər] *n* : curtidor *m*, -dora *f*
tannery ['tænəri] *n, pl* **-neries** : curtiduría *f*, tenería *f*
tannin ['tænən] *n* : tanino *m*
tantalize ['tæntə,laɪz] *vt* **-lized; -lizing** : tentar, atormentar (con algo inasequible)
tantalizing ['tæntə,laɪzɪŋ] *adj* : tentador, seductor
tantamount ['tæntə,maʊnt] *adj* : equivalente
tantrum ['tæntrəm] *n* : rabieta *f*, berrinche *m* ⟨to throw a tantrum : hacer un berrinche⟩
tap[1] ['tæp] *vt* **tapped; tapping 1** : ponerle una espita a, sacar líquido de (un barril, un tanque, etc.) **2** : intervenir (una línea telefónica) **3** PAT, TOUCH : tocar, golpear ligeramente ⟨he tapped me on the shoulder : me tocó en el hombro⟩
tap[2] *n* **1** FAUCET : llave *f*, grifo *m* ⟨beer on tap : cerveza de barril⟩ **2** : extracción *f* (de líquido) ⟨a spinal tap : una punción lumbar⟩ **3** PAT, TOUCH : golpecito *m*, toque *m*
tape[1] ['teɪp] *vt* **taped; taping 1** : sujetar o arreglar con cinta adhesiva **2** RECORD : grabar
tape[2] *n* **1** : cinta *f* (adhesiva, magnética, etc.) **2** → **tape measure**
tape measure *n* : cinta *f* métrica
taper[1] ['teɪpər] *vi* **1** : estrecharse gradualmente ⟨its tail tapers towards the tip : su cola va estrechándose hacia la pun-

ta⟩ **2** *or* **to taper off** : disminuir gradualmente
taper[2] *n* **1** CANDLE : vela *f* larga y delgada **2** TAPERING : estrechamiento *m* gradual
tapestry [ˈtæpəstri] *n, pl* **-tries** : tapiz *m*
tapeworm [ˈteɪpˌwərm] *n* : solitaria *f*, tenia *f*
tapioca [ˌtæpiˈoːkə] *n* : tapioca *f*
tar[1] [ˈtɑr] *vt* **tarred; tarring** : alquitranar
tar[2] *n* : alquitrán *m*, brea *f*, chapopote *m Mex*
tarantula [təˈræntʃələ, -ˈræntələ] *n* : tarántula *f*
tardiness [ˈtɑrdinəs] *n* : tardanza *f*, retraso *m*
tardy [ˈtɑrdi] *adj* **-dier; -est** LATE : tardío, de retraso
target[1] [ˈtɑrgət] *vt* : fijar como objetivo, dirigir, destinar
target[2] *n* **1** : blanco *m* ⟨target practice : tiro al blanco⟩ **2** GOAL, OBJECTIVE : meta *f*, objetivo *m*
tariff [ˈtærɪf] *n* DUTY : tarifa *f*, arancel *m*
tarnish[1] [ˈtɑrnɪʃ] *vt* **1** DULL : deslustrar **2** SULLY : empañar, manchar (una reputación, etc.) — *vi* : deslustrarse
tarnish[2] *n* : deslustre *m*
tarpaulin [tɑrˈpɔlən, ˈtɑrpə-] *n* : lona *f* (impermeable)
tarragon [ˈtærəˌgɑn, -gən] *n* : estragón *m*
tarry[1] [ˈtæri] *vi* **-ried; -rying** : demorarse, entretenerse
tarry[2] [ˈtɑri] *adj* **1** : parecido al alquitrán **2** : cubierto de alquitrán
tart[1] [ˈtɑrt] *adj* **1** SOUR : ácido, agrio **2** CAUSTIC : mordaz, acrimonioso — **tartly** *adv*
tart[2] *n* : tartaleta *f*
tartan [ˈtɑrtən] *n* : tartán *m*
tartar [ˈtɑrt̬ər] *n* **1** : tártaro *m* ⟨tartar sauce : salsa tártara⟩ **2** : sarro *m* (dental)
tartness [ˈtɑrtnəs] *n* **1** SOURNESS : acidez *f* **2** ACRIMONY, SHARPNESS : mordacidad *f*, acrimonia *f*, acritud *f*
task [ˈtæsk] *n* : tarea *f*, trabajo *m*
taskmaster [ˈtæskˌmæstər] *n* **to be a hard taskmaster** : ser exigente, ser muy estricto
tassel [ˈtæsəl] *n* : borla *f*
taste[1] [ˈteɪst] *v* **tasted; tasting** *vt* : probar (alimentos), degustar, catar (vinos) ⟨taste this soup : prueba esta sopa⟩ — *vi* : saber ⟨this tastes good : esto sabe bueno⟩
taste[2] *n* **1** SAMPLE : prueba *f*, bocado *m* (de comida), trago *m* (de bebidas) **2** FLAVOR : gusto *m*, sabor *m* **3** : gusto *m* ⟨she has good taste : tiene buen gusto⟩ ⟨in bad taste : de mal gusto⟩
taste bud *n* : papila *f* gustativa
tasteful [ˈteɪstfəl] *adj* : de buen gusto
tastefully [ˈteɪstfəli] *adv* : con buen gusto
tasteless [ˈteɪstləs] *adj* **1** FLAVORLESS : sin sabor, soso, insípido **2** : de mal gusto ⟨a tasteless joke : un chiste de mal gusto⟩
taster [ˈteɪstər] *n* : degustador *m*, -dora *f*; catador *m*, -dora *f* (de vinos)
tastiness [ˈteɪstinəs] *n* : lo sabroso
tasty [ˈteɪsti] *adj* **tastier; -est** : sabroso, gustoso
tatter [ˈtæt̬ər] *n* **1** SHRED : tira *f*, jirón *m* (de tela) **2 tatters** *npl* : andrajos *mpl*, harapos *mpl* ⟨to be in tatters : estar por los suelos⟩
tattered [ˈtæt̬ərd] *adj* : andrajoso, en jirones
tattle [ˈtæt̬əl] *vi* **-tled; -tling** **1** CHATTER : parlotear *fam*, cotorrear *fam* **2 to tattle on someone** : acusar a alguien
tattletale [ˈtæt̬əlˌteɪl] *n* : soplón *m*, -plona *f fam*
tattoo[1] [tæˈtuː] *vt* : tatuar
tattoo[2] *n* : tatuaje *m* ⟨to get a tattoo : tatuarse⟩
taught → **teach**
taunt[1] [ˈtɔnt] *vt* MOCK : mofarse de, burlarse de
taunt[2] *n* : mofa *f*, burla *f*
Taurus [ˈtɔrəs] *n* : Tauro *mf*
taut [ˈtɔt] *adj* : tirante, tenso — **tautly** *adv*
tautness [ˈtɔtnəs] *n* : tirantez *f*, tensión *f*
tavern [ˈtævərn] *n* : taberna *f*
tawdry [ˈtɔdri] *adj* **-drier; -est** : chabacano, vulgar
tawny [ˈtɔni] *adj* **-nier; -est** : leonado
tax[1] [ˈtæks] *vt* **1** : gravar, cobrar un impuesto sobre **2** CHARGE : acusar ⟨they taxed him with neglect : fue acusado de incumplimiento⟩ **3 to tax someone's strength** : ponerle a prueba las fuerzas (a alguien)
tax[2] *n* **1** : impuesto *m*, tributo *m* **2** BURDEN : carga *f*
taxable [ˈtæksəbəl] *adj* : sujeto a un impuesto
taxation [tækˈseɪʃən] *n* : impuestos *mpl*
tax–exempt [ˈtæksɪgˈzɛmpt, -ɛg-] *adj* : libre de impuestos
taxi[1] [ˈtæksi] *vi* **taxied; taxiing** *or* **taxying; taxis** *or* **taxies** **1** : ir en taxi **2** : rodar sobre la pista de aterrizaje (dícese de un avión)
taxi[2] *n, pl* **taxis** : taxi *m*, libre *m Mex*
taxicab [ˈtæksiˌkæb] *n* → **taxi**[2]
taxidermist [ˈtæksəˌdərmɪst] *n* : taxidermista *mf*
taxidermy [ˈtæksəˌdərmi] *n* : taxidermia *f*
taxpayer [ˈtæksˌpeɪər] *n* : contribuyente *mf*, causante *mf Mex*
TB [ˌtiːˈbiː] → **tuberculosis**
tea [ˈtiː] *n* **1** : té *m* (planta y bebida) **2** : merienda *f*, té *m* (comida)
teach [ˈtiːtʃ] *v* **taught** [ˈtɔt]; **teaching** *vt* : enseñar, dar clases de ⟨she teaches math : da clases de matemáticas⟩ ⟨she taught me everything I know : me enseñó todo lo que sé⟩ — *vi* : enseñar, dar clases

teacher [ˈtiːʧər] *n* : maestro *m*, -tra *f* (de enseñanza primaria); profesor *m*, -sora *f* (de enseñanza secundaria)
teaching [ˈtiːʧɪŋ] *n* : enseñanza *f*
teacup [ˈtiːˌkʌp] *n* : taza *f* para té
teak [ˈtiːk] *n* : teca *f*
teakettle [ˈtiːˌktəl] *n* : tetera *f*
teal [ˈtiːl] *n, pl* **teal** *or* **teals** : cerceta *f* (pato)
team[1] [ˈtiːm] *vi or* **to team up 1** : formar un equipo (en deportes) **2** COLLABORATE : asociarse, juntarse, unirse
team[2] *adj* : de equipo
team[3] *n* **1** : tiro *m* (de caballos), yunta *f* (de bueyes o mulas) **2** : equipo *m* (en deportes, etc.)
teammate [ˈtiːmˌmeɪt] *n* : compañero *m*, -ra *f* de equipo
teamster [ˈtiːmstər] *n* : camionero *m*, -ra *f*
teamwork [ˈtiːmˌwərk] *n* : trabajo *m* en equipo, cooperación *f*
teapot [ˈtiːˌpɑt] *n* : tetera *f*
tear[1] [ˈtær] *v* **tore** [ˈtor]; **torn** [ˈtorn]; **tearing** *vt* **1** RIP : desgarrar, romper, rasgar (tela) ⟨to tear to pieces : hacer pedazos⟩ **2** *or* **to tear apart** DIVIDE : dividir **3** REMOVE : arrancar ⟨torn from his family : arrancado de su familia⟩ **4 to tear down** : derribar — *vi* **1** RIP : desgarrarse, romperse **2** RUSH : ir a gran velocidad ⟨she went tearing down the street : se fue como rayo por la calle⟩
tear[2] *n* : desgarradura *f*, rotura *f*, desgarro *m* (muscular)
tear[3] [ˈtɪr] *n* : lágrima *f*
teardrop [ˈtɪrˌdrɑp] *n* → **tear**[3]
tearful [ˈtɪrfəl] *adj* : lloroso, triste — **tearfully** *adv*
tease[1] [ˈtiːz] *vt* **teased; teasing 1** MOCK : burlarse de, mofarse de **2** ANNOY : irritar, fastidiar
tease[2] *n* **1** TEASING : burla *f*, mofa *f* **2** : bromista *mf*; guasón *m*, -sona *f*
teaspoon [ˈtiːˌspuːn] *n* **1** : cucharita *f* **2** → **teaspoonful**
teaspoonful [ˈtiːˌspuːnˌfʊl] *n, pl* **-spoonfuls** [-ˌfʊlz] *or* **-spoonsful** [-ˌspuːnzˌfʊl] : cucharadita *f*
teat [ˈtiːt] *n* : tetilla *f*
technical [ˈtɛknɪkəl] *adj* : técnico — **technically** [-kli] *adv*
technicality [ˌtɛknəˈkæləṭi] *n, pl* **-ties** : detalle *m* técnico
technician [tɛkˈnɪʃən] *n* : técnico *m*, -ca *f*
technique [tɛkˈniːk] *n* : técnica *f*
technological [ˌtɛknəˈlɑʤɪkəl] *adj* : tecnológico
technology [tɛkˈnɑləʤi] *n, pl* **-gies** : tecnología *f*
teddy bear [ˈtɛdi] *n* : oso *m* de peluche
tedious [ˈtiːdiəs] *adj* : aburrido, pesado, monótono — **tediously** *adv*
tediousness [ˈtiːdiəsnəs] *n* : lo aburrido, lo pesado
tedium [ˈtiːdiəm] *n* : tedio *m*, pesadez *f*
tee [ˈtiː] *n* : tee *mf*
teem [ˈtiːm] *vi* **to teem with** : estar repleto de, estar lleno de
teenage [ˈtiːnˌeɪʤ] *or* **teenaged** [-eɪʤd] *adj* : adolescente, de adolescencia
teenager [ˈtiːnˌeɪʤər] *n* : adolescente *mf*
teens [ˈtiːnz] *npl* : adolescencia *f*
teepee → **tepee**
teeter[1] [ˈtiːṭər] *vi* : balancearse, tambalearse
teeter[2] *n or* **teeter–totter** [ˈtiːṭər-ˌtɑṭər] → **seesaw**
teeth → **tooth**
teethe [ˈtiːð] *vi* **teethed; teething** : formársele a uno los dientes ⟨the baby's teething : le están saliendo los dientes al niño⟩
telecast[1] [ˈtɛləˌkæst] *vt* **-cast; -casting** : televisar, transmitir por televisión
telecast[2] *n* : transmisión *f* por televisión
telecommunication [ˈtɛləkəˌmjuːnəˈkeɪʃən] *n* : telecomunicación *f*
telegram [ˈtɛləˌgræm] *n* : telegrama *m*
telegraph[1] [ˈtɛləˌgræf] *v* : telegrafiar
telegraph[2] *n* : telégrafo *m*
telepathic [ˌtɛləˈpæθɪk] *adj* : telepático — **telepathically** [-θɪkli] *adv*
telepathy [təˈlɛpəθi] *n* : telepatía *f*
telephone[1] [ˈtɛləˌfoːn] *v* **-phoned; -phoning** *vt* : llamar por teléfono a, telefonear — *vi* : telefonear
telephone[2] *n* : teléfono *m*
telescope[1] [ˈtɛləˌskoːp] *vi* **-scoped; -scoping** : plegarse (como un telescopio)
telescope[2] *n* : telescopio *m*
telescopic [ˌtɛləˈskɑpɪk] *adj* : telescópico
televise [ˈtɛləˌvaɪz] *vt* **-vised; -vising** : televisar
television [ˈtɛləˌvɪʒən] *n* : televisión *f*
tell [ˈtɛl] *v* **told** [ˈtoːld]; **telling** *vt* **1** COUNT : contar, enumerar ⟨all told : en total⟩ **2** INSTRUCT : decir ⟨he told me how to fix it : me dijo cómo arreglarlo⟩ ⟨they told her to wait : le dijeron que esperara⟩ **3** RELATE : contar, relatar, narrar ⟨to tell a story : contar una historia⟩ **4** DIVULGE, REVEAL : revelar, divulgar ⟨he told me everything about her : me contó todo acerca de ella⟩ **5** DISCERN : discernir, notar ⟨I can't tell the difference : no noto la diferencia⟩ — *vi* **1** SAY : decir ⟨I won't tell : no voy a decírselo a nadie⟩ **2** KNOW : saber ⟨you never can tell : nunca se sabe⟩ **3** SHOW : notarse, hacerse sentir ⟨the strain is beginning to tell : la tensión se empieza a notar⟩
teller [ˈtɛlər] *n* **1** NARRATOR : narrador *m*, -dora *f* **2** *or* **bank teller** : cajero *m*, -ra *f*
temerity [təˈmɛrəṭi] *n, pl* **-ties** : temeridad *f*
temp [ˈtɛmp] *n* : empleado *m*, -da *f* temporal
temper[1] [ˈtɛmpər] *vt* **1** MODERATE : moderar, temperar **2** ANNEAL : templar (acero, etc.)

temper[2] *n* **1** DISPOSITION : carácter *m*, genio *m* **2** HARDNESS : temple *m*, dureza *f* (de un metal) **3** COMPOSURE : calma *f*, serenidad *f* ⟨to lose one's temper : perder los estribos⟩ **4** RAGE : furia *f* ⟨to fly into a temper : ponerse furioso⟩
temperament [ˈtɛmpərmənt, -prə-, -pərə-] *n* : temperamento *m*
temperamental [ˌtɛmpərˈmɛntəl, -prə-, -pərə-] *adj* : temperamental
temperance [ˈtɛmprənts] *n* : templanza *f*, temperancia *f*
temperate [ˈtɛmpərət] *adj* : templado (dícese del clima, etc.), moderado
temperature [ˈtɛmpərˌʧʊr, -prə-, -pərə-, -ʧər] *n* **1** : temperatura *f* **2** FEVER : calentura *f*, fiebre *f*
tempest [ˈtɛmpəst] *n* : tempestad *f*
tempestuous [tɛmˈpɛsʧʊəs] *adj* : tempestuoso
temple [ˈtɛmpəl] *n* **1** : templo *m* (en religión) **2** : sien *f* (en anatomía)
tempo [ˈtɛmˌpoː] *n, pl* **-pi** [-ˌpiː] *or* **-pos** : ritmo *m*, tempo *m* (en música)
temporal [ˈtɛmpərəl] *adj* : temporal
temporarily [ˌtɛmpəˈrɛrəli] *adv* : temporalmente, provisionalmente
temporary [ˈtɛmpəˌrɛri] *adj* : temporal, provisional, provisorio
tempt [ˈtɛmpt] *vt* : tentar
temptation [tɛmpˈteɪʃən] *n* : tentación *f*
tempter [ˈtɛmptər] *n* : tentador *m*
temptress [ˈtɛmptrəs] *n* : tentadora *f*
ten[1] [ˈtɛn] *adj* : diez
ten[2] *n* **1** : diez *m* (número) **2** : decena *f* ⟨tens of thousands : decenas de millares⟩
tenable [ˈtɛnəbəl] *adj* : sostenible, defendible
tenacious [təˈneɪʃəs] *adj* : tenaz
tenacity [təˈnæsət̬i] *n* : tenacidad *f*
tenancy [ˈtɛnəntsi] *n, pl* **-cies** : tenencia *f*, inquilinato *m* (de un inmueble)
tenant [ˈtɛnənt] *n* : inquilino *m*, -na *f*; arrendatario *m*, -ria *f*
tend [ˈtɛnd] *vt* : atender, cuidar (de), ocuparse de — *vi* : tender ⟨it tends to benefit the consumer : tiende a beneficiar al consumidor⟩
tendency [ˈtɛndəntsi] *n, pl* **-cies** : tendencia *f*, proclividad *f*, inclinación *f*
tender[1] [ˈtɛndər] *vt* : entregar, presentar ⟨I tendered my resignation : presenté mi renuncia⟩
tender[2] *adj* **1** : tierno, blando ⟨tender steak : bistec tierno⟩ **2** AFFECTIONATE, LOVING : tierno, cariñoso, afectuoso **3** DELICATE : tierno, sensible, delicado
tender[3] *n* **1** OFFER : propuesta *f*, oferta *f* (en negocios) **2 legal tender** : moneda *f* de curso legal
tenderize [ˈtɛndəˌraɪz] *vt* **-ized; -izing** : ablandar (carnes)
tenderloin [ˈtɛndrˌlɔɪn] *n* : lomo *f* (de res o de puerco)
tenderly [ˈtɛndərli] *adv* : tiernamente, con ternura
tenderness [ˈtɛndərnəs] *n* : ternura *f*
tendon [ˈtɛndən] *n* : tendón *m*
tendril [ˈtɛndrɪl] *n* : zarcillo *m*
tenement [ˈtɛnəmənt] *n* : casa *f* de vecindad
tenet [ˈtɛnət] *n* : principio *m*
tennis [ˈtɛnəs] *n* : tenis *m*
tenor [ˈtɛnər] *n* **1** PURPORT : tenor *m*, significado *m* **2** : tenor *m* (en música)
tenpins [ˈtɛnˌpɪnz] *npl* : bolos *mpl*, boliche *m*
tense[1] [ˈtɛnts] *v* **tensed; tensing** *vt* : tensar — *vi* : tensarse, ponerse tenso
tense[2] *adj* **tenser; tensest 1** TAUT : tenso, tirante **2** NERVOUS : tenso, nervioso
tense[3] *n* : tiempo *m* (de un verbo)
tensely [ˈtɛntsli] *adv* : tensamente
tenseness [ˈtɛntsnəs] → **tension**
tension [ˈtɛnʧən] *n* **1** TAUTNESS : tensión *f*, tirantez *f* **2** STRESS : tensión *f*, nerviosismo *m*, estrés *m*
tent [ˈtɛnt] *n* : tienda *f* de campaña
tentacle [ˈtɛntɪkəl] *n* : tentáculo *m*
tentative [ˈtɛntət̬ɪv] *adj* **1** HESITANT : indeciso, vacilante **2** PROVISIONAL : sujeto a cambios, provisional
tentatively [ˈtɛntət̬ɪvli] *adv* : provisionalmente
tenth[1] [ˈtɛnθ] *adj* : décimo
tenth[2] *n* **1** : décimo *m*, -ma *f* (en una serie) **2** : décimo *m*, décima parte *f*
tenuous [ˈtɛnjʊəs] *adj* : tenue, débil ⟨tenuous reasons : razones poco convincentes⟩
tenuously [ˈtɛnjʊəsli] *adv* : tenuemente, ligeramente
tenure [ˈtɛnjər] *n* : tenencia *f* (de un cargo o una propiedad), titularidad *f* (de un puesto académico)
tepee [ˈtiːˌpiː] *n* : tipi *m*
tepid [ˈtɛpɪd] *adj* : tibio
tequila [təˈkiːlə] *n* : tequila *m*
term[1] [ˈtərm] *vt* : calificar de, llamar, nombrar
term[2] *n* **1** PERIOD : término *m*, plazo *m*, período *m* **2** : término *m* (en matemáticas) **3** WORD : término *m*, vocablo *m* ⟨legal terms : términos legales⟩ **4 terms** *npl* CONDITIONS : términos *mpl*, condiciones *fpl* **5 terms** *npl* RELATIONS : relaciones *fpl* ⟨to be on good terms with : tener buenas relaciones con⟩ **6 in terms of** : con respecto a, en cuanto a
terminal[1] [ˈtərmənəl] *adj* : terminal
terminal[2] *n* **1** : terminal *m*, polo *m* (en electricidad) **2** : terminal *m* (de una computadora) **3** STATION : terminal *f*, estación *f* (de transporte público)
terminate [ˈtərməˌneɪt] *v* **-nated; -nating** *vi* : terminar(se), concluirse — *vt* : terminar, poner fin a
termination [ˌtərməˈneɪʃən] *n* : cese *m*, terminación *f*
terminology [ˌtərməˈnɑləʤi] *n, pl* **-gies** : terminología *f*
terminus [ˈtərmənəs] *n, pl* **-ni** [-ˌnaɪ] *or* **-nuses 1** END : término *m*, fin *m* **2** : terminal *f* (de transporte público)

termite [ˈtərˌmaɪt] *n* : termita *f*
tern [ˈtərn] *n* : golondrina *f* de mar
terrace[1] [ˈtɛrəs] *vt* **-raced; -racing** : formar en terrazas, disponer en bancales
terrace[2] *n* **1** PATIO : terraza *f*, patio *m* **2** : terraplén *m*, terraza *f*, bancal *m* (en agricultura)
terra–cotta [ˌtɛrəˈkɑt̬ə] *n* : terracota *f*
terrain [təˈreɪn] *n* : terreno *m*
terrapin [ˈtɛrəpɪn] *n* : galápago *m* norteamericano
terrarium [təˈræriəm] *n, pl* **-ia** [-iə] *or* **-iums** : terrario *m*
terrestrial [təˈrɛstriəl] *adj* : terrestre
terrible [ˈtɛrəbəl] *adj* : atroz, horrible, terrible
terribly [ˈtɛrəbli] *adv* **1** BADLY : muy mal **2** EXTREMELY : terriblemente, extremadamente
terrier [ˈtɛriər] *n* : terrier *mf*
terrific [təˈrɪfɪk] *adj* **1** FRIGHTFUL : aterrador **2** EXTRAORDINARY : extraordinario, excepcional **3** EXCELLENT : excelente, estupendo
terrify [ˈtɛrəˌfaɪ] *vt* **-fied; -fying** : aterrorizar, aterrar, espantar
terrifying [ˈtɛrəˌfaɪɪŋ] *adj* : espantoso, aterrador
territory [ˈtɛrəˌtori] *n, pl* **-ries** : territorio *m* — **territorial** [ˌtɛrəˈtoriəl] *adj*
terror [ˈtɛrər] *n* : terror *m*
terrorism [ˈtɛrərˌɪzəm] *n* : terrorismo *m*
terrorist[1] [ˈtɛrərɪst] *adj* : terrorista
terrorist[2] *n* : terrorista *mf*
terrorize [ˈtɛrərˌaɪz] *vt* **-ized; -izing** : aterrorizar
terry [ˈtɛri] *n, pl* **-ries** *or* **terry cloth** : (tela de) toalla *f*
terse [ˈtərs] *adj* **terser; tersest** : lacónico, conciso, seco — **tersely** *adv*
tertiary [ˈtərʃiˌɛri] *adj* : terciario
test[1] [ˈtɛst] *vt* : examinar, evaluar — *vi* : hacer pruebas
test[2] *n* : prueba *f*, examen *m*, test *m* ⟨to put to the test : poner a prueba⟩
testament [ˈtɛstəmənt] *n* **1** WILL : testamento *m* **2** : Testamento *m* (en la Biblia) ⟨the Old Testament : el Antiguo Testamento⟩
testicle [ˈtɛstɪkəl] *n* : testículo *m*
testify [ˈtɛstəˌfaɪ] *v* **-fied; -fying** *vi* : testificar, atestar, testimoniar — *vt* : testificar
testimonial [ˌtɛstəˈmoːniəl] *n* **1** REFERENCE : recomendación *f* **2** TRIBUTE : homenaje *m*, tributo *m*
testimony [ˈtɛstəˌmoːni] *n, pl* **-nies** : testimonio *m*, declaración *f*
test tube *n* : probeta *f*, tubo *m* de ensayo
testy [ˈtɛsti] *adj* **-tier; -est** : irritable
tetanus [ˈtɛtənəs] *n* : tétano *m*, tétanos *m*
tête–à–tête [ˌtɛt̬əˈtɛt, ˌteɪt̬əˈteɪt] *n* : conversación *f* en privado
tether[1] [ˈtɛðər] *vt* : atar (con una cuerda), amarrar
tether[2] *n* : atadura *f*, cadena *f*, correa *f*
text [ˈtɛkst] *n* **1** : texto *m* **2** TOPIC : tema *m* **3** → **textbook**
textbook [ˈtɛkstˌbʊk] *n* : libro *m* de texto
textile [ˈtɛkˌstaɪl, ˈtɛkstəl] *n* : textil *m*, tela *f* ⟨the textile industry : la industria textil⟩
textual [ˈtɛkstʃuəl] *adj* : textual
texture [ˈtɛkstʃər] *n* : textura *f*
Thai [ˈtaɪ] *n* **1** : tailandés *m*, -desa *f* **2** : tailandés *m* (idioma) — **Thai** *adj*
than[1] [ˈðæn] *conj* : que, de ⟨it's worth more than that : vale más que eso⟩ ⟨more than you think : más de lo que piensas⟩
than[2] *prep* : que, de ⟨you're better than he is : eres mejor que él⟩ ⟨more than once : más de una vez⟩
thank [ˈθæŋk] *vt* : agradecer, darle (las) gracias (a alguien) ⟨thank you! : ¡gracias!⟩ ⟨I thanked her for the present : le di las gracias por el regalo⟩ ⟨I thank you for your help : le agradezco su ayuda⟩
thankful [ˈθæŋkfəl] *adj* : agradecido
thankfully [ˈθæŋkfəli] *adv* **1** GRATEFULLY : con agradecimiento **2** FORTUNATELY : afortunadamente, por suerte ⟨thankfully, it's over : se acabó, gracias a Dios⟩
thankfulness [ˈθæŋkfəlnəs] *n* : agradecimiento *m*, gratitud *f*
thankless [ˈθæŋkləs] *adj* : ingrato ⟨a thankless task : un trabajo ingrato⟩
thanks [ˈθæŋks] *npl* **1** : agradecimiento *m* **2 thanks!** : ¡gracias!
Thanksgiving [θæŋksˈgɪvɪŋ, ˈθæŋksˌ-] *n* : el día de Acción de Gracias (fiesta estadounidense)
that[1] [ˈðæt] *adv* (*in negative constructions*) : tan ⟨it's not that expensive : no es tan caro⟩ ⟨not that much : no tanto⟩
that[2] *adj, pl* **those** : ese, esa, aquel, aquella ⟨do you see those children? : ¿ves a aquellos niños?⟩
that[3] *conj & pron* : que ⟨he said that he was afraid : dijo que tenía miedo⟩ ⟨the book that he wrote : el libro que escribió⟩
that[4] *pron, pl* **those** [ˈðoːz] **1** : ése, ésa, eso ⟨that's my father : ése es mi padre⟩ ⟨those are the ones he likes : ésos son los que le gustan⟩ ⟨what's that? : ¿qué es eso?⟩ **2** (*referring to more distant objects or time*) : aquél, aquélla, aquello ⟨those are maples and these are elms : aquéllos son arces y éstos son olmos⟩ ⟨that came to an end : aquello se acabó⟩
thatch[1] [ˈθætʃ] *vt* : cubrir o techar con paja
thatch[2] *n* : paja *f* (usada para techos)
thaw[1] [ˈθɔ] *vt* : descongelar — *vi* : derretirse (dícese de la nieve), descongelarse (dícese de los alimentos)
thaw[2] *n* : deshielo *m*

the[1] [ðə, *before vowel sounds usu* ði:] *adv* **1** (*used to indicate comparison*) ⟨the sooner the better : cuanto más pronto, mejor⟩ ⟨she likes this one the best : éste es el que más le gusta⟩ **2** (*used as a conjunction*) : cuanto ⟨the more I learn, the less I understand : cuanto más aprendo, menos entiendo⟩

the[2] *art* : el, la, los, las ⟨the gloves : los guantes⟩ ⟨the suitcase : la maleta⟩ ⟨forty cookies to the box : cuarenta galletas por caja⟩

theater *or* **theatre** [ˈθi:ət̬ər] *n* **1** : teatro *m* (edificio) **2** DRAMA : teatro *m*, drama *m*

theatrical [θiˈætrɪkəl] *adj* : teatral, dramático

thee [ˈði:] *pron* : te, ti

theft [ˈθɛft] *n* : robo *m*, hurto *m*

their [ˈðɛr] *adj* : su ⟨their friends : sus amigos⟩

theirs [ˈðɛrz] *pron* : (el) suyo, (la) suya, (los) suyos, (las) suyas ⟨they came for theirs : vinieron por el suyo⟩ ⟨theirs is bigger : la suya es más grande, la de ellos es más grande⟩ ⟨a brother of theirs : un hermano suyo, un hermano de ellos⟩

them [ˈðɛm] *pron* **1** (*as a direct object*) : los (*Spain sometimes* les), las ⟨I know them : los conozco⟩ **2** (*as indirect object*) : les, se ⟨I sent them a letter : les mandé una carta⟩ ⟨give it to them : dáselo (a ellos)⟩ **3** (*as object of a preposition*) : ellos, ellas ⟨go with them : ve con ellos⟩ **4** (*for emphasis*) : ellos, ellas ⟨I wasn't expecting them : no los esperaba a ellos⟩

thematic [θiˈmæt̬ɪk] *adj* : temático

theme [ˈθi:m] *n* **1** SUBJECT, TOPIC : tema *m* **2** COMPOSITION : composición *f*, trabajo *m* (escrito) **3** : tema *m* (en música)

themselves [ðəmˈsɛlvz, ðɛm-] *pron* **1** (*as a reflexive*) : se, sí ⟨they enjoyed themselves : se divirtieron⟩ ⟨they divided it among themselves : lo repartieron entre sí, se lo repartieron⟩ **2** (*for emphasis*) : ellos mismos, ellas mismas ⟨they built it themselves : ellas mismas lo construyeron⟩

then[1] [ˈðɛn] *adv* **1** : entonces, en ese tiempo ⟨I was sixteen then : tenía entonces dieciséis años⟩ ⟨since then : desde entonces⟩ **2** NEXT : después, luego ⟨we'll go to Toronto, then to Winnipeg : iremos a Toronto, y luego a Winnipeg⟩ **3** BESIDES : además, aparte ⟨then there's the tax : y aparte está el impuesto⟩ **4** : entonces, en ese caso ⟨if you like music, then you should attend : si te gusta la música, entonces deberías asistir⟩

then[2] *adj* : entonces ⟨the then governor of Georgia : el entonces gobernador de Georgia⟩

thence [ˈðɛn*t*s, ˈθn*t*s] *adv* : de ahí, de ahí en adelante

theologian [ˌθi:əˈlo:ʤən] *n* : teólogo *m*, -ga *f*

theological [ˌθi:əˈlɑʤɪkəl] *adj* : teológico

theology [θiˈɑləʤi] *n, pl* **-gies** : teología *f*

theorem [ˈθi:ərəm, ˈθɪrəm] *n* : teorema *m*

theoretical [ˌθi:əˈrɛt̬ɪkəl] *adj* : teórico — **theoretically** *adv*

theorist [ˈθi:ərɪst] *n* : teórico *m*, -ca *f*

theorize [ˈθi:əˌraɪz] *vi* **-rized; -rizing** : teorizar

theory [ˈθi:əri, ˈθɪri] *n, pl* **-ries** : teoría *f*

therapeutic [ˌθɛrəˈpju:t̬ɪk] *adj* : terapéutico — **therapeutically** *adv*

therapist [ˈθɛrəpɪst] *n* : terapeuta *mf*

therapy [ˈθɛrəpi] *n, pl* **-pies** : terapia *f*

there[1] [ˈðær] *adv* **1** : ahí, allí, allá ⟨stand over there : párate ahí⟩ ⟨over there : por allí, por allá⟩ ⟨who's there? : ¿quién es?⟩ **2** : ahí, en esto, en eso ⟨there is where we disagree : en eso es donde no estamos de acuerdo⟩

there[2] *pron* **1** (*introducing a sentence or clause*) ⟨there comes a time to decide : llega un momento en que tiene uno que decidir⟩ **2 there is, there are** : hay ⟨there are many children here : aquí hay muchos niños⟩ ⟨there's a good hotel downtown : hay un buen hotel en el centro⟩

thereabouts [ðærəˈbaʊts, ˈðærəˌ-] *or* **thereabout** [-ˈbaʊt, -ˌbaʊt] *adv* **or thereabouts** : por ahí, más o menos ⟨at five o'clock or thereabouts : por ahí de las cinco⟩

thereafter [ðærˈæftər] *adv* : después ⟨shortly thereafter : poco después⟩

thereby [ðærˈbaɪ, ˈðærˌbaɪ] *adv* : de tal modo, de ese manera, así

therefore [ˈðærˌfor] *adv* : por lo tanto, por consiguiente

therein [ðærˈɪn] *adv* **1** : allí adentro, ahí adentro ⟨the contents therein : lo que allí se contiene⟩ **2** : allí, en ese aspecto ⟨therein lies the problem : allí está el problema⟩

thereof [ðærˈʌv, -ˈɑv] *adv* : de eso, de esto

thereupon [ˈðærəˌpɑn, -ˌpɔn; ˌðærəˈpɑn, -ˈpɔn] *adv* : acto seguido, inmediatamente (después)

therewith [ðærˈwɪð, -ˈwɪθ] *adv* : con eso, con ello

thermal [ˈθərməl] *adj* **1** : térmico (en física) **2** HOT : termal

thermodynamics [ˌθərmodaɪˈnæmɪks] *ns & pl* : termodinámica *f*

thermometer [θərˈmɑmət̬ər] *n* : termómetro *m*

thermos [ˈθərməs] *n* : termo *m*

thermostat [ˈθərməˌstæt] *n* : termostato *m*

thesaurus [θɪˈsɔrəs] *n, pl* **-sauri** [-ˈsɔrˌaɪ] *or* **-sauruses** [-ˈsɔrəsəz] : diccionario *m* de sinónimos

these → **this**

thesis ['θi:sɪs] *n, pl* **theses** ['θi:ˌsi:z] : tesis *f*

they ['ðeɪ] *pron* : ellos, ellas ⟨they are here : están aquí⟩ ⟨they don't know : ellos no saben⟩

they'd ['ðeɪd] (*contraction of* **they had** *or* **they would**) → **have, would**

they'll ['ðeɪl, 'ðɛl] (*contraction of* **they shall** *or* **they will**) → **shall, will**

they're ['ðɛr] (*contraction of* **they are**) → **be**

they've ['ðeɪv] (*contraction of* **they have**) → **have**

thiamine ['θaɪəmɪn, -ˌmi:n] *n* : tiamina *f*

thick[1] ['θɪk] *adj* **1** : grueso ⟨a thick plank : una tabla gruesa⟩ **2** : espeso, denso ⟨thick syrup : jarabe espeso⟩ — **thickly** *adv*

thick[2] *n* **1 in the thick of** : en medio de ⟨in the thick of the battle : en lo más reñido de la batalla⟩ **2 through thick and thin** : a las duras y a las maduras

thicken ['θɪkən] *vt* : espesar (un líquido) — *vi* : espesarse

thickener ['θɪkənər] *n* : espesante *m*

thicket ['θɪkət] *n* : matorral *m*, maleza *f*, espesura *f*

thickness ['θɪknəs] *n* : grosor *m*, grueso *m*, espesor *m*

thickset ['θɪk'sɛt] *adj* STOCKY : robusto, fornido

thick–skinned ['θɪk'skɪnd] *adj* : poco sensible, que no se ofende fácilmente

thief ['θi:f] *n, pl* **thieves** ['θi:vz] : ladrón *m*, -drona *f*

thieve ['θi:v] *v* **thieved; thieving** : hurtar, robar

thievery ['θi:vəri] *n* : hurto *m*, robo *m*, latrocinio *m*

thigh ['θaɪ] *n* : muslo *m*

thighbone ['θaɪˌbo:n] *n* : fémur *m*

thimble ['θɪmbəl] *n* : dedal *m*

thin[1] ['θɪn] *v* **thinned; thinning** *vt* : hacer menos denso, diluir, aguar (un líquido), enrarecer (un gas) — *vi* : diluirse, aguarse (dícese de un líquido), enrarecerse (dícese de un gas)

thin[2] *adj* **thinner; -est 1** LEAN, SLIM : delgado, esbelto, flaco **2** SPARSE : ralo, escaso ⟨a thin beard : una barba rala⟩ **3** WATERY : claro, aguado, diluido **4** FINE : delgado, fino ⟨thin slices : rebanadas finas⟩

thing ['θɪŋ] *n* **1** AFFAIR, MATTER : cosa *f*, asunto *m* ⟨don't talk about those things : no hables de esas cosas⟩ ⟨how are things? : ¿cómo van las cosas?⟩ **2** ACT, EVENT : cosa *f*, suceso *m*, evento *m* ⟨the flood was a terrible thing : la inundación fue una cosa terrible⟩ **3** OBJECT : cosa *f*, objeto *m* ⟨don't forget your things : no olvides tus cosas⟩

think ['θɪŋk] *v* **thought** ['θɔt]; **thinking** *vt* **1** : pensar ⟨I thought to return early : pensaba regresar temprano⟩ **2** BELIEVE : pensar, creer, opinar **3** PONDER : pensar, reflexionar **4** CONCEIVE : ocurrirse, concebir ⟨we've thought up a plan : se nos ha ocurrido un plan⟩ — *vi* **1** REASON : pensar, razonar **2** CONSIDER : pensar, considerar ⟨think of your family first : primero piensa en tu familia⟩

thinker ['θɪŋkər] *n* : pensador *m*, -dora *f*

thinly ['θɪnli] *adv* **1** LIGHTLY : ligeramente **2** SPARSELY : escasamente ⟨thinly populated : poco populado⟩ **3** BARELY : apenas

thinness ['θɪnnəs] *n* : delgadez *f*

thin–skinned ['θɪn'skɪnd] *adj* : susceptible, muy sensible

third[1] ['θərd] *or* **thirdly** [-li] *adv* : en tercer lugar ⟨she came in third : llegó en tercer lugar⟩

third[2] *adj* : tercero ⟨the third day : el tercer día⟩

third[3] *n* **1** : tercero *m*, -ra *f* (en una serie) **2** : tercero *m*, tercera parte *f*

third world *n* **the Third World** : el Tercer Mundo *m*

thirst[1] ['θərst] *vi* **1** : tener sed **2 to thirst for** DESIRE : tener sed de, estar sediento de

thirst[2] *n* : sed *f*

thirsty ['θərsti] *adj* **thirstier; -est** : sediento, que tiene sed ⟨I'm thirsty : tengo sed⟩

thirteen[1] [ˌθər'ti:n] *adj* : trece

thirteen[2] *n* : trece *m*

thirteenth[1] [ˌθər'ti:nθ] *adj* : décimo tercero

thirteenth[2] *n* **1** : decimotercero *m*, -ra *f* (en una serie) **2** : treceavo *m*, treceava parte *f*

thirtieth[1] ['θərt̬iəθ] *adj* : trigésimo

thirtieth[2] *n* **1** : trigésimo *m*, -ma *f* (en una serie) **2** : treintavo *m*, treintava parte *f*

thirty[1] ['θərt̬i] *adj* : treinta

thirty[2] *n, pl* **thirties** : treinta *m*

this[1] ['ðɪs] *adv* : así, a tal punto ⟨this big : así de grande⟩

this[2] *adj, pl* **these** ['ði:z] : este ⟨these things : estas cosas⟩ ⟨read this book : lee este libro⟩

this[3] *pron, pl* **these** : esto ⟨what's this? : ¿qué es esto?⟩ ⟨this wasn't here yesterday : esto no estaba aquí ayer⟩

thistle ['θɪsəl] *n* : cardo *m*

thong ['θɔŋ] *n* **1** STRAP : correa *f*, tira *f* **2** FLIP-FLOP : chancla *f*, chancleta *f*

thorax ['θorˌæks] *n, pl* **-raxes** *or* **-races** ['θorəˌsi:z] : tórax *m*

thorn ['θɔrn] *n* : espina *f*

thorny ['θɔrni] *adj* **thornier; -est** : espinoso

thorough ['θəro:] *adj* **1** CONSCIENTIOUS : concienzudo, meticuloso **2** COMPLETE : absoluto, completo — **thoroughly** *adv*

thoroughbred ['θəroˌbrɛd] *adj* : de pura sangre (dícese de un caballo)

Thoroughbred *n or* **Thoroughbred horse** : pura sangre *mf*

thoroughfare ['θəroˌfær] *n* : vía *f* pública, carretera *f*

thoroughness ['θəronəs] *n* : esmero *m*, meticulosidad *f*

those → **that**
thou ['ðaʊ] *pron* : tú
though[1] ['ðo:] *adv* **1** HOWEVER, NEVERTHELESS : sin embargo, no obstante **2 as ~** : como si ⟨as though nothing had happened : como si nada hubiera pasado⟩
though[2] *conj* : aunque, a pesar de ⟨though it was raining, we went out : salimos a pesar de la lluvia⟩
thought[1] → **think**
thought[2] ['θɔt] *n* **1** THINKING : pensamiento *m*, ideas *fpl* ⟨Western thought : el pensamiento occidental⟩ **2** COGITATION : pensamiento *m*, reflexión *f*, raciocinio *m* **3** IDEA : idea *f*, ocurrencia *f* ⟨it was just a thought : fue sólo una idea⟩
thoughtful ['θɔtfəl] *adj* **1** PENSIVE : pensativo, meditabundo **2** CONSIDERATE : considerado, atento, cortés — **thoughtfully** *adv*
thoughtfulness ['θɔtfəlnəs] *n* : consideración *f*, atención *f*, cortesía *f*
thoughtless ['θɔtləs] *adj* **1** CARELESS : descuidado, negligente **2** INCONSIDERATE : desconsiderado — **thoughtlessly** *adv*
thousand[1] ['θaʊzənd] *adj* : mil
thousand[2] *n, pl* **-sands** *or* **-sand** : mil *m*
thousandth[1] ['θaʊzəntθ] *adj* : milésimo
thousandth[2] *n* **1** : milésimo *m*, -ma *f* (en una serie) **2** : milésimo *m*, milésima parte *f*
thrash ['θræʃ] *vt* **1** → **thresh 2** BEAT : golpear, azotar, darle una paliza (a alguien) **3** FLAIL : sacudir, agitar bruscamente
thread[1] ['θrɛd] *vt* **1** : enhilar, enhebrar (una aguja) **2** STRING : ensartar (cuentas en un hilo) **3 to thread one's way** : abrirse paso
thread[2] *n* **1** : hilo *m*, hebra *f* ⟨needle and thread : aguja e hilo⟩ ⟨the thread of an argument : el hilo de un debate⟩ **2** : rosca *f*, filete *m* (de un tornillo)
threadbare ['θrɛd'bær] *adj* **1** SHABBY, WORN : raído, gastado **2** TRITE : trillado, tópico, manido
threat ['θrɛt] *n* : amenaza *f*
threaten ['θrɛtən] *v* : amenazar
threatening ['θrɛtənɪŋ] *adj* : amenazador — **threateningly** *adv*
three[1] ['θri:] *adj* : tres
three[2] *n* : tres *m*
3–D ['θri:'di:] *adj* → **three–dimensional**
three–dimensional ['θri:də'mɛnʧənəl] *adj* : tridimensional
threefold ['θri:ˌfo:ld] *adj* TRIPLE : triple
three hundred[1] *adj* : trescientos
three hundred[2] *n* : trescientos *m*
threescore ['θri:'skor] *adj* SIXTY : sesenta
thresh ['θrɛʃ] *vt* : trillar (grano)
thresher ['θrɛʃər] *n* : trilladora *f*
threshold ['θrɛʃˌho:ld, -ˌo:ld] *n* : umbral *m*
threw → **throw**[1]
thrice ['θraɪs] *adv* : tres veces
thrift ['θrɪft] *n* : economía *f*, frugalidad *f*
thriftless ['θrɪftləs] *adj* : despilfarrador, manirroto
thrifty ['θrɪfti] *adj* **thriftier; -est** : económico, frugal — **thriftily** ['θrɪftəli] *adv*
thrill[1] ['θrɪl] *vt* : emocionar — *vi* **to thrill to** : dejarse conmover por, estremecerse con
thrill[2] *n* : emoción *f*
thriller ['θrɪlər] *n* **1** : evento *m* emocionante **2** : obra *f* de suspenso
thrilling ['θrɪlɪŋ] *adj* : emocionante, excitante
thrive ['θraɪv] *vi* **throve** ['θro:v] *or* **thrived; thriven** ['θrɪvən] **1** FLOURISH : florecer, crecer abundantemente **2** PROSPER : prosperar
throat ['θro:t] *n* : garganta *f*
throaty ['θro:ṭi] *adj* **throatier; -est** : ronco (dícese de la voz)
throb[1] ['θrɑb] *vi* **throbbed; throbbing** : palpitar, latir (dícese del corazón), vibrar (dícese de un motor, etc.)
throb[2] *n* : palpitación *f*, latido *m*, vibración *f*
throe ['θro:] *n* **1** PAIN, SPASM : espasmo *m*, dolor *m* ⟨the throes of childbirth : los dolores de parto⟩ **2 throes** *npl* : lucha *f* larga y ardua ⟨in the throes of : en el medio de⟩
throne ['θro:n] *n* : trono *m*
throng[1] ['θrɔŋ] *vt* CROWD : atestar, atiborrar, llenar — *vi* : aglomerarse, amontonarse
throng[2] *n* : muchedumbre *f*, gentío *m*, multitud *f*
throttle[1] ['θrɑtəl] *vt* **-tled; -tling 1** STRANGLE : estrangular, ahogar **2 to throttle down** : desacelerar (un motor)
throttle[2] *n* **1** : válvula *f* reguladora **2 at full throttle** : a toda máquina
through[1] ['θru:] *adv* **1** : a través, de un lado a otro ⟨let them through : déjenlos pasar⟩ **2** : de principio a fin ⟨she read the book through : leyó el libro de principio a fin⟩ **3** COMPLETELY : completamente ⟨soaked through : completamente empapado⟩
through[2] *adj* **1** DIRECT : directo ⟨a through train : un tren directo⟩ **2** FINISHED : terminado, acabado ⟨we're through : hemos terminado⟩
through[3] *prep* **1** : a través de, por ⟨through the door : por la puerta⟩ ⟨a road through the woods : un camino que atraviesa el bosque⟩ **2** BETWEEN : entre ⟨a path through the trees : un sendero entre los árboles⟩ **3** BECAUSE OF : a causa de, como consecuencia de **4** (*in expressions of time*) ⟨through the night : durante la noche⟩ ⟨to go through an experience : pasar por una experiencia⟩ **5** : a, hasta ⟨from Monday through Friday : de lunes a viernes⟩

throughout[1] [θru:ˈaʊt] *adv* **1** EVERYWHERE : por todas partes **2** THROUGH : desde el principio hasta el fin de (algo)

throughout[2] *prep* **1** : en todas partes de, a través de ⟨throughout the United States : en todo Estados Unidos⟩ **2** : de principio a fin de, durante ⟨throughout the winter : durante todo el invierno⟩

throve → **thrive**

throw[1] [ˈθro:] *vt* **threw** [ˈθru:]; **thrown** [ˈθro:n]; **throwing** **1** TOSS : tirar, lanzar, echar, arrojar, aventar *Col, Mex* ⟨to throw a ball : tirar una pelota⟩ **2** UNSEAT : desmontar (a un jinete) **3** CAST : proyectar ⟨it threw a long shadow : proyectó una sombra larga⟩ **4 to throw a party** : dar una fiesta **5 to throw into confusion** : desconcertar **6 to throw out** DISCARD : botar, tirar (en la basura)

throw[2] *n* TOSS : tiro *m*, tirada *f*, lanzamiento *m*, lance *m* (de dados)

thrower [ˈθro:ər] *n* : lanzador *m*, -dora *f*

throw up *v* VOMIT : vomitar, devolver

thrush [ˈθrʌʃ] *n* : tordo *m*, zorzal *m*

thrust[1] [ˈθrʌst] *vt* **thrust; thrusting** **1** SHOVE : empujar bruscamente **2** PLUNGE, STAB : apuñalar, clavar ⟨he thrust a dagger into her heart : la apuñaló en el corazón⟩ **3 to thrust one's way** : abrirse paso **4 to thrust upon** : imponer a

thrust[2] *n* **1** PUSH, SHOVE : empujón *m*, empellón *m* **2** LUNGE : estocada *f* (en esgrima) **3** IMPETUS : ímpetu *m*, impulso *m*, propulsión *f* (de un motor)

thud[1] [ˈθʌd] *vi* **thudded; thudding** : producir un ruido sordo

thud[2] *n* : ruido *m* sordo (que produce un objeto al caer)

thug [ˈθʌg] *n* : matón *m*

thumb[1] [ˈθʌm] *vt* : hojear (con el pulgar)

thumb[2] *n* : pulgar *m*, dedo *m* pulgar

thumbnail [ˈθʌm,neɪl] *n* : uña *f* del pulgar

thumbtack [ˈθʌm,tæk] *n* : tachuela *f*, chinche *f*

thump[1] [ˈθʌmp] *vt* POUND : golpear, aporrear — *vi* : latir con vehemencia (dícese del corazón)

thump[2] *n* THUD : ruido *m* sordo

thunder[1] [ˈθʌndər] *vi* **1** : tronar ⟨it rained and thundered all night : llovió y tronó durante la noche⟩ **2** BOOM : retumbar, bramar, resonar — *vt* ROAR, SHOUT : decir a gritos, vociferar

thunder[2] *n* : truenos *mpl*

thunderbolt [ˈθʌndər,bo:lt] *n* : rayo *m*

thunderclap [ˈθʌndər,klæp] *n* : trueno *m*

thunderous [ˈθʌndərəs] *adj* : atronador, ensordecedor, estruendoso

thundershower [ˈθʌndər,ʃaʊər] *n* : lluvia *f* con truenos y relámpagos

thunderstorm [ˈθʌndər,stɔrm] *n* : tormenta *f* con truenos y relámpagos

thunderstruck [ˈθʌndər,strʌk] *adj* : atónito

Thursday [ˈθərz,deɪ, -di] *n* : jueves *m*

thus [ˈðʌs] *adv* **1** : así, de esta manera **2** SO : hasta (cierto punto) ⟨the weather's been nice thus far : hasta ahora ha hecho buen tiempo⟩ **3** HENCE : por consiguiente, por lo tanto

thwart [ˈθwɔrt] *vt* : frustrar

thy [ˈðaɪ] *adj* : tu

thyme [ˈtaɪm, ˈθaɪm] *n* : tomillo *m*

thyroid [ˈθaɪ,rɔɪd] *n or* **thyroid gland** : tiroides *mf*, glándula *f* tiroidea

thyself [ðaɪˈsɛlf] *pron* : ti, ti mismo

tiara [tiˈærə, -ˈɑr-] *n* : diadema *f*

Tibetan [təˈbɛtən] *n* **1** : tibetano *m*, -na *f* **2** : tibetano *m* (idioma) — **Tibetan** *adj*

tibia [ˈtɪbiə] *n, pl* **-iae** [-bi,i:] : tibia *f*

tic [ˈtɪk] *n* : tic *m*

tick[1] [ˈtɪk] *vi* **1** : hacer tictac **2** OPERATE, RUN : operar, andar (dícese de un mecanismo) ⟨what makes him tick? : ¿qué es lo que lo mueve?⟩ — *vt or* **to tick off** CHECK : marcar

tick[2] *n* **1** : tictac *m* (de un reloj) **2** CHECK : marca *f* **3** : garrapata *f* (insecto)

ticket[1] [ˈtɪkət] *vt* LABEL : etiquetar

ticket[2] *n* **1** : boleto *m*, entrada *f* (de un espectáculo), pasaje *m* (de avión, tren, etc.) **2** SLATE : lista *f* de candidatos

tickle[1] [ˈtɪkəl] *v* **-led; -ling** *vt* **1** AMUSE : divertir, hacerle gracia (a alguien) **2** : hacerle cosquillas (a alguien) ⟨don't tickle me! : ¡no me hagas cosquillas!⟩ — *vi* : picar

tickle[2] *n* : cosquilleo *m*, cosquillas *fpl*, picor *m* (en la garganta)

ticklish [ˈtɪkəlɪʃ] *adj* **1** : cosquilloso (dícese de una persona) **2** DELICATE, TRICKY : delicado, peliagudo

tidal [ˈtaɪdəl] *adj* : de marea, relativo a la marea

tidal wave *n* : maremoto *m*

tidbit [ˈtɪd,bɪt] *n* **1** BITE, SNACK : bocado *m*, golosina *f* **2** : dato *m* o noticia *f* interesante ⟨useful tidbits of information : informaciones útiles⟩

tide[1] [ˈtaɪd] *vt* **tided; tiding** *or* **to tide over** : proveer lo necesario para aguantar una dificultad ⟨this money will tide you over until you find work : este dinero te mantendrá hasta que encuentres empleo⟩

tide[2] *n* **1** : marea *f* **2** CURRENT : corriente *f* (de eventos, opiniones, etc.)

tidily [ˈtaɪdəli] *adv* : ordenadamente

tidiness [ˈtaɪdinəs] *n* : aseo *m*, limpieza *f*, orden *m*

tidings [ˈtaɪdɪŋz] *npl* : nuevas *fpl*

tidy[1] [ˈtaɪdi] *vt* **-died; -dying** : asear, limpiar, poner en orden

tidy[2] *adj* **-dier; -est** **1** CLEAN, NEAT : limpio, aseado, en orden **2** SUBSTANTIAL : grande, considerable ⟨a tidy sum : una suma considerable⟩

tie[1] [ˈtaɪ] *v* **tied; tying** *or* **tieing** *vt* **1** : atar, amarrar ⟨to tie a knot : atar un nudo⟩ ⟨to tie one's shoelaces : atarse los cordones⟩ **2** BIND, UNITE : ligar, atar **3** : empatar ⟨they tied the score : em-

pataron el marcador⟩ — *vi* : empatar ⟨the two teams were tied : los dos equipos empataron⟩
tie[2] *n* **1** : ligadura *f*, cuerda *f*, cordón *m* (para atar algo) **2** BOND, LINK : atadura *f*, ligadura *f*, vínculo *m*, lazo *m* ⟨family ties : lazos familiares⟩ **3** *or* **railroad tie** : traviesa *f* **4** DRAW : empate *m* (en deportes) **5** NECKTIE : corbata *f*
tier ['tɪr] *n* : hilera *f*, escalón *m*
tiff ['tɪf] *n* : disgusto *m*, disputa *f*
tiger ['taɪgər] *n* : tigre *m*
tight[1] ['taɪt] *adv* TIGHTLY : bien, fuerte ⟨shut it tight : ciérralo bien⟩
tight[2] *adj* **1** : bien cerrado, hermético ⟨a tight seal : un cierre hermético⟩ **2** STRICT : estricto, severo **3** TAUT : tirante, tenso **4** SNUG : apretado, ajustado, ceñido ⟨a tight dress : un vestido ceñido⟩ **5** DIFFICULT : difícil ⟨to be in a tight spot : estar en un aprieto⟩ **6** STINGY : apretado, avaro, agarrado *fam* **7** CLOSE : reñido ⟨a tight game : un juego reñido⟩ **8** SCARCE : escaso ⟨money is tight : escasea el dinero⟩
tighten ['taɪtən] *vt* : tensar (una cuerda, etc.), apretar (un nudo, un tornillo, etc.), apretarse (el cinturón), reforzar (las reglas)
tightly ['taɪtli] *adv* : bien, fuerte
tightness ['taɪtnəs] *n* : lo apretado, lo tenso, tensión *f*
tightrope ['taɪt,ro:p] *n* : cuerda *f* floja
tights ['taɪts] *npl* : leotardo *m*, malla *f*
tightwad ['taɪt,wɑd] *n* : avaro *m*, -ra *f*; tacaño *m*, -ña *f*
tigress ['taɪgrəs] *n* : tigresa *f*
tile[1] ['taɪl] *vt* **tiled; tiling** : embaldosar (un piso), revestir de azulejos (una pared), tejar (un techo)
tile[2] *n* **1** *or* **floor tile** : losa *f*, baldosa *f*, mosaico *m Mex* (de un piso) **2** : azulejo *m* (de una pared) **3** : teja *f* (de un techo)
till[1] ['tɪl] *vt* : cultivar, labrar
till[2] *n* : caja *f*, caja *f* registradora
till[3] *prep & conj* → **until**
tiller ['tɪlər] *n* **1** : cultivador *m*, -dora *f* (de la tierra) **2** : caña *f* del timón (de un barco)
tilt[1] ['tɪlt] *vt* : ladear, inclinar — *vi* : ladearse, inclinarse
tilt[2] *n* **1** SLANT : inclinación *f* **2 at full tilt** : a toda velocidad
timber ['tɪmbər] *n* **1** : madera *f* (para construcción) **2** BEAM : viga *f*
timberland ['tɪmbər,lænd] *n* : bosque *m* maderero
timbre ['tæmbər, 'tɪm-] *n* : timbre *m*
time[1] ['taɪm] *vt* **timed; timing 1** SCHEDULE : fijar la hora de, calcular el momento oportuno para **2** CLOCK : cronometrar, medir el tiempo de (una competencia, etc.)
time[2] *n* **1** : tiempo *m* ⟨the passing of time : el paso del tiempo⟩ ⟨she doesn't have time : no tiene tiempo⟩ **2** MOMENT : tiempo *m*, momento *m* ⟨this is not the time to bring it up : no es el momento de sacar el tema⟩ **3** : vez *f* ⟨she called you three times : te llamó tres veces⟩ ⟨three times greater : tres veces mayor⟩ **4** AGE : tiempo *m*, era *f* ⟨in your grandparents' time : en el tiempo de tus abuelos⟩ **5** TEMPO : tiempo *m*, ritmo *m* (en música) **6** : hora *f* ⟨what time is it? : ¿qué hora es?⟩ ⟨it's time for dinner : es hora de comer⟩ ⟨at the usual time : a la hora acostumbrada⟩ ⟨to keep time : ir a la hora⟩ ⟨to lose time : atrasar⟩ **7** EXPERIENCE : rato *m*, experiencia *f* ⟨we had a nice time together : pasamos juntos un rato agradable⟩ ⟨to have a rough time : pasarlo mal⟩ ⟨have a good time! : ¡que se diviertan!⟩ **8 at times** SOMETIMES : a veces **9 for the time being** : por el momento, de momento **10 from time to time** OCCASIONALLY : de vez en cuando **11 in time** PUNCTUALLY : a tiempo **12 in time** EVENTUALLY : con el tiempo **13 time after time** : una y otra vez
timekeeper ['taɪm,ki:pər] *n* : cronometrador *m*, -dora *f*
timeless ['taɪmləs] *adj* : eterno
timely ['taɪmli] *adj* **-lier; -est** : oportuno
timepiece ['taɪm,pi:s] *n* : reloj *m*
timer ['taɪmər] *n* : temporizador *m*, cronómetro *m*
times ['taɪmz] *prep* : por ⟨3 times 4 is 12 : 3 por 4 son 12⟩
timetable ['taɪm,teɪbəl] *n* : horario *m*
timid ['tɪmɪd] *adj* : tímido — **timidly** *adv*
timidity [tə'mɪdət̬i] *n* : timidez *f*
timorous ['tɪmərəs] *adj* : timorato, miedoso
timpani ['tɪmpəni] *npl* : timbales *mpl*
tin ['tɪn] *n* **1** : estaño *m*, hojalata *f* (metal) **2** CAN : lata *f*, bote *m*, envase *m*
tincture ['tɪŋktʃər] *n* : tintura *f*
tinder ['tɪndər] *n* : yesca *f*
tine ['taɪn] *n* : diente *m* (de un tenedor, etc.)
tinfoil ['tɪn,fɔɪl] *n* : papel *m* (de) aluminio
tinge[1] ['tɪndʒ] *vt* **tinged; tingeing** *or* **tinging** ['tɪndʒɪŋ] TINT : matizar, teñir ligeramente
tinge[2] *n* **1** TINT : matiz *m*, tinte *m* sutil **2** TOUCH : dejo *m*, sensación *f* ligera
tingle[1] ['tɪŋgəl] *vi* **-gled; -gling** : sentir (un) hormigueo, sentir (un) cosquilleo
tingle[2] *n* : hormigueo *m*, cosquilleo *m*
tinker ['tɪŋkər] *vi* **to tinker with** : arreglar con pequeños ajustes, toquetear (con intento de arreglar)
tinkle[1] ['tɪŋkəl] *vi* **-kled; -kling** : tintinear
tinkle[2] *n* : tintineo *m*
tinsel ['tɪntsəl] *n* : oropel *m*
tint[1] ['tɪnt] *vt* : teñir, colorear
tint[2] *n* : tinte *m*
tiny ['taɪni] *adj* **-nier; -est** : diminuto, minúsculo
tip[1] ['tɪp] *v* **tipped; tipping** *vt* **1** *or* **to tip over** : volcar, voltear, hacer caer **2** TILT : ladear, inclinar ⟨to tip one's hat : saludar con el sombrero⟩ **3** TAP : to-

car, golpear ligeramente **4** : darle una propina (a un mesero, etc.) ⟨I tipped him $5 : le di $5 de propina⟩ **5** : adornar o cubrir la punta de ⟨wings tipped in red : alas que tienen las puntas rojas⟩ **6 to tip off** : dar información a — *vi* TILT : ladearse, inclinarse

tip² *n* **1** END, POINT : punta *f*, extremo *m* ⟨on the tip of one's tongue : en la punta de la lengua⟩ **2** GRATUITY : propina *f* **3** ADVICE, INFORMATION : consejo *m*, información *f* (confidencial)

tip–off [ˈtɪpˌɔf] *n* **1** SIGN : indicación *f*, señal *f* **2** TIP : información *f* (confidencial)

tipple [ˈtɪpəl] *vi* **-pled; -pling** : tomarse unas copas

tipsy [ˈtɪpsi] *adj* **-sier; -est** : achispado

tiptoe¹ [ˈtɪpˌtoː] *vi* **-toed; -toeing** : caminar de puntillas

tiptoe² *adv* : de puntillas

tiptoe³ *n* : punta *f* del pie

tip–top¹ [ˈtɪpˈtɑp, -ˌtɑp] *adj* EXCELLENT : excelente

tip–top² *n* SUMMIT : cumbre *f*, cima *f*

tirade [ˈtaɪˌreɪd] *n* : diatriba *f*

tire¹ [ˈtaɪr] *v* **tired; tiring** *vt* : cansar, agotar, fatigar — *vi* : cansarse

tire² *n* : llanta *f*, neumático *m*, goma *f*

tired [ˈtaɪrd] *adj* : cansado, agotado, fatigado ⟨to get tired : cansarse⟩

tireless [ˈtaɪrləs] *adj* : incansable, infatigable — **tirelessly** *adv*

tiresome [ˈtaɪrsəm] *adj* : fastidioso, pesado, tedioso — **tiresomely** *adv*

tissue [ˈtɪˌʃuː] *n* **1** : pañuelo *m* de papel **2** : tejido *m* ⟨lung tissue : tejido pulmonar⟩

titanic [taɪˈtænɪk, tə-] *adj* GIGANTIC : titánico, gigantesco

titanium [taɪˈteɪniəm, tə-] *n* : titanio *m*

titillate [ˈtɪtəlˌeɪt] *vt* **-lated; -lating** : excitar, estimular placenteramente

title¹ [ˈtaɪt̬əl] *vt* **-tled; -tling** : titular, intitular

title² *n* : título *m*

titter¹ [ˈtɪt̬ər] *vi* GIGGLE : reírse tontamente

titter² *n* : risita *f*, risa *f* tonta

tizzy [ˈtɪzi] *n, pl* **tizzies** : estado *m* agitado o nervioso ⟨I'm all in a tizzy : estoy todo alterado⟩

TNT [ˌtiːˌɛnˈtiː] *n* : TNT *m*

to¹ [ˈtuː] *adv* **1** : a un estado consciente ⟨to come to : volver en sí⟩ **2 to and fro** : de aquí para allá, de un lado para otro

to² *prep* **1** (*indicating a place*) : a ⟨to go to the doctor : ir al médico⟩ ⟨I'm going to John's : voy a la casa de John⟩ **2** TOWARD : a, hacia ⟨two miles to the south : dos millas hacia el sur⟩ **3** ON : en, sobre ⟨apply salve to the wound : póngale ungüento a la herida⟩ **4** UP TO : hasta, a ⟨to a degree : hasta cierto grado⟩ ⟨from head to toe : de pies a cabeza⟩ **5** (*in expressions of time*) ⟨it's quarter to seven : son las siete menos cuarto⟩ **6** UNTIL : a, hasta ⟨from May to December : de mayo a diciembre⟩ **7** (*indicating belonging or possession*) : de, a ⟨the key to the lock : la llave del candado⟩ **8** (*indicating response*) : a ⟨dancing to the rhythm : bailando al compás⟩ **9** (*indicating comparison or proportion*) : a ⟨it's similar to mine : es parecido al mío⟩ ⟨they won 4 to 2 : ganaron 4 a 2⟩ **10** (*indicating agreement or conformity*) : a, de acuerdo con ⟨made to order : hecho a la orden⟩ ⟨to my knowledge : a mi saber⟩ **11** (*indicating inclusion*) : en cada, por ⟨twenty to the box : veinte por caja⟩ **12** (*used to form the infinitive*) ⟨to understand : entender⟩ ⟨to go away : irse⟩

toad [ˈtoːd] *n* : sapo *m*

toadstool [ˈtoːdˌstuːl] *n* : hongo *m* (no comestible)

toady [ˈtoːdi] *n, pl* **toadies** : adulador *m*, -dora *f*

toast¹ [ˈtoːst] *vt* **1** : tostar (pan) **2** : brindar por ⟨to toast the victors : brindar por los vencedores⟩ **3** WARM : calentar ⟨to toast oneself : calentarse⟩

toast² *n* **1** : pan *m* tostado, tostadas *fpl* **2** : brindis *m* ⟨to propose a toast : proponer un brindis⟩

toaster [ˈtoːstər] *n* : tostador *m*

tobacco [təˈbækoː] *n, pl* **-cos** : tabaco *m*

toboggan¹ [təˈbɑgən] *vi* : deslizarse en tobogán

toboggan² *n* : tobogán *m*

today¹ [təˈdeɪ] *adv* **1** : hoy ⟨she arrives today : hoy llega⟩ **2** NOWADAYS : hoy en día

today² *n* : hoy *m* ⟨today is a holiday : hoy es día de fiesta⟩

toddle [ˈtɑdəl] *vi* **-dled; -dling** : hacer pininos, hacer pinitos

toddler [ˈtɑdələr] *n* : niño *m* pequeño, niña *f* pequeña (que comienza a caminar)

to–do [təˈduː] *n, pl* **to–dos** [-ˈduːz] FUSS : lío *m*, alboroto *m*

toe [ˈtoː] *n* : dedo *m* del pie

toenail [ˈtoːˌneɪl] *n* : uña *f* del pie

toffee *or* **toffy** [ˈtɔfi, ˈtɑ-] *n, pl* **toffees** *or* **toffies** : caramelo *m* elaborado con azúcar y mantequilla

toga [ˈtoːgə] *n* : toga *f*

together [təˈgɛðər] *adv* **1** : juntamente, juntos (el uno con el otro) ⟨Susan and Sarah work together : Susan y Sarah trabajan juntas⟩ **2 ~ with** : junto con

togetherness [təˈgɛðərnəs] *n* : unión *f*, compañerismo *m*

togs [ˈtɑgz, ˈtɔgz] *npl* : ropa *f*

toil¹ [ˈtɔɪl] *vi* : trabajar arduamente

toil² *n* : trabajo *m* arduo

toilet [ˈtɔɪlət] *n* **1** : arreglo *m* personal **2** BATHROOM : (cuarto de) baño *m*, servicios *mpl* (públicos), sanitario *m Col, Mex, Ven* **3** : inodoro *m* ⟨to flush the toilet : jalar la cadena⟩

toilet paper *n* : papel *m* higiénico

toiletries [ˈtɔɪlətriz] *npl* : artículos *mpl* de tocador

token [ˈtoːkən] *n* **1** PROOF, SIGN : prueba *f*, muestra *f*, señal *m* **2** SYMBOL : símbolo *m* **3** SOUVENIR : recuerdo *m* **4** : ficha *f* (para transporte público, etc.)
told → **tell**
tolerable [ˈtɑlərəbəl] *adj* : tolerable — **tolerably** [-bli] *adv*
tolerance [ˈtɑlərənts] *n* : tolerancia *f*
tolerant [ˈtɑlərənt] *adj* : tolerante — **tolerantly** *adv*
tolerate [ˈtɑləˌreɪt] *vt* **-ated; -ating** **1** ACCEPT : tolerar, aceptar **2** BEAR, ENDURE : tolerar, aguantar, soportar
toleration [ˌtɑləˈreɪʃən] *n* : tolerancia *f*
toll[1] [ˈtoːl] *vt* : tañer, sonar (una campana) — *vi* : sonar, doblar (dícese de las campanas)
toll[2] *n* **1** : peaje *m* (de una carretera, un puente, etc.) **2** CASUALTIES : pérdida *f*, número *m* de víctimas **3** TOLLING : tañido *m* (de campanas)
tollbooth [ˈtoːlˌbuːθ] *n* : caseta *f* de peaje
tollgate [ˈtoːlˌgeɪt] *n* : barrera *f* de peaje
tomahawk [ˈtɑməˌhɔk] *n* : hacha *f* de guerra (de los indígenas norteamericanos)
tomato [təˈmeɪt̬o, -ˈmɑ-] *n, pl* **-toes** : tomate *m*
tomb [ˈtuːm] *n* : sepulcro *m*, tumba *f*
tomboy [ˈtɑmˌbɔɪ] *n* : marimacho *mf*; niña *f* que se porta como muchacho
tombstone [ˈtuːmˌstoːn] *n* : lápida *f*
tomcat [ˈtɑmˌkæt] *n* : gato *m* (macho)
tome [ˈtoːm] *n* : tomo *m*
tomorrow[1] [təˈmɑro] *adv* : mañana
tomorrow[2] *n* : mañana *m*
tom–tom [ˈtɑmˌtɑm] *n* : tam-tam *m*
ton [ˈtən] *n* : tonelada *f*
tone[1] [ˈtoːn] *vt* **toned; toning** **1** *or* **to tone down** : atenuar, suavizar, moderar **2** *or* **to tone up** STRENGTHEN : tonificar, vigorizar
tone[2] *n* : tono *m* ⟨in a friendly tone : en tono amistoso⟩ ⟨a greyish tone : un tono grisáceo⟩
tongs [ˈtɑŋz, ˈtɔŋz] *npl* : tenazas *fpl*
tongue [ˈtʌŋ] *n* **1** : lengua *f* **2** LANGUAGE : lengua *f*, idioma *m*
tongue–tied [ˈtʌŋˌtaɪd] *adj* **to get tongue–tied** : trabársele la lengua a uno
tonic[1] [ˈtɑnɪk] *adj* : tónico
tonic[2] *n* **1** : tónico *m* **2** *or* **tonic water** : tónica *f*
tonight[1] [təˈnaɪt] *adv* : esta noche
tonight[2] *n* : esta noche *f*
tonsil [ˈtɑntsəl] *n* : amígdala *f*, angina *f Mex*
tonsillitis [ˌtɑntsəˈlaɪt̬əs] *n* : amigdalitis *f*, anginas *fpl Mex*
too [ˈtuː] *adv* **1** ALSO : también **2** EXCESSIVELY : demasiado ⟨it's too hot in here : aquí hace demasiado calor⟩
took → **take**[1]
tool[1] [ˈtuːl] *vt* **1** : fabricar, confeccionar (con herramientas) **2** EQUIP : instalar maquinaria en (una fábrica)
tool[2] *n* : herramienta *f*
toolbox [ˈtuːlˌbɑks] *n* : caja *f* de herramientas
toot[1] [ˈtuːt] *vt* : sonar (un claxon o un pito)
toot[2] *n* : pitido *m*, bocinazo *m* (de un claxon)
tooth [ˈtuːθ] *n, pl* **teeth** [ˈtiːθ] : diente *m*
toothache [ˈtuːθˌeɪk] *n* : dolor *m* de muelas
toothbrush [ˈtuːθˌbrʌʃ] *n* : cepillo *m* de dientes
toothless [ˈtuːθləs] *adj* : desdentado
toothpaste [ˈtuːθˌpeɪst] *n* : pasta *f* de dientes, crema *f* dental, dentífrico *m*
toothpick [ˈtuːθˌpɪk] *n* : palillo *m* (de dientes), mondadientes *m*
top[1] [ˈtɑp] *vt* **topped; topping** **1** COVER : cubrir, coronar **2** SURPASS : sobrepasar, superar **3** CLEAR : pasar por encima de
top[2] *adj* : superior ⟨the top shelf : la repisa superior⟩ ⟨one of the top lawyers : uno de los mejores abogados⟩
top[3] *n* **1** : parte *f* superior, cumbre *f*, cima *f* (de un monte, etc.) ⟨to climb to the top : subir a la cumbre⟩ **2** COVER : tapa *f*, cubierta *f* **3** : trompo *m* (juguete) **4 on top of** : encima de
topaz [ˈtoːˌpæz] *n* : topacio *m*
topcoat [ˈtɑpˌkoːt] *n* : sobretodo *m*, abrigo *m*
topic [ˈtɑpɪk] *n* : tema *m*, tópico *m*
topical [ˈtɑpɪkəl] *adj* : de interés actual
topmost [ˈtɑpˌmoːst] *adj* : más alto
top–notch [ˈtɑpˈnɑʧ] *adj* : de lo mejor, de primera categoría
topographic [ˌtɑpəˈgræfɪk] *or* **topographical** [-fɪkəl] *adj* : topográfico
topography [təˈpɑgrəfi] *n, pl* **-phies** : topografía *f*
topple [ˈtɑpəl] *v* **-pled; -pling** *vi* : caerse, venirse abajo — *vt* : volcar, derrocar (un gobierno, etc.)
topsoil [ˈtɑpˌsɔɪl] *n* : capa *f* superior del suelo
topsy–turvy [ˌtɑpsiˈtərvi] *adv & adj* : patas arriba, al revés
torch [ˈtɔrʧ] *n* : antorcha *f*
tore → **tear**[1]
torment[1] [tɔrˈmɛnt, ˈtɔrˌ-] *vt* : atormentar, torturar, martirizar
torment[2] [ˈtɔrˌmɛnt] *n* : tormento *m*, suplicio *m*, martirio *m*
tormentor [tɔrˈmɛntər] *n* : atormentador *m*, -dora *f*
torn *pp* → **tear**[1]
tornado [tɔrˈneɪdo] *n, pl* **-does** *or* **-dos** : tornado *m*
torpedo[1] [tɔrˈpiːdo] *vt* : torpedear
torpedo[2] *n, pl* **-does** : torpedo *m*
torpid [ˈtɔrpɪd] *adj* **1** SLUGGISH : aletargado **2** APATHETIC : apático
torpor [ˈtɔrpər] *n* : letargo *m*, apatía *f*
torrent [ˈtɔrənt] *n* : torrente *m*
torrential [tɔˈrɛnʧəl, tə-] *adj* : torrencial
torrid [ˈtɔrɪd] *adj* : tórrido
torso [ˈtɔrˌsoː] *n, pl* **-sos** *or* **-si** [-ˌsiː] : torso *m*

tortilla [tɔr'ti:jə] *n* : tortilla *f* (de maíz)
tortoise ['tɔrṭəs] *n* : tortuga *f* (terrestre)
tortoiseshell ['tɔrṭəs,ʃɛl] *n* : carey *m*, concha *f*
tortuous ['tɔrʧuəs] *adj* : tortuoso
torture[1] ['tɔrʧər] *vt* **-tured; -turing** : torturar, atormentar
torture[2] *n* : tortura *f*, tormento *m* ⟨it was sheer torture! : ¡fue un verdadero suplicio!⟩
torturer ['tɔrʧərər] *n* : torturador *m*, -dora *f*
toss[1] ['tɔs, 'tɑs] *vt* **1** AGITATE, SHAKE : sacudir, agitar, mezclar (una ensalada) **2** THROW : tirar, echar, lanzar — *vi* : sacudirse, moverse agitadamente ⟨to toss and turn : dar vueltas⟩
toss[2] *n* THROW : lanzamiento *m*, tiro *m*, tirada *f*, lance *m* (de dados, etc.)
toss–up ['tɔs,ʌp] *n* : posibilidad *f* igual ⟨it's a toss-up : quizá sí, quizá no⟩
tot ['tɑt] *n* : pequeño *m*, -ña *f*
total[1] ['to:təl] *vt* **-taled** *or* **-talled; -taling** *or* **-talling** **1** *or* **to total up** ADD : sumar, totalizar **2** AMOUNT TO : ascender a, llegar a
total[2] *adj* : total, completo, absoluto — **totally** *adv*
total[3] *n* : total *m*
totalitarian [to:,tælə'tɛriən] *adj* : totalitario
totalitarianism [to:,tælə'tɛriə,nɪzəm] *n* : totalitarismo *m*
totality [to:'tæləṭi] *n, pl* **-ties** : totalidad *f*
tote ['to:t] *vt* **toted; toting** : cargar, llevar
totem ['to:təm] *n* : tótem *m*
totter ['tɑtər] *vi* : tambalearse
touch[1] ['tʌʧ] *vt* **1** FEEL, HANDLE : tocar, tentar **2** AFFECT, MOVE : conmover, afectar, tocar ⟨his gesture touched our hearts : su gesto nos tocó el corazón⟩ — *vi* : tocarse
touch[2] *n* **1** : tacto *m* (sentido) **2** DETAIL : toque *m*, detalle *m* ⟨a touch of color : un toque de color⟩ **3** BIT : pizca *f*, gota *f*, poco *m* **4** ABILITY : habilidad *f* ⟨to lose one's touch : perder la habilidad⟩ **5** CONTACT : contacto *m*, comunicación *f* ⟨to keep in touch : mantenerse en contacto⟩
touchdown ['tʌʧ,daʊn] *n* : touchdown *m* (en futbol americano)
touching ['tʌʧɪŋ] *adj* MOVING : conmovedor
touchstone ['tʌʧ,sto:n] *n* : piedra *f* de toque
touch up *vt* : retocar
touchy ['tʌʧi] *adj* **touchier; -est** **1** : sensible, susceptible (dícese de una persona) **2** : delicado ⟨a touchy subject : un tema delicado⟩
tough[1] ['tʌf] *adj* **1** STRONG : fuerte, resistente (dícese de materiales) **2** LEATHERY : correoso ⟨a tough steak : un bistec duro⟩ **3** HARDY : fuerte, robusto (dícese de una persona) **4** STRICT : severo, exigente **5** DIFFICULT : difícil **6** STUBBORN : terco, obstinado
tough[2] *n* : matón *m*, persona *f* ruda y brusca
toughen ['tʌfən] *vt* : fortalecer, endurecer — *vi* : endurecerse, hacerse más fuerte
toughness ['tʌfnəs] *n* : dureza *f*
toupee [tu:'peɪ] *n* : peluquín *m*, bisoñé *m*
tour[1] ['tʊr] *vi* : tomar una excursión, viajar — *vt* : recorrer, hacer una gira por
tour[2] *n* **1** : gira *f*, tour *m*, excursión *f* **2** **tour of duty** : período *m* de servicio
tourism ['tʊr,ɪzəm] *n* : turismo *m*
tourist ['tʊrɪst, 'tər-] *n* : turista *mf*
tournament ['tərnəmənt, 'tʊr-] *n* : torneo *m*
tourniquet ['tərnɪkət, 'tʊr-] *n* : torniquete *m*
tousle ['taʊzəl] *vt* **-sled; -sling** : desarreglar, despeinar (el cabello)
tout ['taʊt] *vt* : promocionar, elogiar (con exageración)
tow[1] ['to:] *vt* : remolcar
tow[2] *n* : remolque *m*
toward ['tord, tə'wɔrd] *or* **towards** ['tordz, tə'wɔrdz] *prep* **1** (*indicating direction*) : hacia, rumbo a ⟨heading toward town : dirigiéndose rumbo al pueblo⟩ ⟨efforts towards peace : esfuerzos hacia la paz⟩ **2** (*indicating time*) : alrededor de ⟨toward midnight : alrededor de la medianoche⟩ **3** REGARDING : hacia, con respecto a ⟨his attitude toward life : su actitud hacia la vida⟩ **4** FOR : para, como pago parcial de (una compra o deuda)
towel ['taʊəl] *n* : toalla *f*
tower[1] ['taʊər] *vi* **to tower over** : descollar sobre, elevarse sobre, dominar
tower[2] *n* : torre *f*
towering ['taʊərɪŋ] *adj* : altísimo, imponente
town ['taʊn] *n* : pueblo *m*, ciudad *f* (pequeña)
township ['taʊn,ʃɪp] *n* : municipio *m*
tow truck ['to:,trʌk] *n* : grúa *f*
toxic ['tɑksɪk] *adj* : tóxico
toxicity [tɑk'sɪsəṭi] *n, pl* **-ties** : toxicidad *f*
toxin ['tɑksɪn] *n* : toxina *f*
toy[1] ['tɔɪ] *vi* : juguetear, jugar
toy[2] *adj* : de juguete ⟨a toy rifle : un rifle de juguete⟩
toy[3] *n* : juguete *m*
trace[1] ['treɪs] *vt* **traced; tracing** **1** : calcar (un dibujo, etc.) **2** OUTLINE : delinear, trazar (planes, etc.) **3** TRACK : describir (un curso, una historia) **4** FIND : localizar, ubicar
trace[2] *n* **1** SIGN, TRACK : huella *f*, rastro *m*, indicio *m*, vestigio *m* ⟨he disappeared without a trace : desapareció sin dejar rastro⟩ **2** BIT, HINT : pizca *f*, ápice *m*, dejo *m*
trachea ['treɪkiə] *n, pl* **-cheae** [-ki,i:] : tráquea *f*

tracing paper *n* : papel *m* de calcar
track[1] ['træk] *vt* **1** TRAIL : seguir la pista de, rastrear **2** : dejar huellas de ⟨he tracked mud all over : dejó huellas de lodo por todas partes⟩
track[2] *n* **1** : rastro *m*, huella *f* (de animales), pista *f* (de personas) **2** PATH : pista *f*, sendero *m*, camino *m* **3** *or* **railroad track** : vía *f* (férrea) **4** → **racetrack** **5** : oruga *f* (de un tanque, etc.) **6** : pista *f* (deporte) **7 to keep track of** : llevar la cuenta de
track–and–field ['trækənd'fi:ld] *adj* : de pista y campo
tract ['trækt] *n* **1** AREA : terreno *m*, extensión *f*, área *f* **2** : tracto *m* ⟨digestive tract : tracto digestivo⟩ **3** PAMPHLET : panfleto *m*, folleto *m*
traction ['trækʃən] *n* : tracción *f*
tractor ['træktər] *n* **1** : tractor *m* (vehículo agrícola) **2** TRUCK : camión *m* (con remolque)
trade[1] ['treɪd] *v* **traded; trading** *vi* : comerciar, negociar — *vt* EXCHANGE : intercambiar, canjear
trade[2] *n* **1** OCCUPATION : oficio *m*, profesión *f*, ocupación *f* ⟨a carpenter by trade : carpintero de oficio⟩ **2** COMMERCE : comercio *m*, industria *f* ⟨free trade : libre comercio⟩ ⟨the book trade : la industria del libro⟩ **3** EXCHANGE : intercambio *m*, canje *m*
trade–in ['treɪd,ɪn] *n* : artículo *m* que se canjea por otro
trademark ['treɪd,mɑrk] *n* **1** : marca *f* registrada **2** CHARACTERISTIC : sello *m* característico (de un grupo, una persona, etc.)
trader ['treɪdər] *n* : negociante *mf*, tratante *mf*, comerciante *mf*
tradesman ['treɪdzmən] *n, pl* **-men** [-mən, -,mɛn] **1** CRAFTSMAN : artesano *m*, -na *f* **2** SHOPKEEPER : tendero *m*, -ra *f*; comerciante *mf*
trade wind *n* : viento *m* alisio
tradition [trə'dɪʃən] *n* : tradición *f*
traditional [trə'dɪʃənəl] *adj* : tradicional — **traditionally** *adv*
traffic[1] ['træfɪk] *vi* **trafficked; trafficking** : traficar (con)
traffic[2] *n* **1** COMMERCE : tráfico *m*, comercio *m* ⟨the drug traffic : el narcotráfico⟩ **2** : tráfico *m*, tránsito *m*, circulación *f* (de vehículos, etc.)
traffic circle *n* : rotonda *f*, glorieta *f*
trafficker ['træfɪkər] *n* : traficante *mf*
traffic light *n* : semáforo *m*, luz *f* (de tránsito)
tragedy ['trædʒədi] *n, pl* **-dies** : tragedia *f*
tragic ['trædʒɪk] *adj* : trágico — **tragically** *adv*
trail[1] ['treɪl] *vi* **1** DRAG : arrastrarse **2** LAG : quedarse atrás, retrasarse **3 to trail away** *or* **to trail off** : disminuir, menguar, desvanecerse — *vt* **1** DRAG : arrastrar **2** PURSUE : perseguir, seguir la pista de
trail[2] *n* **1** TRACK : rastro *m*, huella *f*, pista *f* ⟨a trail of blood : un rastro de sangre⟩ **2** : cola *f*, estela *f* (de un meteoro) **3** PATH : sendero *m*, camino *m*, vereda *f*
trailer ['treɪlər] *n* **1** : remolque *m*, tráiler *m* (de un camión) **2** : caravana *f* (vivienda ambulante)
train[1] ['treɪn] *vt* **1** : adiestrar, entrenar (atletas), capacitar (trabajadores), amaestrar (animales) **2** POINT : apuntar (un arma, etc.) — *vi* : entrenar(se) (físicamente), prepararse (profesionalmente) ⟨she's training at the gym : se está entrenando en el gimnasio⟩
train[2] *n* **1** : cola *f* (de un vestido) **2** RETINUE : cortejo *m*, séquito *m* **3** SERIES : serie *f* (de eventos) **4** : tren *m* ⟨passenger train : tren de pasajeros⟩
trainee [treɪ'ni:] *n* : aprendiz *m*, -diza *f*
trainer ['treɪnər] *n* : entrenador *m*, -dora *f*
training ['treɪnɪŋ] *n* : adiestramiento *m*, entrenamiento *m* (físico), capacitación *f* (de trabajadores)
traipse ['treɪps] *vi* **traipsed; traipsing** : andar de un lado para otro, vagar
trait ['treɪt] *n* : rasgo *m*, característica *f*
traitor ['treɪt̬ər] *n* : traidor *m*, -dora *f*
traitorous ['treɪt̬ərəs] *adj* : traidor
trajectory [trə'dʒɛktəri] *n, pl* **-ries** : trayectoria *f*
tramp[1] ['træmp] *vi* : caminar (a paso pesado) — *vt* : deambular por, vagar por ⟨to tramp the streets : vagar por las calles⟩
tramp[2] *n* **1** VAGRANT : vagabundo *m*, -da *f* **2** HIKE : caminata *f*
trample ['træmpəl] *vt* **-pled; -pling** : pisotear, hollar
trampoline [,træmpə'li:n, 'træmpə,-] *n* : trampolín *m*, cama *f* elástica
trance ['trænts] *n* : trance *m*
tranquil ['træŋkwəl] *adj* : calmo, tranquilo, sereno — **tranquilly** *adv*
tranquilize ['træŋkwə,laɪz] *vt* **-ized; -izing** : tranquilizar
tranquilizer ['træŋkwə,laɪzər] *n* : tranquilizante *m*
tranquillity *or* **tranquility** [træŋ'kwɪlət̬i] *n* : sosiego *m*, tranquilidad *f*
transact [træn'zækt] *vt* : negociar, gestionar, hacer (negocios)
transaction [træn'zækʃən] *n* **1** : transacción *f*, negocio *m*, operación *f* **2 transactions** *npl* RECORDS : actas *fpl*
transatlantic [,træntsət'læntɪk, ,trænz-] *adj* : transatlántico
transcend [træn'sɛnd] *vt* : trascender, sobrepasar
transcendent [trænt'sɛndənt] *adj* : trascendente — **transcendence** [trænt'sɛndənts] *n*
transcendental [,trænt,sɛn'dɛntəl, -sən-] *adj* : trascendental ⟨transcendental meditation : meditación trascendental⟩

transcribe [træn'skraɪb] *vt* **-scribed; -scribing** : transcribir
transcript ['træn,skrɪpt] *n* : copia *f* oficial
transcription [træn'skrɪpʃən] *n* : transcripción *f*
transfer[1] [trænts'fər, 'trænts,fər] *v* **-ferred; -ferring** *vt* **1** : trasladar (a una persona), transferir (fondos) **2** : transferir, traspasar, ceder (propiedad) **3** PRINT : imprimir (un diseño) — *vi* **1** MOVE : trasladarse, cambiarse **2** CHANGE : transbordar, cambiar (de un transporte a otro) ⟨he transfers at E Street : hace un transborde a la calle E⟩
transfer[2] ['trænts,fər] *n* **1** TRANSFERRING : transferencia *f* (de fondos, de propiedad, etc.), traslado *m* (de una persona) **2** DECAL : calcomanía *f* **3** : boleto *m* (para cambiar de un avión, etc., a otro)
transferable [trænts'fərəbəl] *adj* : transferible
transference [trænts'fərənts] *n* : transferencia *f*
transfigure [trænts'fɪgjər] *vt* **-ured; -uring** : transfigurar, transformar
transfix [trænts'fɪks] *vt* **1** PIERCE : traspasar, atravesar **2** IMMOBILIZE : paralizar
transform [trænts'fɔrm] *vt* : transformar
transformation [,træntsfər'meɪʃən] *n* : transformación *f*
transformer [trænts'fɔrmər] *n* : transformador *m*
transfusion [trænts'fju:ʒən] *n* : transfusión *f*
transgress [trænts'grɛs, trænz-] *vt* : transgredir, infringir
transgression [trænts'grɛʃən, trænz-] *n* : transgresión *f*
transient[1] ['træntʃənt, 'trænsiənt] *adj* : pasajero, transitorio — **transiently** *adv*
transient[2] *n* : transeúnte *mf*
transistor [træn'zɪstər, -'sɪs-] *n* : transistor *m*
transit ['træntsɪt, 'trænzɪt] *n* **1** PASSAGE : pasaje *m*, tránsito *m* ⟨in transit : en tránsito⟩ **2** TRANSPORTATION : transporte *m* (público) **3** : teodolito *m* (instrumento topográfico)
transition [træn'sɪʃən, -'zɪʃ-] *n* : transición *f*
transitional [træn'sɪʃənəl, -'zɪʃ-] *adj* : de transición
transitive ['træntsət̬ɪv, 'trænzə-] *adj* : transitivo
transitory ['træntsə,tori, 'trænzə-] *adj* : transitorio
translate [trænts'leɪt, trænz-; 'trænts,-, 'træns,-] *vt* **-lated; -lating** : traducir
translation [trænts'leɪʃən, trænz-] *n* : traducción *f*
translator [trænts'leɪt̬ər, trænz-; 'trænts,-, 'træns,-] *n* : traductor *m*, -tora *f*
translucent [trænts'lu:sənt, trænz-] *adj* : translúcido
transmission [trænts'mɪʃən, trænz-] *n* : transmisión *f*
transmit [trænts'mɪt, trænz-] *vt* **-mitted; -mitting** : transmitir
transmitter [trænts'mɪt̬ər, trænz-; 'trænts,-, 'træns,-] *n* : transmisor *m*, emisor *m*
transom ['træntsəm] *n* : montante *m* (de una puerta), travesaño *m* (de una ventana)
transparency [trænts'pærəntsi] *n*, *pl* **-cies** : transparencia *f*
transparent [trænts'pærənt] *adj* **1** : transparente, traslúcido ⟨a transparent fabric : una tela transparente⟩ **2** OBVIOUS : transparente, obvio, claro — **transparently** *adv*
transpiration [,træntspə'reɪʃən] *n* : transpiración *f*
transpire [trænts'paɪr] *vi* **-spired; -spiring** **1** : transpirar (en biología y botánica) **2** TURN OUT : resultar **3** HAPPEN : suceder, ocurrir, tener lugar
transplant[1] [trænts'plænt] *vt* : trasplantar
transplant[2] ['trænts,plænt] *n* : trasplante *m*
transport[1] [trænts'port, 'trænts,-] *vt* **1** CARRY : transportar, acarrear **2** ENRAPTURE : transportar, extasiar
transport[2] ['trænts,port] *n* **1** TRANSPORTATION : transporte *m*, transportación *f* **2** RAPTURE : éxtasis *m* **3** *or* **transport ship** : buque *m* de transporte (de personal militar)
transportation [,træntspər'teɪʃən] *n* : transporte *m*, transportación *f*
transpose [trænts'po:z] *vt* **-posed; -posing** : trasponer, trasladar, transportar (una composición musical)
transverse [trænts'vərs, trænz-] *adj* : transversal, transverso, oblicuo — **transversely** *adv*
trap[1] ['træp] *vt* **trapped; trapping** : atrapar, apresar (en una trampa)
trap[2] *n* : trampa *f* ⟨to set a trap : tender una trampa⟩
trapdoor ['træp'dor] *n* : trampilla *f*, escotillón *m*
trapeze [træ'pi:z] *n* : trapecio *m*
trapezoid ['træpə,zɔɪd] *n* : trapezoide *m*, trapecio *m*
trapper ['træpər] *n* : trampero *m*, -ra *f*; cazador *m*, -dora *f* (que usa trampas)
trappings ['træpɪŋz] *npl* **1** : arreos *mpl*, jaeces *mpl* (de un caballo) **2** ADORNMENTS : adornos *mpl*, pompa *f*
trash ['træʃ] *n* : basura *f*
trashy ['træʃi] *adj* : de pacotilla
trauma ['trɔmə, 'traʊ-] *n* : trauma *m*
traumatic [trə'mæt̬ɪk, trɔ-, traʊ-] *adj* : traumático
travel[1] ['trævəl] *vi* **-eled** *or* **-elled; -eling** *or* **-elling** **1** JOURNEY : viajar **2** GO, MOVE : desplazarse, moverse, ir ⟨the waves travel at uniform speed : las ondas se desplazan a una velocidad uniforme⟩

travel² *n or* **travels** *npl* : viajes *mpl*
traveler *or* **traveller** ['trævələr] *n* : viajero *m*, -ra *f*
traverse [trə'vərs, træ'vərs, 'trævərs] *vt* **-versed; -versing** CROSS : atravesar, extenderse a través de, cruzar
travesty ['trævəsti] *n, pl* **-ties** : parodia *f*
trawl¹ ['trɔl] *vi* : pescar con red de arrastre, rastrear
trawl² *n or* **trawl net** : red *f* de arrastre
trawler ['trɔlər] *n* : barco *m* de pesca (utilizado para rastrear)
tray ['treɪ] *n* : bandeja *f*, charola *f Bol, Mex, Peru*
treacherous ['trɛʧərəs] *adj* **1** TRAITOROUS : traicionero, traidor **2** DANGEROUS : peligroso
treacherously ['trɛʧərəsli] *adv* : a traición
treachery ['trɛʧəri] *n, pl* **-eries** : traición *f*
tread¹ ['trɛd] *v* **trod** ['trɑd]; **trodden** ['trɑdən] *or* **trod; treading** *vt* TRAMPLE : pisotear, hollar — *vi* **1** WALK : caminar, andar **2 to tread on** : pisar
tread² *n* **1** STEP : paso *m*, andar *m* **2** : banda *f* de rodadura (de un neumático, etc.) **3** : escalón *m* (de una escalera)
treadle ['trɛdəl] *n* : pedal *m* (de una máquina)
treadmill ['trɛd,mɪl] *n* **1** : rueda *f* de andar **2** ROUTINE : rutina *f*
treason ['tri:zən] *n* : traición *f* (a la patria, etc.)
treasure¹ ['trɛʒər, 'treɪ-] *vt* **-sured; -suring** : apreciar, valorar
treasure² *n* : tesoro *m*
treasurer ['trɛʒərər, 'treɪ-] *n* : tesorero *m*, -ra *f*
treasury ['trɛʒəri, 'treɪ-] *n, pl* **-suries** : tesorería *f*, tesoro *m*
treat¹ ['tri:t] *vt* **1** DEAL WITH : tratar (un asunto) ⟨the article treats of poverty : el artículo trata de la pobreza⟩ **2** HANDLE : tratar (a una persona), manejar (un objeto) ⟨to treat something as a joke : tomar(se) algo a broma⟩ **3** INVITE : invitar, convidar ⟨he treated me to a meal : me invitó a comer⟩ **4** : tratar, atender (en medicina) **5** PROCESS : tratar ⟨to treat sewage : tratar las aguas negras⟩
treat² *n* : gusto *m*, placer *m* ⟨it was a treat to see you : fue un placer verte⟩ ⟨it's my treat : yo invito⟩
treatise ['tri:t̬ɪs] *n* : tratado *m*, estudio *m*
treatment ['tri:tmənt] *n* : trato *m*, tratamiento *m* (médico)
treaty ['tri:t̬i] *n, pl* **-ties** : tratado *m*, convenio *m*
treble¹ ['trɛbəl] *vt* **-bled; -bling** : triplicar
treble² *adj* **1** → **triple 2** : de tiple, soprano (en música) **3 treble clef** : clave *f* de sol
treble³ *n* : tiple *m*, parte *f* de soprano
tree ['tri:] *n* : árbol *m*
treeless ['tri:ləs] *adj* : carente de árboles
trek¹ ['trɛk] *vi* **trekked; trekking** : hacer un viaje largo y difícil
trek² *n* : viaje *m* largo y difícil
trellis ['trɛlɪs] *n* : enrejado *m*, espaldera *f*, celosía *f*
tremble ['trɛmbəl] *vi* **-bled; -bling** : temblar
tremendous [trɪ'mɛndəs] *adj* : tremendo — **tremendously** *adv*
tremor ['trɛmər] *n* : temblor *m*
tremulous ['trɛmjələs] *adj* : trémulo, tembloroso
trench ['trɛnʧ] *n* **1** DITCH : zanja *f* **2** : trinchera *f* (militar)
trenchant ['trɛnʧənt] *adj* : cortante, mordaz
trend¹ ['trɛnd] *vi* : tender, inclinarse
trend² *n* **1** TENDENCY : tendencia *f* **2** FASHION : moda *f*
trendy ['trɛndi] *adj* **trendier; -est** : de moda
trepidation [,trɛpə'deɪʃən] *n* : inquietud *f*, ansiedad *f*
trespass¹ ['trɛspəs, -,pæs] *vi* **1** SIN : pecar, transgredir **2** : entrar ilegalmente (en propiedad ajena)
trespass² *n* **1** SIN : pecado *m*, transgresión *f* ⟨forgive us our trespasses : perdónanos nuestras deudas⟩ **2** : entrada *f* ilegal (en propiedad ajena)
tress ['trɛs] *n* : mechón *m*
trestle ['trɛsəl] *n* **1** : caballete *m* (armazón) **2** *or* **trestle bridge** : puente *m* de caballete
triad ['traɪ,æd] *n* : tríada *f*
trial¹ ['traɪəl] *adj* : de prueba ⟨trial period : período de prueba⟩
trial² *n* **1** : juicio *m*, proceso *m* ⟨to stand trial : ser sometido a juicio⟩ **2** AFFLICTION : aflicción *f*, tribulación *f* **3** TEST : prueba *f*, ensayo *m*
triangle ['traɪ,æŋgəl] *n* : triángulo *m*
triangular [traɪ'æŋgjələr] *adj* : triangular
tribal ['traɪbəl] *adj* : tribal
tribe ['traɪb] *n* : tribu *f*
tribesman ['traɪbzmən] *n, pl* **-men** [-mən, -,mɛn] : miembro *m* de una tribu
tribulation [,trɪbjə'leɪʃən] *n* : tribulación *f*
tribunal [traɪ'bju:nəl, trɪ-] *n* : tribunal *m*, corte *f*
tributary ['trɪbjə,tɛri] *n, pl* **-taries** : afluente *m*
tribute ['trɪb,ju:t] *n* : tributo *m*
trick¹ ['trɪk] *vt* : engañar, embaucar
trick² *n* **1** RUSE : trampa *f*, treta *f*, artimaña *f* **2** PRANK : broma *f* ⟨we played a trick on her : le gastamos una broma⟩ **3** : truco *m* ⟨magic tricks : trucos de magia⟩ ⟨the trick is to wait five minutes : el truco está en esperar cinco minutos⟩ **4** MANNERISM : peculiaridad *f*, manía *f* **5** : baza *f* (en juegos de naipes)
trickery ['trɪkəri] *n* : engaños *mpl*, trampas *fpl*
trickle¹ ['trɪkəl] *vi* **-led; -ling** : gotear, chorrear

trickle[2] *n* : goteo *m*, hilo *m*
trickster ['trɪkstər] *n* : estafador *m*, -dora *f*; embaucador *m*, -dora *f*
tricky ['trɪki] *adj* **trickier; -est 1** SLY : astuto, taimado **2** DIFFICULT : delicado, peliagudo, difícil
tricycle ['traɪsəkəl, -ˌsɪkəl] *n* : triciclo *m*
trident ['traɪdənt] *n* : tridente *m*
triennial ['traɪ'ɛniəl] *adj* : trienal
trifle[1] ['traɪfəl] *vi* **-fled; -fling** : jugar, juguetear
trifle[2] *n* : nimiedad *f*, insignificancia *f*
trifling ['traɪflɪŋ] *adj* : trivial, insignificante
trigger[1] ['trɪgər] *vt* : causar, provocar
trigger[2] *n* : gatillo *m*
trigonometry [ˌtrɪgə'nɑmətri] *n* : trigonometría *f*
trill[1] ['trɪl] *vi* QUAVER : trinar, gorjear — *vt* : vibrar ⟨to trill the *r* : vibrar la *r*⟩
trill[2] *n* **1** QUAVER : trino *m*, gorjeo *m* **2** : vibración *f* (en fonética)
trillion ['trɪljən] *n* : billón *m*
trilogy ['trɪləʤi] *n, pl* **-gies** : trilogía *f*
trim[1] ['trɪm] *vt* **trimmed; trimming 1** DECORATE : adornar, decorar **2** CUT : recortar **3** REDUCE : recortar, reducir ⟨to trim the excess : recortar el exceso⟩
trim[2] *adj* **trimmer; trimmest 1** SLIM : esbelto **2** NEAT : limpio y arreglado, bien cuidado
trim[3] *n* **1** CONDITION : condición *f*, estado *m* ⟨to keep in trim : mantenerse en buena forma⟩ **2** CUT : recorte *m* **3** TRIMMING : adornos *mpl*
trimming ['trɪmɪŋ] *n* : adornos *mpl*, accesorios *mpl*
Trinity ['trɪnət̬i] *n* : Trinidad *f*
trinket ['trɪŋkət] *n* : chuchería *f*, baratija *f*
trio ['tri:ˌo:] *n, pl* **trios** : trío *m*
trip[1] ['trɪp] *v* **tripped; tripping** *vi* **1** : caminar (a paso ligero) **2** STUMBLE : tropezar **3 to trip up** ERR : equivocarse, cometer un error — *vt* **1** : hacerle una zancadilla (a alguien) ⟨you tripped me on purpose! : ¡me hiciste la zancadilla a propósito!⟩ **2** ACTIVATE : activar (un mecanismo) **3 to trip up** : hacer equivocar (a alguien)
trip[2] *n* **1** JOURNEY : viaje *m* ⟨to take a trip : hacer un viaje⟩ **2** STUMBLE : tropiezo *m*, traspié *m*
tripartite [traɪ'pɑrˌtaɪt] *adj* : tripartito
tripe ['traɪp] *n* **1** : mondongo *m*, callos *mpl*, pancita *f Mex* **2** TRASH : porquería *f*
triple[1] ['trɪpəl] *vt* **-pled; -pling** : triplicar
triple[2] *adj* : triple
triple[3] *n* : triple *m*
triplet ['trɪplət] *n* **1** : terceto *m* (en poesía, música, etc.) **2** : trillizo *m*, -za *f* (persona)
triplicate ['trɪplɪkət] *n* : triplicado *m*
tripod ['traɪˌpɑd] *n* : trípode *m*
trite ['traɪt] *adj* **triter; tritest** : trillado, tópico, manido
triumph[1] ['traɪəmpf] *vi* : triunfar
triumph[2] *n* : triunfo *m*
triumphal [traɪ'ʌmpfəl] *adj* : triunfal
triumphant [traɪ'ʌmpfənt] *adj* : triunfante, triunfal — **triumphantly** *adv*
trivia ['trɪviə] *ns & pl* : trivialidades *fpl*, nimiedades *fpl*
trivial ['trɪviəl] *adj* : trivial, intrascendente, insignificante
triviality [ˌtrɪvi'æləṭi] *n, pl* **-ties** : trivialidad *f*
trod, trodden → **tread**[1]
troll ['tro:l] *n* : duende *m* o gigante *m* de cuentos folklóricos
trolley ['trɑli] *n, pl* **-leys** : tranvía *m*
trombone [trɑm'bo:n] *n* : trombón *m*
trombonist [trɑm'bo:nɪst] *n* : trombón *m*
troop[1] ['tru:p] *vi* : desfilar, ir en tropel
troop[2] *n* **1** : escuadrón *m* (de caballería) **2** GROUP : grupo *m*, banda *f* (de personas) **3 troops** *npl* SOLDIERS : tropas *fpl*, soldados *mpl*
trooper ['tru:pər] *n* **1** : soldado *m* (de caballería) **2** : policía *m* montado **3** : policía *m* (estatal)
trophy ['tro:fi] *n, pl* **-phies** : trofeo *m*
tropic[1] ['trɑpɪk] *or* **tropical** [-pɪkəl] *adj* : tropical
tropic[2] *n* **1** : trópico *m* ⟨tropic of Cancer : trópico de Cáncer⟩ **2 the tropics** : el trópico
trot[1] ['trɑt] *vi* **trotted; trotting** : trotar
trot[2] *n* : trote *m*
trouble[1] ['trʌbəl] *v* **-bled; -bling** *vt* **1** DISTURB, WORRY : molestar, perturbar, inquietar **2** AFFLICT : afligir, afectar — *vi* : molestarse, hacer un esfuerzo ⟨they didn't trouble to come : no se molestaron en venir⟩
trouble[2] *n* **1** PROBLEMS : problemas *mpl*, dificultades *fpl* ⟨to be in trouble : estar en un aprieto⟩ ⟨heart trouble : problemas de corazón⟩ **2** EFFORT : molestia *f*, esfuerzo *m* ⟨to take the trouble : tomarse la molestia⟩ ⟨it's not worth the trouble : no vale la pena⟩
troublemaker ['trʌbəlˌmeɪkər] *n* : agitador *m*, -dora *f*; alborotador *m*, -dora *f*
troublesome ['trʌbəlsəm] *adj* : problemático, dificultoso — **troublesomely** *adv*
trough ['trɔf] *n, pl* **troughs** ['trɔfs, 'trɔvz] **1** : comedero *m*, bebedero *m* (de animales) **2** CHANNEL, HOLLOW : depresión *f* (en el suelo), seno *m* (de olas)
trounce ['traʊnts] *vt* **trounced; trouncing 1** THRASH : apalear, darle una paliza (a alguien) **2** DEFEAT : derrotar contundentemente
troupe ['tru:p] *n* : troupe *f*
trousers ['traʊzərz] *npl* : pantalón *m*, pantalones *mpl*
trout ['traʊt] *n, pl* **trout** : trucha *f*
trowel ['traʊəl] *n* **1** : llana *f*, paleta *f* (de albañil) **2** : desplantador *m* (de jardinero)
truant ['tru:ənt] *n* : alumno *m*, -na *f* que falta a clase sin permiso

truce [ˈtruːs] *n* : tregua *f*, armisticio *m*

truck[1] [ˈtrʌk] *vt* : transportar en camión

truck[2] *n* **1** : camión *m* (vehículo automóvil), carro *m* (manual) **2** DEALINGS : tratos *mpl* ⟨to have no truck with : no tener nada que ver con⟩

trucker [ˈtrʌkər] *n* : camionero *m*, -ra *f*

truculent [ˈtrʌkjələnt] *adj* : agresivo, beligerante

trudge [ˈtrʌʤ] *vi* **trudged; trudging** : caminar a paso pesado

true[1] [ˈtruː] *vt* **trued; trueing** : aplomar (algo vertical), nivelar (algo horizontal), centrar (una rueda)

true[2] *adv* **1** TRUTHFULLY : lealmente, sinceramente **2** ACCURATELY : exactamente, certeramente

true[3] *adj* **truer; truest 1** LOYAL : fiel, leal **2** : cierto, verdadero, verídico ⟨it's true : es cierto, es la verdad⟩ ⟨a true story : una historia verídica⟩ **3** GENUINE : auténtico, genuino — **truly** *adv*

true–blue [ˈtruːˈbluː] *adj* LOYAL : leal, fiel

truffle [ˈtrʌfəl] *n* : trufa *f*

truism [ˈtruːˌɪzəm] *n* : perogrullada *f*, verdad *f* obvia

trump[1] [ˈtrʌmp] *vt* : matar (en juegos de naipes)

trump[2] *n* : triunfo *m* (en juegos de naipes)

trumped–up [ˈtrʌmptˈʌp] *adj* : inventado, fabricado ⟨trumped-up charges : falsas acusaciones⟩

trumpet[1] [ˈtrʌmpət] *vi* **1** : sonar una trompeta **2** : berrear, bramar (dícese de un animal) — *vt* : proclamar a los cuatro vientos

trumpet[2] *n* : trompeta *f*

trumpeter [ˈtrʌmpət̬ər] *n* : trompetista *mf*

truncate [ˈtrʌŋˌkeɪt, ˈtrʌn-] *vt* **-cated; -cating** : truncar

trundle [ˈtrʌndəl] *v* **-dled; -dling** *vi* : rodar lentamente — *vt* : hacer rodar, empujar lentamente

trunk [ˈtrʌŋk] *n* **1** : tronco *m* (de un árbol o del cuerpo) **2** : trompa *f* (de un elefante) **3** CHEST : baúl *m* **4** : maletero *m*, cajuela *f Mex* (de un auto) **5 trunks** *npl* : traje *m* de baño (de caballero)

truss[1] [ˈtrʌs] *vt* : atar (con fuerza)

truss[2] *n* **1** FRAMEWORK : armazón *m* (de una estructura) **2** : braguero *m* (en medicina)

trust[1] [ˈtrʌst] *vi* : confiar, esperar ⟨to trust in God : confiar en Dios⟩ — *vt* **1** ENTRUST : confiar, encomendar **2** : confiar en, tenerle confianza a ⟨I trust you : te tengo confianza⟩

trust[2] *n* **1** CONFIDENCE : confianza *f* **2** HOPE : esperanza *f*, fe *f* **3** CREDIT : crédito *m* ⟨to sell on trust : fiar⟩ **4** : fideicomiso *m* ⟨to hold in trust : guardar en fideicomiso⟩ **5** : trust *m* (consorcio empresarial) **6** CUSTODY : responsabilidad *f*, custodia *f*

trustee [ˌtrʌsˈtiː] *n* : fideicomisario *m*, -ria *f*; fiduciario *m*, -ria *f*

trustful [ˈtrʌstfəl] *adj* : confiado — **trustfully** *adv*

trustworthiness [ˈtrəstˌwərðinəs] *n* : integridad *f*, honradez *f*

trustworthy [ˈtrəstˌwərði] *adj* : digno de confianza, confiable

trusty [ˈtrəsti] *adj* **trustier; -est** : fiel, confiable

truth [ˈtruːθ] *n, pl* **truths** [ˈtruːðz, ˈtruːθs] : verdad *f*

truthful [ˈtruːθfəl] *adj* : sincero, veraz — **truthfully** *adv*

truthfulness [ˈtruːθfəlnəs] *n* : sinceridad *f*, veracidad *f*

try[1] [ˈtraɪ] *v* **tried; trying** *vt* **1** : enjuiciar, juzgar, procesar ⟨he was tried for murder : fue procesado por homicidio⟩ **2** : probar ⟨did you try the salad? : ¿probaste la ensalada?⟩ **3** TEST : tentar, poner a prueba ⟨to try one's patience : tentarle la paciencia a uno⟩ **4** ATTEMPT : tratar (de), intentar **5** *or* **to try on** : probarse (ropa) — *vi* : tratar, intentar

try[2] *n, pl* **tries** : intento *m*, tentativa *f*

tryout [ˈtraɪˌaʊt] *n* : prueba *f*

tsar [ˈzɑr, ˈtsɑr, ˈsɑr] → **czar**

T–shirt [ˈtiːˌʃərt] *n* : camiseta *f*

tub [ˈtʌb] *n* **1** CASK : cuba *f*, barril *m*, tonel *m* **2** CONTAINER : envase *m* (de plástico, etc.) ⟨a tub of margarine : un envase de margarina⟩ **3** BATHTUB : tina *f* (de baño), bañera *f*

tuba [ˈtuːbə, ˈtjuː-] *n* : tuba *f*

tube [ˈtuːb, ˈtjuːb] *n* **1** PIPE : tubo *m* **2** : tubo *m* (de dentífrico, etc.) **3** *or* **inner tube** : cámara *f* **4** : tubo *m* (de un aparato electrónico) **5** : trompa *f* (en anatomía)

tubeless [ˈtuːbləs, ˈtjuːb-] *adj* : sin cámara (dícese de una llanta)

tuber [ˈtuːbər, ˈtjuː-] *n* : tubérculo *m*

tubercular [tʊˈbərkjələr, tjʊ-] → **tuberculous**

tuberculosis [tʊˌbərkjəˈloːsɪs, tjʊ-] *n, pl* **-loses** [-ˌsiːz] : tuberculosis *f*

tuberculous [tʊˈbərkjələs, tjʊ-] *adj* : tuberculoso

tuberous [ˈtuːbərəs, ˈtjuː-] *adj* : tuberoso

tubing [ˈtuːbɪŋ, ˈtjuː-] *n* : tubería *f*

tubular [ˈtuːbjələr, ˈtjuː-] *adj* : tubular

tuck[1] [ˈtʌk] *vt* **1** PLACE, PUT : meter, colocar ⟨tuck in your shirt : métete la camisa⟩ **2** : guardar, esconder ⟨to tuck away one's money : guardar uno bien su dinero⟩ **3** COVER : arropar (a un niño en la cama)

tuck[2] *n* : pliegue *m*, alforza *f*

Tuesday [ˈtuːzˌdeɪ, ˈtjuːz-, -di] *n* : martes *m*

tuft [ˈtʌft] *n* : penacho *m* (de plumas), copete *m* (de pelo)

tug[1] [ˈtʌg] *v* **tugged; tugging** *vi* : tirar, jalar, dar un tirón — *vt* : jalar, arrastrar, remolcar (con un barco)

tug[2] *n* **1** : tirón *m*, jalón *m* **2** → **tugboat**

tugboat [ˈtʌgˌboːt] *n* : remolcador *m*

tug–of–war [ˌtʌgəˈwɔr] *n, pl* **tugs–of–war** : tira y afloja *m*
tuition [tuˈɪʃən] *n or* **tuition fees** : tasas *fpl* de matrícula, colegiatura *f Mex*
tulip [ˈtu:lɪp, ˈtju:-] *n* : tulipán *m*
tumble[1] [ˈtʌmbəl] *v* **-bled; -bling** *vi* **1** : dar volteretas (en acrobacia) **2** FALL : caerse, venirse abajo — *vt* **1** TOPPLE : volcar **2** TOSS : hacer girar
tumble[2] *n* : voltereta *f*, caída *f*
tumbler [ˈtʌmblər] *n* **1** ACROBAT : acróbata *mf*, saltimbanqui *mf* **2** GLASS : vaso *m* (de mesa) **3** : clavija *f* (de una cerradura)
tummy [ˈtʌmi] *n, pl* **-mies** BELLY : panza *f*, vientre *m*
tumor [ˈtu:mər, ˈtju:-] *n* : tumor *m*
tumult [ˈtu:ˌmʌlt, ˈtju:-] *n* : tumulto *m*, alboroto *m*
tumultuous [tʊˈmʌltʃʊəs, tju:-] *adj* : tumultuoso
tuna [ˈtu:nə, ˈtju:-] *n, pl* **-na** *or* **-nas** : atún *m*
tundra [ˈtʌndrə] *n* : tundra *f*
tune[1] [ˈtu:n, ˈtju:n] *v* **tuned; tuning** *vt* **1** ADJUST : ajustar, hacer más preciso, afinar (un motor) **2** : afinar (un instrumento musical) **3** : sintonizar (un radio o televisor) — *vi* **to tune in** : sintonizar (con una emisora)
tune[2] *n* **1** MELODY : tonada *f*, canción *f*, melodía *f* **2 in tune** : afinado (dícese de un instrumento o de la voz), sintonizado, en sintonía
tuneful [ˈtu:nfəl, ˈtju:n-] *adj* : armonioso, melódico
tuner [ˈtu:nər, ˈtju:-] *n* : afinador *m*, -dora *f* (de instrumentos); sintonizador *m* (de un radio o un televisor)
tungsten [ˈtʌŋkstən] *n* : tungsteno *m*
tunic [ˈtu:nɪk, ˈtju:-] *n* : túnica *f*
tuning fork *n* : diapasón *m*
Tunisian [tu:ˈni:ʒən, tju:ˈnɪziən] *n* : tunecino *m*, -na *f* — **Tunisian** *adj*
tunnel[1] [ˈtʌnəl] *vi* **-neled** *or* **-nelled; -neling** *or* **-nelling** : hacer un túnel
tunnel[2] *n* : túnel *m*
turban [ˈtərbən] *n* : turbante *m*
turbid [ˈtərbɪd] *adj* : turbio
turbine [ˈtərbən, -ˌbaɪn] *n* : turbina *f*
turboprop [ˈtərbo:ˌprɑp] *n* : turbopropulsor *m* (motor), avión *m* turbopropulsado
turbulence [ˈtərbjələnts] *n* : turbulencia *f*
turbulent [ˈtərbjələnt] *adj* : turbulento — **turbulently** *adv*
tureen [təˈri:n, tjʊ-] *n* : sopera *f*
turf [ˈtərf] *n* SOD : tepe *m*
turgid [ˈtərdʒɪd] *adj* **1** SWOLLEN : turgente **2** : ampuloso, hinchado ⟨turgid style : estilo ampuloso⟩
Turk [ˈtərk] *n* : turco *m*, -ca *f*
turkey [ˈtərki] *n, pl* **-keys** : pavo *m*
Turkish[1] [ˈtərkɪʃ] *adj* : turco
Turkish[2] *n* : turco *m* (idioma)
turmoil [ˈtərˌmɔɪl] *n* : agitación *f*, desorden *m*, confusión *f*
turn[1] [ˈtərn] *vt* **1** : girar, voltear, volver ⟨to turn one's head : voltear la cabeza⟩ ⟨she turned her chair toward the fire : giró su asiento hacia la hoguera⟩ **2** ROTATE : darle vuelta a, hacer girar ⟨turn the handle : dale vuelta a la manivela⟩ **3** SPRAIN, WRENCH : dislocar, torcer **4** UPSET : revolver (el estómago) **5** TRANSFORM : convertir ⟨to turn water into wine : convertir el agua en vino⟩ **6** SHAPE : tornear (en carpintería) — *vi* **1** ROTATE : girar, dar vueltas **2** : girar, doblar, dar una vuelta ⟨turn left : doble a la izquierda⟩ ⟨to turn around : dar la media vuelta⟩ **3** BECOME : hacerse, volverse, ponerse **4** SOUR : agriarse, cortarse (dícese de la leche) **5 to turn to** : recurrir a ⟨they have no one to turn to : no tienen quien les ayude⟩
turn[2] *n* **1** : vuelta *f*, giro *m* ⟨a sudden turn : una vuelta repentina⟩ **2** CHANGE : cambio *m* **3** CURVE : curva *f* (en un camino) **4** : turno *m* ⟨they're awaiting their turn : están esperando su turno⟩ ⟨whose turn is it? : ¿a quién le toca?⟩
turnaround [ˈtərnəˌraʊnd] *n* PROCESSING : procesamiento *m*
turncoat [ˈtərnˌko:t] *n* : traidor *m*, -dora *f*
turn down *vt* **1** REFUSE : rehusar, rechazar ⟨they turned down our invitation : rehusaron nuestra invitación⟩ **2** LOWER : bajar (el volumen)
turn in *vt* : entregar ⟨to turn in one's work : entregar uno su trabajo⟩ ⟨they turned in the suspect : entregaron al sospechoso⟩ — *vi* : acostarse, irse a la cama
turnip [ˈtərnəp] *n* : nabo *m*
turn off *vt* : apagar (la luz, la radio, etc.)
turn on *vt* : prender (la luz, etc.), encender (un motor, etc.)
turnout [ˈtərnˌaʊt] *n* : concurrencia *f*
turn out *vt* **1** EVICT, EXPEL : expulsar, echar, desalojar **2** PRODUCE : producir **3** → **turn off** — *vi* **1** : concurrir, presentarse ⟨many turned out to vote : muchos concurrieron a votar⟩ **2** PROVE, RESULT : resultar
turnover [ˈtərnˌo:vər] *n* **1** : empanada *f* (salada o dulce) **2** : volumen *m* (de ventas) **3** : rotación *f* (de personal) ⟨a high turnover : un alto nivel de rotación⟩
turn over *vt* **1** TRANSFER : entregar, transferir (un cargo o una responsabilidad) **2** : voltear, darle la vuelta a ⟨turn the cassette over : voltea el cassette⟩
turnpike [ˈtərnˌpaɪk] *n* : carretera *f* de peaje
turnstile [ˈtərnˌstaɪl] *n* : torniquete *m* (de acceso)
turntable [ˈtərnˌteɪbəl] *n* : tornamesa *mf*
turn up *vi* **1** APPEAR : aparecer, presentarse **2** HAPPEN : ocurrir, suceder (inesperadamente) — *vt* : subir (el volumen)
turpentine [ˈtərpənˌtaɪn] *n* : aguarrás *m*, trementina *f*

turquoise ['tər,kɔɪz, -,kwɔɪz] *n* : turquesa *f*
turret ['tərət] *n* **1** TOWER : torre *f* pequeña **2** : torreta *f* (de un tanque, un avión, etc.)
turtle ['tərt̬əl] *n* : tortuga *f* (marina)
turtledove ['tərt̬əl,dʌv] *n* : tórtola *f*
turtleneck ['tərt̬əl,nɛk] *n* : cuello *m* de tortuga, cuello *m* alto
tusk ['tʌsk] *n* : colmillo *m*
tussle¹ ['tʌsəl] *vi* **-sled; -sling** SCUFFLE : pelearse, reñir
tussle² *n* : riña *f*, pelea *f*
tutor¹ ['tu:t̬ər, 'tju:-] *vt* : darle clases particulares (a alguien)
tutor² *n* : tutor *m*, -tora *f*; maestro *m*, -tra *f* (particular)
tuxedo [,tək'si:,do:] *n, pl* **-dos** *or* **-does** : esmoquin *m*, smoking *m*
TV [,ti:'vi:, 'ti:,vi:] → **television**
twain ['tweɪn] *n* : dos *m*
twang¹ ['twæŋ] *vt* : pulsar la cuerda de (una guitarra) — *vi* : hablar en tono nasal
twang² *n* **1** : tañido *m* (de una cuerda de guitarra) **2** : tono *m* nasal (de voz)
tweak¹ ['twi:k] *vt* : pellizcar
tweak² *n* : pellizco *m*
tweed ['twi:d] *n* : tweed *m*
tweet¹ ['twi:t] *vi* : piar
tweet² *n* : gorjeo *m*, pío *m*
tweezers ['twi:zərz] *npl* : pinzas *fpl*
twelfth¹ ['twɛlfθ] *adj* : duodécimo
twelfth² *n* **1** : duodécimo *m*, -ma *f* (en una serie) **2** : doceavo *m*, doceava parte *f*
twelve¹ ['twɛlv] *adj* : doce
twelve² *n* : doce *m*
twentieth¹ ['twʌntiəθ, 'twɛn-] *adj* : vigésimo
twentieth² *n* **1** : vigésimo *m*, -ma *f* (en una serie) **2** : veinteavo *m*, veinteava parte *f*
twenty¹ ['twʌnti, 'twɛn-] *adj* : veinte
twenty² *n, pl* **-ties** : veinte *m*
twice ['twaɪs] *adv* : dos veces ⟨twice a day : dos veces al día⟩ ⟨it costs twice as much : cuesta el doble⟩
twig ['twɪg] *n* : ramita *f*
twilight ['twaɪ,laɪt] *n* : crepúsculo *m*
twill ['twɪl] *n* : sarga *f*, tela *f* cruzada
twin¹ ['twɪn] *adj* : gemelo, mellizo
twin² *n* : gemelo *m*, -la *f*; mellizo *m*, -za *f*
twine¹ ['twaɪn] *v* **twined; twining** *vt* : entrelazar, entrecruzar — *vi* : enroscarse (alrededor de algo)
twine² *n* : cordel *m*, cuerda *f*, mecate *m CA, Mex, Ven*
twinge¹ ['twɪndʒ] *vi* **twinged; twinging** *or* **twingeing** : sentir punzadas
twinge² *n* : punzada *f*, dolor *m* agudo
twinkle¹ ['twɪŋkəl] *vi* **-kled; -kling 1** : centellear, titilar (dícese de las estrellas o de la luz) **2** : chispear, brillar (dícese de los ojos)
twinkle² *n* : centelleo *m* (de las estrellas), brillo *m* (de los ojos)
twirl¹ ['twərl] *vt* : girar, darle vueltas a — *vi* : girar, dar vueltas (rápidamente)
twirl² *n* : giro *m*, vuelta *f*
twist¹ ['twɪst] *vt* : torcer, retorcer ⟨he twisted my arm : me torció el brazo⟩ — *vi* : retorcerse, enroscarse, serpentear (dícese de un río, un camino, etc.)
twist² *n* **1** BEND : vuelta *f*, recodo *m* (en el camino, el río, etc.) **2** TURN : giro *m* ⟨give it a twist : hazlo girar⟩ **3** SPIRAL : espiral *f* ⟨a twist of lemon : una rodajita de limón⟩ **4** : giro *m* inesperado (de eventos, etc.)
twisted ['twɪstəd] *adj* : retorcido ⟨a twisted mind : una mente retorcida⟩
twister ['twɪstər] **1** → **tornado 2** → **waterspout**
twitch¹ ['twɪtʃ] *vi* : moverse nerviosamente, contraerse espasmódicamente (dícese de un músculo)
twitch² *n* : espasmo *m*, sacudida *f* ⟨a nervous twitch : un tic nervioso⟩
twitter¹ ['twɪt̬ər] *vi* CHIRP : gorjear, cantar (dícese de los pájaros)
twitter² *n* : gorjeo *m*
two¹ ['tu:] *adj* : dos
two² *n, pl* **twos** : dos *m*
twofold¹ ['tu:'fo:ld] *adv* : al doble
twofold² ['tu:,fo:ld] *adj* : doble
two hundred¹ *adj* : doscientos
two hundred² *n* : doscientos *m*
twosome ['tu:səm] *n* COUPLE : pareja *f*
tycoon [taɪ'ku:n] *n* : magnate *mf*
tying → **tie¹**
type¹ ['taɪp] *v* **typed; typing** *vt* **1** TYPEWRITE : escribir a máquina, pasar (un texto) a máquina **2** CATEGORIZE : categorizar, identificar — *vi* : escribir a máquina
type² *n* **1** KIND : tipo *m*, clase *f*, categoría *f* **2** *or* **printing type** : tipo *m*
typeface ['taɪp,feɪs] *n* : tipo *m* de imprenta
typewrite ['taɪp,raɪt] *v* **-wrote; -written** : escribir a máquina
typewriter ['taɪp,raɪt̬ər] *n* : máquina *f* de escribir
typhoid¹ ['taɪ,fɔɪd, taɪ'-] *adj* : relativo al tifus o a la tifoidea
typhoid² *n or* **typhoid fever** : tifoidea *f*
typhoon [taɪ'fu:n] *n* : tifón *m*
typhus ['taɪfəs] *n* : tifus *m*, tifo *m*
typical ['tɪpɪkəl] *adj* : típico, característico — **typically** *adv*
typify ['tɪpə,faɪ] *vt* **-fied; -fying** : ser típico o representativo de (un grupo, una clase, etc.)
typist ['taɪpɪst] *n* : mecanógrafo *m*, -fa *f*
typographic [,taɪpə'græfɪk] *or* **typographical** [-fɪkəl] *adj* : tipográfico — **typographically** [-fɪkli] *adv*
typography [taɪ'pɑgrəfi] *n* : tipografía *f*
tyrannical [tə'rænɪkəl, taɪ-] *adj* : tiránico — **tyrannically** [-nɪkli] *adv*
tyrannize ['tɪrə,naɪz] *vt* **-nized; -nizing** : tiranizar
tyranny ['tɪrəni] *n, pl* **-nies** : tiranía *f*
tyrant ['taɪrənt] *n* : tirano *m*, -na *f*
tzar ['zɑr, 'tsɑr, 'sɑr] → **czar**

U

u [ˈjuː] *n, pl* **u's** *or* **us** [ˈjuːz] : vigésima primera letra del alfabeto inglés
ubiquitous [juːˈbɪkwət̬əs] *adj* : ubicuo, omnipresente
udder [ˈʌdər] *n* : ubre *f*
UFO [ˌjuːˌɛfˈoː, ˈjuːˌfoː] *n, pl* **UFO's** *or* **UFOs** (*u*nidentified *f*lying *o*bject) : ovni *m*, OVNI *m*
Ugandan [juːˈgændən, -ˈgɑn-; uːˈgɑn-] *n* : ugandés *m*, -desa *f* — **Ugandan** *adj*
ugliness [ˈʌglinəs] *n* : fealdad *f*
ugly [ˈʌgli] *adj* **uglier; -est 1** UNATTRACTIVE : feo **2** DISAGREEABLE : desagradable, feo ⟨ugly weather : tiempo feo⟩ ⟨to have an ugly temper : tener mal genio⟩
Ukrainian [juːˈkreɪniən, -ˈkraɪ-] *n* **1** : ucraniano *m*, -na *f* **2** : ucraniano *m* (idioma) — **Ukrainian** *adj*
ukulele [ˌjuːkəˈleɪli] *n* : ukelele *m*
ulcer [ˈʌlsər] *n* : úlcera *f* (interna), llaga *f* (externa)
ulcerate [ˈʌlsəˌreɪt] *vi* **-ated; -ating** : ulcerarse
ulceration [ˌʌlsəˈreɪʃən] *n* **1** : ulceración *f* **2** ULCER : úlcera *f*, llaga *f*
ulcerous [ˈʌlsərəs] *adj* : ulceroso
ulna [ˈʌlnə] *n* : cúbito *m*
ulterior [ˌʌlˈtɪriər] *adj* : oculto ⟨ulterior motive : motivo oculto, segunda intención⟩
ultimate [ˈʌltəmət] *adj* **1** FINAL : último, final **2** SUPREME : supremo, máximo **3** FUNDAMENTAL : fundamental, esencial
ultimately [ˈʌltəmətli] *adv* **1** FINALLY : por último, finalmente **2** EVENTUALLY : a la larga, con el tiempo
ultimatum [ˌʌltəˈmeɪt̬əm, -ˈmɑ-] *n, pl* **-tums** *or* **-ta** [-t̬ə] : ultimátum *m*
ultrasound [ˈʌltrəˌsaʊnd] *n* **1** : ultrasonido *m* **2** : ecografía *f* (técnica o imagen)
ultraviolet [ˌʌltrəˈvaɪələt] *adj* : ultravioleta
umbilical cord [ˌʌmˈbɪlɪkəl] *n* : cordón *m* umbilical
umbrage [ˈʌmbrɪʤ] *n* **to take umbrage at** : ofenderse por
umbrella [ˌʌmˈbrɛlə] *n* **1** : paraguas *m* **2 beach umbrella** : sombrilla *f*
umpire¹ [ˈʌmˌpaɪr] *v* **-pired; -piring** : arbitrar
umpire² *n* : árbitro *m*, -tra *f*
umpteenth [ˌʌmpˈtiːnθ] *adj* : enésimo
unable [ˌʌnˈeɪbəl] *adj* : incapaz ⟨to be unable to : no poder⟩
unabridged [ˌʌnəˈbrɪʤd] *adj* : íntegro
unacceptable [ˌʌnɪkˈsɛptəbəl] *adj* : inaceptable
unaccompanied [ˌʌnəˈkʌmpənid] *adj* : solo, sin acompañamiento (en música)
unaccountable [ˌʌnəˈkaʊntəbəl] *adj* : inexplicable, incomprensible — **unaccountably** [-bli] *adv*
unaccustomed [ˌʌnəˈkʌstəmd] *adj* **1** UNUSUAL : desacostumbrado, inusual **2** UNUSED : inhabituado ⟨unaccustomed to noise : inhabituado al ruido⟩
unacquainted [ˌʌnəˈkweɪnt̬əd] *adj* **to be unacquainted with** : desconocer, ignorar
unadorned [ˌʌnəˈdɔrnd] *adj* : sin adornos, puro y simple
unadulterated [ˌʌnəˈdʌltəˌreɪt̬əd] *adj* **1** PURE : puro ⟨unadulterated food : comida pura⟩ **2** ABSOLUTE : completo, absoluto
unaffected [ˌʌnəˈfɛktəd] *adj* **1** : no afectado, indiferente **2** NATURAL : sin afectación, natural
unaffectedly [ˌʌnəˈfɛktədli] *adv* : de manera natural
unafraid [ˌʌnəˈfreɪd] *adj* : sin miedo
unaided [ˌʌnˈeɪdəd] *adj* : sin ayuda, solo
unambiguous [ˌʌnæmˈbɪgjʊəs] *adj* : inequívoco
unanimity [ˌjuːnəˈnɪmət̬i] *n* : unanimidad *f*
unanimous [jʊˈnænəməs] *adj* : unánime — **unanimously** *adv*
unannounced [ˌʌnəˈnaʊnst] *adj* : sin dar aviso
unanswered [ˌʌnˈæntsərd] *adj* : sin contestar
unappealing [ˌʌnəˈpiːlɪŋ] *adj* : desagradable
unappetizing [ˌʌnˈæpəˌtaɪzɪŋ] *adj* : poco apetitoso, poco apetecible
unarmed [ˌʌnˈɑrmd] *adj* : sin armas, desarmado
unassisted [ˌʌnəˈsɪstəd] *adj* : sin ayuda
unassuming [ˌʌnəˈsuːmɪŋ] *adj* : modesto, sin pretensiones
unattached [ˌʌnəˈtæʧt] *adj* **1** LOOSE : suelto **2** INDEPENDENT : independiente **3** : solo (ni casado ni prometido)
unattractive [ˌʌnəˈtræktɪv] *adj* : poco atractivo
unauthorized [ˌʌnˈɔθəˌraɪzd] *adj* : sin autorización, no autorizado
unavailable [ˌʌnəˈveɪləbəl] *adj* : no disponible
unavoidable [ˌʌnəˈvɔɪdəbəl] *adj* : inevitable, ineludible
unaware¹ [ˌʌnəˈwær] *adv* → **unawares**
unaware² *adj* : inconsciente
unawares [ˌʌnəˈwærz] *adv* **1** : por sorpresa ⟨to catch someone unawares : agarrar a alguien desprevenido⟩ **2** UNINTENTIONALLY : inconscientemente, inadvertidamente
unbalanced [ˌʌnˈbælənst] *adj* : desequilibrado
unbearable [ˌʌnˈbærəbəl] *adj* : insoportable, inaguantable — **unbearably** [-bli] *adv*
unbecoming [ˌʌnbɪˈkʌmɪŋ] *adj* **1** UNSEEMLY : impropio, indecoroso **2** UNFLATTERING : poco favorecedor

unbelievable [ˌʌnbəˈli:vəbəl] *adj* : increíble — **unbelievably** [-bli] *adv*

unbend [ˌʌnˈbɛnd] *vi* **-bent** [-ˈbɛnt]; **-bending** RELAX : relajarse

unbending [ˌʌnˈbɛndɪŋ] *adj* : inflexible

unbiased [ˌʌnˈbaɪəst] *adj* : imparcial, objetivo

unbind [ˌʌnˈbaɪnd] *vt* **-bound** [-ˈbaʊnd]; **-binding** **1** UNFASTEN, UNTIE : desatar, desamarrar **2** RELEASE : liberar

unbolt [ˌʌnˈbo:lt] *vt* : abrir el cerrojo de, descorrer el pestillo de

unborn [ˌʌnˈbɔrn] *adj* : aún no nacido, que va a nacer

unbosom [ˌʌnˈbʊzəm, -ˈbu:-] *vt* : revelar, divulgar

unbreakable [ˌʌnˈbreɪkəbəl] *adj* : irrompible

unbridled [ˌʌnˈbraɪdəld] *adj* : desenfrenado

unbroken [ˌʌnˈbro:kən] *adj* **1** INTACT : intacto, sano **2** CONTINUOUS : continuo, ininterrumpido

unbuckle [ˌʌnˈbʌkəl] *vt* **-led**; **-ling** : desabrochar

unburden [ˌʌnˈbərdən] *vt* **1** UNLOAD : descargar **2 to unburden oneself** : desahogarse

unbutton [ˌʌnˈbʌtən] *vt* : desabrochar, desabotonar

uncalled-for [ˌʌnˈkɔldˌfɔr] *adj* : inapropiado, innecesario

uncanny [ənˈkæni] *adj* **-nier**; **-est** **1** STRANGE : extraño **2** EXTRAORDINARY : raro, extraordinario — **uncannily** [-ˈkænəli] *adv*

unceasing [ˌʌnˈsi:sɪŋ] *adj* : incesante, continuo — **unceasingly** *adv*

unceremonious [ˌʌnˌsɛrəˈmo:niəs] *adj* **1** INFORMAL : sin ceremonia, sin pompa **2** ABRUPT : abrupto, brusco — **unceremoniously** *adv*

uncertain [ˌʌnˈsərtən] *adj* **1** INDEFINITE : indeterminado **2** UNSURE : incierto, dudoso **3** CHANGEABLE : inestable, variable ⟨uncertain weather : tiempo inestable⟩ **4** HESITANT : indeciso **5** VAGUE : poco claro

uncertainly [ˌʌnˈsərtənli] *adv* : dudosamente, con desconfianza

uncertainty [ˌʌnˈsərtənti] *n, pl* **-ties** : duda *f*, incertidumbre *f*

unchangeable [ˌʌnˈʧeɪnʤəbəl] *adj* : inalterable, inmutable

unchanged [ˌʌnˈʧeɪnʤd] *adj* : sin cambiar

unchanging [ˌʌnˈʧeɪnʤɪŋ] *adj* : inalterable, inmutable, firme

uncharacteristic [ˌʌnˌkærɪktəˈrɪstɪk] *adj* : inusual, desacostumbrado

uncharged [ˌʌnˈʧɑrʤd] *adj* : sin carga (eléctrica)

uncivilized [ˌʌnˈsɪvəˌlaɪzd] *adj* **1** BARBAROUS : incivilizado, bárbaro **2** WILD : salvaje

uncle [ˈʌŋkəl] *n* : tío *m*

unclean [ˌʌnˈkli:n] *adj* **1** IMPURE : impuro **2** DIRTY : sucio

unclear [ˌʌnˈklɪr] *adj* : confuso, borroso, poco claro

Uncle Sam [ˈsæm] *n* : el Tío Sam

unclog [ˌʌnˈklɑg] *vt* **-clogged**; **-clogging** : desatascar, destapar

unclothed [ˌʌnˈklo:ðd] *adj* : desnudo

uncomfortable [ˌʌnˈkʌmpfərtəbəl] *adj* **1** : incómodo (dícese de una silla, etc.) **2** UNEASY : inquieto, incómodo

uncommitted [ˌʌnkəˈmɪtəd] *adj* : sin compromisos

uncommon [ˌʌnˈkɑmən] *adj* **1** UNUSUAL : raro, poco común **2** REMARKABLE : excepcional, extraordinario

uncommonly [ˌʌnˈkɑmənli] *adv* : extraordinariamente

uncompromising [ˌʌnˈkɑmprəˌmaɪzɪŋ] *adj* : inflexible, intransigente

unconcerned [ˌʌnkənˈsərnd] *adj* : indiferente — **unconcernedly** [-ˈsərnədli] *adv*

unconditional [ˌʌnkənˈdɪʃənəl] *adj* : incondicional — **unconditionally** *adv*

unconscious[1] [ˌʌnˈkɑnʧəs] *adj* : inconsciente — **unconsciously** *adv*

unconscious[2] *n* : inconsciente *m*

unconsciousness [ˌʌnˈkɑnʧəsnəs] *n* : inconsciencia *f*

unconstitutional [ˌʌnˌkɑntstəˈtu:ʃənəl, -ˈtju:-] *adj* : inconstitucional

uncontrollable [ˌʌnkənˈtro:ləbəl] *adj* : incontrolable, incontenible — **uncontrollably** [-bli] *adv*

uncontrolled [ˌʌnkənˈtro:ld] *adj* : incontrolado

unconventional [ˌʌnkənˈvɛnʧənəl] *adj* : poco convencional

unconvincing [ˌʌnkənˈvɪntsɪŋ] *adj* : poco convincente

uncouth [ˌʌnˈku:θ] *adj* CRUDE, ROUGH : grosero, rudo

uncover [ˌʌnˈkʌvər] *vt* **1** : destapar (un objeto), dejar al descubierto **2** EXPOSE, REVEAL : descubrir, revelar, exponer

uncultivated [ˌʌnˈkʌltəˌveɪtəd] *adj* : inculto

uncurl [ˌʌnˈkərl] *vt* UNROLL : desenrollar — *vi* : desenrollarse, desrizarse (dícese del pelo)

uncut [ˌʌnˈkʌt] *adj* **1** : sin cortar ⟨uncut grass : hierba sin cortar⟩ **2** : sin tallar, en bruto ⟨an uncut diamond : un diamante en bruto⟩ **3** UNABRIDGED : completo, íntegro

undaunted [ˌʌnˈdɔntəd] *adj* : impávido

undecided [ˌʌndiˈsaɪdəd] *adj* **1** IRRESOLUTE : indeciso, irresoluto **2** UNRESOLVED : pendiente, no resuelto

undefeated [ˌʌndiˈfi:təd] *adj* : invicto

undeniable [ˌʌndiˈnaɪəbəl] *adj* : innegable — **undeniably** [-bli] *adv*

under[1] [ˈʌndər] *adv* **1** LESS : menos ⟨$10 or under : $10 o menos⟩ **2** UNDERWATER : debajo del agua **3** : bajo los efectos de la anestesia

under[2] *adj* **1** LOWER : (más) bajo, inferior **2** SUBORDINATE : inferior **3** : insuficiente ⟨an under dose of medicine : una dosis insuficiente de medicina⟩

under[3] *prep* **1** BELOW, BENEATH : debajo de, abajo de ⟨under the table : abajo de la mesa⟩ ⟨we walked under the arch : pasamos por debajo del arco⟩ ⟨under the sun : bajo el sol⟩ **2** : menos de ⟨in under 20 minutes : en menos de 20 minutos⟩ **3** (*indicating rank or authority*) : bajo ⟨under the command of : bajo las órdenes de⟩ **4** SUBJECT TO : bajo ⟨under suspicion : bajo sospecha⟩ ⟨under the circumstances : dadas las circunstancias⟩ **5** ACCORDING TO : según, de acuerdo con, conforme a ⟨under the present laws : según las leyes actuales⟩

underage [ˌʌndərˈeɪʤ] *adj* : menor de edad

underbrush [ˈʌndərˌbrəʃ] *n* : maleza *f*

underclothes [ˈʌndərˌkloːz, -ˌkloːðz] → **underwear**

underclothing [ˈʌndərˌkloːðɪŋ] → **underwear**

undercover [ˌʌndərˈkʌvər] *adj* : secreto, clandestino

undercurrent [ˈʌndərˌkərənt] *n* **1** : corriente *f* submarina **2** UNDERTONE : corriente *f* oculta, trasfondo *m*

undercut [ˌʌndərˈkʌt] *vt* **-cut; -cutting** : vender más barato que

underdeveloped [ˌʌndərdɪˈvɛləpt] *adj* : subdesarrollado, atrasado

underdog [ˈʌndərˌdɔg] *n* : persona *f* que tiene menos posibilidades

underdone [ˌʌndərˈdʌn] *adj* RARE : poco cocido

underestimate [ˌʌndərˈɛstəˌmeɪt] *vt* **-mated; -mating** : subestimar, menospreciar

underexposed [ˌʌndərɪkˈspoːzd] *adj* : subexpuesto (en fotografía)

underfoot [ˌʌndərˈfʊt] *adv* **1** : bajo los pies ⟨to trample underfoot : pisotear⟩ **2 to be underfoot** : estorbar ⟨they're always underfoot : están siempre estorbando⟩

undergarment [ˈʌndərˌgɑrmənt] *n* : prenda *f* íntima

undergo [ˌʌndərˈgoː] *vt* **-went** [-ˈwɛnt]; **-gone** [-ˈgɔn]; **-going** : sufrir, experimentar ⟨to undergo an operation : someterse a una intervención quirúrgica⟩

undergraduate [ˌʌndərˈgræʤʊət] *n* : estudiante *m* universitario, estudiante *f* universitaria

underground[1] [ˌʌndərˈgraʊnd] *adv* **1** : bajo tierra **2** SECRETLY : clandestinamente, en secreto ⟨to go underground : pasar a la clandestinidad⟩

underground[2] [ˈʌndərˌgraʊnd] *adj* **1** SUBTERRANEAN : subterráneo **2** SECRET : secreto, clandestino

underground[3] [ˈʌndərˌgraʊnd] *n* : movimiento *m* o grupo *m* clandestino

undergrowth [ˈʌndərˈgroːθ] *n* : maleza *f*, broza *f*

underhand[1] [ˈʌndərˌhænd] *adv* **1** SECRETLY : de manera clandestina **2** *or* **underhanded** : sin levantar el brazo por encima del hombro (en deportes)

underhand[2] *adj* **1** SLY : solapado **2** : por debajo del hombro (en deportes)

underhanded [ˌʌndərˈhændəd] *adj* **1** SLY : solapado **2** SHADY : turbio, poco limpio

underline [ˈʌndərˌlaɪn] *vt* **-lined; -lining** **1** : subrayar **2** EMPHASIZE : subrayar, acentuar, hacer hincapié en

underlying [ˌʌndərˈlaɪɪŋ] *adj* **1** : subyacente ⟨the underlying rock : la roca subyacente⟩ **2** FUNDAMENTAL : fundamental, esencial

undermine [ˌʌndərˈmaɪn] *vt* **-mined; -mining** **1** : socavar (una estructura, etc.) **2** SAP, WEAKEN : minar, debilitar

underneath[1] [ˌʌndərˈniːθ] *adv* : debajo, abajo ⟨the part underneath : la parte de abajo⟩

underneath[2] *prep* : debajo de, abajo de

undernourished [ˌʌndərˈnərɪʃt] *adj* : desnutrido

underpants [ˈʌndərˌpænts] *npl* : calzoncillos *mpl*, calzones *mpl*

underpass [ˈʌndərˌpæs] *n* : paso *m* a desnivel

underprivileged [ˌʌndərˈprɪvlɪʤd] *adj* : desfavorecido

underrate [ˌʌndərˈreɪt] *vt* **-rated; -rating** : subestimar, menospreciar

underscore [ˈʌndərˌskor] *vt* **-scored; -scoring** → **underline**

undersea[1] [ˌʌndərˈsiː] *or* **underseas** [-ˈsiːz] *adv* : bajo la superficie del mar

undersea[2] *adj* : submarino

undersecretary [ˌʌndərˈsɛkrəˌtɛri] *n, pl* **-ries** : subsecretario *m*, -ria *f*

undersell [ˌʌndərˈsɛl] *vt* **-sold; -selling** : vender más barato que

undershirt [ˈʌndərˌʃərt] *n* : camiseta *f*

undershorts [ˈʌndərˌʃɔrts] *npl* : calzoncillos *mpl*

underside [ˈʌndərˌsaɪd, ˌʌndərˈsaɪd] *n* : parte *f* de abajo

undersized [ˌʌndərˈsaɪzd] *adj* : más pequeño de lo normal

understand [ˌʌndərˈstænd] *v* **-stood** [-ˈstʊd]; **-standing** *vt* **1** COMPREHEND : comprender, entender ⟨I don't understand it : no lo entiendo⟩ ⟨that's understood : eso se comprende⟩ ⟨to make oneself understood : hacerse entender⟩ **2** BELIEVE : entender ⟨to give someone to understand : dar a alguien a entender⟩ **3** INFER : tener entendido ⟨I understand that she's leaving : tengo entendido que se va⟩ — *vi* : comprender, entender

understandable [ˌʌndərˈstændəbəl] *adj* : comprensible

understanding[1] [ˌʌndərˈstændɪŋ] *adj* : comprensivo, compasivo

understanding[2] *n* **1** GRASP : comprensión *f*, entendimiento *m* **2** SYMPATHY : comprensión *f* (mutua) **3** INTERPRETATION : interpretación *f* ⟨it's my understanding that . . . : tengo la impresión de que . . ., tengo entendido

que . . . 〉 **4** AGREEMENT : acuerdo *m*, arreglo *m*
understate [ˌʌndərˈsteɪt] *vt* **-stated; -stating** : minimizar, subestimar
understatement [ˌʌndərˈsteɪtmənt] *n* : atenuación *f* 〈that's an understatement : decir sólo eso es quedarse corto〉
understudy [ˈʌndərˌstʌdi] *n, pl* **-dies** : sobresaliente *mf*, suplente *mf* (en el teatro)
undertake [ˌʌndərˈteɪk] *vt* **-took** [-ˈtʊk]; **-taken** [-ˈteɪkən]; **-taking 1** : emprender (una tarea), asumir (una responsabilidad) **2** PROMISE : comprometerse (a hacer algo)
undertaker [ˈʌndərˌteɪkər] *n* : director *m*, -tora *f* de funeraria
undertaking [ˈʌndərˌteɪkɪŋ, ˌʌndərˈ-] *n* **1** ENTERPRISE, TASK : empresa *f*, tarea *f* **2** PLEDGE : promesa *f*, garantía *f*
undertone [ˈʌndərˌto:n] *n* **1** : voz *f* baja 〈to speak in an undertone : hablar en voz baja〉 **2** HINT, UNDERCURRENT : trasfondo *m*, matiz *m*
undertow [ˈʌndərˌto:] *n* : resaca *f*
undervalue [ˌʌndərˈvælˌju:] *vt* **-ued; -uing** : menospreciar, subestimar
underwater[1] [ˌʌndərˈwɔţər, -ˈwɑ-] *adv* : debajo (del agua)
underwater[2] *adj* : submarino
under way [ˌʌndərˈweɪ] *adv* : en marcha, en camino 〈to get under way : ponerse en marcha〉
underwear [ˈʌndərˌwær] *n* : ropa *f* interior, ropa *f* íntima
underworld [ˈʌndərˌwərld] *n* **1** HELL : infierno *m* **2 the underworld** CRIMINALS : la hampa, los bajos fondos
underwrite [ˈʌndərˌraɪt, ˌʌndərˈ-] *vt* **-wrote** [-ˌro:t, -ˈro:t]; **-written** [-ˌrɪtən, -ˈrɪtən]; **-writing 1** INSURE : asegurar **2** FINANCE : financiar **3** BACK, ENDORSE : suscribir, respaldar
underwriter [ˈʌndərˌraɪţər, ˌʌndərˈ-] *n* INSURER : asegurador *m*, -dora *f*
undeserving [ˌʌndiˈzərvɪŋ] *adj* : indigno
undesirable[1] [ˌʌndiˈzaɪrəbəl] *adj* : indeseable
undesirable[2] *n* : indeseable *mf*
undeveloped [ˌʌndiˈvɛləpt] *adj* : sin desarrollar, sin revelar (dícese de una película)
undies [ˈʌndi:z] → **underwear**
undignified [ˌʌnˈdɪgnəfaɪd] *adj* : indecoroso
undiluted [ˌʌndaɪˈlu:ţəd, -də-] *adj* : sin diluir, concentrado
undiscovered [ˌʌndɪˈskʌvərd] *adj* : no descubierto
undisputed [ˌʌndɪˈspju:ţəd] *adj* : indiscutible
undisturbed [ˌʌndɪˈstərbd] *adj* : tranquilo (dícese de una persona), sin tocar (dícese de un objeto)
undivided [ˌʌndɪˈvaɪdəd] *adj* : íntegro, completo
undo [ˌʌnˈdu:] *vt* **-did** [-ˈdɪd]; **-done** [-ˈdʌn]; **-doing 1** UNFASTEN : desabrochar, desatar, abrir **2** ANNUL : anular **3** REVERSE : deshacer, reparar (daños, etc.) **4** RUIN : arruinar, destruir
undoing [ˌʌnˈdu:ɪŋ] *n* : ruina *f*, perdición *f*
undoubted [ˌʌnˈdaʊţəd] *adj* : cierto, indudable — **undoubtedly** *adv*
undress [ˌʌnˈdrɛs] *vt* : desvestir, desabrigar, desnudar — *vi* : desvestirse, desnudarse
undrinkable [ˌʌnˈdrɪŋkəbəl] *adj* : no potable
undue [ˌʌnˈdu:, -ˈdju:] *adj* : excesivo, indebido — **unduly** *adv*
undulate [ˈʌndʒəˌleɪt] *vi* **-lated; -lating** : ondular
undulation [ˌʌndʒəˈleɪʃən] *n* : ondulación *f*
undying [ˌʌnˈdaɪɪŋ] *adj* : perpetuo, imperecedero
unearth [ˌʌnˈərθ] *vt* **1** EXHUME : desenterrar, exhumar **2** DISCOVER : descubrir
unearthly [ˌʌnˈərθli] *adj* **-lier; -est** : sobrenatural, de otro mundo
uneasily [ˌʌnˈi:zəli] *adv* : inquietamente, con inquietud
uneasiness [ˌʌnˈi:zinəs] *n* : inquietud *f*
uneasy [ˌʌnˈi:zi] *adj* **-easier; -est 1** AWKWARD : incómodo **2** WORRIED : preocupado, inquieto **3** RESTLESS : inquieto, agitado
uneducated [ˌʌnˈɛdʒəˌkeɪţəd] *adj* : inculto, sin educación
unemployed [ˌʌnɪmˈplɔɪd] *adj* : desempleado
unemployment [ˌʌnɪmˈplɔɪmənt] *n* : desempleo *m*
unending [ˌʌnˈɛndɪŋ] *adj* : sin fin, interminable
unendurable [ˌʌnɪnˈdʊrəbəl, -ɛn-, -ˈdjʊr-] *adj* : insoportable, intolerable
unequal [ˌʌnˈi:kwəl] *adj* **1** : desigual **2** INADEQUATE : incapaz, incompetente 〈to be unequal to a task : no estar a la altura de una tarea〉
unequaled *or* **unequalled** [ˌʌnˈi:kwəld] *adj* : sin igual
unequivocal [ˌʌnɪˈkwɪvəkəl] *adj* : inequívoco, claro — **unequivocally** *adv*
unerring [ˌʌnˈɛrɪŋ, -ˈər-] *adj* : infalible
unethical [ˌʌnˈɛθɪkəl] *adj* : poco ético
uneven [ˌʌnˈi:vən] *adj* **1** ODD : impar (dícese de un número) **2** : desigual, desnivelado (dícese de una superficie) 〈uneven terrain : terreno accidentado〉 **3** IRREGULAR : irregular, poco uniforme **4** UNEQUAL : desigual
unevenly [ˌʌnˈi:vənli] *adv* : desigualmente, irregularmente
uneventful [ˌʌnɪˈvɛntfəl] *adj* : sin incidentes, tranquilo
unexpected [ˌʌnɪkˈspɛktəd] *adj* : imprevisto, inesperado — **unexpectedly** *adv*
unfailing [ˌʌnˈfeɪlɪŋ] *adj* **1** CONSTANT : constante **2** INEXHAUSTIBLE : in-

agotable **3** SURE : a toda prueba, indefectible
unfair [ˌʌnˈfær] *adj* : injusto — **unfairly** *adv*
unfairness [ˌʌnˈfærnəs] *n* : injusticia *f*
unfaithful [ˌʌnˈfeɪθfəl] *adj* : desleal, infiel — **unfaithfully** *adv*
unfaithfulness [ˌʌnˈfeɪθfəlnəs] *n* : infidelidad *f*, deslealtad *f*
unfamiliar [ˌʌnfəˈmɪljər] *adj* **1** STRANGE : desconocido, extraño ⟨an unfamiliar place : un lugar nuevo⟩ **2 to be unfamiliar with** : no estar familiarizado con, desconocer
unfamiliarity [ˌʌnfəˌmɪliˈærət̬i] *n* : falta *f* de familiaridad
unfashionable [ˌʌnˈfæʃənəbəl] *adj* : fuera de moda
unfasten [ˌʌnˈfæsən] *vt* : desabrochar, desatar (una cuerda, etc.), abrir (una puerta)
unfavorable [ˌʌnˈfeɪvərəbəl] *adj* : desfavorable, mal — **unfavorably** [-bli] *adv*
unfeeling [ˌʌnˈfiːlɪŋ] *adj* : insensible — **unfeelingly** *adv*
unfinished [ˌʌnˈfɪnɪʃd] *adj* : inacabado, incompleto
unfit [ˌʌnˈfɪt] *adj* **1** UNSUITABLE : inadecuado, impropio **2** UNSUITED : no apto, incapaz **3** : incapacitado (físicamente) ⟨to be unfit : no estar en forma⟩
unflappable [ˌʌnˈflæpəbəl] *adj* : imperturbable
unflattering [ˌʌnˈflæt̬ərɪŋ] *adj* : poco favorecedor
unfold [ˌʌnˈfoːld] *vt* **1** EXPAND : desplegar, desdoblar, extender ⟨to unfold a map : desplegar un mapa⟩ **2** DISCLOSE, REVEAL : revelar, exponer (un plan, etc.) — *vi* **1** DEVELOP : desarrollarse, desenvolverse ⟨the story unfolded : el cuento se desarrollaba⟩ **2** EXPAND : extenderse, desplegarse
unforeseeable [ˌʌnforˈsiːəbəl] *adj* : imprevisible
unforeseen [ˌʌnforˈsiːn] *adj* : imprevisto
unforgettable [ˌʌnfərˈgɛt̬əbəl] *adj* : inolvidable, memorable — **unforgettably** [-bli] *adv*
unforgivable [ˌʌnfərˈgɪvəbəl] *adj* : imperdonable
unfortunate[1] [ˌʌnˈfɔrʧənət] *adj* **1** UNLUCKY : desgraciado, infortunado, desafortunado ⟨how unfortunate! : ¡qué mala suerte!⟩ **2** INAPPROPRIATE : inoportuno ⟨an unfortunate comment : un comentario poco feliz⟩
unfortunate[2] *n* : desgraciado *m*, -da *f*
unfortunately [ˌʌnˈfɔrʧənətli] *adv* : desafortunadamente
unfounded [ˌʌnˈfaʊndəd] *adj* : infundado
unfreeze [ˌʌnˈfriːz] *v* **-froze** [-ˈfroːz]; **-frozen** [-ˈfroːzən]; **-freezing** *vt* : descongelar — *vi* : descongelarse
unfriendliness [ˌʌnˈfrɛndlinəs] *n* : hostilidad *f*, antipatía *f*
unfriendly [ˌʌnˈfrɛndli] *adj* **-lier; -est** : poco amistoso, hostil
unfurl [ˌʌnˈfərl] *vt* : desplegar, desdoblar — *vi* : desplegarse
unfurnished [ˌʌnˈfərnɪʃt] *adj* : desamueblado
ungainly [ˌʌnˈgeɪnli] *adj* : desgarbado
ungodly [ˌʌnˈgɔdli, -ˈgɑd-] *adj* **1** IMPIOUS : impío **2** OUTRAGEOUS : atroz, terrible ⟨at an ungodly hour : a una hora intempestiva⟩
ungrateful [ˌʌnˈgreɪtfəl] *adj* : desagradecido, ingrato — **ungratefully** *adv*
ungratefulness [ˌʌnˈgreɪtfəlnəs] *n* : ingratitud *f*
unhappily [ˌʌnˈhæpəli] *adv* **1** SADLY : tristemente **2** UNFORTUNATELY : desafortunadamente, lamentablemente
unhappiness [ˌʌnˈhæpinəs] *n* : infelicidad *f*, tristeza *f*, desdicha *f*
unhappy [ˌʌnˈhæpi] *adj* **-pier; -est 1** UNFORTUNATE : desafortunado, desventurado **2** MISERABLE, SAD : infeliz, triste, desdichado **3** INOPPORTUNE : inoportuno, poco feliz
unharmed [ˌʌnˈhɑrmd] *adj* : salvo, ileso
unhealthy [ˌʌnˈhɛlθi] *adj* **-thier; -est 1** UNWHOLESOME : insalubre, malsano, nocivo a la salud ⟨an unhealthy climate : un clima insalubre⟩ **2** SICKLY : de mala salud, enfermizo
unheard–of [ˌʌnˈhərdəv] *adj* : sin precedente, inaudito, insólito
unhinge [ˌʌnˈhɪnʤ] *vt* **-hinged; -hinging 1** : desquiciar (una puerta, etc.) **2** DISRUPT, UNSETTLE : trastornar, perturbar
unholy [ˌʌnˈhoːli] *adj* **-lier; -est 1** : profano, impío **2** UNGODLY : atroz, terrible
unhook [ˌʌnˈhʊk] *vt* **1** : desenganchar, descolgar (de algo) **2** UNDO : desabrochar
unhurt [ˌʌnˈhərt] *adj* : ileso
unicorn [ˈjuːnəˌkɔrn] *n* : unicornio *m*
unidentified [ˌʌnaɪˈdɛntəˌfaɪd] *adj* : no identificado ⟨unidentified flying object : objeto volador no identificado⟩
unification [ˌjuːnəfəˈkeɪʃən] *n* : unificación *f*
uniform[1] [ˈjuːnəˌfɔrm] *adj* : uniforme, homogéneo, constante
uniform[2] *n* : uniforme *m*
uniformed [ˈjuːnəˌfɔrmd] *adj* : uniformado
uniformity [ˌjuːnəˈfɔrmət̬i] *n, pl* **-ties** : uniformidad *f*
unify [ˈjuːnəˌfaɪ] *vt* **-fied; -fying** : unificar, unir
unilateral [ˌjuːnəˈlæt̬ərəl] *adj* : unilateral — **unilaterally** *adv*
unimaginable [ˌʌnɪˈmæʤənəbəl] *adj* : inimaginable, inconcebible
unimportant [ˌʌnɪmˈpɔrtənt] *adj* : intrascendente, insignificante, sin importancia
uninhabited [ˌʌnɪnˈhæbət̬əd] *adj* : deshabitado, desierto, despoblado

uninhibited [ˌʌnɪnˈhɪbət̬əd] *adj* : desenfadado, desinhibido, sin reservas

uninjured [ˌʌnˈɪnʤərd] *adj* : ileso

unintelligent [ˌʌnɪnˈtɛləʤənt] *adj* : poco inteligente

unintelligible [ˌʌnɪnˈtɛləʤəbəl] *adj* : ininteligible, incomprensible

unintentional [ˌʌnɪnˈtɛntʃənəl] *adj* : no deliberado, involuntario

unintentionally [ˌʌnɪnˈtɛntʃənəli] *adv* : involuntariamente, sin querer

uninterested [ˌʌnˈɪntəˌrɛstəd, -trəstəd] *adj* : indiferente

uninteresting [ˌʌnˈɪntəˌrɛstɪŋ, -trəstɪŋ] *adj* : poco interesante, sin interés

uninterrupted [ˌʌnˌɪntəˈrʌptəd] *adj* : ininterrumpido, continuo

union [ˈjuːnjən] *n* **1** : unión *f* **2** *or* **labor union** : sindicato *m*, gremio *m*

unionize [ˈjuːnjəˌnaɪz] *v* **-ized; -izing** *vt* : sindicalizar, sindicar — *vi* : sindicalizarse

unique [jʊˈniːk] *adj* **1** SOLE : único, solo **2** UNUSUAL : extraordinario

uniquely [jʊˈniːkli] *adv* **1** EXCLUSIVELY : exclusivamente **2** EXCEPTIONALLY : excepcionalmente

unison [ˈjuːnəsən, -zən] *n* **1** : unísono *m* (en música) **2** CONCORD : acuerdo *m*, armonía *f*, concordia *f* **3 in ~** SIMULTANEOUSLY : simultáneamente, al unísono

unit [ˈjuːnɪt] *n* **1** : unidad *f* **2** : módulo *m* (de un mobiliario)

unitary [ˈjuːnəˌtɛri] *adj* : unitario

unite [jʊˈnaɪt] *v* **united; uniting** *vt* : unir, juntar, combinar — *vi* : unirse, juntarse

unity [ˈjuːnət̬i] *n, pl* **-ties** **1** UNION : unidad *f*, unión *f* **2** HARMONY : armonía *f*, acuerdo *m*

universal [ˌjuːnəˈvərsəl] *adj* **1** GENERAL : general, universal ⟨a universal rule : una regla universal⟩ **2** WORLDWIDE : universal, mundial — **universally** *adv*

universe [ˈjuːnəˌvərs] *n* : universo *m*

university [ˌjuːnəˈvərsət̬i] *n, pl* **-ties** : universidad *f*

unjust [ˌʌnˈʤʌst] *adj* : injusto — **unjustly** *adv*

unjustifiable [ˌʌnˌʤʌstəˈfaɪəbəl] *adj* : injustificable

unjustified [ˌʌnˈʤʌstəˌfaɪd] *adj* : injustificado

unkempt [ˌʌnˈkɛmpt] *adj* : descuidado, desaliñado, despeinado (dícese del pelo)

unkind [ˌʌnˈkaɪnd] *adj* : poco amable, cruel — **unkindly** *adv*

unkindness [ˌʌnˈkaɪndnəs] *n* : crueldad *f*, falta *f* de amabilidad

unknowing [ˌʌnˈnoːɪŋ] *adj* : inconsciente, ignorante — **unknowingly** *adv*

unknown [ˌʌnˈnoːn] *adj* : desconocido

unlawful [ˌʌnˈlɔfəl] *adj* : ilícito, ilegal — **unlawfully** *adv*

unleash [ˌʌnˈliːʃ] *vt* : soltar, desatar

unless [ənˈlɛs] *conj* : a menos que, salvo que, a no ser que

unlike[1] [ˌʌnˈlaɪk] *adj* **1** DIFFERENT : diferente, distinto **2** UNEQUAL : desigual

unlike[2] *prep* **1** : diferente de, distinto de ⟨unlike the others : distinto a los demás⟩ **2** : a diferencia de ⟨unlike her sister, she is shy : a diferencia de su hermana, es tímida⟩

unlikelihood [ˌʌnˈlaɪkliˌhʊd] *n* : improbabilidad *f*

unlikely [ˌʌnˈlaɪkli] *adj* **-lier; -est** **1** IMPROBABLE : improbable, poco probable **2** UNPROMISING : poco prometedor

unlimited [ˌʌnˈlɪmət̬əd] *adj* : ilimitado

unload [ˌʌnˈloːd] *vt* **1** REMOVE : descargar, desembarcar (mercancías o pasajeros) **2** : descargar (un avión, un camión, etc.) **3** DUMP : deshacerse de — *vi* : descargar (dícese de un avión, un camión, etc.)

unlock [ˌʌnˈlɑk] *vt* **1** : abrir (con llave) **2** DISCLOSE, REVEAL : revelar

unluckily [ˌʌnˈlʌkəli] *adv* : desgraciadamente

unlucky [ˌʌnˈlʌki] *adj* **-luckier; -est** **1** : de mala suerte, desgraciado, desafortunado ⟨an unlucky year : un año de mala suerte⟩ **2** INAUSPICIOUS : desfavorable, poco propicio **3** REGRETTABLE : lamentable

unmanageable [ˌʌnˈmænɪʤəbəl] *adj* : difícil de controlar, poco manejable, ingobernable

unmarried [ˌʌnˈmærid] *adj* : soltero

unmask [ˌʌnˈmæsk] *vt* EXPOSE : desenmascarar

unmerciful [ˌʌnˈmərsɪfəl] *adj* MERCILESS : despiadado — **unmercifully** *adv*

unmistakable [ˌʌnmɪˈsteɪkəbəl] *adj* : evidente, inconfundible, obvio — **unmistakably** [-bli] *adv*

unmoved [ˌʌnˈmuːvd] *adj* : impasible ⟨to be unmoved by : permanecer impasible ante⟩

unnatural [ˌʌnˈnætʃərəl] *adj* **1** ABNORMAL, UNUSUAL : anormal, poco natural, poco normal **2** AFFECTED : afectado, forzado ⟨an unnatural smile : una sonrisa forzada⟩ **3** PERVERSE : perverso, antinatural

unnecessary [ˌʌnˈnɛsəˌsɛri] *adj* : innecesario — **unnecessarily** [-ˌnɛsəˈsɛrəli] *adv*

unnerve [ˌʌnˈnərv] *vt* **-nerved; -nerving** : turbar, desconcertar, poner nervioso

unnoticed [ˌʌnˈnoːt̬əst] *adj* : inadvertido ⟨to go unnoticed : pasar inadvertido⟩

unobstructed [ˌʌnəbˈstrʌktəd] *adj* : libre, despejado

unobtainable [ˌʌnəbˈteɪnəbəl] *adj* : inasequible

unobtrusive [ˌʌnəbˈstruːsɪv] *adj* : discreto

unoccupied [ˌʌnˈɑkjəˌpaɪd] *adj* **1** IDLE : desempleado, desocupado **2** EMPTY : desocupado, libre, deshabitado

unofficial [ˌʌnəˈfɪʃəl] *adj* : extraoficial, oficioso, no oficial

unorganized [ˌʌnˈɔrgəˌnaɪzd] *adj* : desorganizado
unorthodox [ˌʌnˈɔrθəˌdɑks] *adj* : poco ortodoxo, poco convencional
unpack [ˌʌnˈpæk] *vt* : desempacar — *vi* : desempacar, deshacer las maletas
unpaid [ˌʌnˈpeɪd] *adj* : no remunerado, no retribuido ⟨an unpaid bill : una cuenta pendiente⟩
unparalleled [ˌʌnˈpærəˌlɛld] *adj* : sin igual
unpatriotic [ˌʌnˌpeɪtriˈɑt̬ɪk] *adj* : antipatriótico
unpleasant [ˌʌnˈplɛzənt] *adj* : desagradable — **unpleasantly** *adv*
unplug [ˌʌnˈplʌg] *vt* **-plugged; -plugging** **1** UNCLOG : destapar, desatascar **2** DISCONNECT : desconectar, desenchufar
unpopular [ˌʌnˈpɑpjələr] *adj* : impopular, poco popular
unpopularity [ˌʌnˌpɑpjəˈlærət̬i] *n* : impopularidad *f*
unprecedented [ˌʌnˈprɛsəˌdɛntəd] *adj* : sin precedentes, inaudito, nuevo
unpredictable [ˌʌnpriˈdɪktəbəl] *adj* : impredecible
unprejudiced [ˌʌnˈprɛʤədəst] *adj* : imparcial, objetivo
unprepared [ˌʌnpriˈpærd] *adj* : no preparado ⟨an unprepared speech : un discurso improvisado⟩
unpretentious [ˌʌnpriˈtɛnʧəs] *adj* : modesto, sin pretensiones
unprincipled [ˌʌnˈprɪntsəpəld] *adj* : sin principios, carente de escrúpulos
unproductive [ˌʌnprəˈdʌktɪv] *adj* : improductivo
unprofitable [ˌʌnˈprɑfət̬əbəl] *adj* : no rentable, poco provechoso
unpromising [ˌʌnˈprɑməsɪŋ] *adj* : poco prometedor
unprotected [ˌʌnprəˈtɛktəd] *adj* : sin protección, desprotegido
unprovoked [ˌʌnprəˈvo:kt] *adj* : no provocado
unpublished [ˌʌnˈpʌblɪʃt] *adj* : inédito
unpunished [ˌʌnˈpʌnɪʃt] *adj* : impune ⟨to go unpunished : escapar sin castigo⟩
unqualified [ˌʌnˈkwɑləˌfaɪd] *adj* **1** : no calificado, sin título **2** COMPLETE : completo, absoluto ⟨an unqualified denial : una negación incondicional⟩
unquestionable [ˌʌnˈkwɛsʧənəbəl] *adj* : incuestionable, indudable, indiscutible — **unquestionably** [-bli] *adv*
unquestioning [ˌʌnˈkwɛsʧənɪŋ] *adj* : incondicional, absoluto, ciego
unravel [ˌʌnˈrævəl] *v* **-eled** *or* **-elled; -eling** *or* **-elling** *vt* **1** DISENTANGLE : desenmarañar, desenredar **2** SOLVE : aclarar, desenmarañar, desentrañar — *vi* : deshacerse
unreal [ˌʌnˈri:l] *adj* : irreal
unrealistic [ˌʌnˌri:əˈlɪstɪk] *adj* : poco realista
unreasonable [ˌʌnˈri:zənəbəl] *adj* **1** IRRATIONAL : poco razonable, irrazonable, irracional **2** EXCESSIVE : excesivo ⟨unreasonable prices : precios excesivos⟩
unreasonably [ˌʌnˈri:zənəbli] *adv* **1** IRRATIONALLY : irracionalmente, de manera irrazonable **2** EXCESSIVELY : excesivamente
unrefined [ˌʌnriˈfaɪnd] *adj* **1** : no refinado, sin refinar (dícese del azúcar, de la harina, etc.) **2** : poco refinado, inculto (dícese de una persona)
unrelated [ˌʌnriˈleɪt̬əd] *adj* : no relacionado, inconexo
unrelenting [ˌʌnriˈlɛntɪŋ] *adj* **1** STERN : severo, inexorable **2** CONSTANT, RELENTLESS : constante, implacable
unreliable [ˌʌnriˈlaɪəbəl] *adj* : que no es de fiar, de poca confianza, inestable (dícese del tiempo)
unrepentant [ˌʌnriˈpɛntənt] *adj* : impenitente
unresolved [ˌʌnriˈzɑlvd] *adj* : pendiente, no resuelto
unrest [ˌʌnˈrɛst] *n* : inquietud *f*, malestar *m* ⟨political unrest : disturbios políticos⟩
unrestrained [ˌʌnriˈstreɪnd] *adj* : desenfrenado, incontrolado
unrestricted [ˌʌnriˈstrɪktəd] *adj* : sin restricción ⟨unrestricted access : libre acceso⟩
unrewarding [ˌʌnriˈwɔrdɪŋ] *adj* THANKLESS : ingrato
unripe [ˌʌnˈraɪp] *adj* : inmaduro, verde
unrivaled *or* **unrivalled** [ˌʌnˈraɪvəld] *adj* : incomparable
unroll [ˌʌnˈro:l] *vt* : desenrollar — *vi* : desenrollarse
unruffled [ˌʌnˈrʌfəld] *adj* **1** SERENE : sereno, tranquilo **2** SMOOTH : tranquilo, liso ⟨unruffled waters : aguas tranquilas⟩
unruliness [ˌʌnˈru:linəs] *n* : indisciplina *f*
unruly [ˌʌnˈru:li] *adj* : indisciplinado, díscolo, rebelde
unsafe [ˌʌnˈseɪf] *adj* : inseguro
unsaid [ˌʌnˈsɛd] *adj* : sin decir ⟨to leave unsaid : quedar por decir⟩
unsanitary [ˌʌnˈsænəˌtɛri] *adj* : antihigiénico
unsatisfactory [ˌʌnˌsæt̬əsˈfæktəri] *adj* : insatisfactorio
unsatisfied [ˌʌnˈsæt̬əsˌfaɪd] *adj* : insatisfecho
unscathed [ˌʌnˈskeɪðd] *adj* UNHARMED : ileso
unscheduled [ˌʌnˈskɛˌʤu:ld] *adj* : no programado, imprevisto
unscientific [ˌʌnˌsaɪənˈtɪfɪk] *adj* : poco científico
unscrupulous [ˌʌnˈskru:pjələs] *adj* : inescrupuloso, sin escrúpulos — **unscrupulously** *adv*
unseal [ˌʌnˈsi:l] *vt* : abrir, quitarle el sello a
unseasonable [ˌʌnˈsi:zənəbəl] *adj* **1** : extemporáneo ⟨unseasonable rain

: lluvia extemporánea⟩ 2 UNTIMELY : extemporáneo, inoportuno
unseemly [ˌʌnˈsi:mli] *adj* **-lier; -est** 1 INDECOROUS : indecoroso 2 INAPPROPRIATE : impropio, inapropiado
unseen [ˌʌnˈsi:n] *adj* 1 UNNOTICED : inadvertido 2 INVISIBLE : oculto, invisible
unselfish [ˌʌnˈsɛlfɪʃ] *adj* : generoso, desinteresado — **unselfishly** *adv*
unselfishness [ˌʌnˈsɛlfɪʃnəs] *n* : generosidad *f*, desinterés *m*
unsettle [ˌʌnˈsɛtəl] *vt* **-tled; -tling** DISTURB : trastornar, alterar, perturbar
unsettled [ˌʌnˈsɛtəld] *adj* 1 CHANGEABLE : inestable, variable ⟨unsettled weather : tiempo inestable⟩ 2 DISTURBED : agitado, inquieto ⟨unsettled waters : aguas agitadas⟩ 3 UNDECIDED : pendiente (dícese de un asunto), indeciso (dícese de una persona) 4 UNPAID : sin saldar, pendiente 5 UNINHABITED : despoblado, no colonizado
unshaped [ˌʌnˈʃeɪpt] *adj* : sin forma, informe
unsightly [ˌʌnˈsaɪtli] *adj* UGLY : feo, de aspecto malo
unskilled [ˌʌnˈskɪld] *adj* : no calificado
unskillful [ˌʌnˈskɪlfəl] *adj* : inexperto, poco hábil
unsnap [ˌʌnˈsnæp] *vt* **-snapped; -snapping** : desabrochar
unsociable *adj* : poco sociable
unsolved [ˌʌnˈsɔlvd] *adj* : no resuelto, sin resolver
unsophisticated [ˌʌnsəˈfɪstəˌkeɪṭəd] *adj* 1 NAIVE, UNWORLDLY : ingenuo, de poco mundo 2 SIMPLE : simple, poco sofisticado, rudimentario
unsound [ˌʌnˈsaʊnd] *adj* 1 UNHEALTHY : enfermizo, de mala salud 2 : poco sólido, defectuoso (dícese de una estructura, etc.) 3 INVALID : inválido, erróneo 4 **of unsound mind** : mentalmente incapacitado
unspeakable [ˌʌnˈspi:kəbəl] *adj* 1 INDESCRIBABLE : indecible, inexpresable, incalificable 2 HEINOUS : atroz, nefando, abominable — **unspeakably** [-bli] *adv*
unspecified [ˌʌnˈspɛsəˌfaɪd] *adj* : indeterminado, sin especificar
unspoiled [ˌʌnˈspɔɪld] *adj* 1 : conservado, sin estropear (dícese de un lugar) 2 : que no está mimado (dícese de un niño)
unstable [ˌʌnˈsteɪbəl] *adj* 1 CHANGEABLE : variable, inestable, cambiable ⟨an unstable pulse : un pulso irregular⟩ 2 UNSTEADY : inestable, poco sólido (dícese de una estructura)
unsteadily [ˌʌnˈstɛdəli] *adv* : de modo inestable
unsteadiness [ˌʌnˈstɛdinəs] *n* : inestabilidad *f*, inseguridad *f*
unsteady [ˌʌnˈstɛdi] *adj* 1 UNSTABLE : inestable, variable 2 SHAKY : tembloroso
unstoppable [ˌʌnˈstɑpəbəl] *adj* : irrefrenable, incontenible
unsubstantiated [ˌʌnsəbˈstænʧiˌeɪṭəd] *adj* : no corroborado, no demostrado
unsuccessful [ˌʌnsəkˈsɛsfəl] *adj* : fracasado, infructuoso
unsuitable [ˌʌnˈsu:ṭəbəl] *adj* : inadecuado, impropio, inapropiado ⟨an unsuitable time : una hora inconveniente⟩
unsuited [ˌʌnˈsu:ṭəd] *adj* : inadecuado, inepto
unsung [ˌʌnˈsʌŋ] *adj* : olvidado
unsure [ˌʌnˈʃʊr] *adj* : incierto, dudoso
unsurpassed [ˌʌnsərˈpæst] *adj* : sin par, sin igual
unsuspecting [ˌʌnsəˈspɛktɪŋ] *adj* : desprevenido, desapercibido, confiado
unsympathetic [ˌʌnˌsɪmpəˈθɛṭɪk] *adj* : poco comprensivo, indiferente
untangle [ˌʌnˈteɪŋgəl] *vt* **-gled; -gling** : desenmarañar, desenredar
unthinkable [ˌʌnˈθɪŋkəbəl] *adj* : inconcebible, impensable
unthinking [ˌʌnˈθɪŋkɪŋ] *adj* : irreflexivo, inconsciente — **unthinkingly** *adv*
untidy [ˌʌnˈtaɪdi] *adj* 1 SLOVENLY : desaliñado 2 DISORDERLY : desordenado, desarreglado
untie [ˌʌnˈtaɪ] *vt* **-tied; -tying** *or* **-tieing** : desatar, deshacer
until¹ [ˌʌnˈtɪl] *prep* : hasta ⟨until now : hasta ahora⟩
until² *conj* : hasta que ⟨until they left : hasta que salieron⟩ ⟨don't answer until you're sure : no contestes hasta que (no) estés seguro⟩
untimely [ˌʌnˈtaɪmli] *adj* 1 PREMATURE : prematuro ⟨an untimely death : una muerte prematura⟩ 2 INOPPORTUNE : inoportuno, intempestivo
untold [ˌʌnˈto:ld] *adj* 1 : nunca dicho ⟨the untold secret : el secreto sin contar⟩ 2 INCALCULABLE : incalculable, indecible
untouched [ˌʌnˈtʌʧt] *adj* 1 INTACT : intacto, sin tocar, sin probar (dícese de la comida) 2 UNAFFECTED : insensible, indiferente
untoward [ˌʌnˈtɔrd, -ˈto:ərd, -təˈwɔrd] *adj* 1 : indecoroso, impropio (dícese del comportamiento) 2 ADVERSE, UNFORTUNATE : desafortunado, adverso ⟨untoward effects : efectos perjudiciales⟩ 3 UNSEEMLY : indecoroso
untrained [ˌʌnˈtreɪnd] *adj* : inexperto, no capacitado
untreated [ˌʌnˈtri:ṭəd] *adj* : no tratado (dícese de una enfermedad, etc.), sin tratar (dícese de un material)
untroubled [ˌʌnˈtrʌbəld] *adj* : tranquilo ⟨to be untroubled by : no estar afectado por⟩
untrue [ˌʌnˈtru:] *adj* 1 UNFAITHFUL : infiel 2 FALSE : falso
untrustworthy [ˌʌnˈtrʌstˌwərði] *adj* : de poca confianza (dícese de una persona), no fidedigno (dícese de la información)

untruth [ˌʌnˈtru:θ, ˈʌnˌ-] *n* : mentira *f*, falsedad *f*

untruthful [ˌʌnˈtru:θfəl] *adj* : mentiroso, falso

unusable [ˌʌnˈju:zəbəl] *adj* : inútil, inservible

unused [ˌʌnˈju:zd, *in sense 1 usually* -ˈju:st] *adj* **1** UNACCUSTOMED : inhabituado **2** NEW : nuevo **3** IDLE : no utilizado (dícese de la tierra) **4** REMAINING : restante ⟨the unused portion : la porción restante⟩

unusual [ˌʌnˈju:ʒʊəl] *adj* : inusual, poco común, raro

unusually [ˌʌnˈju:ʒʊəli, -ˈju:ʒəli] *adv* : excepcionalmente, extraordinariamente, fuera de lo común

unwanted [ˌʌnˈwɑntəd] *adj* : superfluo, de sobre

unwarranted [ˌʌnˈwɔrəntəd] *adj* : injustificado

unwary [ˌʌnˈwæri] *adj* : incauto

unwavering [ˌʌnˈweɪvərɪŋ] *adj* : firme, inquebrantable ⟨an unwavering gaze : una mirada fija⟩

unwelcome [ˌʌnˈwɛlkəm] *adj* : importuno, molesto

unwell [ˌʌnˈwɛl] *adj* : enfermo, mal

unwholesome [ˌʌnˈho:lsəm] *adj* **1** UNHEALTHY : malsano, insalubre **2** PERNICIOUS : pernicioso **3** LOATHSOME : repugnante, muy desagradable

unwieldy [ˌʌnˈwi:ldi] *adj* CUMBERSOME : difícil de manejar, torpe y pesado

unwilling [ˌʌnˈwɪlɪŋ] *adj* : poco dispuesto ⟨to be unwilling to : no estar dispuesto a⟩

unwillingly [ˌʌnˈwɪlɪŋli] *adv* : a regañadientes, de mala gana

unwind [ˌʌnˈwaɪnd] *v* **-wound** [-ˈwaʊnd]; **-winding** *vt* UNROLL : desenrollar — *vi* **1** : desenrollarse **2** RELAX : relajar

unwise [ˌʌnˈwaɪz] *adj* : imprudente, desacertado, poco aconsejable

unwisely [ˌʌnˈwaɪzli] *adv* : imprudentemente

unwitting [ˌʌnˈwɪt̬ɪŋ] *adj* **1** UNAWARE : inconsciente **2** INADVERTENT : involuntario, inadvertido ⟨an unwitting mistake : un error inadvertido⟩ — **unwittingly** *adv*

unworthiness [ˌʌnˈwərðinəs] *n* : falta *f* de valía

unworthy [ˌʌnˈwərði] *adj* **1** UNDESERVING : indigno ⟨to be unworthy of : no ser digno de⟩ **2** UNMERITED : inmerecido

unwrap [ˌʌnˈræp] *vt* **-wrapped; -wrapping** : desenvolver, deshacer

unwritten [ˌʌnˈrɪtən] *adj* : no escrito

unyielding [ˌʌnˈji:ldɪŋ] *adj* : firme, inflexible, rígido

unzip [ˌʌnˈzɪp] *vt* **-zipped; -zipping** : abrir el cierre de

up[1] [ˈʌp] *v* **upped** [ˈʌpt]; **upping; ups** *vt* INCREASE : aumentar, subir ⟨they upped the prices : aumentaron los precios⟩ — *vi* **to up and** : agarrar y *fam* ⟨she up and left : agarró y se fue⟩

up[2] *adv* **1** ABOVE : arriba, en lo alto ⟨up in the mountains : arriba en las montañas⟩ **2** UPWARDS : hacia arriba ⟨push it up : empújalo hacia arriba⟩ ⟨the sun came up : el sol salió⟩ ⟨prices went up : los precios subieron⟩ **3** (*indicating an upright position or waking state*) ⟨to sit up : ponerse derecho⟩ ⟨they got up late : se levantaron tarde⟩ ⟨I stayed up all night : pasé toda la noche sin dormir⟩ **4** (*indicating volume or intensity*) ⟨to speak up : hablar más fuerte⟩ **5** (*indicating a northerly direction*) ⟨the climate up north : el clima del norte⟩ ⟨I'm going up to Canada : voy para Canadá⟩ **6** (*indicating the appearance or existence of something*) ⟨the book turned up : el libro apareció⟩ **7** (*indicating consideration*) ⟨she brought the matter up : mencionó el asunto⟩ **8** COMPLETELY : completamente ⟨eat it up : cómetelo todo⟩ **9** : en pedazos ⟨he tore it up : lo rompió en pedazos⟩ **10** (*indicating a stopping*) ⟨the car pulled up to the curb : el carro paró al borde de la acera⟩ **11** (*indicating an even score*) ⟨the game was 10 up : empataron a 10⟩

up[3] *adj* **1** (*risen above the horizon*) ⟨the sun is up : ha salido el sol⟩ **2** (*being above a normal or former level*) ⟨prices are up : los precios han aumentado⟩ ⟨the river is up : las aguas están altas⟩ **3** : despierto, levantado ⟨up all night : despierto toda la noche⟩ **4** BUILT : construido ⟨the house is up : la casa está construida⟩ **5** OPEN : abierto ⟨the windows are up : las ventanas están abiertas⟩ **6** (*moving or going upward*) ⟨the up staircase : la escalera para subir⟩ **7** ABREAST : enterado, al día, al corriente ⟨to be up on the news : estar al corriente de las noticias⟩ **8** PREPARED : preparado ⟨we were up for the test : estuvimos preparados para el examen⟩ **9** FINISHED : terminado, acabado ⟨time is up : se ha terminado el tiempo permitido⟩ **10 to be up** : pasar ⟨what's up? : ¿qué pasa?⟩

up[4] *prep* **1** (*to, toward, or at a higher point of*) ⟨he went up the stairs : subió la escalera⟩ **2** (*to or toward the source of*) ⟨to go up the river : ir río arriba⟩ **3** ALONG : a lo largo, por ⟨up the coast : a lo largo de la costa⟩ ⟨just up the way : un poco más adelante⟩ ⟨up and down the city : por toda la ciudad⟩

upbraid [ˌʌpˈbreɪd] *vt* : reprender, regañar

upbringing [ˈʌpˌbrɪŋɪŋ] *n* : crianza *f*, educación *f*

upcoming [ˌʌpˈkʌmɪŋ] *adj* : próximo

update[1] [ˌʌpˈdeɪt] *vt* **-dated; -dating** : poner al día, poner al corriente, actualizar

update[2] [ˈʌpˌdeɪt] *n* : actualización *f*, puesta *f* al día

upend [ˌʌpˈɛnd] *vt* **1** : poner vertical **2** OVERTURN : volcar

upgrade[1] ['ʌp,greɪd, ,ʌp'-] *vt* **-graded; -grading 1** PROMOTE : ascender **2** IMPROVE : mejorar
upgrade[2] ['ʌp,greɪd] *n* **1** SLOPE : cuesta *f*, pendiente *f* **2** RISE : aumento *m* de categoría (de un puesto), ascenso *m* (de un empleado) **3** IMPROVEMENT : mejoramiento *m*
upheaval [,ʌp'hi:vəl] *n* **1** : levantamiento *m* (en geología) **2** DISTURBANCE, UPSET : trastorno *m*, agitación *f*, conmoción *f*
uphill[1] [,ʌp'hɪl] *adv* : cuesta arriba
uphill[2] ['ʌp,hɪl] *adj* **1** ASCENDING : en subida **2** DIFFICULT : difícil, arduo
uphold [,ʌp'ho:ld] *vt* **-held; -holding 1** SUPPORT : sostener, apoyar, mantener **2** RAISE : levantar **3** CONFIRM : confirmar (una decisión judicial)
upholster [,ʌp'ho:lstər] *vt* : tapizar
upholsterer [,ʌp'ho:lstərər] *n* : tapicero *m*, -ra *f*
upholstery [,ʌp'ho:lstəri] *n, pl* **-steries** : tapicería *f*
upkeep ['ʌp,ki:p] *n* : mantenimiento *m*
upland ['ʌplənd, -,lænd] *n* : altiplanicie *f*, altiplano *m*
uplift[1] [,ʌp'lɪft] *vt* **1** RAISE : elevar, levantar **2** ELEVATE : elevar, animar (el espíritu, la mente, etc.)
uplift[2] ['ʌp,lɪft] *n* : elevación *f*
upon [ə'pɔn, ə'pɑn] *prep* : en, sobre ⟨upon the desk : sobre el escritorio⟩ ⟨upon leaving : al salir⟩ ⟨questions upon questions : pregunta tras pregunta⟩
upper[1] ['ʌpər] *adj* **1** HIGHER : superior ⟨the upper classes : las clases altas⟩ **2** : alto (en geografía) ⟨the upper Mississippi : el alto Mississippi⟩
upper[2] *n* : parte *f* superior (del calzado, etc.)
uppercase [,ʌpər'keɪs] *adj* : mayúsculo
upper hand *n* : ventaja *f*, dominio *m*
uppermost ['ʌpər,mo:st] *adj* : más alto ⟨it was uppermost in his mind : era lo que más le preocupaba⟩
upright[1] ['ʌp,raɪt] *adj* **1** VERTICAL : vertical **2** ERECT : erguido, derecho **3** JUST : recto, honesto, justo
upright[2] *n* : montante *m*, poste *m*, soporte *m*
uprising ['ʌp,raɪzɪŋ] *n* : insurrección *f*, revuelta *f*, alzamiento *m*
uproar ['ʌp,ror] *n* COMMOTION : alboroto *m*, jaleo *m*, escándalo *m*
uproarious [,ʌp'roriəs] *adj* **1** CLAMOROUS : estrepitoso, clamoroso **2** HILARIOUS : muy divertido, hilarante — **uproariously** *adv*
uproot [,ʌp'ru:t, -'rʊt] *vt* : desarraigar
upset[1] [,ʌp'sɛt] *vt* **-set; -setting 1** OVERTURN : volcar **2** SPILL : derramar **3** DISTURB : perturbar, disgustar, inquietar, alterar **4** SICKEN : sentar mal a ⟨it upsets my stomach : me sienta mal al estómago⟩ **5** DISRUPT : trastornar, desbaratar (planes, etc.) **6** DEFEAT : derrotar (en deportes)
upset[2] *adj* **1** DISPLEASED, DISTRESSED : disgustado, alterado **2 to have an upset stomach** : estar mal del estómago, estar descompuesto (de estómago)
upset[3] ['ʌp,sɛt] *n* **1** OVERTURNING : vuelco *m* **2** DISRUPTION : trastorno *m* (de planes, etc.) **3** DEFEAT : derrota *f* (en deportes)
upshot ['ʌp,ʃɑt] *n* : resultado *m* final
upside–down [,ʌp,saɪd'daʊn] *adj* : al revés
upside down [,ʌp,saɪd'daʊn] *adv* **1** : al revés **2** : en confusión, en desorden
upstairs[1] [,ʌp'stærz] *adv* : arriba, en el piso superior
upstairs[2] ['ʌp,stærz, ,ʌp'-] *adj* : de arriba
upstairs[3] ['ʌp,stærz, ,ʌp'-] *ns & pl* : piso *m* de arriba, planta *f* de arriba
upstanding [,ʌp'stændɪŋ, 'ʌp,-] *adj* HONEST, UPRIGHT : honesto, íntegro, recto
upstart ['ʌp,stɑrt] *n* : advenedizo *m*, -za *f*
upswing ['ʌp,swɪŋ] *n* : alza *f*, mejora *f* notable ⟨to be on the upswing : estar mejorándose⟩
uptight [,ʌp'taɪt] *adj* : tenso, nervioso
up to *prep* **1** : hasta ⟨up to a year : hasta un año⟩ ⟨in mud up to my ankles : en barro hasta los tobillos⟩ **2 to be up to** : estar a la altura de ⟨I'm not up to going : no estoy en condiciones de ir⟩ **3 to be up to** : depender de ⟨it's up to the director : depende del director⟩
up–to–date [,ʌptə'deɪt] *adj* **1** CURRENT : corriente, al día ⟨to keep up-to-date : mantenerse al corriente⟩ **2** MODERN : moderno
uptown ['ʌp'taʊn] *adv* : hacia la parte alta de la ciudad, hacia el distrito residencial
upturn ['ʌp,tərn] *n* : mejora *f*, auge *m* (económico)
upward[1] ['ʌpwərd] *or* **upwards** [-wərdz] *adv* **1** : hacia arriba **2 ~ of** : más de
upward[2] *adj* : ascendente, hacia arriba
upwind [,ʌp'wɪnd] *adv & adj* : contra el viento
uranium [jʊ'reɪniəm] *n* : uranio *m*
Uranus [jʊ'reɪnəs, 'jʊrənəs] *n* : Urano *m*
urban ['ərbən] *adj* : urbano
urbane [,ər'beɪn] *adj* : urbano, cortés
urchin ['ərtʃən] *n* **1** SCAMP : granuja *mf*; pillo *m*, -lla *f* **2 sea urchin** : erizo *m* de mar
Urdu ['ʊrdu:, 'ər-] *n* : urdu *m*
urethra [jʊ'ri:θrə] *n, pl* **-thras** *or* **-thrae** [-,θri:] : uretra *f*
urge[1] ['ərdʒ] *vt* **urged; urging 1** PRESS : instar, apremiar, insistir ⟨we urged him to come : insistimos en que viniera⟩ **2** ADVOCATE : recomendar, abogar por **3 to urge on** : animar, alentar
urge[2] *n* : impulso *m*, ganas *fpl*, compulsión *f*
urgency ['ərdʒəntsi] *n, pl* **-cies** : urgencia *f*

urgent ['ərʤənt] *adj* **1** PRESSING : urgente, apremiante **2** INSISTENT : insistente **3 to be urgent** : urgir
urgently ['ərʤəntli] *adv* : urgentemente
urinal ['jʊrənəl, *esp Brit* jʊ'raɪnəl] *n* : orinal *m* (recipiente), urinario *m* (lugar)
urinary ['jʊrəˌnɛri] *adj* : urinario
urinate ['jʊrəˌneɪt] *vi* **-nated; -nating** : orinar
urination [ˌjʊrə'neɪʃən] *n* : orinación *f*
urine ['jʊrən] *n* : orina *f*
urn ['ərn] *n* **1** VASE : urna *f* **2** : recipiente *m* (para servir café, etc.)
Uruguayan [ˌʊrə'gwaɪən, ˌjʊr-, -'gweɪ-] *n* : uruguayo *m*, -ya *f* — **Uruguayan** *adj*
us ['ʌs] *pron* **1** (*as direct object*) : nos ⟨they were visiting us : nos visitaban⟩ **2** (*as indirect object*) : nos ⟨he gave us a present : nos dio un regalo⟩ **3** (*as object of preposition*) : nosotros, nosotras ⟨stay with us : quédese con nosotros⟩ ⟨both of us : nosotros dos⟩ **4** (*for emphasis*) : nosotros ⟨it's us! : ¡somos nosotros!⟩
usable ['ju:zəbəl] *adj* : utilizable
usage ['ju:sɪʤ, -zɪʤ] *n* **1** HABIT : costumbre *f*, hábito *m* **2** USE : uso *m*
use¹ ['ju:z] *v* **used** ['ju:zd, *in phrase "used to" usually* 'ju:stu:]; **using** *vt* **1** EMPLOY : emplear, usar **2** CONSUME : consumir, tomar (drogas, etc.) **3** UTILIZE : usar, utilizar ⟨to use tact : usar tacto⟩ ⟨he used his friends to get ahead : usó a sus amigos para mejorar su posición⟩ **4** TREAT : tratar ⟨they used the horse cruelly : maltrataron al caballo⟩ **5 to use up** : agotar, consumir, gastar — *vi* (*used in the past with* **to** *to indicate a former fact or state*) : soler, acostumbrar ⟨winters used to be colder : los inviernos solían ser más fríos, los inviernos eran más fríos⟩ ⟨she used to dance : acostumbraba bailar⟩
use² ['ju:s] *n* **1** APPLICATION, EMPLOYMENT : uso *m*, empleo *m*, utilización *f* ⟨out of use : en desuso⟩ ⟨ready for use : listo para usar⟩ ⟨to be in use : usarse, estar funcionando⟩ ⟨to make use of : servirse de, aprovechar⟩ **2** USEFULNESS : utilidad *f* ⟨to be of no use : no servir (para nada)⟩ ⟨it's no use! : ¡es inútil!⟩ **3 to have the use of** : poder usar, tener acceso a **4 to have no use for** : no necesitar ⟨she has no use for poetry : a ella no le gusta la poesía⟩
used ['ju:zd] *adj* **1** SECONDHAND : usado, de segunda mano ⟨used cars : coches usados⟩ **2** ACCUSTOMED : acostumbrado ⟨used to the heat : acostumbrado al calor⟩
useful ['ju:sfəl] *adj* : útil, práctico — **usefully** *adv*
usefulness ['ju:sfəlnəs] *n* : utilidad *f*
useless ['ju:sləs] *adj* : inútil — **uselessly** *adv*
uselessness ['ju:sləsnəs] *n* : inutilidad *f*
user ['ju:zər] *n* : usuario *m*, -ria *f*
usher¹ ['ʌʃər] *vt* **1** ESCORT : acompañar, conducir **2 to usher in** : hacer pasar (a alguien) ⟨to usher in a new era : anunciar una nueva época⟩
usher² *n* : acomodador *m*, -dora *f*
usherette [ˌʌʃə'rɛt] *n* : acomodadora *f*
usual ['ju:ʒʊəl] *adj* **1** NORMAL : usual, normal **2** CUSTOMARY : acostumbrado, habitual, de costumbre **3** ORDINARY : ordinario, típico
usually ['ju:ʒʊəli, 'ju:ʒəli] *adv* : usualmente, normalmente
usurp [jʊ'sərp, -'zərp] *vt* : usurpar
usurper [jʊ'sərpər, -'zər-] *n* : usurpador *m*, -dora *f*
utensil [jʊ'tɛn*t*səl] *n* **1** : utensilio *m* (de cocina) **2** IMPLEMENT : implemento *m*, útil *m* (de labranza, etc.)
uterine ['ju:t̬əˌraɪn, -rən] *adj* : uterino
uterus ['ju:t̬ərəs] *n, pl* **uteri** [-ˌraɪ] : útero *m*, matriz *f*
utilitarian [ju:ˌtɪlə'tɛriən] *adj* : utilitario
utility [ju:'tɪlət̬i] *n, pl* **-ties** **1** USEFULNESS : utilidad *f* **2 public utility** : empresa *f* de servicio público
utilization [ˌju:t̬ələ'zeɪʃən] *n* : utilización *f*
utilize ['ju:t̬əlˌaɪz] *vt* **-lized; -lizing** : utilizar, hacer uso de
utmost¹ ['ʌtˌmo:st] *adj* **1** FARTHEST : extremo, más lejano **2** GREATEST : sumo, mayor ⟨of the utmost importance : de suma importancia⟩
utmost² *n* : lo más posible ⟨to the utmost : al máximo⟩
utopia [jʊ'to:piə] *n* : utopía *f*
utopian [jʊ'to:piən] *adj* : utópico
utter¹ ['ʌt̬ər] *vt* : decir, articular, pronunciar (palabras)
utter² *adj* : absoluto — **utterly** *adv*
utterance ['ʌt̬ərən*t*s] *n* : declaración *f*, articulación *f*

V

v ['vi:] *n, pl* **v's** *or* **vs** ['vi:z] : vigésima segunda letra del alfabeto inglés
vacancy ['veɪkən*t*si] *n, pl* **-cies** **1** EMPTINESS : vacío *m*, vacuidad *f* **2** : vacante *f*, puesto *m* vacante ⟨to fill a vacancy : ocupar un puesto⟩ **3** : habitación *f* libre (en un hotel) ⟨no vacancies : completo⟩
vacant ['veɪkənt] *adj* **1** EMPTY : libre, desocupado (dícese de los edificios,

etc.) **2** : vacante (dícese de los puestos) **3** BLANK : vacío, ausente ⟨a vacant stare : una mirada ausente⟩

vacate [ˈveɪˌkeɪt] *vt* **-cated; -cating** : desalojar, desocupar

vacation[1] [veɪˈkeɪʃən, və-] *vi* : pasar las vacaciones, vacacionar *Mex*

vacation[2] *n* : vacaciones *fpl* ⟨to be on vacation : estar de vacaciones⟩

vacationer [veɪˈkeɪʃənər, və-] *n* : turista *mf*, veraneante *mf*, vacacionista *mf CA, Mex*

vaccinate [ˈvæksəˌneɪt] *vt* **-nated; -nating** : vacunar

vaccination [ˌvæksəˈneɪʃən] *n* : vacunación *f*

vaccine [vækˈsiːn, ˈvækˌ-] *n* : vacuna *f*

vacillate [ˈvæsəˌleɪt] *vi* **-lated; -lating** **1** HESITATE : vacilar **2** SWAY : oscilar

vacillation [ˌvæsəˈleɪʃən] *n* : indecisión *f*, vacilación *f*

vacuous [ˈvækjʊəs] *adj* **1** EMPTY : vacío **2** INANE : vacuo, necio, estúpido

vacuum[1] [ˈvæˌkjuːm, -kjəm] *vt* : limpiar con aspiradora, pasar la aspiradora por

vacuum[2] *n, pl* **vacuums** *or* **vacua** [ˈvækjʊə] : vacío *m*

vacuum cleaner *n* : aspiradora *f*

vagabond[1] [ˈvægəˌbɑnd] *adj* : vagabundo

vagabond[2] *n* : vagabundo *m*, -da *f*

vagary [ˈveɪgəri, vəˈgɛri] *n, pl* **-ries** : capricho *m*

vagina [vəˈʤaɪnə] *n, pl* **-nae** [-ˌniː, -ˌnaɪ] *or* **-nas** : vagina *f*

vagrancy [ˈveɪgrən*t*si] *n, pl* **-cies** : vagancia *f*

vagrant[1] [ˈveɪgrənt] *adj* : vagabundo

vagrant[2] *n* : vagabundo *m*, -da *f*

vague [ˈveɪg] *adj* **vaguer; -est** **1** IMPRECISE : vago, impreciso ⟨a vague feeling : una sensación indefinida⟩ ⟨I haven't the vaguest idea : no tengo la más remota idea⟩ **2** UNCLEAR : borroso, poco claro ⟨a vague outline : un perfil indistinto⟩ **3** ABSENTMINDED : distraído

vaguely [ˈveɪgli] *adv* : vagamente, de manera imprecisa

vagueness [ˈveɪgnəs] *n* : vaguedad *f*, imprecisión *f*

vain [ˈveɪn] *adj* **1** WORTHLESS : vano **2** FUTILE : vano, inútil ⟨in vain : en vano⟩ **3** CONCEITED : vanidoso, presumido

vainly [ˈveɪnli] *adv* : en vano, vanamente, inútilmente

valance [ˈvælən*t*s, ˈveɪ-] *n* **1** FLOUNCE : volante *m* (de una cama, etc.) **2** : galería *f* de cortina (sobre una ventana)

vale [ˈveɪl] *n* : valle *m*

valedictorian [ˌvæləˌdɪkˈtoriən] *n* : estudiante *mf* que pronuncia el discurso de despedida en ceremonia de graduación

valedictory [ˌvæləˈdɪktəri] *adj* : de despedida

valentine [ˈvælənˌtaɪn] *n* : tarjeta *f* que se manda el Día de los Enamorados (el 14 de febrero)

Valentine's Day *n* : Día *m* de los Enamorados

valet [ˈvæˌleɪ, væˈleɪ, ˈvælət] *n* : ayuda *m* de cámara

valiant [ˈvæljənt] *adj* : valiente, valeroso

valiantly [ˈvæljəntli] *adv* : con valor, valientemente

valid [ˈvæləd] *adj* : válido

validate [ˈvæləˌdeɪt] *vt* **-dated; -dating** : validar, dar validez a

validity [vəˈlɪdət̬i, væ-] *n* : validez *f*

valise [vəˈliːs] *n* : maleta *f* (de mano)

valley [ˈvæli] *n, pl* **-leys** : valle *m*

valor [ˈvælər] *n* : valor *m*, valentía *f*

valorous [ˈvælərəs] *adj* : valeroso, valiente

valuable[1] [ˈvæljʊəbəl, ˈvæljəbəl] *adj* **1** EXPENSIVE : valioso, de valor **2** WORTHWHILE : valioso, apreciable

valuable[2] *n* : objeto *m* de valor

valuation [ˌvæljʊˈeɪʃən] *n* **1** APPRAISAL : valoración *f*, tasación *f* **2** VALUE : valuación *f*

value[1] [ˈvælˌjuː] *vt* **-ued; -uing** **1** APPRAISE : valorar, avaluar, tasar **2** APPRECIATE : valorar, apreciar

value[2] *n* **1** : valor *m* ⟨of little value : de poco valor⟩ ⟨to be a good value : estar bien de precio, tener buen precio⟩ ⟨at face value : en su sentido literal⟩ **2 values** *npl* : valores *mpl* (morales), principios *mpl*

valueless [ˈvæljuːləs] *adj* : sin valor

valve [ˈvælv] *n* : válvula *f*

vampire [ˈvæmˌpaɪr] *n* **1** : vampiro *m* **2** *or* **vampire bat** : vampiro *m*

van[1] [ˈvæn] → **vanguard**

van[2] *n* : furgoneta *f*, camioneta *f*

vanadium [vəˈneɪdiəm] *n* : vanadio *m*

vandal [ˈvændəl] *n* : vándalo *m*

vandalism [ˈvændəlˌɪzəm] *n* : vandalismo *m*

vandalize [ˈvændəlˌaɪz] *vt* : destrozar, destruir, estropear

vane [ˈveɪn] *n or* **weather vane** : veleta *f*

vanguard [ˈvænˌgɑrd] *n* : vanguardia *f*

vanilla [vəˈnɪlə, -ˈnɛ-] *n* : vainilla *f*

vanish [ˈvænɪʃ] *vi* : desaparecer, disiparse, desvanecerse

vanity [ˈvænət̬i] *n, pl* **-ties** **1** : vanidad *f* **2** *or* **vanity table** : tocador *m*

vanquish [ˈvæŋkwɪʃ, ˈvæn-] *vt* : vencer, conquistar

vantage point [ˈvæntɪʤ] *n* : posición *f* ventajosa

vapid [ˈvæpəd, ˈveɪ-] *adj* : insípido, insulso

vapor [ˈveɪpər] *n* : vapor *m*

vaporize [ˈveɪpəˌraɪz] *v* **-rized; -rizing** *vt* : vaporizar — *vi* : vaporizarse, evaporarse

vaporizer [ˈveɪpəˌraɪzər] *n* : vaporizador *m*

variability [ˌvɛriəˈbɪlət̬i] *n, pl* **-ties** : variabilidad *f*

variable[1] [ˈvɛriəbəl] *adj* : variable ⟨variable cloudiness : nubosidad variable⟩

variable[2] *n* : variable *f*, factor *m*
variance [ˈvɛriən*t*s] *n* **1** DISCREPANCY : varianza *f*, discrepancia *f* **2** DISAGREEMENT : desacuerdo *m* ⟨at variance with : en desacuerdo con⟩
variant[1] [ˈvɛriənt] *adj* : variante, divergente
variant[2] *n* : variante *f*
variation [ˌvɛriˈeɪʃən] *n* : variación *f*, diferencias *fpl*
varicose [ˈværəˌkoːs] *adj* : varicoso
varicose veins *npl* : varices *fpl*, várices *fpl*
varied [ˈvɛrid] *adj* : variado, dispar, diferente
variegated [ˈvɛriəˌgeɪṭd] *adj* : abigarrado, multicolor
variety [vəˈraɪəṭi] *n, pl* **-ties** **1** DIVERSITY : diversidad *f*, variedad *f* **2** ASSORTMENT : surtido *m* ⟨for a variety of reasons : por diversas razones⟩ **3** SORT : clase *f* **4** BREED : variedad *f* (de plantas)
various [ˈvɛriəs] *adj* : varios, diversos
varnish[1] [ˈvɑrnɪʃ] *vt* : barnizar
varnish[2] *n* : barniz *f*
varsity [ˈvɑrsəṭi] *n, pl* **-ties** : equipo *m* universitario
vary [ˈvɛri] *v* **varied; varying** *vt* : variar, diversificar — *vi* **1** CHANGE : variar, cambiar **2** DEVIATE : desviarse
vascular [ˈvæskjələr] *adj* : vascular
vase [ˈveɪs, ˈveɪz, ˈvɑz] *n* : jarrón *m*, florero *m*
vassal [ˈvæsəl] *n* : vasallo *m*, -lla *f*
vast [ˈvæst] *adj* : inmenso, enorme, vasto
vastly [ˈvæstli] *adv* : enormemente
vastness [ˈvæstnəs] *n* : vastedad *f*, inmensidad *f*
vat [ˈvæt] *n* : cuba *f*, tina *f*
vaudeville [ˈvɔdvəl, -ˌvɪl; ˈvɔdəˌvɪl] *n* : vodevil *m*
vault[1] [ˈvɔlt] *vi* LEAP : saltar
vault[2] *n* **1** JUMP : salto *m* ⟨pole vault : salto de pértiga, salto con garrocha⟩ **2** DOME : bóveda *f* **3** : bodega *f* (para vino), bóveda *f* de seguridad (de un banco) **4** CRYPT : cripta *f*
vaulted [ˈvɔltəd] *adj* : abovedado
vaunted [ˈvɔntəd] *adj* : cacareado, alardeado ⟨a much vaunted wine : un vino muy alardeado⟩
VCR [ˌviːˌsiːˈɑr] *n* : video *m*, videocasetera *f*
veal [ˈviːl] *n* : ternera *f*, carne *f* de ternera
veer [ˈvɪr] *vi* : virar (dícese de un barco), girar (dícese de un coche), torcer (dícese de un camino)
vegetable[1] [ˈvɛʤtəbəl, ˈvɛʤəṭə-] *adj* : vegetal
vegetable[2] *n* **1** : vegetal *m* ⟨the vegetable kingdom : el reino vegetal⟩ **2** : verdura *f*, hortaliza *f* (para comer)
vegetarian [ˌvɛʤəˈtɛriən] *n* : vegetariano *mf*
vegetarianism [ˌvɛʤəˈtɛriəˌnɪzəm] *n* : vegetarianismo *m*
vegetate [ˈvɛʤəˌteɪt] *vi* **-tated; -tating** : vegetar
vegetation [ˌvɛʤəˈteɪʃən] *n* : vegetación *f*
vegetative [ˈvɛʤəˌteɪṭɪv] *adj* : vegetativo
vehemence [ˈviːəmən*t*s] *n* : intensidad *f*, vehemencia *f*
vehement [ˈviːəmənt] *adj* : intenso, vehemente
vehemently [ˈviːəməntli] *adv* : vehementemente, con vehemencia
vehicle [ˈviːəkəl, ˈviːˌhɪkəl] *n* **1** *or* **motor vehicle** : vehículo *m* **2** MEDIUM : vehículo *m*, medio *m*
vehicular [viˈhɪkjələr, və-] *adj* : vehicular ⟨vehicular homicide : muerte por atropello⟩
veil[1] [ˈveɪl] *vt* **1** CONCEAL : velar, disimular **2** : cubrir con un velo ⟨to veil one's face : cubrirse con un velo⟩
veil[2] *n* : velo *m* ⟨bridal veil : velo de novia⟩
vein [ˈveɪn] *n* **1** : vena *f* (en anatomía, botánica, etc.) **2** LODE : veta *f*, vena *f*, filón *m* **3** STYLE : vena *f* ⟨in a humorous vein : en vena humorística⟩
veined [ˈveɪnd] *adj* : veteado (dícese del queso, de los minerales, etc.)
velocity [vəˈlɑsəṭi] *n, pl* **-ties** : velocidad *f*
velour [vəˈlʊr] *or* **velours** [-ˈlʊrz] *n* : velour *m*
velvet[1] [ˈvɛlvət] *adj* **1** : de terciopelo **2** → **velvety**
velvet[2] *n* : terciopelo *m*
velvety [ˈvɛlvəṭi] *adj* : aterciopelado
venal [ˈviːnəl] *adj* : venal, sobornable
vend [ˈvɛnd] *vt* : vender
vendetta [vɛnˈdɛṭə] *n* : vendetta *f*
vendor [ˈvɛndər] *n* : vendedor *m*, -dora *f*; puestero *m*, -ra *f*
veneer[1] [vəˈnɪr] *vt* : enchapar, chapar
veneer[2] *n* **1** : enchapado *m*, chapa *f* **2** APPEARANCE : apariencia *f*, barniz *m* ⟨a veneer of culture : un barniz de cultura⟩
venerable [ˈvɛnərəbəl] *adj* : venerable
venerate [ˈvɛnəˌreɪt] *vt* **-ated; -ating** : venerar
veneration [ˌvɛnəˈreɪʃən] *n* : veneración *f*
venereal disease [vəˈnɪriəl] *n* : enfermedad *f* venérea
venetian blind [vəˈniːʃən] *n* : persiana *f* veneciana
Venezuelan [ˌvɛnəˈzweɪlən, -zʊˈeɪ-] *n* : venezolano *m*, -na *f* — **Venezuelan** *adj*
vengeance [ˈvɛnʤən*t*s] *n* : venganza *f* ⟨to take vengeance on : vengarse de⟩
vengeful [ˈvɛnʤfəl] *adj* : vengativo
venial [ˈviːniəl] *adj* : venial ⟨a venial sin : un pecado venial⟩
venison [ˈvɛnəsən, -zən] *n* : venado *m*, carne *f* de venado
venom [ˈvɛnəm] *n* **1** : veneno *m* **2** MALICE : veneno *m*, malevolencia *f*

venomous [ˈvɛnəməs] *adj* : venenoso
vent[1] [ˈvɛnt] *vt* : desahogar, dar salida a ⟨to vent one's feelings : desahogarse⟩
vent[2] *n* **1** OPENING : abertura *f* (de escape), orificio *m* **2** *or* **air vent** : respiradero *m*, rejilla *f* de ventilación **3** OUTLET : desahogo *m* ⟨to give vent to one's anger : desahogar la ira⟩
ventilate [ˈvɛntəlˌeɪt] *vt* **-lated; -lating** : ventilar
ventilation [ˌvɛntəlˈeɪʃən] *n* : ventilación *f*
ventilator [ˈvɛntəlˌeɪt̬ər] *n* : ventilador *m*
ventricle [ˈvɛntrɪkəl] *n* : ventrículo *m*
ventriloquism [vɛnˈtrɪləˌkwɪzəm] *n* : ventriloquia *f*
ventriloquist [vɛnˈtrɪləˌkwɪst] *n* : ventrílocuo *m*, -cua *f*
venture[1] [ˈvɛntʃər] *v* **-tured; -turing** *vt* **1** RISK : arriesgar **2** OFFER : aventurar ⟨to venture an opinion : aventurar una opinión⟩ — *vi* : arriesgarse, atreverse, aventurarse
venture[2] *n* **1** UNDERTAKING : empresa *f* **2** GAMBLE, RISK : aventura *f*, riesgo *m*
venturesome [ˈvɛntʃərsəm] *adj* **1** ADVENTUROUS : audaz, atrevido **2** RISKY : arriesgado
venue [ˈvɛnˌjuː] *n* **1** PLACE : lugar *m* **2** : jurisdicción *f* (en derecho)
Venus [ˈviːnəs] *n* : Venus *m*
veracity [vəˈræsət̬i] *n, pl* **-ties** : veracidad *f*
veranda *or* **verandah** [vəˈrændə] *n* : terraza *f*, veranda *f*
verb [ˈvərb] *n* : verbo *m*
verbal [ˈvərbəl] *adj* : verbal
verbalize [ˈvərbəˌlaɪz] *vt* **-ized; -izing** : expresar con palabras, verbalizar
verbally [ˈvərbəli] *adv* : verbalmente, de palabra
verbatim[1] [vərˈbeɪt̬əm] *adv* : palabra por palabra, textualmente
verbatim[2] *adj* : literal, textual
verbose [vərˈboːs] *adj* : verboso, prolijo
verdant [ˈvərdənt] *adj* : verde, verdeante
verdict [ˈvərdɪkt] *n* **1** : veredicto *m* (de un jurado) **2** JUDGMENT, OPINION : juicio *m*, opinión *f*
verge[1] [ˈvərdʒ] *vi* **verged; verging** : estar al borde, rayar ⟨it verges on madness : raya en la locura⟩
verge[2] *n* **1** EDGE : borde *m* **2 to be on the verge of** : estar a pique de, estar al borde de, estar a punto de
verification [ˌvɛrəfəˈkeɪʃən] *n* : verificación *f*
verify [ˈvɛrəˌfaɪ] *vt* **-fied; -fying** : verificar, comprobar, confirmar
veritable [ˈvɛrət̬əbəl] *adj* : verdadero — **veritably** *adv*
vermicelli [ˌvərməˈtʃɛli, -ˈsɛli] *n* : fideos *mpl* finos
vermin [ˈvərmən] *ns & pl* : alimañas *fpl*, bichos *mpl*, sabandijas *fpl*
vermouth [vərˈmuːth] *n* : vermut *m*
vernacular[1] [vərˈnækjələr] *adj* : vernáculo
vernacular[2] *n* : lengua *f* vernácula
versatile [ˈvərsət̬əl] *adj* : versátil
versatility [ˌvərsəˈtɪlət̬i] *n* : versatilidad *f*
verse [ˈvərs] *n* **1** LINE, STANZA : verso *m*, estrofa *f* **2** POETRY : poesía *f* **3** : versículo *m* (en la Biblia)
versed [ˈvərst] *adj* : versado ⟨to be well versed in : ser muy versado en⟩
version [ˈvərʒən] *n* : versión *f*
versus [ˈvərsəs] *prep* : versus
vertebra [ˈvərtəbrə] *n, pl* **-brae** [-ˌbreɪ, -ˌbriː] *or* **-bras** : vértebra *f*
vertebrate[1] [ˈvərtəbrət, -ˌbreɪt] *adj* : vertebrado
vertebrate[2] *n* : vertebrado *m*
vertex [ˈvərˌtɛks] *n, pl* **vertices** [ˈvərtəˌsiːz] **1** : vértice *m* (en matemáticas y anatomía) **2** SUMMIT, TOP : ápice *m*, cumbre *f*, cima *f*
vertical[1] [ˈvərtɪkəl] *adj* : vertical — **vertically** *adv*
vertical[2] *n* : vertical *f*
vertigo [ˈvərtɪˌgoː] *n, pl* **-goes** *or* **-gos** : vértigo *m*
verve [ˈvərv] *n* : brío *m*
very[1] [ˈvɛri] *adv* **1** EXTREMELY : muy, sumamente ⟨very few : muy pocos⟩ ⟨I am very sorry : lo siento mucho⟩ **2** (*used for emphasis*) ⟨at the very least : por lo menos, como mínimo⟩ ⟨the very same dress : el mismo vestido⟩
very[2] *adj* **verier; -est 1** EXACT, PRECISE : mismo, exacto ⟨at that very moment : en ese mismo momento⟩ ⟨it's the very thing : es justo lo que hacía falta⟩ **2** BARE, MERE : solo, mero ⟨the very thought of it : sólo pensarlo⟩ **3** EXTREME : extremo, de todo ⟨at the very top : arriba de todo⟩
vesicle [ˈvɛsikəl] *n* : vesícula *f*
vespers [ˈvɛspərz] *npl* : vísperas *fpl*
vessel [ˈvɛsəl] *n* **1** CONTAINER : vasija *f*, recipiente *m* **2** BOAT, CRAFT : nave *f*, barco *m*, buque *m* **3** : vaso *m* ⟨blood vessel : vaso sanguíneo⟩
vest[1] [ˈvɛst] *vt* **1** CONFER : conferir ⟨to vest authority in : conferirle la autoridad a⟩ **2** CLOTHE : vestir
vest[2] *n* **1** : chaleco *m* **2** UNDERSHIRT : camiseta *f*
vestibule [ˈvɛstəˌbjuːl] *n* : vestíbulo *m*
vestige [ˈvɛstɪdʒ] *n* : vestigio *m*, rastro *m*
vestment [ˈvɛstmənt] *n* : vestidura *f*
vestry [ˈvɛstri] *n, pl* **-tries** : sacristía *f*
vet [ˈvɛt] *n* **1** → **veterinarian 2** → **veteran**[2]
veteran[1] [ˈvɛt̬ərən, ˈvɛtrən] *adj* : veterano
veteran[2] *n* : veterano *m*, -na *f*
Veterans Day *n* : día *m* del Armisticio (celebrado el 11 de noviembre en los Estados Unidos)
veterinarian [ˌvɛt̬ərəˈnɛriən, ˌvɛt̬əˈnɛr-] *n* : veterinario *m*, -ria *f*
veterinary [ˈvɛt̬ərəˌnɛri] *adj* : veterinario
veto[1] [ˈviːt̬o] *vt* **1** FORBID : prohibir **2** : vetar ⟨to veto a bill : vetar un proyecto de ley⟩

veto² *n, pl* **-toes** **1** : veto *m* <the power of veto : el derecho de veto> **2** BAN : veto *m*, prohibición *f*
vex ['vɛks] *vt* : contrariar, molestar, irritar
vexation [vɛk'seɪʃən] *n* : contrariedad *f*, irritación *f*
via ['vaɪə, 'vi:ə] *prep* : por, vía
viability [ˌvaɪə'bɪləṭi] *n* : viabilidad *f*
viable ['vaɪəbəl] *adj* : viable
viaduct ['vaɪəˌdʌkt] *n* : viaducto *m*
vial ['vaɪəl] *n* : frasco *m*
vibrant ['vaɪbrənt] *adj* **1** LIVELY : vibrante, animado, dinámico **2** BRIGHT : fuerte, vivo (dícese de los colores)
vibrate ['vaɪˌbreɪt] *vi* **-brated; -brating** **1** OSCILLATE : vibrar, oscilar **2** THRILL : bullir <to vibrate with excitement : bullir de emoción>
vibration [vaɪ'breɪʃən] *n* : vibración *f*
vicar ['vɪkər] *n* : vicario *m*, -ria *f*
vicarious [vaɪ'kæri:əs, vɪ-] *adj* : indirecto — **vicariously** *adv*
vice ['vaɪs] *n* : vicio *m*
vice admiral *n* : vicealmirante *mf*
vice president *n* : vicepresidente *m*, -ta *f*
viceroy ['vaɪsˌrɔɪ] *n* : virrey *m*, -rreina *f*
vice versa [ˌvaɪsɪ'vərsə, ˌvaɪs'vər-] *adv* : viceversa
vicinity [və'sɪnəṭi] *n, pl* **-ties** **1** NEIGHBORHOOD : vecindad *f*, inmediaciones *fpl* **2** NEARNESS : proximidad *f*
vicious ['vɪʃəs] *adj* **1** DEPRAVED : depravado, malo **2** SAVAGE : malo, fiero, salvaje <a vicious dog : un perro feroz> **3** MALICIOUS : malicioso
viciously ['vɪʃəsli] *adv* : con saña, brutalmente
viciousness ['vɪʃəsnəs] *n* : brutalidad *f*, ferocidad *f* (de un animal), malevolencia *f* (de un comentario, etc.)
vicissitudes [və'sɪsəˌtu:dz, vaɪ-, -ˌtju:dz] *npl* : vicisitudes *fpl*
victim ['vɪktəm] *n* : víctima *f*
victimize ['vɪktəˌmaɪz] *vt* **-mized; -mizing** : tomar como víctima, perseguir, victimizar *Arg, Mex*
victor ['vɪktər] *n* : vencedor *m*, -dora *f*
Victorian [vɪk'to:riən] *adj* : victoriano
victorious [vɪk'to:riəs] *adj* : victorioso — **victoriously** *adv*
victory ['vɪktəri] *n, pl* **-ries** : victoria *f*, triunfo *m*
victuals ['vɪṭəlz] *npl* : víveres *mpl*, provisiones *fpl*
video¹ ['vɪdiˌo:] *adj* : de video <video recording : grabación de video>
video² *n* **1** : video *m* (medio o grabación) **2** → **videotape**²
video camera *n* : videocámara *f*
videocassette [ˌvɪdiokə'sɛt] *n* : videocasete *m*, videocassette *m*
videocassette recorder → **VCR**
video game *n* : videojuego *m*, juego *m* de video
videotape¹ ['vɪdioˌteɪp] *vt* **-taped; -taping** : grabar en video, videograbar
videotape² *n* : videocinta *f*
vie ['vaɪ] *vi* **vied; vying** ['vaɪɪŋ] : competir, rivalizar
Vietnamese [viˌɛtnə'mi:z, -'mi:s] *n* **1** : vietnamita *mf* **2** : vietnamita *m* (idioma) — **Vietnamese** *adj*
view¹ ['vju:] *vt* **1** OBSERVE : mirar, ver, observar **2** CONSIDER : considerar, contemplar
view² *n* **1** SIGHT : vista *f* <to come into view : aparecer> **2** ATTITUDE, OPINION : opinión *f*, parecer *m*, actitud *f* <in my view : en mi opinión> **3** SCENE : vista *f*, panorama *f* **4** INTENTION : idea *f*, vista *f* <with a view to : con vistas a, con la idea de> **5 in view of** : dado que, en vista de (que)
viewer ['vju:ər] *n or* **television viewer** : telespectador *m*, -dora *f*; televidente *mf*
viewpoint ['vju:ˌpɔɪnt] *n* : punto *m* de vista
vigil ['vɪʤəl] *n* **1** : vigilia *f*, vela *f* **2 to keep vigil** : velar
vigilance ['vɪʤələnts] *n* : vigilancia *f*
vigilant ['vɪʤələnt] *adj* : vigilante
vigilante [ˌvɪʤə'lænˌti:] *n* : integrante *mf* de un comité de vigilancia (que actúa como policía)
vigilantly ['vɪʤələntli] *adv* : con vigilancia
vigor ['vɪgər] *n* : vigor *m*, energía *f*, fuerza *f*
vigorous ['vɪgərəs] *adj* : vigoroso, enérgico — **vigorously** *adv*
Viking ['vaɪkɪŋ] *n* : vikingo *m*, -ga *f*
vile ['vaɪl] *adj* **viler; vilest** **1** WICKED : vil, infame **2** REVOLTING : asqueroso, repugnante **3** TERRIBLE : horrible, atroz <vile weather : tiempo horrible> <to be in a vile mood : estar de un humor de perros>
vilify ['vɪləˌfaɪ] *vt* **-fied; -fying** : vilipendiar, denigrar, difamar
villa ['vɪlə] *n* : casa *f* de campo, quinta *f*
village ['vɪlɪʤ] *n* : pueblo *m* (grande), aldea *f* (pequeña)
villager ['vɪlɪʤər] *n* : vecino *m*, -na *f* (de un pueblo); aldeano *m*, -na *f* (de una aldea)
villain ['vɪlən] *n* : villano *m*, -na *f*; malo *m*, -la *f* (en ficción, películas, etc.)
villainess ['vɪlənɪs, -nəs] *n* : villana *f*
villainous ['vɪlənəs] *adj* : infame, malvado
villainy ['vɪləni] *n, pl* **-lainies** : vileza *f*, maldad *f*
vim ['vɪm] *n* : brío *m*, vigor *m*, energía *f*
vindicate ['vɪndəˌkeɪt] *vt* **-cated; -cating** **1** EXONERATE : vindicar, disculpar **2** JUSTIFY : justificar
vindication [ˌvɪndə'keɪʃən] *n* : vindicación *f*, justificación *f*
vindictive [vɪn'dɪktɪv] *adj* : vengativo
vine ['vaɪn] *n* **1** GRAPEVINE : vid *f*, parra *f* **2** : planta *f* trepadora, enredadera *f*
vinegar ['vɪnɪgər] *n* : vinagre *m*

vinegary [ˈvɪnɪgəri] *adj* : avinagrado

vineyard [ˈvɪnjərd] *n* : viña *f*, viñedo *m*

vintage[1] [ˈvɪntɪʤ] *adj* **1** : añejo (dícese de un vino) **2** CLASSIC : clásico, de época

vintage[2] *n* **1** : cosecha *f* ⟨the 1947 vintage : la cosecha de 1947⟩ **2** ERA : época *f*, era *f* ⟨slang of recent vintage : argot de la época reciente⟩

vinyl [ˈvaɪnəl] *n* : vinilo

viola [viːˈoːlə] *n* : viola *f*

violate [ˈvaɪəˌleɪt] *vt* **-lated; -lating** **1** BREAK : infringir, violar, quebrantar ⟨to violate the rules : violar las reglas⟩ **2** RAPE : violar **3** DESECRATE : profanar

violation [ˌvaɪəˈleɪʃən] *n* **1** : violación *f*, infracción *f* (de una ley) **2** DESECRATION : profanación *f*

violence [ˈvaɪlənts, ˈvaɪə-] *n* : violencia *f*

violent [ˈvaɪlənt, ˈvaɪə-] *adj* : violento

violently [ˈvaɪləntli, ˈvaɪə-] *adv* : violentamente, con violencia

violet [ˈvaɪlət, ˈvaɪə-] *n* : violeta *f*

violin [ˌvaɪəˈlɪn] *n* : violín *m*

violinist [ˌvaɪəˈlɪnɪst] *n* : violinista *mf*

violoncello [ˌvaɪələnˈʧɛloː, ˌviː-] → **cello**

VIP [ˌviːˌaɪˈpiː] *n, pl* **VIPs** [-ˈpiːz] : VIP *mf*, persona *f* de categoría

viper [ˈvaɪpər] *n* : víbora *f*

viral [ˈvaɪrəl] *adj* : viral, vírico ⟨viral pneumonia : pulmonía viral⟩

virgin[1] [ˈvərʤən] *adj* **1** CHASTE : virginal ⟨the virgin birth : el alumbramiento virginal⟩ **2** : virgen, intacto ⟨a virgin forest : una selva virgen⟩ ⟨virgin wool : lana virgen⟩

virgin[2] *n* : virgen *mf*

virginity [vərˈʤɪnət̬i] *n* : virginidad *f*

Virgo [ˈvərˌgoː, ˈvɪr-] *n* : Virgo *mf*

virile [ˈvɪrəl, -ˌaɪl] *adj* : viril, varonil

virility [vəˈrɪlət̬i] *n* : virilidad *f*

virtual [ˈvərʧʊəl] *adj* : virtual ⟨a virtual dictator : un virtual dictador⟩ ⟨virtual reality : realidad virtual⟩

virtually [ˈvərʧʊəli, ˈvərʧəli] *adv* : en realidad, de hecho, casi

virtue [ˈvərˌʧuː] *n* **1** : virtud *f* **2 by virtue of** : en virtud de, debido a

virtuosity [ˌvərʧʊˈɑsət̬i] *n, pl* **-ties** : virtuosismo *m*

virtuoso [ˌvərʧʊˈoːsoː, -zoː] *n, pl* **-sos** *or* **-si** [-ˌsiː, -ˌziː] : virtuoso *m*, -sa *f*

virtuous [ˈvərʧʊəs] *adj* : virtuoso, bueno — **virtuously** *adv*

virulence [ˈvɪrələnts, ˈvɪrjə-] *n* : virulencia *f*

virulent [ˈvɪrələnt, ˈvɪrjə-] *adj* : virulento

virus [ˈvaɪrəs] *n* : virus *m*

visa [ˈviːzə, -sə] *n* : visa *f*

vis–à–vis [ˌviːzəˈviː, -sə-] *prep* : con relación a, con respecto a

viscera [ˈvɪsərə] *npl* : vísceras *fpl*

visceral [ˈvɪsərəl] *adj* : visceral

viscosity [vɪsˈkɑsət̬i] *n, pl* **-ties** : viscosidad *f*

viscount [ˈvaɪˌkæʊnt] *n* : vizconde *m*

viscountess [ˈvaɪˌkæʊntɪs] *n* : vizcondesa *f*

viscous [ˈvɪskəs] *adj* : viscoso

vise [ˈvaɪs] *n* : torno *m* de banco, tornillo *m* de banco

visibility [ˌvɪzəˈbɪlət̬i] *n, pl* **-ties** : visibilidad *f*

visible [ˈvɪzəbəl] *adj* **1** : visible ⟨the visible stars : las estrellas visibles⟩ **2** OBVIOUS : evidente, patente

visibly [ˈvɪzəbli] *adv* : visiblemente

vision [ˈvɪʒən] *n* **1** EYESIGHT : vista *f*, visión *f* **2** APPARITION : visión *f*, aparición *f* **3** FORESIGHT : visión *f* (del futuro), previsión *f* **4** IMAGE : imagen *f* ⟨she had visions of a disaster : se imaginaba un desastre⟩

visionary[1] [ˈvɪʒəˌnɛri] *adj* **1** FARSIGHTED : visionario, con visión de futuro **2** UTOPIAN : utópico, poco realista

visionary[2] *n, pl* **-ries** : visionario *m*, -ria *f*

visit[1] [ˈvɪzət] *vt* **1** : visitar, ir a ver **2** AFFLICT : azotar, afligir ⟨visited by troubles : afligido con problemas⟩ — *vi* : hacer (una) visita

visit[2] *n* : visita *f*

visitor [ˈvɪzət̬ər] *n* : visitante *mf* (a una ciudad, etc.), visita *f* (a una casa)

visor [ˈvaɪzər] *n* : visera *f*

vista [ˈvɪstə] *n* : vista *f*

visual [ˈvɪʒʊəl] *adj* : visual ⟨the visual arts : las artes visuales⟩ — **visually** *adv*

visualize [ˈvɪʒʊəˌlaɪz] *vt* **-ized; -izing** : visualizar, imaginarse, hacerse una idea de — **visualization** [ˌvɪʒəwələˈzeɪʃən] *n*

vital [ˈvaɪt̬əl] *adj* **1** : vital ⟨vital organs : órganos vitales⟩ **2** CRUCIAL : esencial, crucial, decisivo ⟨of vital importance : de suma importancia⟩ **3** LIVELY : enérgico, lleno de vida, vital

vitality [vaɪˈtælət̬i] *n, pl* **-ties** : vitalidad *f*, energía *f*

vitally [ˈvaɪt̬əli] *adv* : sumamente

vital statistics *npl* : estadísticas *fpl* demográficas

vitamin [ˈvaɪt̬əmən] *n* : vitamina *f* ⟨vitamin deficiency : carencia vitamínica⟩

vitreous [ˈvɪtriəs] *adj* : vítreo

vitriolic [ˌvɪtriˈɑlɪk] *adj* : mordaz, virulento

vituperation [vaɪˌtuːpəˈreɪʃən, -ˌtjuː-] *n* : vituperio *m*

vivacious [vəˈveɪʃəs, vaɪ-] *adj* : vivaz, animado, lleno de vida

vivaciously [vəˈveɪʃəsli, vaɪ-] *adv* : con vivacidad, animadamente

vivacity [vəˈvæsət̬i, vaɪ-] *n* : vivacidad *f*

vivid [ˈvɪvəd] *adj* **1** LIVELY : lleno de vitalidad **2** BRILLIANT : vivo, intenso ⟨vivid colors : colores vivos⟩ **3** INTENSE, SHARP : vívido, gráfico ⟨a vivid dream : un sueño vívido⟩

vividly [ˈvɪvədli] *adv* **1** BRIGHTLY : con colores vivos **2** SHARPLY : vívidamente

vividness [ˈvɪvədnəs] *n* **1** BRIGHTNESS : intensidad *f*, viveza *f* **2** SHARPNESS : lo gráfico, nitidez *f*

vivisection [ˌvɪvəˈsɛkʃən, ˈvɪvəˌ-] *n* : vivisección *f*
vixen [ˈvɪksən] *n* : zorra *f*, raposa *f*
vocabulary [voːˈkæbjəˌlɛri] *n, pl* **-laries** **1** : vocabulario *m* **2** LEXICON : léxico *m*
vocal [ˈvoːkəl] *adj* **1** : vocal **2** LOUD, OUTSPOKEN : ruidoso, muy franco
vocal cords *npl* : cuerdas *fpl* vocales
vocalist [ˈvoːkəlɪst] *n* : cantante *mf*, vocalista *mf*
vocalize [ˈvoːkəlˌaɪz] *vt* **-ized; -izing** : vocalizar
vocation [voˈkeɪʃən] *n* : vocación *f* ⟨to have a vocation for : tener vocación de⟩
vocational [voˈkeɪʃənəl] *adj* : profesional ⟨vocational guidance : orientación profesional⟩
vociferous [voˈsɪfərəs] *adj* : ruidoso, vociferante
vodka [ˈvɑdkə] *n* : vodka *m*
vogue [ˈvoːg] *n* : moda *f*, boga *f* ⟨to be in vogue : estar de moda, estar en boga⟩
voice[1] [ˈvɔɪs] *vt* **voiced; voicing** : expresar
voice[2] *n* **1** : voz *f* ⟨in a low voice : en voz baja⟩ ⟨to lose one's voice : quedarse sin voz⟩ ⟨the voice of the people : la voz del pueblo⟩ **2 to make one's voice heard** : hacerse oír
voice box → **larynx**
voiced [ˈvɔɪst] *adj* : sonoro
voice mail *n* : correo *m* de voz
void[1] [ˈvɔɪd] *vt* : anular, invalidar ⟨to void a contract : anular un contrato⟩
void[2] *adj* **1** EMPTY : vacío, desprovisto ⟨void of content : desprovisto de contenido⟩ **2** INVALID : inválido, nulo
void[3] *n* : vacío *m*
volatile [ˈvɑlət̬əl] *adj* : volátil, inestable
volatility [ˌvɑləˈtɪlət̬i] *n* : volatilidad *f*, inestabilidad *f*
volcanic [vɑlˈkænɪk] *adj* : volcánico
volcano [vɑlˈkeɪˌnoː] *n, pl* **-noes** *or* **-nos** : volcán *m*
vole [ˈvoːl] *n* : campañol *m*
volition [voˈlɪʃən] *n* : volición *f*, voluntad *f* ⟨of one's own volition : por voluntad propia⟩
volley [ˈvɑli] *n, pl* **-leys** **1** : descarga *f* (de tiros) **2** : torrente *m*, lluvia *f* (de insultos, etc.) **3** : salva *f* (de aplausos) **4** : volea *f* (en deportes)
volleyball [ˈvɑliˌbɔl] *n* : voleibol *m*
volt [ˈvoːlt] *n* : voltio *m*
voltage [ˈvoːltɪʤ] *n* : voltaje *m*
volubility [ˌvɑljəˈbɪlət̬i] *n* : locuacidad *f*
voluble [ˈvɑljəbəl] *adj* : locuaz
volume [ˈvɑljəm, -ˌjuːm] *n* **1** BOOK : volumen *m*, tomo *m* **2** SPACE : capacidad *f*, volumen *m* (en física) **3** AMOUNT : cantidad *f*, volumen *m* **4** LOUDNESS : volumen *m*
voluminous [vəˈluːmənəs] *adj* : voluminoso
voluntary [ˈvɑlənˌtɛri] *adj* : voluntario — **voluntarily** [ˌvɑlənˈtɛrəli] *adv*
volunteer[1] [ˌvɑlənˈtɪr] *vt* : ofrecer, dar ⟨to volunteer one's assistance : ofrecer la ayuda⟩ — *vi* : ofrecerse, alistarse como voluntario
volunteer[2] *n* : voluntario *m*, -ria *f*
voluptuous [vəˈlʌpʧʊəs] *adj* : voluptuoso
vomit[1] [ˈvɑmət] *v* : vomitar
vomit[2] *n* : vómito *m*
voodoo [ˈvuːˌduː] *n, pl* **voodoos** : vudú *m*
voracious [vɔˈreɪʃəs, və-] *adj* : voraz
voraciously [vɔˈreɪʃəsli, və-] *adv* : vorazmente, con voracidad
vortex [ˈvɔrˌtɛks] *n, pl* **vortices** [ˈvɔrtəˌsiːz] : vórtice *m*
vote[1] [ˈvoːt] *vi* **voted; voting** : votar ⟨to vote Democratic : votar por los demócratas⟩
vote[2] *n* **1** : voto *m* **2** SUFFRAGE : sufragio *m*, derecho *m* al voto
voter [ˈvoːt̬ər] *n* : votante *mf*
voting [ˈvoːt̬ɪŋ] *n* : votación *f*
vouch [ˈvæʊʧ] *vi* **to vouch for** : garantizar (algo), responder de (algo), responder por (alguien)
voucher [ˈvæʊʧər] *n* **1** RECEIPT : comprobante *m* **2** : vale *m* ⟨travel voucher : vale de viajar⟩
vow[1] [væʊ] *vt* : jurar, prometer, hacer voto de
vow[2] *n* : promesa *f*, voto *m* (en la religión) ⟨a vow of poverty : un voto de pobreza⟩
vowel [ˈvæʊəl] *n* : vocal *m*
voyage[1] [ˈvɔɪɪʤ] *vi* **-aged; -aging** : viajar
voyage[2] *n* : viaje *m*
voyager [ˈvɔɪɪʤər] *n* : viajero *m*, -ra *f*
vulcanize [ˈvʌlkəˌnaɪz] *vt* **-nized; -nizing** : vulcanizar
vulgar [ˈvʌlgər] *adj* **1** COMMON, PLEBIAN : ordinario, populachero, del vulgo **2** COARSE, CRUDE : grosero, de mal gusto, majadero *Mex* **3** INDECENT : indecente, colorado (dícese de un chiste, etc.)
vulgarity [ˌvʌlˈgærət̬i] *n, pl* **-ties** : grosería *f*, vulgaridad *f*
vulgarly [ˈvʌlgərli] *adv* : vulgarmente, groseramente
vulnerability [ˌvʌlnərəˈbɪlət̬i] *n, pl* **-ties** : vulnerabilidad *f*
vulnerable [ˈvʌlnərəbəl] *adj* : vulnerable
vulture [ˈvʌlʧər] *n* : buitre *m*, zopilote *m* *CA, Mex*
vying → **vie**

W

w [ˈdʌbəlˌjuː] *n, pl* **w's** *or* **ws** [-ˌjuːz] : vigésima tercera letra del alfabeto inglés
wad[1] [ˈwɑd] *vt* **wadded; wadding 1** : hacer un taco con, formar en una masa **2** STUFF : rellenar
wad[2] *n* : taco *m* (de papel), bola *f* (de algodón, etc.), fajo *m* (de billetes)
waddle[1] [ˈwɑdəl] *vi* **-dled; -dling** : andar como un pato
waddle[2] *n* : andar *m* de pato
wade [ˈweɪd] *v* **waded; wading** *vi* **1** : caminar por el agua **2 to wade through** : leer (algo) con dificultad — *vt or* **to wade across** : vadear
wading bird *n* : zancuda *f*, ave *f* zancuda
wafer [ˈweɪfər] *n* : barquillo *m*, galleta *f* de barquillo
waffle [ˈwɑfəl] *n* **1** : wafle *m* **2 waffle iron** : waflera *f*
waft [ˈwɑft, ˈwæft] *vt* : llevar por el aire — *vi* : flotar
wag[1] [ˈwæg] *v* **wagged; wagging** *vt* : menear — *vi* : menearse, moverse
wag[2] *n* **1** : meneo *m* (de la cola) **2** JOKER, WIT : bromista *mf*
wage[1] [ˈweɪʤ] *vt* **waged; waging** : hacer, librar ⟨to wage war : hacer la guerra⟩
wage[2] *n or* **wages** *npl* : sueldo *m*, salario *m* ⟨minimum wage : salario mínimo⟩
wager[1] [ˈweɪʤər] *v* : apostar
wager[2] *n* : apuesta *f*
waggish [ˈwægɪʃ] *adj* : burlón, bromista (dícese de una persona), chistoso (dícese de un comentario)
waggle [ˈwægəl] *vt* **-gled; -gling** : menear, mover (de un lado a otro)
wagon [ˈwægən] *n* **1** : carro *m* (tirado por caballos) **2** CART : carrito *m* **3** → **station wagon**
waif [ˈweɪf] *n* : niño *m* abandonado, animal *m* sin hogar
wail[1] [ˈweɪl] *vi* : gemir, lamentarse
wail[2] *n* : gemido *m*, lamento *m*
wainscot [ˈweɪnskət, -ˌskɑt, -ˌskoːt] *or* **wainscoting** [-skət̬ɪŋ, -ˌskɑ-, -ˌskoː-] *n* : boiserie *f*, revestimiento *m* de paneles de madera
waist [ˈweɪst] *n* : cintura *f* (del cuerpo humano), talle *m* (de ropa)
waistline [ˈweɪstˌlaɪn] → **waist**
wait[1] [ˈweɪt] *vi* : esperar ⟨to wait for something : esperar algo⟩ ⟨wait and see! : ¡espera y verás!⟩ ⟨I can't wait : me muero de ganas⟩ — *vt* **1** AWAIT : esperar **2** DELAY : retrasar ⟨don't wait lunch : no retrase el almuerzo⟩ **3** SERVE : servir, atender ⟨to wait tables : servir (a la mesa)⟩
wait[2] *n* **1** : espera *f* **2 to lie in wait** : estar al acecho
waiter [ˈweɪt̬ər] *n* : mesero *m*, camarero *m*, mozo *m Arg, Chile, Col, Peru*
waiting room *n* : sala *f* de espera
waitress [ˈweɪtrəs] *n* : mesera *f*, camarera *f*, moza *f Arg, Chile, Col, Peru*
waive [ˈweɪv] *vt* **waived; waiving** : renunciar a ⟨to waive one's rights : renunciar a sus derechos⟩ ⟨to waive the rules : no aplicar las reglas⟩
waiver [ˈweɪvər] *n* : renuncia *f*
wake[1] [ˈweɪk] *v* **woke** [ˈwoːk]; **woken** [ˈwoːkən] *or* **waked; waking** *vi or* **to wake up** : despertar(se) ⟨he woke at noon : se despertó al mediodía⟩ ⟨wake up! : ¡despiértate!⟩ — *vt* : despertar
wake[2] *n* **1** VIGIL : velatorio *m*, velorio *m* (de un difunto) **2** TRAIL : estela *f* (de un barco, un huracán, etc.) **3** AFTERMATH : consecuencias *fpl* ⟨in the wake of : tras, como consecuencia de⟩
wakeful [ˈweɪkfəl] *adj* **1** SLEEPLESS : desvelado **2** VIGILANT : alerta, vigilante
waken [ˈweɪkən] → **awake**
walk[1] [ˈwɔk] *vi* **1** : caminar, andar, pasear ⟨you're walking too fast : estás caminando demasiado rápido⟩ ⟨to walk around the city : pasearse por la ciudad⟩ **2** : ir andando, ir a pie ⟨we had to walk home : tuvimos que ir a casa a pie⟩ **3** : darle base por bolas (a un bateador) — *vt* **1** : recorrer, caminar ⟨she walked two miles : caminó dos millas⟩ **2** ACCOMPANY : acompañar **3** : sacar a pasear (a un perro)
walk[2] *n* **1** : paseo *m*, caminata *f* ⟨to go for a walk : ir a caminar, dar un paseo⟩ **2** PATH : camino *m* **3** GAIT : andar *m* **4** : marcha *f* (en beisbol) **5 walk of life** : esfera *f*, condición *f*
walker [ˈwɔkər] *n* **1** : paseante *mf* **2** HIKER : excursionista *mf* **3** : andador *m* (aparato)
walking stick *n* : bastón *m*
walkout [ˈwɔkˌaʊt] *n* STRIKE : huelga *f*
walk out *vi* **1** STRIKE : declararse en huelga **2** LEAVE : salir, irse **3 to walk out on** : abandonar, dejar
walkway [ˈwɔkˌweɪ] *n* **1** SIDEWALK : acera *f* **2** PATH : sendero *m* **3** PASSAGEWAY : pasadizo *m*
wall[1] [ˈwɔl] *vt* **1 to wall in** : cercar con una pared o un muro, tapiar, amurallar **2 to wall off** : separar con una pared o un muro **3 to wall up** : tapiar, condenar (una ventana, etc.)
wall[2] *n* **1** : muro *m* (exterior) ⟨the walls of the city : las murallas de la ciudad⟩ **2** : pared *f* (interior) **3** BARRIER : barrera *f* ⟨a wall of mountains : una barrera de montañas⟩ **4** : pared *f* (en anatomía)
wallaby [ˈwɑləbi] *n, pl* **-bies** : ualabí *m*
walled [ˈwɔld] *adj* : amurallado
wallet [ˈwɑlət] *n* : billetera *f*, cartera *f*
wallflower [ˈwɔlˌflaʊər] *n* **1** : alhelí *m* (flor) **2 to be a wallflower** : comer pavo
wallop[1] [ˈwɑləp] *vt* **1** TROUNCE : darle una paliza (a alguien) **2** SOCK : pegar fuerte

wallop[2] *n* : golpe *m* fuerte, golpazo *m*

wallow[1] [ˈwɑˌloː] *vi* **1** : revolcarse ⟨to wallow in the mud : revolcarse en el lodo⟩ **2** DELIGHT : deleitarse ⟨to wallow in luxury : nadar en lujos⟩

wallow[2] *n* : revolcadero *m* (para animales)

wallpaper[1] [ˈwɔlˌpeɪpər] *vt* : empapelar

wallpaper[2] *n* : papel *m* pintado

walnut [ˈwɔlˌnʌt] *n* **1** : nuez *f* (fruta) **2** : nogal *m* (árbol y madera)

walrus [ˈwɔlrəs, ˈwɑl-] *n, pl* **-rus** *or* **-ruses** : morsa *f*

waltz[1] [ˈwɔlts] *vi* **1** : valsar, bailar el vals **2** BREEZE : pasar con ligereza ⟨to waltz in : entrar tan campante⟩

waltz[2] *n* : vals *m*

wan [ˈwɑn] *adj* **wanner; -est 1** PALLID : pálido **2** DIM : tenue ⟨wan light : luz tenue⟩ **3** LANGUID : lánguido ⟨a wan smile : una sonrisa lánguida⟩ — **wanly** *adv*

wand [ˈwɑnd] *n* : varita *f* (mágica)

wander [ˈwɑndər] *vi* **1** RAMBLE : deambular, vagar, vagabundear **2** STRAY : alejarse, desviarse, divagar ⟨she let her mind wander : dejó vagar la imaginación⟩ — *vt* : recorrer ⟨to wander the streets : vagar por las calles⟩

wanderer [ˈwɑndərər] *n* : vagabundo *m*, -da *f*; viajero *m*, -ra *f*

wanderlust [ˈwɑndərˌlʌst] *n* : pasión *f* por viajar

wane[1] [ˈweɪn] *vi* **waned; waning 1** : menguar (dícese de la luna) **2** DECLINE : disminuir, decaer, menguar

wane[2] *n* **on the wane** : decayendo, en decadencia

wangle [ˈwæŋgəl] *vt* **-gled; -gling** FINAGLE : arreglárselas para conseguir

wannabe [ˈwɑnəˌbiː] *n* : aspirante *mf* (a algo); imitador *m*, -dora *f* (de alguien)

want[1] [ˈwɑnt, ˈwɔnt] *vt* **1** LACK : faltar **2** REQUIRE : requerir, necesitar **3** DESIRE : querer, desear

want[2] *n* **1** LACK : falta *f* **2** DESTITUTION : indigencia *f*, miseria *f* **3** DESIRE, NEED : deseo *m*, necesidad *f*

wanting [ˈwɑntɪŋ, ˈwɔn-] *adj* **1** ABSENT : ausente **2** DEFICIENT : deficiente ⟨he's wanting in common sense : le falta sentido común⟩

wanton [ˈwɑntən, ˈwɔn-] *adj* **1** LEWD, LUSTFUL : lascivo, lujurioso, licencioso **2** INHUMANE, MERCILESS : despiadado ⟨wanton cruelty : crueldad despiadada⟩

wapiti [ˈwɑpəṭi] *n, pl* **-ti** *or* **-tis** : uapití *m*

war[1] [ˈwɔr] *vi* **warred; warring** : combatir, batallar, hacer la guerra

war[2] *n* : guerra *f* ⟨to go to war : entrar en guerra⟩

warble[1] [ˈwɔrbəl] *vi* **-bled; -bling** : gorjear, trinar

warble[2] *n* : trino *m*, gorjeo *m*

warbler [ˈwɔrblər] *n* : pájaro *m* gorjeador, curruca *f*

ward[1] [ˈwɔrd] *vt* **to ward off** : desviar, protegerse contra

ward[2] *n* **1** : sala *f* (de un hospital, etc.) ⟨maternity ward : sala de maternidad⟩ **2** : distrito *m* electoral o administrativo (de una ciudad) **3** : pupilo *m*, -la *f* (de un tutor, etc.)

warden [ˈwɔrdən] *n* **1** KEEPER : guarda *mf*; guardián *m*, -diana *f* ⟨game warden : guardabosque⟩ **2** *or* **prison warden** : alcaide *m*

wardrobe [ˈwɔrdˌroːb] *n* **1** CLOSET : armario *m* **2** CLOTHES : vestuario *m*, guardarropa *f*

ware [ˈwær] *n* **1** POTTERY : cerámica *f* **2 wares** *npl* GOODS : mercancía *f*, mercadería *f*

warehouse [ˈwærˌhaʊs] *n* : depósito *m*, almacén *m*, bodega *f Chile, Col, Mex*

warfare [ˈwɔrˌfær] *n* **1** WAR : guerra *f* **2** STRUGGLE : lucha *f* ⟨the warfare against drugs : la lucha contra las drogas⟩

warhead [ˈwɔrˌhɛd] *n* : ojiva *f*, cabeza *f* (de un misil)

warily [ˈwærəli] *adv* : cautelosamente, con cautela

wariness [ˈwærinəs] *n* : cautela *f*

warlike [ˈwærˌlaɪk] *adj* : belicoso, guerrero

warm[1] [ˈwɔrm] *vt* **1** HEAT : calentar, recalentar **2 to warm one's heart** : reconfortar a uno, alegrar el corazón **3 to warm up** : calentar (los músculos, un automóvil, etc.) — *vi* **1** : calentarse **2 to warm to** : tomarle simpatía (a alguien), entusiasmarse con (algo)

warm[2] *adj* **1** LUKEWARM : tibio, templado **2** : caliente, cálido, caluroso ⟨a warm wind : un viento cálido⟩ ⟨a warm day : un día caluroso, un día de calor⟩ ⟨warm hands : manos calientes⟩ **3** : caliente, que abriga ⟨warm clothes : ropa de abrigo⟩ ⟨I feel warm : tengo calor⟩ **4** CARING, CORDIAL : cariñoso, cordial **5** : cálido (dícese de colores) **6** FRESH : fresco, reciente ⟨a warm trail : un rastro reciente⟩ **7** (*used for riddles*) : caliente

warm–blooded [ˈwɔrmˈblʌdəd] *adj* : de sangre caliente

warmhearted [ˈwɔrmˈhɑrṭəd] *adj* : cariñoso

warmly [ˈwɔrmli] *adv* **1** AFFECTIONATELY : calurosamente, afectuosamente **2 to dress warmly** : abrigarse

warmonger [ˈwɔrˌmɑŋgər, -ˌmʌŋ-] *n* : belicista *mf*

warmth [ˈwɔrm*p*θ] *n* **1** : calor *m* **2** AFFECTION : cariño *m*, afecto *m* **3** ENTHUSIASM : ardor *m*, entusiasmo *m*

warm–up [ˈwɔrmˌʌp] *n* : calentamiento *m*

warn [ˈwɔrn] *vt* **1** CAUTION : advertir, alertar **2** INFORM : avisar, informar

warning [ˈwɔrnɪŋ] *n* **1** ADVICE : advertencia *f*, aviso *m* **2** ALERT : alerta *f*, alarma *f*

warp[1] [ˈwɔrp] *vt* **1** : alabear, combar **2** PERVERT : pervertir, deformar — *vi* : pandearse, alabearse, combarse

warp² *n* **1** : urdimbre *f* ⟨the warp and the weft : la urdimbre y la trama⟩ **2** : alabeo *m* (en la madera, etc.)

warrant¹ [ˈwɔrənt] *vt* **1** ASSURE : asegurar, garantizar **2** GUARANTEE : garantizar **3** JUSTIFY, MERIT : justificar, merecer

warrant² *n* **1** AUTHORIZATION : autorización *f*, permiso *m* ⟨an arrest warrant : una orden de detención⟩ **2** JUSTIFICATION : justificación *f*

warranty [ˈwɔrənti, ˌwɔrənˈti:] *n, pl* **-ties** : garantía *f*

warren [ˈwɔrən] *n* : madriguera *f* (de conejos)

warrior [ˈwɔriər] *n* : guerrero *m*, -ra *f*

warship [ˈwɔrˌʃɪp] *n* : buque *m* de guerra

wart [ˈwɔrt] *n* : verruga *f*

wartime [ˈwɔrˌtaɪm] *n* : tiempo *m* de guerra

wary [ˈwæri] *adj* **warier; -est** : cauteloso, receloso ⟨to be wary of : desconfiar de⟩

was → **be**

wash¹ [ˈwɔʃ, ˈwɑʃ] *vt* **1** CLEAN : lavar(se), limpiar, fregar ⟨to wash the dishes : lavar los platos⟩ ⟨to wash one's hands : lavarse las manos⟩ **2** DRENCH : mojar **3** LAP : bañar ⟨waves were washing the shore : las olas bañaban la orilla⟩ **4** CARRY, DRAG : arrastrar **5 to wash away** : llevarse (un puente, etc.) — *vi* **1** : lavarse (dícese de una persona o la ropa) ⟨the dress washes well : el vestido se lava bien⟩ **2 to wash against** *or* **to wash over** : bañar

wash² *n* **1** : lavado *m* ⟨to give something a wash : lavar algo⟩ **2** LAUNDRY : artículos *mpl* para lavar, ropa *f* sucia **3** : estela *f* (de un barco)

washable [ˈwɔʃəbəl, ˈwɑ-] *adj* : lavable

washboard [ˈwɔʃˌbord, ˈwɑʃ-] *n* : tabla *f* de lavar

washbowl [ˈwɔʃˌbo:l, ˈwɑʃ-] *n* : lavabo *m*, lavamanos *m*

washcloth [ˈwɔʃˌklɔθ, ˈwɑʃ-] *n* : toallita *f* (para lavarse)

washed-out [ˈwɔʃtˈaʊt, ˈwɑʃt-] *adj* **1** : desvaído (dícese de colores) **2** EXHAUSTED : agotado, desanimado

washed-up [ˈwɔʃtˈʌp, ˈwɑʃt-] *adj* : acabado (dícese de una persona), fracasado (dícese de un negocio, etc.)

washer [ˈwɔʃər, ˈwɑ-] *n* **1** → **washing machine** **2** : arandela *f* (de una llave, etc.)

washing [ˈwɔʃɪŋ, ˈwɑ-] *n* WASH : ropa *f* para lavar

washing machine *n* : máquina *f* de lavar, lavadora *f*

washout [ˈwɔʃˌaʊt, ˈwɑʃ-] *n* **1** : erosión *f* (de la tierra) **2** FAILURE : fracaso *m* ⟨she's a washout : es un desastre⟩

washroom [ˈwɔʃˌru:m, ˈwɑʃ-, -ˌrʊm] *n* : servicios *mpl* (públicos), baño *m*, sanitario *m Col, Mex, Ven*

wasn't [ˈwʌzənt] (*contraction of* **was not**) → **be**

wasp [ˈwɑsp] *n* : avispa *f*

waspish [ˈwɑspɪʃ] *adj* **1** IRRITABLE : irritable, irascible **2** CAUSTIC : cáustico, mordaz

waste¹ [ˈweɪst] *v* **wasted; wasting** *vt* **1** DEVASTATE : arrasar, arruinar, devastar **2** SQUANDER : desperdiciar, despilfarrar, malgastar ⟨to waste time : perder tiempo⟩ — *vi or* **to waste away** : consumirse, chuparse

waste² *adj* **1** BARREN : yermo, baldío **2** DISCARDED : de desecho **3** EXCESS : sobrante

waste³ *n* **1** → **wasteland** **2** MISUSE : derroche *m*, desperdicio *m*, despilfarro *m* ⟨a waste of time : una pérdida de tiempo⟩ **3** RUBBISH : basura *f*, desechos *mpl*, desperdicios *mpl* **4** EXCREMENT : excremento *m*

wastebasket [ˈweɪstˌbæskət] *n* : cesto *m* (de basura), papelera *f*, zafacón *m Car*

wasteful [ˈweɪstfəl] *adj* : despilfarrador, derrochador, pródigo

wastefulness [ˈweɪstfəlnəs] *n* : derroche *m*, despilfarro *m*

wasteland [ˈweɪstˌlænd, -lənd] *n* : baldío *m*, yermo *m*, desierto *m*

watch¹ [ˈwɑʧ] *vi* **1** *or* **to keep watch** : velar **2** OBSERVE : mirar, ver, observar **3 to watch for** AWAIT : esperar, quedar a la espera de **4 to watch out** : tener cuidado ⟨watch out! : ¡ten cuidado!, ¡ojo!⟩ — *vt* **1** OBSERVE : mirar, observar **2** *or* **to watch over** : vigilar, cuidar **3** : tener cuidado de ⟨watch what you do : ten cuidado con lo que haces⟩

watch² *n* **1** : guardia *f* ⟨to be on watch : estar de guardia⟩ **2** SURVEILLANCE : vigilancia *f* **3** LOOKOUT : guardia *mf*, centinela *f*, vigía *mf* **4** TIMEPIECE : reloj *m*

watchdog [ˈwɑʧˌdɔg] *n* : perro *m* guardián

watcher [ˈwɑʧər] *n* : observador *m*, -dora *f*

watchful [ˈwɑʧfəl] *adj* : alerta, vigilante, atento

watchfulness [ˈwɑʧfəlnəs] *n* : vigilancia *f*

watchman [ˈwɑʧmən] *n, pl* **-men** [-mən, -ˌmɛn] : vigilante *m*, guarda *m*

watchword [ˈwɑʧˌwərd] *n* **1** PASSWORD : contraseña *f* **2** SLOGAN : lema *m*, eslogan *m*

water¹ [ˈwɔt̬ər, ˈwɑ-] *vt* **1** : regar (el jardín, etc.) **2 to water down** DILUTE : diluir, aguar — *vi* : lagrimear (dícese de los ojos), hacérsele agua la boca a uno ⟨my mouth is watering : se me hace agua la boca⟩

water² *n* : agua *f*

water buffalo *n* : búfalo *m* de agua

watercolor [ˈwɔt̬ərˌkʌlər, ˈwɑ-] *n* : acuarela *f*

watercourse [ˈwɔt̬ərˌkors, ˈwɑ-] *n* : curso *m* de agua

watercress [ˈwɔt̬ərˌkrɛs, ˈwɑ-] *n* : berro *m*

waterfall ['wɔt̬ər,fɔl, 'wɑ-] *n* : cascada *f*, salto *m* de agua, catarata *f*
waterfowl ['wɔt̬ər,faʊl, 'wɑ-] *n* : ave *f* acuática
waterfront ['wɔt̬ər,frʌnt, 'wɑ-] *n* **1** : tierra *f* que bordea un río, un lago, o un mar **2** WHARF : muelle *m*
water lily *n* : nenúfar *m*
waterlogged ['wɔt̬ər,lɔgd, 'wɑt̬ər-,lɑgd] *adj* : lleno de agua, empapado, inundado (dícese del suelo)
watermark ['wɔt̬ər,mɑrk, 'wɑ-] *n* **1** : marca *f* del nivel de agua **2** : filigrana *f* (en el papel)
watermelon ['wɔt̬ər,mɛlən, 'wɑ-] *n* : sandía *f*
water moccasin → **moccasin**
waterpower ['wɔt̬ər,paʊər, 'wɑ-] *n* : energía *f* hidráulica
waterproof¹ ['wɔt̬ər,pru:f, 'wɑ-] *vt* : hacer impermeable, impermeabilizar
waterproof² *adj* : impermeable, a prueba de agua
watershed ['wɔt̬ər,ʃɛd, 'wɑ-] *n* **1** : línea *f* divisoria de aguas **2** BASIN : cuenca *f* (de un río)
waterskiing ['wɔt̬ər,ski:ɪŋ, 'wɑ-] *n* : esquí *m* acuático
waterspout ['wɔt̬ər,spaʊt, 'wɑ-] *n* WHIRLWIND : tromba *f* marina
watertight ['wɔt̬ər,taɪt, 'wɑ-] *adj* **1** : hermético **2** IRREFUTABLE : irrebatible, irrefutable ⟨a watertight contract : un contrato sin lagunas⟩
waterway ['wɔt̬ər,weɪ, 'wɑ-] *n* : vía *f* navegable
waterworks ['wɔt̬ər,wərks, 'wɑ-] *npl* : central *f* de abastecimiento de agua
watery ['wɔt̬əri, 'wɑ-] *adj* **1** : acuoso, como agua **2** : aguado, diluido ⟨watery soup : sopa aguada⟩ **3** : lloroso ⟨watery eyes : ojos llorosos⟩ **4** WASHED-OUT : desvaído (dícese de colores)
watt ['wɑt] *n* : vatio *m*
wattage ['wɑt̬ɪʤ] *n* : vataje *m*
wattle ['wɑt̬əl] *n* : carúncula *f* (de un ave, etc.)
wave¹ ['weɪv] *v* **waved; waving** *vi* **1** : saludar con la mano, hacer señas con la mano ⟨she waved at him : lo saludó con la mano⟩ **2** FLUTTER, SHAKE : ondear, agitarse **3** UNDULATE : ondular — *vt* **1** SHAKE : agitar **2** BRANDISH : blandir **3** CURL : ondular, marcar (el pelo) **4** SIGNAL : hacerle señas a (con la mano) ⟨he waved farewell : se despidió con la mano⟩
wave² *n* **1** : ola *f* (de agua) **2** CURL : onda *f* (en el pelo) **3** : onda *f* (en física) **4** SURGE : oleada *f* ⟨a wave of enthusiasm : una oleada de entusiasmo⟩ **5** GESTURE : señal *f* con la mano, saludo *m* con la mano
wavelength ['weɪv,lɛŋkθ] *n* : longitud *f* de onda
waver ['weɪvər] *vi* **1** VACILLATE : vacilar, fluctuar **2** FLICKER : parpadear, titilar, oscilar **3** FALTER : flaquear, tambalearse
wavy ['weɪvi] *adj* **wavier; -est** : ondulado
wax¹ ['wæks] *vi* **1** : crecer (dícese de la luna) **2** BECOME : volverse, ponerse ⟨to wax indignant : indignarse⟩ — *vt* : encerar
wax² *n* **1** BEESWAX : cera *f* de abejas **2** : cera *f* ⟨floor wax : cera para el piso⟩ **3** *or* **earwax** ['ɪr,wæks] : cerilla *f*, cerumen *m*
waxen ['wæksən] *adj* : de cera
waxy ['wæksi] *adj* **waxier; -est** : ceroso
way ['weɪ] *n* **1** PATH, ROAD : camino *m*, vía *f* **2** ROUTE : camino *m*, ruta *f* ⟨to go the wrong way : equivocarse de camino⟩ ⟨I'm on my way : estoy de camino⟩ **3** : línea *f* de conducta, camino *m* ⟨he chose the easy way : optó por el camino fácil⟩ **4** MANNER, MEANS : manera *f*, modo *m*, forma *f* ⟨in the same way : del mismo modo, igualmente⟩ ⟨there are no two ways about it : no cabe la menor duda⟩ ⟨no way! : ¡de ninguna manera!⟩ **5** (*indicating a wish*) ⟨have it your way : como tú quieras⟩ ⟨to get one's own way : salirse uno con la suya⟩ **6** STATE : estado *m* ⟨things are in a bad way : las cosas marchan mal⟩ **7** RESPECT : aspecto *m*, sentido *m* **8** CUSTOM : costumbre *f* ⟨to mend one's ways : dejar las malas costumbres⟩ **9** PASSAGE : camino *m* ⟨to get in the way : meterse en el camino⟩ **10** DISTANCE : distancia *f* ⟨to come a long way : hacer grandes progresos⟩ **11** DIRECTION : dirección *f* ⟨come this way : venga por aquí⟩ ⟨which way did he go? : ¿por dónde fue?⟩ **12 by the way** : a propósito, por cierto **13 by way of** VIA : vía, pasando por **14 out of the way** REMOTE : remoto, recóndito **15** → **under way**
wayfarer ['weɪ,færər] *n* : caminante *mf*
waylay ['weɪ,leɪ] *vt* **-laid** [-,leɪd]; **-laying** ACCOST : abordar
wayside ['weɪ,saɪd] *n* : borde *m* del camino
wayward ['weɪwərd] *adj* **1** UNRULY : díscolo, rebelde **2** UNTOWARD : adverso
we ['wi:] *pron* : nosotros, nosotras
weak ['wi:k] *adj* **1** FEEBLE : débil, endeble **2** : flojo, pobre ⟨a weak excuse : una excusa poco convincente⟩ **3** DILUTED : aguado, diluido ⟨weak tea : té poco cargado⟩ **4** FAINT : tenue (dícese de los colores, las luces, los sonidos, etc.)
weaken ['wi:kən] *vt* : debilitar — *vi* : debilitarse, flaquear
weakling ['wi:klɪŋ] *n* : alfeñique *m fam*; debilucho *m*, -cha *f*
weakly¹ ['wi:kli] *adv* : débilmente
weakly² *adj* **weaklier; -est** : débil, enclenque
weakness ['wi:knəs] *n* **1** FEEBLENESS : debilidad *f* **2** FAULT, FLAW : flaqueza *f*, punto *m* débil

wealth [ˈwɛlθ] *n* **1** RICHES : riqueza *f* **2** PROFUSION : abundancia *f*, profusión *f*
wealthy [ˈwɛlθi] *adj* **wealthier; -est** : rico, acaudalado, adinerado
wean [ˈwi:n] *vt* **1** : destetar (a los niños o las crías) **2 to wean someone away from** : quitarle a alguien la costumbre de
weapon [ˈwɛpən] *n* : arma *f*
weaponless [ˈwɛpənləs] *adj* : desarmado
weaponry [ˈwɛpənri] *n* : armamento *m*
wear[1] [ˈwær] *v* **wore** [ˈwor]; **worn** [ˈworn]; **wearing** *vt* **1** : llevar (ropa, un reloj, etc.), calzar (zapatos) ⟨to wear a happy smile : sonreír alegremente⟩ **2** *or* **to wear away** : desgastar, erosionar (rocas, etc.) **3 to wear out** : gastar ⟨he wore out his shoes : gastó sus zapatos⟩ **4 to wear out** EXHAUST : agotar, fatigar ⟨to wear oneself out : agotarse⟩ — *vi* **1** LAST : durar **2 to wear off** DIMINISH : disminuir **3 to wear out** : gastarse
wear[2] *n* **1** USE : uso *m* ⟨for everyday wear : para todos los días⟩ **2** CLOTHING : ropa *f* ⟨children's wear : ropa de niños⟩ **3** DETERIORATION : desgaste *m* ⟨to be the worse for wear : estar deteriorado⟩
wearable [ˈwærəbəl] *adj* : que puede ponerse (dícese de una prenda)
wear and tear *n* : desgaste *m*
weariness [ˈwɪrinəs] *n* : fatiga *f*, cansancio *m*
wearisome [ˈwɪrisəm] *adj* : aburrido, pesado, cansado
weary[1] [ˈwɪri] *v* **-ried; -rying** *vt* **1** TIRE : cansar, fatigar **2** BORE : hastiar, aburrir — *vi* : cansarse
weary[2] *adj* **-rier; -est 1** TIRED : cansado **2** FED UP : harto **3** BORED : aburrido
weasel [ˈwi:zəl] *n* : comadreja *f*
weather[1] [ˈwɛðər] *vt* **1** WEAR : erosionar, desgastar **2** ENDURE : aguantar, sobrellevar, capear ⟨to weather the storm : capear el temporal⟩
weather[2] *n* : tiempo *m*
weather–beaten [ˈwɛðər,bi:tən] *adj* : curtido
weatherman [ˈwɛðər,mæn] *n, pl* **-men** [-mən, -,mɛn] METEOROLOGIST : meteorólogo *m*, -ga *f*
weatherproof [ˈwɛðər,pru:f] *adj* : que resiste a la intemperie, impermeable
weather vane → **vane**
weave[1] [ˈwi:v] *v* **wove** [ˈwo:v] *or* **weaved; woven** [ˈwo:vən] *or* **weaved; weaving** *vt* **1** : tejer (tela) **2** INTERLACE : entretejer, entrelazar **3 to weave one's way through** : abrirse camino por — *vi* **1** : tejer **2** WIND : serpentear, zigzaguear
weave[2] *n* : tejido *m*, trama *f*
weaver [ˈwi:vər] *n* : tejedor *m*, -dora *f*
web[1] [ˈwɛb] *vt* **webbed; webbing** : cubrir o proveer con una red
web[2] *n* **1** COBWEB, SPIDERWEB : telaraña *f*, tela *f* de araña **2** ENTANGLEMENT, SNARE : red *f*, enredo *m* ⟨a web of intrigue : una red de intriga⟩ **3** : membrana *f* interdigital (de aves) **4** NETWORK : red *f* ⟨a web of highways : una red de carreteras⟩ **5 the Web** : la web
webbed [ˈwɛbd] *adj* : palmeado ⟨webbed feet : patas palmeadas⟩
Web site *n* : sitio *m* web
wed [ˈwɛd] *vt* **wedded; wedding 1** MARRY : casarse con **2** UNITE : ligar, unir
we'd [ˈwi:d] (*contraction of* **we had, we should,** *or* **we would**) → **have, should, would**
wedding [ˈwɛdɪŋ] *n* : boda *f*, casamiento *m*
wedge[1] [ˈwɛʤ] *vt* **wedged; wedging 1** : apretar (con una cuña) ⟨to wedge open : mantener abierto con una cuña⟩ **2** CRAM : meter, embutir
wedge[2] *n* **1** : cuña *f* **2** PIECE : porción *f*, trozo *m*
wedlock [ˈwɛd,lɑk] → **marriage**
Wednesday [ˈwɛnz,deɪ, -di] *n* : miércoles *m*
wee [ˈwi:] *adj* : pequeño, minúsculo ⟨in the wee hours : a las altas horas⟩
weed[1] [ˈwi:d] *vt* **1** : desherbar, desyerbar **2 to weed out** : eliminar, quitar
weed[2] *n* : mala hierba *f*
weedy [ˈwi:di] *adj* **weedier; -est 1** : cubierto de malas hierbas **2** LANKY, SKINNY : flaco, larguirucho *fam*
week [ˈwi:k] *n* : semana *f*
weekday [ˈwi:k,deɪ] *n* : día *m* laborable
weekend [ˈwi:k,ɛnd] *n* : fin *m* de semana
weekly[1] [ˈwi:kli] *adv* : semanalmente
weekly[2] *adj* : semanal
weekly[3] *n, pl* **-lies** : semanario *m*
weep [ˈwi:p] *v* **wept** [ˈwɛpt]; **weeping** : llorar
weeping willow *n* : sauce *m* llorón
weepy [ˈwi:pi] *adj* **weepier; -est** : lloroso, triste
weevil [ˈwi:vəl] *n* : gorgojo *m*
weft [ˈwɛft] *n* : trama *f*
weigh [ˈweɪ] *vt* **1** : pesar **2** CONSIDER : considerar, sopesar **3 to weigh anchor** : levar anclas **4 to weigh down** : sobrecargar (con una carga), abrumar (con preocupaciones, etc.) — *vi* **1** : pesar ⟨it weighs 10 pounds : pesa 10 libras⟩ **2** COUNT : tener importancia, contar **3 to weigh on one's mind** : preocuparle a uno
weight[1] [ˈweɪt] *vt* **1** : poner peso en, sujetar con un peso **2** BURDEN : cargar, oprimir
weight[2] *n* **1** HEAVINESS : peso *m* ⟨to lose weight : bajar de peso, adelgazar⟩ **2** : peso *m* ⟨weights and measures : pesos y medidas⟩ **3** : pesa *f* ⟨to lift weights : levantar pesas⟩ **4** BURDEN : peso *m*, carga *f* ⟨to take a weight off one's mind : quitarle un peso de encima a uno⟩ **5**

IMPORTANCE : peso *m* **6** INFLUENCE : influencia *f*, autoridad *f* ⟨to throw one's weight around : hacer sentir su influencia⟩

weighty [ˈweɪt̬i] *adj* **weightier; -est** **1** HEAVY : pesado **2** IMPORTANT : importante, de peso

weird [ˈwɪrd] *adj* **1** MYSTERIOUS : misterioso **2** STRANGE : extraño, raro — **weirdly** *adv*

welcome[1] [ˈwɛlkəm] *vt* **-comed; -coming** : darle la bienvenida a, recibir

welcome[2] *adj* : bienvenido ⟨to make someone welcome : acoger bien a alguien⟩ ⟨you're welcome! : ¡de nada!, ¡no hay de qué!⟩

welcome[3] *n* : bienvenida *f*, recibimiento *m*, acogida *f*

weld[1] [ˈwɛld] *v* : soldar

weld[2] *n* : soldadura *f*

welder [ˈwɛldər] *n* : soldador *m*, -dora *f*

welfare [ˈwɛlˌfær] *n* **1** WELL-BEING : bienestar *m* **2** : asistencia *f* social

well[1] [ˈwɛl] *vi or* **to well up** : brotar, manar

well[2] *adv* **better** [ˈbɛt̬ər]; **best** [ˈbɛst] **1** RIGHTLY : bien, correctamente **2** SATISFACTORILY : bien ⟨to turn out well : resultar bien, salir bien⟩ **3** COMPLETELY : completamente ⟨well-hidden : completamente escondido⟩ **4** INTIMATELY : bien ⟨I knew him well : lo conocía bien⟩ **5** CONSIDERABLY, FAR : muy, bastante ⟨well ahead : muy adelante⟩ ⟨well before the deadline : bastante antes de la fecha⟩ **6 as well** ALSO : también **7** → **as well as**

well[3] *adj* **1** SATISFACTORY : bien ⟨all is well : todo está bien⟩ **2** DESIRABLE : conveniente ⟨it would be well if you left : sería conveniente que te fueras⟩ **3** HEALTHY : bien, sano

well[4] *n* **1** : pozo *m* (de agua, petróleo, gas, etc.), aljibe *m* (de agua) **2** SOURCE : fuente *f* ⟨a well of information : una fuente de información⟩ **3** *or* **stairwell** : caja *f*, hueco *m* (de la escalera)

well[5] *interj* **1** (*used to introduce a remark*) : bueno **2** (*used to express surprise*) : ¡vaya!

we'll [ˈwiːl, wɪl] (*contraction of* **we shall** *or* **we will**) → **shall, will**

well-balanced [ˈwɛlˈbælənst] *adj* : equilibrado

well-being [ˈwɛlˈbiːɪŋ] *n* : bienestar *m*

well-bred [ˈwɛlˈbrɛd] *adj* : fino, bien educado

well-defined [ˌwɛldiˈfaɪnd] *adj* : bien definido

well-done [ˈwɛlˈdʌn] *adj* **1** : bien hecho ⟨well-done! : ¡bravo!⟩ **2** : bien cocido

well-known [ˈwɛlˈnoːn] *adj* : famoso, bien conocido

well-meaning [ˈwɛlˈmiːnɪŋ] *adj* : bienintencionado, que tiene buenas intenciones

well-nigh [ˈwɛlˈnaɪ] *adv* : casi ⟨well-nigh impossible : casi imposible⟩

well-off [ˈwɛlˈɔf] → **well-to-do**

well-rounded [ˈwɛlˈraʊndəd] *adj* : completo, equilibrado

well-to-do [ˌwɛltəˈduː] *adj* : próspero, adinerado, rico

Welsh [ˈwɛlʃ] *n* **1** : galés *m*, galesa *f* **2** : galés *m* (idioma) — **Welsh** *adj*

welt [ˈwɛlt] *n* **1** : vira *f* (de un zapato) **2** WHEAL : verdugón *m*

welter [ˈwɛltər] *n* : fárrago *m*, revoltijo *m* ⟨a welter of data : un fárrago de datos⟩

wend [ˈwɛnd] *vi* **to wend one's way** : ponerse en camino, encaminar sus pasos

went → **go**[1]

wept → **weep**

were → **be**

we're [ˈwɪr, ˈwər, ˈwiːər] (*contraction of* **we are**) → **be**

werewolf [ˈwɪrˌwʊlf, ˈwɛr-, ˈwər-, -ˌwʌlf] *n, pl* **-wolves** [-ˌwʊlvz, -ˌwʌlvz] : hombre *m* lobo

west[1] [ˈwɛst] *adv* : al oeste

west[2] *adj* : oeste, del oeste, occidental ⟨west winds : vientos del oeste⟩

west[3] *n* **1** : oeste *m* **2 the West** : el Oeste, el Occidente

westerly [ˈwɛstərli] *adv & adj* : del oeste

western [ˈwɛstərn] *adj* **1** : Occidental, del Oeste **2** : occidental, oeste

Westerner [ˈwɛstərnər] *n* : habitante *mf* del oeste

West Indian *n* : antillano *m*, -na *f* — **West Indian** *adj*

westward [ˈwɛstwərd] *adv & adj* : hacia el oeste

wet[1] [ˈwɛt] *vt* **wet** *or* **wetted; wetting** : mojar, humedecer

wet[2] *adj* **wetter; wettest** **1** : mojado, húmedo ⟨wet clothes : ropa mojada⟩ **2** RAINY : lluvioso **3 wet paint** : pintura *f* fresca

wet[3] *n* **1** MOISTURE : humedad *f* **2** RAIN : lluvia *f*

we've [ˈwiːv] (*contraction of* **we have**) → **have**

whack[1] [ˈhwæk] *vt* : golpear (fuertemente), aporrear

whack[2] *n* **1** : golpe *m* fuerte, porrazo *m* **2** ATTEMPT : intento *m*, tentativa *f*

whale[1] [ˈhweɪl] *vi* **whaled; whaling** : cazar ballenas

whale[2] *n, pl* **whales** *or* **whale** : ballena *f*

whaleboat [ˈhweɪlˌboːt] *n* : ballenero *m*

whalebone [ˈhweɪlˌboːn] *n* : barba *f* de ballena

whaler [ˈhweɪlər] *n* **1** : ballenero *m*, -ra *f* **2** → **whaleboat**

wharf [ˈhwɔrf] *n, pl* **wharves** [ˈhwɔrvz] : muelle *m*, embarcadero *m*

what[1] [ˈhwɑt, ˈhwʌt] *adv* **1** HOW : cómo, cúanto ⟨what he suffered! : ¡cómo sufría!⟩ **2 what with** : entre ⟨what with one thing and another : entre una cosa y otra⟩

what[2] *adj* **1** (*used in questions*) : qué ⟨what more do you want? : ¿qué más quieres?⟩ ⟨what color is it? : ¿de qué color es?⟩ **2** (*used in exclamations*) : qué ⟨what an idea! : ¡qué idea!⟩ **3** ANY, WHATEVER : cualquier ⟨give what help you can : da cualquier contribución que puedas⟩

what[3] *pron* **1** (*used in direct questions*) : qué ⟨what happened? : ¿qué pasó?⟩ ⟨what does it cost? : ¿cuánto cuesta?⟩ **2** (*used in indirect statements*) : lo que, que ⟨I don't know what to do : no sé que hacer⟩ ⟨do what I tell you : haz lo que te digo⟩ **3 what for** WHY : porqué **4 what if** : y si ⟨what if he knows? : ¿y si lo sabe?⟩

whatever[1] [*h*wɑṭ'ɛvər, ˌ*h*wʌṭ-] *adj* **1** ANY : cualquier, cualquier . . . que ⟨whatever way you prefer : de cualquier manera que prefiera, como prefiera⟩ **2** (*in negative constructions*) ⟨there's no chance whatever : no hay ninguna posibilidad⟩ ⟨nothing whatever : nada en absoluto⟩

whatever[2] *pron* **1** ANYTHING : (todo) lo que ⟨I'll do whatever I want : haré lo que quiera⟩ **2** (*no matter what*) ⟨whatever it may be : sea lo que sea⟩ **3** WHAT : qué ⟨whatever do you mean? : ¿qué quieres decir?⟩

whatsoever[1] [ˌ*h*wɑtso'ɛvər, ˌ*h*wʌṭ-] *adj* → **whatever**[1]

whatsoever[2] *pron* → **whatever**[2]

wheal ['*h*wi:l] *n* : verdugón *m*

wheat ['*h*wi:t] *n* : trigo *m*

wheaten ['*h*wi:tən] *adj* : de trigo

wheedle ['*h*wi:dəl] *vt* **-dled; -dling** CAJOLE : engatusar ⟨to wheedle something out of someone : sonsacarle algo a alguien⟩

wheel[1] ['*h*wi:l] *vt* : empujar (una bicicleta, etc.), mover (algo sobre ruedas) — *vi* **1** ROTATE : girar, rotar **2 to wheel around** TURN : darse la vuelta

wheel[2] *n* **1** : rueda *f* **2** *or* **steering wheel** : volante *m* (de automóviles, etc.), timón *m* (de barcos o aviones) **3 wheels** *npl* : maquinaria *f*, fuerza *f* impulsora ⟨the wheels of government : la maquinaria del gobierno⟩

wheelbarrow ['*h*wi:lˌbærˌo:] *n* : carretilla *f*

wheelchair ['*h*wi:lˌʧær] *n* : silla *f* de ruedas

wheeze[1] ['*h*wi:z] *vi* **wheezed; wheezing** : resollar, respirar con dificultad

wheeze[2] *n* : resuello *m*

whelk ['*h*wɛlk] *n* : buccino *m*

whelp[1] ['*h*wɛlp] *vi* : parir

whelp[2] *n* : cachorro *m*, -rra *f*

when[1] ['*h*wɛn] *adv* : cuándo ⟨when will you return? : ¿cuándo volverás?⟩ ⟨he asked me when I would be home : me preguntó cuándo estaría en casa⟩

when[2] *conj* **1** (*referring to a particular time*) : cuando, en que ⟨when you are ready : cuando estés listo⟩ ⟨the days when I clean the house : los días en que limpio la casa⟩ **2** IF : cuando, si ⟨how can I go when I have no money? : ¿cómo voy a ir si no tengo dinero?⟩ **3** ALTHOUGH : cuando ⟨you said it was big when actually it's small : dijiste que era grande cuando en realidad es pequeño⟩

when[3] *pron* : cuándo ⟨since when are you the boss? : ¿desde cuándo eres el jefe?⟩

whence ['*h*wɛnts] *adv* : de donde

whenever[1] [*h*wɛn'vər] *adv* **1** : cuando sea ⟨tomorrow or whenever : mañana o cuando sea⟩ **2** (*in questions*) : cuándo

whenever[2] *conj* **1** : siempre que, cada vez que ⟨whenever I go, I'm disappointed : siempre que voy, quedo desilusionado⟩ **2** WHEN : cuando ⟨whenever you like : cuando quieras⟩

where[1] ['*h*wɛr] *adv* : dónde, adónde ⟨where is he? : ¿dónde está?⟩ ⟨where did they go? : ¿adónde fueron?⟩

where[2] *conj* : donde, adonde ⟨she knows where the house is : sabe donde está la casa⟩ ⟨she goes where she likes : va adonde quiera⟩

where[3] *pron* : donde ⟨Chicago is where I live : Chicago es donde vivo⟩

whereabouts[1] ['*h*wɛrəˌbaʊts] *adv* : dónde, por dónde ⟨whereabouts is the house? : ¿dónde está la casa?⟩

whereabouts[2] *ns & pl* : paradero *m*

whereas [*h*wɛr'æz] *conj* **1** : considerando que (usado en documentos legales) **2** : mientras que ⟨I like the white one whereas she prefers the black : me gusta el blanco mientras que ella prefiere el negro⟩

whereby [*h*wɛr'baɪ] *adv* : por lo cual

wherefore ['*h*wɛrˌfor] *adv* : por qué

wherein [*h*wɛr'ɪn] *adv* : en el cual, en el que

whereof [*h*wɛr'ʌv, -ɑv] *conj* : de lo cual

whereupon ['*h*wɛrəˌpɑn, -ˌpɔn] *conj* : con lo cual, después de lo cual

wherever[1] [*h*wɛr'ɛvər] *adv* **1** WHERE : dónde, adónde **2** : en cualquier parte ⟨or wherever : o donde sea⟩

wherever[2] *conj* : dondequiera que, donde sea ⟨wherever you go : dondequiera que vayas⟩

wherewithal ['*h*wɛrwɪˌðɔl, -ˌθɔl] *n* : medios *mpl*, recursos *mpl*

whet ['*h*wɛt] *vt* **whetted; whetting** **1** SHARPEN : afilar **2** STIMULATE : estimular ⟨to whet the appetite : estimular el apetito⟩

whether ['*h*wɛðər] *conj* **1** : si ⟨I don't know whether it is finished : no sé si está acabado⟩ ⟨we doubt whether he'll show up : dudamos que aparezca⟩ **2** (*used in comparisons*) ⟨whether I like it or not : tanto si quiero como si no⟩ ⟨whether he comes or he doesn't : venga o no⟩

whetstone ['*h*wɛtˌsto:n] *n* : piedra *f* de afilar

whey ['*h*weɪ] *n* : suero *m* (de la leche)

which[1] ['*h*wɪʧ] *adj* : qué, cuál ⟨which tie do you prefer? : ¿cuál corbata prefieres?⟩ ⟨which ones? : ¿cuáles?⟩ ⟨tell me which house is yours : dime qué casa es la tuya⟩

which[2] *pron* **1** : cuál ⟨which is the right answer? : ¿cuál es la respuesta correcta?⟩ **2** : que, el (la) cual ⟨the cup which broke : la taza que se quebró⟩ ⟨the house, which is made of brick : la casa, la cual es de ladrillo⟩

whichever[1] [*h*wɪʧˈɛvər] *adj* : el (la) que, cualquiera que ⟨whichever book you like : cualquier libro que te guste⟩

whichever[2] *pron* : el (la) que, cualquiera que ⟨take whichever you want : toma el que quieras⟩ ⟨whichever I choose : cualquiera que elija⟩

whiff[1] [ˈ*h*wɪf] *v* PUFF : soplar

whiff[2] *n* **1** PUFF : soplo *m*, ráfaga *f* **2** SNIFF : olor *m* **3** HINT : dejo *m*, pizca *f*

while[1] [ˈ*h*waɪl] *vt* **whiled; whiling** : pasar ⟨to while away the time : matar el tiempo⟩

while[2] *n* **1** TIME : rato *m*, tiempo *m* ⟨after a while : después de un rato⟩ ⟨in a while : dentro de poco⟩ **2 to be worth one's while** : valer la pena

while[3] *conj* **1** : mientras ⟨whistle while you work : silba mientras trabajas⟩ **2** WHEREAS : mientras que **3** ALTHOUGH : aunque ⟨while it's very good, it's not perfect : aunque es muy bueno, no es perfecto⟩

whim [ˈ*h*wɪm] *n* : capricho *m*, antojo *m*

whimper[1] [ˈ*h*wɪmpər] *vi* : lloriquear, gimotear

whimper[2] *n* : quejido *m*

whimsical [ˈ*h*wɪmzɪkəl] *adj* **1** CAPRICIOUS : caprichoso, fantasioso **2** ERRATIC : errático — **whimsically** *adv*

whine[1] [ˈ*h*waɪn] *vi* **whined; whining** **1** : lloriquear, gimotear, gemir **2** COMPLAIN : quejarse

whine[2] *n* : quejido *m*, gemido *m*

whinny[1] [ˈ*h*wɪni] *vi* **-nied; -nying** : relinchar

whinny[2] *n, pl* **-nies** : relincho *m*

whip[1] [ˈ*h*wɪp] *v* **whipped; whipping** *vt* **1** SNATCH : sacar (rápidamente), arrebatar ⟨she whipped the cloth off the table : arrebató el mantel de la mesa⟩ **2** LASH : azotar **3** DEFEAT : vencer, derrotar **4** INCITE : incitar, despertar ⟨to whip up enthusiasm : despertar el entusiasmo⟩ **5** BEAT : batir (huevos, crema, etc.) — *vi* FLAP : agitarse

whip[2] *n* **1** : látigo *m*, azote *m*, fusta *f* (de jinete) **2** : miembro *m* de un cuerpo legislativo encargado de disciplina

whiplash [ˈ*h*wɪpˌlæʃ] *n or* **whiplash injury** : traumatismo *m* cervical

whippet [ˈ*h*wɪpət] *n* : galgo *m* pequeño, galgo *m* inglés

whir[1] [ˈ*h*wər] *vi* **whirred; whirring** : zumbar

whir[2] *n* : zumbido *m*

whirl[1] [ˈ*h*wərl] *vi* **1** SPIN : dar vueltas, girar ⟨my head is whirling : la cabeza me está dando vueltas⟩ **2 to whirl about** : arremolinarse, moverse rápidamente

whirl[2] *n* **1** SPIN : giro *m*, vuelta *f*, remolino *m* (dícese del polvo, etc.) **2** BUSTLE : bullicio *m*, torbellino *m* (de actividad, etc.) **3 to give it a whirl** : intentar hacer, probar

whirlpool [ˈ*h*wərlˌpu:l] *n* : vorágine *f*, remolino *m*

whirlwind [ˈ*h*wərlˌwɪnd] *n* : remolino *m*, torbellino *m*, tromba *f*

whisk[1] [ˈ*h*wɪsk] *vt* **1** : llevar ⟨she whisked the children off to bed : llevó a los niños a la cama⟩ **2** : batir ⟨to whisk eggs : batir huevos⟩ **3 to whisk away** *or* **to whisk off** : sacudir

whisk[2] *n* **1** WHISKING : sacudida *f* (movimiento) **2** : batidor *m* (para batir huevos, etc.)

whisk broom *n* : escobilla *f*

whisker [ˈ*h*wɪskər] *n* **1** : pelo *m* (de la barba o el bigote) **2 whiskers** *npl* : bigotes *mpl* (de animales)

whiskey *or* **whisky** [ˈ*h*wɪski] *n, pl* **-keys** *or* **-kies** : whisky *m*

whisper[1] [ˈ*h*wɪspər] *vi* : cuchichear, susurrar — *vt* : decir en voz baja, susurrar

whisper[2] *n* **1** WHISPERING : susurro *m*, cuchicheo *m* **2** RUMOR : rumor *m* **3** TRACE : dejo *m*, pizca *f*

whistle[1] [ˈ*h*wɪsəl] *v* **-tled; -tling** *vi* : silbar, chiflar, pitar (dícese de un tren, etc.) — *vt* : silbar ⟨to whistle a tune : silbar una melodía⟩

whistle[2] *n* **1** WHISTLING : chiflido *m*, silbido *m* **2** : silbato *m*, pito *m* (instrumento)

whit [ˈ*h*wɪt] *n* BIT : ápice *m*, pizca *f*

white[1] [ˈ*h*waɪt] *adj* **whiter; -est** : blanco

white[2] *n* **1** : blanco *m* (color) **2** : clara *f* (de huevos) **3** *or* **white person** : blanco *m*, -ca *f*

white blood cell *n* : glóbulo *m* blanco

whitecaps [ˈ*h*waɪtˌkæps] *npl* : cabrillas *fpl*

white–collar [ˈ*h*waɪtˈkɑlər] *adj* **1** : de oficina **2 white–collar worker** : oficinista *mf*

whitefish [ˈ*h*waɪtˌfɪʃ] *n* : pescado *m* blanco

whiten [ˈ*h*waɪtən] *vt* : blanquear — *vi* : ponerse blanco

whiteness [ˈ*h*waɪtnəs] *n* : blancura *f*

white–tailed deer [ˈ*h*waɪtˈteɪld] *n* : ciervo *f* de Virginia

whitewash[1] [ˈ*h*waɪtˌwɔʃ] *vt* **1** : enjalbegar, blanquear ⟨to whitewash a fence : enjalbegar una valla⟩ **2** CONCEAL : encubrir (un escándalo, etc.)

whitewash[2] *n* **1** : jalbegue *m*, lechada *f* **2** COVER-UP : encubrimiento *m*

whither [ˈ*h*wɪðər] *adv* : adónde

whiting [ˈ*h*waɪt̬ɪŋ] *n* : merluza *f*, pescadilla *f* (pez)

whitish [ˈ*h*waɪt̬ɪʃ] *adj* : blancuzco

whittle [ˈ*h*wɪt̬əl] *vt* **-tled; -tling** **1** : tallar (madera) **2 to whittle down** : reducir, recortar ⟨to whittle down expenses : reducir los gastos⟩

whiz[1] *or* **whizz** [ˈ*h*wɪz] *vi* **whizzed; whizzing 1** BUZZ : zumbar **2 to whiz by** : pasar muy rápido, pasar volando

whiz[2] *or* **whizz** *n, pl* **whizzes 1** BUZZ : zumbido *m* **2 to be a whiz** : ser un prodigio, ser muy hábil

who [ˈhuː] *pron* **1** (*used in direct and indirect questions*) : quién ⟨who is that? : ¿quién es ése?⟩ ⟨who did it? : ¿quién lo hizo?⟩ ⟨we know who they are : sabemos quiénes son⟩ **2** (*used in relative clauses*) : que, quien ⟨the lady who lives there : la señora que vive allí⟩ ⟨for those who wait : para los que esperan, para quienes esperan⟩

whodunit [huːˈdʌnɪt] *n* : novela *f* policíaca

whoever [huːˈɛvər] *pron* **1** : quienquiera que, quien ⟨whoever did it : quienquiera que lo hizo⟩ ⟨give it to whoever you want : dalo a quien quieras⟩ **2** (*used in questions*) : quién ⟨whoever could that be? : ¿quién podría ser?⟩

whole[1] [ˈhoːl] *adj* **1** UNHURT : ileso **2** INTACT : intacto, sano **3** ENTIRE : entero, íntegro ⟨the whole island : toda la isla⟩ ⟨whole milk : leche entera⟩ **4 a whole lot** : muchísimo

whole[2] *n* **1** : todo *m* **2 as a whole** : en conjunto **3 on the whole** : en general

wholehearted [ˈhoːlˈhɑrt̬əd] *adj* : sin reservas, incondicional

whole number *n* : entero *m*

wholesale[1] [ˈhoːlˌseɪl] *v* **-saled; -saling** *vt* : vender al por mayor — *vi* : venderse al por mayor

wholesale[2] *adv* : al por mayor

wholesale[3] *adj* **1** : al por mayor ⟨wholesale grocer : tendero al por mayor⟩ **2** TOTAL : total, absoluto ⟨wholesale slaughter : matanza sistemática⟩

wholesale[4] *n* : mayoreo *m*

wholesaler [ˈhoːlˌseɪlər] *n* : mayorista *mf*

wholesome [ˈhoːlsəm] *adj* **1** : sano ⟨wholesome advice : consejo sano⟩ **2** HEALTHY : sano, saludable

whole wheat *adj* : de trigo integral

wholly [ˈhoːli] *adv* **1** COMPLETELY : completamente **2** SOLELY : exclusivamente, únicamente

whom [ˈhuːm] *pron* **1** (*used in direct questions*) : a quién ⟨whom did you choose? : ¿a quién elegiste?⟩ **2** (*used in indirect questions*) : de quién, con quién, en quién ⟨I don't know whom to consult : no sé con quién consultar⟩ **3** (*used in relative clauses*) : que, a quien ⟨the lawyer whom I recommended to you : el abogado que te recomendé⟩

whomever [huːmˈɛvər] *pron* WHOEVER : quienquiera, quien ⟨marry whomever you please : cásate con quien quieras⟩

whoop[1] [ˈ*h*wuːp, ˈ*h*wʊp] *vi* : gritar, chillar

whoop[2] *n* : grito *m*

whooping cough *n* : tos *f* ferina

whopper [ˈ*h*wɑpər] *n* **1** : cosa *f* enorme **2** LIE : mentira *f* colosal

whopping [ˈ*h*wɑpɪŋ] *adj* : enorme

whore [ˈhor] *n* : puta *f*, ramera *f*

whorl [ˈ*h*wɔrl, ˈ*h*wərl] *n* : espiral *f*, espira *f* (de una concha), línea *f* (de una huella digital)

whose[1] [ˈhuːz] *adj* **1** (*used in questions*) : de quién ⟨whose truck is that? : ¿de quién es ese camión?⟩ **2** (*used in relative clauses*) : cuyo ⟨the person whose work is finished : la persona cuyo trabajo está terminado⟩

whose[2] *pron* : de quién ⟨tell me whose it was : dime de quién era⟩

why[1] [ˈ*h*waɪ] *adv* : por qué ⟨why did you do it? : ¿por qué lo hizo?⟩

why[2] *n, pl* **whys** REASON : porqué *m*, razón *f*

why[3] *conj* : por qué ⟨I know why he left : yo sé por qué salió⟩ ⟨there's no reason why it should exist : no hay razón para que exista⟩

why[4] *interj* (*used to express surprise*) : ¡vaya!, ¡mira!

wick [ˈwɪk] *n* : mecha *f*

wicked [ˈwɪkəd] *adj* **1** EVIL : malo, malvado **2** MISCHIEVOUS : travieso, pícaro ⟨a wicked grin : una sonrisa traviesa⟩ **3** TERRIBLE : terrible, horrible ⟨a wicked storm : una tormenta horrible⟩

wickedly [ˈwɪkədli] *adv* : con maldad

wickedness [ˈwɪkədnəs] *n* : maldad *f*

wicker[1] [ˈwɪkər] *adj* : de mimbre

wicker[2] *n* **1** : mimbre *m* **2** → **wickerwork**

wickerwork [ˈwɪkərˌwərk] *n* : artículos *mpl* de mimbre

wicket [ˈwɪkət] *n* **1** WINDOW : ventanilla *f* **2** *or* **wicket gate** : postigo *m* **3** : aro *m* (en croquet), palos *mpl* (en críquet)

wide[1] [ˈwaɪd] *adv* **wider; widest 1** WIDELY : por todas partes ⟨to travel far and wide : viajar por todas partes⟩ **2** COMPLETELY : completamente, totalmente ⟨wide open : abierto de par en par⟩ **3 wide apart** : muy separados

wide[2] *adj* **wider; widest 1** VAST : vasto, extensivo ⟨a wide area : una área extensiva⟩ **2** : ancho ⟨three meters wide : tres metros de ancho⟩ **3** BROAD : ancho, amplio **4** *or* **wide–open** : muy abierto **5 wide of the mark** : desviado, lejos del blanco

wide–awake [ˈwaɪdəˈweɪk] *adj* : (completamente) despierto

wide–eyed [ˈwaɪdˈaɪd] *adj* **1** : con los ojos muy abiertos **2** NAIVE : inocente, ingenuo

widely [ˈwaɪdli] *adv* : extensivamente, por todas partes

widen [ˈwaɪdən] *vt* : ampliar, ensanchar — *vi* : ampliarse, ensancharse

widespread [ˈwaɪdˈsprɛd] *adj* : extendido, extenso, difuso

widow[1] [ˈwɪˌdoː] *vt* : dejar viuda ⟨to be widowed : enviudar⟩

widow[2] *n* : viuda *f*

widower ['wɪdowər] *n* : viudo *m*
width ['wɪdθ] *n* : ancho *m*, anchura *f*
wield ['wi:ld] *vt* **1** USE : usar, manejar ⟨to wield a broom : usar una escoba⟩ **2** EXERCISE : ejercer ⟨to wield influence : influir⟩
wiener ['wi:nər] → **frankfurter**
wife ['waɪf] *n, pl* **wives** ['waɪvz] : esposa *f*, mujer *f*
wifely ['waɪfli] *adj* : de esposa, conyugal
wig ['wɪg] *n* : peluca *f*
wiggle[1] ['wɪgəl] *v* **-gled; -gling** *vt* : menear, contonear ⟨to wiggle one's hips : contonearse⟩ — *vi* : menearse
wiggle[2] *n* : meneo *m*, contoneo *m*
wiggly ['wɪgəli] *adj* **-glier; -est 1** : que se menea **2** WAVY : ondulado
wigwag ['wɪg,wæg] *vi* **-wagged; -wagging** : comunicar por señales
wigwam ['wɪg,wɑm] *n* : wigwam *m*
wild[1] ['waɪld] *adv* **1** → **wildly 2 to run wild** : descontrolarse
wild[2] *adj* **1** : salvaje, silvestre, cimarrón ⟨wild horses : caballos salvajes⟩ ⟨wild rice : arroz silvestre⟩ **2** DESOLATE : yermo, agreste **3** UNRULY : desenfrenado **4** CRAZY : loco, fantástico ⟨wild ideas : ideas locas⟩ **5** BARBAROUS : salvaje, bárbaro **6** ERRATIC : errático ⟨a wild throw : un tiro errático⟩
wild[3] *n* → **wilderness**
wild card *n* **1** : factor *m* desconocido **2** : comodín *m* (carta o símbolo)
wildcat ['waɪld,kæt] *n* **1** : gato *m* montés **2** BOBCAT : lince *m* rojo
wilderness ['wɪldərnəs] *n* : yermo *m*, desierto *m*
wildfire ['waɪld,faɪr] *n* **1** : fuego *m* descontrolado **2 to spread like wildfire** : propagarse como un reguero de pólvora
wildflower ['waɪld,flaʊər] *n* : flor *f* silvestre
wildfowl ['waɪld,faʊl] *n* : ave *f* de caza
wildlife ['waɪld,laɪf] *n* : fauna *f*
wildly ['waɪldli] *adv* **1** FRANTICALLY : frenéticamente, como un loco **2** EXTREMELY : extremadamente ⟨wildly happy : loco de felicidad⟩
wile[1] ['waɪl] *vt* **wiled; wiling** LURE : atraer
wile[2] *n* : ardid *m*, artimaña *f*
will[1] ['wɪl] *v, past* **would** ['wʊd]; *pres sing & pl* **will** *vt* WISH : querer ⟨do what you will : haz lo que quieras⟩ — *v aux* **1** (*expressing willingness*) ⟨no one would take the job : nadie aceptaría el trabajo⟩ ⟨I won't do it : no lo haré⟩ **2** (*expressing habitual action*) ⟨he will get angry over nothing : se pone furioso por cualquier cosa⟩ **3** (*forming the future tense*) ⟨tomorrow we will go shopping : mañana iremos de compras⟩ **4** (*expressing capacity*) ⟨the couch will hold three people : en el sofá cabrán tres personas⟩ **5** (*expressing determination*) ⟨I will go despite them : iré a pesar de ellos⟩ **6** (*expressing probability*) ⟨that will be the mailman : eso ha de ser el cartero⟩ **7** (*expressing inevitability*) ⟨accidents will happen : los accidentes ocurrirán⟩ **8** (*expressing a command*) ⟨you will do as I say : harás lo que digo⟩
will[2] *vt* **1** ORDAIN : disponer, decretar ⟨if God wills it : si Dios lo dispone, si Dios quiere⟩ **2** : lograr a fuerza de voluntad ⟨they were willing him to succeed : estaban deseando que tuviera éxito⟩ **3** BEQUEATH : legar
will[3] *n* **1** DESIRE : deseo *m*, voluntad *f* **2** VOLITION : voluntad *f* ⟨free will : libre albedrío⟩ **3** WILLPOWER : voluntad *f*, fuerza *f* de voluntad ⟨a will of iron : una voluntad férrea⟩ **4** : testamento *m* ⟨to make a will : hacer testamento⟩
willful *or* **wilful** ['wɪlfəl] *adj* **1** OBSTINATE : obstinado, terco **2** INTENTIONAL : intencionado, deliberado — **willfully** *adv*
willing ['wɪlɪŋ] *adj* **1** INCLINED, READY : listo, dispuesto **2** OBLIGING : servicial, complaciente
willingly ['wɪlɪŋli] *adv* : con gusto
willingness ['wɪlɪŋnəs] *n* : buena voluntad *f*
willow ['wɪ,lo:] *n* : sauce *m*
willowy ['wɪlowi] *adj* : esbelto
willpower ['wɪl,paʊər] *n* : voluntad *f*, fuerza *f* de voluntad
wilt ['wɪlt] *vi* **1** : marchitarse (dícese de las flores) **2** LANGUISH : debilitarse, languidecer
wily ['waɪli] *adj* **wilier; -est** : artero, astuto
wimp ['wɪmp] *n* **1** COWARD : gallina *f*, cobarde *mf* **2** WEAKLING : debilucho *m*, -cha *f*, alfeñique *m*
win[1] ['wɪn] *v* **won** ['wʌn]; **winning** *vi* : ganar — *vt* **1** : ganar, conseguir **2 to win over** : ganarse a **3 to win someone's heart** : conquistar a alguien
win[2] *n* : triunfo *m*, victoria *f*
wince[1] ['wɪn*t*s] *vi* **winced; wincing** : estremecerse, hacer una mueca de dolor
wince[2] *n* : mueca *f* de dolor
winch ['wɪntʃ] *n* : torno *m*
wind[1] ['wɪnd] *vt* : dejar sin aliento ⟨to be winded : quedarse sin aliento⟩
wind[2] ['waɪnd] *v* **wound** ['waʊnd]; **winding** *vi* MEANDER : serpentear — *vt* **1** COIL, ROLL : envolver, enrollar **2** TURN : hacer girar ⟨to wind a clock : darle cuerda a un reloj⟩
wind[3] ['wɪnd] *n* **1** : viento *m* ⟨against the wind : contra el viento⟩ **2** BREATH : aliento *m* **3** FLATULENCE : flatulencia *f*, ventosidad *f* **4 to get wind of** : enterarse de
wind[4] ['waɪnd] *n* **1** TURN : vuelta *f* **2** BEND : recodo *m*, curva *f*
windbreak ['wɪnd,breɪk] *n* : barrera *f* contra el viento, abrigadero *m*
windfall ['wɪnd,fɔl] *n* **1** : fruta *f* caída **2** : beneficio *m* imprevisto
wind instrument *n* : instrumento *m* de viento

windlass [ˈwɪndləs] *n* : cabrestante *m*
windmill [ˈwɪndˌmɪl] *n* : molino *m* de viento
window [ˈwɪnˌdo:] *n* **1** : ventana *f* (de un edificio o una computadora), ventanilla *f* (de un vehículo o avión), vitrina *f* (de una tienda) **2** → **windowpane**
windowpane [ˈwɪnˌdo:ˌpeɪn] *n* : vidrio *m*
window–shop [ˈwɪndoˌʃɑp] *vi* **-shopped; -shopping** : mirar las vitrinas
windpipe [ˈwɪndˌpaɪp] *n* : tráquea *f*
windshield [ˈwɪndˌʃi:ld] *n* **1** : parabrisas *m* **2 windshield wiper** : limpiaparabrisas *m*
windup [ˈwaɪndˌʌp] *n* : conclusión *f*
wind up *vt* END : terminar, concluir — *vi* : terminar, acabar
windward[1] [ˈwɪndwərd] *adj* : de barlovento
windward[2] *n* : barlovento *m*
windy [ˈwɪndi] *adj* **windier; -est** **1** : ventoso ⟨it's windy : hace viento⟩ **2** VERBOSE : verboso, prolijo
wine[1] [ˈwaɪn] *v* **wined; wining** *vi* : beber vino — *vt* **to wine and dine** : agasajar
wine[2] *n* : vino *m*
wing[1] [ˈwɪŋ] *vi* FLY : volar
wing[2] *n* **1** : ala *f* (de un ave, un avión, o un edificio) **2** FACTION : ala *f* ⟨the right wing of the party : el ala derecha del partido⟩ **3 wings** *npl* : bastidores *mpl* (de un teatro) **4 on the wing** : al vuelo, volando **5 under one's wing** : bajo el cargo de uno
winged [ˈwɪŋd, ˈwɪŋəd] *adj* : alado
wink[1] [ˈwɪŋk] *vi* **1** : guiñar el ojo **2** BLINK : pestañear, parpadear **3** FLICKER : parpadear, titilar
wink[2] *n* **1** : guiño *m* (del ojo) **2** NAP : siesta *f* ⟨not to sleep a wink : no pegar el ojo⟩
winner [ˈwɪnər] *n* : ganador *m*, -dora *f*
winning [ˈwɪnɪŋ] *adj* **1** VICTORIOUS : ganador **2** CHARMING : encantador
winnings [ˈwɪnɪŋz] *npl* : ganancias *fpl*
winnow [ˈwɪˌno:] *vt* : aventar (el grano, etc.)
winsome [ˈwɪnsəm] *adj* CHARMING : encantador
winter[1] [ˈwɪntər] *adj* : invernal, de invierno
winter[2] *n* : invierno *m*
wintergreen [ˈwɪntərˌgri:n] *n* : gaulteria *f*
wintertime [ˈwɪntərˌtaɪm] *n* : invierno *m*
wintry [ˈwɪntri] *adj* **wintrier; -est** **1** WINTER : invernal, de invierno **2** COLD : frío ⟨she gave us a wintry greeting : nos saludó fríamente⟩
wipe[1] [ˈwaɪp] *vt* **wiped; wiping** **1** : limpiar, pasarle un trapo a ⟨to wipe one's feet : limpiarse los pies⟩ **2 to wipe away** : enjugar (lágrimas), borrar (una memoria) **3 to wipe out** ANNIHILATE : aniquilar, destruir
wipe[2] *n* : pasada *f* (con un trapo, etc.)
wire[1] [ˈwaɪr] *vt* **wired; wiring** **1** : instalar el cableado en (una casa, etc.) **2** BIND : atar con alambre **3** TELEGRAPH : telegrafiar, mandarle un telegrama (a alguien)
wire[2] *n* **1** : alambre *m* ⟨barbed wire : alambre de púas⟩ **2** : cable *m* (eléctrico o telefónico) **3** CABLEGRAM, TELEGRAM : telegrama *m*, cable *m*
wireless [ˈwaɪrləs] *adj* : inalámbrico
wiretapping [ˈwaɪrˌtæpɪŋ] *n* : intervención *f* electrónica
wiring [ˈwaɪrɪŋ] *n* : cableado *m*
wiry [ˈwaɪri] *adj* **wirier; -est** **1** : hirsuto, tieso (dícese del pelo) **2** : esbelto y musculoso (dícese del cuerpo)
wisdom [ˈwɪzdəm] *n* **1** KNOWLEDGE : sabiduría *f* **2** JUDGMENT, SENSE : sensatez *f*
wisdom tooth *n* : muela *f* de juicio
wise[1] [ˈwaɪz] *adj* **wiser; wisest** **1** LEARNED : sabio **2** SENSIBLE : sabio, sensato, prudente **3** KNOWLEDGEABLE : entendido, enterado ⟨they're wise to his tricks : conocen muy bien sus mañas⟩
wise[2] *n* : manera *f*, modo *m* ⟨in no wise : de ninguna manera⟩
wisecrack [ˈwaɪzˌkræk] *n* : broma *f*, chiste *m*
wisely [ˈwaɪzli] *adv* : sabiamente, sensatamente
wish[1] [ˈwɪʃ] *vt* **1** WANT : desear, querer **2 to wish (something) for** : desear ⟨they wished me well : me desearon lo mejor⟩ — *vi* **1** : pedir (como deseo) **2** : querer ⟨as you wish : como quieras⟩
wish[2] *n* **1** : deseo *m* ⟨to grant a wish : conceder un deseo⟩ **2 wishes** *npl* : saludos *mpl*, recuerdos *mpl* ⟨to send best wishes : mandar muchos recuerdos⟩
wishbone [ˈwɪʃˌbo:n] *n* : espoleta *f*
wishful [ˈwɪʃfəl] *adj* **1** HOPEFUL : deseoso, lleno de esperanza **2 wishful thinking** : ilusiones *fpl*
wishy–washy [ˈwɪʃiˌwɔʃi, -ˌwɑʃi] *adj* : insípido, soso
wisp [ˈwɪsp] *n* **1** BUNCH : manojo *m* (de paja) **2** STRAND : mechón *m* (de pelo) **3** : voluta *f* (de humo)
wispy [ˈwɪspi] *adj* **wispier; -est** : tenue, ralo (dícese del pelo)
wisteria [wɪsˈtɪriə] *n* : glicinia *f*
wistful [ˈwɪstfəl] *adj* : añorante, anhelante, melancólico — **wistfully** *adv*
wistfulness [ˈwɪstfəlnəs] *n* : añoranza *f*, melancolía *f*
wit [ˈwɪt] *n* **1** INTELLIGENCE : inteligencia *f* **2** CLEVERNESS : ingenio *m*, gracia *f*, agudeza *f* **3** HUMOR : humorismo *m* **4** JOKER : chistoso *m*, -sa *f* **5 wits** *npl* : razón *f*, buen juicio *m* ⟨scared out of one's wits : muerto de miedo⟩ ⟨to be at one's wits' end : estar desesperado⟩
witch [ˈwɪʧ] *n* : bruja *f*
witchcraft [ˈwɪʧˌkræft] *n* : brujería *f*, hechicería *f*

witch doctor *n* : hechicero *m*, -ra *f*
witchery [ˈwɪtʃəri] *n, pl* **-eries** 1 → **witchcraft** 2 CHARM : encanto *m*
witch–hunt [ˈwɪtʃˌhʌnt] *n* : caza *f* de brujas
with [ˈwɪð, ˈwɪθ] *prep* 1 : con ⟨I'm going with you : voy contigo⟩ ⟨coffee with milk : café con leche⟩ 2 AGAINST : con ⟨to argue with someone : discutir con alguien⟩ 3 (*used in descriptions*) : con, de ⟨the girl with red hair : la muchacha de pelo rojo⟩ 4 (*indicating manner, means, or cause*) : con ⟨to cut with a knife : cortar con un cuchillo⟩ ⟨fix it with tape : arréglalo con cinta⟩ ⟨with luck : consuerte⟩ 5 DESPITE : a pesar de, aún con ⟨with all his work, the business failed : a pesar de su trabajo, el negocio fracasó⟩ 6 REGARDING : con respecto a, con ⟨the trouble with your plan : el problema con su plan⟩ 7 ACCORDING TO : según ⟨it varies with the season : varía según la estación⟩ 8 (*indicating support or understanding*) : con ⟨I'm with you all the way : estoy contigo hasta el fin⟩
withdraw [wɪðˈdrɔ, wɪθ-] *v* **-drew** [-ˈdruː]; **-drawn** [-ˈdrɔn]; **-drawing** *vt* 1 REMOVE : retirar, apartar, sacar (dinero) 2 RETRACT : retractarse de — *vi* : retirarse, recluirse (de la sociedad)
withdrawal [wɪðˈdrɔəl, wɪθ-] *n* 1 : retirada *f*, retiro *m* (de fondos, etc.), retraimiento *m* (social) 2 RETRACTION : retractación *f* 3 **withdrawal symptoms** : síndrome *m* de abstinencia
withdrawn [wɪðˈdrɔn, wɪθ-] *adj* : retraído, reservado, introvertido
wither [ˈwɪðər] *vt* : marchitar, agostar — *vi* 1 WILT : marchitarse 2 WEAKEN : decaer, debilitarse
withhold [wɪθˈhoːld, wɪð-] *vt* **-held** [-ˈhld]; **-holding** : retener (fondos), aplazar (una decisión), negar (permiso, etc.)
within[1] [wɪðˈɪn, wɪθ-] *adv* : dentro
within[2] *prep* 1 : dentro de ⟨within the limits : dentro de los límites⟩ 2 (*in expressions of distance*) : a menos de ⟨within 10 miles of the ocean : a menos de 10 millas del mar⟩ 3 (*in expressions of time*) : dentro de ⟨within an hour : dentro de una hora⟩ ⟨within a month of her birthday : a poco menos de un mes de su cumpleaños⟩
without[1] [wɪðˈaʊt, wɪθ-] *adv* 1 OUTSIDE : fuera 2 **to do without** : pasar sin algo
without[2] *prep* 1 OUTSIDE : fuera de 2 : sin ⟨without fear : sin temor⟩ ⟨he left without his briefcase : se fue sin su portafolios⟩
withstand [wɪθˈstænd, wɪð-] *vt* **-stood** [-ˈstʊd]; **-standing** 1 BEAR : aguantar, soportar 2 RESIST : resistir, resistirse a
witless [ˈwɪtləs] *adj* : estúpido, tonto
witness[1] [ˈwɪtnəs] *vt* 1 SEE : presenciar, ver, ser testigo de 2 : atestiguar (una firma, etc.) — *vi* TESTIFY : atestiguar, testimoniar
witness[2] *n* 1 TESTIMONY : testimonio *m* ⟨to bear witness : atestiguar, testimoniar⟩ 2 : testigo *mf* ⟨witness for the prosecution : testigo de cargo⟩
witticism [ˈwɪt̬əˌsɪzəm] *n* : agudeza *f*, ocurrencia *f*
witty [ˈwɪt̬i] *adj* **-tier; -est** : ingenioso, ocurrente, gracioso
wives → **wife**
wizard [ˈwɪzərd] *n* 1 SORCERER : mago *m*, brujo *m*, hechicero *m* 2 : genio *m* ⟨a math wizard : un genio en matemáticas⟩
wizened [ˈwɪzənd, ˈwiː-] *adj* : arrugado, marchito
wobble[1] [ˈwɑbəl] *vi* **-bled; -bling** : bambolearse, tambalearse, temblar (dícese de la voz)
wobble[2] *n* : tambaleo *m*, bamboleo *m*
wobbly [ˈwɑbəli] *adj* : bamboleante, tambaleante, inestable
woe [ˈwoː] *n* 1 GRIEF, MISFORTUNE : desgracia *f*, infortunio *m*, aflicción *f* 2 **woes** *npl* TROUBLES : penas *fpl*, males *mpl*
woeful [ˈwoːfəl] *adj* 1 SORROWFUL : afligido, apenado, triste 2 UNFORTUNATE : desgraciado, infortunado 3 DEPLORABLE : lamentable
woke, woken → **wake**[1]
wolf[1] [ˈwʊlf] *vt or* **to wolf down** : engullir
wolf[2] *n, pl* **wolves** [ˈwʊlvz] : lobo *m*, -ba *f*
wolfram [ˈwʊlfrəm] → **tungsten**
wolverine [ˌwʊlvəˈriːn] *n* : glotón *m* (animal)
woman [ˈwʊmən] *n, pl* **women** [ˈwɪmən] : mujer *f*
womanhood [ˈwʊmənˌhʊd] *n* 1 : condición *f* de mujer 2 WOMEN : mujeres *fpl*
womanly [ˈwʊmənli] *adj* : femenino
womb [ˈwuːm] *n* : útero *m*, matriz *f*
won → **win**
wonder[1] [ˈwʌndər] *vi* 1 SPECULATE : preguntarse, pensar ⟨to wonder about : preguntarse por⟩ 2 MARVEL : asombrarse, maravillarse — *vt* : preguntarse ⟨I wonder if they're coming : me pregunto si vendrán⟩
wonder[2] *n* 1 MARVEL : maravilla *f*, milagro *m* ⟨to work wonders : hacer maravillas⟩ 2 AMAZEMENT : asombro *m*
wonderful [ˈwʌndərfəl] *adj* : maravilloso, estupendo
wonderfully [ˈwʌndərfəli] *adv* : maravillosamente, de maravilla
wonderland [ˈwʌndərˌlænd, -lənd] *n* : país *m* de las maravillas
wonderment [ˈwʌndərmənt] *n* : asombro *m*
wondrous [ˈwʌndrəs] → **wonderful**
wont[1] [ˈwɔnt, ˈwoːnt, ˈwɑnt] *adj* : acostumbrado, habituado
wont[2] *n* : hábito *m*, costumbre *f*
won't [ˈwoːnt] (*contraction of* **will not**) → **will**[1]
woo [ˈwuː] *vt* 1 COURT : cortejar 2 : buscar el apoyo de (clientes, votantes, etc.)

wood[1] [ˈwʊd] *adj* : de madera
wood[2] *n* **1** *or* **woods** *npl* FOREST : bosque *m* **2** : madera *f* (materia) **3** FIREWOOD : leña *f*
woodchuck [ˈwʊdˌʧʌk] *n* : marmota *f* de América
woodcut [ˈwʊdˌkʌt] *n* **1** : plancha *f* de madera (para imprimir imágenes) **2** : grabado *m* en madera
woodcutter [ˈwʊdˌkʌt̬ər] *n* : leñador *m*, -dora *f*
wooded [ˈwʊdəd] *adj* : arbolado, boscoso
wooden [ˈwʊdən] *adj* **1** : de madera ⟨a wooden cross : una cruz de madera⟩ **2** STIFF : rígido, inexpresivo (dícese del estilo, de la cara, etc.)
woodland [ˈwʊdlənd, -ˌlænd] *n* : bosque *m*
woodpecker [ˈwʊdˌpɛkər] *n* : pájaro *m* carpintero
woodshed [ˈwʊdˌʃɛd] *n* : leñera *f*
woodsman [ˈwʊdzmən] → **woodcutter**
woodwind [ˈwʊdˌwɪnd] *n* : instrumento *m* de viento de madera
woodworking [ˈwʊdˌwərkɪŋ] *n* : carpintería *f*
woody [ˈwʊdi] *adj* **woodier; -est** **1** → **wooded** **2** : leñoso ⟨woody plants : plantas leñosas⟩ **3** : leñoso (dícese de la textura), a madera (dícese del aroma, etc.)
woof [ˈwʊf] → **weft**
wool [ˈwʊl] *n* : lana *f*
woolen[1] *or* **woollen** [ˈwʊlən] *adj* : de lana
woolen[2] *or* **woollen** *n* **1** : lana *f* (tela) **2** **woolens** *npl* : prendas *fpl* de lana
woolly [ˈwʊli] *adj* **-lier; -est** **1** : lanudo **2** CONFUSED : confuso, vago
woozy [ˈwu:zi] *adj* **-zier; -est** : mareado
word[1] [ˈwərd] *vt* : expresar, formular, redactar
word[2] *n* **1** : palabra *f*, vocablo *m*, voz *f* ⟨word for word : palabra por palabra⟩ ⟨in one's own words : en sus propias palabras⟩ ⟨words fail me : me quedo sin habla⟩ **2** REMARK : palabra *f* ⟨by word of mouth : de palabra⟩ ⟨to have a word with : hablar (dos palabras) con⟩ **3** COMMAND : orden *f* ⟨to give the word : dar la orden⟩ ⟨just say the word : no tienes que decirlo⟩ **4** MESSAGE, NEWS : noticias *fpl* ⟨is there any word from her? : ¿hay noticias de ella?⟩ ⟨to send word : mandar un recado⟩ **5** PROMISE : palabra *f* ⟨to keep one's word : cumplir uno su palabra⟩ **6** **words** *npl* QUARREL : palabra *f*, riña *f* ⟨to have words with : tener unas palabras con, reñir con⟩ **7** **words** *npl* TEXT : letra *f* (de una canción, etc.)
wordiness [ˈwərdinəs] *n* : verbosidad *f*
wording [ˈwərdɪŋ] *n* : redacción *f*, lenguaje *m* (de un documento)
word processing *n* : procesamiento *m* de textos
word processor *n* : procesador *m* de textos
wordy [ˈwərdi] *adj* **wordier; -est** : verboso, prolijo
wore → **wear**[1]
work[1] [ˈwərk] *v* **worked** [ˈwərkt] *or* **wrought** [ˈrɔt]; **working** *vt* **1** OPERATE : trabajar, operar ⟨to work a machine : operar una máquina⟩ **2** : lograr, conseguir (algo) con esfuerzo ⟨to work one's way up : lograr subir por sus propios esfuerzos⟩ **3** EFFECT : efectuar, llevar a cabo, obrar (milagros) **4** MAKE, SHAPE : elaborar, fabricar, formar ⟨a beautifully wrought vase : un florero bellamente elaborado⟩ **5** **to work up** : estimular, excitar ⟨don't get worked up : no te agites⟩ — *vi* **1** LABOR : trabajar ⟨to work full-time : trabajar a tiempo completo⟩ **2** FUNCTION : funcionar, servir
work[2] *adj* : laboral
work[3] *n* **1** LABOR : trabajo *m*, labor *f* **2** EMPLOYMENT : trabajo *m*, empleo *m* **3** TASK : tarea *f*, faena *f* **4** DEED : obra *f*, labor *f* ⟨works of charity : obras de caridad⟩ **5** : obra *f* (de arte o literatura) **6** → **workmanship** **7** **works** *npl* FACTORY : fábrica *f* **8** **works** *npl* MECHANISM : mecanismo *m*
workable [ˈwərkəbəl] *adj* **1** : explotable (dícese de una mina, etc.) **2** FEASIBLE : factible, realizable
workaday [ˈwərkəˌdeɪ] *adj* : ordinario, banal
workbench [ˈwərkˌbɛnʧ] *n* : mesa *f* de trabajo
workday [ˈwərkˌdeɪ] *n* **1** : jornada *f* laboral **2** WEEKDAY : día *m* hábil, día *m* laborable
worker [ˈwərkər] *n* : trabajador *m*, -dora *f*; obrero *m*, -ra *f*
working [ˈwərkɪŋ] *adj* **1** : que trabaja ⟨working mothers : madres que trabajan⟩ ⟨the working class : la clase obrera⟩ **2** : de trabajo ⟨working hours : horas de trabajo⟩ **3** FUNCTIONING : que funciona, operativo **4** SUFFICIENT : suficiente ⟨a working majority : una mayoría suficiente⟩ ⟨working knowledge : conocimientos básicos⟩
workingman [ˈwərkɪŋˌmæn] *n, pl* **-men** [-mən, -ˌmɛn] : obrero *m*
workman [ˈwərkmən] *n, pl* **-men** [-mən, -ˌmɛn] **1** → **workingman** **2** ARTISAN : artesano *m*
workmanlike [ˈwərkmənˌlaɪk] *adj* : bien hecho, competente
workmanship [ˈwərkmənˌʃɪp] *n* **1** WORK : ejecución *f*, trabajo *m* **2** CRAFTSMANSHIP : artesanía *f*, destreza *f*
workout [ˈwərkˌaʊt] *n* : ejercicios *mpl* físicos, entrenamiento *m*
work out *vt* **1** DEVELOP, PLAN : idear, planear, desarrollar **2** RESOLVE : solucionar, resolver ⟨to work out the answer : calcular la solución⟩ — *vi* **1** TURN OUT : resultar **2** SUCCEED : lograr, dar resultado, salir bien **3** EXERCISE : hacer ejercicio

workroom ['wərk,ru:m, -,rʊm] *n* : taller *m*
workshop ['wərk,ʃɑp] *n* : taller *m* ⟨ceramics workshop : taller de cerámica⟩
workstation ['wərk,steɪʃən] *n* : estación *f* de trabajo (en informática)
world[1] ['wərld] *adj* : mundial, del mundo ⟨world championship : campeonato mundial⟩
world[2] *n* : mundo *m* ⟨around the world : alrededor del mundo⟩ ⟨a world of possibilities : un mundo de posibilidades⟩ ⟨to think the world of someone : tener a alguien en alta estima⟩ ⟨to be worlds apart : no tener nada que ver (uno con otro)⟩
worldly ['wərldli] *adj* **1** : mundano ⟨wordly goods : bienes materiales⟩ **2** SOPHISTICATED : sofisticado, de mundo
worldwide[1] ['wərld'waɪd] *adv* : mundialmente, en todo el mundo
worldwide[2] *adj* : global, mundial
World Wide Web *n* : World Wide Web *f*
worm[1] ['wərm] *vi* CRAWL : arrastrarse, deslizarse (como gusano) — *vt* **1** : desparasitar (un animal) **2 to worm one's way into** : introducirse en ⟨he wormed his way into her confidence : se ganó su confianza⟩ **3 to worm something out of someone** : sonsacarle algo a alguien
worm[2] *n* **1** : gusano *m*, lombriz *f* **2 worms** *npl* : lombrices *fpl* (parásitos)
wormy ['wərmi] *adj* **wormier; -est** : infestado de gusanos
worn *pp* → **wear**[1]
worn–out ['worn'aʊt] *adj* **1** USED : gastado, desgastado **2** TIRED : agotado
worried ['wərid] *adj* : inquieto, preocupado
worrier ['wəriər] *n* : persona *f* que se preocupa mucho
worrisome ['wərisəm] *adj* **1** DISTURBING : preocupante, inquietante **2** : que se preocupa mucho (dícese de una persona)
worry[1] ['wəri] *v* **-ried; -rying** *vt* : preocupar, inquietar — *vi* : preocuparse, inquietarse, angustiarse
worry[2] *n, pl* **-ries** : preocupación *f*, inquietud *f*, angustia *f*
worse[1] ['wərs] *adv* (*comparative of* **bad** *or of* **ill**) : peor
worse[2] *adj* (*comparative of* **bad** *or of* **ill**) : peor ⟨from bad to worse : de mal en peor⟩ ⟨to get worse : empeorar⟩ ⟨to feel worse : sentirse peor⟩
worse[3] *n* : estado *m* peor ⟨to take a turn for the worse : ponerse peor⟩ ⟨so much the worse : tanto peor⟩
worsen ['wərsən] *vt* : empeorar — *vi* : empeorar(se)
worship[1] ['wərʃəp] *v* **-shiped** *or* **-shipped; -shiping** *or* **-shipping** *vt* : adorar, venerar ⟨to worship God : adorar a Dios⟩ — *vi* : practicar una religión
worship[2] *n* : adoración *f*, culto *m*
worshiper *or* **worshipper** ['wərʃəpər] *n* : devoto *m*, -ta *f*; adorador *m*, -dora *f*
worst[1] ['wərst] *vt* DEFEAT : derrotar
worst[2] *adv* (*superlative of* **ill** *or of* **bad** *or* **badly**) : peor ⟨the worst dressed of all : el peor vestido de todos⟩
worst[3] *adj* (*superlative of* **bad** *or of* **ill**) : peor ⟨the worst movie : la peor película⟩
worst[4] *n* **the worst** : lo peor, el (la) peor ⟨the worst is over : ya ha pasado lo peor⟩
worsted ['wʊstəd, 'wərstəd] *n* : estambre *m*
worth[1] ['wərθ] *n* **1** : valor *m* (monetario) ⟨ten dollars' worth of gas : diez dólares de gasolina⟩ **2** MERIT : valor *m*, mérito *m*, valía *f* ⟨an employee of great worth : un empleado de gran valía⟩
worth[2] *prep* **to be worth** : valer ⟨her holdings are worth a fortune : sus propiedades valen una fortuna⟩ ⟨it's not worth it : no vale la pena⟩
worthiness ['wərðinəs] *n* : mérito *m*
worthless ['wərθləs] *adj* **1** : sin valor ⟨worthless trinkets : chucherías sin valor⟩ **2** USELESS : inútil
worthwhile [wərθ'*h*waɪl] *adj* : que vale la pena
worthy ['wərði] *adj* **-thier; -est 1** : digno ⟨worthy of promotion : digno de un ascenso⟩ **2** COMMENDABLE : meritorio, encomiable
would ['wʊd] *past of* **will 1** (*expressing preference*) ⟨I would rather go alone than with her : preferiría ir sola que con ella⟩ **2** (*expressing intent*) ⟨those who would ban certain books : aquellos que prohibirían ciertos libros⟩ **3** (*expressing habitual action*) ⟨he would often take his kids to the park : solía llevar a sus hijos al parque⟩ **4** (*expressing contingency*) ⟨I would go if I had the money : iría yo si tuviera el dinero⟩ **5** (*expressing probability*) ⟨she would have won if she hadn't tripped : habría ganado si no hubiera tropezado⟩ **6** (*expressing a request*) ⟨would you kindly help me with this? : ¿tendría la bondad de ayudarme con esto?⟩
would–be ['wʊd'bi:] *adj* : potencial ⟨a would-be celebrity : un aspirante a celebridad⟩
wouldn't ['wʊd'ənt] (*contraction of* **would not**) → **would**
wound[1] ['wu:nd] *vt* : herir
wound[2] *n* : herida *f*
wound[3] ['waʊnd] → **wind**[2]
wove, woven → **weave**[1]
wow ['waʊ] *interj* : ¡guau!, ¡híjole! *Mex*, ¡hala! *Spain*
wrangle[1] ['ræŋgəl] *vi* **-gled; -gling** : discutir, reñir ⟨to wrangle over : discutir por⟩
wrangle[2] *n* : riña *f*, disputa *f*
wrap[1] ['ræp] *v* **wrapped; wrapping** *vt* **1** COVER : envolver, cubrir ⟨to wrap a package : envolver un paquete⟩

⟨wrapped in mystery : envuelto en misterio⟩ **2** ENCIRCLE : rodear, ceñir ⟨to wrap one's arms around someone : estrechar a alguien⟩ **3 to wrap up** FINISH : darle fin a (algo) — *vi* **1** COIL : envolverse, enroscarse **2 to wrap up** DRESS : abrigarse ⟨wrap up warmly : abrígate bien⟩
wrap[2] *n* **1** WRAPPER : envoltura *f* **2** : prenda *f* que envuelve (como un chal, una bata, etc.)
wrapper [ˈræpər] *n* : envoltura *f*, envoltorio *m*
wrapping [ˈræpɪŋ] *n* : envoltura *f*, envoltorio *m*
wrath [ˈræθ] *n* : ira *f*, cólera *f*
wrathful [ˈræθfəl] *adj* : iracundo
wreak [ˈriːk] *vt* : infligir, causar ⟨to wreak havoc : crear caos, causar estragos⟩
wreath [ˈriːθ] *n, pl* **wreaths** [ˈriːðz, ˈriːθs] : corona *f* (de flores, etc.)
wreathe [ˈriːð] *vt* **wreathed; wreathing** **1** ADORN : coronar (de flores, etc.) **2** ENVELOP : envolver ⟨wreathed in mist : envuelto en niebla⟩
wreck[1] [ˈrɛk] *vt* : destruir, arruinar, estrellar (un automóvil), naufragar (un barco)
wreck[2] *n* **1** WRECKAGE : restos *mpl* (de un buque naufragado, un avión siniestrado, etc.) **2** RUIN : ruina *f*, desastre *m* ⟨this place is a wreck! : ¡este lugar está hecho un desastre!⟩ ⟨to be a nervous wreck : tener los nervios destrozados⟩
wreckage [ˈrɛkɪʤ] *n* : restos *mpl* (de un buque naufragado, un avión siniestrado, etc.), ruinas *fpl* (de un edificio)
wrecker [ˈrɛkər] *n* **1** TOW TRUCK : grúa *f* **2** : desguazador *m* (de autos, barcos, etc.), demoledor *m* (de edificios)
wren [ˈrɛn] *n* : chochín *m*
wrench[1] [ˈrɛnʧ] *vt* **1** PULL : arrancar (de un tirón) **2** SPRAIN, TWIST : torcerse (un tobillo, un músculo, etc.)
wrench[2] *n* **1** TUG : tirón *m*, jalón *m* **2** SPRAIN : torcedura *f* **3** *or* **monkey wrench** : llave *f* inglesa
wrest [ˈrɛst] *vt* : arrancar
wrestle[1] [ˈrɛsəl] *v* **-tled; -tling** *vi* **1** : luchar, practicar la lucha (en deportes) **2** STRUGGLE : luchar ⟨to wrestle with a dilemma : lidiar con un dilema⟩ — *vt* : luchar contra
wrestle[2] *n* STRUGGLE : lucha *f*
wrestler [ˈrɛsələr] *n* : luchador *m*, -dora *f*
wrestling [ˈrɛsəlɪŋ] *n* : lucha *f*
wretch [ˈrɛʧ] *n* : infeliz *mf*; desgraciado *m*, -da *f*
wretched [ˈrɛʧəd] *adj* **1** MISERABLE, UNHAPPY : desdichado, afligido ⟨I feel wretched : me siento muy mal⟩ **2** UNFORTUNATE : miserable, desgraciado, lastimoso ⟨wretched weather : tiempo espantoso⟩ **3** INFERIOR : inferior, malo
wretchedly [ˈrɛʧədli] *adv* : miserablemente, lamentablemente
wriggle [ˈrɪgəl] *vi* **-gled; -gling** : retorcerse, menearse
wring [ˈrɪŋ] *vt* **wrung** [ˈrʌŋ]; **wringing** **1** *or* **to wring out** : escurrir, exprimir (el lavado) **2** EXTRACT : arrancar, sacar (por la fuerza) **3** TWIST : torcer, retorcer **4 to wring someone's heart** : partirle el corazón a alguien
wringer [ˈrɪŋər] *n* : escurridor *m*
wrinkle[1] [ˈrɪŋkəl] *v* **-kled; -kling** *vt* : arrugar — *vi* : arrugarse
wrinkle[2] *n* : arruga *f*
wrinkly [ˈrɪŋkəli] *adj* **wrinklier; -est** : arrugado
wrist [ˈrɪst] *n* **1** : muñeca *f* (en anatomía) **2** *or* **wristband** [ˈrɪst-ˌbænd] CUFF : puño *m*
writ [ˈrɪt] *n* : orden *f* (judicial)
write [ˈraɪt] *v* **wrote** [ˈroːt]; **written** [ˈrɪtən]; **writing** : escribir
write down *vt* : apuntar, anotar
write off *vt* CANCEL : cancelar
writer [ˈraɪt̬ər] *n* : escritor *m*, -tora *f*
writhe [ˈraɪð] *vi* **writhed; writhing** : retorcerse
writing [ˈraɪt̬ɪŋ] *n* **1** : escritura *f* **2** HANDWRITING : letra *f* **3 writings** *npl* WORKS : escritos *mpl*, obra *f*
wrong[1] [ˈrɔŋ] *vt* **wronged; wronging** : ofender, ser injusto con
wrong[2] *adv* : mal, incorrectamente
wrong[3] *adj* **wronger** [ˈrɔŋər]; **wrongest** [ˈrɔŋəst] **1** EVIL, SINFUL : malo, injusto, inmoral **2** IMPROPER, UNSUITABLE : inadecuado, inapropiado, malo **3** INCORRECT : incorrecto, erróneo, malo ⟨a wrong answer : una mala respuesta⟩ **4 to be wrong** : equivocarse, estar equivocado
wrong[4] *n* **1** INJUSTICE : injusticia *f*, mal *m* **2** OFFENSE : ofensa *f*, agravio *m* (en derecho) **3 to be in the wrong** : haber hecho mal, estar equivocado
wrongdoer [ˈrɔŋˌduːər] *n* : malhechor *m*, -chora *f*
wrongdoing [ˈrɔŋˌduːɪŋ] *n* : fechoría *f*, maldad *f*
wrongful [ˈrɔŋfəl] *adj* **1** UNJUST : injusto **2** UNLAWFUL : ilegal
wrongly [ˈrɔŋli] *adv* **1** : injustamente **2** INCORRECTLY : erróneamente, incorrectamente
wrote → **write**
wrought [ˈrɔt] *adj* **1** SHAPED : formado, forjado ⟨wrought iron : hierro forjado⟩ **2** *or* **wrought up** : agitado, excitado
wrung → **wring**
wry [ˈraɪ] *adj* **wrier** [ˈraɪər]; **wriest** [ˈraɪəst] **1** TWISTED : torcido ⟨a wry neck : un cuello torcido⟩ **2** : irónico, sardónico (dícese del humor)

X

x¹ *n, pl* **x's** *or* **xs** [ˈɛksəz] **1** : vigésima cuarta letra del alfabeto inglés **2** : incógnita *f* (en matemáticas)
x² [ˈks] *vt* **x–ed** [ˈɛkst]; **x–ing** *or* **x'ing** [ˈɛksiŋ] DELETE : tachar
xenon [ˈziːˌnɑn, ˈzɛ-] *n* : xenón *m*
xenophobia [ˌzɛnəˈfoːbiə, ˌziː-] *n* : xenofobia *f*
Xmas [ˈkrɪsməs] *n* : Navidad *f*
x–ray [ˈɛksˌreɪ] *vt* : radiografiar
X ray [ˈɛksˌreɪ] *n* **1** : rayo *m* X **2** *or* **X–ray photograph** : radiografía *f*
xylophone [ˈzaɪləˌfoːn] *n* : xilófono *m*

Y

y [ˈwaɪ] *n, pl* **y's** *or* **ys** [ˈwaɪz] : vigésima quinta letra del alfabeto inglés
yacht¹ [ˈjɑt] *vi* : navegar (a vela), ir en yate ⟨to go yachting : irse a navegar⟩
yacht² *n* : yate *m*
yak [ˈjæk] *n* : yac *m*
yam [ˈjæm] *n* **1** : ñame *m* **2** SWEET POTATO : batata *f*, boniato *m*
yank¹ [ˈjæŋk] *vt* : tirar de, jalar, darle un tirón a
yank² *n* : tirón *m*
Yankee [ˈjæŋki] *n* : yanqui *mf*
yap¹ [ˈjæp] *vi* **yapped; yapping 1** BARK, YELP : ladrar, gañir **2** CHATTER : cotorrear *fam*, parlotear *fam*
yap² *n* : ladrido *m*, gañido *m*
yard [ˈjɑrd] *n* **1** : yarda *f* (medida) **2** SPAR : verga *f* (de un barco) **3** COURTYARD : patio *m* **4** : jardín *m* (de una casa) **5** : depósito *m* (de mercancías, etc.)
yardage [ˈjɑrdɪʤ] *n* : medida *f* en yardas
yardarm [ˈjɑrdˌɑrm] *n* : penol *m*
yardstick [ˈjɑrdˌstɪk] *n* **1** : vara *f* **2** CRITERION : criterio *m*, norma *f*
yarn [ˈjɑrn] *n* **1** : hilado *m* **2** TALE : historia *f*, cuento *m* ⟨to spin a yarn : inventar una historia⟩
yawl [ˈjɔl] *n* : yola *f*
yawn¹ [ˈjɔn] *vi* **1** : bostezar **2** OPEN : abrirse
yawn² *n* : bostezo *m*
ye [ˈjiː] *pron* : vosotros, vosotras
yea¹ [ˈjeɪ] *adv* YES : sí
yea² *n* : voto *m* a favor
year [ˈjɪr] *n* **1** : año *m* ⟨last year : el año pasado⟩ ⟨he's ten years old : tiene diez años⟩ **2** : curso *m*, año *m* (escolar) **3** **years** *npl* AGES : siglos *mpl*, años *mpl* ⟨I haven't seen them in years : hace siglos que no los veo⟩
yearbook [ˈjɪrˌbʊk] *n* : anuario *m*
yearling [ˈjɪrlɪŋ, ˈjərlən] *n* : animal *m* menor de dos año
yearly¹ [ˈjɪrli] *adv* : cada año, anualmente
yearly² *adj* : anual
yearn [ˈjərn] *vi* : anhelar, ansiar
yearning [ˈjərnɪŋ] *n* : anhelo *m*
yeast [ˈjiːst] *n* : levadura *f*
yell¹ [ˈjɛl] *vi* : gritar, chillar — *vt* : gritar
yell² *n* : grito *m*, alarido *m* ⟨to let out a yell : dar un grito⟩
yellow¹ [ˈjɛlo] *vi* : ponerse amarillo, volverse amarillo
yellow² *adj* **1** : amarillo **2** COWARDLY : cobarde
yellow³ *n* : amarillo *m*
yellow fever *n* : fiebre *f* amarilla
yellowish [ˈjɛloɪʃ] *adj* : amarillento
yellow jacket *n* : avispa *f* (con rayas amarillas)
yelp¹ [ˈjɛlp] *vi* : dar un gañido (dícese de un animal), dar un grito (dícese de una persona)
yelp² *n* : gañido *m* (de un animal), grito *m* (de una persona)
yen [ˈjɛn] *n* **1** DESIRE : deseo *m*, ganas *fpl* **2** : yen *m* (moneda japonesa)
yeoman [ˈjoːmən] *n, pl* **-men** [-mən, -mɛn] : suboficial *mf* de marina
yes¹ [ˈjɛs] *adv* : sí ⟨to say yes : decir que sí⟩
yes² *n* : sí *m*
yesterday¹ [ˈjɛstərˌdeɪ, -di] *adv* : ayer
yesterday² *n* **1** : ayer *m* **2 the day before yesterday** : anteayer
yet¹ [ˈjɛt] *adv* **1** BESIDES, EVEN : aún ⟨yet more problems : más problemas aún⟩ ⟨yet again : otra vez⟩ **2** SO FAR : aún, todavía ⟨not yet : todavía no⟩ ⟨as yet : hasta ahora, todavía⟩ **3** : ya ⟨has he come yet? : ¿ya ha venido?⟩ **4** EVENTUALLY : todavía, algún día **5** NEVERTHELESS : sin embargo
yet² *conj* : pero
yew [ˈjuː] *n* : tejo *m*
yield¹ [ˈjiːld] *vt* **1** SURRENDER : ceder ⟨to yield the right of way : ceder el paso⟩ **2** PRODUCE : producir, dar, rendir (en finanzas) — *vi* **1** GIVE : ceder ⟨to yield under pressure : ceder por la presión⟩ **2** GIVE IN, SURRENDER : ceder, rendirse, entregarse
yield² *n* : rendimiento *m*, rédito *m* (en finanzas)
yin and yang [ˈjɪnændˈjæŋ, -ˈjɑŋ] *n* : yin *m* y yang *f*
yodel¹ [ˈjoːdəl] *vi* **-deled** *or* **-delled; -deling** *or* **-delling** : cantar al estilo tirolés
yodel² *n* : canción *f* al estilo tirolés
yoga [ˈjoːgə] *n* : yoga *m*
yogurt [ˈjoːgərt] *n* : yogur *m*, yogurt *m*
yoke¹ [ˈjoːk] *vt* **yoked; yoking** : uncir (animales)
yoke² *n* **1** : yugo *m* (para uncir animales)

⟨the yoke of oppression : el yugo de la opresión⟩ **2** TEAM : yunta *f* (de bueyes) **3** : canesú *m* (de ropa)

yokel [ˈjoːkəl] *n* : palurdo *m*, -da *f*

yolk [ˈjoːk] *n* : yema *f* (de un huevo)

Yom Kippur [ˌjoːmkɪˈpʊr, ˌjɑm-, -ˈkɪpər] *n* : el Día *m* del Perdón, Yom Kippur

yon [ˈjɑn] → **yonder**

yonder[1] [ˈjɑndər] *adv* : allá ⟨over yonder : allá lejos⟩

yonder[2] *adj* : aquel ⟨yonder hill : aquella colina⟩

yore [ˈjoːr] *n* **in days of yore** : antaño

you [ˈjuː] *pron* **1** (*used as subject — familiar*) : tú; vos (*in some Latin American countries*); ustedes *pl*; vosotros, vosotras *pl Spain* **2** (*used as subject — formal*) : usted, ustedes *pl* **3** (*used as indirect object — familiar*) : te, les *pl* (se *before lo, la, los, las*), os *pl Spain* ⟨he told it to you : te lo contó⟩ ⟨I gave them to (all of, both of) you : se los di⟩ **4** (*used as indirect object — formal*) : lo (*Spain sometimes* le), la; los (*Spain sometimes* les), las *pl* **5** (*used after a preposition — familiar*) : ti; vos (*in some Latin American countries*); ustedes *pl*; vosotros, vosotras *pl Spain* **6** (*used after a preposition — formal*) : usted, ustedes *pl* **7** (*used as an impersonal subject*) ⟨you never know : nunca se sabe⟩ ⟨you have to be aware : hay que ser consciente⟩ ⟨you mustn't do that : eso no se hace⟩ **8 with you** (*familiar*) : contigo; con ustedes *pl*; con vosotros, con vosotras *pl Spain* **9 with you** (*formal*) : con usted, con ustedes *pl*

you'd [ˈjuːd, ˈjʊd] (*contraction of* **you had** *or* **you would**) → **have, would**

you'll [ˈjuːl, ˈjʊl] (*contraction of* **you shall** *or* **you will**) → **shall, will**

young[1] [ˈjʌŋ] *adj* **younger** [ˈjʌŋgər]; **youngest** [-gəst] **1** : joven, pequeño, menor ⟨young people : los jóvenes⟩ ⟨my younger brother : mi hermano menor⟩ ⟨she is the youngest : es la más pequeña⟩ **2** FRESH, NEW : tierno (dícese de las verduras), joven (dícese del vino) **3** YOUTHFUL : joven, juvenil

young[2] *npl* : jóvenes *mfpl* (de los humanos), crías *fpl* (de los animales)

youngster [ˈjʌŋkstər] *n* **1** YOUTH : joven *mf* **2** CHILD : chico *m*, -ca *f*; niño *m*, -ña *f*

your [ˈjʊr, ˈjoːr, jər] *adj* **1** (*familiar singular*) : tu ⟨your cat : tu gato⟩ ⟨your books : tus libros⟩ ⟨wash your hands : lávate las manos⟩ **2** (*familiar plural*) : su, vuestro *Spain* ⟨your car : su coche, el coche de ustedes⟩ **3** (*formal*) : su ⟨your houses : sus casas⟩ **4** (*impersonal*) : el, la, los, las ⟨on your left : a la izquierda⟩

you're [ˈjʊr, ˈjoːr, ˈjər, ˈjuːər] (*contraction of* **you are**) → **be**

yours [ˈjʊrz, ˈjoːrz] *pron* **1** (*belonging to one person — familiar*) : (el) tuyo, (la) tuya, (los) tuyos, (las) tuyas ⟨those are mine; yours are there : ésas son mías; las tuyas están allí⟩ ⟨is this one yours? : ¿éste es tuyo?⟩ **2** (*belonging to more than one person — familiar*) : (el) suyo, (la) suya, (los) suyos, (las) suyas; (el) vuestro, (la) vuestra, (los) vuestros, (las) vuestras *Spain* ⟨our house and yours : nuestra casa y la suya⟩ **3** (*formal*) : (el) suyo, (la) suya, (los) suyos, (las) suyas

yourself [jərˈsɛlf] *pron, pl* **yourselves** [-ˈslvz] **1** (*used reflexively — familiar*) : te, se *pl*, os *pl Spain* ⟨wash yourself : lávate⟩ ⟨you dressed yourselves : se vistieron, os vestisteis⟩ **2** (*used reflexively — formal*) : se ⟨did you hurt yourself? : ¿se hizo daño?⟩ ⟨you've gotten yourselves dirty : se ensuciaron⟩ **3** (*used for emphasis*) : tú mismo, tú misma; usted mismo, usted misma; ustedes mismos, ustedes mismas *pl*; vosotros mismos, vosotras mismas *pl Spain* ⟨you did it yourselves? : ¿lo hicieron ustedes mismos?, ¿lo hicieron por sí solos?⟩

youth [ˈjuːθ] *n, pl* **youths** [ˈjuːðz, ˈjuːθs] **1** : juventud *f* ⟨in her youth : en su juventud⟩ **2** BOY : joven *m* **3** : jóvenes *mfpl*, juventud *f* ⟨the youth of our city : los jóvenes de nuestra ciudad⟩

youthful [ˈjuːθfəl] *adj* **1** : de juventud **2** YOUNG : joven **3** JUVENILE : juvenil

youthfulness [ˈjuːθfəlnəs] *n* : juventud *f*

you've [ˈjuːv] (*contraction of* **you have**) → **have**

yowl[1] [ˈjæʊl] *vi* : aullar

yowl[2] *n* : aullido *m*

yo–yo [ˈjoːˌjoː] *n, pl* **-yos** : yoyo *m*, yoyó *m*

yucca [ˈjʌkə] *n* : yuca *f*

Yugoslavian [ˌjuːgoˈslɑviən] *n* : yugoslavo *m*, -va *f* — **Yugoslavian** *adj*

yule [ˈjuːl] *n* CHRISTMAS : Navidad *f*

yuletide [ˈjuːlˌtaɪd] *n* : Navidades *fpl*

yuppie [ˈjʌpi] *n* : yuppy *mf*

Z

z [ˈzi:] *n, pl* **z's** *or* **zs** : vigésima sexta letra del alfabeto inglés

Zambian [ˈzæmbiən] *n* : zambiano *m*, -na *f* — **Zambian** *adj*

zany[1] [ˈzeɪni] *adj* **-nier; -est** : alocado, disparatado

zany[2] *n, pl* **-nies** : bufón *m*, -fona *f*

zap[1] [ˈzæp] *vt* **zapped; zapping 1** ELIMINATE : eliminar **2** : enviar o transportar rápidamente — *vi* : ir rápidamente

zap[2] *n* **1** ZEST : sabor *m*, sazón *f* **2** BLAST : golpe *m* fuerte

zap[3] *interj* : ¡zas!

zeal [ˈzi:l] *n* : fervor *m*, celo *m*, entusiasmo *m*

zealot [ˈzɛlət] *n* : fanático *m*, -ca *f*

zealous [ˈzɛləs] *adj* : celoso — **zealously** *adv*

zebra [ˈzi:brə] *n* : cebra *f*

zenith [ˈzi:nəθ] *n* **1** : cenit *m* (en astronomía) **2** PEAK : apogeo *m*, cenit *m* ⟨at the zenith of his career : en el apogeo de su carrera⟩

zephyr [ˈzɛfər] *n* : céfiro *m*

zeppelin [ˈzɛplən, -pəlɪn] *n* : zepelín *m*

zero[1] [ˈzi:ro, ˈzɪro] *vi* **to zero in on** : apuntar hacia, centrarse en (un problema, etc.)

zero[2] *adj* : cero, nulo ⟨zero degrees : cero grados⟩ ⟨zero opportunities : oportunidades nulas⟩

zero[3] *n, pl* **-ros** : cero *m* ⟨below zero : bajo cero⟩

zest [ˈzɛst] *n* **1** GUSTO : entusiasmo *m*, brío *m* **2** FLAVOR : sabor *m*, sazón *f*

zestful [ˈzɛstfəl] *adj* : brioso

zigzag[1] [ˈzɪgˌzæg] *vi* **-zagged; -zagging** : zigzaguear

zigzag[2] *adv & adj* : en zigzag

zigzag[3] *n* : zigzag *m*

Zimbabwean [zɪmˈbɑbwiən, -bweɪ-] *n* : zimbabuense *mf* — **Zimbabwean** *adj*

zinc [ˈzɪŋk] *n* : cinc *m*, zinc *m*

zing [ˈzɪŋ] *n* **1** HISS, HUM : zumbido *m*, silbido *m* **2** ENERGY : brío *m*

zinnia [ˈzɪniə, ˈzi:-, -njə] *n* : zinnia *f*

Zionism [ˈzaɪəˌnɪzəm] *n* : sionismo *m*

Zionist [ˈzaɪənɪst] *n* : sionista *mf*

zip[1] [ˈzɪp] *v* **zipped; zipping** *vt or* **to zip up** : cerrar el cierre de — *vi* **1** SPEED : pasarse volando ⟨the day zipped by : el día se pasó volando⟩ **2** HISS, HUM : silbar, zumbar

zip[2] *n* **1** ZING : zumbido *m*, silbido *m* **2** ENERGY : brío *m*

zip code *n* : código *m* postal

zipper [ˈzɪpər] *n* : cierre *m*, cremallera *f*, zíper *m CA, Mex*

zippy [ˈzɪpi] *adj* **-pier; -est** : brioso

zircon [ˈzərˌkɑn] *n* : circón *m*, zircón *m*

zirconium [ˌzərˈko:niəm] *n* : circonio *m*

zither [ˈzɪðər, -θər] *n* : cítara *f*

zodiac [ˈzo:diˌæk] *n* : zodíaco *m*

zombie [ˈzɑmbi] *n* : zombi *mf*, zombie *mf*

zone[1] [ˈzo:n] *vt* **zoned; zoning 1** : dividir en zonas **2** DESIGNATE : declarar ⟨to zone for business : declarar como zona comercial⟩

zone[2] *n* : zona *f*

zoo [ˈzu:] *n, pl* **zoos** : zoológico *m*, zoo *m*

zoological [ˌzo:əˈlɑʤɪkəl, ˌzu:ə-] *adj* : zoológico

zoologist [zoˈɑləʤɪst, zu:-] *n* : zoólogo *m*, -ga *f*

zoology [zoˈɑləʤi, zu:-] *n* : zoología *f*

zoom[1] [ˈzu:m] *vi* **1** : zumbar, ir volando ⟨to zoom past : pasar volando⟩ **2** CLIMB : elevarse ⟨the plane zoomed up : el avión se elevó⟩

zoom[2] *n* **1** : zumbido *m* ⟨the zoom of an engine : el zumbido de un motor⟩ **2** : subida *f* vertical (de un avión, etc.) **3** *or* **zoom lens** : zoom *m*

zucchini [zʊˈki:ni] *n, pl* **-ni** *or* **-nis** : calabacín *m*, calabacita *f Mex*

Zulu [ˈzu:lu:] *n* **1** : zulú *mf* **2** : zulú *m* (idioma) — **Zulu** *adj*

zygote [ˈzaɪˌgo:t] *n* : zigoto *m*, cigoto *m*

Common Spanish Abbreviations

SPANISH ABBREVIATION AND EXPANSION		ENGLISH EQUIVALENT	
abr.	abril	**Apr.**	April
A.C., a.C.	antes de Cristo	**BC**	before Christ
a. de J.C.	antes de Jesucristo	**BC**	before Christ
admon., admón.	administración	—	administration
a/f	a favor	—	in favor
ago.	agosto	**Aug.**	August
Apdo.	apartado (de correos)	—	P.O. box
aprox.	aproximadamente	**approx.**	approximately
Aptdo.	apartado (de correos)	—	P.O. box
Arq.	arquitecto	**arch.**	architect
A.T.	Antiguo Testamento	**O.T.**	Old Testament
atte.	atentamente	—	sincerely
atto., atta.	atento, atenta	—	kind, courteous
av., avda.	avenida	**ave.**	avenue
a/v.	a vista	—	on receipt
BID	Banco Interamericano de Desarrollo	**IDB**	Interamerican Development Bank
Bo	banco	—	bank
BM	Banco Mundial	—	World Bank
c/, C/	calle	**st.**	street
C	centígrado, Celsius	**C**	centigrade, Celsius
C.	compañía	**Co.**	company
CA	corriente alterna	**AC**	alternating current
cap.	capítulo	**ch., chap.**	chapter
c/c	cuenta corriente	—	current account, checking account
c.c.	centímetros cúbicos	**cu. cm**	cubic centimeters
CC	corriente continua	**DC**	direct current
c/d	con descuento	—	with discount
Cd.	ciudad	—	city
CE	Comunidad Europea	**EC**	European Community
CEE	Comunidad Económica Europea	**EEC**	European Economic Community
cf.	confróntese	**cf.**	compare
cg.	centígramo	**cg**	centigram
CGT	Confederación General de Trabajadores *or* del Trabajo	—	confederation of workers, workers' union
CI	coeficiente intelectual *or* de inteligencia	**IQ**	intelligence quotient
Cía.	compañía	**Co.**	company
cm.	centímetro	**cm**	centimeter
Cnel.	coronel	**Col.**	colonel
col.	columna	**col.**	column
Col. *Mex*	colonia	—	residential area
Com.	comandante	**Cmdr.**	commander
comp.	compárese	**comp.**	compare
Cor.	coronel	**Col.**	colonel

SPANISH ABBREVIATION	AND EXPANSION	ENGLISH EQUIVALENT	
C.P.	código postal	**—**	zip code
CSF, c.s.f.	coste, seguro y flete	**c.i.f.**	cost, insurance, and freight
cta.	cuenta	**ac., acct.**	account
cte.	corriente	**cur.**	current
c/u	cada uno, cada una	**ea.**	each
CV	caballo de vapor	**hp**	horsepower
D.	Don	**—**	—
Da., D.ª	Doña	**—**	—
d.C.	después de Cristo	**AD**	anno Domini (in the year of Our Lord)
dcha.	derecha	**—**	right
d. de J.C.	después de Jesucristo	**AD**	anno Domini (in the year of Our Lord)
dep.	departamento	**dept.**	department
DF, D.F.	Distrito Federal	**—**	Federal District
dic.	diciembre	**Dec.**	December
dir.	director, directora	**dir.**	director
dir.	dirección	**—**	address
Dña.	Doña	**—**	—
do.	domingo	**Sun.**	Sunday
dpto.	departamento	**dept.**	department
Dr.	doctor	**Dr.**	doctor
Dra.	doctora	**Dr.**	doctor
dto.	descuento	**—**	discount
E, E.	Este, este	**E**	East, east
Ed.	editorial	**—**	publishing house
Ed., ed.	edición	**ed.**	edition
edif.	edificio	**bldg.**	building
edo.	estado	**st.**	state
EEUU, EE.UU.	Estados Unidos	**US, U.S.**	United States
ej.	por ejemplo	**e.g.**	for example
E.M.	esclerosis multiple	**MS**	multiple sclerosis
ene.	enero	**Jan.**	January
etc.	etcétera	**etc.**	et cetera
ext.	extensión	**ext.**	extension
F	Fahrenheit	**F**	Fahrenheit
f.a.b.	franco a bordo	**f.o.b.**	free on board
FC	ferrocarril	**RR**	railroad
feb.	febrero	**Feb.**	February
FF AA, FF.AA.	Fuerzas Armadas	**—**	armed forces
FMI	Fondo Monetario Internacional	**IMF**	International Monetary Fund
g.	gramo	**g., gm, gr.**	gram
G.P.	giro postal	**M.O.**	money order
gr.	gramo	**g., gm, gr.**	gram
Gral.	general	**Gen.**	general
h.	hora	**hr.**	hour
Hnos.	hermanos	**Bros.**	brothers
I + D, I & D, I y D	investigación y desarrollo	**R & D**	research and development
i.e.	esto es, es decir	**i.e.**	that is
incl.	inclusive	**incl.**	inclusive, inclusively
Ing.	ingeniero, ingeniera	**eng.**	engineer

SPANISH ABBREVIATION AND EXPANSION		ENGLISH EQUIVALENT	
IPC	indice de precios al consumo	**CPI**	consumer price index
IVA	impuesto al valor agregado	**VAT**	value-added tax
izq.	izquierda	**l.**	left
juev.	jueves	**Thurs.**	Thursday
jul.	julio	**Jul.**	July
jun.	junio	**Jun.**	June
kg.	kilogramo	**kg**	kilogram
km.	kilómetro	**km**	kilometer
km/h	kilómetros por hora	**kph**	kilometers per hour
kv, kV	kilovatio	**kw, kW**	kilowatt
l.	litro	**l, lit.**	liter
Lic.	licenciado, licenciada	—	—
Ltda.	limitada	**Ltd.**	limited
lun.	lunes	**Mon.**	Monday
m	masculino	**m**	masculine
m	metro	**m**	meter
m	minuto	**m**	minute
mar.	marzo	**Mar.**	March
mart.	martes	**Tues.**	Tuesday
mg.	miligramo	**mg**	milligram
miérc.	miércoles	**Wednes.**	Wednesday
min	minuto	**min.**	minute
mm.	milímetro	**mm**	millimeter
M-N, m/n	moneda nacional	—	national currency
Mons.	monseñor	**Msgr.**	monsignor
Mtra.	maestra	—	teacher
Mtro.	maestro	—	teacher
N, N.	Norte, norte	**N, no.**	North, north
n/o	nuestro	—	our
n.º	número	**no.**	number
N. de (la) R.	nota de (la) redacción	—	editor's note
NE	nordeste	**NE**	northeast
NN.UU.	Naciones Unidas	**UN**	United Nations
NO	noroeste	**NW**	northwest
nov.	noviembre	**Nov.**	November
N.T.	Nuevo Testamento	**N.T.**	New Testament
ntra., ntro.	nuestra, nuestro	—	our
NU	Naciones Unidas	**UN**	United Nations
núm.	número	**num.**	number
O, O.	Oeste, oeste	**W**	West, west
oct.	octubre	**Oct.**	October
OEA, O.E.A.	Organización de Estados Americanos	**OAS**	Organization of American States
OMS	Organización Mundial de la Salud	**WHO**	World Health Organization
ONG	organización no gubernamental	**NGO**	non-governmental organization
ONU	Organización de las Naciones Unidas	**UN**	United Nations
OTAN	Organización del Tratado del Atlántico Norte	**NATO**	North Atlantic Treaty Organization
p.	página	**p.**	page
P, P.	padre	**Fr.**	father

SPANISH ABBREVIATION AND EXPANSION		ENGLISH EQUIVALENT	
pág.	página	**pg.**	page
pat.	patente	**pat.**	patent
PCL	pantalla de cristal líquido	**LCD**	liquid crystal display
P.D.	post data	**P.S.**	postscript
p. ej.	por ejemplo	**e.g.**	for example
PNB	Producto Nacional Bruto	**GNP**	gross national product
p[o]	paseo	**Ave.**	avenue
p.p.	porte pagado	**ppd.**	postpaid
PP, p.p.	por poder, por poderes	**p.p.**	by proxy
prom.	promedio	**av., avg.**	average
ptas., pts.	pesetas	—	—
q.e.p.d.	que en paz descanse	**R.I.P.**	may he/she rest in peace
R, R/	remite	—	sender
RAE	Real Academia Española	—	—
ref., ref.[a]	referencia	**ref.**	reference
rep.	república	**rep.**	republic
r.p.m.	revoluciones por minuto	**rpm.**	revolutions per minute
rte.	remite, remitente	—	sender
s.	siglo	**c., cent.**	century
s/	su, sus	—	his, her, your, their
S, S.	Sur, sur	**S, so.**	South, south
S.	san, santo	**St.**	saint
S.A.	sociedad anónima	**Inc.**	incorporated (company)
sáb.	sábado	**Sat.**	Saturday
s/c	su cuenta	—	your account
SE	sudeste, sureste	**SE**	southeast
seg.	segundo, segundos	**sec.**	second, seconds
sep., sept.	septiembre	**Sept.**	September
s.e.u.o.	salvo error u omisión	—	errors and omissions excepted
Sgto.	sargento	**Sgt.**	sergeant
S.L.	sociedad limitada	**Ltd.**	limited (corporation)
S.M.	Su Majestad	**HM**	His Majesty, Her Majesty
s/n	sin número	—	no (street) number
s.n.m.	sobre el nivel de mar	**a.s.l.**	above sea level
SO	sudoeste/suroeste	**SW**	southwest
S.R.C.	se ruega contestación	**R.S.V.P.**	please reply
ss.	siguientes	—	the following ones
SS, S.S.	Su Santidad	**H.H.**	His Holiness
Sta.	santa	**St.**	Saint
Sto.	santo	**St.**	saint
t, t.	tonelada	**t., tn.**	ton
TAE	tasa anual efectiva	**APR**	annual percentage rate
tb.	también	—	also
tel., Tel.	teléfono	**tel.**	telephone
Tm.	tonelada métrica	**MT**	metric ton
Tn.	tonelada	**t., tn.**	ton
trad.	traducido	**tr., trans., transl.**	translated

SPANISH ABBREVIATION AND EXPANSION		ENGLISH EQUIVALENT	
UE	Unión Europea	**EU**	European Union
Univ.	universidad	**Univ., U.**	university
UPC	unidad procesadora central	**CPU**	central processing unit
Urb.	urbanización	—	residential area
v	versus	**v., vs.**	versus
v	verso	**v., ver., vs.**	verse
v.	véase	**vid.**	see
Vda.	viuda	—	widow
v.g., v.gr.	verbigracia	**e.g.**	for example
vier., viern.	viernes	**Fri.**	Friday
V.M.	Vuestra Majestad	—	Your Majesty
V^{o}B^{o}, V.^{o}B.^{o}	visto bueno	—	OK, approved
vol, vol.	volumen	**vol.**	volume
vra., vro.	vuestra, vuestro	—	your

Common English Abbreviations

ENGLISH ABBREVIATION AND EXPANSION		SPANISH EQUIVALENT	
AAA	American Automobile Association	—	—
AD	anno Domini (in the year of Our Lord)	**d.C., d. de J.C.**	después de Cristo, después de Jesucristo
AK	Alaska	—	Alaska
AL, Ala.	Alabama	—	Alabama
Alas.	Alaska	—	Alaska
a.m., AM	ante meridiem	**a.m.**	ante meridiem (de la mañana)
Am., Amer.	America, American	—	América, americano
amt.	amount	—	cantidad
anon.	anonymous	—	anónimo
ans.	answer	—	respuesta
Apr.	April	**abr.**	abril
AR	Arkansas	—	Arkansas
Ariz.	Arizona	—	Arizona
Ark.	Arkansas	—	Arkansas
asst.	assistant	**ayte.**	ayudante
atty.	attorney	—	abogado, -da
Aug.	August	**ago.**	agosto
ave.	avenue	**av., avda.**	avenida
AZ	Arizona	—	Arizona
BA	Bachelor of Arts	**Lic.**	Licenciado, -da en Filosofía y Letras
BA	Bachelor of Arts (degree)	—	Licenciatura en Filosofía y Letras
BC	before Christ	**a.C., A.C., a. de J.C.**	antes de Cristo, antes de Jesucristo
BCE	before the Christian Era, before the Common Era	—	antes de la era cristiana, antes de la era común
bet.	between	—	entre
bldg.	building	**edif.**	edificio
blvd.	boulevard	**blvar., br.**	bulevar
Br., Brit.	Britain, British	—	Gran Bretaña, británico
Bro(s).	brother(s)	**Hno(s).**	hermano(s)
BS	Bachelor of Science	**Lic.**	Licenciado, -da en Ciencias
BS	Bachelor of Science (degree)	—	Licenciatura en Ciencias
c	carat	—	quilate
c	cent	—	centavo
c	centimeter	**cm.**	centímetro
c	century	**s.**	siglo
c	cup	—	taza
C	Celsius, centigrade	**C**	Celsius, centígrado
CA, Cal., Calif.	California	—	California
Can., Canad.	Canada, Canadian	—	Canadá, canadiense
cap.	capital	—	capital
cap.	capital	—	mayúscula
Capt.	captain	—	capitán

ENGLISH ABBREVIATION AND EXPANSION		SPANISH EQUIVALENT	
cent.	century	**s.**	siglo
CEO	chief executive officer	—	presidente, -ta (de una corporación)
ch., chap.	chapter	**cap.**	capítulo
CIA	Central Intelligence Agency	—	—
cm	centimeter	**cm.**	centímetro
Co.	company	**C., Cía.**	compañía
co.	county	—	condado
CO	Colorado	—	Colorado
c/o	care of	**a/c**	a cargo de
COD	cash on delivery, collect on delivery	—	(pago) contra reembolso
col.	column	**col.**	columna
Col., Colo.	Colorado	—	Colorado
Conn.	Connecticut	—	Connecticut
corp.	corporation	—	corporación
CPR	cardiopulmonary resuscitation	**RCP**	reanimación cardiopulmonar, resucitación cardiopulmonar
ct.	cent	—	centavo
CT	Connecticut	—	Connecticut
D.A.	district attorney	—	fiscal (del distrito)
DC	District of Columbia	—	—
DDS	Doctor of Dental Surgery	—	doctor de cirugía dental
DE	Delaware	—	Delaware
Dec.	December	**dic.**	diciembre
Del.	Delaware	—	Delaware
DJ	disc jockey	—	disc-jockey
dept.	department	**dep., dpto.**	departamento
DMD	Doctor of Dental Medicine	—	doctor de medicina dental
doz.	dozen	—	docena
Dr.	doctor	**Dr., Dra.**	doctor, doctora
DST	daylight saving time	—	—
DVM	Doctor of Veterinary Medicine	—	doctor de medicina veterinaria
E	East, east	**E, E.**	Este, este
ea.	each	**c/u**	cada uno, cada una
e.g.	for example (exempli gratia)	**v.g., v.gr.**	verbigracia
EMT	emergency medical technician	—	técnico, -ca en urgencias médicas
Eng.	England, English	—	Inglaterra, inglés
esp.	especially	—	especialmente
EST	eastern standard time	—	—
etc.	et cetera	**etc.**	etcétera
f	false	—	falso
f	female	**f**	femenino
F	Fahrenheit	**F**	Fahrenheit
FBI	Federal Bureau of Investigation	—	—
Feb.	February	**feb.**	febrero
fem.	feminine	—	femenino
FL, Fla.	Florida	—	Florida

ENGLISH ABBREVIATION AND EXPANSION		SPANISH EQUIVALENT	
Fri.	Friday	**vier., viern.**	viernes
ft.	feet, foot	—	pie(s)
g	gram	**g., gr.**	gramo
Ga., GA	Georgia	—	Georgia
gal.	gallon	—	galón
Gen.	general	**Gral.**	general
gm	gram	**g., gr.**	gramo
gov.	governor	—	gobernador, -dora
govt.	government	—	gobierno
gr.	gram	**g., gr.**	gramo
HI	Hawaii	—	Hawai, Hawaii
hr.	hour	**h.**	hora
HS	high school	—	colegio secundario
ht.	height	—	altura
Ia., IA	Iowa	—	Iowa
ID	Idaho	—	Idaho
i.e.	that is (id est)	**i.e.**	id est (esto es, es decir)
IL, Ill.	Illinois	—	Illinois
in.	inch	—	pulgada
IN	Indiana	—	Indiana
Inc.	incorporated	**S.A.**	sociedad anónima
Ind.	Indian, Indiana	—	Indiana
Jan.	January	**ene.**	enero
Jul.	July	**jul.**	julio
Jun.	June	**jun.**	junio
Jr., Jun.	Junior	**Jr.**	Júnior
Kan., Kans.	Kansas	—	Kansas
kg	kilogram	**kg.**	kilogramo
km	kilometer	**km.**	kilómetro
KS	Kansas	—	Kansas
Ky., KY	Kentucky	—	Kentucky
l	liter	**l.**	litro
l.	left	**izq.**	izquierda
L	large	**G**	(talla) grande
La., LA	Louisiana	—	Luisiana, Louisiana
lb.	pound	—	libra
Ltd.	limited	**S.L.**	sociedad limitada
m	male	**m**	masculino
m	meter	**m**	metro
m	mile	—	milla
M	medium	**M**	(talla) mediana
MA	Massachusetts	—	Massachusetts
Maj.	major	—	mayor
Mar.	March	**mar.**	marzo
masc.	masculine	—	masculino
Mass.	Massachusetts	—	Massachusetts
Md., MD	Maryland	—	Maryland
M.D.	Doctor of Medicine	—	doctor de medicina
Me., ME	Maine	—	Maine
Mex.	Mexican, Mexico	**Méx.**	mexicano, México
mg	milligram	**mg.**	miligramo
mi.	mile	—	milla
MI, Mich.	Michigan	—	Michigan
min.	minute	**min**	minuto
Minn.	Minnesota	—	Minnesota
Miss.	Mississippi	—	Mississippi, Misisipí
ml	mililiter	**ml.**	mililitro

ENGLISH ABBREVIATION AND EXPANSION		SPANISH EQUIVALENT	
mm	millimeter	**mm.**	milímetro
MN	Minnesota	—	Minnesota
mo.	month	—	mes
Mo., MO	Missouri	—	Missouri
Mon.	Monday	**lun.**	lunes
Mont.	Montana	—	Montana
mpg	miles per gallon	—	millas por galón
mph	miles per hour	—	millas por hora
MS	Mississippi	—	Mississippi, Misisipí
mt.	mount, mountain	—	monte, montaña
MT	Montana	—	Montana
mtn.	mountain	—	montaña
N	North, north	**N**	Norte, norte
NASA	National Aeronautics and Space Administration	—	—
NC	North Carolina	—	Carolina del Norte, North Carolina
ND, N. Dak.	North Dakota	—	Dakota del Norte, North Dakota
NE	northeast	**NE**	nordeste
NE, Neb., Nebr.	Nebraska	—	Nebraska
Nev.	Nevada	—	Nevada
NH	New Hampshire	—	New Hampshire
NJ	New Jersey	—	Nueva Jersey, New Jersey
NM, N. Mex.	New Mexico	—	Nuevo México, New Mexico
no.	north	**N**	norte
no.	number	**n.º**	número
Nov.	November	**nov.**	noviembre
N.T.	New Testament	**N.T.**	Nuevo Testamento
NV	Nevada	—	Nevada
NW	northwest	**NO**	noroeste
NY	New York	**NY**	Nueva York, New York
O	Ohio	—	Ohio
Oct.	October	**oct.**	octubre
OH	Ohio	—	Ohio
OK, Okla.	Oklahoma	—	Oklahoma
OR, Ore., Oreg.	Oregon	—	Oregon
O.T.	Old Testament	**A.T.**	Antiguo Testamento
oz.	ounce, ounces	—	onza, onzas
p.	page	**p.**	página
Pa., PA	Pennsylvania	—	Pennsylvania, Pensilvania
pat.	patent	**pat.**	patente
PD	police department	—	departamento de policía
PE	physical education	—	educación física
Penn., Penna.	Pennsylvania	—	Pennsylvania, Pensilvania
pg.	page	**pág.**	página
PhD	Doctor of Philosophy	—	doctor, -tora (en filosofía)

ENGLISH ABBREVIATION AND EXPANSION		SPANISH EQUIVALENT	
pkg.	package	**—**	paquete
p.m., PM	post meridiem	**p.m.**	post meridiem (de la tarde)
P.O.	post office	**—**	oficina de correos, correo
pp.	pages	**págs.**	páginas
PR	Puerto Rico	**PR**	Puerto Rico
pres.	present	**—**	presente
pres.	president	**—**	presidente, -ta
prof.	professor	**—**	profesor, -sora
P.S.	postscript	**P.D.**	postdata
P.S.	public school	**—**	escuela pública
pt.	pint	**—**	pinta
pt.	point	**pto.**	punto
PTA	Parent-Teacher Association	**—**	—
PTO	Parent-Teacher Organization	**—**	—
q, qt.	quart	**—**	cuarto de galón
r.	right	**dcha.**	derecha
rd.	road	**c/, C/**	calle
RDA	recommended daily allowance	**—**	consumo diario recomendado
recd.	received	**—**	recibido
Rev.	reverend	**Rdo.**	reverendo
RI	Rhode Island	**—**	Rhode Island
rpm	revolutions per minute	**r.p.m.**	revoluciones por minuto
RR	railroad	**FC**	ferrocarril
R.S.V.P.	please reply (répondez s'il vous plaît)	**S.R.C.**	se ruega contestación
rt.	right	**dcha.**	derecha
rte.	route	**—**	ruta
S	small	**P**	(talla) pequeña
S	South, south	**S**	Sur, sur
S.A.	South America	**—**	Sudamérica, América del Sur
Sat.	Saturday	**sáb.**	sábado
SC	South Carolina	**—**	Carolina del Sur, South Carolina
SD, S. Dak.	South Dakota	**—**	Dakota del Sur, South Dakota
SE	southeast	**SE**	sudeste, sureste
Sept.	September	**sep., sept.**	septiembre
so.	south	**S**	sur
sq.	square	**—**	cuadrado
Sr.	Senior	**Sr.**	Sénior
Sr.	sister	**—**	sor
st.	state	**—**	estado
st.	street	**c/, C/**	calle
St.	saint	**S., Sto., Sta.**	santo, santa
Sun.	Sunday	**dom.**	domingo
SW	southwest	**SO**	sudoeste, suroeste
t.	teaspoon	**—**	cucharadita
T, tb., tbsp.	tablespoon	**—**	cucharada (grande)
Tenn.	Tennessee	**—**	Tennessee

ENGLISH ABBREVIATION AND EXPANSION		SPANISH EQUIVALENT	
Tex.	Texas	—	Texas
Thu., Thur., Thurs.	Thursday	**juev.**	jueves
TM	trademark	—	marca (de un producto)
TN	Tennessee	—	Tennessee
tsp.	teaspoon	—	cucharadita
Tue., Tues.	Tuesday	**mart.**	martes
TX	Texas	—	Texas
UN	United Nations	**NU, NN.UU.**	Naciones Unidas
US	United States	**EEUU, EE.UU.**	Estados Unidos
USA	United States of America	**EEUU, EE.UU.**	Estados Unidos de América
usu.	usually	—	usualmente
UT	Utah	—	Utah
v.	versus	**v**	versus
Va., VA	Virginia	—	Virginia
vol.	volume	**vol.**	volumen
VP	vice president	—	vicepresidente, -ta
vs.	versus	**v**	versus
Vt., VT	Vermont	—	Vermont
W	West, west	**O**	Oeste, oeste
WA, Wash.	Washington (estado)	—	Washington
Wed.	Wednesday	**miérc.**	miércoles
WI, Wis., Wisc.	Wisconsin	—	Wisconsin
wt.	weight	—	peso
WV, W. Va.	West Virginia	—	Virginia del Oeste, West Virginia
WY, Wyo.	Wyoming	—	Wyoming
yd.	yard	—	yarda
yr.	year	—	año

Spanish Numbers

Cardinal Numbers

1	uno	28	veintiocho
2	dos	29	veintinueve
3	tres	30	treinta
4	cuatro	31	treinta y uno
5	cinco	40	cuarenta
6	seis	50	cincuenta
7	siete	60	sesenta
8	ocho	70	setenta
9	nueve	80	ochenta
10	diez	90	noventa
11	once	100	cien
12	doce	101	ciento uno
13	trece	200	doscientos
14	catorce	300	trescientos
15	quince	400	cuatrocientos
16	dieciséis	500	quinientos
17	diecisiete	600	seiscientos
18	dieciocho	700	setecientos
19	diecinueve	800	ochocientos
20	veinte	900	novecientos
21	veintiuno	1,000	mil
22	veintidós	1,001	mil uno
23	veintitrés	2,000	dos mil
24	veinticuatro	100,000	cien mil
25	veinticinco	1,000,000	un millón
26	veintiséis	1,000,000,000	mil millones
27	veintisiete	1,000,000,000,000	un billón

Ordinal Numbers

1st	primero, -ra	18th	decimoctavo, -va
2nd	segundo, -da	19th	decimonoveno, -na;
3rd	tercero, -ra		*or* decimonono, -na
4th	cuarto, -ta	20th	vigésimo, -ma
5th	quinto, -ta	21st	vigésimoprimero,
6th	sexto, -ta		vigésimaprimera
7th	séptimo, -ta	22nd	vigésimosegundo,
8th	octavo, -ta		vigésimasegunda
9th	noveno, -na	30th	trigésimo, -ma
10th	décimo, -ma	40th	cuadragésimo, -ma
11th	undécimo, -ca	50th	quincuagésimo, -ma
12th	duodécimo, -ma	60th	sexagésimo, -ma
13th	decimotercero, -ra	70th	septuagésimo, -ma
14th	decimocuarto, -ta	80th	octogésimo, -ma
15th	decimoquinto, -ta	90th	nonagésimo, -ma
16th	decimosexto, -ta	100th	centésimo, -ma
17th	decimoséptimo, -ma	1,000th	milésimo, -ma

English Numbers

Cardinal Numbers

1	one	50	fifty
2	two	60	sixty
3	three	70	seventy
4	four	80	eighty
5	five	90	ninety
6	six	100	one hundred
7	seven	101	one hundred and one
8	eight	200	two hundred
9	nine	300	three hundred
10	ten	400	four hundred
11	eleven	500	five hundred
12	twelve	600	six hundred
13	thirteen	700	seven hundred
14	fourteen	800	eight hundred
15	fifteen	900	nine hundred
16	sixteen	1,000	one thousand
17	seventeen	1,001	one thousand and one
18	eighteen	2,000	two thousand
19	nineteen	10,000	ten thousand
20	twenty	100,000	one hundred thousand
21	twenty-one	1,000,000	one million
30	thirty	1,000,000,000	one billion
40	forty	1,000,000,000,000	one trillion

Ordinal Numbers

1st	first	17th	seventeenth
2nd	second	18th	eighteenth
3rd	third	19th	nineteenth
4th	fourth	20th	twentieth
5th	fifth	21st	twenty-first
6th	sixth	30th	thirtieth
7th	seventh	40th	fortieth
8th	eighth	50th	fiftieth
9th	ninth	60th	sixtieth
10th	tenth	70th	seventieth
11th	eleventh	80th	eightieth
12th	twelfth	90th	ninetieth
13th	thirteenth	100th	hundredth
14th	fourteenth	1,000th	thousandth
15th	fifteenth	1,000,000th	millionth
16th	sixteenth	1,000,000,000th	billionth

Nations of the World

Africa/África

ENGLISH	SPANISH
Algeria	Argelia
Angola	Angola
Benin	Benin
Botswana	Botswana, Botsuana
Burkina Faso	Burkina Faso
Burundi	Burundi
Cameroon	Camerún
Cape Verde	Cabo Verde
Central African Republic	República Centroafricana
Chad	Chad
Comoro Islands	Islas Comores, Comoras
Congo	Congo
Democratic Republic of Congo	Congo, República Democrática del
Djibouti	Djibouti, Djibuti
Egypt	Egipto
Equatorial Guinea	Guinea Ecuatorial
Eritrea	Eritrea
Ethiopia	Etiopía
Gabon	Gabón
Gambia	Gambia
Ghana	Ghana
Guinea	Guinea
Guinea-Bissau	Guinea-Bissau
Ivory Coast	Costa de Marfil
Kenya	Kenya, Kenia
Lesotho	Lesotho, Lesoto
Liberia	Liberia
Libya	Libia
Madagascar	Madagascar
Malawi	Malawi, Malaui
Mali	Malí
Mauritania	Mauritania
Mauritius	Mauricio
Morocco	Marruecos
Mozambique	Mozambique
Namibia	Namibia
Niger	Níger
Nigeria	Nigeria
Rwanda	Ruanda, Rwanda
São Tomé and Principe	Santo Tomé y Príncipe
Senegal	Senegal
Seychelles	Seychelles
Sierra Leone	Sierra Leona
...lia	Somalia
...rica, Republic of	Sudáfrica, República de
	Sudán
...d	Suazilandia, Swazilandia
...a	Tanzanía, Tanzania
	Togo

ENGLISH	SPANISH
Tunisia	Túnez
Uganda	Uganda
Zambia	Zambia
Zimbabwe	Zimbabwe, Zimbábue

Antarctica/Antártida

No independent countries

Asia/Asia

Afghanistan	Afganistán
Armenia	Armenia
Azerbaijan	Azerbaiyán, Azerbaiján
Bahrain	Bahrein
Bangladesh	Bangladesh
Bhutan	Bhután, Bután
Brunei	Brunei
Cambodia	Camboya
China	China
Cyprus	Chipre
Georgia, Republic of	Georgia
India	India
Indonesia	Indonesia
Iran	Irán
Iraq	Iraq, Irak
Israel	Israel
Japan	Japón
Jordan	Jordania
Kazakhstan	Kazajstán
Korea, North	Corea del Norte
Korea, South	Corea del Sur
Kuwait	Kuwait
Kyrgyzstan	Kirguistán, Kirguizistán
Laos	Laos
Lebanon	Líbano
Malaysia	Malasia
Maldive Islands	Maldivas
Mongolia	Mongolia
Myanmar	Myanmar
Nepal	Nepal
Oman	Omán
Pakistan	Pakistán
Philippines	Filipinas
Qatar	Qatar
Saudi Arabia	Arabia Saudita, Arabia Saudí
Singapore	Singapur
Sri Lanka	Sri Lanka
Syria	Siria
Taiwan	Taiwán
Tajikistan	Tayikistán
Thailand	Tailandia
Turkey	Turquía
Turkmenistan	Turkmenistán

ENGLISH	SPANISH
United Arab Emirates	Emiratos Árabes Unidos
Uzbekistan	Uzbekistán
Vietnam	Vietnam
Yemen	Yemen

Europe/Europa

Albania	Albania
Andorra	Andorra
Austria	Austria
Belarus	Belarús
Belgium	Bélgica
Bosnia and Herzegovina	Bosnia y Hercegovina, Bosnia y Herzegovina
Bulgaria	Bulgaria
Croatia	Croacia
Czech Republic	República Checa
Denmark	Dinamarca
Estonia	Estonia
Finland	Finlandia
France	Francia
Germany	Alemania
Greece	Grecia
Hungary	Hungría
Iceland	Islandia
Ireland	Irlanda
Italy	Italia
Latvia	Letonia
Liechtenstein	Liechtenstein
Lithuania	Lituania
Luxembourg	Luxemburgo
Macedonia	Macedonia
Malta	Malta
Moldavia	Moldavia
Monaco	Mónaco
Netherlands	Países Bajos
Norway	Noruega
Poland	Polonia
Portugal	Portugal
Romania	Rumania, Rumanía
Russian Federation	Rusia, Federación de
San Marino	San Marino
Serbia and Montenegro	Serbia y Montenegro
Slovakia	Eslovaquia
Slovenia	Eslovenia
Spain	España
Sweden	Suecia
Switzerland	Suiza
Ukraine	Ucrania
United Kingdom	Reino Unido
[illegible]n City	Ciudad del Vaticano

ENGLISH	SPANISH

North America/Norteamérica

Antigua and Barbuda	Antigua y Barbuda
Bahamas	Bahamas
Barbados	Barbados
Belize	Belice
Bermuda	Bermudas
Canada	Canadá
Costa Rica	Costa Rica
Cuba	Cuba
Dominica	Dominica
Dominican Republic	República Dominicana
El Salvador	El Salvador
Grenada	Granada
Guatemala	Guatemala
Haiti	Haití
Honduras	Honduras
Jamaica	Jamaica
Mexico	México, Méjico
Nicaragua	Nicaragua
Panama	Panamá
Saint Kitts-Nevis	Saint Kitts y Nevis
Saint Lucia	Santa Lucía
Saint Vincent and the Grenadines	San Vicente y las Granadinas
Trinidad and Tobago	Trinidad y Tobago
United States of America	Estados Unidos de América

Oceania/Oceanía

Australia	Australia
Fiji	Fiji
Kiribati	Kiribati
Marshall Islands	Islas Marshall
Nauru	Nauru
New Zealand	Nueva Zelanda, Nueva Zelandia
Papua New Guinea	Papua Nueva Guinea
Solomon Islands	Islas Salomón
Tonga	Tonga
Tuvalu	Tuvalu
Vanuatu	Vanuatu
Western Samoa	Samoa del Oeste

South America/Sudamérica

Argentina	Argentina
Bolivia	Bolivia
Brazil	Brasil
Chile	Chile
Colombia	Colombia
Ecuador	Ecuador
Guyana	Guyana
Paraguay	Paraguay
Peru	Perú
Suriname	Surinam
Uruguay	Uruguay
Venezuela	Venezuela

Metric System: Conversions

Length

unit	number of meters	approximate U.S. equivalents	
millimeter	0.001	0.039	inch
centimeter	0.01	0.39	inch
meter	1	39.37	inches
kilometer	1,000	0.62	mile

Longitud

unidad	número de metros	equivalentes aproximados de los EE.UU.	
milímetro	0.001	0.039	pulgada
centímetro	0.01	0.39	pulgada
metro	1	39.37	pulgadas
kilómetro	1,000	0.62	milla

Area

unit	number of square meters	approximate U.S. equivalents	
square centimeter	0.0001	0.155	square inch
square meter	1	10.764	square feet
hectare	10,000	2.47	acres
square kilometer	1,000,000	0.3861	square mile

Superficie

unidad	número de metros cuadrados	equivalentes aproximados de los EE.UU.	
centímetro cuadrado	0.0001	0.155	pulgada cuadrada
metro cuadrado	1	10.764	pies cuadrados
hectárea	10,000	2.47	acres
kilómetro cuadrado	1,000,000	0.3861	milla cuadrada

Volume

unit	number of cubic meters	approximate U.S. equivalents	
cubic centimeter	0.000001	0.061	cubic inch
cubic meter	1	1.307	cubic yards

Volumen

unidad	número de metros cúbicos	equivalentes aproximados de los EE.UU	
centímetro cúbico	0.000001	0.061	pulgada cúbica
metro cúbico	1	1.307	yardas cúbicas

Capacity

unit	number of liters	approximate U.S. equivalents		
		CUBIC	DRY	LIQUID
liter	1	61.02 cubic inches	0.908 quart	1.057 quarts

Capacidad

unidad	número de litros	equivalentes aproximados de los EE.UU.		
		CÚBICO	SECO	LÍQUIDO
litro	1	61.02 pulgadas cúbicas	0.908 cuarto	1.057 cuartos

Mass and Weight

unit	number of grams	approximate U.S. equivalents	
milligram	0.001	0.015	grain
centigram	0.01	0.154	grain
gram	1	0.035	ounce
kilogram	1,000	2.2046	pounds
metric ton	1,000,000	1.102	short tons

Masa y peso

unidad	número de gramos	equivalentes aproximados de los EE.UU.	
miligramo	0.001	0.015	grano
centigramo	0.01	0.154	grano
gramo	1	0.035	onza
kilogramo	1.000	2.2046	libras
tonelada métrica	1,000,000	1.102	toneladas cortas